Marc Chagall: The Tribe of Asher

(one of the stained-glass windows of the Synagogue of the Medical Center, Jerusalem)

THE NEW STANDARD
JEWISH ENCYCLOPEDIA

The New Standard Jewish Encyclopedia

ORIGINAL EDITION EDITED BY

CECIL ROTH and GEOFFREY WIGODER

NEW REVISED EDITION EDITED BY

GEOFFREY WIGODER, D. Phil.

FIFTH EDITION

DOUBLEDAY & COMPANY, INC.

Garden City, New York

1977

Fifth Edition

ISBN 0–385–12519–4

LIBRARY OF CONGRESS CATALOG CARD NUMBER 76–21965

COPYRIGHT © 1959, 1962, 1966, 1970, 1977 BY ENCYCLOPEDIA PUBLISHING COMPANY, LTD.

PRINTED AND BOUND BY KETERPRESS ENTERPRISES, JERUSALEM

PREFACE

THE NEW STANDARD JEWISH ENCYCLOPEDIA is intended basically as a work of contemporary reference. No comparable work has appeared since before World War II and during this interval three major events have occurred in Jewish history — the destruction of European Jewry, the establishment of the State of Israel, and the emergence of the United States as the outstanding Diaspora community. This work therefore throws special stress on these recent historic developments, although at the same time covering every phase of Jewish life, literature, and thought from their beginning. Particular attention is paid to the American community and its outstanding figures and to the twin pole of modern Jewish life, the State of Israel and the men who are shaping its development. The subject-matter includes prominent Jews from the earliest times down to the present, non-Jews who have made a major impression on Jewish history and scholarship, the history of the Jews in all countries and towns where they have settled in number, summaries of Jewish history, literature, religion, philosophy, etc., the leading concepts of Jewish law, Jewish customs, festivals, and institutions, and general articles on a variety of topics relating to Jewish history and the Jewish way of life.

Conciseness has been a principal aim in compiling the encyclopedia and every endeavor has been made to minimize repetition. Articles should therefore be read in conjunction with the other entries to which reference is made by cross-headings printed in CAPITALS. All this taken in conjunction constitutes the basic article.

The latest available sources have been exploited in preparing this volume. However, present circumstances make it difficult to obtain information from Eastern Europe. In Russia, for instance, the surviving Jewish groups, some of them numerically very large (although exact figures are a matter of conjecture), seldom maintain any Jewish corporate life.

The functions of the American Advisory Board were to assist the editors in the preparation of articles dealing with subjects of special interest to Americans and to ensure accurate and authoritative information on all important phases of Jewish life in the United States. Success would have been impossible without the cooperation of a large number of friends and contributors, to whom we express our wholehearted gratitude.

Hebrew words have been transliterated according to the Sephardi pronunciation (for the system of transliteration, see page 30). They have also been italicized except in certain cases where these words have passed into common usage (e.g. Torah, Midrash, yeshivah, kibbutz). Wherever a Hebrew word appears in the text without explanation, the reader is referred to the relevant entry where the term is translated and explained. A number of common Hebrew and Yiddish phrases have also been included and explained. Yiddish transliteration is in accordance with *YIVO* usage.

The Jewish Publication Society version of the Bible has been used for spellings, translations, and verse-references. The common English forms of all names appearing in the Bible have been maintained; an exception has been made in the cases of persons living in modern Israel (formerly Palestine) where the names are transliterated — thus, readers will find entries on Moses, Moses Maimonides, Moses Mendelssohn, but on Mosheh Sharett. In the case of Israel place-names, the familiar anglicized forms have been retained where such exist (e.g. Jerusalem, Nazareth, Tiberias, Caesarea). The familiar forms Israel and Zion (rather than Yisrael, Tziyyon) have generally been kept, even when transliterating Hebrew (e.g. *Poale Zion*).

Places of birth and death are generally not indicated as it has been found that those given in other works of reference are often conjectural (especially in the case of personalities prior to the modern period) or irrelevant (e.g. when the event took place while traveling).

Capitalization indicates the exact cross-reference, e.g. Isaac IBN EZRA refers the reader to *IBN EZRA*, and SAMUEL BEN ALI to *SAMUEL*.

Non-Jews are indicated by an asterisk (*) prefixed to the entry. No special sign has been adopted for Jews who left Judaism but the fact has generally been mentioned in the text.

Where two or more members of a family appear, their biographies have been consolidated into a single entry which is placed before individual entries of personalities with the same surname; e.g. the entry *ABRAHAMS* family (incorporating Adolphe, Harold, and Sidney) precedes the entries *ABRAHAMS, ISRAEL*; *ABRAHAMS, LIONEL*, etc. Another point of alphabetic order is that where the same word is both a first name and a surname, all entries where it appears as a first name precede entries where it is a family name (e.g. *ABRAHAM, ABRAHAM BEN ALEXANDER*, etc. and then *ABRAHAM, KARL*, etc.).

The editors are hopeful that this volume will fill a long-felt need and provide a concise, accurate, and handy reference book on all major topics of Jewish interest.

Jerusalem, 1958

PREFACE TO THE NEW REVISED EDITION

It is almost twenty years since the STANDARD JEWISH ENCYCLOPEDIA first appeared and these two decades have witnessed many changes, major and minor, in the Jewish world that are fully reflected in this new edition. New entries have been introduced, all the material has been updated, articles revised, and the latest available statistics incorporated. The editors have been gratified at the reception accorded this work since its initial appearance and are confident that this new edition will ensure its continuing role as a standard book of reference.

A few days after the appearance of the last edition, Professor Cecil Roth passed away in Jerusalem. His wise advice and guidance, his encyclopedic knowledge, and his inspired editing are sadly missed but we are glad that this revised edition will ensure the continued use of this Encyclopedia — a major monument to his scholarship.

Alexander Peli
Managing Editor

Jerusalem, January 1977

LIST OF CONTRIBUTORS

ABBADY, BATYA, Jerusalem
Article: Women's League for Israel

ABRAHAMS, Rabbi ISRAEL (the late), Jerusalem
South Africa

AGMON, GALLIA (the late), Jerusalem
Theater

AHIMEIR, Dr. ABBA SHAUL (the late), Ramat Gan
Israel Affairs; Russian Jewry

ALCALAY, Rabbi Dr. ISAAC, New York
Article: Central Sephardic Jewish Community of America

ALLON, YIGAL, Ginnosar
Article: Palmaḥ

ALOUF, YEHOSHUA, Tel Aviv
Sport

ALPERT, CARL, Haifa
US

ALTMANN, Prof. ALEXANDER, Waltham, Mass.
Article: Judaism

ANAT, MOSHEH ARYEH, Pardes Ḥannah
Kabbalah

APPLEBAUM, Prof. SHIMON, Tel Aviv
Classical Period; Contemporary Affairs

ASSAF, Rabbi SIMḤAH (the late), Jerusalem
Rabbinic Literature

ASTOR, Rev. ALEXANDER, Jerusalem
New Zealand

AULICK, JUNE, New York
Article: National Council of Jewish Women

AVI-YONAH, MIKHAEL (the late), Jerusalem
History and Geography of Israel

AVIVI, Dr. PINḤAS, Jerusalem
Article: Physics, Jews in

AVNERI, Dr. TZEVI (the late), Haifa
Germany

BAER, Prof. YITZḤAK, Jerusalem
Article: Ibn Verga

BAMBERGER, Rabbi Dr. BERNARD J., New York
Christianity

BAR-DAVID, MOLLY LYONS, Savyon
Article: Cookery

BAR-LEV, Dr. YOSEPH, Jerusalem
Article: Gratz College

BARON, Prof. SALO W., New York
Article: Community

BARSHAI, BEZALEL, Jerusalem
Hebrew Literature

BEIN, Dr. ALEX, Jerusalem
Article: Theodor Herzl

BELFIELD, E. M., Doylestown, Pa.
Article: National Agricultural College

BELKIN, Dr. SAMUEL, New York
Article: Yeshiva University

BELTH, NATHAN C., New York
Article: Anti-Defamation League

BEN-ISRAEL, Prof. ḤEDVAH, Jerusalem
History

BEN-SHAMMAI, Dr. MEIR HILLEL, Jerusalem
Science

BENTWICH, Prof. NORMAN (the late), London
Modern History

BERMAN, Dr. HYMAN, New York
Labor

BERNSTEIN, PERETZ (the late), Jerusalem
Article: General Zionism

BERNSTEIN, PHILIP, New York
Article: Council of Jewish Federations and Welfare Funds

BERNSTEIN, SAUL, New York
Article: Union of Orthodox Jewish Congregations of America

BINDER, Dr. ABRAHAM W. (the late), New York
Article: Cantor and Cantoral Music

BISGYER, MAURICE (the late), Washington, D.C.
Article: B'nai B'rith

BLOCH, Dr. JOSHUA (the late), New York
US

BLUESTEIN, RICHARD N., Cincinnati, Ohio
Article: Hebrew Union College — Jewish Institute of Religion

BLUM, Dr. KARL (the late), Jerusalem
Rumania

BLUMENTHAL, NAḤMAN, Tel Aviv
Nazi Europe

BOWMAN, Prof. JOHN, Melbourne
Samaritans

BRAWER, Dr. ABRAHAM J. (the late), Tel Aviv
Geography of Israel

BRICKNER, Rabbi Dr. BARNETT R. (the late),
    Cleveland
Article: Chaplains

CARMEL, Dr. HERMAN, New York
Article: Jewish Teachers' Seminary

CARMIN, ITZHAK J., New York
US; Latin America

CASPER, Rabbi BERNARD, Johannesburg
Article: Jewish Brigade

CATANE, Dr. MOSHE, Jerusalem
France

CHIEL, Rabbi ARTHUR A., New Haven
Canada

CLINCHY, Dr. EVERETT, R., New York
Article: National Conference of Christians and Jews

COHEN, ISRAEL (the late), London
Article: Travelers

COHEN, Rabbi JACK J., Jerusalem
Article: Society for the Advancement of Judaism

COHEN, JANUS, London
Article: Humor

COHEN, Rabbi MEYER, New York
Article: Union of Orthodox Rabbis

DAVIS, Prof. MOSHE, Jerusalem
Article: Jewish Theological Seminary

DICKMAN, IRVING R., New York
Article: American Jewish Joint Distribution Committee

DIJOUR, ILJA M., New York
Article: Hias

DIRINGER, Prof. DAVID (the late), Tel Aviv
Hebrew Alphabet

DI-ZAHAV, EPHRAIM (the late), Jerusalem
Music

EICHHORN, Rabbi Dr. DAVID M., New York
Article: Armed Forces, Jews in the

EISENSTEIN, Rabbi Dr. IRA, New York
Reconstructionism

ELKOSHI, Prof. GEDALYAH, Jerusalem
Hebrew Literature

EPSTEIN, BENJAMIN R., New York
Article: Anti-Defamation League

FELDMAN, Prof. LEON A., New York
US

FELIKS, Prof. YEHUDAH, Jerusalem
Article: Hillazon

FERENCZ, BENJAMIN B., New York
Article: Jewish Restitution Successor Organization

FICHMAN, YAAKOV (the late), Tel Aviv
Article: Bialik

FISCHEL, Prof. WALTER J. (the late), Berkeley,
    Calif.
The Orient

FISHMAN, ARYEH, Jerusalem
Article: Bene Akiva

FLUSSER, Prof. DAVID, Jerusalem
Literature of the Second Temple Period

FRAENKEL, JOSEPH, London
Article: Press (General)

FRANKEL, WALTER, Jerusalem
Article: Sport

FRANKFURTER, Justice FELIX (the late),
    Washington
Article: Brandeis, Louis D.

FRIEDMAN, Dr. PHILIP (the late), New York
Nazi Europe

FRIEDMAN, Rabbi Dr. THEODORE, Jerusalem
Rabbinic Law

GARBELL, Prof. IRENE (the late), Jerusalem
Article: Dialects

GARTNER, Prof. LLOYD P., Jerusalem
US

GELBER, Dr. NATAN MIKHAEL (the late),
    Jerusalem
Eastern Europe

GERSHENFELD, Dr. LOUIS, Philadelphia
Article: Nobel Prize Winners

GERSHONY, GERSHON K. (the late), Jerusalem
Art

GINSBERG, Prof. HAROLD L., New York
Apocrypha

GLANZ, Dr. RUDOLF, New York
US

GOLDBERG, Rabbi Dr. AVRAHAM, Jerusalem
Rabbinics

GOLDBERG, HANNAH L., New York
Article: Hadassah

GOLDSTEIN, Rabbi Dr. ISRAEL, Jerusalem
US

GOODMAN, SAUL, New York
Article: Sholem Aleichem

GORDON, Rabbi MORRIS E., New York
Article: Mir

GRADENWITZ, Dr. PETER EMANUEL, Tel Aviv
Music

GRANOTT, Dr. AVRAHAM (the late), Jerusalem
Article: Jewish National Fund

GRAYZEL, Dr. SOLOMON, Philadelphia
Article: Jewish Publication Society of America

GREENESS, Rabbi MORRIS, New York
Mesivta Yeshiva Rabbi Chaim Berlin

GRINZ, Prof. YEHOSHUA M. (the late), Jerusalem
Bible

GRUNWALD, Dr. KURT, Jerusalem
Banking

HABERMAN, Prof. AVRAHAM MEIR, Jerusalem
Jewish Literature and Customs

HALKIN, Prof. ABRAHAM S., Jerusalem
Article: American Academy for Jewish Research

HALPRIN, ROSE L., New York
Article: Hadassah

HAREL, YITZHAK, Jerusalem
Israel

HERLITZ, Dr. GEORG (the late), Jerusalem
Zionism

HESKY, Dr. MOSHE, Tel Aviv
Article: Philately

HEYD, Prof. URIEL (the late), Jerusalem
Turkey

HODES, JACOB (the late), Jerusalem
Zionism

HON, SHAUL, Tel Aviv
Chess

HURWITZ, HENRY (the late), New York
Article: Menorah Journal and Movement

HYMAN, ABRAHAM S., New York
Article: United Jewish Appeal

ISH-SHALOM, Prof. MIKHAEL, Jerusalem
Geography of Israel

JAFFE, BINYAMIN, Jerusalem
Zionism

JAFFE, MAURICE A., Jerusalem
Religious Zionism

JAMMER, Prof. MOSHEH, Ramat-Gan
Article: Mathematics, Jews in

KAHN, Prof. SHALOM J., Jerusalem
American Literature

KALMAN, SOPHIE, Jerusalem
Central Europe and General

KAPLAN, TZEVI, Jerusalem
Rabbinics

KARLINSKY, Rabbi JACOB, New York
Article: Vaad Hatzala Rehabilitation Committee

KATZ, SIMHAH, Jerusalem
Russia

KATZMAN, JACOB, New York
Article: Poale Zion

KELMAN, Rabbi WOLFE, New York
Article: Rabbinical Assembly of America

KEYFETZ, BEN G., Toronto, Canada
Canada

KLAUSNER, Prof. YOSEPH (the late), Jerusalem
Jewish Literature; Second Temple History

KLAVAN, Rabbi ISRAEL, New York
Article: Rabbinical Council of America

KLEIN, Rabbi HYMAN (the late), London
Rabbinics

KOHN, Rabbi Dr. EUGENE, New York
Article: Reconstructionism

KOL, MOSHE, Jerusalem
Israel

KOMLOS, Dr. YEHUDAH OTTO, Jerusalem
Bible

KOPF, Dr. LOTHAR (the late), Jerusalem
Arab Lands

KRESSEL, GETZEL, Holon
Zionism

KUGEL, LILLIAN, New York
Article: Pioneer Women

LAMED, LOUIS, Detroit
Article: Louis LaMed Literary Foundation

LANDMAN, AMOS, Denver
Article: National Jewish Hospital

LANDRESS, SYLVIA, New York
Article: Zionist Archives and Library

LAPIDE, PINHAS, Jerusalem
Article: San Nicandro

LASERSOHN, ELEAZAR, Tel Aviv
Article: El-Al

LEBESON, ANITA L., Winnetka, Ill.
US

LEFTWICH, JOSEPH, London
Article: Glicenstein

LEICHTER, SINAI, Jerusalem
Israel

LESSER, ALLEN, New York
*Article: American Zionist Committee for Public
   Affairs*

LEVIN, NAHUM (the late), Jerusalem
Article: Berit Ivrit Olamit

LEVIN-SHATZKES, ICCHOK, New York
Article: Jewish Socialist Verband of America

LEWISOHN, Prof. LUDWIG (the late),
   Waltham, Mass.
French, German, and American Literature

LIPSCHITZ, Rabbi CHAIM U., New York
Article: Rabbinical Alliance of America

LIPSKY, LOUIS (the late), New York
Article: Chaim Weizmann

LIPTZIN, Prof. SOLOMON, Jerusalem
Yiddish Language and Literature

LIS, YEHUDAH (the late), Jerusalem
Article: Keren ha-Yesod

LISKOFSKY, SIDNEY, New York
Article: United Nations

LIVNEH, ELIEZER (the late), Jerusalem
Article: Cooperatives (Israel)

LOEWE, RAPHAEL, London
English Hebraists

LORCH, Colonel NETANEL, Jerusalem
Article: War of Liberation

MAHLER, Prof. RAPHAEL, Tel Aviv
Article: Council of the Four Lands

MARCUS, Prof. JACOB RADER, Cincinnati
*Articles: American Jewish Archives; American Jewish
   Periodical Center*

MARCUS, Dr. SHIMON, Jerusalem
Middle East

MARKS, Dr. SIDNEY, New York
Article: Zionist Organization of America

MARTON, Dr. YEHUDAH, Jerusalem
Hungary

MAYER, Dr. EUGENE (the late), Jerusalem
Germany

MELAMED, Prof. EZRA ZION, Jerusalem
Article: Rashi

MELTZER, JULIAN L., Jerusalem
Article: Weizmann Institute

MESTEL, JACOB, New York
Yiddish Theater

MEYER, Rabbi ISIDORE S., New York
US

MEYOUHAS, YOSEPH (the late), Jerusalem
Article: Scouts

MICHAELIS, MEIR, Tel Aviv
Israel Army

MINKOFF, ISAIAH M., New York
*Article: National Community Relations Advisory
   Council*

MONTAGU, the Hon. LILY (the late), London
Article: World Union for Progressive Judaism

NARDI, Dr. NOAH, Jerusalem
Education

NEHER, Prof. ANDRÉ, Jerusalem
Bible and Ethics

NEUMAN, Prof. ABRAHAM A. (the late),
   Philadelphia
US

NEWMAN, ARYEH, Jerusalem
Rabbinics

ORNI, EPHRAIM, Jerusalem
Israel Settlements

PARKES, Dr. JAMES, Southampton
Article: Holy Places

PAT, JACOB (the late), New York
Article: Frank Atran

PATAI, Dr. RAPHAEL, New York
History; Folklore

PATERSON, Dr. DAVID, Oxford
Article: Mendelssohn Family

PESSIN, Rabbi NACHUM, New York
Bachad Organization of North America

PLESSNER, Prof. MARTIN (the late), Jerusalem
Islam

POOL, Rabbi Dr. DAVID DE SOLA (the late),
   New York
*Articles: The Union of Sephardic Congregations;
   de Sola Family*

PORUSH, Rabbi ISRAEL, Sydney
Australia

RAANAN, Prof. URI, Boston
Modern History

RABBINOWITZ, Prof. TZEVI MEIR, Tel Aviv
Ḥasídism

RABIN, Prof. CHAIM, Jerusalem
Hebrew Language and Literature

RABINOWICZ, Dr. OSKAR K. (the late), New York
Article: Winston Churchill

RABINOWITZ, Prof. LOUIS ISAAC, Jerusalem
South Africa

RAPHAEL, YITZḤAK, Jerusalem
Article: Aliyah

REGNER, Rabbi SIDNEY L., New York
Article: Central Conference of American Rabbis

ROBACK, Prof. ABRAHAM A. (the late),
Cambridge, Mass.
Article: Languages

RODITI, EDUARD, Paris
Art

ROGEL, NAKDIMON, Jerusalem
Arab Lands

ROLBANT, Dr. SHEMUEL, Tel Aviv
Histadrut

ROSE, Rabbi ISAAC B., New York
Religious Zionists of America, Mizraḥi – Hapoel Hamizraḥi

ROSEN, Dr. PINḤAS, Jerusalem
Article: Genocide

ROSENBERG, LOUIS, Montreal
Canada

ROSENNE, SHABBETAI, Jerusalem
Law

ROTHSCHILD, Prof. SOLOMON, Jerusalem
Article: Sigmund Freud

SACHAR, Dr. ABRAM L., Waltham, Mass.
Article: Brandeis University

SAFFER, LOUIS, Leeds
Rabbinics

SAMUEL, Viscount EDWIN, Jerusalem
State of Israel

SCHAECHTER, MORDKHE, New York
Article: Freeland League

SCHNEIDERMAN, HARRY (the late), New York
US

SCHATZ, JULIUS, New York
Article: Motion Pictures, Jews in

SCHECHTMAN, Dr. JOSEPH B. (the late),
New York
Revisionist Zionism

SCHIFF, Dr. FRITZ (the late), Haifa
Art

SCHOLEM, Prof. GERSHOM, Jerusalem
Article: Zohar

SCHWARTZ, Rabbi S. ALVIN, Chicago
Article: Hebrew Theological College

SEGAL, Rabbi BERNARD, New York
Article: United Synagogue of America

SEGAL, CHARLES M., New York
US

SEGAL, LOUIS (the late), New York
Article: Farband Labor Zionist Order

SCHACHTER, Rabbi YAAKOV (the late),
Jerusalem
Rabbinics

SHALIT, Prof. AVRAHAM, Jerusalem
Second Temple Period

SHAPIRO, Dr. JUDAH J., New York
Article: Hillel Foundation

SHAPIRO, LEON, New York
Demography; World Jewish Population

SHEMEN, NACHMAN, Toronto
Canada

SHERER, Rabbi MORRIS, New York
Article: Agudat Israel

SHIMONI, YAAKOV, Jerusalem
Article: Arab League

SIEGEL, MARC, New York
Mizraḥi Women's Organization of America

SILVER, Rabbi Dr. ABBA HILLEL (the late),
Cleveland
Article: Messiah

SILVER, Rabbi SAMUEL M., New York
*Articles: Union of American Hebrew Congregations
Reform Judaism*

SIMON, Sir LEON (the late), London
Article: Nationalism

SLAWSON, Dr. JOHN, New York
Article: American Jewish Committee

SLOAN, JACOB, New York
US

SOMPOLINSKY, MEIR, Mikveh Yisrael
Scandinavia

SPEAR, OTTO IMMANUEL, Tel Aviv
Philosophy

STEINBACH, Rabbi Dr. ALEXANDER A.,
    Brooklyn, N. Y.
Article: Rabbinical Conferences

TABACHINSKY, BENJAMIN, New York
Article: Jewish Labor Committee

TAL, Prof. YOSEPH, Jerusalem
Music

TARTAKOWER, Prof. ARYEH, Jerusalem
Sociology

TENENBAUM, Dr. JOSEPH L. (the late),
New York
    Nazi Europe

TOLEDO, JACK, New York
Article: Sephardic Brotherhood

TRACHTENBERG, Rabbi Dr. JOSHUA (the late),
    Teaneck, N.J.
US

UNGER, Rabbi JEROME, New York
Article: American Zionist Council

UNTERMAN, BARUCH, Tel Aviv
Article: Bar-Ilan University

URBACH, Prof. EPHRAIM E., Jerusalem
Article: Aggadah

WAXMAN, Prof. MEYER (the late), Chicago
Jewish Literature

WEINGREEN, Prof. YACOB, Dublin
Article: Bible Criticism

WEINSHANKER, YITZHAK, Montevideo
Uruguay

WEINSTEIN, Dr. DAVID, Brooklyn, Mass.
Article: Hebrew Teachers' College

WERBLOWSKY, Prof. R. J. ZVI, Jerusalem
Jewish Philosophy and Religion

WILKINSON, SADIE, Tel-Aviv
Article: Israel Philharmonic Orchestra

WISCHNITZER, Dr. RACHEL, New York
Article: Art

WYDRA, Dr. NAPHTALI, Haifa
Article: Zim

WYLER, MARJORIE, New York
Article: Jewish Theological Seminary of America

WYSCHOGROD, Prof. MICHAEL, New York
US

ZAUSMER, SARAI, Philadelphia
Article: Dropsie College

ZIPRIN, NATHAN, New York
Jewish Press

ABBREVIATIONS

abbr.	abbreviation	*Judg.*	Judges
Arab.	Arabic	*KA*	Ha-Kibbutz ha-Artzi
Aram.	Aramaic	*KM*	Ha-Kibbutz ha-Meuḥad
b.	born	*Lev.*	Leviticus
BCE	Before Common Era (= BC)	*Lam.*	Lamentations
c.	circa (about)	*Lat.*	Latin
CE	Common Era (= AD)	*m.*	mile
cent.	century	*Macc.*	Maccabees
d.	died	*Mal.*	Malachi
Deut.	Deuteronomy	*MH*	Ha-Moetzah ha-Ḥaklait
E	East	*Mic.*	Micah
Ecc.	Ecclesiastes	*Mt.*	Mount
Est.	Esther	*N*	North
Exod.	Exodus	*Neh.*	Nehemiah
Ezek.	Ezekiel	*Num.*	Numbers
fl.	flourished	*PAI*	Poale Agudat Israel
Fr.	French	*PM*	Ha-Poel ha-Mizraḥi
Gen.	Genesis	*Pop.*	Population
Ger.	German	*Prov.*	Proverbs
Gk.	Greek	*Ps.*	Psalms
Hab.	Habakkuk	*R*	Rabbi; River
Hag.	Haggai	*S*	South
Heb.	Hebrew	*Sam.*	Samuel
Hos.	Hosea	*Sp.*	Spanish
IK	Iḥud ha-Kibbutzim	*TM*	Tenuat ha-Moshavim
Is.	Isaiah	*W*	West
It.	Italian	*Y*	Talmud Yerushalmi
Jer.	Jeremiah	*Zech.*	Zechariah
Josh.	Joshua	*Zeph.*	Zephaniah

* indicates a non-Jew.

SYSTEM OF HEBREW TRANSLITERATION

א is not transliterated

ב = b

ב = v

ג,ג = g

ד,ד = d

ה = h

ו = v (where not a vowel)

ז = z

ח = ḥ

ט = t

י = y

כ = k

כ = kh

ל = l

מ = m

נ = n

ס = s

ע is not transliterated

פ = p

פ = ph

צ = tz

ק = k

ר = r

שׁ = sh

שׂ = s

ת,ת = t

ָ = a

ַ = a

ֳ, ֹ = o

וּ = u

short ָ = o

ֵ = e

ֶ = e

ִ = i

ֻ = u

ְ = e

ֺ = o

ֲ = a

vocal *sheva* = e

silent *sheva* is not transliterated

AACHEN (Aix-la-Chapelle): City in W Germany. There was a "Jews' Street" in the city as early as the 11th cent. but information is sparse. The modern settlement dates from 1667. The community, destroyed by the Nazis, was reorganized in 1945, and numbered 155 in 1967.

AARON: Elder brother of Moses and a leading figure in the events of the Exodus. A. was Moses' spokesman in his dealings with Pharaoh, but was persuaded to make the Golden Calf while Moses was on Mt. Sinai. When the Tabernacle was erected, A. and his sons were consecrated to the PRIESTHOOD. He died on Mt. Hor, on the border of Edom, at the age of 123. In rabbinic legend he is regarded as the personification of piety and the spirit of peace.

Aaron: a traditional picture appearing in a number of old Hebrew works.

AARON BEN ELIJAH (1300–1369): Karaite philosopher and exegete who lived in Nicomedia (Asia Minor). Taking Maimonides' *Guide* as his model, he wrote a philosophical basis for Karaism called *Etz ha-Ḥayyim* ("The Tree of Life"). In this he maintains the existence, incorporeality, and unity of God, to whom he ascribes positive (power, knowledge, will, and existence), as well as negative, attributes. The anthropomorphisms in the Bible are interpreted symbolically; the Mosaic Law is regarded as immutable and not to be supplemented by rabbinic accretions. A. also wrote a commentary on the Pentateuch and a work on the precepts of the Bible.

AARON BEN JACOB HA-COHEN (fl. 13th–14th cents.): French talmudist. He emigrated to Majorca after the expulsion of the Jews from France (1306) and there completed his compilation of Jewish laws, *Orhot Ḥayyim* ("Paths of Life"), subsequently abridged as the compendium *Kol Bo* ("All Is In It") which enjoyed wide popularity.

AARON (BEN JACOB) OF KARLIN (1736–1772): Founder of the Karlin-Stolin Ḥasidic dynasty. He is known as "Aaron the Great" to distinguish him from his grandson, Aaron ben Asher (1802–1872).

AARON BEN JOSEPH HA-LEVI (abbr. *R'ah*; fl. 13th cent.): Spanish talmudic authority. He studied under Naḥmanides in Barcelona where he himself subsequently became an important teacher. He is known chiefly for his strictures on Solomon ben Adret's *Torat ha-Bayit,* which he entitled *Bedek ha-Bayit.* Adret wrote *Mishmeret ha-Bayit* in reply.

AARON BEN JOSEPH THE PHYSICIAN, called **THE ELDER** (c. 1250–1320): Karaite philosopher and liturgical poet in the Crimea. His major work, a philosophical commentary on the Pentateuch, revealed his affinity to rabbinic Judaism. Most Karaite congregations adopted his arrangement of the prayerbook. He wrote *Sepher ha-Mivḥar,* a commentary on the Pentateuch.

AARON BEN MOSES BEN ASHER see **BEN ASHER.**

AARON (ABU AHARON) BEN SAMUEL (9th cent.): Mystic and wonder-worker. A. left Baghdad (c. 870) and wandered through Italy, teaching kabbalistic lore. His pupil Moses ben Kalonymos of Lucca carried his teachings to Germany. A. is regarded as the father of kabbalistic study in Europe.

AARON OF LINCOLN (d. 1185): English financier. His business activities extended to at least 25 English counties; his clients included religious houses, abbeys, and cathedrals as well as many of the nobility. On his death, his property was confiscated by the Crown, and a special branch of the Exchequer was set up to exact the debts due him.

AARON OF YORK (d. 1268): English financier; "archpresbyter" of English Jewry, 1236–43. The royal exactions from him were so great that he was compelled to resign his office and ended his days in relative poverty. There are many glimpses of his personality and activities in the writings of the chronicler, Matthew Paris.

AARON SAMUEL BEN ISRAEL KAIDANOVER see **KAIDANOVER**

AARONSON, AARON (1876–1919): Agronomist and Palestinian leader. Born in Rumania and taken to Palestine in 1882 (his father was one of the founders of Zikhron Yaakov), he studied agronomy in France, and from 1895 worked in Metullah as an expert for Baron Edmond de Rothschild. In 1906, he discovered Wild Emmer Wheat *(triticum dicoccoides)* in Palestine and in 1911, founded the agricultural experimental station at Athlit. During World War I, he was chief agricultural adviser to the Turkish commander Jemal Pasha, and at the same time organized (with Avshalom FEINBERG) an underground intelligence service (NILI) in behalf of the Allies as part of the struggle to realize Jewish aspirations in Palestine and end Turkish rule. His sister Sarah was arrested by the Turks while en-

Aaron Aaronson.

gaged in this espionage work, subjected to severe tortures, and eventually killed herself without disclosing any secrets of the Nili (1917). A. served as a staff officer at British army headquarters in Cairo, was adviser to General Allenby, and was sent on several missions. At the Paris Peace Conference (1919) he endeavored to promote Zionist interests. A. was killed in an airplane crash over the English Channel. He wrote many articles and papers on agricultural and botanical subjects.

AB see **AV**

ABARBANEL see **ABRAVANEL**

ABAYE see **ABBAYE**

ABBA (Aram. "father"): Title of honor, often synonymous in the early Rabbinic Period with "Rabbi." It also passed into Christian usage as abbé, abbot, etc. In modern Hebrew, it is the usual word for "father."

ABBA ARIKHA see **RAV**

ABBA MARI BEN MOSES HA-YARHI (Don Astruc of Lunel; 13th–14th cents.): Anti-Maimonist scholar. He was one of the leaders of the Montpellier community and opposed the secular studies of the followers of Maimonides. With Asher ben Jehiel he persuaded Solomon ben Adret to issue a ban (1305) prohibiting students under the age of thirty from studying philosophy, a subject treated in his book *Ha-Yareah*. His opponents, led by Jacob ben Makhir Ibn Tibbon, issued a counter-ban. The expulsion of the Jews from France (1306) put an end to the dispute. A. M. went to Arles and thence to Perpignan where he compiled his book *Minhat ha-Kenaot* ("The Offering of Zeal") on the controversy, incorporating much contemporary correspondence.

ABBA SIKRA (or **SAKKARA**; fl. 1st cent. CE): Zealot leader in Jerusalem during the revolt against the Romans; called elsewhere Ben Batiah. He was a nephew of R Johanan ben Zakkai whom he helped escape from the beleaguered city. It has been suggested that A.S. was a title meaning "Leader of the Sicarii."

ABBAHU (c. 279–320): Palestinian amora distinguished as an aggadist and controversialist. He became head of the rabbinical academy at Caesarea and one of the leading rabbis of the community. His popularity, wealth, and knowledge of Greek made him influential with the Roman proconsular authorities. Though strict in his own observance of the Law, he made concessions to local usages in his legal decisions, but polemized against Christians and other sectarians. He was at the head of a group of scholars known as the Rabbis of Caesarea to whom the redaction of the juridical part of the Jerusalem Talmud has been ascribed.

ABBAYE (real name Nahmani ben Kaylil; often called Nahmani; Abbaye = "little father." 278–338): Babylonian amora, head of the Pumbedita academy, 333–8. He developed talmudic dialectic to its peak, and

Photostat of a section of the Scroll of Abiathar.

his arguments with his colleague, RAVA, left their impress on the entire Babylonian Talmud and became proverbial. In all cases where he and Rava differed, the legal decision was according to Rava, except in 6 instances. Among A.'s contributions to talmudic study was the sharpening of the distinction between *peshat*, the evident meaning of a biblical text, and *derash*, the allegorical interpretation. By profession a wine-dealer and farmer, A. was fond of citing folk tales and customs.

ABBREVIATIONS (Heb. *rashe tevot* — "initials of words"): The use of parts or single letters of words to indicate the whole. A. are found in Hebrew as early as the 2nd cent. BCE on the Maccabean coinage, and the system was common in the talmudic period. In the Middle Ages, it was extremely prevalent in Hebrew as well as European writing, partly because of the urgent necessity to convey as much as possible on a limited amount of writing material. Contractions were indicated by a dot, stroke, or double-stroke over the line. Sometimes, the last letters only (especially in the case of plurals) would be omitted. The characteristic feature of Hebrew a. was the wide use of initials for groups of words (the style has recently become familiar in English, e.g. UNESCO). Entire sentences might sometimes be conveyed largely by this means. Some a. attained the status of words in their own right as applied to authors (e.g. Rashi, Rambam), books (e.g. *Tanakh, Shass)*, and organizations (e.g. BILU). Several handbooks of Hebrew a. have been published, among the most helpful being M. Heilpern's *Notarikon* (Vilna, 1912) and a more recent one by G. Bader (New York, 1951).

*ABDULLAH (1882–1951): Emir, later (1946), king of Transjordan; second son of Hussein, sherif of Mecca (later, king of Hejaz). His support of Britain during World War I led to his nomination as ruler of Transjordan (1923). Credited with a moderate attitude toward Zionism, he negotiated with Chaim Weizmann in 1922 but invaded Israel in 1948. He formally annexed the Arab-held part of Cis-Jordan in 1950 and proclaimed himself ruler of the Hashemite kingdom of Jordan. His attempts to reach an understanding with Israel were nullified by the growing influence of the Palestinian Arabs, and he was assassinated in Jerusalem allegedly at the instance of the Mufti, Haj Amin el-Husseini.

ABEL: Second son of Adam and Eve. He was a shepherd while his elder brother, Cain, tilled the soil (Gen. 4:2). God favored A.'s animal sacrifice, whereupon Cain in envy killed his brother. Some commentators regard the story as a reflection of the ancient antagonism between the cultivator and the shepherd.

ABENAES see **IBN YAISH**

ABENDANA: Sephardi family of Marrano origin with branches in Amsterdam, Hamburg, and London. (1) *DAVID A.* (fl. 16th–17th cents.): He fled the Spanish Inquisition, reverted to Judaism, and settled (c. 1600) in Amsterdam where he became a leader of the Sephardi community. (2) *ISAAC A.* (1650–1710): Scholar. He taught Hebrew at Cambridge and Oxford and translated the Mishnah into Latin (unpublished). (3) *JACOB A.* (1630–1684): Rabbi in Amsterdam and later in London; brother of (2). He translated the Mishnah (unpublished) and Judah Ha-Levi's *Kuzari* into Spanish.

Seal of the Abendana family.

ABIATHAR: Son of Ahimelech, chief priest at Nob.
He escaped the massacre of his family by Saul and took refuge with David who later appointed him high priest. A. remained loyal to David during Absalom's rebellion. In the closing days of David's reign, A. supported Adonijah's claims to the succession, as against those of Solomon who subsequently banished him from Jerusalem and transferred his priestly rights to Zadok (I Sam. 22:19–23; I Kings 2).

ABIATHAR BEN ELIJAH HA-COHEN (c. 1040–
1109): The last Palestinian Gaon. He was exiled
for a period following a violent quarrel with the
Egyptian exilarch David ben Daniel. His account of
his vicissitudes, entitled *Megillat Evyatar* ("Scroll of
A."), was discovered in the Cairo *genizah*. He apparently left Palestine at the time of the First Crusade,
transferring the seat of the Gaonate to Syria.

ABIB see **AVIV**

ABIGAIL: Wife of David, after the death of her first
husband, Nabal. She won David's pardon for
Nabal's churlishness by her gifts and conciliatory
words (I Sam. 25).

ABIHU see **NADAB AND ABIHU**

ABIJAH (or **ABIJAM**): Second king of Judah, son of
Rehoboam, reigned c. 917–915 BCE. He engaged
in continuous warfare with Jeroboam, king of Israel
(I Kings 15; II Chron. 13). Although this feud is taken
in rabbinic literature as evidence of his religious zeal,
the rabbis censure him for his uncharitable attitude
toward Judah's northern neighbors.

*ABIMELECH: Philistine king of Gerar, with whom
Abraham concluded a pact of friendship (Gen. 21).
The account of Abraham's relations with A. (Gen. 20)
resembles, in some respects, the story of the latter's
relations with Abraham's son Isaac (Gen. 26). Because
of his friendly association with both Patriarchs, the
rabbis accorded A. a place in Paradise among the
Pious Heathens.

ABIMELECH: Illegitimate son of Gideon. In an attempt to establish a monarchy in Israel (c. 12th
cent. BCE), he slew his seventy brothers (except
Jotham). He ruled for three years in Shechem, largely
with the support of the chiefs of that city, and was
killed in the ensuing revolt (Judg. 9).

ABIRAM: One of the leaders of the revolt against
Moses in the wilderness (Num. 16): see DATHAN.

ABISHAG: Shunammite maiden who ministered to
David in his old age. Adonijah's request to marry
her after David's death led to his execution by Solomon who interpreted this as a claim to the throne.

ABISHAI: David's devoted general; son of his sister,
Zeruiah. He assisted his elder brother Joab in the
murder of Abner. A. fought heroically on many occasions and saved David's life in battle.

ABITUR, JOSEPH ISAAC IBN see **IBN ABITUR**

ABLUTION: Ritual washing required to remove spiritual impurities before the performance of religious acts or after contact with things considered
unclean. Biblical and rabbinic literature mention three
types of a. (1) Complete Immersion. This is the main
type of a. and must be performed only in a natural
water-source or in a specially constructed ritual bath
(MIKVEH). It was a common feature in the service of
the Temple. After the Destruction, rabbinic law prescribed it only for proselytes on being accepted into
Judaism and for married women following their

Frontispiece of Isaac Aboab's *Menorat ha-Maor*
(Amsterdam, 1722).

periods of menstruation or after childbirth. Nevertheless, pietists (especially Ḥasidim) later continued
to practice immersion as an aspect of spiritual purification. (2) Washing of the Feet and Hands. This was
prescribed only for the priests in the Temple service.
(3) Washing of the Hands. Rabbinic law makes this
mandatory before sitting down to a meal, before prayer, upon rising from sleep, after being in proximity to
a corpse, and after elimination of bodily wastes.

ABNER BEN NER: Uncle of Saul and commander of
his army. After Saul's death, A. supported Ish-
bosheth's claim to the throne. He later joined David's
court, but was killed by Joab in an act of vendetta.
David composed a famous lament for him (II Sam. 3).

ABNER OF BURGOS (later called Alfonso of Valladolid; c. 1270–c. 1340): Spanish convert and anti-
Jewish polemicist. He wrote many bitter attacks on
Judaism, and at his instigation, Alfonso XI of Castile
prohibited the recital of ALENU and prayers allegedly
blaspheming Christianity (1336). His works, extant
only in ms, are cited in Jewish polemics of the period.
They opened a new chapter in the history of medieval
anti-Jewish propaganda.

ABOAB: Widespread family of Spanish origin (sometimes *ABOAF*, etc.): (1) *IMMANUEL A.* (c. 1555–
1628): Scholar and writer. Born of Marrano parents,
he emigrated to Italy, where he reverted to Judaism,

and died on his way to Palestine. His work, intended primarily to win over Marranos to Judaism, included *Nomologia,* a defense in Spanish of the Talmud and rabbinic tradition. (2) *ISAAC A.* (fl. 14th cent.): Author of *Menorat ha-Maor* ("The Candelabrum of Light"), a famous collection of homilies and aggadic teachings intended to emphasize the ethics of Judaism. The book achieved very wide popularity both in the original and in subsequent Spanish, German, and Yiddish translations. It is part of a whole literature of such ethical works that arose at the time as a popular reaction to the prevailing concentration on esoteric and abstruse rabbinic studies. (3) *ISAAC A.* (1433–1493): Talmudic and biblical scholar, called the last Gaon of Castile. He was among the 30 Jewish leaders who journeyed to Portugal in 1492 to request permission for exiled Spanish Jews to enter the country. He settled and died in Oporto. (4) *ISAAC DE FONSECA A.* (d. 1693): The first rabbi in the Western Hemisphere. Born as a Marrano in Portugal, he was taken to Holland as a child and at the age of 21, entered the service of the Amsterdam community. In 1642, he went as rabbi to Recife in Brazil, then under Dutch rule. When the Portuguese recaptured the city (1654), A. and his fellow Jews fled. He returned to Amsterdam where he was appointed *Hakham* and served as head of the religious academy; he was a member of the tribunal which excommunicated Spinoza in 1656. He won fame as a preacher and was influential in persuading the wealthy members of the community to

Frontispiece of Isaac de Fonseca Aboab's book on Hebrew grammar (Amsterdam, 17th cent.).

build the Amsterdam Great Synagogue. He was an adherent of Shabbetai Tzevi (1666). A. published a Spanish translation of the Pentateuch together with a commentary. (5) *SAMUEL A.* (1610–1694): Rabbi in Venice, talmudic scholar, and author of halakhic responsa *(Devar Shemuel)* and ethical writings.

ABOMINATION: English equivalent of three Hebrew terms: (1) *Toevah:* The highest degree of obnoxiousness, applied to such major sins as idolatry, child-sacrifice, and the practice of magic. (2) *Shikkutz,* which is rather less extreme than (1), is applied to idolatrous usages and prohibited animals. (3) *Piggul:* sacrificial flesh that has become putrid.

ABRAHAM (ABRAM): Biblical patriarch to whom both the Jewish people and many Arabian tribes trace their ancestry. According to the biblical account, he was the son of Terah and the father of Isaac (by Sarah) and Ishmael (by his concubine Hagar). He left his birthplace in Ur of the Chaldees and pitched his tent among the Canaanite and Philistine inhabitants of Palestine, visited Egypt, and returned to dwell in Hebron. He fought to deliver Lot from CHEDORLAOMER king of Elam, AMRAPHEL king of Shinar, and their allies. God appeared to him in a vision and promised that his seed would inherit the land "from the river of Egypt to the Euphrates," made a covenant with him, and tested his loyalty by ordering the sacrifice of Isaac. On the death of his wife Sarah, A. purchased the cave of Machpelah as a family burial place. He married a second wife, Keturah. A. died at the age of 175 and was buried in the cave of Machpelah. According to tradition, A. was the founder of monotheism (being called a "prophet" in Gen. 20:7), while later legends refer to him as the repository of all wisdom and science. He is the prototype of humility and kindness, famed for his hospitality. Circumcision is spoken of as "the Covenant of Abraham our Father," and A. is pictured as sitting at the gates of Hell not allowing any circumcised Jew to be brought there. According to hellenistic legends, he was king of Damascus. Arab legends claim he laid the foundations for the sanctuary at Mecca. Modern biblical research is inclined to maintain his historical integrity. It is generally believed that he lived at the beginning of the second millennium BCE.

ABRAHAM, APOCALYPSE OF: Jewish pseudepigraphic work of the late 1st or 2nd cent. CE. The original was written in Hebrew or Aramaic but is extant only in a Slavonic translation. It relates the conversion of Abraham to monotheism, his destiny in heaven, and the ultimate fate of the nations of the world.

ABRAHAM, TESTAMENT OF: Jewish pseudepigraphic book, probably of the 2nd cent. CE, revised by Christians and extant in Greek versions. The work tells of Abraham's initiation into Divine mysteries before his death and of his ascension to paradise.

The Sacrifice of Isaac by Titian (Santa Maria della Salute, Venice).

ABRAHAM ABELE OF GOMBIN (c. 1635–c. 1683):
Polish talmudist and rabbi of Kalish. His authoritative work *Magen Avraham*, a partial commentary on the *Shulḥan Arukh*, exercised a profound influence on Ashkenazi practice.

ABRAHAM BAR ḤIYYA (*Ha-Nasi*, called Abraham Judaeus and Savasorda [*Saḥib es-Sorta:* an official title] in non-Jewish literature; fl. early 12th cent.):
Spanish translator, scientist, encyclopedist, and philosopher. He was author of Hebrew works on astronomy, geography, and moral philosophy, including: *Hegyon ha-Nephesh Ha-Atzuvah* ("Meditation of the Sad Soul"), an ethical work influenced by Neoplatonism, and *Megillat ha-Megalleh* ("Scroll of the Revealer"), which forecast the advent of the Messiah in 1358. He also assisted in the translation of scientific works from Arabic into Latin. A. laid the foundations of Hebrew scientific terminology, and was an important figure in the transmission of Greco-Arab science to the Christian world.

ABRAHAM BEN ALEXANDER KATZ OF KALISK (d. 1810): Ḥasidic rabbi. He studied under Elijah of Vilna but later joined the Ḥasidic movement. He represented the popular elements in Ḥasidism, but the strange rites practiced by his followers aroused widespread opposition. In 1777, he led the emigration of 300 Ḥasidim from Russia to Palestine together with Menahem Mendel of Vitebsk.

ABRAHAM BEN DAVID PORTALEONE see **PORTALEONE**

ABRAHAM BEN DAVID OF POSQUIÈRES (known as *Ravad;* 1120–1198): French talmudist. A wealthy man, he was imprisoned by the lord of Posquières for purposes of extortion, and probably owed his release to the intervention of the count of Carcassonne. A. is particularly famed for his strictures *(Hassagot)* on Maimonides' *Mishneh Torah* to which he strongly objected because he feared that such codes might supplant the study of the Talmud. He composed similar notes on the writings of Alfasi and Zerahiah Ha-Levi.

ABRAHAM BEN ELIJAH OF VILNA (1750–1808): Russian talmudist; son of Elijah of Vilna. He was particularly noted for his enlightened researches into homiletic literature. His edition of *Aggadat Bereshit* contains the first attempt at a complete history of midrashic literature, while his *Rav Pealim* is a critical index to 130 Midrashim.

ABRAHAM BEN ḤASDAI HA-LEVI see **IBN ḤASDAI**

ABRAHAM BEN ISAAC BEN GARTON (fl. 15th cent.): Printer of the first dated Hebrew book—Rashi's commentary on the Pentateuch (Reggio di Calabria, 1475). The only extant copy of this edition (incomplete) is in the Palatine Library, Parma.

ABRAHAM BEN ISAAC OF NARBONNE (known as *Ravad* II; 1110–1179): French talmudist. His *Ha-Eshkol* ("The Cluster") was the first work of codification produced in S France and remained authoritative in France and Italy until the time of Jacob ben Asher.

ABRAHAM BEN MEIR DE BALMES see **BALMES**

ABRAHAM BEN MOSES BEN MAIMON (1186–1237): Court physician to the Sultan Alkamil; son of Moses Maimonides. A. wrote many works in Arabic including *Kitab Kifayat al-Abidin* ("Book of Satisfaction for the Godfearing")—an encyclopedic work on Judaism—and commentaries on the Pentateuch, the Talmud, and his father's books. As *Nagid* of Egyptian Jewry, in succession to his father, he issued ordinances to strengthen the community.

ABRAHAM BEN NATHAN HA-YARḤI (i.e. "of Lunel"; c. 1155–c. 1215): French talmudist. His *Ha-Manhig* ("The Guide") is historically important for its description of special synagogal usages prevalent in France, Germany, England, and Spain and for its literal quotations from many lost rabbinic sources.

ABRAHAM BEN SAMUEL ḤASDAI see **IBN ḤASDAI**

ABRAHAM BEN SAMUEL ZACUT (ZACUTO) see **ZACUTO**

ABRAHAM IBN DAUD see **IBN DAUD**

ABRAHAM IBN EZRA see **IBN EZRA**

ABRAHAM IBN ḤASDAI see **IBN ḤASDAI**

ABRAHAM IBN TIBBON see **IBN TIBBON**

ABRAHAM JOSHUA HESHEL ("The Rabbi of Opatov"; c. 1745–1825): Polish Ḥasidic leader, rabbi of Kolbuszov, Opatov, and Jassy. His sermons were inspired by the Baal Shem Tov's teachings, and stress love for Israel and its unity, as well as the belief in the transmigration of souls. He believed that he himself had passed through various incarnations (high priest, prince, king, etc.).

ABRAHAM, KARL (1877–1925): Psychoanalyst. He was one of the pioneers of psychoanalysis in Germany and was president of the International Psychoanalytic Association.

ABRAHAMS: English family. (1) *SIR ADOLPHE A.* (1884–1967): Physician and author of works on medical and athletic subjects. (2) *HAROLD MAURICE A.* (1899–): Athlete and barrister; brother of (1). He represented Britain at the Olympic games of 1920, 1924 (when he won the 100 meters race), and 1928 (when he captained the British team). He was secretary of the National Parks Commission and from 1969 chairman of the British Amateur Athletic Board. (3) *SIR SIDNEY SOLOMON A.* (1885–1957): Brother of (1) and (2). He was chief justice of Uganda (1933), Tanganyika (1934–6), and Ceylon (1936–9). A. represented Britain at the Olympic games (1906, 1912), and was amateur broad-jumping champion (1913).

ABRAHAMS, ISRAEL (1858–1925): English scholar and Hebraist. With Claude Montefiore, A. founded and edited (1888–1908) the JEWISH QUARTERLY REVIEW. He advanced the cause of Liberal Judaism in England. A. served on the faculty of Jews' College from 1891 until 1902 when he became reader in rabbinics at Cambridge. He was among the early proponents of the idea of a Hebrew Univ. in Jerusalem. His works include *Jewish Life in the Middle Ages* and *Studies in Pharisaism and the Gospels.* He edited *Hebrew Ethical Wills.*

ABRAHAMS, ISRAEL (1903–1973): Rabbi. He held ministerial positions in London and Manchester. From 1937 chief rabbi of Cape Town, and from 1951, of Cape Province. In 1968, he settled in Jerusalem.

ABRAM, MORRIS BERTHOLD (1918–): U.S. attorney. He was born in Fitzgerald, Georgia, and went into legal practice. He was active in the civil rights movement and in 1964 became president of the American Jewish Committee. From 1968–70 he was president of Brandeis University.

ABRAMOWITSCH, SHALOM JACOB (pen-name Mendele Mocher Sephorim; c. 1836–1917). Hebrew and Yiddish author. Born in White Russia, he studied at yeshivot, began to write lyrics, and wandered through Volhynia, eventually (1853) settling at Kamenetz-Podolsk. He began to publish articles in Hebrew periodicals and in 1858, moved to Berdichev. In 1862–

Shalom Jacob Abramowitsch (Mendele Mocher Sephorim), center; at his left — Bialik and Frug, and at his right — An-ski and Ravnitsky.

72, he issued (in Hebrew) his 3-volume *Natural History* which was greatly influenced by Haskalah and positivist views. In 1863, he published in Hebrew his first short story, but then, turning to Yiddish, wrote *The Little Man, The Wishing Ring,* and *Fathers and Sons* (an adaptation of an earlier story in Hebrew), a contemporary love-story describing the clash between orthodoxy and the younger generation. *Fishke the Lame* appeared in 1869, as did the sharply satirical *The Meat Tax* which incurred the wrath of the Berdichev communal leaders. As a result A. had to move to Zhitomir. *The Mare* (1873) was an allegory of Diaspora life and a protest against anti-Semitism. He translated the Psalms into Yiddish and in 1878, brought out (in Yiddish; Hebrew version in 1897) the humorous classic *The Travels of Benjamin III.* From 1881, A. was principal of the Talmud Torah at Odessa where he wrote the Yiddish drama *The Call-Up* and the Hebrew story *The Hidden Place of Thunder* on Jewish life in the pogrom period. His subsequent writings included *Shem and Japhet in the Chariot, No Joy in the House of Jacob,* an autobiographical novel *In Those Days* (Yiddish and Hebrew), and *In the Days of the Storm.* After the 1905 pogroms, he moved to Geneva and in 1908, returned to Odessa where he continued to write and also compiled his memoirs. A. collaborated with Bialik and Ravnitzky in translating the Pentateuch into

Yiddish. A. was the father of artistic prose literature in Hebrew and Yiddish, describing and often satirizing the Jewish masses of Europe in the later 19th cent. He laid the foundations of an artistic Hebrew style far removed from that previously accepted, and strove towards precision and naturalness. His influence was even more marked in Yiddish literature, the prose style of which he helped shape for a long time to come.

ABRAMS, ALBERT (1863–1924): US physician and medical author who practiced in his native San Francisco. The originator of a new method in the treatment of spinal disorders, he also devised a system of diagnosis and treatment of disease now familiar as the *Electronic Reactions of Abrams (ERA).*

ABRAMSON, ABRAHAM (1754–1811): Medalist and lapidary who revived the classical medal in 18th cent. Germany and executed medals for royalty and other leading figures; son of Jacob Abraham. In 1782, he was appointed Prussian court medalist.

ABRAVANEL (also written Abarbanel, etc.): Distinguished family of Spanish origin: the name is a diminutive of Abraham (through Abravam). (1) *ISAAC A.* (1437–1508): Statesman, philosopher, and Bible exegete. A. served as treasurer to Alfonso V of Portugal, but fled to Spain (1483) to escape charges of conspiracy leveled by Alfonso's son and successor against his father's ministers. In Toledo, he entered the service of Ferdinand and Isabella but was unable to avert the decree of expulsion from Spain (1492). He accompanied many of his fellow-exiles to Italy where he was employed by the court of Naples. After further tribulations which brought him to Sicily, Corfu, and Monopoli, he finally settled in Venice (1503), where he tried to negotiate a treaty with Portugal. His main importance derives from his voluminous literary works which include a commentary on the Bible (having considerable influence on 17th and 18th cent. Christian exegesis), philosophical works of an essentially anti-rationalist nature, and religious writings that stressed the primacy for Judaism of the belief in Divine Revelation and the Messiah. The latter works influenced the messianic movements of the 16th and 17th cents. (2) *JUDAH A.* known as Leone Ebreo (c. 1460–c. 1521): Philosopher and physician; son of (1) whom he accompanied to Italy. His *Dialoghi d'Amore* ("Dialogues of Love"; written 1502, first published 1535) strives to combine Neoplatonism and Judaism; it stresses the concept of Love as the foundation of the universe and the key to union with God. The book was translated into a number of languages, including Hebrew, and exercised a great influence on the lyric poetry of 16th cent. Italy, France, and Germany.

Frontispiece of the French translation of Judah Abravanel's *Dialoghi d'Amore* with a cut of the author (Lyons, 1595).

(3) *SAMUEL A.* (1473–1547): Financier; son of (1). He was long the head of the Jewish community in Naples, settling in Ferrara after the expulsion of the Jews from that kingdom (1541). He and his wife Bienvenida (d. 1560) were literary patrons.

ABRAVANEL, DAVID DORMIDO see **DORMIDO, DAVID ABRAVANEL**

ABSALOM: Third son of David. He killed his half-brother Amnon to avenge the rape of his sister Tamar. A. exploited his personal popularity by stirring up a rebellion against David who was obliged to flee across the Jordan. Ultimately, A's. army was vanquished and he himself killed by JOAB after his long hair became entangled in a tree (II Sam. 13–19). In rabbinic literature, his career is cited as a striking example of vanity and rebellion. A monument in the Valley of Kidron outside Jerusalem is traditionally called A.'s tomb (*Yad Avshalom*) but is, in fact, a structure of the 1st cent. BCE or CE.

ABSALOM (d. 66): Patriot leader. At the beginning of the revolt against the Romans he was associated with the Zealot chief MENAHEM BEN JUDAH in the military operations in Jerusalem, but was killed in the subsequent civil disturbances. His followers then became inactive.

ABSTINENCE see **ASCETICISM**

ABU GOSH: Israel Arab village, 9 km. W of Jerusalem; on the site of KIRJATH JEARIM. The Crusader church built on a Roman foundation is still in use. A.G. is named after a robber sheikh who controlled the neighbourhood in the 18th cent. Pop. (1972): 1,910.

ABU IMRAN OF TIFLIS see **TIFLISI, ABU IMRAN**

ABU ISSA AL-ISFAHANI (8th cent.): Persian sectary and pseudo-messiah at Isfahan. A. declared himself the immediate forerunner of the Messiah, prohibited divorce, meat-eating, and the drinking of wine, decreed seven daily prayers (instead of three), and acknowledged the prophecies of Jesus and Mohammed. About 755, he led his supporters, numbering some 10,000, in a rebellion against the Abbasid rulers, failed, and was killed in battle. His followers, however, believed that he had hidden in a cave and would reappear some day to redeem Jews from their oppressors. The sect named after him, the Issawites, was gradually absorbed by the Karaites; a small Issawite community existed in Damascus until the 10th cent.

ABUDARHAM (also **ABUDRAHIM**), **DAVID BEN JOSEPH** (14th cent.): Spanish talmudic scholar whose commentary on synagogue liturgy *Sepher Abudarham* ("The Book of A.") provided a vast store of explanations of the prayerbook culled from a variety of rabbinic sources. The book, first published at Lisbon in 1490, was frequently reprinted.

ABULAFIA: Name of a widespread family of Spanish origin, meaning "Father of Health" (in Arabic): sometimes Bolaffio, Bolaffi, etc. (1) *ABRAHAM BEN SAMUEL A.* (1241–after 1291): Kabbalist and pseudo-

First page of *Sepher Abudarham* (Lisbon, 1490).

messiah. He traveled widely in Palestine, Greece, and Italy, returning to Spain where he proclaimed himself a prophet. In 1280, he went to Rome to attempt the conversion of Pope Nicholas III to Judaism, and was saved from death at the stake only by the pope's sudden decease. A. incurred the enmity of the rabbis, led by Solomon ben Adret, by his prophecies of imminent redemption and his alleged messianic pretensions. He created a new tendency in Kabbalah—a striving for the prophetic spirit through GEMATRIA and the use of abbreviations under the influence of the SEPHER YETZIRAH. (2) *HAYYIM BEN MOSES* (?) *A.* (1660–1744): After serving as chief rabbi of Smyrna (1720–40), he spent the remaining years of his life in restoring the desolated city of Tiberias. (3) *HAYYIM NISSIM A.* (1775–1861): Rabbi and communal leader. He worked to improve the lot of the Jews of Tiberias and Safed, gaining protection for them against unfriendly neighboring sheikhs. He was appointed *Hakham Bashi* in Jerusalem in 1854. (4) *MEIR BEN TODROS HA-LEVI A.* (c. 1170–1244): Talmudic scholar and poet, teaching in Toledo. He opposed Maimonides. (5) *SAMUEL BEN MEIR HA-LEVI A.* (c. 1320–1361): Financier and philanthropist. Treasurer to Pedro the Cruel, king of Castile, he was ultimately arrested and executed for unknown reasons. Several synagogues were built in Castile through his generosity, among them the *Sinagoga del Transito* in Toledo, the walls of which preserve Hebrew inscriptions ex-

tolling his good deeds. His home still stands in Toledo. (6) *SAMUEL HA-LEVI A.* (fl. 13th cent.): Physician and scientist of Toledo. He invented a water-clock and translated a book on the candle-watch from Arabic into Spanish for Alfonso X of Castile. (7) *TODROS BEN JOSEPH A.* (c. 1225–1298): Astronomer and kabbalist. He lived in Toledo, was influential in the court of Alfonso X, and wrote halakhic interpretations and a mystical commentary on talmudic legends. (8) *TODROS BEN JUDAH A.* (1247–after 1295): Hebrew poet whose verses throw much light on contemporary conditions in Castile. More than 1,000 poems have been collected in his diwan, illustrating his tendency to mischievousness, pleasure, and eroticism.

ABYSSINIA see **ETHIOPIA**

ACADEMY (Heb. YESHIVAH; Aram. *metivta*): Name generally given to a higher school of Jewish learning in PALESTINE and BABYLONIA, where rabbinic studies were pursued. The Palestinian schools, which were already in existence in Second Temple times, took on added importance after the fall of Jerusalem, becoming the central authority of the Jewish people. The first academy founded after 70 CE was that set up by JOHANAN BEN ZAKKAI at JABNEH; this succeeded to the authority of the Great Sanhedrin. Later, others sprang up under the leadership of great scholars, such as that at LYDDA under ELIEZER BEN HYRCANUS, and that at PEKIIN under JOSHUA BEN HANANIAH. After the Bar Kokhba rebellion and the catastrophic decline in the population of Judea, the center of Jewish learning moved north, to Galilee. The central school of authority was at USHA, where the pupils of R Akiva were prominent. Later it moved to SHEPHARAM, then to BET SHEARIM, and finally to SEPPHORIS. It was at this last-mentioned place that R JUDAH HA-NASI compiled the Mishnah. After his death, the center moved to TIBERIAS which remained the chief Palestinian school

Interior of the *Sinagoga del Transito* built by Samuel Abulafia.

of Jewish learning for centuries. It was here that the Jerusalem Talmud and, later, the Masorah were compiled. In Babylonia, the principal seats of Jewish learning during tannaitic times were at NISIBIS and NEHAR PEKOD. A flourishing period began in the 3rd cent. when RAV and SAMUEL presided over two schools—Samuel at the academy established after the Bar Kokhba revolt by Palestinian refugees at NEHARDEA, and RAV at the institution which he founded at SURA. The Babylonian tradition of two colleges of equal rank continued almost until the end of the Gaonic Period. After the destruction of Nehardea in 259, a new school was set up at PUMBEDITA. The Babylonian Talmud was edited at Sura by R ASHI and his successor RAVINA at the close of the 5th cent. Throughout the period of the SAVORAIM and GEONIM and until the rise of new Jewish centers of learning in N Africa and Europe, the supremacy of the a.'s at Sura and Pumbedita was recognized by all Jewry. Their real importance ended in the 11th cent., but they continued to exist until the 13th. The title "academy" was given to a Jewish body set up in Ferrara in the 16th cent. and to various poetical societies in Amsterdam in the 17th. In more recent years a.'s for Jewish studies have been active in Germany, Israel, the US, etc.

ACADEMY OF HEBREW LANGUAGE: Official Israel scientific institution founded by Knesset law in 1953. Its function is the direction of the correct development of the Hebrew language, taking over the work of the VAAD HA-LASHON. It has 18 members and its committees work on determining Hebrew vocabulary, syntax, and pronunciation as well as on preparing lexicons, etc. It publishes the journal *Leshonenu*. The president of the A. since its foundation has been N.H.TUR-SINAI.

ACADEMY ON HIGH: The Talmud and later Jewish literature refer to a heavenly A. constituted by those who studied the Torah on earth and those who supported their studies. To be "called to the A. on H." is thus a euphemism for death, and A. itself another name for Paradise. God presides over its deliberations, in which the study of the Law is continued.

ACCAD see **AKKAD**

ACCENTS (Heb. *te'amim, neginot*): System of notation serving in the Hebrew Bible both as punctuation and as musical symbols. A. mark divisions of sentences and indicate stress inasmuch as many of them are placed upon the tone-syllable of the word. They are divided into disjunctive a. *(melakhim)* which indicate various degrees of pause, and conjunctive signs *(mesharetim)* which indicate absence of pause. The sequence of these signs is governed by strict rules. They are of great help for the proper understanding of biblical sentences. As musical notations, each accent conveys a particular grouping of notes, and the type of chant thus produced is called cantillation. Different Jewish communities reflect varying musical styles, the

Sephardim showing oriental influence and the Ashkenazim, European. There is a difference in the cantillation for the Pentateuchal and Prophetical readings, while the system of a. in the books of Psalms, Proverbs, and Job differs from that in other books because of the shorter verses, frequency of tristiches, etc. Tradition attributes both VOCALIZATION and accentuation to Ezra, and certainly the oral transmission of proper pausal stops and musical declamation is very old. The written signs, moreover, date from the second half of the first millennium CE, and resemble the Syriac system of accentuation (itself a development of the Greek system of *ekphonesis* found in lectionaries from the 5th cent. onward). To the three systems of vocalization—Babylonian, Palestinian, and Tiberian—correspond three systems of a. In the first two systems there are only disjunctive a.; it is the third, however, which has obtained general currency.

אֵלוּ שְׁמוֹת הַטְּעָמִים
פַּשְׁטָא מֶנַח זַרְקָא מֶנַח סָגוֹל מֶנַח ו מֶנַח רְבִיעַ
מַהְפַּךְ פַּשְׁטָא זָקֵף קָטֹן זָקֵף גָּדוֹל מֵרְכָא טִפְחָא
מֶנַח אֶתְנַחְתָּא פָּזֵר תְּלִישָׁא קְטַנָּה תְּלִישָׁא
נְדוֹלָה קַדְמָא וְאַזְלָא אַזְלָא גֵּרֵשׁ גֵּרְשַׁיִם דַּרְגָּא
תְּבִיר יְתִיב פְּסִיק ו סוֹף־פָּסוּק : שַׁלְשֶׁלֶת קַרְנֵי־
פָּרָה מֵרְכָא־כְפוּלָה יָרֵחַ בֶּן־יוֹמוֹ :

Ashkenazi names of accents for punctuation and cantillation.

ACCIDENT (legal): An unexpected happening not due to negligence or malfeasance. The basic rule for a. in Jewish law is derived from Deut. 22:27, which indicates clearly that a person is not to be held liable if he commits a criminal offense under the pressure of superior force. An a. is normally regarded as the equivalent of superior force. Accidental homicide, which sometimes entailed the penalty of exile to a City of Refuge, constituted the sole exception to this rule. If a person accidentally causes loss or damage to another person or to property, this does not normally exempt him from liability. Most authorities consider, however, that sheer unforeseeable a. exempts even in this case. Again a. always exempts if the basis of the liability is rabbinic and scriptural. If a mishap—illness or death—prevents one of the parties from fulfilling a condition in a commercial contract, no penalty attaching to non-fulfilment can be enforced. The degree of liability of a bailee for a.'s varies with the status of the bailee. In all cases, initial negligence makes a subsequent plea of a. unacceptable.

ACHAN: Member of the tribe of Judah who, on the capture of Jericho by Joshua, secretly took some of the consecrated spoil (Josh. 7). This sacrilege led to the failure of the Israelites to capture Ai. When A's guilt was discovered by casting lots, he and his family were put to death.

ACHER, MATTATHIAS see **BIRNBAUM, NATHAN**

*ACHISH (fl. 11th–10th cents. BCE): Philistine king. Owing to the proximity of his realm to the frontier of Judah, refugees such as David sought asylum with him. A. led the Philistine army at the battle of Mt. Gilboa in which Saul was killed. He continued to reign after David's conquest of Philistia.

ACHRON, JOSEPH (1886–1943): Composer and violinist. A pupil of Auer, he rapidly acquired a reputation as a virtuoso, but began to devote himself primarily to musical composition. He was a founder of the Society for Jewish Folk Music (1911) in St. Petersburg. A. settled in the US in 1925. His compositions include *Hebrew Melody,* for violin and piano, and violin concertos and string quartets inspired by Jewish motifs.

ACHZIB (Keziv in Mishnah): Ancient Canaanite port, N of Acre. Although allotted to the tribe of Asher, it was only captured for the Israelites by David. In late Second Temple times, it was a stopping-place for travelers and its population mainly Jewish. In modern times A. was the Arab village A-Zib. The site was excavated in 1941–4 and 1959–64. Remains were found from ancient times to the Crusader Period. SE stands the kibbutz of GESHER HA-ZIV.

ACOSTA (DA COSTA), URIEL (originally Gabriel; c. 1585–1640): Religious skeptic: born in Oporto of Marrano parents. With his mother and brothers, he fled to Amsterdam to profess Judaism openly (c. 1615). There, however, he became perturbed because Jewish practice was not in accordance with the literal meaning of Scripture. In 1616, while residing in Hamburg, he wrote in Portuguese and sent to Venice his eleven theses attacking Jewish tradition. A controversy ensued, and A. was excommunicated by the rabbis of Hamburg and Venice (1618), and later by those of Amsterdam. On returning to Amsterdam, he wrote works in which he denied the validity of the Oral Law and the doctrines of immortality, resurrection, and reward and punishment. These were confiscated and destroyed by the Dutch courts, which found them to contain heresies against the basic tenets of Christianity.

Coat of Arms of Acosta (Da Costa) Family.

A. remained under the ban for 15 years, but, impelled by poverty and isolation, he publicly recanted. He soon came under renewed suspicion of heresy and was excommunicated a second time (1633). He again recanted and was forced to undergo the penance of flogging and other degradations (1640). These humiliations were too much for him, and he committed suicide. Shortly before his death, A. wrote a brief but bitter autobiography *Exemplar Humanae Vitae.* The story of A. has formed the subject of several literary works.

ACRA: Fortress in Jerusalem; exact site uncertain but probably on the western hill. After Antiochus IV Epiphanes occupied the city (168 BCE), his commander built A., in which he placed a Greek garrison and in which the hellenized Jews took up residence. When Judah the Maccabee captured Jerusalem (165 BCE), he failed to take A. The fortress continued in Greek occupation until 142 BCE when it was occupied by Simon the Hasmonean, and the Greek garrison and Hellenizers who had escaped there were expelled.

ACRE (Heb. *Akko*): Israel town located at the N extremity of Haifa Bay. Owing to the convenience of its harbor, its situation on an easily fortified peninsula, and its proximity to the Jezreel Valley, A. was an important commercial town in the 15th cent. BCE. It was also a center of glass manufacture and a purple-dyeing industry. Although assigned to the tribe of Asher, it remained in gentile hands and was not included in the sanctified area of the country. A colony of Greek merchants lived there before the time of Alexander the Great and A. subsequently became a hellenistic city. Ptolemy II of Egypt called it Ptolemais by which name it was known until the Moslem conquest (638). It continually persecuted its Jewish neighbors and during the War against Rome, 2,000 Jewish inhabitants were massacred (66 CE). The community was, however, reconstituted in mishnaic times. A., like other coastal towns, declined under the Moslems and became again of importance under the Crusaders, who named it St. Jean d'Acre. From 1191 to 1291 A. was the Crusader capital of Palestine and again harbored a Jewish community. In the 1740's the Bedouin sheikh Dahir al-Ummar, who controlled Galilee, made his capital at A. which he rebuilt. He favored Jewish settlement and A. became the home of a small community. In 1775–1804 it was controlled by the brutal Aḥmed el-Jazzar whose treasurer was the Jew Ḥayyim Farḥi. During this period Napoleon besieged but failed to capture A. owing to the covering fire afforded by British warships (1799). In 1832–40, A. was taken by the Egyptians under Ibrahim Pasha and, in 1918, was captured from the Turks by the British. At the termination of the British mandate (1948), A. was an Arab town of 12,000 inhabitants, most of whom fled during the battle for the city. With its wall, beautiful mosque (erected by el-Jazzar), and view of Haifa Bay,

View of Acre.

it is among the most picturesque of Israel towns. Pop. (1975): 34,800 (of whom c. 9,000 were Arabs).

ACROSTICS: Literary device. Alphabetic a. (probably intended as an aid to memory) are found in the Bible (e.g. Ps. 34, 37; Prov. 31:10–31; Lam. 1–4). Most medieval hymns used alphabetic a. in a variety of combinations (sometimes reversed) or a. to spell out the names of persons, verses from the Bible, etc.; the practice is employed in many of the medieval liturgical compositions. Like other letter-combinations, a. are of especial importance in Kabbalah.

ACSÁDY, IGNÁC (1845–1906): Hungarian historian and journalist who laid the foundations of the modern approach to economic history in Hungary. A prolific writer, the author of novels, essays, and dramas, he also wrote extensively on the history of Jews in Hungary and ardently championed the cause of equal rights for the Jews of his native land.

ACTIONS COMMITTEE: The Zionist General Council; see ZIONISM.

AD MEAH [VE-ESRIM] SHANAH (Heb. "until a hundred [and twenty] years"): Expression of good wishes on the occasion of the birthday anniversary, etc. of an elderly person.

ADAFINA (Arab. "put away"): Word used in medieval Spain and still in N Africa to denote the food eaten by Jews on Sabbath *(Ḥamin)*. Eating a. was regarded by the Inquisition as a symptom of Judaism.

ADALBERG, SAMUEL (1868–1939): Writer and educator; advisor for Jewish religious affairs in the Polish Ministry of Culture and Education (1918). He published (1889–94) a collection of 40,000 Polish proverbs and idioms. He lost his life in a concentration camp.

ADAM: The biblical name of the first man (Heb. *adam*=man) and progenitor of the human race, according to biblical tradition. Made in the image of God from the dust of the earth on the sixth day of creation, he was given dominion over the rest of the animate world. Subsequently, woman was created out of one of his ribs, being intended as "a help meet for him." A. was placed in the Garden of Eden to tend it, and permitted to eat of the fruit of all the trees save that conferring knowledge of good and evil. Seduced by the serpent, both Adam and Eve ate of the forbidden fruit, and became conscious of their nakedness, to cover which they made girdles of fig-leaves. For this act of disobedience (A.'s sin, original sin), they were expelled from the Garden, man was condemned to a life of toil, and woman to the pangs of childbirth. A. lived for 930 years and became the father of many children who lived in different parts of the earth (thus demonstrating the unity of mankind). Talmudic literature abounds with legends connected with A. (e.g. "A. was created from dust gathered from the whole world," "His head was made of earth from the Holy Land, his body from Babylonia, and the various members from different lands"). The Kabbalah also devoted much attention to the subject of ADAM KADMON.

ADAM, BOOK OF: Pseudepigraphic book, probably written originally in Hebrew or Aramaic, extant in Greek, Latin, and Slavonic versions. The book relates the lives of Adam and Eve after the expulsion from Eden, their repentance, death, and promised resurrection. There are also several "Books of Adam" of Christian origin.

ADAM HA-COHEN see **LEBENSOHN, A.D.**

ADAM KADMON (Heb. "Primeval Man"): Kabbalistic term applied to the spiritual prototype of man, existing as an incorporeal intelligence. The Zohar considers A.K. (*Adam Ilaa* in the Zohar) a manifestation of the SEPHIROT (or of one of them), but in the Kabbalah of Isaac Luria it assumes the role of mediator between God (the *En Soph*) and the *sephirot*.

*ADAMS, HANNAH (c. 1755–1831): U.S. author. Her sympathetic *History of the Jews* (1812) was the first such work to be published in America.

Detail from *The Creation of Adam* by Michelangelo. (From the ceiling of the Sistine Chapel, Rome).

ADAR: 12th month of the Jewish religious year, 6th of the civil; approximating to Feb.-Mar. In the event of a leap year, a 13th month, *Adar Sheni* (Second Adar), is intercalated and assumes a superior status to First A. Thus, the holidays associated with the month are transferred from First to Second A. The 7th day of the month, according to tradition, commemorates the birth and death of Moses. The 13th is *Taanit Ester* (The Fast of Esther), the 14th is Purim, and the 15th Shushan Purim. The name A. is of Assyrian origin.

ADAT ISRAEL (or **ADAS YISROEL**): Name of several Orthodox Jewish communities. The one founded in Berlin in 1869 had three synagogues and a school system by 1927. Similar communities were founded in London, New York, and E European Jewish centers.

ADDIR BI-MELUKHAH (Heb. "Mighty in Kingship"): Alphabetic acrostic poem introduced into the Haggadah by Ashkenazim in the Middle Ages. It is based on *Genesis Rabbah* 6:2.

ADDIR HU (Heb. "Mighty Is He"): Alphabetic acrostic prayer for the rebuilding of the Temple, added to the Haggadah in 15th cent. Germany. In Provence it served as a festival song without reference to Passover.

ADDITIONAL SERVICE see **MUSAPH**

ADELAIDE: Capital of S Australia. A pioneer in settling the city was Jacob Montefiore (a brother of Sir Moses Montefiore) who was appointed com-missioner by William IV. The Jewish community was founded in 1848. The synagogue built in 1850, was reconstructed in 1870. Jews were prominent pioneers in commercial spheres, and Sir Vabian L. Solomon, premier of the State in 1899, was a member of the community. Sir Lewis Cohen served as A.'s mayor and lord mayor ten times. Despite immigration, the community's numbers have decreased over the past 50 years. Jewish pop. (1974): 1,600.

ADEN: Port in South Arabia. Jews were resident there from remote times. After the British annexation in 1838, their number rose rapidly through immigration—mainly from Yemen—and at one time there were some 5,000 Jews in the town and perhaps 2,000 more in the remainder of the protectorate. There were serious attacks by the local Arab population in 1947. After the establishment of the state of Israel (when A. served as the base for Operation Magic Carpet), most of the Jews there emigrated. Anti-Jewish manifestations increased as the British protectorate drew to its end and the last Jews left A. at the time of the Arab-Jewish tension in the summer of 1967.

ADIABENE: Ancient district in N Mesopotamia. In the 1st cent. BCE, A. became an independent kingdom. Its queen, Helena, was converted to Judaism (c. 30 CE) with her sons, Kings Monobaz ii and Izates, who supported the Jews during the war against the Romans (66–70). The Tombs of the Kings in Jerusalem was their burial place.

Nathan Marcus Adler.

ADLER: Family of British rabbis and scholars. (1) *NATHAN MARCUS A.* (1803–1890): Of German birth, he was chief rabbi of the British Empire from 1845. A. introduced modern standards into the British ministry and may be regarded as the creator of the British Chief Rabbinate in the present-day sense. His unifying activities led to the establishment of JEWS' COLLEGE (1855) and the creation of the UNITED SYNAGOGUE in London (1870). A. was an early leader of *Hoveve Zion* and a staunch proponent of Orthodoxy. He wrote a Hebrew commentary to Targum Onkelos, *Netinah la-Ger.* (2) *HERMANN A.* (1839–1911): Son and successor of (1), he received his secular education in German universities. He served as principal of Jews' College, 1862–91, succeeding his father as chief rabbi in 1891. A. continued his father's interest in the *Hoveve Zion* movement, visiting Palestine (1885) in its behalf, and was a leading spokesman for British Jewry. (3) *ELKAN NATHAN A.* (1861–1946): Lawyer, bibliophile, and collector of Hebrew mss; youngest son of (1). By virtue of his profession, A. was a world-traveler who acquired on his extensive journeys the greatest Hebrew library in private hands in the world. His entire collection of mss, numbering well over 5,000, was acquired by the Jewish Theological Seminary of America (1923, 1947). His works include a *History of the Jews in London, About Hebrew Manuscripts,* and *Jewish Travelers.*

ADLER: Austrian family. (1) *FRIEDRICH A.* (1879–1960): Socialist; son of (2). After lecturing in physics at Zurich Univ. (1907–11), he returned to Austria, was sentenced to death for his assassination of the Austrian prime minister Count Stürgkh, an act of protest against the war (1916), but was amnestied in 1918. In 1921, he founded the Viennese Socialist International. After the suppression of Austrian Social Democracy (1934), he left Vienna and continued his Socialist activity in Europe and America. (2) *VICTOR A.* (1852–1918): A doctor by profession, he founded the Austrian Social Democratic Party (1888) and led its moderate wing. A., who was baptized, became the editor of the influential Socialist daily *Arbeiter-Zeitung* (1894) and won his greatest political victory when the Imperial government granted universal suffrage (1905). He was a member of the Austrian parliament, 1905–18, and in 1918 served for a few days as foreign minister in the revolutionary government.

ADLER: US family. (1) *FELIX A.* (1851–1933): Founder, leader, and philosopher of the Ethical Culture movement; son of (2). He prepared for the rabbinate, but broke with Judaism after study in Germany. He was professor of Semitics at Cornell Univ., 1874–6, but left the university to form the New York Society for Ethical Culture (1876), later also becoming professor of ethics at Columbia Univ., 1902–28. He considered Ethical Culture an application of Judeo-Christian morality to contemporary life. In keeping with this philosophy, A. pioneered in progressive education, and later was national chairman of the National Child Labor Commission, 1904–21. He became a member of the State Tenement House Commission (1888), and was active in the formation of the committee that exposed corruption in New York in 1901. His most complete statement of his philosophical position is to be found in *An Ethical Philosophy of Life.* (2) *SAMUEL A.* (1809–1891): Reform rabbi. At Alzey, Germany (1842–57), A. played a leading role in the struggle for Jewish emancipation and religious reform. In 1857, he became rabbi of Temple Emanu-El in New York. He wrote numerous monographs, a collection of which appeared under the title *Kovetz al Yad.*

ADLER: US theatrical family. (1) *JACOB A.* (1855–1926): He began his acting career in Russia in 1878 with the Goldfaden troupe. After the Russian government banned the Yiddish theater, he went to London (1883) and thereafter to America (1888) where he became the most important figure on the Yiddish stage. A. first established himself as a romantic lead; but thereafter, in close collaboration with the Yiddish playwright, Jacob Gordin, began to produce and act in plays of a more serious character, thus contributing materially to raising the standard of the Yiddish theater. (2) *LUTHER A.* (1903–), son of (1) and (3), established a reputation in the Group Theater's productions of Clifford Odets' works, and has appeared in many plays and films. (3) *SARAH A.* (c. 1858–1953), wife of (1), was a leading member of her husband's troupe. (4) *STELLA A.* (1902–), daughter of (1) and (3), first appeared in her father's troupe and later became a member of the Group Theater.

ADLER, ALFRED (1870–1937): Austrian psychologist and physician. Originally a disciple of Freud,

Cyrus Adler.

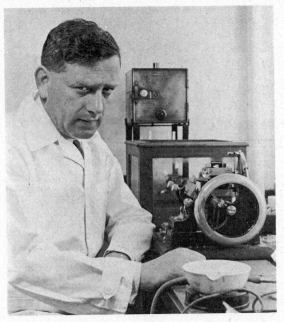

Saul Adler.

he formulated his own theory of "Individual Psychology" which influenced medical, educational, and social theory. In 1934, he settled in the U.S. He taught that human nature is influenced by the conflict between the individual's will to survive and his social feelings; and by the necessity of reaching a compromise between them. The inferiority complex, at its greatest intensity in childhood, results in self-assertive tendencies and opposition to society; this causes psychological disturbances and demoralization. A.'s works include *The Neurotic Constitution* and *The Practice and Theory of Individual Psychology*. He was editor of the *International Journal of Individual Psychology*, 1935–7.

ADLER, CYRUS (1863–1940): US orientalist and communal leader. Instructor in Semitic languages at Johns Hopkins Univ.; director of the Ancient East Department of Washington National Museum, 1888–1909; librarian (1892–1905) and assistant secretary (1905–8) of the Smithsonian Institution. He was founder and member of numerous cultural and scientific societies including the American Jewish Historical Society and the Jewish Publication Society of America; president of the Jewish Theological Seminary, New York, and Dropsie College, Philadelphia; editor of the *Jewish Quarterly Review*, member of the editorial board of the *Jewish Encyclopaedia*, and editor of the *American Jewish Year Book*. He was a founder and president of the American Jewish Committee and the Jewish Welfare Board, and non-Zionist co-chairman of the Jewish Agency. His works include *Jews in the Diplomatic Correspondence of the US* and an autobiography *I Have Considered the Days*. Over a long period, he was one of the foremost influences in estab-

lishing the pattern of American Jewish cultural, philanthropic, and communal life.

ADLER, DANKMAR (1844–1900): US architect and engineer. Born in Germany, he went to the US in 1854. With his partner, Louis H. Sullivan, he promoted a new type of steel-frame building, thus playing an important role in developing the modern skyscraper. Among the buildings he designed were the Chicago Stock Market, Carnegie Hall in New York, and several synagogues.

ADLER, JANKEL (1895–1949): Painter. Born in Lodz, he later taught at the Academy for Modern Art at Dusseldorf. In 1935, he settled in France and ultimately in England. He evolved an artistic style based on Jewish folk tradition, and most of his early works were on Jewish subjects. His paintings are to be found in art galleries in many countries.

ADLER, JULIUS OCHS (1892–1955): US journalist and soldier. Associated with the *New York Times* from 1914, he was the general manager from 1935, retaining his previous positions of vice-president and treasurer, and in 1954 became first vice-president. A. was also president and publisher of the *Chattanooga Times*, 1935–55. Having distinguished himself in active military service in World Wars I and II, he was appointed brigadier-general (1941) and major-general (1948).

ADLER, LARRY (1914–): US harmonica virtuoso. He has elevated the playing of the mouth organ to a musical art, and leading composers have contributed to his repertoire.

ADLER, MAX (1873–1937): Sociologist. Professor of sociology in Vienna, he was a Socialist theoretician who tried to reconcile Marxist and Kantian philosophy. A member of the Austrian parliament 1920–3, in his later years he was attracted to Labor Zionism.

ADLER, NATHAN BEN SIMEON (1741–1800): German talmudist and kabbalist famed for his rigorous asceticism and mystic piety. He established his own yeshivah in Frankfort-on-Main where several rabbis, among them Moses Sopher, received their early training. His disciples constituted themselves a congregation in his home and adopted liturgical practices similar to those of the Ḥasidim. They soon came to believe in A.'s and their own miraculous powers. In 1779, these activities provoked strong rabbinical censure, and a ban was imposed on their prayer-meetings under threat of excommunication. A.'s tenure of a rabbinical position in Boskowitz (Moravia; 1782–5) was cut short by the enmity aroused by his practices. Returning to Frankfort, he reverted to his previous way of life and the ban, reimposed, remained in force until shortly before his death. His published works consist only of marginal glosses on the Mishnah, some of which were edited with a commentary by B. H. Auerbach under the title *Mishnat Rabbi Nathan*.

ADLER, SAUL (1895–1966): Israel parasitologist. He studied tropical medicine in England and conducted research in tropical diseases in Mesopotamia and Sierra Leone, 1921–4. He joined the faculty of the Hebrew Univ. in 1924, becoming professor and dean of the Institute of Parasitology in 1928. A. conducted several scientific surveys in the Near East and made notable contributions to the study of tropical disease.

ADLOYADA (Aram.): Purim carnival. The term derives from the rabbinic pleasantry that on Purim a man should celebrate until he reaches a point where he does not know *(ad de-la yeda)* the difference between Haman and Mordecai. In Israel the carnival usually consists of a parade of decorated floats through one of the city centers.

ADMON (GOROCHOV), YEDIDYAH (1896–): Israel composer. He was one of the first Israel musicians to capture the oriental atmosphere both in compositions (songs, stage music) and in performances.

ADMOR (initials of Heb. *Adonenu Morenu ve-Rabbenu* i.e. "Our Lord, Master, and Teacher"): The general appellation, especially in Hebrew contexts, of the Ḥasidic TZADDIK.

ADON OLAM (Heb. "Lord of the World"): Liturgical hymn to the Unity and Providence of God recited in many rites at the beginning of the morning liturgy, and/or at the close of the morning service, in

Tel Aviv Adloyada.

the night prayers, and also on the deathbed. Its authorship and date of composition are unknown, but it has been ascribed to Solomon Ibn Gabirol. Many musical settings have been composed for its liturgical use.

Adon Olam
(Old melody adapted by Ephraim Di-Zahav)

ADONAI, see **GOD, NAMES OF**

***ADONI-ZEDEK:** King of Jerusalem who led a coalition of five Amorite cities against the Gibeonites for making peace with Joshua at the time of the invasion of Canaan. Joshua defeated them, slaying the five kings who had taken refuge in a cave.

ADONIJAH: Fourth son of David. After Absalom's death he claimed the succession to the throne, with the support of Joab and Abiathar, but was unsuccessful. A. later sought to marry Abishag, David's concubine, but Solomon regarded this as an act of rebellion and had him killed (I Kings 1–2).

ADOPTION: Establishment of a parental relationship between persons other than parent and child. The legal conception is not found in the Bible or Talmud, but there are instances of voluntary a. (cf. Mordecai and Esther). The Talmud maintains exegetically, "Whoever teaches a child Torah has the right to be deemed its father." In the state of Israel, no a. legislation has yet been passed, although a. orders are made for minors in accordance with humane considerations.

ADORNO, THEODOR W. (1903–1969): Philosopher and sociologist. He worked in his native Germany until 1933 and in the U.S. from 1938, returning to Frankfurt in 1956. In his latter years, he exerted considerable influence on radical youth movements. He co-authored *The Authoritarian Personality*, an important analysis of Fascism.

ADOSHEM (=ADONAI+HA-SHEM): Artificially constructed word used in liturgical rehearsals, etc. to avoid pronouncing the Divine name.

ADRET, SOLOMON BEN (IBN) (known as *Rashba*; 1235–1310): Spanish rabbi. He lived in Barcelona and was long regarded as the leader of Spanish Jewry, even being spoken of as the "Rabbi of Spain." His halakhic responsa and decisions, which number well over 1,000 and were regarded as authoritative by later codifiers, constitute a valuable historical and cultural record of the period, since they deal with a wide variety of religious questions that came to him from many communities of Europe, Africa, and Asia Minor. A. was a leading figure in the controversies that agitated his times. He vigorously opposed the mystical excess and messianic pretensions of such men as Abraham

Abulafia. Toward the end of his life, he was drawn into the revived Maimonist controversy. Despite his reverence for Maimonides and his own philosophical interests, he joined the anti-rationalist faction and issued a ban against secular studies by students under the age of 30 (1305). A. also wrote in defense of Judaism against the attacks of the Dominican scholar, Raymond MARTINI, and the Moslem, Ibn Ḥazm, who maintained that the text of the Bible had been corrupted by the Jews.

ADRIANOPLE (Edirne): Turkish city. Jews are said to have been living in A. in the 2nd cent. CE. In the Byzantine period, severe restrictions were imposed on the community as elsewhere in the Empire. When the Turks captured A. (1361), the condition of the Jews improved, and in the 14th and 15th cents. there was a large migration of Jews to A., each national community setting up its own synagogue. Jews expelled from Spain constituted a majority from the 16th cent., and henceforth the other Jews followed Sephardi customs and spoke their language. The A. community became a center of learning and the home of distinguished scholars. The Sabbetaian movement found enthusiastic supporters here and it was the scene of Shabbetai Tzevi's apostasy. At the beginning of the 20th cent., there were 20,000 Jews in A. but by 1973 only 250 remained.

A Jewess of Adrianople. (From N. Nicolay's *Navigations en la Turquie*, 1577).

ADULTERY: As prohibited in the Decalogue (Exod. 20:13; Deut. 5:17), a. is halakhically defined as sexual intercourse between a man's wife and another man; punishment for both sinners is death (Lev. 20:10). In rabbinical law, an adulteress is prohibited both to her husband and to the adulterer; if the wife of a priest, she is prohibited even if the act has been committed against her will. A special ritual was prescribed for a woman suspected of having committed a. (SOTA).

ADUMIM see **ROSSI**

AEGEAN ISLANDS see **GREECE: RHODES**

AELIA CAPITOLINA: Name given by the Romans to Jerusalem when they rebuilt it after the Bar Kokhba revolt (135). It was named after the emperor P. Aelius Hadrianus (Hadrian) and the god Jupiter Capitolinus, in whose honor a temple was erected in the city. Jews were forbidden to enter A.C. except on the fast of *Av* 9.

Coin to commemorate the founding of Aelia Capitolina.

AELYON, SOLOMON see **AYLLON, SOLOMON**

AFAM: Abbreviation for Asti, Fossano, and Moncalvo, three communities in NW Italy, in which the ancient French prayer rite was followed, especially for the New Year and the Day of Atonement.

AFENDOPOLO, CALEB BEN ELIJAH (1464–1525): Karaite scholar who lived in Constantinople. He was a pupil of Mordecai COMTINO who instructed him in secular sciences and introduced him to the works of Maimonides. One of the most prolific of Karaite authors, he wrote on biblical, religious, scientific, philosophical, ethical, and other subjects, as well as composing poems and allegories.

AFGHANISTAN: Moslem kingdom in Central Asia some of the inhabitants of which believe themselves to be descended from the Lost Ten Tribes. The impoverished Jewish community, numbering about 200, is confined chiefly to three cities: Kabul, Herat, and Balkh. Jews were living in A. in early medieval times, but little is known of their fate after the 12th cent. The present community is a 19th cent. extension of the Persian community; most Afghan Jews speak Judeo-Persian, and their religious rites are those of Persian Jewry, but they do not study the Talmud. They have been untouched by modern influences and still live in a medieval atmosphere, confined in their ghettos and distinguishable by their black turbans. It is be-lieved there were some 40,000 Jews in A. a century ago, including many prosperous merchants. Successive governmental measures of repression after 1870 and in the mid-1930's drastically reduced the Jewish population. 4,500 have emigrated to Israel since the foundation of the State in 1948.

AFRICA, NORTH: Jewish history has been associated with this area since biblical days. There were probably Jewish military settlers in the service of the last Pharaohs, and at the time of the destruction of the First Temple (586) numerous fugitives found refuge in EGYPT. Ample records illustrate the life of the Jewish military colony at YEB in the 5th cent. BCE, and it was probably not unique. With the conquest of Egypt by the Greeks, the Jewish element increased very rapidly, Alexander the Great and his successors introducing Jewish settlers to colonize their new cities. ALEXANDRIA thus became, from the 3rd cent. BCE, one of the greatest seats of Jewish life and civilization. From Egypt, Jewish settlements spread westward along the Mediterranean littoral. By the 2nd cent. BCE, there was an important colony in CYRENE, and numerous inscriptions and literary monuments testify to the presence of Jews during the Roman period nearly as far west as the Straits of Gibraltar. Such was their strength and cohesion that the Egyptian Jews were able to organize a revolt after the fall of Jerusalem (70 CE), while those of Cyrene momentarily seized control of the entire province in 115. The intense rivalry between Jew and non-Jew in Egypt was enhanced with the growth and triumph of Christianity. The persecutions at the beginning of the 4th cent., instigated by the Patriarch Cyril, which ended the great tradition of Alexandrian Jewry in the classical age, were imitated elsewhere. Although farther west the Vandal invaders introduced a more tolerant policy (5th cent.), the Byzantine reconquest under Belisarius a century later reversed the process. A persistent tradition tells of the presence at this time of numerous independent or semi-independent tribes professing Judaism, of whom the FALASHAS of Ethiopia are the most prominent survivors. There was a general revival all over N Africa after the Moslem invasion (7th cent.) and the Jewish communities became thoroughly Arabicized in language, customs, and social habits. Egypt again became the seat of an important settlement, especially in the newly-built city of CAIRO. Farther west, KAIROUAN became a great center of Jewish learning. The appearance here of ELDAD HA-DANI (c. 883) suggests the existence at this time, too, of independent Jewish tribes inland. In the middle of the 12th cent., the ALMOHADES forbade the open practice of Judaism in MOROCCO and in the neighboring territories, this persecution leading to a considerable migration eastward to Egypt. In due course, the Almohades lost their power and N African Jewish life revived. The persecution in Spain in 1391 led to a large-

A Moroccan Jewess.

scale emigration across the Straits and introduced a
new Jewish element of a higher talmudic and general
culture. This was reinforced in succeeding years, and
especially in 1492, by more Spanish-speaking exiles
in large numbers. The Moslem anti-Jewish code continued to be enforced throughout N Africa (especially
in Morocco) with great strictness: the Jews were
confined to their own quarter (MELLAH), compelled
to wear black clothing, made to pay heavy taxes, and
treated with contumely. They were excluded from one
or two "Holy" Cities (e.g. Kairouan), and subject to
occasional massacres; however, generally they were
tolerated (if no more). The 19th cent. found them in a
position hardly different in any detail from that of
many generations previously. Meanwhile, the lot of the
Falashas had steadily deteriorated, and when in the
19th cent. relations were opened between them and the
Jews of Europe, they too had long passed their zenith.
The European penetration brought security and emancipation, in a varying degree, to the communities of
N Africa. The Fascist regime, however, led to a serious
reaction in TRIPOLI, even before Italy officially adopted
anti-Semitism in 1938: later, a policy of systematic
discrimination was followed. This was imitated in the
territories under French rule after the Franco-German
armistice of 1940 when the gains of emancipation were
nullified. After the German armies occupied N Africa
in 1941–3, there was a thorough-going persecution,
forced levies and outbreaks of violence occurring
everywhere from Tripoli westwards. The former con-

ditions were nominally restored with the German
defeat, though relations between the Jews and Moslems had by now begun to deteriorate. After 1948, the
Jews of N. Africa left in large numbers, mostly for
Israel or France with some going to Canada. Few Jews
remain in Algeria since 1962, while since the Six-Day
War (1967) the Libyan community has been liquidated
and very few remain in Egypt. The 50,000 Jews in
N. Africa in 1976 were mostly in Morocco and Tunisia
but their numbers were also dropping rapidly.

AFRICA, SOUTH: Jews began to settle there during
the early 19th cent. and the first synagogue was
organized in CAPETOWN in 1841. Many of the Jewish
settlers were traders and peddlers, traveling among the
Boer farmers; later they tended to gravitate to the
towns. Many Jews went to S.A., including a number
from E Europe, after gold was discovered toward the
end of the 19th cent. JOHANNESBURG became the main
center of Jewish settlement. Jews early enjoyed political
equality in Cape Colony and Natal, but obtained it in
the TRANSVAAL only after the second Boer War. A
considerable immigration followed World War I,
stemming mainly from Lithuania. Restrictions imposed during the 1930's limited the influx, although
many German Jews were able to settle in S.A. Since
1939, Jewish immigration has been small. Over 6,000
S African Jews have settled in Israel since 1948. The
organization of S.A. Jewry resembles that of the Jews
of Britain, with the BOARD OF DEPUTIES (founded
1903–4) as the central institution. The rabbis of the
principal congregations in both Johannesburg (Jewish
pop. 57,490) and Capetown (25,650) are styled chief
rabbi, and enjoy wide jurisdiction. A Reform movement was started in Johannesburg in 1933, and has
spread elsewhere. The Zionist movement is strong
although the community has been faced with dilemmas
as a result of Israel's opposition to official S. African
policies. In all, there are about 200 organized Jewish
communities in S.A., most of them very small. Jewish
pop. (1973): 117,990.

AFTERNOON SERVICE see MINHAH

AFULA: Town (pop. (1974): 18,700) situated at the
junction of the roads leading N-S and E-W in the
Valley of Jezreel. Founded in 1925 by the American
Zion Commonwealth society, its growth was retarded
as the surrounding cooperative settlements had no
need for an urban center. It grew markedly after the
War of Independence, absorbing many immigrants in
maabarot and in the new suburb of "Upper A." Its
industrial undertakings include a flour-mill and a
sugar factory.

*AGAG: Amalekite king, captured in battle by Saul
who spared his life. The prophet Samuel regarded
this as a transgression of the Divine command to wipe
out the Amalekites and hewed A. into pieces (I Sam. 15).

AGGADAH (or HAGGADAH): A. can be defined
negatively as that part of the Oral Law distinct

Synagogue in Pretoria.

Zionist Center of Johannesburg.

from HALAKHAH, i.e., that which does not deal with the laws incumbent upon the Jew in his daily activities. From this follows the positive definition: the A. is primarily the sequel to those parts of the Bible which include stories and chronicles, sayings of the wise and moral instructions, and the admonitions and consolation of the prophets. Inasmuch as the A. does deal with laws and commandments, it is limited to an explanation of why they were given and what they teach. A. thus complements *halakhah*: "The *halakhah* is the exemplification and crystallization of the A., while the A. is the crucible of the *halakhah*" (Bialik). There are many facets to A. in both content and form. It includes stories, principles of faith and belief, moral instruction, words of comfort, and a vision of the ideal world of the future. In harmony with its varied and colorful content, the A. is rich in literary forms; parable and allegory; personification and poetic phrase; lyric song, lament, and prayer; biting satire and fiery polemic; idyllic story and dramatic colloquy; metaphor, parable, and word play; fanciful letter combination and its use in word and number symbolism— all these are mixed indiscriminately in the A. "Everything the imagination can conceive is found in the A. with one great exception: idle laughter and frivolity" (Zunz). There is, however, only one subject: to teach the way of the Lord. Historical A. includes additions to the stories of the Bible as well as old legends preserved among the people. It does not, however, recognize the natural boundaries of time and place, and abounds in anachronisms. The A. does not contain the philosophical or theological systems of individual scholars and certainly no unified, developed general approach. There are, however, a number of attempts to answer theological questions, such as the secret of God's providence and rule over creation and man, the nature of idolatry, the origin, nature, and purpose of man, his relationship to God and the universe, the problem of the righteous and the wicked, reward and punishment, the place of Israel among the nations and its mission, the world to come, and the messianic period. The moral teaching of A. reflects not only the points of view and the spiritual outlook of the scholars who strove to improve the moral state of mankind, but also the political, social, and ethical conditions of the periods in which they lived. All strata of society came under critical appraisal, and even the scholars themselves were not exempt. A. is found scattered throughout the Talmud indiscriminately intermingling with *halakhah*. Large portions of the Talmud are aggadic (although there is little A. in the Mishnah). MIDRASHIC LITERATURE, which consists almost entirely of A., grew over a period of a thousand years in countries of various religions and cultures and shows traces of the influence of different periods and localities, e.g. Platonic, Stoic, and Pythagorean ideas, popular superstitions, and beliefs from Babylonia. The arrangement

of the A., and probably even its preservation in written form, began as early as the period of the tannaim. However, no aggadic work edited before the 4th cent. exists. The work of editing and arranging the Midrashim came to an end about the end of the 10th cent. Jacob Ibn Ḥaviv collected the aggadic portions of the Talmud in his *En Yaakov*. An important modern work was completed by Louis Ginzberg in his *Legends of the Jews* (1909–28) which arranges the relevant aggadic material in accordance with the personalities and events described in Scriptures. A Hebrew work that has done much to popularize the A. is the *Sepher ha-Aggadah* ("Book of A.") by Bialik and Ravnitsky.

AGLA (initials of Heb. *Atta gibbor le-olam adonai* i.e., "Thou art mighty forever, O Lord"): Word used among the kabbalists which subsequently entered into currency in Christian Europe.

AGNON (CZACZKES), SHEMUEL YOSEPH (1888–1970): Hebrew novelist and Nobel Prize winner. Born in Galicia, he settled in Palestine in 1909 but lived in Germany 1912–23. A. began to write in his youth and achieved success with the first story he published in Palestine, entitled *Agunot* ("Deserted Wives") from which he derived his name. Subsequently, he produced a series of novels and short stories dealing with life in Galicia and Palestine. A. is regarded as the great epic writer of modern Hebrew literature, his works having a symbolic content mingling reality and imagination. He is free of didactic motives, creating an inner Jewish criterion. *Hakhnasat Kallah* ("The Bridal Canopy") depicting Jewish Galicia in the early 19th cent., like most of A.'s work, incorporated rich folklore and ethnographic material. *Oreaḥ Natah La-lun* ("A Guest for the Night") describes the inner ruin of the Jewish townlet in Galicia between the two World Wars. Most of A.'s heroes are Galicians, even when the setting is Israel (*Temol Shilshom*, etc.). Nevertheless, within the geographical compass of the townlet, A.'s conception is universal. He wrote

S. Y. Agnon.

love-stories, while *Sepher ha-Maasim* ("The Book of Tales") comprises tales of fantasy and horror. He wrote in an original Hebrew style, blending elements from the Bible and talmudic literature. In 1966, he was awarded (together with Nelly SACHS), the Nobel Prize for literature. *Shirah* appeared post-humously.

*AGOBARD (779–840): Archbishop of Lyons. He has been called "the father of medieval anti-Semitism". In four epistles, he called on King Louis le Debonair and the French clergy to forbid Christian-Jewish social intercourse which, he alleged, was endangering the Christian faith. Amolo his successor as archbishop in 841–52, followed his example.

AGRANAT, SHIMON (1906–): Israel jurist. Born in the US he went to Palestine in 1930. He was appointed district judge in 1940, a judge of the high court in 1950, and president of the high court in 1964.

AGRARIAN LAWS: The Pentateuch establishes several a.l. to be observed by the Children of Israel in Canaan. The land is to be divided among the tribes according to lot: "To the more ye shall give the more inheritance, and to the fewer thou shalt give the less inheritance" (Num. 33:54). Each family group was thus assured a proper inheritance according to its needs, and inequality avoided. This balance was further preserved by various laws, especially that of the JUBILEE every 50 years when all fields sold since the previous Jubilee were returned to their original owners. This, in effect, prohibited outright alienation. Moreover, a man selling his inheritance could redeem it even before the Jubilee. The Talmud, however, states that the privilege to redeem was restricted to two years from the date of sale. According to tradition, the laws concerning the Jubilee year and the redemption of land apply only to Palestine and only during those periods when all Jews live there. Several laws concerning the working of the field have their basis in the Bible and are developed in the Talmud. Most apply only in Palestine, and some still have validity. Several laws have strict agricultural reference. Diverse breeds *(kilayim)* may not be sown or planted together. The fruit of trees may not be eaten during the first three years after their planting. A corner *(peah)* of the planted field must be set aside for the needs of the poor. The gleanings *(leket)* which fall aside during the harvest also belong to the poor as do the sheaves which have been forgotten *(shikhhah)* in the fields. Certain offerings must be allotted from all things which grow. *Terumah* ("heave offering"), ordinarily one fiftieth of the produce, must be set aside for the priest; *maaser rishon* ("first tithe"), a tenth, for the levite. In addition, another tenth, *maaser sheni* ("second tithe"), either in the original produce or in its money equivalent, must be brought to Jerusalem to be eaten there. Every third year, however, these second tithes are to be given to the poor and this is called *maaser ani* ("tithe for the poor"). The first fruits of the seven plants and trees

regarded as characteristic of Palestine (Deut. 8:8) are brought to the Temple and distributed among the priests. Every seventh year is a sabbatical rest *(shemittah)* during which the fields may not be worked. Fruit which grows of itself during these years is free to all. The owner of an adjacent plot has first rights in the purchase of a field offered for sale. Real estate is transferred in one of three ways—money payment, purchase deed, or act of possession (i.e., by beginning work on the field). Ownership of a field can be proved by continuous possession of three years during which time the former owner has not offered any protest. A man's real estate is automatically considered security to his creditor. Thus, a creditor who brings written evidence of an unpaid debt can take possession of the debtor's land. If the debtor has sold his real property in the meantime, the creditor is considered as having prior rights and may take away this property from the purchaser.

AGRICULTURAL EXPERIMENTAL STATIONS: The first official a.e.s. in Palestine was founded at Athlit under Aaron AARONSON in 1911. Ben Shemen (1927), Merhavyah (1921–8), and Deganyah (1921–7) also served as a.e.s. The Merhavyah station was later transferred to Gevat (1928) and the one at Ben Shemen to Rehovot which is the central research station, set up in 1932. In 1943, three observation points were established in the Negev for preparatory regional research (Bet Eshel, Revivim, Gevulot). The British maintained a.e.s. at Acre, Sarafand, Jericho, and elsewhere during the period of the Mandate. The Israel government stations are at Rehovot (taken over in 1953), Acre (animal husbandry), Ilanot (forestry), Parod (fodders and cereals), Ashkelon (fodder grasses), Tzemah, and Sarafand. A.e.s. for field crops were established (1950) at En Harod, Gath, and Nirim; for vegetables, at Ramat ha-Sharon. There are four regional experimental stations—Neveh Yaar, Gilat, Bet Dagon, and Tahanat ha-Har.

AGRICULTURAL SETTLEMENT: (1) *Diaspora.* Farming continued to be one of the occupations practiced by Jews after the destruction of the Second Temple. Jewish farmers are known to have existed not only in Palestine but also in Babylonia. Egypt. pre-Islamic Arabia, Ethiopia, and in various European countries. Isolated attempts were also made to promote Jewish settlement on the land, such as that by Joseph NASI in the Tiberias area during the 16th cent. In the course of time, the number of Jewish farmers decreased considerably, chiefly owing to legal restrictions on the acquisition of land and the dangers of settlement in country districts. Modern Jewish settlement had its origins in Russia at the beginning of the 19th cent. From 1804 onward, the Russian government founded a large number of Jewish colonies in the southern and western provinces. By the middle of the century, these numbered almost 240 with a total population of 70,000, and, by the outbreak of World War I, their population had risen to 100,000. After the war, the Soviet authorities resumed Jewish colonizing activities in various parts of the country—Ukraine, White Russia, the Crimea, and BIRO-BIDJAN. Considerable assistance for these activities was furnished by foreign Jewish organizations (AGRO-JOINT, ORT, ICA, and others). By the end of the nineteen-twenties, the Jewish farming population had grown to 250,000, but it sharply declined again owing to the entry of large numbers of villagers into industry. During World War II, the Jewish farms in European Russia were destroyed, but many farmers returned to their holdings when the war was over. Today, however, it is unlikely that the Jewish farming population in the USSR is of any real significance: authoritative figures have not been made available during the past few years. Jewish farm settlement in the US began in the early eighteen-eighties when a number of communal settlements were founded by members of the AM OLAM movement in various parts of the country. None of these, however, lasted very long. At the same time, many Jews tried to establish themselves as individual farmers, and their efforts were greatly assisted by the JEWISH AGRICULTURAL SOCIETY. In 1945, the number of Jewish farmers in the US was estimated at between 80,000 and 100,000; by the 1970s, their number was under 10,000. Jewish farm settlement in Argentina was largely due to the efforts of the noted Jewish philanthropist, Baron Maurice de Hirsch. To further this project, he founded the Jewish Colonization Associa-

tion (ICA) with an aggregate capital of $10 million. His aim was to transfer a million Jews from Russia to Argentina and settle them on the land, but the results failed to justify these high hopes. Jewish colonization in Argentina began in the early eighteen-nineties, and by the turn of the century, the number of Jewish families in the colonies and the nearby townships had reached 4,000 (about 30,000 persons). Although there were subsequent additions to the population,—especially German Jewish refugees after Hitler's rise to power—the numbers as a whole decreased owing to the tendency of members of the younger generation to leave. By 1970 only c.700 Jewish families were in land-cultivation. They are economically well-established, their total assets are estimated at $9 million, and the value of their annual production at $5 million. The total area of Jewish-owned land in Argentina is 750,000 acres, of which about two-thirds are cultivated by Jews. Before World War II, many Jewish agricultural settlements existed in Poland, Bessarabia (Rumania), and Carpatho-Russia (Czechoslovakia). The settlements in Bessarabia and Poland were founded in Czarist times, and those in Carpatho-Russia were among the oldest in Europe. They all had to struggle hard to maintain their existence. Isolated Jewish settlements also existed in other countries (Canada, Germany, Lithuania, Hungary, Cyprus, Brazil, the Dominican Republic, and Uruguay). The total Jewish farming population throughout the Diaspora on the eve of World War II was almost half a million, its main distribution being as follows: USSR, 150,000; Poland,

Jewish farmers in Rumania.

135,000; USA, 100,000; Rumania, 43,000; Czecho-slovakia, 31,000; Argentina, 25,000. Jewish farmers thus accounted for slightly over 3% of the total Diaspora Jewish population (at that time 16 million). (2) *Israel*. Modern agricultural settlement of the Jews in Palestine began in 1855 when Jerusalem Jews bought a parcel of land at Motza, though no immediate use was made of it. About the same time, Sir Moses Montefiore purchased land near Jaffa and financed the planting of citrons, but the experiment proved unsuccessful. In 1870, however, the Alliance Israélite Universelle founded MIKVEH ISRAEL near Jaffa with a view to attracting Jews from the "Old Yishuv" to productive work on the land. In 1878, two groups prepared almost simultaneously to go into agriculture: one group went from Safed to the Upper Jordan Region to found Ge Oni (later ROSH PINNAH), and the other, from Jerusalem to PETAH TIKVAH. Both attempts failed, but they prepared the ground for the revival of those settlements in 1882, the year of the First ALIYAH, when the HIBBAT ZION and BILU movements commenced settlement activities in the country. RISHON LE-ZION, NES TZIYYONAH, and ZIKHRON YAAKOV were founded in the same year, to be followed by other colonies. Lack of experience, limitation of financial means, disease, and Arab attacks threatened speedy disintegration, when Baron Edmond de ROTHSCHILD took the colonies under his protection (1883). Under these auspices, most of them changed from the cultivation of grain to fruit, especially vines. In 1899, he transferred the settlements to the care of the ICA society which sought to return to grain cultivation as the mainstay of the settlers' farms: for that purpose it acquired new land, mainly in Lower Galilee, and founded additional colonies. When the Second Aliyah arrived in the country, early in the 20th cent., the necessity to employ Jewish labor and Jewish guards in the colonies instead of Arabs led to sharp disputes, and, eventually, to the foundation of the *Ha-Horesh* and *Ha-Shomer* organizations — the first as contractor for agricultural work and the second for self-defense. In the same years, the JEWISH NATIONAL FUND began practical work in the country, establishing training and experimental farms on a basis of mixed agriculture. DEGANYAH, the first KEVUTZAH, was founded in 1910, and the first successful experiments with citrus cultivation were made about the same time. In the nineteen-twenties, the KIBBUTZ movement, reinforced by the pioneers of the Third Aliyah, gathered momentum and was instrumental in the collective settlement of the Jezreel and Kinnarot Valleys; NAHALAL was the pioneer of the MOSHAV movement. Citrus cultivation spread speedily in the Coastal Plain and facilitated the close settlement of the Sharon Plain, mainly by private initiative. Settlement gained new impetus with the mass immigration after 1933, and especially after the outbreak of the Arab disturbances in 1936. "Stock-

Cultivation under plastic protection

ade and Watchtower" settlements went up at exposed strategic points; new areas were settled (e.g. the Bet Shean and Huleh Valleys, W Galilee, the Hills of Manasseh, and the N part of the Plain of Zebulun); the foundation of NEGBAH on the eve of World War II began the expansion toward the S Coastal Plain and the Negev. The new regions posed new problems of soil conservation, irrigation, etc. while giving the opportunity to introduce new branches, e.g. fish breeding and tropical fruit. A new type of settlement, called the MOSHAV SHITTUPHI, came into being in the 1930's. The construction of pioneer villages proceeded, despite Arab opposition and the 1939 WHITE PAPER. The outcome of the WAR OF INDEPENDENCE was due, in large measure, to Israel's agricultural settlements, many of which put up a heroic resistance to the Arab invaders. "Stronghold Settlements" were now built all over the country on an unprecedented scale; and the MOSHAV OLIM and KEPHAR AVODAH were introduced. A later innovation is Administrative Farms which grow mainly industrial plants relying on hired labor. A new immigrants' absorption scheme "From Ship to Village" was put into operation in 1954. From the foundation of the state until 1973, 494 villages were set up, as against 277 existing before the war. The aggregate figure of the Jewish agricultural population in Israel was 274,000 compared to 111,000 in 1947. The area under cultivation has greatly expanded during the years of statehood (412,500 acres in 1948; 1,100,000 acres in 1974), as has the irrigated area (439,000 acres in 1974 compared to 72,500 in 1948). The citrus industry has recovered from severe setbacks suffered in 1939–48; grain and fodder production have greatly increased, local wheat covering about a third of the country's needs, and barley, maize, and sorghum providing most of the fodder required by husbandry. New crops include cotton (first shown in 1953 and by 1974 covering 105,000 acres), groundnuts (12,000 acres), and sugar-beet (5,000 acres). 124,000 tons of poultry were produced. The number of milch cows had risen from 19,000 to 91,500, sheep from 20,000 to 105,000, and the annual fish catch from 3,500 to 26,100 tons.

AGRICULTURE: The raising of corn, vines, olives, and livestock in ancient Palestine before the Israelite conquest is attested to by Egyptian sources. Abraham and Isaac, however, are portrayed in the Bible as owners of livestock, practicing a shifting cultivation of cereals. The Bible envisages the domestication of animals and fruit-growing as having preceded crop-cultivation, which emerged separately. Directly after the conquest of Canaan, the a. of the Israelites was restricted to the hill country and was assisted by terracing, a new technique of lime-plastering cisterns, and—from the 11th cent. BCE—by the use of iron tools. The farm-unit was the family holding, a division of the tribal land. The 10th cent. GEZER CALENDAR already indicates a well-regulated agricultural year. Millet, barley, and wheat are known from Bronze Age deposits (4th millennium—1100 BCE) in Palestine, and the Bible also records other crops, as well as a variety of vegetables and gourds. Vines, figs, and olives were planted on the hillsides; other cultivated trees were the walnut, citron, myrtle, pomegranate, almond, date, and apple. Horses, introduced between the 17th and 15th cents. BCE, were bred by Solomon. Nabal and Job were owners of livestock. Poultry is evidenced from the early royal period. In Hezekiah's time the mixed farm for wheat, fruit, and stock was typical, but the kings established the large multiple-branched estate with a specialist hierarchy. Stall-feeding and the use of dung for manure were known by the period of the kings; green-manuring and fallowing may have been introduced either under Philistine or later Greek influence. The plow was a two-beast implement with an iron point producing a shallow tilth; sowing (barley, Oct.-Nov.; wheat, Nov.-Jan.) was frequently preceded by two plowings and followed by a third, a fourth being given after harvest. The winter-summer crop sequence was pre-Israelite, but in the 3rd cent. BCE, summer wheat was being introduced from Syria into Egypt. The hellenistic period witnessed a standardization of a. throughout the Near East and the introduction into Palestine of cotton, lemons, apricots, of new tools, strains of stock, and plants. In the later Second Temple and mishnaic periods, a. was still the principal Jewish occupation; although tenant-farming increased, large units were the exception and the smallholding was characteristic.

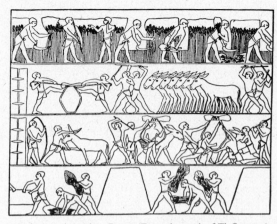

Agriculture in ancient Egypt. (From the tomb of Ti, Saqqara).

Palestine exported wine and olive oil, occasionally corn. A number of vegetables and other plants were introduced from the Roman Empire. While the towns and villages remained agricultural centers, and the Mishnah states that fields in the plains were unenclosed (implying an open-field system with communal features), the mishnaic and talmudic *ir* was a self-sufficient private estate with farm-buildings and slaves on the Roman model. In the talmudic epoch, large tenant-estates under the control of the Patriarchate emerged in Galilee and Transjordan, and a labor shortage created a reaction in favor of stockbreeding. In Babylonia, where elaborate irrigation was practiced, Jewish peasants were numerous. In the Arab countries, Jews continued their agricultural pursuits, wherever toleration permitted, until the 15th cent. In Europe, Jewish agriculturists are recorded almost universally in the first cents. CE, but, generally, the Christian Church and the feudal system made Jewish landholding virtually impossible, the change becoming pronounced by the end of the 10th cent. In Poland, however, such prohibitions were introduced only in the 17th cent. With degrees of emancipation in the 19th and 20th cents., Jews tended to revert in some degree to agriculture, as in Russia, Argentina, the US, and more particularly in Israel. See AGRICULTURAL SETTLEMENT.

AGRIGENTO (medieval GIRGENTI): Town in Sicily. A Jewish community existed there in the 6th cent. and remained one of the most important in the island until the expulsion in 1492.

AGRIPPA I (Marcus Julius or Herod Agrippa I; 10 BCE–44 CE): King of Judea; son of ARISTOBULUS and grandson of HEROD. A. was educated at the court of the emperor Tiberius and was friendly with his son Drusus. After the latter's sudden death, he became involved in various escapades with CALIGULA, the heir-apparent, and was imprisoned by Tiberius for suspected treachery. When Caligula succeeded to the throne, he freed A., appointing him ruler of some of his ancestral territories, including part of Transjordan, with the title of king. In succeeding years, his rule was extended over Galilee, S Transjordan, and, after 41 CE, by decree of the emperor Claudius, over Judea and Samaria. A. was beloved by his Jewish subjects because of his respect for the Jewish religion (e.g. carrying his first fruits to the Temple). He aroused the suspicions of the governor of Syria by convening several other subject kings in Tiberias and by his efforts to strengthen the fortifications of Jerusalem. He died suddenly while attending the games in Caesarea. After his death, his kingdom was again converted into an annex of the province of Syria.

AGRIPPA II (Marcus Julius or Herod Agrippa II; 28 CE–c. 93): Last king of the house of Herod; son of Agrippa I. On the death of his father, Judea reverted to the rule of the Procurators, but in the year 50, A. received the principality of Chalcis and was made responsible for supervising the Temple in Jerusalem. Emperor Claudius gave him the title of king. In 54, A. had to give up Chalcis, receiving in exchange scattered territories in Transjordan and elsewhere. His domain was extended under Nero by the addition of tracts in Galilee, etc. Although not king of Judea, he enjoyed royal prestige there, but his quarrels with the priests and his inscribing of coins with heathen emblems and portraits of the emperors earned him the hostility of the people. When the Jews revolted against Rome (66), he went to Jerusalem to restore calm but had to flee for his life. He accompanied and assisted Titus during the siege of Jerusalem. As a reward, his dominions outside Palestine were further extended. He was brother of BERENICE.

AGRO-JOINT (American Jewish Joint Agricultural Corporation): Organization founded in 1924 by the American Joint Distribution Committee to resettle on the soil in Russia Jews who had been eliminated from their trades and businesses by the Soviet government. Between 1924 and 1938, the A.J. expended close to $16,000,000 and resettled a quarter of a million Jews in colonies in the Crimea and the Ukraine.

AGRON (AGRONSKY), GERSHON (1894–1959): Israel public figure. Born in Russia, he went to the US in 1906, and to Palestine with the Jewish Legion in 1917. He was director of the press office of the World Zionist Organization (1920–1 and 1924–7) and New York editor of the Jewish Telegraphic Agency (1921–4). In 1932, A. founded and edited the *Palestine Post* (from 1950 the *Jerusalem Post*). He was head of the Israel Government Information Services, 1949–50. In 1955, A. became mayor of Jerusalem.

AGUDAT HA-SOPHERIM HA-IVRIIM (Heb. "Hebrew Writers' Association"): Organization founded in Tel Aviv in 1921 to promote Hebrew literature and protect the interests of Hebrew writers. BIALIK headed it until his death. With branches in Tel Aviv, Jerusalem, and Haifa, the society numbers 300 members

(1969). In 1969, it decided to admit members writing in languages other than Hebrew. Since 1930 it has published the literary periodicals, *Moznayim,* and a number of anthologies. It supports the bio-bibliographical institute, *Genazim.*

AGUDAT HA-SOTZIALISTIM HA-IVRIIM (Heb. "Jewish Socialist Union"): The first association of Jewish socialists, founded in London by A. S. LIEBERMANN in 1876. It created the first Jewish trade union, its members being mostly tailors. Its statutes were prepared in Hebrew and the Hebrew language was widely used in its propaganda along with Yiddish. The organization was disbanded the same year as a result of internal dissension and pressure by Anglo-Jewish leaders.

AGUDAT (AGUDAS) ISRAEL (Heb. "Union of Israel"): World organization of orthodox Jews. It was founded at Kattowitz in 1912, chiefly by German, Polish, and Ukrainian Jews, in order to solve in a religious spirit problems concerning Jewry. It opposed Zionism and the MIZRAḤI movement and drew its inspiration from the Samson Raphael Hirsch school of neo-orthodoxy in Germany. During World War I, German rabbis organized considerable numbers of Polish Ḥasidim into an association which subsequently merged with *A.I.* By World War II, *A.I.* had branches in many countries, claiming about half a million members drawn chiefly from Ḥasidic elements. In 1947, an executive committee was constituted under R. Yitzḥak Meir LEVIN with three offices (Jerusalem, London, New York) working together on basic issues. The movement has been responsible for important educational achievements in Europe and in Palestine. It has developed its own press and publishes a daily, *Ha-Modia,* in Jerusalem. Until the emergence of the state of Israel, *A.I.* pursued an extreme anti-Zionist policy and has still not affiliated with the Jewish Agency. In 1948, however, its representatives joined the Provisional Government of Israel. In the First Knesset (1949), *A.I.* and POALE AGUDAT ISRAEL had 6 seats, evenly divided. In the Second Knesset (1951), *A.I.* had 3 and *Poale A.I.* 2; in the Third Knesset (1955), *A.I.* 3, and *Poale A.I.* 3; in the Fourth (1959), *A.I.* and *Poale A.I.* (jointly) 6; in the Fifth (1961), Sixth (1965), and Seventh (1969), *A.I.* 4 and *Poale A.I.* 2 and in the Eighth (1973), 5 (jointly).

AGUILAR, DIEGO D' (formerly Moses Lopez Pereira; 1690–1759): Marrano financier; born in Portugal. After many wanderings, he returned to Judaism, settling in Vienna where he helped to found the local Sephardi community. In recognition of his financial help, he was created baron and was able to assist Jews threatened with expulsion in Moravia and Bohemia. In his latter years, he moved to London.

AGUILAR, GRACE (1816–1847): English poetess and novelist of Marrano ancestry. Her most popular book was *The Vale of Cedars,* a romantic novel de-

Lions carved in ivory. (From the throne of Ahab at Samaria, 9th century BCE).

scribing the tribulations of the Marranos in Spain. Other studies dealing with Jewish experience are included in *Home Scenes and Heart Studies, The Perez Family, The Edict,* and *The Escape.* She wrote *Spirit of Judaism* and *Women of Israel,* the latter a series of delineations of women mentioned in the Bible and in the writings of Josephus.

AGUNAH: A woman whose husband's death is suspected but not proved. She therefore cannot remarry, according to Jewish law. Since early talmudic days, efforts have been made to ease the restrictions by accepting testimony of the husband's death from the wife herself or even from a single witness. Nevertheless, the problem of the a. is still one of the most serious facing rabbinic jurisprudence.

AGUR BEN JAKEH: Compiler of proverbs (Prov. 30). The name was interpreted by the rabbis to be a pseudonym for Solomon.

AHA OF SHABHA (c. 680–752): Babylonian scholar. He settled in Palestine about 750 after a rival candidate was appointed gaon of Pumbedita. A. compiled *Sepher She'iltot* ("Book of Questions"), popular lectures in Aramaic on the weekly pentateuchal portion in which *halakhah* and *aggadah* are skilfully interwoven.

AHAB: King of Israel, son of Omri; ruled c. 876–853 BCE. His wife JEZEBEL, daughter of the king of Sidon, introduced Baal worship into Israel, and a fierce struggle ensued between the royal house and the prophets headed by Elijah. A. defeated Ben Hadad of Damascus in battle and regained several districts previously captured by him. Later, the two formed an alliance and fought the Assyrians near Karkar (853 BCE). A. was subsequently killed while fighting Damascus in alliance with Jehoshaphat of Judah. He is the first king of Israel to be specifically mentioned on Assyrian monuments. Remains of his magnificent palace have been excavated at Samaria.

AHAD HA-AM (pen-name of Asher Ginzberg; 1856–1927): Essayist and philosopher. Born in the Ukraine and educated in a traditional Jewish manner, he early adopted a critical attitude and, though attending universities at Vienna, Berlin, and Breslau

(1882–4), was chiefly self-educated. Settling at Odessa in 1886, he joined *Hoveve Zion,* the policy of which he criticized in essays signed *Ahad Ha-Am* (Heb. "one of the people") in *Ha-Melitz* (1889 ff.). At the same time, he founded the BENE MOSHEH league, of which he was president 1889–91, and in 1892, helped to establish the AHIASAPH publishing society. His collected articles, including criticism of Palestine colonization based on repeated visits to the country, were published as *Al Parashat Derakhim* ("At the Crossroads," 1895–1913). In 1896, he founded HA-SHILOAH (edited by him until 1903), in which he opposed Herzl's "political" Zionism. He resided in London from 1908, and there he wrote *Al Shete ha-Seipim* ("Wavering Between Two Opinions"), also participating in the negotiations leading to the Balfour Declaration (1916–17). In 1922,

Ahad Ha-Am.

he settled in Tel Aviv where he published his correspondence (6 vols. 1923–5) and memoirs. A.H. taught that the nation is the people's "ego" i.e., its internal creative force, which is the sum-total of the combination of its memory and will for survival expressed in its political, religious, and moral beliefs. With Jewish exile, individual replaced national "ego," and the protective armor securing existence in the Diaspora was insufficient for national rejuvenation which could only be effected by renewed aspiration for the national soil. The revival of the Jewish nation must involve the revival of Judaism, beginning with the development (by education and literature) of a morally based "spiritual Zionism" which would foster colonization inspired by the will for redemption. This would lead to the establishment of a "national spiritual center" that would profoundly influence the Jews in the Diaspora. The Jewish State for A.H. was the end rather than the beginning, coming after the regeneration of the nation in Palestine where the Jews must be a majority (although most Jews would not settle there).

AHARONI (AHARONOWITZ), ISRAEL (1882–1946): Zoologist. Born in Lithuania, he settled in Reḥovot, Palestine, in 1901, became lecturer in zoology at the Hebrew Univ. (1930), and wrote pioneer works on Palestinian animal and insect life.

AḤARONIM (Heb. "latter ones"): Designation for recent rabbinic authorities as distinguished from the *rishonim* ("early authorities"). The dividing line is variously placed between the 11th and 16th cents.

AHARONOWITZ, JOSEPH (1877–1937): Writer and labor leader. Born in Padolia, he settled in Palestine in 1906 and worked as an agricultural laborer A prolific publicist and original thinker, he was one of the founders of HA-POEL HA-TZAIR, editing its journal, 1908–22. He served as manager of *Bank ha-Poalim* ("The Workers' Bank"), 1922–37. A. was active in all aspects of the Palestinian labor movement and in the Zionist Organization.

AHASUER(US): Name frequently applied in Christian legend to the WANDERING JEW.

AHASUERUS: King of Persia who figures prominently in the Book of Esther (cf. also Ezra 4:6). Modern scholarship identifies him with Xerxes (reigned 486–465 BCE), son of Darius I.

AHAVAH RABBAH (Heb. "Great Love"): Initial words of the ancient prayer preceding the *Shema* in the morning service of the Ashkenazi ritual. *Ahavat Olam* (Heb. "Everlasting Love") are the initial words of the prayer in the Sephardi ritual and of the corresponding prayer according to both rites in the evening service. The difference arises from a dispute in the Talmud between Rav and Samuel as to which version is preferable.

AHAZ: King of Judah, son of Jotham; ruled c. 735–c. 720 BCE. His kingdom was attacked by Israel and Syria, while the Edomites and Philistines harried his southern territory. Despite the opposition of the prophet Isaiah, A. sought the aid of Tiglath-Pileser of Assyria, who thereupon invaded Syria and Israel (733). Judah, however, became an Assyrian vassal and was also subjected by A. to Assyrian idolatry.

AHAZIAH: (1) Son and successor of Ahab as king of Israel, c. 853 BCE; denounced as an idolator by Elijah (I Kings 22). He was succeeded by his brother Jehoram. (2) Son and successor of Jehoram as king of Judah, c. 844–3 BCE. A Baal-worshiper like his mother Athaliah, he joined his uncle Jehoram of Israel in battle against Hazael of Syria (II Kings 8–9). After Jehoram was wounded, A. visited him at his place of convalescence in Jezreel where both were killed by Jehu.

AḤDUT HA-AVODAH, LE-: Israel socialist party. The original nucleus, largely identical with the majority of the KIBBUTZ HA-MEUHAD movement, was *Si'ah Bet,* a left faction which split from MAPAI in 1944, and in 1946, joined HA-SHOMER HA-TZAIR and the Left POALE ZION to form MAPAM. Largely as a protest against anti-Semitism and anti-Zionism in the Soviet countries, *A.H.* and *Left Poale Zion* broke away from *Mapam* in 1954 to set up a separate group which obtained 10 Knesset seats in the 1955 elections, 7 in 1959, and 8 in 1961. From 1955, it participated in government coalitions and in 1965 accepted an alignment with *Mapai,* which obtained 45 seats in that year's elections. In 1968 it merged with *Mapai* and *Rafi* to form the ISRAEL LABOR PARTY.

AḤDUT HA-AVODAH (Heb. "Labor Unity"): Zionist socialist movement founded in Palestine in 1919, federated to the World Federation of POALE ZION. Its main activities were political and educational. In 1930, it amalgamated with HA-POEL HA-TZAIR to form MAPAI.

AḤER see **ELISHA BEN AVUYAH**

AḤIASAPH: (1) Hebrew publishing house in Warsaw (1893–1926), founded by members of BENE MOSHEH headed by Aḥad Ha-Am. It published many important Hebrew works and translations, the periodical *Ha-Shiloaḥ* (1896–1921) edited during its first years by Aḥad Ha-Am, *Ha-Dor* edited by David Frischmann, and 13 volumes of the *Luaḥ Aḥiasaph,* a literary annual (1893–1904, 1923). (2) Hebrew publishing house in Jerusalem, founded in 1933.

AHIJAH: (1) Son of Ahitub; priest in the reign of Saul who accompanied the Ark into battle against the Philistines. (2) A. the Shilonite (i.e., of Shiloh); prophet during and after the reign of Solomon who foretold that Jeroboam would become king of Israel and later forecast his downfall (I Kings 11:29).

AḤIKAR: Hero of a widespread folk-tale, mentioned in the Book of Tobit and current in various versions in several Semitic languages (Syriac, Arabic, Ethiopic) as well as Slavonic and Hindi. According to the legend, A. was a high court official in Assyria whose position and life were threatened by an adopted son. Ultimately,

A. had the young man thrown into prison where he regaled him with maxims. The form and content of the different versions of the story and the maxims suggest an original Jewish substratum. Fragments of an Aramaic recension of the book were found among the Jewish papyri of the 5th cent. BCE at YEB.

AHIMAAZ BEN PALTIEL (1017–c. 1060): S Italian chronicler. His *Megillat Yuḥasin* ("Scroll of Descent") describes the history of his family including his ancestors AMITTAI, SHEPHATIAH, and Paltiel over a period of two centuries. Although its facts are fantastically interwoven with legend, it remains the most important source for the history of the Jews in Italy at this period.

AHIMELECH: Priest of Nob. When David fled from Saul, he was welcomed by A. who gave him the hallowed bread and the sword of Goliath that were kept in the sanctuary. Saul took revenge by killing A. and the other priests of Nob, the sole survivor being A.'s son, ABIATHAR (I Sam. 21–22).

AHITHOPHEL: David's counselor who joined ABSALOM's revolt. His advice to pursue David was frustrated by David's secret adherent Hushai the Archite. As a result, the decisive battle was postponed and David had an opportunity to organize his forces. A., in despair, hanged himself. Rabbinic sources view him as the archetype of a man destroyed by his own vainglory.

AHLEM: Pioneering German Jewish horticultural school founded by Moritz Simon in 1893 near Hanover. It was closed in 1938.

AHUZAT BAYIT: (Heb. "House Holding"): Society of Jewish residents of Jaffa. In 1909/10, it founded under that name a suburb which became the nucleus of TEL AVIV.

AI: Ancient town N of Jerusalem in the vicinity of Bethel, known in the days of Abraham (Gen. 12:8). After an initial failure due to the sin of ACHAN the city was destroyed by Joshua (Josh. 7–8). The site has not yet been definitely established by archeologists. A. was subsequently rebuilt (cf. Is. 10:28) and was inhabited at the time of the return from Babylon (Ezra 2:28, etc.).

AIJALON: (1) Ancient town of Palestine in the Judean foothills. According to contemporary documents, it was in the kingdom of Gezer in the 15th–14th cents. BCE. Captured by the Israelites under David, it was fortified by Rehoboam to protect Jerusalem. (2) A plain near (1); scene of Joshua's victory over the Gibeonites (Josh. 10:12).

AIX-EN-PROVENCE: Town in S France. Jews lived there from the 5th cent. and formed a large community in the 13th cent. They were given permission in 1282 to own a synagogue and a cemetery. Anti-Jewish riots in 1436 were suppressed by René of Anjou, but further attacks followed his death in 1484. The community was destroyed in the anti-Jewish outbreaks of 1501. A new community was founded by emigrants from Avignon and Carpentras at the end of the 18th cent. and increased in recent years by N. African immigrants. Jewish pop. (1967): 1,000.

AIX-LA-CHAPELLE see **AACHEN**

AKABA: (1) Gulf at the NE end of the Red Sea known in Hebrew as *Miphratz Elath*. (2) The small harbor town on the NE shore of its inner extremity, 4 m. ESE of the present ELATH. It is Jordan's only harbor. See EZION GEBER.

AKAVIA BEN MAHALALEL (1st cent. BCE): Tanna, noted for his wisdom and piety. Only a few of his sayings have been preserved (e.g. *Avot* 3:1). He disagreed with his fellow-sages on various aspects of the law of purity and refused to change his views even when promised the position of president of the court. He was excommunicated for maintaining his opinion, and died under the ban.

AKDAMUT: Mystical poem in honor of the Torah recited by Ashkenazim before the Torah reading on Pentecost: originally an introduction to the Targum, written in Aramaic by Meir ben Isaac of Worms (11th cent.). It is an acrostic of 90 lines containing a double alphabet and the poet's name.

AKEDAH (Heb. "binding"): Traditional designation of Abraham's intended offering of Isaac (Gen. 22), the consummation of which was prevented at the last minute by Divine intervention. The biblical account was elaborated with much detail in later rabbinic literature and was understood as a symbol of complete devotion to God's will. References to the a. and its saving merit abound in medieval liturgical composition, probably as a Jewish counterpoise to the Christian doctrine of the Crucifixion; they are particularly prominent in the services for the High Holidays (Gen. 22 is read as the portion of the Law on the first day of *Rosh ha-Shanah*).

AKIVA (Ben Joseph; c. 50–c. 135): Tanna. His early life is shrouded in obscurity; according to legend he was of humble origin and remained uneducated until the age of 40 when, with the assistance of his wife Rachel, daughter of the rich Kalba Sabbua, he devoted himself to learning. He studied with many leading scholars and developed his own method of biblical interpretation according to which every word and sign in the Bible has a particular significance and can be used to establish a source for accepted halakhic decisions. A. collected and arranged the whole Oral Law according to subjects, and on this basis the Mishnah was later recorded by R Judah Ha-Nasi and his colleagues. A. was regarded as the greatest scholar of his time, and thousands of students studied at his school in Bene Berak. His interest in mystical speculation is reflected in the statement that he was the only one of four rabbis who studied mysticism and remained unscathed. He also participated in political missions, traveling with R Gamaliel, etc. to Rome to secure the

El-Aksa mosque, Jerusalem.

reversal of Domitian's legislation against the Jews and journeying widely among Jewish communities outside Palestine. According to a talmudic tradition, he was one of Bar Kokhba's enthusiastic supporters, saying of him: "This is the king-messiah!" (Y *Taanit* IV, 8). When the Roman government prohibited the study of the Law, A. ignored the decree publicly. He was arrested as a rebel and remained long in prison, being finally executed at Caesarea. His disciples were the spiritual leaders of the Jewish people during subsequent generations, while various later works were falsely ascribed to him in order to lend them authority. No rabbi of the talmudic period made a more profound impression on Jewish history and on the imagination of the Jewish people.

AKIVA, ALPHABET OF RABBI: Late Midrash attributed to R Akiva, based on the letters of the Hebrew alphabet. Three versions are in existence, but the author and date of composition are unknown. Its object was apparently to employ moral sayings for teaching the alphabet to small children.

AKKAD (or Accad): (1) In the Babylonian period, the northern region of the valley between the Euphrates and the Tigris, which contained Babylon, Sippar, and other important cities. (2) Ancient city of Babylonia (mentioned in Gen. 10:10); residence of Sargon the Great.

AKKADIAN: Semitic language. Formerly known as Assyrian owing to the prevalence of A. inscriptions (in cuneiform script) found in Assyria, it is now called after the Akkadians, the first people to use it in writing. A. was spoken from the 4th millennium BCE and served as the language of diplomacy and commerce throughout the Near East until the Greek conquest. A. resembles Hebrew and Aramaic in structure, phonology, and vocabulary but differs from them in the derived forms of its verbs, in the use of tenses, in

syntax, and in the fact that its gutturals lost their distinctive character.

AKKUM: (abbr. for Heb. *oved kokhavim umazzalot,* i.e., worshiper of stars and constellations): Term for idolator, widely introduced into talmudic and rabbinic literature from the 16th cent. onward in place of *goy* (=gentile), etc. It was thus made clear that the reference was not to Christians.

AKNIN, JOSEPH IBN JUDAH IBN see **IBN AKNIN**

AKRON: City in Ohio, US. A Reform congregation has existed since 1865. A. also has 5 Orthodox congregations. Its Jewish Social Service Federation was founded in 1914 and a Jewish Welfare Fund, in 1935. Jewish pop. (1973): 6,500.

AKSA, EL (Arab. "the farthest" i.e., from Mecca): Moslem mosque built in the TEMPLE area of Jerusalem by the caliph abd el-Malik (8th cent.) to mark the site of the legendary flight of MOHAMMED from Mecca to Jerusalem.

AL HA-MISHMAR (Heb. "On The Watch"): Tel Aviv daily newspaper. Founded in 1942, under the name *Mishmar,* as the journal of the *Ha-Shomer ha-Tzair* movement, it became from 1948 the organ of *Mapam.*

AL HA-NISSIM (Heb. "For the miracles"): Opening words of a thanksgiving prayer recited in the *Amidah* and Grace after Meals during ḤANUKKAH and PURIM, with different forms for the two feasts.

AL ḤET (Heb. "For the sin"): Confession of sins repeatedly recited on the Day of Atonement. The sins are listed alphabetically, with a double acrostic, each line beginning "For the sin we have committed by..."

AL TIKRE (Heb. "Do not read"): Talmudic exegetical device by which the meaning of a biblical expression is altered through a small change in rendering, e.g. "Do not read 'Ye shall observe *matzot* (unleavened bread)' (Exod. 12:17) but 'Ye shall observe *mitzvot* (commandments)'": teaching that a Divine commandment, such as that concerning unleavened bread is diminished by procrastination and should be performed immediately.

ALABAMA: US state, formerly under French rule as part of Louisiana. The BLACK CODE excluded Jews from this area after 1724. There is evidence in MOBILE of three Jewish merchants who bought several plantations in the neighborhood in 1777. In 1840, Congregation Shaarai Shamayim was organized in Mobile. When A. entered the Union, Jews from the neighboring states began to move there. German Jews settled in A., especially in Selma, from 1840–50, and E European Jews, from 1880–90. A. had 9,140 Jews in 1973, more than one-half of whom were living in BIRMINGHAM, Mobile, and Montgomery.

ALABARCH: Title of fiscal officer in Egypt in the Roman period (perhaps=Arabarch—"ruler of the Arabs" or from *Arabon*=Heb. *eravon*—"deposit").

The office was sometimes held by wealthy Jews, such as Alexander Lysimachus, brother of Philo.

ALASKA: US state in NW America. American Jews, especially from San Francisco, played an important role in its transformation from Russian to American territory. They reorganized the Alaska Company which dominated the fur trade, A.'s most important industry. Jewish merchants in A. supplied the needs of the resident population. There has been no organized Jewish community, but religious services were held as early as 1868. Ernest GRUENING was governor of A., 1939–53 and senator 1958–68. Jewish pop. (1973): 630

ALAV (fem. **ALEHA**) **HA-SHALOM** (Heb. "Peace be on him [her]"): Phrase uttered when mentioning a deceased person.

ALBA IULIA see **KARLSBURG**

ALBALAG, ISAAC (IBN) (fl. c. 1300): Spanish philosopher. He translated into Hebrew Al-Ghazzali's *Maqasid al-Falasifa* ("Tendencies of the Philosophers"), with an exposition of his own views where they differ from those of the author. In this he developed the "double truth" theory which had been evolved by Christian theologians, and already introduced into Jewish philosophy by Judah Ha-Levi. According to this theory there are two sources of knowledge: philosophical thinking and prophetic intuition (or revelation).

ALBANIA: Balkan republic. Jewish communities established themselves in the coastal ports (Durazzo, Valona, etc.) after the expulsion from Spain and S Italy (15th–16th cents.); they have since died out. The principal Jewish center in the 17th cent. was Berat. Shabbetai Tzevi spent his last years in A., and it is reported that an organized Shabbetaian group existed in Tirana into the 20th cent. There was also a small community in Scutary before World War II but only c. 200 Jews without any organized religious life are left in A. (1974).

ALBANY: Capital of New York State, US. Portuguese Jews visited A. in the late 17th cent. The oldest existing congregation in the state outside New York City, Beth El (now Beth Emeth), was founded in 1838. The city now has 4 congregations, and a Jewish Community Council founded in 1938. Jewish pop. (1973): 13,500.

ALBECK, HANOKH (1890–1972): Talmudic scholar; son of Shalom A. (1858–1920), a noted researcher into rabbinical literature. A. was born in Poland and taught at the Hebrew Univ. from 1936. He published critical editions of rabbinic works, a commentary on the Mishnah, and studies of midrashic literature.

ALBERTA: Province in W Canada. Jews began to settle in 1889 and by 1906 sizable Jewish communities existed in CALGARY and EDMONTON where congregations were established in that year. In 1973, there were some 7,500 Jews in A., of whom 4,000 were in Calgary, 2,700 in Edmonton, 210 in Lethbridge, and 140 in Medicine Hat. A number of Jews are located in the rural areas.

ALBIGENSES: Christian sectaries, fl. S France, 12th–13th cents. They were friendly to the Jews and it was popularly (though erroneously) thought that their doctrines were influenced by Judaism. The movement therefore stimulated the Church's reaction against the Jews at the close of the 12th cent., and during its suppression many Jews were massacred (especially at Béziers, 1209).

ALBO, JOSEPH (c. 1380–c. 1435): Spanish religious philosopher. He was a pupil of Hasdai Crescas and took part in the Disputation of Tortosa (1413–4). In his *Sepher ha-Ikkarim* ("Book of Dogmas"), he reduced the foundations of religion to three primary principles: Divine Existence, Divine Revelation, and Reward and Punishment. From these, secondary dogmas (which A. calls *shorashim* "roots") are deduced. To negate any of these is heresy. There are other dogmas called *anaphim* ("branches") such as creation *ex nihilo,* the coming of the Messiah, and Resurrection, to doubt which is not heretical. By basing Judaism on

First page of *Sepher ha-Ikkarim* by Joseph Albo. 15th cent. illuminated ms in Library of Accademia dei Concordi, Rovigo, Italy.

The symbol of the philosopher's stone, containing garbled Hebrew words.

general religious principles, A.'s system has considerable significance as an apologetic (particularly anti-Christian) theology. A.'s originality has been questioned, but his work achieved great popularity among both scholars and laymen.

*ALBRIGHT, WILLIAM FOXWELL (1889–1971):
US archeologist and historian; director of the American School of Oriental Research in Jerusalem 1921–9 and 1933–6, and from 1929 professor of Semitic languages at Johns Hopkins Univ., Baltimore. He conducted archeological excavations in various parts of the Middle East, and was one of the pioneers of modern research methods in Palestinian archeology and historical geography. His many works on biblical and archeological subjects include *From the Stone Age to Christianity, Archeology and the Religion of Israel,* and *The Archeology of Palestine.*

ALCALAY see **ALKALAI**

ALCHEMY: Chemical experimentation chiefly aimed at the transmutation of metals. Though not of Jewish origin, a. was in former times widely ascribed to Jews, and the alchemical writer Moses of Alexandria was probably Jewish. Maria Hebrea, an early alchemist, invented chemical apparatus still in use and perhaps discovered hydrochloric acid. It is controversial whether there are references to a. in the Talmud. The strong connection between a. and gnosticism in Alexandria was renewed in the link between a. and the Kabbalah: medieval alchemists claimed knowledge of Kabbalah which became closely associated with a. in Christian eyes. The Zohar bears traces of a. in its views on metals and contributed to alchemical studies its use of numerical and letter combinations; such influence can be discerned in the works of Raymound Lull (13th–14th cents.) and von Rosenroth (17th cent.). The great alchemist Artephius (12th cent.) was a converted Jew; other Jewish alchemists were Jacob Aranicus (13th cent.), Isaac "Hollander" and his son (15th–16th cents.), and Benjamin Jesse (18th cent.). The

family of Leone Modena (17th cent.) conducted experiments in a., as did the *Baal Shem* of London, Samuel de Falk (18th cent.). Few Jewish works on the subject have survived. Maimonides and Gershon ben Solomon (12th–13th cents.) were skeptical of a. which was attacked by Judah Ha-Levi and other Jewish scholars.

ALCIMUS (Greco-Roman form of Hebrew *Eliakim*):
High priest during the Maccabean revolt, 162–159 BCE. An ardent Hellenizer, but of priestly stock, he was appointed by the Syrian king, Demetrius I, to succeed Menelaus after the first victories of Judah the Maccabee, in the hope that he would be able to win back the country's allegiance. He had some measure of success and at the outset gained the confidence of the Hasideans but died (perhaps in battle) three years later.

ALDANOV (LANDAU), MARK (1889–1957): Author. Of Russian birth, he emigrated to France in 1919. Originally a physical chemist, he later turned to literature, publishing biographies and historical novels.

ALENU (for *alenu le-shabbeah:* Heb. "It is our duty to praise"): Prayer proclaiming the sovereignty and unity of God, probably composed by Rav in Babylonia (3rd cent.) for the New Year, now recited at the conclusion of every synagogue service. In the Middle Ages, it was the martyrs' prayer. Its vigorous affirmation of monotheism made it the object of onslaught by those who saw in it an attack on Christianity, and its recital was prohibited in Aragon (1336), Prague (1399), etc. In Prussia in 1703 the cancellation of one passage (still omitted in the Ashkenazi rite) was officially ordered. Among the Ashkenazim, A. is chanted during the additional service of the High Holidays to a solemn traditional tune.

ALEPH (א) First letter of the Hebrew alphabet; numerical value 1. It is not a vowel but a consonant sounded as a glottal stop. In Hebrew, no word can begin with a vowel unless an *a.* precedes. In some biblical words, however, *a.* is not pronounced, and in later times became silent altogether, and was used as a vowel-letter to indicate a long *a* (as in "father"). The name means "ox," and in the oldest form of the Hebrew script the letter had the shape of an ox's head.

ALEPH-BES (or *-Bet,* Heb.): The alphabet; figuratively, the most elementary knowledge.

ALEPPO: City in Syria. It was called by the Jews Aram-Zobah (Ps. 60:2), and its Jewish community is one of the oldest in the world. The Al-Ḥayyat mosque was formerly a synagogue, dating from the 6th cent. Benjamin of Tudela found 1,500 Jews there (c. 1170), and later in the Middle Ages the community assumed some importance, being the home of many men of learning. Spanish Jews settling there after 1492 reinvigorated the community. Before 1914, there were 14,000 Jews in A., but the number dwindled by emigration, mainly to America and England. After the UN decision of Nov. 1947 to partition Palestine, anti-Jewish riots took place in A. and many Jews fled. The community numbers 1,200 (1975), its main occupations are trade and peddling. The Jewish quarters contained many ancient synagogues, the oldest being the Mustaribah (destroyed in 1947 riots), the main part of which dated from the 4th cent.; here a famous 10th cent. masoretic codex of the Bible, now in Israel, corrected by Ben Asher was formerly preserved.

ALESSANDRIA: City of N Italy. Jews are first mentioned there in 1457, and A. was the only place in the duchy of Milan where Jews were allowed to remain after the expulsion of 1591; they remained after the city passed under the rule of Piedmont in 1706. In 1914, the synagogue was destroyed by the Fascists, and only 90 Jews lived there in the early 1970s.

*ALEXANDER: Name of 3 Russian czars in the 19th cent. (1) *ALEXANDER I*, reigned 1801–25. His initial Jewish policy was liberal, and during his reign, the first Jewish agricultural colonies were established in S Russia. His ultimate object was not, however, the amelioration of the position of the Jews but the undermining of their religious individuality. Later, he changed his approach, imposing restrictions on Jews and ordering their expulsion from various regions. (2) *ALEXANDER II*, reigned 1855–81. At the beginning of his reign, he alleviated some of the anti-Jewish decrees of his father, Nicholas I, and this encouraged emancipatory elements in Russian Jewry. However, toward the close of his reign, an anti-Semitic tendency paralleled the general reaction. (3) *ALEXANDER III*, reigned 1881–94. His reign was marked by harsh anti-Jewish measures including the MAY LAWS, expulsions from villages and from Moscow, *numerus clausus* in universities, and widespread pogroms. The consequence was mass Jewish emigrations to the West and a fillip to the Zionist movement in Russia.

ALEXANDER (c. 80–48 BCE): Son of Aristobulus II. He was taken captive with his father by the Romans in 63 BCE, escaped, and organized further unsuccessful resistance in Judea. He was later beheaded at Antioch by order of Pompey.

ALEXANDER (c. 35–7 BCE): Son of Herod and Mariamne. Herod, at the instigation of his son Antipater and his sister, Salome, had him and his brother Aristobulus executed at Sebaste on charges of treachery. His descendants abandoned Judaism.

ALEXANDER JANNAEUS see **ALEXANDER YANNAI**

ALEXANDER LYSIMACHUS (fl. 1st cent. CE): Wealthy Alexandrian, brother of PHILO and father of TIBERIUS JULIUS ALEXANDER. He was ALABARCH in the Roman fiscal administration in Egypt and plated the Temple gates in Jerusalem with gold and silver.

*ALEXANDER THE GREAT: King of Macedonia, 336–323 BCE. His personality made a deep impression on the Jews: Josephus describes his visit to Jerusalem, the honor which he paid to the high priest Jaddua, and the privileges accorded to the Jews of Palestine and the Diaspora. It is beyond doubt, however, that A. never visited Jerusalem, although the Talmud's traditions of a meeting between him and the Jews at (what was later) Antipatris may well be historical. The traditions may have grown up on the background of his suppression of a Samaritan revolt which gave the Jews of Jerusalem the occasion to stress their own loyalty. A. figures prominently in talmudic, midrashic, and medieval Jewish legend.

ALEXANDER, TIBERIUS JULIUS (fl. 1st cent. CE): Roman official. The son of ALEXANDER LYSIMACHUS and nephew of PHILO, he was born in Alexandria. Completely assimilated, even in a religious sense, he served in the Roman army and administration. As procurator of Judea (46–8), he showed great severity. Appointed prefect of Egypt in 66, he savagely suppressed a Jewish riot in Alexandria. He took part in the siege of Jerusalem (70) as chief of Titus' staff.

ALEXANDER YANNAI (= Jonathan: Gk. Jannaios [Jannaeus]): King and high priest in Judea, reigned 103–76 BCE; son of John Hyrcanus. He proved a despotic, violent ruler who maintained his authority with the aid of foreign mercenaries. He set about annexing those Greek cities of Palestine whose inhabitants still refused to acknowledge Hasmonean rule. After suffering some setbacks, he succeeded in adding the entire coastal region to his kingdom. His political aspirations ran counter to the religious outlook of a large section of the Judean population. In his reign, therefore, occurred the final breach between the Crown and the Pharisees, apparently as a result of A.'s flouting their susceptibilities while officiating in the Temple. In 94, civil war broke out, the Pharisees soliciting the aid of Demetrius III of Syria who defeated A. near Shechem (88). 6,000 Jews serving in Demetrius' army, realizing the implications of the situation, went over to A. who succeeded in regaining his hold upon the country and in taking a ferocious vengeance on his former opponents. At the end of his reign, A. tried to complete his conquests in Transjordan and died while besieging Ragaba.

ALEXANDER MOSES (1853–1932): Govenor of the state of Idaho. 1915–9. An immigrant from Germany, he was the first foreign-born Jew to hold such office in the US.

ALEXANDER, SAMUEL (1859–1938): Philosopher. Of Australian birth, he was professor at Manchester from 1893. He was an exponent of metaphysical realism, metaphysics being for him the descriptive science of reality. He regarded space-time as the primordial element of the universe and showed how in successive stages of emergence it developed all the content of the universe from the physical to the Divine. The most original aspect of his metaphysics is his emipirical deduction of the categories, properties which are part of reality and not modes of thought. In later life, he turned his attention to the nature of artistic (including literary) creation. His writings include: *Moral Order and Progress; Locke; The Basis of Realism; Space, Time and Deity; Spinoza and Time; Beauty and other Forms of Value.* He was awarded the Order of Merit in 1930.

ALEXANDRA: Daughter of Aristobulus II. After her father's death (49 BCE), she married Philippion, son of Ptolemy of Chalcis (Lebanon) where she had taken refuge. Ptolemy subsequently engineered his son's death and then himself married A.

ALEXANDRA (d. 28 BCE): Daughter of Hyrcanus II; wife of Alexander son of Aristobulus II; mother of Aristobulus III, and of Mariamne who married Herod. When Herod had Aristobulus III drowned, A. complained to Antony. Herod succeeded in exonerating himself, but his animosity toward A. increased. After the execution of Mariamne, Herod was thought to be dying. A. took the opportunity to attempt to seize power, but Herod, learning of her design, had her executed.

ALEXANDRA SALOME see **SALOME ALEXANDRA**

ALEXANDRIA: Egyptian port. According to Josephus, Jews settled there from the 3rd cent. BCE. In the Roman period, they constituted a considerable proportion of the population, two of the city's five districts being inhabited by Jews. The community was autonomous, but its legal position deteriorated under Roman rule. The Jews aspired to civic rights while the pagan Alexandrians, strongly anti-Jewish, objected; against this background, grave riots broke out in 38 CE against the Jews. In 66, under the influence of the rebellion in Judea, disturbances broke out among the Jews, but were suppressed with cruelty by the Roman governor, the convert Tiberius Julius ALEXANDER. In 115–7, at the time of the general Jewish revolt, the Alexandrian Jews were heavily attacked and punished, their great synagogue being burnt down. As a result of these risings, the Jewish population diminished. Their condition deteriorated further with the establishment of Christian predominance. In 414, owing to the inflammatory preaching of the Patriarch CYRIL, they were expelled from the city, but many evidently returned, as at the Arab conquest (642) their number was again considerable. Subsequently, the community was numerically and intellectually unimportant, leadership now passing to Cairo. The community grew in the 19th cent. when there was a considerable Italian influx, and numbered some 15,000 until 1956. Thereafter there was a steady exodus and by 1976, very few remained.

The Jews of ancient A., living in a Greek environment, acquired Greek language and manners and attempted to place the intellectual values of HELLENISM within the framework of Judaism. From this compromise arose the Jewish-Hellenistic culture which brought Judaism to the pagan world and Greek achievements to the Jews. It found expression in a Jewish Alexandrian literature in Greek whose starting point was the SEPTUAGINT. Jewish authors of A. included Philo the poet (who composed *Jerusalem,* an epic on the Homeric model), Ezekiel the playwright (author of a drama called *The Exodus),* nationalist writers (e.g., authors of WISDOM OF SOLOMON; probably Books III and IV of the SIBYLLINE ORACLES; III MACCABEES, etc.), apologists and philosophers (e.g. PHILO) who directly and indirectly influenced subsequent intellectual and religious movements in Judaism and Christianity.

ALFASI, DAVID (fl. 10th cent.): Karaite grammarian and commentator. Born in Fez, he spent a number of years in Jerusalem and composed a Hebrew-Arabic lexicon to the Bible, which displays a profound knowledge of Hebrew philology.

ALFASI, ISAAC BEN JACOB (known as *Rif.* 1013–1103): Talmudic scholar. He lived and taught at Fez, N Africa (hence his name Al-Fasi=Man of Fez). At the age of 75, he was the victim of malicious slander and had to leave Fez, escaping to Spain. Both in Africa and Spain he had numerous disciples and penned authoritative responsa. His compendium of the legal discussions of the Babylonian Talmud, *Sepher ha-Halakhot* ("Book of Legal Decisions": generally called *Alfas*) is the main collection of its type prior to the work of Maimonides and still enjoys classical status. It was used to advantage in the days when the Talmud itself was suppressed.

ALFAYYUMI, JACOB (fl. 12th cent.): Scholar and leader of Yemenite Jewish community to whom Maimonides addressed his *Letter to the Yemen* in 1172.

ALFONSI, PETRUS (formerly Moses Sephardi; c. 1062–1110): Spanish apostate and translator. He traveled widely and for some time lived in England. He wrote in dialogue form a bitter polemic against Judaism, but is best remembered for his collection of pious anecdotes for the use of preachers, *Disciplina Clericalis* ("Training for the Clergy"), which introduced many oriental fables and tales to European readers.

ALFONSO DE SPINA see **SPINA, ALFONSO DE**

ALGERIA: Country of N Africa. Jews possibly accompanied Carthaginians to this area, and under the Romans there were certainly Jewish communities of which relics (inscriptions, catacombs, etc.) are preserved. Some local Berber tribes apparently embraced Judaism. The condition of the Jews deteriorated when the Roman Empire became Christian, but new colonies were established under Arab rule from the 7th cent. onward. After the rise of the Almohades (12th cent.), the open practice of Judaism was temporarily forbidden. Refugees from the Spanish massacres (1391) and expulsion (1492) revivified the community which was henceforth where, during this period, occurred the Kishinev and Homel pogroms and the failure of the 1905 revolution. Many of the newcomers were motivated by socialist idealism. 35,000–40,000 Jews entered during this period, many from E Europe and oriental countries. A number left the country after a time but in 1914 the Jewish population was 90,000, falling to 50,000 by the end of World War I. The Balfour Declaration gave the impetus to the Third A. (1919–23) in which the youthful element predominated, members of HE-HALUTZ being prominent. In 1920, free immigration was permitted to persons with means of subsistence, craftsmen, those joining their families, and Talmud students whose upkeep was assured; in addition, a quota was fixed for immigrants whose maintenance was guaranteed by the Zionist Organization. These regulations were modified the following year but the principle remained. Annual immigration figures for 1920–3 averaged 8,000 and at the end of the period the country's Jewish population was again c. 90,000. 80,000 more entered during the period of the Fourth A. (1924–31), the great majority in 1924–5. The main source was Poland where Jews suffered from fiscal restrictions. Many of the newcomers were middle-class, some "capitalists" (i.e., owners of £500, later £1,000). A number left, especially during the 1926 depression, but there were 190,000 Jews in Palestine in 1931. The Fifth A. (1932–40) fell into two periods; (a) 1932–5, covering the beginning of the Nazi persecutions, saw 144,000 immigrants (62,000 in 1935 alone) and was followed by economic prosperity. During this time YOUTH ALIYAH was founded. (b) 1936–40, coinciding with the Arab riots and economic depression, when *a*. was restricted by the Mandatory government, first for economic, later for political reasons. Nevertheless in 1936–38, there were 53,000 immigrants. In 1939, the MacDonald White Paper recommended that only 75,000 further Jews be allowed admission during the next 5 years and then *a*. would be dependent on Arab agreement. However, 36,000 immigrants entered during the second phase of the Fifth *a*. including 15,000 "illegal" immigrants (i.e., without government permits) in 1939–40. The Sixth A. (1941–7) was a period of struggle against restrictions on immigration. Many tragic incidents were recorded (cf. EXODUS; PATRIA; STRUMA) and during the latter years many intending immigrants were interned in Cyprus. 85,000 Jews arrived in this time, of whom 28,000 were "illegal immigrants." There were 750,000 Jews in Israel when the state was established. Free Jewish immigration was immediately proclaimed and the period of mass-*a* inaugurated. The survivors of Nazi rule in Central Europe, the internees in Cyprus, the Jewries of countries behind the Iron Curtain, and the communities under Arab rule (e.g. the Yemen, Iraq) were transferred to Israel under the auspices of the Jewish Agency's Immigration Department.

Immigrants disembarking in Haifa.

Total immigration figures for the period 1948–75 were as follows: 1948–101,819 immigrants; 1949–239,076; 1950–169,405;

1951–173,901;	1952–23,375;	1953–10,347;
1954–17,471;	1955–36,303;	1956–54,925;
1957–69,733;	1958–25,919;	1959–22,987;
1960–23,487;	1961–46,571;	1962–59,473;
1963–62,086;	1964–52,193.	1965–28,795;
1966–13,610;	1967–12,275;	1968–18,156;
1969–23,207;	1970–22,470;	1971–25,578;
1972–55,888;	1973–54,886;	1974–31,979;
1975–19,756.		

By continents of origin (1948–74): Eastern Europe–557,858; Western Europe–85,929; Asia–331,668; Africa–397,562; America–98,383; Australasia–3,186.

ALJAMA (Arabic: "the gathering"): Term applied in Christian Spain and Sicily to the community of the Jews (and Moslems); sometimes also to the Jewish quarter.

ALKABETZ, SOLOMON BEN MOSES (c. 1505–1584): Hebrew poet and kabbalist. Born in Salonica, he later lived in Adrianople and Safed where he was a colleague of Joseph Caro. Noted for his writings on biblical and kabbalistic topics as well as for his religious poems, A.'s best-known composition is *Lekhah Dodi* ("Come my beloved"), a hymn welcoming the Sabbath, which is recited in all rites on Friday evenings.

ALKALAI: Family originating in Alcala, Castile, important branches being in Salonica, Serbia, and Bulgaria. Its members included: *ABRAHAM BEN SAMUEL A.* (1749–1811) author of a commentary on Jacob ben Asher's *Turim; MOSES BEN DAVID A.* (1843–1901) writer and Hebrew pedagogue; *ISAAC* a center of Sephardi life and produced some notable scholars. From the 16th cent., under Turkish rule, conditions were generally good. A number of Jews from Italy (especially Leghorn) settled in A., controlling a great part of its foreign trade: they established a community which long retained a separate existence. The growth of the independent authority of the beys of A., always rapacious and relentless, reacted unfavorably on the condition of the Jews. In the 18th and early 19th cents., the political history of the Jews of A. revolved around that of the two rival families of BACRI and BUSNACH, members of which succeeded one another as lay head (*Mukkadem*) of the community. More than one member of these families fell victim to mob violence (e.g. a riot in 1804) or the ruler's whim. The French occupation in 1830 introduced a new spirit, and in 1870, the CREMIEUX DECREE conferred French citizenship on the Jews of A. Antipathy persisted, however, both among the new French settlers and the Moslems, and there were violent anti-Jewish outbreaks in 1884–7 and 1897–8. With the fall of France in 1940, the Vichy government introduced anti-Semitic laws into A. and abrogated the Crémieux Law, and when the German forces were in occupation (1942–3), the Jews suffered. The former state of affairs was thereafter slowly restored, though the growth of nationalist feelings has reacted adversely on the Jewish position. The chief center of Jewish population in A. was Algiers (30,000 in 1961), which after World War II attracted many Jews from the interior. On the attainment of independence, almost the entire Jewish community of 130,000 emigrated—in its greatest number to France, others went to Israel. By 1974 only 1,000 (in Algiers and Constantine) remained.

ALGIERS see **ALGERIA**

ALHARIZI, JUDAH (c. 1170–c. 1235): Spanish Hebrew poet and translator. He traveled widely through Mediterranean countries. His wanderings are reflected in his writings, the most important of which is his *Tahkemoni* (Heb. "The Wise One") consisting of 50 *makamot* (narratives in rhymed prose), a literary form introduced by A. into Hebrew under the influence of Arabic poetry. The book is of historical importance, as it describes the communities visited by R. and gives appreciations of contemporary Hebrew poets. A. translated many books from Arabic into Hebrew, including the writings of the Arabic poet Al-Hariri (which inspired his own *Tahkemoni*) and Maimonides' *Guide to the Perplexed*. He occupies a special place in medieval Hebrew literature because of his light, humorous style and the variety of his topics.

ALIYYAH (*Aliyah*, Heb. "ascent"): (1) A "calling up" to read the Scroll of the Law in the synagogue during worship. Originally, each person read his particular section, but later a special reader was appointed for this purpose and those called up recited solely the blessings. To receive an a. is traditionally considered

Yemenite immigrants being flown to Israel – Operation "Magic Carpet".

a great honor. (2) The immigration of Jews to Israel. From the destruction of the Second Temple until modern times, only isolated instances are recorded of group immigration. In 1121, some 300 Jews went to Palestine from France and England; Nahmanides in 1267 and Obadiah of Bertinoro in 1488 were both followed by groups of disciples; while as a result of the Spanish expulsion in 1492, many Sephardi Jews—including an important kabbalistic circle—entered the country. Joseph Nasi's resettlement attempt in 1564 brought groups from Italy, while in 1700, 1,500 arrived from E Europe in response to R Judah Hasid's call. In the latter 18th cent., there was a considerable influx of both Hasidim and followers of the Vilna Gaon. In the thirty years (1850–80) preceding the BILU, it is estimated that 20,000–30,000 Jews settled in Palestine. Organized a., mainly influenced by ZIONISM, began in 1882. The First A. (1882–1903) commenced under the shadow of Russian pogroms and was led by the *Bilu*. In 1882, 300 families and additional smaller groups arrived from Russia, 450 pioneers from Rumania, and a few dozen from the Yemen. An attempt by the HOVEVE ZION to coordinate immigration resulted in the KATTOWITZ CONFERENCE of 1884. Despite difficulties created by the Turkish authorities, a. proceeded, and an increasing number of AGRICULTURAL SETTLEMENTS were founded. Further persecutions in 1890 sent thousands of Russian Jews to Palestine, but the number dwindled during the rest of the decade. It is estimated that 25,000 Jews immigrated during the First A. but a number subsequently emigrated. The Second A. (1904–14) also derived chiefly from Russia

Rabbi Judah Solomon Ḥai Alkalai.

BEN ABRAHAM ALCALAY (1881–) chief rabbi of Yugoslavia and the first Jewish senator in Yugoslavia. On the German occupation in 1941, he escaped to the US where he became chief rabbi of the Union of American Sephardi Congregations; and *JUDAH SOLOMON ḤAI A.* (1798–1878) rabbi and proto-Zionist. Brought up in Jerusalem, he was appointed in 1825 rabbi to the Sephardi community at Zemun, near Belgrade. After the Damascus Affair (1840), he began to conduct propaganda for the settlement of Palestine. He tried to win support for his views among the Jews of W Europe but without success. In 1874, A. settled permanently in Jerusalem and continued to work for the colonization of the land. His writings insisted that natural precedes supernatural redemption, and he thus paved the way for Zionism within the framework of religion.

ALKAN, CHARLES (real name Charles Henri Valentine Morhange; 1813–1888): French pianist, teacher, and composer. His compositions enlarged the technical scope of the piano and are still used for pedagogical purposes and recitals.

ALLEGORY: Exposition of an implied meaning; extended metaphor. Allegories may be read into literal texts for scientific, apologetic, or mystic motives. A. is already found in the Bible and Apocrypha. It was widely used by the Alexandrian Jews (e.g. Philo) who interpreted the Bible allegorically to convey hellenistic doctrines. A. was also a favorite rabbinic device and occurs frequently in the Midrash. Many medieval Jewish philosophers (e.g. Maimonides and Ibn Gabi-

rol) utilized allegorical interpretations of biblical passages, but others (e.g. Saadyah and Albo) issued warnings against excessive allegorization. Both Christianity and Islam tended to regard the Torah as allegorical (see ANTINOMIANISM). The Kabbalah held that the Bible clothed an inner reality, and presented extensive a. as a means for deducing its true meaning. There are also many examples in modern Hebrew literature (e.g. M.H. Luzzatto, Mendele Mocher Sephorim).

*ALLENBY, EDMUND HENRY HYNMAN, VISCOUNT (1861–1936): British military leader. In World War I, he commanded the Egyptian Expeditionary Force (from June 1917). In Oct. 1917, he launched a successful attack on the Turkish forces in the Gaza-Beersheba sector and on Dec. 9 entered Jerusalem. A. renewed his offensive in Sept. 1918, and won a decisive victory over the Turks near Megiddo (Sept. 19), sweeping northward to Damascus and Aleppo. After the allied conquest of Palestine, A. headed the Military Administration (until 1919). Although cool toward Zionist aspirations while in Palestine, he later evinced a more favorable attitude, traveling to Jerusalem in 1925 to attend the opening of the Hebrew Univ.

ALLENTOWN: City in Pennsylvania, US. Jews appeared in the 18th cent., but the Jewish community began in 1830, a dozen families from Germany arriving a decade later. Jews from E Europe began to settle there in the 1860's. A.'s Jewish Federation was founded in 1948. Jewish pop. (1973): 3,900.

ALLGEMEINE ZEITUNG DES JUDENTUMS (Ger. "General Journal of Judaism"): German Jewish journal, founded by Ludwig PHILIPPSON in 1837 and edited by him until his death in 1889. The first periodical to deal with current Jewish affairs, it fought for Jewish emancipation and religious reform. It was instrumental in establishing major cultural institutions such as the publication society, *Institut zur Forderung der Israelitischen Literatur* (1853) and the *Hochschule für die Wissenschaft des Judentums* (1872). From 1890 to 1921, when it ceased publication, the journal was the organ of moderate assimilation.

ALLIANCE ISRAELITE UNIVERSELLE: Organization with headquarters in Paris. It was founded in 1860 as a result of the MORTARA CASE to defend Jewish civil and religious liberties, to provide vocational and other training for backward Jewish communities, and to defend Jews from attack and help them in disaster. Its noteworthy stands included opposition to Swiss discrimination against French Jewish-businessmen and to anti-Semitism in the Balkans. It helped victims of the Russian pogroms (1881 ff), Jewish sufferers from famine in Europe (1896), European Jewish victims of World War I, Russian Jewish famine victims (1922), etc. A.I.U. established an educational network, strongly French in feeling, in various lands of the Balkans, Asia, and N Africa, as well as

Palestine, where it founded the pioneer agricultural school at MIKVEH ISRAEL (1870). Its educational influence in oriental countries declined after World War

Seal of the Alliance Israélite Universelle.

II, but Alliance schools in Israel, Morocco, Tunisia, Syria, the Lebanon, and Iran had 21,000 pupils in its schools in 1968, including 4,828 in 13 schools in Israel. Its presidents have included Adolphe Crémieux, Narcisse Leven, Sylvain Lévi, Salomon Munk, and René Cassin.

ALLIANZ, ISRAELITISCHE, ZU WIEN: Austrian society for assistance to needy Jews and defense of their civil rights. Originally founded as a branch of the Alliance Israélite Universelle (1873), it subsequently became an independent organization. The A. alleviated Jewish suffering, particularly in E Europe, until its activities ceased with the Nazi occupation in 1938.

ALLITERATION: Recurrent use of initial letter or sound. The device is frequently utilized in the Bible and later (including modern) Jewish literature, sometimes with an onomatopoeic effect. It is particularly common in the hymns of KALLIR.

ALLON, GEDALIAH (1902–1950): Historian. Emigrating to Palestine from Europe in 1926, he became lecturer at the Hebrew Univ. and wrote a standard work on the history of the Jews in Palestine in mishnaic and talmudic times.

ALLON, YIGAL (1918–): Israel military commander. He was one of the founders of the PALMAH and fought with the Allies in Syria in 1942. He was commander of the *Palmah* 1945–8, and commanded Israel armies on various fronts during the War of Independence, conducting the operation that led to the conquest of the S Negev and the occupation of Elath. In 1954, he became one of the leaders of the newly-formed *Le Ahdut ha-Avodah Poale Zion* party which he has represented in the Knesset since 1955. In 1961 he became minister of labor. From 1968, Allon was deputy prime minister. He was also minister of absorption (1968–9), minister of education (1969–74), and foreign minister (1974–).

ALMAN, SAMUEL (1877–1947): Liturgical composer. Born in Russia, he was in England from 1903

and choirmaster in London synagogues. He published two volumes of synagogue music.

ALMANZI, JOSEPH (1801–1860): Italian Hebrew writer and bibliophile. He was in close touch with the Jewish scholars of his day (especially S.D. Luzzatto) and wrote Hebrew poetry. His valuable collection of Hebrew mss was purchased by the British Museum.

ALMEMAR (or **ALMEMOR**): Name given among the Ashkenazim to the raised place in the synagogue on which the reading-desk is situated (in Hebrew *bimah* = platform). It derives from the Arabic *alminbar* (platform) which passed into general use in the Middle Ages in S Europe, but the application is unknown to the Sephardim who term the synagogal platform *tebah* (Heb. "box"). In parts of Central and E Europe, the *a.* attained architectural importance, being incorporated in the central column which supported the roof.

ALMOGI, YOSEPH AHARON (1910–): Israel labor leader. Born in Poland, he settled in Palestine in 1930. Among the positions he held were minister of housing 1963–5, minister of labor 1968–74, mayor of Haifa 1974–6, and chairman of the Zionist Executive from 1976.

ALMOHADES: Moslem sectaries who rose in N Africa in the 12th cent. and conquered S Spain in 1149–74. In both areas they compelled all non-Moslems to become converted. Though N African Jewry ultimately recovered from the blow, in Spain it brought final disaster to the communities living under Moslem rule, who embraced Islam or fled to Christian Spain.

ALMOSNINO, MOSES (c. 1516–1580): Rabbi at Salonica. With the help of Joseph Nasi, he secured a firman from Sultan Selim II in 1568 confirming the

Yigal Allon.

rights of the Salonica community. A. wrote on philosophy, astronomy, and ethics. His account of Constantinople (published in Spanish, Madrid, 1638) is an important historical source.

AL-MUKAMMAS, DAVID BEN MARWAN (fl. probably c. 900): Philosopher; of Mesopotamian birth. Writing in Arabic, he was the first to introduce the methods of the Arab religious philosophy (*Kalam*) into Jewish philosophy. Part of his writings has survived in ms.

ALNAKAWA: (1) *EPHRAIM A.* (d. 1442): Rabbi, poet, and physician; son of (2). He was born in Spain but migrated to N Africa after 1391: he first lived in Morocco, then settled in Honain (Algeria) and finally at Tlemçen. He is still venerated throughout the communities of N Africa as a saint and miracle-worker; (2) *ISRAEL BEN JOSEPH A.* (martyred 1391): Spanish scholar. He composed the ethical work *Menorat ha-Maor* ("Candlestick of Light") published (1929–31) by Enelow who maintained that A.'s work served as the model for Isaac Aboab's classical book of the same name.

ALPHABET: A system of writing which expresses single sounds (as opposed to word-scripts and syllabic scripts), hence the most highly developed and most easily adaptable system of writing. It is now generally agreed that all the alphabetic scripts derive from one original a. Various theories have been advanced to explain the origin of the a. The solution may come from Palestine where several inscriptions belonging to the 18th–13th cents. BCE have been discovered since 1929. Though these Early Canaanite inscriptions are not yet fully deciphered, they are clearly alphabetic. The most probable theory of the origin of the a. appears to be that which considers the a. an indigenous invention of the NW Semitic population of Palestine and Syria. It may be that the a. arose before the middle of the 2nd millennium BCE. The N Semitic a. remained almost unaltered for many centuries; the phonetic value, number, and order of the modern Hebrew letters being a continuation of the original a. created more than 3,500 years ago. The Semitic a. represents only consonants. In the late 2nd millennium and the early 1st millennium BCE three main branches arose out of the original a.—the Canaanite, the Aramaic, and the S Semitic. The Canaanite branch is subdivided into the Phoenician and the Early Hebrew: the latter was employed by the Hebrews roughly in the pre-exilic period (thus being the original script of the Bible), but its use continued for some further centuries and lingered on till the 2nd cent. CE when it was employed by Bar Kokhba on his coins. It is still used by the Samaritans. In post-exilic times, the Early Hebrew was gradually replaced by the

Development of the Hebrew alphabet.

Square Script which was a distinctive Palestinian Jewish descendant of the Aramaic a. It is from this script that the modern Hebrew letters eventually, though gradually, developed. In the evolution of the Hebrew a. three fundamental types of writing can be traced: (1) the Square Script which during its bi-millennial history gradually developed into the neat, well-proportioned printing type of modern Hebrew; (2) the cursive literary or book-hands which were employed by the medieval Jewish savants in many local varieties (in the Levant, Morocco, Spain, Italy, France, and Germany), the best known being the rabbinic, so-called RASHI SCRIPT; and (3) the current hands, also in many local varieties, of which the Polish-German form became the Hebrew hand of today. Besides giving rise to the Square Script, the Aramaic a. also developed into the Arabic, Syriac, various Persian, and Indian a.'s (including the widely used Devanagari a.) and various Mongolian scripts. From the Early Canaanite or Phoenician a. was borrowed the Greek a., which in turn gave rise to the Latin, the Russian "Cyrillic," and various oriental scripts. The cuneiform a. used for UGARITIC was probably also based on the Early Canaanite. The Hebrew a. has 22 letters, though it is probable that some (ה,ע,שׂ) expressed more than one sound. In the Square Script, five letters (פ,נ,מ,צ,כ) have different forms at the end of a word. There are no capitals. All letters are consonants, but ,ו,י and more rarely א came to be used for a rather imperfect representation of vowels before VOCALIZATION was invented.

ALROY, DAVID (real name: Menahem ben Solomon; fl. 12th cent.): Leader of a messianic movement in Persia. The movement began before 1121 among the "Mountain Jews" in NE Caucasia, the background of the movement lying in the invasion of the nomadic Kipchaks from the steppes of the Black Sea, the sufferings and poverty of the Jews, and the greater possibility of conquering Palestine after the Crusades. The movement was first led by A.'s father, and A., who was physically and intellectually outstanding, was proclaimed Messiah. After an initial defeat, A. transferred the center of the revolt to the mountains of Kurdistan, trying to gain a firm foothold in the fortified city of Amadia. However, he was killed by secret assassins (possibly his father-in-law, instigated by the Moslem governor of the city; probably in 1135, although his death has also been dated in 1160). Some of A.'s followers in Azerbaijan remained loyal to him after his death and were called Menahemites. Benjamin Disraeli's novel *The Wondrous Tale of David Alroy* is unhistorical.

ALSACE: French province. Traditionally the Jews reached A. in the Roman period, but reliable information on a Jewish community derives only from the 12th cent. In the 13th cent., Jews were settled in most of the smaller towns of A. and engaged in moneylending to

Alsatian Jew of the 14th century.

the lesser nobility, being dependent on the favor of the religious and secular princes. In the 13th and 14th cents. the Jews of A., like those of the rest of Germany, were subject to blood libels and physical assaults which reached their peak in the ARMLEDER attacks (1336–38). In 1348, there were widespread accusations of well-poisoning in A. and many Jews were massacred (e.g. in Strasbourg). The Jewish settlement was later tolerated, although from the 15th to the 17th cent. blood libels, massacres, and expulsions continued. When A. came under French rule in the 17th cent., the Jews were allowed to remain. Their legal position was a central point of discussion at the time of the French Revolution and they were emancipated in 1791. The *Décret Infâme* of Napoleon (1808) imposed serious restrictions on them which lasted until 1818. After this date, the Alsatian Jews had, in general, full civic rights and became the backbone of French Jewry. During the period of the annexation of A. to Germany, (1871–1918), many Jews migrated. In 1931, the Jewish community numbered over 28,000. In 1940, the whole community was expelled by the Nazis, thus escaping immediate annihilation, though many eventually perished. The population in 1968 was 20,000 of whom 13,000 were in Strasbourg. Jews still live in some 40 village communities but only 18 of these were functioning as communities.

ALSHEKH, MOSES BEN ḤAYYIM (c. 1507–c. 1600): Biblical commentator and talmudic codifier. A pupil of Joseph Caro, he settled and taught in Safed winning fame through his homilies (especially on the Pentateuch) and his responsa.

ALTALENA: Pseudonym of Vladimir JABOTINSKY, used as the name of the ship in which the *Irgun Tzevai Leumi* attempted to bring arms to Israel in June, 1948. The vessel arrived during a cease-fire and its unloading was forbidden by the Israel government.

The order was resisted and the vessel destroyed off Tel Aviv with some loss of life.

ALTAR: Place of offerings to a deity. The importance of sacrifices in early religion caused the a. to occupy a prominent position, both in temples and in the open (especially on hilltops and in groves). The "horns" of the a. (Ps. 118:27, etc.) may be remnants of stones placed on it. The Pentateuch allowed only one central a., a condition fulfilled by the Tabernacle and subsequently by Solomon's Temple (where it took the form of a bronze table). After the return from the Babylonian exile, an a. of stone was set up before the Temple was rebuilt. Separate from the a. for burnt-offerings was the incense a. which was overlaid with gold and stood before the veil of the inner sanctum. No a. is found in the synagogue, its central place being taken by the Ark containing the Torah-scrolls.

ALTENBERG, PETER (pseudonym of Richard Engländer; 1859–1919): Author. He wrote short stories and impressionistic sketches depicting Viennese life in the late 19th and early 20th cent.

ALTER OF GUR: Dynasty of Ḥasidic rabbis whose residence was in the townlet of Gur near Warsaw. (1) *ISAAC MEIR A.* (1799–1866): Founder of the dynasty. His learning was renowned and his followers numbered tens of thousands. A number of his halakhic works were published. (2) *JUDAH ARYEH LOEB A.* (1847–1905): Nephew of (1). Owing to his influence, the Polish Ḥasidim refrained from joining the Zionist movement. (3) *ABRAHAM MORDECAI A.* (1864–

Stone altar with "horns". Megiddo (Israelite period).

1948): Eldest son of (2). An enthusiastic collector, he amassed a huge library of rare books and mss. He was active as a leader of *Agudat Israel,* and urged his followers to participate in building Palestine where he settled after the Nazi catastrophe. (4) *ISRAEL A.* (1895–). Son and successor of (3). He is resident in Jerusalem.

ALTERMAN, NATAN (1910–1970): Poet and translator. Born in Poland, he went to Palestine in 1925 and became one of the leading Hebrew poets. An innovator in style, he made liberal use of everyday Hebrew and was a master of topical verse, reacting sharply and satirically to contemporary social and political events. Some of his work has been collected in *Tur Shevii* ("Seventh Column") and other volumes. He translated plays by Shakespeare and other classics for the Hebrew theater.

ALTMAN, BENJAMIN (1840–1913): Philanthropist who revolutionized New York shopping in 1906 by moving his business closer to the newer middle-class residential areas. His art collection, valued at $20,000,000, was the largest single bequest ever received by the Metropolitan Museum. He established the Altman Foundation ($30,000,000) to provide funds for philanthropic purposes and to advance employee profit-sharing plans.

ALTMANN, ALEXANDER (1906–): Scholar. He was rabbi and lecturer in the Berlin Rabbinical Seminary 1931–8, communal rabbi in Manchester 1938–59, and professor of Jewish philosophy at Brandeis Univ. since 1959.

ALTNEULAND see **HERZL, THEODOR**

ALTNEUSCHUL: Oldest extant synagogue in Europe, possibly founded in the 11th cent. although the present building is probably of the 14th cent.

ALTONA: German town near (now in) Hamburg. Its Jewish community dates from 1641 when Sephardi Jews received a residence charter and commercial and shipbuilding privileges from Christian IV of Denmark. Ashkenazi Jews soon superseded the Sephardim in numbers and importance. A.'s trade and shipping and whaling industries were greatly stimulated by Jewish enterprise in the succeeding two centuries. In 1664, the three neighboring Ashkenazi communities of A., Hamburg, and Wandsbeck were united under the jurisdiction of the chief rabbi of A. The city became famous for such rabbinical leaders as Tzevi Ashkenazi, Jonathan Eibeschütz, Jacob Emden, and Jacob Ettlinger. The union of the three communities was dissolved in 1812. In 1933, there were some 5,000 Jews in A; only a few score returned after World War II.

ALTSCHULER: (1) *DAVID A.* (fl. 17th cent.): Bible commentator; lived in Prague. He commenced a commentary on the Prophets and Hagiographa which was continued by his son. (2) *JEHIEL HILLEL A.* (fl. 18th cent.): Rabbi of Yavorov (Galicia); son of

(1). He completed his father's biblical commentary (except for the Hagiographa) and arranged it in two volumes: *Metzudat David* ("Stronghold of David") which explains each word literally, and *Metzudat Tziyyon* ("Stronghold of Zion") which explains difficult words as they occur. This commentary, distinguished by its clarity and simplicity, became very popular and is printed in many editions of the Hebrew Bible.

AM HA-ARETZ (Heb. "People of the Land"): Biblical phrase denoting the masses of the people (as distinct from certain aristocratic classes), or the people generally. M. Sulzberger tried to show that the term was used to designate "the ancient Hebrew Parliament." In talmudic times it was applied to the common people who did not adhere to the rabbinic regulations as regards the laws of purity, tithe-separation, etc. Ultimately, it acquired the connotation of "ignoramus."

AM OLAM (Heb. "Eternal People"): Organization founded by Jewish youth in Russia after the massacres in 1881. Their object was to emigrate, and they stressed the pursuit of agriculture as a means to national regeneration. Although interested in settlement in Palestine, their main activity was in the US where they founded (1883) the "New Odessa" colony in Oregon: this broke up in 1886 owing to ideological disagreements. The *A.O.* group from Kremenchug founded in 1882 two colonies in S Dakota, which lasted until 1885.

AM OVED (Heb. "Working People"): Tel Aviv publishing house operated under the auspices of the *Histadrut*. Founded in 1941, its chief editor until 1944 was Berl Katznelson. By 1976, it had issued over 1,500 original publications and translations including the monthly paperback series of classics *Sifriyyah la-Am* (Popular Library).

AMALEK: Ancient people mentioned several times in the Bible, almost always as hostile to Israel. A nomadic folk wandering between S Palestine and Canaan, they attacked the Israelites in the desert near Rephidim shortly after the exodus, annihilating the weak and weary. However, they were eventually defeated by the Israelite army under Joshua (Exod. 7: 8–13; Deut. 25:17–19). Israel consequently regarded A. as an eternal foe, the extermination of which was a national mission (Exod. 17:13–16), incompletely carried out later by Saul (I Sam. 15). During the period of the Judges (12th-11th cents. BCE), A. penetrated W Palestine at various points and their presence was a standing threat to the peace of the country. In David's time, A. invaded S Judea, burning the town of Ziklag. David fought and defeated them heavily, only 400 escaping (I Sam. 30). In the reign of Hezekiah (720–690 BCE) the tribe of Simeon overwhelmed the Amalekites and settled in their territory. The name remained in rabbinic literature as a symbol of everlasting enmity to Israel, and Haman "the Agagite" (Est. 3:1) is regarded as a descendant of Agag, king of A. (I Sam. 15:33).

AMARNA, TEL EL: Arabic name of the site of the capital of Pharaoh Amenhotep IV (Akh-en-Aton) in Middle Egypt. In 1887, many cuneiform tablets were discovered there (including letters from kings in Asia Minor) from the archives of Amenhotep III (c. 1413–1377 BCE) and Amenhotep IV (c. 1377–1361). Others were found later. Of special interest are several scores of letters from vassal kings in Canaan (the kings of Ascalon, Acre, Jerusalem, Megiddo, Sidon, Gebal, etc.). These complain of the disorder prevailing in the country following the incursion of the ḤABIRU (probably Hebrews) and the frequent wars among Pharaoh's vassal kings, and request Egyptian assistance. Almost all the letters are written in Akkadian, a few in Hurrian and Hittite, and some have glosses in Canaanite.

AMASA: Commander of Absalom's army in his rebellion against David. After the suppression of Absalom's rising, David appointed A. as his general. When Sheba ben Bichri revolted, David ordered A. to mobilize the men of Judah within 3 days, but A. acted slowly. Later, Joab killed him at Gibeon, perhaps from jealousy, perhaps out of suspicion of his loyalty. David on his deathbed bade Solomon avenge this murder.

AMATUS LUSITANUS (i.e., A. the Portuguese: Hebrew name probably Ḥaviv; 1511–1568): Medical scholar. Born in Portugal of Marrano parents as Joao Rodriguez, he studied medicine at Salamanca. About 1533, he went to Antwerp where he published his annotations on Dioscorides (1536). From there he went to Ferrara where free worship and research were permitted; here, for a time he taught anatomy at the university. In 1547, he moved to the Papal States where his patients included Pope Julius III. He was living in Ancona when the Marranos were persecuted there (1555), but escaped, settling as a professing Jew in Ragusa and then Salonica. His major work was *Centuriae curationum* in 7 volumes, each describing 100 case-histories and treatments. He was the first to suggest the connection of the heart-valves with the circulation of the blood.

AMAZIAH: King of Judah; reigned 796–c. 780 BCE. He succeeded his father, Joash, on his assassination, and put his murderers to death. A. pursued a vigorous policy and gained a victory over Edom, but, challenging Samaria, was heavily defeated and held prisoner for a time. He was killed in a palace revolution.

AMEN (Heb. "So be it"): Expression of affirmation used as response to prayers and benedictions. The word occurs 14 times in the Bible. A longer formula was preferred in the Temple, but A. was adopted in the synagogue as a symbol of congregational participation, and its utterance after every blessing was made obligatory. It has passed into use in Christian and (to a lesser degree) Moslem worship.

AMERICA: Although the Jewish origin of Christopher COLUMBUS is controversial, Jews and Marranos were intimately associated with the origin of his expedition, and his interpreter Luis de Torres, a converted Jew, was the first European to set foot on American soil. From the beginning of the colonization in the New World in the 16th cent., Marranos settled in both the Spanish and the Portuguese colonies, notwithstanding the Inquisition. When BRAZIL was under Dutch rule (1630–54), the first openly Jewish communities were founded by native Marranos and immigrants from Holland. The Portuguese reconquest dispersed its members who established settlements throughout the British and Dutch WEST INDIES and, in 1654, in New Amsterdam (NEW YORK). Further communities were founded on the N American mainland in the course of the next generation. From the beginning of the 19th cent., with the improvement in transatlantic communications and the opening-up of the Middle West, the UNITED STATES, which from the time it achieved independence had established full religious freedom for the first time in the modern world, attracted a growing number of immigrants from Europe. By 1880, the Jewish population had grown to some 250,000, mainly of German origin: there was also a small settlement in CANADA. After the pogroms of 1881, a vast stream of Russian refugees arrived, changing the entire aspect of American Jewry. The immigration continued unabated until 1914 and thereafter, on a smaller scale. Communities were now formed in Latin America also, including Baron de Hirsch's agricultural colonies in ARGENTINA. The stemming of the immigration to the US in the legislation of 1924 directed an increasing stream to Canada and S America, where the communities were further increased from 1933 onward by refugees from Germany and Central Europe. Spanish-speaking Sephardi immigrants from the Mediterranean countries, moreover, were attracted by linguistic affinities. With the annihilation of a large part of European Jewry in 1939–45, the Jews of A., numbering in all over 6,901,545 (1973), became by far the most numerous portion of the Jewish people. Apart from the US (5,800,000), the communities of Argentina (with 475,000 Jews), of Canada (305,000), and of Brazil (155,000) were henceforth numbered among the largest in the world. No country in America is now without its organized Jewish community.

AMERICA-ISRAEL CULTURAL FOUNDATION: Organization founded in 1941 by Edward A. Norman, as the American Fund for Palestine Institutions, to be the sole fund-raising agency in the US for 81 Israel educational, cultural, and social welfare institutions.

AMERICAN ACADEMY FOR JEWISH RESEARCH: Institution organized in 1919–20 (incorporated 1929) to foster Jewish learning and research in America. It holds meetings at which scholarly papers are read, publishes an annual volume of *Proceedings* and other works, and grants money for research purposes and subventions for publications.

AMERICAN ASSOCIATION FOR JEWISH EDUCATION: Organization founded in 1939 to foster Jewish education in the US and Canada. The Association offers services in the field of educational research, community organization for Jewish education, pedagogics and curricula, personnel training, and welfare. The Association sponsors the National Board of License for Jewish Teachers, the National Council on Jewish Audio-Visual Materials, and publishes special conference materials and studies on Jewish education. Its publications include *Jewish Education Newsletter* (bi-monthly) and *Trends and Developments* (annually). It co-sponsors with the National Council for Jewish Education the publication of the quarterly *Jewish Education*.

AMERICAN COUNCIL FOR JUDAISM: Organization founded in 1943, maintaining that Judaism is a religion of universal values—not a nationality. It seeks for "Americans of Jewish faith," an increasing civic, cultural, and social integration in US life. The Council's active program aims at enabling American Jews to meet obligations in public affairs, religion, and philanthropy in ways "compatible with Jewish belief rather than in the Jewish nationalist pattern of Zionism." It works from the premise that nationality and religion are separate and distinct; that no Jew or group of Jews can speak for all American Jews; and that Israel is the "homeland" of its own citizens only and not of all Jews.

Medal commemorating 250th anniversary of Jewish settlement in America.

Hester Street (c. 1898). Scene characteristic of early Jewish settlement in New York City.

President Eisenhower at the American Jewish Tercentenary Dinner, 1954.

American Jewish Committee delegation in Washington, 1911.
From l. to r.: Louis Marshall, Herbert Friedenwald, Judge Mayer Sulzberger, Harry Cutler, Oscar S.
Straus, Judge Leon Sanders, Henry M. Goldfogle, Samuel Dorf, Leon Kamaiky.

AMERICAN HEBREW: Weekly newspaper in English, founded by Philip Cowen in New York in 1879. It formerly served as a leading forum for the writings of eminent Jewish literary figures. Its editors have included F. de Sola Mendes, Herman Bernstein, Joseph Jacobs, and Isaac Landman.

AMERICAN ISRAELITE: Oldest surviving Jewish periodical in the US, founded by Isaac Mayer Wise in Cincinnati in 1854. It provides news and information on Judaism to widely-scattered Jewish communities, and was the unofficial organ of Reform Judaism for many years. Wise edited it until his death in 1900, and the periodical remained in the hands of his family until 1930.

AMERICAN JEWISH ARCHIVES: National depository, organized in 1947 at the Hebrew Union College, Cincinnati, to preserve records dealing with the life and history of US Jewry. It has originals, photostats, and microfilms, including volumes of minute books of early congregations and Jewish societies. It has been publishing the semi-annual *American Jewish Archives* since 1948. It was directed from its foundation by Jacob R. MARCUS.

AMERICAN JEWISH COMMITTEE: Organization founded in 1906 "to prevent the infraction of the civil and religious rights of Jews in any part of the world," and "to secure for Jews equality of economic, social, and educational opportunity." In 1911, the Committee initiated a movement to bring about the abrogation of the Russo-American commercial treaty of 1832 in consequence of Russian discrimination against Jewish holders of US passports. At the beginning of World War I, the Committee joined the Zionist Organization of America in extending emergency aid to the Jews in Palestine and brought about the creation of the American Jewish Relief Committee, the most important constituent of the American Jewish Joint Distribution Committee. Later, the AJC headed the opposition to the establishment of a permanent AMERICAN JEWISH CONGRESS but agreed to a congress for the sole purpose of working for rights for Jews in all lands at the Paris Peace Conference. It fought for the retention of the open-door immigration policy in the US and, when restrictive legislation was enacted, tried to mitigate the effects. During the Hitler period, the AJC concentrated on exposing the aims of Nazism and on countering anti-Jewish propaganda in the US. After World War II, the Committee actively encouraged legislative, judicial, and social action for eliminating discrimination and prejudice against minorities and improving intergroup relations in the US. The AJC has led in the systematic application of the social sciences to the study of anti-Semitism and other forms of prejudice. Although the Committee has always been non-Zionist, it has had a consistently favorable attitude to Palestine and Israel. In 1969, the Committee had about 43,000 members in more than 500 cities throughout the US. Its publications are the *American Jewish Year Book* (issued jointly with the Jewish Publication Society of America since 1909), *Commentary*, a monthly magazine, and *Present Tense*. Its presidents have included Mayer Sulzberger, Louis Marshall, Cyrus Adler, Joseph M. Proskauer, Morris B. Abram, and Arthur J. Goldberg.

AMERICAN JEWISH CONFERENCE: Organization founded in 1943 to coordinate American Jewish efforts in behalf of Palestine and other Jewries. In 1948, the Conference attempted to organize an American Jewish Assembly as its successor, to function also in the area of domestic problems. The Conference was dissolved in 1949 when the plan was rejected by several major organizations.

AMERICAN JEWISH CONGRESS: Organization founded in 1917 for the purpose of securing, in cooperation with the Jewish communities among the Allied Powers, the recognition of Jewish civil, political,

and religious equal rights in Central and E Europe, as well as to secure and protect Jewish rights in Palestine. Founded by Zionists, it later also received non-Zionist support. It consisted of designees of organizations together with delegates elected by communities. It sent a delegation to the Peace Conference in Paris headed by Julian W. Mack and Louis Marshall. After the Peace Conference, the AJC adjourned *sine die*. A number of the delegates and groups, however, joined to form a permanent organization under the same name in 1922 with Nathan Straus as president. Subsequent presidents have been Stephen Wise, Israel Goldstein, Joachim Prinz, Arthur J. Lelyveld and Arthur Hertzberg. The Congress, which is a membership organization representing affiliated national bodies, played an important role in the fight against Nazism, in the organization of the WORLD JEWISH CONGRESS in 1936, in supporting Zionism, as well as in the defense of civil rights in the US.

AMERICAN JEWISH HISTORICAL SOCIETY: Research organization founded in 1892, on the initiative of Cyrus Adler and Oscar S. Straus, to promote the study of American Jewish history. Since its inception, it has issued its proceedings in the *Publica-*

Guests of honor at American Jewish Joint Distribution Committee's Dinner, 1954.
Seated (l. to r.): Adolph Held, Bernard Semel, James N. Rosenberg, Senator Herbert H. Lehman, Paul Baerwald.
Standing (l. to r.): Rabbi David de Sola Pool, Alexander Kahn, Dr. Bernard Kahn, Alex A. Landesco, Baruch Zuckerman, I. Edwin Goldwasser, Rabbi Jonah B. Wise.

tions of the American Jewish Historical Society which. since 1948, appears as a quarterly. It also publishes monographs in its series *Studies in American Jewish History* and *American Jewish Communal Histories*. Its headquarters are now situated on the campus of BRANDEIS UNIVERSITY.

AMERICAN JEWISH JOINT AGRICULTURAL CORPORATION see **AGRO-JOINT**

AMERICAN JEWISH JOINT DISTRIBUTION COMMITTEE (popularly known as the "Joint" or JDC): American Jewry's overseas relief and rehabilitation agency. It was created (1914) by a committee representing relief organizations established by the American Jewish Committee, orthodox groups, and labor elements. Up to 1976 it has expended more than $1,079,126,000, including $585,000,000 in 1948–67. It now receives its funds from the UNITED JEWISH APPEAL. Felix M. Warburg was its first chairman, and Paul Baerwald and the former's son, Edward M.M. Warburg, were chairmen during the years of its greatest activity. The history of the JDC can be divided into seven periods: 1) World War I (1914–18), when relief and medical care were provided for the Jews of E and Central Europe, uprooted and impoverished by warfare, and for the Jews of Palestine; 2) post-war emergency (1919–21), especially in E Europe where pogroms, disease, and hunger ravaged the Jewish population; 3) reconstruction (1921–5). during which time emphasis was placed on helping E European, especially Polish, Jews, with medical care, vocational training, loan funds, credit cooperatives, and assistance for their educational, religious, and communal institutions; 4) economic crisis (1925–32), mostly in Poland, requiring emergency relief, etc.; 5) pre-war Nazism (1933–9), assisting German Jewry with relief and vocational retraining and facilitating emigration; 6) World War II (1939–45), when rescue and relief work was carried out; 7) post-war years, during which the major tasks were assistance to Displaced Persons, emigration to Israel, reconstruction of Jewish life in Europe, care of the ill, aged, and disabled in Israel (through MALBEN), and relief and communal help to Jews in Moslem countries. The JDC extended very considerable aid to the Jews in Russia and E Europe before the war through AGRO-JOINT and thereafter directly. This did not prevent the Soviet calumny (1952: disowned, 1953) that the JDC had engineered the murder of prominent Russian officials. In 1957, the JDC was invited to recommence its activities in Poland but was again excluded ten years later. In general the JDC continued to be regarded with suspicion and hostility in E Europe and its director Charles H. Jordan died in mysterious circumstances in Prague in 1967.

AMERICAN JEWISH PERIODICAL CENTER: Institute established in 1956 at the Hebrew Union College, Cincinnati, to microfilm the c. 1,200 newspapers, journals, and serials of Jewish interest published in the US, 1823–1925, as well as selected examples from later years.

AMERICAN JOINT RECONSTRUCTION FOUNDATION: Organization established in 1924 by the American Joint Distribution Committee and ICA to assist in the economic reconstruction of the Jews in Central and E Europe. The Foundation was formally liquidated in 1948.

AMERICAN ZION COMMONWEALTH: A land-purchasing agency organized in 1914 by the Zionist Organization of America. It was responsible for the redemption of land in Israel and developing Jewish settlement there. It was dissolved in 1931 after transferring its properties to Zionist national funds and private individuals.

AMERICAN ZIONIST COUNCIL: Body organized by the various Zionist groups in the US as the American Zionist Emergency Council in 1939, reorganized under its present name in 1949. Its public relations program seeks to impart to Americans a knowledge of Israel's problems, achievements, and aims. The AZC sponsors the Student Zionist Organization and Zionist Youth Council.

AMIA (Sp. *Asociación Mutual Israelita Argentina*): Argentine body founded in 1894. Originally a *Ḥevrah Kaddisha,* it developed from a relief organization into a cultural and educational body with a membership of 43,680 (1972); since 1956, the A. has extended its activities to include cultural ties with Israel.

AMIDAH see **EIGHTEEN BENEDICTIONS**

AMIEL, MOSES AVIGDOR (1883–1946): Rabbi and *Mizraḥi* leader. After occupying posts in his native Poland and Antwerp, he was elected chief rabbi of Tel Aviv in 1936. His published works include novellae and sermons.

AMITTAI: Name of two synagogal poets who lived at Oria (S Italy) in the 9th cent., one, the father, the other, the son of SHEPHATIAH: a hymn by one of them is included in the *Neilah* service according to the Ashkenazi rite. Their family history is related with much embellishment in the rhymed chronicle of their descendant, AHIMAAZ BEN PALTIEL.

AMMAN see **RABBATH AMMON**

AMMI BAR NATHAN (fl. c. 300): Palestinian amora. Probably born in Babylon, he became head of the Tiberias academy. He was the friend and companion of R Assi with whom he toured the villages of Palestine to encourage sacred study and organize the judiciary. A. and Assi were called "the judges of Palestine," and their names constantly figure together.

AMMON: Ancient people and country in Transjordan; capital — RABBATH AMMON (modern Amman). They were a Semitic tribe, according to the Bible, related to the Israelites (Gen. 19:38). A.'s main period of development was the 13th–8th cents. BCE, following which they declined, being eventually absorbed into

Amorite types (bas-relief).

Arab tribes. After the Israelites occupied Canaan, they were frequently attacked by the Ammonites who suffered defeats at the hands of Jephthah and Saul. David annexed their kingdom but they regained their independence and attacked Judah on several occasions (II Chron. 20; 27:5; II Kings 24:2). After the destruction of the First Temple, Baalis, king of A., instigated the murder of Gedaliah, presumably to weaken Judah still further (Jer. 40:14). On the return from Babylon, A. joined Judah's enemies and Tobiah the Ammonite supported Sanballat in his opposition to Nehemiah (Neh. 2:10). During the Hasmonean rising, the Ammonites aided the Syrian forces and were defeated by Judah the Maccabee (163 BCE). Few details are known of Ammonite culture as no literary remains survive, but excavations in Transjordan indicate a developed kingdom with fortified frontiers, artistic tastes, and advanced agriculture. They worshiped fertility gods, the chief being Milkom.

AMNON (also Aminon): Eldest son of David by Ahinoam the Jezreelite. He became enamored of his half-sister, TAMAR, and raped her. Two years later, Tamar's brother, Absalom, had A. killed for his crime (II Sam. 13).

AMNON OF MAINZ: Legendary martyr (10th–11th cents.). Commanded by the bishop of Mainz to become converted, A. requested a three-day respite to consider. When he failed to appear, he was brought before the bishop, and made the request that his tongue should be cut out for not immediately refusing. Instead, the bishop ordered that his limbs should be mutilated. On the New Year, he was taken to the synagogue where, before expiring, he recited the *U-Netanneh Tokeph* prayer which thereafter figured prominently in the Ashkenazi liturgy. In fact, the prayer had been composed much earlier, and has been found in the Cairo *genizah*.

AMON: King of Judea; reigned 642–640 BCE. He ascended the throne at the age of 22 in succession to his father Manasseh and ruled for 2 years before being killed by conspirators.

AMORA (from Heb./Aram. *amar* = speak): Title given to the Jewish scholars in Palestine and especially Babylonia in the 3rd–6th cents. Their intellectual activity is recorded in the TALMUD. The a. was originally a lecturer who expounded the views of previous scholars or interpreted them for the masses. Later, the a. himself explained the MISHNAH and its application to practical issues. On occasion, he initiated laws which were accepted as equal in authority to earlier legislation. The amoraim taught in the period after the conclusion of the Mishnah, their work being comprised in the GEMARA. There were two principal types of amoraic scholars—those distinguished for erudition and those noted for logical acumen. The amoraic method was entirely original and necessitated extensive preparation. Specific training was a prerequisite to acceptance into the academy; after entering, the student was required to gain thorough experience in halakhic discussion before he was able to make legal decisions. Many amoraim were noted for their aggadah. The influence of the amoraim derived from the originality, literary construction, and effective delivery of their ideas. The amoraim, of whom over 3,000 are known by name, were honored by the people and their judicial decisions were authoritative. They were not paid for their teaching but earned their living independently. There was constant contact between Palestinian and Babylonian sages throughout the entire amoraic period, but for external reasons, the influence of those in Palestine declined rapidly after the end of the 4th cent.

AMORITES: One of the biblical names for the inhabitants of Canaan before the Israelite conquest. The name is applied to (1) the entire population of the country at that period; and (2) one of the ancient peoples of the country, annihilated or assimilated by the Israelites. The name is also mentioned in both cuneiform and hieroglyphic sources where its significance is not constant: on some occasions it is an ethnographic term, probably denoting the W Semitic tribes, and on others it is a geographical term, denoting the whole area of Syria and Palestine. From the middle of the 2nd millennium BCE, there was an Amorite state in central and S Syria incorporating the Lebanese Mountains and important harbor towns. It constituted an important link between Egypt and Mesopotamia and, after a long struggle between Egypt and the Hittite kingdom, was annexed to the latter. The A. are mentioned in the Bible from patriarchal times. They were settled on both sides of the Jordan, especially in mountainous regions. Moses is credited with the conquest of two Amorite kingdoms (Heshbon and Bashan). At this period, the A. were no longer a pure W Semitic element but mixed with other strains in Palestine, especially the Horites and Hittites. "The ways of the Amorite" is a term applied in rabbinic and medieval literature to folk-practices alien to the spirit of Judaism.

AMOS (fl. 8th cent. BCE): Prophet. Of Judean origin (a herdsman and sycamore-pruner from Tekoa near Bethlehem), his main center of activity was in the northern kingdom. Although Israel was enjoying a period of prosperity under Jeroboam II, A. sensed that the calm was temporary and that grave danger threatened from Assyria. Moreover, he was acutely conscious of the internal corruption of the kingdom arising from the sharp antagonism between the wealthy upper classes and the exploited masses. A. prophesied at Bethel, the royal sanctuary, not encountering opposition until he foretold the destruction of the land of Ephraim, its shrines, and its royal house. Amaziah, the priest of Bethel, regarded this as treason and ordered A. to return to Judah, but the prophet insisted on fulfilling his Divine mission. Nothing further is known of his life. The Book of A., the third of the 12 minor prophets, consists of 9 chapters, the central theme being the conception of social morality as a historical and determining factor in the life of Israel and other peoples. The book is couched in a simple style with a wealth of imagery drawn from nature and from peasant life.

AMPAL (abbr. of "American-Palestine Trading Company"): American Jewish trading corporation, organized in 1942 to develop trade between the US and Israel, and to aid banking, credit, industry, and agriculture in Israel. Its affiliates include shipping, industrial, and financial enterprises in Israel. The controlling interest is held by the HISTADRUT.

AMRAM: Son of Kohath; grandson of Levi. He was the father of Moses, Aaron, and Miriam.

AMRAM BAR SHESHNA: Gaon and head of the Sura academy, 856–74; author of responsa. *Seder Rav Amram,* a liturgical compilation with pertinent halakhic prescriptions for the whole year, was ascribed to him. Prepared at the request of Spanish communities, this became a standard guide in matters of ritual law and practice; many modifications were, however, introduced into the ms in the course of time, and the original text is difficult to establish.

*AMRAPHEL: King of Shinar; one of the five kings who united to attack the rulers of Sodom and were defeated by Abraham (Gen. 14). The identification of A. with the Babylonian king, Hammurabi, is now thought unlikely.

AMSTERDAM: Largest city of HOLLAND. At the end of the 16th cent., Marranos from Spain and Portugal began to migrate to A. The Sephardi congregation was openly established not later than 1608. Some of the newcomers were large-scale merchants who helped to develop Dutch overseas trade. Many Jews arrived in A. from Germany during the Thirty Years' War and from E Europe after the persecutions of 1648-9. Thus, by the second half of the 17th cent., the Ashkenazim outnumbered the Sephardim. Nevertheless, the latter remained pre-eminent for their wealth and culture, and the synagogue they consecrated in 1675 was one of the monuments of the city. Up to the end of the 18th cent., the Amsterdam community was the most important and wealthy in W Europe, and a focus of Jewish scholarship. In 1626/7, MANASSEH BEN ISRAEL set up a Hebrew printing-press, and A. was henceforth a great center of Hebrew printing. A. Jewry was influential in all economic spheres, including diamond-polishing which was almost entirely in the hands of Jewish craftsmen and workers until the 20th cent. The community maintained particularly close relations with

Seal of Portuguese community of Amsterdam.

those of Hamburg and London. In 1797, the first reformed congregation in Europe, *Adath Jeshurun,* was established at A. Throughout the 19th cent., the community, with its splendidly organized institutions, its great libraries, and its staunch Jewish loyalties, remained among the most important in the western world. In 1941, it numbered some 86,000 (including 5,000 Sephardim). The Jews suffered terribly during the Nazi occupation, and mass deportations were carried out from July, 1942. The community (14,000 in 1973) is still the largest in Holland.

Frontispiece of Passover Haggadah printed in Amsterdam, 1695.

AMULET (Heb. *kamea*): Object worn as charm against evil, consisting usually of sacred letters or symbols: names of angels or demons are often written in geometric patterns, etc. Such charms were common in the ancient Middle East and have been found frequently in excavations in Palestine. In the talmudic and gaonic periods, a.'s were widely worn and their use was recognized, though not specifically approved, by rabbis. With the development of the later Kabbalah and its insistence on the efficacy of combinations of letters of the Divine names, the vogue of a.'s became universal, and their preparation was regarded as a rabbinic function. They were inscribed on paper, parchment, or metal, and comprised kabbalistic diagrams, biblical verses, and various letter-combinations: sometimes they were worn on the person, sometimes hung on the wall, etc. In this category, charms against LILITH for use in the birth-chamber are still common. In Italy, the silver or gold containers for the a.'s (usually bearing on the outside the Divine name *Shaddai*, by which they were known) often attained a high degree of artistic achievement. See also MAGIC, SUPERSTITION.

AMZALAK, MOSES BENSABAT (1892–): Portuguese economist; director, then rector, of the Institute of Economic Sciences at the Univ. of Lisbon, and author of many works on economic and Jewish subjects. He is the leading figure in Portuguese Jewish life, having for many years headed the Lisbon community. He was president of the Portuguese Academy of Sciences.

ANACLETUS II (Piero Pierleoni): Antipope (1130–8) in opposition to Innocent II. Descendant of a converted Jewish financier, Piero Leoni, A. encountered bitter opposition within the Church (e.g. from Bernard of Clairvaux), partly as a result of his Jewish extraction. Nevertheless he was able to maintain himself in Rome until his death. It is likely that his career engendered the widespread medieval legend of a Jewish pope, Andreas.

ANAGRAM: A word or phrase formed by the transposition of the letters of another word or phrase. Employed in rabbinic hermeneutics, it became a favorite literary device in medieval Hebrew. It occurs frequently in kabbalistic writings, and is particularly practiced in connection with the use of Divine and angelic names appearing on amulets and charms.

ANAKIM: People who according to biblical tradition lived in Canaan before its conquest by the Israelites. They inhabited the mountainous area of Judah and also the S coastal zone, but were exterminated in the time of Joshua. The A. have not yet been identified; they were tall in stature (Num. 13:32–3) and the word a. in Hebrew has come to denote giants.

ANAN BEN DAVID (second half of 8th cent.): Founder of the sect of KARAITES. He is said to have been the oldest son of the Babylonian exilarch and

Arm amulet, Persia, 18th century.
(Bezalel Museum, Jerusalem).

learned in Jewish law, but apparently tended to one of the messianic sects then prevalent in Babylon. The heads of the academies refused to install him as his father's successor, preferring his younger brother Hananiah whose appointment was approved by the caliph (c. 760). A. refused to yield and proclaimed himself exilarch. Imprisoned as a rebel (767), he pleaded that he and his supporters held a religion different from that of other Jews, and he was therefore not rivaling the official exilarch. On being released, he became the leader of a separate Jewish sect (at first called Ananites) whose main feature was opposition to the talmudical tradition. In his *Sepher ha-Mitzvot* ("Book of Precepts," only portions of which survive), A. postulated that the Bible was the sole basis of Judaism, his interpretations being stringent (e.g. prohibition of leaving the house on Sabbath, interdiction on wine and meat, and the institution of numerous fasts). Later Karaite teachers were less severe in their interpretations.

ANANIAS (d. 66 CE): High priest. He was appointed by Herod of Chalcis in 47, deposed by Agrippa II in 59, and killed by the extremists at the outset of the rebellion against Rome. A. took a leading part in the prosecution of the apsotle Paul (Acts 24).

ANATHEMA: Greek term applied, like the Heb. *ḥerem,* both to the process of EXCOMMUNICATION and to an object on which a curse lies and which is therefore considered untouchable. Thus, property of idolators (Deut. 7:26) or even of sinful Jews (Ezra 10:8) was in certain cases considered *ḥerem,* and no enjoyment was to be derived from it.

ANATHOTH: Town in the territory of Benjamin, NE of Jerusalem. Abiathar the priest settled in A. after being deposed by Solomon. It was also the birthplace of Jeremiah. A. has been identified with the Arab village Anata.

ANATOLI, JACOB BEN ABBA MARI (c. 1194–1246): Preacher, philosopher, and Hebrew translator. A native of Provence, he settled in Naples and, under the patronage of the emperor Frederick II (with whom he was in personal contact), made an important contribution to Western learning through his Hebrew translations of Arabic philosophical and astronomical works, particularly those of Averroes, later rendered into Latin. A. preached popular sermons, collected in his *Malmad ha-Talmidim* ("A Goad to Students"), in which he adapted the rationalism of Maimonides to the interpretation of Scripture and to contemporary ethical and religious problems.

ANATOLIA see **ASIA MINOR**

ANATOMY: Although there is no scientific a. in the Bible, there is much use of anatomical data, both in determining the names of the parts of the body and their forms, and in idioms and metaphors which have their origin in a. This data is close to being accurate and is based upon correct observation. The preoccupation with dietary laws, blemishes, menstruation, ritual impurity, etc. necessitated extensive anatomical knowledge among the talmudic scholars. The dissection of the carcasses of animals in order to examine their ritual fitness led to direct observation of natural data. The Talmud even postulates—although it rejects—the possibility of dissecting a human body for the purpose of criminal investigation *(Ḥullin* 11*b).* The sages themselves made examinations or relied on the testimony of an authoritative medical witness. The number of 248 members (bones) and 365 sinews (totaling 613, the number of the precepts) is famous in rabbinic tradition *(Oholot* 1:8). The former does not, in fact, correspond to the number of bones in an adult body which amounts to only 200. The naming of the bones in the Talmud was exact and aimed at anatomical differentiation. The a. of the Talmud is rich in detail and serves to explain the structure of the body in its normal and diseased states, contrasting with the Greek theory of the humors. The details are sometimes extraordinary in their accuracy—to the extent of the recognition of the small cartilages in the structure of the windpipe, discovered in the West only in the 18th cent. There are, of course, certain deficiencies; there was no systematic presentation, and material is only given

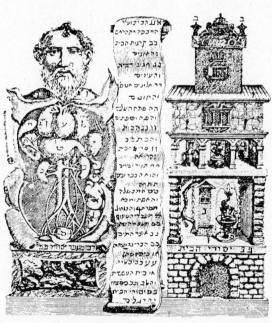

בית חרש

Anatomy of the human body compared to the structure of a house. From the book *Maaseh Toviyah* by Tobias Cohen. (Venice, 1707).

incidentally to the extent required for the elucidation of some halakhic problem. Side by side with imaginary opinions (e.g. the "nut" at the foot of the spine) are found the beginnings of a scientific approach in the use of direct examination and the dissection of the bodies of living creatures. As in Greek a., there is inexactitude of terminology as a result of the occasional use of analogy and metaphor. In the Middle Ages, the Jewish physicians shared the anatomical opinions of their neighbours. Vesalius was, however, assisted in his work on a. in the 16th cent. by the Jew Lazarus de FRIGEIS. The reluctance of Jews to submit bodies for dissection led to complications and ill-feeling in the universities (e.g. at Padua in the 17th–18th cent.; E Europe in the 20th). According to modern Israel law, bodies can be used for medical dissection if unclaimed or if so specified by will. Autopsies may be conducted when needed for reasons of civil law, to establish causes of death, to save lives, and in cases of hereditary disease. Although the Israel Law of Anatomy and Pathology was approved by the Chief Rabbis, there has been opposition among the more extreme Orthodox to the conducting of autopsies.

ANAV or **ANAU** (Heb. *Min Ha-Anavim*): Italian family prominent since the 10th cent. and legendarily settled in Rome by Titus. The usual Italian form of the name is (Dei) Piatelli, sometimes (Delli) Mansi. Its members have included scholars and communal leaders, among them *BENJAMIN BEN ABRAHAM*

A., physician, talmudist, commentator, and liturgical poet; and his brother *ZEDEKIAH A.* (both fl. Rome 13th cent.), author of *Shibbole ha-Leket* ("Gathered Sheaves"). This work, comprising ritual law and regulations gathered from other sources and containing useful social and literary material, became the standard for ritual observances in Italy, also in an abbreviated form entitled *Tanya*. *JEHIEL BEN JEKUTHIEL A.* (13th cent.), author and copyist, wrote liturgical poems, including one on the burning of the Rome synagogue in 1268, and a popular ethical work, *Maalot ha-Middot*, often reprinted. *JUDAH BEN BENJAMIN A.* (c. 1215–c. 1290) wrote a commentary on Alfasi's Code. *PHINEHAS HAI A.*, known as Felice Umano (1693–1768), rabbi of Ferrara, was a famous preacher and pietist. His monumental *Givat Pinḥas*, containing his responsa, remains unpublished.

ANCHEL, ROBERT (1880–1951): French historian. An archivist at the Archives Nationales, he published a number of important historical monographs on general and Jewish history, including a volume on Napoleon and the Jews, and a collection of essays on French history.

ANCIENT OF DAYS see **GOD, NAMES OF**

ANCIENT ORDER OF MACCABAEANS see **MACCABAEANS, ANCIENT ORDER OF**

ANCONA: Port of E coast of Italy. It was one of the centers from which Jewish loan-bankers spread through central Italy in the 13th–14th cents. A colony of Marranos established itself there in the 16th cent., but was brutally uprooted in 1555–6 when 24 were burnt at the stake. When the Jews were expelled from the smaller centers of the Papal States in 1569, they were allowed to remain only in Rome and A., which continued to be one of the largest Italian Jewish communities until the end of the Ghetto Period. The Jews were temporarily emancipated under Napoleon, and finally when the city became part of the kingdom of Italy (1861). The community, once numbering 2,000, had 300 Jews in 1970.

ANCONA D': Italian family of scholars. *ALESSANDRO D'A.* (1835–1914), professor at the Univ. of Pisa, was a foremost literary historian and authority on the origins of the Italian theater. Of his brothers, *CESARE D'A.* (1832–1901) was professor of geology and paleontology in Florence and active in Jewish life, and *VITO D'A.* (1825–1884) was a well-known painter. Alessandro's son *PAOLO D'A.* (1878–1964) of the Univ. of Milan was an art historian and authority on medieval manuscript illumination.

ANDREAS (POPE) see **ANACLETUS II; ELHANAN**

ANGEL (Gk. ἄγγελος, used in the Septuagint to translate the Heb. *malakh* "messenger"): The word is now used for numerous types of supernatural beings mentioned in the Scriptures (CHERUBIM, SERAPHIM, heavenly host, etc.), but the Bible does not suggest any kinship between these classes, at least in the period prior to the Babylonian exile. Thus, only the angels *(malakhim)* appear in human form; as emissaries they convey God's words to mortals (Abraham, Manoah, etc.) and even perform practical missions (precede the Israelites in the Exodus, smite Sennacherib's army, etc.). The place of the a.'s is heaven (Jacob's dream); in their human guise they are not always recognized by mortals. Reverence to a.'s is due to them only as the envoys of God. Although their superhuman character often inspires awe (cf. Is. 6; Ezek. 1), this attitude does not extend to individual a.'s. Until the Second Temple period, no a. has a personal name, though he may sometimes exercise a permanent function ("the angel who redeems me from all evil," Gen. 48:16). Names were first mentioned in the Book of DANIEL (Gabriel and Michael) and increased in the hellenistic period when they included a group (sometimes listed as consisting of seven and sometimes four, of whom the best-known are Gabriel, Michael, Uriel, and Raphael) permanently close to God (archangels). The differentiation between the various categories gradually disappeared. The importance of angelology grew under foreign influence. The heavenly host was now arranged

Doors of Ark. Italian synagogue, Ancona.

Cherubim guarding the Tree of Life. (From a 15th cent. ms, British Museum, London).

and Ezek. 3:12, is incorporated in the KEDUSHAH, PIYYUTIM, and SELIHOT while a popular hymn, *Shalom Aleikhem,* greets the ministering a.'s on the Sabbath eve.

ANGEL OF DEATH (Heb. *malakh ha-mavet*): Divine messenger who takes the soul from the body. Like all ANGELS he is, in principle, the personification of a particular Divine will, act, or function. Again, like other angels, the A. of D. developed from a particular functional expression of God to a relatively independent personality with a distinct character of his own. He appears as such in rabbinic literature whereas in the Bible he is one of the host of "destroying angels." Since death is normally experienced by man in its negative and destructive aspects, the A. of D. became associated with DEMONS. This trend is particularly noticeable in folklore and in midrashic and kabbalistic literature. Since in Jewish tradition death is associated with sin, evil, and punishment, while the future world is expected to be free of death and evil, the A. of D. is part of a cluster of negative personifications such as SATAN, the Tempter, the Accuser, the Evil Inclination *(yetzer ha-ra)*, and SAMAEL, the prince of demons; often, these are identified. Midrashic legend contains lurid descriptions of the A. of D. but also tells stories of his deception by mortals. Theologically, however, the stress in rabbinic literature is on the positive function of the A. of D. in the Divine scheme as an instrument of the Creator's will.

ANGLO-JEWISH ASSOCIATION: Organization founded in 1871 in imitation of the Alliance Israélite Universelle for political and educational work in

into divisions (e.g. Enoch 61) but without uniformity or system. Occasionally, the stars appear as a.'s, while natural phenomena (e.g. clouds, hail) were presided over by a.'s. Each of the seventy nations of the world had its own a. who protected it. Other a.'s conveyed human prayers to God, serving as mediators between man and the transcendental Divinity. Despite their participation in mundane affairs, there is no trace of any cult of a.'s. A special group was the fallen a.'s — the sons of God who had taken the daughters of men (Gen. 6:2); they taught mankind evil ways but were eventually punished (see SATAN). In midrashic and talmudic literature, all previous trends are recorded and new ones added. The characteristics of the a.'s are partly human (they speak Hebrew), partly superhuman. They participate in the important events of human life (pregnancy, birth, etc.). God consults his household (i.e., the a.'s) on every subject. Nevertheless, the righteous man may attain angelic rank and rise even higher. Medieval philosophers do not reject the reality of a.'s but interpret their nature in harmony with their general opinions (often identifying them with the Higher Intelligences of Aristotle). The Kabbalah greatly extended the theory of a.'s, the number of personal names increasing vastly; each man has an a. of luck who decides his fate. In the Jewish liturgy, the praise of God by the ministering a.'s, based on Is. 6:1–3

Joshua before the commander of the heavenly host. Illuminated page from a 15th cent. Haggadah at the Schocken Library, Jerusalem.

behalf of the Jews of backward areas. The most important of its institutions is the Evelina de Rothschild school in Jerusalem. From 1881 to 1944, its political activities were conducted in association with the Board of Deputies of British Jews in the Conjoint (Joint) Foreign Committee. In 1917, Claude G. Montefiore, as president of the AJA, opposed the Balfour Declaration. Though no longer anti-Zionist, it later consolidated its work as the organ of the non-Zionist element in Anglo-Jewry. By the terms of the will of Baron de Hirsch, it is closely associated in the control of ICA.

ANGLO-PALESTINE BANK see **BANK LEUMI LE-ISRAEL**

ANGOLA: W. African country (former Portuguese colony'. A few Portuguese Marranos settled there 16–17 cents.). In 1911–13, a plan was broached by the Jewish Territorial Organization for Jewish settlement in the colony but was abandoned owing to the refusal of the Portuguese government to grant a concession to a Jewish organization.

ANGORA see **ANKARA**

ANHALT: Former German state, since 1945 part of Saxony (Sachsen-Anhalt). The Jewish settlement in A. dates from the Middle Ages. In the 17th and 18th cents., communities flourished in Köthen, Jessnitz, and DESSAU. Its Jewish community, numbering in 1933 over a thousand, was exterminated by the Nazis. Since World War II, only a few Jews have resided there.

ANILAI AND ASINAI: Two outlaw brothers of Nehardea (Babylonia), who founded a small state on the Upper Euphrates and ruled in c. 20–40 CE. They were supported by Artabanus III, king of Parthia. Their raids led to anti-Jewish feeling among the Babylonian populace, and their prestige declined as a result of friction between them and their subjects. Anilai was defeated by Mithridates, son-in-law of the Parthian king, and his supporters were annihilated. His defeat had disastrous results for the Jews of SELEUCIA.

ANILEWICZ, MORDECAI (1919–1943): Leader of the WARSAW Ghetto revolt. A member of *Ha-Shomer ha-Tzair,* he was arrested by the Soviet authorities in Sept. 1939 for organizing the emigration of Jews to Palestine. Upon release (1940), he went to Vilna and to Czestochowa to organize resistance. Appointed commander-in-chief of the Jewish Fighters' Organization in 1942, he led the uprising in the Warsaw Ghetto where he was killed.

ANIM ZEMIROT see **SHIR HA-KAVOD** ,

ANIMALS, HUMANENESS TO (Hebr. *tzaar baale hayyim*): Kindness to animals is an obligatory religious duty in Jewish law which lays down that cruelty to animals is forbidden by the Torah (Deut. 22:4). The Bible forbids the muzzling of an ox while threshing and commands that animals be given rest on the Sabbath. An animal that falls down under its load must be helped to rise. Animals may not be gelded or

Statue of Mordecai Anilewicz at Yad Mordekhai, Israel.
(Sculptor: Natan Rapoport).

cross-bred. Slaughter for food, though permitted, must be humane, and even here special limitations are enforced. Further extension of the principle of kindness to animals is found in rabbinic legislation. A man may not eat unless he has first given food to his animals, nor may a man buy an animal for which he cannot assure a proper supply of food. Rabbis of a later period prohibited hunting because of the cruelty involved. The Israel rabbinate bases certain of its decisions (e.g. the permissibility of plucking feathers from a live bird) on whether cruelty is involved.

ANINUT (Heb.): Period between death and burial during which the mourner is called *onen*. The *onen* may not partake of bread or wine and does not pray or wear *tephillin*.

ANJOU: Former duchy in France. In the Middle Ages, Jews were living at Angers, Baugé, Saumur, and Segré. The community suffered heavily from Crusaders in 1236. Later in the 13th cent., Charles I and Charles II of A. patronized Jewish scholars and translators but imposed serious restrictions on the Jewish communities; Charles II ultimately ordered their expulsion. Jews returned to A. in the 14th cent. and a few lived there until the expulsion from France in 1394.

ANKARA (ANGORA): Capital of Turkey. An organized Jewish community was founded by exiles from Spain (1492), their chief occupation being the silk trade. It has increased in importance since A. became the Turkish capital in 1923, and numbers 1,000 (1973).

ANNENBERG, WALTER HUBERT (1908–): US publisher, philanthropist, and diplomat. His father, Moses A. (1865–1942), built up a big publishing enterprise which was developed by his son whose papers included the *Philadelphia Inquirer, TV Guide, Seventeen,* and *Daily Racing Form.* A. made many donations to educational and charitable causes, financing buildings and institutions at universities and colleges. in 1969–75, A. was US ambassador to London.

ANOINTING: The everyday use of oils as an unguent was common in Palestine in biblical and post-biblical times. Fragrant unguents were used on joyous occasions and feast days, but the use of oil was prohibited on fast days and to mourners generally. The most important function of a. was in religious rites and to consecrate kings, priests, and the sacred vessels of the Tabernacle. Thus, David was anointed by Samuel; and the descendant of David who would traditionally redeem Israel at the End of Days was called the MESSIAH (Heb. *mashiah,* i.e. "The Anointed One").

ANOKHI, Z.I. see **ARONSOHN, ZALMAN**

AN-SKI, S. (pen-name of Solomon Seinwil Rapoport; 1863–1920): Russian author and dramatist. He was

S. An-Ski.

active in the Russian socialist movement. From 1904, he began to write regularly in Yiddish (his poems included *Die Shvueh* — the hymn of the Bund) and collected Jewish folklore material. During World War I, he visited Jewish communities in the area of hostilities and collected material for his 3-volume work on *The Destruction of the Jews of Poland, Galicia, and Bukovina.* His most famous play, *The Dibbuk,* based on a Jewish folk legend, has been produced with great success in Hebrew (by the *Ha-Bimah* theater, in a translation by Bialik) and other languages. After the 1917 Bolshevik revolution, A. left Russia, living in Vilna and later Warsaw.

ANTHROPOMORPHISM: the ascription to GOD of human form and characteristics. Biblical phraseology is sometimes anthropomorphic and refers, for instance, to God's hand, fingers, etc. The desire to minimize the risks run by the allegorical and symbolic use of a. is already apparent in the biblical emendations of the *Sopherim,* and is intensified in the early translations (into Aramaic and Greek) where, e.g., the notion of the "word of God" *(memra* or *logos)* is frequently introduced to soften biblical a. As all Divine ATTRIBUTES (e.g., mercy, jealousy) contain an element of a., Philo's conception of God, under Greek influence, is devoid of attributes, but rabbinic fancy continued to ascribe human attributes to God (e.g., He

Samuel anointing David.
(From a 9th cent. manuscript).

puts on phylacteries each day). The 9th cent. composition *Shiur Komah* actually indicates the dimensions of the various parts of God. The problem of Divine attributes occupied the medieval Jewish philosophers, and Maimonides postulated Divine incorporeality as a basic Jewish dogma. Nevertheless, a. continued to enter Jewish thought, especially in Kabbalah.

ANTICHRIST: In Christian belief, the adversary of Christ. From a very early period, the conception of the A. received an anti-Jewish color. Certain Church Fathers maintained that he would come from the tribe of Dan, and the A. was sometimes identified with the Messiah expected by the Jews. Medieval Christian writings describe in detail the birth of the A. from a Jewish family. In Jewish apocalypse, ARMILUS corresponds in a certain fashion to the A.

ANTI-DEFAMATION LEAGUE (of B'NAI B'RITH): US organization founded in 1913 to fight anti-Semitism, protect Jews from the effects of bigotry and DISCRIMINATION, and to secure for them equal rights and opportunities. As part of this task, the ADL seeks the extension of civil rights for all Americans. It carries on a broad educational program to combat organized anti-Semites and anti-Semitism, to improve intergroup relations and understanding, and to win public support for civil rights reforms.

ANTI-NAZI BOYCOTT: Movement, principally in the US, to secure the boycotting of German goods and services during the Hitler regime in Germany. In 1936, the Jewish Labor Committee joined the American Jewish Congress in a Jewish Joint Boycott Council. The boycott movement spread to Great Britain and other countries. In 1939, the Joint Boycott Council was joined by the Volunteer Christian Committee, and the American Boycott Against Aggressor Nations, while other cooperating agencies were the Jewish War Veterans and the B'nai B'rith Boycott Committee. The boycott in the US continued until the US entry into World War II.

ANTIGONUS (MATTATHIAS): Last Hasmonean king, ruled 40–37 BCE; son of Aristobulus II. On Pompey's capture of Jerusalem (63), he was taken as hostage to Rome. Obtaining permission to return to Judea in 49, he took refuge at the court of Chalcis. With the support of the Parthians, he captured Jerusalem (40), put to death Herod's brother Phasael, and mutilated his own uncle Hyrcanus so as to disqualify him for the high priesthood. He then ruled as king of Judea and high priest. When the Romans drove the Parthians from Syria (39), Herod attacked A. who, despite popular support, was defeated in battle. A. fortified himself in Jerusalem, but was captured after a five months' siege and put to death.

ANTIGONUS OF SOKHO: (fl. c. 200 BCE): Early mishnaic sage. The sole aphorism of his to be preserved is "Be not like servants who serve their master in the hope of receiving a reward, but be like those

Coin of Antigonus.

servants who serve their master with no expectation of receiving a reward; and let the fear of Heaven be upon you" (*Avot* 1:3). His pupils, ZADOK and Boethus, are reported to have taken this saying as a repudiation of the belief in retribution (*Avot de-Rabbi Natan* 5:2; see BOETHUSIANS).

ANTIN, MARY (1881–1949): US author. Her best-known work, *The Promised Land,* contrasted her early days in White Russia with her new life in America, to which she emigrated in 1894.

ANTINOMIANISM: Opposition (on various grounds) to the old Law (i.e., particularly to the Torah and the practical commandments). In hellenistic Egypt, many Jews interpreted biblical law allegorically and neglected its practical aspects. JESUS observed the Law and only rejected certain regulations on moral grounds. A. in CHRISTIANITY begins with PAUL who opposed all demands to make the observance of the ritual commandments obligatory on Christians. The Church Fathers treated the Torah as an allegory foretelling the advent of Jesus, but generally accepted its Divine origin. The Christian gnostics of the 2nd–4th cents. distinguished between the lower demiurge (Creator God = the God of the Old Testament) and the most-High God who had sent the savior. Certain gnostics considered the demiurge as evil, and therefore, that the Old Testament was evil. In some sects, the rejection of the Law took the form of license and the rejection of all morality. The Reformation elevated the authority of the Bible and gave rise to "judaizing" sects which tended to accept some parts of the Old Testament. Luther rejected the validity of Jewish law but acknowledged its educative value; Johann Agricola, on the other hand, regarded the Law as a mistaken attempt to instruct man by threats. The resultant struggle within the PROTESTANT church ended with the victory of the opponents of a. In the KABBALAH, the theory is propounded that the Torah changes its meaning cyclically; an old rabbinic saying foresees the lapse of the commandments in the world to come; and a third view held that only the esoteric meaning of the Law was valid. These three trends led to the radical a. of the Sabbetaians who evolved an antinomistic theology, and in some circles and successor groups (e.g., the Frankists) to complete license. Antinomistic traits can be discerned today in certain liberalizing branches of Judaism.

ANTIOCH: Ancient Syrian city, now in S Turkey. Jews were living there at the beginning of the 2nd cent. BCE, and it had a synagogue in which some

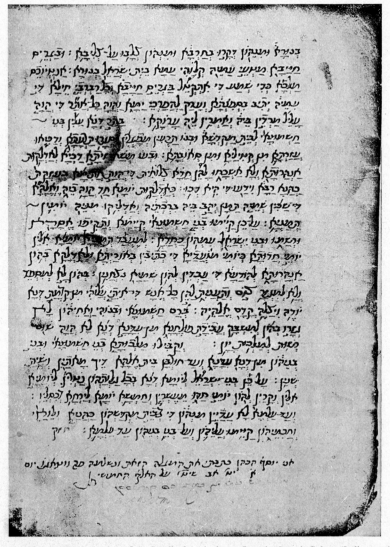

Last page of the Aramaic version of the Scroll of Antiochus written by Joseph Cohen. (Italian ms 1559).

Temple vessels plundered by Antiochus Epiphanes were eventually deposited. In the 1st cent. CE, the Jewish population was large, and many gentiles attended Jewish worship. At the time of the revolt against Rome (66–70), conditions deteriorated, and for a time, Jewish observances were suppressed. Jewish influence on the Christians was considerable in the 4th cent. when a gerousiarch controlled Jewish life. From the 5th cent., the Jews suffered from mounting ecclesiastical intolerance, and there were outbreaks against them in the reign of Zeno (474–91). In 608, before the Persian invasion, the Jews of A. revolted and were suppressed only after bitter fighting. Massacre and exile followed, and the community ceased to be of importance. Benjamin of Tudela found only 10 Jewish families there in 1170. In 1930, 200 Jews resided in A., but by 1964, few remained.

*ANTIOCHUS: Name of 13 Greek kings of the House of Seleucus who ruled Syria in the Hellenistic Period. *ANTIOCHUS III* (reigned 223–187 BCE): He transferred 2,000 Jewish families from Babylon to Lydia and Phrygia. After his capture of Jerusalem in 198 BCE, he treated the Jews with understanding. *ANTIOCHUS IV EPIPHANES* (reigned 175–163 BCE): Turned back by Rome on his second expedition against Egypt (168 BCE), he occupied Jerusalem, plundered the Temple treasure, and endeavored to hellenize Judea by force in order to convert it into a reliable frontier-province. This brought about a rising which A. suppressed with great cruelty; thousands of Jews were killed and many sold into slavery. A. brought gentile settlers into Jerusalem and fortified the ACRA as a stronghold of the Hellenizers to dominate the city. He now began a fierce religious persecution of the Jews, forbidding circumcision and observance of the Sabbath, desecrating the Temple altar, setting up pagan altars in the provincial towns, and compelling the Jews to participate in pagan ceremonies. His excesses caused the HASMONEAN uprising. His son, *ANTIOCHUS V* (reigned 164–162) continued the war against the Jews until 163 BCE, when he granted them religious and some political autonomy in return for their acceptance of his rule. *ANTIOCHUS VII SIDETES* (reigned 138–128 BCE) reasserted the Seleucid claims on Judea. After an initial repulse in 138 BCE, he again invaded Judea and besieged Jerusalem in 135–4 BCE. John Hyrcanus was forced to surrender, destroy the walls of Jerusalem, cede his conquests outside Judea, and pay tribute; but after A.'s death in 129, he reasserted his independence. *ANTIOCHUS IX CYZICENUS* (reigned intermittently 125–95) was severely defeated in 107 when endeavoring to assist Samaria which was under siege by a Jewish army.

ANTIOCHUS, SCROLL OF: A Hebrew account of the Hasmonean revolt, written in biblical style, probably in the 7th cent. CE. Although the work is valueless as a historical source, it entered into the Italian and Yemenite rituals for Ḥanukkah, sometimes being read from a scroll, with a benediction before its recital.

ANTIPAS, HEROD (20 BCE–c. 39 CE): Son of Herod and Malthace of Samaria. After his father's death (4 BCE), he became tetrarch of Galilee and Perea. He founded a new capital on the Sea of Galilee and named it Tiberias in honor of the emperor Tiberius. His marriage to Herodias, wife of his brother Herod, aroused public feeling against him. When John the Baptist publicly rebuked him for his offense against the Mosaic law, A. had John put to death. This marriage eventually led to a disastrous war (35–6) against Aretas IV, king of the Nabateans, who was father of A.'s first wife now divorced by him. During Caligula's reign, A. was accused of plotting against Rome and exiled to Gaul, where he died.

ANTIPATER: (1) Father of Herod and ruler of Judea from 63 to 43 BCE; son of (2). He attained great influence by supporting Hyrcanus in his war against his brother Aristobulus. Later, he assisted the Romans. A. promptly joined Julius Caesar after his victory over Pompey, recruiting Jewish and Nabatean troops for his army. Caesar made A. financial administrator of Judea (47) and he became effective ruler of the country, appointing his sons, Phasael and Herod, to the chief administrative posts. He was poisoned during a carouse. (2) Ruler of Idumea (fl. 1st cent. BCE). Of obscure origin, he became governor of Idumea for Alexander Yanai and Salome Alexandra. He grew rich from trade with Arabia. (3) Eldest son of Herod by his first wife Doris (d. 5 BCE). After Herod had killed his sons Alexander and Aristobulus (7 BCE), A. was marked for the succession, but on discovering a plot

Anti-Semitic caricature.

to poison him, Herod ordered A.'s execution, five days before his own death.

ANTIPATRIS: Fortified city in Judea, built by Herod (1st cent. BCE) near the springs of the Yarkon to protect the narrow pass between the Yarkon and the nearby mountains. He called it after his father Antipater. During the Roman-Jewish wars A. remained loyal to the Romans who left it untouched. A. is identified with Rosh Ha-Ayin near Petaḥ Tikvah.

ANTI-SEMITISM: A term (derived from *Semites*= descendants of the biblical Shem, and *anti*= against) used since the close of the 19th cent. to designate the organized movement or other manifestations against the Jews: more loosely, hatred of the Jews generally. Its characteristic feature is its direction not only against persons professing Judaism, but also against those of Jewish extraction. It thus is basically different from the medieval anti-Jewish prejudice which was religious in nature and could generally be obviated by conversion to Christianity. On the other hand, it has some affinities with the anti-Jewish prejudice in ancient Alexandria and, later, against the Marranos in Spain. The "theory" of modern a. was ultimately based on the distinction between the Aryan and Semitic language-groups, first realized at the close of the 18th cent., which (partly through the advocacy of Ernest RENAN) gave rise to the unsound theory of Aryan and Semitic "races." Later, the attribution of different characteristics to Aryans and Semites developed, the former being identified especially with the Teutonic peoples—who were depicted as the elite of humanity—and the latter represented by the Jews, who were regarded as its antithesis. This viewpoint was put forward with special brilliance by the French writer Count GOBINEAU. The conception naturally became popular in Germany, the classical land of medieval Jew-baiting. Here the progress of the Jews during the course of the 19th cent. in all walks of life and activity had been particularly marked, and created general resentment and jealousy. But in the ostensibly tolerant religious atmosphere of the age it was impossible to base the resultant prejudice overtly on religious grounds, and moreover, the social advance of the Jews had weakened their religious ties. Hence wide popularity was achieved by the term "Anti-Semitism," coined in 1879 by the journalist Wilhelm MARR to designate the anti-Jewish movement. This had been spreading rapidly in the country since 1873, when the wave of speculation after the Franco-Prussian war had resulted in the inevitable crash, blamed gratuitously on Jewish financiers. A number of agitators such as Eugen DÜHRING now seized the opportunity to publish works inveighing against Jewish "supremacy" in German life and clamouring for corrective measures. It has been suggested that in 1879, the movement received a sudden impetus through the secret support of the German chancellor BISMARCK, who

Anti-Semitic exhibition *The Jew and France* (Bordeaux, 1942).

hoped thereby to discredit the Liberal opposition to his regime, in the leadership of which Jews were active. The historian TREITSCHKE lent the prestige of his name to the tendency, and a court chaplain, Adolph STÖCKER, organized the Christian Social Union as its instrument. Later, a demagogue named Hermann Ahlwardt, who took his place as the leader of the movement, received for a time the overt support of the Conservative party. An Anti-Semitic League had by that time been organized, and in 1881, a petition which bore no fewer than 255,000 signatures was presented, demanding the disenfranchisement of the Jews. Anti-Jewish rioting broke out in some parts of the country. At Xanten, etc. ritual murder charges in the medieval style were leveled and the anti-Semitic party gained 15 seats in the Reichstag in 1893. From Germany, the movement spread to other countries of Europe. In Russia, the German example was partly responsible for the renewal in 1881 of religious persecutions which, however, was essentially medieval in conception. The wave of Russian refugees which swept through Europe provided a powerful impetus for reaction in other countries. In Austria, an anti-Semitic party was organized in parliament in 1882 by Georg von Schönerer and from 1895 onward there was a declared anti-Semitic administration in Vienna headed by Karl LUEGER. In Hungary, the agitation was responsible for the ritual murder charge in TISZA-ESZLAR in 1882. Even in France, the pioneer of Jewish emancipation in Europe, there was a virulent outburst of propaganda, largely due to Paul Bontoux, a ruined speculator, and Edouard DRUMONT, author of *La France Juive* (1886) which achieved a vast circulation. This agitation culminated in the DREYFUS case which convulsed French life between 1894 and 1899. Even countries such as England, Italy, and the US did not remain completely unaffected. In 1882, there was held at Dresden the first of a series of international anti-Semitic conferences at which fantastic restrictions on the Jews were demanded. The settled conditions of the first decade of the 20th cent. resulted in a considerable lessening of the tension. However, Houston Stewart CHAMBERLAIN, English by birth, now provided a philosophical basis for the new racial conceptions, placing the Germans at the summit of humanity and the Jews at the nadir. After World War I, the reactionary identification of Judaism with BOLSHEVISM, and the publication of the preposterous Protocols of the Learned ELDERS OF ZION, purporting to prove an international Jewish conspiracy to control the world, led to a revival of anti-Semitic propaganda in the new style in many countries. Among the consequences were the outbreak of violence against the Jews in Hungary on the suppression of the Bolshevik administration in 1920, and the assassination of Walter Rathenau, the German foreign minister, in 1922. Fresh anti-Semitic groups meanwhile sprang up in some

Shield of David branded on the heads or foreheads of Jews by Germans.

A German soldier clipping the beard of a Jew. (From an official German Army photograph).

Plundering of the ghetto in Frankfort-on-Main (1614). Etching by H. Merian.

countries, and in the US the automobile manufacturer Henry FORD, for a time, lent his name and financial support to the movement. In the course of the following decade, the strength of the old prejudices, resentment at defeat in the field, and the craving to find a scapegoat, stimulated by the widespread economic distress and the resentment of the reactionaries against liberal ideas and policies, played into the hands of Adolf HITLER who made anti-Semitism one of the principal planks of the program of his NATIONAL SOCIALIST (Nazi) Party, officially organized in 1920. After his advent to power in 1933, he exploited the more or less latent anti-Semitism to be found in other lands to cloak and forward German expansionist aims, and ultimately (after 1939) to weaken the resistance of other nations. Even in the traditional homes of liberalism in W Europe and America, there was a menacing growth of anti-Semitism, using the new vocabulary and a modern technique, organized in parties such as the CAGOULARDS in France, the Rexists in Belgium, the ARROW CROSS in Hungary, the British Union of Fascists (under Sir Oswald Mosley) in England, the Silver Shirts and similar bodies in America—all exploiting anti-Jewish prejudice for remoter, ultimately disloyal, political objects. An anti-Semitic administration under Octavian Goga was in office in Rumania for some months in 1937–8, and in Italy, the Fascist government officially adopted an anti-Semitic policy in 1938. In all countries, the influx of refugees from Central Europe (and later from other lands)

stimulated the growth of prejudice. In Germany, the movement was fantastically elaborated under government auspices, with publications, "scientific" journals, research institutes, great libraries, and a vast organization for propaganda abroad, centered at Erfurt. The whole of German history was re-written from an anti-Semitic angle: it was included in the schools as a basic principle of German nationhood, and counter-arguments were savagely suppressed as treason to the state. The implementation of the policy of a. was seen in the annihilation first of German and then of large parts of European Jewry (the Holocaust). Its gradual extension from theory to practice is to be traced in the successive stages of increasing barbarity which have been the tragic landmarks of European Jewish history in the past generation—the NUREMBERG LAWS, 1935; the occupation of Austria, March 1938; the pogrom throughout Germany and burning of synagogues, Nov. 9–10, 1938; the introduction of the Jewish BADGE in E Europe 1939, Germany 1941, France, etc., 1942; the creation of GHETTOS, at first in E Europe, from 1940; deportations to E Europe from 1941; the decision to "liquidate" the Jews, 1941; the annihilation of European Jewry, 1942–45. Even the downfall of Nazi Germany did not end the movement which had been so painstakingly propagated. Neo-Nazi and Neo-Fascist parties are still active in various parts of the world. But the most recent dangerous symptoms of an anti-Jewish reaction have made it apparent that it is to be found, perhaps with some difference in emphasis, in

Soviet Russia and other E European countries and, often cloacked as "anti-Zionism", is a frequent manifestation in the more extreme left-wing circles in many parts of the world. Moreover anti-Semitism is being consciously fostered by Arab propaganda in Africa, S. America, and elsewhere, where the Protocols of the Elders of Zion are being regularly disseminated.

ANTOKOLSKY, MARK (1843–1902): Russian sculptor. He took many of his subjects from Russian and general history, but a number of his themes were specifically Jewish. A. enjoyed the favor of the Imperial court, and gained an international reputation. He abandoned the conventional attitude of the contemporary Russian artists for a realistic approach, stressing the social and humanitarian aspects of his subject-matter. Owing to the attacks made upon him by anti-Semites, A. left Russia toward the end of his life and settled in Paris. He was the author of numerous essays on art and an autobiography.

ANTONIA: Citadel in Jerusalem in the days of the Second Temple, built by Simon the Hasmonean. Situated to the NW of the Temple, it was originally called the *Birah*. The A. was extended by Herod who renamed it after Mark Antony. Under the procurators, a Roman garrison occupied A. until it was seized by the Jews in 66 CE.

*ANTONINUS PIUS: Roman emperor; ruled 138–161. He was a kindly ruler and rescinded Hadrian's legislation against Judaism (prohibition of circumcision, etc.). Talmudic legends speak of a Roman emperor "Antoninus" and of his discussions with R Judah Ha-Nasi. Whatever their truth, they reflect the amicable relations between the Jews and the Romans in the time of A. There is no unanimity of opinion as to the identity of the Talmudic A. but present opinion tends to believe the A. in question was Caracalla.

ANTWERP: Belgian port. The first mention of Jews in A. dates from the 15th cent., and the city became a very important center for Marranos from Portugal in the 16th cent., though no open community was formed. Jews from Germany began to settle in A. in the 18th cent. and Jews from E Europe arrived after the Russian pogroms of 1881, many embarking from A. for America. A large section of the Jewish population earned its living in the diamond industry. In 1939, the Jewish community numbered 60,000 most of whom were annihilated during the Nazi occupation. The community of 13,000 (1974) has many institutions and a high proportion of orthodox Jews (over 10% hasidic) and 85% of the children go to Jewish day schools.

ANUSIM see **MARRANOS**

APAM see **AFAM**

APHEK: Palestinian town. (1) Possibly on the site of the modern Afula; scene of the crushing defeat of the Israelites by the Philistines (c. 1000 BCE; I Sam.

29:1). (2) Today Rosh ha-Ayin, near Petaḥ Tikvah. It was the site of the Philistine camp when the ark was captured from the Israelites (I Sam. 4).

APHIKIM: Kibbutz W of the Jordan 2 m. S of the Sea of Galilee, founded 1932, by settlers from Russia. Originally affiliated with *Ha-Kibbutz ha-Meuḥad*, it joined *Iḥud ha-Kibbutzim* in 1952. One of the largest (1,352 settlers in 1972) and most prosperous settlements in Israel, its entire land is under irrigation, and it maintains a plywood factory and a motor repair workshop.

APHIKOMAN: Name applied to the piece taken from the middle of the three *matzot* (pieces of unleavened bread) used in the *Seder* ceremony on Passover eve. The *a.* is regarded as symbolizing the paschal lamb in imitation of which it is eaten at the conclusion of the meal. It is customary for the *a.* to be hidden by the children present, from whom it is then ransomed. The word is apparently derived from the Greek, but the original form and meaning are uncertain.

APIKOROS or **EPICURUS:** Rabbinical term for an unbeliever or skeptic, derived from the name and followers of the Greek philosopher E. whose adherents polemized against Judaism. The term, which first occurs in the Mishnah, has come to be applied loosely to skeptics not adhering to Jewish religious belief and practice.

*APION (fl. 1st cent. CE): Alexandrian hellenistic writer and orator. He traveled widely, lecturing on Homer, and was author of an Egyptian history which has not survived. Part of this book, containing traditional anti-Jewish material with some original additions, was directed against the Jews. JOSEPHUS refuted A.'s attacks in his apologetic treatise *Contra Apionem* ("Against Apion"). A. participated in an anti-Jewish delegation from Alexandria to the emperor Caligula in 37 CE, in opposition to a Jewish delegation headed by PHILO.

APOCALYPSE: A revelation of the future, particularly of the End of Days and the DAY OF JUDGMENT. The classical period for the Jewish literature of this nature is from the 2nd cent. BCE to the 2nd cent. CE. It deals with revelation of secrets beyond the bounds of normal human knowledge, such as the mysteries of the heavens and the secrets of the world's governance, the function of angels and evil spirits, details of the end of the world, of the soul's existence in heaven and hell, etc. As the authors of the A. believed that prophecy had ceased before their time, they usually attributed the authorship of their books to personalities of the biblical period. Until the discovery of the DEAD SEA SCROLLS, only certain types of such pseudepigraphic literature, mainly included in the APOCRYPHA and especially the Pseudepigrapha, were known, but others are now recognized, such as apocalyptic discussions, hymns of apocalyptic writers, and commentary on certain biblical books. The authors of

Rubens' *Judith with the head of Holofernes,* based on the Apocryphal book of Judith.

apocalypses generally felt that they were living in the last days of the world, and ESCHATOLOGY therefore occupies a central place. Cosmic and social upheavals were regarded as close at hand and ineluctable; hence the call for immediate repentance. The anticipation of decisive changes in the world spurred the writers to visions of future events. The sacred books of an apocalyptic nature include the Book of DANIEL, the apocalyptic sections of which were composed at the beginning of the Hasmonean revolt. In the Hasmonean period, an important apocalyptic movement arose producing works like the Book of ENOCH and many others which have not survived. From this movement probably sprang the Dead Sea sect which in its writings developed a complete apocalyptic cosmic conception. The books of this movement contain the first records of Jewish mysticism. The *Assumption of Moses* dates from the period of Roman rule in Judea. The tension between Rome and the Jews is discernible in the Small Apocalypse (Mark 13; Matthew 24; Luke 21) which forms part of the Gospels. After the destruction of the Second Temple, the New Testament Apocalypse of John was written by Christians in a spirit of Jewish resentment against the destroyers of the Temple. Jewish apocalypses echoing the destruction are the second Book of ESDRAS, the Syriac *Apocalypse of Baruch,* and the Sibylline Oracles. In the first two cents. CE, apocalypses were composed (in Hebrew, Aramaic, or Greek) akin in spirit to the first Jewish mystics and the gnostics. The influence of the apocalyptic writings on talmudic literature is considerable from both the eschatological and mystical aspects. Apocalypses continued to be composed by Jews in the Middle Ages, and Jewish A. exercised a great influence on Christian thought and art.

APOCRYPHA AND PSEUDEPIGRAPHA: Noncanonical Jewish literature written during the period of the Second Temple and for some time after its destruction (approximately until the Bar Kokhba revolt of 132–5 CE). The works included in the A. are for the most part akin to those which constitute the Bible, but were not admitted to the Scriptures because they were not included in the canon, or were composed after the closing of the Bible, or were written in Greek. The term A. is normally applied only to the nonbiblical books incorporated in the Septuagint which were canonized by the Catholic Church, while the other non-canonical works are called Pseudepigrapha. This distinction, however, is accidental. Moreover, the name Pseudepigrapha properly denotes books ascribed to imaginary authors and is not confined to those books rejected by the Church. The books of the A. were excluded from the canon of the Protestant churches at the Reformation. The authors of most of them are unknown, or the writings are ascribed to historical figures, generally of the biblical period. With the exception of the Book of ECCLESIASTICUS (most of which is preserved in medieval Hebrew copies) and the fragments now discovered among the DEAD SEA SCROLLS, the Hebrew and Aramaic A. have not survived in their original languages. The oldest of the A. are thought to be the Books of JUDITH (composed in Hebrew) and TOBIT (composed in Hebrew or Aramaic). Both are evidently pre-Hasmonean, with ancient subject-matter. The Second Book of ESDRAS seems also to be a product of the pre-Hasmonean period. Important as historical sources are the two first Books of the MACCABEES, composed in the 2nd cent. BCE; the original language of the first was Hebrew, of the second, Greek. The third Book of the Maccabees is not an historical record but a fable on the rescue of the Jews of Egypt from persecutions by an evil king; while the fourth Book is a Greek oration commemorating the martyrs of the time of Antiochus. In the Greek translation of the Scriptures, there sometimes occur additions to the Hebrew version, which are also reckoned as part of the A. The supplements to the Scroll of Esther comprise imaginary documents in which Haman appears as a Macedonian. The Greek version of the Book of Daniel contains interpolated stories of Daniel proving the worthlessness of paganism to the king, and also the story of SUSANNAH AND THE ELDERS. Two of the works are Wisdom Literature, viz. Ecclesiasticus (written in Hebrew) and the WISDOM OF SOLOMON, the work of an Alexandrian Jew which is saturated with the influence of Greek philosophy. The story of the translation of the Septuagint is related in the letter of ARISTEAS. Other compositions were also written in the form of letters, such as the Letter of Jeremiah; some appear under the form of testaments attributed to the heroes of the Bible or of their visions and life-histories. This form is especially used in APOCALYPTIC literature which ascribes contemporary visions and doctrines to the periods of patriarchs and prophets. The Book of Jubilees, for example, was allegedly dictated to Moses by an angel and recounts the history of the world from the Creation to the time of Moses. The PSALMS OF SOLOMON, on the other hand, are ascribed to Solomon only in the title: the book itself was probably originally written in Hebrew and is a product of Pharisaic piety. Although the books of the A. were composed by and for Jews, they were completely unknown to Jewish schol-

ars in the Middle Ages, being preserved only by the Church.

APOLLONIA: Coastal city of Palestine, built by the Greeks in Second Temple times on the site of the Canaanite city, RISHPON. After being conquered by Alexander Yannai, A. remained Jewish until taken by Pompey in 63 BCE. Under Arab rule, it was called Arsuf, and had a Samaritan settlement. It was held by the Crusaders 1101–87 and 1191–1265, when it was destroyed by the Mameluke sultan Baibars. In the 17th cent. Arsuf was a large village where Jewish merchants lived. The ruins can be seen N of Herzliyyah.

*APPOLONIUS MOLON (fl. 1st cent. BCE): Greek rhetorician and writer who lived at Rhodes. He wrote a violently anti-Jewish treatise, fragments of which have been partly preserved in Josephus' *Contra Apionem* and Eusebius' *Praeparatio Evangelica*.

APOLOGETICS: Argumentative defense of religion. Traces of Jewish a. may be found in the Talmud, in the records of discussions between various rabbis and pagan (or Christian) "philosophers," etc. and there is some material in the writings of Philo. The first systematic Jewish apologetic treatise is Josephus' *Contra Apionem* in which he defends the Jews and Judaism against current calumnies. In the Middle Ages, various Jewish philosophers and commentators (e.g. Judah Ha-Levi, David Kimḥi) provided in their writings counter-arguments against Christian and Moslem theology. In the medieval DISPUTATIONS, the Jewish and Christian protagonists were brought face to face, and the record of their discussions is an important element in apologetic literature. Later, systematic treatises against Christianity began to make their appearance (see POLEMICS). Hebrew records of this literature have been collected by J.D. Eisenstein in his *Otzar Vikkuḥim* ("Thesaurus of Disputations") and the Christian counterparts described in A. Lukyn Williams' *Adversus Judaeos*. From the 17th cent., ex-Marrano scholars in Amsterdam, etc. and the rabbis administering to them (e.g. Orobio de Castro, S.L. Morteira) began a new tradition of polemics in Spanish and Latin, based on a more profound knowledge of Christian theological sources. Manasseh ben Israel's *Vindiciae Judaeorum,* published in 1656 to refute the anti-Jewish charges brought up at the time of his mission in England, initiated a new type of non-aggressive and non-theological Jewish a., intended specifically for gentile readers. This example was followed in the 18th cent. by Moses Mendelssohn. A considerable literature appeared in this field in the 19th cent. as a result of the discussion regarding Emancipation and in the 20th to counter anti-Semitism; these championed Judaism against calumny (e.g. the Ritual Murder libel) and vindicated the place of the Jew in the modern world.

APOSTASY: Abandonment or change of a religious faith: the apostate who leaves Judaism is called in

Hebrew *meshummad* or *mumar*. Apostates are found in Jewish history in the hellenistic period, while in the 1st cent. CE, Tiberius Julius ALEXANDER abandoned Judaism before entering the Roman service. After Christianity became dominant, the process was very marked, and it is probable that the great reduction in the number of the Jews in the early Middle Ages was due to large-scale conversions from Judaism. A. to Islam was also common. Jewish law and sentiment distinguished between converts through pressure or force *(anusim)* such as the MARRANOS, and voluntary converts who in the Middle Ages often distinguished themselves by the virulence with which they attacked their former coreligionists. It was due to apostates of this type, for example, that the Blood Libel received currency in the Middle Ages and that the Talmud was condemned to be burned in the 13th and 16th cents. According to Jewish law, the apostate remains a Jew, albeit a sinner, and no formal ceremony is required if he returns to Judaism. Nevertheless, for psychological reasons a ceremony was sometimes considered desirable, prayers for the occasion figuring in some modern rituals.

APOSTLE: Emissary; perhaps a Jewish institution (see MESHULLAH), adopted by primitive Christianity. According to the New Testament, Jesus selected some of his disciples to spread his doctrine. There were 12 a.'s (corresponding to the 12 tribes of Israel) but Luke adds another 70 (corresponding to the nations of the world; possibly a late addition). The most noteworthy was Simon bar Jonah, later called Cephas or Peter, who played a major part in the history of Christianity. He was apparently imaginative and a fervent believer but unlearned. The others were Andrew, James and John (sons of Zebedee), Philip, Bartholomew, Matthew (or Levi), Thomas (or Didymus), James (son of Alphaeus), Jude, Simon the Cananaean (also called "the Zealot"), and Judas Iscariot (replaced by Matthias). After the crucifixion, Jesus' brother James was regarded as an a. Jesus sent the 12 a.'s to the towns of Israel with his message, expressly ordering them not to approach the gentiles (Matthew 10:5). According to Jewish custom, they traveled in pairs and without any money or possessions. They spread the doctrines of Jesus, stories of miracles, and even exorcised spirits in his name. After the crucifixion, they scattered from fear of persecution, but returned in the company of Mary, mother of Jesus, his brothers, and the female disciples. Later, under the influence of Paul ("the Apostle to the Gentiles"), missions were undertaken to non-Jewish communities.

APT, RABBI OF see **ABRAHAM JOSHUA HESHEL**

APTOWITZER, AVIGDOR (Victor; 1871-1942): Scholar. He was born in Tarnopol, and taught at the Vienna Rabbinical Seminary before emigrating to

The Twelve Apostles (Early Christian art).

Palestine in 1938. Though almost blind in his later years, A. published monographs on many aspects of rabbinic literature and Jewish history, including works on R Eliezer ben Joel Ha-Levi, the Sanhedrin, and Maccabean politics.

APULIA: Region of SE Italy including several towns closely associated with Jewish life from classical times. Under Byzantine rule and in the Dark Ages, they were among the principal centers of Jewish scholarship in Europe. From 1290 onward, there was a series of persecutions which drove many communities into apostasy; under the name NEOFITI, the descendants of the converts maintained their individuality and Jewish sentiment for many generations thereafter. The Apulian communities revived in the 15th cent. under the Aragonese royal house, suffered greatly at the time of the French invasion (1495), and were expelled finally after the Spanish conquest in 1529. There was no further Jewish settlement in the region until the war of 1939-45, when many refugees (largely Yugoslav Jews) established themselves temporarily in A., with their center in Bari. A group of converts to Judaism from SAN NICANDRO in A. emigrated to Israel.

AQUILA (Akylas; fl. 2nd cent. CE): Translator of the Bible into Greek. According to Christian sources, he was a relative of the emperor Hadrian, by whom he was appointed in 128 to participate in the rebuilding of Jerusalem. Later, he was converted to Christianity and ultimately to Judaism, studying under R Akiva. Large portions of his Bible translation survive. They demonstrate its faithfulness to the Hebrew original, even at the expense of the Greek idiom. In a measure, the translation reflects Akiva's method of biblical interpretation. The Babylonian and Palestinian Talmud, as well as the Tosephta, report several traditions connected with A. which are attributed to ONKELOS, author of the Aramaic version of the Pentateuch. Some scholars therefore conjectured that the same person was responsible for both versions.

ARAB HIGHER COMMITTEE: Central council of the Arab National Movement in Palestine, 1936–48. Led by the mufti of Jerusalem, Hajj Amin el-HUSSEINI, its aim was to fight Zionism and the Palestinian Jews. The A.H.C. organized the Arab disturbances in 1936 and on this account was outlawed by the British Mandatory government in 1937, its leaders being exiled to the Seychelles. It was re-established in 1945 and organized the disturbances of 1947–8. After the establishment of Israel in 1948, the king of Jordan abolished the A.H.C., but the mufti endeavored unsuccessfully to revive it as the "Palestine Government" in the Gaza Strip.

ARAB LEAGUE: Political organization, founded in 1945 by Egypt, Syria, the Lebanon, Iraq, Jordan (then called Transjordan), Saudi Arabia, and the Yemen; Libya joining in 1953. British statesmen had been largely responsible for the preparatory discussions (1943–5) and their realization. Although hailed as a step towards ultimate all-Arab Federation, the A.L. is in fact based on full recognition and mutual guarantees of the separate independence of its member-states. These states are bound only by such decisions of the League as they support and accept. It is thus no more than a loose alliance of sovereign states which serves a convenient political bloc, but all its attempts at cooperation in practical and constructive fields have failed. Egypt has so far been dominant; the A.L. secretariat being situated in Cairo, and its secretary general an Egyptian. The main issue uniting the A.L. is common enmity toward Israel—although even in the joint war against Israel (1948–9), disruptive rivalries overshadowed that unity. Subsequently, it was essentially a tool of President Nasser, but its position in the Arab world has been increasingly nominal.

ARABAH (Heb. *aravah*="steppe"): Rift valley between the Dead Sea and the Gulf of Elath, 106 m. long. In biblical times the name was applied also to the valley N of the Dead Sea, particularly around Jericho (Josh. 4:13). See ISRAEL (geography).

ARABIA: Peninsula of SW Asia. Traditions suggest a Jewish settlement, especially in the S, even in biblical times, but the first definite information on Jews in any part of A. dates from the 1st cent. CE. It is not clear whether compact communities were established at that time. At first, the number of Jews was small (the figure for the YEMEN in the first cents. CE is estimated at 3,000, scattered all over the country), but it rapidly increased through conversion of ARABS to Judaism, especially in the S where even some rulers, e.g. DHU NUWAS, embraced Judaism. In the 6th and early 7th cents., there was a considerable Jewish population in HEJAZ, and particularly in MEDINA and its vicinity. According to local Jewish tradition, Judaism spread from Medina to the S. Smaller Jewish communities also existed in BAHREIN, at Makna on the Gulf of Akaba, at Adhruh between Maan and Petra, and further N at Jarba. After the rise of Islam, these Jews and those of Yemen were allowed to survive on the payment of special taxes, but most of the Hejazi Jews were either expelled or annihilated. Henceforth, the Jewish settlement in A. was almost wholly concentrated in the Yemen, HADRAMAUT, and ADEN. The former Jews of N Arabia in particular, though living in isolated communities, had become strongly assimilated to their Arab neighbors not only in language and culture but also in manners and customs, social organization, and mentality. The Arabic verses composed by their poets hardly differed in any respect from other Arabic poetry, and they expressed the contemporary notions, views, and feelings of Arabic society. Only a few hundred Jews are now left in the entire peninsula of A., the overwhelming majority having emigrated to Israel.

ARABIC: Semitic language. A. has borrowed many Jewish-Aramaic words, while the style of the KORAN (mid-7th cent.) betrays Hebrew influence. A. literature had already begun in the 5th–6th cent. CE with pre-Islamic poets, among them a JEW, SAMUEL IBN ADIYA. In the Middle Ages, A. was the literary language of a flourishing mixed Hellenistic-Persian

Arabian Jews in prayer.

culture which profoundly influenced Hebrew philosophy, poetry, and grammar. From the 9th cent., Jews in Moslem countries used A. (except for liturgy and religious poetry), and c. 925 Saadyah Gaon translated the Bible into A. Jews usually wrote A. in Hebrew script (with some diacritic dots and A. vowel-signs) and took hardly any part in general A. literary activity. Thus, the extensive Jewish-Arabic literature remained a thing apart. Many works by eminent Jews who wrote in A. were translated into Hebrew, as were numerous writings by Moslem authors, especially those dealing with science and philosophy. Most of these translations were made c. 1150–1350. Many A. words as well as words coined in imitation of A., originally employed by the translators, are still used in Hebrew. In the 11th–12th cents., numerous Jews helped Christian scholars to translate A. works into Latin, thus contributing to the development of the European scientific renaissance. Jews in A.-speaking countries developed local Jewish A. dialects. Even after the cessation of Jewish writings in literary A. (in the 14th cent.), popular literature continued in these dialects. Some Jews—such as the Egyptian dramatist Abu Naddara—took an active part in the 19th cent. A. literary revival. A. is the mother-tongue of about a quarter of Israel's Jews, and is recognized as an official language for the Arab minority.

ARABS: Semitic people. From earliest historical times they inhabited the Arabian peninsula and certain adjacent regions but shortly after the advent of ISLAM, burst forth from their homeland to conquer the greater part of the then civilized world. Their language (ARABIC) is cognate to Hebrew and forms a branch of the SEMITIC LANGUAGES. The A. and their homeland are mentioned repeatedly both in biblical and talmudic literature. It is possible that some A. were already settled in Palestine in the time of the Second Temple. The affinity between Hebrews and A. found its expression in the genealogical traditions of both peoples. According to Gen. 10, Eber was the forefather of Abraham as well as of Joktan, the ancestor of the southern A., and several Arab tribes are enumerated among the descendants of Abraham. The A. themselves trace their origin to Ishmael. Jews were found in Arabia by the 1st cent. CE. Expelled from N Arabia shortly after the rise of Islam, they continued to live in the S in considerable numbers until recent times. Jewish-Arab symbiosis, thus initiated at the earliest period of Arab history and Jewish diaspora, continued for many centuries in several countries and under various and changing conditions. The Islamic conquests extended to a number of countries with ancient Jewish communities, where the A. were generally welcomed by the Jews who even assisted in the conquest and occupation of the respective areas. This fact is expressly admitted by Arab historians of Spain, Palestine, and Syria. The conquerors usually treated

An Arab working in the fields.

the Jews well and assured them protection and freedom of religion against payment of the poll tax, as prescribed by the Pact of OMAR. The Jews—like all non-Moslems—were subjected to certain restrictions. Outright persecutions occurred not infrequently, especially in countries under sectarian rule, but in general, their position in the Arab world during the Middle Ages tended to be somewhat better than in Christian Europe. Notwithstanding the provisions of Islamic law, Jews sometimes filled high governmental office, e.g. in Spain and Fatimid Egypt. In Spain, Jewish life under Arab rule reached a hitherto unrivaled climax, especially in the cultural field. On the other hand, medieval conditions continued to dominate the Arab world after the age of Enlightenment began in W Europe. Under western European influence, conditions greatly improved in most areas (though not in the Yemen, etc.) in the 19th-20th cents. The position of the Jews was, however, adversely affected by the anti-European tendency and rising nationalism of the past generation, the reaction against Zionism being a pretext rather than the sole cause of the deterioration of the Jewish status. The emigration partly resulting from this, since the creation of the Jewish state, has virtually ended the Jewish settlement in most parts of the Arab world. An Arab minority numbering 476,900 lives in Israel and about another million came under Israel administration as a result of the Six-Day War in 1967.

ARAD: Negev town mentioned in the Bible as captured by Joshua. The site has been excavated by Yoḥanan Aharoni and discoveries include ancient fortifications, a Canaanite temple, and inscribed sherds. The modern town of A., founded in 1960, has been built some distance from the ancient site. Pop. (1974) 8,000.

Modern Arad: the beginnings.

ARAD: City in W Rumania (formerly Hungary).
Jewish settlement dates from 1717 and the first
synagogue was built in 1759. Through the efforts of
Aaron Chorin, who officiated there from 1790, the
city became the center of the Hungarian Reform
movement. The community suffered relatively little
during World War II, and the Jewish population in
1970 numbered 4,000 as against 12,000 following the
war.

ARAGON: Former state in NE Spain (capital: SARA-
GOSSA) in which Jews were resident from its establishment in the 10th cent. In 1137, it was united with
Catalonia, which had important communities, especially BARCELONA and GERONA. Henceforth, A. is
reckoned to have had the densest Jewish population in
Europe. The Jewish communities flourished especially
under James the Conqueror (reigned 1213–76), but
under the influence of the Dominicans their condition
deteriorated from the close of the 13th cent. Their
numbers were drastically diminished as a result of the
massacres of 1391 and the Forced Conversions in the
early 15th cent., and only 10,000 Jews left A. at the
time of the final expulsion from Spain in 1492.

ARAKHIN (Heb. "Estimations"): Fifth tractate of
the Mishnah order of *Kodashim* with *gemara* in the
Babylonian and Palestinian Talmuds. It discusses the
valuation, for purposes of redemption, of men and
things vowed to the sanctuary (cf. Lev. 27:2–29).

ARAM, ARAMEANS: Group of Semitic tribes who
apparently invaded the Fertile Crescent in the
second half of the 2nd millennium BCE and roamed
between the Persian Gulf and the Amanus Mountains.
According to the Bible (Gen. 10:22), Aram and Israel
had a common ancestry and the Israelite patriarchs

were of Aramaic origin and maintained ties of marriage with the tribes of Aram. Apart from the Bible,
the earliest light is shed by Akkadian sources of the
12th cent. BCE. The A. achieved considerable political
importance not long after when independent Aramean
states and princedoms (e.g., ARAM-DAMMESEK, ARAM-
NAHARAIM, ARAM-ZOBAH) came into being in Syria
and Mesopotamia. At the end of the 11th cent.,
Assyria was threatened with invasion by Aramean
tribes, and only at the end of the 10th did she finally
succeed in averting the danger. Intermittent war with
these powers was a constant feature of the 9th-8th
cents. BCE. In 743–2, the Aramean states in Syria were
overthrown and turned into Assyrian dependencies,
rebellions being punished by the deportation of the
inhabitants to distant countries. The ARAMAIC lan-

Aramean warrior from Haran (c. 9th cent. BCE).

guage thus spread among the peoples in whose midst the A. dwelt and became current throughout W Asia. The principal Aramean deity in Syria was Hadad, god of wind, rain, thunder, and lightning.

ARAM-DAMMESEK: The most important Aramean kingdom in Syria in the 10th–8th cents. BCE, called after its capital DAMASCUS (in Heb. *Dammesek*). After the division of Solomon's kingdom, A.D. constituted a constant danger to the neighboring kingdom of Israel which it frequently exploited in its recurrent disputes with Judah. It joined the kings of Israel, Judah, and Syria in opposing the Assyrians (853, 848, and 845 BCE). In 805, the Assyrians besieged Damascus and forced the king to pay a heavy tribute. The kings of Israel now took the opportunity to win back areas conquered by A.D. and even to annex A.D. for a time (Jeroboam II). In 738 BCE, A.D. allied itself with Israel against Assyria. During the subsequent campaign conducted by Tiglath Pileser (733–2), the country was plundered, its population exiled, and its existence as an independent state ended.

ARAM-NAHARAIM (i.e., "Aram of the Two Rivers"): The biblical appellation for the NE area of Mesopotamia. A.N. is the land of origin of the patriarchs, and nearly all the names of the ancestors of Abraham (e.g. Serug, Nahor, Terah) correspond to place-names in this region.

ARAM-ZOBAH: Aramean Kingdom in S Syria. In the 10th cent. BCE, HADADEZER, king of A.Z. formed a political and military alliance with other Aramean kingdoms to check Israel's expansion. David inflicted three severe defeats on A.Z., after which it disappears from the biblical record. From the Middle Ages, the name was applied in Hebrew to Aleppo.

ARAMA, ISAAC BEN MOSES (c. 1420–1494): Spanish scholar. He served as rabbi in various Spanish communities until the expulsion of 1492, when he went with his family to Naples. His best-known work is *Akedat Yitzhak* ("The Binding of Isaac"), a philosophical commentary on the Pentateuch and the Five Scrolls, in the form of sermons. The work, which incidentally criticizes certain philosophical ideas current among the Spanish Jews, became extremely popular and is still frequently reprinted.

ARAMAIC: North-Semitic language (erroneously known as Chaldaic), still in restricted use. It is divided into 3 principal dialect groups: (1) Ancient A. (found on inscriptions of the 1st millennium BCE, and in the ELEPHANTINE papyri) used in the Bible (Dan. 2:4–7:28; EZRA 4:8–6:18; 7:12–26; Jer. 10:11). (2) Intermediate A., comprising western A. (the language of the Palestinian Talmud, the aggadic Midrashim, TARGUM Jonathan, and the Samaritan translation of the Pentateuch) and eastern A. (including Syriac and the A. of the Babylonian Talmud). (3) New A., still spoken by the Nestorian Christians in the Kurdish districts of Syria, Iraq, Turkey, Persia, and Russia and

also by Jews who have settled in Israel from these regions. A. is closer to HEBREW than the other SEMITIC LANGUAGES and has influenced it considerably. It emerged as an international language—especially for commerce—from the period of the late Assyrian and Persian kingdoms (6th cent. BCE) as evidenced by the many inscriptions found in Asia Minor, Egypt, India, and in other places where it was never native. A. was for many centuries the Palestinian vernacular, and biblical readings were translated into A. in the synagogues for the benefit of congregants who did not understand Hebrew. It long persisted as a literary tongue and was the language of the Zohar and of later kabbalistic poetry.

ARANNE (AHARONOWITZ), ZALMAN (1899–1970): Israel labor leader. A. went to Palestine from Russia in 1926 and worked in agriculture and construction until 1930. He served as director of the *Histadrut's* school for Trade Union leaders, 1936–47, and secretary-general of *Mapai*, 1948–51. Member of the Knesset from 1949 to 1969, he was minister without portfolio 1953–5 and minister of education and culture 1955–60 and from 1963 to 1969.

Zalman Aranne.

ARARAT: Ancient name of Armenia, mentioned in the Bible (II Kings 19:37, etc.). According to Gen. 8:4, Noah's ark came to rest on the mountains of A. There are various traditional identifications of the site.

שמע ישראל יי אלהינו
יי אחד
ARARAT
A City of Refuge for the Jews
founded by MORDECAI MANUEL NOAH in the Month Tizri 5586
1825 is in the 50ᵗʰ year of American Independence

Foundation stone of Ararat, the proposed refuge for Jews planned by Mordecai Manuel Noah in 1825.

ARARAT: Name given by Mordecai Manuel NOAH to his proposed refuge for Jews on Grand Island in the Niagara River NW of Buffalo.

ARAVAH see **ARABAH**

ARBA KANPHOT see **TZITZIT**

ARBA KOSOT (Heb. "four cups"): Four cups of wine drunk at the *Seder* service. See HAGGADAH.

ARBEITER RING see **WORKMEN'S CIRCLE**

ARBITRATION: Voluntary agreement to settle a dispute by the decision of a person or persons not a party to it. Talmudic law provides for the settlement of certain disputes by two arbitrators appointed respectively by either side, who elect a neutral chairman. Under the rule of the Romans, neither Jews nor Christians willingly resorted to pagan courts. In the Middle Ages, the Jewish tribunals to which cases were submitted often arbitrated between the parties. The *Din Torah,* i.e., a. before a rabbi or a group of rabbis, became an accepted method. In modern times as well, a. courts have served the Jewish community. The London *Bet Din,* under the supervision of the chief rabbi of the British Commonwealth, is a voluntary court of a. THE JEWISH CONCILIATION BOARD OF AMERICA functions in New York, and similar courts exist in other American cities. Jews (e.g. Brandeis) have been active in introducing a. into labor disputes.

ARCHA: The "chest" which was established in the principal English cities from 1194 to hold duplicates of all documents concerning debts contracted with Jews. Each a. was in the charge of 2 Jewish and 2 Christian "chirographers," and the Central EXCHEQUER OF THE JEWS in Westminster coordinated their work. There were about 27 such archae throughout the country.

ARCHANGEL see **ANGEL**

ARCHELAUS: Ruler of Judea from 4 BCE to 6 CE; son of Herod and Malthace the Samaritan. Under Herod's last will, A. was appointed ruler over the greater part of Herod's kingdom with the title of king. When A. went to Rome to obtain Augustus' ratification of Herod's will, disturbances broke out all over Pales-

tine, and a Jewish delegation requested Augustus to dethrone the Herodian dynasty. Augustus abolished the title of king but confirmed A. as "ethnarch" of Judea, Idumea, and Samaria. A.'s rule was marked by a severity which led to his removal from office by Augustus and his exile to Gaul where he died (c. 16 CE).

ARCHEOLOGY: The investigation of ancient cultures through their material remains. In Palestine, a. began with the attempted re-identification of biblical sites by E. Robinson (1838) and a growing stream of travelers in the 19th cent. F. de Saulcy carried out the first excavation (the Tombs of the Kings in Jerusalem) in 1850–1; the (English) Palestine Exploration Fund (1865) initiated C. Warren's Jerusalem excavations (1867) and a survey of W Palestine (1872–8) by Conder and Kitchener, coinciding with important work by C. Clermont-Ganneau, G. Schumacher, and others. In 1890, W. Flinders Petrie at Tel el-Hesi devised the system of pottery-dating by stratification and cross-dating with Egyptian finds, thereby initiating the methods used subsequently at Gezer, Samaria, etc.

Representation of a *menorah*. Found in the ruins of Gadara.

From the Middle Paleolithic (Old Stone) Age, Palestine has yielded the Carmel and Nazareth skeletons, intermediate between Neanderthal man and *Homo Sapiens*. Mesolithic (Middle Stone) culture is represented by the Natufian cave-dwellers, the first cultivators (c. 8000 BCE), and Neolithic, most strikingly by the Yarmukian settlement (Shaar ha-Golan). By 5000 BCE, walled village settlement had evolved (Jericho); the use of copper begins c. 4500, initiating the Chalcolithic age (Jericho, Telulat Ghassul, and in the Beersheba district); and in the Bronze Age (Early: 3200–2100; Middle: 2100–1500; Late: 1500–1100 BCE) walled towns spread, as revealed by excavations at Bet Yerah, Megiddo, Jericho, Bet Shean, Tel Bet Mirsim, etc. Research has evidenced the Hyksos (18th cent. fortresses at Hazor, Shechem) and Horite or Hurrian (17th cent.) migrations and growing Mediterranean contacts under Egyptian rule (Bet Shean) 1500–1100. Bible study is illuminated by a. both in and outside Palestine. Mesopotamian discoveries (Ur) indicate a period of great floods reflected in the biblical Flood Story. Both the Egyptian Execration (20th–19th cents. BCE) and the Mari (Euphrates, 19th–18th cents.) texts illustrate the patriarchal period. Transjordan researches show contemporary Middle Bronze Age life as semi-nomadic. While the TEL EL-AMARNA tablets (14th cent.) illumine the Israelite advent, the Hammurabi (18th cent.) and similar legal codes provide the background of Mosaic legislation, and especially of the legal habits of the patriarchal period. Nelson Glueck's Transjordan survey is taken by some scholars to show that the Israelite entry did not precede the 13th cent., while the Merneptah stele (c. 1231 BCE) sets a *terminus ad quem* for the Exodus. Similar deductions resulted from the researches at Jericho, Bethel, Lachish, Tel Bet Mirsim, Hazor, etc. Pottery study has identified the Philistines, and work at Gibeah (Tel el-Ful) and Jerusalem (Zion) has cast light on Saul's and David's reign, just as digs at Tel el-Hesi, and elsewhere may have revealed Solomon's chariot-stables, and Tel el-Khalife (Ezion Geber), his trade and mining. The UGARIT (Ras Shamra) discoveries include old Canaanite texts (1880–1200 BCE) which shed light on the earliest poetical parts of the Bible. Similarly, epigraphical finds (SINAI, GEZER CALENDAR, SILOAM, the MOABITE STONE, LACHISH LETTERS, the Arad ostraca etc.) have clarified the development of the Hebrew alphabet. A. in Samaria has uncovered the palaces of Omri, Ahab, and Jeroboam II and shown the Phoenician affinities of their culture. Various sites (e.g. Megiddo, Lachish) have elucidated the dates and extent of the destruction that preceded the Babylonian exile. Excavations at Samaria, Beth Zur, Marisa, Beth Shean, and the Transjordan Tobiad palace (2nd cent. BCE) date from the hellenistic period (3rd–1st cents. BCE). The later Second Temple Period has invited researches into the tombs and ossuaries of the Jerusalem area and into Herodian structures (e.g. the southern and western walls of the Temple area, the Jerusalem Citadel, Mamre) and Masada with its remains of Herod's palace, Zealot living-quarters and Roman siege-lines. To about the 1st cent. belong the DEAD SEA SCROLLS with their impact on Bible study and knowledge of Jewish sectarianism. Another important recent find in caves of the Judean desert is the correspondence of the Bar Kokhba period. Roman sites investigated include Samaria, Gerasa, Sepphoris, and Caesarea; synagogues of the 2nd–6th cents. (e.g. Capernaum, Bet Alpha, Bet Shearim, Nirim) have been extensively studied, and the catacombs at Bet Shearim have shed light on Jewish art, language, and religion of the 2nd–5th cents. In the Negev, Byzantine sites have been tested, including Subeita, Auja el-Hafir, and Abde. The Israel Government Department of Antiquities has, since 1949, carried out the supervision and protection of antiquities, investigation of chance finds, and systematic excavations. Among its more notable work may be mentioned investigations at Bet Yerah, Shaar ha-Golan, Caesarea, Tel el-Kasile (Tel Aviv), Emek Hever (Dead Sea), and regional surveys. The Israel Exploration Society has worked at Bet Shearim and Masada. Outside Palestine, archeological discoveries that have illustrated Jewish history include: in Egypt, the 5th–4th cent. BCE Aramaic PAPYRI at Elephantine (Yeb), numerous Greek (and a few Hebrew) papyri of hellenistic and Roman times, the Edfu ostraca, and the Jewish temple at Leontopolis. Jewish inscriptions of the hellenistic or Roman periods exist in most Mediterranean lands;

Pitcher with a Greek decoration found at Taanach.

Head of a clay statue from the Neolithic period,
found at Jericho.

notable are Jewish catacombs in Rome and Carthage
and tombstones in the Crimea. Synagogues of the
classical period have been found in Greece, Yugoslavia, Italy, Asia Minor, and Syria especially DURA-
EUROPOS, remarkable for its biblical frescoes.

ARCHISYNAGOGOS: Honorary title found among
pagan and Christian communities but especially
common in Jewish congregations of the Roman and
Byzantine Empires. The A. (rendered as "Ruler of the
Synagogue" in the English New Testament) was the
official head of the congregation and was generally a
man of intellectual attainments capable of supervising
the services.

ARCHITECTURE: Israelite building in Palestine presumably began at the period immediately after the
conquest of the country. Major developments are recorded, however, only with the reign of Solomon and
his ambitious building program in Jerusalem and elsewhere, including the TEMPLE and the royal palaces.
One of the earliest specimens of Israelite a. now extant
is the stables ascribed to his reign which have been
excavated at Megiddo. There is, however, no reason to
imagine that at this period any native Hebrew a.
emerged, buildings being generally in the style of
neighboring lands and sometimes erected by foreign
craftsmen. The reigns of Ahab, Jehu, and Omri were
also periods of intensive building, particularly at
Samaria, where important relics of the royal palace
have been excavated. During the period of the Second
Temple, before the Maccabean revolt, building was on
a modest scale but later, there was much activity, the
Greco-Roman styles becoming firmly established.
Under Herod, the temple was rebuilt, and further
architectural achievements included his palace, fortifications, amphitheaters, gymnasia, etc. The decline
in Jewish building in Palestine after 70 CE reflects the
dwindling of the Jewish population. There are, however, especially in Galilee, the impressive remains of
SYNAGOGUES in the classical style dating from the 3rd–
6th cents. CE. The buildings of the Jews in the Diaspora did not differ architecturally from those of their
neighbors. Originality can only be traced in interior
synagogue designs, especially the Ark and, in E
Europe, the ALMEMAR. There have been many prominent Jewish architects in the 19th and 20th cents.,
including Erich Mendelsohn, one of the leaders of the
modern functional school; Oscar Kaufmann, who
influenced theater and cinema design; Alfred Messel,
an innovator in the design of department stores; and
Leopold Edlitz whose work is marked by a monumental approach. In Israel, a new style of a. based on
European standards but adapted to climatic conditions is now beginning to evolve through the works of
Aryeh Sharon, Alexander Baerwald, Abba Elḥanani,
Richard Kaufmann, Leopold Krakauer, Zeev Rechter,
etc. Some of the structures especially worthy of note
are the Hebrew University campus, the Knesset building, the Haifa Technion campus, the Israel Museum,
and the Mann auditorium. In America, the growth of
new Jewish communities in the suburbs of the larger
cities has brought about a great increase in new synagogues and community centers, many of which are

Hadassah's medical Center in En Kerem, Jerusalem. Designed by J. Neufeld.

Cultural Center, Elath. Designed by A. Elhanani.

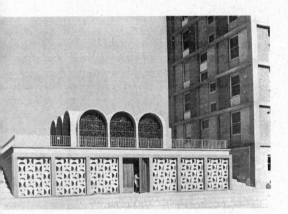

The Synagogue at Hadassah's Medical Center (with Chagall's stained-glass windows), En Kerem, Jerusalem. Designed by J. Neufeld.

'El Al' Building, Tel-Aviv. Designed by Carmi, Melzer, Carmi

Baltimore Hebrew Congregation. Designed by P. Goodman.

Mordekhai Ardon: *The Story of a Candle.*

built in an advanced architectural style. The leading synagogue architect in the US is Percival Goodman.

ARCHIVES: Local a. were kept in Palestine even before the Israelite conquest. Later, laws, contracts, annals, and political documents were deposited in the Temple. From the time of David, reference is made to a recorder *(sopher)* who was a royal official. Diaspora Jews kept records of their privileges in Greek and Roman times, and some communities maintained a record office. Jewish communities of the Middle Ages kept records, but few of their original documents have survived. In many places where Jews lived in medieval times, the general a. have preserved Jewish records (especially in Italy, Spain, Germany, Austria, France, and England). The most complete medieval a. on Jews extant is that of the English Exchequer of the Jews (13th cent.). After the period of Emancipation, only a few specialized files were kept on Jews and Jewish life, and the relevant information has to be sought in the general records. With the growth of anti-Semitism, Jewish files reappeared in lands of oppression (especially those under Nazi domination). Jewish communal records have been preserved continuously since the 16th or 17th cent. in a number of countries (e.g. Italy, Holland) and comprise especially minute-books and registers. Though the register *(pinkas)* of the Council of the Four Lands is no longer extant, that of the Lithuanian Council from 1623 to 1761 has been preserved and published. The *Memorbuch* (Commemoration Book) of German Jewish communities is also an invaluable source. In the 19th cent., national Jewish organizations, philanthropic societies and international Jewish political bodies (e.g. the Bund, the Zionist Organization) maintained systematic records. In the 20th cent., attempts were also made to set up national Jewish a. (e.g. Germany, 1906). Some of the most important modern Jewish a. are: the Central Zionist Archives (established in Berlin, 1919; transferred to Jerusalem, 1933); the Yivo Archives (established Vilna, 1926; transferred to New York, 1940); the Bund Archives, now in New York; the General Jewish Historical Archives in Jerusalem; and the American Jewish Archives at Cincinnati. A number of a. have collected material relating to the European Jewish catastrophe of 1939–45; they include the Institute of Jewish Affairs set up by the World Jewish Congress in New York, 1940; the Wiener Library in London; the *Centre de Documentation Juive Contemporaine* in Paris; the records of the Rescue Committee of the Jewish Agency, established in Jerusalem, 1947; and the archives of *Yad va-Shem* in Jerusalem.

ARCHIVOLTI, SAMUEL (1515–1611): Italian scholar who lived in Bologna, Venice, and (from 1568) Padua. His grammatical work *Arugat ha-Bosem* ("Bed

Padua. His grammatical work *Arugat ha-Bosem* ("Bed of Spices," 1602) attained great popularity. A. also wrote responsa, poetry, and hymns.

ARDON (BRONSTEIN), MORDEKHAI (1896–):
Israel painter. After teaching in Germany, he emigrated to Palestine in 1933. From 1940–52, A. directed the Bezalel School of Arts in Jerusalem, and 1952–62, the Arts Division of the Israel Ministry of Education and culture.

ARENDT, HANNAH (1906–1975): US writer and political philosopher. German-born, she lived in France 1933–41 and from 1941 in New York. Her major work is *The Origins of Totalitarianism. Eichmann in Jerusalem* created a stir for its criticism of the conduct of the Eichmann trial and of aspects of Jewish behavior in Nazi Europe.

*ARETAS IV: King of the Nabateans, ruled c. 9 BCE–39 CE. He led a contingent to join the Roman campaign against Judea after Herod's death (4 BCE). Later, his daughter married Herod Antipas who subsequently divorced her to marry Herodias, thereby involving himself eventually in an unsuccessful war with A.

ARGENTINA: S American republic. Marranos arriving there in the 16th cent. were ultimately absorbed into the Christian population. In the 19th cent., the first groups of Jewish traders came from the countries of western and central Europe. The first Jewish community in A., at BUENOS AIRES, was founded in 1862. The main influx of E European Jews began only in the 1880's. Greatly increasing after World War I, a large, Spanish-speaking sephardi immigration from Mediterranean lands was also stimulated by the similarity of language. 240,000 Jewish immigrants entered A. 1881–1951. In 1975, the Jewish pop. was between 350,000 and 450,000. A. has the largest Sephardi segment in Latin America (c. 80,000). In 1889, 136 Jewish families arrived from the Ukraine with the intention of settling on the land. In 1891, Baron de HIRSCH's plan for the mass-settlement of Jews on the soil of A. was initiated (see ICA). In spite of the large amount of capital invested, the scheme was not successful. In 1940, there were 25 Jewish colonies in A. with 28,000 settlers, but during the economic boom of the 1940's, many moved to the towns, and by 1970, only c. 700 families cultivated the land. The Jews of A. play an important part in the development of industry and commerce. A considerable percentage lives by petty trading, often with the primitive village population. The political representation of Argentine Jewry and its connection with other Jews are in the hands of a delegation of Jewish organizations, *Daia* (abb. for *Delegacion de Asociaciones Israelitas Argentinas*), a representative body of Argentine Jews, formed in Buenos Aires by 11 organizations in 1934 as a committee to fight anti-Semitism; it now deals with political matters of common Jewish interest and maintains ties with Jewish communities in other countries. Over 100 organizations are affiliated, and every section of Jewry is represented. The central Ashkenazi body is AMIA. The *Vaad ha-Kehillot,* the national organization of Jewish communities, founded in 1952, has 145 affiliates, mostly Ashkenazi. 15,000 children attended full-time Jewish schools and kindergartens (1973). The *Vaad ha-Hinnukh ha-Rashi,* established in 1939, supervises Jewish education in schools and kindergartens, as well as two teachers' training seminaries. Argentine Jewry maintains a number of Yiddish cultural institutions, including a theater, a Yiddish daily, a Yiddish monthly, and other publishing enterprises, and the Zionist movement also is active in various spheres.

ARGOB: Region of Bashan in N Transjordan. It possessed 60 fortified cities when conquered in Moses' time (Deut. 3); it was then included in the territory of half the tribe of Manasseh. A. belonged to the sixth province of Solomon's kingdom (I Kings 4). It was later known as TRACHONITIS.

ARI see LURIA, ISAAC

ARISTEAS, LETTER OF: Pseudepigraphic work describing the glories of Jerusalem and Judaism and the legendary origin of the Septuagint. It takes the form of a Greek letter, supposedly written by Aristeas, a Greek official of Ptolemy II of Egypt (285–246 BCE). In reality, it was probably composed in the 2nd cent. BCE by an unknown Egyptian Jew who, although steadfast in his Judaism, was also an admirer of Greek culture. While emphasizing the national distinctiveness of the Jews as expressed by the performance of the commandments, he wished to demonstrate the merits of Judaism to the hellenistic world.

ARISTOBULUS (c. 35 BCE–7 BCE): Judean prince; son of Herod and Mariamne. As a result of intrigues at Herod's court, he was accused, together with his brother Alexander, of conspiring to murder his father and was killed by strangulation.

ARISTOBULUS I (Judah; reigned 104–103 BCE):
High priest and possibly first king of Judea; eldest son of John Hyrcanus. According to his father's testament, A. was to have been high priest, the administration of the state being left in his mother's hands. A., however, murdered his mother and his brother Antigonus and imprisoned his other brothers. He extended the northern boundaries of Judea. An admirer of Greek culture, he called himself *Philhellene.*

ARISTOBULUS II (reigned 67–63 BCE): King of Judea; younger son of Alexander Yannai and Salome Alexandra. After Salome's death, her elder son, HYRCANUS II, became king, but A. usurped the throne. Civil war ensued, and in 63, the two brothers appeared in Damascus to urge their respective claims before Pompey who ordered A. to surrender all the Judean strongholds, including Jerusalem. A. was forced to agree, but his supporters refused to comply. Pompey laid siege to the Temple hill, and after three months, captured the Temple (63). This marked the end of Judea's political independence. A. was taken prisoner and sent to Rome. Together with his son, Antigonus, A. escaped (56) and returned to Judea. The Romans besieged him in the fortress of Makhvar (Machaerus in Transjordan) and took him prisoner, sending him again to Rome. When Julius Caesar rose to power, A. was released (49) and promised two legions with which to attack Pompey's supporters in Syria. He was poisoned before being able to embark.

ARISTOBULUS III (Jonathan; d. 35 BCE): Last Hasmonean high priest; grandson of Aristobulus II and brother of Mariamne, wife of Herod. Herod was suspicious of A., but, for fear of the intervention of Mark Antony, he appointed A. high priest at the age of 17. The affection with which the populace openly greeted A. when he appeared on the Feast of Tabernacles in priestly robes aroused Herod's jealousy, and he had A. drowned in a swimming pool at Jericho.

*ARISTOTLE: (384–322 BCE): Greek philosopher who, according to his disciple Clearchus of Soli, had profitable conversations with a Jew in Asia Minor. From the 10th cent., A.'s system gained ground among Jewish philosophers. Its main Jewish exponents were Abraham Ibn Daud, Maimonides, Levi ben Gershon, Hillel ben Samuel, Judah Messer Leon, Abraham Bibago, and Isaac Abravanel. Aristotelianism introduced into Judaism the concept of scientific knowledge and of Nature as the essence of organic growth. This signified a departure from the traditional way of thinking. On the other hand, A.'s doctrines of the temporal infinity of the universe and the eternity of matter were resisted by Jewish philosophers. A.'s notion of God as the pure act of self thinking was generally adopted. The resultant conflict within Jewish ranks was severe, especially after the rise of the Kabbalah. Jewish Aristotelianism became extinct in the 16th cent.

ARIZONA: US state. In 1871, Herman Bendell was appointed by President Ulysses S. Grant superintendent of Indian affairs in the territory which six years later had 48 Jews. By 1897, A. had 2,000 Jews, but their numbers dwindled to 500 in 1907. Jews played an active part in the state's economic and political life. In 1973, there were 21,240 Jews in A., divided between Phoenix (14,000) and Tucson (7,000), where there are Jewish Community Councils, established in 1940 and 1942 respectively.

ARK: Receptacle containing the Scrolls of the Law in the SYNAGOGUE. The corresponding Hebrew term is *aron, aron kodesh* ("holy ark") among the Ashkenazim, and *hekhal* ("shrine": frequently transliterated *Ehal*) among the Sephardim. The difference in terminology reflects the architectural divergences: the Sephardim originally incorporated the a. as an architectural feature in the building, while to the Ashkena-zim it was a supplementary feature, at one time portable. The a., situated at the east wall *(mizrah)*, was the most important feature in the synagogue, and great care was lavished on it. It was usually placed on a platform and sometimes rose to a considerable height; frequently, it was adorned by a crown symbolizing the Crown of the Law and by an appropriate biblical phrase. In western countries, it has become usual to surmount the a. with tablets bearing the Ten Commandments (in abbreviated form). The NER TAMID is suspended before the a. In front of the doors of the a. (in some Sephardi congregations, inside it), there generally hangs a decorative curtain *(parokhet)* embroidered with religious symbols.

ARK OF THE COVENANT: The chest in which the two Tablets of the Law were kept. Its exact description is given in Exod. 25:10–22. Made of acacia wood, both inlaid and covered with gold, it was $2\frac{1}{2}$ cubits in length, $1\frac{1}{2}$ in breadth, and $1\frac{1}{2}$ in height. A molding of gold surrounded it and 4 gold-overlaid wooden staves were placed through 4 rings on its sides. A cover of gold was placed over it, two golden cherubim with outstretched wings screening the ark cover. Various scriptural verses indicate that the golden cover and cherubim symbolized the place where the *Shekhinah* ("Divine presence") dwelt, whereas the a. itself, containing the Tablets of the Law, stood for the Covenant between God and His people. The sacredness of the a. was such that even the high priest could

16th cent. Italian ark. (Jewish Museum, London).

Ark in the Forest Hills (New York) Jewish Center. Designed by Arthur Szyk.

behold it but once a year and even then, only under "a cloud of incense" (Lev. 16:1–6). From the time of Moses until the construction of Solomon's Temple, the a. was taken out from the Holy of Holies in case of national need to lead the people on their journey and help them in battle. During the period of the First Temple, the a. found a permanent place in the Holy of Holies and was never removed. There is no mention of the a. among the vessels carried away and later returned from Babylon. Talmudic tradition held that it had been hidden "in its place" by Josiah. The miraculous qualities of the a. and the incidents connected with it inspired many poetical utterances in the Talmud and Midrash.

ARKANSAS: US state with a Jewish population (1973) of 3,090. Its largest and oldest Jewish community (founded 1838) is at Little Rock, and numbers 1,260. Communal organizations include 14 congregations, 8 of which maintain religious schools. There is a Jewish Welfare Agency of Little Rock. The Leo N. Levi Memorial Hospital was founded at Hot Springs in 1914 by B'nai B'rith.

ARLES: French town where a Jewish community existed at least from the 5th cent. In the Middle Ages, it was of great importance and the home of noted scholars. Attacks on the Jews became common after a Ritual Murder accusation in 1344, and they were expelled in 1493. A small settlement started after the French Revolution but no community now exists.

ARLOSOROFF, CHAIM (Victor; 1899–1933): Zionist leader and writer. Born in the Ukraine, as a child he migrated with his parents to Germany. Here, he became active in the *Ha-Poel ha-Tzair* party and in 1923, was elected a member of the Zionist General Council. In 1924, he went to Palestine and served as secretary of the *Ha-Poel ha-Tzair* party. In 1930, A. was appointed editor of *Aḥdut ha-Avodah,* the monthly

Haim Arlosoroff.

journal of *Mapai.* In 1931, he was elected to the Jewish Agency Executive, heading its political department in Jerusalem, and succeeded in mitigating the tension between the Zionist movement and the British authorities which followed the 1929 disturbances. On Hitler's accession to power (1933), A. devoted himself to aiding the immigration of German Jews to Palestine and transferring their property. He was murdered by unknown assailants on the Tel Aviv seashore. Suspicion fell on some members of the Revisionist movement, who were subsequently acquitted in court. A.

wrote extensively on financial, economic, and sociological subjects related to Zionism and the Jews in Palestine.

ARMAGEDDON (Gk. form of Heb. *Har Megiddo* i.e., Mt. Megiddo): Site of ultimate battle between the forces of good and evil, according to Christian tradition (Revelations 16:16).

ARMED FORCES, JEWS IN: The original Jewish tribal system involved a mass levy of every fit male, when necessary, the unit of mobilization being the tribe divided into *mishpaḥot* (families) and *bate avot* (clans). The need for military leadership against the Philistines produced the Israelite monarchy, under which, by Solomon's time, a standing army evolved, equipped with chariots stationed in fortresses and also including foreign mercenaries. In the period of Ezra and Nehemiah, on the other hand, defense was again in the hands of a citizen militia. The first part of the Maccabean struggle was conducted by peasant partisan groups, but the brilliant Hasmonean leadership ultimately developed a regular organization. The Hasmonean army became hellenized in arms and tactics, able to undertake sieges, and ultimately was established on a permanent basis. Herod's forces were partly Jewish, but by 70 CE, Jewish fighting capacity was impaired by lack of organization and training; tradition attributes to Bar Kokhba improvement of both. Jews served as garrison troops from the 6th cent. BCE in Egypt (Elephantine) where they were mercenaries and military settlers under the Ptolemies. A special Jewish military district was established in the 2nd cent. BCE at Leontopolis. Jewish participation in the Roman forces was slight, despite traditions to the contrary, and in the 5th cent., Jews lost the right to serve. In N Africa, the half-legendary warrior-queen Dahia Al-Kahinah (6th cent.) was the subject of many legends. Samuel Ibn Nagrela commanded the forces of Granada in the field in the 11th cent. In the Moslem-Christian wars, Jews served on both sides, and later, Marranos participated in the Spanish conquest of the New World. In the Middle Ages, for obvious reasons, Jews in regular service were exceptional. In Germany, Jews could bear arms till the end of the 13th cent., sometimes successfully fighting off Christian assault (e.g. Halle, 1096); in some towns they bore a part in urban defense and acquitted themselves well; a number served in the Thirty Years' War. Berek Joselowicz raised a Jewish regiment in Poland in 1794. Jews began to enlist sporadically in England from the 17th cent. and in France, after the Revolution, when they became subject to conscription. With growing emancipation, they were well represented in all European forces, many attaining high rank and distinction, (e.g. Ottolenghi, Singer, Huntziger, Kornhaber, Kisch, Monash). In World War I, Jewish enlistments and casualties proportionately exceeded those of non-Jews in many countries. World War I witnessed the raising of

Reform Jewish Service at West Point Military Academy.

the Zion Mule Corps (Gallipoli, 1915) and the Jewish regiment (3 battalions) for the British campaigns in Palestine. For the growth of Jewish military organization culminating in the Israel Defense Force see HA-SHOMER; HAGANAH; JEWISH BRIGADE; TZEVA HA-GANAH LE-ISRAEL. In World War II, JEWISH PARTISAN groups and ghetto fighters displayed particular bravery. 1,300,000 Jewish soldiers fought in the allied forces in this war. 400,000 were in the Soviet forces, including commanders and soldiers of distinction. Jews have served in all American wars since the Revolution and figured notably in the Civil War, World Wars I and II, and the wars in Korea and Vietnam. Of the 550,000 Jews in the US armed forces during World War II, (Army–58%, Air Force–23%, Navy and Marines–19%), 53,000 were decorated for bravery. There were 23 US Jewish generals and admirals.

ARMENIA: Area in W Asia, E of Caspian Sea, divided today among the Soviet Union, Turkey, and Iran. The largest sector constitutes the Armenian Soviet Republic. According to Armenian historians, Jews arrived in A. as early as the period of the destruction of the First Temple. Ties existed between Jews in A. and Palestine during Second Temple days.

One of Herod's grandsons, Aristobulus, was made king of Little A. by Nero, while two other grandsons ruled Greater A. Many Jews settled in the country during succeeding generations. The Talmud mentions a R Jacob of A. and a school at Nisibis. From the 4th cent., the Jewish population dwindled as a result of exile and emigration. Medieval travelers, however, found a number of small Jewish communities, notably at Nisibis.

ARMILUS: Legendary enemy of the Messiah. He became prominent in Midrashim of an apocalyptic nature from the 7th cent. onward. According to these sources, A. was to slay the anticipatory Messiah (Ben Joseph) and rule the world until overcome by the true Messiah (Ben David) and Elijah. His name is perhaps derived from "Romulus."

ARMISTICE AGREEMENTS see **RHODES AGREEMENTS**

ARMLEDER (Ger. "arm-leather"): Name given to the leaders of attacks on the German Jews in 1336–9; perhaps so called from the strips of leather they wore around their arms. They were responsible for massacres in over 100 places in Alsace, Swabia, and Franconia.

ARNHEM: Capital of Gelderland (Holland). Its medieval Jewish settlement came to an end at the time of the Black Death massacres (1348), and some Jews who resettled were expelled in 1545. A new community was organized in the 18th cent., and after 1881, A. was the seat of the chief rabbinate of the province. The community, formerly numbering 1,400, suffered severely under the Nazis. Jewish pop. (1970): 350.

ARNON: River flowing into the Dead Sea on its E shore. In biblical times, it was the frontier of Moab. After the Israelite settlement, it constituted the S border of the tribe of Reuben and the boundary of the Holy Land in Second Temple times.

ARNSTEIN, FANNY VON (1757–1818): Austrian society leader; daughter of Daniel ITZIG. Her charm, tact, and generosity made her home a center of Viennese society, especially during the Congress of Vienna (1814–5). Her philanthropic efforts were directed toward hospital work and the encouragement of music and the arts.

ARON KODESH see **ARK**

ARON, RAYMOND (1905–): French political scientist. In 1947, he became a columnist for *Figaro* and professor at the Paris Institute of Political Science. He wrote on sociology, philosophy, and politics.

ARONSOHN, ZALMAN YITZHAK (pseudonym *Onochi;* 1876–1947): Hebrew and Yiddish novelist and playwright. Born in White Russia, he went to Argentina in 1923 and subsequently to Palestine. A.'s early stories were written in Hebrew and made a considerable impression. Nevertheless he turned to Yiddish, reverting to Hebrew only in his later years. The best-known of his stories is *Rabbi Abba.*

ARONSON: (1) *BORIS A.* (1898–): Painter and scenic designer. He studied art in Kiev and was a stage designer for the Yiddish theater in Moscow. A. went to the US in 1923 and rapidly became recognized as scenic designer for Yiddish and English plays. He later turned to painting and art criticism. (2) *SOLOMON A.* (1862–1935): Rabbi; father of (1). An early leader of the *Hoveve Zion* in Russia, he served as rabbi in Kiev. After the 1905–6 pogroms, he led a delegation of protest to the Minister of the Interior, and was subsequently received by the czar. During the Bolshevik Revolution, he fled to Berlin and later settled in Tel Aviv where he was chief rabbi from 1923.

ARPACHSHAD: One of the sons of Shem and ancestor of the Hebrews. The name was applied to a region – perhaps a province in the vicinity of Mosul or the Armenian province of Albak.

ARRAGEL, MOSES (fl. 1st part of 15th cent.): Translator of the Bible into Spanish. On the invitation of Luis de Guzman, master of the Order of Calatrava, A. translated the Bible into Castilian with the aid of two Christian scholars, adding a short commentary (1422–33). The ms, now known as the Alba Bible, is preserved in Madrid and contains 334 illus-

Moses Arragel presenting his translation to the Grand Master of Calatrava. (From the Alba Bible).

trations, some of which reflect a Jewish tradition.

ARROW, KENNETH JOSEPH (1921–): US economist. He was professor of economics at Stanford and from 1968 at Harvard. In 1972, he was awarded the Nobel Prize for Economics.

ARROW CROSS: Hungarian Fascist and anti-Semitic organization which became active in 1936. It was responsible for many atrocities against the Jews when Hungary entered World War II in 1941. In Oct. 1944, after the abortive attempt to extricate Hungary from the German alliance, its leader Ferenc Szálasi exercised supreme power and was responsible in the ensuing months for the death of tens of thousands of Jews.

ART, JEWISH: The only knowledge of the art of the Hebrews in the earliest period of their history comes from the descriptions of the construction and ornamentation of the Tabernacle in the Wilderness and, at a later period, of Solomon's Temple in Jerusalem. Later, with the growth of prosperity in Samaria, rich animal and floral decorations in metal and ivory (specimens of which have been discovered in recent excavations) resembling contemporary Phoenician work began to appear. While few relics of the earlier part of the Second Temple period have been preserved, the age of the Hasmoneans and of Herod witnessed a great development manifested in coins, funerary monuments, and buildings, all in the Romano-Greek style. This tradition was also followed in the syna-

A prophet or scribe. Fresco from the Dura-Europos
Synagogue (3rd cent. CE).

Ivory plate of hybrid creature; possibly a cherub.
(Samaria, 9th cent. BCE).

Part of an illuminated *megillah*. (Germany, early 18th cent.).

Jacob wrestling with the Angel. Woodcarving by the Israel artist, Rubin.

gogues erected in Palestine and elsewhere in the succeeding centuries; of these, massive remains still stand. They were decorated with mosaics (as at Bet Alpha) and frescoes (as at Dura Europos) depicting biblical episodes and the familiar cult-symbols (*etrog, lulav, menorah,* etc.). Under Moslem rule and influence, the figurative motifs were abandoned. In the Hebrew illuminated mss produced in Egypt, Palestine, and Syria in the 9th–14th cents., emphasis was placed on penmanship and geometric ornamentation. Jewish art received a new impetus in Christian Spain, France, Germany, and Italy. French and German synagogues of the 12th cent. were decorated with wall-paintings. The Passover Haggadah, prayer-books, and Bibles were illustrated with miniatures. With the introduction of printing, woodcuts and engravings were substituted for the illuminations. The illustration cycles created in Prague, and later in Venice and Amsterdam, were

Torah Scroll and case (designed by Ludwig Wolpert) presented to President Harry S. Truman
by Israel's first president, Dr. Chaim Weizmann.

copied in Germany in the 17th–18th cents. and modified by self-taught limners in Moravia and Hungary.
The Scroll of Esther *(megillah)* and the marriage contract *(ketubbah)* were favorite subjects for illumination. The walls of synagogues in Galicia, Russian
Poland, and the Ukraine were decorated with allegorical animals, views of the Holy City, the zodiac,
etc. in the style of a peasant baroque. The furnishings
of the synagogues were adorned with carved wood-
work. Names of some Jewish synagogue builders,
painters, carvers, embroiderers, and workers in brass
have been preserved. In the middle of the 18th cent., a
group of artists arose from the ranks of privileged
Jews in Germany and Austria and their descendants.

Outstanding were the medalists Jacob Abraham and Abraham Abramson and the painters Judah and Solomon Pinḥas. Later, Eduard Magnus, Philip Veit, and Eduard Bendemann obtained teaching and museum positions at the price of baptism. Solomon Hart in England and Moritz Oppenheim in Germany turned to Jewish themes, which Joseph Israels was the first to treat realistically. The sculptor Mark Antokolsky was diverted from his original interest in Jewish life by commission from the imperial court for figures from Russian history. In Paris, Camille Pissarro was a foremost exponent of impressionism. Isaac Levitan in Moscow came to be regarded as the most gifted interpreter of the Russian landscape. Max Liebermann was the acknowledged leader of the German impressionists. Lesser Ury, Hermann Struck, and Ephraim M. Lilien found inspiration in Judaism, the latter two particularly in the Zionist cause. In the 20th cent., Jews from many countries became disproportionately prominent as exponents of the advanced schools, which had their center in Paris. The expressionist movement, nurtured by the grim realities of World War I, was represented by Issachar Ryback, Ludwig Meidner, and Jacob Steinhardt who contributed to the revival of graphic arts. Marc Chagall used cubism as a means of communicating his mystical experiences. Lev Bakst was the stage designer of the Russian Ballet in Paris. Amadeo Modigliani, Jules Pascin, Moïse Kisling, Chaim Soutine, and Mané Katz subordinated subject-matter to design and color values. The sculptor Hannah Orloff attained unusual power of characterization through simplification of forms. Arthur Szyk used the old technique of book-illumination with notable success. In England, where the tradition began in the 18th cent., Simeon Solomon was a gifted member of the pre-Raphaelite school, while S. J. Solomon became president of the Royal Society of British Artists and William Rothenstein (who was at one time attracted by the Jewish scene) achieved distinction as a portraitist. In the US, Jewish artists appear late. Solomon Carvalho and Henry Mosler, painters, and Moses Ezekiel, the sculptor, belong to the 19th cent. Abraham Manievich was an impressionist landscape painter; Ben Shahn and Jack Levine are absorbed by the American social panorama which they comment upon in caustic terms. Joseph Hirsch, Aaron Bohrod, and the Soyer brothers emphasize topical interest without sacrificing esthetic values. Morris Kantor, Francis Criss, and Max Weber may be called surrealists. Gentler moods are represented by Abraham Walkowitz, Emanuel Romano, Jacques Zucker, William Meyerowitz, and Elias Newman. Public mural projects were executed by Maurice Sterne and others. Ben Zion has interpreted biblical themes with vigor. Aline Bernstein, John Wenger, and Boris Aronson are stage designers. Ilya Schorr is an illustrator, painter of still life, and silversmith.

In sculpture, Enrico Glicenstein, trained in the realistic school, struggled for a simplified monumental style. Jo Davidson was a noted portraitist. Jacob Epstein challenged all conventions in his interpretation of religious and symbolic subjects. Elie Nadelman has charmed his admirers by the high finish of his figurines. Chaim Gross and Bernard Reder have in common an increased feeling for design and volume which in Jacques Lipchitz' and William Zorach's work has led to semi-abstract compositions.

Contemporary Israel a. originates from the foundation of the BEZALEL SCHOOL OF ARTS by Boris Schatz assisted by E. M. Lilien (1906); teachers there during the initial period included Hirzenberg, Pann, and the brothers Goldberg. In the course of time, it became a school of arts and crafts, directed successively by Yoseph Budko and Mordekhai Ardon, fostering a native style which fused oriental and European traditions. At first, many ornamental motifs were used, but the recent trend in the decoration of sacred objects, etc. has been more severe. The variety and brightness of the Israel landscape have attracted many artists, e.g. Ardon, Aschheim, Blum, Nahum Gutman, Holzmann, Mokady, Zaritsky, Jancu, Levanon, Litvinovsky, Sigart, Yoḥanan Simon, Steinhardt, Sima, Sobel, Kosonogi, Castel, and Rubin, working in oil, gouache, pastel, and water-color; while Anna Ticho and Krakauer have drawn chiefly in black and white. Originality is the keynote of many of the book illustrations (N. Gutman, Navon, Stern). Younger artists of prominence include the painter Yaacov Agam and the painter-sculptor Igael Tumarkin.

ARTAPANUS (fl. 2nd cent BCE): Hellenistic author. Fragments of his writings are preserved in the works of the Church Fathers. His object was to show that the Patriarchs, especially Moses, laid the foundations of human culture.

*ARTAXERXES: Name of three Persian kings. *A. I Longimanus* (reigned 465–421 BCE), *A. II Mnemon* (reigned 404–359 BCE), and *A. III Ochos* (reigned 358–338 BCE). The first of these is to be identified with the A. (Artachshasta) of the memoirs of Ezra and Nehemiah. According to Josephus, A. III exiled many Jews to Hyrcania.

ARTEMION: Leader of the Jewish revolt in Cyprus in 115 CE. He seized control of a large part of the island, but Trajan sent Roman reinforcements which defeated the Jews, and A. was ultimately killed.

ARTOM, ISAAC (1829–1900): Italian statesman; secretary and confidant of Cavour. In 1876, he was appointed Italian ambassador in Copenhagen. He served as deputy foreign minister 1870–6, and was the first Jew elected to the Italian Senate (1877). A. published a number of political and historical works.

ARUKH see **NATHAN BEN JEHIEL**

ARYEH LEIB BEN ASHER (c. 1695–1785): Talmudist; rabbi in Pinsk, Minsk, Volozhin, and (from 1765) Metz. He was the author of *Shaagat Aryeh,* a collection of halakhic responsa.

ASA: King of Judah, 915–875 BCE; son of Abijam.

To repel the invasion of Baasha, king of Israel, he was compelled to call for help from Aram-Dammesek, but ultimately succeeded in reestablishing the independence of the country. He fortified Geba (of Benjamin) and Mizpah, making them key fortresses in a line of frontier posts along the border with Israel. A. won a decisive victory over Zerah the Ethiopian who invaded Judah and penetrated as far as Mareshah (II Chron. 14). A. abolished heathen cults in his kingdom.

ASAPH BEN BERECHIAH: One of the levites appointed by David to supervise the music in the Sanctuary. Twelve psalms (50, 73–83) are attributed to him. The "Sons of A." served as singers in the Temple under the kings of Judah and also in the time of Ezra and Nehemiah.

ASAPH THE PHYSICIAN (*Ha-Rophe*): Author of ancient Hebrew medical treatise, *Sepher Asaph ha-Rophe* ("Book of Asaph the Physician"), which though much later in date, was ascribed to ASAPH BEN BERECHIAH. The author apparently flourished in Syria or Mesopotamia between the 7th and 9th cents. BCE, and if so, this is the earliest specific medical work to survive in Hebrew literature. A. is the first medical writer who seems to have realized the hereditary character of certain maladies.

ASCALON (Heb. *Ashkelon*): Ancient Mediterranean port in S Israel. It is mentioned in the Egyptian execration texts (19th cent. BCE). At the end of the

Ascalon: archeological findings from the Byzantine Period.

13th cent. BCE, A. was captured by the Philistines and became one of their five chief towns. It retained its independence during the period of the Israelite kingdom but was captured by Assyria in 734 BCE. In hellenistic times, A. was a center of Greek culture, remaining independent during the Hasmonean Period. Herod adorned A. with gardens and fine buildings, although it was not under his rule. Jews lived there in mishnaic and talmudic times, but it was considered outside the boundaries of Palestine. Its Jewish community survived its capture by the Crusaders in 1153, and the city was destroyed by the sultan Baibars (1270). The ruins were partially excavated in 1921–2 and many remains found. Modern A. has been developed since the establishment of the State of Israel and incorporates the former Arab town of Migdal and the "Afridar" section partly developed by the S. African Zionist Federation. It is a tourist resort and also the terminal of an oil pipeline from Elath. Pop. (1974): 46,700.

ASCAMA, ASCAMOT see **HASKAMAH**

ASCETICISM: Self-mortification practiced for religious ends. A. has sometimes been adopted as a way of life by Jewish individuals and even groups (e.g. ESSENES, THERAPEUTAE). Nevertheless, the general temper of Judaism is opposed to it, regarding all things in life as good when enjoyed within limits and under discipline. In this way, even material pleasures can be spiritualized. Celibacy was especially opposed, as the first commandment is "be fruitful and multiply." Maimonides condemned extreme a. as observed in non-Jewish faiths and pointed out that the various restrictions on diet and sex in Jewish law are in themselves sufficient spiritual discipline. However, a. was highly valued and to some extent practiced by the German Hasidim, certain kabbalists, and later Hasidim, despite its rejection by the Baal Shem Tov.

ASCH, SHOLEM (1880–1957): Yiddish novelist and playwright; born in Poland. His early stories, pessimistic in character, were published in Hebrew, but his major writings were in Yiddish and many of them have been translated into other languages. He achieved popularity through his idyllic novel *The Town.* Among his other early novels were *America* and *Motke the Thief.* His play *The God of Vengeance* was produced in several languages and was the forerunner of other successful Yiddish plays. He established himself in the US immediately after his arrival in 1910 and there wrote some of his leading novels which gained for him world-wide recognition. His *Three Cities* describes Jewish experience in E Europe during the early years of the 20th cent. *Salvation* depicts Hasidic life in Poland, while American Jewish life is the subject of his *East River.* His late novels on leading figures linked with the early history of Judaism and Christianity endeavored to present in fictional form the Jewish-Christian idea of the mes-

Sholem Asch.

sianic salvation of mankind. In these works *(Moses. The Prophet* [Deutero-Isaiah], *Mary, The Nazarene,* and *The Apostle*), A. aimed at bringing Jews and Christians closer by demonstrating their common spiritual heritage. Some views he expressed in these works aroused violent criticism especially in Orthodox Jewish circles. In 1955, he settled in Israel.

ASCOLI: Italian family, ultimately deriving from A. (Piceno) near Ancona, from which the Jews were expelled in 1569. Among its members were: (1) *ALDO A.* (1882–), Italian officer; from 1930. commander of the Italian fleet in the Aegean Sea. The racial laws under Mussolini forced his retirement

in 1938. (2) *DAVID A.*, who was imprisoned in Rome for publishing in 1559 an "Apology for the Jews" in protest against anti-Jewish legislation, (3) *ETTORE A.* (1873–1943). Italian general. After distinguished service, he was compelled to resign in 1938, (4) *GRAZIA-DIO ISAIA A.* (1829–1907), professor of Semitic languages and a leading Italian philologist who published an important monograph on the Jewish inscriptions of S Italy. He occupied the chair of comparative philology at the Milan Academy. From 1889, he was a member of the Italian senate. (5) *GIULIO A.* (1843–1896), mathematician: from 1879, professor at the polytechnic school in Milan. He introduced the notion of quasi-uniform convergence and dealt with the theory of functions and with problems of calculation. (6) *MAX A.* (1898–), political scientist. Professor of law at the Univ. of Genoa (1926–31), he migrated to the US where he lectured at the New School for Social Research, New York. He edited and published *The Reporter*, an influential American weekly (1949–68).

ASENATH: Daughter of Poti-phera, priest of On: wife of Joseph, and mother of Ephraim and Manasseh (Gen. 41:45–50). The name is Egyptian and apparently connected with the goddess Neith.

ASHAMNU (Heb. "we have trespassed"): Initial word of alphabetic confession of sin recited on the Day of Atonement.

ASHDOD: One of the five chief Philistine cities in ancient Palestine, 20 m. S. of Jaffa. It was a Philistine center by the 11th cent. BCE, site of a temple of Dagon. In 711 BCE, it became the capital of an Assyrian province (cf. Is. 20:1), but after the return of the Jews from Babylon it was again autonomous and the center of the Philistine remnants. It was captured by the Hasmoneans. Pompey took it from the Jews in 63 BCE but it was returned to Herod in 30 BCE and was an important Jewish center in Roman times. The ancient city has been excavated in

Marble lattice work from the Ashdod Synagogue, 6 th. cent. CE.

The construction of Modern Ashdod.

recent years. In the British Mandatory period, A. was a large Arab village. In 1948, the Egyptian advance along the coast was stopped here after hard fighting. A new town, founded in 1956, developed quickly and had a population of 55,000 in 1975. It has a deep-water harbor serving southern Israel, and an industrial area.

ASHDOT YAAKOV: Two kibbutzim in the Jordan Valley. The original settlement, founded in 1922, was transferred to its present site in 1933. Political disputes among the members led to a split in the settlement (1952); Ashdot Yaakov Aleph (IK; pop. [1967] – 530); and Bet (KM; pop. 530) now stand side by side. After the Six-Day War, they became frequent targets for attacks from Jordanian territory.

ASHER: Tribe of Israel, traditionally descended from A., eighth son of Jacob and the second of his concubine Zilpah. When the Israelites took possession of the Land of Canaan, A.'s fertile territory extended from W Galilee to the S of Carmel.

ASHER BEN JEHIEL (known as the *Rosh*; c. 1250–1327): Codifier. Born in Germany, A. was the outstanding pupil of R Meir of Rothenburg and after his master's death, was regarded as the spiritual leader of German Jewry. Owing to the deterioration of conditions in Germany, A. left in 1303 and was ultimately appointed rabbi in Toledo. He was soon recognized as the chief rabbinic authority in the peninsula. His responsa (of which over 1,000 survive) are a primary source for the history of the Jews in Spain in the early 14th cent. His decisions (*Piske ha-Rosh*), a halakhic compendium, are still standard. Out of his teachings evolved the *Tosephot ha-Rosh*

("The Additions of A."), covering the greater part of the Talmud. A. displayed intellectual independence in his legal rulings and strongly opposed the tendency of some Spanish Jews to place secular learning above religious study. His sons, Jehiel and Jacob, were distinguished scholars.

ASHERAH: (1) Canaanite goddess of fertility. The cult of A. penetrated into Judah (through Maachah, mother of King Asa) and Israel (through Jezebel). (2) Wooden ritual object symbolizing the goddess A. It is believed to have taken the form of a tree-trunk or pillar near the goddess' altar.

ASHI (c. 335–c. 427): Editor of the Babylonian Talmud. For 56 years, A. headed the academy of Sura which he re-established at Mata Mehasya. In this capacity, he twice went over the entire Mishnah and the relevant discussions of the amoraim. Thus, in effect, he was responsible for the arrangement and editing of the Babylonian Talmud. Most of the sayings of the early amoraim were available to him in definitive and classified form, but he had the task of further editing them and reconciling the variations in the texts. The theory that A. completed the Talmud is disproved by the fact that sages of a later date figure in it. He was presumably aided in his tremendous task by the large group of scholars attached to his academy.

ASHKELON see **ASCALON**

ASHKENAZI, ASHKENAZIM: Member(s) of a biblical people (cf. Gen. 10:3; Jer. 51:27); since the 9th cent. applied to the Germans. The German Jews and their descendants were therefore called Ashkenazim in contrast to the SEPHARDIM. After the

Crusades, Ashkenazi Jews tended to migrate to E European countries, assimilating those whom they found there and thence passing at a later period to W Europe and America. Their Hebrew pronunciation differs from that of the Sephardim, and, in some particulars, their ritual is distinctive, being closer to the ancient Palestinian tradition. Until the 20th cent., the overwhelming majority of Ashkenazi Jews spoke Yiddish. Equal or perhaps inferior in number to the Sephardim in the Middle Ages, they constituted before 1933 some nine-tenths of the Jewish people (about 15,000,000 out of 16,500,000). Owing to the massacres of 1939–45 the proportion was lowered (9,500,000 out of 11,500,000).

ASHKENAZI, BERMAN (Issachar ben Naphtali Ha-Cohen; fl. c. 1586): Polish rabbi. Author of *Matenot Kehunnah* (a standard commentary on *Midrash Rabbah*), and *Mareh Cohen* (a key to scriptural references in the Zohar).

ASHKENAZI, BEZALEL (d. c. 1590): Talmudist. As chief rabbi in Cairo, he was responsible for the abolition of the office of NAGID. He later settled in Jerusalem but traveled widely to collect funds for religious and charitable institutions. His main work is a compendium of commentaries on most of the Talmud gathered from medieval sources and known as *Shittah Mekubbetzet* ("Collected Opinion").

ASHKENAZI, JACOB (c. 1550–1626): Devotional author. He was born in Janow (Poland) and died in Prague. A. wrote in Yiddish the *Tz'enah u-Re'enah* ("Go forth and see, ye daughters of Jerusalem," Song of Songs 3:11), consisting of rabbinical commentaries and legends on the Pentateuch. This gained widespread popularity among Jewish women. A companion volume *Sepher ha-Maggid* ("Book of the Preacher") is based on the Prophets and Hagiographa.

ASHKENAZI, SOLOMON (c. 1520–1602): Turkish physician and diplomat. Born in Italy, he studied medicine at Padua and became physician to Sigismund Augustus, king of Poland. In 1564, he settled in Turkey, where he entered the service of the grand vizier, Mehemet Sokolli, who employed him in peace negotiations with Venice after the battle of Lepanto. In 1574, he was sent to Venice as Turkish ambassador on a special mission; on his return to Constantinople, he continued to be one of the most influential persons at Court. He advised the grand duke of Tuscany on policy and was partly responsible for the election of Henri de Valois to the Polish throne in 1573; later he endeavored to secure the election of the duke of Ferrara. In 1591, he was concerned in the appointment of a new ruler in Moldavia.

ASHKENAZI, TZEVI (known as Ḥakham Tzevi; c. 1660–1718): Talmudist. Born in Moravia, he studied under Sephardi teachers in Salonica, being,

Tzevi Ashkenazi. (From a drawing formerly in the Museum of the Berlin Jewish Community).

therefore, generally known by the title of *Hakham*. After prolonged wanderings, he became head of the rabbinical academy (*klaus*) in Altona, where he taught for 18 years, eventually being appointed rabbi of the united communities of Altona, Hamburg, and Wandsbeck (1707). Owing to a controversy, he soon relinquished this office, and in 1710, was called to Amsterdam as rabbi of the Ashkenazi community. In this capacity, he issued a ban against Nehemiah ḤAYYON, who was carrying on Sabbetaian propaganda. Ḥayyon appealed to the secret Sabbetaian, Solomon Ayllon, *Ḥakham* of the Sephardi community, who in turn issued a ban against A. In the course of the subsequent polemics, the municipal authorities intervened and A. was compelled to resign (1714). After a triumphant visit to London, he went to Poland and became rabbi of Lvov (Lemberg) shortly before his death. Although his literary output was small (except for his remarkable collection of responsa), he enjoyed in his day an unrivaled reputation for his upright character and learning. He was the father of Jacob EMDEN.

ASHKENAZI, VLADIMIR (1938–): Pianist. Born in Moscow, he won the Tchaikovsky piano competition in 1962. The following year, while on a foreign tour, he announced that he would no longer live in the USSR and settled in England.

ASHRE: Initial word of Ps. 84:5 ("Happy are those [who dwell in Thy house]"). This is prefixed (with Ps. 144:15) to Ps. 145 and recited in the traditional morning and afternoon liturgy.

ASHTORETH (or Astarte): Fertility goddess worshiped by the Canaanites and Phoenicians. Many A. figurines have been found in Canaanite and Israelite cities. Temples were dedicated to A. in the Canaanite cities of Beth Shean, Ascalon, and even in Jerusalem between the reigns of Solomon and Josiah.

ASIA: The earliest stages of Hebrew and Jewish history were centered in western A., the only non-Asian power that enters into early Hebrew records being Egypt. The conquest of Alexander the Great in the 4th cent. BCE brought PALESTINE and the Jews for the first time into the European orbit. Although from c. 200 CE the hub of Jewish life within A. shifted from Palestine to BABYLON, A. remained the center of Jewish life and productivity throughout the mishnaic, talmudic, and early gaonic periods down to c. 1000. The history of Jews in A. continued uninterrupted and was not disturbed by any widespread persecution. From Babylon, PERSIA, and surrounding areas migration eastward led to the formation of Jewish communities in INDIA, CHINA. etc. In the YEMEN and other parts of ARABIA, the the Jewish settlement was continuous at least from Second Temple times. The Jewish settlement in Palestine, too, was constant, though on a small scale. After the expulsion from Spain (1492) the communities in western A. were reinforced by new Sephardi elements. Although no large-scale disaster occurred in these areas, there were in some parts consistent maltreatment and a growing intellectual sterility. The opening of Palestine to outside influences in the 19th cent. followed by the beginnings of Zionism, brought about a revival of Jewish life in western A., Israel again becoming the main center of Jewish life in the Old World, containing (1975) all but 100,000 of A's 2,907,000 Jews (constituting over 15% of the world's total). The development of the USSR has led to a considerable dispersal of Jews through Asiatic RUSSIA (not included in the above total.).

ASIA MINOR (Anatolia): Peninsula in SW Asia. Jews were settled in this area before it passed under Roman rule in the 2nd cent. BCE, and important communities existed in all the principal towns, such as EPHESUS, Pergamum, etc. One of the charges brought against L. Valerius Flaccus in 59 BCE for maladministration as *Propraetor* of Asia related to his confiscation of moneys collected by the Jews of this region for the Temple in Jerusalem. The Jewish communities retained some significance in the early Byzantine Period but later dwindled. They again became important after 1492 under the Turks, with the influx of refugees from Spain (especially in BRUSA and SMYRNA), but began to decline in the period after World War I.

Emigration to Israel has now depleted the area of much of its remaining Jewish population.

ASIDEANS see **HASIDEANS**

ASKENAZY, SIMON (1867–1937): Polish historian and statesman. He published several standard works on Polish history. In 1921, A. was appointed Polish delegate to the League of Nations but was recalled under pressure of Polish anti-Semites, despite his assimilationist philosophy.

ASKNAZI, ISAAC LVOVICH (1856–1902): Russian painter. His subjects were taken mainly from the Bible, Jewish history, and contemporary Jewish life. He was elected to the St. Petersburg Academy in 1885.

ASMAKHTA (Aram. "support"): Talmudic term designating (1) a biblical citation used to strengthen a rabbinic interpretation or enactment; (2) a submission to a disproportionate penalty or forfeiture in the event of breach of contract. This was not enforceable at law.

ASMODEUS (Heb. *Ashmedai*): Evil spirit, king of the demons, frequently mentioned in aggadic literature. Most scholars maintain that the name is derived from *Aêshma Daêva*, the Persian god of anger: the derivation from the Hebrew *sh-m-d* ("destroy") is improbable. A. is first mentioned in the Apocryphal Book of Tobit.

ASSAF, SIMHAH (1889–1953): Israel scholar. After serving as head of Odessa yeshivah (1914–19), he migrated to Palestine in 1921. From 1925, A. taught

Simha Assaf.

gaonic and rabbinic literature at the Hebrew Univ., where he was professor from 1936, and rector 1948–50. He was the author of many works on the Gaonic Period, the history of Jewish jurisprudence, medieval culture, and the history of the Jewish settlement in Palestine. In 1948, he was appointed an Israel Supreme Court Justice. A. was active in many public bodies, especially in the field of education.

ASSEMBLY, GREAT see **KENESET GEDOLAH**

ASSEMBLY OF NOTABLES see **SANHEDRIN, GRAND**

ASSER: Dutch family, noted for its contributions to jurisprudence. *MOSES SOLOMON A.* (1754–1826) was a member of the first Legislative Council of the Batavian Republic in 1798 and one of the three jurists who drew up a commercial code for Holland in 1808. His son *CAREL A.* (1780–1836) was a delegate to the Napoleonic Sanhedrin in 1807, a leader of the Reform Movement in Holland, and author of legal works. *TOBIAS MICHAEL CAREL A.* (1838–1913) was professor of international law at the Univ. of Amsterdam (1862–93) and a member of the International Arbitration Court at The Hague from 1900. He received the Nobel Peace Prize in 1911.

ASSI: Name of several scholars in the talmudic period, the best-known of whom are (1) Babylonian amora of the 3rd cent., a colleague of Rav; (2) Palestinian amora of the 3rd–4th cents., a colleague of R Ammi, with whom his name is constantly associated.

ASSIMILATION: Loss of national or religious identity by absorption into the environment. Among Jews it is applied somewhat loosely to: (1) the abandonment of external "foreign" characteristics—e.g. in clothing or speech; (2) the abandonment of national identity by regarding Judaism as a religion and nothing more; and (3) the abandonment of all Jewish identity without (as in cases of apostasy) formally embracing another faith. The first of these is a natural process, but in certain environments (e.g. in parts of E Europe in the 19th cent.) it led to a more far-reaching a. The second was a product of the 19th cent. Reform movement in Judaism, not, however, being confined to the Reform element. Although advocated by zealous Jews of the type of Claude G. MONTEFIORE and I. M. WISE, this denial of national identity proved difficult to maintain, especially in the light of the new anti-Semitism; the profound feelings of Jewish solidarity on the part of some of its exponents showed that they themselves upheld it only theoretically. The third type of a. was discernible in ancient Alexandria, but attained serious proportions in modern times in Europe and America with the general loosening of the religious bond. There were many instances of a complete, though informal, abandonment of Jewish beliefs and observances followed by intermarriage and, ultimately, by complete absorption into the surrounding population—sometimes even in a religious sense—the next generation having no more than a vague notion of its Jewish extraction. This process made great inroads before 1933 throughout W Europe, being largely responsible, for example, for the virtual disappearance of large segments of the older English and French Jewries. It has been stemmed to some extent by the Zionist movement on the one hand, and on the other, by the virulent development of anti-Semitism (which paid no attention to this process, considering all persons of Jewish extraction as Jews). It remains the greatest threat to Jewish survival in the Western World.

ASSYRIA: Ancient state of W Asia. Its people (Semites) established an aggressive kingdom in the 20th cent. BCE, expanding rapidly in the 13th and 10th cents. The successes of David and Solomon against the Aramean states in Mesopotamia and Syria probably contributed to A.'s subsequent recovery. Ashurbanipal II (reigned 883–59 BCE), having effected a tactical revolution in the Assyrian army, overran Syria and the Phoenician cities in 876. When, in 853, Shalmaneser III attacked Ben-Hadad II of Damascus, Ahab of Israel supported the latter in the indecisive battle of Karkar. Shalmaneser's second attack in 848 likewise failed, but after the liquidation of the house of Ahab in 842, his successor Jehu paid tribute, although Damascus itself held out (841). Her capture in 806 freed Israel from Damascus' control. In 803–2, however, Adad–Nirari III (810–783) compelled the submission of Ben-Hadad III of Damascus. The subsequent successes of Jehoash of Israel and his son Jeroboam II against Ben-Hadad III may have been due to the passivity of Shalmaneser IV (782–72) under pressure of the kings of Ararat, and of Ashur-Dan III (772–59). After the death of Jeroboam II of Israel,

King Ashurnazirpal of Assyria accompanied by a "far-covering cherub" (cf. Ezek. 28:14).

Lion hunting in Assyria.

Uzziah became head of the W anti-Assyrian alliance. The Assyrian decline which made this possible was ended by Tiglath-Pileser III (745–27) who overthrew the Syrian confederacy. In 735, Ahaz, attacked by Pekah of Israel in alliance with Damascus, Philistia, and Edom, appealed for help to Tiglath-Pileser; as a result, Israel lost its territory in Transjordan and Galilee, while Philistia, Tyre, Moab, and Edom became Assyrian provinces. The attempt of Hosea of Israel (726) to throw off the yoke led to Shalmaneser V's siege of Samaria and its capture in 721 by his successor, Sargon. The latter annexed the country, deported 27,290 Israelites to A. and Media, and replaced them with Syrian and Babylonian prisoners. The revolt of Ashdod, supported by Hezekiah of Judah, was suppressed (715), but on the accession of Sennacherib in 705, an uprising broke out throughout the Assyrian Empire, and Hezekiah reasserted his independence. Sennacherib, marching south, subdued the Phoenician cities one by one and, defeating the Egyptian forces at Eltekeh (701), took Ascalon and Joppa, sacked Lachish, and invested Jerusalem (700). Judah was ravaged, but Hezekiah was able to hold out and obtained moderate terms by paying tribute and ceding some territory. Later, Sennacherib was forced by a plague in his army to return home. Manasseh of Judah was exiled to A. in 652 as a result of complicity in a plot against Ashurbanipal (669–26). After this time, A. declined rapidly and was succeeded by BABYLON.

ASTARTE see **ASHTORETH**

ASTI: Town in NW Italy in which Jews expelled from France settled in the 14th cent. It was one of the three AFAM communities where the ancient French rite was followed. The Jewish settlement is now virtually extinct.

ASTROLABE: Instrument for measuring the position of heavenly bodies. Originally an Alexandrian invention, it was used and perfected primarily by medieval Arab and Jewish astrologers. Jewish writings of the Middle Ages abound in descriptions of this instrument, terming it "Rule of planets," "Seer's scales," etc. Abraham Ibn Ezra wrote a special treatise

on this subject. The names of Abraham ZACUTO and Joseph VECINHO are associated with improvements in the a. in the 15th cent., while the instruments made by the Jewish experts in Majorca were famous.

ASTROLOGY: The belief that heavenly bodies influence terrestrial events which are thereby predictable. The prophets condemn a. (cf. Is. 47:13; Jer. 10:2, etc.). The Book of Daniel calls Babylonian astrologers "Chaldeans," and this term is found in the Talmud. The Sibylline Oracles praise the Jews for rejecting a. together with war and immorality as the sins which the Nephilim brought upon mankind. Nevertheless, belief in the influence of stars upon the fate of men and upon the history of nations was prevalent among the great majority of Jews during the talmudic period and after. Josephus relates (*Wars*, VI: 5, 3) that Jews were encouraged in their stubborn resistance during the period of the revolt against Rome by heavenly signs, favorably interpreted. Even the rabbis of the Talmud, for the most part, believed in a. as a science. The Talmud relates several stories about astrologers whose forecasts came true, although many astrologers were also said to have failed to read the

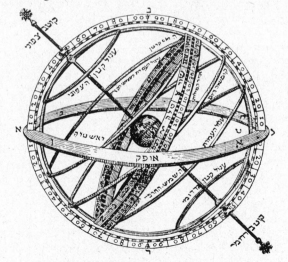

Astrolabe. From Tobias Cohen's *Maaseh Toviyah* (Venice, 1707).

stars correctly. Every person, indeed every blade of grass, was born under a special star which determined his or its fate. Some rabbis saw significance in the day of the week on which a person was born, others in the hour of the day. Yet the rabbis, while admitting the effect of the stars upon the nations, taught that Israel stood above stellar influence. During the Middle Ages, many rabbis and philosophers studied a., and Jews were regarded by the occidental world as masters of the art, a considerable number serving as court astrologers, especially in Spain. Among those who regarded a. as a true science may be mentioned Saadyah Gaon, Shabbetai Donnolo, Abraham bar Ḥiyya, Abraham Ibn Ezra, Samuel Ibn Nagrela, Solomon Ibn Gabirol, and Abraham ben David of Posquières. Maimonides was the sole medieval figure to combat categorically the prevailing belief in a., declaring it forbidden by Scripture and bordering on idolatry. He was, nevertheless, not successful in eradicating the belief, and subsequent thinkers, including Naḥmanides, Levi ben Gershon, Ḥasdai Crescas, Isaac Abravanel, and the Vilna Gaon gave it recognition, while Abraham Zacuto was among the foremost astrologers of his day. The notorious Nostradamus was also of Jewish descent. On the other hand, Joseph Nasi, duke of Naxos, wrote a book condemning a. Astrological observation did much to advance scientific ASTRONOMY. The Zohar, and kabbalistic literature in general, show familiarity with and belief in a. A number of Jewish customs, mentioned in medieval codes, have an astrological basis, e.g. not starting a project on Mondays or Wednesdays. The popular greeting *mazzal tov* is of astrological origin.

ASTRONOMY: The science treating of the heavenly bodies and the laws controlling them. Notwithstanding the use of such general phrases as "the ordinances of the heavens" (Job 38:33) etc., there is in the Bible no specific reference to a. as such. Planets mentioned in the Bible are Saturn (Amos 5:26), Venus (Is. 14:12), and Jupiter (Is. 65:11). There are references also to perhaps six constellations, but the commentators differ as to the exact interpretation of each. In apocryphal literature, the Books of Enoch and Jubilees deal with astronomical questions, such as the length of days, months, and years. Talmudic literature assumes the importance of astronomical calculations for determining the New Moon and, hence, the dates of festivals, etc. R Gamaliel had for this purpose a chart which showed 36 different phases of the moon. The amora Samuel was also learned in a. and maintained that its study would obviate the necessity of having witnesses to determine the date of the New Moon. The Talmud followed contemporary belief in considering the earth as the center of the universe. The heavens were thought to be a vault enclosing the flat disc of the earth. In all, seven heavens were assumed, the sun, moon, and stars being fixed in the

second heaven. A distance of 500 walking years separated the earth from the first heaven, this being also the measurement of the thickness of the heavens and of the space between them. An interesting difference of opinion between Jewish and non-Jewish sages on the question of whether the planets or the spheres revolve is recorded in the Talmud *(Pesaḥim* 94b*)*. The different times and places for the rising and setting of the sun during the year were picturesquely explained by the statement that the sky has 182 windows in the east, 182 in the west, and one in the center. The earth itself was depicted as a round disc surrounded by water. Jews became important in astronomical study only after the rise of Islam and the revival of Greek science: their main interest was, however, its implication for ASTROLOGY. They translated many important astronomical works from Arabic into Latin and Spanish, and, in some instances, added commentaries. They were the chief compilers of the various astronomical tables drawn up in Spain. Over 250 Jewish astronomers who flourished before 1500 are known by name. Abraham bar Ḥiyya (12th cent.) wrote in Hebrew on a.; his writings in Latin translation contributed to the development of a. in Europe. Others who wrote on a. were Abraham Ibn Ezra, Isaac Israeli, Jacob ben Makhir, and Levi ben Gershon; the two last-named invented improvements for the quadrant. During the Renaissance period, an outstanding name was Abraham Zacuto, famous for his astronomical tables (published by his pupil, Joseph Vecinho) which were used by Columbus. In the post-Renaissance period, David Gans worked with Tycho Brahe. In modern times, important Jewish names are Wilhelm Beer, Hermann Goldschmidt, Arthur Schuster, Maurice Loewy, Edmund Weiss, Samuel Oppenheim, and Karl Schwarzschild. It is believed that the English astronomer, Sir William Herschel, was of Jewish extraction. Modern cosmology is based to a great extent on Einstein's general theory of relativity.

ASTRONAUTS see **AVIATION**

ASTRUC LEVI (fl. c. 1414): Spanish scholar. Rabbi at Alcañiz, he participated in public disputation there with Joshua LORKI in 1412, when the latter first produced his anti-Jewish writings. In 1413–4, he represented his community at the disputation of TORTOSA, where he was the outstanding orator among the Jewish spokesmen.

***ASTRUC, JEAN** (1684–1766): French biblical scholar and medical historian. In an anonymous work (1753), he expressed the view that while Moses composed the Law, he utilized various older sources. He is regarded, together with Spinoza, as the father of the Higher Criticism of the Bible.

ASYLUM see **CITIES OF REFUGE**

ATHALIAH: Queen of Judah from 842 to 836 BCE; daughter of Ahab and Jezebel. On the death of her son Ahaziah, who reigned only one year, she ex-

Crusaders' castle in Athlit.

terminated the entire royal family except for her grandson, Joash (saved by his aunt Jehosheba). A. now seized power and introduced the Baal cult into Judah. After she had ruled for six years, a successful revolt broke out in favor of Joash, and A. was put to death.

ATHENS: Capital of Greece. The Athenians granted Hyrcanus II a gold crown in recognition of his protection of Athenians visiting Judea, while inscriptions were set up acknowledging favors to the city from Herod, Agrippa I, and Berenice. The apostle Paul preached in a synagogue at A. (Acts 17:17). Few Jews lived in the city until the early 20th cent. In 1939, there were 4,000 Jews in A. and in 1942 they were joined by 4,000 refugees from Salonica. Owing to the sympathy of the Orthodox patriarch, the Jews in A. suffered less than those elsewhere in Greece during the German occupation, and 5,000 survived (1944). Jewish pop. (1973): 2,800.

ATHIAS: Sephardi family of Marrano origin. *ABRA-HAM A.* (Jorge Mendez de Castro; d. 1665) was burned at Cordova by the Inquisition; his son *JO-SEPH A.* (d. 1700) became a distinguished Hebrew printer at Amsterdam, his famous Bible of 1661 receiving a government award. He also published many other noteworthy works in Spanish, etc. as well as in Hebrew. *YOMTOV A.* (fl. 16th cent.), formerly Jeronimo de Vargas, was co-publisher of the Ferrara Bible of 1553 and other important works in Spanish and Portuguese. *YSHAC (ISAAC) A.* (fl. 16th–17th cents.) was *Hakham* of the Sephardi community in Hamburg and published a work on Jewish practice, *Tesoro de Preceptos* (1627). Other members of the family lived in Italy, Turkey, etc.

ATHLETICS see **SPORT**

ATHLIT: Israel moshavah founded by ICA in 1903, 8.5.m. S of Haifa, near the site of an Arab village of the same name and the ruins of successive ports of the Canaanites, Israelites, and Romans. As Castellum Peregrinorum it was the port of Christian pilgrims in the Middle Ages but was destroyed in 1291 together with the other Crusader harbors. In 1911, Aaron Aaronsohn founded an agricultural experimental station there which during World War I was a center of NILI. During the last stages of the British Mandatory government, it was a detention camp for "illegal" immigrants, and later, a refugee reception center. It is now an agricultural and fishing village, with some 2,467) inhabitants (1972), and the site of a plant for extracting salt from sea-water. The massive ruins of a Crusaders' castle dominate the area, in which there are also prehistoric caves.

ATLAN, JEAN (1913–1960): Painter. Born in Algeria, he studied at Paris under the Nazi occupation and first exhibited in 1944. His abstract compositions, with their vivid coloring, reflect his N African background.

ATLANTA: Capital of Georgia, US. The first Jewish settler, Jacob Haas, arrived in 1846, and a Jewish free loan association existed prior to the Civil War. The first congregation was founded in 1867, and a synagogue built 10 years later. There are now a Jewish Welfare Fund and Jewish Community Council; also a weekly paper, the *Southern Israelite,* founded in 1925. Jewish pop. (1973): 18,000.

ATLANTIC CITY: City in New Jersey, US. The first Jewish settlers came from Philadelphia in 1880. The city's first congregation, Beth Israel, was organized in 1889. In 1973, A.C. had 10,000 Jews with five synagogues, a Federation of Jewish Charities founded in 1924, and a weekly paper, *The Jewish Record,* published since 1939.

ATONEMENT: The expiation of a sin and its consequent forgiveness through appropriate repentance and reparation. The Hebrew word for "atone" *(kapper)* can have the connotation of both "ransoming" *(kopher)* and "washing away of sin" (the Babylonian *kuppuru*). In the Bible, a. is connected with sacrifice (Lev. 5:14–26). The tendency to look upon sacrifice as sufficient a. in itself was strenuously opposed by the prophets. Without advocating the abolition of sacrifice, they stressed the moral and ethical aspects of a.; sacrifice without righteousness is worthless, and forgiveness may be achieved without sacrifice where there is sincere repentance and the resolve to refrain from sin. In addition to sacrifice, prayer and fasting are also specified in the Bible as methods of seeking a.; they attained overwhelming importance after the destruction of the Temple and the consequent cessation of sacrifice. Charity, too, was regarded as a means of attaining a. The rabbis taught "Prayer, repentance, and charity avert the Judgment" (Y. *Taanit* II, I). In addition to conscious efforts, the rabbis considered suffering, poverty, exile, sickness, and death as achieving a. The sufferings or death of the righteous vicariously atone for the sins of the people. In the Middle Ages, partly under the influence of the Kabbalah, self-inflicted suffering and ascetic practices were common ways of making a.

ATONEMENT, DAY OF (Heb. *Yom Kippur*): Solemn fast-day observed on *Tishri* 10, described in Lev. 23:32 as a "Sabbath of solemn rest" (literally "Sabbath of Sabbaths"). Though listed in the Bible among the series of festivals, it is distinguished as a day on which a man must cleanse himself of all sin (Lev. 16:30). According to rabbinic tradition *(Bava Batra* 121*a),* it is the day on which Moses came down from Mt. Sinai with the second tablets of the law and announced to the people the Divine pardon for the sin of the Golden Calf. Besides cessation of all manner of work and abstention from food, drink, and sexual intercourse, the day was outstanding for the elaborate Temple ceremonial (fully described in the talmudic tractate *Yoma*). This included the dispatch of the scapegoat to the wilderness "for AZAZEL." Only on the D. of A. was the high priest allowed to enter the Holy of Holies clad—not in his golden vestments—but in white linen, symbolic of purity and humility. On his appearance at the conclusion of the service, he was greeted with rejoicing by the people, confident that their sins had been forgiven. Except for the absence of priestly ceremonial, the observance of this day in late Judaism is similar in character to that of Temple procedure. An essential part of the Additional Service on the D. of A. is a description of the sacrificial service performed on this occasion in the Temple. Another characteristic is the confession of sin as prescribed for the high priest. It is phrased in the plural because of the mutual responsibility of all Jews *(Shevuot* 39*a).* The confession enumerates ethical lapses exclusively and covers almost the whole range of human failings. Especially impressive are the Evening Service (called KOL NIDRE, from its opening formula canceling rash vows between man and God) and the Concluding (NEILAH) Service which ends with the invocation of the *Shema* and the declaration: "Next year in Jerusalem." Reform Judaism retains the general structure of the traditional services.

Synagogue in Atlanta, Georgia, US.

Frank Atran.

ATRAN, FRANK Z. (1885–1952): US industrialist and philanthropist. Born in Russia, he delivered arms for the Jewish self-defense organization during the period of the Czarist pogroms. A sharp critic of the Bolsheviks, he left Russia and lived in Berlin, Paris, and Brussels where he directed large textile enterprises. In 1940, he went to the US where he established the Atran Foundation which, among many projects, contributed $1,000,000 for a laboratory at Mt. Sinai Hospital, New York, established a chair in Yiddish at Columbia Univ., and presented the Atran Center for Jewish Culture to the Jewish Labor Committee.

ATTAR, HAYYIM BEN MOSES BEN (or Abu; 1696–1743): Kabbalist. Born in Morocco, he became famous as a preacher. In c. 1732, he set out for Palestine. On the way, he spent considerable time at Leghorn, where he found a wide circle of admirers. He received substantial donations for a great yeshivah in Jerusalem which he established after settling there in 1742. He wrote several works of rabbinic scholarship, including a commentary on the Pentateuch, *Or ha-Ḥayyim*, and is the hero of many legends.

ATTRIBUTE (Heb. *toar*): Permanent quality which does not form part of the essence. The Bible ascribes to God many qualities and traits (jealousy, mercy, belligerency, etc.) which, for a more philosophical mode of thought, implied the ascription to God of change, passion or even incomplete unity. The problem of interpreting such statements without ascribing to God a.'s distinct from His essence occupied all medieval Jewish philosophers. By eliminating poetical and anthropomorphic biblical statements, they severely limited the number of applicable a.'s and further divided those remaining into apparent a.'s resulting from linguistic habit (a.'s of action, like merciful or just; a.'s of relation) and those that constitute essential a.'s (living, omnipotent, omniscient, etc.). These latter were either declared identical with God's essence (Saadyah) or else negative, i.e., denials of imperfection in God's nature (Maimonides and others). Later medieval philosophers from Hasdai Crescas onward admitted a limited number of positive a.'s, thus coming closer to popular faith. The Kabbalah applied the term "a." to ten Divine potencies (SEPHIROT) which represent the manifest Deity (see ANTHROPOMORPHISM).

ATZERET see **SHAVUOT**

ATZMON: Mountain in Lower Galilee opposite Sepphoris; site of a battle between Jews and the Roman commander Gallus in 66 CE. In the 19th–20th cents. the name was erroneously applied to Mt. Meron.

AUCKLAND: New Zealand city. Jews settled there early in the 19th cent. A community was organized in the early 1840's and a synagogue built in 1855. The first two mayors of A. were Jews. Jewish pop. (1973): 2,000.

AUER, LEOPOLD (1845–1930): Hungarian violinist. A pupil of Joachim, he was a concert artist, professor of violin at St. Petersburg (1886–1917), conductor, and the founder of a famous quartet. Tchaikovsky dedicated his violin concerto to A. In 1918, he emigrated to the US. A. was converted in youth to the Russian Orthodox Church.

AUERBACH, BERTHOLD (1812–1882): German author and a leader of Jewish emancipation. A. prepared for the rabbinate. He turned to literature after being expelled from the university and arrested for revolutionary activities. A. attained a European reputation through a series of short stories on peasant life in S Germany, *Schwarzwälder Dorfgeschichten* ("Village Tales from the Black Forest," 1843–61) which represented a new literary genre in Germany. In later years, he acted as literary adviser to the Prussian queen and wrote patriotic literature; at the same time, he advocated a liberal German nationalism. Throughout his life, he was deeply interested in Jewish problems.

AUGSBURG: German city. Definite information on Jewish settlement in A. dates from 1212. The community was annihilated at the time of the Black Death (1349) but renewed the following year. In 1438, however, the Jews were expelled from the city. During the ensuing centuries, few lived there, although it was the seat of a Hebrew printing press c. 1514–44. The community, refounded in 1803, numbered 1,100 in 1933, but was wiped out during the Nazi regime. Jewish pop. (1966): 230.

*AUGUSTUS: Roman emperor; ruled 31 BCE– 14 CE. His attitude toward the Jews of Palestine and the Diaspora was correct but not friendly. He

Jews being taken to the gas-chambers in Auschwitz.

confirmed the kingship of Herod and returned to him the areas which had been taken away through the influence of Cleopatra. Herod named the cities of Sebaste (Greek for A.) and Caesarea in his honor. A. confirmed Herod's will dividing his territory among his three heirs (Archelaus, Philip, and Antipas) but later converted Judea into a region governed by a procurator residing at Caesarea.

AUSCHWITZ: (Polish: Oswiecim; Yiddish: Ush-
pitzin): Town in Poland, 30 m. W of Cracow; site of the largest Nazi extermination camp. The original Jewish community, numbering some 4,000, was expelled or annihilated in 1940, and the camp established in the spring of that year. It had three large components: A. I, the *Stammlager* ("main camp"), A. II, *Birkenau,* A. III, the *Aussenkommandos* ("outside groups"); later, the large synthetic rubber plant, Buna-Werke, was added to the A. administration, which also supervised forced labor in about 40 subsidiary installations comprising munitions factories, coal mines, highway construction, farms, and a scientific hygiene institute. Prisoners of virtually every occupied European nation were interned there, as well as Jews of all nationalities. Most non-Jewish prisoners were assigned to slave labor; but up to 90% of the Jews were selected on their arrival for immediate extermi-

nation, the remainder being gradually destroyed by hunger, disease, and maltreatment. Gassing, first experimented with in Sept. 1941, superseded earlier methods of mass killing (shooting, beating, poisonous injections) in the summer of 1942 with the installation of four modern gas chambers and crematoria capable of processing thousands of human beings daily. It has been estimated that about 4–5,000,000 prisoners passed through A., including c. 1,500,000 Jews almost all of whom perished. Russian troops liberated the camp on Jan. 27, 1945 and found some 5,000 survivors.

AUSLANDER, JOSEPH (1897–1965): US poet, anthologist, and translator. After teaching at Harvard and Columbia Univs., he served as consultant in English poetry to the Library of Congress (1937–43). A. wrote *Sunrise Trumpets* and translated Petrarch's sonnets.

AUSTRALIA: British dominion. In 1817, the nucleus of its first congregation was established in SYDNEY. Jews were among the early settlers in the other principal cities (MELBOURNE, ADELAIDE, BRISBANE, etc.) where communities were organized shortly after their foundation. The discovery of gold in the middle of the 19th cent. led to a considerable Jewish immigration, though some congregations established in that period are now extinct. Australian communal life is largely

Sir Isaac Isaacs as governor-general of Australia.

patterned on that of English Jewry. Most of the congregations recognize the jurisdiction of the chief rabbi
of the British Empire and are traditional in character,
but liberal movements have emerged in Sydney and
Melbourne. The Jewish population has more than
doubled since 1935, mainly through immigration from
Europe, and numbers (1973): 72,000: 97% of the Jews
live in the metropolitan areas. Until its recent growth,
the numerical weakness and the isolation of the
community were marked. However, religious and cultural life has been strengthened of late. The Zionist
movement is well-organized and active. Jews have at
all times enjoyed full equality and freedom. Anti-
Semitism has never assumed organized proportions,
and Jews have been prominent in all walks of life:
thus, Sir Isaac ISAACS was the first Australian-born
governor-general and Sir John MONASH commanded
the Australian Expeditionary Force in World War I.
The Jews in each state have their elected Representative Board, and these Boards elect the Executive
Council of Australian Jewry, which is the official
representative body of the community.

AUSTRIA: Central European republic. Its first Jewish
settlers probably came with the Romans, but the
first specific mention of them is in a document of
c. 906 placing Jewish and Christian merchants on the
same footing. Persecutions in Germany drove numbers
of Jews to A., and in 1204, there is reference to a

synagogue in VIENNA. In 1238, the emperor Frederick
II granted a charter to the Jews of Vienna, taking them
under his protection. In 1244, Duke Frederick the
Quarrelsome gave the Jews a new charter *(Privilegium
Fredericianum)* which subsequently served as a model
elsewhere. The period between the 13th and 15th cents.
was marked by serious persecutions culminating in
1420 when, as a result of a charge of ritual murder, all
the Jews of A. were either burned, expelled, or forcibly
baptized *(Wiener Gezerah)*. They did not disappear,
however, and were subject to further restrictions and
local expulsions until 1670, when another general
expulsion was decreed through the influence of the
Spanish-born empress, Margaret Theresa. Jews reappeared the following century but suffered from the
hostility of Maria Theresa. The Edict of Toleration
(1782) of her successor, JOSEPH II, was designed to
enforce emancipation and hasten assimilation, but the
Jews received full rights only in 1867. In 1938, there
were about 200,000 Jews in A. The Nazi annexation
led to an unprecedented persecution; c. 80,000 emigrated (1938–40), but c. 100,000 were annihilated.
Jewish pop. (1973): 10,000, of whom 9,000 are in
Vienna.

AUSTRO-HUNGARY see **AUSTRIA; HUNGARY**

AUTOBIOGRAPHIES: The earliest autobiography
in Jewish literature is that of Nehemiah, included
in the Bible, followed by Josephus' apologetic *Vita*.
In the Middle Ages, the little material extant deals only
with specific episodes or stages of the writer's life—
e.g. the Scroll of Abiathar, the *Megillat Evah* of Yom-
Tob Lipmann Heller, or the travel-diary of David

Jewish gravestone of Vienna (1630).

Reuveni. The earliest Hebrew autobiography in the proper sense of the word is that of Leone Modena (17th cent.). Others of outstanding Jewish interest are by Glückel of Hameln, Solomon Maimon, Ber of Bolochov, Jacob Emden, Isaac Hirsch Weiss, Shemaryahu Levin, Abe Cahan, Chaim Weizmann, etc. Many Hebrew and Yiddish writers have written a., including J. L. Gordon, Mendele Mocher Sephorim, and H. N. Bialik. The Jewish catastrophe in Europe produced a large number of personal recollections, as have events in Israel since the modern period of colonization. Many selections from Jewish a. are contained in Leo W. Schwarz's *Memoirs of my People* (1943) and from those bearing on Palestine, in A. Yaari's *Zikhronot Eretz Yisrael* (1947). Much American Jewish autobiography is contained in J. R. Marcus' *Memoirs of American Jews* (3 vols. 1955/6). See also DIARIES.

AUTO-DA-FE (Portuguese "act of faith"; in Spanish *Auto-de-Fé*): Ceremony at which the sentences of the Inquisition were announced to the victims. These were regarded as ceremonial occasions, attendance

St: Dominic presiding over an Auto-da-fè.
(From a painting by Alonso Berruguete).

being encouraged by promises of spiritual benefit. After a solemn procession through the streets of the city, the condemned heretics were brought to the scene of the a. in the public square where a sermon was preached. The sentences were then proclaimed. In the case of the "impenitent" or "relapsed," these would normally result in their being handed over to the secular authorities. They were then taken to a site (Quemadero), generally outside the city walls, where they were burned. The preliminary "mercy" of strangulation was accorded to "penitents." The bones or effigies of those who had evaded their fate by death or flight were also burned. It is estimated that over 2,000 a.'s took place in Spain, Portugal, and their dependencies between 1480 and 1825, and some 30,000 persons (mostly judaizers) were put to death, with perhaps as many as 400,000 receiving lighter sentences ranging from penance to the galleys. A.'s also took place in other countries subject to Roman Catholic control.

AUTO-EMANCIPATION see **PINSKER, LEO**

AUTONOMY: Some degree of self-government was enjoyed by Jews almost everywhere even after the fall of the Jewish state in 70 CE. In Roman Palestine, Jewish courts continued to exist, and the NASI exercised considerable authority. In Babylonia, the EXILARCH had greater powers, including that of imposing taxation. Throughout the Middle Ages, the desire of the Jews to judge civil cases according to talmudic law and the official exploitation of the Jewish communities to raise bloc-taxation ensured a certain degree of a. in every land. The regulations enacted by the communities, extending far beyond the religious sphere, were termed TAKKANOT. In Spain, the Jewish courts imposed physical and, at one period, even capital punishment. Here, and in some other countries, the officially-recognized head of the Jewish COMMUNITY was called the NAGID. Sometimes, this a. extended over wide areas, as in the case of the Polish COUNCIL OF FOUR LANDS. A. was consolidated by means of the lavish employment of excommunication and through the support of the secular government whose wish was that the Jewish community be an efficient fiscal entity. The spread of emancipation, the end of separate taxation, and the abolition of the KAHAL in Russia (1844) ended the last traces of Jewish a. in Europe. A movement for cultural a. in Europe was launched by Simon Dubnow and received much support after World War I, having important temporary results in the Ukraine and Lithuania. Following its principle of granting a. to minorities, the USSR by the 1930's had five autonomous Jewish districts, three in the Ukraine and two in the Crimea. BIROBIDJAN was declared a Jewish autonomous region in 1934, and represented in the USSR Council of Nationalities. There is, however, no longer any Jewish a. in the Soviet Union. A. never appreciably penetrated into

Tishah be-Av by Leopold Horowitz.

America. Some degree of a. was enjoyed by Palestinian Jewry, under the VAAD LEUMI, before independence.

AV: Fifth month of the Jewish religious year and 11th of the civil. It lasts 30 days and falls in July-Aug. *Av 9 (Tishah be-Av)* is the fast commemorating the destruction of the First and Second Temples. *Av 15* was formerly celebrated as a holiday. A., by euphemism, is generally known as *Menaḥem A.* ("A. the Comforter").

AV, FIFTEENTH OF: Day of rejoicing in Second Temple times. The last date for bringing wood-offerings for the altar, it became a joyous holiday with the maidens dancing in the vine-yards. There are still some liturgical observances on this date.

AV, NINTH OF (in Heb. *Tishah be-Av*): Fast day already observed at the beginning of the Second Temple period (cf. Zech. 8:19) commemorating the destruction of the First and second Temples, both on approximately this date. The Book of Lamentations is read after the Evening Service (and also in the Morning Service according to certain rituals). *Kinot* (dirges) are recited after or during the Morning Service. These include compositions dealing with tragedies in later Jewish history. The fast resembles that of the Day of Atonement in its restrictions upon eating, drinking, anointing, etc. Phylacteries are only worn during the afternoon prayers, ornamentation is removed from the synagogue, and the worshipers sit on the floor or on low benches. If *Av 9* falls on a Sabbath, the fast is postponed to the following day. *Av 9* is also traditionally the anniversary of the fall of Betar in 135 CE, the expulsion from Spain in 1492, and other national calamities.

AV BET DIN (Heb. "Father of the Court"): Vice-president of the Supreme Court (*Bet Din ha-Gadol*) in Jerusalem during the Second Temple period. He probably handled court procedure. The Talmud records detailed rules of precedence in which the *A.B.D.* immediately follows the president *(Nasi)* and precedes the "sage" *(Ḥakham)* who was the third member of presidium. In the gaonic period, the *A.B.D.* was assistant to the Gaon, while in modern times, the title is given to communal rabbis, as heads of the religious courts (see BET DIN).

AV HA-RAḤAMIM (Heb. "Father of Mercy"): Opening words and name of a medieval dirge in memory of martyrs recited during Sabbath prayers in the Ashkenazi rite.

AVADIM (Heb. "Slaves"): Minor tractate incorporated in Talmud editions. Its 3 chapters contain a discussion of laws regarding the purchase and manumission of bondsmen, and allied legislation.

AVDAT (Abde): Ancient city in the Negev, near Sedeh Boker. Originally a caravan stop, it was first built by the NABATEANS in the 1st cent. CE and was destroyed in the 7th century. The well-preserved remains have been reconstructed and include Byzantine baths, a Roman camp, burial caves, and churches.

AVELE ZION (Heb. "Mourners for Zion"): Jews who led an ascetic existence in mourning for the destruction of the Temple and the Jewish state. The Talmud called them *perushim* (abstainers) because they refused meat and wine. They again became an important element in Jewish life after the rise of Karaism. There is no trace of them after the destruction of the Jerusalem community at the close of the 11th cent.

AVENGER OF BLOOD (Heb. *goel ha-dam* = "blood redeemer"): Next of kin of a murdered man, upon whom rests the responsibility for avenging the murder (Deut. 19:6). Such family obligation existed among most ancient peoples; biblical legislation, however, made a distinction between willful murder and accidental manslaughter, alloting six CITIES OF REFUGE as asylums in cases of accident.

AVERAH (Heb. "transgression"): A trespass, especially breach of a religious injunction (e.g. of the Sabbath). A. is the opposite of MITZVAH.

AVIATION: Jews have played a significant part in the development of a. David Schwarz began to build a rigid airship in 1890; this was tested by the German government in 1897 and inspired Zeppelin's invention. Emile Berliner and his son designed the first practical helicopter in the US. The aircraft engine designer Harold Caminez and the aerodynamicist Benedict Cohn made important contributions. Theodor von Karman, of Hungarian birth but in the US since 1930, is prominent in aerodynamics. In England, H. M. Levy and S. Brodetsky were active in the same field, while Sir Ben Lockspeiser has been director of aircraft production and director-general of scientific research (air) at the Ministry of Supply. Sydney Goldstein was chairman of the Aeronautical Research Council of Great Britain (1946–9). The foundations of aeronautics in Italy were laid by Leonino de Zara. Lena Bernstein (France) established various records in international flying, while Henri Deutsch de la Meurthe founded the aeronautical school of St. Cyr. In the US, eight university schools of a. were established by Daniel Guggenheim and his son Harry F. between 1925 and 1930. The Daniel Guggenheim Foundation also made possible basic research in a., including some of the earlier experiments in jet propulsion. Martin Summerfield, of Princeton Univ., developed the rocket engine. The first Jewish cosmonaut was the Russian BORIS VOLYNOV. The pioneer of Jewish flying in Palestine was the Aviron Co. founded in 1936. Its Piper Cub monoplanes brought aid to isolated settlements during the disturbances of 1936–9 and were the nucleus of the Israel Air Forces formed in 1948. The latter counteracted Egyptian bombing of Israel, supported land forces, and bombed Arab capitals. The force is today modeled on advanced lines and includes jet craft. It proved its effectiveness in the SINAI CAMPAIGN (1956), the SIX-DAY WAR (1967) when it destroyed the Egyptian and Jordanian air forces on the ground, and the YOM KIPPUR WAR. Civil a., to and from Israel, is controlled by EL AL, while the Arkia company operates within the country.

AVIDOM (MAHLER-KALKSTEIN), MENAḤEM (1908—): Israel composer. Born in Galicia, he settled in Tel Aviv in 1935. His style is influenced by modern French music and oriental nuances. His works include the opera *Alexandra the Hasmonean*, *Folk Symphony*, the symphony *David*, chamber music, and songs.

AVIGDOR-GOLDSMID, SIR OSMOND ELIM D' (1877–1940): English leader. He served as a director of the Economic Board for Palestine, president of the Anglo-Jewish Association (1921–6) and of the Board of Deputies of British Jews (1926-33), and joint chairman, European Council of the Jewish Agency (1933–5). His son, *SIR HENRY D'AVIGDOR GOLDSMID* (1909–1976) was active in Anglo-Jewish life and like his father, president of ICA. He was a Conservative member of parliament 1955–74.

AVIGNON: City of S France which, from the 14th to the 18th cents., was, together with the adjacent COMTAT VENAISSIN, under Papal rule. The Jews, who had settled there from the early Middle Ages, were thus enabled to remain after they were expelled from the rest of France in the 14th cent. From the 16th cent., they were confined in a ghetto known as the CARRIERE DES JUIFS. Decadence set in rapidly after the French Revolution. Jews from Alsace found refuge there in World War II but the modern community is based on the influx from N. Africa in the 1950's and early 1960's; the community numbered 2,000 in 1968 and maintains the circular synagogue (1844).

AVIḤAYIL: Israel smallholders' settlement (TM) N of Netanyah, founded in 1932 by veterans of the Jewish Battalions of World War I. Bet ha-Gedudim at A. contains a museum of the JEWISH LEGION. Pop. (1972): 633.

AVILA: Town in Old Castile (Spain) where a Jewish community existed at least from the 13th cent. Here, there appeared in 1295 the so-called "Prophet of Avila" who persuaded the local Jews that he was a messenger of God. On a date announced by him, the community gathered in the synagogue to await the arrival of the Messiah. The Christians asserted that crosses mysteriously appeared in the houses of the Jews, many of whom became converted to Christianity. The community suffered during the anti-Jewish disturbances of 1391 and 1412 but retained its importance throughout the 15th cent.

AVINOAM (GROSSMAN), REUBEN (1905–1974): Hebrew poet and author. Born in Chicago, he emigrated to Palestine in 1929. He published several volumes of original poetry, a novel *A Father* *and his Daughter,* and translations from English authors. Since the establishment of the state of Israel, A. devoted himself to publishing the literary and artistic works of soldiers who fell in the Israel War of Independence.

AVINU MALKENU (Heb. "Our Father, Our King"): Prayer of supplication recited during the Ten Days of Penitence and on public fast days. It originated in Mishnaic times but later underwent changes and additions. It has 25 verses in the Sephardi ritual, 44 in the Ashkenazi.

AVIV or **ABIB** (Heb. "spring"): Period of the ripening of the corn.

AVODAH (Heb. "service," "prayer"): Term applied to the Temple sacrificial service and to the Day of Atonement ritual of the high priest. It also refers to an impressive section of the Additional *(Musaph)* Service on the Day of Atonement describing the Temple service on that day with its repeated confession of sins. Many medieval liturgists wrote such compositions.

AVODAH ZARAH (Heb. "Idolatry"): Eighth tractate in the Mishnah order of *Nezikin* containing 5 chapters, with both Babylonian and Palestinian Talmud commentary. It deals with idols, prohibitions connected with various types of idolatry, and regulations to prevent close contact with idolators.

AVOT see **PATRIARCHS**

AVOT (Heb. "Fathers"): Tractate of the Mishnah in *Nezikin* having no Talmud commentary. It contains the sayings and religio-ethical teachings of the sages from the 3rd cent. BCE to the 3rd cent. CE. Because of its great ethical importance, A. (or *Pirke Avot* — "Chapters of the Fathers") has been incorporated in the liturgy and is read in Ashkenazi communities every Sabbath afternoon during the summer, while the Sephardim recite it only at home on the Sabbaths between Passover and Pentecost. Its sixth and last chapter *(kinyan torah* or *Perek Rabbi Meir)* is a later addition. An expanded version is the AVOT DE-RABBI NATAN. The language is precise and clear, the form occasionally resembling biblical aphorisms. Many commentaries have been written on A. It has been translated into other languages and has made a wide impression outside the confines of Judaism.

AVOT DE-RABBI NATAN: One of the small tractates usually printed with the Babylonian Talmud; a kind of Tosephta or midrashic expansion of AVOT, preserved in two versions stemming from a common ancient source. It is ascribed to R Nathan the Babylonian, a contemporary of R Meir, although it certainly belongs to a later period.

AVTALION see **SHEMAIAH**

AVUKAH: US students' Zionist federation established in 1925 with the support of the Zionist Organization of America. A. carried on important educational and cultural work until it was succeeded in 1945 by the INTERCOLLEGIATE ZIONIST FEDERATION OF AMERICA.

AXELROD, JULIUS (1912–): US physiologist. He taught at the National Institute of Mental Health, Bethesda, and was awarded a Nobel Prize in 1970 for his work on the mechanism of nerve cells.

AXELROD, PAVEL (1850–1928): Russian revolutionary. When the Russian Social Democratic party, of which he was a founder, divided into the Mensheviks and the Bolsheviks (1903), A. was among the leaders of the former. After the revolution of Oct. 1917, he settled in Germany.

AXENFELD, ISRAEL (1787–1866): Russian Yiddish writer. Originally a Hasid, he joined the ranks of the *maskilim* and went to live in Odessa, where he was a notary. A. wrote some thirty novels and plays (mostly unpublished) inveighing against obscurantism and the hypocrisy of the Hasidim.

AYELET HA-SHAHAR: Israel kibbutz (IK) in Upper Galilee, founded in 1918 by members of *Poale Zion.* It is the site of a museum containing discoveries from nearby HAZOR. Pop. (1972): 760.

AYIN (ע): Sixteenth letter of the Hebrew alphabet; numerical value 70. Oriental Jews pronounce it like Arabic *'ain* with compression of the lowest part of the throat immediately above the vocal cords (voiced pharyngeal fricative). Among European Sephardim it is pronounced *ng* as in "king"; among Ashkenazim and in Israel mostly like *aleph.* In Yiddish, it stands for the vowel *e* (as in *get*).

AYLLON (AELYON), SOLOMON BEN JACOB (1660–1728): Rabbi and kabbalist. Going to Europe from Palestine to collect donations for the community, he served as Hakham in London and Amsterdam. His hardly-concealed proclivity toward Sabbetaianism involved him in fierce controversies, in particular with Tzevi ASHKENAZI.

AZARIAH see **UZZIAH**

AZAZEL: Name possibly designating the "scapegoat" or the "demon" to whom the scapegoat was sent (Lev. 16). On the Day of ATONEMENT, two goats were prescribed as sin-offerings for the people. The high priest cast lots and designated one goat "for the Lord" and the other "for Azazel." The latter was sent into the wilderness and cast over a precipice. In apocryphal and midrashic sources, A. is variously represented as a fallen angel or an arch-demon, the personification of impurity. The origin of the name is uncertain. The term is used in modern Hebrew as an imprecation.

AZEFF, YEVNO FISHELEVICH (1869–1918): Russian police agent. A. was the classic example of the *agent provocateur,* serving both the Social Revolutionary party and the Czarist secret police. Periodic suspicions of A. in the Social Revolutionary party, which he helped organize, were allayed by his successful terrorist activity. When his treacherous role was discovered in 1908, he was tried *in absentia* by a revolutionary tribunal, but escaped to Germany.

AZERBAIJAN: Region now divided between Russia and Iran. Artaxerxes III settled Jewish prisoners in Hyrcania within the area of A. in 342 BCE. Jews lived in the town of Berdea in the 7th and from the 10th cent., and in the 11th–12th cents. occupied important positions; many were adherents of the pseudo-messiah ALROY. They continued to flourish under the Moguls (13th cent.) but after the latter embraced Islam, most of them apostatized. In 1926, there were in A. some 19,000 European Jews, largely at Baku, and 7,500 "mountain Jews" speaking a Persian dialect. In 1959, there were 40,204 Jews in A.

AZHAROT (Heb. "exhortations"): Liturgical poems devoted to the enumeration of the 613 biblical PRECEPTS (which is also the numerical value of the Hebrew letters of the word *azharot*). The name is derived from the initial word of the first composition of this nature ("Exhortations didst Thou give to Thy people of old"), written in the gaonic period. Saadyah Gaon and Solomon Ibn Gabirol were among the many authors of a. that have been incorporated in the *Shavuot* liturgy, especially in the Sephardi rite.

AZRIEL OF GERONA (fl. 13th cent.): Spanish kabbalist; younger colleague of Ezra of Gerona. His mystical writings are marked by original ideas and terminology and evidence a strong philosophical bent.

AZULAI: (1) *ABRAHAM A.* (1570–1643): Kabbalist. He was born in Fez and emigrated to Hebron at the beginning of the 17th cent. He wrote a commentary on the *Zohar* and an original kabbalistic work *Ḥesed le-Avraham*. (2) *ḤAYYIM JOSEPH DAVID A.* (abbr. *Ḥida*; 1724–1806); Rabbi, kabbalist, and bibliographer.

Hayyim Joseph David Azulai.

He traveled widely as emissary of the Hebron community, finally settling at Leghorn, where he died. He described his journeys in a diary entitled *Maagal Tov*, which is of great historical importance. In the course of his travels, he consulted and copied ancient works and mss, and was one of the first Jewish scholars to investigate Hebrew mss in Italian and French libraries. Said to have published 71 volumes, his most important work is a bibliographical lexicon *Shem ha-Gedolim* ("Name of the Great"), containing the biographies of 1,300 scholars and writers and a description of 2,200 works and mss.

B

BAAL: Heb. for "husband," "owner," "lord"; among the Canaanite peoples taking on the connotation of the proper name of one principal god of the sky and fertility (cf. Babylonian BEL). The term was originally applied to various local gods, generally represented in the form of a bull or a man, with the main common characteristic of being worshiped as gods of fertility, both of the field and of the womb; these attributes were absorbed by the central deity. After the Israelites entered Canaan, they tended to adopt the deities *(Bealim)* of the local inhabitants, notwithstanding the vehement protests of the prophets. The conflict is one of the principal themes of the historical accounts of the Book of Kings. B. was later identified with the Greek Zeus; the "Abomination of Desolation" set up in the Temple by Antiochus was that of B. Shamin, i.e., "Lord of Heaven."

BAAL DIMYON see **SHTIF, NOCHUM**

BAAL HA-BAYIT (Heb. "master of the house"): Landlord; also, derogatively, a property-conscious bourgeois. In Yiddish *balebos* (feminine: *baleboste,* an efficient housewife).

BAAL HA-TURIM see **JACOB BEN ASHER**

BAAL KORE (properly *Baal Keriah* — "master of reading"): Term applied among Ashkenazim to the reader of the pentateuchal portion *(sidrah)* from the Scroll of the Law in the synagogue.

BAAL MAKHSHOVES see **ELYASHEV, ISIDOR**

BAAL NES (Heb. "miracle master"): Term applied to reputed miracle workers and to several specific rabbis; particularly to R MEIR, whose tomb at Tiberias was a center of pilgrimage.

BAAL PEOR: Local Canaanite deity, worshiped with sexual orgies on Mt. Peor in Moab. The Israelites were temporarily attracted to this cult during their wanderings in the desert (Num. 25).

BAAL SHEM (Heb. "master of the Divine Name"): Title given to men to whom was ascribed the power to work miracles by utilizing the Divine Name. The first to be so known was the poet Benjamin ben Zerah (11th cent.). The title was not infrequent in Poland and other lands in the 17th-18th cents., where it sometimes implied a quack who prepared magic amulets, etc.

BAAL SHEM, ELIJAH OF CHELM see **ELIJAH BEN JUDAH OF CHELM**

BAAL SHEM TOV, ISRAEL BEN ELIEZER (c. 1700–1760): Founder of HASIDISM. Born in Podolia, he inclined to solitude at an early age — studying Practical Kabbalah in the countryside. He was successively a children's teacher, lime burner, and ritual slaughterer. About 1735, because of his miraculous cures, he became known as *Baal Shem* or *Baal Shem Tov* (initials, *Besht*). From c. 1740 until his death, he lived at Medzibozh, Podolia, where disciples flocked to study his doctrines; at his death, his followers numbered some 10,000. He did not record his teachings, but they were published 20 years

Baal of the Lightning.

The Baal Tekiyah. Relief by Boris Schatz.

after his death by his pupil Jacob Joseph of Polonnoye. His doctrines were largely based on the kabbalistic teachings of Isaac Luria and his school, but with important innovations. Nature is the vestment of the Deity and man's thoughts must always seek a cleaving to or communion with the Divinity —(DEVEKUT)— so as to perceive the spirituality which is within Matter. *Devekut* is attained through prayer with DEVOTION *(Kavvanah),* and with fervor eventually attains to ecstasy. Communion with God can also be attained by study but this, too, requires fervor. The most important principles in Divine worship are religious feeling, joyful observance of the commandments, trust in God and love of God, the Torah, and Israel. The highest human manifestation of spiritual power is, in Ḥasidic thought, the *tzaddik*, the saintly rabbi who mediates between the Upper and Lower Worlds. These teachings, which are the basis of Ḥasidism, appealed strongly to the masses, and the movement rapidly swept over large areas of E Europe.

BAAL TEKIYAH (Heb. "master of blowing"): The person who sounds the *shophar* in the synagogue during the services on New Year and during the penitential period.

BAAL TESHUVAH see **REPENTANCE**

BAAL ZEBUB: Canaanite deity adopted by the Philistines. His shrine was at Ekron, and when Ahaziah, king of Israel, fell sick, he sent messengers to consult this oracle (II Kings 1). In the New Testament, B. Z. is transformed into Beelzebub, chief of the demons. The name may derive from *Baal Zevul* (= "Lord of heavenly habitation").

BAALBEK: Lebanese town and cult-center of the Phoenician sun-god Baal; the ancient Heliopolis. Magnificent temples to Jupiter Heliopolitanus,

Bacchus, and Venus were erected in Roman times. Arab legend ascribed part of its imposing ruins to a fortress built by King Solomon, and B. is mentioned in the Mishnah. There was a Jewish community in B. from the 16th cent.

BAASHA: King of Israel, son of Ahijah; reigned c. 908–885 BCE. B. declared himself king after killing Nadab, son of Jeroboam, and exterminating the latter's family. He waged war on Asa of Judah in alliance with Ben-Hadad of Aram, who, however, changed sides, so that B. was defeated and had to cede some territory.

BABA BUCH see **BAVA BUCH**

BABEL see **BABYLON**

BABEL, ISAAC (1894–1941?): Russian author. During and after the Russian civil war, he served as political commissar in the Soviet cavalry. From 1923, he devoted himself to literature. In 1939, he was accused of Trotskyism and he died in a concentration camp. His literary work, small in quantity, includes stories and plays, chiefly on two themes: the civil war and life in his native city of Odessa, especially among assimilated Jews.

BABEL, TOWER OF: Building intended to reach to heaven erected in Shinar by the descendants of Noah after the Flood. God frustrated the work by confusing their languages, this leading to the diversity of tongues (Gen. 11:1-9). Modern scholars have seen a similarity between the tower and the Sumerian *Ziggurat,* or step-temple.

BABI YAR: Ravine outside Kiev where tens of thousands of Jews were killed in September 1941. The horror of the massacre together with the fact that no memorial was erected in memory of the Jewish victims turned B. Y. into a symbol of anti-Semitism. It was used by the Soviet poet Evgeni Yevtuschenko in his poem "Babi-Yar" (1962), later incorporated by Shostakovitch into his 13th symphony. It was also the subject of a novel by Anatoly Kuznetzov.

BABYLON, BABYLONIA: Ancient state of W Asia. also known in the Bible as the land of Shinar or of the Kasdim (Chaldees). The Book of Genesis regards B. as the cradle of humanity and as the scene of man's first revolt against God (see BABEL, TOWER OF). Many of the early biblical stories find a parallel in Babylonian literature (see FLOOD). Abraham was born in Ur of the Chaldeans, but migrated to Palestine where he later fought Amraphel king of Shinar (Gen. 14). The identification of Amraphel with the great Babylonian lawgiver, Hammurabi, now seems unlikely. B. was to the prophets a symbol of insolent pagan tyranny, and the symbolism was later adopted by writers of the Apocalypse and New Testament. The Babylonian Nebuchadnezzar II (604–561 BCE) inherited the Assyrian Empire and after his conquest of Judah (597 and 586), exiled many Jews to B. In

The Tower of Babel by Pieter Brueghel the Elder.

association perhaps with members of the Ten Tribes exiled previously, they constituted a large Jewish population, many of whom remained in B. even after Cyrus permitted a return to Palestine. Certain towns (e.g. Nehardea, Nisibis, Mahoza) had an entirely Jewish population. Their position remained favorable during successive regimes. In the 1st cent. BCE a Jewish state was set up around Nehardea by two brothers, ANILAI (Anilaos) and Asinai (Asinaios), and this lasted for some years. The Jews of B. remained in constant touch with the Jews of Palestine and even supplied some of their leaders (e.g. Hillel). During the Roman occupation, the Babylonian Jews rose against the emperor Trajan, the revolt being bloodily suppressed by his commander, Lucius Quietus (116). Under both Persian and Parthian rule, the Jews of B. enjoyed an extensive measure of internal autonomy, being headed by an EXILARCH of Davidic descent who was the king's representative, while the community was governed by a council of elders. The great literary creation of the Jews of B., the Babylonian TALMUD, reflects a society preponderantly based on agriculture and crafts. They were learned in Jewish studies and had produced works of literary merit (Ezekiel, Daniel, Tobit). At the beginning of the 3rd cent., B. became the main center of rabbinic studies, academies being founded by Samuel at Nehardea and by Rav at Sura, while in the later 3rd cent., the academy of Pumbedita was founded to replace that at Nehardea (destroyed

261). The importance of these schools was further enhanced with the abolition of the Palestinian patriarchate in 425, when B became the spiritual center for all Jewry. Persecutions in the 5th cent. led to the Jewish revolt under Mar Zutra II who held out for 7 years but was finally captured and killed. The Talmud was concluded about this period. The position of the Jews continued to be difficult until the Arab conquest (7th cent.). See further IRAQ.

BABYLONIAN EXILE see **EXILE, BABYLONIAN**

BABYLONIAN PUNCTUATION see **VOCALIZATION**

BABYLONIAN TALMUD see **TALMUD**

BACH, ALEXEI NIKOLAYEVICH (1857–1946): Russian chemist and revolutionary. In 1920 he became director of the Biochemical Institute of the Commissariat of Health. He conducted research into oxidation processes in living organisms.

BACHARACH: German city on the Rhine where Jews lived from the 12th cent. Repeated attacks on them took place during the Crusader, Armleder, and Black Death persecutions. Heine's famous work *The Rabbi of Bacharach* describes the persecution in the town during a blood libel.

BACHARACH, JAIR HAYYIM (1638–1702): Talmudist. A member of a distinguished rabbinical family, he served as rabbi at Coblenz, Mainz, and Worms, experiencing much personal and religious suffering in his life. His many works include *Havvot*

Yair (responsa demonstrating an extensive knowledge of secular subjects), *Ma Kashisha* on talmudic method, liturgical poems, and prayers. He also engaged hesitantly in Kabbalah and showed great interest in Shabbetai Tzevi.

BACHE, JULES SEMON (1862–1944): Banker and director of commercial and industrial enterprises. An art-connoisseur, B. presented his rich collection of paintings to the state of New York.

BACHER: (1) *SIMON B.* (1823–1891): Hungarian Hebrew poet. He was influenced by the Haskalah and wrote original poetry, as well as translating into Hebrew from various languages. (2) *WILHELM B.* (1850–1913): Hungarian Semitic scholar; son of (1). He was professor at the Budapest Rabbinical Seminary from 1877, and from 1907, its director. B. published many books and nearly 700 studies on various aspects of Jewish scholarship, including a series of works on talmudic Aggadah, which are still standard. He also wrote on early Hebrew grammarians, Bible exegesis in the medieval period, Judeo-Persian literature, etc,

*BACON, ROGER (1214–1294): English philosopher. He advocated the study of Hebrew as an essential prerequisite for the translation of the Bible and himself prepared a Hebrew grammar. He sought the aid of Jewish scholars in his study of Hebrew, while his writings avoid the common disparagement of Jews and oppose conversionist activity.

BACRI: Jewish family in Algiers, prominent with that of BUSNACH in the late 18th and early 19th cents. Its members supplied the French expedition to Egypt in 1801, and the non-payment by the Dey of the vast sums of money they advanced to him was a reason for the French occupation of Algeria in 1830. The founder of the family was *JOSEPH B.* (1740–1811), official head *(Muqaddem)* of Algerian Jewry, who died in exile. His son, *DAVID B.* (1770–1811), who made the family business one of the most important in the Mediterranean area, was put to death by the Dey on a flimsy pretext. *JACOB B.* (1763–1836) was appointed lay head of the Jewish community after the French occupation.

BADEN: Former state of SW Germany. The first information on Jews in B. dates from the 13th cent., conditions being similar to those in the rest of Germany. A central community at Karlsruhe was organized at the end of the 17th cent. Riots followed a promise of religious equality in 1848, but restrictions on Jews were removed in 1862. The Jewish population numbered 24,000 in 1925 but dropped to 16,800 by 1936. About 500 Jews returned after World War II and in 1969, 1,094 were living there.

BADER, GERSHOM (1868–1953): Hebrew and Yiddish author; he lived in Cracow and Lvov, and from 1912, in the U.S. He contributed to the Yiddish press and edited several Hebrew and Yiddish journals, including the *Tageblatt* (1904–06), the first Yiddish daily paper in Galicia. His literary output was prolific.

BADGE, JEWISH: Moslem rulers, from the 7th cent., ordered that Jews and Christians should wear special clothing to distinguish them from "believers," and this was strictly applied in Egypt in the 10th cent. The conception was officially introduced into Christian Europe by the Fourth Lateran Council (1215) which ordered that Jews (and other infidels) should be distinguished from Christians by their clothing. Sporadically, this was made obligatory

Part of a page from Roger Bacon's Hebrew Grammar.

Rabbi Leo Baeck. (Painting by Eugen Spiro).

henceforth throughout Europe, becoming firmly established—especially in Italy—after the Counter-Reformation (1555 onwards). The color of the b. was normally yellow. In medieval England, it took the form of the two Tablets of the Law. In France, Spain, and elsewhere, it was a circular patch known as the *ruota* (Ital. "wheel") and in Germany, down to the 18th cent. it was a large yellow circle. In Italy, where the b. was not considered sufficiently prominent, a hat of distinctive color was enforced — red in Venice, yellow in Rome. The wearing of the b. (or hat), even in reactionary countries, fell into disuse in the 18th cent. and although re-enacted in Rome as late as 1797, was abolished in the Napoleonic era. The b. was revived by the Nazis and made compulsory in Germany and throughout the occupied areas of Europe in the form of a yellow Shield of David with the letter *J* (or the word *Jude* or its equivalent) inside it.

BADHAN (Heb.): A jester, particularly at the traditional Jewish wedding of E Europe.

BAECK, LEO (1873–1956): Rabbi and theologian; son of Samuel B. (1834–1912), rabbi and author of a history of the Jews and Jewish literature. B. ministered at Oppeln (1897–1907), Düsseldorf (1907–1912), and Berlin (from 1912) where he also lectured in Midrash and homiletics at the *Hochschule fur die Wissenschaft des Judentums*. He became the spiritual leader of German Reform Jewry and from 1922, was chairman of the *Rabbinerverband*. After the advent to power of Hitler (1933), B. was elected head of the *Reichsvertretung der Juden in Deutschland* and remained at his post with his congregation until its liquidation. In 1943, he was sent to the Theresienstadt concentration camp, but survived until its liberation (1945) when he settled in London. He was president of the World Union for Progressive Judaism, established at his initiative, and was repeatedly visiting professor at the Hebrew Union College, Cincinnati. B. was the leading spiritual figure of modern liberal Judaism. According to B., Judaism is the supreme expression of morality; it is the "classical" religion of action as distinct from the "romantic" religion of feeling exemplified by Christianity. Judaism is universal in its content and teaching, but particularistic and bound to a particular nation in its historic expression. B. wrote on Jewish philosophy and theology (including *The Essence of Judaism*) as well as on Midrash and the New Testament.

BAER, MAX (1909–1959): US boxer; world heavyweight boxing champion 1934–5.

BAER, SELIGMANN (1825—1897): Masoretic scholar; lived in Germany. He collaborated with Franz Delitzsch in his masoretic edition of the Bible (1869–95; incomplete). He also published an edition of the prayer-book, *Seder Avodat Israel* (1868), which has become a standard work, and other books on the liturgy.

BAER, YITZHAK (Fritz; 1888—): Historian. He was born in Germany and has been professor of Jewish medieval history (1930) and of general medieval history (1932) at the Hebrew Univ. His works on the Jews in Christian Spain are authoritative. Latterly, he has devoted himself to religious history in the period of the Second Temple. B. is co-editor of *Zion*, the journal of the Israel Historical Society.

BAERWALD, PAUL (1871–1961): US communal leader. Born in Germany, he settled in the US in 1896. After a successful career as a banker in New

Paul Baerwald.

York, he retired to devote himself to Jewish community affairs. He was treasurer (1917–32) and then (1932–45) chairman of the American Joint Distribution Committee.

BAGHDAD: Capital of IRAQ. Its Jewish community, dating from the time of the town's foundation (763), soon became the largest in the country and the seat of the Exilarchate and, ultimately, of the Gaonate also. Benjamin of Tudela (c. 1170) states that he found 40,000 Jews there, including many distinguished scholars. There were also poets, physicians, and talmudists. Under Mongol rule, from 1258, the Jews were favored, many achieving high administrative positions. A reaction and massacre followed in 1291. The community was reconstituted in due course, but when Tamerlane captured B. in 1400, most of the Jews fled. It became prominent again only in the period of Turkish domination, from the 17th cent. onwards. By 1939, the Jewish population numbered some 80,000, playing an important role in economic life. The rebellion of Rashid Ali (1941) was accompanied by pogroms in which hundreds of Jews were killed or wounded. After the establishment of the State of Israel, most of B.'s Jews migrated to Israel, a few to other countries. Only some 5,000 remained and these had dwindled to c. 500 by 1973. They were subject to severe restrictions and nine were publicly hanged in 1969 after charges of spying for Israel. In the 19th cent., B. was the mother-community of the new Jewish settlements of India and the Far East.

BAGINSKY, ADOLF (1843–1918): German pediatrician. He was one of the foremost pioneers in the clinical and scientific study of children's diseases and a voluminous writer on the subject.

*BAGOAS (BAGOHI): Persian governor of Judea, fl. c. 400 BCE. When the high priest Johanan murdered his brother Jeshua, B. entered the Temple and imposed a fine on all offerings for the next seven years. The Elephantine papyri contain an appeal from the Jews of Yeb to B. for permission to rebuild their temple (411 BCE).

BAGRITSKY, EDUARD (pen-name of Eduard Dzyobin; 1895–1934): Russian poet. His works reflect the atmosphere of the Bolshevik Revolution and contain an open Soviet propagandist element.

BAHAI: Religion deriving from the Babi sect in Persia, whose adherents were exiled to Acre in 1868. The center was later transferred to Haifa where an imposing mausoleum was erected over the body of the teacher of the faith, Mirza Ali Mohammed. Haifa is still the residence of the leader of this religion which has adherents throughout the world, although few in Israel.

BAHIA (or **SALVADOR**): Brazilian port. Its earliest Jewish settlers (16th cent.) consisted of Marranos from Portugal. From 1580, they began to suffer from the Inquisition. During the Dutch occupation (1624–5), 200 Marranos returned to Judaism, suffering for this after the Portuguese reconquest. Jewish immigration to B., chiefly from E Europe, was resumed in 1881, and by 1973 the community numbered 140 families.

BAHIR: The oldest classical text of kabbalistic literature. It was known in S France at the end of the 12th cent., but the date of composition and authorship remain problematical. B. consists of a collection of sayings attributed to various tannaim and amoraim, anonymous views, and traditions. It is mainly concerned with mystical interpretations of the letters of the alphabet, accents, etc. The language is a mixture of Hebrew and Aramaic, but the style is obscure and the treatment unsystematic. It is the first source to teach the specifically kabbalistic doctrine of the Divine "attributes" or ten spheres symbolically. The last part of the book is a rewriting of *Raza Rabbah*, an ancient mystical work, to which gnostic elements have been added. Kabbalistic circles regarded B. as an ancient and authoritative source, but some of its opponents considered it heretical. B. was ascribed to R Nehunyah ben Ha-Kanah, author of the first tradition it reports.

BAHREIN ISLANDS: British protectorate in the Persian Gulf. Jews, originating from Iraq, Iran, and India, first settled there in the late 19th cent. Their existence was peaceful until 1947, when there were anti-Jewish demonstrations. In 1956, 400 Jews lived there, but by 1970 they numbered only 100.

Mausoleum of Mirza Ali Mohammed, founder of the Bahai faith, on Mt. Carmel, Haifa.

BAHUR (Heb. "young man"): Term used in the Bible to designate a picked fighting-man and, in rabbinic literature (and still colloquially), in reference to an unmarried man. It came to be applied in the Middle Ages to the advanced yeshivah student (*yeshivah bokhur* in Yiddish).

BAHUR ELIJAH see **LEVITA, ELIJAH**

BAHYA BEN ASHER IBN HALAWA (d. 1340): Spanish biblical exegete and homilist; pupil of Solomon ben Adret and younger contemporary of Nahmanides. He followed the latter in utilizing Kabbalah for biblical exegesis. His most famous work is his frequently published commentary on the Pentateuch in which he followed the fourfold method of interpretation: literal, philosophical, homiletical, and mystical (see PARDES). He also wrote *Kad ha-Kemah*, an ethical work with kabbalistic tendencies.

BAHYA BEN JOSEPH IBN PAKUDA (?c. 1050–?c. 1120): Religious philosopher. Nothing is known of his life except that he was a *dayyan* at Saragossa in Spain. He is famous for his book *Hovot ha-Levavot* ("Duties of the Hearts") written in Arabic and translated into Hebrew by Judah Ibn Tibbon and Joseph Kimhi (most of the latter version being lost). In this, he examines the duties of the heart and conscience (trust in God, humility, asceticism, love of God, etc.) which, according to B., are not less important than the practical commandments. His philosophy was largely Neoplatonic and his asceticism has strong spiritual affinities with the Arab mystics. The work became immensely popular and profoundly influenced subsequent Jewish moralists and mystics; it was translated into English by Moses Hyamson.

BAILMENT: Movable property given in trust by the owner (bailor) to another (bailee). Talmudic law (based upon Exod. 22:6–14) on this subject covers several chapters in the tractate *Bava Metzia*. The Mishnah *(Bava Metzia 7:8)* enumerates four types of bailee *(shomer)*: *shomer hinnam* (the unpaid guardian), *shomer sakhar* (the paid guardian), *sokher* (the hirer), and *shoel* (the borrower). The degrees of responsibility (3 in number) vary from the minimum in the case of the *shomer hinnam* to the maximum in the case of the *shoel*.

BAKKASHAH (Heb. "supplication"): Term applied in Sephardi usage to a type of synagogal hymn included especially in the New Year and Day of Atonement liturgies.

BAKST (ROSENBERG), LEON (1866–1924): Russian artist, noted for his theater décors, especially those which he executed in Paris for Diaghilev's Russian ballet. His bright, rich coloring had a great influence on theater design. Baptized in youth, he later returned to Judaism.

BAKU: Caspian port in Azerbaijan, USSR. Jews originally from Persia began to settle there in the 18th cent. Jewish pop. (1970): 29,716.

Leon Bakst. Costume painting for "Scheherazade".

*BALAAM:** Heathen prophet invited by Balak, king of Moab, to curse the Israelites when they approached his country during their wanderings in the wilderness. Divinely inspired, B. uttered blessings in place of curses (Num. 22:5). On his advice, the Midianites invited the Israelites to worship Baal Peor and B. was killed by the Israelites on the battlefield (Num. 31:16; Josh. 13:22). B. possesses the characteristics of a Mesopotamian priest and soothsayer but also appears as a faithful servant of God. The rabbis, while associating B. with Israel's lapse into immorality, classed him among the seven prophets who spoke to heathen nations. The biblical report of B.'s reproof by his ass is interpreted by Maimonides as a vision.

BALABAN, BARNEY (1887–1971): US motion picture executive. He helped develop the motion picture industry in Holywood and was president of of Paramount Pictures from 1936. He was active in Jewish communal affairs.

BALABAN, MEIR (1877–1942): Historian. In 1920, he became director of the "Taḥkemoni" rabbinical seminary in Warsaw, and in 1928–39, taught at the Warsaw Institute of Jewish Studies and the Univ. of Warsaw. His writings deal primarily with the internal history of the Jews in Poland and Russia. He died in the Warsaw ghetto.

*BALAK: King of Moab. When the Israelites wandering in the desert, approached his borders, he requested BALAAM to curse them, but the curse was turned into a blessing (Num. 22-23).

BALCON, SIR MICHAEL (1896—): British film director and producer. He founded Gainsborough Pictures Ltd., directed Ealing studios, and has produced many British film successes. He also wrote an autobiography.

Lord Balfour.

Foreign Office,
November 2nd, 1917

Dear Lord Rothschild,

I have much pleasure in conveying to you, on behalf of His Majesty's Government, the following declaration of sympathy with Jewish Zionist aspirations which has been submitted to and approved by the Cabinet.

His Majesty's Government view with favour the establishment in Palestine of a national home for the Jewish people and will use their best endeavours to facilitate the achievement of this object it being clearly understood that nothing shall be done which may prejudice the civil and religious rights of existing non-Jewish communities in Palestine, or the rights and political status enjoyed by Jews in any other country.

I should be grateful if you would bring this declaration to the knowledge of the Zionist Federation.

The Balfour Declaration.

BALEARIC ISLANDS: Mediterranean archipelago belonging to Spain. In MINORCA there was in the Roman period a Jewish settlement forced into baptism by Bishop Severus (417). Jews were found in the Islands when they were reconquered from the Moslems by the kings of Aragon in the 13th cent. The principal settlement at this time was in MAJORCA, which, in the 14th cent., was the center of activity of a distinguished band of Jewish makers of maps and nautical instruments, such as Judah Cresques. The massacres of 1391, repeated on the pretext of a Ritual Murder accusation in 1435, drove the great mass of the Jews in the islands into baptism, and the survivors were expelled in 1492. Secret Jews, known as CHUETAS, retained their individuality in Majorca, continued to be persecuted by the Inquisition, and can still be identified. Under British rule, in the 18th cent. a Jewish community openly existed for a time in Minorca.

*BALFOUR, ARTHUR JAMES, LORD (1848–1930): British statesman and philosopher. He was head of the government with which Herzl negotiated in 1902–3, and later was strongly impressed by the personality and Zionist philosophy of Chaim Weizmann. As foreign secretary in 1917, he issued the BALFOUR DECLARATION. He opened the Hebrew Univ. in 1925 and remained outspokenly devoted to the Zionist ideal.

BALFOUR DECLARATION: Official statement issued on Nov. 2, 1917, by the British foreign secretary Arthur James BALFOUR, declaring that the

British government favors "the establishment in Palestine of a national home for the Jewish people, and will use their best endeavors to facilitate the achievement of this object, it being clearly understood that nothing shall be done which may prejudice the civil and religious rights of existing non-Jewish communities in Palestine, or the rights and political status enjoyed by Jews in any other country." This statement was the result of long negotiations initiated by Chaim Weizmann, Nahum Sokolow, and others shortly after the outbreak of World War I, with the support of Herbert Samuel, Chief Rabbi J. H. Hertz, the Haham Moses Gaster, etc. There was much discussion on both the formula of the Declaration and its timing. Balfour's visit to the US in the spring of 1917 and his meeting with President Wilson, who supported the efforts of the American Zionists headed by Brandeis, expedited the final decision of the British government. However, the presidents of the Board of Deputies of British Jews and of the Anglo-Jewish Association (D. L. Alexander and C.G. Montefiore) issued a statement that the Zionist aspirations were calculated to endanger the Jewish position in all countries. There were strong Jewish protests against this action by Jewish representatives and Alexander had to resign from the Board of Deputies. This opposition made the government more cautious, and the moderate formula submitted by the Zionist leaders to recognize Palestine as "the national home of the Jewish people" and for providing a "Jewish National Colonizing Corporation" for the resettlement and economic development of the country was not accepted. The Declaration, after having finally been approved by the British cabinet, was sent to Lord (Walter) Rothschild who was asked to convey it to the Zionist Federation. The document was approved by other Allied governments and incorporated in the Mandate in 1922.

BALFOUR FOREST: Pine forest planted on the slopes of the Nazareth hills. It was the gift of British Jewry in honor of Lord BALFOUR (1929). More than half-a-million trees have been planted in an area of 400 acres.

BALFOURIYYAH: Israel smallholders' settlement (TM), named after Lord Balfour in the E Valley of Jezreel, founded in 1922 by settlers from Europe and the US with the aid of the American Zionist Commonwealth Corporation. Pop. (1974): 216.

BALLIN, ALBERT (1857–1918): German industrialist. He rose from small beginnings to be managing director of the *Hamburg-Amerika* Line, the largest shipping company in Germany, with a fleet of 400 vessels. B. was responsible for the American-German shipping agreement of 1912 and for other agreements designed to eliminate unnecessary competition. He committed suicide after Germany's military collapse in World War I.

West German postage stamp commemorating centenary of Albert Ballin's birth.

BALMES, ABRAHAM BEN MEIR DE (c. 1440–c. 1523): Italian physician, poet, and grammarian. He was rabbi at Padua and is said to have lectured on philosophy at the university. B. translated works by Averroes into Latin and published a standard work on Hebrew grammar *Miskneh Avraham* (also in Latin) which posits a philosophical basis to grammar.

BALTIMORE: City in MARYLAND, US. The first Jews settled there in the latter 18th cent., and the Baltimore Hebrew Congregation was incorporated in 1830. In 1835, there were about 300 Jews in the city, mostly of German origin. B.'s first Reform group, the Har Sinai Congregation, was formed in 1842 by Jews newly arrived from Germany. During the Civil War, B.'s Jews, reflecting current sentiments, were divided in their sympathies, and Rabbi David EINHORN was forced to leave because of his abolitionist convictions. By 1880, the Jewish population had increased to 10,000. By the end of the 19th cent., large numbers of Russian Jews were coming to B.; in 1900, it had 5 synagogues and a number of Jewish periodicals in Yiddish and English. Jews took an active part in civic affairs from the early 19th cent. B.'s Jewish educational facilities include an institution for higher Jewish learning and a teachers' training school. In 1920, the Associated Jewish Charities was formed by a merger of existing organizations. In 1941, the Jewish Welfare Fund was established. The *Jewish Times* has been published there weekly since 1919. Jewish pop. (1973): 94,000.

BALTIMORE, DAVID (1938–): US medical researcher, working at the Center for Cancer Research, Massachusetts Institute of Technology. He was awarded a Nobel Prize in Medicine in 1975 for his work on the interaction between tumor viruses and the genetic material of cells.

BAMBERG see **BAVARIA**

BAMBERGER, LOUIS (1855–1944): Philanthropist, merchant, and communal figure in Newark, New Jersey. B. and his sister, Mrs. Felix Fuld, gave (among other benefactions) $5,000,000 for the establishment of the Institute for Advanced Study, at Princeton (1929).

Bronze plaque of Louis Bamberger.

BAMBERGER, LUDWIG (1823–1899): German economist and statesman. A noted writer on political and economic topics, he took part in the 1848 revolution and was sentenced to death but escaped abroad, becoming a banker in Paris (1853). Subsequently, he returned to Germany and, in 1871, was elected to the first Reichstag. He was one of the leaders of the German liberal party.

BAMBERGER, SELIGMANN BÄR (Isaac Dov; 1807–1878): Leader of German Orthodoxy. It was largely through his advocacy that the Orthodox cause triumphed at a conference called by the Bavarian government in 1836. From 1840 to his death, he was rabbi in Würzburg, where he founded a teachers' college which exercised a great influence in Germany.

BAMBERGER, SIMON (1847–1926): US industrialist and political leader. He went from Germany to the US in 1861. Originally a mine owner, banker, and railroad builder, B. entered politics and by 1902 was a Democratic state senator. He was governor of Utah 1916–20, the first Democrat and the first non-Mormon to hold that position. B. was also active in Jewish community life.

BAMBUS, WILLI (1863–1904): German Zionist. In 1894, he helped to form the Ezra society in Berlin to support colonization in Palestine, on which he wrote several works. He opposed Political Zionism, advocating settlement activity under any circumstances. B. was a co-founder of the Hilfsverein der deutschen Juden (1901).

BAN see **EXCOMMUNICATION**

BANCO, ANSELMO DEL (in Heb. Asher Levi Meshullam; d.c. 1532): Founder of the Venice community. Head of a family established at Padua which controlled a chain of loan-banks throughout Venetian territory, he took refuge in Venice at the time of the German invasion in 1508. His financial assistance to the government and adroitness in negotiations resulted in the formal recognition of the community.

BANDES (MILLER), LOUIS E. (1866–1927): US Yiddish journalist. Born in Russia, B. migrated in 1886 to the US where he became a leader in the Socialist movement. He was a founder of the first Yiddish Marxist weekly, *Die Arbeiter Zeitung* (1890), and when this came under the control of a radical group he helped establish the labor daily, *Forverts* (1897). He later founded *Die Varheit* (1905) which gradually shifted its position from Socialism to Zionism. B. also wrote books and plays.

BANETH: (1) *DAVID TZEVI HARTWIG B.* (1893–1973): Orientalist; son of (2). He settled in Palestine in 1924 and lectured in Arabic language and literature at the Hebrew Univ. from 1926. B. published researches, particularly on the influence of Arab thought on medieval Jewish philosophy. (2) *EDUARD B.* (1855–1930): Rabbi and scholar; grandson of (3). He was born in Poland, was rabbi at Krotoshin 1882–95, and then lecturer at the *Hochschule für die Wissenschaft des Judentums* in Berlin. B. was the author of various studies on talmudic subjects. (3) *EZEKIEL B.* (1773–1854): Hungarian rabbi and yeshivah head. Although famed for his learning, he left no writings and prior to his death destroyed his commentary on the Tosephta. B. lived in ascetic seclusion and was the subject of a number of legends.

BANISHMENT: Temporary or permanent exclusion from one's native soil. The Bible regarded b. primarily as a Divine punishment (e.g. in the cases of Adam and Cain). Accidental slayers were banished to CITIES OF REFUGE where they found asylum from the avenger of the blood. During the Second Temple period, there are occasional references to this punishment for misdeeds or for political reasons. In the Middle Ages, b. was not uncommonly imposed by Jewish courts to protect the community from harmful individuals. See EXPULSIONS.

BANK LEUMI LE-ISRAEL: Bank established in 1903 by the JEWISH COLONIAL TRUST as the Anglo-Palestine Company with a capital of £40,000. It soon became the central bank of Palestinian Jewry. Closed as a British concern during World War I by the Ottoman government, it nevertheless survived and developed. It was known as the Anglo-Palestine Bank Ltd. from 1931 until 1951, when its entire business was transferred to a new body, the Bank Leumi le-Israel Ltd., incorporated in Israel with share capital and open reserves (1956) of I£5,250,000. In 1975 its share capital and reserves amounted to IL645,344,000. In 1948–54, it acted as banker to the Israel government.

BANK OF ISRAEL: The Israel national bank, established in 1954 with a capital of I£10 million and reserve fund of I£10 million. Its purpose is to administer the currency system and regulate the credit and banking system in accordance with governmental economic policy. In 1974 its assets and liabilities balanced at I£20,551 million. The bank's first president *(Nagid)* was David Horowitz.

BANKING: The use of deposited money for credit purposes. The role of Jews in this branch was un-important until the 18th cent., their finance-credit activities during the 11th–13th cents. in Europe being based on the resources of individuals or of small groups of individuals. Jews were absent from the N Italian trading-republics when b. in the modern sense had its origins there. The growth of world economy in the 18th cent. led to the rise of the private banks of the Rothschilds, Worms, Sterns, Bischoffsheims, etc., who were merchant-bankers, financing trade and in-dustry internationally. The Jewish merchant banks did not themselves provide the capital so much as make it mobile and available for industrial expansion. Their decline set in with the revolution of 1848, and with the introduction of public subscriptions to state loans. Another factor was the growth of joint stock banks, pioneered by the Jewish brothers Péreire who founded the *Société du Crédit Mobilier* in France, and by Sir David Salomons, a founder of the Westminster Bank in England. The Jewish lead in the British foreign exchange business of the late 19th cent. had vanished by the mid-20th. World War I hastened the decline of private banks. In the US in the early 19th cent., a number of Jewish merchants founded banks (e.g. the Lazards, Erlangers, Guggenheims), and several (e.g. Kuhn-Loeb, Speyer) contributed considerably to rail-road development. See OCCUPATIONS.

BANU KAINUKA: One of the three Jewish tribes in MEDINA. Possessing no land, they lived from com-merce and as goldsmiths. They were the first to suffer from the hostile attitude adopted by MOHAMMED after his failure to win the Jews over to Islam. They were attacked and besieged in their strongholds, probably in 624, and were forced to surrender after 15 days. Mohammed first wished to have all the men executed but spared them on condition that they quit the town, leaving all their property in the hands of the Moslems. They first migrated to the Jewish centers in Wadi-I-Kura and later further N to Adhriat.

BANU KURAIZA: One of the three Jewish tribes in MEDINA. They inhabited several villages to the S of the town, and their main occupation was agriculture. At the rise of Islam, they numbered 750 fighting-men and held some fortified positions in the neighborhood.

The B.K. were the last Jews to be attacked by Moham-med who charged them with treason. When forced to surrender, they were treated more cruelly than their two fellow-tribes, the men being executed and the women and children sold into slavery. Raihana, a woman of the tribe, was married to Mohammed. Among the B.K. were several poets, some of whose Arabic verses are extant.

BANU-L-NADIR: One of the three Jewish tribes in MEDINA in the vicinity of which they owned landed estates and strongholds. Through cultivation of the soil, moneylending, and trading in weapons and jewels they accumulated considerable wealth. They were besieged in their forts by Mohammed and surrendered after about two weeks (c. 626); their immovable pro-perty was confiscated, but they themselves were per-mitted to depart. They left for the N and founded new settlements, partly in Khaibar and partly in Syria.

BAPTISM: Ablutionary rite symbolizing purification or consecration. Such immersion played an im-portant part in Judaism, apart from the frequent ablutions enjoined both on priests and laymen by the Bible, and acquired great significance in the rites of the ESSENES and HEMEROBAPTISTS. An essential part of the rite of conversion to Judaism in case of either sex is immersion in water to the accompaniment of special prayers. This rite, followed by John the Baptist, was subsequently taken over by the Christian Church.

BAPTISM, FORCED: From Pope Gregory the Great onward, the Catholic Church condemned forced baptisms. But the definition of force is elastic, and it was widely held that baptism was valid even when improperly conferred. Moreover, Christian popular feeling was opposed to the return to Judaism of persons baptized by whatever means. Hence, f.b., sometimes on a large scale, remained a recurrent problem in Jewish history. The outstanding cases were those in Visigothic Spain in the 7th cent. and in the same country and in Portugal in the 14th–15th cents., the latter instance giving rise to the MARRANO problem. The question also arose whether a child of immature years should be baptized without the parents' consent. Though this was condemned by the Popes, Benedict XIV in 1747 declared that, once performed, it was valid. The clandestine baptism of children was hence-forth one of the terrors of Jewish life in parts of Italy, the most famous instance being the MORTARA case of 1858.

BAPTISTS: Protestant sect, successors of the Ana-baptists. In the 17th cent., the English B., strongly opposed by all other sects, developed a philosophy of universal toleration, extending also to Jews. The out-standing exponents of this view were Leonard Busher *(Religion's Peace,* 1614), John Murton *(Objections Answered,* 1615), John Wemys *(Four Degenerate Sonnes,* 1636), and Roger Williams *(Bloudy Tenent of Persecution,* 1644). Williams introduced these conceptions into the charter of the early American colony of Rhode Island.

BAR: Aramaic for "son"; frequently appearing in personal names.

BAR: Ukrainian town. Jews first settled there in the 16th cent., receiving special privileges from Sigismund Augustus of Poland in 1556, but the community was almost completely exterminated in the Chmielnicki massacres of 1648. Before the Nazi invasion, there were about 6,000 Jews in B.

BAR GIORA (= "son of the convert"?), **SIMON** (1st cent. CE): A leader of the Jewish war against Rome, 66–70. In the early stages of the fighting he led a band of Zealots and helped to defeat the forces of the Syrian governor Cestius Gallus. He was an extreme democrat, proclaiming the equality of all and liberating the slaves. Quarreling with the provisional government in Jerusalem, he set up his headquarters for a time in the vicinity of Masada. As his forces increased, he was able to overrun large areas of S Judea, attacking settlements which he regarded as disloyal to the revolt. The opponents of John of Giscala invited B.G. in 69 to Jerusalem with his army; he seized the upper city and civil war raged until the city was besieged by Titus, when B. G. acted as one of the leaders of the defense. After Jerusalem fell in 70, he was taken by the Romans to be displayed in Titus' triumphal procession and then executed.

BAR GIORA: Defense organization (named after Simon Bar Giora) set up in Palestine in 1907 by

Rabbi Meir Bar-Ilan.

members of the Second Aliyah, before the establishment of HA-SHOMER.

BAR-HANINA (end of the 4th cent). Palestinian scholar. He lived in Bethlehem and was a teacher of Jerome who relates that he had to receive B. in his cell at night so as not to be publicly associated with a Jewish scholar. B. has not been precisely identified but from Jerome's writings, it appears that he exercised an influence on the VULGATE translation and was responsible for introducing certain rabbinic exegesis to the Church Fathers.

BAR-HEBRAEUS, GREGORIUS (1226–1286): Syrian scholar of Jewish origin; from 1264, primate of the Jacobite church in Persia. B.H. wrote extensively in Syriac and Arabic, his works including a Syriac grammar, commentaries on the Bible and Aristotle, and a world history (translated into English).

BAR-ILAN (formerly **BERLIN**), **MEIR** (1880–1949): Rabbi and orthodox Zionist leader. A son of Naphtali Tzevi Judah BERLIN, he joined the Zionist movement in his youth, becoming secretary of the *Mizraḥi* World Executive and editor of its weekly *Ha-Ivri*. In 1914, he went to New York, where he became president of the *Mizraḥi* in the US and renewed publication of *Ha-Ivri*. For many years he was president of the *Mizraḥi* movement. In 1926, he settled in Jerusalem, and in 1937, founded the Tel Aviv daily paper *Ha-Tzopheh* as an organ of the *Mizraḥi* and *Ha-Poel ha-Mizraḥi*. He was an initiator and editor of the *Talmudic Encyclopedia* (1947 ff), and author of an autobiography *From Volozhin to Jerusalem*.

BAR-ILAN UNIVERSITY: Israel university near Ramat Gan, founded in 1955 under the auspices of the American *Mizraḥi* organization and named after R. Meir BAR-ILAN. Its object is to produce scholars

Bar-Ilan University, Ramat Gan, Israel.

Letter by Simeon Bar Kokhba (real name: Bar or Ben Kosiba) found in Wadi Merubaat in. the Desert of Judah (1952).

steeped in Jewish tradition while at the same time possessing a good secular education. In 1974 there were 7,000 students and 417 lecturers. The first president was Pinkhos CHURGIN and since 1958, Joseph Lookstein.

BAR KAPPARA (early 3rd cent.): Palestinian scholar believed to be the son of R Eleazar Ha-Kappar. He collected a number of leagal traditions and arranged them in *Mishnat Bar Kappara* ("The Mishnah of B. K."). B.K., an eloquent conversationalist, was a noted teller of fables and, on one occasion, related 300 stories about foxes. He respected the Greek esthetic sense and adopted a positive attitude to natural science. He headed an academy near Lod (Lydda).

BAR KOKHBA (Heb. "son of the star," real name Bar or Ben Kosiba), **SIMEON** (d. 135 CE): Revolutionary leader. Little is known of his life. He was the nephew of R Eleazar of Modiin and reputedly of Davidic descent. On the outbreak of the revolt against Hadrian (132), which he led, R Akiva acclaimed him as the Messiah, but not all rabbis accepted this view. Talmudic anecdotes represent him as of great personal strength, autocratic, and irascible, traditions borne out by letters from B. K. recently discovered near the Dead Sea. The causes of the revolt are unclear; probably the rebuilding of Jerusalem as a Roman colony and the prohibition of circumcision were contributory factors, but it had been fermenting for a considerable period. B.K.'s forces captured Jerusalem but it is improbable that they annihilated a legion, as is sometimes claimed. The minting of Jewish COINS with the names Simeon and Eleazar the Priest indicates an established revolutionary régime. In 133, the Roman counterattack, with an army of 35,000 under Hadrian and the commander

Julius Severus, began. Talmudic extracts suggest they first entered Galilee, then fought actions for the Valley of Jezreel, Ephraim, and the Judean Hills, eventually retaking Jerusalem. In 134–5, the Romans invested B.K.'s last stronghold BETAR and gradually reduced the remaining hill and cave strongholds. B.K. was killed when Betar fell by storm; records speak of the destruction of 50 fortresses and 985 villages, and of 580,000 Jewish casualties besides those who died of hunger and disease. As a result of the revolt, Judea fell into desolation, its population was annihilated, and Jerusalem was turned into a heathen city, barred to Jews. B.K.'s personality has been blurred by subsequent censorship, but he must be credited with military ability in organizing a nearly total popular revolt which engaged the best Roman forces for over 3 years.

BAR-LEV, ḤAYYIM (1924–): Israel soldier. Born in Yugoslavia, he went to Palestine in 1939. He served in the *Haganah* and *Palmaḥ* and from 1948 in the Israel Defense Forces. He commanded an armored division in the 1956 Sinai Campaign. After occupying senior military positions he was chief of staff of the Israel army 1968–71. He is a Labor Knesset member, minister of commerce and industry since 1972.

BAR MITZVAH (Heb. "one who is obliged to fulfil the commandment"): Ceremony marking the initiation of a boy at the age of 13 into the Jewish religious community and into observance of the precepts

Hayyim Bar-Lev.

of the Torah. The first definite reference to the custom dates from the 13th cent., but rabbinic literature contains allusions which may indicate the existence of such a ceremony at a much earlier date. The central feature is the calling-up of the boy to the reading of the Law. According to ancient custom, the father recites the BARUKH SHE-PETARANI blessing, thanking God for being freed of legal responsibility for the child's actions. During the Middle Ages, it was customary for the boy to give a talmudic discourse on the occasion. The Sephardim term the ceremony "entering into MINYAN." In some oriental communities, the climax of the celebration is the first wearing of the phylacteries. Among the Ashkenazim, the ceremony occurs on a Sabbath but in other communities on weekdays. Reform Judaism has introduced a parallel ceremony of confirmation for both boys and girls, which has been adopted by some traditional communities. The B.M. has become the occasion for extensive festivities.

BAR-YEHUDA (originally **IDELSON**), **YISRAEL** (1895–1965): Israel political leader. Born in Russia, he settled in Palestine in 1926. A prominent figure in the socialist movement, he sat in the Knesset from 1949. After the split in *Mapam* (1954), he became a member of the *Aḥdut ha-Avodah — Poale Zion* party. He was minister of the interior 1955–9, and 1962–5 minister of communications.

BARABBAS (1st cent. CE): Jewish rebel against Rome who, according to the New Testament, about to be crucified together with Jesus, was pardoned by Pontius Pilate at the request of the Jews.

BARAITA (Aram. "external"): Tannaitic sayings not included in the Mishnah. The name occurs repeatedly in the Babylonian TALMUD but only once in the Jerusalem Talmud. The latter consistently, and the Babylonian Talmud frequently, uses the term *Matnita* (Aram. for Mishnah) to designate extra-mishnaic *halakhot*. *Baraitot* (plural form) are introduced by the formulas: *teno rabbanan* ("the rabbis taught"), *tanya, tena,* ("it was taught"); and in the Jerusalem Talmud by *tane* (see TANNA). The greatest collection of extra-mishnaic *halakhot* is the TOSEPHTA. A great number of uncollected *baraitot* are scattered throughout both Talmuds. The halakhic Midrashim are in a certain

The Bar Mitzvah Speech by Moritz Oppenheim.

Asher Barash.

sense *baraitot,* since they are extra-mishnaic *halakhot.*
The term *b.* occurs also in the name of certain collections. These include: (1) *B.* on *Avot,* also called
Perek Kinyan ha-Torah or *Perek of R Meir.* This chapter is generally included in the Mishnah treatise *Avot.*
(2) *B.* of *R Adda,* dealing with the calendar. (3) *B.* of
R Eliezer; another name for *Pirke de-Rabbi Eliezer.*
(4) *B.* on the erection of the tabernacle. (5) *B.* of the 49
hermeneutic rules (for spiritual exegesis). (6) *B.* of *R
Ishmael,* which contains the 13 hermeneutic rules of
R Ishmael. (7) *B.* of the 32 rules, explaining 32 rules
of scriptural interpretation. (8) *B. de-Sod ha-Ibbur,* explaining the intercalation of the calendar. (9) *B. de-
Niddah,* containing both halakhic and aggadic expansion of Lev. 15:19–33, is of ancient origin and represents the view of the *halakhah* as taught by Shammai.

BARAK BEN ABINOAM: Commander of the Israelite tribes, with Deborah the prophetess, in their
war against the Canaanites (c. 12th cent. BCE).
He led the forces of Naphtali and Zebulun which
defeated the army of Sisera.

BARAM: Israel communal settlement (KA), near the
Lebanese border. It was founded in 1949 on the
lands of the Maronite village Kafr Birim, whose
inhabitants fled to Gush-Ḥalav. In the deserted village
there are ruins of a beautiful 3rd cent. CE synagogue.

BARANY, ROBERT (1876–1936): Physician and
aurologist. Born in Vienna, he was awarded the
Nobel Prize in 1914 for his work on the physiology
and pathology of the vestibular apparatus. From
1917, B. was professor at Uppsala Univ. (Sweden).

BARASH, ASHER (1889–1952): Hebrew author. He
was born in Galicia and in 1914 settled in Palestine
where he engaged in teaching and contributed to the
Hebrew press. B.'s literary output increased after
World War I and included novels, short stories, poems,
essays, and translations. His main success was in the
field of the novel and short story; his tales chiefly
described life among Galician Jewry during the first
quarter of the present century, but he also wrote about
the pioneering effort in Palestine. Some of B.'s best
novels are on historical themes.

BARBADOS: Island of the British WEST INDIES. Its
Jewish community was founded in 1655 by refugees
fleeing from Brazil after the Portuguese conquest.
More Jews arrived from Cayenne in 1664 after the
cession of the French colony to Holland. For a time,
they controlled the island's sugar industry. In the 18th
cent., there were communities in Bridgetown and
Speightstown. B. was the first British possession to
grant full political emancipation to Jews (act of the
local government, 1802; confirmed by British parliament, 1820). In the second half of the 19th cent., the
economic decline of the island led to the complete
disappearance of the Jewish community. Since 1934,
Jews have settled in B. and in 1973, the community
numbered 30.

BARCELONA: Spanish city (in ARAGON). The presence of Jews is recorded from the 9th cent. Later
it became one of the most important communities in
Spain, being the home of scholars such as Judah Al-
Bargeloni (i.e. "of B."), Abraham bar Ḥiyya, and
Abraham ben Ḥasdai, the financiers of the De la
Caballeria family, and rabbinical authorities like Solomon ben Adret. The famous DISPUTATION of B. between Naḥmanides and Pablo Christiani took place in

Hebrew inscription on a house in the former
Jewish quarter of Barcelona.

1263, and on its conclusion, James I harangued the Jews in the synagogue to convert them to Christianity. The Jews were attacked in 1348, at the time of the Black Death, and in the massacres of 1391 the community was wiped out. Jews, both Sephardi and Ashkenazi, have recently reestablished themselves in B., the community numbering c. 3,100 (1973).

BARENBOIM, DANIEL (1942–): Musician. Born in Buenos Aires, he moved to Israel in 1952 having made his debut as a pianist at the age of seven. From 1954 on, he toured in many parts of the world and later achieved an additional reputation as a conductor. B., who lives in England, married the cellist Jacqueline du Pré.

BARI: Seaport in SE Italy. Jews probably settled there in Roman times, and in the Dark Ages, it became one of the great centers for the diffusion throughout Europe of the Jewish learning received from the East. The phrase "for Torah comes forth from B." was long proverbial. The community lost much of its importance in the later Middle Ages, and persecutions at the end of the 13th cent. drove many of its members into Christianity. There were destructive riots in 1463 and 1495, and the community came to an end with the expulsion from the kingdom of Naples in 1541. At the end of World War II, B. was a great refugee center and a community of some thousands, mainly fugitives from Yugoslavia, temporarily existed. The medieval Jewish quarter still stands.

BARKAI: Israel communal settlement (KA) in the NW Samaritan foothills. Founded in 1949, its settlers originate from the US, Canada, S. Africa, Rumania, and Poland.

BARMINAN (Aram. "Far from us"): An exclamation, used among Sephardim, to ward off ill-fortune; equivalent to the Ashkenazi *lo alenu* ("not on us"). The term b. is sometimes used among Ashkenazim for a corpse.

BARNATO, BARNETT ISAACS (properly Isaacs: 1852–1897): English financier. Going in 1873 to S Africa where he earned his living as a conjurer ("Barnato" being his stage name), he became an outstanding diamond magnate and with Cecil Rhodes founded the De Beers Consolidated Diamond Mines. Later, he turned his attention to gold-mining. After his death by suicide, his nephews of the Joel family (especially Jack Joel, 1862–1940 and Solomon Joel, 1865–1939) took over his financial interests.

BARNAY, LUDWIG (1842–1924): Actor and producer. He was born in Hungary and gained his first success in Leipzig as William Tell (1867–8). In 1883, he helped to found the *Deutsches Theater* and later directed the *Berliner Theater* and the Hanover State Theater. B., who was baptized, founded the German Actors' Association and was its first president.

BARNERT, NATHAN (1838–1927): US industrialist. Born in Germany, B. went to the US in 1849,

Statue of Nathan Barnert, Paterson, New Jersey.

settling in Paterson in 1858 and helped to develop the silk industry in that city. He served as its mayor 1883–91 and made many notable benefactions to the city and to its Jewish community.

BARNETT, LIONEL DAVID (1871–1960): British orientalist. B. was keeper of oriental books and mss at the British Museum and lectured at the School of Oriental Studies, London. He made important contributions to the history of the Sephardim in England. His son *RICHARD DAVID B.* (1909–) is keeper of Egyptian and Assyrian antiquities in the British Museum.

BARON, BERNHARD (1850–1929): British philanthropist. In his youth, he went from Russia to England where he later modernized cigarette manufacture, amassing a vast fortune and devoting the greater part (amounting to more than £2,000,000) to charity, both Jewish and non-Jewish.

BARON, DEVORAH (1887–1956): Hebrew novelist; born in White Russia, she settled in 1911 in Palestine where she married Joseph AHARONOWITZ. Her stories deal mostly with life in the small Jewish communities of White Russia.

BARON, SALO WITTMAYER (1895–): Jewish historian. Born in Galicia and educated in Vienna, B. went to the US in 1926 to lecture at the Jewish Institute of Religion, New York. In 1930 he was appointed professor of Jewish history, literature, and institutions at Columbia Univ. Until 1967 he was head of the American Academy for Jewish Research. He founded and edited the quarterly *Jewish Social Studies*.

Salo Baron.

As a scholar, B. has brought to his historical work a vast Jewish and secular erudition, an unusual linguistic range, and a mastery of the social sciences. His works include *A Social and Religious History of the Jews, Modern Nationalism and Religion,* and *The Jewish Community.*

BARON DE HIRSCH FUND: Trust foundation incorporated in New York State in 1891 to serve Jews fleeing E Europe and migrating to the US. The Fund offered protection for immigrants through port work, relief, temporary aid, promotion of suburban industrial enterprises, removal from urban centers (through the INDUSTRIAL REMOVAL OFFICE), land settlement, agricultural training, and trade and general education. In 1894, the Baron de Hirsch Agricultural College was opened in Woodbine, New Jersey—the first school in the US to impart secondary education in agriculture. In 1895, the Fund established the Baron de Hirsch Trade School to teach mechanical trades to young men. During 1936–43, the Fund spent large sums of money for German Jewish relief. Later its chief activity was support of the JEWISH AGRICULTURAL SOCIETY, created in 1900 by the Fund and its European counterpart, the JEWISH COLONIZATION ASSOCIATION, to promote the Jewish farm movement.

BARONDESS, JOSEPH (1867–1928): US Zionist and labor leader. Born in Russia, he migrated to the US and settled in New York in 1888, becoming a pioneer labor organizer. A founder of the American Jewish Congress, he was a member of its delegation which was responsible for the incorporation of safeguards for Jewish minority rights in the Versailles Peace Treaty.

BARRIOS, DANIEL LEVI (MIGUEL) DE (1635–1701): Marrano poet. Born in Spain, he adopted Judaism in Italy, took part in an unsuccessful colonizing attempt in the W Indies, entered the Spanish army in the Low Countries, and ultimately settled in Amsterdam. In his later years, he became a devoted adherent of Shabbetai Tzevi. He published large numbers of Spanish poems which contain extensive information regarding contemporary Jewish life and personalities in Amsterdam and elsewhere.

BARROS BASTO, ARTURO CARLOS DE (1887–1961): Portuguese soldier and religious leader. Of Marrano descent, he became attracted to Judaism and in 1919, was formally converted. He henceforth threw himself into the work of bringing about a revival of traditional Judaism among the Portuguese Marranos, establishing a synagogue in Oporto, founding a seminary, editing a periodical *(Ha-Lapid),* and conducting missionary journeys among the Marrano centers.

BARSIMSON, JACOB (17th cent.): An early, if not the earliest identified, Jewish settler in New Amsterdam (New York). Of Dutch or German origin, he arrived at least a month before the first group of 23 Jews who went from Brazil in 1654. A champion of equal rights for the Jews in New Amsterdam, he insisted upon his right to render guard duty in place of paying a fine or tax.

BARTH: (1) *AARON B.* (1890–1957): Israel banker, lawyer, and *Mizraḥi* leader; son of (2). Born in Germany, he settled in Palestine in 1931, and from

Joseph Barondess.

1947, was director of the Anglo-Palestine Bank (later the Bank Leumi). B. wrote several works on the contemporary relevance of Jewish orthodoxy. (2) *JACOB B.* (1851–1914): German Semitic scholar. He was lecturer in Hebrew exegesis and religious philosophy at the Berlin Rabbinical Seminary from 1874 and professor of Semitic languages at the Univ. of Berlin from 1880. His most important work dealt with the noun structure of Semitic languages.

BARTHOLDY, FELIX MENDELSSOHN see **MENDELSSOHN-BARTHOLDY, FELIX**

*BARTOLOCCI, GIULIO (1613–1687): Italian scholar. As *scriptor* at the Vatican library, he prepared *Bibliotheca Magna Rabbinica* (4 vols. 1675–93), the first work to give the Christian world a comprehensive idea of Hebrew literature. The publication was completed and supplemented after B.'s death by his pupil Carlo Giuseppe Imbonati. See BIBLIOGRAPHY; HEBRAISTS, CHRISTIAN.

BARUCH: Scribe of Jeremiah. Jeremiah dictated his prophecies of disaster to B. who later read them to the people of Jerusalem (Jer. 36). After the assassination of Gedaliah, B. accompanied Jeremiah to Egypt (Jer. 43:6) and according to legend later moved to Babylon. He figures prominently in Jewish folklore as a paragon of piety, and a number of apocryphal and pseudepigraphic writings are ascribed to him.

BARUCH, APOCALYPSE OF: Several works attributed to BARUCH. They include: (1) *The Syriac A. of B.* dealing with the destruction of Jerusalem, the Messiah and the messianic kingdom, and theological problems. It is the work of one author who wrote in Hebrew; the book was translated into Greek and thence into Syriac. Baruch in this work is more exalted than Jeremiah, serving as mediator between God and the prophet. It appears to have been written c. 115. (2) *The Greek A. of B.* relates Baruch's ascension to heaven and contains a description of the five spheres above the earth. It contains Greek and Jewish mythological elements and betrays a gnostic influence; there are Christian interpolations. The date of composition is uncertain and is not before the 2nd cent. (3) *The Ethiopic A. of B.* contains stories of Baruch and Jeremiah at the period of the destruction of Jerusalem. It entered the canon of sections of the eastern Christian church, and Christian additions have been incorporated. It may have been written after the failure of the Bar Kokhba revolt.

BARUCH, BOOK OF: Apocryphal work probably written in Hebrew but preserved in Greek. The book is not a unit, being partly in prose and partly in poetry. The prose section relates how BARUCH wrote the work in Babylon and read it to Jehoiachin and the exiles who thereupon confessed their transgressions and sent money to Jerusalem to purchase sacrifices for the altar. The lyrical part comprises a hymn to the wisdom of the Law, lamentations, and consolation.

The date of composition is uncertain but is generally placed after the destruction of the Second Temple.

BARUCH BEN SAMUEL OF MAINZ (d. 1221): Codifier and liturgical poet. He was a dayyan at Mainz, and his responsa were incorporated in *Sepher ha-Hokhmah* ("The Book of Wisdom") which has not survived. B. wrote commentaries to several talmudic tractates and *piyyutim* on the tribulations of his times.

BARUCH BEN SAMUEL OF SAFED (d. 1834): Physician and rabbinical emissary. He was born in Russia, settled in Palestine in 1819, and in 1830, went to the Yemen in search of the Ten Tribes. Reaching Sanaa in 1833, he was appointed court physician but was put to death by the king.

BARUCH OF MEDZIBOZH (c. 1757–1810): Hasidic rabbi, son of Odel, daughter of the Baal Shem Tov. He lived most of his life at Tulchin (Ukraine), and was also known as B. of Tulchin. For over 30 years, he headed the Hasidic community of Podolia and lived in luxurious splendor, even keeping his own court-jester—Hirschel OSTROPOLER. He behaved contemptuously towards other Hasidic rabbis, regarding the Hasidim as his personal property inherited from his grandfather. B. was the first to institute payments to the *tzaddik* from the Hasidim, a practice he justified on mystical and ideological grounds.

BARUCH OF SHKLOV (Schick; 1752–1810): Talmudist and scientist. After his rabbinical ordination, he studied medicine in England, going later to Berlin where he wrote on astronomy, mathematics, and medicine. His latter years were spent at Slutzk where he was dayyan to the community and physician to Prince Radziwill.

BARUCH OF TULCHIN see **BARUCH OF MEDZIBOZH**

BARUCH YAVAN (d. 1780): Polish financier. Through his connections with the powerful minister, Count Brühl, he was able to exercise considerable influence at the Polish court, which he used to protect his coreligionists and to discredit the Sabbetaians and Frankists.

BARUCH: (1) *BERNARD MANNES* (1870–1965): US financier and public official; son of (2). B. was a leading figure in the organization of the American economy during World War I when he served on various control commissions and was chairman of the War Industries Board (1918–9) which directed the industries of the entire nation. After the war, he was an economic adviser for the American Peace Commission. He advised successive presidents on economic problems and, as a confidential adviser to President Franklin D. Roosevelt, helped plan the National Industrial Recovery Act of 1933 and other "New Deal" legislation, as well as the mobilization of the country's economic resources during World War II. He was widely regarded as the "elder statesman" of the US. In 1946–7, he was US representative to the UN Atomic

Bernard Baruch.

Energy Commission, in which capacity he submitted a much-discussed plan for the control of atomic weapons. (2) *SIMON B.* (1840–1921): Physician. Of German birth, he migrated as a young man to the US and served as surgeon in the Confederate army. B. was a pioneer in the surgery of the appendix, in the study of malaria and typhoid fever, and in hydrotherapy.

BARUKH HA-BA (Heb. "Blessed be he who comes"; cf. Ps. 118:26): Greeting of welcome to a visitor or newly-arrived acquaintance.

BARUKH SHE-AMAR (Heb. "Blessed be He who spoke"): Opening words of the introduction to the *pesuke de-zimra* ("verses of song") in the Morning Service. The formulation is old, although not mentioned before the early 9th cent. It was at first recited antiphonally and, in gaonic times and later in the Prague synagogue, by trained choirs. The Ashkenazi and Sephardi forms differ.

BARUKH SHE-PETARANI (Heb. "Blessed be He who absolved me"): Blessing recited by the father of a BAR MITZVAH boy in which he gives thanks for being absolved from further responsibility for his son's observance of the precepts of the Torah.

BARZILAI: Italian family. *GIUSEPPE B.* (1824–1902) was a Semitic scholar and secretary of the Trieste Jewish community. His son *SALVATORE B.* (1860–1939), statesman, worked constantly for the union of Trieste with Italy, was cabinet minister in 1915–6, and a signatory of the Treaty of Versailles in 1919. In 1920, he was appointed senator.

BARZILLAI: A wealthy Gileadite who supplied David and his army during Absalom's rebellion. After its suppression, David invited him to his court at Jerusalem but B. refused on account of his age and sent his son Chimham in his stead.

BARZILLAI (originally **EISENBERG**), **YISRAEL** (1913–1970): Israel labor leader. He was born in Poland and settled in Palestine in 1934. A leading member of *Ha-Kibbutz ha-Artzi* and *Mapam,* he was a member of the Knesset 1955–65, minister of health 1955–61 and 1966–9, and deputy speaker 1963–5.

BASCH, VICTOR GUILLAUME (1863–1944): Philosopher. Born in Budapest, he studied in France and became professor of esthetics and art history at the Sorbonne. B. was among the most active champions of Alfred Dreyfus and a leader of the League of the Rights of Man. He was murdered with his wife by the Vichy government.

BASEVI: Italian family, stemming from Verona where for centuries they occupied an important position in Jewish communal life. Mattathias, Abraham, and Abraham Joseph B. were active printers at Verona and Salonica c. 1590–1605. Gioacchino B. (1780–1867), lawyer, defended the Tyrolese patriot Andreas Hofer when he was tried by the French. Some of the family settled in London, in particular Giacomo (James) B. Cervetto (1682–1773), musician, who introduced the cello into England. In the next generation, George B. (1794–1845), who was baptized, was an outstanding British architect in the neo-classical tradition.

BASHAN: Region of Transjordania, now included in Syria. Broadly speaking, B. contains HAURAN, the Argob region, GOLAN as far as Mt. Hermon, and NE Gilead as far as the Yarmuk. In ancient times, it was on the trade-route from Damascus to Arabia and the Red Sea ports. Its original inhabitants, according to the Bible, were the REPHAIM who were succeeded by the Amorites. In the Exodus period, it was ruled by OG who was defeated and slain by the Israelites. B., then noted for its oak woods and fertile pasture, was settled by half the tribe of Manasseh. Tiglath-Pileser III of Assyria overran B. in 732 BCE. It was subsequently under the rule of the Persians (4th cent. BCE), Seleucids (2nd cent BCE), and Romans (from the 1st cent. BCE). Augustus gave it to Herod who settled Idumeans and Jews from Babylon there to guard the country from desert robbers. Later, a Ghassanide Arab state under Roman protection was set up in B.; Jews continued to live there until the end of the Middle Ages, but the land itself deteriorated into desert tracts. Today, most of the population are Syrian Arabs, with Druzes living in E Bashan (Jebel Druze) and Circassians and Turkomans in the W.

BASHEVIS SINGER, ISAAC see **SINGER**

BASHYAZI, ELIJAH (c. 1420–1490): Karaite *hakham* in Adrianople and Constantinople. His legal code *Aderet Eliyahu,* expounding the ceremonial precepts of the Torah, comprises also a philosophical formulation of the ten principles of the Karaite faith. This work was the last of the Karaite religious classics.

BASLE: Town in Switzerland. Its Jewish community, traceable from the 12th cent., shared in the Middle Ages the history of German Jewish communities. It came to a tragic end during the Black Death massacres when the whole community was martyred by burning on an island in the Rhine (Jan. 16, 1349). Although a decree of the town council forbade the Jews to live in B. for another 200 years, a fresh settlement existed later in the 14th cent., coming to an end in 1397. Jews began to settle permanently again only at the beginning of the 19th cent. but suffered from serious disabilities until 1864, after which the community rapidly developed. Several Zionist Congresses, including the First (1897), were held in B. A Jewish museum was opened in 1966. Jewish pop. (1968): 2,300.

BASLE, COUNCIL OF: CHURCH COUNCIL for disciplinary reform, held 1431–49. At its 19th session (Sept. 7, 1434) it passed a series of severe regulations aimed at cutting off all personal relations between Jews and Christians and forbidding the study of the Talmud.

BASLE PROGRAM: The basic program of Zionism adopted at the First Zionist Congress at Basle in 1897. It began: "The aim of Zionism is to create for the Jewish people a home in Palestine secured by public law." It went on to define the means of realization, viz. agricultural and industrial settlement, the united organization of World Jewry, the strengthening of Jewish national consciousness, and preparatory work to obtain international approval. The draft of the first clause was arrived at after various proposals representing several currents; Nordau's group proposed "a homeland secured by law," in deference to Turkey; Motzkin and others demanded "by international law"; Herzl's compromise was "public law." The expression "Jewish state" was omitted for diplomatic reasons.

*BASNAGE, JACQUES (1653–1723): French Protestant divine. His *Histoire des Juifs depuis Jésus-Christ jusqu'a présent* (7 vols., 1706–11), which he wrote while living in exile in Holland, was the first attempt to give an account of the development of the Jewish people throughout the ages. Though of little value, it enjoyed great popularity and was the basis for later more informed Jewish histories.

BASRA: Port in Iraq. The city was founded in the 7th cent. and a Jewish community is attested from the 9th, numbering 2,000 in the time of Benjamin of Tudela (c. 1170). There was at this period a synagogue named after Ezra who was traditionally held to be buried in the vicinity. In the 18th cent., the Jews of B. occupied an important economic position but were persecuted in the late 18th and early 19th cents. The community, which included a high proportion of merchants, physicians, and lawyers, and was regarded as among the wealthiest in the Middle East, numbered 11,000 in 1939. Most of them emigrated to Israel in 1950–1. Only about 200 remained in 1969.

BASS, SHABBETAI BEN JOSEPH (1641–1718): Father of Hebrew BIBLIOGRAPHY. Born in Poland, where his parents were killed in the Cossack rising, he went to Prague and sang in the synagogue choir (hence his name). Later he published at Amsterdam various works, including an elucidation of Rashi's commentary on the Pentateuch and *Siphte Yeshenim* (1680), a bibliographical handbook comprising 2,200 titles which served as the basis for all later works in this field. In 1680, B. set up a printing press at DYHERNFURTH. This led to attacks on him by the Jesuits, in consequence of which he was imprisoned in 1712.

BASSANI, GIORGIO (1916–): Italian writer. Born in Bologna, he lived mainly in Ferrara until 1943 when he moved to Rome. He edited the international literary review *Bolteghe Oscure* 1948–60. He has published verse but is best known for his novels including *The Gold-Rimmed Spectacles* and *The Garden of the Finzi-Continis*.

BASSEVI (VON TREUENBERG), JACOB (1570–1643): The first Austrian Jew to be ennobled. From 1590, he was the "Court Jew" of the Emperor Rudolph II, acting as tax-farmer to the governor of Bohemia and supplying gold to the state mint. For these services he received his title from Ferdinand II (1622). B. headed the Prague Jewish community and used his influence to protect the Jews during the Thirty Years' War. In his last years, he was stripped of his fortune and died impoverished.

BAT KOL (Heb. "daughter of a voice," i.e., quiet sound, echo): Expression found in rabbinic literature to denote a Divine voice. It differed from the Holy Spirit in that it could manifest itself to any individual or group of individuals and not merely to a select few. The *B.K.* was sometimes said to give heavenly approval to halakhic decisions although its pronouncements were not necessarily accepted.

BAT YAM: Israel coastal town, being the S continuation of Jaffa. Founded in 1926 and originally called Bayit va-Gan, it is noted for its bathing beach. Pop. (1968): 62,000.

BATH-SHEBA: Wife of David. In order to marry her, David engineered the death in battle of her husband, URIAH the Hittite, for which he was severely rebuked by the prophet Nathan. Her first son by David died (II Sam. 11–12). Their second son was SOLOMON whose succession to the throne was ensured by her intervention (I Kings 1–2).

BATHING: Apart from ritual purification (see ABLUTION, MIKVEH), b. has always been important to Jews. Physical cleanliness was cultivated because, as Hillel taught, the body is the receptacle which holds the soul. B. on Fridays in honor of the approaching Sabbath was almost universal in Judaism. Ritual b., on the other hand, was not necessarily connected with personal cleanliness but symbolized spiritual purification. It was a daily and constant requirement in all on the other hand, was not necessarily connected with personal cleanliness but symbolized spiritual purification. It was a daily and constant requirement in all aspects of the Temple service, and certain groups, such as the Essenes, made it a cult. In post-Temple days, the significance of ritual b. declined. It was revived among kabbalists and various Ḥasidic sects, some of whom practiced a routine immersion before morning prayers 310 times a year *(Shai tevilot)*.

BATHYRA: Military colony of Jewish soldiers from Babylonia, founded in Transjordania by Herod to defend the area against raiders. It has been suggested that the BENE BETERA originated from B.

BATLAN (Heb.): Term applied in the Talmud to men who were able to spare time for communal business, especially synagogue attendance. It has since come to denote an idler or dilettante.

BAUER, OTTO (1881–1938): Austrian socialist leader and political writer. He was Austrian foreign minister Nov. 1918–Aug. 1919 and member of parliament until 1933. B. helped to organize the socialist rising in Vienna in 1934 when he was wounded but succeeded in escaping to Czechoslovakia. He was one of the great theoreticians of the Austrian Social Democrats and was a leader of the Austro-Marxist school which composed the left wing of the Socialist International.

BAUM, VICKI (1888–1960): Novelist. She was born in Austria but lived in the US from 1932. Her *Grand Hotel* was both dramatized and filmed.

BAVA: Aramaic for the "gate"; used to denote a section of a book. The first tractate of the Mishnah order of *Nezikin* was later divided into three sections, each of ten chapters and all with commentary in the Babylonian and Palestinian Talmud. They are: (1) *Bava Kamma* ("first part"), which discusses damage caused by property or agents (by an ox, pit, cattle-grazing, or fire), or by a man himself (theft, assault, robbery). (2) *Bava Metzia* ("middle part"), dealing with the laws of chattels, lost and found property, the four types of caretakers (unpaid, paid, the hirer, and the borrower), embezzlement, fraud, interest, rights of hired laborers, partnership, etc. (3) *Bava Batra* ("last part"), which deals with laws concerning real estate, inheritance, partnership, usucapion, procedure for drawing up legal documents, etc.

BAVA-BUCH: Yiddish adaptation made (c. 1507) by Elijah LEVITA of the Anglo-French romance *Sir Bevis of Hampton*. The Yiddish phrase *"Bobe Maiseh"* (=Old Wife's Tale) is probably derived from this. The book proved especially popular among Jewish women.

BAVARIA: S German state, now part of the German Federal Republic. Jews have lived in B. from at least the 10th cent. Major communities included NUREMBERG, AUGSBURG, REGENSBURG, FÜRTH, MUNICH, PASSAU, and Bamberg, most of which figure significantly in German Jewish history. The Jews were

excluded from Upper B. in 1276, suffered severely in the Rindfleisch (1298) and ARMLEDER (1336–8) persecutions, were almost exterminated at the time of the Black Death in 1348–9, and were excluded altogether from 1551 to the 18th cent. In the first half of the 19th cent., unfavorable conditions in B. led to a particularly large Jewish emigration to the US. In 1969, 4,700 Jews were living in B.

BAVLI, HILLEL (1893–1961): US Hebrew poet. Born in Lithuania, he migrated to the US in 1912. His poems, mainly lyrical, have been collected in several volumes. He also translated into Hebrew Shakespeare's *Antony and Cleopatra* and Dickens' *Oliver Twist*. B. taught Hebrew literature at the Jewish Theological Seminary, New York, from 1937, and wrote autobiographically in *Ha-Doar* and other Hebrew periodicals.

BAYONNE: Seaport of SW France. Its proximity to the Spanish frontier made it a refuge for fugitive Marranos from the early 17th cent. It was also a center for small congregations in neighboring towns (e.g. Bidache, Peyrehorade). The Jews played an important part in local economic life, but it was only in the 18th cent. that they were officially permitted to profess Judaism openly. The community continued to flourish and preserve its former traditions until the German occupation in 1940. The community numbered 700 in 1970.

BAYONNE: City in New Jersey, US. Its first Jewish congregation was founded in 1885. Most of B.'s 8,500 (1973) Jews are of Russian origin. Since 1938, the entire community has been affiliated with the Jewish Community Council.

BAYREUTH: City in S Germany with a Jewish community from the 13th cent. Expulsions were frequent until the early 18th cent. The condition of the Jews improved after 1810 when B. was joined to Bavaria. At the advent of the Nazi régime (1933), there were over 400 Jews in B. A small community (numbering 40 in 1968) was reestablished after World War II.

BAZELON, DAVID L. (1909–): US jurist. He became assistant attorney-general of the US in 1946 and a member of the US Court of Appeals in 1949.

BEACONSFIELD, BENJAMIN DISRAELI, EARL OF (1804–1881): British statesman; son of Isaac D'ISRAELI. When he was 13, his father (who had become estranged from the synagogue) had him baptized. After unsuccessful ventures in business, he made a reputation by his brilliant novel, *Vivian Grey* (1826). In 1828–31, he traveled through the Mediterranean, spending some time in Palestine. On his return to England, he entered politics and after initial failure, was elected to parliament in 1837 as a Tory. Though at first howled down in the House of Commons, he became the spokesman of the inarticulate Protectionist right-wing when the official Conservative Party under

Benjamin Disraeli.

Peel went over to Free Trade in 1845. In the course of the next few years, he revived the Party and became its official parliamentary leader. Meanwhile, he continued his literary career, publishing a series of outstanding political novels. In 1852, 1858–9, and 1866–8, he was chancellor of the exchequer and leader of the House of Commons in Conservative governments, and in 1868 and 1874–80 served as prime minister. In this capacity, he acquired the deep affection of Queen Victoria (who became Empress of India under his premiership), represented Great Britain at the Berlin Congress (1878), dazzled the country with his Imperial vision, acquired for England a dominant holding in the Suez Canal Company, introduced social legislation, and saved the Conservative Party in England from reactionary development. In 1878, he was created Earl of Beaconsfield. Throughout his career, he never ceased to proclaim his sympathy with and admiration for the Jewish people, to which he was proud to trace his origin. He championed Jewish Emancipation in parliament, almost identified himself with a medieval messianic pretender in his early work *Alroy*, delineated an idealized Rothschild as "Sidonia," a principal character in his novels *Coningsby* and *Tancred*, spoke of Christianity as a development of Judaism, and ascribed exaggerated qualities to the Jewish "race."

BEAME, ABRAHAM DAVID (1906–): New York's first Jewish mayor. After holding various civic posts, he was elected mayor in 1973 and was in office during the city's financial crisis in 1975.

BEARD: The growing of the b. was considered in the Orient a sign of male dignity, and to cut it off was a disgrace (cf. II Sam. 10:4–5). The Bible explicitly forbids the elimination of the corners of the b. (Lev. 19:27). Hence, in later Jewish life the b. was thought to be religiously prescribed, the Talmud regarding it as "the ornament of the face" and the mystics ascribing to it esoteric significance. In European Jewish life, the emphasis shifted from the obligation to wear a b. to the prohibition of SHAVING, which was circumvented by clipping. Portraits of medieval Jews often show them with bare chins or trimmed beards, although the oppressive Spanish code of 1408 forbade Jews to be beardless. The full b. is now uncommon among Western Jews, even the most orthodox generally removing it by clipping (e.g. by electric razor) or by depilatories.

BEARSTED, MARCUS SAMUEL, 1st VISCOUNT (1853–1927): English industrialist. He was responsible for the creation and subsequent development of the Shell Oil Company and its important subsidiaries. He was lord mayor of London in 1902–3 when he refused to entertain officially the representative of the anti-Semitic Rumanian government. He was raised to the peerage in 1920. His son, *WALTER HORACE*, 2nd *VISCOUNT B.* (1882–1948) was active in philanthropic work, especially for the relief of refugees from Nazi Germany.

BECK, KARL ISIDOR (1817–1879): Austrian poet and publicist. His rhetorical German and Hungarian verse, which agitated for Hungarian independence, the rights of the proletariat, and (although he was baptized) Jewish Emancipation, was widely recited. After 1848, he gave up his revolutionary tendencies.

BEDERSI: Family originating from Béziers (S France). (1) *ABRAHAM BEN ISAAC B.* (c. 1230–c. 1300). Hebrew grammarian and poet who spent much of his life in Perpignan. B. was the author of many poems and satires (including a parody on the Passover Haggadah) which throw interesting light on contemporary Jewish history. He also compiled *Ḥotam Tokhnit*, the first dictionary of biblical synonyms. (2) *JEDAIAH B.* (styled *Ha-Penini*=Dispenser of Pearls; c. 1270–c. 1340): Physician, poet, and philosopher; son of (1): lived in Perpignan and Barcelona. He wrote many works, the best-known being the popular *Beḥinat Olam* ("Examination of the World"; reprinted over 80 times), an ethical book stressing the worthlessness of this world and indicating the way to attain eternal happiness. His poetic works include a prayer *Eleph Alaphim*, each of the 1,000 words of which begins with the letter *aleph*. His *Iggeret Hitnatzelut* ("Apologetic Letter"), addressed to Solomon ben Adret, championed philosophical studies.

BEDIKAH (Heb. "examination"): Term used in connection with various inspections, e.g. *bedikat ḥametz*, the search for leaven before Passover; *bedikat ha-edim*, the questioning of witnesses by a court, etc. The term is applied especially to the examination of a slaughtered animal to ensure that it is not suffering from a serious disease. See BODEK.

BEELZEBUB see **BAAL ZEBUB**

Ben-Gurion University, Beersheba

BEER TUVYAH: Israel smallholders' settlement (TM) on the S coastal plain. Pop. (1972): 659. Founded by Baron Edmond de Rothschild in 1887, it was gradually abandoned but was taken over as a model colony by the Ḥoveve Zion in 1896. The number of settlers diminished constantly and after the 1929 Arab riots it was abandoned and destroyed. Refounded in 1930, it has become the center of a flourishing region.

BEER: (1) *MICHAEL B.* (1800–1833): German playwright; brother of the composer Giacomo Meyerbeer and of (2). His best plays were *Struensee* and *Der Paria,* the latter being performed in Weimar at Goethe's suggestion. B.'s ballads include *Der Fromme Rabbi.* (2) *WILHELM B.* (1797–1850): German astronomer. He collaborated in mapping the mountains of the moon, one of which was named after him.

BEER, ELIJAH see **ELIJAH BEER**

BEER, GEORGE LOUIS (1872–1920): US historian. B. served on the American Peace Commission as chief of the colonial division (1918) and is believed to have coined the term "mandate" in its present sense. He was later a member of the Mandates Commission of the League of Nations.

BEER, SAMUEL FRIEDRICH (1846–1912): Sculptor; lived in Paris, Florence, etc. He was a friend of Theodor Herzl and struck a medal to commemorate the First Zionist Congress.

BEER-HOFMANN, RICHARD (1866–1945): Playwright, poet, and novelist. Born in Vienna, he emigrated to New York after the Nazi occupation of Austria (1938). He wrote little, but much of his work deals with Jewish themes. From the character of Red Ike in his most successful play, *Der Graf von Charolais* through his *Jaákobs Traum* and *Der junge David,* he illustrated eloquently the inner spirit of Judaism. Especially memorable is his *Schlaflied für Mirjam,* a lullaby for his daughter.

BEERI: Israel communal settlement (KM) in the Negev, founded 1946. B. was successfully defended against the Egyptians in 1948. Pop. (1972): 510.

BEEROT YITZḤAK: Israel communal settlement (PM), N of Lydda. Originally founded in 1943 near Gaza, it suffered heavy losses but was successfully defended in the 1948 fighting. After the war, the survivors moved to its present site. Pop. (1972): 288.

BEERSHEBA: Israel town. It is mentioned in connection with all three Patriarchs. In biblical times, it was the southernmost administrative, religious, and judicial center of Palestine, and the place of gathering for the south of the country. It was settled by re-

Beersheba.

patriated Jews after the return from Babylon (Neh. 11:27, 31). After the destruction of the Second Temple, it became a fortified frontier-post against the Nabateans, and a Roman garrison was stationed there. It was deserted in the later Middle Ages and rebuilt by the Turks in 1900. Jews lived there in modern times until 1929. In 1948 the all-Arab population of 5,700 abandoned the town and B. became the chief Jewish town of the Negev district. It has developed rapidly and has been connected to the national railway system (1956) and the Mediterranean-Elath oil pipeline and is the site of Ben-Gurion Univ. Pop. (1974): 93,400.

BE-EZRAT HA-SHEM (Heb.: "With the help of the Name" i.e., of God). Customarily written at the beginning of letters and uttered as an expression of pious hope (cf. "Please God").

BEHAR, NISSIM (1848–1931): Educator. A native of Jerusalem, he organized schools in the Near East in behalf of the Alliance Israélite Universelle and from 1882–7, directed their school in Jerusalem. Here he introduced Hebrew as a spoken language, his teachers including Eliezer Ben-Yehudah and David Yellin. In 1901, he settled in New York and was managing director of the National Liberal Immigration League, 1906–24.

BEHEMOTH: Animal described in Job 40:24, thought to be the hippopotamus. In rabbinic and medieval lore, the feast from the flesh of the B. was to be a feature of messianic days.

BEHRMAN, SAMUEL NATHANIEL (1893–1973): US dramatist. *The Second Man* (1927) started his career as a successful writer of comedies. His plays include *Amphitryon* 38 and *No Time for Comedy*. His autobiography *The Worcester Account* describes his childhood environment among Jewish immigrants in Massachusetts.

BEIGIN, MENAHEM (1913–): Israel leader. Born in Poland, he joined the BETAR movement in his youth and was its head in Poland. He reached Pales-

Menahem Beigin.

tine in 1942 with the Polish army and became commander of the IRGUN TZEVAI LEUMI the following year. In 1944–8, he led the *Irgun's* underground war against the British with the aim of forcing them to leave Palestine. In the summer of 1948, he founded the ḤERUT party, which he led in the Knesset and from 1965 was a leader of the GAHAL party. From 1967 to 1970 was a member of the National Unity government as minister without portfolio. Subsequently he opposed returning the areas occupied as a result of that war. A lawyer by profession, he has written autobiographical works (*The Revolt, White Nights*).

BEILINSON, MOSHEH (1889–1936): Hebrew writer and journalist. Born in Russia, he became a physician in W Europe and was for a time active in Italy. He became increasingly absorbed in Zionist work and settled in Palestine in 1924. He was a member of the editorial board of *Davar* from its foundation in 1925. B. was one of the leaders of the Labor Movement in Palestine and wrote works on the history of socialism.

BEILIS, MENAHEM MENDEL (1874–1934): Victim of ritual murder libel. In 1911, the body of a boy was found at Kiev and B. was charged with ritual murder. The investigation lasted two years and was accompanied by violent anti-Jewish propaganda in the Russian and anti-Semitic press and by a wave of protest in Jewish and liberal circles throughout the world. In 1913, the trial was held and B. acquitted. He went to Palestine and later (1920) to the US. His story was the subject of the study *Blood Accusation* by Maurice Samuel and the novel *The Fixer* by Bernard Malamud.

BEIN, ALEX (1903–): Zionist historian and archivist. He emigrated to Palestine from Germany in 1933, working as assistant director (and from 1956, director) of the Central Zionist Archives in Jerusalem. In 1956, he was appointed state archivist. His writings include a biography of Herzl and a history of the modern settlement in Palestine.

BEIRUT (BEYROUTH): Capital of the republic of LEBANON. The Jewish settlement is thought to be ancient, for the town received benefactions from Herod. A synagogue was in existence in the 6th cent., but there is no evidence of a large community, and in the 12th cent. only 50 Jewish families lived there. Nothing is known of Jews in the 14th and 15th cents., but the community was renewed on a small scale with the arrival of exiles from Spain. The number grew only at the end of the 19th cent. There were 6,000 Jews in 1940, mostly of the middle class, and excellently organized. After 1948, numerous Jews who fled from Syria settled in B. However many left subsequent to the 1967 Six-Day War. Pop. (1975) c. 1,000, most of whom left during the Civil War of that year.

BEISAN see **BET SHEAN**

BEIT, SIR ALFRED (1853–1906): Financier, benefactor. Born in Hamburg, he emigrated to S Africa and became closely associated with Cecil Rhodes in the development of the diamond and gold mines. His far-reaching bequests included the foundation of thirty scholarships for medical research. His parents adopted Christianity before he was born.

BEIT JIBRIN see **BET GUVRIN**

BEKHOR SHOR, JOSEPH BEN ISAAC (12th cent.): Tosaphist, Bible commentator, and liturgical poet; lived at Orleans, France. His commentary on the Pentateuch is marked by originality and a critical rationalizing tendency. He knew Latin and engaged in disputations with non-Jewish scholars.

BEKHOROT (Heb. "Firstlings"): Fourth tractate in the Mishnah order of *Kodashim* dealing in 9 chapters with laws relating to the first-born, both of men and animals. The laws are amplified in the Babylonian Talmud.

BEKIIN see **PEKIIN**

BEL: Babylonian deity; the name is related to the Phoenician word BAAL. B. was the chief god of the Babylonians, and is mentioned as such by Isaiah and Jeremiah. The apocryphal work *B. and the Dragon* (in Greek) consists of two stories of Daniel's exposure of the falsity of pagan cults. It is thought to have been composed in the 5th or 4th cent BCE.

BELASCO, DAVID (1859–1931): US actor-manager and dramatist. Son of an English Jew and a gypsy mother, he began acting as a child. After many years of theatrical activity in California, he moved to New York in 1882. B. was famous as one of the foremost producers of his generation, a discoverer and trainer of "stars," and an adapter of plays. He paid particular attention to the mechanical details of the stage. In 1907, he opened his own theater, the "Belasco." He was the author of *Madame Butterfly* and *Girl of the Golden West*, both of which were set to music by Puccini.

BELAYA TSERKOV: Town in the Ukraine, USSR. 600 Jewish families were massacred there by the Cossacks in 1648. Settlement was renewed in 1721 and a further massacre perpetrated by the Haidamaks in 1768. In World War II, the Jews of B. (numbering some 20,000) were murdered by the Nazis and the Ukrainians. Jewish pop. (1975): c. 15,000.

BELFAST: Capital of N IRELAND. Jews settled there in the 18th cent., but a community was founded only in 1870. Sir Otto Jaffe was lord mayor in 1904–5. Jewish pop. (1974): 1,200.

BELGIUM: European kingdom. A few Jews were present in the area which constitutes the present B. —Brabant and Hainault—from the 13th cent., but were almost exterminated at the time of the Black Death (1348): a fresh settlement in Brabant—especially BRUSSELS—was wiped out in 1370 as the result of a Host Desecration charge. In the 16th cent., many Marranos settled in ANTWERP which, under Spanish rule, had become a great center of the spice trade, the leading family being the banking-house of MENDES. There were occasional judicial inquiries (1531–2, 1540–1, 1550, etc.), but the secret settlement retained its importance until the open community was formed at Amsterdam. In the 17th and 18th cents., Amsterdam Jews frequently traveled in B. for trade, and there was a semi-overt synagogue in Antwerp. Ashkenazi Jews began to settle in the 18th cent., when the area was under Austrian rule, and became formally organized under French (1794–1814), and then Dutch (1814–30) rule. When the kingdom of B. was constituted in 1830–1, religious equality became part of the fundamental law of the state, as in Holland, and Belgian Jewry was organized under a consistory with its center in Brussels. Antwerp, however, because of its great diamond industry, was the largest community. The Jews of B. suffered severely during the German occupation (1940–4), the usual anti-Semitic legislation being introduced, and 53,000 out of about 100,000 were deported. There are 40,000 Jews in B. (1973), the community of Brussels (24,500) being larger than that of Antwerp (13,000); small centers exist in Charleroi and Ostend, with semi-organized groups also in Ghent, Liège, and Arlon.

BELGRADE: Capital of YUGOSLAVIA. Although Jews were in the region from Roman times, there was no permanent community until the 16th cent. when Sephardim, penetrating from the Dalmatian coast and from Salonica, settled there. In the sieges and captures of the city from 1688 onward, the Jewish community inevitably suffered. It began to increase in importance after B. became the capital of the kingdom of Serbia in the 19th cent., and of Yugoslavia in the 20th. By 1939, the Jewish population was c. 8,000 (including 2,000 Ashkenazim). They suffered severely in World War II and were all massacred or deported by 1942. A community was reestablished in 1946 and numbered 1,600 in 1973.

BELIAL: Biblical term of uncertain etymology applied to subversive individuals *(bene belial*—"sons of Belial," cf. Deut. 13:14); in rabbinic and apocryphal literature, often synonymous with Satan.

BELKIN, SAMUEL (1911–1976): US scholar and educator. He was born in Poland, studied at the Radin yeshivah, and migrated to the US in 1929. In 1935, he joined the faculty of Yeshiva College (now Univ.), becoming professor in 1940, and later its dean (1941), president (1943), and chancellor (1975). He has been instrumental in the growth and expansion of the institution. B. is the author of several works on the Hellenistic Period and on religious questions.

BELKIND, ISRAEL (1861–1929): Zionist leader He was born in White Russia and was a leader of the first *Bilu* group to go to Palestine (1882), settling in Rishon le-Zion. Forced to leave after heading the opposition to the officials of Baron Edmond de Rothschild, he founded the first Hebrew school in Jaffa in

Saul Bellow

1889, and later, the agricultural training institution "Kiryat Sepher" near Lydda for orphans of the 1903 Kishinev pogrom. After World War I, he set up another agricultural institution at Shepheyah for orphans of the Ukrainian pogroms. B. was the author of Hebrew, Yiddish, and Russian textbooks on Jewish topics.

BELLOW, SAUL (1915–): US author. A native of Canada, he has taught at various American univerties. His novels include *The Adventures of Augie March, Herzog, Mr. Sammler's Planet* and *Humbolt's Gift*. Regarded as the most distinguished US novelist of the post-War period, he was awarded the Nobel Literature Prize in 1976. His account of a visit to Israel appeared in *To Jerusalem and Back*.

BELLS: The usual English term for the decoration on the finials of the Scrolls of the Law; otherwise RIMMONIM.

BELMONT (originally **SCHONBERG), AUGUST** (1816–1890): US diplomat and banker. Born in Germany, he settled in the US in 1837 as agent for the Rothschilds and became a successful banker. An active Democrat, he was US minister to the Netherlands (1855–8). B. was a patron of the turf and an art collector.

BELMONTE: Dutch Sephardi family of Marrano extraction. (1) *JACOB ISRAEL B.* (1570–1629), poet, settled in 1610 in Amsterdam where he became a leader in communal life. (2) *ISAAC* or *MANUEL DE NUÑEZ B.* (1673–1705) was from 1664, agent-general and from 1674, diplomatic representative of Spain in the Netherlands. In 1693, he was created a count palatine. He wrote Spanish verses and founded two literary academies in Amsterdam. He was succeeded in his title and office by his nephew *FRANCISCO DE XIMENES B.* (d. 1713) and the latter by his son *EMMANUEL B.* (d. 1729). (3) *ISAAC NUÑEZ B.* (18th cent.) of Smyrna was an outstanding rabbinical authority. (4) *JACOB DE B.* (c. 1653–1717), grandson of (1), entered the Dutch diplomatic service under the name of Franz von Schoonenberg. From 1678–1703, he represented William of Orange in Spain and played a part in the diplomatic struggle surrounding the Spanish succession.

BELOFF, MAX (1913–): British historian. Professor of government at Oxford and from 1974 principal, University College, Bucks. Author of many works, including *The Foreign Policy of Soviet Russia*.

BELSHAZZAR: The last king of Babylon, according to the Book of Daniel. During a feast in his palace, at which the Temple utensils were being utilized, the inscription *Mene Mene Tekel Upharsin* miraculously appeared on the wall. This was interpreted by DANIEL to foretell the capture of Babylon by the Persians, which actually occurred the same night, B. being slain. According to Babylonian records, the last king of Babylon was Nabonidus (reigned 556–539 BCE) whose eldest son B. acted as viceroy during his father's lengthy stays in Arabia. B. is not mentioned in Greek sources but both Herodotus and Xenophon mention that Babylon fell on a feast-day.

BELTESHAZZAR see **DANIEL**

BELZ: E Galician town, now in the Soviet Ukraine. Jews are known to have lived there from the beginning of the 16th cent., and the community was the most important of the region during the 16th–18th cents. Before World War II, there were 2,000 Jews in B.—half the town's population—but they were annihilated during the Nazi occupation. R Shalom ben Eleazar Rokeah lived at B. from 1816–56 and founded a Hasidic dynasty. He was succeeded by his son Joshua, grandson Issachar Dov, and great-grandson Aaron. The last-named (d. 1957) escaped from the Nazis and settled in 1944 in Israel, where he renewed his activity. His seven children were killed in Europe and he was succeeded by his grandson.

BELZEC: Polish village selected by the Nazis as an extermination camp for Jews. Victims arrived almost daily between 1942 and 1944, many of them from Galicia. Almost 600,000 were shot or gassed. See CAMPS, CONCENTRATION.

BELZER (SPIVAK), NISSAN (1824–1906): Cantor in Belz, Kishinev, and Berdichev. He was one of the leading *hazzanim* of his time and wrote liturgical compositions.

BEN: Hebrew for "son" or "son of"; frequently appearing in personal names.

BEN-AHARON, YITZHAK (1906–): Israel public figure. Born in Austria, he went to Palestine in 1928. A representative of *Ahdut-Avodah — Poale Zion* in the Knesset, he was minister of communications 1959–62 and secretary-general of Histadrut, 1969–73. It was on his suggestion that various labor parties merged or aligned in the ISRAEL LABOR PARTY.

BEN-AMI, JACOB (Jacob Shieren; 1890–): US actor and director. Born in Russia, he organized a Yiddish theater in Odessa with Peretz Hirshbein (1909–12). B. went to the US in 1912 and appeared there on the Yiddish stage, later also on the English stage and in motion pictures.

BEN-AMMI (pseudonym of Mordecai Rabinowicz; 1854–1932): Russian and Yiddish author. Of Ukrainian birth, he lived in Odessa from 1864 and was one of the organizers of the first self-defense movement among Russian Jews at the time of the Odessa pogroms (1881). After the 1905 pogroms, he migrated to Geneva, and in 1923, settled in Palestine. He was one of the first writers to inveigh in the Russian Jewish press against assimilation. His writings, which tended to be

Rabbi Issachar Dov of Belz.

Jacob Ben-Ami.

naïve, called on educated Jews to turn to their own culture.

BEN ASHER, AARON BEN MOSES (fl. 10th cent.):
Masoretic scholar, according to some a Karaite; last of a famous family of Masoretes. He lived at Tiberias and died in Jerusalem, devoting many years to preparing an accurate biblical manuscript incorporating vocalization and accentuation in accordance with his school of tradition. His version was a model for subsequent copyists and forms the basis of the accepted Bible text, though changes intruded in later centuries. The victory of this version was assured by the recommendation of Maimonides. The third edition of Kittel's *Biblia Hebraica* is based on B.A.'s tradition. B.A. also wrote grammatical works crystallizing the masoretic tradition of the Tiberias scholars.

BEN-AVI, ITTAMAR (1882–1943): Hebrew journalist. The son of Eliezer Ben-Yehudah (initials *Avi*), he assisted his father in editing Hebrew newspapers. In 1919, he founded in Jerusalem and edited until 1929 the paper *Doar ha-Yom*. He wrote stories on Palestinian life and advocated the use of Latin characters for Hebrew, even publishing a Hebrew newspaper in Latin type.

BEN AVIGDOR (pen name of Abraham Leib Shalkovitz; 1867–1921): Hebrew writer and publisher. After an Orthodox education, he was attracted by Haskalah and settled in Warsaw where he founded *Siphre Agorah* ("Penny Books"). These small booklets, containing Hebrew *belles-lettres*, aspired to introduce current European literary trends (especially naturalism) into Hebrew literature. B.A. published several of his own realistic stories in this series. In 1893, he helped to establish the Aḥiasaph publishing company. He left it to set up the Tushiyyah company which published hundreds of Hebrew books. In 1901, he founded the children's weekly *Olam Katan* and in 1913, the *Ahisepher* publications.

BEN AZZAI, SIMEON (fl. early 2nd cent. CE):
Tanna. In order to devote himself entirely to study, he remained unmarried. B.A. died in his prime, and a tradition, which numbers him among four scholars who engaged in mysticism, connects his premature death with esoteric study *(Ḥagigah 14b)*. Another report lists B.A. as one of the ten sages martyred in the Hadrianic persecutions.

BEN-GURION (originally **GRUEN**), **DAVID** (1886–1973): Israel statesman. Born in Plonsk, Poland, and joined the Zionist movement early, he settled in Palestine in 1906. The same year, he served as chairman of the foundation conference of the Palestine *Poale Zion*, being elected to its central committee. After working as an agricultural laborer and watchman in several settlements, he went in 1910 to Jerusalem where he helped to organize the *Poale Zion* party and its weekly newspaper *Ha-Aḥdut*. He studied law in Constantinople 1912–14, returned to Palestine in 1914,

David Ben-Gurion.

but was expelled by the Turkish authorities in 1915 and left for the US. Here he was active in Labor Zionist politics and in organizing the volunteer movement for the Jewish Legion. Returning to Palestine in 1918 as a soldier, he was among the labor leaders who founded the Aḥdut Ha-Avodah party in 1919 and Mapai in 1930. From 1921–35, B.G. was general secretary of the *Histadrut*. He was chairman of the Zionist executive and of the Jewish Agency executive 1935–48. On his initiative, the Zionist movement adopted in 1942 his program for the establishment of a Jewish commonwealth in Palestine as a feature of the post-war settlement (the "Biltmore Program"). It was his leadership that was largely responsible for the implementation of the UN resolution of Nov. 1947, recommending the establishment of a Jewish state in part of Palestine. In April 1948, he was placed at the head of the provisional government which, on May 14, 1948, proclaimed the creation of the state of Israel. In the government, he served as prime minister and minister of defense, in the latter capacity organizing the Israel army that decisively defeated the invading Arab forces. B.G. held these offices in the various coalition governments until Dec. 1953 when he resigned from governmental duties and lived in the settlement of Sedeh Boker in the Negev. He rejoined the government as minister of defense in Feb. 1955 and resumed the premiership later that year until 1963, when he resigned from office although continuing to play an active role in political events. In 1956, he was responsible for the SINAI OPERATION. In 1965 he led a dissident group which separated from MAPAI and formed the RAFI list. However, he refused to join the rest of the Rafi party when they became part of the Israel Labor party. B.G. was a noted orator and a prolific journalist, many of his speeches, articles, and memoirs having been published in book form.

*BEN-HADAD: Name of three kings of Aram-Dammasek mentioned in the Bible. (1) Reigned c. 908–886 BCE. He was an ally of Baasha of Israel until bribed by Asa of Judah to attack the northern kingdom (Kings 15:16–21). (2) Reigned middle of 8th cent. BCE; son or grandson of (1). He declared war on Israel (c. 856) but was defeated and captured. He was freed by Ahab with whom he allied himself in the war against Shalmaneser III of Assyria (853). Later, he defeated Ahab at Ramoth Gilead where the latter fell (I Kings 22:1–40). (3) Reigned end 9th—early 8th cents. BCE. He was thrice defeated by Jehoash of Israel who recaptured the towns previously ceded to Aram (II Kings 13:25).

BEN-ḤAIM (FRANKENBURGER), PAUL (1897–): Israel composer and teacher. Born in Germany, he settled in Tel Aviv in 1933. His early works betray the influence of Central European modernism, but his style changed after he became familiar with oriental folksongs. His works include two symphonies, an oratorio *Joram,* a piano concerto, and chamber music.

BEN KALBA SABBUA: Citizen of Jerusalem at the time of the Roman siege (70 CE). According to the Talmud, he possessed in his granaries sufficient grain to feed Jerusalem for several years, but this was destroyed by Zealots. He is said to have been the father-in-law of R Akiva.

BEN KOZIBA see **BAR KOKHBA**

BEN NAPHTALI, MOSES BEN DAVID (c. 10th cent.): Masoretic scholar, resident probably in Tiberias. Like his contemporary Aaron ben Moses BEN ASHER, from whom he differed in small details in about 900 instances, he edited—according to the tradition of his school—the punctuation and accentuation of the Hebrew Bible. B.N. may not have been the name of an individual but only of a masorelic tradition.

BEN SHEMEN: Two Israel settlements near Lydda at the edge of the coastal plain, one an agricultural school for youth (pop. 679 in 1972), the other a moshav (TM) (pop. 236 in 1972). It was the farm of one of the earliest groups working Jewish National Fund land (1907) and is the site of the HERZL FOREST. A village was first erected there in 1921 while the youth village (directed by Siegfried Lehmann until his death in 1958), opened in 1927, began to absorb Youth Aliyah children in 1934. Rumanian immigrants expanded the moshav in 1952.

BEN-SIRA (or Ben Sirach; fl. c. 170 BCE): Sage.
In Hebrew his first name is given as Simeon, in Greek as Jeshua or Jesus. Little can be adduced concerning his life apart from the facts that he lived in Jerusalem, belonged to the class of learned men or scribes, traveled widely, taught in his own school, and at one time narrowly escaped with his life from a plot hatched by his enemies. He was the author of the work known as the *Wisdom* (also Book, Proverbs, Sayings) *of Ben Sira* or *Ecclesiasticus* which was translated into Greek by his grandson in 132 BCE and incorporated in the APOCRYPHA. The book chiefly contains wise axioms in poetic parallelism, similar in form to the Book of Proverbs. It lays down moral precepts, advising against extremism and advocating moderation. It also includes a number of liturgical poems and psalms. The original Hebrew text was lost for centuries but mss covering most of the work were found in the Cairo *genizah* (1896 ff) and in scrolls from the Judean desert. From these, M.H. Segal published the complete work in Hebrew with the missing sections reconstructed (1943).

BEN SIRA, ALPHABET OF: Popular medieval work known from the 11th cent., consisting of folklore, proverbs, and aphorisms alphabetically arranged and ascribed without authority to Ben Sira. From its Arabic linguistic elements, it appears to have been composed in a Moslem environment.

BEN-TZEVI, YITZḤAK see **BEN-ZVI**

BEN-TZEVI, ZE'EV (1904–1952): Israel sculptor, noted for his portraits and busts. He was born in Poland and settled in Palestine in 1924.

BEN-YEHUDAH (PERELMANN), ELIEZER (1858–1922): Pioneer of the modern Hebrew renascence. Born in Lithuania, he went to Paris in 1878 to study medicine. The following year, he began to publish articles advocating Jewish settlement in Palestine. In

Eliezer Ben-Yehudah.

1881, B.Y. settled in Jerusalem where he taught and edited a succession of Hebrew journals. He determined to speak only Hebrew and to fight for its acceptance as a spoken language. This obstinate persistence was one of the chief factors in the establishment of Hebrew as the language of the Jewish population in Palestine. For many years, he was one of the principal personalities in Jewish life in Jerusalem. Although he attacked the HALUKKAH system, he supported Baron de Rothschild in his conflict with the Jewish farmers; later, he advocated the Uganda scheme. From 1915-9, B.Y lived in the US. His main publication was a comprehensive dictionary of ancient and modern Hebrew, in which he coined many words to meet modern exigencies. The volumes covering the letters *aleph* to *mem* appeared in his lifetime, and the work was continued after his death by his widow and other leading philologists. B.Y. founded in 1888, the *Vaad ha-Lashon ha-Ivrit* ("Hebrew Language Council") and served as its chairman until his death.

BEN ZAKKAI see **JOHANAN BEN ZAKKAI**

BEN-ZEEV (BENSEW), JUDAH LÖB (1764–1811):
Hebrew grammarian and lexicographer. He was born in Poland, lived for some time in Berlin where he met leading Haskalah scholars, and later, in Breslau, Cracow, and Vienna. His writings include a Hebrew grammar (which achieved widespread popularity), a biblical lexicon with German translation, an introduction to the Bible, the critical spirit of which aroused the opposition of Orthodox circles, and a Hebrew translation of Ecclesiasticus. He also wrote Hebrew poetry, including a collection of liturgical parodies for Purim.

BEN-ZION SIMHAH (pseudonym of Simhah Alter Gutmann; 1870–1932): Hebrew author. He was

Yitzhak Ben-Zvi.
Bust by Batyah Lishanski.

Simha Ben-Zion.

born in Bessarabia where he wrote stories of small-town life. After he settled in Palestine in 1905, his work became lyrical and symbolist. Besides fiction and drama, he published textbooks and translated German classics into Hebrew.

BEN ZOMA, SIMEON (fl. early 2nd cent. CE):
Tanna, noted for his brilliant scholarship and biblical expositions. He studied mystical lore, as a result of which he lost his reason *(Hagigah* 14*b)*.

BEN-ZVI (formerly **SHIMSHELEVITZ**), **YITZHAK** (1884–1963): Second president of Israel. Born in Poltava (Ukraine), he joined the Zionist movement in his youth and was one of the pioneers of the *Poale Zion* movement in Russia before settling in Palestine in 1907. He organized the *Poale Zion* party in Palestine and was prominent in the Jewish self-defense movement. In 1912–4, he studied law at the Univ. of Constantinople. When World War I broke out, he returned to Palestine but was deported by order of the Turkish government and went to the US where he helped to organize the *He-Halutz* organization. He returned to

Palestine in 1918 as a soldier in the Jewish Legion and in 1919, was among the founders of the *Ahdut ha-Avodah* party, in 1920, of the *Histadrut,* and in 1930, of Mapai. From 1931–48, he was president of the *Vaad Leumi.* B.Z. was a *Mapai* member of the Knesset from 1949 until elected to succeed Chaim Weizmann as president of Israel in Dec. 1952. He was also active as a journalist and scholar, publishing researches on several aspects of Jewish history, especially on the Samaritans, oriental communities, and the Jewish settlement in Palestine. He founded the Ben-Zvi Institute for Research of Jewish Communities in the Middle East. His wife, *RAHEL YANAIT B.Z.* (1886–) was also a pioneer of the Palestinian labor and Jewish self-defense movement, being particularly active in women's agricultural training. She wrote an autobiography *Coming Home.*

BENAIAH BEN JEHOIADA: One of David's warriors; commander of the CHERETHITES AND PELETHITES. He was noted for his bravery, and stories are reported of his outstanding exploits (II Sam. 23:20–23; I Chron. II:22–5). Following David's death, he supported Solomon. After killing Adonijah, Joab, and Shimei ben Gera at Solomon's behest, B. was appointed commander of his army (I Kings 2).

BENAMOZEGH, ELIJAH (1823–1900): Rabbi of Leghorn and theologian. He wrote Hebrew works in defense of the Kabbalah and apologetic books in Italian and French defending Jewish morality and religion. He is regarded as the last Italian Jewish Kabbalist, and his writings greatly influenced Aimé PALLIÈRE.

BENDA, JULIEN (1867–1956): French philosopher and critical writer. His works include *L'ordination,* an analytic novel, and *La trahison des clercs,* an attack on anti-intellectualist schools of thought.

BENDAVID, LAZARUS (1762–1832): German philosopher and mathematician. An enthusiastic Kantian, he lectured in Berlin and Vienna, and directed the Jewish *Freischule* in Berlin 1806–26. He suggested the abolition of the practical commandments and for their substitution the emphasis on moral Jewish values. In his later days, he devoted himself principally to Bible research, publishing several critical studies.

BENDEMANN, EDUARD (Julius Friedrich; 1811–1889): German painter. Converted to Christianity in 1835, he became professor of painting at Dresden in 1838, and director of the Düsseldorf Academy in 1859. B. was one of the most successful historical painters of his day. Some of his paintings depict biblical themes, such as *Jeremiah at the Fall of Jerusalem* and *Jews in the Babylonian Exile.*

BENE AKIVA (Heb. "Sons of Akiva"): Religious Zionist pioneering youth movement affiliated with HA-POEL HA MIZRAHI. Founded in 1929, it had 18,600 members in 1968, in Israel and in 25 other countries.

Its motto is *Torah va-Avodah* ("Religion and Labor"). Members are trained for settlement on the land and are required to study for at least one year at a yeshivah. The movement has founded 3 *kibbutzim* — En Tzurim, SAAD and Alumim-Urim. Its general secretariat is situated in Tel Aviv. The movement in the Diaspora maintains close contact with Israel, and the B.A. Organization of N America runs summer camps, educational seminars, etc.

BENE BERAK: (1) Ancient Palestinian city, 3 m. NE of Jaffa. It was designated for the tribe of Dan but was in the hands of the Philistines for long periods until captured by Sennacherib (701 BCE). B.B. became an important Jewish center in the 1st–2nd cents. CE and was the seat of R Akiva's academy. A settlement called Kephar ha-Mesubbim was founded on the site in 1951. (2) Israel town, 5 m. NE of Tel Aviv. Founded as an agricultural colony in 1924 by religious Polish Jews, it has become an industrial town with a population of 81,000 (1974). The town has maintained its religious character and there are several yeshivot in B.B.

BENE BERIT (Moledet): Israel cooperative smallholders' settlement (TM) in Lower Galilee, founded in 1937 on land bought with contributions provided by the US B'nai B'rith movement. Pop. (1972): 422.

BENE BETERA (Heb. "sons [or elders] of Bathyra"): Group of scholars, possibly living at the fortress-town of BATHYRA in Transjordan, prominent from the 1st cent. BCE. They were associated with the appointment of Hillel as president of the Sanhedrin. Several tannaim are referred to as B.B.

BENE BINYAMIN (Heb. "sons of Benjamin"): Organization of farmers in Palestinian moshavot, active 1921–39. It was responsible for founding Netanyah, Kephar Aharon, Even Yehudah, and part of Herzliyyah.

BENE DAROM: Israel communal settlement (PM) founded in 1949 on the S coastal plain by members of Kephar Darom which had been evacuated in 1948 after a heroic resistance. The settlers came from the US, Germany, Egypt, Britain, India, etc. Pop. (1972): 194.

BENE ISRAEL: Ancient Jewish community in INDIA whose origin is unknown. Their own tradition holds that they came from the N and were shipwrecked on the Indian coast, settling near Colaba, adopting Marathi dress and language, and engaging principally in agriculture and oil-pressing. For many centuries, they were without contact with the rest of the Jewish world, and their religious observances deviated considerably from accepted Jewish practice. In the 18th–19th cents., teachers from Cochin and Baghdad brought them into line with traditional Judaism. Under the British rule, the B.I. began to concentrate in Bombay, also serving in the British Maratha regiments. Later, they began to enter the liberal professions, trades, and "white-collar" occupations. There are four B.I. synagogues in Bombay and several in other centers; a few B.I. live in Pakistan. Their estimated number is 17,000–18,000. Most have migrated to Israel.

BENE MOSHEH (Heb. "sons of Moses"): An exclusive order within HOVEVE ZION. It was founded in 1889 at Odessa by AHAD HA-AM and Joshua Barzilai as a result of their dissatisfaction with the Zionist leadership which, they alleged, was neglecting popular education and giving no intellectual guidance. The central office was originally located in Odessa, later in Warsaw, and finally in Jaffa. Its first leader was Ahad Ha-Am, and the number of its members never exceeded a hundred. The group broke up on the foundation of the Zionist Organization (1897). Its activities included the foundation of Hebrew schools in the Diaspora and in Jaffa and the establishment of the AHIASAPH publishing house in Warsaw.

*BENEDICT XIII: Anti-pope, 1394–1417/23. In 1413/4, he presided over the Disputation at TORTOSA between Jewish and Christian representatives in the endeavor to strengthen his wavering position through mass-conversions. The dispute lasted 21 months and resulted in a Bull placing extensive restrictions on Jewish life.

BENEDICT, SIR JULIUS (1804–1885): Composer. Of German birth, he lived in England from 1835, and wrote oratorios and operas of which the best-known is *The Lily of Killarney* (1862). He was converted to Christianity.

BENEDICTIONS (Heb. *berakhot*): Formulas of praise and thanks established and regulated, according to talmudic tradition, by the men of the Great Synagogue. Recitations of b. constitute a great part of the prayer service, whether at the synagogue or in individual prayer. Such formulas are found occasionally in the Bible, e.g. "Blessed be the Lord" (Gen. 14:20, etc.) and "Blessed art Thou, O Lord" (Ps. 119:12, etc.). The latter phrase is incorporated into every blessing. The rabbis taught that a man should recite a hundred blessings daily. There are four categories of b.: (1) Blessings of pleasure which are recited before every act of eating, drinking, etc. The concluding phrase of the b. (the opening section "Blessed art Thou, O Lord our God, King of the Universe" is common to all) for fruit is "who createst the fruit of the tree"; for vegetables "who createst the fruit of the ground"; for bread "who bringest forth bread from the earth"; for cooked grains "who createst various sorts of foods"; for things which do not grow upon the ground or for ordinary liquids "at whose word all things were created": for wine "who createst the fruit of the vine." Concluding formulas of Grace were also established. For pleasures of smell the appropriate blessing is "who createst various kinds (or "trees") of spices." (2) Blessings recited before the performance of a commandment. The common formula here is "Blessed art Thou, O Lord our God, King of the Universe, who has sanctified us with His commandments and has commanded us to..." Examples of such b. are those recited before wrapping oneself in a *tallit*, laying *tephillin*, and taking the *lulav*. (3) Blessings of praise and thanks. These are recited in connection with natural phenomena, e.g. lightning and thunder, falling stars and earthquakes, the appearance of the rainbow, etc. B. are also recited over good and bad news, and on seeing persons distinguished for their position or wisdom. Two special b. are those of deliverance *(ha-gomel)* from sickness, danger, etc. and of *sheheheyanu* ("who has kept us alive... to this season") for all new things or on the incidence of a seasonal holiday. B. of this nature are recited before the reading of certain biblical portions. (4) Blessings forming part of prayer. These include b. contained in the *Amidah* prayer, etc.

BENEDIKT, MORITZ (1849–1920): Austrian journalist. From 1881, he was chief editor of the Vienna newspaper *Neue Freie Presse*. An anti-Zionist, he opposed the publication of the *Jewish State* by Herzl (who was one of his contributors). Active in the Liberal Party, B. was appointed to the Austrian Upper House *(Herrenhaus)* in 1917.

BENET, MORDECAI (Marcus Benedikt; 1753–1829): Talmudist. After serving as rabbi in several communities in Hungary and Moravia, he was appointed in 1789 chief rabbi of Moravia, in which position he did much to organize Jewish education. B. was noted for his broad secular knowledge and his temperate attitude toward the Reform movement and Haskalah. He was the author of several works of responsa, novellae, etc.

BENFEY, THEODOR (1809–1881): Philologist and Sanskrit scholar. In 1848, he was converted to Christianity and became lecturer and, then, professor (1862) of classical philology and comparative linguistics at Göttingen. He made important contributions to the study of Sanskrit.

BENGHAZI: Capital city of Cyrenaica. Jews were first settled here by the Ptolemies probably in the

Benediction for wine. (From Passover plate, Ancona, 1616).

3rd cent. BCE. Inscriptions of 24 and 56 CE mention their synagogue, communal council of 7–10 archons, and "amphitheater" (perhaps a gathering place). The community probably was refounded with the renewal of the town in the 15th cent. Nearly all the 2,500 Jewish inhabitants emigrated to Israel after 1948 and those that remained left after the 1967 Six-Day War.

BENISCH, ABRAHAM (1814–1878): Journalist and scholar. While a student at the Univ. of Vienna, he helped form a secret society with the object of re-establishing a Jewish state in Palestine. In connection with this, he went in 1841 to England where he settled. He was largely responsible for the development of the JEWISH CHRONICLE, which he edited 1854–69 and 1875–8, and helped to found the Anglo-Jewish Association (1871).

BENJACOB, ISAAC EISIK (1801–1863): Hebrew author and bibliographer; lived in Vilna. He published many Hebrew texts including an edition of the Bible (prepared with Abraham Lebensohn) incorporating Mendelssohn's German translation, and was the author of original essays, poems, etc. in Hebrew. His main work was *Otzar ha-Sepharim,* a bibliography—still standard—listing and describing 17,000 Hebrew books.

BENJAMIN: The twelfth and youngest son of Jacob and the second son of Rachel who died in childbirth when he was born. The exceptionally strong mutual devotion of Jacob and B. played a prominent part in the events which ended with Jacob's migration to Egypt. The tribe of B. occupied territory between Ephraim and Judah which included Jerusalem. On one occasion, it was almost exterminated in a war with the other tribes (Judg. 19–21). Saul, the first king of Israel, was a Benjamite. The territory was a bone of contention between the kingdoms of Israel and Judah after the division of the kingdom and eventually, was partitioned between the two.

BENJAMIN II (real name Israel ben Joseph Benjamin; 1818–1864): Traveler. Born in Rumania, he journeyed widely in the Near East, Asia, N Africa, and N America in order to examine the position of Jews and to discover the lost ten Tribes. In reminiscence of Benjamin of Tudela, he published an account of his experiences under the name of B. II. His travel book, *Drei Jahre in Amerika* (1862, also translated into English), is the first comprehensive report on Jewish communities throughout the US.

BENJAMIN BEN MOSES NAHAVENDI (fl. 9th cent.): Karaite scholar resident at Nahavend (Persia). He was responsible for establishing Karaite principles and methods of biblical investigations stressing the importance of independent study of the Bible without reliance on predecessors. B. was the first Karaite scholar to write in Hebrew and was responsible for the term "Karaites" replacing "Ananites" to designate the sect.

BENJAMIN OF TUDELA (fl. 12th cent.): TRAVELER. A resident of Tudela in N Spain, he set out on his travels about 1165, returning 1172/3. He visited about 300 places in France, Italy, Greece, Syria, Palestine, Iraq, the Persian Gulf, Egypt, and Sicily. His book of travels (first published 1543), compiled from his notes, is a major source for Jewish history of that period and an important work in geographical literature. B. was interested not only in the Jewish communities but also in economic and political conditions generally, and collected information on many places which he did not himself visit.

BENJAMIN, ERNEST FRANK (1900–1969): British officer. He served in Malaya, Madagascar, Italy, and the Middle East, commanding the JEWISH BRIGADE Group 1944–6.

BENJAMIN, JUDAH PHILIP (1811–1884): US statesman. Of W Indian birth, he became a successful lawyer in Louisiana and was elected to the state legislature in 1842. This was the beginning of a political career which led him ten years later to the US Senate. He withdrew in 1861 when his state seceded from the Union, and he was at once named attorney-general of the Confederacy. He also held the post of acting secretary of war, an office he was forced to resign, and from 1862 until the collapse of the Confederacy was its secretary of state. After the Civil War, he took up a legal career in England, became a distinguished barrister, and wrote the standard legal work on *Sales of Personal Property.*

BENNETT, SOLOMON (1761–1838): Copper engraver and author. He was born in Russia and after becoming a member of the Royal Academy in Berlin, settled in England in 1799. Here he continued his artistic activity, also conducting a polemic with the chief rabbi Solomon Herschell, publishing apologetic works, and beginning a new English translation of the Bible.

BENSH (Yidd.): (1) To say the Grace after Meals; (2) to bless the children. The word is believed to derive from the Latin *benedi(ce)re* (=bless) through the Old French.

BENSUSAN, SAMUEL LEVY (1872–1958): British author and journalist. He published numerous novels, plays, and sketches, mainly on English country life.

BENTOV (originally **GUTTGILD**), **MORDEKHAI** (1900–): Israel labor leader. A founder of *Ha-Shomer ha-Tzair* in Poland, he settled in Palestine in 1920 and became a leader of *Ha-Kibbutz ha-Artzi*. B. was minister of labor and reconstruction in the provisional government (1948–9), *Mapam* member of the Knesset 1949–65, minister of development 1955–61 and of housing 1966–9. He was a founder and editor of the *Mapam* daily *Al ha-Mishmar.*

BENTWICH: English family. *HERBERT B.* (1856–1932), lawyer, was a leader of the *Ḥoveve Zion* and later of the Zionist movement in England. He edited the *Law Journal*. His son, *NORMAN DE MATTOS B.* (1883–1971), lawyer and public worker, worked as an inspector of courts in Egypt, served in World War I, and was attorney-general in Palestine 1920–31, until his strong Zionist sympathies resulted in his resignation. He then became professor of international relations at the Hebrew Univ. (1932–51). Meanwhile, he was active in relief work for the victims of Nazi persecution and was director of the British High Commission for German Refugees, 1933–6. He was co-editor of the *Jewish Review* 1910–3, and has published much on legal, Palestinian, and Jewish subjects, including works on Philo, Josephus, Hellenism, biographies of S. Schechter and Y.L. Magnes, and autobiographical books. His wife *HELEN CAROLINE B.* (1892–1972) was chairman of the London County Council, 1956–7; his brother *JOSEPH B.* (1902–) was headmaster of the *Bet Sepher ha-Reali* in Haifa, and active in education in Israel.

BENVENISTE (originally Aben [Ibn] Veniste): Spanish family. (1) *ABRAHAM B.* (c. 1390–1456): Financial agent to John II of Aragon. Enjoying great influence at court, he was able to avert a Ritual Murder charge brought against the Jews and to strengthen their communal organization. In 1432, the king appointed him chief rabbi (*Rab de la Corte*), and in this capacity he convened a synod at Valladolid which reorganized Jewish education on a secure foundation. (2) *HAYYIM BEN ISRAEL B.* (1603–1673): Turkish talmudist. He lived first in Constantinople and after 1635 in Smyrna, where he was rabbi from 1663. Originally a supporter of Shabbetai Tzevi, he later claimed that this was imposed on him by violence, and underwent penance. His main work, *Kneset ha-Gedolah* (1658), is a guide to the halakhah embodying decisions made after the completion of the *Shulḥan Arukh* and is regarded as authoritative. (3) *IMMANUEL B.* (17th cent.): Hebrew printer in Amsterdam. His outstanding production was an uncensored edition of the Talmud (1644–8). (4) *ISAAC BEN JOSEPH B.* known as Don Zag (13th cent.): Physician to James I of Aragon. He was favored by Pope Honorius II and in 1214–5, was the leading spirit in the Jewish synod held in S France to avert persecutory Church legislation. (5) *SHESHET BEN ISAAC B.* (d. 1210): Physician, poet, and communal leader in Barcelona; perhaps son of (4). Some of his medical writings are extant in ms. Owing to his knowledge of Arabic, he was used by Alfonso II of Aragon on diplomatic missions.

BENZAQUEN, LEON (1905–): Moroccan public figure. A physician by profession, he was minister of posts and telegraphs in the Moroccan government 1955–8. In 1967 he headed the Casablanca Jewish community.

BEOBACHTER AN DER WEICHSEL (Ger. "The Observer by the Vistula"): First weekly Jewish newspaper in Poland, in Hebrew letters (with a section in Polish), published in Warsaw by Anton Eisenbaum in 1823–4. It advocated assimilation and equal rights for Jews and received financial support from the Polish government.

BER OF BOLECHOV (Ber Birkenthal; 1723–1805): Autobiographer. He lived in Galicia and earned his livelihood from the wine-trade. One of the first *maskilim*, he took part in the debate with the Frankists at Lvov (1759) and wrote a polemical work against Sabbetaians and Frankists. His memoirs, written in Hebrew (published by Mark Wischnitzer in 1922), constitute a major source for the study of the economic and cultural situation of the Jews of E Galicia in the 18th cent.

BER OF LIUBAVICH see **LIUBAVICH**

BER OF MEZHIRICH see **DOV BER OF MEZHIRICH**

BERAB (BERAV), JACOB (c. 1475–1546): Talmudist. He was born in Spain and lived in N Africa before settling in Safed where he headed a yeshivah. B. initiated the plan to reintroduce ORDINATION *(semikhah)* by Palestinian scholars in order to unite the Jewish people under one authoritative leadership and reconstitute the Sanhedrin, thereby hastening redemption. He was supported by the rabbis of Safed but the leading Jerusalem scholar, Levi Ibn Haviv, opposed him on halakhic grounds. A violent controversy ensued, and B. had to take refuge in Damascus for a time; his scheme died with him.

BERAKHAH see **BENEDICTIONS**

BERAKHOT (Heb. "Blessings"): First tractate of the Mishnah order of *Zeraim*, consisting of 9 chapters, with commentary in the Babylonian and Palestinian Talmuds. It deals with the recitation of the *Shema*, blessings, and prayer in general.

BERDICHEV: City in the Ukrainian Soviet Republic. Jewish settlement commenced in the 16th cent. and by the 19th cent. 80% of the total population were Jews. The community was of great significance— being called the "Jerusalem of Volhynia"—and from the time R LEVI ISAAC settled there (c. 1780), became a Ḥasidic stronghold. Later it was a center of Haskalah, and its famous printing press published many of the classics of the Enlightenment movement. Books of religious import were also printed in B., including a one-volume Babylonian Talmud. Pogroms led to a decline in the Jewish population, but the community still numbered c. 40,000 before World War II. The Nazis set up a ghetto in B. which was the scene of large-scale massacres in 1941. Estimated Jewish pop. (1970): 15,000.

BERDICHEVSKY, MICAH JOSEPH see **BIN GORION**

BERECHIAH (ben Ḥiyya; fl. 4th cent.): Palestinian amora and Bible homilist. Few names appear in midrashic literature so frequently, and he is considered one of the greatest masters of aggadah.

Berek Joselowicz.

BERECHIAH BEN NATRONAI HA-NAKDAN (12th
–13th cents): Fabulist. He wrote *Mishle Shualim*
("Fox Fables"), mainly collected from non-Jewish
medieval tales, to which he added stories from Hebrew
sources. The book was very popular and was frequently republished. He also translated into Hebrew the
Quaestiones Naturales of Abelard of Bath, and was
the author of ethical works. B. lived in S France and
also visited England. He has been identified with
Benedict le Pointur (= *Nakdan*, i.e., Punctuator) who
lived in Oxford in 1194.

BERECHIAH (BENEDICT) OF NICOLE (=Lin-
coln; d. 1278): English financier and scholar; son
of R Moses of London. In 1255, he was arrested in
connection with the Hugh of Lincoln Ritual Murder
charge but was released through the intervention of
the Castilian ambassador. Many of his halakhic decisions have been preserved.

BEREK (BERKO) JOSELOWICZ (c. 1765–1809):
Polish military hero. He was born in Lithuania,
settled in Warsaw, and during Kosciuszko's rebellion
(1794) organized a volunteer battalion of Jewish cavalry, most of whom fell in the defense of the city. After
the rising was suppressed, B. escaped to France, took
on the establishment of the duchy of Warsaw (1807),
returned to Poland, being appointed commander of a
battalion of Polish cavalry. He fell in battle leading a
charge against the Austrians. B. became a folk hero,
figuring in Polish song and legend.

BERENICE: (1) Judean princess (late 1st cent. BCE–
1st cent. CE); daughter of Herod's sister Salome.
She married her cousin Aristobulus and, after his
death, Herod's brother-in-law, Theudion. She was
mother of Herod Agrippa I and Herodias. (2) Judean
princess (28 CE–after 79); daughter of Herod Agrippa
I and Cypros, daughter of Phasael, and granddaughter
of (1). She was betrothed at the age of 13 to Marcus son
of the Alexandrian alabarch Alexander, but after he
died, married her uncle Herod of Chalcis. Following
his death (48 CE), her close association with her
brother Agrippa I drew the imputation of incest and
she was induced to marry Polemon II of Cilicia. In 60,
she rejoined Agrippa, supporting his efforts to prevent
the outbreak of the great Revolt (66) and later fleeing
with him to the Romans. She became mistress of
Titus and followed him to Rome, but was forced by
Roman popular opinion to leave him. On Vespasian's
death she unsuccessfully attempted reconciliation with
Titus.

BERENSON, BERNARD (1865–1959): Art historian.
Born in Lithuania and educated in America, he
lived most of his life in Italy and was baptized there.
He wrote many works, especially *Italian Painters of
the Renaissance*.

BERESHIT see **GENESIS**

BERESHIT RABBAH see **GENESIS RABBAH**

BERGELSON, DAVID (1884–1952): Russian author.
His early work was in Russian and Hebrew; then
turning to Yiddish, he wrote novels, plays, stories, and
criticism. He somberly described the Jewish Russian
townlet in the early 20th cent. in an impressionistic
style. Returning to Russia in 1933, after 11 years in
Berlin, he published a series of realistic novels with a
marked pro-communist emphasis. He was imprisoned
and put to death, along with other Yiddish writers,
in the last years of Stalin's rule.

BERGEN-BELSEN: Site of German concentration
camp. Opened in Aug. 1943, there were 18,000

Bergen-Belsen.

Henri Bergson.

inmates by 1944. Conditions deteriorated in Dec. 1944 when B. became a center for prisoners from more easterly camps. By Mar. 1945, there were 42,000 prisoners, rapidly succumbing to typhus, but newcomers continued to arrive. On Apr. 15th, the liberating British army found there 55,000 prisoners and 13,000 unburied corpses; another 13,000 detainees died within the next three days. Altogether 30,000 Jews perished in B.-B.

BERGER, VICTOR (1860–1929): US socialist. He helped found the American Socialist Party and in 1911 was the first Socialist to sit in Congress. Jailed for anti-war sentiments in 1919, sentence was quashed by the Supreme Court.

BERGMAN, SAMUEL HUGO (1883–1975): Philosopher. Born in Prague, he was active in the Czech Zionist movement, being influenced by Ahad Ha-Am, Buber, and A.D. Gordon in his conception of Zionism as a movement of the spiritual and moral rebirth of the Jewish people. In 1920, he settled in Palestine and directed the National and University Library, Jerusalem 1920–35. From 1928, he taught philosophy at the Hebrew Univ. of which he was rector 1936–8. B. wrote widely on philosophical topics.

BERGMANN, ERNST DAVID (1900–1975): Israel chemist. He migrated to Palestine in 1934 and was scientific director of the Daniel Sieff Institute, Rehovot 1934–49, director of the Weizmann Institute of Science 1949–51, and was head of the planning sections of the Israel Ministry of Defense and of the Israel Atomic Energy Commission 1951–66.

BERGNER, ELISABETH (1897–) Actress; a native of Vienna. She appeared under Max Reinhardt's direction, excelling in Shakespearean roles. Her performance of Shaw's *St. Joan* was also outstanding. From 1933, she acted on the stage and in films in England and the US. After World War II she reappeared in Germany.

BERGSON, HENRI (1859–1941): French philosopher. He taught at the Collège de France from 1900–21, was elected to the French Academy in 1914, and received the Nobel Prize for literature in 1927. His works represent a reaction against the exclusive domination of the intellect, in which he saw merely man's aptitude for grasping and mastering the physical world. His almost mystical view of intuition influenced many important minds of his day, including Marcel Proust. B.'s most famous works are *L'Evolution créatrice* (translated as "Creative Evolution"), *Matière et Mémoire* ("Matter and Memory"), *Le Rire* ("Laughter"), *L'Energie spirituelle* ("Mind-Energy"), and *Durée et Simultanété* ("Duration and Simultaneity"). Though remote from Jewish life, he protested against the anti-Jewish legislation of the Vichy government after the fall of France in 1940.

BERIT (Ashkenazi *bris;* Heb. "Covenant"): Abbr. for *Berit Milah,* the ceremony of CIRCUMCISION.

BERIT IVRIT OLAMIT (Heb. "World Hebrew Union"): World movement dedicated to the dissemination of Hebrew as a spoken language and of Hebrew culture. It was founded at a convention held in Berlin in 1931, and organized world congresses in Jerusalem in 1950 and 1955. The seat of its directorate is in Jerusalem. All national Hebrew organizations in the Diaspora are affiliated to it. The *B.I.O.* publishes *Am va-Sepher* and *Megillat ha-Sepher.*

BERIT SHALOM (Heb. "Peace Covenant"): Jewish society founded in Palestine in 1926 by Arthur Ruppin to work for peace between Arabs and Jews in the country. It recommended an Arab-Jewish binational state based on equality of rights of both sides (irrespective of numerical relationship). The group, headed by Y.L. MAGNES, came to an end in 1940, its place being taken by IHUD. See also BI-NATIONALISM.

BERIT TRUMPELDOR see **BETAR**

BERKMAN, ALEXANDER (c. 1870–1936): Anarchist. Migrating to the US from Russia in 1888, he became a colleague of Emma Goldman in the anarchist movement. B. was imprisoned from 1892 to 1906 for the attempted assassination of Henry C. Frick, a steel magnate, as a protest against labor conditions in the steel industry and was convicted in 1917 of obstructing military conscription. In 1919, B. was deported to Russia, but repudiated the communist dictatorship. He left for Berlin in 1922 and went to France in 1925.

BERKOVITZ, YITZHAK DOV (1885–1967): Hebrew writer, editor, and translator. Born in White Rus-

Yitzhak Dov Berkovitz.

sia, in 1914 he migrated to the US where he edited Hebrew periodicals. He settled in Palestine in 1928. B.'s short stories and novels are realistic and humorous and notable for their precise style. Until settling in Palestine, he wrote about Jewish life in E Europe and the Jewish immigrants in America. His later work includes two novels *Menahem Mendel be-Eretz Yisrael* ("Menahem Mendel in Palestine") and *Yemot ha-Mashiah* ("Days of the Messiah") and several plays. He translated from Yiddish into Hebrew the writings of his father-in-law, SHOLEM ALEICHEM, whose personality constitutes a central element in B.'s five volumes of reminiscences.

BERKOWICZ, JOSEPH (1789–1846): Polish military hero; son of BEREK JOSELOWICZ. He served with his father in Napoleon's army and took part in the invasion of Russia (1812). Joining the patriot army during the Polish 1830 revolution, he issued a manifesto calling on the Jews of Poland to enroll. After the suppression of the rising, he escaped to Paris and went from there to England.

BERKOWITZ, HENRY (1857–1924): Reform rabbi in Philadelphia 1892–1921. He founded the JEWISH CHAUTAUQUA SOCIETY in 1893, and was the author of popular religious and devotional literature.

BERL BRODER see **BRODER, BERL**

BERLIN: Chief city of GERMANY. Jews settled there at the end of the 13th cent. They suffered during the Black Death persecutions of 1349, but settlement flourished again shortly thereafter. The community came to an end in 1510 after a Host Desecration charge at Bernau, near B., and the general expulsion from Brandenburg, but was renewed in 1539. In 1571, popular violence drove the Jews out again from all Brandenburg. Settlement recommenced when refugees from Vienna were admitted to Brandenburg in 1670, the commercial ability of the Jews inducing the authorities

to protect them against the townspeople. In 1714, a synagogue was inaugurated. Although financial transactions were officially prohibited to the Jews, they were unofficially countenanced and Jewish mint-masters helped finance the Seven Years' War. The period of Enlightenment was ushered in by Moses Mendelssohn in B., and Jewish salons were prominent in B. society in the late 18th cent. This resulted in a wave of conversion, one Jew in ten embracing Christianity. In 1808, the Jews were recognized as town-citizens. A congregation introducing liturgical modification came into existence in 1815, and the Society for Jewish Culture, in 1819; the latter provided the framework for Leopold Zunz's pioneer researches. The Hochschule für die Wissenschaft des Judentums was established in 1872, largely due to the initiative of Abraham Geiger, the communal rabbi. The Orthodox seceded in 1869 and in 1873 founded the ADAS ISRAEL congregation and the BERLIN RABBINICAL SEMINARY directed by Israel Hildesheimer. Many Jews immigrated to B. from the province of Posen and from E Europe. Under the Nazis, the Jews of B., numbering 160,564 in 1933, suffered the same fate as the rest of German Jewry. Some returned after World War II, and in 1973, there were 6,000 Jews in West B. with synagogues and other organizations; and 430 registered Jews in East B.

BERLIN, CONGRESS OF see **CONGRESS OF BERLIN**

BERLIN RABBINICAL SEMINARY (*Rabbinerseminar für das orthodoxe Judentum*): Rabbinical institute founded in 1873 by Israel Hildesheimer. It was one of the leading Orthodox seminaries in Europe until closed by the Nazis in 1938.

BERLIN (BALINE), IRVING (1888–): US composer. Born in Russia, he went to the US in 1893. Since 1911, when he composed *Alexander's Ragtime Band*,

First page of the Minute Book of the Berlin community. 1723.

he has written a series of popular songs (including *God Bless America*) and also the scores for many revues, musical plays, and films.

BERLIN, SIR ISAIAH (1909–): British political scientist; professor of social and political theory at Oxford. He served as first secretary in the British embassy in the US 1942–5. In 1966–74 he was the first president of Wolfson College, Oxford and from 1974 president of the British Academy. B. has written works on philosophy and political thought.

BERLIN, ISAIAH BEN JUDAH LOEB (also known as Isaiah Pick; 1725–1799): German talmudist. B.'s writings are distinguished not only for their erudition in talmudic literature but also for their critical intuition which paved the way for the correction of talmudic texts. His emendations have been added in Talmud editions since 1800. B.'s writings touch on almost every aspect of rabbinic literature.

BERLIN, MEIR see **BAR-ILAN, MEIR**

BERLIN, NAPHTALI TZEVI JUDAH (known as *Ha-Natziv*; 1817–1893): Talmudist. From 1853, he was head of the Volozhin yeshivah. His educational system, based on the principles advocated by the Vilna Gaon, included the rejection of *pilpul*, the fullest understanding of the text, and a minute knowledge of sources. He was one of the first rabbis to support Zionism, being elected a leader of the *Hoveve Zion* in 1887. B.'s main work is *Haamek Sheelah* on the *Sheiltot* of Aḥa of Shabḥa, which demonstrated his great knowledge of exegetical literature and his keen critical sense in the use of mss, etc. He also wrote responsa and *Haamek Davar,* a commentary on the Pentateuch. B. was the father of Meir BAR-ILAN.

BERLIN, NOAH ḤAYYIM TZEVI HIRSCH (1737–1802): Rabbi of Mainz (1784) and Altona (1792). He was exceptional among German talmudists for his reliance on the Palestinian Talmud and his familiarity with the New Testament.

BERLIN, SAUL (1740–1794): Rabbi and reformer. Son of Hirschel Löbel, rabbi of Berlin, he favored reforms in Jewish religious practice and opposed the excessive casuistry characteristic of rabbinic education in his time. He was discredited and, in 1793, was forced to resign as rabbi at Frankfort-on-Oder following a personal attack on a respected colleague and his forgery of a volume of responsa containing radical ideas which he attributed to Asher ben Jehiel. He died in London where his father had been rabbi.

BERLINER: (1) *EMILE B.* (1851–1929): Inventor. He was born in Hanover, and lived in the US from 1870. His many remarkable inventions include the microphone (1877), a gramophone, perhaps anterior to Edison's (1887), and improvements to the telephone, now in general use. He was also a foremost advocate of mild pasteurization. His publications include *Conclusions* in which he reveals his agnosticism. (2) *HENRY A. B.* (1895–), son of (1), assisted his father in

Abraham Berliner.

designing a pioneer helicopter and has manufactured planes and plane parts in the US.

BERLINER, ABRAHAM (Adolf; 1833–1915): Literary historian. He was born in Posen province and taught at the Berlin Rabbinical Seminary. His publications included an edition of Rashi's commentary on the Pentateuch, general works on Rashi and medieval Bible commentators, an edition of Targum Onkelos, studies on the liturgy and on Jewish life in the Middle Ages, and a history of the Jews in Rome.

BERMAN, JACOB (1901–): Polish politician. He was deputy minister for foreign affairs in the Polish Communist regime 1945–7, and then state secretary and a deputy premier until his removal in 1956.

BERMANN, ISSACHAR (17th–18th cents.): Pioneer of the Yiddish folk-theater. In 1708, he founded at Frankfort-on-Main a Yiddish theater group, the actors being mainly yeshivah students. Here he produced his play *Mekhirat Yoseph* ("The Selling of Joseph") which was widely performed, especially at Purim time.

BERMUDA CONFERENCE: Conference summoned at the instance of President Franklin D. Roosevelt. Representatives of a number of Allied nations met in Bermuda (April 19–30, 1943) to consider methods of rescuing Jews trapped under Nazi occupation. The proceedings were kept secret and no concrete suggestions resulted.

*BERNADOTTE, FOLKE, COUNT (1895–1948): Swedish diplomat. He was associated in the negotiations with the Germans toward the end of World War II to rescue Jewish survivors. In May, 1948, he was appointed UN mediator in the Jewish-Arab conflict in Palestine. His plan for a settlement accepted the severance of Jerusalem from the Jewish state. He was assassinated in Jerusalem and a Jewish terrorist organization, a splinter group of *Lohame Herut Israel,* claimed responsibility for his death.

*BERNARD OF CLAIRVAUX (1090–1153): Benedictine preacher, one of the prime movers of the Second Crusade (1146–7). When the monk Radulf attacked the Jews in the Rhineland, B. insisted that they should not be molested and, in several places, succeeded in stopping the persecution. He bitterly opposed the "Jewish" anti-pope ANACLETUS II.

BERNARD: (1) *JEAN-JACQUES B.* (1888–1972): French playwright and novelist (became a Catholic); son of (2). His stylistically elegant and psychologically penetrating plays include *Le feu que reprend mal, Martine,* and *L'Invitation au voyage.* (2) *TRISTAN B.* (1866–1947): French humorist. His comedies, stories, and essays, which are concerned with exposing the follies of the middle class and of man in general, influenced contemporary French literature. His works include *L'Anglais tel qu'on le parle, Triplepatte,* and the novel *Mémoires d'un jeune homme rangé.*

BERNARD, LAZARE see **LAZARE**

*BERNARDINO DA FELTRE (1439–1494): Italian Franciscan preacher. From 1475, he inveighed against the Jews throughout N Italy, advocating the enforcement of all legal restrictions against them and pleading for the establishment of public loan-banking establishments *(monti di pietà)* to make their presence superfluous. His agitation was responsible for the Ritual Murder accusation at TRENT in 1475.

BERNAYS: (1) *ISAAC B.* (1792–1849): German rabbi. In 1821, he became rabbi ("chacham") of Hamburg. He was one of the first Orthodox rabbis in Germany to preach in German, and introduced German as the language of instruction in the Hamburg Talmud Torah. B. was one of the leaders of the opposition to religious reform and to revision of the prayer-book. (2) *JACOB B.* (1824–1881): Classical

Medallion presented to Rabbi Isaac Bernays
after 25 years of service in Hamburg.

Simon Bernfeld.

philologist; son of (1). He lectured in classical languages and German literature at the Breslau Rabbinical Seminary (1853) and was professor at Bonn from 1866. B. published many studies on Greek philosophy. (3) *MICHAEL B.* (1834–1897): Student of German literature; son of (1). He was baptized in 1856 and became professor in Leipzig and Munich, his lectures being famous throughout Germany.

BERNE: Capital of Switzerland. Jews are recorded in B. from 1259; they suffered heavily in 1294 as the result of a blood-libel charge which is commemorated by a relief on a 16th cent. monument in the city. In 1349, at the time of the Black Death, the Jews were expelled, and again in 1427, a new community being established only in 1855. The community numbers 800 (1973).

BERNFELD, SIMON (1860–1940): Scholar. Of Galician birth, he was chief rabbi of Belgrade 1886–94, and thereafter lived in Berlin. His numerous articles and books, most of which were written in Hebrew, included *Daat Elohim* ("Knowledge of God") which is a history of Jewish religious philosophy, *Sepher ha-Demaot* ("Book of Tears"), a documentation of Jewish martyrdom, studies in the Haskalah movement, Jewish religious reform, the origins of Islam and of the Crusades, and a literary and historical introduction to the Bible. Among his German writings is a work on the Talmud and a translation of the Bible.

BERNHARD, GEORG (1875–1944): German journalist and economist. He edited the commercial section of the *Berliner Zeitung* (1898–1903) and in 1904, founded the journal *Plutus,* devoted to economic affairs, which he edited until 1925. B. was also chief editor of the influential daily *Vossische Zeitung.* In 1928, he was elected to the Reichstag representing

Sarah Bernardt in stage costume.

the Democratic Party. After 1933, he edited the emigré daily paper *Pariser Tageblatt* in Paris. During World War II, he fled to New York where he died.

BERNHARDT, SARAH (1844–1923): French actress. A half-Jewess, she was educated as a Catholic. In 1866 she began to appear in leading roles at the Odéon theater, later playing in classical and romantic dramas at the Comédie Française. From 1879, she toured widely in Europe and America. In 1915, one of her legs was amputated but she continued acting until•her death.

BERNHEIM, ISAAC WOLFE (1848–1945): Industrialist and philanthropist. He went to the US from his native Germany in 1867 and settled in Kentucky where he founded a great distillery. He was treasurer of the American Jewish Committee 1915–25. A vigorous opponent of Zionism, he advocated the formation of a "Reform Church of American Israelites" and the discarding of the term "Jew."

BERNHEIMER, CHARLES LEOPOLD (1864–1944): US merchant, arbitration expert, and explorer. He was born in Germany and went to the US in 1881. A successful businessman, he pursued interests in widely varied fields, ranging from labor arbitration, in which he was responsible for progressive legislation, to exploration. He organized and took part in archeological expeditions to Central America and the American southwest. In politics, he was one of three founders of the Fusion Reform Party in New York City (1913).

BERNSTEIN: (1) *AARON B.* (1812–1884): German writer on political and scientific subjects. He was among the first to delineate Jewish life in fiction in a non-Jewish language. In 1849, he founded a liberal journal in Berlin and for several decades wrote its leading articles. He published his collected political writings in three volumes and his popularization of science in 21 parts. His novels *Vögele der Maggid* and *Mendel Gibbor* described life in a small Jewish town and were widely translated. B. was one of the founders of the Reform congregation in Berlin. (2) *EDUARD B.* (1850–1932): German socialist leader; nephew of (1). From 1872, he was active in the Social Democratic Party. On the suppression of the German socialist movement, he went to Zurich (1878) where he edited the first Marxist periodical *Sozial-Demokrat*. Expelled from Zurich on the insistence of Bismarck (1888), he settled in England. Here, his observation of social and economic development convinced him of the falsity of Marx's doctrine of the imminent end of capitalism. He therefore evolved "Revisionism," basing socialism not on class war and revolution but on reforms and slow evolution within the existing order. B. returned to Germany in 1901, engaged in journalistic work, and was a member of the Reichstag (1902–6, 1912–8, 1920–8). He took up a pacifist stand in World War I. After the war, he was sympathetic to Zionist work in Palestine.

BERNSTEIN, HENRY (1876–1953): French playwright. He wrote successful melodramas, two of which deal with Jewish subjects—*Israel,* directed against anti-Semitism in France, and a historical play, *Judith.*

BERNSTEIN, HERMAN (1876–1935): US diplomat and journalist. For a time he was special European correspondent for the *New York Times.* He founded and edited the New York Yiddish daily *Der Tog,* 1913–6, and *The American Hebrew,* 1916–8. After World War I he informed US public opinion of the sufferings of the Jews of Poland and conducted a press campaign against anti-Semitic articles appearing in Henry Ford's *Dearborn Independent.* From 1925–9 he edited the *Jewish Tribune.* In 1930–2, he was US minister to Albania.

Leonard Bernstein.

BERNSTEIN, IGNAZ (1836–1909): Ethnographer. He lived in Warsaw and devoted himself to collecting proverbs and sayings in all languages, traveling extensively for the purpose. He amassed an enormous library on the subject and published a Polish catalogue of all his books of proverbs (2 vols. 1900). His main work was on Yiddish proverbs and expressions, and he also compiled a volume of *Erotica et Rustica* in Yiddish.

BERNSTEIN, KARL (1842–1894): Jurist. From 1877, he was professor of law at the Univ. of Berlin and published legal studies.

BERNSTEIN, LEONARD (1918–): US conductor and composer. He became assistant conductor of the New York Philharmonic Orchestra in 1943, conductor of the New York City Symphony in 1945, and permanent conductor of the N.Y. Philharmonic Orchestra 1957–69. He has conducted the Israel Philharmonic Orchestra both in Israel and the US. His compositions include the *Jeremiah* and *Kaddish* symphonies, *The Age of Anxiety* (Symphony No. 2), the ballets *Facsimile* and *Fancy Free*, a violin concerto, and scores for the musical shows *On the Town, Wonderful Town, Candide,* and *West Side Story.*

BERNSTEIN, PERETZ (Fritz; 1890–1971): Israel leader. Formerly president of the Dutch Zionist organization, he edited its weekly magazine. B. settled in Palestine in 1936. In 1946–8, he headed the Jewish Agency's department of commerce and industry and was minister of commerce and industry in Israel governments (1948–49; 1953–55). From 1937–46, he

edited the Tel Aviv daily *Ha-Boker.* He became president of the General Zionist Party in 1948 and was a member of the Knesset from 1949.

BERNSTEIN, SIMON (1882–1962): Hebrew author. He was secretary of the executive of the World Zionist Organization in Berlin, Copenhagen, and London 1912–22. He directed the Jewish Agency's Palestine Bureau in New York 1922–49 and edited the Zionist Yiddish organ *Dos Yiddishe Folk* 1922–53. B. published many works on medieval Hebrew poetry, including an annotated edition of the sacred poems of Moses Ibn Ezra.

BERR: French family. (1) *BERR ISAAC B.* (Berr de Turique; 1744–1828): Jewish leader and tobacco manufacturer. He headed the delegation which presented the case of the Jews of Alsace and Lorraine to the States-General (1789). In 1792, he was elected to the municipal council of his native town of Nancy. B., who advocated religious reform, was a member of the Assembly of Notables (1806) and of the Napoleonic Sanhedrin (1807). (2) *MICHEL B.* (1781–1843) son of (1), was France's first Jewish advocate but devoted himself to literature, writing bibliographical and apologetic works. He served as secretary of the 1807 Sanhedrin. (3) *HENRI B.* (1861–1954) was a historian and philosopher, writing many books and editing the series *L'Evolution de l'Humanité.*

BERSHADSKI (DOMASHEVITZKY), ISAIAH (1871–1908): Hebrew novelist. He lived in Russia, earning his living by teaching and journalism. His novel *Be-en Mattarah* ("Without an Aim") is a realistic work, noteworthy for its psychological analysis and lucid style. The romance *Neged ha-Zerem* ("Against the Current") reflects Zionist ferment in a typical Russian Jewish community. B. is regarded as the father of the naturalistic school of Hebrew literature.

*BERSHADSKI, SERGEI ALEXANDROVICH (1850–1896): Historian. Of Cossack origin and son of a priest, he became interested in Jewish questions and wrote historical works on the Jews of medieval Russia, Poland, and Lithuania.

BERTINORO, OBADIAH (YARE) OF (c. 1450–c. 1510): Commentator. Born at Bertinoro in N Italy, he lived at Citta di Castello until he emigrated to Palestine in 1485. The journey lasted 2½ years, and he settled in Jerusalem where he founded a yeshivah. His graphic letters to his father describing his journey and conditions in Palestine are among the classics of Hebrew travel-literature. His most important composition is a commentary on the Mishnah, which incorporates explanations from Rashi and Maimonides and became very popular for the lucidity of its exposition. It was printed in almost all subsequent editions of the Mishnah and was translated into Latin.

BERUR (BEROR) ḤAYIL: Israel communal settlement (IK) in S coastal plain. It was founded
in May, 1948 by immigrants from Egypt later joined
by newcomers from Brazil. Pop. (1972): 568. There
was a Jewish settlement on the site in mishnaic times,
R Johanan ben Zakkai's academy having been
situated there for some time. Oil was struck in the
vicinity in 1957.

BERURYAH (fl. 2nd cent. CE): Wife of R Meir;
daughter of R Hananiah ben Teradyon. She is
the only woman mentioned in the Talmud who
participated in legalistic discussion, her opinion on
one occasion being decisive. Her fortitude in the
face of severe family misfortunes (her parents were
martyred, and her two children died on the same
day) aroused the admiration of the rabbis.

BESAMIM (Heb.): Spices, especially those used in
the HAVDALAH ceremony at the end of the Sabbath.
The box containing the b., often in tower-form and
made of silver, has been a favorite object of Jewish
ritual art. It is sometimes termed *"Hadas"* (= myrtle).

BESANÇON: City in central France. A Jewish
community existed there from at least the 13th
cent. In the 14th cent., B. — then a free city —
admitted Jews expelled from other parts of France.
Although subject to restrictions, they were allowed
to trade freely until the 15th cent. when the community came to an end. Jews resettled after the French
Revolution, and a small community still exists
numbering c. 900 in 1970.

BESHT see **BAAL SHEM TOV**

BE-SIMAN TOV (Heb. "In a good omen"): The
Sephardi equivalent of MAZZAL TOV.

BESSARABIA: Province, formerly Rumanian, now
in the Ukrainian Republic, USSR. Jews were
resident there when B. was annexed to Russia in
1812. Between 1839 and 1858, they were forbidden
to live within 50 *versts* of the frontier and, in common
with gypsies, could not be government officials. B.
remained a focus of anti-Semitism (see KISHINEV).
90,000 Jews escaped from Soviet Russia through B.
in 1919–25, and many Jews emigrated from there,
a large number to Brazil. About 250,000 Jews were
living in B. in 1941 when 100,000 of them were
driven into Transdniestria. The overwhelming majority
of those who did not escape to Russia were murdered
by the Germans and Rumanians, but a remnant in
the Kishinev ghetto was liberated by the Red Army
in 1944.

BESSIS, ALBERT (1885–): Tunisian public figure.
After being secretary of the Tunisian Supreme
Council and municipal councilor in Tunis, he was
for a time minister of reconstruction and planning
in the first independent Tunisian cabinet (1955).

BET (ב): Second letter of the Hebrew alphabet;
numerical value, 2. Pronounced like *b* when it
has *dagesh* (בּ) and in most dialects of Hebrew like *v*,
when it has no *dagesh* (ב).

BET ALPHA: Israel communal settlement (KA) in
the Valley of Jezreel, founded in 1922. Pop. (1972):
837. The mosaic floor of a 6th cent. CE synagogue,
unearthed on the site, depicts the sun-carriage, the

Synagogue mosaic floor at Bet Alpha (Detail).

Document of the Bet Din at Kairouan, 977–8 CE.

wheel of the zodiac, the sacrifice of Isaac, ritual symbols, etc. with Hebrew, Greek and Aramaic inscriptions.

BET(H) (HA-)ARABAH: Biblical site (Josh. 15:61).
The name was given to a former communal settlement (KM), founded in 1939 near the N shore of the Dead Sea, where vegetables were cultivated despite the highly saline soil. It was evacuated in May, 1948, and destroyed by the Arabs.

BET DAGAN: Israel village 3 m. SE of Tel Aviv; probably the biblical Beth Dagon (Josh. 15:41). It was a Philistine town named after the god Dagon. In Byzantine times, B. D. was inhabited mainly by Samaritans, while the Crusaders built a castle there. The Arabs living there abandoned it in 1948 and it was subsequently resettled by Jewish immigrants. Most of its inhabitants are employed in Tel Aviv. Pop. (1972): 2,819.

BET(H) DIN (Heb. "House of judgment"; pl. *batte din*): Rabbinic court of LAW with jurisdiction in civil, criminal, and religious matters. In the Temple Period, the Sanhedrin, made up of 70 or 71 members, was the *Bet Din Gadol,* the "High Court," which exercised final authority on questions of religious law, appointed judges of the lower courts, and legally was entrusted with selecting kings and declaring war.

There were also lower courts of 23 members to adjudicate criminal cases, and local courts of at least 3 members for civil cases. Even with the end of Jewish AUTONOMY in Palestine (70 CE), the Sanhedrin (originally set up at Jabneh) was the central religious authority for all Jews. After the decline of Palestinian Jewry, no such body was reorganized because it was held that only the scholars of the Holy Land had the authority to confer the ordination requisite for membership in a strictly constituted *b. d.* In subsequent centuries, every center of Jewish population had a system of local courts, generally presided over by the chief rabbi or the dayyan, which exercised religious authority and adjudicated upon the internal affairs of the communities. In Spain, they also had criminal jurisdiction delegated by the king. There were late medieval instances of special *batte din* for guilds of bankers and merchants, and up to 1764, the Council of Four Lands constituted a court of final appeal for the Jews of Poland. The Emancipation of the Jews in the 19th cent. and the resultant breakdown of communal autonomy limited the *b. d.* to voluntary arbitration and jurisdiction in ritual matters. Under the Ottoman millet system, the *b. d.* was the Jewish equivalent of the Moslem *shari'a* court and had jurisdiction over Jews in cases of personal status. In Israel, the state has accorded rabbinical courts exclusive jurisdiction in matters of personal status, such as marriage, divorce, and inheritance.

BET(H) EL see **BETHEL**

BET(H) (HA-)EMEK: Israel communal settlement (IK) founded in 1949 NE of Acre, W of the biblical B.E. (Josh. 19:27). Its members came from Hungary, Britain, and Holland. Pop. (1972): 326.

BET GUVRIN: Israel communal settlement (KM) founded in 1949 in the Judean foothills, near the deserted Arab village of Beit Jibrin which stood on the site of the historic B. G. built in 40 BCE. In talmudic times, it was a commercial and administrative center; its population was predominantly gentile but several leading rabbis lived there in the 2nd–3rd cents. Septimius Severus (193–211) gave it the status of a free city, and it was renamed Eleutheropolis. B. G. continued to be of importance in the Middle Ages but declined after the defeat of the Crusaders. In the neighborhood are extensive caves which were inhabited in prehistoric times. Many remains, including mosaic floors and the remnants of a synagogue, have been found in B. G. The ruins of Mareshah (Marissa) — birthplace of Micah — have been discovered $1\frac{1}{2}$ m. to the S. Large-scale settlement of the region commenced in 1955.

BET HA-ARAVAH see **BET(H) ARABAH**

BET HA-EMEK see **BET(H) (HA-)EMEK**

BET(H) HA-KENESET see **SYNAGOGUE**

BET(H) HA-MIDRASH (Heb. "House of study"): School for higher rabbinic learning where students gathered for study, discussion, and prayer. In the Second Temple Period, the most important school was the "Great *Bet Midrash*" which stood in the Temple Hall. In the Talmud, the term generally denotes an academy presided over by a distinguished halakhic teacher. In subsequent centuries, most synagogues had their own *b.m.* or were themselves used as places of study and became identified with the *b.m.* It was equipped with a rabbinic library and was often the home of the local yeshivah. In Germany, the *b.m.* was known as the *klaus* (from the Latin *claustrum,* cloister); in E Europe, *kloiz* and also as *shtiebel* ("little room"). More recently, the term has been applied to synagogues utilized as popular study-centers.

BET HA-MIKDASH see **TEMPLE**

BET ḤAYYIM (Heb. "House of life" or "house of the living"): Euphemism for a cemetery.

BET HILLEL AND BET SHAMMAI (Heb. "School of Hillel"; "School of Shammai"): Two schools of tannaim during the first cent. CE, which differed in their decisions on more than 300 legal interpretations. In most cases, the School of SHAMMAI took the more stringent view, but in some instances, the rigorous view was held by the School of HILLEL. Cases are also recorded where the School of Hillel eventually adopted the view of the School of Shammai. The differences of opinion at one time almost led to a miniature civil war (*Shabbat* 13*b*, 17*a*, *Y Shabbat* I), but these may have reflected the differing outlooks of the schools with regard to revolt against the Roman power, the School of Shammai representing an ultra-nationalistic party. The doctrines of the

School of Hillel eventually became accepted in most cases in Jewish law, legend telling of a proclamation to this effect by a BAT KOL.

BET(H) HORON: Two ancient Palestinian towns (Upper B. H. and Lower B. H.) in the territory of Ephraim (Josh. 16:3, 5). They commanded important strategic positions and were therefore the scene of battles from the time of Joshua (Josh. 10:10) until Allenby. The two towns were fortified by Solomon and captured during the reign of Rehoboam by Sheshak of Egypt. Judah the Maccabee here defeated the Syrian army (166 BCE). The sites have been identified 9½ m. NW of Jerusalem.

BET NETOPHA: Town in Lower Galilee, mentioned in the Mishnah. It gave its name to the surrounding Plain of B. N. The W part of the plain is now a reservoir containing water pumped from the Jordan until it is conveyed to the coastal plain and the Negev.

BET SHAMMAI see **BET HILLEL**

BET(H) SHEAN (Beisan): Israel town, center of the B.S. plain. B.S. is mentioned in Egyptian inscriptions of the 2nd millennium BCE and was an Egyptian military and administrative center during the Egyptian occupation of Palestine at that time. After the Israelite conquest, it was allotted to the tribe of Manasseh but was only captured during the period of the monarchy. Later it was a hellenistic city called Scythopolis allegedly after the Scythians, said to have captured it in the 7th cent. and settled there. John Hyrcanus conquered the town and it remained in Jewish hands until the time of Pompey (63 BCE) who restored its autonomy as a member of the DECAPOLIS. Its Jews were in a minority, and many were massacred in 66 CE. The Jewish community was refounded and existed until the Middle Ages. Jews lived there again from the end of the 19th cent. until 1936. Excavations on the imposing mound N of the present town have revealed 18 strata, while the remains of a Roman hippodrome are clearly visible nearby. The Roman theater has been excavated. The town was a center of Arab nationalism during the British Mandate. The Arabs left in 1948 and the town was resettled by Jews (mainly recent immigrants). Pop. (1974): 12,000.

BET(H) SHEAN, PLAIN OF: Israel region, part of the Jordan Rift interposing between the hills of SE Galilee and Mt. Gilboa; known after its chief inhabited point, BET(H) SHEAN. Its area is 62 sq. m. It falls from a height of 330 ft. below sea-level by several terraces to the Jordan, 850 ft. below sea-level. The land has numerous springs and is agriculturally rich. In ancient times it was known as "the gate of paradise" but in the Middle Ages became a desert controlled by a few Bedouin and infested with malarial swamps. The Egyptians reinstituted cultivation there in 1832. The Turkish government

The mound of ancient Bet Shean—a view from the Roman theatre.

Carved *menorah* in rock-cut tomb at Bet Shearim.
To right: painted epitaph.

annexed the plain to its domains but did little to prepare the soil for settlement. In 1930, the Jewish National Fund purchased part of the land at a high price from its Arab owners and Jewish settlement commenced in the midst of the 1936–9 disturbances. In 1948, the few remaining Arabs fled. Recently the area has been developed for cotton-growing.

BET SHEARIM: Israel smallholders' settlement (TM) in the W Valley of Jezreel, founded in 1936. Pop. (1972): 309. The ancient town of B.S., which lay 3 m. W of the settlement, became a spiritual center in 170 CE when Judah Ha-Nasi transferred his academy and Sanhedrin there from Shepharam Judah Ha-Nasi was buried in B. S. which was a centra burial-place for Jews from the Diaspora as well as Palestine. Excavations since 1936 have revealed a synagogue and hundreds of rock-tombs of the 2nd–4th cents. (including perhaps those of R Judah and his sons, Simeon and Gamliel) with inscriptions in Hebrew, Aramaic, Greek, Palmyrene, etc.

BET(H) SHEMESH (Heb. "House of the Sun," a Canaanite god): Name of several ancient Palestinian cities of which the best-known was in the Shephelah and was also known as Ir Shemesh. In the time of Samuel the ark was brought there after being retrieved from the Philistines (I Sam. 6:13). B. S. was the scene of the defeat of Amaziah of Judah by Jehoash of Israel, c. 790 BCE (II Kings 14:11–13). Excavations have revealed the city wall, subterranean tanks, etc. In 1950, a settlement was founded at B. S., most of the settlers being employed in nearby Hartuv. Pop. (1974): 11,200.

BET TZAYYADA (BETHSAIDA): A fishing town NE of the Sea of Galilee in Second Temple times. Philip, son of Herod, built a city on the site which he called Julias. B. is mentioned frequently in the Gospels.

BET YERAH: Ancient city on SW shore of the Sea of Galilee. Excavations since 1936 have revealed traces of habitation from the 5th millennium BCE, particularly intensive between 4000 and 2300 BCE. It has been identified with the hellenistic Philoteria, conquered by Alexander Yannai. B. is mentioned in the Talmud as inhabited by a mixed Jewish and Gentile population. A large 5th cent. synagogue has been excavated there. An agricultural school (*Oholo*) and a study center in memory of Berl Katznelson have been built in B. Y.

BET YOSEPH see **CARO**

BETAIRA see **BATHYRA**

BETAR: Ancient town, today Bittir, 5 m. WSW of Jerusalem. Although not mentioned in the Bible, it is listed in the Septuagint as a city of the tribe of Judah. It was inhabited c. 1000 BCE but is famous as the last stronghold of BAR KOKHBA (134–5 CE). Its walls, enclosing some 4 acres, are traceable on a hill, 2,200 ft. above sea-level, surrounded by a Roman siege-dike. Evidence of two large Hadrianic Roman marching camps has been detected. The Talmud exaggerates B.'s population and the numbers killed at its capture.

BETAR (initials of Heb. *Berit Yoseph Trumpeldor*, i.e., "Yoseph Trumpeldor League"): Youth organization of the Zionist REVISIONIST party (now of the HERUT movement). It originated in Latvia in 1923 and was at first a scout movement, holding its first world congress in Danzig in 1931. The principles of the movement are a non-socialist Zionism, the building of Israel on a national, and not sectoral, basis, militarism, and the fostering of discipline. The E European branches were liquidated in World War II and the center is now in Israel, with branches in W Europe, America, S Africa, and Australia. Members of B. set up in Palestine the *Histadrut ha-Ovedim ha-Leumit* ("National Workers' Organization"), have founded several settlements, and played prominant roles in the IRGUN TZEVAI LEUMI and LOHAME HERUT ISRAEL. B. was led by Vladimir JABOTINSKY until his death (1940): its present leader is Menahem BEIGIN.

BETH see **BET**

BETH ARABAH, etc. see **BET ARABAH,** etc.

BETHEL: Ancient Israelite city, 10 m. N of Jerusalem and formerly called LUZ. Abraham erected an altar near the site (Gen. 12:8) and later, it was the scene of Jacob's dream, as a result of which it received the name B. ("House of God"; Gen. 28:17). After the conquest of Canaan, the tabernacle and ark rested in B. for a period (Judg. 20:26–7). Its importance as a center of pilgrimage dwindled after Solomon built the temple in Jerusalem, but was renewed when Jeroboam of Israel set up a new shrine with the image of a calf. This shrine, which was denounced by the prophets, survived the fall of Israel and was destroyed by Josiah (621 BCE; II Kings 23:15). The town was ravaged by the Babylonian army (587 BCE), but there are records of subsequent settlement. The remains of B. have been excavated at Beitin near the Jerusalem–Nablus road.

BETHLEHEM: Name of two ancient Palestinian towns, the better known being $5\frac{1}{4}$ m. S of Jerusalem. This was the birthplace of David and the background of the Book of Ruth. Christians ascribe special sanctity to B. as the scene of Jesus' birth and few references are found to Jews there after that time. The first Christian Roman emperor, Constantine, and his mother Helena, built the Church of the Nativity in B. in 330. JEROME lived there when translating the Bible into Latin. Catholic, Orthodox, Armenian, and Coptic religious institutions are maintained there. In 1948, B. had 10,000 inhabitants (7,500 Christians, 2,500 Moslems). From 1948–67, B. was under Jordanian rule. In the Six-Day War it was captured by Israel. In 1968, it had 32,000 inhabitants. The other B. (B. of Galilee; Josh. 19:15), 7 m. NW of Nazareth, is the site of a moshav ovedim with a population of 275.

BETHSAIDA see **BET TZAYYADA**

BETHULIA: Ancient Palestinian town near the Valley of Jezreel; scene of the main action of the Apocryphal Book of Judith. Its identity is uncertain.

BETROTHAL see **MARRIAGE**

BETTELHEIM: Hungarian family of rabbis, physicians, etc. *BERNARD JEAN B.* (1811–1869), converted to Christianity, became a missionary in the Orient, translated parts of the Bible into Chinese and Japanese, and settled in the US as a physician.

Bethlehem.

ALBERT SIEGFRIED B. (1830–1890) was a rabbi, educator, and editor in Hungary; he moved to the US in 1867 and held pulpits in Philadelphia, Richmond, San Francisco, and Baltimore. His son, *FELIX ALBERT B.* (1861–1890), was a physician who practiced in the US and Panama and pioneered in the study of tropical diseases. *ANTON B.* (1851–1930) was an author and editor in Vienna. *KARL B.* (1840–1895), a practicing physician in Vienna, wrote extensively on diseases of the blood and circulatory organs. *SAMUEL B.* (1873–1942), communal leader, was active in the Zionist movement and edited Jewish periodicals in Hungarian and German. He lived in the US, 1915–7 and 1922–7, and helped to organize the American branch of *Agudat Israel* and the Federation of Hungarian Jews in America. A native of Pressburg, he died in Budapest. *ERNEST B.* (1873–1944), a native of Budapest, served as a judge in Vienna from 1900, and was president of the Austrian Court of Appeal 1918–38. Professor of law at the Univ. of Vienna, he was author of several works on patent and international law. *BRUNO B.* (1903–), educator, went to the US from Austria in 1939. He is the author of *Dynamics of Prejudice.*

BETZAH (Heb. "Egg"): Seventh tractate in the Mishnah order of *Moed*, containing 5 chapters. It has both Babylonian and Palestinian Talmud. The present name is derived from the first word in the tractate, but the original name was *Yom Tov* ("festival day"). It deals with the laws applicable to festivals. The tractate includes a long list of differences of opinion between the Schools of Hillel and Shammai.

BEUR see **MENDELSSOHN, MOSES**

*BEVIN, ERNEST (1881–1951): British trade union leader and statesman. As foreign secretary in the Labor government of 1945, he continued the restrictive policy limiting Jewish immigration to Palestine (initiated by the Conservative government in the WHITE PAPER of 1939) and adopted repressive measures toward the Jewish resistance movement there. In 1945, B. set up the Anglo-American Joint Committee of Enquiry for Palestine but refused to implement its recommendations without US participation. He then sponsored the "Morrison Plan" (suggesting cantonization), on the rejection of which he referred the problem to the UN. This step led to the termination of the British Mandate in 1948.

BEVIS MARKS SYNAGOGUE: The oldest existing synagogue in England, called after the street in Central London in which it stands. It was built by the London Sephardi community in 1701 and is registered as a historical monument.

BEYROUTH see **BEIRUT**

BEZALEL: Craftsman of the tribe of Judah, responsible (with Oholiab) for the construction of the tabernacle in the wilderness (Exod. 35:30). He also designed the sacred vessels and the decorations.

BEZALEL: (1) School of Arts and Crafts in Jerusalem founded by Boris Schatz in 1906. The school at first concentrated on the manufacture of sacred objects, silver work, and embroidery, seeking to develop a national Jewish art-style on the basis of the folk-motifs of Jewish handicraft from ancient times down to the 19th cent. Until 1915 the school was maintained by a society headed by Otto Warburg. It was closed during World War I being subsequently reopened with the assistance of the Zionist Organization. Closed again in 1929, it was renewed in 1935 as the New Bezalel School for Arts and Crafts under the direction of Yoseph Budko, who was later succeeded by Mordekhai Ardon (1940–52) and Yaakov Steinhardt (1953–7). (2) The National MUSEUM of Jerusalem. Founded in 1906 by Boris Shatz in association with the Art School, it became an independent institution in 1925 under the direction of Mordekhai Narkiss. It moved to a new site as part of the ISRAEL MUSEUM complex in 1965. The B. Museum possesses a comprehensive collection of exhibits connected with Jewish ritual art, tradition, and custom, illuminated mss, works by Jewish and non-Jewish artists, and an art library.

BEZIERS: Town in S France, known in Hebrew as Beders, whence the surname Bedersi. There are traces of Jewish settlement in B. from the 5th cent. The community, in which resided well-known scholars, prospered in the 12th cent. under the protection of the viscounts. In 1209, the crusade against the Albigenses led to a massacre in which 200 Jews were butchered. Henceforth, the position of the Jews deteriorated; they were expelled in 1306, and again in 1394. A small community was refounded in B. in the 19th cent. and was augmented in the 1950s and 1960s by immigrants from N Africa. In 1969, the community numbered 400.

BIALIK, HAYYIM NAHMAN (1873–1934): Hebrew poet. He was born at Zhitomir and studied at the Volozhin yeshivah. He moved to Odessa in 1891, publishing his first poem there the same year. After spending four years at Korostyshev as a timber-trader, he taught at Sosnowice 1897–1900. There he completed *Ha-Matmid* ("The Perpetual Student"), marking his revolt against the traditional environment, *Akhen Hatzir ha-Am* ("Surely the People is Grass"), bitterly critical of Jewish society, and his first prose

Hayyim Nahman Bialik.

story, *Aryeh Baal Guph*. As a result, he was invited to Odessa where he wrote *Mete Midbar* ("The Desert Dead") in revolt against the Diaspora, worked as a teacher, and helped to found the Moriah publishing house. Together with Y. H. Ravnitzky, he published *Sepher ha-Aggadah* classifying midrashic material according to subject-matter. In 1903, his poem *Be-Ir ha-Haregah* ("In the City of Slaughter") stirred the Jewish youth to organize self-defense in reaction to the Kishinev pogrom. B. was literary editor of *Ha-Shiloah* 1904–9. His poem *Ha-Berekhah* ("The Pool") contrasted the world of beauty with the storms of reality, and his *Megillat ha-Esh* ("The Scroll of Fire") reflected the Jewish spiritual problem against the background of the Russian 1905 revolution. B.'s visit to Palestine (1909) marked the beginning of his folk-songs and his autobiography *(Saphiah*—"Aftergrowth"). In 1921, he left Russia for Berlin where he founded the Devir publishing house, later, with Moriah, transferred to Tel Aviv. He himself settled there in 1924, becoming the center of Hebrew cultural activity and the creator of the ONEG SHABBAT. Here he published stories and children's tales and edited the poems of Ibn Gabirol and Moses Ibn Ezra. His poetry expresses the national revival and his model style, deriving from all periods of Hebrew, includes both simple lyrics and fervent utterances of prophetic caliber. B. developed Hebrew metrics and revived biblical parallelism. As the editor of anthologies, he devoted himself to folk-literature, its influence being felt in his children's poetry. He was chairman of the *Vaad ha-Lashon* ("Hebrew Language Council"), and active in the composition of the Hebrew Technical Dictionary (1929). As translator *(Don Quixote, William Tell,* the *Dibbuk,* Shakespeare, etc.), he set a Hebrew stamp on his material while preserving the spirit of the original. His Tel Aviv home is now the B. Museum.

BIALYSTOK: Polish city. Until World War II, the majority of its prominent textile industry was in Jewish hands. A pogrom occurred there in 1906. The town was a center of Zionism and of Hebrew education. At the outbreak of World War II, there were 39,115 Jews. The Jewish population was herded into a ghetto by the Nazis in 1941. Despite attempts at resistance, the entire Jewish population was transferred to various extermination camps and liquidated by 1943. Only a few Jews now live there.

BIBAGO, ABRAHAM BEN SHEMTOV (fl. 15th cent): Spanish philosopher and author. Head of a yeshivah at Saragossa, he participated in religious disputations with Christian clergy. He wrote on the principles of Judaism (in his *Derekh Emunah*) and on Creation, as well as commentaries on Aristotle. In his works, he criticized both the ultra-orthodox critics of Maimonides and freethinkers.

BIBLE (lit. ("book"; in Heb. *mikra, kitve-kodesh,* or TANAKH): The sacred canonical books. The Hebrew B., originally divided into 24 books, contains 3 sections *(Torah, Neviim, Ketuvim,* i.e., "Pentateuch, Prophets, Hagiographa"). The Pentateuch contains

King David (Kennicott Bible, Bodleian Library, Oxford).

Bialystok: monument to the victims of the 1906 pogrom.

five books, the Hebrew names of which are taken from the first significant word in each book, while the non-Hebrew names derive from the SEPTUAGINT. GENESIS relates the creation of the world, human history until the time of Abraham, and the story of the patriarchs; EXODUS tells of the departure from Egypt, the giving of the Law at Mt. Sinai, and the construction of the tabernacle; LEVITICUS is concerned with sacrificial and priestly laws. The wanderings of the Israelites in the desert and additional laws are contained in NUMBERS; DEUTERONOMY recapitulates the Sinaitic legislation and records Moses' last addresses. The Prophetic books are divided into the Former and the Latter Prophets. The Former Prophets relate Israelite history from the conquest of Canaan to the destruction of the First Temple; they consist of the Book of JOSHUA, describing the conquest and partition of Canaan among the tribes; JUDGES continues the story until after the period of Samson; SAMUEL (now divided into two books) portrays the lives of the prophet Samuel and the first two kings, Saul and David; and KINGS (now I and II) spans the period from the accession of Solomon to the destruction of the Temple in 586 BCE, incorporating the histories of both Hebrew kingdoms, Israel and Judah. The Latter Prophets include the utterances of 3 major prophets, ISAIAH, JEREMIAH, and

Opening page of Leviticus with commentaries:
published by D. Bomberg, Venice, 1525.

First Temple and Jerusalem by the Babylonians (read on *Av* 9: see Av, NINTH OF); ECCLESIASTES, meditations on human fate (read on Tabernacles); and ESTHER, the story of a persecution under the Persian king Ahasuerus (read on Purim). The other books are DANIEL, tales from the Babylonian Exile and apocalyptic vision; EZRA–NEHEMIAH (traditionally a single work) relating events after the return from the Babylonian Exile; and CHRONICLES (now subdivided into two), a summary of history down to the end of the Babylonian Exile with particular stress on the monarchy of Judah; parallel with the Book of Kings but written from a different view-point and with greater emphasis on the acts of the levites. Christian tradition added a number of other Jewish writings of the Second Temple period (APOCRYPHA) calling the entire collection the "Old Testament with the addition of the NEW TESTAMENT (which consists of purely Christian writings). Most of the Pentateuch, the Former Prophets, and the historical sections of the Hagiographa are in prose; the other books are written in a poetic style. The prose, solemn and rhythmic; the POETRY is built on parallelism and is expressed in a variety of forms. The B. was written in the HEBREW LANGUAGE with the exception of solitary words in Genesis and Jeremiah and a few chapters in Ezra and Daniel written in Aramaic.

Covering a period of time exceeding a thousand years (the earliest traditions date from the time of Hammurabi while the latest are contemporary with Pericles), the B. reflects several of the most significant epochs of ancient civilization. The nomadic existence of tribes inhabiting the deserts and the trade-routes of the Middle East constitutes the background to the Pentateuch. The shadows of the Egyptian, Phoenician, Babylonian, and Assyrian empires fall across the historical and prophetic books. The Persian period, with the advent of Greece on the horizon, covers the last works of the canon. The B. is thus a valuable mine of information on ancient cultural and political history. Despite the progress of historical and archeological research, much of contemporary culture (Philistine civilization, Phoenician Baal-worship) is known principally from this source. Another aspect of biblical unity is its essentially religious structure. The B. throughout is presented as an inspired document. The Word of God echoes everywhere — its object is not metaphysical speculation but human instruction. God communicates with man through the medium of Prophecy. The collection, arrangement, and final redaction of the biblical books were traditionally carried out in the Persian Period *(Bava Batra* 14*b)* by the "men of the GREAT ASSEMBLY." The tripartite division of the B. was known by the beginning of the Hasmonean Period (as is evidenced by the first Greek translator of Ecclesiasticus) when the Pentateuch was already being read in the synagogue

EZEKIEL; while the other 12 prophets were regarded as a single book—the MINOR PROPHETS. The Hagiographa has 12 books: PSALMS is a collection of prayers and hymns, many taken from the Temple service; PROVERBS collects parables and sage counsel; JOB is a poetic philosophical work written in dialogue-form and concerned with the problems of reward and punishment. They are followed by the five scrolls *(megillot)*, each read in the synagogue (in most rites) on a special occasion — the idyllic story of RUTH relating to the period of the Judges (read on Pentecost); the SONG OF SONGS, a collection of love-poems which have been interpreted allegorically (read on Passover); LAMENTATIONS, elegies on the destruction of the (at first apparently over a seven-year cycle, later reduced to three years, but in Babylon annually — as subsequently became the general custom) and so were weekly selections from the prophetic books *(haphtarot)*. In some places, excerpts from the Hagiographa were also recited. The books were originally written on parchment scrolls and this usage has survived for copies of the Pentateuch and the Book of Esther read in the synagogue. Later, the books were copied in volume-form for schools and private usage. The ancient script was Phoenician; the transformation to the square Aramaic letters occurred gradually (but traditionally in the time of Ezra). Only the Samaritans retain the old writing. The B. has played a vital part in the spiritual and political life of the Jews. In post-biblical times it remained an unfailing source of guidance. The synagogue institutions drew much of their inspiration from the B., the liturgy being saturated with quotations from it. Readings from the Scriptures are a regular feature of the service, while the arrangement of the prayers is founded on biblical sacrificial legislation. The SHEMA (Deut. 6:4–9, etc.) has been recognized as the basic formulation of Jewish creed. The transmission of the holy text was the responsibility of the SCRIBES *(sopherim)* who created the textual traditions (MASORAH) which determined the reading, VOCALIZATION, and punctuation of the Hebrew text. Partial vocalization by vowel-letters was inserted for popular usage and is found, e.g., in biblical fragments among the Dead Sea documents. Later, systems of pointing were introduced — the Palestinian method, the Babylonian (supralinear), and the Tiberias system

Extract from the Petropolitanus Codex, 916 CE.

which became generally adopted. Other minor differences distinguished the Palestinian and Babylonian traditions. The first translation of the B. was the Aramaic TARGUM. The Greek Septuagint (3rd cent. BCE) was extremely influential, and other Greek versions were made by AQUILA, SYMMACHUS, and THEODOTION; all were recorded by ORIGEN in his *Hexapla* (3rd cent. CE). The Syriac translation — the PESHITTA — was edited in the 2nd cent. CE while JEROME'S Latin VULGATE (4th cent. CE) was adopted by the Roman Catholic Church. SAADYAH GAON translated the B. into Arabic (10th cent.), Moses ARRAGEL into Spanish (1422), and Yiddish versions appeared from the 15th cent. Outstanding translations include Martin Luther's German version (1523–32), The Spanish Ferrara version (1553), the English Authorized Version (1611, based on earlier works) and Revised Version (1885), Moses MENDELSSOHN'S German translation (1780), the translation of the Jewish Publication Society of America (1917; new translation of Pentateuch, 1962), and the German translation by M. Buber and F. Rosenzweig (1925–38). A number of polyglot versions from the 16th cent. onward include translations into various languages. The best-known printed Hebrew B. accompanied by the standard commentaries *(Mikraot Gedolot)* was first published in Venice (1524–5) at the Bomberg press under the editorship of Jacob ben Hayyim. In 1952, an edition of the biblical text by Kahle appeared at Strasbourg embodying the 10th cent. ms (now at Leningrad) of the masorete Aaron Ben Asher. See also BIBLE COMMENTATORS; BIBLE CRITICISM.

BIBLE COMMENTATORS: There have been two basic Jewish methods of Bible interpretation: (1) according to the plain meaning of the text *(peshat)*; and (2) the homiletic exposition of underlying meanings, not always logically deducible *(derash)*. Three periods of Jewish textual interpretation can be discerned: I. Before the age of the geonim (i.e., to the 6th cent.): II. From the geonim to the Haskalah (6th–18th cents.): III. From the Haskalah to modern times. The first period had already begun in Bible times when the oral law supplemented the written law and aided its interpretation according to both *peshat* and *derash*. Traces of interpretation can be discerned by comparing parallel passages in the Books of Kings and Chronicles. Systematic interpretation began with Ezra (cf. Neh. 8:8): *Derash* developed out of the need to find scriptural authority for traditional customs. Hence, the MIDRASH appeared, developing under the tannaim and treating both the legal (halakhic Midrash) and the narrative (aggadic Midrash) sections of the Bible. This necessitated principles of interpretation (MIDDOT) formulated initially by Hillel and later extended by R Ishmael and R. Eliezer ben Yose. Among the tannaim, there were two methods of *derash,* one close to the *peshat* (developed by R Ishmael) and the other far-fetched (R Akiva). *Derash* and *peshat* were regarded as complementary rather than contradictory. Hellenistic Jews (such as Philo) evolved the allegorical method which was used to adapt Judaism to Greek thought. In the second period, i.e., in the Middle Ages, further methods of Bible commentaries supplemented the old. Saadyah Gaon, faced by Moslem and Karaite criticism, broke free of the homiletic interpretation and wrote an objective commentary, utilizing contemporary secular knowledge and applying philological and independent philosophical investigation for the first time. This method developed especially in Spain; historical criticism was also evolved, and all elements were fused by Abraham Ibn Ezra. In France, Rashi relied on the literal meaning, generally having recourse to Midrash only where the text warranted; his comments were logical, clear, and based on contemporary philology. David Kimḥi and Naḥmanides combined the Spanish and French systems, Naḥmanides, however, introducing kabbalistic interpretations, i.e., the search for mystical symbolism behind the text, which spread with the publication of the Zohar. In the 14th cent., Jewish exegesis tended to become restricted to the more exaggerated method and declined in consequence, although Isaac Abravanel's discursive commentaries were an exception. A renascence began with Moses Mendelssohn's German Bible translation and commentary, which used the best works of the medieval period but directed attention to secular research at the expense of tradition. Jews began to study the Bible according to Christian standards of criticism. The most recent tendency of Jewish scholars has been to relink tradition with the latest scientific and archeological deductions. The Christian commentators, for their part, inherited the Septuagint and the allegorical method of Philo; their desire to find in the Old Testament a foreshadowing of Jesus led them to evolve the allusive and the allegorical methods; both, based partly on corrupt translation, lasted through the Middle Ages. Humanism encouraged the study of Hebrew and Jewish commentary, resulting in the polyglot Bibles, comparison of various translations with the source, and skepticism toward the Hebrew traditional version which was subjected to philological and historical criticism. Christian comment has not completely freed itself from anti-Jewish prejudice, the German school in particular having seriously distorted Judaism. The Karaites, rejecting rabbinical methods, also sought their own criteria; though free from traditional restrictions, their innovations were few and their methods, based on *peshat* and *derash,* used several rabbinical principles. They stressed philological research but, in fact, remained dependent on the rabbis, and their work was distorted by polemical motives. Among the best Karaite commentators was Japhet ben Ali.

BIBLE CRITICISM: The critical study of the Hebrew BIBLE falls into two main categories— (a) Literary or Higher Criticism and (b) Textual or Lower Criticism. The former deals with questions of the authorship, date of composition, style, and specific interests of the various literary elements which make up the Bible. The latter is confined to problems of a purely textual nature and attempts to establish, where difficulties are encountered, the true wording of texts. (a) Spinoza (d. 1677) is generally regarded as the founder of Higher Criticism, for he challenged the rabbinic assertion that the Pentateuch, with the exception of the last eight verses, was written by Moses and suggested that Ezra was the compiler of this and the historical books. A critical spirit was abroad centuries earlier, not only among Christian scholars but also among Jews. Abraham Ibn Ezra (d. 1167) mentions, and rejects, the theory that Gen. 36:31 ff. was written during the time of Jehoshaphat and, while noting the awkward interpolation at the end of Gen. 12:6, comments "he who is wise will be silent." After Spinoza, the non-Jewish French physician Jean Astruc (d. 1766) found two main sources in Genesis characterized respectively by the use of *Yhwh* and *Elohim* to designate the Divine name. De Wette (d. 1848) identified Deuteronomy as the book which was found in 621 BCE during the reign of Josiah (II Kings 22:8), while Graf and Wellhausen, in the second half of the 19th cent., developed the documentary theory. The general conclusions of the critical school are that the Hexateuch (i.e., the Pentateuch and Joshua) consists of four main sources, denoted by the symbols J (Jahwist or Yahwist, i.e., using the Divine name *Yhwh,* 9th cent.), E (Elohist, i.e., using the Divine name *Elohim,* 8th cent.). D. (Deuteronomist, i.e., author of Deuteronomy, 7th cent.), and P (Priestly, the author of the priestly code, 5th cent.), while JE denotes the combination of J and E by a redactor (7th cent.). Within P is the H (Holiness) code (part of Leviticus), while further subdivisions of the main sources are denoted by J^1, J^2, etc. Some scholars go further and isolate some of the subdivisions by giving them special symbols, as L (for Lay, by Eissfeldt) and S (for Seir, or South, by Pfeiffer), thereby indicating their special character or origin. Each original document is held to have its own distinctive style and interests forming the criteria by which they may be identified and disentangled from associated strands. A clear distinction is made, however, between the date assigned to the publication of each source and the age of the material it contains, for the primary material is much older. (b) For the critical study of the text of the Hebrew Bible the main materials are: (1) comparison of duplicated passages; (2) the evidence of the Samaritan Pentateuch, the ancient translations especially the Septuagint, and now the Dead Sea biblical scrolls, etc.; (3) the rules of parallelism in ancient Hebrew poetry; and (4) recurring types of scribal error. Of the latter, the most common are confusion of letters of similar form (in both the ancient and square scripts), accidental transportation of letters within a word, wrong division of words, dittography or the accidental duplication of a letter or group of letters and, conversely, haplography or the failure to repeat a letter or group of letters. The presence of scribal errors was recognized early by the rabbis, as is evidenced by their directives for oral correction *(ketiv* and *kere,* etc.). Modern textual studies also distinguish categories of glosses incorporated into the text. While many discrepancies may be due to faulty copying, some reflect variant traditional readings. Within recent years, many textual difficulties have been solved without recourse to emendation, for lost meanings of words have been restored by the comparative study of Semitic languages. Thus, a more conservative attitude prevails among scholars today in the handling of biblical texts.

BIBLE, LOST BOOKS OF: Works cited in the Bible which have not survived. The oldest was the *Book of the Wars of the Lord,* apparently a collection of epic poems and panegyrics relating to the wars of the Israelites under Moses. The second work was the *Book of* JASHAR. The *Chronicles of the Kings of Israel* and the *Chronicles of the Kings of Judah* described the monarchic period and were the chief sources for the biblical Book of Kings. Other works from that time include the *Book of the Words of Solomon,* the *Words of Iddo the Seer,* and a "Midrash" on the Book of Kings. The Books of Judges and Samuel are also based on earlier sources.

BIBLIOGRAPHY: The description of books and of their making, embracing the subjects and divisions of all branches of learning. As applied to books of Jewish interest, it includes Hebraica (works written or printed in Hebrew) and Judaica (works by or about Jews in other languages). The first bibliographical work in which Hebrew books were included was Conrad Gesner's *Bibliotheca Universalis* (Zurich, 1545–55). After various experiments, the first systematic b. of Hebrew books was included in the *Bibliotheca Magna Rabbinica* by Giulio BARTOLOCCI (Rome, 1675–93) which was supplemented by his pupil Carlo Giuseppe IMBONATI (1694). Shabbetai BASS, in his *Siphte Yeshenim* (Amsterdam, 1680), presents in alphabetical order 2.200 titles of Hebrew books both printed and in ms. It served as a model for the compilation of later works. Johann Christian WOLF, Giovanni Bernardo de ROSSI, and Hayyim Joseph David AZULAI continued the tradition of the earlier bibliographies. Among the leading bibliographers of the modern period were Julius FÜRST (*Bibliotheca*

Judaica, Leipzig, 1848–63), Isaac BEN-JACOB *(Otzar ha-Sepharim,* Vilna, 1880) and especially the father of modern Hebrew b., Moritz STEINSCHNEIDER, author of many bibliographical works, including his great Bodleian catalogue (1852–60) which refers also to works not in the Bodleian Library. An attempt to describe modern Hebrew works was made by William ZEITLIN in his *Bibliotheca Hebraica Post-Mendelssohniana* (Leipzig, 1891–5). More recently, H. D. FRIEDBERG's *Bet Eked Sepharim* (1928–31; second enlarged edition, 1949–55) contains the names of all books printed in Hebrew type. Some of the world's great libraries with collections of Hebraica and Judaica have published catalogues of their Hebrew books. Joseph ZEDNER's *Catalogue of the Hebrew Books in the British Museum* (London, 1867) is a model of accuracy. The first bibliographical journal was *Hebraische Bibliographie* which was published by Moritz Steinschneider (Berlin, 1858–82), to be succeeded by the *Zeitschrift für Hebraische Bibliographie,* ed. H. Brody and A. Freimann (Berlin 1896–1923), *Journal of Jewish Bibliography* (New York, 1938–44), and *Studies in Jewish Bibliography and Booklore* (Cincinnati, since 1953). The standard bibliographical journal at present, listing all works of Hebraica and Judaica as they appear, is *Kiryat Sepher,* the quarterly of the National and University Library (Jerusalem, 1926 ff). S. Shunami's *Bibliography of Jewish Bibliographies* (Jerusalem, 1965; supplement 1975) is an indispensable general handbook.

BICKERMAN, ELIAS J. (1897–): Scholar. A native of Russia, he taught in Berlin and Paris before settling in the US. He was research fellow in hellenistic literature at the Jewish Theological Seminary and then professor of ancient history at Columbia Univ., New York. He has written several standard works on the Maccabees.

BIEN, JULIUS (1826–1909): Cartographer and lithographer. A native of Germany, he went to America in 1849. He made maps for the US War Department, his productions including an atlas of Colorado and numerous lithographed maps for state geological surveys. He was president of the National Lithographers' Association 1886–96, and active in Jewish life.

BIKKUR ḤOLIM see **VISITING THE SICK**

BIKKURE HA-ITTIM (Heb. "First-Fruits of the Times"): Title of Hebrew annual devoted to literature and science, published in Vienna 1820–31. It attracted leading Hebrew writers and disseminated Haskalah, especially in Galicia.

BIKKURIM see **HARVEST FESTIVALS**

BIKKURIM (Heb. "First-Fruits"): Eleventh and final tractate in the Mishnah order of *Zeraim.* It contains 3 chapters and has Palestinian, but not Babylonian, Talmud commentary. It deals with the offering of the first-fruits in the Temple (Exod. 23:19;

Bringing the First Fruits. From the
Prague Haggadah (1527).

Deut. 26:1–11) and contains a vivid description of the
first-fruits ceremony in the Second Temple.

BILHAH: Concubine of Jacob, mother of Dan and
Naphtali. Originally, she was the maidservant of
Rachel who gave her to Jacob when she herself was
barren (Gen. 30:18; 35:25–6).

BILL OF DIVORCEMENT see **DIVORCE**

BILTMORE PROGRAM: Platform adopted by the
Zionist conference meeting at the Biltmore Hotel,
New York, in May, 1942. It denounced the British
WHITE PAPER of 1939, called for the reopening of
Palestine's gates to Jewish immigration, and asked for
the establishment of Palestine as "a Jewish commonwealth integrated in the structure of the new democratic world." The statement was adopted at the
insistence of David Ben-Gurion who appeared at the
conference to urge a more activist Zionist program.
This was the first official Zionist pronouncement that
Zionism's goal was statehood in Palestine; previously
the phrase "Jewish National Home" had been used.

BILU (initials of *Bet Yaakov lekhu ve-nelkhah* "O
house of Jacob, come ye and let us go," cf. Is. 2:5):
First modern Zionist pioneering movement. It was
founded in 1882 at Kharkov by Jewish students
reacting against the wave of Russian pogroms. There
were several branches numbering 525 members, of
whom only a few dozen eventually went to Palestine.
The first group, consisting of 15 men and women,
reached Jaffa in the summer of 1882 and the others,
later that year. The *B.* constituted the main nucleus
of the First ALIYAH and experienced severe hardship.
Some of them settled on the land in various colonies
and others went to Jerusalem to master handicrafts.
Their vision of social reform antagonized various
circles of *Ḥoveve Zion,* but they received the support
of Jehiel Michael Pines on whose initiative some of
them settled the colony of Gedera (1884).

BIMAH (Heb.): Among Ashkenazim, the dais or
platform in the synagogue where the reading desk
is placed. See ALMEMOR.

**BIN-GORION (BERDICHEVSKY), MICHA JO-
SEPH** (1865–1921): Hebrew novelist and thinker.
Born in the Ukraine, he studied philosophy in Breslau
and Berlin. Under Nietzsche's influence, he declared an
ideological war under the slogan "a change of values."
He held that Judaism's universal outlook was the
reason for exile and, consequently, redemption from
exile involved the negation of Judaism. B. G. urged
that Hebrew literature draw its inspiration from
life and nature and thereby heal the rift in the soul of
the younger generation struggling between Judaism
and humanism. B. G. opposed Aḥad Ha-Am who
stressed the fundamental value of the spirit of Judaism.
His novels reflect his own predicament—that of a
young Jew, far from his family, wandering in the
alien but enchanting western world. These stories
represented a great innovation in Hebrew literature by
revealing the constant ferment underlying the apparently idyllic and intellectual Jewish townlet and
depicting the Jew as a human being with sensuous
passions. His researches into Hebrew and Yiddish
folk-stories form the basis of extensive published
anthologies. His last work was concerned with the
origins of Judaism.

BINATIONALISM: The doctrine that Jewish-Arab
differences in Palestine were to be solved by the
establishment of a joint state in which both communities cooperated on a parity basis while retaining
internal autonomy. It was advocated by the BERIT
SHALOM and the circle led by Y. L. MAGNES. HA-
SHOMER HA-TZAIR published a detailed plan for a
binational state in 1946. The program remained
abortive since Arab response was lacking and Jewish
support was weak.

BINDER, ABRAHAM WOLF (1895–1966): US
musician. B. was musical director of the New York
YM- and YWHA, professor of synagogue music at
the Hebrew Union College—Jewish Institute of
Religion School of Sacred Music, and musical director
of the Stephen Wise Free Synagogue. He composed
many works with a special interest in synagogue and
folk music.

BINDING OF ISAAC see **AKEDAH**

BINYAMINAH: Israel village in the N Sharon plain,
founded by PICA in 1922. Pop. (1972): 2,700. Its
economy is largely based on citrus plantations.

BIOGRAPHIES: To a certain extent the chronicles
of the reign of David embodied in the Book of
Samuel, and apparently based in part on an independent work by the prophet Nathan (I Chr. 29:29),
may be considered as a biography. The earliest
specific biography in Jewish literature was of Isaac
Abravanel by Baruch Hazachetto (Forte) prefixed to
the former's *Maayane ha-Yeshuah* (Ferrara, 1551). No

really important b. in Hebrew or in the sphere of Jewish studies were written until the 19th cent. Now, biographical studies have appeared of most of the greatest figures of recent history, though not so many are available for earlier periods.

BIOLOGY: The science of living organisms. Its basis was laid by Aristotle — whose writings were reintroduced to the European world largely through the medium of medieval Jewish translators — and Dioscorides, whose most eminent Renaissance commentator was Amatus Lusitanus. Jewish contributions to b. date from the period when Garcia D'Orta (c. 1500–70) revolutionized botanical study. Later, important researches were carried out in Germany by Leopold Auerbach (1828–97) in cellular biology and histology, while Robert Remak (1815–65) probed into the general problems of cellular development in animal life. Heinrich Caro's (1834–1910) discovery of synthetic dyes facilitated research by making possible the coloring of tissues and organisms. Ferdinand Julius Cohn's (1828–98) investigations of bacteria helped to dispose of the theory of spontaneous generation and thus prepared the ground for epoch-making advances. In Italy, Paolo Enriques (1878–1932) studied the mechanics of heredity, formulating a fourth law of independent variability in addition to the three of Mendel. Leading Jewish biologists in the US include Jacques Loeb (1859–1924) who headed the department of experimental biology in the Rockefeller Institute for Medical Research and conducted basic experiments in artificial fertilization; Gregory Pincus (1903–) of Harvard who has con-contributed much to experimental embryology and has studied the factors activating the process of fertilization; and Herman Joseph Muller (1890–1967) who did important work in genetics and heredity, and, for his work on the artificial transmutation of the gene through X-rays, was awarded a Nobel Prize.

BIRMINGHAM: English city. Jews settled there about 1750, and in the following century it was — with Liverpool — the most important provincial Jewish community in England. After 1881, however, it attracted a relatively small immigration, and the city now has the smallest proportion of Jews of any city of its size in the English-speaking world. There is a unified Orthodox community maintaining four synagogues, as well as a Liberal congregation. Jewish pop. (1973): 6,000.

BIRMINGHAM: City in Alabama, US. B. has had Jewish inhabitants since its foundation in 1871. In addition to a community center, there are three congregations of which the oldest is Temple Emanu-El, founded in 1882. There is also a United Jewish Fund established in 1937. Jewish pop. (1973): 4,000.

BIRNBAUM: (1) *NATHAN B.* (pseudonym Mathias Acher; 1864–1937): Political and philosophical writer. Born in Vienna of a Hasidic family, he studied law but turned to journalism. His writings from 1882 advocated Jewish nationalism and B. was the first to use the term "Zionism" in its modern connotation. He was among the founders of the Jewish students' nationalist society "Kadimah" (1883), and his writings evolved a basis for Zionist ideology several years before the appearance of Herzl on the Jewish scene. Initially, B. cooperated with Herzl and was the first general secretary of the World Zionist Organization. From about 1897, he (like Ahad Ha-Am) inclined to an "organic" Zionism to grow naturally from Jewish life, as contrasted with Herzl's political methods. He therefore opposed the belief that settlement in Palestine would solve the Jewish problem. After the Third Zionist Congress (1899), he left the Zionist movement and became its opponent, advocating cultural and political autonomy in the Diaspora as the method of securing Jewish national existence. At the same time, he emphasized the importance of E European Jewry and the value of the Yiddish language and was one of the convenors of the Conference at Czernowitz (1908) which proclaimed Yiddish as the Jewish national tongue. A further metamorphosis in his views was apparent from 1912 when B. turned to Orthodoxy. Henceforth his writings included plans for a religious order to realize the messianic idea in a Jewish community based on Torah and labor. In 1919, he joined *Agudat Israel,* becoming its chief secretary, but left after a short time because of its lack of flexibility. After the Nazi advent to power, he moved to Holland (1934) and died there in poverty. (2) *SOLOMON B.* (1891–): Scholar; son of (1). Lecturer at London Univ. in Hebrew paleography, he has studied the paleographic aspects of the Dead Sea Scrolls. B. is also an authority on the Yiddish language.

BIRNBAUM, EDUARD (Asher Anschel; 1855–1920): Liturgical composer and cantor at Beuthen (1874–9) and Königsberg (1879–1920). He published pioneer studies on Jewish music.

BIROBIDJAN: USSR autonomous region in E Siberia. In 1928, the Soviet government, on the initiative of President Kalinin, allotted B. for Jewish settlement and Yiddish was recognized as an official language there. Of the 20,000 Jewish inhabitants who went there in the early days of the experiment, over 11,000 had left by 1934 and the government began to recruit new settlers. In 1939, the Jewish population amounted to 23,000 — 20% of the total: in 1951 there were 40,000 Jews ($26\frac{1}{2}$%). Yiddish was in the course of time largely supplanted by Russian and the small Yiddish theater was closed in the early 1950's. A Yiddish newspaper *Birobidjaner Shtern* (founded 1930) continues to appear three times a week. The project to set up a Jewish autonomous region has been abandoned. Its Jewish population in 1970 was 11,452.

BIRTH: In biblical literature, b. pangs are considered the legacy of Eve's disobedience. Childbirth ritually defiles the mother for a period of several weeks. Rabbinic literature contains considerable scientific discussion, based on direct experience and the study of Greek sources, of problems connected with b. The rabbis, following Hippocrates and Galen, believed that a 7-month b. would survive, but not an 8-month b. The first-born child delivered by Caesarean operation, which is not considered genuine b. in halakhah, is accorded neither the rights nor the duties of the first-born. Many superstitious practices connected with b., such as the use of charms and amulets, were known in talmudic times and abounded in the Middle Ages. In modern times, it has become customary for mothers to visit the synagogue and recite a special prayer of thanks soon after childbirth. In both biblical and rabbinic traditions, b. connotes spiritual regeneration, especially of repentant sinners and proselytes who are regarded as "newly born."

BIRTHRIGHT: The privilege of the first-born male to lead the family and to receive a double share of the INHERITANCE is an ancient practice reflected in the Bible. In patriarchal times, the father could confer the b. on any of his sons (cf. Isaac, Jacob, and Joseph), although generally the first son born to the father received the special privileges. Rabbinic legislation obliges the first-born to contribute proportionately of his inheritance in settling debts of the estate, and he had to provide the female heirs with dowries, but these obligations could be avoided by renouncing the b. Talmudic law provides for the disposal of property prior to death in accordance with parental preference so that the biblical inheritance laws should not be applied. This practice later came into increasing vogue (see WILLS). The law of inheritance in the state of Israel makes no special provision for the first-born heir.

BISCHOFFSHEIM: Family of bankers and philanthropists, originating in Mainz. *LOUIS RAPHAEL B.* (1800–1873) established himself in Paris, and his brother *RAPHAEL JONATHAN B.* (1808–1883), founder of the *Banque Nationale de Belgique,* in Brussels; and in the next generation *HENRY B.* (1828–1907), in London. *ELLEN, COUNTESS OF DESART* (1858–1933), a daughter of Henry B., became a senator of the Irish Free State. See also HIRSCH, MAURICE DE.

BISHOP OF THE JEWS (Latin; *Episcopus Judaeorum*; Norman-French, *l'eveske*): Term used in medieval England as equivalent to the Hebrew *Cohen*. In Germany, it was sometimes applied to a rabbi.

*BISMARCK, OTTO VON (1815–1898): German statesman. The Jewish liberal leaders, such as L. BAMBERGER and E. LASKER, generally supported his work for achieving German unity but broke with him subsequently because of his reactionary domestic policy. B., who had shown dislike of Jews in his younger days, now seized the opportunity of stigmatizing liberalism in politics as "Jewish" and was alleged to have secretly encouraged the organization of the anti-Semitic movement.

BITZARON (Heb. "Fortification"): US Hebrew monthly devoted to philosophy, literature, and current affairs. It was founded in 1939 by Chaim Tchernowitz who edited it until his death in 1949, when a board of editors assumed responsibility.

BIUR see **MENDELSSOHN, MOSES**

BIUR HAMETZ (Heb. "Elimination of leaven"): The burning of all leaven on the morning preceding the Passover holiday. This follows the search for leaven (*bedikat hametz*: see BEDIKAH) the previous evening. An Aramaic formula recited after the burning declares all leaven *batel* ("annulled").

BLACK CODE (Fr. *code noir*): Code to regulate slavery, instituted in the French W Indian islands in 1685 and introduced into Louisiana in 1724. Its first article ordered the expulsion of all Jews, and article III prohibited the practice of any religion other than Roman Catholicism. The B.C., which put an end to the Jewish settlement in the French W Indies, remained in force on the mainland until 1803 when the Louisiana Purchase brought the territory into the US. The prevailing opinion is that the B.C. was never strictly enforced on the mainland, as there is no further mention of it in the Louisiana records and Jews lived in the colony even before 1803.

BLACK DEATH: Epidemic which killed a great part of the population of Europe and led to murderous attacks on many Jewish communities, particularly in GERMANY, in 1348–9. The superstitious masses readily gave ear to charges originating in Savoy that Jews had caused the disease by poisoning wells. The fact that the Jews were less exposed to the plague because of their enforced segregation and their dietary and hygienic practices lent weight to the charges. Pope Clement VI issued a bull condemning the libel and ordering the Jews to be protected. Nevertheless, hardly a single Jewish community from Alsace eastward was spared. Emperor Charles IV condoned the attacks in return for a share in the booty. The hatred of the guilds for the lower nobility and the lower patrician classes was diverted against their Jewish supporters. Moreover, those who owed money to Jews welcomed the opportunity to kill their creditors. In Germany alone, attacks took place on the Jews in about 350 places, while 60 large and 150 small communities were exterminated. Many towns thereafter banished the Jews for all time, although some soon changed their minds. This was the greatest disaster which occurred to German Jewry in the Middle Ages. Attacks on a smaller scale took place also in Poland, Catalonia, and N Italy.

BLACK HUNDREDS (Russ. *Chornaya Sotnya*): The name popularly given to the local branches of the

Soyuz Russkavo Naroda ("Union of Russian People"), an organization which came into being after 1905 to suppress the liberal movement in Russia. They were violently anti-Semitic and were largely responsible for the pogroms in the succeeding years.

BLANK, SAMUEL LEIB (1892–1962): Hebrew author. Born in Russia, B. settled in the US in 1922. One of the more prolific and important Hebrew prose writers in America, he produced more than a score of novels. The major theme of his early works is life in the Jewish peasant villages of his native Bessarabia.

BLASER, ISAAC BEN MOSES SOLOMON (1837–1907): Rabbi. A child prodigy, he studied in Kovno with R Israel SALANTER. He founded a yeshivah in the suburb of Slobodka, teaching Talmud, codes, and the doctrines of Israel Salanter. After the latter's death (1883), B. was regarded as the leader of the MUSAR MOVEMENT. In 1904, he settled in Jerusalem.

BLASPHEMY (Heb. *gidduph*): Reviling of God. B. is forbidden in the Pentateuch and was punished by stoning; in later times, this punishment was replaced by excommunication. The Mishnah restricts b. to cases where the Divine Name was actually pronounced. During a trial for b., witnesses were not allowed to quote the offending words verbatim until the closing stages when the public was excluded from the court. One of the witnesses then repeated the b. and the judges rent their garments.

BLAU, AMRAM (1895–1976): Leader of the Jerusalem group of NATORE KARTA. Born in Jerusalem, he led the group of extreme Orthodox Jews which broke away from AGUDAT ISRAEL. Regarding the state of Israel as a contradiction of the Jewish religion, he has conducted frequent demonstrations against religious profanation. His marriage in 1965 with a convert from Catholicism created a storm among his followers.

BLAU, LAJOS (Ludwig; 1861–1936): Scholar and talmudist. Teacher at the Budapest Rabbinical Seminary from 1887, B. succeeded Wilhelm Bacher as its director in 1913. He edited the periodical *Magyar Zsidó Szemle* ("Hungarian Jewish Review") after 1891, and was co-founder, with Simon Hevesi, of the Hebrew review *Ha-Tzopheh* which he edited 1910-31. B. wrote standard works on Jewish history and literature.

BLAUSTEIN, LOUIS (1869–1937): Oil industrialist. In 1910, he founded the American Oil Co. and pioneered in methods of gasoline distribution. His son, *JACOB B.* (1892–1970) succeeded him in the firm and also became active in Jewish community affairs. He was elected president of the American Jewish Committee in 1949 and was co-chairman of the Consultative Council of Jewish Organizations.

BLECH, LEO (1871–1958): German conductor and composer. He conducted at the Royal Opera and

Jacob Blaustein.

later at the State Opera, Berlin. He left Germany in 1939, but returned after World War II.

BLEICHRÖDER, GERSON VON (1822–1893): German banker and philanthropist. Succeeding in 1855 to the banking business of his father, Samuel B., he became the friend and confidant of Bismarck and was ennobled in 1872 in recognition of his economic advice during and immediately after the Franco-Russian war. At the Congress of Berlin (1878), he worked in behalf of the persecuted Balkan Jews. His sons, who inherited his banking house, became converted.

BLEMISH (Heb. *mum*): Biblical term, referring to a physical or ritualistic defect, debarring a person from the Temple service and rendering an animal unfit for sacrifice. According to the Bible, any of 12 external physical defects disqualifies a priest from the performance of his duties (Lev. 21:16–23), but the halakhah extends this list to 142. Physical defects which disqualify an animal for sacrifice are also enumerated (Lev. 22:20–25) and are extended to 73 in rabbinic law. A temporary b. disqualifies a priest from his duty and an animal for sacrifice only as long as the b. exists. Ritualistic b.'s are paralleled by moral b.'s: thus, a priest known to have had improper sex relationships can no longer serve in the Temple, while an animal which has been set aside for idolatrous worship cannot be brought for sacrifice. In rabbinic law, a physical b. of either husband or wife can in certain instances invalidate a marriage-contract.

BLESSING see **BENEDICTION**
BLESSING OF THE NEW MOON see **NEW MOON**
BLIOCH, IVAN see **BLOCH, JAN**

Ernest Bloch.

BLITZSTEIN, MARC (1905–1964): US composer. His works include operas *(The Cradle Will Rock, The Little Foxes)*, other works for stage, a choral symphony *(The Airborne)*, and music for films.

BLOCH, ERNEST (1880–1959): Composer. Born in Switzerland, he was professor of composition at Geneva Conservatory 1911–5. In 1917, he settled in the US. A specific "Hebrew idiom" is inherent in much of B.'s music, although he seldom actually used folk themes. His works include the operas *Macbeth* and *Jezebel*, chamber music, symphonic poems, *Israel* symphony, *America* symphony, concertos, *Shelomoh* rhapsody for cello and orchestra and a setting of the Sabbath service *(Avodat ha-Kodesh)*.

BLOCH, FELIX (1905–): US physicist. Born in Switzerland, he settled in the US in 1934. Associate professor (1934–6) and professor (since 1936) of physics at Stanford Univ., he shared the 1952 Nobel Prize in physics for his work in measuring nuclear magnetic fields.

BLOCH, IVAN (1872–1922): German physician. He was one of the founders of modern sexology and wrote important works in that field.

BLOCH (BLIOCH), JAN (IVAN) STANISLAVO-VICH (Jean de; 1836–1901): Polish pacifist. His 6-volume work *The War of the Future* (1898) stressed the horrors of modern weapons as well as the tremendous economic burden of war.

BLOCH, JEAN-RICHARD (1884-1947): French author. Some of his early works deal with Jewish problems and the Jewish position in the contemporary world, e.g., *"Lévy"* and *"...Et Cie"* (English translation *"...& Co"*.). He subsequently became a Marxist and lived in Moscow from 1941 to 1945.

BLOCH, JOSEPH SAMUEL (1850–1923): Austrian rabbi and publicist. After serving as rabbi to several communities, he became lecturer at the Vienna *Bet ha-Midrash*. In 1882, he accused August ROHLING of perjury in his allegation of blood libel against the Jews. Rohling sued B. but withdrew the suit, being then dismissed from his post in the Univ. of Prague. B. was a member of the Austrian parliament 1883–5, 1891–5. In 1884, he founded the *Osterreichische Wochenschrift* in which he continued to fight anti-Semitism. In 1885, he established the Union of Austrian Jews to combat anti-Semitism. His works included his much-quoted defense of Judaism, *Israel and the Nations*.

BLOCH, JOSHUA (1890–1957): US librarian. Born in Lithuania, he went to the US in 1907. B. was chief of the Jewish division of the New York Public Library 1923–1956, and wrote monographs on aspects of Jewish and Semitic literatures and bibliography.

BLOCH, KONRAD (1912–): Biochemist. Born in Germany, he went to the US in 1936. Professor of biochemistry at Harvard, he was awarded the 1964 Nobel Prize for medicine for his work on cholesterol molecules and their production in animal cells.

BLOCH, MARC (1886–1944): French historian. Professor at the Univ. of Strasbourg and later at the Sorbonne, B. was the outstanding authority on

Felix Bloch.

feudalism and the economic history of the Middle Ages. A member of the French resistance movement in World War II, he was captured, tortured, and later shot by the Germans.

BLOCH, MARCUS ELIEZER (1723–1799): German physician and ichthyologist. His main work is a monumental 12-volume history of fishes, superbly illustrated (1781–96). B. built up a private natural science museum, including an aquarium which, after his death, became part of the Berlin Zoological Museum.

BLOIS: Town in central France, scene of the first Ritual Murder charge on the continent of Europe (1171), as a result of which 31 Jewish men and women were burned at the stake. The tragedy is commemorated in several dirges. There was subsequent Jewish settlement in the town until recent years. Jewish pop. (1964): 175.

BLONDES, DAVID: Victim of Blood Libel charge in Vilna, 1900. His Christian maidservant complained he had wounded her to extract blood for *matzot*. The inquiry was prolonged and the Jewish population lived in fear of pogroms. At the trial, B. was acquitted of the Blood Libel accusation but sentenced to imprisonment for wounding his servant. On appeal (1902), he was completely vindicated of all charges.

BLONDHEIM, DAVID SIMON (1884–1934): US scholar. He taught Romance laguages at Johns Hopkins Univ. from 1913, and published major studies on the Judeo-Romance dialects, including Rashi's use of Old French.

BLOOD: B. is regarded in the Bible as the seat of life or even as life itself. The prohibition of its consumption is one of the seven laws given to Noah and is repeated several times. The punishment for violating this prohibition is to be "cut off" from the people. The draining of b. from a slaughtered animal is one of the fundamentals of the system of *shehitah* and the subsequent preparation of meat before it is eaten. The sprinkling of b. on the altar formed the crux of sacrificial rites symbolic of atonement; this is based on the passage "I have given (the b.) to you upon the altar to make an atonement for your souls; for it is the life of all flesh" (Lev. 17:11,14).

BLOOD LIBEL: The allegation that Jews murder Christians in order to obtain blood for the Passover or other rituals. The first mention of such a libel occurs in Josephus *(Against Apion* II, viii 95) who attributed to Apion the charge that Jews sacrifice a Greek every year in connection with the Temple service. The Greek writer, Democritus, stated that the Jews sacrifice a stranger once every seven years. It was only many centuries later, however, that the b. l. charge took on serious dimensions, being used to stir up the masses against the Jews. In the Christian world, the original charge was that at Easter the Jews

martyred a young boy in mockery of the Passion of Jesus. Owing to the approximate coincidence of Easter and Passover, the elaboration was later added that the blood was used in the preparation of the *matzot* or in the *seder* rites. The first instance of such a charge was in 1144 in connection with a Christian child named William, at NORWICH in England. The first continental case was at Blois in 1171. During the following century, blood accusations against Jews became frequent, one of the best-known being that of HUGH OF LINCOLN (1255). The case of SIMON OF TRENT (1475) is also notorious. Although no proof was ever produced, confessions were extracted from Jews by torture, and "miracles" in connection with the dead body were taken as proof that death was due to Ritual Murder. Many Christians, however, fought the blood-murder charge and declared its absurdity. Pope Gregory X defended the Jews in his bull *Sicut Judaeis* (1272) and other popes did likewise. In 1758, Cardinal Lorenzo Ganganelli (later Pope Clement XIV) drew up a memorandum condemning the libel. This was reaccepted by Pope Pius XI in 1935. Christian scholars who have written refutations include Strack, Nöldecke, Franz Delitzsch, Renan, and Thomas Masaryk. Nevertheless, the charge has persisted and in the 19th cent. there were 42 instances, the most notorious being the DAMASCUS AFFAIR (1840), TISZA-ESZLAR (1882), Corfu (1891), Xanten (1891), and POLNA (1899). In the 20th cent., the KISHINEV massacre (1903) followed the spreading of a blood accusation, while the BEILIS trial in Kiev (1913) shocked the world. Ritual Murder charges appeared in Poland (1928), Lithuania (1929), and Bulgaria (1934). The Nazis made great efforts to revive the libel during their period of hegemony.

BLOOD REDEEMER see **AVENGER OF BLOOD**

BLOOM, SOL (1870–1949): US public figure. B. was Democratic congressman from New York City 1923–49, chairman of the House of Representatives Foreign Affairs Committee 1940–7, 1949, and US delegate to the Anglo-American Conference on Refugee Problems in 1943. He directed the George Washington Bicentennial Exposition (1932) and the US Constitution Sesquicentennial Exposition (1937–9). B. was a member of the US delegation to the conference which established the UN Organization in 1945.

BLOOMFIELD: (1) *LEONARD B.* (1887–1949): US philologist; son of (2). He was professor at Ohio 1921–7, Chicago 1927–40, and Yale 1940–9. His main contribution was in general philology and in the study of American Indian languages. His standard work *Language* developed a new approach to linguistics. (2) *MAURICE B.* (1855–1928): US Sanskrit scholar; professor at Johns Hopkins Univ. from 1881. His major work was a study of the *Vedas* of which he composed a concordance, besides numerous important studies in Sanskrit literature and religion.

Solomon Bloomgarden.

BLOOMGARDEN, SOLOMON (pen-name Yehoash; 1870–1927): Yiddish poet and author. Born
in Lithuania, B. went to the US in 1890. He was a
prolific writer of dramas, poems, fables, folktales,
and stories, usually in a lyrical romantic vein, and
greatly enriched Yiddish literature by his creative
use of vocabulary. His outstanding work is his
Yiddish version of the Bible, regarded as a milestone
in the development of modern Yiddish literature. He
also translated *Avot* into Yiddish, as well as masterpieces of English, German and American literature.

BLOWITZ, ADOLPHE OPPER (or Henri Georges
Stephan de; 1825–1903): Journalist. Born in
Bohemia, he settled in France and became closely
connected with Thiers, helping him to suppress the
Marseilles commune. He served as Paris correspondent
of the *Times* (1871–1902) and was the first journalist
to feature interviews with prominent personalities. B.
was converted to Christianity.

BLUM, JULIUS (1843–1919): Financier. Of Hungarian birth, he lived in Egypt where he was
appointed director of the Austro-Egyptian bank in
1869, and finance minister from 1879 until 1890 when
he moved to Vienna to direct the Austrian Cre-
ditanstalt. He was widely known as Blum Pasha.

BLUM, LÉON (1872–1950): French statesman. At
first a literary critic and author, he became interested in the socialist movement, was elected a
deputy in 1919, and headed the French Socialist Party
from that year. He was premier in the Popular Front
government of 1936–7, vice-premier 1937–8, and again
premier for a short period in 1938. Imprisoned by
Pétain (1940), he was brought to trial at Riom (1942)
where his courageous bearing made a deep impression.
He was handed over to the Germans who deported
him to Buchenwald (1943), but was liberated in 1945.

In 1946–7, he headed a brief interim government and
was again vice-premier for a short period in 1948.
He was active in certain Jewish affairs, serving on the
council of the Jewish Agency and taking an interest in
the Jewish labor movement.

BLUM, LUDWIG (1891–1974): Painter. Of Czech
birth, he settled in Palestine in 1923. B. specialized
in still-life and portraiture.

BLUMBERG, BARUCH S. (1925–): US medical
researcher; prof. at Univ. of Pennsylvania from
1970. He was awarded the 1976 Nobel Prize in Medicine for his work on a test to detect hepatitis.

BLUME, PETER (1906–): US painter. Born in
Russia, he went to the US in 1911. His work
includes a number of "problem" pictures, being
surrealist in style and allegorical in character.

BLUMENFELD, KURT YEHUDAH (1884–1963):
Zionist leader. He was president of the German
Zionist Organization from 1924 until he settled in
Palestine in 1933. B. was active in the work of *Keren
ha-Yesod* and to a large extent was responsible for
introducing Zionist ideas into academic circles in
Central European Jewry.

BLUMENTHAL, NISSEN (1805–1903): Cantor. He
was *ḥazzan* of the Brody synagogue in Odessa
from its foundation (1841) for 55 years. His liturgical
compositions, although unpublished, were sung in
many E European synagogues.

B'NAI B'RITH (Heb. "Sons of the covenant"):
Jewish service organization (see FRATERNAL SO-
CIETIES) founded in New York in 1843. Its objectives
are moral, social, philanthropic, and educational. Its
first overseas lodge was instituted in Berlin in 1882,
and by 1970, it had over 500,000 members in 40
countries. In the US there are 190,000 men in 1,300
lodges and 150,000 women in 906 lodges. 80,000

Léon Blum.

The National Executive of B'nai B'rith meeting at the White House in 1910 with President Taft.
To his right is the B'nai B'rith president at the time, Adolf Kraus.

members are enrolled in 525 lodges in Latin America, Europe, Australia, Africa, and Israel. 38,000 young men and women belong to the B. B. youth organizations. During the period of mass Jewish immigration to the US (1880–1920), the B. B. helped in the absorption of newcomers and established several welfare institutions. Women's chapters were inaugurated in 1909, the ANTI-DEFAMATION LEAGUE in 1913, the HILLEL FOUNDATIONS in 1923, the B. B. Youth Organization (including Aleph Zadik Aleph for boys aged 14–18, B. B. Girls aged 14–19 in 1924), the Career and Counciling Service in 1938, and the Department of Adult Jewish Education in 1953. B. B. publishes the *National Jewish Monthly*. The B. B. International has its headquarters in Washington. B. B. fights for Jewish political rights, supports Israel, encourages cultural work among World Jewry, etc. B. B. in Palestine was founded in 1888, and in Israel numbers 200 lodges with 5000 members.

BNAI ZION see **FRATERNAL SOCIETIES**

BOARD OF DELEGATES OF AMERICAN ISRAELITES: The first "defense agency" for American Jews. Founded in 1859, as a reaction to the Mortara Case, the organization was created by representatives of various congregations for the purpose of upholding the good name of the Jew and combating bigotry. The Board cooperated with similar groups of other countries in protesting anti-Jewish measures, and was instrumental in persuading President LINCOLN to rescind the anti-Semitic Order of General Grant expelling Jews from the military district of Tennessee. In 1878, the Board was absorbed by the Union of

American Hebrew Congregations and was dissolved in 1925.

BOARD (properly, **LONDON COMMITTEE) OF DEPUTIES OF BRITISH JEWS:** The representative body of English Jewry. It was first organized

B'nai B'rith building in Washington, D.C.

in 1760 at the time of accession of George III, as a result of cooperation between the Ashkenazi and Sephardi communities of London, and secured the adhesion of other London synagogues as they were formed. In the 19th cent., it was extended to provincial and even overseas communities. Although primarily based on religious organizations, a number of non-religious bodies (e.g. Friendly Societies) have secured representation in more recent years. Relatively small up to the end of the 19th cent., it now comprises some 450 members. Its proceedings partly follow British parliamentary procedure. A number of committees (e.g. for Foreign Affairs, Eretz Israel, Charity Registration, Jewish Defense, etc.) deal with individual problems, periodically reporting to meetings of the full Board. From 1881 to 1946, the Board was associated with the Anglo-Jewish Association in the JOINT FOREIGN COMMITTEE, but it now deals with foreign affairs independently. It is financed by levies payable by affiliated bodies, etc. Oligarchic in control and tendency until 1917, it has since become more representative of the popular currents in English Jewish life, and strongly Zionist.

BOARD OF DEPUTIES, SOUTH AFRICAN JEWISH: The representative body of S African Jewry. The Jewish Board of Deputies for the Transvaal and Natal was founded in 1903 and was followed the next year by a similar organization in Cape Province. The two bodies were merged in 1912. The offices of the Board are in Johannesburg where the executive sits; there are provincial committees in Cape Town, Durban, Bloemfontein, and Port Elizabeth. It performs important work in connection with the defense of Jewish rights and the coordination of communal activities in S AFRICA, and has, of recent years, increasingly participated in international activities in the Jewish cause.

BOAS, FRANZ (1858–1942): Anthropologist, regarded as the father of American anthropology. He was born in Germany and participated in a meteorological expedition to Baffin Land (1883) where he became interested in Eskimos. From 1886, he was in the US and took part in several anthropological expeditions among the Indian tribes of the US, Canada, Mexico, and Puerto Rico, and from 1896–1937, taught anthropology at Columbia Univ. Many of his studies were devoted to problems of race, and in opposition to German "racial" theories, he maintained that bodily characteristics change under the influence of the environment. B. wrote on many important anthropological subjects, including problems of culture, language, art, etc.

BOAS, ISMAR ISIDOR (1858–1938): German physician; one of the leading modern specialists on gastroenterology. He discovered the frequent presence of lactic acid in the stomachic fluid of patients suffering from cancer of the stomach and (together with his teacher C.A. Eswald) introduced the technique of the test meal for examining the action of the bowels ("Boas-Eswald breakfast test").

BOAZ: (1) Husband of Ruth; ancestor of David. He lived at Bethlehem and was a man of property. (2) A column in Solomon's Temple: see JACHIN.

BOBE (Yidd.): An old woman, grandmother.

BOBEMEISE (Yiddish *Bobe*—grandmother; *meise*—story: or from BAVA-BUCH): An old wives' tale.

BODEK (Heb. "examiner"): Official who inspects a slaughtered animal to ensure that it has had no disease to render it ritually unfit for consumption. A licensed ritual slaughterer is generally termed *Shohet u-Vodek*.

BODENHEIM, MAXWELL (1895–1954): US poet and novelist. One of the founders of the Imagist movement, his works (*Minna and Myself, Against the Age, Naked on Roller Skates*, etc.) had a great vogue in the 1920's. Later, he lived in poverty and was murdered by a deranged ex-convict.

BODENHEIMER: (1) *MAX ISIDOR B.* (1865–1940): Lawyer and Zionist leader. He joined the *Hoveve Zion* in Cologne in his youth, and was one of the first to support Herzl, being on the committee which drafted the Basle Program. In 1898, he was a member of the delegation headed by Herzl which visited Palestine. From 1897 to 1921 he was a member of the general council of the World Zionist Organization and drew up the statutes of the Jewish National Fund, of which he was director 1907–14. He later joined the Revisionist movement but left it when the Revisionists withdrew from the Zionist Organization. From 1935, he lived in Jerusalem. (2) *SHIMON B.* (1897–1959): Israel zoologist; son of (1). He settled in Palestine in 1922 and was director of the department of entomology at the Agricultural Experimental Station, Rehovot. He taught zoology and entomology at the Hebrew Univ. 1928–53.

BODO (9th cent.): French proselyte. Of noble family, and high in the royal service, he became converted to Judaism in 839, under the name Eleazar, while ostensibly on a pilgrimage to Rome. He then settled in Spain where he engaged in religious polemic with Paolo Alvarez of Cordova on behalf of his faith.

BOETHUSIANS: Jewish religious political party during the century preceding the destruction of the Second Temple; closely associated with the high priesthood. Tradition attributes their origin to Boethus, a pupil of ANTIGONUS OF SOKHO, but more probably they were connected with Simeon ben Boethus (high priest in 25–24 BCE, Herod's father-in-law, and a Sadducee leader). The views of the B. were similar to, but not always identical with, those of the Sadducees. An inscription suggests that the family of Boethus belonged to the BENE HEZIR.

BOGEN, BORIS DAVID (1869–1929): US social worker. Born in Russia, B. settled in the US in 1888.

He was director of Jewish charities in Cincinnati 1904–10, director-general of the American Joint Distribution Committee during World War I, and international secretary of B'nai B'rith 1925–9.

BOGORAZ, VLADIMIR GERMANOVICH (1865–1936): Russian revolutionary and ethnographer. Banished to Siberia in 1888–96, he investigated the Chukchees and later participated in expeditions to the N Pacific. He took part in the 1905 revolution and was after 1917, curator of the Museum of Anthropology and Ethnography at Leningrad.

BOGROV: (1) *DMITRI B.* (1888–1911): Russian anarchist and secret police agent; grandson of (2). In 1911, he assassinated the Russian premier, Stolypin, for which he was executed. (2) *GRIGORI B.* (1825–1885): Russian author. He wrote historical novels, some of which *(A Jew's Notes, Kidnapped)* sharply criticized Jewish leadership and advocated radical reforms. B. tended to assimilation, supporting Jacob Gordon's "Spiritual Biblical Brotherhood" which held that Jews should abandon the Talmud as a precondition for receiving equal rights. He was baptized shortly before his death.

BOHEMIA see **CZECHOSLOVAKIA**

BÖHM, ADOLF (1873–1941): Zionist historian and leader. He was born in Bohemia and settled in Vienna where he was one of the first Zionists advocating practical work in Palestine. B. published several works on Palestinian financial and agrarian problems, edited the German monthly for Palestinography *Palästina,* and wrote a monumental history of Zionism (down to 1926). He was for many years on the board of the Jewish National Fund.

BOKHARA: Province of the Central Asiatic republic of UZBEKISTAN, USSR (see also TURKESTAN). Jews were first recorded in B. in the 13th cent., probably originating from Persia. During the 17th–18th cents. they possessed an independent cultural life. Notable among them were Yusuf Yahudi, Benjamin ben Mishal, Elisha ben Samuel, and Ibraham ibn Abu al-Khair who constituted a school of poets in Judeo-Persian. Bokharan Jewry was nevertheless on the decline until their Jewish life was revived by R Joseph Maaravi, sent to them from Palestine in 1793, and by refugees from Meshed, Persia, in 1839. The community was composed mainly of traders and craftsmen and had a monopoly of the silk trade, widely ramified in the 19th cent. Immigration to Palestine began in the 1880's. Jewish pop. (1970): c. 12,000.

BOLECHOV: Town in W Ukraine. Jews received equal rights with Christians in its foundation charter (1612). They were largely cattle- and wine-dealers, this being the profession of the autobiographer BER OF B. In the 19th cent., under Austrian rule, B. constituted the center of a parliamentary district in which the Jews were in the majority. The Jewish population predominated until the Nazi invasion (1941) when those who did not escape to the interior were exterminated.

BOLECHOV, BER OF see **BER OF BOLECHOV**

BOLIVIA: S American republic. Jewish immigration from Europe began in 1905 but was negligible until the 1920's when it came mainly from Poland and, after 1933, from Germany. The Jewish population (1973) numbered 2,000, chiefly in La Paz and Cochabamba. The *Comité Central Judio de Bolivia* is the representative body of the entire community. The *Vaad ha-Ḥinnukh* maintains Jewish schools. The Jewish press consists of two German monthlies.

BOLOGNA: City of N Italy. The first authentic information relating to Jews is an expulsion order of 1171. In the 14th cent., B. became a center for the loan-bankers, mainly from Rome, on whose activities there were no restrictions. Notwithstanding occasional anti-Jewish acts (enforcement of Jewish badge, 1421; riots, 1530), B. in the 15th and 16th cents. was one of the most important Jewish communities of Italy, many famous scholars being associated with it. A printing-press was set up there in 1477. Reaction came in the middle of the following century; a ghetto was established in 1556, and the Jews expelled in 1569. The community was temporarily re-established 1586–93, but thereafter lapsed until the 19th cent. B. was the scene of the kidnapping of Edgardo MORTARA (1858). The community suffered severely during the Nazi persecution but has been reconstituted and numbers about 250.

BOLSHEVISM: Political theory propounded by the left-wing majority of the Russian Social Democratic Party, which crystallized under Lenin in 1903. Its forerunner, the "Group for the Emancipation of Labor" (1883), was led by the Jewish socialist, Pavel AXELROD. The Bolshevik wing, in agreement with MARX, held that revolution must come by armed uprising and the dictatorship of the industrial proletariat. Chief among Lenin's Jewish collaborators were KAMENEV and ZINOVIEV; TROTSKY joined the Bolsheviks only in 1917. In 1903, Lenin, supported by MARTOV, opposed the retention within the party on a federal basis of the Jewish BUND (to which the Social Democratic Party largely owed its foundation in 1898). Lenin stated that the Jews were not a nation as they had no territory and he advocated their assimilation. This became the Bolshevik attitude, later only partly modified (although the Bund was readmitted as a distinct body in 1906), as the assimilated Jewish Bolsheviks were indifferent to Jewish loyalties. The Bolshevik Party initially set its face against anti-Semitism, dubbing it "the tool of reaction." See also COMMUNISM.

BOMBAY: Indian port. European Jews, mainly associated with the London Sephardi community, settled there in the 17th cent. and apparently established a short-lived community in the 18th. B. was also the greatest center of the BENE ISRAEL. In the 19th cent., Jews from Baghdad went to B., forming their own community. The city had a Jewish population of 3,607 in 1974, but many of these subsequently emigrated to Israel.

*BOMBERG, DANIEL (d. 1549): Hebrew printer. Born in Antwerp, he established a Hebrew publishing house in Venice in 1516. During the 32 years of his press's existence, about 200 books were published, including the first complete editions of the Palestinian and Babylonian Talmuds, the Tosephta, the Rabbinic Bible, etc.; his pagination of the Talmud has become standard. B. cut a new Hebrew typeface, and Hebrew scholars assisted him as advisers and readers. In 1539, he returned to Antwerp, but the press continued to function under the direction of his son David until 1548.

BONAPARTE see NAPOLEON

BONDI, AUGUST (1833–1907): US abolitionist. Born in Austria, B. participated in the 1848 revolutionary movement and on its failure, went to the US. In 1855, B. and his partners, Jacob Benjamin and Theodore Weiner, joined the military company organized in Kansas by John Brown and fought under him against the pro-slavery forces in the battles of Black Jack and Osawatomie. After serving throughout the Civil War, B. held various public offices in Salina, Kansas.

BONET DE LATTES see LATTES, BONET DE

BONFILS, IMMANUEL (or B. of Tarascon; fl. 14th cent.): S French astronomer. He wrote many works

August Bondi.

on mathematics, astronomy, and astrology. His *Shesh Kenaphayim* ("Six Wings"; cf. Is. 6:2) was translated into Latin and became known in E Europe where it introduced new astronomical and mathematical conceptions.

BONFILS (Heb. *Tov Elem*), **JOSEPH BEN SAMUEL** (fl. 11th cent.): French talmudist; born in Narbonne and active in Limoges and Anjou in Central France. His literary compositions were many-sided, including religious poems, biblical and talmudic commentaries, and codifications.

BONN, MORITZ JULIUS (1873–1965): Political economist. He was professor at Munich and later in the US and London. His works include *The Crisis of European Democracy* and *The American Experiment*. His autobiographical *Wandering Scholar* is rich in observations on Jewish life and anti-Semitism in Germany.

BOOK: The Hebrew word *sepher* originally meant any written document, even a letter, but in due course, it came to denote a b. in the modern sense. Originally b.'s were written in the form of a scroll (MEGILLAH); later, under Roman influence, the volume (codex) form was adopted. Older Hebrew b.'s (such as those of the Bible) were small, but the tendency was to increase them in size by bringing smaller compilations together. Henceforth, a number of Jewish books were of very great dimensions – e.g. the Talmud which was sometimes comprised in a single volume. This was possible only through writing in a small hand with lavish use of abbreviations. In the later Middle Ages, illuminations were common in some Hebrew b.'s, e.g. the Passover HAGGADAH. The Jews were among the pioneers in medieval Europe in the use of paper instead of parchment for writing b.'s. They were interested in PRINTING from the outset, and it was considered a "holy craft." Italy, then Amsterdam, and later E Europe became the great centers of Jewish book-production and diffusion. In medieval mss and the earliest printed b.'s there is no title-page, details regarding the production of the work being embodied in the colophon after the text; in some INCUNABULA this is arranged to give artistic effects. The earliest title-page in Hebrew printing appears in Italy, c. 1520. To lend b.'s for study was regarded among the Jews as highly meritorious, and the Ḥasidim held that b.'s were to be found even in heaven. There have been many notable Jewish book-collectors some of whose LIBRARIES are now in various public collections.

BOOK OF JASHAR see JASHAR, BOOK OF

BOOK OF LIFE: Divine book in which God is believed to inscribe the righteous "who are to be recorded for life." In the Bible, omission from the Book of Life (or the Book of God) is synonymous with death (Exod. 32:32; Ps. 69:29). Apocryphal works speak of the Book of Life and the Book of

Bookplates of Jewish interest.

Death but tend to interpret the concepts eschatologically. The Jewish liturgy retains the literal meaning and associates the annual "writing" of individuals in the Books of Life and Death with the New Year and the "sealing" with the Day of Atonement.

BOOK OF THE WARS OF THE LORD see **BIBLE, LOST BOOKS OF**

BOOKPLATES: Although b. of Christian Hebraists embodying Hebrew words are known from the early 16th cent. (H. Pomar, 1525) no b. of Jews occur before the 18th cent.; the earliest recorded is that of Isaac Mendes of London, engraved by the Jewish artist Benjamin Levi in 1746. The first b. of a Jew bearing Hebrew lettering is ascribed to the same artist. B., sometimes embodying Jewish symbols and motifs, became common among Jews in the 19th and 20th cents. Among the better-known designers of such

Jewish b. are E. M. Lilien and H. Struck. In Israel, b. bearing only Hebrew lettering are common. An exhibition of Jewish b. held in Jerusalem in 1955 comprised 800 items.

BOOKS, BURNING OF: The systematic attack on Jewish literature in the Middle Ages began with the Disputation of Paris (1240), which was followed by the condemnation of the Talmud and the burning of 24 cartloads of Hebrew books in Paris on June 17, 1242. There were similar onslaughts later – e.g. in Rome (Pentecost, 1322). The attack on Jewish literature was renewed in 1553, when on New Year's day (Sep. 9) thousands of volumes were burned in Rome. This example was followed in succeeding years all over Italy, sometimes even copies of the Bible being destroyed. Burning on a smaller scale took place after searches in the Jewish quarters until

Torah Scrolls from the Worms synagogue burned by the Nazis.

the end of the Ghetto Period. In 1757, copies of the Talmud were burned in Poland after the disputation with the Frankists. On May 10, 1933, vast numbers of books and volumes, many by Jewish authors, were burned by the Nazis throughout Germany.

BOOKS, PROHIBITED: The campaign of the Catholic Church against Jewish literature began in the 13th cent. at the time of the Disputation of Barcelona, but it is accurate to speak of Prohibited Books only from the period of the publication of the *Index Librorum Prohibitorum* by the Council of Trent in 1564. This included "the Talmud, its glosses, annotations, interpretations, and expositions," although for a time censored editions were permitted. Generally speaking, however, the *Index* was concerned only with books in Latin or European languages, those in Hebrew being dealt with by the CENSORSHIP. Within the Jewish community, attempts were made to ban the writings of Maimonides because of their rational tendencies (13th cent.), of Immanuel of Rome because of their sensuousness (16th cent.), and of Azariah Dei Rossi because of their spirit of criticism (16th cent.). None of these attempts was, however, permanently successful and, on the whole, such suppression was alien to the Jewish spirit.

BOOTHS see **TABERNACLES**

BORAISHA, MENAHEM (1888–1949): Yiddish poet and journalist. He was born in Poland and went to the US in 1915. A prolific writer, his poems, marked by spiritual and mystical qualities, appeared in many publications.

BORCHARDT, GEORG (pseudonym Georg Hermann; 1871—c. 1943): German novelist and art critic. He depicted Jewish life in mid-19th cent. Berlin in *Jettchen Gebert* and its sequel *Henriette Jacoby*. His *Die Nacht des Dr. Herzfeld* expresses

his staunch adherence to liberal Judaism. With the advent of Hitler, he fled to Holland but was arrested by the Germans in 1940 and deported to his death. His brother, *LUDWIG B.* (1863–1938), was a noted Egyptologist who discovered the famous bust of Queen Nefertiti.

BORCHARDT, RUDOLF (1877–1945): German poet and translator. He achieved a distinguished if archaistic, German style. Although a fervent assimilationist and German patriot, he died a refugee in the Tyrol.

BORDEAUX: Port of SW France. Jews are first mentioned there in the 6th cent. At the end of the 11th cent., they dwelt in a special quarter, but were later permitted to live in the city. Under English rule (1152–1453), their condition was superior to that of the Jews in the rest of France. In the 16th–18th cents. the commercial importance of B. attracted large numbers of fugitive Marranos who continued to live under the disguise of Christianity although their full observance of Judaism was generally known. In 1706, freedom of worship was granted. The arrival of some Jews from Avignon and Alsace in the 18th cent. led to friction within the community which lasted until the granting of civil rights after the French Revolution (1790). The community, still officially Sephardi, numbers (1973): 6,000.

BORN, MAX (1882–1970): Physicist. Dismissed from his post at Göttingen by Nazis in 1933, he went to England, returning to Germany after 1945. An authority on the quantum theory, atomic structure, the dynamics of matter, and relativity, he was awarded the Nobel Prize in physics in 1954. He wrote an autobiography *My life and My Views*. B. did not identify himself with Judaism.

BÖRNE, LUDWIG (originally Löb Baruch; 1786–1837): Memeber of the "Young Germany" movement and essayist who, with Heine, originated the feuilleton and aroused the German press from its lethargy. He rebelled against his traditional background and studied at various universities. In 1813, he was forced out of his municipal post in Frankfort-on-Main, submitted to baptism (1818), and emigrated to Paris in 1830. From then on, especially in his *Briefe aus Paris*, he poured his libertarian convictions into a style of such brilliance and acuteness that his collected works became a minor classic of German literature, appearing in many editions, but proscribed by the Bundestag in 1835. His zeal for mankind included the Jews as individuals, but not as a people nor as members of a faith.

BOROCHOV, DOV BER (1881–1917): Founder and leader of the *Poale Zion* party. Born in the Ukraine, he early joined the Russian Social Democratic Party but later became a Zionist, playing an important role in the opposition to the Uganda project. He helped to organize the workers' Zionist

Dov Ber Borochov.

movement, being among the founders of POALE ZION in 1906, and the secretary of the World Confederation of *Poale Zion* most of the time from its foundation in 1907 until his death. He left Russia in 1907, and from 1914 continued political activity in the US where his analysis of Jewish strike activity was important to the labor movement. He died in Russia, after having returned to participate in the Congress of Minorities convened by the Kerensky regime. His chief ideological contribution was his Marxist analysis of the economic structure and social situation of the Jewish people, pointing to the physical inevitability of territorial concentration in Palestine as a means of occupational redistribution and economic normalization. B. also made contributions to Yiddish philology.

BOSNIA AND HERZEGOVINA: Former Turkish, then Austro-Hungarian province, now in Yugoslavia. Jews of Sephardi origin are first mentioned in B. (SARAJEVO) in 1551. In the 19th cent., they received equal rights from the Turkish government, and some were elected to the parliament at Constantinople. Ashkenazi Jews settled in Sarajevo when B. was ruled by Austro-Hungary (1878/1908–18). At the beginning of World War II, there were in B. and H. 14,000 Jews, the great majority of whom were annihilated by the Nazis and local anti-Semites.

BOSTANAI BEN ḤANINAI (c. 620—c. 675): First Babylonian exilarch after the Arab conquest. The caliph Omar confirmed his succession to the exilarchate (previously held by his father), appointed him a member of the Council of State, and gave him as wife a daughter of the former Persian king, Chosroes. After prolonged controversy, her children

were recognized as legitimate. Many remarkable legends are reported in connection with B.'s birth and career.

BOSTON: US city. Individual Jews lived there during the last half of the 17th cent. About 1830, a few Algerian Jews are said to have settled in B. A decade later, Jewish immigrants from Germany, Poland, and Austria laid the foundation for a permanent community life. This group of settlers included several small manufacturers, as well as merchants and peddlers. The first congregation, Ohabei Shalom, was formed in 1843, and in 1852, a synagogue was erected. A secession in 1854 resulted in the establishment of a second congregation composed mostly of German Jws. In 1858, a Hebrew school was founded and existed for 5 years. Tremendous growth in B.'s Jewish population as a result of the arrival of E European immigrants, helped B. to develop culturally, educationally, and communally from 1880 on. In 1973 B. had 180,000 Jews with nearly forty congregations and an organized Hebrew school system, supervised and directed by the Bureau of Jewish Education, culminating in the Hebrew Teachers' College, now located in Brookline. B.'s Jewry maintains a large number of institutions and is an important factor in the city's political life. The Associated Jewish Philanthropies was established in 1895 and the Jewish Community Council in 1944. In recent years, a tendency has become apparent for Jews to move to suburbs and transfer their institutions there from the older Jewish population centers. A weekly

Zionist House, Boston, Mass.

newspaper, *The Jewish Advocate*, published in B. since 1903, serves the Jewry of E New England.

BOTANY: Branch of BIOLOGY concerned with plants. About 100 plant names are mentioned in the Bible, almost all being common to Palestine and Egypt. The Mishnah refers to 180, all in connection with various aspects of the halakhah, such as the mixture of heterogeneous species and the grains permitted for making the unleavened bread. Most of these plant names are borrowed from the Greek. Classification systems in the Bible and talmudic literature are elementary (such as in the different ritual blessings for "fruit of the tree" and "fruit of the ground"), but Maimonides succeeded in presenting a fairly full and systematic classification (*Mishneh Torah; Kilayim* 1:8–9). Jewish scholars of the Middle Ages helped to transmit the Greek writing on b.: thus, in the 10th cent., Ḥasdai Ibn Shaprut collaborated in translating Dioscorides' work on b. into Arabic. The earliest scientific description of a large number of plants is in the *Colloquies* of the Marrano physician Garcia d'Orta (16th cent.). Outstanding modern Jewish botanists have included Ferdinand Cohen, Julius von Sachs, Nathaniel Pringsheim, and Eduard Strasburger.

BOTVINNIK, MIKHAIL (1911–): Russian chess master. At the age of 13, he participated in the All-Russian tournament at Leningrad. In 1931, he first won the all-Russian championship. He was world chess-champion, 1948–57, 1958–60, and 1961–3.

BOXING see **SPORT**

BRAFMAN, JACOB (c. 1825–1879): Russian convert and anti-Jewish author. He taught Hebrew at the seminary for priests in Minsk, later serving as censor of Hebrew books at Vilna and St. Petersburg. In 1869, he published *Kniga Kagala* ("Book of the Kahal") purporting to reproduce the resolutions of the Minsk Jewish community between 1789 and 1869. The work, extensively utilized by anti-Semites, contained an element of truth distorted by inaccurate quotations and forgeries.

BRAGANÇA: Town in N Portugal. A Jewish community, first mentioned in 1279, existed in B. in the Middle Ages. Later, there was a large Marrano element in its population. It is now the most important Marrano center in Portugal, with a loosely-organized religious life.

BRAHAM (originally **ABRAHAM**), **JOHN** (c. 1774–1856): English singer. Formerly a choirboy at the Great Synagogue in London, he became famous as the finest English tenor of his age. He also made unsuccessful experiments in theatrical management. His daughter Frances (1821–1879), later Lady Waldegrave, was a leading political hostess. B. left Judaism.

BRAHINSKI, MANI LEIB (pen-name Mani Leib; 1883–1953): US Yiddish poet and journalist.

Born in Russia where he was early involved in the revolutionary movement, B. went to the US in 1905. His verse is characterized by a lyric mood, and some of his poems, set to music, became popular songs. He translated several Russian novels into Yiddish. B. was on the editorial staff of *Forverts* 1916–53, and edited a number of Yiddish literary periodicals.

BRAININ, REUBEN (1862–1939): Hebrew author. A native of White Russia, he lived in Vienna and Berlin, engaging in fertile literary activity, chiefly as journalist, literary critic, and editor. At the beginning of the 20th cent., he was among the cheif spokesmen in Hebrew criticism demanding the enrichment of Hebrew literature through the infusion of "general human" topics and new literary forms. From 1909 until his death, he lived, with few interruptions, in the US and Canada. During his later years, B. devoted himself to Hebrew and Yiddish journalism and sympathized with Jewish settlement in the Russian province of Birobidjan which he had occasion to visit. He edited several Hebrew and Yiddish periodicals.

BRAMPTON (originally **BRÃNDAO**), **SIR EDWARD** (c. 1440–1508): Medieval adventurer. Born in Portugal, he was baptized in England, achieved success as a soldier of fortune at the close of the Wars of the Roses, and was governor of Guernsey 1482–5. He later returned to Portugal where he founded a noble family.

BRAMSON, LEON (1869–1941): Russian communal worker. He was active in the Society for the Propagation of Enlightenment among the Jews of Russia and was from 1894, inspector of its schools. In 1899–1906, he directed ICA in Russia and conducted a statistical survey of the economic position of Jews in the Pale (2 vols., 1904). In 1906, B. was elected to the Duma of which he later wrote a history. From 1908, he directed ORT in Russia. He settled in Berlin in 1920 and headed ORT's world center. In the Nazi period, he moved to France.

BRANDEIS, LOUIS DEMBITZ (1856–1941): Justice of the US Supreme Court and Zionist leader. He was born in Louisville, Kentucky, to parents who had fled Bohemia in 1848 to find liberty in America. After a long and successful career at the bar in Boston, he was appointed to the Supreme Court by President Wilson in 1916 and served until his retirement in 1939. He played a leading part in American Zionism, being honorary president of the Zionist Organization of America 1918–21, and of the World Zionist Organization 1920–1, resigning after differences of opinion with Chaim Weizmann. His wide experience at the bar helped to make him an expert in the growing complexities and implications of a large-scale industrial society. B. became an effective champion of the common interest against the "curse of bigness." He defended the public interest against encroachments by the utilities,

Louis D. Brandeis.
(Bust by Eleanor Pratt, presented to the US Supreme Court
in behalf of the American Bar).

insurance companies, and railroads. His efforts eventually secured passage of legislation to fix minimum wages and maximum hours. By the manner of his presentation, he changed the direction of constitutional argument before the Supreme Court. As formulator of a protocol agreement in the New York Ladies' Garment Industry (1910–16), he laid the groundwork for mediation and arbitration in the Jewish industries. As judge, B. maintained and developed the same unrelenting insistence on facts and the same humble acceptance of them; the same unswerving following where reason led. With his colleague, Justice Oliver Wendell Holmes, he insisted that the Supreme Court must not shackle with dogmas of the past the legislative efforts – whether of individual states or of the American nation – to meet new public needs in new situations by new means. But he would not allow legislative majorities to become strong enough to override the liberties of individual men, however unpopular. Indifferent to things Jewish during most of his life, he became sympathetic to Zionism about 1910, when he was induced to help settle the great cloakmakers' strike in New York. Sympathy soon passed into commitment and impassioned activity in behalf of the Zionist cause, particularly after European Jewry was divided by World War I. His elevation to the Supreme Court inevitably curtailed his activity but not his concern or his devotion. He had scant patience with those who feared the collision of loyalty and feeling in being an American Zionist. The sternest days of World War II left his faith in Zion unshaken.

BRANDEIS CAMP INSTITUTE: Institute established in 1941. Originally sponsored by the American Zionist Youth Commission, the BCI became an independent organization in 1948. It conducts a large youth camp, a children's camp, and institutes for adults in Santa Susana, Calif.

BRANDEIS UNIVERSITY: US educational institution named for Louis Dembitz BRANDEIS. It was opened in 1948 as a corporate contribution of American Jewry to American higher education. A coeducational liberal arts college, it is located in

Julius Kalman Science Center at Brandeis University.

Waltham, Mass., near Boston. The campus covers over 250 acres and has over 70 major faculties, with several others planned. The University's undergraduate College of Arts and Sciences is composed of four schools: Science, Social Science, Humanities, and Creative Arts. It granted its first BA degrees in 1952. The Graduate School of Arts and Sciences, opened in 1953, now offers Master of Arts, Master of Fine Arts, and Doctor of Philosophy degrees in 19 areas of study: chemistry, English and American literature, history of ideas, biology, music, Near Eastern and Judaic studies, mathematics, biophysics, chemistry, American civilization, anthropology, Mediterranean studies, philosophy, physics, sociology, and psychology. It also conducts an institute in Near Eastern studies in Israel. In 1976 there were 3,264 students. Abram Leon Sachar, its first president became chancellor in 1968. Marvin Bronstein has been president since 1972.

BRANDENBURG: Former state in E Germany. Jewish settlement is recorded from the 13th cent. The community flourished until the 15th cent. when agitation led to its expulsion (1446). A charge of Host Desecration at Berlin led to the execution of several Jews and a further expulsion (1510). The Jews were readmitted, but an allegation that the elector Joachim II had been killed by his Jewish mint-master, Lippold, led to their being expelled again (1573). The community was renewed in 1670. For the following period, see PRUSSIA.

BRANDES: (1) *CARL EDVARD (COHEN) B.* (1847–1931): Danish author and statesman. One of the chief spokesmen of the Radical Party, he was minister of finance 1909–10, 1913–20. B. was the author of plays, mainly on social themes, and was a leading dramatic critic (chiefly in the daily paper *Politiken* which he helped to found), writing two works on contemporary actors. He translated parts of the Bible into Danish. (2) *GEORG B.* (Morris Cohen; 1842–1927): Danish critic; brother of (1). Under the influence of Taine, he emphasized the sociological groundwork of art but later modified this view. He fought for the recognition of new writers from Ibsen, Björnsen, and Strindberg to Nietzsche. His most famous work is *Hovedströmminger i det 19de Aarhundredes Literature* ("Main Currents of Nineteenth Century Literature," 4 vols. 1872–5); he also wrote monographs on Lassalle, Disraeli, Shakespeare, Goethe, Voltaire, Michelangelo, Julius Caesar, etc. His last work denied the historicity of Jesus. Indifferent to Judaism until late in life, he raised his voice for Dreyfus and for the oppressed Jews of E Europe. After World War I, he embraced Zionism with characteristic courage and fervor.

BRANDSTÄTTER, MORDECAI DAVID (1844–1928): Galician Hebrew novelist. After an Orthodox upbringing, he became interested in Haskalah,
and from 1869, contributed to Smolenskin's journal *Ha-Shaḥar*. His stories contain descriptions of Hasidic life in Galicia, which introduced an element of humor into Hebrew literature.

BRANN, MARCUS (1849–1920): Historian. He succeeded Graetz in the chair of history at the Breslau Rabbinical Seminary, which he held from 1891 until his death. He was co-editor of *Germania Judaica*, a topographical encyclopedia of German Jewish history, and author of many works on Jewish history, literature, and bibliography.

BRATISLAVA (Ger. Pressburg; Hung. Pozsony): Capital of SLOVAKIA. Jewish martyrs are recorded there in the 13th cent. During the next two centuries, the Jews were serfs of the king. There were 3,000 Jews in B. in 1526 before their expulsion by Maria of Hapsburg. A ghetto was enforced 1712–1840. The community was famed as a center of rabbinic learning; strictly Orthodox, all secular learning was rigorously opposed. The Jews developed culturally and economically during the period of the Czechoslovak Republic and B. was the seat of all Jewish organizations in Slovakia. The Nazis entered in 1939 and by 1942 the community had been completely

Bratislava: Entrance to the Bet Din.

destroyed. It was reconstituted after World War II. Jewish pop. (1970): 1,500.

BRATZLAV: Town in the Ukraine where Jews are said to have been settled in the 14th cent. The community defended the town against the Mongols in 1551 but was annihilated in the Chmielnicki uprising (1648). After Naḥman (of B.) settled there (1802), the town became an important Ḥasidic center.

BRAUDES, REUBEN ASHER (1851–1902): Hebrew author. Born in Vilna, he wandered through S Russia in his younger days and from 1875, lived in Warsaw where he edited the monthly *Ha-Boker Or* 1876–9. In 1882–4, he was in Rumania and edited a Yiddish paper in Bucharest. He subsequently lived in Lvov and in 1896, settled in Vienna. B. was one of the leading Hebrew novelists of his time, and his *Shete ha-Ketzavot* ("Two Extremes") stresses the shortcomings of the two extremes – Haskalah and unbending Orthodoxy – and advocates Jewish nationalism. His stories reflect the intellectual changes taking place in E European Jewish society at the end of the 19th cent. and display psychological insight. B. was for some time editor of the Yiddish version of the official Zionist weekly, *Die Welt*.

BRAUNSTEIN, MENAḤEM MENDEL (pen-name Mibashan; 1858–1944): Hebrew author. He propagated Hebrew culture in his native Rumania and settled in Palestine in 1914. His works include poems, stories, feuilletons, and translations.

BRAZIL: S American country. Fernando de Noronha, the Brazilian pioneer (1503), is thought to have been a Marrano. Later Marrano immigrants from Portugal, some deported by the Inquisition, fostered the sugar and tobacco industries and developed rice and cotton plantations. Inquisitional visitations in 1591–5 and 1618 led many Marranos to emigrate. Some Jews went to Bahia from Holland during its brief period of Dutch rule (1624–5). When the Dutch conquered the Pernambuco region (1631), the Marranos returned openly to Judaism, and numerous immigrants came from Holland. Communities now flourished in Itamaracá and Recife, where Isaac Aboab served as rabbi. After the Portuguese capture of Recife (1654), the Jews had to leave, some returning to Holland, others establishing Jewish communities throughout the W Indies and in New York, etc. In 1822, with the proclamation of Brazilian independence, some Marranos reverted to Judaism. Thereafter, European Jews began to immigrate and communities were established in Belem, São Paolo, Recife, Bahia, Manaos, and especially Rio de Janeiro. Immigration was considerable after World War I. ICA was active in B. from 1903. German Jews arrived from 1933, and many individual immigrants went there after World War II. The 1973 Jewish pop. was 155,000 (including 15,000 Sephardim), mainly merchants, manufacturers, factory and property owners, and professional workers. The Confederation of Jewish Organizations, established in 1951, represents the Jewish communities of Rio de Janiero (Jewish pop. 60,000), São Paolo (c. 70,000), Porto Alegre (10,000), Curitiba (2,000), Recife (1,000), and smaller communities. There are 38 Jewish schools with an enrollment of over 14,000 of whom 4,000 were in kindergarten. The remainder accounted for 20% of Jewish children of school age. There are 14 Jewish newspapers and periodicals.

BREAD: In the Bible b. is considered the main element of any meal. The benediction prescribed by the rabbis before partaking of b. takes precedence over that for any other solid food. Thus, the blessing over the Sabbath b. (the *ḥallah*) became a feature of the Sabbath ritual. The full grace after meals is recited only when b. has been eaten with the meal.

BREAKING OF THE VESSELS (Heb. *shevirat ha-kelim*): Kabbalistic term referring to a primordial catastrophe that occurred in the early stages of Creation. According to Isaac Luria, the Divine light emanating from Adam Kadmon into Creation, burst the vessels which were to "contain" it and many of the Divine sparks fell into chaos. Since then the whole cosmos is in need of restoration or redemption (Tikkun).

BREASTPLATE: One of the sacred garments of the high priest. It consisted of a square gold frame in

Torah breastplate. (Breslau, 18th cent.).

Yoseph Ḥayyim Brenner.

which were set twelve gems of different colors representing the tribes of Israel and holding the URIM AND THUMMIM. The b. was worn by the high priest over the ephod and attached to it. The term is now applied to the silver ornament (*tas*) placed in front of the *Sepher Torah*, sometimes made in a similar form.

BREMEN: German port. Jews are mentioned there from the early 14th cent. when their occupations were restricted by law to money lending. Jewish residence was forbidden in 1373, and renewed only during the French occupation in the early 19th cent. Most were expelled, notwithstanding international protests, in 1820, but from 1848, their presence was permitted and in 1876, a synagogue was opened. 1,314 Jews lived in B. in 1933, but the community was liquidated under the Nazis. Jewish pop. (1969): 150.

BRENNER, VICTOR DAVID (1871–1924): US medalist. Born in Russia, B. went to the US in 1890 and became a leading designer of medallions, plaques, and tablets, renowned for his mastery of bas-relief portraiture. He created the head of Lincoln on the one-cent coin.

BRENNER, YOSEPH ḤAYYIM (1881–1921): Hebrew author. Born in the Ukraine, he began to edit the Bund newspaper in Homel in 1898. His first sketches describing Jewish poverty in Russia appeared in 1900. Shortly afterwards, his novels *Ba-Ḥoreph* ("In Winter") and *Mi-Saviv ha-Nekuddah* ("Around the Point") came out in serial form in *Ha-Shiloaḥ*. In 1904–7, he lived in London working as a printer's compositor and publishing the monthly Hebrew journal *Ha-Meorer* which attacked the barren verbosity of Jewish political life. Later, B. went to

Lvov where he edited the collection *Revivim* (subsequently continued in Jerusalem and Jaffa). In 1909, he settled in Palestine where he worked as a laborer, but before long returned to journalism and became a leader of the workers' movement. His stories realistically depict contemporary Palestinian life. He also published critical essays and translated world classics into Hebrew. In 1919, B. began to edit *Ha-Adamah*, the journal of *Aḥdut ha-Avodah*. In 1921, he was murdered by Arabs near Jaffa.

BRENTANO, AUGUST (1831–1886): US bookseller whose business, founded in 1858, developed into one of the largest bookselling chains in the US.

BRESLAU: Capital of Silesia. Jews lived there from the 12th cent., enjoying ducal privileges, but the community was wiped out at the time of the Black Death (1349). In 1453, an accusation of Host Desecration instigated by the Franciscan John of Capistrano led to the martyrdom of 41 Jews and the banishment of the rest. A new community was founded in the 17th cent. and prospered after Silesia was annexed to Prussia in 1741; it was reorganized in 1754 and later held a key position in the modernist movement. As in the rest of Prussia, the status of the Jews improved in the course of the 19th cent. The foundation of the conservative BRESLAU RABBINICAL SEMINARY in 1854 made B. a center of Jewish intellectual life in Germany. Before 1933, there were in B. 20,200 Jews. B., renamed Wrocław, is now under Polish rule, and its Jewish community (now of Polish origin) numbers 3,000 (1973).

BRESLAU RABBINICAL SEMINARY: The first rabbinical seminary in Germany. It was founded in 1854 with funds left by Jonas Fränckel and propagated "historical" Judaism. Its first president was Zacharias FRANKEL. In 1938, it was closed by the Nazis.

BRESSLER, DAVID M. (1879–1942): Social worker. Born in Germany, B. went to the US as a child. Admitted to the bar in 1901, he turned to social welfare work and was manager of the INDUSTRIAL REMOVAL OFFICE, a position he held till 1916 when he became the first secretary of the American Joint Distribution Committee, later being appointed to the New York State Planning Board. He served as a non-Zionist member of the council of the Jewish Agency.

BREST-LITOVSK (BRISK): Town in White Russia, USSR. In 1388, the Jews of B. received extensive privileges from the duke of Lithuania. Their legal position deteriorated at the end of the 15th cent., and in 1495, they were expelled together with the rest of the Lithuanian Jews. In 1503, they returned, and in 1511, the charter of 1388 was confirmed. The community flourished materially and intellectually throughout the 16th cent., its yeshivah being renowned. The Jews of B. played a considerable role in the

Council of the Four Lands, and from 1623, in the Council of Lithuania. They were massacred during the Chmielnicki pogroms (1648–9) and, although communal life was slowly reconstructed, the hegemony of Jewish life in Lithuania passed to Vilna. Nevertheless, important scholars lived there in the 18th–19th cents., and in 1914, two-thirds of the town's 60,000 inhabitants were Jews. B. suffered severely in World War I, and by 1939, the Jewish population was reduced to 20,000 (50% of the total). The vast majority of these were destroyed by the Germans and the few survivors dispersed. Jewish pop. (1970): 2,000.

BREUER: (1) *ISAAC B.* (1883–1946): Leader of Orthodox Jewry; son of (2). He lived in Frankfort on the Main and settled in Palestine in 1936. A qualified rabbi and a lawyer by profession, he was among the founders and leaders of *Agudat Israel* and published a number of works on Judaism and Jewish problems. (2) *SOLOMON B.* (1850–1926): Leader of Orthodox Jewry. Born in Hungary, he succeeded his father-in-law Samson Raphael Hirsch in 1889 as rabbi of the Orthodox community in Frankfort on the Main. B. founded the *Verband orthodoxer Rabbiner* ("Union of Orthodox Rabbis") in Germany and led the extremist wing within *Agudat Israel.*

BREUER, JOSEPH (1842–1925): Viennese neurologist. He collaborated with Sigmund Freud, but differed with him on the theory of psychoanalysis.

BRIBERY: The conveyance of a gift in order to prevent judgment. B. is stated in the Pentateuch to "blind the eyes of the wise and prevent the words of of the righteous" (Deut. 16:19) and is repeatedly condemned in biblical and talmudic sources. Bribes taken for upholding justice are equally reprehensible. A judge is morally disqualified from adjudicating a case by the slightest – even accidental – favor (e.g. if one of the parties helps him to alight from a ferry). Judges could take payment for loss of time only if it came from both parties. When judges received a salary, they were paid one year in advance from the communal purse so as to ensure their independence. The law of the state of Israel makes both the offering of a bribe to a public servant and its acceptance punishable offenses.

BRICKNER, BARNETT ROBERT (1892–1958): US rabbi. He was one of the founders of the Young Judea movement (1910). From 1925, he was rabbi of the (Reform) Euclid Ave. Temple, Cleveland, now the Fairmount Temple. B. wrote a *History of Jews in Cincinnati.*

BRIDEGROOM OF GENESIS see **SIMHAT TORAH**

BRIDEGROOM OF THE LAW see **SIMHAT TORAH**

BRIDGEPORT: City in Connecticut, US. In 1857, there was only a handful of Jews in B., but two years later the first congregation, B'nai Israel, was organized; in 1890, a second congregation was formed, and since 1900, nine others. In 1935, the B. Jewish Community Council was organized; it sponsors the United Jewish Campaign. In 1973, B. had a Jewish population of 14,500. It has a Jewish day school.

BRIGADE, JEWISH see **JEWISH BRIGADE**

BRILL, ABRAHAM ARDEN (1874–1948): Psychiatrist. He was born in Galicia and from 1929, lectured at Columbia Univ., New York, on psychoanalysis and psychosexuality. He was the first to translate the works of Freud into English.

BRILL, JEHIEL (1836–1886): Hebrew journalist. As a young man he went to Palestine where he edited the journal *Ha-Levanon* 1863–4. The periodical reappeared in Paris (1865) and later in Mainz (1872) under his editorship. *Ha-Levanon* was the organ of the extreme religious group which attacked the Haskalah movement and all religious reform. Although at first opposing Zionism, B. was converted by the 1881 pogroms and went to Palestine, helping to found the colony of Ekron. As the result of a dispute, he left the country and settled in London (1884) where he founded a Jewish newspaper *Ha-Shulamit* and, shortly before his death, renewed publication of *Ha-Levanon.* B. also published medieval texts.

BRILL, JOSEPH (1839–1919): Hebrew author whose nom-de-plume was "Iyyov (= Job) of Minsk." A frequent contributor to the Hebrew press, he was noted for his satirical feuilletons and parodies modeled on talmudic and midrashic texts.

BRIS see **BERIT**

BRISBANE: Capital of Queensland, Australia. The Jewish community, founded in 1865, now consists of 2 congregations. It has recently been somewhat increased by immigration, and numbers (1973) 1,000.

BRISCOE, ROBERT (1894–1969): Irish communal leader. He was active in the Irish Republican Movement during the struggle for independence and sat in the Dail 1927–65. B. was closely associated with the New Zionist (Revisionist) Organization. In 1956–7 and 1961–2, he was lord mayor of Dublin.

BRISK see **BREST-LITOVSK**

BRISTOL: English port. Jews are first recorded there c. 1150, a hostel for converted Jews was founded there in 1154, and there was an accusation of Ritual Murder in 1183. In the 13th cent., B. was the seat of an ARCHA for the registration of Jewish debts. King John imprisoned all of English Jewry at B. in 1210 in order to exact a levy of 66,000 marks. In the 16th cent., a Marrano group resided at B. The modern community, dating from about 1750, flourished in the 19th cent. but now numbers only some 410 (1973).

BRITAIN see **ENGLAND; SCOTLAND; WALES**

BRIT SHOLOM see **FRATERNAL SOCIETIES**

Max Brod.

BRITISH COLUMBIA: Province on the W coast of Canada. Jews first arrived during the gold rush of 1858 in Fraser River Valley. Among these pioneers were the Oppenheimer, Franklin, Sutro, and Gabit families, all of whom settled in Victoria where in 1863 they established a synagogue. The first Jew to sit in Canada's House of Commons was Henry Nathan, elected as a member for Victoria in 1871. With the completion of the Canadian Pacific Railway and the founding of VANCOUVER in 1885 large numbers of Jewish settlers were attracted. In 1973, Vancouver's Jewish population was 11,000, Victoria's 190, and there were small numbers of Jews in outlying towns of the province.

BRITTANY: Province of NW France. Except at NANTES, the Jewish population in B. was never large. There were massacres and forced conversions at the time of the Crusades in 1235–6 culminating in expulsion in 1239–40. After B. became part of France, a general expulsion of the Jews was decreed (1391). In the 17th cent., Nantes was a center for Marranos escaping from Spain and Portugal.

BRNO (BRÜNN): Capital of MORAVIA. The first Jewish community, important in the 13th cent., was expelled in 1454. A new community was founded at the end of the 18th cent. and grew to over 10,000 by the beginning of the 20th, when it was the chief center of Moravian Jewry. After the Nazi occupation in 1939, many Jews fled and those who remained suffered persecution and deportation. Jewish pop. (1969): c. 700.

BROCH, HERMANN (1886–1951): Austrian novelist. Director of a Viennese textile concern, he only began to publish late in life and his trilogy *Die Schlafwandler* brought him widespread recognition. In 1938 he emigrated to the US. His prose-poem *Der Tod des Vergil* aroused great interest. From 1949, he was a professor at Yale.

BROD, MAX (1884–1968): Author and composer. He left his native Prague and settled in Palestine in 1939 after attaining an important position in German letters. His many works include a trilogy of historical novels (*Tycho Brahe's Way to God*; *Reubeni, Prince of the Jews*; *Galileo in Bondage*), *Unambo*, a story of the Israel war of independence, and books interpreting religion, especially Judaism. B. was the friend, discoverer, and biographer of Franz KAFKA whose works, diaries, and letters he edited. He was dramaturgic director of the *Ha-Bimah* theater in Tel Aviv. B.'s musical compositions were performed in Israel and elsewhere.

BRODER (real name: **MARGULIES), BERL** (c. 1815–1868): Yiddish composer and singer. He organized in Brody a troupe known as the "Broder Singers" which toured the Jewish communities of Galicia and Rumania entertaining the public with Yiddish folk-songs, many written by B. himself.

BRODERSON, MOSES (1890–1956): Yiddish poet. He founded in Lodz a "Young Yiddish" group which introduced new expressionist tendencies into Polish Yiddish literature. B.'s work in the Yiddish theater continued after his escape to Soviet Russia in 1939. He was arrested by the Soviet authorities in 1950, but released shortly before his death.

BRODETSKY, SELIG (1888–1954): Mathematician and Zionist leader. Born in the Ukraine, he was taken to England at the age of 5, educated at Cambridge, and was professor at Leeds 1920–49. A member of the World Zionist Executive and of the Jewish Agency Executive from 1928, he took a leading part in their political activities. He served as president of the Board of Deputies of British Jews

Selig Brodetsky.

1940–49. In 1949, he was appointed president of the Hebrew Univ., Jerusalem but returned to England in 1952. He made important contributions to aeronautics.

BRODIE, SIR ISRAEL (1895–): Chief rabbi of the United Hebrew Congregations of the British Commonwealth 1948–65. Born in Newcastle-on-Tyne, he served as chaplain to the British forces in both World Wars, was minister in Melbourne 1922–37, lecturer in homiletics at Jews' College 1939–48, and Senior Jewish Chaplain 1944–8.

BRODSKI: Wealthy Russian family, originating from the town of Brody. Its outstanding members were *ABRAHAM B.* (1817–1884) who became a leading merchant in Odessa; and his brother *ISRAEL B.* (1823–1889) who settled at Kiev and was a pioneer of the Ukrainian sugar industry further developed by his sons *LAZAR B.* (1848–1904) and *LEV B.* (1853–1923), both notable philanthropists.

BRODY: Galician town. Jews lived there from the end of the 16th cent. and, in 1699, received from the Polish crown a charter which served as the basis of their communal organization until the annexation of the city by Austria in 1772. From 1702, B. was controlled by the Potocki family under whom the town's entire trade passed into Jewish hands. The community was also an intellectual center, playing a prominent role in the opposition to Frankism and Ḥasidism, and it was a center of the Haskalah movement. The abolition of its status as a free town (1880) weakened its economic position, and the Jewish population dwindled. After World War I, B. came under Polish rule, and the condition of its Jews deteriorated. The entire community (except 50 souls) was exterminated by the Nazis 1941–4.

BRODY, HEINRICH (Ḥayyim; 1868–1942): Editor of medieval Hebrew poetry. Of Czech birth, he was appointed chief rabbi of Prague in 1912. He settled in Palestine in 1934 and headed the Schocken Institute for Hebrew Poetry. B. was co-founder (1896) and editor (till 1906) of the *Zeitschrift für hebräische Bibliographie* and edited the poems of Judah Ha-Levi, Moses Ibn Ezra, Immanuel of Rome, etc.

BRONFMAN, SAMUEL (1891–1971): Canadian industrialist, philanthropist, communal leader. A distilling magnate, he has been president of the Canadian Jewish Congress since 1940. B. was a founder of the Palestine Economic Corporation of Canada and its board chairman, and has been a member of the board of governors of the Canadian Welfare Council, and the central committee of the Canadian Red Cross. He is honorary president of the Zionist Organization of Canada. His brother ALLAN B. (1895–) has been active in Jewish communal affairs especially in the Zionist Organization, the Friends of the Hebrew University, and in companies investing in Israel.

BRONSTEIN, LEO see **TROTSKY**

BROOK OF EGYPT see **NAḤAL MITZRAYIM**

BROOK OF SOREK see **NAḤAL SOREK**

BROWN, HAROLD (1927–): Physicist and statesman. In 1959, succeeded Edward TELLER as head of California's Livermore Radiation Laboratories. One of the "whiz kinds" in Robert McNamara's Defense Dept., he was air force secretary under President Johnson. From 1969 he was a member of the US *Salt* delegation. In 1977, he became secretary of defense in the Carter administration.

*BRUCH, MAX (1838–1920): German composer. His compositions include *Kol Nidre* variations for cello and orchestra and *Hebrew Melodies*.

BRÜLL, IGNAZ (1846–1907): Pianist and composer. A native of Moravia, he composed operas, notably *The Golden Cross*, and instrumental works.

BRÜLL, NEHEMIAH (1843–1891): German scholar; from 1870, rabbi of the Reform synagogue in Frankfort on the Main. He founded and edited 1874–1890) the *Jahrbücher für jüdische Geschichte und Literatur* in which he published many Jewish studies.

BRÜNN see **BRNO**

BRUNNER, ARNOLD W. (1857–1925): US architect and author. Though much of his life was spent as a town-planning expert, he is best known for designing such structures as Lewisohn Stadium, New York, several buildings of Columbia Univ., Mount Sinai Hospital in New York, and a number of synagogues.

BRUNNER, CONSTANTIN (pseudonym of Leopold Wertheimer; 1862–1937): German philosopher. An enthusiastic Spinozist, he opposed the Kantian epistemology. He distinguished three possibilities of human thought: the practical mind (ego), with which every man is endowed; the spirit, which is found in few men; and superstition, which is widespread and manifested in religion, metaphysics, and ethics. He regarded Jesus as the representative of pure Judaism.

BRUNSCHVICG, LEON (1869–1944): French philosopher. He was professor at the Sorbonne from 1909 and became a member of the *Académie des sciences morales et politiques* in 1919. Influenced by Kant and Spinoza, B.'s chief work was in rational ethics and the philosophy of science. He was a leader of the intellectual movement in France.

BRUNSWICK: Capital of former German duchy of the same name. Jews are mentioned there from the 13th cent. and a Jewish quarter from the beginning of the 14th; a massacre took place at the time of the Black Death (1349). The Jews of B. were fully emancipated when it was part of the kingdom of Westphalia in 1807–13 and again in 1832. Before 1933, B. had about 1,100 Jews. A small community

Interior of the Synagogue, Brussels.

was refounded after World War II and numbered 43 in 1967.

BRUSA (BURSA): City in Anatolia, Turkey, where Jews have lived since the 1st cent. BCE. The community increased in importance with the influx of Spanish refugees after 1492, and a famous yeshivah existed in the 16th and 17th cents. There were 3,500 Jews in B. before World War I, but the number has dwindled to 350 (1970) as the result of emigration, mainly to America and Israel.

BRUSSELS: Capital of BELGIUM. The presence of Jews is reliably reported from the 13th cent. The community suffered at the time of the Black Death (1348), was thereafter reestablished, but was exterminated in 1370 after being accused of Host Desecration. Under Spanish and Austrian rule there were occasional Jewish visitors, but no community was reconstituted until the 19th cent. when B. became the administrative center of Belgian Jewry and seat of its central consistory. Since World War II, B. has had the largest Jewish community in Belgium, numbering (1973) some 24,000.

BRUTZKUS: (1) *BORIS* (*BER*) *B.* (1874–1938): Agricultural economist. He was born in Lithuania and taught at the Agricultural High School in Leningrad 1907–22, and from 1936, was professor of agricultural economy at the Hebrew Univ. He was an expert in Russian agrarian economy and the economic and social problems of E European Jewry. (2) *JULIUS B.* (1870–1952): Historian; brother of (1). One of the chief spokesmen of the Zionist press in Russia, he was in 1921 appointed minister for Jewish affairs in Lithuania. His latter years were spent in Berlin, Paris, and New York. B. was the author of several monographs on E European Jewish history.

BUBER: (1) *MARTIN B.* (1878–1965): Religious philosopher; grandson of (2). Born in Vienna, he passed his youth in Lvov and studied in German universities. In 1898, he joined the Zionist movement, being appointed editor of its organ *Die Welt* in 1901. He strongly advocated practical Zionist work and was among the organizers of the DEMOCRATIC FRACTION. B. helped to found the *Jüdischer Verlag* publishing house. From 1903, he devoted himself primarily to literary activity, but during World War I organized the Jewish National Council in Berlin. In 1916, he founded the German monthly *Der Jude*. B. exercised a profound influence on Zionist ideology, especially on the youth movements. Together with FRANZ ROSENZWEIG, B. published a German translation of the Bible. From 1924 to 1933, he was professor of the philosophy of Jewish religion and ethics at Frankfort on the Main. In 1938, he settled in Jerusalem as professor of the sociology of religion at the Hebrew Univ. With Y.L. Magnes, he was a warm advocate of Judeo-Arab understanding. B.'s attitude to Judaism was largely influenced by Ḥasidism, which he interpreted to the Western world. B. conceived religious faith as a dialogue between man and God. This conception ("I and Thou") has deeply influenced contemporary Christian theology.

Martin Buber.

According to B., Israel exemplifies this "dialogual relationship" on a collective, national level. The Bible is the record of this experience in which Israel knows itself to be "addressed" by the Divine and tries to "respond," i.e., to listen and to obey. B.'s most important works which have appeared in English include *I and Thou*, *For the Sake of Heaven*, *Mamre*, *Moses*, *Between Man and Man*, *Tales of the Hasidim*, *Israel and the World*, *Hasidism*, *The Prophetic Faith*, *Paths in Utopia*, and *Two Types of Faith*.
(2) *SOLOMON B.* (1827–1906): Talmudic scholar; lived in Lvov where he was engaged in business. His investigations brought to light many ancient Midrashim which he discovered in ms; these he published in comprehensive critical editions. B. also edited important works by medieval scholars (Rashi, Saadyah Gaon, etc.) and wrote on the history of the Jews in Poland.

BUBLICK, GEDALIAH (1875–1948): Yiddish writer. Born in Lithuania, he lived in Argentina from 1900 to 1904 when he went to New York and joined the staff of the Yiddish *Daily News*, becoming its editor in 1915. When it ceased publication in 1928, he wrote for the *Morgen Journal*. He was among the founders of the American Jewish Congress and of the *Mizrahi* Organization of America of which he was president 1928–32.

BUCHAREST: Capital of RUMANIA. Jewish merchants from Turkey first settled in B. in the 16th cent. and Ashkenazi Jews – mainly craftsmen – in considerable numbers in the 18th and 19th cents. No synagogue was officially permitted until 1787. Throughout the 19th cent., the community was subject to attacks and economic discrimination, and many Jews left as a result. Although the Rumanian Jews nominally received equal rights after World War I, their condition did not greatly improve. A unified community was organized in 1921. During World War II, B. became the seat of the central office of the Jews of Rumania; although subject to pogroms and confiscations, the Jews of B. suffered less than those in the rest the country. On the establishment of the Rumanian People's Republic (1948), all Zionist activity was prohibited and Jewish communists took control of the community. However, the community retained its identity and services including religious activities and a Yiddish theater. Jewish pop. (1973): 50,000.

BUCHENWALD: Town in Germany, 5 m. NW of Weimar. In 1937, the Nazis established a CONCENTRATION CAMP there to provide slave labor for factories in central Germany. The first large shipment, 10,000 German Jews, arrived in Nov. 1938. In subsequent years, Jews from various European countries were sent there; the camp held an average of 30,000 prisoners, but the figure rose to 98,000 in 1944. Political prisoners, including the former French premier Léon Blum, were interned in a special barrack. 51,572 inmates, among them many Jews, died of hunger, disease, and maltreatment, or were executed. When B. was liberated by US troops on Apr. 11, 1945, some 21,000 survivors were found.

BÜCHLER, ADOLF (1867–1939): Historian and theologian. He was born in Hungary and went to London as principal of Jews' College in 1906, continuing to fill the position until his death. He wrote many discerning monographs in German and English, mainly on religious and social history in Palestine at the beginning of the Christian era. In particular, he took issue with the treatment of this period by Christian theologians.

BUDA see **BUDAPEST**

BUDAPEST: Capital of HUNGARY. A Jewish community is first mentioned at Buda in the 12th cent., and Jews were expelled from the city during the Black Death (1348). The community of Buda grew in importance from the beginning of the 15th cent., while Sephardi influence increased during the period of Turkish rule (16th–17th cents.). In 1783, Jews were permitted to live in Pest – at first temporarily, later permanently. A Jewish congregation was established there in 1821 and a rabbinical seminary in 1877. A number of prominent Jewish leaders came from B., including Herzl and Nordau. The community flourished during the early 20th cent.; its political and economic situation deteriorated after World War I, although intellectually it remained active. There were 250,000 Jews in B. before World War II of whom a great proportion were deported by the Nazis. In 1956, there were 95,000 Jews left, but

Budapest: Obuda synagogue.

many of them fled at the end of that year, and in 1973 the Jewish pop. was estimated at 80,000. The Budapest Rabinical Seminary is now directed by Alexander Scheiber.

BUDKO, YOSEPH (1888–1940): Painter and engraver. Of Polish birth, he lived in Berlin from 1910 to 1933 when he settled in Jerusalem. Here he

Engraving by Yoseph Budko.

reestablished the Bezalel School of Arts (1935) and served as its director until his death. Most of B.'s works are derived from Jewish life, including the E European townlet and scenes of Jerusalem. He made a significant contribution to book illustration and designed a Hebrew type face.

BUENOS AIRES: Capital of ARGENTINA. The first Jewish community in B. A., composed of French, English, and German Jews, was organized in 1862. From the 1880's, many Jews immigrated from E Europe, while Sephardi Jews arriving from the Middle East established a separate congregation in 1897 and at present number c. 75,000, constituting 20% of the total. Many German Jews escaped to B. A. after 1933. The Chevra Kaddisha Ashkenazit, founded in 1894, fulfilled the functions of a community council until 1949 when it was converted into the Ashkenazi Community of B. A. It now has a membership of c. 50,000 and maintains the rabbinate and a ramified educational system with 68 Hebrew and Yiddish schools with c. 16,000 students. A teachers seminary has 250 students. B. A. has over 50 synagogues and houses of worship and a rich cultural and social life. There is a large Yiddish press which includes one daily, four weeklies, five fortnightlies, and 17 monthlies in addition to periodicals in Spanish, Hebrew, German, and Hungarian. The Jewish community of B. A., numbering 350,000 (1973), is one of the largest in the world.

BUERGER, LEO (1879–1943): US surgeon and urologist. B. first described the arterial condition known as Buerger's Disease (1908) and invented urologic instruments.

BUFFALO: City in New York state, US. The first Jews to settle there arrived from Germany in 1837. In 1847, they formed an organization for religious and cultural activities, but Polish Jews built the city's first synagogue in 1850. Between 1890 and 1914 large numbers of E European Jews settled in B. It was near B. that Mordecai Manuel NOAH planned to establish his Jewish colony of ARARAT in 1825. The weekly *Buffalo Jewish Review* has appeared since 1919. Jewish pop. (1973): 23,500.

BUKOVINA: Region now divided between Rumania and the USSR. The first reliable information on Jewish settlement dates from the 14th cent. when communities appeared along the great trade routes. The wine and spirit trade was concentrated in their hands from the 16th cent. and, thereafter, many Jews immigrated to B. from Poland and the Ukraine. There were 650 families at the time of the Austrian conquest (1775); restrictions reduced the number to 175 families by 1785. When these were eased, many E Galician Jews immigrated, and by 1890, the community numbered 90,000. They had received civil rights in 1867. Up to World War I, their economic position was stable and the region was a center of

Yiddishism. After the war, B. was annexed to Rumania and the Jews shared the fate of Rumanian Jewry. In 1939, there were in B. 150,000 Jews most of whom were annihilated during World War II. After the War, B. was partitioned.

BUL: Ancient Hebrew name (I Kings 6:38) for the eighth month, now *Marheshvan*.

BULAN (fl. 7th cent.): King of the KHAZARS. He and his nobility became converted to Judaism after a religious discussion c. 640. Another source dates the event c. 740. As a Jew, B. apparently adopted the name Sabriel.

BULAWAYO: Town in Rhodesia. Jews settled there shortly after its foundation in 1894, and the community numbers 2,000 (1973).

BULGARIA: Balkan state. Jews settled in this area in the Roman period. In the early Middle Ages, when the Bulgarians were Christianized, their new religion showed a marked Jewish influence. The official attitude was favorable, and many Jews fleeing from central Europe found refuge in B. In the Middle Ages, the area was in the orbit of Byzantium. The queen of Ivan Alexander, Czar of B. 1331–55, was the former Jewess, THEODORA. After the expulsion from Spain (1492), new Sephardi communities, stemming in part from Salonica, were established in B., those of SOFIA, Nicopolis, and Plevna being the most important. The newcomers quickly absorbed the other elements in the country, and for centuries Bulgarian Jewry was a typical Turkish community. Religious equality was laid down as a condition for the forerunner of the present B. by the CONGRESS OF BERLIN in 1878, and (notwithstanding the persistence of some prejudices) was generally observed. Even when allied to Nazi Germany in World War II, the Bulgarian government refused to carry out the German anti-Semitic policies except in minor matters, and the Bulgarian community was the only one in occupied Europe (beside Finland) which escaped mass-deportations, etc. The Zionist movement was strong in B. and after 1948, almost the entire community transferred itself, with the approval of the government, to Israel. Jewish pop. (1973): 7,000 (out of a former 48,000) with a communal life directed by a central consistory.

BULLS, PAPAL see **POPES**

BUND (abbr. of *Allgemeiner Yiddisher Arbeterbund in Lite, Poilen un Russland* – "General Federation of Jewish Workers in Lithuania, Poland, and Russia"): Jewish Socialist Party, founded at a conference in Vilna in 1897, out of a Jewish workers' movement which had existed in Russia from the end of the 1880's. The first branches were nearly all in Poland and Lithuania, but the B. soon spread to Jewish centers in Russia proper. Serving at first as both a trade-union and a political party, it struggled for better working conditions and for popular education, especially in social problems. It was outlawed in Czarist Russia and its members were severely punished if discovered by the police. The B. joined the Russian Socialist Party after the right to organize its own branches had been recognized. The influence of the B. grew after the 1905 revolution, and similar parties arose in Galicia, Rumania, England, and the

"Bund" convention at Riga, Latvia.

US. The Soviet régime nurtured communist groups within the B., the Ukraine B. going over to the Communist Party in 1919, and the Russian B. in 1920. Only the Polish B. retained importance, lasting until the Nazi invasion of 1939. After the cessation of World War II, it renewed its activities, but was compelled to merge with the Polish Communist Party in 1947. The small B. groups in other lands established a world federation in 1947 with an executive located in New York, but they no longer constitute a significant factor in Jewish life. The B. did not create its own ideological values and its ideals approximated to those of the German socialist movement at the end of the 19th cent. As a Jewish workers' party, it denied the cohesion of the Jewish people throughout the world as one body, maintaining that Jews were permanently bound to their countries of residence and were obliged to fight alongside their fellow-citizens for freedom and democracy. The B. was strongly Yiddishist and violently opposed Zionism, regarding it as a nationalist movement of the middle-class. Before World War I, however, it began to claim the Jewish right to cultural autonomy in each country, under the influence of Austrian socialist thought. The B.'s positive contributions included the organization of Jewish workers in E Europe, its efforts to obtain and safeguard an adequate minimal standard of living, and a program for popular education.

BUNIN, ḤAYYIM ISAAC (1875–1943): Polish scholar. He wrote studies and essays in Hebrew and Yiddish and published the Hebrew periodical *Shear Yashuv* in Lodz (1921). A follower of the HABAD movement, his lifework *Mishneh Ḥabad* (10 vols., uncompleted) described *Ḥabad* doctrines and endeavored to adapt them to modern life. B. was murdered by the Nazis.

BURG YOSEPH (1909–): Israel political leader. Born in Germany, he settled in Palestine in 1939 as a teacher. A leader of *Ha-Poel ha-Mizraḥi*, he has sat in the Knesset since 1949 and served as deputy speaker (1949–51), minister of health (1951–2), minister of posts (1952–8), and minister of social welfare 1959–70, minister of interior from 1970.

BURGENLAND: Austrian province (before 1920, in Hungary). Up to the 18th cent. B. was an important center of Jewish learning. Especially noted were the "Seven Communities" with a considerable Jewish population of which Mattersdorf was the oldest and Eisenstadt the most important. These communities from c. 1690 were under the protection of the Counts Eszterházy. The Jewish community, then numbering 4,000, disappeared with the Nazi annexation of Austria in 1938.

BURGLARY: Breaking into a house to commit a felonious act; punishable by death or imprisonment. In Scripture, housebreaking by night is regarded as a graver offense than ordinary theft (Exod. 22:1), because danger to life is involved. The owner is exonerated if he slays a thief in the act of breaking in at night, but if it occurs by day, the owner is culpable. The Talmud expresses the view (*Sanhedrin 72a*) that the burglar is liable to restore the stolen article (or its equivalent) but without any additional fine. In post-talmudic times, b. hardly figures in rabbinic law, as such cases fell under civil jurisdiction. Laws relating to b. in the state of Israel, as in the case of other criminal offenses, are based on Mandatory legislation (of 1936) founded on English law.

BURGOS: Capital of Old Castile (Spain). Its Jewish community was important from the early 11th cent., and in the 13th cent., their relations with the Christian inhabitants were newly regulated. In 1367, they supported King Pedro against his half-brother Henry and severely suffered in consequence. There was a violent attack on the Jews during the 1391 massacres, and many were driven into Christianity. A community continued nevertheless to exist until the expulsion of 1492. The apostates Paul and Gonzalo de Santa Maria were bishops of B. in the 15th cent.

BURGUNDY: French province. As early as the time of the *Lex Burgundionum* (516) there was a large Jewish population in the region. Later, the Jews were particularly numerous in Dijon, Mâcon, and Chalon, but were found in all towns and many villages of the province. In 1196, the duke proclaimed them his "serfs" – which meant in effect that he took them under his protection – and during the 13th cent. they played an important role in trade. The special tax imposed in 1256 was the first of a series of oppressive measures. As in the rest of France, the Jews were expelled from B. in 1306, being readmitted in 1315, and expelled finally in 1394. A new community, mainly of Alsatian origin, was founded in the 19th cent.

BURIAL AND BURIAL SOCIETIES: Burial is regarded by Jews as a basic duty to be performed for all, including criminals, suicides, and enemies. Jewish burial practice has always been to place the corpse in an earthen grave or in a rock-cut cave. Often in antiquity, burial was first in the ground; after the disintegration of the body, the bones were collected and placed in stone OSSUARIES in the family burial cave. In the Second Temple Period, tombs standing on their own and rock-cut graves, fronted by architectural façades, were common. The practice of constructing burial-galleries underground, later exemplified at Bet Shearim in Galilee, gave rise to the CATACOMB system in Rome adopted also by the early Christians. Cremation and embalming were not Jewish customs. The body was, whenever possible, buried on the day of death; burials were hastened on

A burial in the Amsterdam Sephardi cemetery.
(Engraving by Novelli after Picart).

Fridays and on the eve of festivals. At one time, bodies were sometimes dressed in costly garments, but this led to much abuse. R. Gamaliel, therefore, gave instructions to bury his corpse in a simple linen garment, and this became standard Jewish custom. The use of a coffin is not universal among Jews, oriental Jews, for example, burying their dead without coffins. Where coffins are used, they are generally made of simple wood. The only known excavated Jewish flat cemetery (late Second Temple Period) is at Khirbet Kumran, near the Dead Sea. Participation in a funeral is regarded as a primary good deed (*mitzvah*). With the growing complexity of the Jewish community, a HEVRAH KADDISHA ("holy society") was organized to provide for all the rites and details of burial. The functions of these societies are to help read the deathbed confession (*viddui*), wash and dress the corpse, carry out the burial services and actual burial and provide for the special meal given to the mourners after the funeral. Jews aspired to be buried in Palestine in preparation for the day of resurrection; from this arose the practice of placing some Holy Land soil in the coffins of Jews buried in the Diaspora.

BURLA, YEHUDAH (1886–1969): Israel novelist. Born in Jerusalem, he has written a series of novels around Sephardi and oriental Jewish life. B. brought eastern folklore into Hebrew literature, combining it with the realism of the modern European novel.

BURMA: Country of SE Asia. Jews first arrived there in the mid-19th cent., the early settlers coming from Calcutta, Cochin, and Persia. A congregation was organized in Rangoon in 1857 by Jews

Yehudah Burla.

of Baghdadi origin. Before World War II, there were c. 200 Jews in B., but they fled during the Japanese occupation. The community now (1973) numbers c. 200, mostly in Rangoon.

BURNHAM, LORD see **LAWSON**

BURNING BUSH: The desert shrub from which the angel of God appeared to Moses, prior to his Divine call. The bush was aflame, but miraculously was not consumed (Exod. 3:2–4). The rabbis considered this to be symbolic of the history of the Jewish people.

BURNS, ARTHUR FRANK (1904–): US economist. Born in Stanislav, Austria, he went to the US as a child. He taught at Rutgers and Columbia; from 1969 was chairman of the US National Reserve Board.

BURNT OFFERING see **SACRIFICE**

BURSA see **BRUSA**

BURTON, SIR MONTAGUE (1885–1952): English industrialist. He devoted part of his wealth, derived from his chain of tailoring-shops, to the foundation of chairs in industrial and international relations in English universities and at the Hebrew Univ.

BUSH, ISIDOR (1822–1898): Author, editor, and communal leader. Upon his arrival in New York from Austria, he founded (1849) the first American Jewish weekly, *Israels Herold*, which lasted three months. He then moved to St. Louis where he entered upon a successful business career. B. was active as abolitionist, public servant, and Jewish communal leader. He served in the Civil War with the rank of captain. In later life, he engaged in viticulture.

BUSNACH: Family in Algiers who – with their associates, the BACRI family – long dominated local Jewish life. *NAPHTALI B.* (c. 1750–1805) who received the monopoly of the grain trade from the Dey and was lay head of Algerian Jewry, was assassinated in 1805. Another member of the family, *WILLIAM BERNARD B.* (1832–1907), made a reputation in Paris as a playwright.

BUSTANAI see **BOSTANAI**

BUTENSKY, JULES LEON (1871–1947): US sculptor. Born in Russia, B. emigrated to the US in 1904. His works, devoted primarily to Jewish themes, are noted for their spiritual depth and power.

BUTTENWIESER, MOSES (1862–1939): US biblical scholar. Born in Germany, B. went to the US in 1896 and was professor of Bible at the Hebrew Union College, Cincinnati 1897–1934. His contributions include studies in the Prophets, Psalms, and Job.

***BUXTORF:** German family of Hebraists whose members included: (1) *JOHANNES B.* (Senior; 1564–1629): Professor of Hebrew at the Univ. of Basle, he edited *Biblia hebraica rabbinica*, the Hebrew Bible with rabbinic commentaries (Basle 1618–9),

Bird from the mosaic floor of the 4th cent. CE
Byzantine synagogue at Hamam-Lif.

compiled the *Bibliotheca rabbinica* (a pioneer rabbinic bibliography), and wrote a Hebrew grammar and a Hebrew and Aramaic lexicon. His works on the Hebrew language and on Jewish customs and culture were important sources for Christian scholars. (2) *JOHANNES B.* (Junior; 1599–1664): Son of (1). Professor of Hebrew and of Bible exegesis at the Univ. of Basle, he published his father's works and wrote on the Hebrew alphabet and punctuation. He translated Maimonides' *Guide* and Judah Ha-Levi's *Kuzari* into Latin.

BYBLOS (the biblical *Gebal*): Ancient Phoenician coastal city. It supplied builders for Solomon's Temple (I Kings 5:32) and was a center for the export of Lebanese cedar and a shipbuilding port (Ezek. 27:9). Excavations have revealed a number of Semitic inscriptions, dating from the 2nd and 1st millennia BCE, which are valuable for the study of the early evolution of Semitic alphabets and languages.

Greek and Hebrew inscriptions show that Jews lived in B. in the Roman Period. Benjamin of Tudela (c. 1170) found 150 Jews there.

BYZANTIUM: The E Roman Empire with its capital in CONSTANTINOPLE, extending over a varying geographical area; up to 637, including Palestine. Jews were present in B. from its foundation in the 4th cent. As the Eastern emperors developed their specific religious attitudes, the position of the Jews, especially their religious life, deteriorated. JUSTINIAN (527–65), besides including elaborate anti-Jewish laws in his Code, issued a decree in 553 which interfered with the conduct of the synagogue services. Heraclius is reported (c. 614) to have issued an edict ordering the conversion of the Jews. The practice of Judaism was formally forbidden by successive emperors – by Leo in 723, by Basil I in 873–4, by Romanus Lucapenus in 932–6, etc. But on each occasion Jewish life reestablished itself, and Benjamin of Tudela (c. 1170) found communities throughout the Empire, though he emphasized that in Constantinople itself they were treated with contempt. Jews remained in the attenuated Byzantine Empire until the last remnant was conquered by the Turks in 1453. The former Byzantine communities had their own rite of prayer, akin to the Italian rite, known as the *Mahzor Romania*. This, printed more than once in the 16th–17th cents., became almost extinct in the 18th, except in Corfu and Kaffa.

Lion from the Byzantine synagogue at Hamam-Lif.

CABALA see **KABBALAH**

CABALLERIA, DE LA (in Heb. called [Ibn] Labi): Aragonese family. *JUDAH* (c. 1260), *VIDAL* (c. 1360), and especially *BENVENISTE* (d. 1411) *DE LA C.* were prominent in financial administration. *VIDAL (GONZALO) DE LA C.* (d. c. 1455), Hebrew poet who translated Cicero from Latin into Spanish, and *PEDRO (BONAFOS) DE LA C.* (c. 1450), high financial official and author of the anti-Jewish work, *Zelus Christi adversus Judaeos,* were converted to Christianity.

CACERES: Sephardi family, deriving from Caceres in Spain. (1) *SAMUEL DE C.* (1628–1660): Scholar and spiritual leader of Amsterdam Jewry. He edited and revised a Spanish translation of the Bible (1661). C. married a sister of Spinoza. (2) *SIMON DE C.* (d. 1704): Leader of the London Marrano community. He was a signatory of the petition of 1656–7 requesting toleration for the practice of Judaism in England.

CAECILIUS OF CALACTE (fl. 1st cents. BCE and CE): Writer and rhetorician. Born of slave parents in Calacte, Sicily, he lived in Rome and wrote on rhetoric, literary criticism and history and essays on Demosthenes, Plato, etc.

CAESAREA: Ancient city on the Mediterranean coast of Palestine. It first appears in history in the 4th cent. BCE as the "Tower of Straton." A flourishing port in the hellenistic period, it was captured by Alexander Yannai but separated from Judea by Pompey. Herod received it from Augustus and transformed it into a large city with a safe harbour (12–9 BCE), calling it C. in the emperor's honor. When Judea became a Roman province, C. was its capital and, as such, a rival of Jerusalem; the disputes between its Jewish and gentile inhabitants were one of the causes of the war with Rome, 66–70. Vespasian made C. a Roman colony *(colonia)*; it remained the capital of the province Palestina until, as the last of the Byzantine strongholds, it was conquered by the Arabs (640). Despite its pagan character, C. had a great Jewish community in the 3rd–4th cents. Christianity was early established there; in the 2nd–4th cents., it was a famous center of Christian learning, the home of Origen and Eusebius, and noted for

Caesarea: the Roman Theater in the course of Reconstruction.

its Bible library. C. continued to exist throughout Crusader times until destroyed by Baibars in 1291. In 1878, C. was resettled by Bosnian Moslems and in 1940, by the Jewish settlement of SEDOT YAM. The extensive ruined site, enclosed by a semi-circular wall and once served by two aqueducts, has recently been the scene of excavations which have yielded interesting Roman, Byzantine and Crusader remains, as well as the ruins of a synagogue. The excavated Roman theater has been reconstructed and is again used for artistic performances. The Israel government's Fisheries Research Station is at C. as is Israel's only golf course.

CAFTAN (Turkish): Long gown or under-tunic with waist girdle, worn by oriental and E European Jews.

CAGOULARDS (Fr. "Hooded men"): A secret French organization uncovered in 1937. Strongly anti-Semitic, it aimed at overthrowing the Republic and establishing a dictatorship. See ANTI-SEMITISM.

CAHAN: Variant form of the name COHEN.

Page from Bible manuscript in Karaite synagogue, Cairo: now in Leningrad Library.

CAHAN, ABRAHAM (1860–1951): US Yiddish journalist and editor. Born in Lithuania, he went to the US in 1882 with the *Am Olam* group. He settled in New York and became known as an eloquent orator and popularizer of Marxian socialism among Jewish workers. He organized the first Jewish tailors' union. C. founded Yiddish periodicals to propagate his theories of socialism and Americanization. From 1897, he was (except for 1898–1902) editor-in-chief of New York's largest Yiddish daily, the *Forverts,* wielding great influence upon the Yiddish sector of American Jews and American labor in general. His English novel, *The Rise of David Levinsky,* became a classic in American immigrant literature.

CAHAN, ISRAEL MEIR see ḤAPHETZ ḤAYYIM

CAHAN (COHEN), YAAKOV (1881–1960): Hebrew author. Born in White Russia, he lectured at the Institute for Jewish Studies in Warsaw 1927–33, and settled in Palestine in 1934. His first book of poems (1902) placed him among the foremost contemporary Hebrew poets. C. has written lyrics, ballads, and epic poems, while his works include also folk stories,

novels, and "dramatic symphonies" in verse and prose.

CAIAPHAS, JOSEPH: High priest c. 18–36 CE. Appointed by the procurator Valerius Gratus, he served also under Pontius Pilate. The New Testament represents him and his father-in-law Annas as chiefly responsible for the prosecution of Jesus and the arrest of the apostles. He was removed by the Syrian governor, Vitellius.

CAIN: Eldest son of Adam and Eve. When God rejected his offering consisting of the "fruit of the earth" while accepting the animal sacrifice of his brother ABEL, C. slew the latter. Condemned to wander over the land of Nod, E of Eden, he built a town called Enoch and was the progenitor of several peoples (Gen. 4). Scholars have seen in the Cain-Abel conflict a relic of the struggle between the nomadic shepherd and the settled agriculturalist. According to the Midrash, C. was accidentally slain by his blind grandson, Lamech.

CAIRO: Capital of modern EGYPT. Jews lived in Old Cairo (Fostat) from the period of the Arab invasions and in the new city since its foundation in the 10th cent. C. has since then always been the greatest center of Egyptian Jewry, being the seat of the local Exilarchs in the 11th–12th cents., and later of the NAGID. A frustrated attempt of the local pasha to persecute the Jews in 1524 gave rise to the Purim of Cairo. The Cairo GENIZAH was found in 1896 in the ancient Ezra synagogue in Fostat. The community shared in the economic expansion and westernization of C. in the 19th–20th cents. Before 1948, it numbered nearly 40,000, including 2,000 Karaites, with a network of charitable and educational institutions. From 1948, their position and numbers declined. Jewish schools and communal institutions were destroyed in the riots of "Black Saturday" (Jan. 26, 1952) and there were mass expulsions in 1956–7. By 1975, only c. 250 Jews remained in C. The old Jewish quarter was destroyed in various mob attacks from 1946 on and is now occupied by Arabs.

CAISERMAN, HANANE MEIER (1884–1950): Communal worker. He was born in Rumania and emigrated to Canada where he was active in the trade union movement among Jewish workers. C. helped found the Canadian Jewish Congress (1917–19), the Canadian Zionist Organization (1925–6), and various institutions for Jewish popular education.

CALABRIA see ITALY

CALATAYUD: Town in Aragon (Spain). where a Jewish community flourished from the 12th cent. There was a Jewish quarter within the fortifications, which included a castle for defense. The community seems to have escaped during the massacres of 1391, but lost many members through conversion in the early 15th cent. and thereafter was of little importance.

CALCUTTA: Indian city. Although Jews visited C. in the 17th cent., a permanent community was formed only in the 19th cent. by Baghdad Jews who transplanted thither the traditions of Iraq. Outstanding were the Ezra and Gubbay families, closely associated with the Sassoons of Bombay. There are now five synagogues and several institutions. Jewish pop. (1973): 700.

CALEB: A member of the KENIZZITE family; one of the leaders of the tribe of Judah during the wandering in the desert. He and JOSHUA were the only spies out of the twelve dispatched by Moses to reconnoiter the land of Canaan who brought back a favorable report. As a reward, they were the sole survivors of the exodus from Egypt to enter Palestine. Promised an inheritance at Hebron, C. captured the place and expelled its inhabitants, the Anakim. A region of the Negev and a leading family of Judah were long known by his name.

CALENDAR: The Jewish c. is a "bound lunar" type: it consists of twelve months calculated according to the moon, but in order to celebrate the agricultural festivals in their proper season, the difference between the lunar year (354 days) and the solar year (365¼ days) is made up by adding (intercalating) a full month after *Adar* in the 3rd, 6th, 8th, 11th, 14th, 17th, and 19th year of each 19-year cycle (5730 began such a cycle). The month so added is called *Adar Sheni* ("Second *Adar*") and the year, a leap year. The year commences at the New Moon of *Tishri* (Sept.-Oct.) but its beginning may be shifted by a day for various reasons, among them the rule that the Day of Atonement must not fall on Friday or Sunday, or the 7th day of Tabernacles on a Sabbath. Thus non-leap years can have 353, 354, or 355 days, leap years 383–385 days. The months are counted (following the biblical custom) from *Nisan*. Only a few biblical month-names are known *(Abib* and *Ziv* in the spring; *Bul* and *Ethanim* in the fall); the present ones are of Babylonian origin:

HEBREW NAME	BABYLONIAN NAME	LENGTH	
1. *Nisan*	Nisannu	30	days
2. *Iyyar*	Ayaru ("Bud")	29	"
3. *Sivan*	Simânu	30	"
4. *Tammuz*	Du'ûzu (Name of a god)	29	"
5. *Av*	Abu	30	"
6. *Elul*	Ulûlu ("Purification")	29	"
7. *Tishri*	Tashrêtu ("Beginning")	30	"
8. *Marḥeshvan (Heshvan)*	Arakhshamna	29 or 30	"
9. *Kislev*	Kislîmu	29 or 30	"
10. *Tevet*	Tabêtu ("Flooding")	29	"
11. *Shevat*	Shabâtu ("Beating")	30	"
12. *Adar*	Addaru	29	"
		(in leap year 30)	

This constant c. was probably officially introduced by the patriarch Hillel II (330–65). Before that time, witnesses had to report each month the appearance of the new moon to the Sanhedrin which announced the date by fire-signals, and later by messengers (because of the uncertainty involved, it became customary for countries in the Diaspora to celebrate certain holidays for 2 days); the Sanhedrin also determined each year whether intercalation was to take place. Some sectarians, whose views are preserved in the Book of Jubilees, etc., advocated a purely solar calendar (probably 12 months of 30 days and 4 extra days). The Jewish year is reckoned from the Creation of the World, calculated on biblical data to coincide with 3760 BCE. AM *(=Anno Mundi)* 5000 began Sept. 1, 1239. For calculations since 1240 CE: to find AM, deduct 1240 from Common Era (CE) and add 5000 (for dates in Sept.-Oct. to Dec. add another year): e.g. 1958—1240+5000=5718; i.e., 1958 CE= AM 5717–8. To find CE: delete the 5 from AM and add 1240 (for dates in *Tishri-Tevet,* deduct one year).

In giving Hebrew dates, it is customary to use Hebrew letters for numbers, and to omit the thousands from the year number. Often the day of the week and the name of the weekly biblical portion

Calendar in ancient Hebrew discovered at Gezer.

of the following Sabbath are given by way of a date. The printed calendar *(luah)* indicates correspondence between Jewish and civil dates, dates of festivals, weekly portions, etc., and generally the times of the beginning and end of Sabbaths and festivals in the country of publication.

CALENDAR REFORM: The movement to change the existing (Gregorian) calendar in order to secure greater regularity. C. R. in general is not of special concern to Jews, but plans currently urged (a year of 364 days, with a "blank" day that would not be reckoned part of any week and two "blank" days in a leap year) would cause the Sabbath to fall on different days of the week every year, with resulting hardship to conscientious Sabbath observers. The US League for Safeguarding the Fixity of the Sabbath (founded 1929) is among the Jewish organizations which have taken action opposing c. r.

CALF, GOLDEN: Golden idol constructed by Aaron on the demand of the Israelites who had become impatient during Moses' long absence on Mt. Sinai. The calf was burnt by Moses who ground the gold to dust and subsequently obtained Divine forgiveness for the Israelites (Exod. 32). The sin of the G. C., immediately after the giving of the law, was regarded as the primary offense of the Hebrew people.

CALF WORSHIP: Calves or young bulls were regarded as symbols of strength and fertility among ancient Semitic peoples. Traces of c. w. are discernible in the Bible in the stories of the Golden Calf constructed by Aaron at Mt. Sinai (Exod.32), and the golden calves set up at Dan and Bethel by Jeroboam (I Kings 12:28–30) and presumably destroyed by Josiah (II Kings 23:15).

CALGARY: Canadian city. Jewish settlement began in 1889, and the first Jewish religious service was held in 1894. In 1906, the Chevra Kadisha Congregation was organized and in 1912, Beth Jacob Synagogue built. C. has a thriving Jewish community of 4,000 (1973) with a large community center-synagogue and two Jewish day schools.

CALICUT: Seaport on W coast of India. A Jewish trading community with autonomous privileges existed there during the 15th and 16th cents.

CALIFORNIA: US state. It was not until the gold rush of 1849 that Jews reached C. in considerable numbers. The main foreign influx at that time came from Germany, the rest from Poland, Russia, England, and France. A community was established forthwith at SAN FRANCISCO. During the decade 1850–60, other groups and congregations appeared all over C., in mining camps as well as cities. The first Jewish periodical on the Pacific coast, *The Gleaner,* appeared in San Francisco in 1855. Jewish communities arose in other cities of C., including SAN DIEGO (1850), Sacramento (1850), Stockton (1855), OAKLAND (1874), and San José (1875). LOS ANGELES' first synagogue was erected in 1873. Jewish settlement in C., especially in the Los Angeles area, has increased rapidly during the last fifty years. In 1973 C. had 666,610 Jewish inhabitants.

*CALIGULA (Gaius Julius Caesar Germanicus): Roman emperor 37–41. He gave Agrippa, grandson of Herod, the tetrarchy of NE Palestine and the title of king. His insistence on being worshiped as a divinity caused consternation among the Jews and was used as an excuse for anti-Jewish disturbances at Alexandria on the occasion of Agrippa's visit (38). Philo headed the Jewish delegation sent to intercede with C., and has recorded a graphic impression of his court. C.'s assassination prevented serious consequences in the Jewish world.

CALMANN-LEVY: French publishing house founded by Michel Lévy (1821–1875) who was associated with and succeeded by his brother, Calmann Lévy (1819–1891).

CALUMNY see **SLANDER**

CALVIN, MELVIN (1912–): US biochemist and Nobel Prize winner. Born in St. Paul, Minnesota, he studied and taught at the University of California at Berkeley (professor, 1947). In 1961 he was awarded the Nobel Prize for Chemistry for his work using carbon–14 isotopes as radioactive tracers to study photosynthesis.

CAMBRIDGE: English university town. A small Jewish community, with an ARCHA for the registration of debts, existed in C. in the 12th–13th cents. The Jews were expelled by the queen mother Eleanor in 1275. A small community was again founded in the 18th cent. and numbers about 250 (1973). Organized religious life centers around the Jewish undergraduates. The Cambridge Univ. library contains considerable collections from the Cairo *genizah*.

CAMDEN: City in New Jersey, US. Most of its community are descendants of Russian immigrants who began arriving in the last decade of the 19th cent. C.'s first synagogue was founded in 1894, and there are now 5 synagogues, a community center, and a Jewish Federation founded in 1952. Jewish pop. (1973): 21,000 (including surrounding area).

CAMONDO, ABRAHAM (1785–1873): Turkish financier. He gained the confidence of the Austrian, Italian, and Turkish governments, was ennobled by Victor Emmanuel of Italy, and was the founder and first president of the Central Consistory of Turkish Jewry.

CAMPS, CONCENTRATION AND EXTERMINATION: Immediately after the accession to power of the NATIONAL SOCIALISTS in GERMANY in 1933. C. C. were established for the detention of opponents of the new regime, especially the active leaders of the Socialist and Communist parties. In the course of time, individuals were sent there on a detention order from the *Gestapo* (State Secret Police); later, entire groups were arrested and committed to C. C. The first general action directed against Jews in Germany was in Nov. 1938 when c. 20,000 male Jews were placed in camps (especially DACHAU and BUCHENWALD). From Mar. 1938, many Austrian Jews were detained. Most of the Jews arrested at this period were allowed to emigrate on the surrender of a great part of their property. In the camps, they were confined in special blocks, under conditions inferior to those of the non-Jewish prisoners. The explanation for the arrests was either punishment for general crimes or "protective custody." The deportation of Jewish masses eastward from Germany, Austria, and Czechoslovakia in 1941 bore a different character. The Jews sent in these transports were first held in the GHETTOS established in the occupied areas of Poland and Russia (e.g. Warsaw, Lodz, Riga). Sometimes, the Jews were sent directly to labor camps and thence to extermination camps. From the spring of 1942, the transports were dispatched directly to the latter. From the end of 1942, Jews were sent to their death from all occupied areas in W and SE Europe, e.g. France, Belgium, Holland, Greece, and Norway. The last transports were sent from Hungary in May-July 1944. The concentration camp of THERESIENSTADT was regarded by the Germans as a "model ghetto" but it was for most of the inmates only a way-station to the extermination camps and over 34,000 Jews lost their lives there. In some of the C. C., particularly the extermination camps, gas chambers were installed in which members of the transports were poisoned. Occasionally, people fit for work (the young or specialists in certain occupations) were selected from the transport to be sent to labor camps, and only later to extermination camps. While in labor camps, they lived and worked under inhuman conditions on a starvation diet; brutally ill-treated and forced to overwork, many perished as they labored. Those who became unfit for work were killed. On the evidence of witnesses quoting EICHMANN, 4,000,000 Jews were exterminated in German C. C. The greatest number perished at AUSCHWITZ (Oswiecim), viz. 1,500,000, including 400,000 from Hungary. 2,000,000 Jews were killed in other death camps situated in the Polish sector at Treblinka (730,000 Jewish victims), Belzec (600,000), Maidanek (200,000), Sobibor (250,000), and Chelmno (340,000). The remainder died in other camps throughout the Reich area, notably Buchenwald (51,500), Dachau (10,200), Mauthausen (121,000), and Bergen-Belsen (30,000). Other camps in occupied areas included Compiègne, Drancy, Vélodrôme d'Hiver in France, Westerbork in Holland, Fossoli in Italy, Kloga in Estonia, Minsk in White Russia, etc. Altogether, c. 1,000 camps were established by the Nazis. The prisoners constituted an important source of income. Those in forced labor either worked unpaid for German or German controlled enterprises or, alternatively, their wages were paid to the central SS Office for Economic Administration in Berlin. All possessions (money, valuables, even gold teeth extracted from corpses) belonging to victims were transferred to the Reichsbank; clothing, etc. was sent to be reprocessed or delivered to the Nazi Welfare Office. Hair cropped from women was used in the mattress industry or for manufacturing rope. The ashes of cremated bodies were utilized as field manure and for insulating material. Unburnt bones were ground in special mills, and the bonemeal sold to industrial concerns. When the final defeat of Germany became inevitable, HIMMLER stopped the mass annihilation of Jews (Nov. 1944) but took measures to prevent the release or escape of detainees, moving them back from potential front-line areas. The authorities made efforts to delete traces of their crimes by burning interred bodies on pyres. Special crematoria had been built, e.g. at Auschwitz, and selected prisoners, supervised by trained Storm Troopers, were engaged in burning the corpses before being themselves exterminated. Prior to the entry of Allied troops, some — but not all — gas-cells,

Seti I of Egypt attacking Canaanite city.

crematoria, etc. were blown up and efforts made to destroy relevant documents, many of which were nevertheless preserved.

CAMPS, DETENTION: Camps set up by the British administration for Jewish immigrants who entered Palestine in contravention of the Mandatory regulations and for those accused of political offenses. From Jan. 1940, such immigrants were confined at Athlit, but from Aug. 1946, most were sent to Cyprus, Athlit continuing to serve for clearance. Alleged members of Jewish terrorist organizations were sent to Latrun (Palestine), Kenya, and Eritrea. In 1940, one group of 1,500 Jewish immigrants was deported to Mauritius where they were detained under difficult conditions until Aug. 1945. The members of the Jewish Agency arrested in June 1946 were confined at Latrun, while a number of suspected members of the *Haganah* were held at Rafa (S Palestine).

CAMPS, IMMIGRANT: Camps erected in Israel to accommodate newcomers until they were absorbed into permanent settlement. The first such camp was set up by the Jewish Agency in 1948 in Raananah to receive the arrivals from the Cyprus detention camps. By the end of 1950, the number of such camps reached 35, with a population of 95,000. The inmates stayed for prolonged periods and semi-permanent institutions developed. From 1951, immigrants were directed to Maabarot and at the peak these, together with the I.C., numbered 133, housing 257,000 people. From 1948, over 550,000 newcomers from 60 countries passed through I.C. After Aug. 1954, the new arrivals went directly to permanent settlements.

CANA see **KAFR KANNA**

CANAAN: Youngest son of Ham, son of Noah (Gen. 9–10). On account of his father's transgression, he was condemned by Noah to servitude to Shem and Japheth. Medieval Jews applied the name C. to the Slavonic countries.

CANAAN, LAND OF: Name for Syria in the 15th–13th cents. BCE; in a more restricted sense, applied to the coast of PALESTINE. Prior to the Israelite conquest, the country was divided into small city-states. The Israelites called the land *Eretz Yisrael* ("The Land of Israel"), and the northern part *Aram* (i.e., Syria).

CANAAN, MOUNT: Mountain in Israel NE of Safed in Upper Galilee; height: over 3,250 ft. It is frequented as a summer resort.

CANAANITES: Inhabitants of the land of Canaan; traditionally descended from Canaan, son of Ham. They were divided into 11 peoples who occupied the area between the Nile and the Euphrates (Gen. 10:15–19). The derivation of the name is uncertain. It appears in inscriptions from the 15th cent. BCE, and from the 14th cent., the inhabitants of Syria applied it to themselves. By origin, the C. appear to have been a mixture of Horites, Hittites, and Hebrews, dating back to the Hyksos period (17th cent.). The C. were almost entirely obliterated or assimilated by the Israelites (c. 13th cent.), the Philistines along the coast (12th cent.), and the Arameans in the N (11th cent.). The remnants were subjected by David and Solomon and subsequently absorbed. Later, the name was preserved only among the Sidonians and Phoenicians.

CANADA: N American country. Under French rule, professing Jews were not allowed to live in C., although the GRADIS family of Bordeaux had an important share in the development and defense of the colony. After the British conquest, a handful of Jews settled in MONTREAL and in 1768, established a congregation, most members of which were Sephardim closely associated with the London community. As in the mother-country, their political rights were limited. In 1807, Ezekiel HART was elected to the QUEBEC Assembly but not permitted to take his seat. A lengthy struggle ensued but in 1832, a bill was passed by the Quebec Assembly granting Jews full civil rights. Ashkenazim from England, Germany, and Poland began arriving during the decades preceding 1850. Their first congregation came into being in 1858. In 1862, a further Ashkenazi congregation was formed in TORONTO. Jews appeared on the west coast in British Columbia during the gold rush in 1858. In the economic life of C., Jews have participated significantly in commercial trade, the merchant marine, fishing, telegraph communications, clothing manufacture, and the fur and tobacco industries. Thousands of Jewish general-store merchants who settled in small railroad towns across C. made their contribution to the land's economy. Several thousand Jews settled in Saskatchewan under the auspices of the Jewish Colonization Association. A great influx of Jewish settlers in C. began after the Russian pogroms of 1881. In the decade following 1900, C.'s Jewish population increased from 16,000 to 75,000 due to immigration from Russia and Rumania. Their numbers were further augmented by later immigration waves after World War I and World War II; in the latter period, C. was one of the few countries in the world where immigration was relatively free. Some 67,000 Jews immigrated to Canada 1946–63, many of them from Israel and later from North Africa. A dynamic Canadian Jewish community of 305,000 has developed a comprehensive education system (95 Jewish schools including over 30 day schools attended by some 40,000 children), influential religious and cultural institutions (including 3 teachers' seminaries and 4 yeshivot), a strong Zionist movement, a Jewish press, and a representative body in the CANADIAN JEWISH CONGRESS. There are 206 Jewish congregations in the country, of which 138 are in Montreal, Toronto, and WINNIPEG, in which three cities lives the overwhelming majority of Canadian Jewry. During the last decades, Canadian Jewry has begun to develop advanced communal institutions, the ill-organized conventicles giving place in many cities to great modern synagogues.

CANADIAN JEWISH CONGRESS: National representative body of Canadian Jewry, founded in 1919 and reorganized in 1934. It seeks to safeguard the status, rights, and welfare of Jews in Canada and throughout the world; to combat anti-Semitism; and promote better understanding among all ethnic and religious groups. It is affiliated with the WORLD JEWISH CONGRESS, and its overseas relief and rehabilitation activities are channeled through the American Joint Distribution Committee, the ORT, the OSE, and the Alliance Israélite Universelle. In partnership with the Zionist Organization of Canada, it has organized and financed the Canada-Israel Corporation which purchases in Canada supplies needed by the government of Israel and the Jewish Agency. The CJC has a department of public relations, in partnership with the Canadian B'nai B'rith lodges, and departments of Jewish education and culture, youth and adult education, and community organ-

Sinai Sanatorium for Tuberculosis, St. Agathe des Montes, Quebec, Canada.

Delegation of the United Zionist Council and Canadian Jewish Congress to meet Prime Minister Diefenbaker, Aug. 28, 1957.

ization, national archives, and a bureau of social and economic research.

CANARY ISLANDS: Island group off the Atlantic coast of Africa, belonging to Spain. Its Jewish community originally consisted of Marranos against whom a branch of the Inquisition was established in 1499/1564. Their traces disappeared in the first half of the 17th cent. A number of the founders of the London Jewish community at this period originated from the C. I.

CANDELABRUM see **MENORAH**

CANDIA see **CRETE**

CANON see **BIBLE**

CANOPY see **ḤUPPAH**

CANTARINI (Heb. *Min Ha-Ḥazzanim*): Italian family prominent from the 16th cent. distinguished as rabbis and physicians. *ISAAC COHEN C.* (1644–1723) of Padua described in his *Pahad Yitzḥak* the attacks on the Jews of that city which led to the institution of the local celebration known as the Purim of Buda. He combated the Ritual Murder libel in a Latin work *Vindex Sanguinis.*

CANTERBURY: English cathedral city. A Jewish community is first mentioned in C. in 1160. In the 13th cent., it was the seat of an ARCHA for the registration of. Jewish debts. In 1261, and again in 1264, attacks were made on the Jewish quarter (the present Jewry Lane). A detailed inventory of the property left by the Jews on the expulsion of 1290 is extant. Jews again settled in C. in the 18th cent. and a synagogue was built in 1763, but the community is now extinct.

CANTICLES see **SONG OF SONGS**

CANTILLATION see **ACCENTS; CANTORAL MUSIC**

CANTONISTS: Term applied in Czarist Russia to adolescent conscripts; the system was in force 1805-56. Jews became subject to this decree from 1827, and a disproportionately high number of Jewish children were taken away with the implicit intent of converting them to Christianity. The Jewish communities were bound to supply annually a certain number of recruits between the ages of 12 (or even 8) and 25: service lasted 25 years and was not reckoned until the recruit had passed the normal conscription age of 18. The Jewish recruits were educated at special institutions outside the Pale of Settlement and then sent to distant places (e.g., the eastern provinces, Siberia). Thousands were converted and assimilated, while many died of hardship. Most of the C. were children of poor families, as the wealthy bought out their children. The brutal police functions imposed on the Jewish communal authorities in the selection (known popularly as "kidnapping") of recruits led to widespread corruption and deep resentment on the part of the poorer Jews.

CANTOR (*Ḥazzan*) and **CANTORAL MUSIC** (*Ḥazzanut*): In the Temple in Jerusalem, the liturgy was intoned by the priests and levites, but in the synagogues, a learned and prominent member of the community was usually selected to lead the PRAYERS. He was called the *sheliaḥ tzibbur* ("emissary of the congregation"). The prayer modes, which were in a contemporary musical style, were uniform and known to all. In many cases, therefore, when PIYYUTIM eventually became a feature of the synagogue service, the poets (*paytanim*) themselves were *hazzanim*, feeling that they were best qualified to interpret their own songs, often improvised. R Yehudai Gaon, head of the academy of Sura (760-4), was one of the leading precentors of his time and is credited with codifying and arranging the musical tradition of the Babylonian synagogues. He favored the new practice of professional *hazzanut*. The influence of Italy's musical development at the end of the Middle Ages was felt throughout Europe, and reached the synagogue as well. Cantors increasingly introduced into the service secular melodies and also the style that was heard from traveling singers and troubadours. In the 14th and 15th cents., traveling *hazzanim* carried melodies and customs from one community to another, thus contributing to the stabilization and unification of the musical tradition of the synagogue. On the other hand, a profound difference had by now developed between the more restrained Sephardi tradition, somewhat affected by Arab influences, and the more florid Ashkenazi tradition. The impact of musical progress in the 18th cent. made itself felt among the *hazzanim*, many of whom began to study music and instrumental playing. Influenced by the musical style of the period, they began to bring into the synagogue the popular melodies of the day. Aaron Beer, who became a cantor in Berlin in 1765, was one of the first cantors with a technical musical training. In 1826, the Viennese community dedicated a new temple, and Solomon Sulzer was brought to Vienna to officiate. Instead of "*hazzan*," Sulzer called himself "cantor." His chief contribution to the cantoral chant and to synagogue music was form, which had been lacking up to that time. Louis Lewandowski of Berlin, choir director and composer, influenced the cantoral renditions of his period through two volumes of synagogue music which became standard works throughout Europe and, later, America. Samuel Naumbourg of Paris was also one of the major influences in *hazzanut* in Europe during his time. *Hazzanim* who combined outstanding musical gifts, learning, and piety became great celebrities, e.g. Solomon Kashtan (1781-1829), many of whose works were preserved by his son, Hirsh Weintraub (1811-1882). Another cantoral light of that time was Bezalel Shulsinger (c. 1791-1860), otherwise known as Bezalel Odesser. Another 19th cent. cantor was Yeruchom Blindman who composed many works steeped in the synagogue musical tradition. His contemporary, Nissen Spivak, also known as Nissi Belzer, has gone down in cantoral history as

one of the greatest *hazzanim* of his time. In the 19th and 20th cents., outstanding cantors have included Joseph Rosenblatt, Zavel Kwartin, Mordecai Hershman, David Roitman, Aryeh Leib Rutman, Moshe Kussevitsky, and Leib Glantz. Cantoral training was until the 19th cent. personal and casual. The first school for the training of cantors in America, the Hebrew Union College School of Sacred Music, was founded in 1948. It has organized an American Conference of Certified Cantors and founded the Sacred Music Press. This was followed by the Cantors' Institute of the Jewish Theological Seminary, organized in 1953, and later by a cantoral school under the auspices of Yeshiva Univ. US and Canadian Conservative cantors founded the Cantors' Assembly of America in 1947. 300 cantors belong to the Jewish Ministers Cantors' Association of America. In England, cantors are trained at Jews' College, and similar facilities exist in other countries. Among the more important collections of cantoral music (besides those published by persons mentioned above) are those by Consolo (Italian Sephardi rite), Crémieux (Comtat Venaissin), and Mombach, Hast, and Alman (England).

CANTOR, BERNARD (1892-1920): US rabbi and social worker. With his colleague Israel Friedlaender he was murdered by bandits in the Ukraine while a member of an American Joint Distribution Committee relief delegation.

CANTOR, EDDIE (Edward Israel Iskowitz; 1892-1964): US comedian. Prominent in every

Eddie Cantor.

medium of entertainment, he was president of the Jewish Theatrical Guild, the Screen Actors' Guild, and the American Federation of Radio Artists.

CANTOR, MORITZ BENEDICT (1829—1920): German mathematician. Professor at Heidelberg from 1877, he was a specialist in the history of mathematics on which he wrote his classic *Vorlesungen über Geschichte der Mathematik*.

CAPA, ROBERT (1913–1954): Photographer, of Hungarian origin, he settled in the US and became especially well-known for his photos of various wars. He was killed when covering the Indochina war. His brother *CORNELL C.* (1918–) is also a noted photographer who has been associated with *Life* magazine.

CAPE PROVINCE: Province of Union of S Africa. Marranos and converted Jews were among the first Europeans to reach the Cape, and in the 17th and 18th cents., officials of the Dutch East India Co. included baptized Jews. Conforming Jews settled at Cape Town early in the 19th cent. in 1841, Tikvat Israel, S Africa's first Jewish congregation, was founded in Cape Town. Communities were subsequently formed at Port Elizabeth (1857), Kimberley (1873), Oudtshoorn (1883), and East London (1901). In 1970, there were 32,670 Jews in C.P. The main institutions are the Cape Bet Din, the United Council of Hebrew Congregations of the Cape, the Cape Jewish Aged Home, and the Cape Jewish Orphanage. The Western and Eastern Provinces have separate committees of the Board of Deputies and councils of the Zionist Federation.

CAPE TOWN: Legislative capital of the Union of S Africa and of Cape Province. The first congregation in C. (and in S Africa) was Tikvat Israel, established in 1841. The community numbers 25,650 (1973), possesses 12 Orthodox congregations and one Reform temple, and is highly organized in its religious, Zionist, cultural, and philanthropic activities. Its major institutions include the S African Jewish Board of Deputies (Cape Committee), Western Province Zionist Council, the Cape Board of Jewish Education, the United Council of Hebrew Congregations, the Cape Bet Din, the Union of Jewish Women, the Bnoth Zion Association, and the Herzlia day school.

CAPERNAUM (Heb. *Kephar Naḥum*): Ancient township on the NW shore of the Sea of Galilee. Jesus visited the place and preached in the synagogue. The Jewish settlement continued probably until the 6th cent. It is identified with the present Tel Hum with its well-preserved remains of a fine synagogue consisting of a large hall and courtyard, dated between the 2nd and 4th cents. In 1894, Franciscan monks acquired the site, built a monastery, and restored part of the synagogue.

CAPHTOR: Place of origin of the Philistines according to the Bible (Gen. 10:14 *et al*); Jeremiah (47:4) calls it an island. Although the old translations identify C. with Cappadocia, several other Bible texts associate the Philistines with the Cherethites (Cretans according to the Septuagint – I Sam. 30–14, etc.), and C. is generally thought to be Crete.

*CAPISTRANO, JOHN OF (1386–1456): Italian Franciscan preacher. He was one of the inspirers of the reaction against the Jews in Sicily, Italy, and Central Europe in the middle of the 15th cent. and was directly responsible for the burning of Jews in Breslau (1453) and for many other persecutions and expulsions.

CAPITAL PUNISHMENT: The following are the main offenses for which biblical law decrees c.p.: murder, certain sexual crimes (including incest and adultery), blasphemy, idolatry, Sabbath-desecration, witchcraft, kidnapping, and dishonor of parents. However, according to talmudic law there can be no capital conviction unless two eye-witnesses testify to the crime. In addition, the perpetrator must have been previously warned concerning the crime and its punishment. Only a court of 23 judges is permitted to try cases where the punishment is death. The Bible mentions only three types of c.p.: stoning, burning, and slaying with the sword. Rabbinic law finds biblical basis for a fourth, strangulation. This last was the method of execution applied in all cases where the mode of c.p. is not specifically prescribed in the Bible. Hanging, mentioned in Deut. 21:22, is regarded by the rabbis as referring to exposure after death practiced in the case of idolators and blasphemers. The manner of burning was a matter of dispute between the Sadducees and Pharisees. Stoning is primarily the act of throwing the convicted person from an elevation. C. p. in general was only rarely carried out and was suspended under Roman rule; later, many rabbis advocated its total abolition. Nevertheless, it was known in exceptional cases even in the Middle Ages. The state of Israel has abolished c. p. in all cases except treason in time of war and genocide.

CAPITALISM: The devotion of privately owned resources to large-scale production for profit through private enterprise, or the social system created by such. With the rise of a free economy in Holland in the 17th cent., Jews were active in applying merchant capital to imports which expanded production. They were thus associated with the origin of investment capital. Jews had little to do directly with the 19th cent. industrial revolution. Nevertheless, for a short time in the 19th cent., Jews were important to the growth of c. as the main holders of liquid capital in Central Europe (especially in Germany), where the development of industry owed much to Jewish private BANKING. Jews made contributions to industrial development in most countries (e.g. the diamond industry in S Africa, textiles and metal manufacture in the US, sugar in Russia prior to 1917, textiles in Poland, etc.) In Israel, private capital has played its share in opening up the country (e.g. Palestine Potash Company, Palestine Electric Company, etc.). After World War I, conditions in E and Central Europe led to the gradual elimination of Jewish capitalists owing to their exclusion from markets and the difficulty of obtaining raw materials as a result of internal competition and state control. The Bolshevik Revolution of 1917, the Nazi era (1933–45), and the communist regime in the satellite countries since 1945 have completed the elimination of the Jewish capitalist in E and Central Europe.

CAPITATION TAX see **POLL TAX**

CAPON, AUGUSTO (1872–1943): Italian admiral, to which rank he was promoted in 1931 after serving with distinction in the Italian-Turkish War and World War I. Wearing his medals, he was deported by the Germans from Rome to his death in Auschwitz.

CAPP, AL (1909–): US cartoonist. His cartoon strips, chief among them *Li'l Abner*, are widely syndicated in the American press.

CAPPADOCIA: Ancient province of Asia Minor; under Roman rule from 1st cent. BCE. Jews are first mentioned there in the 2nd cent. BCE and Glaphyra, princess of C., married Alexander, son of Herod 1. The Jews of C., some of whom were engaged in the linen trade, were in close touch with Palestine and a number settled in Jaffa, Sepphoris, and Tiberias. A large community existed in Mazaca and several amoraim came from C.

CAPSALI, ELIJAH (c. 1483 – c. 1555): Historian. He was head of the Jewish community in Crete. His works include histories of Turkey and of Venice, neither yet published in full, containing valuable information on the exiles from Spain and the Jewish communities in N Italy.

CAPSALI, MOSES (c. 1420 – c. 1497): Scholar. He was dayyan in Constantinople, and after the Turkish capture of the town in 1453 was appointed chief rabbi *(Ḥakham Bashi)* of the Ottoman Empire.

CAPTIVE: The only biblical legislation specifically concerning c.'s is that governing a woman taken in battle and desired in marriage by the victorious Israelite (Deut. 21:10–14). If her captor should change his mind after cohabitation, she must be set free. In talmudic times and afterwards, Jewish law concerned itself with Jewish captives and the duty of ransoming them, this being given priority over any other *mitzvah*. The ransoming of a Jewish woman who suffered captivity was given precedence owing to the threat to chastity involved. In medieval times, Jews were frequently incarcerated and ransoms extorted. A Society for Redeeming the Captives (*Ḥevrat Pidyon Shevuyyim*) was established by members of the Sephardi community of Venice in the 17th cent. for ransoming captives taken by Mediterranean pirates and the Knights of Malta. This was subsequently imitated in many other communities, some of which appointed special Wardens of Captives (*Parnassim dos cautivos*) to collect funds for the purpose.

CAPUA: Town in S Italy. Its Jewish community dates back to Roman times, and it was the home of notable medieval Jewish scholars. The Jews were expelled in 1510, returned shortly afterwards, and were finally driven out on the expulsion from the kingdom of Naples in 1541.

*CARACALLA, MARCUS ANTONINUS AURELIUS: Roman emperor, ruled 211–7. Like his father, Septimius Severus, he tended to favor the Jews and has been identified by some with ANTONINUS, the friend of Judah Ha-Nasi. In 212, he extended Roman citizenship to all inhabitants of the Roman Empire, including Jews.

CARCASSONNE: Town in SW France in which Jews were residing by the 6th cent. They flourished under the protection of the viscount of C. until the Albigensian Crusade (1229). Thereafter, their condition deteriorated and they were temporarily expelled in 1253, again in 1306, and finally in 1394. The town was a center of Jewish scholarship and several Jewish families bear the name of C. 75 Jews were living there in 1970.

CARDIFF: Welsh city. Jews were present there in the 18th cent. and a community was founded in 1840. There are 2,500 Jews (1973) with three synagogues (one Reform) and numerous charitable and educational institutions.

CARDOZO (CARDOSO): Sephardi family with many branches (Aboab C., Nuñez C., etc.). Its most important members were: *AARON NUNEZ C.* (1762–1834): Diplomat. He was head of the Jewish community of Gibraltar, enjoyed the friendship of Nelson, and on various occasions conducted diplomatic negotiations between Great Britain and the Moslem states of N Africa. *ABRAHAM* (formerly Miguel) *C.* (c. 1630–1706): Marrano physician and mystic. After a youth devoted to pleasure, he reverted to Judaism in Italy. He then became a devoted adherent of Shabbetai Tzevi, carrying out unremitting propaganda in behalf of his pretensions even after his apostasy, and expounding Sabbetaian doctrines in a number of books which circulated in ms. After practic-

Stop blessing the Moon! It is an artificial one !! (A caricature by Y. Bass.).

ing as a physician in various parts of the Mediterranean, he was killed by his nephew in a family quarrel in Cairo. *ISAAC* (formerly Fernando) *C.* (c. 1615–1681): Marrano physician; brother of Abraham. Born in Portugal, and formerly a royal physician in Madrid, he settled in Verona (Italy) as a professing Jew. He published a number of books, a famous apologetic work in Spanish, *Las Excellencias de los Hebreos.* The first of the C.'s to settle in the US was *AARON NUNEZ C.* who left London in 1752. *DAVID NUNEZ C.* (1752–1835) and *ISAAC NUNEZ C.* (1751–1832) fought against the British in the American Revolutionary War as members of the Charleston Militia of Carolina. *JACOB N.C.* (1786–1873): S Carolina journalist and economist was author of *Notes on Political Economy* and editor of *The Southern Patriot* 1823–45. *ALBERT JACOB C.* (1828–1885) was elected to the Supreme Court of New York State in 1867, but five years later resigned, following a recommendation for his impeachment as a result of Tammany scandals. His son, *BENJAMIN NATHAN C.* (1870–1938), was named in 1914 to the New York Court of Appeals, became chief judge in 1927, and in 1932, succeeded Oliver Wendell Holmes on the Supreme Court of the US where he served with distinction until his death. Justice Cardozo earned a reputation as a liberal, as well as for his humane approach to the law, and for the literary style of his decisions. He was a devoted, though not an observant, Jew.

CARICATURES: The earliest c. of Jews may be certain terra cotta figures of the Roman period with exaggerated Semitic features. The first known caricature, in the modern sense, of a group of Jews is found in an English Exchequer Roll of 1233. Very gross anti-Jewish c. in various media were common in Germany at the close of the Middle Ages, and engraved c. received wide popularity after the discovery of printing. In England, c. were published at the time of the Readmission controversy (1655–6) and the "Jew Bill" (1753). The English periodicals such as *Punch* commented regularly in the early Victorian age on the struggle for Jewish Emancipation, at first in an unfavorable spirit; while in France, the Dreyfus Case engendered a great spate of c., both for and against. In Germany, the tradition of fierce anti-Jewish c. persisted throughout the 19th cent., and reached a climax in the pornographic publications in Streicher's *Der Stürmer* in the Nazi Period. Jews prominent as caricaturists include: William Gropper, Frederick B. Opper (Opp), Al Capp, and Herbert Block (Herblock) in the US; in Great Britain, Victor Weisz (Vicky); and Aryeh Navon, Cariel Gardosh (Dosh), Yaakov Farkash (Ze'ev), and Yoseph Bass in Israel.

CARIGAL (also **CARREGAL, KARIGAL,** etc.), **RAPHAEL HAYYIM ISAAC** (1929–1777): Palestinian rabbi and emissary. On his two visits to the US (1761–4 and 1772–3), he became friendly with Ezra Stiles, later president of Yale, who mentions him frequently in his *Diary*. He died in Barbados.

CARLEBACH: (1) *AZRIEL C.* (1908–1956): Israel journalist; grandson of (3). After working in Yiddish and German journalism in Europe, he settled in Palestine (1936). He founded and edited the evening papers *Yedioth Aḥaronot* (1939) and *Maariv* (1948). (2) *JOSEPH C.* (1883–1944): Rabbi; son of (3). After

Ancient Caves on mount Carmel.

teaching in Jerusalem, he founded the first Hebrew secondary school in Kovno and succeeded his father as rabbi of Lübeck, later becoming chief rabbi, first of Altona, then of Hamburg. He was murdered by the Nazis near Riga. (3) *SOLOMON C.* (d. 1919): Rabbi of Lübeck.

CARMEL (1) Mountain range in Israel, between the Valley of Jezreel, the Haifa coastal plain, and the Mediterranean. Its highest point is 1,742 ft. above sea level. Haifa's modern suburbs extend up its slopes. The Bible frequently mentions C. which is included in the borders of Asher. It was the site of Elijah's victory over the prophets of Baal (I Kings 18–19 ff) and of Elisha's residence (II Kings 4:25) and is a symbol of beauty and fruitfulness. Carmel wine is mentioned in the Talmud *(Niddah 21a)*. In Crusader times, its numerous caves attracted solitary anchorites who organized themselves in the 12th cent. as the "Society of the Carmelites"; their monastery at the top of the mountain was built over an ancient cave, traditionally Elisha's. At the foot of the hill is the "Cave of Elijah," sacred to Jews, Christians, and Moslems since early times. (2) Ancient town in Judah; home of Nabal and Abigail (I Sam. 25).

CARMEL, MOSHEH (1911–): Israel political leader. Born in Poland, he settled in Palestine in 1924, and since 1939, has been a member of kibbutz Naan. He was an officer in the *Haganah* and later, the Israel army, commanding the northern district 1948–50, with the rank of brigadier-general. An Israel Labor Party (formerly *Aḥdut ha-Avodah*) member of the Knesset, C. was minister of communications 1955–9 and from 1965 to 1969.

Raphael Hayyim Carigal.

CARMIEL: Israel urban settlement in Lower Galilee.
It was founded in 1964 as part of the plan for Jewish settlement in the area. The settlers are mostly veteran Israelis and immigrants from E Europe. Pop. (1974): 6,300.

CARMOLY, ELIAKIM (1802–1875): German scholar.
Rabbi of Brussels for some years, he published many works and documents (a history of Jewish physicians, descriptions of travels to Palestine, etc.), the reliability, and sometimes the authenticity, of which have been impugned.

CARMONA: Turkish family of financiers. (1) *BEHOR ISAAC C.* (1773–1826) was court banker during the reign of Sultan Mahmoud II, but the accusations of his enemies led to his execution by strangling. He supported religious and charitable institutions. (2) *DAVID C.* (fl. 19th cent.), son of (1), was appointed senator by Sultan Abdul Hamid and presided for ten years over the *Mejlis Jismani* (Jewish Community Council). (3) *SOLOMON (CORMANO) C.*: Agent of Solomon Ibn-Yaish, duke of Mytilene, on whose behalf he went to London in 1592 on a mission to Queen Elizabeth.

CARO, GEORG MARTIN (1867–1912): Economic historian. Born at Glogau, he taught in Zurich and wrote on Jewish economic and social history.

CARO, HEINRICH (1834–1910): German chemist.
He revolutionized the dyeing industry by his discoveries of aniline red, methylene blue, and phosgene dyes.

CARO, JOSEPH (1488–1575): Codifier. Born in Toledo, he was taken by his parents from Spain on the expulsion (1492), and after much wandering they settled in Constantinople (1498). He moved to Adrianople c. 1518, and in 1525, went to Palestine, founding a yeshivah at Safed. Here he wrote his code *Bet Yoseph* ("House of Joseph"; 1550–9), a commentary on JACOB BEN ASHER'S *Arbaah Turim,* and also compiled its classical abbreviation, the *Shulhan Arukh* ("The Prepared Table"; 1564–5), collecting the views of previous codifiers and giving his own decisions on disputed points. C.'s codes were greeted with sharp opposition, especially by Ashkenazi scholars who claimed that they were based on the codifications of Spanish rabbis, ignoring the French and German traditions. Particularly critical was MOSES ISSERLES in his *Darkhe Mosheh* and *Ha-Mappah.* Nevertheless, the *Shulhan Arukh,* printed together with Isserles' strictures, became the authoritative code and is still recognized by Orthodox Jews throughout the world. C. was a zealous supporter of Jacob BERAB's ordination scheme and was one of the first rabbis to be ordained by him. He was also interested in Kabbalah and claimed that religious secrets were divulged to him by an angel *(maggid).*

CARO, NIKODEM (1871–1935): German chemist.
Together with Adolf Frank, he developed the cyanamide process for the fixation of nitrogen.

CARPATHO-RUSSIA: Region on the S slopes of the Carpathian mountains, now in the Ukrainian Soviet Republic. Jews lived there from the 17th cent., and the region was a stronghold of Hasidism. Their numbers before World War II (when C. was part of Czechoslovakia) exceeded 100,000 (14%), of whom a fifth were engaged in agriculture. Under German rule they were transferred to Auschwitz and massacred.

CARPENTRAS: Principal Jewish community of the former COMTAT VENAISSIN where Jews were allowed by the Popes to remain after their expulsion from the rest of France in the 14th cent. The community first came into prominence in the 13th cent. and maintained its importance until the close of the 18th., although from 1460 it was forced into a ghetto (CARRIÈRE). It followed its own liturgy which contained many local historical reminiscences. The community numbers 150 (1971) and the synagogue (built 14th cent., restored 18th cent.) is a national monument.

CARREGAL see **CARIGAL**

CARRIÈRE (DES JUIFS): French term applied in Avignon and the Comtat Venaissin to the ghetto: the local Jews called it by the Hebrew term *Mesillah* (which they pronounced *Mefilla).*

CARRION, SANTOB DE (fl. 14th cent.): Poet writing in Hebrew and Spanish. His collection of aphorisms *Proverbios Morales,* dedicated to King Pedro of Castile, is the principal work by a medieval Jew to enter Spanish literature. Recently, it has been proved that he is identical with the Hebrew poet Shem Tov Ibn Ardutial.

CARTHAGE (from the Punic *Karta Hadatta* = "New Town"): Settlement founded by Phoenicians in N Africa; possibly the biblical Tarshish. Jews are first mentioned there c. 200 CE but were then already long-established. The Jewish cemetery of the Roman Period had 3,000 tombs, and Jewish proselytization was apparently active in the 3rd and 4th cents. The community declined due to persecution after the conquest by Justinian (535). The Talmud mentions various scholars from C.

CARTOGRAPHY: The drawing of maps. One of the centers of c. in the Middle Ages was the Mediterranean island of Majorca, where Abraham Cresques (d. 1387) was "Master of Maps and Compasses" to the Infant Juan of Aragon, and his son Jahuda (later baptized forcibly as Jayme Ribes) was also outstanding. Their productions included the monumental Catalan Atlas in the Bibliothèque Nationale, Paris. The knowledge of the Mediterranean shown by these and other Majorcan Jewish cartographers (e.g. Hayyim ibn Rish) was remarkable. About 1500, Judah Abenzara of Alexandria and Safed produced important maps. The first Jewish map of Palestine with Hebrew lettering appeared in the Amsterdam Haggadah (1695).

CARVAJAL, ANTONIO FERNANDEZ (Abraham Israel; c. 1590–1659): A founder of the modern

Casablanca: École de l'Habitat Israélite.

English Jewish community. He furnished the Parliamentary forces with supplies during the Civil War, and through his foreign connections, was able to give valuable political intelligence to Cromwell. C. headed the crypto-Jewish community founded by Manasseh ben Israel in London and led it when it emerged into the open.

CASABLANCA: Moroccan port. Jews have lived there in numbers since the 8th cent. The community grew rapidly after the French occupation in 1907: at that time they numbered 5,000; in 1940, 20,000; and in 1960, 72,000. Since then it declined and in 1973 numbered 30,000. The increase was due to the high birthrate and the influx from the interior of the country. It is still the largest Jewish community of N Africa and a center of communal life. The Alliance Israélite Universelle, which founded the first Jewish school there in 1897, now maintains a school system. The condition of the great majority of the Jews is abject, most of them being crowded into the miserable *mellah*, but their position is being improved as a result of systematic welfare work by European and American organizations such as ORT.

*CASIMIR III (THE GREAT): King of Poland (reigned 1333–70) who welcomed Jewish refugees from Germany and became known as "King of the Serfs and the Jews." He ratified and extended the privileges enjoyed by the Jews in Poland (1334, 1364, 1367), these becoming henceforth their basic charter of liberty. His benevolence may have been due to the influence of his mistress Esterka, the daughter of a Jewish tailor in Opoczno, who bore him two sons and a daughter.

CASPI, JOSEPH BEN ABBA MARI (c. 1280– c. 1340): Commentator, philosopher, and grammarian; born in L'Argentière, lived at Tarascon (S France). Many of his works have been lost but of those known, the most important are two commentaries on Maimonides' *Guide*. In his philosophy, C. was a follower of Aristotle and Averroes, equating their teachings with Judaism. His daring conclusions evoked the opposition of many rabbis who regarded his views as heretical. His Bible commentary is a combination of literal and homiletic expositions in which miracles are explained by natural phenomena.

CASSEL: German city. The first information on Jewish settlement in C. dates from the end of the 13th cent. The community suffered during the Black Death persecutions (1349) and was expelled in 1524. Only individual Jews lived there until the 18th cent. when a synagogue was opened (1714). Jews played a considerable role in developing the city's commerce and industry (e.g. paints, textiles) in the 19th cent. The community, numbering 2,300 in 1933, ended under the Nazis. Jewish pop. (1970): 106.

CASSEL: (1) *DAVID C.* (1818—1893): German scholar. He taught at various institutions and

Sir Ernest Cassel.

from 1872, was lecturer at the Lehranstalt für die Wissenschaft des Judentums in Berlin. C. published many works on Judaica including a history of Jewish literature, German translations of the Apocrypha and of Judah Ha-Levi's *Kuzari*, and critical editions of several Hebrew classics. (2) *PAULUS STEPHANUS C.* (1821–1892): German convert to Christianity and missionary; brother of (1). His writings include a history of the Jews, essays on Judaism, and biblical studies.

CASSEL, SIR ERNEST (1852–1921): Financier and philanthropist. Born in Cologne, he went to England as a young man, rose to great wealth, and made benefactions on a vast scale. He was on terms of close friendship with Edward VII.

CASSIN, RENE (1887–1976): French lawyer, statesman, and Nobel Prize winner. He was professor at Lille and at the Sorbonne and French

René Cassin.

delegate to the League of Nations 1924–38. In 1940, C. was among the first to join the Free French, becoming national commissioner for justice and education under General de Gaulle 1941–3. He was a French delegate to the UN General Assembly 1946–51, and from 1944, head of the Conseil d'Etat. In 1968, he was awarded the Nobel Peace Prize. C. was president of the Alliance Israélite Universelle.

CASSIRER: German family. (1) *ERNEST C.* (1874–1945): German philosopher; taught at Hamburg, Oxford, Göteborg, Yale, and Columbia. Starting out as an epistemologist on a neo-Kantian basis, he developed his theory of symbolic forms to embrace all phenomena of human culture. His works include *The Philosophy of Symbolic Forms* and *An Essay on Man.* (2) *PAUL C.* (1871–1926): German art dealer. His Berlin salon was a notable artistic center.

CASSIUS DIO see **DIO CASSIUS**

CASSUTO, MOSES DAVID (Umberto; 1883–1951): Biblical scholar and historian. Born in Florence, he was appointed chief rabbi in 1922 and director of the Collegio Rabbinico Italiano there in 1925. From 1933, he was professor of Hebrew at the Univ. of Rome and from 1939, professor of Bible at the Hebrew Univ., Jerusalem. C. evolved an approach to Bible research which utilized modern scientific discoveries to demonstrate the uniformity of the text. He was editor-in-chief of the *Entziklopedia Mikrait* ("Biblical Encyclopedia," 1950 ff), and prepared the Jerusalem Bible for publication (1953). His articles on Ugaritic are outstanding. He wrote a monograph on the Jews in Florence during the Renaissance.

CASTEL, MOSHEH (1909–): Painter. Born in Jerusalem of a Bokharan family, he has sought to express Bokharan traditions in his art and has painted vivid pictures of synagogues and ceremonial life. His later work has tended to the abstract.

CASTELNUOVO-TEDESCO, MARIO (1895–1968): Italian composer who settled in the US in 1939. His compositions include operas, several overtures to plays by Shakespeare, a violin concerto, a concertino for harp and seven instruments, Sephardi songs, and chamber works.

CASTILE: Largest province of Spain, formerly (from 1037) an independent kingdom; after 1230 united with Leon. Jews resided in C. almost from the beginning of its political history. With the conquest of Toledo in 1085, C. became the most important center of Spanish Jewry, and its subsequent expansion southward brought more Jews under its rule. In 1146, C. received large numbers of Jews expelled from Andalusia by the ALMOHADES. As in its sister kingdom of ARAGON (where the Jewish population was denser) the Jews were treated relatively well in the early

Mosheh Castel.

Balthasar (Isaac) Orobio de Castro.

Middle Ages, but later their condition deteriorated. The arrest of the Jews of C. in 1281 in order to exact a levy, Gonzalo Martinez's foiled attempt at their expulsion in 1339, the overthrow of their patron King Pedro in 1360, the massacres of 1391, and the conversionist sermons of Vincente Ferrer in 1411, etc. marked successive stages in the decline of the status and security of Castilian Jewry. Nevertheless, down to the 15th cent. Jewish notables were influential in the Castilian court.

CASTRO, DE: Family of Spanish origin, later established in France, Egypt, Turkey, Holland, Germany, England, and the US. (1) *ABRAHAM DE C.:* Master of the mint in Cairo in the 16th cent. His warning to Sultan Suleiman II of Turkey of a plot by Pasha Aḥmad Shaitan to make himself independent ruler of Egypt and the subsequent averting of Aḥmad's anti-Jewish designs resulted in the establishment of a local Cairo Purim. (2) *BALTHASAR (ISAAC) OROBIO DE C.* (1620–1687): Philosopher and physician. For three years he was imprisoned and tortured by the Inquisition in Spain. Subsequently, he went to Toulouse where he openly professed Judaism. He wrote numerous polemical works in Latin and Spanish, including an attack on the ethics of Spinoza. (3) *BENEDICT (BARUCH) NEHAMIAS DE C.* (1597–1684): After practicing medicine in Hamburg from 1625,

he became physician to the queen of Sweden (1645). For some time, he was president of the Portuguese-Jewish congregation at Hamburg, and became a zealous follower of Shabbetai Tzevi. (4) *DAVID HENRIQUES DE C.* (1832–1898): Dutch bibliophile, numismatist, and historian of Amsterdam Jewry. (5) *HENRY DE C.* (1786–1861): Texas pioneer. He organized the emigration of over 5,000 colonists from the Rhineland for settlement in Texas. (6) *ISAAC DE C. TARTAS* (1623–1647): Martyr. His heroism at the stake in Lisbon, with the *Shema* on his lips, became legendary. (7) *JACOB DE C.* (1758–1815): English actor whose memoirs throw much light on stage history and English Jewish life. (8) *JACOB (HENRIQUE) DE C. SARMENTO* (1691–1761): Marrano physician who was active for a short period in the life of the Jewish community in London from 1720. He was elected a Fellow of the Royal Society in 1725 and was one of the earliest English advocates of vaccination. (9) *MOSES DE C.* (16th cent.): Egyptian rabbi who settled in Jerusalem in 1530, and successfully opposed Jacob Berab on the question of ORDINATION. (10) *RODRIGO DE C.* (1550–1627): Marrano physician who settled in Hamburg in 1594. His work on diseases of women, published in 1612, was the starting point of modern gynecology.

Fresco in the Jewish catacombs at Villa Torlonia, Rome.

CASUISTRY see **PILPUL**

CATACOMBS: Subterranean burial galleries with side recesses for tombs, such as were used by the early Christians in Rome. The system apparently originated with the Jews in Palestine where the recently-discovered c. of Bet Shearim seem to have served as a central burial place between the late 2nd and 4th cents. In Rome, six separate systems of Jewish c. of the Classical Period, containing many hundreds of inscriptions, have been found. Jewish c. are also known elsewhere in Italy (especially in Venosa) and in N Africa.

CATALONIA: Spanish province, formerly an independent county with its capital at Barcelona; later, incorporated in the kingdom of Aragon. Jews were settled in this area from the Arab Period, and in the later Middle Ages. C. is believed to have had the densest Jewish settlement in all Europe. The greatest strength of Aragonese Jewry derived from this nucleus. It suffered with special severity in the persecutions of 1391. Catalonian congregations were established after 1492 in Rome, Salonica, etc., and, in the latter place, preserved their own liturgy.

CATECHISM: Instruction, especially in religious doctrine, by question and answer. The method was introduced into Jewish literature in Abraham Jaghel's *Lekah Tov* (Venice 1587: often republished) but never became popular until the Emancipation Period, when many c.'s were published. S.I. Cohen's *Elements of Faith for the Use of the Jewish Youth* (Hebrew and English: London 1815) occasioned much controversy because of its views on Orthodoxy but continued in use for a long time. Many c.'s appeared at this period also in German, French, Italian, etc. C.'s on the laws of *shehitah* were common long before this time in Hebrew and in other languages.

CATECHUMENS, HOUSE OF (*Casa dei Catecumeni*): Hostel for Jewish converts set up in Rome in 1548. It was supported by taxation on the Jewish community of Rome. No professing Jew was allowed to pass under its windows lest he should communicate with the inmates. Similar institutions existed in other Italian cities.

***CATHERINE:** Name of two Russian empresses. *C. I*, ruled 1725-7, and in May 1727, expelled all Jews resident in Little Russia. This order was countermanded after her death. *C. II* ("*the Great*") ruled 1762–96, and her Jewish policy was marked by a combination of liberalism and coercion. On the one hand, Jews were allowed to register in the merchant and urban classes (1780), but permission was restricted to White Russia (1786); this marked the beginning of the Pale of Settlement. During her last years, which were marked by reaction (1789–96), she prevented the extension of Jewish settlement and in 1795, prohibited Jewish residence in rural areas.

CATHOLICISM see **CHRISTIANITY; CHURCH COUNCILS; POPES**

CATTAUI: Prominent Egyptian family. *YAKOUB C.* (19th cent.) was master of the Egyptian mint. His son *MOSES C.* (d. 1924) was president of the Cairo Jewish community from 1883 until his death. Another son *JOSEPH ASLAN C.* (1861–(1943) was Egyptian senator (1923), minister of finance and communications (1924), and president of the Jewish community (1924).

CAUCASUS: Region now in S Russia. Its Jewish population in 1940 consisted of (1) 40,000 Ashkenazi Jews who arrived from Russia after

Jews of the Caucasus.

1859. Their language is Russian and their main centers are at BAKU, TIFLIS, Kutaisi, and Batum. (2) 21,105 Jews from GEORGIA, speaking Georgian and living there since antiquity; and (3) 25,866 Mountain Jews known as Dag Chufut, residing chiefly in AZERBAIJAN and Daghestan and speaking Judeo-Tati; of Persian origin, they have lived there since the 6th cent. More recently they have left the mountains and live in the cities of the Kabadrin-Balkar Autonomous Republic. According to the 1959 records, 125,000 Jews were living in the C. The Jews of C. were mentioned by Pethahiah of Regensburg (latter 12th cent.), while 14th cent. Russian chronicles mention a "Land of Jews" in the C. Many Jews there were compelled to embrace Islam in the 17th–18th cents. The community suffered during the civil was of 1918–1921.

CAVAILLON: Small town in the Comtat Venaissin (Provence) where Jews were living in the 5th cent. They were allowed to remain in the area, which was under Papal rule, after the expulsion from the rest of France. C. was one of the "Four Communities" (with Avignon, Carpentras, L'Isle) maintaining a special rite of prayer. The Jewish community has become extinct within the past generations. The synagogue was rebuilt in 1774 over the ghetto gateway.

CAYENNE (French Guiana): French colony on N coast of S America named after the adjacent island. Jews first settled there under Dutch rule in 1654 after the Portuguese reconquest of Brazil. Jewish civil law was accorded recognition in the charter given to David Nassy by the Dutch West India Company in 1659. About 150 Jews migrated there from Leghorn in 1660. Jews left the colony when it came under French control (1664), and there has been no Jewish settlement since. Devil's Island, scene of the confinement of Alfred DREYFUS, is off the coast of C.

CEJTLIN, HILLEL see **ZEITLIN, HILLEL**
CELIBACY. see **ASCETICISM**
CELLER, EMANUEL (1888–): US public figure. He was congressman from New York 1923–72 and was chairman of the House Judiciary Committee 1949–52. He wrote an autobiography *You Never Leave Brooklyn.*

CEMETERY (called in Hebrew *Bet Olam,* i.e., "Eternal Home," *Bet Kevarot* i.e., "House of Graves," or euphemistically *Bet Ḥayyim* i.e., "House of Life"): In ancient times, the c. usually consisted of a series of vaults in natural caves, royalty having burial places separate from those of the ordinary people. According to Jewish law, the c.'s were to be located fifty ells from the city, a special benediction was recited on entering, and they were forbidden to priests in order to prevent ritual defilement. Buildings for discharging burial rites were usually attached. The graves were customarily visited on anniversaries or fast days and during the month preceding *Rosh ha-Shanah,* but a frequenter of c.'s was regarded as demented or as a sorcerer. In the Middle Ages, Jewish c.'s were often referred to as the Jews' Gardens. The Jewish c.'s of

Military Cemetery, Jerusalem.

Prague, Amsterdam, and Venice, containing ancient artistic monuments, are especially famous.

CENSORSHIP: The campaign against Hebrew literature in the Middle Ages began with the Disputation of Paris (1240) followed by the condemnation and burning of the Talmud. The first traces of a less sweeping c. were after the Disputation of Barcelona (1263), when the Jews were ordered to delete references to Jesus from all copies of Maimonides' *Code*. Systematic censorship began in Italy, after the burning of the Talmud, with the Papal Bull of 1554 which specified that works other than the Talmud might be owned by Jews if they contained no blasphemies against Christianity. Henceforth, in most of Italy, Hebrew books could be retained only if they had been examined and signed by the Christian censor (generally an apostate from Judaism), who tore out pages and blackened out passages to which he objected. For safety, the Jewish Synod at Ferrara (1554) instituted a pre-censorship by the rabbinical authorities to ensure that nothing objectionable should be published. In some areas (e.g. Venice), books had to be submitted to the secular authorities before publication. Similar c. of Jewish literature applied in the Austrian dominions in the 17th–18th cents. and in Russia after 1790. Many copies of early Hebrew books still bear the censor's marks. In Israel, censorship of publications is maintained in matters affecting national security.

CENSUS: Enumeration of a people. The Bible records several counts, two of them by Moses, in which every male who had reached the age of 20 contributed half a shekel. The counting of the shekel gave the number, a direct c. being considered sinful. Such a c. carried out by David was followed by an epidemic in which thousands died. The traditional attitude was the main cause for the Jewish opposition to a Roman c. Estimates of Jewish population since biblical times have generally been only speculative. In relatively recent years, however, Jewish population figures have become more reliable, partly due to the fact that many modern states record religious faith in their c. counts. A c. of the population of the state of Israel was taken in 1972. (See STATISTICS).

CENTRAL BRITISH FUND FOR JEWISH RELIEF AND REHABILITATION: Jewish charitable organization founded in 1933 as the Central British Fund for German Jewry, later, the Central Council for Jewish Refugees. It was the main English Jewish organization from 1933 onward for the relief of fugitives from Nazi persecution.

CENTRAL CONFERENCE OF AMERICAN RABBIS: Reform rabbinical association, established in 1889 by I. M. Wise. It has (1969) a membership of over 1,000 rabbis, most of them graduates of the Hebrew Union College—Jewish Institute of Religion. Its early strong anti-Zionism was modified to a neutral position on the Zionist issue, and in the "Columbus Platform" (1937) it affirmed the obligation of all Jewry to aid in the upbuilding of Palestine not only as a haven of refuge but also as a center of Jewish culture and spiritual life. In recent decades, it has inclined toward the re-introduction of traditional usage in modified form, the creation of new ceremonials for synagogue and home, and an increased use of Hebrew in the service. The *Union Prayer Book* (2 vols.), which the CCAR edits and publishes, has become the standard ritual used in Reform synagogues. Among the other publications of the Conference are the *Union Hymnal*, the *Union Haggadah*, the *Union Home Prayer Book*, a *Rabbi's Manual*, the *CCAR Journal*, and a *Yearbook*. The Conference works in close association with the UNION OF AMERICAN HEBREW CONGREGATIONS.

CENTRAL SEPHARDIC JEWISH COMMUNITY OF AMERICA, INC.: Organization of Sephardim in Greater New York. It was founded in 1941 by Nissim Ovadia, who was succeeded as religious leader by Isaac Alcalay. Under the community's leadership, several cultural and religious institutions, such as centers, Talmud Torahs, and a home for aged have been established. The Community encompasses 24 affiliated congregations and societies.

CENTRAL YIDDISH CULTURE ORGANIZATION (CYCO): Society founded in New York, 1935, to coordinate the cultural activities of the Workmen's Circle (*Arbeiter-Ring*), Jewish National Workers' Alliance (*Farband*), Yiddish Writers Union, and other groups. In 1940, it took over the *Yiddish Encyclopedia*, formerly published in Paris, and continued it both in Yiddish and English (*The Jewish People, Past and Present*; 4 vols. by 1956). In 1941, CYCO revived the monthly *Zukunft*. In 1943, it established a publishing house issuing works by outstanding Yiddish authors.

CENTRAL YIDDISH SCHOOL ORGANIZATION (CYSHO): Organization founded in Poland in 1921 by Jewish educational and cultural groups to stimulate the growth of Yiddish schools and coordinate their curricula, etc. Under its auspices were a teachers' seminary and a network of schools attended by over 20,000 pupils. CYSHO's activities ended with World War II.

CENTRAL-VEREIN DEUTSCHER STAATSBÜRGER JÜDISCHEN GLAUBENS (Ger.: "Central Union of German Citizens of the Jewish Faith"): Organization of German Jews, founded in Berlin in 1893, and dissolved by the Nazis in 1938. Its objectives were to fight anti-Semitism, to protect and strengthen Jewish civic and social status, and to unite all Jews regardless of their religious and political views and foster their German patriotism. The name was changed in Oct. 1935 to *Central-Verein der Juden in Deutschland* ("Central Union of the Jews in Germany"). The C. established the publishing house, PHILO VERLAG.

CENTRE DE DOCUMENTATION JUIVE CONTEMPORAINE (Fr. "Center of Contemporary Jewish Documentation"): Body founded in 1943 in Occupied France, under the presidency of Isaac Schneersohn, to gather documents dealing with the Nazi persecution of the Jews. After the liberation of France, the *Centre* was installed in Paris. It has published an important series of documentary works and furnished information during the trials of Nazi war-criminals. The *C.* was largely responsible for the monument to the "unknown Jewish martyr," dedicated in Paris in 1956.

CEREMONIAL LAWS (known as *mitzvot maasiyyot* "practical observances"): Rites and observances prescribed biblically and rabbinically (e.g. the ceremonies connected with Sabbaths and festivals, dietary laws, circumcision, marriage, death). The prophets and rabbis saw their importance not so much in the outward observance as in their beneficent influence on those who performed them (Amos 5:21–4; Gen. Rabbah 44.1), holding the c. l. responsible for the sanctification of Jewish life and the development of self-discipline. The recurrent rituals of everyday life (connected with prayer, food, etc.) were meant to remind man continually of his allegiance to God. Biblical and rabbinic literature lay particular stress on the practical performance of the ceremonials. Study of the law without practice of the precepts is not meritorious (*Yevamot* 109*b*). The observance of the ceremonials was regarded as of great pedagogical value, giving external expression to profound religious and moral truths. The c. l. were codified by a number of medieval rabbis, notably Maimonides, Moses of Coucy, Jacob ben Asher, and Joseph Caro (see LAW, CODIFICATION OF). The 19th cent. Reform movement challenged the efficacy of the c. l., stressing the ethical element in Judaism as crucial. Samuel Holdheim even rejected the entire ceremonial law. The modern Reform movement is less radical than its predecessors, maintaining certain ceremonies as permanently binding, while rejecting others as outmoded. Conservative Judaism permits reinterpretation in some instances.

CERF, BENNETT ALFRED (1898–1971): US publisher. He was president of Random House publishers. C. edited a number of anthologies, especially of humorous stories.

CERFBERR, HERZ (c. 1726–1794): Alsatian Jewish leader. As an army contractor, he received governmental permission to live in Strasbourg despite the opposition of the citizens who forbade Jews to reside there. C. sent Moses Mendelssohn a memorandum on Jewish life in Alsace (1780) which was utilized by Dohm in his work advocating an improvement in Jewish rights. C. was largely instrumental in securing equal rights for Jews from the Constituent Assembly.

CERNAUTI see **CHERNOVTSY**

CEYLON (SRI LANKA): Island S of India. *Genizah* documents evidence a Jewish mercantile settlement in C. during the Middle Ages, but otherwise there was no Jewish community.

CHAGALL, MARC (1887–): Artist. A native of Vitebsk, he left Russia in 1922, settling in Paris and rapidly making his reputation as one of the leading painters of the surrealist school. His lively fantasy, powerful use of color, and remarkable technical ability give his work a distinctive quality. He has sought his inspiration largely in the life of the E European Ḥasidim and village communities. The stained-glass windows at the Hadassah Medical Center in Jerusalem, the ceiling of the Paris Opera House, the frescoes for the Metropolitan Opera, New York, a glass window for the UN building, New York, tapestries for the Knesset, Jerusalem and a stained-glass panel for the Vatican audience hall (the first commission given by the Vatican to a Jewish artist), are later examples of his work.

CHAIBAR see **KHAIBAR**

CHAIN, SIR ERNST BORIS (1906–): Biochemist. Born in Germany, he went to England in 1933 and lectured in chemical pathology at Oxford. In 1945, he was awarded the Nobel Prize for physiology and medicine for his part in the discovery of the curative properties of penicillin. He was director of the International Research Center for Chemical Microbiology in Rome 1949-60 and professor of biochemistry at London Univ. from 1960.

CHAIR OF ELIJAH see **CIRCUMCISION**

CHAJES: (1) *TZEVI HIRSCH C.* (1805–1855): Galician scholar; rabbi at Zolkiev (1829–52) and Kalish (1852–5). Together with Naḥman Krochmal and Solomon Judah Rapoport, he was among the Galician pioneers of the scientific study of Judaica, but as a traditional Jew, his approach was less critical than theirs and his conclusions were never extreme. He wrote on the principles of the written and oral law, on the Targums and Midrash, an introduction to the Talmud, etc. (2) *TZEVI (HIRSCH) PERETZ C.* (1876–1927): Scholar; grandson of (1). After teaching at the rabbinical seminary in Florence, he was appointed chief rabbi at Trieste (1912). From 1918 until his death, he was chief rabbi of Vienna. C. was chairman of the Zionist General Council 1921–5. A gifted orator and scholar in many branches of Jewish studies, his works include books on biblical exegesis, archeology, Talmud, and medieval Hebrew poetry.

CHALCIS see **ITUREA**

Marc Chagall *The Chicken Slaughterer.*

CHALDEA, CHALDEANS (Heb. *Kasdim*): Semitic tribe which migrated to S Babylonia and adopted the ancient Babylonian culture. They gradually gained supremacy over the native inhabitants and gave their name to the entire area. Attempts were made, initially under Merodach-Baladan, to overthrow Assyria, and they finally succeeded in the 7th cent. BCE under Nabopolassar and his son Nebuchadnezzar who established an empire extending from Assyria to the Egyptian border. This was conquered by the Persians in 539. The fame of the Chaldeans as astrologers made the terms synonymous long after their empire had vanished. Aramaic has been called Chaldaic (or Chaldee), but this is a misnomer.

CHAMBER THEATER: Tel Aviv Hebrew theater group, founded in 1945 by the producer Yoseph Millo. Its repertoire includes classics, modern plays, and original Hebrew drama.

*CHAMBERLAIN, HOUSTON STEWART (1855–1927): Anti-Semitic writer. Son of a British admiral, C. became a German subject. His pseudo-scientific *Foundations of the 19th Century* (1898) developed fantastic anti-Semitic racial theories.

CHAMPAGNE: Region of NE France. Its international fairs attracted Jews from an early date and, according to legend, a Jewish community existed in Vitry-en-Perthois in 279. By the 10th cent., there were many Jews in the province, especially in its capital Troyes, home of Rashi; many of the latter's pupils (the tosaphists) taught at various places in C. (at Ramerupt, Dampierre, Vitry, etc.). The Jews were subjected by the counts of C. to severe taxation in the 12th cent. but in the 13th cent., increasingly enjoyed royal protection and acted as financiers to nobles, monasteries, etc. The general French expulsion orders of 1306–1394 affected them, and Jews reappeared in C. only in the 17th cent. At present, there are communities at Châlons, Rheims, Chaumont, Troyes, Epernay, and Vitry-le-François.

CHANTING see **ACCENTS; CANTOR**

CHAO: The principal family among the native Chinese Jews of Kai-Feng Fû. The surname was first conferred on the physician Yen Ch'êng in 1423. He was probably an ancestor of Chao Yng Ch'êng (in Hebrew, Moses ben Abram) the physician (17th cent.), who was the most outstanding Chinese Jew. He entered public service as a mandarin, occupied various high offices, suppressed a band of brigands in Fukien, and established schools for the common people. Going on leave to Kai-Feng-Fu (about 1660) after his father's death, he took the leading part in restoring the synagogue, destroyed in the floods of 1645, and in reassembling the sacred scrolls. He described this work in a book, now lost, and also edited a collection entitled *Records of the Hall of the Four Bamboos*. He was assisted in his work by his younger brother, the magistrate Chao Ying Tou. Their efforts were gratefully commemorated in a stele in the synagogue.

CHAPBOOKS: Unbound popular booklets sold by itinerant dealers. Ephemeral by nature, they seem originally (in the 18th cent.) to have been a regular feature of Jewish life in E Europe where hawkers sold, in the streets and market-places, vast numbers of poorly-printed works of popular appeal in Hebrew or Yiddish, including wonder-tales of Ḥasidic rabbis, ethical treatises intended especially for women, etc. Specific religious works (e.g. the Passover Haggadah or *Seliḥot*) were sometimes distributed in the same form, often with Yiddish translation. Later, popular works of fiction also appeared in a similar style. C. of this type, somewhat better produced, were published in the Balkans and N Africa. Stories about the "Wandering Jew" were the most popular c. of Jewish interest appearing in European languages. Hebrew c. were seldom illustrated except in the case of the Haggadah.

CHAPLAINS: The first Jewish military c. called to service were probably those appointed in the US army during the Civil War when four Jewish c. were appointed to serve in the Union army and its hospitals. During World War I, 25 US rabbis served as full-time Jewish c. in uniform. During World War II, a chaplaincy committee of the National Jewish Welfare Board was organized, consisting of an equal number of rabbis representing the Orthodox, Conservative, and Reform bodies. A total of 311 Jewish c. in uniform served both in the US and overseas; some lost their lives, others were wounded, and many were decorated for distinguished service. Notable for heroism was Chaplain Alexander Goode, one of the four American c. who lost their lives on the American military transport SS *Dorchester*. After World War II, 20 full-time Jewish c. remained in the armed forces. During the Korean War (1950–3), an average of 112 US Jewish c. were on duty. In 1973, the number was 71. In addition, there were full-time c. in the Veteran Administration hospitals and rabbis serving on a part-time basis as auxiliary c. at military installations. Chaplaincy services exist in other countries (Italy, France, formerly in Germany), but have not been so elaborately organized as in the US. In England, a Jewish minister was appointed acting chaplain to the Jews in the army (1892), but Jewish c. first served in the field in World War I. In World War II, c. served in every theater of the war. A Jewish chaplaincy system for hospitals and prisons is organized in most western countries. In the Israel army, the chaplaincy is a department of the manpower division. It supervises, among other things, *kashrut* and burials. Each regional command and brigade has a *ketzin rabbanut* (chaplain) and each battalion, a *sammal dat* (chaplain-sergeant).

The Four Chaplains on the S.S. Dorchester by Dudley.

CHARIOT MYSTICISM see **MAASEH BERESHIT AND MAASEH MERKAVAH**

CHARITY (Heb. *tzedakah* ["righteousness"; now used not in the biblical sense of righting wrongs but with the primary connotation of alms-giving] and talmudic *gemilut ḥasadim* ["doing of loving kindnesses," referring especially to such personal services as burying the dead and visiting the sick].): The Jewish conception from the earliest times has been that the needy are entitled to help, i.e., that the giving of c. is not a virtue but a duty. The biblical regulations regarding c. are adapted to a restricted agricultural society. They particularly prescribe succor of the widow, orphan, and stranger, the support of the aged being presumably the special care of the family. Regulations, such as those reserving the corner of the field (PEAH) for reaping by the needy, gave practical effect to ethical generalizations. In the Talmudic Period, the institution of c. was also made to cover education, this being long a characteristically Jewish conception. The principle was laid down that c. should also extend to non-Jews. Rabbinic legislation extended the obligatory aspects of c. beyond the bounds of an agricultural society. The Mishnah already assumed a well-defined system of organized relief. A c. box *(kuppah)* existed in every community, out of which the town poor were given money for 14 meals a week. Transient poor received a daily allocation. There was also a food-bowl *(tamhui)* from which food prepared in advance was distributed. Distinguished members of the community were c. administrators, known as *gabbaë tzedakah.* The trusteeship of the c. box was in the hands of three men who constituted a special court to decide on its proper disposal. Any individual resident in the community for 30 days automatically became obligated to contribute to the c. box. C. is one of the three bases of the world (*Avot* 1:2) and ranks among religious duties of special merit, "the profits of which man enjoys in this world, but the principal remains for the world to come" (*Peah* 1.1). Among the characteristic charitable activities for which provision was made were the dowering of poor brides, the burial of the indigent dead, and the ransoming of captives which was considered a paramount duty; the rabbis stipulate that in the highest form of c., donor and recipient are unknown to each other. Maimonides enumerates eight different degrees of giving c., the highest being to help the needy individual support himself in some occupation. In the Middle Ages, philanthropic institutions such as the hospice, etc., became firmly established; in the Ghetto Period, most communities maintained an elaborate system of charitable institutions which covered all emergencies. In the 19th cent., after Emancipation, Jews began to take a prominent part in all philanthropic work, applying to general c. not only the spirit but also some of the institutions that had developed in the Ghetto Period. In certain aspects — e.g. education, housing — the Jewish participation was particularly marked. The names of the Montefiore, Rothschild, and Sassoon families in the Old World, and of Rosenwald, Guggenheim, Straus, Schiff, and Warburg in the New, illustrate the Jews' philanthropic activities in recent times. Charitable organizations, served by professional instead of volunteer staffs, began to appear in Europe in the mid-19th cent. The persecution of Jews in Russia in the 1880's stimulated the creation of national organizations in central and western Europe, as well as in the US, for the relief of the suffering and the aid of those seeking refuge. The process was further stimulated in the early 20th cent. by the Kishinev and succeeding pogroms (1903–5) and the ensuing mass emigration from Russia. Funds were collected on a larger scale than ever before, especially in the US, where there was now organized the first of the "drives" which have become a familiar part of American Jewish communal life. The outbreak of World War I brought into existence three nation-wide relief committees in the US, which combined to create the AMERICAN JOINT DISTRIBUTION COMMITTEE. From this period onward, except for a relatively quiet interlude in the 1920's, the charitable demands on Jews throughout the free world have known no intermission: first to face the Nazi persecutions in Germany, then to deal with the manifold emergencies created by World War II, then to assist the creation and consolidation of the state of Israel and the absorption there of refugees from lands of actual or potential persecution. In the US and Canada, fund-raising for aid to Jews in other countries was greatly facilitated by the fact that the relevant machinery had been established in virtually every Jewish community, beginning in Cincinnati in 1896. The initial function of the community c. federations was to take over from the constituent societies the burden of fund-raising, but later the federation also influenced the communities to eliminate duplication and raise standards of administration. In some communities, however, there exist separate "welfare funds," etc. for aiding local organizations.

Mother lifting her child to deposit a coin into a Meir Ba'al Ha-Nes charity box. Boris Schatz, 1904.

The development of welfare activities by the state (e.g. care for the aged, national health insurance) is profoundly affecting the traditional direction of Jewish c.

*CHARLEMAGNE: Frankish king from 768, and the first Holy Roman Emperor 800–814. He patronized the Jews and encouraged their immigration, granting them security of life and property, freedom of religion, and exemption from excise taxes. He is known to have employed Jews in his court and on missions, and various legends were preserved in Jewish lore of favors bestowed by him.

CHARLESTON: City in S Carolina, US. Because of the state's liberal constitution, Jews were already living in C. in the late 17th cent. Immigrants from London and a few from Barbados, France, the Netherlands, Jamaica, etc. made up the bulk of the Jewish population in the 18th cent. In 1749, C.'s Jews founded Kahal Kadosh Beth Elohim, the oldest congregation in the state and the fourth oldest in N America. During the Revolutionary War, a third of Captain Richard Lushington's militia company was composed of Jews. There were 400 Jews in C. in 1791. It was here that the first Jewish reformed group in America came into being in 1824. After the Civil War, C.'s Jewish community began to decline, many going north. The last two decades of the 19th cent. saw E European and German immigrants assume numerical superiority. The community has 3 synagogues – one

Orthodox, one Conservative, and one Reform. Jewish pop. (1973): 3,000.

CHARNEY: (1) *DANIEL C.* (1888–1959): Yiddish poet and author; brother of (2). A native of Lithuania, he settled in the US in 1940. His works include poems, an autobiography, children's stories, and articles descriptive of E European Jewish life. (2) *SAMUEL C.* see *NIGER S.*

CHASANOWITSCH, LEON (pen-name of Kasriel Schub; 1882–1925): Labor Zionist leader and Yiddish journalist. Lithuanian born, he spread the *Poale Zion* ideology in various countries including Argentina, Austria, and the US. C. was very active in mobilizing support for Zionism at international socialist conferences and conventions.

CHASTITY: Abstention from unlawful or immoral sexual acts. Unchaste rites were a feature of many ancient religions, and the biblical emphasis on sexual purity is constantly linked with the condemnation of idolatry (cf. Lev. 18). Unchastity is the reason given for the expulsion of the Canaanites from Palestine. Four of the 12 curses listed in Deut. 27 are directed against sexual sins. Prophetic and Wisdom literature describe the dire consequences of unchastity. The rabbis, too, listed adultery with idolatry and murder as those cardinal sins which must not be committed even under pain of death. Early marriage was regarded as the best safeguard against sexual impurity.

CHATTANOOGA: City in Tennessee, US. Its first Jews settled there in 1858. In 1866, a Reform congregation, now called Mizpah, was formed. The first Orthodox congregation, B'nai Zion, was organized in 1888. C. now has 2 Orthodox and 2 Reform congregations with affiliated Hebrew schools. Its Jewish Welfare Federation was founded in 1931. Jewish pop. (1973): 2,250.

***CHAUCER, GEOFFREY** (c. 1340–1400): English poet. "The Prioress's Tale" in his *Canterbury Tales* is based on the Blood Libel, and at the end, there is a pious reference to HUGH OF LINCOLN.

CHAZANOVITZ, JOSEPH (1844–1919): Zionist and founder of the Jewish National Library. A physician by profession, he practiced in his native Grodno (Lithuania) and later at Bialystok and Yekaterinoslav where he died in poverty. One of the first members of *Hoveve Zion,* and later active in political Zionism, he conceived the establishment of a central Jewish library at Jerusalem. C. devoted his energies to gathering the nucleus of a collection which, in 1920, was recognized as the NATIONAL LIBRARY.

CHAZARS see **KHAZARS**

***CHEDORLAOMER:** King of Elam (Gen. 14). Together with his confederates, he overcame five Canaanite kings in S Palestine, but was defeated by Abraham who recaptured the spoil and liberated his captive nephew, Lot.

CHELKIAS (Heb. *Ḥilkiyyah*): Egyptian general. He and his brother Ananias (Hananiah), sons of the exiled high priest ONIAS IV, commanded the forces of Cleopatra in Palestine against her son, Ptolemy Lathyrus, king of Cyprus (102 BCE). It was due to their influence that Cleopatra confirmed Alexander Yannai's rule over Palestine.

CHELM: Polish town. Its Jewish settlement, dating from the 15th cent., was destroyed during the Cossack massacres of 1648 but subsequently was refounded. The community numbered 7,615 before World War II; some escaped to Russia in 1939, the remainder being killed by the Nazis. The naïve inhabitants of C. figure in many anecdotes of Jewish folk-humor.

CHELMNO (Kulmhof): Polish village, site of a Nazi CONCENTRATION CAMP. 300,000 Jews were killed there until it ceased operations late in 1942.

CHEMISTRY: The greatest center of chemical progress and discovery during the 19th and early 20th cents. was Germany where Jews made many important contributions in this field. Adolph von Baeyer (1835–1917), who discovered eosin, artificial indigo and many aniline dyes, and who won the Nobel Prize in 1905, was a half-Jew. Another Nobel Prize winner (1919) was Fritz Haber (1868–1934), inventor of a method for producing ammonia from hydrogen and from the unlimited nitrogen in the air. This discovery helped Germany obtain the necessary fertilizer which kept her from starving during World War I. Haber had based his work upon foundations laid by Nikodem Caro (1871–1935) who had perfected a method of obtaining nitrogen from the air. Caro's collaborator, Adolf Frank (1834–1916), worked out techniques for obtaining potash and calcium cyanide and founded the potash industry. Victor Meyer (1848–1897) did important work in stereo-chemistry and invented an apparatus for determining vapor-densities. In 1882, he discovered the sulphur-containing compound thiophine in impure benzine and thus helped to secure cheap industrial chemicals. Jews also made contributions to the discovery of the aniline dyes. Heinrich Caro (1834–1910) discovered aniline red, induline, Manchester brown, and Victoria blue. Richard Willstätter (1872–1942) won fame both in research which helped the dye industry and in organic chemistry. He showed the relationship between plant chlorophyll and the hematin of the blood. Lothar Julius Meyer (1830–1895) was one of the founders of biological chemistry and famed for his discovery of the fact that the absorption of oxygen in the blood is through chemical action on the hemoglobin. Several important Jewish chemists also worked in England. Ludwig Mond (1839–1919) revolutionized the chemical industry by his process for the recovery of sulphur from alkali waste, and his son Alfred, Lord Melchett, founded the Imperial Chemical

Industries. Raphael Meldola (1849–1915) discovered important compounds and coal-tar dyes, while Chaim Weizmann (1875–1952) made a number of discoveries, especially the extraction of glucose. US Jewish chemists have included Morris Loeb, Albert E. Woolf, and Carl L. Alsberg, the last-named, the creator of a new field in biochemistry relating to nutrition.

CHEMOSH: God of the Moabites, mentioned in the Bible and on the Moabite Stone. Solomon, in his old age and under the influence of his wives, built a shrine to C. which stood for 400 years until destroyed by Josiah.

CHERETHITES AND PELETHITES: David's bodyguard of foreign mercenaries (II Sam. 8:18, etc.). They probably were Cretans and Philistines.

CHERNIAKOV, ADAM (Abraham; 1881–1942): Engineer and labor leader who headed the organization of Jewish craftsmen in Poland after World War I. Under the Nazi occupation, he was appointed chairman of the council of the Warsaw Ghetto by the Germans. In 1942, confronted by a demand to supply an unceasing number of Jewish names for deportation, he committed suicide. His diary is an important source of information on life in the Warsaw Ghetto.

CHERNIGOV: Capital of a Ukrainian province of the same name. Jews were living there in the 17th cent. but were massacred by the Cossacks in 1648. The community grew in the 19th cent. and was the scene of a pogrom in 1905 and again after World War I. When the city was occupied by the Nazis in 1941, 300 Jews who remained were exterminated, but the rest — about 25,500 — succeeded in fleeing to the Russian interior. Jewish pop. (1970): 4,000.

CHERNOBYL: Ukrainian townlet in the province of Kiev, famous as the seat of the TWERSKY dynasty of *tzaddikim*. Jewish pop. (1970): 150 families.

CHERNOVTSY (Cernauti; Ger.: Czernowitz): Town in the Soviet Ukraine. Its Jewish community was in existence when C. passed under Austrian rule in 1774 but only received citizenship in the 1867 constitution. A Yiddish conference held in C. in 1908 proclaimed Yiddish as the Jewish national language. The Jewish position deteriorated when C. was annexed to Rumania (1918). There were over 50,000 Jews in the city in 1940, the great majority of whom were deported to their death in 1941–2 during the Nazi occupation. An influx of Jews from various parts of the USSR after World War II brought the Jewish population to 37,459 in 1970 for C. province.

CHERUB (Heb. *keruv*): Winged figure (with human, animal. or bird's head and body), probably derived from a Semitic (Babylonian) prototype; frequently mentioned in the Bible. Cherubim guarded the gates to the Garden of Eden, and in the Tabernacle their images were placed on either side of the Ark. Later, they were used in decorating the Temple. Ezekiel, in his vision, describes a group of four cherubim carrying the Divine throne (Ezek. 1). In post-biblical Jewish literature, cherubim have come to be identified with a category of angels similar to seraphim, etc. The conception of the c. popularized by European artists has no support in Jewish tradition.

CHESS: Jews are known to have been among the first in Europe to have cultivated the game of c. They learned it from Arabs who had in turn acquired it from the Persians. The Spanish Jews, in particular, produced some enthusiastic players, the best-known being Abraham IBN EZRA, one of whose poems describes the game. Other poets who wrote similar descriptions, include R Solomon ben Mazal-Tov, Bonsenior Ibn Yahya, and Jacob EICHENBAUM. After the Arab conquest of Spain, c. traveled northward in the path of trade, and everywhere it found keen Jewish adherents, some of whom enriched it by devising new moves. This interest encountered some opposition in religious circles who considered it a dangerous distraction from study. From the mid-19th cent., there arose a number of outstanding Jewish players who left their mark upon the game. Wilhelm STEINITZ introduced into c. a new concept on the lines of military strategy. As a result of this approach, he won the world championship, and retained his title for 28 consecutive years. His pupil, Emmanuel LASKER, won the world title from him and held it for 27 consecutive years. Michael BOTVINNIK of the USSR held the world championship in recent rears as did Mikhael TAL, Boris SPASSKY and Bobby FISCHER. Other prominent Jewish players include David Bronstein, Samuel RESHEVSKY, Reuben FINE, and M. Neudorff (Argentina).

CHICAGO: City in Illinois, US. Individual Jews began settling there in the 1830's. The late 1840's saw the arrival of Jews from Bohemia, Hungary, and Poland. C.'s first Jewish congregation, the KAM (Kehilath Anshe Maarib) Temple, was organized in 1847. A second congregation, B'nai Sholom (now part of Temple Isaiah Israel), was founded in 1852 by Polish Jews. In 1861, Sinai Congregation (Reform) was organized. In pre-Civil War years, C. Jews were active in the cause of abolitionism. In 1862, the community — then numbering 1,000 — recruited and outfitted a 96-man company and raised $11,000 to give each volunteer a bonus. This Jewish company, as part of the 82nd Illinois infantry, distinguished itself at Gettysburg and elsewhere. The fire of 1871 destroyed 3 synagogues and the Jewish hospital, while that of 1874 inflicted severe losses on the Polish Jewish community. In addition to the Michael Reese Hospital dedicated in 1880, C.'s Jewish community founded a number of cultural, philanthropic, and social groups, notably the Zionist Literary Society and the United

Gates of Ark, South Shore Temple, Chicago
(Milton Horn, sculptor).

Hebrew Relief Association. In the last two decades of the 19th cent., 100,000 Jews from E Europe went to C., and by 1900, there were 50 congregations. The Jewish Federation, which supports local philanthropic causes, was founded in 1900; the Welfare Fund (founded 1936) raises money primarily for overseas causes. In 1973, C.'s metropolitan area had a Jewish population of 253,000, with 17 Reform, 17 Conservative, and close to 100 Orthodox congregations. Many Jewish communities have grown up in the suburbs. Two Jewish weeklies are published there. The institutions of higher learning include the (Orthodox) Hebrew Theological College, the Jewish People's Institute, and the College of Jewish Studies.

CHIEF RABBINATES: There has been a constant tendency in recent Jewish history to establish central rabbinates representing the Jews of a country in their relations with the secular authorities. Such were known in various countries in the Middle Ages (see CROWN RABBI), and there was a prolonged dispute in 14th cent. France caused by the attempt of Johanan ben Mattathias to establish himself as chief rabbi of the country. In Turkey, the ḤAKHAM BASHI enjoyed a high status from the 15th cent. In the modern world, the conception was introduced by the regulations of Napoleon who, in the hope of establishing a subservient Jewish hierarchy to carry out certain civil functions, set up in 1807 an elaborate system of CONSISTORIES presided over by the *grand rabbin* of France. This institution still prevails, though no

longer under governmental auspices. In Germany, c. r., vaguely inspired by the French model, existed in the various provinces, but there was no central institution of the sort. In England, the chief rabbinate (officially "of the United Hebrew Congregations of the British Commonwealth") grew up informally, at the beginning of the 19th cent., out of the office of the rabbi of the Great Synagogue, London, whose authority had come to be generally recognized. The institution in Israel resulted from the British Mandatory ordinance of 1920 setting up two chief rabbis. one each for the Ashkenazi and Sephardi communities.

CHIERA, ESTHER (c. 1520–1593): Turkish court favorite who exercised considerable influence on state policy. Her undue interference with appointments, by which she enriched herself, resulted in her gruesome murder by the Janissaries.

CHILD SACRIFICE: The Bible refers to the sacrifice of children, particularly first-born, as a propitiatory rite to the gods prevalent among heathen nations, e.g. Moab and Canaan. On rare occasions, Israel and Judah lapsed into these practices, incurring the wrath of the prophets. The Mosaic code replaces such barbaric rites by symbolic and vicarious redemption or consecration to the service of God. The "binding of Isaac" (AKEDAH) marks for Judaism the supersession of c. s.

CHILE: S American republic. Marranos settled in C. (chiefly in Santiago) during the early period of Spanish rule, but the Inquisition, introduced in 1570, prevented any open observance of Judaism. Religious liberty followed the attainment of independence in 1810 and Jews began to immigrate, although in 1914 their number did not exceed 3,000. A Jewish community was formally organized after World War I and there are now 12 synagogues, 6 in Santiago. Jewish immigration from Germany reached a considerable scale after 1933 but, from 1939 to 1952, was restricted to 200–300 annually. C.'s Jewish community, the fourth largest in Latin America, numbers 30,000 (1973), 90 % in Santiago. The Comité Representativo is the central body of all Jewish organizations. The Jewish day schools (3 in Santiago and 1 in Valparaiso) are attended by 1,350 children. There are two Jewish weeklies.

CHINA: Asian country. The oldest Jewish settlers in C. arrived, probably from Persia, about 1000. Their main community at KAI FENG FU became completely assimilated to Chinese customs and mores, virtually disappearing at the end of the 18th cent. In the mid-19th cent., Jews, mainly stemming from Baghdad and associated with the Sassoon family business, set up Sephardi communities in Hong Kong and SHANGHAI. The latter flourished especially in the period between World Wars I and II, when it absorbed large numbers first of

Russian, and then of German, refugees. Russian Jews, moreover, founded communities in HARBIN, Tientsin, Peiping, and elsewhere. The peak Jewish population in C. was 26,000 during World War II. The Harbin community dwindled when Manchuria was occupied by the Japanese who introduced anti-Semitic restrictions in 1941–5 in all areas occupied by them. The community recovered to some extent from this but not from the subsequent Chinese Communist regime when almost the whole of Shanghai Jewry emigrated (partly to Israel). In 1974, there was a community of 200 under the British rule in Hong, Kong, now virtually the only one in C. The number of Jews in the rest of C. dwindled rapidly and the community is no longer existent.

CHIOS: Aegean Island. Jews lived there from the 11th cent. and, in the 12th, Benjamin of Tudela found 400 families. The Sabbetaian movement had strong support in C. in the 17th cent. Most of the Jewish population fled to Smyrna at the time of the Greek revolt in 1822. The small remnant was exterminated by the Nazis during World War II.

CHIPKIN, ISRAEL SOLOMON (1891–1955): US educator. He organized the American Association for Jewish Education and served as its executive director. C. was later vice-president in charge of research of the Jewish Education Committee of New York.

*CHMIELNICKI (KHMELNITSKY), BOGDAN (1593–1657): Cossack leader. In 1648, he headed the rising of the Cossacks and Ukrainian masses directed against the Polish landowners, the Catholic clergy, and the Jews. The rebellion initially made headway and resulted in the annihilation of hundreds of Jewish communities and the brutal murder of hundreds of thousands of Jews, only those accepting baptism being spared. The exact number cannot be ascertained but one contemporary source affirms that 744 communities were wiped out. The horror of these events sent a shock throughout Jewry and the consequent messianic impulse served to gather support for Shabbetai Tzevi. The Ukrainians regard C. as a national hero.

CHOIR: An organized c. of levites participated in the Temple service. In the Second Temple, this consisted of at least twelve voices, more being added as desired. The levites apparently sang without accompaniment until they reached some pause, when instrumental music was introduced. After the destruction of the Temple, the rabbis, as a sign of mourning, prohibited all music. This decision was eventually modified and songs in praise of the Creator permitted. In the 9th cent., a c. took part in Babylonia in the ceremony for the installation of the exilarch. In the period of the Renaissance, despite some opposition in various places, synagogue c.'s began to be introduced — though not regularly — e.g. in Italy, and in a more organized fashion, in Prague. The HAZZAN in Ashkenazi communities was often accompanied by a bass and boy's voice. It was only in the 19th cent., however, that the c. became generally accepted in occidental synagogues. At approximately the same time, the Hasidic groups introduced unaccompanied congregational singing as a feature of the service. Reform synagogues adopted the organ into the synagogue, as well as a mixed c. consisting of men and women.

CHOMSKY: (1) *NOAM AVRAM C.* (1928–): US linguist; son of (2). An outstanding theoretical linguist, he pioneered the field of "algebraic linguistics." From 1957 he was professor of linguistics at the Massachusetts Institute of Technology. (2) *WILLIAM C.* (1896–): Educator. Born in Russia, he went to the US in 1913. He joined the faculty of Gratz College, Philadelphia, in 1924 and became chairman of the faculty in 1949. C. has published various works on Hebrew grammar and the Hebrew language.

CHORIN see **HORIN**

CHOSEN PEOPLE: The concept that Israel has been elected by God to carry the message of His Law to the world. It is based on the covenant between God and Abraham (Gen. 15) and renewed in that of Sinai (Exod. 19:5) where the election is conditional on observance of the Torah (Deut 7:6), Israel being declared "a kingdom of priests and a holy nation" (Exod. 19:6). The prophets stressed that election was conditional on social righteousness; Isaiah (42:6; 53) describes the image of Israel as the chosen servant of mankind whose suffering will bring salvation to the world. Ezekiel saw the Divine purpose in the unification of the world, with Israel as the instrument; Isaiah and Micah envisaged Jerusalem as the future center of the peoples and Israel as mediator between them and God. In Jewish hellenistic literature, Israel is God's servant drawing the Gentiles to the Law, but the pseudepigraphic writings state the paradox between the election of Israel and its sufferings. The Jewish revolutionary movements of the earlier 2nd cent. BCE appear to have aimed at the destruction of sinful Gentile society (cf. the Sibylline Oracles). Christianity, as molded by Paul, attempted to transfer the claim to election from the Jews, who had rejected the divinity of Jesus, to the latter's followers. In Mishnah and Talmud the role of Israel as the teacher of other nations is stressed; the potential equality of the other peoples with Israel is expressed by the Midrash (*Mekhilla Yitro*) which states that God offered the Torah to all of them, but only Israel accepted it.

Tanḥuma states that the preservation of the conception of God is inseparably bound up with the salvation of Israel. The Jewish idea of the C.P. implies not superiority over others, but superiority of responsibility and moral duty. The Diaspora-centered trend of early Reform Judaism did not favor the C.P. idea, seeing in dispersion the instrument for transmitting the ethical teachings of Judaism. Zionism stressed Jewish reconcentration in the land of Israel and the realization of a moral Jewish society on independent Jewish terms as indispensable to the maintenance of Jewish values.

*CHOSROES II: King of Persia, ruled 590–628 CE. With Jewish support, led by Benjamin of Tiberias, he conquered Palestine from the Byzantines in 614. After 15 years, the Persian army was forced to withdraw by Heraclius, the Byzantine emperor.

CHRIST see **JESUS**

CHRISTIANI, PABLO (d. 1274): Apostate and anti-Jewish agitator. Born in Montpellier, he became a Dominican and a violent anti-Jewish propagandist. C. was the Christian protagonist at the DISPUTATION of Barcelona in 1263. He later carried on anti-Jewish activities in France.

CHRISTIANITY: The Christian religion grew out of JUDAISM. JESUS and all his followers were Jews; so was PAUL, the architect of Gentile C., and, according to some scholars, the Jewish origin of many Christian doctrines has been illustrated by the Dead Sea Scrolls. The Christians regarded the Hebrew Scriptures as authoritative and adopted much of the traditional interpretation. The CHURCH was a natural outgrowth of the SYNAGOGUE, and its ancient liturgies go back to Jewish models. The early APOSTLES regarded themselves as Jews committed to the belief that Jesus was the Messiah; but with the growth of Gentile C., the JEWISH CHRISTIANS eventually became a minority. The NEW TESTAMENT preserves memories of the struggle between old loyalties to the Jewish people and tradition and the view that C. is a distinctive faith completely superseding Judaism. Paul held that the Christians are the true heirs of the promise to Abraham but anticipated the eventual conversion of the Jews. The Fourth Gospel is uncompromisingly hostile to everything Jewish. Some CHURCH FATHERS went so far as to deny that Israel had ever been the CHOSEN PEOPLE. The separation between Judaism and C. was hastened by the fall of the Jewish state, the destruction of the Temple, and the disastrous Bar Kokhba rebellion. This separation was emphasized by the substitution of Sunday ("The Lord's Day") for the traditional Sabbath and by the adoption of rules for the dating of EASTER so that it should no longer coincide with Passover. After C. became the official religion of the Roman Empire, long established rights were taken from the Jews and many restrictive and discriminatory enactments were devised to limit their influence and degrade them. Nevertheless, Judaism remained a problem for Christian thinkers and leaders. While non-Christian religions were outlawed and Christian heresies banned, Judaism had a status of its own. Jews were usually tolerated in medieval Europe, though their position was both humiliating and precarious. It was widely held that the Jews must be permitted to exist, but in abject degradation as a warning of the terrible fate overtaking those who rejected salvation through the Christian savior. Much of the persecution of the Jews was rooted in Christian religious intolerance, notably the massacres during the CRUSADES, the charges of Ritual Murder (see BLOOD LIBEL) and DESECRATION OF THE HOST, the activities of the INQUISITION, culminating in the expulsion from Spain, and the GHETTO system introduced with the Counter-Reformation. The POPES often protected the Jews against persecution by local clergy or secular officials and repeatedly denounced the Blood Libel and other accusations as baseless. The DISPUTATION between Jewish and Christian theologians, organized at intervals during the Middle Ages and down to the beginning of modern times, were avoided by the Jews whenever possible. Their purpose was not so much to convince as to embarrass the Jews who could not speak frankly. But despite threats and CENSORSHIP, the Jews produced an extensive polemical literature (see POLEMICS), in which the claims of C. were vigorously refuted. Notwithstanding, there was much friendly contact between Jews and Christians, even between religious leaders. Many Jews adopted the Christian religion under pressure (see APOSTATES); on the other hand, some Christians became PROSELYTES to Judaism, though in lesser numbers, in almost every country and century. There was in fact a steady mutual influence between the two religions. Such customs as the *Yahrzeit* and prayers of intercession for the dead, now firmly entrenched in Judaism, were doubtless influenced by Christian example. In modern times, there have been many borrowings from Church practice in organization, forms of worship, liturgical music, etc. Judaism has likewise influenced C. The scholasticism of the medieval Church depended on Latin translations of Aristotle and his commentators, partly provided by Jewish translators. The philosophers Albert Magnus and Thomas Aquinas frequently cite Maimonides, while Duns Scotus turned repeatedly to Ibn Gabirol. During the Renaissance, many Christians studied Hebrew under Jewish masters, a circumstance which contributed in some measure to the Protestant REFORMATION. The Church was inclined to attribute this, as well as numerous heresies, to Jewish influence. Nevertheless, the early Reformation leaders, such as Martin LUTHER, showed no greater tolerance than the Roman Catholics. In many cases, however, judaizing heresies were inspired by study of the Bible, sometimes in Hebrew, though there was little or no contact with living Jews. This was the case also with the English and American Puritans. Jewish thinkers from the Middle Ages onward distinguished sharply between paganism, on one hand, and C. and/or Islam, on the other. The latter are monotheistic faiths, deriving from the Bible, and may therefore be regarded as the means by which the heathen world will gradually be won for the true religion. This was the view of Maimonides, and was expressed more recently by Solomon Formstecher, Samuel Hirsch, and Franz Rosenzweig. The last-named assigned a specially important role to C. within the framework of a Jewish philosophy. Some Christian leaders opposed the emancipation of the Jews on the ground that Jews must be aliens in a Christian state, but others such as Abbé GREGOIRE fought valiantly for the acceptance of Jews as citizens. Some outstanding Christian teachers of the 19th and 20th cents. opposed anti-Semitism as essentially un-Christian. In the US and, to some extent, in W Europe there has been interfaith activity intended to bring about better understanding and joint activity by church and synagogue groups for civic betterment and social justice.

CHRONICLES (Heb. *Divre ha-Yamim*): Biblical book. In the Hebrew Bible it appears as the very last book, at the end of the Hagiographa, but in the Septuagint, Vulgate, and English Bible, it is among the historical books, placed between Kings and Ezra. Originally a unit, it has become customary to divide the book into two parts, following the Greek translations. C. contains: (1) genealogical lists of the Israelite tribes from Adam until the time of David (I Chron. 1–9): (2) an account of David's rule, differing from the parallel account in the Book of Samuel by omitting his misdeeds and adding details of his projects and state organization (I Chron. 10–29): (3) an account of the reign of Solomon, emphasizing the building of the Temple (II Chron. 1–9): (4) the history of the kingdom of Judah down to its destruction, differing in both details and attitude from the parallel account in the Book of Kings (II Chron. 10–36). Scholars are divided as to the date of composition, some placing it at the end of the 6th cent. BCE, others maintaining that it forms a unit with the Book of Ezra and was written in the latter 7th cent., while certain scholars have dated it as late as the Hellenistic Period (c. 300 BCE) but this now appears unlikely.

CHRONOLOGY: The Bible has no uniform system of dating but uses events like the Flood and the Exodus, the reigns of kings, and the Babylonian Exile as determining dates for its c. The method of counting that became universally accepted among Jews is according to the number of years that have traditionally elapsed since the Creation (*li-ytzirah*). This era begins 2760 years before the Christian Era. This system, based on various data in the Bible, is first mentioned in the *Seder Olam Rabbah* (2nd cent. CE) but did not become popular until the 10th cent. The accepted system of Jewish reckoning prior to this was the Seleucid CALENDAR (beginning 312 BCE), known as *minyan shetarot* ("era of documents") as legal documents were dated in accordance with this calendar. It prevailed among eastern Jews until the 16th cent. and is still used by those from Yemen. Dates of the Hasmonean and Bar Kokhba victories are found on coins of these two periods. Jewish dates were occasionally reckoned from the destruction of the Second Temple (68 CE in former Jewish tradition). In western countries, Jews use the accepted c. but substitute BCE ("Before Christian [or "Common"] Era") and CE ("Christian [or "Common"] Era") for the familiar BC and AD.

*CHRYSOSTOM, JOHN (347–407): Church father; patriarch of Constantinople. His vituperative *Homilies against the Jews* was one of the first endeavors to create popular Christian anti-Semitism.

CHUETAS (Majorean: "pork" or "Jews"): The crypto-Jews or MARRANOS in Majorca, descended from the victims of the Forced Baptism in 1391 and 1435. Inquisitional persecutions, particularly in 1678 and 1691, suppressed the practice of Judaism among them, but they continued nevertheless, to be wholly excluded from normal life and subjected to all manner of social discrimination which to some extent still continues. It is doubtful whether they retain any traces of Jewish religious belief or custom.

CHURCH see **CHRISTIANITY; POPES**

CHURCH COUNCILS: Councils of the Church can be either Regional or General (Ecumenical). The former frequently had occasion to occupy themselves with the Jews, almost always in connection with the local enforcement of accepted anti-Jewish regulations. The earliest instance is the Council of Elvira in Spain (312) which endeavored to prevent familiar intercourse between Jews and Christians, particularly in rural areas. So, too, successive Councils of Toledo were responsible for the bitter campaign against Judaism in Spain in the 7th cent. More significant were the General Councils, the decisions of which sometimes greatly affected the course of Jewish history; that of Nicaea (325) widened the breach between Christianity and Judaism by forbidding the celebration of the Christian Sabbath on Saturday and tried to prevent the coincidence of Easter and Passover. The Third

Lateran Council (1179) reverted to the Jewish question and re-enacted some restrictive measures. This prepared the way for the sweeping anti-Jewish legislation of the Fourth Lateran Council (1215) which endeavored to erect an impassable barrier between Jews and Christians. Its innovations included the Jewish Badge. Though its legislation was not immediate or universally obeyed, it established a standard of conduct for the future. The Council of Basle at its 19th session passed a code of extreme severity, repeating and strengthening the former anti-Jewish legislation, condemning the Talmud, and recommending conversionist sermons (1434). In effect, this program was carried out by papal legislation in the second half of the 16th cent., and later General Councils did not occupy themselves with Jewish questions. The Council of Trent (1545–63), however, dealt incidentally with the printing of the Talmud, but took no extreme attitude. The Second Vatican Council (1962–5) passed a schema on non-Christian religions which included a section on the Catholic attitude to Jews. This stated that the blame for the death of Jesus must be attributed only to some of his Jewish contemporaries and the Jewish people as a whole cannot be blamed. The declaration also deplored anti-Semitism.

CHURCH FATHERS: Teachers and writers of the Christian Church from the period immediately following the New Testament writers to some time in the Dark Ages (Pope Gregory the Great, d. 604, is often considered the last of the Fathers). Some of the Fathers were biblical specialists and have preserved important Jewish material in this field. ORIGEN's massive *Hexapla* provides information as to the pronunciation of Hebrew in 3rd cent. Palestine and preserved many of Aquila's renderings. Much similar information is contained in the Bible commentaries of JEROME who studied Hebrew under Jewish teachers and frequently quotes biblical interpretations in their name. The C. F. were familiar with aggadah and viewed numerous biblical episodes and characters in the light of aggadic interpretation. Other interpretations were acquired by later Fathers through conversation with Jews in their own day. The patristic writings record not only legend and interpretations also found in Jewish sources, but much similar material, not otherwise preserved and undoubtedly of Jewish origin. Moreover, many obscure statements of the Fathers may be clarified by reference to rabbinic parallels and *vice versa*. The Fathers quote extracts from hellenistic Jewish writers whose works are not otherwise preserved — EUSEBIUS, for example, cites Artapanus, Demetrius, Eupolemus, and the lost *Hypothetica* of Philo. Moreover, many facts of Jewish history were recorded by the C.F. The pseudo-messiah, Moses of Crete, is known only from the *Ecclesiastical History* of Socrates (5th cent.). The Fathers engaged in frequent polemic against Judaism. One of the oldest patristic documents is JUSTIN MARTYR's *Dialogue with the Jew Tryphon* (2nd cent.). The tone of this dialogue is relatively friendly; other Fathers who wrote about the Jews (Tertullian, Aphraates) were more bitterly hostile. The famous preacher John CHRYSOSTOM used his oratorical powers to stir up anti-Jewish feeling in Antioch (4th cent.). The polemic writings of the Church often illuminate passages of rabbinic literature. The rabbis rarely engaged in direct attacks on the views of their opponents, but many an aggadic homily acquires fuller meaning when understood as a rejoinder to hostile statements by a Christian contemporary. The possibilities in this vast field for the enrichment of Jewish studies were opened up by the historian Graetz; more recent scholars, such as Samuel Krauss and Louis Ginzberg, have also made major contributions.

*CHURCHILL, SIR WINSTON (1874–1965): British statesman. He strenuously opposed restrictive legislation on immigration into England, mainly affecting Jews, 1904–5; supported the Saturday Closing and Sunday Opening Bills; and fought for specific Jewish educational rights. As early as 1908, he expressed his "full sympathy with the historical aspirations of the Jews" to restore "a center of racial and political integrity" in Palestine. As colonial secretary, he virtually cut off Transjordan from the Palestine Mandated territory (1921), and in the Churchill WHITE PAPER (1922) formulated what he believed would remain the basis of Anglo-Jewish cooperation. His subsequent attacks against the measures proposed in the Passfield White Paper (1930), the Partition Scheme (1937), and the White Paper of 1939 were based on the premise that they constituted a breach of an agreed policy expressed in his White Paper. Under his premiership during World War II, Britain maintained her restrictive policy in Palestine, but his *Memoirs* reveal that while concentrating singlemindedly on winning the war and wishing to avoid disagreement with his colleagues, he maintained his pro-Jewish attitude throughout. He was one of the first in Britain to insist on recognition of the State of Israel.

CHURGIN, PINKHOS M. (1894–1957): Scholar; founder and first president of BAR-ILAN UNIV. 1955–7. Before going to Israel, he was professor of Jewish history and literature at Yeshiva Univ., New York, and dean of its teachers' institute. He wrote works of biblical and rabbinic scholarship, particularly on the Hasmonean Period.

CHWOLSON, DANIEL (1819–1911): Russian orientalist. After baptism (1855), he became professor of oriental languages at the Univ. of St. Petersburg and later also lectured at the Greek Orthodox and Roman Catholic theological seminaries there. In 1910, he was elected to the Russian Academy of Sciences.

Sir Winston Churchill.

C. Published studies on Semitic subjects including a corpus of Jewish inscriptions and a monograph on the Last Supper (in which he endeavored to show that the court which sentenced Jesus consisted of Sadducees, not Pharisees), etc. He fought anti-Semitism and the Blood Libel, frequently intervened with Russian authorities in behalf of Jews, and was respected by Orthodox Jewry. His valuable library is in the Asiatic Museum of Leningrad.

*CICERO, MARCUS TULLIUS (106–43 BCE): Roman statesman and orator. In his defense of L Valerius Flaccus (59 BCE), who as governor of Asia had confiscated Jewish Temple contributions, C. attacked Judaism and the Jews of Rome.

CILICIA: Region in Asia Minor. Jews are first mentioned there in the 1st cent. BCE, the chief groups being at Tarsus, where the career of the apostle Paul evidences close links with Palestine, and Corycos, where many funerary inscriptions have been found, as also in Seleucia, Olba, etc. Jews from C. maintained a synagogue in Jerusalem. The community was connected with textile and perfume manufacture and gold working, many Cilician products being mentioned in the Talmud. Inscriptions suggest Jewish influence on paganism in C. Polemon II of C. married Berenice, sister of Herod Agrippa II.

CINCINNATI: City in Ohio, US. The first Jewish settlers came from England and later, in the 1830's, from Germany. The first congregation, Bene Israel, was formed in 1824 and the first synagogue dedicated in 1836. C.'s second congregation, Bene Jeshurun, was organized in 1841 with the arrival of more German Jews. Isaac Mayer WISE was rabbi of Bene Jeshurun from 1854, and C. became the center of REFORM JUDAISM in the US. Orthodoxy, however, continued to be strongly represented. In 1875, the HEBREW UNION COLLEGE was established in C. to train Reform rabbis. The oldest existing American Jewish weekly in English, the *American Israelite*, was founded there by I. M. Wise in 1854. The community supports a large number of social and philanthropic institutions united since 1896 in the United Jewish Social Agencies, the oldest federation of its kind in the US. Since 1928, all organizations in the community have been represented in the Jewish Community Council. Jewish pop. (1973): 30,000.

CIRCUMCISION (Heb. *milah*; sometimes *berit milah* "covenant of circumcision"): Ceremony of cutting away the foreskin practiced by many peoples including the Semites. Among the Jews, c. is performed on the eighth day after birth. C. is often called "the covenant of Abraham," as Abraham's c. was made the sign of his covenant with God. Male proselytes to Judaism must undergo c. In biblical times and later, male slaves were also circumcised. An uncircumcised person was excluded from participation in important Jewish rites, such as eating the paschal lamb. C. has taken on added significance in Jewish history because of the martyrdom suffered for its sake during the persecutions of Antiochus Epiphanes and later, of the Romans. It became a symbol distinguishing the Jew from the idolator. Conversely, Jewish hellenists, wanting to assimilate to the Greek way of life, underwent operations to obliterate the sign of c. To prevent the possibility of effacing the sign of the covenant, the rabbis emphasized the act of

Circumcision ceremony. (From a Haggadah in the British Museum).

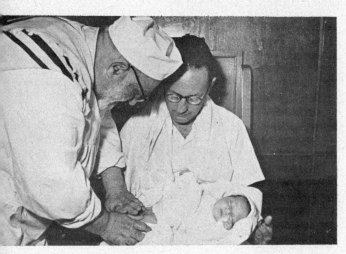

Circumcision ceremony: the Sandak is holding the child, while the Mohel is performing the Ritual.

periah (pushing back the skin to lay bare the *glans*) as an indispensable feature of the operation. The ceremony must be performed on the eighth day, even if it falls on the Sabbath or Day of Atonement. Postponement is permitted only when the health of the child would be endangered. The ceremony early took on a festive character, and in the Gaonic Period was transferred to the synagogue (a custom still prevalent in some places). The chief participants in the ritual, in addition to the child, are the *mohel* (performer of the rite), the father (who recites a special blessing), and the *sandak* (godfather, from the Greek *synteknos*) who holds the child in his lap during the operation. A chair on which the child is placed before being circumcised is known as the Chair of Elijah. Appropriate blessings follow the operation, being recited over a cup of wine while the child is given his name.

CITIES OF REFUGE: Places of asylum. Scripture provides for c. of r. in which an accidental killer was to be safe from the vengeance of the murdered man's kinsmen, and where he was required to stay until the death of the reigning high priest (Exod. 21:13; Num. 35:11ff). Six such cities were allotted — three E and three W of the Jordan. The inviolability of the refuge is expressly repudiated in cases of wilful murder. The story of Adonijah and Joab (I Kings 2:28) indicates that the Sanctuary was also considered an asylum for political fugitives but provided inadequate protection. The Talmud records detailed measures to safeguard the refugees, but emphasized that the city of refuge is a place of expiation and only operative in cases of contributory negligence. Sheer accident required no expiation, while grave carelessness could not be adequately atoned for by seeking sanctuary.

CITROEN, ANDRÉ-GUSTAVE (1878–1935): French industrialist. Of Dutch extraction, he was a pioneer both in the automobile industry and in desert exploration. C. gave generously to ORT.

CITRON see **ETROG**

CITY OF DAVID see **JERUSALEM**

CIVIL RIGHTS: Privileges and duties attached to the full membership of a state. In ancient Israel such rights were limited to those known to belong by blood to a given tribe; they consisted of rights to ownership of land and to the protection of the Torah (e.g. in case of enslavement), which did not apply to non-Jews. They also involved participation in the cult and the discharge of religious duties. In due course, the principle of blood was replaced by that of faith, insofar as proselytes also received such rights. In the Greek and Roman world, c.r. were bound up with membership of a city; individual Jews became citizens of Greek cities or obtained Roman citizenship, but Jews as such never held bloc rights in these bodies until the Edict of Caracalla (212 CE) gave citizenship to all free members of the Empire except those recently conquered. On the other hand, outside Judea Jewish communities enjoyed, from the first, internal religious and juridical AUTONOMY. With the triumph of Christianity in the 3rd–4th cents., Jews began to be excluded from full citizenship. During the Middle Ages, the prevailing status of Jews in Europe was that of royal dependents rather than free citizens, and their exclusion from the feudal pattern made their protection depend on being the direct property of a powerful person, or on their acquiring a charter from a sovereign or city. Nevertheless, in some areas Jews were regarded as citizens without active political rights, and REUCHLIN argued that the Jews were citizens of the Holy Roman Empire. The acquisition of c.r. by European and American Jews began in the late 18th cent. simultaneously with the rise of responsible government and the conception of equality of all before the law (See COMMUNITY, DISABILITIES, EMANCIPATION, etc.).

CLASSICAL LITERATURE, JEWS IN: In the later 4th cent. BCE when the Greeks first encountered the Jews, their notion of them was influenced by the aspiration to find among exotic peoples social and philosophical solutions; hence Theophrastus Clearchos of Soli, and later Megasthenes and Hermippus all regarded the Jews as philosophers and star-gazers possessed of all knowledge. Hecataeus of Abdera (4th–3rd cents. BCE) was better informed; in his *On the Jews,* he describes Moses' legislation and the Jewish priesthood favorably, attributing the Exodus to the Egyptian exclusion of foreign cults. The Egyptian priest Manetho (3rd cent. BCE), on the other hand, was the first writer known to have incorporated anti-Semitic folk-tales in his works: he ascribes the foundation of Jerusalem to Hyksos, and identifies the Jews with lepers expelled from Egypt after they had persecuted the Egyptian religion and oppressed the country. These accounts influenced the entire subsequent hellenistic literature which, under the impact of the Hasmonean attack on Hellenism, developed a strongly anti-Semitic school. The general trend was to regard Judaism as a barbarous cult, and to interpret Jewish rejection of the Greek deities as "atheism," while mocking circumcision, the dietary laws, and the Sabbath. It was also common to charge the Jews with unsociability and misanthropy (Apollonius Molon, Lysimachus, etc.). Menetho's leper story was elaborated by Lysimachus, Chairemon (1st cent. CE), Diodorus Siculus (1st cent. BCE), and later by Tacitus and Justin (2nd cent. CE), while Apollonius Molon also accused the Jews of lack of ability. In addition, Mnaseas (3rd cent. BCE) originated the legend of Jewish ass-worship, repeated by Damocritus who wrote *On the Jews* (1st cent. BCE or CE) and by Plutarch who derived the Jews from the Egyptian evil spirit Typhon, and (like Tacitus) attributed to them bacchic rites. More dangerous was the Ritual Murder libel, originated by Damocritus and Apion (1st cent. CE), who ascribed to Jews the taking of an oath to hate all gentiles. Only Poseidonius (135–51 BCE) made a defense of Judaism, claiming that its (in Greek eyes) undesirable aspects were the result of degeneration from a high and lofty faith. Apion's criticism, political in aim and directed against the Jewish claim to Greek citizenship, culminated in the question why, if the Jews were citizens, they did not worship the cities' gods. The Roman writers of the 1st cent. BCE — 3rd cent. CE, even including men like Tacitus, were on the whole ignorant of Judaism, despite personal contacts with Jews, and even the more intelligent were hostile. Cicero called it a "barbarous superstition" and the Jews, "a nation born to slavery"; the Roman satirists found in the Jewish proletariat of Rome ample material for mockery, Horace gibing at their credulity, Juvenal at the Sabbath, circumcision, Jewish occupations, mendicancy, and poverty, which also was a butt to Martial; Juvenal believed Jews worshiped the clouds, and both Pliny and Apuleius regarded them as adepts at magic. Petronius held that they worshiped the pig. Quintilian regarded Jews as injurious to mankind, and Persius alludes deprecatingly to the Sabbath, which Petronius, Suetonius and Justin all believed to be a fast day. Among the more serious writers, Seneca accused the Jews of ignorance of the foundations of their own ceremonies, and the Sabbath of being a source of sloth; Tacitus, who

seems genuinely to have tried to grasp the nature of Jewish monotheism (Hist. V 17–24), nevertheless attacked the Jews for refusal to recognize the Roman gods, and said that their institutions were tainted with knavery, and that they were "enslaved to superstition and opposed to religion." Terentius Varro (1st cent. BCE) favored Judaism for its imageless worship, but thought this an impracticable ideal, Galen (129–?200 CE) also retained an objective attitude to Judaism, according to Arab reports. The 3rd cent. pagan writers Celsus and Porphyry were concerned in the fight against Christianity, and in their writings found the opportunity also to attack Judaism, on which they were better informed than earlier authors; both, on the whole, were anti-Jewish, but both preferred Judaism to Christianity, regarding it as more consistent in its monotheism. A comprehensive collection of texts of classical authors about the Jews and Judaism, with French translation, was published by T. Reinach (1895).

*CLAUDIUS, TIBERIUS (Tiberius Claudius Germanicus Nero): Roman emperor 41–54 CE. His accession was largely due to the aid of his friend Herod Agrippa I, whom he approved as king, adding Judea to his kingdom and uniting under him the whole area ruled by Herod. C. at once issued edicts reaffirming Jewish religious autonomy in Alexandria. In 44, on Agrippa I's death, C. placed Judea under a procurator, but in 49, he gave Agrippa's son (Agrippa II) regions of N Palestine to rule. In 49–50, he expelled a number of Jews from Rome, apparently as a result of a Jewish-Christian conflict.

CLEAN ANIMALS: Animals whose flesh may be eaten and whose milk may be drunk according to the Jewish DIETARY LAWS. Clean and unclean animals are first mentioned in the Bible in connection with Noah who took seven pairs of the former and only two of the latter into the ark. Detailed description and lists of clean and unclean animals are given in Lev. 11:1–47 and in Deut. 14:3–20. Clean quadrupeds are those which both chew the cud and have cloven hooves. Marine animals which may be eaten are those having both fins and scales. This makes permissible almost all true fishes, but prohibits shellfish. Clean fowl are those birds not specifically listed as unclean; almost all fowl, other than birds of prey, are thus permitted. Reptiles and insects are all prohibited, with the exception of four types of locust.

CLEANLINESS see **ABLUTION; PURITY, RITUAL**

*CLEMENCEAU, GEORGES-BENJAMIN (1841–1929): French statesman. One of Dreyfus' leading defenders, he edited the newspaper *L'Aurore* in which Zola's *J'accuse* appeared. After

Fairmount Temple, Cleveland.

World War I, he supported Jewish claims at the Versailles conference (minority rights, national home in Palestine). His book of short stories *Au pied du Sinaï* deals with Jewish themes.

CLERMONT-FERRAND: French town. In 576, after the Jews of C.-F. demonstrated against a convert, Bishop Avitus gave them the choice of baptism or expulsion. The community reappeared in the 13th cent. and is said to have lasted until 1615. A synagogue was reopened in 1780 and there has been a community since then numbering 800 in 1970; during World War II, it harbored the Paris Rabbinical Seminary for a brief period.

CLEVELAND: City in Ohio, US. C.'s oldest congregation, known today as the Euclid Ave. Temple, began in 1846 as the Anshe Chesed Society. It was followed in 1850 by Tifereth Israel. Both were Reform groups. C.'s third congregation, B'nai Jeshurun (today better known as the Heights Temple) was founded by Hungarian immigrants in 1865. The first school for Jewish children was established in 1880 by Tifereth Israel. In the 1902's, a Hebrew school system developed under the supervision of Abraham H. Friedland. In 1929–38, an Orthodox rabbinical seminary existed in C., and after World War II, the Tels

yeshivah made its home there. A Jewish Community Federation has been in existence since 1903. The *Cleveland Jewish News* (founded 1964) appears weekly. In 1973, C. had 80,000 Jews.

CLUJ (Hung. Kolozsvar; Ger. Klausenburg): Town in Rumania since 1918 (except for 1940–44 when restored to Hungary). Jews settled there permanently c. 1770. The town was the center of Jewish and Zionist life in Transylvania. Its Jewish community (about 15,000 before World War II) was herded into a ghetto under Nazi occupation and wiped out in 1944. Jewish pop. (1970): 1,100 (down from 6,500 in 1947).

COATS OF ARMS: The Midrash describes the flags of the Twelve Tribes on the basis of the Blessings of Jacob (Gen. 49) and of Moses (Deut. 33), and some of these (e.g. the Lion of Judah) became family badges among the Jews in the Middle Ages. Moreover, priestly families inscribed on tombstones, etc. the symbol of hands spread in blessing, while levites portrayed the laver and basin. Many Italian Jewish families also had distinctive badges from the 16th cent. onward. In the modern and technical sense, however, c. of a. are found among Jews only from the 17th cent. when various Marrano families escaping to other lands continued to use their c. of a. Later, other families belonging to this group adopted the c. of a. of noble Spanish and Portuguese families of the same name, their claims being sometimes confirmed by the official colleges of heraldry. Their example was followed from the 18th cent. by some wealthy Ashkenazi families in England, etc. Subsequently, when a number of Jewish families were ennobled in European countries, c. of a. became necessary. They occasionally embodied certain traditional elements but, more often, closely imitated non-Jewish models. In a few cases (e.g. the Montefiore and Sassoon families), a Hebrew motto was incorporated.

COBLENZ: German city. Jews are first mentioned there c. 1135–59, and were protected by the archbishop of Trier (Trèves) who gave them a charter in 1265. They were important financiers for the Rhine region, lending money to the city, the burghers, and the archbishop of Cologne and leasing the Rhine customs toll at C. between 1339 and 1345. The community suffered persecutions in 1265, 1281, and 1287, and from the *Armleder* attacks in 1337, and was destroyed during the Black Death massacres of 1349. Jews returned by 1356 but were expelled from the entire province of Trier in 1418. During the 16th cent., they were alternately admitted and expelled on several occasions but eventually allowed to remain. The community numbered over 700 before its elimination by the Nazis. Jewish pop. (1967): 100.

COCHIN: Port and former state on the Malabar coast in S India. Refugees transferred themselves to C. after Cranganore was captured by the Portuguese in 1523, after which the area became the center of this branch of Indian Jewry. This native element ("Black Jews") was later reinforced by new immigrants ("White Jews") from Syria, Turkey, etc. who under the influence of the Indian caste system, kept themselves rigidly separate from the others. A third element of "Freedmen," descended from converted native slaves, added a further gradation. Though suffering during the Portuguese incursions, the Jews of C. flourished under Dutch, and later British, rule and many made military careers. Notwithstanding their isolation, they maintained a vigorous Jewish intellectual life. The Jews of C. preserved their own liturgy for various occasions (e.g. marriage, *Simḥat Torah*). Most of the Jews from C. emigrated to Israel. About 100 were left in 1968 when Cochin Jewry celebrated the 400th anniversary of its synagogue at a special service attended by the Indian prime minister Mrs. Indira Gandhi.

CODES see **LAW, CODIFICATION OF**

COELE SYRIA: Geographical term, first mentioned in the 4th cent. BCE, applying to the country between Cilicia, the Euphrates, and the Syrian coast down to Egypt; after the time of Alexander the Great, it was used for Syria S of the Orontes.

COHEN see **PRIEST**

Jewish girls from Cochin in Israel.

COHEN (Heb. "Priest"): Common Jewish family name found among descendants of priestly families; also as Cahan, Cohan, Kagan, Kahn, Kogen, Kohn, etc.

COHEN (or **KOHEN**) **TZEDEK** (Heb. "Priest of righteousness," i.e. "righteous priest" based on Ps. 132:9): Epithet applied to one of priestly family; in gaonic times, used as a name. It was abbreviated to *K. Tz.* which as Katz became a surname in the modern period.

COHEN: US family of Richmond (Va.), Philadelphia, and Baltimore. *JACOB I. C.* (1744–1823) went to the US from Germany in 1773, and after serving in the Revolutionary Army settled in Richmond. His brother, *ISRAEL I. C.* (1750–1803), went to Richmond about 1784. Their descendants, into the 20th cent. included prominent bankers, railroad executives, physicians, and public officials. *JACOB I. C. JR.* (1790–1869), the eldest of Israel I. C.'s sons, set up a banking house in Baltimore and was conspicuous in the fight for the civic and political rights of the Jews in Maryland (1826).

COHEN, ABRAHAM (1887–1957): English scholar and communal leader. After many years as chief minister of the Birmingham Hebrew Congregation (1913–49), he was president of the Board of Deputies of British Jews (1949–55). He wrote works on Jewish literature and edited a commentary in English on the entire Bible, compiled from ancient sources.

COHEN, ALBERT (1895—): French author; a native of Corfu. He was an official in international organizations at Geneva and edited the *Revue juive*. C. has written poems and colorful novels on Cephalonian Jewry including *Solal of the Solals* and *Mangeclous*.

COHEN, ALFRED MORTON (1859—1949): US communal leader. An attorney, he was president of the B'nai B'rith 1925–38, and chairman of the board of governors of Hebrew Union College 1918–37. C. was active in Ohio Democratic politics, serving in the Ohio Senate for two terms.

COHEN, SIR ANDREW BENJAMIN (1909—1968): British colonial administrator. He was assistant under-secretary of state in the Colonial Office from 1947, governor of the Uganda Protectorate 1951–6, British representative on the UN Trusteeship Council 1956–61, and secretary, Ministry of Overseas Development 1964–8. His sister, *RUTH LOUISA C.* (1906–), economist, has been principal of Newnham College, Cambridge since 1954.

COHEN, BENJAMIN ALBERTO (1896–1960): Chilean diplomat. At first a journalist, he entered the Chilean foreign service and served as ambassador to Bolivia 1939–45, and then to Venezuela (1945). He was assistant secretary general of the United Nations in charge of the Public Information Department 1946–54, and was in charge of Trusteeships and Information from Non-Self-Governing Territories 1954–8.

COHEN, BENJAMIN VICTOR (1894—): US government official. He was one of the original members of Roosevelt's "brains' trust," and as a lawyer, drafted much of the New Deal legislation. From 1948 to 1952, he was alternate representative of the US to the United Nations. C. was counsel to the American Zionist delegation to the Paris Peace Conference in 1919.

COHEN, GERSON D. (1924–): US Jewish historian. He was librarian of the Jewish Theological Seminary of America and prof. of history at Columbia Univ. and The Seminary. In 1972 he was appointed chancellor of The Seminary. He published a critical edition of IBN DAUD's *Sefer ha-Kabbalah.*

COHEN, HENRY, LORD (1900—): English physician; professor of medicine at Liverpool Univ. (1934) and writer on medical subjects. He was president of the British Medical Association 1950–1, chancellor of Hull Univ. from 1970 and noted in diagnosis and medical administration.

COHEN, HENRY (1863–1952): US rabbi and civic leader. He was rabbi of Temple Bnai Israel, Galveston, Texas, 1888–1949. C. established a nationwide reputation for his broad-minded humanitarianism and advocacy of prison reform.

COHEN, HENRY EMANUEL (1840–1916): Australian statesman. C. was elected to the New South Wales parliament in 1874 and 1877, serving as colonial treasurer (1874) and minister of justice (1883–5) and being appointed a judge of the Supreme Court of NSW in 1896. He was president of the Great Synagogue, Sydney, 1884–6.

Hermann Cohen.
(Drawing by Max Liebermann).

COHEN, HERMANN (1842–1918): German philosopher; founder of the so-called Marburg School of Neo-Kantianism. On the basis of a reinterpretation of Kant, C. founded his own system in *Die Logik der reinen Erkenntnis, Die Ethik des reinen Willens, Die Aesthetik des reinen Gefühls*, etc. In 1880, C. began to return to Judaism and to defend the Jewish faith and the Jewish people against the anti-Semitic historian Treitschke. Even before leaving his Marburg chair (1912), he lectured at the Lehranstalt für die Wissenschaft des Judentums in Berlin and after his resignation from the university, taught there exclusively. His influence on several generations of Jewish thinkers and scholars has been immense, even though he harshly repudiated Zionism as reactionary. Among his specifically Jewish works are *Religion und Sittlichkeit, Das Gottesreich, Der Nächste*, and, above all, the posthumously published *Religion der Vernunft aus den Quellen des Judentums*.

COHEN, ISRAEL (1879–1961): English author. A member of the secretariat of the Zionist movement 1910–40, he traveled widely in behalf of Jewish causes and described his experiences in several books. His works include *Jewish Life in Modern Times, History of the Jews in Vilna, Contemporary Jewry*, and *A Short History of Zionism*.

COHEN, LIONEL LEONARD, LORD (1888–1973): English lawyer. He was a justice of the High Court of Chancery in 1943, lord justice of appeal in 1946, and lord of appeal in ordinary, 1951. He was vice-president of the Board of Deputies of British Jews 1934–8, and president of the Jewish Historical Society 1951–3. He has presided over several important Royal Commissions.

COHEN, MAXWELL (1910–): Canadian jurist. Born in Winnipeg he has taught at McGill Univ., Montreal since 1946 and in 1964 was appointed dean of its law school. In 1959–60 he was a member of the Canadian UN delegation. C. is also active in Jewish communal affairs.

COHEN, MORRIS RAPHAEL (1880–1947): US philosopher. He went to the US from Russia in 1892 and was professor of philosophy at City College, New York 1912–38, and at the Univ. of Chicago 1938–42. He wrote a number of works, especially on the logic of the natural and social sciences and the philosophy of law, including *Reason and Nature* and *Law and the Social Order*. He was cofounder (1933) and president of the Conference on Jewish Relations, and from 1938, an editor of *Jewish Social Studies*. His son, *FELIX S. C.* (1907–1953), attorney, helped redraft legislation affecting Indians.

COHEN, NAPHTALI BEN ISAAC (1649–1719): Rabbi and kabbalist. Rabbi successively at Ostrog, Posen, and Frankfort-on-Main, he gained a reputation as a "practical kabbalist." He was forced to resign his post when it was alleged that his kabbalistic experiments were responsible for the destruction of the Frankfort ghetto by fire. After wandering from community to community, he died at Constantinople on his way to Palestine. C. was among the chief opponents of the Sabbetaians.

COHEN, RAPHAEL see **RAPHAEL BEN JEKUTHIEL**

COHEN, SIR ROBERT WALEY (1877–1952): English oil magnate and communal leader. He was managing director of the Shell Transport and Trading Co. (from 1907) and chairman of the Palestine Corporation. A dominant figure in English Jewry for a quarter of a century, C. was president of the United Synagogue and vice-president of the Board of Deputies. His son, *SIR BERNARD WALEY COHEN* (1914–) was lord mayor of London 1960–1.

COHEN, SHABBETAI see **SHABBETAI BEN MEIR HA-COHEN**

COHEN, SHALOM BEN JACOB (1772–1845): Hebrew poet. Of Polish birth, he went to Berlin as a youth and joined the circle of Hebrew *maskilim*. In 1809, he revived the journal *Ha-Measseph* which appeared until 1811 as *Ha-Measseph he-Ḥadash*. He eventually settled in Vienna, founding the annual *Bikkure ha-Ittim* in 1821. The English edition of his catechism of Judaism, *Elements of Faith* (London, 1814), aroused much controversy. From 1836 until his death, he lived in Hamburg. He was one of the most influential Hebrew poets of his time, and his poems, lyrical in tone, included several on biblical themes. C. wrote various textbooks, among them a history of the Jews from the Hasmonean Period.

COHEN (COHN), TOBIAS (1652–1729): Physician and Hebrew author. He was born in Metz and studied medicine at Padua before settling in Poland where he became a well-known practitioner. Later he went to Turkey and finally to Palestine. C. wrote *Maaseh Tovyah* on philosophy, natural science, and medicine, incorporating in it documents on the Sabbetaian movement.

COHEN, YAAKOV see **CAHAN, YAAKOV**

COHN, EDWIN J. (1892–1953): US biological chemist. He taught at Harvard from 1922. His researches into blood components were the basis for the discovery of gamma globulin and other life-restoring blood fractions. C. developed a blood fractionation machine which revolutionized the use of blood plasma.

COHN, FERDINAND JULIUS (1828–1898): German botanist. Professor at Breslau Univ. where he founded the Institute of Plant Physiology. A. discovered the nature of bacteria, was the first to employ the term "bacillus," and made important contributions to combating plant disease and pests. His researches finally disposed of the former widespread belief in "spontaneous generation."

COHN, ḤAIM HERMANN (1911–): Israel jurist. Born in Lübeck, Germany, he went to Palestine in 1930. C. was Israel's attorney-general for most

Samuel S. Cohon.

of the period 1948–60, and was minister of justice for a short time in 1952. In 1960 he was appointed a supreme court judge. C. wrote a study on the trial of Jesus.

COHN, LEOPOLD (1856–1915): German classical philologist; lecturer, later librarian, at the Univ. of Breslau. His works on Greek literature and lexicology included research on Philo.

COHN, OSCAR (1869–1934): German socialist politician. First elected to the Reichstag in 1912, he was under-secretary of state for justice for a short time after World War I. He left Germany in 1933 and died in Geneva.

COHN, TOBIAS see **COHEN, TOBIAS**

COHNHEIM, JULIUS (1839–1884): German pathologist. Professor of pathological anatomy at Kiel (1868), Breslau (1872), and Leipzig (1876), C. was noted for his revelation of the nature of pus, which revolutionized pathology.

COHON, SAMUEL SOLOMON (1888–1959): US rabbi and educator. A native of Russia, C. went to America in 1904. From 1923, he was professor of Jewish theology at Hebrew Union College, Cincinnati. C. wrote extensively on religious problems from a Reform viewpoint.

COINS: The basic unit of Jewish weight was the SHEKEL (Ezek. 45:12) which was later equivalent to 4 Greek drachmas. No Jewish coinage existed in most of the Biblical Period. The earliest coin thought to be Jewish is a half-shekel, imitated from 5th cent. BCE Greek coinage, attributed to Nehemiah as governor of Judah. In the 4th cent., c. appear inscribed "Yahud" but it is uncertain whether they were issued by the Persian or the Jewish authority. The Hasmonean coins reveal a national spirit expressed in the archaic Hebrew inscriptions and in the symbolism (cornucopiae, *lulav, etrog,* chalice, palm, flowers, etc.). After Simon and until the end of Jewish independence, only bronze issues are known. John Hyrcanus (135–104 BCE) coined as high priest in the name of "the Jewish Council(?)" and Alexander Yannai (103–76 BCE) was the first Hasmonean to call himself king on his currency. Under Mattathias Antigonus (40–37 BCE), when the candlestick symbol first appears, considerable debasement took place, a feature repeated under Herod (37–4 BCE). His house adopted purely Greek inscriptions, but avoided the representation of human figures in Judea. Herod's son, Philip, was the first Herodian dynast to place the Roman emperor's head on his issues. The last ruler of the family, Agrippa II (50–93) at first reproduced his own image, but later was only permitted to strike the image of the Roman emperors. In the war of 66–70, the Jewish patriots issued silver shekels containing Hasmonean symbolism and archaic Hebrew inscriptions. Many of Bar Kokhba's coins (132–5) were overstruck Roman issues defaced for propaganda purposes; the rebuilt Temple is shown, with *lulav, etrog,* and the musical instruments of the cult; the legends are "The liberation of Israel"; later: "The (or 'For the') liberation of Jerusalem." Between 1927 and 1947, the British Mandatory government in Palestine issued a

Coinage of the State of Israel.

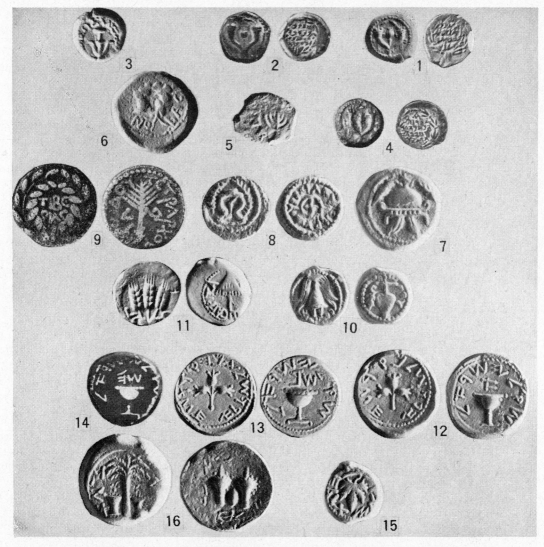

Ancient Hebrew coins from the Hasmonean Period to the Destruction of the Second Temple.
Hasmonean Dynasty: 1. John Hyrcanus I; 2.–3. Jonathan (Alexander Yannai); 4. John Hyrcanus II; 5.–6. Mattathias (Antigonus). *Herodian Dynasty*: 7.–8. Herod; 9. Antipas; 10. Archelaus; 11. Agrippa I. *From the Great Revolt against Rome*: 12. Shekel of year 1; 13. Shekel of year 2; 14. Shekel of year 5; 15. Second Year (copper); 16. Fourth Year (copper half Shekel).

neutral coinage on which the Hebrew initials of E(retz) Y(israel) appeared beside "Palestine" in Hebrew, English, and Arabic letters. The pound was divided into 1,000 *mils* (Heb. *perutah* after 1948). With the re-establishment of the state of Israel, the currency remained denominationally the same as under the Mandate (copper and nickel coinage up to 100 *perutah*) with the addition of 25 and 250 *perutah* nickel pieces; paper was also issued from 250 *perutah* upward. In 1960 the *perutah* was abolished in favor of the *agorah* whose value is 100th of a pound. With this change a new coinage was issued.

COLLECTIVES see **AGRICULTURAL SETTLE-MENTS; COOPERATIVE MOVEMENTS**

COLLEGE OF JEWISH STUDIES: Chicago institution founded in 1924 by the Chicago Board of Jewish Education in order to foster Jewish studies in various spheres and train teachers. It grants Bachelor of Hebrew Literature degrees and conducts graduate school leading to the degrees of Master and Doctor of Hebrew literature. Its president (1968) is David Weinstein.

COLLEGES see **UNIVERSITIES**

COLLEGIO RABBINICO ITALIANO: The earliest modern rabbinical seminary, established at Padua in 1829 as Instituto Convitto Rabbinico. It was closed in 1871, but revived in Rome in 1887, subsequently flourished in Florence, and in 1930, returned to Rome.

Closed during the later Fascist Period, it reopened in 1955.

COLMAR: Town in Alsace where Jews were living as early as 1278. The Jews were generally protected by the emperor, but in 1349, the community was annihilated. By the end of the 14th cent., 29 families had resettled there, but this community was short-lived. Jews were again in C. at the end of the 17th cent., and the town became the seat of the consistory and chief rabbinate of the Upper Rhine in 1823. It is still one of the principal Alsatian communities with 1,100 Jews in 1970.

COLOGNE: W German city. Its Jewish community is the only one known in Germany during Roman times. In 321, Constantine canceled the Jewish exemption from membership in the city council which was responsible for taxation. At that time the community was already well-organized. Nothing is known of its subsequent history until the 11th cent. when Jews lived there under the protection of the archbishop and had their own quarter and synagogue. In 1096, they were decimated by rioters who plundered their property and desecrated the synagogue; the community, however, was soon refounded. Some of its members lived in a special quarter of the city, and an adjacent gate ("Jews' gate") was entrusted to their supervision in 1106. The Jews received a charter of rights in 1331, being granted broad juridical autonomy while obligated to pay heavy taxes. Till the end of the 13th cent., they engaged in trade and participated in the local fairs but, later, their economic activity was limited to monetary transactions. The town council endeavored to protect the Jews during the Black Death massacres of 1349, but the mobs grew out of hand and the entire community was destroyed. Some Jews returned from 1372 but were expelled in 1384, and the synagogue was turned into a church. A considerable community now sprang up in the neighboring Deutz. Settlement in C. was only resumed in 1798 and the Jews numbered 14,816 in 1933. They were annihilated under the Nazis, but a small community was later re-established. Jewish pop. (1973): 1,352.

COLOMBIA: S American republic. Marranos settled in Barranquilla and Cali early in the 16th cent. but were eliminated by the Inquisition. Some Jews returned in the middle of the 19th cent. but came in number only after World War I when immigrants arrived from E Europe, Palestine, and (during the Nazi period) Germany. Jewish immigration was forbidden in 1939. Most of the Jews live in Bogota (c. 7,000), Cali Barranquilla, and Medellin. Jewish pop. (1973): 12,000.

COLON, JOSEPH (c. 1420–1480): Rabbinic scholar. Born in France, he served as rabbi in several Italian communities. His responsa constitute a rich source of information on halakhic problems as well as on contemporary conditions in Italy.

COLONIES, AGRICULTURAL see **AGRICULTURAL SETTLEMENTS**

COLORADO: US state. The earliest Jewish settlers who reached DENVER in 1858 came from Germany. Jews took part in the gold rush during the 1860's; others, like Simon GUGGENHEIM, were later prominent in developing additional mineral resources, such as silver and lead. The Jewish population (1973) is 27,455 Denver, with 26,000 Jews, is the largest center, with other communities in Colorado Springs and Pueblo. The National Jewish Hospital, the Jewish Consumptives' Relief Society, and other major health institutions are located in Denver.

COLUMBUS: City in Ohio, US. Its first Jews settled there in 1838. In 1852, the first Jewish congregation, B'nai Jeshurun (later Temple Israel), was founded by adherents of Reform Judaism, and an Orthodox congregation, Agudath Achim, came into being in 1883. A group of Hungarian Jews formed the Conservative congregation, Tifereth Israel, in 1901. The weekly *Ohio Jewish Chronicle* has appeared in C. since 1922. Its United Jewish Fund was established in 1925 and its Community Council in 1940. Jewish pop. (1973): 13,000.

*COLUMBUS, CHRISTOPHER (c. 1446–1506): Discoverer of America. Numerous scholars have endeavored to demonstrate that he was of Jewish or Marrano extraction. No positive evidence has as yet been discovered, but the fact that, though born in Italy, his mother-tongue was Spanish makes the latter suggestion not impossible. Moreover, he boasted cryptically of his remote origins and clearly tried to conceal something of his immediate background. His mysterious signature, to which he attached much importance, is also capable of a Jewish interpretation; in one place, he uses an inaccurate Jewish chronological tradition, and he seems to have avoided sailing on the ill-fated day of Av 9. Hypothesis aside, he certainly found encouragement and financial help from Jews and Marranos and his first reports of success were addressed to his Marrano patrons. It was formerly believed that five members of his crew were of Jewish origin, but recent research has shown that this is true of only one, the interpreter Luis de Torres.

COMITÉ DES DÉLÉGATIONS JUIVES (Fr. "Committee of Jewish Delegations"): Body that came into existence in Paris in Mar., 1919 for the purpose of presenting the Peace Conference with the demand for Jewish national rights in certain countries, especially in the newly established "succession states" in Central and E Europe. The Committee was formed to avoid separate representations by the various Jewish delegations from different countries, though the delegates of W European communities and the American Jewish Committee did not join it. With Leo Motzkin at its head, the committee continued to function throughout the Peace Conference and succeeded in obtaining some of its demands. It remained in existence for the protection of Jewish rights during the next decades, mainly financed by the Zionist Organization. Motzkin headed it till his death, and later it evolved into the WORLD JEWISH CONGRESS.

COMITÉ REPRESENTATIF DES ISRAELITES DE FRANCE see **CRIF**

COMMANDMENT see **MITZVAH**

COMMANDMENTS, TEN (referred to in Deut. 4:13; 10:4, etc. as the Ten Words [Decalogue]: Fundamental laws proclaimed by God on Mt. Sinai and transmitted through Moses to Israel. The T. C. are regarded in Jewish literature as the fountainhead of all other laws. They are given in Exod. 20:2–14 and repeated with slight variations in Deut. 5:6–18. The main difference between the two versions concerns the law of the Sabbath which in Exod. is motivated by God's resting on the seventh day of creation, while in Deut. the reason given is the deliverance from Egypt. The division into ten commandments is not apparent in the Hebrew original and the Christian tradition regarding this differs slightly at the outset from the Jewish (maintaining that the first verse is not a commandment and dividing into two

Moses with the Ten Commandments
(From the Sarajevo Haggadah).

either the second or tenth commandment). According to Jewish tradition, the first five commandments describe man's duties to God, the latter five his responsibilities to his fellow-man. They were written on two tablets of stone, which were broken by Moses in his indignation over the worship of the Golden Calf. After Moses reascended Mt. Sinai he brought down a second set, which was placed in the Ark, henceforth known as the Ark of Testimony or the Ark of the Covenant. The T. C. were recited daily in the Temple just before the *Shema,* forming an integral part of the morning service. The practice was, however, abolished when the *Minim* (sectarians) asserted that the Decalogue alone had been given to Moses on Mt. Sinai. The fundamental importance of the T. C. was emphasized by the rabbis and medieval Jewish philosophers.

COMMENTATORS see **BIBLE COMMENTATORS; TALMUD COMMENTARIES**

COMMERCE: International c. was not highly developed among the Hebrews in the Biblical Period. The commercial peoples mentioned in the Bible are the Ishmaelites (Gen. 37:25) or Midianites (Gen. 37:28), the Phoenicians (Is. 23), and the Canaanites (Hos. 12:8), "Canaanite" and "merchant" being synonymous (Prov. 31:24). Solomon, however, made his realm an entrepôt of international trade. He also dispatched ships once every 3 years from Ezion-Geber to Ophir. After his reign, it was not until the Maccabean era that international c. began to play an important role in Jewish life. Simon the Hasmonean took Joppa (Jaffa), and Herod built Caesarea to provide ports for international trade. Jews living in hellenistic Egypt also began to show interest in shipping and wholesale merchandizing activity. The great impetus for the development of Jewish trade came after the rise of Islam. Jews served as the middlemen in the trade between Islamic countries and those of Christian Europe. The RADANITES, for example, carried on trade from China and India in the East to the countries of W Europe. The Venetians during the 10th cent. were the first to try to suppress Jewish trade in Europe; but the most restrictive period was during the Crusades in the 12th and 13th cents. Jews were excluded from the merchant guilds which monopolized trade. This forced them to turn to usury and petty trading for their livelihood. Nevertheless, large-scale Jewish c. still continued to flourish in various areas. The Marranos later developed trade between Europe, America, and the Levant, helping to make Amsterdam the commercial center of Europe in the 17th cent. In Central Europe, Jews were active in the great FAIRS of Leipzig, etc. The fur trade was largely in Jewish hands. During the heyday of CAPITALISM, Jewish influence was felt in Central Europe, especially in railroad construction, banking, and foreign trade. In the American colonies,

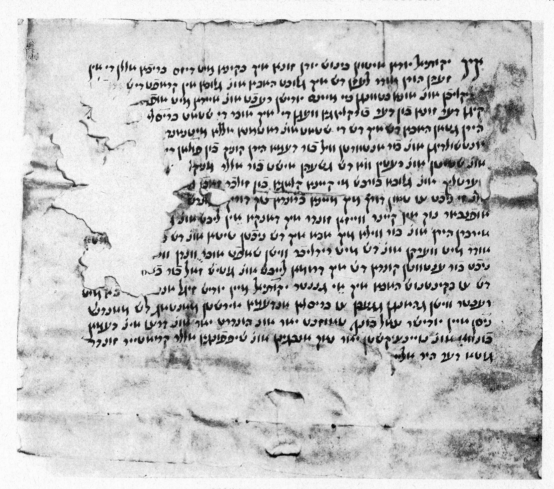

Yiddish promissory note of 1435.

Jews participated in a triangular c. involving England, the colonies, and the W Indies. This trade was impaired by the American Revolution and its W Indian link completely paralyzed by the War of 1812. With the settlement of the western US after 1812, Jewish peddlers moved to the interior of the country to supply the new settlers and eventually set up stores. Jewish wholesale firms supplied the retail stores, particularly in the West. The Jewish merchant in the US has played an important role in the mail order business, as well as in department store development. In Israel, the Jewish occupational structure tends to parallel the general structure in other countries, rather than that of the Jews in the Diaspora (see OCCUPATIONS). In 1966, 13.5% of the Jewish population in Israel was engaged in c.

COMMITTEE FOR JEWISH CLAIMS ON AUSTRIA: Body established in 1953 by major Jewish organizations throughout the world concerned with refugee problems. Its objectives are (1) to improve benefits to Jewish victims of Nazism from Austria under the terms of the Austrian compensation laws, and (2) to obtain from Austria funds for the relief of those who are in need. In 1955, the C.J.C.A. concluded a settlement of Jewish indemnification claims with the Austrian government by which an Aid Fund *(Hilfsfond)* was to be created to distribute $21 million from the Austrian government over a 10-year period.

COMMUNISM: The movement which aims at the proletarian control of society by revolution. It originated in the doctrines of Karl MARX. (For C. prior to 1917, see BOLSHEVISM). At the time of the Russian Revolution (1917), practically all Jewish socialist parties (including the BUND) opposed C., while C. came to look upon Zionism as the tool of British imperialism and a reactionary movement calculated to divert the Jewish working-class from socialism. Jews were not numerous in the Communist Party, but some of the leaders were of Jewish origin (e.g. TROTSKY, ZINOVIEV, KAMENEV, RADEK, and LITVINOV) while the communist opposition to anti-Semitism caused many Jews to support the regime. The party set up a special Jewish department (the

Yevsektzia) which acknowledged Yiddish as the Jewish language. In 1923, the communist government initiated schemes to colonize Jews in autonomous areas, thus conceding their national identity. Jews were prominent in the Trotskyist faction. During the 1936–38 purges, many veteran Jewish leaders of the Communist Party were executed. In 1957 KAGANOVICH was removed from his position. Veniamin E. Dymshyts was appointed (1962) Soviet Deputy Premier and Chairman of the State Planning Committee, the first Jew since Kaganovich to hold high office. In Germany, Jews were prominent in the nascent Communist Party of 1918, but some of the leading ones were assassinated (Rosa LUXEMBURG) and others left the party. In Hungary, the communist regime of 1919 was headed by Béla KUN. In the US, Jewish communists founded a daily Yiddish newspaper *Freiheit* (1922) and also organized a fraternal society, the International Workers' Order (1930), to compete with the Workmen's Circle, but this organization was ordered disbanded by the NY State Insurance Department in 1952. In other countries also, a number of Jews joined the Communist Parties between the two World Wars, motivated by the economic depression, the growth of anti-Semitism, and the communist opposition to Nazism. This tendency was checked by the Moscow-Berlin pact (Aug. 1939). After 1945, communist control extended to the satellite states of E Europe; these followed the Russian lead in supporting the establishment of the state of Israel (1947–8) and subsequently in attacking Zionism because of Israel's close association with the US. Russia's policy toward its Jews was severely criticized by Western Communist parties in the 1960's. In Israel, the Communist Party has never been important; its chief strength is among the Arab population. In recent years, it has split into two — MAKI attracting in particular the Jewish Communists, and RAKAH, the Arabs who have always provided the main strength for C. in Israel.

COMMUNITY, JEWISH: For more than twenty-five centuries the Jews have maintained their communal AUTONOMY with varying degrees of independence and authority. In First Temple times, even Palestinian Jews, living in outlying communities, must have gathered in assemblies for prayer to replace sacrificial worship, e.g. in the period of Manasseh's persecution of the prophetic party and his desecration of the Temple (II Kings 21). Thus, the foundations were laid for the SYNAGOGUE. The c. underwent a crucial test during the Babylonian Exile when the exiles laid the foundations for their fully self-governing institutions clustered around the synagogue (cf. Ezek. 11:16, etc.). This development was stimulated by the restoration to Palestine. Although relatively little is known about the Babylonian c. until the 3rd cent. CE, the patterns developed during the Exile served as the foundations of Jewish communal structure in other countries. The Second Temple Period helped in the process of adjustment, since Jews had for long periods lived as minorities in Palestinian cities which, until the Maccabean revolt, were not under Jewish control. When the Maccabeans unified the country, many of these minority communities became regular Jewish municipalities. But many others retained their minority character, especially in the "Greek" cities. The presence of a Jewish garrison c. with priests and a temple between the 7th and 4th cents. BCE at Elephantine, Egypt, implies a considerable degree of communal organization, The Jews of Alexandria had their corporation at least from the 2nd cent. BCE, involving the right to elect officers and a council *(gerousia)*, to conduct their affairs according to Jewish law, to erect synagogues, to maintain a records office, and to send the Temple tax to Jerusalem. Throughout the hellenistic world nearly all Jewish c.'s had similar organizations modeled on that of the Greek cities, normally granted by the hellenistic kings on the basis of the right "to use their ancestral laws"— a privilege given by Antiochus III to the Jews of Palestine as a whole (201 BCE). Under the Roman Empire these institutions spread to the W (e.g. Rome). While the emperors prohibited associations with political potentialities, purely religious organizations and municipal corporations were permitted. The existing Jewish communal organization in the E, which was quasi-municipal in character, was not interfered with. In the 2nd cent. CE the municipal organizations of Jewish towns in Palestine (Tiberias, Sepphoris) were de-judaized, and the minority status of the Jews, even in Palestine became ever more pronounced. For this reason, the talmudic legislation of the Palestinian as well as the Babylonian Talmud became applicable to townships where the Jews were in the majority as well as in those more numerous ones where they were but a tolerated minority. Since the Greco-Roman world was filled with voluntary associations of all kinds, Jews, too, were able to pioneer along new paths. While Palestine and Babylonia were directed by central authorities, the Jewries of the other countries had to emphasize local autonomy. In Palestine after the destruction of the Temple the leadership was taken over by "patriarchs" *(nesiim)* working together with the supreme council, the Sanhedrin. Until its formal suppression about 425, the patriarchate claimed supremacy over the whole Jewish people and exercised considerable control over all Jewish communities in the Empire. However, because of the great distances involved, patriarchal interventions were as a rule limited to extraordinary occasions. Babylonia, on the other hand, was headed by a dynasty of EXILARCHS which claimed descent from the kings of Judah, exiled by

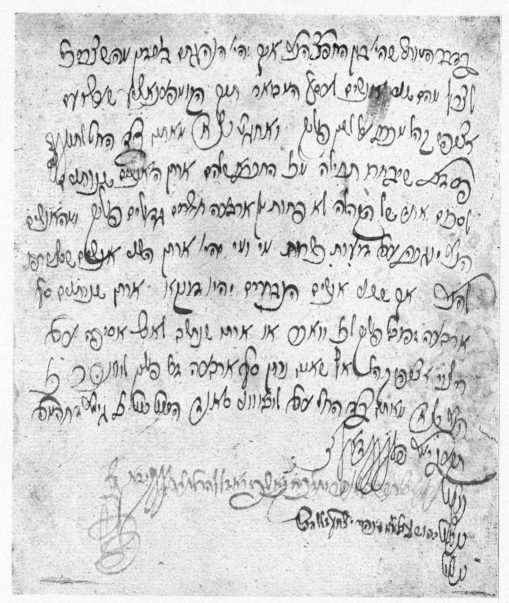

Page from the Minute Book of the Pinsk community.

Nebuchadnezzar. They achieved great eminence under Sassanian rule (from 226 CE) but during the turbulent 5th-6th cents., became embroiled in domestic political struggles. Mar Zutra II was executed and his son, Mar Zutra III, had to emigrate to Palestine (about 491). Under Islam, the exilarchate was revived and achieved an unrivaled position. From Bostanai to Hezekiah (c. 640–1058) the "prince of captivity" exercised fairly effective control over the Jewries of the Great Caliphate, and, after its dissolution, over the Jewish c.'s of Babylonia and its vicinity. Even after Hezekiah, the exilarchate continued for another two centuries until the Mongolian destruction

of Baghdad. Members of the exilarchate family meanwhile established themselves in other communities including Palestine, Egypt, Aleppo, and Mosul. They thus joined the increasingly independent provincial leaders, exemplified in particular by the Egyptian *negidim* who were indirect successors to the ancient Egyptian ethnarchs. The origins of the Egyptian, Kairouanian, and Spanish *negidim* are shrouded in legend, but by the end of the 10th cent., these provincial chiefs enjoyed considerable authority. In Egypt, the office was entrusted, for more than two centuries, to the descendants of Maimonides. In the meantime, the western communities emerging from the dissolution of the ancient Roman Empire continued with their chaotic, but creative, communal life. Under the changed conditions of the new Christian regimes with their manifold restrictive laws, each c. strove for the implementation of its religious and cultural programs as best it could. Without the guidance of central authorities, most communities had to develop some new forms of organization which fostered a preponderant element of self-reliance, pioneering, and essentially democratic cooperation. Whether in Byzantium, Italy, France, Germany, England, or later also in Christian Spain or Poland-Lithuania, the "sovereignty" really rested with the communal assembly which only delegated its responsibilities to elected officials and appointive religious, educational, and judicial executives. While many leaders possessed rabbinic training, the rabbinate became fully professionalized in the West only from the 14th cent. But since everyone was encouraged to devote himself to study, there were no social obstacles to entry into the highest echelons of this "aristocracy of learning" which, to all intents and purposes, was another form of democracy. Governments tried to make use of the Jewish c. for their own purposes. The c., which already under Roman and Persian domination had been used as a tax-collecting agency for the state, now became a principal source of royal revenue. Many princes promoted Jewish autonomy for no other reason than to have the communal organs exert more effective authority over the members' fiscal contributions. At times, the states tried to organize their Jewries on a countrywide basis. The Jewish "archpresbyters" in England, the chief rabbis of Aragon, Castile, and, for a time, of France, were in reality more treasury agents than ecclesiastical chiefs. For this reason, both German and Polish-Lithuanian Jews fiercely resisted attempts by emperors and kings to impose upon them such chief rabbinates. Because of Germany's imperial weakness, German Jewry succeeded in staving them off. Polish Jewry, on the other hand, compromised with the government and established, instead, in the middle of the 16th cent. a collegiate body, the so-called COUNCIL OF FOUR LANDS, consisting of representatives of the major Jewish communities. The Polish Council, together with the Lithuanian Council which split off it in 1623, exerted great influence on the internal and cultural affairs not only of Polish Jewry but also of neighboring lands. In the meantime, the large Jewish population concentrated in the rapidly expanding Ottoman Empire in the 15th and 16th cents. was reorganized along traditional eastern patterns under a single chief, the *hakham bashi* of Constantinople. Under him functioned many provincial chief rabbis, replacing even the Egyptian *negidim* whose office was suppressed by the conquering Turks in 1517. This system prevailed in the Ottoman possessions until the 20th cent. Elsewhere, Jewish communal life underwent a radical transformation under the impact of Emancipation. Now, equality of rights of all citizens required the dissolution of the various estates and, with it, also the restriction of Jewish communal autonomy to matters of purely religious concern. Only with the rise of modern Jewish nationalism at the end of the 19th cent. were postulates formulated to supplement Jewish equality by Jewish national minority rights on a broader secular basis. Out of the turmoil of conflicting interests and ideologies, there emerged in the modern era several new forms of communal life, all maintaining some sort of continuity with the traditional Jewish KEHILLAH, but none approaching it in compass and authority. Most radical was the break in those western countries where Jewish Emancipation was combined with separation of State and Church. In extreme forms, as during the French revolutionary Religion of Reason, the government actually combated Jewish and Christian religious groups. In most periods, however, the governments remained sympathetic, but inactive, observers of what the religious c.'s did of their own volition. The US government has supported all religious groups through tax exemptions and other indirect methods. It has also allowed them to organize congregations of their own and to enjoy within each group complete autonomy. Although such freedom threatened communal chaos, in practice in the US and, to a lesser extent in 20th cent. France and elsewhere, the separation of State and Church has largely accrued to the benefit of the Jewish c., and most Jews have fought for its continuation. This system required a great many adjustments, but here the Jewish people's spirit found outlets through new institutions and methods of democratic cooperation. In America, such organs as federations of charities, Jewish centers and camps, defense agencies to protect Jewish rights in the country and abroad, cultural and educational groups, as well as strong religious bodies have taken over the main functions of organized Jewish life. Such organizations, though weak as compared with the medieval c., have, nevertheless, set the pace for Jewish life under fully emancipated conditions. At the other extreme, there emerged the "people's community," a national secular organization demanded by Jewish nationalists since the end of the 19th cent. After the Russian Revolution of 1917, such people's communities were established in the Soviet Union and some adjoining countries. In the 1920's, they seemed to hold out great promise of achievement in Jewish cultural autonomy. However, because of the anti-religious, anti-Zionist, and anti-Hebraic policies of the Soviet government, and the generally outspoken opposition of the majority of the peoples and governments in the other countries (except Czechoslovakia and Esthonia) to the curtailment of their "sovereignty" by minority rights, these national c.'s declined in the 1930's and practically went out of existence during World War II. Only in Palestine before and after the establishment of the Mandate did the c.'s, under the leadership of their National Council *(Vaad Leumi)*, function as effective organs of Jewish self-government. Between these extremes, the Jewish c.'s in many major countries of Jewish settlement, Poland, Germany, Austria, Hungary, and more recently Italy, etc. maintained a greater measure of continuity with the pre-Emancipation organizational forms. Greatly curtailed in their educational and judicial authority, they nevertheless carried on religious and cultural work under the sanction of public law. Among the more important legislative enactments were those of Prussia in 1847 and 1876, of Austria in 1890, and of Poland in 1927. In Italy, where after 1871 the state withheld its support from all religious organizations, there was a re-assertion of such unity after the Lateran Treaties of 1929. Here, as well as in Germany, the Jewish c.'s were federated in a central *Unione* or the various *Landesverbände* of German states. Under the Nazi regime, there even emerged for a time a central organization, the *Reichsvertretung der deutschen Juden*. Less sharply defined was the position in public law of the British c.'s, although the Board of Deputies of British Jews, as well as the chief rabbinate, have long enjoyed considerable recognition on the part of both government and public opinion. Since 1935, the evolution has been beclouded everywhere by the uncertainties of the divided world, the destruction of many centers of Jewish life and, on the other hand, by a certain revival of religious forces throughout the western world. Because of the Israel-Arab conflict, Jewish c.'s in Moslem countries which had, on the whole, preserved their old organizational forms have been facing uncertainties of a new kind.

COMMUNITY CENTERS see **JEWISH COMMUNITY CENTERS**

COMMUNITY COUNCILS: An adaptation of the European *kehillah* to US conditions. Jewish c. c. have come to the fore in the past twenty years. The method of organization varies widely, though all attempt to create a body representing every point of view in the community. In most instances, members are nominated by existing organizations recognized as basically Jewish in their interests and activities. In many cities, the older welfare fund has been incorporated into the c. c. Its activities embrace the fields of philanthropy, community relations, education, and internal Jewish affairs. The c. c. usually serve as the spokesmen of the community and as their liaison with public and/or other bodies.

COMMUNITY RELATIONS: Since about 1940, Jewish communities in the US have developed an organized program of activities designed to promote better relations between the Jews and the general community in which they live. C. r. committees, frequently associated with a Jewish Community Council, have sought to combat discrimination in employment, education, housing, public facilities, etc. and to fight anti-Semitism in the various forms in which it manifests itself. Their program involves use of educational methods, promotion of legislation, etc. C. r. activity opposes tendencies against all minority groups and encourages inter-cultural understanding. The National Community Relations Advisory Council, founded in 1944, coordinates these activities for its affiliated agencies; the Anti-Defamation League of B'nai B'rith and the American Jewish Committee work separately.

COMPOSERS see **MUSIC**

COMTAT VENAISSIN: District in Provence, formerly under Papal rule, where Jews were allowed to remain in the "Four Communities" of AVIGNON, CARPENTRAS, CAVAILLON, and L'Isle after they were expelled from the rest of France. They maintained their own traditions and distinctive *Comtadin* liturgy.

COMTINO, MORDECAI BEN ELIEZER (fl. 15th cent.), Turkish scholar. He wrote a commentary to the Pentateuch, called *Keter Torah*, and works on rabbinic and scientific subjects. The Karaites incorporated two of his hymns into their liturgy.

CONCENTRATION CAMPS see **CAMPS, CONCENTRATION**

CONCORDANCES see **DICTIONARIES**

CONCUBINE see **POLYGAMY**

CONDUCTORS see **MUSIC**

CONFERENCE OF PRESIDENTS OF MAJOR AMERICAN JEWISH ORGANIZATIONS: Central coordinating agency of US Jewry representing 22 national organizations and their local counterparts. It was founded in 1954 and acts as a forum for exchanging information and as a body that speaks on behalf of the community particularly with regard to Israel and the position of Jews in other countries.

CONFERENCE ON JEWISH MATERIAL CLAIMS AGAINST GERMANY: Organization established in 1951 to secure funds for the relief, rehabilitation, and resettlement of Jewish victims of Nazism; to obtain compensation for property sequestrated by the Nazis; and to secure indemnification for physical and economic disabilities suffered in concentration camps. In 1952, after lengthy negotiations in which the Israel government participated, the Claims Conference and the German Federal Republic concluded an agreement whereby $107 million would be allotted to the Claims Conference for the relief, rehabilitation, and resettlement of the Jewish victims living outside Israel. Payments were to be made annually over a period of from 12 to 14 years. The Claims Conference allotted considerable sums of money, mainly in Europe and America, for Jewish intellectual and educational purposes, including schools, academies, and learned projects.

CONFERENCE ON JEWISH SOCIAL STUDIES: US organization (until 1955, the Conference on Jewish Relations) founded by Morris Raphael Cohen and Salo W. Baron in 1933 to promote a better understanding of the position of Jews in the modern world. It sponsors studies in American Jewish demography, the history and nature of anti-Semitism, and the problems of Jews in other countries. Its publications include *Jewish Social Studies,* a quarterly journal (since 1939).

CONFERENCES, RABBINICAL see **RABBINICAL CONFERENCES**

CONFESSION OF SIN (Heb. *vidduy*): Confession (direct to God and not through any human intermediary) is a prominent feature of Jewish liturgy. It is a chief element in the Day of Atonement and also figures in the daily services (except on Sabbaths and holidays) being especially prominent on Mondays and Thursdays. The Bible frequently mentions the efficacy of both public and individual c. (e.g. Lev. 16:21; II Sam. 12:13). Sin offerings (always accompanied by verbal c.) played an important role in the Temple sacrificial service. Originally there was no fixed form of c., but the Talmud records certain formulas. The best-known examples in the liturgy are the alphabetic enumerations of various types of sins in the *Al Het* and *Ashamnu* prayers of the Day of Atonement. The latter has also found its way into the daily service in certain rites. A common custom is for the bridegroom to recite the c. on the day of his wedding. A special formula is prescribed for a deathbed c. *(Shabbat 32a).*

CONFIRMATION see **BAR (BAT) MITZVAH**

CONFORTE, DAVID (1618—c. 1690): Talmudic scholar and literary historian. He was born in Salonica, studied in Jerusalem, and eventually settled in Cairo where he served as dayyan. His book *Kore ha-Dorot* surveys Hebrew literature from the Talmudic Period down to the author's own times.

CONGO (ZAIRE): African country. Jews settled there early in the 20th cent. from S. Africa but these were eventually outnumbered by Sephardi Jews, mainly from Rhodes. The community of 2,500 in 1959 was depleted by emigration during the unrest in the early 1960's. The 1973 population was 250.

CONGRATULATIONS: The most common Hebrew forms of c. are *mazzal tov* ("good luck"), *mazzal u-verakhah* ("luck and blessing"), or among Sephardim *be-simman tov* ("in good omen"). On performing a religious duty (e.g., being called to the law in synagogue), the form of c. among Ashkenazim is *yeyasher koah* ("May He [i.e., God] straighten [i.e., increase] [your] strength," usually in a contracted form) and

among Sephardim *hazak u-varukh* (= "[be thou] strong and blessed"). The Sephardim also commonly use the c. *tizkeh le-mitzvot* ("may you have [the merit to perform] commandments"). As a toast, the c. *le-hayyim* ("for life") is universal. A birthday greeting is *ad meah (ve-esrim) shanah* (or in Yiddish *biz a hundert [tzvantzig]*, i.e., "[may you live] to a hundred [and twenty]").

CONGRESS see **ZIONIST CONGRESS**

CONGRESS FOR JEWISH CULTURE: Organization founded in the US in 1948 to promote Yiddish culture throughout the world. It publishes a Yiddish periodical *Zukunft* and aids Jewish institutions in various countries.

CONGRESS OF BERLIN: Conference convoked by BISMARCK in 1878 to deal with the differences between Russia and Turkey and to settle the Eastern Question; one of the dominant figures was the Earl of BEACONSFIELD. Among the questions discussed was the position of the Jews in the Balkan states. On the initiative of the French delegate, the recognition of the independence of Bulgaria, Serbia, and Rumania was made conditional on the granting of full civil and political rights to the subjects of these countries, irrespective of religious belief. Rumania, however, found a technical loophole in the treaty and continued to deprive her Jews of rights.

CONGRESS OF VIENNA: Conference held in 1814–5 for the reorganization of Europe after the Napoleonic wars. It was the first such congress at which the Jewish question was specifically considered and to which Jewish representatives were sent to watch over Jewish interests. Metternich, the Austrian chancellor, and Hardenberg, the Prussian delegate, favored the maintenance in all the various German states of the Emancipation achieved during the period of French domination. The delegates of the smaller states – Bavaria, Saxony, and the Free Cities – were, however, opposed. A compromise resolution was finally adopted whereby the Confederate Diet of the proposed German Federation was instructed to take steps to grant citizens' rights to Jews.

CONIAH see **JEHOIACHIN**

CONJOINT FOREIGN COMMITTEE (or **JOINT FOREIGN COMMITTEE**) see **ANGLO-JEWISH ASSOCIATION**

CONNECTICUT: US state. Individual Jews lived there from the mid-17th cent. At the time of the Revolution, many went there from New York and Rhode Island to escape from the British. Thereafter, down to the late 1830's when Jews from Germany settled in NEW HAVEN and HARTFORD, and a little later at BRIDGEPORT, there were no Jews in C. In 1843, the statutes of C. were amended to sanction the organization of Jewish congregations. In 1947, about 2,500 Jewish families were living on farms and tilling about 25,900 acres. Abraham RIBICOFF was governor of the state 1955–60. Jewish pop. (1973): 99,930.

CONSCRIPTION: In the Israelite tribal period, military service devolved on all able-bodied males from the age of 20 (Num. 1:3), although grounds for exemption were allowed (Deut. 20:5–8). The kings retained power of levy (II Kings 25:19). Although there was no general exemption of Jews in the Roman Emipre, circumstances made them few in the Roman army until the 3rd cent.; in the 4th cent. they were legally excluded from the forces. In medieval Europe, Jews were generally forbidden to bear arms, although they were obliged to participate in the defense of the Rhenish cities in the 12th cent. In most of Europe, Jews became liable to c. at the period of the French Revolutionary Wars. In Russia before 1827, however, Jews paid a tax in lieu of service; subsequently c. was imposed with the aim of assimilating them and the Jewish conscripts suffered much hardship (see CANTONISTS). In Israel, c. is applicable to males between the ages of 18 and 29 and females between 18 and 26. See ARMED FORCES.

CONSECRATION: The dedication of a person or thing for special – usually holy – use. Personal c. ceremonies are mentioned in the Bible in connection with kingship and priesthood. This ceremony consists in anointing with oil, and, in the case of priests, also with the blood of a sacrifice. The Bible speaks of the c. of vessels intended for use in the Tabernacle by anointing them with oil. The altar was of special importance, and sacrificial offerings formed part of its c. ceremony, while special sacrifices were offered at the dedication of the Second Temple (Ezra 6:16–17). The rededication of the desecrated altar in the days of the Maccabees is commemorated in the name *Ḥanukkah* ("dedication") given to the yearly celebration in honor of the event. In post-biblical times, there are records of c. ceremonies at the establishment of new synagogues. A Jewish custom, still widely observed, is the *ḥanukkat ha-bayit* ("dedication of the house") ceremony held shortly after entering a new home. Another custom, which can be traced back to rabbinical times is connected with the initiation of children to religious study. The *Bar Mitzvah* ceremony marks the c. of the adolescent boy to the observance of the commandments. In Reform synagogues, this is replaced by a service for both boys and girls.

CONSERVATIVE JUDAISM: Trend in American Judaism representing the concurrence of varying forces. The first, purely ideological, derives from the point of view developed by such scholars as Naḥman Krochmal, Zacharias Frankel, and Heinrich Graetz who maintained that in its most creative epochs Judaism was responsive to the changing religious, moral, social, and economic needs of the Jewish people. Later researches demonstrated the influence of social and economic factors upon the growth of halakhah. C. J. maintains that Judaism, in its periods of vitality, far from being a static self-contained datum, was the developing religious culture of a people that could assimilate influences from other cultures and yet retain its distinctive ethos. Another force is the fact that the founders and leaders of C. J. (notably Solomon SCHECHTER) spent their youth within the orbit of the traditional Judaism of pre-World War I E European Jewry. They insisted that Judaism, to be true to its own nature, had to reckon with the reality of Jewish peoplehood as well as its individual aspects and it has, therefore, supported Zionism. C.J. opposes extreme changes in traditional observances. However, it permits certain modifications of halakhah, e.g. in the text of the traditional *ketubbah*, and the sitting of men and women together during worship. These changes have been opposed by Orthodox Judaism. The influence of the American scene is clearly visible in the practices of the Conservative congregation. The liturgy used in Conservative congregations follows the traditional Ashkenazi version with some abbreviations and a few changes in text. The typical Conservative synagogue provides for weekday activities that include a religious school, a youth program, women's groups, etc. Recently, increasing emphasis has been placed on Jewish study for adults. See also JEWISH THEOLOGICAL SEMINARY OF AMERICA; RABBINICAL ASSEMBLY; UNITED SYNAGOGUE OF AMERICA.

CONSISTORY (Fr. *Consistoire*): The main feature in the reorganization of the Jews of France introduced by Napoleon in 1808 (perpetuated also in Belgium). Local consistories represent the Jews of a particular area and send delegates to Paris to the central body *Consistoire Central des Israélites de France* which is responsible for the maintenance of the chief rabbinate and the rabbinical seminary. The system was extended to Algeria. There are now 12 French consistories. The c.'s of Strasbourg, Colmar, and Metz are independent of the central c.

CONSOLATION see **MOURNING**

CONSTANCE: City in Baden (Germany), with a Jewish settlement at least from the 13th cent. The entire community was burned at the time of the Black Death (1349), while in 1429 and 1433, there were Ritual Murder accusations. A new community was established in the 19th cent.

CONSTANTINE: Algerian city. Early Jewish settlement is indicated by tombstones from the 1st cent. CE. In the 4th cent., the advent of Christianity forced the Jews to leave, not to return until the local Nefzaona bedouin tribe adopted Judaism. Except for persecutions under the Almohades, the Jews did not suffer under Moslem rule and many noted scholars lived there. Many Spanish Jewish refugees arrived in the 14th and 15th cents. The community suffered greatly under Spanish rule (1509–55), but later, conditions improved somewhat under the French. The Jewish population (1959: 14,000) disappeared almost entirely as the result of emigration on the eve of Algerian independence (1962).

*CONSTANTINE I ("The Great"): First Christian emperor of Rome; ruled 312–337. The so-called edict of toleration which he issued at Milan in 312 in effect established the supremacy of Christianity. Hence, in 315, his decrees took an anti-Jewish turn, canceling Jewish exemptions from municipal office and prohibiting proselytization or interference with Jewish converts to Christianity. C.'s legislation initiated the legal degradation of Jews characteristic of the Middle Ages.

CONSTANTINOPLE (Istanbul): Turkish city. In the Byzantine Period, the Jewish community suffered continuous persecution. Benjamin of Tudela found there, c. 1165, 2,000 Jews and 500 Karaites. After its capture by the Turks (1453), the number of Jews increased through transfer from various Ottoman provinces and the arrival of Spanish exiles. The Jews were organized in 44 distinct congregations – divided into Greek, Spanish (and Italian), and Karaite; the Ashkenazim constituted a small minority. In the early and late Ottoman periods, there was a chief rabbi (*hakham bashi*) resident in the city, and the Hebrew printing presses of C. were noted from the end of the 15th cent. Jews developed the city's commerce, while others were distinguished as physicians and in court circles. The 19th cent. saw the economic and cultural decline of the community, weakened by political reforms and the establishment of modern schools. The Jewish population exceeded 90,000 in 1919, but was reduced to 22,000 by 1973.

CONSULTATIVE COUNCIL OF JEWISH ORGANIZATIONS: Body formed in 1946, with its seat in New York, by the American Jewish Committee, the Anglo-Jewish Association, and the Alliance Israélite Universelle. It has consultative status with Unesco which it assists and advises on problems relating to human rights and matters pertaining to Jews.

CONTRACT: Although a promise is morally binding in Judaism, it cannot be enforced in the Bet Din unless there has been symbolic acquisition of the rights involved before two proper witnesses through what is known as *kabbalat kinyan* ("acquiring possession"). This is the act whereby obligation is effected through one of the parties taking up or pulling at a garment (e.g. a handkerchief) or other object belonging to the other. C.'s between Jews which violate Jewish law are invalid. There is no uniformity in the written form of c.'s – known as *sepher* ("book")

in the Bible and *shetar* ("deed") in the Talmud – with the exception of marriage c.'s and bills of divorce.

CONTRACTION see TZIMTZUM

CONTROVERSIES, RELIGIOUS (Internal): The forms and outlook of modern Judaism are the outcome of a long series of c. going back far into Jewish history, many of them leaving permanent traces. The oldest in post-biblical Judaism is that with the SAMARITANS which continued down to the Middle Ages and revolved ultimately around the questions whether Judaism was to be based on the Pentateuch alone or on the prophetical writings as well. In the Hellenistic Period, there were two main subjects of religious controversy, of which, however, only sparse literary traces have been preserved; first, whether the Jewish faith could be reinterpreted in pagan forms, and later, whether it could be allegorized in accordance with Greek philosophy. The controversy between PHARISEES and SADDUCEES reflected political, social, and economic problems; the main issue, however, was whether Judaism was to be interpreted by the priests, basing themselves narrowly on the Bible, or by the newly-emerged rabbis and their wide tradition. The differences between the schools of HILLEL and SHAMMAI dealt only with the application of certain laws, but they were in agreement on basic principles. The Dead Sea Scrolls appear to reflect a religious controversy between the main Jewish center at Jerusalem and a dissident sect. In the 8th cent., the KARAITE movement reverted to or revived the Sadducee viewpoint, rejecting the Oral Law and rabbinic tradition. This was the last serious challenge to Talmudic Judaism for a thousand years (the dispute over the writings of Maimonides centered on the interpretation of forms and doctrines accepted by both sides). The controversy with the Sabbetaians in the 17th–18th cents. (facets of which were the EMDEN-EIBESCHÜTZ and the FRANKIST c.) was, however, fundamental. The controversy that followed the rise of ḤASIDISM was bitter for a short time, but the rift between the Ḥasidim and the MITNAGGEDIM tended to narrow. The REFORM controversy of the 19th cent., which was particularly marked in Germany and the US, has lost a good deal of its bitterness in some countries, but is still unsolved.

CONVERSION, FORCED: The idea of f. c. to the dominant faith became common only after the rise of Christianity with its concept of exclusive salvation. Local instances of f. c. enforced by mob violence were known all over the Roman Empire in the 4th–6th cents. F. c. because state policy in the Byzantine Empire under Heraclius (c. 611) who was imitated in France (626), Lombardy (c. 620), and especially Visigothic Spain (616 ff.). There was a renewal in the Byzantine Empire, including S Italy, in 723 and 867. Local f. c. to Islam took place in the

Conversionist sermon to Jews in Rome, 1829. Watercolor by H. Hess, Basle Museum.

Arabian Peninsula after the beginning of the activity of Mohammed; and in the 12th cent. the ALMOHADES carried out f.c. over large areas of N Africa and Spain. F. c. to Islam took place also in Persia, especially at Meshet, in the 17th and 19th cents., giving rise to the class of crypto-Jews known as JEDID AL ISLAM. The most notorious instance of f. c. to Christianity occurred in the Iberian Peninsula in the 14th–15th cent.; in SPAIN from 1391 onward, there was a series of mass conversions induced by violence, while in Portugal in 1496–7, almost the entire Jewish population was baptized by force without being given the alternative of exile or even of death. These events in Spain and Portugal gave rise to the class of crypto-Jews known as MARRANOS.

CONVERTS FROM JUDAISM see **APOSTASY**

CONVERTS TO JUDAISM see **PROSELYTES**

COOKERY, JEWISH: Dishes of the Jewish people in various parts of the world, conforming to the laws of *kashrut* and usually traditional to the Sabbath or other Jewish festivals or celebrations (circumcisions, weddings). Oriental (broadly referred to as Sephardi) and occidental (generally called Ashkenazi) c. differ as much from each other as do the dishes of the general population in the respective areas where, indeed, most Jewish dishes were inspired. Sephardi (and all other oriental) Jewish communities use much olive oil, rice, pulses, and lamb in their cuisine, as well as herbs and hot spices. The Ashkenazi communities prefer beef and bland vegetables, the flavors of which are brought out with fats, sugar, onions, etc. Both communities have many similar fowl and pastry dishes. The names of dishes are generally Yiddish or Spanish (or Arabic or Persian), Hebrew seldom figuring. A distinctive feature of J. c. is that meat and milk products are never intermingled, in conformity with the talmudic interpretation of biblical law. Legends and symbolism abound. On Purim, *Hamantashen* are eaten in memory of Haman. On the New Year, honey cakes are served to symbolize a sweet year ahead. A dish called *cholent* in the West and *ḥamin* in the East is typical for the Sabbath since it cooks overnight on a small flame and provides a hot meal not requiring preparation on the day of rest. Milk dishes are associated with Pentecost (*Shavuot*). Typical Israel dishes are also emerging, suitable for the climate and employing ingredients native to the land.

SOME TYPICAL DISHES OF JEWISH COOKERY FROM EAST AND WEST

(A = Ashkenazi; S = Sephardi).

ARAINAWDOOS: stuffed artichoke hearts with tomato or eggplant or minced meat. (S)

BAGEL: A crusty, doughnut-shaped bun.

BANIZA DE SPINACA: Spinach pastry. (S)

BAMYA: Okra stewed in tomatoes and spiced sauce served with rice. (S)

BAKLAWA: Turkish pastry, very flaky and nutty.

BELEK: Goose breasts. (A)

BLINTZES: (known among Jews of Polish and Russian origin as Mliniza): Pancake filled with cheese or meat, folded and fried. With cheese and sour cream used as *Shavuot* dish. (A)

BOJAS: Crushed *matzah* cakes. (S)

BOREKAS or FEELUS: A rolled or triangular crisp dough for Sabbath morning, usually stuffed with salt cheese or spinach or eggplant or meat. (S)

BORSHT: Soup using cabbage, tomatoes, beets, and greens, cooked with meat for hot dish, or without meat for cold dish when it is served with sour cream. (A)

BRUMOELOS: Soft *matzot* with egg, lemon, etc. (S)

BURGHUL: Cracked wheat served with gravy as a side dish to meat. (S)

CHOLENT: Similar to Oriental Ḥamin but made of beans, fat meat, potato, kugel, pearl barley, and sometimes prunes and seasonings. (A)

CHRAIN: Horseradish in vinegar; beet relish may be added. (A)

CHREMZLACH: A Passover dessert of *matzah*-meal pancake filled with fruit. (A)

DICHT: Goose leg. (A)

DILL PICKLES: Small cucumbers pickled in brine with garlic and dill and/or grape leaves. (A)

DOLMA: Same as *Praakes*, but rolled in grape leaves; the latter type by Oriental Jews. (S)

ELMONTI: Pentecost dish of dough, flour, eggs, nuts, etc. (S)

FARFEL: A soup garnish made of roasted noodle flakes. Used also for *kugel*. (A)

FELAFEL: Oriental fried balls of chick peas and spices, eaten in a *pitah* with pickles. (S)

FISCHON or FISOLES: Beans fried with onions. (S)

FOLDEN: Purim cake made of layers of pastry filled with nuts, fruit, poppy-seeds, and honey. (A)

FRANKIS ENCHIDAS: Stuffed tomatoes eaten on ceremonial occasions. (S)

FRUIT SOUP: Cold soup made of fruits in season and slightly thickened with colored cornflour. (Israel)

FRUTAS: Variety of fruits eaten on *Tu-bi-Shevat*. (S)

FUL: Green broad beans, cut up with pods and stewed in olive oil with dill. (S)

GEFILLTE FISH: Sabbath minced-fish dish, boiled with carrots, onion, and pepper. (A)

GEHAKTE (= chopped) HERRING: Herring with apple, onion, egg, etc. *Hors d'oeuvre*. (A)

GEHAKTE LEBER: Liver with chicken fat. The liver is broiled and ground, onions, egg, etc. are added. (A)

GOLDENE YOICH (Yidd. "golden soup"): Chicken-soup eaten by newly-wed couples. (A)

GOSHT TAKHARI: Meat curry from India. (S)

GRIEBENES (also known as GRIEVEN): Cracklings of fowl. Used in *knishes* and as side dish to salad. (A)

GUVETCH: Balkan vegetable mixture, in tomato sauce, sometimes using fish or sausage; popular in Israel.

HALA AND BEBE: A Persian dish meaning "Aunt and Gandma" who discuss what to put in the stew. A variety of vegetables and pulses, highly peppered and seasoned with garlic.

HALLAH: The Sabbath or festival loaves, usually braided, baked with egg and sugar and sprinkled with poppy-seed.

HALVAH: Israel and Near Eastern confection made of sesame seeds. (S – Israel).

HAMAN: Smoked meat on Purim. (A)

HAMANTASHEN: Triangular Purim pastry of yeast dough filled with poppy seed (A): in Italy called *Orecchi di Aman*.

HAMIN: Similar to *cholent*, but also using hard-boiled eggs and meat-balls. Sabbath luncheon hot dish. (S)

HAROSET: Passover Seder dish made of fruits (apple) and nuts and wine to imitate the clay used for brickmaking by the Hebrews in Egypt. (S–A)

HELZEL: Stuffed neck of fowl. (as in *kishke*). (A)

HOLUBZES: Stuffed cabbage eaten on the Festival of Tabernacles. (A)

HUMMUS: Chick peas pounded to a paste with *tahina*, etc. and spiced. (S)

INGBERLACH: Passover delicacy for tea, made of *matzah* meal, ginger, nuts, honey, etc. (A)

JIBNEH: Usually goat's salty cheese (S)

Making dumplings for Passover in Alsace.
(Lithograph by Alphonse Lévy).

KAILAK: A peppery Persian dish of potatoes and onion in oil.

KASHA: Buckwheat groats cooked with gravy. (A)

KEBAB: See *Shish-Kebab*.

KEFTA BRINJI: Persian meat dumpling made with ground rice and herbs.

KESTANE SEKERI: Turkish chestnut dessert, popular in Near East.

KICHLACH: A dry cookie, very plain. (A)

KISHKE: Derma or intestine stuffed with flour and onions in oil.

KNAIDEL: A suet pudding or dumpling used in soups or with *cholent*. (A)

KNISHES: Yeast dough filled with meat and/or potatoes or cheese or fruit and baked. (A)

KOLATCHEN: A cinnamon yeast cake. (A)

KREPLACH or VARENIKIS: Dough filled with meat, cheese, groats, or fruit, shaped into triangles or hearts and boiled. (A)

KRUPNIK: Barley broth. (A)

KUGEL: A baked or boiled pudding made of vegetables, rice, potatoes or macaroni, with eggs and fat (sometimes sweetened), used as side dish or dessert. (A)

KUSKUS: A N African dish, usually made of semolina granules, steamed and served with soup of chick peas and vegetables with meat or fowl.

LATKES: Pancakes or patties made of potatoes for Hanukkah, or *matzah* meal for Passover; also with other ingredients. (A)

LEBENIYAH: Israel-type yoghurt, made from cow's milk. (Israel)

LEBKUCHEN: A cookie with nuts and fruits. (A)

LEYKACH: Honey cake for New Year and Sabbath or other festive occasions. (A)

LOKSHEN: Noodles, usually home-made, using eggs and flour only. (A)

LOKSHENKUGEL: Pudding made of noodles. (A)

LOX: Smoked salmon, usually served Sunday morning with cream cheese and *bagel* in N America. (A)

MAHSHI: Stuffed tomatoes, peppers, eggplant, or marrows – usually filled with meat, rice, and herbs or spices such as mint, celery, onion, or cinnamon. (S)

MALAI: Maize-bread, of Rumanian origin. (A)

MAMALIGI (also known as *Polenta*): Cornmeal dish from Rumania and Italy, made sweet with milk as dessert or with gravy for meat.

MAMOUL: Filled pastries. Nuts, fruits, and rose water are used in preparation. An Egyptian dish.

MANDELBRODT or KOMISHBRODT: Nut (usually almond) cookies. (A)

MANDELN: Fried dough in almond shapes for soup garnish. (A)

MESE: Roasted nuts, apples, etc. (S)

MILTZ: Stuffed spleen; filled with flour and raw onions and roasted. (A)

MJEDDARAH: A combination of lentils and *burghul*. (S)

MON SQUARES: Poppy-seed and honey candy for Purim. (A) (*mon* = poppy seed).

NAHIT: Chick peas cooked Rumanian style as side dish. Sometimes eaten as salted nuts. (S–A)

ORIENTAL SALATAH: Many vegetables diced, much mint and parsley added, seasoned with garlic, onion, pepper, and dressed in olive oil. Served with olives. (S)

OWAK RISHTUK: A lentil mess of pottage made with noodles and aromatic herbs. (S)

PAN D'ESPAGNA: A variation of *ḥallah*. (S)

PAPRAS ENCHIDAS: Stuffed paprika eaten on ceremonial occasions. (S)

PESTELA: Pastry filled with minced meat, pine nuts, and onion, and sprinked with sesame. Sabbath *kiddush* delicacy to commemorate the manna in the wilderness. (S)

PICKLED FISH: Marinated fish dish used on Sabbaths and other festivals as *hors d'oeuvre*. (A)

PICKLED HERRING: Marinated herring served with onions, black olives, and oil. (A)

PILAV: Sabbath dish from Bokhara with layer of meat or fowl, carrots, pepper, rice, raisins, fried onion, cooked in sealed casserole.

PIROGEN: Outsize *Piroshki*. (A)

PIROSHKI: Baked dumplings served with soup or meat course. (A)

PITA: Thin, flat, well-baked Arab bread.

PITCHA: Jellied calf's foot or jellied chicken, with egg slices, garlic, and vinegar flavored. (A).

POJOS ARAINAWDOOS: Roast chicken, stuffed with rice and grilled liver. (S)

PONTCHIKES: Doughnuts. (A)

POSTRAMI: Smoked cured beef, well-prepared. (A)

PRAAKES or HOLISHES: Chopped meat with rice, rolled in cabbage. (A)

REGENWURMER: Dough-strips eaten in soup on *Shemini Atzeret*. (A)

RICE AND KIBBEI HAMOUD: Sabbath eve dish of Aleppo. Comprises stuffed sour meat-balls and rice. (S)

RICE AND SPINACH: Served by all Sephardim on Passover as two of the main dishes because they are within the means of even the poorest.

RIZZ AND ASSAL: A rice and honey dish used on the Feast of Tabernacles. (S)

ROSKITAS DI GUEVE: Biscuits. (S)

ROSSEL: Fermented beetroot juice for Passover *borsht*. (A)

ROULLADEN: Rolled shoulder steak. (A)

SHAFRE FISH: Jellied fish in sauce with vegetables. (A)

SHNITZEL: Egged and breaded thin shoulder steaks. (A)

SHASHLIK: Near Eastern dish of lamb pieces grilled on skewers over coals. (S)

SHISH-KEBAB: Oriental dish of chopped lamb with parsley grilled over coals. (S)

Histadrut Sick Fund's Hospital, Kephar Saba.

SHLATTEN: Shallots. Eaten by Hamburg Jews on Friday evenings. (A)

SLIUSNEHN: A Syrian delicacy eaten on the occasion of a baby's first tooth; made of whole wheat, nuts, and fruits. (S)

STRUDEL: Pastry, usually flaky, filled with fruits, meat, or cheese, rolled and baked. (A)

SUM-SUM SQUARES: Confection made of sesame seeds and nuts. (S)

SWEET-SOUR FISH: Fish cooked with vinegar, sugar, raisins, yolks, cinnamon. (A)

TAḤINA: Sesame oil mixed with water, lemon, etc. used either as a dressing or *hors d'oeuvre*. (Oriental)

TAYGLACH: A nut, honey, and ginger confection for Purim. (A)

TILTAK: Persian poor man's dish. Onion soup and dry bread with radishes and olives.

TZIMMES: Sweet side-dish for meat or dessert, usually made of carrots or prunes or other dried fruits. Vegetables are well roasted and almost glazed. (A)

VARENYE: Confiture of fruit. Served as a syrup with tea. (A)

COOPERATIVE MOVEMENTS: 1. *Diaspora*: The cooperative movement among Jews grew up at the beginning of the present century. Three factors

hastened its development: the tradition of previous generations (mutual assistance which had existed in the medieval ghetto), the deteriorating economic situation of E European Jewry, and the worldwide spread of the cooperative idea. In 1914, there already existed in Russia 678 Jewish cooperatives with more than 400,000 members, constituting together with the members of their families about a third of the Russian Jewish population. With few exceptions, these institutions were credit cooperatives and their members were recruited chiefly from the middle class, i.e., from merchants and shopkeepers (36% in 1914), craftsmen (32.6%), and farmers (7.4%). These characteristics were retained by Jewish cooperatives in Europe in subsequent years. The movement was liquidated in the USSR by order of the authorities, but c. m. in Poland, Lithuania, and Rumania were of great importance and additional ones were set up in the other countries of Central and E Europe. Their total at the beginning of the 1930's reached 1,200 with 550,000 members. The majority were credit cooperatives; only in Poland were attempts made to set up producers' cooperatives of Jewish workers, all of which ended in failure. Several cooperatives of Jewish farmers were also established in Poland for the sale of produce, and these were (to some extent) successful. This movement received much assistance before World War I from the Jewish Colonization Association; after the war, the American Joint Reconstruction Foundation, a joint institution of this company and of the American Joint Distribution Committee, was set up and invested considerable resources in the development of Jewish cooperatives in E Europe. This movement was completely destroyed during World War II. Several attempts were subsequently made to re-establish a number of cooperatives, but none lasted long under the new conditions. In Poland, some 200 producers' cooperatives were established for Jewish craftsmen and workers, but when Jewish life was regimented in that country, these institutions also ceased to be Jewish. In the US, there has been little trend toward a special cooperative movement among Jews, though Jews have been active in the general cooperative movement which is widespread, particularly among the Jewish farmers and trade unionists. On the other hand, the Jews of Argentina have shown much initiative in this sphere. At the beginning of the century, cooperatives were established in the Jewish colonies for the marketing of produce, and these developed rapidly. No less important are the achievements of the urban population. Cooperative warehouses of Jewish shopkeepers have a large turnover and there are more than 40 Jewish People's banks in the state (and in other Latin-American lands).

2. *Israel*: The cooperative movement began among the Jews of Palestine at the end of the 19th cent. Its pioneers were the vintners' association which took over the wine production at Rishon le-Zion and Zikhron Yaakov from Baron de Rothschild, and the *Pardes* society which began the organized export of citrus. Credit cooperation began some time later and eventually crystallized in the *Halvaah ve-Ḥissakhon* ("Loan and Saving") society. The Second Aliyah gave the cooperative movement a strong impulse, especially when its pioneers passed to independent economic activity. Between 1910 and 1914 were founded the first agricultural KEVUTZOT, MOSHEVE OVEDIM, the *Kupat Ḥolim* (cooperative sick-fund) which afterwards became part of the HISTADRUT or General Federation of Labor, and urban cooperatives, chiefly in the printing trade. With the founding of the *Histadrut* in Dec. 1920, the cooperative framework was systematically extended in various fields To the KIBBUTZ and MOSHAV, which embraced tens of thousands of people, was added, in the early thirties, the MOSHAV SHITTUPHI. Small cooperatives in the sphere of transport combined into large regional and countrywide bodies (*Egged, Shelev, Dan, Ha-Mekasher*, etc.). *Ha-Mashbir*, founded during World War I, became the purchasing center of a consumers' cooperation combining many branches; and the agricultural villages of the labor movement established *Tenuvah*, a cooperative society for the processing and marketing of produce. The most prominent undertak-

Tenuvah central dairy, Tel Aviv

The Rejoicing of the Law festival at the Copenhagen synagogue. By Joel Balin, 1841.
(Oil painting in Museum of Jewish Community, Copenhagen).

ing under cooperative initiative is *Solel Boneh*. This developed as a cooperative society (in 1923) from the public works office of the *Histadrut* and became in time the largest contractor and industrialist in the country. The cooperative and other enterprises of the *Histadrut* are loosely federated in *Hevrat ha-Ovedim* (the "Workers' Company"). The kibbutz movement is divided into four countrywide federations, according to lines of party and politics (IHUD HA-KIBBUTZIM, HA-KIBBUTZ HA-ARTZI, HA-KIBBUTZ HA-MEUHAD, HA-KIBBUTZ HA-DATI). The credit cooperation of the *Histadrut* is concentrated by *Bank ha-Poalim* ("The Workers' Bank"). Outside the *Histadrut* framework, the cooperative movement has also spread considerably, the most important achievement being the "cooperative villages" (*Kepharim Shittuphiyim*) federated in their own countrywide framework, and the cooperatives for the marketing of agricultural produce (*Tene, Amir*).

COORDINATING BOARD OF JEWISH ORGA-NIZATIONS: Body founded in 1947, and composed of B'nai B'rith, the Board of Deputies of British Jews, and the South African Board of Deputies, having consultative status with several UN bodies as a non-governmental organization.

COPENHAGEN: Capital of DENMARK. Jews settled in the first half of the 17th cent. as suppliers to Christian V. They were Ashkenazim originating from Altona and were responsible for the first congregation. In the 18th cent., a small Sephardi community was founded. Full civil rights were granted in 1814. Later in the 19th cent. there was a trend toward assimilation and baptism. Many immigrants from E Europe arrived in the early 20th cent. Most of the Jews of C. were rescued from the Nazis in 1943 by a flight to Sweden carried out as a spontaneous secret operation. Jewish pop. (1974): 6,000.

COPENHAGEN BUREAU see ZIONISM

COPLAND, AARON (1900–): US composer. He has lectured and written on music and is a member of the faculty of the Berkshire Music Center, Tanglewood, and a board member of the Koussevitzky Foundation. His compositions include symphonies, ballets (*Appalachian Spring*, *Rodeo*), film scores

Aaron Copland.

(*Louisiana Story*, *The Red Pony*), orchestral works (*El Salon Mexico*), an opera (*Tender Land*), and chamber music (*Vitebsk*, a study on a Jewish melody).

COPPER SCROLL: *Dead Sea Scroll made of copper, discovered in 1952, and now kept in Amman. Its contents include minute but cryptic descriptions of places where treasure has been hidden. Speculation as to the nature of the treasure has varied from that of the Kumran Community to that of the Temple in Jerusalem.

CORDOVA: Spanish city. In the 10th cent., when C. was the capital of the Western Caliphate, its Jewish community (of which little previous history is known) was the most important in the peninsula and was the center of the activity of Ḥasdai Ibn Shaprut. Moses ben Enoch established there the first talmudical college in Spain (c. 972). The city's predominance ended with the fall of the caliphate in 1002, but its Jews remained important. They were expelled or converted after the capture of C. by the Almohades in 1148, but the community revived after the Christian conquest (1236). It suffered severely in the massacres of 1391, and in the following century, there were violent outbreaks against the Marranos (henceforth numerous there), especially in 1473. The Jews were expelled from the bishopric of C. in 1483, before the general expulsion from Spain. A square in C. is named after Maimonides who was born in C., and a synagogue built in 1315 is still preserved as a national monument.

CORDOVERO, MOSES BEN JACOB (known as *Ramak*; 1522–1570): Kabbalist. A pupil of Joseph Caro, he was chief of the Safed mystics before the advent of Isaac LURIA in 1569. His criticisms are logical and he imparted a contemplative nature to kabbalistic studies. His chief work, *Pardes Rimmonim*, covers a wide range of problems of the KABBALAH. C. maintained all creation to be a unity, no division separating God from the ten SEPHIROT, which C. regarded as spiritual vessels. From the *Sephirot* emanate the upper worlds and the corporeal world, but the Divinity is unaffected by these emanations. The human soul contains the image of all the upper worlds: the aim of morality is to secure the unification of all the powers of the soul and place them under the control of Divine wisdom.

CORFU: Largest of the Ionian Islands. Benjamin of Tudela (c. 1165) found only one Jew there but, thereafter, the community grew through immigration from the Greek mainland. Later, there was an influx from S Italy and Spain. The older community adhered to the Greek rite (*Minhag Corfu*) which ultimately survived nowhere else. The Venetian administration was relatively favorable to the Jews, no ghetto being established in C., and it was the only place in the western world where Jews were allowed to practice law. During the various Turkish attacks (1537, 1716), the Jews collaborated in the defense of the island. The Jews were emancipated under French occupation (1797–9, 1806–15), lost their rights under the British protectorate, and regained them when C. was united with the kingdom of Greece in 1864. The local Greek population was unfriendly and there were Ritual Murder accusations in 1861, 1864, and 1891, the last leading to large-scale emigration from the island

A street in the old Jewish quarter (the juderia) of Cordova.

and the decay of the distinctive traditions of the community. In 1939, there were 1,750 Jews in C., but the majority were deported and only 175 survived in 1945, 98 in 1968.

CORINTH: Greek town. A vigorous Jewish community existed there in the 1st cent. when Paul visited the town, and an inscription and other remains of a synagogue of the Classical Period have been found. Benjamin of Tudela found about 300 Jews there (c. 1165), but the community subsequently died out.

CORMANO see **CARMONA**

CORNERS see **PEAH**

CORPORAL PUNISHMENT: Physical chastisement (*makkot, malkot*) administered as legal punishment. Although it is one of the oldest forms of punishment known to Jewish law, special provision was made to protect the person sentenced from excessive pain. Thirty-nine lashes were the maximum which could be inflicted for any one offense, but this figure could be lessened (in multiples of 3) in certain cases. Three judges were always present at the time of punishment, one ordering the lashes, a second counting them, and a third reading the relevant verse from Deut. 28:58–9. The convict was tied to a post by his hands, and his back and breast were bared. The lashes administered with fourfold thongs were alternated, two on the back and one on the breast. The rabbis taught that biblical law permitted the administering of c. p. only in Palestine, but they made provision for *makkat mardut* (beating for disobedience) even outside Palestine. Maimonides enumerates 207 cases to which c. p. by lashes is applicable.

CORPSE: In Jewish law, the dead body of a human being renders ritually unclean all persons and things which come in contact with it or which are under the same roof. Special purification by the ashes of the Red Heifer (Num. 19) was required by one thus rendered ritually unclean before he could enter the Sanctuary or eat sanctified food. The Mishnah tractate *Oholot* deals with impurity occasioned by a dead body. In later religious law, the restrictions on coming into proximity to a corpse applied only to a *Cohen*, but all individuals close to a c. are required to wash their hands.

CORRUPTION AND BRIBERY see **BRIBERY**

CORSICA: Mediterranean island. There is no record of Jews there either in antiquity or in the Middle Ages, though attempts were made to attract a Jewish settlement in the 18th cent. In recent years, a small community (mainly Sephardi) has been organized in Bastia and in 1969 numbered 150.

CORWIN, NORMAN (1910–): US radio writer. Since 1938, he has written and produced a large number of radio and television dramas. In 1949, he was appointed to take charge of special UN radio projects. He later left and turned to film writing.

COS: Island in Aegean Sea. Jews lived there in the Classical Period. They were expelled by the grand master of Rhodes in 1500. A very small Sephardi community, re-established in the 17th cent., was liquidated by the Germans in 1944.

COSMOGONY AND COSMOLOGY: Speculations dealing with the origin and structure of the world. JUDAISM has only one generally accepted cosmogonical dogma: that God created the world. Whether it was created from existing formless matter or from nothing *(creatio ex nihilo)* is left open by the Bible, but Philo, the rabbis, and the medieval philosophers insist more or less strictly on creation from nothing. The rabbis — like the Stoics — did not exclude the possibility that our world was preceded by others. Certain biblical statements were interpreted as meaning that the world would one day cease to exist, although Maimonides taught that it would be permanent. Though the "making" of the world plays a role in most ancient mythologies, Judaism was the first religion to make it a central principle of its faith and a basis for its system of ethics. All other aspects of Jewish cosmological thought seem to be adaptations of views held also by others and underwent changes in the course of time. The biblical structure of the world closely resembles that appearing in Babylonian myths. The rabbis of the Talmud accepted gnostic ideas of c., interpreting biblical statements accordingly. The more advanced speculations on the nature of the visible universe (MAASEH BERESHIT) and the transcendental world *(Maaseh Merkavah)* were, however, not publicly taught. Some inkling of these teachings, proving their gnostic character, can be gathered from works such as *Midrash Konen,* the *Hekhalot* writings, and *Pirke de-Rabbi Eliezer.* The world of the Jewish medieval philosophers was that of Ptolemy, with the earth in the center surrounded by concentric spheres which were conceived as incorporeal (i.e., not subject to laws of physics), and gifted with intellect. In details, each philosopher followed the general school to which he adhered. Maimonides stated that the world derived its existence from God. This formulation, which covers both creation and Divine providence, is omitted in the hymn *Yigdal* based on his teaching, which thus omits Divine creation from Jewish belief. Cosmological speculation abounds in the Kabbalah. In the Zohar, the "world of separate things" mirrors the transcendental world, and within each thing a good and an evil "side" correspond to each other. In the mysticism of Isaac Luria, c. occupies a central position; the problem of evil is tied up with the BREAKING OF THE VESSELS which occurred during the creation of the world, and the coming of the Messiah will be the TIKKUN of the cosmos, the restoration of its perfect state. Through ascribing to man the power to further the *tikkun* by prayer and action, Luria, and even more Ḥasidim, made the Jewish individual an active cosmological force. (See PHILOSOPHY).

COSSACKS see **CHMIELNICKI; HAIDAMAKS**

COSTA, DA: Family of Marrano origin; its branches included the families of Mendes da Costa, Nuñes da Costa, etc. *BENJAMIN DA C.* (17th cent.) of Martinique introduced the cultivation of sugar and of cocoa to the W Indies. In England, *BENJAMIN MENDES DA C.* (1704–1764) was a philanthropist and communal leader, and his kinswoman *CATHE-RINE DA C.* (d. 1756) was an artist. *DANIEL MENDES DA C.* (c. 1728) was a prominent member of the New York community. *DUARTE NUNES DA C.* (Jacob Curiel; b. 1587) was Portuguese chargé d'affaires in Hamburg from 1640; his descendants continued to fill the office for the next 160 years, other members of the family performing similar functions in Amsterdam. *EMMANUEL MENDES DA C.* (1717–1791) of London was a distinguished conchologist and mineralogist, and secretary of the Royal Society. ISAAC DA C. (1798–1860) of Amsterdam, who became a fervent Christian, was a foremost Dutch poet and wrote monographs on Dutch Jewish family history. *JOSEPH MENDES DA C.* (1864–1939) was one of the pioneers of modern art in Holland. For Uriel da C., see ACOSTA, URIEL.

COSTA RICA: Republic of Central America. Sephardi Jews immigrated to C. R. from Curaçao at the end of the 19th cent. After World War I, Jews arrived from Turkey, Poland, and, later, from Germany; Ashkenazi Jews now constitute a majority. Most live in the capital San José and are engaged in trade and the shoe and clothing industries. Jewish pop. (1968): 1,500.

COSTUME: The dress of the Hebrews in the Biblical Period was similar to that of neighboring peoples. Details may be derived from the Bible, and from representations on certain Egyptian, Assyrian, and Babylonian monuments. Among the upper classes, Greek and Roman c. became prevalent from the Hasmonean age. The wearing of the *tzitzit* on the four corners of the robe differentiated the zealous Jew from his neighbor, though later it became usual to relegate these to synagogal and intimate wear (see TALLIT). The institution of the Jewish BADGE as a distinguishing mark in the 13th cent. proves how alike Jewish and non-Jewish clothing were at this time in Europe. Nevertheless, Jews sometimes continued to wear the costumes of the countries from which they came (e.g. Moslem c. for some time in Christian Spain). Moreover, they generally tended to be conservative in their clothing. In Europe, a pointed hat (*pileum cornutum*) was considered in the 13th cent. to be specifically Jewish, and it was long customary for the Jews to wear a special coat (*sarbal*) on holidays. In E Europe, the fur-trimmed hat (*streimel*), long kaftan, and in certain cases knee-breeches and buckle-shoes, reflected long-forgotten Polish fashions which came to be regarded as sacrosanct. Distinctive c. was abandoned in W Europe, and was never known in America except among small ultra-Orthodox groups. In the Moslem countries of N Africa, the prohibition of the wearing of bright colors by Jews resulted in the evolution of the black robe and skull-cap, later considered characteristic Jewish garb. In certain Mediterranean areas, Jews until recently continued to wear the Spanish fashions introduced by the Sephardi exiles in 1492. Extravagance in c. was checked in many Jewish communities by SUMPTUARY LAWS.

*COUGHLIN, CHARLES EDWARD (1891–): US Roman Catholic priest from Michigan who began using radio in the late 1930's to stir up hatred against the Jews and organized labor. In 1942, the Church ordered C. to discontinue his broadcasts.

COUNCIL OF FOUR LANDS (in Heb. *Vaad Arba Aratzot*): The autonomous central organization of Polish-Lithuanian Jewry, taking its name from the "four provinces" into which it was originally divided: Major Poland, Minor Poland, Red Russia, and Lithuania. Though its beginnings reach back to the middle of the 16th cent., the first known record of the C.'s resolutions is dated 1580. In 1623, the Jews of Lithuania seceded and formed a council of their own (see COUNCIL OF LITHUANIA). Nevertheless, the traditional name was retained. The C. met twice yearly, at the fairs of Lublin and Yaroslav (in the 18th cent. only once) generally at the town where the Polish finance minister resided. It consisted of

Part of page from the Minute Book of the Council of the Four Lands.

Workshop for elderly people maintained by the Council of Jewish Federations and Welfare Funds.

deputies of the "provinces" and autonomous towns, about 20 in number in the 17th cent. and 40 in the 18th. The C. elected its marshals, syndics, secretaries, and treasurers. A similar organization was introduced in the Councils of the Provinces (*Vaad ha-Galil*) into which each of the Councils was subdivided. Delegates occasionally met with representatives of the Lithuanian Council at the fair of Leczna (near Lublin). The C.'s main task was the assessment of the state taxes of the Jewish population. The overall sum of the Jewish poll-tax was distributed among the "provinces," and the provincial councils in turn divided their quotas among the individual communities. In addition to this fiscal function, the C. settled conflicts between "provinces" and communities, issued regulations concerning economic life (e.g. limiting competition), the system of elections, and the prohibition of luxury, supervised schools and charities (including aid for the Jews in Palestine), and exercised control over religious life (e.g. censorship of books). In the 18th cent., a steady disintegration of the system set in. The impoverished Jewish population, burdened with heavy taxes, displayed growing insubordination. The number of "provinces" of the C. was increased from the original "Four Lands" to 20. From without, the central

organization was undermined by the Polish nobility who interfered with its functions in order to "safeguard" the interests of their personal protégés. Finally, in 1764, in connection with the financial reorganization of the Polish state, the *Seym* (Diet) ordered the exaction of the poll-tax directly from each Jewish COMMUNITY according to the size of the Jewish population. The central and provincial Jewish AUTONOMY thus became superfluous for fiscal purposes and was dissolved by the same decree.

COUNCIL OF JEWISH FEDERATIONS AND WELFARE FUNDS: Association of central community organizations in the US and Canada, established in 1932. Its membership (1968) is 220 Federations, Welfare Funds, and COMMUNITY COUNCILS, serving almost 800 communities. It represents its member organizations in joint action on regional, national, and international problems and serves them in strengthening fund-raising for the major local, national, and overseas needs, etc.

COUNCIL OF LITHUANIA: The former autonomous central organization of Lithuanian Jewry. Originally LITHUANIA was one of the provinces represented in the COUNCIL OF FOUR LANDS. In 1623, a separate Council was formed, the organization and activities of which were similar in every respect to those of the greater Council. It consisted of the elected representatives and rabbis of the three chief communities — Brzesć, Grodno, and Pinsk — to which Sluck and Vilna were later added. In the 17th cent., plenary meetings were held, on the average, every three years, but in the 18th, every ten. The Council, like that of the Four Lands, came to an end in 1764.

COUNCILS AND SYNODS: Of the recorded Jewish synods in ancient times, the most memorable was that held at Usha (c. 138 CE) to reorganize Jewish life after the Hadrianic persecutions. Occasional local or regional synods were held in the Middle Ages. Noteworthy were the synods of the N French communities summoned by R Tam c. 1150 and 1160 to consider problems arising from the Crusades. A synod of the Castilian communities at Valladolid in 1432, summoned by the chief rabbi Abraham Benveniste, devoted its attention to problems of education and organization. A series of synods was held in Italy in the 15th cent. (Bologna 1416, Forli 1418, Perugia 1423, Florence 1428) to concert action against anti-Jewish Church legislation; that of Forli, moreover, passed a series of SUMPTUARY LAWS and other regulations to discipline the inner lives of the Jewish communities. In 1554, to meet the threat of the Catholic reaction, a synod at Ferrara instituted pre-censorship of Hebrew books. In Poland, Lithuania, etc., synods took a permanent form in the COUNCIL OF FOUR LANDS, etc. During the 19th cent., a number of restricted RABBINICAL CONFERENCES were held in Germany and America (e.g. Brunswick 1844, Pittsburg 1885) for establishing the principles of Reform Judaism. In the US, assemblies of the Reform, Conservative, and Orthodox rabbinates now take place annually.

COUNTING OF THE OMER see **OMER, COUNTING OF**

COURANT, RICHARD (1888–): Mathematician. Born in Poland, he was professor at Göttingen 1920–33 and emigrated to the US in 1934, becoming professor at New York Univ.

COURLAND (also **KURLAND**): Former duchy on Baltic coast. When annexed to Poland in 1561, restrictions were imposed on Jewish commerce. In 1617, Jews were admitted to the bishopric of Pilten in West C. Many Jews found refuge in C. from the Chmielnicki massacres (1648). C. was united to Russia in 1795 and the rights of its Jews confirmed in 1799, but thereafter they shared the lot of Russian Jewry. All the Jews were evacuated to the Russian interior in 1915, and few returned when C. became part of LATVIA in 1918.

COURNOS, JOHN (1881–): US author. C., who was baptized, has written novels, translated from Russian, and has been a frequent contributor to literary publications.

COURT JEWS (Ger. *Hofjuden*): Jews who served as financial or other agents of rulers (chiefly advancing credit as tax-farmers and as organizers of commissariat) in Central and E Europe during the 17th–18th cents. They were men of wealth and played an important role at court especially in the period after the Peace of Westphalia (1648). These Jews enjoyed special privileges; were exempted from wearing the Jewish badge, and could live anywhere, maintaining the necessary Jewish religious functionaries in their place of residence. C.J. were especially prominent in the Vienna court, two of the most notable being Samuel OPPENHEIMER and Samson WERTHEIMER; some however met disaster, such as Joseph Süss OPPENHEIM of Württemberg. C. J., because of their position, were influential in obtaining rights and privileges for their fellow-Jews and were men of great power in the Jewish community. The office was sometimes hereditary.

COURTS see **BET DIN; LAW; SANHEDRIN; TRIBUNALS**

COVENANT (Heb. *berit*): Agreement of friendship between persons or nations. In early biblical times, a c. was effected by a ceremonial, such as passing between the two halves of a sacrificed animal (Gen. 15:9–11). The special relationship between God and individuals or nations is also termed c., accompanied as a rule by an external symbol (*ot* "sign"). The c. made with Noah is symbolized by the rainbow (Gen. 9:13); that with Abraham, by the act of circumcision (Gen. 17:10); that with the Children of Israel at Sinai by the Sabbath (Exod. 31:13), and also by the Torah and the Ten Commandments, called "the book of the covenant" (Exod. 24:7) and "the tables of the covenant" (Deut. 9:9). In addition, God made a special c. with the house of Aaron of the tribe of Levi to assure them the priesthood (Num. 25:12–13), and with David to assure the monarchy to his descendants (II Sam. 23:5).

COVERING OF THE HEAD: Rabbinic law finds biblical sanction for the covering of the hair by a married woman, while mishnaic law regards bareheadedness on the part of a married woman as grounds for divorce. Bareheadedness in men was not considered unseemly, and head-coverings were used only when special dignity and respect were required. Babylonian Jewry, however, placed particular emphasis on the covering of the head by men, and this stringency later was adopted by other Jewries. The Mohammedan influence in Spain also contributed toward the adoption of this custom. In France and Germany, as late as the 12th cent., men could be called up to the Reading of the Law bareheaded, and only the one reciting grace at the table was required to cover his head. It was not until the 17th cent. that R David Ha-Levi of Ostrog found religious basis for the custom in the prescription to avoid *ḥukkat ha-goy* ("gentile custom"). Traditional Jews in the modern period cover their heads during prayers, while the strictly Orthodox go with head-covering at all times. Reform Jews have abolished the custom altogether, even in the synagogue.

COWEN, SIR FREDERICK HYMEN (1852–1935): British musician. He was a prolific composer, writing songs, instrumental music, operas, oratorios, etc. He was the conductor of the London Philharmonic Society (1887–92, 1900–7) and of the Liverpool Philharmonic Orchestra (1896–1914).

COWEN, JOSEPH (1868–1932): English Zionist leader. A London businessman, he participated in the First Zionist Congress and became the friend and confidant of Herzl whom he accompanied on his mission to the sultan in 1901. C. was a founder of the Jewish Colonial Trust.

COWEN, PHILIP (1853–1943): US editor and publisher. He was co-founder, managing editor, and publisher of *The American Hebrew* 1878–1905.

***COWLEY, SIR ARTHUR ERNEST** (1861–1931): English Hebraist. Librarian at the Bodleian Library, Oxford, he published translations and texts of various Hebrew works (Ecclesiasticus, Judith, etc.), a catalogue of the Hebrew books in the Bodleian Library, and the Aramaic papyri of Elephantine.

CRACOW: Polish city. Its Jewish community developed from the 14th cent., but was subject to increased restrictions and eventually, in 1495, was expelled to the neighboring townlet of Kazimierz. This town was destroyed in 1655 during the period of the Polish-Swedish war when the Poles accused the Jews of treason, forcing them to pay compensation and subjecting them to serious pogroms, especially in 1664 and 1682. On the partition of Poland in 1772, Kazimierz fell to Austria and C. to Poland, thereby preventing the flow of trade between them. In 1776, Kazimierz was restored to Poland and this resulted in a renewal of the previous rivalry between Jewish and Christian merchants in C. The Austrians occupied C. in 1796, and when the city was included in the duchy of Warsaw in 1806, the Jews were expelled and again restricted to Kazimierz. Their situation changed little during the period when C. was a Free City, 1815–46. The city was annexed to Austria in 1847 and the Jewish position improved with the adoption of the liberal constitution of 1867. The community lived a rich cultural life and played an important role in Polish Jewish autonomy. Outstanding rabbis and scholars flourished there, including many Polish Jewish intellectual leaders of the 16th–18th cents. In the 18th cent., C. showed initial opposition to Ḥasidism and Haskalah, but both succeeded in making inroads. From 1890, there was a strong Zionist movement in C. and several important Hebrew periodicals were published there. The Jewish

Badges of the Butchers' and Cobblers' Guilds, Prague, 18th cent.

pop. before World War II was c. 50,000. A ghetto was set up by the Nazis in 1941 and liquidated by 1943. Survivors returned to C. in 1945, but most of them left shortly thereafter. Jewish pop. (1970): 700.

CRAFTS: Craftsmen existed among Jews from the earliest times. The Bible refers to many, especially in connection with the construction of the Tabernacle and Temple. It mentions, for instance, workers in brass, iron, gold, silver, linen, and wool; as well as refiners, smiths, potters, masons, and stone-cutters. In the Talmud, the range is even greater. Moreover, craftsmanship is looked upon with great favor by the rabbis. According to R Judah, one of the specific duties of a father toward his son is to teach him a trade (*Kiddushin* 29a). Worshipers were seated in the great synagogue at Alexandria according to guilds. The chief c. for which Jews were noted in the Middle Ages were wool and silk weaving, dyeing, goldsmithery, and glass manufacture. In more recent times, Jews became prominent also in tailoring, diamond cutting, shoe-making, and as furriers.

CREATION see **COSMOGONY AND COSMOLOGY**

CREATION, BOOK OF see **SEPHER YETZIRAH**

CREDIT see **LOANS**

CREED: Authoritative summary of religious belief. Unlike the two other great monotheistic faiths, Judaism does not have any abstract formulation of c. in the form of DOGMA or CATECHISM. However, certain basic principles of belief characterize Judaism, and major thinkers have attempted to draw up articles of faith ever since the time when Judaism came into contact with speculative Greek thought. Philo set out five chief articles of faith. Maimonides listed 13, and this exposition won the greatest popularity. Ḥasdai Crescas differentiated between fundamental beliefs, true beliefs, and opinions. Albo also accepted the division of articles of faith into different categories: primary roots, secondary roots, and branches. The primary roots number only three: existence of God, revelation, and retribution. Despite these formulations, Judaism was always a religion of practice with its dogma deducible from Jewish forms of living and prayer. The main elements of Jewish prayer, the *Shema* and the *Shemoneh Esreh*, proclaim the unity of God and belief in His providence and in resurrection.

CREIZENACH: (1) *MICHAEL C.* (1789–1842): German pedagogue. From 1825, he taught in the Philanthropin school at Frankfort-on-Main. He joined the group demanding religious reforms and published several works which made a deep impression. Together with Jost, he edited the scholarly periodical *Zion.* (2) *THEODOR C.* (1818–1877): Poet and historian of literature; son of (1). Like his father, he taught in the Philanthropin school and was active in the Reform movement. In 1854, he became a Protestant. C. wrote extensively on literary subjects and was an authority on Goethe.

CREMATION: The burning of bodies was never a common practice among the Hebrews who buried their dead in graves or sepulchers. Burning, however, is mentioned in the Bible as the punishment for certain transgressions. The rabbis deplored the burning of the dead, explaining the three years' famine in David's reign as punishment for the burning of Saul's body by the inhabitants of Jabesh-Gilead. In modern times, there has been much discussion in rabbinic circles regarding the permissibility of c. Though still forbidden by the Orthodox, c. is occasionally practiced by Reform Jews.

CRÉMIEU, CRÉMIEUX (Heb. *Karmi*): French family originating from the village of Crémieu in Dauphiné. Among its members were many rabbis at Avignon and Carpentras in the 17th–18th cents. They included *ÉLIE C.* who edited the local liturgy *Seder ha-Tamid* (Avignon, 1767). His son *SEMÉ-C.* was kidnaped and baptized in 1762 and, as Joseph Vignolli, became bishop of Foligno. *MARDOCHÉE C.* (1749–1821) with his brother *SALOMON C.* and the latter's son *MOISE C.* of Aix (1766–1837), all prolific writers were the last eminent scholars of the Jewries of the Comtat Venaissin; the religious music of the Comtat was published in 1885 by *JULES SALOMON C.*, and *MARDOCHÉE C. HECTOR-JONATHAN CRÉMIEUX* (1828–1892), dramatist, wrote the libretto for Offenbach's *Orpheus in the Underworld. GASTON CRÉMIEUX* (1836–1871), socialist leader, in 1871 became president of the Marseilles departmental administration. Despite his opposition to the extremism of the Paris *Commune*, he was shot after the overthrow of the *Commune* of Marseilles. *ANDRÉ CRÉMIEU-FOA* (1857–1892), officer, fought duels against anti-Semites, and subsequently distinguished himself in battles in Africa.

CRÉMIEUX, ISAAC-ADOLPHE (1796–1880): French statesman. A lawyer by profession, he successfully fought for the abolition of the OATH MORE JUDAICO (1827–46). He was elected president of the Central Consistory of French Jews in 1843 but resigned in 1845 after the conversion of his children to Christianity. On several occasions, C. intervened with the French government in behalf of Jews persecuted in various parts of the world; at the time of the DAMASCUS AFFAIR, he journeyed to the Middle East with Sir Moses Montefiore and, while in Egypt, founded Jewish schools which he personally supported. A deputy from 1842, he became minister of justice when the French Republic was proclaimed in 1848, being responsible for numerous humanitarian reforms. During the Second Empire, C. directed the opposition movement of the Freemasons among whom he held a high position. In the republican government of 1870, he again became minister of justice and, in this capacity, signed the decree granting French nationality to the Jews of Algeria (see CRÉMIEUX DECREE). In 1875, he was appointed to the Senate for life. From 1863 to 1880 (except for a brief interval in 1867), he was president of the Alliance Israélite Universelle and obtained concessions ameliorating the position of Jews in Rumania, Turkey, and Russia.

CRÉMIEUX DECREE: Decree issued for the French government on Oct. 24, 1870 by Isaac-Adolphe CRÉMIEUX, as minister of justice, which conferred French citizenship on the Jews of ALGERIA. Although the reform had been approved before he took office, Crémieux was accused of favoring his coreligionists. The Vichy government abrogated the decree in 1940, but General de Gaulle restored it in 1943.

CREMONA: City in Lombardy (Italy). Jewish loan-bankers are first mentioned in C. in 1278. When in 1387, Giov. Galeazzo Visconti invited Jewish financiers from Germany to settle in the duchy of Milan, C. became — with Pavia — their most important settlement. It was a major seat of learning, and many Hebrew books were printed there 1556–67. The expulsion of the Jews from the duchy of Milan was ordered by the king of Spain more than once but took effect only in 1591. No Jewish community has since been re-established in C.

CRESCAS, ḤASDAI BEN ABRAHAM (c. 1340–c. 1410): Philosopher and CROWN RABBI of Aragon. He lost his son in the massacres of 1391, which he briefly described in a Hebrew account. He also wrote, to win back apostates, a Spanish criticism of the Christian faith (of which only extracts have been preserved in Hebrew translation). His main work *Or Adonai* ("The Light of the Lord") is a refutation of Maimonides along strictly philosophical lines. In it, he argues that the essence of Judaism lies neither in holding correct beliefs about the nature of creation (he even admits that the world may be eternal) nor in intellectual grasp of God's essential features. In discussing free will, C. states that human will is influenced by causality like everything else, but that nevertheless man is responsible for his actions. He closely approaches modern ideas, e.g. in his criticism of Aristotle's system of physics, and applies procedures of talmudic discussion to Aristotle's arguments with telling effects (cf. H. A. Wolfson. *Crescas' Critique of Aristotle*). C. paid much attention to the problem of the articles of faith, reducing Maimonides' thirteen articles to six, and preparing the ground for the further treatment of this subject by his pupil Joseph Albo. (See also CREED.)

CRESQUES, ABRAHAM (d. 1387): Majorcan cartographer; "Master of Maps and Compasses" to the king of Aragon. In 1376–7, he made the famous Catalan Atlas which was sent as a gift to the king of France and is now in the Bibliothèque Nationale, Paris. In this work he was assisted by his son *JUDAH (JAHUDA) C.*, known as the Map Jew. In the persecutions of 1391, the latter was forced to adopt Christianity under the name of Jayme Ribes. He later entered the service of the king of Portugal and, as Jacomo de Majorca, became the director of the nautical observatory at Sagres.

CRESQUES DE VIVERS (d. 1391): Spanish astrologer; probably born in S. France. Count astrologer to King John of Aragon. He was killed in the anti-Jewish outbreaks of 1391, after which his family converted to Christianity.

CRESSON, WARDER (Michael C. Boaz Israel; 1798–1860): US convert to Judaism. He belonged to a Quaker family of Philadelphia but after his term of office as first US consul in Jerusalem (1844–8), he embraced Judaism. He successfully fought his family's efforts to have him declared insane, returned to settle in Palestine where he lived a strictly Orthodox life, and endeavored to promote Jewish colonization.

CRESTOHL, LEON DAVID (1900–1963): Canadian public figure and lawyer. One of the leaders of the Canadian Zionist Organization, he was a member of the Canadian parliament 1950–63.

CRETE (from the 13th cent., called after its capital, Candia): Greek island, probably the biblical Caphtor (Amos 9:7, etc.). Jews were established there before the beginning of the Christian era. In 440, a false messiah promised to redeem the Jews who thereupon followed him into the sea. At the close of the Middle Ages, under Venetian rule, there were communities at Canea, Candia, and Retimo, etc.; at their head was a "constable," this office being quasi-hereditary in the family of CAPSALI. Many refugees from Spain settled in C. after 1492, so that the traditions of the original Byzantine community

were superseded by the Sephardi rite. After the island was conquered by the Turks (1669), conditions became identical with those elsewhere in the Ottoman Empire. The community, already greatly reduced, dwindled further after the 1896 disturbances. In 1939, there were 275 Jews in C. almost all of whom lost their lives in 1942 when the ship in which they were being deported by the Germans was scuttled. The last Jewish residents left the island in 1968.

CRIF (abbr. of *Conseil représentatif des Juifs de France*): Representative organization founded in Lyon, 1943, to which the principal Jewish institutions nominated delegates. On a similar model, Orthodox Jewry in France founded CRJTF (*Conseil représentatif du Judaïsme traditionnel de France*) in 1952 to deal with religious problems.

CRIMEA: Russian peninsula in the Black Sea. Evidence of Jewish settlement dates from the 1st cent. BCE and several Jewish inscriptions from succeeding centuries have been discovered. From the 7th cent. to 1117, eastern C. was controlled by the KHAZARS. A large Karaite population lived there from the 12th cent., centered at Eupatoria; at Theodosia (Kaffa) the Jewish community preserved the Byzantine rite of prayer. Many Jews became Moslems under Tatar rule, i.e., from the end of the 13th cent. The Genoese, who ruled southern C. in the 15th cent., prohibited interference with internal Jewish affairs. Under Turkish rule (1475–1783), Chufut-Kale was the Jewish center. Many Jewish captives from the Ukraine were sent to C. after 1648. Following the Russian conquest of 1783, numerous Ashkenazi Jews settled there. In 1863, the Russian authorities granted the Karaites equal rights, but other Jews continued to suffer from disabilities until the 1917 Revolution. In the late 1920's, thousands of Jews were settled in C. under a plan to establish an autonomous Jewish agricultural center. In 1939, the Jewish population numbered 50,000 including 40,000 Ashkenazim, 6,000 KRIMCHAKS, and 4,000 Karaites. These were mostly wiped out by the Germans in 1941, and only a few, including some 300 Karaites, survived. Jewish pop. (1970): 25,614.

CRITICISM, BIBLICAL see **BIBLE CRITICISM.**

CROATIA see **YUGOSLAVIA.**

CROISSET, FRANCIS DE (pseudonym of Franz Wiener; 1877–1937): French author. He was born in Belgium and lived in Paris where he wrote novels and dramas. C. was one of the last representatives of the wit of the 19th cent. Paris boulevards.

CROLL, DAVID ARNOLD (1900–): Canadian public figure. C. was mayor of Windsor 1930–4 and 1939–40, and minister of public welfare, municipal affairs, and labor 1934–7 for the province of Ontario, being the first Jewish cabinet minister in Canada. After serving 10 years in the Canadian parliament (1945–55), he was appointed senator in 1956.

*CROMWELL, OLIVER: Lord Protector of England, 1653–8. A Puritan, he was inclined to view the Jews, the people of the Old Testament, with sympathy. He strongly supported the readmission of the Jews to England and favored the petitions submitted to the English government in 1654 by Manuel Martinez Dormido. MANASSEH BEN ISRAEL's mission to England to secure permission for Jews to live there (1655) was probably at C.'s own suggestion, and his various petitions were presented to the Lord Protector in person. Unable to carry the council of state with him, C. convened the WHITEHALL CONFERENCE to consider the problem (Dec. 1655), presided over the opening session, but dissolved it when the probability arose that its decisions would be negative. Considering it unwise to utilize his prerogative to secure his object, he henceforth "connived" at the presence of the Jews in the country, and gave up the attempt to readmit them formally.

CROWN RABBI: A rabbi appointed by the secular authority to represent the Jewish community in its dealings with the state, not always selected for his intellectual qualifications. The PRESBYTER JUDAEORUM in medieval England was of this type. In Spain, the functionary had the title of *Rab de la Corte* ("court rabbi"); in Portugal, *Arrabi-Mor* ("grand rabbi"); in Sicily, *Dienchelele* (i.e., *dayyan kelali*–"general judge"). In 19th cent. Russia, the crown (*Kazyonnay*) rabbi, appointed to satisfy the government's requirements as regards registration, regulations, etc., functioned side by side with the recognized rabbi of the community.

CRUCIFIXION: Form of capital punishment by nailing or tying to a cross, common among the ancient Greeks and Romans, and derived from Persia, but unknown to Jewish law. The custom was introduced into Palestine by the Romans and was the usual punishment inflicted by them upon rebels. Many Jews suffered this fate under Roman rule. The New Testament description of the c. of Jesus clearly shows that the Roman procedure was followed.

CRUSADES: The name given to the wars waged by Christian rulers in the Middle Ages to win Palestine from the Moslems. The consequent stimulation of religious passion resulted in serious consequences for the Jews. In the course of the preparations for the First Crusade (1096–9), attacks were made on the Jews in N France and especially in the Rhineland where massacres occurred in many cities (Mainz, Worms, Speyer, Cologne, etc.). Similar attacks took place in Prague and, later, in Salonica where the reports of the Crusade gave rise to a messianic ferment. When Jerusalem was captured in 1099, Jews and Karaites were massacred. Nevertheless, in the Crusading Kingdom which was now established, toleration was extended to the Jews. In the course of the Second Crusade, organized to succor the Crusading Kingdom (1147–9), similar outbreaks took place

in France and the Rhineland as the results of the agitation of a monk called Rudolf. They were, however, restricted in scale through the humanitarian efforts of Bernard of Clairvaux. At the outset of this Crusade, the Pope urged that the debts of crusaders to the Jews should be remitted, and this became henceforth a regular demand on such occasions. The Third Crusade (1189–92) commanded, for the first time, wide support in England where it led to preliminary attacks by the assembled crusaders on the Jews in various places, especially York (1190). Later c. involved the Jews only incidentally, though the so-called Shepherds' Crusade in 1320 resulted in widespread attacks on the Jews in S France and N Spain. The c. may be said to have begun the age of unmitigated suffering for medieval Jewry. Moreover, through the impetus which they gave to the Italian maritime republics and to international intercourse, they helped to displace the Jewish merchants from their former favored position and thus stimulated the economic decline of the Jews. On the other hand, the demand for credit on the part of the participants stimulated Jewish financial operations in some countries of Europe.

CRYPTO-JEWS: Persons who, while outwardly professing another religion (generally adopted by themselves or their ancestors under compulsion), continue to adhere secretly to Judaism. Such were the MARRANOS of Spain and Portugal, the CHUETAS of Majorca, the JEDID-AL-ISLAM in Persia, the NEOFITI of S Italy, and (with somewhat different antecedents) the DONMEH of Salonica.

CUBA: Island of W Indies. Jewish settlement in C. dates back to the 16th cent. when Marranos immigrated from Spain but the Inquisition prevented open observance of Judaism. The history of the Jews in C. properly begins at the end of the 19th cent. with the appearance of Jews from the US, mainly from Florida. In 1904, the United Hebrew Congregation was founded, and the Union Hebrea Shevet Ahim, consisting of Sephardim from Turkey, Syria, and Mexico, in 1914. After World War I, Jews immigrated from E Europe and (after 1933) from Germany and Austria, many intending to proceed to the US. Jewish immigration was almost completely stopped in 1947. In 1959, C. had 8–10,000 Jews of whom 90% lived in Havana. Considerable emigration followed the establishment of the Castro regime, primarily motivated by the new economic policy. Jewish pop. (1973): 1,500, of which 1,400 were in Havana.

CUKERMAN, YITZHAK ("Antek"; 1915–): Resistance leader. A native of Vilna, he was active in the Zionist youth organization *He-Halutz*. In 1942, he helped to establish the WARSAW Jewish resistance organization of which he was deputy commander and later, commander. After the Warsaw Ghetto rising, he escaped from the city and set up Jewish

Battle of Jaffa, 1102 by Serrur.

partisan units. Reaching Palestine in 1947, he was among the founders of the settlement Loḥame ha-Gettaot. His wife, Tzivia Lubetkin, also took an active part in the Warsaw Ghetto uprising.

CULTURAL ZIONISM see **ZIONISM**

CUMANUS VENTIDIUS see **PROCURATORS**

*CUMBERLAND, RICHARD (1732–1811): English playwright. His once-famous drama *The Jew*, which took an outwardly uncouth Jew as its hero, marked an epoch in English literary attitudes towards Jews. His other writings include a comic opera *The Jews of Mogador* and a novel *Nicholas Pedroza* in which he touches on the life of the Marranos.

CUNEIFORM (Lat. *cuneus* = "wedge"): Writing used in Babylon for the Sumerian and Akkadian languages; it was adopted for other tongues in neighboring lands (Horite, Hittite, etc.). C. was generally written with a wedge-shaped stylos on clay tablets. The signs were originally pictographic but became syllabic. C. was used by Palestinian scribes in the period prior to the Israelite conquest.

CURAÇAO: Island of the Dutch W Indies. In 1652, a charter was granted to David NASSY to encourage Jewish settlement there, and with the arrival of refugees from Brazil in 1654, a congregation was organized. In the 18th cent., the community enjoyed great prosperity, and even after its decline the Jews continued to play a very prominent part in local economic life. The Sephardi synagogue built in 1732 is the oldest in the Western Hemisphere and a Reform congregation was established in 1863. The Dutch monthly *Mikve Israel* has been published since 1940. Jewish population (1973): 700. Amba, the second small island of the Dutch W Indies, has a Jewish pop. of 100 (1973).

CURSES: The Bible has at least six different words for cursing, and the Talmud adds almost as many more. The Bible specifically prohibits the cursing of God, one's parents, the authorities, and the deaf. The penalty in the case of the first two is death. The Talmud expresses a strong belief in the efficacy of a curse, permitting it in certain cases where inspired by

Cyprus internment camp, 1947.

a religious motive. However, any curse invoking the Divine name is rigidly forbidden.

CUSH: (1) Son of Ham; brother of Mizraim (=Egypt), Put (=Libya and Morocco), and Canaan (Gen. 10:6). The list of his sons seems to refer to tribes in Africa and S Arabia. He is also the father of NIMROD, and scholars identify this C. either with the Cosseans or with the city of C. which, in Babylonian tradition, was one of the first cities built after the Flood. (2) Region S of Egypt (Nubia, Ethiopia) in Hebrew and other ancient languages. It extended S from Elephantine and Syene (the modern Assouan).

CUSPIUS FADUS see **PROCURATORS**

CUSTOM (Heb. *minhag*): C. plays an important role in Judaism. Many aspects of Jewish tradition belong neither to the written nor the oral law, but have binding force because they have been customarily observed by the Jewish people. The rabbis of the Talmud taught "Give heed to the custom of your fathers," but not everything commonly observed was certified by the rabbis as binding, and certain c.'s were abolished. Binding c.'s are those linked to religious life which were introduced or sanctioned and considered worthy of preservation because of their closeness to the character and spirit of Jewish law. Such c.'s were accepted even after the final editing of the Talmud, and incorporated in the halakhic codes. Certain c.'s found acceptance only among limited groups, and this accounts for the variations in Jewish tradition in the different lands of the Diaspora. The Talmud, for instance, notes usages of Babylonian Jewry which differed from those observed in Palestine. Varying c.'s between Sephardi and Oriental Jews on the one hand and Ashkenazi Jews on the other still exist. These have been noted by the codifiers; thus, Joseph Caro in the *Shulhan Arukh* cites the c.'s of Spanish Jewry, while Moses Isserles in his glosses to this work mentions those of the Ashkenazim. There are also differences in c.'s among the Jewish oriental groups themselves, while among the Ashkenazim, there are differences between the western and eastern European traditions, the latter being further divided into Hasidim and Mitnaggedim. C. can play an important part in determining the character of a law about which there is difference of opinion, and it has been said (Y Yevamot 12:1) "Custom cancels law." C. is of binding character in Jewish civil law, and "the custom of the land" is, for instance, the determining factor in the relationship between employer and employee.

CYCO see **CENTRAL YIDDISH CULTURE ORGANIZATION**

CYPRUS: Mediterranean island; the biblical "land of the Kittim," (Is. 23:1, etc.) in modern Hebrew usage *Kaphrisin.* Jews were probably established there before the Christian era, and in New Testament times, there were important communities at Salamis and Paphos. In 117, the Jews of C. under ARTEMION took part in the universal Jewish revolt against Rome and slew many of the general population. The revolt was bloodily suppressed, and Jews were henceforth excluded from the island. Some, however, returned and inscriptions evidence the existence of communities in the late Classical Period. Benjamin of Tudela (c. 1165) found heretics there who observed the Sabbath on Sundays. At a later date in the Middle Ages, there were communities at Nicosia, Paphos, and especially Famagusta. Joseph Nasi was partly responsible for the conquest of C. by the Turks in 1571 but was not created king as had been anticipated. Jews were later deported from Safed to help repopulate C., but there is little record of Jews there under Turkish rule. At the end of the 19th cent., under the British, several attempts were made to establish Jewish agricultural settlements in C. but with limited success. C. was a center for the deportation of "illegal immigrants" from Palestine in 1945–9, 11,000 being interned there. There are 25 Jews on the island (1974). There is no rabbi in C. The cemetery is at Margo near Nicosia (another at Larnaca is disused).

CYRENAICA: Province of LIBYA (capital: Cyrene).

It was colonized by Greeks from the 7th cent. BCE. Under the Ptolemies, Jews were present as soldiers and cultivators in the principal towns and also in the villages. There was an uprising here in 73 CE, headed by fugitives from Palestine. In 115–7, a Jewish revolt, connected with simultaneous risings in Egypt, Cyprus, etc., devastated the country. Its suppression led to the almost total annihilation of the community. Jews are again found in C. in the 4th cent. when the Berber tribes of neighboring Tripo-

litania seem to have included Jewish elements. Jews were at Barca in the 9th cent. and new communities grew up in the 15th cent. at BENGHAZI, etc. In 1908, the country was investigated by the Jewish Territorial Organization with a view to Jewish settlement. The Jewish population in 1935 was 3,192, but from 1945, most of these migrated to Israel, and the last Jews left C. in 1967 after anti-Jewish demonstrations at the time of the Six-Day War.

*CYRIL: Bishop of Alexandria, c. 412–44. His frenzied hostility to Judaism resulted in the expulsion and destruction of the Alexandrian community.

*CYRUS II (d. 529 BCE): King of Persia. In the course of his conquests, he overran the Babylonian Empire, including Palestine. He pursued an enlightened policy towards his subject peoples and in 538, granted permission to the exiles of Judah in Babylon to return to their homeland and rebuild the Temple (Ezra 1:1–44; II Chron. 36:22–3). The Jewish exiles regarded C. as a Divine agent (cf. Is. 44:28; 45:1).

CYSHO see **CENTRAL YIDDISH SCHOOL ORGANIZATION**

*CZACKI, TADEUSZ (1765–1813): Polish stateman.

He was a member of the commission that inquired into the position of the Jews (1788–92), and recommended the removal of disabilities. C. subsequently wrote on the history of the Jews of Poland and Lithuania.

CZECHOSLOVAKIA: Jews are known to have lived in Bohemia from the 10th cent., PRAGUE being probably the oldest settlement. In the Crusading

Inscription in Roman bath at Cyrene recording its reconstruction after the Jewish revolt 115–7 CE.

Period, from 1096 onward, they suffered severe persecutions and many were forcibly baptized. Their position improved in the 13th cent. under Ottokar II but deteriorated in the 14th, especially under Charles IV. A number of decrees directed against the Jews and their economic position were issued during the 15th and 16th cents., and Jews were expelled on several occasions, even from Prague, by now one of the greatest European Jewish centers. Many Jews fled to C. from E Europe at the time of the Chmielnicki pogroms (1648) but ghetto regulations continued to be enforced and even the number of marriages was restricted by law (see FAMILIANTEN LAW). Maria Theresa decreed in 1744 a general expulsion of the Jews which was enforced to some extent the next year. From 1781 to 1919, the history of the Jews merged with that of AUSTRIA. After World War I, Jews enjoyed full rights under the Czechoslovak republic which was the first country to recognize Jewish nationality. The community numbered 357,000 in 1935, RUTHENIA, which was formerly part of Hungary, having 105,000 Jews, SLOVAKIA 150,000. Bohemia and MORAVIA 80,000, (and also c. 40,000 refugees from Germany). After the German occupation in Mar. 1939, the Jews suffered severely; there was large-scale emigration, and those remaining behind were systematically annihilated in 1942–5. Only 42,000 remained at the end of World War II; of these, 24,000 emigrated to Israel 1945–53. Jews were prominent in the post-war regime, but the SLANSKY trial of 1952 had an anti-Semitic element and thereafter the number of leading Jews dwindled. The American Joint Distribution Committee was banned in 1950 and the Zionist Organization closed in 1951. In 1953, a Council of Jewish Communities was set up; all communal activities have to conform with government requirements. A more liberal attitude to Jews was manifested by the Dubcek regime in 1968 but the Russian invasion of that year brought

The Old Synagogue (Altneuschul), Prague.

anti-Semitic undertones and many Jews left the country. Jewish pop. (1973): 14,000.

CZERNOWITZ see **CHERNOVTSY**

CZESTOCHOWA: Polish city. Jacob FRANK was imprisoned there 1760–73, and traces of Frankism remained until World War I. Its early Jewish settlement was restricted (1829–62) to certain streets. The Nazis established a ghetto in C. in 1940. Only about 800 Jews out of the pre-war 25,000 (c. 30% of the total population) survived when the city was liberated in World War II.

D

D', DA, DE: For names beginning with these, see the second element (e.g. Da Costa see Costa, D'Orta see Orta, etc.).

DACHAU: Town in Bavaria (Germany), site of one of the first Nazi CONCENTRATION CAMPS, established in 1933. Originally intended to accommodate 8,000 prisoners, it held 32–50,000 in 1944–5. More than half the inmates died of starvation, ill-treatment, and typhus, or were executed. Various medical experiments were carried out on prisoners. Of the 1,672 members of the prison-staff charged with crimes against humanity, 260 were condemned to death, and 498 to imprisonment.

DAGESH (etymology dubious): In Hebrew punctuation, a dot in a consonant. There are two types: *D. kal* (Latin: *D. lene*) indicating that the letter (*Bet, Gimel, Dalet, Kaph, Pe,* or *Tav*) in which it occurs is to be pronounced with a plosive or "hard" sound; and *D. ḥazak* (Latin: *D. forte*) which can occur in all consonants except *Aleph, He, Ḥet, Ayin,* and *Resh,* showing that a consonant is to be pronounced double. In the punctuation of the Bible other kinds of *d.* sometimes appear, the phonetic effect of which is not clear.

DAGGATUN: Berber tribe in Sahara region of Morocco. Although Moslems, they observe some apparently Jewish rites, and according to their traditions are of Jewish origin.

DAGHESTAN see **CAUCASUS**

DAGON (? from *dagan* – "corn"): Ancient Semitic deity whose cult was adopted by the Philistines when they entered Canaan. Shrines to D. are mentioned at Gaza (Judg. 16:12 ff), Ashdod (I Sam. 5:1–7), and Beth Shean (I Chron. 10:10). D. occupied an important place in the Ugaritic pantheon. He was a god of the soil and plant-growth and widely worshiped in the Middle Eastern countries.

DAHIA AL-KAHINAH (d. 703/4): Queen of judaizing Berber tribes (the Jerua) of the Aurez mountains (Algeria), apparently the last of a dynasty founded in the 4th cent. She led her tribes successfully against Moslem invaders until defeated and killed in battle.

DAIA see **ARGENTINA**

DAICHES: English family: (1) *DAVID D.* (1912–): Critic; son of (3). After teaching at US universities,

he taught English at Cambridge and (from 1961) the Univ. of Sussex. D. has written critical works on English literature and an autobiography. (2) *ISRAEL ḤAYYIM D.* (1850–1937): Rabbi. Born in Lithuania, he was rabbi in Leeds from 1901 and wrote several works of talmudic scholarship. (3) *SALIS D.* (1880–1945): Rabbi; son of (2), officiated at the Edinburgh Hebrew congregation from 1918. (4) *SAMUEL D.* (1878–1949): Rabbinical scholar; son of (2), lecturer in Bible and Talmud at Jews' College, London. He was author of biblical studies and works on Assyriology.

DAIGES (Yiddish from Heb. *deagot*): Worries.

DAINOW, TZEVI HIRSCH ("The *Maggid* of Slutzk"; 1832–1877): Preacher. He was born in Russia, became an adherent of Haskalah, and in his brilliant sermons, which attracted large crowds, advocated secular studies. D. left Russia in 1873 because of persecution by Orthodox opponents and spent his last years in London.

DALET (ד): Fourth letter of the Hebrew alphabet; numerical value: 4. Pronounced now in all dialects (except Yemenite and Iraqi which have retained the ancient pronunciation) as *d*, it originally had the sound of *th* in "this" when without a *dagesh*.

DALIYAH: Kibbutz (KA) founded 1939 in the hills of Manasseh. It engages in dairying and orchard and grain cultivation. D. is noted for its folk-dancing festival. Pop. (1972): 612.

DALLAS: City in Texas, US. Its first Jewish community organization, the Hebrew Benevolent Association, dates from 1872. From this developed the Reform congregation Emanu-El which received its charter in 1874. A Conservative congregation, Shearith Israel, was formed in 1884. D. also has 3 Orthodox congregations. The Jewish Welfare Federation was founded in 1911. Jewish pop. (1973): 20,000.

*DALMAN, GUSTAF HERMANN (1855–1941): German orientalist. From 1902–26, he directed the German Evangelical Institute for the Archeology of the Holy Land in Jerusalem, and thereafter headed an Institute of Palestinology bearing his name at the Univ. of Greifswald. He wrote numerous studies on archeology, biblical criticism, etc.

DAMAGES see **TORTS**

DAMASCUS: Capital of Syria. Its Jewish associations date back to the reign of David in whose
realm it was comprised. It was the capital of Aram-
Dammesek which figured prominently in the period
of the Kings as alternately friend and foe of Israel.
The city had a large Jewish population in the time
of Herod who built there a theater and gymnasium.
Many of its Jews were killed in the disorders in the
early stages of the Jewish Revolt against Rome in
67 CE. The community continued to exist throughout
succeeding centuries and did not suffer from the Arab
conquest (635). In the 9th–10th cents., D. was a
Karaite center. In c. 1170, Benjamin of Tudela
found there 200 Karaites and 3,000 Rabbinite Jews.
The Jewish population was further increased by
Spanish exiles after 1492. The Turkish capture of the
city in the 16th cent. led to an improvement in the
status of the Jews who comprised many wealthy
merchants. After the Damascus Affair (1840),
many Jews left D. and the progressive decline of
the community commenced. In 1848, Benjamin II
found 4,000 Jews there but no traces of the Karaites.
The emigration of Jews was hastened after World
War I as a result of Arab nationalist feeling, and
many moved to Palestine, Lebanon, as well as more
distant countries. Of the 10,000 Jews there in 1940,
only some couple of thousand remained in 1973,
most of them impoverished materially and intellectually and subject to severe restrictions.

DAMASCUS AFFAIR: Blood Libel raised in 1840
when the disappearance in Damascus of the superior
of the Franciscan convent and his servant led to a
search of the Jewish quarter on the instigation of the
local Catholics supported by the French consul.
The torture of leading Jews (one of whom died under
the ordeal) elicited a confession of murder. The
investigations were accompanied by a campaign of
incitement against Jews. The public outcry in the
western world and the personal intervention of Sir
Moses Montefiore and Adolphe Crémieux (who went
to Alexandria to interview Mehemet Ali, ruler of
Syria) led to the quashing of the charges and the
release of the survivors. Montefiore then visited the
sultan in Constantinople and procured a *firman*
condemning the Ritual Murder libel and confirming
Jewish rights. The episode had important consequences
in stimulating the political consciousness and organization of W European Jewry.

DAMASCUS DOCUMENTS see **ZADOKITE
DOCUMENTS**

DAMROSCH: Family of musicians. (1) *FRANK
HEINO D.* (1859–1937): Conductor; son of (2).
A native of Germany, he settled in the US in 1871,
conducted many musical societies, especially choral,
and in 1905, founded the Institute of Musical Art,
New York which he directed until his death. (2)

LEOPOLD D. (1832–1885): Musician. A violinist
of distinction, he turned to conducting and founded
the Breslau Orchestral Society of which he was
director until going to New York in 1871. Here, he
founded and conducted the Oratorio Society (1874)
and the Symphony Society (1878). (3) *WALTER
JOHANNES D.* (1862–1950): Conductor and composer; son of (2). In 1885, he succeeded his father
as director of the Oratorio Society and Symphony
Society of New York. In 1894, he formed the
Damrosch Opera Co. which toured the US for five
years presenting Wagnerian opera and D.'s own
Scarlet Letter. He conducted the New York Symphony Soc. Orchestra from 1903 to 1927.

DAN: (1) Fifth son of Jacob. His mother was Bilhah,
the handmaid of Rachel. (2) One of the twelve
tribes. After the conquest of Canaan, D. was allotted a
portion S of Jaffa, but was thrust back into the hill-
country by the Amorites, only a part of the tribe
remaining in the coastal region. The greater part of
D. was forced to migrate northward where it eventually wrested from the Phoenicians a settlement
area around Laish (Judg. 18:27–9 also mentioned
in the Mari tablets) or Leshem (Jos. 19:47), the
name of which became Dan. The situation of the
rest of the tribe grew serious after the arrival of the
Philistines, despite the heroism of Samson, until
the period of Saul and David. The northern part of
D. was the site of a temple (Judg. 18:26–30) at which
the descendants of Manasseh (or perhaps of Moses)
acted as priests. This became one of the chief cult
centers in the kingdom of Ephraim, and Jeroboam
erected in it the image of a calf to deflect worshipers
from the sanctuary at Jerusalem. D. was captured
by Ben Hadad of Syria during the rule of Baasha
(c. 900 BCE). (3) Israel communal settlement (KA)
at the foot of Mt. Hermon, near the source of the
River Dan. It was founded in 1939 by pioneers of
Rumanian origin and withstood a heavy Syrian
attack in the War of Independence. The nearby
tel, site of the biblical city of Dan (Laish), has been
excavated by Avraham Biran.

*DANBY, HERBERT (1889–1953): English Hebraist.
He was librarian and, later, canon of St. George's
Cathedral in Jerusalem (1919–36). In 1936, he was
appointed Regius professor of Hebrew at Oxford.
Besides original research, he translated many books
from Hebrew into English, including the Mishnah,
works by Maimonides and Bialik, and Klausner's
Jesus of Nazareth.

DANCE: Dance, like music, has an ancient tradition
in Jewish life and cult. In ancient Israel, meals,
wine festivals, weddings, funerals, and ceremonials
were accompanied by appropriate dancing, generally
executed by women and children. The Bible relates
several instances, e.g. the dances of Miriam and "all
the women" (Exod. 15:20) and Jephthah's daughter

The Dance of Miriam.
(Above: Passage through the Red Sea)
From the Sarajevo Haggadah.

(Judg. 11:34), which illustrate the prominence of women in the d. This may explain Michal's reproach directed at David's "unseemly" dancing before the Ark (II Sam. 6:20); male dancing was usually processional and solemn, while ecstatic religious d.'s were reserved for women. The d.'s were always accompanied by singing and instruments (drums,

Inbal ballet.

flutes, and lyres) generally played by the dancing women, but also by musicians. In the Maccabean Period, the Jews adopted Greek and Roman d.'s (e.g. sword d.'s and mime) while ritual and wedding d.'s are frequently mentioned in rabbinic times. The Temple ritual on Tabernacles at this period included a torch d. executed at night in the Temple court with the participation of illustrious scholars. In the Middle Ages, Jews were considered outstanding practitioners of the art of dancing and frequently executed formal d.'s on state occasions. From the 14th cent. onward, Jews throughout Italy were forbidden to maintain dancing academies or to teach dancing on the grounds that this engendered too intimate relations with non-Jews. Guglielmo da Pesaro, who taught dancing at the court of Lorenzo de' Medici, composed one of the earliest practical dancing treatises extant. German Jewish communities frequently had a *Tanzhall* at which wedding d.'s were held, but mixed dancing by the two sexes was disapproved of or forbidden on moral grounds. The constant reiteration of the prohibition, from the Middle Ages onward, makes it clear that it was not consistently observed. In modern times, many Jews have been prominent as dancers, choreographers, designers, etc., including Ida Rubinstein, Marie Rambert, Markova, David Lichine, and Leon Bakst. In Israel leading d. groups are those of Batsheva de Rothschild and the Yemenite ballet of Sara Levi (*Inbal*). Many folk d.'s have been evolved in Israel embodying d.'s of the various communities in the country (e.g. Ḥasidic, Rumanian, Circassian, oriental, etc.).

DANIEL: An individual known for his sense of justice and mentioned in conjunction with Noah and Job in Ezek. 14:14. This is probably an echo of an ancient story which has been discovered in a Ugaritic text. The fame of the ancient sage, D. is referred to in Ezek. 28:3 (which is the source of the phrase "A Daniel come to judgment" in Shakespeare's *The Merchant of Venice*). Aspects of this tradition may well have been woven into the story of D. who figures in the biblical book of that name.

DANIEL: Name of biblical book, included in the Hagiographa, and of its central character whose history and visions comprise the book's contents. There are 12 chapters: 1–6 relate the story of D., a Judean exile in Babylon, and the miraculous experiences that occur to him and his pious friends, Hananiah, Mishael, and Azariah at the courts of Nebuchadnezzar, Darius the Mede, and Belshazzar. Most modern critics hold the stories to be legendary, composed c. 300 BCE; some maintained that the central figure is derived from the wise and just DANIEL cited in the Bible and in Ugaritic texts. Chaps. 7–12 are apocalyptic; the visions relate nominally to ancient times, but the reference seems

Story of Daniel in the Lions' den on the mosaic floor in the synagogue at Naaran near Jericho.

to be to the four persecuting kingdoms of Babylonia, Media, Persia, and Greece. They allude to historical events down to the period of Antiochus Epiphanes of Syria (not mentioned explicitly) whose wicked rule is to be succeeded by the kingdom of heaven. Critics have placed the composition of this section in Palestine at the beginning of the Maccabean revolt (c. 165 BCE). The Book of D., (of which chaps. 2:4–7:28 are in Aramaic) exercised a profound influence on subsequent mysticism.

DANIEL BEN MOSES AL-KUMISI (or Al-Damagani; fl. latter half of 9th cent.?): Karaite scholar; of Persian birth. Originally an admirer of Anan, the founder of the Karaite sect, he later changed his views and called him a fool. Nevertheless, his writings were highly valued by later Karaite scholars. Nothing is known of his life, and his works, written in Hebrew, have survived only in citations. They include a biblical commentary on selected passages considered from the philosophical, religious, eschatological, and polemic viewpoints. He inclined to literal interpretation but rejected the existence of angels.

DANIEL, YULI MARKOVICH (1925–): Soviet writer; son of the Yiddish author M. Daniel (pseudonym of Daniel Meyerovich). Known in USSR chiefly as a translator, he aroused official anger by smuggling to the West and publishing short stories that were critical of the Soviet Union. In 1966 he was tried, together with the author Andrei Sinyavski, and sentenced to five years hard labor. In 1968 his wife was sentenced to prison for protesting the Soviet invasion of Czechoslovakia.

DANZIG (Polish: Gdansk): Polish Baltic port. Jewish settlement in D. was prohibited in the Middle Ages. A few Jews lived in the suburbs in the 16th cent., but were subject to persecution, expulsion, and pogroms until 1773 when the Prussian king gave a general charter to the Jews of the region. At the end of the 18th cent., 1,300 Jews were living in D. The community grew throughout the 19th cent., but its numbers declined in the early 20th cent. D. was an important embarkation port and 60,000 Jews sailed from there for the US and Canada between 1920 and 1925. After D. was declared a Free City (1919), Jewish refugees from Soviet Russia settled there and the community numbered over 10,000 in 1929. After 1933, many Jews left D. and the remainder were annihilated by the Nazis after its annexation to Germany in 1939. Jewish pop. (1964): 100.

DANZIG, ABRAHAM BEN JEHIEL MICHAEL (1748–1820): Rabbinic scholar. Born at Danzig, he eventually settled at Vilna where he became dayyan. He wrote several compilations of which the best-known are *Ḥayye Adam* ("Human Life") and *Ḥokhmat Adam* ("Human Wisdom"), popular and concise presentations of the first two parts of the *Shulḥan Arukh* code. In his decisions, D. generally followed the latest codifiers and opposed extreme severity.

DAPHNAH: Israel kibbutz (KM) at foot of Mt. Hermon, founded 1939. It engages in trout breeding, and maintains a physical training establishment. D. is situated near the site of Daphne mentioned by Josephus. Pop. (1967): 550.

*DARIUS: Name of 3 kings of ancient Persia. *DARIUS I* (reigned 522–486 BCE) inherited the throne of CYRUS. At the beginning of his reign, he permitted Zerubbabel and the Jews who had returned to Jerusalem to resume reconstruction of the Temple.

DARMESTETER: (1) *ARSÈNE D.* (1846–1888): French philologist. At the age of 20, he published a remarkable essay on the Talmud, and his lifework was a study of ancient French words cited as glosses in medieval Hebrew works, notably in the writings of Rashi. From 1877, he was professor of the history of medieval French language and literature at the Sorbonne, and was co-author of a French dictionary. (2) *JAMES D.* (1849–1894): French orientalist; brother of (1). A specialist in oriental languages, he was appointed professor of Persian language and literature at the Collège de France in 1885. D. wrote also on Jewish subjects, including a short history of the Jews and an outstanding work on the prophets. He also translated into and from English.

Seal of Darius I.

DARMSTADT: W. German town. The first information on Jews in D. is an order of 1585 decreeing
the expulsion of 11 Jewish residents. Jews were
compelled to attend sermons by Christian clergy in
the 16th and 17th cents. Oppressive laws adopted
in 1629 harassed the Jews until the end of the 17th
cent. when public religious services were first
authorized. Jews were eventually admitted to citizenship in 1820. The community of 1,500 (1933) was
wiped out in the Nazi era. Jewish pop. (1968): 70.

DARMSTADT HAGGADAH: Illuminated codex of
the Passover Eve service executed in W Germany
about 1430, now in the public library of Darmstadt.
It is considered by some authorities to be the most
beautiful Jewish illuminated ms of the Middle Ages.
It was reproduced in colored facsimile in 1927.

DAROM (Heb. "South"): Area of Israel. Ezekiel
applied the term to the NEGEV, while in the
Talmud, it generally means the area around Lydda,
or between Lydda and Hebron. It now refers to the
area S of Beer Tuvyah down to the Negev.

DARSHAN (Heb. "Expounder"): Name applied
to a teacher either of halakhah or aggadah,
referring in particular to a public teacher or preacher
in the synagogue. The tradition of the *d.* is ancient
and can be traced back to the time of Ezra. From
talmudic times, it was almost a universal custom
for the *d.* to preach and teach in the synagogue on
Sabbaths and festivals. Originally, the exposition
of the halakhah was an essential part of the synagogue lecture; later, however, the study of the halakhah became formalized in smaller groups, and
the function of the *d.* was to expound the aggadah,
with the prime purpose of stressing morality and
observance of religious obligations. The SERMON was
normally delivered in the vernacular.

DATHAN AND ABIRAM: Heads of families of the
tribe of Reuben who, together with 250 "princes
of the congregation," joined KORAH in his rebellion.
They attacked Moses for assuming the leadership
which they claimed for themselves, evidently as the
descendants of Jacob's eldest son. D. and A. perished
with the other rebels, being swallowed up by the
earth (Num. 16).

DAUBE, DAVID (1909–): Jurist. He was born in
Germany and taught at Cambridge before becoming professor of jurisprudence at Aberdeen, Regius
professor of civil law of Oxford (1955), professor at
Univ. of California (1970). His writings deal largely
with the legal background of the Bible.

DAUGAVPILS (formerly **DVINSK**): Latvian city,
now in the USSR. Jews settled in D. in the 18th
cent. and soon constituted a majority of the city's
inhabitants. In 1913, it had over 55,000 Jews, but
the number rapidly dwindled during and after World
War I. The 11,000 Jews who lived there in 1939
were herded into a ghetto by the Nazis. 10,000 were de-

Illuminated page from the Darmstadt Haggadah.

ported to Zolotaya Gorka in Nov. 1941 and massacred. Jewish pop. (1970): 2,000.

DAUGHTER OF ZION (Heb. *Bat Tziyyon*): Biblical
phrase, meaning sometimes Jerusalem and sometimes the Jewish people personified.

DAUPHINÉ: Former French province. Jews lived in
D. (especially at Vienne) probably from Roman
times. Expelled in 1253 after a Blood Libel at Valréas,
they returned in 1289 and were allowed to remain
throughout the succeeding centuries. Jews from other
parts of France found refuge there after the 14th
cent. expulsions. They suffered, however, from severe
restrictions, and few remained by the 16th cent. At
present, there is a community in Grenoble.

David. Sculpture by Verrocchio.
(National Museum, Florence).

DAVAR (Heb. "Word"): Israel daily newspaper. published since 1925 by the *Histadrut*. Its first editors and formative influences were Berl Katznelson, Zalman Shazar (Rubashov), and Mosheh Beilinson. It also publishes a children's weekly *Davar li-yeladim*.

DAVEN (Yiddish term of uncertain origin): To pray.

DAVID: King of Israel c. 1000–c. 960 BCE; youngest son of Jesse. Born at Bethlehem, he became, at the age of 25, armor-bearer to Saul, friend of his son Jonathan, and – after displaying his military prowess in war with the Philistines – husband of Saul's daughter, Michal. Saul's jealousy of D. caused the latter to seek refuge with Achish, king of Gath. D. returned to Israel after Saul and three of his sons had been defeated and killed at the battle of Mt. Gilboa. He settled in Hebron and declared himself king of Judah. At first, Saul's general, Abner, sided with Saul's son Eshbaal whom he crowned king at Mahanaim, but after Eshbaal's murder all the tribes accepted D. as king. In the eighth year of his reign, D. captured the Jebusite stronghold of Jerusalem which he proclaimed his capital and to which he eventually moved the Ark. He succeeded in breaking the Philistine military power and annexing the entire coastal belt. His defeat of the Edomites gave the Israelites an outlet to the Red Sea at Ezion-Geber. He crushed Ammon and Moab, which became subject to Israel, and decisively defeated Aram (Syria), annexing large tracts of territory, including Damascus, as far as the Euphrates. D. signed treaties with Tyre and Sidon and extended the Israelite frontiers to an extent never again attained. Internally he made energetic preparations for building a central temple and organized the national administration. In his old age, his son Absalom rebelled against him and was killed in the revolt; the succession was eventually secured by his son Solomon. The Bible depicts D.'s virtues and vices. On occasion he was ruled by his passions (e.g. in his conduct with Bathsheba). Nevertheless, in the course of time he became a religious symbol and the Jewish messianic hope was attached to his descendants. Jewish tradition has magnified him to the point of saying "King D. still lives" (*Rosh ha-Shanah 25a*), and has attributed to him the composition of the whole Book of Psalms, many of which were certainly ascribed to him from a very early date. Christianity and Islam have derived from Judaism their admiration for D.

DAVID, CITY OF see **JERUSALEM**

DAVID, SHIELD (STAR) OF see **MAGEN DAVID**

DAVID, TOMB OF: According to I Kings 2:10, David was buried in "the city of David," equated by modern archeologists with a site E of the present Old City of Jerusalem. The modern identification of the Tomb of David with a site SW of the Old City derives from a medieval tradition. Especially after 1948, it attained great prominence as a place of Jewish pilgrimage.

DAVID BEN ABRAHAM ALFASI see **ALFASI, DAVID**

DAVID BEN SAMUEL HA-LEVI (c. 1586–1667): Codifier. He served as rabbi in Posen, Ostrog, and Lvov. His chief work is a commentary on the

Shulḥan Arukh called *Ture Zahav* ("Rows of Gold"), and he is often referred to as *Taz* from its initials. This book was accepted as authoritative by rabbis throughout the Diaspora and still forms the basis of halakhic decisions. After D.'s death it was criticized by SHABBETAI BEN MEIR HA-COHEN by defended by D.'s grandson Joel bar Gad in *Maginne Zahav*.

DAVID BEN SOLOMON IBN ZIMRA see **ZIMRA**

DAVID BEN ZAKKAI (d. 940): Exilarch in Babylonia. After appointing Saadyah to the gaonate in 928, D. quarreled with him and deposed him. Saadyah, in return, attempted to appoint a new exilarch. After a long dispute, the two parties were reconciled (937), Saadyah securing the succession to the gaonate for D.'s son after his father's death.

DAVID IBN MERWAN AL-MUKAMMAS see **AL-MUKAMMAS**

DAVID: One of the first Jewish families to settle in Canada after the British conquest in 1763. *LAZARUS D.* (1734–1776), born in Wales, was a founder of Congregation Shearith Israel in Montreal. His son, *DAVID D.* (1764–1824), was a founder of the Bank of Montreal and a charter member of the Montreal Board of Trade. Another son, *SAMUEL D.* (1766–1824), was commander of the 2nd Montreal battalion in the War of 1812–4. *AARON HART D.* (1812–1882), son of Samuel, was one of the first Jewish physicians in Canada, and dean of the faculty of medicine of the present McGill Univ.

DAVID, FERDINAND (1810–1873): German violinist and composer. A friend of Felix Mendelssohn, he gave the first performance of his violin concerto. D. published ancient violin music and had a profound influence as a teacher, many of the outstanding violinists of the 19th cent. (including Joachim) being among his pupils.

DAVIDOVICH, JUDAH LÖB see **BEN-DAVID**

DAVIDSON, ISRAEL (1870–1939): Scholar. Born and educated in Russia, he migrated in 1888 to the US where he completed his studies. From 1905, D. taught medieval Hebrew literature at the Jewish Theological Seminary, New York. His numerous works dealt mainly with aspects of medieval Hebrew poetry and culminated in his great 4-volume *Thesaurus of Medieval Hebrew Poetry* (1924–33) with 35,000 entries.

DAVIDSON, JO (1883–1952): US sculptor. He achieved an international reputation as the sculptor of busts of famous personalities. His busts of Woodrow Wilson and Anatole France are in the Luxembourg Museum in Paris. Shortly before his death, he worked for a time in Israel where he modeled the heads of representative personalities.

DAVIN (DAVID) DE CADEROUSSE (fl. 15th cent.): Earliest known Jewish printer, who in 1444 – before the beginning of Gutenberg's activity – negotiated a contract at Avignon with Procopius

Waldwogel for making letters of the Hebrew alphabet according to "the new art of writing." No specimen of his printing has survived.

DAVIS, SAMMY, JUNIOR (1925–): Negro entertainer. Born a Catholic in Harlem, he became a Jew in 1954. His life and career on the stage and films is described in his autobiography *Yes I Can*.

DAVKA (Aram. "Exactness"): Term (used in Heb. and Yiddish) to emphasize the accuracy of a fact or to draw attention to something unexpected. It also indicates contrariness or obstinacy.

DAWISON, BOGUMIL (1818–1872): Actor. Appearing first in Poland, later in Germany and the US, he was one of the leading actors of his day, noted for his portrayal of tragic roles.

DAY, THE see **TOG, DER**

DAY OF ATONEMENT see **ATONEMENT, DAY OF**

DAY OF JUDGMENT: Period when God decides the fate of people or individuals. Although the Bible refers to an eschatological day of Divine judgment (see APOCALYPSE, ESCHATOLOGY, MESSIAH), the first reference to periodical days of judgment is in the Mishnah where it is stated that the world is judged at four different periods during the year (*Rosh ha-Shanah* I, i). In Jewish liturgy, the first of *Tishri*, considered the New Year, took on the aspect of an annual day of judgment (*yom ha-din*) for all mankind, the decrees being finally sealed on the Day of Atonement.

DAY OF THE LORD, THE: The day on which, according to ESCHATOLOGY, God will reveal His power to mortal eyes, finally defeat his enemies, and judge the wicked of Israel for their evil deeds. Israel will be rescued from affliction and be created anew, while paganism will end and the world-reign of the Almighty will begin.

DAYAN: (1) *MOSHE D.* (1915–): Israel public figure; son of (2). He joined the *Haganah* in his youth and was a founder of the PALMAH. In 1941, he lost an eye while serving in the British army on Lebanese territory. During the Israel War of Independence, his unit repelled the Syrian army from the Jordan Valley and in Aug. 1948, he was appointed commander of the Jerusalem region. He was chief of general staff of the Israel army 1953–8 and in 1956, was responsible for the SINAI OPERATION. Elected to the Knesset in 1959 as a *Mapai* member, he was minister of agriculture 1959-64. In 1965 he joined RAFI. Just before the Six-Day War, he joined the government as minister of defense. He resigned in 1974 following public criticism concerning his responsibility for setbacks in the early part of the Yom Kippur War. (2) *SHEMUEL D.* (1891–1968): Israel agricultural pioneer and labor leader. Born in Russia, he migrated to Palestine in 1908 and was among the founders of Deganyah and Nahalal. D.

Moshe Dayan.

was a leader of the moshavim cooperative settlement organization, and represented *Mapai* in the Knesset 1949–59.

DAYTON: City in Ohio, US. The first congregation, B'nai Jeshurun (now Temple Israel) dates from 1854. The Orthodox congregation, Beth Jacob, was organized in 1875. Beth Abraham, also Orthodox, dates from 1895. D. has a Jewish Community Council, founded in 1943. Jewish pop. (1973): 6,300.

DAYYAN: (Heb. "Judge"): Judge of a rabbinical court. Not all rabbis are qualified to serve as dayyanim. Whereas the ordinary rabbi may decide only on matters of a specifically religious nature, the d. is also qualified to judge money matters and problems of civil law brought before a Jewish court. In England, the title d. is given to rabbis of the chief rabbi's court.

DAYYENU (Heb. "It would have sufficed us"): Refrain of a hymn (probably of the Gaonic Period) in the Passover HAGGADAH. The phrase became proverbial.

DE HAAS, DE LA CABALLERIA, etc. see under **HAAS, CABALLERIA,** etc.

DEAD, PRAYERS FOR see **KADDISH; YIZKOR**

DEAD SEA (Heb. *Yam Ha-Melah* = "the Salt Sea"): The southernmost and largest of the Palestinian lakes; also known as the Sea of the Arabah (Deut. 3:17, etc.), the East Sea (Ezek. 47:18, etc.), the Sea of Sodom, the Sea of Lot, and the Sea of Death (the last name was based on the ancient belief that nothing could live in it). It covers at present only part of its ancient area which, according to geologists, previously extended 80 m. N (including the Sea of Galilee) and 62 m. S of its present shores. It now lies within the Jordan depression between the mountains of Moab on the E and the Judean hills on the W. Its length is 47½ 49 m., its width 11 m., and its total area 390 sq. m. Its surface is about

Salt encrusted branches on the shore of the Dead Sea.

Fragment from the commentary on the Book of Habakkuk.
(From the Dead Sea Scrolls).

1,300 ft. below sea-level (the lowest point on earth) and its average depth, 462 ft. (the measurements are not constant). It derives its water mainly from the Jordan and Arnon rivers. On account of the great heat, there is a high rate of evaporation. The bottom of the Sea and the shore area contain an immense quantity of pitch. The waters are rich in salinity (28–33%), and the Palestine Potash Co. extracts salts (potash, bromine compounds) at its plant at Sodom to the S of the D. S.

DEAD SEA SCROLLS: Ancient manuscripts the first of which, found at Khirbet KUMRAN, $7\frac{1}{2}$ m. from Jericho, were revealed in 1947. Archeological exploration later discovered in the neighborhood a cemetery of over 1,000 graves, a central building, and central caves containing fragments of old documents. The coins found on the site showed it to have been lived in approximately from the time of John Hyrcanus, but there is evidence of an earlier period of occupancy. It was apparently destroyed by an earthquake in 31 BCE and rebuilt not long thereafter. The writers of the scrolls lived there until c. 68 CE. Both the contents of the scrolls and the archeological finds show that these people belonged to a Jewish sect. Great importance attaches to the scrolls – or fragments of scrolls – of the Bible, including 2 complete copies of Isaiah and fragments of nearly every other book of the Bible. These discoveries have advanced the study of the Hebrew text of the Bible, as the previous known oldest versions date from the Middle Ages. Generally speaking, the scrolls justify a conservative approach to biblical study with the exception of a fragment from the Book of Samuel which resembles the version known to the Greek translators. Fragments have also been found of the Apocrypha and Pseudepigrapha and of books hitherto unknown as well as of familiar works; the latter include the Book of Tobit, the Hebrew version of Jubilees, the Aramaic version of the Book of Enoch, etc. Of the sectarian books, a commentary on the Book of Habakkuk, and part of a commentary on the Books of Micah, Nahum, etc. have been found. These commentaries explain the prophetic writings in relation to the history of the sect. Another scroll includes the plan of the struggle of "the sons of light" (i.e., the members of the sect) against "the sons of darkness," which was to begin with the conquest of Palestine and to end forty years later with the conquest of the whole world. The "Scroll of Thanksgivings" comprises religious hymns which develop in poetic fashion the sect's theological doctrines. One scroll deals with the sect's organization and teachings; in addition there are fragments of the ZADOKITE DOCUMENTS, the greater part of which had previously been found in the Cairo *genizah*. The COPPER SCROLL describes hidden treasure and the TEMPLE SCROLL contains a minute description of the Temple. Several identifications have been suggested for the sect, the most widely accepted being that it was a group akin to the ESSENES. As a

Shrine of the Book, housing the Dead Sea Scrolls.

Procession around the bier, prior to burial. (B. Picart *Cérémonies et coutumes religieuses, Amsterdam* 1723).

result of their dualist outlook, which beheld the power of good ruling in the world in opposition to the power of evil, they saw themselves as the chosen "sons of light" elected as such by God. With the aid of the Holy Spirit which had been granted to them, they attained to a knowledge of "Divine secrets" and their apocalyptic circles, among whom the Book of Enoch and similar works were composed, probably influenced the beginnings of Christianity, especially the circles close to Paul and John the Evangelist. Some of the scrolls came into the possession of the Hebrew Univ. through E. L. SUKENIK who was responsible for the first publication of selections from their contents. Others went to the US where they were published by Burrows. Brownlee, etc. and were subsequently purchased for the government of Israel largely through the agency of Sukenik's son, Yigael YADIN. They are housed in the Shrine of the Book in the ISRAEL MUSEUM.

DEARBORN INDEPENDENT see **FORD, HENRY**

DEATH: Many passages in the Bible indicate that the early Hebrews looked upon d. as rejoining one's fathers. Although d. was not an evil in itself. premature d. was regarded as a great misfortune and the blessing pronounced over the righteous was to die "in a good old age." After d., a certain type of existence still continued in SHEOL, and the dead were considered to possess certain psychic powers. In later Hebrew eschatology, d. came to be considered a prime evil; at the end of days, d.

would cease and all the dead would rise. The idea of RESURRECTION became a fundamental doctrine of Pharisaic Judaism. The classical liturgy reiterates faith in God as the "quickener of the dead." D. came to the world, according to the rabbis, because of sin – either that of Adam, from which mankind still suffers, or else personal sin. Various rabbinic legends convey a belief that the dead carry on some connection with the living and even take an interest in their affairs. The practice of praying for the intercession of the dead is considered by the rabbis as of early origin. The last act of the dying Jew is the recitation of the *Shema*. After d., the body is washed and watched until it is placed in the earth. BURIAL, according to the rabbis is to take place quickly and be conducted with simplicity.

DEATH PENALTY see **CAPITAL PUNISHMENT**

DEBIR: Canaanite city; previously called Kiriath-Sepher. In ancient times, it was inhabited by the ANAKIM. There are two biblical traditions, one that it was captured by Joshua (Josh. 10:38–9) while according to the other it was taken by Othniel son of Kenaz (Josh. 15:17). D. is included in the list of priestly cities (Josh. 21:15).

DEBIR see **TEMPLE**

DEBORAH: (1) Nurse of Rebekah, buried beneath a tree known as ALLON-BACUTH (Gen. 35:8). (2) Prophetess, c. 1150 BCE; wife of Lapidoth. She roused the Israelite tribes to revolt under Barak son of Abinoam against the Canaanite king Jabin of

Hazor and Sisera, his ally and commander (Judg. 4). The song of victory attributed to her (Judg. 5) is regarded as one of the oldest compositions preserved in Hebrew.

"DEBORAH": German language weekly publication, appearing in Cincinnati 1855–1900, edited by I. M. WISE, as a supplement to the AMERICAN ISRAELITE. D. was reissued, afte Wise's death, as a monthly (1901–2) but lost its function with the decline of the German-speaking Jewish population in the US.

DEBRECZEN: Hungarian city. Jewish settlement was only permitted after 1840 but over 10,000 Jews were living there before World War II when it was the third largest community in Hungary. The community suffered greatly in World War II. In 1970 it had 1,200 Jews.

DEBT: Biblical law is notable for its many provisions to ease the burden of d. No interest may be collected; d.'s are automatically canceled every seven years; chattels may not be seized for failure to repay. Practical experience, however, forced certain modifications of these liberal provisions so as to facilitate credit for the ultimate benefit of the borrower himself. Hillel introduced the PROSBUL to overcome the Sabbatical year cancellation, and when ownership of real property declined among Jews, the rabbis ordained that chattels too could become security for d.

DECALOGUE see **COMMANDMENTS, TEN**

DECAPOLIS (Gk. "League of the Ten Towns"): Confederation of ten Greek cities chiefly in Palestine in the Roman Period. Though its towns were much older, the D. was possibly created in 63 BCE by Pompey and consisted of Philadelphia (Rabbath-Ammon), Raphana (or Raphon), Scythopolis (Beth Shean), Gadara, Abilene, Hippos (Susita), Dion, Pella (Peḥal), Gerasa (Jerash), and Kanatha. (A listing by Pliny substitutes Damascus for Abilene.) All (except Philadelphia and Kanatha which were held by Nabateans) were taken from Jewish control and handed to the direct supervision of the Roman governor of Syria. The D. towns retained a certain measure of internal autonomy, including the right of coinage. In the course of time, changes took place in the structure, and the number of member-cities reached 14. During the Roman war (66–70), there were bloody clashes between the citizens of the D. and the resident Jews. The significance of the D. was its control of the trade-route from Arabia to Syria and its links with Palestine.

DEED: A document attested by two witnesses confirming a conveyance of property, contract of marriage. bill of divorce, etc. In the Bible, it is known as *sepher* ("book") but in rabbinic literature as *shetar* or *get*, the latter word, however, usually having limited application to bills of divorce. An important variety of d. is the *shetar ḥov* ("debt-contract"), a sealed bond acknowledged by two witnesses. This type of bond, unlike a note of hand or verbal promise, made liable for seizure all property held at the time of the giving of the bond, even if the propery were subsequently sold.

DEGANYAH A: Israel communal settlement (IK) immediately S of the Sea of Galilee. First founded in 1908 at Umm-Juni by a workers' group from

Deganyah on the shore of the Jordan River.

nearby Kinneret, it was finally established on its present site in 1909. D. was a pioneer settlement known as the "mother of *kevutzot*" and was the home of A. D. GORDON. Although originally intended as a "family commune" with a membership not to exceed 20, it had a population of 448 in 1972. During the Israel War of Independence, Syrian troops reached the periphery of D. before being thrown back. Its sister-settlement *DEGANYAH B* (IK) was founded in 1920 when Deganyah A preferred to cut its holdings rather than increase its membership. Its founders were of Russian origin. Pop. (1972): 534.

DEGGENDORF: Town in Lower Bavaria; scene in 1338 of a charge of Host Desecration leading to a massacre of Jews which subsequently spread throughout S Germany.

DEINARD, EPHRAIM (1846–1930): Hebrew writer and bibliographer. He traveled widely in Europe and the Orient, collecting books, many of which were purchased by M. Sulzberger and the libraries of Congress and Harvard. In addition to journalism and accounts of his journeys, he wrote bibliographical studies, including *Kohelet America* (1926), listing all Hebrew books published in the US.

DEITY see **GOD**

DELAWARE: US state. From the mid-17th cent. until the beginning of immigration from E Europe in the 1880's, there were only individual Jews in D. Jewish religious services were first held in WILMINGTON in 1881. In 1883, the Moses Montefiore Benefit Society, forerunner of D.'s first congregation, Adas Kodesh, was incorporated; Adas Kodesh received its charter in 1889. D. had 9,000 Jews in 1973, nearly all of them in Wilmington where the English-Yiddish *Jewish Voice* is published bimonthly.

DELILAH: Woman of the Valley of Sorek, loved by SAMSON. Learning the secret of his strength, she had his locks shaved and handed him over to the Philistines (Judg. 16).

DELITZSCH: (1) *FRANZ D.* (1813–1890): German philologist and Hebrew scholar. An expert on Hebrew and rabbinical literature, his most important work in this field was a history of Jewish poetry (*Zur Geschichte der jüdischen Poesie*, 1836) containing the first scientific evaluation of the subject. D. wrote commentaries on several books of the Bible and translated the New Testament into Hebrew. Although he defended the Jews against anti-Semitic attacks, he was active in missionary work. (2) *FRIEDRICH D.* (1850–1922): German Assyriologist; son of (1). His works dealt mainly with Assyrian grammar and the lexicography of Assyrian, Hebrew, and Sumerian. He was one of the first to discover the connection between Assyrian and Hebrew and the influence of Assyrian and Babylonian culture on biblical civilization. In his *Babel und Bibel*, he sought to prove that all the ideas of the Bible were drawn from Babylon. This aroused bitter controversy, and D. eventually adopted a stand of unconcealed hatred for the Jews and the Bible, especially in his *Die grosse Täuschung*.

DELLA REINA, JOSEPH see **REINA**

DELMEDIGO: Cretan family of German origin. (1)*ELIJAH BEN MOSES ABBA D.* (1460–1497): Philosopher and talmudist. He was born in Crete and lived in Italy where he is reported to have taught philosophy at the Univ. of Padua. His pupils included Pico della Mirandola under whose auspices he settled in Florence and became prominent in philosophical circles. D. translated some of the works of Averroes into Latin. His chief work is *Beḥinat ha-Dat* ("Examination of Religion") which claimed that there was no clash between philosophy and faith, and distinguished in Jewish tradition between halakhah, which is obligatory on every Jew, and aggadah, which conveys the private views of the talmudic sages. He criticized the kabbalists and concluded that the *Zohar* was written at a late period. His philosophy was largely influenced by Averroes and Maimonides. He returned to Crete before his premature death. (2) *JOSEPH SOLOMON BEN ELIJAH D.* (known as *Yashar*; 1591–1655): Astronomer, mathematician, philosopher, and talmudist. He was born in Crete and studied astronomy (under Galileo), philosophy, medicine, and mathematics at the Univ. of Padua. He traveled widely, visiting Egypt, Turkey, Poland (where he was personal physician to the Lithuanian duke, Radziwill), Germany, Holland, and Bohemia; he was employed as teacher by the Sephardi communities of Hamburg and Amsterdam, was physician of the community at Frankfort-on-Main, and finally settled in Prague where he died. His opinions oscillated between Kabbalah and scientific knowledge, with many consequent contradictions in his views. He wrote several books on both religious and scientific topics, some of his writings being collected in *Sepher Elim*.

DELOS: Greek island in the Aegean Sea. Jews were settled there in 138 BCE and Josephus mentions their exemption from military service in 49 BCE. The ruins of a synagogue, probably of the 1st cent. BCE, have been excavated near the coast. D. has been uninhabited since the Middle Ages. It was part of the territory controlled by Joseph Nasi as duke of Naxos.

DEMAI (Heb. "Dubious Produce" with reference to tithes): Third tractate in the Mishnah order of *Zeraim*, consisting of 7 chapters. It has *gemara* in the Palestinian, but not the Babylonian, Talmud. It deals with the requirements for tithing produce where there is doubt whether the proper tithes have already been given.

DEMBITZ, LEWIS NAPHTALI (1833–1907): US lawyer. Of German birth, he settled in the US while a youth. Engaging in the practice of law, he lived, from 1853 to the end of his life, in Louisville. A staunch adherent of Orthodox Judaism, he nevertheless aided in the organizaton of the Union of American Hebrew Congregations. He was also prominent in civil and Jewish affairs in Kentucky. His writings include both monographs on aspects of law and studies in Jewish lore.

DEMBITZER, ḤAYYIM NATHAN (1821–1892): Rabbi and historian. He was born in Cracow, where he served as dayyan. D. published several studies in Jewish history including *Kelilat Yophi* comprising biographies of the rabbis of Lvov and neighboring communities.

***DEMETRIUS:** Kings of Syria. *DEMETRIUS I* (Soter), reigned 162–150 BCE. He supported the pro-hellenistic Alcimus' appointment as high priest at Jerusalem. In 161, his general, Nicanor, was defeated by Judah the Maccabee, but subsequently another of his generals, Bacchides, defeated and killed Judah. In 153, when threatened by the pretender

Coin of Demetrius II.

Alexander Balas, he recognized Jonathan the Hasmonean who, however, preferred Alexander's support. D. was later killed in battle. *DEMETRIUS II* (Nicator), regned 145–138 BCE; son of Demetrius I. He expelled Alexander Balas who was supported by Jonathan the Hasmonean. Jonathan, however, came to terms with D. who recognized his high priesthood and his right to part of Samaria. When Tryphon rose against D. in the name of Balas' son, Antiochus, he gained Jonathan's support. After Jonathan's murder, his brother Simon helped D. who granted Judea remission of taxes and virtually acknowledged its independence.

DEMOCRACY: Form of government in which political power resides in all who have civic rights. The ancient Hebrew polity, whether under priesthood, judges, or monarchy, cannot be called democratic. Nevertheless, the Pentateuch laid down fundamental principles which had to be followed by the ruler in governing his "brethren" (cf. Deut. 17:20), there being, therefore, important elements of limited or constitutional monarchy, i.e., the ruler was subject to law. According to one opinion, the *Am ha-Aretz* or "People of the Land," who had a strong political influence from time to time in the period of the First Temple, was the "Ancient Hebrew Parliament." The prophets, most of whom were derived from the masses, exercised continual pressure to modify legislation in favor of the common man. The exact nature of the *Ḥever ha-Yehudim* or "Commonalty of the Jews," referred to on Hasmonean coins is obscure, but it should be noted that Simon's rule was by popular consent. The later Hasmonean monarchy, however, was absolute, restricted only by the imprecise authority of the Sanhedrin. In later generations, political d. was out of the question for the Jewish people, living constantly under alien rule. In the medieval communities, authority tended to be vested in the wealthy; sometimes the poor had no controlling rights at all, and sometimes there was a tripartite division, each of the three economic ranges (wealthy, middle-class, poor) having an equal voice. It is questionable whether the paupers figured in this scheme. Nevertheless, the egalitarian tendencies of Jewish religion and life fostered democratic feelings at all times, and the rights of the poor were always respected. In the 19th cent., the Jews of Europe, long excluded from privilege and clearly forming no part of the aristocracy, threw their weight everywhere on the side of d. They were thus active in movements of this period, both "revolutionary" and constitutional, to secure the establishment of democratic government in all countries. The recent experiences of the Jews under totalitarian regimes have reinforced this tendency. Throughout E and Central Europe in the 19th and 20th cents., commencing with the Haskalah movement and strengthened by current socialist trends, a continuous struggle was waged by some intellectuals and working class "representatives" to destroy the alleged monopoly of wealth and Orthodoxy over Jewish public life. Thus a more democratic direction became established in Jewish community organization though, where contributions for communal purposes are voluntary, the wealthier elements inevitably have disproportionate authority. The influence of the Bible in establishing democratic tendencies in 17th cent. England and 18th cent. America was incalculable. In modern Israel, the VAAD LEUMI and, after it, the KNESSET were from the beginning spontaneously organized on a fully democratic basis.

DEMOCRATIC FRACTION: An organized group which appeared at the 5th Zionist Congress (1901) and consisted of about 37 delegates, including a number of notable figures such as Leo Motzkin, Chaim Weizmann, Berthold Feiwel, Victor Jacobson, and Martin Buber. The group opposed the policy of waiting for diplomatic events, urged a deepened nationalism, greater cultural activity, a larger measure of democracy in the leadership of the movement, and more regard for the youth. While generally sympathetic with the somewhat vague ideas of the youthful group, Herzl feared that the organized opposition might lead to a breach in the unity of the movement and succeeded in postponing discussion of the "cultural" question until the election of the Zionist Council (Actions Committee) at the conclusion of the Congress. The D. F. disappeared thereafter.

DEMONOLOGY: The Greek word "demon" originally signified a higher being, also a god. In later usage, demons came to mean non-Divine beings who can wield power and influence – mainly of a destructive kind – over human fate. In the Bible, all angels were originally merely messengers (Heb. *malakh*) and *ad hoc* expressions of the Divine will and as such could be good or evil according to the purpose for which they were sent (help, punishment, etc.). The "negative" aspects were in due course personified as demons in the accepted sense. The Bible already knows a fringe of demonic beings who, unlike SATAN or the "lying spirit" (Job 1:6; I Kings 22:21 ff), are not members of the Divine household but demons proper (cf. Is. 13:21; 34:14). An important source of d. is the myth of the fallen ANGELS which probably preserves remnants of earlier stories concerning rebellious and vanquished gods. Also, the obscure passage of Gen. 6:1–4, greatly elaborated in apocryphal and aggadic literature, was interpreted as the story of fallen angels who were seduced by the beauty of the daughters of man. Stories like these made it possible for a great deal of pagan d. to enter Judaism. A different version of the story of the Fall of Angels recounts the fall of one of the highest angels together with his retinue through rebellious pride and disobedience. Under the influence of these ideas, Satan became a devil and king of the evil spirits. Similarly, many words which in the Bible have no connection with d. became proper names of demon princes (Azazel, Belial, etc.). Other angelic beings with a negative character or activity were also demonized in due course, e.g. the ANGEL OF DEATH or the guardian angels of the gentile nations. The fully-developed dichotomy appears again in medieval Kabbalah where two parallel but antagonistic systems (the Divine and the demonic spheres) are presented as two cosmic principles. The demons of folklore and legend are less forbidding. ASHMEDAI, the king of demons of the Solomon legend (*Gittin* 68a and Midrash) though not active as a Divine angel-messenger, is certainly not evil. In fact, demons could be both good and evil and often were merely mischievous. Generally, however, they were malicious and dangerous, necessitating all kinds of precautionary measures (AMULETS, magic formulas, etc.). Though of little importance in official religion, which tended to deprecate both angels and demons for the sake of the exclusive and immediate sway of God

Himself, demons (e.g. LILITH the baby-snatching queen of demons), etc. had great significance in the life of the masses.

DENMARK: European country. No Jews lived in D. in the Middle Ages, but in 1622, Sephardi Jews were invited to Glückstadt (then Danish) in order to develop commerce. In 1657, Frederick III permitted Sephardim to settle freely in D., although German Jews still needed special permission. Full civic, but not political, rights were accorded in 1814 and full equality, in 1849. Jews achieved distinction in many branches of public and literary life. In the 20th cent., the community was augmented by refugees from E Europe. The relations with the non-Jewish community are friendly and the people of D., led nobly by Christian X, made great efforts to save Danish Jewry during World War II and assisted most of them to escape to Sweden. Jewish pop. (1973): 7,000 nearly all in COPENHAGEN.

DENUNCIATION: Closely pressed by a hostile world, Jews in past ages always regarded d. to the gentile authorities as a heinous crime. A bitter prayer in condemnation of such "slanderers" (*malshinim*) was included in the daily *Amidah* prayer from the 1st cent. In the Middle Ages, with the elaboration of anti-Jewish legislation, the problem became even more serious. In Spain, the civil authority realized that the practice of d. could undermine Jewish communal life and actually empowered the Jewish authorities to seek the death-penalty against offenders. The term *malsin* (verb *malsinar*) entered the Spanish vocabulary. The same problem presented itself in different forms in all parts of the Jewish world, where the term *moser* ("slanderer") became the greatest reproach that could be leveled against a Jew. A difficulty, however, remained in cases of actual criminality. Although a Jew might deserve condemnation for anti-social actions, he would suffer during his trial and subsequently as a result of his faith, and there was consequent reluctance to testify against a fellow-Jew in any circumstances. Nevertheless, the Jewish community would on occasion invoke the secular authority to help root out criminal tendencies which threatened the general well-being.

DENVER: City in Colorado, US. Its first Jewish organization was formed in 1861 in order to aquire a cemetery. By 1866, there were about 100 Jews in D. In 1876, German Jews founded the first synagogue, Temple Emanuel, with a congregation of 28 members, which increased rapidly in subsequent years. Since 1899 when the NATIONAL JEWISH HOSPITAL for tuberculosis was established, D. has become the foremost Jewish health center in the US. Its Allied Jewish Community Council, founded 1936, coordinates fund-raising for domestic and overseas needs. The weekly *Intermountain Jewish News* has

Denver. Jewish National Home for Asthmatic Children.

been published there since 1913. In 1973, D. had 26,000 Jews.

DERASH see **MIDRASH**

DERASHAH see **HOMILETICS**

DEREKH ERETZ (Heb. "Way of the land"): Common courtesy, respect.

DEREKH ERETZ RABBAH: One of the lesser tractates appended to the Babylonian Talmud at the end of tractate *Nezikin*. Its contents, largely of tannaitic origin, are varied and include laws of personal status, moral sayings, a list of sins which cause eclipses of the sun and moon, etc.

DEREKH ERETZ ZUTA: One of the lesser tractates appended to the Babylonian Talmud at the end of tractate *Nezikin*. It is normally printed after *Derekh Eretz Rabbah*, but there is no connection between them. *D.E.Z.* contains moral sayings, the last section being in praise of peace.

DERENBOURG: (1) *HARTWIG D.* (1844–1908): French orientalist; son of (2). Professor of Arabic and Semitic languages in Paris at the *École des Langues Orientales* (1875) and the *École des Hautes-Études* (1885), he was the author of many articles on Arabic grammar, literature, and religion, as well as on Semitic mss and inscriptions. D. was one of the founders of *La Grande Encyclopédie* and was active in Jewish life as president of the *Société des Études Juives*, etc. (2) *JOSEPH D.* (1811–1895):

French orientalist; son of (3). From 1852, he was proof-reader of oriental texts at the *Imprimerie Nationale* and from 1877, professor of Hebrew at the *École des Hautes Études*. In 1871, D. was elected a member of the *Académie des Inscriptions et Belles-lettres* as a tribute to his scientific studies, notably on the relation of Arabic and Hebrew literature. He published an edition of Maimonides' commentary on Mishnah *Tohorot*, a corpus of Semitic inscriptions (with his son, Hartwig), and commenced an edition of the complete works of Saadyah Gaon (5 vols.). D. was also active in Jewish affairs, being vice-president of the Alliance Israélite Universelle. (3) *TZEVI HIRSCH D.* (Denburg; 1760–1836): Hebrew author. He wrote a drama *Yosheve Tevel* ("Inhabitants of the World") which satirized personalities in the Mainz community of which he was a member.

*DERZHAVIN, GAVRIIL (1743–1816): Russian poet and statesman. His report on the economic condition of the Jews in White Russia (1800), although generally unfriendly, contained certain positive proposals for furthering Jewish enlightenment.

DES MOINES: City in Iowa, US. German Jews began to arrive in D.M. in the 1840's. In 1872, the first congregation (Reform), B'nai Jeshurun, was established. An Orthodox congregation, B'nai Israel, was founded in 1876. The Conservative congregation, Tifereth Israel, dates from 1901. The

Detroit. Ark of the Beth Aaron Synagogue.

Jewish Welfare Fund was founded in 1914. Jewish pop. (1973): 3,000.

DESART, ELLEN ODETTE see **BISCHOFFSHEIM**
DESECRATION OF THE HOST see **HOST, DESECRATION OF**
DESECRATION OF THE NAME see **HILLUL HA-SHEM**
DESSAU: German town. Jews first settled there in the 17th cent. but until 1848, were allowed to live only in the suburb of Sandvorstadt. In 1687, they were permitted to build a synagogue, and an important Hebrew printing press existed there 1696–1704. Moses Mendelssohn was born in D. A Jewish school was founded in 1804, and in 1806, the first Jewish monthly in German (*Sulamith*) appeared in D. The community was destroyed during World War II and only a few Jews settled there subsequently.
DETENTION CAMPS see **CAMPS, DETENTION**
DETROIT: City in Michigan, US. A number of Jewish settlers, mostly from Bavaria, migrated to D. in the 1850's. The first congregation in the state, Beth El, formed in D. in 1850; it inclined to Reform. An Orthodox offshoot (now Conservative) was established in 1869 and called Shaarey Zedek. The Jewish population increased rapidly in the first quarter of the 20th cent., coinciding with the expansion of the automobile industry. Most of the new arrivals were from E Europe. The Jewish Welfare Federation was organized in 1926, and a Community Council founded in 1937 with a membership of over 260 local organizations. The United Hebrew Schools administer a Hebrew school system. The *Detroit Jewish News* (founded 1942) appears weekly. Jewish pop. (1973): 80,000, with 23 Orthodox, 6 Conservative and 4 Reform synagogues.
DEUTERO-ISAIAH see **ISAIAH**
DEUTERONOMY: Fifth and last book of the Pentateuch; known in Hebrew as *Devarim* ("Words") after the initial phrase, but also called *Mishneh Torah* ("Repetition of the Law") of which *Deuteronomion* is the approximate Greek translation. It is divided into 34 chapters comprising: (1) introduction (Chaps. 1–4) containing Moses' review of the events since Sinai; (2) Moses' ethical exhortation (including a repetition of the Ten Commandments) and a summary of the legislation accepted by the Israelites (5–26); (3) Moses' final speeches (27–30); and (4) Moses' last acts, his farewell song and blessing, and an account of his death (31–4). The book differs

in style from its predecessors and on occasions even contradicts them (e.g. in Exodus the cult-place has no permanent home; in D. it has one fixed home chosen by God). Critics have therefore concluded that some of the laws in D. were derived from a special ("Deuteronomic") group to which they also assign parts of other Pentateuchal books. They differ as to the date of its redaction; most recent views are more conservative than those previously prevalent, some scholars going so far as to assign it to the period of Samuel and Judges or even in the main to Mosaic authorship. D. has been identified by some scholars with the book found by Josiah (II Kings 22–3).

DEUTERONOMY RABBAH: Midrash on the Book of Deuteronomy; part of MIDRASH RABBAH. It consists of 27 expositions of identical structure, each beginning with a halakhic statement. The text incorporates fragments from the Palestinian Talmud, *Genesis Rabbah*, and *Leviticus Rabbah*. Scholars have surmised that it was compiled c. 900 in a Greek-speaking country.

DEUTEROSIS (Gk. "Repetition"): Term applied by the Byzantine emperor Justinian to the rabbinic interpretation which he forbade to be incorporated in the synagogue liturgy (553). It has been variously interpreted as Targum, Mishnah, and Midrash, but probably connotes all rabbinic exposition.

DEUTSCH, BABETTE (1895–): US author. A poet of liberal views, she has also written novels and criticism (*Poetry in Our Time*). With her husband, Avrahm YARMOLINSKY, she has published many

Babette Deutsch

translations from German and Russian poets (notably, Rilke, Pushkin, and Blok).

DEUTSCH, BERNARD SEYMOUR (1884–1935): US political leader. He played an important role in New York city politics, serving as president of the board of aldermen. D. became president of the American Jewish Congress in 1929.

DEUTSCH, EMANUEL OSCAR MENAHEM (1829–1873): German orientalist. In 1855, he assumed a position in the oriental department of the British Museum. He wrote a number of essays, including one on the Talmud which was often republished and greatly stimulated interest in the subject.

DEUTSCH, GOTTHARD (1859–1921): Historian. After serving as rabbi at Brünn (Austria), he became professor of Jewish history and the philosophy of religion at the Hebrew Union College, Cincinnati (1891). He was an editor of the *Jewish Encyclopedia* to the success of which his articles contributed, but he published no major work except his collection of essays *Scrolls*.

DEUTSCH, LEO (1855–1941): Russian social democrat. In 1877, he was a leader of a revolt of Ukrainian peasants. He was exiled to Siberia in 1884 but escaped in 1901. Later, he edited a workers' journal in the US. D. returned to Russia in 1917 but opposed Bolshevism. In 1923, he began to publish in Berlin his work on Jews in the Russian revolutionary movement.

DEUTSCH, MORITZ (1818—1892): Cantor. A pupil of Sulzer, he was cantor in the Great Synagogue, Breslau, from 1844 until his death and from 1855, lectured on Jewish liturgical music at the Breslau Rabbinical Seminary. He established (1859) and directed a cantors' institute at Breslau and published several volumes of liturgical compositions.

DEVARIM see **DEUTERONOMY**

DEVARIM RABBAH see **DEUTERONOMY RABBAH**

DEVEKUT (Heb. "Cleaving unto"): Intense love of God. The term is based on the phrase "love the Lord your God... and cleave unto Him" (Deut. 11:22). The concept of *d.* played an important role in the Kabbalah. "A man should always remember God and His love, never ceasing to think of Him, so that even when he is talking to his fellow-men, his heart is with God" (Nahmanides). In the doctrine of Abraham Abulafia, *d.* took on the meaning of ecstasy. The Hasidim, in particular, gave *d.* contemplative and ecstatic duality, Dov Ber of Mezhirich holding that "the principal elements of Divine worship are *d.* and awe."

DEVIR: Hebrew publishing-house founded in 1922 in Berlin by H. N. Bialik, Shemaryahu Levin, and Y. H. Ravnitsky. The following year, it acquired the rights of the MORIAH publications (at Odessa).

Since 1924, it has operated in Tel Aviv, publishing hundreds of works in all branches of Hebrew literature and scholarship.

DEVOTION (Heb. *kavvanah*): According to Jewish belief, a man's religious actions and particularly his prayers must be conducted with inner d. This is stressed in the Bible (e.g. Is. 29:13 ff) and the Talmud, while Maimonides said that a man when praying should turn his heart from all secular thoughts and regard himself as standing before God. The Talmud discusses whether a man fulfils his religious obligations if performing them without d. D. is of special importance in the Kabbalah and Hasidism where a prayer pronounced with d. influences the upper worlds – the *sephirot*. According to kabbalists, *kavvanah* in prayer is produced by various combinations of the letters of the Tetragammaton, as described at length in the teachings of R Isaac Lurie and his pupil, R Hayyim Vital. The adage "prayer without d. is like a body without a soul" was often inscribed on the walls of synagogues.

DEVOTIONAL LITERATURE: Apart from the liturgy intended for statutory synagogue services, there is in Jewish literature a great mass of material intended for private devotion. This may be divided into (i) the services for supernumerary prayer-meetings such as became popular especially in Italy from the close of the 16th cent. (e.g. TIKKUN HATZOT): among the most successful compositions of this type is Joseph Jedidiah Carmi's hymn collection *Kenaph Renanim* (Venice, 1626); (ii) private devotions and meditations for various occasions, such as those collected by Nathan Hannover in his *Shaare Zion* (Prague, 1662; frequently republished); (iii) pious writings, intended for personal edification but which attained general popularity, such as Solomon Ibn Gabirol's *Keter Malkhut*, or Jedaiah Bedersi's *Behinat Olam*. Such literature being especially important for women, whose Hebrew knowledge was deficient, many collections were made for their benefit in the vernacular (Yiddish, Ladino), comprising prayers before lighting the Sabbath candles, etc. In recent times, many devotional handbooks have appeared in the various European languages, among the most popular being *Prayers and Meditations* by Hester de Rothschild (1856).

DHU NUWAS (d. 525 CE): Arabian king; the last ruler of the independent Himyarite kingdom. He embraced Judaism under the name Yusuf (Joseph) after ascending the throne (c. 518). An Arabic tradition holds that his subjects also became converts. According to legend, in retaliation for the persecution of Jews in the Byzantine empire, he put to death some Byzantine merchants who came to his kingdom. On the surrender to his forces of the Christian city of Najran (probably in 523), he invited the inhabitants to embrace Judaism and when they refused, executed many of them. He was killed and his kingdom destroyed in a combined attack by Abyssinia and Byzantium.

DIALECTICS see **PILPUL**

DIALECTS, JEWISH: The d. spoken by Jewish groups in different parts of the Diaspora are divided into two main classes: (1) autochthonous (i.e., locally developed) d. of the language of the country or region, e.g. Judeo-Aramaic, Judeo-Arabic, Judeo-Persian, Judeo-German (*Jüdisch-deutsch*), Judeo-Italian, and Judeo-Provençal (of which only traces remain). D. of this kind differ from the vernacular of the regions in which they arose chiefly by reason of the preservation of old forms of speech, the varying admixture of Hebrew words and — in certain regions — of elements borrowed from the language of other communities with which the local Jews came into contact. (2) Languages brought by Jews from one region to another. An instance of this is the Judeo-German (YIDDISH) language spoken among the Jews of Europe and their descendants in other countries. Similarly, Judeo-Spanish (LADINO or, more correctly, Español), is spoken in the Balkans, Asiatic Turkey, and to some extent, in Morocco. Neither Yiddish nor Ladino is homogeneous; both represent a mixture of former local d. brought by Jews migrating from other countries. At the same time, they both display regional variations due, apparently, to the predominance of particular elements or d. in different localities. Apart from Hebrew elements (numerous in Yiddish, fewer in Ladino), both languages contain a large number of words and forms borrowed from the language of the country. A feature common to the d. is a certain carelessness with regard to pronunciation and sentence-structure. This may be attributed to the particular social conditions to which the Jews in the Diaspora were subjected.

DIAMOND, DAVID LEO (1915–): US composer. His works include violin concertos, symphonies, chamber music, ballets, film scores, and choral work (including *Young Joseph* after the book by Thomas Mann).

DIARIES: D. in the modern sense are a recent phenomenon, and none of any importance is known in Jewish literature before Hayyim AZULAI's *Maagal Tov* (1753–78), which records details of his travels while collecting money for the Holy Land. Many d. of 19th cent. Jews are known but not all of them have Jewish significance. Of great importance, however, are the travel-diaries of Sir Moses MONTEFIORE (published only in part) and the d. of Theodor HERZL, giving a day-to-day account of his Zionist activities. Selections from d. of Jews may be found in Leo W. Schwartz' *Memoirs of My People* (1943) and A. Yaari's *Zikhronot Eretz Yisrael* (1947). See AUTOBIOGRAPHIES.

Exile by Samuel Hirschenberg.

DIASPORA: Greek word meaning "dispersion," applied since classical times to the Jewish settlement outside Palestine. The existence of such Jewish groups goes back to the close of the First Temple period. These settlements came to be of great importance at the time of the overthrow of the kingdom of Judah (6th cent. BCE) when large-scale deportations were carried out by the Babylonian conquerors. A large number – perhaps a majority – of the "exiles" did not avail themselves of the subsequent opportunity to return to Palestine. They were later scattered (according to the Book of Esther) throughout the 127 provinces of the Persian Empire. The Elephantine papyri illustrate the vitality of the Jewish colony in Egypt in the 5th cent. BCE. The cultural unification of the entire E Mediterranean area through the conquests of Alexander the Great, as well as the later deportations and colonizing movements, extended the area of Jewish settlement. The groups in Egypt were of major significance and already in the 2nd cent. BCE extended westward into Cyrene. To the N, Jews were to be found all over Syria and Asia Minor, and they penetrated into Greece and even as far as Rome in the same period. Subsequently, the Roman conquest of Palestine brought the Jews into the Latin orbit. The settlements in Italy now became numerous, and others extended in the Roman Imperial period all over Europe – certainly as far west as Spain, into N France and the Rhineland, and all along the coast of N Africa. D. Jewry spoke for the most part Greek and/or Latin; the fullest account of their organization may be found in the works of Salo Baron (in English) and Jean Juster (in French). There remained all this time a strong Jewish settlement in Babylonia (Iraq) which was united, after the rise and conquests of Islam, with the Greco-Roman or Mediterranean D. In the course of the Middle Ages, the D. became strong in N and W Europe, reaching England. The persecutions and expulsions of the later Middle Ages brought its center of gravity to E Europe (Poland, Turkey). The maritime discoveries caused it to move westward again and the Russian persecutions of the late 19th cent. made America one of its greatest centers, besides extending it to Australia, S Africa, etc. The Zionist movement implied a vital change in the attitude toward the D. The Nazi persecutions almost wiped out the D. on the continent of Europe, thus increasing the relative importance of the transoceanic communities. But at the same time, the creation of the state of Israel and the return of $1\frac{1}{2}$ million Jews has changed the conception of the D., now no longer an "exile" (*gola*) but a voluntary decentralization (*tephutzot*).

DIBBUK (Heb. "Adhesion"): In kabbalistic folklore, the soul of a sinner which, after his death, transmigrates into the body of a living person. The *d.* can be expelled by conjuring the Divine name, and such exorcism was practiced in the circle of Isaac Luria and, later, by wonder-workers and Ḥasidic *tzaddikim*. A famous play was written on the subject by S. An-Ski.

DIBON: Ancient city, $12\frac{1}{2}$ m. E of the Dead Sea. It was captured by Sihon, king of the Amorites, from Moab (Num. 21:30). Rebuilt by the tribe of Gad it was nevertheless reckoned among the cities of Reuben (Josh. 13:17). After the death of Ahab, Mesha of Moab captured D. and rebuilt it. A place called D. is also mentioned in the Negev (Neh. 11:25).

DICK, ISAAC MEIR (c. 1807–1893): Yiddish and Hebrew author; lived at Vilna. His early works were written in Hebrew and included *Masekhet Aniyut* ("Tractate Poverty"), a satire on Russian Jewish society in the form of a talmudic parody. Turning to Yiddish, he published hundreds of tales in that language. D. introduced the sentimental story, the historical tale, and the humorous sketch into Yiddish literature. His stories always possess a moral motive and are based on acute observation of Jewish life in E Europe.

DICTIONARIES, BIBLE: Works dealing in alphabetical order with names, things, and ideas of the Bible in the light of archeological and historical research, etc. Their range is indicated by the title of the oldest, *Dictionnaire historique et critique, chronologique, géographique et littéraire de la Bible* (Paris, 1772) by Auguste Calmet, which was soon outdated by Blasius Ugolini's *Thesaurus antiquitatum sacrarum* (Venice, 1744–69). The rapid advance of oriental archeology in the 19th cent. led to the chief modern works of this type: *Encyclopaedia Biblica*, ed. T. K. Cheyne and J.S. Black (London, 1899–1903); *Dictionary of the Bible,* ed. J. Hastings (Edinburgh, 1898–1904); *Dictionnaire de la Bible,* ed. F. Vigoroux (Paris, 1891–1912), brought up to date by the *Supplement*, ed. L. Pirot, since 1928. The various Jewish encyclopedias were *inter alia* also B. d. The first all-Jewish Bible dictionary, as also the most modern, is the *Entziklopedia Mikrait* published since 1950 by Mosad Bialik, Jerusalem (6 vols. by 1975).

DICTIONARIES AND CONCORDANCES, HEB-REW: The first Hebrew dictionary was the *Egron* ("Compilation"), written in 912 by Saadyah Gaon. It gave the words without translation, first in alphabetical order of the first letters, then again in the order of the last letters, so as to help in making rhymes. In a later edition, Saadyah added translations of the words into Arabic. In contrast to most later dictionaries (until modern times), he gave both biblical and post-biblical words. Little of it is preserved, but most of the material has passed into the *Jami al-Alfaz* by the 10th cent. Karaite David ben Abraham Alfasi (ed. by S. L. Skoss, New Haven, 1936–45). About the same time Menahem ben Saruk wrote his *Mahberet* in Spain. There too, Ibn Janah (10th–11th cents.) wrote his *Sepher ha-Shorashim.* The results of the Spanish school are summed up in David Kimhi's *Mikhlol* which was long the standard work. All these deal only with biblical Hebrew. Toward the end of the 11th cent., Nathan ben Jehiel

of Rome treated the Aramaic and Hebrew of the Talmud in his *Arukh*. The only dictionary ever written exclusively on mishnaic Hebrew is by Tanhum Yerushalmi (13th cent.) and is still unpublished. In the Renaissance Period, Elias Levita produced his *Tishbi* which was published by Fagius (Isny, 1541–42) with a Latin version, this being the first Hebrew dictionary in the modern sense. Non-Jewish Hebrew lexicography started with Johannes Buxtorf's *Lexicon Hebraicum* (1607) and *Lexicon Chaldaicum, Talmudicum et Rabbinicum* (1639). Biblical lexicography was placed on a new basis by W. Gesenius whose *Handwörterbuch* (1810–12) is still used in the editions revised by F. Buhl (1915) and Brown, Driver, and Briggs (1906). The classic dictionaries covering mishnaic Hebrew are Jacob Levy's *Neuhebräisches und chaldäisches Wörterbuch* (1876–89) and M. Jastrow's *Dictionary of the Talmud* (1903). The first attempt to include all periods of Hebrew was Eliezer Ben-Yehudah's *Thesaurus Totius Hebraitatis*. Later dictionaries notably those by Y. Grazovsky-Goor (1935–1947), A. Even-Shoshan (1944–52), M. Medan (1954), the Hebrew-English dictionary by M. H. Segal (1946), the English-Hebrew dictionary by Y. Kaufmann (1929), and the "Picture Dictionaries" by D. Ettinger, endeavor to keep pace with the new words being created in Israel. Much lexicographical work has been done through the technical dictionaries of the Academy of Hebrew Language which decided in 1954 to prepare a comprehensive Academic Dictionary, on which work is proceeding.

DIEMENSTEIN, SIMON see **DIMANSTEIN**

DIENCHELELE (Heb. *dayyan kelili* = "general judge"): Name given to the crown rabbi of the Jews of Sicily. The office was organized in 1396 and abolished at the petition of the Jewish communities in 1447.

DIESENDRUCK, TZEVI HIRSCH WOLF (1890–1940): Philosopher. He was born in Galicia, lectured in Jewish philosophy at the Hebrew Univ. 1928–30, and taught at the Hebrew Union College, Cincinnati 1930–40. He wrote philosophical essays and studies, chiefly on the theory of consciousness and morals, and published studies on Maimonides. He also translated several of Plato's dialogues into Hebrew.

DIETARY LAWS: Biblical laws, interpreted in the Oral Law, prohibit certain foods from the diet of Jews. These comprise (a) meat from animals and birds biblically "unclean" or from "clean" animals and birds not ritually slaughtered or found defective in one of their vital organs; and certain parts of the "clean" beasts, such as the *helev* (abdominal fat of the cattle), the sinew of the hip, parts cut from living animals, the blood, and meat from which the blood has not been extracted by the process of salting called *melihah*; (b) meat and milk foods

Examining a chicken for its fitness according to dietary laws. (Painting by Meir de Haan).

intermingled or eaten in proximity; this originates from the biblical prohibition (noted three times) of seething a kid in its mother's milk, interpreted in detail in the Talmud and the codes; (c) fish that have no fins and scales. With the exception of the prohibition of blood (Lev. 17:10–14), no definite reason is given for these prohibitions either in the Bible or in rabbinic literature. Various explanations have, however, been advanced from time to time. The motives, however, of the d. l. have been traditionally interpreted as (1) holiness, as a regulating principle in everyday life; (2) as a means of preventing the Jew from close and intimate association with "heathens"; and (3) as a lesson in self-discipline. Hygienic and folkloristic reasons have also been suggested. Wine known or suspected to have been touched by an idolator is also forbidden for use. These laws are not regarded as binding by Reform Jews.

DIJON: French town. Jewish tombstones found there date from the 10th cent., while documentary records concerning the community survive from the 12th cent. The Jews were expelled in 1306, 1322, and 1394. Alsatian Jews re-established a community after the French Revolution and there is still a small Jewish congregation numbering 1,000 in 1970.

DIMANSTEIN (or DIMENSTEIN), SIMON (1886–1937): Russian communist. Although an ordained rabbi, D. joined the Bolsheviks in 1904. Twice arrested for revolutionary activities, he fled to France in 1913. Returning to Russia after the 1917 revolution, he subsequently became commissar for Jewish affairs, establishing various Yiddish communist newspapers, including EMES. During the civil war, he was commissar for labor in Lithuania and White Russia, later holding high posts as an expert on national minority problems. D. was active in the BIROBIDJAN settlement scheme. He was executed in the Stalinist purges.

DIMONAH: Israel urban center, 19 m. SE of Beersheba. Established in 1955, it is a center for Negev industries and the site of an atomic reactor. Pop. (1974): 26,900.

DIMSHITS, BENJAMIN (1908–): Russian economist. He was USSR minister for the construction of metal and chemical industries 1955–7, first deputy chairman of Gosplan 1959–62. In 1962 he became a deputy premier and head of the economic council of the USSR, and in 1965, chairman of the State Committee for Material and Technical Supply.

DIN: Hebrew for "judgment" (cf. BET DIN). The term is also applied to a law (both secular and religious), a legal decision, or a lawsuit.

DIN TORAH (Heb. "Judgment of the Law"): A hearing taking place according to Jewish law.

DINAH: Daughter of Jacob and Leah. Her rape by Shechem was avenged by her brothers, Simeon and Levi, who annihilated the inhabitants of the town of Shechem (Gen. 34). Some scholars of the critical school believe that this story indicates the beginning of the conquest of Canaan by Israelite tribes.

DINESOHN, JACOB (1856–1919): Yiddish novelist. Under the influence of Haskalah, he began his literary career in the Hebrew press but turned to Yiddish, his first novel being confiscated by the Russian censor (1877). He then wrote *Der Shvartzer Yungermanchik* ("The Dark Young Man") which attained wide success. In 1885, he settled in Warsaw and published a series of sentimental novels. During World War I, D. devoted himself to establishing orphanages and Yiddish schools.

DINUR (formerly **DINABURG**), **BEN ZION** (1884–1973): Israel historian and statesman. Born in the Ukraine, he settled in Palestine in 1921, teaching at (and later directing) the Teachers' Seminary at Bet ha-Kerem, Jerusalem. From 1936, he lectured at the Hebrew Univ., becoming professor of Jewish history in 1947. D. was elected to the first Knesset (1949–51) as a *Mapai* delegate and in 1951–5, was minister of education and culture. D. has written extensively on aspects of Jewish and Zionist history and edited the Jewish historical quarterly *Zion*.

*DIO CASSIUS (Cassius Dio Cocceianus; c. 150–235): Roman historian. His narrative of the Jewish war of 66–70 complements Josephus' description; he also describes the Jewish risings against Trajan and Hadrian for which he is the most important source. His approach is reasonably objective; anti-Jewish touches may have been introduced by the writer of the abridgment, in which form his work has been partly preserved.

DISABILITIES: The conception of Jewish d. did not arise until the 18th cent., as before that date (except in the Roman Empire) the rights accorded to Jews were limited and they had no political pretensions or expectations. Only after their emergence from the ghetto were they able to aspire to rights from which they were excluded. The constitution of the US (1787) expressly laid down that no political d. should be imposed on any person because of his

Ben Zion Dinur.

religious beliefs. The French Revolution admitted Jews to full equality for the first time in Europe, although Napoleon reimposed certain d. in 1807. In most parts of Europe, d. prevailed until late in the 19th cent. They ranged from extreme severity in parts of Germany, Italy, and especially Russia, to relatively slight d. (confined in the end to exclusion from parliament) in England. Some parts of Germany were more retrograde than others and the removal of d. was piecemeal, becoming final in 1871. In Italy, the process was on the whole more dramatic, the unification of the various regions into the kingdom of Italy during the 19th cent. bringing about automatically the emancipation of the Jews from a condition of inferiority. The same was the case in Russia at the time of the 1917 Revolution. In the 20th cent., the reimposition of d. in Germany in 1933 proved the prelude to the cancellation of personal as well as political rights and eventually to the Nazi policy of extermination. The Jews still suffer from some d. in certain Moslem areas (N Africa, etc.). Recent experiences have, however, shown that the removal of d. does not necessarily involve the achievement of equality of opportunity. See also EMANCIPATION.

DISCIPLINE SCROLL (or "Manual of Discipline"; Heb. *Serekh ha-Yaḥad*): One of the DEAD SEA SCROLLS describing the organization and some of the beliefs of the Dead Sea sect.

DISCRIMINATION: Unfair distinction based on race, religion, color, and national origin. While still practiced in the US in the fields of employment, housing, education (see NUMERUS CLAUSUS), and hotel accommodation, it is being steadily reduced as a result of legislation and education. 11 states have enacted effective legal safeguards against employment d. directed against Jews and other religious minorities or racial groups. The President's Committee on Government Contracts is charged with the responsibility of enforcing a provision in government contracts against employment d. Much progress has been achieved in the elimination of d. by the educational work of the ANTI-DEFAMATION LEAGUE of B'nai B'rith and similar community relations organizations. An increasing number of US colleges have dropped from their application forms questions seeking information with respect to religion.

DISKIN, YEHOSHUA LEIB (1818–1898): Religious leader. Born in Grodno, he was rabbi in various Russian cities, and opposed the civil authorities on questions of religious principle, being persecuted for his attitude. In consequence, he settled in Jerusalem (1877) where he founded an orphanage and the *Ohel Mosheh* yeshivah.

DISPENSATION: Action by competent authority to allow certain rules to be relaxed or abolished in order to modify the hardships which would arise from a strict application of the law. In Jewish rabbinic practice, d. is called "giving a *heter* (i.e., 'permission')" and is generally limited to laws having only rabbinic validity or arising from custom. Thus, the Israel chief rabbinate has found ways to permit agriculture during the Sabbatical year, since its observance today is considered to have only rabbinic stringency. Similarly, rabbis have permitted the eating of lentils and rice on the Passover holiday during years of hardship. Among Ashkenazim, the "dispensation of a 100 rabbis" permits a man to marry a second wife in certain cases where the first cannot be divorced. However, legal devices have been resorted to upon occasion even in matters of biblical compulsion. Most famous of these is Hillel's introduction of the PROSBUL to permit the collection of debts even after the Sabbatical year.

DISPLACED PERSONS: Term introduced during World War II when, in an unparalleled operation, millions were forcibly removed from their homes by the Nazis, many being deported from their countries to other lands under Nazi occupation for serf-labor. By the end of the War, it was estimated that one-tenth of the population of Europe was displaced. When Germany was occupied by the Allies, 14 million foreign subjects were living there in desperate conditions. It was a primary function of the first United Nations specialized agency, the Relief and Rehabilitation Administration (UNRRA), to assist their repatriation. That work was executed in 1945-7 with the help of the Allied military forces. Those who could not be repatriated received assistance to establish themselves elsewhere. The Jewish D. P.'s, survivors of the concentration and labor camps, for the most part did not want to return to their former homes. They were treated on the same terms as REFUGEES who had fled from their countries because of political or religious persecution and were resettled by the INTERNATIONAL REFUGEE ORGANIZATION (IRO) which in 1947 replaced UNRRA. The resettlement was carried out with the help of the Jewish Agency for Palestine and the American Joint Distribution Committee. A fund of about $8,000,000 from the non-monetary gold seized in Germany was applied to this purpose. Between 1948 and 1950, the bulk of the 450,000 Jews in the D. P. camps emigrated from Europe. The majority went to Israel, and about 80,000 were admitted to the US under the Displaced Persons Act of Congress which permitted an exceptional immigration of 400,000 persons. D. P.'s enjoy in their new homes the benefit of the international conventions on the status of refugees. By the 1950's, most of the D. P.'s in Europe (Poles, Balts, etc.) had emigrated or been integrated into the economies of the European countries.

DISPUTATIONS: Organized verbal arguments between adherents of different religions. These are to be found in Jewish history from a very early date. They were common in hellenistic Alexandria, and there are reports in the Talmud and Midrash of those conducted against "philosophers" and pagan protagonists. They attained a different character with the growth of Christianity as a missionary religion, and henceforth there are many records of them. One of the earliest instances is the Dialogue of Justin Martyr (d. 165) with "Tryphon the Jew." This was the forerunner of an entire literature, generally centered upon the same subjects of argument – the Virgin Birth, the nature of the messianic prophecies and their fulfillment, and the divinity of Jesus. The title "d." is, however, generally applied

Disputation between a Christian and a Jew. (From a Dresden ms of the "Sachsenspiegel").

to religious discussions in which Jews were compelled to defend their religion against Christian protagonists in the presence of secular authorities. The Jews inevitably were on the defensive and unable to put forward their counter-arguments freely. Such a disputation is said to have taken place in Rome in 314 between Pope Sylvester I and the Jew Zambri in the presence of the emperor. The disputation became a regular feature of Jewish history in the Middle Ages. The earliest formal instance was in 1240, when Jehiel of Paris, Moses of Coucy, and other rabbis were compelled to defend the Talmud against the accusations of the apostate, Nicholas Donin, in the presence of members of the royal court, including the queen mother, Blanche of Castile. The result of this was the burning of the Talmud in Paris, after its formal condemnation, in 1242. In 1263, a disputation took place at Barcelona in the presence of King James I of Aragon between Moses ben Naḥman (Naḥmanides) and the apostate Pablo Christiani, backed by the Dominican, Raymon de Peñaforte and other Christian scholars: in the sequel, the Jewish protagonist had to seek safety in exile in Palestine. The most elaborate of the medieval d. was held at Tortosa in 1413–4, under the auspices of the anti-pope Benedict XIII, between his physician Mestre Geronimo de Santa Fé (formerly Joshua Lorki) and a group of Jewish scholars including Joseph Albo and Astruc Levi of Alcañiz, in the presence of the entire papal curia; it was hoped that this would secure a great moral triumph in the eyes of the Christian world by bringing about mass baptism. John of Capistrano, the Dominican zealot, forced a religious disputation on the Jews of Rome in 1450. Other d. of a less formal nature took place between Abraham Farrisol and some monks at the court of Ferrara in 1503–4, between Gumprecht Levi and a certain apostate at the court of Hanover in 1704, etc. In June 1757 and July 1759, two d. in the medieval spirit took place under Church auspices in Poland, at Kemieniec-Podolsk and Lvov between the representatives of rabbinic Judaism and the Frankists who rejected the Talmud in favor of the Zohar. Records of d. have been collected by the Christian Hebraist J. C. Wagenseil in his *Tela Ignea Satanae* (Altdorf, 1681) and J.D. Eisenstein in his *Otzar Vikkuḥim* ("Thesaurus of Disputations"; New York, 1928). Religious d. between Jews and Moslem protagonists were less formal.

DISRAELI, BENJAMIN see **BEACONSFIELD, EARL OF**

D'ISRAELI, ISAAC see **ISRAELI, ISAAC D'**

DISSECTION see **ANATOMY**

DIVINATION: The universal human desire to penetrate the future and thereby to gain greater security gave rise to techniques and methods supposedly serving this end. The large and apparently specialized d. terminology known to the Bible (cf. Lev. 19:26, 31; Deut. 18:10–11) shows that these practices were highly developed and widely spread. Some were local Palestinian (i.e., Canaanite) while others were of Babylonian origin (cf. Ezek. 21:26). All forms of d., augury, soothsaying, charming, and conjuring the spirits of the dead (cf. I Samuel 6:2; 15:23) are strictly prohibited by the Bible, though in practice they were not wholly eradicated. PROPHECY and prophetic dreams were considered the Divinely-approved alternatives to pagan soothsaying (cf. Deut. 18:13ff; 13:2; I Sam. 28:6). The URIM AND THUMMIM (cf. Exod. 28:30 and I Sam. 28:6) and the EPHOD (cf. I Sam. 23:6 ff) are instances of oracular practice condoned in Israel. Talmudic, rabbinic, and kabbalistic texts confirm the folklorists' opinion that belief in oracles and omens flourished in all these periods and that various forms of d. were pursued in spite of official discouragement and disapproval.

DIVINE SERVICE see **PRAYER**

DIVORCE: The act of dissolution of the marriage-tie between husband and wife is effected in Jewish law by a bill of divorcement termed *sepher keritut* in the Pentateuch (Deut. 24:3) or *get* in the Talmud. This bill, which the husband writes or orders to be written expressly for the purpose, is handed by him to his wife together with a formal declaration in the presence of witnesses. Although the Torah granted the husband the right to divorce his wife, this privilege cannot be exercised arbitrarily. A husband cannot summarily send his wife away by word of mouth or in any other similar fashion. Marriage cannot be dissolved except by a formal and judicial bill of divorcement which requires the sanction of a court and involves stringent and protracted proceedings, the consequent delay affording an opportunity for reflection and reconciliation. The fulfillment of the conditions stipulated in the *ketubbah* or marriage contract also tends to render d. infrequent. The grounds on which the pentateuchal law permits d. are termed the finding of an "unseemly thing" in the woman (Deut. 24:1). This cryptic phrase was diversely interpreted by talmudic authorities. According to the School of Shammai, it means "a thing of indecency"; hence marriage could be dissolved only on grounds of unchastity on the part of the wife. The School of Hillel interpreted it to mean "anything unseemly," i.e., anything that may involve the disruption of domestic harmony. (The question is discussed at length in the talmudic tractate *Gittin* which deals with questions of d.). Barrenness on the part of the wife was accepted as sufficient reason for d. Though in theory the power of d. is vested in the husband, in many cases his power was considerably restricted. In such circumstances as apostasy, leprosy, misbehavior, dishonest occupation, or even uncontrollable temper the husband can be compelled to grant a *get* (*Ketubbot* 76*a*). This, however, can only apply where rabbinic courts have legal power to enforce their decisions. Jewish d.-laws have in the course of the ages developed in the direction of greater equality between husband and wife. As early as 1000 CE., R Gershom decreed that a man may not divorce his wife without her consent. Maimonides in his code (*Ishut* 13:3) extends the woman's rights still further: "if the husband debars his wife from participating in certain joyous functions, she may sue for and be granted a d." Again, if she pleads that her husband is repulsive to her and that she cannot cohabit with him, the husband is forced to divorce her, because, as Maimonides maintains, "she is not like a captive woman who is compelled to consort with a man against her will." In occidental countries, both the civil and religious laws of d. are strictly safeguarded, and, as in the case of civil marriage, civil d. can be recognized by Jewish law only when it is supplemented by d. according to religious procedure. Thus, while religious courts insist on civil d. prior to annulment by *get*, a civil annulment of marriage without a religious dissolution is not regarded as valid for the purpose of remarriage. In Israel, d. among Jews is possible only under rabbinic auspices. Judaism generally looked upon d. as a calamitous necessity. The prophet Malachi condemns the practice (Mal. 2:13–16), while the rabbis say "for him who divorces his first wife the very altar sheds tears" (*Sanhedrin* 22*a*). The rabbis were bidden to exhaust every possible expedient to further the integrity of the Jewish family and endeavor to adjust any misunderstanding that might arise. In the US, a revised *ketubbah* was instituted in 1953 by the Conservative Movement. Under its terms, both husband and wife agree before marriage to present domestic difficulties to a National Bet Din before resorting to d. action. The innovation was opposed by the Orthodox on legal grounds.

DIVRE HA-YAMIM see **CHRONICLES**

DIZENGOFF, MEIR (1861–1936): Zionist leader and first mayor of Tel Aviv. Born in Bessarabia, he joined the *Hibbat Zion* movement in his youth. After living for a time in Palestine, he managed a glass factory in Odessa 1897–1905. He founded the *Geulah* company to buy land for settlement in Palestine (1904) and returned there the following year. D. joined the *Ahuzat Bayit* Society which was responsible for the foundation of Tel Aviv in 1906. He laid the cornerstone of the future city in 1909, and was henceforth intimately associated with its development. During World War I, D. was expelled by the Turkish authorities. From 1921 until his death (except from 1925–8), D. was mayor of Tel Aviv and played a leading part in the city's life,

Meir Dizengoff.

founding a number of economic concerns and cultural institutions, including the museum.

DJERBA see **JERBA**

DNEPROPETROVSK (formerly **YEKATERINOSLAV**): City in the Ukraine, USSR. Jews have lived there since the end of the 18th cent. It was the scene of several pogroms between 1883 and 1905, and during the Civil War (1919–20). Its Jewish population, at one time nearly half of the total, rose to about 100,000 in 1940, but was severely reduced during the Nazi invasion. In 1970, 69,287 Jews lived in D. drovince.

DÖBLIN, ALFRED (1878–1956): German author. A physician by profession, he left Germany in 1933, settling in the US in 1940, and returning to Germany in 1945. In his books, he attacked the ossification of ethical and religious values and called for social reforms. At the end of World War I, D. severed his contacts with Judaism, but regained interest in Jewish affairs after a visit to Poland and Lithuania (1925). Following Hitler's rise to power, he wrote *Jüdische Erneuerung* and *Flucht und Sammlung des Judenvolkes*. He then became a Catholic, and subsequent writings bear the imprint of his conversion.

DOEG THE EDOMITE: Saul's chief herdsman who betrayed David when he took shelter at Nob with the priest, Ahimelech. When Saul ordered his followers to punish Ahimelech, only D. obeyed, killing him and 84 other priests (I Sam. 22).

DOGMA: A formulation of faith to which all members of a religious group are required to adhere. Abstract d.'s are not in harmony with the essential nature of Judaism, and it was not until Judaism came into contact with Greek thought that such formulations were attempted. Even here, their main purpose was to serve as a protective barrier against antagonistic theological systems. Philo was the first to lay down articles of faith; Karaism and Mohammedan polemics brought forth new formulations of Jewish d. by Saadyah, R Hananel, and others. Maimonides' famous version was influenced by Arab scholasticism, dominant in his day. Similarly, the complicated and elaborate system of d. worked out by Albo met the challenge of Christian doctrine. The Mishnah and Talmud contain occasional discussions of what may be called d., but these are secondary to both the content and spirit of the Talmud where the chief emphasis is on the practice of Judaism. See also CREED.

*DOHM, CHRISTIAN WILHELM VON (1751–1820): German writer and champion of Jewish Emancipation. He was archivist at the government archives in Berlin. At the request of his friend, Moses Mendelssohn (who had been approached by the communities of Alsace), D. wrote *Uber die bürgerliche Verbesserung der Juden* ("Concerning the Civil Improvement of the Jews," 1781–3), in which he maintained that the inferior status of the Jews in Europe was due to Christian prejudices, and urged that they be given general equality of rights. This was the first specific plea for Jewish Emancipation and aroused great interest in its day.

DOLITZKI, MENAHEM MENDEL (1856–1931): Hebrew and Yiddish poet and writer. He lived in Moscow 1882–92, and subsequently in the US where he edited the Yiddish monthly, *Die Zeit*. His early Hebrew poems expressed Zionist sentiments.

DOME OF THE ROCK see **OMAR, MOSQUE OF**

DOMINICAN REPUBLIC (Santo Domingo): Jews, at first W Indian Sephardim, later from European countries, began immigrating in the latter 19th cent. As a result of the EVIAN CONFERENCE, a colony of over 1,000 European Jewish refugees was established in Sosua, but most of them emigrated after World War II, and only 200 remain. D. R. in 1938 announced its willingness to admit 100,000 Jewish refugees but the project made little progress. Jewish pop. (1973): 110, in Santo Domingo, Sosua and a few elsewhere. The Parroquia Israelita is the central Jewish body. There are two synagogues, one in Santo Domingo and one in Sosua.

DOMINICANS: Religious order founded by St. Dominic in 1215 to protect the Christian faith against attack. Later, it commenced activities against the Jews. The "preaching friars" were thus especially associated with conversionist sermons, the censorship of Hebrew books. disputations, the Inquisition, and similar activities of the Catholic Church in the Middle Ages and after. The deterioration in the position of the Jews in Europe from the 13th cent. onward was largely due to the constant propaganda and activity of the D. Their rivals, the Franciscans (founded by St. Francis of Assisi in 1209), worked mainly among the poor, came into less contact with the Jews, yet were principally responsible for the reaction against the Jewish loan-bankers in Italy in the 15th cent.

DOMUS CONVERSORUM (Lat. "House of converts"): Name given to the hostel for converted Jews established by Henry III in London in 1232. In 1280, the number of inmates was 96. After the expulsion of the Jews from England (1290), the institution continued its work, receiving mainly apostates who went to England to enjoy its benefits. 51 persons are known to have been admitted after 1290, the last being in 1606. Thereafter the institution ceased to function, though surviving in name until the 19th cent.

DONIN, NICHOLAS (fl. 13th cent.): French apostate. Excommunicated for Karaite leanings by R Jehiel of Paris, he eventually became baptized. He participated in the persecution of French Jews in 1236 and, three years later, denounced the Talmud to Pope Gregory IX who ordered an investigation. In 1240, a disputation on its character took place in Paris between D. and four rabbis (including R Jehiel), as a result of which the Talmud was condemned and 24 cartloads of Hebrew mss were burned.

DÖNMEH: (Turkish: "Apostates"): Judeo-Moslem sect derived from the followers of SHABBETAI TZEVI. These followed him into ostensible Islam while still retaining many Jewish observances and their belief in him as messiah. They were accused of antinomian tendencies and sexual orgies. Ultimately, the sect was divided into two or more groups, their main center being Salonica. Some of the D. (e.g. Djavid Bey, 1875–1926, repeatedly minister of finance) took a leading part in the Young Turk revolution of 1909. Outwardly Turkish Moslems, they were uprooted from Salonica in the course of the interchanges of population between Turkey and Greece in 1923. Though still forming recognizable groups in Constantinople, Izmir, etc., they now have no established center. Their liturgies in Judeo-Spanish, centering upon the messiahship of Shabbetai Tzevi, were long kept in profound secrecy, but have recently been brought to light and partly published. These show the D. to have been much closer to Jewish tradition than was previously imagined.

DONNOLO, SHABBETAI (913–c. 984): Physician. Born in Oria (S Italy), he was taken prisoner in a Saracen raid and then traveled widely to study. He later achieved a considerable reputation as a medical authority, serving as personal physician to the Byzantine governor in Calabria and to Church dignitaries. D., who also composed a commentary on the *Sepher Yetzirah*, was the first medical writer in post-classical Europe.

DOR: Israel smallholder settlement (TM) on the Carmel coast; founded in 1949 by recent immigrants from Greece. Their economy is based on mixed

Coins from Dor, 111 CE.

farming and sea fishing. In the second millennium BCE, the site was a Phoenician harbor, passing under Israelite rule in the period of David and Solomon, and captured by the Assyrians in 732 BCE. The city then returned to the Phoenicians and was generally independent thereafter. It was a bishopric in the 7th cent. CE. Many remains dating from the Late Bronze to the Crusader Period have been found. Pop. (1974): 174.

DORI (DOSTROVSKI), YAAKOV (1899–1973): Israel soldier. Originally a building engineer, he was one of the heads of the *Haganah* organization from 1929 and, from 1938, chief of its general staff. During the War of Independence, D. was chief of the general staff of the Israel armed forces. He was president of the Institute of Technology (the Technion) in Haifa 1951–65.

DORMIDO, DAVID ABRAVANEL (formerly Manuel Martinez D.; d. 1667): Pioneer of Jewish settlement in England. He was born in Portugal, settled in Brazil and – on its conquest by the Por-

Yaakov Dori.

tuguese – in London. Here in Nov. 1654, he petitioned for assistance in recovering his lost property and for the authorization of Jewish settlement. This was one of the preliminaries to the establishment of the London Jewish community of which D. was an early warden.

D'ORTA, GARCIA see **ORTA, GARCIA D'**

DORTMUND: German town. Jews are first known there c. 1235. During the Black Death (1349), the community was destroyed, those not murdered being expelled. Settlement was soon resumed and continued until an expulsion in 1596. The community was reconstituted in the mid-18th cent. and numbered 4,000 before its destruction by the Nazis. Jewish pop. (1970): 350.

DOSA BEN SAADYAH (c. 930–1017): Babylonian scholar. As his father, Saadyah Gaon, died when D. was a child, he did not succeed him and was only appointed gaon of Sura when over 80 years old (1013). He wrote responsa, philosophical works, and a life of his father.

DOSITHEUS (Dostai; fl. c. beginning of the Common Era): Samaritan pseudo-messiah and founder of a sect which, in certain respects, resembled Judaism. The sect was never numerous and eventually disappeared.

DOSTAI see **DOSITHEUS**

DOTHAN: Ancient Palestinian city in the mountains of Ephraim. It is mentioned in the story of the selling of Joseph (Gen. 37:17). It is associated with the story of Elisha (II Kings 6:13–14) and often mentioned in the Book of Judith.

DOV BER OF MEZHIRICH ("The *Maggid* of Mezhirich"; c. 1710–1772): Ḥasidic leader. Originally an austere *maggid* (folk preacher), he fell under the influence of Israel Baal Shem Tov and became his most influential disciple. After the Baal Shem Tov's death (1760), D. B. became the leader of the Ḥasidim and the center of the movement was accordingly transferred from Medzibozh to his residence at Mezhirich. He attracted scholars, rabbis, and kabbalists – in addition to the masses – and almost all Ḥasidic leaders of the next generation were his disciples. He was responsible for the growth of Ḥasidism in the Ukraine, Lithuania, and Galicia, sending preachers round the various communities to spread his doctrines. D. B. wrote no books, but his teachings were collected and published by his disciple, R Solomon of Lutsk. The central role of the *tzaddik* in Ḥasidism and his function as a mediator between man and God is largely due to D. B.'s teaching.

DOWRY: The marriage portion (*nedunya*) brought by the bride to her husband. The Bible mentions gifts brought by the husband to the bride (cf. the Arabic *mohar*) and also by the wife to the husband. The practice of giving a d. was well-established in talmudic times, Jewish law even specifying the amount a daughter could claim from her deceased father's inheritance at the time of her marriage. The d. was recorded in the marriage-contract and reverted to the wife upon divorce or the death of the husband.

DRACH, DAVID PAUL (1791–1865): Scholar. Born at Strasbourg, he was baptized in 1823, and in 1827, became librarian of the Papal Propaganda at Rome. Before his conversion, D. edited the Passover Haggadah, and later wrote on Samaritan and Aramaic, as well as missionary material.

DRACHMAN, BERNARD (1861–1945): US rabbi. A leading exponent of Orthodoxy, D. was a founder of the Jewish Theological Seminary, New York (1886), where he was professor of Bible and codes 1887–1908. He established (1905) and headed the Jewish Sabbath Alliance, of America, and was president (1908–20) of the Union of Orthodox Jewish Congregations.

DRAMA see **THEATER**

DREAM: Like other ancient peoples, the Hebrews attached prophetic importance to d.'s which were regarded as Divinely-inspired and often conveying a message of national significance. Joseph and Daniel were noted for their power of interpreting d.'s. Varying views are presented in the Talmud, ranging from the prophetic view to the psychological explanation that "a d. is a reflection of the heart" (*Berakhot* 55*b*). The rabbis regarded a bad d. as preferable to a good one since it puts fear into the heart and leads to repentance. It became customary to fast after a troubled d. (*taanit ḥalom*—"dream-fast"), and a fast of this nature was observed even on the Sabbath. A special prayer was also recited after a bad d. In modern times, Jewish psychologists, notably Sigmund FREUD, have taken a leading part in the psychological interpretation of d.'s.

DREIDEL (or *trendel*): Top, bearing the initials of the Hebrew phrase "A great miracle happened there" (in Israel, "here" for "there"). It is spun in a traditional *Hanukkah* game.

Community seal, Dresden.

DRESDEN: E German city. Jews are first mentioned as resident in 1375 and were expelled in 1448 on charges of counterfeiting coins and sympathizing with the Hussites. From the 18th cent., they lived in the Altstadt district despite the opposition of the townspeople. The community was officially recognized in 1837, and a synagogue consecrated in 1840. Later in the 19th cent., the community was augmented by arrivals from Austria-Hungary, Poland, and Russia. The Jewish population in 1930 was 5,500 but was destroyed by the Nazis. A small community was reorganized after World War II numbering 100 in 1970.

DRESS see **COSTUME**

Statue of Alfred Dreyfus.

DREYFUS, ALFRED (1859–1935): French soldier. A brilliant and efficient captain on the French general staff, he was accused – partly from motives of anti-Semitism – of having sold secret documents to Germany and in 1894, was condemned to life imprisonment, the verdict being influenced by invalid documents which had not been communicated to the defense. D. protested his innocence both at his public degradation in Paris and from his cell in

Dropsie College, Philadelphia.

Devil's Island, off the coast of French Guiana, but the campaign demanding a revision of the sentence, instigated by his brother Mathieu and the publicist, Bernard Lazare, initially met a series of rebuffs. The real traitor, ESTERHAZY, was acquitted by a further tribunal (1898). Emile ZOLA, in his famous article *J'accuse* published in CLEMENCEAU'S paper *L'Aurore*, attacked the judgments of both tribunals but was himself sentenced to prison for defamation. The same year, however, the French officer, Colonel Henry, was forced to admit that he had forged a document to implicate D. and committed suicide under arrest. A retrial of D. took place in 1899 at Rennes in an atmosphere verging on civil war. A verdict of guilty was again returned, but on this occasion, it was not unanimous and extenuating circumstances were admitted. D. was pardoned by President Loubet, and eventually the Court of Cassation pronounced him completely innocent (1906). The "Dreyfus Affair" stirred and divided all France; the Catholic clergy, the military, and the right-wing refused to recognize a miscarriage of justice which would lower the prestige of the army, and did not hesitate to exploit anti-Semitism to buttress their position. The "Dreyfus Affair" contributed to the separation of the Church and the State of France (1905), the rise of the Socialist Party, and – by its influence on Herzl – to the development of Zionism. D. himself was rehabilitated and resumed his career in the army, retiring with the rank of lieutenant-colonel.

DREYFUS, FERDINAND-CAMILLE (1851–1905): French journalist. He was founder of the liberal newspaper *La Nation*, general secretary of *La Grande Encyclopédie*, and was twice elected to the Chamber of Deputies (1885, 1889). D. engaged in several duels with anti-Semites, being seriously wounded by E. DRUMONT.

DRINK OFFERING: Wine offering added to every sacrifice in the Temple. The quantities varied from a fourth part of a *hin* of wine for a lamb, to a third part for a ram, and a half part for a bullock (Num. 15:5–9).

*DRIVER, SAMUEL ROLLES (1846–1914): English Hebraist and professor of Hebrew at Oxford. His works included a revolutionary monograph on the Hebrew tenses, commentaries on various biblical books (especially Samuel), and collaboration (with F. Brown and C. A. Briggs) in the revised edition of Gesenius' Hebrew Dictionary. His son, *SIR GODFREY ROLLES D.* (1892–1975), professor of Semitic philology at Oxford, wrote widely on subjects connected with the Hebrew language, and took part in the investigation of the DEAD SEA SCROLLS.

DROHOBYCZ: Former Polish town, now in the USSR Ukrainian Republic. Jewish settlement was prohibited until 1635, but by the beginning of the 18th cent., the entire trade of the town was in Jewish hands. After the discovery of petroleum wells nearby in the 1840's, the Jews of D. controlled the industry, and thousands of them worked in the oil fields. Before World War II, the Jewish population numbered c. 15,000, about 40% of the total. D. was the scene of a massacre by the Nazis in Aug. 1941. The Jewish labor camp in the oil fields was liquidated in 1944.

DROPSIE UNIVERSITY (formerly **College for Hebrew and Cognate Learning**): Philadelphia institution in branches of Jewish studies and Semitic

Israel Druze.

studies. It was established through the will of Moses Aaron Dropsie (1821–1905), a Philadelphia lawyer, son of a Jewish father and a Christian mother, who adopted Judaism at the age of 14 and remained a devout Jew. A charter was obtained in 1907 and the college opened in 1909 with two major departments, Bible and rabbinics, to which the department of Hebrew and cognate languages was added shortly afterward. A department of history was established in 1913. The first president was Cyrus Adler (1909—40), succeeded in 1941 by Abraham A. Neuman and in 1967 by Abraham Katsh. After World War II, the College was expanded, and additional departments included Jewish philosophy, Hebrew language and literature, history of Semitic civilization, comparative religion, and two subordinate schools, – the school of education (1945) and the institute for Israel and the Middle East (1948). About a third of the student body is non-Jewish. The official organ of the College is the JEWISH QUARTERLY REVIEW. The College is sponsoring a new edition and translation of the Apocrypha and Pseudepigrapha. Its library consists of about 68,000 volumes. The College conducts an extension department in New York City; also a summer session during the months of June and July.

*DRUMONT, EDOUARD-ADOLPHE (1844–1917): French anti-Semite. After publishing various historical books, he issued the violently anti-Jewish *La France Juive* in 1886. This work, which had a vast circulation, led to strong protests and a series of duels and contributed to the growth of anti-Semitism in France which culminated in the Dreyfus Case. D. continued to write against the Jews both in books and in the journal, *La Libre Parole* which he founded in 1892.

DRUYANOW, ALTER (1870–1938): Hebrew author. An early member of the *Ḥibbat Zion* movement, and secretary of its Odessa committee 1890–1905, he lived in Palestine 1906–9, 1923–38. D. was one of the leading Hebrew journalists of his time, edited the Zionist organ *Ha-Olam* 1909–14, and wrote a 3-volume history of *Ḥibbat Zion*. His interest in folklore led him to publish in Hebrew a collection of over 3,000 Jewish jokes (*Sepher ha-Bediḥah veha-Ḥiddud*, 3 vols., 1932–5).

DRUZE: Religious sect deriving from Islam with members in Syria, the Lebanon, and Israel. Benjamin of Tudela (c. 1170) was one of the first Europeans to describe the D. and their religion to the western world. Out of a total of 200,000 (plus 20,000 who migrated overseas), 38,000 live in Israel and are concentrated in 18 villages in W Galilee and on Mt. Carmel. The D. cooperated with the Israel forces during and since the War of Independence and D. representatives sit in the Knesset. They have their own religious courts which administer Druze religious law.

DUALISM: (1) The doctrine of a cosmic struggle between the powers of GOOD AND EVIL in the world, taught in the ancient religion of Persia and later by the gnostics. Even in biblical times, this teaching was opposed by the prophets who insisted that God alone is the source of light and darkness, good and evil (Is. 45:7). The talmudic teachers, equally zealous for the monotheistic principle, condemned those who recognized *shete reshuyyot* (two divine powers). From time to time, dualistic trends affected Jewish thinkers. Such books as Jubilees and the Testaments of the Twelve Patriarchs depict a demonic being (Mastema, Beliar) who stands in opposition to God; no doubt this was one reason why these books were rejected by the leaders of Judaism. In rabbinic literature, Satan is not a devil in rebellion against God but an agent of Divine justice whose task is to accuse and punish sinners. In some kabbalistic works, notably the Zohar, there is a revival of dualistic thinking; but the effort was made to reconcile such notions with MONOTHEISM by the assumption that the forces of evil emerge through the inscrutable will of the supreme Deity. (2) The doctrine of a radical difference and opposition between matter and spirit, body and soul. This philosophical d. stems from Greek thought, chiefly that of Plato and his later interpreters. Its logical outcome is ASCETICISM. This type of d. exerted considerable influence on Philo and, in its Christian and Moslem versions, left an imprint on medieval Jewish thought and life. The ethical and religious teaching of the Bible implies the primacy of spiritual values over materialistic self-seeking and self-indulgence; but this does not mean a contempt for the body as the "prisonhouse" of the soul and the source of evil. The talmudic rabbis insist that the physical universe, as God's creation, is good, and that its beauties and pleasures must be gratefully enjoyed. Though the Evil Inclination is sometimes equated with the sexual impulse, the rabbis insist that the evil inclination is not wholly bad and must be disciplined to the service of God. Marriage is a religious duty, and celibacy is condemned as sinful.

DUBINSKY, DAVID (1892–): US labor leader. Born in Poland, he went to the US in 1911. D. has been president of the International Ladies' Garment Workers' Union since 1932 and vice-president of the American Federation of Labor 1934–6, and since 1945. An outstanding leader of of Jewish labor movement, D. has pioneered in programs for industrial stability and labor education.

He was one of the founders of the American Labor Party in New York State (1936) but broke away (1944) to found the Liberal Party after communist elements took over the A.L.P. He was co-founder of the Jewish Labor Committee.

DUBLIN: Capital of the republic of Ireland. There are vague indications that Jews lived there in the Middle Ages. Some ex-Marranos settled in D. in the middle of the 17th cent., and a Sephardi community, afterwards augmented and ultimately absorbed by Ashkenazim, was later organized. The community was temporarily dissolved in 1791 but was revived in 1822 and, after 1880, was greatly reinforced by immigrants from E Europe. The Jewish pop. (1973) is 3,600, with 6 Orthodox synagogues and one Reform, a chief rabbinate, a Jewish Representative Council etc.

DUBNO: Polish town. A Jewish center from 1532, it was a seat of Jewish scholars and sent representatives to the Council of the Four Lands. Its communal register from 1700–1815 has been preserved and contains valuable historical information. Before World War II, half its total population of 10,000 was Jewish. Its Jews were massacred by the Nazis in Oct. 1942.

DUBNO, SOLOMON (1738–1813): Bible commentator, masoretic scholar, and Hebrew poet. He was born at Dubno, and pursued advanced studies at Amsterdam (1767–71) before moving to Berlin where he taught Hebrew to the son of Moses

David Dubinsky.

Simon Dubnow.

Mendelssohn. D. inspired Mendelssohn to publish the Pentateuch with its German translation in Hebrew type and undertook to add a Hebrew commentary. He later ceased his collaboration with Mendelssohn, only his commentaries on Genesis and part of Exodus appearing, and left Berlin in 1781 for Vilna. He died at Amsterdam.

DUBNOW, SIMON (1860–1941): Historian. Born in White Russia, he worked in St. Petersburg 1880–4 and 1906–22, Odessa 1890–1903, Vilna 1903–6, Berlin 1922–33, and Riga 1933–41. D. wrote a universal history of the Jewish people in 10 vols. which appeared in Russian, Hebrew, etc. In this, he attempted, in opposition to Graetz, to emphasize social as against intellectual factors and to give proper stress to E European developments. His researches into Jewish history in Russia, Poland, and Lithuania were of major importance, while his historical method marked a turning-point in Jewish historiography due to its sociological conception of Jewish history in the Diaspora. He distinguishes one period from another by the hegemony of various Jewish centers. D. divided post-biblical history into two great eras – one oriental and the other occidental – holding that the Jewish people was now completely westernized. He propounded the doctrine of National Autonomism according to which the Jews are a nation intellectually and aspire to social and cultural – but not political or territorial –

independence, the Jewish problem in the Diaspora being soluble only through national and cultural AUTONOMY in the states where they live. D.'s other works include a shorter Jewish history, a history of the Jews in Russia and Poland, and a history of Ḥasidism. He was murdered by the Nazis in Riga.

*DÜHRING, EUGEN (1833–1921): German philosopher and anti-Semite. In his writings, notably the widely-read *Die Judenfrage als Frage des Rassencharakters*, he viciously attacked the Jews, as well as Christianity, regarding the latter as a manifestation of the Jewish spirit.

DUKAS, PAUL (1865–1935): French composer. His works include overtures, a symphony, piano compositions, the opera *Ariane et Barbe-Bleu*, the ballet *La Péri*, and — best-known of his pieces — the scherzo for orchestra *L'Apprenti Sorcier*, based on a ballad by Goethe.

DUKER, ABRAHAM GORDON (1907–): Historian. Born in Poland, D. settled in the US in 1923. He was managing editor of the *Contemporary Jewish Record* 1938–41, and of *Jewish Social Studies* from 1952. In 1956, he was appointed president of the College of Jewish Studies in Chicago and from 1963 was professor of history Yeshiva University, New York, and then (from 1972) at Brooklyn College.

DUKES, LEOPOLD (1810–1891): Jewish literary historian. He was born in Slovakia, traveled widely to consult mss and rare books (spending many years in England) and in 1869, settled in Vienna. His works embrace all fields of medieval Jewish literature, especially synagogal poetry. D. translated Rashi's commentary on the Pentateuch into German.

DUKHAN (Heb.): Platform; in the Temple, the priests' stand, hence, as a verb, to pronounce the priestly benediction (colloquial among Ashkenazim).

DULUTH: City in Minnesota, US. The first Jewish family went to D. from Hungary in 1870. D.'s first Jewish congregation, Temple Emanuel (Reform) was founded in 1891. D. has a Jewish Federation and Community Council founded in 1937. Its Jewish population in 1973 was 1,100 with 4 synagogues and an educational center.

DÜNABURG see **DAUGAVPILS**

DUNASH BEN LABRAT (c. 920–c. 990): Hebrew poet and grammarian. Born in Baghdad, he studied at Fez and then settled in Cordova. Here, under the patronage of Ḥasdai Ibn Shaprut, he devoted himself to philological studies. Writing both religious and secular verse, he was the first to introduce Arabic meter into Hebrew poetry. D. was the author of 200 criticisms (80 in rhyme) of MENAHEM BEN SARUK'S views on grammar and biblical interpretation. These strictures led to a violent controversy which beneficially influenced the development of Hebrew philology and grammar.

DUNASH BEN TAMIM (c. 900–960): Scholar; probably a native of Kairouan. He gained distinction as a philologist, grammarian, and Bible commentator and also wrote on philosophy, astronomy, and medicine. A commentary on the *Sepher Yetzirah*, written in Arabic, is attributed to him.

DÜNNER, JOSEPH HIRSCH (1833–1911): Rabbi and scholar. He was born in Cracow, became principal of the Dutch Rabbinical Seminary (1862), and Ashkenazi chief rabbi of Amsterdam (1874). He published critical notes on many talmudic tractates and an enquiry into the origin of the Tosephta.

DURA-EUROPOS: Former city on the Euphrates. In 1932–5, the ruins of a synagogue built in 245 CE were discovered on the site in a remarkable state of preservation. The walls were covered with frescoes depicting scenes from the Bible, etc. These, together with the mosaic of Bet Alpha, provided the first substantial evidence that a pictorial art existed among the Jews in antiquity and was, perhaps, the basis of Christian religious art.

DURAN: Family of scholars originating in Provence.

(1) *PROFIAT D.* (pen-name Ephodi; 14th–15th cents.): Philosopher, grammarian, and polemicist. Living at Barcelona, he was forced to feign Christianity during the 1391 persecutions but escaped to S France where he openly reverted to Judaism. Thence he wrote a letter *al tehi kaavotekha* ("Be not like your fathers") to a friend who had become converted; this sharp satire on Christianity was misunderstood by some Christians who at first imagined that *Alteca Boteca* (as they called it) supported their beliefs. At the invitation of Ḥasdai Crescas, D. composed *Kelimmat ha-Goyyim*, an anti-Christian work which uses the

Frescoes from the western wall of the synagogue at Dura-Europos.

Gospels to show that Jesus had no intention of establishing a new religion. D. also wrote a commentary on Maimonides *Guide*, a Hebrew grammar *Maaseh Ephod* which is a pioneer work in the scientific study of the Hebrew language, a book on astronomy, and a chronicle (now lost). (2) *SIMEON BEN TZEMAH D.* (known as *Rashbatz*; 1361–1444): Codifier, kabbalist, and religious philosopher. Born in Majorca, he settled in Algiers after the 1391 persecutions, being appointed rabbi of the community in 1408. D. played a large part in fostering Jewish studies in N Africa and introduced important innovations, including permission for rabbis to receive a salary. His responsa are of great importance from the halakhic, historical, and cultural viewpoints; he was, moreover, the author of works covering many branches of Jewish studies including the philosophical book *Magen Avot.* (3) *SOLOMON BEN SIMEON D.* (known as *Rashbash*; c. 1400–1467): Rabbi and codifier; son of (2). He lived in Algiers. His works included *Milhemet Mitzvah*, a defense of the Talmud directed especially against the views of the apostate Geronimo de Santa Fé.

DURBAN: Capital of province of Natal, S Africa. The first Jewish religious services there were held in 1882. Sir Matthew Nathan, governor of Natal, was president of the community 1907–10. There are 3 synagogues (one Reform), a day school, many communal institutions, and a Jewish pop. of 5,990 (1973).

DURKHEIM, DAVID ÉMILE (1858–1917): French sociologist; professor of sociology at Bordeaux (1887) and Paris (1902). He founded and edited *L'année sociologique* and originated a school of sociology emphasizing the role of philosophical criticism and anthropology in sociology.

DUSCHAK, MORITZ (1815–1890): Scholar, He was rabbi in Gaya, Moravia, then preacher in Cracow, and later settled in Vienna, B. wrote books on talmudic and other Jewish subjects.

DUSHKIN, ALEXANDER (1890–1976): Educator. He held important positions in education both in the US and Israel including that of professor of educational administration at the Hebrew Univ.

DÜSSELDORF: German town. The original date of Jewish settlement is unknown. The community was expelled in 1438 and only returned in the late 16th cent. A synagogue was consecrated in 1712. In the 19th cent., the Jews of D. were prominent in its commerce and finance. Before annihilation by the Nazis, 5,000 Jews lived there. Jewish pop. (1973): 1,574.

DUTCH WEST INDIES see **CURAÇAO**

DUVEEN: British family of art-dealers and patrons founded by *SIR JOSEPH JOEL D.* (1843–1908). His son, *JOSEPH* (from 1933, Lord) *D.*, (1869–1939) active also in America, was a benefactor of the British Museum, the Tate Gallery, and the National Portrait Gallery in London.

DUVERNOIS, HENRI (pseudonym of Henry Schwabacher; 1875–1937): French author. He wrote realistic novels, plays, and stories (*Faubourg Montmartre, Le journal d'un pauvre homme*, etc.).

DVINSK see **DAUGAVPILS**

DYBBUK see **DIBBUK**

DYER, LEON (1807–1883): US soldier. Born in Germany, he went to Baltimore at an early age. As acting mayor was responsible for quelling the "bread riots" in that city in 1834. He fought for Texas in battles following the Alamo, and during the Mexican War 1846–8) was a colonel and served as quartermaster-general in the US army. In 1848, he was special envoy to Prussia. Settling in San Francisco, he established the first congregation on the Pacific Coast. His brother *ISIDORE D.* (1813–1888) organized the first religious services in Galveston.

DYHERNFURTH: Town in Silesia. Its Jewish community, founded in the 17th cent. and extinct by 1916, was unimportant, but D. was memorable in the history of Hebrew printing. The first privileged Hebrew printer there was Shabbetai BASS (1689), and the press continued to exist under various managements until 1834. A Yiddish newspaper, the *Dyhernfurther Privilegirte Zeitung*, was published in D. 1771–2.

DYKAAR, MOSES (1885–1933): Sculptor. He was born in Vilna, studied in Paris, and went to the US in 1916. D was a noted portraitist.

DYMOV, OSSIP (pseudonym of Joseph Perelmann; 1878–1959): Russian and Yiddish author. His Russian writings (plays, humoresques, feuilletons, etc.) were popular in E Europe before World War I. In 1913, he settled in New York. Several of his plays achieved outstanding success on the Yiddish stage.

E

EASTER: Christian festival perpetuating the tradition of Passover but marking the Feast of the Resurrection of Jesus. The Church Council of Nicaea (325) readjusted the calendar in an attempt to avoid the coincidence of E. and Passover, but it nevertheless occasionally still continued to occur. It was a widespread custom throughout the Christian world to attack Jews during the E. period in order to avenge the Passion, and in some places Jews were subjected to beatings every E., often with fatal consequences. Owing to the proximity of Passover, these attacks were often connected with Blood Libels. During the Ghetto Period, the Jews were confined in their quarters during Eastertide from Holy Thursday onward.

EASTON: City in Pennsylvania, US. The origins of its Jewish community go back to 1750. There are now three congregations (Reform, Conservative, and Orthodox). The Jewish Community Council (founded in 1939) represents all Jewish organizations. Jewish pop. (1973): 1,675.

EBAL see **GERIZIM**

EBAN (in Heb. **EVEN**), **ABBA (AUBREY) SOLOMON** (1915–): Israel diplomat. Born in Capetown, he worked in the political dept. of the Jewish

Abba Eban.

Agency from 1946, and was a member of the Jewish Agency delegation to the UN 1947–8. E. represented Israel at the UN 1948–59, and was also Israel ambassador to the US 1950–9. He was deputy-chairman of the UN assembly in 1953. E. was president of the WEIZMANN INSTITUTE 1958–66. Elected as a *Mapai* delegate to the Knesset in 1959, he was appointed minister without portfolio. He was minister of education and culture 1960–3, deputy prime minister 1963–6, and foreign minister 1966–74. He wrote *My People*, a history of the Jews.

EBED-MELECH (6th cent. BCE): Cushite eunuch who persuaded his master, Zedekiah, king of Judah (597–586), to rescue Jeremiah from the mud-pit into which he had been thrown. In gratitude, Jeremiah prophecied that E. M. would be saved when disaster befell Jerusalem (Jer. 38:7–13; 39: 15–18). In the Midrash he is identified with BARUCH.

EBER: Grandson of Shem (Gen. 10–11). His descendants formed a group of Semitic peoples and tribes, including the Israelites who are therefore, according to one view, called Hebrews.

EBERS, GEORG (1837–1898): Egyptologist; of Jewish origin. Professor of Egyptology at Leipzig, he was one of the first to demonstrate the connection between the ancient Egyptian and Greek cultures.

EBIONITES (probably from Heb. *evyon* = "poor"): Judeo-Christian sect in Palestine, fl. 2nd–4th cents. Its members observed the Mosaic law (e.g. circumcision, Sabbath) but rejected sacrifices; they believed in Jesus as the Messiah, though denying his divinity and opposing Pauline doctrine. They considered poverty a basic principle of Christianity and held their property in common. Most members of the sect lived in Transjordan and E Syria.

EBREO, LEONE see **ABRAVANEL, JUDAH**

ECCLESIASTES (Heb. *Kohelet* from its second word: the word E. is the Greek for "congregant," the Septuagint translation of *Kohelet*): One of the five scrolls in the Hagiographa section of the Bible. It contains twelve chapters, generally of a pessimistic nature. The author seeks to discern the purpose of human life with all its trials, but finds no spiritual support in either faith or intellect, and at times even adopts a bluntly hedonistic outlook. His motto is "vanity of vanities, all is vanity." The last few verses of the book are optimistic in outlook, and are regarded by some scholars as a later addition. E. includes counsel on human conduct, based on the assumption that all is preordained, and that man should reconcile himself to oppression and injustice. This doctrine is so contrary to the spirit of biblical thought that the rabbis endeavored to suppress the book, but the ascription of its authorship to "Kohelet, son of David" (identified with Solomon) secured its inclusion in the canon. Modern scholars regard the name Kohelet as pseudonymous and ascribe the composition of the book to the Second Temple Period (3rd cent. BCE?). The prose is uniform, precise, and lucid, the language bearing the closest resemblance to mishnaic Hebrew found in the Bible, while the style is that of the WISDOM literature. The Scroll of E. is read in the synagogue during Tabernacles.

ECCLESIASTES RABBAH (Heb. *Kohelet Rabbah*): Midrash written on the Book of Ecclesiastes; part of the collection known as MIDRASH RABBAH. It utilizes various older Midrashim. Generally dated as post-talmudic.

ECCLESIASTICUS see **BEN SIRA**

ÉCLAIREURS ISRAÉLITES see **SCOUTS**

ÉCOLE RABBINIQUE DE FRANCE see **SEMINAIRE ISRAÉLITE**

ECUADOR: Jews have lived in E. only in the 20th cent. Immigration increased during the Nazi Period, most of the newcomers settling in Quito. Since 1945, however, many have left the country for economic reasons. The Jews of Quito (numbering c. 800) are organized in the Asociacion de Beneficencia Israelita, and those of Guayaquil (110) in the Centro Israelita. A newspaper *Informaciones* (in German and Spanish) appears in Quito. Jewish pop. (1973): 1,000.

EDELMAN, GERALD (1929–): US immunologist; professor of biochemistry at Rockefeller University, N.Y. He was awarded the 1972 Nobel Prize in medicine for discovering the chemical structure of antibodies.

EDELS, SAMUEL ELIEZER (known as the *Maharsha*; 1555–1631): Polish talmudist, called after his mother-in-law Edel who founded a yeshivah for him in Posen. He was subsequently rabbi in Chelm, Lublin, and Ostrog. His main work *Ḥiddushe Halakhot* ("Halakhic Novellae") became a classic and was incorporated in most editions of the Talmud.

EDEN, GARDEN OF (Heb. *Gan Eden*): Original abode of Adam and Eve (Gen. 2–3). It was watered by a river which divided into four streams, the Pishon, Gihon, Tigris, and Euphrates. Adam and Eve were eventually excluded from the garden for their disobedience. Ezekiel (28:11–19; 31:8–9, 16–18) locates E. on a mountain consecrated to God and describes the expulsion of a cherub from it.

In later Jewish literature, E. is the abode of the righteous after death.

EDER, MONTAGUE DAVID (1866–1936): British psychologist and Zionist leader. He was a follower of Freud and one of the founders of the British Psychoanalysts' Association. He was active in Jewish affairs and joined the Jewish Territorial Organization in 1905. After 1917, he supported Zionism and in 1918–21, was in Palestine with the first Zionist Commission. E. was a member of the Zionist Executive in London and Jerusalem 1921–3 and 1927–8.

EDESSA (now Urfa): City in Asiatic Turkey, where Jews have lived since Second Temple times. They suffered massacre in Trajan's time (116 CE) and under Julian (363). In the 19th cent., a third of the population was Jewish, but their numbers dwindled, especially after World War I. Few are now left. Emigrants from E. living in Jerusalem have their own synagogue.

EDINBURGH: Capital of SCOTLAND. Individual Jews appeared in E. from the 17th cent. but no community existed until the close of the 18th. The main Jewish immigration to Scotland after 1881 was atttacted to Glasgow, but E. has a well-organized, unified community, with charitable, educational, and social institutions. Jewish pop. (1973): 1,100.

EDINGER, LUDWIG (1855–1918): German neurologist; professor at Frankfort Univ. from 1914. His researches led to advances in the knowledge of brain-anatomy.

EDIRNE see **ADRIANOPLE**

EDMAN, IRWIN (1896–1954): US philosopher; professor of philosophy at Columbia Univ. from 1935. He wrote many books and articles on philosophy, esthetics, literature, and education.

EDMONTON: Canadian city. The first Jews went there in the last decade of the 19th cent. The first congregation (Orthodox) was founded in 1906, and its Beth Israel synagogue built in 1911. A Reform congregation was established subsequently. Jewish pop. (1973): 2,700.

EDOM (IDUMEA): Country in SE Palestine, also called Mount SEIR. Its terrain was mountainous and easily fortified and its land was fertile. E. lay S of the Dead Sea and bordered on the Red Sea at Elath and Ezion Geber. The Edomites were of Semitic origin, traditionally descendants of Esau, and lived by hunting. They dispossessed the Horite inhabitants of Seir and organized themselves along tribal lines headed by a chieftain (called *allooph*), later consolidating into a monarchy. The Edomites were traditional enemies of the Israelites; they fought Saul and were defeated by David who partly annexed their land. The Edomites regained their independence during the reign of Jehoram, but wars between the two states were frequent. In the 8th

School for Yemenite children, Lachish.

cent. BCE, the Edomites became vassals of Assyria. At the time of the destruction of the First Temple, they plundered and looted in association with the Babylonians, and, being driven out from Seir by the Nabateans, occupied S Judah during or after the period of the Exile. The Edomites were conquered by John Hyrcanus who forcibly converted them to Judaism, and from then on they constituted a part of the Jewish people, Herod being one of their descendants. During Titus' siege of Jerusalem, they marched in to reinforce the extreme elements. killing all they suspected of peace tendencies. Thereafter, they ceased to figure in Jewish history. The name in the Talmud is a synonym for an oppressive government, especially Rome: in the Middle Ages, it was applied to Christian Europe.

EDREI: Ancient city of Transjordan in the Bashan region; today Deraa (Syria). Formerly the capital of Og (Num. 21:33), it was later in the territory of the tribe of Manasseh (Josh. 13:31). A Jewish community survived there until the 14th cent.

EDUCATION: The constant reiteration in the Pentateuch of the duty to teach the Divine precepts to the people, and especially to the young, must have stimulated some sort of religious e. among the Hebrews at a very early period. Even in the age of the Judges, a young man, casually encountered, was able to write (Judg. 8:14). The Lachish letters illustrate relatively widespread literacy at the end of the period of the First Temple. Religious e. at this time was apparently conducted by levites sometimes dispatched expressly from Jerusalem (II Chr. 7:7ff). The religious revival under Ezra centered on the regular reading of and instruction in the Torah which inevitably entailed the extension of organized e. According to tradition, local schools were first organized systematically in ancient Palestine by Simeon ben Shetaḥ (1st cent. BCE), while elementary e. was instituted for boys of six or seven by the high priest Joshua ben Gamla (c. 64–5 CE). Before the fall of the Jewish state, the pagan philosopher Seneca stated that the Jews were the only people who knew the reasons for their religious observances, while Josephus observed that "our principal care is to educate our children well." A comprehensive system of e., open to all, was fundamental to the organization of Jewish life in the Talmudic Period when the rabbis maintained that the entire world was "poised on the breath of schoolchildren." The patriarch Judah I sent a commission throughout Palestine to ensure that there should be teachers of the Bible and of the Oral Law in every place. There was opposition to female e., but some women were nevertheless well versed even in advanced Jewish learning. The elementary school was termed the *Bet ha-Sepher* to distinguish it from the advanced school, the

BET HA-MIDRASH, which was generally in immediate proximity to the synagogue. No teacher was supposed to instruct a class of more than 25 pupils. Apart from the instruction in the *Bet ha-Midrash*, there was something approximating to universal adult e. in the Sabbath discourses in the synagogue, besides sermonic instruction. This system was the basis of subsequent Jewish educational organization. In the Middle Ages and Ghetto Periods, there was universal and generally free Jewish e., and an illiterate male was seldom encountered in the medieval community. In the small local communities characteristic of this period, elementary e. was generally in the hands either of the father or of a professional elementary teacher who might at the same time be one of the communal functionaries or a scribe or copyist. Advanced instruction in Talmud would be volunteered as a meritorious deed by learned householders. Adults would continue throughout their lives to participate in study-groups, almost as their sole diversion. For business purposes, some elementary mathematical instruction was obviously a necessity. In larger communities, e. was more formally and elaborately organized. A full account has survived of the educational reform introduced for the Castilian communities by a synod which met at Valladolid in 1432. In this period, the essential aspect of the duty of the rabbi – especially in Central and E Europe – was to maintain and conduct a YESHIVAH, those who studied in it being supported at public expense. Though only the Talmud and Jewish lore were taught, the wide ramifications of purely Jewish study contained many of the elements of general e. In Renaissance Italy, the scope of Jewish e. widened to include versification, philosophy, the rudiments at least of the vernacular, and even Latin. Elementary e. in the Italian communities was often conducted by women and more advanced e. by private tutors. It was then that Jews began to enter universities for general e., particularly in medicine. In 1366, the Sicilian Jewish communities attempted to establish a university of their own, while in 1583, David Provenzale of Mantua planned an institution for providing, in a Jewish atmosphere, preparatory training before entering the universities. The educational system of the Italian Jewish communities in the Ghetto Period was well organized, a special society (*ḥevra*) having charge of the Talmud Torah (as the elementary institution was henceforth generally called). Feminine e. also began to make headway at about this time, a Talmud Torah for girls being reportedly established in Rome in the 15th cent. The combination of Jewish and general e. was perfected in the famous and lavishly supported Talmud Torah of the Sephardi community in Amsterdam where, in the 17th cent., Spanish and Latin were taught besides Hebrew, and the advanced class spoke only Hebrew. In Germany and E Europe, however, the old educational system continued almost unmodified. It was confined to talmudic study and to some extent neglected even the Bible in favor of the Talmud. Elementary instruction was given in the ḤEDER, sometimes by poorly qualified teachers; this institution long survived among immigrant Jews in W Europe and America. In the second half of the 18th cent., the system was subjected to attack by Haskalah writers, such as Naphtali Herz Wessely whose proposal for a drastic Jewish educational reform and the inclusion of secular subjects led to bitter controversy. In the course of the next generation, schools giving instruction in general, as well as Jewish subjects, were established in many countries; the Jews' Free School, founded in London in 1817, was at the close of the century the largest elementary school in Europe, if not in the world. In such institutions, general e. tended gradually to predominate, only rudimentary Jewish instruction being normally given. However, with the spread of universal e. in the western world in the 19th cent., separate Jewish schools began to be superseded, and "Sunday schools" or "Hebrew and religious classes" were set up in most Jewish communities to give a modicum of Jewish instruction. This tended to be most elementary and to end with the age of *Bar-mitzvah*, girls being often wholly neglected for this reason. In recent years, there has been an increasing tendency in some countries to revert to Jewish Day Schools or "parochial schools," in which a more advanced and comprehensive Jewish e. can be given in the framework of general e. At the same time, bodies such as the London Board of Jewish Religious Education, the Jewish Education Committee in New York, and the Commission on Jewish Education of the Union of American Hebrew Congregations, have done much to set Jewish e. on a sounder footing by providing training colleges, modern textbooks, etc. Zionism has often resulted in the introduction of modern Hebrew into the curriculum. It is nevertheless estimated that about one-half of the 1,800,000 Jewish children in the western world receive no Jewish e. whatsoever. The prohibition of public religious instruction in the USSR has been the most potent factor in the decline of Judaism there since 1917. See also RABBINICAL SEMINARIES.

The state of Israel inherited from the British Mandatory period a network of Jewish schools run by the *Vaad Leumi*, a governmental network of Arab schools, as well as private schools, yeshivot, etc. The Jewish schools were divided into three "trends": general, labor, and religious, to which an extreme religious trend was added after the establishment of the state. E. is supervised by the Ministry of Education and culture (see ISRAEL, STATE OF). In 1949, e.

was made compulsory for children between 5 to 13. The differing trends were abolished in 1953, and only two types of schools recognized – state and state religious. Permission was however given to opt out of the state system and most of the extreme religious educational institutions withdrew, although they still receive state support. 740,000 (Jewish and Arab) pupils attended recognized schools in 1967–8; in addition, 46,000 (Jews and Arabs) attended private educational institutions (under Jewish Christian or Moslem auspices). Secondary e., which is not compulsory, is given at high schools, gymnasia, vocational centers, and, with certain qualifications, yeshivot. Institutes of higher education which grant degrees are the HEBREW UNIVERSITY, Jerusalem, the TECHNION or Israel Institute of Technology, Haifa, TEL AVIV UNIVERSITY, and BAR-ILAN UNIVERSITY, Ramat Gan. The government has also recognized the WEIZMANN INSTITUTE (incorporating the Sieff Institute), Reḥovot.

EDUYYOT (Heb. "Testimonies"): Seventh tractate in the Mishnah order of *Nezikin*, containing 8 chapters. It has no *gemara* in either the Babylonian or the Palestinian Talmud. The name is derived from the testimonies given before the high court at Jabneh concerning statements of older authorities. In the Babylonian Talmud, the name of the tractate is *Beḥirta* ("chosen"). Most of the contents of E. are found again in other tractates.

EFROS, ISRAEL (1890–): Hebrew poet, scholar, and educator. Born in Poland, he migrated to the US in 1906, and served as rabbi and teacher in Baltimore and Buffalo. E. was also professor of Hebrew at Dropsie College and Hunter College. Like other Hebrew poets in America, he elicits the influence of the folk sources of American poetry, particularly evident in *Wigwamim Shotekim* ("Silent Wigwams"). He is the author of studies in medieval Jewish philosophy, and co-author of a standard English-Hebrew dictionary. E. translated Shakespeare's *Hamlet* and *Timon of Athens* into Hebrew and much of Bialik's poetry into English. In 1954, E. settled in Israel as rector of the Tel Aviv Univ. (till 1959) and dean of its humanities department.

EGER: Rabbinical family. (1) *AKIVA BEN MOSES E.* (1761–1837) was rabbi at Märkisch-Friedland (1791) and from 1814, at Posen where his yeshivah attracted many students. Recognized as one of the foremost rabbinical authorities in Europe, he led opposition to religious reform and secular education. E. published many works including novellae, responsa, and glosses on the Mishnah, Talmud, and Maimonides' *Mishneh Torah*. (2) *AKIVA BEN SIMḤAH BUNEM E.* (1729–1758), grandfather of (1), was rabbi at Zülz (Upper Silesia) and from 1756, headed the yeshivah at Pressburg. (3) *JUDAH LEIB E.* (1816–1888), son of (5), founded the Lublin dynasty of Ḥasidic rabbis. (4) *SAMUEL LEVIN*

Rabbi Akiva Eger (1761–1837).

(PERETZ ZABEL) BEN JUDAH LEIB E. (1769–1842), grandson of (2), was rabbi in Brunswick from 1809. He was one of the outstanding scholars of his generation, and rabbinical inquiries (some relating to the Reform movement) were directed to him from many lands. (5) *SOLOMON BEN AKIVA E.* (1786–1852), son of (1). After serving as rabbi of Kalish, he succeeded his father in Posen. E. reorganized the collections for Ḥalukkah Jewry in Palestine and wrote on talmudic and halakhic topics.

EGLAH ARUPHAH: Heifer, the neck of which was to be broken on the occasion of an unsolved murder (Deut. 21:1–9). The entire court of the city nearest to the crime had to wash their hands over the heifer's body and affirm their innocence. The Mishnah (*Sota* 9, 9) states that when murders became more frequent, this ceremony was stopped.

*EGLON (c. 12th cent. BCE): King of Moab. With the aid of the Amalekites, he conquered parts of Israelite territory but was killed cunningly by EHUD (Judg. 3). Talmudic legend depicts him as the father of RUTH.

EGYPT (Heb. *Mitzrayim*): Country in NE Africa. The history of the Jewish people from its very outset has been connected with E. The patriarchs all visited the country, and the beginnings of Hebrew history are bound up with the bondage in E. and the Exodus. It is probable that the first Hebrew immigration into E. was connected with the period of domination there of the Semitic Hyksos dynasty (18th–16th cents. BCE). E. was at that period closely involved in Palestinian affairs, as is shown by the Tel el-AMARNA letters which illustrate the background of, and perhaps allude to, the first Israelite incursions there. The scholar A. S. Yahuda has shown the

Egyptian captives from the neighboring lands of Lidya, Ethiopia (?) and Canaan. The temple of Sahure (c. 2750 BCE).

close influence of Egyptian civilization on the Pentateuch. Throughout the period of the Monarchy, there were constant Judeo-Egyptian relations. Solomon married an Egyptian princess and concluded a trade treaty; the pharaoh Shishak attacked Jerusalem (c. 930) to assist the newly-established Northern kingdom; Josiah was killed in 608 when attempting to check the march of Pharaoh Necho through his territory; his successor, Jehoahaz, was deported, and Jehoiakim installed in his place by the Egyptians. Even before the fall of the First Temple, there was a Jewish colony in E., and the prophet Jeremiah was taken there shortly after. Jewish military colonies existed in E., particularly in pharaonic days. In YEB, a vast mass of papyri has been found, minutely illustrating local life and showing the existence of a Jewish temple under the Persians in the 5th cent. BCE. With the conquest by Alexander the Great (333 BCE), Jews formed a large proportion of the new immigrants who streamed into the country, some spontaneously, some as deportees. There is evidence of synagogues from the 3rd cent. BCE. The community was to a great extent hellenized in speech and culture. The focus of Jewish life was ALEXANDRIA, the seat of the great hellenistic Jewish civilization, the best-known exponent of which was the philosopher PHILO, but there were many lesser centers. The total of Egyptian Jews at this period has been estimated as high as 1,000,000. For a long time, the Ptolemies of Egypt were in control of Palestine where they were generally popular. During the dark period before the Maccabean revolt, the refugee high priest Onias founded a Temple in Heliopolis. This was the period of the completion at Alexandria of the first Greek translation of the Bible (SEPTUAGINT) which had enormous influence. On the other hand, there was a great deal of anti-Jewish feeling among the Greek populace, expressing

itself sometimes in riots and necessitating the periodic intervention of the Roman authorities. In 71 CE, after the destruction of Jerusalem, zealot refugees stirred up a Jewish revolt in E. and another uprising there assumed considerable proportions in 115-7. HELLENISM may have weakened the resistance of Egyptian Jewry to Christianity, and there are many obvious Alexandrian-Jewish elements in early Christian literature and thought. The condition of Egyptian Jewry deteriorated with the Christianization of the Roman Empire, and riots in Alexandria, instigated by the bishop Cyril in 415, drove masses of Jews to baptism. At the time of the Arab invasion of 640, the Egyptian Jewish community was unimportant. Under Moslem rule, the former traditions of hellenistic Egypt were submerged. The community, centered in the new city of CAIRO, was wholly Arab in character and culture. Its life is minutely illustrated in the mass of documents of the Cairo GENIZAH. Saadyah Gaon was a native of the Fayyum. The organization of Mesopotamian Jewry under an exilarch (later *nagid*) was imitated in E., and there were distinguished academies of learning. An important Karaite community flourished, surviving to modern times. Generally, under the Moslems, conditions were fairly favorable, though normally the traditional Moslem anti-Jewish code was enforced, and under Caliph Ḥakim (996–1021), there was an interlude of almost ferocious persecution. Moses MAIMONIDES, arriving in E. in the second half of the 12th cent., found a congenial environment. His descendants long continued to serve as *nagid* of Egyptian Jewry. After the Turkish occupation in 1517, conditions improved somewhat. The record of Egyptian Jewry was tranquil, undistinguished, and unenlightened until the 19th cent. when the penetration of western influences made for rapid occidentalization among the upper strata, and families such as those of Cattaui and Mosseri played some part in public life. The anti-European reaction of the mid-20th cent. involved the Jews, many of whom had European citizenship. This became linked ultimately with the adoption of an anti-Zionist policy, though Zionism had formerly been favored. In 1948, as a result of the war in Palestine, many Jews were placed in concentration camps and attacks made on Jewish homes. A great emigration of Jews from E. ensued and their number dropped from 90,000 in 1947 to c. 30,000 in 1955. In 1954, there were still 11 Jewish day schools with 1,750 pupils. Following the SINAI OPERATION, NASSER dispossessed and expelled many Jews from E. Most of the others left in the following years and by 1966, only 2,500 remained, 1,800 in Cairo and the rest in Alexandria. Most of the remaining males of Egyptian nationality were arrested at the time of the Six-Day War in 1967 and the other Jews emigrated. Pop. (1973): 500.

EHAD MI YODEA (Heb. "Who knows one?"):
Medieval Hebrew "riddle of numbers" extending from 1 to 13 appended to the Passover Haggadah in certain rites.

EHRENBURG, ILYA GRIGORYEVICH (1891–1967): Russian novelist. He was born at Kiev, and in 1909, was exiled for revolutionary activity. Returning in 1917, he opposed the Bolsheviks and from 1921, lived for a time in W Europe. Later adapting himself to the regime, he became Stalin's semi-official spokesman. His attitude to Jews and Zionism varied according to the policy of the Soviet authorities, and from 1941, he wrote against Nazi anti-Semitism and served on the Jewish Anti-Fascist Committee. His anti-Zionist article in *Pravda* in 1948 heralded the Soviet swing away from active support of Israel and the anti-Zionist drive in the Soviet satellite countries. He was awarded the Stalin Prize in 1942 for his novel *The Fall of Paris* and in 1948, for *The Storm*. His autobiography appeared in 6 volumes.

EHRENKRANZ, BENJAMIN WOLF (known as Velvel Zbarazer; 1819–1883): Hebrew and Yiddish folk-poet. He was born in Galicia and wandered throughout E Europe rendering his songs, many of which were satirical parodies reflecting the views of the Haskalah. E.'s last years were spent in Constantinople.

EHRENPREIS, MARCUS (Mordecai; 1869–1951): Rabbi, essayist, and pioneer Zionist. He served as rabbi in Croatia 1896–1900, chief rabbi of Bulgaria 1900–14, and chief rabbi of Sweden 1914–51. E. was one of Herzl's chief assistants in the preparation of the First Zionist Congress.

EHRLICH, ARNOLD BOGUMIL (1848–1919): Biblical scholar. Born in Russia, he studied oriental languages at Berlin where he helped Franz Delitzsch translate the New Testament into Hebrew. In 1878, he went to the US. His biblical commentaries in Hebrew (published 1899 ff) display critical acumen with radical tendencies.

EHRLICH, PAUL (1854–1915): German biochemist. He directed the Institute for Experimental Therapy at Frankfort-on-Main from 1899 and was professor at Frankfort Univ. from 1914. He was noted for his diagnostic methods in hematology and bacteriology (e.g. the dyeing of tissues and bacteria), and his theoretical and practical contributions to immunology. Above all, he created modern chemotherapy by the discovery of salvarsan ("606"), a cure for syphilis, thus opening a new chapter in the history of medicine. In 1908, he was awarded a Nobel Prize.

EHUD: One of the Judges, belonging to the tribe of Benjamin. He saved Israel from the oppression of Eglon, king of Moab (Judg. 3).

EIBESCHÜTZ, JONATHAN (c. 1690–1764): Talmudist and kabbalist. He headed a yeshivah in Prague and in 1741, became rabbi at Metz. From 1750 until his death, he officiated in the triple community of Altona, Hamburg, and Wandsbeck. As early as 1724, he was suspected of being a follower of Shabbetai Tzevi. To clear himself of suspicion, he signed the ban placed by the Prague rabbinate on Sabbetaianism. E. was again accused in Altona in 1751 on the evidence of amulets he distributed to ward off sickness. He again denied the connection, swearing an oath to this effect in the Altona synagogue. Nevertheless a bitter and prolonged controversy ensued with ramifications throughout Europe where Jewish communities were divided between supporters of E. and his opponents led by Jacob EMDEN. Even Christian scholars participated in the literary dispute that developed and which was accompanied by abuse, mutual excommunications, and, in some instances, by the intervention of the civil authorities. The argument only subsided with E.'s death, but the riddle of his Sabbetaianism has never been solved. Some hold he was never a Sabbetaian; others believe that he belonged to the sect in his youth but left after the ban of 1725; still others maintain he was a lifelong crypto-Sabbetaian. E. was one of the greatest talmudic scholars of his time. His son *BENJAMIN WOLF E.* (18th cent.), an adventurer, claimed at one time to be the messiah, amassed considerable wealth, and lived in a castle at Dresden, calling himself Baron von Adlerstal.

EICHENBAUM, JACOB (1796–1861): Russian Hebrew poet. In 1844, he became principal of the government Jewish school at Kishinev and in 1850, was appointed inspector of the rabbinical seminary at Zhitomir. His Hebrew writings include works on mathematics and chess.

*EICHMANN, ADOLF OTTO (1906–1962): Nazi official. In 1940, he became head of the German Central Emigration Office and of the Jewish section

Eichmann on Trial.

of the Gestapo. The former was the organizational headquarters responsible for the liquidation of Jewry throughout Europe. Hence, though not high in the Nazi hierarchy, E. was directly responsible for all Jewish deportations and exterminations. In 1945, he went into hiding but in 1960 was brought by Israelis from Argentina to Israel to stand trial. E. was charged with crimes against humanity and against the Jewish people, his defense counsel being Dr. Servatius, a German lawyer. Found guilty by the Jerusalem District Court, after a trial that attracted worldwide attention, he was sentenced to death. His appeal before the Israel Supreme Court having been rejected, he was hanged at Ramlah prison. His body was cremated and his ashes scattered into the sea.

EIGHTEEN BENEDICTIONS (Heb. *shemoneh esreh*): The principal prayer, also known as *tephillah* ("prayer") or *amidah* ("standing," so called because recited while standing). The E.B. were not all assembled at one time and the text reflects the political and economic situation at the dates of composition. Traditionally, they were decreed by the men of the Great Assembly, and some definitely originate from Second Temple times. Others were added and some redacted after the destruction of the Second Temple, one of them, the benediction directed against the sectaries (*birkat ha-minim*), being inserted by R Gamaliel in Jabneh. In Babylon (but not in Palestine), the "blessing of David" was added, bringing the number of blessings to 19. In public prayer, except at the evening service, the E. B. are recited by the congregation and repeated by the precentor, the KEDUSHAH being inserted during the repetition in No. 3, and the PRIESTLY BLESSING on certain occasions in No. 19. The name is wrongly also applied to the *amidah* on Sabbaths and festivals when the number of benedictions is far less.

A First Blessings: Praise
1. *Commemoration of the patriarchs*
2. *Mightiness of God in natural phenomena*
3. *Sanctification of God*

B Intermediate blessings: prayer for
4. *Understanding*
5. *Penitence*
6. *Forgiveness*
7. *Redemption*
8. *Healing*
9. *Blessing of the harvest ("Years")*
10. *Ingathering of the exiles*
11. *Restoration of the judges*
12. *Destruction of the sectaries*
13. *Rewarding of the righteous*
14. *Rebuilding of Jerusalem*
15. *Restoring of the Kingdom of David*

C Last blessings: Praise and thanksgiving
16. *Acceptance of prayer*
17. *Restoration of Temple service*
18. *Thanksgiving*
19. *Blessing of priests, prayer for peace*

Additions are inserted in the blessings on special occasions, e.g. end of Sabbath, *Av* 9, fasts, and the new moon.

EINHORN, DAVID (1809–1879): Reform rabbi. In 1849, he succeeded Ignaz Einhorn as rabbi of the Pest Reform Synagogue. In 1855, he emigrated to the US where he was minister successively in Baltimore, Philadelphia, and New York. E. led the extreme Reform wing of US Jewry, his liturgy *Olat Tamid* ("Perpetual Offering") being introduced in all Reform synagogues. E. was prominent in the anti-slavery movement and was an eloquent preacher in German. His devotion to German language and culture limited his influence within American Jewry and brought him into conflict with more moderate English-speaking religious reformers.

EINHORN, IGNAZ (pseudonym: Eduard Horn; 1825–1875): Hungarian religious reformer and economist. In 1847, he founded a Reform congregation in Pest and served as its rabbi, introducing extreme reforms including the transfer of the Sabbath to Sunday. He participated in the 1848 Revolution. and, on his initiative, the Hungarian National Assembly granted equal rights to Hungarian Jewry. After the suppression of the rising, he settled in Paris where he published works on economic problems. In 1867, he returned to Budapest, was elected to the Hungarian parliament, and shortly before his death, was appointed assistant minister of commerce (1875).

EINHORN, MAX (1862–1953): Gastroenterologist. Born in Poland, he went to the US in 1885 and taught at the New York Post-Graduate Medical School from 1888 (professor 1899). He gained an international reputation from his various innovations for the treatment of stomach diseases and was the first to describe the duodenal ulcer.

EINHORN, MOSES (1896–1966): US physician. He founded (1926) and edited *Ha-Rophe ha-Ivri* which played an important role in Hebrew medical journalism.

EINSTEIN, ALBERT (1879–1955): Physicist. He was born in Ulm, Germany, educated in Switzerland, and worked as an engineer in the patent office at Berne (1902–9) and after receiving his degree was appointed instructor at Berne Univ. Later, he was professor at Zurich and Prague. In 1914, E. became professor of physics at Berlin Univ. and director of the Kaiser Wilhelm Institute of Physics. He remained there until the rise of Nazism in 1933 when he settled in the US (becoming an American

Albert Einstein.

citizen in 1940) and he was subsequently appointed professor of theoretical physics at the Princeton Institute of Advanced Study. E. expounded the theory of relativity which revolutionized concepts of space and time in the fields of both physics and philosophy and, consequently, the foundations of the exact sciences. He began to develop his theory in 1905 and in 1913–6 published his general, or extended, theory of relativity. He developed a new view on the "Brownian motion" of tiny particles and by his interpretation of "photoelectric effects" contributed to the foundation of the quantum theory (for which he was awarded a Nobel Prize in 1921). His theory of relativity was subsequently confirmed experimentally in many fields and paved the way for advances in atomic physics. From 1929, he advanced his unified field theory (expressed mathematically in 1950) which, however, did not win general acceptance. E. was a conscious Jew and an active supporter of Zionism. After the death of Weizmann (1952), he refused an invitation to stand for election as president of Israel. He showed keen interest in Israel scientific institutions, especially the Hebrew Univ. of which he was a trustee and to which he donated the manuscripts of his theory of relativity. A pacifist during World War I, he remained outspoken on current questions, especially as a champion of academic and democratic freedom. Apart from his scientific papers, he wrote on various humanistic and Jewish topics.

EINSTEIN, ALFRED (1880–1952): German musicologist. Editor of the *Zeitschrift für Musikwissenschaft* (1918–33), he left Germany in 1933. eventually settling in the US where he was professor at Smith College 1939–50. His works include *History of Music*; *Mozart, His Character, His Work*; and *The Italian Madrigal*.

EINSTEIN, LEWIS (1877–1967): US diplomat and author. He entered the diplomatic service in 1903, and represented the US in Costa Rica 1911–3, Turkey 1915, Bulgaria 1915–6, and Czechoslovakia 1921–30. Retiring in 1930, he continued to write books on Renaissance history, modern diplomacy. and his memoirs entitled *A Diplomat Looks Back*.

EISENDRATH, MAURICE NATHAN (1902–1973): US rabbi. He was rabbi in Charleston, W Va., and in Toronto until 1943, when he became president of the Union of American Hebrew Congregations. He was active in many Jewish and interfaith organizations.

*EISENMENGER, JOHANN ANDREAS (1654 1704): German anti-Jewish author. After studying Talmud and Midrash for 19 years with Jewish scholars, he published (1700), for purposes of blackmail, his *Entdecktes Judentum* ("Judaism Revealed") which maligned the Jews and collected rabbinical quotations allegedly directed against Christianity. The edition was sequestered on the representations of the Jewish community, but the book was reprinted in 1711. It has since served as a handbook for anti-Semites.

EISENSTADT: Capital of the province of Burgenland in E Austria. Its Jewish community dates from the 14th cent., and was the chief of the "seven communities" of Burgenland. The Jewish quarter was preserved up to 1938 and possessed special privileges, such as the closing of its gates to traffic on the Sabbath. In 1938, there were 500 Jews there, but after the advent of the Nazis, the community was destroyed, and subsequently only a few families returned.

EISENSTADT, BENZION (1873–): Rabbi and Hebrew author. He was born in White Russia and settled in the US in 1903. E. has published several lexicographic and biographical works on contemporary rabbis and writers.

EISENSTADT, MEIR BEN ISAAC (known as *Maharam Ash*; 1670–1744): Talmudist. He was rabbi successively at Szydlowiec (Poland), Prossnitz (Moravia) and, from 1714, at Eisenstadt (Hungary) where he founded a yeshivah. His main work was *Panim Meirot* containing novellae on the Talmud.

EISENSTEIN, JUDAH DAVID (1854–1956): Hebrew author and editor. Born in Poland, he settled in New York in 1872. He published and edited the first major Jewish encyclopedia in Hebrew, *Otzar Yisrael* (10 vols., NY, 1907–13). E. assembled many collections of Jewish literature including *Otzar Midrashim* which comprises 200 short Midrashim; *Otzar Massaot*, an anthology of Jewish travel literature; and *Otzar Vikkuḥim*, a collection of disputations between Jewish and Christian scholars.

EISLER: (1) *GERHARD E.* (1896–1968): Communist leader. A member of the German Communist Party until 1933, he entered the US in 1941. Here he became embroiled with the authorities in 1947; in 1949, he escaped to E Germany, being appointed minister of information, but was removed in Dec. 1952. Later, he was chief of the E German radio commission. (2) *HANNS E.* (1898–1962): German composer who lived in the US 1937–48; brother of (1). He wrote choral and film music, an opera *Goliath*, and a suite based on Jewish folksongs.

EISLER, MORITZ (1832–1902): Moravian pedagogue. He published (3 vols.; 1870–83) one of the first systematic studies of medieval Jewish philosophy.

EISLER, RUDOLPH (1873–1926): Austrian philosopher. He wrote on various philosophical problems and compiled a dictionary of philosophical expressions.

EISNER, KURT (1867–1919): German workers' leader. An editor of the Social Democratic newspaper *Vorwärts* from 1898 to 1905, he left the Social Democrats during World War I on account of his pacifism and founded the leftist Independent Social Democratic Party (1917). On the collapse of the German monarchial regime in Nov. 1918, E. headed the revolutionary movement in Munich and became first premier of the Bavarian republic. He was assassinated the following February. E. was an essayist of note, writing especially on art and sociology.

EKHAH see **LAMENTATIONS**

EKHAH RABBATI see **LAMENTATIONS RABBATI**

EKRON: Most northerly of the five Philistine cities in ancient Palestine. It is mentioned in Assyrian and Egyptian sources as well as in the Bible where the local god is called Baal Zebub. The city was captured by Sargon in 711 BCE. Alexander Balas gave E. to Jonathan the Hasmonean in 147 BCE, and according to Eusebius, it was a large village inhabited by Jews in the 3rd cent. CE. The modern Israel settlement of Mazkeret Batyah, in the vicinity of what is believed to have been the ancient site, was originally called E.

EL see **GOD, NAMES OF**

EL AL (Heb. "On high"): Israel airline, established in 1949 and now running services to four continents, including regular flights to Europe, New York, and Johannesburg. E. A., using Boeing planes, is a member of the International Air Transport Association and has concluded interline agreements with other airlines so as to provide its passengers with facilities to fly to most parts of the world. It also operates an air-freight service.

EL-ARISH, WADI: River and coastal town close to the border of Sinai and Palestine. In 1903, the British colonial secretary, Joseph Chamberlain, offered E.-A. to Herzl for Jewish settlement. A commission of the Zionist Organization visited the area, but the project came to nothing because of the refusal of Lord Cromer, viceroy of Egypt, to allot Nile water for irrigation. The area was under Israel control Nov. 1956–Jan. 1957 as a result of the SINAI OPERATION. It was again conquered by Israel during the Six-Day War of 1967. A census taken later that year put its population at 30,000.

EL ELYON: The "Most-High God" whose priest, in Abraham's time, was Melchizedek. See GOD, NAMES OF.

EL MALE RAḤAMIM (Heb. "God, full of compassion"): Prayer (probably dating in its present form from the 17th cent.) for the repose of the dead, customarily recited by the Ashkenazim in memorial services. A shorter form is known as YIZKOR. The corresponding Sephardi prayer is termed HASHKABA.

EL PASO: City in Texas US. German Jewish immigrants settled there prior to the Civil War. The first Jewish congregation, Mount Sinai Association, was founded in 1887, and its temple dedicated in 1899. An Orthodox synagogue was established in 1902 and a Jewish Community Council founded in 1939. Jewish pop. (1973): 4,500.

EL SHADDAI see **GOD, NAMES OF**

ELAH: King of Israel; son of Baasha. He ruled for two years (c. 886–885 BCE) and was murdered by the captain of his chariots, Zimri, while the Israelite army was besieging the Philistine city of Gibbethon.

ELAM: Ancient state E of Babylonia (the modern Khuzistan); capital: Susa (the Shushan of the Book of Esther). The Elamites, as several other non-Semitic peoples, are classed by the Bible as children of Shem (Gen. 10:22). CHEDORLAOMER King of E., together with three confederates, attacked the kings of S Canaan in the neighborhood of the Dead Sea and was in turn defeated by Abraham (Gen. 14). Elamites participated in Sennacherib's siege of Jerusalem in 704 BCE (Is. 22:6), and Ashurbanipal transferred part of the population of E to Samaria after 639 BCE (Ezra 4:9–10). Jews may have lived in E. from the period of the Babylonian Exile (Is. 11:11). Under Persian rule, their numbers were considerable; they were still of importance several centuries later (cf. Acts 2:9), and remained significant in and after the Gaonic Period.

ELATH: (1) Gulf at the N extremity of the Red Sea. Length: 117 m.; breadth at widest point: 9 m.; maximum depth; 1,080 ft. It is bounded by four states: Saudi Arabia, Jordan, Israel, and Egypt. At its S entrance lies the island of TIRAN. (2) Settlement near the site of EZION-GEBER. The town was built by Amaziah and his son Uzziah but was captured by Rezin, king of Aram, in the reign of Ahaz and became an Edomite city. It was of importance when the Jewish settlement was renewed under Islam, and remained so until the 10th cent. The city was destroyed by the Crusaders in 1116. During the period of the Palestine Mandate, the British developed the neighboring port of AKABA in the territory of Transjordan. The modern Israel settlement of E. was founded after its occupation in Mar. 1949. It expanded rapidly after the Gulf of E. was opened to Israel shipping by the 1956 SINAI OPERATION. E. has a port connecting with E Africa and Asia, an oil pipeline terminus, and a tourist center. It is also the site of a desalination plant. Pop. (1974): 14,900.

ELATH (formerly **EPSTEIN**), **ELIAHU** (1903–): Israel diplomat. Born in Russia, he went to Palestine in 1925 and headed the Middle East division of the Jewish Agency 1934–45, and its Washington political department 1945–8. He was the first Israel representative (later ambassador) to the US (1948–50) and Israel minister, later ambassador, to Great Britain 1950–9. He was president of the Hebrew Univ. 1962–8.

ELAZAR, DAVID (1925–1976): Israel soldier. Born in Yugoslavia he went to Palestine in 1940. He was responsible for the capture of the Golan Heights in the Six-Day War. C-in-C from 1972, he led the army to victory in the Yom Kippur War but resigned in 1974 following criticism of army unpreparedness at the War's outbreak.

ELAZARI-VOLCANI (formerly **WILKANSKI**), **YITZHAK AVIGDOR** (1880–1955): Agronomist. He was born in Lithuania and settled in Palestine in 1908, becoming one of the leaders of the *Ha-Poel ha-Tzair* party. An advocate of mixed farming, he founded and directed the workers' farms at Ben Shemen and Huldah, 1910–18. He also founded and directed the Agricultural Experimental Station at Ben Shemen in 1921 (transferred to Rehovot, 1927), and was professor at the Hebrew Univ.

ELBOGEN, ISMAR (1874–1948): Scholar. He taught in Italy and at the Lehranstalt für die Wissenschaft des Judentums in Berlin from 1902 until 1938 when he migrated to New York. A scholar in many spheres of Jewish learning, E.'s major research was in the history of the Jewish liturgy, his *Der jüdische Gottesdienst in seiner geschichtlichen Entwicklung* being a standard work. His *A Century of Jewish Life* (1848–1939) was a supplement to Graetz' history. E. also produced important studies on the history of German Jewry.

ELDAD: One of the 70 Israelite elders appointed by Moses to aid him in governing the people (Num. 11:2 ff). E. and Medad aroused the suspicion of

Elath.

Joshua by prophesying within the camp, but their conduct was approved by Moses.

ELDAD HA-DANI (fl. late 9th cent.): Traveler. His origins and personality still remain a riddle. He claimed to belong to the tribe of Dan, and that it, together with the tribes of Naphtali, Gad, and Asher, ruled over a large area in Africa. In 880–5, E. visited Jewish communities in N Africa and Spain, exciting their imagination by his fantastic accounts of the Ten Tribes who, he averred, were living a free, nomadic existence. E. also cited strange halakhic practices which, he maintained, were in vogue among them. The Kairouan community requested the gaon Tzemah's advice regarding this information. Many medieval Jewish scholars believed his tales, and some tried to reconcile the contradictions between these customs and those accepted in Jewish communities. His seemingly fantastic story may have had a basis of fact in the judaizing tribes (e.g. Falashas) to be found in Africa at that time.

ELDER (Heb. *zaken*): In biblical times, a member of the authoritative group of the nation. The e.'s were influential in shaping the form of government and served as judges and chief representatives of the people down to the period of the Second Temple. *Zaken* was the title given to communal councillors in some areas throughout the Middle Ages (e.g. Sicily).

"ELDERS OF ZION", PROTOCOLS OF: Anti-Semitic fabrication. The origins go back to a document circulated in Russian official circles at the close of the 19th cent. purporting to reveal the covert Jewish motives of history. This ultimately developed into an account of a plan made by a secret Jewish "government" for the overthrow of Christian society in association with Liberals, Freemasons, etc. This was published in Russian (c. 1902) as an appendix to a work by Sergei Nilus. In 1919, the protocols were introduced into W Europe by Russian emigrés and obtained a remarkable vogue, being translated into most languages, running through many editions, and being taken seriously by politicians. Philip Graves, the Constantinople correspondent of the London *Times*, demonstrated in 1921 that in essentials the work was clumsily plagiarized from a satire on Napoleon III, written by a non-Jewish journalist, M. Joly, *Dialogue aux enfers entre Machiavel et Montesquieu* (Brussels, 1865). Although this utterly destroyed their credit in responsible circles, the protocols have remained in circulation in many countries, played a great part in Nazi propaganda, and are still being reprinted. On several occasions, they have been condemned in legal actions (e.g. at Berne, 1934–5). Recently they have been frequently reprinted and widely distributed by Egypt in Arab and African countries.

ELEAZAR: Third son and successor of Aaron.
The high priests of the house of Zadok were descended from E.

ELEAZAR (called Auran; d. 163 BCE): HASMONEAN warrior; brother of JUDAH THE MACCABEE. At the battle of Bet Zechariah, E. stabbed an elephant of the enemy's army in the belief that its rider was the Syrian ruler Antiochus Eupator; he was crushed to death when the animal fell on him.

ELEAZAR BEN ARAKH (fl. late 1st cent.): Tanna.
A favorite pupil of R Johanan ben Zakkai, he left his colleagues after his teacher's death and went to Emmaus where he died at an early age.

ELEAZAR BEN AZARIAH (fl. 1st–2nd cents.): Tanna. Of distinguished birth (being descended from Ezra), he was extremely modest, despite his wealth. When Gamaliel was temporarily deposed from the patriarchate, E. was elected in his place notwithstanding his youth (according to tradition, he was then 16 or 18). In 95–6, he went on a mission to Rome with R Gamaliel, R Joshua, and R Akiva. He was expert in the Scriptures, the Mishnah, halakhah, and, especially, in aggadah. His halakhic teachings were based on the principle "the Torah is written in everyday language."

ELEAZAR BEN DINAI (fl. 1st cent.): Patriot leader in Palestine. He was involved in border conflicts with the Ammonites and the Samaritans. By means of a ruse, E. and his band were captured by the procurator Felix (52–60) and he was sent as a prisoner to Rome where he probably perished.

ELEAZAR BEN JAIR (d. 73 CE): Patriot leader.
After the assassination in 66 of the Zealot leader, Menahem ben Judah, E. led the remnant of his forces back to the fortress of Masada and held it for seven years. When it was completely surrounded by the Romans, he persuaded the defenders to kill their families and themselves, so as to avoid capture.

ELEAZAR BEN JUDAH OF WORMS (c. 1160–1238): Codifier, kabbalist, and liturgical poet. A native of Mainz, his wife and two daughters were slaughtered by Crusaders before his eyes in 1196. From 1201, he was rabbi at Worms. His works, based on the system of his master, Judah Hasid, popularized the Ashkenazi theory of "practical" Kabbalah which stressed the doctrine of repentance. His ethical teachings are embodied in his code *Sepher ha-Rokeah* ("The Book of the Spice-Dealer"), after which he is known as Eleazar Rokeah.

ELEAZAR BEN PEDAT (fl. latter part of 3rd cent.): Amora. Of Babylonian birth, he went to Palestine in his youth. Colleague and successor of R Johanan in Tiberias, E. was noted for his saintliness and frugality.

ELEAZAR BEN SHAMMUA (fl. mid-2nd cent.): Tanna; pupil of R Akiva. His disciples included R Judah Ha-Nasi. He lived to very old age, and, according to a late Midrash, was one of the TEN MARTYRS.

ELEAZAR BEN SIMEON (fl. 2nd cent.): Tanna, son of R Simeon ben Yohai. According to legend, he hid twelve years in a cave from the Romans, together with his father. Subsequently he studied under R Simeon ben Gamaliel. His awe of authority led him to become an informer, but he repented of his behavior before his death.

ELEAZAR BEN SIMON: Zealot leader in the Jewish war of 66–70 CE. Of priestly family, he took an important part in the defeat of Cestius Gallus. E. was probably responsible for inviting Idumeans to Jerusalem and the subsequent massacre of opponents of the Zealots. He fought against John of Gischala till the beginning of the siege of the city by Titus.

ELEAZAR ROKEAH see **ELEAZAR BEN JUDAH OF WORMS**

ELEGY see **KINAH**

ELEPHANTINE see **YEB**

ELEUTHEROPOLIS see **BET GUVRIN**

ELHANAN (ANDREAS): Legendary Jewish pope.
According to the story, E., son of R Simeon the Great of Mainz, was kidnapped by monks, bap-

tized, educated in a monastery, entered the priest-hood, and eventually became pope. Discovering his Jewish origin and becoming convinced of the truth of Judaism, he ascended to the top of a tower, preached against Christianity, and then threw himself down to the ground. According to another version, he reverted to Judaism.

ELI: High priest at the shrine of Shiloh and one of the last Judges (11th cent. BCE); mentor of Samuel. He succeeded to the high priesthood at the age of 58 and died forty years later as a result of falling from his chair on hearing of the Philistine capture of the Ark (I Sam. 4:13 ff.) His family was subsequently deprived of the high priesthood (I Kings 2:26–7), the Bible ascribing this to the immoral conduct of his sons Hophni and Phinehas (I Sam. 2:11–36; 3:11–14).

ELI ZION (Heb. "Lament, O Zion"): Lamentation arranged in alphabetical order, recited on *Av* 9. The traditional tune was used for one of Byron's *Hebrew Melodies*.

ELIAKIM see **JEHOIAKIM**

ELIAS, JULIUS SALTER see **SOUTHWOOD**

ELIAS, NEY (1844–1897): British explorer and diplomat. He traveled from Pekin to Russia over the Gobi Desert at great risk, discovered the sources of the Oxus, fulfilled political missions in India, and from 1891, was British consul-general in Persia.

ELIASHIB: High priest in the time of Ezra and Nehemiah (5th cent. BCE). He played a major part in rebuilding the wall of Jerusalem (Neh. 3:1).

ELIEZER: (1) of Damascus. Abraham's servant and steward of his household (Gen. 15:2) identified with the servant sent to bring a wife for Isaac (Gen. 24). (2) Second son of Moses (Exod. 18:4). (3) Prophet from Mareshah who denounced Jehoshaphat's alliance with Ahaziah (II Chron. 20:37).

ELIEZER BEN HYRCANUS (fl. c. 100): Tanna; pupil of R Johanan ben Zakkai and teacher of R Akiva. He was reputed to have had a phenomenal memory and to have adhered closely to his master's teachings. He followed R Johanan ben Zakkai to Jabneh but later set up his own academy at Lydda. In 95–6, he accompanied the patriarch, R Gamaliel, on an official mission to Rome. A patrician, most of his legal rulings were in the spirit of the school of Shammai, but his views were not accepted by his colleagues. When he insisted upon having his way, they excommunicated him "in order not to foment dissension within Israel" at a critical hour. Upon his death, the ban was revoked, and he was buried with honor.

ELIEZER BEN JOEL HALEVI (known as *Rabiyah*: c. 1140–c. 1225): German scholar. Although regarded as the spiritual leader of German Jewry, he refused for many years to accept a rabbinical appointment in order not to derive material benefit from his learning, but in 1200, he agreed to become rabbi of Cologne. His principal work is *Sepher ha-Rabiyah* (also known as *Avi ha-Ezri*), an important halakhic work replete with material for social history.

ELIEZER BEN NATHAN OF MAINZ (known as *Raben*; c. 1090–1170): Codifier and liturgical poet. His chief work is *Even ha-Ezer* ("Stone of help"; cf. I Sam. 7:12) incorporating halakhic material adapted to practical requirements. The book contains much material bearing upon Jewish life at the time. His *Even ha-Roshah* ("Keystone") is virtually an abridgment of *Even ha-Ezer*. He also composed a number of liturgical poems which were incorporated in the Ashkenazi ritual.

ELIEZER BEN YOSE HA-GALILI (fl. 2nd cent.): Tanna. After the Hadrianic persecutions, he helped to establish the colleges of Jabneh and Usha. E. was a well-known aggadist and laid down 32 rules for expounding the Scriptures which have been preserved in a separate *baraita*.

ELIEZER OF TOUQUES (fl. 13th cent.): French tosaphist. He edited most of the *tosaphot* incorporated in the standard editions of the Babylonian Talmud. E. also wrote a commentary on the Pentateuch, now lost.

ELIJAH (fl. 9th cent. BCE; known as "the Tishbite"): Prophet in the kingdom of Israel during the reign of Ahab and Ahaziah. Striving to restore the purity of Divine worship, he intensified his efforts when Ahab's wife, Jezebel, introduced the cult of Baal. E.'s zeal aroused the opposition of the royal court which, for political reasons, tolerated the cults of the neighboring peoples in the country. E. was forced to flee, taking refuge in the desert. The climax of his efforts to free Divine worship from alien influences was the great assembly on Mt. Carmel when E. turned to the people asking "How long halt ye between two opinions?" (I Kings 18:21) and eventually, with the help of his supporters, slew the prophets of Baal. E. also fought strenuously in the interests of social justice, rebuking Ahab for murdering Naboth in order to obtain possession of his vineyard. According to the biblical account, E. did not die but ascended to Heaven in a fiery chariot. He occupies a prominent place in Jewish lore. According to Malachi (3:23–4), E. will reconcile fathers and children "before the coming of the great and dreadful day of the Lord." This led to E.'s being depicted in later tradition as the harbinger of the Messiah. At the Passover Seder, a glass of wine is traditionally poured for E. (see ELIJAH, CUP OF), and at the circumcision ceremony, a chair is prepared for him. He is popularly believed to come to the help of Jewish communities, and also individuals, in dire distress and it is believed that he will clarify all obscurities in talmudic law upon his return. E.

Chair of Elijah

also figures prominently in Christian and Moslem legend.

ELIJAH, APOCALYPSE OF (*Sepher Eliyahu*): Hebrew messianic work, possibly of the Gaonic Period (6th–10th cents.). It describes the archangel Michael's account to Elijah of the end of Rome, the destruction of the wicked, the last judgment, the heavenly Jerusalem, etc. A similar document in Ethiopic (*Makbeba Abba Elias*) exists among the Falashas.

ELIJAH, CHAIR OF: Symbolic chair set aside for the prophet Elijah at the circumcision ceremony. Chairs specially made for this purpose are to be found in many synagogues. In Central Europe, they were generally double seats, one being reserved for the prophet while the infant was ceremonially placed on the other.

ELIJAH, CUP OF: Cup of wine placed on the Seder table during the Passover meal but not drunk. The linking of this with the name of E. stems from a talmudic dispute as to whether four or five glasses of wine are to be drunk at the Seder. The decision was left "for Elijah to determine in messianic times." A similar cup is used in some countries in the circumcision ceremony. Sometimes specially-made receptacles are utilized for this purpose.

ELIJAH BAḤUR see **LEVITA, ELIJAH**

ELIJAH BE'ER BEN SHABBETAI (Elijah Sabot; fl. 15th cent.): Italian physician. One of the best-known practitioners of his age, he taught at Padua, was in the service of successive popes and of numerous other Italian rulers, and was accorded the honor of knighthood. When summoned to England in 1410 to attend on Henry IV, he was empowered to bring ten retainers who constituted a *minyan* for religious services.

ELIJAH BEN JUDAH OF CHELM, BAAL SHEM (1514–1583): Rabbi and kabbalist, known for his miracle cures by means of charms and amulets. According to tradition, he created a *Golem*.

ELIJAH BEN SOLOMON ZALMAN ("The Vilna Gaon"; 1720–1797): Talmudist. He was born in Lithuania and was early famed for his scholarship. From 1740–5, he traveled among the Jewish communities of Poland and Germany, settling in Vilna where he taught and later founded his own academy. Although refusing rabbinic office and living in seclusion, his reputation as a saint and scholar was widespread. The weight of his authority became apparent when he led the opposition to the Ḥasidim in Lithuania, ordering their excommunication and the destruction of their literature. His obdurate attitude checked the spread of Ḥasidism in Lithuania. When he was about 60, E. set out unaccompanied for Palestine but, for unexplained reasons, returned before reaching his destination. His reputation lies primarily in the field of halakhah; he sought to establish critical texts of the authoritative rabbinic writings, resorting also to emendations. By these methods, he avoided *pilpul* and based his views and rulings upon the plain meaning of the text. He regarded highly the early kabbalistic works, and was extremely critical of philosophy. E. was interested in secular studies insofar as they threw light on the Torah, but he opposed the Haskalah. His numerous works, all published posthumously, include commentaries on the Bible, annotations on the Talmud, Midrash, and Zohar, works on mathematics, the geography of Palestine, Hebrew grammar, etc. E. exercised a vast influence on his own and succeeding generations, the Mitnaggedim regarding him as their spiritual leader.

ELIMELECH: Husband of Naomi and father-in-law of Ruth. A native of Bethlehem, he moved to Moab during a period of famine and died there (Ruth 1).

ELIMELECH OF LIZENSK (1717–1787): One of the founders of Ḥasidism in Galicia; disciple of Dov Ber of Mezhirich. Numerous legends tell of his penances and his ecstasy in prayer. In his book *Noam Elimelekh* ("Elimelech's Delight") E. stresses the role of the *tzaddik* in Ḥasidism, particularly his holiness and absolute perfection which have influence in the terrestrial as well as the spiritual realm, and thereby laid the theoretical foundations for the establishment of "dynasties" of *tzaddikim*.

*ELIOT, GEORGE (pen-name of Mary Anne Evans; 1819–1880): English novelist. Her later novels included *Daniel Deronda* (1876) which, in consonance with her sympathy for the persecuted, showed the Jews as a progressive historical factor and advocated the re-establishment of a Jewish national home in Palestine.

ELIPHAZ: (1) Eldest son of Esau. (2) *E. THE TEMANITE*: one of Job's three friends.

ELISHA (fl. 9th cent. BCE): Israelite prophet.

He flourished during and after the reign of Jehoram. The biblical stories reflect the esteem in which he was held by the people; numerous miracles are attributed to him, including resurrection of the dead. His chief importance is that he was the disciple and successor of Elijah, and, like Elijah, is depicted as earnest, brave, and forceful. Interested in politics, he foretold Hazael's accession to the Syrian throne and he anointed Jehu king over Israel. His activity as a prophet lasted some 60 years.

ELISHA BEN AVUYAH (fl. early 2nd cent. CE): Tanna; teacher and friend of R Meir. After his adoption of heretical opinions, the rabbis always referred to E. as *Aher* ("the other"). It is difficult to reconstruct his character from the fragmentary aggadic references. He doubted the unity of God, reward and punishment, and the resurrection of the dead. During a period of persecution (Hadrianic?), he profaned the Sabbath, inciting others to follow his example, and also to neglect the study of the Torah in favor of heretical literature. When he wished to repent, a Divine voice is reported to have said "All may repent, except Aher!" His enigmatic personality forms the subject of several compositions of the Haskalah Period as well as Milton Steinberg's novel *As a Driven Leaf*.

ELISHEVA (real name: Yelizaveta Zhirkova; 1888–1949): Hebrew poet. Born in Russia of a Russian father and an Irish mother, her early poems were in Russian, but later, she wrote in Hebrew, publishing poems and critical essays. In 1925, she settled in Palestine.

ELIZABETH: City in New Jersey, US. The first Jewish settlers, consisting of families from Bohemia and Germany, date from the third quarter of the 19th cent. E.'s first congregation, B'nai Israel, was formed in 1881. Most of the subsequent arrivals were from E Europe. In 1888, the Orthodox congregation of Holche Yosher was founded. E. had 16,500 Jews in 1971; its Jewish Council was founded in 1940.

*ELIZABETH: Empress of Russia 1741–62. Desiring, as she said, "no profit from the enemies of Christ," she decreed the expulsion of the Jews from Russia in 1742, denying them even the right of temporary residence and refusing to countenance their readmission.

ELKAN, BENNO (1877–1960): Sculptor and medalist.

He lived and worked mainly in Germany until 1933 when he settled in London. He produced numerous monuments and sculptured many distinguished portraits and bronzes. E. executed many works of Jewish interest including a historical candelabrum for the Knesset in Jerusalem.

ELKANAH (c. 11th cent. BCE): Father of the prophet Samuel. Probably an Ephraimite and of levitical origin, E. lived in Ramathaim Zophim.

ELKASAITES or **ELKESAITES:** Sect existing from the 2nd cent. CE in Transjordan, with adherents also in Syria and Rome; connected with the ESSENES. They stressed ritual purification and, unlike the Essenes, the duty of fertility. The E. believed in elemental power and regarded Jesus as one of a series of reincarnations of the Messiah. Under persecution, they feigned conversion to paganism and are not heard of after the 4th cent.

EL-KUDS (Arab. "The sanctuary"): Arabic name for Jerusalem.

ELKUS, ABRAM ISAAC (1867–1947): US lawyer and diplomat. During World War I, he was US ambassador to Turkey (1916–7) directing the aid of US Jewry to the local communities and helping to relieve the plight of Palestinian Jewry. In 1919, he was appointed associate judge of the New York Court of Appeals.

ELLSBERG, EDWARD (1891–): US naval officer and engineer. During World War I, he was in charge of the refitting of confiscated German liners and subsequently became the acknowledged expert in raising sunken vessels, etc. having invented several

Benno Elkan: Granite monument in Mainz (destroyed by the Nazis).

devices for such work. He has written sea-novels and works on salvaging. E. became chief engineer of an oil company in which capacity he devised improved techniques.

ELMAN, MISCHA (1891–1967): US violinist. He was born in Russia and gave his first concert at the age of five. He resided in the US from 1923. E. made many violin transcriptions and composed songs and pieces for the violin

Mischa Elman.

ELOESSER, ARTHUR (1870–1938): German dramatic critic, essayist and literary historian. His main work is a history of German literature from the baroque period down to modern times (1930).

ELOHIM see **GOD, NAMES OF**

ELOHISTIC CODE see **BIBLE CRITICISM**

ELON: Israel communal settlement (KA) in W Galilee, founded in 1938 as an outpost to prevent the infiltration of armed gangs from the Lebanon.

ELON (or *Elone* [pl.] **MOREH** (Heb. "Oak [terebinth] of Moreh"; authorized version: "Plain of Moreh"): Place near Shechem regarded as sacred by the ancient Israelites and associated with Abraham (Gen. 12:6–7).

ELSBERG, CHARLES ALBERT (1871–1948): US neurologist. He was responsible for various innovations in the treatment of heart wounds and in brain surgery and was surgical director of the New York Neurological Institute.

ELUL: 6th month of the Jewish religious calendar, and last of the civil. It has 29 days. The name is Babylonian and first occurs in Neh. 6:15. As it immediately precedes the High Holiday season, E. has become the traditional month of penitence and spiritual preparation for the Day of Judgment, and the *shophar* is sounded after morning service on weekdays throughout *E.*

ELVIRA: Former town near Granada, Spain, the scene of a Church Council which prohibited Christian-Jewish familiarity and intermarriage (312).

It was the first Church Council to concern itself with Jews and constitutes one of the earliest evidences of extensive Jewish settlement in Spain.

ELYASHEV, ISIDOR (pseudonym: *Baal Makhshoves*; 1873–1924): Yiddish and Hebrew critic. He devoted himself mainly to Yiddish journalism in Russia and Poland and, from 1922, in Berlin. He was the founder of modern esthetic criticism in Yiddish.

EMANATION: Philosophical theory explaining the plurality and multiplicity of the sensible world as a "flowing out" from a primary source. It was taken over from the Neoplatonists by the Arab Aristotelians. The theory can be traced in the Apocrypha, Philo and especially in medieval Jewish philosophy (e.g. Ibn Gabirol), although with modifications. The doctrine of e. passed over into the Kabbalah where it became an essential part of the theory of the 10 *sephirot.*

EMANCIPATION: Term applied to the removal, particularly in the western world in the 18th–20th cents., of the DISABILITIES imposed on Jews. There was normally no specific anti-Jewish religious discrimination in the Roman Empire, and the Jews had benefited from the Edict of Caracalla (212) which extended universally the rights and duties of citizenship. From the 4th cent. onward, the Christian Empire enacted an elaborate system of discrimination against the Jews which was adopted and intensified in medieval Europe as well as in the Islamic world. It was brought to its climax by the GHETTO system which aimed at the complete expulsion of the Jews from gentile society. Nevertheless, the new settlements established by the cultured and Europeanized Marrano settlers in N Europe in the 17th cent. enjoyed a considerable degree of social e., and the same may be said of the influential "Court Jews" who played a prominent role in Germany at that time. In the less rigid environment of the New World, the atmosphere was even more favorable. In the British colonies in N America, Jews tended to intermingle with their neighbors on equal terms; they were admitted to the franchise (not without difficulty) in the 18th cent. and took part freely in the events leading up to the American Revolution. Virginia established full religious freedom in 1785, and the constitution of the US (1787) formally completed e. (without, however, contemplating the Jews specifically) in stipulating that no religious test should be required as a qualification for any public office. Full e. in individual states, however, was delayed (Maryland 1825, N Carolina 1868, New Hampshire 1876–7, etc.). In France, Jewish e. was a natural corollary of the Declaration of the Rights of Man (1789) but, though it was extended (1790) to the long-established Jews in Avignon and the Sephardim of Bordeaux, etc., it was only with great difficulty that the Germanized Jews of Alsace were brought within its scope (1791). Napoleon's *décret infâme* of 1808 restricted Jewish municipal (though not political) rights, especially in Alsace. But it was not renewed on its expiration in 1818. In 1831, the process of e. in France was completed by the official recognition of Judaism (like the Christian Churches) as a subsidized state religion. The armies of the French Revolution had introduced the conception of Jewish e. into the countries they conquered. The Jews of Holland, already to a great extent socially assimilated, were formally emancipated in 1796, and so continued thereafter, as did the Jews of Belgium when its independence was established in 1830. E. was also introduced in the Revolutionary and Napoleonic era into those parts of Italy and Germany occupied or influenced by the French (e.g. Westphalia, 1807, Frankfort 1811), while, influenced by this, Prussia conceded a qualified e. in 1812. In the reaction following the fall of Napoleon, all these concessions were rescinded or diluted in varying degrees, the Jews being expelled from some towns in Germany and the ghetto system being restored in Rome and various other parts of Italy. In the 19th cent., there was a see-saw process, Jewish e. being introduced by revolutionary movements and canceled during periods of reaction. It was, however, gradually established in Germany (Hesse-Cassel 1833; Brunswick 1834; Prussia in a modified degree 1850; Baden 1862; Saxony 1868, etc.) and was embodied in the constitutions of the N German Federation (1869) and of the German Empire (1871). It was introduced into Austro-Hungary in 1867. In Italy, the kingdom of Piedmont had established it in 1848, and as this state gradually embraced the whole of Italy, the principle was accordingly extended, being completed on the occupation of Rome in 1870. Denmark began the process in 1814, granting municipal e. in 1837 and political e. in 1848. The other Scandinavian countries followed somewhat later. The Swiss cantons, most of which had maintained a highly intolerant policy hitherto, modified their attitude from the mid-19th cent. and the Federal constitution of 1874 proclaimed full religious liberty. In England, the ghetto system had never obtained and the Jews enjoyed a high degree of personal liberty in the 17th and 18th cents. With the e. of the Catholics in 1829, a movement began for extending the process to Jews, but it was implemented only gradually. Such disabilities as existed were removed piecemeal; Jews were admitted to municipal offices 1830–55, and to parliament, after a long struggle, in 1858. E. had already been established in the British colonies (Barbados 1802/20, Jamaica 1831, Canada 1831–2), while in S Africa and Australia there was at no time any legal discrimination on religious grounds. Disabilities of the most stringent and inhuman sort

continued in the Russian Empire throughout this period, being intensified by the May Laws of 1882. Full legal e. immediately followed the Russian Revolution of 1917, although the results were far from what had been anticipated. E. had been imposed on the Balkan states by the Berlin Conference of 1878, but in the case of Rumania, the obligations were evaded. In the "succession states" set up in Central and E Europe after World War I Jewish equality was established as a basic constitutional principle, though this was fully carried out only in Czechoslovakia. Nominally, however, the Jews were excluded from full rights after this period only in certain Moslem states. In 1933, the Nazi regime in Germany reversed the process, taking as its criterion not religion but race. This reaction extended during the following years and comprised in the end the greater part of the continent of Europe, over which the Nazi occupation or influence extended. The cancelation of e. was the preliminary to the subsequent campaign of annihilation. On the overthrow of the Nazis, former conditions were reestablished, and in all countries of the occidental world (though not in some Moslem states) Jews now enjoy, here and there with some trivial reservations, the same political and civil rights as their neighbors. Among the champions of Jewish e. (not all of whom, however, envisaged political e.) may be mentioned John TOLAND and T. B. MACAULAY in England, Abbé GREGOIRE in France, C.W. von DOHM in Germany, and M. d'Azeglio in Italy.

EMANUEL, DAVID (1744–1808): Sixth governor of Georgia, US (Mar.–Nov. 1801). Emanuel County, Georgia, is named after him. He was probably baptized.

EMDEN: Seaport in Lower Saxony, Germany. The first reference to Jews there dates from the 16th cent. Civil rights were conferred by Louis Bonaparte in 1808. These were annulled in 1815 when the Jewish right of residence was curtailed, being restored only in 1842. Before the Nazi era, the community numbered c. 1,000.

EMDEN, JACOB ISRAEL (known as *Yavetz*; c. 1697–1776): Rabbinical scholar; son of Tzevi Hirsch ASHKENAZI. He was rabbi at Emden (1728–32), whence his name. Out of a desire to be independent and also on account of difficulties with various personalities, he left the rabbinate in 1733 and returned to his birthplace, Altona, where he opened a printing-press and engaged in commerce. A man of wide rabbinic knowledge and a highly developed critical faculty, his emphatic views led him into frequent conflicts. He expressed the view that parts of the Zohar were late and not to be attributed to R Simeon ben Yoḥai. E. regarded Sabbetaianism, which in his time had penetrated several countries of Europe, as a danger to the

Charm used by Jacob Emden in his book *Sepher Shimush*, printed at his press in Amsterdam and Emden, 1757–1767.

existence of Judaism and treated it with exaggerated suspicion. His fierce and prolonged dispute on this score with Jonathan EIBESCHUTZ was notorious. He wrote some forty books on halakhic subjects, including *Leḥem Shamayim* (a commentary on the Mishnah), twenty-five polemical pamphlets written

during his controversy with Eibeschütz, and an autobiography *Megillat Sepher*.

EMEK: Hebrew for "valley" or "plain." Today, *Ha-Emek* is primarily used to refer to the Valley of Jezreel.

EMEK BET SHEAN see **BET(H) SHEAN**

EMEK HA-YARDEN (Heb. "Jordan Valley"): The Jordan rift from its sources near Dan to the S end of the Dead Sea; also called in Heb. *Kikkar ha-Yarden*. Applied in a more restricted sense to the plain of the R Jordan, S of the Sea of Galilee to Naharayim, bounded on the W by the Lower Galilean hills. Its area is about 20 sq. m. and its climate tropical. The Jordan Valley is intensively cultivated and irrigated. It constitutes a rural district with local self-government. The Rutenberg power station (Tel Or; now in disuse) is at Naharayim in the Jordan Valley.

EMEK ḤEPHER: Stretch of the Israel coastal plain between Tel Aviv and Haifa. The tract, at the time highly malarious, was acquired by the Jewish National Fund in 1929 and is now the site of over 40 fertile agricultural settlements. The regional council of E. Ḥ. is situated in its largest village, Kephar Vitkin.

EMEK YIZREEL see **JEZREEL, VALLEY OF**

EMEK ZEVULUN (Heb. "Plain of Zebulun"): The coastal plain between Mt. Carmel (Haifa) and Acre, bounded on the E by the entrance to the Valley of Jezreel and by the Galilean hills to the NE and N. Its area is c. 145 sq. m. E. Z. is the basin of the rivers Kishon and Naaman and includes the industrial area and residential suburbs N of Haifa, Kephar Atta, and a number of agricultural villages.

River scene in Emek Ḥepher.

En Gedi.

EMES, DER (Yidd. "The Truth"): Yiddish daily paper, the official organ of the Russian Communist Party relating to Jewish affairs. Founded in 1918 by the *Yevsektzia*, it was published (with a short interval) until 1940. Its first editor was S. Diemenstein.

EMET VE-EMUNAH (Heb. "True and trustworthy"): Opening words of the blessing in the evening service immediately following the three paragraphs of the *Shema*.

EMET VE-YATZIV (Heb. "True and valid"): Opening words of the prayer immediately following the three paragraphs of the *Shema* in the morning service. The phrase became proverbial.

EMIGDIRECT (*Emigrations-Direktion*): Office set up by the Jewish Emigration Conference at Prague in 1921, to assist and organize Jewish emigration from Europe, particularly Russia. Its activities and connections were extended in 1925; in 1935, it merged with ORT-OSE.

EMIGRATION see **MIGRATION**

EMIM: Ancient inhabitants of the land of Moab (Gen. 14:5; Deut. 2:10–11).

EMIN PASHA (real name: Eduard Schnitzer; 1840–1892): Traveler and explorer. Born in Germany and baptized in childhood, he practiced medicine in Albania, then under Turkish rule, became a Moslem, and took a Turkish name. He served under General Gordon, governor of the Equatorial Provinces, who nominated E. as his successor in 1878. On the outbreak of the Mahdi's rebellion. E. was cut off from the outside world (1883) and compelled to retire with his force into Central Africa where he was eventually relieved by a British ex-

peditionary force under Stanley. In 1890, he transferred to German service and set out to acquire areas near Lake Victoria for Germany. He was murdered in the Congo by slave-traders whose activities he had opposed. He was responsible for important investigations into the ornithology, ethnography, and meteorology of Central Africa.

EMMAUS: Ancient city in Judea, first mentioned in I Macc. as the site of the camp of the Seleucid army defeated by Judah the Maccabee (166 BCE). The Talmud described it as a resort. In 221 CE, it received the privileges of a Roman city and was called Nicopolis. After the foundation of Ramlah (717), E. declined in importance. The ruins of E. were excavated at Kubeiba (Latrun) in 1924–5.

EN (or **EIN**): Hebrew for "well". A common component of place-names both in biblical and modern times.

EN DOR: Israel communal settlement (KA) in Lower Galilee founded in 1948 by Israelis and immigrants from the US, Bulgaria, Turkey, and Germany. Pop. (1972): 616. The biblical E. D., probably on the same site, was a village of the tribe of Issachar (Jos. 17:11) and the residence of the witch who raised Samuel's ghost (1 Sam. 28:7).

EN GANNIM: Israel settlement, now merged with Petah Tikvah. It was the first workers' smallholder village in the country, having been founded in 1908 by the Russian *Hoveve Zion*.

EN GEDI: Israel communal settlement, founded in 1953, near an oasis on the W shore of the Dead Sea. It was a desert town at the time of Joshua's invasion (Josh. 15:62), and David hid there from

En Gev: on the shores of Lake Kinnereth.

Saul (I Sam. 24:1–2). Its vineyards were famed (Song of Songs 1:14). In Second Temple times, an Essene settlement existed nearby, and abundant remains have been found from the Late Bronze Age to the Byzantine Period, while scroll fragments were among the many discoveries made in nearby caves.

EN GEV: Israel settlement (IK) on the E shore of the Sea of Galilee. Founded in 1937, its epic defense during the War of Independence secured Israel a footing on the E shore of the Sea. Its economy is based on fishing and tropical fruit plantations An annual music festival is held there during Passover week. Until the 1967 Six-Day War, it was dominated by the nearby Syrian frontier and was frequently the object of bombardment. Pop. (1972): 305.

EN HA-RA (Heb.): The evil eye. *Beli en ha-ra* (in Yiddish, *kinanhora*) "without the evil eye" is a phrase to ward off the supposed ills resulting from praise or from the admission of good fortune.

EN ḤAROD: Israel communal settlement in the Valley of Jezreel, founded in 1921 near the spring of Harod where Gideon tested his men before the battle with the Midianites (Judg. 7:4–6). The settlers drained the surrounding swamps, and in 1929,

transferred to a permanent site nearby. E. Ḥ. became a well-developed agricultural community with highly intensive and diversified farming, workshops, dairy, etc. as well as a printing-press, art-gallery, and museum. The settlement was severely affected by the split in the *Kibbutz ha-Meuḥad* movement in 1951. Considerable ill-feeling developed between the two parties and in 1956, E. Ḥ. divided into two settlements, one affiliated to KM (pop. 808) and the other to IK (666). (1972).

EN HA-SHOPHET: Israel communal settlement (KA) founded in the Hills of Manasseh in 1937 by N American and Polish settlers and named for Justice (*shophet*) BRANDEIS. Pop. (1974): 623.

EN K-ELOHENU: First words ("There is none like unto our God") of an ancient hymn which attained great popularity, especially in the Sabbath

En Kelohenu
(Traditional)

En ke-lo – he –nu en ka-do-ne – nu en ke-mal-ke –nu en kemoshi-e –nu
D.c.
mi khe-lo-he – nu mi khado-ne –nu mi khe-mal-ke –nu mi khemoshi-e —nu

additional service. Its original form was an acrostic constituting the word "Amen."

EN KEREM: Village in Israel in the Jerusalem municipal area. It is noted for its vineyards and orchards and revered by Christians as the traditional birthplace of John the Baptist. Its Arab population fled during the War of Independence (1948), and the Jewish inhabitants living there are mainly recent immigrants and artists. Excavations in the neighborhood have revealed a HIGH PLACE of the period of the Israelite monarchy.

EN SOPH (Heb. "Infinite"): Name of God used particularly in kabbalistic circles.

EN YAAKOV (Heb. "Fountain of Jacob"): Popular compilation of aggadic passages from the Babylonian and Palestinian Talmuds, by Jacob, father of Levi IBN ḤAVIV. First published in 1515-6, it became favorite reading also among the less scholarly.

ENCYCLOPEDIA: General surveys of knowledge were attempted in the Middle Ages by ambitious Jewish scholars such as the Spaniard Abraham bar Ḥiyya, while the *Paḥad Yitzḥak* of the 18th cent. Italian Isaac Lampronti is, in fact, a talmudic e. A plan for a Jewish e. in German was launched by M. Steinschneider and D. Cassel in 1844, some of the articles subsequently figuring in a separate section of the *Allgemeine Encyklopädie* of Ersch and Gruber. In 1870-84, J. Hamburger produced his *Real-Encyklopädie für Bibel und Talmud*. The first comprehensive Jewish e. was the *Jewish Encyclopaedia* edited by I. Singer (12 vols. New York, 1901-6) which remains, in many respects, the best in this field. This was followed by *Yevreyskaya Entziklopedia* edited by Y. L. Katzenelson in Russian (16 vols. St. Petersburg, 1906-13) and (on a smaller scale) the *Jüdisches Lexikon*, ed. G. Herlitz and B. Kirschner (5 vols., Berlin, 1927-30). J.D. Eisenstein issued in Hebrew the *Otzar Yisrael* (N.Y., 1906—13); Aḥad Ha-Am had already planned a work of this type as early as 1894. The ambitious *Encyclopaedia Judaica* (ed. J. Klatzkin, in German, 1928-34) had published only 10 vols. (and 2 vols. of the Hebrew counterpart *Eshkol*) when it had to cease publication. A number of one-volume e.'s also appeared in German, English, Hungarian, etc. In 1939-43, the *Universal Jewish Encyclopedia* appeared in 10 vols. in New York under the editorship of Isaac Landman. This was largely the basis of the *Enciclopedia Judaica Castellana* (ed. E. Weinfeld and I. Babani; 10 vols., Mexico City, 1948-51), useful especially for contemporary S American and Spanish entries. The 16-vol. *Encyclopaedia Judaica* in English (ed. C. ROTH and G. Wigoder) appeared in Jerusalem in 1972. The *Encyclopaedia Hebraica*, one of the biggest cultural enterprises of Israel, under the general editorship of Professors Y. KLAUSNER, B. Netanyahu, Y. Leibowitz and Y. Prawer and the direction of A. Peli (Jerusalem, 1949 ff) is a thirty-two volume general e. covering all branches of knowledge but paying special attention to Jewish and Israel matters. Large-scale talmudic and biblical encyclopedias of great scientific importance are also now appearing in Israel.

En Kerem.

END OF DAYS see **ESCHATOLOGY**

ENDEKS (Abbr. of Polish: "National Democrats"):
Former Polish anti-Semitic political party. Recruited from the middle-class, its members were a leading factor in the steady elimination of Jews from Polish economic and intellectual life in the 1930's.

ENELOW, HYMAN GERSHON (1877–1934): US
Reform rabbi and scholar. Born in Russia, he went to the US at a very early age. From 1912, he was rabbi of Temple Emanu-El, New York. He discovered and edited Israel Alnakawa's *Menorat ha-Maor* and the Midrash of hermeneutic rules ascribed to R Eliezer.

ENGEL, JOSEPH (1815–1901): Hungarian sculptor.
His work and subjects were predominantly classical, but he also executed portraits, including royal figures.

ENGEL, YOEL (1868–1927): Composer. He studied
composition with Taneiev and Ippolitov-Ivanov at Moscow, and for many years was a music critic for the Russian press. In 1908, he founded in Moscow the Society for Jewish Folk Music, and from 1924, he resided in Tel Aviv. His compositions include the incidental music to An-Ski's play *The Dibbuk*.

ENGLAND: There is no positive evidence for the
presence of Jews in England until the Norman conquest (1066) after which a handful of financiers followed William the Conqueror from the Continent. During the course of the next generation, communities were established in LONDON, YORK, BRISTOL, CANTERBURY, etc. They traded, lent money to the baronage, and, above all, advanced funds for current needs on the security of the revenue to the Crown, which therefore protected them. They were not molested at the time of the first two Crusades, though in 1144, the first recorded Ritual Murder accusation was brought against them in NORWICH. At the time of the Third Crusade (1189–90), there were riots all over the country accompanied by much bloodshed, especially in London and York where their business bonds were burned. To avoid the recurrence of this and the consequent loss to the Exchequer, a system of registration of Jewish debts was set up (1194), with ARCHAE or chirograph chests in all the principal cities under the control of a central EXCHEQUER OF THE JEWS. This made possible the systematic exploitation of Jewish resources by merciless taxation during the reigns of John (1199–1216) and Henry III (1216–1277). The enforced sternness of Jewish creditors in exacting their dues now resulted in growing unpopularity evidenced in the Ritual Murder case of HUGH OF LINCOLN (1255) and the attacks made on them during the Baron's Wars (1263–5). The competition of the Italian bankers was by now making their services superfluous. Hence, their rights were progressively restricted from 1269 onward and, in 1290, they were expelled from the country. There is much information on the activities of medieval

English Jewry whose numbers probably never exceeded 5,000. In the "Middle Period" of English Jewish history (1290–1655), no Jews lived officially in the country, though in the 16th cent. there was a Marrano colony which was broken up in 1609. In 1655, MANASSEH BEN ISRAEL went to negotiate with CROMWELL for the readmission of the Jews. He had only a partial success, but henceforth, the presence of the new Marrano group was connived at and received official recognition in 1664. The original Sephardi community was reinforced by Ashkenazi immigrants from Germany and Central Europe who established their first synagogue in London in 1690 and thence spread to the rest of the country. There were no important restrictions on the Jews, and no ghetto system was enforced. Violence against them was virtually unknown, even the JEW BILL controversy of 1753 leading to no serious molestation. In the 19th cent., with the activity of Sir Moses MONTEFIORE, English Jewry took a leading part in Jewish philanthropy. Disabilities, not very irksome, were removed slowly from 1829 onward, culminating in the admission of Lionel de ROTHSCHILD to parliament in 1858. From 1881, the older community was strongly reinforced by an immigration of refugees from Russian persecutions; these soon adapted themselves to the English-Jewish way of life under the CHIEF RABBI, BOARD OF DEPUTIES OF BRITISH JEWS, and, in London, the UNITED SYNAGOGUE. New communities of importance henceforth existed in LEEDS, GLASGOW, MANCHESTER, etc. A further influx, arriving from Germany in 1933–9, helped to stimulate a weak and short-lived organized anti-Semitic movement. E. was the only important European country to escape the Nazi persecutions, but the air bombardment of the principal cities and consequent scattering of the Jewish population changed and, to some extent, weakened the traditional Jewish life. The Jewish population of Great Britain (with N Ireland) is estimated (1973) at 410,000.

ENLIGHTENMENT see **HASKALAH**

ENNERY, ADOLPHE PHILIPPE D' (1811–1899):
French dramatist. He wrote personally or in collaboration (with Alexandre Dumas and others) about 300 popular plays from which he made a fortune. He was the author of libretti for operas by Auber and Massenet.

ENOCH (Heb. *Ḥanokh*): Father of Methuselah
(Gen. 5:18–24). The biblical account ("And Enoch walked with God, and he was not; for God took him") was traditionally interpreted to mean that he did not die naturally but was transported to heaven in his lifetime on account of his righteousness. Several apocalyptic books centered around his decease, while the early Christians utilized the accepted views on E. to expound the immortality of Jesus. This led to a reaction among the rabbis, some of

whom even denied E.'s righteousness. Only after the Christians had become quite distinct from the Jews did E. regain his popularity in Jewish lore, being identified with the angel Metatron, and a mystical literature grew up around his personality. Some modern critics maintain that E.'s 365 year lifespan corresponds to the 365 days of the Babylonian calendar and that the story of E. was originally a Babylonian sun-myth.

ENOCH, BOOK OF (1) *Abyssinian version*: An apocryphal work in 108 chapters attributed to Enoch, son of Jared (Gen. 5:18–24) but probably composed during Hasmonean Period (2nd–1st cents. BCE). Much of the book contains apocalyptic visions, messianic yearnings, and moral discourses. The original, which must have been in Hebrew or Aramaic, is lost. The Abyssinian translation (probably made in the 6th cent. from the Greek version) was found in 1769 and, subsequently, parts of the Greek text were discovered. (2) *Slavonic version*: An apocryphal work first discovered at Belgrade in 1886. It describes Enoch's ascent, his journey through the Seven Heavens, his return to earth, his address to his son, and his second ascent. It is thought to have been written in Hebrew in Palestine during the 2nd–1st cents. BCE and to have been translated into Greek in the 1st–2nd cents. CE.

ENOCH BEN MOSES (950–1024): Spanish rabbi. He succeeded his father MOSES BEN ENOCH as head of the academy at Cordova. Some of his responsa have been preserved.

EPHAH: Ancient Hebrew dry measure frequently mentioned in the Bible. It is equivalent to a tenth of a *homer*, and is itself ten times as large as an *omer*. The size of the e. differed in biblical and mishnaic times. In the former, it appears to have been about 2,600 c.c. (0.8 bushel); in the latter, 1,700 c.c. (0.57 bushel).

EPHOD: Upper garment worn in ancient Israel for sacred service, especially by the high priest (Exod. 28:6–8). It was held together by a girdle and two shoulder-straps. At the point where the latter were joined together in the front, two golden rings were placed to hold the breastplate (*Hoshen*) which bore the URIM AND THUMMIM. The term e. is used broadly for the entire oracular vestment. The practice of consulting the Divine Will through the e. is not mentioned after David's time.

EPHRAIM: Younger son of Joseph; also the name of an Israelite tribe, and a term applied to the more northern of the two Israelite kingdoms. E. included the hill-country in central Palestine and was noted for its fertility. In the period of the Judges, E. claimed priority among the Israelite tribes, partly because their religious center was situated at Shiloh in its territory. The secession of the northern tribes after Solomon's death centered on the tribe of E.,

to which Jeroboam, the first king of the northern kingdom of Israel, belonged. The prophets later spoke of the House of Judah and the House of E. as representing the two branches of the Hebrew people.

EPHRAIM, MOUNT: Geographical term applied to: (1) the area occupied by the tribe of Ephraim in the hill regions from Bethel northward; and (2) at the time of Solomon, the entire region occupied by the tribes of Ephraim and Manasseh in the center of Palestine.

EPHRAIM BEN ISAAC OF REGENSBURG (d. c. 1175): German tosaphist and liturgical poet. His hymns are noteworthy for their depth of feeling, and his decisions for their reluctance to recognize post-talmudic authority in matters of law.

EPHRAIM BEN JACOB OF BONN (1132–c. 1200): German liturgical poet and historian. His chronicle of Jewish persecutions during the Second and Third Crusades (including the massacre at York in 1190) was widely used by later historians.

EPHRAIM BEN SHEMARIAH (c. 975–c. 1060): Leader (*haver*) of the Palestinian Jewish community in Fostat (Cairo) from 1020. Part of his correspondence with Palestinian *geonim* was found in the Cairo *genizah*.

EPHRAIM MOSES HAYYIM OF SADILKOV see **MOSES OF SADILKOV**

EPHRAIM, VEITEL HEINE (d. 1775): German financier. He succeeded his father as court jeweler in Berlin, and Frederick the Great made him mint-master. He was responsible for large financial transactions during the Silesian war and worked to develop the Prussian silk industry. From 1749, he headed the Berlin Jewish community and endowed several of its educational establishments.

EPHRON: Hittite. He sold Abraham a site including a cave (MACHPELAH) near Hebron as a burial plot (Gen. 23).

EPHRON, ELIA (1847–1915): Russian publisher. Together with P. Brockhaus, he founded the Brockhaus-Ephron publishing house which became one of the largest in Russia, publishing a general Russian encyclopedia in 86 volumes and participating in the 16-volume Russian Jewish encyclopedia *Yevreyskaya Entziklopedia*.

EPICUREAN see **APIKOROS**

EPIGRAPHY see **ARCHEOLOGY; WRITING**

EPIPHANES, ANTIOCHUS see **ANTIOCHUS**

EPISCOPUS JUDAEORUM see **BISHOP OF THE JEWS**

EPITAPH: Inscription on a tomb. Although familiar in other countries of antiquity, hardly any Jewish e.'s are known until the 1st cent. BCE when they begin to be relatively common on graves and ossuaries. Very large numbers dating from the early centuries of the Christian era have been found in Palestine and elsewhere, especially in the Roman CATACOMBS; most have been collected by J. B. Frey in his *Corpus Inscriptionum Iudaicarum*. They range from single words to long verse inscriptions; even in Palestine, Greek was frequently used, although the Hebrew word *shalom* very often figures and the e. is frequently embellished by Jewish symbols (especially the seven-branched candlestick). In the Middle Ages, e.'s were almost invariably in Hebrew, becoming longer and more eulogistic in the course of time; many are extant from Spain, France, Germany, etc. In the 16th cent., elaborate rhymed e.'s became frequent, sometimes embodying an acrostic. In the 17th cent. the Spanish and Portuguese communities in Venice, Amsterdam, London, New York, etc. introduced the use of Spanish (sometimes unaccompanied by Hebrew) in e.'s, and the vernacular began to figure in most western countries – often exclusively – in the 19th cent.

EPSTEIN: (1) *YITZHAK E.* (1862–1943): Author and pedagogue. He was born in Russia and settled in Palestine in 1886, leaving to study at Lausanne (1902–8). He headed the Alliance school at Salonica 1908–15. After World War I, he returned to Palestine and engaged in educational activities. He was a pioneer in teaching Hebrew by the direct method on which he published a textbook *Ivrit be-Ivrit* (1901). E. wrote considerably on Hebrew language problems, while his article advocating approchement with the Arabs in Palestine (1907) made a deep impression. (2) *ZALMAN E.* (1860–1936): Hebrew author; brother of (1). He served as secretary to the Odessa *Hoveve Zion* 1890–1900, and settled in Palestine in 1925. E. wrote on Zionist problems, on Hebrew and general literature, etc. A romantic admirer of Jewish tradition, he nevertheless strove for its fusion with the best in European culture.

EPSTEIN, ABRAHAM (1841–1918): Rabbinical scholar. A businessman, he lived from 1876 in Vienna, devoting himself to Jewish learning, and publishing works on Jewish medieval scholars, midrashic literature, and the history of Rhenish Jewry. His penetrating monographs on Eldad Ha-Dani are still authoritative.

EPSTEIN, ABRAHAM (1880–1952): Hebrew critic. He was born in White Russia and went to the US in 1925. E.'s critical essays on Hebrew literature appeared in European and American periodicals.

EPSTEIN, ISIDORE (1894–1962): Rabbi and scholar. Born in Kovno, he went to England in 1911 and was rabbi in Middlesborough 1921–8. In 1928, he was appointed lecturer in Semitics and librarian at Jews' College, London, of which he was principal 1945–61. E. edited the English translation of the Talmud (published by the Soncino Press, 1935–52) and wrote scholarly works on medieval responsa

as well as popular books on Jewish religion and ethics.

EPSTEIN, SIR JACOB (1880-1959): Sculptor. He was born in New York and settled in England in 1904. E. was influenced by the work of Rodin and by ancient Egyptian and negro art. His sculptures aroused strong controversy among English art critics, some of whom saw in them both an infringement of public morality and esthetic failings, but the opposition to his style decreased with time and the importance of his art was widely recognized. His works include eighteen figures decorating the former building of the British Medical Association in London, the tomb of Oscar Wilde in Paris, the W. H. Hudson memorial, London; a series of symbolic figures ("Genesis," "Madonna and Child," "Adam," "Ecce Homo," "Jacob and the Angel," etc.); busts of leading personalities (Einstein, Weizmann, Churchill, Ramsay MacDonald, Shaw); illustrations to Baudelaire's *Fleurs du Mal*, etc. His autobiography *Let there be Sculpture* appeared in 1940.

EPSTEIN, JACOB NAHUM (1878–1952): Talmudist. He was born in Lithuania, lectured at the Berlin Hochschule für die Wissenschaft des Judentums, and from 1926, was professor of Talmud at the Hebrew Univ. E. published many studies on Mishnah and Talmud, his chief contribution being a work on the text of the Mishnah which illustrates his great powers of textual criticism. He was the first editor (1929–52) of the learned quarterly *Tarbitz*.

EPSTEIN, JEHUDO (1870–1945): Painter. He was born in White Russia and studied in Vilna and Vienna, eventually settling in S Africa (1934). His paintings are distinguished by realism and colorful impressionism.

EPSTEIN, LOUIS M. (1887–1949): US rabbi; born in Lithuania. He served as rabbi in Dallas, Toledo, and Boston (Congregation Kehillath Israel, 1925–47), and was the author of several scholarly works on Jewish marriage laws and problems.

ERDHEIM, JACOB (1874–1937): Austrian pathologist, professor at Vienna Univ. He contributed to knowledge of the pathology of the hemal glands and the bones, and made important discoveries relating to parathyroid tetany and craniopharyngioma ("Erdheim's tumors").

ERETZ YISRAEL (Heb. "Land of Israel"): See **ISRAEL, LAND OF**

EREV: Hebrew for "evening". Used to refer to the eve of Sabbath and festivals (*Erev Shabbat, Erev Yom Tov*).

ERFURT: E German city. Its Jewish community is known from the 12th cent. and, despite anti-Jewish riots in 1221, continued to develop throughout the 13th cent. After the Black Death massacre in 1349, the survivors were expelled. The Jews were briefly allowed to return in 1357 and in the 15th

Jacob Epstein: *Night.*

cent., the community became a center of rabbinic scholarship. In 1458, the Jews were again expelled. The community, refounded in the 19th cent. and numbering 831 in 1933, was destroyed by the Nazis. Jewish pop. (1961): 120.

ERIE: City in Pennsylvania, US. Jews settling there in the 1849's formed its first congregation, the Anshe Chesed Society, soon after their arrival. In 1875, this group was incorporated as a Reform congregation. A Conservative congregation, B'rith Sholom, was founded in 1874. The Jewish Community Welfare Council was established in 1946. In 1973, E. had 1,700 Jews.

ERLANGER, CAMILLE (1863–1919): French composer. The best-known of his many operas is *Le juif polonais.* He also wrote orchestral music, songs, etc.

ERLANGER, JOSEPH (1874–1965): US physiologist; professor at the Univ. of Wisconsin 1906–10, and at Washington Univ. 1910–46. His work on blood-mechanics and neurology gained him a Nobel Prize in 1944. In collaboration with Herbert S. Gasser he wrote *Electrical Signs of Nervous Activity.*

ERTER, ISAAC (1791–1851): Hebrew writer. Born in a Galician village, he early came under the influence of the *Haskalah.* In 1823, he published his first work, the satire *Mozne Mishkal* ("Balances"), directed against the rabbis and Ḥasidim. He studied medicine at Budapest Univ., and then settled in Brody, earning his living by medical practice. His chief literary work consists of five satires and a polemical article, later collected in *Ha-Tzopheh le-Vet Yisrael* ("The Observer of the House of Israel"). E. was the leading Hebrew satirist of his generation, and directed his sharp humor principally against Ḥasidic superstition.

ERUSIN see **MARRIAGE**

ERUV: (Heb. "mixture" or "amalgamation"):
Technical term for the rabbinical provision which permits the alleviation of certain Sabbath restrictions. These include carrying on the Sabbath (permitted through *Eruv Ḥatzerot*, i.e., amalgamating individual holdings), walking further than the permitted 2,000 cubits beyond the inhabited area of the town (through *Eruv Teḥumim*, i.e., amalgamating boundaries), and cooking for the Sabbath on a festival day falling on Friday (through *Eruv Tavshilin*, i.e., amalgamating meals). In all these cases, the *e.* is made by a formality such as setting aside food prior to the Sabbath or holiday.

ERUVIN (Heb. "Amalgamations"): Second tractate in the Mishnah order of *Moed*, containing 10 chapters. It has *gemara* in both the Babylonian and Palestinian Talmuds. It deals with the laws of ERUV. The last chapter is a collection of miscellaneous laws concerning the Sabbath.

*ESARHADDON: King of Assyria, reigned 680–669 BCE. Son of Sennacherib, he was a wise and courageous ruler under whom Assyria became a great power. In accordance with Assyrian practice, he transferred populations, in one instance sending eastern settlers to Samaria. Manasseh, king of Judah, was among the kings who paid him tribute and sent him gifts for the rebuilding of his palace at Nineveh (673 BCE).

ESAU: Son of Isaac; elder twin-brother of Jacob. After Jacob obtained his birthright and the first-born's blessing, E. became Jacob's enemy, seeking to kill him. Jacob fled to Haran but on returning, twenty years later, was received affectionately by E. (Gen. 35 ff). The Bible identifies E. with EDOM (Gen. 36:1), Jacob becoming Israel (Gen. 32:25–9). The story of the two brothers thus symbolized the relationship between the two nations, developing to the point of hostility. In the Talmud, E. was synonymous with villainy and violence. The word E. in late Hebrew literature implies a coarse materialist.

ESCHATOLOGY: Doctrine of the end of days, referring to the fundamental changing of the present world by Divine plan at a period determined by God. The eschatological world is not necessarily one that has never previously existed; the view is sometimes advanced that on the last day the world, which was entirely good at creation and only corrupted by human deviations, will be restored to its pristine condition. Such views were common in the ancient Orient and are found in Greek literature. Eschatological opinions cannot be classified in an orderly system according to logical laws of development. Varied and sometimes contradictory outlooks were held successively or even simultaneously. A general line is nevertheless discernible in Jewish e. from its very beginnings in the early sections of the Bible. Originally, eschatological theory was an expression of popular faith in the glorious future anticipated for the nation after a period of suffering. In its full development, it possessed a religious and moral content, and was introduced by the great Hebrew prophets into their teachings, albeit with their own moral coloring which transformed the naïve folk beliefs. The popular conception of the eschatological era was of a period when the renewed people of Israel would wreak vengeance on their foes and set up a great, powerful kingdom; this victorious period was called "the Day of the Lord." The prophets, however, added moral content and threatened catastrophe in the absence of genuine repentance; thus, the Day of the Lord became a day of doom. This transition is patently clear in Amos and recurs in various forms and degrees in the writings of the other great prophets. But disaster was not the only element in prophetic e.; the final day was also envisioned as the great day when God would reform the world and reign over all peoples in justice. A new heaven and earth will be created, while God will renew His covenant with Israel and establish His throne in Zion. This trend is particularly apparent in the latter chapters of Isaiah. However, no distinction between the present world and the world to come is known to prophetic e. which recognizes only this world. The resuscitation of the Jewish people and the land of Israel and the appearance of the king-messiah are described as events which will occur in the real world. But as reality became ever more remote from the expected glory, so the accounts of the Day of the Lord became more glowing, exaggerated, and imaginative. E. was thus transformed into apocalyptic beliefs (see APOCALYPSE) as can be seen in the Book of Ezekiel and the visions of Zechariah. A new element is thought by many scholars to have been introduced into Jewish e. by the Book of Daniel, which they date in the Maccabean Period. The persecutions of Antiochus Epiphanes depressed the nation's religious groups, and the messianic kingdom, receding from this world, took on the aspect of a kingdom beyond human reality. The change is symbolized by the figure of the "son of man" who descends from the heavens and proclaims the proximity of the kingdom of God. At the threshold of the new epoch stand the resurrection of the dead and Judgment Day when evil will be outlawed and the wise will receive their due reward. The APOCRYPHA (including pseudepigraphic literature) and aggadah provide an unfailing source of information on eschatological outlooks during and after Second Temple times, reflecting all shades of religious opinion. The development of the apocalyptic aspect of the eschatological beliefs, adumbrated under Antiochus Epiphanes, eventually encompassed the nation as a whole, in addition to its individuals, and this proved of particular importance in the early stages of Christianity. The eschatological thinker comprehends the entire world, knowing the period of its duration and the events of its latter days. The "end" will be an era of suffering and catastrophes under the rule of the ANTI-CHRIST. The apocalyptic sources, from the Book of Daniel onward, regard the "end" as a sign of the advent of the MESSIAH. They speak of "the agonies of the Messiah," a terrible last war – the war of GOG AND MAGOG — ranging over Jerusalem. According to one view, the Messiah Son of Joseph, the forerunner of the Messiah Son of David, will fall in this war. But the forces of evil will be defeated, whereupon Elijah will appear and announce the advent of the Messiah and this will be the signal for the ingathering of the Diaspora and the freedom of Israel from subjection to gentile kingdoms. A new Jerusalem will arise, and Israel's glory will be manifest to the world. The duration of the messianic kingdom is, however, restricted; it will be succeeded by the Kingdom of God and Judgment Day when the just and wise (generally meaning Israel) will receive their reward, and the wicked (generally the gentiles who have oppressed Israel) will descend to Gehinnom "to everlasting abhorrence."

Levi Eshkol.

ESDRAELON see **JEZREEL**

ESDRAS: Two apocryphal books ascribed to Ezra (of which E. is the Greek form). They are known as III Esdras and IV Esdras (the Book of Ezra and Nehemiah being called I Esdras and II Esdras). III Esdras contains a history of Israel from the time of Josiah to the reading of the Law by Ezra. It is largely based on the biblical books of Chronicles, Ezra, and Nehemiah, but there are significant omissions, changes, and additions. The main original section relates the story of Zerubbabel winning the favor of Darius and receiving his permission to return to Palestine. The book was apparently composed in the 1st cent. BCE or perhaps earlier. IV Esdras or the Apocalypse of Ezra is one of the profoundest books in apocalyptic literature. It was written in Hebrew, translated into Greek, and thence into Syriac, Abyssinian, Latin, etc. The Hebrew original and the Greek translation have not been preserved. Chapters 3–13 constitute the original book, the rest being later Christian additions. The subject-matter deals with the problem of human suffering, a vindication of God's actions, and especially the fate of Israel and the advent of the Messiah. Shaltiel "who is Ezra" complains to God of the vicissitudes of the world and his perplexities are answered by the angel Uriel in a vision. The heathens will vanish from the world and Israel will be established on the Final Day. The end of evil is at hand and the wicked will receive their deserts with the advent

of the Messiah. On the angel's command, Ezra hides for forty days and dictates the Lord's words to five scribes in 94 books of which 24 are revealed (the Bible) and 70 reserved for those learned in esoteric lore. IV Esdras was probably written in the period of despair following the destruction of the Second Temple (perhaps in the time of Domitian, c. 90 CE).

ESHBAAL see **ISH-BOSHETH**

ESHET ḤAYIL (Heb.): A woman of character.
The phrase occurs in Prov. 31:10 which, with succeeding verses, is recited in the Jewish home on Friday evenings by the head of the house.

ESHKOL: Jewish publishing house, founded in Berlin in 1923 by Nahum Goldman and Jacob Klatzkin, and publishing works dealing with medieval Jewish literature, etc. Its publications of Jewish encyclopedias in Hebrew (*Eshkol*) and German (*Encyclopaedia Judaica*) had to be abandoned after the advent of the Nazi regime.

ESHKOL (SHKOLNIK), LEVI (1895–1969): Statesman and third premier of Israel. He was born in Oratovo in the Ukraine and studied in Vilna. In 1914 he settled in Palestine where he first worked as a laborer in Petaḥ Tikvah. During World War I, he served in the Jewish Legion. After the war he was among the founders of Deganyah Bet and then moved into public service, helping to plan and develop Jewish settlement in the Jezreel Valley and Emek Hefer. In 1944 he was appointed secretary of the Tel-Aviv Council and in 1948 became director-general of the Israel Defense Ministry. He represented *Mapai* in the Knesset from 1949. In 1949, as the period of large-scale Jewish immigration began, E. was elected to the executive of the Jewish Agency serving as head of its settlement department and from 1950 as its treasurer. In 1951, he joined Ben-Gurion's government as minister of agriculture and development and in 1952 became minister of finance. In 1963 he succeeded Ben-Gurion as prime minister and minister of defense (relinquishing the latter portfolio to Moshe Dayan on the eve of the Six-Day War in 1967). While he was premier, diplomatic relations were established with West Germany, the military administration of areas inhabited by Arabs was abolished, and the various labor parties united to form the ISRAEL LABOR PARTY. The outstanding events of his period as premier were the establishment of the government of national unity, the Six-Day War, and the succeeding international struggle for secure boundaries. E. was noted for his abilities as a conciliator and his success is holding together disparate elements in his party and government.

ESNOGA (from **SINAGOGA**): Among Sephardim, a synagogue.

ESSEN: Town of W Germany where Jews are first mentioned in the 13th cent. They were expelled at the time of the Black Death (1349) and although they later returned, the community ceased to exist by the 16th cent. Substantial resettlement began in the 19th cent. and in 1933, there were over 5,000 Jews, but the community was destroyed after the Nazi rise to power. Jewish pop. (1970): 170.

ESSENES (etymology obscure; possibly from Syriac *Ḥasya* "pious"): Religious sect in Palestine at the close of the Second Temple Period. In religious outlook, they were close to the Pharisees but had their own specific beliefs and customs. They believed in the immortality of the soul and in reward and punishment but not in physical resurrection. They opposed slavery and private property, and lived an abstemious communal life. Before meals they immersed themselves in water. Celibacy was common but some married in order to perpetuate mankind. Their chief occupation was farming; they opposed animal sacrifice and brought only offerings of flour and oil to the Temple. Novices underwent a 3–year initiation and were only admitted as full members after swearing not to reveal the sect's secrets. The group was not altogether remote from political life, even taking part in the wars against the Romans. In the time of Philo, they numbered 4,000 and lived in several towns and villages; Pliny the Elder mentions their settlement near En Gedi. Nothing is heard of them after the destruction of the Second Temple.

Information on the E. comes mainly from Philo and Josephus, who endeavored to represent them as a philosophical sect on the hellenistic pattern. The discovery of the DEAD SEA SCROLLS, the precise implications of which are still being debated, may cast a new light on the nature and beliefs of the E. or some sect closely associated with them, and possibly on their relations with early Christianity which seems to have owed a great deal to them.

*ESTERHAZY, COUNT MARIE CHARLES FERDINAND WALSIN- (1847–1923): French officer stemming from a noble Hungarian family. As a result of the debts incurred by his extravagant and dissipated mode of life, he sold French military secrets to Germany. When the leak was discovered, DREYFUS was suspected and condemned. When the supporters of Dreyfus first accused E., he was tried and acquitted by a military tribunal, but after the suicide of Col. Henry (1898), one of Dreyfus' accusers, he fled to London.

ESTERKE (Esther): Mistress of Casimir the Great, king of Poland 1333–70. According to tradition, she bore Casimir 4 children, influenced his pro-Jewish policy, and was the victim of a pogrom after his death. E. was first mentioned by the 15th cent. Polish historian Dlugosz and the veracity of the story is doubtful. She is the subject of several Hebrew and Yiddish works.

ESTHER: Daughter of Abihail and central character in the biblical book or scroll named after her (*Megillat Esther*). The subject of the work is the deliverance of the Jews of Persia in the time of King Ahasuerus, on account of which the reading of the Scroll of E. and the festival of Purim were instituted. According to the story, E. was married to Ahasuerus and, through her intervention with him, and with the aid of her kinsman Mordecai, succeeded in averting the annihilation of the Persian Jewish community planned by the king's adviser, Haman. Scholars are divided as to the historical value of the work. The date of its composition is generally placed in the Persian Period – i.e., before 330 BCE. In Second Temple times, the Scroll of E. was already apparently included in the canon. Its reading on Purim was made obligatory, and a special talmudic tractate was written on the relevant regulations. As it was customary for congregants in the synagogue to follow the reading from a written text in the form – but not subject to the same meticulous regulations – as that used by the reader, it became one of the favorite objects of Jewish folk-art. The earliest-known illustrated *Megillah* is of the 16th cent., but the tradition probably goes back to the Middle Ages. The same subjects (e.g. the hanging of the sons of Haman or rejoicings at the deliverance) constantly recur. From the 17th cent., scrolls with copper-plate borders were published with the text written by hand. The

Scroll of Esther

Scroll was frequently enclosed in a decorative case, of ivory, silver, or even gold.

ESTHER (pen-name of Malkah Lifschitz; c. 1880–1937): Russian labor leader and Yiddish author. Arested several times for revolutionary activities, she was exiled to Astrakan during World War I. After the Communist Revolution, she returned to her native Minsk and continued Bundist activities but, in 1919, joined the Communists and was largely responsible for liquidating the Bund in Russia. From 1921, she was active in the *Yevsektzia* in Moscow. She was nevertheless arrested by the Soviet authorities and died in prison.

ESTHER, FAST OF: Fast on *Adar* 13, the day preceding Purim. If this date falls on a Sabbath, the fast is observed on the previous Thursday. The institution of the fast is of comparatively late origin, not finding mention in halakhic literature until the 8th cent. It has no connection with the fasting of Esther recorded in the Bible which, according to rabbinical tradition, was in the month of *Nisan*. Probably it was instituted as a counterbalance to the merrymaking on Purim. The fast attained symbolic importance among the Marranos.

ESTHER CHIRA see **CHIRA, ESTHER**

ESTHER RABBAH: Midrash to the Book of Esther. It originally consisted of seven chapters (ten in later editions), of which the first six are of an early compilation, drawing upon the Palestinian Talmud and the Midrash *Leviticus Rabbah*. The last chapter contains elements of a much later date.

ESTHONIA: Baltic Soviet republic. Jews reached E. in the 18th cent., and the community numbered about 5,000 on the outbreak of World War II. They lived mostly in the towns, engaging especially in trade, industry, and the liberal professions. In independent E. (1917–40), they enjoyed cultural autonomy, but there was serious anti-Semitism in the 1930's. Its 1970 Jewish pop. was officially given as 5,300.

ESTORI HA-PARHI see **FARHI**

ETERNAL LIGHT see **NER TAMID**

ETHAN THE EZRAHITE: Sage and poet, to whom the authorship of Ps. 89 is attributed. According to the Talmud, the name is a pseudonym for the patriarch Abraham.

ETHICAL LITERATURE see **MUSAR**

ETHICAL WILLS: Testaments expressing the moral instructions of the deceased to his family. Instances of verbally communicated e. w. occur in the Bible (e.g. of Jacob, Moses, David), Apocrypha (Testaments of the Twelve Patriarchs, etc.), and Talmud. During and after the Middle Ages, they became a relatively common phenomenon and are historically important for the light they throw on contemporary moral aspirations as well as on the details of daily life. Thus, the ethical will of Eleazer "the Great" of Worms (11th cent.) is especially notable for its elevated moral counsel; that of Judah Ibn Tibbon (12th cent.), for advice on the care of books; that of Judah ben Asher (14th cent.), for the light it casts on the status of the Spanish rabbinate, while successive generations of the Horowitz family (16th–17th cents.) laid particular stress on the study of the Torah. Others emphasized the importance of the performance of ritual precepts (e.g. Naphtali Cohen, 1718). A selection of e. w. with English translations was published by Israel Abrahams (1927).

ETHICS: Jewish religious teaching is essentially of an ethical character. From biblical times onward, e. have marked the principles and goal of Judaism. Although not presented as a moral treatise, the Bible throughout has an ethical purpose. Its theological sections reject the ancient religious conceptions of a plethora of powers hostile to each other and to man, substituting the belief in a single God, sovereign creator of the entire universe, just, good, and, above all, making known His will to man. The Divinely-revealed Torah expounds the path to be followed. Man is free to obey or disobey the Law, and by his choice can acquire ethical merit. This is reinforced by the legislative parts of the Bible which link the standards of individual and social life to the necessity of imitating God in His goodness and justice. Purely legal, economic, or sociological injunctions are rare; man is almost always appealed to on moral grounds —

equity, truth, love, charity, etc. The prophetical and historical books of the Bible link e. with the core of religious life, and present history not as a mere succession of events but as a moral drama where God causes the ultimate triumph of Good. Jewish hellenistic literature remained faithful to this attitude, whether in its praise of the virtuous man (in the Wisdom literature) or in stressing the struggle of Good and Evil in history (the Apocalypse) or in the first systematic sketch of Jewish e. by Philo. The legislative preoccupations of the Talmud are never the last word – "the essential is not learning but doing" is an axiom of *Avot*, a tractate which is an anthology of moral dicta. E. in the Talmud are not treated solely as abstract principles but as everyday experience; the talmudic sages in their lives exemplify ideals of ethical conduct. Theoretical and practical e. are developed by later writers; they are systematized by Jewish philosophers, both medieval (e.g. Saadyah, Ibn Gabirol – whose *Tikkun Middot ha-Nephesh* expounds an autonomous e. unconnected with religious dogmas – and Maimonides, whose introduction to *Avot* is a classic work of Jewish e.) and modern (e.g. Moritz Lazarus in his *Die Ethik des Judentums*). Parallel to these works, another trend of literature marks the medieval and modern development of Jewish e. reflecting individual or collective experience, sometimes of a very unusual nature, viz., the thought of the Kabbalah and other mystical currents which has had a considerable influence on ethical works (Bahya's *Hovot ha-Levavot*, the 13th cent. *Sepher Hasidim*; M. H. Luzzatto's *Mesillat Yesharim*). These books achieved remarkable popularity and were accepted in the most diverse Jewish circles, e.g. by both Hasidim and Mitnaggedim. In the 19th cent., under the influence of Israel Salanter, the MUSAR movement developed, bringing back ethical notions into the over-intellectualized atmosphere of the yeshivot. Despite the close connections between religion and e. in the history of Jewish thought, the content of Jewish e. is neither uniform nor simple. Two main tendencies can be distinguished. One identifies e. with the Middle Way in accordance with the ideal outlined in the Book of Proverbs and some of the Psalms. This conforms to the main trends of Judaism in the Hellenistic Period and in Palestine during the rabbinical epoch; it condemns excess in either direction, e.g. avarice or extravagance, debauchery or abstinence. The second tendency, exemplified in the Books of Job and Ecclesiastes, criticizes the Middle Way, which the Mishnah calls "the way of Sodom" (*Avot* 5:13); this was personified in the actions of certain rabbis who gave their entire fortunes to the poor (R Yeshevav), practiced celibacy (Ben Azzai), passed long periods in prayer (R Hanina ben Dosa), and even lived according to monastic ideals (cf. the Essenes, the *Manual of*

Discipline discovered in the Dead Sea Scrolls). ASCETICISM characterizes the work of Bahya, M. H. Luzzatto, the *Sepher Hasidim*, and much of the thought inspired by mysticism.

ETHICS OF THE FATHERS see AVOT

ETHIOPIA (Abyssinia): Country of NE Africa; possibly identical with the biblical CUSH. Strong biblical and Jewish elements are to be found in the practices of the Abyssinian Church. The emperors of the country claim descent from Menelik who was, according to their tradition, born to Solomon and the queen of Sheba, in token of which they use the title "Lion of Judah." A small Jewish community has recently established itself in E., but Judaism is chiefly represented in the country by the native FALASHAS. There are a few Abyssinians in Israel, grouping about a church in Jerusalem. The number of Jews (including Falashas) in E. in 1973 was estimated at 12,000.

ETHNARCH (Gk. "ruler of a people"): Title, implicitly denying independent status, which was given in classical times to the head of a national community. It was thus conferred on Simon the Hasmonean by the people of Judea. Hyrcanus II and his heirs got the title from Julius Caesar and Archelaus, son of Herod, from Augustus. The title was used also with reference to the head of a Jewish community in the Diaspora, e.g. in Alexandria in the 1st cent. BCE.

ETHRONGES (or **ATHRONGAIOS**): Leader with his four brothers, of the Jewish revolt against the Romans in 4 BCE; believed to be identical with Ben Batiah mentioned in the Talmud. A shepherd of great physical strength, according to Josephus he aspired to be king. After defeating a Roman force at Emmaus, he was captured by Archelaus.

ETROG (a word of Indian origin): The citron (*citrus medica* Linn); one of the FOUR SPECIES used in the synagogue service on the Feast of Tabernacles. In the Classical Period, it was a popular Jewish symbol on coins, graves, synagogues, etc. During the Middle Ages, the difficulty of its acquisition in N Europe, etc. gave rise to serious problems. Various folk-practices (use as a handle for circumcision knife, etc.) were associated with the e. after its ritual use. Silver boxes for the e. were a common object of Jewish ritual art.

ETTINGER, AKIVA YAAKOV (1872–1945): Agronomist. After working for ICA in Bessarabia and S America, he settled in Palestine in 1918. He established the first example of hill settlement in Palestine at Kiryat Anavim near Jerusalem and played an important role in developing new forms of villages.

ETTINGER, SOLOMON (c. 1801–1856): Polish Yiddish author. Trained as a physician, he eventually settled as a farmer at Zhdanov near

Zamosc. E. wrote Yiddish parables, poems, and plays in the spirit of the Haskalah, his best-known work being the comedy *Serkele*.

ETZ ḤAYYIM (Heb. "tree of life"; cf. Prov. 3:18): Term applied to the wooden staves about which a Scroll of the Law is rolled, and hence, to the silver finials which surmount them.

ETZEL see **IRGUN TZEVAI LEUMI**

EUCHEL, ISAAC (1756–1804): Hebrew author. Born in Copenhagen, he settled in Berlin (1787) where he helped to found *Ha-Measseph* and was one of the fathers of the Hebrew revival. His works include a comedy satirizing Orthodoxy and the Yiddish language, a biography of Moses Mendelssohn, and the translation of and commentary on the Book of Proverbs in Mendelssohn's *Biur*.

EULOGY, FUNERAL: Funeral or memorial oration. To lament and praise the dead has been a Jewish custom since ancient days. The Bible preserves David's poetic e.'s over Saul and Jonathan (II Sam. 1:17–27) and over Abner (II Sam. 3:33–34). Talmudic literature also contains fragments of funeral orations which reveal poetic beauty and striking imagery. In later times, the e. took the form of the *Hesped* at the time of the funeral and (among the Sephardim) a talmudic discourse after the expiration of the thirty days' mourning period (*Sheloshim*).

EUPHEMISM: The substitution of an unoffending word for one of unpleasant association; known in Hebrew as *lashon nekiyyah* ("clean speech"). E.'s are most usual in the Bible and talmudic literature with reference to sexual intercourse. However, even words like "unclean" are sometimes avoided. The Talmud is also careful not to use expressions betokening misfortune. A blind man is referred to as "abundant in light," while a cemetery is still called "house of the living."

EUPHRATES (Heb. *Perat*): The westerly of the two rivers (the other being the Tigris) enclosing Mesopotamia, the "Land of the Two Rivers." Gen. 2:14 puts its source inside the Garden of Eden. According to Gen. 15:18, the river E. was to form the ultimate boundary of the Israelites. Solomon exercised suzerainty up to the river (I Kings 5:4). Many Jewish communities lay along the E. in talmudic times and after; thus, on its lower course, were the centers of Babylonian scholarship, including Sura, Nehardea, and Mahoza.

EUROPE: The Jews seem to have first come into contact with European culture about the period of the destruction of the First Temple when various references to "the isles of the sea" (i.e., the Greek coastlands?) appear in the Bible. The conquest of Palestine by Alexander the Great brought the mass of the Jewish people into the European orbit. In the Maccabean Period, before the middle of the 2nd cent. BCE, the presence of Jews in GREECE is proved by inscriptions as well as literary sources, and there were Jews in ROME as early as 139 BCE. From 57 BCE, Palestine was under Roman control, and as the result of political intercourse, trade, war, and captivity there was an increasing tendency for its inhabitants to become scattered throughout the Empire. They were in SPAIN and Gaul even before the destruction of the Second Temple, and on the Rhineland at least as early as the 4th cent. European Jewry of this period left few traces of cultural life, save what may be deduced from the inscriptions in the catacombs of Rome and elsewhere. After the Christianization of the Roman Empire in the 4th cent., their position greatly deteriorated, and it appears that large numbers were driven into baptism; in the 7th cent., attempts were made to enforce wholesale conversion in BYZANTIUM, N ITALY, Gaul and, especially, in Spain. Thereafter, communities reestablished themselves – partly through the advance of Islam, which brought the Jewish reservoirs of population in Mesopotamia into intimate contact with the West, partly through the encouragement of the Carolingian rulers in FRANCE, and partly through the fact that the new political circumstances had made the Jews the most important international trading element with contacts both in the Islamic and Christian worlds. By c. 1000, the center of gravity of the Jewish people had been removed into the European region. Great independent cultural centers now emerged there — humanistic in Spain, talmudic in France and GERMANY. This was in spite of the comprehensive anti-Jewish code which was elaborated at this time by the Church. In N Europe (to a far less degree in the S), the force of circumstances drove a great part of the Jewish community ultimately into the profession of moneylending. The First Crusade (1096) was initiated by a wave of massacres on the Rhineland, and henceforth, the record of European Jewry was punctuated by such outbreaks. The Fourth Lateran Council of 1215 intensified the ecclesiastical campaign against the Jews, the enforcement of which was pressed for by the friars of the newly-established Dominican order. The ultimate result was a series of expulsions – from England (1290), from France (1306, 1322, 1394), from Spain (1492), from PORTUGAL (1497); while in Germany local expulsions were reinforced by wholesale massacres, especially at the time of the BLACK DEATH (1348–9). The only country where the record was generally somewhat better was Italy – in the S before, in the N after, the 13th cent. Here the Jews, to some extent protected by the POPES from the worst excesses of fanaticism, played a consistent part in cultural life. Both there and in Spain, the Jewish medieval participation in the re-awakening of intellectual life by the transmission of Greco-Arab culture in translation was of the utmost significance. The 16th

Bull of Pope Innocent III against the Blood Libel, 1274.

cent. found the mass of European Jewry driven eastward, to POLAND and TURKEY. From that time, however, Jewish life in the newly-dominant countries of W Europe began to reassert itself – partly because of the vitality of the remaining communities of Germany and Italy, and partly through the pioneering colonies established by the crypto-Jews or MARRANOS of Spain and Portugal in the countries of the Atlantic seaboard, especially HOLLAND and ENGLAND. These new communities, Europeanized culturally, linguistically, and socially through the circumstances of their past history, formed the nucleus of important new settlements of the same type. These were constantly recruited from Central Europe and later from Poland where, after the Chmielnicki massacres in 1648–9, the Jewish position, though culturally advanced, was politically and economically miserable. The French Revolution and its aftermath brought EMANCIPATION to these European Jewries and those who desired to follow their example; except in RUSSIA, this was the keynote of Jewish history in the age of European economic and geographical expansion in the 19th cent. The Jewish communities of W Europe, constantly recruited from the East (especially after the pogroms of 1881 ff), now began to take a leading part in European social, literary, cultural, and even political life, providing the occidental countries with writers, statesmen, scientists, physicians, pioneers, explorers, and humanitarians in disproportionate numbers. This was, however, in many cases at the expense of Jewish national and religious loyalties; and though E. produced an occidentalized renewal of Jewish culture in the form of the *Jüdische Wissenschaft*, Jewish, and especially rabbinic, studies declined tragically. In E Europe, emancipation brought about at last by the Russian Revolution of 1917, was followed by the establishment of the communist system which, in effect, entirely suppressed Jewish national and cultural life. In Central Europe, the jealousy aroused by Jewish progress after emancipation contributed to the rise of the Nazi movement. At first re-enforcing certain anti-Jewish restrictions, in the end this movement embarked on a campaign of extermination, in the course of which between 5,000,000 and 6,000,000 Jews perished out of some 11,000,000 living in E. in 1939. Apart from the 2,680,000 survivors in Russia, now deprived of Jewish life, there are left in Europe fewer than 1,500,000 Jews, or about 14% of the effective Jewish population of the world, as against about 90% a century ago and 60% in 1939. The former European Jewish predominance, which lasted for nearly 1,000 years, has now ended.

*EUSEBIUS (260–339): Church Father and bishop of Caesarea. In his *Praeparatio Evangelica*, he demonstrates the superiority of Judaism over pagan Hellenism in the style of the Jewish Alexandrian apologists, but in his *Demonstratio Evangelica*, he attacks the Jews for distorting Scriptures and neglecting the New Testament. E. wrote an important work on biblical place-names. His writings contain numerous quotations from otherwise lost Alexandrian Jewish authors and are invaluable for the study of Jewish history and literature in the Classical Period.

EVANS, MARY ANNE (MARIA) see **ELIOT, GEORGE**

EVANSVILLE: City in Indiana, US. Its first Jews arrived in the late 1830's, and the first congregation, B'nai Israel, was organized in 1857. The Jewish Community Council was founded in 1936. E. had 1,000 Jews in 1973 with 3 synagogues.

EVE (Heb. *Havvah*): The first woman; wife of Adam (Gen. 2–4). Created out of Adam's rib to be "a helpmeet for him," she lived with him in the Garden of Eden until seduced by the snake into eating – and leading Adam to eat – fruit from the tree of the knowledge of good and evil, expressly forbidden by God. In punishment, they were expelled from Eden and E. was condemned to suffer pangs at childbirth and be subservient to her husband. She was the mother of Cain, Abel, and, later, Seth.

EVEL RABBATI (Heb. "Great Mourning"; euphemistically termed *Semaḥot* "Joyful Occasions"): Minor tractate dealing with death, mourning customs, etc. included in Talmud editions. It was written in Palestine during the period of the Tannaim, with later accretions added from the amoraic and gaonic eras.

EVEL ZUTRATI (or *Semaḥot of R Ḥiyya*): Minor tractate included in Talmud editions containing a number of discourses on mourning customs.

EVEN, ABBA see **EBAN, ABBA**

EVEN HA-EZER see **JACOB BEN ASHER**

EVEN SHETIYYAH (Heb. "stone of foundation"): Rock projecting on the summit of the Temple hill in Jerusalem. Hebrew legend relates that on this rock the world was founded and Isaac bound for sacrifice. According to the Mishnah, the ark and Tables of the Law were placed upon it in the First Temple and, in the Second Temple, it supported the censer. It is still to be seen in the Mosque of Omar.

EVEN-SHOSHAN (originally **ROSENSTEIN**), **AV-RAHAM** (1906–): Hebrew lexicographer. He was born in Minsk and settled in Palestine in 1925. He has edited an illustrated dictionary of modern Hebrew (5 vols., 1941–52).

EVEN YEHUDAH: Israel village of private holders in S Sharon, founded in 1932 by the *Bene Binyamin*. Its economy is based mainly on citrus cultivation. Pop. (1972): 3,829.

EVENING SERVICE see **MAARIV**

EVIAN, CONFERENCE OF: Conference on the REFUGEE problem with the participation of 32 nations called by President F.D. Roosevelt in July 1938 because of conditions in Germany and the inadequacy of the League of Nations and voluntary bodies to tackle the problem. Only the Dominican Republic offered to accept sizable numbers of refugees; but an Inter-Governmental Committee for Refugees was established and continued to operate until the outbreak of World War II.

EVIDENCE: Proof supporting an allegation. The regulations concerning e. are very strict in Jewish law. All circumstantial e. is ruled out whether in criminal or civil cases. Biblical law specifically calls for the testimony of at least two witnesses in criminal cases (Deut. 19:15; 17:6). Rabbinical law limited the suitability of witnesses by disqualifying usurers, gamblers, and others of improper character. Near relatives of either the husband or wife could not testify, nor was testimony accepted from non-Jews, slaves, women, or minors. These restrictions apply also to civil law, except that documents and direct testimony are acceptable where witnesses are not available. The severity of the rules of e. was mitigated by the rabbis in the case of the *agunah* – a widow who could not prove the death of her husband. Here the testimony of a single witness, or of a relative, woman, minor, slave, or non-Jew was held sufficient. Witnesses were not under any special oath, but were admonished by the judges concerning the gravity of bearing false witness. All witnesses had to be cross-examined by the judges, although there was greater leniency in civil than in criminal cases.

EVIL see **GOOD AND EVIL**

EVIL EYE (Heb. EN HA-RA; Aram. *ena bisha*): The belief that certain individuals can harm by a jealous or spiteful glance was widespread among all ancient and medieval peoples. Although not mentioned in the Bible, it is found in the Talmud and Kabbalah. Many customs were prevalent for

The *Even Shetiyyah*.

Amulet to protect women from the "Evil Eye"
after childbirth.

averting the power of the "evil eye," especially in medieval times; these included the use of AMULETS. Most of these were simply Jewish adaptations of non-Jewish superstitions.

EVIL INCLINATION see **GOOD AND EVIL**; **MAN**

*EVIL-MERODACH: Son and successor of Nebuchadnezzar II; reigned 562–56 BCE. He released Jehoiachin, king of Judah, from prison (II Kings 25:27).

*EWALD, GEORG HEINRICH AUGUST (1803–1875): German orientalist and theologian. His works include a biblical commentary, a Hebrew grammar, and a history of the Jews. His approach to the traditional text of the Bible was conservative. He regarded Jewish history from Moses to Ezra as the unfolding of Providence in bequeathing monotheism to the world.

EXCAVATIONS see **ARCHEOLOGY**

EXCHEQUER OF THE JEWS: Central organ of administration for the Jews of England in the Medieval Period. It developed out of the reorganization effected by the ministers of Richard I in 1194. A number of local chirograph chests (*archae*) for registering Jewish debts was set up, with a central authority under the direction of a small number of officials (generally four), subsequently known as the Custodians or Justices of the Jews. The organization over which they presided – a branch of the Great Exchequer – was not merely a financial institution, but also had important judicial and administrative functions.

EXCOMMUNICATION: Severance from (religious) fellowship; the corresponding Hebrew term is *ḥerem* (see ANATHEMA). In talmudic times, this was commonly employed as a weapon against Jews considered responsible for teachings dangerous to the community. It involved the complete severance of personal, business, social, and religious intercourse with the culprit until he repented. There was also a milder form termed *niddui* which initially applied for thirty days only. In the Middle Ages and after, e. came to play a prominent part in Jewish life, being imposed, for example, during the Maimonist controversies as a weapon to prevent the study of philosophy, or applied by R Gershom and others as a sanction to prevent anti-social actions. In the 16th cent., it was used so commonly in learned controversies as almost to lose its significance; later, in Italy, it became a means to enforce the payment of communal taxation.

EXECUTION see **CAPITAL PUNISHMENT**

"EXECUTION, JEWISH": In the Middle Ages, capital sentences against Jews were frequently carried out in an especially brutal manner, the victims being hung not by the neck but by the heels in such a way as to cause the maximum suffering. Frequently, dogs were strung up on either side. Traces of the

Execution of Jews in Mantua, 1607.
(Contemporary Italian engraving).

"J.E." are found in Spain, the Balearic Islands, N Italy, and especially Germany. It was known until the 17th cent.

EXEGESIS see **BIBLE COMMENTARIES**

EXETER: English cathedral town. A Jewish community, with an *archa* for the registration of debts, existed there in the Middle Ages. A fresh settlement (the original nucleus of which came from Italy) was established in the 18th cent. and the present synagogue built 1763–4. 70 Jews now live in E.

EXILARCH (Aram.: *Resh Galuta* i.e., "head of the exile"): Title of the head of Babylonian Jewry. *Seder Olam Zuta* (c. 800) gives a list of e.'s beginning with the exiled king Jehoiakim, but reliable information starts with Nahum at the beginning of the 2nd cent. CE. The office was hereditary and its holder legendarily of the house of David. The e. was recognized by the court and held an honored place in the king's council, living in royal state and acting as chief tax-collector among the Jews who enjoyed a great measure of autonomy until the 5th cent. He appointed judges and exercised criminal jurisdiction among his people. Later, there were frequent conflicts between the e. and the holders of the Office of GAON, owing to the latter's superior learning. Jewish autonomy and the exilarchate were abolished for a short period toward the end of the 5th cent., while a further interruption followed the attempt of the e., MAR ZUTA, to found an independent Jewish principality early in the 6th cent. The Arab conquest (642) inaugurated a new period of brilliance, beginning with BOSTANAI and lasting until the secession of Anan led to the founding of the Karaite sect (late 8th cent.). HEZEKIAH (d. 1040) was long believed to have been the last e., but it is now known that the office continued in at least nominal existence until the 13th cent., or even later. From the 11th cent., the office was imitated, frequently under the same name, in Egypt and elsewhere.

EXILE see **DIASPORA**

EXILE, BABYLONIAN (Heb. *galut bavel*): The period between the destruction of the kingdom of Judea by Nebuchadnezzar and the return from captivity in 538 BCE. As the duration of the B. E. is traditionally reckoned as 70 years (cf. Jer. 29:10), its beginning must be calculated not from the fall of Jerusalem in 586 but from the debacle of the monarchy after the death of Josiah in 608, or else must be reckoned to have lasted until the dedication of the Second Temple (515 BCE). The Exile, however, was not complete; a nucleus of Jews remained in Palestine under the rule of GEDALIAH, and some elements of the population survived there after his assassination (their relative importance is disputed among historians). The deportees in Mesopotamia, mostly peasants and craftsmen, with their main center at Tel Abib near the Great Canal, were encouraged by the confident counsels of Jeremiah, and later inspired by the ecstatic prophecies of Ezekiel. Hence, they were able to maintain and even fortify their religious identity. The circumstances of the B. E. seem to have given rise to the institution of the SYNAGOGUE and, as a corollary, to the beginnings of the prayer-book and of the canonization of the Scriptures. Some light is thrown on their economic life by the records of the banking-house of MURASHU at Nippur. The condition of the exiles improved when the ex-king Jehoiachin was released from prison and accorded royal honors in 561 BCE, and it is possible that the institution of the *Resh Galuta* (EXILARCH) as head of Babylonian Jewry goes back to this period. Less favorable conditions apparently prevailed under Besharuzur (Belshazzar). He was, however, overthrown in 538 by Cyrus of Persia who permitted his Jewish subjects to return to Palestine if they so desired.

EXODUS (Gk. "road out"): The departure of the Israelites from Egypt. Biblical chronology (cf. I Kings 6:1), supported by some archeological findings, suggests that the e. took place c. 1445 BCE. On the other hand, the circumstances of Egyptian

Scenes from the Exodus. (From a Spanish Haggadah in the British Museum).

history indicate a period during the reign of Pharaoh Merneptah (1225–15).

EXODUS, BOOK OF (called in Heb. from its opening phrase *Shemot* – "names"): Second book of the Pentateuch. There are 40 chapters: 1–17 narrate the oppression of the Israelites by the Egyptians, the rise of Moses, the ten plagues, and the exodus from Egypt; 18–24 comprise the Divine revelation and legislation of Sinai and the covenant between God and Israel; 25–50 include the episode of the Golden Calf and its sequel. Some of the laws have parallels in other ancient codes, notably the legislation of Hammurabi of Babylon (18th–17th cents. BCE), but are permeated with greater humanity. As with the other books of the Pentateuch, Jewish tradition regards Moses as the author. Critics believe it to be compounded from various sources but the prevailing view is to assign an early date at least to Exod. 20–25.

EXODUS RABBAH: Midrashic work on the Book of Exodus included in MIDRASH RABBAH. Its present form dates from the 11th–12th cents. but it embodies extracts from more ancient Midrashim.

"EXODUS 1947": Ship (formerly the "President Warfield") which carried 4,554 Jewish refugees to Palestine under *Haganah* auspices in 1947. It was seized by the British in the Mediterranean after a battle in which 3 Jews were killed. The refugees, returned forcibly from Haifa to Port de Bouc, France, refused to land there; in spite of their resistance they were disembarked at Hamburg by British soldiers. The incident did much to swing world opinion against Britain's Palestine policy.

EXORCISM: The driving out of an evil spirit. There is only indirect evidence of e. in the Bible but it occurs in the Apocrypha (Tobit's expulsion of a demon), New Testament, and Talmud. Its use is also evidenced by AMULETS bearing magic names, still used among some Jews. The use of magic formulas was condemned by Maimonides and other authorities but flourished among the people. The e.

Refugees' ship "Exodus 1947".

practiced by the later kabbalists and Hasidim is less concerned with DEMONS than with living persons "possessed" by the souls of the dead; an example is depicted in An-Ski's play *The Dibbuk*. See also DIBBUK.

EXPLORERS: Although the characteristic contribution of the Jews to the great voyages of exploration at the close of the Middle Ages was the provision of maps and nautical instruments, there was some degree of personal collaboration as well, exemplified in the career of Gaspar DA GAMA. Since the 19th cent., Jewish e. have included Nathaniel ISAACS, the pioneer of Natal; EMIN PASHA (Central Africa); Eduard GLASER and Hermann Burchardt (Arabia); Aurel STEIN (Central Asia); and Arminius VAMBERY (Persia). Other African e. were Angelo Castelbolognesi, Eduard Foa, Louis Binger, and Henry Aaron Stern. Arctic e. included Rudolf SAMOILOVICH, Isaac Israel Hayes, and August Sontag.

EXPULSIONS: Local e. of Jews are recorded from antiquity, e.g. from Rome in 139 BCE, 19 CE, and 49/50 CE. With the growth of religious intolerance in the early Middle Ages, FORCED CONVERSION to the dominant faith, usually without the alternative of exile, was frequent, e.g. in the Byzantine Empire. The e. from certain areas of Jews who refused conversion became common from the 12th cent., e.g. from the royal dominions of France in 1182. The first general expulsion of Jews from an entire country was from ENGLAND (1290), followed by FRANCE (1306, 1322, 1394) and large areas of GERMANY after the BLACK DEATH massacres (1348/9). Professing Jews were excluded from Andalusia in 1484 and expelled from Spain and Spanish dominions (including Sicily and Sardinia) in 1492. This was followed by the e. from Portugal 1497 (accompanied by Forced Conversion), Navarre 1498, Provence 1512, and the kingdom of Naples 1541. In 1569, the Jews were expelled from the smaller centers of the papal dominions both in Italy and in France. The Jews were expelled from Little Russia in 1727, 1739, and 1742, and periodically in the 19th cent. from areas outside the PALE OF SETTLEMENT. The Nazis, while seldom expelling the Jews from Germany and the subject areas, compelled the emigration of persons of Jewish ancestry (regardless of religion) by means of ferocious persecution before embarking on their policy of deportation and extermination.

EXTERMINATION CAMPS see **CAMPS, CONCENTRATION AND EXTERMINATION**

EZEKIEL (fl. 6th cent. BCE): Prophet. Probably a member of the priestly family of Zadok, he may have served in the Temple before its destruction in 586 BCE. E. was among those exiled before that date to Tel Abib on the river Kebar in Babylonia where he prophecied over a period of at least 22

The Vision of the Prophet Ezekiel by Raphael, c. 1518. (Palazzo Pitti, Florence).

years (592–570). At first, he rebuked those Jews who had remained in Judah for their evil ways and their confidence that they would resist the Babylonians. He foresaw the utter destruction of Jerusalem, after which, he maintained, the people of Israel would rehabilitate itself. After Jerusalem was destroyed, he consoled and encouraged the survivors with visions of redemption, describing in detail the rebuilt Temple and the redeemed nation (Ezek. 40–5). E. attributed the catastrophes that had befallen Israel to a deliberate moral purpose – the re-establishment in the world of the rule of justice which had been weakened by the sins of Israel. The redemption of Israel would not be conditional on repentance but would occur to prevent the desecration of God by the nations. He also assured the exiles that every generation was responsible only for its own deeds and would not have to bear responsibility for the actions of its ancestors. His graphic prophecies are written in a majestic, poetic prose, excelling in metaphor and frequently describing the prophet's own symbolic actions. They include a description of the Divine throne (Ezek. 1), which provided a basic text for later mystics. The Book of E., the third of the Major Prophets, is divided into 48 chapters: 1–24, mainly prophecies and rebukes uttered before the destruction of Jerusalem; 25–32, prophecies of castrophes to the gentiles; 33–9, consolation to Israel (after the destruction of Jerusalem); 40–8, visions of the reconstructed Temple and reconstituted kingdom. It is written throughout in the first person, but some critics believe it to have been assembled by E.'s pupils.

EZEKIEL: (1) *JACOB E.* (1812–1899): US public writer. He fought legislation discriminating against Jews and obtained the modification of a treaty between the US and Switzerland because of Swiss anti-Jewish legislation. He was secretary to the board of governors of the Hebrew Union College, Cincinnati, 1876–96. (2) *MOSES JACOB E.* (1844–1917): US sculptor, son of (1). He served as a Confederate soldier in the Civil War and then devoted himself to art, studying in Berlin and settling in Rome. His sculptures include religious subjects and public monuments in various parts of the US.

EZEKIEL, MORDECAI JOSEPH BRILL (1899–): US agricultural economist and statistician. He has developed new methods of statistical analysis.

EZION BLOC see **KEPHAR EZION**

EZION GEBER: Ancient port at the head of the Gulf of AKABA from which Solomon's ships sailed to Ophir. After being captured by Edom, E. G. was recovered by Jehoshaphat whose fleet was wrecked as it sailed to Ophir. Uzziah moved the port to a new site at ELATH although E. G. still continued to be used. Remains identified with E. G. were excavated by Nelson Glueck.

EZRA (fl. 5th cent. BCE): Refounder of Palestinian Jewry and reformer of Jewish life. A member of the priestly family of Zadok, he served as a scribe in the employ of the Persian government. When word reached him of the spiritual deterioration of the Jewish community in Palestine, reorganized some sixty years previously by a group of Jews returned from Babylon under Zerubbabel, E. decided to lead a new party of settlers who would firmly establish the Mosaic law in Judah. In 458, he received the requisite permission from Artaxerxes I of Persia and went to Jerusalem with 1,754 returning exiles. E., together with NEHEMIAH, persuaded the people to keep the Torah, to observe the Sabbath and the sabbatical year, to pay their Temple dues, and to reject intermarriage with gentiles (444). The Talmud credits E. with reintroducing biblical law after it had been forgotten and ascribes to him and his entourage many ancient laws as well as the introduction of the square Hebrew characters, the precise determination of the text of the Pentateuch, and the establishment of the Great Assembly (*Kneset ha-Gedolah*). Biblical critics from the time of Spinoza have regarded E. as the compiler of the Pentateuch, but this view is no longer widely held. According to legend, he died while on his way back to Susa to confer with the Persian king. According to a Jewish tradition, his tomb is in a Babylonian village on the Tigris. The rabbis compared his spiritual level with that of Moses. The biblical books of Nehemiah and Ezra were originally a unit, and the first Hebrew ms which divides them dates from 1448. The Book of E. now contains 10 chapters relating events from the return of Zerubbabel (537 BCE) until after the return of Ezra in 458 (1–4; the first return from Babylon and the commencement of the building of the Second Temple; 5–6: the continued rebuilding of the Temple and its inauguration; 7–10: E.'s return and work). The book is a compilation from previous sources (including E.'s memoirs) and part (4:7–6:18; 7:12–26) is in Aramaic. The continuation of E.'s career is to be found in the Book of Nehemiah. Many scholars believe the Books of E., Nehemiah, and Chronicles to have been written by a single hand in the 5th–4th cents. BCE.

F

FABLE (usually called in Heb. *mashal*, i.e. "parable"):
Moral allegory in which beasts, etc. speak like
human beings. The outstanding biblical example is
that of the trees choosing their king (Jud. 9:8–15).
Numerous f.'s occur in the Talmud and Midrash,
and it is possible that the rabbis knew the f.'s of
Kybises (corrupted in the printed text to *kovesim* =
washermen). In the Middle Ages, popular collections
of f.'s largely deriving from Arab sources, were made
by BERECHIAH HA-NAKDAN. Isaac IBN SAHULA. etc.
The f.'s of Bidpai, which had great influence on me-

dieval folklore and fairy-tales, were introduced into
Europe though the medium of Jewish translators,
especially John of Capua. Some modern Hebrew
authors have written f.'s e.g. J.L. Gordon, and Judah
Steinberg.

FAIRS: Markets held periodically for the sale of com-
modities. The rapid development in the Middle
Ages of the Jewish communities in Champagne (N
France) is undoubtedly connected with the famous
international f. held in this region. In Poland, the
great conflux of Jews to the annual f. held in the spring
in Lublin and in the early summer in Jaroslav was responsible for the development in the 16th cent. of the
Council of the Four Lands. The f. of Lemberg and
Lublin were favorite occasions for arranging marriages. In W Europe, f., in which street amusements
predominated, were frequently held in the Jewish
quarters on Purim.

FAITH, CONFESSION OF see **SHEMA**

FAITH, THIRTEEN ARTICLES OF see **CREED**

FAITLOVITCH, JACQUES (1880—1955): Expert on
the FALASHAS. He was born in Poland and lived in
France, Switzerland and Israel. From 1904, he visited
Ethiopia regularly and worked to acquire support in
Europe and America for bringing the Falashas back into the orbit of traditional Judaism. He was also
responsible for considerable educational work among
them and published books on their literature.

FAJANS, KASIMIR (1887—): Chemist. Born in
Warsaw, he was professor of chemistry at the
Universities of Munich (1917–35) and Michigan
(1936—). He discovered Uranium X2 (brevium),
formulated the theory of isotopes, and has written a
number of books on chemical influences in atomic
structure.

FALAQUERA (or Ibn Falaquera), **SHEMTOV BEN
JOSEPH** (c. 1225—c. 1295): Philosopher, translator, and Hebrew poet; member of a distinguished
Toledo family. An expert in Arabic philosophy, the
object of his philosophical writings was to prove the
harmony of religion and philosophy. His works include a defense of Maimonides' *Guide*, Hebrew
abridgments of works by Avicenna. Averroes, etc.,
and a poetical introduction to knowledge, entitled
Sepher ha-Mevakkesh.

Wood-cut illustrations from Isaac Ibn Sahula's book of fables
Meshal ha-Kadmoni, Brescia, 1491.

Falasha youngsters visiting Israel are received
by President Ben-Zvi

FALASHAS: Abyssinian tribes observing a form of
Judaism, living N of Lake Tana. The term F.
probably means "immigrants." Legends and reports
regarding semi-independent Jewish tribes in ETHIOPIA
were current in Europe from the early Middle Ages,
but authentic information was first made available by
James Bruce in 1790. The F. live in a number of village
communities, mainly practicing handicrafts and
agriculture. They are dark-skinned and their way of
life is in most respects similar to that of their
neighbors, whose dialects they speak. Their religion is
based on an almost literal obedience to Old Testament
injunctions, and they know nothing of post-biblical
Hebrew literature; their knowledge of Hebrew is
confined to a very few words, their Scriptures being in
Ge'ez (Old Ethiopic). Sacrifices are offered on certain
occasions by the priests, some of whom live in
monastic communities maintaining rigorous purifi-
catory rites. While observing the biblical feasts, they
have no Ḥanukkah, Purim, etc. They are in all probability descended from converts to Judaism, possibly
before the beginning of the Christian era. There are
persistent legends among them of a former independent status, and at one time they were certainly
more powerful and more widely spread, having
suffered in recent times as a result both of war and
of missionary propaganda. From 1904 onward,
J. FAITLOVITCH carried on intensive activity to bring
the F. into touch with the main currents of Jewish

life and Pro-Falasha committees were established
in Europe and America which trained teachers
and maintained schools at Addis Ababa, etc. Since
1948, similar activity has been carried on systematically by the Jewish Agency. The number of F. is not
established but is estimated at c. 12,000 .

FALK: US family of industrialists and philanthropists.
MAURICE F. (1866—1946) and his brother *LEON
F.* (1870—1928) organized the Duquesne Redaction
Co. which was later merged with Federated Metals
Corp., now the American Smelting and Refining
Corp. In 1928, they founded the Univ. of Pittsburgh's
Falk Medical Clinic for the free treatment of the
needy. The following year, they donated $10 million to
establish the Maurice and Laura F. Fund for religious,
educational, and welfare projects. During and after
World War I. they played major roles in the relief of
European Jews. *LEON F. JR.* (1901-), son of Leon
F., is also active in public affairs and Jewish philan-
thropy.

FALK, ḤAYYIM SAMUEL JACOB (c. 1708–1782):
Kabbalist; known as the Baal Shem of London. He
was born in Podolia but after attaining fame in
Europe, settled in England about 1742. He made a
reputation in non-Jewish as well as Jewish circles as a
miracle-worker and many remarkable tales were told
of his achievements.

FALK (or **WALK**). **JOSHUA BEN ALEXANDER
HA-COHEN** (c. 1550—1614): Codifier. He lived
at Lvov where he founded a yeshivah. F. was the
author of *Bet Yisrael*, a commentary on Jacob ben
Asher's *Turim*, and *Sepher Meirat Enayim* on the
Shulḥan Arukh (*Ḥoshen Mishpat*) which amends and
interprets Joseph Caro's text and was incorporated
into almost all subsequent editions. Many of F.'s
responsa have also been published but his commentaries on the Pentateuch and on 14 tractates of
the Talmud have been lost.

FALL OF MAN: The teaching that death, labor,
and pain were brought into the world by Adam
who sinned in transgressing the Divine command
by eating the fruit of the tree of knowledge. The
biblical narrative describing how the happy state
of the human race as first created came to be
changed is certainly innocent of the extreme theological conclusions later derived from it. Christian
theology has fashioned out of this story the doctrine of
original sin, which teaches the inherent depravity of
the human race. Some trace of this teaching can
already be found in late Apocryphal and Pseudepigraphic literature where mention is first made
that men die because of Adam's original sin. The
generally accepted rabbinic view is that Adam's sin
doomed all men to death, regardless of individual
freedom from sin, although there is reference to a
moral blemish imparted to Eve by the serpent and
transmitted by her to all her descendants. The ac-

ceptance of the Torah at Sinai, however, restored man's original state which was again lost by the worship of the golden calf. R Ammi differed from the majority view and held that every death is caused by actual sin (*Sabbath* 55a).

FALL RIVER: City in Massachusetts, US. A few German Jews settled there in the 1860's. Russian Jews, arriving in the 1880's, founded the first congregation, Adas Israel. The community now has four synagogues. Jewish pop. (1973): 3,300. The F. R. Jewish Community Council was formed in 1938.

FALL, LEO (1873–1925): Viennese operetta composer. His 25 stage works include *The Dollar Princess* and *Madame Pompadour*.

FAMILIANTEN: Term applied to those Jews in Bohemia, Moravia, and Silesia who, in accordance with the policy of restricting the Jewish population, were legally allowed to marry. The maximum number of families with this privilege, which was limited to the eldest son, was fixed by law in 1726. In 1789, they numbered 8,600 in Bohemia and 5,400 in Moravia. Younger sons were compelled to emigrate or remain single. The *Familiantengesetz* was abrogated in 1849, revived in 1853, and finally abolished in 1859.

FAMILY AND FAMILY LIFE: The Israelite family of the biblical period differed from the Jewish family in later times in two important respects. It was more comprehensive, including all male descendants as well as various dependents; and it was based on POLYGAMY. The household of Jacob exemplifies both these facets. On the other hand, Isaac had one wife only, and in later tradition, his household was represented as ideal. So, too, the panegyric of the house wife in Prov. 31 suggests a monogamous family,

Jewish family with guest for the Passover Eve meal by Moritz Oppenheim.

while filial piety is the theme of the Apocryphal Book of Tobit. Talmudic literature reflects, with rare exceptions, a monogamous society and the idealization of the family in the modern sense, emphasizing the duty of the father to educate his sons and train them for some useful trade, the veneration of motherhood, and the biblical precept of honoring parents. The talmudic ideals and, perhaps still more, its legislation governed the Jewish conceptions of family life in the Middle Ages and later. Monogamy became firmly established in N Europe as a result of the *Takkanah* of R Gershom, c. 1000. Marital relations were controlled and, in a way, hallowed by the strict restrictions connected with the menstrual period. Marital fidelity, moreover, was firmly established if only because of the obvious limitations within a restricted "ghetto" society and the savage secular penalties attached to association with gentile women (or *vice versa*). The education of the young came to be recognized as the primary parental duty. The intimate nature of Jewish home observances, in particular those connected with the Sabbath, resulted from and at the same time profoundly strengthened Jewish family life. Family solidarity (the continued attachment of married children to their parents, responsibility of members of the family for one another) was developed to an extent unusual among non-Jews. Although at the outset of modern times, occidental Jewish family life continued in the old pattern, gradual assimilation has led to an increase in divorce, a diminution in the birth rate, and the dwindling of internal solidarity, so that the family pattern has approached that of the environment.

FANO: Port on E coast of Italy, with a flourishing Jewish community from the 13th cent. It produced numerous scholars and physicians. The printer Geronimo Soncino worked there in the early 16th cent. The municipal council protected the Jews from a Ritual Murder charge in 1492, but the community came to an end with the expulsion of the Jews from the Papal States in 1569.

FANO: Italian family. (1) *AVIGDOR F.* (fl. 15th cent.), poet, wrote an apology for the female sex. (2) *GIULIO F.* (1856—1930) was the most eminent Italian physiologist of his day and was appointed senator in 1911. (3) *JACOB F.* (fl. 16th cent.), poet, was punished by the Church authorities for his elegy commemorating the burning of the Marranos in Ancona in 1556. (4) *JOSEPH DA F.* (c. 1550 — c. 1630), of Mantua, was created marquis of Villimpenta, probably being the first European Jew ennobled. (5) *MENAHEM AZARIAH DA F.* (1548—1620), rabbi at Mantua, popularized the study of the Kabbalah in Italy and subsidized the publication of various mystical works. His most important original composition was *Asarah Maamarot* ("Ten Sayings") of which three sections were published in his lifetime.

FARBAND LABOR ZIONIST ORDER: Zionist educational and mutual benefit organization in the US and Canada. Organized in 1913 (as the Jewish National Workers' Alliance), by 1957 it had 300 branches and a family unit membership of 30,000. The F. pioneered in the establishment of Zionist-oriented Jewish folk schools, helped to establish the Jewish Teachers' Seminary and People's University, and has been active in relief and fund-raising, particularly for the *Histadrut*.

FARBSTEIN: (1) *DAVID TZEVI F.* (1868—1953): Zionist and socialist leader. He was born in Warsaw and settled in Switzerland where he did much to organize the Jewish communities. A leader of the Swiss socialist movement, he was the first Jew to be a member of the Swiss National Council. (2) *JOSHUA HESCHEL F.* (1870—1948): Polish Zionist leader; brother of (1). F. was president of the Zionist Organization of Poland 1915–8, and of the Polish *Mizrahi* 1918–31. He was a delegate to the Seym 1919–27 and president of the Warsaw Jewish community 1926–31. He settled in Palestine in 1931 and was a member of the Jewish Agency Executive 1931–3.

FARHI (PARHI), ESTORI (c. 1280—c. 1355): Explorer of Palestinian topography. He was born in S France and after studying medicine and rabbinics, went to Palestine (1312) where he settled at Beisan (Bet Shean). His book *Kaphtor va-Pherah*, completed in 1322, presents the results of his biblical scholarship and travels throughout the country; it determines the names of Palestinian towns and villages, describes the geography, natural history, numismatics, etc., and identifies with remarkable accuracy some 180 ancient sites.

FARHI, HAYYIM MU'ALLIM (c. 1760—1820): Statesman. He succeeded his father as finance minister to the Pasha of Damascus, later settling in Acre where he became financial adviser to the tyrannous pasha, Jazzar. F. organized the city's successful defense against Napoleon (1799), but aroused the jealousy of Jazzar who mutilated and deposed him. He was restored under Jazzar's successor, Suleiman (ruled 1805–18), but Suleiman's successor, Abdullah, had him strangled and confiscated his property. In the period of his greatness, F. was the protector of the Jews of Palestine.

FARJEON: English family of N African origin. Among its members were *BENJAMIN LEOPOLD F.* (1838—1903) who, after a career in Australian journalism, returned to England and published melodramatic novels; his sons *HERBERT F.* (1887—1945), wit, dramatist, and critic, and *JOSEPH JEFFERSON F.* (1883–1955), playwright and novelist; and his daughter *ELEANOR F.* (1881—1965), novelist, poet, dramatist, and author of works for juveniles.

FARMER see **AGRICULTURAL SETTLEMENTS; AGRICULTURE**

FARRISOL, ABRAHAM (c. 1451—1526): Hebrew author. Born in Avignon, he lived in Florence, Mantua, and Ferrara, earning his living as a *hazzan* and scribe. Large numbers of works beautifully copied by him are extant. His works include a commentary on Job; the polemical *Magen Avraham* resulting from a religious disputation at the court of Ferrara; and a geographical composition *Iggeret Orehot Olam* — the first Hebrew work to mention the discovery of America.

FASCISM: Italian political movement, organized by Benito Mussolini in 1919. Some Jews were associated with it from its inception when it showed no anti-Semitic tendencies other than those usually associated with a totalitarian and reactionary movement. When it seized power in 1922, Jewish life was barely affected, and some Jews rose to high position under the regime. Mussolini began to turn against the Jews when they proved not wholly subservient and when he came to consider Zionism a pro-British movement. In 1938, his rapprochement with Hitler resulted in his adoption of a thorough-going anti-Semitic policy. In Sept.-Nov. of that year racial laws modeled after the German Nuremberg Laws were introduced with the object of excluding Jews from Italian life. Nevertheless, Italian anti-Semitism never reached the appalling excesses of its German model, and after the entry of Italy into World War II in 1940, the Italian authorities, both at home and abroad, did their best to restrain German brutality. On the other hand, the Republican Fascist movement set up by the Germans in N Italy in 1943 collaborated in the deportation of Jews to the extermination camps. Outside Italy, the various Fascist parties have invariably been anti-Semitic.

FAST (Heb. *tzom* or *taanit*): Voluntary abstention from food. In Judaism, it is practiced for spiritual ends, as a sign of repentance or mourning, or to request Divine assistance. The f. in Judaism involves complete abstention from food and drink. The fasts of the Day of Atonement and *Av* 9 last from sunset to sunset and include the additional prohibitions of anointing, wearing shoes, and sexual intercourse; the other public fasts last only from sunrise to sunset. On public f.-days, special prayers are customary, and in earlier times those fasting used to sit on the ground, dress in sackcloth, and put ashes on their heads. The first f. commanded to Israel was the Day of Atonement (Lev. 23:27–32), while the Bible also refers to the f.'s of *Tishri* 3, *Tevet* 10, *Tammuz* 17, and *Av* 9 (Zech. 8:19). The Jews of Shushan were ordered to fast 3 days and one night (Est. 4:16) but the Fast of Esther, instituted at a later date, was, like the other public f.'s, for one day only. The *anshe maamad* (community representatives during the daily Temple sacrifices) fasted for 4 days *(Taanit 27b)*. Pious individuals in former times fasted on three days (Monday, Thursday, Monday) following the festivals of Passover and Tabernacles to ask forgiveness for sins committed during the festival period. Some pietists (imitated by the Marranos) fasted every Monday and Thursday. F.-days falling on Sabbath are postponed, with the exception of the Day of Atonement. Isaiah rebuked those who fasted out of hypocritical virtue as well as those who believed that a f. without a change of heart brought forgiveness (Is. 58:3–6). After the destruction of the Second Temple, the number of f.'s increased among the Jews (f. of the first-born, f.'s after bad dreams, f.'s to overcome unfavorable decrees, the f. of the bridegroom and bride on their wedding-day, f.'s on the *Yahrzeit*, etc.). The Talmud contains treatise *Taanit* dealing with f.'s, while *Megillat Taanit* lists those days on which fasting is forbidden because traditionally miracles occurred on these dates.

TRADITIONAL FAST-DAYS

3 Tishri	Fast of Gedaliah	Commemorates assassination of Gedaliah
10 Tishri	Day of Atonement	Atonement for sins
10 Tevet		Siege of Jerusalem begun by Nebuchadnezzar
13 Adar	Fast of Esther	Commemorates fast decreed by Esther
14 Nisan	Fast of the First-born	Commemorates the last of the ten plagues
17 Tammuz		Walls of Jerusalem breached by Nebuchadnezzar and by Titus
9 Av		Destruction of First and Second Temples

FAST, HOWARD (1914–   ): US author. His books include *Citizen Tom Paine, Freedom Road,* and *My Glorious Brothers* (based on the story of the Maccabees), as well as a biography of Haym Salomon. A former sympathizer with causes endorsed by the American Communist Party, since 1957 he has broken with them and described his disillusionment in *The Naked God.* Fast also wrote *The Jews,* a history of the Jewish people.

FATALISM: The belief that all things have a fixed destiny over which man has no control. This belief had wide circulation in the ancient world and is still important in the religions of India and many Moslem sects. Biblical teaching can be adduced both for (Deut. 30:19) and against (Exod. 7:3) free will. The Pharisees taught that "all things are in the hands of Heaven except the fear of Heaven" (*Berakhot* 33*b*). Man has free will and can determine his actions within certain limits. An unfavorable Divine decree can be modified by "penitence, prayer, and charity." This represented a moderate attitude between the extremes held by the other Jewish sects, the Sadducees and Essenes, as described by Josephus. The former denied Divine interference in human affairs, while the latter held it to be the controlling force in every aspect of life. Maimonides pointed out that whereas man is born with certain tendencies, his acts are entirely under his own control, and a fatalistic approach would make meaningless the commandments and the doctrine of reward and punishment. In antiquity and the Middle Ages, f. was often identical with astrological beliefs in determinism by the stars. The rabbinic negations of f. therefore often took the form of denying the power of the stars over Israel, which is subject to the exclusive province of God.

FAUDEL-PHILLIPS, SIR GEORGE see **PHILLIPS, SIR GEORGE FAUDEL-**

FEAST OF THE COMMANDMENT see **SEUDAT MITZVAH**

FEASTS see **HOLY DAYS**

FEDER, TOBIAS GUTTMANN (c. 1760–1817): Hebrew author, poet, and grammarian; pioneer of Haskalah in Galicia. He was noted for his Hebrew style and is considered one of the forerunners of Hebrew literary criticism. He engaged in satire against the Ḥasidim and in other controversies.

FEDERATIONS see **WELFARE FUNDS**

FEFER, ITZIK (1900–1952): Russian Yiddish poet. The main theme of his work is the effect of the 1918–20 Russian civil war (in which F. participated) on Jewish life. He visited western countries during World War II as a representative of the Jewish Anti-Fascist Committee but, like many other Russian Jewish authors, was murdered during the latter days of Stalin.

FEIERBERG, MORDECAI ZE'EV (1874–1899): Russian Hebrew author. He wrote essays and several lyrical novels of which the best-known is *Le'an* ("Whither?"). In his novels, which show the influence of Aḥad Ha-Am, F. expresses the struggle of E European youth at the end of the 19th cent., disappointed by Haskalah and yet unable to remain within the bounds of traditional Judaism.

FEIGENBAUM, BENJAMIN (1860–1932): Yiddish journalist. He left his native Poland in the early 1880's, worked in Belgium and England, and arrived in New York in 1891. Here he wrote for the labor publication *Arbeiter Zeitung.* He edited the *Zukunft* 1904–5, and when *Forverts* was founded, joined its editorial staff. Most of his writings deal with socialism, but also include volumes of anti-religious discourses.

FEINBERG, AVSHALOM (1889–1917): Palestinian Nili leader. Together with A. AARONSOHN, he founded the *Nili* movement but was killed by Bedouin in the Sinai desert while on his way to Egypt to establish contact with the British. His remains were discovered in 1967 after the Six-Day War when Israelis had access to Sinai. A. palm-tree had grown out of a date-pit in his pocket at the time of his death. He was reburied on Mt. Herzl in Jerusalem.

*FEISAL IBN HUSSEIN (1885–1933): King of Iraq from 1921; eldest son of Hussein, sherif of Mecca. He led the Arab "rising" against Turkey

(1916–18) and was designated king of Syria. F. was at first sympathetic to Zionism from which he hoped to receive aid in building his future kingdom. He met Dr. Weizmann in Transjordan (1918) and Paris (1919) where they reached an agreement on mutual aid, conditional on the implementation of British promises to the Arabs. Later, owing to his expulsion from Syria by the French (1920) and the influence of the Palestinian Arab leaders, his attitude to Zionism became hostile.

FEIWEL, BERTHOLD (1875–1937): Zionist leader.

He was one of Herzl's closest assistants, helping to organize the First Zionist Congress and to edit the Zionist newspaper, *Die Welt,* in Vienna. He was a founder of the DEMOCRATIC FRACTION in 1901. F. was one of the first western Zionists to appreciate the vitality of E European Zionism. He translated Hebrew and Yiddish works into German to convey the suffering of the Jewish masses and was a founder of the Jüdischer Verlag in Berlin, which published these and other books of Jewish interest. After World War I, he resided for a time in London where he directed the *Keren ha-Yesod* 1920–6. In 1933, F. settled in Palestine.

FELDMAN, HERMAN (1894–　): US sociologist.

He has taught at several universities and acted as government consultant on social and industrial affairs, specializing in labor relations, unemployment, and personnel programs.

FELIX ANTONIUS see **PROCURATORS**

FELIX LIBERTATE (Lat. "happy through freedom"): Name of an association formed by Jews in Amsterdam in 1795 to secure political emancipation and (later) certain religious reforms.

FELIX, ARTHUR (1887–1956): Bacteriologist and immunologist. Born in Poland, he was bacteriologist for the Hadassah Medical Organization in Palestine 1921–7 and from 1927 held posts in London at the Lister Institute (1927–45) and public health services. He was joint discoverer of the Weil-Felix reaction for the diagnosis of typhus fever.

FELIX, ELISA RACHEL (stage-name "Rachel"; 1820–1858): French actress. First appearing on the stage at the age of 13, she made her name at the *Comédie Française* and gained a world reputation as a tragic actress, particularly in French classical drama. Her best-known part was Racine's *Phèdre* which she played in many countries.

FELS: US family. *JOSEPH F.* (1853–1914), industrialist, gained wealth as a manufacturer of naphtha soap in Philadelphia. He later became a leader in land reform movements in the US and England, championing Henry George's "single tax" theories. His wife, *MARY F.* (1863–1953), carried on his philanthropic work as head of the Joseph Fels Foundation which promoted goodwill between Jews and non-Jews and also assisted Palestinian settlement. Joseph's brother, *SAMUEL F.* (1860–1950), established a $12,000,000

Elisa Rachel Felix, the actress "Rachel."

foundation to further scientific and educational projects largely in the field of medicine.

FELSENTHAL, BERNARD (1822–1908): Rabbi.

He was born in Germany and settled in the US in 1854, serving in Chicago as rabbi of the Sinai (1861–4) and Zion (1864–87) congregations. Though one of the pioneer Reform rabbis in the US, F. took a moderate position and was an early supporter of the Zionist movement. He was a founder of the Jewish Publication Society of America and of the American Jewish Historical Society.

FEODOSIA see **KAFFA**

FERBER, EDNA (1887–1968): US novelist and playwright. She has described her Wisconsin childhood in her autobiography, *A Peculiar Treasure* and her later life in *A Kind of Treasure.* F. wrote many popular short stories, plays (*Dinner at Eight, Stage Door*), and novels (*So Big, Saratoga Trunk, Giant*); some of the latter were dramatized (*Cimarron, Show Boat*).

FERDINAND AND ISABELLA see **SPAIN**

FERENCZI, SÁNDOR (1873–1933): Psychoanalyst; of Hungarian birth. One of the first collaborators of Freud, he wrote on hypnosis, transference, the ego, and genitality.

FERRARA: N Italian city. Jews are first mentioned there in 1275, the early settlers being in part native Italians and in part immigrants from Germany. In the

Renaissance Period, it was one of the most important Italian Jewish centers, a printing-press being set up as early as 1477. Spanish refugees were welcomed there after 1492, and Portuguese Marranos congregated in F. in the middle of the 16th cent.; the works published for their benefit in Spanish and Portuguese (1552–8) constitute the first publications of Jewish vernacular literature. The Marrano settlement was broken up in 1581 and the ghetto system introduced in 1597 when F. passed under papal rule; nevertheless, the city continued to be a center of Jewish intellectual life. Emancipation was granted with the French occupation in 1796, was canceled with the papal restoration of 1814, and renewed with the annexation to the kingdom of Italy (1860). Thereafter, the community declined and it suffered severely during the German occupation of 1943–5 when the ancient synagogues were sacked. In 1970, there were 150 Jews in F.

*FERRER, VICENTE (1350—1419): Spanish Dominican. In 1411–3, he traversed Spain with a following of flagellants, preaching to the Jews in the synagogues. This resulted in widespread conversions, sometimes of entire communities.

FESTIVAL PRAYERS: As on Sabbaths, an additional prayer (*Musaph*) is added on festivals to the regular morning prayer, corresponding to and describing the additional sacrifice offered on these days during the Temple Period. Appropriate verses are selected for the readings from the Pentateuch and Prophets. Special commandments peculiar to the festival are the occasion for special prayers (e.g. taking the *lulav*, blowing the *shophar*). Since the end of talmudic times, it has become customary to recite special hymns (*piyyutim*) in honor of the festival. The book containing f.p. is called MAHZOR.

FESTIVALS see HOLY DAYS

FESTSCHRIFT: A collection of learned essays in honor of a scholar. Many have been published in the sphere of Jewish scholarship — most of them formerly in Germany, now in America and Israel. An index to Jewish *Festschriften* was published by J. R. Marcus and A. Bilgray (Cincinnati, 1937).

*FETTMILCH, VINCENT (d. 1616): German agitator. In 1614, he led a mob against the Jews of Frankfort-on-Main, expelling them from the town, where he seized control. Ultimately, he was over-

The execution of Fettmilch.

thrown and executed. On their return, the Jews instituted an annual celebration of this event (*Purim Vintz*) on *Adar* 20.

FEUCHTWANGER, LION (1884—1958): Novelist and dramatist. Born in Germany, he emigrated to France in 1933, and to the US in 1940. F. gained an international reputation with his historical novels *Jew Süss* and *The Ugly Duchess* and the modern novel *Success*. On the rise of Nazism, he wrote *The Oppermanns* about a German Jewish family. His outstanding achievement is a historical trilogy on the life of Josephus.

FEUERMANN, EMANUEL (1902—1942): Cellist. Of Galician birth, from 1917 to 1933 he taught in Germany and in 1938, settled in the US.

FEYMAN, RICHARD P. (1918–): US physicist. After working on nuclear research at Los Alamos, he became professor of physics at Cornell Univ. and since 1951 at the California Institute of Technology. In 1965, he was co-recipient of the Nobel physics prize for transforming the "exchange play" between elementary particles to hard mathematical facts.

FEZ: Moroccan town. Its Jewish community, like the city itself, dates from the 9th cent. and swiftly became a major intellectual center, producing many outstanding rabbinical scholars, notably Isaac Alfasi. Persecutions were instituted by the Almohades and Jews rejecting Islam were executed in 1146, but many of the conversions were nominal. The anti-Jewish *Marabout* movement occurred during the 13th cent., and at the end of that century, Jews were allotted a special quarter popularly termed the MELLAḤ. Refugees from Spain joined the community in 1391 and many more after 1492. The Jews suffered severely in various Spanish invasions of Morocco. During the French Protectorate, in the 20th cent., their position improved. Most of them emigrated after 1948 and in 1970 only 1,000 remained.

FICHMAN, YAAKOV (1881–1958): Hebrew poet, author, and translator. He was born in Bessarabia and divided his time between Palestine and Europe, engaging in literary activities. He settled in Palestine in 1925. He edited literary periodicals, anthologies, textbooks, etc.

FIDEL PITA see **FITA**

FIEDLER, ARTHUR (1894–): US conductor. F. has led the Boston "Pops" Orchestra since 1930.

FIEDLER, LESLIE A. (1917–): US critic and author. Born in Newark, he was appointed professor of English at Montana State Univ. in 1941 and later at New York State Univ. at Buffalo. His pungent critical writings have included *Love and Death in the American Novel* and *The Image of the Jew in American Fiction*. He has also written novels, stories, essays, and poems.

FILENE: (1) *EDWARD ALBERT F.* (1860–1937): US merchant. He is considered the father of the credit union movement in the US; he also promoted the development of consumer cooperatives. (2) *A. LINCOLN F.* (1865–1957): Merchant; brother of (1) and his partner in a Boston department store. He was active in the New Deal and in behalf of liberal economies.

FILIPOWSKI, HERSCHELL PHILLIPS (Tzevi Hirsch F.; 1816–1872): Mathematician and Hebraist. Born in Russia, he worked in England and Scotland from 1839. In addition to his mathematical writings, he printed and published a number of medieval Hebrew texts (e.g. Zacuto's *Sepher Yuḥasin*) in a fine type, establishing in 1851 an antiquarian society (*Ḥevrat Meorere Yeshenim*) for the purpose.

FILM see **MOTION PICTURES**

FINALY CASE: The case of Robert and Gerald Finaly, two Jewish orphans who were the subjects of a legal struggle in France, 1950–3. Their parents having died in a Nazi concentration camp, they were baptized in 1948 in a Catholic children's home at Grenoble which refused to give them up despite the decision of a French court awarding the boys to their nearest relative, an aunt in Israel. They disappeared in Feb. 1953, and were later traced to Spain. 10 persons, including 4 Catholic priests, were arrested in connection with the kidnapping. The children were returned to France by agreement with Catholic leaders, who were influenced by the public outcry, and immediately afterward taken to Israel. The episode aroused violent controversy in France.

FINANCE see **BANKING; CAPITALISM; CREDIT; MONEYLENDING**

FINCK, HERMAN (1872–1939): British conductor and composer. He composed numerous orchestral works, piano pieces, and songs of which the best-known is *In the Shadows*.

FINDING OF PROPERTY: According to the Bible, lost property must be returned to the rightful owner wherever possible (Exod. 23:4; Deut. 22:3). The finder must make public announcement of his find. In Temple times, this announcement was made regularly over a period covering the three festival celebrations, and a special stone existed at Jerusalem from which lost and found property was proclaimed. Later, synagogue announcements over shorter periods were considered sufficient. Lost property, however, is not to be returned without proper identification by the owner. Property which has no identifying marks, or property lost under such unusual circumstances that the owner has certainly given up hope of recovering it (*veush bealim*) need not be returned or even announced. Pious Jewish practice, however, calls for the return of lost property even where the proper owner cannot make the identification required by law. No reward may be claimed for the return of lost property, although the finder is entitled to reimbursement for expenses entailed in caring for it.

Rabbi Louis Finkelstein conferring honorary doctorate of Jewish Theological Seminary on David Ben-Gurion.

FINE: There are only four instances where the Bible places a fixed sum as the punishment for wrongdoing, but these are payments to the injured party and not to the state. The cases are: 50 shekels for ravishing a virgin, the same for seducing a virgin, 100 shekels for falsely accusing one's wife of prenuptial unchastity, and 30 shekels for the killing of a slave by an ox. At a later date, rabbinical courts adopted the practice of imposing f.'s payable to the community fund for certain public offenses, such as the keeping of false weights. The regulations of Jewish communities before the Emancipation Period stipulated f.'s as punishment for refusing communal office or synagogal honors and sometimes even for absence from services or communal meetings.

FINE, REUBEN (1914–): US chess master. Champion of the US in 1934, he was victor in a long series of international tournaments. He wrote several books on chess openings, the middle game, and basic endings. Later he became professor of psychology at City College, New York.

FINEMAN, IRVING (1893–): US novelist. Originally an engineer, he turned to literature and established his reputation with *This Pure Young Man* and *Hear Ye, Sons*, the story of a Polish Jew in New York.

FINKELSTEIN, LOUIS (1895–): US scholar. He studied at the Jewish Theological Seminary in New York from which he graduated as rabbi in 1919 and where he subsequently taught Talmud and theology. He became provost (1937), president (1940), and chancellor (1951) of the Seminary, greatly extending its activities and scope. F.'s major writings have been largely in the field of Jewish history and literature in the Mishnaic Period. In particular, he has shown the social and economic basis of the dispute between the Pharisees and Sadducees.

FINLAND: Baltic republic. Jews first settled there in the mid-19th cent. and were fully emancipated with the achievement of Finnish independence from Russia in 1917. It was the only part of Europe in the Nazi orbit where no anti-Jewish measures were taken in World War II. Jewish pop. (1973): 1,200, most of whom are in HELSINKI, with communities also in Tampare and Turku.

FINTA (Sp. "fine"): The assessment for dues payable to Sephardi congregations in Holland, England, etc.

FINZI (etymology uncertain): Italian family. Its outstanding members have included: *ANGELO (MORDECAI) F.* (fl. 15th cent.), loan-banker and scientific scholar in Mantua. He wrote extensively on mathematics and astrology, besides translating into Hebrew. He had close relations with contemporary non-Jewish scientists. *MOSES F.* (fl. 16th cent.), probably rabbi of Imola, translated the Aristotelian writings of Themistius from Hebrew into Latin. *GIUSEPPE F.* (1815–1886), Italian patriot, participated in the wars of the Risorgimento and was closely associated with Mazzini and Garibaldi. He was the first Italian Jew appointed senator (1886). *ISAAC RAPHAEL F.* (1728–1812), rabbi of Padua and a renowned preacher, was a vice-president of the Napoleonic Sanhedrin. *SOLOMON F.* (fl. c. 1800), rabbi of Elba, was imprisoned on a charge of attacking Catholicism in an Italian poem on the coming of the Messiah. *GERALD F.* (1901–1956), English musician, was professor of composition at the Royal Academy of Music and wrote songs as well as choral, orchestral, and chamber music.

FIRKOVICH, ABRAHAM (1785–1874): Karaite scholar. He held posts in various communities in the Crimea and in the course of his extensive traveling systematically purchased ancient manuscripts, especially of the Bible. These became the nucleus of the great Leningrad collections. He also published works on Karaite history. In these, he endeavored to demonstrate the great antiquity of the sect. In consequence, he forged or falsified dates, thus undermining confidence even in his more scholarly writings.

FIRST-BORN: In ancient Hebrew tradition, special privileges and the preponderant part of the father's estate passed to the eldest son, this being the origin of rivalry between Jacob and Esau (Gen. 27). The special distinction automatically belonging to the f. b. is also implied in Jacob's blessing (Gen. 49:3). According to the Pentateuch, a double share of the father's inheritance belongs to the f. b. (Deut. 21:17), and this privilege could not be withdrawn or withheld under any circumstances. These privileges were linked with the responsibility of the f. b. regarding the care of the other children (cf. the action of Reuben in the story of Joseph; Gen. 37:22, 29–30). Modern Israel legislation has adopted the Ottoman law of inheritance which

Page of *Ezekiel* from codex No. 1283 of the Firkovich collection, Leningrad.

grants no special privileges to the f. b. See FIRST-BORN, REDEMPTION OF; INHERITANCE.

FIRST-BORN, FAST OF THE: The custom of the first-born fasting on the day preceding Passover was a late (gaonic) innovation instituted to commemorate the deliverance of the Israelite first-born from the tenth plague (*Sopherim* 21:3). It was later somewhat modified by permitting the breaking of the fast at a SEUDAT MITZVAH. It therefore became customary to conclude the study of a talmudic treatise on *Nisan* 14 so as to permit the holding of a feast.

FIRST-BORN, REDEMPTION OF THE (Heb. *pidyon ha-ben*): According to biblical injunction, every first-born of the womb, whether of man or beast, is considered as belonging to the Lord (Exod. 13:11–16); humans must be redeemed and clean animals sacrificed (Lev. 27:26). The redemption consists in the payment of 5 shekels, or its equivalent in goods, to the priest thirty days after the birth of the first-born son. However, since redemption is considered a release from Temple service, originally destined for the first-born but later given to the levites (Num. 3:12–13; 45–51), the first-born of priests or levites, or even of a woman of priestly or levitical birth married to an ordinary Israelite, need not be redeemed. Nor does redemption apply to one born in a Caesarean operation or subsequent to a miscarriage. The ceremony of the Redemption of the First-Born on the 30th day after birth by paying a sum of silver to a *Cohen* (who generally devotes the amount to charity) is accompanied by the recital of a special formula and blessing. Clean animals were given to the priest who offered them as sacrifices. First-born animals which developed blemishes were considered profane and could be eaten by anyone. The restrictions against making profane use of first-born animals apply even after the destruction of the Temple. For this reason, it is customary for an Orthodox Jew to "sell" an animal to a gentile prior to her first delivery in order to circumvent the difficulties in making use of a male first-born. The first-born of unclean animals are profane, except that of the ass which, if not killed by cervical dislocation, must be redeemed by a sheep or its monetary equivalent.

FIRST FRUITS (Heb. *bikkurim*): Biblical legislation called for the bringing of the first choice fruits of field and tree to the Temple and the recitation upon this occasion of the "Declaration" in Deut. 26:5–10. The f. f. could be brought any time between the Feast of Weeks (also called the Feast of the First Fruits) and Ḥanukkah, but the Declaration could not be said after the Feast of Tabernacles. The third chapter of the Mishnah tractate *Bikkurim*, which deals with the f. f., describes the stages of the custom from the time of the fruits' ripening until it was offered at the Temple. "When a man goes down into his field and notices a ripening fig or cluster of grapes, he ties reed-rope around them and says 'Let these be First Fruits.'" The fruit was later carried in great pomp to Jerusalem from the chief district towns, known as towns of the *Maamad*. The night was spent out of doors and in the early morning the call came: "Arise ye and let us go up to Zion unto the Lord our God" (Jer. 31:6). An ox bedecked with gold and olive-leaves led the way. At Jerusalem, the officers of the Temple came to meet the pilgrims, and craftsmen stopped their work to rise and greet them (*Bikkurim* 3:1–3). The f. f. were then presented at the altar to the accompaniment of the Declaration.

*FIRUZ: Sassanid king of Persia 459–83. A fanatical Zoroastrian, he used the alleged murder of two Magi at Isfahan in 468 as a pretext for a bitter persecution. Half of the local Jews were put to death, while the children were handed to the Magi for education. The exilarch, Huna bar Zutra, and several rabbis were sentenced to death and the practice of Judaism forbidden. The revolt of Mar ZUTRA may have been provoked by these events.

FISCHEL, HARRY (1865–1948): US philanthropist. He established in Jerusalem the Harry Fischel Foundation for Research in Talmud (1933) and endowed a post-graduate school for the Yeshiva College, New York (1945). He was treasurer of HIAS for over 50 years.

FISCHER, ROBERT (BOBBY; 1943–): US chess master. While in his teens he was US champion. He defeated SPASSKY for the world championship in 1972 but refused to defend it in 1975. He joined a Christian Sabbatarian sect.

FISCHER, LOUIS (1896–1970): US journalist. Writing largely about European and Asian political problems, he at first championed Soviet Russia. He described his subsequent disillusionment with communism in *The God That Failed* (1949).

FISCHER, SAMUEL (1859–1934): Publisher. Of Hungarian birth, he settled in Berlin in 1886. Here he founded a leading publishing house and the literary journal *Die Neue Rundschau*. After his death, the firm passed to his son-in-law Gottfried Bermann and received the name Bermann-Fischer. It published in Vienna from 1936–8 and subsequently in Stockholm New York, and Frankfort-on-Main.

FISCHHOFF, ADOLF ABRAHAM (1816–1893): Austrian statesman and physician. He was prominent in the 1848 revolution in Vienna, becoming president of the committee of public security. He was arrested after the failure of the revolution but later amnestied.

FISCUS JUDAICUS (Lat. "Jewish Fund"): Poll tax imposed by the Romans on the Jews after 70 CE in place of the half-shekel formerly paid to the Temple in Jerusalem. Its exaction was harsh under Domitian and modified humanely by Nerva, but the tax continued to be collected, probably until the 4th cent. It was renewed in the Middle Ages (1342) as the *Opferpfennig* exacted by the Holy Roman Emperors.

FISHBEIN, MORRIS (1889–1976): US physician. He edited the *Journal* of the American Medical Association 1924–49, and writes and lectures on medical and public health topics.

FISHBERG, MAURICE (1872–1934): US physician and anthropologist. Born in Russia, he emigrated to the US in 1890. He was an outstanding authority on pulmonary tuberculosis. As an anthropologist, he is best known for his work *The Jews*, in which he contended that modern Jews are derived from a variety of racial stocks.

FISHMAN, JACOB (1876–1946): Yiddish journalist. Born in Poland, he migrated in 1890 to the US where he edited Yiddish journals, including the *Morgen Journal* (1916–38). He was a leading figure in the American Zionist movement. F. designed the first Hebrew typewriter.

Eleazar Fleckeles.

FITELBERG: (1) *GRZEGORZ F.* (1879–1953):
Polish conductor and composer. He conducted in
Warsaw from 1907 with intervals as conductor of
the Vienna Opera (1911–4) and in Russia (1914–20).
F. composed symphonic works, chamber music, and
songs. (2) *JERZY F.* (1903–1951): Polish composer;
son of (1). In 1933, he settled in Paris and in 1940,
in the US. His compositions include symphonic and
chamber music and works for the piano.

FLACCUS see **PROCURATORS**

FLAG (Heb. *degel*): Each tribe of Israel had its
individual banner (Num. 2). The Midrash (*Numbers Rabbah* 2) describes them as having the colors
of the 12 precious stones in the high priest's breastplate,
and makes the emblem of every tribe correspond
to the appropriate reference in the blessings of Jacob
(Gen. 49) and Moses (Deut. 33). The Maccabees in
their revolt are said to have carried a banner on
which were inscribed the initial letters of the words
"Who is like unto Thee among the gods, O Lord!"
F.'s of various designs are carried by children in the
synagogue on the Festival of the Rejoicing of the Law.
Herzl suggested a f. of seven golden stars, symbolizing
the proposed seven-hour working day. The f. adopted
by the Zionist movement, however, consists of a
central Shield of David set off by two broad blue
horizontal stripes upon a white background. The
stripes and white background are said to have been
inspired by the *tallit*. This f., with minor modifications,
later became that of the State of Israel.

FLAGELLATION: Corporal punishment (*makkot*,
malkot) administered by lash. The Mishnah
enumerates a partial list of 50 biblical transgressions
of which the punishment is f., but Maimonides makes
a specific reckoning of 207. The maximum number of
stripes which could be given for any single offense
was 39 (i.e., 40–1; cf. Deut. 25:3); the court, however,
had the discretion to reduce this number. They
were administered upon the right shoulder, breast,
and left shoulder in turn. Limitation of the number
of stripes did not apply, however, in the case of
makkat mardut ("punishment for rebellion") instituted
in Babylonia and given in special cases of disobedience
to a court order. Punishment by f. was permitted in
Palestine during the period of the British Mandate
but was abolished in the state of Israel. The mystics
reintroduced f. as a voluntary penance, practiced
especially on the eve of the Day of Atonement.

FLAVIUS CLEMENS see **CLEMENS, FLAVIUS**

FLAVIUS JOSEPHUS see **JOSEPHUS**

FLECKELES, ELEAZAR BEN DAVID (1754–1826):
Talmudist and preacher; senior dayyan at Prague.
His works include several homiletical books, responsa,
and commentaries to the Haggadah and *Avot*.

FLEG, EDMOND (1874–1963): French poet and
playwright. Even among his earlier works, Jewish
subjects are treated. In his maturity he turned entirely
to Jewish interests and produced such works as *Le
Mur des Pleurs*; *Pourquoi je suis Juif*; *Ma Palestine*;
Écoute Israel, and *L'Anthologie juive*. His other works
include lives of Moses and Solomon based on
midrashic sources.

FLEISCHER, MAX (1885–1972): US cartoonist. He
was associated with the development and, later, the
improvement of methods for producing motion
picture cartoons (e.g., Popeye).

FLESCH, CARL (1873–1944): Hungarian violinist.
He taught in Bucharest, Amsterdam, and Berlin
before settling in London in 1934. F. published books
on violin technique and composed violin studies.

FLEISHIG see **MILCHIG**

FLEXNER: US family. (1) *ABRAHAM F.* (1866–
1959): Educator. Noted for his studies of American
universities and especially for his surveys of medical
education, he was the first head of the Institute for
Advanced Study at Princeton (1930–9). His wife,
Anne, was a successful playwright. (2) *BERNARD F.*
1865–1945): Lawyer and economist, brother of (1)
and (3). He was active with Brandeis in the Zionist
Organization of America and was a member of the
Zionist delegation to the Paris Peace Conference in
1919. F. was one of the founders of the Palestine
Economic Corporation and a member of the council
of the Jewish Agency. (3) *SIMON F.* (1863–1946):

Raising of the Israel flag at UN headquarters. New York, May 1949
(David Hacohen, Abba Eban, Arthur Lourie, Moshe Sharett).

Florence synagogue.

Pathologist; brother of (1) and (2). He discovered the germ which causes polio, wrote extensively on snake poison, made important discoveries in connection with dysentery, and from 1903–35 was director of laboratories at the Rockefeller Institute for Medical Research.

FLIESS, WILHELM (1858–1928): German physician. His theories of time-cycles of life and of bisexuality acquired prominence. He was a friend of Freud who first propounded the development of his psychoanalytical theories in letters to F. (published 1955).

FLOOD: Deluge brought by God to destroy mankind because of its wickedness (Gen. 6–9). The central figure in the narrative is NOAH who, as the one righteous man on earth, is bidden to make an ark in which to shelter his family and male and female specimens of all living creatures, so that mankind may begin afresh after the catastrophe. The f. lasted for 150 days and the ark eventually came to rest on Mt. Ararat. This story is closely paralleled in the eleventh tablet of the Babylonian Gilgamesh epic, the phenomenon being native to Babylonia, although it should be noted that the biblical f. was due to rain and not inundation. The historical background of the tradition of the f. was thought to have been demonstrated by Sir Leonard Woolley in his excavations at Ur (1927–9) and other places but the evidence of floods discovered are now known to have been entirely local. The f. legend is common among many peoples.

FLORENCE: Italian city. The Jewish community was founded in 1437 when Jews were invited to establish loan-banks for the benefit of the poor. Despite occasional outbreaks of violence (1458, 1471) and expulsions (1495, 1527), they flourished under the Medici. Grand Duke Cosimo I enforced the papal policy of repression, including the Jewish badge (1567) and the ghetto (1571), the latter continuing until the invasion of the French revolutionary armies at the end of the 18th cent. In 1849, the Jews were partly emancipated, the process being completed in 1860. F. was the seat of a Jewish spiritual revival early in the 20th cent. and the Collegio Rabbinico Italiano was situated there from 1899 to 1930. During the German occupation of 1943–5, nearly 300 Jews were deported to the death camps and the beautiful synagogue was severely damaged. Jewish pop. (1973): 1,400.

FLORIDA: US state. In 1819, Moroccan-born Moses Levy acquired in F. 60,000 acres of land on which he planned to settle European Jews. His son David (YULEE) was the first Jew to sit in Congress and later in the US Senate. Few Jews lived in F. until after the Civil War. The first Jewish community was established in JACKSONVILLE in 1850; it disbanded before 1875 and was reorganized in 1880. The oldest existing Jewish congregation in F. is Temple Beth El in Pensacola, founded in 1874. The number of Jews in F. remained small until MIAMI began developing as a winter resort. F. had 300,000 Jews in 1973, mostly in Miami, with several thousands each in Jacksonville, Tampa, St. Petersburg, West Palm Beach, and Hollywood.

FLORUS GESSIUS see **PROCURATORS**

FOA: N Italian family, perhaps of French origin; some members subsequently settled in Bordeaux, etc. (1) *ELEAZAR NAḤMAN F.* (fl. 17th cent.), kabbalist, was rabbi at Reggio and published a

Printer's mark Tobias Foa.

commentary on the Passover Haggadah. (2) *MOSES BENJAMIN F.* (b. 1729), court agent to the dukes of Modena, was among the most eminent bibliophiles

Michelangelo, *The Flood.* (From the ceiling of the Sistine Chapel, Rome).

and bookdealers of the 18th cent. (3) *PIO F.* (1848–1923), professor of pathological anatomy at Padua and Turin, was the outstanding Italian anatomist of his day. In 1908, he was appointed to the senate. (4) *TOBIAS F.* (fl. 16th cent.) founded and ran the important printing house at Sabbionetta 1551–9, later working in Cremona and Mantua. (5) *EDOUARD F.* (1862–1901), French explorer, traveled adventurously through the Dahomey and Congo regions and discovered the sources of the Zambesi.

FOLKISTEN: Jewish political party in Poland founded in 1916, and most active in the 1920's. It advocated Jewish national and cultural autonomy in Poland and equal rights for Jews as individuals and as an ethnic group. It insisted on full implementation of Jewish minority rights and on state support for Jewish educational and cultural institutions. Its organ was the Yiddish monthly *Das Folk* and its parliamentary spokesman. Noah PRILUZKY.

FOLKLORE: The study of popular beliefs, arts, and customs. Much material of this type is incorporated in the Bible, not infrequently reflecting universal usage and the beliefs of the ancient Mediterranean peoples; this has engaged the attention of many scholars, such as Sir James Frazer (*Folklore in the Old Testament,* 1918). Less attention has been paid to the vast amount of f. embodied in talmudic literature. The Midrash recounts stories and legends still preserved orally in the f. of Arabs in Palestine while the Talmud (both Babylonian and Palestinian) describes or prescribes many practices which were similarly rooted in the environment. Sometimes, when these were grossly superstitious or objectionable, they were stigmatized by the rabbis as "the way of the Canaanite," which the Jews should eschew. Other practices, on the other hand, not infrequently entered into Jewish ritual, being regarded in due course as an integral part of religious observance. In the Diaspora, the f. of the Jews may be divided into two categories. In the first place, there were the practices of the environment (including folk medicine, ballads, music, etc.) which were adopted or shared by the Jews; on occasions, these were taken by the latter into exile, becoming distinctively Jewish in their new homes. This was the case, for example, with many of the usages as well as the balladry of the Jews of Salonica, which were basically Spanish rather than Jewish. On the other hand, many such practices, in general closely bound up with the minutiae of religious observance, may be regarded as native to the Jewish communities. Occasionally, ancient Palestinian usages are preserved; thus, for example, the very old Near Eastern custom of placing keys in graves persisted among the Jews of Spain late in the Middle Ages. The scientific study of Jewish f. in the modern period began at the close of the 19th cent., the most active worker in this sphere being Max GRUNWALD who established a periodical

on the subject. With the liquidation of Ashkenazi Jewry in E Europe and of Sephardi Jewry in the Balkans, the opportunities for recording Jewish f. have greatly contracted. At the same time, Israel, with its vast ingathering of representatives of all branches of the Jewish people (although they are rapidly losing their distinctiveness), at present offers extensive opportunities for the study of the subject, to which have been devoted the periodicals *Edot* (1945–8) and, on a more popular level, *Yeda Am* (since 1948).

FONSECA: Sephardi family of Marrano origin, found in Hamburg, London, Amsterdam, New York, etc. *ABRAHAM F.* (d. 1675) was rabbi at Glückstadt and Hamburg; and two other men of the same name (d. 1727 and d. 1809) were physicians in Holland. *ANTONIO (RODRIGO) DA F.* (fl. 17th cent.), physician, taught medicine in Pisa and Padua and wrote a standard work on fevers (1623). *DANIEL DA F.* (17th–18th cents.), born in Portugal and educated for the priesthood. openly adopted Judaism after leaving Portugal and became physician to the sultan in Constantinople; in 1730, he settled in Paris where he was friendly with Voltaire. *ANTONIO LOPEZ DIAS DE F.* (1776–1857), who left Judaism, was a soldier and military writer. One branch of the F. family, raised to the rank of marquis in Portugal, became members of the Venetian nobility in the 17th cent.; some of their descendants later reverted to Judaism and may still be traced in the US.

*FORD, HENRY (1863–1947): US automobile manufacturer. One of the first to undertake anti-Jewish agitation in the US, he launched in his *Dearborn Independent* a series of articles based on the *Protocols of the Elders of Zion*, some of which were collected in a book entitled *The International Jew.* After a lawsuit brought by Aaron Sapiro, F. withdrew his allegations and forbade the reprinting of his anti-Semitic writings.

FORGIVENESS: Forgiveness of sin is one of the biblical attributes of God's mercy (Exod. 34:6). Essential requisites for such f., however, are man's repentance and the resolve not to repeat the sin. The final sections of the treatise *Yoma* deal with the functions of REPENTANCE and of the Day of Atonement ritual in obtaining f. Emphasis is laid upon the fact that the f. of sins committed against a fellow-man cannot be obtained before the wrong is righted and his pardon solicited.

FORT WAYNE: City in Indiana, US. Its first Jews, mostly of German origin, founded Congregation Achdut Ve-Sholom in 1848. The community was augmented during the latter 19th cent. by immigrants from E Europe. The F. W. Jewish Federation (founded 1922) centralizes fund-raising activities. Jewish pop. (1973): 1,250.

FORT WORTH: City in Texas, US. Jews first settled there in 1876, the first congregation Ahavath Sholom (Orthodox) being formed in 1890 and followed by a Reform congregation, Beth El, in 1902. A Jewish Federation of F.W. was founded in 1936 and the weekly *Texas Jewish Post* established in 1947. In 1973, F. W. had 2,850 Jews.

FORTAS, ABRAHAM (1910–): US jurist. He was under-secretary of the Interior 1942–6, and then partner in a Washington law firm until appointed to the Supreme Court in 1965. In 1968 he was nominated by President Johnson as president of the Supreme Court, but in view of Republican opposition his candidature was withdrawn at his request. He resigned from the Supreme Court in 1969 following charges of unethical conduct.

FORVERTS (Yidd.: "Forward"): New York Yiddish daily. Founded in 1897, it has the largest circulation among the non-English newspapers of the US. It began as the organ of the Jewish labor movement and of the Jewish socialists. Its best-known editor was Abraham CAHAN.

FOSS, LUKAS (originally Lothar Fuchs; 1922–): Pianist and composer. Born in Germany, he settled in the US in 1937. His works include biblical cantatas, orchestral and piano music, and chamber works.

FOSSOLI: Village in N Italy near which, in 1943, a concentration camp was set up under the control of the SS. Many Italian Jews were imprisoned there before deportation and extermination.

FOULD, ACHILLE (1800–1867): French statesman. A proprietor of the Fould-Oppenheim Bank, he was in 1842, elected to the Chamber of Deputies where he supported the conservative Guizot. Louis Napoleon appointed him minister of finance (1849) and, subsequently, senator and minister of state. F. was again minister of finance 1861–7. In 1857, he was elected to the Academy of Fine Arts.

FOUNDATION FUND see **KEREN HA-YESOD**

FOUR SPECIES (Heb. *arbaah minim*): Term applied to the four plants held and waved during the Festival of TABERNACLES – the ETROG, palm, myrtle, and willow. See also LULAV.

FRANCE (Heb. *Tzarephat*): Individual Jews are known to have lived in what is now F. before 70 CE, and it is certain that organized Jewish communities existed there in the period of the Roman Empire. Their position deteriorated with the triumph of Christianity, Church Councils taking steps to enforce the conventional anti-Jewish codes. Some Jews occupied prominent positions at court under the Merovingians. From the 8th cent., under the protection of Charlemagne and his house, Jewish merchants began to settle in F. for purposes of trade, importing foreign luxuries and establishing new communities up the Rhone Valley and into CHAMPAGNE. In the 9th cent., S France was the main center of the activity of the international traders, the RADANITES. In the 11th–12th cents., the Jewish communities of N France were the most densely settled and perhaps culturally the most

important in Europe — if not in the world. The Talmud was the main branch of study, and here was the seat of RASHI and the TOSAPHISTS. The exclusion of the Jews from trade and handicrafts drove them more and more into moneylending which in N France became their economic stand-by. In PROVENCE, however, the Jewish communities were economically and intellectually under a very strong Spanish influence. The spread of the Crusading spirit and the religious reaction in its wake influenced the position of the Jews adversely. Murderous attacks became common after the First Crusade (1096), the Blood Accusation often providing the motive after the case at BLOIS in 1171. The anti-Jewish legislation of the Fourth Lateran Council (1215) was speedily enforced, while the Talmud was burned after the DISPUTATION of Paris in 1240. The condition of the Jews further deteriorated under Louis IX (1226–70), and in 1306, they were brutally expelled. A handful, incapable of reviving the past intellectual distinction, was allowed back for a brief and troubled period 1315–21, and again 1361–94. In Provence, where the royal authority was not yet effective, they were allowed to stay until the beginning of the 16th cent., and even after this, a few remained under papal rule in AVIGNON and the COMTAT VENAISSIN. The legal exclusion of the Jews was further qualified from the 16th cent. by the establishment of semi-organized Marrano groups in BORDEAUX, BAYONNE (Saint-Esprit), etc., and by the presence of Ashkenazi communities in ALSACE and Lorraine which passed under French rule in the 16th-18th cents. The French Revolution brought full emancipation (1790–1) after which Jews (especially from Alsace) spread into the remaining areas of France. The communities were elaborately organized by NAPOLEON in a system of CONSISTORIES following the Assembly of Notables in 1806 and the SANHEDRIN of 1807. The restored monarchy maintained the policy of Jewish Emancipation, the few remaining slight disabilities being now removed. In the 19th cent., the Jews of F. took a lead — with those of England — in philanthropic movements for the benefit of Jewry, the ALLIANCE ISRAÉLITE UNIVERSELLE being organized in 1860 for this purpose. Toward the end of the century, however, anti-Semitism spread and gave rise to the DREYFUS case (1894—1906). Jews, however, remained prominent in French life as exemplified in the careers of Léon BLUM, René MAYER, Pierre MENDÈS-FRANCE, and others who have served in the highest ministerial offices. To some extent from 1881, but more after World War I, the former predominantly Alsatian character of French Jewry was modified by a large immigration from E Europe and the Balkans. The fall of F. and the rule of the VICHY government in 1940 entailed disaster for the Jews. Even in the area left for a time nominally under French rule, anti-Semitism triumphed and elaborate anti-Jewish legisla-

The synagogue of Cavaillon, Southern France, in 1733
(Romanticized drawing by G. Loukomsky).

tion was enforced. The Germans carried out their invariable policy of confiscation and brutality, culminating in wholesale deportations: 90,000 Jews were deported from the country to the death-chambers. Many French communities did not recover from the blow. Jewish pop. (1973): 550,000, PARIS being to an overwhelming extent the center of French Jewish life and organization, which in recent years has been augmented and transformed by immigration from N Africa, especially Algeria. A period of close cooperation between Israel and France inaugurated in the mid.-1950's, was abruptly terminated by president de Gaulle at the time of the 1967 Six-Day War.

FRANCES: (1) *IMMANUEL BEN DAVID F.* 1618–c. 1710): Italian rabbi and poet. His works included responsa, poems in Hebrew, Spanish, and Italian, and *Metek Sephataim* on Hebrew prosody. Fiercely attacked for his opposition to the Kabbalah, he lived for a time in Algiers. (2) *JACOB BEN DAVID F.* (1615–1667): Italian poet and talmudist; brother of (1). Together with his brother, he combated Sabbetaism in various diatribes which aroused such opposition that he was forced to leave Mantua for Florence. Only one complete copy of his satirical poem against the Kabbalah escaped destruction.

FRANCHE-COMTE: Former French province. Jews expelled from other parts of France were admitted in 1181, and many engaged in financial occupations. They served the nobles, but the Church insisted on limiting their influence and on their wearing a badge. More Jews entered F.-C. after the expulsion from France in 1321. They suffered outbreaks during the Black Death period, although protected by the pope and the duke of Burgundy. The provincial community was expelled with the rest of French Jewry in 1394, but that in Besançon (which was independent) only gradually dissolved during the 15th cent. It was reconstituted after the French Revolution.

FRANCHETTI, BARON ALBERTO (1860–1942): Italian composer. He wrote several operas, a symphony, and chamber music.

FRANCK, ADOLPHE (1809–1893): French philosopher. Member of the Institut and professor at the Collège de France, he took a deep interest in the defense of Judaism. In his work on the Kabbalah, he upheld the antiquity of the Zohar.

FRANCK, JAMES (1882–1964): Physicist. An authority on nuclear physics and photochemistry in pre-Hitler Germany, he was awarded the 1925 Nobel Prize in physics. In 1935, he went to the US and has been on the faculties of Johns Hopkins Univ., Baltimore (1935–8) and the Univ. of Chicago (1938–64). He investigated the structure of matter, especially the kinetics of electrons.

FRANCO-MENDES, DAVID (1713–1792): Dutch Hebrew poet and playwright. Fluent in several languages, he engaged in trade and, late in life, became honorary secretary of the Amsterdam Spanish and Portuguese community. He contributed poems, riddles, and articles to the *Ha-Measseph* miscellanies. F.-M. was the author of two historical dramas, *Gemul Atalyah* ("Athaliah's Punishment") after Racine and *Teshuat Yisrael bi-de Yehudit* ("Judith saves Israel") after Metastasio.

FRANK, ADOLF (1834–1916): German chemist. He founded the German potash industry by his discovery of the use for potash fertilizers of waste salts overlying brine deposits, also developing the use of its commercial by-products which formed the basis of further industries. He devised a method for extracting nitrogen from air.

FRANK, ANNE (1929–1945): Dutch child writer. While in hiding during the Nazi occupation of Holland, she wrote in 1942–44, a remarkable "Journal" displaying great literary ability and psychological insight. This, discovered after her death in the concentration camp of Bergen-Belsen, has been published in many languages, and, in its dramatized form, produced on the stage in many parts of the world.

FRANK, BRUNO (1887–1945): Author. His literary career was established in Germany and continued in the US after 1933. F. wrote novels, plays, and poems.

*****FRANK, HANS** (1900–1946): German Nazi leader. A lawyer by profession, he became Bavarian minister of justice in 1933 and Reich minister without portfolio in 1934. As governor-general in Poland, he was responsible for the deportation and massacre of millions of Jews. F. was executed in accordance with the verdict of the Nuremberg tribunal.

FRANK, JACOB (1726–1791): Pseudo-messiah; founder of the Frankist movement. He declared himself the Messiah and the successor of Shabbetai Tzevi. He attracted many followers in Podolia. His mystical festivities were alleged to be accompanied by sexual orgies, the function of which was to bring redemption through impurity. The rabbis excommunicated F. and his followers in 1756, whereupon the Frankists appealed to the anti-Semitic bishop Dembovsky at Kamenetz-Podolsk, who agreed to protect them on condition that they renounced the Talmud. The Frankists accepted and, in addition, announced that they accepted the Trinity, one of three divinities being the "Messiah who had come" (for them, Shabbetai Tzevi or F.). The bishop ordered a public disputation between the Frankists and the rabbis; this was held in Kamenetz-Podolsk in 1757 and ended with the burning of the Talmud at the bishop's command. A second debate was held in Lvov in 1759, at the conclusion of which the Frankists led by F. were baptized. When the Polish authorities learned that the Frankists continued to revere F. as their "Lord of Holiness," he was tried ecclesiastically and secluded in a monastery but his followers maintained contact with him as the "suffering Messiah." Released by the Russians after the partition of Poland (1772), he settled at Offenbach where his home continued to be the center of the sect. F.'s place after his death was taken by his daughter, Eve, who in later life was entangled in debt and died in poverty in 1817. Many of the baptized Frankists became prominent members of the Polish nobility and in the course of time, were absorbed into Polish society.

FRANK, JEROME NEW (1889–1957): US lawyer, jurist, and administrator. He was one of the active leaders of the New Deal in Washington in the 1930's. From 1941, he was a member of the US Circuit Court of Appeals. He served on the faculty of Yale Univ. and wrote standard works on law and economics.

FRANK, JOSEPH (1885–): Austrian architect and city-planner. He built the Museum of E Asiatic Art at Cologne and notable buildings in Sweden, Vienna, etc.

FRANK, WALDO (1889–1967): US novelist, critic, lecturer, and editor. His novels, experimental and avant-garde in form, include *The Dark Mother*, *Rahab*, *City Block*, and *Holiday*. F. achieved considerable reputation as a student and interpreter of Latin American culture.

FRANKAU: English literary family. *JULIA F.* (1859–1916), sister of the dramatist James Davis, was a successful novelist under the pseudonym of Frank Danby, satirizing middle-class Jewish life. She edited the weekly publication *Jewish Society* 1889–1901. Her son, *GILBERT F.* (1884–1952) and the latter's daughter *PAMELA F.* (1908–1967), both novelists, had no connection with Judaism.

FRÄNKEL, AVRAHAM HA-LEVI (1891—1965): Mathematician. He was professor of mathematics at Marburg and Kiel before settling in Palestine (1929) in a similar position at the Hebrew Univ. where he was rector 1938–40. F. published works on mathematics and philosophy.

FRANKEL, BENJAMIN (1906–1973): British composer. He wrote music for stage and films and also composed symphonic works (including *Music for Youth*), a violin concerto, *Sonata ebraica* for cello and harp, *Elegie juive* for cello and piano, etc.

FRÄNKEL (MIRLES), DAVID BEN NAPHTALI HIRSCH (1707–1762): German rabbi and scholar. He was rabbi at Dessau (where Moses Mendelssohn was his pupil) and (from 1743), Berlin, being chief rabbi of Prussia and Pomerania. His main studies were on the Palestinian Talmud on which he wrote a pioneer commentary.

FRANKEL, LEE KAUFER (1867–1931): US communal leader. A chemist by training, he became interested in social service, insurance, and public health. He was vice-president of the Metropolitan Life Insurance Co. and took a leading role in Jewish overseas relief work.

FRANKEL, ZACHARIAS (1801–1875): Rabbi and scholar. After serving at Leitmeritz and Teplitz, where he was the first Bohemian rabbi with a modern secular education, he became chief rabbi at Dresden

Zacharias Frankel.

(1836). Here he fought anti-Jewish legislation, publishing a study on the Jewish oath which led to its abolition in Saxony and other German states. In 1851, he founded the scholarly periodical MONATSSCHRIFT FÜR GESCHICHTE UND WISSENSCHAFT DES JUDENTUMS which he edited until 1868. From 1854 until his death, he directed the BRESLAU RABBINICAL SEMINARY, exerting a profound influence on its development. F. endeavored to combine Jewish religious tradition with the European enlightenment. He opposed religious reform (especially prayer in the vernacular and the deletion of references to sacrifice and the return to Zion) but he nevertheless sought to introduce certain liturgical reforms not involving a deviation from the historical spirit of Judaism. In the controversy between the Reform group of Geiger and the Orthodox school of S. R. Hirsch, F. took up an intermediate position which satisfied neither sector. He participated in the 1845 Assembly of Reform Rabbis at Frankfort-on-Main but withdrew after the majority decided that Hebrew prayer should not be obligatory. F. published many learned works, notably the fundamental study *Darkhe ha-Mishnah* ("The Ways of the Mishnah," 1859), and monographs on the Targums, Septuagint, Talmud, etc.

FRANKFORT-ON-MAIN: German town. The first record of Jewish settlement dates from the 12th cent. The community was annihilated in 1241 and again by the Flagellants in 1349. Jews had returned and secured privileges by 1365, and a ghetto was established in 1458 after earlier attempts had proved unsuccessful. From the 14th cent., Jews were principally engaged in money transactions. Though few in number (c. 100 toward the end of the 15th cent.), they were subject to heavy levies and forced loans. One of the many tribulations was caused by Johann PFEFFERKORN, while the FETTMILCH riots in 1614 led to a temporary expulsion. Their economic position deteriorated in the 18th cent., and the war of 1796 resulted in the destruction of a large part of the ghetto. At the same time, several restrictions were revoked and the more enlightened elements endeavored to introduce reforms. The Philanthropin school was opened; two delegates were sent to the Napoleonic Sanhedrin and an Emancipation Order was issued in 1811. Recognition of Jewish citizenship was given in 1824 and full equality obtained in 1864. The Reform movement led in 1851 to the formation of a separate orthodox community, granted corporation status in 1864. As a result, F. Jewry reorganized its religious institutions, combining both elements under a united administration. The Jews of F., foremost among them the ROTHSCHILD family, played a prominent part in the development of the city and its emergence as an international financial center. Throughout its entire history, the community was a seat of distinguished rabbis and scholars. From the

17th cent., F., together with the neighboring Offenbach and Rödelheim, was an important center of Hebrew printing. There were about 30,000 Jews in F. in 1933. In Aug. 1942, the German press reported the town as *judenrein*. In 1973, the reconstructed community numbered 4,950.

FRANKFORT-ON-ODER: German town. Jews were living there at the end of the 13th cent. and partly engaged in handicrafts. They were expelled (with the rest of Brandenburg Jewry) in 1510, returned in 1546, and were again expelled in 1573. During the Thirty Years' War, some Polish Jews were allowed to reside in F. because of their economic importance, and the number gradually grew. The Hebrew press at F., founded in 1675, existed until 1826, producing three editions of the Babylonian Talmud between 1697 and 1739. From the 18th cent., Polish Jews were prominent in the F. fairs. In 1861, a "Society for the Settlement of Palestine" — the first of its kind — was founded at F. by Ḥayyim Lorjé. 800 Jews lived there before the Nazi persecution. The community was revived after World War II, but declined from its 1958 pop. of 200.

FRANKFURTER, DAVID (1909–): Yugoslav who killed the Nazi leader Wilhelm Gustloff at Davos, Switzerland, on Feb. 4, 1936. F. was given the minimum sentence of 18 years for premeditated murder but was released in 1946 and later settled in Israel.

FRANKFURTER, FELIX (1882–1965): US jurist; associate justice, US Supreme Court, 1939–62. He continued the liberal tradition established on the bench by Holmes, Brandeis, and Cardozo. Prior to 1912, he served in the US justice and war depts. While a professor at Harvard Law School (1914–39),

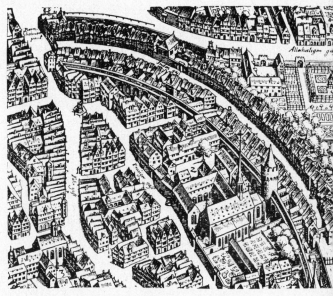

View of Frankfort-on-Main with ghetto and synagogue (in the curved street) c. 1460.

he was a consultant to successive presidents of the US. Many of his students became important government officials, especially in the New Deal administration. As a teacher, his original interpretation of the "commerce clause" in the Constitution opened up new fields of activity for administrative agencies; thus, he was instrumental in devising Wage and Hour and other labor laws as well as the Natural Securities Act. He was founder of the American Civil Liberties Union and took an active part in many civil liberties cases. As Supreme Court justice, he sustained this interest and was equally concerned with necessary limitations on civil liberties and with preserving the prerogatives of lower courts and state government. Before 1921, F. was associated with Brandeis in the leadership of the Zionist Organization. In 1919, he was legal adviser to the Zionist delegation at the Paris Peace Conference and collaborated closely with Chaim Weizmann in his negotiations with Emir Feisal, the Arab leader.

FRANKIST MOVEMENT see **FRANK, JACOB**

FRANKL, LUDWIG AUGUST, RITTER VON HOCHWART (1810–1894): Austrian poet. From 1838, he served as secretary and archivist of the Viennese Jewish community and in 1842, founded the literary periodical *Sonntagsblätter* which he edited for six years until it was banned by the government. His revolutionary poem *Die Universität* was distributed in half-a-million copies and set to music 27 times. After the failure of the revolution of 1848, he devoted himself to literature, writing poems, satires, and stories, some based on Jewish tradition. In 1853, he published his history of the Jews in Vienna. The following year, he visited Jerusalem and founded the

Felix Frankfurter.

Lämel school — the first secular school for Jewish children in Palestine. F. was ennobled in 1876 on the occasion of the dedication of a Jewish school for the blind in Vienna the founding of which he had initiated.

FRANKLIN: English family. Its outstanding members have included *JACOB ABRAHAM F.* (1809–1877), founder and editor of *The Voice of Jacob* (1841–8), the earliest effective Anglo-Jewish periodical in the English language; his nephew *ARTHUR ELLIS F.* (1857–1938), banker, who built up an outstanding collection of Jewish ritual art (now in the Jewish Museum, London); and the latter's brother *SIR LEONARD F.* (1862–1944), banker and Liberal member of parliament.

*FRANKLIN, BENJAMIN (1706–1790): US statesman. As a believer in full freedom of conscience, he displayed a friendly interest in the Jews and in their teachings. In the 1930's, there was widely distributed what purported to be an extract from Charles Pinckney's journal of the proceedings of the US Constitutional Convention of 1789, in which a vicious anti-Jewish statement is attributed to F. The historian Charles A. Beard exposed this in 1935 as a crudely conceived and barefaced forgery, the alleged Pinckney Diary being itself mythical.

FRANKS: Family prominent in England, the US, and Canada in the 18th cent. *JACOB F.* (1688–1769), merchant, helped to construct New York's first synagogue. Best known of his children were: *MOSES F.* (1719–1789) who represented the family's business

Benjamin Franklin.

interests in England. *DAVID F.* (1720–1793) who remained loyal to England when the Revolutionary War broke out, and was imprisoned by the Americans. After the war, he returned to public life as a merchant and publisher. Other family members who achieved distinction were *REBECCA F.* (1760–1823), daughter of David, who was one of the belles of British society in the Colonies; *ISAAC F.* (1759–1822) who fought in the American army under Washington and later rose to the rank of lt.-colonel; and *DAVID SALISBURY F.* (18th–19th cents.) who lived in Montreal but threw in his lot with the Americans, serving in the US army with distinction, and thereafter acting for the US on diplomatic missions abroad.

FRANZOS, KARL EMIL (1848—1904): German novelist. His account of Galician Jewish life *Aus Halb-Asien* and his novel *Die Juden von Barnow* were translated into many languages. Other works of his are *Judith Trachtenberg* and *Ein Kampf Ums Recht*. F. was an observant delineator of Jewish life as well as an able editor and literary scholar.

FRATERNAL SOCIETIES: Jewish social and mutual aid societies existed in Europe from the close of the Middle Ages. They were organized along trade lines and had religious aspects, some having exclusive religious aims. Friendly societies of a modern type first emerged in England in the late 18th cent. To meet the needs of immigrants to the US for social, fraternal, and benevolent activities, as well as to provide outlets for philanthropic and cultural work, a number of F. S. were created in the 19th and early 20th cents. They were modelled largely after non-Jewish fraternal groups, then popular. At first, most of these societies were of the LANDSMANNSCHAFT type, being composed of immigrants from the same areas, and offering insurance and burial benefits. More than a score of such organizations came into being during the period of large-scale immigration from E Europe, some engaging in significant social, cultural, and philanthropic programs. Less than half of these now survive. Most operate under the careful supervision of state insurance law, and some have accumulated large financial reserves which have operated to keep the organizations in existence long after membership interest has otherwise lapsed. Oldest, largest, and most active of the Orders is B'NAI B'RITH which was created in 1843. Others which have survived include: FREE SONS OF ISRAEL (1849) which maintains a cultural and philanthropic program; Brith Abraham (1887), oldest of the Orders organized by E European immigrants, which has a philanthropic foundation; Progressive Order of the West (1896), centered largely in the St. Louis area; the WORKMEN'S CIRCLE (1900); Brith Sholom (1905), largely centered in the Philadelphia area; B'nai Zion (1910) which carries on a program of Zionist activity, including projects in Israel; the FARBAND, Labor Zionist Order (1913) which operates a network of Jewish schools and promotes the Labor Zionist movement (previously known as the Jewish National Workers' Alliance); and the SEPHARDIC JEWISH BROTHERHOOD OF AMERICA (1915). The similar societies in Great Britain are organized in the Association of Jewish Friendly Societies. They include the Orders Achei Brith and Shield of Abraham (1888); Ancient MACCABEANS (1891); Achei Emeth (1897); and Sons of Jacob (1900).

FRATERNITIES, COLLEGE: The failure of most American c. f. to accept Jewish members led to the formation of Jewish "Greek letter" societies which imitated the organization and activities of the others. Their interests have for the most part been social, though some have undertaken cultural and philanthropic activities. In recent years, almost all have become non-sectarian by constitution, though the membership continues to be Jewish. The major Jewish c. f. are: Pi Lamda Phi, established 1895; Zeta Beta Tau, 1898; Phi Alpha, 1914; Phi Epsilon Pi, 1904; Phi Sigma Delta, 1909; Sigma Alpha Mu, 1909; Beta Sigma Rho, 1910; Tau Delta Phi, 1910; Tau Epsilon Phi, 1910; Kappa Nu, 1911; Alpha Epsilon Pi, 1913. Major sororities are: Iota Alpha Pi, 1903; Alpha Epsilon Phi, 1909; Phi Sigma Sigma, 1913, Delta Phi Epsilon, 1917; Sigma Delta Tau, 1917. There are also professional fraternities and sororities.

FREE SONS OF ISRAEL: One of the oldest of Jewish FRATERNAL SOCIETIES in the US, founded in New York by German Jews in 1849. It developed as an outgrowth of the order B'nai B'rith which had set the pattern for the mode of organization and ritual. The early lodges of the F. S. adopted biblical names. Its Noah Lodge No. 1, while still in existence as the Noah Benevolent Society, is no longer affiliated with the order.

FREE WILL: The ability to decide upon a course of action independent of Divine or material determination or predestination. The Jewish point of view is that freedom of decision definitely exists with regard to moral and spiritual conduct. Scripture emphasizes the power of the individual to choose between the good and the bad, the concepts of punishment and reward being postulated upon freedom of will in this respect. The Talmud posits Divine omniscience in all matters but unequivocally states that man has the power to choose his own way of moral living. Thus, although everything occurs by Divine decree, "everything is in the hands of Heaven except the fear of Heaven." (*Berakhot* 33*b*). The rabbis did not discuss the apparent contradiction between f. w. and Divine omniscience and providence, but Jewish philosophers in the Middle Ages, influenced by the treatment of the problem among the Islamic sects, paid much attention to it and offered various solutions. Some limited omniscience, holding that only after man's will is made up does it become part of Divine knowledge

(Saadyah, Judah Ha-Levi). Others (e.g. Crescas) limited freedom of will. Maimonides differentiated between the human concept of knowledge and Divine knowledge, holding that man can no more understand the nature of God's knowledge than he can His essence.

FREE WILL OFFERING (Heb. *nedavah*): Gift to the Temple given spontaneously and not as a result of obligation or vow. The term is used in connection with the gifts brought during the construction of the Tabernacle, the Temples, etc. Such an offering might be a burnt-offering or a peace-offering (Lev. 22:18, 21). These sacrifices were especially numerous during the festival periods since the meat of the peace-offering could be eaten.

FREELAND LEAGUE: Movement, first established in Europe and reorganized in the US in 1935, with the object of creating a Jewish settlement in some unoccupied area for Jews who seek a new home and cannot or will not go to Israel. Its founder was BEN ADDIR who was succeeded by I. N. STEINBERG. The League publishes English, Yiddish and Spanish periodicals and has sections and sympathizers in several countries. See JEWISH TERRITORIAL ORGANIZATION.

FREEMASONRY: A non-sectarian world-wide brotherhood with a secret ritual and code of morality veiled in allegory and permeated with symbolism. Some of the words and phrases used in its ritual are derived from Hebrew terms, and Solomon's Temple plays a role in its symbolism. It is said that F. is an outgrowth of the medieval building guilds, though its legendary lore assumes its existence as early as the days when Solomon's Temple was erected with the aid of Hiram, king of Tyre. Jews began to find their way into its membership in Holland and England during the 17th and 18th cents., and the coat of arms of the English Grand Lodge was designed by J. J. Leon Templo. Early European Jewish settlers in the US were among the most enthusiastic masons and the first lodge in Newport, R. I., was organized in 1780 by Moses M. Hays. F. was established in Palestine before World War I, and the Grand Lodge of Israel (dedicated 1953) has a membership of over 3,500 (1970).

FREIDUS, ABRAHAM SOLOMON (1867–1923): Librarian and bibliographer. He was born in Latvia, went to Palestine in 1887 and to the US in 1889, becoming chief of the Judaica and Hebraica divisions of the New York Public Library. Under his guidance, the department became one of the most important Jewish collections in the world. F. worked out a classification of Jewish books which has been accepted in many Jewish libraries.

FREIHEIT (Yidd. "Freedom"): New York Yiddish daily. founded 1922; the organ of Jewish communists in the US.

FREIMANN: German family of scholars. (1) *AVRAHAM ḤAYYIM F.* (1899-1948): Jurist; son of (4). A native of Moravia, he lectured on Jewish law at the Hebrew Univ. (1946–8). His works include *Jewish Marriage Law in the Middle Ages* and studies on Maimonides. He was killed by Arabs when travelling in a convoy to Mt. Scopus. (2) *ARON F.* (1871–1948): Historian and bibliographer; son of (3). Librarian of of the Jewish department in the Frankfort-on-Main municipal library 1897–1933. he was an editor of the bibliographical journal *Zeitschrift für hebräische Bibliographie* and of the German-Jewish topographical encyclopedia *Germania Judaica*. He wrote many studies on the history of Jewish culture, especially on the Jewish book. After the Nazi advent to power, he went to the US, lecturing at the Yeshiva College, New York. (3) *ISRAEL MEIR F.* (1830-1884): Rabbi. He seved communities in the province of Posen and published a critical edition of the *Ve-Hizhir* midrashic work. (4) *JACOB F.* (1866–1937): Scholar; cousin of (2). He was rabbi in Moravia 1890–1913, Posen 1914–28, and Berlin 1928–37, and published critical editions of medieval rabbinical texts.

FREJKA (FREUND), LUDVIK (1904–1952): Czech politician. Born in Germany, he settled in Czechoslovakia and in 1948, became head of the economic division of the presidential chancellery, in which capacity he prepared the Czech Five Year Plan. He was purged with SLANSKY in 1951, tried, and executed in 1952.

FRENK, AZRIEL NATHAN (1863–1924): Polish Hebrew author. He wrote sketches and stories on Polish Jewish life and sudies on the history of Polish Jewry. F. translated Polish literary works into Hebrew and Yiddish.

FRENKEL, FEIVUSCH see **BAR TUVYAH**

FRESS (Yidd.): Gobble; eat gluttonously.

FREUD, SIGMUND (1856–1939): Founder of psychoanalysis. He spent most of his life in Vienna which he left for London after the Nazi invasion in 1938. After a successful scientific career as a neuropathologist and clinical neurologist, F. began to interest himself in hypnosis and especially in the cathartic method of treating neuroses by hypnosis. From 1892–5, he developed the technique of "free-association" which requires the patient to speak whatever comes to his mind. This paved the way for the discoveries on which F. based psychoanalysis. For many years, F. encountered misunderstanding and bias, especially when Jewish students began to gather around him at the turn of the century. In some of this criticism, F. saw manifestations of anti-Semitism which, as a child and later during his academic career, he often experienced. He himself considered all religion, including the Jewish faith, as an irrational manifestation of the human mind traceable, by the aid of psychoanalysis, to early personal internal conflicts,

Sigmund Freud.

like other individual neuroses. The year of his death marked the appearance of the controversial study *Moses and Monotheism* in which F. presents data based on psychoanalytical concepts to prove that Moses was an Egyptian and discusses the nature of religion. His daughter *ANNA F.* (1895–), born in Vienna, and living in London since 1938, has specialized in child psychology. His grandson, *LUCIEN F.* (1922–), who lives in England, is a noted painter.

FREUND, ERNST (1863–1946): Austrian chemist. He established his reputation by his researches on the chemical changes of blood in disease, being joint discoverer of a cancer-reaction test. He served as director of the Pearson Research Laboratory, first in Vienna, and from 1938, in London.

FREUND, WILHELM (1806–1894): German philologist. A teacher and school director until 1870, he is best remembered for his monumental Latin dictionary. He also prepared a German-Latin-Greek school dictionary and introductory school volumes to the Greek and Latin classics.

FREYER, RECHA (1892–): Founder of YOUTH ALIYAH. A teacher in Germany, she began in 1932 to aid Jewish youth to prepare for agricultural life. After 1933, she organized such training outside Germany, directing trainees to Palestine where she settled in 1941.

FRIED, ALFRED HERMANN (1864–1921): Austrian pacifist. He founded the German and Austrian peace societies and edited pacifist publications. In 1911, he was awarded the Nobel Peace Prize.

FRIEDBERG, ABRAHAM SHALOM (nom-de-plume Har Shalom; 1838–1902): Hebrew author. He was born in Lithuania and settled in Warsaw where ne taught, worked on the editorial board of *Ha-Tzephirah*, and was active in the Ḥibbat Zion movement. In 1888, he edited the Hebrew encyclopedia *Ha-Eshkol* of which only a few parts appeared. F.'s main work is *Zikhronot le-Vet David* ("Reminiscences of the House of David"; 4 vols.), a cycle of stories from Jewish history. He also wrote a romantic novel based on Grace Aguilar's *Vale of Cedars,* a history of the Jews of Spain, and a book of memoirs containing valuable historical and ethnographical material

FRIEDBERG, BERNHARD (Ḥayyim Dov Berish 1876–1961): Hebrew writer and bibliographer. He was born in Cracow and lived in Frankfort-on-Main 1900–11, Antwerp 1911–40, and France 1940–6, settling in Palestine in 1946. His works include *Bet Eked Sepharim,* a Hebrew bibliographical lexicon and studies on the history of Jewish printing.

FRIEDBERG, HEINRICH VON (1813–1895): Prussian statesman and jurist. He was baptized in 1836 and ascended the state legal hierarchy until he became minister of justice (1879). He prepared the German penal code of 1873.

FRIEDELL, EGON (1878–1938): Austrian writer and critic. He wrote plays and essays, while his *Cultural History of the Modern Age* became a classic. He committed suicide on the Nazi annexation of Austria.

FRIEDENTHAL, KARL RUDOLPH (1827–1890): Prussian statesman. A convert to Christianity, he became a member of the N German Reichstag (1867). He participated in the drafting of the German constitution in 1870, and was minister of agriculture 1874–9. F. founded the German *Reichspartei.*

FRIEDENWALD: Family of physicians and public workers in Baltimore, US. *AARON F.* (1836–1902), ophthalmologist, was a leader of his profession, serving also as professor in the College of Physicians and Surgeons in Baltimore for almost 30 years. He was prominent in the *Ḥoveve Zion* movement and was among the founders of the Jewish Theological Seminary, the Jewish Publication Society, and the American Jewish Historical Society. His sons include: *HARRY F.* (1864–1950), ophthalmologist and president of the Federation of American Zionists 1904–18, and author of many works on Jewish medical history. He left his great library on the subject to the Hebrew Univ., Jerusalem; *JULIUS F.* (1866–1941), gastroenterologist and professor in that field at the Univ. of Maryland School of Medicine; and *EDGAR BAR F,* (1879–1966), pediatrician, was associated with the Univ. of Maryland from 1910. *HERBERT F.* (1870–1944), nephew of Aaron, was the first secretary of the American Jewish Historical Society and edited the *American Jewish Year Book* 1908–13. *JONAS STEIN F.* (1897–1955), son of Harry, was associate professor

of ophthalmology at Johns Hopkins Univ. and author of many works on the subject.

FRIEDJUNG, HEINRICH (1851–1920): Austrian historian. He was professor of history at Vienna 1873–81, but was removed for his pro-German views. He inspired the German nationalist party in Austria but, although a convert, was excluded from it because of his Jewish birth. An outstanding Austrian historian, his most important writings deal with the 19th cent.

FRIEDLAENDER, ISRAEL (1876–1920): Schoiar. Born in Poland and educated in Germany, he became professor of biblical literature and exegesis at the Jewish Theological Seminary, New York, in 1903. F. was a distinguished Arabist and did important research on Islamic sects and Judeo-Arabic literature. In his works on the Bible, he adopted a conservative attitude. He also translated Dubnow's *History of the Jews in Russia and Poland* into English and Aḥad Ha-Am's essays into German. F. was murdered by bandits in the Ukraine during a relief mission in behalf of the American Joint Distribution Committee.

FRIEDLAND, ABRAHAM HYMAN (1892–1939): US Hebrew writer and educator. His textbooks and children's stories contributed to the advancement of Hebrew education in America. He wrote and lectured extensively in behalf of the Hebrew cultural movements in the US and wrote fiction, mainly about Jewish immigrant life.

FRIEDLÄNDER, DAVID (1750–1834): German Reform leader. Settling in Berlin in 1771, he founded a successful silk-factory and became the son-in-law of Daniel Itzig and intimate friend of Moses Mendelssohn. He was one of the founders of the Jewish Free School in Berlin (1778) which became a model for secular schools in other cities. F. led the fight for equal rights for Prussian Jewry and after Mendelssohn's death, was leader of the German Jewish Enlightenment movement. In 1809, he was elected to the Berlin City Council, the first Jew so honored. In accordance with his rationalist attitude, he championed extreme religious reform, being prepared to give up the Talmud and abolish practical observances. His aim was complete cultural assimilation into European society. In an anonymous letter, he even announced the readiness of several Berlin Jewish families to adopt Christianity if they were not asked to accept dogmas incompatible with their reason. In an anonymous pamphlet on synagogue ritual (1812), he rejected messianic belief and advocated the substitution of German for Hebrew as the language of prayer. In another pamphlet (1819), he advocated the solution of the problem of Polish Jewry by assimilatory reform. All the members of his own family became Christians, some in his lifetime.

FRIEDLÄNDER, LUDWIG (1824–1909): German philologist and historian. A convert to Christianity, he taught at the Univ. of Königsberg and was professor at Strasbourg from 1892. His work on Roman life and manners (*Sittengeschichte Roms*) is the best known study in its field.

FRIEDLÄNDER, MAX (1852–1934): German scholar; professor of music in Berlin 1903–21. His chief work was on 18th cent. German vocal music. He discovered over 100 unknown *lieder* by Schubert.

FRIEDLÄNDER, MICHAEL (1833–1910): Scholar. Born in Prussian Poland, he was principal of Jews' College, London 1865–1906. His chief works were on the writings of Abraham Ibn Ezra, an English translation of Maimonides' *Guide*, and a handbook of Judaism.

FRIEDLÄNDER, MORITZ (1842–1919): Scholar. Born in Hungary, he became secretary of the Vienna Israelite *Allianz* in 1875, and organized a Jewish school system in Galicia under the auspices of the Baron de Hirch Fund. F. wrote on the relations of Hellenism and Christianity to Judaism.

FRIEDMAN, ELISHA MICHAEL (1889–1951): US economist and economic consultant to several US government agencies. He was an active Zionist and supporter of the Hebrew Univ. His many books included *Survival or Extinction*, a discussion of the Jewish problem.

FRIEDMAN, IGNAZ (1882–1948): Pianist. Born in Poland, he lived in Berlin, Copenhagen, and Australia. F. achieved an international reputation and was composer of piano works and songs.

FRIEDMAN, LEE MAX (1871–1957): US lawyer and historian. A bibliophile, he wrote many studies on American Jewish history. He was a founding member of the American Jewish Historical Society in 1893 and its president 1948–53.

FRIEDMAN, MILTON (1912–): US economist. Born in New York, he was appointed professor in Chicago in 1947. He is leader of the "Chicago school" of economics which attacked the theories of Keynes and stressed the importance of money supply. His influential writings have included *A Program for Monetary Stability* and *A Monetary History of the United States*. Nobel Prize for Economics, 1976.

FRIEDMANN, DAVID ARYEH (1889–1957): Hebrew critic. An oculist by profession, he was in the Russian Army in World War I and settled in Palestine in 1925. His first critical studies appeared in *Ha-Shiloaḥ* in 1912, and hundreds were published subsequently on aspects of Hebrew and world literature. Later, he wrote on art criticism and on the history of Jewish medicine.

FRIEDMANN, DAVID BEN SAMUEL (R David of Karlin; 1828–1917): Russian rabbi, living in Karlin from 1868. One of the greatest halakhic authorities of his generation, he was the author of *Pirke Halakhot*, a comprehensive work on ritual. Although originally a supporter of *Ḥibbat Zion*, he became an opponent of Zionism from the 1890's.

FRIEDMANN, MEIR see **ISH-SHALOM**

FRIEDMANN-YELLIN, NATHAN see **MOR**

FRIEDSAM, MICHAEL (1858–1931): US merchant. Active in the civic and commercial life of New York, he was in 1925 chairman of a New York state commission which led to increased state aid for education. The F. Foundation (1932) administers his estate for the educational benefit of the young and for the care and comfort of the aged.

FRIENDLY SOCIETIES see **FRATERNAL SOCIETIES**

FRIGEIS, LAZARO DE (fl. 16th cent.): Italian physician. He was one of two Jews assisting Vesalius (who refers to him as his intimate friend) in the compilation of his Anatomical Tables.

FRINGES see **TZITZIT**

FRISCHMANN, DAVID (1861–1922): Hebrew and Yiddish author. He was born in Poland and his first publications, written in the spirit of Haskalah, appeared there in 1878. His story *Be-Yom ha-Kippurim* ("On the day of Atonement"), published in 1880, describes the esthetic and emotional awakening of a Jewish girl in the ghetto. Subsequent writings included satires, critical essays (notably on contemporary Hebrew literature), poems (*Alim*, etc.), and feuilletons—especially in the first Hebrew daily *Ha-Yom*, of which F. was assistant editor (St. Petersburg, 1886–7), as he was of the Yiddish daily *Heint* (Warsaw, 1908 ff.). He also published translations of European literature. He worked in journalism, serving as editor of a number of periodicals, miscellanies and anthologies and contributing widely to the Hebrew press. F. also wrote stories and poems in Yiddish. One of his last works was a series of biblical stories *Ba-Midbar* ("In the Wilderness"). F. introduced into Hebrew literature values of W European literature and was largely

David Frischmann.

responsible for liberating Hebrew fiction from the artificial plot characteristic of the Haskalah Period.

FROHMAN: *CHARLES F.* (1860–1915) and his brother *DANIEL F.* (1851–1940), US theatrical managers, staged hundreds of plays in New York and sent numerous stock companies on the road in the period between 1885 and World War I. Charles died in the sinking of the *Lusitania* and his brother then retired from the theater.

FROMM, FROOM (Yidd. from German): Pious; strict in Jewish religious observance.

FROMM, ERICH (1900–): US author and psychoanalyst. Born in Frankfort-on-Main he went to the US in 1934. He taught at Mexico University from 1951 and New York University from 1961. His writings include *The Art of Loving* and *Be Ye like Gods.* A neo-Freudian, he applies psychoanalysis to problems of culture and society.

FRUG, SIMON SAMUEL (1860–1916): Russian poet. His first poems were published in 1880 in Russian and achieved a reputation. In 1885, he began to write in Yiddish and toward the end of his life, in Hebrew. The main themes of his poetry are the sufferings of the Jewish people and its yearnings for Zion. His work, mostly in ballad form, influenced Hebrew and national poetry. He also wrote Yiddish satires, feuilletons, and stories.

FRUMKIN, ARYEH LEIB (1845–1916): Scholar and Zionist pioneer. He was born in Lithuania and made his first journey to Palestine in 1871. After serving as rabbi near Kovno, he returned to Palestine in 1883, being among the pioneers who renewed the settlement of Petaḥ Tikvah. In 1894, he went to London but returned to Palestine in 1911. F.'s main work was *Toledot Ḥakhme Yerushalayim* ("History of the Sages of Jerusalem") which contains valuable information on the history of the Jewish population in Palestine from 1490. He also edited the *Seder Rav Amram* ("Ritual of AMRAM Gaon").

FRUMKIN, ISRAEL DOV (1850–1914): Palestinian Hebrew journalist. In 1870, he renewed the Jerusalem periodical *Ḥavatzelet* which he edited until 1911. While not rejecting traditional values, he fought for the spread of Enlightenment, severely criticizing religious formalism and the oppressive administration of *Ḥalukkah.* From the mid-1880's, he retreated from his struggle with the fanatics of the old community and began a sharp campaign against the *Ḥibbat Zion* movement, especially opposing Aḥad Ha-Am and the *Bene Mosheh.* He was the brother of Michael Levi RODKINSON.

FUCHS, EMIL (1866–1929): Artist. A native of Vienna, he lived in London from 1896 to 1915 when he moved to New York. A painter, sculptor, and medallist, his works were acquired by prominent galleries, including the Metropolitan Museum of Art, New York.

Israel Dov Frumkin.

FUCHS, EUGEN (1856–1923): German jurist. A prominent barrister, he was executive member of the German Barristers' Association and wrote important legal works. F. led the anti-Zionist *Central-Verein deutscher Staatsbürger jüdischen Glaubens.*

FULD, FELIX (1869–1929): Merchant. Arriving in the US from Germany he entered upon a successful business career. He distributed more than $2,500,000, most of it anonymously, for philanthropic and cultural purposes.

FULDA: Town of Hesse-Nassau, Germany. Its Jews were the victims of a Ritual Murder charge in 1235; many further persecutions are recorded in the 14th and 16th cents. Notwithstanding a brief expulsion, from 1671 onward F. was the home of several distinguished rabbis. 1,137 Jews lived there before 1933; 17 in 1967.

FULDA, LUDWIG (1862–1939): German poet and playwright. He wrote comedies and satirical dramas on social problems and published poetry and epigrams. F. was a leader of the *Freie Bühne* dramatic movement and translated works of Molière, Ibsen, Shakespeare, etc. into German. He was a pioneer in using the theater as a medium for directing public attention to current problems.

FULVIA: Roman aristocrat; converted to Judaism in the reign of Tiberius (14–37 CE). Her contributions to the Temple were unscrupulously diverted to their own use by four Jews, an incident which contributed to the expulsion of Jews from Rome by the emperor (c. 19 CE).

FUNERAL see **BURIAL**

FUNK, CASIMIR (1884–1967): Biochemist. Born in Poland, he went to the US in 1915. His discovery of vitamins resulted from his search for a cure to beriberi, carried out at the Lister Institute in England. Another of his major discoveries was the use of sex hormones

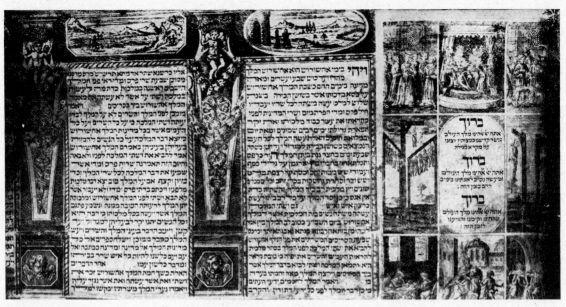

Fulda library: Scroll of Esther.

for the treatment of certain ailments. He was research consultant for the US Vitamin Corporation from 1936, and was president of the Funk Foundation for Medical Research.

FÜNN, SAMUEL JOSEPH (1818–1890): Hebrew scholar. From 1856, he was superintendent of Jewish schools in the Vilna region. His many writings include a general Jewish history, a Jewish biographical lexicon, a Hebrew dictionary, and especially a history of the Jews of Vilna. In addition, F. translated works into Hebrew, was active in the *Ḥibbat Zion* movement, and edited the periodical *Ha-Karmel*.

FÜRST, JULIUS (1805–1873): German historian, bibliographer, and lexicographer. He taught oriental languages at the Univ. of Leipzig where, in 1840, he founded the scholarly Jewish periodical *Orient*. His many publications included *Bibliotheca Judaica,* a 3-volume bibliography of Jewish books and books on Judaism in all languages (1862–9), a history of Karaism, a Bible concordance, a Hebrew and Aramaic lexicon, and a history of Jewish literature.

FÜRSTENTHAL, RAPHAEL JACOB (1781–1855): Author and translator; lived in Germany. A master of Hebrew poetry, he is best remembered for his *Song of Zion*. His translations from Hebrew into German included Maimonides' *Guide*, Baḥya's *Ḥovot ha-Levavot*, and Aboab's *Menorat ha-Maor*, as well as Jewish liturgical works.

FURTADO, ABRAHAM (1756–1817): French communal leader. Son of Marrano parents, he was a merchant at Bordeaux, interested also in agriculture and literature. He was chosen president of the Assembly of Notables convened by Napoleon (1806) and was on the committee of nine appointed to draw up its recommendations which he defended before the Paris Sanhedrin (1807). On several occasions he made representations to Napoleon in behalf of underprivileged Jewries. A philosopher and man of society, he favored civic and cultural assimilation.

FÜRTH: German town. Its Jewish community was founded early in the 16th cent., and received a liberal charter in 1719. The first synagogue was consecrated in 1617, while the yeshivah gained renown during the 17th cent. A Hebrew printing press operated there 1690–1868. Jews were active in the commercial life of the city. They numbered 2,500 before the Nazi catastrophe but in 1970, only 200.

Abraham Furtado
(Engraving by L. C. Ruotte, 1806).

G

GABBAI (Heb. "collector"): Originally a collector of dues and charitable contributions; later, an official of a Jewish congregation.

*GABINIUS, AULUS (d. 48/7 BCE): Roman governor of Syria 57–54 BCE. He drastically reduced the territory of Judea (then ruled by HYRCANUS II who lost the title of ethnarch), dividing it into five regions. G. frustrated the attempt of Aristobulus II and his son Alexander to regain power in Judea.

GABIROL see **IBN GABIROL**

GABOR, DENNIS (1900–): Physicist. Born in Hungary, he lived in England from 1933. He was awarded a Nobel Prize in 1971 for pioneer work in holography. He taught at Imperial College, London.

GABRIEL: Archangel; with MICHAEL, the only ANGEL mentioned by name in the Bible (Dan. 8–10). In apocryphal and rabbinic literature, G. is always described as a leader of the angelic host and one of the four (or seven) highest angels in the celestial hierarchy (also described as the "angel of the presence"). G. (under the name "Jibril") has attained prominence in Islamic legend and folklore.

GAD: Ancient Semitic god of fortune. G. was worshiped by Jews in Babylonia (Is. 65:11) and shrines are recorded at Palmyra and Petra. The name occurs in both Canaanite and Jewish personal and place-names in Palestine.

GAD: Son of Jacob and Zilpah (Gen. 30:10–11): ancestor of the tribe of G. which settled in Gilead and Central Transjordan where they gained a warlike reputation (Num. 32; Josh. 13:24). They flourished during the rule of Saul and their position was consolidated under David. After the split in the kingdom, G. belonged to the N kingdom (Samaria) and suffered severely from Syrian attacks. In 732, the region was devastated by Tiglath-Pileser III and most of its inhabitants exiled; later it was occupied by the Ammonites.

GAD: Seer of David, whom he accompanied at Adullam, remaining at his court when it moved to Jerusalem. A lost book, "The Words of Gad the Seer," is ascribed to him (I Chron. 29:29). The apocalyptic book of the same name is medieval.

GADARA (Heb. *Geder*): Ancient town near the river Yarmuk in Transjordan. First mentioned as a Greek city in the time of Antiochus III, it was taken by Alexander Yannai but from 63 BCE was one of the ten cities forming the DECAPOLIS. The town was an important center of Greek culture, but its hot springs attracted Jews. Archeological discoveries here have included two theaters, a 4th–6th cent. synagogue, and Jewish graves.

GADNA (Heb. abbr. of *gedude noar*, i.e., "youth battalions"): Israel movement for the preliminary training of youth between the ages of 14 and 18.

Mosaic floor in the nave of the synagogue at Gadara
(4th–6th cents. CE).

Galicia: Street in Kazimierz, the historic Jewish centre (Cracow).

Set up by the *Haganah* as an underground organization in 1939, it passed under Israel government sponsorship in 1949, and since 1953, its administration has been divided between the Ministries of Education, Labor, and Agriculture under army supervision.

GAHAL (Heb. abbr. for "Herut-Liberal bloc"):
Alignment of LIBERAL and HERUT parties formed in 1965, receiving 26 seats in the Sixth and Seventh Knessets. and 39 (with allied parties) in the Eighth.

It joined the Coalition government formed on the eve of the Six-Day War in 1967.

GALANTE: (1) *ABRAHAM G.* (1873–1961): Turkish historian. An active member of the Young Turk movement, he was elected to the first Turkish National Assembly after World War I and to the Turkish parliament in 1943. In 1914, he was appointed lecturer in Semitic languages, later professor of the history of the ancient east, in the Univ. of Constantinople. His very numerous monographs established the history of Turkish Jewry on a new basis. (2) *ABRAHAM BEN MORDECAI G.* (d. 1588): Kabbalist. He was born in Rome but settled in Safed in his youth. G. wrote a commentary on the Zohar. (3) *MOSES BEN JONATHAN G.* (1620–1689): Palestinian rabbi; grandson of (4). He was chief rabbi in Jerusalem 1667–8 and then went as emissary to Turkey and Hungary. He was the author of responsa, comments on the Bible, etc. (4) *MOSES BEN MORDECAI G.* (c. 1520–c. 1612): Scholar in Safed; brother of (2). He wrote responsa and works of kabbalistic interest.

GALATIA: Ancient country of Asia Minor. Its Jewish population was widespread in the 1st cent. CE. Classical sources and inscriptions tell of communities at Ankyra, Germa, Pessinus, etc. and the Talmud mentions Galatian rabbis. The legal and economic position of the community resembled that of the rest of ASIA MINOR.

GALICIA: Region of Central Europe, N of the Carpathian Mountains. Its first Jewish settlement dates from the 11th cent.; for their history until 1722 see POLAND. In 1772, G., which then had 225,000 Jews (9.6% of the population), was annexed by Austria, and in 1782–9, Joseph II introduced legislation aimed at the forced assimilation of the Jews (abolition of communal autonomy and the validity of rabbinical courts, liability to military service, compulsory education in government schools, tax on *kasher* meat, etc.). In succeeding years, the Austrian government tried to integrate the Jews by turning them to agriculture and ending their isolation; the policy failed owing to the Jewish masses' loyalty to tradition. This period was marked by a flourishing of rabbinic scholarship and by a severe struggle between the Hasidim and Mitnaggedim ending with the victory of the former and the consolidation of G. as a Hasidic citadel. A further conflict developed in the mid-19th cent. between Hasidism and Haskalah. From 1849, the Jews of G. began to receive equality of political rights and these were embodied in the Austrian constitution of 1867. G. was an important center of neo-Hebrew literature during the 19th and 20th cents.; many scholars worked there and many Hebrew periodicals were published in G. However, a considerable section of the *maskilim* displayed pronounced tendencies to assimilation, first to German, later to Polish, culture. The Jewish national movement in the late 19th cent. appealed to the Jews of G. which was the birthplace of *Ḥibbat Zion*. A Jewish workers' movement originated in G. early in the 20th cent. About that time, the Poles and Ukrainians began to push the Jews out of the economic sphere and their general plight, always depressed, deteriorated. This led to extensive emigration, especially to the US. During World War I, many Jews fled from G. to Hungary, Austria, and Bohemia. G. was again part of Poland from 1918.

GALILEE: District of N Israel. The name is derived from the Hebrew *"galil* (i.e., circuit) of the gentiles" (Is. 8:23), a district at the N border of Israel. Occupied by the tribes of Naphthali and Asher, it was separated from Israel by Tiglath-Pileser III of Assyria in 732 BCE, but remained largely Jewish in population. G. was re-attached to Judea by Aristobulus I in 104 BCE and became one of the three districts of the Jewish state under Herod and the Romans and a center of national and religious zeal. Jesus was bred in G. and began his preaching there. In the Roman war, G. joined the revolt and was unsuccessfully defended by Josephus against the army of Vespasian; this phase of the war ended with the fall of Jotapata. G. does not seem to have taken an active part in the revolt of Bar Kokhba. After the disaster that ensued for the Jews of Judea, it became the main center of Judaism in Palestine, the seat of the patriarchate and of the talmudic academies (Tiberias, Sepphoris, etc.). The Jewish peasantry remained attached to the soil, though in decreasing numbers, through the Persian and Arab conquests and into the Crusader Period. From the 16th–17th cents., Safed was an important rabbinic and kabbalistic center. Joseph Nasi attempted to establish an autonomous settlement at Tiberias (1565). Jewish colonization of the soil of G. was resumed with the foundation of Rosh Pinnah in 1882 and Deganyah in 1909. In the British Mandatory period, the Jordan Valley, the Valley of Jezreel, the Ḥuleh area, and the sea coast were gradually colonized by Jews. G. passed entirely into Israel hands in the War of Independence (Jul.-Oct. 1948). The area of G. is defined on the W by the Mediterranean, on the S by the Valley of Jezreel, on the E by the Jordan Valley; the physical N boundary follows the Litani river, the political, the N boundary of Israel. G. measures 27 miles from N to S, 30 from W to E; its total area (including surrounding valleys) being 1,414 sq. m. The mountains of Upper G. reach 3,724 ft. (Mt. Meron). G. is part of the N district of Israel (cap.: Nazareth) and in its center is a core of Arab villages, surrounded by Jewish settlements. Its principal products are fish from the Sea of Galilee, olive-oil, and tobacco. Large-scale irrigation projects have been carried out in the valleys, including numerous fishponds. Iron ore has been found in the mountains of Naphthali; fruit growing and afforestation are extensive.

GALILEE SKULL: Incomplete prehistoric skull, discovered in 1925 by the British archeologist F. Turville Petre in a cave W of the Sea of Galilee. It is akin to the European Neanderthal but closer to modern man, forming a link between subhuman races and *Homo Sapiens*.

Landscape in Galilee.

GALILI, ISRAEL (1911–): Israel public figure. He is a leader of the *Ha-Kibbutz ha-Meuhad* movement and a founder of kibbutz Naan. A member of the *Haganah* from his youth, he became chief of its national command and helped to form the *Palmah*. He represented *Mapam* (of which he was a founder) in the First Knesset and *Le-Ahdut Avodah – Poale-Zion* in the Third Knesset. In 1966, he became minister without portfolio, holding that post in successive governments.

GALITZIANER: A Jews from Galicia.

GALLAH (Heb. "shaveling"): A Christian priest.

GALLICO: Italian family of French origin. Its members included *ABRAHAM JAGEL BEN HANANIAH G.* (16th–17th cents.), who was mint-master of the prince of Correggio. His *Ge Hizzayon* ("Valley of Vision") was a remarkable imitation of Dante's *Divine Comedy*. He wrote also the first Jewish catechism *Lekah Tov* (c. 1595, often reprinted and translated).

GALLIPOLI: Turkish port. Benjamin of Tudela found 200 Jews there c. 1165. Their number grew after the expulsion from Spain, and the community was a center of Shabbetai Tzevi's activity in the 17th cent. Only 200 Jews are now left in G. In World War I, the ZION MULE CORPS was in action in the G. peninsula.

GALLUS CESTIUS see **PROCURATORS**

GALUT (Heb. "exile"; in Ashkenazi pronunciation and in Yiddish, *golus*): Term applied to the state of the Jewish people in the period of dispersal, with connotation of misery, degradation, and persecution. See DIASPORA.

GALVESTON: City in Texas, US. Jews were living there in 1840, and religious services were first held in a private home in 1856. Ten years later, the Hebrew Benevolent Society was organized. In 1868, a Reform congregation, B'nai Israel, was formed. Orthodox services were first held in 1887. G. now has 2 synagogues and a G. County United Jewish Welfare Association founded in 1936. Jewish pop. (1973): 610.

GALVESTON PLAN: Project seeking to steer immigrants from E Europe away from the east coast of the US by directing them via Galveston, Texas, to less populous centers. The project, initiated by the JEWISH TERRITORIAL ORGANIZATION and partly financed by Jacob Schiff, resulted in the settlement in the southern states of the US of c. 10,000 immigrants between 1907 and 1914.

GAM ZO LE-TOVAH (Heb. "this also is for good"): An expression of resignation to misfortune, frequently uttered by R NAHUM OF GIMZO.

GAMA, GASPAR DA (original name unknown; c. 1440–c. 1510): Traveler. Born in Posen (Poland), he made his way to Egypt, was taken prisoner, and sold as a slave in India. When Vasco da Gama arrived at Anchediva, near Goa, he was greeted by G. in a friendly fashion. The explorer seized him by treachery and compelled him to embrace Christianity, conferring on him the name of Gaspar da Gama. He now had to pilot the Portuguese fleet in Indian waters. Subsequently, he was taken back to Portugal and accompanied Cabral on his voyage to the east in 1502. G. took part in the Portuguese expedition against Calicut in 1510 when, it is believed, he died.

GAMALA: (1) Ancient city situated in Upper Galilee. It was the home of JUDAH THE GALILEAN. (2) Ancient city E of the Sea of Galilee. A natural stronghold, it was fortified by Josephus in 66 CE and taken by storm by Vespasian the following year.

GAMALIEL: Name of six Palestinian rabbis, descendants of Hillel. The most important were (1) *G. THE ELDER* (fl. early 1st cent.): President of the Sanhedrin at Jerusalem; grandson of Hillel. He corresponded with Jewish communities in Palestine and the Diaspora and framed several regulations directed at social improvements, including the betterment of the legal position of women. He is sympathetically mentioned in the New Testament as a teacher of Paul (Acts 22:3). (2) *G. II (BEN SIMEON)* or *G. OF JABNEH* (fl. late 1st-early 2nd cent.): President of the Sanhedrin at Jabneh after the death of Jonathan ben Zakkai (c. 80); grandson of (1). He worked for the consolidation of the authority of Jabneh and endeavored to determine a uniform, clear halakhah, binding all sections of the Jewish people. In matters in dispute between the schools of Hillel and Shammai, he decided according to the former. His dictatorial attitude (e.g. harsh use of the ban against scholars who did not accept majority decisions, including his own brother-in-law, Eliezer ben Hyrcanus) aroused the opposition of the older scholars, who deposed him, putting Eleazar ben Azariah in his place. G. was, however, later reinstated. He was one of the most important scholars of his generation, being responsible for the final version of the EIGHTEEN BENEDICTIONS, the obligation to pray thrice daily, etc. He also represented the Jews before the emperor at Rome and succeeded in securing the abolition of several hostile decrees. He conducted ideological debates with Roman philosophers and early Christians. (3) *G. III* (3rd cent.): President of the Sanhedrin; eldest son of Judah Ha-Nasi. The compilation of the Mishnah was finally conducted during his period of office.

GAMORAN, EMANUEL (1895–1962): Educator. A native of Russia, he settled in the US in 1907. G. exerted a wide influence on the development of Reform religious schools in the US as educational director (from 1923) of the Union of American Hebrew Congregations.

GAN YAVNEH: Israel moshavah in the S coastal plain, 4 m from the historical Jabneh. It was founded in 1931 by American Zionists (the Ahuzah Society of New York), few of whom settled permanently. Greatly extended after the War of Independence, its population in 1972 numbered 2,698.

GANDZ, SOLOMON (1887–1954): Scholar. He was born in Galicia and settled in the US in 1923, becoming librarian and professor of Arabic and medieval Hebrew at Yeshiva College, New York. From 1942, he was professor of Semitic culture at Dropsie College, Philadelphia. Many of his studies dealt with the history of mathematics among the Jews.

GANEF (Yidd. from Heb. *gannav*): Thief, rascal.

GANS, DAVID BEN SOLOMON (1541–1613): Historian and astronomer. After studying with Moses Isserles in Cracow, he settled in Prague (1564) where he became an intimate of the astronomers Kepler and Tycho Brahe. His best-known works are *Tzemaḥ David* (1592), an abbreviated Jewish and general chronicle down to his own time (translated into Latin and Yiddish) and *Neḥmad ve-Naim* on astronomical and mathematical problems.

GANS, EDUARD (1798–1839): German jurist. Enthusiasm for Hegel pervaded his legal researches including his main work (uncompleted) on the law of inheritance and its historical development. Together with Leopold Zunz and Moses Moser, he founded in 1819, the Society for Jewish Culture and Learning of which he was president. His attitude to Judaism called for a synthesis with world culture and an abandonment of national individuality. When his attempts to secure academic standing failed, he adopted Christianity (1825) and was subsequently appointed professor of law at Berlin.

GANZFRIED, SOLOMON (1804–1886): Rabbinical scholar in Ungvár (Uzhgorod). He is best known for his abridgment of the *Shulḥan Arukh* code called *Kitzur Shulḥan Arukh* (1864) which achieved wide popularity and was translated into several languages (English by Michael Friedländer, 1915 and Hyman E. Goldin, 1928).

GAON (pl. *geonim*): The intellectual leaders, often with considerable temporal power, of the Babylonian Jewish community in the post-talmudic period (6th–11th cents.). They headed the two leading academies, SURA and PUMBEDITA, and their influence extended for the greater part of this period over all Jewry. Their title *gaon* ("eminence, pride") derives from their position as *resh metivta geon Yaakov* ("head of the academy which is the pride of Jacob"). The basic source for information on this period is the historical "letter" of SHERIRA GAON. The GENIZAH, however, has more recently also served as a prime source for gaonic history both before and after his day. Sherira lists Mar (= Master) Ḥanan as the first g. of Pumbedita, taking office in 589, and R Mar bar Huna as the first in Sura, appointed in 591.

The academies were ancient institutions, dating from the early amoraic days of Rav and Samuel. Their geographical location, however, did not always remain in the cities after which they were called. Thus at the end of the 9th cent., both academies moved to Baghdad, while retaining their distinctive names. Although Sura was given formal primacy through the influence of R Ashi (the main formulator of the Talmud) and also because of its special connection with the exilarch, there were several periods in which the rival institution exerted the dominant influence. Important geonim in the early history of Sura were MAR SAMUEL (730–48) and R YEHUDAI BEN R NAḤMAN (760–3), both originally from Pumbedita but appointed by the exilarch to the gaonate of the rival college. The succeeding geonim in the course of the 130-year ascendancy of the Sura academy were R Ḥanina (pupil of R Yehudai), R Jacob ha-Cohen, R Zadok ben Jesse, R Moses ben Jacob, R Cohen Tzedek, R SAR SHALOM, R NATRONAI, R AMRAM, and R NAḤSHON. The most famous g. of this academy was SAADYAH, appointed in 928. On his death in 942, the academy remained closed for 45 years, but was reopened with the appointment of R Tzemaḥ of Pumbedita, to be followed by SAMUEL BEN HOPHNI (1003–13). The last four geonim of this academy were Dosa, son of Saadyah (1013–17), Israel, son of Samuel ben Hophni (1017–34), Azariah Ha-Cohen (1034–8), and Isaac. The ascendancy of the Pumbedita academy began with PALTOI (842–58), the first of the geonim from this academy to make contact with N African Jewry, hitherto connected only with Sura. His prominent successors were his son Tzemaḥ (858–76), Cohen Tzedek, and Nehemiah. The most important period of the academy was the 70 years when it was headed by Sherira (968–98) and his son HAI (998–1038). According to the medieval chronicler Abraham Ibn Daud, the gaonate came to an end after a two-year period when it was administered by the exilarch Hezekiah. Newly-discovered documents show that this was not the case. The academies having removed to Baghdad were now united and continued their existence for another 150 years. Among the heads of the Baghdad academy were Hezekiah ben David (1058), Isaac ben Moses (1070), Eli, and SAMUEL BEN ALI (d. c. 1207). This last also took over the prerogatives of the exilarch. The influence of the later geonim was primarily local, for the new Jewish centers in the Diaspora had by this time developed their own spiritual leadership. In addition, competing influence from a rival academy set up in Palestine, also under a nominal gaon, toward the end of the 9th cent., drew away much Diaspora support. The Palestinian gaonate, of which little was known until the discovery of the *genizah*, was founded in the early 10th cent. in rivalry to the Babylonian, but never enjoyed great authority outside Palestine. The attempt of Aaron ben Meir (c. 920) to establish its supermacy was defeated by Saadyah. The names of about 18 incumbents of the office during the next two centuries are known. On the capture of Jerusalem by the Seljuks in 1071, the gaon Elijah ben Solomon (1062–83) transferred his seat to Tyre. He was succeeded by his son EBIATHAR, on whose death in 1109 the "Palestinian" gaonate disintegrated. Although gaonic literature was primarily in the field of halakhah, many geonim made contributions to the understanding of the language of the Talmud, the development of the liturgy, biblical exegesis, and religious philosophy. Important religious decisions, occasionally even the amendment of a talmudic law, were often taken by the geonim at the Talmud discussions during the KALLAH months.

GAON, SOLOMON (1912–): Rabbi. Born in Yugoslavia and educated in England, he was appointed Haham of the Sephardi community of London in 1949.

GARDEN OF EDEN see **EDEN, GARDEN OF**

GARDOSH, KARIEL ("Dosh"; 1921–): Israel cartoonist. Born in Budapest, he went to Israel in 1948 and from 1953 his political cartoons appeared regularly in the afternoon newspaper *Maariv*. His characterization of Israel as a young boy came to symbolize the young state.

*GARSTANG, JOHN (1876–1956): British archeologist. He directed the Palestine Department of Antiquities 1920–6, and excavated at Ascalon, Jericho, and Hazor. His books include *The Heritage of Solomon* and *Joshua, Judges* which tend to confirm the biblical account.

GARY: City in Indiana, US. Its first Jewish settlers came from Chicago and were mostly of Hungarian and Russian origin. An Orthodox congregation was founded in 1908. The Welfare Federation was established in 1940. In 1973, G. had 6,500 Jews.

GASCONY: Former French province. The oldest Hebrew inscription found in France (c. 700) was discovered in Auch. Nothing is known of the Jews who were in G. before the 13th cent. In 1275 and 1281, Edward I of England, who was duke of G., intervened to protect them, but a series of expulsion orders beginning in 1305 culminated in the general expulsion of 1394. The community had suffered severely at the time of the Shepherds' Crusade in 1320, only a few of its members surviving. Many

Dosh: To the limit . . .

Marranos who went to G. in the 15th–16th cents. openly adopted Judaism, and these formed a group of small communities, especially at Saint-Esprit, near BAYONNE.

GASTER: (1) *MOSES G.* (1856–1939): Rabbi and scholar. He was born in Bucharest, and lectured in Rumanian language and literature at the university there from 1881–5. In 1885, owing to his protests against the treatment of the Jews, he was expelled from Rumania. He settled in England where he was appointed Haham of the Sephardi community in 1887, playing a prominent role in Jewish and general intellectual life. He was also active in the Zionist movement and was a vice-president of the First Zionist Congress; his opposition to the "Uganda" Project, however, brought him into opposition to Herzl. In 1917, owing to disagreement with his community, he retired from the position of Haham. He assembled a great library, including large numbers of mss, which he sold in 1925 to the British Museum. His works covered many branches of learning, including comparative folklore, Samaritan literature and history, English-Jewish history, biblical studies, etc. (2) *THEODOR HERZL G.* (1906–): Folklorist; son of (1). Professor of comparative religion at Dropsie University, Philadelphia, since 1944, he has written on folklore and published a translation of the Dead Sea Scrolls.

GASTON-MARIN (originally **GROSSMAN**), **GHE-ORGHE** (1919–): Rumanian statesman. At first active in Zionist Movements, he turned to communist activities. In 1949, he became minister of electrical energy, in 1954 first vice-chairman of the State Manning Commission, and in 1962–5, deputy premier responsible for the country's industrialization program.

GATH: One of the five Philistine cities in the S coastal plain. The home of Goliath, G. was captured by David, fortified by Rehoboam, but lost to the Assyrian king, Sargon, in the 8th cent. BCE. A communal settlement was founded in 1942 by E European youth near the presumed site. The townlet of KIRYAT-GAT is in the same vicinity but the identification of the traditional *tel* of Gath with the biblical city is doubtful.

GAZA (Heb. *Azzah*): Ancient Palestinian city on the S coastal plain, 2 m. from the sea. Commercially it was noted for its black pottery and in Nabatean times was an entrepôt of trade passing from the Red Sea to the Mediterranean. G. is mentioned in Egyptian documents of the 15th–13th cents. BCE when it served as a base for Egyptian expeditions to the N. In the 12th cent., it was captured by the Philistines and remained the most important of their five coastal cities, also housing the temple of Dagon. Although allotted to the tribe of Judah, it remained in Philistine hands and was the place of the imprisonment and death of Samson. In 720

Jewish symbols carved on marble pillar of a 2nd cent. CE synagogue; now in the mosque at Gaza.

BCE, it was annexed by Sargon of Assyria and in 521, by Cambyses of Persia. Alexander the Great recolonized it as a hellenistic city in 332. After his death, it was disputed between the Egyptian Ptolemies and the Syrian Seleucids until annexed by Antiochus III of Syria in 198. It became independent in 110, was captured by Alexander Yannai in 96, but declared a free city by Pompey in 61. A Jewish population lived in G. throughout the Middle Ages, as did a Samaritan community until its capture by Napoleon in 1799. G. was a center of Sabbetaism in the 17th cent. Its Jewish inhabitants left in 1917; the few subsequently returning departed during the 1929 Arab disturbances. It became the main city in the GAZA STRIP, its 1949 population of 30,000 being swollen by many refugees. G. was captured in Nov. 1956 by Israel forces who remained there until Mar. 1957. It again passed under Israel rule during the Six-Day War in 1967. A census taken later that year gave its population at 119,000.

GAZA STRIP: Tongue of land including the town of Gaza, extending from the E border of Egypt northward along the Palestinian coast for 22 m.; average width 8 m. It was the result of the Egyptian advance into the Negev in May 1948, and the Israel offensives of Oct.-Dec. 1948 which drove them out of the entire area, with the exception of the G.S. The area remained under Egyptian rule according to the Armistice Agreement of 1949. The G.S. became the focus of military and political tension in 1955, and in Nov. 1956, was captured by Israel forces in the course of the SINAI OPERATION. Under UN and, especially, US pressure, Israel returned the G.S. in Mar. 1957, when Egyptians resumed control with a UN Emergency Force stationed along the border with Israel. In May 1967 the UN secretary-general U Thant acceded to a demand by NASSER to withdraw the UN force thereby precipitating the events leading to the Six-Day War when the G.S. again passed under Israel control. The 1967 census found 352,260 in the G.S. of whom 172,520 were refugees.

GEDALIAH: Governor of Judah. Of a noble Jewish family, he was appointed by the Babylonians as governor of the population which remained in Judah after the destruction of the First Temple in 586 BCE. He set up the seat of his administration at Mizpah but shortly thereafter was murdered by the commander Ishmael ben Nethaniah and his followers who were apparently planning a revolt against Babylon in concert with neighboring powers. After the murder, G.'s supporters fled to Egypt (II Kings, 25:25–26; Jer. 41).

GEDALIAH, FAST OF: Fast held on the day after *Rosh ha-Shanah* (*Tishri* 3) to commemorate the assassination of GEDALIAH, which destroyed any hope of holding a Jewish community together in Palestine after the Babylonian conquest.

GEDERAH: Israel village in S Judean plain. Founded in 1884 by *Bilu* pioneers, it was for several years the only settlement independent of Baron de Rothschild's administration. Its economy is largely based on intensive farming. Pop. (1974): 5,700.

GEDUD HA-AVODAH (Heb. "Labor Battalion"): Palestinian labor organization. Formed near Tiberias in 1920, and joined by members of the

Members of of Gedud Ha-Avodah in Migdal, near Tiberias.

settlement of Kinneret and of HA-SHOMER, it became a large collective which undertook pioneering work – e.g. road-making – all over the country. In 1921, members of the *G. H.* began to settle the E Valley of Jezreel, and were the exponents of the large kibbutz (En ḤAROD, TEL YOSEPH). Hard hit by the economic crises of 1924–6 and resulting left extremism, *G. H.* split in 1928, its remnants joining *Ha-Kibbutz ha-Meuḥad* in 1929.

GEHAZI: Servant of Elisha. His vulgar behavior is illustrated in the stories relating his attempts to repel the Shunammite woman (II Kings 4) and to obtain Naaman's gifts by cunning; for the latter offense, he was cursed with leprosy (II Kings 5).

GEHINNOM (Ge-Hinnom or Ge-ben-Hinnom = "Valley of Hinnom"; also Gehenna): Valley SW of Jerusalem, opposite the City of David. Children were sacrificed there to Moloch at a site called Tophet and the name G. became synonymous with hell – the place where the wicked are condemned after death.

GEIGER: (1) *ABRAHAM G.* (1810–1874): German scholar and religious reformer. In 1832, he became rabbi at Wiesbaden where he instituted liturgical reforms and began to publish the *Wissenschaftliche Zeitschrift für jüdische Theologie* (appearing 1835–9, 1842–7). In 1837, he convened the first conference of Reform rabbis. G. moved to Breslau in 1840, to Frankfort-on-Main in 1863, and in 1870, to Berlin, helping to establish there the *Hochschule für die Wissenschaft des Judentums* where he taught until his death. His scholarship embraced most aspects of Judaism. He sought to link Jewish with European culture and opposed Orthodoxy as over-legalized and unesthetic. G. emphasized the prophetic nature of Judaism which he regarded as a religion with a world mission; he therefore sought to eliminate the national element, including the concept of universal Jewish identity and the use of Hebrew in the synagogue (in the latter respect he later modified his attitude). His chief scholarly works were on the Bible and its translations (in which he analyzed the development of Jewish religious thought), Sadducees and Pharisees, Judaism and its history, mishnaic Hebrew, Maimonides, Judah Ha-Levi, etc. (2) *LAZARUS G.* (1829–1870): Philosopher and philologist; nephew of (1). From 1861, he taught at the Jewish school in his native Frankfort-on-Main. His chief works were on the birth of language. (3) *LUDWIG G.* (1848–1919): Historian of culture and literature; son of (1) and an extreme assimilationist. From 1880, he was assistant professor of German history at Berlin Univ. His main studies concerned the Renaissance and the Weimar period of German literature. G. also wrote several Judaic studies, founded and edited (1886–92) the *Zeitschrift für die Geschichte der*

Abraham Geiger.

Juden in Deutschland and edited the *Allgemeine Zeitung des Judentums* from 1905.

GELBER, NATAN MIKHAEL (1891–1966): Historian. Born in Galicia, he lived in Vienna where he was chief secretary of the Austrian Zionist Organization 1921–1930. In 1933, he settled in Palestine. G. has published many works on Jewish history (especially in Poland) and Zionism.

GELILAH (Heb. "rolling"): The rolling-up of the Scroll of the Law after it has been read in the synagogue.

GELLMAN, ARYEH LEON (1887–1973): Yiddish editor and *Mizraḥi* leader. Born in Russia, G. went to the US in 1910. Active in *Mizraḥi* leadership since 1914, he headed the US organization (1935–49) and the world organization (since 1949) In 1949, he settled in Israel.

GELL-MANN, MURRAY (1929–): US physicist. He taught at Princeton, Chicago, and then at the California Institute of Technology in Pasadena. His discoveries, for which he won a Nobel Prize in 1969, concern the classification of elementary particles. He is noted for his theory concerning the smallest particle in the universe (omega minus).

GEMARA see **TALMUD**

GEMATRIA (Gk. *geometria?*): Method of biblical exegesis, etc. based on the interpretation of a word or words according to the numerical value of its letters in the Hebrew alphabet. It first appears among tannaim in the late 2nd cent. CE. An example is the explanation that the "318 members" of Abraham's household (Gen. 14:14) is a reference to Abraham's servant, Eliezer (numerical value of Eliezer = 318). It is chiefly found in the later Midrashim and in certain kabbalistic writings (12th–13th cents. onward). Jacob ben Asher's biblical commentary is largely based on g. The usage was criticized by Abraham Ibn Ezra and opponents of the Kabbalah.

GEMILUT ḤESED (Heb. "doing kindness"): CHARITY in the broadest sense. The specific connotation given to the term in the halakhah is personal kindness: e.g. visiting the sick and burying the dead, in contrast to the good done with money. The Mishnah lists this type of kindness among those things for which "no measure is prescribed" (*Peah* I. 1), whereas charity in money need not exceed a fifth of one's possessions. Because of the special merit of personal kindnesses, the Mishnah lists them among "things the fruit of which a man enjoys in this world while the principal remains for the world to come" (ibid).

GENEALOGY: The study of the descent of families.
Much genealogical material is embodied in the Bible (especially the Pentateuch and Chronicles), demonstrating the descent of the Jewish people from the patriarchs (and ultimately from Adam). The priests claimed their g. from Aaron. G.'s from remote antiquity were maintained in Second Temple times. In the talmudic age, the tradition weakened, though the patriarchs in Palestine and (down to the 13th cent.) the exilarchs in Babylonia were believed to possess unbroken descent from David. Although later some families continued to claim Davidic origin, authentic g.'s bridging the ages were unknown. In the medieval and post-medieval period, descent from famous scholars was prized. Recent historians have turned attention to g. and on the basis of communal records, inscriptions etc., have traced certain families back for some centuries (e.g. Gompertz, Montefiore, Rothschild). It is improbable that the g. of any Jewish family today can be demonstrated authentically beyond the late Middle Ages.

GENERAL ZIONISTS: Zionist political party. At the beginning of the 20th cent., when socialist and religious parties emerged in the World Zionist Organization, a movement developed favoring the formation of a general, undefined group. It incorporated two trends, one aiming at a supra-party approach and the other at the crystallization of a specific center group. Within these ranks one section ("A") urged that Diaspora Zionism should not single out any group in Palestine for special support but should concern itself only with the general political and practical interests of Jewish settlement in Palestine. A second section ("B") felt the necessity of encouraging private initiative and middle-class settlement in Palestine. The REVISIONISTS seceded from the G. Z. in the 1920's. In Palestine, two parties emerged within the movement; they united after World War II,

Opening page of the Book of Genesis with Masorah.
(From a 13th cent. ms).

but after 1948, the PROGRESSIVE PARTY broke away as a separate entity with emphasis on liberal tendencies. The G. Z. party had 7 delegates to the First Knesset in 1949 (22,661 votes), 20 to the Second in 1951 (111,394), 13 to the Third in 1955 (87,099) and 8 to the Fourth in 1959. From 1952–5, they participated in the government coalition. In 1961, the G. Z. and the Progressives in Israel re-united, to form the LIBERAL PARTY. This however split in 1965 with the G. Z. uniting with the HERUT Party to form GAHAL In 1946, the World Confederation of G. Z. was established, representing all G. Z. groups in the Diaspora and Israel. It set up a Constructive Fund to support agricultural settlement in Israel. Tensions in the World Confederation reflected the split of the Israel G. Z. and in 1958, it divided into two confederations.

GENESIS (Gk. "Creation"; called in Heb. after its first word *Be-Reshit* "In the beginning"): The first book of the Bible. Its subject-matter consists of: the creation of the world and the beginning of mankind (chapters 1–6:8); the ten generations to Abraham, including the story of the Flood (6:9–11:32); Abraham as the progenitor of the people of Israel (12–20); Abraham and his son Isaac (21–25:18); Isaac and his son Jacob (25:18–36:43); Jacob and his sons (37:1–47:27); the last years of Jacob and of Joseph (47:28–50:26). The first two sections reflect Mesopotamian traditions transformed by the monotheistic outlook, while the rest of the book relates the specific history of the forefathers of the Jewish people. The main teachings of G. are that God, the sole Deity, Creator and Ruler of the material world, has laid down a moral world-order and that man will be rewarded or punished according to his obedience to that order. As only Abraham, Isaac, and Jacob accepted this conception of monotheism and agreed to observe Divine law, they were rewarded by a convenant in which they became God's people and heirs to the Land of Canaan. Bible critics do not regard the book as a homogeneous composition but as the product of three authors, styled J, E, and P (see BIBLE CRITICISM). Other schools regard the work as a unified composition based on a consistent philosophy, the duplications being a conscious literary device. Scholarly opinion is also divided on the date of final redaction.

GENESIS RABBAH: Midrash on the Book of Genesis; the first work in MIDRASH RABBAH. It incorporates 100 sections, each headed by a quotation from Genesis leading to a chain of interpretative *aggadot*. The language of G. R. is W Aramaic, like that of the Palestinian Talmud, interspersed with Greek words, flowery expressions, and folk sayings. Its date of composition cannot be ascertained, but it is clearly one of the earliest Midrashim and seems to have been edited in Palestine not later than the 6th cent. The text was scientifically edited by J. Theodor and H. Albeck (1903–36).

GENESIS ZUTARTA (Aram. "Lesser Genesis"): See JUBILEES.

GENEVA: Swiss town. Its small medieval Jewish community was expelled in 1490. In the 18th cent., Jews were permitted to settle in the suburb of Carouge (which was under the rule of the House of Savoy), settlement in G. itself being authorized only in the 19th cent. Jewish pop. (1973): 3,250.

GENIZAH (Heb. "hiding"): Depository for used sacred books, etc. In mishnaic and talmudic times, holy utensils and writings which had passed out of use but were too sacred to be destroyed were hidden. In the Second Temple Period, sacred writings were apparently hidden in caves in times of danger (see DEAD SEA SCROLLS). Subsequently, used documents were buried in the ground or deposited in the walls, foundations, or attics of synagogues.

The best-known *g.* was discovered in the synagogue of Fostat, Cairo, built in 882. Its large store of mss was first seen in 1763. Firkowitz, Elkan Adler, and other visitors obtained a number of mss, and in 1896, some leaves were brought to Cambridge to Solomon SCHECHTER who recognized part of the lost Hebrew version of the Book of Ecclesiasticus. With the aid of Cambridge Univ., he traveled to Cairo where he acquired some 100,000 leaves; many more have found their way to other libraries throughout the world. The Cairo *g.* revealed many lost Hebrew works, including extracts from Aquila's Greek translation of the Bible, the Zadokite Documents, ancient liturgies and synagogue poetry from Palestine, Babylonia, and Spain, and documents and letters of important persons. It threw light on the history of the gaonate, the Jews of Egypt and Palestine between 640 and 1100, and the Karaites. The oldest dated ms was from 750 CE. Searches in *genizot* in Crimea, Poland, N Africa, etc., have been less successful for climatic reasons, but documents in Judean caves have been preserved by the dry atmosphere and remarkable finds have been made there in recent years.

GENNESARET see **SEA OF GALILEE**

GENOA: Italian town. Jews were apparently settled in G. from Roman times. At the end of the 5th cent., the synagogue was destroyed in a mob outbreak. The trading republic of the Middle Ages, apprehensive of Jewish competition, attempted to exclude the Jews, and Benjamin of Tudela found only two Jews there (c. 1165). Starving Jewish refugees from Spain arrived at the port in 1492, but were not allowed to remain. In the 16th cent., a handful were admitted from time to time under strict limitations. Marrano merchants were invited to the city in 1648 to stimulate trade, and a ghetto was established in 1660, but the importance of the community was slight. In 1752, a new charter extended Jewish rights and after the union of the republic with the kingdom of Sardinia (later of Italy), the position of the Jews improved considerably. In World War II, the community suffered severely, many of its members being deported to death. Jewish pop. (1967): 800.

GENOCIDE: The extermination of a race. The term was first used by Raphael Lemkin in his report to the Fifth International Conference for the Unification of Penal Law held in Madrid in 1933. In the UN convention on the Prevention and Punishment of the Crime of Genocide, the term signifies a coordinated set of acts, intended to destroy a national, ethnic, racial, or religious group, as such. The passing of this convention was preceded by a long struggle against many difficulties and objections both in the political and legal spheres. The Nazi atrocities, of which the main victims were Jews, weighed most

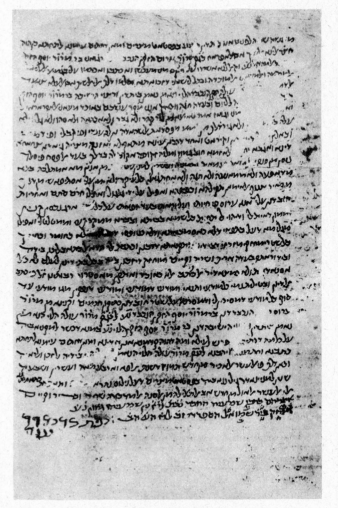

12th cent. legal document from the Cairo Genizah.

strongly in favor of such a convention which furnished new legal provisions extending the field of international crimes beyond those previously understood. An important extension had already been made by the charter of the International Military Tribunal in reaction to the general abhorrence roused by the Nazi crimes. This charter, and later the trials at Nuremberg, dealt with the Nazi crimes in Germany before the war only insofar as they formed part of the general Nazi conspiracy against peace. Therefore, in 1946, a resolution was adopted in the United Nations calling for international cooperation in preventing such crime, not as a war crime, but as a crime against modern international law as such, even if perpetrated in time of peace or within the boundaries of a sovereign state against its own subjects. These were embodied in the convention which came formally into force on Jan. 12, 1951, after having been ratified or acceded to by 27 governments. Israel ratified the convention on Mar. 2,

1950 and was among the first states to enact the requisite legislation.

GENTILE: Non-Jew; in Hebrew *nokhri* or *goi*,

According to Jewish law, every one whose mother is a non-Jewess is considered a non-Jew, regardless of whether the father is Jewish. The seven Noachian laws, but not the commandments of the Torah, are binding on a g. A non-Jew who converts to Judaism is considered a Jew. Jewish law does not recognize as binding any marriage between Jew and g., all marital relationship between them being prohibited. A g. could offer sacrifices to God and such sacrifices were offered at the Temple. The non-Jew, however, was prohibited from eating the paschal lamb as well as certain other offerings. A g. might not be appointed king over Israel or to any other governing position over Jews. A Jew was forbidden to sell land to a non-Jew in Palestine. Toward the end of the Second Temple Period, during the time of tension between the Jews and Rome, the rabbis enacted several decrees to diminish contact between Jew and non-Jew; these included the prohibition of drinking wine belonging to a g. Other rabbinical enactments, however, were intended to further peaceful co-existence with non-Jewish neighbors; e.g. non-Jewish invalids were to be visited and non-Jewish poor supported together with the Jewish poor. To defraud a g. was stigmatized as a special sin (*Ḥillul ha-Shem*). The rabbis taught that the "righteous among the nations of the world (i.e., the gentiles) have a share in the world to come."

Moses ben Gershom Gentile.
(Engraving in his *Melekhet Maḥashevet*, Venice, 1710).

GENTILE: (Heb. *Ḥephetz*): N Italian Jewish family, prominent in and around Verona. *MOSES BEN GERSHOM G.* (1663–1711) was rabbi in Venice and author of *Melekhet Maḥashevet*, a philosophical commentary of the Pentateuch. He also wrote *Ḥanukkat ha-Bayit* on the structure of the

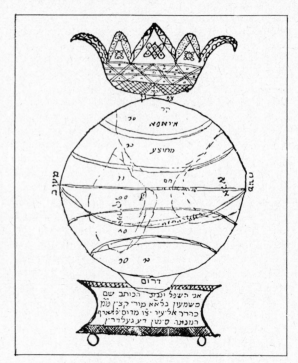

Drawing of a globe by the 18th cent. traveler,
Simon von Geldern.

Second Temple. His son *GERSHOM G.* (1683–1700) published a rhyming dictionary, *Yad Ḥaruzim*.

GEOGRAPHY AND GEOGRAPHERS: The Jewish geographical horizon early included Egypt, Chaldea, and Babylon, while Solomon's trading expeditions extended knowledge southward. The growth of the Diaspora brought Jews into contact with Greece, W Asia, and the Roman Empire. Under Byzantium and Islam, Jews traded from the Rhone through the Mediterranean or Central Europe to India and China, until interrupted by the Crusades (11th cent.) and the rise of gentile trade. Jews nevertheless pioneered the routes from N Africa to the Niger (14th–15th cents.). The Bible and Apocrypha reflect the belief that the world was a circle of land surrounded by sea. The concept that Jerusalem was the center of the world was shared with Christianity, but the knowlege of the earth as a sphere came to Jews via Islam in the 10th cent., while the Zohar (13th cent.) knew that the world revolves on its axis. The Jewish CARTOGRAPHERS of Majorca showed in their maps a remarkable knowledge of the g. and trade-routes of the Mediterranean and N Africa. The first systematic g. in Hebrew was by ABRAHAM BAR ḤIYYA (c. 1100). The geographical knowledge derived from new discoveries was communicated to Jews by Abraham FARISSOL (16th cent.). Jewish travel books are known from the 10th cent., the most important being that of BENJAMIN OF TUDELA (12th cent.)

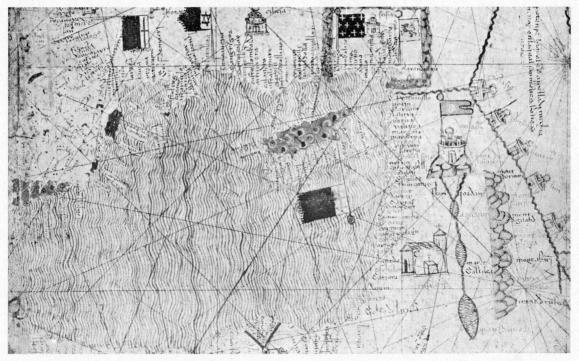

Part of the "Catalan" Atlas of Judah Cresques (14th cent.).

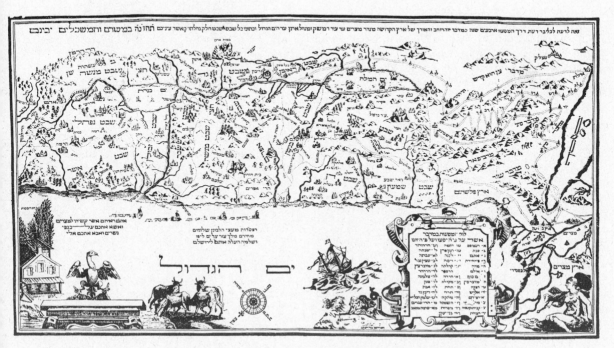

Map of Palestine by the proselyte Abraham ben Jacob. Printed in the Amsterdam Haggadah, 1695.

Mosaic from the 6th cent. CE synagogue at Gerasa.

while his contemporary, PETHAHIAH OF REGENSBURG, wrote on his own journey to E Europe and the Orient. After the 13th cent., accounts of Palestine are common. In the 18th cent. Hayyim Joseph David AZULAI described Jewish communities throughout the world and in the 20th cent., Jacob SAPIR added information on Yemen, etc. The first modern Hebrew geographical text-books were published in the 18th cent. based on German sources (Samson Ha-Levi, *Shevile Olam*, 1825) while Hillel Kahana's *Gelilot Aretz* (1880) laid the foundation for the textbooks and terminology used in Israel today. See also EXPLORERS.

GEORGE, MANFRED (1893–1965): Journalist and biographer. On leaving Germany in 1938, he settled in the US where he edited *Aufbau*, a German Jewish weekly journal.

GEORGIA (Russian *Gruzia*): Soviet republic in the Caucasus. The origins of its Jewish community are shrouded in legend. Before the 12th cent., the Jews of G. were under the religious authority of the Babylonian exilarch. They suffered persecution in the 14th cent.; this was intensified in the 15th when they became dependent on and partly enslaved to the great landlords, a situation which continued until the Russian annexation in the 19th cent. Some European Jews now settled in G. Georgian Jews began to emigrate to Palestine in 1863, 1,700 having arrived by 1921. Jews received equal rights when the republic of G. was established in 1918; in 1926, there were 21,105 in the Soviet republic, maintaining a communal organization. A Jewish ethnographic museum was established at Tiflis (now Tbilisi) in 1933. The Jewish population increased considerably as a result of the Second World War and numbered 55,382 in 1970. After that date many Jews left G. and emigrated to Israel.

GEORGIA: US state. When the colony was founded in 1733, Jews constituted a third of the white inhabitants. The second ship bearing colonists from England contained about 40 Jews of Sephardi origin and others from Germany. Most of them remained in SAVANNAH. Many were granted lots and farms, but some entered the coastal trade or opened stores.

They received full civil rights. The hard life in the colony caused a general exodus so that by 1740 only a few Jews remained. At the outbreak of the Revolutionary War, G. had about 40 Jewish families, who played an active part in the conflict. In the second half of the 19th cent., Jewish immigrants from Germany and other parts of the US settled in G., chiefly in Albany, Augusta, ATLANTA, Columbus, and Macon. G. had 27,150 Jews in 1973.

GER see **PROSELYTE**

GERAR: Ancient Palestinian city in the W Negev.
It was visited by Abraham and Isaac when its king was Abimelech. It is not mentioned in the later Biblical Period, but reappears in Byzantine times as a bishopric located on the imperial domain. Its actual site is doubtful.

Gerasa coin of the period of Hadrian.

GERASA: Ancient city of Transjordan, now Jerash.
Reputedly founded by the Macedonians, it was captured by Alexander Yannai and later became part of the DECAPOLIS (63 BCE). In the Roman War, its Jews were protected by the Greeks (68 CE), and a community existed there at least until the 6th cent.

GERBA see **JERBA**

GERIM (Heb. "Proselytes"): Minor tractate appended to the Talmud. It consists of 4 chapters containing short halakhic statements concerning the acceptance of proselytes, the manner of conversion, etc.

GERIZIM: Palestinian mountain (ht. 2,907 ft.) in the hills of Ephraim facing Mt. Ebal (3,102 ft.). Shechem (Nablus) is situated in the intervening valley. When the Israelites entered Canaan, a ceremony was held at which the people assembled on Mt. G. blessed all who observed the law, and those on Mt. Ebal cursed those who profaned it (Deut.

11:29–30; 27:11–13; Josh. 8:30–5). Mt. G. came to be especially venerated by the SAMARITANS whose entire religious life was bound up with what they called the "Chosen Mount." At the beginning of the Second Temple Period, they erected an altar and Sanballat built a temple on G. which constituted their religious and political center until Antiochus IV converted it into a temple of Zeus; this was destroyed by John Hyrcanus in 129 BCE. The sanctity of Mt. G. was emphasized in passages interpolated into the Samaritan Pentateuch, including the Ten Commandments. The Samaritans still perform their paschal sacrifice on G.

GERMANY: European country, now divided into two republics. In 321 CE, the emperor Constantine issued regulations which indicate the existence of an organized Jewish community with rabbis and elders at COLOGNE, and it is probable that Jews were settled elsewhere on the Rhineland at the time. Archeological finds also demonstrate the presence in the Roman Period of Jews in what is now G. It has even been suggested that there were Jewish soldiers in the Roman garrisons. Whether these communities were able to maintain their continuity during the period of the Barbarian invasions is unknown. In the 8th–9th cents., the Carolingian royal house adopted a pro-Jewish policy and encouraged the settlement of Jews in its dominions with the object of developing trade. New Jewish communities now began to make their appearance in the principal commercial centers. In the 9th cent., mention is found of them in AUGSBURG and METZ; in the 10th, at WORMS, MAINZ, MAGDEBURG, RATISBON, etc. The densest settlement was in the Rhineland (Mainz, SPEYER, Worms, Cologne, etc.) where an intense intellectual life developed in the 11th cent. under Franco-Jewish influence. Conditions were generally not unfavorable, though the persecution recorded in 1012 was probably not unique. In 1096, however, the Crusaders massacred the Jews throughout the Rhineland and the adjacent areas. Henceforth, the moral atmosphere changed, and at all times of unrest or excitement in G., the Jews were attacked. As elsewhere in Europe, this contributed to the process which drove them out of trade and forced them increasingly into the profession of moneylending. On the other hand, the political fragmentation of G. made impossible unified action against the Jews such as destroyed the continuity of Jewish history in other countries of Europe; if they were driven out of one area, another could receive them. G. figures pre-eminently in Jewish history as the land of martyrdom where expulsion was resorted to only locally and sporadically in order to complete the work of extermination. The 1298 massacres inspired by a knight named RINDFLEISCH, those of 1336 led by leather-jerkined fanatics nick-

Jew taking oath on sow's skin, as prescribed by law in Breslau.
(From a 17th cent. copper engraving).

named ARMLEDER, and especially those of 1348/9 at the time of the BLACK DEATH (which the Jews were accused of deliberately propagating), were on the widest possible scale and perpetrated with extreme barbarism; in the last-mentioned series, over 350 localities suffered, and over 200 communities were utterly wiped out. In the second half of the 14th cent., the survivors were kept perpetually impoverished by the imperial authorities' cancellation of the debts due to them. Nevertheless, a sturdy Jewish intellectual life manifested itself in G. throughout the Middle Ages centering mainly on talmudic study, while individual Jews participated in certain aspects of German life. Toward the close of the Middle Ages, most of the larger German cities banished the Jews; after the beginning of the 16th cent., the only communities of importance left were those of FRANKFORT-ON-MAIN and Worms. Nevertheless, settlements still existed in a large number of small places under the protection of local barons, etc., sometimes only a few miles away from the former great centers to which the Jews resorted to transact business. The Protestant Reformation seemed at first to offer the prospect of a notable amelioration in the Jewish position, but LUTHER ultimately reverted to the traditional German anti-Semitic standard. The Jews greatly benefited from the circumstances which developed in G. in the 17th cent. after the Thirty Years' War when a large number of competitive states, vying with one another in petty magnificence, began to emerge. Many of these employed Jews as factors, military purveyors, financial advisers, etc. and conferred on them privileged positions as COURT JEWS, around whom new communities began to establish themselves. The Jews of HAMBURG came to be of prime importance after a Marrano colony was established there in the early 17th cent. PRUSSIA (Brandenburg) attracted important new colonies (especially in BERLIN) when it began its period of expansion; its absorption in the 18th cent. of SILESIA and (later) parts of Poland brought further old-established Jewish centers into its orbit. With Moses MENDELSSOHN, Jews began to enter the main stream of German cultural life and society. Nevertheless, non-privileged Jews throughout the country continued to suffer from the severest discrimination, some important cities and even entire provinces (e.g. NUREMBERG, SAXONY) excluding them entirely. The French Revolution and its aftermath brought equality to the Jews of western G., now either annexed to or dependent on France. In the rest of the country, this example resulted in a considerable degree of EMANCIPATION — e.g. in Prussia in 1812, on the eve of the War of Liberation. After the fall of Napoleon, this amelioration was everywhere qualified, sometimes canceled, and there was a wave of violence against the Jews (the "HEP! HEP!" riots) in 1819. By now, the Jews had come to constitute part of German life, and their full emancipation was an integral feature of the Liberal program, achieved temporarily in the periods of revolution (1830, 1848), thereafter nullified, but slowly advancing toward consolidation. Universal emancipation in G. was achieved as a constitutional principle in 1869. Meanwhile, the Jews had begun to enter German life in every aspect – literary, cultural, scientific, political – with brilliant success, and to a degree unknown in any other land. In the scholarly sphere, this had its parallel in the innovation of the scientific study of Jewish history, theology, etc. (WISSENSCHAFT), while the attempt to adjust religious forms to German life resulted in the emergence in 19th cent. G. of Reform Judaism. This rapid progress on the part of the German Jews stimulated jealousy and resentment which found expression in the organization and rapid spread of the new radical

ANTI-SEMITISM, as well as in the *de facto* exclusion of professing Jews from political, military, and academic appointments. The downfall of the German Empire in 1918 and the establishment of the Republic led to real equality. Under the Weimar Republic, the Jews of G. attained great achievements in all spheres. Anti-Semitism of the most extreme type had, however, become the motive-force of the Nazi movement under Adolf HITLER who attained power in 1933. The process of excluding Jews from German life and the organization of CONCENTRATION CAMPS began immediately, resulting in a large-scale emigration from the country. In 1935, conditions were made even worse by the NUREMBERG LAWS; but with admirable courage and resourcefulness, German Jewry began to adjust its life to the changed circumstances. However, the riots on Nov. 9–10, 1938 ("the Night of Broken Glass"), accompanied by the destruction of almost all synagogues, wholesale arrests, and the imposition of a confiscatory levy, ended the possibility of maintaining an organized Jewish life. Emigration was limited by the outbreak of World War II in Sept. 1939. In Sept. 1941, the wearing of the "Jewish Badge" was enforced in G. In Oct. wholesale deportations to Poland started, where in the following year the policy of physical annihilation began to be carried into effect. The Jewish pop. of Greater G. in 1938 was approximately 540,000; by Sept. 1939, the number had been halved. In 1975 there were 27,668 Jews in Germany including 1,300 in East Germany. Many Jews now in Germany came from E European countries after World War II. Communities are to be found in Berlin, Frankfort, Munich, and several other places; they are organized under a Central Council with its center in DUSSELDORF. In Sept. 1952, a REPARATIONS agreement was signed whereby Western G. paid $822 million compensation to the Jewish people for the material losses of German Jews at the hands of the Nazis; Eastern G. refused to consider a similar agreement. In 1965 diplomatic relations were established between Israel and Western G.

GERÖ (originally Singer), **ERNÖ** (1898–): Hungarian politician. He was minister of communications 1945–9, minister of finance and the interior until 1954, and then first deputy-premier. In 1956, G. became secretary of the Hungarian Communist Party, but was relieved of his position after the uprising later that year. In 1962, he was expelled from the party.

GERONA: Town in Catalonia (Spain). An important Jewish community is recorded from the beginning of the 11th cent. and there is minute information from both Jewish and official sources regarding its organization. It suffered very severely in the persecutions of 1391 but recovered afterward, continuing to exist down to the expulsion of 1492. It was the home of many notable scholars, including Naḥmanides. Part of the medieval Jewish quarter still stands.

GERONDI: Surname applied to persons whose families originated in GERONA (formerly Gerunda), N Spain. Among those bearing the name were (1) *ISAAC BEN ZERACHIAH G.* (fl. 12th cent.): Liturgical poet. (2) *JONAH BEN ABRAHAM G.* known as "the pious" (d. 1263): Talmudist; cousin of Naḥmanides. Having been induced, while living at Montpellier, to sign the ban which led to the burning of the works of Moses Maimonides, he vowed to go on a pilgrimage to Palestine to seek forgiveness on the latter's grave, but was induced to remain in Toledo and head a yeshivah there. He wrote novellae on many talmudic tractates, much used by later writers and sometimes incorporated in their works, as well as ethical treatises which are still widely read. (3) *NISSIM BEN REUBEN G.* (known as *Ran*; d.c. 1380): Talmudist, physician, and astronomer. One of the foremost halakhists of his age, he wrote commentaries, essentially practical and non-theoretical, on the writings of Alfasi and on many talmudic tractates, that on *Nedarim* being his most significant work. His responsa are important both historically and halakhically. He played a foremost part in the communal life of Barcelona, where the secular records refer to him as Magister Nescim. About 1367, he was imprisoned, probably in connection with an accusation of Host Desecration. (4) *ZERACHIAH BEN ISAAC G.* (*HA-LEVI*) (d. 1186?): Talmudist. Originating in Gerona, he settled in Lunel. His *Sepher ha-Maor* on Alfasi aroused comment because of its relentless critical spirit, while his *Sepher ha-Tzava* is an original introduction to the methodology of the Talmud. He also wrote liturgical poems. See also GHIRONDI.

GERONIMO DE SANTE FÉ see **LORKI**

GERSHENSOHN, MICHAEL OSIPOVICH (1869–1925): Russian philosopher, critic, and literary historian. After the Bolshevik Revolution, he was dean of the historical faculty of the State Academy of Sciences and Arts. A violent opponent of western culture, he was the intellectual spokesman of the Slavophil movement, and wrote books on the history of Russian literature and studies of Russian culture in the 19th cent.

GERSHOM BEN JUDAH (known as Rabbenu [= "Our Teacher"] Gershom *Meor ha-Golah*, i.e., "Light of the Diaspora"; c. 965–1028): Rabbinic authority. The earliest notable W European Jewish scholar, he was born in Metz and lived at Mainz where he directed an academy. One of the first commentators on the Talmud, he corrected many copyists' errors and also transcribed the biblical Masorah to ensure accurate reading. According to tradition, he wrote a commentary on the entire Talmud, but only fragments have survived. G.'s legal decisions and regulations (*takkanot*) were accepted as binding by European Jewry; they included bans on polygamy, divorcing a woman without her consent, reading letters directed to others, cutting pages out of books, and mocking converts who had returned to Judaism. His son (and possibly his wife) was forcibly baptized in 1012, and G. wrote a number of penitential prayers expressing his grief.

GERSHON BEN SOLOMON (fl. 13th cent.): French scholar. He wrote the encyclopedic work *Shaar ha-Shamayim*, devoted to natural sciences, astronomy, and mathematics. This incorporates many quotations from Latin and Arab scientific literature translated into Hebrew.

George Gershwin.

GERSHWIN, GEORGE (1898–1937): US composer. He introduced the jazz and blues style into symphonic music (*Rhapsody in Blue*, *American in Paris*), writing an American Negro opera (*Porgy and Bess*) as well as musical comedies, a piano concerto, and film scores. The lyrics of many of his successful works were written by his brother *IRA G.* (1896–).

GERSONIDES see **LEVI BEN GERSHON**

GERTLER, MARK (1892–1939): English artist. Born in poor circumstances and originally a factory worker, he achieved considerable fame which has increased since his untimely death by his own hand.

GERUNDI see **GERONDI**

GERUSIA (Gk.): The council of elders, numbering 71, which assisted the high priest; later more often referred to as the SANHEDRIN. The Jews of Greek Alexandria also had a g. and presidents of

Gezer Calendar.

the *g.* of synagogues are recorded in Italy and else-where in the Classical Period.

*GESENIUS, WILHELM (1786–1842): German orientalist. From 1811 professor at Halle, he laid the foundation of the modern comparative study of the Hebrew language. His larger works, a comparative and critical grammar (1817) and the lexicon *Thesaurus Philologicus-criticus* (1829–58), as well as his history of the Hebrew language and script (1815), did much to further Hebrew studies. He also wrote two practical handbooks which are still the basis of the most widely used works of reference for the study of biblical Hebrew: a grammar (1813), and a dictionary, on which is based the standard Hebrew-English biblical lexicon by Brown, S. R. Driver, and Briggs (Oxford, 1907; 2nd ed., 1953).

GESHER HA-ZIV: Israel communal settlement (IK) in W Galilee. It was founded near ACHZIB in 1949 by pioneers who had been forced to leave BETH ARABAH and a group from English-speaking countries. The name (literally "bridge of splendor") commemorates 14 *Haganah* members killed on the site in 1946 while blowing up the bridge over the Keziv river as part of a protest against British policy in Palestine. Pop. (1972): 380.

GESSIUS FLORUS see **FLORUS GESSIUS**
GET see **DIVORCE**
GEVAT: Israel communal settlement (KM) in W Jezreel Valley. It was founded in 1926 by immigrants from Poland who participated in draining the Jezreel Valley swamps. Pop. (1972): 664.
GEZER: Town in Palestine. It was a Canaanite center in the 3rd and 2nd millennia BCE. The king of G. was among the rulers vanquished by Joshua, but the Israelite hold did not last. The Egyptian pharaoh gave the town to Solomon as dowry for his daughter, but it was captured from Rehoboam by Pharaoh Shishak. Jews were among the population of the late First Temple and Second Temple times, the city being captured by Simon the Hasmonean. In the Middle Ages, it was the site of Mont Gisart, a Crusader castle. A settlement (IK) was founded there in 1945 by Youth Aliyah graduates from Central Europe. Pop. (1972): 18,000 The ancient town was excavated by R.A.S. Macalister 1902–5, 1907–9, and revealed evidence of occupation from the Chalcolithic to the Arab Period. Further excavations have been carried out in recent years under William G. Dever.
GEZER CALENDAR: The oldest known Hebrew inscription. Written in Canaanite script, it contains a list (incomplete) of agricultural seasons and the work associated with them. It was found on a limestone tablet in a late 10th cent. BCE stratum at Gezer. The original is in the Istanbul archeological museum.
GEZERAH (Heb.): A decree, an anti-Semitic law; hence by extension, a disaster.
GHAZZATI, NATHAN BENJAMIN see **NATHAN OF GAZA**
GHETTO: Jewish quarter; strictly, a quarter set up by law to be inhabited only by Jews. The name derives from the foundry or *Ghetto* in Venice

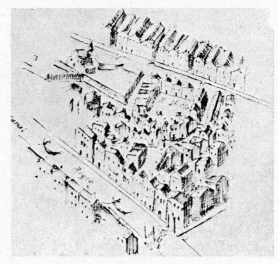

The Venetian Ghetto. (From an 18th cent. plan).

where the Jews were segregated in 1517. However, the idea of the segregation of the Jews, implicit in earlier Church legislation, goes back to the Lateran Councils of 1179 and 1215 which forbade Jews and Christians to live together in close contact. In Spain, the Jews lived at least from the 13th cent. in *juderias* provided with walls and gates for their protection. From the 15th cent., the friars in Italy began to press for the effective segregation of the Jews, and in 1555, Pope Paul IV ordered that Jews in the Papal States should be forced to live in separate quarters. This was immediately carried into effect in Rome and became the rule throughout Italy in the course of the next generation. The name "ghetto" (already accepted in Venice) was now universally applied. The institution was common (under the name *Judengasse*, etc.) also in Germany, Prague (where the *Judenstadt* was famous), and in some Polish cities. It was a town within a town, enjoying a certain degree of autonomy and a vigorous spiritual and intellectual life. But it was insalubrious, overcrowded (since the area was not allowed to expand) and subject to frequent fires. Moreover the g. system was often accompanied by forced baptism, the wearing of the Jewish Badge, conversionist sermons, occupational restrictions, etc. It was abolished in Italy in the French Revolutionary Period, reintroduced locally in the 19th cent., and came to an end when Rome united with the kingdom of Italy in 1870. In other countries, the record was similar. One of the features of the new settlements in W Europe from the 16th cent. onward was that the g. system was not introduced.

Original Moslem law contained no provisions restricting non-Moslem areas of residence. The deterioration came in the 18th cent. when Jews were required to move from the vicinity of mosques and were restricted in the size of their houses; with economic decline, these Jewish quarters became slums. In the E Moslem area (e.g. Persia), Shi'ite fanaticism from the outset enforced distinct Jewish quarters, closed at night and on Sabbaths. These were extended also to Yemen and Morocco where the g.'s were called respectively *Qa'at al-Yahud* (or *Masbattah*) and MELLAḤ. Many Moroccan g.'s are still inhabited.

The g.'s set up by the NAZIS in E Europe (1939–42) were not intended to be permanent Jewish quarters but were part of their plan of liquidation aiming to concentrate, isolate, and break the spirit of their occupants prior to annihilation. Between 1939 and 1942, Jews from Poland, Germany, Czechoslovakia, and elsewhere were transferred mainly to the WARSAW and Lublin areas. G.'s were instituted there and at other places (e.g. Lodz, Minsk, Vilna, Cracow, Bialystok, Lvov, Riga, Sosnowiec). The population of the Warsaw G. rose ultimately to 445,000, and

there were 200,000 in the g. of Lodz. The g.'s, already overcrowded at the outset, were steadily restricted in area. All were ultimately enclosed and exit, except with permission, was punished by death. Control was in the hands of the Gestapo and SS which appointed Jewish councils to carry out their orders through the medium of a Jewish police force. The councils organized social welfare and schools, maintained courts of law, and had to raise a labor force for the Germans. As Nazi liquidation plans became clear, both councils and Jewish police passed increasingly into the hands of collaborators who formed a privileged group. The g. contained industrial centers working for Germany at nominal wages. The Nazis steadily starved the g's and available relief could only be financed at the expense of the Jews themselves. Despite destitution and demoralization, the Jews maintained widespread cultural activity, schools, and mutual aid; from this moral resistance were born the Ghetto Revolts of 1943. Systematic liquidation of the g.'s began with the successive removal of groups for annihilation in 1941. The Warsaw G. was liquidated in 1943 and the remaining g.'s by 1944.

"GHETTO BENCHES": Separate benches for Jewish students at Polish universities. These were instituted on the demand of extremist representatives of the student body between the two World Wars, but the Jewish students refused to accept segregation and serious clashes ensued. Similar manifestations occurred in Rumania and Hungary.

GHIRONDI: Italian family, originating in Gerona (Spain) from where they moved to Turkey. Its outstanding member was *MORDECAI SAMUEL G.* (1799–1852), rabbi in Padua from 1831; he was co-author with H. Neppi of the biographical dictionary of Italian Jewish scholars, *Toledot Gedole Italia*.

GIANTS: Mythological g. are apparently referred to by the Bible as Nephilim, Anakim, and Gibborim (Gen. 6:4; Num. 13:28). Og, king of Bashan, is described as of prodigious stature, being the last of the Rephaim (Deut. 3:11). Later g. were Goliath whose stature was 6 cubits and a span (I Sam. 17) and Ishbi-benob (II Sam. 21:16).

GIBEATH BENJAMIN (= Gibeah of Benjamin): Ancient Palestinian city situated between Jerusalem and Mt. Ephraim. It was the central town of the Benjamites, being destroyed by the other Israelite tribes for the gruesome crime committed there (Judg. 19:20). Rebuilt at the end of the period of the Judges, it served as Saul's royal city, being called henceforth Gibeath Saul. It declined after his death and was probably destroyed in the reign of Jeroboam, but was again inhabited under Asa and in the Second Temple Period. The site has been excavated and remains of fortifications, etc. discovered.

GIBEON: Ancient priestly city N of Jerusalem in the territory of the tribe of Benjamin (Josh. 18:25; 21:17). Before the Israelite conquest, the city had been occupied by HIVITES who tricked Joshua into making a treaty with them. When their duplicity was discovered, they were condemned to be slaves of the sanctuary and, according to talmudic traditions, were the ancestors of the NETHINIM. Their persecution by Saul was regarded by David as an infringement of the original treaty, and in atonement, he handed over seven of Saul's sons whom they killed forthwith. G. was the site of a high place where Solomon sacrificed and subsequently experienced a Divine vision (I Kings 3:4–14). The site was excavated in 1956, when the pool mentioned in II Sam. 2:12 ff. was discovered.

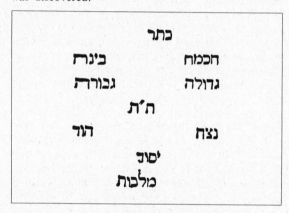

The Ten *Sephirot* ("emanations").
(From *Shaare Orah* by Joseph Gikatilla).

GIBRALTAR: There were Jewish associations with G. in the Middle Ages, and in 1473, an attempt was made to establish there a center for fugitive Marranos. Jews from N Africa began to settle in G. immediately after the British conquest (1704), but it was not until after 1749 that a community was officially formed. The Jews played a prominent part in local commerce and in the 19th cent., their number rose to 2,000, with four synagogues and many institutions. The number is reduced to 552 (1972), but there is still and active communal life. Sir Joshua HASSAN was first chief minister 1964–69 and again from 1972.

GIDEON (also called Jerubaal; fl. 12th cent. BCE): Judge of Israel for forty years. A member of the tribe of Manasseh, he defeated the Midianites near En Harod using a group of picked volunteers. He was subsequently offered the kingship, but refused out of loyalty to the principle that God is king of Israel (Judg. 6–8).

GIDEON, SAMSON (original name: Abudiente; 1699–1762): English financier. During the Anglo-French wars in the mid-18th cent., he was the principal agent for the raising of government loans, and his advice was largely instrumental in preserving the financial stability of the country during the Jacobite rebellion in 1745 and the Seven Years' War. In his later days, he drifted away from Judaism, although he continued to contribute to synagogue funds in secret. His son, Lord Eardley (1745–1824), had no contact with Judaism.

GIHON: (1) One of the four rivers issuing from the Garden of Eden, which encompassed the land of Cush (Gen. 2:10–13). The Septuagint and Josephus identified it with the Nile. (2) Spring in the Kidron Valley, E of Jerusalem, near which Solomon was anointed king (I Kings 1:33–5). When Sennacherib besieged Jerusalem, Hezekiah cut a tunnel to direct the waters of G. to the pool of SILOAM.

GIKATILLA (Chiquitilla; Arabic, Jiqatila): Family which produced many scholars, notably: (1) *ISAAC G.* (10th–11th cents.): Poet and grammarian; lived at Lucena. (3) *JOSEPH BEN ABRAHAM G.* (1248–c. 1325): Kabbalist and liturgical poet; lived in Castile. He wrote in 1274, *Ginnat Egoz*, following the kabbalistic system of Abraham Abulafia; an abridgement was made by Eliakim of London. The book influenced Moses de Leon. Later, G. adopted Moses de Leon's system which he followed in his main mystical work *Shaare Orah* ("Gates of Light"). (3) *MOSES BEN SAMUEL G.* (fl. 11th cent.): Rationalist, philologist, and Bible commentator; lived in Cordova. His commentaries are lost but quotations from them were collected by S. Poznanski. He wrote a treatise on irregularities in Hebrew nouns and translated into Hebrew two Arabic grammatical works by Hayyuj (being probably the first translator from Arabic into Hebrew) as well as the Book of Job into Arabic.

GILBOA: Palestinian mountain ridge, SW of Bet Shean. It is 10½ m. long, 5 m. wide, and its highest point is 1,709 ft. above sea-level. G. was the site of the Philistine victory over the Israelites when Saul and three of his sons, including Jonathan, were killed.

GILEAD: (1) Region of Transjordania, settled by the tribes of Reuben, Gad, and half the tribe of Manasseh (Num. 32; Josh. 22:9, 15). After Solomon's reign, G. was part of the northern kingdom and, in 732, was captured by Assyria, its inhabitants being sent into exile. Its boundaries were not stable, and the area has not been precisely determined. (2) Ancient city in the region of the same name (Judg. 10:17, etc.).

GILELS, EMIL (1916–): Russian pianist. He first aroused attention at the All-Ukrainian congress of pianists in 1931. In 1936, he was awarded second prize at an international competition in Vienna, and in 1938, first prize at the Ysaye competition in Brussels. G. is regarded as one of the greatest contemporary Russian pianists.

GILGAL: Name of various holy places in ancient Palestine. The best-known was the first camp of the Israelites after crossing the Jordan, where Joshua set up twelve commemorative stones and the Israelites were circumcised after celebrating there their first Passover in Canaan (Josh. 4:19–20; 5:2–10). The site has not been identified.

GILGAMESH EPIC: Ancient Babylonian creation myth. Several parallels with the biblical narrative (especially the story of the Flood) indicate that the ancestors of the Jews may have brought a knowledge of the epic with them from Babylon to Canaan. However, the contrast between the consistent monotheism of the Bible and the crude, pagan polytheism of the Babylonian version is striking.

GILGUL see **METEMPSYCHOSIS**

GIMBEL: US family of merchants and philanthropists. The founder of the family, *ADAM G.* (1817–1896) went to the US from Germany in 1835. His dry goods store founded in 1842 in Vincennes, Ind., served as the basis for a chain of stores, developed by his sons *JACOB G.* (1851–1922), *ISAAC G.* (1857–1931), *CHARLES G.* (1861–1932), and *ELLIS G.* (1865–1950) and grandsons, especially *BERNARD F. G.* (1885–1966) in the 20th century.

GIMMEL (ג): Third letter of the Hebrew alphabet; numerical value 3. Pronounced like *g* in *good* (by Yemenite Jews like *j*); when without *dagesh*, some communities sound it like the French *r* ("*gh*").

GINAEA see **JENIN**

GINNEGAR: Israel communal settlement (IK) in the Valley of Jezreel. It was founded in 1922 by pioneers of the Third Aliyah and is in the vicinity of the BALFOUR FOREST. Pop. (1972): 440.

GINNOSAR: Israel communal settlement (KM) on the W shore of the Sea of Galilee; founded in 1937. Pop. (1972): 411. A town of G. existed in talmudic times in the Vale of G. (or Ginossar) praised by Josephus for its fertility. It was still known in the Middle Ages. The Sea of Galilee was formerly called also Lake Gennesaret, after G.

GINSBERG see also **GÜNZBURG**

GINSBERG, ALLEN (1926–): US poet. Born in Newark, he became one of the outstanding literary figures of the "beat" generation. His best-known works include *Howl*, *Kaddish*, and *Sandwiches*.

GINSBERG, ASHER see **AHAD HA-AM**

GINSBERG, HAROLD LOUIS (1903–): US Semitic scholar. Born in Canada, G. went to the US in 1936 when he joined the faculty of Jewish Theological Seminary, New York, as instructor (later professor) in Bible. He has written extensively, notably studies on Ugaritic and contributions to biblical philology.

GINSBERG, MORRIS (1889–1970): British sociologist. He taught philosophy at Univ. College, London (1914–23) before being appointed professor of sociology at the London School of Economics in 1929. His publications deal with sociology and its psychological aspects.

GINSBURG, CHRISTIAN DAVID (1831–1914): Bible scholar. He was born in Warsaw, was baptized in 1846, and emigrated to England where he worked as a missionary. He re-edited the text of the Masorah, publishing it in 4 large volumes. In connection with this, he produced two editions of the Bible based on ms texts (1894, 1911) with an introduction (1897) and a series of facsimiles (1897–8). He also wrote commentaries on Ecclesiastes, etc. and studies on the Karaites, Essenes, and the Kabbalah.

GINSBURG, JEKUTHIEL (1889–1957): Hebrew writer and mathematician; founder and editor of *Scripta Mathematica* from 1932. Brother of Pesaḥ and Shimon GÜNZBURG. Born in Poland, G. went to the US in 1912, and was on the faculty of Yeshiva College (now Univ.) from 1928.

GINSBURG, SAUL (1866–1940): Journalist and scholar. His work on the Yiddish folk-songs of Russia (published jointly with Peretz Marek) is still one of the most comprehensive on the subject. In 1903, he helped found at St. Petersburg the first Yiddish daily in Russia, *Der Freint* (circulation 50,000), and subsequently edited Jewish historical periodicals. After the Bolshevik Revolution, he had access to the rich official archives in Russia. In 1930, he left Russia and in 1932, settled in the US. His *Historical Works* (3 vols., 1937) contains valuable material on 19th cent. Russian Jewry.

GINZBERG, LOUIS (1873–1953): Rabbinic scholar. Born in Lithuania, he settled in the US in 1899 and was a leading contributor to the *Jewish Encyclopedia* (1901–6). From 1902 until his death, he was professor of Talmud at the Jewish Theological Seminary. His earliest interest was in aggadah on which he published several outstanding works, notably *Die Haggada bei den Kirchenvätern* and the masterly compilation *The Legends of the Jews* (7 vols.). He made major contributions to the study of the Gaonic Period (*Gaonica* and *Genizah Studies in Memory of Solomon Schechter*) and the Palestinian Talmud (*Perushim ve-Ḥiddushim ba-Yerushalmi*, 3 vols.). Important shorter studies were collected in *Students, Scholars, and Saints* and *Jewish Law and Lore*. G. was one of the founders of the American Academy for Jewish Research and its president from 1929 to 1947. His son ELI G. (1911–) is a noted US economist; since 1935 professor at Columbia Univ. His works include *Human Resources, The Ineffective Soldier*, and *The Nation's Children* as well as a biography of his father *Keeper of the Law*.

GINZBURG, NATALIA (1916–): Italian author. Her novels, which tend to be pessimistic, are centered around characters who are often lonely and persecuted. The best-known one, *Family Sayings*, has an autobiographical theme. Of her plays, *The Advertisement* has been presented by the National Theatre in London.

GIRGASHITES: One of the seven peoples living in Canaan before its conquest by Joshua. It has been conjectured that they originated in Asia Minor.

GIRGENTI see **AGRIGENTO**

GISCALA see **GUSH ḤALAV**

GITTIN (Heb. "Bills of Divorcement"): Fifth tractate in the Mishnah order of *Nashim*, containing 9 chapters. It has *gemara* in both the Babylonian and Palestinian Talmuds. It deals with the laws of divorce (Deut. 24:1–4).

GIVAT BRENNER: Israel communal settlement (KM) in the Judean plain. It was founded in 1928 by pioneer immigrants from Lithuania and Central Europe, who developed a number of industrial undertakings and a convalescent home. Pop. (1972): 1,572.

GIVATAYIM: Israel township in the Judean plain E of Tel Aviv; created in 1942 by the unification of five suburbs. Pop. (1974): 49,900.

GLANZ, LEIB (1898–1964): Cantor. Born in Russia, he officiated as cantor from the age of eight. He went to the US in 1927 and in 1953, settled in Tel Aviv. A leading virtuoso-cantor, he composed many cantoral recitatives.

GLASER, DONALD A. (1926–): US physicist. Professor at the University of California, Berkeley, he was awarded the 1960 Nobel Prize in physics for his work on the development of the bubble chamber to photograph the atom.

GLASER, EDUARD (1855–1908): Bohemian explorer. Unsupported by any scientific institution. he made four journeys to Yemen between 1883 and 1894, during which he determined the location of Sanaa, thus providing the key to the position of other settlements on the Yemenite plateau. He discovered many inscriptions (including over 1,800 in Sabean), archeological remains, and ancient Arabic mss.

GLASER, JULIUS ANTON (1831–1885): Austrian jurist; baptized in his youth. He was minister of justice (1871–9), in which capacity he introduced a new penal code. He was later attorney-general at the Vienna Court of Cassation. G. was the author of many works on legal subjects.

GLASGOW: Town in Scotland. The first record of a Jew there dates from 1812, and a synagogue was established in 1823, but the rate of increase remained slow until the 1880's when many Jews from Russia settled in G. The Jewish population is estimated (1973) at 13,400 with about 15 synagogues. The early immigrants were concentrated in tailoring industries, but the economic basis of the community is now much wider.

GLATSTEIN, JACOB (1896–1971): Yiddish author and critic. Born in Lublin, he settled in the US in 1914. A gifted poet, he was among the founders of *Insich*, the poetic introspective current of the 1920's, editing a journal of that name. In his daily column in *Der Tog—Morgen Journal*, he dealt largely with current experiences in Jewish cultural life.

GLATZER, NAHUM NORBERT (1903–): US scholar. Born in Lemberg, he taught in Frankfort and in 1938 he went to the US where he was chief editor of Schocken Books and later professor at Brandeis Univ. His books include studies of Franz Rosenzweig and Leopold Zunz.

GLEANINGS: The remains of the crop (*leket*) after the harvest; these are left for the poor (Lev. 19:9–10; Deut. 24:20–21). The Book of Ruth (2:2) describes the gathering of the g. by the poor who followed the harvesters. The custom of leaving g. for the poor was also observed by Jews in Babylonia, although there the injunction had only rabbinic validity. The regulations for g. are to be found in the Talmud tractate *Peah*.

GLICENSTEIN, ENRICO (1870–1942): Artist. The son of a tombstone carver, he was born near Lodz, lived in Italy, and from 1928, in the US. Best known as a sculptor, he was also outstanding in etching (dry-points), pen drawing, and water color

Enrico Glicenstein: *The Pioneer*. Terra Cotta.

and was noted for some fine oil painting. His works are in leading galleries in many parts of the world. He was an ardent Zionist, and a museum in Safed containing his books was posthumously called after him. He was the father of the painter and sculptor Enrico Romano (1897–).

GLICK, HIRSCH (1922–1944): Yiddish poet. The youngest member of the Yiddish literary group *Yung Vilna*, he composed in the Vilna ghetto in 1943 the *Partizanenlied*, a testament of hope and heroism. Transported to the Esthonian concentration camp at Goldfield, he escaped to join the partisans but was never heard of again.

GLICKSON, MOSHEH (1878–1939): Hebrew author and Zionist leader. He was born in Lithuania and during World War I, edited the weekly (later daily) *Ha-Am* in Moscow and the Odessa miscellanies *Olamenu* and *Massuot*. He settled in Palestine in 1919 and was the chief editor of *Ha-Aretz* 1922–37. G. wrote monographs on Aḥad Ha-Am, Maimonides, etc.

GLOSSARIES: From R Gershom (10th cent.) onward, commentators on the Bible and Talmud have occasionally explained words by giving their equivalents in the vernacular language in Hebrew script. The habit seems to be restricted to Ashkenazi Jewry and may have been inspired by similar practices current among European Christians from before 700 CE. It lasted into modern times: *Kitzur Shulḥan Arukh* (1864) is still accompanied by such translations. They are called glosses (Heb. *leazim*). The most important glossator was Rashi who gives 967 glosses on the Bible and 2,190 on the Talmud; most of these are into French, but some are German. They form an important source for modern knowledge of Old French. Greek glosses are found in *Midrash Lekaḥ Tov* by Tobiah ben Eliezer. Biblical g., following the order of the text, were made in the later Middle Ages in French, Italian, etc., written in Hebrew characters.

GLOUCESTER: English port. A Jewish community existed there in the 12th–13th cents. and was the seat of an ARCHA. In 1168, one of the earliest Blood Accusations is recorded in G. The Jews were expelled in 1273, before the general expulsion from the country. A small community existed also in the 18th–19th cents.

GLÜCKEL OF HAMELN (1646–1724): German memoir-writer, living mainly in Hamburg. After her husband's death (1689), she eased her widowhood by writing her memoirs in Yiddish (English translation by Marvin Lowenthal, 1932). These charming reminiscences are valuable for the light they shed on contemporary German life, the status of women at that period, the circle of Court Jews and wealthy German merchants in the 17th cent., the impact of Shabbetai Tzevi, and the history of Yiddish.

Nelson Glueck.

GLUCKMANN, HENRY (1893–): S African physician. He lectured at Witwatersrand Univ. 1923–45, was elected to parliament in 1938, and was minister of health under Smuts, 1945–8.

GLUCKSTEIN: English family closely associated with the restaurant-chain catering organization, J. Lyons and Co. (1) *SIR LOUIS HALLE G.* (1897–) served in World War I and II and was Conservative member of parliament 1931–45. In 1968, he was chairman of the Greater London Council. (2) *SIR SAMUEL G.* (1880–1958) was mayor of Westminster 1920–1.

GLUECK, NELSON (1900–1971): US archeologist and educator. He directed the American School of Oriental Research at Jerusalem (1932–3 1936–40, 1942–7) and at Baghdad (1933–4). His topographical survey of archeological sites in Transjordan (*Explorations in Eastern Palestine*, 4 vols.) is a work of prime importance. One of his spectacular discoveries was the site of Solomon's mines at Ezion Geber. In 1952, he commenced an archeological survey of the Negev which disclosed the intensive settlement of that region in ancient times. In 1947, G. became president of the Hebrew Union College, Cincinnati (from 1950, of the merged Hebrew Union College—Jewish Institute of Religion). He was the author of studies of Transjordan, the Negev, the Nabateans, etc.

GLUECK, SHELDON (1895–): US criminologist. He has taught at Harvard Univ. since 1925 (professor since 1931). His specialties are psychoanalysis and correctional procedures.

GLUSBERG, SAMUEL see **ESPINOZA, ENRIQUE**

GNESEN see **GNIEZNO**

GNESSIN, URI NISAN (1879–1913): Hebrew novelist. He was born in Russia and led a life of wandering and frequently of hardship which brought on his early death. His most important literary output consisted of four stories with an autobiographical basis describing the psychological suffering of the rootless Jewish intellectual in the Russian Pale. G. also wrote poems and translated into Hebrew. His brother *MENAḤEM G.* (1882–1957), actor, was a founder of the HABIMAH Company. He lived in Palestine 1903–12 and from 1923.

GNIESSIN, MICHAEL FABIANOVICH (1883–1957): Russian composer. His early compositions were influenced by literary symbolism, many being characterized by pessimism and a preoccupation with death. In 1913, he founded the Society for Jewish Music, and continued his interest in Jewish folklore after the Russian Revolution. In 1936, he became professor at the Leningrad Conservatoire. His works include the operas *The Maccabeans* and *The Youth of Abraham*.

GNIEZNO (Ger. Gnesen): Polish town. Its medieval Jewish settlement was confined to a special "Jewish street." The economic position of the Jews deteriorated in the latter part of the 17th cent., but the community flourished under Prussian rule after 1793. It dwindled after G. was annexed to Poland in 1919 and by 1931 was non-existent.

GNOSTICISM (from Gk. *gnosis* "knowledge"): Religious movement, flourishing in the hellenistic East in the 2nd–3rd cents. Its origins (in the 1st cent.) are somewhat obscure, but it contained oriental mythological motives combined with Greek philosophical ideas having a monotheistic basis. According to the gnostics, the material world is not the work of a benevolent Creator but the result of a primeval fall, viz. the work of an intermediary fallen from the Divine sphere. G. is known mainly in its Christian form. References in Talmud and Midrash leave no doubt that gnostic DUALISM was regarded by the rabbis as a serious danger. Many polemical utterances against MINIM seem to refer not to Christians but to heretical gnostics. It is not known whether g. originally arose in Jewish circles or penetrated from outside, but further study of the Dead Sea Scrolls may throw more light on the subject. G., though extruded from official Judaism, continued to influence Jewish mysticism. It is a major element of the *Merkavah* mysticism of the tannaitic and later periods, of the classical KABBALAH (12th–13th cents.), and of Lurianic kabbalism (16th cent.).

*GOBINEAU, JOSEPH-ARTHUR, COMTE DE (1816–1882): French diplomat and traveler. His *Essai sur l'inégalité des races humaines* (1853–5) held that human races were unequal, the white race – especially the Nordic – being superior. Although G.'s attitude to the Jews was sympathetic, his book formed a basis for subsequent racialist ideology, including anti-Semitism.

GOD: The Supreme Being. Although the concept of a Creator G. is present in many primitive societies and although monotheistic tendencies have been at work in many polytheistic cultures, only the biblical idea of G. proved sufficiently dynamic and vital to survive and to impose itself on other civilizations; this was due to the extraordinary purity. power, and richness of the Hebrew idea. The biblical G. is already unique by virtue of His non-mythological character; He has no body, no kindred, no human needs. All depends on Him and He on nothing. In due course all the great phenomena of nature and life in which man experiences the Divine power were related to the one Creator and only G. Like every truly religious reality, G. was experienced as ambivalent, evoking different, even contradictory (i.e. complementary) responses; He is majestic and condescending, terrible and kind, destructive and loving, punishing and forgiving, etc. In His presence man feels lowly and humble, but man also seeks His nearness and the closest possible communion with Him (cf. e.g. the Psalms). G. is transcendent and non-human, but at the same time is intensely personal and voluntaristic. It is His will or "word" which in relation to nature is called Creation (see COSMOLOGY) and in relation to man is REVELATION. G. is thus not merely the Maker or First Cause (Deism) but the Lord of History and of the fate of all mankind as well as of every individual. The biblical concept of G. was not reached by rationalization or deduction, but by immediate experience and "pictorial thinking" (e.g., G. as father, king, lover, shepherd, etc.). Only under the impact of Greek PHILOSOPHY did Jewish thinkers, particularly in Alexandria, begin to translate traditional symbols into abstract terms. In this way the monotheistic tendencies of philosophy (first cause, cosmic principle, ultimate reality, etc.) crystallized; the coalescence of the two traditions proved of far-reaching consequence for western civilization as a whole. For the philosophers the Divine ATTRIBUTES (goodness, strength, greatness, etc.) posed a serious problem as they seemed to be modelled too closely on human forms of thought (ANTHROPOMORPHISM). They therefore stressed G.'s utter transcendence which can only be approached (though never completely) in the ecstasy of contemplation. The biblical anthropomorphic tradition was continued by the rabbis, who believed that only by adhering to such imagery would the full relevance and meaningfulness of the transcendent G. be brought out. On the one hand, the rabbis (in the Midrash and Aggadah) use different circumlocutions for G. in order to increase respect for His holy name (see GOD, NAMES OF); on the other, they were at pains to bring the Divine near to even the humblest heart and understanding. Thus, G. suffers together with His children, weeps over the destruction of the Temple, rejoices over piety and good works, takes part in learned discussions about points of ritual law, eagerly looks forward to receiving prayers, etc. More particularly He demonstrates moral values in order to teach His children the proper way of the "Imitation of G."; e.g. "even as He is merciful, so be ye merciful; even as He visiteth the sick, so go ye and visit the sick" (*Sotah* 14*a*). The rabbinic idea of G. is essentially the elaboration on a more popular and homiletic level of the prophetic concept (although the prophets, speaking at the time of Israel's greatness and decadence, preached judgment, whereas the rabbis, addressing a persecuted and harassed people, stressed the Divine love for Israel and the message of hope and comfort). The antidote to the popular tendencies of rabbinic teaching was provided by the medieval thinkers under the influence of the rediscovery and development of Greek philosophy by the Arabs. In the wake of the Moslem thinkers who examined their own faith in terms of the new philosophy, the Jewish theologians discussed fundamental Jewish beliefs in the light of Neoplatonism or Aristotelianism and with the rigorous discipline of philosophical logic. The greatest of medieval Jewish philosophers, Maimonides, was also the most extreme in his doctrine of Divine transcendence which actually denied the human capacity of saying anything meaningful about G. The existence of G., he thought, could be proved, but the meaning and nature of this existence were beyond human comprehension; everything man, or even Scripture, can say about G. is merely allegorical or negative. Other thinkers, like Judah Ha-Levi, felt the aridity of this philosophically purified and abstract G. and insisted on the vital experience of Divine action in history (e.g. the Exodus) as the basis of Jewish theology. Ha-Levi distinguished between the "G. of Aristotle" and the "G. of Abraham." An interesting, albeit difficult, attempt to overcome the tension between the transcendent, absolutely unique G. of philosophy and the vital, real and dynamic G. of religious experience was made in the medieval KABBALAH in its doctrine of the two aspects of the Godhead: the infinite, inaccessible "Mystery of Hiddenness" and the ten SEPHIROT or realm of Divine manifestation. This profound and daring conception often came under criticism for harbouring the seeds of heretical deviations. More recent Jewish speculation on G. is indebted to the problems posed and the terminologies provided by the various modern systems of philosophy. Thus there are theologies bearing the imprint of Kant, of Hegel, and – more recently – of existentialist thought. All these are of significance to JUDAISM (as distinct from their significance to philosophy as such) to the extent that they do not merely speculate about G. but attempt to relate the possibilities of contemporary thought to the fundamental experiences, attitudes, and symbols enshrined in Jewish religion and tradition.

GOD, NAMES OF: The most important of these are the names contained in the Bible; others arose later as a result of rabbinic, philosophical, and kabbalistic usage. Many words denoting G. are not names proper but circumlocutions or epithets used instead of a name. The most important are: *El* (etymology uncertain), occurring in all Semitic languages. In the Bible it appears relatively rarely for God but is an element in proper names (e.g., *El*eazar, Nethan*el*); *Eloah* (etymology uncertain), generally poetic, occurs far less frequently than its (probable) plural *Elohim* which is used both in the plural (for gods, idols, etc.) and singular (God). *YHVH* (the TETRAGRAMMATON or *Shem ha-Mephorash*) was the particular name of the God of Israel and occurs nearly 7,000 times in the Bible. Its original pronunciation is unknown (*Yahweh* has been conjectured). By the time of the Septuagint (2nd cent. BCE) it was no longer pronounced (except by the high priest on the Day of Atonement), but read as *Adonai* (Heb. "My Lord(s)"; hence the "Lord" YeHoVaH). The vowel points of this latter word were inserted in the name (thereby creating the English misnomer Jehovah). Sanctity subsequently became attached to *Adonai*; in writing (and printing), there are generally substituted for it two letters *yod* (ׯ) originally with a stroke between them, or else the letter *he* (ה) as an abbreviation of *Ha-Shem* (i.e. "The Name") or else the letter *dalet* (ד) from the second character of *Adonai*. *Yah* is probably an abbreviation of *Yhvh*, *Shaddai* (mainly poetical) is possibly of Akkadian origin. Other biblical terms include *Elyon* ("the Most High"), which was the Canaanite appellation for their supreme deity, *Kedosh Yisrael* ("The Holy one of Israel"), *Abbir Yaakov* ("Champion of Jacob"), and *Attik Yomin* (Aram. "Ancient of Days"), an apocalyptic term which occurs frequently in later literature, and was taken up by kabbalistic literature. Rabbinic names include *Ha-Makom* ("the place" i.e., of the *Shekhinah* ["Divine presence"]), *Ha-Kadosh Barukh Hu* ("the Holy One blessed be He"), *Ha-Gevurah* ("the Strength"), etc. Other names and appellations occur mainly in liturgical texts, e.g. *Ha-Raḥaman* ("the Merciful") or "Our Father in Heaven." A rich variety of other terms was coined by the medieval poets (*paytanim*) and kabbalists.

GODEFROI, MICHAEL HENDRIK (1813–1882): Dutch jurist and statesman. He was elected to the Dutch parliament in 1849, drafted a new juridical code for Holland (1860), and was minister of justice 1860–2. He used his influence to defend Jewish rights in countries trading with Holland.

GODOWSKY, LEOPOLD (1870–1938): Pianist and composer. Born in Vilna, he settled in the US in 1914. G. traveled widely as a virtuoso and was also renowned as a teacher. His son LEOPOLD G. JR. (1900–) is a noted violinist and a chemist who made important contributions to color photography.

*GOEBBELS, JOSEF (1897–1945): German Nazi leader. In 1933, with the Nazi accession to power, G. became minister of propaganda; one of his main tasks was the psychological preparation of Germany, and later of the conquered peoples, for the extermination of the Jews. He was one of Hitler's chief abettors in the extermination of European Jewry. He committed suicide with Germany's final defeat in World War II.

GOEL see AVENGER OF BLOOD

*GOERING, HERMAN (1893–1946): German Nazi leader. Responsible for Germany's war-economy, he was one of the chief executors of the spoliation of Jewish property, especially art treasures. He committed suicide shortly before the time fixed for his hanging as a WAR CRIMINAL.

GOG and MAGOG: King (Gog) and country (Magog) mentioned in the Bible (Ezek. 38–9). Ezekiel foretells the downfall of G. "in the latter years" after his attack upon the Land of Israel at the head of the armies of many peoples. The Talmud holds that the wars of G. and M. will precede the advent of the Messiah. The concept also figures in Christian and Moslem legend.

GOIDO, ISAAC (pseudonym: Bernard Gorin; 1868–1925): Hebrew and Yiddish author. He wrote first in Hebrew, but changed over to Yiddish and published at Vilna a series of popular Yiddish editions. In 1894, he settled in New York and introduced a realistic element into Yiddish literature in the US. G. was a theater critic and dramatist and wrote a history of Yiddish drama.

GOITEIN, SHELOMOH DOV (1900–): Historian, who left Germany for Palestine in 1923. He has lectured at the Hebrew Univ. and at the Univ. of Pennsylvania on the history of Islam and the Moslem peoples. He has specialized in the history of Yemenite Jewry and on the Cairo *genizah*.

GOLAH (Heb. "exile"; see DIASPORA; GALUT): Term applied to the collectivity of the Jewish people outside Palestine (originally to those of Babylonia).

GOLAN: (1) Ancient town of W Bashan; one of the cities of refuge (Josh. 20:8). It was the capital of a region in Second Temple times and had a Jewish settlement until the 5th cent. CE. (2) W region of Bashan, named after its chief town. It was known in Greek as Gaulanitis. Upper G. (called in the Bible Beth-Maachah), stretching from Mt. Hermon

Landscape in the Golan Heights.

Arthur Goldberg receives his Honorary Doctorate from the Hebrew University on Mt. Scopus, Jerusalem.

to the Sea of Galilee, was pasture land, sparsely populated, whereas Lower G. (the biblical Geshur) was rich and fertile until the Arab invasion. The Golan Heights from which the Syrians bombarded kibbutzim along the upper Jordan Valley, was occupied by Israel troops in the 1967 Six-Day War. Its population in 1968 was 6,400.

GOLD, ZE'EV (Wolf; 1889–1956): Zionist leader. He served as rabbi in various American towns and was a founder of the American *Mizraḥi* organization, becoming its president in 1931. G. settled in Palestine in 1935 and was a member of the Jewish Agency Executive from 1946. In 1955, he was elected joint president of the *Ha-Poel ha-Mizraḥi* and *Mizraḥi* World Center.

GOLDBERG, ABRAHAM (1883–1942): Journalist and Zionist leader. Born in Russia, he lived from 1901 in New York. He was co-founder of *Poale Zion* in the US, and editor of its paper *Freie Shtimme*. In 1909, G. became editor of the New York Zionist journal *Dos Yiddishe Folk*, and in 1920, of the Hebrew monthly *Ha-Toren*. He was one of the leaders of the Hebrew-speaking movement in the US.

GOLDBERG, ARTHUR JOSEPH (1908–): US labor leader. Born in Chicago, he became general counsel for the United Steel-Workers of America and the C.I.O. in 1948, was responsible for the merger of the C.I.O. and A.F.L., and was noted for his skill as arbiter in labor disputes. He was secretary of labor in the Kennedy administration

1960–2, Supreme Court justice 1962–5, and senior US delegate to the UN 1965–8. In 1968–9 he was president of the AMERICAN JEWISH COMMITTEE.

GOLDBERG, DOV BER (1801–1884): Scholar. Born in Poland, he devoted himself to the publication of Jewish mss stored in European libraries. For this purpose, he visited Berlin, Oxford, and London, and from 1852, resided in Paris. Besides his editions, he wrote many articles in contemporary Hebrew periodicals.

GOLDBERG, ISAIAH NISSAN see **YAKNEHAZ**

GOLDBERG, LEA (1911–1970): Hebrew poet. She was born in Kovno and settled in Palestine in 1935. Her poems from 1939 were greatly influenced by the European Jewish tragedy and were imbued with melancholy and disappointment, although possessing a positive message. G. was also a noted critic, particularly of drama, and a translator. Her play *Lady of the Castle* scored a success in Tel Aviv. She was appointed lecturer (subsequently, professor) in comparative literature at the Hebrew Univ. in 1957.

GOLDBERG, REUBEN LUCIUS ("Rube"; 1883–1970): US cartoonist. His work, often depicting ingeniously complicated inventions, appeared in hundreds of American newspapers.

GOLDBERGER, JOSEPH (1874–1929): US pathologist. He first proposed a successful cure for pellagra which he showed to be caused by diet deficiencies. Vitamin B_2 was discovered by him.

GOLDEN BOOK: Zionist roll of honor (instituted 1902), kept at the headquarters of the Jewish National Fund in Jerusalem. The inscribing of a name is accompanied by the donation of a fixed sum, raised by public subscription, etc., to the Fund.

GOLDEN CALF see **CALF, GOLDEN**

GOLDEN RULE: Term applied to the aphorism of Confucius (5th cent. BCE): "What thou dost not like when done to thyself, do not unto others." In Jewish lore, this was the reply of HILLEL when asked by a scoffer to condense the whole of the Torah in one sentence (*Shabbat* 31a). Jesus phrased the rule positively ("Do unto thy neighbor as thou wouldst be done by" – Matt. 7:12), in which form it is also found in contemporary Jewish literature (e.g. The Testament of Twelve Patriarchs, Tobit, etc.). The more succinct form, "Thou shalt love thy neighbor as thyself," quoted by Jesus from Lev. 19:18, was regarded by R Akiva as the fundamental rule of the Torah.

GOLDEN, HARRY (1902–): US editor and author. He published and edited *The Carolina Israelite*, (1941–68) excerpts from which appeared in *Only in America* and other books.

GOLDENBERG, ELIEZER (1846–1916): Russian socialist. Arrested while a student in St. Petersburg, he escaped to London where he was cofounder

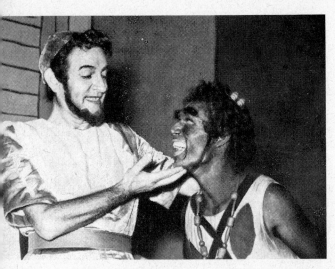

Scene from Abraham Goldfaden's *Shulamit* at the Ohel theater.

with Aaron Liebermann of the Society of Hebrew Socialists.

GOLDENTHAL, JACOB (1815–1868): Orientalist. From 1849, he was professor of Semitic languages and rabbinics at Vienna Univ. He edited medieval philosophical and rabbinic texts written by Jews in Arabic, and composed an Arabic primer in Hebrew.

GOLDENWEISER, ALEXANDER (1880–1940): Anthropologist. Born in Russia, he was in the US from 1900. After lecturing at Columbia Univ. and the New School for Social Research, New York, he became professor at the Univ. of Oregon (1930). His numerous works included studies of American Indian life.

GOLDFADEN, ABRAHAM (1840–1908): Founder of the Yiddish theater. In 1876, he set up in Rumania the first modern Yiddish theatrical company in which he served as actor, producer, and playwright. He traveled widely in Europe with the company and spent several years in the US where he died. G. wrote about 50 plays, many of them in the form of operas and operettas imbued with sentiment and imagination. His dramas (e.g. *The Witch, Shulamit, Bar Kochba*) reached all Yiddish-speaking centers, his arias (e.g. *Rozhinkes mit Mandlen*) becoming folk-songs and some of his types (*Shmendrick, Kuni Lemmel*) passing into popular speech. G. also wrote a Hebrew play *David at War.*

GOLDING, LOUIS (1895–1958): English novelist. He established a reputation by his war-poems and his novels of Manchester Jewish life such as *Forward from Babylon.* His *Magnolia Street* (1932) gave him a world-wide reputation. His later novels included the cycle beginning with *Five Silver Daughters.* He also wrote essays and travel-books, some dealing with Palestine (*Those Ancient Lands, In the Steps of Moses*) and the widely circulated *The Jewish Problem.*

GOLDMAN, EDWIN FRANKO (1878–1956): US conductor and composer; leader of the Goldman Band from 1919. G. wrote over 100 marches and other compositions for bands, etc.

GOLDMAN, EMMA (1869–1940): Anarchist. Long a stormy figure in the anarchist movement, she was deported from the US to her native Russia in 1919 for her pacifist activity during World War I. Afterwards, she left Russia and wrote on her disillusionment with it.

GOLDMAN, SOLOMON (1893–1953): US rabbi. Born in Russia, G. went to the US in 1900 and served as Conservative rabbi in Cleveland 1919–29 and Chicago 1929–53. He was president of the Zionist Organization of America 1938–40. His works included *The Jew and the Universe*, a study of Maimonides' philosophical system, and an unfinished series on the Bible.

GOLDMANN, NAHUM (1894–): Zionist leader. Born in Russia, he was educated in Germany and in 1923, helped to found the Eshkol Publishing Co., participating in the publication of the *Encyclopedia Judaica.* He represented the Jewish Agency at the League of Nations in Geneva 1935–9. G. became chairman of the executive of the World Jewish Congress and was its president from 1953. From 1949, he was joint chairman of the Jewish Agency, and in 1955–68, president of the World Zionist Organization. G. played a decisive part in reaching the REPARATIONS agreement with W Germany in 1952. In 1940, he settled in the US. later in Switzerland and Israel.

Nahum Goldmann.

GOLDMARK: (1) *KARL G.* (1830–1915): Composer. Born in Hungary, he lived in Vienna from 1850. Best-known for his opera *Die Königin von Saba*, he also wrote symphonies and chamber music. (2) *RUBIN G.* (1872–1913) US composer; nephew of (1). A noted teacher and lecturer, he was director of the composition department at the Juilliard School of Music, New York, from 1924.

GOLDSCHMIDT, LAZARUS (1871–1950): Orientalist and bibliophile. Of Lithuanian birth, he lived most of his life in Berlin but went to London after 1933. G.'s early work was on the Ethiopic language and literature. His greatest achievement was a complete translation of the Babylonian Talmud into German (9 vols., 1896–1936). He also wrote bibliographical studies. Much of his library, which included many incunabula, was purchased by the Royal Library, Copenhagen.

GOLDSCHMIDT, MEIR AARON (1819–1887): Danish physician, novelist and journalist. He founded, edited, and largely wrote the political and cultural journal *Nord og Syd*. G. wrote many novels and plays, mostly on Jewish subjects, and was largely responsible, with Georg BRANDES, for opening Danish intellectual life to modern ideas.

GOLDSCHMIDT, RICHARD BENEDICT (1878–1958): Zoologist and biologist. He was director of the Kaiser Wilhelm Institute for Biology at Berlin from 1921 until 1936 when he emigrated to the US, becoming professor of zoology at the Univ. of California. G.'s main research was on sex-determination, and he formulated the physiological theory of the genes, covering the concepts of gene, chromosome, and mutation.

GOLDSCHMIDT, VIKTOR MORITZ (1888–1947): Mineralogist and crystallographer. Professor at Oslo, he was smuggled to England after the German invasion of Norway (1940) and participated in atomic research. He is regarded as the father of modern geochemistry and explained the distribution of the chemical elements on the earth's surface.

GOLDSMID: English family of bankers and communal workers. Its founder *AARON G.* (d. 1781) settled in England before 1747. His two younger sons, *BENJAMIN G.* (1755–1808) and *ABRAHAM G.* (1756–1810), were among the leading members of the London money-market and played an outstanding role in the Jewish community. Both committed suicide. *ALBERT G.* (1794–1861), son of Benjamin, abandoned Judaism and rose to the rank of general in the army. *SIR ISAAC LYON G.* (1778–1859), grandson of Aaron G., made a large fortune, was created Baron de Palmeira in Portugal, 1846, and was the first Jewish baronet in England (1841). He was prominent in the struggle for Jewish political emancipation, and helped to found Univ. College, London (1825). His elder son, *SIR FRANCIS*

Sir Isaac Lyon Goldsmid.

HENRY G. (1808–1878) was the first Jewish barrister in England. *ALBERT EDWARD WILLIAMSON G.* (1846–1904) was descended from the family in the female line. A soldier by profession, he adopted Judaism only on reaching manhood. He was a leading member of the *Hoveve Zion*, and administered the Jewish colonies in Argentina 1892–4. He is said to have inspired George Eliot's *Daniel Deronda*. See also AVIGDOR-GOLDSMID.

GOLDSMITH, LEWIS (1763–1846): English writer. One of the first English political journalists, he was alternately or even simultaneously in the service of the British and French governments at the time of the Napoleonic wars. His daughter, Georgina (1807–1901), as Lady Lyndhurst, was a distinguished political hostess.

GOLDSTEIN, EUGEN (1850–1930): German physicist. He discovered canal rays and the second helium spectrum. His pioneer work influenced atomic research.

GOLDSTEIN, ISRAEL (1896–): US rabbi and Zionist leader. He served from 1918 as rabbi in Bnai Jeshurun Congregation, New York. G. was president of the Zionist Organization of America, the World Confederation of General Zionists, and the Jewish National Fund in the US. He is a member of the Jewish Agency Executive and was its treasurer 1948–9. He was also chairman of the Western Hemisphere Executive of the World Jewish Congress, president of the American Jewish Congress, cochairman of the United Palestine Appeal, and one of the sponsors of Brandeis Univ. (1946). In 1960,

Israel Goldstein.

he settled in Israel becoming chairman of *Keren Ha-Yesod* (until 1971). He wrote a *Century of Judaism in New York*, etc.

GOLDSTEIN, KURT (1878–1965): Neurologist and psychiatrist; settled in the US in 1935. He propounded the neurobiological theory known as "holism" which – in contrast to mechanism – conceives the mind as a single unit in all the functions of which the total personality is reflected. He summarized his philosophical views in *The Nature of Man*.

GOLDSTÜCKER, EDUARD (1913–): Czech literary historian. He was the first Czech minister to Israel, but in 1952 was accused at the SLANSKY trial and imprisoned for several years; rehabilitated in 1963. He was prominent in the 1968 liberalization movement when he became head of the Czech Authors Association but on the Russian invasion, went to England to lecture at the University of Sussex.

GOLDSTÜCKER, THEODOR (1821–1872): Sanskrit scholar. Leaving Germany for political reasons, he settled in London and was professor of Sanskrit at Univ. College 1851–72. His works include many studies on Sanskrit language, grammar, and literature.

GOLDWYN (originally Goldfish), **SAMUEL** (1882–1974): US film producer. He was an original partner in Metro-Goldwyn-Mayer (MGM) but later organized his own company, Goldwyn Productions Inc. G. introduced many leading stars to the screen.

GOLDZIHER, IGNAZ (1850–1921): Hungarian orientalist. From 1872, he taught at the Univ. of Budapest and from 1899, also at the Budapest Rabbinical Seminary. Specializing in the study of Islam, on which he was one of the greatest experts

of modern times, his main achievement was his research into the development of oral tradition (*ḥadith*) and his studies into the history of Koran exegesis.

GOLEM (Heb. "shapeless mass" – cf. Ps. 139:16): An automaton, especially in human form, unnaturally created by magical means, more particularly by the use of Holy Names. The concept is common to many ancient peoples. Its development among the Jews is associated with the magical interpretation of SEPHER YETZIRAH and with the belief in the creative power of the Holy Names. The Talmud relates stories of the creation of a g. (cf. *Sanhedrin* 65b), and they recur in Jewish literature from the 12th cent. on. The German Ḥasidim of the 12th–13th cents. regarded the creation of the g. as an ecstatic experience following a solemn ceremonial. From the 15th cent., the g. in Jewish legend (under the influence of alchemical beliefs) became a real, rather than symbolic, creature fulfilling tasks imposed upon it and also able to bring about destruction and ruin. Power to create an actual g. was ascribed to R Elijah of Chelm (16th cent.), and this story was later associated with the personality of R Judah Löw ben Bezalel of Prague (*Maharal*). The g. has been a favorite topic in Jewish literature; Leivik's play on this theme is well-known. The word is used in Yiddish for a stupid person.

Samuel Goldwyn.

GOLGOTHA (Aram. *Gulgulta*, "skull," i.e., skull-shaped hill): Place near Jerusalem in Second Temple times where Jesus was crucified (Matt. 27:33 etc.). It is also called Calvary (Luke 23:33). Its site has not been precisely identified but it is thought to have been NW of the city walls. The traditional Christian identification with the Church of the Holy Sepulcher is not generally accepted by scholars.

GOLIATH: Philistine giant from Gath slain by David in single combat (I Sam. 17; 21:10). According to another tradition, G. was killed by Elhanan the Bethlehemite (II Sam. 21–19).

GOLL, IWAN (1891–1949): Alsatian poet and novelist. He wrote expressionist poems in both German and French, some of them (*Naomi, Jean Sans Terre*) on Jewish themes. He translated Joyce's *Ulysses* into German. His wife *CLAIRE G.* (1901–) has written novels in French and German.

GOLLANCZ: English family of scholars, founded by *SAMUEL MARCUS G.* (1820–1900), *ḥazzan* of the Hambro Synagogue in London from 1854. Of his sons, *SIR HERMANN G.* (1852–1930) became a rabbi in London and was at the same time professor of Hebrew at Univ. College, London. He published a number of books on Hebrew and allied subjects. He was the first English rabbi to have been knighted. His younger brother, *SIR ISRAEL G.* (1864–1930), was an outstanding scholar in the realm of Anglo-Saxon and English literature, professor of English at King's College, London, 1905–30, and one of the foremost Shakespearian experts of his day. He was the organizer of the British Academy and its secretary from its foundation in 1902 until his death. *SIR VICTOR G.* (1893–1967), a nephew of Hermann and Israel G., was a successful publisher and leader of left-wing political thought in England.

GOLOMB, ELIYAHU (1893–1945): One of the creators of the HAGANAH. Born in White Russia, he settled in Palestine in 1909. During World War I, he helped to smuggle arms to the Jews in Palestine and was among the leaders of the movement to enlist in the British forces (1918). In 1921, he became a member of the Defense Committee of the *Histadrut* and in 1922–4, was in Europe procuring arms and educating pioneer youth. From 1931, he was the chief figure on the national command of the *Haganah*, establishing its broad popular basis. Responsible for the self-restraint policy of 1933–9 (HAVLAGAH), G. supported recruiting for the British forces in World War II but was also among the creators of the *Palmaḥ*.

GOLUS (Yidd. or Ashkenazi = *galut*): The DIAS-PORA, chiefly in the sense of oppression and denial of rights.

GOMBINER, ABRAHAM ABELE see **ABRAHAM ABELE OF GOMBIN**

GOMEL, BLESSING OF: Special blessing of thanks for personal deliverance from peril or illness, recited in the synagogue. It is said after being called up to the reading of the Torah. To the blessing, which thanks "Him Who recompenseth (*ha-gomel*) good to the undeserving," the congre-

Samuel Gompers.

gation responds: "May He Who gave you recompense of all good give you good recompense ever."

GOMEZ: Marrano family. Its members included *ANTONIO G.*, professor of medicine at Coimbra from 1584, penanced as a Judaizer by the Inquisition in 1619; and *ANTONIO ENRIQUEZ* (de Paz) *G.* (1600–1660), a popular playwright and poet in Spain who, after being burned in effigy by the Inquisition in 1660, openly returned to Judaism at Amsterdam. He was father of *DIEGO ENRIQUEZ BASURTO*, also a poet and playwright. *DUARTE G.* (d. 1608), martyr, who returned from Salonica to Portugal and taught his fellow-Judaizers there, was burned at an auto-da-fé. *VIOLANTE G.* (16th cent.) was mistress of the Infante Luiz of Portugal and thus mother of Don Antonio (d. 1595), pretender to the Portuguese throne. *DUARTE G. SOLIS* (16th–17th cents.) was an outstanding economist and author of a remarkable *Discourse on the Commerce of the Indies. LEWIS (LUIS) MOSES G.* (1654–1740), born in Spain or Portugal as a Marrano, emigrated via England to New York, arriving there in 1705. He prospered as an importer and exporter and also traded with the Indians. The house he built as a trading post near Newburgh is one of the oldest in the country. He helped acquire the site for the Mill Street Synagogue in New York in 1730. His great-grandson *BENJAMIN G.* (1769–1828) was the first Jewish bookseller in N America.

GOMORRAH: One of the five cities of the plain, destroyed in the time of Abraham. See SODOM.

GOMPERS, SAMUEL (1850–1924): US labor leader. London born, he went to the US in 1863, became active in the cigarmakers' union, and emerged as a leader of workers' rights. He was elected president of the newly-formed American Federation of Labor in 1886, and, with the exception of one year, held that office until his death, building it up into a powerful organization. His name has become synonymous with collaboration between labor-unions and employers.

GOMPERTZ: English family. In the first half of the 19th cent., four brothers attained distinction. *ISAAC G.* (1774–1856) was a poet and man of letters. *EPHRAIM G.* (1776–1867) was a political economist and mathematician. *BENJAMIN G.* (1779–1865), mathematician and actuary, became president of the Astronomical Society. He was the author of "Gompertz' Law," laying down the principles regarding the decline of resistance to death which became the foundation of the actuarial tables used by Life Insurance Companies. He also drafted a scheme of poor relief for the Jewish charities in London, *LEWIS G.* (1784–1861), a mechanical inventor, devoted his life to the welfare of animals on which he published various works. He was one of the founders of the Society for the Prevention of Cruelty to Animals and for a time, its honorary secretary, but was ejected when the Society was reorganized as a Christian body.

GOMPERZ: (1) *HEINRICH G.* (1873–1942): Philosopher; baptized son of (2). He was professor at the Univ. of Vienna until 1934 and then settled in the US. He wrote on epistemology, adopting an empirical attitude. (2) *THEODOR G.* (1832–1912): Historian of ancient philosophy. Professor of classical philology at the Univ. of Vienna from 1873, he wrote many studies, notably a 3-vol. work on Greek thinkers.

GOOD AND EVIL: In the Bible, it is GOD's will which determines G. and E. and the terms must consequently be understood as meaning "good or pleasing in the eyes of the Lord" and "evil and displeasing in the eyes of the Lord." G. and E. in a wider sense are what the Divine order has determined as ultimately advantageous or harmful to man (cf. Deut. 30:15. The story in Gen. 2–3 concerning the Tree of Knowledge of G. and E. is too obscure to allow safe interpretation). The metaphysical problem posed by G. and E. touches the roots of religion. In the view which considers all opposites or phenomena of variety to be mere illusion, the problem is merely denied. On the other hand, it is resolutely tackled by Zoroastrianism which poses two primeval principles (G. and E. = light and darkness) locked in mortal combat. DUALISM results from a logically consistent and ethically perfect good God. Judaism rejected this solution in the pointedly polemical utterance of Isaiah (45:7) "I form the light and create darkness; I make peace and create evil; I am the Lord that doeth all these things." Only in a monotheistic religion does the problem of the origin and continued existence of evil become acute. The God who tolerates evil can never be acquitted of complicity: either He is not omnipotent or else is not perfectly good. The answers to this dilemma vary from the simple and naïve assumption that evil, as suffering, is merely punishment for evil as wickedness (cf. the friends of Job who are reprimanded by God Himself), to the denial of evil as a positive reality, i.e., defining evil as the "absence of good" (as in Neoplatonism). Others again consider evil to be the result of a Divine self-limitation whereby God grants full freedom to His creatures. But freedom to do good also implies freedom to do evil and presupposes the reality of both alternatives. The profoundest and most daring treatment of G. and E. in Jewish theology was probably given by the kabbalists who taught that evil is ultimately grounded in the manifestations of the Divine essence known as the 10 SEPHIROT. If the *sephirah* of judgment is dissociated from other aspects (e.g. Divine mercy), the equilibrium is broken and evil manifests itself as an independent force. Kabbalistic speculations on evil were developed in Isaac LURIA's doctrine of the *kelippot* ("husks").

*GOODENOUGH, ERWIN RAMSDELL (1893–1965): US scholar. Professor of the history of religion at Yale from 1934, G. was an authority on hellenistic Judaism and on Philo and wrote a monumental work on *Jewish Symbolism in the Greek and Roman Period* (1954 ff).

GOODHART, ARTHUR LEHMAN (1891–): Jurist. Born in the US, he settled in England, teaching at Cambridge (1919) and becoming professor of jurisprudence at Oxford (1931). In 1952–63 he was master of Univ. College, Oxford, the first Jew to head an Oxford college. He has written on legal subjects and edited the *Law Quarterly Review*.

GOODMAN, BENNY (1909–): US musician. A popular band-leader and an outstanding jazz and swing clarinetist, G. is also noted for his performances of classical music. He wrote an autobiography *The Kingdom of Swing*.

GOODMAN, PAUL (1875–1949): British communal worker. He was secretary of the London Spanish and Portuguese Synagogue and active in Zionist politics and journalism, editing the *Zionist Review* from 1920. G. wrote many studies on Jewish topics.

GOODMAN, PERCIVAL (1904–): US architect and artist; since 1945, professor at Columbia Univ., New York. He has designed several synagogues.

GOOR (GRAZOVSKY), YEHUDAH (1862–1950): Hebrew lexicographer. Born in White Russia, he settled in Palestine in 1887 and was a pioneer in the direct method of Hebrew instruction. He was the author of numerous textbooks and of a standard Hebrew dictionary.

GORDIN, JACOB (1853–1909): Yiddish playwright. Under the influence of Tolstoy, he founded the sect of the *Bibleitzy* ("Bible brotherhood") preaching an ethical Judaism on scriptural foundations with practical expression in physical labor, primarily agriculture. Jewish circles looked on the sect as Christological and it broke up after the pogroms of 1881. G. then made an unsuccessful effort to found a Jewish agricultural colony in Russia and failed in a similar attempt in the US after settling there in 1891. In the US, he wrote over 80 plays, many of them adaptations, of uneven literary merit but of expert technique, which revolutionized the Yiddish theater.

GORDIS, ROBERT (1908–): US scholar; rabbi of Temple Beth El, Rockaway Park, New York, since 1931; associate professor of Bible at the Jewish Theological Seminary since 1941 and adjunct professor of religion, Columbia Univ. (1948–57). Among his published works are *Judaism for the Modern Age, Koheleth*, and a new edition of the Conservative prayer-book (1957).

GORDON, AHARON DAVID (1856–1922): Zionist philosopher. Born in Russia, he worked as an official on the estate of Baron Horace Günzburg and was an enthusiastic member of the *Hoveve Zion* movement. In 1904, he settled in Palestine and worked as an agricultural laborer in various settlements until his death at Deganyah. His teachings exerted a great influence in the Palestinian Jewish labor movement, especially the *Ha-Poel ha-Tzair* party. G. regarded physical labor as the basis of human existence. Culture is the elevated creation of man but, for various reasons, man has become removed from the source – i.e., nature – and culture now works to man's detriment. The solution is a return to a close association with nature. Labor is a psychological and spiritual necessity, a condition for the development of personality. To avoid exploitation, the soil and tools of work must not be the property of the individual; this change is to be accomplished not by altering the mechanics of economic life, as the Marxists advocate, but by a new attitude to work and the elimination of the passion for power. The nation, too, must liberate itself from the greed of exploitation and enrichment at the expense of other nations. Self-realization is the duty of every man, as influence can be exerted only by the living example and not by verbal precept.

GORDON, CYRUS HERZL (1908–): US orientalist. He has taught at several colleges including Dropsie College, Philadelphia, and Brandeis Univ. G. wrote the standard grammar and lexicon of UGARITIC (1947). In 1957, he claimed to have deciphered the "Linear A" Cretan script which he identified as a Semitic tongue. He traced connections between the early Semitic and Hellenistic cultures.

GORDON, DAVID (1831–1886): Hebrew journalist. He was born in Lithuania, and lived for a few years in England before settling at Lyck in E Prussia (1858) as editor of the Hebrew weekly *Ha-Maggid*. He already published Zionist articles in the 1860's and in the 1880's; *Ha-Maggid* became the mouthpiece of the *Hoveve Zion* movement (of which G. was a leader).

GORDON, LORD GEORGE (1751–1793): English agitator; convert to Judaism. Third son of the duke of Gordon, he entered parliament in 1774 and organized the Protestant Association to oppose the relief of Roman Catholic disabilities. In 1780, he headed a disorderly mob which presented a petition to Parliament. G. was tried for high treason but acquitted. In 1787, he adopted Judaism and lived an observant Jewish life. The following year, he

Aharon David Gordon.

Lord George Gordon.

was convicted of libeling the queen of France and sentenced to imprisonment. In Newgate prison, where he died, he surrounded himself with foreign Jews and held regular religious services in his apartments.

GORDON, JUDAH LÖB (known as *Yalag*; 1830–1892): Hebrew poet. As a young man, he was one of the leading *maskilim* in his native Vilna and from 1853 taught at Jewish government schools. His early works, e.g. the historical poem *Ahavat David u-Michal* ("The Love of David and Michal") bore a romantic stamp. He also published a collection of fables, mostly taken from La Fontaine and Krylov. His poem *Hakitzah Ammi* ("Wake, my people") became the credo of Russian Haskalah. Thereafter, the element of reproof and criticism increased in his

Judah Löb Gordon.

work and he attacked the supremacy of religion in Jewish life. A number of historical poems (e.g. *Ben Shinne Arayot* – "In the Lions' Teeth") marked the completion of the transition to realism and criticized Jewish communal organization. In 1872, G. went to St. Petersburg as secretary to the Jewish community; he was exiled for a few months in 1879 as a result of an accusation brought against him by the Hasidim and, though it was proved false, he was not reinstated in his post. Despair and disappointment characterize his subsequent work. G. was the creator of Hebrew realist poetry. His series of poems *Korot Yamenu* ("Events of our Days"), which includes such well-known works as *Kotzo shel Yod* ("The Point of a *Yod*") and *Shene Yoseph ben Shimon* ("Two Joseph ben Simons"), sarcastically attacks the Jewish pundits and privileged classes and expresses sympathy for underprivileged sections, especially the Jewish woman. G. made a great contribution to the revival

of Hebrew, using it precisely and realistically. He was also one of the first to write Hebrew novels and feuilletons.

GORDON, MICHEL (1823–1890): Writer. Always poor, he wandered through the Ukraine, earning his living as a private tutor. He wrote articles and books in Hebrew but was chiefly known for his humorous Yiddish folk poems, written in the spirit of the Haskalah.

GORDON, SAMUEL LÖB (known as *Shelag*; 1867–1933): Hebrew author and Bible commentator. He lived most of his life in Warsaw but was in Palestine from 1898 to 1900 and after 1924. G. was one of the first teachers to introduce spoken Hebrew into Diaspora schools and edited Hebrew youth journals. He published Hebrew poems and translations from world literature. His main achievement was the publication of the Bible with his own popular commentary in which he took account of the views of textual critics.

GORDONIA: Pioneer scouting youth movement, called after A.D. GORDON. Founded in Poland in 1925, it spread to other countries and in 1928, held a world conference at Danzig. Ideologically, it was identified with the HA-POEL HA-TZAIR party in Palestine and the HITAHDUT in the Diaspora, its aim being education and the realization of labor Zionism. Members of the movement founded several settlements in Israel, now its headquarters, where it is part of HA-TENUAH HA-MEUHEDET—HA-BONIM.

GOREN, SHELOMO (1918–): Israel rabbi. He was a member of the *Haganah* and with the establishment of the Israel ·Defense Forces was appointed chief chaplain. In this capacity he was responsible for decisions concerning the duties of the religious soldier and he set up the army's religious services. In 1968 he was elected chief rabbi of Tel Aviv and in 1972 chief rabbi of Israel.

*GORGIAS (fl. 2nd cent. BCE): Syrian commander. He was defeated by Judah the Maccabee near Emmaus (166) and fled westward where he repelled an attack by Judah's commanders. He opposed Judah again in an indecisive battle in Edom (165).

GORIN, BERNARD see **GOIDO, ISAAC**

GOSHEN: Fertile district of ancient Egypt, allotted by Pharaoh to Joseph's family (Gen. 47:6, 11). It is thought to have been situated E of the Nile delta.

GOSPELS: The four books of the NEW TESTAMENT which relate the life and teachings of JESUS. The first three books (Matthew, Luke, and Mark) are called the Synoptic G. and deal with the narrative material from similar viewpoints; Mark is regarded as the most authentic while the fourth book, John, is the latest. The G. throw much light on Palestinian Jewish conditions in the 1st cent. CE. Matthew is traditionally believed to have been composed originally in Hebrew (though modern scholars tend to question

Maurycy Gottlieb: *Self Portrait.*

this) and Hebrew versions of all have been published since the 16th cent.

GOTTHEIL: (1) *GUSTAV G.* (1827–1903): Rabbi. A Prussian by birth, he received his academic and rabbinic training at Berlin where he entered the ministry as assistant to Samuel Holdheim. From 1860–73, he was rabbi of the Reform congregation in Manchester. He then went to New York, first as assistant to, then as successor of, Samuel Adler in the rabbinate of Temple Emanu-El. He was active in the promotion of Zionism in America. His *Sun and Shield*, an anthology of Jewish teachings, is one of the earliest publications of its kind to appear in the US. (2) *RICHARD JAMES HORATIO G.* (1862–1936): Orientalist and Zionist; son of (1). Born in Manchester, England, he went to New York with his parents in 1873. In 1886, he was appointed lecturer, later professor, of Semitic languages at Columbia Univ. and from 1896, headed the oriental department of the New York Public Library. Active in Zionism, he was the first president (1898–1904) of the Federation of American Zionists and attended several of the early Zionist Congresses.

GOTTLIEB: (1) *LEOPOLD G.* (1883–1934): Painter. He was born in Galicia and settled in Paris in 1908. His landscapes and figure (especially female) compositions were famous. (2) *MAURYCY G.* (1856–1879): Painter; brother of (1). He lived in Lvov, Vienna, Munich, and Cracow. He succeeded in completing only a fraction of his paintings, many of which are on Jewish themes. G. also painted Christian subjects, scenes from Polish history, portraits, and genre-pieces. He was one of the outstanding Jewish artists of the 19th cent.

GOTTLOBER, ABRAHAM BÄR (pen-name Mahalalel; 1810–1899): Hebrew and Yiddish author. He wandered through E Europe and died in poverty at Bialystok. G. wrote poems, drama, works on the history of the Karaites, Kabbalah, and Ḥasidism (mostly re-editions of scholarly German works), stories, memoirs, and translations. He published the monthly *Ha-Boker Or*, first at Lvov, later at Warsaw. After the 1881 pogroms, he joined the *Ḥoveve Zion* and was the author of Zionist poems.

GOTTSCHALK, MAX (1889–): Belgian educator and social worker. He played a prominent role in refugee work in Belgium until World War II. For nine years he served on the research staff of the American Jewish Committee in New York, and then returned to Belgium where he became professor of sociology at Brussels Univ. He has been president of the International Association of Social Progress and is president of the Brussels National Center of Jewish Studies.

GOUDCHAUX, MICHEL (1797–1862): French statesman. A banker by profession and an adherent of the republican opposition, he was twice minister of finance after the 1848 Revolution. Elected a deputy in 1857, he refused to take an oath to the emperor Napoleon III and was therefore excluded from the Chamber. He devoted his last years to philanthropic activities, especially in behalf of the Jewish community in his native town of Nancy.

GOULD, MORTON (1914–): US musician. He has conducted orchestras for the leading radio networks in the US and has composed symphonies, concertos, scores for musical revues and films, and semi-popular music.

GOULD, SAMUEL B. (1910–): US educator. Born in New York, G. was professor of radio and speech at Boston Univ. (1947–53), president of Antioch College 1954–8, chancellor of the University of California, Santa Barbara, 1959–62, and president of New York Univ. 1964–70. G. became a Christian while a college student.

GOY (Heb.): Non-Jew. Originally meaning a nation, the word was later applied in the plural (*goyyim*) to the (gentile) nations of the world.

GRACE AFTER MEALS (to say g. is known popularly among Ashkenazim as to *"bentsh"*): Blessing recited after meals, considered a biblical injunction on the basis of Deut. 8:10. The rabbis laid down that the eating of food the size of an olive or greater, should be followed by grace. The halakhic requirement limits the obligation to a meal including bread with which it is therefore customary to commence. If only fruit or certain cooked food is eaten, a shorter version of grace is said. The rabbis established three blessings to be recited as grace. After the destruction of the Temple, a fourth blessing was added (*hatov-vehametiv*) having only rabbinic compulsion. The oldest extant formulation of the grace after meals is that found in the prayer book edited by Saadyah Gaon (later adopted by Maimonides). This seems to follow the early Palestinian ritual. The version found in the prayer book of Amram Gaon belongs to a fuller formulation; after undergoing further amplification, this passed into all rituals. Grace must be recited at the place where the meal has been consumed. Three or more males who have eaten together are required to say grace as a group. One leads by inviting his companions to join in the blessing; this is called *zimmun* ("invitation"). The invitation formula is: "Let us Bless Him from Whose food we have eaten." The reply given by the others is: "Blessed be He from Whose food we have eaten." Where there are ten or more males the words "our God" are introduced into both invitation and reply formulas. Poetic versions of the grace have been found in the *genizah* and a much shortened form (originally for children) is widely used. The grace is preceded on weekdays by Ps. 137 and on Sabbaths by Ps. 126. At circumcisions and wedding feasts, poetic additions are made. There is a special form of the fourth blessing, in a house of mourning.

GRADE, ḤAYYIM (1910–): Yiddish poet. A native of Vilna, he headed the group of young Yiddish poets called "Young Vilna." In 1941, he escaped to the USSR and reached New York in 1948. His poetry mainly reflects the former traditions of Polish Jewry.

GRADIS: Family of 18th cent. French traders of Spanish origin. *DIEGO RODRIGUES G.* (fl. mid-17th cent.), born in Bordeaux, was the family's founder. His son, *DAVID G.* (1665–1751), bought his own ships which traded with the French possessions in the Caribbean. David's son, *ABRAHAM G.* (1699?–1780), extended the trade to Canada where he organized *La Société du Canada*. During the Franco-British wars, he provided the French in Canada with food, often saving them from starvation. His ships brought valuable war supplies to the French

and he was active in the exchange of French prisoners held in England. Uprisings in the French West Indies and the French Revolution brought about the downfall of the house although the family retained its prominence in Bordeaux.

GRADNAUER, GEORG (1866–1946): German socialist leader. He was a Saxon deputy in the German Reichstag 1898–1928, and edited the *Dresdner Volkzeitung* 1906–18. He was a member of the Saxon cabinet from 1918 to 1921 when he entered the Reich government as minister of the interior.

GRAETZ, HEINRICH (1817–1891): German historian and Bible scholar. From 1854, he lectured in Jewish history at the Breslau Rabbinical Seminary and from 1869, also at Breslau Univ. His great *History of the Jews*, which appeared in 11 volumes (1853–75), was based on all authorities available at the time (including many ms sources), scientifically treated and presented in a fluent, literary style. The influence of this work on subsequent Jewish historians – even those who disagreed with G.'s historical approach — was immense. He emphasized the phenomena of Jewish suffering and stressed Jewish national aspirations and devotion to the Torah. His lack of sympathy with mysticism (e.g., Kabbalah and Ḥasidism) is readily apparent. In addition, his characteristic continental 19th cent. prejudices led him to overestimate the tranquillity of Jewish life in the Moslem as opposed to the medieval Christian world. He also paid too little attention to economic and social factors. Nevertheless, his history remains one of the most remarkable products of a single

Heinrich Graetz.

individual in the entire course of Jewish literature. G. also wrote Bible studies and edited (1869–87) the *Monatsschrift für die Geschichte und Wissenschaft des Judentums* in which he published hundreds of studies.

GRAMMAR see **HEBREW LANGUAGE**

GRAMMARIANS: Some knowledge of Hebrew grammatical categories was found among the amoraim. Later, the study of grammatical forms went hand in hand with the establishment of a standard Bible text by the MASORETES. They recorded their findings partly in mnemonic aphorisms and in lists of passages which exhibit similar peculiarities. Some old treatises, e.g. *Dikduke ha-Te'amim*, are based on their work which shows points of contact with the grammatical science of the E Syrians. The great achievements of Arabic philology in the 8th–9th cents. served as a model for Hebrew scholars, beginning with SAADYAH GAON (d. 940) in Babylonia and MENAHEM BEN SARUK and DUNASH BEN LABRAT (both 10th cent.) in Spain. The dependence of Hebrew philology on Arabic is limited by the fact that accidence is the least developed field with the Arabs, while the highly refined methods of Arabic syntax dealt with cases and moods which do not exist in Hebrew. A sound basis for Hebrew grammar was created by the discovery of the triliteral nature of weak roots by Judah ḤAYYUJ of Fez, and the elaboration of his system by Jonah IBN JANAḤ of Cordova (both 10th–11th cents.). The conclusions of these and numerous other Spanish Hebrew g. (who mostly wrote in Arabic) were systematized by Abraham IBN EZRA (d. 1167) in a series of short handbooks and by David KIMḤI (d. 1235) in his *Mikhlol*. Apart from the philosophical grammarian Profiat DURAN (fl. c. 1400), all grammatical writers until modern times adapted old material. In NW Europe, too, there was a school of g. mainly concerned with fixing the correct biblical readings, among them being the English Jew Moses ben Isaac Ha-Nessiah (13th cent.). Some Christian scholars in the Middle Ages knew Hebrew, but the first grammar (based on Kimḥi) by a non-Jewish scholar was that of J. REUCHLIN (1506). The Italian Jewish scholar Elijah LEVITA (d. 1549) did much to acquaint Christians with the work of Hebrew g. Between J. BUXTORF (d. 1629) and W. GESENIUS (d. 1842), many grammars were written but no progress achieved. Modern scientific Hebrew grammar began with Gesenius' *Elementarbuch* – in its 2nd English ed. (1910) still the standard work. Since then, the use of the comparative method (first employed by Judah IBN KURAISH in the 9th–10th cents.) and modern descriptive methods have made biblical Hebrew one of the best-studied languages. The grammatical study of mishnaic Hebrew began in 1822, and was put on a scientific basis by M. H. SEGAL (1927); the

first grammar of medieval Hebrew was written by M. Goshen-Gottstein (1951). Apart from numerous school grammars, the works of M.B. Sznejder (1923, 1939), D. Yellin (1942), Y. Livni (1951), and Z. Har-Zahav (1951, etc.) are the first attempts in Israel to deal in a more ambitious way with the Hebrew language as a whole.

GRANADA: City in S Spain. Jews are said to have garrisoned G. after the Arab invasion of 711 CE. The community rose to importance in the 11th cent. when it was the residence of SAMUEL IBN NAGRELA, who was vizier to the king of G. The Jews, however, shared the unpopularity of Samuel's son and successor Joseph, and were attacked and expelled on his downfall in 1066. Though the community later re-established itself, it was again uprooted by the Almohadan invasion (1144) and never again achieved importance. The expulsion of the Jews from Spain was decreed from G. in Mar. 1492.

GRAND RAPIDS: City in Michigan, US. Its Jewish settlement dates from 1852. In 1857, a benevolent and burial society was formed, and in 1871, the first Reform congregation, Emanuel, was organized. G. R. also has an Orthodox synagogue. The Jewish Community Fund of G. R. was founded in 1940. Jewish pop. (1973): 1,500.

GRANDVAL (originally Hirsch-Ollendorf), **GILBERT** (1904–): French administrator. A leader of the French resistance movement during World War II, he governed the Saar 1945–55 and was resident-general in Morocco, June-Aug. 1955. In 1962–6, he was minister for foreign trade.

GRANOTT (GRANOVSKY), AVRAHAM (1890–1962): Zionist leader. Of Bessarabian birth, he settled in Palestine in 1922 and in 1934, was appointed managing director of the Jewish National Fund, in 1945, chairman of its board of directors and in 1960, president. He sat in the Knesset as a Progressive member 1949–51. G. published works on aspects of land settlement in Israel.

GRATZ: Family distinguished in the early history of the US. The family business and name were first established by two brothers who emigrated to the US from Germany: *BARNARD G.* (1738–1811) and *MICHAEL G.* (1740–1811) who engaged in coastal shipping and interior trading. They became suppliers and financiers of the revolutionary cause. Both were active in Jewish communal affairs in Philadelphia. Their published correspondence is of great importance for 18th cent. American economic and social history. Of Michael G'.s 12 children, best known were *HYMAN G.* (1776–1857) whose trust fund was responsible for the establishment of GRATZ COLLEGE in 1893; *REBECCA G.* (1781–1869), founder of the Jewish Sunday-school movement in the US (at Philadelphia) who was said to have been the prototype for Sir Walter Scott's

Rebecca Gratz.

characterization of Rebecca in *Ivanhoe*; and *JACOB G.* (1790–1856), merchant, who entered politics and served in both the Pennsylvania State Legislature and State Senate.

GRATZ COLLEGE: First Jewish teachers' training college in the US. It was founded in Philadelphia in 1893 and named for Hyman GRATZ who had helped endow it. There are two departments: the Normal Dept. (for instruction in Judaica in English) and a College Dept. which prepares students for the degree of Bachelor of Hebrew Literature. A preparatory school trains pupils for higher Hebrew studies. Principals of G. C. have included Julius H. Greenstone and William Chomsky.

GRAVES see **BURIAL; CATACOMBS; EPITAPH; OSSUARIES; TOMB**

GRAYZEL, SOLOMON (1896–): US scholar. A native of Russia, he went to the US in 1908. He was rabbi in Camden NJ 1921–6 and registrar of Gratz College 1928–43. He was editor of the Jewish Publication Society 1939–67. His publications include *The Church and the Jews in the 13th Century* and A *History of the Jews*.

GRAZ: Austrian provincial city; former capital of Styria. Jews settled there in the 13th cent., and in the 15th there was a flourishing community (interrupted 1439–47) until 1496. A new community was organized in 1867, and destroyed by the Nazis. Before 1938 there were 2,000 Jews in G.

GREAT ASSEMBLY (Heb. *Keneset Gedolah*): The institution which embodied the spiritual leadership of the Jewish people at the beginning of the Second Temple Period and constituted the supreme authority in matters of religion and law. It was considered the link between the last of the prophets and the first of the rabbis. The size and composition of the G. A. varied from time to time; legendarily, it had 120 members drawn from the most prominent Jewish scholars of the period (known as "the men of the G. A."), who drew up *inter alia* the main text of the accepted liturgy. The body is perhaps to be identified with the G. A. of the people in the Temple Court, presided over by Ezra, which accepted the binding authority of the Torah (Neh. 8–9).

GREAT BRITAIN see **ENGLAND; SCOTLAND; WALES**

GREECE (Heb. *Yavan*): Country in SE Europe. The Jews seem to have come into contact with the inhabitants of G. in biblical times, and it is certain from inscriptions, etc. that they were settled on the Greek mainland by the 2nd cent. BCE. In the 1st cent. CE, synagogues and organized communities were found by the apostle Paul in all the principal cities. They suffered the same vicissitudes as Jews in the remainder of the BYZANTINE EMPIRE, attempts to enforce wholesale conversion being made from the 7th cent. Benjamin of Tudela (c. 1165) found Jews in many parts of the country engaged largely in silk-weaving, with some in agriculture. At the end of the 15th cent., the vast influx of refugees from Spain overwhelmed the local communities which lost their former character and became henceforth entirely Sephardi in culture. Only in CORFU was the original Greek rite of prayer ultimately preserved.

Greek rite. (Miniature from the Corfu Maḥzor [1700] for Tabernacles).

Hayyim Greenberg.

SALONICA attracted the greatest number of new settlers, but there were many other communities, especially in the seaports. The kingdom of G., created in the early 19th cent., had small and unimportant Jewish communities in ATHENS and elsewhere which suffered from intermittent anti-Semitic attacks. The capture of Salonica in 1912 brought under Greek rule one of the largest Jewish communities of the Mediterranean. The subsequent interchanges of population between Greece and Turkey reduced the proportionate importance and economic value of the Jewish element. In the period of the German occupation of G., wholesale deportations took place (1941–3), many communities losing up to 90% of their numbers, and the losses amounting to 60,332 out of a former total of 76,420. The community of Salonica, reduced to 1,300, now lost its importance. Over 2,000 Greek Jews immigrated to Israel after the establishment of the state. Jewish pop. (1973): 6,500.

GREENBERG, ḤAYYIM (1889–1953): Labor Zionist theoretician and journalist; of Russian birth. In 1921–4, he edited in Berlin, *Ha-Olam*, the official organ of the World Zionist Organization. After his arrival in the US in 1924, he edited the *Yiddisher Kemfer* (1924–53) and the *Jewish Frontier* (1934–53), both issued by the Labor Zionist Organization of America. G. was a member of the Jewish Agency Executive from 1946 until his death.

GREENBERG, HENRY ("Hank"; 1911–): US baseball player. During his career he played for the Detroit Tigers and Pittsburgh Pirates ball clubs, and was later a manager and owner.

GREENBERG, LEOPOLD (1885–1964): S African jurist. In 1924, he was appointed a judge (from 1938, judge-president) of the Transvaal Supreme Court and in 1943–55, was judge of the S African Court of Appeal.

GREENBERG, LEOPOLD JACOB (1861–1931): British journalist and Zionist leader. An advertising agent active in Jewish communal life, he became one of Herzl's most devoted adherents, representing him in negotiations with British statesmen, serving on the commission which investigated the EL ARISH scheme, and initiating the negotiations with Chamberlain over the UGANDA offer. G. was among the founders of the English Zionist Federation. In 1907, he became editor of the London JEWISH CHRONICLE which he converted into a militant, though unattached, Zionist organ, thus helping to create in England the atmosphere which elicited the BALFOUR DECLARATION. G. later fought violently against the policies of Weizmann, especially the enlarged Jewish Agency and the acceptance of the Churchill WHITE PAPER. His son, IVAN MARION G. (1896–1966), edited the *Jewish Chronicle* 1936–46.

GREENBERG, URI TZEVI (1894–): Hebrew poet. Born in Galicia, he wrote mostly in Yiddish until 1923, when settling in Palestine, he devoted himself entirely to Hebrew. He was associated with the Third Aliyah pioneers and wrote for the labor press. In 1928, an ideological change is discernible in his writings, as a result of his disappointment with the official Zionist movement. His poetry was now

Uri Tzevi Greenberg.

exclusively topical and G. became one of the central personalities and intellectual spokesmen of the Revisionist movement. His main work of this period was *Sepher ha-Kitrug veha-Emunah* ("Book of Indictment and Faith," 1937), an attack on the Jewish Agency's policy of *havlagah* ("self-restraint") and an exposition of his vision of a fighting Jewish youth. G. supported the underground movements which fought the British in Palestine and was himself a *Herut* member of the First Knesset (1949–51). After World War II, he published many poems on the European Jewish catastrophe, most of which were collected in *Reḥovot ha-Nahar* ("Streets of the River").

GREENSTONE, JULIUS HILLEL (1873–1955): US educator and author. Born in Russia, G. taught at Gratz College, Philadelphia, 1905–33 and was its principal 1933–45. His publications include *The Messiah Idea in Jewish History, The Jewish Religion*, and commentaries on *Numbers* and *Proverbs*.

GREETINGS: A normal greeting in the biblical period, as illustrated in Ruth 2:4, was "The Lord be with you," the answer being: "The Lord bless you." *Shalom Aleikhem* ("Peace be with you") with the answer *Aleikhem Shalom*, later became usual; it was prescribed when two men had not seen one another for three days, and became the formula by which Jews identified one another in a gentile environment. (A similar form exists in Arabic). The shorter *Shalom* ("Peace") is used in Israel on all occasions. On the Sabbath, *Shabbat Shalom* ("A Sabbath of Peace") is universal, though among the Ashkenazim *Gut Shabess* ("Good Sabbath") is commonly heard, while on festivals their *Gut Yomtov* ("Good Festival") has as its Israel equivalent *Ḥag Sameaḥ* or *Moadim le-Simḥah*, all with a similar meaning. The New Year greeting is "May you be inscribed for a Good Year." On *Av* 9 and in the house of mourning, any greeting is discouraged. Specific g. in Hebrew are usual on the completion of a religious duty (e.g. being summoned to the reading of the Torah); among the Ashkenazim *Yishar* (or *Yeyasher*) *Koaḥ* ("May [your] strength increase"), and among Sephardim *Ḥazak Barukh* ("[Be] strong, blessed").

*GREGOIRE, HENRI (Abbé Grégoire; 1750–1831): French ecclesiastic and politician. He wrote a famous essay advocating Jewish Emancipation, and as a member of the Revolutionary Assemblies from 1789 played an important part in procuring equal rights for Jews (1790–1).

*GREGORY I: Pope, 590–604. He rigidly enforced canonical anti-Jewish restrictions, strongly objected to the observance of any ceremony that savored of Judaism, and approved the initial stages of the reaction against the Jews in Spain under the Visigoths. On the other hand, he insisted that the Jews be treated with humanity, condemning forced baptism and the destruction of synagogues. G.'s Jewish policy in both aspects set the model for that of the medieval papacy as a whole.

GREGORY, SIR THEODOR (1890–1971): British economist. He taught at the London School of Economics from 1913 (dean, 1927–30) and at London Univ. 1927–37. He then served as economic adviser to the government of India and as British representative on the Greek Currency Committee. His principal publications deal with banking and tariffs.

GREIDIKER, EPHRAIM (middle 18th cent.): Jewish folk-jester in Poland. His jokes were partly influenced by German and Italian motifs and greatly resemble those of the German folk-hero Till Eulenspiegel although possessing a pronounced Jewish coloring.

GREINER, LEO (1876–1928): Austrian author. He wrote poems and plays, compiled anthologies, and edited German literary journals.

GRODNO: Polish town. Its Jewish community dated from the 14th cent. and in the 17th cent., was reckoned with Brest-Litovsk and Pinsk as one of the three chief communities of Lithuania. It was the seat of many distinguished rabbis and in 1789, the first Jewish printing press in the country was set up there. On the Russian conquest in 1793, Jews constituted 85% of the 4,000 inhabitants. Economic conditions grew less favorable from the close of the 19th cent. and before World War II, the Jewish community of 20,000 represented 30% of the population. The Nazis herded c. 40,000 Jews (including those from neighboring centers) into two ghettos in G. whence they were deported to their deaths in 1942–3.

GRONINGEN: Town in Holland. Jews lived there in the 16th cent. but were generally excluded, and no permanent community was established until c. 1733. In the mid-19th cent., a Reform synagogue existed for a time. The community, once of 2,500, numbered 150 in 1970.

GROPPER, WILLIAM (1897–): US artist distinguished for his incisive social satire. His lithographs, paintings, and murals are to be seen in many Amercian museums and public buildings.

GROSS, CHAIM (1904–): US sculptor. Born in Carpatho-Russia, he has lived in the US since 1921. G. is particularly noted for his wood sculpture.

GROSS, CHARLES (1857–1909): US historian; taught at Harvard from 1888. An outstanding authority on medieval English administrative and economic history, he also wrote on the EXCHEQUER OF THE JEWS.

GROSS, HEINRICH (1835–1910): Scholar. Born in Hungary, he was rabbi at Augsburg from 1875 until his death. He specialized in medieval French Jewish texts, his main work being *Gallia*

Judaica (1897), a topographical encyclopedia of French Jewish literary history.

GROSSMAN, ELIAS MANDEL (1898–1947): US artist. A native of Poland, he went to the US in 1911. Virtually all his themes are drawn from Jewish life.

GROSSMAN, MEIR (1888–1964): Zionist leader; of Russian birth. He collaborated with Jabotinsky in founding the Jewish Legion during World War I, and subsequently was a leader of the Revisionist and Jewish State parties. In 1953, he joined the General Zionists. He settled in Palestine in 1934 and was a member of the Jewish Agency Executive 1948–61.

GROSSMAN, VASILY SEMYONOVICH (1905–1964): Russian novelist. After working as an engineer in the Donbas area, he established his reputation with a novel on the life of the miners in that region. His trilogy *Stefan Kolchugin* and his story *The Old Miner* are of Jewish interest. After World War II, he wrote an epic novel about the defense of Stalingrad.

*GROTIUS, HUGO (1583–1645): Dutch jurist and Bible commentator. In 1615, he composed a report on the conditions under which refugee Jews might be allowed in the United Provinces, and this provided the basis for their ultimate communal organization. In 1640–4, while ambassador of Sweden at Paris, he published his commentary on the Old and New Testaments which displayed a considerable knowledge of Judaism and Jewish sources, partly derived from his friend Manasseh ben Israel. In 1636, he scathingly denounced the Lublin Blood Libel trials.

GRUENBERG, LOUIS (1884–1964): US composer. His works include operas (*Jack and the Beanstalk, Emperor Jones*), occasional pieces, and orchestral and chamber works.

GRUENING, ERNEST (1887–1974): US journalist and public administrator. He was governor of Alaska 1939–53, and its senator from 1958 to 1968. He was editor of several influential papers in Boston and New York, including *The Nation* and the New York *Tribune*.

GRÜNBAUM, HENRY (1911–): Danish statesman. He was a journalist and trade union economic expert. In 1964 he became minister for economic affairs in the Social Democratic government.

GRÜNBAUM, MAX (1817–1898): German scholar. After directing the Hebrew Orphanage Asylum in New York from 1858 to 1870, he settled in Munich where he devoted himself to literary studies. G. was one of the pioneer investigators of the Yiddish language and its structure and also wrote on Ladino literature, aggadah, etc.

GRÜNBAUM, YITZHAK (1879–1970): Zionist leader, and writer. Born in Warsaw, he edited the weekly *Ha-Olam* and during World War I lived

Yitzhak Grünbaum.

at St. Petersburg. After the war, he returned to Warsaw, became the leader of Polish Zionism and was elected to the *Seym*. In 1933, he was elected to the Jewish Agency Executive and settled in Palestine. In 1948–9, he was minister of the interior (representing the General Zionist Party) in the Israel provisional government. Subsequently, he contributed to the more extreme left-wing press. G. published books on Polish and Zionist history and current affairs. He edited the *Encyclopaedia of the Jewish Diaspora* (1953 ff).

GRÜNBERG, CARL (1861–1940): Political economist. A native of Rumania and baptized, G. was professor of political economy in Vienna and from 1924, director of the Institute for Social Research in Frankfort-on-Main. He founded the *Archiv für die Geschichte des Sozialismus und der Arbeiterbewegung*.

GRUNWALD, MAX (1871–1953): Rabbi and folklorist. In 1895, he was rabbi at Hamburg and in 1903–30, at Vienna, settling in Palestine in 1938. He founded the Society of Jewish Folklore and the Hamburg Jewish Museum (1897). G. published the German periodical *Mitteilungen zur jüdischen Volkskunde* (1897–1922) which was the central organ of Jewish folkloristic study. His works included many studies on Jewish folklore and a history of the Hamburg community.

GRUSENBERG, OSCAR (1866–1940): Russian barrister. He gained prominence as defense counsel in political cases, especially those involving Jews (e.g. the Blondes and Beilis Blood Libels, the trials after the Kishinev pogroms, etc.). The Kerensky government appointed him senator in 1917, but he left Russia after the Communist Revolution and later lived in Riga and Nice.

GRYNSZPAN, HERSCHEL (1921–c. 1942): Anti-Nazi. Deeply affected by the sufferings of his parents and other deportees from Germany in a no-man's land on the Polish frontier, he shot Ernst Vom Rath of the German embassy in Paris (Nov. 7, 1938). In revenge, the Nazis subjected the Jews of Germany to the persecutions of the "Night of Broken Glass" (Nov. 9/10), including mass arrests, synagogue burnings, and a collective fine of a billion marks. G. was killed by the Germans during World War II.

GUADALAJARA: Spanish city. Jews lived there from the time of the Arabs until the expulsion of 1492. The greatest importance of G. in Jewish life was its Hebrew printing-house, the first in Spain, established in 1476.

GUARDIAN: The talmudic term *epitropos* (from the Greek) has the connotation of guardian trustee, and administrator combined, but refers almost exclusively to the care of property of minors, deaf-mutes, or persons of unsound mind. A father may appoint anyone he deems fit to care for his minor children, but a court is obliged to seek a learned or pious man of full legal age. As the function of the g. is considered to be a religious duty, he is also required to give account of his administration under severe oath. He is permitted, however, to act according to his own best judgment in behalf of his wards and is therefore only liable for loss due to negligence.

GUATEMALA: Central American state. The first Jewish immigration to G. stemmed from Germany in 1848. Further groups followed from other countries but the rate from Germany increased 1930–40, and German Jews constitute the majority of the community. The Jewish population (1973) of 1,900, nearly all residing in Guatemala City, is represented by the Comunidad Israelita which maintains a synagogue.

GÜDEMANN, MORITZ (1835–1918): German rabbi and scholar; from 1894, chief rabbi of Vienna. G. wrote major works on Jewish cultural history, especially a history of education and culture among western Jews in the Middle Ages. He led the rabbinical opposition to Herzl's Zionism, regarding Judaism as essentially religious.

GUEDALLA, PHILIP (1889–1944): English author and scholar. He wrote a series of witty historical and biographical works especially covering the 19th and 20th cents.

GUGGENHEIM: US family. After success in the copper industry, they branched out into mining, smelting, and refining other metals. Thereafter, almost every member of the family devoted much of his fortune to philanthropy and to the establishment of foundations which have distributed an aggregate of tens of millions of dollars. Head of the family and founder of its fortunes in the US was *MEYER G.* (1828–1905), who eventually drew all his seven sons into business with him. They included *ISAAC G.* (1854–1922), director of the Mexican Union Railway; *DANIEL G.* (1856–1930), who established foundations for the promotion of aeronautics and the advancement of social welfare; *SOLOMON ROBERT G.* (1861–1949), distinguished as a patron of the arts (the Guggenheim museum in New York was named for him); and *SIMON G.* (1867–1941), who served as US senator from Colorado 1907–13, and in 1925, set up a foundation to award fellowships for research and creative work. *HARRY FRANK G.* (1890–1971), son of Daniel, was US ambassador to Cuba 1929–33.

GUGLIELMO DA PESARO (fl. 15th cent.): Italian dancing-master. His treatise on the art of dancing (c. 1463) is one of the most memorable works of its kind produced in Renaissance Italy. G. was ultimately converted to Christianity.

GUILDS: Associations of artisans. G. of apothecaries, goldsmiths, etc. in Jerusalem are mentioned at the beginning of the period of the Second Temple (cf. Neh. 3:8, 31–2), and before 70 CE there were also g. of weavers, coppersmiths, etc. In the Mishnaic Period, g., sometimes maintaining their own synagogues, are mentioned in other cities of Palestine. In the Great Synagogue in Alexandria, special sections were reserved for members of the various g. Artisans' associations were familiar also among the Jews of Babylonia. Inscriptions have

Illumination from a treatise on dancing by
Guglielmo da Pesaro.

been found of the g. of weavers and dyers in Hierapolis in Asia Minor, while in Rome there was a separate congregation of the g. of *calcarenses* or lime-burners. In the medieval cities where Jews formed small minorities, the numbers of those engaged in single callings were generally insufficient for them to form their own g. The development of Christian g. with monopolies in certain branches of manufacture was an important factor in the exclusion of the Jews from handicrafts. In S Europe, however, the number of Jewish artisans remained great enough for them to have their own organizations. Thus in various places in Spain (e.g. Saragossa) there were g. of Jewish weavers, leather-workers, carpenters, etc., the last-named guild existing also in Sicily. Among E European Jews, too, a strong g. organization developed, being especially powerful in Prague. In Poland, Jewish g., e.g. of tailors, furriers, jewelers, were found in all the principal cities from the 17th cent. The regulations of some are preserved; they are not unlike those of non-Jewish g. With a less rigid organization, such g., with mutual assistance as their main object and still frequently maintaining their own synagogues, continued to exist in E Europe until recent times, sometimes forming the first basis of trade-union organizations.

GUILT-OFFERING (Heb. *asham*): Sacrifice which atoned for certain types of sin, such as wrongs committed against a fellow-man (provided proper restitution had been made before the sacrifice) and the improper use of Sanctuary property.

GUITERMAN, ARTHUR (1871–1943): US poet and librettist; chiefly known for his light verse. Many of his ballads deal with American history and legend.

GUMPLOWICZ, LUDWIG (1838–1909): Polish sociologist. After working in law and journalism and publishing works on Polish Jewish history, he devoted himself to political and social problems, lecturing at Graz Univ. from 1875. G. exercised a profound influence on the development of sociology which he established as an individual science. He regarded sociology as the science of human groups and their mutual relationship, the individual being passive and of no influence. The history of civilization is a ceaseless series of struggles, the state being a result of the conflict between races until one triumphs and annihilates or absorbs the others. G. was converted to Christianity.

GUNDOLF (originally **GUNDELFINGER**), **FRIEDRICH** (1880–1931): German literary critic and biographer. He lifted literary studies out of their usual philological context and exercised great influence, his Shakespeare translations being famous. G. belonged to the circle of Stefan George of whom he wrote a study. His other subjects included Paracelsus, Shakespeare, Goethe, and Kleist.

GÜNZBURG: Russian family of philanthropists. (1) *JOSEPH YOZEL G., BARON* (1812–1878) accumulated great wealth and settled in Paris in 1857, continuing his financial activities in Russia. He founded a bank in St. Petersburg, and participated in the building of railways and the development of Siberian gold mines. A founder of the Society for the Promotion of Culture among the Jews, he supported Jewish education and agriculture. He was created a baron in 1874 by the grand duke of Hesse-Darmstadt. (2) *HORACE G., BARON* (1833–1909), son of (1), conducted the bank founded by his father. A supporter of the arts, he was one of the principal spokesmen of Russian Jewry and succeeded his father as head of the St. Petersburg Jewish community. (3) *DAVID G., BARON* (1857–1910), son of (2), was a scholar of oriental languages. He published various works and studies, was an editor of the *Yevreyskaya Entziklopedia* (the Russian Jewish encyclopedia) and established courses in oriental subjects at the Institute of Jewish Studies in St. Petersburg (1908). G. was one of the leaders of Russian Jewry. His superb library included many mss.

GÜNZBURG: (1) *PESAH G.* (1894–1947): Hebrew writer and journalist. Born in Volhynia, he lived in the US 1912–4, Scandinavia 1914–7, London 1917–22, and in Palestine from 1922. He published poems and stories and translated many works from English and the Scandinavian languages into Hebrew. (2) *SHIMON G.* (1890–1944): Hebrew poet and critic; brother of (1). He was born in Volhynia and lived in the US 1912–33, and in Palestine from 1933. His collected poems appeared in 1931 and his biblical poem *Ahavat Hoshea* ("The Love of Hosea") in 1936. He edited the plays and letters of Moses Hayyim Luzzatto. (3) *JEKUTHIEL G.*; brother of (1) and (2). See GINSBURG, JEKUTHIEL.

GÜNZBURG, ILYA (1859–1939): Russian sculptor. His artistic talents were discovered by the sculptor Antokolsky, and he was sent by Baron Horace Günzburg to study at the St. Petersburg Academy of Art. In 1911, he received the title of academician. One of the best Russian realist sculptors of the country, his works consist chiefly of genre-studies of child life, statues (some on literary themes), and busts of prominent Russian personalities. After 1917, he sculpted revolutionary subjects.

GÜNZBURG, MORDECAI AARON (1795–1846): Hebrew author. Born in Lithuania, he was attracted to Haskalah and settled in Vilna where he founded a secular school for Jewish children (1841). He published original and translated works in various fields including general history, works on Jews and Judaism, and also dictionaries. His books were very popular and their simple Hebrew, free from quotation and elaborate language, paved the way for the new Hebrew style. His most important

Gush Halav: Lower part of the lintel of the entrance to a 3rd cent. synagogue.

work was his autobiography *Aviezer*, which vividly depicted Jewish life in Lithuania.

GUNZENHAUSER, AZRIEL BEN JOSEPH (fl. 15th cent.): Hebrew printer. Born in Germany, he settled in Naples and founded its first Hebrew press, in 1486. The press was closed in 1494 when the Jews in Naples were under attack.

GÜNZIG, AZRIEL (1868–1931): Rabbi and scholar. He was born in Cracow, served as rabbi in Czechoslovakia and (from 1921) in Antwerp. He edited and published the literary miscellany *Ha-Eshkol* 1899–1913.

GURWITSCH, ALEXANDER (1874–1954): Russian biologist. He was professor at the Univ. of Simferopol 1919–24 and Moscow 1925–9 and directed the Moscow Institute of Histology and the Leningrad Laboratory of Experimental Biology. G. achieved fame for his experimental studies in embryology and in the mechanics of evolution and heredity. He received a Stalin Prize in 1941.

GUSH ḤALAV (Giscala): Small fortified town in Upper Galilee. First mentioned in historical sources in the 1st cent. CE, it was the birthplace of the Zealot leader John (Johanan) who fortified the city at the time of the Roman war. When it was besieged by Titus, John and his followers escaped by night, the citizens then surrendering to the Romans. A Jewish population continued in the town at least until the 13th cent. Today it is the Arab village El Jish (pop. 1,400, mostly Maronites), 5 m. N of Safed, containing the ruins of two ancient synagogues.

GUTMACHER, ELIJAH (1796–1874): Zionist precursor. Rabbi in the province of Posen, his kabbalistic studies led him to the conclusion that the return of the Jews to their own land was necessary to purify them from the pollution of exile. He participated in the Thorn conference (1860) which discussed problems of Palestinian colonization, and worked with R Tzevi Hirsch Kalischer to encourage settlement work in Palestine. G. was the author of rabbinic studies.

GUTMAN, NAḤUM (1898–): Israel painter and author; son of Simḥah Ben-Zion. His main work is in graphic art and illustration. G. has also written books for children.

GUTMANN, SIMḤAH ALTER see **BEN-ZION SIMḤAH**

GUTMANN, WILHELM VON (1825–1895): Austrian industrialist and philanthropist. Together with his brother David (1834–1912), he became one of the leading coal magnates in the country. They generously supported Jewish causes, including the Vienna Rabbinical Seminary. They received Austrian titles of nobility in 1879.

GUTT, CAMILLE (1884–1971): Belgian statesman and financial expert. He was a minister of finance 1934–5 and held various posts in the Belgian government-in-exile during World War II. In 1946, he was appointed chairman of the board of directors of the International Monetary Fund.

Rabbi Elijah Gutmacher.

GUTTMANN: (1) *JACOB G.* (1845–1919): Rabbi and scholar. He officiated at Hildesheim and Breslau and published numerous studies on medieval Jewish philosophy. (2) *JULIUS G.* (1880–1950): Philosopher; son of (1). He lectured at Breslau 1910–19, the Berlin Hochschule für die Wissenschaft des Judentums 1919–34, and was professor at the Hebrew Univ. from 1934. His writings (notably *Die Philosophie des Judentums*) trace the development of Jewish philosophical thought and its connection with other cultures. He also wrote on general philosophical and sociological subjects.

GUTTMANN, JACOB (1811–1860): Sculptor and engraver. Born in Hungary, he lived in Vienna, Rome, London, and Paris. He executed sculptures of mythological and biblical subjects.

GUTTMANN, MICHAEL (Jehiel; 1872–1942): Hungarian talmudic scholar. He taught at the rabbinical seminaries of Breslau and Budapest. His chief work was a talmudic lexicon *Maphteaḥ ha-Talmud* of which 4 volumes appeared; the material for the other volumes was prepared but was lost during the Nazi occupation of Hungary. G. wrote many studies on aspects of Jewish scholarship.

GUYANA: Country in S America. Marranos settled there in the 17th cent. Under Dutch rule (see SURINAM) a Jewish settlement, New Middleburg, was established on the Pomeroon (1648). Most of the Jews emigrated to the British W. Indies or were absorbed into the general population. There is now no organized Jewish community in the former British Guiana and 500 Jews in Surinam.

HAAPALAH see **MAAPILIM**

HA-ARETZ (Heb. "The Land"): Hebrew daily newspaper. It was founded by a group of Hebrew writers in Jerusalem in 1919 as *Ḥadshot ha-Aretz* but in 1922, removed to Tel Aviv where it was edited by Mosheh Glickson until 1937. In 1936, it was acquired by S. Z. SCHOCKEN and subsequently edited by his son Gershom Schocken. The oldest extant Hebrew daily in Israel and independent in its views, it publishes a weekly youth magazine (*Ha-Aretz Shelanu*).

HAAS, JACOB DE (1872–1937): Zionist leader and journalist. Born in London, he was an early disciple of Herzl and settled in the US in 1902 to carry on Zionist work. He became a leading figure in early American Zionism, being closely associated with Louis Brandeis and later with Stephen S. Wise. He served as an American Jewish Congress delegate to the Versailles Peace Conference (1919). From 1920–4, he was secretary of the Palestine Development League and the Palestine Development Fund; and from 1930, a member of the administrative committee of the Zionist Organization of America. H. wrote a biography of Herzl and edited *The Encyclopedia of Jewish Knowledge*.

HAAS, LUDWIG (1875–1930): German statesman. He was first elected to the Reichstag in 1912 and in 1918, was minister of the interior in the Baden provisional government. From 1919, he was a leader of the Democratic Party in the Reichstag.

HAASE, HUGO (1863–1919): German socialist leader. He was first elected to the Reichstag briefly in 1897 in behalf of the Social Democratic Party and continually from 1907. On being expelled from this party in 1916 for his opposition to the war, he founded in 1917 the Independent Social Democratic Party. After the war H. became a member of the provisional government and for a time shared the presidency of the Council of the People's Deputies. He was assassinated by a German nationalist.

ḤABAD (initials of *Ḥokhmah Binah va-Daat*; Heb. for "wisdom, understanding, and knowledge"): Hasidic movement. In contrast to the popular attraction of the simple unlearned ḤASIDISM, which spread throughout Volhynia and the Ukraine, H.'s attraction was intellectual and its main support came from White Russia. Its founder was SHNEOUR ZALMAN of Lyady, who was strongly opposed by the Ḥasidic leaders of Volhynia (e.g. Baruch of Medzibozh and Abraham of Kalish) as well as the Mitnaggedim led by the Vilna Gaon. As a result of persecution, Shneour Zalman was twice imprisoned but after his release, the movement grew rapidly. The chief doctrines of H. on the soul and moral conduct are contained in his TANYA and on creation and the Deity, in his discourse *Shaar ha-Yiḥud veha-Emunah*. Its religious pantheistic philosophy teaches that "there is no vacuum in which God is not present." The world was created *ex nihilo* by Divine power which continues to sustain it: should this Active Force ("Divinity") remove itself from the object acted upon ("creation"), all would return to nothingness. Ethical teachings are directed to people of "middle quality" – neither entirely wicked nor entirely good. Man must gain mastery over his evil desire, the product of his animal soul, by means of "wisdom, understanding, and knowledge." A "higher fear" results from the contemplation of God's exalted qualities: from this, a man proceeds to "love" and to "cleaving" (DEVEKUT) to God. The emphasis is upon Torah study and intellectual contemplations, not emotional ecstasy. H. Ḥasidim stressed the observance of the commandments but opposed excessive ascetic practices and fasts. Humility, saintliness, joy, and melody all play an important part in the system. The *tzaddik* was a spiritual leader but not a miracle worker. The H. Ḥasidim have a special rite and follow the legal code laid down by Shneour Zalman. Their leaders (see SHNEERSOHN) have included Dov Ber (d. 1828), Menahem Mendel of LIUBAVICH (d. 1866), Shalom Dov Ber (d. 1920), and Joseph Isaac (d. 1952) who was imprisoned for a time in Soviet Russia (released 1927) and eventually settled in New York, which is the home of the present leader, Menahem Mendel. Followers of H. are to be found in many parts of the world (including the US, Canada, Australia, N Africa) as well as in Israel where – besides their urban centers – they have founded the agricultural settlements Kephar Ḥabad and Shaphrir.

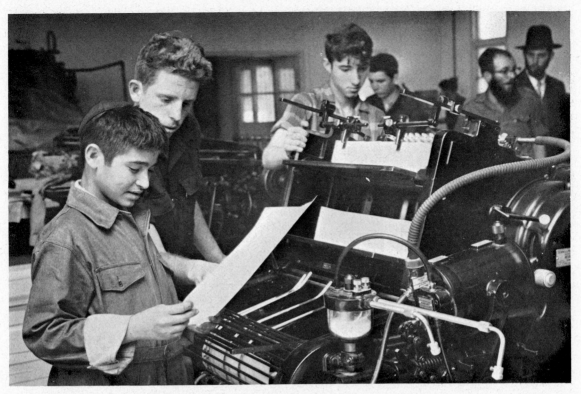

A Printing School in Kephar Ḥabad.

HABAKKUK: Prophet. The book of H. (eighth of the Minor Prophets) contains no information concerning his life or person. It is believed that he prophesied at the time of the Chaldean siege of Nineveh (612 BCE). The boqk consists of three chapters containing an outcry against the victory of the Chaldeans and the rule of iniquity in the world; God's reply; a prayer; and a description of the Day of the Lord. A midrashic commentary on the first two chapters of H. was found among the DEAD SEA SCROLLS.

HABE, HANS (1911–): Author. Born in Hungary, he fled the country in 1940 and joined the US army. In 1945 he founded the newspaper *Neue Zeitung* in Munich. His works include *Death in Texas* about the murder of President Kennedy and *The Mission*, a novel about the EVIAN CONFERENCE. His novel *The Poisoned Stream*, about a man who kills young girls, was coincidentally published shortly after the murder of his own daughter.

HABER, FRITZ (1868–1934): German chemist. From 1911, he headed the Kaiser Wilhelm Institute for physical chemistry at Dahlem , Berlin. Although baptized, H. was dismissed from his post by the Nazis in 1933 for refusing to discharge his Jewish assistants and he went into exile. One of the leading chemical technologists of his generation, his most important achievement was the synthesis of ammonia from its elements. This discovery, besides aiding Germany vitally during World War I (when H. was head of the German war chemical services), made unlimited supplies of natural fertilizer available for the soil. In 1918, he received the Nobel Prize for chemistry.

HABERMANN, AVRAHAM MEIR (1901–): Bibliographer; librarian of the Schocken library in Zwickau, Germany, from 1923, and from 1934, in Jerusalem. In 1969 he was appointed professor of medieval Hebrew literature at Tel Aviv Univ. He has published many studies on Jewish bibliography, the history of Hebrew printing, and medieval Hebrew poetry.

ḤABIB see **IBN ḤABIB**

HA-BIMAH (Heb. "The Stage"): Hebrew theater company, since 1958 the Israel National Theater. It was founded in Moscow in 1917 by a group of amateur actors who interested the producer Stanislavsky in their work. He delegated as permanent instructor the producer Vachtangov under whose guidance they prepared their première which took place in Oct. 1918. At the end of 1919, they staged their first major success, David Pinski's *The Wandering Jew*, and in 1922, they put on An-Ski's *The Dibbuk* in Bialik's translation. Owing to the opposition of the *Yevsektzia*, their subsidy was abolished and their financial position became precarious. In 1926,

Ha-Bimah foremost actors Hanna Rovina and Aharon Meskin
in *Death of a Salesman* by Arthur Miller.

the company left Russia and toured Europe and
America until, in 1928, most of the actors went to
Palestine. (A small group remained in the US,
but broke up after a short period). In 1929–31, *H.*
was in Europe again but thereafter has been in
Palestine (except for brief foreign tours). In 1945,
its own building in Tel Aviv was opened. Perfor-

Illustration for Ḥad Gadya. (From an 18th cent. Haggadah).

mances are given regularly in other centers throughout
the country. *H.*'s repertoire includes original Israel
and Jewish works as well as translations both of
classics and modern successes.

HABIRU: Designation of mercenaries or slaves,
used in the Tel el Amarna tables and in other
documents of the 15th–14th cents. BCE. Many
scholars are of the opinion that the word *H.* is
identical with *Ivri(i)m* ("Hebrews"), and some
believe that the reference in the Tel el Amarna
tablets to the threat of the *H.* to Canaanite cities
alludes to one of the stages in the Israelite conquest
of Canaan.

HA-BONIM (Heb. "The Builders"): World organization of Zionist youth movements. Founded
in Great Britain in 1929 as a group to undertake
youth education, it spread to S Africa (1931), India
(1936), and Australia (1943). In the US, it resulted
from a reorganization of the Young *Poale Zion*
(1935). The Dutch movement affiliated in 1951,
when the World Organization was set up; this was
also joined by the HA-TENUAH HA-MEUḤEDET. The
movement, now "*H.–Tenuah Meuḥedet*," has a
pioneering objective and has helped to establish
settlements in Israel, including Kephar Blum, Kephar
ha-Nasi, Maayan Barukh, Tzorah, Urim, and Moshav
ha-Bonim. The general secretariat is in Tel Aviv.

HACKER, LOUIS MORTON (1899–): US historian.
In 1935, he joined the faculty of Columbia Univ.,
becoming dean of its School of General Studies in
1952. H. has lectured in history and economics at a
number of universities in the US and abroad. Among
his works is *The United States and Its Place in World
Affairs, 1918–43* (with Allan Nevins).

HA-COHEN: (1) *DAVID H.* (1898–): Israel public
figure; son of (2). He was a founder of the
Histadrut contracting company *Solel Boneh* and
represented *Mapai* in the Knesset 1949–69, except in
1953–5 when he was Israel minister to Burma. (2)
MORDECAI BEN HILLEL H. (1856–1936): Hebrew
author. Born in White Russia, he published articles in
Hebrew journals from the age of 18. Although a pioneer of the *Ḥoveve Zion*, he criticized their colonization
work after a visit to Palestine in 1891. H. was the
first delegate to address the First Zionist Congress in
Hebrew. In 1907, he settled in Palestine, was a
founder of Tel Aviv, an organizer of credit cooperation, and initiator of the *Agudat ha-Sopherim*
(authors' association). He wrote topical articles
on Zionist questions with emphasis on economic
matters as well as memoirs (historical and cultural)
and stories.

HA-COHEN, SHALOM see **COHEN, SHALOM**

ḤAD GADYA (Aram. "One kid"): Aramaic song
which concludes the Passover Haggadah in the
Ashkenazi ritual; perhaps introduced in order to
keep the children awake until the end of the *Seder*

Hadassah's medical center in En Kerem near Jerusalem.

service. A children's song, on the style of *The House that Jack built*, its theme may nevertheless be interpreted as the moral order of the universe in which a man inevitably reaps the consequences of his action. The song seems to have been composed in the 15th cent. on a German model, unless, as some believe, it was itself the model for the ditties of this type found in various literatures. It has been interpreted also as an allegorical description of Israel's fate among the nations.

HADAD: (1) Chief god of the ancient Semitic pantheon. Often regarded as the god of justice and augury, he was especially the patron of rain and thunder. He is sometimes identified with Baal, but it is thought that H. was his main name and Baal a title denoting lordship of the world. (2) Name of several kings of Edom.

*HADADEZER (or **HADAREZER**): King of Aram-Zoba, at the end of the 11th cent. BCE. He headed the coalition of Syrian states which suffered a decisive defeat at the hands of David (II Sam. 10:7-19; I Chron. 19:6-19).

HADAMARD, JACQUES SALOMON (1865-1963): French mathematician; professor at the Collège de France from 1909. His chief works concern the calculus of variations.

HADAR see **HADAR RAMATAYIM**

HADAR RAMATAYIM (HOD HA-SHARON): Israel township in S Sharon; originally three separate settlements, viz. Ramatayim (founded 1925), Hadar (founded 1929), and Ramat Hadar (founded 1938). Its economy is based on citrus plantations, farming, trade, and small industry. Pop. including Magdiel (1974): 15,100.

HADASSAH (Heb. "Myrtle"): Alternative (Jewish) name for Esther (Est. 2:7).

HADASSAH: The Women's Zionist Organization of America. It has 318,000 members in 1,200 chapters and groups, organized in every state of the US and in Puerto Rico; in 1965, its budget exceeded $10,000,000. It was founded in 1912 by Henrietta Szold with a threefold object – to raise the standard of health in disease-ridden Palestine; to encourage the development of Jewish life in America; and to foster the Jewish ideal. The concept of educating a population to understand its medical problems and to demand a high standard of medical services, both preventive and curative, was one of H.'s most significant contributions to Palestine, later to become incorporated in Israel's medical and public health programs. Today in Israel, H. conducts a health and social welfare program, which includes a network of diagnostic, curative, and preventive medical services and health stations; a Youth Aliyah program; vocational education; and land redemption projects. Together with the Hebrew Univ., H. runs the only medical school in Israel, which is an integral part of the H.-Hebrew Univ. Medical Center. A new medical center has been built at En Kerem near Jerusalem to replace the Rothschild-H. Hebrew Univ. hospital on Mt. Scopus which was inaccessible 1948-67. With the return to Mt. Scopus after the Six-Day War, preparations were made to reopen the buildings there. In the US,

H. conducts a general and Jewish education program. H. policy is the responsibility of the entire membership represented in an annual National Convention, and is carried out by a National Board. Junior H. (organized 1920) is the Young Women's Zionist Organization including girls between the ages of 17 and 25.

HADASSI, JUDAH BEN ELIJAH (fl. 12th cent.): Turkish Karaite scholar. He was called *Ha-Avel* ("mourner") because he practiced the customs of the AVELE ZION. His chief work *Eshkol ha-Kopher* (or *Sepher ha-Peles*; begun 1148), was a rhymed encyclopedia in which the achievements of Karaite literature in all scholarly spheres were traced to the Ten Commandments.

HADASSIM: Israel agricultural school ("youth village") in S Sharon plain. It was founded by the Canadian Hadassah movement (affiliated to WIZO) and opened in 1947. 500 pupils are educated in all branches of agriculture and special courses are given for children from Canada.

ḤADERAH: Israel township in N Sharon, founded in 1891 by *Bilu* immigrants. The extensive swamps, flanked by sand dunes, were the source of malaria which before World War I caused the death of nearly half the settlers. On Baron Edmond de Rothschild's initiative, eucalyptus trees were planted and drainage canals dug, as a result of which the danger to health disappeared. An important junction, Ḥ.'s economy is now based on intensive agriculture, trade, and industry. Pop. (1974): 34,800.

HA-DOAR (Heb. "The Post"): New York Hebrew weekly. It was founded in 1922 as a daily under the editorship of M. Lipson and ceased publication after 202 numbers had appeared. Revived as a weekly in 1923, Menahem Ribalow was its editor for 30 years (until 1953). Its literary section is influential and has attracted leading American and overseas Hebrew authors as contributors.

HADRAMAUT: Country of S Arabian peninsula, E of Aden. Its very ancient Jewish settlement, with distinctive traditions and strongly marked physical type, became known to the outside world only in the 1940's. The small community emigrated to Israel after the foundation of the state.

*HADRIAN (P. Aelius Hadrianus): Roman emperor 117–138. His initial eastern policy (removal and execution of the savage governor of Judea, Lucius Quietus; support of Egyptian Jewry in disputes with Greeks, etc.) created a favorable impression on the Jews. However, his prohibition of sexual mutilation was extended to circumcision and thus into an attack on a fundamental rite of Judaism. As a result of his visit to Palestine in 130 and the implacable attitude of the Jews with whom he negotiated, he decided to commence the hellenization of the country by converting Jerusalem into a Roman colony to be called after himself, Aelia Capitolina. The Jews rebelled under BAR KOKHBA and the ensuing war (132–5), was the most difficult of H.'s reign. After his victory, H. received the title Imperator. Judea became a consular province called Syria-Palaestina. The ruins of Jerusalem were reconstructed as a pagan city, and an equestrian statue of H. erected on the site of the Holy of Holies.

ḤADYAV see **ADIABENE**

HA-EMET (Heb. "The Truth"): First Hebrew socialist periodical. Three numbers appeared in Vienna in 1877 under the editorship of Aaron Samuel Liebermann.

HAFFKINE, WALDEMAR MORDECAI WOLFF (1860–1930): Bacteriologist. He was born in Odessa and worked at the Pasteur Institute, Paris, where he discovered a serum against cholera and bubonic plague. In 1893, he was called to India where he fought epidemics and directed the Bombay plague research institute named for him. H., who was profoundly religious, was active in Jewish affairs and left a large bequest to yeshivot.

ḤAG see **FESTIVAL**

ḤAG SAMEAḤ (Heb. "joyful feast"): The usual GREETING in Israel on a religious holiday.

HAGANAH (Heb. "defense"): Clandestine organization for Jewish self-defense in Palestine. It succeeded HA-SHOMER in 1920 and existed until 1948 when its members were transferred to TZEVA HAGANAH LE-ISRAEL. The establishment of the H. was due to the realization of the inadequacy of the protection given to the Jewish population under the British administration, and also to the conscious determination to entrust security to a popular volunteer organization. The H. combined an illegal organization with individual Jewish participation in the government's security forces and even had certain legal formations. Intensive efforts to strengthen the H. followed the 1929 Arab riots which resulted in a British policy of appeasement of the Arabs. In 1931, the H. split and the minority, chiefly right-wing groups, formed a separate organization; these reunited with the H. in 1936 but certain elements remained outside and formed the nucleus of the IRGUN TZEVAI LEUMI. The H. was considerably strengthened during the 1936–9 disturbances by the establishment of the Supernumerary Police Force (Heb. *noterim*) which numbered 20,000 in 1939. This force was recruited by the H. command and operated as far as possible under its instructions. At this period, the "Special Field Companies" were raised (by Yitzḥak SADEH) and the "Night Squads" established (by Orde WINGATE). The H. also executed settlement operations ("STOCKADE AND TOWER"), organized "illegal" immigration (HAAPALAH), and even set up its own secret plant for manufacturing equipment. The chairman of the Jewish Agency

Haganah forces taking over the Rosh Pina Police station.

Executive, David Ben-Gurion, ensured that the H. should operate as the security arm of the executive and at its instructions. During World War II, the H. directed its members to enroll in Jewish units within the framework of the British army, and 30,000 men and women volunteered. In 1941, military commando units (the PALMAH) were set up, at first in collaboration with the British, but later independently. After the War, H. operations were directed against the British with the object of obtaining the withdrawal of the 1939 WHITE PAPER. These operations centered largely around the transport of unauthorized immigrants to Palestine. In June 1946, the British administration undertook an extensive counter-operation; although this did not succeed in attaining its objectives, the H. did not resume its struggle against the British. From the end of 1947, H. concentrated on defense against the mounting Arab attacks. Generally, the relations between the H. and other underground Jewish groups (*Irgun Tzevai Leumi* and LOHAME HERUT ISRAEL) were strained, although there were periods of cooperation in 1945–6 and 1947–8.

HAGAR: Egyptian handmaid of Sarah; mother of Ishmael. Sarah, being barren, gave her to Abraham but H. ran away when pregnant to escape her mistress' jealousy. H. returned on the guidance of an angel. Later, after Sarah had a son, Isaac, H. was again expelled but was miraculously rescued in the wilderness together with her son. The object of the biblical story is to stress the relationship between the Israelites and Ishmaelites and to account for the nomadic nature of the latter.

HAGBAHAH (Heb. "elevation"): The ceremonial raising of the Scroll of the Law in the synagogue before or after reading.

HAGGADAH, PASSOVER: Ritual recited in the home on the first Passover evening (in the Diaspora, the first two evenings). Originally the narration (i.e., *haggadah*, cf. Exod. 13:8) of the story of the Exodus by the father to his children accompanied the meal of the paschal lamb (on *Nisan* 15). After the cessation of sacrifice, the only aspect of the meal still valid was the partaking of unleavened bread, while the eating of bitter herbs was observed as a rabbinical commandment. The rabbis defined this as a festive meal, therefore requiring the drinking of four cups of wine (interpreted symbolically by later generations) and the recitation of *Hallel*. They also introduced the reading of Deut. 26:5–9 with its Midrash. Other additions included four questions asked by the youngest present and the explanation of the distinguishing foods of the evening. The order (SEDER) of the ritual developed into established custom, and the *H.* already approximated its present form by the close of the Talmudic Period. Amoraic additions included the Midrash on the Four Sons and excerpts from the *Mekhilta*. The *H.* is contained in the prayer books of Amram Gaon (8th cent.), Saadyah Gaon (10th cent.), etc. indicating that it

Jews of Hadramaut celebrating the *Seder*.

was originally included in the general prayerbook. Before the 12th cent., it began to be copied separately, being practically uniform in all rituals except for such later liturgical additions as the concluding folk-songs (in the Ashkenazi version). The *H.* became extremely popular and was the subject of many commentaries. It has been one of the chief objects of Jewish ritual art, and many finely illuminated examples have been preserved, in addition to illustrated editions (Prague, 1527; Mantua, 1560; Venice, 1629; Amsterdam, 1695; the Szyk H., 1940) which appeared after the invention of printing.

HAGGAI (fl. c. 520 BCE): Post-exilic prophet. The book of H., the tenth of the Minor Prophets, comprises in two chapters four prophecies made in the second year of Darius I. H. calls for the rebuilding of the Temple, questions the priests regarding the laws of uncleanness, and foretells the glory of the Temple and the greatness of Zerubbabel.

HAGIGAH (Heb. "Festival Offering"): Twelfth (eleventh in some codices) tractate in the Mishnah order of *Moed,* containing 3 chapters. It has *gemara* in both the Babylonian and Palestinian Talmuds. It deals with the Temple sacrificial obligations of the individual during the three pilgrim-festivals. In addition, it discusses what constitutes improper topics for public teaching and discussion.

HAGIOGRAPHA (Gk.=Holy Writings: in Heb. *ketuvim,* i.e., "writings"): Third and last section of the Bible (after the Pentateuch and Prophets) containing 11 books, usually in the order: Psalms, Proverbs, Job, Song of Songs, Ruth, Lamentations, Ecclesiastes, Esther, Daniel, Ezra and Nehemiah, Chronicles.

ḤAGIZ: (1) *JACOB Ḥ* (1620–1674): Palestinian scholar. He was principal of the Bet Yaakov yeshivah in Jerusalem from 1657, being responsible for the introduction of secular studies there. Ḥ. was the author of a number of scholarly works on talmudic subjects. He was one of Shabbetai Tzevi's sharpest opponents. (2) *MOSES Ḥ.* (1672–c. 1760): Palestinian scholar; son of (1). He spent many of his earlier years in Europe where he resided in Italy, Amsterdam, and Altona, returning to Palestine in 1738 and settling in Safed. Ḥ. violently combatted Sabbetaianism, and while in Amsterdam, helped Tzevi Ashkenazi in his campaign against Nehemiah Ḥayyon. Well-versed in both Jewish and general knowledge, he wrote many books on Jewish subjects.

HAGUE, THE: City in HOLLAND. Both Sephardi and Ashkenazi Jews began to settle there early in the 17th cent., but it was not until the close of the cent. that the latter community was organized, while the Portuguese group built its synagogue only in the 18th cent. The outstanding Portuguese families, such as that of Lopes Suasso, played a brilliant role for a time in the city's social and intellectual life. Before World War II, the community attained its peak population of c. 12,000, but it never rivaled the importance of Amsterdam. The German persecutions in 1940–5 reduced the total drastically, the Sephardi community now ceasing to exist. Jewish pop. (1973): 2,500.

HAHAM see ḤAKHAM

HAHN, MICHAEL (1830–1886): US public official and editor. He was elected to the US Senate where he served briefly (1863) and was governor of Louisiana 1864–5. From 1884 until his death, H. was a Republican member of Congress.

HAHN, REYNALDO (1875–1947): French composer. Chiefly noted for his vocal music which included operas, operettas, and song cycles, he also composed orchestral and chamber works.

HAI (939–1038): Last gaon of PUMBEDITA; son of SHERIRA Gaon. From his youth, he assisted his father in teaching and in administering the academy. He was appointed head of the Bet Din in 986 and in 998, became gaon in succession to Sherira who retired in extreme old age. Despite the decline of Babylonian Jewry, Sherira and H. raised the prestige of the Pumbedita academy, and under H. it became the leading contemporary center of Jewish learning, attracting students from all parts of the world. Jewish scholars from many countries submitted their queries to H. and he issued thousands of responsa covering all branches of halakhic literature, continuing to write and teach until his death in his hundredth year. He

wrote, in Arabic, commentaries on the Bible and Talmud.

HAIDAMAKS: Ukrainian bands, chiefly in the provinces of Kiev and Podolia, hostile to the Poles and Jews, 1708-70, demanding the complete extermination of the latter. Their activity reached a peak in 1768 with an appalling massacre at Uman. The anarchic nature of the outbreaks led to their suppression by the Russian and Polish authorities.

HAIFA: Israel city, It appears first in history after the 1st cent. as the home of various Jewish scholars and as the S limit of the coast on which the purple snail was caught; in the 4th cent., it was a fishing village called Epha. In 1071, the seat of the Jerusalem academy was temporarily transferred there; in 1100, the Jews defended H. against the crusaders. The modern rise of H. began only in the second half of the 19th cent. with the sanding-up of Acre harbor and the establishment of a European colony; it was much advanced by the selection of the town as the Mediterranean terminus of the Hejaz railway (1905), which deflected the Hauran grain trade from Acre. Soon afterwards, the Jewish quarter of Hadar ha-Carmel was established, and in 1925, the Hebrew Technical College (Technion) began to operate. Under the British Mandate, the deep-water harbor was completed (1933) and the refineries in the bay,

Haifa: view from Mt. Carmel toward the Bay.

connected by pipeline with the Kirkuk oil fields. The development of the Jezreel Valley settlements and the establishment of the principal Jewish industries in the vicinity (Nesher cement works, Shemen oil factory, etc.) added their impetus to the development of H. which spread into Haifa Bay and over Mt Carmel. The city was taken over on Apr. 22, 1948 by the Haganah and the Arab population fled almost in its entirety. Since then, it has remained the principal port of Israel and a center of industrial development; the population has risen (1974) to over 225,000. It serves as the base for Israel ships, both of the navy and the merchant fleet and is also the main gateway for immigration into Israel by ship. The city area includes traditional religious sites such as the Cave of Elijah. It also contains the magnificent tomb of Baha Effendi and is the religious center of the BAHAI.

HAINT (Yidd. "Today"): Yiddish daily newspaper, appearing in Warsaw 1908-39. It was founded and edited by Samuel Jacob Jackan. From 1920, it was edited by Abraham Goldberg and after 1933, by an editorial board. Originally non-party, it became a Zionist organ during World War I. It ceased publication with the German invasion of Poland in 1939.

HAITI: Caribbean island. The first European to set foot in H. was Luis de TORRES, the Marrano interpreter to Columbus (1492). Jewish immigrants arrived from Spain after World War I and a few families from Germany and Poland came during World War II. Jewish life in H. is undeveloped. In 1973, the community numbered 150.

HA-KADOSH BARUKH HU (Heb. "The Holy One, Blessed be He"): Reverential periphrasis common in rabbinic literature; used in order to avoid "mentioning the name of God in vain" i.e., for non-liturgical purposes.

HAKHAM (also *Haham;* Heb. "wise man"): Originally an officer of the ancient rabbinic courts in Palestine and Babylonia, the term was later applied in Sephardi communities to an officiating rabbi. The title is frequently amplified as *Hakham ha-Shalem* ("Perfect Sage"). The title Haham is applied in England to the rabbi of the Spanish and Portuguese congregation in London.

HAKHAM BASHI (Heb. and Turk. "chief sage"): Title in the 15th cent. and modern times of the chief rabbi of the Turkish Empire, residing in Constantinople; also applied to principal rabbis in provincial towns.

HAKHNASAT KALLAH (Heb. "dowering [lit: introducing] the bride"): The custom of helping toward a bride's dowry is an ancient Jewish tradition. It was considered by the rabbis an outstandingly meritorious act, being classed among the commandments which bring reward both in this world and the next. Especially during the Middle Ages, and to a lesser extent today, communal societies were and are

organized for this purpose, often bearing the name *Hevrat H. K.*

HAKHNASAT ORHIM (Heb. "entertaining wayfarers"): Hospitality. A primary commandment of Judaism, as is illustrated in the historical narratives of the Bible (cf. Abraham, Laban, Jethro, and Rahab; the sin of Sodom, in contrast, was traditionally described as lack of hospitality). The rabbis regarded *H. O.* even higher than matters of pure spirit ("the reception of the Divine Presence"). The invitation issued at the *Seder* meal — "let all who are hungry come in and eat" — was originally the daily exhortation before meals of R Huna (3rd cent.). Hospitality was a general communal responsibility as well as being a private virtue. During the Middle Ages and after, when many Jews were reduced to itinerant trading and mendicancy, the custom arose of providing special lodging for the vagrant poor in a *bet hakhnasat orehim* (guest-house), later known also as *hekdesh* ("sanctuary").

HAKHSHARAH (Heb. "preparation"): Training or preparation, both intellectual and physical, for settlement in Israel. In pioneering movements, applied particularly to training in physical labor, especially farming, in the Diaspora.

HA-KIBBUTZ HA-ARTZI HA-SHOMER HA-TZAIR: Kibbutz federation of HA-SHOMER HA-TZAIR in Israel. Founded in 1927, its ideology is based on Zionism, Marxist socialism, and kibbutz life. Another principle is "ideological collectivism", i.e., unanimous acceptance of the official views of *Ha-Shomer ha-Tzair* (now part of *Mapam*). In 1970, 75 kibbutzim were affiliated, with a total area exceeding 140,000 acres of land and a population of 30,000. A number of industries are run in partnership with private enterprise. Its supreme institution is its council, and the executive is the *Vaad ha-Poel* situated at Merhavyah. It is active educationally and culturally, issuing periodicals, books, etc.

HA-KIBBUTZ HA-DATI (Heb. "The Religious Settlement"): Israel settlement movement to which are affiliated all collective settlements founded by HA-POEL HA-MIZRAHI. These settlements, 13 in number (1970) with 4,000 members, follow the same principles of economic and social organization as other kibbutzim, but in addition adhere to the Orthodox forms of Jewish religious life (three daily services, *kashrut*, etc.) and allot periods to religious study. Settlements of this movement include Yavneh, Tirat Tzevi, Sedeh Eliyahu, and En ha-Natziv. New members are often recruited from the ranks of the youth movements of *Torah va-Avodah* and *Bene Akiva.*

HA-KIBBUTZ HA-MEUHAD (Heb. "United Kibbutz"): Organization of Israel collective settlements. It was founded in 1927 by Kibbutz EN HAROD and the remnants of GEDUD HA-AVODAH, adopting from them the program of the kibbutz as a centralized colonizational mass-movement, KIBBUSH AVODAH, wage-work, and the combination of agriculture with industry in the large collective. Originally with a strong *Mapai* majority, its left-wing crystallized as an opposition (*Siyah Bet*) in the later 1930's, leading to the 1951 split when the *Mapai* members, now a minority (40%), left to form their own organization IHUD HA-KEVUTZOT VEHA-KIBBUTZIM). *K. M.* constitutes the main nucleus of the AHDUT AVODAH party. It was closely associated with the development of the PALMAH (1940–7), and pioneered in many spheres (quarrying, fishing, seafaring). Its headquarters and press are at En Harod. The Diaspora youth movements *Deror* and *He-Halutz ha-Tzair* are affiliates. In 1970, it had c. 25,000 members in 60 villages.

HAKKAPHOT (Heb. "circuits"): Processional circuits. (1) During the *Hoshanah* service on the Feast of Tabernacles, the reader and members of the congregation walk around a Scroll of the Law carrying *lulav* and *etrog*. It recalls the procession around the altar in the Temple. (2) On *Hoshanah Rabbah*, a similar circuit is made seven times. (3) On the Feast of the Rejoicing of the Law, repeated *H.* take place, sometimes until every adult person in the congregation has carried a Scroll of the Law around the synagogue. They are often joined by children carrying flags inscribed with appropriate biblical verses. A similar procession takes place upon the dedication of a synagogue. (4) In Sephardi and Hasidic communities, mourners walk round a coffin seven times before interment. (5) In some communities, the bride encircles the bridegroom three (or seven) times before the wedding ceremony. (6) A medieval Jewish custom was to walk around a cemetery, encircling it with a thread, when praying for the sick.

HA-KOAH (Heb. "The Strength"): Jewish sports society founded in Vienna in 1909. It developed from a small soccer club into a strong Austrian sports federation with Zionist proclivities. Its emblem was the Shield of David. Ceasing to function in the 1930's, it was refounded in Palestine (in 1942) and other centers, confining its interests chiefly to soccer.

HALAKHAH (Heb. "law" derived from *halakh* "to go," "follow"): The legal part of talmudic and later Jewish literature, in contrast to Haggadah or AGGADAH, the non-legal elements. In the singular, *h.* means "law" in all-inclusive, abstract sense, or else a specific regulation; in the plural, *halakhot* refers to collections of laws. *H.* refers especially to the ORAL LAW, i.e., the accepted tradition of interpretation of the written law. Collections of oral laws existed long before the compilation of the Mishnah at the end of the 2nd cent. CE. Various tannaim had their own collections of *h.* The most famous was that of R Akiva which was in turn handed down in separate traditions by his four leading disciples—R Meir,

R Judah, R Yose, and R Simeon; R Judah Ha-Nasi, in arranging the Mishnah, utilized these collections, especially that of R Meir. The Mishnah was not basically a formulation of binding law, for (at least in its present form) it contains many conflicting *halakhot*, but its main object was to give an orderly presentation of the *h.* as such, without necessarily deciding which version of any particular law was binding. The Mishnah became the prime text of discussion in the academies both in Palestine and Babylonia, the amoraim formulating rules to determine the binding version of the *h.* as well as expanding it in many ways. After the Talmudic Period, the geonim in their responsa interpreted and developed the law. For codification of *h.*, see LAW, CODIFICATION OF.

HALAKHOT GEDOLOT (Heb. "Great Laws"): A codification of talmudic law arranged according to the order of the tractates, made in Babylonia during the 8th cent. by Simeon Kayyara. Only laws which have relevance in the post-Temple period are included. *H. G.* was the first book to enumerate the 613 PRECEPTS.

HALAKHOT PESUKOT (Heb. "Decided Laws"): Talmudic code said to have been written in the 8th cent. by Yehudai Gaon; also called *Hilkhot Reu*. Originally written in Aramaic, it is now known in Hebrew translations. Sources are not given for the talmudic decisions incorporated in the work.

HALBERSTADT: German city. The date of its original Jewish settlement is unknown, but in 1261, the town promised the Jews protection "as formerly." In 1493, the community was expelled; they returned in the 16th cent. and were again driven out in 1594. Shortly thereafter, Jews resettled and opened a synagogue which was destroyed during the Thirty Years' War. A charter of rights was granted the Jews in 1650, and the government protected them against the hostility of Christian traders. In 1712, permission was again received to build a synagogue. The community of 900 was destroyed by the Nazis and was not reestablished.

HALBERSTAMM, HAYYIM (1793–1876): Rabbinical scholar. He served as rabbi in Nowy Sadz (Galicia) from 1830. While there, he was attracted to Hasidism and founded a dynasty (the "Sanzer"), his ultimate aim being to merge Hasidism with Rabbinism. In 1869, he became involved in a dispute with the Sadagora dynasty, and the controversy was accompanied by mutual recriminations and virtual excommunications. H. was the author of responsa and works on talmudic subjects.

HALBERSTAMM, SOLOMON ZALMAN HAYYIM (1832–1900): Polish Hebrew scholar and bibliophile. A merchant by trade, he amassed a valuable library of printed books and Hebrew mss, some of which he published in critical editions. After his death, most of his mss passed to the Judith

Montefiore College, Ramsgate, and are now housed at Jews' College, London.

HALDEMAN-JULIUS, EMANUEL (1889–1951): US publisher and author. H. was a pioneer in the mail-order book business and publisher of the *Little Blue Books* which sold over 200 million copies.

HALEVAI (Aram. "may it be so"): An interjection expressing a wish for a desirable event.

HA-LEVANON (Heb. "Lebanon"): Hebrew periodical. It was edited by Jehiel Brill and published in Jerusalem (1863), Paris (1865–7), Mainz (1871–81), and London (1886). Of a conservative nature, it opposed the colonization of Palestine.

HALÉVY: French family. *ÉLIE H.* (or Halfan; c. 1760–1826), Hebrew author and poet, went to Paris as a young man and became cantor and clerk of the community. He gained a reputation as a poet with his *Shir ha-Shalom* ("Hymn of Peace") in honor of Napoleon I (1801). He edited *L'Israélite Français* (1917–9) which advocated the ideas of Haskalah and preached French patriotism. His son was *JACQUES FRANÇOIS FROMENTAL H.* (1799–1862), the composer whose most famous work is the opera *La Juive* (1835); he wrote about 20 other operas as well as cantatas, etc. H. taught at the Paris Conservatoire from 1827, his pupils including Gounod and Bizet. Élie H.'s other son *LÉON H.* (1802–1883), author, dramatist, and disciple of Saint Simon, wrote a history of the Jews, but his main works consist of novels, plays, and memoirs. Léon's son, *LUDOVIC H.* (1834–1908), dramatist who wrote the libretto for Offenbach's *Orpheus in the Underworld* and (in collaboration) *La Belle Hélène* and Bizet's *Carmen*, and his grandsons, the historian *ÉLIE H.* (1870–1937), author of *A History of the English People in the Nineteenth Century*, and the essayist *DANIEL H.* (1872–1962), had no connection with Judaism.

HALEVY (originally Rabinowitz), **ISAAC** (1847–1914): Talmudist and historian. For many years, he engaged in commerce in Vilna, settling later in Hamburg to devote himself to research. His principal work was *Dorot ha-Rishonim,* an uncompleted Jewish literary history, of which five volumes appeared posthumously, covering the period from the Hasmoneans to the close of the gaonic era. The work is written from a traditional viewpoint and although defective linguistically and scientifically, excels in its critical mastery of talmudic literature.

HALÉVY, JOSEPH (1827–1917): French Semitic scholar. He taught at schools of the Alliance Israélite Universelle in Turkey and Rumania and in 1868, went at the request of the Alliance to Ethiopia where he visited the Falashas. Subsequently, the Académie des Inscriptions et Belles-Lettres sent him to Yemen where, disguised as a native rabbi, he succeeded in collecting 686 Sabean inscriptions (1869–70). He was appointed professor of Ethiopic

at the École des Hautes Études of Paris in 1879. He wrote many works on Semitic philology, epigraphy, archeology, and biblical exegesis.

HALFAN, ELIJAH HALÉVY see **HALÉVY, ÉLIE**

HALICZ: Town of E Galicia. Its Jewish population, mentioned in 1488, was augmented shortly thereafter by Karaites who maintained a separate community from 1578. In 1921, there were 1,000 Jews and 100 Karaites (together a third of the total population), mostly agriculturalists. They were exterminated during the Nazi occupation.

ḤALITZAH (Heb. "taking off"): Biblically prescribed ceremony (Deut. 25:9–10), performed when a man refuses to marry his brother's childless widow. The ceremony, without which the widow is forbidden to remarry, involves her removing her brother-in-law's shoe and reciting the biblical formula "so shall be done to the man who will not build his brother's house." Abuse and hardship caused by inaccessibility or the brother's refusal to perform the ceremony have led to sanctions against recalcitrants. Israel legislation (1953) provides for imprisonment of the deceased husband's brother if he refuses to grant *h.*

HALKIN: (1) *ABRAHAM S. H.* (1903–): US educator and orientalist. Born in White Russia, he went to the US in 1914. He has taught Hebrew and Semitics at Columbia Univ. and Brooklyn College, and is professor of Hebrew at the College of the City of New York and of Jewish history at the Jewish Theological Seminary. He edited and contributed studies of Judeo-Arabic history and literature. H. was the first teacher of Hebrew in New York municipal colleges. He settled in Jerusalem in 1970. (2) *SHEMUEL H.* (1897–1960): Yiddish poet in the USSR; cousin of (1) and (3). One of the few Yiddish Communist writers in the Soviet Union who did not decry Jewish tradition, he was arrested during the campaign against Yiddish writers in 1948 but released in 1955. He wrote plays and poems. (3) *SHIMON H.* (1899–): Hebrew author; brother of (1). He was born in White Russia and emigrated to the US in 1914. He lived in Palestine from 1932 to 1939, and after a further stay in the US became professor of modern Hebrew literature at the Hebrew Univ. (1949). His works include poetry, novels (several about American Jewry), critical essays, and translations.

ḤALLAH (Heb.): Portion of dough, donated in Temple times to the priest (Num. 15:17–21). In post-Temple times, the rabbis ordained that the *h*— which had to be at least the size of an olive—must be separated and burnt. The *h* should be given from wheat, barley, spelt, oats, and rye used when baking bread. If the *h* is not taken from the dough, it must be removed from the bread. According to the rabbis, a private individual gave 1/24th and a shopkeeper 1/48th of the loaf. Separation of the *h* was one of the main commandments obligatory on women. The term *ḥ* is used today to refer to the Sabbath loaf, from which *ḥ* has presumably been removed.

ḤALLAH (Heb. "Dough-Offering"): Ninth tractate in the Mishnah order *Zeraim,* containing 4 chapters. It has *gemara* in the Palestinian, but not the Babylonian, Talmud. It deals with the setting aside of the ḤALLAH.

HALLE: German city. Jewish settlement is definitely known from the second half of the 12th cent. The Jews were under the protection of the archbishop of Magdeburg but suffered the hostility of the townspeople. A massacre, followed by expulsion, took place in 1206. Returning later in the century, they underwent many persecutions and were annihilated during the Black Death (1349). The succeeding community was expelled in 1493, and Jews were only permitted to resettle at the end of the 17th cent. A synagogue was opened in 1700 and a Hebrew press operated 1709–14. 1,400 Jews lived there before the Nazi era. About 50 Jews were living there in 1967.

HALLEL (Heb. "praise"): Term referring to Ps. 113–18 in liturgical use. The Talmud regards these psalms as a single composition; another theory holds them to have been assembled for liturgical use at the rededication of the Temple after the Maccabean wars, and later to have become accepted for all three pilgrim festivals. The rabbis regarded the reading of *H.* as a commandment and ordained opening and closing blessings. On Passover eve it is recited in the synagogue in some rites and during the *Seder* service. H. is recited in the morning service

Rose Halprin.

on the first day (2 days in the Diaspora) of Passover, and on Pentecost, Tabernacles, and Ḥanukkah. In Babylon, *H.* was recited — with the omission of two sections — on the New Moon, and this custom has been retained ("half H.") and extended to the latter days of Passover. Ps. 113–18 are called by the rabbis the Egyptian *H.* (cf. Ps. 114–8) whereas Ps 136 was termed the Great *H.*

HALLELUJAH or **HALLELUYAH** (Heb. "praise ye the Lord"): Refrain at the beginning and end of certain psalms. This refrain was used also as the congregational response during the reading of the Great *Hallel* in the Talmudic Period. The Aramaic form is *Allelujah,* and in this form found its way, through the influence of the Septuagint, into Christian liturgy.

HALPER, ALBERT (1904–): US novelist. During the 1930's he utilized personal experience to write about life among the working class (*Union Square, The Foundry, The Little People*).

HALPER, BENZION (1884–1924): Scholar. Born in Lithuania, he settled in the US in 1911 and taught at Dropsie College, Philadelphia, from 1914. His published works were on Hebrew and Arabic, including an anthology of post-biblical Hebrew literature and a catalogue of Cairo *genizah* documents.

HALPERT, SAMUEL (1884–1930): US painter. Born in Russia, he was taken to the US in 1890. Following studies in Europe, he returned to the US after 1914 and pioneered in the development of modern art in America.

HALPRIN, ROSE LURIA (c. 1900–): US Zionist. She was national president of Hadassah 1932–4 and 1947–52. From 1946 to 1968 she was a member

The Hallel prayer. (From the 15th cent. Nuremberg Haggadah.)

of the executive of the Jewish Agency. In 1969 she was appointed to head the American division of the World Jewish Congress.

ḤALUKKAH (Heb. "division"): The distribution of collections made abroad for the support of the poor in Palestine. "*Ḥ*. Jews" were those living on such contributions. This type of charity is ancient and already in the time of the tannaim, monies were collected even in Europe for the support of the academies and scholars in Palestine. The new settlement set up in Jerusalem from the 13th cent. onward and the academies established there were entirely supported by *Ḥ*. Emissaries sent from Palestine to collect money abroad were known as *meshullaḥim* or *shadarim*. In the 17th and 18th cents., these emissaries were sent only from the four "holy cities" of Jerusalem, Hebron, Safed, and Tiberias. They were usually men of great piety and learning and made a profound impression; among the most noted were Ḥayyim Joseph David Azulai and Moses Ḥagiz. Originally the Sephardi group sent most of the emissaries, and much of the money came from Turkey, Algeria, and Morocco. Later, with the increase of the Ashkenazim, most of the monies came from Europe. Many countries had their own *kolel* or national group supported by the communities in the countries of origin. The system of *Ḥ*. continued to the present century.

ḤALUTZ (Heb.): A pioneer, especially in agriculture, in Israel. See He-Ḥalutz.

HAM: Son of Noah. On account of his unseemly behavior toward his father, his descendants, the Canaanites, were cursed and condemned to servitude (Gen. 9:20 ff.). H. was "father" of Cush (Nubia and Ethiopia), Put (Libya and Morocco), Mizraim (Egypt), and Canaan (Syria and Palestine). In philology, the languages of Africa S of Egypt which are related to Semitic are called Hamitic.

HA-MABBIT (Heb. "The Onlooker"): Hebrew weekly literary journal, edited by Peretz Smolenskin in Vienna, Feb.–Oct. 1878.

HAMADAN: Town of Iran; identified with Ecbatana where Cyrus issued his decree permitting the Jews to rebuild the Jerusalem Temple (Ezra 6:2). An ancient Jewish tradition identifies H. with Shushan and regards a mausoleum in the city as the tomb of Esther and Mordecai: it is more likely that of Queen Sushan-dukht of Susa, Jewish wife of Yazdegerd I (4th cent.), the reputed founder and builder of H. Hebrew inscriptions indicate that the tombs were built or reconstructed by a pious Jewess of the 13th cent. H. was early the seat of a Jewish community. Although Benjamin of Tudela's estimate (c. 1170) of their number at 50,000 is an exaggeration, H. was certainly, along with Isfahan, the cultural center of Persian Jewry and the seat of a celebrated yeshivah. 17th cent. chronicles describe the persecution and forced

Inscription and monument in the traditional tombs of Esther and Mordecai, Hamadan.

conversion of its Jews under the Sefavid shahs, but under the Kajars, H. continued to be a leading Jewish center, despite discrimination and occasional outbursts of Moslem fanaticism. Many of its Jews have immigrated to Israel. Jewish pop. (1970): 400.

HA-MAGGID (Heb. "The Narrator"): First Hebrew weekly journal. It was founded in 1856 in Lyck (E Prussia) by Eliezer Lipmann Silbermann; David Gordon (who had been assistant editor from 1858) edited it 1880–6. It continued to appear (in its later years in Berlin, then Cracow) until 1903, its name being changed to *Ha-Maggid he-Ḥadash, Ha-Maggid le-Yisrael,* and *Ha-Shavua.* It was noted for its moderation and was influential both in Haskalah and Orthodox circles. Zionist in outlook from the 1860's, it was the first organ of *Ḥibbat Zion.*

ḤAMAM-LIF (ancient Naro): Town in Tunisia. Remains of a 4th cent. synagogue with a remarkable mosaic floor have been discovered there.

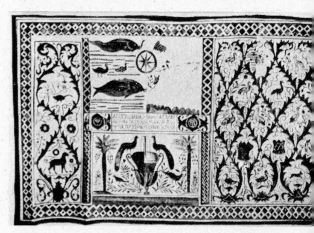

Mosaic floor from the 4th cent. synagogue at Ḥamam-Lif.

HAMAN: Chief minister of Ahasuerus, king of
Persia (Est. 3–9). His resentment of the independent attitude of Mordecai led him to detest all Jews
and he planned their annihilation. His scheme having
been frustrated by Esther, H. and his sons were
hanged. In memory of their deliverance, the Jews
observe the festival of PURIM. H. is called "the
Agagite" which was interpreted by the rabbis to
indicate his descent from Agag, king of Amalek.
Scholars differ as to his historicity. The name H.
has become synonymous with an enemy of the Jews.

HAMAT GEDER see **GADARA**

HA-MAVDIL (Heb. "who differentiates" i.e., between the sacred and the secular): A hymn in
both the Ashkenazi and Sephardi liturgies chanted
at home after the HAVDALAH on the conclusion of
the Sabbath. It was written by the otherwise unknown Isaac Ha-Katan possibly for the conclusion
of the Day of Atonement. Another hymn for this
latter occasion, forming the acrostic "Isaac," has
the same opening.

HAMBOURG, MARK (1879–1960): Pianist. Born
in Russia, he settled in England in 1894 and
achieved world renown.

HAMBURG: German city. Wealthy Marranos
deriving from Spain and Portugal were living there
at the end of the 16th cent. The citizens demanded
their expulsion but the city council realized their
economic value and protected them. These Jews were
financiers (some helping to found the Bank of Hamburg in 1619), shipbuilders, importers, etc. Ashkenazi
Jews lived in the neighboring town of ALTONA from
1622 and began to settle in H. in 1627. Most of the
Ashkenazim were expelled in 1649 as a result of
clerical agitation and moved to Altona, under Danish
rule, going daily to H. to trade. A handful resettled
in H. after some years and were reinforced by refugees
from E Europe. The three neighboring Ashkenazi
congregations of H., Altona, and Wandsbeck were
united in 1671. As a result of the drastic increase in
taxation in 1697, many of the wealthy Sephardim
moved to Altona or Amsterdam. Distinguished
scholars lived in H., Tzevi Ashkenazi maintaining
his *klaus* there and Jonathan Eibeschütz officiating
from 1750. GLÜCKEL of Hameln in her memoirs
vividly describes Jewish life in 17th cent. H. In 1812,
the triple Ashkenazi community was abolished and
a single community established. Under the French
occupation (1811–14), Jews were granted equality
but the restrictions were reimposed in 1814 and
confirmed by the Congress of Vienna. In 1817–8, the
Israelitischer Tempelverein was founded and adopted
liturgical reforms which were bitterly opposed by
the traditional section of the community. Jews
suffered during the HEP! HEP! riots of 1819, but
in 1850, were again recognized as citizens, largely
through the efforts of Gabriel REISSER. Communal

Haman leading Mordecai.
(From an illuminated Megillah.)

life was full and varied, and Jewish elementary and
secondary schools were founded in the 19th cent.
In 1933, there were 16,885 Jews, but these either left
or were annihilated under the Nazi regime. The
community was reorganized after World War II, and
in 1973 numbered 1,485.

HAMBURGER, JACOB (1826–1911): German
scholar; from 1859, chief rabbi of Mecklenburg-
Strelitz. He published the first encyclopedia of Jewish
subjects in German (*Real-Encyclopädie für Bibel und
Talmud,* 1883–6) and other works on Judaica.

HA-MEASSEPH (Heb. "The Gatherer"): The first
secular Hebrew monthly journal, appearing from
1783 to 1829 (with numerous interruptions). Founded
at Königsberg by young Jewish *maskilim,* it was
subsequently published in Berlin, Altona, Dessau,
and Breslau. It filled an important function in the
history of the Hebrew Enlightenment movement and
its literature and gave its name to a literary school,
the MEASSEPHIM.

HA-MEIRI (originally **FEUERSTEIN**), **AVIGDOR**
1890–1970): Hebrew poet and novelist. He was
born in Carpatho-Russia, and settled in Palestine in
1921. A fertile author, he published hundreds of poems
and stories (many on topical themes), translations,

Document issued in 1708 by the Senate of Hamburg
forbidding members of the Portuguese community to
leave the communal organization.

Oscar Hammerstein II.

critical articles, etc. Two collections of his tales, *Ha-Shiggaon ha-Gadol* ("The Great Madness") and *Gehinnom shel Mattah* ("Hell Below"), describe his experiences as a Hungarian soldier and Russian prisoner in World War I.

HA-MELITZ (Heb. "The Advocate"): Hebrew periodical appearing 1860–1904, originally weekly; from 1886, daily. It was founded by Alexander Zederbaum-Erez who was its editor until 1893 when he was succeeded by Leon Rabbinovitz. The central organ of Russian Jewry, it appeared in Odessa 1860–71 and St. Petersburg 1871–3, 1878–1904. *H.* was moderately conservative in tone and was very influential. It issued a Yiddish supplement, *Kol Mevasser.*

HAMELN, GLÜCKEL OF see **GLÜCKEL OF HAMELN**

ḤAMETZ see **LEAVEN**

HA-MEVASSER (Heb. "The Herald"): (1) First Hebrew weekly journal in Galicia; appeared in Lvov 1861–6. (2) Hebrew political and literary weekly, edited by Vladimir Jabotinsky; appeared in Constantinople 1910–11.

HAMILTON: Canadian city. Jews lived there from the mid-19th cent. The Orthodox congregation Anshe Sholem came into being in 1863. By the time its synagogue was erected in 1882, it had become Reform, the first of its kind in Canada. There are 4 Orthodox synagogues in H. and a Council of Jewish Organizations, established in 1934. Its United Jewish Welfare Fund was organized in 1939. Jewish pop. (1973): 4,000.

ḤAMISHAH ASAR BI-SHEVAT see **SHEVAT, FIFTEENTH OF**

HAMMERSTEIN: (1) *OSCAR H. I.* (1847–1919): Impresario. Born in Germany, he went to the US in 1863. Though best remembered as a New York opera producer and builder of theaters, he was also an inventor, composer, and journalist. He attempted unsuccessfully to popularize grand opera in England. (2) *OSCAR H. II* (1895–1960): US librettist; grandson of (1). Among the musicals for which he wrote the librettos were *Rose Marie, Show Boat, Oklahoma,* and *South Pacific.*

*HAMMURABI: W Semitic king ruling in Babylon 1728–1686 BCE. His famous legal code was discovered at the beginning of this century. It concerns various aspects of social life, and its penalties are generally severe, enforcing the Jus Talionis. There is much resemblance between this code and biblical legislation and it has been surmised that both arose from a uniform legal tradition rooted in Mesopotamian culture. However, there are significant differences resulting from the secular and political nature of H.'s legislation, which is based on custom and obedience to the king's will, in contrast to the religious and ethical nature of the Pentateuch with its appeal to the human conscience. The identification of H. with Amraphel (Gen. 14) is now generally rejected.

HAMNUNA: Name of several Babylonian amoraim in the 3rd and 4th cents. CE including (1) *H.* (fl 4th cent.), a distinguished scholar frequently consulted by the exilarch; author of the saying "study of the Torah takes precedence even over good deeds" and of the benediction recited at the public Reading of the Law (*"asher baḥar banu"*); (2) *H. SABA*

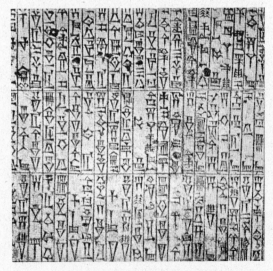

Fragment of the Laws of Hammurabi.

("H. the Elder"), who was either identical with (1) or (more probably) was an amora of the following generation; and (3) *H. ZUTA* ("H. the lesser"), a younger contemporary of (2), who composed a potential prayer incorporated into the Day of Atonment liturgy (*Elohai ad she-lo notzarti*).

HA-MOTZI (Heb. "who brings forth" i.e., bread from the earth, cf. Ps. 104:14): Blessing over bread, called after its first distinctive word. It falls under the "blessings of enjoyment," derived from the principle that a man should not enjoy anything without uttering a BENEDICTION, and is recited irrespective of the amount eaten. On the other hand, a concluding benediction is only required if bread at least equivalent in size to an olive has been consumed.

HANANEL BEN ḤUSHIEL (990 — c. 1055): N African talmudist. He was born at Kairouan and succeeded his father as head of the academy there. He composed a commentary — one of the first — on most of the Babylonian Talmud, distinguished for its clarity and brevity and reflecting its author's broad erudition. The extant fragments are printed in the outer margin of the standard editions. H. paid special attention to the establishment of the correct text. He also wrote a commentary on the Pentateuch, of which only isolated fragments have survived, and halakhic works.

HANANIAH (Ḥanina; fl. c. 135): Tanna. On the advice of his uncle and teacher, R Joshua, he emigrated after the Bar Kokhba revolt from Palestine to Babylonia where he founded an academy at Nehar Pekod. Because the Sanhedrin had ceased to function, he introduced his own calendar deciding on intercalation and dates of the new moon. After Hadrian's death, however, the Sanhedrin was reconstituted and called on H. to recognize its authority. Eventually he agreed, urging all the Babylonian congregations not to secede from the Palestinian Sanhedrin.

HANANIAH (HANINA) BEN ḤAKHINAI (40–135?): Tanna. He was one of the few sages of Jabneh who, though not ordained, were permitted to argue cases before the rabbis. According to tradition, he was one of the TEN MARTYRS, meeting his fate at the age of 95.

HANANIAH BEN TERADYON (fl. 2nd cent.): Tanna. His school at Siknin in Galilee had a reputation for authoritative decisions. He publicly defied the Hadrianic decree forbidding religious teaching, and for this was condemned to death by the Romans, being wrapped in a Torah scroll and burned. His daughter BERURIAH became the wife of R Meir.

HANDICRAFTS see **CRAFTS**

HANDLIN, OSCAR (1915–): US historian. He has taught at Harvard since 1939 (professor, 1955). His writings include *The Uprooted* (for which he was awarded a Pulitzer Prize), *Race and Nationality in American Life*, and *The Americans*.

ḤANINA BAR ḤAMA (d. c. 250): Palestinian amora; lived in Sepphoris. A noted halakhist and aggadist, he was author of the saying "everything is in the power of Heaven except the fear of Heaven."

ḤANINA BEN DOSA (fl. 1st cent.): Tanna. He was noted for his extreme piety and many miracles. He taught that fear of sin should precede learning and that good works stand above learning (*Avot* 3, 9). His prayers for the sick were considered of great efficacy (*Berakhot* 34*b*). He lived in extreme poverty, and of him it was related that a Divine voice proclaimed daily "The whole world is fed by the merits of H. my son, but H. himself is satisfied with a measure of carobs from one Sabbath eve to the next" (*Berakhot* 17*b*).

HANKIN, YEHOSHUA (1864–1945): Zionist pioneer. Born in the Ukraine, he settled in Palestine in 1882. As early as 1897, he tried to acquire from the Arabs land in the Valley of Jezreel where he first successfully negotiated a land purchase in behalf of the Jewish National Fund in 1909. In 1920, he acquired there an extensive tract making possible large-scale Jewish colonization. From 1932, H. was director of the Palestine Land Development Co.

HANNAH: Mother of Samuel; wife of Elkanah. When barren, she vowed that if she became mother of a son, he would be consecrated to the service of God. Her prayer being answered, she brought the child Samuel to serve Eli the priest. H.'s prayer (I Sam. 2:1–10) is regarded by some scholars as being of late origin.

HANNAH AND HER SEVEN SONS see **MACCABEES**

HANNOVER, NATHAN NATA (d. 1683): Kabbalist and chronicler. He was born in Volhynia from which he fled during the Cossack rising of 1648 and subsequently served as rabbi in several centers including Leghorn, Jassy, and Ungarisch-Brod (Moravia) where he was killed during a Turkish siege. H. is the author of the chronicle *Yeven Metzulah* ("Deep Mire," 1653), a major historical source for the Chmielnicki pogroms of 1648–52. Some of the beautiful kabbalistic prayers in his *Shaare Zion* became generally accepted.

HA-NOAR HA-OVED (Heb. "The Working Youth"): Junior group of the Israel General Federation of Labor (*Histadrut*). Founded in 1924, it numbers some 100,000 members (1974) aged between 10 and 18. It has settlement projects and maintains handicraft schools. Its members are organized into crafts sections affiliated with the parallel trade unions in the *Histadrut*. Some of the older members prepare for agricultural settlement. It has Jewish and non-Jewish members.

HA-NOAR HA-TZIYYONI (Heb. "The Zionist Youth"): Pioneering Zionist youth movement. It originated in E Europe, and in the early 1930's, its

World Organization was established, with head-quarters in Poland. From the same period, it founded kibbutzim in Palestine and later was responsible for setting up the settlements of the HA-OVED HA-TZIYYONI movement. After the establishment of the state of Israel, its members helped to form the PROGRESSIVE Party. Most of the Diaspora membership perished during World War II, and it has since developed chiefly in Latin America and W Europe. The headquarters are now in Tel-Aviv, and it has 2,000 members in Israel, where it has 6 kibbutzim.

HA-NOTEN TESHUAH (Heb. "He who gives salvation"): Opening words of prayer recited in many countries for the welfare of the government (originally, of the king) during the Sabbath and festival morning service. The prayer, probably stemming from Spain, became customary in the 14th cent. It is frequently recited by the rabbi, holding a Scroll of Law. In Israel, a prayer for the state replaces *H. T.*

HANOVER: German city. Jews are first mentioned there in 1292. They contributed to the well-being of the city by their moneylending, and this function was recognized in the municipal law of 1303. The Jews of H. nevertheless suffered during the Black Death massacres (1349). Few Jews lived there subse-

quently, although a small congregation was organized in 1499. An edict banning them from Hanoverian territory was issued in 1553, but when the province came under the control of the dukes of Brunswick in 1584, Jews were readmitted. In the 17th cent. their numbers grew, the rabbi being given authority over the outlying communities from 1687. In 1755, a Hebrew printing-press was established in H. There were 4,839 Jews there in 1933 but they either left or were annihilated by the Nazis. A community was re-established after World War II and in 1966, it numbered 455.

ḤANUKKAH (Heb. "dedication"): Eight-day cele-bration (*Kislev* 25 — *Tevet* 3) commemorating the victory of JUDAH THE MACCABEE over Antiochus Epiphanes and the subsequent rededication of the Temple and altar. Judah and his brothers assigned this period to praise of the Lord and thanksgiving. After the destruction of the Temple, the festival was linked with the miracle of the cruse of oil which burned for 8 days (*Shabbat* 21*b*), and the duty of kindling lights was instituted (see MAOZ TZUR). One light is kindled on the first night and an extra one added each succeeding night. The 8-branched lamp (*menorah*) constructed to hold these lights has often been the object of artistic design. Work is not prohib-

Bronze Hanukkah lamp. France 14th–15th cents. (Roth Collection, Toronto).

Brass Hanukkah lamp. Eastern Europe, 18th cent. (Museum of Art, En Harod).

ited. The dedication-offering of the princes (Num. 7:1–8:4) is read from the Pentateuch in the synagogue, while in the liturgy, HALLEL is recited and a description of the H. miracle inserted in each *Amidah*. It is usual to spend the evenings in various games (e.g. spinning the H top, known as the *dredel* or *trendel*).

HA-OLAM (Heb. "The World"): Hebrew weekly journal of topical and literary content; published by the World Zionist Organization. It appeared in Cologne 1907–8, Vilna 1908–12, Odessa 1912–4, London 1919–20, 1924–36, Berlin 1923–4, and Jerusalem 1936–50.

HA-OVED HA-TZIYYONI (Heb. "The Zionist Worker"): Israel labor organization now called The Liberal Workers' Movement. Founded as the General Zionist Worker's section of the *Histadrut*, it has, as affiliates, 6 kibbutzim, 13 *moshavim* and 5 *moshavim shittuphiim* with 5,400 members (1968). Since 1948 it has been associated with the Progressive (later, Independent Liberal) Party.

HAPAX LEGOMENA (Gk.): Words occurring only once in the Bible. Many were at one time common words, some foreign, and a few, apparently, misspellings. The exact meaning of many h. l. is difficult to establish, unless they also happen to occur in later Hebrew or other Semitic languages. Saadyah and other medieval grammarians wrote studies on these words.

ḤAPHETZ ḤAYYIM (real name Israel Meir Kahan; 1835–1933): Talmudist. Born in Poland, he became one of the leaders of E European Orthodox Jewry, founding and conducting a yeshivah at Radin in Lithuania. In his later years he was active in *Agudat*

Israel. He was the author of many books on halakhah and morals, notably *Ḥaphetz Ḥayyim* ("Desiring Life"), an ethical and religious work discussing at length misdemeanors such as gossip and slander. He was subsequently known by its title.

HAPHTARAH (Heb. "conclusion," sometimes pronounced *Haphtorah*): Selection from the prophetic books of the Bible read in the synagogue on Sabbaths,

Page from an illuminated Yemenite Pentateuch, with Haphtarah readings, signed by the copyist Mosheh ben Amram, 1409.

festivals, and afternoons of fast days, after the reading from the Pentateuch. These selections are chosen either because of their connection with the pentateuchal reading for the day or because of their special appropriateness to the particular holiday or special Sabbath. The origin of the practice is uncertain but is doubtless very ancient. In talmudic times, it was customary to read also a selection from the Hagiographa during the Sabbath afternoon service. The *H.* is chanted according to a special system of cantillation by a member of the congregation (frequently as part of the BAR-MITZVAH ceremony, or in Sephardi communities, by a child). One special benediction is recited before reading the *H.* and four on its conclusion.

HA-POEL (Heb. "The Worker"): Israel workers' sports organization affiliated to the HISTADRUT. The first branch was founded in 1924 and the association established in 1926. In 1974, it had 500 branches throughout the country with 90,000 members. It sponsors regular championships in most sports and is also concerned with the organization of recreation and sporting activities at places of employment. It is affiliated with the Workers' Sports International.

HA-POEL HA-MIZRAHI (Heb. "The *Mizrahi* Worker"): Religious Zionist labor movement. It was officially established in Jerusalem in 1921, and its objectives defined as the building of Palestine with the right of labor assured, and the development of religious feeling among the workers. Beginning as part of the MIZRAHI movement, it is responsible for 70 cooperative settlements (60 moshavim and 11 kibbutzim), organized in the *Igud ha-Moshavim* and HA-KIBBUTZ HA-DATI movement. It conducts labor exchanges, educational institutions (together with *Mizrahi*), cooperatives, etc. From its foundation it has been part of the Zionist Organization and since 1948, it has participated in most Israel coalition governments. In the First Knesset (1949), it had 6 members; in the Second (1951), 8; in the Third (jointly with *Mizrahi*), 11; in the Fourth and Fifth (jointly), 12; in the Sixth, 11 (jointly), in the Seventh, 12 (jointly) and in the Eighth 10 (jointly). Groups also exist outside Israel, with the World Head Office of *Mizrahi* and *Ha-Poel ha-Mizrahi* in Jerusalem. Its Women's Organization is responsible *inter alia* for children's homes and social welfare, the building and upkeep of kindergartens, etc. Its youth movement is BENE AKIVA. After amalgamating with *Mizrahi* in 1955, its functions became those of a religious trade union dealing specifically with labor problems, all other activities being transferred to the National Religious Party, *Mizrahi—Ha-Poel ha-Mizrahi.*

HA-POEL HA-TZAIR (Heb. "The Young Worker"): (1) Palestinian Zionist labor party. Founded at Petah Tikvah in 1905, it stood for personal settlement on the soil and the rights of Jewish labor. It opposed class-struggle and rejected adherence to the international workers' movement. Its members founded the first *kevutzah* at Deganyah and the first *moshav ovedim* at Nahalal. It prompted much creative cultural activity and influenced Zionist youth in the Diaspora, especially the *Tzeire Zion* movement with which it combined to form the *Hitahdut.* The party merged with *Ahdut ha-Avodah* to form MAPAI in 1930. (2) Weekly journal, organ of the *Ha-Poel ha-Tzair* party and then *Mapai*; appearing since 1907.

HARAN: (1) Brother of Abraham; father of Lot. He lived and died at Ur of the Chaldees (Gen. 11:26–31). (2) Trading town of NW Mesopotamia; center of a moon cult. It is mentioned several times in Genesis with reference to the patriarchs. Assyrian inscriptions from this time mention a Habiru (Hebrew?) settlement in the vicinity which some scholars link with Terah's residence there. In the 12th cent., Benjamin of Tudela found a small Jewish community in H.

HARBIN: Town in Manchuria, China. A few Jews settled there in the early 19th cent. and the community became numerous with the immigration of Russian refugees after 1917. It dwindled during the Japanese occupation and most of the last survivors settled in Israel.

HARBY: (1) *LEAH COHEN H.* (1849–1918): US writer, born and died in Charleston, S C; granddaughter of (3). Among her writings are *The Earliest Texas* and *The Tejas: Their Habits, Government, and Superstitions.* (2) *LEVI MYERS H.* (1793–1870): US naval officer; brother of (3). He entered the US navy at an early age and was a British prisoner in the War of 1812. H. was dismissed from the navy for participating in the Texas struggle for independence, but later was reinstated and rose to the rank of captain. He fought with the S in the Civil War. (3) *ISAAC H.* (1788–1828): US editor, author, and playwright. In 1824, he helped in the founding at Charleston SC of the Reform Society of Israelites which started the Reform movement in American Judaism.

HARDEN, MAXIMILIAN (originally Felix Witkowski; 1861–1927): German essayist and political polemicist. He founded the influential periodical *Die Zukunft,* largely written by himself. H. opposed World War I and accepted—though not uncritically—the Weimar Republic, thereby arousing the hostility of the neo-nationalists which culminated in an attempt at his assassination. Although baptized in his youth, he maintained an interest in Jewish affairs.

HA-REUVENI, EPHRAIM (1881–1953): Israel botanist. He was born in Russia and in 1906 settled in Palestine, being appointed lecturer in biblical botany at the Hebrew Univ. in 1935. In 1912, he founded the Museum of Biblical and Talmudical Plants which, in 1936, was transferred to the Hebrew Univ. H. published numerous studies on the flora of

Avraham Harman.

Palestine, some in collaboration with his wife Hannah (d. 1956).

HARKAVY: (1) *ALBERT H.* (Abraham Elijah; 1835–1919): Russian orientalist and from 1877, librarian of the Hebrew department in the Imperial Public Library of St. Petersburg. He published over 400 studies on various branches of Judaica, utilizing unknown mss chiefly concerning the gaonic era and the evolution of Jewish sects, especially the Karaites. H. also wrote pioneer studies in the history and languages of Russian Jewry. He gained widespread recognition by his work on ancient Jewish tombstones in the Crimea, which exposed the fabrications of the Karaite scholar, Abraham Firkovich. (2) *ALEXANDER H.* (1863–1939): Lexicographer. Born in Russia, he went in 1882 to the US where he joined a collective agricultural colony which failed. For several years he supported himself by manual labor while experimenting with Yiddish papers (all short-lived), first in Montreal and then in Baltimore. In 1887, he settled in New York and compiled textbooks and dictionaries of the English language from and into English, Hebrew, Yiddish, Russian, and Polish, all designed as aids in the Americanization of immigrants.

HARMAN, AVRAHAM (1914–): Israel diplomat. Born in London, he settled in Palestine in 1940. He occupied diplomatic positions in Canada and New York, was a member of the Jewish Agency Executive 1955–9, and Israel ambassador in the US 1959–1968. In 1968 he was appointed president of the Hebrew University. His wife *ZINA H.* (1914–), also born in England, was chairman of the executive board of *Unicef* in 1964; *Mapai* Knesset member 1969–73.

HAROSET: Food eaten on *Seder* night (for ingredients see COOKERY). The bitter herb is dipped into *h.* to render it less harsh. The rabbis interpreted the *h.* as symbolizing the mortar with which the Israelites worked in Egypt.

HARP (Heb. *nevel*): Stringed instrument mentioned in the Bible; its exact identification is still uncertain. It was played by prophets in Samuel's time (I Sam. 10:5), accompanied the removal of the Ark to Jerusalem (I Chron. 13:8), and was popular in the Temple (*Y. Sukkot* 5, 6). In Israel, an international harp contest is now held biennially.

HARRIS, SAM HENRY (1872–1941): US theatrical producer. At first in partnership with George M. Cohan and from 1920, independently, he was one of Broadway's best-known producers.

HARRISBURG: City in Pennsylvania, US. Its Jewish community goes back to the 1840's. In 1852, the first congregation Ohev Sholom was established by German immigrants: at first Orthodox, it became Reform in 1867. In 1884, an Orthodox synagogue was established; in 1904, a Hasidic; and in 1926, a Conservative. In the 1880's, Jews arrived from Russia and Poland. A United Jewish Community was founded in 1933. Jewish pop. (1973): 4,600.

HARRISSE, HENRY (1829–1910): US historian and bibliographer. H. was born in Paris, and returned there after teaching at North Carolina State and Georgetown universities. He was one of the founders of the modern school of historical research in connection with the period of discovery and exploration in America.

HART: Canadian family. *AARON H.* (1724–1800) went to Quebec from England in the army of General Amherst which captured Montreal in 1760. Upon leaving the army he settled in Three Rivers, Quebec, and eventually became one of the largest landowners in Canada. He was largely responsible for developing Three Rivers into an important trading city, establishing there a number of business ventures. His second son, *EZEKIEL H.* (1770–1843), entered politics, was elected in 1807 and 1809 to represent Three Rivers in the Assembly of Lower Canada but was not allowed to sit on either occasion because he refused to take the Christian oath. This caused a protracted controversy which lasted until 1832 when the disability imposed on Jews to hold office was removed by an act of the Canadian House of Commons. Descendants of the H. family have been prominent in various branches of Canadian life.

HART, AARON (1670–1756): English rabbi. Born in Breslau, he went to England about 1704 as rabbi of the newly-established Ashkenazi community,

A modern version of the First-Fruits festival in an Israel Kibbutz.

officiating in the Great Synagogue in London until his death. He is regarded as the first of the English chief rabbis.

HART, ERNEST ABRAHAM (1835–1898): English physician and humanitarian. A specialist in ophthalmics, he founded and edited the *British Medical Journal* (from 1866). His strenuous advocacy was responsible for the enactment of the Infant Life Protection Act and the establishment of the Metropolitan Asylums Board.

HART, JACOB see **ELIAKIM BEN ABRAHAM OF LONDON**

HART, MOSS (1904–1961): US playwright. His plays include *Lady in the Dark*, and (with George S. Kaufmann) *You Can't Take it With You, The Man Who Came to Dinner*, etc. He also wrote an autobiography *Act One*.

HART, SOLOMON ALEXANDER (1806–1881): English painter. The son of a Plymouth silversmith, he was professor of painting at the Royal Academy 1854–63. He was noted for canvases depicting dramatic episodes of English history, among them the 1655 Whitehall Conference to discuss the readmission of the Jews.

HARTFORD: City in Connecticut, US. Jews lived in H. as early as 1659. In the late 1830's, immigrants from Germany began to arrive, and the Beth Israel congregation was organized in 1843. Many Russian Jews settled there from the 1880's on. A United Jewish Social Service Agency exists in H. The weekly *Connecticut Jewish Ledger* was founded in 1929. In 1973, H. had 23,000 Jews with 22 synagogues and a Jewish Federation founded in 1945.

HARTMANN, MORITZ (1821–1872): Austrian author and liberal agitator. His revolutionary poems, novels, and political writings had great influence, and he was a delegate to the German Parliament at Frankfort-on-Main in 1848. From 1868, he was an editor of the Vienna *Neue Freie Presse*.

HARTOG: English family. *NUMA EDWARD H.* (1846–1871) became senior wrangler (in mathematics) at Cambridge. His inability to graduate because he was a Jew stimulated the abolition of university tests in England in 1871. His brother, *SIR PHILIP JOSEPH H.* (1864–1947), after lecturing in chemistry at Manchester Univ., was vice-chancellor of the Univ. of Dacca (India), chairman of the education committee of the Indian Statutory Commission, and one of the recognized English experts on university education.

HARTUV see **BET SHEMESH**

HARVEST, HARVEST-FESTIVALS: In biblical times, as now, harvesting in Palestine began immediately after Passover, i.e., in April-May, especially in the Jordan Valley. In the coastal plain and hill regions, it continued throughout the summer. First came the gathering-in of barley and wheat, followed by olives and the vintage (see GEZER CALENDAR). There were three harvest-festivals: the Omer festival when the barley-flour offering was brought to the Temple (Passover); the first-fruit (BIKKURIM) festival seven weeks later, when the wheat ripened (Feast of Weeks); and the feast of the ingathering *(Asiph)* marking the conclusion of the entire harvest (Tabernacles). The agricultural significance of the festivals has been re-emphasized in modern Israel by special observances, particularly in the villages.

ḤAS VE-SHALOM (Heb. "forbear and [hold your] peace": also *Ḥas ve-Ḥalilah*): Expression of apprehension of an undesired occurrence (= "God forbid").

ḤASDAI see **IBN ḤASDAI**

ḤASDAI CRESCAS see **CRESCAS**

ḤASDAI IBN SHAPRUT see **IBN SHAPRUT**

HA- SHAHAR (Heb. "The Dawn"): Name of several Hebrew journals, the most important being a literary monthly appearing in Vienna 1868–85. The editor (except for the last four numbers) was Peretz Smolenskin. It played an important part in awakening Zionist consciousness among the *maskilim* and contributed significantly to the development of modern Hebrew literature.

HA-SHEM (Heb. "The Name"): Metonym commonly used to avoid mentioning the name of God, especially in phrases such as *be ezrat ha-Shem* ("with the help of God"); *barukh ha Shem* ("Blessed be God," used as an affirmative reply to an inquiry after health, etc.); *im yirtze ha-Shem* ("God willing").

HA-SHILOAḤ (Heb. "Siloam"): Hebrew literary monthly appearing 1896–1927. Published by the Aḥiasaph society, its editors included Aḥad Ha-Am, Bialik, Klausner, and Fichman. Until 1920, it was edited in Odessa (except for a short period in Warsaw) and thereafter, in Jerusalem. Under Aḥad Ha-Am, its content was exclusively Jewish and it polemicized against Herzl's political Zionism. After Klausner took over the editorship (1903), general topics were also discussed. It was long the central organ of Hebrew literature and exercised an immense influence.

HASHKAMAH (Heb. "early rising"): An early service held before the official morning prayers.

HASHKAVAH (often pronounced *ascava*; Heb. "Laying to rest"): Name given by the Sephardim to the memorial prayer, corresponding to the Ashkenazi YIZKOR.

HA-SHOMER (Heb. "The Watchman"): Organization of Jewish workers in Palestine founded in 1909 and commanded by Israel Shochat; it performed the dual function of defense of Jewish settlements and struggle for the employment of Jewish workers (KIBBUSH AVODAH). It was anticipated by the *Ha-Ḥoresh group* (1907) and the *Bar Giora* society (1908). H. originated the concept of a "labor legion" and participated in the establishment of several labor settlements during World War I and of the GEDUD HA-AVODAH subsequently. After the British conquest, it collaborated with the Upper Galilee police force

Ha-Shomer watchmen in Galilee.

and directed self-defense activities during the riots of 1920–1. Its functions were taken over by the HAGANAH.

HA-SHOMER HA-DATI (Heb. "The Religious Watchman"): Religious pioneering youth movement. Founded in Warsaw in 1929, it was chiefly active in E Europe and the US. It was affiliated to HA-POEL HA-MIZRAḤI and is now incorporated in BENE AKIVA.

HA-SHOMER HA-TZAIR (Heb. "The Young Guard"): Zionist youth organization and former Palestinian political party. Its first groups were formed in Galicia in 1913, and were reorganized in Vienna in 1917. They were influenced by the revolutionary ferment of the period, as well as by the German youth movements, and stirred by the heroism of *Ha-Shomer* in Palestine. They immigrated with the Third Aliyah (1919–21) and subsequently, and their settlement organization (HA-KIBBUTZ HA-ARTZI) was founded in 1927. Their ideology became revolutionary Marxist and demanded "ideological collectivism" (identity of doctrine among its members). Outside Palestine, it adopted scouting techniques and physical preparation for pioneering; the largest movement of its kind, its chief strength lay in Central and E Europe. Its political program, rejecting class-collaboration and advocating the joint organization of Arab and Jewish workers, led to the secession (1931) of sections favoring a united labor party. Before the UN partition vote of Nov. 1947, it favored a binational state to solve the Palestinian problem. In 1946, it formally became a political party, and in 1948, participated in the formation of MAPAM.

ḤASID, JUDAH see **JUDAH ḤASID HALEVI**

ḤASIDE ASHKENAZ (Heb. "The Ḥasidim (pietists) of Germany"): Medieval religious movement fostering a profound awareness of morality and its practical application. Its central figures were R SAMUEL, his son R JUDAH BEN SAMUEL HE-ḤASID (d. 1217), and R ELEAZAR ROKEAḤ (d. 1238). The teachings of the German Ḥasidim were assembled in *Sepher Ḥasidim* containing anecdotes, sayings, and practical advice on subjects of religious and social morality. The basis of the movement was (1) asceticism: by expurgating sin, doing penance, physical mortifications, and fasts (notably on Mondays and Thursdays); (2) humility: expressed in the rejection of honors, and the grateful acceptance of insults; (3) moral law: by basing conduct not on strict talmudic or common law but on moral considerations.

HASIDEANS or **ASIDEANS** (Greek form of *Ḥasidim* = the pious): Jewish religious sect. Its precise date of origin is unknown but it is first recorded during the persecutions of Antiochus Epiphanes in the 2nd cent. BCE when its members suffered martyrdom rather than desecrate the Sabbath and formed the backbone of the Hasmonean revolt. The Mishnah and Talmud mention their meticulous

Ḥasidim in a Polish town.

observance of the commandments, their frequent prayers which they would not even renounce on the approach of physical danger, and their rigid Sabbath observance. They ceased to support the Maccabees when the latter's secular political aims became clear. It has been suggested that they were the forerunners of the PHARISEE party.

ḤASIDISM: I. *History*: Ḥ is a religious and social movement founded by Israel BAAL SHEM TOV (1699–1761) in Volhynia and Podolia. It had no connection with previous movements of the same name, being the outgrowth of the depressed state of E European Jewry in the 18th cent. following the Chmielnicki massacres and Church persecutions. Internal Jewish life was also in a catastrophic condition owing to the oligarchic rule of the community and the disillusionment engendered by the Sabbetaian fiasco. The unlearned Jewish populace was speedily attracted by the Baal Shem Tov's preaching and doctrines. He taught that all are equal before the Almighty (the ignorant no less honored than the learned), that purity of heart was superior to study, and that devotion to prayer and the commandments was to be encouraged but ascetic practices eschewed. The new movement spread rapidly through E Europe and many who had been disappointed by the failure of the messianic movements turned to Ḥ. The Baal Shem Tov on his death was succeeded by Dov BER OF MEZHIRICH (d. 1773) who systematized Ḥasidic teaching, bringing it into line with the doctrine of Isaac Luria, and was responsible for the wave of adherents (many from the learned and influential classes) in Lithuania. Fierce opposition was evinced by the Lithuanian rabbis and communal heads, especially to the apparent pantheism of Ḥasidic theology. Dov Ber taught that the "saint must go down to the place of the husks to separate the good from the bad, redeeming the holy sparks from the husks." His antagonists (MITNAGGEDIM), led by the Gaon of Vilna, regarded these teachings as heretical and reminiscent of the reasoning by which Shabbetai Tzevi justified his apostasy. This opposition was intensified after SHNEOUR ZALMAN OF LYADY (d. 1813) became leader of the Ḥasidim. He founded the ḤABAD current, a philosophical and rationalizing movement within Ḥ. which attracted the scholars of White Russia and Lithuania. In 1784, the Mitnaggedim issued a manifesto against the Ḥasidim, prohibiting ritual slaughter performed by a Ḥasid and refusing to allow any member of the sect to hold public office. The bans were frequently reissued, and great bitterness was engendered throughout Lithuania. Elsewhere, however, there was far less opposition and Ḥ. branched into three main divisions. 1. The popular Ukrainian branch. This carried on the traditions of the original. Ḥ: elevation of the simple man, devotion in prayer, song and dance, and faith in the TZADDIK. To this branch belonged Nahum of Chernobyl (d. 1797) from whom sprang the TWERSKY family dynasty, LEVI ISAAC OF BERDICHEV (d. 1802), and NAḤMAN OF BRATZLAV (d. 1810). From Dov Ber of Mezhirich was descended ISRAEL OF ROZHIN and the ensuing dynasties (Chortkov, Sadagora). 2. The *Ḥabad* branch (see above). 3. The Polish-Galician branch, founded by ELIMELECH OF LIZENSK (d. 1786) who elevated the *tzaddik* to the role of intermediary between man and God, and Michel of Zloczov (d. 1786), noted for his saintly simplicity. Leading Polish *tzaddikim* included Jacob Isaac "the seer" of Lublin and Israel the maggid of Kozniece, who were the ancestors of the dynasties of Przysucha, Kotzk, and Gur. Polish Ḥ. was characterized by the stress on learning. The movement spread widely during the 19th cent. when the opposition of the Mitnaggedim abated, while the Ḥasidic dynasties exerted influence on social and cultural life. At the same time, the inner decline of Ḥ. began. Leadership became a matter of inheritance from father to son; the various dynastic groups fought among themselves for hegemony and influence over the Jewish masses. In Russia and Poland, the Ḥasidim turned increasingly to study and founded yeshivot. They joined hands with the Mitnaggedim to combat the common enemy — the Haskalah, whose writers (e.g. Perl, Erter) mocked the Ḥasidim and accused them of superstitious practice and blind faith. During the Nazi holocaust, all Ḥasidic centers were destroyed in Poland and Russia. Only a few of the *tzaddikim* escaped and re-established their "courts." These included R Aaron Rokaḥ of Belz

(in Tel Aviv), R Abraham Mordecai of Gur (Jerusalem), and R Joseph Isaac of Liubavich (New York).

II. *Doctrines*: The philosophic basic for Ḥ. is the Kabbalah as expounded by Isaac Luria, but whereas the Kabbalah concerned itself chiefly with cosmological considerations, Ḥ. (except possibly the *Ḥabad* stream) was primarily concerned with morality and religion. God — or the *Shekhinah* — incorporates all creation, including inorganic matter and vegetable, animal, and human life. Everything perceived is an illusive cover for Divinity. Evil is merely a cover for good, and all evil will eventually be turned into good. Man's function is to redeem the evil in nature and bring it within the radius of Divine Light. Evil thoughts must be sublimated. Everything — thoughts, words, and deeds — must be integrated for the sake of God who is all-pervasive. This approach leads to DEVEKUT and ecstasy, which must stem from both love and fear. Man must strive to attain that freedom from sensuality in which he will be unconscious of the lower world and only be conscious of the forms of the higher world, viz. angels and seraphim. Prayer in particular must be characterized by *devekut*. The basic principle of daily conduct is love of Israel. No man — even the wicked — must be despised, but only the evil quality within him. The Ḥasid must be joyful when he sees things are well with the Jewish people, and if the reverse, he must participate in their sorrow. Special emphasis is laid on humility. A basic premise is that evil desire can only be overcome by joy, and not by melancholy. For this reason, melody is exalted, having the power to draw the heart of man to God. The *tzaddik* plays a central role in Ḥ., being linked to God and bringing life to the world. Even the *tzaddik's* casual actions are raised to holiness, and his secular conversation has a Divine intent. Any apparent decline from his high state is only to redeem the sparks from the husks.

III. *Way of Life*: The *tzaddik* (or ADMOR, or simply *rebbe*) stood at the center of the movement. At first the *tzaddikim* were chosen for their piety and leadership, and this continued in Poland until the middle of the 19th cent. In the Ukraine, however, dynasties of *tzaddikim* were established from the outset. The Ḥasidim would travel to the *tzaddik* for the Sabbath to listen to his teaching and seek his advice. Before departing home, they would leave a *pitka* ("written slip" containing a list of the members of the family and their requests) and attached would be a *pidyon* ("ransom," i.e., money-offering). On Sabbaths and holidays, the Ḥasidim sat at the table of the *tzaddik*. Dressed in white, the *tzaddik* would begin to chant a melody. After the meal, he would expound Ḥasidic teaching. From each course of the meal he would leave *shirayim* ("left-overs") which would be seized by the Ḥasidim as a *segullah* ("good-fortune charm"). The meal of the *tzaddik* was regarded as an "altar" and a sacrifice. Ecstasy was particularly pronounced during the third Sabbath meal (*seudah shelishit*) when the Ḥasidim would sit in the closing darkness listening to the words of the *rebbe* and singing songs of *devekut*. The greatest number of Ḥasidim would congregate at festival-time, when their comradely affection (*dibbuk ḥaverim*) was especially strong. After prayer or a meal, the Ḥasidim would start to dance, the *rebbe* joining— and even leading— on occasion. After the death of a *tzaddik*, an OHEL would be built over his grave and visited by thousands of Ḥasidim on the anniversary of his death, which would be celebrated with drink and joy as a *yom de-hillula* ("day of celebration"). Some *tzaddikim* lived in poverty, distributing all their "ransom" money to the needy; others lived in luxurious style eventually leading to a degeneration which contributed to the decline of the movement. However, although much reduced numerically, H. is still widespread. Its teachings have become widely known in the occidental world mainly through the works of Martin Buber, both through his retelling of Ḥasidic anecdotes and through his philosophy which has been termed "neo-Ḥasidic."

HASKALAH (Heb. "Enlightenment"; the term was coined in 1832 by Judah Jeiteles): The movement for spreading modern European culture among Jews, c. 1750–1880. The H. school believed that Jewish Emancipation required intellectual and social conformity with the non-Jewish population and that the latter could be achieved by modernized and westernized Jewish religion and customs (including the active literary use of the Hebrew language). It thus attempted to mediate between unyielding Orthodoxy and radical assimilation. H. was transitory largely because the merely partial conformity and the Hebraism which it preached were insufficient or superfluous in the countries where it flourished. However, H. paved the way for Zionism by creating a stratum of secularized middle-class Jews imbued with Hebrew culture and faithful to their historic traditions, yet also permeated by the political and social ideas of the western world. While Jewish participation in western culture and interest in the sciences were cultivated in 18th cent. Orthodoxy by the Gaon of Vilna and his circle, they were regarded solely as aids to a more perfect knowledge of sacred tradition. The innovation of H. consisted in proclaiming such western education as necessary for the masses. A further important feature of H. was a strong element of national and linguistic romanticism which became the chief preoccupation of many of its literary representatives. The cradles of H. were the somewhat westernized Jewries in Holland and Italy as early as the 17th cent., but H. as a movement began in Berlin. There, mercantilism had produced a small Jewish capitalist class and, under Frederick II

(1740–86), European Enlightenment attitudes were dominant. The first manifestation of H. was the weekly *Kohelet Musar*, published for 2 weeks in 1750 by Moses MENDELSSOHN and T. Bock in imitation of the *Tatler* and *Spectator*. In 1783, Mendelssohn published his German translation of the Pentateuch in Hebrew characters with a rationalist commentary (*Biur*), the work of a group which included several young men from E Europe. The same group, the Association of Friends of Hebrew, started a Hebrew quarterly, HA-MEASSEPH (1784–1811). In spite of its insipid contents and reliance on translations from the German, this publication had a profound effect —especially outside Germany, for in that country full cultural assimilation rapidly outstripped the efforts of the *maskilim* (i.e., those engaged in H.). Only in Breslau did the Hebrew H. last until about 1830. When, in 1782, the Austrian emperor Joseph II initiated a policy of Emancipation linked by his Edict of Tolerance with the Germanization of the Jews of Galicia, N. H. WESSELY, a leader of the Berlin circle, greeted this fervently. Herz HOMBERG hastened to help by putting the proposals into practice and between 1787 and 1800, founded over 100 German-Jewish schools. The westernizing policy in Galicia was resisted by the Orthodox leaders (J. Orenstein, rabbi of Lemberg, imposed the ban on leading *maskilim* in 1816) and especially by the strong Ḥasidic community. The scanty literary activity of Galician H. consisted mainly of satirical writings directed against Ḥasidism (J. PERL, I. ERTER), but its chief achievement was the initiation of historical studies under the leadership of N. KROCHMAL and S. J. RAPOPORT. This was served by several Hebrew scholarly periodicals (BIKKURE HA-ITTIM, 1820–31; HE-ḤALUTZ, 1852–89; KEREM ḤEMED, 1853–57). In S Russia, also a stronghold of Ḥasidism, H. seems to have had an easier course. In contrast to Germany and Galicia, Russian *maskilim* used Yiddish in addition to Hebrew for their propaganda. The talmudist Manasseh Ilyer (1767–1831) published Yiddish booklets. In 1817, a Yiddish translation of *Die Entdeckung Amerikas* by the educator J. H. Campe was published at Berdichev; and in 1823, a Hebrew translation by M. A. GUNZBURG appeared at Vilna. A school for arts and crafts was founded by J. Perl at Tarnopol (then Russia) in 1819; in 1826, a similar school was opened at Odessa to which was added a girls' section in 1836 — education of women was previously almost unknown. By the early 1840's most larger communities had modern schools. In the 1830's, a Society of Lovers of Light and Enlightenment was founded at Berdichev; in 1841 six such societies conferred at Vilna and proposed, *inter alia*, that talmudic study be restricted to future rabbis. The central figure of S Russian H. was I. B. LEVINSON. The real home of H., however, was Lithuania, especially Vilna. Its

Soldiers of Antiochus at the siege of Jerusalem by Lebrun.

early leaders were M. A. Günzburg and A. LEBEN-SOHN. The latter, in particular, gave Hebrew H. literature its romantic and nationalist trends, which reached their peak in the writings of his son M. J. LEBENSOHN, J. L. Gordon in his earlier period, and the first Hebrew novelist A. MAPU. Here biblical Hebrew, the chosen vehicle of all H., was written most successfully, and the world of the Bible was made to illumine the ghetto. Under Catherine II and, especially, Paul and Alexander I, the Russian government seemed disposed to improve the Jew's position and favored the first steps of H. From 1815 onward, and, in particular, under Nicholas I (1825–55) this was replaced by a policy of repression aimed at securing mass conversion. In 1840–3, an attempt was made, with the help of the German rabbi Max LILIENTHAL, to employ the H. movement for furthering this purpose. The conflict thus engendered between H. and Orthodoxy developed in the 1850's, reinforced by the growing social rift within the community. The literary expression of the new aggressive H. was the realist movement which had the distinction of being the first Hebrew literary trend to develop in close association with contemporary European tendencies. Its chief representatives were Mapu (whose *The Hypocrite*, 1857–61, was the first novel of contemporary Jewish life), J. L. Gordon in his epic

poems, M. L. Lilienblum, and S. J. ABRAMOVICH ("Mendele Mocher Sephorim") in his first novel *Fathers and Sons* (1868). The H. was slowly strangled by tendencies to full cultural assimilation and also by the realization that its program of internal Jewish reform could not bring about Jewish Emancipation. The pogroms of 1881 marked the real beginning of Zionism and of new viewpoints in Hebrew literature. Soon P. SMOLENSKIN, originally a realistic H. writer, denounced H. as a betrayal of Jewish identity; this negative judgment was widely accepted, and a more positive view of H. has set in only in recent years.

HASKAMAH (Heb. "approval"): Authorization sometimes prefixed to Hebrew books. The usage became established after the decision of the Synod of Ferrara in 1554 that Hebrew books should be approved by the local Jewish authorities to avoid difficulties with the Church. Later, the *h.* was sought by the author as an indication of scholarship as well as of orthodoxy, and several 'from different rabbis would frequently be prefixed to the same work. *H.* (often pronounced *ascama*, pl. *ascamot*), is also the name given among Sephardim to a communal regulation.

HASMONEANS: Name of priestly family and dynasty founded by MATTATHIAS of Modiin; and called *Hashmonai* (Hasmonean) perhaps after his ancestor Hashmon, but it may derive from a place-name (cf. Josh. 15:27). Mattathias and his five sons JUDAH THE MACCABEE, JONATHAN, SIMON, JOHN, and ELEAZAR directed the popular revolt against the hellenizing policy adopted in Palestine by the Syrian king ANTIOCHUS EPIPHANES. In 166–164 BCE, the H. fought a number of successful battles against the Syrians and in 164, Judah captured Jerusalem and rededicated the Temple. This was followed by a series of raids to rescue the Jewish populations of Ammon, Idumea, Gilead, and Galilee. Though defeated in 163 at Bet Zechariah, where Eleazar was killed, the H. were able, owing to dynastic distractions in Syria, to obtain terms securing Jewish religious freedom, but Judah and his party, aspiring for political freedom, continued the fight and Judah fell at Elasa in 160. John was murdered shortly thereafter and Jonathan took over the leadership. By playing off Syrian pretenders against each other, Jonathan was able to secure the high priesthood (152) and governorship of Judah (150). Simon succeeded in gaining exemption from tribute (147). He was confirmed by the people as hereditary high priest, ethnarch, and general in 142. He was murdered in 135. His son John HYRCANUS, who succeeded him, suffered a crushing defeat by Antiochus VII Sidetes, Jerusalem being taken by the Syrians after a prolonged siege and Judea once more becoming a Seleucid province. But after the defeat of Antiochus in his war against Parthia, John launched a successful offensive against Transjordan, Samaria, and Idumea, marking the transition of the H. to a semi-hellenized secular military dynasty. This led to his repudiation of the PHARISEES and his adherence to the aristocratic SADDUCEE party. He was succeeded by his sons Judah ARISTOBULUS (105–4) and ALEXANDER YANNAI (104–76), one of whom was the first to adopt the royal title. Yannai set up a standing mercenary army and conquered Transjordan, Idumea, and the coastal plain. His antagonism to the Pharisees, who opposed his war policy, led to civil war in which he was victorious after a bloody struggle, but the Pharisees were in the ascendant during the reign of his widow SALOME ALEXANDRA (76–69). With her death, the H. declined. The strife between her sons HYRCANUS II and ARISTOBULUS II led to the intervention and eventual domination of ANTIPATER and his son HEROD, with Roman assistance. POMPEY drastically reduced the country's territory in 63. Hyrcanus remained a puppet, while the efforts of Aristobulus II and his sons ALEXANDER and ANTIGONUS MATTATHIAS to regain power failed. Hyrcanus' granddaughter MARIAMNE married Herod but was put to death by him (29) as were the surviving H., viz. ARISTOBULUS III (35), Hyrcanus II (30), and Mariamne's sons ALEXANDER and ARISTOBULUS (7).

HASSAN, SIR JOSHUA ABRAHAM (1915–): Gibraltar public figure. He was chairman of the city council of Gibraltar from 1945 (mayor, from 1955). He was chief minister of Gibraltar's Legislative Council, 1964–9 and again from 1972.

ḤASSENEH (Heb. *ḥatunah*): A wedding.

ḤATAM SOPHER see **SOPHER, MOSES**

ḤATAN (Heb.): A bridegroom.

ḤATAPH: Common name of the signs ־ (*Ḥataph Pataḥ* or *Ḥatuph*), ־ (*Ḥataph Segol* or *Segol Ḥatuph*), ־ (*Ḥataph Kamatz* or *Kamatz Ḥatuph*) which show that the SHEVA after the letters *aleph, he, ḥet, ayin* is pronounced respectively as an *a, e, o*. *Ḥataph* (Aramaic *ḥitpha*) is an old name for *sheva* mobile. In old mss the *sheva* sign is written inside the consonant.

HA-TEKUPHAH (Heb. "The Age"): Hebrew quarterly appearing 1918–50 (vols. 1–3, MOSCOW; 4–23, Warsaw; 24–5, Berlin; 26–9, Tel Aviv; 30-5, New York). Besides original contributions, both literary and scientific, it contained translations of major works of world literature.

HA-TENUAH HA-MEUḤEDET (Heb. "The United Movement"): Israel pioneer youth movement, organized in 1950 by *Mapai* supporters who split from MAḤANOT OLIM. In 1951, it joined the World HA-BONIM Organization.

Hatikva

Kol od ba-le-vav pe — ni—mah nephesh ye-hu-di   ho — mi-yah ule-
pha-a—te miz-rah ka—di-mah a-yin le—tzi-yon   tzo — phi—yah
od lo aveda tik-va—te—nu ha-tik-vah shenot al-pa-yim   lihyot amhophshi
be — ar—tze——nu   e-retztziyon ye-rushalayim

HA-TIKVAH (Heb. "The Hope"): Hymn of the Zionist movement and now the national anthem of Israel. The words, composed by Naphtali Herz IMBER and first published in 1886, express the hope of Jews for redemption and their yearning to return to Zion. The last lines of the refrain have been modified to correspond to modern developments. The melody echoes a Sephardi hymn as well as a tune in Smetana's *Vltava*.

HA-TOREN (Heb. "The Mast"): New York Hebrew journal, published 1913–25. It dealt with current and literary questions, and its editors included Shemaryahu Levin, Y. D. Berkovitz, Reuben Brainin, and Simon Bernstein.

HATTARAT HORAAH see **ORDINATION**

HA-TZEPHIRAH (Heb. "The Dawn"): Hebrew periodical founded by Ḥayyim Selig Slonimsky, appearing intermittently in Warsaw from 1862 to 1931 (in Berlin 1874–5). Its initial object was to disseminate

Silver spice-boxes for Havdalah from Central and E. Europe, 17th, 18th and 19th cents.
(Formerly in Howitt Collection).

a knowledge of the natural sciences and mathematics in Hebrew circles. In 1879, Nahum Sokolow joined the editorial board (editor, 1904) and under his influence political essays, stories, feuilletons, etc. were incorporated. When the journal became a daily in 1886, the scientific section was omitted. It was the organ of the Polish Zionist Organization after World War I when its appearance was, however, irregular.

HA-TZEVI ("The Hind"): Hebrew periodical appearing in Jerusalem 1884–1900 and 1909–10 under the editorship of Eliezer Ben-Yehudah. The first modern political journal in Palestine, it opposed religious extremists and advocated the revival of spoken Hebrew.

HA-TZOPHEH (Heb. "The Observer"): (1) Hebrew daily paper appearing in Warsaw 1903–5. (2) Tel Aviv daily newspaper, organ of *Mizraḥi* and *Ha-Poel ha-Mizraḥi*. It was founded by R Meir Bar-Ilan in 1937.

HA-TZOPHEH BA-ERETZ HA-ḤADASHAH (Heb. "The Observer in the New Land"): First American Hebrew periodical 1871–6, founded and edited by Tzevi Hirsch Bernstein.

HA-TZOPHEH LE-ḤOKHMAT ISRAEL (Heb. "The Observer of Jewish Science"): Hebrew scholarly quarterly appearing in Budapest; edited by Ludwig Blau, 1921–31. From 1912–5, it had appeared as *Ha-Tzopheh me-Eretz Hagar*.

HAURAN: Region E of Jordan; today part of Syria. The area of BASHAN and GOLAN was known in later antiquity as H. (Gk. Auranitis). It was extremely fertile and densely populated; its biblical capital was EDREI.

HAVANA see **CUBA**

ḤAVATZELET (Heb. "Lily"): One of the first Hebrew periodicals in Palestine. It appeared in Jerusalem for a short period in 1863 and renewed regular publication in 1870. From 1873, its editor was Israel Dov FRUMKIN. It ceased publication in 1911. The policy of the paper initially was moderate, opposing fanaticism and the *Ḥalukkah* system. From the middle 1880's, it adopted a militant religious attitude and bitterly opposed the Zionist settlement.

HAVDALAH (Heb. "distinction"): Ceremony marking the end of the Sabbath. It consists of blessings over wine, spices, flame, and the main blessing which refers to the distinction between holy and profane, between light and darkness, between Israel and other peoples, and between the day of rest and the six working days. In addition to this home ritual, a special prayer with substantially the same content is recited in the *Amidah* in the evening service at the conclusion of the Sabbath. The *H.* ceremony has been the inspiration for many folk songs as well as artistry in the design of spice (BESAMIM) boxes, candle-holders, etc. Folklore, as expressed in various hymns, associates the *H.* with the coming of Elijah the prophet as harbinger of the Messiah.

ḤAVER (Heb. "companion"): Title occasionally given to a scholar. The Talmud uses the term for members of associations of pietists, first appearing in the 2nd cent. BCE, who pledged themselves to maintain stricter standards of ethical and ritual purity than those obtaining among the general public. Their code, which allowed for various degrees of observance from novice upward, was characterized by meticulous concern to eat only tithed produce, maintain ritual cleanliness, avoid base callings (such as tax-farming); and generally to keep apart from the *am ha-aretz*. The term is now used to mean "friend" or "comrade."

HAVLAGAH (Heb. "self-restraint"): The official policy of the Jewish Agency and the *Haganah* during the Arab revolt of 1936–9 in Palestine, viz. self-defense without retaliation or attacks on Arabs not known to be implicated in the outbreaks.

HAWAII: US state in the Pacific Ocean. Jews have lived in H. since the early 19th cent. The present community, dating from World War I, numbers 1,500 (1973) concentrated in Honolulu.

HAYES, ISAAC ISRAEL (1832–1881): US Arctic explorer. From 1853–5, he was the surgeon attached to the second Grinnell Arctic expedition. In 1860, he himself led an expedition to the Polar regions, and in 1869, he traveled through Greenland in search of an open Polar sea. H. described his explorations in several books.

HA-YOM (Heb. "The Day"): Name of several journals including the first Hebrew daily paper, appearing in St. Petersburg 1886–8. It was published and edited by Judah Löb Kantor, assisted by David Frischmann. Another *H.* was also the organ of Israel's GAḤAL party, succeeding *Ha-Boker* (of the General Zionists) and *Ḥerut* and appearing 1966–70.

HAYS: US family prominent in the 18th-19th cents. Five brothers, Jacob, David, Solomon, Judah, and Isaac, emigrated from Holland in the Colonial Period and their descendants took a prominent part in Jewish and community life in both the US and Canada. Among the more distinguished members were *DAVID H.* (1732–1812) who served in Washington's forces and helped supply the American troops. *ANDREW H.* (18th cent.) who founded the Canadian branch of the family; *JACOB H.* (1772–1849) high constable of New York 1802–49; *MOSES MICHAEL H.* (1739–1805) one of the early leaders of the Masonic movement in America; *ISAAC H.* (1796–1879), a leading ophthalmologist, an editor of the *American Journal of the Medical Sciences,* and a founder of the American Medical Association; and his son *ISAAC MINIS H.* (1847–1925) also editor of the *American Journal* and for 28 years secretary of the American Philosophical Society.

HAYS, ARTHUR GARFIELD (1881–1954): US lawyer. He made a fortune as representative of large corporations but earned his reputation as a fighter for civil rights. Among the famous cases in which he participated as defense attorney were the Reichstag fire trial in 1933 and in the US, the Scopes trial (1925), and the Sacco-Vanzetti case (1927). From 1912 until his death, he was general counsel of the American Civil Liberties Union.

HAYYIM BEN ISAAC OF VOLOZHIN (1749–1821): Talmudist; founder of the VOLOZHIN yeshivah. After the death of his teacher, the Vilna Gaon, he was recognized as the leader of Lithuanian Jewry. He founded the yeshivah in 1802 to counteract the influence of Haskalah and Ḥasidism. His teaching methods followed those of the Vilna Gaon, viz. avoidance of *pilpul* and determination of the accurate talmudic text.

HAYYON, NEHEMIAH (c. 1655–c. 1730): Kabbalist and Sabbetaian adventurer. Born probably in Safed, he studied at Hebron and was appointed rabbi at Uskub (now Skopije, Yugoslavia). Later he adopted a wandering existence, preaching, teaching and, according to his enemies, even thieving. He joined the Sabbetaians and was denounced by the rabbis in Smyrna as a charlatan. He lived for a time in Italy, Prague, and Berlin, publishing kabbalistic works and advocating a new type of Sabbetaism based on a trinity of the First Cause, the Infinite, and the Holy Father (the last being implicitly identified with Shabbetai TZEVI). When he went to Amsterdam to circulate his books, a controversy broke out which re-echoed throughout the Jewish world. H. and his works (which had been printed with forged rabbinical approval) were banned by leading European rabbis and he was eventually forced to leave Amsterdam, settling in N Africa where he died in poverty. His son became converted to Christianity in Rome and leveled spiteful accusations against the Jews.

HAYYUJ, JUDAH (YAḤYA) BEN DAVID (c. 940 –c. 1010): Hebrew grammarian. He was born in N Africa and lived most of his life in Spain. He wrote a work on Hebrew punctuation and a philological commentary on the biblical books Joshua to Ezekiel. His fame rests mainly on two treatises, one on verb-roots containing a *vav, yod,* or *aleph,* the other on verbs the second and third root-letters of which are identical. He showed that these roots consisted of three consonants and differed from regular verbs only because of certain phonetic rules. The previous view, that all weak roots consisted of two consonants only, had led to many misinterpretations and wrong forms. His work was completed by IBN JANAḤ. H wrote in Arabic, but his two main grammatical works were translated into Hebrew, perhaps in his lifetime, by Moses Gikatilla, being probably the first Arabic books to be translated into Hebrew.

*HAZAEL: King of Aram-Dammesek, c. 842–808 BCE. In his victorious campaigns he reduced the kingdom of Israel to vassaldom and limited its armed forces. Joash, king of Judah, subsequently saved Jerusalem from attack by paying tribute.

Ḥayyim Hazaz.

ḤAZAK (Heb. "be strong") or **ḤAZAK VE-EMATZ**
(Heb. "be strong and of good courage" — Josh.
1:9): Phrase said at the completion of a piece of work.
Among Sephardim, *Ḥazak (u-) Barukh* ("be strong
and blessed") is said in congratulating the performer of
a *mitzvah*. The response is *barukh tihyeh* ("be you
blessed").

ḤAZAKAH (Heb. "taking hold"): Talmudic term
designating (1) the act of taking possession of
property whether movable or immovable; (2) fact
of undisturbed possession (in case of land, 3 years)
creating presumption of legally acquired title. In the
Ghetto Period, this gave rise in Italy to an elaborate
system safeguarding tenant rights (see JUS GAZAGA);
(3) presumed legal or ritual state of person or object
as derived from the last known condition of facts
(until evidence to the contrary is adduced); (4) an
axiom of human behavior, e.g. "It is a presumption
(*ḥazakah*) that no man pays his debts before they
are due."

ḤAZARS see **KHAZARS**

ḤAZAZ, ḤAYYIM (1897–1973): Hebrew novelist.
Born in the Ukraine and, after several years
in Paris, settled in Palestine in 1931. H. is one of the
leading modern Hebrew stylists. A realistic novelist he depicted Jewish life in various countries
(Ukraine, Yemen, Israel, etc.) and in different eras
(e.g. Second Temple times, the period of Shabbetai
Tzevi). His works include the novels *Be-Yishuv shel
Yaar* ("In a Forest Settlement") set in a Russian
townlet before the Revolution, *Yaish,* a vivid picture
of Yemenite Jewry and *Be-Kolar Eḥad* ("In the one
collar") based on an incident in the fight of the
underground movements against the British.

ḤAZER (from Heb. *ḥazir*): Swine; obnoxious
person.

ḤAZON ISH see **KARLITZ, AVRAHAM YE-
SHAYAHU**

ḤAZOR: The name of several ancient sites in
Palestine. The best-known is situated in NE Galilee
and was a hill-fort defended by formidable ramparts.
It was mentioned in Egyptian inscriptions from the
19th cent. BCE and was burnt by Joshua (Josh. 11:10).
H. was the center of the league led by Jabin which
was defeated by Barak (Judg. 4). It was rebuilt by

Hazor: a Canaanite shrine, stele with relief and a figurine sculptured in basalt.

Solomon (I Kings 9:15), captured by Tiglath-Pileser III (II Kings 15:29), and was the site of a battle between Jonathan the Maccabee and Demetrius II of Syria. Garstang undertook trial excavations here in 1928 and large-scale diggings were executed by Yigael Yadin 1955–8 and 1968–9. The excavations include an altar and the ancient water system. Many of his findings are housed in the Ḥ museum in the nearby kibbutz of Ayelet ha-Shaḥar. There is a modern communal settlement (KA) of the same name in the S coastal plain. It was founded in 1946 by a group of Palestinian youth and Youth Aliyah graduates, later joined by settlers from the US and Bulgaria. Pop. (1972): 483. There is also the town of H. in Lower Galilee. Pop. (1974): 5,400.

HA-ZOREA: Israel communal settlement (KA) in the Valley of Jezreel. It was founded in 1936 by settlers from Germany (members of the *Werkleute* movement). It houses the Wilfred Israel Museum for art and antiquities. Pop. (1972): 730.

ḤAZZAN (Heb. "cantor"): In modern times, the precentor; originally, a Temple functionary. In talmudic times, he was an executive command official whose functions included the preservation of order, the security of the town, and the administering of flagellation. He decided who should officiate as CANTOR and reader of the Law, took the Scrolls of the Law from the ark, rolled them, and sometimes taught the children. In many places, he was also the moral instructor. In still earlier times, when the prayers began to be supplemented by hymns, the *h*. was the poet, reciting his compositions in public (which sometimes led to complaints against the lengthiness of the prayers). For this reason, he stood beside the cantor and in the course of time took his place. It is not known when the title was transferred to the precentor. In the Middle Ages, the *h*. was generally the only one to know the prayers or possess a *maḥzor*, and the congregation consequently was dependent on him. As cantor, he had to be of unblemished personality, and although a good voice was highly esteemed, considerations of character took precedence. The office of *h*. has been abolished in many Reform communities, especially in Europe.

ḤAZZANUT see **CANTORAL MUSIC**

HE (ה): Fifth letter of the Hebrew alphabet; numerical value 5. It is a consonant having the phonetic value of h. As an abbreviation it stands for *Ha-Shem*, the Name of God. At the end of words, it is silent unless bearing a dot (*mappik*).

HEATHEN see **GENTILE**

HEAVE-OFFERING (Heb. *terumah*): General name for an offering to the Sanctuary or to the priests. It most frequently refers to the produce tithes but is also used for the priest's dough-offering and the half-shekel that had to be contributed to the Sanctuary.

HEAVEN: In biblical COSMOLOGY, the upper part of the universe or the firmament dividing the upper from the lower (terrestrial) waters. H., as that which surrounds man and his factual universe on all sides and which looks down on him whichever way he turns, naturally became the abode of the transcendent, all-seeing, omnipotent, and omniscient GOD. The God of H. is surrounded by His court, the Host of H.—a conception in which ideas about the heavenly bodies and about heavenly beings merge. Man turns to H. in prayer or "raises his hands to H." whence God looks down. The concept of Divine abode in H. is balanced by the notion of the immanence of God's spirit in man and in creation, as well as by the belief in His "presence" in a particular place, e.g. the Temple. The tension between these ideas is reflected in Solomon's prayer (cf. I Kings 8:27). In due course, H. became synonymous with God in such expressions as "the fear of H.," the "kingdom of H." (i.e., decreed by God) or "for the sake of H." Parallel to hellenistic notions of a gradual ascent of the soul from the material, lower world to progressively higher, more spiritual, and "purer" spheres, there appears a plurality of heavens (seven or ten in rabbinic and apocryphal literature) inhabited by the various orders of the angelic hierarchy. Sometimes Paradise—to which the righteous souls ascend after death—was located in one of these H.'s. The idea that the lower world was ruled by evil forces, while God had retired to H., communicating with the world through angelic mediation, added further pungency to the identification of H. and God. Nevertheless, in rabbinic literature, God's sovereign rule over the universe, though often veiled, is never compromised.

HEBRAISTS, CHRISTIAN: At the close of the Classical Period, JEROME, who worked in Palestine, had a considerable knowledge of Hebrew and consulted Jews while preparing the Vulgate version of the Bible. In the earlier Middle Ages, knowledge of Hebrew among Christians was rare. It has recently been established, however, that Hugh, abbot of the monastery of St. Victoire in Paris in the 12th cent., studied the Hebrew Bible intensively with the aid of Jewish scholars. This practice continued among his followers and students elsewhere, such as the Englishmen HERBERT OF BOSHAM, and, to a lesser degree, Roger BACON. In the late 13th cent., the Dominicans began to advocate the study of Hebrew as an instrument to assist their religious controversies, and some, such as Raymond MARTINI, became highly proficient. Similarly, the Franciscan Nicholas de LYRA used Rashi methodically in his biblical commentaries. Through the advocacy of Raymond Lull, the Council of Vienna in 1305 ordered the institution of chairs of Hebrew at the major universities, but this remained almost a dead letter. The revival of Hebrew studies dates from the period of the Renaissance, when some Italian humanists began to study the language as part of the general classical revival. Pica Dells MIRANDOLA'S enthusiasm · for the Kabbalah gave the process a great impetùs, and it was carried to Germany by J. REUCHLIN. Here the study of Hebrew as an instrument for the understanding of the Bible, became general among the reformers, and during the 16th cent., it was widespread in northern countries, as exemplified by LUTHER and S. MÜNSTER in Germany, BROUGHTON in England, etc. The 17th and 18th cents. produced Hebraists of the caliber of J. Lightfoot, the BUXTORFS, J. C. WAGENSEIL, and, in Italy, the bibliophiles BARTOLOCCI and De ROSSI. Germany with GESENIUS, STRACK, DELITZCH, KITTEL, KAHLE, and many more was the great center of Christian Hebrew scholarship in the 19th–20th cents., but France produced RENAN, England, the DRIVERS, H. DANBY, A. COWLEY, and Travers HERFORD, and America G. Foot MOORE. C. H. have greatly advanced the study of Hebrew philology and the scientific approach to the Bible.

HEBREW IMMIGRATION AID SOCIETY see **HIAS**

HEBREW LANGUAGE: Hebrew, together with Moabite and Phoenician, belongs to the Canaanite branch of Semitic languages. The Tel el Amarna letters prove that Hebrew was spoken in Palestine before the Israelite conquest. Pre-exilic biblical Hebrew (B. H.) was a standardized literary language with distinct idioms for prose and poetry, full-sounding, rich in vocabulary and rhetorical devices. It borrowed many words from surrounding languages. Little is known of the underlying spoken dialects. There seems to have been a slightly different standard language in the N kingdom. After the exile, B. H. continued in use for over 500 years, but showed many signs of decay and uncertainty in usage. The reasons were, firstly, the influence of Aramaic, from 539 to 331 the language of officialdom and spoken by many Jews; and, secondly, the emergence of mishnaic Hebrew as a new colloquial language (from at least 200 BCE). Mishnaic Hebrew (M.H.) is not derived from B. H., but probably from some pre-exilic colloquial dialect. It became a literary language through the tannaim in the 1st cent. CE., but its spoken use declined after the wars of 66-70 and 132–5. It was more sober, simple, and brief than B. H. and better suited for precise expression. The prayers composed during the Tannaitic Period combine B. H. vocabulary with M. H. grammar. Almost all later styles mix the two dialects. After 200, even the Jews of Palestine stopped using Hebrew and wrote in Aramaic and Greek. About 500, a literary revival began which led to the use of Hebrew in its written form throughout the Middle Ages. It started in Palestine with the *piyyutim*. Their authors extensively enriched Hebrew by inventing new words and made some daring grammatical innovations. Through *piyyut* and Midrash, the use of Hebrew soon spread to the whole Diaspora. From 900–1400, Jews of NW Europe wrote only Hebrew. In Moslem countries, including Spain, B. H. was employed for artistic writing, Arabic for other purposes. The extensive translation from Arabic (1100–1400) produced a strongly arabicized scientific style. Both this and the B. H. poetical style survived after 1500 in Italy, and later in Holland. E European Jewry used a harsh, ungrammatical semi-Aramaic language, while women and the uneducated read and wrote Yiddish. The Haskalah (1750–1880) revived the use of B. H., but was unsuccessful in adapting it to modern thought and life. It created, however, a modern secular literature in Hebrew. With the rise of Jewish nationalism in 1880, the modern period of Hebrew set in. It became a spoken language again; the first daily paper appeared in 1886; and in 1913, the Jewish community in Palestine enforced its exclusive use in Palestinian schools. In 1921, it was one of 3 languages recognized by the Palestine Mandate and in 1948, became the official language of Israel. Between the wars, some 100,000 children were educated in Hebrew-speaking *Tarbut* schools in E Europe. Now the speaking of Hebrew outside Israel is fostered by the Jewish Agency, the BERIT IVRIT OLAMIT, and has become an essential feature of the curriculum in all Jewish schools. Modern Hebrew is a combination of all previous stages of Hebrew, though it has taken over from each only the elements that suit it. Expressions derived from different periods often serve as synonyms or stylistic alternatives (like Germanic and Romance words in English). Its syntax is strongly influenced by European languages. Besides an average standard written style and a colloquial style, there are literary styles tending toward the biblical and the midrashic-talmudic. Words for modern concepts have been created either by giving old words new meanings or by newly-formed words. Many European words have been naturalized in Hebrew (e.g. *telephon,* "telephone," *telephonit* "by phone," *letalphen* "to phone"). Important work in this connection is done by the ACADEMY OF THE HEBREW LANGUAGE (until 1953, the *Vaad ha-Lashon*) which works out word-lists for technical subjects.

Hebrew grammar is dominated by the fact that the consonants (the "root") carry the meaning, the vowels (with some prefixes and suffixes) provide the form (e.g. B-R-KH "bless"; *barukh* "blessed," *berekh* "he blessed," *berakhah* "blessing"). In pre-exilic times, Hebrew writing expressed consonants only. Later, the vowels *i*, more rarely *e*, were expressed by *yod*, *u* and *o* by *vav*. In the masoretic Bible text, this method was only applied for long vowels but short vowels were sometimes written in the same way in texts for private use (e.g. the Dead Sea Scrolls). A more precise indication of vowels, was achieved about the 8th cent. CE, by a system of diacritical points above or below the consonants. Known systems include the Babylonian, the Palestinian, the Samaritan, and the Tiberian; the last, the only one still in use, represents Palestinian pronunciation in the 9th cent. CE. The consonant spelling has hardly changed since pre-exilic times (see ALPHABET); the changes undergone by Hebrew pronunciation are thereby obscured, but they can to some extent be traced through transliterations of words into Assyrian (9th–6th cents. BCE), Greek (4th cent. BCE–4th cent. CE), etc. (e.g. Ass. *Khazaqiyahu*, Gk. *Ezekias*, Tiberian Heb. *Ḥizkiyyahu*). Ancient Hebrew possessed guttural (*aleph*, *he*, *ayin*, *ḥet*) and emphatic (*tet*, *koph*, *tzade*) consonants and long and short vowels. Most of the gutturals disappeared in Europe and in the traditional pronunciation of the Samaritans. In Europe, *sh* and *s* were confused until c. 1100 CE. The Yemenite pronunciation has continued the Babylonian tradition whereas the Ashkenazi and Sephardi pronunciations reflect the Tiberian and Palestinian pronunciation respectively. Each has numerous sub-varieties.

EXAMPLES OF PRONUNCIATION			
	Sephardi	*Ashkenazi*	*Yemenite*
Kametz (ָ)	a	o	o
Ḥolam (ֹ)	o	au, oi, etc.	öw
Tzere (ֵ)	e	ei, ai,	e, ei
Segol (ֶ)	e	e	a (=*pataḥ*)
Tav (without *Dagesh*)	t	s	th

True Sephardi and Yemenite Hebrew display variations of the gutturals and emphatics. The Ashkenazi disregards nearly all the gutturals and all the emphatics. The Israel pronunciation has the vowel sounds of Sephardi Hebrew but (except for *tav*), the consonants of the Ashkenazim. Schools, the radio, and the League for Speech Culture are endeavouring to introduce the distinctive sounds of consonants, as well as of the *sheva na* and the *dagesh ḥazak*.

HEBREW LANGUAGE ACADEMY see **VAAD HA-LASHON**

HEBREW LITERATURE: (1) *Period of the Bible.*
Even Higher Criticism acknowledges at least parts of the Pentateuch to be the oldest work of H. L.; however, certain poems quoted in the Pentateuch (see POETRY) are probably older than the text in which they are quoted. Similarly, the Song of Deborah (Judg. 5) is older than the Book of Judges. It has been conjectured that a national epos existed before the prose stories of the Pentateuch, Joshua, Judges, and Samuel; the "Book of Jashar" (Josh. 10:13; II Sam. 1:18) may have belonged to this literature. The historical books quote lost chronicles and other works. Israel thus had a considerable

literature, of which the BIBLE is a selection. The style and composition of the biblical literature, too, bear witness to established literary practices which in many ways, both in technique and in themes, correspond with those of the surrounding civilizations — the Babylonian, Canaanite, Egyptian, etc. Direct influence from all these is likely but is still disputed. Three types of books in the Bible constitute "literature" in the narrow modern sense: (a) Wisdom Literature (Proverbs, Job, Ecclesiastes); (b) religious poetry (Psalms, Lamentations); (c) love poetry (The Song of Songs). The Latter Prophets, which from a modern point of view would be classed as political writings, show a high degree of literary finish.

(2) *Seond Temple Period.* As the earlier biblical books are a selection from H. L. before the Babylonian Exile, so the later books (Chronicles, Ezra, Nehemiah, Esther, Daniel, etc.) are a selection from post-exilic literature. Some other contemporary works such as the APOCRYPHA AND PSEUDEPIGRAPHA have been preserved as a result of their inclusion in the Bibles of certain Christian communities. Again, most of these are political; only ECCLESIASTICUS and perhaps the PSALMS OF SOLOMON can be reckoned as literature in the modern sense. To this period belong also the DEAD SEA SCROLLS, in their nature not very different from the Pseudepigrapha; among these only the "Thanksgiving Psalms" can claim literary merit.

(3) *The Tannaitic and Amoraic Periods.* Rabbinic literature began during the second cent. BCE; it is thus partly contemporaneous with the previous literature. The formulation of many *halakhot* is believed to date back to Maccabean times; some tractates of the MISHNAH (e.g. *Tamid, Sanhedrin*) are thought to have been almost complete before 70 CE. The first truly literary creation is the oldest parts of the daily prayers, which are in a literary language of their own, constructed to strict form. Throughout Jewish history, prayers remained an important and highly developed form of literary production. A somewhat later type of rabbinic literature was MIDRASH, which grew out of the synagogue sermon. The tannaitic and amoraic Midrashim consist of small independent paragraphs, often — especially in the amoraic GENESIS RABBAH and TANḤUMA — highly polished in structure and style. According to recent discoveries (mainly by Y. Schirman), the poetry of the PIYYUT type began in the Amoraic Period in Palestine. It combined, in a way, prayer and Midrash, and was the highest Hebrew literary achievement of the period. The best-known creations of this time are the MISHNAH, TOSEPHTA, and the two TALMUDS. As legal works (except for their many midrashic passages), their importance lies in the history of Jewish thought rather than of literature in the strict sense, but all these works have literary merit resulting from their polished phrasing. The Talmud, especially,

often contains considerable literary artifice and lively wit. The legal literature, like the early Midrash, is formless.

(4) *The Gaonic Period*. The period from 500–900 saw the redaction of the Babylonian Talmud, followed by much exegetical activity based upon it, both in legal lectures (*Sheiltot*), legal collections (*Halakhot, Maasim*), and especially in answers to legal inquiries (RESPONSA), which remained for a long time (and to some extent are today) a topical and interesting form of Jewish literature, throwing much light on Jewish life and thought. The famous responsum of SHERIRA GAON is a chief source for the history of Jewish law. *Piyyut* continued to flourish during that period (according to some, it only began then), among its outstanding names being YOSE BEN YOSE, YANNAI, KALLIR, and SAADYAH. Many additions were made to the prayer-book, especially the services for the festivals (*Mahzor*). Midrash entered a new stage, becoming real books arranged according to a central plan (*Pirke Rabbi Eliezer, Tanna de-ve Eliyahu*) and became more narrative and rhetorical. This period is marked by two general major developments: (a) the beginning of Arabic influence (which in many respects was only disguised hellenistic Greek culture) affecting those fields which may be called literature proper, and (b) the shift westward. The end of the gaonic period saw centers of H. L. in Greece, Italy, N Africa, Spain, S France, and Central Germany. S Italy, in particular, became a center of *piyyut* and Midrash, and was the scene of the beginning of historical literature (JOSIPPON) and scientific writing (ASAPH, DONNOLO).

(5) *Medieval Period*. The literature of this period is ramified and heterogeneous. It had many geographic centers and reflected the life and culture of different environments. Besides legal works, it includes grammar, lexicography, poetry, exegesis, philosophy, and science. Philology began with the work of the MASORETES who flourished in Tiberias and elsewhere in the 7th–8th cents. and were concerned with the preservation and VOCALIZATION of the Bible text. In Babylonia, Saadyah compiled the first Hebrew lexicon, *Egron,* and also wrote in Arabic the first Hebrew grammar. In N Africa, Judah IBN KUREISH wrote on the relation of Hebrew to other Semitic languages. The study of Hebrew philology was translated to Spain, where the main contributions to the science of the Hebrew language were by MENAHEM BEN SARUK and his opponent DUNASH IBN LABRAT. They were followed by Judah HAYYUJ, the creator of the system of Hebrew grammar, Jonah IBN JANAH, and Abraham IBN EZRA. Of importance are the works of Joseph KIMHI and his son David who wrote an extensive grammar, *Mikhlol,* and a well-constructed dictionary, *Sepher ha-Shorashim.* In later centuries, Elijah LEVITA distinguished himself as grammarian

and lexicographer. The interest in the science of the Hebrew language gave an impetus to the development of biblical exegesis, which, on the whole, followed two methods: PESHAT and DERASH, the latter being a development of Midrash. The former prevailed in Babylonia and Spain, the latter in France and Germany. In addition, there were two minor currents, viz. the philosophical-allegorical and the mystic. The leading commentators were: Saadyah who translated the entire Bible into Arabic with commentaries in the same language, SAMUEL BEN HOPHNI, Judah IBN BALAM, Moses IBN GIKATILLA and Abraham IBN EZRA, the leading Spanish exegete. Solomon ben Isaac, known as RASHI, was the greatest of the Franco-German school of exegetes. His commentaries on the entire Bible blended both methods. He was followed by his grandson, SAMUEL BEN MEIR, David Kimhi, Moses BEN NAHMAN or Nahmanides, and LEVI BEN GERSHON or *Ralbag* who combined the *peshat* and philosophic methods. Outstanding among the later commentators is Isaac ABRAVANEL who included historical introductions to the books of the Bible. *Piyyut* continued for a time, expressing the suffering of the people as well as their hopes for redemption. Leading *paytanim* in Italy, France, and Germany were MESHULLAM BEN KALONYMOS, SIMEON BEN ISAAC, and the cantor MEIR BAR ISAAC. In Spain, where *piyyut* was also written, its place was soon taken by poetry in Arabic meters, which was used both for religious and secular themes. Spanish Hebrew poetry is the first type of H. L., which was in spirit and pattern comparable with the literature of the Greeks and Romans and of Europe. The leading Spanish poets were SAMUEL IBN NAGRELA, Solomon IBN GABIROL, Moses IBN EZRA, and Judah HA-LEVI. From Spain, the new poetry spread to S France and Italy (IMMANUEL OF ROME) and to Palestine (Israel NAJARA). Throughout this period, there was great productivity in the field of rabbinics. Responsa still played an important role. An important early collection are the responsa of the "Sages of France and Lorraine" of the 11th cent. Leading writers in this field were SOLOMON BEN ADRET, 3,000 of whose responsa have survived, MEIR BEN BARUCH of Rothenburg, Joseph ben Solomon COLON, and others. From the 11th cent., there was great activity in this field in N Africa, Italy, N France, Germany, and later in Poland. The leading talmudic commentators included HANANEL and NISSIM in N Africa. Outstanding was Rashi whose commentaries cover almost the entire Talmud. He was followed by his grandsons Solomon ben Meir and JACOB BEN MEIR, known as Rabbenu Tam. The latter headed a group of scholars known as the TOSAPHISTS whose novellae, comments, and analytical remarks cover the entire Talmud. MAIMONIDES wrote a commentary on the complete Mishnah. The major codifiers were Isaac ALFASI,

Maimonides whose great code *Mishneh Torah* covers the entire Oral Law, ASHER BEN JEHIEL, his son Jacob, author of the code known as the *Turim,* and Joseph CARO whose code, the *Shulḥan Arukh,* became accepted by all Jews, after the addition of the copious notes of Moses ISSERLES of Poland. The KARAITE sect, founded by ANAN BEN DAVID, also produced its literature. The leading scholars of the sect included — besides Anan who wrote the code *Sepher ha-Mitzvot* — BENJAMIN BEN MOSES NAHAVENDI the author of a book of precepts and of commentaries on several books of the Bible; JOSEPH ABU JACOB (Al Basir), the philosopher; and Judah ben Elijah HADASSI, author of the encyclopedic *Eshkol ha-Kopher.* Among the later Karaite authors were the Bible commentator AARON BEN JOSEPH; the philosopher AARON BEN ELIJAH whose *Etz Ḥayyim* is the most distinguished Karaite philosophic work; Elijah BASHYAZI who wrote a legal compendium; and CALEB AFENDOPOLO, author of scientific treatises and commentaries on the Book of Psalms. Along with these studies, there arose in the Jewish centers under Islamic domination intensive activity in the field of PHILOSOPHY, the main purpose of which, as in Arabic philosophy, was to reconcile the tenets of religion with the principles of reason and science. The activity began in Babylonia with Saadyah's *Emunot ve-Deot.* It was further developed in Spain where there arose a number of thinkers, including Solomon Ibn Gabirol, BAḤYA IBN PAKUDA, Judah Ha-Levi with his *Kuzari,* Abraham IBN DAUD whose *Emunah Ramah* bears the stamp of Aristotelian philosophy, and Maimonides whose *Guide to the Perplexed* became for later Jewish generations almost synonymous with philosophy. Later philosophers include LEVI BEN GERSHON — a devoted follower of Aristotle, Ḥasdai CRESCAS, the first Jewish critic of Aristotle, and his pupil Joseph ALBO. Alongside the current of philosophy, ran a current of mysticism of which the two leading works were SEPHER YETZIRAH and the Aramaic ZOHAR, the latter ascribed to the 2nd cent. tanna Simeon ben Yoḥai but "revealed" at the end of the 13th cent. by the Spanish scholar Moses de LEON, who was probably the author. Later works in this field include the *Pardes Rimmonim* of Moses ben Jacob Cordovero, *Maggid Mesharim* of Joseph Caro, and above all, the writings of the school of Isaac LURIA (especially *Etz Ḥayyim* by Ḥayyim VITAL) which also had great influence upon the prayer-book (e.g. the hymn *Lekhah Dodi*). Typical of the Middle Ages are the works of moral instruction (MUSAR) including JEDAIAH BEDERSI'S *Beḥinat Olam,* JUDAH BEN SAMUEL HE-ḤASID'S *Sepher Ḥasidim,* Israel Nakawa's *Menorat ha-Maor* and the work of the same name by Isaac ABOAB, Isaiah HOROWITZ'S *Shene Luḥot ha-Berit,* and Moses Ḥayyim Luzzatto's *Mesillat Yesharim*; the two last-named are colored by mysticism. Works

were produced in other branches of literature, such as history (Ibn Daud's *Sepher ha-Kabbalah,* a survey of Jewish history from creation to the 11th cent., and Abraham ZACUTO'S *Yuḥasin,* a chronicle of Jewish history to the end of the 15th cent.), medicine and science (works by Abraham bar Ḥiyya, Abraham Ibn Ezra, Isaac ISRAELI, and Maimonides). There also was a certain amount of artistic prose (usually rhymed), such as that by Joseph ZABARA, the animal fables of BERECHIAH HA-NAKDAN, Isaac IBN SAHULA'S *Meshal ha-Kadmoni,* Abraham IBN ḤASDAI'S *Ben ha-Melekh veha-Nazir,* and, especially, the great imitation of the Arabic *Makamas,* Judah AL-ḤARIZI'S *Taḥkemoni,* and the similar work, *Maḥberot Immanuel* by Immanuel of Rome. There was no narrative literature, although among the surrounding Christian peoples verse and prose story-writing were in great vogue. The nearest to a novel is perhaps the *Megillah* of the paytan *Ahimaaz* in S Italy. Only at the end of the period are continuous narratives to be found in the Ḥasidic parables and stories of pious men.

(6) *Modern Period and Neo-Hebrew Literature*: In the mid-18th cent., a need was felt in W Europe, especially Germany, for a change in Jewish life. This was expressed in the rise of the HASKALAH movement aiming at the adjustment of Jewish life to the culture of the modern environment. The means chosen was a renaissance of the Hebrew language and literature along secular and modern lines. The movement was headed by Moses MENDELSSOHN who devoted much energy to the spiritual improvement of the Jews. Others joined him, and in 1783, there appeared *Ha-Measseph,* a monthly Hebrew journal serving as a rallying point for poets, essayists, scholars, biographers, and even satirists and humorists. The Haskalah movement made headway and a literature began to develop. Conditions in Germany were not favorable, but it struck root in other lands, first the Austrian province of Galicia, and later, in Russia where the renaissance movement came to full bloom. Hebrew poetry of the modern period began with Moses Ḥayyim Luzzatto whose historical drama *Maaseh Shimshon* and the allegorical dramas *Migdal Oz* and *La-Yesharim Tehillah* are modern in content and form. His dramas reflect the conflict between the various emotions in the individual as well as the struggle between good and evil in society. He was followed by Naphtali Herz Wessely whose *Shire Tipheret* in twenty cantos is the first attempt to produce a biblical epic on a large scale. The leading poets of the later Haskalah period were Abraham LEBENSOHN, his son Micah LEBENSOHN, and Judah Leib GORDON. A vein of seriousness permeates the poems of all three poets. The poems of the elder Lebensohn are more contemplative than emotional. His son's work is characterized by both deep thought and stirring feeling, especially in his

biblical and historical poems. Gordon dominated the poetic horizon of the period. He mastered all forms of poetry and wrote on historical and polemical themes and even composed fables. His long narrative poems of a didactic nature exerted great influence at the time. The poetry of the period of nationalism, from the 1880's on, surpasses that of the Haskalah in quantity and quality; the outstanding poets are Hayyim Nahman BIALIK, Saul TSCHERNIKHOVSKY, Zalman SHNEOUR, Yaakov CAHAN, David SHIMONI, and Yaakov FICHMAN. Bialik was called the national poet, for he gave voice to the ramified life of the people, to its tragedy, suffering, scholarship, and its hopes. Tschernikhovsky excelled in idylls and poems of a humanistic character. Shneour evinces a strong personality in his poems in which he sings of strength in life and in nature. Cahan, Shimoni, and Fichman represent the Israel center of H. L. They made their debut in Russia, but their long residence in Palestine left its mark on them. Other important poets are Avraham SHLONSKY, Yitzhak LAMDAN whose poem *Masadah,* glorifying the pioneering spirit, made a great impression, Uri Tzevi GREENBERG who gave stirring voice to Jewish suffering, Shin SHALOM, Nathan ALTERMAN who distinguishes himself in short humorous and topical poems, Avigdor HA-MEIRI, Reuven AVINOAM (Grossman) whose elegiac poems at the death of his son killed in the Israel war are outstanding, Yoseph Lichtenbaum, Yehudah Amihai, and Miriam bat-Yokhevet. The Hebrew fiction of the modern period begins with Abraham MAPU whose novels *Ahavat Zion* and *Ashmat Shomron* present masterly portrayals of Jewish life in Jerusalem and Samaria in the time of Isaiah. He was followed by many others, among whom Peretz SMOLENSKIN, Reuben Asher BRAUDES, and SHALOM JACOB ABRAMOVITSCH, better known by his pseudonym, Mendele Mocher Sephorim, are outstanding. The important novelists and short story writers of the nationalistic period are David FRISCHMANN, Mordecai Tzevi FEIERBERG, Judah STEINBERG, and S. BEN ZION. These are mostly short story writers and can be called the romantic group. Their stories breathe love and reverence for traditional life and note the tragedy of its passing. To the realistic school belong the novelists Isaiah BERSHADSKI and Yoseph Hayyim BRENNER, and also the short story writers Yitzhak Dov BERKOWITZ and Gershon SCHOFFMAN. Their works depict primarily the life of the Jewish youth in conflict and struggle. Aharon KABAK in several novels portrayed the life of the pioneers in Palestine and wrote on historical subjects. Shemuel Yoseph AGNON in his stories immortalized the ideal aspect of Jewish life in the ghetto in the recent past as well as the early period of Zionist settlement in Palestine; the award to Agnon of the Nobel Prize was regarded as international recognition of the new Hebrew literature.

Other Israel authors include Asher BARASH, Avigdor Ha-Meiri, Yehudah BURLA, Mosheh SMILANSKI, and Hayyim HAZAZ, all of whom concentrated on depicting phases of life in Israel — Hazaz specializing in portraying the life of the Yemenite Jews — Yoseph Arikha, Yehudah Yaari, and Yitzhak SHENHAR. After the War of Independence, a whole group of *Tzabra* (Israel-born) writers made its appearance portraying the life of Israel youth and its rugged thought and speech. They have been followed by a new generation whose emphasis has been more international. There has also been a spate of Israel plays, mostly of the lighter variety.

Numerous scholars made important contributions in the fields of history, literary criticism, and essay-writing. Solomon RAPOPORT wrote the history of important Jewish centers in the form of biographies of their moving spirits. Nahman KROCHMAL's *Moreh Nevukhe ha-Zeman* is an important contribution to the philosophy of Jewish history and the history of Jewish literature. Samuel David LUZZATTO was a poet, grammarian, and biblical exegete who also wrote essays on the philosophy of Judaism. Isaac Hirsch WEISS composed a history of Jewish tradition and its literature from early times to 1500 CE. Some of the works of the historian Simon DUBNOW were written in Hebrew. The leading literary critics of the period are David Frischmann, Baruch KURZWEIL, Yoseph KLAUSNER, Fischel LACHOWER, the last two writing histories of modern H. L. There were numerous Hebrew essayists in this period, the most distinguished being Peretz Smolenskin who in his essay championed the cause of nationalism and the cultivation of the Hebrew language; Eliezer BEN-YEHUDAH who was an outstanding proponent of Hebrew as a spoken language; Asher Ginzberg, known as AHAD HA-AM, the propounder of cultural Zionism which emphasized the role of Palestine as a cultural rather than political center; and the publicist Nahum SOKOLOW. Also distinguished were Micah Joseph BERDICHEVSKI, champion of changing values in Jewish life, Moses Leib LILIENBLUM, an exponent of Zionism, Elhanan Löb LEWINSKY, a brilliant feuilletonist, Alter DRUYANOW, and RABBI BINYAMIN, who wrote essays on philosophical and literary subjects. American Jewry has a share in the growth of modern H. L. Important poets are Gershon Rosenzweig, Benjamin SILKINER, Ephraim LISITZKI, Shimon HALKIN, and Israel EFROS (the last two now in Israel). Leading novelists and short story writers are Yohanan TWERSKY (later in Israel) and Samuel Leib BLANK. Critics and essayists, literary and historical, include Abraham GOLDBERG, Menahem RIBALOW, Abraham EPSTEIN, Daniel PERSKI, and Zevi SCHARFSTEIN.

HEBREW TEACHERS' COLLEGE: Boston institute established in 1921. The College graduates Jewish teachers and offers graduate degrees in education

Hebrew Union College, Cincinnati.

and Hebrew literature. It also conducts a four-year pre-college high school and a department for adult studies.

HEBREW THEOLOGICAL COLLEGE: Traditional rabbinical college in Chicago founded in 1922. In addition to ordination, it offers degrees of Doctor and Master of Hebrew Literature. Its campus is in Skokie, Ill., and includes a liberal arts college.

HEBREW UNION COLLEGE—JEWISH INSTITUTE OF RELIGION: US rabbinical seminary. In order to strengthen and advance the cause of American Reform Judaism, Isaac Mayer Wise founded the Hebrew Union College in Cincinnati, Ohio, in 1875. With similar objects, Stephen Wise founded the Jewish Institute of Religion in New York in 1922. The two schools were merged in 1950 as the Hebrew Union College — Jewish Institute of Religion. The presidents of the Hebrew Union College have been: Isaac Mayer Wise, 1875–1900; Moses Mielziner, 1900–1903; Gotthard Deutsch, Feb.–June 1903; Kaufmann Kohler, 1903–1921; Julian Morgenstern, 1921–1947. S. Wise was president of the Jewish Institute of Religion, 1922–1948. Nelson Glueck 1947–1971 (of the Jewish Institute of Religion from 1948, and of the combined school from 1950) and Alfred Gottschalk from 1971. HUC-JIR graduates about 30 rabbis a year after a 5-year course. It is dedicated to the preservation of Judaism in the spirit of Reform. The Cincinnati school has ordained over 800 rabbis and the New York school over 300. The Cincinnati school is housed in a campus of approximately 18 acres. It has a library, with over 200,000 volumes and 6,000 mss, besides a further 3,000 mss of Jewish music. It publishes the *Hebrew Union College Annual* and *Studies in Bibliography and Booklore*. In 1947, it established the American Jewish Archives with the primary purpose of furthering the study of American

Jewish history. It also maintains a museum of Jewish interest. The New York school also houses the Hebrew Union School of Education for the training of principals and teachers for Jewish religious education and the Hebrew Union School of Sacred Music, which trains cantors in a four-year course and has a library of over 50,000 volumes. The HUC has also a branch in Los Angeles and an Israel center in Jerusalem.

HEBREW UNIVERSITY: University in Jerusalem.

The proposal to found a Hebrew university was first mooted by Hermann Schapira in the Hebrew press in 1882-4, and afterward at the First Zionist Congress (1897). The 5th Zionist Congress (1901) passed a resolution (moved by Chaim Weizmann) advocating that the Zionist Actions Committee should examine the possibility of establishing a Hebrew

The new building of the Jewish National
and University Library.

college for higher studies. At the 11th Congress (1913), Weizmann spoke on the problems of the establishment of a Hebrew university, and a committee was elected to implement the project. In 1914, an area of land on Mt. Scopus was purchased by the *Hoveve Zion* of Odessa and the philanthropist Y. L. Goldberg. In July 1918, the foundation stones were laid by Dr. Weizmann and in Apr. 1925, the University was officially opened by Lord Balfour. At its head, first as chancellor (1925–35) and later (1935–48) as president, stood J. L. Magnes. Magnes was succeeded by Selig Brodetsky (1949–52), Binyamin Mazar 1953–61), Eliahu Elath (1961–8), and Avraham Harman since 1968. In 1973, the H. U. had seven faculties (Humanities, Social Sciences, Science, Law, Medicine, Dental Medicine, Agriculture) and four schools (Education, Pharmacy, Social Work, and the Graduate Library School). There were 16,000 students including 3,000 from overseas, and 2,000 academic workers. The Hadassah Hospital serves as the University Hospital. There exist also several ancillary institutions, including the Jewish National and University LIBRARY. Under the H. U.'s auspices the Magnes University Press publishes original and translated learned works, and also the quarterlies *Tarbitz* (on the humanities; founded 1929), and *Kiryat Sepher* on bibliography (founded 1924). The H. U. has also set up a university extension scheme in various centers outside Jerusalem. The controlling authorities of the H. U. are (a) the board of governors which is the supreme directing body; (b) the executive council which conducts the affairs of the H. U. in Israel; and (c) the senate which directs the academic affairs of the H. U. The budget is derived from fees and from contributions collected for the purpose all over the world (from "Friends of the H. U."). The government of Israel participates in the budget. The War of Independence (1948) gravely affected the work of the H. U. which was cut off from its buildings, laboratories, and libraries on Mt. Scopus, and was compelled to use various temporary premises in central Jerusalem. In 1954, work commenced on a second permanent site at Givat Ram in the W suburbs of Jerusalem, the first buildings being opened in 1955 and the campus in 1958. Access to Mt. Scopus was opened again after the Six-Day War in 1967 and the H. U. is now developing both campuses. In addition the University has its Medical and Dental School at En Karem, and its Agriculture Faculty at Rehovot, A number of faculties are being transferred from Givat Ram to Mt. Scopus which will also house the Truman Center for the Advancement of Peace, the Baker Center for Adult Education, and eventually provide residential accommodation for up to 8,000 students and faculty. The Mount Scopus campus will eventually be the center for the Humanities and the Givat Ram campus for the Sciences.

General view of Hebron

HEBREWS: English form of Heb. *Ivrim*, denoting either a descendant of Eber, grandson of Shem (Gen. 10:24) or one who comes from the other side of the River [Euphrates] (Heb. *ever ha-nahar*). Abraham is called "the Hebrew" (Gen. 14:13) and the term was later sometimes used interchangeably with Israelites (Exod. 9:1, etc.). It is disputable whether the HABIRU and H. are identical. In the 19th cent., "Hebrew" was occasionally used in preference to "JEW" as implying greater dignity, though on the Continent of Europe "Israelite" was more common. H. was the origin of *ebreo* and *Yevrei*, the usual Italian and Russian words.

HEBRON (in the Bible also called Kiriath-Arba): Ancient city of Judah, 18 m. S of Jerusalem. Before Abraham's time, it was under the control of Hittites. Abraham bought from them a plot of land (the Cave of MACHPELAH) in H. in which to bury Sarah; today a mosque stands on the reputed site. Joshua assigned H. to Caleb, and it became a levitical city and a city of refuge. David reigned there for seven and a half years before transferring his capital to Jerusalem. A Jewish community continued in H. in the Byzantine Period and under Arab rule. The modern city is situated somewhat to the E of the historical location and was (together with Jerusalem, Tiberias, and Safed) one of Palestinian Jewry's four sacred towns. Jews lived there throughout recent centuries and in 1890, numbered 1,500 with yeshivot and religious schools. For economic reasons, their number subsequently declined, although the great Lithuanian yeshivah of Slobodka was transferred there in 1925. In 1929, the Arabs massacred many Jews of the town (then numbering 700), and the survivors fled. About 30 Jewish families returned in 1931, but after the Arab riots of 1936, no Jews lived in H. After the Six-Day War of 1967, a number of Jews again settled in H. establishing the Kiryat Arba quarter. Its population in 1967 was 38,310.

*HECHLER, WILLIAM H. (1845–1931): Zionist sympathizer. A British Protestant clergyman who served as chaplain to the British embassy in Vienna and later as tutor to the children of Grand Duke Frederick of Baden, he became inspired by Zionist ideals and advised Herzl on political matters. H. assisted Herzl in making contacts, especially through Grand Duke Frederick, an uncle of the German kaiser William II. He wrote *The Restoration of the Jews to Palestine* (1884).

HECHT, BEN (1894–1964): US author. His first novel *Erik Dorn* was experimental, but it was succeeded by a number of sensational novels (*The Florentine Dagger*, *A Jew in Love*). In 1945–8, he actively supported the *Irgun Tzevai Leumi*. He wrote a personal Jewish credo *A Guide for the Bedevilled* and an autobiography *A Child of the Century* (1954). H. also wrote plays and film scenarios.

ḤEDER (Heb. "room"): A school for teaching children the basis of Jewish religious observance. The *ḥ* was a prominent feature of traditional Jewish education in E Europe. The term is now sometimes applied to the school attached to a synagogue.

HE-ḤALUTZ (Heb. "The Pioneer"): Federation formed by *ḥalutz* (pioneering) youth movements. It is responsible for *ḥalutz* education, training farms for *ḥalutz* movements, and immigration to Israel of youth movement members within a framework created by the *Histadrut*. The first *H.* group was founded in the US in 1915 by David Ben-Gurion and Yitzḥak Ben-Zvi; many of its members fought in the Jewish Legion against the Turks. In E Europe, *H.* was inspired by Yoseph Trumpeldor after World War I, and was closely bound up with Jewish self-defense. Similar groups were formed throughout Europe in 1919–21, and were combined into a world organization in 1924. *H.* supplied the bulk of pioneering labor for the upbuilding of Palestine, especially in agriculture, and is responsible for the growth of new social forms there. From 1933, it became strong in Germany and grew rapidly in Central Europe. World War II swept away the Central and E European movements, which were prominent in Jewish resistance in Warsaw and elsewhere. During the later 1920's and more particularly in the 1930's, the pioneering ideal developed in affiliated youth movements (e.g. HA-SHOMER HA-TZAIR, GORDONIA, HA-BONIM, BENE AKIVA) and pioneers emigrated to Palestine from N and S Africa, W Europe, the US, etc.

HEIDELBERG: German town. Jews are mentioned there in the late 13th cent. The community was martyred during the Black Death massacres (1349), but renewed from 1360 to 1391. Individuals settled there from the late 15th cent. and in 1714, a synagogue was consecrated. The number of Jews grew in the 18th cent. against the wishes of the local population, and in 1819, *Hep! Hep!* riots broke out. The 1933 Jewish community, numbering 1,400, was annihilated. Jewish pop. (1968): 140.

HEIDENHEIM, WOLF BENJAMIN (1757–1832): German liturgical scholar. In 1799, he set up a press at Rödelheim where he printed important Hebrew works. The festival prayer-book which he published (1800) with commentary and German translation (in Hebrew letters) became the standard text, while his daily prayer-book went through over 100 editions.

Jasha Heifetz.

HEIFETZ, JASCHA (1901–): Violinist. Born in Vilna, he began to make concert appearances before he was 5. After the 1917 Russian Revolution, he settled in the US. In 1926, he donated a concert hall to Tel Aviv. H. has transcribed many pieces for the violin, and written a number of original compositions.

HEIJERMANS, HERMANN (1864–1924): Dutch author and playwright. He published short stories, novels, and plays, many devoted to unsparing criticism of the social order. Some of his works depict Jewish life.

HEILBRON, SIR IAN MORRIS (1886–1959): British chemist. He was professor at the Univs. of Liverpool, Manchester, and London and held several government appointments as scientific adviser. In 1950, he became chairman of the Advisory Council for Scientific and Industrial Research.

HEILBRONN: German town. The first definite information on its Jews dates from 1298 when 200 were martyred in the RINDFLEISCH massacres. During the Black Death persecutions (1349), the Jews were murdered or expelled. A new synagogue was consecrated by 1357, and thereafter, the Jews were alternately expelled and restored until 1476, from which time no Jews lived in H. until 1831. A congregation was founded in 1851. The community numbering 1,000 disappeared under Nazi rule.

HEILPRIN: (1) *ANGELO H.* (1853–1907): US geologist, paleontologist, and explorer; son of (2). He taught in American colleges and universities, and made a number of exploring voyages for geological study. He ascended Mt. Pelée during an eruption, and in 1892, led the Arctic expedition for the relief of Peary. (2) *MICHAEL H.* (1823–1888): Author and journalist. Of Polish birth, he went to Hungary in 1842. In the 1848 rebellion, he was appointed secretary of the Ministry of the Interior's press office. After the suppression of the rebellion, he escaped abroad and in 1856, settled in the US where he taught in Jewish schools in Philadelphia and was active in the anti-slavery movement. H. was an editor of *Appleton's Encyclopedia of American Biography* and wrote works on the Bible. He worked indefatigably to establish farm colonies for the Jewish migrants going to the US from Russia after 1881. (3) *LOUIS H.* (1851–1912): Editor; son of (2). He wrote the *Historical Reference Book* (1884), edited *Nelson's Encyclopedia,* and together with (1) edited *Lippincott's New Gazetteer* (1905).

HEILPRIN, JEHIEL BEN SOLOMON (c. 1660–1746): Scholar. He was rabbi at Glusk (White Russia) and, from 1711, at Minsk. His best-known work was *Seder ha-Dorot* comprising a chronology down to 1696, an alphabetical list of tannaim and amoraim, and a catalog of post-talmudic Hebrew authors and books. Besides his rabbinical knowledge, H. had a wide secular education and was a student of Kabbalah.

HEIMANN, MORITZ (1868–1925): German author. As chief editor of the S. Fischer publishing house, he influenced Hauptmann and Wassermann. H. was

Heinrich Heine.

the author of novels and plays (the latter including *Das Weib des Akiba*).

HEINE, HEINRICH (1797 or 1799–1856): German poet and writer. After qualifying as a lawyer, he submitted to baptism in 1825. A frequenter of the fashionable Berlin salons, H. soon displayed his talents in *Die Harzreise* (1826) and *Das Buch der Lieder* (1827). A sojourn in Heligoland inspired the *Nordsee* poems and a visit to Italy, the *Italienische Reise*. Welcoming the 1830 revolution in France, he settled in Paris the following years and became the intimate of leaders of French literature. His many works include *Die Romantische Schule, Der Salon, Deutschland, ein Wintermärchen, Atta Troll, Romanzero,* and *Neue Gedichte*. From 1847, he was attacked by a spinal disease and became a helpless invalid confined to his "mattress grave," but bore his sufferings heroically. His early poems thrilled an enormous public and were set to music by Schubert, Schumann, Rubinstein, and Brahms; subsequently, however, their popularity waned. His later works include several lyrical masterpieces. His prose-style was the most brilliant in German since Lessing and was unequaled until Nietzsche. His political insight was extraordinarily pertinent, while the humor and satire of some of his works entitle H. to be ranked with Rabelais and Swift. His relationship to Judaism varied; during his illness, he recanted the rather showy Hellenism of earlier years. He recovered a deep sense of the grandeur and compelling power of the Hebrew scriptures, yet could not write a Jewish poem without breaking the mood by an ironic note.

His works of Jewish interest include *Hebräische Melodien* and the unfinished novel *Der Rabbi von Bacherach*.

HEINEMANN, YITZḤAK (1876–1957): Scholar of philosophy. From 1919, he lectured at the Breslau Rabbinical Seminary, from 1920 editing the *Monatsschrift für die Geschichte und Wissenschaft des Judentums*. In 1939, he settled in Palestine. His works emphasize the individual characteristics of classical Jewish, in contrast to Greek and Roman, thought. He participated in (and from 1915, edited) the German translation of Philo.

HEIR see **INHERITANCE**

HEJAZ: Coastal province in NW ARABIA. The origin of permanent Jewish settlement is obscure, but there is evidence of the presence of Jews between the 1st and 4th cents. CE. In ancient poetry of the region, the Jews are depicted chiefly as traders and wine-merchants. The most important Jewish community was that of MEDINA. Several Jewish colonies were also found N of Medina including KHAIBAR, Fadak, Wadi 'l-Qura, and Taima. The Jewish population increased through the conversion of Arabs to Judaism. Some Jews lived in Mecca, at least temporarily, before the rise of Islam. Shortly after the arrival of MOHAMMED, almost all the Jews of Medina were expelled or massacred. Mohammed subdued the Jewish colonies N of the city but permitted the inhabitants to stay. Under the reign of OMAR, the Jews were expelled from Khaibar and Fadak and possibly from Wadi 'l-Qura. In the latter place, however, they reappeared in the 10th cent. There are no subsequent traces of Jews in H.

HEKHAL (Heb. "shrine"): The forward part of the central TEMPLE building of Jerusalem (I Kings 7; II Chron. 4), the inner part being the *Devir*. Among the Sephardim, the term refers to the Ark in the synagogue (written *Ehal* in N Europe).

HEKHALOT, BOOKS OF: Early mystical Midrashim of the Amoraic and Gaonic Period. Most of them are attributed to R Ishmael ben Elisha and contain descriptions of the dangerous ascent to heaven to behold the Divine Chariot (MERKAVAH), the Heavenly Palaces (*hekhalot*, hence the generic name of the literature), and the Throne of Glory. The descriptions reflect the ecstatic experiences of visionary mystics and abound with powerful hymns in praise of the Divine majesty. Many have been incorporated in the Ashkenazi liturgy for the High Holidays.

HELENA (d. 56 CE): Queen of ADIABENE; wife of MONOBAZ I. She was converted to Judaism c. 30 CE, following the example of her son Izates. She built herself palaces in Jerusalem and Lydda and is reported to have checked a famine in Judea by her bulk purchases of food from abroad. Her piety and generosity to the Temple were proverbial. H. was buried in the so-called "Tombs of the Kings," N of Jerusalem; her inscribed sarcophagus, found in 1863, is in the Louvre, Paris.

HELETZ: Israel smallholder settlement (TM) in the S coastal plain founded in 1950 by newcomers from Yemen. In 1955, it was the site of the first successful oil boring in Israel and is now an oil field. Pop. (1972): 587.

HELIOPOLIS see **ON**

HELL see **GEHINNOM**

HELLENISM: The form of Greek civilization which was diffused over the Mediterranean and the Middle East after the end of the 4th cent. BCE as a result of the conquest of Alexander the Great. About that time, Palestine fell under Greek rule and Judea was surrounded by a ring of hellenized cities; simultaneously, the Jewish DIASPORA was expanding rapidly in Egypt, Cyrenaica, Syria, and Asia Minor, which were all in a process of hellenization. By the 3rd cent. BCE, the Jews of Egypt had adopted Greek and the SEPTUAGINT translation of the Bible had been completed. Antagonism between the traditional and hellenizing Jews in Jerusalem (the latter led by the TOBIADS) brought on Antiochus IV Epiphanes' attempt to suppress Judaism and the Hasmonean revolt. John Hyrcanus and Alexander Yannai broke the power of the Greek cities of Palestine, but later these were restored and strengthened as a result of Roman intervention aided by the Herods. By the Mishnaic Period, Jewish material life in Palestine was predominantly hellenistic although hellenization had ceased to be the political program of any Jewish faction. Both the Mishnah and Talmud contain hundreds of Greek words which had become absorbed into Hebrew and Aramaic and tomb inscriptions were in Greek (e.g. at BET SHEARIM). In a few cases, Jewish scholars (e.g. ELISHA BEN AVUYAH) fell away from Judaism under the influence of Greek philosophy. In the Diaspora, Judaism was first tolerated by the Greeks, and the organ of Jewish religious and juridical autonomy, the *politeuma,* essentially Greek in form, was recognized by the hellenistic kings: however, Jews frequently had recourse to the Greek courts. Their aspirations to Greek gymnasium education and Greek citizenship caused a violent civil struggle in EGYPT which only ended with the revolt of 117 CE. Jewish contacts with H. gave rise to a variegated Judeo-Hellenistic literature, one school of which advocated a Greco-Jewish rapprochement and held Greek philosophy to be Jewish in origin. The writings were propagandist, apologetic, literary, historical, and ethical; the leading authors were PHILO and JOSEPHUS. There were also translations into Greek, e.g. of works of the APOCRYPHA and APOCALYPSE, while synagogue decoration and architecture were influenced by Greek art. The Greeks as a whole, however, learned little about Judaism, and Jewish monotheism to them was atheism. The Jewish rejection of polytheism, with which the Greek city was bound up, prevented the Jews' general acceptance into Greek life despite the assimilation of a few wealthy Jews and the desire of the Jewish upper class to be regarded as Greeks. Jewish life, although influenced by H., therefore remained fundamentally apart.

HELLER: (1) *JAMES H.* (1892–1971): Rabbi and Zionist; son of (2). He was rabbi of the Isaac Mayer Wise Temple, Cincinnati, 1920–52 and then became president of the Labor Zionist Organization of America. H. was also a musician and composer, and lectured in musicology at the Cincinnati Conservatory of Music 1935–52. (2) *MAXIMILIAN H.* (1860–1929): US rabbi. He served Temple Sinai, New Orleans, for more than 40 years and was one of the pioneers of Zionism in the American Reform rabbinate.

HELLER, CHAIM (1879–1960): Scholar. Rabbi in Lomza, Poland, he moved in 1917 to Berlin where he founded a yeshivah combining modern systematic study with the traditional approach. Later, he went to the US. He wrote on Bible versions (particularly the Syriac and Samaritan translations) and halakhic problems and published an edition of Maimonides' *Book of the Commandments*.

HELLER, YOM-TOV LIPMANN (1579–1654): Talmudist. He was born in Bavaria and at the age of 18 was appointed dayyan at Prague. In 1629, he was fined heavily on a charge of libeling the state and Christianity, and forbidden to act as rabbi in Prague. He served in various communities, being in Cracow during the Chmielnicki massacres of 1648–9 on which he composed penitential psalms and commemorative prayers. His chief rabbinic work is a commentary on the Mishnah, *Tosephot Yom Tov* ("The Additions of Yom Tov"), printed in many subsequent editions of the Mishnah, characterized by its profundity, simplicity, and logical approach. H. wrote many other works on religious subjects and secular compositions on mathematics and natural science.

HELLMAN, LILLIAN FLORENCE (1905–): US playwright. Among her successful plays are *The Children's Hour*, *The Dark Angel*, *The Little Foxes*, and *Watch on the Rhine*.

HELSINGFORS CONFERENCE: Conference of Russian Zionists held at Helsingfors, Nov. 1906, under the chairmanship of Jehiel Tschlenow. A program was accepted recognizing the Jewish nationality and urging autonomy in Jewish national life, respect for Jewish religious observances, etc. The Conference affirmed that the ultimate goal of Zionism was Palestine.

HELSINKI (formerly Helsingfors): Capital of FINLAND. It was one of the three Finnish cities (the others being Viipuri and Abo) to which Jews were admitted under Russian rule. Jewish pop. (1973): 970.

HEMAN: (1) Son of Mahol, called the Ezrahite; famous sage, apparently author of parables (I Kings 5:11). Psalm 88 is attributed to him. His date is unknown. (2) Son of Joel; a levite and member of the group of singers established by David in the Jerusalem sanctuary (I Chron. 6:18).

HEMEROBAPTISTS: Jewish sect whose central feature was ablution at the beginning of the day. These "bathers at dawn" recorded by the Church Fathers are possibly identical with the *tovele shaharit* mentioned in the Talmud.

HENRIQUES: Sephardi family, of Marrano extraction, found in Holland, Italy, England, the W Indies, the US, etc. The best-known branch is that of Quixano H., which emigrated to England from Jamaica in the 18th cent. and included (1) *SIR BASIL LUCAS QUIXANO H.* (1890–1961): Social worker. He was active in welfare work in London as founder and leader of the Bernhard Baron St. George's Jewish settlement and was an authority on juvenile delinquency. He was a leading advocate of Liberal Judaism. (2) *HENRY STRAUS QUIXANO H.* (1865–1925): Lawyer. He was a king's counsel and active in Jewish life, being president of the Board of Deputies of British Jews 1922–5. His works include the standard *The Jews and the English Law*. (3) *ROBERT DAVID QUIXANO H.* (1905–1967): Soldier and author. After a successful army career, he achieved a literary reputation by a series of distinguished novels and *Hundred Hours to Suez*, an account of Israel's Sinai Operation.

HENSCHEL, SIR ISIDOR GEORGE (1850–1934): Musician. German born, and first known as a baritone singer, he conducted the Boston Symphony Orchestra 1881–4, and thereafter lived in England. H., who left Judaism, composed an oratorio, operas, etc.

HEP! HEP!: Anti-Jewish slogan used during the riots in Germany in 1819. The cry was then said to be of Crusader origin, being formed from the initials of the words *Hierosolyma est perdita* ("Jerusalem is lost").

HEPHETZ BEN YATZLIAH (fl. 10th cent.): Scholar in Mosul. Little is known of his life, but one one tradition states that he was blind. He wrote (in Arabic) *Sepher ha-Mitzvot* ("Book of Commandments") enumerating the 613 precepts and interpreting them according to talmudic sources. Although frequently cited in medieval literature, the original work had long been lost until rediscovered in the Cairo *genizah*.

HEPHKER (Heb.): Ownerless property. Most cases where property is rendered ownerless are due to its being renounced or unclaimed. According to Jewish law, anyone may acquire such property by taking possession. In Yiddish usage the word denotes lawlessness.

HERBERG, WILL (1906–): US writer. In the 1920's, he was active in the Young Communist League and edited Communist Party publications. In the mid-1940's he abandoned communism and henceforth his Jewish interests developed. He is author of *Judaism and Modern Man; Protestant, Catholic, Jew,* etc.

*HERBERT OF BOSHAM (fl. c. 1159–1190): English Hebraist; author of an independent commentary on Psalms derived basically from Rashi and older rabbinical sources. He was one of the earliest Christian commentators to utilize Jewish exegesis directly.

HERBSTEIN, JOSEPH (1897–): S African jurist. He was appointed judge of the S African Supreme Court in 1946. He settled in Israel after his retirement in 1963.

HEREM (Heb.): Ban, boycott, EXCOMMUNICATION.

HERESY: The erroneous doctrines of a religious sect. Although sects such as the KARAITES were known among the Jews, the connotation of h. in the Christian sense did not apply to them since Judaism, while imposing a physical discipline, did not attempt to define belief and doctrine precisely nor did it insist that deviation involved eternal punishment. Nevertheless, the denial of certain fundamental beliefs (resurrection, revelation, etc.) was held to forfeit a man's share in the world to come. In Christian doctrine, Judaism was not h., not being a sect of Christianity but a separate faith the profession of which, although in ignominy, was tolerated by the Church. Hence, professing Jews did not come under the jurisdiction of the Inquisition, although Marranos,

having been baptized, constituted its chief preoccupation.

*HERFORD, ROBERT TRAVERS (1860–1950): English theologian. A Unitarian minister, he became librarian of the Dr. Williams' Library, London, and devoted himself to fostering a better understanding of Pharisaic Judaism among Christians, particularly in his *Pharisaism* and *The Pharisees.* His *Pirke Aboth* includes an English translation of and commentary on the tractate *Avot.*

HERMANN, GEORG see BORCHARDT, GEORG

HERMENEUTICS, TALMUDIC: The rules for the determination of the exact meaning of the Bible are termed *Middot* ("measurements," "rules") in the Talmud. Various collections of these rules existed in tannaitic times; the three extant are the seven rules of Hillel, the thirty two rules of R Ishmael, and the thirteen rules of R Eliezer ben R Yose ha-Galili (the last is found only in post-talmudic works). The seven *middot* of Hillel are: (1) *Kal va-Ḥomer.* An *a fortiori* inference. (2) *Gezerah Shavah.* Inference from the analogy of words. (3) *Binyan Av mi-Katuv Eḥad.* A principle derived from a particular verse and applied generally. (4) *Binyan Av mi-Shene Ketuvim.* A principle derived from two verses and applied generally. (5) *Kelal u-Pherat u-Pherat u-Kelal.* A general statement limited by a particular which follows, or a particular limited by a following general one. (6) *Ka-Yotze Bo be-Makom Aher.* Exposition by reference to another similar passage. (7) *Davar ha-Lamed me-Inyano.* Inference from the context. The 13 rules of R Ishmael are an extension of these, in a different arrangement and with the addition of *Shene Ketuvim —* two verses which seemingly contradict one another and are reconciled by reference to a third verse. In addition to these standard rules, certain principles of exposition were accepted, the principal ones being: (1) Special interpretation of superfluous words, prefixes, and suffixes. (2) Different interpretations derived from the written text as opposed to the vocalized text. (3) Use of the numerical value of the letters of a word (GEMATRIA). (4) Taking certain words as abbreviations for complete phrases (NOTARIKON). (5) Attaching special meaning to words, the letters of which are dotted in Bible mss. There was a difference of opinion among the tannaim as to how far special meanings could be read into "superfluous" words and letters. R Akiva, who inherited the tradition of R Nahum of Gimzo, taught that every marking on every letter was open to interpretation. R Ishmael, however, laid emphasis on logical derivation rather than on the form of the text, teaching that "the Torah speaks in human language." See BIBLE COMMENTATORS.

HERMON: Mountain range in Lebanon; since 1967, partly under Israel rule. The highest point, 9,232 ft. above sea-level, is always snow-capped. Its ample

A view of snow-capped Mt. Hermon.

streams and melting snow feed the Jordan and Ḥuleh plain throughout the year.

HEROD I (known as "the Great"; 73 BCE–4 BCE):
King of Judea, etc.; son of ANTIPATER the Idumean by his Nabatean wife, Cypros. While still a young man, he was appointed governor of Galilee by his father, immediately showing a strong hand by executing dissidents. For this he was summoned by the Sanhed-

Coin of Herod I.

rin and only saved from death by the intervention of Hyrcanus and Sextus Caesar, governor of Syria. After his father's death, he defeated an attempt by Antigonus, son of Aristobulus II, to establish himself in Galilee. When the Parthians made Antigonus king (40 BCE), H. escaped to Rome and was appointed king of Judea by the senate. He captured Jerusalem in 37 with the help of a large Roman force, Antigonus being put to death. Earlier that year, he married the Hasmonean Mariamne, granddaughter of the high priest, Hyrcanus. H. received a free hand in internal affairs, but was prohibited from conducting an independent foreign policy. He was an energetic ruler, mercilessly suppressing opposition, which was widespread because of the people's attachment to the Hasmoneans. Taxation was heavy not only because of H.'s extravagance but also on account of the large sums Mark Antony demanded from his protégé. During the conflict between Antony and Octavian, H. turned against the Nabateans whom he defeated. After the battle of Actium, he was confirmed by Octavian in his kingdom and his territory was enlarged. H. murdered all possible rivals to his power, including his brother-in-law, Aristobulus III, the last Hasmonean high priest. As a result of palace intrigues, he put to death his wife Mariamne, their two sons Alexander and Aristobulus, and in the end, his firstborn, Antipater. The New Testament associates him with the Massacre of the Innocents. On the other hand, partly through his commercial operations, he greatly enhanced the wealth of his state. He rebuilt the Temple in Jerusalem on a magnificent scale and erected the two new cities of Sebaste and Caesarea. Outside Palestine, he was regarded not only as a generous patron, but also as a spokesman and protector of the Jews. In his will, H. partitioned his kingdom among his sons Archelaus, Herod Antipas, and Philip.

HEROD AGRIPPA I see **AGRIPPA I**
HEROD AGRIPPA II see **AGRIPPA II**

HEROD ANTIPAS see **ANTIPAS**
HEROD ARCHELAUS see **ARCHELAUS**
HEROD OF CHALCIS (d. 48 CE): Son of Aristobulus, grandson of Herod; brother of Agrippa I. He was appointed king of Chalcis (Syria) by Caligula in 41, and received pretorian rank. His first wife was Mariamne, granddaughter of Herod, and their son Aristobulus was appointed by Nero to reign in Lesser Armenia. H. later married his niece, Berenice. H. deposed and appointed a succession of high priests. He was succeeded by his nephew Agrippa II.

HERODIANS: Group mentioned in the New Testament as opponents of Jesus (Matt. 22:16; Mark 3:6; 12:13). Their identity is uncertain, the most acceptable theory holding that they were members of Herod's party who conducted propaganda among the masses in favor of the hated king and continued their activity after the death of Herod.

HERODIAS (fl. first part of 1st cent. CE): Daughter of Aristobulus, son of Herod and Berenice; sister of Agrippa I. Her first husband was her uncle Herod, whom she left after bearing him a daughter Salome. She then married the tetrarch Herod Antipas whom she accompanied when he was exiled to Gaul.

HERSCHELL (HIRSCHEL), SOLOMON (1762–1842): English rabbi; son of Hirschel LEVIN. Born in London, he returned there in 1802 as rabbi of the Great Synagogue. His authority as chief rabbi was formally recognized by the Ashkenazi communities of the whole country.

HERSCHMANN, MORDECAI (1886–1941): Cantor. He officiated in his native Volhynia and in Vilna and, from 1920, in the US. He was noted for his improvisations based on traditional melodies.

HERTZ: (1) *GUSTAV H.* (1887–1975): German physicist; nephew of (2). Professor at Halle and Berlin, director of the Siemens Research Laboratory, in Russia 1945–54, head of Physics Institute, Leipzig, 1954–61. With James FRANCK, he investigated the kinetics of electrons and shared with him the 1925 Nobel Physics Prize. In 1932, he discovered a new method of isolating isotopes. (2) *HEINRICH RUDOLPH H.* (1857–1894): German physicist; professor at Kiel, Karlsruhe, and Bonn. He conducted research into electro-magnetic waves, discovering the elements of modern radiotechnics. He also originated the investigation of photoelectric phenomena. H. discovered electric waves of large amplitude (known as "hertzian waves").

HERTZ, JOSEPH HERMAN (1872–1946): Rabbi. Born in Slovakia, he studied in New York and in 1898, went to officiate in Johannesburg from which he was expelled during the Boer War for his proBritish views. In 1913, H. was appointed chief rabbi of the British Empire, thenceforth residing in London and becoming the religious and spiritual leader of British Jewry. An enthusiastic Zionist, he played a part in the negotiations leading to the Balfour Declaration. His publications include English commentaries on the Pentateuch and prayer-book and the popular anthology *A Book of Jewish Thoughts.*

HERTZKA, THEODOR (1845–1924): Austrian economist and author. After being economic editor of the Viennese *Neue Freie Presse,* he founded the daily *Wiener Allgemeine Zeitung* in 1880, editing it until 1886. From 1889, he edited the economic journal *Zeitschrift für Staats- und Volkswirtschaft* in which he advocated free trade. Besides his economic studies, H. wrote *Freiland,* a utopian romance set in an imaginary African state, which influenced Herzl.

ḤERUT (Heb. "Freedom"): Israel political party associated with the *Ḥerut* Federation of Zionist Revisionists outside Israel. It was founded in 1948 by veterans of the IRGUN TZEVAI LEUMI and members of the REVISIONIST party and the BETAR movement. The leader is Menaḥem BEGIN and its objectives are territorial integrity ("a state of Israel on both banks of the Jordan"), unselective ingathering of the exiles, and liberalism in internal and economic policies. H. obtained 14 seats in the First Knesset in 1949 (49,782 votes), 8 in the Second in 1951 (46,651 votes), 15 in the Third in 1955 (107,190 votes), 17 in the 4th (130,515 votes, 17 in the 5th (138,599). In 1965, it cooperated with the LIBERAL party to form a political alignment called GAḤAL.

HERZ: (1) *HENRIETTE H.* (1764–1847): German society figure; wife of (2), and daughter of Benjamin De Lemos, a Sephardi physician from Hamburg. Her great beauty, wide culture, and deep understanding of contemporary intellectual currents converted her Berlin salon into an intellectual meeting place. After her husband's death, she was left in poverty. She was baptized in 1817. (2) *MARCUS H.* (1747–1803): German physician and philosopher. He practiced medicine at the Jewish Hospital, Berlin, and was regarded as one of the finest physicians of his day, receiving the title of professor of medicine in 1787. He published many philosophical works, while his correspondence with Kant, his teacher, is a major source for understanding the development of Kant's *Critique of Pure Reason.* H. was an intimate of Moses Mendelssohn and was active in promoting the civic and cultural welfare of Prussian Jewry.

HERZEGOVINA see BOSNIA; YUGOSLAVIA

HERZFELD, LEVI (1810–1884): German rabbi and historian; from 1842, district rabbi of the state of Brunswick. He was one of the moderate Reform group and an initiator of the Brunswick Rabbinical Conference (1884). His studies include a history of the Second Temple and an economic history of the Jews in antiquity.

HERZL, THEODOR (Benjamin Ze'ev; 1860–1904): Founder of Political Zionism. Born at Budapest, he studied at Vienna 1878–84, and devoted himself

Theodor Herzl.

to free-lance writing from 1885, achieving success as a social dramatist. In 1891–5, he was Paris correspondent for the Vienna *Neue Freie Presse.* He became increasingly interested in the Jewish problem, first advocating assimilation as the solution, but his drama *Das Neue Ghetto* (1894) expressed his reversion from this view, and the Dreyfus trial in the same year spurred him to more decisive action. After an unsuccessful interview with Baron de Hirsch (1895), he wrote his *Der Judenstaat* ("The Jewish State," published 1896). Here he defined the Jews as a people whose assimilation was impracticable and whose plight would deteriorate owing to its social and economic position: the solution was the founding of a Jewish state by international agreement. The territory must be chosen by the Jews but H. favored Palestine. Although opposed initially by both assimilationists and ultra-Orthodox, his book rallied the HIBBAT ZION movement and the youth. He returned to Vienna as literary editor of the *Neue Freie Presse* but devoted himself primarily to ZIONISM. He established contacts with the duke of Baden (1896) and with the Turkish grand vizier, offering financial assistance for Turkey in return for an independent Jewish Palestine. He substituted a request for a charter of land-settlement, but both proposals were rejected and, failing to win the Jewish financiers, H. convened the First ZIONIST CONGRESS (Basle, Aug. 1897) to mobilize Jewish popular aid. Here was founded the World Zionist Organization of which H. served as president until his death. Despite strong criticism, H. devoted himself to obtaining the agreement of Turkey and the great powers to the establishment of a Jewish national home in Palestine, and to strengthening the Zionist Organization to negotiate and carry on settlement work. In 1899, the JEWISH COLONIAL TRUST was founded. After the Second Congress, H. secured the temporary sympathy of the German kaiser William II, whom he met at Constantinople and again on his visit to Palestine (1898); in 1901, he was received by the sultan Abdul Hamid but lacking the backing of Jewish financiers, achieved nothing. Later (1902), he refused the sultan's offer of Jewish settlement in Turkey outside Palestine. H. then began negotiations with Britain to obtain a charter for Jewish settlement in Cyprus, Wadi EL ARISH in the Sinai peninsula, or (later) E Africa ("UGANDA"); a commission sent to Wadi el Arish reported negatively. In 1903, H. visited Russia to enlist the support of the Czar's minister Von PLEHVE in the negotiations with Turkey; here he received news of Britain's approval of Jewish settlement in Uganda as suggested by Joseph CHAMBERLAIN. The proposal, submitted to the 6th Zionist Congress, aroused a strom of protest and evoked H.'s declaration that Palestine remained the ultimate aim. He continued negotiations in that direction by contacts with Von Plehve, the pope, and the king of Italy but maintained touch with Britain. Opposition to Uganda, headed by Ussishkin, Tschlenow, Ahad Ha-Am, and the *Tziyyone Zion*, compelled him to affirm his loyalty to Palestine in a plenary session of the Zionist Actions Committee (Apr. 1904), thus preventing a split in the organization. The controversy had affected his heart, already weak, and he died at Edlach (Austria). His remains were reinterred on Mt. Herzl, W of Jerusalem, in 1949. His novel *Altneuland* presents his Zionist ideas as embodied in a utopian Jewish state in Palestine.

HERZL FOREST: Forest in Israel. When HERZL died in 1904, the Zionist Organization decided to commemorate his name by planting forests in Palestine. At first, olive and almond trees were planted, but these were found impracticable and were soon superseded by pine forests planted in his name at Huldah and Ben Shemen.

HERZLIYYAH: Israel municipality in S. Sharon, founded in 1924 by sons of settlers from established moshavot. It is a leading holiday-resort and the site of film studios. Pop. (1974): 45,700.

Rabbi Yitzhak Ha-Levi Herzog.

HERZOG, YITZHAK HA-LEVI (1888–1959): Rabbi and scholar. Born in Poland, he was educated in England and France. He officiated at Belfast 1915–9 and Dublin 1919–36, being appointed chief rabbi of the Irish Free State in 1925. In 1936, he was elected Ashkenazi chief rabbi in Palestine. His works include *The Main Institutions of Jewish Law*. Of his two sons, *HAYYIM H.* (1918–) was chief of intelligence in the Israel army 1948–50, 1959–62 military commentator and Israel ambassador to the UN (1975); and *YAAKOV H.* (1921–1972) served in senior posts in the diplomatic service (minister to US 1957–60, ambassador to Canada 1960–3) and government (director-general of the prime minister's office 1966–72).

HESCHEL, ABRAHAM JOSHUA (1907–1972): Philosopher. Educated in Berlin, he went to the US in 1940. After teaching at the Hebrew Union College, he became professor of Jewish ethics and mysticism at the Jewish Theological Seminary in 1945. He wrote works dealing with various phases of religion and philosophy, many bearing the stamp of neo-Hasidism. H. played a leading role in humanitarian causes including the Civil Rights campaign and the movement to support Soviet Jewry.

HESHVAN see **MARHESHVAN**

HESPED see **EULOGY**

HESS, MOSES (1812–1875): German social philosopher and Zionist precursor. Under the influence of Hegel and Spinoza, he published at 25 the *Heilige Geschichte der Menschheit* ("The Holy History of Humanity") and in 1841, *Die Europäische Triarchie* ("The European Triarchy") which first proposed a United State of Europe. In the same year, he joined other left-wing Hegelians in founding the *Rheinische Zeitung* of which Karl Marx became the editor. Sharp differences arose between H. and both Marx and Engels, and the breach became complete on the publication of the *Communist Manifesto* in 1848. H., as his further development showed, could reconcile himself neither to the materialistic interpretation of history nor to the doctrine of class-war. Hence, he withdrew from the movement and took up his residence first in Geneva, later in Paris, occupying himself increasingly with the Jewish people's history, character, and destiny. The fruit of these studies was *Rome and Jerusalem* (1862), the first Zionist classic, which explicitly stated or foreshadowed all the chief ideas of the movement. Although at first it made little impression, this remarkable work was to influence Pinsker, Ahad Ha-Am, and Herzl. During the last years of his life, H. became influential in the work of the Alliance Israélite Universelle.

HESS, DAME MYRA (1890–1965): English pianist. She appeared with many major orchestras as soloist and in chamber recitals. During World War II, she organized the National Gallery lunch-time concerts in London.

HESSE: State in W Germany. Jews lived there from the late 12th cent. and by the mid-14th cent., were resident in over 70 localities. Most of them suffered during the Black Death persecutions (1349), but settlement was soon resumed. From the time of Louis the Bavarian (1314–47), the kings tended to transfer the protection of Jews to nobles and, as a result, communities also sprang up in townlets and villages. Under Duke Philip, there was a brief expulsion (1524) and, under ecclesiastical pressure, the right of criminal jurisdiction was withdrawn from rabbis and the rate of interest on loans restricted (1539). From 1567, the country was divided into H.-Cassel and H.-Darmstadt. Jews received favorable treatment in the former, where a chief rabbinate was set up in 1656. Although certain trades were restricted, the Jews prospered. In 1808–13, H.-Cassel was incorporated in the kingdom of Westphalia and Jews received civic rights, which were renewed by the duke of H.-Cassel in 1833, but restricted 1852–66. Developments in H.-Darmstadt were similar: here, the Jews received full civic equality in 1848. There were 17,888 Jews in H. in 1933, but they disappeared under the Nazis. After World War II, communities were established in FRANKFORT-ON-MAIN (which is now incorporated in H.), WIESBADEN, CASSEL, DARMSTADT, and Nauheim. Jewish pop. (1970): 1,508.

HESSEN, JULIUS (1871–1939): Russian historian. He first wrote stories and feuilletons but from 1900, devoted himself to Jewish history, concentrating in particular on Russian Jewry in the 18th–19th cents. He wrote a history of the Jews of Russia and was an editor of the Russian Jewish encyclopedia *Yevreyskaya Entziklopedia*.

ḤET (ח) Eighth letter in the Hebrew alphabet; numerical value 8. It is pronounced by Oriental Jews with a rough breathing sound, by western Jews like *ch* in Scottish *loch*.

ḤEVER HA-KEVUTZOT (Heb. "League of Kevutzot"): Organization of Palestinian Jewish collective villages, founded 1926. It consisted of the smaller kevutzot (see KEVUTZAH) which desired to retain the intimate group, avoiding over-centralization, industry, and external wage-work. Originally without party affiliation, the organization tended to take up a position on the right-wing of *Mapai*. In 1951, after the split in *Ha-Kibbutz ha-Meuḥad*; *Ḥ. K.* merged with the dissident minority to form IḤUD HA-KEVUTZOT VEHA-KIBBUTZIM.

HEVESI (originally Handler), **SIMON** (1868–1943): Hungarian rabbi. A noted preacher, he officiated at Kassa 1894–7, Lugos 1897–1905, and Budapest 1905-43 (chief rabbi from 1927). From 1905, he lectured in homiletics and religious philosophy at the Budapest Rabbinical Seminary. H. was the author of many works of Jewish scholarship, including a Hungarian translation of the liturgy.

HEVESY, GEORG KARL VON (1885–1966): Chemist. Of Hungarian birth, he taught at Freiburg, Copenhagen, and from 1943, at Stockholm. He was a co-discoverer of the chemical element hafnium (1923) and was the first to introduce radioactive isotopes (of phosphorus) into the investigation of biochemical processes in living bodies, for which he received the 1943 Nobel Prize in chemistry.

ḤEVRAH (or ḤAVURAH) KADDISHA (Heb. and Aram. "sacred society"): Title applied to charitable confraternities, now generally limited to those for the visiting of the sick, the burial of the dead, and the comforting of the bereaved. Among the Sephardim, the *Ḥ.K.* is generally called the *Ḥ.K., Ḥessed ve-Emet* ("kindness and truth": Gen. 47: 29).

HEXAPLA see **ORIGEN**

*HEYDRICH, REINHARD (1904–1942): German Nazi leader who devised the plan for annihilating European Jewry. While heading the Nazi Security Police, Security Service, and Criminal Police, and while serving as acting protector of Bohemia-Moravia, H. was responsible for the evacuation and murder of millions of Jews. He was assassinated near Prague by a Czech partisan. He was known as *Der Henker* ("The Hangman").

HEZEKIAH: King of Judah, 720–692 BCE. In contrast to his father, Ahaz, he aimed at breaking the country's dependence on Assyria. To this end, he freed religious worship from Assyrian influence, purged the palace and Temple of images and pagan altars, and renewed the pure monotheistic religion. These reforms were supported by the prophets, especially Isaiah who wielded great influence in affairs of state. H. allied himself with neighboring rulers,

Engraved goblet of the Eisenstadt Ḥevrah Kaddisha, 1712, showing funeral scenes.

fortified Jerusalem, and constructed the SILOAM tunnel to improve its water-supply. In 712, he joined the neighboring states in their uprising against Assyria. Sargon II thereupon dispatched a punitive expedition which captured the Philistine cities but, for unknown reasons, did not enter Judah, Edom, or Moab. After Sargon's death in 705, H. led a league of states (including Edom, Moab, Sidon, and the Philistine cities), supported by Egypt and Babylon, to cast off the Assyrian yoke. In 701, Sennacherib and his army invaded Judah, calling on H. to surrender. After beating off an Egyptian challenge to his rear, Sennacherib invested but for some reason, did not occupy Jerusalem. Nevertheless, H. was forced to pay a large indemnity and cede 43 cities. After Sennacherib returned home, H. recaptured these towns from the Philistines to whom they had been consigned. There are several contradictions in the reports of the events as transmitted in the Bible and in Assyrian sources, and some scholars believe that Sennacherib attacked Judah a second time, but then had to desist on account of a plague in his camp, as recounted in II Kings 19:35–37. Talmudical legend exalts H. whom it praises for his fostering of religion and study.

HEZEKIAH (first part of the 11th cent.): Babylonian exilarch from 1021, and after the death of Hai (1038), also head of the Pumbedita academy. The legend that H. held his post for only two years and was then put to death by the caliph has been discredited.

HEZIR: Ancient priestly family of Jerusalem, mentioned at the time of David (I Chron. 24:15) and Nehemiah (Neh. 10:21). The tomb (? 1st cent. BCE) of the Bene Hezir discovered in the Valley of Kidron, outside Jerusalem, has revealed some of the oldest inscriptions in modern Hebrew characters, including a number probably of the allied Boethus family. See BOETHUSIANS.

HIAS ("Hebrew Sheltering and Immigrant Aid Society"): US society created in New York in 1909 by the merger of the Hebrew Sheltering House Association (founded 1884) and the Hebrew Immigrant Aid Society (founded 1902). Its object was to assist Jewish immigrants to the US. The organization rapidly expanded and during World War I, offices were opened in the Far East to assist immigrants *en route* to the US. After the war, a network of agencies was established in E Europe, and hundreds of thousands of Jews were helped in their journeys to the US, Canada, and S America. In 1927, H. helped to create HICEM; when the latter was dissolved in 1945, H. took over its migration agencies in c. 50 countries. In 1954, H. merged with the United Service for New Americans and the Overseas Migration Services of the American Joint Distribution Committee to create the United Hias Service. H. is also active in Israel.

ḤIBBAT ZION (Heb. "Love of Zion"): Zionist movement arising in Russia in 1882, deriving its strongest impulse from the 1881 pogroms. The slogan "To Palestine" aroused tremendous enthusiasm and societies were organized in Russia, Poland, Rumania, and England to purchase land in Palestine for settlement by their members. Jewish student youth inclined toward the movement (in their organizations *Aḥvat Zion* and BILU) but most of the religious leaders initially stood aside. Opposition came from assimilated elements in Russian Jewry, while many in W Europe also opposed the movement. The greatest obstacle was the Turkish authorities who in Apr. 1882 imposed a prohibition on Jewish settlement in Palestine. Nevertheless, practical work commenced and colonies in Palestine were founded in the same year. Baron Edmond de Rothschild extended financial support, but at the cost of undue dependence upon his assistance. The Zerubbabel society, founded in Odessa in 1883 under the leadership of Leon Pinsker and M. L. Lilienblum, became the hub of activity, while an important part was played by the Warsaw committee under Saul Pinhas Rabbinowitz. At the KATTOWITZ CONFERENCE (1884) the federation of the societies was commenced, at first under the name of *Mazheret Mosheh,* and from the second conference (at Droskiniki in 1887) as *Hoveve Zion.* This conference also endeavored to reconcile the movement's secular leadership with its religious opposition. The gap widened in 1888–9 over the problem of cultivation in Palestine during the sabbatical year. The third conference, held in Vilna in 1889, extended the religious influence and representation in the movement. Many of the secular leaders found a cultural expression for their Zionism in the BENE MOSHEH order founded by Aḥad Ha-Am in 1889. In 1890, the Turks rescinded the ban on Jewish settlement in Palestine, while the Russian authorities approved the existence of the *H. Z.* movement. This evoked widespread fervor and the numbers grew rapidly. At the fourth conference (Odessa, 1890), a central committee was established under Pinsker and an office was opened in Jaffa. The work of practical colonization continued and many Russian Jews immigrated to Palestine in 1890–1. The resultant land speculation led the Turkish authorities again to forbid Jewish immigration. The Jaffa executive of the *H. Z.* was closed in 1891 after suffering considerable financial loss, and practical work was restricted thenceforward to supporting existing colonies and Hebrew schools. After 1891, several currents flowed among the *H. Z.,* the main one being the "practical" trend, led by Lilienblum, which advocated the foundation of Palestinian colonies as the main activity. The others were the intellectual trend, centering around the *Bene Mosheh,* which insisted on the priority of cultural work, and the religious Zionists. In 1897, nearly all the *H. Z.* societies joined the newly-founded World Zionist Organization, and led the demand for practical work in Palestine. The movement continued to exist separately and was headed by Ussishkin from 1906 to 1919. However, after the Zionist Organization accepted the principle of practical work, the differences between it and the *H. Z.* were minor and the latter declined rapidly. It was formally dissolved in Russia in 1920 by order of the communist authorities.

HICEM: Emigration association set up in 1927 jointly by HIAS, ICA, and EMIG-DIREKT, becoming known as Hicem, from the initials of the three agencies. Emig-Direkt severed its connections in 1934, and the association was thereafter also known as HIAS-ICA. Its purpose was to serve as an information and assistance office for Jews emigrating from Europe. With the creation of the German refugee problem, H. extended its program and sought countries of haven in various parts of the world. Toward the end of World War II, ICA was forced to withdraw from the association because of lack of funds, and in 1945, H. was dissolved, its offices and activities being transferred to HIAS.

ḤIDDEKEL see **TIGRIS**

ḤIDDUSHIM see **NOVELLAE**

ḤIDKA, FEAST OF RABBI (in Heb. *seudat rabbi Ḥidka*): Term applied to a light repast eaten by some Jews in addition to the three obligatory Sabbath meals. It is called after R. Ḥidka, who maintained that four meals should be eaten on the Sabbath *(Shabbat 117b).*

HIGGER, MICHAEL (1898–1952): Scholar. He went to the US from Lithuania in 1915. He edited the minor treatises of the Talmud and compiled the talmudic *Baraitot* in 10 vols.

HIGH COMMISSIONER FOR REFUGEES see **LEAGUE OF NATIONS; REFUGEES**

HIGH COMMISSIONERS OF PALESTINE: Chief executive officials in Palestine under the British MANDATE. The appointment of Sir Herbert SAMUEL (1920–5) evoked great hopes among Jews, especially as he was known to be a supporter of Zionism. His initial task was complicated by the delay in confirming the Mandate and by Arab violence. The suspension of Jewish immigration after the 1921 Arab riots, the benevolence shown to the anti-Jewish mufti of Jerusalem, and the 1922 White Paper which detached Transjordan from Palestine came as disappointments to the Jewish community. On the other hand, Samuel erected the structure of the new Palestine, creating a solid governmental machinery and turning a chaotic country into an organized state. The foundations of the Jewish National Home were firmly laid during his term of office. Lord Plumer (1925–8) refused to restrict Jewish immigration and displayed much administrative energy. Under his rule, Palestine citizenship provisoes were laid down, a water-supply for Jerusalem installed, and public works schemes inaugurated to meet the threat of unemployment. Sir John Chancellor (1928–31) condemned in outspoken terms the 1929 Arab massacres (which occurred while he was away on leave) but later inclined to temporize. Sir Arthur Wauchope (1931–7) was sympathetic to Jewish aspirations while being scrupulously fair to the Arabs. During his period of office, the stream of immigrants rapidly increased. This led to Arab restiveness which he tried to pacify by promising a Legislative Council. His failure to quell the Arab revolt of 1936 at the outset led to an unhappy conclusion to his rule. His successor, Sir Harold MacMichael (1938–44), was in office during World War II when his refusal to admit refugees from Europe made him unpopular with the Jewish population. Viscount Gort (1944–5), although unable to make a fundamental change in the British government's policy, was sympathetic. The last H. C., Sir Alan Cunningham (1945–8), governed the country throughout the eventful happenings which culminated in the British withdrawal from Palestine.

HIGH PLACE: Place for worship, usually on a hill or mountain, where an altar was built, a pillar erected, and a sacred tree (*sherah*) planted in the vicinity. Sanctuaries of this nature were common among the Canaanites and other ancient neighbors of the Israelites, while the early Hebrew patriarchs followed the custom. Moses, however, fearing an imitation of pagan customs, imposed a strict ban on all such localities and the destruction of those already existing, also insisting on the centralization of Divine worship in one place (Deut. 12:2 ff.). In effect, worship on the High Places remained widespread until the establishment of the Temple at Jerusalem and the intensification of the prophetic struggle against paganism. They were finally removed by Hezekiah and Josiah, the latter obliterating them also in Samaria. Remains have been found in Palestinian excavations.

HIGH PRIEST: Chief official in the Temple. The office of h. p. was conferred on Aaron and his descendants who held it until the reign of Herod when it became dependent on the will of the Jewish rulers and the Roman procurators. During the war with Rome (66 CE), the post was filled by lot, Phinehas ben Samuel being the last h. p. During the First Temple Period, there were traditionally 18 h. p.'s, while c. 60 h. p.'s served in Second Temple times. Apart from the regular priestly garments — the breeches, tunic, girdle, and miter — the h. p. also wore a robe, *ephod,* breastplate, and frontlet. Attached to the breastplate was the Divine oracle — the URIM AND THUMMIM, consisting of four rows of three precious stones on which were inscribed the names of the tribes. These garments were worn when the h. p. conducted the service, which occurred whenever he chose; he donned white linen on the Day of Atonement for the solemn and unique moment when he entered the Holy of Holies to burn incense. He was only permitted to marry a virgin and forbidden to become defiled by proximity to a corpse or to mourn the dead.

HILDESHEIM: W German town. Jews lived there from the first half of the 14th cent. and were subject to both the town and the bishop. They were persecuted during the Black Death (1349) and expelled from the entire diocese in 1457. A few individuals returning after 1520, were exiled 1595–1601; they received a charter in 1662. 650 Jews lived there in 1933; 63 in 1961 but most of them left in the following years.

HILDESHEIMER: (1) *AZRIEL (ISRAEL) H.* (1820–1899): German rabbinical scholar. He officiated as rabbi at Eisenstadt 1851–69 and Berlin 1869–99. A foremost opponent of Reform, he aspired to combine traditional Judaism with European culture ("neo-orthodoxy"), for this purpose founding the BERLIN RABBINICAL SEMINARY (1873) which he directed until his death. H. published many studies, notably a critical edition of *Halakhot Gedolot.* (2) *MEIER H.* (1864–1934): German rabbi; son of (1). He was preacher to the Berlin Orthodox congregation *Adat Israel* and director of its religious schools. H. was a leader of *Agudat Israel* and published several studies on Jewish subjects.

HILFERDING, RUDOLPH (1877–1941): German socialist statesman. A physician by training, he became one of the chief theoreticians of the German Social Democratic Party. After the party split, he led the Independent Socialists and was German minister of finance in 1923, 1928–9. He left Germany in 1933, but was handed over to the Nazis by the Vichy authorities in 1941 and died in prison.

HILFSVEREIN DER DEUTSCHEN JUDEN (Ger. "German Jews' Aid Society"): The central charitable society of German Jewry to assist Jews in E Europe and oriental countries. Founded in Berlin in 1901, it continued to exist until 1941. Besides extending financial aid to Jews in various countries, it assisted Jewish emigration from E Europe. After 1933, it concentrated on helping Jews to leave Germany, aiding 90,000 persons up to 1941. The organization maintained a network of schools in Palestine and the Balkan countries from 1903 to 1918. It participated in establishing the Haifa Technion where the decision to teach technical subjects in German led to a "language-war" (1913–4) as a result of which German ceased to be the language of instruction in any Palestinian school. After World War I, it supported Jewish schools in E Europe.

ḤILLAZON: Creature mentioned in the Talmud as the source for the blue dye used for the fringes of the TALLIT. According to the rabbis, it was a rare creature found on the Mediterranean coast. To obtain the requisite color, it had to be captured alive. The *ḥ.* may have been the sea snail *murex* from which the ancients derived blue and purple dyes. Early in the 20th cent., the rabbi of Radin stated that the dye was derived from the *sepia officinalis* and his followers adopted the custom of using this dye for their *tallit,* although the identification was opposed by most scholars.

HILLEL (called "The Elder"; fl. 1st cent. BCE): Scholar; founder of the school known as the

"House of H." (BET HILLEL) and ancestor of a dynasty of patriarchs which held office until the 5th cent. Of Babylonian birth, he settled in Palestine and earned a slender living by manual labor while studying with Shemaiah and Avtalyon. In due course, he was appointed president of the Sanhedrin and together with his friend and ideological opponent SHAMMAI constituted the last of the pairs (ZUGOT) of scholars. Unlike Shammai, H. was noted for his humility and tendency to leniency. Although the two men differed in their decisions only on a few halakhot, their schools ("House of H." and "House of Shammai") diverged in many instances, but legal practice ultimately went in almost all cases according to the decision of the House of H. Few decisions are cited in H.'s name but they include the institution of the PROSBUL. He laid down the seven rules of Bible interpretation (see HERMENEUTICS). Many stories illustrate his virtues and he is credited with the authorship (in its negative form) of the so-called GOLDEN RULE "Do not do unto others that which you would not have them do unto you" (*Shabbat* 31a).

HILLEL II: Patriarch of Palestinian Jewry (c. 330–365). In 359, he published a system of intercalation to equalize the solar and lunar years, thus making it possible for the Jewish calendar to be determined without actual observation of the lunar phases. This system, complicated but extremely accurate, is still the accepted Jewish calendar. H. was in correspondence with the emperor JULIAN who addressed him as "my brother, the venerable patriarch."

HILLEL BEN SAMUEL ("of Verona"; c. 1220– c. 1295): Italian physician and philosopher. An admirer of Maimonides, he was one of the first scholars to introduce philosophical studies among Italian Jewry and tried to re-establish peace when Maimonides' writings were attacked. His principal work *Tagmule ha-Nephesh* discusses the nature of the soul (following the Arab Neoplatonists and the Aristotelians) and reward and punishment in the next world (concluding that their nature is spiritual, not material).

HILLEL FOUNDATIONS: Organization founded in 1923 and supported by B'NAI B'RITH. It offers (1972) religious, cultural, communal, and counseling services to some 300,000 Jewish students at 270 colleges and universities in the US, Canada, Israel, England, S Africa, Australia, Switzerland, and Holland. A professional staff directs the program at the institutions of higher learning.

HILLER, FERDINAND (1811–1885): German musician; founder (1850) and director of the Cologne conservatoire. He composed over 200 works including 6 operas, several oratorios (*The Destruction of Jerusalem* and *Saul*), cantatas, etc. H. was an influential musical critic and a noted pianist.

Sidney Hillman.

HILLMAN, SIDNEY (1887–1946): US labor leader. He went to the US from Russia in 1907. While president of the Amalgamated Clothing Workers' Union (1915–46), he made his reputation as a moderate who found the interests of labor reflected in the welfare of industry as a whole. He constantly advocated "constructive cooperation" between labor and management. He was politically close to President Franklin D. Roosevelt who appointed him member of the National Industrial Recovery Board and chairman of the labor division of the War Production Board. H. was a founder of the American Labor Party in New York State and a vice-president of the CIO.

HILLQUIT, MORRIS (1869–1933): US socialist. Born in Riga, he went to the US in 1887. Here, he joined Daniel de Leon's Socialist Labor Party but broke with him and eventually was a founder of the more moderate Socialist Party. H. learned Yiddish in order to participate in the immigrant Jewish socialist and trade union movement. As a lawyer, he defended many socialists and trade unionists who were brought to trial.

ḤILLUL HA-SHEM (Heb. "profanation of the Name" i.e., of God; cf. Mal. 1:11–12): The public desecration of the Divine Name (the opposite of KIDDUSH HA-SHEM). A Jew must avoid such desecration not only for its own sake but also to set an example to other peoples and to unlettered Jews. Thus it is a grave *Ḥillul ha-Shem* for a Jew to rob a non-Jew. In certain instances, *Ḥillul ha-Shem* was punished by excommunication. The phrase came to denote any action likely to bring disgrace on Judaism or on the Jews generally.

HILSNER, LEOPOLD see **POLNA CASE**

*HIMMLER, HEINRICH (1900–1945): German Nazi leader; principal agent in the annihilation of European Jewry. He was head of the SS, chief of the German police, and minister of the interior. On his instructions, millions of Jews were herded into ghettos and later transported to their deaths in extermination camps. He committed suicide on his capture by the British forces.

HINDUS: *MAURICE GERSHON H.* (1891–1969): US writer; of Russian origin. He was the author of several works on the Societ Union. His nephew *MILTON H.* (1916–), critic and teacher, has written on Proust, Whitman, Céline, etc., and has been professor of English at Brandeis Univ. since 1948.

HINNOM, VALLEY OF see **GEHINNOM**

HIPPOS see **SUSITA**

*HIRAM (fl. 10th cent. BCE): (1) King of Tyre. He extended his kingdom to Cyprus and Libya and maintained friendly relations with David to whom he sent wood and craftsmen for his palace. He contributed wood, gold, and craftsmen to Solomon's Temple and residences, as well as sailors to his Red Sea fleet, receiving in exchange wheat, oil, and 20 Galilean cities. (2) Tyrian metal-worker, responsible for the metal-fittings of Solomon's Temple.

HIRSCH OSTROPOLER see **OSTROPOLER**

HIRSCH: (1) *EMIL GUSTAV H.* (1852–1923): Reform rabbi; son of (2). Born in Luxemburg, he settled in the US in 1866, becoming rabbi of the Sinai Congregation at Chicago in 1880 and in 1892, professor of rabbinic literature and Jewish philosophy at the Univ. of Chicago. H. advocated extreme reforms in Judaism including the observance of the Jewish Sabbath on Sunday. He produced various publications devoted to Reform and was an editor of the *Jewish Encyclopedia*. (2) *SAMUEL H.* (1815–1889): Rabbi. He was chief rabbi of Luxemburg 1843–65. He then went to the US as rabbi of the Congregation Keneseth Israel, Philadelphia, where he introduced a number of reforms. He presided at the 1869 Reform rabbinical conference in Philadelphia which helped to determine the development of Reform Judaism in the US. H. wrote on Jewish theology in the spirit of Hegelian philosophy.

HIRSCH, BARONESS CLARA see **HIRSCH, BARON MAURICE DE**

HIRSCH FUND see **BARON DE HIRSCH FUND; JEWISH COLONIZATION ASSOCIATION**

HIRSCH, BARON MAURICE DE (1831–1896): Banker and philanthropist. A native of Munich, he went to Brussels in 1851, engaged in banking, and later settled in Paris. In 1869, he received a railroad concession from the Turkish government and also

Baron de Hirsch.

built railroads in Russia and Austria, adding to his large inherited fortune. His philanthropies, especially to Jewish causes, were proverbial. In 1873, he made a contribution to the Alliance Israélite Universelle to found Jewish schools in Turkey, and from 1880, covered the Alliance's annual deficits. In an effort to improve the economic situation of E European Jewry, he offered £2,000,000 in 1888 to found craft and agricultural schools for Russian Jews. When this scheme was opposed by the Russian government, H. decided that the only hope for Russian Jewry was emigration and in 1891, set up the JEWISH COLONIZATION ASSOCIATION (ICA) with £2 million capital, almost entirely contributed by himself, to establish Jewish agricultural colonies in Argentina and elsewhere. He also founded in 1891 the Hirsch Fund for agricultural and crafts schools in Galicia (foundation capital £1,000,000) and in New York, the BARON DE HIRSCH FUND for the technical and agricultural training of immigrants. His total benefactions exceeded $100,000,000. His wife, *BARONESS CLARA DE HIRSCH* (1833–1899), was a member of the BISCHOFFSHEIM family. She participated in her husband's philanthropies and continued them after his death.

HIRSCH, MAX (1832–1905): German economist and labor leader. In 1868, he founded the League of German Workers and edited its periodical. He began the organization of the German trade unions and was elected to the Reichstag four times.

HIRSCH, SAMSON RAPHAEL (1808–1888): German leader of Jewish Orthodoxy. He officiated at Oldenburg (1830) and Emden (1841), was chief rabbi of Moravia (1846), and from 1851, rabbi of the separatist Orthodox community of Frankfort-on-Main, the influence of which greatly increased during his period of office. Under his leadership, Frankfort became the center of Orthodox Judaism in Germany. His main views are expressed in his work *Nineteen Letters of Ben Uzziel* and *Horeb*. He maintained that until the advent of the Messiah, the Jews are not a people but a group of believers performing the obligations of the written and oral law. The Torah is above place and time and no observance, however small, is to be renounced. Religious reform leads to the degeneration of Judaism and empties it of content. The modern generation should be raised to the Torah and not the Torah lowered to the generation. Loyalty to the Torah does not prevent a man from identifying himself with national and political communities. H. is regarded as the progenitor of neo-Orthodoxy in western countries, aspiring to fuse European culture with unqualified loyalty to rigorously observed traditional Judaism.

HIRSCH, SOLOMON (1839–1902): US diplomat. A merchant in Portland, Oregon, he served in both the Senate Legislature and State Senate and was US minister to Turkey 1889–92.

HIRSCHBEIN, PERETZ (1880–1948): Hebrew and Yiddish author. Born in Lithuania, he began writing Hebrew poems and plays at an early age. In 1906, he turned his attention to Yiddish, writing plays

Peretz Hirschbein.

of a mystical and symbolic nature. Two years later, he founded a Yiddish dramatic troupe at Odessa. His play *The Idle Inn* (1911) marked a turning-point in his writings and he subsequently wrote a series of successful plays based on the life of simple Jews in Russian villages. These were frequently performed on the Yiddish stage. From 1911, he made his home in the US. H. was the author of Yiddish poems and a 3-volume Yiddish novel *Babylon* on Jewish life in America.

HIRSCHEL LEVIN see **LEVIN, HIRSCHEL**

HIRSCHEL, SOLOMON see **HERSCHELL**

HIRSCHFELD, GEORG (1873–1942): German author. A representative of the naturalistic movement, he wrote fiction and drama, the latter including several plays on Jewish topics.

HIRSCHFELD, HARTWIG (1854–1934): Orientalist. A native of Prussia, he settled in England in 1889, teaching first at the Judith Montefiore College, Ramsgate, later at Jews' College and London Univ. He wrote mainly on Judeo-Arabic literature and edited Ha-Levi's *Kuzari* which he translated into English and German.

HIRSCHFELD, MAGNUS (1868–1935): German psychiatrist. His studies of homosexuality led him to regard it as an intermediate sexual stage, and he demanded alleviations of the penalties imposed when it was detected. In 1918, he founded in Berlin the first Institute for Sexual Science ("The Hirschfeld Institute") in the world; it was subsequently closed down and destroyed by the Nazis, while H. himself found refuge in France.

HIRSZENBERG, SAMUEL (1865–1908): Polish artist. He was well-known in his day for his historical and sentimental paintings, strongly Jewish in feeling (e.g. *Uriel Acosta*, *Golus*). In his later years, he taught in the Bezalel School, Jerusalem.

ḤISDA (c. 217 — c. 309): Babylonian amora. He and R HUNA were called "the pious men of Babylonia" and greatly enhanced the reputation of the Sura academy. H. was a master of dialectic and devoted much attention to the interpretation of biblical texts. He instituted the prayers to be recited by travelers.

HISTADRUT (abbr. of Heb. *Ha-Histadrut ha-Kelalit shel ha-Ovedim be-Eretz Yisrael* — "The General Federation of Workers in Israel"): Israel labor federation; founded in 1920. The *H.* is a federation of trade unions, of which the basic organizational unit is the workers' committee in the place of employment, the second — the trade union, the third — the labor council (elected by the local workers) which looks after union, economic, and cultural affairs, and the fourth — the national organizations and the countrywide professional associations. The central institutions are (1) the *H.* conference with delegates elected by the totality of the membership according to party lists; (2) the *H.* council, elected at the *H.* conference, and constituting the supreme body in the period between conferences; and (3) the executive (*vaad ha-poel*) elected by the council. The labor councils and countrywide federations are responsible to the executive, the local trade union groups to the labor council, and the workers' committees to the trade union groups. Every member entering the *H.* also enters the *Ḥevrat Ovedim* ("Workers' Company") which is the COOPERATIVE society of the entire body of workers, embracing and coordinating all the economic and cooperative institutions of the *H.*; its directorate is elected by the *H.* executive and consists of 58 members, representing all branches of *H.* economy. In the *H.* are federated both the physically and intellectually occupied urban and rural workers, wage-workers, and independent earners. In 1973, it had 1,259,200 members including 89,000 Arabs and Druse. Its *Kupat Ḥolim* ("Sick Fund") serves over two million people including members of *Ha-Poel ha-Mizraḥi* and *Poale Agudat Yisrael*). The *H.* embodies the totality and the workers' agricultural settlements. The occupational distribution is: agriculture, industry, and crafts—42%; building, public works, and transport—26%; office work, medicine, and the free professions—32%. The result of the election of 1973 were Israel Labor Party 58.3%; *Gaḥal*—22.74%; Independent Liberals—5.97%; Religious Workers—4.2%; *Rakaḥ*—2.41%; Moked—1.72%: Within the *H.* are the *Berit Poale Eretz Yisrael* ("League of Palestinian Workers"), common to Jewish and Arab workers, aiming to create support among the Arabs for cooperation between the two peoples; *Noar Oved* ("Working Youth") for the Jewish working youth; and the HA-POEL sports organization. It also maintains the *Amal* network of schools for vocational training, a cultural center for the dissemination of Hebrew; artistic activities, including the OHEL theater and the *Telem* dramatic touring company. The *H.* press includes the daily DAVAR and OMER, the weekly illustrated *Devar ha-Shavua*, the children's *Davar li-Yladim*, and the Arabic *Ḥaqiqat al-Amr*. It also maintains a correspondence course institute, the AM OVED publishing house, a school for officials, etc.

HISTADRUT HA-OVEDIM HA-LEUMIT (Heb.

"National Workers' Organization"): Israel non-socialist labor organization affiliated with the HERUT movement with 88,000 members (1973). It was founded in 1926 as the Organization of Zionist Revisionist and *Betar* Workers, receiving its present name in 1934. In 1933, the National Workers' Sick Fund (*Kupat Ḥolim Leumit*) was founded and caters for 280,000 persons.

HISTADRUTH IVRITH OF AMERICA: US organi-

zation of Hebraists, founded at New York in 1916. Since 1922, it has published the weekly HA-DOAR. It organizes Hebrew study for adults, sponsors Hebrew cultural activities, and publishes the works of Ame-

Histadrut Building, Jerusalem.

rican Hebrew authors through the publishing house Ogen.

HISTORY AND HISTORIOGRAPHY: The Pen-

tateuch, purporting to give the history of mankind as a whole in relation to the origins of the Hebrew race, is the earliest instance in literature of a consistent philosophy of world history. The historical books of the Bible (Joshua, Judges, Samuel, Kings, Chronicles) maintain this tradition in presenting the history of the Hebrews from their occupation of Palestine down to the Babylonian Exile. These works are memorable not only for their broad sweep but also for their force in style, conciseness of expression, and power of description. The internal proportions are inconsistent, partly because sections of earlier works now lost, dealing, e.g. with the life of David and the house of Ahab, were incorporated *in extenso*. In addition, the Bible contains historical monographs covering single events or periods, such as the Books of Ruth and Esther. The Books of Ezra and Nehemiah (the latter incorporating Nehemiah's autobiography) continued this tradition into the post-exilic period. Other historical works, now lost — e.g. the Book of the Wars of the Lord (Num. 21:14), or the Book of the Acts of

Solomon (I Kings 11:41) — are also mentioned in the Bible. In the Apocrypha, the parallel accounts of the Hasmonean revolt in the two Books of Maccabees (the latter by Jason of Cyrene) perpetuate the biblical traditions. JOSEPHUS, who carries the story down to the fall of the Jewish state, may be reckoned one of the great historians of antiquity — not so much for his style, often mediocre, as for the breadth of his outlook and his graphic descriptions. His *Jewish Antiquities,* besides retelling Bible history, is virtually the only surviving source for the history of the Hasmonean and Herodian dynasties, as is his *Jewish Wars* for the Revolt of 66–70 and the siege of Jerusalem. Josephus used other works, now lost, which dealt with this period — the court chronicle of Herod's reign by NICHOLAS OF DAMASCUS and a patriotic account of the Revolt by JUSTUS OF TIBERIAS. Historical interest dwindled in the Rabbinic Period, although the composition ascribed to JOSEPH BEN GORION, based on Josephus, became very popular in the Middle Ages, notwithstanding its insignificance as an independent record. Medieval Jewish historiography was restricted to histories of tradition (e.g. *Seder ha-Kabbalah* of Abraham IBN DAUD, *Sepher Yuhasin* of Abraham ZACUTO) and stories of persecution (e.g. the parallel accounts of the Rhineland massacres of 1096, etc.); the S Italian family chronicle known as the Chronicle of AHIMAAZ may be included in the former category. Profiat DURAN (15th cent.) compiled a history of Jewish persecutions, now lost. Historical interest revived during the Renaissance Period. Solomon USQUE wrote in Portuguese a great poetical survey of his people's martyrdom; IBN VERGA approached the subject from a different angle in his *Shevet Yehudah*; JOSEPH HA-COHEN used and supplemented these accounts in his *Emek ha-Bakha*; Elijah CAPSALI concentrated on more recent events in his two works on Venetian and Turkish history; while David GANZ summarized Jewish chronology in his *Tzemah David.* From this time, brief accounts of local persecutions and deliverances, often associated with imitative Purims, etc., began to be produced in relative profusion in Italy and Germany. But the first attempt to write a comprehensive history of the Jews from ancient times down to the modern period was made by the Protestant pastor BASNAGE in the early 18th cent., to be followed by the American Hannah ADAMS in the early 19th. In effect, these examples did not penetrate the Jewish world until the WISSENSCHAFT period when JOST produced his history of the Jews (1820–8) and his history of Judaism and its sects (1857–9). These pioneering works were superseded by the great, but uneven, achievement of H. GRAETZ (1853–70); this was rivalled, though not displaced, in the 20th cent. by the work of S. DUBNOW, which paid attention to certain aspects (e.g. social and economic, E European Jewish history) largely overlooked by

former writers. This period saw the emergence of numerous historians who dealt with individual countries and communities (e.g. BERLINER, D. KAUFMANN, Vogelstein, Rieger, ARONIUS, Kracauer, KOHUT, ELBOGEN for Germany; CASSUTO, ROTH for Italy; LOEB, I. LEVY, and GROSS for France; JACOBS, WOLF, HYAMSON, Roth for England; KAYSERLING, FIDEL FITA, NEUMAN, and BAER for Spain; ROSANES and GALANTE for Turkey; I. Markens, C. P. Daly, A. Lebensohn, L. M. FRIEDMAN, and J. R. MARCUS for the US, etc.), and also writers on social and cultural history such as M. GUDEMANN and I. ABRAHAMS. The Greco-Roman Period, which had long engaged the attention of Christian scholars such as SCHURER, was scientifically treated on the basis of Jewish sources by A BUCHLER, Y. KLAUSNER, G. ALLON, A. TCHERIKOVER, and S. ZEITLIN. The mass of material on the Gaonic Period and oriental Jewish history discovered in the Cairo *genizah* was digested in the works of J. MANN, S. D. GOITEIN, and others. Social and economic aspects of Jewish history throughout the ages have been dealt with by S.W. BARON in a series of masterly studies and B. DINUR has devoted himself especially to the history of the development of the national idea. At the same time, specific societies for the study of Jewish history were established in England, America, Czechoslovakia, etc. Before the catastrophe of 1939–45, E European Jewish historiography reached a high state of development. A substantial group of historians followed the pioneering work of S. Dubnow in writing the history of Jewry in Slavic lands with emphasis upon communal, social, and economic history. The leaders were M. BALABAN, I. SCHIPPER, M SCHORR, and among their survivors and successors were J. Shatzky, I. Halperin, R. MAHLER, and E. Tscherikover. More attention has been paid recently to the history of Palestine and its Jewish settlement, pre-eminently by scholars such as Y. BEN ZVI who established an institute in Jerusalem for the study of the history of the Jews in the Orient. A large-scale collaborative history of the Jews, edited by an international group of scholars, is now appearing. In the US, local historiography received some impetus from the tercentenary celebration of 1954, as a result of which various monographs were published and a comprehensive documentary history planned. Historiography in Israel has been strongly influenced by the progress of archeological research, as well as by a desire to perpetuate the memory of E European Jewry, by great attention to Jewish political and military history, and by a revival of interest in the Oriental communities.

HITAHDUT (abbr. of *Hitahdut Olamit shel Ha-Poel ha-Tzair u-Tzeire Tziyyon*—"World Union of HA-POEL HA-TZAIR and TZEIRE ZION"): Zionist labor party founded in 1920 by the amalgamation of the Palestinian *Ha-Poel ha-Tzair* with the Diaspora

Hittite women wearing long robes of the period.

Tzeire Zion. The *H.* was particularly active in Central and E Europe, and the GORDONIA movement was its offshoot. In 1932, it amalgamated with POALE ZION.

*HITLER, ADOLF (1889–1945): German NATIONAL SOCIALIST leader. Of Austrian birth, he joined the National Socialist German Workers' Party after serving in World War I and built it up into a major force exploiting ANTISEMITISM in GERMANY. After becoming German chancellor in 1933, he imposed on the state a totalitarian regime with extreme militaristic tendencies. CONCENTRATION CAMPS were set up for Jews and political opponents. His invasion of Poland in 1939 led to World War II. H. committed suicide as Russian troops were advancing through Berlin. His paranoiac hatred of the Jews stirred his followers and adherents to unspeakable excesses and was responsible for the extermination of 6 million Jews in Europe.

HITTIN see **KEPHAR HITTIN**

HITTITES: Ancient people inhabiting Asia Minor From the 15th cent. BCE, their power extended southward to Syria. Even after the main kingdom fell c. 1200, small Hittite kingdoms continued to flourish in N Syria and in the vicinity of the Euphrates. These states were eventually overrun by the Armenians and the Assyrians. The Bible connects the H. with the Canaanites (Gen. 10:15) and indicates that some dwelt in Palestine at an early period. Abraham purchased the cave at Machpelah from H., while Esau took wives from among them. The H. were one of the seven peoples from whom the Israelites conquered Canaan. Later, David had Hittite warriors, and Solomon, Hittite wives.

HITYASHVUT (Heb.): AGRICULTURAL SETTLEMENT in Israel.

ḤIVI AL-BALKHI (fl. latter part of 9th cent.): Persian Bible exegete; born in Balkh (now in Afghanistan). He wrote a work containing two hundred queries on the Bible. Although the book is lost, quotations have survived showing Ḥ. to have been a daring and free-thinking scholar who sought to explain biblical miracles naturally and detected later additions in the biblical text. His views aroused intellectual ferment among oriental Jewry and Saadyah Gaon published a refutation.

HIVITES: One of the "seven nations" inhabiting Canaan when the Israelites took possession of the country. GIBEON was one of their main cities (Josh. 9:17). Joshua was fraudulently forced to enter into a league with the Gibeonites which was extended to the other Hivite cities. Some of the H. inhabited N Canaan, near Mt. Hermon (Josh. 11:3).

ḤIYYA (called "the Great"; fl. 2nd cent. CE): Palestinian tanna; of Babylonian birth. A pupil of R Judah Ha-Nasi, he was a leading halakhist. He and his pupil Hoshaiah were responsible for the collection of *Baraitot* known by their name. H. participated in the compilation of the Tosephta.

ḤIYYA BAR ABBA (fl. 3rd cent. CE): Palestinian amora; of Babylonian birth. An outstanding halakhist, he traveled considerably, lecturing on talmudic problems.

*HOCHHUTH, ROLF (1931–) German playwright. His play *The Deputy* created a furore in 1963 for its attack on the Catholic Church, and especially Pope Pius XII, for failing openly to condemn the extermination of the Jews by the Nazis in World War II.

HOCHSCHULE (or **LEHRANSTALT** [1883–1922; 1934–42]) **FÜR WISSENSCHAFT DES JUDENTUMS** (Ger. "High School for Jewish Knowledge"): Berlin institution of higher Jewish learning founded in 1870 to advance Jewish studies and to train teachers and rabbis. It existed until 1942, its last principal being LEO BAECK.

HOD HA-SHARON see **HADAR RAMATAYIM**

HOD, MORDEKHAI (1926–): Israel military leader. He was born in Deganyah, joined the Haganah, and in 1949 was one of the first Israel-trained pilots in the Israel Air Force. He occupied various positions in the air force and in 1966 was appointed its commander. In this capacity he was in charge of the air strike at the outset of the 1967 Six-Day War which destroyed the Egyptian, Jordanian, and Syrian air forces paving the way for the Israel victory.

HOFFMAN, DAVID TZEVI (1843–1921): Scholar. Of Slovakian birth, he was lecturer in the Berlin Rabbinical Seminary (1873) and from 1899, its director. He opposed the Reform movement and published articles defending the Talmud and *Shulḥan Arukh* against their anti-Semitic detractors. H. attacked the Wellhausen school of biblical criticism.

His published studies include commentaries on parts of the Pentateuch and an introduction to tannaitic Midrashim.

HOFJUDE see **COURT JEWS**

HOFMANNSTHAL, HUGO VON (1874–1929): Austrian poet. The son of a converted banker, he early achieved fame for his lyrics and was a leader of the neo-romantic *Jung-Wien* group of writers. He wrote libretti (*Salome, Elektra, Der Rosenkavalier, Ariadne auf Naxos*) for operas by Richard Straus, and his *Everyman* was long the center of the Salzburg Festivals.

HOFSTADTER, ROBERT (1915–): US physicist. Professor of physics at Stanford Univ., he was awarded the 1961 Nobel Prize for physics for his researches into methods of controlling nuclear reactions for peaceful purposes.

HOL HA-MOED (Heb. "weekday of the festival"): Term applied to the intermediate days of Passover and Tabernacles on which only essential work may be pursued. Their status derives from the fact that the Pentateuch endows them with a festive character but does not prohibit work. No marriages are solemnized during these periods, in accordance with the principle of not superimposing one celebration upon another. Mourning is forbidden, the special holiday prayers are recited, while Sephardi and some Ashkenazi rites omit the wearing of the phylacteries. In modern Israel, these days are observed more strictly by the oriental communities and are the occasion for pilgrimages to holy sites.

HOLDHEIM, SAMUEL (1806–1860): Leader of Reform Judaism. After a traditional education, he was appointed rabbi at Frankfort-on-Oder in 1836 and chief rabbi of Mecklenburg-Schwerin in 1840. At first inclined to moderate religious reform, he later joined the extreme reformers and advocated basic changes, including the observance of Sabbath on Sundays and the abolition of the second days of festivals. From 1847, he headed the Berlin Reform congregation.

HOLIDAYS see **HOLY DAYS**

HOLINESS: The Hebrew word *kedushah* denotes "separation" in its primary meaning, but the connotation which has become dominant is "separation for Divine purposes." A holy person, therefore, is one who lives in accordance with Divine prescription with regard to both ceremonial and ethical matters. H. as an aspect of the ethical life is stressed in Lev. 19 (the so-called "Holiness Code") with its motto "Ye shall be holy; for I the Lord your God am holy." As an aspect of ceremonial practice, it finds repeated mention in connection with dietary laws, physical purity, etc. H. is not something required of the few, but is demanded of the entire Jewish people who are spoken of in the Bible in connection with various observances as a "holy people." Similarly, Palestine is the "holy land," while special h. attaches to the Temple and its servants — the priests and levites. The way to h., the great ideal of rabbinic ethics, is outlined by R Phinehas ben Jair in the concluding section of the talmudic treatise *Sotah*: "Scrupulousness in the observance of the commandments leads to cleanliness, cleanliness leads to purity, purity leads to a withdrawal from the profane and a withdrawal from the profane leads to holiness."

HOLLAND: Jews lived in some regions of what is now H. in the Middle Ages under the same precarious conditions as in Germany, but the effective history of Dutch Jewry begins at the close of the 16th cent. when, with the decline of ANTWERP, Marranos began to settle in AMSTERDAM. They received freedom of worship in the early 17th cent. The expansion of Dutch trade gave them great opportunities and freed them from almost all restrictions. Before long there were three Sephardi synagogues in Amsterdam (later unified), soon to be followed by Ashkenazi congregations, founded by German immigrants. Communities spread to other Dutch cities; at the HAGUE, ROTTERDAM, etc. both Sephardim and Ashkenazim were represented. Some cities however (e.g. UTRECHT) excluded the Jews. The upper strata (especially among the Sephardim) were physicians, brokers, wholesale traders, gem-merchants, etc., taking an important part in the activities of the Bourse and in export trade. Amsterdam remained the principal center, its community in the 18th cent. numbering 10,000 — the largest body of Jews in W Europe. Through this community with its flourishing intellectual life, its active printing-presses, its learned rabbis, its thronged academies, H. became one of the nerve-centers of Judaism. The Sephardi community in particular provided eager votaries of SHABBETAI TZEVI and recovered only with difficulty from the disappointment of his failure. Dutch Jewry played a great part in the establishment of the communities of London, New York, etc. With the occupation of H. by the French Revolutionary armies in 1796, Dutch Jewry was formally emancipated. This was an easy process as their former disabilities were slight; and in H. — alone in Europe — there was no qualification of or recession from the policy of Jewish equality thereafter. From 1815, Jewish ministers of religion, like the Christian, were paid by the state. H. was moreover the first country in the modern world where Jews were not only admitted to parliament (1797) but also appointed to high public office. In the 19th cent., with the development of huge Jewish centers elsewhere in the western world, the relative importance of Dutch Jewry (especially the once-glorious Sephardi community) began to decline, but it continued to be a vital center. In 1870, a Central Commission for Jewish affairs was set up to coodinate communal life. At the outbreak of World War II, there were in H. c. 140,000 Jews (apart from refugees), and over half of them in Amsterdam. The general population opposed the German annihilation program to the best of its ability, and many Dutch workmen died in the protest riots in Amsterdam in Feb. 1941. Nevertheless, owing to the protraction of the German hold on H. until the last days of the war, the overwhelming proportion of its Jews, both Sephardi and Ashkenazi, perished; the main transit-camp for extermination was at Westerbork. There are left in the country some 30,000 Jews (1973), the only important communities being Amsterdam (15,700), The Hague (2,500), and Rotterdam (1,500).

HOLOCAUST see **NATIONAL SOCIALISM**

ḤOLON: Israel municipality 2 m. S of Tel Aviv-Jaffa.

Of the 6 districts of which H. is composed, the earliest and largest is Kiryat Avodah, founded in 1936. Pop. (1974): 110,300.

HOLOPHERNES see **JUDITH**

HOLY CITY see **JERUSALEM**

HOLY DAYS (Heb. *yamim tovim, ḥaggim, moadim*):
The Bible mentions the following festivals: the three pilgrim festivals (when every male was bound to appear in the Temple), viz. PASSOVER, PENTECOST, and TABERNACLES, which were harvest-festivals as well as commemorations of historical events; and days of solemnity, viz. the NEW YEAR and DAY OF ATONEMENT. The first and last days of Passover and Tabernacles are considered festive days, but the intermediate days non-festive (ḤOL HA-MOED) when work, the neglect of which would involve loss, is permitted. On all holy days work is forbidden, but — except on the Day of Atonement — the prohibition is not as rigid as on the Sabbath (e.g. fire may be used, vital food prepared, and carrying is permitted). In the Diaspora, all the festive days (except the Day of Atonement) are doubled, according to an ancient practice originating from a doubt in determining the exact calender (the observance of the second day, has been abolished among Reform Jews and is regarded as unnecessary by the Conservatives). The post-biblical festivals of ḤANUKKAH and PURIM are working-days from the point of view of Jewish law.

HOLY LAND see **ISRAEL**

HOLY OF HOLIES see **TEMPLE**

HOLY PLACES: Term used in three senses: (1) loosely to cover such Palestinian shrines, Jewish, Christian, or Moslem, ancient or modern, as are associated with biblical or koranic incidents, or commemorate saints of the religion concerned; such shrines are very numerous; (2) more strictly, to describe centers of pilgrimage, of which the most famous are the TEMPLE area, the mosque at Hebron, the WESTERN ("Wailing") WALL, and the Churches of the Holy Sepulcher and the Nativity; many others are scattered through the country, such as the Christian churches at Nazareth and the Jewish shrines at

Meron; (3) politically, to describe nine shrines the use of which is shared or disputed by members of different religions, or denominations within one religion, and which are the subject of special regulations. These are (in the Jerusalem area) the Holy Sepulcher and its area including Deir-es-Sultan, the Sanctuary of the Ascension, the Tomb of the Virgin, and the Western Wall: (in the Bethlehem area) the Church of the Nativity, the Milk Grotto, and the Shepherds' Fields. Their ultimate ownership remained by Moslem law in the hands of the government. Their disposal has been governed by the "Status Quo," a Turkish decree issued in 1757 and confirmed in 1852. By the Treaty of Paris (1853) at the conclusion of the Crimean War, the European Powers undertook to maintain its provisions. The United Nations in Nov. 1947 recommended that unrestricted access to the H. P. should be given both by Israel and the Arab states. The principal recognized Jewish H. P. are the Western Wall (on the former Temple site), to which the Jews at all times until 1967 had only restricted access, and Rachel's Tomb, outside Bethlehem — which alone was in Jewish hands. When these were in Jordan territory they were barred to Jews. In addition, there were all over the country, — particularly in Galilee — tombs, etc. traditionally associated by the Jews with leading biblical figures and with rabbis of the Talmudic Period. These were throughout the Middle Ages places of pilgrimage, and various descriptions of them were compiled under the title *Yiḥuse ha-Tzaddikim* ("The Genealogies of the Righteous"), etc. The most famous of these tombs is that of R Simeon ben Yoḥai at Meron.

HOLY SPIRIT (Heb. *ruaḥ ha-kodesh*; Gk.: *pneuma hagion*): The term is found in the Bible (Is. 63:10, 11; Ps. 51:13) where it means "Divine Spirit." In rabbinic literature, however, it means "Divine inspiration" in particular. Thus, a person who speaks with it gives utterance to the very words of God. The criterion determining the acceptance of a book in the biblical canon was whether it had been inspired by the H. S. According to rabbinic teaching, the H. S. is not communicated by chance but merited only by a long religious discipline of spiritual ascent.

ḤOMAH U-MIGDAL (Heb. "Stockade and Tower"):
Name given to a method of settlement adopted in Palestine 1936–45 in answer to Arab violence and

Hanitah, a *Ḥomah u-Migdal* settlement on the Lebanese border, 1938.

(from 1939) the White Paper restrictions. The camps, forming the nucleus of villages, were usually erected in one day from prefabricated parts, their main features being a watchtower and a stockade. They were set up according to a strategic plan for consolidating continuous areas of Jewish settlement.

HOMBERG, HERZ (1749–1841): Pedagogue and author. He was chief inspector of Jewish schools in Galicia in behalf of the Austrian government from 1787 to 1800, and incurred the enmity of the Orthodox Jews, particularly because his opinion contributed to the imposition of a tax on Sabbath candles. From 1806 to 1814, he was censor of Hebrew books in Vienna, and from 1814, government inspector of Jewish schools in Bohemia. His writings include the commentary on Deuteronomy in his friend Mendelssohn's *Biur,* other biblical commentaries, and textbooks of Judaism.

HOMEL: Town in White Russia. Jews were living there in 1537, and 2,000 were massacred by Cossacks in 1648. At the end of the 19th cent., over half of its population of 46,500 were Jews, and H. was a center of the *Ḥabad* movement and later of Zionism and of socialism. A pogrom occurred in 1903. In 1940, H. had 38,000 Jews, but the community was annihilated by the Germans.

ḤOMETZ BOTEL (Heb. *bittul ḥametz —* "annulment of leaven"): The removal of leaven before Passover.

HOMICIDE see **MURDER**

HOMILETICS: The art of preaching. In rabbinic times, the system of h. as reflected in the MIDRASH began with a verse which was, in turn, illustrated from another verse. A devious chain of exegesis, legend, etc. would bring the preacher back to his original text and lead to some ethical lesson or ritual prescription which the preacher wished to emphasize. Occasionally, fantastic statements would be made in order to rivet the attention of the audience. The researches of Jacob Mann have shown that the preliminary verses were in all probability chosen from the sections of the Pentateuch, Prophets, and Hagiographa associated with the week. In Italy, the biblical text was followed by a talmudic passage, the preacher's art consisting in bringing the two into relation. In 19th cent. Jewish h., a biblical verse chosen from the Pentateuchal portion of the week usually served as text, being illustrated by midrashic teachings. The great exponent of this system was Adolf JELLINEK. Modern preachers in some countries tend to concentrate on current events in their weekly SERMON.

HONDURAS: Central American Republic. Jewish settlers arrived from E Europe in 1930. The community in 1973 numbered 200, mostly in the capital Tegucigalpa; Jewish immigration is now restricted. In 1939–40, there was an abortive plan to establish Jewish refugees in British H.

HONG KONG: British crown colony in S. China. Jews arrived there after the British conquest in 1842. They have been prominent in banking and mercantile life. Notable Jewish families include the *SASSOONS* and the *KADOURIES.* Jewish pop. (1973): 200, mostly of Iraqi and European origin.

ḤONI HA-MEAGGEL (Heb. "Ḥoni the Circle-Drawer"; fl. 1st cent. CE): Sage and wonderworker. His prayers for rain were considered efficacious, and his name is thought to have originated from his habit of drawing a circle around him from which he refused to emerge until his petition was answered. Another theory, however, relates the name to his place of origin. During the civil war between Hyrcanus and Aristobulus, the supporters of the former requested him to curse their opponents, but when he prayed for the welfare of both sides, they stoned him to death. According to talmudic legend, H. slept for seventy years and on awakening found the world so changed that he sought death.

ḤONYO see **ONIAS**

HOOK, SIDNEY (1902–): US philosopher and educator. He has taught philosophy at New York Univ. since 1927 (professor, 1939), also at Columbia Univ. and the New School of Social Research. H. is a leading exponent of John Dewey's philosophy and an authority on Marxism; he has written voluminously on civil liberties, academic freedom, and progressive education.

HOPHNI AND PHINEHAS: Priests at Shiloh; sons of Eli. The Bible describes their evil behavior and their deaths in battle at the hands of the Philistines (I Sam. 1–4).

HOR, MOUNT: (1) Mountain on the frontier of Edom, scene of Aaron's death (Num. 20:22–9). (2) A northerly frontier-mark of Israel (Num. 34:7). Neither site has been definitely identified.

HORA: Israel folk-dance. It originated in the Balkans, but took root in Palestine shortly after World War I and has remained the country's most popular

Dancing the Hora at the Western Wall.

folk-dance. Many Israel composers have composed songs in h. rhythm.

HORAYOT (Heb. "Decisions"): Tenth tractate in the Mishnah order of *Nezikin,* containing 3 chapters. It has *gemara* both in the Babylonian and Palestinian Talmud. It deals with decisions in matters of religious law made in error by the high priest or the Sanhedrin (Lev. 4:1–21).

HORE-BELISHA, LESLIE (ISAAC), LORD (1895–1957): British statesman. A Liberal (later National Liberal) member of parliament from 1923, he was minister of transport 1934–7, minister of war 1937–40, and minister of national insurance in 1945.

HOREB: Mountain at the foot of which Moses saw the burning bush (Exod. 3). In Deut., the name replaces SINAI, and the two mountains have become identified. The name H., being associated with revelation, has been applied to various religious periodicals.

ḤORIN (CHORIN), AARON BEN KALMAN (1766–1844): Pioneer of Reform Judaism in Hungary. Rabbi of Arad from 1789, he was constantly engaged in controversies with Orthodox rabbis because of his liberal views. In 1804, after advocating the modification of certain traditional laws, he was called before a rabbinical court and forced to retract. The condemnation, however, was later annulled by the government. He welcomed the early 19th cent. Reform movement and advocated worship with uncovered head, use of the organ, the recital of certain prayers in the vernacular, and riding on the Sabbath under certain circumstances.

HORITES: Ancient people, originating S of the Caucasian mountains, who invaded Syria and Palestine in the 17th cent. BCE. They fused Akkadian mythology with their own tradition and were responsible for transmitting Sumero-Akkadian culture to the Hittites. They dwelt near Mt. Seir in Abraham's time but their territory was conquered by the Edomites (Gen. 14:6; 36:20–30; Deut. 2:12, 22). Egyptian documents from the 16th cent. call Palestine "Ḥaru" whereas previously it had been known as "Rutenu." Scholars have identified the Ḥaru with the H. and believe that they were pushed back by the Amorites and Canaanites to the Mt. Seir region whence they were later driven by the Edomites.

HORNER, HENRY (1878–1940): US public official. He was judge of the probate court in Cook Country, Illinois 1914-33, and Democratic governor of Illinois 1933-40.

HORODETZKY, SHEMUEL ABBA (1871–1957): Scholar. A native of the Ukraine, he lived in Berdichev, Berlin, and Switzerland before settling in Palestine in 1939. One of the leading modern scholars of kabbalah and Ḥasidism, he wrote on mysticism, Ḥasidism (especially in *Ha-Ḥasidut veha-Ḥasidim,* 4 vols., 1923), the history of Polish Jewry, biographies of medieval rabbis, etc.

HOROVITZ: (1) *JOSEPH H.* (1874–1931): German orientalist; son of (2). He traveled throughout the Middle East and from 1907, taught Arabic at the Moslem Anglo-Oriental College in Aligarh, India. From 1914, he was professor of Semitic philology at the Univ. of Frankfort-on-Main. He wrote on Islamic literature and culture, and was regarded as a leading authority on the Koran. (2) *MARCUS H.* (1844–1910): Rabbi. Of Hungarian birth, he officiated at Frankfort-on-Main from 1878, becoming one of the most respected religious leaders of German Jewry. Although a conservative, he opposed the separatism of the ultra-Orthodox. His writings include four volumes of biographies of Frankfort rabbis.

HOROVITZ, SAUL (1859–1921): Scholar. Born in Hungary, he became rabbi at Bielitz (Silesia) in 1885 and lecturer at the Breslau Rabbinical Seminary in 1896. He edited the *Siphre,* published studies on the influence of Greek and Arabic philosophy on medieval Jewish literature, and wrote on the language and sources of the Midrash.

HOROWITZ: (1) *ELEAZAR* (Lazar) *H.* (1803–1868): Rabbi; great-grandson of (2). Born in Bavaria, he officiated in Vienna from 1828. Although sharply opposing the Reform movement, he inclined to make concessions in order to preserve Jewish unity. He engaged in dispute with anti-Semites and successfully advocated the abolition of the JEWISH OATH. (2) *PHINEHAS H.* (c. 1730–1805): Author and kabbalist. A pupil of Dov Ber of Mezhirich, he was appointed rabbi and head of the yeshivah at Frankfort-on-Main in 1772. He fought Haskalah and Reform and condemned Mendelssohn's German translation of the Bible for its deviation from tradition. His chief work is *Haphlaah,* novellae on parts of the Talmud.

HOROWITZ, DAVID (1899–): Israel economist. Born in Drohobycz, Poland, he settled in Palestine in 1920 and was active in *Ha-Shomer Ha-Tzair.* He was director of the Jewish Agency's economic department 1935–48, director-general of the Israel Ministry of Finance 1948–52, and the governor of the Bank of Israel from its establishment in 1954 to 1971. He wrote many works on economics and finance.

HOROWITZ, HIRSCH BER see **BERNARD, HERMANN**

HOROWITZ, ISAIAH (known as the *Sheloh* from the initials of his chief book; c. 1565–1630): Scholar and kabbalist. He officiated in various communities in Poland, Lithuania, and Volhynia and, from 1606 to 1614, was rabbi and head of the yeshivah at Frankfort-on-Main. In 1615, H. removed to Prague and in 1621, to Jerusalem where he became rabbi of the Ashkenazi community. In 1625, he was imprisoned with other Jerusalem rabbis but escaped to Safed, later moving to Tiberias where he died. His

Vladimir Horowitz.

chief work is *Shene Luḥot ha-Berit* ("Two Tablets of the Covenant"), a deeply ethical but unsystematic work, of kabbalistic tendencies, on Jewish laws and customs. It opposed *pilpul* and advocated the study of Hebrew grammar.

HOROWITZ, JACOB ISAAC ("The Rabbi of Lublin"; d. 1815): Ḥasidic rabbi. Originally from Galicia, he moved to Lublin c. 1800. His saintliness was legendary and the Ḥasidim believed him to be possessed of the Holy Sprit, calling him *Ha-Ḥozeh* ("The Seer"). H. wrote works on the Bible and emphasized the importance of the *tzaddik*.

HOROWITZ, LEOPOLD (1839–1917): Painter. A native of Slovakia, he lived in Warsaw 1869–93 and Vienna 1893–1917. H. painted the Austrian royal family, but his reputation rests on his pictures of Jewish life.

HOROWITZ, MOSES HA-LEVI (1844–1910): Yiddish playwright. In 1878, he organized a Yiddish troupe which traveled and performed plays in various European countries. In 1886, he settled in New York and wrote for the Yiddish stage. H. introduced the operetta into the repertoire of the American Yiddish theater.

HOROWITZ, VLADIMIR (1904–): Pianist. Of Russian birth, he began his European tours in 1924. In 1928, he made his debut in the US where he settled.

HOS, DOV (1894–1940): Palestinian labor leader. Born in White Russia, he settled in Palestine in 1906. He helped to found the labor party *Aḥdut ha-Avodah*, the *Histadrut* contracting organization *Solel Boneh*, the sports society *Ha-Poel*, and was deputy mayor of Tel Aviv from 1935 until his death in an automobile accident.

HOSEA (fl. 8th cent. BCE): Prophet. He lived and prophesied in the kingdom of Israel, apparently from the reign of Jeroboam II (744) but chiefly in the last years of the kingdom (i.e., up to 722). His book of prophecies, the first in the Minor Prophets, contains 14 chapters: 1–3, the relationship between God and Israel; and 4–14, a prophecy rebuking Israel, followed by promises of consolation and salvation. H. conceives the bond between God and Israel as an almost physical love, and compares Israel's defection with a wife's marital unfaithfulness (which some commentators believe to be founded on personal experience). He forecasts Israel's exile but comforts it with visions of restoration after the people's repentance.

HOSHAIAH (OSHAIAH) RABBAH (called "the great"; fl. c. 200): Palestinian amora. He conducted an academy at Sepphoris, later removing to Caesarea. H. was styled "father of the Mishnah" because of his ability to expound the mishnaic code. He was noted both as halakhist and aggadist and was the author of the opening homily of *Midrash Rabbah*.

HOSHA-NA (Heb. "Save now"): (1) Refrain, taken from Ps. 118:25, in the special liturgical poems recited during the feast of Tabernacles in the daily procession around the synagogue with *lulav* and *etrog*. (2) The popular name given to the willow branch, one of the FOUR SPECIES that figure in the Tabernacles ritual, especially on the 6th day (7th in the Diaspora), i.e., *Hosha-na Rabbah*. The word passed into European usage as Hosanna.

HOSHA-NA RABBAH (Heb. "The great Hosha-na"): Popular name for the seventh day of Tabernacles. Special observances were held on this day from early times, and in the Temple seven circuits were made around the altar, instead of one as on other days of the feast, by worshipers carrying willow branches. The Talmud refers to it as *Yoma de-Aravta* ("willow day"), and this is commemorated in the custom, which has survived, of beating the willow-branch at the end of the prayer. In origin a joyful festival, like the rest of Tabernacles, it was particularly associated with prayers for rain and water. Furthermore, the link created between the New Year and *H. R.* and the view that the Judgment decreed on the Day of Atonement became irrevocable on *H. R.*, gave the day a solemn character connected with the aspect of judgment and this influenced its liturgy. Sabbath psalms and the full *kedushah* are recited, the melodies of the High Holy Days chanted, and white robes worn. In the Middle Ages, the conclusion of the service was similar to that of the Day of Atonement. During the morning service, worshipers make seven circuits around the synagogue carrying the *lulav* and *etrog*. In Sephardi synagogues, penitential prayers are recited in the morning, and in some congregations, the *shophar* is sounded after every circuit. In preparation for *H. R.*, it became

Illustration of popular superstition connected with Hoshana Rabbah. (From *Minhagim Buch*, Amsterdam, 1707.)

customary from the 16th cent. to spend the previous night reading selections from sacred literature (see TIKKUN).

HOSHEA: Last ruler of the kingdom of Israel; reigned 732–724. H. conspired against PEKAH, assassinated him, and seized the throne (II Kings 15:30). Assyrian sources relate that H. ascended the throne with Assyrian help, his kingdom being confined to the surroundings of Mt. Ephraim. Eventually, he rebelled against Assyria, and was imprisoned by Shalmaneser who then besieged and captured Samaria (II Kings 17:1–6).

ḤOSHEN MISHPAT see **JACOB BEN ASHER**

HOSPITALITY see **HAKHNASAT OREḤIM**

HOSPITALS: Occasional references are found to h. in the medieval period, especially in Germany but h. in the modern sense developed late in the Jewish community. Portuguese Jews founded one in London in 1747 and others were established in Berlin and Metz in the course of the 18th century. The first Jewish hospital in the U.S. was the Jews' Hospital (later called Mount Sinai Hospital) in New York, founded in 1852. The Hebrew Hospital in Philadelphia was founded in 1864. Since then many Jewish hospitals have been established in the US and elsewhere. However, modern trends toward socialized medicine, in various forms, have lessened the need for the Jewish community to make separate provision for its sick. Israel in 1974 had 157 h. run mainly by the government, the HISTADRUT'S *Kupat Ḥolim*, HADASSAH and MALBEN.

HOST, DESECRATION OF THE: Accusation that the Jews defiled or tortured the elements consecrated by the priest in the Catholic ceremony of the Mass. This charge became current in Europe after the recognition of the doctrine of Transubstantiation by the Fourth Lateran Council in 1215. It was based on the conception that the Jews wished in this fashion to renew the agonies of the passion of Jesus. These accusations were frequently the pretext for persecution and massacre. The first known occasion was at Belitz (Germany) in 1243. There were later famous instances in Paris in 1290, Brussels in 1370, and Segovia in 1410; that at Deckendorf in 1337 led to a wave of massacres in Germany. It is believed that the presence of the minute scarlet fungus, MICROCOCCUS PRODIGIOSUS, may have been responsible for the idea that the Host actually bled on such occasions.

HOUDINI, HARRY see **WEISS, ERICH**

HOUSTON: City in Texas, US. Its Jewish settlement dates from the 1820's. In 1847, Jacob de Cordova from H. was a member of the Texas Legislature. Organized services were first held in a private home in 1854, and Congregation Beth Israel was founded in 1860. Russian and Polish Jews began arriving in the 1880's. In 1889, the first Orthodox congregation, Adath Yeshurun, was established. A Jewish Community Council to coordinate the activities of all H. organizations was formed in 1937. The journal *Jewish Herald-Voice* appears weekly. H. has 5 major congregations. Jewish pop. (1973): 22,000.

ḤOVEVEI ZION see **ḤIBBAT ZION**

HUBERMANN, BRONISLAW (1882–1947): Violinist; born in Poland. One of the great violinists of his day, he founded in 1936, the Palestine Symphony

Bronislaw Hubermann.

Draining Lake Ḥuleh.

Orchestra (later the ISRAEL PHILHARMONIC ORCHESTRA), initially composed of eminent European refugee musicians.

HUEBSCH, ADOLPH (1830–1884): Rabbi. After studying in Europe, he went from Prague to the US in 1866 and served as rabbi of Congregation Ahavath Chesed (now the Central Synagogue), New York. H. was a moderate religious reformer and published sermons and philological studies in German.

*HUGH OF LINCOLN (d. 1255): Alleged victim of a Ritual Murder accusation at Lincoln, England, as a result of which nearly 100 Jews were executed. H. was popularly considered a saint. The story is used in Chaucer's *Prioress's Tale*.

HUHNER, LEON (1871–1957): US historian. A lawyer, he was for many years curator of the American Jewish Historical Society and wrote extensively on Jewish history in the US.

ḤUKKAT (Ashkenazi *Ḥukkas*) **HA-GOY** (Heb. "law of the gentile"): A specifically non-Jewish practice (e.g. in worship or domestic habits) which the pious Jew tries to avoid.

ḤULATA: Israel communal settlement (KM) in Upper Galilee, founded 1936, and on its present site since 1946. It was a frontline settlement facing fire in the Israel War of Independence. Pop. (1972): 380.

HULDAH (fl. 7th cent. BCE): Prophetess in Jerusalem at the time of Josiah. She foretold the catastrophic fall of Judah and that Josiah would die prior to the calamity.

HULDAH: Israel communal settlement (IK) on the border of the Judean Plain; site of the HERZL FOREST. One of the first purchases (1905) of the Jewish National Fund, it was founded as a laborers' training and research farm (1909). The present settlement group dates from 1930. Pop. (1972): 307.

ḤULEH: District in Upper Galilee. The name appears in the works of Josephus as Oulatha and in the Talmud as Ḥulata; it covered the uppermost reaches of the Jordan Valley from Dan down to (and including) the Ḥ. Lake (known in Josephus as Lake Semechonitis and in the Talmud as *Yam Samkho* ["sea of Samkho"]). The excellent quality of the soil and the abundance of water have led to a series of attempts to settle this valley densely, most of them defeated by endemic malaria. In antiquity, the upper reaches of the valley were occupied by the tribe of Dan; later, they belonged to the hellenistic city of Paneas and were known as the Valley of Antiochus. The area was conquered by Alexander Yannai and subsequently belonged to Herod and his dynasty. In the Talmudic Period, rice was cultivated there by Jews. The region was much fought over by the crusaders and their adversaries; it deteriorated almost completely under the Turks. In 1934, the Jewish National Fund acquired most of the land of the upper valley. Between 1939 and 1948, these lands were settled, and since 1948, the marshes and lake have been drained and the water area reduced; the first crops on the drained area were harvested in 1955.

ḤULLIN (Heb. "Profane Matters"): Third tractate in the Mishnah order of *Kodashim*, containing 12 chapters. It has *gemara* in the Babylonian, but not the Palestinian, Talmud. It is called also *Sheḥitat Ḥullin* ("slaughtering for profane use"). It treats primarily of the laws of ritual slaughtering and other regulations connected with the preparation of animal food and is thus the basic authority for matters concerning *sheḥitah*.

ḤUMASH (Heb. from *ḥamesh* — "five"): The five books of the Pentateuch; a volume containing these.

HUMOR: Satire and irony are to be found in the Bible (cf. Elijah's taunts to the false prophets of Baal in I Kings 18:27, and Is. 44:12–17). The Talmud and Midrash contain parables and anecdotes illustrating characteristics with which modern Jewish h. is associated. A few medieval Jewish classics (e.g. *Taḥkemoni*) are noted for their h. The *Bet ha-Midrash* was a fertile breeding-ground for anecdotes and *bon mots*. As there was a constant interchange between the *Bate Midrash* situated all over E Europe, these sayings spread quickly over a wide area. Simultaneously, in various districts there flourished a number of famous humorists such as Motke Ḥabad and Sheike Fifer in Lithuania and Hershel Ostropoler in S Russia. There were also a number of rabbis who were renowned for their *siḥat ḥullin* ("light talk") which was redolent with wit and epigrams. All this paved the way for the giants of Jewish humor, e.g. SHOLEM ALEICHEM and MENDELE MOCHER SEPHORIM. In Israel, Ephraim KISHON is the leading humorous author. Because the Jews have lived among so many and varied peoples with diverse cultures, their h. has had a rich and versatile foundation and has enjoyed a continual stream of influences. The humor of Jewish groups of the Sephardi world and the Orient has as yet been imperfectly studied and recorded.

HUNA (or Hona; c. 216–297): Babylonian amora. A member of the family of the exilarch, he became the leading rabbinical authority in Babylon. Originally poor, he later prospered and spent his wealth generously, the daily invitation to his home — "he who is hungry, let him come and eat" — being incorporated in the *Seder* service. H. was head (*Resh Metivta*) of the Sura academy from 256 and maintained its 800 students at his own expense. He was noted both as halakhist and aggadist.

HUNGARY: E European country. Its first known Jewish grave dates from the 2nd cent. CE. There are indications of the presence of Jewish communities in the 9th cent. In the 13th cent., the decrees of the Lateran Council segregating the Jews from their neighbors were put into effect and the wearing of a distinctive badge was instituted. During the reign of Béla IV (1235–70) many Jews settled in H. as his property. They enjoyed good relations with their neighbors, and were often minters of coins, some of which bore Hebrew inscriptions. Despite pressure by the Pope, the position of the Jews remained good until 1349 when they were expelled for the first time. A second expulsion took place in 1360. Many Jews immigrated from the neighboring countries when the edict was revoked in 1364. A year later the office of "judge of the Jews" was established to collect taxes from the Jewish population and protect their interests; the last judge was appointed in 1440. The 15th and 16th cents. were marked by recurrent charges of Ritual Murder and the cancellation of debts owed to Jews. For nearly a century and a half (until 1686), the Jews of Buda and southern H. enjoyed a large measure of civic equality and religious liberty under the occupying Ottoman regime, although subject to heavy taxes. The restoration of Hungarian sovereignty brought in its wake expulsions and the exclusion of Jews from agriculture and the professions. At the same time, some nobles protected the Jews whose numbers were augmented by refugees from Vienna in 1670. The arrival of Jews from Moravia and Poland in the first half of the 18th cent. further increased the Jewish population. The Polish immigrants brought the study of the Talmud to H., establishing important centers of learning. During Maria Theresa's reign, various new methods were devised for exacting money from the Jews. The rule of JOSEPH II (1780–90) brought the right to establish schools, lease lands, engage in all trades and professions, and live in the royal cities. The Jewish badge was abolished, and the Jews had to adopt German surnames. All this was nullified at Joseph's death. The subsequent struggle for legal rights was accompanied by increased Magyarization of the Jewish community. Wholehearted support for the 1848 revolution brought severe reprisals by the Austrians. In 1867, the Jews were finally granted full civic and political rights. Shortly afterward, Hungarian Jewry became divided in its religious life into two opposing camps of orthodox and liberal Jews. The rapid integration of the Jews into the country's life received a brief setback with the rise of 19th cent. anti-Semitism, culminating in the TISZAESZLAR Ritual Murder libel. Jews played a prominent part in the cultural life of H. before World War I. Because of their disproportionate participation in the Communist Revolution of 1919, they suffered heavily after the collapse of the Bela KUN regime, and discrimination of various kinds was instituted against them. After the advent of Nazism in Germany, the scope of anti-Jewish measures enacted by the government

Marriage ceremony under a *ḥuppa*. (From Nuremberg Haggadah now in Schocken Library, Jerusalem.)

increased. These also applied to the 300,000 Jews in territories which the Hungarians annexed from Czechoslovakia, Yugoslavia, and Rumania during World War II. In 1944, the Nazis overran H., imposing ghettos, concentration-camps, and deportations to extermination centers. Of H.'s 725,000 Jews, c. 400,000 were killed. After the liberation, all pre-war organizations were re-established. The accession to power of the communists in 1948 led to the nationalization of Jewish institutions, and religious organizations were centralized under one authority. Some 20,000 Jews fled the country after the 1956 revolution. Jewish pop. (1973): 80,000. However, Jewish communal and religious life has continued undisturbed and there is a Jewish high school in Budapest.

ḤUPPAH (Heb. "canopy"): The wedding ceremony; also the portable canopy under which the ceremony is held. Originally the word referred to the bridal chamber itself, of which the modern canopy is considered a symbolic representation. The term also has a definite legal meaning in talmudic terminology, indicating the coming of a woman into the legal domain of her husband. In some communities, a *tallit* is held as a *ḥ.* over the bridal couple.

HUROK, SOL (1890–1974): Impresario. A native of Russia, he settled in the US in 1905. He was responsible for introducing many of the world's leading artists to the US, and presenting American artists abroad.

HURRIANS see **HORITES**

HURST, FANNIE (1889–1968): US novelist; author of many popular novels (*Lummox*, *Back Street*, *Great Laughter,* etc.). She was active in many liberal causes, e.g., the New York Urban League.

HURWICZ, SAUL ISRAEL (1860–1922): Hebrew author. A native of White Russia, he published in 1904 an article forecasting the destruction awaiting Jewry unless it again became a normal nation living on its own soil. This extreme rejection of the Diaspora characterized his other writings. He settled in Berlin where he founded a literary miscellany *He-Atid* and published several scholarly works.

HURWITZ, HENRY (1886–1961): US editor. Born in Lithuania, he studied law at Harvard, where in 1906 he founded the first MENORAH Society, subsequently expanding it into the Intercollegiate Menorah Association. In 1915, he founded the quarterly *The Menorah Journal* — the first and, for long, the only Jewish literary periodical of its type in English — which he edited till his death when it ceased publication.

HUSHAI THE ARCHITE : Supporter of David. After Absalom's revolt, he remained in Jerusalem on David's request to observe the rebel's plans. By counteracting the influence of AHITHOPHEL, he prepared the way for Absalom's downfall (II Sam. 15–17).

ḤUSHI, ABBA (1898–1969): Israel labor leader. Born in Galicia, he settled in Palestine in 1920. He was secretary of the Haifa Labor Council 1938–51, *Mapai* member of Knesset 1949–51, and mayor of Haifa 1951–69.

ḤUSHIEL BEN ELHANAN (10th–11th cents.): Talmudist. He migrated from Italy and settled in Kairouan. The traditional story is that Ḥ. was one of four shipwrecked scholars from Bari who were ransomed in various communities, but evidence discovered in the Cairo *genizah* shows that Ḥ. went voluntarily to Kairouan where he headed a great yeshivah. Under his influence, Kairouan became an important center of Jewish learning.

HUSIK, ISAAC (1876–1939): Philosopher. From 1911, he taught philosophy (professor, 1922) at the Univ. of Pennsylvania. H. wrote particularly on

Fannie Hurst.

medieval Jewish philosophy, including a general survey of the subject and an English edition of Albo's *Ikkarim*.

*HUSSEIN (1935–): King of Jordan. He succeeded to the throne in 1952. He removed British officers from his Arab Legion in 1956 and signed a pact with Egypt and Syria but later that year refrained from joining the fighting during the SINAI CAMPAIGN. Although often isolated he maintained his throne and in 1967 attacked Israel at the time of the Six-Day War. His army was decisively defeated and had to retreat from Eastern Palestine. Subsequently his position was threatened by Arab terrorist organizations with whom he had a major showdown in Sept. 1970. From 1975, he drew close to Syria.

*HUSSEINI, HAJJ MOHAMMED AMIN EL- (1893–1974): Arab leader. In 1921, the high commissioner, Sir Herbert Samuel, appointed him mufti of Jerusalem and head of the Supreme Moslem Council. In 1936, as chairman of the Arab Supreme Council, he organized the Palestine disturbances for which he was sentenced to exile in 1937. He fled to the Lebanon, and during World War II, participated in Rashid Ali's pro-Axis coup in Iraq before going to Europe, where he assisted Hitler and was largely responsible for the liquidation of the Jews in the Moslem areas of Bosnia. In 1946, he escaped to Egypt. After 1948, he set up a short-lived "Palestine Government" in Gaza (later in Cairo).

HUSSERL, EDMUND (1859–1938): German philosopher; founder of the phenomenological school. H., who was baptized, was professor at Göttingen 1901–16 and Freiburg 1916–28. According to his doctrines, logic becomes a pure *a priori* science based on mental intuition and independent of sensory experience.

HUTZPAH (Heb.): Insolence, shamelessness.

HUTZPIT HA-METURGEMAN (fl. 2nd cent. CE): Tanna. He served as "interpreter" at the Sanhedrin in Jabneh under R Gamaliel. According to Midrash Lamentations (2:4), he was one of the Ten Martyrs put to death by the Romans.

HUYAYY IBN AKHTAB (d. 627): Chief of the BANU NADIR tribe in the Hejaz. In revenge for MOHAMMED's expulsion of the Banu Nadir from the vicinity of Medina in 626, H. attempted to organize Mohammed's foes. These included the Banu Kureiza whom Mohammed beleaguered and forced to surrender, putting all the males to death including H. H.'s daughter was subsequently captured at Khaibar, adopted Islam, and became one of Mohammed's wives.

HYAMSON, ALBERT MONTEFIORE (1875–1954): English civil servant and historian. From 1921–34, he directed the British mandatory government's department of immigration in Palestine. H. published many works, especially on English Jewish history.

He edited the *Dictionary of Universal Biography* and was co-editor of *Vallentine's Jewish Encyclopaedia*.

HYAMSON, MOSES (1862–1949): Rabbi and scholar. Educated in England, he officiated in various communities, and ultimately became *dayyan* of the London *Bet Din*. After his unsuccessful candidacy for the English chief rabbinate in 1912, he took up a rabbinic position in New York and served as professor of codes at the Jewish Theological Seminary. His writings include English translations of Bahya's *Duties of the Heart* and of parts of Maimonides' *Mishneh Torah*.

HYGIENE: Whatever the purpose of the ritual prescriptions of the Mosaic code, there can be no doubt that many of them had a considerable hygienic importance, e.g. circumcision, frequent ablutions, segregation of persons suffering from certain diseases, prohibition of the flesh of an animal found dead. The stringent regulations for complete rest on one day of the week also had considerable health significance. The Talmud amplified all such regulations in a spirit, perhaps uncritical, which incidentally served to strengthen their hygienic importance. Thus, for example, the dietary prohibition was extended to animals suffering from serious disease, while the extended periods of menstrual separation are believed to have contributed to the relative freedom of Jewish women from certain forms of cancer. Even some regulations which ostensibly had a superstitious origin — the avoidance of "spirits" which lurked in certain places — entailed the avoidance of filth, flies, etc.; similarly a "religious" importance was attached to the regular movement of the bowels. The Talmud lays down regulations regarding the sites of unpleasant industries and public works, the size of school-classes, maintenance of roads, avoidance of ordure, and the location of latrines; these rules could be assembled into a comprehensive code of h. perhaps unexampled in its age. In the Middle Ages, the talmudic prescriptions, yet further extended, secured in the Jewish quarters a minimal standard of h., in some ways far above those of their neighbors. This may have been the reason for the relative freedom from epidemics such as the Black Death. On the other hand, this was sometimes canceled out by the appalling overcrowding imposed by the ghetto system. With Emancipation and the assimilation of the Jewish way of life to that of their neighbors its distinctive quality has passed, together with some of its undoubted advantages.

HYKSOS: Semitic peoples who overran Egypt after the destruction of the Middle Kingdom. Excavations in Egypt have revealed royal H. scarabs, etc. bearing names similar to Hebrew, while H. remains have also been uncovered in Palestine. The H. ruled in Egypt c. 1720–1580 BCE, and during this period, the Children of Israel entered the country and were favorably treated; the period of bondage is believed to have begun after the expulsion of the H. The word H. is apparently Egyptian, meaning "rulers of the foreign lands"; it was first applied to his people by MANETHO who erroneously took the word to mean "shepherd kings."

HYMAN, JOSEPH C. (1889–1949): US relief administrator. He held various leading positions in the directorship of the American Joint Distribution Committee 1924–46. He also served as secretary of the American Society for Farm Settlements in Russia and was a member of the council of the Jewish Agency. He helped found the Dominican Republic Settlement Association.

HYMANS, PAUL (1865–1941): Belgian statesman. He was professor of constitutional history at Brussels Univ. (1896) and in 1900, was elected a Liberal deputy. H. served as foreign minister (1918–20, 1924–5, 1927–34, 1934–5) and minister of justice (1926–7). He headed the Belgian delegation to the Versailles Conference (1919) and was the first president of the League of Nations Assembly (1920).

HYRCANUS, JOHN: Son and successor of Simon the Hasmonean; ruled 135–104 BCE. During Simon's lifetime, H. was governor of Gezer, but after the murder of his father and two brothers by his brother-in-law Ptolemy, escaped to Jerusalem, where he seized power before Ptolemy could gain control. He besieged Ptolemy in the fortress of Dok but had to desist on account of the sabbatical year; Ptolemy escaped after murdering H.'s mother whom he had been holding as hostage. In 135–4, Antiochus Sidetes captured Jerusalem; H. was confirmed as high priest but had to accept harsh peace-terms which made the Hasmonean state again tributary to Syria. H. participated in the Parthian campaign of Antiochus Sidetes. After the defeat of Syria and the death of Antiochus, he freed himself from Syrian suzerainty and regained territory he had been obliged to cede. He attacked the Samaritans, capturing Shechem and Mt. Gerizim and destroying their temple. H. then overran the territory of the Idumeans and forced them to embrace Judaism. It is probable that H. largely conquered Galilee, with his son Aristobulus only completing the conquest. Shortly before his death, his sons defeated the Samaritans and gained control of Bet Shean and part of the Valley of Jezreel. Domestically, H. was at first allied with the Pharisees but, as his state expanded, he drew nearer to the Sadducees who constituted the backbone of his army and state administration. Eventually, there was an open breach between H. and the Pharisees. H. thereupon abolished several Pharisaic regulations and suppressed the subsequent uprising. Ultimately, he managed to calm the country, his last years being tranquil.

HYRCANUS II (d. 31 BCE): Eldest son of Alexander Yannai. He succeeded his mother Salome Alexandra (67 BCE) but was driven from the throne and the high priesthood by his brother Aristobulus. Helped by ANTIPATER to escape to Petra, he there obtained support from Aretas the Nabatean and returned to defeat Aristobulus. The dispute between the brothers was referred to Pompey when he reached Syria, but Aristobulus, knowing that Pompey was about to decide in favor of his opponents, left for Jerusalem, firmly determined to fight the Roman invaders. Pompey pursued him and after a three-month siege, captured the Temple mount, deposed Aristobulus, and appointed H. high priest, with limited political authority but without the title of ethnarch. After the death of Pompey, H. supported Julius Caesar who restored him as ethnarch and enlarged his territory. Real power, however, was in the hands of Antipater and his sons. When the Parthians invaded Judea in 40, H. was taken prisoner, maimed so as to disqualify him for the priesthood, and sent to Parthia. Here he was greatly honored by the Babylonian Jewish communities. He, however, insisted on returning to Judea, where Herod was now king, and at first was treated with respect. In the tension after the battle of Actium, Herod accused him of treason and had him executed.

I

IBN: Arabic term (="son") occurring before many Sephardi family names, sometimes in the form *aben*. It does not necessarily denote immediate paternity and is occasionally used in conjunction with a place-name.

IBN ABITUR, JOSEPH BEN ISAAC (10th–11th cents.): Spanish scholar. He was a pupil of Moses ben Enoch at Cordova and was disappointed when his master's son Enoch succeeded to the rabbinate. I. A. ultimately attempted to displace Enoch, but after a bitter dispute, he was forced into exile and traveled to N Africa, Pumbedita, and Damascus where he died. He wrote a commentary in Arabic on the Talmud, now lost, and a Hebrew commentary on the Psalms of which fragments survive. Over 200 of his liturgical poems are known.

IBN ADRET, SOLOMON BEN ABRAHAM see **ADRET**

IBN AKNIN, JOSEPH BEN JUDAH (c. 1160–1226): Scholar and physician. Born in Barcelona, he settled in Fez. He was the author of poems, talmudic commentaries, a commentary on the Song of Songs, and works on medicine, ethics, and philosophy (mostly in Arabic). He was subsequently confused with the Joseph b. Judah to whom Maimonides dedicated his *Guide of the Perplexed,* who, in fact, was Maimonides' disciple Joseph b. Judah Ibn Shimon.

IBN AVI ZIMRA, DAVID BEN SOLOMON see **ZIMRA**

IBN BAKUDA see **BAHYA**

IBN BALAM, JUDAH BEN SAMUEL (10th–11th cents.): Spanish commentator and grammarian. His commentaries (in Arabic) on most of the Bible are remarkable for their philological method and use of comparison with Arabic. He wrote books on verbs derived from nouns and on the Hebrew particles and was the first writer on the stylistic devices of the Bible in his work called *Tajnis* (Paranomasia, i.e. the use of similar words with different meanings).

IBN BARUN, ISAAC BEN JOSEPH (11th–12th cents.): Spanish grammarian. He explained many difficult biblical passages by reference to related Arabic words and constructions. His activity marks the highest achievement of the comparative studies initiated by IBN KURAISH.

IBN DANA see **ABENDANA**

IBN DAUD, ABRAHAM (c. 1110 — c. 1180): Spanish philosopher and historian. The Arabic original of his main philosophical work is lost, but two Hebrew translations are extant, one of which has been published as *Emunah Ramah* ("Sublime Faith"). I. D. was the first purely Aristotelian Jewish philosopher. To solve the problem of free will, he discusses physics, metaphysics, and psychology, concluding that God restricts His omnipotence and omniscience deliberately so as to allow man freedom of choice. Ceremonial law is less important than ethics. Scientific and religious truth are absolutely identical; thus, e.g. Ps. 139 expounds the ten categories. I. D. regarded Ibn Gabirol as his chief opponent. Of the Arab philosophers, Avicenna influenced him most. In the same year that he wrote *Emunah Ramah* (1161), he completed *Sepher ha-Kabbalah* ("Book of Tradition") in a vivid Hebrew style and in the Arabic rhetorical tradition of historiography, relating the history of talmudic scholarship to his own day. This work is of singular importance for the history of Spanish Jews. He also wrote brief histories of the Second Temple and of Rome. Of his work on astronomy, completed in 1180, nothing is known. He was martyred at Toledo.

IBN EZRA, ABRAHAM (1089–1164): Scholar and poet. He lived in Spain until 1140 but thereafter journeyed extensively, visiting Italy, France, England, and perhaps Palestine. Almost all his extant writings, which are in Hebrew, date from the period of his travels. He wrote secular and sacred poems, riddles, and epigrams (collected and published notably by D. Kahana and H. Brody), much of his penitential poetry being incorporated in the liturgy. His Bible commentaries, based on linguistic and factual examinations of the text and occasionally even including daring hints that foreshadow Bible criticism, excel in depth and clarity of thought. I. E. was also a Hebrew grammarian of importance, translating pioneer works from the Arabic and writing several original grammatical compositions. Two of his shorter books deal, from a Neoplatonic standpoint, with philosophical problems and these figure prominently in his Bible commentary. He was also a scientist and the author of several studies on astrology in which he firmly

The last page of Moses Ibn Ezra's collection of poems. (Photostat from a ms at Oxford.)

believed. His son Isaac was also a poet, who lived for many years in the Near East and for a period, professed Islam.

IBN EZRA, MOSES (1055 — after 1135): Spanish Hebrew poet. He was a close friend of Judah Ha-Levi whose poetic gifts he encouraged. After the Almoravides captured his native town of Granada (1090), he led a life of wandering filled with suffering and disappointments. I. E. wrote religious and secular poetry (published by H. Brody, 2 vols., 1942–5). Of his sacred poems, the most important are his *seliḥot*: the secular poems bear the imprint of the author's personal hardships, except for the happy youthful songs written while he was still in Granada. I. E. wrote in Arabic a work on poetry describing the methodology and meter of Hebrew and Arabic poetry which also contains useful material on the history of Hebrew poetry and poets in Spain. I. E. was the author of an Arabic philosophical work in the spirit of Neoplatonism.

IBN GABIROL, SOLOMON (c. 1021 — c. 1056): Spanish poet and philosopher. Orphaned in childhood, he was supported by philanthropy, and his physical sickliness made him lonely and depressed. His earliest surviving poems were written at the age of 16. His self-confidence resulted in frequent clashes even with his supporters, such as the Jewish statesman Jekuthiel Ibn Ḥasan, and he left his native Saragossa c. 1046. Little is known of his subsequent life, except some unreliable legends. His considerable poetic legacy was collected in the 19th cent. and published by Bialik and Ravnitzky in 1924–32. Distinguished by the wealth and elasticity of the language, it is influenced by earlier Spanish Hebrew poetry, mystical literature, and Muslem Sufism. The secular poems are lively and gay, dealing with love, drinking, and nature and include subjective verses voicing dissatisfaction with the ravages of time and the world which refused to acknowledge his greatness. His sacred poetry, on the other hand, expresses humble submission and reverence for God and the suffering of the Jewish people and their longing for redemption. Many of these poems have been incorporated into the liturgy. Outstanding is his *Keter Malkhut* ("Crown of Divine Kingship"), written in rimed prose, which is in part a lofty panegyric of the God of the cosmos and in part the confession of a man struggling with his passion and realizing his insignificance. Two of his philosophical works, both originally written in Arabic, have survived — *Mekor Ḥayyim* ("Source of Life," well known in Latin translation as *Fons Vitae*) and *Tikkun Middot ha-Nephesh* ("Improvement of the Moral Qualities"). In the 19th cent., the French scholar Solomon Munk identified I. G. as the author of *Fons Vitae*. Previously it had been ascribed to an Arab "Avicebron." One of the few medieval Hebrew works to confine itself to general — and not Jewish —

The poem *Grief and Desire*. (From a 12th cent. collection by Solomon Ibn Gabirol.)

philosophical problems, it is a product of Neoplatonism and expounds a detailed plan of creation by emanation, which influenced Christian scholasticism, Spinoza, etc.

IBN GIKATILLA see **GIKATILLA**

IBN ḤASAN, JEKUTHIEL BEN ISAAC (d. 1039): Spanish statesman and philanthropist. A supporter and patron of Solomon Ibn Gabirol, he was vizier in the Moslem state of Saragossa. He was put to death for unknown reasons.

IBN ḤASDAI, ABRAHAM BEN SAMUEL HA-LEVI (fl. first part of 13th cent.): Hebrew translator; lived at Barcelona. His many translations from the Arabic include Maimonides' *Letter to Yemen* and the story of *The Prince and the Dervish*. He endeavored to induce the anti-Maimonists to give up their opposition to Maimonides' teachings.

IBN ḤAVIV (ḤABIB): (1) *JACOB I. Ḥ.* (c. 1460–1516): Scholar. A native of Spain, after the 1492 expulsion he settled in Portugal where he was forcibly baptized in 1497, and then in Salonica where he reverted to Judaism. He was the author of EN YAAKOV, an annotated compilation of the aggadic sections of the Palestinian and Babylonian Talmuds. The work achieved wide popularity, was frequently republished, and became the subject of special study-circles. Only the first two (out of six) parts were published in I. Ḥ.'s lifetime and the work was completed by his son. (2) *LEVI I. Ḥ.* (c. 1480–1545): Scholar; son of (1). He completed his father's *En Yaakov*. Later he settled in Jerusalem, becoming its chief rabbi and opposing Berab's plan to revive ORDINATION. His youthful apostasy was used in arguments against him. Besides his Jewish knowledge, he was well-versed in the sciences, particularly astronomy.

IBN JANAḤ, JONAH (c. 990 — c. 1050): Spanish philologist. After his native town of Cordova was sacked in 1012, he settled in Saragossa, practicing as a physician. He wrote on Hebrew philology and biblical exegesis. His main contribution to Hebrew grammar was *Sepher ha-Dikduk* which includes an alphabetical list of Hebrew roots, interpreted with reference to biblical and rabbinic literature as well as by comparison with other Semitic languages. This work, which was translated from Arabic into Hebrew by Judah Ibn Tibbon, formed the basis of subsequent Hebrew grammatical research.

IBN KILLIS, YAKUB BEN YUSUF (c. 930–991): Statesman. At an early age he went from Baghdad to Syria and later settled in Egypt, becoming converted to Islam in 969. He was the chief minister to successive caliphs and reorganized the state's economy.

IBN KURAISH, JUDAH (fl. 10th cent.): Philologist. Born in Morocco, he was by profession a physician. He addressed a letter in Arabic to the Jews of Fez protesting against the abolition of the recitation of the Aramaic Targum. The letter points out that comparison with Aramaic words often helps to establish the meaning of rare and difficult biblical expressions. He shows that similar benefit can be derived from late Hebrew expressions found in the Mishnah, etc. In a third part, he gives a list of words explicable by reference to Arabic. He thus laid the foundation of a method which later, in the hands of Ibn Balam and Ibn Barun, proved to be of much help in solving problems of biblical vocabulary.

IBN LABRAT, DUNASH see DUNASH

IBN LATIF, ISAAC BEN ABRAHAM (c. 1220–1290): Spanish philosopher, kabbalist, and physician. He passed his latter years in Palestine. I. L. created a new method of Kabbalah based on Aristotelian philosophy and the natural sciences and also used a new kabbalistic terminology derived from philosophy and mathematics. Unlike other contemporary kabbalists, he was an admirer of the works of Maimonides.

IBN MIGAS, JOSEPH BEN MEIR HA-LEVI (1077–1141): Spanish codifier. He studied at Lucena with Isaac Alfasi who appointed I. M. as his successor in the rabbinate and as head of the academy he had founded. I. M. was an outstanding scholar who composed responsa and talmudic novellae, only a few of which have been printed.

IBN NAGRELA (NAGDELA) see SAMUEL IBN NAGRELA

The shepherd. (From an illustrated 15th cent. German ms of Ibn Sahulah's *Meshal ha-Kadmoni*, Munich State and University Library.)

IBN PAKUDA, BAḤYA see BAḤYA

IBN PALQUERA, SHEMTOV BEN JOSEPH see FALAQUERA

IBN POLEGAR (erroneously Pulkar or Pulgar), **ISAAC BEN JOSEPH** (fl. 14th cent.): Spanish author. His many works (mostly still in ms) include a polemical reply to the convert Abner of Burgos' anti-Jewish *Minḥat Kenaot*. This work — entitled *Ezer ha-Dat* — aims at reconciling faith and philosophy.

IBN SAHULAH, ISAAC BEN SOLOMON (fl. 13th cent.): Spanish Hebrew author. A physician at Guadalajara, he wrote a kabbalistic commentary on Canticles but is best-known as the author of *Meshal ha-Kadmoni* ("Easterner's Parable"), a book of rimed fables; his illustrations to his original version were copied in later mss and printed editions.

IBN SHAPRUT, ḤASDAI (or Ḥisdai; c. 915 — c. 970): Spanish statesman. A physician by profession, he served at the courts of the caliphs Abd er-Raḥman III and Ḥakam II at Cordova. His linguistic ability and adroitness in negotiation made him useful in diplomatic relations, and he was employed with brilliant success on foreign missions. His generous support of Jewish scholars and scholarship was an important factor in the great progress made by Jewish culture in Spain in his day. He used his high political office to defend Jewish communities and was widely regarded as the protector and spokesman of Jewry. His well-known letter to the king of the KHAZARS, dispatched through the medium of two Slavic Jews visiting Cordova on a mission, expressed his joy at their independent Jewish kingdom. I. S. was a scholar in his own right, with a knowledge of several languages, and collaborated in translating a work of Dioscorides into Arabic.

IBN SHAPRUT, SHEMTOV BEN ISAAC (14th–15th cents.): Spanish scholar and physician. In 1375, he conducted a disputation in Pamplona with the future Pope Benedict XIII. To combat apostasy, he wrote the polemical *Even Boḥan* ("Touchstone"). He was also the author of a commentary on Avicenna, a supercommentary to Ibn Ezra's Bible commentary, and a philosophical explanation of the talmudic aggadah.

IBN SHEMTOV: (1) *JOSEPH BEN SHEMTOV I. S.* (c. 1400 — c. 1460): Spanish author; son of (2). He lived for some years in Valladolid and was physician and treasurer at the court of the prince of Asturias. His position aroused jealousy, and he was murdered under obscure circumstances. Of his numerous books, only three have been published including *Kevod Elohim* ("The Glory of God"), a theological work endeavoring to find a compromise between the views of Maimonides and the anti-philosophical attitude of several contemporary Jewish scholars, including his own father. (2) *SHEMTOV I. S.* (d. 1430): Spanish kabbalist. His main work *Sepher ha-Emunot* ("Book of Beliefs") criticizes Jewish philosophers and philosophy, which he regards as leading to apostasy and conversion, in contrast to Kabbalah, the genuine interpretation of tradition.

IBN TIBBON: Family of Jewish scholars who performed a significant role in the development of Hebrew language and literature as translators and commentators. The family had its origin in Granada and its most important members were (1) *JACOB BEN MAKHIR* (Don Profiat) *I. T.* (c. 1230–1312): Astronomer, physician, author, and translator; grandson of (4). He was born at Marseilles and lived most of his life at Montpellier where he is reported to have taught medicine at the university. His translations from Arabic to Hebrew include works by Euclid, Averroes, and Al-Ghazzali. His astronomical tables, composed in 1300, were translated into Latin and used by Dante for his *Divine Comedy*. He staunchly defended Maimonides in the controversy that raged

about his works. (2) *JUDAH BEN SAUL I. T.* (c. 1120 — after 1190): Physician and translator. Forced by persecution to leave his birthplace of Granada in 1150, he settled in Lunel. He translated several Jewish classics from Arabic to Hebrew including Saadyah's *Beliefs and Opinions,* Baḥya's *Duties of the Heart,* and Judah Ha-Levi's *Kuzari.* His translations are overliteral but are important for their coinage of philosophical terminology. His ethical will to his son Samuel, including advice on the care of books, is famous. (3) *MOSES BEN SAMUEL I. T.* (d. c. 1283): Author and translator; son of (4). He resided at Marseilles where he practiced medicine and translated many philosophic and scientific books from Arabic to Hebrew, including Ibn Tzaddik's *Olam Katon* and works by Maimonides. His original compositions include commentaries on the Bible and rabbinical works. (4) *SAMUEL BEN JUDAH I. T.* (c. 1150 — c. 1230): Translator, scholar and physician; son of (2). He traveled widely, finally settling at Marseilles. His classic translation is of Maimonides' *Guide,* executed with the author's approval and guidance. He also translated other works by Maimonides and was the author of philosophical commentaries on the Bible.

IBN TZADDIK, JOSEPH BEN JACOB (c. 1075–c. 1149): Philosopher and poet; dayyan at Cordova from 1138. Little of his poetry has survived and his reputation rests largely on his philosophical work *Olam Katon* ("Microcosm"; known only in the Hebrew translation of the Arabic original) which discusses cosmology, the nature of man, and his relation to the external world. Man's soul is a microcosm of the world and in order to attain full awareness of the Divinity, man must first honor himself. The views are strongly Neoplatonic with an admixture of Aristotelianism.

IBN VERGA: (1) *JUDAH I. V.* (fl. latter half of 15th cent.): Chronicler. At the time of the expulsion from Spain (1492), he fled from Seville to Lisbon where he was martyred (apparently in 1497). His historical writings are included in *Shevet Yehudah* (see below); he also composed works on arithmetic and astronomy. (2) *SOLOMON I. V.* (fl. 15th–16th cents.): Historian; probably son of (1). On the capture of Malaga in 1487, he was sent by the Spanish communities to collect money for the ransom of Jewish prisoners. After the expulsion from Spain, he went to live in Portugal and was apparently forced to become a Marrano in 1497. He later reverted to Judaism in Italy where he wrote his famous work *Shevet Yehudah* ("Rod of Judah"), called after (1). The book was first printed in Adrianople in 1550 with additions written by Solomon's son, Joseph. It comprised a collection of narratives describing persecutions and disputations which the author gathered from earlier Hebrew sources or from hearsay.

He displays a remarkable knowledge of contemporary Spanish and Italian literature. The work is an important historical source, especially for the events of the period of the expulsion from Spain.

IBN YAHIA: Sephardi family, said to have been ennobled by the kings of Portugal for services in battle. Outstanding members include (1) *DAVID BEN JOSEPH I. Y.* (1465–1543) who settled in Italy after the expulsion from Spain and became rabbi in Naples, Bologna, etc. He wrote grammatical works as well as an autobiographical fragment. (2) *DAVID BEN SOLOMON I. Y.* (1440–1524), one of the most distinguished Portuguese rabbis at the time of the expulsion. He wrote biblical commentaries (on Proverbs, etc.) as well as grammatical and halakhic works. He died in Constantinople after many wanderings. (3) *GEDALIAH BEN JOSEPH I. Y.* (1515–1587), loan-banker in Imola, etc., who wrote many historical works, of which only his *Shalshelet ha-Kabbalah* ("Chain of Tradition") has been published. This is a history of Jewish scholars, so replete in legendary elements that it was dubbed a "Chain of Lies." Nevertheless, it is of great importance for history as well as folklore. (4) *JACOB TAM I. Y.* (d. 1542), son of (2), born in Portugal, became rabbi and court physician in Constantinople; many of his responsa are preserved. (5) *JOSEPH I. Y.* (1494–1534), son of (1) and father of (3), rabbi in Italy, was author of biblical commentaries and philosophical works, including *Torah Or.* (6) *JUDAH* ("*Negro*") *I. Y.* (14th cent.), poet, fled from Toledo to Portugal after the 1391 massacres. Later members of the family in Italy, where they produced rabbis and communal workers, were known as "Iacchia."

IBN YAISH (Abenaes), **SOLOMON** (d. 1603): Statesman and merchant. A Portuguese Marrano by birth (under the name Alvaro Mendes), he eventually returned to Judaism in Turkey. Attaining prominence at the Porte, he was created duke of Mytilene and became an important figure in international diplomacy as organizer of the Anglo-Turkish alliance against Spain. He obtained the renewal of Joseph Nasi's concession for Tiberias, sending his own son Jacob to develop the town.

IBN ZABARA, JOSEPH (c. 1140 — c. 1200): Spanish Hebrew poet, who practiced medicine in his native Barcelona. His *Sepher Shaashuim* ("Book of Delights"; Engl. translation by M. Hadas) comprises rimed anecdotes, parables, etc. which the author claimed to have collected on his travels.

IBN ZERAH, MENAHEM (d. 1385): Spanish codifier. Orphaned and maimed in the attack on the Jews of Navarre in 1328, he settled in Toledo and devoted himself to study. His *Tzedah la-Derekh* was a concise handbook of essential Jewish religious laws for the use of busy Jews in attendance at the royal court.

IBRAHIM BEN YACUB AL-ISRAILI (fl. latter 10th cent.): Traveler. Starting from Spain c. 965, he traveled through Central Europe, visiting the court of Otto I of Germany and reaching Stettin. His descriptions of his travels have only survived in quotations.

*IBRAHIM PASHA (1789–1848): Egyptian general. He overran Palestine and Syria in 1831, ruling these areas efficiently until 1841 when he was compelled to withdraw. He favored the Jews, who honored him and for some time celebrated at Hebron the "Purim of I. P." to commemorate his capture of the town.

ICA see **JEWISH COLONIZATION ASSOCIATION**

ICHABOD (11th cent. BCE): Son of Phinehas and grandson of Eli the priest. His father and uncle Hophni were killed when the Israelites were defeated by the Philistines. His grandfather and mother died of shock on receiving the news, the latter in giving birth to I. whose name means "There is no glory" (I Sam. 4:10–22).

ICOR: Organization founded in the US in 1924, and run by Jewish communists, to promote Jewish colonization in the Soviet Union. After 1928 it concentrated its efforts on Biro-Bidjan and conducted a fund-raising program to provide agricultural machinery and to finance cultural activities. As the Biro-Bidjan experiment faded, the I. program collapsed, and the organization disappeared before the end of World War II.

IDAHO: US state. Jews first settled there in the 1860's. The largest community is in Boise with a Jewish population of about 200 and the only active congregation and school in the state. Moses Alexander served two terms as governor of I. (1915–19). The Jewish pop. (1973) is 630 of whom 120 were in Boise.

IDELSOHN, ABRAHAM ZVI (1882–1938): Musicologist. He was born in Courland, settled in Palestine in 1906, and moved to the US in 1922. In 1924, he was appointed professor of Jewish music and liturgy at Hebrew Union College, Cincinnati. I. collected and published oriental melodies and conducted research into the origin of oriental music (Jewish and Arabic). Among his musical compositions is an opera *Jephthah*. His books include *Jewish Music in its Historical Development* and a corpus of Hebrew oriental music (10 vols. 1914–32).

IDOLATRY: Judaism was the only religion in the ancient world to oppose idol-worship. However, foreign influences introduced idolatrous practices among the Jews against which the prophets struggled continually. I. made the heaviest inroads in the Northern Kingdom where the worship centered around the golden calves set up by Jeroboam. During the Babylonian Exile, i. seems to have disappeared altogether from among Jews, and the rabbis maintained that whoever rejected i. is considered as having acknowledged the whole Torah. Rabbinic law as recorded in the Mishnah treatise *Avodah Zarah* deals, therefore, not with Jews serving idols but with rabbinic prohibitions against contact with idolators. Thus, commerce with an idolator is prohibited before an idolatrous holiday so that the Jew may not even have an indirect share in preparations for such. The rabbis prohibited the selling or leasing of land or houses in Palestine to an idolator, nor was it permitted to sell animals to an idolator, or to eat at the same table with him. Moreover, they forbade the eating of his bread, oil, or wine and declared all gentile wine as "wine of idolatrous libation."

IDRA see **ZOHAR**

IDUMEA see **EDOM**

*IGNATIEV, NICOLAI (1832–1908): Russian statesman. As minister of the interior, he was responsible for the formulation and enforcement of Russia's anti-Semitic policy, particularly as manifested in the MAY LAWS of 1882.

IGNATOV, DAVID (1885–1954): Yiddish writer; born in the Ukraine, settled in the US in 1906. One of the the creators of the modern Yiddish novel, he wrote about the lives of Jewish workers in the US. I. reworked Ḥasidic tales and medieval Jewish fables as well as writing stories for children.

IGRAT BAT-MAḤLAT: An evil night spirit who, according to the Talmud, was rendered powerless by Abbaye.

IḤUD (Heb. "Unity"): Jewish organization founded in Palestine in 1942 with the object of fostering cooperation between Jews and Arabs in the country and its conversion into a binational Jewish-Arab state. Ideologically it was the successor of BERIT SHALOM. Since the establishment of the state of Israel it has advocated the rights of the Arab minority, the return of the refugees, and territorial concessions by Israel. Its membership is small. The leaders of *I.* have included Y. L. MAGNES, RABBI BINYAMIN, and Ernst SIMON. See also BI-NATIONALISM.

IḤUD HA-KEVUTZOT VEHA-KIBBUTZIM (Heb. "Union of kevutzot and kibbutzim"): Organization of Israel collective villages founded in 1951 by the fusion of the dissident minority of HA-KIBBUTZ HA-MEUḤAD with ḤEVER HA-KEVUTZOT. While not identified with a single party, most of its members belong to *Mapai.* In 1971, 76 villages, with a population of 26,900 were affiliated.

IKRITI, SHEMARIAH (1275–1355): Philosopher and biblical commentator. Brought up in Crete (whence his name), he spent most of his life in Italy. I. wrote a philosophical commentary on the Bible at the invitation of Robert of Naples (only extracts survive). He went to Spain in 1352 on an unsuccessful mission to reconcile the Karaites and Rabbinites.

Here he was accused of messianic pretensions and died in prison. His works include *Sepher ha-Mora,* a cosmological polemic, and *Eleph ha-Magen* on talmudic legends.

ILANIYYAH (formerly Sejera): Israel moshavah. It was the first modern Jewish settlement in Lower Galilee, being the site of an agricultural training farm in 1899 (destroyed in World War I) and of a moshavah in 1902. The first attempt to set up a workers' "collective" was made there in 1907 and among the members was D. Ben-Gurion. In 1909, HA-SHOMER was founded in I. Population (1972): 174.

ILF (FAINZILBER), ILYA (1897–1937): Soviet Russian humorist and journalist. He was co-author of the satirical novels, *Diamonds to Sit On, The Little Golden Calf*, and *Little Golden America* written after a trip to the US (1936).

ILLEGITIMACY: The issue of any union prohibited in the Bible and for which the punishment is *karet* ("excision") is considered illegitimate in Jewish law. Such issue is designated *mamzer.* A *mamzer,* according to Jewish law, may not marry an Israelite but is permitted to marry one of the same status as himself or a proselyte. The children of *mamzerim* are still considered to be of the same status as far as the prohibition of marrying a proper Israelite is concerned. A child merely born out of wedlock, however, where both parents could have entered into a legal marriage, is considered legitimate. Such child, moreover, even has a share in his father's heritage, if paternity is admitted.

ILLINOIS: US state. Individual Jews appeared there in the mid-18th cent. and began to settle in CHICAGO in the 1830's. The first Jewish community

Hillel House, Evanston, Illinois.

outside Chicago was established in Peoria in 1847. Jewish immigrants settled in Pontiac in 1856, Aurora in 1860, and Moline in 1866. Communities in Cairo, Urbana, Champaign, Frankfort Station, Bloomington, Quincy, and SPRINGFIELD date from the latter half of the 19th cent. More than 100,000 Jews from E Europe went to I. between 1880 and 1900, nearly all settling in Chicago. There are now Jewish communities in about 30 cities and towns in I. Henry HORNER was governor of I. 1932–40. Jewish pop. (1973): 269,000.

ILLUY (Heb.): An outstanding scholar or genius, especially a young prodigy; usually applied to talmudic scholars.

ILPHA (Ḥilphai; in the Palestinian Talmud; fl. 220–250): Palestinian amora. An aggadist of note, his keen intellect was legendary. He had the reputation of working miracles.

IM YIRTZEH HA-SHEM (Heb.): If the Name (viz. God) wills; used in discussing future events (similar to "God willing").

IMAGES see **IDOLATRY**

IMBER: (1) *NAPHTALI HERZ* (1856–1909): Hebrew poet. He wandered through Galicia, Rumania, and Turkey where he met Laurence OLIPHANT whom he accompanied to Palestine as his secretary. I. remained there from 1882 to 1887. From 1892 until his death he lived in the US. He published three volumes of poetry besides other writings. His poetry is sentimental and is saturated with national ideals. His most famous poem is HA-TIKVAH, the Israel national anthem. (2) *SAMUEL JACOB I.* (1889–

Naphtali Herz Imber.

Page from the first edition of *Maḥberot Immanuel* printed by Gershom Soncino, Brescia, 1491.

1942): Galician Yiddish poet; nephew of (1). He published several collections of lyrical verse, notably the historical poem *Esterke,* and essays and critical works in Yiddish, as well as in Polish. He was killed by the Nazis in World War II.

IMMA SHALOM (fl. 1st cent. CE): Sister of R Gamaliel II and wife of R Eliezer ben Hyrcanus. One of the few women whose name occurs in talmudic literature, she was praised for her knowledge and her devotion to both her brother and her husband.

IMMANUEL BEN SOLOMON OF ROME (1260–c. 1328): Italian poet. He wandered about Italy, teaching and writing. He composed philosophical commentaries on several parts of the Bible, only partly published. He was a prolific writer of poetry, much of it erotic but including also hymns, etc.; he introduced Spanish metrical forms into Italy and the sonnet form into Hebrew. In 1321, he composed the earliest-known imitation of Dante's *Divine Comedy.* This with the rest of his occasional verses, was collected within a rough narrative framework in rimed prose in his *Maḥberot Immanuel* ("The Compositions of Immanuel") the reading of which was forbidden by some rabbis because of its low moral standard. I. was also an Italian poet, under the name Manoello Giudeo many of his verses (including a sonnet on Dante's death) being preserved.

IMMIGRANT CAMPS see **CAMPS, IMMIGRANT**

IMMIGRATION see **ALIYAH; MIGRATION**

IMMORTALITY OF THE SOUL: In religion the direct belief in a continued existence after death; in philosophy, the idea that there is some part of the human personality the eternity of which can be proved or at least made acceptable to reason. Primitive religions generally consider life as whole and indivisible; their concept of an after-life therefore refers to the personality as a whole and not to the SOUL in the narrower sense. The dead exist in a state of lowered vitality; this kind of bleak shadow-life in the underworld was known, for instance, to the Greeks (*Hades*) and the ancient Hebrews (*Sheol*). When the spirit of life has departed, man continues to exist in the land of the shadows, but "the dead praise not the Lord, neither any that go down into silence" (Ps. 115:17). On the other hand the soul is regarded as an immaterial substance whose relation to a particular body is more or less incidental. According to this view, existence before birth and after death is a matter of course and it is the soul's descent into matter and the mortal body that requires explanation. The moral and religious task of life is then to protect the soul from losing its purity while in the material world. These ideas were already current in Hellenism and appear as commonplaces in rabbinic literature. A further possibility within this range of ideas is METEMPSYCHOSIS. Another approach to immortality, preserving the older conception of life as a totality of body and soul, is manifest in the belief of the RESURRECTION of the body, which became an article of faith in Judaism and was incorporated into Maimonides' 13 Articles. The conflation of the two kinds of belief yielded the traditional Jewish concept of a Hereafter where the departed souls are rewarded (paradise, garden of Eden, etc.) and the wicked punished (hell, Gehinnom) for their deeds in this life until the great day of the Resurrection when the final judgment will be followed by a completely new era (*olam ha-ba*).

IMPURITY see **PURITY, RITUAL**

INBER, VERA (1890–1972): Russian poet and novelist. Her experiences in the siege of Leningrad in World War II form the background to much of her subsequent work, of which the diary *Almost Three Years* was awarded a Stalin Prize.

INCENSE: In the Temple, i. accompanied all sacrifices except the sin-offering of the poor and the meat-offering of the leper. On the Day of Atonement, it was solemnly burned by the high priest in the Holy of Holies. The ingredients, prescribed briefly in Exod. 30:34–8, are given in detail in the Talmud (cf. *Keritot* 6*a*: PITTUM HA-KETORET, which entered the liturgy). According to Maimonides, its object was to animate the spirits of the priests and to neutralize the odors of the sacrifice.

First page of a Bible printed in Naples by Joshua Soncino in 1492.

INCUNABULA: Books printed before 1500. Approximately 150 Hebrew i. are known, some surviving in unique copies or fragments. About two-thirds were printed in Italy where the first dated Hebrew books appeared in 1475. The most prolific printers of Hebrew i. were the Soncino family in Italy. Several Hebrew i. appeared in Spain and Portugal, including the earliest specimens of printing in

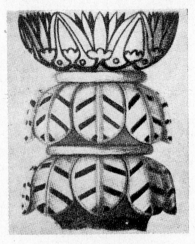

Stone brazier for burning incense.
(Megiddo, 11th cent. BCE.)

The oldest document of Indian Jewish History. Charter of Privileges for Joseph Rabban on a bronze plate. (?750 CE.)

those countries. A single i. is known to have been printed in Constantinople (1493); this is the first book printed in the Levant. Important collections of Hebrew i. are those in the Bodleian Library, Oxford; the British Museum, London; the Jewish Theological Seminary of America, New York; and the Schocken collection in the Hebrew Univ., Jerusalem.

INDEPENDENCE DAY see **YOM ATZMAUT**

INDEPENDENT LIBERAL PARTY see **PROGRESSIVE PARTY**

INDEX LIBRORUM PROHIBITORUM see **BOOKS, PROHIBITED**

INDIA: The relations of the Hebrews with I. go back to the time of Solomon (I Kings 9:26–8). Later, a number of distinct strands can be traced in the history of the Jews there. (1) The COCHIN Jews. First established in Cranganore probably in the 6th cent. CE, they removed to Cochin and its neighborhood in the 16th and were later reinforced by immigration from Europe and Syria. (2) BENE ISRAEL, in the neighborhood of BOMBAY. Ethnically Indian, their origin is uncertain. In the 18th cent. their Jewish observance was at a low ebb, but they have since returned to a whole-hearted observance of Judaism. (3) Iraqi Jews, who began to arrive from Baghdad, etc. in the early 19th cent. and established Arabic-speaking communities in Bombay, CALCUTTA, etc.

Some of them, such as the SASSOON family, have attained great prominence. They numbered c. 3,000 in 1948. (4) European Jews (including German refugees) who settled in some numbers during the later period of British rule. They have never established any communal organization. In addition to these categories, there were in the Middle Ages Jewish communities in CALICUT and other places, and from the 16th cent. ex-Marranos and their descendants (via London or Amsterdam) appeared in various places, including Madras where there was an organized congregation. Most Indian Jews have settled in Israel and by 1973 only 6,134 were left. See also PAKISTAN.

INDIANA: US state. Jewish fur traders penetrated into the area in the 1760's. Individual Jews settled there soon after homesteaders started staking their claims in 1810. The first Jewish settlement was established at Rising Sun about 1825. A Jewish community of substance did not develop until the late 1840's when large numbers of Jews reached the territory. In 1848, I.'s first congregation was founded in FORT WAYNE, and the following year, Temple Israel was established in Lafayette. I.'s largest Jewish communities are located in INDIANAPOLIS, GARY, South·Bend, EVANSVILLE, Hammond, and FORT WAYNE, Jewish pop. (1973): 26,215.

INDIANAPOLIS: City in Indiana, US. Its first Jewish settlers arrived from England in 1850. The I. Hebrew Congregation was founded in 1856. The Ladies' Hebrew Benevolent Society, established in 1859, was succeeded in 1905, by the Jewish Welfare Federation which maintains all Jewish social services. The Jewish Educational Association conducts Hebrew religious schools. The weekly *National Jewish Post* (founded in 1935), is published in I. In 1973 there were 10,740 Jews with 5 synagogues.

INDONESIA: Asian republic. Jews from Baghdad spread into the Dutch E Indies in the mid-19th cent., and for a short time there were communities at Batavia and Semarang. After World War I, there were reckoned to be 2,000 Jews in Java, including some from Holland, but their communal organization was weak. Subsequently, an influx from E Europe strengthened Jewish life, and further refugees arrived during World War II. With the end of Dutch rule, the numbers dwindled from 3,000 to 100 (1973). Most of the Jews and a synagogue are in Surabaya, 20 Jews live in Jakarta, and a few in Bandung.

INDUSTRIAL REMOVAL OFFICE: US organization that received funds from several sources, notably the Jewish Colonization Association. It sought to encourage new immigrants in the US to leave the large population centers on the E seaboard and settle in the interior. The office functioned 1901–22 (with the exception of the World War I Period).

INFELD, LEOPOLD (1898–1968): Polish scientist. A student of Einstein and Max Born, he became a

אויבי אלביש בושת ועליו יציץ נזרו

זלמלשׁצנים אל יהי תקוה וכלם כדגע יאבדו וכל שונאי לעשר מחוח לכרתו

A Jewish caricature against informers (Modena, Italy, mid-18th cent. Roth Collection).

member of the Institute for Advanced Study at Princeton (1936) and professor of applied mathematics at Toronto (1939). After World War II, he returned to Poland. His works include *The World in Modern Science, The Evolution of Physics,* and his autobiography *Quest* (1941).

INFORMER: Owing to the circumstances of Jewish life in past times, the greatest crime that a Jew could commit against his coreligionists was to denounce them to the secular authorities, whether with or without justification, for the infringement of some arbitrary and unjust regulation. No punishment for such a person was considered excessive. In Spain, the secular authorities, realizing that such action undermined the basis of Jewish life, authorized the Jews to demand capital punishment in these cases. Here, the i. was called in Spanish *Malsin* (Heb.

malshin—slanderer), whence the modern Spanish verb *malsinar*. Among the Ashkenazim, the usual term, which was considered one of the greatest expressions of obloquy which could be proffered against a Jew, was *moser* (Heb. "betrayer").

INGATHERING FESTIVAL (Heb. *ḥag haasiph*): Name given to the Feast of Tabernacles which falls at the end of the agricultural year (Exod. 23:16).

INGATHERING OF THE EXILES see **KIBBUTZ GALUYYOT**

INHERITANCE (Heb. *yerushah, naḥalah*): The Bible accepts the principle of primogeniture, and the case of ZELOPHEHAD's i. determined that daughters should inherit where there are no sons (Num. 27:8–11). The rabbis determined the order of legal heirs: (1) sons and their descendants (the first-born receiving a double portion); (2) daughters and their descendants;

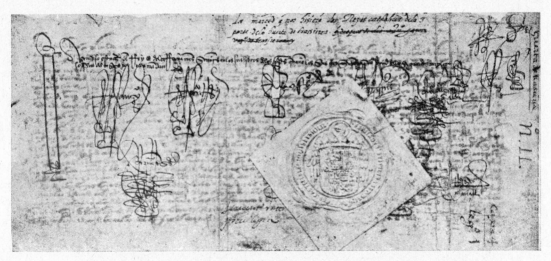

Back of a deed of gift from 1485 handing over the estate of the poet Juan Alfonso de Baena.
confiscated by a court of the Inquisition, to a monastery in Cordova.

(3) the father; (4) brothers and their descendants; (5) sisters and their descendants; (6) the father's father; (7) the father's brothers and their descendants; (8) the father's sisters and their descendants; (9) the father's father's father, etc. In general, only a son born of a slave or of a non-Jewess was excluded, but this could be circumvented by making him a specific gift. The Bet Din may deprive a person of the right of i. where it sees fit. A controversy raged between the Pharisees and Sadducees before the view of the former was accepted to the effect that a son and all his descendants, whether male or female, precede the daughter in the right of i. However, the rabbis made maintenance of an unmarried daughter a prime charge upon the estate of the deceased. If the estate were small, the unmarried daughters had to be supported even if the sons had to beg. A husband inherits his wife's property after her death; a wife does not inherit from a husband, but her support remains a first charge on his estate as long as she does not remarry. By levirate marriage, a man becomes sole heir to his brother's estate (unless the father is living): in the event of *halitzah,* however, he shares the estate with other brothers. Possession by the heirs, if they are of age, takes place immediately after the death of the deceased; if minors, a trustee (*epitropos*) is appointed for them. A man cannot disinherit his son or appoint a stranger in place of a legal heir. He may, however, prefer one legal heir to another or give his estate to a stranger in his lifetime in the form of a gift; this, however, was disapproved of by the rabbis.

INITIALS see **ABBREVIATIONS**

*INNOCENT III: Pope, 1198–1216. Although confirming the protective papal bulls in favor of the Jews, he also renewed all the former restrictive legislation against them and was responsible for the repressive decrees enacted at the fourth LATERAN COUNCIL in 1215 which marked the acme of medieval anti-Jewish reaction.

INQUISITION: Name given to the ecclesiastical tribunal ("Holy Office") which grew out of the various punitive measures taken by the Catholic Church from an early date for the correction of "heresy." In the Middle Ages, when under the control of the Dominicans, it concerned itself with Jews only incidentally. It was, however, revived in Spain under royal auspices by a Papal Bull of 1478 for the express purpose of dealing with the MARRANOS. The first inquisitors were appointed in 1480, Thomas de TORQUEMADA becoming inquisitor-general in 1483. In 1481, an AUTO DA FÉ was held at Seville—the first of a long series which continued until the 19th cent. In 1483–4, the I. was extended, in the teeth of determined opposition from the Marranos, to Aragon. In 1540, after prolonged delays due to the agitation and intrigues of the New Christians, the I. began activities in Portugal; later, it was introduced, always primarily to cope with the problem of fugitive Marranos, into the Spanish and Portuguese dependencies overseas, as far as Goa in India, 1561, and Peru in the New World, 1570; Mexico, 1571, etc. In due course, its attention was extended to ex-Moslems and later to Protestants, while it also dealt with offenses such as witchcraft, bigamy, etc., and issued certificates of *limpieza* or purity of blood (from Jewish or Moorish admixture) to those who sought certain offices. Nevertheless, the Marranos continued to remain its principal objective. In Spain, except in Majorca, the I. managed to stamp out the native Judaizers almost entirely by the end of the 16th cent.; their place was taken by refugees from Portugal who henceforth provided a great proportion of the victims. In the middle of the 18th cent., the activity of the I. diminished, partly because of the effectiveness of its work and the dwindling number of Judaizers, partly because of the spread of humanitarian ideas and partly because of the jealousy aroused by its wealth. The reforming Portuguese minister Pombal restricted the power of the I. in Portugal where the last public auto da fé was held in 1765: the institution was formally abolished there, after prolonged inactivity, in 1821. In Spain it was abolished in 1808 during the French domination, reinstituted with the Restoration, claimed a last human victim (not a Jew) in 1826, and was finally swept away in 1834. In a less highly-organized sense, the I. was active also in other Catholic countries, being responsible for occasional onslaughts on converts relapsed to Judaism (e.g. in Italy — not only in the Papal States). In 1605, it was given authority over the Roman ghetto; it still exists for the suppression of "heretical" literature.

INSCRIPTIONS see **ALPHABET; ARCHEOLOGY**

INSPIRATION: In theology, the working or influence of the Divine power which guarantees that a written or spoken utterance originates from God and remains free of human error or falsehood. In a wider sense, it refers to the influence of the Divine power which enables man to perform acts normally beyond his capacity (cf. Judg. 11:29; 13:25). There is no exact equivalent to i. in Hebrew which speaks of the Holy Spirit or the SHEKHINAH descending or resting upon a man. The Jewish philosophers in Alexandria stressed the passivity of man and compared him to a lyre, the strings of which were moved by the wind (i.e., the Divine Spirit). Rabbinic tradition seems always to have distinguished various levels of i. as, e.g., when distinguishing between the verbal i. of the Pentateuch and the lesser holiness of other biblical texts. There is a similar distinction between prophecy (see PROPHETS) and i. (by the Holy Spirit). The most extreme conception of i. is fundamentalism which defends the inspired character of every letter, vowel, and even musical accent of the biblical text. Modern liberal theology tends to substitute the somewhat vague concept of i. for the traditional REVELATION. On the other hand, the Jewish medieval philosophers hardly ever considered i. as such but focused all their discussions and theories on the concept of prophecy, and under the latter term subsumed such ideas as perfect knowledge, communion with God, state of illumination, etc.

INSTITUTE FOR THE STUDY OF HEBREW POETRY: Institute founded in 1930 at Berlin by Salman Schocken for the study and publication of medieval Hebrew poetry. It was headed by Ḥayyim Brody until his death in 1942. Since 1934, it has been located in Jerusalem.

INSTITUTUM JUDAICUM: Christian institute for Jewish study founded at Berlin in 1883 by H.L. STRACK and later associated with the theological faculty of the university under the direction of Hugo Gressman. It published works in the field of postbiblical Judaism and Talmud. Several missionary institutes also existed under the name. I. J., the earliest being founded at Halle in 1728. One of the most important, named for its former director Franz DELITZSCH, was in Leipzig.

INTERCOLLEGIATE ZIONIST FEDERATION OF AMERICA see **STUDENT ZIONIST ORGANIZATION**

INTERMARRIAGE: Marriage between a Jew and a non-Jew. This phenomenon was rare before the Emancipation Period and one of the partners in such cases was inevitably converted to the other's religion. In the 19th cent., with the establishment of civil marriage in most countries, the practice considerably increased in W Europe and America. In some communities, e.g. in Italy, the proportion of mixed marriages (including those in which conversion took place) rose to nearly two-thirds of all marriages by Jews. In 1932, 60 mixed marriages took place in Germany for every 100 Jewish marriages. In the US, the rate of i. is very high in some smaller communities, though its incidence is checked in the larger towns by the more intense Jewish social life. In most cases accurate statistics are not available. However, it is clear the phenomenon is on the increase. I. continues to be one of the main threats to continued Jewish existence outside Israel and seriously endangers some European Jewish communities. In the vast majority of cases, the children of mixed marriages are lost to Judaism.

INTERNATIONAL REFUGEE ORGANIZATION (IRO): A temporary agency of the UN with head office at Geneva. In 1947, it was entrusted with the care of REFUGEES and DISPLACED PERSONS previously under the charge of UNRRA and before that, of an international committee. In 1950, 15 states were affiliated. The office of the High Commissioner for Refugee Affairs took over the international protection of refugees after IRO ceased to operate at the end of 1951. IRO assisted, among others, 250,000 Jewish refugees and aided the entry to Israel of those who expressed the desire to settle there, cooperating for this purpose with the Jewish Agency.

IONIAN ISLANDS: Chain of islands lying off the W coast of Greece. Jewish communities existed in CORFU and ZANTE.

IOWA: US state. The first Jewish settler arrived in Dubuque in 1833, and in the late 1830's, Jewish peddlers from Poland and Germany reached I. The first Jewish community was formed in Keocuic in 1855. Congregations were organized in Dubuque and Burlington in 1857. Russian, Polish, and — to a lesser extent — German Jews began arriving there in the decade following the Civil War. During the first decade of the 20th cent., 1,500 E European immigrants were sent to 64 towns and cities in I. by the INDUSTRIAL

REMOVAL OFFICE. I.'s largest Jewish communities are in DES MOINES and Sious City. Jewish pop. (1973): 6,590

IRAN see **PERSIA**

IRAQ (formerly Mesopotamia): Country in SW Asia; for its pre-Moslem history see BABYLONIA. I. was conquered by the Arabs in 637, when its large and ancient Jewish community favored and even assisted the Arab advance in the hope that it would afford them deliverance from Sassanid persecution. Shortly after the Arab occupation, Jews expelled from Arabia settled in Kufa. For centuries, I. continued to be the center of Jewish life. The authority of both the EXILARCH and the GAON was recognized throughout the Diaspora. Jews from all parts of the world submitted their religious problems to the geonim whose answers were accepted as binding. The exilarch, although still officially recognized as head of the Jewish community, was limited in power and enforced his verdicts mainly by means of the religious ban and the imposition of fines. Moreover, the position of the Jewish authorities was undermined by the rivalry between the exilarchs and geonim which sometimes led to the interference of the caliph — to the detriment of both institutions. Internal Jewish strife was also accentuated by newly-founded sects (Issawites, Yudganites) and especially by the rise of Karaism. In the 10th and early 11th cents., the gaonate experienced a flourishing period with Saadyah as gaon of Sura, and Sherira and Hai in Pumbedita, but with the cessation of the gaonate and the closing of the two famous academies (Pumbedita in 1040), I. lost her central position in the Jewish world, although geonim are recorded in BAGHDAD as late as the 13th cent. The exilarchate was suspended in 1040, but was restored for a short period about two centuries later. The position of the Jews during the first centuries after the Arab conquest seems to have been generally good. They suffered from the restrictions laid down by OMAR, but the fact that some of these regulations had to be proclaimed anew by various caliphs indicates that they were not stringently enforced. The ordinance that Jews should be excluded from public offices was officially altered by an edict of the caliph Al-Muktadir (908) admitting them to two state offices: as physicians and bankers. The Jews also benefited from the development of Arabic culture, as is evidenced by their outstanding physicians, scientists, and scholars. A great change in the Jewish social structure took place after the Arab conquest. Because of heavy taxation on cultivated land, the Jews tended to leave agriculture and concentrate in the larger towns, especially Baghdad, BASRA, and MOSUL, where they mostly became traders and craftsmen. Some were financiers or participated in international commerce. When Benjamin of Tudela visited I. (c. 1170), he reported places with up to 15,000 Jewish inhabitants.

With the invasion of the Mongols (2nd half of the 13th cent.), who were free from religious prejudice, the condition of the Jews improved inasmuch as they were no longer discriminated against because of their faith, and even the highest state offices were now open to them. But Mongol rulers soon became converted to Islam and reintroduced discriminatory laws. The assassination in 1291 of the influential Jewish administrator and physician, SAAD ad-Daula was followed by a general attack on the Jews of I. For the following centuries, information is scanty. During the invasion of Timur (end of 14th cent.), the Jews suffered severely like the rest of the population, but the Turkish conquest (1534) seems to have bettered their condition, at least economically. Nevertheless maltreatment at the whim of local administrators was not infrequent. Turkish domination lasted, with slight interruption, until 1917, when the British took over. I.'s Jews were then largely concentrated in Baghdad where they gained a dominating position in commerce and were prominent in the professions. Jews were appointed to high government offices, and some served in the Iraqi army. The attainment of Iraqi independence in 1932 was accompanied by persecutions of the Jews. Hundreds of Baghdad Jews were killed and wounded in a pogrom during the revolt of Rashid Ali (1941). Iraqi troops participated in the 1948 attack on Israel on the central front. Despite their defeat, I. never concluded an armistice agreement with Israel. The great majority of Iraqi Jews subsequently left the country, chiefly for Israel in OPERATION EZRA AND NEHEMIAH, and their property in I. was confiscated. 123,500 reached Israel since 1948. Those that remained were subject to severe restrictions especially after the Six-Day War when the treatment of Iraqi Jews led to international protests. Jewish pop. (1976): c. 400, chiefly in Baghdad.

IRELAND: Island W of Britain. Jews may have lived in I. in the 12th and 13th cents. but none survived the expulsion of 1290. A few ex-Marranos settled in DUBLIN after 1660 and more arrived as military purveyors after the 1689 revolution. The original Sephardi group was displaced by Ashkenazim, but in the 18th cent., this community, too, declined and in 1816, there were only 3 Jewish families in Dublin and a few in the rest of I. The Dublin community was reconstituted in 1822, and there were 400 in I. in 1880. The number grew with the emigration from E Europe at the end of the 19th cent., and communities appeared at Cork, Waterford, Limerick, BELFAST, etc. The chief rabbinate was founded in 1918, its first incumbent being Yitzhak Halevi HERZOG. Jewish pop. (1973): Republic of Ireland: 4,000, mainly in Dublin; Northern Ireland, 1,400, mainly in Belfast.

IRGUN TZEVAI LEUMI (Heb. "National Military Organization"; also known from its initials as *Etzel*): Palestinian Jewish underground organization.

THE binding of Isaac to the altar as portrayed on the mosaic floor of the 6th cent. CE synagogue at Bet Alpha. *From left to right*: the two young men waiting with the ass, the ram caught in the thicket, divine intervention in the form of a hand, and Abraham laying Isaac on the altar.

It was founded in 1937 by members of BETAR as well as REVISIONISTS in the Haganah. Its original aim was retaliation against Arab attacks, but on the publication of the 1939 WHITE PAPER its target became the British authorities in Palestine, by attacking administrative personnel and executing acts of sabotage. The *Irgun* was outlawed by the Mandatory government, while the Jewish Agency dissociated itself from its activities. The organization declared a truce on the outbreak of World War II in 1939 and its leader David RAZIEL was killed in Iraq in 1941 on a British mission; he was succeeded in 1943 by Menaḥem BEIGIN. In 1944, the *Irgun* renewed its anti-British activities as a consequence of the continuing ban on Jewish immigration and organized "illegal immigration" from Europe. The British, in reply, arrested and exiled many of the movement's members. The 1946 Anglo-American Commission of Enquiry estimated its membership at 3,000–5,000. After Nov. 1947, the *Irgun* carried out a number of attacks on Arab villages but announced its entry into the Haganah on the proclamation of the state. Its military framework was completely dismantled in Sept. 1948, after a period of serious tension with the government. The successor movement in the political field was ḤERUT.

IRO see **INTERNATIONAL REFUGEE ORGANIZATION**

ISAAC: The second of the three patriarchs. His forthcoming birth was announced by angels to his parents, Abraham and Sarah, when they were advanced in years. He was circumcised when eight days old and saved by Divine intervention on Mt. Moriah when Abraham, in obedience to Divine command, was about to offer him as a sacrifice (AKEDAH). At the age of forty he married Rebekah and was sixty when his twin sons, Jacob and Esau, were born. Famine moved him from the Negev to the Philistine country, but he did not leave the Land of Israel. In his old age, his sight failed, and this enabled Jacob instead of Esau to obtain his blessing. According to tradition, he introduced the afternoon prayer (*minḥah*). Some modern critics maintain that I. was originally more prominent in the Bible story but was suppressed in favor of Abraham and Jacob.

ISAAC: Jew of Aachen, presumably a merchant, who accompanied as interpreter the embassy sent by Charlemagne to the caliph Haroun-al-Rashid in Baghdad in 797. He alone survived to deliver to the emperor, in 802, a report and the caliph's gift of an elephant.

ISAAC ARAMA see **ARAMA**

ISAAC BEN ABBA MARI (c. 1122 — after 1193): French codifier. His *Ittur Sopherim* (or *Sepher ha-Ittur*), which expounds civil and religious law, was regarded as authoritative until superseded by Jacob ben Asher's *Tur*.

ISAAC BEN ABRAHAM TROKI see **TROKI**

ISAAC BEN JOSEPH OF CORBEIL (also called *Baal ha-Ḥotem* i.e., "the man with the nose"; d. 1280): French codifier. He wrote a work on the law called *Ammude ha-Gola* or *Sepher Mitzvot Katan* ("Small Book of Precepts," generally known from its initials as *Semak*). This was an imitation of MOSES OF COUCY'S *Sepher Mitzvot Gadol* (*Semag*); it attained enormous popularity.

Illuminated page from *Shaare Dura* by Isaac ben Meir of Düren. (From a ms of 1477.)

ISAAC BEN MEIR (or **REUBEN**) **OF DÜREN** (fl: 14th cent.): German codifier, His *Sepher Shearim* (generally known as *Shaare Dura* or *Issur ve-Hetter*) was the authoritative code determining dietary laws until the publication of Caro's *Shulḥan Arukh*.

ISAAC BEN MOSES OF VIENNA (also known after his main work as Isaac *Or Zarua*; c. 1180–c. 1260): Codifier. He was born in Bohemia, studied in France and Germany (with the tosaphists), resided in several European towns, and died at Vienna. His massive *Or Zarua,* arranged on the basis of the Talmud, contains commentaries on talmudic subjects as well as earlier codifications and responsa. It carefully cites all sources quoted and makes full use of the Palestinian Talmud. It contains much material concerning the life of medieval Jews in Germany, France, and Italy.

ISAAC BEN SAMUEL OF ACRE (c. 1250–1340): Palestinian kabbalist. Leaving Acre when it was sacked in 1291, he traveled to Spain to inquire into the origins of the Zohar. There he met Moses de LEON who assured him that the original ms was in his house at Avila, which I. visited in 1305. As a result of his inquiries, he questioned the antiquity of this work, expressing his doubts in his diary *Sepher ha-Yamim*. His *Meirat Enayim* (unpublished) is an important source for the development of early Kabbalah. I. was also an exponent of "Practical Kabbalah" on which he wrote several works (all unpublished). He died in Toledo.

ISAAC BEN SAMUEL OF DAMPIERRE (or Isaac ha-Zaken, i.e., Senior; before 1115 — after 1184): French tosaphist. He succeeded his uncle Rabbenu Tam as head of the Ramerupt yeshivah and later settled at Dampierre. His *tosaphot* are quoted by his pupils, while his responsa are scattered through many contemporary works. His commentary on the Pentateuch has not survived. Interested in mysticism, he was in touch with the kabbalists of S France. His scholarly son ELHANAN was martyred in his lifetime.

ISAAC BEN SHESHET BARFAT (known as *Ribash;* 1326–1408): Spanish codifier. As a result of the 1391 persecutions, he left Spain and settled as rabbi in Algiers. His halakhic works were regarded as authoritative, and he was the author of many responsa which shed much light on contemporary circumstances among Spanish Jewry and the condition of the exiles in Africa. He opposed the study of philosophy and Kabbalah. His grave near Algiers is still a center of pilgrimage.

ISAAC ELHANAN see **SPECTOR**

ISAAC ELHANAN YESHIVA see **YESHIVA UNIVERSITY**

ISAAC THE BLIND (12th–13th cents.): Kabbalist; son of Abraham ben David of Posquières. I. was one of the earliest recorded kabbalists in Provence and Spain. Most of his teachings were transmitted orally, although a commentary on the *Sepher Yetzirah* exists in ms.

ISAAC, JULES (1877–1963): French historian. His seven-volume *Cours d'histoire* was a basic textbook in French schools and colleges. In 1936, I. was appointed inspector-general of education for France. His family was killed by the Nazis in World War II and this turned his attention to the Christian roots of anti-Semitism about which he wrote in *Jésus et Israel* and *Genèse de l'antisémitisme*. These made a significant impact in catholic circles and had an influence on Pope John XXIII in introducing the Jewish Schema in the Second Vatican Ecumenical Council.

ISAACS: US family. *SAMUEL MYER I.* (1804–1878), arrived in New York from England in 1839 and was the first minister of the B'nai Jeshurun synagogue and from 1847 of the Shaaray Tefila congregation. In 1857, he founded the first English weekly, *The Jewish Messenger,* which advocated traditional Judaism and supported the abolition of slavery. His son,

MYER SAMUEL I. (1841–1904), a judge in New York City and lecturer at New York Univ. Law School, was active in Jewish affairs. Another son, *ABRAM SAMUEL I.* (1852–1920), was professor of Hebrew and later of German at New York Univ. He was rabbi of B'nai Jeshurun congregation, Paterson, N. J., and succeeded his father as editor of *The Jewish Messenger* in 1878. *STANLEY MYER I.* (1882–1962), son of Myer Samuel I., a lawyer, was president of the borough of Manhattan, 1938–41. He has been active in Jewish and general social work in New York.

ISAACS, SIR ALFRED ISAAC (1855–1948): Australian statesman. After a distinguished career in law and politics (acting premier of Victoria, 1897; attorney-general 1905–6; High Court justice 1906–30; chief justice, 1930–1), he was the first elected governor-general of AUSTRALIA 1931–6.

ISAACS, NATHANIEL (1804–1872): British explorer. In 1825–32, he explored Natal, gaining the friendship of the Zulu king who bestowed on him the title of chief and a large tract of land (1828). His *Travels in Eastern Africa* (1836) is a classic.

ISAACS, RUFUS see **READING**

ISAIAH: Prophet. He prophesied in Jerusalem from the death of Uzziah until the middle of Hezekiah's reign (740–701 BCE). Of noble family, he was closely connected with the royal court and, especially under Hezekiah, was prominent in public affairs. According to legend, he was put to death by Manasseh. The prophet protests strongly against moral laxity; kindness, pity, and justice to the poor and underprivileged are more significant to God than offering sacrifices. The hand of God is predominant in all historical events, even Assyria serving only as an instrument of Divine anger. He opposes all treaties with neighboring states; Israel as the people of God must trust solely in Him. The people of Israel will be punished for its sins but not exterminated; a remnant will return and renew the link between God and the Land of Israel. I. is the seer of eternal peace at the end of the days when the Lord's Anointed shall judge the nations. Scholars generally divide the Book of I. into two main sections: chaps. 1–39 and 40–66. Authorship of the latter has been ascribed to a second ("deutero") I. writing during the Babylonian exile. (Some scholars maintain that a third I. wrote chaps. 56–66). In subject-matter, the Book is divisible into chaps. 1–12, prophecies to Israel and Judah and promises of a glorious future, c. 761–740 BCE; 13–23, visions concerning other nations; 24–27 are apocalyptic prophecies on the future Day of Judgment; 28–33 deal chiefly with the campaign of Sennacherib; 34–5, a short apocalypse incorporating a vision of Edom; 36–9 (= II Kings, 18:13–20:19), historical chapters in prose describing the march of Sennacherib and the mission of Merodach Baladan; 40–66, chapters of consolation and promise of future redemption. This is interrupted (52:13–53:12) by the vision of the Suffering Servant, interpreted by most Jewish commentators as referring to the Jewish people, but considered by the Christian Church as foretelling the Passion of Jesus. I.'s prophecies of redemption and comfort have been of supreme importance both in Judaism and Christianity.

ISAIAH, ASCENSION OF: Greek apocryphal book.
The first part is based on a talmudic legend that Isaiah was sawed in two on King Manasseh's orders; the second part describes the scenes witnessed by the prophet as he traverses the seven firmaments. The two sections were apparently written at different times, and date from the 2nd–3rd cents. CE. The thought is entirely Christian although embodying Jewish traditions and legends. D. Flusser has tried to trace the influence of the Dead Sea Sect in this work.

ISAIAH OF TRANI see **TRANI**

ISFAHAN: Town of W Persia. The Talmud ascribes the foundation of I. to Jews exiled by Nebuchadnezzar. Jews were settled there by the Persian Jewish Queen SHUSHAN-DUKHT. I. was the center of the pseudo-messiah ABU ISSA AL-ISFAHANI (c. 700). Its largest quarter was known as Yahudiyyah in the 10th cent. and in the 12th cent., Benjamin of Tudela reported 15,000 Jews there. In the 17th cent., the Jews were persecuted and a number forcibly converted to Islam. The present Jewish population engages in crafts and trade; its cultural situation was depressed until the liberalization of the regime and the establishment of a school by the Alliance Israélite Universelle. Jewish pop. (1969): 2,500.

ISFAHANI see **ABU ISSA AL-ISFAHANI**

ISH-BOSHETH (11th cent. BCE): Fourth son of Saul; originally called Esh-Baal. He was the only son of Saul to survive the battle of Gilboa and was crowned king of the Israelite tribes by Abner. Acceptance of David by Judah led to indecisive war between the two claimants to the throne. I. was eventually deserted by Abner and murdered by two of his generals, Baanah and Rechab, who were executed by David for regicide.

ISH-SHALOM (FRIEDMANN), MEIR (1831–1908): Scholar. A native of Slovakia, he taught Midrash at the Vienna Rabbinical Seminary and prepared critical editions of midrashic and aggadic works.

ISHMAEL: Eldest son of Abraham, his mother being Sarah's Egyptian handmaid Hagar. He was named by Divine command and was circumcised when 13 years old. After he and his mother had been excluded from Abraham's home, he lived at Paran but joined Isaac in burying Abraham. His daughter married Esau. He is traditionally the ancestor of the Arab peoples to whom the name I. was applied in the Middle Ages.

ISHMAEL BEN ELISHA (fl. 2nd cent. CE): Tanna.

He made his home in S Palestine, at Kephar Aziz near the Idumean border. He is noted for his 13 rules of exegetical interpretation of the Pentateuch (see HERMENEUTICS). He taught that "the Torah speaks in human language" and that too much should not be inferred from an apparently extraneous word or phrase. A great part of the halakhic Midrashim, including the *Mekhilta* and the *Siphre* to Numbers, comes from his school and illustrates his exegetical approach. According to some sources, he was martyred.

ISHMAEL BEN NETHANIAH (fl. 6th cent. BCE):

Military officer; murderer of GEDALIAH. After the destruction of Jerusalem by the Babylonians, he fled to Baalis, king of the Ammonites, who had for political reasons incited him to kill Gedaliah. After the murder, I. endeavored to take the remnants of the Jewish community to Ammon, but was prevented by Jonathan ben Kareah (Jer. 40–1).

ISHMAEL OF UKBARA (fl. first half of 9th cent.):

Babylonian sectarian. He founded a religious group known as the Ukbarites which seceded from the Karaite community because of differences of doctrine. I. inclined to leniency in Sabbath observance and regarded the accepted Bible text as distorted.

ISHMAELITES: People, divided into twelve tribes (Gen. 25:12 ff.), who lived in N Arabia between Egypt and the Assyrian border. The Bible refers several times to their trade with Egypt. Traditionally they are the Arab descendants of ISHMAEL and modern Arabs still claim this descent.

ISIDOR, LAZARE (1814–1888): French rabbi. He was chief rabbi of Paris from 1847 and of France from 1867. His main preoccupations were the amelioration of the conditions of Algerian Jewry and opposition to the Reform movement. He was partly responsible for the abolition of the Jewish oath in France.

*ISIDORE OF SEVILLE (c. 570–636): Archbishop of Seville; one of the fathers of anti-Jewish doctrines in the Church. About 620, he wrote *Contra Judaeos* to prove the fallacies of Judaism.

ISLAM: Form of monotheism conveyed to the ARABS by MOHAMMED, which became a world religion as a result of the Arab conquests. As in Judaism, religion and law are inextricably interwoven in I. Another parallel is that I., too, derives from a Written Law (KORAN) which is developed further in Oral Law (*ḥadith*). Traditionally, Mohammed's original legislation was markedly similar to Jewish *halakhah,* but when the Jews of MEDINA failed to acknowledge his mission, he introduced laws calculated to emphasize the differences between I. and Judaism. Biblical personages occupy a considerable place in the Koran, Abraham being regarded as the founder of monotheism and the builder of the Ka'ba, and Noah, Moses, David, and Solomon as well as Jesus are among other prophets who were the fore-runners of Mohammed. The reputed tombs of many biblical personalities (notably the Cave of Machpelah at Hebron) are revered in I. According to Moslem tradition, the mosque on the Temple mount at Jerusalem was the "farthest mosque" reached by Mohammed on his famous night journey: it is therefore regarded as a Holy Place. Islamic legend absorbed much material from the Midrash. Many religious laws are common to both Islam and Judaism (prohibitions against pigs, images; fixed times for prayers, etc.). The clashes between Mohammed and the Jews of ARABIA resulting in the latter's expulsion or extermination did not alter the basic attitude of I. toward Jews and Judaism. The Jews were not regarded as infidels against whom a Holy War was to be waged, but — like the Christians and others — as a "people of the Book" who should enjoy religious freedom in Moslem territory in return for payment of a POLL TAX. Some sects, e.g. the Shi'a, were more stern in their attitude. I. has had its influence on Judaism; the formulation of a Jewish CREED was a result of developments in I., while the medieval philosophers reflected current Arab philosophy. An extensive polemical literature developed between Jews and Moslems. The persecution of Jews by Moslems for religious reasons was rare, even discriminatory legislation often remaining unenforced.

ISPAHAN see **ISFAHAN**

ISRAEL (Latin *Palaestina* hence PALESTINE): Country in Asia. I. *Geography.* Its frontiers as determined in the Bible are approximately: on the W the Mediterranean Sea; on the E the Syrian Desert; on the S the Brook of Egypt (Wadi El-Arish) to Kadesh Barnea, thence to the Brook of Zin as far as the Valley of Zoar S of the Dead Sea, and in Transjordan from the river Arnon to Mt. Hermon, and to the Valley of Iyon. Its total surface is 17,500 sq. m. of which c. 45% is in TRANSJORDAN. The extent of the Promised Land reached the Pelusium arm of the Nile Delta, the Gulf of Elath, and the Euphrates opposite Aleppo in the E; it included most of Syria and altogether covered c. 58,000 sq. m. This entire area was occupied by the Israelites under David and Solomon (I Kings 5:4). The actual area under Jewish control fluctuated, and there were extensive gentile enclaves within Jewish territory. The Jewish National Home under the British Mandate embraced only the area W of the Jordan excluding part of Upper Galilee N of the Ladder of Tyre which was given to Lebanon. The S Negev beyond the Rafiah — Gulf of Elath line had been handed over by the Turkish government to Egypt for administration in 1906. The UN resolution of Nov. 29, 1947 recommended the establishment of a Jewish state in the larger part of the mandated area of W Palestine, although with a complex frontier. The armistice agreements of 1949 left Israel with 8,000 sq. m. — a larger area than envisioned, although still with complicated borders. After the 1967 Six-Day War she was in occupation of all Judea and Samaria, the Golan, heights, and the Sinai desert up to the Suez Canal. The greater part of the geological strata of I. are calcareous deposits of later Cretaceous and early Tertiary formations in the highlands and of Diluvial and Alluvial in the low plains. Pliocene and Pleistocene eruptions have covered all Transjordan N of the river Yarmuk and most of E Lower Galilee with a deep stratum of basalt. Some basalt belts occur in the Carmel, in E Upper Galilee, and in Transjordan S of the Yarmuk. Deep soil is found in the coastal plain and in the Jordan Rift; in the highlands, the soil-layer is thin and rocks occur over wide areas. Historical I. consists of 4 longitudinal belts — the coastal plain, the W highlands, the Jordan Rift, and the E highlands. The coastal plains are twice interrupted — by the Carmel promontory and the Ladder of Tyre. The natural regions of the coastal area are 1) the Negev plain from the S frontier to the Brook of Besor (Wadi Gaza), 2) the plain of Judea — the ancient Philistia (Pelesheth) to the Ramlah–Jaffa road, 3) the Sharon to the Crocodile River, 4) the Carmel coast to Haifa, 5) the plain of Haifa Bay (or the plain of Lower Galilee), 6) the plain of Acre to the Ladder of Tyre (now the armistice frontier), and 7) the plain of Tyre. The breadth of the coastal plain in the Negev averages 25 m., in Judea, 13 m., in the Sharon, 11 m., and elsewhere only a few miles. From the S frontier to Jaffa, sand-dunes extend 3–4½ miles inland. N of Tel Aviv there is continuous flat sand. The soil of the Negev coastal plain — where not sandy — is loess; further N it is generally red, sandy loam (suitable for citriculture). Swamps in the Sharon and Haifa Bay areas have been drained in the present century. The W highlands are divided by the plain of Jezreel and the Beersheba valley into 3 parts: Galilee, Samaria with Judea, and the Negev. Galilee is divided by a line from Acre to a point NE of Kephar Ḥananiah on the Sea of Galilee into Upper and Lower Galilee, the former being higher (Mt. Meron — 3,682 ft.) and consisting mostly of dissected highlands, hence the difficulty of movement and the ability of religious and ethnic groups to maintain an isolated existence. The highest points in Lower Galilee are only c. 1,850 ft. The region is divided into ridges by valleys running E–W; the largest of these, at Natopha, has recently been made into a reservoir for the irrigation of the lowlands. S of this valley are the Nazareth hills. Mt. Tabor (1,793 ft.) stands detached from them at the NW extremity of the Valley of Jezreel. The hot springs of Tiberias preserve a trace of former volcanic activity. The triangular Valley of Jezreel connects the coastal plain with the Jordan Valley and is of great international importance as a communications route. Its area (c. 155 sq. m.) is fertile, but water was scarce until modern irrigation: the only two sizeable brooks are the Kishon flowing into the sea near Haifa, and the Harod, discharging into the Jordan. The mountains of Samaria are more broken than those of Judea, but small valleys opening into the coastal plain make them more accessible. Samaria has a higher rainfall and hence a denser vegetation. From the Samarian highlands, Mt. Carmel (1,660 ft.) and Mt. Gilboa (1,525 ft.) extend to the NW and NE respectively. One of the valleys traversing Samaria is that of Shechem, commanded by Mt. Ebal (2,860 ft.) on the W and Mt. Gerizim (2,685 ft.) on the S; this valley is the most suitable for passage from the Sharon to the Jordan valley. The Judean hills are higher than the Samarian, ranging from 3,345 ft. near Hebron to 2,935 ft. near Jerusalem. The lower western hills of Judea are the biblical Shephelah. A few miles E of the watershed is the Judean Desert, which falls sharply to the Dead Sea. The Negev highlands consist of many ridges stretching SW–NE with gentle slopes on the NW side and a steeper descent to the SE. The highest ridges (3,050 ft.) are in the Desert of Paran; the crests of some of the ridges contain MAKHTESHIM. The Negev also includes extensive plains, notably around Beersheba. The Jordan Rift extending from the Iyon Valley to the Gulf of Elath (Akaba) is about 265 m. long (109 m. to the Dead Sea; the Dead Sea 50 m.; the Arabah 106 m.); its maximum width is 9.5 m. at Jericho. It is entirely set within mountains to the E and W (except in the vicinity of Bet Shean). Transjordan is a high plateau dissected at its W extremity; besides the mountains created by erosion there are hills formed by lava eruption. Its three natural regions are (1) Bashan in the N from the historic frontier to the river Yarmuk; an area of 4,350 sq. m. covered with basalt and divisible from W to E into Golan, the plain of Bashan, and the mountains of Bashan (the last including Trachonitis, 320 sq. m. of late lava terraces). It is separated from the next area by the river Yarmuk, the largest of the Jordan tributaries. (2) Gilead and Moab; Gilead is 62 m. long and 37 m. wide at its greatest width; total area — 1,970 sq. m., and reaching a height of 3,750 ft. at its center. The river Jabbok runs through it in a deep gorge. Gilead retains slight traces of the woodlands which existed there until the 19th cent. Moab is a plateau through the middle of which flows the river Arnon; S Moab rises to 3,800 ft. and then falls steeply to the river Zered. (3) The Mount of Edom (Seir) rises in its center to 5,720 ft. In the N of Israel, precipitation favors agriculture and the growth of forest trees. The S part and the territory to the E are desert.

II. *History*. I. is associated with the earliest stage in the history of humanity by prehistoric relics discovered in the Jordan Valley and by the GALILEE SKULL, while recent excavations in JERICHO have produced the oldest evidence of organized city life.

The first known inhabitants of I. in historic times were the CANAANITES from whom the land long took its name. By c. 3000–2500 BCE the inhabitants seem to have been largely Semitic speaking; they introduced the use of bronze and developed cities. The Bible mentions seven tribes which dominated the country. The long struggle for its control between the South (Egypt) and the North (Assyria), which — in varying political forms — was to dominate the local scene down to the 19th cent. had already begun at this time. The country was now divided into large numbers of warring city-states ruled over by petty "kings." It first enters into Jewish history with the immigration of ABRAHAM whose descendants continued to consider it their home. The TEL EL AMARNA letters throw much light on conditions in Palestine in the 15th cent. BCE and on the conquests of the Semitic "HABIRU," perhaps denoting or comprising incursions by the Israelite tribes. The latter's invasion of Palestine gave the country (henceforth "the land of Israel") its unity and historic significance. Except during the brief Crusading interlude (1099–1187), the concept of Palestine has in fact existed only in relation to Israelite and Jewish history. The Israelites' invasion was a slow and difficult process; they first established themselves in the plains, and only gradually obtained control of the hill-country; the process was completed with the capture by DAVID of Jerusalem in c. 1000 BCE. Meanwhile, the disunited and sometimes warring Israelite tribes, ruled over by regional JUDGES, were the prey of other invaders from the N and E. The most dangerous were the PHILISTINES, sea-invaders from the Aegean who obtained firm control of the Maritime Plain in the 12th cent. BCE and thence pushed inland. For a time, it seemed probable that they would subdue the whole country. But the threat forced union on the Israelite tribes at last, largely through the spiritual dominance of SAMUEL and the military genius of SAUL who established a monarchy embracing the entire country. His work was completed by his son-in-law David who finally crushed the Philistine menace and extended the boundaries of the state in all directions. The latter's son SOLOMON raised the kingdom to a great pitch of magnificence by his maritime enterprises, his lavish court, and his ambitious buildings, including a TEMPLE at Jerusalem to serve as a religious center. The heavy taxation which all this necessitated resulted in widespread discontent, and after Solomon's death, the northern tribes revolted. Henceforth, the Land of Israel was divided for many years into two rival and sometimes warring states — the smaller kingdom of JUDAH in the south, and the larger, more luxurious and more powerful kingdom of Israel (or Samaria) to the north. The latter, weakened by internal dissensions between rival dynasties and recurrent wars with the kingdom of Syria (Damascus), succumbed in 721 to the Assyr-

ians, its inhabitants being to a great extent deported and replaced by new settlers. The kingdom of Judah, more secluded geographically and more staunch spiritually and politically, for the moment escaped but succumbed in 586 before the Babylonians. Jerusalem was now destroyed, large numbers of the inhabitants deported, and the monarchy abolished. An attempt to renew organized political life in subordination to Babylonia under GEDALIAH, a member of the old royal house, was ended by his assassination (582 BCE). On the overthrow of the Babylonian Empire, the Persian king Cyrus permitted the children of the exiles, who had continued to cherish the recollection of their former land, to return and set up an autonomous center in the former territory (539). Reestablishment proved a long and painful process, and the center became, to some extent, firmly established only with the advent from the Persian court of EZRA and NEHEMIAH. The mixed population of the northern part of the country (SAMARITANS) were excluded from participation in the southern colony, which, it was feared, they would contaminate or even dominate. Henceforth, Judea (as the southern part was to be termed) was a semi-autonomous Persian vassal state, administered by the high priest of the Jerusalem Temple, while the Samaritans had their center on Mt. Gerizim. The invasions of Alexander the Great, which replaced Persian by Greek dominance, resulted in the establishment of Greek colonies along the coastal plain and around the Jordan valley and in giving the entire country a European rather than Asiatic orientation. The general political circumstances were, however, unchanged under the alternate control of the Ptolemies of Egypt and the Seleucids of Syria. This continued until in the 2nd cent. BCE the attempt of ANTIOCHUS EPIPHANES of Syria to hellenize the country by force, religiously as well as culturally, led to the HASMONEAN revolt (165) and the reestablishment for the first time since 586 of full independence under the Hasmonean house (142) which converted its rule into a monarchy (104). Successive wars of conquest, particularly under JOHN HYRCANUS (135–104), extended its rule over the whole of historic Palestine. Henceforth, though the Greeks were strong on the coastal plain, etc. and the Samaritans in the central hill-country, almost all Palestine was Jewish, GALILEE in particular being now a center of patriotic sentiment. In 63 BCE, the expansion of the Romans in the Middle East brought Palestine into their political orbit. For a period of many centuries, it was part of the Roman Empire, whether administered nominally by members of the Hasmonean dynasty, by the house of HEROD, or directly by the Roman PROCURATORS and proconsuls. There were interludes only in 55–49, when it was a vassal kingdom under Parthian control, and during the two great Jewish revolts of 66–70 CE and

General view of Valley of Jezreel.

132–5. These resulted in the depopulation of great parts of the country, non-Jewish settlers being introduced and many districts, particularly in the S, losing their Jewish character. Nevertheless, a solid Jewish life continued to maintain itself (after 135, principally in Galilee) based as formerly on AGRICULTURE and increasingly controlled by the intellectual leaders and the "Patriarchs" (presidents of the SANHEDRIN) whose authority was in due course recognized by the Roman government also. This was the period of the intense intellectual life reflected in the Mishnah, Palestinian Talmud, and Midrash. But increasing areas of the country now had a distinctly pagan aspect: for example the new administrative center on the coast, CAESAREA, in which the Jews were a minority, was one of the hubs of Roman-Greek intellectual life, and some cities of the DECAPOLIS in the N were centers of philosophical study. The Christianization of the Roman Empire in the 4th cent., the moral pressure and waves of violence which succeeded it, and the anti-Jewish legislation henceforth adopted by the emperors resulted in the complete undermining of the position of Jews in Palestine, now a focus of Christian piety. The abolition of the Patriarchate in 425 reflected as well as stimulated this process. Although the Jewish element in the population remained strong and there was considerable intellectual activity (evidenced in the development of poetry, the Midrash, and the Masorah), Jews were now a minority in the country, henceforth in most respects indistinguishable from any other Roman (or in due course Byzantine) province. The Jews assisted the Persian invaders in 614/28 and suffered when they were ejected. Under the Moslems, who conquered the country in 635/40, their role was unimportant, though an attempt was made to revive intellectual life by the establishment of a Gaonate, in imitation of that of Babylonian Jewry. Under the Ummayad caliphs, ruling from Damascus, the country prospered. Palestine was, however, neglected when the Abbasid dynasty transferred its capital to more distant Baghdad. Henceforth, once again it became the perennial bone of contention of the rival rulers of Egypt and Iraq, the consequent depopulation finally reducing the Jewish population to insignificance. The incursion of the Crusaders in 1099 was followed by the setting up of a western feudal state in the country which lasted, in a turmoil of war, only until 1187, and in 1291, the last Christian stronghold (at Acre) fell. The incursion of the Tatars in the 13th cent. added to the devastation. The country was now under Egyptian rule and without political importance. In 1517, it was conquered (with Egypt) by Turkey for whom it was usually a remote and unimportant province regarded as little more than a source of revenue. This was the period of the renewal of the Jewish settlement on any scale — in part through the arrival

after 1492 of refugees from Spain and Portugal, in part through the emergence of SAFED as the great kabbalistic center, and, to a minor extent, through the attempt of Joseph NASI (and after him Solomon IBN YAISH) to establish an autonomous center around TIBERIAS. Connection between I. and the Diaspora was maintained by the EMISSARIES from the "Four Holy Cities" of Jerusalem, Safed, Tiberias, and Hebron who traveled abroad to collect alms for the maintenance of the Jewish institutions. Local pashas were frequently corrupt and oppressive (e.g. Muhammad Ibn Farukh, Pasha of Jerusalem, who barbarously maltreated the Jews there in 1625). On the other hand, local rulers who established a firmer government (e.g. the Beduin sheikh Dahir al-Umar, who rebuilt Tiberias in 1740 with Jewish participation led by R Ḥayyim ABULAFIA, or Aḥmed al-Jazzar, governor of Acre 1775–1804) were unable to perpetuate it. In the late 18th cent., the Jewish settlement was greatly reinforced by an Ashkenazi immigration — first of Ḥasidim (1777), followed by Mitnaggedim (Perushim) whose early settlements were mainly in Galilee. Napoleon's campaign in 1799, in the course of which he called on the Jews to rally to his armies and help free the Holy Land from the Turks, proved only a momentary disturbance. The firm administration of MEHEMET ALI of Egypt, which made a promising beginning in 1831, was ended by the Powers (England, Austria, Prussia, Russia) after only 9 years. The establishment of more peaceful conditions in the Mediterranean in the 19th cent., accompanied by a vast improvement in communications, opened up Palestine more and more to outside influence. Its importance in international politics was enhanced both by the cutting of the Suez Canal and by the southerly advance of Russia. Visitors to and settlers in Palestine now became more common. Religious institutions of all faiths were established in great profusion. The Jewish population rapidly increased. The restrictions on the settlement of Jews in Jerusalem were removed, that city attaining before long a Jewish majority. Sir Moses MONTEFIORE and others began to attempt the founding of Jewish agricultural colonies. In 1882, the BILU settlers initiated a new chapter in the history of colonization (see also ZIONISM) backed up by the resources of Baron Edmond de ROTHSCHILD, while the Second ALIYAH from 1904 onward placed Jewish rural life in I., supported by a Hebrew-speaking culture, on a firm social basis. The British campaigns of 1917–18, in the course of World War I, led to the termination of Turkish rule. The administration was now entrusted by the League of Nations to Great Britain as the Mandatory Power with the object of implementing the BALFOUR DECLARATION, Sir Herbert SAMUEL becoming the first HIGH COMMISSIONER (1920–5). But in 1922, an arrangement negotiated for political reasons by Winston CHURCHILL, then the

British colonial secretary, detached Transjordan from the historic Palestine, setting it up as a separate emirate in which Jewish settlement was forbidden. The British administration, at first enthusiastically hailed by the Jewish population, proved to be temporizing. Jewish political rights were restricted, Arab objections sometimes favored if not fostered, and immigration and expansion arbitrarily limited. Nevertheless, the labor of the Jewish immigrants and the influx of Jewish capital into the country after 1918 — sometimes restricted, sometimes lavish, but never ceasing — changed the face of the country. New settlements were founded, swamps drained, forests planted, and cities created or vastly expanded (e.g. TEL AVIV). The condition of the Arab population, especially in the towns, was also benefited enormously, though in the countryside the landowning *effendi* rather than the hard-working peasant enjoyed the advantage. This economic expansion was given a powerful stimulus after the beginning of Nazi persecution in Europe in 1933 when, in spite of all obstacles, Jewish immigration, and the consequent investment of capital, increased still further. In 1936, Arab rioting stimulated by the German and especially Italian Fascist governments, anxious to embarrass England in the Middle East, developed into guerrilla warfare which lasted sporadically for some three years, but the development of the country continued without interruption. Owing to the increasing restrictions imposed by the British authorities, "illegal immigration," carefully organized, assumed considerable proportions from 1940. By 1936, the total population of Palestine was 1,367,000 of whom 384,000 were Jews. The British obstruction, even after the European tragedy of 1939–45, of the Jewish right of settlement in I. implicitly guaranteed by the Balfour Declaration, led to an intensification of activity for the establishment of a fully autonomous Jewish state. From 1945 onward, there was increasing tension, mounting bloodshed, and the beginning of large-scale clashes with the British forces, used to prevent immigration, as well as with the Arab guerrillas. Ultimately, the British government referred the problem to the UNITED NATIONS which recommended the division of Palestine into independent Arab and Jewish states (Nov. 1947). The British MANDATE terminated on May 15, 1948. The previous day the state of Israel had been proclaimed (see ISRAEL, STATE OF). The WAR OF INDEPENDENCE against the Arab coalition resulted in the extension of the area of the state beyond the boundaries proposed by the United Nations. It comprised the whole of the coastal plain, Galilee, part of Samaria, and the Negev, together with the new parts of Jerusalem and a "corridor" leading up to it. The rest of the country—including the Old City of Jerusalem and virtually the whole of Transjordan— was annexed by the kingdom of Jordan and the GAZA STRIP by Egypt. The nature of the country was changed by the flight of most of its Arabs and the arrival of a million and a half Jewish immigrants, extensive soil conservation, the foundation of settlements, extension of irrigation schemes, establishment of industries, etc. In particular, great expanses of the NEGEV have been systematically developed and settled, resulting in the extension of the effective area of the Land of Israel for the first time in the modern period over much of the south, including an outlet to the Indian Ocean, via the Red Sea, at Elath.

ISRAEL, KINGDOM OF: The northerly of the two kingdoms into which Palestine was divided after the revolt led by JEROBOAM against REHOBOAM, Solomon's son and successor, in 933 BCE. It is sometimes called the kingdom of SAMARIA after the city which became its capital c. 890. The seceding tribes were led by Ephraim, which remained predominant and to which most of the kings belonged; the other tribes were Manasseh, Issachar, Zebulun, Naphtali, Asher, Dan and (in Transjordan) Reuben, Gad, and part of Manasseh. The extent of the kingdom of I. was thus far larger than that of the kingdom of JUDAH, and its wealth and political importance correspondingly greater. On the other hand, born in violence, it perpetuated this tradition and was the subject of constant revolution. In the course of its existence of 210 years it had 19 kings, belonging to 9 dynasties, of whom 10 died by violence and 7 ruled for less than two years. Settled conditions were established only under the House of OMRI, which maintained itself under 4 successive monarchs (887–843), and the five rulers of the House of JEHU (843–744). At this period, the kingdom reached its greatest power, conducting successful campaigns against neighboring states, enjoying much luxury, and at one time extending its sway as far as the Gulf of Akaba. But its strength was sapped in consequence of perpetual warfare with the kingdom of Damascus (Syria), and both ultimately fell before the advancing power of Assyria. The capture of Samaria by Sargon in 721 BCE ended the history of the kingdom of I., though some of its traditions were preserved thereafter by the SAMARITANS. The religious life of the king-

KINGS OF ISRAEL :

Jeroboam (933–912)	Jehoahaz (816–800)
Nadab (912–911)	Jehoash (800–785)
Baasha (911–888)	Jeroboam II (785–745)
Elah (888–887)	Zechariah (744)
Zimri (887)	Shallum (743)
Omri (887–876)	Menahem (743–736)
Ahab (876–853)	Pekahiah (736–735)
Ahaziah (853)	Pekah (735–730)
Jehoram (853–843)	Hoshea (730–721)
Jehu (843–816)	

The Proclamation of the Establishment of the State of Israel being read by David Ben Gurion.
Tel Aviv, 14 May, 1948.

dom of I. was on a relatively low level—partly as a result of the deliberate policy of its first rulers who set up local sanctuaries in order to divert their subjects from Jerusalem. Only a minority of the biblical prophets (e.g. Hosea and Amos) worked in the N kingdom; however, the Book of Kings gives lengthy accounts of Elijah and Elisha's endeavors to check idolatry and social injustice

ISRAEL, STATE OF: *History:* In its early years I. was faced by formidable problems. The first was that of defense. I.'s long land frontiers made her particularly vulnerable to assault—either by direct attack or infiltration. Sabotage and theft originating mainly from the Gaza Strip and from Jordan were a constant nuisance, and did not cease despite Israel reprisal raids. Against direct attack, immense efforts were made to build up and equip the armed forces (TZEVA HAGANAH LE-ISRAEL). Its efficiency was shown in the SINAI CAMPAIGN, the SIX-DAY WAR, the YOM KIPPUR WAR, etc.: the defeat of the Egyptian forces, the destruction of Egypt's bases, and the capture of large quantities of war material on the first two occasions deferred the assault on I. from three sides planned by President Nasser and gave I. much needed breathing-spaces. It also won I. much popular sympathy throughout the world and opened up to shipping the Gulf of Elath twice blocked by Egypt.

However, Arab pressures—especially after 1973—led to considerable international isolation. I.'s population grew rapidly. At its inception, I. adopted a unique law conferring citizenship on every Jew immediately upon landing on I. soil. Within the first three years the Jewish population was doubled (from 650,000 to 1,300,000) through mass immigration (ALIYAH). This was accompanied by severe economic difficulties that were overcome only to some extent after a prolonged struggle. Immense sums had to be spent on settlement without an immediate increase in production. Inflation was rampant and the public services were overworked. Nevertheless, the new immigrants were slowly integrated with the former Jewish residents. I.'s own Arab population of some quarter million was also slowly integrated but the accretion of a million further Arabs, many of them refugees, after the Six-Day War posed new problems and led to new tensions, fostered by external Arab forces. New towns and villages were built and large areas of land brought under cultivation for the Jewish population throughout the entire period. In the selection, transportation, and settlement of immigrants, the JEWISH AGENCY played a leading part, as also in the raising of the necessary sums abroad. Some capital, especially for industry, was provided by private investors, but much of the development was

The Atomic Reactor at Nahal Soreq, where nuclear energy is harnessed in the service of Peace.

undertaken by the government and other public bodies. Their aim was to increase I.'s capacity to absorb new immigrants (e.g. through extension of irrigation, the opening up of the Negev to agriculture, and exploitation of minerals) and to extend its public services and utilities (such as roads, railways, and electric power production and distribution) in order to keep up with the rapidly expanding population. A constant effort was made to increase self-sufficiency in raw materials and agriculture as well as in manufactured goods. The vast capital required was raised the raising of the necessary sums abroad. Some from a variety of sources—private investment, US grants, German REPARATIONS until the mid-1960's, the sale of I. government bonds (particularly in the US), loans from foreign banks, and large sums in gifts from Jewish communities in the Diaspora. In consequence, Israel's production slowly increased, as

did its exports, which rose from $28.6 million in 1949 to $1,000 million in 1972. I.'s external debt stood at $5,000 million in 1973 and it was rising. Much effort was needed in the first years of the new state to establish a stable and effective government on a secular and democratic basis. A single-chamber legislative assembly, the KNESSET, was created with a broad franchise. Owing to the adoption of an extreme form of proportional representation, a multiplicity of political parties was returned, with inevitable Cabinet coalitions. The MAPAI party remained the strongest single political party, obtaining a majority in the Knesset by successive coalitions with the religious parties, some of the parties of the right, and then of the left. In the late 1960's it consolidated its position by merging with other left-wing groups to form the ISRAEL LABOR PARTY. In the 1973 general elections, it obtained (together with MAPAM), 51 seats. The

executive was kept under popular control and
a fiscal and budgetary system laid down. A new
administration was recruited and trained, while the
independence of the judiciary was assured. The social
services were developed and unemployment kept
within bounds. Compulsory and free elementary
education was introduced, while the Hebrew language
was spread among the new immigrants. Higher
education was fostered and many advances achieved
in the fields of LITERATURE, the fine arts, ARCHI-
TECTURE, and MUSIC.

Structure: The state of Israel is a democratic republic. The first president, elected by the Knesset,
was Chaim Weizmann (1948–52), who was succeeded
by Yitzhak Ben-Zvi (1952–63), Zalman SHAZAR
(1963–73) and Aharon Katzir (from 1973). The seat of
government is in Jerusalem where the Knesset sits.
There is no written constitution, but the functions of
the president, the Knesset, and the courts are defined in
special laws. The judiciary consists of three grades of
courts that have both civil and criminal jurisdiction.
The lowest rank is composed of 17 magistrates' courts
in 16 towns; the middle rank consists of 3 district
courts; the apex is the Supreme Court with judges sitting collectively or in panels. The Supreme Court also
sits as a high court to hear cases against the government. There are no juries. The magistrates act as examining magistrates for criminal cases heard in the
district courts. The judiciary is appointed by the
president on the recommendation of a special nomin-
ating committee.

Population: The population of I. in Nov. 1948,
was 782,000 of whom 713,000 were Jews. The figure
in 1975 was 3,490,000 of whom 2,953,000 were Jews.
The rapid increase of the Jewish population is due
largely to immigration. In spite of an intensive "back
to the land" movement, the majority of the Jewish
population lives in towns and cities: the majority of
the Arab population lives in villages. The largest cities
are Tel Aviv-Jaffa, Haifa, the capital, Jerusalem, and
Ramat-Gan. There are 15 other towns. Of the
476,000 Arabs in Israel, 75% are Moslem and the remainder Christian. About 40% of the Christian Arabs
are Greek Catholic, the rest are mostly Greek Orthodox. There are also 33,000 Druze. *Agriculture*: The
Jewish villages are of three types: (a) the moshavot (see
MOSHAVAH); (b) the MOSHAVE OVEDIM; and (c) the
KIBBUTZIM and Kevutzot (see KEVUTZAH). The
numbers of each type are as follows:

Type	No. of settlements	No. of inhabitants
a) Moshave Ovedim, and Moshavim Shittuphiyyim	376	134,300
b) Kibbutzim and Kevutzot	235	102,654

(See also AGRICULTURAL SETTLEMENT.) The largest landowners prior to 1948 were the JEWISH
NATIONAL FUND, the Palestine government, and the
Awqaf (Moslem religious trusts). Since 1948, large
areas of abandoned Arab land have been taken over
by the I. government in trust and leased to the Jewish
National Fund.

AGRICULTURAL PRODUCTION — SELECTED ITEMS

in tons, except where otherwise designated

	1948/49	1961/62	1971/2
Wheat	21,200	51,700	301,400
Barley and oats	20,900	49,500	32,800
Sorghum	3,000	43,400	40,400
Hay	40,600	103,600	132,500
Green fodder and silage	372,800	1,616,400	15,000
Groundnuts	300	12,400	19,800
Cotton lint	—	16,070	40,300
Tobacco	600	2,240	1,000
Sugar beet	—	221,000	248,500
Vegetables and potatoes	106,000	391,500	806,800
Citrus fruit	272,700	532,500	1,552,800
Grapes (table and wine)	17,800	72,500	88,400
Olives	10,700	44,800	27,000
Bananas	3,500	49,200	41,500
Other fruit	7,200	87,500	206,600
Milk (kilolitres)	85,950	359,400	519,200
Eggs (thousands)	242,500	1,273,000	1,404,700
Poultry	5,040	66,400	142,100
Beef	2,010	22,450	33,700
Fish	3,500	16,400	27,100

Industrial Raw Materials: I. has no known iron or
coal of commercial value. Petroleum deposits covering a small percentage of the country's annual consumption have been discovered near the S coastal
plain. Under the Ottoman regime, industry in Palestine
was limited to olive oil pressing, weaving of woolen
textiles, flour milling, lime burning, and salt evaporation. Under the British Mandate, potash evaporation
at both ends of the Dead Sea was developed by a
concession company that has now been taken over by
the I. government and operates solely at the S end
of the Dead Sea near Sodom. The copper waste
from the ancient mines near Elath were processed
abroad to produce copper concentrates but the mines
were closed in 1976. The low-grade phosphate
deposites in the Negev are being exploited and
a heavy chemicals industry has been established
at Haifa where the refineries, built under the Mandate to refine oil brought by pipeline from Iraq,
now refine oil brought by sea. Other mineral raw
materials are exploited for the building industry—
such as the manufacture of cement for which
three factories have been established. The low
grade of many deposits, their distance from the coast,
and the absence of rail facilities in the south often
impede profitable exploitation. Many industries—
such as the metal industries—depend on imported
materials; others, such as the fruit- and vegetable-
canning industries, use mainly local materials. Others

such as the textile and clothing, paper, and pharmaceutical industries depend partly on local but mainly on imported raw materials. As in Europe, the diamond industry is based on imported materials.

Industrial Production: The value in Israel pounds of industrial products manufactured in 1958 and 1963 was as follows:

ESTIMATED VALUE OF INDUSTRIAL OUTPUT

in IL millions 1965 *prices*

	1964	1971
Machinery and metal products	869.5	1,908
Foodstuffs	1,400	2,705
Textiles	805.5	1,309
Wood and wood products	374	447
Chemicals	464.5	1,316
Diamonds	367	1,175
Paper, printing and publishing	279	624
Rubber and plastics	170.5	612
Leather and leather goods	159	132
Mining and quarries	142	339
Total	5,031	10567

Capital: Under the Ottoman regime, capital accretion was low in Palestine, being almost entirely agricultural. There was some Jewish and non-Jewish investment in Palestine's industries under the Mandate. The government in the early years preferred public to private investment. The Government Investment Center has, however, done much to encourage private investment in I. through tax exemptions, guarantees of repatriation of dividends and capital, and other facilities. Mixed companies are increasingly popular, the foreign participants providing the machinery, the raw materials, and the experience, the I. participants providing the land, the buildings, and the labor. Many of I.'s infant industries have only been able to withstand competition from cheaper imported products by means of a tariff wall and this has had to be cut as a result of the agreement with the Common Market.

Banks: In 1973, 21 commercial banks operated in I. Outstanding are the BANK LEUMI LE-ISRAEL, Palestine Discount Bank, Union Bank of I., and Workers' Bank, while foreign banks are represented by Barclays Bank and Holland Bank Union. Supplementing the activities of these banks were 18 cooperative credit societies. The BANK OF I. opened in 1954 as the national central bank while the Post Office bank receives and makes payments in behalf of the government.

Labor: Most of I.'s labor force consists of immigrants who have had to be retrained for their new jobs. There is no scheme of unemployment insurance. There are laws for the protection of women and children in industry and for compulsory insurance against industrial accidents under a national insurance scheme. The HISTADRUT (General Federation of Labor) enters into periodic wage agreements with the MANUFACTURERS' ASSOCIATION and these ensure automatic increases when the cost-of-living index rises. The Histadrut in addition to being a federation of trade unions is itself an agricultural and industrial producer on a very large scale. Nearly all the COOPERATIVES are affiliated with the *Histadrut*. Other unions include *Ha-Poel ha-Mizrahi* which cooperates closely with the *Histadrut,* the National Workers' Organization, and the *Poale Agudat Israel.*

Trade: I., since its inception, has been subjected to an Arab blockade on all its land frontiers and to interference by Egypt with its shipping using the Suez Canal and the Gulf of Akaba. It has managed, nevertheless, to develop new markets and find new supplies. It has entered into trade agreements with many countries, sometimes on a barter basis. As a country in process of development, I. imports considerable quantities of capital goods. Until its exports increase, there must inevitably be a heavy adverse trade balance. This has been partly covered by receipts from the tourist traffic, I. shipping and air lines, foreign investment, loans, gifts and German reparations. I., nevertheless, has been chronically short of foreign exchange, even for the purchase of raw materials for its industries. Food was rationed for several years but the controls were lifted after 1953.

Communications: I.'s main road system was largely inherited from the Mandate, with important additions since 1948. Most of the bus services are owned by cooperatives composed of the bus-drivers themselves. The railroads are state-owned and were inherited from the Mandate and have been extended into the Northern Negev. The total length of line in operation is only 425 miles which makes it very expensive to run. Road transport competition is also severe. The main port of the country is at Haifa, built under the Mandate but since improved through additions on the Kishon river. It includes a 10,000 ton floating dock and a large grain silo. The port at Elath has been expanded and handles trade with Asia and E Africa. The Ashdod port started operation in 1965 and by 1972 handled 40% of the country's total. On its inauguration, the Tel Aviv and Jaffa ports were closed. I.'s merchant marine has been built up almost entirely since 1948, to a large extent through the use of German reparation funds. In 1973 there were ships with a capacity of 3,435,076 tons. The main civil airport of I. at Lydda (Lod) was built by the Mandatory Government and has since been expanded. There are subsidiary airfields at Haifa, Tel Aviv, Jerusalem, Elath, etc.

Health: The rapid influx of immigrants with little medical control before arrival did not lead to any epidemics after the creation of the state. There have

Pupils in Israel Vocational School studying by television.

Schools: 7,000, Orthodox yeshivot: 19,000; Higher Education: 50,000.

Culture: Hebrew is the language of the country, although Arabic is officially recognized in the Arab areas, in the Knesset, and the law courts. Book printing and publishing are well developed in I. Israel ranks second in the world for the number of titles in proportion to the population. Over 3,000 books are published annually, of which 25% are translations. Several theater companies play, mostly in Tel Aviv, of which the oldest and largest is *Ha-Bimah*. There are some ballet groups, while folk dancing and choral singing are popular, especially in the villages. The Israel Philharmonic Orchestra has a world-wide reputation. There are smaller orchestras in Jerusalem, Haifa, Ramat Gan, and in certain rural areas. The many motion picture theaters in the towns and larger villages are well attended. A few films are produced each year in I. The large amount of building is leading to the establishment of a specific type of ARCHITECTURE, using local materials and adapted to Mediterranean climatic conditions. The larger cities have ART museums and art schools.

Imbal dance group performing before participants at Rehovoth Conference for Developing Countries

always been many hospitals in Palestine run by voluntary organizations, including the *Histadrut's Kupat Ḥolim*, the Hadassah Organization, and religious (both Jewish and Christian) bodies. Some of these continue till today; others have been acquired by the state which has built additional hospitals. Health insurance in I. dates from Mandatory days and is voluntary through *Kupat Ḥolim* and smaller organizations. Special attention is devoted to endemic diseases, such as ophthalmia, typhoid, diphtheria, tuberculosis, and polio. Malaria and polio have been almost stamped out and tuberculosis has shown a great decrease.

Education (for schools and universities see EDUCATION): Many newcomers to I. spend the first four months after arrival learning Hebrew in intensive courses (*Ulpanim*), some residential, publicly maintained in different parts of Israel. In addition there are especially in Jerusalem many *yeshivot*, etc. of the traditional type for talmudic study. Adult education is highly developed. The numbers of students in 1973 were as follows: Kindergarten: 137,000; Elementary Schools: 528,000; Secondary Schools: 65,000; Vocational Schools: 65,000; Agricultural

Press and Radio: There is a vigorous PRESS. The most influential periodicals are in Hebrew but many papers appear in other languages for Arabs and for new immigrants who are still learning Hebrew. The number of newspapers published is as follows:

	Hebrew	*Other Languages*
Dailies	11	13
Other publications	310	240

The Israel Broadcasting Authority supervises the television service (in Hebrew and Arabic) and the broadcasting programs. It has its head offices in Jerusalem and branch offices in Tel Aviv and Haifa (it broadcasts programs for listeners in Israel, an Arabic service, and programs beamed overseas); and *Gale Tzahal* (the Defence Forces station), operated for the troops by the I. army. Television for schools started in 1966 and is supervised by the Ministry of Education.

Foreign Relations: I. maintained diplomatic and consular relations with over 100 countries but many of these severed relations around the time of the Yom Kippur War and in 1974 Israel had relations with 70 countries. I. is represented abroad by 60 embassies and other missions as well as by a delegation at the UNITED NATIONS. I. participates in the work of the various United Nations agencies (*UNESCO, ILO, FAO, WHO*, etc), making use of experts supplied by these agencies. I.'s experts are also serving in other countries under similar auspices.

Public Finance: The ordinary annual budget for the year 1974 amounted to IL 35 billion. An increasing proportion of the budget is raised through income tax and other forms of direct taxation. The rapid increase of population in the first few years of the state, unaccompanied by an immediate and comparable increase in production, produced severe inflation. The I. pound, once at parity with the pound sterling (IL 1 = $2.80) has fallen and at the end of 1976 IL 8.75 = $1.00. The heaviest expenditures are on defense, education, health and social welfare, and the promotion of agriculture, industry, and exports.

Local Government: The primary unit of self-government is the village; most have elected committees with elementary powers of taxation. The large villages and smaller towns have local councils, many dating from the early days of the Mandate. The cities and larger towns have municipal councils, some dating from the Ottoman regime. Since the establishment of the state, an increasing number of villages has been grouped under elected rural district councils. There are no elected councils for the local government of larger areas.

ISRAEL LABOR PARTY: Israel workers' party formed in 1968 by a merger of the Alignment for the Unity of Israel's workers (an alignment of the MAPAI and AHDUT AVODAH parties formed in 1965) and RAFI. In 1969 it signed an alignment with MAPAM. At its foundation I.L.P. controlled 59 seats in the KNESSET (51 in 1973) and was the dominant party in the Israel coalition government.

ISRAEL (formerly Palestine) **LAND DEVELOPMENT COMPANY:** Company founded in 1908 by the World Zionist Organization, after the opening of the Palestine Office in Jaffa by Arthur Ruppin. Its main task was to purchase land from the Arabs for the Jewish National Fund and for private investors. When the state of Israel was established in 1948, some 45% of all Jewish-owned land had been redeemed by the Company. Its share capital amounted in 1945 to LP. 318,000 plus LP. 111,000 of the Jewish National Fund and the *Keren ha-Yesod*. The land purchasing activities of the company extend to both rural and urban districts, the latter for the establishment of workers' quarters. Among the main undertakings of the I.L.D.C. is the acquisition of the Huleh concession, which was sold to the Jewish National Fund soon after the establishment of the state. Its central office is now in Jerusalem, and its administration is largely influenced by the Jewish National Fund and the *Keren ha-Yesod*.

ISRAEL MUSEUM: Museum in Jerusalem opened in 1965. It includes the BEZALEL Museum, the Billy Rose Garden of modern sculpture, the Samuel Bronfman Biblical and Archeological Museum, and the Shrine of the Book housing the DEAD SEA SCROLLS.

General view of the Israel Museum, Jerusalem.

The Israel Philharmonic Orchestra performing at the opening ceremony of the Mann Auditorium in Tel Aviv, 1957.

ISRAEL PHILHARMONIC ORCHESTRA: Orchestra founded in 1936 (as the Palestine Symphony Orchestra) by the violinist Bronislaw HUBERMANN and inaugurated by Arturo Toscanini. It comprises an average of 100 musicians, many of them former first-desk players from leading European orchestras. Its center is Tel Aviv but it gives concerts throughout the country. Its guest conductors and soloists include world-famous musicians, and the ensemble has an international reputation. The IPO has toured outside I. on many occasions.

ISRAEL BEN ELIEZER see **BAAL SHEM TOV**

ISRAEL BEN SAMUEL ASHKENAZI OF SHKLOV (c. 1770–1839): Talmudist. A pupil of the Vilna Gaon, he was preacher in Shklov and co-editor of the Gaon's glosses to the *Shulḥan Arukh*. In 1809, he settled in Palestine, opening a yeshivah at Safed. I. was head of the Safed group of the Gaon's disciples who were called *perushim* to distinguish them from the local Ḥasidim. In 1837, he moved to Jerusalem where he became rabbi of the Ashkenazi community. His chief work, *Peat ha-Shulḥan,* supplements the *Shulḥan Arukh* with a codification of laws appertaining to life in Palestine which had been omitted by Joseph Caro.

ISRAEL BEN SHABBETAI OF KOZIENICE ("The Kozienicer Maggid"; c. 1737–1814): Ḥasidic leader and scholar. He settled in the townlet of Kozienice in central Poland and became famous for his wonder-cures effected by means of prayers and amulets. Ḥasidic legend ascribes the failure of Napoleon's Russian expedition to I.'s prayers.

ISRAEL OF RUZHIN see **RUZHIN**

ISRAEL, JAMES ADOLF (1848–1926): German surgeon. He was responsible for important developments in internal surgery, especially of the kidneys.

ISRAELI, ISAAC BEN JOSEPH (d. after 1330): Spanish scholar and astronomer. He was the author of *Yesod Olam,* an encyclopedic survey of contemporary astronomical and cosmographical knowledge together with mathematical information, an explanation of the Jewish calendar, and a chronology of Jewish history.

ISRAELI, ISAAC BEN SOLOMON (known in the Middle Ages as Isaac Judaeus; c. 850 — c. 950): Philosopher, biblical commentator, and physician. A native of Egypt, he was court physician to the caliphs there and in Kairouan. At the request of Caliph Ubaid-Allah he wrote (in Arabic) eight medical works, including standard treatises on pharmacology, fevers, and ophthalmology, which were subsequently translated into Hebrew, Latin, and Spanish and were widely reputed in the Middle Ages. He also wrote on logic and psychology as well as a commentary to *Sefer Yetzirah,* now thought to have been written by his pupil Dunash Ben Tamim. I. was one of the first Jewish medieval philosophers and endeavored to reconcile Jewish and Neoplatonic traditions.

ISRAELI, ISAAC D' (1766–1848): English author; son of an Italian-born merchant. His first essays, published in 1786, were among the earliest Jewish contributions to English prose-literature. His most important works include *Curiosities of Literature,*

Jozef Israels: *Self-portrait* (Amsterdam Municipal Museum).

which earned him a great reputation, and *Commentary on the Life and Reign of Charles I.* In 1813, D. was fined by the Sephardi synagogue in London for refusing to serve as warden. He later withdrew from the congregation and had his children (including the future Earl of BEACONSFIELD) baptized. His *Genius of Judaism* (published anonymously) was written in an unfriendly spirit.

ISRAELITES see **ISRAEL**

ISRAELITISCH - THEOLOGISCHE LEHRAN-STALT: Rabbinical and teachers' seminary in Vienna, founded in 1893. It continued in existence until the annexation of Austria by Germany in 1938. Its approach to Judaism was traditional.

ISRAELITISCHE ALLIANZ ZU WIEN see **ALLIANZ**

ISRAELS, JOZEF (1824–1911): Dutch painter. After studying in Holland and Paris, he began to paint historical subjects but later turned for his subject-matter to the life of the peasants and fisherfolk. He is considered the most significant figure in Dutch art since the 17th cent., and nearest in spirit to Rembrandt, on whom he modeled himself. He was consciously Jewish, and from the 1880's several of his best-known paintings dealt realistically with Jewish themes (e.g. *The Torah Scribe, Jewish Wedding,* etc.). His son *ISAAC I.* (1865–1934) was a sophisticated impressionist painter.

ISRU ḤAG (Heb. "Bind the festival offering"; cf. Ps. 118:27): Term applied to the semi-festal day after Passover, Pentecost, and Tabernacles. In Second Temple times it was the day when the pilgrims left Jerusalem for their homes.

ISSACHAR: Fifth son of Leah by Jacob. His descendants numbered 64,309 at the end of the desert wanderings, constituting the third largest tribe. They inherited land between Mt. Tabor and the Jordan including much of the fertile Valley of Jezreel. Apparently some of the tribe was saved from the Assyrian exile, and men of I. answered Hezekiah's summons to celebrate Passover at Jerusalem.

ISSERLEIN, ISRAEL BEN PETHAHIAH (1390–1460): German talmudist. He was rabbi at Marburg and from 1445, at Wiener-Neustadt which, through him, became a center of learning. His principal work is the collection of responsa *Terumat ha-Deshen.* I. was the leading halakhic authority of his time.

ISSERLES, MOSES (known as *Rema*; c. 1525–1572): Codifier. A man of means, he founded and maintained a yeshivah in his native Cracow and presided over it until his death. Upon the appearance of Joseph CARO's *Bet Yoseph,* which was a halakhic codification based on Sephardi authorities and tradition, I. wrote *Darkhe Mosheh* expounding the viewpoint of Ashkenazi scholars. When Caro's popular abridgement *Shulḥan Arukh* (i.e., "The Prepared Table") appeared, I. wrote his *Mappah* ("Tablecloth") incorporating the Ashkenazi practice. It was through I.'s additions to the *Shulḥan Arukh*

Salom Italia's etching of Manasseh ben Israel.

The ark in the Sephardi synagogue at Pesaro.

that the work was eventually accepted as authoritative among the Ashkenazim. I. also wrote on Kabbalah, philosophy, etc.

ISTANBUL see **CONSTANTINOPLE**

ITALIA, SALOM (fl. 17th cent.): Artist and miniaturist. Member of a family of printers at Mantua, he settled in Amsterdam where he engraved portraits of Manasseh ben Israel, etc. as well as copper-plate borders for the *Ketubbah* and *Megillah*.

ITALY: The only country of W Europe in which the settlement of the Jews has been continuous from before the Christian era to the present day. Jews were first settled there in the 2nd cent. BCE–at first in ROME and thereafter in the southern ports and along the trade routes. The presence of Jews is known in at least 40 places before the close of the Classical Period. CATACOMBS provide graphic evidence of their way of life and high degree of cultural assimilation. Their condition seriously deteriorated with the Christianization of the Roman Empire in the 4th cent. Nevertheless, they were protected by the POPES against the worst excesses and their fundamental rights were maintained. In the Dark Ages the great center of Jewish life was in the south, in BARI, etc., and I. played a great part in the transmission of talmudic scholarship to N Europe. The S Italian communities were mainly engaged in wholesale trade, from which they were later eliminated by the Venetians, and in handicrafts, particularly dyeing and silk-weaving. In SICILY, there was a large proletarian community of manual laborers. At the end of the 13th cent., persecution in the kingdom of NAPLES drove large numbers of Jews to Christianity. At this period, however, Jewish loan-bankers began to be invited for the public convenience into the towns of central and N Italy. This was the origin of the famous

Italian Jewish family in the 15th century. (From a painting of the school of Mantegna, formerly in the church of the Madonna della Vittoria at Mantua.)

communities of FLORENCE, VENICE, MANTUA, FERRARA, etc. In 1492 the Spanish authorities expelled the Jews from Sicily and in 1541, from the kingdom of Naples to which they never returned. Elsewhere in this period the Jews lived on the whole in affluent and comfortable conditions and both influenced and were influenced by the RENAISSANCE. With the Counter-Reformation their position deteriorated. Pope PAUL IV's bull *cum nimis absurdum* (1555) instituted the GHETTO and the concomitant oppression in Rome and the Papal States, this policy being later imitated all over the country. The Ghetto Period lasted until the end of the 18th cent. EMANCIPATION was introduced at the time of the French Revolutionary Wars (1796–7), was canceled on the fall of Napoleon (1814–5), and was reestablished with the consolidation of united I. (1840–70). In the course of the next generation, Jewish emancipation was more complete in I. than in any other country of Europe. The position of the Jews was on the whole maintained in the early years of FASCISM (1922 ff.) but in 1938, after MUSSOLINI concluded an alliance with Nazi Germany, a thoroughgoing anti-Semitic policy was adopted, Jews being removed from office and many emigrating. I. did not imitate Nazi brutality, but during the German occupation of N Italy in 1943–5 violent persecution began and some thousands of Italian Jews were deported to the death-camps. The blow seriously affected Italian Jewish life. Some 3,000 Italian Jews have settled in Israel. Jewish pop. (1973): 33,000.

ITHAMAR: Priest. Together with his brother Eleazar, he succeeded his father Aaron in the priestly office.

ITO see **JEWISH TERRITORIAL ORGANIZATION**

ITUREA: Ancient Syrian state. The Bible refers to the sons of Jetur who fought those Israel tribes settled in Transjordan (I Chron. 5:19). The Itureans became independent in the following cent., their territory including part of Galilee and the towns of Chalcis (the capital) and Heliopolis. Pompey and Mark Antony, however, reduced its extent, the beneficiaries being Herod and his descendants. The country was later absorbed into Syria.

ITZIG, DANIEL JAFFE (1723–1799): German financier. Together with two Jewish partners, he minted coins in behalf of the Prussian state during the Seven Years' War. In 1771, he was the sole purveyor to the Prussian mint and in 1797, court banker. I. was a lover of learning and amassed an important collection of Jewish books and mss. In 1764, he became *parnas* of the Berlin Jewish community and was subsequently the representative of all Prussian Jewry. He was responsible for the foundation in 1778 of the Jewish Free School *Ḥinnukh Nearim*.

IVRIT BE-IVRIT (Heb. "Hebrew in Hebrew"): Method of teaching Hebrew by actual speaking without the intermediacy of another language. It was first introduced c. 1874 in an Alliance Israélite Universelle school at Constantinople upon the initiative of Nissim BEHAR. Behar introduced the method into Palestine in 1883 where it was widely taken up by Jewish educational institutions under the inspiration

Daniel Jaffe Itzig.
(Medal by A. Abrahamson.)

of Eliezer BEN-YEHUDAH. By the beginning of the 20th cent. it had become accepted in many Jewish schools outside Palestine as well.

IYYAR: Second month of the religious calendar and the eighth month of the civil calendar; it consists of 29 days. In the Bible it is also called "the month of Ziv." *Iyyar* 5 is Israel INDEPENDENCE DAY; "Second Passover" falls on *Iyyar* 14: LAG BA-OMER on *Iyyar* 18.

IZATES II (d. 55 CE): King of ADIABENE, son of HELENA and Monobaz I. Converted to Judaism, he influenced his mother to follow his example and sent his sons to Jerusalem to be educated.

IZFA see **STUDENT ZIONIST ORGANIZATION**

IZMIR (Smyrna): Turkish port. Its Jewish community is mentioned in the New Testament. Its numbers dwindled in the Middle Ages but grew with the settlement of Spanish refugees after 1492. In the 17th and 18th cents., the Jews occupied a pivotal position in the city's economy, and their cultural life was on a high level. Many distinguished scholars resided there. Shabbetai Tzevi was born in I. which became a center of his movement. The community declined from the late 19th cent., especially after World Wars I and II, many of its members emigrating to Israel. Jewish pop. (1973): 2,000.

J

JABBOK: River rising from a spring near Rabbath Ammon, crossing Gilead, and flowing into the Jordan at Damya, a distance of 62 m. Jacob wrestled with the angel by the ford of the J. (Gen. 32) and the river marked the frontier between the Ammonites and Amorites (Deut. 2:31–7; 3:16). It is now entirely within the kingdom of Jordan.

JABESH GILEAD: Ancient Palestinian city situated in the Gilead region of Transjordania. Because its inhabitants refused to join the Israelite tribes in the war with Benjamin (Judg. 21), they were all put to the sword with the exception of 400 virgins who were given to the ·remnants of the Benjamites in order to perpetuate the tribe. In the 11th cent., Saul saved its citizens from the threat of Nahash the Ammonite that he would put out their right eyes. After Saul's death at the hands of the Philistines, the people of J. G., in gratitude, rescued his body from indignity.

JABIN: Name of two kings of Hazor who fought against the Israelites. The first commanded the coalition of kings who were defeated by Joshua in N Palestine. The later king headed another coalition whose army, commanded by Sisera, was defeated by some of the Israelite tribes led by Deborah and Barak. Some scholars hold that these two episodes are varying traditions referring to the same incident.

JABNEEL: Israel village in E Lower Galilee. Founded by ICA in 1901, its development was slow until water was discovered in the vicinity in the 1930's. Pop. (1972): 1,427. Two towns of that name are mentioned in the Bible (Josh. 15:11; 19:33); the one in Galilee was fortified by Josephus in the war against Rome, while the other one corresponded to the later JABNEH.

JABNEH (Gk. Jamnia): Ancient Palestinian city S of Jaffa. Mentioned in the Bible as JABNEEL, it lay in the territory of Judah and was fortified by Uzziah as a barrier against Philistine expansion. J. became hellenized in the Second Temple Period, was an object of strife during the Hasmonean wars, and was constituted an autonomous city under Pompey. After the destruction of the Second Temple, R Johanan ben Zakkai opened an academy there; he assembled a group of scholars and reestablished the Sanhedrin which sat in J. until the Bar Kokhba revolt. From the late 2nd cent., the number of Jews in J. diminished and after the Arab conquest, the community was preponderantly Samaritan. The Crusaders conquered the town (which they called Ybelin), and it remained an important commercial center in the Middle Ages. It was colonized by Jewish immigrants in 1948, its 1974 population numbering 10,600. The modern kevutzah (PM) of J. (Yavneh), 4 m. to the S, was founded in 1941. An important yeshivah has been established on the adjacent hill of Givat Washington (Bet Rabban) in commemoration of the ancient institution.

JABOTINSKY, VLADIMIR (Ze'ev; 1880–1940): Writer, orator, and Zionist leader. Of Russian birth, he served as Rome correspondent for Odessa

Vladimir Jabotinsky. (Bust by Alfred Hüttenbach.)

newspapers under the pen-name "Altalena," 1898–1901. Beginning his Zionist activities in Russia in 1903, he became a leading force in the struggle for Jewish self-defense units, civic and minority rights, and the revival of Hebrew. In World War I, he advocated the recruiting of Jewish regiments to fight on the Palestine front; this led to the establishment of the ZION MULE CORPS (1915). In 1917, the British government consented to the formation of Jewish battalions, in one of which J. served. He organized the first Jewish self-defense in Jerusalem and led it during the Arab onslaught in 1920. For this he was sentenced by the British Military Tribunal to 15 years' imprisonment but was soon reprieved. In 1921, J. joined the Zionist Executive but resigned in 1923, accusing it of failing to oppose British policy with sufficient vigor. In 1925, he formed the World Union of Zionist REVISIONISTS in opposition to official Zionism (later also the youth organization *Berit Trumpeldor* – BETAR). When the Zionist Organization coopted non-Zionists into the Jewish Agency (1929) and refused to define the aim of Zionism as a Jewish State (1931), J. began to advocate secession; the "discipline clause," introduced in 1935 precipitated the formation by J. of a dissident "New Zionist Organization." From 1936, he urged the speedy evacuation of E European Jewry to Palestine. J. was the spiritual father and nominal head of the *Irgun Tzevai Leumi*. When World War II broke out, he again demanded a Jewish army. His literary works include: in Russian – translations from Bialik's poetry, novels (*Samson* and *The Five*), and poetry; in Hebrew – translations from Dante and Poe, *Autobiography*; in English – *Turkey and the War* and *The Jewish War Front*. In 1964, J.'s body was reburied on Mt. Herzl, Jerusalem.

JACHIN: Right-hand pillar at the entrance to the First Temple corresponding to BOAZ on the left (I Kings 7:21). Similar pillars were discovered in a Canaanite shrine excavated at Hazor.

JACKSONVILLE: City in Florida, US. Jews appeared there shortly after its founding in 1816. The first Jewish community in Florida was established in J. about 1850. Its first congregation, Ahavath Chesed, was organized in 1882. Jews from Lithuania, Rumania, etc. began settling in J. about the end of the 19th cent., and in 1901, organized an Orthodox congregation. The Jewish Community Council was established in 1935. The *Southern Jewish Weekly* (founded 1924), is published in J. Jewish pop. (1973): 6,000 with 3 congregations.

JACOB: Third of the patriarchs and the younger of the twin sons of Isaac and Rebekah. After buying his brother Esau's birthright from him for a mess of pottage, then, with Rebekah's help, securing for himself the blessing Isaac intended to bestow on Esau, he left home for fear of his brother's wrath.

Opening page of *Arbaah Turim* by Jacob ben Asher.
(Soncino, 1485.)

At Haran, he married his uncle Laban's two daughters, Rachel and Leah. By them and their handmaids Bilhah and Zilpah, he had twelve sons – progenitors of the twelve tribes – and a daughter Dinah. While returning home with property accumulated during his absence of twenty years, he struggled with a heavenly emissary and overcame him, being then given the name Israel. After resettling in Canaan, the disappearance of his young son Joseph left him inconsolable, but they were eventually reunited in Egypt where Joseph had become Pharaoh's chief minister. J. settled in Goshen in E Egypt, dying there at the age of 147. He was buried in the Cave of Machpelah at Hebron. Rabbinic legend adds that J. spent 14 years studying Torah under Eber, the son of Shem, before leaving for Haran; that the "man" he overcame was Esau's guardian angel; and that he introduced the evening prayer. Some modern critics claim that incidents in the early life of a tribe were attributed to an eponymous ancestor. The name J. has been discovered in Akkadian and Egyptian sources.

JACOB BEN ASHER (c. 1270–c. 1343): Codifier; son of Asher ben Jechiel (*Rosh*). He was born in Germany and in 1303, went with his father to Spain, residing first in Barcelona and later in Toledo. All his life he lived in poverty and sickness. His great work was the code *Arbaah Turim* ("Four Rows"; cf. Exod. 39:10) from which he is known as the *Baal ha-Turim*. J. collected the decisions of both

Talmuds, the geonim, and previous commentators and codifiers (especially his father), indicating the source in each case. The book is divided into four parts: (a) *Orah Hayyim*, dealing with daily conduct, including prayers, Sabbaths, holidays, etc.; (b) *Yoreh Deah*, including dietary laws; (c) *Even ha-Ezer*, governing personal and family matters; and (d) *Hoshen Mishpat*, describing civil law and administration. This work combined the learning of the French, German, and Spanish rabbinical traditions and formed the basis of subsequent codifications, especially the works of Joseph Caro and Moses Isserles. Its warm humanity and literary quality secured it wide popularity. J. also wrote a commentary on the Pentateuch replete with fanciful explanations based on *gematria*.

JACOB BEN JACOB MOSES OF LISSA (d. 1832): Talmudist; rabbi at Kalisz, Lissa, and Stryj. One of the leading rabbis of his time, he was in the forefront of the opposition to the Reform movement and to Hasidism. J. published numerous works, the best-known being his brief compendium of Jewish religious practice, *Derekh ha-Hayyim*, printed in many prayer-books.

JACOB BEN MEIR TAM (or Rabbenu Tam i.e., "Our Perfect Master"; cf. Gen. 25:27; c. 1100–1171): French tosaphist; grandson of Rashi and brother of Samuel ben Meir (*Rashbam*). He resided at Ramerupt until his home was destroyed by Crusaders in 1147 and he himself narrowly escaped death. J. then settled at Troyes where in 1160, the first conference of French rabbis met under his leadership. Many of his *tosaphot* and novellae were collected in his *Sepher ha-Yashar* which aimed at the correction of textual corruptions in the Talmud. The outstanding rabbinical authority of his day, he also wrote on grammar and Bible interpretation and composed liturgical poems. An independent codifier, he disagreed with Rashi on the order of the verses inscribed in the *tephillin* and some Orthodox Jews to this day alternately wear two pairs of *tephillin*, one according to Rashi and the other according to Rabbenu Tam.

JACOB BEN MOSES HA-LEVI MÖLLN (known as *Maharil*; c. 1360–1427): German codifier. He succeeded his father as rabbi of Mainz and in his later years lived in Worms. J. was regarded as a leading authority on Jewish customs, especially on the liturgy. His published responsa are important. His religious habits and usages were carefully noted by his disciple Zalman of St. Goar in the *Sepher Maharil* which became a standard work. This throws much light on Jewish social history of the period as well as on J.'s warm and pious personality.

JACOB BEN REUBEN (fl. 12th cent.): Karaite exegete; lived in the Byzantine Empire. His Bible commentary *Sepher ha-Osher* (still in ms) contains excerpts from earlier Karaite authors, particularly Japheth ben Ali.

JACOB BEN SAMSON: (fl. first half of 12th cent.): French tosaphist; disciple of Rashi. Besides his novellae on the Talmud, he wrote commentaries on *Avot*, *Seder Olam*, etc.

JACOB BEN WOLF KRANZ ("The *Maggid* of Dubno"; c. 1740–1804): Preacher and scholar. He officiated in Poland, Galicia, and at Dubno (Volhynia) but traveled widely, gaining a reputation as the outstanding preacher of his period. His sermons were spiced with epigrams and parables. His writings were published posthumously.

JACOB BEN YAKAR (d. 1064): Talmudist. He was a pupil of R Gershom *Meor Ha-Golah* and headed a yeshivah at Worms. Here his students included Rashi who often cites his views. J. wrote glosses on several talmudic tractates.

JACOB ISAAC OF PRZYSUCHA (1766–1814): Polish *tzaddik*. He inaugurated a Hasidic trend based upon speculative study of the Torah and Hasidism and opposed the more popular kind of Hasidism with its belief in miracles.

JACOB JOSEPH OF POLONNOYE (d. 1782): Hasidic writer and ideologist. At first inclined to asceticism, he was rabbi at Sharagrod (Volhynia) but had to leave his post after becoming an adherent of Israel Baal Shem Tov. Subsequently, he was rabbi at Rashkov, Nemirov, and Polonnoye. He attacked contemporary rabbis for their remoteness from the community and was persecuted by the Mitnaggedim, his *Toledot Yaakov Yoseph* leading the Vilna Gaon to issue a ban on Hasidism. This book is the primary source for the teachings of Israel Baal Shem Tov. J. J.'s other works include *Ben Porat Yoseph, Tzaphenat Paneah*, and *Ketonet Passim*. He taught that everything exists in a Unity, nothing in the world being separate from Divinity. Man must raise himself above the "material and visible" world and achieve Devekut with the hidden Divinity.

JACOB JOSHUA BEN TZEVI HIRSCH FALK (1680–1756): Talmudist. He officiated in various Polish and German cities, and his yeshivah at Lvov was the center of rabbinical scholarship in Poland. In 1730, he became rabbi in Berlin but had to leave as a result of a conflict with an influential congregant, while he later gave up his post in Frankfort-on-Main because of his support of Jacob Emden. He wrote *Pene Yehoshua*, novellae on the Talmud.

JACOB OF DUBNO see **JACOB BEN WOLF**

JACOB, BENNO (1862–1945): Bible commentator. Rabbi at Gottingen and Dortmund, he published several works defending the Pentateuch against the criticism of the Wellhausen school; these included a pentateuchal commentary and a history of the Hebrews in the Biblical Period. He spent his last years in England.

JACOB, FRANÇOIS (1920–): French geneticist. Professor of cellular genetics at the Collège de France, he was a co-recipient of the 1965 Nobel Prize in medicine for research into the mechanisms by which genes regulate biochemical processes.

JACOB, MAX (1876–1944): French author. A surrealist, he achieved a reputation with his poetry and prose. Although he was converted to Catholicism and lived in a monastery, he died in the deportation camp of Drancy.

JACOBI: (1) *KARL GUSTAV JACOB J.* (1804–1851): German mathematician. A convert, he was professor of mathematics at Königsberg and Berlin. He constructed the theory of transcendental – especially elliptical – functions. (2) *MORITZ HERMANN J.* (1801–1874): Physicist; brother of (1). Also a convert, he was professor at Dorpat in Esthonia and from 1837, at St. Petersburg where he was ennobled. He discovered the technique of galvano-plastics, applied electromagnetism as a motive power, and pioneered in electrotyping.

JACOBI, ABRAHAM (1830–1919): Pediatrician. He was imprisoned in his native Germany for revolutionary activities (1851–3), thereafter settling in New York where he taught 1860–92 at several medical schools. He founded the first free childrens' clinic in America and pioneered in scientific pediatrics. He invented the laryngoscope.

JACOBI, FREDERICK (1891–1952): US composer. Formerly assistant conductor at the Metropolitan Opera House, New York, he taught composition at the Juilliard School of Music (1936–51). His works including two Sabbath Eve Services and chamber music were based on Jewish subjects.

JACOBOWSKI, LUDWIG (1860–1900): German author. His outstanding works consist of poems and the novel *Werther der Jude*.

JACOBS, JOSEPH (1854–1916): Historian and folklorist. Born in Australia, he studied in England and turned to medieval English Jewish history to which he made important contributions (e.g. *The Jews of Angevin England*). He also wrote on Spanish Jewish history and on Celtic folklore, was editor of *Folk Lore* and the *Jewish Year Book*, and secretary of the Russo-Jewish Committee. In 1900, he settled in the US as revising editor of the *Jewish Encyclopedia*, also teaching at the Jewish Theological Seminary, and editing *The American Hebrew*.

JACOBS, LOUIS (1920–): English rabbi. Born in Manchester, he occupied various pulpits in London. His critical views especially concerning the Divine origin of the Pentateuch, led to the disqualification by Chief Rabbi Brodie of his candidacy for the post of principal of Jews' College and later for a pulpit in a London synagogue. J. thereupon founded his own congregation – the New London Synagogue (1964). His books include theo-logical studies (*Jewish Values, We have reason to believe*), a study of the 613 precepts (*Principles of the Jewish Faith*), etc.

JACOBS, SAMUEL WOLF (1871–1938): Canadian public figure and lawyer. Prominent in civil rights legislation, J. was member of parliament from 1917 to his death. From 1934–8, he served as president of the Canadian Jewish Congress.

JACOBSOHN, SIEGFRIED (1881–1927): German dramatic critic and political writer. In 1905, he founded the periodical *Die Schaubühne*, for literary and theatrical criticism; from 1918, this appeared as *Die Weltbühne*, an influential organ of the Radical Democrats.

JACOBSON, DAN (1929–): Novelist. Born in Johannesburg, he was brought up in Kimberley. He lived for a time in Israel and the US before settling in London. His novels, mostly with S. African setting, include *The Beginners, The Price of Diamonds, A Dance in the Sun*, and *The Rape of Tamar*.

JACOBSON, ISRAEL (1768–1828): German Reform pioneer. As president of the Jewish consistory in the Napoleonic kingdom of Westphalia, he worked for the reform of Jewish education and the synagogue liturgy, being of the opinion that this would help Jewish-Christian understanding. In Seesen, Brunswick, he founded in 1801 the Jacobson School for Jewish and Christian pupils, which existed until the Nazi era. In 1810, he set up a Reform synagogue modeled on Protestant usage with an organ and with sermons delivered in German. J. later removed to Berlin, where he held Reform services in his home, himself sometimes acting as reader and preacher.

JACOBSON, JULIUS (1828–1889): German ophthalmologist. He taught at Königsberg Univ. and secured the recognition of ophthalmology as an independent branch of medicine.

JACOBSON, LUDWIG LEWIN (1783–1843): Danish anatomist. He discovered a nasal organ in certain creatures which is largely responsible for the sense of smell ("Jacobson's organ"). He refused the professorship offered him by the Univ. of Copenhagen becaused it involved baptism.

JACOBSON, VICTOR (1869–1934): Zionist. A native of the Crimea, he was elected to the Zionist Executive in 1899. J. became manager of the Beirut branch of the Anglo-Palestine Bank in 1906 and in 1908, political representative of the Zionist Organization at Constantinople. During World War I, he conducted the Zionist Office in Copenhagen and from 1925, was permanent representative of the Zionist Organization to the League of Nations.

JACOBY, ḤANOKH (Heinrich; 1909–): Israel composer. A native of Germany, he settled in Jerusalem in 1934 as a teacher and viola-player. J. has written chamber, orchestral, and choral works.

Jaffa port and Jaffa hill: Rock of Andromeda on the left.

JACOBY, JOHANN (1805–1877): German statesman.

A physician by profession, he became a member of the Prussian National Assembly in 1849 and of the Chamber of Deputies in 1858. Imprisoned several times for his outspokenness, he was detained in 1870 for opposing Bismarck's annexation of Alsace-Lorraine. In later life, he became a socialist. J., a strenuous worker for Jewish Emancipation, advocated religious reform.

JADASSOHN, SALOMON (1831–1902): German composer. He taught at the Leipzig Conservatory and wrote on musical theory.

JAEL (fl. 12th cent. BCE): Wife of Heber the Kenite.

After the forces of Jabin of Hazor were defeated by the Israelites, the fleeing commander Sisera sought refuge in J.'s tent She killed him in his sleep (Judg. 4–5).

JAFFA (Joppa; Heb. *Yapho*): Israel city. It is mentioned in Egyptian documents from the time of the 19th Egyptian dynasty (16th cent. BCE) and also in Assyrian documents. Its position on a slight promontory jutting out from the straight coastline of S Palestine makes it a natural anchorage. In biblical times, it marked the boundary of the Philistines, although in theory it was within the tribal area of Judah. In the period of Solomon and again after the return from the Babylonian captivity, the cedars of Lebanon were floated to the "sea of J." on their way to Jerusalem: unloading may have been at Tel Kasileh (recently excavated N of Tel Aviv). In the Persian Period, J. belonged to the Phoenicians; in the Hellenistic, it was an independent city with a non-Jewish population. Judah the Maccabee avenged a massacre of the Jewish community there; his brothers, Jonathan and Simon, took J. and replaced the foreign population with Jews, after which it served as the principal Jewish port until the destruction of Jerusalem in 70 CE. It remained one of the main harbors on the coast in Roman times (when it was renamed Flavia Ioppe) and in the Crusader Period and from the 17th cent. onward, it was again the principal port of pilgrims for Jerusalem. In antiquity, the legend of Andromeda and Perseus was located there and the Bible mentions that Jonah sailed from J. In the 19th cent., it profited from the developing belt of surrounding Jewish colonies, but the Arab riots in 1921–2 forced the Jews to leave for TEL AVIV, the neighboring city which had been founded as a suburb of J. The development of Haifa harbor undermined the economic position of J., although it continued to share the orange exports. In 1946, its population was 101,000, 30% of whom were Jews. During the War of Independence, the Arab sections of J. capitulated (May 14, 1948) and almost all its Arabs left, their places being taken by new immigrants. J. was joined with Tel Aviv into one city (Tel-Aviv–J.). Its port was closed in 1965. One quarter has been developed as an artists' colony.

JAFFE, DANIEL see **ITZIG, DANIEL**

JAFFE, JOSEPH (1865–1938): Yiddish poet. He was born in Lithuania and settled in New York in 1892. His verse, dealing mainly with love, differs from that of most of his Yiddish contemporaries in its humor and serenity.

JAFFE, LEIB (1876–1948): Zionist leader. A native of Lithuania, he participated in the First Zionist Congress (1897), was a founder of the DEMOCRATIC

FRACTION (1901), and later a leader of the *Tziyyone Zion*. In 1919, he settled in Palestine where he edited *Ha-Aretz* 1919–22, and from 1923, devoted himself to work in behalf of the *Keren ha-Yesod*, serving on its directorate from 1926. He was killed in a bomb-attack on the Jewish Agency building in Jerusalem. J. wrote poetry in Russian, Yiddish, and Hebrew.

JAFFE, MEIR BEN ISRAEL (fl. latter part of 15th cent.): German copyist and book-binder. He executed a fine illuminated Haggadah now in Cincinnati, and also bindings of high artistic merit for the Nuremberg city council.

JAFFE, MORDECAI BEN ABRAHAM (c. 1530–1612): Codifier. He was born in Prague, studied in Poland and Italy, and served as rabbi in Grodno, Lublin, Kremenetz, Prague and Posen. His major work is *Levush Malkhut* (in brief, *Levush*), a partial commentary on Jacob ben Asher's *Tur*, giving clear reasons for each decision and citing the views of Polish and German scholars. This commentary, regarded by many as authoritative, provoked criticism.

JAFFE, SIR OTTO (1846–1929): British industrialist. Hamburg-born, he was a leader of the linen industry in Belfast where was lord mayor 1899–1900 and 1904–5.

JAFFE, TZEVI HIRSCH (1853–1927): Russian mathematician. He invented a calculating machine and wrote on mathematical theory and chronology. He was also a talmudic scholar and authority on the Jewish calendar.

JAGEL, ABRAHAM see **GALLICO, ABRAHAM ISRAEL**

JAHRZEIT see **YAHRZEIT**

JAIR: (1) Israelite hero of the Exodus Period. He captured a group of villages in N Gilead from the Amorites which were thenceforward known as the "villages of J." (Num. 32:41). (2) Israelite judge (Judg. 10:3), originating from Gilead.

JAKOBOVITS, IMMANUEL (1921–): British rabbi. Born in Germany, he went to London at an early age. In 1949 he was appointed chief rabbi of Ireland; in 1958 rabbi of the Fifth Avenue Synagogue, New York; and in 1966 chief rabbi of the British Commonwealth. His publications include *Jewish Medical Ethics*.

JAMAICA: Island in W Indies. When the English occupied J. in 1655, some Portuguese Marranos were probably already residents. Numerous Sephardim of Marrano origin established themselves shortly thereafter, and in the course of the 18th cent., when the island's economy flourished, the Jewish settlement developed, benefiting from the immigration of Portuguese Marranos and of Jews, Sephardi as well as Ashkenazi, the latter from Europe, mainly from England. They were however, subjected to various restrictions until 1831, since when they have played a prominent part in the life of J., filling every public office. With the decline in the island's prosperity in the 19th cent., the Jewish community diminished, now contributing some of the outstanding families in Jewish life in England (e.g. the Henriques). There were formerly communities in Spanish Town, Falmouth, and Montego Bay, but the only one remaining is that of Kingston where the majority of the island's 600 (1974) Jews resides.

JAMNIA see **JABNEH**

JANCU, MARCEL (1895–): Painter. Of Rumanian birth, he studied in Paris and founded Dadaism, together with Picasso and Tristan Tzara. In 1941, he settled in Palestine where he founded the artists' colony at En Hod. J. is a cubist painter and architect, who has concentrated increasingly on Israel landscapes.

JANNER, BARNETT, BARON (1892–): British public figure. He was a Liberal member of parliament in 1931–5 and a Labor member 1945–70. J. is president of the British Zionist Federation and, from 1955 to 1964, of the Board of Deputies of British Jews.

JANOWSKY, OSCAR (1900–): US educator. He was professor of history at City College, New York, from 1924, and directed its department of graduate studies. J. has written on Jewish history and sociology especially concerning the US scene.

JAPAN: The Jewish settlement dates only from 1861 when two brothers named Marks arrived in Yokohama. By 1869 there were some fifty families, mainly originating from Poland. At the end of the cent. a community, mainly of Russian origin, was established at Nagasaki. From 1941–5, J. applied German anti-Semitism in a modified form and the feeble Jewish life further declined, to be revived, however, with the US military occupation. Jewish pop. (1973): 750, mostly in Tokyo.

JAPHETH: Son of Noah. In his father's blessing, he was promised wide territories. The Bible (Gen. 10:2) regards him as the progenitor of 14 peoples (mostly in the Indo-European language group) ranging from the Caucasus to the Aegean.

JAPHETH BEN ALI HA-LEVI (c. 920–after 1005): Karaite scholar. He originated from Basra and resided in Jerusalem. He translated the Bible into Arabic and his commentary, which embodies unique sources shedding light on the history of the older Karaite literature, is regarded as the major Karaite scriptural commentary. His references to Hebrew grammar and philology are of particular significance.

JAROSLAV: Polish town. Jews are mentioned in 1434, but in 1571, only 2 families were allowed to live there. Many Jews participated in the town's famous fair, and in 1608–90, is was one of the regular seats of the COUNCIL OF THE FOUR LANDS. A community was founded toward the end of the 17th cent.; as the 1676 charter again restricted the Jewish population to two families, the others lived in the Ruthenian suburb. In 1737, several Jews were executed on a Blood Libel charge. Before World War II over 8,000 Jews (30% of the total) lived there, but nearly all were massacred by the Nazis in 1941.

JASHAR, BOOK OF: Ancient work mentioned in Josh. 10–13, II Sam. 1:18, and I Kings 8:53 (Septuagint version). The book seems to have contained poems concerning events and historical personalities from the time of Joshua to the commencement of the Royal Period. The collection was made in the time of Solomon, but was lost in ancient times. A popular medieval compilation of biblical legends going by the same name, based on Midrashim to the Pentateuch, was probably composed in 11th cent. Spain.

JASON (= Joshua): High priest 175–2 BCE; son of the high priest Simon II. A leader of the hellenizing party, he replaced his brother Onias III in the high priesthood by bribing Antiochus IV, but after sweeping innovations, was ousted by the extreme hellenizer, Menelaus. After receiving rumors of Antiochus' defeat in Egypt (170), he attacked Jerusalem, but was defeated by popular resistance and fled to Ammon.

JASSY: Capital of Moldavia. Jews are recorded there from the 15th cent. In 1717, when under Turkish rule, they received a constitution according to which their head was a chief judge (*Staroste*) under whom there was (until 1832) a virtually hereditary *Ḥakham Bashi* with authority over the whole country. Jews were divided into indigenous, privileged, and foreign elements until 1832, when J. came under Russian rule which treated all Jews as foreigners or – if without property – as vagabonds to be expelled. The Austrian occupation of 1853 brought a measure of relief, but from 1864, the Jewish community was no longer recognized as a juridical entity. When Bucharest became capital of Rumania in 1861, J. declined; it was a center of anti-Semitism and the scene of several pogroms. The community numbered c. 45,000 in 1939. About 14,000 Jews were shot in and near J. by German and Rumanian troops in June 1941. Subsequently, many Jews were driven into J. from the country towns. In 1946, there were 38,000 Jews and in 1959, 18,000 but many emigrated to Israel. Jewish pop (1969): 2,000 families.

JASTROW: (1) *JOSEPH J.* (1863–1944): US psychologist; son of (2). Professor at the Univ. of Wisconsin, he specialized in abnormal and child psychology. J. wrote many scientific and popular works on psychology. (2) *MARCUS J.* (1829–1903): Rabbi and philologist. While rabbi in Warsaw, his Polish patriotism during the 1861 anti-Russian ferment led to his arrest and expulsion by the Russian authorities. After a brief incumbency in Worms he became rabbi of the Rodeph Shalom congregation,

Jacob K. Javits.

Philadelphia, where he opposed drastic liturgical reforms. J.'s main work was the monumental *Dictionary of the Targumim, the Talmud Babli and Yerushalmi, and the Midrashic Literature* (2 vols. 1886–1903). He was an editor of the Talmud department of the *Jewish Encyclopedia*. (3) *MORRIS J.* (1861–1921): Orientalist; son of (2). In 1892, he was appointed professor of Semitic languages (from 1898 also librarian) at the Univ. of Pennsylvania. He wrote extensively on biblical and Assyriological topics.

JASTROW, IGNAZ (1856–1937): German sociologist, economist, and historian. He was professor in Berlin and wrote prolifically, especially on social policy. His works include *A History of the Dreams of United Germany* and *A History of the World*.

JAVITS, JACOB KOPPEL (1904–): US public official. He was Republican member of Congress from New York 1946–54, attorney general of NY state 1954–6, and elected to the US Senate in 1956. J. is a spokesman for the liberal wing of the Republican Party.

JAWITZ, ZE'EV (Wolf; 1847–1924): Historian. Born in Poland, he worked in Palestine in 1888–98 as teacher, rabbi and journalist. He then returned to Russia where he helped to found the *Mizraḥi* movement. Later, he lived in Berlin and Antwerp and from 1914, in London. J. published many works in a pure biblical Hebrew. The most important was a 13-volume history of the Jews from the earliest times written from a strongly conservative standpoint. It retains its value for the Rabbinic Period of which J. had comprehensive knowledge.

JEBUSITES: Canaanite people settled in Palestine prior to the Israelite conquest. They lived in the hill region, principally around Jerusalem which they called Jebus. Although Joshua defeated a Jebusite-led coalition, Jerusalem was occupied only in the reign of David (II Sam. 5:6–7). The last Jebusite king was apparently Araunah (II Sam. 24:15). The J. remained in the city under David and became tributary under Solomon. In the course of time, they appear to have been assimilated.

JECONIAH see **JEHOIACHIN**

JEDAIAH HA-PENINI see **BEDERSI, JEDAIAH**

JEDID AL-ISLAM (Arab. "New Moslems"): Name given to the secret Jews of Meshed (Persia), whose ancestors were ostensibly converted to Islam during the persecutions of 1839. Outwardly devout Moslems, they still meticulously observe Jewish rites.

JEDUTHUN: David's seer (II Chron. 35:15). His descendants were levitical musicians in the Temple. Psalms 39, 62, and 77 are attributed to him.

JEHIEL BEN JOSEPH OF PARIS (d. before 1267): French talmudist. In 1224, he succeeded his teacher, Judah Sir Leon, as head of the talmudical school in Paris, where he is reported to have had 300 disciples. He wrote *tosaphot* on several tractates of the Talmud, and his legal decisions commanded great respect. He is notable especially for the leading part he took in the DISPUTATION of Paris in 1240, where he courageously defended the Talmud against the charges of Nicolas DONIN. Thereafter, he emigrated to Palestine where he died.

JEHIEL MICHAL OF ZLOCZOV ("The Maggid of Zloczov"; 1726–1786): Hasidic leader in Galicia. A disciple of Israel Baal Shem Tov, he

Ze'ev Jawitz.

preached in various communities and was famed for his ascetic way of life. J.M. suffered from the persecution of the Mitnaggedim. His teachings are often cited and are marked by a lofty morality. All his five sons founded Hasidic dynasties.

JEHOAHAZ (or **JOAHAZ**): King of Israel, son of Jehu; reigned 815–c. 800 BCE. In his time, Aram in effect reduced Israel to a tributary, restricting her army and controlling large tracts of her territory (II Kings 13:1–9).

JEHOAHAZ (originally Shallum): King of Judah for 3 months in 609/8 BCE; son of Josiah. He was crowned by the people after his father was killed fighting the Egyptians. J. apparently belonged to the pro-Babylonian party since he was deposed and arrested by Pharaoh Necoh, dying in captivity in Egypt (II Kings 23:29–34).

JEHOASH see **JOASH**

JEHOASH see **BLOOMGARDEN**

JEHOIACHIN (originally Coniah or Jeconiah): King of Judah, son of Jehoiakim; reigned 597 BCE. Succeeding to the throne at the age of 18 during the Babylonian siege of Jerusalem, he reigned for 3 months and 10 days before capitulating to Nebuchadnezzar. He was taken to exile in Babylonia, remaining in detention until the accession of Evil-Merodach (561) when he was released (II Kings 24–5; II Chron. 36:8–10). Official Babylonian records relating to his captivity have been recovered.

JEHOIADA (fl. 9th cent.): High priest in Jerusalem. On the assassination of King Ahaziah, his mother Athaliah seized power in Judah, putting to death the members of the Davidic family. J.'s wife Jehosheba, a sister of Ahaziah, rescued her brother's year-old child Joash, hiding him in the Temple. When Joash reached the age of seven, J. declared him king and had Athaliah slain, proceeding to act as regent until the young king's majority. Under J.'s influence the Baal cult was prohibited, its sanctuaries destroyed, and the Temple in Jerusalem restored. According to Chronicles, he died at the age of 130 and was buried in the royal tomb.

JEHOIAKIM (originally **ELIAKIM**): King of Judah, son of Josiah; reigned 608–598 BCE. He was made king by Pharaoh Necoh in succession to his brother JEHOAHAZ. For three years, he was subject to Egypt but after the defeat of Necoh at the decisive battle of Carchemish (605), became a Babylonian vassal. In 601, he joined the pro-Egyptian party in Judah in opposition to the advice of Jeremiah who depicts J. as a tyrannical oppressor. J. died while Jerusalem was under siege by the Babylonians (598).

JEHONADAB BEN RECHAB see **RECHABITES**

JEHORAM (**JORAM**): King of Israel, son of Ahab; reigned 853–842 BCE. Succeeding his elder brother Ahaziah, he joined Jehoshaphat of Judah in the war against Mesha of Moab in which Moab regained its independence. J. waged wars with Aram to recover towns in Gilead but was wounded in battle at Ramoth-Gilead; upon his return to Jezreel, he was killed by Jehu.

JEHORAM (JORAM): King of Judah, son of Jehoshaphat; reigned c. 850–843 BCE. In obtaining the succession, he put his brothers and many of the leading men of state to death. Under the influence of his wife ATHALIAH, he introduced the Baal cult into Judah. His reign was marked by the successful revolt of the Edomites and by invasions of Philistines and Arabs who plundered Jerusalem. J. died after a prolonged illness (II Kings 8).

JEHOSHAPHAT: King of Judah, son of Asa; reigned 874–850 BCE. The first king of Judah to make a treaty with the kingdom of Israel, he strengthened the ties by marrying his son Jehoram to Athaliah, daughter of Ahab of Israel. He fought unsuccessfully with Ahab against Aram and, with Ahab's son Jehoram against Mesha of Moab. J. endeavored to revive sea-commerce, but his craft were wrecked at Ezion-Geber (I Kings 22). The Bible praises his piety.

JEHOSHAPHAT, VALLEY OF: Place where – according to Joel 4:2 – the Lord will gather all nations and plead with them for His people Israel. From the 4th cent., this was identified with the central part of the Kidron Valley, which contained the "Cave of Jehoshaphat" wrongly believed to be situated in the tomb-cave near "Absalom's Tomb." The Last Judgment was consequently located there by both Christian and Moslem tradition.

JEHOVAH: Traditional but wholly inaccurate Christian reading of the Hebrew TETRAGRAMMATON. It resulted from overlooking the fact that the vowel-points with which the letters of the Divine name YHVH were provided by the Masoretes are those of ADONAI. See also GOD, NAMES OF.

JEHU: King of Israel; reigned 842–814 BCE. While the commander-in-chief of Jehoram, he conspired with the army and, with the support of Elisha, annihilated the royal family including Jehoram, Ahaziah of Judah, and the queen-mother Jezebel as well as the priests of Baal. J. was unsuccessful in his wars with Aram and paid tribute to Shalmaneser III of Assyria to obtain his protection (the Black Obelisk of Shalmaneser depicts J. paying tribute). On repelling the Assyrian threat, Hazael of Aram deprived J. of much of his territory. The dynasty of J. continued to reign for a century.

JEITELES (or **JEITTELES**): Prague family which produced several scholars during the 18th–19th cents. They included: (1) *AARON* (*ANDREAS*) *LUDWIG JOSEPH HEINRICH J.* (1799–1878): Physician and author; son of (6). After baptism, he became professor of medicine at the Univ. of Olmütz. Beethoven composed settings for several of his

German poems. (2) *ALOIS J.* (1794–1858): Physician and poet; grandson of (5). Beethoven set to music his song-cycle *An die ferne Geliebte*. He wrote many plays and edited several German periodicals, including (together with (4) the short-lived Jewish weekly *Siona* (1819). (3) *BARUCH* (*BENEDICT*) *J*: (1762–1813): Physician and talmudist; son of (5). He maintained a yeshivah in Prague but later inclined to the Haskalah movement, for which he was persecuted by the Orthodox members of the community. His writings include halakhic novellae as well as Hebrew poetry, translations, etc. He died of an infection caught while tending the wounded after the battle of Dresden. (4) *IGNAZ J.* (1783–1843): Author; son of (3). He wrote prolifically on literature, philosophy, history, and statistics as well as poems and satires. His chief work was a *Lexicon of Esthetics*. (5) *JONAS J.* (1735–1806): Physician and public figure. In 1763, he was appointed to the Prague Jewish hospital and in 1784, received permission to attend all patients, regardless of their religion. (6) *JUDAH J.* (1773–1838): Orientalist; son of (5). He contributed to Hebrew periodicals and wrote an Aramaic grammar in Hebrew. (7) *MOSES WOLF J.* (18th–19th cents.): Hebrew and Yiddish author who wrote pioneer works on the history of Prague Jewry.

JELLINEK: (1) *ADOLF J.* (c. 1821–1893): Scholar. He was rabbi in Leipzig from 1845 and in Vienna from 1856. J. was widely reputed as a preacher and his sermons (many of which were published), with their subtle midrashic expositions, attracted multitudes of hearers, Jewish and gentile, and exercised a profound influence on Jewish homiletics. A fertile scholar in various fields of Judaica, especially the history of Kabbalah and medieval Jewish philosophy, he published numerous works, including editions of many smaller Midrashim in his *Bet ha-Midrash*. He also produced bibliographical booklets on medieval Jewish history and literature. (2) *GEORG J.* (1851–1911): Jurist; son of (1). Professor of law at Vienna, Basle, and Heidelberg, he wrote studies on civil law. He converted to Christianity. (3) *HERMANN J.* (1822–1848): Writer on political and philosophical subjects; brother of (1). He was executed for participating in the 1848 Austrian Revolution.

JENIN: Palestinian town. Mentioned as Gina in the Tel el Amarna tablets, it is probably the biblical En Gannim (Josh. 19:21); in Roman times it was called Ginaea. J. had a small Jewish community in the 17th cent. It was a center of Arab nationalist fanaticism in the 1930's. It was part of Jordan 1948–67. Pop. (1967): 8,346 apart from 5,019 Arab refugees in the vicinity.

JEPHTHAH (fl. c. 12th cent. BCE): Israelite judge. He lived in Gilead which was threatened by the Ammonites. J. decisively defeated them and also the Ephraimites who opposed his leadership. He acted as judge for six years. The Bible relates that before fighting the Ammonites he vowed to sacrifice whatever came first from his home should he return safely; he was met by his daughter and, with her consent, performed his vow (Judg. 11).

JERBA: Island off the coast of Tunisia containing a Jewish community legendarily dating from Bible times. The first reliable evidence of Jewish residence comes from the 10th cent. From the 18th cent., J. was a live cultural center and two Hebrew presses existed there until recently. The community consisted mainly of traders and craftsmen. In 1943, it was saved from extermination at the hands of the Nazis by paying a gold ransom. Some 1,500 of its Jews left for Israel in 1949 ff. Some 1,500 remained in 1970, mostly pious and some deeply learned and many of them left subsequently. The main settlements are at the villages of Hara Kebira and Hara Saghira. The ancient synagogue in the former place is a renowed center of pilgrimage and the subject of many legends.

JEREMIAH (fl. 7th–6th cents. BCE): Prophet. Belonging to a priestly family of Anathoth near Jerusalem, he began to prophecy in 625. At first, he rebuked the nation for idolatry and after Josiah's reform (621), warned it to keep the covenant then made with God. His gloomy prophecies aroused bitter resentment, but during the reigns of Jehoiakim and Zedekiah, he found supporters among leading personalities and priests. Baruch – a member of a prominent family — now joined him as a faithful friend and scribe. When Nebuchadnezzar ascended the Babylonian throne (605), J. forecast that he would conquer Judah. Jehoiakim, fearing the effect of this prophecy on the populace, ordered the arrest of J. who went into hiding until the country submitted to Nebuchadnezzar the following year (597). Zedekiah thought highly of J. although he did not follow his advice and joined an anti-Babylonian alliance. J. foretold their defeat and advocated surrender; he was imprisoned for a time and later consigned to a pit, being saved only by Zedekiah's personal regard. After the fall of Jerusalem, Nebuchadnezzar's officials, aware of J.'s pro-Babylonian attitude, accorded him protection, but after Gedaliah's murder, the panic-stricken survivors forced him and Baruch to accompany them in their flight to Egypt. J.'s last recorded prophecy is a condemnation of Egyptian Jewry for their idol-worship. His subsequent history has been the subject of Jewish and Christian legend. Jewish tradition ascribes to him the authorship of the Book of Kings and (more plausibly) Lamentations. His prophecies, recorded by Baruch at J.'s dictation, were assembled in the Book of J., the second of the Latter Prophets in the Bible. It consists of 52 chapters: 1–18, prophecies, mostly from time of Josiah; 19–36, prophecies and narrative from various periods,

mostly in the reigns of Jehoiakim, Jehoiachin, and Zedekiah; 37–44, historical narrative from the time of Zedekiah to the journey into Egypt; 45–51, various prophecies mostly concerning other nations; 52, a recapitulation of the last chapter of the Book of Kings. The Book of J. was edited by Baruch but variant readings between the masoretic text and the Septuagint evidence subsequent re-editing. Its final redaction has been placed in the 2nd cent. BCE.

JEREMIAH (fl. 4th cent.): Palestinian amora. A native of Babylonia, he eventually headed the Tiberias academy. He praised the Palestinian method of talmudic study, in contrast to the Babylonian which he termed "darkness." He excelled in posing difficult, even fantastic, halakhic problems, many of which remained unanswered.

JEREZ (XERES) DE LA FRONTERA: Town in S Spain, with a Jewish community going back to the Moorish Period. When Alfonso X captured J. in 1264, a number of houses were reserved for the Jews. The Jewish quarter contained two synagogues and two merchants' halls. The community existed until the expulsion of 1492.

JERICHO: Palestinian city in S Jordan valley, 825 ft. below sea level. One of the oldest settlements in the world, its first city wall goes back to the Neolithic Period (5000 BCE). It was inhabited throughout Chalcolithic and Canaanite times until destroyed by Joshua (Josh. 6). Its area was left desolate, being revived only during the reign of Ahab (c. 870 BCE) by Hiel the Bethelite (I Kings 16:34). In the time of Herod, the city was transferred from its former position near the spring to another, further S. There Herod built himself a palace where he died. J. was destroyed by the Romans 68 CE; later it was rebuilt at its present location. J. derives

Decorative stone-work in the court of Hisham's palace at Jericho.

its economic position from the surrounding plantations which have been irrigated by streams from the Judean mountains since the Hellenistic Period. A center of balsam groves, it was known as the "City of Palms"; it is now surrounded by orange groves and banana plantations. The population (3,000 in 1946) was much augmented by Arab refugees in 1948 and numbered 61,000 in 1961. Most of the refugees fled over the Jordan before Israel troops arrived during the Six-Day War, and some 9,000 remained at the time of the 1967 census. The archeological excavations in the mound started in 1906 and were pursued regularly from 1930.

JEROBOAM I: King of Israel c. 930–910 BCE. An Ephraimite, he acted as a superintendent of forced labor during the reign of Solomon but later led the revolt against the burden imposed on the people by the monarchy. His revolutionary movement was at first suppressed, and he took refuge in Egypt. After Solomon's death, he led a delegation representing the northern Israelite tribes which met Rehoboam at Shechem, demanding changes in the system of taxation and forced labor. When the request was refused, the northern tribes declared their independence and anointed J. as their king. J.'s capital was first at Shechem, but was later removed to Penuel in Transjordan and finally to Tirzah. Five years after his accession, 60 towns of his territory were ravaged by an Egyptian invasion. To combat the influence of the Jerusalem Temple, he set up new shrines at Bethel and Dan with a similar cult but centering round the symbols of golden calves. The Bible and talmudic sources are violently hostile to J. who "sinned and caused Israel to sin."

JEROBOAM II: King of Israel 784–744 BCE. Under his rule, the northern kingdom attained the climax of its economic, military, and political prosperity. He exploited Aram's weakness after the defeat by Assyria by recapturing all areas detached from Israel and annexing Aramean towns. Internally, his rule was marked by corruption and the pursuit of pleasure and profit, which were denounced by the prophets Hosea and Amos.

*JEROME (c. 340–420): Church Father. He eventually settled in Bethlehem where he studied Hebrew with Jewish scholars while preparing his Latin translation of the Bible. This became (except for the Psalms) the basis of the VULGATE. His biblical commentaries, though indulging in anti-Jewish sentiments, are relatively free of Christian allegorical tendencies and show acquaintance with rabbinic exegesis. His *De viris illustribus* contains (among others) biographies of Philo, Josephus, and Justus of Tiberias.

JERSEY CITY: City in New Jersey, US. Jews began arriving there in 1858. The Ephraim Congregation was formed in 1874. E European Jews who went to J. C. in the last two decades of the 19th cent. laid the foundation for the city's Orthodox congregations. The weekly *Jewish Standard* appears in J.C. Jewish pop. (1973): 10,000.

JERUBAAL see **GIDEON**

JERUSALEM: Capital of Israel; situated roughly in the center of the Judean Mountains. The original city was slightly E of the watershed between the Mediterranean and the Dead Sea, on the E slope of a plateau; recently, however, the New City has spread across the watershed into a series of ridges and valleys facing west.

Geography: The area occupied by ancient J. (and by the Old City today) consists of two ridges circumscribed by two valleys, the KIDRON Valley on the E and the HINNOM Valley on the W; a central valley (called Tyropoeon, or the Valley of the Cheese-Makers, in the time of the Second Temple; now partly filled in) formerly passed between the two ridges. Of the two, the western, called the Upper City in the time of the Second Temple and (erroneously) "Mt. Zion" to-day, is the higher and broader ridge (sloping from 2,816 ft. to 2,505 ft.). The eastern is much narrower and lower (2,502 ft. to 2,054 ft.); as it had on its eastern slope the only spring in the area, it was chosen as the area of earliest settlement. The fact that both ridges are surrounded by deep valleys added to their strength in ancient times, so that the city could only be attacked from the N. J. has the mountain variety of the Mediterranean climate, with a dry season of seven months (May-Oct.) and a rainy one of five months (Nov.-April). The only water source in the J. area is the Gihon spring. From ancient times, the water supply has been supplemented by cisterns, the Temple area alone having 37. In addition, there are several pools: Amygdalon (erroneously called "Hezekiah's Pool") in the Old City, Hamman es-Sitt Maryam, Mamillah, and the Serpents' Pool. All these have, however, been insufficient in periods of rising population and have been supplemented by aqueducts. In 1935, a 47-mile pipeline was established from the Rosh ha-Ayin springs in the coastal plain. This line was cut by the Arabs in 1948, but was soon repaired and extended.

"Holy Jerusalem" inscribed on a silver shekel together with three pomegranates (68 CE).

Jerusalem: A general view.

Names: The name "Jerusalem" appears first as *U[r]ushamem* in the Execration Texts from the time of the Egyptian 12th Dynasty (19th–18th cents. BCE); in Akkadian it is called *Urusalim* in the Tel el Amarna letters (15th cent. BCE). The name is now commonly assumed to be derived from the verb *yarah* ("cast" the foundation stone, i.e., "founded") and the name of the Semitic god Shalem. In the early books of the Bible J. is also called Jebus, after the people inhabiting it before David. It is sometimes called ZION, after David's fortress, and was also known as the City of David. The Bible abounds in poetic names for the city, such as the "city of righteousness," the "faithful city" (Is. 1:26), the "city of God" (Ps. 46:5), the "holy city" (Is. 48:2), "city of truth" (Zech. 8:3), "Ariel" (Is. 29:1), etc. The name Jerusalem (*Hierosolyma* in Latin, Ἱεροσολύμα in Greek) is derived from the Hebrew *Yerushalayim*. The Roman colony founded by Hadrian on the ruins of Jewish J. was called AELIA CAPITOLINA, which name persisted into the Arab Period; but the common Arab name is EL-KUDS ("the Holy," sometimes *Beit el-Makdes*, "The House of Holiness," cf. Heb. *Bet ha-Mikdash* i.e., "temple").

History: The earliest evidence of man in the J. area belongs to the Paleolithic (Old Stone) Age, but the actual foundation of the city can be assigned to the Early Bronze Age (c. 3500 BCE — 2000 BCE), i.e., to the period when the Canaanites first established themselves in the country. In the ensuing Middle Bronze Age (2000–1550 BCE), J. appears as the capital of a Canaanite city state. It is apparently identical with the Salem ruled by Melchi-zedek "priest of the most high god" who was honored by Abraham (Gen. 14:18–19). The Hyksos revolution left behind in J. elements of Hittite and Hurrite habitation; in the Tel el Amarna Period (15th cent. BCE), the city was ruled by a king who was menaced by the HABIRU invaders and appealed to his suzerain, the pharaoh, for help; the Egyptians seem to have maintained a Cushite garrison in J. At the time of Joshua's conquest (c. 1320 BCE), Adoni-zedek, king of J., was defeated at Aijalon, but his city remained an independent enclave between the tribal

Jerusalem: view of the Israel Museum and the Shrine of the Book.

areas of Benjamin and Judah. In the 12th cent., Jebus–Jerusalem maintained its independence with Philistine help, until its capture by David c. 1010 BCE. J. now became the capital of united Israel (II Sam. 5:6–8; I Chron. 11:4–6); David dealt leniently with the JEBUSITES, but established himself in the city, adding the fortress of Zion and also a "House of Heroes" for his guard. He also constructed a tomb inside the city for himself and his dynasty; this might correspond to a rock-cut tomb in two tiers found in 1914 in "The City of David" (now called OPHEL). By transferring the Ark of the Covenant there, David made J. the religious center of Israel; by his conquests, he made it the capital of an empire reaching from the Red Sea to the Euphrates. Solomon (970–930 BCE) enriched the city from his commercial ventures and heavy taxation (I Kings 10:27–9). He enlarged the city by adding the Palace and the TEMPLE, while filling the gap between them and David's City with the MILLO ("filling"). The erection of the Temple transformed Jerusalem definitely into the permanent center of the Jewish religion, notwithstanding all later separatist efforts. After Solomon's death and the secession of the Northern tribes, J. remained the capital of Judah and of the Davidic dynasty down to its destruction in 586 BCE. During this period, the city was often threatened by the kings of Israel (one of whom, Joash, made a breach in its wall in 785 BCE) and the kings of Aram; it was plundered by Shishak of Egypt (905 BCE). Sennacherib of Assyria besieged it in 701 BCE; it was in preparation for this siege that Hezekiah cut the tunnel (named after him) by which the waters of the Gihon were permanently diverted from SILOAM into the "Lower Pool" inside

the city. The city walls were strengthened during this period by Uzziah (who added towers and "engines"), Jotham, and Hezekiah who made the "other wall" to encompass his pool. The fall of the city to the Babylonian ruler Nebuchadnezzar (586 BCE) was followed by the deportation of most of the population and the destruction of the Temple and Royal Palace. After an interval of fifty years, some of the exiles returned and renewed the Temple worship (519 BCE). J. became the capital of a Persian province, autonomous in internal matters, under the rule of the high priest of the House of Zadok. In the 5th cent. BCE, its walls were repaired by Nehemiah, while Ezra effected a spiritual reform. By decree, all the nobles and a tenth of the people were brought to fill the half-empty city. The theocratic rule continued in hellenistic times, during which the city prospered materially. This was due in part to the growth of a Jewish Diaspora which regarded J. as its spiritual center. The growing Hellenization, first under Ptolemaic rule (312–198 BCE) and then under the Seleucids, led to an attempt to establish a parallel Greek city on the western ridge. The intervention of Antiochus IV in favor of the Hellenizers led to desecration of the Temple and a religious persecution which brought about the Hasmonean revolt. After two years of struggle, Judah the Maccabee occupied the Temple Hill and restored the Temple service (Hanukkah, 164 BCE). The hellenistic fortress ACRA remained in alien hands until 141 BCE, although Jewish rule in J. itself was restored under Jonathan in 152 BCE. In the Hasmonean Period, J. again became the capital of the whole Land of Israel. In 63 BCE, the Roman general Pompey profited from internecine warfare between the Hasmoneans, Hyrcanus and Aristobulus, to occupy J. After a troubled period, during which the city was captured by the Parthians (40 BCE), it fell — following a long siege — to Herod (37 BCE) who ruled it as a Roman vassal until his death in 4 BCE. Herod built a palace in the NW quarter of the city, protecting it with three great towers; the base of one of these, the tower Phasael, popularly called the "Tower of David," is still visible; he also rebuilt the Temple on a vast scale, erecting a huge surrounding esplanade (parts of his outer wall are known as the WESTERN [or Wailing] WALL); at the NW corner of the esplanade he erected the fortress ANTONIA. After Herod's death and the deposition of his son and successor, Archelaus (6 CE), the city was ruled by Roman PROCURATORS, except for the brief reign of Agrippa I (41–44) who began to build a Third Wall to the N. During the rule of one of these procurators, Pontius Pilate, Jesus was crucified in J. (29 CE). In the end, Roman rule proved unbearable and the people revolted (66). After three years of independence, the city was besieged by the Romans under

Titus and fell despite a heroic resistance (70); the Temple and most of the buildings were destroyed and a Roman garrison encamped on its ruins. After another revolt under Bar Kochba (132–5), during which J. was liberated for a time, the Roman emperor Hadrian rebuilt it as the Roman colony, Aelia Capitolina, forbidding Jews to approach it under pain of death. With the Christianization of the Roman empire under Constantine, J. became a Holy City for the new religion; after a visit by the emperor's mother, Helena (325), the Church of the Holy Sepulcher was built (335). J. now became a city of churches and monasteries, of pilgrimages and religious disputes. In 363, the emperor Julian made an unsuccessful attempt to restore the Temple. In 614, it was occupied for some years by the Persians, assisted by a Jewish force; but in 628, Byzantine rule was restored by the emperor Heraclius. In 638, the city fell to the caliph Omar who set up a place of prayer in the Temple esplanade; this was magnificently rebuilt in 691 as the DOME OF THE ROCK by the Umayyad caliph Abd-el Malik. Under Arab rule, the Jews were allowed to return; but the city began to decay after the transfer of the center of Abbasid rule to Baghdad (750). The Fatimids (11th cent.) built the second principal mosque, *El-Aksa*, on the Temple site. In 1099, J. was stormed by the Crusaders under Godfrey of Bouillon; they established it as a capital of the Latin Kingdom. In 1187, the Ayyubid sultan Saladin retook the city for Islam and it henceforth remained in Moslem hands, save for a few years in the middle of the 13th cent., despite

A boy of the Orthodox Jewish community in Jerusalem with traditional earlocks and *tzitzit*.

all Christian efforts in successive crusades. In the Mameluke Period (14th–15th cents.), many new buildings were erected and the water supply improved. Under Ottoman rule it decayed, till in the 18th–19th cents. the city reached its nadir: its population sank below 10,000 and part of its area lay in ruins. The Jewish community, destroyed by the Crusaders and still almost non-existent in the 13th cent., was reinforced by pious immigrants from many lands, especially after the expulsion from Spain in 1492; its numbers were, however, artificially restricted by the government. In 1625, they were brutally despoiled by the local pasha Muḥammad ibn Farukh. The increase of European influence in the 19th cent. and the influx of Jewish immigration brought about a revival, the population rising from 11,000 (3,000 Jews) in 1838 to 68,000 (50,000 Jews) in 1910; new quarters outside the Old City wall were built (pioneered by Sir Moses Montefiore) from 1855. In the 1880's, J. was connected with Jaffa by a railway line. In 1898, the German emperor William II visited the city through a breach made in its wall near the Jaffa Gate in his honor; he was greeted on this occasion by Herzl in behalf of the Zionist Organization. The development of J. was interrupted by World War I, during which the population fell to 50,000. In Dec. 1917, the city was occupied by General Allenby at the head of a British army. British rule under the Mandate was a period of rapid growth, especially due to Jewish immigration; in 1946, the population reached 165,000 of whom 100,000 were Jews. The city expanded and the Hebrew Univ. was erected on Mt. Scopus. The political situation during the British Mandatory period affected J. in particular. The Arab riots in 1922, 1929, and 1936–9 claimed many victims among the Jewish population, but were usually followed by a renewed spurt of building and consolidation. In the period of Jewish resistance to the Mandatory Government (1945–8), several buildings were damaged and the city outside the walls transformed into a patchwork of "security" zones. The UN partition resolution of Nov. 29, 1947 provided for the creation of an independent area of J. under UN administration. Arab outbreaks which soon reached the dimensions of regular warfare between the *Haganah* and the Arabs (first local bands and then the Arab Legion of Transjordan) put an end to the internationalization scheme. The struggle lasted from Dec. 1947 until July 1948; in its course the Jewish quarter in the Old City had to be evacuated and was destroyed; on the other hand, all the New City (with the exception of the Arab quarters N of the walls) fell into Jewish hands. The attempt of the Arab Legion to shell and starve the Jews of J. into surrender was foiled by the fortitude of the population and by the opening of the "Burma Road" which restored the connection between Jewish J. and the coast. In 1949, the government and Knesset were transferred to J.

The city from 1948 was divided into two parts. The Israel section included the whole of the W and S part of the New City, including "Mount Zion" and an enclave on Mt. Scopus. The city extended westward by the construction of the Knesset and Government quarter (*Ha-Kiryah*) with the National Museum and University campus nearby. New housing projects (of which Kiryat Yovel is the largest) were constructed. Herzl and other Zionist leaders were reinterred on a mountain W of the city (Mt. Herzl), the slopes of which were laid out as a cemetery for soldiers who died on active service. New rabbinical centers were also erected. The industrial development lagged behind that of other cities, although a number of factories were set up; but the city was the administrative center of the country. At the outset of the Six-Day War (June 5, 1967), Jordanian troops in the Old City and Jordanian sections of the city bombarded the New City. The Israel army reacted and two days later the entire city came under Israel control. One of the first reactions was mass visits to the Western Wall which had been prohibited to Jews for almost 20 years. On June 29, 1967, the Israel government formally united the two sections of the city and the barriers that had divided them were removed. The population of the eastern portion of the city—including 93,000 Moslems and Christians—have been incorporated into the total population of 344,200 (1974). While there were examples of Arab-Jewish cooperation in the city, there were also regular cases of sabotage which tended to exacerbate relations. These were encouraged by outside elements and Arab states continued to press for a reversion to the pre-1967 situation. Meanwhile the Jewish administration proceeded with development plans including the renewed expansion of the institutions on Mount Scopus, the restoration of the Old City's Jewish quarter which had been razed by the Jordanians and the building of new suburbs. The excavations which had been carried out at the site of the City of David were now supplemented by diggings around the western and southern walls of the Temple enclosure.

JERUSALEM POST: Israel English newspaper founded (as the *Palestine Post*) by Gershon Agron in 1932 and edited 1955–74 by Ted Lurie. It is the chief non-Hebrew organ in the country and played a particularly significant role as the mouthpiece of the official Jewish agencies under the British Mandate.

JERUSALEM TALMUD see **TALMUD**

JERUSALEM, WILHELM (1854–1923): Philosopher. He lectured at the Univ. of Vienna and the Vienna Rabbinical Seminary. He wrote on the psychology of language and thought, the theory of consciousness, problems of logic, etc.

JESHUA BEN DAMNA: High priest c. 61–63 CE. He was appointed by Herod Agrippa II and later displaced by Joshua ben Gamla with whom he commenced a factional struggle. Toward the end of the siege of Jerusalem (70 CE) he fled to the Romans with other members of the priestly families.

JESHUA BEN JUDAH (fl. 11th cent.): Karaite scholar; lived probably in Jerusalem. He translated the Pentateuch into Arabic with a commentary and wrote a halakhic work of which only a section on personal status has been preserved. His legal rulings, generally less stringent than those of his predecessors, are still observed by the Karaites.

JESHURUN: Poetic name of the Jewish people; probably an artificial name or hypocoristic abbreviation of Israel (in the sense *ish yosher*—"man of uprightness").

JESI, SAMUEL (1789–1853): Italian artist, working principally in Milan. His engravings of paintings by Raphael, etc. were famous in their day.

JESOFOWICZ: (1) *ABRAHAM J.* (1448–1519): Lithuanian financier. He was appointed in 1505, after baptism, governor of Minsk and later of Smolensk. He was elevated to the nobility by Sigismund I and from 1510, was finance minister of Lithuania. (2) *MICHAEL J.* (d. 1531): Lithuanian financier; brother of (1). In 1514, Sigismund I appointed him "Elder and Judge" of Lithuanian Jewry, chief collector of their dues, and their representative at court. In 1525, he was ennobled.

JESSE (fl. 11th–10th cents. BCE): Father of David; grandson of Ruth and Boaz. He lived in Bethlehem but for fear of Saul dwelt for a time in Moab. The royal house of David is known as "the stock (or root) of J." (cf. Is. 11:1, 10).

JESSEL: English family. *SIR GEORGE J.* (1824–1883), jurist, after a brilliant legal career entered Parliament and in 1871, was appointed solicitor-general, being the first professing English Jew to hold political office. In 1873–81, he was Master of the Rolls. He was one of the great formative influences in English law in the 19th cent. His second son, *HERBERT MERTON J.* (1866–1950) was active in Conservative politics and was created a peer. *EDWARD HERBERT J.* (1904–), 2nd Baron J., takes no part in Jewish life. *RICHARD FREDERICK J.* (1902–) has had a distinguished naval career and is vice-president of the Jewish Maritime League.

JESSEL, GEORGE (1898–): US entertainer. He has appeared in vaudeville, motion pictures, radio, and television. J. has been active in raising funds in behalf of Israel. He wrote an autobiography *So Help Me*.

JESSNER, LEOPOLD (1878–1946): German theatrical producer. A pioneer in expressionist production, he directed the Berlin State and Schiller theaters from 1919. He left Germany in 1933 and settled in Los Angeles in 1936.

JESURUN DE MESQUITA see **MESQUITA**

JESURUN, ISAAC (17th cent.): Blood Libel victim.

A merchant at Ragusa, he was accused there in 1622 of the Ritual Murder of a Christian girl. His three years of suffering were described in Hebrew and Spanish accounts and entered into Jewish folklore. Subsequently banished, J. died in Palestine.

JESURUN, REUEL (fl. 17th cent.): Marrano poet.

Portuguese-born, as Paul de Pina, he was dissuaded from entering a religious order at Rome and settled as a Jew in Amsterdam. His dialogue-play in honor of Judaism *Dialogo de los Montes* was produced in Amsterdam (Pentecost 1624) and later published.

JESUS (Gk. equivalent of Joshua; d. 29 CE): Founder of CHRISTIANITY. There are no independent Jewish sources for the life of Jesus of Nazareth. A reference in Josephus is at least in part a Christian interpolation; allusion in the Talmud and the post-talmudic TOLEDOT YESHU are of value only as an indication of later Jewish attitudes. The only source of information about J. is thus the NEW TESTAMENT Gospels. Analysis of the Gospels has shown that certain sections seem to reflect ideas and situations in the developing Christian Church rather than those of J.'s own day. To determine the facts of his career and his actual teachings is therefore not easy. The following outline is thus probable rather than certain: J. was a Galilean Jew who as a young man was influenced by the ascetic JOHN THE BAPTIST and became a wandering teacher and preacher. With a small band of followers, he roamed the country, announcing that the "Kingdom of God" was at hand and urging men to repent before the final judgment. In the year 29, he and his group went to Jerusalem for the Passover; messianic honors were paid him by his disciples and it is probable that J. himself claimed to be the Messiah. As the potential leader of a revolt against Rome, he was arrested and crucified by order of the Roman procurator, Pontius Pilate, at the age of about thirty-five. The devoted followers (APOSTLES), who believed that he rose from the dead, formed the core of the earliest Christian church. The reports contained in the Synoptic Gospels (Matthew, Mark, Luke) indicate that in form and content, Jesus' preaching was closely akin to that of the Pharisaic preachers. Many striking parallels exist between the sayings of J. and those of the rabbis. Like them, he made effective use of parables, and inculcated a noble and selfless morality. J., however, laid greater stress on the imminent end of the age; he therefore tended to be indifferent to family and community obligations, since he expected the contemporary social order to disappear swiftly. Moreover, he taught the doctrine of non-resistance to evil, which is not found in classic Jewish sources. The Gospels depict J. and the Pharisees as mutually hostile, but also report many friendly associations between them. Most of his ethical-religious doctrine is thoroughly Pharisaic. It seems likely, therefore, that the growing antagonism between the young Church and official Judaism was referred back to the time of J. This is most plainly evident in the accounts of his execution. It is possible that Jewish officials, nominees of the Romans and anxious for their favor, brought the incipient messianic movement to the attention of the Roman authorities. But the Gospels represent the entire Jewish people as eager for the death of J., rejecting Pilate's proposal to release him, and taking the responsibility of his blood on themselves and their descendants. This story reflects the anti-Jewish sentiment of the early Christians and also the desire to absolve the Romans from guilt in the death of their savior. The Fourth Gospel (John) represents J. as, throughout his career, bitter and contemptuous toward his fellow-Jews. The growing breach between Judaism and Christianity led to similar distortions from the Jewish side. *Toledot Yeshu* and the talmudic stories about Jesus express this animosity by casting aspersions on the origin and character of J. In modern times, however, many Jews have written sympathetically about J. (e.g. C. G. Montefiore, Y. Klausner) and have made important contributions to New Testament scholarship.

JESUS BEN SIRA see **BEN SIRA**

JETHRO: Midianite priest and father of Zipporah, Moses' wife (Exod. 2–3). Moses lived for a considerable period in J.'s home, tending his flocks. After the Exodus, J. visited Moses at Rephidim and advised him on legal administration (Exod. 18). J.'s son Hobab accompanied Moses to Canaan, his family eventually settling in Galilee; from him was descended JAEL. In two places, J. is called Reuel, which may have been his personal name, J. being a sobriquet. The Druze honor him as Nebi Shu'aib at the shrine near Kephar Hittin.

JETURITES: Itureans. See ITUREA.

JEW: A member of the Jewish faith. The English word derives from the Old French *giu* (German *Jud*) which in turn comes from the Latin *Judaeus* (from *Yehudah* = Judah). The word J. is sometimes used as a verb in English in a pejorative sense.

JEW BILL: Name popularly given to the Jewish Naturalization Bill passed by the English parliament in May 1753 to facilitate the naturalization and encourage the immigration of foreign Jews. It did not affect the position of the native-born. An artificially stimulated wave of opposition swept the country and in consequence, it was repealed in Dec. 1753.

JEWISH ACADEMY OF ARTS AND SCIENCES: US society of Jews distinguished in the arts and professions. Founded in 1927, it holds four public meetings yearly, publishes papers, and encourages achievement in scholarship and the arts and sciences.

JEWISH AGENCY FOR ISRAEL: The authority and functions of the J.A. prior to the establishment of Israel were outlined in Article IV of the British Mandate over Palestine, which provided that "an appropriate Jewish agency shall be recognized as a public body for the purpose of advising and cooperating with the administration of Palestine in such.... matters as may affect the establishment of the Jewish National Home and the interests of the Jewish population in Palestine," and that "the Zionist Organization.... shall be recognized as such agency." With the establishment of the state of Israel in May 1948, the J.A. automatically ceased to be the spokesman for "the interests of the Jewish population" in that country whose internal and external affairs were now conducted solely by its sovereign government, but it continues as an international non-governmental body which functions as the coordinator of all Jewish overseas efforts in Israel. An Israel Law on Status of 1952 sets forth the authority and functions of the J.A. This Law reads in part: "The World Zionist Organization, which is also the J.A. for Palestine, deals, as hitherto, with immigration and directs the projects of absorption and settlement in the state. The state of Israel recognizes the World Zionist Organization as the authorized agency which shall continue to work in the state of Israel for the development and colonization of the activities in Israel of Jewish institutions and associations operating in these fields." The title, originally the J.A. for Palestine, was formally adopted in 1929 when recognized non-Zionist leaders (e.g. Louis Marshall, Léon Blum, Lord Melchett) joined the executive of an enlarged J.A. whose president was also the president of the World Zionist Organization. Cooperation between the executive and non-Zionist groups has continued, notably in the US through the UNITED JEWISH APPEAL. The World Zionist Executive has headquarters in Jerusalem and New York and offices in London and Paris. Its activities are carried out through the departments for Immigration, Youth Aliyah, Absorption, and Agricultural Settlement, which have aided over 1,500,000 Jews to settle in Israel since 1948, in addition to those assisted before the establishment of the state. These departments direct agricultural settlement work and train immigrants for agriculture. The Department of Education and Culture maintains seminars in Israel and abroad for Hebrew school teachers from the Diaspora and for non-Jewish scholars of Hebrew, and has helped to establish Israel institutions in universities outside Israel; the Department for Torah Education and Culture provides a similar service for religious education. The Economic Department's objective is the encouragement of capital investment in Israel by overseas investors. The information Department provides Zionist educational material and publishes English translations of Zionist and Hebrew literature. The Youth and Pioneer Department conducts Israel work-study and pioneer-training workshops in Israel to train Jewish youth for leadership. It also helps training farms in the Diaspora. The Latin American Department supplies educational and informational material to Latin America. A reorganization in the early 1970s put the J.A. in charge of "practical" work in Israel and the W.Z.O. of work in the Diaspora.

JEWISH AGRICULTURAL SOCIETY: Organization formed in 1900 by the Baron de Hirsch Fund to promote farming among Jews in the US. The Society has settled about 4,000 families on farms, placed nearly 22,000 farm employees in 31 states, and extended almost $15,000,000 in loans to farmers in 41 states. It conducts an extensive farm education program, grants scholarships for the study of agriculture, and also publishes a monthly journal *The Jewish Farmer*.

JEWISH BRAILLE INSTITUTE OF AMERICA: Organization founded in 1931 to assist the Jewish blind. In 1945, the Institute undertook to formulate a Yiddish Braille alphabet, and in 1950, published a Hebrew Braille Bible.

JEWISH BRIGADE: Infantry brigade group formed, as part of the British army, in Sept. 1944, in answer to the insistent demand of the Jewish Agency for the establishment of a separate Jewish fighting force. At the outbreak of World War II, Weizmann wrote to the British prime minister, Neville Chamberlain, offering the facilities of the Jewish Agency in mobilizing Jewish manpower and other resources, with particular reference to the Jews in Palestine, on the side of Gt. Britain and France. In subsequent negotiations, the Jewish Agency asked for a Jewish division; but for political reasons, the British govern-

Emblem of the Jewish Brigade in the second World War

ment conceded only a Palestinian regiment, composed of separate Jewish and Arab battalions, apart from other Palestinian (Jewish) companies. Finally, the infantry brigade group was formed, based on the three Jewish battalions of the Palestine Regiment, to which were added supporting and ancillary (Palestinian Jewish) units. Under the command of Brigadier E. F. BENJAMIN, the first HQ was set up at Burg el-Arab in Egypt from where it was soon moved to Italy. The J. B. went into action in Feb. 1945, on the river Senio in N Italy, as part of the Eighth Army. Later the Brigade was moved to the Italo-Austrian-Yugoslav border where it was able to make the first contact with Jewish survivors of the concentration camps and Jewish underground movements in the interior of Europe. The presence of the J. B. at this strategic point undoubtedly encouraged surviving Jews as far away as Poland and greatly facilitated the beginning of their surge southward into Italy, with a view to leaving Europe for Palestine. In Sept. 1945, the J. B. was transferred to Belgium and Holland, and its units were spread over the lines of communication between Brussels and Amsterdam. This period was marked by a growing bitterness and frustration in the face of the British policy toward Palestine. The J. B. was finally returned to Palestine and disbanded in Feb. 1946. 44 men of the Brigade were killed in action or died of wounds.

JEWISH CHAUTAUQUA SOCIETY: US educational and interfaith organization established in 1893 by Henry BERKOWITZ. It sends lecturers to universities and summer church camps. sponsors resident lectureship programs on college campuses, and donates Jewish reference books to college libraries. It is supported by individual membership and, since 1939, has been sponsored by the National Federation of Temple Brotherhoods.

JEWISH CHRISTIANS: (1) The earliest followers of Jesus under the leadership of James, the brother of Jesus. They opposed Paul's policy of seeking and accepting gentile converts who did not adopt the full obligations of Jewish practice. The growth of gentile Christianity soon made this group a minority sect. The New Testament Epistle of James may reflect their viewpoint before the sharp break with catholic Christianity. During the war with Rome, they abandoned their headquarters in Jerusalem and established a settlement in Transjordan. Sundered from the Jewish community as well as from the main body of the Christian Church, they gradually dwindled and eventually disappeared. Their most distinguished figure was the Bible translator SYMMACHUS; a considerable part of the pseudo-Clementine literature is also of Jewish-Christian origin. The Jewish Christians are also known as EBIONITES and Nazarenes. (2) In modern times the term Jewish Christians or Hebrew Christians is sometimes applied by Christians to

Jews who have adopted Christianity, while continuing to stress their Jewish origin and even using Hebrew in their services. They have organizations in the US and other countries with the avowed purpose of bringing the Christian gospel to the Jews.

JEWISH CHRONICLE: Oldest extant Jewish periodical, founded in London in 1841. It was raised to a commanding position through the work of successive editors of great ability, in particular A. BENISCH (1855–69, 1875–8), Asher MYERS (1878–1902), and L. J. GREENBERG (1907–31); under the last-mentioned, it advocated uncompromising Zionism. Since 1958 the J. C. has been edited by William Frankel.

JEWISH COLONIAL TRUST: The first bank of the Zionist Organization, established in 1899 in accordance with a decision of the First Zionist Congress. It began to operate in 1902 through its offshoot, the Anglo-Palestine Bank (see BANK LEUMI). The J.C.T. has assisted in the colonization of Palestine and participated in the establishment of the Workers' Bank (*Bank ha-Poalim*), the Palestine Electric Co., etc. Originally registered in Britain, it became an Israel company in 1955.

JEWISH COLONIZATION ASSOCIATION (ICA): Philanthropic society, the object of which is to assist Jews to emigrate from countries, where they are persecuted or economically depressed, and to settle them elsewhere in productive employment. It was founded in 1891 by Baron Maurice de HIRSCH as a joint stock company with a registered capital of £2,000,000 (= $10,000,000) which after a time increased to £8,000,000 (= $40,000,000). Hirsch's primary intention was to assist the Jews of Russia and Rumania to escape persecution and settle in colonies in ARGENTINA. After his death in 1896, the shares were divided among the Anglo-Jewish Association, the Jewish communities of Frankfort-on-Main and Berlin, and the management of the Brussels synagogue, the chief office being in London. ICA's main work has been in Argentina where in 1966, there were 11 agricultural colonies supporting a population of 8,000 and possessing 750,000 acres of land. The movement, however, did not attain the popular proportions that Baron de Hirsch had envisaged. At the beginning of the cent., ICA acquired land in Brazil and also assisted Jewish farmers in Canada and the US (supporting the INDUSTRIAL REMOVAL OFFICE). It supported Jewish farms in Russia under the Czarist regime and during the early period of Communist rule aided Jewish settlements in Biro-Bidjan and — until World War II — in Bessarabia and Poland. In addition, it helped Jewish credit institutions in E Europe (and until 1921 also in Turkey), establishing loan and saving funds, cooperatives, craft schools. etc. Originally regarding settlement in Palestine unfavourably, it evinced interest in Zionist activities

Young Men's and Young Women's Hebrew Association of NY. (Founded 1874, the oldest YMHA in existence.)

from 1896, and in 1899, Baron Edmond de Rothschild transferred to ICA all the settlements he had founded together with 15 million francs to complete their consolidation. In 1923, all Baron de Rothschild's settlements, by agreement between him and ICA, were transferred to a new company (see PICA). In 1927, ICA, the EMIGDIRECT and HIAS established HICEM. In 1933, ICA resumed direct activities in Palestine, especially in settlement establishment and consolidation.

JEWISH COMMUNITY CENTER: American Jewish communal institution (originally known as the Young Men's Hebrew Association [YMHA] or Young Women's Hebrew Association [YWHA], names still used in a few of the oldest units of the J.C.C. movement). These centers aim at perpetuating Judaism through a program of recreation, health education, and education in Jewish culture to serve the needs of all age groups. They trace their origin to Jewish young men's literary societies established in various American cities in the 1840's. In 1854, the first YMHA was established under that name in Baltimore. The name YWHA first appeared in 1888 when the New York YMHA organized an auxiliary for women. Other cities followed this example. The first independent YWHA was established in New York in 1902, but like all the other YWHA's it has since merged with a YMHA. In the late 1930's, the YM–and YMHA's, which had been primarily youth-serving agencies, broadened their programs to include other elements in the Jewish community. The change in name to Jewish Community Centers followed. In 1976, there were 450 such Centers in more than 225 cities of the US and Canada. Membership was estimated

at over 875,000, and annual attendance at Center activities reached 41,025,933. These Centers sponsored over 275 summer day camps, 50 summer resident camps, and more than 125 nursery schools; they reported annual expenditures of about $82,000,000 and owned buildings valued at more than $121,000,000. Professionally trained workers employed by the Centers numbered more than 1,600. Activities vary according to the needs and interests of the community but generally include a program of arts and crafts, dramatics, health and physical education, musical activity, lectures, forums, concerts, etc. Membership is open to all Jews and in most communities to non-Jews as well.

Two abortive efforts to unite the YM–YWHA's into a national body were made in the 1880's and 1890's, but national unity was not achieved until 1913 when leaders of 175 YM–YWHA's formed the National Council of Young Men's Hebrew and kindred Associations. In 1917, this Council's Army and Navy Committee helped bring into being the NATIONAL JEWISH WELFARE BOARD (JWB). In 1921, the Council and the JWB merged and since then the JWB has served in the dual capacity of national association of Jewish Community Centers and YM–YWHA's and as the government-authorized agency for religious and welfare services to Jewish military personnel.

The World Federation of YMHA's and Jewish communities established in 1947 coordinates Centers in Israel and 19 other countries.

JEWISH COMMUNITY ORGANIZATION see **COMMUNITY**

JEWISH CONCILIATION BOARD OF AMERICA: Tribunal for adjudicating and conciliating Jewish disputes. It has functioned as a voluntary social service agency in New York since 1930, handling about 400 cases a year. Each case is heard by 3 judges consisting of a rabbi, a lawyer, and a businessman. When the litigants sign an agreement to abide by the decision, it is enforceable under the Arbitration Laws of the state.

JEWISH CULTURAL RECONSTRUCTION: Organization founded in 1947 by representative Jewish bodies to recover and redistribute Jewish cultural property which had been looted under the Nazi government during World War II. By Mar. 1952, when the organization concluded its program, some half-million ownerless and heirless books and periodicals had been distributed to Jewish and non-Jewish libraries all over the world. In addition, more than 10,000 ceremonial objects and more than 500 Torah scrolls were recovered, as well as some archival material. Of the property, 40% went to Israel, 40% to the Western Hemisphere, and 20% to other countries.

JEWISH DAILY FORWARD see **FORVERTS**

JEWISH EDUCATION COMMITTEE OF NEW YORK: Organization founded in 1939. It is the central community service agency for Jewish education in New York City, supported mainly by the Federation of Jewish Philanthropies of New York City. It aims to increase the number of children receiving Jewish education and to improve the quality of Jewish teaching. It serves Orthodox, Conservative, Reform, Hebrew, and Yiddish schools, and reaches about 718 schools in Greater New York, comprising 140,219 pupils in 1968.

JEWISH HISTORICAL SOCIETY OF ENGLAND: Organization for the study of English Jewish history, established in London in 1893, among its founders being Lucien Wolf and Joseph Jacobs. Owing to the munificence of F. D. Mocatta, the Society was equipped with a comprehensive library of English Judaica, housed by Gustave Tuck at University College, London. The building and collection were destroyed by bombing in 1940 but reconstructed and reopened in 1954. The J. H. S. publications include volumes of *Transactions*.

JEWISH INFORMATION BUREAU: New York agency founded in 1932 by Bernard Richards, rendering a free source of information on all Jewish affairs and community interests. Supported by voluntary contributions from individuals and co-operating organizations, the J.I.B. maintains a reference library and publishes a bulletin, *The Index*.

JEWISH INSTITUTE OF RELIGION see HEBREW UNION COLLEGE

JEWISH LABOR COMMITTEE: US organization founded in 1934 by representatives of all branches of the Jewish labor movement in the US. Before World War II, the J. L. C. organized an anti-Nazi boycott. During the War, it helped rescue over 1,500 Jewish labor leaders from Europe. After 1945, the Committee was active in Europe, assisting Displaced Persons and organizing the absorption of Jewish workers into various countries, notably Canada. The J. L. C. strongly supports Israel and has established a number of projects there. Inside the US, the Committee conducts an extensive anti-discrimination campaign. The chairmen of the J. L. C. have included Baruch Charney Vladek (1934–8) and Adolph Held (1938–69).

JEWISH LEGION: Jewish military formation founded during World War I to assist the Allied efforts to oust Turkey from Palestine. The concept originated simultaneously in Zionist circles of several European countries and the US. It was effectively propagated in Egypt among Jewish refugees from Palestine by JABOTINSKY and TRUMPELDOR. The British military authorities only permitted the raising of the ZION MULE CORPS which served in Gallipoli, 1915–6. Jabotinsky continued his efforts in several countries. At first, he encountered strong opposition not only from the British War Office but also from the British Zionist leadership who feared the reaction on the Jewish population in enemy countries. After the British decided in 1917 to recruit Russian subjects resident in Britain for the British army, the advocates of a J. L. achieved their objective. In the same year, the first Jewish fighting battalion (the 38th Royal Fusiliers) commanded by Col. J. H. Patterson, was raised. It left in 1918 for Palestine via Egypt, where it was reinforced by Jews who had meanwhile enrolled in the US and Canada (the 39th battalion under Col. Margolin) and the liberated areas of S Palestine (the 40th battalion under Col. F. D. Samuel). The 38th battalion participated in the British attacks on the Turkish army in 1918 and especially in the crossing of the Jordan. In 1919, the three comprised some 5,000 troops. Contrary to the will of the soldiers, the J. L. was soon disbanded and the undertaking to settle its veterans in Palestine was not observed.

JEWISH MEMORIAL COUNCIL: English institution established in London after World War I as the Jewish War Memorial. Its objects are to coordinate and foster Jewish education and to improve the moral and material status of the Jewish ministry.

JEWISH NATIONAL FUND (called in Heb. *Keren Kayemet le-Yisrael* i.e., "The Perpetual Fund for Israel"): Institution of the World Zionist Organization for the acquisition, development, and afforestation of land in Palestine. It was founded at the 5th Zionist Congress (1901) on the proposal of Theodor Herzl according to the principles worked out by Hermann Schapira. The objects of the J.N.F. are redemption of the land by popular contributions, to be the people's property in perpetuity; prohibition of the sale of such lands, which are only given in hereditary leasehold; enabling workers without capital to settle on the land; guaranteeing Jewish labor; supervision of the land's use; and prevention of speculation. The J.N.F. began to acquire land in 1905. Large-scale activity began in 1921 with the acquisition of zones in the Valley of Jezreel; in 1925, tracts were acquired in the Plain of Zebulun; in 1929, in the Plain of Ḥepher; in 1930, in the Bet Shean Plain. From that time onward the scope of the project grew continuously despite the restrictions of the British Mandatory government's Land Ordinance of 1940. Lands were acquired in Galilee, the Ḥuleh Plain, Samaria, and the Negev. At the establishment of the state the J.N.F. owned 235,523 acres. In 1940–50, the Israel government transferred to it 606,097 acres of abandoned soil, mostly agricultural. In 1960 an agreement between the Israel government and the J.N.F. (between them owning over 90% of all Israel's area) established a Land Authority for administration and a Land Development Authority to function within the J.N.F. framework. Since the beginning of its activity the

J.N.F.: Planting a new forest.

J.N.F. has engaged also in the development of the land by its preparation of agricultural settlement, its planning for the needs of housing and industry, the draining of swamps, and afforestation. On the establishment of the state, these development works expanded in scope while the previous urgency of land acquisition decreased. Down to 1973, the J.N.F. had reclaimed some 250,000 acres of land, half by drainage. Large-scale swamp-drainage was carried out by the J.N.F. in the Valley of Jezreel, the Plain of Hepher, the Plain of Zebulun, and in the Huleh Basin. In the same period the Fund planted 125,000 acres of trees and built 1,900 miles of roads in frontier regions and sparsely peopled areas. The objectives of the Fund are the creation of settlements to absorb newcomers on the land, to establish blocs of settlements which will be of political and security significance, and to stabilize agricultural economy by concentrating the land in state ownership. The first directorate of the J.N.F. was set up at Vienna under the leadership of Johann KREMENETZKY. It was later transferred successively to Cologne, the Hague, and Jerusalem, where it was headed successively by Menaḥem USSISHKIN, Avraham GRANOTT, and Yaakov TZUR. By a Knesset bill of 1953 the J.N.F. was registered as an Israel company. It collects funds in 52 countries, accompanying its fund raising with educational activities. Traditional means of collection are the Blue Box (used since 1904), registration in memorial books (the Golden Book, etc.), the planting of trees, and "living legacies."

JEWISH OATH (Oath *more judaico*): Special form of oath imposed on Jews during and after the Middle Ages. It was generally taken over the *Sepher*

Decree issued by the Duke of Brunswick in 1753 concerning the Jewish Oath

Torah (or, later, the *tephillin*) and invoked the most elaborate curses in case of perjury. In some places in Central and E Europe it was accompanied by degrading formalities, such as standing on a sow's skin. The J. O. persisted in France until abolished through the efforts of Isaac Adolphe Crémieux in 1846; it disappeared in Germany during the 19th cent., but persisted longer in E Europe. No special J. O. has been known in England or the US in modern times, though the normal oath was modified in law-courts to a form acceptable to the conscience of Jews (in England, in 1667).

JEWISH OCCUPATIONAL COUNCIL: US organization founded in 1939 to coordinate local and national organizations which have a direct function or an interest in problems of Jewish economic adjustment. Services include vocational guidance, psychological testing, employment, and vocational rehabilitation.

JEWISH PUBLICATION SOCIETY OF AMERICA: A non-profit membership organization founded in 1888 to promote the dissemination of Jewish literature in the English language. It was the successor to two short-lived bodies, with similar objects, 1845–51 and 1873–1875. Since its establishment, the Society has published over 500 titles in every field of Jewish literature including fiction and juvenilia. Since 1899, it has issued annually (jointly with the American Jewish Committee since 1909) the *American Jewish Year Book*. In 1917, the Society published a Jewish translation of the Bible into English and in 1963 commenced the publication of a further translation. Other publications of the Society include an English translation of Graetz's *History of the Jews*; Louis Ginzberg's *Legends of the Jews*; and the *Schiff Classics* illustrative of Jewish literature from the Talmud to the works of M. H. Luzzatto. The business affairs of the Society are conducted by a board of trustees; the selection of books to be published is made by the publication committee on the basis of recommendations by the editor and readers. Its editors have included Henrietta Szold, Ben Zion Halper, Isaac Husik, Solomon Grayzel, and Chaim Potok. Chairmen of the Publication Committee have included Mayer Sulzberger, Cyrus Adler, and Louis E. Levinthal. The headquarters of the Society are in Philadelphia.

JEWISH QUARTERLY REVIEW: Journal of Jewish scholarship. Founded in England by Israel Abrahams and Claude G. Montefiore in 1888, it was

Bible Committee of the Jewish Publication Society of America. *Seated l. to r.*: Dr. B. J. Bamberger, Dr. E. A. Speiser, Dr. H. M. Orlinsky, Dr. H. Freeman and Dr. M. Arzt. *Standing l. to r.*: E. Wolf, Judge L. E. Levinthal, L. Zussman and Dr. S. Grayzel. *Inset*: Dr. H. L. Ginsberg.

adopted by Dropsie College as its organ in 1909. Cyrus Adler was editor until his death in 1940, and after them the joint editors were Abraham A. Neuman and Solomon Zeitlin. Formerly it was one of the main publications dealing with studies relating to the *genizah* documents. In recent years, the J.Q.R. has been a principal vehicle for the controversy led by S. Zeitlin on the authenticity of the Dead Sea Scrolls.

JEWISH RECONSTRUCTIONIST FOUNDATION
see **RECONSTRUCTIONISM**

JEWISH RESTITUTION SUCCESSOR ORGA-NIZATION (JRSO): Organization recognized by the US authorities in 1948 with the function of recovering unclaimed, presumably heirless, Jewish property in the US Zone of Germany. In 1950, a corresponding agency, the Jewish Trust Corporation, was authorized in the British Zone, and in 1952, a Jewish successor organization was appointed in the French Zone. A total of over $22,000,000 was recovered by the end of 1956. Principal JRSO beneficiaries are the Jewish Agency for Palestine, the American Jewish Joint Distribution Committee, and a number of organizations in Israel engaged in aiding Nazi victims.

JEWISH SCIENCE: A movement to promote religious renaissance among the Jews. It was founded in 1921 by Morris LICHTENSTEIN in an effort to combat the inroads among Jews of Christian Science, though it partook of almost none of the elements of the latter movement. J. S. emphasized the spiritual aspects of Judaism, the essential goodness of God, and the efficacy of earnest prayer. After the death of the founder, his wife, Tehilla Lichtenstein, assumed the leadership of the group whose adherents are mostly in New York and Los Angeles.

JEWISH SOCIALIST VERBAND OF AMERICA: Organization founded in 1921 when, because of its anti-Communist stand, the Jewish Socialist Federation (Yiddish-speaking section) left the Socialist Party. In 1936, when the Socialist Party adopted a too radical declaration, the Verband joined the Socialist Democratic Federation. The Verband is still militantly democratic socialist and anti-Communist. It has 8 branches in New York City and 16 throughout the US. The Verband publishes the Yiddish monthly *Der Vecker*.

JEWISH STATE PARTY: Zionist party founded in 1933. It split from the REVISIONISTS when the latter left the Zionist Organization, refraining from doing likewise, but rejoined them in 1946 on their return. Its leaders included Meir Grossman and Robert Stricker.

JEWISH TEACHERS' SEMINARY AND PEO-PLE'S UNIVERSITY: New York institution founded in 1918. It graduates teachers for Yiddish and Hebrew schools in the US and provides opportu-nities for adult education. Its Institute for Jewish Social Service and Studies is named after Hayyim Greenberg.

JEWISH TELEGRAPHIC AGENCY: News-gathering agency providing daily service of news of Jewish interest. From The Hague, where it was founded in 1917, its headquarters were transferred to London and later to New York. It maintains its own offices and correspondents on every continent and also provides a feature service. In the US, it is a non-profit communal organization administered by a group of directors.

JEWISH TERRITORIAL ORGANIZATION (I.T.O.): Organization devoted to finding any suitable territory for Jewish settlements on an auto-nomous basis. It was founded in Basle in 1905 by 40 dissident members of the Seventh Zionist Congress after the rejection of the UGANDA scheme. The leader was Israel ZANGWILL and its head-office was established in London with societies in Europe, America, Australia, and S Africa. A geographical committee was appointed to decide on the most suitable territory for settlement ("Ito-land") and investigations were made into the possibility of settling Jews in various lands (British E Africa, Australia, Angola, Cyrenaica, Iraq, etc.) but without success. The attitude of the Zionist movement was negative. Some of the I.T.O. leaders returned to the Zionist Organization after the promulgation of the Balfour Declaration in 1917 and the I.T.O. was dissolved in 1925. When immigration restrictions were imposed in Palestine, several successor groups to the I.T.O. (e.g. the Freeland League) were formed, but none was able to make any progress in obtaining land for settlement.

JEWISH THEOLOGICAL SEMINARY OF AMERICA: Rabbinical institution founded in New York in 1886. The first classes met in the Shearith Israel synagogue, where Sabato MORAIS, first Seminary president, and H. Pereira MENDES, its co-founder, instructed them; it later acquired its own building. Solomon SCHECHTER was brought from Cambridge in 1902 to become second president of the J.T.S. During his incumbency the Seminary library was established by Mayer SULZBERGER, and Alexander MARX began a long career as librarian. The library containing 220,000 volumes and 10,000 mss was severely damaged by fire in 1966. Under Schechter, the ideology of the J.T.S.A. became crystallized as CONSERVATIVE JUDAISM, of which it served as the nerve center. Upon Schechter's death in 1915, Cyrus ADLER succeeded to the presidency. The Seminary moved into the buildings, which it still occupies, on Morningside Heights in 1929. The Teachers' Institute was expanded to include a youth and adult education department, the Israel Fried-laender classes, later called the Seminary School of

Valley of Jezreel and Mt. Tabor.

Jewish Studies. The UNITED SYNAGOGUE OF AMERICA, founded by Schechter in 1913 as an association of synagogues affiliated with the Seminary, took permanent shape; and the RABBINICAL ASSEMBLY, formerly an alumni body of the Seminary, opened its membership lists to graduates of other schools in America and abroad who wished to associate themselves with the Conservative group. Louis FINKELSTEIN became president in 1940 and Gerson D. Cohen in 1974. The Ramah Camps were developed, and in 1938, the Institute for Religious and Social Studies was founded. The Cantors' Institute and a program of joint study with Columbia Univ. were inaugurated in 1952. The Seminary now has a combined enrollment of more than 2,000 students in all of its schools including the University of Judaism, the West Coast branch of the Seminary in Los Angeles (opened 1947). In Jerusalem the Seminary has a student center and is also responsible for administering the Schocken Library. The Jewish Museum in New York was opened in 1947 as a separate institution under the auspices of the J.T.S.A. The Seminary has produced such programs as the *Eternal Light* on radio and *Frontiers of Faith* on television. The Seminary Israel Institute, established in 1952, was a joint project of the Seminary and the Jewish Agency. By 1975, the Seminary had graduated 999 rabbis and about 1,200 teachers.

JEWISH WAR VETERANS OF U.S.A.: Organization of Jewish men and women who have served in the armed forces of the US. Established in 1896 as the Hebrew Union Veterans Organization by 67 Jewish veterans of the Civil War, it later merged with other groups and adopted the present name in 1929. It is the oldest active war veterans organization in the US. JWV is the official agency for the care of sick and wounded Jewish members of the armed forces, under the US Veterans' Administration. It also aids the families of deceased Jewish veterans.

JEWISH WELFARE BOARD see **NATIONAL JEWISH WELFARE BOARD**

JEWS see **ISRAEL; DIASPORA**

JEWS' COLLEGE: English rabbinical seminary. Founded in London in 1856 by Nathan Marcus ADLER, its principals have included L. LOEWE, B. Abrahams, M. FRIEDLÄNDER, A. BÜCHLER, I. EPSTEIN, and H. J. ZIMMELS. Its courses lead to the ministerial and rabbinic diploma. It also has a cantoral training department. Its library includes the important Montefiore collection of mss formerly in Ramsgate.

JEZEBEL (d. 843 BCE): Wife of AHAB; daughter of Ethbaal, king of Sidon. Of a forceful and vindictive character, she exercised considerable influence over Ahab. By introducing her native Baal cult into Israel, she aroused the anger of the religious elements led by ELIJAH. She is depicted vividly in the Bible (I Kings 16:31 — II Kings 9) as a bloodthirsty woman who persecuted the prophets of the Lord and unjustly brought about the death of NABOTH. J. was killed in the uprising of Jehu. The name has become proverbial in English, though not in Hebrew.

JEZREEL (Heb. *Yizreel*): Name of two ancient cities. The better-known was at the foot of Mt. Gilboa, in the territory of the tribe of Issachar. It was the winter resort of the royal household of Omri and scene of the crime against Naboth (I Kings 21). Joram and his mother Jezebel were killed there by Jehu (II Kings 9). The modern collective settlement of J., founded 1948, is believed to be on the same site. Another ancient city called J. was situated in Judah (Josh. 15:56) but its exact location is unknown.

JEZREEL, VALLEY OF (Gk. Esdraelon): Plain and valley of N Israel dividing the Mts. of Samaria and Carmel from those of Lower Galilee. It runs NE-SW from Haifa Bay to the plain of Beth Shean. Its total area is 156 sq. m. Most of its waters are carried by the Kishon river to Haifa Bay; on the E the Harod river descends to the Jordan. The V. of J. is the main communication route from the maritime plain (ultimately from Egypt) to Transjordan and hence has always been of major strategic importance and the scene of many battles.

JOAB (fl. 10th cent. BCE): David's nephew and commander-in-chief. On David's accession, he was appointed to head the army. A courageous and resourceful commander, he gained a decisive victory over the Ammonites and conducted the campaign against Absalom whom he killed in defiance of David's orders. During the revolt of Sheba, son of Bichri, he was replaced as commander-in-chief by another of David's nephews, Amasa, whom, however, he killed, after which he proceeded to stamp out the insurrection. J. supported Adonijah's claim to succeed David, and was put to death by Solomon in accordance with David's testament.

JOACHIM, JOSEPH (1831–1907): Violinist and composer. He was born in Hungary, studied under Mendelssohn, and first appeared publicly at Leipzig in 1843. Liszt made him concert-master at Weimar in 1849, and in 1853, he filled a similar position in Hanover (where he was baptized). From 1868, he directed the Musical Academy in Berlin. The leading violinist of his time, J.'s compositions include three violin concertos and *Hebrew Melodies* for viola and piano.

JOASH (or **JOHOASH**): King of Judah 836–797 BCE. When he was a year old, the throne was seized by his grandmother Athaliah who had all members of the house of David murdered. J., rescued by his aunt Jehosheba (wife of the high priest Jehoiada), was kept hidden in the Temple for six years. Jehoiada then crowned J. king, had Athaliah put to death, obliterated the Baal cult, and acted as regent until J.'s majority. J. continued in the priestly tradition and restored the Temple but later, according to Chronicles, deviated from his former uprightness. During his reign, the country was invaded by Hazael of Aram who was bought off with a large indemnity. J. was killed by conspirators.

JOASH (or **JEHOASH**): King of Israel c. 800–785 BCE. He exploited the weakness of Aram after her defeat by the Assyrians and recaptured several towns ceded by his father Jehoahaz. When Amaziah of Judah attempted to throw off Israelite suzerainty, J. captured Jerusalem, plundered the Temple and royal treasures, and again reduced the country to vassaldom (II Kings 13:10–13). He is mentioned in an Assyrian inscription (discovered in 1968) as paying tribute to the king of Assyria.

JOB: (1) Name and chief character of the third book in the Hagiographic section of the Bible. The book seeks to answer the problem of the suffering of the righteous. The prose narrative framework (chaps. 1–2, 42:7–17) relates the temptation of the righteous Job (a native of Uz) by Satan, his afflictions, fidelity, and finally his vindication and rehabilitation with God's blessing. The rest of the work consists of philosophical discussions written in poetry between J. and his friends (at first Eliphaz the Temanite, Bildad the Shuhite, and Zophar the Naamathite, later also Elihu) who come to comfort him. The friends hold that J.'s suffering must be a result of his wickedness, but he staunchly maintains his righteousness. Finally, God speaks from a whirlwind and majestically emphasizes the magnitude of the Divine cosmic order and the pettiness of human understanding. The authorship of the work is unknown: its particular style, difficult in language and devoid of Jewish coloring, has led some scholars to suggest an Edomite basis. The date of its composition has been variously placed between Mosaic and early Second Temple times. The Book of J. was recited by the high priest on the eve of the Day of Atonement, and is still customarily read in the house of mourning and by the Sephardim on the Ninth of *Av*. The view is expressed in the Talmud that J. never lived but was a parable. (2) A just non-Jew who figures in Israelite folklore. The Bible (Ezek. 14:14) classes him with Noah and Daniel.

JOB, TESTAMENT OF: Pseudepigraphic book on Job, extant in Greek, dating from the early 1st cent. CE. Its theme is the problem of pagan rule in the world. Job suffers a series of severe trials inflicted by Satan but is comforted by his faith in the reward of the righteous in the World to Come.

JOCHEBED: Wife of Amram, mother of Moses, Aaron, and Miriam. To save Moses from Pharaoh's decree against Hebrew male children, she concealed him for three months and then placed him in a chest of reeds by the bank of the Nile. The child was rescued by Pharaoh's daughter who gave him to J. to nurse without knowing she was the real mother. J. figures prominently in mishnaic and talmudic legend.

JOCHELSON, VLADIMIR (1856–1937): Russian revolutionary and ethnologist. Arrested by the authorities in 1884 for revolutionary activity, he was exiled for ten years to Siberia where he devoted himself to local ethnological research the results of which he published after his return to St. Petersburg. He took part in expeditions to the Pacific, E Asia, and Alaska and in 1919, was appointed professor of ethnology at Leningrad.

Michelangelo, Joel.
(Detail from the ceiling of the Sistine Chapel, Rome.)

JODPAT see **JOTAPATA**

JOEL: Second in order of the Twelve Minor Prophets.
The text does not clearly indicate his date, which has been placed as early as the 9th cent. BCE, and (more probably) as late as the 4th. The book contains 4 chapters; 1–2 describe a locust plague; 3–4 treat of the "Day of the Lord" when God will restore his people from captivity and punish their enemies in the plain of Jehoshaphat.

JOEL: (1) *KARL J.* (1864–1934): Philosopher; nephew of (2). Professor of philosophy at Basle from 1897, he sought to fuse the romantic and idealistic outlook of Schelling and Fichte with the classical idealism of Greek philosophy and propounded his own doctrine linking the concepts of "organism" and "free will." J. also wrote on the history of philosophy. (2) *MANUEL J.* (1826–1890): Scholar. From 1854 he lectured at the Breslau Rabbinical Seminary and in 1863, was elected to succeed Abraham Geiger as rabbi in Breslau. A moderate reformer, his prayer-book (1872) restored mention of Zion and the sacrificial cult, which had been omitted by Geiger. J. wrote studies on medieval Jewish philosophy.

JOEL FAMILY see **BARNATO**

JOEZER, SON OF BOETHUS (fl. 1st cent. BCE — 1st cent. CE): High priest; brother of Mariamne II, wife of Herod. Herod appointed him shortly before his death in 4 BCE, but J. was removed at popular demand by Archelaus the same year. Later reappointed, he influenced the Jews to cooperate in the census (6 CE) conducted by the Roman governor Quirinius who deposed him soon afterwards.

JOFFE, ABRAM FEDOROVICH see **YOFFE, ABRAM**

JOFFE, ADOLPH ABRAMOVICH see **YOFFE, ADOLPH**

JOHANAN ("Gadi"; d. 161 BCE): Son of Mattathias the HASMONEAN. He participated with his brothers in the rising against the Syrians, but was ambushed and killed while on a mission to the Nabateans.

JOHANAN BAR NAPPAHA (fl. 3rd cent.): Palestinian amora. He founded the Tiberias academy where his brother-in-law, R Simeon ben Lakish,

was his colleague. After the death of Rav and Samuel in Babylonia, he was considered the leading rabbinic authority, and pupils flocked to study with him. His teachings are frequently cited in both Talmuds and are characterized by their high ethical standards, praise of study, and devotion to the Holy Land.

JOHANAN BEN KAREAH (fl. 6th cent. BCE):
Military commander in Judah at the time of the destruction of the First Temple (Jer. 40–43). He supported Gedaliah and warned him unsuccessfully of Ishmael ben Nethaniah's treacherous intentions. After Gedaliah's murder, he prevented Ishmael from carrying away prisoners, but for fear of Babylonian reprisals, fled to Egypt taking with him the remnants of Judah, including the reluctant Jeremiah.

JOHANAN BEN NURI (fl. 2nd cent.): Tanna. He lived in great poverty until appointed to a post at the Jabneh academy. Many halakhic disputes are recorded between J. and R Akiva.

JOHANAN BEN ZAKKAI (fl. 1st cent. CE):
Palestinian tanna. Pupil and intellectual heir of Hillel, he was distinguished for his immense erudition. A leader of the Pharisees, he frequently engaged in controversy with the Sadducees and determined a number of halakhic rulings. Most of his sayings that have been preserved are in the fields of aggadah and ethics, reflecting the nobility and humility of his character. During the rebellion against Rome (66–70), he was among the peace party in Jerusalem, and was conveyed from the city by his pupils in a coffin. According to legend, he then approached Vespasian and predicted his accession to the Imperial throne; as a reward he was permitted to resume his teaching. He founded the yeshivah at Jabneh which became the spiritual center of Judaism and the seat of the Sanhedrin after the fall of Jerusalem. Under his influence, Judaism survived the cessation of the temple cult. He also set up a yeshivah at Beror Hayil. The most admired rabbi of his time, J. was dubbed *Rabban*. His pupils — who included R Akiva and R Joshua — were the leaders of Jewish intellectual life in the following generation.

JOHANAN HA-SANDELAR (i.e., "the shoemaker," although the name may be an ellipsis of his birthplace, Alexandria; fl. 2nd cent. CE): Palestinian tanna. A pupil of R Akiva, he survived the Hadrianic persecutions and transmitted his teacher's traditions.

JOHANNESBURG: Largest city in S Africa and (with Cape Town) the center of its Jewish life. Jews were attracted to J. on the discovery of gold in 1886, and a congregation was formed in that year, a few weeks after the proclamation of the city. Jewish pioneers were extremely active from the first in the development of the area and its industries, and have continued prominent in its civic, commercial, and cultural life. J. is the seat of national Jewish institutions such as the S African Jewish Board of Deputies, S

African Zionist Federation, S African Board of Jewish Education, the Federation of Synagogues of the Transvaal, etc. There are 28 Orthodox and three Reform congregations and also the King David day school. Jewish pop. (1973): 57,490.

JOHLSON, JOSEPH (1773–1851): German teacher and scholar. J., who taught from 1813–30 at the Philanthropin school, Frankfort-on-Main, was one of the first to base Hebrew linguistic teaching on grammar and also drew up a systematic plan for the teaching of Judaism. The textbooks he wrote included a history of the Jews in Bible times, a biblical dictionary, and a German translation of the Bible.

JOHN HYRCANUS see **HYRCANUS**

JOHN (JOHANAN) OF GISCALA (Gush-Ḥalav; fl. 1st cent. CE): Military leader. He was a landowner engaged in the production of olive-oil. After Giscala was destroyed by the Syrians, he conducted retaliatory raids, returning to fortify the town. Severe friction broke out between him and Josephus after the latter's arrival in Galilee (66) to conduct its defense against the Roman army. J., suspecting Josephus' loyalty, unsuccessfully recommended his removal. After Vespasian conquered Galilee, J. fled with his men to Jerusalem and became the outstanding leader among the defenders. After internecine strife, he wrested control of the Temple from the extremist Zealots (Passover 70), who fought

Jonah being cast into the sea. (From an illustrated German *mahzor*. Kaufmann collection, Budapest Academy of Sciences.)

under his command during Titus' subsequent siege. J. succeeded at first in destroying the Roman embankment and engines and utilized the consecrated oil when famine threatened – a deed described by Josephus as "one of the dreadful acts of the tyrant." After desperate fighting, he was captured by the Romans and appeared in Titus' triumphal procession. J. was sentenced to life imprisonment and died in a Roman prison.

JOHN THE BAPTIST (fl. early 1st cent. CE): Religious ascete. From the meager information that has survived, it appears that he preached repentance and proclaimed the imminence of the messianic age. He taught an austere and ascetic doctrine, stressing the importance of ritual bathing ("baptism") as a symbol of spiritual purification. It has been supposed that his viewpoint was similar to that of the ESSENES, his activity being centered in the wilderness of Judah. J. was put to death by Herod Antipas, Josephus and the New Testament disagreeing as to the reason for his execution. Among those whom he baptized was JESUS, and consequently he is prominent in Christian doctrine.

JOIADA see **JEHOIADA**

JOIAKIM see **JEHOIAKIM**

JOINT DISTRIBUTION COMMITTEE see **AMERICAN JEWISH JOINT DISTRIBUTION COMMITTEE**

JOINT FOREIGN COMMITTEE see **ANGLO-JEWISH ASSOCIATION**

JOKNEAM: Israel village in W Jezreel Valley. J. was a fortified Canaanite town before the Israelites' entry into the country, and is mentioned among the places conquered by Pharaoh Thutmose III. After Joshua's conquest, it was assigned to the levites. In Byzantine times, it was called Kammona, a name still preserved by the Arabs. Remains of a Crusader fortress are still visible. The modern settlement was founded in 1935. Pop. (1972): 3,845.

JOLOWICZ, HEYMANN (1816–1875): German religious reformer. He was preacher in various German towns, finally at Königsberg. Belonging to the extreme wing of the Reform movement, he led a group that held services in German on Sundays. J. wrote on Jewish theology, etc., and, together with David Cassel, translated Judah Ha-Levi's *Kuzari* into German.

JOLSON, AL (1886–1950): US entertainer. J. starred as a cantor (his father's profession) in the first musical sound-picture *The Jazz Singer* (1927). He was a star of stage, screen, and radio.

JONADAB see **RECHABITES**

JONAH (fl. 8th cent. BCE): Prophet; a native of Gath-hepher in the territory of Zebulun. He foretold the extension of the frontiers of Israel to be secured by Jeroboam (II Kings 14:25). The fifth book of the minor prophets relates an episode in

Joseph Jonas.

Abraham Jonas.

his life (including the well-known incident of Jonah and the fish) but, unlike similar works, contains no prophetic material. It illustrates the power of repentance and Divine mercy for all living creatures, even animals. Estimates of its date range from the 8th to the 4th cent. BCE. It reflects the evolution of a universalist outlook among the Jews in the Biblical Period.

JONAH (4th cent.): Palestinian amora. Together with R Yose, he headed the Tiberias academy. He is frequently cited in the Palestinian Talmud, and his authority was also respected in Babylonia.

JONAH GERONDI see **GERONDI**

JONAH IBN JANAH see **IBN JANAH**

JONAS: US family. *JOSEPH J.* (1792–1869), born in Exeter (England), was in 1817 the first Jew to settle in Cincinnati. He was active in civic affairs and in the new Jewish community there. His brother *ABRAHAM J.* (1801–1864) was a member of the Kentucky State Legislature, a leader in the Masonic movement, and a friend of Abraham Lincoln. Abraham's son, *BENJAMIN FRANKLIN J.* (1834–1911), served in both houses of the Louisiana State Legislature and in 1879–85, as a member of the US Senate.

JONATHAN: Eldest son of Saul. His bravery in the wars with the Philistines won him popularity with the people who saved him on one occasion after he had unwittingly incurred the death penalty (I Sam. 13–14). His devoted friendship with David, whom he defended against his father's anger, became proverbial. Together with Saul, J. was killed in battle against the Philistines on Mt. Gilboa, and news of their death occasioned David's famous lament (II Sam. 1:17–27).

JONATHAN (called Apphus): Head of Jewish state 161–142 BCE; fifth son of Mattathias the HASMONEAN. On the death of Judah the Maccabee, J. took over leadership of the anti-Syrian revolt. He built up the movement, exploiting the unpopularity of the Jewish hellenizers and dynastic differences inside Syria. Alexander Balas conceded to him the title of high priest (153) and recognized him as governor of Judah (150). J. extended his territory in several directions, defeated Demetrius II at Hazor, administered Coele-Syria, and made a treaty with Rome. Ultimately he was treacherously captured by the pretender Tryphon at Acre and put to death.

JONATHAN: Name of many tannaim and amoraim including: (1) *JONATHAN* (fl. 2nd cent. CE): Palestinian tanna, frequently quoted in halakhot of the school of R Ishmael. He emphasized simple, literal interpretations. (2) *JONATHAN* (or *NATHAN*) *BEN JOSEPH* (fl. 2nd cent.): Palestinian tanna, indentified by some with (1). (3) *JONATHAN BEN MESHULLAM* (fl. 2nd cent.): Palestinian tanna; pupil of R Akiva. (4) *JONATHAN BEN AMRAM* (fl. 2nd–3rd cents.): Palestinian amora; pupil of R Judah Ha-Nasi. (5) *JONATHAN* (fl. 3rd cent.): Palestinian amora; one of the famed masters of aggadah. His teachings had an apologetic tendency, seeking to remove any taint that may have attached to great biblical figures (e.g. Reuben, David, Solomon). (6) *JONATHAN BEN HAGGAI* (fl. 4th cent.): Palestinian amora mentioned only in aggadic collections.

JONATHAN BEN DAVID HA-COHEN OF LUNEL (d. early 13th cent.): French scholar. His works include a commentary on Alfasi's *halakhot* (of which

Sources of the Jordan.

only a part exists). An admirer and correspondent of Maimonides, he wrote a defense (that has not survived) of the *Mishneh Torah*.

JONATHAN BEN UZZIEL (fl. 1st cent. CE):
Palestinian tanna; pupil of Hillel. Though his reputation was considerable, none of his halakhot has been preserved. It is doubtful whether his translation of the prophetic books of the Bible into Aramaic is identical with the Targum commonly known by his name.

JOPPA see **JAFFA**

JORAM see **JEHORAM**

JORDAN (Heb. *Yarden* from *yarad* "to descend"):
Chief river of Palestine, running from Mt. Hermon to the Dead Sea, a distance of c. 87 m. directly but c. 200 m. following its winding course. It is fed by four chief sources, viz. the Banias, rising below Mt. Hermon, the Leddan, the Ḥasbani – the largest of the four – and the Barrighit. The waters of these streams unite N of Lake Ḥuleh, 250 ft. above sea-level, whereas they enter the Dead Sea, 1,292 ft. below sea-level. This considerable gradient makes the river a source of electric power. A hydro electric project was begun by the Palestine Electric Co. under the British Mandate at Naharayim but this has been in abeyance since the 1948 war due to its being situated on the Israel-Jordan border. The J. flows 7.5 m. to Lake Ḥuleh, thence with a strong current for some 11 m. to the Sea of Galilee along the Jordan Valley (EMEK HA-YARDEN). Thence it cuts its channel down to the Dead Sea, receiving numerous tributaries particularly from Transjordania, of which the most important are the Yarmuk, the Jabbok, and the Ḥeshbon. At low water, the J. can be crossed on foot at 31

fords and, in addition, it has been spanned by 6 bridges. The river has played an important part in Jewish and Christian tradition. In 1964, Israel began to draw water from the J. to irrigate the Negev (*via* the National Water Carrier). The Arab states, which had threatened war over the issue, decided that they would instead divert those springs of the J. rising in their countries (viz. Syria, Lebanon) and work on this diversion was commenced in 1965. The dispute over the Jordan water lasted until the Six-Day War of 1967. As a result of that conflict Israel controlled the entire west bank of the Jordan which became the scene of frequent clashes, between the Sea of Galilee and the Dead Sea.

JORDAN, HASHEMITE KINGDOM OF see **TRANSJORDAN**

JORDAN VALLEY see **EMEK HA-YARDEN**

JOSE see **YOSE**

JOSELEWICZ, BEREK see **BEREK JOSELEWICZ**

JOSELMAN (JOSEL) OF ROSHEIM (in Hebrew, Yoseph ben Gershom Loanz; 1480–1544): German communal leader and writer. Elected in 1510 by the Alsatian communities as their *parnas u-manhig* ("warden and leader"), he remained until his death the representative of German Jewry before the secular authorities, interceding for his coreligionists in time of danger and becoming a familiar figure at Imperial diets. In 1532, he tried to stem the dangerous activities of Solomon MOLKHO; in 1543, he defended the Jews against the attacks of LUTHER.

JOSEPH: Eleventh son of Jacob: first-born of Rachel. The favoritism shown him by Jacob as well as his own ambitions aroused his brothers' jealousy and they sold him to Ishmaelites traveling to Egypt.

There, he was bought as a slave by Potiphar, chief of Pharaoh's household, but imprisoned on a false accusation brought by Potiphar's wife. His reputation as an interpreter of dreams eventually reached the king who released him from prison and was so impressed that J. was appointed viceroy. Joined by his father and brothers, he received grazing land in Goshen, thus beginning the Israelite settlement in Egypt. J. died at the age of 110, and his body was later brought by the Israelites to Palestine for reburial. The story of J. has been dated during the Hyksos domination of Egypt (18th–16th cents. BCE).

JOSEPH (d. 322/3): Babylonian amora; colleague of Rabbah. He headed the Pumbedita academy during the last two years of his life, and was called "Sinai" because of his erudition. His chief pupils were Rava and Abbaye; the latter helped J. after an illness in which he lost his sight to recall those teachings he had forgotten.

*JOSEPH II (1741–1790): King of Germany and Holy Roman Emperor. As part of his general program of reform he introduced in 1782 the TOLERANZPATENT which greatly ameliorated the position of Austrian Jewry, though more in law than in fact.

JOSEPH ABU JACOB (BEN ABRAHAM AL-BASIR) see **JOSEPH BEN ABRAHAM**

JOSEPH BAR ḤIYYA: Gaon of Pumbedita 827–33. He was involved in a dispute for the office of gaon with the incumbent Abraham ben Sherira. The Babylonian scholars eventually obtained an agreement and J. resigned his claim to the gaonate during his rival's lifetime.

JOSEPH BEKHOR SHOR see **BECHOR SHOR**

JOSEPH BEN ABRAHAM HA-COHEN (Arab. Abu Ya'kub Al-Basir; first half of 11th cent.): Karaite author. He lived in Babylonia or Persia and despite his blindness (whence his sobriquet *Ha-Roeh* = The Seer) traveled widely, apparently with the object of making converts to Karaism. A noted scholar, he was versed in rabbinic studies and wrote many religio-legal and philosophical works.

JOSEPH BEN GORION (1st cent. CE): Military leader in Jerusalem in the revolt against Rome, 66 CE. His name became associated with the authorship of JOSIPPON.

JOSEPH BEN ISAAC HA-LEVI (fl. 17th cent.): Religious philosopher. He was born in Lithuania and lived most of his life at Prague. His works include a commentary on Maimonides' *Guide* with glosses by his pupil Yom-Tov Lipmann Heller.

JOSEPH BEN ISAAC KIMḤI see **KIMḤI**

JOSEPH BEN JACOB BAR SATYA (fl. 10th cent.): Gaon of Sura. When Saadyah was deposed by the exilarch David ben Zakkai, J. was appointed in his place (930). Saadyah was reinstalled in 937, but J. resumed the post after his death in 942; he was,

however, inferior in learning to Saadyah and the reputation of Sura declined. J. was persuaded to close the academy (c. 944) and retired to Basra.

JOSEPH BEN JACOB IBN TZADDIK see **IBN TZADDIK**

JOSEPH BEN JOSHUA HA-COHEN (1496 — c. 1575): Historian. Born to a family of Spanish exiles, he was brought up in Italy where he practiced medicine, mainly in and around Genoa. J. wrote two important works in biblical Hebrew; one, a world history ("History of the Kings of France and Turkey") stressing the struggle between the Christians and Moslems from the period of the Crusades; the other, *Emek ha-Bakha* ("Valley of Weeping") detailing the tribulations of the Jews in the Middle Ages. The latter utilizes many sources otherwise unknown and, with its supplement written by another hand, is of particular value for Jewish history in the 16th cent.

JOSEPH BEN JUDAH IBN AKNIN see **IBN AKNIN**

JOSEPH BEN MATTATHIAS see **JOSEPHUS**

Scenes from the story of Joseph. (From the 15th cent. Nuremberg Haggadah; now in Schocken Library, Jerusalem.)

Josephus before Vespasian. (From a 12th cent. ms.)

JOSEPH BEN NATHAN (fl. 13th cent.): French polemicist. Born of a family in close contact with the local nobility (hence their French sobriquet, later surname, "Official"), he and his circle frequently had religious arguments with them. J. gave a somewhat idealistic account of these in his *Sepher ha-Mekanne* (published only in part).

JOSEPH BEN SHEMTOV see **IBN SHEMTOV**

JOSEPH BEN TANḤUM YERUSHALMI (b. 1262): Egyptian Hebrew poet. Some of his poetry, much of which has been lost, was collected and covers most of the forms practiced by Hebrew poets in Spain. It has little originality but is written in a simple style of a high literary standard.

JOSEPH DELLA REINA see **REINA**

JOSEPH: Canadian family. *HENRY J.* (1755–1832) developed Canada's freight traffic. His son, *JACOB HENRY J.* (1814–1907), helped to construct an early railway system (1836) and pioneered in telegraphic communications. His brother, *JESSE J.* (1817–1904), was active in Montreal business and cultural affairs and served as Canadian consul for Belgium.

JOSEPH, SIR KEITH (1918–): British statesman, son of Sir Samuel J. (1888–1944) who was lord mayor of London. A Conservative member of Parliament from 1956, J. was minister of housing and Welsh affairs, 1962–4 and minister of health and social services, 1970–4.

JOSEPH, MORRIS (1848–1930): English theologian. He officiated at the Reform Synagogue in London from 1893. His *Judaism as Creed and Life* emphasized the ethical basis of Jewish observances.

JOSEPHSON, BRIAN (1940–): British physicist, working at the Cavendish Laboratories, Cambridge. He won the 1973 Nobel Prize for his work on electronic development.

JOSEPHSON, ERNST (1851–1906): Swedish painter. As a young man he introduced Impressionism from Paris into Sweden. A romanticist in a period of realism, he turned for his subject-matter largely to Swedish sagas, but also to the Bible.

JOSEPHUS FLAVIUS (Heb. name: Yoseph ben Mattityahu ha-Cohen, c. 38–c. 100 CE): Politician, soldier, and historian. A Palestinian Jew of priestly family, he seems to have received a fair general education and in 64, went to Rome on a semi-public mission. In consequence, when the Jews of Palestine revolted and temporarily regained their independence in 66, he was regarded as an expert in political affairs and was sent as representative of the Revolutionary Government to Galilee where he subsequently assumed the supreme military command. He quarreled violently with the patriotic extremists who accused him of temporizing tendencies. When the Romans attacked Galilee in 67, he directed the resistance and was besieged in Jotapata, but on the capture of the city went over to the Romans, henceforth calling himself Flavius, the family name of Vespasian. He accompanied Vespasian and Titus during the siege of Jerusalem and attempted to persuade the Jews to abandon their resistance. After the crushing of the revolt, he was given some confiscated estates in Judea, but henceforth lived in Rome. The precise role he played in all these events is difficult to determine as the only authority is his own writings in which he attempted simultaneously to demonstrate his integrity as a patriotic leader and his devotion to the Roman cause. These are, nevertheless, the main authority for the history of the Jews in the first cents. BCE and CE and of the War of 66–70. They consist of (1) *The Jewish War*, written toward the end of Vespasian's reign, and based probably on a previous work written by J. in Aramaic: (2) *The Antiquities of the Jews,* giving the history of the Jews from the beginning to the outbreak of the War with Rome (written in 93): (3) *Autobiography*, defending himself against the allegations of a rival historian, Justus of Tiberias, that he had been responsible for the Jewish War; the account of his part in the events of 66–70 given in this differs in many respects from that in the first-named work: (4) *Against Apion*, defending the Jewish people against the accusations of the Alexandrian sophist, APION.

JOSHUA (Heb. *Yehoshua*): Israelite commander and successor of Moses. Originally called Hoshea (Num. 13:8), Moses prefixed the Divine name *Yah* (Num. 13:16). J. commanded the Israelites in the war with the Amalekites (Exod. 17:14–16). Later, he was the representative of the tribe of Ephraim among the 12 spies sent to reconnoiter the land of Canaan; he and CALEB were the only ones to bring back an encouraging report. Moses, before his death, laid his hands on J. and bade him lead the people in the conquest of Canaan. After crossing the Jordan, J. defeated the alliance of southern kings headed by the king of Jerusalem, and then of northern kings led by the king of Hazor, capturing most of what became the Land of Israel (except the valley areas and the coast). He then brought the Tabernacle to Shiloh and divided the territory among the 12 tribes by lot. J. died at the age of 110 and was buried in the mountains of Ephraim. The biblical book called after him is the first of the Former Prophets and is divided into 24 chapters. The first part is a narrative describing J.'s conquests, and the second section details the division of the land. Scholars tend to regard the material, especially the geographical details, as ancient and of great historical importance. Some have suggested that it was compiled from the same sources as the Pentateuch and call the combined books the Hexateuch.

JOSHUA (JESHUA) BEN GAMLA (d. 68 CE): High priest 63–5 CE. His appointment led to street-fighting between his supporters and those of his predecessor, Joshua ben Damna. The Talmud relates that J.'s appointment was due to the bribery of Agrippa II by Martha, daughter of Boethus. Even after his deposition and replacement by Mattathias ben Theophilus, he remained influential, opposing the Zealots during the early period of the Roman War. He was murdered by the Idumeans after unsuccessfully attempting to persuade them not to enter Jerusalem.

JOSHUA BEN HANANIAH (fl. 1st–2nd cents.): Palestinian tanna. He achieved a reputation for scholarship before the destruction of the Temple, in which as a levite he served as one of the singers. During the siege of Jerusalem, he helped to effect the escape of his teacher, R Johanan ben Zakkai. J. was regarded favorably by the Roman officials, and used his influence to secure the easing of unpopular decrees, traveling repeatedly to Rome with other scholars on national missions. When the *Nasi* R GAMALIEL II humiliated him, the scholars were so indignant that Gamaliel was deposed, though J. secured his restoration shortly thereafter. After Gamaliel's death (c. 110), J. became head of the Bet Din, but without the title of *Nasi*. J. devoted much of his time to polemics with Christians. He

Roman mosaic (2nd–5th cents.)
showing Joshua's meeting with the Angel (Josh. 5:13).

opposed the ascetic practices adopted by some groups after the destruction of the Temple, and was noted for his wisdom, gentleness, and humility. For a time, he had his school in Pekiin. He opposed the movement which led to the Bar Kokhba revolt.

JOSHUA BEN JEHOZADAK (fl. 6th cent. BCE):
High priest who went to Jerusalem with Zerubabel; grandson of Seraiah, the chief priest executed by Nebuchadnezzar. With the encouragement of the prophets Zechariah and Haggai, he set up the altar as a beginning of the reconstruction of the Temple. His descendants remained in office until Hasmonean times.

JOSHUA BEN KORḤA (fl. 2nd cent.): Palestinian tanna. His reported teachings are almost all aggadic. He defended Judaism in debates with Christians and sectaries.

JOSHUA BEN LEVI (fl. 3rd cent.): Palestinian amora. He was born and studied in Lydda and became the recognized head of the Jewish community in Palestine, traveling on special missions to Caesarea, the seat of Roman authority in the country, and to Rome. J. was one of the great masters of aggadah, and became, in time, the subject of many legends, which relate his meetings with Elijah, his visits to Paradise, etc. He is one of the few amoraim whose sayings are included in the Mishnah (cf. *Avot* 6:2, *Uktzin* 3:12).

JOSHUA BEN PERAḤYAH (fl. 2nd cent. BCE):
Head of the Sanhedrin. He, together with Nittai the Arbelite, form the second of the "pairs" (ZUGOT). When the Maccabean high priest John Hyrcanus became a Sadducee, J. — who was a Pharisee — fled to Alexandria, but was recalled after peace had been restored under Salome Alexandra.

JOSHUA HESHEL BEN JACOB OF LUBLIN (d. 1663): Polish rabbi. A noted halakhic authority, he directed yeshivot at Brest-Litovsk and Lublin before his election as chief rabbi of Cracow in 1654. He spent several years in Moravia and Vilna assisting the survivors of the Chmielnicki massacres.

JOSHUA LORKI see **LORKI**

JOSIAH: King of Judah 637–608 BCE. Following the murder of his father, Amon, the populace had the eight-year old J. crowned king. On attaining manhood, he began a program of religious reform, removing foreign cults which had taken hold in Judah and re-establishing the pure monotheistic religion. His actions were facilitated, and perhaps motivated, by the decline of Assyrian influence over the country, and doubtless received the support of the contemporary prophets (including Nahum, Zephania, and Jeremiah). In the course of repairing the Temple, the high priest Hilkiah announced the discovery of a Book of the Law which so influenced J. that he convened an assembly of the entire people during Passover (621 BCE) at which a solemn covenant was made with God. Many scholars have identified this book with Deuteronomy. J. removed the high places and centralized worship at the Jerusalem Temple. His reign was one of cultural, religious, and political prosperity. In 608, he attempted to bar the passage of the Egyptian army under Necoh which was moving to assist Assyria against his Babylonian allies. In a battle at Megiddo, J.'s army was defeated and he himself mortally wounded. His religious reforms were of far-reaching importance for the development of Judaism and formed a basis for the work of Ezra and Nehemiah.

JOSIAH BEN ZAKKAI (fl. first part of 10th cent.):
Babylonian exilarch. His brother David was deposed from the office of exilarch by Saadyah as the result of a quarrel and J. appointed in his stead. The caliph intervened in favor of David, and J. was banished to Chorassan where he died shortly afterward.

JOSIPPON (properly Josephon): The name generally given to a popular chronicle of Jewish history ascribed to JOSEPH BEN GORION. Written in a pure, vivacious Hebrew, it deals with the period from the

Title-page of an English edition of Josippon. (London, 1653.)

return from the Babylonian exile to 70 CE, concentrating especially on the Hasmonean rulers, Herod, the war against Rome, and the siege of Jerusalem. It is based mainly on Josephus, probably through the medium of the Latin Hegesippus. It is generally believed to have been compiled in S Italy in the 8th cent., but there has lately been a tendency to ascribe to it a greater age and authority. Jews of the Middle Ages regarded it as more authoritative than Josephus. The misnomer J. was applied to the work by Christian scholars of the 16th–17th cents., with whom (especially in England) it was popular.

JOST, ISAAC MARCUS (1793–1860): Historian. A teacher in the Jewish school of Frankfort-on-Main, he published many educational works, including a German translation of the Mishnah; he also edited the *Israelitische Annalen* and a Hebrew periodical *Zion*. His history of the Jews from the Maccabean Period to contemporary times (9 vols., 1820–47) was the earliest serious work of this type, of Jewish authorship. His history of Judaism and its sects (3 vols., 1857–9) concentrated on religious history, the rise of the Karaites, etc. Though soon superseded by the history of Graetz, these works have not wholly lost their importance.

JOTAPATA: Ancient town in Galilee, fortified and held by Josephus against the Romans in the war of 66–70, CE, and made famous by his account of the siege.

JOTHAM (fl. c. 12th cent. BCE): Youngest of Gideon's seventy sons and the sole survivor of Abimelech's massacre of his brothers (Judg. 9). From Mt. Gerizim, he uttered a parable rebuking the people of Shechem for electing Abimelech king.

JOTHAM: King of Judah 751–735 BCE. His reign commenced during the lifetime of his father Uzziah who had fallen sick with leprosy. J. fought and defeated the Ammonites and resisted the pressure of the king of Aram to join an anti-Assyrian alliance.

JUBAL: Son of Lamech, described as "the father of all such as handle the harp and pipe" (Gen. 4:19–21).

JUBILEE see **SABBATICAL YEAR AND JUBILEE**

JUBILEES, BOOK OF (also called Lesser Genesis): Pseudepigraphical work. It consists of a history of mankind related by an angel to Moses on Mt. Sinai with specifications of the jubilee of each event. The author assumes the Torah to have been current from the earliest human period but forgotten until Moses was reminded of it. The book embodies many stories concerned with the patriarchs but all with a halakhic intent; it is thus a valuable source for the study of ancient halakhah. It may have come from an early Essene group — perhaps similar to the circles from which the Dead Sea Scrolls originated — and probably dates from the middle of the reign of John Hyrcanus (c. 120 BCE). The author, although

The *Judaea Capta* coin.

austere, was not a Pharisee. Originally written in Hebrew, it has survived in an Ethiopic translation (from a Greek rendering) and in Latin excerpts; a Hebrew fragment has been discovered at Kumran.

JUDAEA CAPTA (Lat. "Judea taken"): Legend on a coin issued by Vespasian and his immediate successors, bearing a representation of a female figure bowed in chains under a palm tree.

JUDAH: Fourth son of Jacob and Leah. He persuaded his brothers to sell Joseph to passing Ishmaelites rather than leave him to die in a pit (Gen. 37). Despite the seniority of Reuben, Simeon, and Levi, he received Jacob's patriarchal blessing (Gen. 49:8). The area received by the tribe of J. was one of the largest in Canaan and it eventually absorbed also the inheritance of Simeon in the Negev. David belonged to this tribe and his accession signaled its assuming a leading position over other tribes. When the kingdom split after the death of Solomon, J. supported his son Rehoboam and was predominant in the southern kingdom (JUDAH, KINGDOM OF).

JUDAH, DESERT OF: Region SE of Jerusalem extending to the Dead Sea; composed of the steeply falling E slope of the Judean hills. Some 60 m. N–S by 15 m. E–W, it falls from c. 3,000 ft.

Desert of Judah.

above sea-level to c. 1,300 ft. below. It is cut by deep gorges and includes the biblical deserts of Ziph, Jeruel, En Gedi, and Tekoa. Geological conditions account for the presence of caves, which were the refuge of mystics, fugitives, and rebels, as well as the hiding place of the Dead Sea Scrolls, etc.

JUDAH, KINGDOM OF: The southerly of the two kingdoms into which Palestine was divided in 933 after the death of Solomon, the northerly being the kingdom of ISRAEL. It comprised, besides the tribe of Judah, most of Benjamin and presumably absorbed the tribe of Simeon which was isolated in the extreme S. Without normal access to the sea, commanding no great trade-route, and occupying no more than a third of the area of the northern kingdom, it was poor and unimportant as compared with the latter. On the other hand, for these reasons, it did not become involved to the same extent in international rivalries, and its existence was more tranquil. Moreover, partly owing to the presence in its territory of Jerusalem and its Temple, it preserved Mosaic monotheism in a purer form. Until toward its last days, J.'s dynastic history was more settled, the monarchy generally passing peacefully from father to son in the Davidic house, except for the usurpation of Athaliah 843–37. A period of political and commercial expansion under Jehoshaphat (875–51), in alliance with Ahab of Israel, ended badly. Hezekiah (720–692) and Josiah (637–608) were especially associated with periods of religious revival. The Assyrian expansion, which had overwhelmed the N kingdom, was checked before the walls of Jerusalem in 701, but the city and state succumbed to the Babylonians in 586, large numbers of the inhabitants being deported. An attempt to perpetuate a subject state under Gedaliah, a member of the former royal house, ended with his assassination in 582. The descendants of the exiles in Babylonia continued to cherish their national and religious ideals so steadfastly as to make possible the renewal of Jewish life after 539 BCE in the area of the former kingdom of J. In contrast to its relative political obscurity, the intellectual and spiritual life of J. was extraordinarily rich. It was there that most of the canonical prophets carried on their activity, great parts of the Bible were

KINGS OF JUDAH:

Rehoboam (933–917)	Jotham (740–735)
Abijam (917–915)	Ahaz (735–720)
Asa (915–875)	Hezekiah (720–692
Jehoshaphat (875–851)	Manasseh (692–638)
Jehoram (851–844)	Amon (638–637)
Ahaziah (844–843)	Josiah (637–608)
Athaliah (843–837)	Johoahaz (608)
Joash (837–798)	Jehoiakim (608–598)
Amaziah (798–780)	Jehoiachin (598–597)
Azariah (Uzziah) (780–740)	Zedekiah (597–586)

composed, and the essential traditions of Judaism were developed and preserved.

JUDAH, MOUNTAINS OF see **JUDEAN HILLS**

JUDAH AL-ḤARIZI see **AL-ḤARIZI**

JUDAH BAR EZEKIEL (d. 299 CE): Babylonian amora; pupil of Rav and Samuel, whose teachings he recorded. He founded the academy at Pumbedita in 259. While earning his livelihood as a wine-seller, J. specialized in halakhah and developed a new dialectical system. He spent much time reviewing his studies, even at the expense of prayer.

JUDAH BEN ASHER (1270–1349): Talmudist; son of Asher ben Jehiel. He was born in Germany but settled in Spain serving as deputy (1321) to his father who was rabbi in Toledo and succeeding him after his death (1327). J. was noted for his firmness, and zealously safeguarded the autonomy of Castilian Jewish communities and courts. His writings included responsa and a moving ethical will.

JUDAH BEN BARZILLAI AL-BARGELONI (i.e., "of Barcelona"; 11th–12th cents.): Spanish scholar. He wrote many halakhic works containing clear summaries of talmudic discussions and incorporating valuable gaonic material. J. also wrote a commentary on the *Sepher Yetzirah* and compiled a formulary of legal documents (*Sepher ha-Shetarot*).

JUDAH BEN BATHYRA: Name of two tannaim. (1) Lived at Nisibis, Babylonia, in the 1st cent. (2) Palestinian scholar; possibly grandson of (1). During the Hadrianic persecutions, he left Palestine for Nisibis where he founded an academy which achieved distinction.

JUDAH BEN BAVA (1st–2nd cents.): Palestinian tanna. A leading member of the Jabneh academy, he was noted for his saintliness. He was responsible for the law permitting a widow to remarry even if only one witness testifies to her husband's death. J. was put to death by the Romans during the Hadrianic persecutions for ensuring the continuance of rabbinic tradition by ordaining the five chief pupils of his martyred colleague, R Akiva.

JUDAH BEN ILAI (fl. 2nd cent.): Palestinian tanna. He was a pupil of his father, as well as of R Tarphon, and R Akiva, and his records of his masters' teachings were copiously used by his disciple R Judah Ha-Nasi in compiling the Mishnah. He taught in the form of halakhic midrashim and was the original author of the *Siphra*. J. was also a noted aggadist. After the Hadrianic persecutions, he and a handful of colleagues established an academy in his native Usha. J. was treated favorably by the Roman authorities because of his moderate views. His humble way of life won him a saintly reputation.

JUDAH BEN ISAAC (called Sir Leon of Paris; 1166–1224): French tosaphist; grandson of Rashi. He refounded the great Paris yeshivah when Jews returned to the city in 1198 after a 16-year ban.

His main literary work was the composition of *tosaphot* to nearly all the Talmud, based on the teachings of his master, Isaac ben Samuel of Dampierre.

JUDAH BEN JEHIEL see **LEON**

JUDAH BEN KALONYMOS (fl. 11th cent.): Talmudist. He lived at Spire where he wrote *Yihuse Tannaim va-Amoraim* ("Genealogies of the Tannaim and Amoraim"), a mammoth work, only partly published, giving the biographies and views of talmudic rabbis.

JUDAH BEN SAMUEL HE-ḤASID OF REGENS-BURG (d. 1217): German rabbi and mystic. A distinguished rabbinic scholar, he devoted himself chiefly to kabbalistic studies, becoming the subject of many contemporary legends. The chief work attributed to him is the *Sepher Hasidim* ("Book of Saints"), one of the major medieval Hebrew ethical works. The book is in fact a compilation based chiefly on the writings of J., his pupil Eleazar of Worms (author of the *Rokeah*), and his father Samuel. J. also edited the itinerary of PETHAHIAH OF REGENSBURG.

JUDAH BEN SIMON (fl. 4th cent.): Palestinian amora. Son of a leading aggadist, he too was an outstanding homilist. His teachings reflect contemporary tribulations.

JUDAH BEN TABBAI (fl. 1st cent. BCE): Scholar; together with his colleague, Simeon ben Shetah, he formed the third of the "pairs" (ZUGOT) and headed the Pharisee party during the reign of Alexander Yannai.

JUDAH HA-LEVI (c. 1075–1141): Spanish Hebrew poet and religious philosopher. He was born in Toledo and resided in several towns in Christian and Moslem Spain, chiefly in Cordova. A physician by profession, he lived a life of affluence and honor, surrounded by friends and disciples. However, in his old age, his meditations led him to leave Spain and settle in Palestine. Despite the perils of the journey — it was the period of the Second Crusade — he set out between 1135 and 1140 and reached Egypt where he stayed for six months. His departure for the Holy Land was delayed and he died in Alexandria. According to legend, he was killed by an Arab horseman near the Western Wall, but recent *genizah* discoveries render this improbable. J. gained a reputation as a poet while still a young man. Intimately acquainted with Arabic poetry, he introduced its forms, content, meter, etc. into Hebrew verse. His own work is distinguished by strict meter, skillful rimes, graphic symbolism, imaginative similes, and the ingenious introduction of biblical and rabbinic quotations. Its themes at first were typical of contemporary poetry — love, friendship, nature, epithalamia, dirges, etc. The serious political developments in Spain during the early 12th cent. — when Christians and Moslems were fighting desperately for suzerainty, with the Jews suffering from both sides — indelibly affected J.'s sensitive mind. He passed through a religious crisis, as a result of which he took up a negative attitude toward philosophy and earthly pleasures and ultimately became profoundly religious. Individual and secular motifs were replaced by religious and national poetry which constitute his greatest verse, ranging over the entire gamut of Judaism and infused with depth of feeling and power of expression. All forms of *piyyut* are represented. Simple in construction, they are embroidered with aggadic and religious allusions and imbued with deep faith in the approaching redemption of the Jewish people. The basic motifs are the value of Judaism and the contrast between the destiny and actual plight of the Jewish people. His songs of Zion ("Zionides") express Israel's yearning for its ruined homeland. J.'s sacred poems have found their way into many liturgies; his secular verse was collected in the 19th cent. The entire *Diwan* was first published by H. Brody, etc. (Berlin, 1894–1930). J.'s national, religious, and philosophical views are also contained in *Ha-Kuzari* ("The Khazar"), written by J. in Arabic shortly before his departure from Spain. Fundamentally concerned with the problem of the Jewish fate and exile, the book expounds many problems and their solution. The framework to which they are attached (the work is written in dialogue form) is the story of the disputation conducted before the king of the Khazars by a rabbi, a Christian and a Moslem scholar, and an Aristotelian philosopher, as the result of which the king accepted Judaism. Unlike most medieval Jewish philosophers, J. does not seek to correlate Judaism and philosophy, as he maintains that Judaism needs no logical proof, being based on incontrovertible revelation. His criticism of Aristotelianism was influenced by the Arab philosopher Al-Ghazzali. The Jewish people, he holds, are the heart of all nations, feeling their pain and bearing their sicknesses. The sufferings of Exile cleanse them of their sins and prepare them for their restoration to their homeland, after which they will bring the world salvation. This redemption is dependent on the united will of the people and is brought nearer by settlement in the Holy Land. The *Kuzari*, in the Hebrew translation of Judah Ibn Tibbon, was of great influence among Jewish readers and is regarded as one of the classics of Judaism.

JUDAH HA-NASI (c. 135 — c. 220): Patriarch (NASI) of Palestinian Jewry and redactor of the MISHNAH; son and successor of R Simeon ben Gamaliel II. His learning and personal piety impressed his contemporaries so deeply that he was known during his lifetime as *Rabbenu ha-Kadosh* ("our holy teacher") and is usually referred to in rabbinic literature simply as "Rabbi." He was political as well as religious head of the Palestinian Jewish community and was therefore obliged to maintain close relations with the Roman authorities. His vast wealth, derived in part from his estates and in part from taxation and voluntary levies, enabled him to invest his establishment with great dignity. Within the community, his wealth was used to advance the welfare of scholars and the study of the Torah; he regarded ignorance as the cause of all troubles that befell the Jews. Many stories are preserved of a personal friendship between him and the "Emperor" ANTONINUS. J.'s major contribution is the redaction of the Mishnah. The pupils of R Akiva had made great progress in collecting and collating details of the Oral Law, but they had worked independently. J.'s authority and prestige, coupled with his knowledge of the Law ("If 'Rabbi' differs from any of his colleagues, the opinion of 'Rabbi' is the norm" says a later rule), enabled him to secure the cooperation of all contemporary scholars of note in the preparation of the Mishnah which became, after the Bible, the basic textbook of Jewish law and thought. Most of his active life was spent in Galilee, first at Bet Shearim and then at Sepphoris. His household spoke pure Hebrew and gave the language new life. He was buried in the family tomb at Bet Shearim, recently excavated.

JUDAH ḤASID (=the Pious) **HA-LEVI** (1638–1700): Kabbalist. Born in Podolia, he founded a group which stressed penitence and enthusiastic prayer. Believing in the imminence of redemption, J. and about 1,500 followers set out for Palestine. After an adventurous journey in which many lost their lives, the group reached Jerusalem in 1700. J. died a few days after his arrival; his followers were persecuted on suspicion of Sabbataianism, and many returned to Europe.

JUDAH IBN BALAM see **IBN BALAM**

JUDAH LÖW BEN BEZALEL (known as Der Hohe Rabbi Löw or the *Maharal*; c. 1525–1609): Kabbalist and scholar. After serving as chief rabbi of Moravia 1553–73, he settled in Prague where he remained until his death except for two periods (1584–8, 1592–8) in Posen. A recognized leader of Ashkenazi Jewry, he was much admired for his rabbinical and mystical learning and was active in all aspects of Jewish communal life, particularly education. J. wrote many books of commentary, ethics, halakhah, etc. Himself of a philosophical turn of mind, he opposed the study of philosophy. Many legends grew up around him, and in the 18th cent., the tale of the GOLEM was associated with his personality. In 1917, a statue of J. was erected near the Prague city hall.

JUDAH NESIAH (fl. 250 CE): Palestinian *Nasi*; son of R Gamaliel III. The first *Nasi* to settle in Tiberias, he was assisted by R Johanan, who was head of his Bet Din, and Resh Lakish. J. promulgated several regulations motivated by the grave economic conditions, e.g. permission to utilize oil prepared by gentiles and the imposition of taxes on scholars.

JUDAH THE GALILEAN (d. 6 CE): ZEALOT leader. Son of the insurgent Hezekiah (d. 47 BCE), he temporarily occupied Sepphoris in 4 BCE, after Herod's death. Later, together with a Pharisee named Zadok, he founded the Zealots. J. met his death when he opposed the census conducted in Judea by Quirinius, claiming that Roman rule was unlawful as Israel owed allegiance solely to God. His sons Jacob and Simon were crucified by the Roman governor of Judea (48 CE); his third son MENAHEM was killed by his opponents in Jerusalem at the beginning of the Roman War (66).

JUDAH THE MACCABEE (d. 160 BCE). Patriot; eldest son of Mattathias the HASMONEAN. Succeeding his father as leader of the revolt against Antiochus Epiphanes (167/6 BCE), he inflicted successive defeats on Syrian armies by his exploitation of ambush, rapid movement, and night-attack. After occupying Jerusalem in 164, he purified the Temple

Bas-relief of Judah the Maccabee in the Academic Board Room at West Point Military Academy.

and brought assistance to Jewish communities in Transjordan and Galilee. He was defeated by overwhelming forces under Lysias in 163 at Bet Zechariah, but dynastic difficulties in Syria forced Lysias to recognize Jewish religious freedom. J., however, maintained his resistance, insisting on political freedom, and was killed in battle at Elasa. He has become the prototype of heroism among the Jews and was regarded by the Christians as one of the military celebrities of antiquity. The meaning and derivation of the name "Maccabee" is disputed.

JUDAISM: The Jewish religion is conceived as having originated with the Divine call which bade Abraham leave his native land in order to become the Father of a nation. Since then, J., the faith in the God of Abraham, has undergone many phases, absorbed and resisted many civilizations, and still remains strong and vigorous after 4,000 years of history. Jewish religious experience is recorded in a series of sacred books which are more in the nature of a living growth than a finished literary product. First and foremost among them is the Hebrew BIBLE with the Pentateuch (Genesis to Deuteronomy) as its focal point. From this sprang, a thousand years after the Scriptural canon was established, a large body of rabbinic traditions (the TALMUD), itself the fountain-head of fresh development in the form of commentaries and codes. The 13th cent. witnessed the appearance of a group of mystical writings, chiefly the ZOHAR, in which the esoteric traditions of J. crystallized under the impact of Neoplatonism, and which gave rise to a succession of mystical movements culminating in 18th cent. HASIDISM. J. has been rightly described as a religion without a dogmatic system. The formulation of dogmatic propositions presupposes theological thinking, and theology arose in J. only late, after the absorption, in the Middle Ages, of the Greek philosophical tradition. When this happened, there no longer existed a central Jewish authority, and great Jewish theologians like Maimonides in the 12th cent. who expressed the tenets of the Jewish faith in the form of "root-principles," did so in their private capacities. Thus, Maimonides' Thirteen Principles conquered the Synagogue and became embodied in the liturgy (see PRAYER), but they by no means barred discussion and dissent. With the rise of Jewish mysticism, theology became increasingly steeped in esoteric doctrines which by their very nature defied expression in terms of a popular creed. Moreover, J. places the emphasis on practical religion rather than on dogma. The prophets of Israel insisted that only he who showed justice, love, and mercy really "knew" God, and the Pentateuch demands the "doing of all the words of this Law" rather than probing of "secret things which are the Lord's." Right action rather than contemplation has been the central theme of J.,

notwithstanding the fact that contemplation does play a great part in its mystical tradition. It is noteworthy that schisms occurred in J., not so much as a result of divergences in theology but from opposition to rules of conduct regulating the religious life. There is, on the other hand, sufficient warrant for the belief that the rules of conduct or "Divine commandments," which J. prescribes and defines with such loving care, are the true reflection of an unuttered and perhaps unutterable theology; that they are replete with religious significance made articulate in action rather than in words. The search for their deeper meaning fills the pages of many a philosophical and mystical tract, but what matters most is the religious fervour which the fulfillment of the Divine commandments engendered in the hearts of simple, unsophisticated Jews throughout the ages. The pattern of Jewish life provided the touchstone also of Jewish theology whenever and in whichever form it arose. That "God is one" — the fundamental affirmation of Jewish monotheism — has no meaning unless it is understood in terms of man's surrender to God's sovereign Will. The Psalmist prays "Make one my heart that I may fear Thy name" (Ps. 86:11), knowing that unless the heart is one, unified, and wholly committed to God, man cannot speak in truth of God's oneness. Jewish philosophers (see PHILOSOPHY) and mystics (see KABBALAH) interpreted the unity of God in terms of the Neoplatonic One, the Absolute beyond "human comprehension," but they did not lose sight of the personal God in whom the heart finds unity and repose by the imitation of His Goodness. The problem of evil is much debated in Jewish literature. It occasioned many daring theories but did not seriously endanger the faith in a moral ordering of the world. It rather served as a challenge to man's own power for good and helped to underline his task of "completing the work of creation" by the exercise of his human potentialities for aiding God as it were in the act of salvation and redemption; for the ultimate Jewish answer to the problem of evil and of moral order is the messianic one — that Divine justice will manifest itself in history once it can be seen as a whole. The role of the Jewish people in that messianic process was regarded as preordained by God, who had chosen Israel for the hard duty of leading mankind to an age when "the world will be perfected unto the Kingdom of Heaven." The Jew has clung to the belief in his world-redeeming mission in spite of all the persecutions — "Though He slay me, yet will I believe in Him" (Job 13:15), and the task of preserving the Jewish people until the end of days has been considered one he must not shirk, at whatever cost. It would appear that in spite of the considerable inroads which the modern age with its secularizing tendencies has made upon the Jewish way of life,

Jews still feel committed to their ancient faith. Dissensions have arisen as to the validity of the traditional pattern of life in a changing world. J. has been split into a variety of groups, ranging from strict Orthodoxy, guardian of the unabridged tradition, to radical Reform. Zionism has tended to shift the emphasis to the ideal of a renascence of Hebrew culture in the reborn state of Israel. But underneath it all there remains discernible a passionate affirmation of J. as a living faith destined to benefit not only Jews but the whole of the human race. See also CONSERVATIVE JUDAISM; ORTHODOXY; RECONSTRUCTIONISM; REFORM JUDAISM.

JUDAS MACCABEUS see **JUDAH THE MAC-CABEE**

JUDEA (from Judah): Name given by the Romans to the vassal kingdom (later, province) in Palestine which came under their rule in 63 BCE. It was renamed *Palaestina* (*Prima* and *Secunda*) in 135. The name J. is also applied to the S part of the country, in distinction from Samaria in the center and Galilee in the N. For the history of J. see HAS-MONEANS; HEROD, etc.; PROCURATORS.

JUDEA CAPTA see **JUDAEA CAPTA**

JUDEAN HILLS: The mountainous region of central Palestine. Fertile and populous in biblical days, they were subsequently neglected and suffered severely from soil erosion. Modern resettlement of the area began in 1894 with the foundation of Motza, but from 1948 to 1967, only a small area of the J.H. (the "Jerusalem Corridor" and some of the foothills) was incorporated in Israel, the rest being in the kingdom of Jordan.

JUDENREIN (Ger. "clear of Jews"): Term applied by the Nazis to a locality from which Jews had been eliminated.

JUDENSTAAT see **HERZL**

JUDEO- see **DIALECTS**

JUDGE: The Hebrew terms are *shophet* and *dayyan*. The latter appears first in this sense in the Book of Ezra (7:25), its previous usage (cf. I Sam. 24:16) applying only to God. Before the settlement in Canaan, the elders of the community acted as judges. Afterward, the soldier-leader, priest, or prophet assumed in addition to his chief function that of j. Thus, the prophet Samuel traveled from place to place to administer justice (I Sam. 7:15–17). Similarly, after the establishment of the monarchy, the king acted in the capacity of final j. (II Sam. 12:1–16; 15:2). David is stated by the Chronicler to have appointed 6,000 levites as officers and judges (I Chron. 23:4). Jehoshaphat set up a special court in Jerusalem, of which the judges were taken from among the priests, the levites, and heads of fathers' houses (II Chron. 19:8–11). This perhaps corresponds to the Great Sanhedrin of 71 judges in the time of the Second Temple, the injuction for the establishment of which

can be assumed from Deut. 17:8–11. Its functions were to judge disputes from all parts of the country. In addition to the Great Sanhedrin sitting at Jerusalem, lesser Sanhedrins of 23 judges sat in towns with a certain minimum population (*Sanhedrin* 1:4–6). The judges of these were appointed by the Great Sanhedrin. Courts of Three (Bet Din) for the adjustment of civil disputes existed in all towns, appointments being made by the president of the Sanhedrin (*Nasi*). The Great Sanhedrin lost its authority to decide on capital cases about 30 CE (*Sanhedrin* 41a). After the Bar Kokhba revolt (135 CE), even cases involving fines or corporal punishment could not be heard, for Roman law prohibited the ordaining of judges (*Sanhedrin* 14a). Later, however, and during the Middle Ages, when in most countries rabbis judged members of their own community, its was felt necessary to reestablish authority to impose fines, and, in extreme cases, even the death penalty. Jewish law sets high moral, intellectual, and even physical requirements for a j., especially in one of the higher courts. It requires strict impartiality, disqualifying a j. to decide in any case where there may be the slightest possibility of bias. In the state of Israel, magistrates and district judges are appointed by the minister of justice (the latter on the recommendation of a special committee) and Supreme Court justices by the president of the state (also on the recommendation of a special committee). See also DAYYAN.

JUDGES, BOOK OF: Second book in the prophetical section of the Bible. It describes the acts of the "Judges," i.e., the leaders of Israel in the period from the death of Joshua until before the time of Eli and Samuel (c. 1220–1050 BCE). It consists of 21 chapters containing: (1) 1–3:6, an introduction to the period of the Judges (many scholars regard chap. 1 as an alternative account to the Book of Joshua of the conquest of Canaan); (2) 3:7–16:31, stories of the Judges, of whom six (OTHNIEL, EHUD, DEBORAH, GIDEON, JEPHTHAH, and SAMSON) are related in detail, and six (Shamgar, Tola, Jair, Ibzan, Elon, and Abdon) mentioned in passing; (3) 17–21, two appendices, viz. the story of the statue stolen by the Danites on their journey to Laish and the story of the concubine of Gibeah. The Judges generally headed only their own tribe or an alliance of tribes. The book contains extremely ancient sections, e.g. the Song of Deborah (chap. 5). Samuel is traditionally regarded as the book's author although critics place its date of composition later.

JUDGMENT, DAY OF see **DAY OF JUDGMENT**

JÜDISCHE RUNDSCHAU (Ger. "The Jewish Review"): Weekly journal published in Berlin by the German Zionist Organization 1902–38. It had formerly appeared on an independent basis (from 1896) as *Israelitische Rundschau*.

The story of Judith in a 14th cent. ms.

JÜDISCHE WISSENSCHAFT see **WISSENSCHAFT**

JÜDISCHER VERLAG: German publishing house founded in Berlin in 1902, and taken over by the Zionist Organization in 1907. It published over 300 books, mostly in German, on Jewish and Zionist subjects (including the 5-volume *Jüdisches Lexikon*) before its liquidation in 1938.

JUDITH, BOOK OF: Book of the Apocrypha. It tells of the siege of Bethulia in N Samaria, and of the flight of the besieging Assyrians after the beautiful Judith succeeded in beheading their general, Holofernes. Most scholars regard the work as an unhistorical composition of the Hasmonean era, written to encourage the Jewish people in their struggle for liberty. Recently, views have been expressed that it is older, and dates from the Persian Period. Originally written in Hebrew, it is preserved only in Greek. A number of late Midrashim and hymns also relate the story which was associated with the Ḥanukkah period and festivity.

JUDITH MONTEFIORE COLLEGE: Seminary founded in 1869 by Sir Moses Montefiore near his home in Ramsgate, England, in memory of his wife. Since 1953, it has been developed, with the participation of the Jewish Agency, into an institution for the rabbinical training of N African youths.

*JULIAN ("The Apostate"): Roman emperor 361–3. His opposition to Christianity culminating in his attempt to restore paganism led him to regard the Jews favorably. In 362, he announced his intention of restoring the Jerusalem Temple and appointed an official named Alypius in charge of the building operation. This stopped after a short time, probably because of the political uncertainties created by J.'s Persian campaign, although Christian sources attributed it to a miraculous fire. On J.'s death in 363, the plan was abandoned.

*JULIUS CAESAR (c. 100–44 BCE): Roman soldier and statesman. After the battle of Pharsalus (48 BCE), he received assistance from Hyrcanus II and Antipater during the Alexandrian war, and on entering Judea revised administrative arrangements to Jewish advantage, confirmed Hyrcanus as Roman ally, hereditary high priest, and ethnarch, and Antipater as procurator (i.e., chief administrator) of Judea. He also safeguarded Jewish freedom of worship in Asia and Rome where the Jews deeply mourned his death.

JUNG: (1) *LEO J.* (1892–): Rabbi. Born in Moravia, he studied in England. Since 1922, he has been rabbi of the Jewish Center, New York, and is a leader of Orthodox Jewry. He has written many books and pamphlets and is editor of *The Jewish Library*. J. has been professor of ethics at Yeshiva Univ. since 1931. (2) *MOSES J.* (1891–1960): Educator; brother of (1). He went to the US from Europe in 1922. J. specialized in comparative religion

Sandro Botticelli: Judith and her maid carrying the head of Holofernes.

Rabbi Leo Jung.

and gave courses in interfaith relations. From 1952, he lectured at Columbia Univ.

JUNG, GUIDO (1876–1949): Italian politician. He was finance minister in Mussolini's cabinet 1932–5. The only minister of the Fascist regime to return to an important position in post-war Italy, he became president of the National Institute of Foreign Commerce.

JUS GAZAGA (from Latin. *jus* = law and Heb. *ḥazakah* = right by usage): Term applied in Italy in the Ghetto Period to the tenant right to houses occupied but, owing to legal restriction, not owned outright by Jews. The *j.g.* could be alienated or bequeathed and was recognized by the Catholic authorities.

JUS (or *Lex*) **TALIONIS:** Law of retaliation, stated three times in the Pentateuch ("an eye for an eye, a tooth for a tooth," etc. in Exod. 21:24; Lev. 24:20; Deut. 19:21). According to the rabbinic interpretation, the biblical texts were never meant to be taken literally, money payments being made in lieu of bodily mutilation.

JUSTER, JEAN (1886–1914): Historian. Rumanian by birth, he studied in France. His great work on the juridical condition of the Jews in the Roman Empire, which was cut short by his death in action in World War I, showed promise of remarkable achievement.

JUSTICE: The biblical Hebrew words for j. (*tzedek*, *tzedakah*, *mishpat*) possess many shades of meaning (justice, righteousness, proper behavior, fairness, integrity, etc.; *tzedakah* also came to mean kindness and hence charity) and it is often doubtful which particular meaning is to be attributed to the biblical terms in the various contexts. Generally speaking, it can be said that j. and righteousness are synonymous concepts, basic to biblical ethics ("Justice, justice shalt thou pursue" — Deut. 16:20). The recognition of man's rights and their protection in those instances where they are most likely to be abused (the weak, the fatherless, the widow, the stranger) are a major concern of biblical legislation and prophetic preaching. Since a narrow conception of j. may often amount to injustice, the rabbis insisted that j. (*din*) should be tempered with mercy (*raḥamim*), this being how God Himself acted in His creation and government of the universe. The ideal — i.e., the righteous — ruler is the subject of many biblical passages and similarly the talmudic sages stressed the great responsibility of the Divinely-charged administration of j. ("A righteous judge is the partner of God in the work of Creation" *Shabbat* 10a).

*JUSTINIAN: Byzantine emperor 527–65. His intolerant attitude to religious minorities resulted in a thoroughgoing anti-Jewish policy. Jews were not allowed to serve in civil or military posts, to own Christian slaves, to give evidence against Christians, or to celebrate Passover at the same time as Easter. In 553, he issued an edict regulating the synagogue service and forbidding the "Deutero-sis" (i.e., rabbinic expositions). In Africa, J. outlawed synagogues (535) and forcibly converted the Jews of Borion. An unsuccessful revolt by Samaritans and Jews against his rule occurred at Caesarea in 556.

JUSTUS OF TIBERIAS (fl. 1st sent. CE): Historian; political and literary rival of Josephus. He belonged to the upper social stratum of Tiberias and evidently to the moderate party in the city which desired peace with Rome. He opposed Josephus' actions in Galilee and, together with his father Pistus and others, was arrested and taken to Tarichaea. Later, he fled to Beirut where Agrippa II appointed him his private secretary. J. did not participate in the actual fighting against Rome but wrote a book on it with a different emphasis from Josephus' history, describing the doubtful role played by Josephus in Galilee. Josephus answered the charges in his autobiography. J.'s book on the war and another composition on the Jewish monarchy are known, apart from Josephus' mention, only from information in the works of the Early Church Fathers and from Byzantine authors.

KA'B AL-AḤBAR (d. 652 or 655): Jewish convert to Islam who spread a knowledge of Jewish traditions among the Moslems. A native of Yemen, he went to Medina shortly after Mohammed's death and, though advanced in age, there embraced the new faith. He was held in high esteem and often questioned about Jewish traditions mentioned in the Koran or in sayings of Mohammed. He is frequently quoted as an authority on Moslem theological literature.

KABAK, AHARON AVRAHAM (1880–1944): Hebrew novelist. Born in White Russia, he lived at Odessa and Constantinople before settling in Jerusalem in 1911. His novels include a tetralogy against a background of the Zionist movement in the first part of the 20th cent.; a historic trilogy about Solomon Molcho; *Ba-Mishol ha-Tzar* ("On the Narrow Path"), centering around the personality of Jesus; and his unfinished *Toledot Mishpaḥah Aḥat* ("One Family's History"; 4 vols.) reflecting the intellectual struggles of an E European Jewish family during the past century.

KABBALAH (Heb. "tradition"): The mystical religious stream in Judaism. The term K. originally denoted the oral tradition which was transmitted alongside the Written Law, but in the 12th cent., it was adopted by mystics to denote the alleged continuity of their mystical "tradition" from early times. Mysticism in general strives for a vital, intensive contact with the Divinity, and in Jewish mysticism, too, this desire for immediate awareness of and communion with God is basic. On a philosophical level, K. also seeks to explain the connection between God and creation, the existence of good and evil, and to show the road to spiritual perfection. In all periods it was influenced by foreign spiritual currents, such as GNOSTICISM and NEOPLATONISM; nevertheless, it always preserved its basic Hebrew character. Although originally an esoteric and, indeed "aristocratic" movement, it succeeded in appealing to the masses, becoming a popular religious movement in the 16th cent. and again, later, in Ḥasidism. A distinction was usually made between theoretical and practical K.; the latter consisted of the use of Divine or Holy Names, the permutation and combination of Hebrew letters, magical formulae (amulets), etc. for healing the sick

and other practical purposes and also for eschatological and genuinely mystical ends (hastening the advent of the Messiah, inducing states of mystical or ecstatic experience, etc.). The first signs of Jewish mysticism can be found in the 1st cent. while the study of the Dead Sea Scrolls may date knowledge on the subject even earlier. The religious syncretism (the mingling and fusion of various oriental religions, mythologies, semi-philosophical notions, etc.) of the period as well as the messianic speculations encouraged by the national and political disasters in Palestine fostered a special kind of interest in the Bible which stressed its eschatological and mystical tendencies. Apocalyptic writings, such as the Book of Enoch and IV Ezra, are typical of this period. Closed circles from among the pupils of R Johanan ben Zakkai (1st–2nd cents.) concerned themselves with the mysteries of Creation and the nature of the Divine Throne or "Chariot" (MAASEH BERESHIT and MAASEH MERKAVAH). These gnosticizing types of study were termed PARDES. Few passages have survived from these mystical writings but, at a later period, they contributed to the creation of the HEKHALOT literature. Babylonia and Byzantium in the 7th–8th cents. were important centers of mystical life, and major works (e.g. the "Greater" and "Lesser" *Hekhalot, Shiur Komah, The Letters of R Akiva, Midrash Konen*) were composed there. These works depict seven celestial *hekhalot* ("palaces" or worlds) populated by angels praising and serving the Deity; in the last or seventh palace, the throne of Divine glory rises. Prepared by a rigorous mystical discipline, and sanctified through fasting and religious ecstasy, the adepts or — as they were called — "viewers of the *Merkavah* (Divine chariot)" experienced the ascent of their soul through worlds and heavens, amid lurking dangers, from palace to palace, until they reached the point where they beheld the radiance of the Divine presence and the Divine throne. To the soul which achieves this vision are revealed the secrets of creation, the ways of the angels, and the date of Redemption and of the advent of the Messiah. *Merkavah* literature is influenced by Gnosticism although not embodying its dualistic beliefs. The *Hekhalot* hymns and accounts are exclusively concerned with the ecstatic ascent to the higher spheres and the overwhelming, terrifying

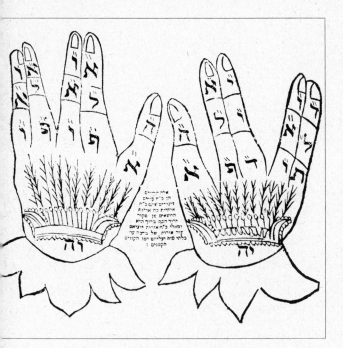

The hand as a cosmic symbol.
(From *Shepha Tal* by Shabbetai Horowitz, Hanau, 1712.)

vision of the Divine majesty. The influence of this literature is still discernible in the liturgy (e.g. the KEDUSHAH prayer). The SEPHER YETZIRAH belongs to the same period; it expounds the creative force of the letters of the Hebrew alphabet and propounds the doctrine of ten SEPHIROT through which the world came into being. The mystic tradition of the *Hekhalot* literature was transmitted in the 9th cent. by Aaron ben Samuel of Baghdad to S Italy and thence found its way to Germany. Here, a particular brand of mystical piety reached its zenith in the teaching of the 12th cent. *Haside Ashkenaz* ("the devout of Germany"), particularly in the *Sepher Hasidim* ("Book of the Devout"). The leading figures of this movement were R Judah He-Hasid (d. 1217) and R Eleazar of Worms (d. 1238). This school preached asceticism and, especially, DEVOTION (*kavanah*) and indifference to honors, worldly emotions, desires, and passions. They distinguished between the hidden transcendent God who is beyond comprehension and His created *Kavod* ("glory") or Cherub — the manifestation of the Divine. To the latter must be ascribed all the ATTRIBUTES of God mentioned in the Bible, including revelation to the prophets. Mystical teachings were also transmitted via Italy to Provence, and it was here that the decisive form of Jewish mysticism, K., developed. The leading kabbalists were R Abraham ben David and his son R Isaac the Blind. One of the earliest kabbalistic texts, the Book BAHIR, circulated among these kabbalists; it contained earlier mystical gnostic ideas and already implied the doctrine of the *Sephirot*, according to

which ten Divine potencies or *Sephirot* emanated from *En Soph*, the hidden God. From Provence the K. reached Spain (12th–13th cents.) with centers in Gerona, Burgos, and Toledo. The teachings of Azriel of Gerona are clearly indebted to Neoplatonism and attempt to give abstract philosophical explanations of kabbalistic concepts. For the kabbalists of Gerona the goal of man is to achieve DEVEKUT or communion with God through concentration in prayer and the mediation of the *Sephirot*. Gerona Kabbalism is also represented in Nahmanides' famous Bible commentary. Alongside these mystics, who formulated the theosophical foundation of K., existed a mystic stream striving to attain the renewal of prophecy and Divine revelation through ecstasy, achieved by a technique of meditation using the letters of the Bible and the Divine names; this group, which included Abraham Abulafia, provoked the antagonism of Solomon ben Adret and rabbinic leadership generally. The climax of Spanish kabbalism was the appearance of the ZOHAR, connected with Moses de LEON (d. 1305). All later kabbalistic systems derived from the Zohar, which teaches the self-manifestation or revelation of God through the Divine *sephirot* which He emanated. *En-Soph*, the transcendent God, remains forever beyond the grasp of the human mind which can only comprehend the *sephirot*. The order of the *sephirot* is (1) *Keter* ("crown"); (2) *Hokhmah* ("wisdom"), the first real manifestation of the *En Soph*, containing the ideal plan of all the worlds; (3) *Binah* ("intelligence"), i.e., Divine intelligence in which the hidden pattern achieves concreteness and form; (4) *Hesed* ("lovingkindness") from which flow the merciful qualities of God; (5) *Gevurah* ("power"), the source of divine judgment and law; (6) *Tipheret* ("beauty") mediating between (4) and (5) to bring harmony and compassion upon the world; (7) *Netzah* ("eternity"); (8) *Hod* ("majesty"); (9) *Yesod* ("foundation") which concentrates all the higher powers and influences; (10) *Malkhut* ("kingdom"), the receptive or "female" potency which distributes the Divine stream to the lower worlds. The *sephirot* were charted and depicted by kabbalists in various ways, e.g. in the form of triangles, in the form of the body of ADAM KADMON, and in the form of a tree and its branches. The fate of the "Lower World" is the reflection of the dynamic operation of the *sephirot*; thus peace and good are brought about by the influence of *Hesed*, war and hunger by *Gevurah*. But the life of the *sephirot* is affected by human action, and a reciprocal relationship is established between the *sephirot* and mankind. Increase of sin forces the *Shekhinah* ("Divine presence" equated with the tenth *sephirah*, *Malkhut*) into exile and with it the people of Israel. The righteous endeavor by good deeds — prayer and the performance of *mitzvot* — to deliver the *Shekhinah* from exile. The human organs correspond to the ten *sephirot* and man must insure the dominion of the higher *sephirot* in order to achieve *devekut* with God. Man was originally created in a state of constant *devekut* but this was destroyed by Adam's sin which drew death and evil upon the world. After death, the human soul is judged and allotted to paradise, hell, or transmigration in human or animal form in order to make restitution and be cleansed. The Zohar traces all K. to the Pentateuch, interpreting every word or letter mystically. These teachings spread in the 14th–15th cents. in Spain, Italy, and Poland but remained a movement of individuals until the expulsion from Spain (1492) which awoke messianic longings and aroused mass interest in the K. with its doctrine of the redemption of Israel. Safed, where were concentrated the leading kabbalists, e.g. Eliezer Askari, Solomon Alkabetz, Joseph Caro, Moses Cordovero, and Isaac Luria, became the center of the kabbalistic renaissance in the 16th cent. CORDOVERO (d. 1570) was the theoretician of the movement, dealing in particular with the differences between pantheism and K. (God is all reality but not all reality is God). No barrier separates God and the *sephirot*. All the spiritual and physical worlds (*Atzilut* the world of emanation, *Beriah* the world of creation, *Yetzirah* the world of formation, *Asiyah* the world of making) are one. Isaac LURIA (d. 1572) wrote nothing himself but impressed his personality on the development of K. His teachings, of a distinctly gnostic character, were recorded by his pupil Hayyim Vital (d. 1620). Their central doctrines were *Tzimtzum* ("contraction"), *Shevirat ha-Kelim* ("breaking of the vessels"), and *Tikkun* ("restoration"). The problem of the creation of the material world from God is answered by *Tzimtzum*, i.e., God, who originally is "all in all," contracts "from Himself into Himself" leaving a vacuum in which Creation can then take place by an emanation or a spiritual beam flowing from the *En Soph*. This process is constant. *Shevirat ha-Kelim* answers the problem of evil. The Divine light was too strong for more than the three first *sephirot* ("the vessels"); the impact of the light shattered the other *sephirot* leading to confusion and to the mingling of light and darkness, of the spiritual and the material; evil and darkness thereby entered the world. Man must restore the damage by releasing the holy sparks from defilement (*Tikkun*). The complete restoration will lead to redemption and the advent of the Messiah. *Tikkun* is accomplished by observance of the commandments, study of the Torah, and mystic meditation. The Safed K. introduced new ceremonies, customs, and prayer rites. Its messianic character profoundly influenced the ideology and heretical theology of the movement connected with SHABBETAI TZEVI (1625–1676) who retained his hold on large numbers even after his apostasy which was mystically interpreted as a descent of the Redeemer to the sphere of sin and the unholy in order to redeem the Divine sparks. This led the way to the antinomism of the extreme Sabbetaians and the Frankists. After the Sabbetaian crisis, the centers of K. were in Jerusalem and Poland. Lurianic kabbalism was absorbed into the doctrines of HASIDISM which popularized the mystic teachings, being less concerned with kabbalistic theosophy than with mystical piety and adherence to the presence of God (*devekut*). Among later Jewish thinkers influenced by K. mention should be made of R Avraham Yitzhak Ha-Kohen KOOK, whose system centered around the soul of the Jewish nation, its rises and falls being viewed from an angle of mystical nationalism. Outstanding among contemporary scholars of K. is G. SCHOLEM, whose researches have put the study of K. on a firm scientific basis by careful philological analysis of the texts and sources, and by viewing the movement against the background of historical conditions and spiritual influences both in the outside world and in Judaism.

KABBALAT SHABBAT (Heb. "reception of the Sabbath"): Prayer service recited in most synagogues on Friday evenings with the approach of Sabbath. The following is the order of service: Ps. 95–99; 29, LEKHAH DODI, and Ps. 92–3. Some rites add the prayer *Anna be-Khoah* after Ps. 29. The recitation of Ps. 92–3 at the inauguration of the Sabbath is designated as "ancient" in medieval literature; but the other psalms and *Lekhah Dodi* were only introduced in the 16th cent., initially by the Safed kabbalists.

KABRONIM (Heb. from *kavar*, "bury"): The gravediggers of the Jewish community — frequently organized as a *hevrah* or society.

KADDISH (Heb. "consecration"): The most famous Jewish liturgical doxology. Its origin is ancient, and it was known during Second Temple times. Its central formula ("May His great Name be blessed for ever and for all time" recited by the entire congregation formerly figured at the close of aggadic expositions (*Berakhot* 3a). The present version is almost entirely in Aramaic. The *k.* was recited before and after prayer or reading the Torah. In more recent times, a mourner's *k.* has been introduced at the end of the prayer. This custom, apparently originating in Germany c. 1200, is based on a legend that R Akiva taught an orphan to recite *k.* and *barekhu*, proving a pious upbringing, in order to save the boy's father from perdition. The varieties of *k.* are (1) *half-k.*, recited in the morning service before the blessings of the *Shema*, after reading the Law, etc.; (2) *mourners'* k. (same as (1) with the addition of one sentence in Aramaic and another in Hebrew) said by mourners and those observing *Yahrzeit*; (3) *full k.* (same as (2) with an added petition in Aramaic for the acceptance of the prayer), read after the *Amidah*; (4) *k. de-rabbanan* ("rabbis' k."). (same as (3) with an additional prayer for students) recited on the completion of study; and (5) *extended k.* specifically referring to the Resurrection and the

Kaddish preceding the prayers for dew and rain, according to the Polish rite followed in Galicia. (c. 1850).

rebuilding of the Temple, said at burials and on the conclusion of the study of a talmudic *masekhta* and in the Sephardi rite on *Av* 9; Yemenite Jews recite it daily after studying the Mishnah following prayer.

KADESH: Name of several ancient places in Palestine.

One of the best-known was in the Wilderness of Zin and was a stopping-place for the Israelites in their wanderings (Num. 33:36). It was situated on the frontier of Edom, near the later Petra. See also KADESH-BARNEA.

KADESH BARNEA: Oasis in the wilderness of Paran; camping-place of the Israelites on their journey from Egypt (Num. 13:26). It was one of the southern-most points of the territory of the Land of Israel as envisaged by Moses and Joshua. The Israelites dwelt there for a considerable period, during which Moses dispatched the Twelve Spies. The site is believed to be in east central Sinai.

KADIMAH: First Jewish students' nationalist society, founded in Vienna in 1882 by students from E Europe with the aim of fighting assimilation and working for Palestinian colonization. K. supported Herzl in 1896 and played an important part in Zionist work in Vienna.

KADOORIE: Family, originating in Baghdad, which rose to great wealth in China. *SIR ELLIS K.* (1865–1922) left among other bequests $300,000 for teaching agriculture in Palestine and this was used to establish a school for Arabs (at Tulkarm) and one for Jews (near Mt. Tabor). The Marrano synagogue at Oporto (Portugal) bears his name.

KAFFA (Feodosiya): Coastal city in Crimea (ancient Theodosia). A synagogue already existed there in 909, and a strong Jewish community was reported

Wadi-el-Kuderat in Sinai, identified as Kadesh Barnea.

during the 13th–15th cents. The local synagogue followed a variant of the ancient Byzantine rite of prayers (*Maḥzor Kaffa*, published in 1793) now extinct. After the 18th cent., the Jewish population declined and before World War II numbered about 2,000.

KAFKA, FRANZ (1883–1924): Czech author. His symbolical or allegorical fiction (edited by Max Brod) established him posthumously as a major figure in European literature. His chief works (all in German) are *The Trial*, *The Castle*, *America*, and *In a Penal Colony*. His apparent realism is loaded with symbolic meaning and dream-psychology. He depicts the fear and despair of western man who feels himself in the grip of anonymous, wicked, and stupid superior powers, bureaucratic, impenetrable, and despotic, which forever keep him away from God, salvation, and happiness. The publication of his diaries and other fragments have shown K.'s Jewish consciousness.

KAFR KANNA: Arab village NE of Nazareth. It contains the remains of the mosaic pavement of a synagogue from the 5th–6th cents. Jews continued to live there until the 16th cent. Since Byzantine times it has been believed that the miracle of Cana in Galilee (John 2:2, etc.), took place there; as a consequence numerous churches were erected in the village. Pop. (1974): 5,900 (all Christian).

KAGANOVICH, LAZAR MOISEYEVICH (1893–): Russian leader. He joined the Bolshevik wing of the Social Democrats in 1911 and in 1917, was elected to the central executive of the USSR, helping to organize the Red Army 1918–9. From 1920, he was active in economic organization and from 1930, directed industrialization. In 1935–7, he was commissar of transportation, in which capacity he was responsible for the building of the Moscow subway.

Kafr Kanna.

A close collaborator of the Russian ruler, Josef Stalin, he was in 1937 appointed commissar of heavy industry. During World War II, he coordinated transport, and subsequently was deputy minister of trade (1945). In 1952, he became a member of the Communist Party presidium and in 1955, as first deputy prime minister, was made adviser of the Council of Ministers on questions of labor and wages. In 1957, he was dismissed by Khrushchev and relegated to an obscure position in Asiatic Russia.

KAHAL (Heb.): A Jewish congregation, generally *kahal kadosh* (= Holy Congregation: abbreviated sometimes as *k.k.*); among Ashkenazim colloquially, *kehillah*. In E Europe the term was applied to the organized Jewish Community having autonomous rights and responsible for taxation; this was abolished in the 19th cent.

KAHAN, ISRAEL MEIR see ḤAPHETZ ḤAYYIM

KAHANA: Name of several Babylonian amoraim, including: (1) a contemporary of Rav and R Assi (fl. 3rd cent.) who spent his latter years in Palestine. (2) A pupil of Rav (fl. 3rd cent.). On being forced to flee from Babylon, he went to Palestine but after a short period returned to his home. He is frequently quoted in the Babylonian Talmud. (3) A pupil of Rava (fl. 4th cent.). He visited Palestine on several occasions, eventually settling there. (4) Head of the Pumbedita academy (fl. 4th cent.). His pupils included R Ashi.

KAHANA, AVRAHAM (1874–1946): Scholar. After living in the Ukraine, he settled in Palestine in 1923, working as teacher and librarian. He was the author of many studies on Jewish literature and history, including collections of source-material, contributions to Italian Jewish history, a Russian-Hebrew dictionary, etc. He published the Bible (1904 ff.) with a commentary (by himself and other leading scholars), combining Jewish tradition with a modern critical approach, and an annotated Apocrypha (by himself and others 1937) in Hebrew translation.

KAHANA, DAVID see **KOGAN, DAVID**

KAHANOVITZ, PHINEHAS (pseudonym "Der Nister"; 1884–1952): Russian Yiddish author. His novels and poems were characterized by an original style, imbued with mysticism and romanticism. In 1939, he began to publish his realistic historical novel of Ukrainian Jewish life *House of Crisis,* of which two volumes had appeared by 1948. He fell victim to the Stalinist purges.

KAHINA see **DAHIYA**

*KAHLE, PAUL (1875–1964): German orientalist. He taught at Giessen and Bonn, and in 1939, settled in Oxford. K.'s classic investigations of the Babylonian and Palestinian systems of vocalization made a major contribution to the study of the development of Hebrew punctuation. By editing the Leningrad ms of the Bible for the third edition of Kittel's *Biblia Hebraica* (1937), he laid a new foundation for the study of the

Tiberian masoretic tradition, freeing it from the accretions of the Middle Ages.

KAHN, ALBERT (1869–1942): US architect. As a leading industrial architect, K. pioneered in the use of reinforced concrete. He designed 1,000 buildings for the Ford Motor Co. and over 500 industrial buildings for Russia's first 5-year plan.

KAHN, BERNHARD (1876–1955): Communal worker. From 1904–21, he was general secretary in Berlin of the Hilfsverein; 1921–4, director of the refugee office of the Joint Distribution Committee; and 1924–39, director of its European office. In 1939, he settled in New York where he continued his connection with the Joint Distribution Committee (vice-chairman from 1950).

KAHN, ELY JACQUES (1884–1972): US architect. Professor of design at Cornell (1915), he has designed many public edifices, large office and apartment buildings, and leading department stores in New York State. K. was chairman of the board of the Beaux Arts Institute of Design (1930) and president of the Municipal Art Society of New York (1938). He wrote *Design in Art and Industry*.

KAHN, GUSTAVE (1859–1936): French poet of the symbolist school; one of the founders of the "free verse" movement. His best-known books are *Les palais nomades* and *Le livre d'images*. The latter influenced the Anglo-American "imagists."

KAHN, OTTO HERMANN (1867–1934): Banker and art patron. German-born, he arrived in the US via England in 1893. He made his fortune as partner in the banking firm of Kuhn, Loeb, and Co. and helped E. M. Harriman reorganize the western railroad. K. was noted as a patron of theater, music, and the arts. He was chairman of the board (1903–17) and then president (1917–31) of the Metropolitan Opera Co. in New York.

KAHN, REUBEN LEON (1887–): US bacteriologist. He has studied and written extensively on immunology. In 1923, he originated the Kahn blood test for syphilis. From 1923, he taught at the Univ. of Michigan Medical School.

KAHN, ZADOC (1839–1905): French rabbi. He was appointed chief rabbi of Paris in 1868 and of France in 1889. An outstanding preacher and a leading personality in W European Jewry and the *Hoveve Zion* movement, he was active in combating anti-Semitism in France, particularly during the Dreyfus Case. He exerted himself in behalf of E European Jewry during the pogroms at the beginning of the century. K. published collections of sermons and other works.

KAI-FENG-FÛ: Town in Central China; seat of the only known historic Chinese Jewish community. Its synagogue, destroyed by floods, was rebuilt by the Jewish mandarin CHAO Yng Ch'êng in 1652 and fell into decay in the 19th cent. Chinese of Jewish descent still live in K. F. F.

The "Seat of Moses" in the Kai-Feng-Fû Synagogue.

KAIDANOVER: (1) *AARON SAMUEL K.* (known as *Maharshak*; 1614–1676): Talmudist. He officiated in various Polish and German communities, and was recognized as an outstanding authority. He was wounded in the Cossack massacres when his two daughters were killed and some of his mss lost. His published works include talmudic novellae written in a critical spirit, sermons, and responsa. (2) *TZEVI HIRSCH K.* (d. 1712): author; son of (1). He was imprisoned for 4 years in Vilna on a false charge. Later, at Frankfort-on-Main, he published his father's writings. His ethical book *Kav ha-Yashar*, which he himself translated into Yiddish, achieved enormous popularity.

KAINUKA see **BANU KAINUKA**

KAIROUAN: Town in N Africa, near Tunis. Jews settled there shortly after its foundation in the 7th cent. For a considerable period, it was the leading Jewish intellectual center in the West, the "sages of K." including Hushiel ben Elhanan and his son Hananel. It was to this place that the famous historical epistle of R Sherira was addressed. The community decayed after the rise of the Almohades (12th cent.), and until the late 19th cent. no Jew was allowed to live in the city. None lives there now.

KAL VA-ḤOMER (Heb. "light and heavy"): An inescapable *a fortiori* conclusion. The phrase became proverbial. See HERMENEUTICS.

KALICH, BERTHA RACHEL (1874–1939): Actress. She went to the US from E Europe in 1895 and

Bertha Rachel Kalich.

quickly became a star of the Yiddish theater, also establishing a reputation on the English-speaking stage.

KALININGRAD see **KÖNIGSBERG**

KALISCHER, TZEVI HIRSCH (1795–1874): Rabbi and Zionist pioneer. A pupil of Akiva Eger, for 50 years he served as rabbi at Thorn, Prussia, in an honorary capacity. He was a strong opponent of Reform and advocated a rational basis for faith. In 1832, he proclaimed that the redemption of the Jews from oppression would come about by natural agencies. K. saw in the return of the Jews to Palestine the possibility of resuming the practical observances bound up with residence there, including the offering of sacrifices. His book *Derishat Zion* (1862) advocates the formation of a Jewish agricultural society in Palestine. These ideas influenced Moses Hess and became the ideological basis of *Ḥibbat Zion*. K. established several societies for colonization and

Tzevi Hirsch Kalischer.

pressed the Alliance Israélite Universelle to assist agriculture in Palestine by opening the Mikveh Israel School. In 1864, he was responsible for the founding in Berlin of the Central Committee for Palestine Colonization. His writings dealt with both rabbinic and Zionist topics.

KALISH: Polish town, Jews were settled in the neighborhood in the 13th cent. and a series of persecutions is recorded from the 14th. In 1656, the community was destroyed by the Polish general Czarniecki. Settlement was soon renewed and the Jews excelled in commerce and crafts. K.'s pre-war population of c. 12,000 was annihilated during the Nazi occupation.

KALISHER, ABRAHAM see **ABRAHAM BEN ALEXANDER KATZ OF KALISH**

KALKILIYAH: Arab village in S Sharon. Between 1948 and 1967 it was in the kingdom of Jordan close to the Israel frontier. Pop. (1967) c. 8,926. In Roman times, it was a station commanding the coastal road.

KALLAH (Heb.): (1) A bride. (2) Late Hebrew tractate dealing with marital relations, now included in Talmud editions. Besides the shorter form (one chapter) included in older editions of the Talmud deriving from the HALAKHOT GEDOLOT, a larger work (10 chapters) is printed in some modern editions.

KALLAH (etymology uncertain): Name given in Babylonia to the study-courses in the months of *Elul* and *Adar* when students gathered from all parts of the country for intensive study at the academies of Sura and Pumbedita. The custom originated in amoraic times and continued throughout the gaonic period. Since agricultural work was minimal during these months, the time was especially suitable for such gatherings. A different tractate of the Talmud was discussed at each session, having been previously prepared by the participants. *Resh Kallah* (head of K.) later became an honorific title.

KALLEN, HORACE MEYER (1882–1974): US philosopher. A pupil and friend of William James he was professor of philosophy at the New School for Social Research, New York, from 1919. K. was the leading exponent of the concept of "cultural pluralism" in the US. His works include *Judaism at Bay*, *A Free Society*, *Art and Freedom*, and *Ideals and Experience*.

KALLIR (or **BEN KALLIR**), **ELEAZAR:** Medieval Hebrew poet. No details are known of his life, but it is now generally believed that he lived in Palestine in the 7th cent. He composed some 200 *piyyutim*, most of which were accepted in various rites (though not by Sephardi communities). They include poems for the festival liturgy and laments for *Av* 9. The content is based on Midrash and talmudic aggadah; the language is rich, difficult, and, on occasions, faulty. K. introduced external innovations into Hebrew poetry, chiefly rhyme, and was much imitated by later *paytanim,* although controversy raged over the merits of his work.

KALMANOVITCH, ZELIG (1881–1943): Yiddish philologist. After a literary and scholarly career in Russia, Lithuania, Latvia, and Germany, he became editor-in-chief of *Yivo-Bletter.* He worked in Vilna until the Nazi liquidation of the ghetto in Sept. 1943, when he was deported to an extermination camp. His Hebrew *Diary of the Nazi Ghetto in Vilna* is an important historical document.

KALONYMOS BEN KALONYMOS (called Maestro Calo; 1286–after 1328): French Hebrew author and translator. He lived in various French centers and in Rome. K. translated many philosophical and scientific works from Arabic into Hebrew and Latin for King Robert of Naples. His original works include *Even Boḥan,* a moral work in rhymed prose, and *Masekhet Purim,* a satiric parody of a talmudic tractate.

KAMATZ: (Sign (ָ) for two Hebrew vowels: (1) *K. gadol,* sounded *a* in Sephardi, *o* in Ashkenazi and Yemenite pronunciation (original short *a*); (2) *K. katan* (also, wrongly *Ḥataph Kamatz*), sounded *o* (in English Sephardi pronunciation often *a*), occurs only in closed unstressed syllables (original *u*).

KAMENETZ-PODOLSK: Town of Soviet Ukraine. Jewish residence was prohibited until 1447 and for a long time afterward existed on a small scale. The community suffered severely in the Chmielnicki massacres of 1648 when, according to one source, 10,000 families were killed. Under Turkish rule (1672–99), the Jewish population grew and their role in commerce was prominent. K. was the scene in 1757 of the debate with the FRANKISTS which resulted in the burning of the Talmud. The Jews suffered from pogroms in 1905 and 1918–9. The pre-war Jewish population of c. 13,000 was massacred by the Nazis, and in Aug. 1941, 11,000 Jews from Carpatho-Ruthenia were killed in the vicinity.

KAMENEV, LEO (originally Lev Borisovich Rosenfeld; 1883–1936): Russian revolutionary. After being arrested for revolutionary activities, he fled to Paris in 1902 and became one of the chief Bolshevik theoreticians. In 1914, K. returned to Russia, was exiled to Siberia in 1915, but released after the 1917 Revolution. Active in the Communist Party 1918–27, he joined Stalin and Zinoviev in a triumvirate ruling the country and opposing Trotsky. Later, he opposed Stalin, was imprisoned in 1934, and in 1936, together with Radek, Zinoviev, etc., was tried and shot.

KAMIA see **AMULET**

KAMINER, ISAAC (1834–1901): Hebrew poet. A physician by profession, he lived in the Ukraine and published satirical poems and feuilletons in most of the contemporary Hebrew periodicals. Under the influence of Russian radical literature he tended to socialism and, in his later years, became an enthusiastic

Ida Kaminska.

Zionist and protagonist of agricultural labor in Palestine.

KAMINKA, ARMAND AHARON (1866–1950): Scholar. Born in the Ukraine, he served as rabbi in Frankfort-on-Oder, Prague, and Esseg (Slavonia) before settling in Vienna as secretary of the *Allianz* and lecturer at the Vienna *Bet ha-Midrash.* In 1938, he moved to Tel Aviv. He was a prolific author in Hebrew and other languages. His biblical studies sought a scientific basis for traditional views. He translated a number of Greek and Latin classics into Hebrew.

KAMINSKI: (1) *ESTHER RACHEL K.* (1870–1925): Yiddish actress. Together with her husband, the noted Yiddish actor Abraham Isaac K. (1867–1918), she toured Poland, being noted especially for her portrayal of matronly roles. (2) *IDA KAMINSKA* (1900–): Actress; daughter of (1). After World War II, she was the outstanding actress on the Yiddish stage in Poland until she left Poland during the anti-Semitic campaign of 1968. She won international acclaim for her role in the movie *The Shop on Main Street.* (3) *JOSEPH K.* (1903–1972): Israel composer and violinist; son of (1). He studied in Europe and led the Warsaw String Quartet before settling in Palestine in 1937 as a member of the Palestine Symphony (later Israel Philharmonic) Orchestra. His compositions include a violin concerto, trumpet concertino, and orchestral works.

KAMMERKNECHTSCHAFT (Ger. "servitude to the [imperial] Chamber"): Term applied to the juridical status of the Jews in Medieval Germany as serfs to the Holy Roman emperors, regarded as successors to Titus. This implied exclusive jurisdiction and the right of exacting the OPFERPFENNIG as a poll-tax. The *K.* was beneficial to the Jews inasfar as it protected them from violence or the arbitrary jurisdiction of local authorities. On the other hand, the emperors not infrequently conceded their rights in the Jews to the latter. The *K.* stimulated the assertion of similar rights by rulers of countries other than Germany over the Jews, as *servi camerae regis* (Lat. "serfs of the Royal Chamber").

KANAH, BOOK OF (*Sepher ha-Kanah*): Kabbalistic work on the commandments. It is believed to have been written in Spain in the second half of the 14th cent. The same author composed *Sepher ha-Peliah* ("Book of Wonder"). A central figure in both works is the wonder-child Nahum who is said to have received a Divine revelation at the age of 5. The books are written in the form of dialogues between the boy and his father Kanah. The writer proclaims that the literal meaning of the rabbinical sources is to be found in the kabbalistic interpretation. Both works are basically collections using as sources both the Spanish Kabbalah and the German "practical" Kabbalah. They are characterized by a strong anti-talmudic and anti-rabbinic tendency and their antinomian mysticism seems to have influenced Shabbetai Tzevi.

KANN, JACOBUS HENRICUS (1872–1945): Dutch Zionist leader and banker. An early associate of Herzl, he participated in the First Congress and continued to play a prominent part in the Zionist executive until 1911 and, thereafter, in the opposition. He died in Theresienstadt.

KANSAS: US state. Jewish merchants went to K. in the 1850's, first settling in Leavenworth, where Congregation B'nai Jeshurun was formed in 1859. Communities also sprang up in Lawrence, Atchison, and Topeka. A number of Jews, notably August Bondi, actively participated in the K. civil strife on the side of the free-staters. Individual Jews went to Ogden, WICHITA, Newton, and Fort Scott between the 1860's and 1880's. In the 1870's and 1880's, Jews also settled in Abilene, Hutchinson, Kansas City, Manhattan, and Pittsburg, Jewish immigrants from E Europe unsuccessfully tried to establish agricultural colonies in 7 places in K. between 1882 and 1892. Few of the 465 Jewish immigrants sent to K. by the INDUSTRIAL REMOVAL OFFICE in 1901–15 settled on farms. In 1973, K. had 11,095 Jews.

KANSAS CITY: City in Missouri, US. Its Jewish settlement dates from the late 1850's, when store-keepers moved there from Weston and Independence, Missouri. K. C.'s first congregation, B'nai Jehudah, was formed in 1870, and its second, Beth Shalom, in 1878. Jews, at first from Central and later from E Europe, settled there in the latter 19th cent. The Jewish Federation and Council were founded in 1933, and the *Kansas City Jewish Chronicle* is published weekly. Jewish pop. (1973): 22,000.

KANTOR, JUDAH LEIB (1849–1915): Author and editor. After working in an editorial capacity on Jewish papers in Hebrew, Yiddish, and Russian in Berlin and St. Petersburg, he founded the first Hebrew daily HA-YOM and edited it throughout its existence (1886–8). In his latter years, he served as Crown rabbi in Libau 1890–1904, Vilna 1905–8, and Riga 1909–15.

KANTOROVICH, LEONID (1912–): Soviet economist, representing the mathematical school in Soviet economic research. He was awarded the 1975 Nobel Prize in Economics as well as Lenin and Stalin Prizes.

KAPH (כ): Eleventh letter in the Hebrew alphabet; numerical value 20. When with a *dagesh* (כּ), it is pronounced *k,* otherwise it is an unvoiced, fricative *kh* sound (כ).

KAPLAN, ELIEZER (1891–1952): Labor Zionist. One of the founders of the *Tzeire Zion* in Russia, he was prominent in the Labor Zionist movement in Europe and, from 1923, in Palestine. From 1933, he was a member of the Jewish Agency Executive and headed its finance department until the establishment of the state of Israel, when he became minister of finance. Shortly before his death, he was appointed deputy premier. K. was a *Mapai* Knesset member.

KAPLAN, JACOB (1895–): French rabbi. A veteran of two world wars, he was appointed chief rabbi of Paris in 1950 and of France in 1955.

KAPLAN, MORDECAI MENAHEM (1881–): US rabbi and philosopher. Born in Lithuania, he was taken to the US while a child. He founded and is the foremost exponent of the RECONSTRUCTIONIST MOVEMENT, and his books include *Judaism as a Civilization,*

Mordecai Menahem Kaplan.

The Meaning of God in Modern Jewish Religion, and *The Future of the American Jew,* as well as prayer books and essays. He taught at the Jewish Theological Seminary, New York, from 1909, and was the founder, and for many years dean, of its Teachers' Institute. K. created the idea of the JEWISH CENTER. He was the founder and leader (1922–43) of the Reconstructionist SOCIETY FOR THE ADVANCEMENT OF JUDAISM. K. has been a foremost intellectual leader in American Judaism. In 1971, he settled in Jerusalem.

KAPLANSKY, SHELOMOH (1884–1950): Labor Zionist; of Polish birth. From 1913–9, he was in charge of settlement affairs at the Jewish National Fund's head office in The Hague. In 1919–21, he directed the Zionist Executive's financial and economic council in London, and was a founder of the *Keren ha-Yesod.* In 1924, K. settled in Palestine and for a time headed the settlement department of the Zionist Executive in London. K. was director of the Haifa Technion from 1932 until his death. He tended to left-wing socialism and in his latter years, left *Mapai* and supported *Mapam.*

KAPPARAH (pl. *kapparot* or popularly *kappores*; Heb. "atonement"): The custom on the eve of the Day of Atonement of swinging a fowl over the head while praying that the fowl, when slaughtered, serve as a substitute for the individual. A cock is taken for a male and a hen for a female. K. is first mentioned in the Gaonic Period, but since medieval times, religious authorities have differed whether to sanction or ban the custom.

KARA, ABIGDOR BEN ISAAC (d. 1439): Scholar. A resident of Prague, he witnessed the massacre of its Jewish community in 1389, writing a penitential

Gravestone of Abigdor ben Isaac Kara, Prague.

psalm on the event. Besides religious poetry, he was the author of rabbinical and kabbalistic works. According to legend, he was friendly with Wenceslaus IV.

KARA, JOSEPH BEN SIMEON (c. 1060–c. 1130): French Bible commentator; probably lived in Troyes. His commentary covers almost the entire Bible and is similar in style to that of his contemporary, Rashi, except that K. only quotes aggadic interpretations by way of illustration and never relies on them to explain the text.

KARAITES: Jewish sect rejecting the Oral Law. It originated in the 8th cent. in and around Persia where the Jewish community was not long established and did not accept the discipline of the Babylonian gaonite. Auxiliary factors in the evolution of such dissident groups were the messianic hopes aroused by local conditions (Arab conquest of Persia, 640; the fall of the Umayyad dynasty, 750, etc.) and the urge toward social justice and asceticism. The most ancient Karaite document preserved is the *Sepher ha-Mitzvot* of ANAN BEN DAVID, written in the 760's. He interpreted the Bible literally and attempted to deduce therefrom a code of life without reference to the Oral Law. Few accepted his authority, but during the next two centuries various groups rejecting the Oral Law sprang up in this area. The most important of their leaders was BENJAMIN BEN MOSES NAHAVENDI, author of the first systematic book of observances and regulations in this spirit. Sharp differences of opinion prevailed among the groups themselves as well as between them and Anan's teachings. Preachers traveled extensively as far as Egypt in order to make converts to their doctrine, but they were hampered by schism, the paucity of scholars backing their views, and the austerity of their asceticism. In view of their lack of success, the rabbis avoided controversy with the K. until Saadyah Gaon (d. 942) attacked them violently and sought to exclude them from the Jewish community. In the face of this onslaught the various groups closed their ranks and united. Moreover, Saadyah's great erudition required an answer in kind, and men of education and ability emerged among the K. inaugurating the Golden Age of Karaite literature in both Arabic and Hebrew, producing polemical works, grammars, Bible commentaries, and codes. Saadyah failed to expel the K. from the community and intermarriage between the K. and the Rabbinites was common. Many Karaite scholars, despite the controversy, studied with the rabbis and were influenced by them; on the other hand, Abraham Ibn Ezra was the only rabbi to quote Karaite sources. The greatest Karaite scholar of the first part of the 10th cent. was KARKASANI, whose numerous works reveal familiarity with Hebrew, Arabic, and Christian literature. In the same century, new communities sprang up in the Byzantine Empire (Asia Minor, the Balkans),

Abraham Firkovich, a Karaite leader in the 19th century.

Syria (Damascus), Cyprus, and Moslem Spain (Toledo, etc.). The Palestinian and Egyptian centers surpassed those of Persia and Babylonia, which dwindled and degenerated. Part of this success may the attributed to the lenient marriage regulations generally adopted in the 11th cent. superseding the stringent rules laid down by Anan and the early Karaite scholars. The Palestinian K. were particularly austere, settling in Jerusalem and adopting the customs of the *Avele Zion* who mourned for the Temple and prayed continually for redemption. The Diaspora communities accepted the authority of the Jerusalem scholars. SAHL BEN MATZLIAH and other emissaries of the Palestinian community journeyed widely, urging the K. to join them in prayer in Jerusalem. The spread of Karaism was checked in the 12th cent. The verbal dispute which raged in Spain for 150 years came to an end when Judah Ibn Ezra utilized his secular authority in Castile to suppress the K. The position of the K. in Palestine was weakened with the advent of the Seljuk Turks and the Crusaders. Maimonides curbed Karaite activity in Egypt. The leadership of the sect therefore passed to the Byzantine Empire (Constantinople, Adrianople, etc.) where outstanding scholars (AARON BEN ELIJAH, Elijah BASHYAZI) supplemented the traditional literature. Karaism spread to the Crimea (12th cent.), Lithuania (Troki in the 13th cent.), and Volhynia (Luzk). After the Russian annexation of Lithuania and Crimea in the 18th cent., Russian K. received from the Czars privileges and rights denied the Rabbinites. The Russian Revolution cut off the Crimean K. from the dwindling body of their coreligionists elsewhere. In World War II, the K. of Europe suffered, but a community numbering 350 survived in Eupatoria (Crimea) and the Russian 1970 cencus put the Karaite pop. of the USSR at 4,571. The Jerusalem and Damascus communities progressively dwindled, many migrating to Egypt. Since 1948, the K. in Egypt have moved to Israel settling in MATZLIAH and elsewhere. In 1972 there were 10,000 Karaites in Israel with 9 synagogues.

Karaite doctrine is conservative and more stringent than rabbinical teaching (e.g., it forbids levirate marriage and all Sabbath illumination and is stricter on laws of purity). Differences in laws of ritual slaughter prevent social intercourse with the Rabbinites. The K. do not celebrate Ḥanukkah (as post-biblical) nor do they use *tephillin* or *mezuzot*. In the course of time, their own Oral Law has evolved, in some instances overlapping rabbinical tradition. The sole difference in principles of faith between Karaism and rabbinical Judaism is on the sanctity of the Oral Law. Karaite literature deals chiefly with practical observances and seldom discusses ethics and metaphysics. The only Karaite author attempting to formulate a philosophical basis for the sect was Aaron ben Elijah, who was influenced by Maimonides. Anan, endeavoring to adapt Karaite prayer to Temple practice, abolished the afternoon prayer. This encountered opposition, but his objection to the post-biblical prayers accepted by the Rabbinites prevailed. To replace them Anan composed prayers constructed from biblical verses. The Karaite liturgy was finally determined in its main lines in the 13th cent., especially by AARON BEN JOSEPH, who introduced some of his own compositions as well as *piyyutim* by rabbinical authors. In some respects, however, considerable latitude and differences persisted.

KARINTHY, FRIGYES (1888–1938): Hungarian author. K., who adopted Christianity, wrote plays and satirical poems, some of which have been translated into other languages.

KARKASANI, ABU YUSUF YAKUB (fl. 10th cent.): Karaite scholar. Originating from Karkasan, near Baghdad, he traveled widely in oriental lands taking particular interest in religious customs. In writings (all in Arabic), he reports objectively the contemporary plight of the Karaites, who were split into several small groups. His book of Karaite observances (937) contains important information on Jewish sects and has preserved quotations from books now lost. His other works included commentaries on Job and Ecclesiastes as well as philosophical and theological studies.

KARKUR: Israel moshavah in N Sharon. Settlement began in 1926 and its pop. (1967) was 2,950. It is the site of a Dew Research Station. In 1969, K. merged with PARDES HANNAH.

Rabbi A. Y. Karlitz (Hazon Ish).

KARLITZ, AVRAHAM YESHAYAHU (known after his chief work as *Hazon Ish*; 1878–1953): Rabbi. Born in the province of Grodno, he long resided in Vilna and in 1935, settled at Bene Berak in Palestine where he founded a yeshivah. One of the great modern codifiers, he wrote his books anonymously under the title *Hazon Ish*. Although he occupied no official position, he was widely consulted on halakhic problems.

KARLSBURG (Alba Julia): Rumanian town. Turkish Sephardim settled there from 1623 and outnumbered the Ashkenazim until the 18th cent., after which they disappeared. The community was comparatively untouched during World War II. Some 2,000 Jews were living there after World War II but most subsequently left.

KARLSRUHE: W German town. Jews settled there immediately after its foundation in 1715. Their numbers were limited in 1738, and restrictions were maintained throughout the 18th cent. Conditional civic rights were conferred in 1809, and became absolute in 1862. In 1819, there were HEP! HEP! riots in the city. About the same time, a Reform congregation was founded and a Jewish school was opened. Hebrew presses were maintained in K. 1755–1840. There were 3,119 Jews in 1933, but these had disappeared by the end of World War II. Jewish pop. (1969): 246.

KARMINSKI, SIR SEYMOUR EDWARD (1902–1974): English jurist. In 1951, he was appointed a judge of the High Court of Justice and in 1969, a Lord Justice of Appeal.

KARO, JOSEPH see **CARO, JOSEPH**

KARPELES, GUSTAV (1848–1909): Scholar. From 1890, he edited in Berlin the *Allgemeine Zeitung des Judentums* and played a prominent part in establishing and running the Society of Jewish History and Literature. He published numerous literary studies (a history of world literature, works on Heine, Börne, etc.) and a history of Jewish literature.

KARPF, MAURICE J. (1891–1964): Social worker. He was head of the Graduate School of Jewish Social Work in New York, 1925–41 and director of the Federation of Jewish Welfare Organizations in Los Angeles, 1941–7.

KASHE (colloquial Yidd. from Aram. *kushya* "a difficult question"): A problem; a talmudic query; a question.

KASHER see **DIETARY LAWS, KASHRUT**

KASHER, MENAHEM (1895–): Talmudist. He was a founder and director of the *Metivta* yeshivah in Warsaw, 1915, and in 1925, went to Jerusalem to direct the *Sephat Emet* yeshivah. Since 1939, he has been living in the US. K. has compiled the monumental corpus *Torah Shelemah* (22 vols. by 1968) which collates diverse interpretations and commentaries on each verse of the Pentateuch.

KASHRUT (Heb. from *kasher* "fit"): Regulations determining the Jewish DIETARY LAWS. The basic laws in the Pentateuch are developed in the Oral Law and by rabbinic regulation. The talmudic tractate HULLIN deals largely with the laws of *k.* as does *Yoreh Deah* (the second part of the *Shulhan Arukh* code). According to these laws, only a small proportion of living creatures are permitted, and every precaution is taken to avoid the consumption of blood or the partaking of meat with milk products. Other prohibited foods include bread from which the dough-offering has not been separated, first-year fruit, and milk derived from a prohibited animal. Special Passover *k.* laws prohibit the eating throughout the festival of leaven and leaven products.

KASSOVSKY (KOSSOVSKY), HAYYIM YEHO-SHUA (1873–1960): Israel rabbinical scholar. He produced concordances on the Bible, Targum Onkelos, the Mishnah, Tosephta, the Babylonian Talmud, etc.

KASTEIN, JOSEPH (pen-name of Julius Katzenstein; 1890–1946): Author. A native of Germany, he later lived in Switzerland and from 1933, in Palestine. He wrote in German (and later in Hebrew) poems, plays, tales, and novels, his reputation resting largely on his monographs on Jewish personalities (*The Messiah of Izmir, Uriel Acosta,* etc.). K. also wrote a one-volume Jewish history (1931).

Mané Katz: *Humility* (Tel Aviv Museum).

KATCHALSKY see **KATZIR**

KATOWICE (KATTOWITZ): Polish town. Jews settled there to any extent only in the 19th cent. Their numbers grew, especially after World War I, and reached c. 12,000 at the time of the Nazi invasion. Only a handful are now left. K. was early a Zionist center and the scene of the KATTOWITZ CONFERENCE.

KATSH, ABRAHAM I. (1908–): Educator. Born in Poland, he went to the US in 1925. He was professor of education at New York Univ. from 1944. From 1967 he had been president of DROPSIE University.

KATTOWITZ see **KATOWICE**

KATTOWITZ CONFERENCE: First conference of the HIBBAT ZION movement. 36 delegates attended its sessions (Nov. 11–16, 1884), the opening address being by Leo Pinsker. Its object was to unify all Zionist bodies, and a permanent committee was established with headquarters at Odessa and a subcommittee at Warsaw.

KATZ see **COHEN TZEDEK**

KATZ, BEN-TZIYYON (1875–1958): Hebrew author. In 1903, he founded and edited the Hebrew periodical *Ha-Zeman* which appeared first at St. Petersburg and later at Vilna. In 1916, K. published in Moscow a Hebrew weekly, *Ha-Am*. Settling in Berlin after World War I and in Palestine in 1931, he continued his activities in Hebrew journalism. K. published works on Russian Jewish history.

KATZ, SIR BERNARD (1911): British physiologist teaching at University College, London. He was awarded a Nobel Prize in 1970 for work on the nature of the nerve-impulse.

KATZ, MANÉ (1894–1962): Painter. Born in Russia, he settled in France in 1921, and exhibited extensively in Europe and in the US where he lived during World War II. Originally a painter of biblical scenes and somber ghetto types, he later developed a more cheerful vein.

KATZ-SUCHY, JULIUSZ (1912–1971): Polish diplomat. Escaping to England in World War II, he served in the Polish government 1944–6. K.-S. represented Poland in the United Nations, 1947 ff, served as vice-chairman of the UN Economic Commission for Europe, and in 1957, was appointed Polish ambassador to India. Subsequently he taught diplomatic history but was dismissed in the anti-Semitic purges of 1968 and went to Denmark.

KATZENELLENBOGEN, MEIR see **PADUA, MEIR**

KATZENELSON, BERL (1887–1944): Palestinian labor leader. A native of White Russia, he commenced socialist Zionist work at an early age and in 1909, went to Palestine, where he rapidly became a

Berl Katzenelson.

leading personality and ideologist in the labor movement. In 1919, he was among the founders of the *Aḥdut ha-Avodah* party and, in 1920, of the *Histadrut*. K. occupied prominent positions in the Zionist Organization and was an eloquent journalist, editing several labor journals, including the *Histadrut* daily, *Davar*. In 1930, he helped to found *Mapai*.

KATZENELSON, ISAAC (1886–1944): Hebrew poet and playwright; lived and taught in Lodz. One of the pioneers of the modern Hebrew theater, he wrote plays and poems distinguished by their humor, lightness, and *joie de vivre*. During World War II, he continued to write in Warsaw and elsewhere, and his works of that period (in Hebrew and Yiddish) movingly describe the disaster that befell European Jewry. His mss were partially preserved and posthumously published. He perished in Auschwitz.

KATZENELSON, JUDAH LÖB BENJAMIN (pseudonym Buki ben Yogli; 1847–1917): Hebrew and Russian author. A physician by profession, he played a prominent part in Jewish communal life in St. Petersburg. K. wrote articles, stories, and fables, notable for their polished biblical style. In opposition to the *Ḥoveve Zion*, he supported Baron de Hirsch's efforts to create Jewish agricultural colonies in Argentina. His medical writings contributed to the formulation of a Hebrew medical terminology. K. was a chief editor of the Russian Jewish encyclopedia.

KATZIR (KATCHALSKY): (1) *AHARON K.* (1913–1972) Israel biophysicist. Born in Poland, he went to Palestine in 1925. He was professor of physical chemistry at the Hebrew University, Jerusalem, and director of the scientific committee of the Weizmann Institute, Rehovot. He was president of the Israel National Academy of the Sciences and Humanities.

Aharon Katzir.

He was killed at Lydda airport in an attack by Japanese terrorists. (2) *EPHRAIM K. (KATCHALSKY)* (1916–) is head of the biophysical section of the Weizmann Institute. In 1973 he was chosen as Israel's fourth president.

KAUFMAN, GEORGE S. (1899–1961): US playwright. Beginning as a newspaper columnist and dramatic critic, he started his playwright career in 1918, usually working in collaboration. His plays, often comic and satirical, included *Of Thee I Sing, You Can't Take It with You, Dinner at Eight, Stage Door,* and *The Man Who Came to Dinner.*

KAUFMANN, DAVID (1852–1899): Scholar; from 1877, professor at the Budapest Rabbinical Seminary. He published a wealth of studies on many aspects of Judaica, notably Italian Jewish history and medieval Jewish philosophy. From 1892–9, he was joint editor of the *Monatsschrift für die Wissenschaft des Judentums*. His library, including a notable collection of mss, is now in the Budapest Academy of Sciences.

KAUFMANN, HENRY (1860–1955): US philanthropist. He was co-founder of a leading Pittsburgh department store, founder of the Irene Kaufmann Settlement in that city, and donated millions of dollars to charitable causes.

Isidor Kaufmann: *A lesson in Arithmetic.*

KAUFMANN, ISIDOR (1854–1921): Hungarian painter. He lived mostly at Vienna where he enjoyed the patronage of Emperor Franz Joseph among others. At first a painter of historical compositions, he altered his ideas after a visit to Galicia, becoming a pioneer in the depiction of traditional E European (especially Jewish) types and genre scenes. His son, *PHILIP K.* (1888–1969), who emigrated from Vienna to England, was also a painter.

Danny Kaye.

KAUFMANN, YEḤEZKEL (1889–1963): Bible scholar and philosopher. Born in Russia, he settled in Palestine in 1920 and became professor of Bible studies at the Hebrew Univ. in 1949. His numerous publications include *Golah ve-Nekhar*, a study of Jewish history in which he argued that Jewish nationality was preserved by religion and preached a return to Zion, and *Toledot ha-Emunah ha-Yisre'elit* ("A History of the Israelite Faith"; 8 vols. by 1956) in which K. challenged many of the theories of biblical criticism and maintained that monotheism, far from being a late product of historical evolution, is an original concept dating from the outset of Jewish history.

KAUNAS see **KOVNO**

*KAUTZSCH, EMIL FRIEDRICH (1841–1910): German theologian; professor of Protestant theology at Basle, Tübingen, and Halle. A Bible scholar of the Wellhausen school, K. edited a scientific, critical translation of the Bible into German. He also published a revision of Gesenius' Hebrew grammar, philological studies, works on the Apocrypha and apocalyptic literature, etc.

KAVVANAH see **DEVOTION**

KAYE (originally **KAMINSKI**), **DANNY** (1913–): US comedian. He achieved international popularity first on Broadway and then in films as an actor, dancer, and singer of exceptional wit and versatility.

KAYSERLING, MEYER (Moritz; 1829–1905): Rabbi and historian. He officiated in Aargau (Switzerland) 1861–70, and later in Budapest. K. wrote copiously on various aspects of Jewish history, his many studies on the history and literature of the Marranos being fundamental.

KAYYARA, SIMEON (fl. 9th cent.): Babylonian scholar. He is generally considered to have been the compiler of the HALAKHOT GEDOLOT.

KAZIN, ALFRED (1915–): US author and educator. He has taught literature at various colleges including the New School for Social Research, New York. His books include *On Native Ground*, an autobiography *A Walker in the City*, and studies of Scott Fitzgerald. Dreiser, Emerson, and Melville.

KEDAR: Arab tribe (Is. 21:16) related to the Ishmaelites (Gen. 25:13). They dwelt in the Arabian desert, and their distinctive black tents (Song of Songs 1:5) were familiar to the Israelites. They were noted for their large flocks and were skilled archers (Is. 21:17). During the Babylonian exile, the tribe apparently occupied areas in S Judah.

KEDUSHAH (Heb. "sanctification"): In the Mishnah, name given to the third of the EIGHTEEN BENEDICTIONS; in later rabbinical literature and in popular usage, an addition to the third blessing in which the public responds to the precentor's introduction and connecting text with verses praising God. There are different forms of the *k.* in the various liturgical rites and certain amplifications on special occasions. *Kedushah Rabba* ("the great *k.*"), which includes the first verse of the *Shema*, is recited in the Additional Service (*Musaph*) and on the Day of Atonement in the Ashkenazi rite in all prayers, and in other rites in the Concluding Service (*Neilah*) only. The congregational responses in the *k.* are not mentioned in the Talmud, and scholars differ in assigning their date of origin: they probably originated in mystical circles in the Gaonic Period. Apparently, *k.* was only recited in Palestine on Sabbaths and festivals, but in Babylon daily. There are two other *kedushot* embodying the same verses — one included in the *yotzer* prayer and the other, the *k.* *de-sidra* in the *u-va le-tziyyon* prayer.

KEHILLAH (Heb.): An organized Jewish community or congregation.

KEHILLAH MOVEMENT IN THE US: Numerous attempts have been made to form central COMMUNITY organizations in the US, adapting the *Kehillah* of E Europe to American life. Most ambitious was the effort in New York where steps were first taken in 1908 to call into being a representative body composed of delegates from leading Jewish organizations. For about 10 years, under the leadership of J. L. Magnes, it sought to direct community affairs in the fields of education, sociology, religion, industrial problems, and general public relations. The size of of the community made efficient operation of the *Kehillah* almost impossible, and the body disintegrated. In the ensuing years, most of the other large Jewish communities in the US had greater success with the establishment of Jewish Community Councils.

KELAL ISRAEL (Heb. "Community of Israel"): Phrase used to denote the entire people of Israel. It also has the connotation of the general community of Israel, from the privileges of which a Jew may be barred by improper conduct

KELIM (Heb. "Utensils"): First tractate in the Mishnah order of *Tohorot*, containing 30 chapters. There is no *gemara* either in the Babylonian or Palestinian Talmud. It discusses the ritual uncleanness of vessels (Lev. 11:32; Num. 19:14; 31:20), specifying the laws of ritual impurity which affect vessels of metal, wood, earthenware, glass, etc.

KELLNER, LEON (1859–1928): Literary historian and philologist. He taught English language and literature at the universities of Vienna and Czernowitz. K. wrote a biography of his close friend Theodor Herzl and edited the first edition of Herzl's collected works in German (1904).

KELM, THE MAGGID OF (Moses Isaac; 1828–1899): Lithuanian preacher. His homiletic talents were revealed in his youth, and he studied under R Israel Salanter at Kovno, becoming the envoy and preacher of the MUSAR movement. He traveled throughout the Pale of Settlement and also lived for a time in London.

KENE-HORA (Yidd. corruption of *Kein en hara,* "no evil eye"): Phrase popularly used to ward off the evil eye.

KENESET see **KNESSET**

KENESET GEDOLAH see **GREAT ASSEMBLY**

KENESET ISRAEL (Heb. "Congregation of Israel"): Phrase frequently found in the Talmud and midrashic literature denoting the collectivity of Israel, usually in a religious and spiritual sense. Phrases such as "The *K. I.* said before the Holy One, Blessed be He" are very common. The phrase ·*K. I.* corresponds to, and may have originated, the Christian expression "Church of God," etc.

KENESET ISRAEL: The organizational framework of the Palestinian Jewish community during the period of the British MANDATE. It embraced all sections with the exception of the extremely Orthodox *Agudat Israel*. In Nov. 1917, a provisional council was elected under Bezalel Jaffe. 314 delegates were elected to the *Asephat ha-Nivharim* ("Representative Assembly") which first met in Oct. 1920. A *Vaad Leumi* ("National Council") of 36 members was chosen to represent the Jewish community, both internally and externally: a directorate of 13 was elected under the presidency of Yitzhak Ben-Zvi, Jacob Thon, and David Yellin. Further general elections were held in 1925, 1931, and 1944. Presidents of the *Vaad Leumi* during this period were David Yellin (1926–9), Pinhas Rutenberg (1929–31), and Yitzhak Ben-Zvi (1931–48). The Palestine Government in 1928 ratified the constitution of *K. I.*, recognizing it as an organic body. Within the framework of the *K. I. kehillot* (communities) were organized in all places possessing not less than 30 adult Jews; they engaged in matters of education, health, social work, citizenship, and immigration. The *K. I.* was financed by a special voluntary tax. Its supreme religious authority was the council of the Chief Rabbinate. It sat until the convening of the provisional council of the state of Israel on May 14, 1948, when the *K. I.* was abolished and its powers transferred to the state.

KENITES: Tribe inhabiting the Negev and the Sinai desert, bordering on the territory of the Amalekites (I Sam. 15:6). The Israelites had a treaty with them from Moses' time and Reuel (i.e., JETHRO), apparently derived from the K. Reuel's son Hobab, guided the Israelites in the desert and, after the conquest, settled with part of his tribe on the borders of the city of Arad (Judg. 1:16). One group of K. headed by Heber (husband of JAEL) departed for the north (Judg. 4:11). The Israelites kept faith with the K. wherever they settled (cf. 1 Sam. 15:6; 30:30) and probably eventually absorbed them.

KENIZZITES: Ancient nation in the Promised Land (Gen. 15:19); possibly a Central Syrian people mentioned in Egyptian and Hittite inscriptions.

*KENNICOTT, BENJAMIN (1718–1783): English Hebraist. An Oxford theologian, he collated hundreds of biblical mss throughout the world with the aid of many scholars (some of them Jewish) in order to produce a scientific text of the Hebrew Bible (Oxford, 1776–80).

KENTUCKY: US state. Until the 1830's only scattered Jews were to be found in K. In 1836, there were about a dozen Jewish families of German and Polish origin in LOUISVILLE. By the 1860's, Jewish communities appeared in Paducah, Owensboro, Newport, Ashland, Henderson, Lexington, and Frankfort. Many of these newcomers were from Germany. After 1880, their numbers were augmented by Jews from E Europe. In 1968, the Jewish population of K. was 11,525, with 9,200 living in Louisville and 1,200 in Lexington.

KENYA: Country in E Africa. Its Jewish community was founded in 1904, though some Jews lived there earlier. The Nairobi synagogue was erected in 1912; the only other synagogue was in Nakuru, and small groups of Jews resided in Mombasa and Eldoret-Kitale, the site of the "UGANDA" SCHEME proposed to Herzl by the British government. The number of Jews has declined in recent years; some 400 were living there in 1973 (almost all in Nairobi).

KEPHAR (Heb.): A village. In Palestine frequently used as a prefix in place-names. The Arabic form is *kafr*.

Kephar Ezion — Reestablished.

KEPHAR (KIRYAT) ATTA: Israel municipality near Haifa. Founded in 1925, it was abandoned for a while in 1929 when neighboring Arabs destroyed its buildings. It developed rapidly after the opening of the *Atta* textile works in 1934 and, later, of smaller industrial undertakings. Pop. (1974): 28,500.

KEPHAR AVODAH (Heb. "work village"): Form of transitional settlement evolved in Israel, 1950–6, to place immigrants on the soil directly on their arrival in the country. To some extent, it replaced the MAABARAH. The *K. A.* was the concentration point for a future permanent village. The inhabitants were initially employed by the Jewish National Fund in land reclamation, afforestation, etc., simultaneously building their own homes and receiving agricultural training from instructors. Ultimately, the *K. A.* became a MOSHAV OVEDIM.

KEPHAR BLUM: Israel communal settlement (IK) in the Ḥuleh valley. It was founded in 1943 by settlers from Baltic countries and members of the *Ha-Bonim* movement from Great Britain. Besides agriculture, its economy is based on industrial workshops. Pop. (1972): 564.

KEPHAR DANIEL (Bet Ḥever): Israel smallholders' settlement (TM) near Lydda. The group was founded in 1949 by veterans of the Israel War of Independence, later joined by settlers from Great Britain, S. Africa, etc. Pop. (1972): 155.

KEPHAR EZION: One of four settlements in the Hebron hills which were destroyed in 1948. K. E. was reestablished as a kibbutz (PM) after the Six-Day War in 1967. The other three settlements were Massuot Yitzhak, En Tzurim, and Revadim. The first attempt to settle in the area was made in 1927 by Jews from Iraq but they had to abandon their village in 1929. K. E. was founded in 1943 by pioneers from Poland. The area fell into the Arab sector of Palestine according to the November 1947 U.N. resolution and was the subject of constant attack until forced to surrender the following May.

KEPHAR GILADI: Israel communal settlement (KM) in Upper Galilee, founded in 1916 by members of *Ha-Shomer* to secure a strategic position on the northern frontier and to grow food for the starving Palestinian Jewish population. In 1920, K. G. and the neighboring settlement of Tel Ḥai (founded 1917) were attacked by Arabs revolting against the French mandatory authorities. TRUMPELDOR and seven others fell in the defense of Tel Ḥai, which had to be evacuated along with K. G., but their defense influenced the Great Powers to include the Ḥuleh Valley in the territory under the British Mandate in Palestine. In 1926, Tel Ḥai was incorporated in K. G. Pop. (1967): 711.

KEPHAR HA-BONIM: Israel smallholders' settlement on the coast, S of Haifa. It was founded in 1949 by veterans of the Israel War of Independence from S Africa and other English-speaking countries. Pop. (1972): 165.

KEPHAR HA-NASI: Israel communal settlement (IK) in Upper Galilee. It was founded in 1948, while intensive fighting was raging in the neighborhood, by settlers from the *Ha-Bonim* movement in Great Britain and other English-speaking contries. Pop. (1972): 431.

KEPHAR HA-ROEH: Israel smallholders' settlement (PM) in Emek Ḥepher. It was founded in 1934 by immigrants from E Europe and is the site of an agricultural school and a yeshivah under the auspices of the *Bene Akiva* movement. Pop. (1972): 738.

KEPHAR ḤASIDIM: Israel smallholders' settlement (PM) near Haifa. It was founded by elderly Ḥasidim from Poland in 1924 under the leadership of the rabbis of Kozienice and Yablonov. They drained the surrounding swamps and built up their settlement under difficult conditions. In 1950, Kephar Ḥasidim B and a *maabarah* were established on the settlement's land. In vicinity is the site of the biblical Harosheth-Goiim (Judg. 4). Pop. (1973): Kephar Ḥasidim A: 328; Kephar Ḥasidim B: 330.

KEPHAR ḤITTIM: Israel smallholders' (TM) settlement in E Galilee. Pop. (1972): 196. In the 19th cent., Jews planted citron groves there. In 1906, the Jewish National Fund acquired its first land holdings in Palestine on this site. Several attempts at settlement failed (1914, 1919, 1924, 1933) until 1936 when the land was occupied by the present group, originating from Bulgaria. Here the *moshav shittuphi* was first practiced. K. Ḥ. (or Kephar Ḥittaya) was inhabited by Jews in the talmudic epoch. In the vicinity is the traditional grave of Jethro (Shu'eib) venerated by the Druze sect. It is near the "Horns of Hittin," an old volcanic crater, where Saladin won his decisive victory over the Crusaders in 1187 CE.

KEPHAR MENAḤEM: Israel communal settlement (KA) on the S coastal plain. It was founded in 1937 during the Arab disturbances. Its original settlers moved to Kephar Warburg and were replaced by the present group, the members of which originated from the US, Poland, and Central Europe. Pop. (1972): 576.

KEPHAR MONASH: Israel smallholders' settlement (TM) in the Sharon plain, founded in 1946 by veterans of World War II. It possesses a photolithographic printing press. Pop. (1972): 308.

KEPHAR MORDEKHAI: Israel smallholders' settlement (MH) in the Judean plain. It was founded in 1950 and its settlers originate from Great Britain. Pop. (1972): 218.

KEPHAR NAHUM see **CAPERNAUM**

KEPHAR SAVA: Israel township in the S Sharon plain, near the ruins of ANTIPATRIS. The land was purchased in 1892. Four years later, Baron Edmond de Rothschild tried to foster the cultivation of medical herbs at K. S., but this proved a failure. Actual settlement began in 1903, but at first the village made little headway. In 1918, British troops under General Allenby broke the German-Turkish front at this point, the village being destroyed. In 1921, it was pillaged by rioting Arabs. During the 1920's, the settlement developed rapidly and became a center of citriculture. K. S. is still based mainly on agriculture but also has many industrial undertakings. It is the site of a hospital. Pop. (1974): 30,500.

KEPHAR SHMARYAHU: Israel smallholders' settlement (MH) in the S Sharon plain. It was founded in 1936 by immigrants from Germany. Pop. (1972): 1,310.

KEPHAR SILVER: Israel agricultural school near Ashkelon, founded in 1952 by the Zionist Organization of America and named for Abba Hillel Silver. Pop. (1972): 178.

KEPHAR SYRKIN: Israel smallholders' settlement (TM) near Petaḥ Tikvah named for Nahman Syrkin. It was founded in 1936 by veteran agricultural laborers of E European and German origin. Pop. (1972): 551.

KEPHAR SZOLD: Israel communal settlement (KM) E of the Ḥuleh Valley; named for Henrietta Szold. It was founded in 1942 by a group hailing from Hungary, Austria, and Germany. In the War of Independence, it withstood repeated attacks by the Syrian army and its proximity to the Syrian border brought it under frequent attack until the Six-Day War. Pop. (1972): 495.

KEPHAR TAVOR: Israel village at the foot of Mt. Tabor. Founded in 1901 by settlers of Rumanian and Russian extraction, water shortage has retarded its development. Pop. (1972): 295.

KEPHAR TRUMAN: Israel smallholders' settlement (TM) near Lydda. It was founded in 1949 by veterans of Israel's War of Independence and named for President Harry S Truman. Pop. (1972): 299.

KEPHAR VITKIN: Israel smallholders' settlement (TM) in the Central Sharon plain. Its settlers, agricultural laborers originating from E Europe, were the first to enter the region and drain its swamps. This was in 1930 after the Jewish National Fund had acquired the land, with Canadian aid. The settlement was founded in 1933. Pop. (1972): 789.

KEPHAR YASSIF: Village in W Galilee. The site was once that of an ancient Jewish village, as is evidenced by the remains of a mosaic pavement and stones with Jewish emblems. K. Y. was traditionally the estate of Josephus. The Jewish settlement in K. Y. was revived in the 16th cent. and continued until the mid-19th. The Jews of nearby ACRE were buried in the vicinity because K. Y. was regarded as inside the boundaries of the Land of Israel and Acre was outside. Pop. (1972): 3,808 (DRUZE and Christian Arabs).

KERCH: Crimean port. A Greek inscription evidences Jewish settlement in 80–1 CE. The name K. was perhaps given by the Khazars who controlled it from the 7th cent. The modern community originated after 1885, and was the victim of a pogrom in 1905. Before World War II, there were c. 10,000

Jews, who were murdered by the Germans at the end of 1941. Jewish pop. (1970): 5,000.

KEREM ḤEMED (Heb. "Vineyard of Delight"): Hebrew journal, published 1833–43 by Samuel Goldberg; it was successor to BIKKURE HA-ITTIM, and was continued by Senior Sachs 1854–6. The journal opposed both Ḥasidism and excessive talmudism.

KEREN HA-YESOD (Heb. "Foundation Fund"): The financial arm of the Zionist Organization. The decision to create the *K. H.* was taken in 1920 and based originally on the conception of a fixed obligatory annual tax to be contributed by every Jew toward the building of Palestine; today, the collections of the *K. H.* are regarded as purely voluntary. It was registered as a company in 1921 with its chief objects defined as (1) the execution of all activities necessary to realize the Balfour Declaration in respect of the establishment of a Jewish National Home in Palestine; and (2) channeling contributions, loans, legacies, etc. and investing them in constructive projects in the country. In 1929, with the establishment of the enlarged JEWISH AGENCY, the *K. H.* became its chief financial instrument. Until the establishment of the state of Israel, the *K. H.* financed all the Agency's activities in Palestine (e.g. settlement, education, security, etc.). After 1948, many of the Agency's projects passed to the government of Israel, and the *K. H.* has concentrated its resources on financing immigration, settlement, and absorption. The 23rd Zionist Congress in 1951 reaffirmed the *K. H.* as the sole fund of the Zionist organization. The *K. H.* — with the additional title United Israel Appeal — is active in over 70 countries. At the beginning of 1956, the *K. H.* and the United Israel Appeal were registered as an Israel company. Its authorized bodies are the directorate, elected by the Zionist Congress or by the Zionist Executive, and the executive, elected by the directorate. The headquarters are in Jerusalem. (See ZIONISM).

KEREN KAYEMET LE-ISRAEL see **JEWISH NATIONAL FUND**

KERI U-KHETIV (Heb. "read and written"): Instructions for the correct readings of those words which were regarded as deviations from the original text of the Bible but were not altered because of veneration for the standard version. These variants, numbering over 1,300, were originally transmitted orally but were noted by the masoretes in the margins of Bible mss not used for synagogal readings.

KERITOT (Heb. "Excisions"): Seventh tractate in the Midrash order of *Kodashim*, containing 6 chapters. It has *gemara* in the Babylonian, but not the Palestinian, Talmud. It deals with the biblical punishment of *karet* ("cutting off") and enumerates the offenses to which this applies.

KERN, JEROME DAVID (1885–1945): US composer. He composed the music for over sixty shows and films including *Sunny, Show Boat,* and *Roberta.*

KEROVAH (from Aram. *kerova* "precentor"; collective plural, under French influence, *kerovetz*): Poems incorporated in the EIGHTEEN BENEDICTIONS. *Kerovot* were written for Sabbaths and festivals, as well as Purim, fast-days, etc. On Sabbaths and festivals, *kerovot* generally extend over the first three blessings; on other occasions over all the Eighteen Benedictions.

KERR (originally **KEMPNER**), **ALFRED** (1867–1948): German dramatic critic and author. He worked on the *Berliner Tageblatt* and his critical essays were widely acclaimed K. also wrote several books of travel. A cycle of twelve of his poems was set to music by Richard Straus. He left Germany in 1933 and eventually settled in England.

KERSH, GERALD (1909–1968): English author. He wrote film scripts and served as a war correspondent. His novels achieved wide popularity, among them being *Night and the City, Jews Without Jehovah,* and *They Died With Their Boots Clean.* He settled in the US in the 1950's.

KESSEL, JOSEPH (1898–): French author. Born in Argentina, he was brought up in Lithuania, and went to France in 1913. His best known book is *The Lion.* In 1964, he was elected to the French Academy.

KESTENBERG, LEO (1882–1962): Pianist and pedagogue. He was born in Slovakia and from 1919, was music counselor at the Ministry of Culture in Berlin. From 1933, he directed the Czech Society for Musical Education. In 1939, K. settled in Tel Aviv where he was artistic director of the Palestine Symphony Orchestra 1939–45.

KETUBBAH (Heb. "writing"): The document embodying the obligations of the bridegroom toward his bride, which in rabbinic law is a prerequisite of marriage. The document must bear the signatures of at least two witnesses and is drawn up in Aramaic. It is carefully preserved by the bride. The economic clauses, formerly fluid, now generally follow a stereotyped formula. Additional clauses (*tenaim* = "conditions") were formerly often appended to the *k.* In some western countries a synopsis in the vernacular is now added, emphasizing the husband's moral obligations; Conservative Jews have introduced certain modifications while Reform Jews have abrogated the *k.* The talmudic tractate KETUBBOT deals with the document and its preparation. Owing to its importance and the festive occasion associated with it, the *k.* was frequently engrossed on parchment with illuminated borders. Some decorated early fragments have been found in the Cairo *genizah*, and one fine German specimen of 1392 is extant. But the art of the illuminated *k.* is associated especially with Italy, where from the Renaissance Period onward

Ketubbah from Padua, 1696.

some magnificent specimens were produced, each town ultimately developing its own artistic tradition.

KETUBBOT (Heb. "Marriage Contracts"): Second tractate in the Mishnah order of *Nashim*, containing 13 chapters. It has *gemara* in both the Palestinian and Babylonian Talmud. It deals primarily with the money to be received by the wife in case of widowhood or divorce. It includes a discussion of a father's rights in regard to his daughter and the mutual rights and duties of husband and wife.

KETUVIM see **HAGIOGRAPHA**

KEVUTZAH (Heb. "group"): Cooperative agricultural group in Israel working a common farm on national land. Production and purchase are collective, consumption being based on the principle of satisfying needs within the ability of the economy.

The k. bears responsibility for housing, health, and education. The earliest group working on these principles was Deganyah (1910). In 1930, those groups tending (unlike the KIBBUTZIM) to greater selectivity and restriction of membership and also desiring to to avoid outside wage-work, centralization, or the introduction of industries, became organized in ḤEVER HA-KEVUTZOT which since 1952 has merged in IḤUD HA-KEVUTZOT VE-HE-KIBBUTZIM. The distinction between k. and kibbutz has progressively decreased. The original principle of outside labor has been, to some extent, infringed in recent years.

KHAIBAR: Oasis, N of MEDINA. The origins of its Jewish community, as of others in HEJAZ, are obscure. In 628, K. was subdued by MOHAMMED, but the Jews were allowed to stay and retain their lands, giving half their produce to the Moslem conquerors. Mohammed adopted this policy because there were no other trained agriculturalists in the region. When slave labor from conquered countries became available, the Jews of K. were expelled by OMAR (641).

KHARKOV: City in the Ukraine, USSR. Its Jewish community dates from the end of the 18th cent. It was outside of the Pale of Settlement, but Jews settled there in number from the late 19th cent. and totaled c. 120,000 in 1939. The great majority fled at the advance of the Germans in 1941; those that remained were annihilated. Its Jewish population in 1970 was c. 80,000.

KHAZARS: A Turkish or Finnish tribe which settled in the lower Volga region. Their capital was Itil in the Volga delta. The Russian chronicles called them White Ugrians (in contrast to the Hungarians who were Black Ugrians). In the 8th–10th cents., the Khazar state was powerful; it extended westward as far as Kiev, and its royal house intermarried with that of Byzantium. In the 8th cent., a powerful judaizing movement manifested itself among the K. Ultimately, about 786–809, their king BULAN and 4,000 of his nobles accepted Judaism, the prince Obadiah being active in securing their Judaization. The legendary disputation which resulted in the conversion of the K. constitutes the theme around which Judah Ha-Levi wrote his *Kuzari*. HASDAI IBN SHAPRUT, believing the K. to belong to the Lost Ten Tribes, is said to have entered into correspondence with their last king, Joseph, in 950, but the authenticity of the documents has been the subject of much discussion, and few scholars are inclined to accept the K. king's reputed reply as genuine. Another important document, found in the Cairo *genizah*, gives a completely different but equally romantic account of the origin of Judaism among the K. How far this extended is problematical, but it is probable that only the king with a good proportion of the nobility and some of his people became converted,

Khazars meeting in a *kubitka* (*tent*).

the Jewish element in the country always constituting a minority. There were, however, separate judicial systems for the members of the various faiths. The once-extensive power of the K. was broken on the Volga by the Russian archduke Yaroslav in 1083. The remnants of the K. on the Volga disappeared in the Tatar invasion of 1237. Italian merchants in Crimea referred to "Gazaria" until the 15th cent. Descendants of the K. probably survived among the Crimea Karaites, the Krimchaks, and other Jews of E European origin.

KHERSON: City of the Ukraine, USSR. It was founded in 1778 and by 1781, possessed a Jewish community. The Jews developed the timber and grain trades and founded agricultural colonies in the

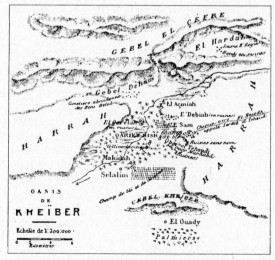

Charles Huber's map of Khaibar (1884) showing the ruins of a number of Jewish castles (Selalim, Qasr Marhaba).

neighborhood. It was the scene of pogroms in 1905 and 1919. In 1941–2 those Jews who did not escape into the Russian interior were exterminated by the Nazis. Jewish pop. (1959): 9,500.

KHMELNITZKI see **CHMIELNICKI**

KHOSROES see **CHOSROES**

KI LO NAEH (Heb. "for to Him it is befitting"): Alphabetic eulogy chanted by Ashkenazim at the end of the *Seder* service. Its author is unknown. It is first found in an English ms of the 13th cent.

KIBBITZER (probably from German): An observer who tenders unsolicited advice.

KIBBUSH AVODAH (Heb. "conquest of labor"): Concept coined by Palestinian pioneers. It meant (1) the acquisition by Jews of the practice of productive manual labor (as expounded by A. D. GORDON); and (2) the obtaining of work with Jewish employers by Jewish laborers. *K. A.* was a major objective of the HA-SHOMER movement and of the HISTADRUT which organized bodies such as YAKHIN and SOLEL BONEH to facilitate the employment of Jewish labor.

KIBBUTZ (Heb. "gathering-in"): Israel collective village. Its main principles resemble those of the KEVUTZAH. The form originated during the Third Aliyah (1918–21) when the creation of large workers' groups undertaking contract work and the need to develop wide tracts of land engendered the broadening of the kevutzah concept to incorporate industry, wage labor, and the removal of restrictions on the size of the group. The plan involved the inclusion of villages in a national organization, which ultimately crystallized as HA-KIBBUTZ HA-MEUHAD (1927). The kibbutzim of the *Ha-Shomer ha-Tzair* movement (organized in 1927 as KIBBUTZ HA-ARTZI HA-SHOMER HA-TZAIR) originally maintained numerical restrictions, but have not rejected wage labor and industry. See also HA-KIBBUTZ HA-DATI.

KIBBUTZ GALUYYOT (Heb. "ingathering of the exiled communities"): Conception involving the regathering of the Jewish nation in Israel. Originating with the Babylonian EXILE (Ezek. 34:37), the belief was strong from the 2nd cent. BCE and especially after the destruction of the Second Temple (70 CE). The return to Palestine of the Ten Tribes is also foretold by the Mishnah (*Sanhedrin* 10:3). The concept became increasingly linked with the messianic idea, and consequently was associated with the aims of many pseudo-messiahs from Serenus to Shabbetai Tzevi and Judah Hasid. Maimonides regarded political restoration in Palestine as indivisible from the messianic era (*Hilkhot Teshuvah*, 9, 2). Whereas 19th cent. Reform Judaism tended to excise the notion of *k. g.* from the liturgy, its long-standing presence there (e.g. grace after meals; *Shemoneh Esreh*) led R Hirsch Kalischer to declare redemption as involving the return to Palestine. It has become an important concept in Zionist and Israel political

Kibbutz Galuyot at the gates of Jerusalem following the advent of the Messiah. (From Venice Haggadah, 1609.)

philosophy and the right of entry of Jews to the country is a fundamental law of the state. See ALIYAH; APOCALYPSE; ESCHATOLOGY; MESSIAH; ZIONISM.

KIBBUTZNIK (Heb., with Russian suffix): Member of a KIBBUTZ.

KIDDUSH (Heb. "sanctification"): Ceremonial blessing recited on Sabbaths and Holy Days. It is composed of the ordinary benediction over wine or bread and a benediction proclaiming the holiness of the occasion. K. is recited in the home before the evening and morning meals, and was introduced into the synagogue at the end of the evening service (except on *Seder* night) for the benefit of travelers who ate their meals in the synagogue precincts. Formerly omitted in Reform liturgies, it has now been reintroduced in many communities.

KIDDUSH HA-SHEM (Heb. "sanctification of the [Divine] Name"): Term originally connoting martyrdom but later extended to apply to any act of strict integrity and uprightness which reflects

Kiddush over wine
(Woodcut from the
Prague Haggadah, 1527.)

creditably on Jews and Judaism in the eyes of non-Jews. Its opposite is HILLUL HA-SHEM.

KIDDUSH LEVANAH see **MOON, BLESSING OF THE**

KIDDUSHIN (Heb. "Betrothals"): Seventh and last tractate in the Mishnah order of *Nashim*, containing 4 chapters. It has *gemara* in both the Babylonian and Palestinian Talmud. It deals with all the regulations concerning betrothal, including prohibited marriages.

KIDRON: Valley separating the Temple Mount from the Mount of Olives, E of Jerusalem. In Neh. 2:15 and elsewhere it is called "the Valley" in view of its importance in defending the city from the N and E. Jerusalem's only spring, the Gihon, rises in the W flank of the K. valley. In Second Temple times, the K. was crossed by one or, possibly, two bridges. The necropolis of ancient Jerusalem was cut in its lower flanks ("Absalom's Tomb," etc.). Beyond Jerusalem the K. traverses the Wilderness of Judah; its steep borders housed numerous hermits' caves and monasteries, the most famous being that of Mar Saba.

KIELCE: Polish town. Jews were forbidden to reside in K. until the 19th cent. The community grew rapidly after the complete abolition of restrictions in 1862 and before World War II, numbered 19,000 (33% of the total), most of whom were annihilated by the Nazis. K. was the scene of pogroms before the War and, again, in 1946, when 43 survivors were killed by a mob.

KIERA, ESTHER see **CHIERA**

KIEV: Russian city; capital of the Ukraine, founded in the 8th cent., possibly by the Khazars. Jewish merchants visited the town in the 9th and 10th cents. The Jewish population grew steadily, despite persecutions which commenced in 1113, and scholars from K. are known from the 12th cent. The community was destroyed by the Tatars in 1240. From the end of the 14th cent., Jews were encouraged to return, and both a Rabbinite and Karaite community existed there during the 15th cent. Expulsions were decreed in 1495 and 1619. Peter the Great permitted Jews to trade in K. from 1708. In 1827, K. was excluded from the PALE OF SETTLEMENT. Resettlement dated from 1857, and K. became one of the largest Russian communities. It was the scene of pogroms in 1881 and 1905 and of the BEILIS Ritual Murder trial in 1913. 1,200 families were expelled in 1910. 350,000 Jews lived in K. in 1939; most of those trapped by the Nazi advance were massacred in 1941 (see BABI YAR). In the postwar period, Soviet antisemitism has been felt particularly strongly in K. Estimated Jewish pop. (1970): 152,006.

KILAYIM (Heb. "Diverse Kinds"): Fourth tractate in the Mishnah order of *Zeraim*, containing 9 chapters. It has *gemara* in the Palestinian, but not

The necropolis of ancient Jerusalem in the Kidron valley.

in the Babylonian, Talmud. It deals with the prohibitions of mingling different species of plants, animals, and clothing (Lev. 19:19; Deut. 22:9).

KIMBERLEY: Diamond center in S Africa. Jews — including the BARNATO family — were associated with its early development. A congregation formed in 1869 numbers 400 (1973).

KIMḤI (or **KAMḤI**): Family of Hebrew grammarians and translators originating in Spain and living in Narbonne (S France). They included: (1) *DAVID K.* (or *Redak*; c. 1160–1235): son of (2). His *Mikhlol* ("Compendium"), which assembled the researches of the Spanish Jewish grammarians and philologists, consisted of a grammar and a biblical dictionary (*Sepher ha-Shorashim* "Book of Roots"). His biblical commentaries were incorporated into standard editions of the Hebrew Bible, translated into Latin, and extensively used by the translators of the Bible into European languages. His comments fuse the Spanish speculative, philological, and philosophical traditions with the rabbinical midrashic method and the plain interpretation of Rashi. His style is lucid and simple. K. also participated in the Maimonist controversy as a supporter of Maimonides. (2) *JOSEPH K.* (c. 1105–1170): He settled in France as a refugee from the Almohad persecutions and inaugurated a fresh approach to the study of the Hebrew language and to Bible commentary, which was

developed by his sons. His works include grammars (he was the first to divide Hebrew vowels into 5 long and 5 short), commentaries on biblical books (specializing in the philological approach), religious poems (some of which were incorporated into the rites of Spain, S France, etc.), translations from Arabic (including Baḥya's *Duties of the Heart*), and a polemical work *Sepher ha-Berit* ("Book of the Covenant"). (3) *MOSES K.* (fl. 12th–13th cents.): son of (2). Author of *Mahalakh Shevile ha-Daat*, the first printed Hebrew grammar (Soncino, 1489). It was translated into Latin and widely utilized by Christian scholars during the Reformation Period. K. was also the author of commentaries on Proverbs, Ezra, and Nehemiah (long ascribed to Abraham Ibn Ezra) and liturgical poems.

יכלו ויכלאה ּּ	יונשא חמת ולא	יעלו דונכם	מח נכואה מו
ירחו ויחנועיה ּּ	עולס כחייתם	מעול נויתם	הבר יל יחונקם
לא ישם יה יוא	כלכו ועש אחר	אמן כיראל	סחף פלשתם
כזוון ישעיה ּּ	עורה ככיחור	יבל חני אול	וחפ כס קחתי

אמר דוד כל יוסף קמחי הספרדי זל חרבעה הספרס הא׳ שהס ישעיה ירמיה יחזקל תרי עשר הם נכוחת ותוכחה ונחמות לנרל נס יש כהם נבוחות לחומות העולם על פורעמותם ולפי שהרש לנרל נבתכו כן הנבוחת ככתכי הקקַ פ מין צבחו הנביחים עליהס לה׳ידיע כי יבקם הא חיהם נקאת בנ יבל ויעעיה ונח כיני חרכעת פלכים לה נס חוצע עוֹם בינח בימי חרבעת פלכים לה וכהוצ זכר יוכנעם כן יוח מלך ירל ולפי שנתנח על חרכן

Part of a page from David Kimḥi's commentary on the Prophets (Guadalajara, Spain, 1481).

KIMḤI (originally **MELLER**), **DOV** (1889–1961): Hebrew novelist and translator. He was born in Galicia and settled in Palestine in 1908. His novels, which have a pronounced romantic and lyrical trend, deal mostly with life in Israel during the 20th cent.

KINAH (Heb. "lamentation"): Dirge over the dead, customary in biblical, mishnaic, and talmudic times. It was extended to lamentations over the fate of the nations (Amos 5:1–2). In the Middle Ages, the name was applied to a special type of *piyyut* for *Av* 9, treating of the loss of the Temple and national independence, later also of contemporary persecutions, and concluding with the hope of the Messiah and redemption. The best-known author of *kinot* was Eleazar Kallir whose compositions still figure in the Italian and Ashkenazi rites. The former custom of reciting *kinot* on *Av* 9 during the Eighteen Benedictions survives only in the Italian rite; elsewhere they are said immediately after that prayer (Sephardi, Yemen) or after the reading of the Law (Ashkenazi). At one time the *kinot* grew so numerous that prayer lasted till midday; only a selection is now normally recited. Formally, they resemble SELIḤOT and the distinction is often very fine. A special type of *k.* in the Ashkenazi rite is the Zionide, which centers on Zion. See also LAMENTATIONS.

KING, KINGSHIP: The Israel monarchy was the culmination of the process of replacing tribal chiefs by leaders with broader jurisdiction, an intermediate stage being occupied by the Judges. The kingship was finally established, with prophetic sanction in the face of a military necessity, in the person of Saul. The k. was both a judge and a military leader possessing a standing force. However, his rule was never absolute as he was faced with prophetic criticism (e.g. David with Nathan, Ahab with Elijah), besides being subordinate to law (Deut. 17:14–19). The prestige of the house of David perpetuated its rule in Judah until the Babylonian Exile and was the basis of the authority of the exilarchs in Babylonia until the 14th cent. CE. From the 2nd cent. BCE. the Divine sanction of the Davidic house, symbolized by the act of anointing was developed in the conception of the MESSIAH. While the Hasmonean kings were also high priests, Jewish revolutionary movements of the 1st–2nd cents. CE produced claimants to messianic kingship (e.g. Andreas, Lukuas, Bar Kokhba). The Zealots rejected any kingship but that of God. The belief in Divine kingship reasserted itself in medieval pseudo-messiahs. The Hebrew notion of Divine sanction affected the Christian monarchies (cf. the British coronation service), while the limitations of Deut. 17:14–19, strongly influenced the Puritan revolutionary movement of the 17th cent. The position, rights, and limitations of the k. are specified in the Mishnah (*Sanhedrin* 2:2–5) and in a special section of Maimonides' *Mishneh Torah*.

KINGS, BOOK OF (Heb. *sepher melakhim*): Last of the four books in the Former Prophets section of the Bible. The book is generally divided into two parts — I Kings and II Kings (called III Kings and IV Kings in the Septuagint where the Book of Samuel is regarded as I and II Kings) but it is a single work, being a direct continuation of the Book of Samuel. K. relates the history of Israel and Judah from the death of David until the liberation of Jehoiachin during the Babylonian captivity. The material is derived from several sources, some cited by the author (e.g. The Book of the Chronicles of the Kings of Israel, the Book of the Chronicles of the Kings of Judah), while the others include works and memoirs derived from prophetic circles (especially those of Elijah and Elisha) and, to some extent, also from the priesthood. This is all united by one historical conception reflecting history in the spirit of the scribes and prophets who held that catastrophe was a consequence of sinfulness, in particular, of pagan worship. Its authorship was ascribed by the Talmud to Jeremiah and by some more recent scholars to Jeremiah's pupil, Baruch. Some authorities maintain that the final redaction was post-exilic.

KINGSLEY, SIDNEY (1906–): US playwright. His successes include *Men in White* and *Dead End.*

KINGSTON: Chief city of JAMAICA, British W Indies. The Jewish community, dating back to the 17th cent., is the only one now remaining on the island. The Sephardi and Ashkenazi communities merged in 1921. Jewish pop. (1973): c. 500.

KINNAROT VALLEY: Section of the deep Jordan Rift Valley comprising the SEA OF GALILEE and some of its adjacent land. It is 14 m. long and averages 3.5 m. in width.

KINNERET: Israel settlement (IK) and village on the SW shore of the Sea of Galilee. An ancient town of that name is mentioned as subject to Pharaoh Thutmose III and was assigned by Joshua to the tribe of Naphtali. The Palestine Office of the Zionist Organization founded a training and experimental farm there in 1908. A group of laborers from K., who wished to take over the farm on their own responsibility without an administrator, conceived the idea of communal settlement and set out to found DEGANYAH. In 1913, K. became an autonomous laborers' farm where the group of *Ha-Ikar ha-Tzair*, which laid the groundwork of the first *moshav ovedim*, worked. A training farm for girls was operated in K. under Hannah Meisels-Shochat. After World War I, a group of the *Gedud ha-Avodah* was stationed there, and the principles of the "large and growing kibbutz" were formulated. K. is now an agricultural and cultural center. Pop. (1972): 730. The adjacent village of K. was founded in 1909 on land acquired with the aid of Baron Edmond de Rothschild, but the fertile soil was not properly exploited until

Beginnings of the colony Kinneret on the shore of the Sea of Galilee.

ownership was transferred to the farmers themselves in 1944. Pop. (1972): 183.

KINNERET, LAKE OF see **SEA OF GALILEE**

KINNIM (Heb. "Bird Nests"): Eleventh and last tractate in the Mishnah order of *Kodashim*, containing 3 chapters. It has no *gemara* either in the Babylonian or Palestinian Talmud. It deals with the regulations for the bringing of an offering after childbirth (Lev. 12:8) or by the poor who might commit the offenses enumerated in Lev. 5. Parts of the treatise deal with cases where sacrifices are interchanged.

KIRCHHEIM, RAPHAEL (1804–1889): German scholar. Originally he was an extreme opponent of religious reform, but under the influence of Abraham Geiger, his attitude changed to enthusiastic adherence. K. wrote on various aspects of Judaism and published editions of several medieval Hebrew works.

KIRIATH JEARIM: Ancient Palestinian town in the territory of Benjamin (Josh. 15:60). Before the Israelite conquest, it was a Hivite settlement and a center of Baal worship. During the conquest of Canaan, K. J., with its allies the Gibeonites, succeeded in concluding a treaty with Joshua. The Ark was kept there for 20 years before David took it to Jerusalem. A youth village is now situated on the site, 10 m. W of Jerusalem. Pop. (1972): 154.

KIRJAT(H) SEPHER: Ancient Palestinian city in the territory of Judah, mentioned in an Egyptian source of the 13th cent. BCE; in the Bible also called DEBIR.

KIRKISANI, JACOB see **KARKASANI**

KIRYAT AMAL see **KIRYAT TIVON**

KIRYAT ANAVIM: Israel collective settlement (IK) near Jerusalem. Founded in 1920 by pioneers from E Europe, it was the first Jewish agricultural settlement in the hills. Despite incessant hardship, the settlers cultivated the site under the guidance of Akiva ETTINGER and produced unirrigated grapes, deciduous fruit, olives, and vegetables, while becoming the main dairy suppliers of Jewish Jerusalem. In the Israel War of Independence, K.A. was defended

Youth Village of Kiriath Jearim.

Kiryat Anavim.

stubbornly against repeated attacks and served as the springboard for the opening of the "Jerusalem Corridor." Pop. (1972): 328.

KIRYAT ATTA see **KEPHAR ATTA**

KIRYAT BIALIK: Israel municipality in the Zebulun plain. It was founded in 1934 by immigrants from Central Europe, and lies in the "residential belt" of the regional development scheme for Haifa Bay. To each house at K. B. is attached a garden and, often, an auxiliary farm. On its outer fringe is Kephar Bialik, a smallholders' settlement associated with *Ha-Moetzah ha-Ḥaklait* (middle-class settlers' organization). Pop. (1974): 21,400.

KIRYAT BINYAMIN: Israel settlement in the "residential belt" in the Zebulun plain. Five autonomous quarters were merged into this larger unit, which grew considerably after 1948 by the integration of new immigrants. Now part of KIRYAT ATTA.

KIRYAT GAT: Israel settlement in the S coastal plain founded in 1956 as the urban center of the Lachish development area. Various industrial plants were established there including textile and plastic plants. Pop. (1974), 21,100.

KIRYAT MOTZKIN: Israel municipality in the "residential belt" in the Zebulun plain. It was founded by middle-class settlers, mainly from E Europe, in 1934, and has grown considerably since 1948. Most of its inhabitants are employed in urban occupations in Haifa or in neighboring industrial undertakings. Pop. (1974): 20,000.

KIRYAT ONO: Israel suburban settlement near Tel Aviv, founded in 1939. Some of the veteran residents and the newcomers who settled here in large housing projects after the Israel War of Independence keep auxiliary farms, but their main occupation is in industry and commerce in the Tel Aviv area. Pop. (1974): 18,400.

KIRYAT SEPHER (Heb. literally "City of a book"): Hebrew quarterly journal devoted to Jewish bibliography, published since 1924 by the National and University Library in Jerusalem.

KIRYAT SHEMONAH: Israel rural settlement in the Ḥuleh Valley. Previously the Arab village of Khalisa, it was abandoned by its inhabitants in the Israel War of Independence and settled by new immigrants in May 1949. It has been developed as a center for the region based on agricultural produce. It has often been the target of artillery attack from nearby Lebanon. Pop. (1974): 15,500.

KIRYAT TIVON: Israel suburban settlement near Haifa. Founded as Kiryat Amal in 1937 as a "garden city," it has become a center of tourism and recreation and in 1958 was joined with the neighboring garden city of Tivon. Pop. (1974): 10,600.

KIRYAT YAM: Israel municipality founded in 1946, in the "residential belt" on the coast of the Zebulun plain. Pop. (1974): 23,500.

KISCH: Prague family prominent especially in medicine, deriving from Chiesch (Czechoslovakia). Its outstanding members have included: (1) *AB-*

Kiryat Shemonah.

Kiryat Tivon.

RAHAM K. (1725–1803): Physician, one of the first Jews to be graduated from the Univ. of Halle. He taught Moses Mendelssohn Latin. (2) *ALEXANDER K.* (1848–1917): Rabbi of Prague, author of works on Bohemian Jewish history. (3) *BRUNO ZACHARIAS K.* (1890–1966): Physiologist; son of (2). He lectured at Cologne Univ. from 1918, and from 1938 lived in the US, teaching at Yeshiva Univ., New York. K. was responsible for important discoveries, especially in cardiology and biochemistry. (4) *EGON ERWIN K.* (1885–1948): Left-wing journalist. Leaving Germany in 1933, he settled in the US in 1934, in Mexico in 1942, and returned to Czechoslovakia in 1946. His exclusion from Australia on political grounds in 1934 was a *cause célèbre* at the time. (5) *GUIDO K.* (1889–): Jurist and historian; son of (2). Formerly professor of law at Königsberg and Halle, he devoted himself mainly to Jewish history after settling in 1937 in the US where he taught at the Jewish Institute of Religion, New York. He founded and edited the journal *Historia Judaica* and wrote on the legal position of the Jews in medieval Germany.

KISCH: Family settled in England since the close of the 18th cent. (1) *SIR CECIL K.* (1884–1961): economist; son of (4). He was deputy undersecretary of state for India (1933–43), British delegate to various international conferences, and a writer on banking and economic questions. (2) *DANIEL MONTEFIORE K.* (1839–1898) emigrated to S Africa and became auditor-general of the Transvaal and adviser to the Zulu king Lobengula. (3) *FREDERICK HERMANN K.* (1888–1943): British soldier and Zionist; son of (4). In World War I, he served on the British General Staff and was on the staff of the British embassy in Paris during the Versailles Conference. In 1922, he joined the Zionist Executive in Jerusalem, resigning in 1931 but continuing to live in Palestine. He rejoined the British army in 1939, reached the rank of brigadier, and was killed in action while clearing a minefield in N Africa. (4) *HERMANN MICHAEL K.* (1850–1942): Indian civil servant. He was deputy-secretary to the government of India, postmaster-general of Bengal, and later active in English Jewish affairs.

KISHINEV: Capital of Soviet Moldavia, previously BESSARABIA. The Jewish community was already in existence in the early 19th cent. and grew rapidly. The pogrom of Apr. 1903 — in which 47 Jews were killed and 92 severely wounded — caused a universal protest and led to the establishment of Jewish self-defense. A further pogrom occurred in 1905. In 1940, 80,000 out of the total population of 113,000 were Jews, many of whom were expelled to Russia. From 1941, the remaining Jews were concentrated in a ghetto and deported to Transnistria where they were murdered. Jewish pop. (1970): 49,905.

Zodiacal sign of the month of Kislev. (From the 15th cent. Nuremberg Haggadah.)

KISHON: River traversing the Valley of Jezreel and entering the Mediterranean 2 m. N of Haifa. Its total length is 27 m., only the last quarter of which is a permanent stream. The river mouth has been recently deepened and transformed into an auxiliary port. In the Bible, the K. is sometimes called "the river that is before Jokneam" (Josh. 19:11), or "the Waters of Megiddo" (Judg. 5:19); but its proper name appears both in the prose and poetic account of Israel's victory over Sisera (Judg. 4:13; 5:21). On its banks near Mt. Carmel, Elijah slaughtered the priests of Baal.

KISHON, EPHRAIM (1924–): Humorist. Born in Hungary, he moved to Israel in 1949 and has written many satires (books, plays, films, articles) reflecting Israel life (*Look Back Mrs. Lot, Noah's Ark, Tourist Class, The Blaumilch Canal, Sallah Shabbati,* etc.).

KISLEV: Ninth month of the Hebrew religious calendar, third of the civil calendar; coinciding with Nov.–Dec. It has 29 or 30 days, the festival of HANUKKAH beginning on the 25th of K.

KISLING, MOISE (1891–1953): Painter. He was born in Poland but lived in Paris from 1910, except for the period of World War II when he was in the US. He excelled in painting nudes, flower-pieces and portraits of women and children.

KISS, JOSEPH (1843–1921): Hungarian poet. Many of his poems deal with Jewish subjects, including *Against the Storm* (1882) inspired by the Tisza-Eszlár blood libel. He was the first Jew to make a strong impression in Hungarian literature.

KISSINGER, HENRY (1923–): US political scientist. Born in Fürth, Germany, he went to the US in 1938. He was appointed professor in Harvard in 1962. K., an expert in defense policy, was an adviser to President Kennedy 1961–2 and was one of the closest political advisers to President Nixon from his assumption of office in 1969. In 1973–7 he was Secretary of State and played a key role in international affairs of the period (including the YOM KIPPUR WAR and its aftermath). He was awarded a 1973 Nobel Prize for Peace for his work in helping to end the Vietnam War. His books include *Nuclear Weapons and Defence Policy* which stressed the danger of massive retaliation.

KITTEL (Yidd. from German): White garment worn as a shroud and, because of its solemn associations, by the officiants (and many individuals) in the synagogue during service on the New Year, the Day of Atonement, etc. It is sometimes also worn at the SEDER service and by bridegrooms. In Germany, this garment was called *sargenes*.

*KITTEL, RUDOLPH (1853–1929): German Protestant theologian and Bible scholar; professor at Breslau and Leipzig. His biblical and historical studies represented the moderate Wellhausen schools. His main work was a history of the Jews in biblical times. He also translated into German several books of the Bible, the Apocrypha, and the apocalyptic literature accompanied by commentaries. In collaboration with a group of scholars, he published a critical edition of the Hebrew Bible (*Biblia Hebraica*), quoting textual variants and conjectured emendations.

KLACZKO, JULIAN (1825–1906): Author. From his youth, he wrote Hebrew and Polish poetry. In 1849, he settled in Paris, where he was converted to Catholicism and continued his literary activities in Polish and French. An ardent Polish patriot, he lived from 1888 in Cracow.

KLAPPER, PAUL (1885–1952): US college president. He taught pedagogics at City College, New York 1907–37 and was the first president of Queens College, New York, 1937–48.

KLATZKIN, JACOB (1882–1948): Hebrew editor and philosopher. Born in Poland, he pursued his university education in Germany where he actively participated in Zionist affairs. After World War I, he founded, together with Nahum Goldmann, the *Eshkol* publishing house, which produced Hebrew books, and the *Encyclopaedia Judaica* under K.'s editorship. After the Nazi rise to power, he moved to Switzerland. K.'s philosophy was based on biological foundations, and emphasized the dangers threatening the soul of modern man from the domination of reason. He based Zionism on biological and ethnic factors of existence and upon an uncompromising rejection of the Diaspora. He predicted that the reconstitution of Jewish national life in Israel would weaken instead of strengthening the Jewish existence in the Diaspora by creating a distinct Jewish type quite unlike the accepted stereotype of the Jew, thus cleaving the nation in two. His books include a thesaurus of Hebrew philosophical terminology.

KLAUS(E) (Ger. "enclosure"): Name given from the 16th cent. in Central and E Europe to an institution, usually with a synagogue attached, where the Talmud was studied perpetually by adults. Among the most famous were those maintained at Vienna by Zerahiah Ha-Levi from 1656 and at

Yoseph Klausner.

Hamburg by Tzevi Ashkenazi around 1700. The Ḥasidim applied the name k. ("kloiz") to their synagogue.

KLAUSENBERG see **CLUJ**

KLAUSNER, YOSEPH GEDALIAH (1874–1958): Scholar. A native of Lithuania, he settled in Odessa as a child and lived there until 1919 when he went to Palestine, being appointed professor of modern Hebrew literature (1926) and of Second Temple history (1945) at the Hebrew Univ. His vast literary output commenced in 1893 from which time on he published hundreds of scholarly works and articles on various aspects of Jewish history and literature. In this way, and as editor of *Ha-Shiloah* 1903–27, he exercised a great influence in Jewish scholarship. His six-volume history of modern Hebrew literature laid the foundations for the systematic study of the subject from the beginning of the Haskalah Period down to the end of the 19th cent. His other writings include a history of the Second Temple Period (5 vols.); a history of the development of the messianic idea among the Jews until the close of the Mishnah Period; *Jesus of Nazareth* and *From Jesus to Paul* which trace the evolution of Christianity, using Jewish sources; philological studies, including a modern Hebrew grammar; monographs on outstanding Hebrew authors, particularly Bialik and Tschernikhovski; essays; and philosophical works.

From 1950, he was editor-in-chief of the *Encyclopaedia Hebraica*. An adherent of the Revisionist, and later *Ḥerut*, party he was a candidate for election as president of Israel in 1949.

KLEIN, ABRAHAM M. (1909–1972): Canadian poet. A lawyer by profession, he was for some years visiting lecturer in poetry at McGill Univ. His poetry appeared in *Hath Not a Jew, The Hitleriad, The Rocking Chair*, etc. He wrote *The Second Scroll*, a work of symbolic fiction.

KLEIN, SHEMUEL (1886–1940): Scholar. Of Hungarian birth, he served as rabbi in Bosnia and Slovakia, and from 1928 was professor of Palestinography at the Hebrew Univ. He wrote numerous studies in Hebrew, German, and Hungarian on the land of Israel and its former Jewish settlement.

KLEINMANN, MOSHEH (1871–1948): Author and editor. In 1904–7, he edited at Lvov the Yiddish daily *Togblat* and the Hebrew daily *Ha-Yom*. From 1908 to 1916, he was in Odessa, playing a prominent part in the Zionist movement and editing local Yiddish journals. He left Russia in 1921, eventually settling in Israel. He edited the Zionist weekly organ *Ha-Olam* 1923–48.

KLEMPERER, OTTO (1885–1973): Conductor and composer. He was general musical director of the Kroll Opera, Berlin, until 1933 when he moved to the US being conductor of the Los Angeles Symphony Orchestra 1935–40. After World War II, K. settled in Switzerland. He was one of the world's most respected conductors, being especially noted for his interpretations of Beethoven.

KLEY, EDUARD (1789–1867): German preacher and pedagogue. In 1817, he was appointed director of the Hamburg Free School. He preached in the Hamburg Temple 1818–40, his innovations including a choir and organ, German songs (of which he published a collection), and sermons in the vernacular. His published sermons were widely used as models.

KLOTZ, LUCIEN LOUIS (1868–1930): French politician. A deputy from 1898, he was a member of various governments in 1910–11 and 1917–20, generally as minister of finance. In 1928, he was appointed to the Senate but in the same year, was imprisoned for fraud.

KLUGER, SOLOMON BEN JUDAH AARON (1783–1869): Rabbinic scholar. Rabbi in Brody, E Galicia, he was a fertile halakhic authority and codifier, inclining to austere interpretations except in cases of *Agunah* where he tended to leniency.

KLUTZNICK, PHILIP MORRIS (1907–): US lawyer and communal leader. He has held leading positions in local and federal housing agencies. K. was international president of B'nai B'rith 1953–9, and has served on the boards of many world and national Jewish bodies. In 1961–2, he was a member of the US delegation to the UN.

Philip Morris Klutznick.

KNESSET (Heb.): Israel's single chamber parliament. The K., created in 1949, has 120 seats which are filled by proportional representation based on the total vote in the country. All men and women with Israel citizenship, above the age of 18, have the right to vote. Candidates for election must be above the age of 25. There is no property or residential qualification. The K. formerly met in Tel Aviv but, in 1949, when Jerusalem was threatened with internationalization, it moved to temporary accommodation in that city. A permanent building was opened in 1966. Members of the K. have certain privileges and immunities, especially immunity from arrest, which can only be waived by the K. as a whole. The language of debate is Hebrew, but a running translation is provided individually for Arab members. Speeches made in Arabic are publicly translated into Hebrew. Bills are discussed in principle on first reading and are then passed to one of the standing committees (house committee, constitution, legislation, and law committee, finance committee, foreign affairs and security committee, labor committee, economic committee, education and culture committee, home affairs committee, and public service committee). The details of bills as amended in committee are discussed on second reading. There is no presidential power to veto laws passed by the K., nor has the Israel Supreme Court the power of the US Supreme Court to declare a law unconstitutional. as there is no complete written constitution.

KNOPF, ALFRED A. (1892–): US publisher. He is the head of the US publishing firm bearing his name.

DISTRIBUTION OF SEATS AFTER SEVEN ELECTIONS

	1949	1951	1955	1959	1961	1965	1969	1973
MAPAI (Israel Labor Party)	46	45	40	47	42	45	56	51
AHDUT AVODAH — POALE ZION	19	15	9	9	9	8		
MAPAM (United Workers' Party)			10	7	8	10		
RAFI (Israel Workers' List)								
HERUT	14	8	15	17	17	26	26	39
GENERAL ZIONISTS (Liberals)	7	20	13	8	17			
INDEPENDENT LIBERALS (Progressives)	5	4	5	6		5	4	4
Religious Parties (MIZRAHI, HA-POEL HA-MIZRAHI, AGUDAT ISRAEL, POALE AGUDAT ISRAEL)	16	15	17	18	18	17	18	15
Communists (MAKI, RAKAH)	4	5	6	3	5	4	4	5
Arab Parties (Affiliated to MAPAI)	2	5	5	5	4	4	4	3
Others	7	3	0	0	0	1	8	3

KNOXVILLE: City in Tennessee, US. Although a number of Jewish families lived there just prior to the Civil War, they had no organization until 1864 when the Hebrew Benevolent Society (from 1877, Temple Beth El) was formed. Its Orthodox members left when the group decided to conduct Reform services in 1875, and in 1881 they organized Congregation B'nai Yeshurun which lasted 5 years. The Orthodox congregation Heska Amuna, still in existence, was founded in 1890. The Jewish Welfare Fund was established in 1939. Jewish pop. (1973): 950.

KOBRIN, LEON (1873–1946): Yiddish dramatist and novelist. A native of Russia, he went to the US in 1892. Here he worked at first in a sweatshop. From 1894 he published realistic sketches and tales and after 1899 also wrote a series of successful plays. His memoirs mirror the life of Jewish immigrants in Philadelphia and New York.

KODASHIM (Heb. "Holy Things"): Fifth Order (*Seder*) of the Mishnah, consisting of 11 tractates, 9 of which have *gemara* in the Babylonian, but not in the Palestinian, Talmud. The tractates in *K.* deal with the law of ritual slaughtering, sacrifice, and other subjects connected with the Temple ritual.

KOENIG, LEO (pseudonym of Leib Yaffe; 1889–1970): Yiddish and Hebrew author. Born in Odessa, he lived in London from 1914 until 1952 when he settled in Israel. K. wrote critical essays on

The Knesset.

Jewish writers and artists, poems, and novels, mainly in Yiddish. He was one of the first to write art criticism in Yiddish.

KOESTLER, ARTHUR (1905–): Author. Of Hungarian birth, he traveled widely before settling in England in 1940. A communist during the 1930's, he repudiated communism in 1938, describing his disillusion in *The God that Failed*. K. is the author of topical novels, essays, and reminiscences, including *Darkness at Noon*, a criticism of communist totalitarianism; *Thieves in the Night*, a novel of kibbutz life in Palestine; and *Promise and Fulfilment*, on Zionism. His autobiography appeared in 2 vols., *Arrow in the Blue* (1952) and *Invisible Writing* (1954).

KOGAN (KAHANA), DAVID (1838–1915): Scholar; lived in Odessa. He wrote many studies on Jewish history and literature, and his *History of the Kabbalists, Sabbetaians and Ḥasidim* laid the foundations of a new outlook on the development of Jewish mysticism.

KOHELET see **ECCLESIASTES**

KOHELET RABBAH see **ECCLESIASTES RABBAH**

KOHEN TZEDEK see **COHEN TZEDEK**

KOHEN TZEDEK BEN JOSEPH: Gaon of Pumbedita 917–36. According to the epistle of Sherira, he was appointed gaon by the exilarch David ben Zakkai, but the scholars of the academy refused to recognize him and elected R Mevasser Kahana. A compromise was reached in 922 with each heading his own college, but after Mevasser's death in 926, K. Tz. was accepted as sole gaon. (A different account of the events is given by Nathan the Babylonian). During his period of office, he raised the prestige of the Pumbedita academy, which he succeeded in establishing officially on the same status as Sura. He supported David ben Zakkai in his quarrel with Saadyah.

KOHLER: (1) *KAUFMANN K.* (1843–1926): Leader of Reform Judaism. He was born and studied in Germany, going to the US in 1869. He served congregations in Chicago and New York until called to the presidency of the Hebrew Union College in 1903, holding that post for 18 years. K. was the leading personality at the Pittsburgh Conference where the radical Reform "Pittsburgh Platform" was adopted. He was a prolific writer in the fields of philosophy and theology and a vigorous opponent of Zionism. K. guided the development of Reform Judaism in the US for many years and was its foremost scholar. He was one of the editors of the American Jewish translation of the Bible and of the *Jewish Encyclopedia*. The best known of his many works is *Jewish Theology Systematically and Historically Considered*. (2) *MAX JAMES K.* (1871–1934): Lawyer and historian; son of (1). He was especially active in safeguarding the rights of immigrants to the US. He wrote on American Jewish

history and Jewish rights at international congresses. (3) *ROSE K.* (1873–1947): Sculptor and painter; daughter of (1). Her works include busts and portraits of eminent Jewish leaders. She is best-known for her medallion *The Spirit of the Synagogue*.

KOHN, ABRAHAM (1807–1848): Rabbi. He officiated from 1833 at Hohenems (Austria) where he introduced innovations into the liturgy. In 1844, he was appointed to a progressive congregation in Lvov where his reforms aroused the opposition of the Orthodox Jews. When he and his son died suddenly, the Orthodox were suspected of having poisoned them, but the charge was not proved.

KOHN, HANS (1891–1971): Historian. Of Czechoslovakian birth, he settled in the US in 1937. He taught at a number of American universities, and since 1949 has been professor of history at City College, New York. K. is an authority on nationalism which constitutes the subject of his principal works.

KOHN, SAMUEL (1841–1920): Hungarian scholar. He officiated as rabbi at Pest from 1866 and lectured at the Budapest Rabbinical Seminary 1899–1905. His many studies dealt especially with the Samaritans and Hungarian Jewish history.

KOHUT: (1) *ADOLPH K.* (1848–1917): Journalist and author. Of Hungarian birth, he edited the *Berliner Zeitung* and other German newspapers in Breslau, Dresden, and Düsseldorf. He wrote prolifically on history, culture, and Jewish affairs, including a history of the Jews in Germany. (2) *ALEXANDER K.* (1842–1894): Rabbi and scholar; brother of (1). Born and educated in Hungary, he served in various Hungarian pulpits. He was elected to the Hungarian parliament, but, instead, went to the US (in 1885) as rabbi of Congregation Ahavath Chesed, New York. He helped to inspire a revival of traditional Judaism in America, and was one of the founders of the Jewish Theological Seminary. K.'s greatest scholarly achievement was the *Arukh Completum* (9 vols. 1878–92), an amplified edition of the talmudic dictionary of Nathan ben Jehiel. (3) *GEORGE ALEXANDER K.* (1874–1933): Educator; son of (2) whom he accompanied to the US in 1885. He was active in a variety of American educational projects and as a bibliophile, bibliographer, and patron of Jewish scholarship. (4) *REBEKAH K.* (1864–1951): US welfare worker; second wife of (2). She was active in many branches of Jewish and general social work and education in New York, serving on a number of employment commissions. She wrote several volumes of reminiscences.

KOIGEN, DAVID (1879–1933): Philosopher and sociologist. Of Russian birth, he lived mainly in Berlin although he lectured at Kiev Univ. 1918–21. His philosophical teaching stressed the relationship between civilization and democracy. He also endeavored to establish sociology on an independent scientific basis, founding for this purpose the Berlin periodical *Ethos*. K. regarded the covenant between man and God as the characteristic of Judaism, symbolizing the identity of human goodness with the Divine Will.

KOITEIN see **GOITEIN**

*KOKOWZOFF, PAVEL (1861–1942): Russian orientalist; pupil of Daniel Chowolson and his successor as professor at the Univ. of Leningrad. He published numerous studies in the field of Semitic philology, on the history of the Khazars, etc.

KOL BO (Heb. "compendium"): Name of a medieval Jewish legal codification. The name is also given to editions of the *maḥzor* designed for the cantor. A work called *Yad Kol Bo* (Frankfort, 1726) also incorporated the Pentateuch with commentaries.

Melody for the chanting of *Kol Nidre*.

KOL NIDRE (Aram. "all vows"): Formula for the annulment of vows, recited on the eve of the Day at Atonement. The custom originated in the early Gaonic Period, probably not in Babylonia, and from the 9th cent. the Babylonian geonim protested against its utterance; nevertheless, its use persisted. According to the original version, it annuls all vows and oaths made during the preceding year and incumbent solely on the vower, i.e., excluding vows affecting another person. The text nevertheless aroused the accusation among non-Jews that a Jewish oath was not to be trusted. In the 12th cent., R Jacob Tam changed the formula to refer to vows in the forthcoming year (without altering the rest of the text), and this is customary among the Ashkenazim; the Italians retain the original version, while the Sephardim (and Ashkenazim in Israel) combine the two. The language is Aramaic for the Ashkenazim and Sephardim, but Hebrew in R Amram Gaon's liturgy, and the Roman and Byzantine rites. The connection with the Day of Atonement is difficult to establish clearly, but the prayer has become firmly rooted in Jewish tradition (the eve of the Day of Atonement being popularly called *K. N.*), and endeared to Ashkenazim by the added reason of its ancient melody.

KOLIN: Town in Czechoslovakia. Its Jewish community was established by the 14th cent. when Jews lived there without restriction. They were expelled in 1541 but returned in 1566. In the latter 18th cent., K. was the largest Bohemian community after Prague and possessed a wide measure of auto-

Theodor Kollek.

nomy; its Jews controlled the local tobacco trade. The old community, numbering some 500 before 1939, ended with the Nazi occupation.

KOLLEK, THEODOR (Teddy; 1911–): Israel public figure. Born in Vienna, he went to Palestine in 1934 and became a member of kibbutz En Gev. During and after World War II he worked for the political department of the Jewish Agency and for the Haganah, in Europe and the US. He was Israel minister in Washington 1950–2 and director-general of the prime minister's office from 1952. Here he played a major role in building up Israel's tourist industry and in founding the ISRAEL MUSEUM. In 1965 he was elected mayor of Jerusalem as a member of the RAFI party (later, the ISRAEL LABOR PARTY. He made special efforts to promote Jewish-Arab cooperation in the city following the reunification of Jerusalem in 1967.

KOLOSZVAR see **CLUJ**

KOMPERT, LEOPOLD (1822–1886): Austrian novelist. He sought to bring the life of Eastern Jewry to the sympathetic attention of the West in *Geschichten aus Ghetto* and *Böhmische Juden*, etc. His other novels deal with problems of intermarriage and racial anti-Semitism. He took an active interest in Jewish education.

KÖNIGSBERG: City of E Prussia (now Kaliningrad, USSR). Its Jewish settlement dates from the late 17th cent. In 1782, there was inaugurated in K. the

Hebrew language society *Doreshe Leshon Ever*, which two years later founded HA-MEASSEPH. Hebrew presses were maintained at K. 1755–65, 1845–79. The Jewish population numbering 3,170 in 1933 was wiped out by the Nazis.

KÖNIGSWARTER: Austrian family of bankers, founded at Fürth in the 18th cent. by JONAS HIRSCH K. of Königswart in Bohemia. His son *BARON JONAS MARCUS VON K.* (1807–1871) moved first to Frankfort-on-Main and then to Vienna and made the banking-house one of the most important in Central Europe. He was active in Jewish life and was president of the Viennese community (1868–71). His son, *BARON MORITZ VON K.* (1837–1893), for a time exercised a dominant influence in the Austrian financial administration. The firm, which played a great part in railway development, had branches in many European capitals.

KONITZ (Chojnice): Polish (formerly German) town. The first Jew settled there in 1767. Its small community was shaken in 1900 by a Blood Libel and even after the acquittal of the accused, the Jews were threatened and boycotted. Many left at this period and when the city was annexed to Poland few remained.

KOOK, AVRAHAM YITZHAK (1865–1935): Rabbinic thinker and chief rabbi of Palestine. He applied his extensive Jewish learning to current problems and emphasized the religious aspect of Zionism. All his writings stress the centrality of Jewish nationalism and Palestine in Judaism. He began his literary career in 1888 by editing and publishing a rabbinical journal called *Ittur Sopherim*. In 1891, he published anonymously *Havash Pe'er* on the proper wearing of the phylacteries. His article *Teudat Yisrael u-Leummiyuto* became the ideological basis of the *Mizrahi* movement with which he was closely associated. He was rabbi in Zimel, Lithuania, 1888–95; Boisk, Latvia 1895–1904; and Jaffa from 1904. He evinced understanding even of the most secular elements. In 1909, he permitted certain agricultural work to be done during the Sabbatical year. Leaving for Europe in 1914, his return to Palestine was prevented by the outbreak of World War I and he officiated at St. Gallen, Switzerland (1914–6) and London (1916–9). In 1919, he went to Jerusalem, becoming chief rabbi of the Ashkenazi community in Palestine on the establishment of the office in 1921. He then established a yeshivah, now called *Merkaz ha-Rav*. His later literary works include *Orot* on the aspect of holiness in the newborn nationalism, *Orot ha-Teshuvah*, on repentance, and *Halakhah Berurah* on halakhic problems.

KOPH (ק): Nineteenth letter of the Hebrew alphabet; numerical value 100. It is sounded by oriental Jews as uvular ("back") *k*, but by western Jews is not distinguished from *kaph*.

KOPLIK, HENRY (1858–1927): Physician. Born in New York, he discovered the diagnostic spots of measles, later referred to as "Koplik's spots." He established the first milk station in the US. K. was the founder of the American Pediatric Society and wrote on children's diseases.

KORAH: A levite related to Moses, who — together with Dathan and Abiram of the tribe of Reuben and 250 Israelite notables — rose against Moses and Aaron (Num. 16), intending to seize the leadership and the high priesthood. However, the earth opened and swallowed them, only K.'s sons surviving (Num. 26:11). One of the three groups of Temple poets and instrumentalists was known as the "sons of K." (II Chron. 20:19), the traditional authors of Ps. 42–9, 84–5, 87–8. Some of the "sons of K." served as Temple gatekeepers (I Chron. 9:19; 26:1).

KORAN: The holy book of ISLAM containing the utterances of MOHAMMED during his prophetic career. The great influence exercised by Judaism on the growth of Islam reveals itself in the K. which reproduces many Jewish ideas and religious notions, mentions several precepts of Jewish law, and even contains Hebrew loan-words. Biblical tales and allusions to events in ancient Hebrew history are frequent, but the biblical narratives are permeated with midrashic elements. Biblical personalities figure prominently, especially Moses and Abraham, the latter being considered the first adherent of the "true religion" which, after numerous distortions, was reestablished through Islam.

Rabbi Avraham Yitzhak Kook.

KORCZAK, JANOS (real name Henrick Goldschmidt; 1878–1942): Polish author and educationalist. His pedagogical method was founded on a
psychological understanding and respect for the
child. K.'s books for children were well-known in
Poland. He conducted a children's institution in
the Warsaw ghetto and went to his death with his
charges.

KORN, ARTHUR (1870–1945): Electronics pioneer.
His research and experiments laid the basis for
the radio transmission of photographs. He sent the
first photo by wire in 1904 and across the Atlantic
in 1922. Leaving his native Germany, he took up
residence in the US in 1939.

KORNBERG, ARTHUR (1918–): US scientist.
Professor of biochemistry at Stanford Univ., he
was in 1959 awarded the Nobel Prize for medicine.

KORNFELD, JOSEPH SAUL (1876–1943): US
rabbi and diplomat. He was Reform rabbi in
various communities (1898–1921, 1925–34) and US
minister to Persia 1921–4.

KORNGOLD, ERICH WOLFGANG (1897–1957):
Composer. Son of the Viennese music critic
Julius Leopold K. (1860–1945), his pantomime *The
Snowman* was performed at the Vienna Court Opera
when he was eleven years old. He worked as musical
adapter and conductor for Max Reinhardt productions
and after settling in the US in 1934, composed for
motion pictures. He wrote operas, chamber music, a
symphony, a violin concerto, etc.

KORTNER, FRITZ (1892–1970): German actor.
Leaving Germany in 1934 he went in 1938 to the
US where he directed and wrote plays and participated
in films. After World War II, he returned to Germany.

KOSHER see **KASHRUT**

KOSSOVSKY see **KASSOVSKY**

KOSTELANETZ, ANDRÉ (1901–): US conductor.
He was chorus master at the St. Petersburg
Grand Opera from 1920 to 1922 when he settled in
the US. Since 1929, he has conducted his own concert
orchestra. K. is noted for his orchestration of popular
music.

KOTEL MAARAVI see **WESTERN WALL**

KOUFAX, SANDY (1935–): US baseball player.
Born in New York, he played with the Brooklyn
Dodgers 1955–7 and the Los Angeles Dodgers 1958–
64. An outstanding pitcher, he broke many records,
establishing various major league records. His most
successful season was in 1963 when he brought the
Dodgers to a 4–0 victory in the World Series.

KOUSSEVITZKY, SERGE (1874–1951): Conductor.
Born in Russia, he first achieved renown as a
double-bass virtuoso, and made his conducting debut
at Berlin in 1907, and from 1910 to 1918 directed the
Koussevitzky Symphony Orchestra in Russia. He
conducted the Boston Symphony Orchestra 1924–49,
and established the Koussevitzky Music Federation

to assist composers. In 1934, he organized the
Berkshire Music Festival at Tanglewood, Mass.

KOVEL: Town in Soviet Ukraine, formerly in
Poland. Jews settled there in the 16th cent. and
encountered various vicissitudes, suffering heavily
in the Chmielnicki invasion of 1648. By 1660, the
community was rehabilitated and Jewish craftsmen
were members of Christian guilds. The Jews numbered
c. 15,000 before World War II, but were exterminated
by the Nazis. Jewish pop. (1970): 250.

KOVNER, ABBA (1918–): Hebrew author. Born
in the Crimea, he was educated at Vilna and
during World War II led the Jewish partisans who
left the Vilna ghetto. In 1945, he settled in Palestine.
His poems and novels have been largely devoted
to the Jewish partisans during the Nazi period and
to Israel's War of Independence.

KOVNER, ABRAHAM URI (1842–1909): Hebrew
and Russian author. His booklet *Ḥeker Davar*,
which criticized contemporary Hebrew writings
and condemned Haskalah literature for its remoteness
from everyday life, aroused bitter controversy. In
his *Tzeror Peraḥim* he attacked Hebrew as a dead
tongue. In 1870, he settled in St. Petersburg and
contributed weekly feuilletons to the Russian journal
Golos. After four years' exile in Siberia for a criminal
offense, he adopted Christianity. His last years were
spent at Lomza, Poland, from where he corresponded
with many leading Russian literary figures.

KOVNO (Kaunas): Lithuanian city. Jews lived
there in the 15th cent., were expelled in 1495, but
returned in 1501. There were also expulsions in
1753, but the community survived, receiving equal
rights in 1858, and by the early 20th cent. numbered
50% of the total population. It was a distinguished
center of Jewish learning, and in the mid-19th cent.
R Israel SALANTER founded the MUSAR MOVEMENT
and the SLOBODKA yeshivah there. During the period
of Lithuanian Independence (1918–40), K. was an
intellectual hub with a Hebrew school system, Ort
technical college, Yiddish and Hebrew press, etc.
Before World War II, there were c. 25,000 Jews in
K. (25% of the total population). In 1941, they
were herded into a ghetto by the Nazis and 10,000
killed in a single day (Oct. 28, 1941). The survivors
were joined by 7,000 deportees from Germany and
Lithuania but nearly all were exterminated by 1944.
Jewish pop. (1959): 4,792.

KRAKAUER, LEOPOLD (1890–1954): Artist and
architect. Of Moravian birth, he settled in Palestine in 1925. Much of his work depicts the landscape
of Jerusalem.

KRANZ, JACOB BEN WOLF (DUBNER MAGGID)
see **JACOB BEN WOLF**

KRAUS, KARL (1874–1936): Austrian satirist and
critic. In 1899, he founded *Die Fackel* ("The
Torch"), largely written by himself, in which he

held up to scorn the cultural and political degeneration of his time, especially as exhibited in the press. His accusations culminated in the massive play *Die letzten Tage der Menschheit* ("The Last Day of Humanity"), a merciless exposition of the causes and character of World War I. He converted to Catholicism in 1898.

KRAUS, PAUL (1904–1944): Orientalist. He studied at Prague, Jerusalem, and Berlin and was *privatdozent* at Berlin Univ. After 1933, he lived for some years in Paris and then became lecturer at Cairo. He was an accomplished Assyriologist but devoted most of his work to the history of science and philosophy in the Islamic Period. His main work was on the medieval chemist Jabir ibn Hayyan.

KRAUSKOPF, JOSEPH (1858–1923): Rabbi. He emigrated to the US from Germany as a child. For more than 35 years he served in Philadelphia and introduced many Reform innovations, including Sunday services. In 1896 he founded what later became the National Agricultural College in Doylestown, Pa.

KRAUSS, SAMUEL (1866–1948): Hungarian scholar. He lectured at the Budapest Rabbinical Seminary 1894–1905 and the Vienna Rabbinical Seminary from 1906 (principal from 1932). In 1938, he escaped to England and settled in Cambridge. A comprehensive scholar, his studies ranged over many fields including philology, history, Bible, Talmud, Christianity, and medieval literature. His major works, most in German, include *Greek and Latin Loan-Words in the Talmud, Midrash and Targum*, *The Archeology of the Talmud*, *Greeks and Romans in Talmudic Sources*, and *Synagogal Antiquities*.

KREBS, SIR HANS ADOLF (1901–): Biochemist. Born in Germany, he settled in England in 1933, being appointed professor of biochemistry at Sheffield in 1945 and at Oxford in 1954. In 1953, he was awarded the Nobel Prize for his researches on the conversion of food-elements into energy.

KREIN: Family of Russian composers. (1) *ALEXANDER K.* (1883–1951): His compositions, influenced by Russian and Jewish folklore, include operas, symphonic and chamber music, the symphonic cantata *Kaddish*, and music for the Jewish theater. (2) *GRIGORI K.* (1886–), brother of (1), has also written works on Jewish themes including *Hebrew Rhapsody* for clarinet and orchestra. (3) *JULIAN K.* (1913–), son of (2), composed *Spring Symphony*, program music, etc.

KREISKY, BRUNO (1911–): Austrian statesman. When the Nazis entered Austria in 1938, K. escaped to Sweden and remained there until 1946 when he returned to Austria and entered its foreign service. In 1956 he was elected to parliament for the Socialist Party (chairman, 1967) and was Foreign Minister 1959–70 and Premier from 1970.

KREMENETZ: Town of Volhynia, Poland. The first information on its Jews dates from 1433, and an organized Jewish community existed by 1536. For the nest century, it was one of the chief communities in Volhynia, and leading rabbis and scholars lived there. In 1648, many Jews were killed in K. by Chmielnicki's hordes, but a number survived and continued to reside there under difficult conditions, including the enmity of the general population. Their lot improved during the 19th cent. They suffered in World War I, but after K.'s annexation to Poland their educational and economic life flourished. Almost the entire population of 15,000 was exterminated by the Germans during two days in Aug. 1942.

KREMENETZKY, JOHANN (1850–1934): Zionist leader. An electrical engineer by profession, he lived in Vienna where he was the helper and friend of Herzl. An ardent supporter of Hermann Schapira's advocacy of the Jewish National Fund, he served as chairman of the Fund's first directorate 1905–7. K. established the Fund's head office in Vienna and laid the foundation for its educational activities.

KREMS: Austrian town with an ancient Jewish community, which in the 13th–14th cents. was larger than that of Vienna. Most of the Jews were massacred by the populace in 1349. Jews were expelled in 1421 and only reorganized in the latter 19th cent. In 1938, there were c. 500 Jews there.

KREMSIER see **KROMERIZ**

KRIMCHAKS: Name given to the "orthodox" aboriginal Jews of the Crimea, as distinguished on the one hand from the Karaite sectaries and on the other, from the recent Ashkenazi immigrants from the interior of Russia. Their language was a Turkish (Tataric) dialect and their dress and many of their customs were also Turkish. Before World War I, they numbered about 7,500 but declined after the Bolshevik Revolution and were all but exterminated by the Germans in World War II.

KROCHMAL: (1) *ABRAHAM K.* (1817–1888): Scholar; son of (2). He lived in various places in Russia and Poland, often in great poverty, and died in Germany. He was a founder of and leading contributor to the *He-Halutz* miscellanies in Brody (1852–9). K. wrote studies on the Talmud and Bible, philosophical works on religion in general and Judaism in particular, and topical articles advocating religious reform. These exercised considerable influence on Haskalah literature, especially on J. L. Gordon and M. L. Lilienblum. (2) *NACHMAN K.* (abbr. *Ranak*; 1785–1840): Historian and philosopher. He lived as a merchant in Tarnopol and Zolkiev (Galicia) and devoted himself to inquiry into the historical fate of the Jewish people. He attracted a group of pupils, on whom he had great influence,

Tombstone of Nachman Krochmal in Tarnopol.

but few of his writings were published in his lifetime. His most famous book *Moreh Nevukhe ha-Zeman* ("Guide to the Perplexed of the Time," ed. Leopold Zunz, 1851) philosophically explains the course of Jewish history by the theory that each people has its own "spirituality," i.e., a spiritual talent inherent in it from the outset of its history, which characterizes all its intellectual creations. The special quality of Jewish "spirituality" is its generality and absoluteness; moreover it is religious and cannot be conceived except in religious terms. Thus, K. supplied a philosophical basis for the traditional faith in a Jewish mission. By taking as his subject the Jewish people and not merely Judaism, he enlarged the scope of Jewish religious philosophy. The work serves at the same time as a general introduction to the critical study of Jewish history and literature.

KROLL, LEON (1884–): US artist. Born in New York City, he studied in France and first exhibited in the US in 1910. In 1936, he won first prize at the Carnegie International Exhibition, as a result of which he was commissioned to paint murals for the Department of Justice Building. He is notably a landscape and portrait painter.

KROMERIZ (Ger. Kremsier): City of Czechoslovakia. In 1322, the privilege of keeping and "protecting one Jew in K." was granted to a bishop. Its first synagogue was erected in the 15th cent. For over 500 years, K.'s Jewish community was under the sole protection of the Catholic priests, its center and synagogue displaying the coat of arms of the archbishop with cross and cardinal's hat. Although nearly destroyed during the Thirty Years' War (1618–48), the community was again flourishing 40 years later.

KROTOSHIN: Polish town. Jews are recorded there from the 14th cent. 350 out of its 400 Jewish families were massacred by the Polish general Czarniecki in 1656. The community grew during the 18th cent. but declined under Prussian rule from the mid-19th, and in 1918, most of the remaining Jews left for Germany. K. was the home of Jewish scholars and of an outstanding Hebrew printing press.

KU KLUX KLAN: US secret society. It flourished in the American South after the Civil War, was revived in the 20th cent., and during the 1920's attained enormous popularity with a program which was anti-Negro, anti-Jewish, and anti-Catholic. Its vigilante activities were characterized by the burning of fiery crosses and the wearing of hooded sheets by its members. Within a decade, public opinion turned sharply against the KKK, and for a time it disappeared as a political or social factor of any significance but came into new prominence with the civil rights struggle of the mid-1960's.

KUBBUTZ (properly *kibbutz*): Hebrew vowel (ֻ), sounded as *oo* in foot, in some traditions also like German *ü*; in biblical spelling often confused with *Shuruk*, to which it is the short equivalent.

KUH, EPHRAIM MOSES (1731–1790): German poet. He went to Berlin to make his fortune but soon joined the literary circle of Moses Mendelssohn and Lessing. In his epigrams, madrigals, and songs, he was profoundly influenced by Catullus and Anacreon and in his verse-satires by Matrial, whom he translated into German.

KULISHER, MICHAEL (1847–1919): Russian jurist, ethnographer, and historian. In 1879, he founded and edited the Russian Jewish weekly journal *Rasviet*. K. published a controversial life of Jesus, whom he regarded as a mythical figure, and wrote on the gentile attitude to the Jews, which he maintained was determined by the economic situation. His sons include *EUGEN K.* (1881–1940), jurist and professor of law in Berlin; and *JOSEPH K.* (1878–) who taught economics at the Univ. of Leningrad.

KUMRAN, KHIRBET: Site on the NW shore of the Dead Sea. Excavations (since 1949) have revealed buildings believed to have been occupied by the owners of the DEAD SEA SCROLLS found in the nearby caves of Wadi Kumran. Adjacent to the buildings is an extensive cemetery.

KUMSITZ (Yidd. "come and sit"): In modern Israel usage, an impromptu party.

KUN, BÉLA (1886–1939): Hungarian revolutionary. Taken prisoner-of-war by the Russians in 1915, he joined the Bolsheviks in 1918 and in the following years was returned to Hungary. With the establishment of the Hungarian Communist government in March 1919, he became commissar for foreign affairs and effective dictator of the sanguinary new regime. On its fall in Aug. 1919, he returned to Russia from where he conducted agitation in Germany and Hungary. In 1937, he was indicted and imprisoned for criticism of Communist policy; and later was executed. K. was the author of several works on socialist problems.

KUNFI, ZSIGMOND (1879–1929): Hungarian politician. From 1907 a member of the Social Democratic Party, he became minister of welfare and then of education in the revolutionary government of 1918 and later commissar of education under Béla Kun. In 1919, he fled to Vienna where he edited left-wing papers and wrote on socialist problems. K. committed suicide.

KUNTRAS (or *Kontres*; derivation uncertain): Medieval Hebrew term for a writing- and notebook, usually applied by the tosaphists to Rashi's commentary on the Talmud and used also in France as a general term for collected commentaries.

KUPAT HOLIM see **COOPERATIVES**

KUPAT HOLIM HA-AMAMIT see **HISTADRUT HA-OVEDIM HA-LEUMIT**

KURAIZA see **BANU KUZAIZA**

KURANDA, IGNAZ (1812–1884): Statesman and journalist. After founding the clandestine revolutionary journal *Grenzboten* and leading the Liberal Party in the 1848 Frankfort pre-Parliament, he settled in Vienna and edited the *Ostdeutsche Post* until 1866. From 1867, he was a member of the Austrian Legislative Assembly where he headed the German Nationalist Party. K. served as president of the Vienna Jewish community 1871–84.

KURANTEN (*Dienstagishe* and *Freitagishe*): The first Yiddish periodical. It appeared twice weekly in Amsterdam Aug. 1686–Dec. 1687.

KURDISTAN: Mountainous region now divided among Turkey, Iran, and Iraq. According to tradition, the first Jewish settlers went to K. as early as the time of Ezra. The early beginnings of Jewish immigration are attested by the Aramaic dialect spoken by Kurdish Jews up to modern times: it is close to the language of the Babylonian Talmud and the speech of the Nestorian Christians in K. Toward the end of the 19th cent., the Jewish community was estimated to number 12–18,000, scattered in numerous villages and townlets and living chiefly as merchants, peddlers, and craftsmen. During the 20th cent., their number increased considerably, amounting in Persian K. alone to 12–14,000. After 1948, the great majority of Kurdish Jews, from all areas, emigrated to Israel, many of them in or near Jerusalem.

KURLAND see **COURLAND**

Baruch Kurzweil.

KURZWEIL, BARUCH (1907–1972): Israel literary critic. Born in Moravia he went to Palestine in 1939. In 1955 he was appointed professor in modern Hebrew literature at Bar-Ilan University. He was responsible for new critical approaches by stressing the mission of modern Hebrew literature and the spiritual crisis consequent upon the breakdown of religious values. His works include *Siphrutenu he-Hadeshah, Hemshekh O Mahapekhah* ("Our new literature — continuation or revolution?").

KUSEVITSKY, MOSHEH (1899–1966): Cantor. Of Polish birth and member of an outstanding family of cantors, he was chief cantor at the main synagogue in Warsaw. K., living in the US from 1947, made concert tours throughout the world.

KUTIM: Talmudic term for Samaritans, alluding to their reported origin (see II Kings 17:24); the term was used occasionally to denote any person or group rejecting the Oral Law. It is also the name of one of the minor tractates appended to the Talmud in which the relationships between Samaritans, Jews, and Gentiles are discussed.

KUZARI see **JUDAH HA-LEVI**

KUZNETS, SIMON (1901–): US economist. He was a professor at the University of Pennsylvania and from 1960 at Harvard. He was awarded the Nobel Prize in Economics in 1971.

KWARTIN, ZAVEL (1874–1953): Cantor. Born in Russia, K. showed his talent while still a child and began to officiate at an early age. In 1903 he went to Vienna and later to the great Tabak Temple in Budapest. In the US from 1919, he became cantor of Temple Emanuel of Borough Park, Brooklyn. He was in Palestine 1926–37.

L

LAAZ: Term deriving from Ps. 114:1, applied to vernacular glosses (especially in a Romance language) used by the medieval Jewish commentators. In the writings of Rashi alone some thousands of glosses are preserved, these being among the earliest extant specimens of Old French vocabulary. Much scientific work on *l.* has been done by scholars such as D. Blondheim, L. Brandin, and A. Darmsteter. The interpretation of *l.* as representing the initials of *leshon am zar* ("language of a foreign people") is recent and erroneous. See GLOSSARIES.

LABAN: Brother of Rebekah, father of Leah and Rachel; resident at Haran in Aram Naharaim. Apparently in accordance with local custom, he gave his sister Rebekah in marriage to Isaac (although his father was still alive). Many years later, he consented to the marriage of his daughter Rachel to Jacob, but substituted her sister Leah at the wedding; subsequently, he also gave him Rachel in exchange for a further seven years of service by Jacob. After Jacob fled secretly, he was pursued by L. but they made a covenant at their encounter on Mt. Gilead. In aggadah and popular Jewish folklore, "L. the Aramean" is synonymous with deceiver.

LABAND, PAUL (1838–1918): German jurist. An expert on the historical sources of German law, L. (who was baptized) taught at Heidelberg and Königsberg and became professor at Strasbourg in 1872. His work on German public law is a classic in its field.

LABOR: The Jewish attitude as expressed in the Bible and Talmud is that physical l. is both necessary and of spiritual value. The Books of Psalms and Proverbs contain numerous passages in praise of l. (e.g. Ps. 128:1–4), re-echoed in the Apocrypha (e.g. *Ben Sira* 7:15) and later works. Manual workers earning wages are the subject of protective legislation. From the Second Temple period, when their number had grown because of land-famine and peasant indebtedness, two types are distinguished, viz. *sekhirim* (skilled workers employed on contract for a fixed period, normally 3 years) and *poalim* or *sekhire yom* (day laborers). There were also landless workers permanently dependent on estate-owners (*laketot*).

The Bible enjoins fair treatment of laborers (Deut. 24:14) and obligates the payment of laborers on the day of work (Lev. 19:13). These passages served as the basis for mishnaic and talmudic legislation which discusses employer and laborer relations in detail (e.g. *Bava Metzia* 9:11;10:5). A contract between employer and employee was regarded as a type of lease, but the freedom of the employee was safeguarded, e.g. in certain conditions he could withdraw from the contract, but was still entitled to his wage for the hours worked. The employer was bound to provide his worker with food, and the worker was permitted to partake of the produce on which he was working. The Babylonian Talmud discusses cases of the liability of employer and employee when work was interrupted for various reasons. The employer's liability for injuries incurred by the worker during work was recognized. Maimonides and others held that a craftsman did not acquire potential ownership of an object commissioned by a customer, but this view was disputed. The Mishnah and Talmud distinguished free l. from slave l., but the latter was not sufficiently common in the Second Temple or subsequent periods in Palestine to endanger the status of the free laborer. L.- organization was of course nonexistent, although CRAFTSMEN were organized. Papyri evidence numerous Jews as manual workers in Ptolemaic and Roman Egypt, and the Jewish occupational structure was normal till the early Middle Ages (see OCCUPATIONS). Jewish agricultural laborers remained relatively numerous in the Levant, Persia, etc. down to the 12th cent., but in Europe the crystallization of the Christian guilds and feudal land-system drove Jews increasingly into the skilled crafts and trade. Jewish manual workers nevertheless persisted in Spain and Sicily in the Middle Ages and in E Europe until the birth of industrialization in the 19th cent. created a Jewish industrial proletariat (see SOCIALISM: TRADE UNIONS). The appreciation of the social spiritual importance of manual l. was restated by the HASKALAH and HIBBAT ZION movements; it was the core of the philosophy of the "Prophet of Labor" A.D. GORDON, and forms one of the main planks of L. Zionism.

LABOR BATTALION see **GEDUD HA-AVODAH**
LABOR MOVEMENT see **SOCIALISM; TRADE UNIONS**
LABOR ZIONISM see **POALE ZION**
LACHISH: Ancient Canaanite town mentioned in the 15th cent. BCE in the Tel el Amarna letters. L. was captured by Joshua and assigned to the tribe of Judah. It was fortified by Rehoboam. In 701 BCE, Sennacherib besieged and took the town; the siege is represented on reliefs found at Nineveh. Nebuchadnezzar destroyed the city some time before the fall of Jerusalem. It continued to exist as a Persian residence and as a village until Byzantine times. Excavations, conducted by J. L. Starkey in 1933–8, uncovered the remains of a city wall, a temple destroyed c. 1320 BCE, part of the Israelite city, a Persian

taught in German universities and became research professor at Princeton in 1931.
LADINO: Name generally given to the Judeo-Spanish dialect spoken by the Sephardim of the Mediterranean and written in Hebrew characters. Its basis is medieval Castilian, but it also contains elements of other Spanish dialects (including Portuguese), many Hebrew words and expressions, and other details absorbed in the Levant from Greek, Turkish, etc. The extraneous elements are however, smaller than is the case with Yiddish (Judeo-German). Texts in L. are extant from the Middle Ages, but its first printed book appeared in Constantinople in 1510. Ethical and religious works (e.g. *Me-Am Loez*) were published in some number in L. in the 16th–18th cents. and in the 19th, were followed by novels,

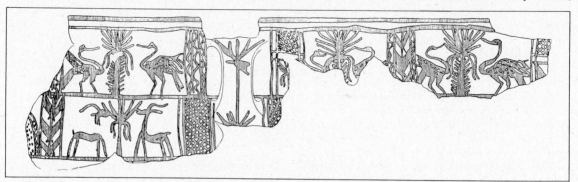

Ornamentation on pottery remains found at Lachish.

palace, and, in a burnt gatehouse, 21 letters written on potsherds (the LACHISH LETTERS). The name of L. has now been applied to a district of Israel.
LACHISH LETTERS: Group of 21 incribed potsherds found in the excavation on the site of LACHISH in 1935 and now in the British Museum. They date probably from 589 BCE, when the Babylonians threatened Lachish, and contain letters in Hebrew from local commanders to their superior officer, name-lists, and business records.
LACHOVER, YERUḤAM FISHEL (1883–1947): Hebrew literary scholar. He edited several journals and miscellanies at Warsaw until 1927 when he settled in Palestine. L. was the author of many essays and studies on Hebrew and general literature, but his life work was a history of modern Hebrew literature (4 vols., 1928–48, incomplete). He also wrote a comprehensive monograph on Bialik.
LADENBURG: German family of financiers, originating from Ladenburg, Baden. To this family belonged *ALBERT L.* (1842–1911), chemist, who was professor at Kiel (1872) and lived at Berlin from 1889. He investigated the organic compounds of silicon and synthesized the first alkaloid, coniine. L. was the author of a history of chemistry. His son *RUDOLF WALTER L.* (1882–), also a chemist,

newspapers, etc. Spoken along the S and E shores of the Mediterranean, its great center until World War II was Salonica. It is still widely used in Israel and the Balkans.
LAEMMLE, CARL (1867–1939): US film producer. He founded the Universal Film Co. and was a pioneer of the Hollywood film industry.
LAG BA-OMER (among Sephardim *Lag la-Omer*): The 33rd (Heb. *lag*) day of the OMER period falling on *Iyyar* 18. According to legend, an outbreak of plague among the pupils of R Akiva in the 2nd cent. ended on this date. It is hence considered the "scholars' feast," the *Omer* period's regulations for half-mourning (prohibitions of marriage, cutting the hair, etc.) being suspended. Schoolchildren are given a holiday and formerly used to conduct a mock-battle with bow and arrow. In Israel, the day is marked by the lighting of bonfires and a mass pilgrimage to the tomb at Meron of R Simeon ben Yoḥai who is said to have died, transmitting his mystical lore, on this day.
***LAGARDE, PAUL DE** (1827–1891): German orientalist; professor at Göttingen from 1869. He published important studies of the Septuagint text and editions of the Targum to the Prophets and Hagiographa. L. drew up a program for the solution

of the Jewish problem for the German Conservative Party; the Jews, he maintained, were aliens in Germany who contaminated German blood and must be harassed by legislation until forced to emigrate.

LAGUNA, DANIEL ISRAEL LOPES (1653–1723): Marrano poet. After persecutions by the Inquisition, he escaped first to Bordeaux and then to Jamaica. He introduced several references to his sufferings into his translation of the Psalms into Spanish verse, *Espejo de Vidas*, one of the most remarkable works of Marrano literature.

LAISH see **DAN**

LAKE KINNERET see **SEA OF GALILEE**

LAMBERT, MAYER (1863–1930): French scholar. He qualified as rabbi in 1886 and thereafter taught Semitic languages at the Séminaire Israélite in Paris and from 1903, also at the École des Hautes Études. He wrote a Hebrew grammar, studies on Saadyah, etc.

LAMDAN (Heb.): A person steeped in talmudic learning.

LAMDAN, YITZHAK (1899–1954): Hebrew poet. The Ukrainian pogroms, which he witnessed after World War I, left an indelible impression on him. Settling in Palestine in 1920, he published from 1933 the literary monthly *Gilyonot*. His poem *Masadah* expressed the struggles of the Third Aliyah and was enthusiastically received. His later verse was written under the shadow of the extermination of European Jewry.

Yitzhak Lamdan.

LAMECH: According to one genealogical tree, descendant of Seth and father of Noah (Gen. 5:4–29); according to another (Gen. 4:18–24), descendant of Cain. He had two wives, Adah and Zillah, and three sons (Jabal, Jubal, and Tubal Cain), the founders

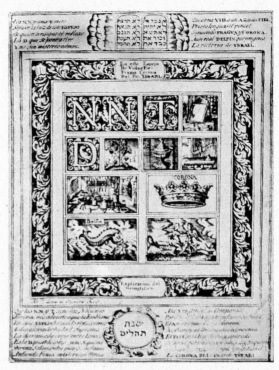

Engraving in Lopes Laguna's *Espejo de Vidas*. London, 1720

of civilization. A poem is ascribed to him in which he boasts of slaying a man, but its meaning is obscure.

LAMED (ל): Twelfth letter in the Hebrew alphabet; numerical value 30. It is pronounced *l*.

LAMED VAV (two Hebrew letters the numerical value of which is thirty-six): The thirty-six righteous men who traditionally (*Sukkot* 45 *b*) exist in every generation, and on whom the continued existence of the world depends. Such a person is referred to as a "*Lamed-vovnik*" (Yiddish) or *Nistar* (Heb. "secret saint").

LAMED, LOUIS see **LOUIS LAMED**

LÄMEL, SIMON VON (1766–1845): Bohemian merchant. He established a factory for wool-production in Prague and was ennobled in 1812 for his services to Austria in the war against Napoleon. He was a notable benefactor of Jewish causes, and the first secular Jewish school in Jerusalem (founded in 1856) bears his name.

LAMENTATIONS (In Heb. *Ekhah* from its initial word): Third of the five scrolls in the Hagiographa section of the Bible. It contains 5 chapters of elegies and mourning over the destruction by the Babylonians of Judah, Jerusalem, and the Temple. Chaps. 1–4 are written in dirge meter (3 long, 2 short stresses), and the first four chapters are alphabetic acrostics, the third being a triple acrostic; other meters also occur. According to rabbinical tradition, the author was Jeremiah but scholars differ as to its authorship,

Silver Sabbath lamp. (Germany, 18th cent.).
Jewish Museum, New York.

some maintaining it to be composite. It is read in the synagogue on the fast of *Av* 9.

LAMENTATIONS RABBATI: Midrash on the Book of Lamentations included in MIDRASH RABBAH. It comprises homiletical interpretations of the text and legends concerning the destruction of the Temple. It was edited in Palestine at an early period and based on older compilations.

LAMM, NORMAN (1927–): US Orthodox Scholar. He taught Jewish philosophy at Yeshiva University of which he was appointed president in 1976.

LÄMMLEIN, ASHER (c. 1500): Pseudo-messiah. Little is known about him except that he lived in Istria and aroused fervent expectations.

LAMP, SABBATH: Oil-lamp formerly kindled on Friday night by the housewife to symbolize the radiance of the Sabbath. In European countries, it was generally of brass, copper, pewter, or silver and consisted of a bowl hanging from the ceiling by a rod or chains. The traditional German form resembled a star with elongated points (generally seven) for the wicks. It sometimes embodied a serrated device for convenience in lowering. In recent times, candles have been almost universally substituted.

LAMPRONTI, ISAAC BEN SAMUEL (1679–1756): Italian talmudist. He lived and practiced medicine in Ferrara, becoming rabbi of the community in 1738. His chief work was *Paḥad Yitzḥak*, a huge talmudic encyclopedia, in which the halakhic material is arranged alphabetically, each article citing relevant material from rabbinic sources.

LAMPS: The central illumination in the Tabernacle and Temple was given by the seven oil l. included in the MENORAH: in Solomon's Temple there were 10 other l. Smaller l. were also in use both for houses and public buildings. Many Palestinian clay l. of the Roman Period are extant, some of them bearing Jewish symbols (*menorah*, etc.) deriving from ancient tombs and synagogues. The kindling of the Sabbath LAMP became obligatory at an early date. The 8-branched *Ḥanukkah*-lamp, some examples of which are preserved in clay, later began to be made in metal, and was manufactured in a great variety of artistic forms from the Middle Ages on. The synagogue was illuminated by l. hanging from the ceiling, the perpetual lamp (NER TAMID) being kept constantly burning, generally before the Ark. It is customary to light a lamp during mourning and on the anniversary of a parent's death (*Yahrzeit*).

LANCASTER: City in Pennsylvania, US. Individual Jews settled there and maintained a synagogue in the 18th cent. The Shaarai Shomayim cemetery dates back to 1747; the congregation of the same name was chartered in 1856. In addition to 3 synagogues, L.'s Jewish community numbering 1,700

Bronze lamp from Syria, with ornamental *menorah* and *Shophar*. (Private collection, New York.)

(1973) has a United Jewish Community Council founded in 1928.

LANDA, ABRAM (1902–): Australian statesman; of Irish birth. He entered the New South Wales Legislative Assembly in 1930 and from 1953 held various portfolios in Labor administrations. In 1965, he was appointed NSW agent-general in London.

LANDAU: (1) *EDMUND GEORG HERMANN L.* (1877–1938): Mathematician; son of (2). He taught at the Univs. of Berlin 1901–9, Göttingen 1909–34, and Jerusalem 1934–8. He investigated the functions and the theory of numbers. (2) *LEOPOLD L.* (1848–1920): Gynecologist. From 1876, he taught at the Univ. of Berlin. Together with his brother Theodor L. (1861–1932), he established the Berlin Gynecological Hospital which became a pioneer center of research. He helped to found the Academy for Jewish Studies in Berlin.

LANDAU, ADOLPH (1841–1902): Russian editor and publisher. Believing that the Jewish problem in Russia could be solved by progress and education, L. published and edited the "Jewish Library" collection from 1871. In 1881, he founded the monthly VOSKHOD which he edited till 1898, also producing the weekly *Voskhod Chronicle* from 1882.

LANDAU, EZEKIEL BEN JUDAH (1713–1793): Talmudist; from 1755, rabbi of the Prague community. An outstanding halakhist, his learning is shown in his responsa *Noda bi-Yhudah*. He endeavored to mitigate the conflict between Jacob Emden and Jonathan Eibeschütz, fought fiercely against Sabbetaism, and strongly opposed Ḥasidism, ordering the public burning of Jacob Joseph of Polonnoye's *Toledot Yaakov Yoseph*. He further objected to Mendelssohn's German translation of the Bible. L. issued many regulations in Prague, including SUMPTUARY LAWS and instructions for the religious behavior of Jewish conscripts.

LANDAU, JACOB (1892–1952): Journalist and publisher. Born in Austria, L. founded the Jewish Telegraphic Agency at the Hague in 1917 and headed it until his death. In New York, he founded and directed (1924–36) the *Jewish Daily Bulletin* and the *Overseas News Agency* (1940).

LANDAU, JUDAH LEO (Leib; 1866–1942): Rabbi and Hebrew author. As a boy in Galicia, he made his name as talmudist and writer of Hebrew belles-lettres. After studying in Vienna and a brief rabbinate in Manchester, he was appointed in 1903, rabbi in Johannesburg (later, chief rabbi) where he consolidated the community and continued his literary work in Hebrew, German, and English. His works include Hebrew poems, essays on modern Hebrew literature in English.

LANDAU, LEV DAVIDOVITZ (1908–1968): Soviet physicist. He was imprisoned in 1937 but released in 1939. He specialized in low temperature physics and the theory of thermodynamics. L. also perfected the microscopic theory of the appearance of liquid helium at a temperature approximating to absolute zero. In 1962, he was awarded the Nobel Prize for physics. The same year he was gravely injured in a car accident. Although apparently dead, he was revived and partially recovered but never resumed his scientific work.

LANDAU, ZISHO (1888–1937): Yiddish poet. He arrived in the US from Poland in 1906. He extensively translated Russian and German poetry into Yiddish. L. gathered young Yiddish poets into a group called *Die Yunge* which opposed the dominant realistic and socialistic Yiddish lyric, preaching art for art's sake and laying emphasis on form and imagery rather than content.

LANDAUER, GUSTAV (1870–1919): German social philosopher and critic. A staunch believer in the ethical values of socialism, he opposed the existence of the state and advocated associations and cooperatives of small consumers and producers. Besides his socialist writings, L. was the author of novels and philosophical and literary essays, and translated Wilde, Shaw, etc. into German. He held office in the Bavarian Soviet Republic and was killed by anti-revolutionary troops. His letters were published in 1938 by Martin Buber who had greatly influenced his thinking.

LANDAUER, SAMUEL (1846–1937): German orientalist. He taught at the Univ. of Strasburg until 1918 when the French replaced all German members of the staff. Thereafter, he lived at Augsburg, devoting himself to research. L. published the Arabic original of Saadyah's *Emunot ve-Deot* and a standard edition of the works of the Persian poet Firdausi.

LANDESMANN, HEINRICH (pseudonym, Hieronymus Lorm; 1821–1902): Author. Born in Moravia, he lived in Austria and Germany before settling in Brünn. Although deaf and blind from youth, he succeeded in establishing communication with the world and developed an enormous literary productivity in the fields of fiction, philosophy, and poetry. His collected poems contain moving and melodious lyrics.

LANDESRABBINER (Ger.): Title applied in Germany, etc. from the 17th cent. to the government-appointed or -recognized rabbis, with authority over an entire political region, generally with civic rather than religious functions in view. They became frequent in 17th cent. Germany with its many political divisions.

LANDLORD AND TENANT see **TENANCY**

LANDMAN, ISAAC (1880–1946): Rabbi. He went to the US from Russia in 1890. A Reform rabbi in New York, L. long edited *The American Hebrew*, and projected and edited the *Universal Jewish Encyclopedia*. He was executive secretary of the National Farm School 1906–16.

LANDOWSKA, WANDA (1877–1959): Polish harp-
sichordist. A pioneer of the renaissance of the
harpsichord, she toured widely and in 1927, founded
near Paris a school for the study of ancient music.
In 1940, she went to the US. L. published works on
the interpretation of ancient music.

LANDSBERG, OTTO (1869–1942): German statesman. A lawyer in Magdeburg, he was elected to
the Reichstag in 1912, was member of the provisional
German government in 1918, minister of justice in
1919, delegate to the Versailles Conference, minister
to Belgium 1920–3, and member of the Reichstag
1924–33. L. left the Jewish faith.

LANDSBERGER, BENNO (1890–1968): Assyriologist. Born in Austria, he taught in Germany until
the Nazi era, then in Turkey, and from 1948 at the
Oriental Institute in Chicago. He laid the foundations
for the study of Assyriology.

LANDSHUTH, ELIEZER (1817–1887): Scholar of
Jewish history and liturgy. He was supervisor of
the Berlin Jewish cemetery. His main work was
Ammude ha-Avodah, a history of Jewish liturgical
poets and their works. He also wrote biographies of
outstanding Jews, notably the rabbis of Berlin.

LANDSMANNSCHAFTEN (Ger.): Societies or associations the membership of which is composed
of persons from the same town or province in the
country of origin. Such l. were set up in the US and
elsewhere (England, S Africa) to help solve the social,
economic, and cultural problems caused by the vast
influx of Jews from Europe, especially in the latter
part of the 19th cent. Many l. also had synagogues
with members drawn from the same city (as was the
case also in Salonica and elsewhere after the expulsion
from Spain). These societies fulfilled three basic
functions: they satisfied the gregarious instincts
of the immigrants; they served as media for maintaining contact with, and later, for providing assistance
to, the former home town; and they helped create
resources and experience for mutual help through
loan funds, etc. In most cases, the language of the
societies has been Yiddish, and their warm spirit
has helped members endure adverse circumstances
and low economic standards. Hundreds of these
groups existed as independent local organizations,
though some banded together to form loose national
associations. A similar phenomenon has sprung up,
for example, in Los Angeles among Jews who have
moved there from other US cities, such as Chicago.
The l. have been variously known as Mutual, Benevolent, Fraternal, Social and Aid Associations, and
many have had ladies' auxiliaries. Many of these l.,
having lost their original motivation, are now social
organizations seeking an outlet for their accumulated
funds. Similar societies have been founded in Israel
(*Hitahdut Ole Britannia, Hitahdut Ole America
ve-Canada,* etc.).

LANDSTEINER, KARL (1868–1943): Austrian bacteriologist, biologist, and pathologist. L., who
was baptized, was professor of pathology at Vienna
1910–20, The Hague 1919–22, and a member of the
Rockefeller Institute for Medical Research. His main
field of research was immunology and hematology,
and he was awarded the Nobel Prize in Medicine in
1930 for his discovery of isoagglutination and the
human blood groups, which had practical application
in blood transfusion, forensic medicine, determination
of parents, and interracial relationship.

LANGER, FRANTIŠEK (1888–1963): Czech novelist
and playwright. His works, noted for their elegant
style, deal mainly with social and psychological
problems: best known are his plays *The Camel
through the Needle's Eye* and *The Outskirts.* A physician by profession, he was an extreme assimilationist.

LANGUAGES OF THE JEWS: With the continual
dispersion since the First Exile, the Jews naturally
accepted the vernacular of the peoples among whom
they dwelt. Nevertheless, the influence of Hebrew,
kept alive through religious practices, and also of
older or regional strata of the local languages, brought
about modifications and substitutions, as well as
divergences in pronunciation of the adopted languages,
thus forming in most cases, until modern times, what
was virtually a new DIALECT. Even the Aramaic of
the Talmud and Targum can scarcely be regarded as
having had currency among non-Jews. The Jews of
Persian Azerbaijan and also of Iraq and Persian
Kurdistan continued to speak the eastern Neo-
Aramaic dialect. By the 3rd cent. BCE, so many Jews,
especially in Egypt, were no longer conversant with
Hebrew that the Bible had to be translated into
Greek; but this Greek version is not free from
Hebraisms and Aramaisms. To a greater extent, this
is true of the New Testament which is Semitic in style
and idiom. Persian became a vehicle of communication among the Jews after the conquest of Cyrus, but
their dialect contained old Persian forms and vocables
even after Pehlevi, or Middle Persian, was in use by
the rest of the population. To this day, the language
of the Caucasian mountain Jews is a species of Tat,
which is a derivate of certain medieval Iranian
dialects. Tat or Farsi Tat, in its Caucasian form, has
acquired some literature (religious readings, folklore,
and folksongs). Tajaiti, another Iranian dialect, is
used by the Jews of Central Asia. In Georgia, the infiltration of Hebrew expressions and forms sets off
the language employed by the Jews from that of their
"Gruzinian" compatriots. Judeo-Arabic emerged
under the impact of the Islamic conquest in the 7th–
8th cents. In each of the countries where Arabic has
gained supremacy, the Jewish vernacular exhibits
considerable variations from the common speech.
Some of the greatest Jewish works were written in
Arabic. There are many Arabic-speaking Jews in

N Africa. Until recently there were also many in Iraq and in Yemen. In Ethiopia, the Falashas normally use Kuarena, although they are versed in Amharic and conduct their religious ceremonies in a variation of Ge'ez. Low Latin, spoken among the Jews of the W Roman Empire, gave way in due course to Old French, to Italian in its various dialects, to Provençal, and above all to Spanish of which the Castilian form ultimately predominated. All of these developed their characteristic Jewish forms or dialects — especially the last-named which gave rise to LADINO. The establishment of Marrano colonies in W Europe and America gave Portuguese a very wide currency in the 16th–18th cents. Spanish is once again the native tongue of increasing numbers of Jews in S and Central America. German, which began to be spoken by Jews toward the end of the 9th cent., developed into YIDDISH, which has grown to the stature of a language of consequence by virtue of its wide currency, creative force, and important literature. In modern times, but especially during the last century, W European languages obtained an ever-stronger hold among Jews, increasing as Yiddish lost its currency. Today, the most widely spoken is English, current among some 6,000,000 Jews in the US and British Commonwealth; 3,000,000 in the USSR speak Russian or to a decreasing extent, Yiddish; and Hebrew is used by some over 2,000,000 in Israel.

LANGUEDOC: Former S French province. Jews were living in this region from the early cents. CE. The Jews of L. were persecuted by the Visigoths in the 6th–7th cents. but were protected by the nobles, and later joined their Christian compatriots in the fight against Arab invasion. They earned their living largely as agriculturists, but there were also tax-gatherers, bailiffs, etc. Toulouse, Narbonne, Lunel, Béziers, Posquières, Nîmes, and especially Montpellier were centers of talmudic study. The Albigensian Crusade in the 13th cent. provoked massacres and restrictions. The Church objected to Jews holding high office and endeavored to enforce the wearing of the Jewish Badge and prevent any social contact between Jew and Christian. However, neither the rulers nor the general population observed the restrictions very seriously and Jewish physicians, for example, were widely respected. Measures were taken against Jewish moneylenders from the 13th cent., and Philip the Fair adopted confiscatory steps. The Jews were expelled in 1306, returned in 1315, and were finally excluded in 1394.

LAPIN, BERNARD (1888–1952): Yiddish poet. A native of Russia, he eventually settled in the US. His earliest poems were published in 1903. He also translated much Russian verse into Yiddish, while his *Neie Lieder* include translations from British and American poetry. In his own verse, he manifests a consistent pessimism.

LARA, DAVID COHEN DE (1602–1674): Ḥakham of the Hamburg Sephardi congregation. His talmudic lexicon *Keter Kehunnah* (printed only up to the letter *yod*) reveals his wide culture and familiarity with Greek, Latin, and ancient Semitic and modern European languages. He also translated ethical works from Hebrew into Spanish.

LA-SHANAH HA-BAAH BI-YERUSHALAYIM see **NEXT YEAR IN JERUSALEM**

LASKER: (1) *ALBERT DAVIS L.* (1880–1952): US advertizing executive and philanthropist; son of (5). He rose to be chairman of the Lord & Thomas advertizing agency in Chicago. From 1921–3, he headed the US Shipping Board. In 1928, he established the Lasker Foundation to pursue research into illnesses affecting middle-aged people. (2) *EDUARD L.* (1829–1884): German statesman. A lawyer, he participated in the 1848 revolution and from 1867, was a member of the German parliament, being a founder and leader of the National Liberal Party and a fierce antagonist of Bismarck. He fought in Prussia for Jewish equality of rights and for the right of any Jew to leave the Jewish community without leaving the Jewish religion *(konfessionslos)*. (3) *FLORINA L.* (1884–1949): US communal worker; daughter of (5). She was active in immigration matters. (4) *LOULA DAVIS L.* (1888–1961): US communal worker; daughter of (5). She promoted the welfare of immigrants to the US, and was also prominent in Jewish charitable work. (5) *MORRIS L.* (1840–1916): Public figure; brother of (2). He went to the US from Germany in 1856, fought in the Confederate Army in the Civil War, and served in the Texas State Senate.

LASKER, EMANUEL (1868–1941): Chess master. He was born in Germany and became world chess champion when he defeated Steinitz in 1894, holding the title until 1921. After the rise of Hitler, he emigrated to the US. He wrote on chess, mathematics, philosophy, etc. and invented the electric breast pump.

LASKER-SCHÜLER, ELSE (1876–1945): German poet; settled in Palestine in 1936. Inspired by her native Rhineland, she was one of the leading lyrical poets in Germany during the first decades of the 20th cent. Her ecstatic Jewish poems, especially the *Hebräische Balladen,* are deeply influenced by the prophetic tradition. She herself illustrated several of her books.

LASKI: English family. (1) *HAROLD JOSEPH L.* (1893–1950): Political economist; son of (3). From 1926, he lectured at the London School of Economics, contributing greatly to its development. A leader of the Fabian Society and executive member of the Labor Party from 1936 (chairman 1945–6), L. belonged to the left intelligentsia of the Party and was its most prominent theoretician. His numerous works on

Hayyim Laskov.

political theory include a study of the US constitution. (2) *MARGHANITA L.* (1915–): Novelist; daughter of (4). She is the author of several witty novels. (3) *NATHAN L.* (1863–1941): Communal worker. Head of a textile firm, he played a leading role in the Manchester Jewish community. (4) *NEVILLE JONAS L.* (1890–1969): Barrister and communal worker; son of (3). In 1935, he was appointed recorder of Burnley, in 1953, judge of appeal in the Isle of Man; and in 1956, recorder of Liverpool. L. was president of the Board of Deputies of British Jews 1933–40.

LASKOV, ḤAYYIM (1919–): Israel soldier. In the Israel War of Independence, L. led units in the Latrun sector and Galilee. In 1951–3, he headed the Israel air force and in 1955, became assistant chief-of-staff. During the SINAI OPERATION, he commanded Israel's armored units. In 1958–60, L. was chief-of-staff. After his retirement, he became head of the country's Harbor Authority.

LASKY, JESSE L. (1880–1958): US film producer. He was associated with several of the leading Hollywood companies and produced a number of outstanding films.

LASSALLE, FERDINAND (1825–1864): German socialist, at first inclined to literature. He participated in the 1848 risings. One of Germany's outstanding lawyers, his latter years were devoted to organizing a political party of German workers, culminating in the foundation of the *Allgemeiner Deutscher Arbeiter-Verein* (1863) of which he was elected president. The following year, he died as a result of injuries sustained in a duel arising from a love-affair. His writings adopt some ideas from MARX. Unlike the latter, L. insisted that the true function of the state is to help the development of the human race toward freedom. Such a state must be based on majority rule — i.e. universal and equal suffrage. Modern industrial evolution makes workers the most important class in the state, and the accession of the proletariat to power would be a victory for humanity. Credit union and cooperative societies do not offer a real solution of the social problem which lies in the "iron law of wages"; the only way out is for the worker to become his own producer.

LASZLO (de Lombos), **PHILIP** (Alexius) **DE** (1869–1937): Artist. Hungarian-born and baptized, he settled in England and became a fashionable painter of society portraits.

LATERAN COUNCILS: Ecclesiastical synods held in the Lateran in Rome. Of importance for Jewish history were the Third L. C. (1179) which re-enforced older Church legislation forbidding Jews to employ Christians or followers of the two faiths to dwell together: and especially the Fourth L. C. (1215), under Pope INNOCENT III, which strengthened the anti-usury laws, excluded Jews from all positions which could give them authority over Christians, and introduced the Jewish BADGE. This marked the climax of medieval anti-Jewish church legislation and affected adversely the status of Jews.

LATIF, IBN see **IBN LATIF**

LATRUN: Monastery and police post on the Jerusalem–Jaffa road. The name derives from the Crusader castle called Le Toron des Chevaliers (Castrum Boni Latronis), which was destroyed in 1191 by Saladin. The strategic post of L. was the scene of very heavy fighting during the Israel War of Independence in 1948, and was held by the Arab Legion despite strong Israel attacks. It remained in no man's land between Israel and Jordan until taken by Israel forces in the Six-Day War of 1967.

LATTEINER, JOSEPH (1853–1935): Yiddish dramatist. Of Rumanian birth, he went to New York in 1884. He adapted works for the Yiddish theater and first succeeded with *Die Tzvey Shmelkes*. L. wrote about 100 plays, comedies, and musicals which, though theatrical pot-boilers, displayed skilled theatrical craftsmanship and served as vehicles for the stars of the day.

LATTES: French and Italian family, ultimately deriving from the town of Lates in S France. Outstanding members are (1) *BONET* (Jacob ben Immanuel) *DE L.* (15th–16th cents.): Physician to Popes Leo X and Clement VII, rabbi to the Roman community, and astronomer. He invented a ring-dial for determining the height of the heavenly bodies, which he described in a frequently reissued Latin treatise dedicated to Clement VII. (2) *DANTE L.* (1876–1965): Scholar. Trained as a rabbi, he dedicated himself to the promotion of Jewish culture among Italian Jewry, editing various Jewish periodicals and translating Hebrew classics, etc., as well as publishing numerous original works. (3) *ISAAC BEN JUDAH L.* (13th–14th cents.): Talmudist and physician. He wrote astronomical and scientific works as well as a commentary on the Talmud and participated successively on both sides in the controversy over the writings of Maimonides. (4) *ISAAC JOSHUA BEN IMMANUEL L.* (d. c. 1570): Rabbi. He lived in various places in S France and Italy, at one time being tutor in the house of the Abravanel family in Ferrara. A devotee of the Kabbalah, he encouraged the publication of the Zohar in 1558–9. His responsa throw much light on contemporary conditions. (5) *JUDAH BEN JACOB L.* (fl. 13th cent.): Talmudist. He compiled *Baal Asuphot,* a collection of rabbinical decisions and responsa. (6) *MOSES L.* (1846–1883): Scholar. He published the first selection of the history of Elijah CAPSALI, a catalogue of Hebrew mss in the Marciana Library in Florence, and historical and lexicographical monographs.

LATVIA: Soviet republic. Individual Jews lived in COURLAND from the 16th cent.; 2,000 resided there in 1795 when it was annexed to Russia. In 1835, Courland and Livland were excluded from the Pale of Settlement. In 1919, L. achieved independence, and national minorities possessed autonomy until 1931; the Jews were thus able to develop a Hebrew and Yiddish school system, divided into Orthodox, Zionist, and Yiddish trends. About 85,000 Jews were living there in 1940 when Russia overran L. and deported a considerable number belonging to the wealthy classes or intelligentsia to N Russia. The next year, L. was conquered by the Germans who established ghettos at RIGA, DVINSK, LIBAU, etc. and annihilated the Jews. In 1970, its Jewish population was officially given as 36,680.

LATZKY-BERTHOLDI, JACOB WOLF (1881–1940): Socialist leader. At first active in the Russian revolutionary movement, he was attracted by Aḥad Ha-Am to Jewish nationalism and, together with Naḥman Syrkin, founded the journal *Ha-Am* in Berlin. He participated in the foundation of the Zionist socialist party S. S. In 1918, he was minister for Jewish affairs in the Ukraine, later removing to Riga where he edited the daily *Frimorgen*. In 1934, he settled in Palestine.

LAUFER, BERTHOLD (1874–1934): Orientalist whose specialty was Chinese culture and archeology. Born and educated in Germany, he participated in numerous expeditions to Asia. He was curator of anthropology at the Field Museum of Natural History in Chicago 1915–34.

LAUTERBACH, JACOB ZALLEL (1873–1942): Talmudist. Of Galician birth, he was educated in Germany and went to the US in 1903. He contributed

The Trappist monastery at Latrun.

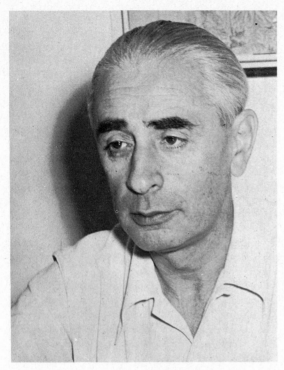

Pinḥas Lavon.

to the *Jewish Encyclopedia* and was professor of Talmud at the Hebrew Union College, Cincinnati 1911–34. He edited the *Mekhilta* and translated it into English.

LAUTERPACHT, SIR HERSCH (1897–1960): Jurist. Born in Galicia, he taught at London Univ. from 1927 and became professor of international law at Cambridge in 1938. In 1954, L. was appointed judge of the International Court at The Hague.

LAVADORES (Ladino): Among the Sephardim, the members of the communal burial society or *Ḥevrah Kaddisha*.

LAVI: Israel communal settlement (PM) in E Lower Galilee. It was founded in 1949 by members of the *Baḥad* mobement from Great Britain near the destroyed Arab village Lubia, scene of violent battles during Israel's War of Independence. There are in the vicinity many traces of buildings of the talmudic and medieval periods. Pop. (1972): 447.

LAVON (LUBIANIKER), PINHAS (1904–1976): Israel labor leader. He was born in Poland where he founded the Gordonia youth movement in 1924. Settling in Palestine in 1929, he was secretary-general of the *Histadrut* 1949–51 and 1956–61, minister of agriculture 1950–51, minister without portfolio 1952–54, and minister of defense 1954–55. L. was a *Mapai* member of the Knesset 1949–61. He was the central figure in a dispute within *Mapai* (the "Lavon Affair") which had wide repercussions, led to a general election and to a split in the party.

LAVRY, MARC (1903–1967): Composer. A native of Latvia, he lived in Palestine from 1935 and directed the music department of the *Kol Zion la-Golah* radio 1950–58. His compositions include an opera *Dan the Guard,* a setting of the Sabbath morning service, symphonic poems (e.g. *Emek*), oratorios (e.g. "Song of Songs"), music for the stage, etc.

LAW, CODIFICATION OF: Since the Gaonic Period, the Talmud has been accepted as the code book for the regulation of Jewish life. However, it does not have the outward form of a code since, besides lacking strict schematic arrangement, it contains long extraneous discussions and presents a variety of opinions among which the practical decision is not always readily apparent. In contrast, logically ordered books of law codifying talmudic and later decisions were composed at different periods. The earliest such compilations are the gaonic HALAKHOT PESUKOT and HALAKHOT GEDOLOT, in which the order of the laws is based on talmudic sequence. The important and still popular codification of Isaac ALFASI, also based on talmudic order, gives a synopsis of talmudic law in the original language, omitting the surrounding discussions. Where a difference of opinion is recorded in the Talmud, Alfasi mentions the one he accepts as *halakhah*. He omits those aspects of legislation which are not applicable in post-Temple Diaspora life. The most comprehensive codification is the *Mishneh Torah* of MAIMONIDES which includes all talmudic law — even that applicable solely during Temple times in Palestine. The material is rearranged according to subject-matter and the language is lucid, approximating to mishnaic Hebrew. The abstract of halakhic material by ASHER BEN JEHIEL is patterned after the example of Alfasi, with the addition of the views of later authorities. His son JACOB BEN ASHER compiled the code *Arbaah Turim* which arranged the laws logically, giving first the various opinions expressed in the Talmud and by codifiers (*posekim*) and then the author's own views, generally based on his father's decisions. This formed the basis for the shorter and more summary *Shulḥan Arukh* of Joseph CARO. Caro follows Alfasi, Maimonides, and Asher ben Jehiel and in the event of a difference of opinion, sides with the two who agree. Moses ISSERLES added to this work supplementary notes called *Mappah* giving the views of Ashkenazi scholars and incorporating their customs, omitted by Caro. On occasions when Isserles differs from Caro, Ashkenazi Jews follow the former and Sephardim the latter. The combined codes of Caro and Isserles have been accepted as standard by all Orthodox Jews. Subsequent legal codifications have not found general acceptance.

LAW, ORAL: From early times in Israel there existed a tradition of interpretation and analysis of the Written Law, and this was handed down orally from

Reading of the Law at a Latrun outpost in the Israel War of Independence, 1948.

generation to generation. The importance of this O. L. was emphasized by the tradition that it was given to Moses on Sinai together with the Written Law. During the Second Temple Period, the ancient oral tradition was upheld by the Pharisees and supported by the majority of the populace. It was not recognized by other sects — the Sadducees and the Essenes — who, however, possessed their own traditions regarding the interpretation of the Written Law. With the disappearance of these sects after the destruction of the Temple, the Pharisaic view won national acceptance, and the O. L. was studied in the various ACADEMIES. The manner of instruction differed; in some places it was taught as a commentary on the relevant section of the Written Law, in others, in a systematic and topical arrangement. Each teacher gave his own interpretation and the Sanhedrin was occasionally called upon to decide between conflicting opinions. The majority view was accepted in practice, but those views rejected continued to be taught theoretically. In time, individuals recorded privately parts of the O. L. which they feared might be forgotten. A complete outline, known as the MISHNAH, apparently incorporating earlier versions, was compiled by R Judah Ha-Nasi and became the basis for study. The discussion of these laws, however, remained oral and was only recorded several centuries later as the TALMUD (GEMARA). After the redaction of the Talmud, study centered around the written text, still known as the O. L. because its roots lie in the oral tradition. During the Gaonic Period, the

KARAITES rejected the O. L. and denied the validity of the Talmud.

LAW, READING OF THE (Heb. *keriat ha-Torah*):
Public reading from the Pentateuch in the synagogue; one of the most ancient portions of the service. The reading is declared obligatory in Deut. 31:10, and the Bible refers to Josiah's and Ezra's public reading (II Kings 23:1–3; Neh. 8:2–18). Ancient tradition ascribes the readings on Sabbaths, festivals, and the New Moon to Moses; on Mondays and Thursdays and at the afternoon service on Sabbaths to Ezra. The Mishnah and Talmud mention R. of the L. on the days which are still customary. Readings are also held on Ḥanukkah, Purim, and fast-days. The complete Pentateuch is read on Sabbaths in the course of one year, concluding on *Shemini Atzeret* (*Simḥat Torah*), in accordance with the ancient Babylonian rite. It is divided into 54 *parashiyyot* (some being joined together when required). In Palestine, the reading of the Pentateuch took 3 years, a cycle still extant in the 12th cent. and revived in some congregations. Originally (and today among Yemenite Jews), each congregant called up read his own section, but eventually a reader was appointed. At first, an introductory blessing was recited by the first person and a concluding blessing by the last; later both blessings were recited by each person called up. Three people are called up (ALIYYAH *la-Torah*) on Mondays, Thursdays, Ḥanukkah, Purim, fast-days, and Sabbath afternoons; four on New Moons and intermediate days of festivals; five on festivals; six

Engraved silver case for The Scroll of Law. Persia, 1764.
(Jewish Museum, New York.)

on the Day of Atonement; and seven on Sabbaths (in each case the first three are respectively a priest, a levite, and an Israelite, i. e., one neither priest nor levite). On Sabbath afternoons, as well as on Mondays and Thursdays, a portion is read from the following week's reading (*sidra*), while appropriate selections are read on holidays, etc. An extra person is called up on Sabbaths, festivals, and fast-days for the *maphtir* and he reads first from the Pentateuch and then from the prophetical books. In mishnaic times, an Aramaic translation was recited after each verse in the Pentateuch and after each three verses in the Prophets, but this survives only among the Yemenites and, for certain occasions, in the Italian rite.

LAW, REJOICING OF THE see **SIMḤAT TORAH**

LAW, SCROLL OF (Heb. *Sepher Torah*): The manuscript of the Pentateuch for public reading in the synagogue. It is written by a trained scribe (**SOPHER**), according to carefully prescribed regulations, on strips of vellum or parchment which are sewn together to form a long roll, each end being wound on a wooden stave. In the Orient, the scroll is enclosed in a wooden or metal case (*tik*). Among Ashkenazim, it is generally covered with a mantle (*me'il*) and the ends of the staves surmounted with silver finials; (*rimmonim*, see **TORAH ORNAMENTATIONS**). On special occasions, as many as three scrolls are used for different readings in the same service. Most congregations had a very large number of scrolls, and to present one to the synagogue was considered highly meritorious; occasionally, a stipulation was made that it should be used for the reading on some specific occasion in the year. The scrolls are kept in the synagogue in the ARK (*aron, hekhal*), at the E end. Their extraction for the public reading and their subsequent replacement are generally effected with great solemnity, and the congregation shows reverence to them as they are taken to and from the reading desk. The open scroll is displayed to the congregation before (among the Sephardim) or after (among the Ashkenazim) the reading. In former times, the scroll sometimes had to be held by Jews in taking the OATH MORE JUDAICO.

LAW, TABLES OF THE: Two tablets on which were inscribed the TEN COMMANDMENTS (Exod. 31:18ff). Moses received the tablets from God but, on hearing of the sin of the Golden Calf, shattered them in his wrath. Subsequently, he prepared two more tablets, reascended Mt. Sinai, and rewrote the Commandments. The new tablets were placed in the Ark (consequently called the Ark of the Covenant) which was placed in the Holy of Holies, initially of the Tabernacle and eventually of the Temple. In medieval England, the Jewish Badge was in the traditional form of the Tables which subsequently figured frequently as a symbol in Jewish ritual art. Two silver tablets are the legal insignia of Jewish chaplains in the US army.

LAWS OF NOAH: Seven laws which the rabbis hold binding upon all mankind, derived from early chapters of Gen. (e.g. 9:4–7). Six of these laws are negative, prohibiting idolatry, blasphemy, murder, adultery, robbery, and the eating of flesh cut from a living animal. The single positive commandment is that requiring the establishment of courts of justice. The "Noachian Laws" were much discussed by European scholars in the 17th cent. in connection with the Law of Nations.

LAWSON (Levy-Lawson): Family of British newspaper proprietors. Its founder was *JOSEPH MOSES LEVY* (1811–1888), printer, who in 1855 opened a new chapter in British journalism by establishing the *Daily Telegraph,* the first London penny paper. He was succeeded in its control by his son, *EDWARD L. L.* (Lord Burnham; 1833–1916) who developed it into one of the leading British newspapers. He was not a professing Jew and the family, which retains its newspaper interests, no longer has any association with the Jewish community.

LAZARE, BERNARD (1865–1903): French author.
A distinguished publicist, he rallied to the support of Dreyfus and was active henceforth in Jewish and Zionist life. His character evoked a noble eulogy from the Catholic poet Charles Péguy.

LAZARON, MORRIS SAMUEL (1888–): Rabbi of the Baltimore Hebrew Congregation 1915–49. As vice-president of the American Council for Judaism, L. has been an articulate opponent of Zionism.

LAZARUS, EMMA (1849–1887): US poet. Her accomplished, though conventional, poetry *Admetus and Other Poems* gained her the friendship of Emerson, and she was also on friendly terms with Browning, Turgenev, Henry George, etc. The Russian persecutions and the flight of Jews to America awakened her Jewish consciousness. Her verse gained vigor and precision in *Songs of a Semite* and *By the Waters of Babylon*. L. learned Hebrew and translated poems by Judah Ha-Levi and other poets of the Spanish Period. Her essays in *The Century* and the *American Hebrew* establish her as a pioneer American Zionist. Her sonnet *The New Colossus* is inscribed on the Statue of Liberty, New York.

LAZARUS, MORITZ (1824–1903): German philosopher. As professor of psychology at Berne from 1860 and at Berlin Military Academy from 1873, he made important contributions to the new field of "psychology of the nations." An orator and writer on Jewish topics, he presided over the Berlin branch of the Alliance Israélite Universelle and over the German Jewish synods of Leipzig, 1869

Emma Lazarus.

and Augsburg, 1871. He opposed Jewish nationalism and regarded the Jews solely as a religious group. L.'s most important work on Judaism was *Ethik des Judentums*. His second wife, *NAHIDA RUTH L.* (1849–1928), born a Christian, was a noted German author whose *Ich Suchte Dich* describes her religious odyssey ending in Judaism.

LEAGUE FOR SAFEGUARDING THE FIXITY OF THE SABBATH see **CALENDAR REFORM**

LEAGUE OF NATIONS: International political organization set up after World War I. It exercised theoretical supervision over the Palestine MANDATE through its Mandates Commission, and over the Minority Treaties entered into by the various nations of E and SE Europe (see MINORITY RIGHTS). The Mandates Commission was increasingly critical of Britain's implemention of her obligation toward the Jewish National Home but was unable to effect any change. The L. of N. could do nothing when most of the E European countries disregarded their minority obligations, and in 1934, Poland refused to remain bound by the L. of N. minorities supervision. As the European Jewish situation deteriorated, and with the increasing barbarity of Nazi persecutions in Germany, the League appointed a High Commissioner for REFUGEES, but the practical results were negligible. With the outbreak of World War II, the League became defunct.

LEAH: Daughter of Laban. Although Jacob intended to marry L.'s younger sister Rachel, local custom did not permit a younger daughter to be married before the elder and Laban substituted L. for Rachel at the nuptials. She bore Jacob six sons (Reuben, Simeon, Levi, Judah, Issachar, and Zebulun) and a daughter (Dinah).

LEAP YEARS see **CALENDAR**

LEAVEN (Heb *ḥametz*): Fermented dough made from flour of the primary grains (wheat, rye, barley, spelt, oats). L. is prohibited during the Passover holiday and was forbidden for use as a meal-offering in most of the Temple sacrifices. (See also LEAVEN, SEARCH FOR).

LEAVEN, SEARCH FOR (Heb. *bedikat ḥametz*): The ceremonial search for all remaining traces of leaven on the evening preceding the Passover holiday. It is made by the light of a candle and preceded by an appropriate blessing. To ensure that the search is not in vain, small pieces of bread (10 in number according to kabbalistic tradition) are placed in various parts of the house to be collected during the search and put aside for burning on the morrow. After the search and again after the burning, an Aramaic formula is recited disowning possession of any leaven which may not have been found.

LEBANON: Middle Eastern republic. The Bible refers to the mountains of L., famed for their cedars; the western part of these mountains is known as L.,

the eastern as Anti-Lebanon of which HERMON marks
the S extremity. The Jewish population is ancient.
It is now chiefly concentrated in BEIRUT; others live
in Tripoli, TYRE, and SIDON. Most of them engage
in commerce, but some are in the liberal professions,
etc. During the Israel WAR OF INDEPENDENCE — when
Lebanese forces invaded Israel — some discriminatory
regulations were imposed on the Jews but removed
after the fighting ceased. In 1944, there were 6,261
Jews in the L. Their numbers were augmented after
1948 by Jews from Syria, and the community in
1964 was estimated at 5–7,000. After 1967, the community diminished. Most of the 1,000 remaining in
1975 left during the Civil War. See ITUREA; PHOENICIA.

LEBENSOHN: (1) *ABRAHAM DOV L.* (known as
Adam Ha-Cohen; c. 1794–1878): Hebrew poet.
He was born and lived most of his life in Vilna where
he engaged in teaching and brokerage. A central
figure in the Haskalah movement in Lithuania, he
was regarded as the outstanding Hebrew poet of his
time. His intellectual poetry posed problems of
suffering, the inadequacy of human understanding,
and the inevitability of death (occasioned by the
premature decease of his son Micah Joseph L. and
several of his other children). L.'s main ideal was the
revival of Hebrew and the safeguarding of the purity
of the language. His own style left a profound mark
on 19th cent. Hebrew literature. His poems were
collected in *Shire Sephat Kodesh* ("Poems in the
Holy Tongue," 3 vols.). Together with Isaac Benjacob,
he published the Bible edition *Mikrae Kodesh* with
a German translation of the text and Mendelssohn's
Biur together with L.'s own notes. He was the author
of several works of biblical commentary and Hebrew
grammar. (2) *MICAH JOSEPH L.* (known as *Michal*;
1828–1852): Hebrew poet; son of (1). Tubercular from
an early age, the knowledge of approaching death
filled him with profound melancholy, although not
breaking his spirit. Influenced by European writers,
especially Schiller, he devoted many of his poems to
universal problems. In 1849, he published a Hebrew
translation (from the German) of part of Virgil's
Aeneid. Thereafter, he turned to subjects from Hebrew
literature, his poems on Jewish themes being collected in *Shire Bat Tziyyon* ("Songs of the Daughter
of Zion"). His lyrics were published posthumously in
Kinnor Bat Tziyyon ("Lyre of the Daughter of Zion").

LEDERBERG, JOSHUA (1925–): US scientist.
Professor at Wisconsin 1948–59, and since 1959
at Stanford Univ., he was awarded a Nobel Prize in
1958 for his research into the genetics of bacteria.

LEDERER, EMIL (1882–1939): Economist and
sociologist. Born in Bohemia, he taught at Heidelberg Univ. from 1912 and at the New School for
Social Research in New York from 1938. While
severely criticizing Marxian Socialism, he was nevertheless influenced by some of the views of Marx.

Isaac Leeser.

LEE (originally **LAZARUS**), **SIR SIDNEY** (1859–
1926): English historian. He edited the *Dictionary
of National Biography*. Earlier, he had become known
as a Shakespearean scholar, his researches into the
background of Shylock leading him to pioneering
work on the secret Jewish settlement in England in
the 16th cent.

LEEDS: English town. A Jewish community was
established in 1823, but remained on a small scale
until after 1881, when the tailoring industry attracted
large numbers of Jews from E Europe. The community
is third in magnitude in England and the largest in
proportion to the general population (5%). It has
8 synagogues and a Jewish Representative Council.
Jewish pop. (1973): 18,000.

LEESER, ISAAC (1806–1868): Rabbi and author.
He went to the US from his native Germany in
1824. From 1829, he officiated as *Ḥazzan* in Philadelphia where he was a founder of the first Jewish
congregational Hebrew school and the Maimonides
rabbis' training college. As editor of *The Occident
and Jewish Advocate* he influenced Jewish communities
throughout the US and is generally held to be the
spiritual father of Conservative Judaism in America.
He rendered the Hebrew Bible into an independent
English translation and edited prayer books which
continued in use for many years. He was the first to
introduce English sermons in the American synagogue.

LEFIN, MENAHEM MENDEL see **LEVIN, MEN-
DEL OF SATANOV**

LEFSCHETZ, SOLOMON (1884–1972): Mathematician. Born in Russia, and in the US from 1906,
he was professor at Princeton from 1924. He was a
pioneer in the field of topology and algebraic geometry

and contributed to the theory of multiple periodic functions.

LEGACY see **INHERITANCE**

LEGEND see **AGGADAH**

LEGHORN (Livorno): Italian port. When it was developed into·a free port by the grand dukes of Tuscany from 1593 onward, Jews were expressly invited to settle there, those who had formerly professed Christianity (i.e., Marranos) being promised immunity. By the middle of the 17th cent., the Jewish community was among the most important in W Europe. In accordance with the undertaking made in 1593, the ghetto system (including the Jewish badge, etc.) was never introduced into L., unlike the rest of Italy, and many settlers were therefore attracted from the rest of the peninsula. In the 18th cent., L. was a great rabbinic and intellectual center, and there was also a vigorous literary activity in Spanish. The importance of the community began to dwindle with the unification of Italy and the loss of L.'s free port privileges. Notwithstanding persecution and the destruction of the monumental synagogue during World War II, communal life still continues and in 1962, the restored synagogue was dedicated. Jewish pop. (1967): 600.

LEGION, JEWISH see **JEWISH LEGION**

LEGISLATION see **LAW**

LE-HAKHIS (Heb. "to anger"): Maliciously; in order to rpovoke. *Mumar le-hakhis*: Apostate out of spite.

LE-HAVDIL (Heb. "to distinguish" taken from the HAVDALAH service): A word interpolated to distinguish honorably one person or category from another of low esteem mentioned in the same context.

Herbert Lehman.

LE-ḤAYYIM (Heb. "to life"): The normal Hebrew expression accompanying a toast.

LEḤI see **LOḤAME ḤERUT ISRAEL**

LEHMAN: (1) *HERBERT HENRY L.* (1878–1963): US statesman. Long a partner in the banking and investment firm of Lehman Bros., he was Democratic lieutenant-governor (1928–32) and governor (1932–42) of New York State and from 1943–6 served as first director-general of the United Nations Relief and Rehabilitation Agency (UNRRA). L. was US senator from New York 1949–57. L.'s political career was marked by vigorous espousal of the New Deal political philosophy. As governor of New York, he furthered social security, unemployment insurance, and public regulation, and was re-elected three times. During his years in the Senate, L. was noted for his efforts in behalf of civil rights and freer immigration. He unrelentingly opposed the political hysteria of the day. He was also active in Jewish and general social welfare, in the American Jewish Committee, and, in his later years, in supporting Israel. (2) *IRVING L.* (1876–1945): US jurist; brother of (1). He was justice of the New York Supreme Court 1908–23, and then of the State Court of Appeals (chief judge from 1939). L. was a judicial liberal who believed that the scope of the law must expand in keeping with the social necessities of the time. For some 20 years he was president of the Jewish Welfare Board. L. was active in affairs of the Union of American Hebrew Congregations and the American Jewish Committee.

LEHMANN, BEHREND (Issachar Bermann; 1661–1730): German financier. He supplied Frederick August I of Saxony with the funds required to secure his election as king of Poland (1697). L. was granted the title "royal commissioner" and used his influence to improve the legal position of the Jews. In 1696, he was responsible for reprinting the Babylonian Talmud at Frankfort-on-Oder, distributing over 5,000 copies to students. Later, he lost his wealth.

LEHMANN, MARCUS (Meyer; 1831–1890): German rabbi; from 1854, officiated at Mainz. In 1860, he founded *Der Israelit*, in the columns of which he published polemics against the Reform movement as well as Jewish historical romances with an edifying content. His stories were widely translated and circulated.

LEHRANSTALT FÜR DIE WISSENSCHAFT DES JUDENTUMS see **HOCHSCHULE FÜR DIE WISSENSCHAFT DES JUDENTUMS**

LEHRER, LEIBUSH (1887–1964): Yiddish educator. Of Polish birth, in 1909 he went to the US where he influenced Yiddish education by his writings on psychology and pedagogical problems and by his direction of the Sholem Aleichem Schools.

LEIBOWITZ, SAMUEL SIMON (1893–): US jurist. He established a reputation as a criminal lawyer. Noted for his defense of the Scottsboro Boys, 1934–7,

H. Leivick.

he was elected a judge of the Kings County Court in New York in 1940.

LEIBZOLL: Special tax paid by Jews in Germany from the 16th cent. upon crossing frontiers or entering cities. It was abolished in Alsace in 1784 and in Prussia in 1787–8. Surviving elsewhere until the early 19th cent., it was then abrogated in several places through the efforts of Wolf Breidenbach, financial agent of the grand duke of Darmstadt.

LEICHTENTRITT, HUGO (1874–1951): German musicologist and composer. He taught in Berlin until 1933 when he became lecturer at Harvard. L. wrote many books on musical subjects.

LEINSDORF, ERICH (1912–): Conductor. Of Viennese birth, he conducted in Europe before going to the Metropolitan Opera House, New York, in 1937. In 1943, he became conductor of the Cleveland Orchestra, in 1947, of the Rochester Philharmonic Orchestra, and in 1961, of the Boston Symphony Orchestra.

LEIPZIG: E German city. In the mid-13th cent., it had a community with a synagogue; the Jews' main livelihood was moneylending. They were annihilated in the Black Death massacres (1349). After 1490, Jews from many parts of Europe visited the L. fair. Jewish settlement — apart from individuals — was only renewed at the end of the 18th cent., and a congregation was organized in 1820. A Reform synod was held there in 1869. The Jews helped to develop the city's fur trade, and this attracted coreligionists from Russia and Poland. There were 11,654 Jews there in 1933, but these were destroyed during the Nazi period. A small community was refounded after World War II. In 1968 it numbered 110, mostly survivors from Poland and Theresienstadt in World War II.

LEISERSON, WILLIAM MORRIS (1883–1957): US economist. He held various positions in the Federal and State governments, particularly under the New Deal when he was a member of the National Labor Relations Board. He also taught economics at Antioch College.

LEIVICK, H. (pseudonym of Leivick Halper; 1888–1962): Yiddish poet and dramatist. After being exiled to Siberia, he settled in the US in 1913. His dramas *Der Golem* and *Shmattes* were successes. Profoundly affected by the fate of the Jews in World War II, he expressed his feelings in the moving poetic volume *In Treblinka Bin Ich Nit Geven* and the symbolic plays, *Maharam Fun Rutenberg* and *Di Chasene in Fernwald.*

LEKAH TOV (Heb. "Good Teaching"): Midrashic commentary to the Pentateuch and the Five Scrolls composed by Tobiah ben Eliezer of Castoria (Bulgaria) in the 11th cent. It is called *Midrash Lekah Tov* since the word *tov* ("good") is used to open every section. It is erroneously known at *Pesikta Zutarta.*

LEKERT, HIRSH (1879–1902): Russian revolutionary. A member of the Bund, he was executed for shooting the governor of Vilna province who had been responsible for the manhandling of Jewish workers. His courageous bearing in his last days made a deep impression on the contemporary Jewish labor movement, and he was the hero of several literary compositions.

LEKHAH DODI (Heb. "Come my beloved"): Song of greeting for the Sabbath, ingeniously incorporating biblical verses, written at Safed c. 1540 by Solomon Alkabetz. It was soon incorporated in the Sabbath eve service in almost all rites, and is sung to a variety of tunes. The custom of "greeting the Sabbath," picturesquely devoloped in the 16th cent., was derived from the saying "Come, let us go out to meet Queen Sabbath" (*Shabbat* 119*a*). It is customary for the congregation to turn toward the entrance while reciting the last verse.

LEL SHIMMURIM (Heb. "night of watching"; cf. Exod. 12:42): Term applied to the first night of Passover, which was believed to be free from personal danger. It was formerly the custom for that reason not to bolt the doors and to omit the recital of the night-prayer.

LELYVELD, ARTHUR (1913–): US rabbi. After serving in various Reform pulpits, he was director of the B'nai B'rith Hillel Foundations 1948–56. In

1958 he was appointed to the Fairmount Temple, Cleveland. In 1966–72, L. was president of the American Jewish Congress.

LEMBERG see **LVOV**

LEMKIN, RAPHAEL (1900–1959): Jurist. After a successful legal career in Poland, he went to the US in 1941 and from 1948, was professor at Yale. He was prominent in the struggle to have the UN adopt a convention on GENOCIDE (a word which L. coined).

LEMON, HARTOG (c. 1750–1823): Physician and protagonist of Jewish rights in Holland. He lived in Amsterdam and was a leader of the FELIX LIBERTATE society which fought for Jewish rights. L. was a deputy in the second national assembly of the Batavian Commonwealth 1797–8, and a delegate to the Napoleonic Sanhedrin in Paris, 1807. He was imprisoned in 1813–4 for anti-French activities.

LENCHITZ see **LUNCHITZ**

LENCZYCA see **LUNCHITZ**

LENGYEL, EMIL (1895–): Author. He was born in Hungary and settled in the US in 1921. He has written books dealing with contemporary European and Near Eastern affairs and has served as a journalist. Since 1937, L. has taught at the school of education at New York Univ.

LENINGRAD (formerly St. Petersburg or Petrograd): Russian city. In the 18th cent., baptized Jews lived there and L.'s first cemetery dates from 1802; expulsions occurred in 1831 and 1838. Horace Günzburg helped to develop the city in the period of Alexander II (1855–81). The community directorate was established in 1878 and a flourishing cultural life ensued although special permission was required for residence. L. was the center of the Jewish press in Russian. In 1900, it had 20,000 Jews; in 1941, 210,000; in 1970, 162,587.

LENSKY, HAYYIM (1905–1942): Hebrew poet in the USSR. In 1925–35 he lived in Leningrad and wrote Hebrew poems which he succeeded in transferring out of the country. Even after he was exiled to Siberia in 1935 he continued to send his work to Palestine. He returned to Leningrad in 1940 and was arrested again, imprisoned near Leningrad, and probably sent back to Siberia, where he died. His poems describe his childhood and his Siberian exile and they express his yearning and his faith in Hebrew and the Jewish people.

*LEO X: Pope from 1513 to 1521. A member of the house of Medici, he favored the Jews and Jewish scholarship, protecting REUCHLIN, authorizing the publication of the Talmud, and employing Jewish physicians such as Bonet de LATTES and musicians such as Giovanni Maria. Roman Jewry reached the zenith of its well-being under his rule.

LEO BAECK INSTITUTE: Research institute founded in 1955 to promote research into the history of German-speaking Jewry. Its *Year Book* contains scholarly monographs and it also furthers the publication of relevant books. Its main offices are in New York, Jerusalem, and London.

LEON: Spanish kingdom, united with Castile from 1218. Its Jewish communities included Leon, Sahagun, Paredes, Mansilla, and Bembibre. The charter of L. (1091) explicitly restricted Jewish rights, notably in the judicial sphere. The protection of the kings of L., however, enabled the Jews to play an active commercial role. The famous Hilleli codex of the Bible was preserved in the synagogue of the town of L. until it was sacked in 1196.

LEON (SIR LEON) OF PARIS see **JUDAH BEN ISAAC**

LEON OF MODENA see **MODENA**

LEON, JUDAH MESSER (fl. 15th cent.): Rabbi and physician in Mantua. His *Nophet Tzuphim* (c. 1478) on rhetoric, showing a considerable knowledge of classical literature, was the first Hebrew book printed while its author was still alive. L. was expelled from Mantua in consequence of a quarrel with Joseph COLON. His son, David Messer Leon, was rabbi at Avlona (Albania) and wrote a querulous account of the disputes between the various sections of the community.

LEON, MOSES (BEN SHEMTOV) DE (1250–1305): Spanish kabbalist. He lived in Guadalajara until removing to Avila in 1290. M. wrote some 20 kabbalistic works of which only two (*Ha-Nephesh ha-Ḥakhamah* and *Shekel ha-Kodesh*) have been printed. His chief fame lies in his revelation of the ZOHAR, attributed to R Simeon ben Yoḥai. According to kabbalists, the book was sent by Naḥmanides from Palestine to Spain, where it reached the hands of L. After L.'s death, R Isaac of Acre went to Avila to see the ms of the Zohar but could not find it. Numerous researches have been written on the authorship of the Zohar; many scholars assign a 13th cent. date to its composition or redaction and assume that L. was its true author, wholly or in part. (See KABBALAH.)

LEON TEMPLO, JACOB JUDAH ARYEH (1603–1675): Rabbi and scholar. Born in Hamburg of a Spanish Marrano family, he officiated at Middelburg, Holland, and from 1643, taught at Amsterdam. He constructed a model of Solomon's temple and published an exposition in Spanish, which was translated into several languages and earned for its author the sobriquet "Templo." He also produced a model and exposition of the Tabernacle. He is believed to have designed the escutcheon of the English Grand Lodge of Free Masons.

LEONARD (originally **LEINER**), **BENNY** (1896–1947): US boxer. From 1917 to 1924 he was the world lightweight boxing champion, retiring undefeated.

LEONE EBREO see **ABRAVANEL, JUDAH**

LEONTOPOLIS: Ancient Egyptian town; site of a temple built c. 170 BCE with the permission of Ptolemy VI by the ex-high priest Onias IV after his flight from Jerusalem. The building, clearly modeled on the Jerusalem Temple, continued to function until closed by the Romans in 71 CE. The remains were excavated by Flinders Petrie in 1906.

LERNER, MAX (1902–): US political scientist and essayist. He served as managing editor of the *Encyclopedia of Social Sciences* (1927), editor of *The Nation* (1936–8), and columnist for the *New York Post*. He has taught at Williams College (1938–43) and Brandeis Univ. (1949–). As a teacher, he has stressed the integration of the social sciences.

LE-SHANAH HA-BAAH BI-YRUSHALAYIM see **NEXT YEAR IN JERUSALEM**

LESHON HA-RA (Heb. "tongue of ill," commonly *loshen hore*; cf. Ps. 34:14): Common phrase denoting SLANDER or unfounded gossip.

LESSER, ERNST JOSEPH (1879–1928): German biochemist. An advocate of scientific research at hospitals, he himself conducted a research laboratory at the Mannheim municipal hospital where he devoted himself largely to the cure of diabetes, paving the way for the discovery of insulin.

*LESSING, GOTTHOLD EPHRAIM (1729–1781): German critic, poet, and dramatist. He brought his career to a climax with the philosophic drama *Nathan the Wise* (1779). Its theme was religious tolerance and universal brotherhood, and the hero was modeled after L.'s friend, MOSES MENDELSSOHN. His plea for tolerance toward Jews had already found dramatic expression in his early play *The Jews* (1749). Thereafter, he engaged in bitter theological disputes, but he realized that he could reach a much wider audience through the medium of the stage and in *Nathan the Wise* sought to demonstrate through representatives of Christianity, Islam, and Judaism that nobility of soul was not the monopoly of any one religion.

LESSING, THEODOR (1872–1933): German social philosopher. Baptized in his youth, he returned to Judaism in 1900. While teaching at the Hanover Technical High School, he published works on the philosophy of Schopenhauer, Wagner, and Nietzsche, on the theory of values, and on the decline of the West, anticipating Spengler. Owing to his criticism of Hindenburg, he was forced to suspend his teaching activity by nationalist tumult in 1926. His last work *Der jüdische Selbsthass* ("Jewish Self-Hate") is a trenchant blending of psychological analysis and skilful biography. L. left Germany in 1933 but was murdered by Nazis in Czechoslovakia.

LESTSCHINSKY, JACOB (1876–1966): Sociologist. He was born in Russia, and most of his early investigations were into the sociology of E European Jewry. In 1921, he went to Germany, in 1938 to the US, and to Israel in 1958. L. was associated with *Yivo* and the World Jewish Congress and was best known for his extensive writings in the Yiddish press and elsewhere on the sociology and economic status of the Jewish people.

LETTER OF ARISTEAS see **ARISTEAS**

LETTERIS, MEIR HA-LEVI (c. 1800–1871): Hebrew author. He was born in Galicia and in his youth was acquainted with Naḥman Krochmal and S. J. Rappaport who influenced his intellectual development. In 1830-9, he lived in Vilna, 1840-8 in Prague, and thereafter in Vienna. His popular poetry, characterized by light and fluent versification, is imbued with tenderness and religious feeling. Some of his poems have become folk-songs (e.g. *Yonah Homiyah*). His Hebrew translations of plays by Racine, Goethe's *Faust*, Byron's *Hebrew Melodies*, etc. tended to be free and even inexact renditions but represented pioneer work in their field. L. also wrote an autobiography and edited the Hebrew Bible for the British and Foreign Bible Society.

LETTERS: Some official documents in the style of l. are embodied in the later books of the Bible (e.g. in Ezra and Nehemiah), but the earliest authentic Hebrew examples extant are the LACHISH LETTERS written in the last years of the First Temple Period. Somewhat later are the official l. in Aramaic relating to the Jewish military colony at YEB (5th cent. BCE). Official l. are also included in the Books of Maccabees and the writings of Josephus, while letters of Jews exist among 3rd and 2nd cent. BCE papyri found in Egypt. Some original l. of Bar Kokhba have recently been discovered in MERUBAAT, and l. are cited in talmudic literature. A vast amount of personal and official correspondence was revealed in the Cairo *genizah*, and in the Middle Ages, the rabbinic RESPONSA were frequently couched in letter form. From the 16th cent. onward, large numbers of original Hebrew l. are preserved. In Italy in particular, letter writing was a highly developed form of literary art, and many model collections were preserved, some being printed. Of the letter collections of historic importance that have been published, the most important are those of Leone MODENA (17th cent.) and a collection of intercepted l., largely in Judeo-German, written during the siege of Prague in 1623. The writing of l. in the vernacular became usual in Europe only from the 18th cent. Collections of letters of Jewish interest have been published by F. Kobler (1952), C. Roth (1939; Anglo-Jewish), and A. Yaari (1943; Hebrew, Palestinian interest). See also BOOKS.

LEVANDA, LEO (Yehudah Leib; 1835–1888): Russian author. From 1861–86, he was advisor on Jewish affairs to the governor of Vilna. He wrote stories in Russian describing Jewish life in the Pale of Settlement. After the 1881 pogroms, L. became an enthusiastic supporter of the *Ḥoveve Zion*.

LEVANON, MORDEKHAI (1901–1968): Painter. Of Hungarian origin, he settled in Palestine in 1921. His Jerusalem landscapes are outstanding.

LEVANT, OSCAR (1906–1972): US pianist and composer. An exponent of classical and jazz music, he was noted for his interpretation of Gershwin. He wrote two volumes of autobiography.

LEVAYAH (Heb. from *lavveh* — "accompany"): A funeral.

LEVEN, NARCISSE (1833–1915): French public figure. He was closely associated with Adolphe Crémieux and Gambetta and was from 1879 a member of the Paris municipal council (vice-president in 1882). L. was a founder of the Alliance Israélite Universelle and its president from 1898. He was also president of ICA from 1891.

LEVERTIN, OSCAR IVAR (1862–1906): Swedish poet, critic, and literary historian. He was professor of the history of literature at Uppsala. His poetry combined universalistic, patriotic Swedish, and Jewish trends.

LEVI: Third son of Jacob and Leah. Together with his brother Simeon, he avenged the dishonoring of his sister Dinah by slaying the men of Shechem (Gen. 34). For this deed they were rebuked by Jacob who forecast that their descendants would be scattered throughout Israel (Gen. 49:7). Nevertheless, in the Second Temple Period when all contact with gentile women was eschewed, the act of L. and Simeon was extolled (cf. Judith 9:2). L. had one daughter, Jochebed (mother of Moses) and three sons, Gershom (Gershon), Kohath (whose son Amram was the father of Moses), and Merari. L. died in Egypt at the age of 137. See also LEVITES.

LEVI BAR SISI (fl. 2nd-3rd cents.): Palestinian amora; pupil of Judah Ha-Nasi. He had his own compilation of *baraitot,* mentioned several times in the Talmud. He eventually went to Babylonia where he was received with great honor, and settled in Nahardea.

LEVI BEN ABRAHAM BEN ḤAYYIM (d. after 1314): French talmudist and philosopher. He lived most of his life in poverty, wandering among the towns of S France and earning his livelihood as a teacher. L. is the author of the encyclopedic *Livyat Ḥen* which deals with various branches of science and includes the author's religious and philosophical views. His allegorical Bible interpretations and his rational interpretation of miracles led to his persecution by anti-Maimonists. Solomon Ibn Adret criticized him as a "heretic and unbeliever."

LEVI BEN GERSHON (or Gershom; known also as Gersonides or by his initials as *Ralbag*; 1288–1344): Philosopher, mathematician, astronomer, Bible commentator, and talmudist. Nothing is known of his life and profession except that he lived at one time in Avignon. His main work is *Milḥamot Adonai*

("Wars of the Lord") in 6 books; its main themes are: (1) Immortality of the soul. This depends on each person's degree of philosophical knowledge, or contact with the Active Intellect; (2) Divination and Prophecy. Prophecy is the highest degree of contact with the Active Intellect; (3) Divine Omnipotence; (4) Divine Providence, which extends only over species and general matters, not over individuals, since God cannot know the particular; (5) Astronomy; (6) Creation and Miracles; God created the world from formless primal matter and miracles are caused by the Active Intellect. L. displays his outstanding knowledge of Aristotelian philosophy in his super-commentaries to the "middle" commentaries of Averroes on the major part of Aristotle's treatises. This is especially remarkable as L. knew no Arabic and little Latin, having to rely entirely on Hebrew translations. L. presented his philosophy in a more moderate form in his Bible commentaries which enjoyed widespread popularity. He also wrote a commentary on the Thirteen Rules of Interpretation of R Ishmael. In an astronomical treatise incorporated in the *Milḥamot* (but omitted in the printed editions) L. sharply criticized current theories. He wrote important works on arithmetic, geometry, harmonic numbers, and especially trigonometry where his system (as enlarged by Regiomontanus in 1464) forms the basis of modern trigonometry. He developed the use of the camera obscura and invented "Jacob's Staff," an important nautical instrument.

LEVI BEN JAPHETH (fl. 10th–11th cents.): Karaite scholar; son of Japheth ben Ali. He probably lived in Jerusalem, but no details of his life are known. His Arabic *Book of the Precepts* (completed 1007) is a major source for Karaite law. He also wrote a brief commentary on the Bible.

LEVI ISAAC OF BERDICHEV (1740–1809): Hasidic leader. A pupil of Dov Ber of Mezhirich, he officiated in Pinsk, Zhelikhov, and Berdichev. His central doctrine was "love for Israel," and he uttered fervent prayers as a defense advocate asking Divine mercy for the Jewish people. His prayers and Yiddish poems and songs were widely repeated and his book *Kedushat Levi* is a Hasidic classic. Because of their high regard for him, the community of Berdichev elected no successor after his death. L. I. was the subject of many legends.

LEVI, CARLO (1902–1975): Italian novelist. Trained as a physician, he was also a versatile painter. Deported as an anti-Fascist to S Italy in 1935-6, he depicted the miseries of local life in his *Christ Stopped at Eboli*. In 1963, he became a senator representing the Communist Party.

LEVI, DAVID (1742–1801): English author. Earning a penurious living as a hat-maker, he rendered portions of the Jewish liturgy into English, published a Hebrew grammar and dictionary *Lingua Sacra*

(3 vols., 1785–7), and engaged in spirited polemics with critics of Judaism such as Joseph Priestley. He was the first native-born English-Jewish scholar of repute.

LEVI DELLA VIDA, GIORGIO (1886–1967): Italian orientalist. Professor of Arabic in Naples (1914), Turin (1916), and Rome (1926–31), his best-known work deals with the history and religion of the Semitic Orient. He coedited the *Annali dell'Islam*.

LEVI, EDWARD H. (1911–): US educator. Son of a rabbi, he became professor of law at the University of Chicago of which he was appointed president in 1967. His work on atomic energy legislation provided the basis for the establishment of the Atomic Energy Commission. US attorney-general, 1975.

LEVI, HERMANN (1839–1900): German conductor. Friend and adviser of Richard Wagner, he conducted the first performance of *Parsifal* at Bayreuth in 1882. L. was baptized.

LÉVI, ISRAEL (1856–1939): French rabbi He was professor of Jewish history and literature at the Paris Rabbinical Seminary from 1892, and taught talmudic literature at the École des Hautes Études from 1896. In 1919, he was elected chief rabbi of France. A noted scholar and author of many historical and philological studies, L. was secretary of the *Société des Études Juives* and edited its *Revue*, in which many of his writings appeared.

LEVI, PAUL (1883–1930): German socialist. A founder of the left revolutionary Spartacus-Bund, in 1918, he became leader of the German Communist Party which he left in 1921 over his opposition to revolutionary violence. He joined the Independent Socialist Party, which merged with the Social Democrats in 1922, and was a Reichstag deputy from 1920. L. committed suicide.

LÉVI, SYLVAIN (1863–1935): French orientalist. One of the outstanding modern Indologists, he was professor of Sanskrit at the Collège de France 1894, director of the Institute for Indian Studies at the Sorbonne 1904, founder of the French School for the Far East at Hanoi, and director of the Franco-Japanese Institute at Tokyo 1926–8. L. was president of the Alliance Israélite Universelle from 1920 and represented French Jewry in the negotiations preceding the Versailles Treaty. His works include an encyclopedia of Buddhism and a standard book on the Indian theater.

LEVI-BIANCHINI, ANGELO (1877–1920): Italian Zionist. A naval officer in World War I, he became interested in Zionism, was appointed a member of the Zionist Commission, and served as Italian military attaché on Allenby's staff 1918–20. In 1920, he influenced the Italian delegation at the SAN REMO CONFERENCE to support the Zionist position. Returning to Palestine, he was murdered in Syria, while on an official mission, by Arabs who mistook him for a Frenchman.

LEVI-CIVITA, TULLIO (1873–1942): Italian mathematician; professor at Padua 1898–1918, and Rome 1918–38. His researches in mathematics and theoretical physics were outstanding. His main innovations were in the sphere of absolute differential calculus and its application in physics and geometry, especially to Einstein's theory of general relativity.

LEVI-STRAUSS, CLAUDE (1908–): French ethnologist and sociologist. Born in Brussels, he participated in anthropological expeditions to South America and Asian countries. From 1935–9 he was professor of sociology at Sao Paolo (Brazil). He returned to France, escaped to the US in World War II, and since 1959 has been professor of social anthropology at the Collège de France. He is the leader of the Structural School of anthropology which based progress on the meeting of cultures and finds all cultures — whether so-called "civilized" or "primitive" — of equal significance.

LEVIAS, CASPAR (1860–1934): Orientalist. He taught at Hebrew Union College, Cincinnati, 1895–1905, and at the Plaut Memorial School, Newark, 1910–20. He wrote numerous studies in the field of Semitic philology, including a grammar of talmudic Aramaic and lexicons of Hebrew medical and philological terms.

LEVIATHAN: Sea-monster described in Job (40–1). Ancient writings (e.g. the Aggadah and Apocrypha, cf. also Ps. 74:14) compare the l. to a sea-animal male and female, made by God on the fifth day of creation. The male is called the serpent Bariaḥ and the female, the serpent Akallaton (Is. 27:1; alternately the male is Behemoth and the female Leviathan). As they threatened to destroy the world, God emasculated the male and preserved the female. In time to come, God will make war on the l. or will cause it to fight Behemoth. The righteous will participate in the struggle and will feast off the flesh of both. A similar legend is found in Ugaritic sources where "the serpent Bariaḥ and the serpent Akallaton" are depicted as huge monsters who assisted Mot (believed to be the death-god) against the fertility-god.

LEVIN (LOEBEL), HIRSCHEL (in England, Hart Lyon; 1721–1800): Rabbi and author. Of Galician birth, he officiated in London as rabbi of the Great Synagogue 1756–63, then in Halberstadt and Mannheim and from 1772, in Berlin. He approved of Mendelssohn's *Biur* but sharply opposed N. H. Wessely's proposed reforms in Jewish education. He was the father of Solomon HERSCHELL.

LEVIN, JUDAH LEIB (1894–1971): Russian rabbi. Born in Yekaterinoslav, was rabbi in various Russian towns including his birthplace and in Georgian communities. In 1957 he succeeded Rabbi Schleifer at the Great Synagogue, Moscow. In

Hirschel Levin (or Loebel).
(Engraving by Abramson, 1798.)

1968, his visit to the US was surrounded with controversy.

LEVIN (or **LEFIN**), **MENDEL** (also called Mendel Satanover; c. 1749–1826): Hebrew author. He was born in Podolia and was attracted to Haskalah, going to Berlin in 1780 to meet Mendelssohn and his circle. He subsequently lived in various Russian centers and became one of the chief advocates of Haskalah in Galicia. In 1792, he published a booklet in French advocating the imposition of Enlightenment upon Polish Jews by the government. He wrote in Hebrew on natural sciences, etc. and translated various classics. L. also made a popular Yiddish translation of several books of the Bible.

LEVIN, MEYER (1905–): US novelist. L. has retold Hasidic legends and written stories of Israel (where he lives). His best-known works include *The Old Bunch, Citizens, Compulsion, Eva, Gore and Igor* and his autobiography *In Search*.

LEVIN, RACHEL (1771–1833): German intellectual leader; wife of the author-diplomat Varnhagen von Ense. Her salon was a center of cultural and political life in Berlin. She had original ideas on children's education and feminine rights and was a fervent admirer of Goethe. L. was baptized before her marriage.

LEVIN, SHEMARYAHU (1867–1935): Hebrew and Yiddish writer and Zionist leader. Born in Russia where he pursued rabbinical studies, L. received a secular university education in Germany. From 1896 to 1906, he was crown rabbi in Grodno, Yekaterinoslav, and Vilna, where he stressed the ideals of the Hebrew and Zionist revivals. Representing Vilna in the Russian Duma, he distinguished himself in speeches in behalf of Russan Jewry, but had to flee to Germany because of his opposition to the dissolution of the Duma. L. played an active part in the founding of the Haifa Technion. Participating in nearly all Zionist Congresses he was a member of the Zionist Executive 1911–8. During and after World War I, he promoted Zionism in the US, Canada, and England. L. was a noted and witty speaker. From 1922, he worked for the Devir Publishing Company of Berlin (from 1924, Tel Aviv), which he founded together with Bialik. L. contributed regularly to Hebrew and Yiddish periodicals and published memoirs, essays, etc.

LEVIN, YITZHAK MEIR (1894–1971): Orthodox Jewish leader. Born in Poland, he settled in Palestine in 1940. Chairman of the *Agudat Yisrael* World Executive since 1939, and member of the Knesset since 1949, he served in the Israel provisional government 1948–9 and as minister for social welfare in coalition governments, 1949–52.

LEVINÉ, EUGEN (1883–1919): Revolutionary. A native of Russia, he participated in the 1905 revolution and, after 3 years' imprisonment, settled in Germany. There he was active in the communist movement and was executed for his part in the revolutionary post-war regime in Munich.

LEVINE, JACK (1915–): US painter. As a war artist he developed a macabre style of moral comment which he uses to criticize social injustice.

Yitzhak Meir Levin.

LEVINSOHN, ISAAC BER (1788–1860): Russian Hebrew author and Haskalah pioneer. In 1820, he published two satires on the Ḥasidim, devoting himself henceforth to the dissemination of Enlightenment. Despite physical frailty and a lonely existence, he persevered in his work and was supported by influential Russian authorities, including government circles, who protected him from Ḥasidic persecution. In 1852, the Russian government purchased from him 2,000 copies of his *Bet Yehudah* for distribution in synagogues and Hebrew schools. L., the first great protagonist of Haskalah in Russia, has been dubbed the Russian Mendelssohn. His books, many of which were published posthumously, sought on the one hand to extol the virtues of Enlightenment and manual labor, especially agriculture, and on the other to combat anti-Semitism. His style is simple, his arguments calm and persuasive, frequently based on proofs from traditional Jewish literature with which he was intimately acquainted. L.'s most important works are: *Teudah be-Yisrael, Bet Yehudah,* and *Zerubbabel,* the last disputing the views of the Irish missionary Alexander McCaul in his *Old Paths.* His other writings included *Ephes Damim* against the Blood Libel and *Die Hefker Velt,* a Yiddish satire on the Ḥasidim.

LEVINSON, SALMON OLIVER (1865–1941): US lawyer and pacifist. He drafted a plan for the outlawing of war which was the basis of the abortive anti-war agreement known as the pact of Paris or Kellogg-Briand pact (1928).

LEVINTHAL: US family. *BERNARD L.* (1865–1952): went to the US from Russia in 1891 and, until his death, was head of the Orthodox rabbinate in Philadelphia. He was among the founders of the Union of Orthodox Rabbis of the US and Canada and of the Mizraḥi Organization of America. His son, *ISRAEL HERBERT L.* (1888–), rabbi of the Brooklyn Jewish Center since 1919, has been active in religious and Zionist affairs and has written a number of books on Jewish topics. Another son, *LOUIS EDWARD L.* (1892–1976), was president of the Zionist Organization of America 1941–3, and was judge of the Court of Common Pleas in Philadelphia 1937–59. After his retirement from the bench, he spent much of his time in Israel where he was chairman of the board of governers of the Hebrew University.

LEVIRATE MARRIAGE: Marriage with a brother's childless widow (*yibbum*). The widow is called *yevamah,* and the brother obliged to marry her is the *yavam.* Although it is forbidden to marry a brother's widow where there are children (Lev. 18:16), such marriage is commanded where the brother has left no offspring (Deut. 25:5). Release from such obligation is made possible through the ceremony of ḤALITZAH, described in Deut. 25:7–10. In the Talmu-

dic Period, many rabbis, fearing improper motives in the fulfillment of this commandment, gave preference to *ḥalitzah,* although subsequently there have been differences of opinion on this question. During the Gaonic Period, l. m. was customary in Sura, but *ḥalitzah* was general in Pumbedita. Maimonides upholds the customs of l. m., and is followed in this respect by the Sephardi communities in Africa, Yemen, Babylonia, and Persia. Rabbenu Tam, however, gave preference to *ḥalitzah,* and this became the accepted custom among Ashkenazi communities. It became usual in some communities for the brother of the bridegroom at the time of the wedding formally to agree to the *ḥalitzah* in case of necessity, thus enabling the widow to remarry. The regulations covering l. m. are contained in the talmudic tractate YEVAMOT.

LEVITA (Baḥur), **ELIJAH** (c. 1468–1549): Grammarian and lexicographer. He was born in Germany and spent most of his life in Italy at Padua, Venice, and Rome, earning his living by teaching Hebrew, mainly to Christian humanists; these included Cardinal Egidio da Viterbo, who was his chief patron. In his later years, he was proof-reader for the Protestant Hebraist Paul Fagius at Isny, returning to Venice where he died. L. was the author of several important works on Hebrew grammar, distinguished for their clarity and method. Most of them were translated into Latin. He was the first to prove that biblical vocalization was post-talmudic, a viewpoint that aroused the opposition of the Orthodox. L. also wrote lexicographical works including *Tishbi* (a talmudical lexion) and the first-known Yiddish-Hebrew dictionary. He composed Hebrew and Yiddish poetry and translated into Yiddish the books of Psalms and Job and the Italian romance on Buovo d'Antona (originally the English *Sir Bevis of Hampton*) as the henceforth classical *Bava Buch.*

LEVITAN, ISAAC ILYITCH (1860–1900): Russian painter. He is regarded as the first Russian landscape artist and the founder of a new style of painting which greatly influenced subsequent Russian artists.

LEVITES: Descendants of the tribe of LEVI, consecrated by Moses to serve in the cult of the Tabernacle and to instruct the people. In ancient times, the first-born of each family served as priest, but because of the loyalty of the l. during the incident of the Golden Calf, they replaced the first-born. Each family of l. was assigned specific duties connected with the transport and assembly of the parts of the Tabernacle in the wilderness. The family of AARON was singled out for service within the Tabernacle (later, the Temple) as PRIESTS in the fullest sense. After the conquest of Palestine, the l. were enjoined to teach the Torah to the people, being therefore excluded from any territorial inheritance but receiving 48 towns with their environs throughout the country, as well as a tithe of the agricultural produce. This arrangement worked somewhat differently in practice. Certain towns assigned to the l. were only captured a long time after the conquest, or not at all, and there is no evidence to show how effective was the collection of tithes. Consequently, some of the l. served at High Places (cf. e.g. Judg. 17), especially in the Northern Kingdom after Jeroboam had instituted independent worship. In his utopian Temple plan, Ezekiel replaced the non-Jewish NETHINIM with the l., but this scheme was never executed. According to Chronicles, when the Temple service was organized, traditionally by David, the l. were divided into groups, each engaging in different work (singers, instrumentalists, gatekeepers, assistants to the priests during the sacrifice, etc.). Like the priests, every group was divided into 24 sections, each serving for a week at a time. In Second Temple times, the priests outnumbered the l. and apparently shared their tithe. In *halakhah*, the levite is regarded as second to the priest (e.g. at the Reading of the Law), and has the privilege of laving the priest's hands before the latter blesses the people.

LEVITICUS (Heb. *Va-Yikra*, from its opening word; formerly known as *Torat Kohanim* "The priestly code"): Third book of the Pentateuch, containing the legislation dictated to Moses after the erection of the Tabernacle and covering chiefly the laws of sacrifice and impurity as well as moral instruction and social regulations not given in Exodus. It contains 27 chapters: 1–7, sacrificial laws; 8–10, installation of priests; 11–16, physical purity and a list of unclean animals; 17, prohibition against eating non-sacrificed meat; 18–22, moral instruction; 23, the festivals; 24, regulations connected with the Tabernacle; 25, sabbatical and jubilee years; 26, the blessings for observance and curses for non-observance; 27, valuations and devotion to sacred usage. Some scholars believe the work to be composed of isolated commandments originally written down individually. Some extreme critics have held that the entire work postdates the Babylonian exile, but internal evidence has been cited to date at least parts from the Sinaitic period.

LEVITICUS RABBAH: Third work in MIDRASH RABBAH. One of the earliest of the Midrashim, it dates from the 5th–6th cents. and is homiletical rather than exegetical in character. Containing 37 chapters, its discussions hinge on what were the opening verses of the weekly Torah-reading according to the triennial cycle then current in Palestine.

LEVONTIN, ZALMAN DAVID (1856–1940): Zionist. He went to Palestine from Russia in 1882 and acquired the land on which Rishon-le-Zion was built, but economic conditions forced him to return to Russia the following year. One of Herzl's earliest collaborators, he was the first director of the Jewish Colonial Trust. On his initiative, the Anglo-Palestine Bank was founded in Palestine in 1903, L. acting as its director until 1924.

LEVY: US printers. *LOUIS EDWARD L.* (1846–1919): introduced new methods of photo-engraving and improved printing processes. He wrote *The Russian Jewish Refugees in America* and edited and published *The Jewish Year*. His brother, *MAX L.* (1857–1926) was associated with him in the photo-engraving business in Philadelphia. In 1887, they produced the first successful half-tone screen, which became the basis for the printing of photographs. He made a number of other technical inventions relating to precision instruments and the counting of blood-corpuscles.

LEVY, AARON (1742–1815): Merchant. He went to the US from Holland in 1760, engaged in trade, and acquired large tracts of land in Pennsylvania. The town of Aaronsburg, which he laid out, is named after him. He extended supplies and credit to Washington's troops.

LEVY, ABRAHAM ARMAND (1794–1841): French mathematician and mineralogist; lived and taught in France, Belgium, and England. He discovered a number of minerals (of which "Levyn" was called after him), published books on power-systems and specific weights, and was an editor of the *Encyclopaedia Britannica*.

LEVY, ALPHONSE (1843–1918): French artist. His works include a series of lithographs on Alsatian Jewish life and paintings of Algerian Jews.

LEVY, ASSER (d. 1681): Pioneer of US Jewry. He was one of the first Jews who arrived in New Amsterdam in 1654 and the first *shoḥet*. By his insistence on burgher rights and the privilege of personal guard duty he set the precedent for full citizenship rights for Jews in the New World.

LEVY, BENJAMIN (d. 1704): Founder of the Ashkenazi community of London. Hamburg-born, he went to England c. 1670, rapidly made a large fortune, and was one of the "proprietors" of New Jersey. At first a liberal supporter of the Sephardi synagogue, he purchased in 1690 a cemetery for his fellow-Ashkenazim who thereafter became organized in a separate community.

LEVY, BENN WOLFE (1900–1973): English dramatist. He wrote and adapted a number of successful plays, particularly comedies. From 1945–50, he was a Labor member of parliament.

LÉVY, CALMANN see **CALMANN-LÉVY**

LEVY, SIR DANIEL (1873–1937): Australian statesman. A lawyer by profession, he was successively minister of justice, speaker, and judge in New South Wales.

LEVY, HYMAN (1889–1975): British mathematician. He taught at the Royal College of Science in London from 1920 (professor 1923, dean 1946–50). He has written extensively on the history and sociology of science from a Marxist viewpoint. In 1958, he published *Jews and the National Question,* an attack on Soviet anti-Jewish discrimination.

LEVY, JACOB (1819–1892): German lexicographer; rabbi at Breslau. In his dictionaries to the Targum (1867–8) and to the Talmud and Midrash (1876–89) — both with notes by H. L. Fleischer — he laid the foundation for the scientific study of talmudic Aramaic.

LEVY, MORITZ ABRAHAM (1817–1872): German scholar. He taught for 30 years at the Breslau Synagogen-Gemeinde. Specializing in Semitic paleography and epigraphy, his publications included a history of Jewish coins and popular textbooks on Jewish history, religion, etc.

LEVY, REUBEN (1891–1966): British orientalist. He lectured in Persian at Oxford 1920–3, taught biblical literature at the Jewish Institute of Religion, New York, 1923–6 and taught Persian at Cambridge since 1926 (professor, 1950). L. published works on Persian and Arabic literature as well as on Deutero-Isaiah.

LEVY, URIAH PHILLIPS (1792–1862): US naval officer. He began his naval career as a boy, served in the merchant marine, fought through the War of 1812,

Uriah Philips Levy. (Painting by T. B. Reed.)

and eventually became flag officer of the Mediterranean squadron, then the highest post in the US Navy. He is credited with fathering the law for the abolition of corporal punishment in the US Navy. He purchased Jefferson's home "Monticello," and through his son it was preserved as a national monument.

LÉVY-BRUHL, LUCIEN (1857–1939): French philosopher and sociologist. Devoting himself to the study of primitive societies, he endeavored to explain the formation of moral ideas historically and scientifically by tracing the belief in supernatural forces which form the background of the life of backward peoples. He was professor at the Sorbonne and taught philosophy at the Paris Rabbinical Seminary.

LEWALD, FANNY (1811–1889): German novelist. L., who was an ardent feminist, wrote many realistic novels including *Clementine, Prinz Louis Ferdinand,* and *Die Familie Darner.* She was baptized in 1828.

LEWANDOWSKI, LOUIS (1823–1894): German liturgical composer and conductor. A supporter of the Reform movement, he composed and arranged traditional music in the style of his own period, greatly influencing synagogue music.

LEWIN, BENJAMIN MANASSEH (1879–1944): Scholar. He was born in White Russia and settled in Palestine in 1912. Devoting himself to research in gaonic literature, he produced the (unfinished) corpus *Otzar ha-Geonim* (12 vols., 1928–43), a collection of the teachings of the geonim of Sura and Pumbedita.

LEWIN, JUDAH LEIB (pseudonym *Yehalel*; 1845–1925): Russian Hebrew poet. A regular contributor to *Ha-Shaḥar,* he introduced social and economic problems into Hebrew literature. L. was sympathetic to early Jewish socialism, but after the 1881 pogroms became an ardent adherent of *Ḥibbat Zion* writing extensively on Zionism and other topical subjects. L. remained in Russia after the 1917 revolution, which he welcomed, and died at Kiev in great poverty.

LEWIN, KURT (1890–1947): Psychologist. He was professor of psychology and philosophy at Berlin and in 1932 went to the US. In 1944, he established and headed the Research Center for Group Dynamics at the Massachusetts Institute of Technology. A keen student of minority group problems, he conducted basic research into their social psychology. L. founded the system of topological psychology on which he wrote extensively and which he used in explaining authoritarian and democratic group behavior.

LEWIN, LOUIS (1850–1929): Pharmacologist. Of Russian birth, he lived most of his life in Berlin where he lectured and conducted research on toxication as well as narcotics, pioneering in immunity against poisoning.

Ludwig Lewisohn.

LEWINSKY, ELHANAN LÖB (1857–1910): Russian Hebrew author. He worked on the journal *Ha-Melitz* and was an active member of the *Bene Mosheh* society, later supporting political Zionism. From 1896, he lived in Odessa but traveled extensively through Russia recording his impressions in a series of charming and humorous feuilletons.

LEWIS, BERNARD (1916–): British orientalist. He has taught oriental studies at London Univ. (professor, 1949) and Princeton. He has written on Arab and Middle Eastern history.

LEWIS, SIR GEORGE HENRY (1833–1911): English lawyer. He enjoyed a great reputation for his complete integrity and reticence, his clients including Edward VII. Humane in outlook, he was largely responsible for the establishment of the Court of Criminal Appeal.

LEWISOHN, ADOLPH (1849–1938): US philanthropist. He made a fortune in the mining business and devoted much of his wealth to cultural and philanthropic causes. He donated the Lewisohn Stadium to the College of the City of New York. He took an active part in prison reform and in the American ORT movement.

LEWISOHN, LUDWIG (1883–1955): US author and translator. From 1911 he was professor of German at Ohio State Univ. and from 1948, professor of comparative literature at Brandeis Univ. Among his novels are a number of Jewish import (*The Island Within* and *The Last Days of Shylock*). His works include criticism (*Expression in America, The Magic World*), autobiography and ideological Jewish and Zionist books (*Israel, Mid-Channel, Theodore Herzl — A Portrait for This Age*).

LEWY, ISRAEL (1841–1917): Talmudist. He was born in Russia, and lectured on Talmud at the Berlin Hochschule für die Wissenschaft des Judentums 1872–83, and the Breslau Rabbinical Seminary 1883–1917. His critical approach greatly influenced the scientific study of the Talmud.

LEXICOGRAPHY see **DICTIONARIES**

LIBATION: The offering of a liquid sacrifice (drink offering). Oil and wine were constituents of almost every sacrificial ceremony. The oil was usually offered with the meal offering, being mingled with it, poured out over it, or soaked with it, depending upon the nature of the sacrifice. Every animal oblation required a wine l., different measures being set for the various types of animals offered (Num. 15:1–16). See also WATER-DRAWING, FEAST OF.

LIBEL see **SLANDER**

LIBERAL JUDAISM see **REFORM**

LIBERAL PARTY: Israel party formed in 1961 by a merger of the GENERAL ZIONISTS and PROGRESSIVE PARTY. In the 1961 general election, it obtained 17 seats in the Knesset. In 1965, the former General Zionists formed an alignment with HERUT (GAHAL) while the former progressives constituted the Independent Liberal Party.

LIBERAL WORKERS MOVEMENT see **HA-OVED HA-TZIYYONI**

LIBERMAN, EVSEI (1897–): Russian economist. Born in Volyn (the Ukraine), he became professor of economics at the Kharkhov Engineering Institute in 1959. His advocacy of greater emphasis on profitability in order to increase plant efficiency and quality led to a major modification in Russian economic policy, especially from 1956.

LIBIN, Z. (Zalman; 1872–1955): Yiddish writer. Born in White Russia, he settled in 1893 in New York where for many years he worked as a cap maker, at the same time writing plays and short stories on New York Jewish life.

LIBRARIES: The most ancient Jewish l. known are those recently discovered in the neighborhood of the Dead Sea (Wadi Kumran) belonging to sectaries of the Second Temple Period. There were certainly l. in the academies of Babylonia after the Talmud was compiled, but there is no detailed information about them. Samuel Ibn Nagrela's library is perhaps the first known great private Jewish library, and he was generous in affording its facilities to others. Judah Ibn Tibbon, in his Ethical Will, gave his son detailed instructions regarding the treatment of his books. The size and scope of private Jewish l. in the Middle Ages may be judged from the auction catalog of that of Leone Mosconi of Majorca (15th cent.). Many important Jewish l. were formed at the time

The National and University Library, Jerusalem.

of the Renaissance, among them that of A. S. Graziani of Modena. Especially great private collections have since been built up by David Oppenheim, Giuseppe Almanzi, D. Kaufmann, Baron de Günzburg, H. J. Michael, S. J. Halberstamm, S. Schocken, E. N. Adler, M. Gaster, D. S. Sassoon, as well as by the Christian Hebraist G. B. de Rossi. The great Hebrew l. of the world include those of the British Museum, Vatican, Parma (Palatine Library), National Library of Paris, Bodleian Library (Oxford), the University Library, Cambridge (with *genizah* material); together with those of the Hebrew University in Jerusalem, the Jewish Theological Seminary of America, N. Y., the Hebrew Union College, Cincinnati, and Jews' College, London.

LIBRARY, JEWISH NATIONAL AND UNIVERSI-TY: Library in Jerusalem. Developed from a small collection, started in 1884, it received a large collection of books from Joseph CHAZANOWITZ in 1895. In 1920, the Library passed under the control of the World Zionist Organization and from 1925, of the Hebrew Univ. It was transferred to Mt. Scopus in 1930 but its 450,000 volumes were cut off between 1948 and 1967. A parallel library was established in the University's other campus in Jerusalem and numbers about 1,500,000 volumes. Since 1924, the Library has been publishing the bibliographical review KIRYAT SEPHER.

LIBYA (Heb. *Luv*): Country of N Africa, including CYRENAICA and TRIPOLITANIA. It is mentioned in the Bible in connection with the Egyptian levies who fought against Judah, and in the Talmud because of its agricultural products. Jews were settled in the area from pre-Roman times. After 1948 over 30,000 Jews left L. for Israel. At the time of the Six-Day War in 1967, there were demonstrations against the country's 6,000 Jews who all left shortly thereafter.

LICHT, FRANK (1916–): US jurist. Born in Providence, he held various judicial posts and in 1956 became a justice of the Supreme Court of Rhode Island. He was a Rhode Island State senator 1948–56 and in 1969 to 1972 was governor of the State of Rhode Island.

LICHTENSTEIN, HILLEL (1815–1891): Rabbi. He officiated in several communities in his native Hungary and from 1867, at Kolomea in Galicia. L. was a leader of the extreme Orthodox group and a fiery opponent of any change in Jewish tradition. He was an influential preacher, and his sermons and responsa were published.

LICHTENSTEIN, MORRIS (1889–1938): Rabbi. In 1907, he went to the US from E Europe. He inaugurated the JEWISH SCIENCE movement largely to counteract the inroads of Christian Science among Jews. Although he attracted a considerable personal following in New York, the organization failed to grow. On his death, the movement was continued by his wife Tehilla.

LIDZBARSKI, MARK (1868–1928): Semitic philologist. Born in Poland, he went to Germany at the age of 14 and was baptized while a student. He was professor of oriental languages at Greifswald 1907–17 and Göttingen 1917–28. L. was the author of fundamental studies on Semitic epigraphy.

LIEBEN, ROBERT VON (1878–1913): Viennese physicist and pioneer aircraft designer. As a result of his experiments with x-rays he invented a device for amplifying alternating current in long distance telephone and radio. He also invented an early type of radio amplifying tube.

LIEBERMAN, HERMAN (1870–1941): Socialist. He was a member of the Polish parliament 1919–30 and took an active part in the leadership of the socialist movement. During World War II, he joined the Polish government-in-exile in London as minister of justice.

LIEBERMAN, SAUL (1898–): Scholar. Of Polish birth, he taught Talmud at the Hebrew Univ. Jerusalem 1931–6, and directed the Fischel Institute there 1935–40. Since 1940, he has been professor of Palestinian literature at the Jewish Theological Seminary, New York. In 1967, he was appointed president of the American Academy of Jewish Research. An outstanding talmudist and authority on Jewish Hellenism, he has published editions of the Tosephta (in progress) and works on the Palestinian

Saul Lieberman.

Talmud and on Greek influences in Palestine in the Talmudic Period.

LIEBERMANN: (1) *MAX L.* (1847–1935): German painter; initiator and leader of the German Impressionist school. He developed into an impressionist somewhat late in life under the influence of

Max Liebermann: *Woman with Goats.*

Jozef and Isaac Israels. A noted wit and active polemist in Berlin's intellectual and artistic life, L. was in 1899 elected president of the *Sezession* group of Berlin painters and, after World War I, of the Academy of Fine Arts in Berlin. Under the Nazi regime he was forbidden not only to exhibit but even to paint. He found his best subjects in aspects of the life of the poor and underprivileged. (2) *ROLF L.* (1910–): German composer; grandnephew of (1). His works include operas. After directing the Hamburg Opera from 1959, he became director of the Paris Opera in 1972.

LIEBERMANN, AARON SAMUEL (1844–1880): Hebrew author and pioneer socialist. He became involved in socialist work in the rabbinical seminary in Vilna, but when this was discovered by the authorities he fled to London. In 1876, he published a pioneer Hebrew socialist manifesto, founded the first Jewish socialist society, and organized a Jewish trade union. Returning to Vilna the following year, he started *Ha-Emet,* the first Hebrew socialist periodical. He committed suicide in America after an unfortunate love-affair.

LIEBMAN, JOSHUA LOTH (1907–1948): US Reform rabbi. He was rabbi of Temple Israel, Boston, from 1939, and an active Zionist and public speaker. In 1946, he published *Peace of Mind,* a best-selling volume on popular psychology.

LIEBMANN, JOST (d. c. 1704): Court jeweler and mint-master to Frederick William and Frederick III of Brandenburg. The only court-Jew of his time in Berlin, he exercised his influence in behalf of his family and endeavored to make himself ruler of the Berlin community.

LIEGNITZ (Legnica): Town in Silesia, now Poland. Jews lived there from 1301 and were expelled in 1453 as a result of incitement by John of Capistrano. Apart from a short interval in the 16th cent., they were excluded until 1812. The community thereafter remained small but attracted many Poles repatriated from the USSR in 1957. Jewish population in 1958 was 4,800 but nearly all of them subsequently left.

LIEME, NEHEMIAH DE (1882–1940): Dutch economist and Zionist leader. He was active in life insurance and educational schemes for workers in Holland. In 1913, he became chairman of the Dutch Zionist Federation and in 1919–21, was president of the Jewish National Fund. Owing to differences of opinion with other Zionist leaders, his Zionist activity ended in the early 1920's.

LIESSIN, ABRAHAM (1872–1938): Yiddish poet. He left his native Russia in 1897 to settle in the US. His early works were based on revolutionary themes, but later, in New York, he wrote extensively on Jewish martyrdom and nationalism.

LIFSCHITZ, JOSHUA MORDECAI (d. 1878): Russian Yiddish writer and lexicographer; a pio-

neer of the modern Yiddish cultural movement. His Yiddish-Russian dictionaries preserve Volhynian usage.

LIFSHITZ, NEHAMA (1927–): Singer. Born in Kovno, she escaped to Uzbekistan during World War II, returning to Lithuania in 1946. She specialized in Yiddish and Hebrew folksongs and gave her first concert in 1951. Thereafter, she appeared frequently throughout the USSR and as one of the few permitted expression of Jewish culture, aroused great enthusiasm among Russian Jewry. In 1969, she left Russia and went to Israel.

LIGHTS, FEAST OF see ḤANUKKAH

LILIEN, EPHRAIM MOSES (1874–1925): Artist. Of Galician birth, he resided most of his life in Germany. He created a special style of pen-and-ink drawing, excelling in his black-and-white technique. He illustrated the Bible and many other books, both of Jewish and general interest. An ardent Zionist, he graphically depicted aspects of the early stages of the Zionist movement and of Palestinian colonization.

LILIENBLUM, MOSES LEIB (1843–1910): Hebrew author and Zionist pioneer. After receiving an Orthodox education, he was attracted to Haskalah and in 1868, published the article *Oreḥot ha-Talmud* which advocated religious reform. His campaign aroused the anger of religious circles and in 1869, he settled in Odessa. In 1871, he decided that not religious reform but a revolution in the Jewish economic structure — notably the teaching of productive occupations to the youth — would solve the Jewish

Ephraim Moses Lilien: *Good Tidings for Zion.*

Moses Leib Lilienblum.

problem. His autobiography *Hattot Neurim* ("Errors of Youth"; 1876) gives expression to his socialist inclinations and impatience with the impractical approach of Haskalah. A further change in his views was occasioned by the 1881 pogroms. He became an outstanding protagonist of Zionism, publishing articles in Hebrew, Yiddish, and Russian. In 1883, together with Pinsker, he founded the Zerubabel Zionist society and the following year was elected secretary of the central committee of the movement at the Kattowitz Conference. He remained in this position until his death, being the moving spirit of all the practical activities of *Hibbat Zion* and its ideological guide.

LILIENTHAL, DAVID ELI (1899–): US industrial consultant and public official. He was a director of the Tennessee Valley Authority 1933–46 (chairman 1941–6), and served as chairman of the US Atomic Energy Commission 1946–50. L. is known as an exponent of liberal policies in politics and economics.

LILIENTHAL, MAX (1815–1882): Rabbi. The Russian government invited him in 1840 to persuade Russian Jews to accept a system of Government Jewish schools in which secular, as well as religious, subjects would be taught. He was unsuccessful and eventually realized that the government's real intentions were anti-Semitic. In 1844, L. left for the US where he began a new and successful career in the

rabbinate. He was among the early founders of Reform Judaism in the US, and from 1855 occupied the pulpit of Bene Israel Congregation in Cincinnati being prominent in civil affairs.

LILITH (according to popular etymology the "demon of the night"): Feminine demon; of Babylonian origin. She is mentioned in Is. 34:14. In the Talmud, L. is described as having a human face, long hair, and wings (*Niddah* 24b), but the term L. also occurs as a noun denoting (female) demons generally. In mystical literature, she became the queen of demons and the consort of Satan-Samael. According to one legend, L. was Adam's first wife, and Eve was created after L. had left Adam and refused to return. She tries to kill all new-born children who, in many parts of the Jewish world, are still allegedly protected against her by characteristic AMULETS. According to another version of the legend, she forced Adam to cohabit with her after the Fall, and the offspring of this union were demons and evil spirits. In kabbalistic literature, L. is the symbol of sensual lust and sexual temptation.

LINCOLN: English town. Jews settled there in the 12th cent. and in the 13th, it was the most important community in England after London. The Ritual Murder accusation of 1255, associated with the name of "Little St. Hugh," claimed many victims, and the Jewish quarter was sacked again in 1264 and 1266, but the community remained of importance until the expulsion of 1290. A small community existed there again in the 18th cent. The medieval synagogue and a neighboring Jewish house are still standing.

LINCOLN: Capital of Nebraska, US. Jews settled there in 1868; a Reform congregation, B'nai Jeshurun, was organized in 1884, and the Orthodox congregation, Tifereth Israel, was founded two years later. Its Jewish Welfare Federation was created in 1931. Jewish pop. (1973): 1,000.

*LINCOLN, ABRAHAM (1809–1865): US president. Records contain many anecdotes of his relationship with Jews. He had several Jewish friends, the closest being Abraham Jonas. L.'s intercession resulted in the immediate revocation of an order issued by General Grant in 1862 expelling Jews from the military department of Tennessee.

LINETZKI, ISAAC JOEL (1839–1935): Yiddish author. After a Hasidic upbringing, he was attracted to Haskalah and settled in Odessa. His popular novel *Dos Poylische Yingel* ("The Polish Boy") humorously criticized not only the ignorant Hasidim but also other strata of the Jewish public, including the maskilim. His subsequent works attracted little attention, and this embittered his latter days.

LINOWITZ, SOL MYRON (1913–): US businessman and public figure. Born in Trenton, he was a successful attorney. In 1959 he became chairman of the Xerox Corporation which expanded rapidly under his direction. From 1966 to 1969 he was US ambassador to the Organization of American States. He is active in communal and Jewish affairs in his home town of Rochester N. Y.

LIPCHITZ, JACQUES (1891–1973): Sculptor. Born in Lithuania, he settled in France in 1909 but escaped to the US in 1941 and made his home there. He developed a cubist style and pioneered in translating the concept of abstract painting into sculpture. His works often portray movement and mythology. A number of his works concern Jewish subjects and the State of Israel.

LIPMANN, FRITZ ALBERT (1899–): Biochemist. Born in Germany, he worked in Denmark 1932–9 and then in the US. He shared the 1953 Nobel Prize for Medicine with Hans KREBS for his discovery of coenzyme A.

LIPKIN, ISRAEL see **SALANTER, ISRAEL**

LIPMAN, JACOB GOODALE (1874–1939): Soil chemist. Of an immigrant family of Russian Jewish farmers, he was director of the New Jersey Agricultural Experiment Station 1911–39, dean of Rutgers Agricultural College 1915–39, founder and editor of *Soil Science*, and the author of many scientific books.

LIPPMANN, YOMTOV BEN SOLOMON see **MÜHLHAUSEN.**

LIPPE, KARPEL (1830–1915): Zionist. A physician by profession, he lived in Jassy and was one of the leaders of Rumanian Jewry. He wrote much on Jewish affairs in Hebrew and other languages. One of the first *Hoveve Zion* in Rumania, L. was the senior delegate to the First Zionist Congress where he opened the proceedings.

LIPPMANN, EDMUND OSCAR VON (1857–1940): Chemist. He helped develop the German sugar industry and headed the great sugar project at Halle 1889–1926. From 1916, he taught the history of chemistry at Halle Univ.

LIPPMANN, GABRIEL (1845–1921): Physicist. Professor at the Sorbonne, he was awarded the 1908 Nobel Prize for his inventions in the field of color photography. He invented the capillary electrometer, a highly sensitive instrument for measuring minute differences of electric motive power.

LIPPMANN, WALTER (1889–1974): US social philosopher. From 1914–9, he was associate editor of *The New Republic* and after World War I — during which he was assistant to the Secretary of War — helped Col. House in preparing data for the Versailles Peace Conference. Until 1931, he edited the liberal *New York World* but turned to a more conservative opinion after its demise. His works include *A Preface to Morals, A Preface to Politics, The Good Society,* and *The Public Philosophy*. He published an influential political column in the *New York Herald Tribune* and other journals.

Louis Lipsky.

LIPSCHUTZ, ISRAEL BEN GEDALIAH (1782–1860): Talmudist. He was rabbi in several Prussian communities and from 1837, in Danzig. His best-known work is *Tipheret Yisrael,* a lucid commentary on the Mishnah.

LIPSCHÜTZ, JACOB (1838–1922): Writer. The secretary and chief assistant of Isaac Elhanan Spektor, rabbi at Kovno, he fought against the Haskalah and subsequently against Zionism. His reminiscence *Zikhron Yaakov,* written from an extreme religious viewpoint, shed important light on Russian Jewish history.

LIPSKY, LOUIS (1876–1963): US Zionist leader. He founded *The Maccabean,* the first official organ of the Zionist Organization of America, in 1899, and was among the foremost leaders of the Zionist movement in the US. He founded and edited *The New Palestine,* and was president of the Zionist Organization of America, vice-president of the American Jewish Congress, co-founder of the World Jewish Congress, etc.

LIPTZIN, SOLOMON (1901–): Educator and author. A native of Russia, he went to the US in 1910. L. was professor of comparative literature at the College of the City of New York and at Yeshiva Univ. In 1962, he settled in Israel. His numerous works include books on German and Yiddish literature.

LISBON: Capital of PORTUGAL. The Jewish community, apparently established under the Moors, flourished after the Christian recapture of the city in the 12th cent. Notwithstanding anti-Jewish out-breaks in 1373, 1449, and 1482, Jews were prominent at court as physicians, astronomers, and tax-farmers, and the Hebrew printing-press in 1489–97 was the first press in the country. L. was the main scene of the Forced Conversion of the Portuguese Jews in 1497. Thereafter, the city was a Marrano center and saw the great "slaying of the New Christians" in Apr., 1506. In the 16th–18th cents., L. was the most active seat of the Portuguese Inquisition. Partly owing to the alliance with England, Jews — mainly from Gibraltar — settled in L. from the close of the 18th cent., and a community was formed in 1813. There are now two synagogues, an Ashkenazi and a Sephardi (the former mainly consisting of recent immigrants). Jewish pop. (1973): 565.

LISITZKY, EPHRAIM E. (1885–1962): Hebrew poet. At the age of fifteen, he went from Russia to the US, where he entered upon a career in Jewish education. He wrote several volumes of Hebrew verse, some of which concern aspects of Indian life, and did Hebrew translations of Shakespeare's *Julius Caesar* and *The Tempest*.

LISSA (Leszno): Polish town. An autonomous community existed there from 1534, many of its members engaging in handicrafts and being organized

Street in the former Jewish quarter in Lisbon.

in guilds. The Jews held key positions in trade, maintaining comprehensive commercial links with other countries. They suffered severely in the 17th–cent. Swedish wars and from other causes; their numbers dwindled from 5,000 in 1790 to a few hundred before World War II.

LISSAUER, ERNST (1882–1937): German lyric and dramatic poet. He was author of the notorious *Song of Hate Against England* in World War I, historical dramas, and many moving lyrical poems in *Die ewigen Pfingsten* and other collections.

LISSITZKI, ELIEZER (1891–1941): Russian painter. After the Russian revolution, he experimented in abstract and constructivist art. L. is believed to have died in a Soviet concentration camp.

LITERATURE see **CLASSICAL LITERATURE, JEWS IN**; **HEBREW LITERATURE**; **WORLD LITERATURE, JEWS IN**

LITERATURE, JEWISH CHARACTERS IN: References to Jews occur in Greek and Roman literature (see CLASSICAL LITERATURE), but not until the Middle Ages did Jews become important as a literary theme. They were admired as the Chosen People but accused of the death of Jesus as a result of which they had been condemned to wander eternally. The theme of the Wandering Jew ("Ahasuerus") was treated with grandeur, but in Mystery and Miracle Plays, the stage-Jew was a diabolical type to be reviled and consigned to hell. Folk-songs and folk-ballads — e.g. Chaucer's *Prioress' Tale* — popularized stories of boy-martyrs whose blood was supposedly needed for Passover. The theological approach toward the Jew was retained as the substratum upon which other attitudes were imposed, such as the picture of the Jew as usurer. This reached its climax in Christopher Marlowe's Barabas in *The Jew of Malta* (1589) and Shakespeare's Shylock in *The Merchant of Venice* (1598). With the rise of Enlightenment, a virtuous but exotic Jew came to the fore in literature, best illustrated in Germany by Gotthold Ephraim Lessing's drama *Nathan the Wise* (1778) and in England by Richard Cumberland's *The Jew* (1794). Puritan literature in America portrayed the Jews as "the beloved people." Romanticists, revolting against literary stereotypes, saw in the Jew and in the gypsy two strange, picturesque types and paid special attention to the beautiful, virtuous suffering Jewess. In Walter Scott's *Ivanhoe* (1819), the new Romantic attitude of sympathy exists side by side with older, less favorable attitudes. In Charles Dickens, the contradictions were most glaring: the diabolical Fagin of *Oliver Twist* (1838) and the impossibly faultless Riah of *Our Mutual Friend* (1864). Realistic fiction depicted the Jew as old-clothes peddler, ragpicker, and radical. The anti-Semitic genre in fiction attained vogue in Gustav Freytag's *Debit and Credit* (1855). George Eliot's *Daniel Deronda* (1876) introduced the heroic Jew, the

Zionist with faith in a Jewish rebirth. Jewish writers such as Leopold Kompert, Karl Emil Franzos, and Israel Zangwill brought ghetto scenes and types to popular attention. 20th cent. literature retained traces of all approaches from the anti-Semitic genre, in vogue in Central Europe during the 1930's, to the prose epic of Jewish heroism, as in John Hersey's *The Wall* (1950). The 1960's saw a surge of interest in fiction on Jewish themes by US Jewish authors (e.g. Bernard Malamud, Philip Roth, Saul Bellow).

LITHUANIA: Soviet Baltic republic. The first information on Jews there dates from 1321. In 1398, a community — mostly composed of Karaites — existed at TROKI, and in 1495, Jews living in VILNA, GRODNO, and KOVNO totaled 10,000. They received a charter in 1529 guaranteeing freedom of movement and employment, and soon monopolized foreign trade and tax-farming. In 1495–1502, they were excluded from L., and in 1566–72, the Jewish badge was introduced and Jews disqualified from giving evidence. Originally represented in the COUNCIL OF THE FOUR (then five) LANDS, the Jews of L. formed the separate COUNCIL OF L. in 1623 when a separate tax-system was established. L. was part of Russia 1795–1918, and during this time was of major Jewish cultural importance, home of distinguished yeshivot and leading rabbis, seat of the MUSAR movement, and a center of Haskalah. During World War I, c. 100,000 Jews were expelled or emigrated to the Russian interior. In independent L., Jews received national AUTONOMY (1918–24) and a Jewish national council was established under a Ministry for Jewish Affairs, the communities having the right to levy taxation under government auspices. The loss of Vilna to Poland in 1919 weakened the Jews of L. and after 1924, autonomy was restricted solely to religious matters, while the economic position of the Jews deteriorated in the subsequent years. In 1923, there were 300 Jewish elementary schools, the majority teaching in Hebrew, a minority in Yiddish. The Jewish pop. at the outbreak of World War II numbered c. 175,000. About 25,000 were deported by the Russians from L. and Latvia in July 1940. The remaining Jews of L. were massacred by the Germans and Lithuanians by 1943. The Jewish pop. in 1970 was officially given as 23,564.

LITTAUER, LUCIUS NATHAN (1859–1944): US philanthropist. He made a fortune as a glove manufacturer, served in Congress 1897–1907, but was best known for his generous gifts for the advancement of education and medicine. Outstanding — apart from his Jewish benefactions — was his establishment of the Graduate School of Public Administration at Harvard and of the Littauer Foundation to promote the welfare of mankind and better international understanding.

LITURGY see **PRAYER**

LITVAK: A Jew from Lithuania.

LITVAKOV, MOSES (1875–c. 1938): Russian Yiddish writer. At first a Zionist, he went over to the BUND. He was one of the founders of the *Yevsektzia*. After World War I, L. edited the communist Yiddish daily *Emes*, viciously fighting Zionism, Judaism, and Hebrew culture. He disappeared during the purges of 1937 ff.

LITVINOV, MAXIM (originally Meir Wallach; 1876–1951): Soviet leader. Born in Bialystok, he joined the revolutionary movement at an early age. He lived mainly outside Russia, conducting communist propaganda from 1908–17, especially in London. From 1918–30, L. was the Russian deputy foreign minister and foreign minister from 1930. A supporter of collaboration with non-communist states, he conducted negotiations in Washington in 1933 which led to American recognition of Soviet Russia. L. represented Russia at the League of Nations 1934–8, vigorously advocating the principle of collective security. Dismissed from his post as foreign minister shortly before Russia's alignment with Nazi Germany in 1939, he returned to the political arena after the Germans attacked Russia and was Russian ambassador to the US 1941–3. L. served as deputy foreign minister for a short period in 1946, but the widening breach between Russia and the West resulted in his retirement from public life. His grandson, Pavel, L. (1939–), physicist, was exiled in 1968 for five years for demonstrating against the Russian invasion of Czechoslovakia.

LITVINOVSKY, PINHAS (1894–): Israel painter. He was born in Russia and in 1919 settled in Palestine, where he was among the founders of the modern school of painting. His work is colorful, and has been widely exhibited.

LIUBAVICH: Russian village near Mohilev; the former center of ḤABAD Ḥasidism. Dov Ber (1773–1828), the influential son and successor of the *Ḥabad* leader Shneour Zalman of Lyady, settled there and was succeeded by Menaḥem Mendel SHNEERSOHN. His descendants lived there until 1916 when Shalom Dov Shneersohn removed to Rostov-on-Don.

LIUZZI, GIORGIO (1896–): Italian soldier. He fought in World War I but was dismissed by Mussolini in 1939. Reinstated in 1944, he was chief of staff of the Italian army 1956–8.

LIVERIGHT, HORACE (1886–1933): US publisher. He entered the book publishing business in New York in 1918 and was responsible for the introduction of the *Modern Library* edition of classics. He was also a theatrical producer.

LIVERPOOL: English port. Its Jewish community was founded c. 1750 and in the early 19th cent. was the most important in England outside London. Although reinforced by immigration from Russia after 1881, it was soon outstripped by Manchester,

Leeds, etc. L. has a flourishing and well-organized Jewish life, with 8 synagogues and a Jewish representative council. Jewish pop. (1973): 6,500.

LIVORNO see **LEGHORN**

*LLOYD GEORGE, DAVID (1863–1945): British statesman. He became familiar with Zionist aspirations when, as a rising lawyer, he acted for the Zionist Organization at the time of the UGANDA negotiations in 1903. He was prime minister of the government which issued the BALFOUR DECLARATION in 1917. L. G. thereafter retained his Zionist sympathies, nurtured by his strong biblical background, on occasion leading the protest both in parliament and in the press against the negative policies of British governments in Palestine.

LOANS: Jewish law obligates Jews to assist the needy. The borrower has to return the loan at a definite fixed time; if he fails, the lender may recover the value of the loan from the property of the borrower. When the loan is made by promissory note, the lender may even recover from property sold by the debtor after the date of the note. Debts are canceled by the SABBATICAL YEAR; Hillel, however, instituted the PROSBUL according to which debts could also be collected after the Sabbatical Year. L. with interest are strictly forbidden in the Bible. Later, however, permission was given to receive interest under certain conditions, if the transaction was for business purposes.

LOANS (LOANZ), ELIJAH BEN MOSES (1564–1636): German scholar and kabbalist; grandson of Josel of Rosheim. Rabbi in Worms and other German communities, he wrote and edited several halakhic, liturgical, and kabbalistic works, including extensive commentaries on the Zohar (unpublished). He was known as BAAL SHEM and was the subject of many legends.

LOCKER, BERL (1887–1972): Zionist. A native of Poland, he was prominent in the *Poale Zion* movement and settled in Palestine in 1936. He was on the Jewish Agency executive 1931–56, serving as its Jerusalem chairman, 1947–56. In 1955–61, he was a *Mapai* member of the Knesset.

LOCKSPEISER, SIR BEN (1891–): British aeronautical scientist. After serving in the Ministry of Aircraft Production and the Ministry of Supply, he was secretary for scientific research to the Privy Council 1949–56, head of the European nuclear research organization from 1956, and scientific adviser to the Israel ministry of development.

LOD see **LYDDA**

LODZ: Polish city. Jews are first recorded there in 1785, and the community dates from 1809. They played a large part in all branches of the textile industry which caused the rapid development of the city. Many Jews arrived after the Russian pogroms of 1881 ff. and by 1939, the Jewish population was c. 200,000 (30%). L. was a Jewish cultural center in the 20th cent. with a well-organized educational system, a Yiddish theater, a Jewish press, etc. Under the Nazis a ghetto was set up for the Jews of the district in 1940, and some German Jews were also concentrated there before being sent to the extermination camps. The ghetto was finally liquidated in 1944. After World War II, a community was reconstituted and 17,500 Jews resided in the province of L. in 1946, but many of these subsequently emigrated to Israel. In 1964, it had 4,000 Jews but by 1973 only 2,000 were left.

LOEB OF SPOLA (1725–1812): Ukrainian Ḥasidic *tzaddik*. Reputed a miracle-worker, he attracted to Ḥasidism many Jewish peasants, who called him *Sabba* ("grandfather"). A dispute between him and Naḥman of Bratzlav was continued by their followers after their deaths.

LOEB SARAHS (c. 1730–1791): Russian Ḥasidic *tzaddik*. He wandered extensively and was the subject of many legends.

LOEB: US family. An original partner in the banking firm of Kuhn, Loeb & Co. was *SOLOMON L.* (1828–1903) who went to the US from Germany in 1849. Two of his daughters married Jacob H. Schiff and Paul M. Warburg. One son, *JAMES L.* (1867–1933), early retired from banking to devote himself to the patronage of the arts. He founded the Loeb Classical Library and established music centers in New York and at Harvard. Another son, *MORRIS L.* (1863–1912), was professor of chemistry at New York Univ. He was also active in Jewish communal life, especially in assisting immigrants to the US and in Jewish agricultural settlement.

LOEB, ISIDORE (1839–1892): French rabbi and scholar. He helped to build up the Alliance Israélite Universelle of which he was secretary from 1869. L. wrote works on Jewish history and edited the *Revue des Études Juives*.

LOEB, JACQUES (1859–1924): US physiologist. Born in Germany, he studied and worked there until 1891. He taught at the Univ. of Chicago 1892–1910, subsequently heading the division of general physiology of the Rockefeller Institute. He succeeded in developing larvae from the unfertilized eggs of sea urchins and worms.

LOEB, LOUIS (1866–1909): US painter. He was noted for his illustrations, portraits and, especially, landscapes.

LOEW, MARCUS (1870–1927): US film executive. He began as a film exhibitor, established the nationwide chain of Loew Theaters, and then became a producer. His company expanded into the firm of Metro-Goldwyn-Mayer.

LOEWE: English family of scholars. *LOUIS L.* (1809–1888) was born in Silesia, settled in England, and became orientalist to the duke of Sussex. Later, he was secretary to Sir Moses Montefiore whom he accompanied on his journey to the East in 1840, his wide linguistic knowledge proving invaluable. He was the first principal of the Judith Montefiore College in Ramsgate and of Jews' College in London. He wrote Montefiore's life and works on oriental languages, including Circassian, Nubian, and Egyptian. His grandson *HERBERT MARTIN JAMES L.* (1882–1940), orientalist, taught rabbinics at Oxford and Cambridge and published works on various aspects of rabbinics and Jewish history, besides collaborating with C. G. Montefiore in his *Rabbinic Anthology.*

LOEWE, FREDERICK (1904–): US composer of Viennese birth, he went to New York in 1924. Composer of some of the most popular music of his time, his successes include *Brigadoon, Camelot, Gigi,* and especially *My Fair Lady* (book by Alan Jay Lerner, based on Shaw's *Pygmalion*) which had record runs in many countries (including Israel) and was made into a prize-winning movie.

LOEWE, HEINRICH (Eliakim; 1869–1951): Scholar and Zionist leader. In 1890, he founded in Berlin the *Society of the Lovers of Hebrew* and in 1892, the first German Zionist society "Young Israel." In 1893–1908, he edited several German Zionist periodicals. L. was a representative of the Palestinian colonists at the First Zionist Congress in 1897. The following year, he became librarian of the Berlin Univ. library. In 1933, he settled in Palestine and was librarian of the Tel Aviv municipal library 1933–48. L. wrote several books on Jewish studies, notably folklore.

Otto Loewi.
(Painting by Eugene Spiro.)

LOEWE (BRILL), JOEL BEN JUDAH LOEB (1762–1802): German Hebrew scholar. A headmaster in Berlin and a prominent member of Haskalah circles, he edited *Ha-Measseph* 1788–90 and wrote commentaries on Psalms and the Five Scrolls.

LOEWI, OTTO (1873–1961): Pharmacologist. Born in Germany, he lectured at Graz 1909–38, settling thereafter in the US where he was research professor at the New York College of Medicine. In 1936, he and his collaborator Sir Henry Dale received the Nobel Prize for their researches on the chemical transmission of nervous impulses. His discoveries were instrumental in the advancement of medical therapy.

LOEWISOHN, SOLOMON (1788–1821): Hebrew poet and scholar. He was born in Hungary, studied at Prague, and settled in Vienna where he worked as a proof-reader. Disappointment in love and dismissal from his job intensified his mental instability, and he died shortly after returning to his native Moór. L. was one of the outstanding Hebrew authors of the Haskalah Period, his chief work being *Melitzat Yeshurun,* an exposition of biblical poetry. He was also the author of *Mehkere Aretz,* first modern lexicon of biblical geography.

LOHAME HERUT YISRAEL (Heb. "Fighters for the Freedom of Israel" or *Lehi,* known by its opponents as the "Stern Gang" after its founder Avraham Stern): Revolutionary Jewish organization. *L.H.Y.* split in 1940 from the Irgun Tzevai Leumi, maintaining that Britain must be fought notwithstanding the war effort against the Germans. After Stern was killed, the group was led by its ideologist Yisrael Scheib (Eldad), its tactician Nathan Mor (Friedmann-Yellin), and its operational commander Yitzhak Jazarnitsky (Shamir), Its membership was estimated at 300, and among the acts attributed to them were the murders of Lord Moyne, the British minister in the Middle East, in 1944, and of Count Bernadotte in 1948. After the latter deed, the organization ceased to be active although it returned one member to the First Knesset (1949–51) before disbanding.

LOMBROSO, CESARE (1836–1909): Italian physician. Professor of medical jurisprudence at Turin, he described the nervous relationships of pellagra, revolutionized criminology by demonstrating the pathological and hereditary aspects of crime, and in his *Man of Genius* endeavored to prove that genius is allied to lunacy and epilepsy.

LONDON: Capital of England. The first reliable mention of Jews there dates from c. 1100, and of a community from 1130 when it was fined on a preposterous accusation. It was the largest community in medieval England. There was a murderous attack on the Jews at the time of the coronation of Richard I in 1189, others during the Barons' Wars in 1263/6,

Celebration of the Feast of Tabernacles (*Sukkot*) in the New Synagogue, London.

and Ritual Murder accusations in 1238, 1244, and 1276. After the expulsion of the Jews in 1290, a Home for Converts continued to exist in L., the inmates coming from abroad. There was a secret Marrano community almost throughout the 16th cent., coming virtually into the open in the reign of Elizabeth. Marranos began to settle again under the Commonwealth, and partly through the abortive efforts of Manasseh ben Israel formed themselves into a semi-overt Sephardi community in the summer of 1656. Ashkenazim from Germany, etc. soon followed and established a synagogue in 1690; this element of the community rapidly increased, and further synagogues were founded in rapid succession. The communal aristocracy were brokers, gem-merchants, etc., the proletariat were pedlars and old-clothes men. Although from c. 1740 small communities began to appear in the provinces, L. maintained unquestionable numerical and moral supremacy, the rabbi of its Great Synagogue coming to be recognized as the chief rabbi of English Jewry. L. was the center of all other communal joint activities — e.g. of the foundation of the BOARD OF DEPUTIES by the communities there in 1760. In the mid-19th cent., L. witnessed the establishment of the Reform Synagogue, of the Jewish Board of Guardians for poor relief, of JEWS' COLLEGE for training ministers, and of the English-Jewish press. In 1870, its Ashkenazi communities were associated into the UNITED SYNAGOGUE, to be followed in 1887 by the looser organization into the Federation of Synagogues of the smaller communities formed by

recent immigrants in the East End. The immigration from Russia after 1881 brought the Jewish population up (1881–1905) from 47,000 to 150,000, introducing with it the Yiddish theater, the trade union movement, etc. Immigration was checked by the Aliens Act of 1905, stopped by World War I, and renewed on a large scale after the beginning of the Nazi persecutions in 1933, which resulted in the strengthening of extreme organized Orthodoxy in the community, though — unexpectedly — not in any marked measure of intellectual life. The German bombing of L., 1939–45, resulted in large-scale evacuation, the momentary scattering of the community, the destruction of much of the East End in which traditional Jewish life had centered, and consequently the dispersal of the Jewish area of settlement in fresh areas of the metropolis and in the remoter suburbs, emphasizing the already existing trend to concentrate in the N. This has resulted in the creation of new problems, as yet only partly solved (e.g. in Jewish education). The Jewish pop. of Greater L. is estimated at 280,000 (1973).

LONDON, MEYER (1871–1926): Socialist leader.

He went in 1891 from Russia to the US. He was elected to the US Congress, serving 1914–8, 1920–2. L. opposed US entry into World War I. He was spokesman and legal counsel for the Jewish garment unions from their beginnings.

LONZANO, MENAHEM DI (d. after 1608): Scholar.

Born probably in the Levant, he lived a nomadic existence in Palestine, Turkey, and Italy. He wrote works on the masoretic text of the Bible and on Hebrew grammar, prosody, and lexicography and published some hitherto unknown Midrashim, especially in his *Shete Yadot*.

LOOKSTEIN, JOSEPH HYMAN (1902–): US rabbi.

Born in Russia, he was taken to the US in 1910. Since 1923 he has been rabbi of Kehilath Jeshurun Congregation, New York and since 1931, professor of homiletics and sociology at Yeshiva University. In addition he has been president of BAR-ILAN UNIVERSITY since 1958.

LOPEZ, AARON (1731–1782): Merchant. A Portuguese Marrano by birth, he went to Newport, R. I., in 1752. With his father-in-law, Jacob Rodriguez Rivera, he formed a partnership which promoted the whaling industry and developed Newport's commercial standing in other ways. In 1763, he laid the cornerstone of the Newport synagogue. In 1777, when the British captured Newport, L., his family, and other coreligionists, moved to Leicester, Mass.

LOPEZ, RODERIGO (1525–1594): Marrano physician. Born in Portugal and educated in Spain, he settled in England and became physician to Queen Elizabeth. Although titularly a Christian, his Jewish sympathies were notorious. Having been caught up in political intrigues, he was accused of being involved in a plot to poison the queen and was barbarously executed to the accompaniment of a minor anti-Jewish storm.

LORD OF HOSTS see **GOD**

LORIA, ACHILLE (1857–1943): Italian economist. Professor at Turin and author of much-translated works, he exercised great influence through his economic theories, his exposition of non-Marxist historical materialism, and his views on the economic basis of the social constitution.

LORKI, JOSHUA (properly [De] Lorca; 14th–15th cents.): Convert and polemist. Born at Lorca, Spain, as Joshua ben Joseph Ibn Vives, he became converted to Christianity under the name Geronimo de Santa Fé and henceforth indulged in frenzied anti-Jewish propaganda. As physician to the anti-Pope Benedict XIII, he was largely responsible for and took the leading part in the Disputation of TORTOSA (1413–4).

LORM, HIERONYMUS see **LANDESMANN, HEINRICH**

LORRAINE see **METZ; NANCY**

LOS ANGELES: City in California, US. Jews began meeting there for public worship in 1854, at which period the Hebrew Benevolent Society was organized. Congregation B'nai Brith was founded in 1862 by Orthodox Jews from Central Europe; in 1884, it became Reform. The L. A. Jewish community at first increased slowly, but large numbers of Jews arrived from other parts of the country after World War I. The Federation of Jewish Welfare Organizations, organized in 1911, coordinates the philanthropic activities of the community. Most Jewish organizations in L. A. are represented in the L.A. Jewish Community Council founded in 1934. The community supports about 50 synagogues (some Sephardi) and affiliated schools. The Jewish Theological Seminary and the Hebrew Union College have branches in L.A. Four weeklies appear in L. A.: the *B'nai B'rith Messenger*, the *California Jewish Voice*, the *Los Angeles Reporter*, and *Heritage*. The Jewish population of L. A. has grown rapidly since World War II and in 1973 numbered 463,000—second only to New York. Jews play a conspicuous part in the film industry in L. A.

LOST TEN TRIBES see **TRIBES, LOST TEN**

LOT: Son of Abraham's brother Haran. He journeyed with his uncle from Aram-Naharaim to Canaan, but as a result of a quarrel between their respective shepherds over pasture land, they parted company. L. settled at Sodom, where he was captured by the five kings who had attacked the country, but was rescued by Abraham. The Bible relates his escape from Sodom, the misfortune of his wife, and how his daughters conceived from him—while he was drunk—two sons, Ammon and Moab. In popular Jewish folklore, the name L. is synonymous with a drunkard not responsible for his actions.

LOTS see **PURIM**

LOUIS LAMED LITERARY FOUNDATION: Created in 1939 by Louis LaMed, Detroit communal leader, to stimulate creativity in Hebrew and Yiddish. Annual awards are given for outstanding works published in each of these languages on the American continent. In 1955, the foundation established a chair for Jewish Studies at Wayne Univ., Detroit.

LOUISIANA: US state. From 1728 to 1803, when the territory became part of the US, the BLACK CODE, prohibiting the practice of any religion other than Roman Catholicism, was in force. Nevertheless, there were individual Jews in L. from 1719. In 1828, the first synagogue in L., Shaaray Chesed, was founded in NEW ORLEANS. In the Old City of Lafayette (now Upper New Orleans), Congregation Shaaray Tefilah was organized about 1845. More than 200 L. Jews served in the Confederate armies during the Civil War. L. sent 3 Jews to the US Senate: Judah P. BENJAMIN (1853–61), Michael HAHN (1865, also governor of L. 1864–65), and Benjamin F. JONAS (1879–85). In 1881, an agricultural colony of 173 Russian Jews was established at Sicily Island in the Mississippi but a flood wiped out the settlement a year later. L.'s largest Jewish communities are in New Orleans, SHREVEPORT and Baton Rouge. In 1973, there were 15,775 Jews in L.

LOUISVILLE: City in Kentucky, US. Although Jewish businessmen from Pennsylvania were partly instrumental in the founding of L. by the Clark Expedition, only individual Jews lived there until the 1830's. In 1834, a Jewish benevolent society was formed. Two years later, L's Jewish community numbered about a dozen families of Polish and German origin. Kentucky's first synagogue, Temple Adath Israel, was founded in L. in 1843, and an Orthodox congregation, Beth Israel, was organized in 1856. The Univ. of L. has 8 departmental libraries established by Brandeis, a native of the city. L.'s Conference of Jewish Organizations was founded in 1934. The *Kentucky Jewish Post and Opinion*, founded in 1931, appears weekly. In 1973, L. had 9,200 Jews with 5 main synagogues.

LÖW: (1) *IMMANUEL L.* (1854–1944): Rabbi and scholar; son of (2). He succeeded his father as rabbi of the Szeged community and led the moderate liberal trend of Hungarian Jewry which he represented in the Hungarian Upper Chamber 1927–40. L. published studies in the field of Hebrew and Aramaic philology and a great work on the *Flora of the Jews* (4 vols. 1923–34). (2) *LEOPOLD L.* (1811–1875): Scholar. He was rabbi in several Hungarian communities, officiating at Szeged from 1850. A powerful preacher and the first rabbi to give sermons in Hungarian, he inclined to extreme religious reform and engaged in fierce controversies with Hungarian

Orthodox elements. L. published a journal of Jewish studies *Ben Ḥananiah* 1858–67, and was the author of pioneer works on the history of Hungarian Jewry.

LÖW, ELEAZAR (1758–1837): Talmudist. He officiated in various communities in his native Poland and, in his later years, in Hungary. L. was a noted teacher and a recognized authority on rabbinical subjects, playing an active role in the opposition to the Reform movement.

LOW: (1) *SIR MAURICE L.* (1869–1929): English journalist. As Washington correspondent of the London *Morning Post,* he interpreted England to America, especially at the beginning of World War I, and America to England in his study *The American People.* (2) *SIR SIDNEY L.* (1857–1932): Historian; brother of (1). He wrote on the British constitution and edited the *Dictionary of English History.*

*LOWDERMILK, WALTER CLAY (1888–1974): US soil conservationist. His book *Palestine, Land of Promise* (1944) expounded a plan for the irrigation of Palestine by utilizing its rivers and subterranean water resources. In 1952–3, L. carried out a detailed survey of the soil in Israel. He was professor of soil conservation at the Haifa Technion 1954–7.

LOWE, ELIAS AVERY (1879–1969): US paleographer. After teaching at Oxford, he became professor of paleography at Princeton in 1936. He made fundamental contributions to the study of medieval Latin paleography, particularly the Beneventan script.

LÖWENBERG, JACOB (1856–1929): German poet. An educator in Hamburg, he reacted to German anti-Semitism by emphasizing Jewish themes in his poems and tales. His anthology of modern German poets *Vom goldnen Überfluss* (1902) had a wide popularity.

LOWENTHAL, MARVIN (1890–1969): US author. His writings include a history of German Jewry, a Jewish travel-guide to Europe, a reconstruction of the autobiography of Montaigne, etc. He was closely associated with many American Jewish periodicals and reviews, including the *Menorah Journal, American Zionist,* etc.

LOZOVSKY, SOLOMON ABRAMOVICH (1878–1952): Soviet politician. He was originally a blacksmith, and embarked on revolutionary activities and after arrest, escaped in 1909 to Paris where he edited the publications of the Russian Social Democratic party. Returning to Russia in 1917, he joined the Bolsheviks, was active in trade union organization, served as deputy foreign minister, 1939–41, and helped to direct Russian propaganda during World War II. He disappeared with other prominent Jews toward the end of Stalin's life and his death was admitted several years later.

LUAH see **CALENDAR**

LUAH AḤIASAPH see **AḤIASAPH**

LUAḤ ERETZ ISRAEL: Hebrew literary almanac published in Jerusalem 1896–1915, by A. M. Luncz. It contained ethnographic, cultural, and bibliographical material on Palestine and was a pioneer project both in Hebrew literature and in Palestinography.

LÜBECK: W German city. Jews settled there in 1680, but were expelled in 1699. During its annexation to France (1811–13), 66 families entered but were excluded, notwithstanding international opinion, in 1815. Only after the 1848 Revolution did Jews return to L., a synagogue being consecrated in 1850. The community, numbering 497 in 1933, was destroyed by the Nazis but was refounded on a small scale after World War II.

LUBIN, DAVID (1849–1919): US agriculturist. Russian-born, he went to the US in 1855. Engaging in fruit-growing in California, he became involved in the agrarian revolt against the railroads and middlemen and, after pioneering a fruit-growers' organization in California, became convinced that only international cooperation could solve the farmer's plight. He obtained the support of the king of Italy and this resulted in 1905, in the founding by 40 nations at Rome of the International Institute of Agriculture, which L. headed.

LUBIN, ISADOR (1896–): US economist. L. has held various governmental positions as an expert in statistics and economics and has served as US representative on UN commissions. He was industrial commissioner of NY state 1955–9.

LUBITSCH, ERNST (1892–1947): Film producer. He went to the US from Germany in 1922 and directed numerous witty pictures.

LUBLIN: Polish city. Jews lived there from the 15th cent., but their residence was long restricted to the area around the palace hill. Jewish merchants attended the famous L. fairs, and the city was one of the meeting-places of the Council of the Four Lands. Many distinguished scholars and physicians lived there, and its yeshivah and printing press were famous. About 2,000 Jews were massacred in L. during the Polish-Swedish war in 1656. A severe conflict with the Christian merchants led to the departure or expulsion of most of the Jewish population in 1761 and 1783. In 1862, the Jews returned to the interior of the town, settling in the old city. It rapidly became one of the main Polish Jewish cultural centers. Its 37,000 Jews were herded by the Germans into a ghetto in 1941 and liquidated by 1942. 870 Jews emerged from hiding on liberation.

LUBLIN, MEIR BEN GEDALIAH OF (known as *Maharam* Lublin; 1558–1616): Polish talmudist. In 1582, he founded a yeshiva at Lublin. He was rabbi at Cracow 1587–95, and then at Lvov until 1613 when, owing to a dispute, he was forced to return to Lublin. A noted teacher and recognized authority, his book *Meir Ene Ḥakhamim* contains novellae on the entire Talmud and was appended to many Talmud editions. 140 of his responsa were collected in *Manhir Ene Ḥakhamim*.

LUBLINSKI, SAMUEL (1868–1910): German critic and playwright. He wrote on the history of religion, stressing the Jewish origin of Christianity. He engaged in polemics with Aḥad Ha-Am on Zionist topics.

LUCCA: Italian city. In the 9th cent., its Jewish community was among the most important in N Italy, being associated with scholars such as R Kalonymos and later, Abraham Ibn Ezra. It was one of the Three N Italian communities mentioned by Benjamin of Tudela c. 1165. In the 15th cent., it had a community of loan-bankers.

LUCENA: Town in S Spain. In the Moorish Period its Jewish population was so important that it was called "Jews' Town." It was then one of the greatest centers of Jewish intellectual life in the west, being the residence of Isaac Alfasi, etc. The community was forced into Islam by the Almoravides in 1107 and thereafter played little part in Jewish life.

LUCK: Town in Soviet Ukraine, formerly Poland. The Jewish community is mentioned in 1388 and obtained a charter in 1432. Jews were excluded from the town 1495–1503. A Karaite group lived there from 1506. The Jewish predominance in trade and crafts led to conflict with the Christian populace. Many were killed in the Chmielnicki massacres of 1648. L. was a prominent community and its numbers grew to c. 25,000 (including 50 Karaites) in 1939, but these were nearly all exterminated by the Nazis.

LUDOMIR, MAID OF (c. 1815—c. 1905): Ḥasidic leader; real name Hannah Rachel, daughter of R Monesh Werbermarcher. Already enjoying a reputation for piety from childhood, she began to follow Ḥasidic customs after her recovery from a severe illness. She built her own synagogue and put on phylacteries daily. Thousands of Ḥasidim gathered to hear her teachings. Toward the end of her life, she journeyed to Palestine where she died.

LUDWIG (COHN), EMIL (1881–1948): Biographer and dramatist. Born in Germany, he spent most of his life in Switzerland and his last years in the US. The subjects of his biographies include Goethe, Bismarck, Napoleon, Jesus, Lincoln, and Beethoven. He applied a biographical technique to his books on the Nile and the Mediterranean.

***LUEGER, KARL** (1844–1910): Austrian anti-Semite. Mayor of Vienna from 1897, he dismissed Jewish officials, introduced segregation into municipal schools, etc.

LUFTMENSCH (Ger. "man of the air" i. e., rootless person): Expression coined by Max Nordau to describe the large class of Jews of contemporary E Europe without stable or productive occupations who lived on peddling and petty speculation.

LUKACS, GEORG (1885–1971): Hungarian philosopher. Commissioner of education in the Bela KUN government; in exile from 1919 until after World War II. His Marxist interpretations of literature proved highly influential.

LUKUAS or **ANDREAS** (d. c. 117 CE): Leader (king, according to Eusebius) of the Jews of Cyrene in their great revolt against Rome in 115. He invaded Egypt and devastated the countryside but was ultimately defeated and killed. According to a later tradition, he died in Judea.

LULAV (Rabbinic Heb. = "sprout"): Name universally applied to the palm-branch prescribed (Lev. 23:40) to be taken on the feast of Tabernacles together with the ETROG, myrtle, and willow, called together the FOUR SPECIES (*Arbaah Minnim*): the *l.* and the other vegetation being held in the right hand, the *etrog* in the left. It is customary to carry them during the recital of the *Hallel* (at specified points of which the *l.* is shaken in all directions consecutively) and of the *Hoshanot*: in some communities, also at other parts of the service. The *l.* was considered in the Classical Period one of the symbols of Judaism. At the beginning of the period of the Second Temple, and still among the Karaites, palm-branches were used for covering the Tabernacle. Some Ashkenazim save the *l.* for the following year to be used in fastening the myrtle and willows to the new *l.*

LUMBROZO, JACOB (d. c. 1665): Physician. Born in Lisbon, he was the first "Jew doctor" known in Maryland. Following a conversation with a missionary in 1658, in which he stated his disbelief in Christian doctrine, he was sentenced to death. However, when Oliver Cromwell became lord protector of England, a general amnesty was issued and L. was released.

LUNCHITZ (Lenczyca): Polish town. It was the scene of a Blood Libel in 1639, and the alleged martyrdom was exploited by the local monastery. 3,000 Jews were slaughtered there in 1656 by the Cossacks under Chmielnicki. A small community was later re-established.

LUNCHITZ, SOLOMON EPHRAIM (d. 1619): Talmudist. He headed the Lvov yeshivah and from 1604, was chief rabbi at Prague. L. wrote on many aspects of talmudic study and composed liturgical poems, including an elegy on the persecution of 1611.

LUNCZ, ABRAHAM MOSES (1854–1918): Palestinographer. Born in Lithuania, he lived in Jerusalem from 1869. L. devoted himself to the study of Palestine and the history of its Jewish community. Although blind from 1879, he continued his researches and published the collections *Jerusalem* (13 vols.

1882 ff.) and the *Luah Eretz Yisrael* ("Palestine Almanac," 19 vols. 1895/6 ff.). His books include guides to Palestine and editions of early sources on Palestinography.

LUNEL: French town. Its Jewish community is ancient. In c. 1165, Benjamin of Tudela found there 300 Jews including eminent scholars in comfortable circumstances. The rabbis of L. admired the writings of Maimonides and supported them in the controversy they engendered. The community ceased to exist after a series of expulsions at the beginning of the 14th cent. Many leading Jewish sages, including the Ibn Tibbon family, lived in L., some being known as Yarḥi (from Heb. *yareaḥ* = French *lune* i.e., moon).

LUNEL, ARMAND (1892–): French novelist. A teacher of philosophy by profession, he has written a series of picturesque novels centered around Provençal life, particularly its Jewish community. L. wrote librettos for Darius Milhaud's operas *Esther de Carpentras* (based on his own novel) and *David*.

LUNGE, GEORG (1839–1923): German chemist. He lived for a time in England and then taught at Zürich 1876–1907. He invented the nitrometer and gasvolumeter and wrote many textbooks, all of which he translated into English.

LURIA, ISAAC BEN SOLOMON (known as "Ashkenazi," in abbreviation *Ari*; 1534–1572): Palestinian kabbalist. He was born in Jerusalem and educated in Egypt. Living in Safed from 1570, he became renowned for his ascetic life and saintly character. His identification of ancient graves in Galilee conferred on them sanctity which has persisted to the present day among the Orthodox. His teachings, received by his disciples orally, were posthumously recorded by his pupil Ḥayyim VITAL in *Etz Ḥayyim, Peri Etz Ḥayyim, Sepher ha-Gilgulim,* and other works. L.'s teaching deeply influenced subsequent mystical thought; it was founded on the three basic doctrines of *tzimtzum, shevirat ha-kelim,* and *tikkun* (see KABBALAH). The unity of God and creation is a fundamental assumption of the Lurianic system. L.'s personality, the subject of many legends which emphasize his supernatural powers, made a profound impression on his contemporaries and on posterity, and the neo-kabbalistic movement which he launched had a vast impact on Jewish life, particularly in the Mediterranean area and in Europe.

LURIA, SALVADOR (1912–): US scientist. Born in Turin, he settled in the US in 1940 and from 1959 headed the Microbiological Department of the Massachusetts Institute of Technology. In 1969 he was a recipient of the Nobel Prize for Medicine for contributions in the field of molecular genetics involving virus structures and bacteria infection which laid the foundation of modern molecular biology.

LURIA, SOLOMON BEN JEHIEL (known as *Maharshal*; c. 1510–1573): Rabbi and codifier. He officiated in several Lithuanian and Polish communities, latterly at Lublin. His approach to the classic text was simple and rational, and he devoted special attention to determining accurate readings. His chief work *Yam shel Shelomoh* criticized the *Shulhan Arukh* for relying on the codifiers instead of going to the source, the Talmud, which he regarded as the sole halakhic authority. His independent and critical views made him many opponents, but the greatness of his learning was undisputed.

*LUTHER, MARTIN (1483–1546): German religious reformer and founder of one of the most important streams of Protestantism. His German translation of the Bible is an outstanding event in German religious and literary history. At the outset of his reforming activity, he spoke favorably of the Jews and condemned their maltreatment by the Catholic Church, hoping that they would be attracted by his new presentation of Christianity. Disappointed in this he later wrote of them with extreme virulence, applauding everything that could be done to persecute and humiliate them. His anti-Jewish attitude helped to inspire later German anti-Semitism.

LUXEMBURG: Independent European grand duchy. The presence of Jews is known in the town of L. from 1276, and though they were attacked and massacred in 1349, a community continued to exist until 1391. After the French Revolution, a new community was established, which increased in the 19th cent. It was reconstituted after the Nazi occupation, when 750 persons perished, and numbers 1,000 (1973). There are synagogues also at Esch, Grevenmacher, Ettelbruck, and Mondorf.

LUXEMBURG, ROSA (1870–1919): Revolutionary. Of Polish birth, she settled in Germany, engaging in socialist journalism. Imprisoned in 1915–8 for her opposition to World War I, she continued to agitate in writing and was associated with Liebknecht as leader of the Spartacus League (from 1918, the German Communist Party). She and Liebknecht were murdered by soldiers after the unsuccessful communist rising of Jan. 1919. Her political and economic studies included *The Accumulation of Capital,* which developed Marx's ideas and evolved a theory on imperialism. Fifty years after her death, her ideas had a strong influence on the New Left movement.

LUZ: Pre-Israelite name of BETHEL (Gen. 28:19). The Israelites captured the city at the beginning of the period of the Judges, and one of the original inhabitants, spared by the Israelites, emigrated to the "Land of the Hittites" (N Syria or Asia Minor) where he built another city of the same name. According to talmudic legend, the Angel of Death has no authority in L. (*Sota* 46b).

LUZ, KADISH (1895–1972): Israel agriculturist. He went to Palestine from Russia in 1920 and was prominent in the kibbutz movement. A *Mapai*

Kadish Luz.

member of the Knesset, 1951–69, he was minister of agriculture 1955–59 and speaker of the Knesset 1959–69.

LUZKI, JOSEPH SOLOMON BEN MOSES (1777–1844): Russian Karaite scholar; from 1802 leader of the Eupatoria community. In 1827, he participated in a mission to Nicholas I which obtained the exemption of Karaites from military service. An account of the proceedings is given in his *Iggeret Teshuat Yisrael* (1840). L. was the author of religious poems, some of which were incorporated in the Karaite liturgy, and of works of Hebrew grammar and Bible commentary.

LUZKI, SIMḤAH ISAAC BEN MOSES (d. 1766): Russian Karaite author and bibliographer. He was widely read in rabbinic and kabbalistic, as well as Karaite, literature and greatly admired the Zohar. His writings include *Oraḥ Tzaddikim,* a history of the Karaites and their literature.

LUZZATTI, LUIGI (1841–1927): Italian statesman. Member of an ancient Venetian family, he taught political economy at Milan and introduced the cooperative movement into Italy. Entering politics, he was repeatedly minister of the treasury 1891–1906, of agriculture in 1909, and in 1910–11 prime minister. While not a conforming Jew, he identified himself with Jewry and protested to Rumania against her persecution of the Jews.

LUZZATO: Italian family, especially associated with Venice and Padua, ultimately deriving from Lausitz in E Germany. One branch became known as LUZZATTI.

LUZZATTO, MOSES ḤAYYIM (abbr. as *Ramḥal*; 1707–1747): Kabbalist and poet. Born and educated in Padua, he gathered around him a circle of students of the esoteric, practiced with them mystical austerities, and apparently considered himself the forerunner of the Messiah or actually the Messiah. He believed himself to be in communication with the spirits of the heroes of the Bible, who dictated to him secret doctrines; these he communicated in turn to his disciples. The Italian rabbinate, led by that of Venice, recollecting the damage done to Judaism by the claims of Shabbetai Tzevi, at first persuaded and then ordered him to desist. In the end, he migrated to Frankfort-on-Main and thence to Amsterdam, where he earned his living as a diamond polisher, and in 1743, went to Palestine. He died of the plague at Acre. His poetical works included psalms in the biblical style, much occasional poetry, a drama on the life of Samson, and two allegorical plays *Migdal Oz* and *La-Yesharim Tehillah,* written under the influence of Guarini. These works, though perpetuating on the one hand the old literary tradition of Italian Jewry, on the other hand marked the beginning of a new era in N Europe and the inception there of modern Hebrew literature. In particular, his influence on subsequent Hebrew poetry was immense. Besides other smaller works (on prosody, grammar, etc.), L. wrote *Mesillat Yesharim* ("The Way of the Righteous"), an ethical work of extreme beauty, which became a classic and is still widely studied.

LUZZATTO, SAMUEL DAVID (known from his initials as *Shadal*: 1800–1865): Italian scholar; from 1829, professor at the Padua Rabbinical College. A many-sided scholar, he occupied a central place in 19th cent. Hebrew literature. The subjects on which he wrote included the Bible, Hebrew grammar and philology, Jewish liturgy, Hebrew poetry, and Jewish philosophy. His writings stress the supremacy of Jewish traditional culture over that of other nations and develop Judah Ha-Levi's distinction between Judaism, the source of good, and Hellenism, which fosters external grace and beauty. He attacked several Jewish authors — e.g. Maimonides. Ibn Ezra, and Spinoza — whom he regarded as unduly influenced by Hellenism. An opponent of mysticism, he opposed the Kabbalah as alien to the true Jewish spirit. L. took up a negative attitude to the contemporary fight for civil rights, sensing the ultimate dangers of assimilation and annihilation, but stressed that Judaism, besides being a religion, involved national consciousness, loyalty to Jewish tradition, and love of the Hebrew language. A pioneer student of medieval Hebrew literature, he edited the poems of Judah Ha-Levi. He translated parts of the Bible into Italian, composing a commentary in Hebrew. L. acknowledged the inspiration of Scripture but not the sanctity of the accepted text (apart from the Pentateuch) which he did not hesitate to amend. Living in Italy, he had special opportunities for collecting and consulting rare books and mss, and his correspondence with Jewish scholars in other lands is of importance. He also wrote poetry in Hebrew in the traditional Italian style.

LUZZATTO, SIMONE (in Heb. Simḥah; c. 1580–1663): Venetian rabbi. Modern in outlook and well-versed in secular literature, he published, besides some Hebrew trivia, two works in Italian: *Socrate* in which he insisted on the importance of revelation to assist human reason; and a Discourse (*Discorso*) on the Jewish people in which he demonstrated their economic and social utility in the modern state. This work, the first of its type, was much used by subsequent apologists.

LVOV (Lemberg): Capital of Galicia, now in the USSR. Jews lived there from the end of the 13th cent. and in 1364 received privileges from Casimir the Great. There were two communities, one inside and one outside the city, and most of the eastern commerce was in their hands. They suffered during the Chmielnicki war (1648–9) but the townspeople paid an indemnity rather than surrender the Jews. Nevertheless, there was continual friction between the Jews and the populace, and from 1759, the Jews were confined to the ghetto and only permitted to reside in other areas in 1867. Treatment under Austrian rule was favorable. Many distinguished rabbis as well as leaders of the Haskalah lived in L., which was the political and cultural focus of Galician Jewry and from 1880, a center of the Zionist movement. The community suffered during World War I, and the Jewish quarter was almost completely destroyed in a pogrom in 1918. Nevertheless, an intensive Jewish life flourished under Polish rule from 1918 to 1939 when the Jews numbered c. 130,000. During the Nazi occupation, they were confined to a ghetto which was finally liquidated in 1943. Its Jewish pop. in 1970 was 21,721 (L. province). The sole synagogue was ordered closed in 1962.

LVOVICH, DAVID (1882–1950): Public worker. Of Russian birth, he was among the founders of the Jewish Socialist Party SS. He lived in Berlin 1921–32, Paris 1932–9, and then in the US. L. devoted himself to the work of ORT, acting as vice-chairman of its World Federation from 1921. After World War II, he organized occupational training projects in Displaced Persons' camps.

LYADY: White Russian townlet. Its Jewish community dates from the 18th cent., and after the Hasidic leader SHNEOUR ZALMAN settled there in 1802, it became a center of the HABAD movement. In 1897, its Jewish population was 4,000 (83%). Those of its Jews who did not escape during World War II were exterminated by the Nazis.

LYCK (Elk): Polish town, formerly German. Jews were excluded until the 18th cent. In 1856, the first Hebrew newspaper HA-MAGGID appeared there, and Hebrew printing-presses existed in L. until 1901. The much-diminished community numbered c. 200 before World War II.

LYDDA (Heb. *Lod*): Israel town. It is mentioned in Egyptian documents as "Rethen." The Bible (I Chron. 8:12) ascribes its building to the tribe of Benjamin. The town grew in importance during the Second Temple Period. Jonathan the Hasmonean added it to Judea in 145 BCE. The Jewish population was decimated by the Romans after their participation

Capture of Lydda airport by Israel forces in 1948.

in the war of 66–70 CE. Later, it was the seat of an academy where R Eliezer ben Hyrcanus, R Akiva, and other distinguished authorities taught. It was also an industrial center, producing textiles, ceramics, etc. From the 3rd cent., it was called Diospolis. After a rising in 352 CE, the Jews were nearly exterminated by Constantius Gallus and thereafter, Christians constituted the majority of the population. The town is considered the home of St. George, in whose honor it was renamed Georgiopolis, a Byzantine church being erected there in his name. After the Arab conquest, L. became the capital of Palestine until 700 CE, when the capital was transferred to newly-built Ramleh nearby. In recent years L. has become a communications center, particularly because of its airport. Most of its Arab inhabitants left when the town was captured by the Israel army in 1948. Since then, large numbers of immigrants have settled there. Pop. (1974): 33,900.

LYON, ABRAHAM DE: Viticulturist; early settler in Georgia, US. He went from Spain or Portugal to the colony of Georgia the year it was founded and settled in Savannah in 1733. He introduced viticulture to the colony.

LYON, HART see **LEVIN, HIRSCHEL**

LYON-CAEN, CHARLES (1843–1935): French jurist. He taught at Paris Univ. from 1872, being elected to the Académie des Sciences Morales et Politiques in 1884 (permanent secretary, 1918). He was also president of the Carnegie Foundation for World Peace at The Hague. His specialty was commercial law.

LYONS: French city. Its Jewish settlement goes back almost certainly to Roman times. In the 9th cent., restrictions against the Jews were demanded by Agobard and Amulo, successive bishops of L., who claimed that the Jews were excessively privileged by the king and that the market-day had been changed from Saturday to suit their convenience. There was a succession of expulsions in the later Middle Ages (1251–1420). Jews from the Comtat Venaissin began to settle in L. in the early 18th cent. The community suffered severely during the German occupation in the 1950's, but became a center of settlement for Jews from N. Africa. In 1966, it became the seat of a regional consistory. Pop. (1974): 25,000.

*LYRA, NICHOLAS DE (c. 1270–1349): French exegete. His much-studied Latin Bible commentaries, though markedly antagonistic to the Jews, depend very largely on those of Rashi. There is no ground for the belief that L. was a converted Jew.

*LYSIAS (d. 162 BCE): Syrian general. In 166/5, while acting as Antiochus Epiphanes' deputy, he was ordered to suppress Judah the Maccabee. After an expedition despatched by him under Gorgias had been repulsed at Emmaus, he himself advanced with an army but was defeated by Judah at Bet Tzur. On the death of Antiochus, he remained effective ruler and invading Judea in 164/3, defeated Judah at Bet Zechariah and besieged Jerusalem. His attention distracted by dynastic problems in Syria, he now granted the Jews religious freedom and autonomy, in return for acknowledgment of Seleucid suzerainty. He was murdered the following year by the pretender Demetrius Soter.

*LYSIMACHUS (prob. 1st cent. BCE): Hellenistic anti-Jewish writer; probably from Alexandria. Josephus cites the slander from his book on Moses that the Jews were expelled from Egypt because they were lepers.

M

MAABARAH (Heb. "transit camp"): Type of temporary village erected in Israel during the period of mass immigration commencing in 1948. Located near towns and villages, their residents found work in the neighborhood and remained in the *m.* until permanent housing was provided, often in the vicinity. From 1950 the *m.* was replaced by the KEPHAR AVODAH and the *maabarot* were gradually liquidated.

MAAMAD see **MAAMADOT; MAHAMAD**

MAAMADOT (Heb. "stands" i.e. "posts"): Groups of non-priestly Israelites attending the Temple sacrifice. The people was divided into 24 lots of priests, levites, and Israelites, each being assigned a specific time to serve in the Temple. Every one of the priests and levites went in his appointed week of service. The Israelites, however, sent only a few representatives to be present at the sacrifices, the rest of the group assembling in their own cities to read prayers and the first chapter of Genesis. In post-Temple times, the custom of reciting these special selections was, to a certain extent, retained (cf. Mishnah *Taanit* 4:2–4). Selections, including biblical and talmudic passages for the use of priests, are included in some modern prayer-books.

MAAPILIM (Heb.): Jews who endeavored to reach Palestine despite difficulties and obstructions; more particularly, those defying the restrictions imposed by the British mandatory government. The name is based on the story of those Israelites who "presumed" to enter the country (Num. 14:44). The movement was called *haapalah*. Transports were organized from 1934 by the Polish HE-ḤALUTZ and the Revisionist movement. Immigration — mostly from Poland — began on a large scale in 1938 chiefly under the auspices of the kibbutz movements in cooperation with the *Haganah*. In 1939, when numerous *m.* arrived from Germany and Austria, British countermeasures grew stricter. When European sources were largely cut off (1939–42), Jews began to enter Palestine "illegally" from Middle Eastern countries in numbers. Large-scale *haapalah* from Europe was resumed with the Nazi retreat and a strong organization set up (with the assistance of Jewish Palestinian army units and members of the PALMAḤ) which in 1945–6 moved 95,000 Jews from E Europe into Germany and Austria, and brought 23,000 Jews to Palestine in 1946, mainly through Italy. From Aug. 1946, the British deported any intercepted *m.* to DETENTION CAMPS in Cyprus, and in the case of

Transit Camp ("Maabarah") for new immigrants before 1950.

Maapilim departing from an Italian port, 1946.

the "EXODUS 1947" even returned them to Germany.

MAARIV (Heb. "who brings in the evening"; from one of the opening words: also called *Arevit*): Evening prayer. Unlike the other daily prayers, *m.* did not originate as a substitute for sacrifice but arose from the spiritual need to pray after the evening repetition of the *Shema* laid down by the Torah (Daniel also prayed thrice daily cf. Dan. 6:11). Traditionally, *m.* was ordained by Jacob. The Talmud records a controversy as to whether the evening prayer is obligatory or optional, but in the course of time it became obligatory. It includes the *Shema* and its blessings and the Eighteen Benedictions (which are not, however, repeated by the Reader). In the Middle Ages, liturgical poems called *maaravot* were composed for *m.*, especially at festivals and are still recited in some Ashkenazi communities.

MAARIV: Israel afternoon mass-circulation newspaper founded in 1948 by Azriel Carlebach who edited it until his death in 1956.

MAASEH (Heb. "deed"): In Yiddish usage, a story, particularly one that is far-fetched.

MAASEH BERESHIT and **MAASEH MERKAVAH** (Heb. lit. "work of creation" and "work of [the] chariot"): Term used to refer to Gen. 1 (the story of the Creation) and Ezek. 1 (vision of the Divine throne-chariot), the exposition of which constituted the principal subject-matter of early Jewish mysticism. Fearing gnostic and philosophical interpretations, the Mishnah restricted the expositions of these chapters (*Hagigah* 2:1). A few early tannaim — pupils of R Johanan ben Zakkai — concentrated on these subjects and the fragments preserved of their teachings formed the basis of the HEKHALOT literature (see KABBALAH). Maimonides, adopting a rational approach, held that *M. B.* is physical science and *M. M.*, theology. See COSMOLOGY.

MAASEH BOOK: A work containing a collection of stories, generally with a miraculous element and/or an ethical object. The stories are derived from the Talmud and medieval folklore and occasionally from non-Jewish sources. Several collections of this sort were made in Yiddish and a comprehensive English corpus was edited by M. Gaster. Somewhat similar collections were current among Sephardi communities (particularly in the Mediterranean area) under the title *Maaseh Nissim* ("Miracle Tales").

MAASER see **TITHE**

MAASER SHENI (Heb. "Second Tithe"): Eighth tractate (seventh in some codices) in the Mishnah order of *Zeraim,* containing 5 chapters. It has *gemara* in the Palestinian, but not the Babylonian, Talmud. *M. S.* deals chiefly with the tithes eaten in Jerusalem (Deut. 14:22–7) and how they could be redeemed for money.

MAASEROT or **MAASER RISHON** (Heb. "Tithes" or "First Tithe"): Seventh (eighth in some codices) tractate in the Mishnah order of *Zeraim,* consisting of 5 chapters. It has *gemara* in the Palestinian, but not the Babylonian, Talmud. *M.* deals with the tithe given to the levite (Num. 18:21).

MAAYAN BARUKH: Israel communal settlement (IK) in the Ḥuleh Valley. It was founded in 1947 by Israel pioneers and World War II veterans demobilized from the S African army.

*MACALISTER, ROBERT ALEXANDER STEWART (1870–1950): Irish archeologist. He directed excavations for the Palestine Excavation Fund 1898–1909 and 1924, his most important work being at Gezer, Marissa, and Ophel in the Davidic City of Zion. His researches at Gezer laid the foundations for the knowledge of early Palestinian pottery and Philistine culture.

*MACAULAY, THOMAS BABINGTON, LORD (1800–1859): English statesman and historian. His speech advocating the removal of Jewish disabilities delivered in the House of Commons on Apr. 17, 1833, as well as his essay on the subject in the *Edinburgh Review* for Jan. 1831, created a profound impression. They were translated into many languages.

MACCABAEANS, ANCIENT ORDER OF: Friendly society established in London in 1896. Its c. 2,000 members throughout the British Isles are organized in 25 Beacons.

MACCABEE: The additional name given to JUDAH, son of Mattathias, military leader of the revolt against Syria in 168 BCE (see JUDAH THE MACCABEE). The name M. is also applied loosely to other members of the family and to the HASMONEAN dynasty as a whole. Its derivation is unknown.

MACCABEES: Name given in Christian tradition to the seven children martyred by Antiochus Epiphanes when they refused to commit idolatry. Shrines to their memory and that of their mother Salome (in Jewish tradition Hannah) were established in many parts of the Christian world.

MACCABEES, BOOKS OF THE: Books of the APOCRYPHA. I Maccabees (or the First Book of the Hasmoneans) describes the history of the Hasmonean family from the persecution of Antiochus Epiphanes down to the early days of John Hyrcanus' reign. It was composed in the time of John Hyrcanus or Alexander Yannai. The factual and straightforward account is obviously written by an admirer of the Hasmoneans. The original Hebrew — still known in the 4th cent. — has been lost, but the Greek translation has survived in the Septuagint. II Maccabees is an abbreviation of a parallel work written in Greek by a hellenistic Jew, Jason of Cyrene. Centered around the personality of Judah the Maccabee, it describes many miracles but is an important historical source containing authentic documents and describing the events leading to the Hasmonean rising. Its date is unsettled but may possibly be 2nd cent. BCE. III Maccabees is unconnected with the Hasmoneans; it describes the alleged persecution of the Jews by Ptolemy IV Philopator of Egypt. Some scholars date it about the beginning of the Christian era; others

hold it to reflect events in Egypt under Caligula. It was originally written in a refined, rhetorical Greek of little literary value. IV Maccabees is a philosophical essay on the power of reason over the passions. The name seems to derive from quotations from II Maccabees cited in the work. It is written in a rhetorical Greek typical of the late hellenistic period and dates from the late 1st cent. BCE or 1st cent. CE. Its philosophical content reflects Jewish religious views and incorporates Stoic elements.

MACCABI: World union of Jewish athletic organizations. The first branches were founded in 1895 in Berlin, Constantinople, Bucharest, and St. Petersburg. The German movement later received official Zionist support, and Berlin became the headquarters of the World Union (established 1921), which later moved to London and is now in Tel Aviv. M. has 200,000 members in 38 countries including 40,000 in Israel. Under its auspices, the MACCABIAH is held regularly.

MACCABIAH: International Jewish sports festival under the auspices of the MACCABI World Union. It has been held in Czechoslovakia (1929), Belgium (1931), and Palestine (Israel) (1932, 1935, 1950, 1953, 1957, 1961, 1965, 1969 and 1973).

The Eighth Maccabiah

The Herodian outer wall of the Cave of Machpelah at Hebron.

MACDONALD WHITE PAPER see **WHITE PAPER OF 1939**

*McDONALD, JAMES GROVER (1886–1964):
US diplomat. He was League of Nations' high commissioner for refugees 1933–5 and a member of the Anglo-American Commission of Inquiry in Palestine, 1946. In 1948–51, M. was the first US minister (later ambassador) in Israel.

MACEDONIA: Region of SE Europe now divided among BULGARIA, CREECE, and YUGOSLAVIA. The apostle Paul visited synagogues in SALONICA and Beroea. The former "Romaniot" Jews of M. spoke Greek, but after the expulsion from Spain, Sephardi immigrants gradually absorbed the Romaniots: the major community was at Salonica; others, far smaller, were at Cavalla, Castoria, Drama, etc. Most of the 60,000 Jews in the Greek area of M. were exterminated during World War II.

MACHAERUS: Ancient stronghold E of the Dead Sea. It was fortified by Alexander Yannai, destroyed by GABINIUS (57–54 BCE), but rebuilt by Herod who made it a royal citadel and prison. John the Baptist is reputed to have been executed there. M. was a Zealot center during the Roman War and was captured by Lucius Bassus in 71 CE.

MACHPELAH: Place near Hebron, including a field and a cave, purchased by Abraham from Ephron the Hittite as a burial plot for Sarah (Gen. 23). Subsequently Abraham, Isaac, Rebekah, Jacob and Leah were also interred there. During the Byzantine period, M. was marked by a church, after the Arab conquest by a synagogue, but from the 12th cent., Arabs prohibited the entry of non-Moslems, except under special circumstances. Since the Six-Day War, it has been a popular place of pilgrimage for Jews. The cave, which is blocked, is surrounded by a building, the foundations of which date back to Second Temple times.

MACK, JULIAN WILLIAM (1866–1943): US jurist and Zionist leader. He taught law at several universities, was judge of the Circuit Court of Cook County, Illinois, and from 1913 till his death, US

Julian Mack.

Circuit Court judge. He was president of the Zionist Organization of America 1918–21, and leader of the "Brandeis-Mack group" which favored a program of investment and industrial development in Palestine. M. was the first president of the American Jewish Congress (1917) and the first chairman of the Comité des Délégations Juives at Versailles (1919).

McMAHON CORRESPONDENCE: Exchange of letters in 1915 between Sir Henry McMahon, British commissioner in Egypt, and Sherif Hussein and his son Feisal. They contain a promise of British support for Arab independence in return for an Arab revolt against the Turks. Palestine was not mentioned, as Britain had not yet reached agreement on this subject with France. The Arabs, however, claimed that Palestine was included in the area for which independence was promised. Sir Henry McMahon stated explicitly in 1937 that his pledge was meant to exclude the area of Palestine and that this was fully realized at the time by Hussein.

MADABA MAP: The only extant ancient representation of Palestine; found on a mosaic pavement in the Byzantine church of Madaba (Transjordan) in 1884. Now fragmentary, it occupied the transepts of the church before the altar, the original size being probably 32 × 75 yards. It dates from 542–565 CE.

MADISON: City in Wisconsin, US. There were 17 Jewish families from Central Europe living in M. in the 1850's. They founded the now defunct Congregation Shaare Shomayim in 1859. E European Jews began to arrive in M. at the turn of the century. The M. Jewish Welfare Fund was founded in 1940. In 1973, M. had 2,900 Jews with 3 synagogues.

MADRID: Capital of Spain. In the Middle Ages, when of little importance, it had a small Jewish community which suffered in the massacres of 1391. Later, it became a Marrano center and seat of an Inquisitional tribunal, a secret synagogue being discovered there in 1720. Declared Jews began to settle in M. in the second half of the 19th cent., and there is now a small community and a synagogue opened in 1959 and dedicated in 1968. Jewish pop. (1973): 3,000.

MAGDALA: Ancient city on the shore of the Sea of Galilee, 3 m. N of Tiberias. In Second Temple times, it was one of the four large towns in Galilee. Jesus' disciple, Mary Magdalene (i.e., of M.), hailed from this town. During the Roman War, it was fortified by Josephus but captured by Titus in 67 and destroyed. After the destruction of the Temple and especially after the Bar Kokhba revolt, the priestly order of the section of Ezekiel settled there. The modern settlement of MIGDAL now stands near the site.

MAGDEBURG: City of E Germany. In 965, Emperor Otto the Great delivered "the Jews and other merchants" to the jurisdiction of the head of the local monastery. Later, the archbishop of M. took over the protection of the Jews and defeated an attempt of the

city to impose a special tax on them. The Jews passed from trade to moneylending, but their wealth provoked acts of robbery and murder. The community was completely destroyed in 1349 during the Black Death outbreaks. The archbishop again afforded protection in 1372 but in 1493, expelled the Jews from M. The congregation was only renewed in the 19th cent. and in 1851, a synagogue was consecrated. Nearly 2,000 Jews lived there in 1933, but none was left by World War II. 100 Jews were living there in 1966.

MAGDIEL: Israel village in the S Sharon plain. Founded in 1924 by middle-class settlers, it became a center of citriculture. See HADAR RAMATAYIM.

MAGEN DAVID (Heb. "Shield of David"): Mystical symbol consisting of two superimposed triangles forming a star or hexagram; today regarded as a Jewish symbol. Although occurring in the Capernaum synagogue (3rd cent. CE), it was in ancient times predominantly a non-Jewish decorative motif (e.g. on Roman mosaic pavements), and is found in Christian churches in the Middle Ages, while absent from con-

Magen David in the Seal of Jacob Daniel of Trier.

temporary Jewish decoration and not mentioned in rabbinic literature. The name figures from the 13th cent. in the "practical Kabbalah," where it is a magic symbol associated with the pentagram or "Star of Solomon" (with which it is frequently confused). The origin and period of its adoption as a Jewish symbol is a matter of dispute. It occurs in a specifically Jewish context in Prague in the 17th cent. The *M. D.* was adopted by the First Zionist Congress (1897) as a symbol, and figures on the flags of the Zionist Organization and of the state of Israel. It was used by the Nazis, in the form of a yellow star, as the Jewish "BADGE of shame."

MAGEN DAVID ADOM (Heb. "Red Shield of David"): Israel first-aid organization founded in 1930 in Tel Aviv as the medical wing of *Haganah*. By 1974, it had 63 branches and first-aid stations and 420 ambulances as well as first-aid squads in about

Judah L. Magnes, delivering his address as Chancellor of the Hebrew University at a graduation ceremony in 1932.

half of all Israel villages. The annual budget is provided in part from "Friends of M.D.A." outside Israel, chiefly in the form of gift ambulances. The activities of the M.D.A. as a national first-aid society are governed by an Israel law of July, 1950.

MAGGID (Heb. "preacher"): Name given to a popular preacher by Jews in Poland. The m. *(maggid mesharim,* "who preaches upright things") or the *mokhiaḥ* ("reprover") preached frequently, on both Sabbaths and on weekdays, encouraging the study of the Torah and observance of the commandments. Their descriptions of the terrors of hell awaiting sinners were meant to arouse the people to repentance. They also heartened the people with words of comfort, hope for redemption, and anticipation of the advent of the Messiah. Of special fame was the *M.* JACOB BEN WOLF KRANTZ (d. 1804), noted for his parables. The Ḥasidic movement, in particular, had recourse to *maggidim* and "reprovers" in order to spread its teachings in Poland and Russia. These itinerant preachers went to the people whom they influenced both by their popular sermons expounding the basic principles of Ḥasidism and by their ethical manner of living. Outstanding Ḥasidic *maggidim* included Dov Ber of Mezhirich, Judah Leib "the *mokhiaḥ* of Polonnoye" and Nahum of Chernobyl. In Kabbalah, *m.* was a supernatural being who conveyed information to scholars.

MAGIC: The practical application of certain dynamistic beliefs. Jewish religion is in principle opposed to m. because the ultimate source of everything is the absolutely free and sovereign will of God which can never be coerced. The only proper attitude is therefore PRAYER; in religion, as distinct from m., it is always unpredictable whether God will accede to prayer or not. In practice, however, the line between religion and m. is difficult to draw (cf. the pouring of water on the altar during the Festival of Tabernacles and the prayers for rain), and the Bible, Talmud, and later literature attest a widespread belief in the practice of m. Sorcery and m. are prohibited by the Bible (Exod. 22:17) but the Talmud, while proscribing the practice as heathenish, admits its efficacy. Members of the Sanhedrin were supposed to have had a thorough knowledge of m. and sorcery, and legends are told of rabbis using "white" m. Healing by m. is condemned only when specifically pagan or idolatrous. The m. of names (Divine names, Tetragrammaton, names of angels, permutations and combinations of Hebrew letters or scriptural quotations), whether in AMULETS or spoken formulas, flourished at all times but particularly under the influence of Kabbalah. In the Middle Ages, etc., Jewish magicians were known in many countries. Some scholars believe that the *tephillin* and *mezuzah* originated as amulets. Exorcisms, too (cf. DIBBUK), were practiced in many circles. Generally, however, the rabbis tried to render the belief in m. innocuous by teaching that the study of Torah and the performance of good works produce immunity against all evil influence.

MAGISTER JUDAEORUM (Lat. "Master of the Jews"): Palace official appointed by the Carolingian sovereign in France to supervise and safeguard the Jews. The sympathetic attitude of the M. J. in the early 9th cent. aroused the resentment of AGOBARD, archbishop of Lyons.

MAGNES, JUDAH LEON (1877–1948): US rabbi and first president of the Hebrew Univ. While Reform rabbi in Brooklyn, he was secretary of the American Zionist Federation. He was rabbi for four years in Temple Emanuel, New York, and then giving up the Reform ministry, threw himself into the organization of that vast Jewish community as a KEHILLAH with representative educational, religious and social organs. For a few years, it was a powerful body. M.'s pacifist activity during World War I weakened his authority both in the Kehillah and the Zionist Federation. In 1921, he settled in Palestine, devoting himself to building up the Hebrew Univ. In 1924, he established the Institute of Jewish Studies, and after the university was opened in 1925, became its chancellor, and from 1935, president. His devotion was largely responsible for its establishment on a sound basis. His humanitarian ideas and devotion to spiritual Zionism led him to oppose official Zionist policies as threatening conflict with the Arabs. He inspired the BERIT SHALOM, and later the IḤUD movement, advocating Arab-Jewish understanding and a bi-national Jewish and Arab commonwealth in Palestine.

MAGNUS: English family. *SIR PHILIP M.* (1842–1933) as a young man was minister of the Reform Synagogue in London. He interested himself in science, becoming an expert on technical education and ultimately a member of parliament representing the University of London. His wife *KATIE (LADY) M.* (1844–1924) wrote several books, including *Outlines of Jewish History,* for children. Their son *LAURIE M.* (1872–1933) published a number of works on European literature. Strongly anti-Zionist, he founded and edited *The Jewish Guardian* 1919–31.

MAGNUS-LEVY, ADOLF (1865–1955): Medical scientist. Born in Berlin, he taught in German universities before going to the US in 1940. He discovered the basic processes of metabolic action and pioneered in the study of diabetes.

MAGOG see **GOG**

MAH NISHTANNAH (Heb. "why is it different?"): Opening of the four questions included in the HAGGADAH and asked at the Passover SEDER service.

MAH TOVU (Heb. "How goodly"): Prayer (called after its initial words) composed of various biblical passages (Num. 24:5; Ps. 5:8, 26:8; 69:14; 95:6) recited on entering the synagogue.

MAḤAL (Heb. initials of *Mitnaddeve ḥutz la-Aretz;* i.e., "overseas volunteers"): Overseas volunteers in the Israel Defense Army during the War of Independence (1948–9). Most came from English-speaking countries, others were from France, Holland, Switzerland, etc. The number of volunteers has been estimated at 3,000–4,000, and 150–200 fell in action. Some settled in Israel after demobilization, their villages including Kissuphim, Kephar Daniel, and Moshav Ha-Bonim.

MAHAMAD: Traditional transliteration in the Sephardi communities of Amsterdam, London, etc. of the Hebrew *maamad* (see MAAMADOT). The term was applied in Sephardi synagogues to the governing body of the congregation. In the 18th–19th cents., the m. was the executive of the autonomous Jewish community, with judicial functions, the right to impose penalties, censor books, etc.

MAHANAIM: Place in Gilead where Jacob encountered a troop of angels (Gen. 32:3). On the division of the country, M. was in the territory of Gad, the town being assigned to the levites. In Solomon's time, it was the capital of an administrative region. It is now the name of an airfield in Galilee.

MAḤANOT HA-OLIM (Heb. "the camps of the ascenders"): Israel pioneer youth movement founded in 1927 by the pupils of the Herzliyyah secondary school, Tel Aviv. Its members founded several kibbutzim.

MAHARAL see **JUDAH LÖW BEN BEZALEL**

MAHLER, EDUARD (1857–1945): Hungarian orientalist. He taught oriental languages at Budapest Univ. from 1898 (professor, 1914) and wrote astronomical researches, publishing the standard work on Jewish chronology. M. survived the Nazi persecutions and died in Hungary.

MAHLER, GUSTAV (1860–1911): Austrian composer and conductor. He began his conducting career in 1881, and in 1897, after embracing Catholicism, joined the Vienna Imperial Opera. As its musical director, he was responsible for a series of outstanding artistic triumphs. He traveled widely, conducting opera and symphonic concerts. His compositions, which are influenced by Wagner and the romantic movement, consist of 9 symphonies, song-cycles with orchestra (including *Lied von der Erde, Kindertotenlieder),* and songs.

MAHLER, RAPHAEL (1899–): Historian. He taught in Warsaw from 1924 to 1937, subsequently living in the US and Israel where he is professor at Tel Aviv University. M.'s works, which include a history of the Jews in modern times and books on the Jews in Poland, the Karaites, and Galician Jewry, approach Jewish history from a Marxist standpoint.

MAHOMET see **MOHAMMED**

MAḤOZA: Jewish center in Babylonia. Its inhabitants were known for their intelligence and charity as well as for their luxurious and frivolous way of living. An important academy was established there by Joseph bar Ḥamma in the mid-3rd cent., after the destruction of Nehardea, attaining prime importance under the direction of his son Rava. Destroyed by the emperor Julian in 363, it was later rebuilt and in 513–20, was capital of the independent area established by the exilarch Mar ZUTRA II.

MAḤZOR (Heb. "cycle"): Festival prayer-book. At first, the *m.* contained prayers for the entire year (including week-days and Sabbaths) in chronological order: such *maḥzorim* still exist for the use of the cantor and a few rites (e.g. the Italian) maintain this arrangement. Most Ashkenazi *maḥzorim* contain only festival prayers, being distinguished from the *siddur* (which contains the weekday and Sabbath prayers, etc.). The oldest *m.* so-called is the *Maḥzor Vitry* arranged by R Simḥah of Vitry, a pupil of Rashi. This primarily includes only the general prayers with the laws relating to the liturgy, etc. and a few hymns added. Early Palestinian *piyyutim,* as well as Italian and Ashkenazi ones of similar origin, have found their way into Ashkenazi *maḥzorim* and, to a certain extent, into the rites of Rome and "Romania" (i.e., the Byzantine Empire; this rite is no longer extant). The Ashkenazi ritual is divided into the *minhag ashkenaz* (the western ritual) and *minhag polin* (Polish or eastern ritual). The N French ritual, which resembled the *minhag ashkenaz,* ceased to exist in the 14th cent., when the Jews were expelled from that area; a remnant long existed in the *m.* of the three Italian towns of Asti, Fossano, and Moncalvo for the New Year and Day of Atonement. *Piyyutim* flourished among the Spanish Jews and many were incorporated into the ritual until the codifiers reacted and excluded most of them from the *m.* Consequently the Spanish *m.* (and the closely-related Yemenite rite) has relatively few *piyyutim:* the N African Sephardi groups have, however, retained large numbers of special hymns.

MAIDANEK: Nazi CONCENTRATION CAMP 3 m. from Lublin. First established in the fall of 1941 as a prisoner of war camp, it was enlarged in 1942 to house about 150,000 prisoners. In 1942, four gas cham-

Solomon Maimon.

bers and crematoria were installed, and in Apr. and May of that year about 10,000 Jews from Slovakia, Bohemia, France, and Greece were shipped there for extermination. Mass transports of Polish Jews began in the summer of 1942, and in the spring and summer of 1943, between 30–50,000 Warsaw Jews were sent to M. On Nov. 3, 1943, about 18,000 inmates were killed. By June 22, 1944, when the Nazis evacuated the camp, an estimated 360,000 prisoners had been exterminated, among them some 200,000 Jews.

MAILER, NORMAN (1923–): US novelist. His novel of World War II, *The Naked and the Dead,* achieved a spectacular success. His later writings include novels, poetry, and documentary reporting. M. was strongly identified with experimental causes.

MAIMON BEN JOSEPH (c. 1110–1165): Scholar; father of MAIMONIDES. A pupil of Joseph IBN MIGAS, he was dayyan in his native Cordova and author of an Arabic commentary on the Bible (now lost). In 1148, he left Spain with his family, because of persecution, and went to Fez where he wrote the *Iggeret ha-Neḥamah* (1161) upholding the faith of those Jews who had been forced to convert to Islam. Eventually, he settled in Egypt.

MAIMON, ABRAHAM BEN MOSES see **AB-RAHAM BEN MOSES BEN MAIMON**

MAIMON, SOLOMON (1754–1800): Philosopher. Son of a Lithuanian village inn-keeper, he was a

Page from a 15th cent. Ashkenazi *Maḥzor.*
(Municipal Library, Hamburg).

typical boy prodigy; married at the age of 14, he was a father at 15. He made great efforts to teach himself to read German. At the age of 25, he left for Germany where he became a wandering beggar. Finally, however, he succeeded in being admitted to Berlin and, with the help of Moses Mendelssohn, entered intellectual circles. After reading Kant, he wrote his first work *Versuch über die Transzendentalphilosophie* ("Essay on Transcendental Philosophy"), concerning which Kant stated "Of all my critics, M. has understood me best." From then on, M. wrote considerably, despite his material straits. Eventually, he was taken into the estate of Count Kalkreuth where he remained until his death. His autobiography, which has been translated into English, is one of the most vivid works in Jewish literature.

MAIMON (originally **FISHMAN**), **YEHUDAH LEIB** (1876-1962): Rabbi and MIZRAḤI leader. He officiated as rabbi in his native Bessarabia and was early active in the Zionist movement, taking part in the *Mizraḥi* founding conference in 1902. In 1913, he settled in Palestine, transferring there after World War I the *Mizraḥi* World Executive, which he headed, and also helping to organize the chief rabbinate. A member of the Jewish Agency Executive 1935-48, he was Israel minister for religious affairs 1948-51, and a *Mizraḥi* delegate to the Knesset 1949-51. M. wrote extensively on folklore and on talmudic and Zionist themes. He directed the MOSAD HA-RAV KOOK which he initiated.

Rabbi Yehudah Leib Maimon.

MAIMONIDES see **MOSES BEN MAIMON**

MAINE: US state. Individual Jews lived there before the 1880's when E European immigrants founded communities in Auburn, Bangor, Biddeford, Lewiston, and Waterville. In 1973, most of M.'s 7,945 Jews lived in Portland (3,500), Lewiston–Auburn (1,750), and Bangor (1,300).

MAINZ (Mayence): W German town. Jews probably lived there in the Roman Period, but definite information only dates from the 10th cent. when it was the principal community of N Europe and the main center for the diffusion of rabbinic learning. In 1012, the Jews were expelled from M. but soon returned. The community obtained protection from the archbishop on the advent of the crusaders in 1096, but hundreds were nevertheless murdered. In 1209, the emperor conceded to the archbishop his rights over the Jews. A further series of massacres occurred at the time of the Black Death (1349). Expulsion edicts were issued in 1438, 1462, and 1470-1. In the 10th–11th cents., the Jews were prominent in commerce but from the 12th, moneylending became a main occupation. There was an elaborate communal organization and from the 12th cent. the Jews of M. united, for many purposes, with the neighboring communities of Spire and Worms (the group was called *Shum* after the Hebrew initials). Despite vicissitudes, M. was a center of Jewish learning, especially of talmudic study, until the expulsion of 1473. Jews began to trickle back from 1583 and the community was re-established. Full emancipation came after the French Revolution. Until the Nazi Period, its Jewish population numbered c. 3,000. Jewish pop. (1970): 122.

MAJORCA: Largest of the BALEARIC ISLANDS, belonging to Spain. Jews may have lived there in Roman times, and in the Middle Ages the communities of PALMA and Inca were important, many documents regarding their organization and privileges being preserved. In the 14th cent., M. was the center of a school of Jewish map-makers headed by the CRESQUES family. The Jews suffered during the massacres of 1391, many fleeing to N Africa. On the occasion of a Ritual Murder accusation in 1435, the community was again attacked and its surviving members forced to accept Christianity. The Inquisition was active against their descendants, known in M. as CHUETAS, who suffered appallingly in the autos-da-fé of 1678 and 1691. There have been no known manifestations of Judaism in M. subsequently, but in Palma the Chuetas are still recognizable and subject to some social discrimination.

MAKHIR BEN ABBA MARI (fl. 14th cent.?): Exegete, probably French. His *Yalkut ha-Makhiri* collects, from various sources, aggadot on the books of the Prophets and Hagiographa.

MAKHSHIRIN (Heb. "Predisposings"): Eighth tractate in the Mishnah order of *Tohorot*, containing 6 chapters. It has *gemara* neither in the Babylonian nor Palestinian Talmud. It treats of the laws of ritual impurity in connection with foods which are susceptible to such impurity when wet (Lev. 11:34, 38).

MAKHTESH (Heb. "mortar"): A deep cirque in the crest of mountain ridges. There are several in the Negev of which the largest is in the Paran highlands and is known a M. Ramon. It is 22.5 m. long, c. 5 m. wide and about 430 yards in depth below its rim. Smaller and more enclosed are two others in the N Negev, *Ha-Makhtesh ha-Gadol* and *Ha-Makhtesh ha-Katan.*

MAKI (initials of *Ha-Miphlagah ha-Kommunistit ha-Yisre'elit*): Israel Communist Party. Its predecessor, the Palestine Communist Party (PKP) was founded in 1919. Until 1948, it regarded Zionism as a reactionary agent of British imperialism and its own function as the liberation of the Arab masses from both, with the assistance of Jewish workers. In the 1949 Knesset it received 15,148 votes (4 seats), in the 1951 Knesset, 27,334 votes (5 seats), in 1955, 38,492 votes (6 seats), in 1959, 27,374 (3 seats), and in 1961, 42,111 votes (5 seats). In 1965, the party split into two and in the 1965 and 1969 elections the faction which derived its main support from the Arab areas (RAKAH) received 3 seats and the "Jewish" faction (MAKI) 1 seat; in 1973 *Rakah* 4, *Maki* (which merged with *Moked*) 1. The party's newspapers are *Kol ha-Am* and *Ittihad* (in Arabic).

MAKKEPH (Heb.): A hyphen (written level with the top of the Hebrew letters) connecting two, three, or four words, only the last bearing an accent. The vocalization of some words changes when followed by an *m.* (e.g. *et, kol*).

MAKKOT (Heb. "Stripes"): Fifth tractate in the Mishnah order of *Nezikin*, containing 3 chapters. It has *gemara* in both the Babylonian and the Palestinian Talmud (except for the final chapter in the Palestinian). Originally part of the tractate *Sanhedrin*, it treats of lashings administered following a court decision (Deut. 25:1–3). It contains an elaborate discussion of false witnesses (Deut. 19:15–21) and cities of refuge (Num. 35:9–28).

MALABAR see **COCHIN**

MALACHI (fl. c. 460–450 BCE): Prophet. The name M. (literally "my messenger") may be an abbreviation of Malakhiah, but the rabbis early expressed the view that this was in effect a sobriquet, and some identified him with Ezra. Many modern scholars also hold the view that M. is not a proper name. The prophet protests against transgressions in matters of sacrifice and tithes. The priest must turn the multitude from sin and himself maintain a high level of morality. M. also complains of mixed and broken marriages. His eschatology contains an important and influential innovation, viz. the vision of the "Day of the Lord" preceded by the advent of Elijah.

MALAGA: Spanish port. In the 11th cent., its community was important and it was the home of Solomon Ibn Gabirol and, for a time, of Samuel Ibn Nagrela. M. was captured by the Christians only in 1487, when persecution of the Marrano refugees began, while the other Jews, sold into slavery with the rest of the inhabitants, were ransomed by their Spanish

coreligionists. A small community has been reestablished in modern times and numbered 150 in 1969.

MALAKH HA-MAVET see **ANGEL OF DEATH**

MALAMUD, BERNARD (1914–): US novelist. He has taught at Oregon State College since 1949 (professor, 1961). His books include *The Natural, The Assistant, A New Life, Pictures of Fidelman* and a short-story collection *The Magic Barrel.* His novel *The Fixer,* a fictional reconstruction of the BEILIS affair, won a Pulitzer Prize in 1967.

MALBEN: AMERICAN JOINT DISTRIBUTION COMMITTEE Services in Israel for the care of handicapped immigrants. Founded in 1950, it had by 1968 given aid to 250,000 chronically ill, disabled or aged immigrants. M. administers 12 homes, villages, and infirmaries for aged, housing 3,000 residents; 4 hospitals for chronic diseases; a hospital for chest diseases; a youth rehabilitation center; 2 schools for nurses, etc.

MALBIM, MEIR LEIBUSH (1809–1879): Rabbinic scholar. Of Volhynian birth, he officiated at Wreschen (Posen) 1838–45, Kempen (Prussia) 1846–60, and from 1866–71, at Bucharest where his opposition to Reform Judaism led to his imprisonment. Later, he had to leave Mohilev when the wealthy community leaders denounced him to the authorities for alleged political offenses. His last years were spent at Königsberg. M.'s best-known work is his commentary on the Bible, designed to show the unity of the Written and Oral Law and to base the traditional aggadic interpretations on the literal meaning — both objectives directed against Reform views. He searched for special significance in every biblical synonym.

MALSIN see **MOSER**

MALTA: Mediterranean island. Jews were there in the Classical Period. In the Middle Ages, there were communities both in M. and the neighboring island of Gozo, both coming to an end when the Jews were expelled from Sicily in 1492. After 1530, when the island was handed over to the Knights of St. John, numerous Jewish prisoners captured in raids on Turkish shipping and sea-ports were taken to M. where they were kept until ransomed. Hence, there was for a long time a community of slaves with its synagogue and burial-ground, organized by the Christian representative of the "Fraternity for Ransoming Prisoners" in Venice. At the close of the 18th cent., voluntary immigrants began to establish themselves on the island, and there is still a small Sephardi community numbering 50 (1973).

MALTER, HENRY (1864–1925): Scholar. He was born in Galicia, studied in Germany, and taught talmudic literature and medieval philosophy at Hebrew Union College, Cincinnati (1900–7) and then, at Dropsie College, Philadelphia (1909–25). M. wrote several works on rabbinic literature and medieval philosophers, including the standard biography of Saadyah.

MAMMELOSHEN (Yidd. "mother" and Heb. *lashon* = tongue, language): Colloquial expression for Yiddish; by extension, plain comprehensible talk.

MAMRAN or **MAMREM** (?Lat. *membrana* = parchment): A legal document similar to a check which was used by Jews in E Europe from the 16th to 19th cents., to meet credit needs. The *m.* was a simple document, one side bearing the signature of the debtor and the other, the amount of the debt and the date when due. It required no witnesses and was transferable without endorsement, thus serving a useful need for Jewish merchants.

MAMRE (or "Oaks of M."): Locality in the immediate vicinity of Hebron named after one of Abraham's friends (Gen. 14:13). The oak was displayed in Second Temple times and attributed to the era of the Creation. A Herodian wall has been uncovered in excavations on the site, while Hadrian set up a large building there which Constantine turned into a Christian basilica (its remains are known as "The House of Abraham"). An ancient oak, 2 m. from Hebron, is popularly called "Abraham's oak."

MAMREM see **MAMRAN**

MAMZER (Heb.): A bastard (also colloquially). According to Jewish law, only the offspring of a forbidden relationship is a *m.*

MAN: In the Bible m. is represented as part of material creation ("dust from the earth") but endowed with a Divine "form" in virtue of which he is the creative master of the earth. His relation to God is determined by his status as a free and responsible moral agent but also by his apparent inability to persevere in the right path. The personal bond between God and m. (humanity, Israel) is described as the COVENANT. Whereas the Bible considers m. an indivisible whole, the rabbis accepted the division into body and SOUL. The latter is pre-existent, returning to its celestial home after death to render account for its life on earth. According to one rabbinic saying, body and soul are again joined together for judgment as only their union represents the concrete human, moral existence. Generally, the soul is conceived as originally pure; man's proneness to evil and his capacity for GOOD are accounted for by the doctrine of the good and evil inclination *(yetzer)*. The evil inclination is expressed in lusts and desires; the good inclination must rule the evil in accordance with the Divine Will as embodied in the Torah (and in reason). Human destiny is variously conceived as life in an ideal community with God ("The Kingdom of God") or as the bliss of the immortal soul (see IMMORTALITY; ESCHATOLOGY). According to the kabbalists, man's nature corresponds so closely to the Divine that his life is vital to the cosmos as a whole and to God Himself; m. as a complete microcosm has a redeeming mission in this world. Modern interpretations of the Jewish doctrine of m. are influenced by contemporary philosophical and anthropological (rationalist, social, existentialist, etc.) views.

MAN OF LIES (Heb. *ish ha-kazav*): An opponent of the TEACHER OF RIGHTEOUSNESS in the DEAD SEA SCROLLS. He was apparently a recognized teacher of the Law whose teaching was widely accepted by the people. The sect accused him of knowingly perverting the meaning of the Law. Groups of Men of lies are frequently mentioned in most of the scrolls. Sometimes they are called "interpreters of smooth things."

MANASSEH: First son of Joseph and Asenath (Gen. 41:50–1). In blessing Joseph's two sons, Jacob conferred on them an equal portion with his own sons in the division of Canaan. The tribe descended from M. was divided into seven families, one called Machir and the other six claiming kinship with Gilead. Half the tribe (together with those of Reuben and Gad) requested territory in Transjordania, which was granted by Moses on condition that they accompany the remaining tribes in the conquest of the land as scouts preceding the main body. This half-tribe received Gilead, Bashan, and Argob. After the conquest of Canaan, the other half received territory in the west of the country around the Valley of Jezreel. Both these areas were highly fertile. Tiglath-Pileser III and Sargon exiled much of the population from both sections but part remained. A Jewish population (partly descended from the tribe of Simeon) still existed in the West M. region in the earlier Second Temple Period.

MANASSEH: King of Judah 692–638 BCE. He succeeded his father Hezekiah at the age of 12 and is depicted in the Bible as one of the worst Jewish monarchs. He canceled his father's reforms, reintroduced pagan practices, and so shocked the faithful that the destruction of the Temple was attributed to his wickedness (II Kings 21:11–17). Apparently, he was forcefully opposed by the loyal monotheists, many of whom he put to death. M. paid tribute to Esarhaddon and Assurbanipal of Assyria and, according to one report, spent some time as a captive in Babylon (II Chron. 33:11–19). It has been suggested that his pagan innovations were the result of Assyrian pressure.

MANASSEH, PRAYER OF: Short prayer (included in the Apocrypha) attributed to Manasseh, king of Judah, who uttered it allegedly while captive in Babylon. It praises God's compassion for the repentant, with whom the petitioner begs to be numbered. The prayer is first found in the 4th cent. Christian work *Didascalia,* from which it was incorporated in Greek and Latin Bible versions. It was originally written in Greek, apparently in Egypt, and the association with the name of Manasseh is late.

MANASSEH BEN ISRAEL (1604–1657): Dutch rabbi. Born of Marrano parentage as Manoel Dias Soeiro, he was taken as a child to Amsterdam, achieved fame as an infant prodigy, and at the age of 18 was appointed rabbi, first of the Neveh Shalom congregation and, from 1629, as one of the rabbis of the unified community. In 1632, the first part of his *Conciliador*, reconciling discordant passages of the Scripture, won him fame in non-Jewish circles. Henceforward, he represented Jewish scholarship in the Christian world, adding to his reputation in a series of expositions of Jewish doctrine published in Spanish and in Latin. He also founded in 1627 the Jewish printing-press in Amsterdam, in which he continued active. His correspondents included many leading Gentile scholars. M.'s *Hope of Israel* (1650), in Spanish, Hebrew, Latin, and English, dealt with the reputed discovery by Aaron Levi Montezinos of the Lost Ten Tribes in S America. This was taken up by English mystics who were interested in the return of the Jews to England and encouraged M. to concern himself with this. After prolonged negotiations, he went to London in Sept. 1655 and presented a petition to Oliver CROMWELL, as a result of which the latter convened the WHITEHALL CONFERENCE in December. The results of this were indeterminate, but M. remained in London where he continued his effforts and published his *Vindiciae Judaeorum* in defense of the Jews (Apr. 1656). Disappointed with the trivial outcome of his efforts, he returned to Holland with a grant from Cromwell in the autumn of 1657, dying shortly after his arrival. Although his mission was ostensibly unsuccessful, it prepared the way for the resettlement of the Jews in England under circumstances better than he had hoped.

MANASSEH BEN JOSEPH OF ILYE (1767–1831): Talmudist. A pupil of the Vilna Gaon, he was proficient in mathematics and mechanics as well as rabbinics. Because of his progressive views, which included the dissemination of Enlightenment and handicrafts among Jews, he was persecuted by the Orthodox who also censured his works. His friendship with Shneour Zalman of Lyady brought upon him the wrath of the *Mitnaggedim*. He refused to accept any permanent rabbinical position and wandered through Lithuania and Germany.

MANCHESTER: English city. A Jewish community was first organized there about 1780. It increased in the middle of the 19th cent., a Reform synagogue being established in 1856 and a Sephardi congregation, recruited mainly from the E Mediterranean, in 1871. At the period of the Russo-Jewish persecutions after 1881, M. (with the adjoining Salford) attracted more settlers than any other provincial city in Great Britain. The community, whose economy was originally centered on the cotton and tailoring trades, has now found a broader basis. There are about 40 synagogues (3 Sephardi) organized under a communal rabbinate and synagogue council, a Jewish hospital, and a representative council. Its community, the largest in Great Britain after London, numbers 35,000 (1973).

British troops leaving Palestine upon termination of the Mandate in May, 1948.

MANCHURIA see **CHINA**

MANCROFT, ARTHUR MICHAEL SAMUEL, BARON (1877–1942): British public figure. He was lord mayor of Norwich 1912–13, Conservative member of parliament 1918–37, and minister for overseas trade 1924–7. His son *STORMONT MANCROFT SAMUEL, BARON MANCROFT* (1914–) was in 1957–8 minister without portfolio in the Conservative government.

MANDATE, PALESTINE: The BALFOUR DECLARATION was an undertaking by Britain to facilitate the establishment of a Jewish national home in Palestine, and was endorsed by other Powers. There was considerable delay in a final decision owing to outside differences. On April 24, 1920, it was formally decided by the Supreme Council of the Principal Allied Powers at the conference in SAN REMO that Britain should administer Palestine and be responsible for the implementation of the Balfour Declaration. Differences among the Powers led to further delay, and it was not until July 24, 1922, that the P. M. was approved by the Council of the League of Nations meeting in London. The draft prepared by Britain in 1920 had been fully discussed by the League and in the final approved form the Balfour Declaration is quoted in the preamble, thereby giving "recognition to the historical connection of the Jewish people with Palestine and to the grounds for reconstituting their national home in that country." The body of the M. contains a number of articles, seven of which have a direct bearing on the Jewish national home. According to Article II the Mandatory Power was responsible for placing the country under such political, administrative, and economic conditions as would secure the establishment of the Jewish national home and the development of self-governing institutions; also for safeguarding the civil and religious rights of all the inhabitants of Palestine, irrespective of race and religion. Article IV provided for an appropriate Jewish Agency to be recognized as a public body for advising and cooperating with the administration of Palestine on economic, social, and other matters affecting the Jewish national home and the interests of the Jewish population and, subject to the control of the Administration, to assist and take part in the development of the country. The Zionist Organization was recognized as the Jewish Agency as long as the Mandatory considered it appropriate. The other relevant articles provided for the facilitation of Jewish immigration by the Mandatory Power, while ensuring the rights and status of the other sections of the community, and for encouraging settlement of the Jews on the land, including unrequired state and waste lands; for enacting a national law to enable Jews taking up their residence in Palestine to acquire Palestine citizenship; the recognition of English, Arabic, and Hebrew as the official languages of Palestine; and the recognition of the holy days of the respective communities as legal days of rest. Article 25 of the M. delimits the borders of the country, excluding Transjordan from Palestine. The P. M. ended on May 15, 1948, with the withdrawal of the British administration.

MANDEL (originally Rothschild), **GEORGES** (1885–1944): French statesman. From 1903, he collaborated with Clemenceau in his journalistic projects and was his *chef de cabinet* 1906–9, 1917–9. A rightwing deputy 1919-24, 1928–40, he served as minister of posts and telegraphs 1935–6, minister of colonies 1938–40, and minister of the interior in 1940. After the fall of France, he refused to surrender and tried to secure the formation of a government in N Africa. After this failed, he was arrested and handed over to to the Germans. He was murdered by Vichyist militia near Paris.

MANDEL, MARVIN (1920–): US public figure. Born in Baltimore, he studied law and in 1953 entered the Maryland State Legislature, serving as speaker from 1963. In 1969 he became governor of Maryland.

MANDELKERN, SOLOMON (1846–1902): Hebrew poet and scholar. He was assistant state rabbi at Odessa 1873–80, thereafter residing at Leipzig. One of the first *Hoveve Zion*, M. was a regular contributor to *Ha-Shahar;* writing on biblical subjects in a flowery style and translating European classics (including Byron's *Hebrew Melodies*) into Hebrew. For 20 years, he was engaged in compiling his comprehensive standard Bible concordance *Hekhal ha-Kodesh* (1896). His other works included a history of Russia, a history of Russian literature (in German), and a German-Russian dictionary. In his latter years, he was mentally unbalanced.

MANDELSTAMM: (1) *BENJAMIN M.* (c. 1805–1886): Russian Hebrew author. He was a protagonist of Haskalah and religious reform, in the interest of which he proposed to prohibit the printing of the Talmud for a number of years. His writings include travelogues and parables. (2) *LEON M.* (1809–1889): Russian Hebraist; brother of (1). He was the first Jew to receive a university degree in Russia, graduating in St. Petersburg in 1844. He administered Jewish education in Russia 1845–57, later living in Germany where he engaged in unsuccessful business ventures and published most of his works. His writings included a Russian translation of the Bible and notes on the German translation of the Bible (24 vols. 1852). (3) *MAX EMANUEL M.* (1839–1912): Russian ophthalmologist and Zionist; nephew of (1) and (2). From 1868–80, he lectured in ophthalmology at Kiev Univ. A member of the *Hoveve Zion,* he was one of the Russian Zionist leaders who assisted Herzl. Supporting the Uganda scheme, he left the Zionist movement in 1903 to create, with Zangwill, the Jewish Territorial Organization.

MANÉ KATZ see **KATZ, MANÉ**

*MANETHO** (fl. 3rd cent. BCE): Egyptian priest and author. His history of Egypt included the story of the expulsion of the lepers from Egypt at Divine behest. It is uncertain whether the identification of the lepers with the Israelites stemmed from M. or from Alexandrian anti-Semites.

MANGER, ITZIK (1901–1969): Yiddish poet. After a childhood in Germany, he learned Yiddish at the age of fourteen in his native Rumania. Soon he displayed his poetic talent in ballads and plays which revealed the influence of German lyricists and of the *badchonim* such as Eliakum Zunser. His satiric *Khumesh-Lieder* and *Megilla-Lieder* are most original. A bohemian by temperament, he lived in London during and after World War II and moved to the US in 1951 and later to Israel.

MANIN, DANIEL (1804–1857): Italian patriot, descended from the Jewish family of Medina. Jews played a prominent part in the revolutionary Venetian republic of 1848–9 which he headed.

MANITOBA: Canadian Province. Canada's first permanent Jewish settler, Ferdinande Jacobs, coming from England, entered the employ of Hudson's Bay Company as fur trader in 1732 and worked in this region. WINNIPEG attracted the first permanent settlers. Communal religious services were held there from 1879. A large immigrant group fleeing the Czarist pogroms arrived in the early 1880's, and this city has continued to attract the overwhelming majority of M.'s Jews. The Jewish pop. of M. in 1970 was c. 20,000.

MANKEWICZ: (1) *HERMAN JACOB M.* (1897–1953): US writer. He was a journalist and critic who wrote film scenarios and later produced pictures. His best-known screen-play was *Citizen Kane.* (2) *JOSEPH LEO M.* (1909–): US film director; brother of (1). He also began as a writer, but later became producer.

MANKOWITZ, WOLF (1929–): English writer. His novels, plays, and films (*A Kid for Two Farthings, The Bespoke Overcoat*) — many with an E London Jewish background — have achieved wide popularity.

MANN, JACOB (1888–1940): Historian. Born in Galicia, he completed his studies in London, afterward teaching history at the Hebrew Union College, Cincinnati. He exhaustively utilized *genizah* material in a series of monographs on the history and literature of the Gaonic Period, notably *The Jews of Palestine and Egypt under the Fatimids; Texts and Studies in Jewish History and Literature;* and *The Bible as Read and Preached in the Old Synagogue.*

MANNA: Food eaten by the Israelites in the desert (Exod. 16:4–35). It was found on the ground every morning except the Sabbath (a double portion was collected on Fridays), and as much as could be eaten was collected by the people. In form it was thin and rough, white in color, and tasted like honey-cake. As a memorial, a jar of m. was placed permanently before the Sanctuary. M. was formerly believed to be a shallow-rooted plant carried by storms: modern botanists have discovered sugary secretions on the *tamarix mammifera* caused by insects. According to the aggadah, m. existed from the first Sabbath eve of creation (*Avot* 5:9).

MANNE, MORDECAI TZEVI (1859–1886): Lithuanian Hebrew poet and painter. One of the first poets of the national renascence, his poetry tended to the didactical though he composed many moving lyrics. M. also wrote essays on aspects of esthetics.

MANNES, DAVID (1866–1959): US musicologist. He established his career as a concert violinist but concentrated on musical education, founding the Mannes School of Music in New York and pioneering in musical education for negroes. His son Leopold M. (1899–1964), a distinguished pianist, was responsible (with Leopold Godowsky Jr.) for developing the Kodachrome process of color photography.

MANNHEIM: W German city. Jewish families settled there in the mid-17th cent. They were subordinate to the jurisdiction of the Worms community until 1660 when the count palatine granted them a charter and permission to open a synagogue. They prospered economically and were protected from molestation. In the mid-18th cent., under the early influence of Emancipation, they were obliged to keep their records in German. A Jewish elementary school was opened in 1816. The Jews were prominent in the grain and tobacco trade and in banking. The community of 6,400 (1933) dwindled under the Nazis. On Oct. 22, 1940, 2,000 were expelled to a camp in France and the rest were subsequently liquidated. After World War II, a community was refounded and numbered 386 in 1970.

MANNHEIM, KARL (1893–1947): Sociologist. A native of Hungary, he was professor of sociology at Frankfort-on-Main 1930–3, thereafter settling in England and lecturing at London Univ. His chief works dealt with education toward democratic society and the relationship of modes of thought to forms of life.

MANNHEIMER, ISAAC NOAH (1793–1865): Reform rabbi. Of Danish birth, he officiated from 1824 in Vienna where he introduced moderate liturgical changes (confirmation, omission of prayers for the restoration of the sacrificial system). M. was a member of the Austrian parliament and fought for Jewish rights.

MANTINO, JACOB (1490–1549): Physician and translator. Born in Spain, he practised medicine in Italy, especially at Venice, his clientele including several patricians and ambassadors who secured him special privileges. Pope Clement VII had him appointed nominal lecturer at Bologna Univ., and he taught also at Rome while physician to Pope Paul III. He translated into Latin several scientific and philosophical texts, especially of Averroes, and his opinion on biblical interpretation was consulted at the time of the "divorce" of Henry VIII of England. A rationalist, he sternly opposed the pretensions of Solomon Molcho.

MANTUA: City in N Italy, formerly capital of a duchy. There must have been a small Jewish settlement in M. in 1145 when Abraham Ibn Ezra resided there. The record of the organized community begins, however, only in 1386 when groups of loan-bankers — Italian and German — were authorized to operate in M. During the Renaissance Period, the community was among the most flourishing in Italy, with a remarkable intellectual life, as indicated by a printing press from 1476, the Jewish theater group headed by Leone de' Sommi performing at court, musicians of whom the most illustrious was Salomone de' Rossi, and enlightened scholars such as Azariah dei Rossi. The introduction of the ghetto system into M. through papal pressure in 1612 and the temporary German occupation of 1630 ended the golden age. It remained, nevertheless, one of the most important Jewish communities in Italy with a population of c. 2,000 until the 19th cent., when its numbers began to dwindle, almost disappearing during the German military occupation and persecution in 1943–5. About 150 Jews were living there in 1970.

MANUAL OF DISCIPLINE see **DISCIPLINE SCROLL**

MANUFACTURERS' ASSOCIATION OF ISRAEL: Israel organization founded in 1923 to represent the interests of industrialists. It endeavors to improve production and efficiency, protects home industries, encourages investment, and organizes exhibitions by local manufacturers in Israel and elsewhere. The M. A. represents industrialists in negotiations with labor and other bodies on wage problems, etc. It publishes a monthly journal in Hebrew and English *(Israel Export Journal)*. The headquarters of the organization are in Tel Aviv and it is represented in the US by the American-Israel Chamber of Commerce and Industry.

MANUSCRIPTS: Until recently, the earliest known ms in Hebrew was the NASH PAPYRUS, a fragment containing the *Shema* and Ten Commandments, probably dating from the 1st cent BCE. The discovery of the DEAD SEA SCROLLS has now, however, provided a mass of biblical, exegetical, and sectarian mss also believed to date from the 1st cent. BCE. The Cairo GENIZAH mss, largely housed at Cambridge, cover in bulk the period from the 8th cent. onward. The oldest complete Hebrew Bible codex, the Codex Petropolitanus, is of the 10th cent. From the 12th cent. onward, Hebrew mss of European origin (particularly from Spain, France, and Germany) have survived in great number. Unlike the oriental mss of the earlier Middle Ages, these are generally on parchment or velum and sometimes of great beauty. Illuminated mss are preserved only from the 13th cent., but they were probably produced earlier. Hebrew mss of the Middle Ages cover every type of literature, but those of the Talmud are scarce owing to its frequent burnings, particularly in the 13th cent. The heyday of the Hebrew ms was reached in the 15th cent. With the advent of Hebrew PRINTING in 1475, the importance of the ms passed, although the earliest printed books slavishly imitated the ms, and for some purposes (e.g. for the Scroll of the Law or Scroll of Esther) printing was not permitted. The great collectors of Hebrew mss include David OPPENHEIM, G. B. De' Rossi, E. N. ADLER, D. KAUFMANN, and D. S. SASSOON. The most important public collections of Hebrew mss are in Oxford, Cambridge, and the British Museum; the Bibliothèque Nationale, Paris; the Vatican and Parma Libraries in Italy; and the library of the Jewish Theological Seminary of America, New York.

MAOT ḤITTIM (Heb. "wheat money"): Collections made before Passover to assure a supply of flour for unleavened bread for the poor. From talmudic days, this was considered a stringent compulsory community tax and even those exempt from other taxes had to participate. In modern times, the term has acquired the broader significance of providing all the holiday needs of the poor at Passover.

MAOZ TZUR (Heb. "Fortress rock"): Song sung by Ashkenazi Jews after lighting the candles on Ḥanukkah. It was composed by Mordecai, an otherwise unknown 13th cent. liturgical poet. The familiar setting is influenced by a German folksong or church melody.

MAPAI (initials of Heb. *miphleget poale eretz yisrael* "Israel Workers' Party"): Israel labor party. In 1930, HA-POEL HA-TZAIR united with AḤDUT HA-AVODAH to form *M*. The foundation platform said *inter alia:* "The Palestine Workers' Party *(M.)* recognizes that the Palestine Labor Movement is united by the historic aim of devotion to the rebirth of the Jewish nation in Palestine as a free laboring people, rooted in all branches of the agricultural and industrial

Illuminated page from the Farhi Bible, a manuscript of the 14th century (Sassoon Collection, Letchworth, England).

economy and independently developing its Hebrew culture; by membership in the working class of the world in its struggle for the abolition of class oppression; by the aspiration to transfer natural wealth and the means of production to the control of all workers and to build a society based on labor, equality, and liberty." In the Diaspora, the World Confederation of *Poale Zion* merged in 1931 with the TZEIRE ZION *(Iḥud Olami)* and *M.* entered the Second International. Its influence was originally preponderant in the kibbutz organization of HA-KIBBUTZ HA-MEUḤAD and subsequently, both in the ḤEVER HA-KEVUTZOT and the Moshav movements. In 1935, it became the strongest party in the Zionist Organization, a position it has since retained. In the elections to the first Knesset (1949) it polled 35.82% of the votes (46 members of the Knesset out of 120), in 1951, 37% (45 members), in 1955, 30% (40 members), in 1959, 38% (48 members); in 1961, 33.7% (42 members), and in 1965 together with *Aḥdut Avodah*) 36.7% (45 members). In 1965, the party split and the dissidents led by David BEN GURION founded the RAFI party. In 1968 *M.* merged with *Aḥdut Avodah* and *Rafi* to form the ISRAEL LABOR PARTY. Throughout the entire period of statehood, *M*. has been the largest single party and the dominant factor in successive government coalitions. In 1944, the leftist *Siyah Bet* ("Group B") split from *M.*, and in 1946, entered MAPAM. The *M*. minority (40%) of *Ha-Kibbutz ha-Meuḥad* merged with *Ḥever ha-Kevutzot* to form IḤUD HA-KEVUTZOT VEHA-KIBBUTZIM. *M*. is the largest group in the HISTADRUT.

MAPAM (Initials of Heb. *miphleget poalim meuḥedet* i.e., "United Workers' Party"): Israel socialist party formed in 1948 by the fusion of HA-SHOMER HA-TZAIR and AḤDUT HA-AVODAH — Left POALE ZION. It stands left of MAPAI, stressing the Marxist dogma, the importance of class-conflict, and originally demanding an alliance with the Soviet bloc. It advocates a more generous policy in respect of the Israel Arab minority and presses for greater emphasis on pioneering. *Aḥdut ha-Avodah — Poale Zion* seceded in 1954, partly because of *Ha-Shomer ha-Tzair's* insistence on voting as a bloc, partly as a result of the Soviet bloc's attack on Zionism. Later, as a result of *M.'s* increasing inability to accept the Soviet line on Zionism, a small group under Mosheh SNEH broke away and eventually joined MAKI. It polled 64,018 votes for the First Knesset in 1949 (19 members), 86,095 votes for the Second Knesset (15 members) in 1951, and — after the split — 62,401 votes for the Third Knesset (9 members) in 1955, 69,468 for the Fourth (9 members) in 1959, 75,654 for the Fifth (9 members) in 1961, and 79,985 for the Sixth (8 members) in 1965. Representatives sat in the provisional government 1948–9, and in coalition governments 1955–61 and from 1965. From 1969, it aligned with the ISRAEL LABOR PARTY, and had 8 seats in the Seventh Knesset.

MAPHTIR (Heb.; more fully *maphtir ba-navi*): The person who reads the HAPHTARAH; also applied colloquially to the *haphtarah* itself.

MAPPAH (Heb. "cloth"): (1) The binder round a Scroll of the Law. (2) The decorated desk-cover in a synagogue. (3) The commentary on the *Shulḥan Arukh* by Moses ISSERLES.

MAPPIK: Dot inside a *He* at the end of a word showing that the letter is sounded as *h*.

MAPU, ABRAHAM (1808–1867): Hebrew novelist. Born in Lithuania, he received a traditional education, became a tutor, and studied European languages. From 1844, he lived in his native Slobodka. His historical romance *Ahavat Tziyyon* ("Love of Zion," 1853), set in the period of Hezekiah, was the first Hebrew novel and had a great influence. His realistic romance *Ayit Tzavua* ("The Hypocrite") satirized the contemporary Lithuanian Jewish community. His other novels were *Ashmat Shomron* ("The Guilt of Samaria"), set in the period of Ahaz, and *Ḥozeh Ḥezyonot* ("Seer of Visions"), about the period of Shabbetai Tzevi. M. also wrote textbooks. His historical novels vividly recaptured the Biblical Period

while reflecting the aspiration of Hebrew Haskalah to a tranquil life in natural surroundings and to political and intellectual freedom. M. was one of the first modern Hebrew writers to depict love for nature and love between man and woman.

MAR (Aram. "master"): Title given to some Babylonian amoraim and especially to EXILARCHS; used in modern Hebrew as "Mr.".

MAR SAMUEL see **SAMUEL**

MAR ZUTRA see **ZUTRA**

MARBITZ TORAH see **RABBI**

MARBURG: (1) Former Austrian city, now Maribor in Yugoslavia. Individual Jews lived there from the 13th cent., and by the 14th cent. the autonomous community occupied a special quarter. Although suffering from persecutions and plundering (1310, 1371, 1397), the Jews flourished economically (wine-trading, viticulture, agriculture, horse-dealing, money-lending), while the rabbis of M. included several outstanding figures. On the instigation of the burghers, the Jews were expelled in 1496. A few Jews have lived there since the late 19th cent. (2) M. in Hesse Nassau had a Jewish community from the 14th cent. expelled c. 1450, and later renewed.

MARCEAU, MARCEL (1923–): French mime. Born in Strasbourg, he made his debut in 1947 and achieved international recognition as the outstanding mime of his time. He created the character Bip and appeared in one-man performances throughout the world.

Colonel David Marcus.

MARCUS, DAVID (1902–1948): US soldier. A graduate of West Point, he studied law and in 1931, was appointed assistant US attorney in the southern district of New York. He served with distinction in World War II. In 1948, he went to Palestine as military adviser to the *Haganah* and was killed in action in the Jerusalem area during the Israel War of Independence. He was subject of the novel and film *Cast A Giant Shadow*.

MARCUS, JACOB RADER (1896–): US historian and rabbi. Since 1920 he has taught at the Hebrew Union College, Cincinnati. In 1946, he became professor of Jewish history. He established the AMERICAN JEWISH ARCHIVES in 1947. After early writings dealing with German Jewry, he concentrated on American Jewish history, publishing *Early American Jewry* (2 vols.) and *Memoirs of American Jews* (3 vols.).

MARCUS, RALPH (1900–1956): US scholar. He taught hellenistic culture at Chicago from 1943 (professor, 1950) and published numerous monographs dealing with hellenistic Jewish history and literature. M. edited volumes of JOSEPHUS and PHILO for the Loeb Classics.

MARCUS, SIEGRIED (1831–1898): German inventor; lived in Austria. A versatile engineer, he invented a number of electrical, telegraphic, and gas devices. In 1864, he built a horseless carriage and in 1875, the first gasoline-driven vehicle ignited by a magneto, embodying the essentials of the automobile.

MARCUSE, HERBERT (1898–): Philosopher. He taught in Germany and from 1934 in the US (at Brandeis Univ. 1954–65, and Univ. of California, San Diego, from 1965). His Marxist humanism made him popular in New Left circles.

MARCZALI (MORGENSTERN), HENRIK (1856–1940): Hungarian historian. Professor at Budapest from 1895, he wrote major works on the history of Hungary.

MARDUK see **MERODACH**

MARETZEK, MAX (1821–1897): Conductor. He conducted orchestras in several European cities but established his major reputation as an opera impresario in New York where he directed the Academy of Music.

MARGOLIN, ELIEZER (1875–1944): Soldier. Of Russian birth, he lived in Palestine 1893–8, and then emigrated to Australia. In World War I, as lt.-col. he commanded the 39th Jewish battalion in Palestine. After the battalion was disbanded, he commanded a Jewish volunteer unit defending Tel Aviv from Arab attacks in 1921, for which he lost his command.

MARGOLIOUTH: English family of orientalists, many of whom were converted. (1) *DAVID SAMUEL M.* (1858–1940): English orientalist; professor of Arabic at Oxford from 1889. He wrote extensively on oriental subjects. M. argued that the Hebrew text of *Ben Sira* was a retranslation from Persian and the Elephantine Papyri were modern forgeries. (2) *GEORGE M.* (1853–1924): Bibliographer. He was curator of Hebrew books in the British Museum, and his main work is a monumental catalogue of its ms collections.

MARGOLIS, MAX LEOPOLD (1866–1932) Scholar. Born in Lithuania, he studied in the US and taught Hebrew and Bible at the Hebrew Union College and Dropsie College. He wrote commentaries to Micah and Zephaniah and a work on Bible versions, supervised the translation of the Bible published by the Jewish Publication Society of America, and collaborated with Alexander Marx in *The History of the Jewish People*. Of his projected critical edition of the Septuagint, only the Book of Joshua was completed.

MARGOSHES, SAMUEL (1887–1968): Yiddish journalist. Born in Galicia, he went to the US in 1905. As columnist (since 1923) and editor of the Yiddish daily *Tog* (1924–44) he vigorously supported Zionism in the US. M. was prominent in the American Jewish Congress and Zionist activities.

MARGULIES, SAMUEL HIRSCH (Tzevi; 1858–1922): Italian rabbi. Born in Galicia, he studied and officiated in Germany. In 1890, he was appointed rabbi of Florence and was responsible for a revival of Jewish life throughout Italy. He renewed the Collegio Rabbinico Italiano in 1899, founded the Pro-Falasha Committee, and interested the king of Italy in Zionism.

MARḤESHVAN (also known as *Ḥeshvan*): Second month of the Jewish religious year and eighth of the civil one. It can have either 29 or 30 days, an extra day being occasionally added in order to prevent the Day of Atonement of the following year from falling on a Friday or Sunday.

MARI: Ancient Mesopotamian city. Excavations in 1933–8 revealed a palace of the 18th cent. BCE containing a rich Akkadian library which throws valuable light on the events and conditions of life depicted in Genesis.

MARIA HEBRAEA: Allegedly an alchemist in Egypt in the 1st cent. CE. She is credited with the authorship of three important alchemist treatises and with the invention of a smelting oven, of the *Bain-Marie* (for heating substances by means of hot water) which was named after her, and of hydrochloric acid.

MARIAMNE (or Mariamme; d. 29 BCE): Hasmonean princess; second wife of HEROD. The daughter of Alexander son of Aristobulus II, she was wedded to Herod at an early age and bore him three sons and two daughters. M. led a wretched married life, loathed by Herod's Idumean family whom she regarded as upstarts, and hating her husband who had murdered her kinsfolk. Herod's sister Salome ceaselessly incited the king against her and eventually succeeded in convincing him that she was an adulteress. For this, M. was condemned and executed.

MARIAMNE II (fl. late 1st cent. BCE): Wife of HEROD. She was the daughter of Simon, son of Boethus, whom Herod had appointed high priest. M., who was renowned for her beauty, bore one son. When Herod discovered that she had been involved in Antipater's plotting, he divorced her and expunged her son's name from his will.

MARINOFF, JACOB (1869–1964): Yiddish writer. A native of Russia, he settled in the US in 1892. In 1909, he established in New York *Der Groisser Kundes,* a humorous weekly which ceased publication in 1927.

MARIX, ADOLPH (1848–1919): US naval figure. Born in Germany, he entered the US navy in 1868. In 1893, he became captain of the battleship *Maine.* As the leading authority on maritime law, he was judge-advocate at the investigation of the *Maine* disaster, his findings precipitating the Spanish-American War. M. was the first Jew ever to be appointed rear-admiral in the US navy (1908). He took an active interest in Jewish life.

MARKENS, ISAAC (1848–1928): US journalist. In the 1880's, he published a series of articles on "Hebrews in America" which was subsequently revised and republished in book form, this being one of the earliest efforts in American Jewish historiography. His other works include *Abraham Lincoln and the Jews.*

MARKISH, PERETZ (1895–1952): Yiddish novelist and poet. Born in Volhynia, he lived in Warsaw 1921–8 and was a leader of modernist Yiddish poetry and editor of Yiddish literary journals. In 1928, he settled in the USSR where he was a central figure in Yiddish literature. He was executed in the anti-Yiddish purge during the last years of Stalin. His fertile output is daring in form and communist in spirit. His poetry includes the epic *War* invoked by the Jewish catastrophe of World War II while his two outstanding novels are *Generations Come and Go* and *One by One.* M. also wrote plays.

MARKON, ISAAC DOV BER (1875–1949): Scholar. Born in Russia, he taught Semitics at the Universities of St. Petersburg and Minsk before becoming librarian of the Hamburg community in 1926. He spent his last years in England. M.'s writings dealt especially with Karaite history and literature and associated subjects.

MARKOVA, DAME ALICIA (Lilian Alicia Marks; 1910–): English ballerina. She started with the Diaghilev ballet in 1925, joined the Vic-Wells company in 1932, and in 1935, founded her own company together with Anton Dolin.

MARKS, DAVID WOOLF (1811–1909): English religious reformer. Minister of the London Reform synagogue from its foundation for nearly seventy years,

he greatly influenced the development of Reform Judaism in England.

MARKS, SAMUEL (1850–1920): S African industrialist. Born in Lithuania, he migrated first to England and in 1868, to S Africa. There he attained great wealth, being responsible for the introduction of many industries into the Transvaal. He was intimate with President Kruger. The reports of his outstanding commercial success did much to stimulate Lithuanian emigration to S Africa.

MARKS, SIMON, BARON (1888–1964): British Zionist leader. Together with his brother-in-law, Israel SIEFF, he developed the Marks and Spencer Ltd. chain-stores. A close friend of Chaim Weizmann, he was active in British Zionism and contributed liberally to Zionist and other causes.

MARMOREK: (1) *ALEXANDER M.* (1865–1923). Bacteriologist. A native of Galicia, he worked at the Pasteur Institute, Paris, where he discovered a serum for treating scarlet fever and also pursued anti-tubercular research. A friend of HERZL. M. was a leader of French Zionism, founding the French Zionist journal *L'Echo Sioniste.* (2) *OSCAR M.* (1863–1909): Architect; brother of (1). He designed many important buildings in Austria. One of Herzl's principal lieutenants, he was member of the commission that investigated settlement possibilities at EL ARISH. He committed suicide on his mother's grave.

MARMORSTEIN, ARTHUR (1882–1946): Scholar. He was rabbi in Austro-Hungary until 1912, after which he lectured in Bible and Talmud at Jews' College, London. M. was a prolific writer on history, halakhah, and folklore, with special interest in Jewish sectarianism and gnosticism.

MAROR: Bitter herb eaten in the SEDER Service. (See HAGGADAH).

*****MARR, WILHELM** (fl. 19th cent.): German anti-Jewish writer who in 1879 coined the word "Anti-Semite." The statement that he was himself a Jew has been disproved.

MARRANOS (Sp. "swine"; in Heb. *anusim,* i.e., "coerced"): Term applied in Spain and Portugal to the descendants of baptized Jews suspected of secret adherence to Judaism. This class became numerous in Spain after the 1391 massacres and the Dominican campaign led by Vicente Ferrer at the beginning of the 15th cent. and was henceforth very prominent socially, economically, and politically. To cope with them, the INQUISITION was introduced into Spain in 1480 and began a pitiless campaign of repression, which continued unremittingly after the expulsion of the Jews from the country in 1492. The Forced Conversion in Portugal in 1497, which converted almost the whole body of Portuguese Jewry into titular but insincere Christians, augmented the number of M.; the Inquisition was introduced there in 1540, and Portuguese immigrants formed a principal object of persecution in Spain down to the close of the 18th cent. Meanwhile, in spite of difficulties and prohibitions, fugitive M. escaped overseas, to Italy, N Africa, and especially Turkey, where they joined the existing communities; outstanding figures were Gracia MENDES, Joseph NASI, and Solomon IBN YAISH. In Italy, the main Marrano centers were Ancona, Ferrara, Venice, and Leghorn. A secret Marrano colony established itself in Antwerp in the 16th cent. when the city was under Spanish rule, but after Holland achieved her independence, the center of immigration shifted to Amsterdam, where from c. 1600 all disguise was thrown off; there were subsidiary communities in The Hague, Rotterdam, etc. In somewhat similar circumstances, communities were organized in Hamburg, Bordeaux, and Bayonne. In England, fugitive M. settled in the reign of Henry VIII and seem to have maintained some sort of organized religious life in secret; many left England when Catholicism temporarily triumphed under Mary (1553) but they reappeared under Elizabeth. An internal quarrel led to their banishment in 1609, but a fresh settlement began shortly thereafter. Manasseh ben Israel's mission to England was in great part intended to find a place of refuge for Marrano fugitives from the Inquisition. In the New World, meanwhile, M. had penetrated into all Spanish and Portuguese colonies, but were followed by the Inquisition and savagely persecuted. With the occupation of Brazil by the Dutch in the first half of the 17th cent., open communities were founded there but were uprooted by the Portuguese reconquest; the refugees, recruited before long from the Old World, set up the earliest Jewish communities in the Dutch and English possessions in the W Indies and N America (e.g. at New York 1654; Newport, R. I. 1658). The Marrano communities played a very important part in international commerce, and began by their very numerous publications in Spanish and Portuguese the tradition of a vernacular literature among European Jews. They comprised great numbers of men of distinction in every intellectual field (e.g. SPINOZA, Isaac PEREYRE). Down to the late 19th cent., they continued to be augmented by immigrants from Spain and Portugal brought up in the secret Marrano tradition. This, however, decayed, and it was long imagined that it had died out, but in 1920, it was discovered that there was still in N Portugal a great number of "New Christians" still conscious of their Jewish descent and maintaining their crypto-Jewish traditions, now hardly recognizable. Under the leadership of Capt. A. C. de Barros Basto, a movement was begun to bring them into touch with Jewish tradition, and a synagogue was established for them at Oporto. The descendants of the former secret Jews of Majorca, locally known as CHUETAS, are still a recognizable and despised class, though it is questionable whether most have retained

any Jewish tradition. Local parallels to the Marranos may be found in the Moslem world in Persia (the JEDID EL-ISLAM), etc.

MARRIAGE: Judaism makes obligatory the requirement to reproduce and continue the human race (see SEX). The first commandment in the Bible is "be fruitful and multiply" (Gen. 1:22). Men are therefore obligated to marry in order to fulfill this commandment. There are, however, certain prohibited relationships. A *Cohen* (priest), for example, may not marry a divorcee. In certain cases, the marriage is not recognized *ab initio,* e.g. marriage with a mother, sister, daughter, non-Jewess, or wife of another man. According to Jewish practice since early times there are two stages in the marriage ceremony: betrothal and m. Betrothal (*erusin* or *kiddushin*) is the ceremony whereby a woman becomes the wife of the betrother so that she may be married to no one else (unless her husband die or divorce her). This ceremony must take place before witnesses and legally may be performed in one of three ways: (1) By money: i.e., the betrother gives the woman a symbolic sum or its equivalent as a token of betrothal. (2) By deed: i.e., the betrother gives the woman a document confirming the betrothal in writing. (3) By intercourse: the betrother enters a private chamber with the woman, informing witnesses beforehand that the intercourse which will take place is to be considered an act of betrothal. Early teachers disapproved of this last manner of betrothal, and it is not found as a Jewish practice. The second manner of betrothal is very rare nowadays. The most common manner today, as always, is the first-mentioned. Betrothal is performed by the man, but has no validity unless the woman gives her consent. The second stage of the m. ceremony is *nissuim,* which is the act of availing oneself of the rights obtained in the act of betrothal, i.e., bringing the woman into the home in order to live a marital life with her. The rabbis ordered a series of blessings to be recited both on *erusin* and *nissuin.* In early times, long periods often intervened between *erusin* and *nissuin;* later it became customary for *nissuin* to follow the betrothal ceremony immediately. The accepted ceremony of marriage — including both *erusin* and *nissuin* — is as follows: the bride and groom stand under a canopy *(ḥuppah).* Ten people are normally required to be present. One of these, usually a rabbi, recites the blessings of *erusin.* The groom places a gold ring without a stone upon the finger of the bride saying as he does so "I betroth you (literally: you are hereby sanctified into me) with this ring in accordance with the religion of Moses and Israel." The KETUBBAH is then read, generally by the rabbi. Finally, the "seven benedictions" of *nissuin* are recited. In some communities, the custom prevails of having the bride walk round the groom seven times before the ceremony actually begins. It is also customary to recite the blessings of *erusin* and *nissuin* over a cup of wine, from which both bride and groom drink, as well as for the groom to break a glass, traditionally a sign of mourning over the destruction of the Temple. The bride and groom usually fast until after the ceremony and immediately after the ceremony go into a separate room where they eat together. It was formerly customary (and is still observed by the Orthodox) to prepare a marriage feast for each day of the following week (the "seven days of feasting") during which the "seven benedictions" are repeated at table. Special features were added to the service when the bridegroom attended synagogue on the Sabbath following his m.

MARSEILLES: French port. Its Jewish community is ancient (in 576, it received refugees expelled from Clermont) and contributed to the town's prosperity, receiving special privileges during the Medieval Period. Despite being subject to heavy taxes and discriminatory measures from the 13th cent. on, Jews were not molested and were recognized as an autonomous community within their own quarters *(carrière)*, evolving an elaborate communal organization. Their connections with the Middle East enabled them to play a significant role in the town's commerce. M. became a center of Hebrew studies from the 12th cent., partly due to its relations with Spain and S Italy, and many distinguished scholars lived there. In 1481, however, it passed under the rule of the French king and the Jews were excluded by 1501. They began to return in the 18th cent., and their settlement was officially countenanced by the French revolutionary regime. In the 20th cent., more Jews from the Balkans and N Africa settled there, and the population was artificially swollen during the period of the Vichy government. In the 1950's and early 1960's M. became one of the main centers of settlement for Jews from N. Africa. Jewish pop. (1974): 70,000.

MARSHAK, SAMUEL (1887–1964): Russian author and translator. Four times winner of a Stalin Prize, M. was a noted author of children's literature, especially verse. As a translator, he specialized in renderings from the English, notably of Shakespeare and Burns.

MARSHALIK (Yidd. from Ger. *marschal* = "royal chamberlain"): Jester at E European weddings, who sang appropriate humorous songs and announced the gifts in verse.

MARSHALL: (1) *JAMES M.* (1896–): Lawyer; son of (2). He was president of the New York City Board of Education 1928–42, and engaged in many communal activities. (2) *LOUIS M.* (1856–1929): US jurist and communal leader, also eminent as an appellate lawyer and defender of civil liberties. A founder (1906) and president (1912–29) of the American Jewish Committee, he played a leading part in its successful campaign to obtain the abrogation of the US–Russian commercial treaty of 1832. M. was a member of the *Comité des Délégations Juives* at the

Louis Marshall.

Versailles Peace Conference and helped to secure the inclusion of minority-rights clauses in the treaties establishing the new states of Central and E Europe. Although a Reform Jew, he was chairman of the board of the Conservative Jewish Theological Seminary. It was to M. that Henry Ford in 1927 directed his apology for the *Dearborn Independent's* notorious articles on "The International Jew." He was not a Zionist but welcomed the Balfour Declaration and supported Palestine as a Jewish spiritual center and as a refuge. Shortly before his death, M. concluded an agreement with Chaim Weizmann for the participation of non-Zionists in the Jewish Agency.

MARSHALL, DAVID SAUL (1908–): Singapore statesman. A lawyer, he led the Labor Front Party in the 1955 elections and served as chief minister and minister of commerce 1955–6.

*MARTI, KARL (1855–1925): Swiss Bible scholar. He wrote some 120 books and studies, mostly on biblical subjects, and from 1907, edited the *Zeitschrift für die Alttestamentliche Wissenschaft*. In cooperation with other scholars, he edited a scientific commentary on the Bible.

*MARTINEZ, FERRAND (fl. 14th cent.): Archdeacon of Ecija (Spain). From 1478, he frenziedly agitated against alleged illegally constructed synagogues in the diocese of Seville. This resulted in outbreaks against the Jews there on Mar. 15 and June 4, 1391, which spread devastatingly throughout Spain.

*MARTINI (MARTI), RAIMUN(D) (c. 1225–1284): Spanish Hebraist. A Dominican, he was present at the Disputation of Barcelona in 1263. In 1278, he composed the anti-Jewish *Pugio Fidei* ("Dagger of Faith"), intended, like the Disputation, to demonstrate the truth of Christianity from Jewish literature. The work contains excerpts from midrashic and rabbinical writings which are important in some instances for establishing correct readings. Many of the passages are unknown from any other source, and scholars still dispute their authenticity.

MARTINIQUE: French W Indian island. Jewish refugees from Brazil, etc. settled there in the mid-17th cent. In 1671, the French minister Colbert established religious and economic liberty for them, but the BLACK CODE of 1685 extruded them. In the 18th cent., Jews from Bordeaux established themselves in M. and received legal protection, but no permanent community resulted.

MARTOV, JULIUS (1873–1923): Russian revolutionary; grandson of Alexander ZEDERBAUM. In 1900, he went to Switzerland where, with Lenin and Plekhanov, he edited the Social Democrat journal *Iskra*. In 1903, he broke with Lenin and headed the moderate Mensheviks. He returned to Russia after the 1917 February Revolution but in 1920, left for Berlin, where he edited the Menshevik journal. His works include a history of Russian social democracy.

MARTYRS: The protomartyrs of Judaism are the seven sons of Hannah, killed by Antiochus III during the Hasmonean revolt (see MACCABEES). Jews recall with especial veneration the TEN MARTYRS of the Bar Kochba period. In Judaism a martyr was termed "one who had died" for the Sanctification of the (Divine) Name, and it was customary to designate him as *kadosh*, i.e., holy. In the Middle Ages, regulations for those who died for their faith and even the benediction they were to recite were specified by the rabbis. Lists of m. are comprised in the German MEMORBUCHER, and in Sephardi communities there was a special form of memorial prayer (HASHKAVAH) for those m. burned by the Inquisition.

MARTYRS' FOREST: Project initiated in 1951 by the Jewish National Fund to commemorate the Jews who perished during the Nazi terror, by planting a memorial forest of six million trees in the Judean mountains. The Forest is divided into 18 sections, dedicated to 18 persecuted Jewries.

MARX BROTHERS: US comedy team starring in vaudeville and motion pictures. They consist of *LEONARD (CHICO) M.* (1891–1961); *ARTHUR (HARPO) M.* (1893–1964); and *JULIUS (GROUCHO) M.* (1895–): A fourth brother *HERBERT (ZEPPO) M.* (1901–), left the team in 1935.

MARX, ADOLF BERNHARD (1796–1866): German composer. He founded and edited the *Berliner Allegemeine Musikalishe Zeitung* (1824 ff.) and helped to found the *Sternsches Konservatorium* music-school. He wrote on musical theory.

MARX, ALEXANDER (1878–1954): Historian and bibliographer. Of German birth, he went to New York as a young man to teach at the Jewish Theological

Karl Marx.

Seminary of which he also became librarian. M. built up its library to its position as the world's greatest Jewish collection. His writings (including two volumes of collected essays) dealt mainly with details of history and bibliography and he collaborated with Max Margolis in a one-volume *History of the Jewish People*.

MARX, KARL HEINRICH (1818–1883): German social philosopher. His parents were Jewish, but they abandoned Judaism before his birth and had him baptized at the age of six. After failing to obtain a teaching position because of his radical views, he turned to journalism, editing the liberal Cologne daily *Rheinische Zeitung* 1842–3. In 1843, he moved to Paris where he struck up his life-long friendship with Friedrich Engels. He was expelled from France as a result of his attacks on the Prussian government and went to Brussels where he renounced his Prussian citizenship and became "stateless." M. cooperated with the "League of the Just" (later "of Communists") long before becoming a member in 1847. At its second Congress, held in London at the end of 1847, the League invited M. and Engels to elaborate a new program. This appeared in Feb. 1848 under the title of *The Communist Manifesto,* and rapidly became the classic work of Marxian socialism. *The Manifesto* is a testament of the economic interpretation of history, ending with the words "Workers of the World, unite!" After further wanderings, M. settled in London (1849) where he gathered material for his main work: *Das Kapital; Kritik der politischen Oekonomie* (Vol. I, 1867;

Masada, view from the air.

Vol. II, 1885; Vol. III, 1893). He had a profound and powerful mind, but his work is the more difficult to understand as his *magnum opus* remained unfinished, and certain aspects of his doctrine are only slightly sketched. His (and Engels') system — Marxism — is also known under the name of "economic" or "materialistic" determinism, "dialectical materialism" or "scientific" (as opposed to "utopian") socialism. The basic assumption of Marxism is that history is essentially the account of class struggles between the oppressing and the oppressed. He had no expert knowledge of any Jewish problems because he studied none of them. His attitude toward the Jews was characterized by antipathy and contempt, and he described Judaism and the Jews in terms similar to those used by many anti-semites. From 1848 on, M. envisaged the Jews chiefly as a financial reactionary group.

MARYLAND: US state. Because of a law requiring acknowledgement of Jesus, there were few Jews in M. until after the Revolutionary War. It was not until 1826 that a bill was passed permitting Jews to hold office. About the same time, Jews began holding regular services in a home in BALTIMORE. A congregation (lasting until 1904) was also formed in Fell's Point in 1838. M.'s Jewish population in 1973 was 226,610.

MASADA: Stronghold, 1 m. W of the Dead Sea, situated on a lofty, isolated rock: today in Israel territory. Originally probably fortified by ALEXANDER YANNAI rather than by Jonathan the Hasmonean as thought, it served as a refuge for Herod's family in 40 BCE when it was unsuccessfully besieged by Antigonus Mattathias. Later, Herod built a palace there. The Roman garrison was annihilated by Eleazar ben Jair in 66 CE and M. was a Zealot fortress until 73 when the garrison of 960 under Eleazar committed suicide to avoid capture by the Romans. In later centuries, it was the site of a Roman post, a Byzantine chapel, and a Crusader stronghold. A survey in 1955-6 uncovered the remains of Herod's palace as well as another palace dating from the Hasmonean Period. In 1963-5, extensive excavations were undertaken — under Yigael YADIN — and the finds included scroll fragments and the site of the earliest known synagogue.

MASEKHET (Heb,; Aram. *masekhta*, lit. "woven fabric"): A treatise of the Mishnah or Talmud.

MASHAL see **FABLE**

MASHGIAH (Heb. "supervisor"): Overseer appointed to supervise the observance of *kashrut* laws in the preparation of food.

MASHIAH see **MESSIAH**

MASHIV HA-RUAH U-MORID HA-GASHEM (Heb. "who causeth the wind to blow and the rain to descend"): Phrase added to the second of the EIGHTEEN BENEDICTIONS during the winter, from *Shemini Atzeret* (when it is first recited solemnly in the prayer for RAIN) until Passover. A corresponding phrase for summer-time (*morid ha-tal,* i.e., "who causeth the dew to fall"), current in Palestine, was not adopted in all rites.

MASKIL see **HASKALAH**

MASLIANSKY, TZEVI HIRSCH (1856—1943): Preacher. Of Russian birth, he was early stirred by *Hibbat Zion* which he advocated from synagogue pulpits throughout Russia. He was one of the finest preachers of his day. Leaving Russia in 1895, M. settled in New York, becoming preacher for the Educational Alliance and active in US Zionist and religious affairs. He wrote several volumes of sermons and an autobiography.

MASORAH (Heb.; literal meaning uncertain): The body of traditions regarding the correct spelling, writing and reading of the Hebrew Bible. The Dead Sea Scrolls and the Samaritan Hebrew Pentateuch display something of the diversity of mss of the Bible current in the Second Temple Period. To stem such changes in the sacred text, normative Judaism has it that the SOPHERIM already "counted every letter in the Pentateuch" and such lists have survived, showing, e.g. the number of times each letter occurs in the Bible. The text which the M. tries to preserve is one showing many irregular spellings and difficulties, and the main effort of the M. is to prevent these being regularized or replaced by easier readings. Indeed, R Akiva used such irregularities for deriving halakhah. The Masoretes (i.e., those who preserved the M. tradition) marked such forms by short notes at the side of the text (Marginal M.; Small M.); they also made lists of such forms (Final M.; Large M.). They noted some 1,300—1,400 cases in which a form was written one way but read another (KERI U-KHETIV), as well as cases where a possible reading was not to be used (*sevir*) and of letters written large or small, dotted letters (the dots apparently denote doubt as to the correct reading), inverted letters, etc. Furthermore the M. fixed places where a space was to be left or a new line to be started, the correct way of writing certain poetical passages, and so on. In the Tannaitic and Amoraic Periods, many words were still written differently from the text now used. A stricter M. was established in the Gaonic Period; this may be connected with the rise of the Karaites and the discussions they engendered about the meaning of the text. There was an Eastern (Babylonian) school, called *Medinha'e,* and a Western (Palestinian), or *Maarva'e.* The Palestinian school had at least two branches, called by the names of the families Ben Asher and Ben Naphtali at Tiberias. In the end, the Ben Asher school won the day, when Maimonides in his *Code* (1170—80) recommended as a model the ms written in 930 CE by Aaron Ben Asher, which was long kept at Aleppo and is now in Jerusalem. During the Gaonic Period the Masoretes also invented further methods for keeping the exact traditions of reciting the text: the marking of verse-divisions, the VOCALIZATION, and the ACCENTS, originally intended to show the logical divisions of the verse, but soon also employed as guides for CANTILLATION. Here, again, Jewry accepted in the end the Tiberian vocalization and accents in the way they were fixed by the Ben Asher school, only the Yemenites using the Babylonian vocalization, however in a form adapted to the Ben Asher tradition. The last features to be introduced were the division into chapters and the numbering of verses, both taken over from the Latin Bible of the Christians in the 16th cent. During the Middle Ages, both text and vocalization underwent further changes. The M. was not understood, and used merely to decorate the mss, being often written so as to form shapes of animals or plants. Numerous variant readings have been collected from medieval mss by such scholars as B. Kennicott, G.B. de' Rossi (both 18th cent.) and C.D. Ginsburg (1894; 1926). This diversity called forth a M. literature, most important amongst which are *Minhat Shai* by Jedidiah Solomon of Norsa (Norzi) and *Masoret ha-Masoret* by Elijah Levita. A fixation of the text was achieved by the Bible printed by D. Bomberg (a Christian) at Venice in 1524—5 and edited by Jacob ben Hayyim, from which were copied (more or less faithfully) all printed Bibles until the 3rd edition of the *Biblia Hebraica* by R. Kittel and P. Kahle, Stuttgart 1929—37. The vocalization and accents were further systematized by W. Heidenheim and S. Baer in the 19th cent. The work of the Masoretes produced the Masoretic Text ("M. T.") of the Bible, i.e., the current Hebrew text as distinct from that of the Dead Sea Scrolls, the Samaritans, or that from which the ancient versions were translated. The variations within this text described above are numerous but slight, and hardly ever affect the meaning of the Hebrew. There is also a M. for the Targum Onkelos.

MASSACHUSETTS: US state. Because of Puritan intolerance, Jews were rare in M. during the 17th cent. A number of Jewish merchants and ship-owners were in and out of BOSTON up to the Revolutionary War. After the Revolution, there was still only a handful of Jews in M., mostly in Boston, and no organized community. Jewish immigrants from Austria, Germany, and Poland in the 1840's laid the foundation for Jewish community life. The Jewish population grew rapidly with the advent of large numbers of immigrants from E Europe in the 2 decades prior to the outbreak of World War 1. Two-thirds of M.'s Jews lived in Greater Boston. There are also large communities in Lynn, WORCESTER, SPRINGFIELD, BROCKTON, FALL RIVER, Framingham and NEW BEDFORD. In 1973, there were 271,340 Jews in M.

MASSADA: Israel publishing house, founded by Meir and Berakhah PELI at Tel Aviv in 1931; it has developed into one of the largest publishers in the Jewish world. Its initial major undertaking was a six-volume general encyclopedia, and other publications have included a *Youth Encyclopedia,* the complete works of Yoseph Klausner, David Shimoni, Asher Barash, etc. and a number of works in English. Its books are printed, bound, and dispatched in its own plant and largely distributed through its own bookshops. M. was the initiator of the *Encyclopedia Hebraica* and has founded the Barash Prize, awarded annually to encourage young authors.

MASSARY, FRITZI (1882—1969): Austrian actress; wife of MAX PALLENBERG. She played the lead in many successful musical comedies. In 1939, she went to the US and returned to Vienna after World War II.

MASSORAH see **MASORAH**

MATATE (Heb. "Broom"): Tel Aviv theater 1928 —54. Its productions generally satirized facets of life in Israel.

MATHEMATICS, JEWS IN: Since the early Middle Ages, when a Jew is said to have introduced the Arabic numerals from India, the science of m. has been considerably enriched by Jews. In the 12th cent., the work of Spanish Jewish scholars such as Abraham Ibn Ezra, John of Seville (Avendeath), and Abraham bar Hiyya was of paramount importance and served as the basis for the transmission of Arabic m. to the Christian world. Later, contributions, eagerly taken up by the outside world, were made in Provence by Jacob ben Makhir, Levi ben Gershon, and Immanuel ben Jacob (Bonfils) of Tarascon. Simeon Ibn Motot (15th cent.) invented the pure equation of the 3rd and 4th degrees and solved the problem of asymptotes. Modern m. is indebted to Carl Gustav Jacob Jacobi for his researches on elliptic functions (based on *theta*-functions) and the calculus of variations. Double *theta*-functions and Abellian functions of two variables were the subject of Johann Georg Rosenhain's investigations. Leopold Kronecker wrote on elliptic functions as well as on quadratic forms and the theory of functions. His successor was Immanuel Lazarus Fuchs, famous for his work on linear differential equations. James Joseph Sylvester taught m. both in England (as Savilian professor of geometry at Oxford) and in America (Johns Hopkins Univ.). He was the first editor of the *American Journal of Mathematics* (1878) His main contribution was the development of the theory of invariants, initiated by Siegfried Heinrich Aronhold and Paul Gordan. To Georg Cantor m. owes the theory of the linear continuum and the

theory of sets which form the foundations of modern analysis and had a decisive influence upon the development of the philosophy of m. and metamathematics. Cantor's work was followed by Felix Hausdorff's (Paul Mongré) theory of dimensions, Felix Bernstein's principle of equivalence, and Avraham Adolf Fränkel's investigations of the axiomatics of the theory of sets. Jacob Rosanes and Eugen Netto made important contributions to the development of algebra. Adolf Hurwitz, Fredrich Shur, and Isai Schur, as well as Edmund G.H.Landau, enriched the theory of functions, the theory of integral equations, and modern mathematical analysis in general. Hermann Minkowski contributed to the mathematical formulation of Einstein's theory of relativity. In Italy, Luigi Cremona, Guido Ascoli, Salvatore Pincherle, Corrado Segre, Guido Castelnuovo, Vito Volterra, Tullio Levi-Civita, Federigo Enriques, Gino Loria, and in France, Georges-Henri Halpern, Paul Emile Appell, Jacques Hadamard, S. Mandelbrojdt, and Paul Lévy are mathematicians of international reputation. In the US, Solomon Lefschetz, Solomon Bochner, Richard von Mises, Otto Szasz, Norbert Wierer, Wallie Abraham Hurwitz, and in the USSR, Sergey Bernshteyn, P.S. Uryssohn, Landau, Frumkin, Vainrib, Spivak, Liubarsky, Rabinovitch, Lusternik, and Shnirelman have made important contributions.

MATMID (Heb. "one who persists"—Yidd. *masmid*): A "perpetual student," devoted to the Talmud. The poet Bialik gives a striking description of this devotion to talmudic learning in a poem of the same name.

MATTAN TORAH (Heb. "giving of the Law"): The giving of the Torah by God to Moses at Mt. Sinai. Traditionally the contents incorporated in the Pentateuch and the ORAL LAW.

MATTANIAH see **ZEDEKIAH**

MATTATHIAS (d. 167/6 BCE): Patriot; father of the HASMONEAN brothers. A priest and landowner of Modiin, his action in slaying the royal official sent to enforce worship of Zeus created a focus for the revolt against Antiochus Epiphanes. M. now took over the leadership of the revolt in the Judean hills, waging guerilla war on the Syrians. After his death, he was succeeded by his son Judah the Maccabee. Rabbinic tradition remembers him inaccurately as "Mattathias son of Johanan the Hasmonean high priest" but overlooks his children.

MATTATHIAS HA-YITZHARI (fl. c. 1414): Spanish scholar. He was one of the representatives of the Saragossa community at the Disputation of TORTOSA, which he mentions in his commentary on Ps. 119.

MATTUCK, ISRAEL ISIDOR (1883–1954): Rabbi. Educated in the US, he was in 1912, appointed to the Liberal Synagogue in London, leading Liberal Judaism in England over a period of 40 years. M. organized (1926) and was chairman of the World Union of Progressive Judaism.

MATYAH BEN ḤARASH (fl. mid-2nd cent.): Tanna. After the Hadrianic persecutions, he left Palestine for Rome where he founded the earliest known rabbinical academy in Europe. His piety and strong moral character form the subject of legends.

MATZAH see **PASSOVER**

MATZEVAH (Heb.): Monument; usually a gravestone.

MATZLIAḤ: Israel smallholders' settlement in the Judean plain, near Ramlah. It was founded in 1950 by Kairaites from Egypt. Pop. (1972): 662.

MAURITIUS: Island in the Indian Ocean. In 1940, 1,500 "illegal" Jewish immigrants to Palestine were deported to M. and kept there until 1945 under harsh conditions. There is no Jewish community in M.

MAUROIS, ANDRÉ (originally Emile Hertzog; 1885–1967): French author. He achieved his reputation with *Les Silences du Colonel Bramble* and his lively biographies of Shelley *(Ariel)*, Disraeli, etc. M. has also written histories of France, England, and the US. His autobiography appeared as *Call No Man Happy*. He was elected a member of the Académie Française in 1938.

MAUSOLEUM: The use of freestanding monuments as or in front of TOMBS became common in Palestine in the Hellenistic Period. The tomb of Queen Helena of Adiabene (1st cent. CE), N of Jerusalem, adorned by three pyramids was an impressive example. The monuments known as the tombs of Zechariah and Absalom (1st cent. BCE–1st cent. CE) are connected with nearby rock-cut tombs. A large square masonry structure stood in front of the tomb of Herod. Other instances have been uncovered at Bet Shearim (late Roman Period). Although m.'s were rare among Jews in the Middle Ages, the custom was reintroduced in the US in the 19th cent. and has increased in popularity.

MAUTHNER, FRITZ (1849–1923): Philosopher. Born in Bohemia, he settled in Berlin in 1876. He began by writing prose parodies and continued with novels which anticipated Berlin Naturalism. His *Beitrage zur Kritik der Sprache* questioned the value of language as a medium for final insight. His main scholarly works include *Wörterbuch der Philosophie* and *Der Atheismus und seine Geschichte im Abendlande.*

MAVDIL see **HA-MAVDIL**

MAY LAWS: Legislation enacted by the Russian government on May 3, 1882, prohibiting Jews from living or acquiring property except in towns in the PALE OF SETTLEMENT. The M. L. were revoked in effect in 1915, and legally in Mar. 1917, after the Russian Revolution. The M. L., resulting in recurrent local expulsions, intolerable overcrowding, and the blocking of economic opportunities, were largely responsible for the wholesale Jewish emigration from Russia during the period they were in force.

MAYBAUM, SIEGMUND (1844–1919): Preacher and scholar. Of Hungarian birth, he officiated and taught in Berlin from 1881. For many years he was chairman of the German Rabbinical Association. In 1897, he was one of the PROTEST RABBIS who objected to the holding of the First Zionist Congress. M. wrote extensively on Jewish religion and homiletics.

MAYENCE see **MAINZ**

MAYER, DANIEL (1909–): French statesman. Active in the socialist movement from his youth, he clandestinely reorganized the French Socialist Party after 1940, becoming its secretary-general after the Liberation. He served as minister of labor in successive governments, 1947–9, and subsequently as president of the parliamentary committee for foreign affairs. He left parliament in 1958 to devote himself to his position as president of the League for the Rights of Man.

MAYER, LEO ARI (1895–1959): Orientalist and archeologist. A native of Galicia and educated in Vienna, he settled in Palestine in 1921 and was inspector of the Government Antiquities Department (1921–9) and professor (1932) of eastern art and archeology at the Hebrew Univ. (rector, 1943–5). He wrote authoritative works on Moslem art and architecture.

MAYER, LOUIS BURT (1885–1957): US film producer. In his early years in Hollywood, he formed a series of production companies which in 1924, merged with the Metro Pictures Corp. and in 1928, with the Goldwyn Co. to form Metro-Goldwyn-Mayer, headed by M. for many years.

MAYER, RENÉ (1895–1972): French statesman and economist. A moderate radical socialist, he served as minister of transport 1944, high commissioner for German affairs 1945–6, finance minister 1947–8, defence minister 1948, and minister of justice 1949. M. was prime minister of France, Dec. 1952–May 1953, basing his coalition on close association with Great Britain and the European Defense Community. He was chairman of the High Authority of the European Coal and Steel Community 1955–7.

MAYZEL (MEISEL), NAḤMAN (1887–1966): Editor. He began his literary career in Hebrew and Yiddish and from 1921, edited Yiddish periodicals in Warsaw. After settling in New York in 1937, he became the central figure of the *Yiddisher Kultur Farband (Ykuf)* and editor of its monthly *Yiddisher Kultur*. M. produced nostalgic studies of Jewish life in Poland and Russia. He settled in Israel in 1964.

MAZAR (MAISLER), BINYAMIN (1906–): Israel scholar. A native of Russia, he settled in Palestine in 1929. Joining the staff of the Hebrew Univ. in 1943, he was appointed professor of biblical history in 1950, and was president of the Univ. 1953–61. He has excavated at Ramat Rachel, En Gedi, Tel el Kasile, Bet Shearim, etc. Since 1968, he has been excavating the Southern and Western walls of the Temple Compound in the Old City of Jerusalem. His major works

Binyamin Mazar.

include a history of Palestine up to the period of the monarchy and a historical atlas of the country.

MAZZAL (Heb.): Constellation; hence, by astrological association, luck, *Mazzal tov* — good luck, the usual greeting on festive occasions.

MAZZIK (Heb. "harmer"): Term synonymous with *shed* ("demon"), *ruaḥ* ("[evil] spirit"), etc. The name clearly expresses the dangerous, harmful, and mischievous though not necessarily diabolic nature of DEMONS in Jewish folk belief.

MEAL-OFFERING (in Heb. *korban solet*): An offering made of flour. When used as a thanksgiving offering *(korban minḥah),* it was mixed with oil and frankincense and seasoned with salt, but when a sin-offering, it was without oil or frankincense. Part was offered upon the altar, and the rest belonged to the priest.

ME'ASSEPHIM: Participants in the Hebrew monthly HA-ME'ASSEPH founded by I. Euchel, M. M. Bresselau, and the brothers Friedländer in 1783; published 1784–6 at Königsberg (3 vols.), 1788–90 in Berlin (3 vols.), one vol. ibid. 1794–7, and again 1809–11 under the editorship of Shalom Cohen at Berlin, Altona, and Dessau. The aims of the *M.* were to publish poetry and essays, explanations of biblical passages and grammatical matters, historical studies, book reviews, and topical discussions. Largely, however, the *M.* were concerned with elegance of style and sentiment; the paucity of original literary work was compensated by numerous translations from world literature. They were widely read in E Europe, where they brought a taste of the HASKALAH. The major modernist thinkers of the time, Mendelssohn and

Solomon Maimon, contributed little; N. H. Wessely wrote frequently until 1791. The chief *M.* were minor literary figures, such as A. Wolfsohn-Halle, J. Loewe, J. L. Bensew, I. Satanov, D. Friedrichsfeld, and D. Franco Mendes.

MECKLENBURG: Former German state. The first information on Jews there dated from the latter 13th cent. when several held important financial posts. A Host Desecration charge was leveled in the early 14th cent., and most of the community was destroyed during the Black Death outbreaks (1350). Settlement was renewed after a time, the Jews now being regarded as the sole property of the duke, but the nobles and burghers eventually forced him to expel them. In 1492, 27 Jews were burnt in Sternberg on a Host Desecration charge and the entire community was again expelled from M. Only in 1679 did Jews return, and their rapid increase drew protests from the local citizens. Despite the opposition of the Estates, the government of Schwerin granted civic rights to the community in 1813, but these were rescinded in 1817. With the founding of the N German Federation in 1869, Jews finally became citizens. Some 1,000 Jews lived in M. in 1933. They suffered severely in the 1938 Nazi riots and none was left by 1942. After World War II, a community was refounded in Schwerin.

MEDAD see **ELDAD**

The Israel Medal of Heroism.

MEDALS: The Midrash has a fanciful account of m. struck to honor the Patriarchs. An enigmatic medal of 1502(?) for Benjamin ben Elijah Beer is the first known in modern times, and there were two or three more in the 16th cent. (e.g. by Pastorini for Garcia Mendes II, c. 1555). A medal with a portrait and Hebrew inscription, struck in 1735 on the appointment of Eliezer Brody as rabbi of Amsterdam, occasioned much controversy. From the close of the 18th cent., m. on historic occasions (e.g. the Napoleonic Sanhedrin, the First Zionist Congress) or historic personalities (Moses Mendelssohn, Moses Montefiore) were relatively common. Many Jews (e.g. Abraham ABRAMSON) were prominent medallists in the employ of the German and other governments. A series of medals has been issued in Israel by the coins and medals department of the Prime Minister's Office.

MEDEM, VLADIMIR (1879–1923): Russian socialist leader. His father had him baptized at birth, but M. declared himself a Jew in 1901. Shortly thereafter, he became one of the leading figures and ideologists in the Bund. He lived in Poland 1914–18, and in the US from 1921.

MEDIA: Ancient Asiatic country. The Pentateuch refers to the Medes as sons of Japheth. The Medes cooperated with the Babylonians in the 6th cent. BCE but were defeated by Cyrus of Persia. Biblical sources — like ancient Greek writers — confuse the Medes with the Persians.

MEDICINE: The Bible evidences the existence of physicians in the time of the First Temple (Jer. 8:22), while the Book of Ecclesiasticus contains a remarkable panegyric of the medical art. The Talmud, which contains extensive incidental medical information, mentions some rabbis who practiced medicine. The Roman Celsus (1st cent. CE) and Greco-Byzantine writings describe the curative prescriptions of Jewish physicians — e.g. the patriarch GAMALIEL. In the Middle Ages, Jews — despite official restrictions — frequently served throughout Europe as court physicians. They also constituted the intermediaries between eastern and western m., especially as TRANSLATORS of the Greco-Arabic medical classics. Great Jewish physicians of this period include ASAPH, author of the first known Hebrew medical work, Shabbetai DONNOLO, Isaac ISRAELI, and MOSES BEN MAIMON whose medical treatises were translated into many languages. With the decline of Arab and Judeo-Arab medical predominance, the role of the Jews changed. In Renaissance times, many noted Jewish physicians, often Marranos, were prominent in W Europe. They were, however, educated in European universities and wrote in Latin (e.g. Garcia d'ORTA, AMATUS LUSITANUS, and ZACUTUS LUSITANUS). Medieval regulations forbidding Christian patients to be attended by Jewish doctors were reinforced with the Counter-Reformation. As a result of social and economic circumstances as well as university restrictions, fewer Jews attained prominence in m. in the 17th–18th cents. Notable exceptions were Marcus Eliezer BLOCH and Tobias COHEN. The position improved with Emancipation, and Jews eventually rose to professional rank in the universities and were responsible for major discoveries, many receiving NOBEL PRIZES. Outstanding pioneers have included Sigmund FREUD, founder of psychoanalysis, Paul EHRLICH, discoverer of Salvarsan, Ferdinand COHN, father of bacteriology, Elie Metchni-

Physician and patient (From a Hebrew ms at Cambridge University Library).

View of the excavations at Megiddo

koff (of Jewish descent), discoverer of phagocytes, Waldemar HAFFKINE, pioneer of inoculation against cholera and bubonic plague, August von WASSERMAN, who determined the syphilis test, the pathologist Julius COHNHEIM, the cancer-researcher Otto WARBURG, Ernst Boris CHAIN, co-discoverer of penicillin, Selman WAXMAN, discoverer of streptomycin, and Jonas SALK and Albert SABIN, discoverers of anti-polio serums. The number of Jews in the medical profession has been disproportionately large in the 20th cent. In Israel, where many eminent European physicians have established themselves, medical services are conducted mainly through the Ministry of Health, the HADASSAH medical organization, and the *Kupat Holim*. The Hadassah medical school, in association with the Hebrew Univ., trains doctors as does Tel Aviv University. In the US, medical training is part of the curriculum of Yeshiva Univ. at its Albert Einstein School of Medicine.

MEDIGO, DEL see **DELMEDIGO**

MEDINA (Heb.): A country or neighborhood.

MEDINA (formerly Yathrib): Town in ARABIA. It became important when MOHAMMED settled there in 622, at which time M. and its immediate neighborhood harbored the largest Jewish community of N Arabia. The origin and previous history of these Jews is unclear, but they may have arrived shortly after the destruction of the Second Temple. They formed three main tribes, BANU-L-NADIR, BANU KAINUKA, and BANU KURAIZA, who occupied themselves mainly with the cultivation of palm-groves but also exercised other callings. Numerous quarrels and feuds forced them to erect forts for protection. A few years after the arrival of Mohammed, who at first was friendly to them, all the Jews were either expelled or massacred. No Jews have since been allowed there.

MEDINA, SIR SOLOMON DE (c. 1650–1730): English financier. Born probably in France, he settled in England c. 1670. During the wars with France, he built up a great fortune as an army contractor, and was knighted by William III; he was the first professing English Jew to be so honored. Accusations that he had bribed the duke of Marlborough were investigated in 1711, and were partly responsible for Marlborough's dismissal. M. passed his last years, impoverished, in Holland.

MEDINI, HAYYIM HEZEKIAH (1833–1904): Halakhist. Born in Jerusalem, he was rabbi at Constantinople and later officiated in the Crimea. From 1889, he resided in Palestine, being appointed *Hakham Bashi* in Hebron in 1891. His humility and saintly conduct endeared him to the masses. M. was the author of *Sede Hemed*, a talmudical encyclopedia in 18 vols.

MEDZIBOZH: Village in Podolia, Russia. It became a center of Hasidism in the 18th cent. when Israel BAAL SHEM TOV settled there.

MEGIDDO: Ancient fortified town in Israel in the Valley of Jezreel. It was inhabited from the 4th millennium BCE to 500 BCE. It stood in a strategic position controlling the pass which connected Egypt with Mesopotamia. M. is mentioned in Egyptian inscriptions and was the site of the victory of Pharaoh Thutmose III over the king of Kadesh. It was the scene

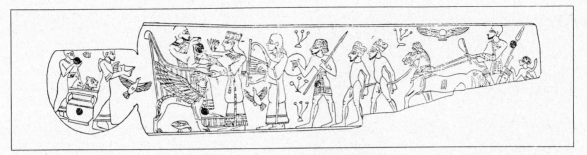

Ivory plaque depicting a victory celebration (Megiddo, 12th cent. BCE).

of many battles, including Deborah's victory over the Canaanites, Josiah's defeat by the Egyptians, encounters in the time of Tiglath-Pileser, the Roman War, and the Crusades. The place was so noted as a battle ground that the New Testament places the apocalyptic war between the forces of good and evil at Har Megiddo (Armageddon). In excavations between 1909 and 1939, over 20 strata of settlement were uncovered, one of which contained stables from early in the First Temple period. When Pope Paul VI visited Israel in 1964, he was received by President Shazar at M. A communal settlement (KA) was founded nearby in 1949 by immigrants from Poland.

MEGILLAH (Heb.): Scroll; a long letter. See SCROLLS, THE FIVE.

MEGILLAH (Heb. "Scroll"): Tenth tractate in the Mishnah order of *Moed,* containing 4 chapters. It has *gemara* in both the Babylonian and Palestinian Talmuds. It deals with the reading of the Scroll of Esther on Purim, enumerating Scriptural readings for particular Sabbaths, festivals, and fastdays. It also lists regulations for the care of synagogues and holy objects.

MEGILLAT TAANIT (Heb. "Scroll of the Fast"): Early work in Aramaic, one of the first tannaitic compositions committed to writing. It lists month by month the days in the calendar which commemorate miracles and joyous events, and on which it is therefore forbidden to fast. A valuable historical source, it is cited in the Mishnah and must have been largely compiled before 70 CE. The reasons for the celebrations are explained in the Hebrew glosses subsequently appended; most of them seem to deal with the period of the Second Temple. The historical background has been elucidated by S. Zeitlin and others.

MEHUTTAN (Heb.): (1) A relative by marriage. (2) A wedding guest.

MEIER, JULIUS L. (1874–1937): US public figure. A business man, he was governor of Oregon 1931–4.

ME'IL (Heb. "mantle"): The covering of a Scroll of the law, sometimes richly decorated.

ME'ILAH (Heb. "Trespass," i.e., in regard to "holy things"): Eighth tractate in the Mishnah order of *kodashim,* containing 6 chapters. It has *gemara* in the Babylonian, but not the Palestinian, Talmud. It deals with the laws concerning trespass in the sense of making profane use of things consecrated for holy use (Lev. 5:15–16).

MEIR (fl. 2nd cent.): Palestinian tanna. A pupil of R Akiva, he was a member of the Sanhedrin at Usha after the Hadrianic persecution. His Mishnah formed the basis of the accepted Mishnah of R Judah Ha-Nasi, it being axiomatic that a ruling stated

Me'il: Dutch (Sephardi) 17th cent. (Jewish Historical Museum, Amsterdam).

Golda Meir

anonymously in the Mishnah was derived from it *(Sanhedrin* 86a). His brilliance was generally recognized, and it was said that when the decision of the rabbis differed from M.'s opinion it was "because his colleagues could not plumb the depth of his reasoning" *(Eruvin* 13b). He was outstanding also as a preacher, noted for his parables and fables. In addition, he was a Torah scribe. His aggadot are also reported, and stories are related as to how his personal conduct exemplified his teachings. His wife BERURIAH was a scholarly authority.

MEIR BAAL HA-NES, RABBI (Heb. "Rabbi Meir the miracle-worker"): Appellation applied to R MEIR on account of miracles ascribed to him in aggadic literature. The traditional charity boxes in the Diaspora for collecting funds for poor Jews in Palestine were called after M.B.H.

MEIR BEN SAMUEL (c. 1069–after 1135): French tosaphist; son-in-law of Rashi. Originally from Lorraine, he settled in Worms and later removed to Ramerupt where he established his own school. His son, R. Tam, quotes his tosaphot.

MEIR OF PRZEMYSLANY (1780–1850): Ḥasidic leader. He won fame as a miracle-worker, and thousands of Ḥasidim streamed to receive his blessing and hear his teachings which were spiced with humor. M. lived frugally and distributed his income among the poor.

MEIR (BEN BARUCH) OF ROTHENBURG (c. 1220–1293): German talmudist. The outstanding rabbinic authority of his generation, his legal rulings (transmitted through his responsa, the halakhic compendia of his pupils R Asher ben Jehiel and R. Mordecai ben Hillel, etc.) exerted a decisive influence on Jewish law and custom throughout Europe. In 1286, Emperor Rudolf imprisoned him at Ensisheim, Alsace, for attempting to emigrate to Palestine. He died a prisoner in 1293, having refused to let himself be ransomed lest European rulers begin to blackmail communities by imprisoning their rabbis. His body was ransomed fourteen years later. A complete edition of his extant works has begun to appear in Israel.

MEIR (formerly **MEYERSON**), **GOLDA** (1898–): Israel statesman. She was born in Russia, went to the US as a child, and settled in Palestine in 1921. Active in Labor Zionism, she held important posts in the *Histadrut* and Jewish Agency. In 1948, M. was the first Israel minister to the USSR. A *Mapai* member of the Knesset since 1949, she was minister of labor in successive governments 1949–56, and foreign minister 1956–66. From 1966 to 1968, she was secretary of *Mapai*. In 1969 she was chosen to suceed Levi ESHKOL as Israel's prime minister, in which capacity she served during the YOM KIPPUR WAR. She was reelected at the end of 1973 but retired in 1974. She wrote *My Life.*

MEIR, YAAKOV (1856–1939): Palestinian rabbi. A native of Jerusalem, he was a Zionist and worked for the revival of spoken Hebrew. In 1906, he was elected *Ḥakham Bashi,* but resigned the same year. From 1908 to 1919, he was chief rabbi of Salonica and in 1921, on the establishment of the Palestinian chief rabbinate, was elected Sephardi chief rabbi.

MEIRI, MENAHEM BEN SOLOMON OF PERPIGNAN (Vidal Salomon; c. 1249–1306): French talmudist. He refused to ban philosophy but favored secular studies only when the Talmud had been mastered. He wrote clear, logical commentaries on parts of the Bible and *Bet ha-Beḥirah* on the Talmud.

MEISEL, MORDECAI MARCUS (1528–1601): Philanthropist. Court banker to the Imperial house, he made great benefactions to the Jewish community in Prague where he founded a synagogue called by his name. After his death, his estate was confiscated.

MEISEL, NAḤMAN see **MAYZEL**

MEISELS, DOV BERUSH (1798–1870): Rabbi and Polish nationalist. His contacts with the Polish nobility led him to occupy an important position in Jewish life under the Cracow Republic (1816–46). In 1832, he was elected rabbi and represented the Jewish Council to the government. M. participated in the 1848 delegation which petitioned the emperor for a special status for Galicia, and supported the Polish demands while a member of the first Austrian parliament (1848–9). In 1856, he was elected rabbi in Warsaw and took a large share in the events leading to the Polish rebellion of 1863. For his political activities M. was expelled from Poland 1861–4 (except for the period of the rising). He was the author of a commentary on Maimonides' *Sepher ha-Mitzvot.*

MEISSNER, ALFRED (1871–?): Czech jurist. A Social Democrat member of the Czech parliament, he was minister of justice 1920–9, and of social welfare 1934. He helped to draw up the Czech constitution in 1918.

MEITNER, LISE (1878–1968): Physicist. Born in Vienna, she taught in Berlin until the Nazi Period when she went to Stockholm. Together with Otto Hahn, she discovered in 1917 the element protactinium and later proved the existence of other radioactive elements. She investigated thorium and actinium, while her researches on the splitting of the uranium nucleus are of fundamental importance in the exploitation of atomic energy. In 1960, she settled in Cambridge, England.

MEIYERS, EDUARD MAURITS (1880–1954): Dutch jurist. Professor at Leyden from 1910, his removal by the Nazis in 1940 caused a protest which led to the closing of the University. He returned to his post in 1945, when he became president of the Dutch Academy of Jurisprudence, and was entrusted with the redrafting of the Dutch Civil Code.

MEKHILTA (Aram. "measure"): Name applied in ancient times to certain midrashic works. It was also used as a synonym for *"masekhet"* i.e., tractate of the Mishnah or Talmud. There exists a halakhic Midrash to Exodus known as *M. de Rabbi Yishmael* ("R Ishmael's *M.*" or just "M.") originating from R Ishmael's school. Recently part of a *M. de Rabbi Shimon ben Yoḥai* has been discovered and published; it belongs to the school of R Simeon ben Yoḥai.

MEKHLIS, LEV ZAKHAROVICH (1889–1953): Soviet leader. He fought prominently in the Red Army in the Civil War, became editor of *Pravda* in 1930, a member of the Supreme Soviet and vice-commissar of defense 1937, and a member of the central committee of the Communist Party 1939. In World War II, he was minister of state control and supervised the financing of the Soviet war-effort.

MEKHULLEH (Heb. "destroyed"): Bankrupt.

MEKITZE NIRDAMIM (Heb. "Rousers of the Slumbering"): Society founded in 1864 for publishing old Hebrew works hitherto unprinted. In 1934, its headquarters were transferred from Germany to Jerusalem.

MELAMED, SAMUEL MAX (1885–1938): Author and journalist. A native of Lithuania, he went in 1914 to the US where he edited several periodical publications, such as the *American Jewish Chronicle* (1914–18) and *The Reflex* (1928–36). Among his books

are *Der Staat im Wandel der Jahrtausende, Psychologie des Jüdischen Geistes,* and *Spinoza und Buddha.*

MELAMMED (Heb. "teacher"): A private teacher or assistant in a *Ḥeder.*

MELAVVEH MALKAH (Heb. "accompanying the Queen" i.e., Sabbath): The concluding Sabbath meal (obligatory according to R Johanan). This, under kabbalistic and Ḥasidic influence, is prolonged by the singing of melodies to delay the end of Sabbath, when the wicked go back to hell and the "additional" Sabbath soul returns to heaven.

MELBOURNE: Capital of Victoria, Australia. The first Jewish congregation was founded in 1841, six years after the city itself, and the community was augmented at the end of the century by immigrants from E Europe. The community now the largest in Australia, supports a Jewish Day School and many organizations. Jewish pop. (1973): 29,800.

MELCHETT see **MOND**

MELCHIOR: Family in Denmark and Germany. The brothers Moses, Samson, and Wolf M. migrated from Hamburg to Copenhagen where they founded a business house, still managed by their descendants. Members of the family have included (1) *KARL JOSEPH M.* (1871–1933), judge and then banker in Hamburg and economic adviser to the German government; (2) *MORITZ GERSON M.* (1816–1884), member of the Danish Upper Chamber and a founder of the Privat-banken in 1857; and (3) *NATHAN GERSON M.* (1811–1872), professor of ophthalmology at Copenhagen; brother of (2).

***MELCHIZEDEK:** King of Salem. When Abraham returned from his pursuit of five Mesopotamian kings, M. blessed him in the name of "God the Most High" (Gen. 14:18–20). Tradition (cf. Ps. 76:3) and scholars identify Salem with Jerusalem.

MELDAR (etymology dubious): Among Sephardim, to read sacred literature.

MELDOLA: Family, descended from *SAMUEL M.* (17th cent.), a learned Ashkenazi physician of Verona: the family is now, however, reckoned Sephardi. *RAPHAEL M.* (1685–1748) of Leghorn was rabbi at Bayonne and published several works, including a volume of responsa. His son *DAVID M.* (1714–1818), rabbi in Amsterdam, was noted for his mathematical ability. *MOSES HEZEKIAH M.* (1725–1791), another son of Raphael, taught Semitic languages in Paris. His son *RAPHAEL M.* (1754–1828) was Haham in London from 1803 and published poems and grammatical treatises. On his death, he was succeeded as spiritual head of the community (though not formally as rabbi) by his son *DAVID M.* (1797–1853), one of the founders of the London *Jewish Chronicle. RAPHAEL M.* (1849–1915), son of the preceding, was a scientist, and authority on photo-chemistry, a distinguished biologist, and the inventor of several synthetic dyes.

The Memorbuch of the Jewish Community of Frankfort-on-Main.
(Feinberg Collection, Detroit.)

MELITZAH: In biblical Hebrew "an aphorism"; in the Middle Ages "elegant style." It now denotes a style, popular in the Haskalah Period, which is based on the artful combination of flowery phrases from the Bible.

MELLAH (etymology uncertain): Name applied to the Jewish quarter in Morocco; apparently originating in Fez where the term is first encountered in the 15th cent.

MELTZER, SHIMSHON (1909–): Israel poet. He was born in Galicia and went to Palestine in 1924. His Hebrew poetry is influenced by Ḥasidic legend and Jewish folklore. He translated the works of Peretz, etc. from Yiddish into Hebrew.

MEM (מ): Thirteenth letter in the Hebrew alphabet; numerical value 40. It is pronounced *m*.

MEMEL: Town of Lithuania, now USSR. There are references to Jews in the 16th cent., but modern settlement dates from 1664, while the community was only organized in 1862. Under Lithuanian rule after World War I, the Jewish population grew and flourished. The town was governed by German elements from 1935 and Nazi legislation was introduced. Some 15,000–16,000 Jews lived there in 1938 but were killed by 1943. Jewish pop. (1970): Under 1,000.

MEMMI, ALBERT (1920–): Tunisian novelist. His autobiographical novel, *La Statue de Sel,* describes life in the ghetto of Tunis and under the German occupation of Tunisia. He also wrote his Jewish credo in *Portrait d'un Juif* and *La Libération du Juif.*

MEMORBUCH: Name given by German Jews to the books containing memorial prayers and lists of martyrs, communal benefactors, etc. which were read on anniversaries. Some of these contain valuable historical material, in particular on the medieval persecutions from the First Crusade onward: the most famous is the "Nuremberg" M. (ed. S. Salfeld, 1898). The name is believed to derive from the Latin *memoria.*

MEMORIAL SERVICE see YIZKOR

MEMPHIS: City in Tennessee, US. Its Jewish community is the oldest and largest in the state. Members of old southern families settled there in the 1840's. The Hebrew Benevolent Society was organized in 1850 to administer a cemetery acquired by the community 3 years earlier. The Society conducted services on the High Holy Days until Congregation B'nai Israel was formed in 1853. The first Jewish welfare agency was organized in 1864, a Federation of Jewish Welfare Agencies was founded in 1906, and a Jewish Welfare Fund, in 1934. The weekly *Hebrew Watchman* has been published in M. since 1925. In 1973, the city had 9,000 Jews with 4 synagogues.

MEMRA see LOGOS

MENAHEM: King of Israel c. 744–735 BCE. He gained the throne by killing Shallum. His brutal treatment of the citizens of Tiphsah, who refused to open the gates of the city, is recorded in II Kings 15:16. When Tiglath-Pileser III invaded Syria and Israel, M. was forced to pay him a heavy tribute.

MENAHEM AV see **AV**

MENAHEM BEN JUDAH THE GALILEAN
(d. 66 CE): Leader of *Sicarii* in the Roman War. He successfully attacked Masada, thence moving on Jerusalem where he led to victory the forces besieging the Romans in Herod's palace. Subsequently, he comported himself like a king, perhaps posing as the messianic ruler. He thereby antagonized Eleazar ben Hananiah and his supporters, who attacked and killed M. Some scholars identify him with the TEACHER OF RIGHTEOUSNESS.

MENAHEM BEN SARUK (c. 910–c. 970): Spanish Hebrew lexicographer. He was secretary to Hasdai Ibn Shaprut, but was dismissed and persecuted, allegedly for heretical opinions. He described his sufferings in a pathetic letter. M. wrote the *Mahberet (Mahbarot)*, the first Hebrew-Hebrew dictionary (ed. by H. Filipowski, London 1854), which was used extensively by Rashi. His work was bitterly attacked by DUNASH BEN LABRAT. M.'s grammatical system is antiquated (he lists roots of one and two consonants), but his own pupil HAYYUJ, and IBN JANAH, pupil of his pupil Isaac ben GIKITILLA, created the classic system of Hebrew GRAMMAR.

MENAHEM IBN ZERAH see **IBN ZERAH**

MENAHEM MENDEL OF LIUBAVICH see **LIUBAVICH**

MENAHEM MENDEL OF PRZEMYSLANY
(d. 1772): Hasidic rabbi; pupil of Israel Baal Shem Tov. He held the foundations of Hasidism to be prayer with DEVEKUT, saying "May it be granted me to pray but one prayer properly during my lifetime." In 1764, he emigrated to Palestine with a group of followers and settled in Tiberias. His example stimulated other Hasidim to leave E Europe for the Holy Land.

MENAHEM MENDEL OF RYMANOV (d. 1815):
Hasidic rabbi. Thousands visited him at Rymanov, Galicia, where he preached the importance of retaining all customs which had won acceptance among Jews, even in dress. During the Napoleonic Wars, he was hopeful of the imminent advent of the Messiah.

MENAHEM MENDEL OF VITEBSK (1730–1788):
Hasidic rabbi; pupil of Dov Ber of Mezhirich. When the Vilna Gaon pronounced a ban on Hasidism, M. M. went to Vilna with Shneour Zalman to justify the movement, but the Gaon refused to receive them. In 1777, he left Russia together with 300 Hasidim, and settled in Safed, later in Tiberias. His teaching tended to be philosophical. Thus, he taught that God is omnipresent through the process of *tzimtzum* (contraction). Man must cleave to the manifestations of the Deity in material creation and redeem the Divine presence from its exile.

MENAHEM NAHUM OF CHERNOBYL (1730–1789): Hasidic rabbi. He was at first given to fasting and ascetic practices but, after studying with the Baal Shem Tov, became an itinerant *maggid*, spreading Hasidism in Russia and the Ukraine. He lived a frugal life but collected considerable sums of money for ransoming Jewish captives and for other charitable objects. M. N. taught the importance of DEVEKUT and the position of the *tzaddik* as the link between God and the world. He founded a noted dynasty.

MENAHEM THE ESSENE (fl. late 1st cent. BCE):
Scholar. According to Josephus, he foretold that Herod would become king and when the prophecy was fulfilled, was treated with honors by the monarch. M. was associated with Hillel, but there are indications that he disagreed with his colleagues and retired from the Sanhedrin.

MENAHOT (Heb. "Meal-offerings"): Second tractate in the Mishnah order of *Kodashim* containing 13 chapters. It has *gemara* in the Babylonian, but not Palestinian, Talmud. It deals primarily with preparation of the meal-offering (Lev. 2:1–14; 5:11–13), also discussing the shewbread (Lev. 24:5–9) and the two loaves brought on the Feast of Weeks (Lev. 23:17).

MENANDER: Putative author of a collection of sayings preserved in Syriac (in a British Museum ms) probably in translation from the Greek. The date is uncertain and it is unknown whether the original was in Hebrew.

MENDELE MOCHER SEPHORIM see **ABRAMOWITCH, SHALOM JACOB**

MENDELSOHN, ERICH (1887–1953): Architect. He lived in his native Germany until 1933, and subsequently in England, Palestine, and (from 1941) the US. His work was influenced by new social trends which he sought to express by freeing materials and functions of old styles and molding buildings to new uses. Notable among his designs were the Einstein tower in Potsdam, the Schocken general store in Chemnitz, factories in Leningrad, the Hadassah Hospital on Mt. Scopus, Jerusalem, the Weizmann home at Rehovot, and monumental synagogues in Cleveland and elsewhere.

MENDELSSOHN: German family. *MOSES M.* (1729–1786) was born in Dessau, and in 1743, he followed his teacher, David Fränkel, to Berlin and studied philosophy, mathematics, Latin, French, and English — a most unusual scope for a young Jew at that time. After seven years of privation, he was engaged by a rich silk manufacturer, Isaac Bernhard, as tutor to his children. Four years later he became Bernhard's bookkeeper, then his representative, and finally his partner. M.'s brilliance gradually won him renown. In 1763, he became a protected Jew, the Berlin community exempting him from all taxes. He was introduced by Gumperz to Maupertuis, the president of the Berlin Academy, and then to LESSING who profoundly influenced his development. M.'s first literary attempt in German, a letter to Gumperz, defended the honor of the Jews against critics of Lessing's *Die Juden*. Lessing anonymously published M.'s *Philosophische Gespräche* without the knowledge of the author (1755). In the same year, an anonymous satirical treatise *Pope ein Metaphysiker* appeared written jointly by Mendelssohn and Lessing in defense of Leibnitz's teachings, while M.'s *Briefe über die Empfindungen* (1755) became the basis of esthetic criticism in Germany. With his translation in 1756 of Rousseau's *Discours sur l'inéqualité parmi les hommes*, M. made his reputation as a leading German stylist. In the journal *Bibliothek der schönen Wissenschaften und der freien Künste*, M. reviewed works on esthetics and literature as well as publishing his own studies which made an important contribution to pre-Kantian ethics. M. won the Berlin Academy of Sciences' prize for the best essay on a metaphysical subject, in spite of theses submitted by Thomas Abbt and Immanuel Kant. The consequent correspondence with Abbt on the destiny of man resulted in the composition of M.'s *Phädon* (1767), a discussion on immortality modeled on Plato's dialogue, which earned its author the title "the German Socrates." Drawn into a tedious and distasteful theological dispute with Johann Kasper Lavater, a preacher in Zürich, from which he finally emerged with his dignity unimpaired but at the cost of his health, M. embarked upon the second period of his activity, in which his concern for Judaism and

Moses Mendelssohn.

the Jews made him his people's foremost representative. His attempt in 1750 to bring out a Hebrew weekly *Kohelet Musar* failed, but in 1770, he published an annotated edition of *Ecclesiastes* and composed a commentary on Maimonides' *Logic* entitled *Millot ha-Higgayon*. His German translation of the Pentateuch with Hebrew commentary, the *Biur*, was completed by 1783 — the commentaries on the five parts being mainly composed respectively by S. Dubno, M. himself, N. H. Wessely, A. Yaroslav, and H. Homberg. This work proved of great significance in the process of Jewish Enlightenment. To the same class belong his translations of the *Psalms* and the *Song of Songs*. M.'s personal prestige enabled him to counteract threatened oppression of the Jews in Switzerland and Dresden. At his instigation, C. W. Dohm composed his famous work *On the Civil Amelioration of the Jews*, while M. Herz translated into German Manasseh ben Israel's *Vindiciae Judaeorum* to which M. added a preface (1782). In answer to the criticism aroused by this, M. composed his *Jerusalem* (1783), renowned for its analysis of Judaism and its vigorous defense of tolerance. For all his advocacy of Jewish civil rights, however, his attitude toward Judaism remained conservative. After Lessing's death in 1781, M. in two works defended his friend from the charge of pantheism. His own influence in the cause of Jewish Emancipation and enlightenment was immeasurable, while his character is enshrined as the prototype of the hero in Lessing's *Nathan the Wise*. Of his children, *JOSEPH M.* (1770–1848) founded the banking firm of Mendelssohn and Co., Berlin. Highly talented, of wide education, and an intimate friend of Alexander von Humboldt, he was largely responsible for the biographical sketch of his father published by his own son G. B. M. Another son of Joseph's, *ALEXANDER M.* (d. 1871), was the last Jewish descendant of the family. *ABRAHAM M.* (1776–1835), the father of Felix MENDELSSOHN-BARTHOLDY, was for a time Joseph's partner in the banking firm. *NATHAN M.* (1792–1852) devoted himself to the study of mechanics, manufacturing various instruments, some of his own invention. *DOROTHEA M.* (1764–1839), a woman of high intelligence and forceful personality, married the Berlin banker Veit but after 15 years eloped with Friedrich von Schlegel, whom she later married after embracing Christianity. *RECHA M.* (1776–1831), once wife of Mendel Mayer, established a boarding school for girls in Altona. *HENRIETTA M.* (1768–1831), who remained unmarried, taught in several boarding schools including her sister's and conducted a salon for scholars and artists in Paris. In spite of her indignation at her sister Dorothea's change of faith, she later became a bigoted Catholic.

MENDELSSOHN-BARTHOLDY, FELIX (Jacob Ludwig; 1809–1847): German composer; son of the banker Abraham M., grandson of Moses M. M.,

Felix Mendelssohn-Bartholdy.
(Painting by Eduard Magnus).

who was brought up as a Christian, early showed musical talent and was a brilliant pianist. At the age of 17, he wrote the overture to *A Midsummer Night's Dream,* the same youthful gaiety appearing in the rest of his incidental music written 17 years later. He helped to renew interest in Bach by his revival of the *St. Matthew Passion.* M. conducted extensively in England, while his visits to Scotland are commemorated in his *Hebrides* overture and *Scottish* symphony. in 1843, he founded the Leipzig Conservatoire of Music. His delicate health deteriorated after the death of his beloved sister, Fanny, in 1847, and he died shortly afterward. His compositions include 5 symphonies, concertos for violin and piano, *Elijah* and other oratorios, theater music, the miniatures for piano *Songs Without Words,* and chamber and vocal music.

MENDES: Family of Marrano origin. Among its outstanding members were: (1) *ALVARO M.* See IBN YAISH, SOLOMON; (2) *DIOGO M.* (d. 1543): Portuguese banker. He established an important financial and trading house at Antwerp c. 1500 and long headed the Marrano community of that city. He was brother-in-law of Gracia NASI. (3) *FERNANDO M.* (d. 1724): Marrano physician. Accompanying Catherine of Braganza when she went to England to marry Charles II, he founded a noted English-Jewish family. (4) *MOSES M.* (d. 1758): English author; grandson of (3). M., who was baptized, wrote poems and plays.

MENDES, CATULLE (1841–1909): French poet and playwright. He was one of the founders of the Parnassian school of poetry and long adhered to classic execution. His later works were written in a lighter vein. M. was an early admirer of Wagner.

MENDES, GRACIA see **NASI, GRACIA**

MENDES, HENRY PEREIRA (1852–1937): US Sephardi rabbi. Born and educated in England, M. was rabbi of Congregation Shearith Israel, New York. He was one of the founders of the Zionist Organization of America, the Union of Orthodox Jewish Congregations, the New York *Kehillah,* and the Jewish Theological Seminary of which he was president 1897–1902.

MENDES-FRANCE, PIERRE (1907–): French statesman, belonging to an old Bordeaux Sephardi family. A lawyer by profession, he was elected to the French parliament in 1932, and in 1938, was deputy minister of finance in Leon Blum's government. During World War II, he served in the Free French Air Force and was appointed by Gen. de Gaulle as finance commissioner in Algeria. M. was executive director of the International Bank for Reconstruction and Development (1946) and French governor of the International Monetary Fund. He served as radical socialist premier of France from June 1954–Feb. 1955 during which time he negotiated an armistice in Indo-China, introduced a vigorous N Africa policy, and produced a far-reaching economic plan. In 1956, he served for a few months as vice-premier under M. Mollet. He has written autobiographical novels as well as political and economic studies.

MENDOZA, DANIEL (1764–1836): English pugilist. Entering the boxing ring in 1784, he innovated "scientific pugilism" and was champion of England

Fernando Mendes.
(Painting by Catherine da Costa, 1722).

1792–5. He published an autobiography and a work on boxing.

MENE MENE TEKEL U-PHARSIN: The writing which appeared on the wall during Belshazzar's last feast (Dan. 5:25). It was interpreted by Daniel to mean that the king's deeds had been weighed in the scales and found wanting, for which his kingdom would be divided. The literal translation is generally accepted as "It has been counted and counted, weighed and cut up," although some see in it names of coins of descending value.

MENELAUS (d. 162 BCE): High priest in the time of Antiochus Epiphanes. Apparently, he was not of a priestly family but belonged to the TOBIADS and obtained the high priesthood in 171 BCE by bribery. M. was an extreme Hellenizer, supporting Antiochus' persecution of Judaism and plundering the Temple in the king's behalf. He seems to have played a part in the peace arrangement between Judah the Maccabee and Lysias in 165 but in 162, was accused by Lysias of responsibility for the war and executed.

MENES, ABRAM (1897–1969): Historian. Born in Poland, he lived in Germany and France before settling in the US in 1940. M. contributed to *Yivo* publications and co-edited the *Yivo* volume on the history of the Jewish labor movement and also the *General Yiddish Encyclopedia*.

MENGS, ANTON RAPHAEL (1728–1779): Painter. Son of the Dresden court miniaturist Ishmael M. (1690–1765) and brought up as a Christian, he worked with brilliant success in Germany, Italy, England, and especially Spain, where he was greatly favored by the royal court. In his paintings he blended and revived the traditions of the Italian 16th cent. masters. His reputation in his day was enormous and his influence (exercised also through his writings) permeated European painting for a generation. Several of M.'s children were also painters of repute.

MENKEN, ADAH ISAACS (1835–1868): US actress. She was a star of the New York, London, and Paris stage. Her poetry, some of which dealt with Jewish themes, stood in marked contrast to her sensational public and personal career. It attracted the interest of prominent literary figures. It is uncertain whether she was a born Jewess or a convert to Judaism.

MENORAH (Heb.): Candelabrum. The golden seven-branched *m.* was one of the most prominent features of the Tabernacle and Temples. The *m.* from the Second Temple was taken to Rome by Vespasian and is portrayed on the Arch of Titus. The term *m.* is also applied to the *Ḥanukkah* lamp (which, however, is seldom a candelabrum). The *m.* was the symbol of Judaism in the 1st cent. CE and is frequently portrayed on tombs and monuments of every description.

MENORAH MOVEMENT: US organization for fostering Jewish culture. It grew out of the Menorah Society founded in 1906 at Harvard, followed

Yehudi Menuhin.

by the establishment of similar societies in other colleges and universities in the US and Canada. leading in 1913, to the foundation of the Intercollegiate Menorah Association (from 1929, The Menorah Association Inc.) *The Menorah Journal* (1915), a magazine of Jewish learning, literature, and art, was edited by Henry HURWITZ, chancellor (head) of the Association from its inception. The Association ceased with Hurwitz' death in 1961.

MENSTRUATION see **NIDDAH**

MENUHIN, YEHUDI (1916–): US violinist. He made his debut at the age of eight and rapidly earned a world-wide reputation. He retired from public per-

Stone relief of a menorah from the 2nd cent. synagogue at Hammat near Tiberias.

formances in order to study, 1936–7, and since then, has been regarded as one of the world's outstanding violinists. Many of his recitals have been given in conjunction with his pianist sister *HEPHZIBAH M.* (1920–).

MEPHIBOSHETH (fl. c. 1000 BCE): Name given in the Book of Samuel to Meribaal or Merib Baal, son of Jonathan (i.e., substituting *boshet* — "a shameful thing" for the word Baal). Aged 5 at his father's death, he fled with his nurse but in the haste was dropped and lamed. When David established himself at Jerusalem, he restored M. to favor and put at his disposal Saul's former servant Zoba. At the time of Absalom's rebellion, M. remained in Jerusalem, whereas Zoba accompanied David. After the uprising was quelled, M. pleaded that he had been misled by Zoba, and David treated him mildly.

MERCHANT: In the agricultural society of the Biblical Period, the calling of m. was left largely to non-Hebrews, as is shown by the synonym Canaanite and m. (Zech. 14:21; Prov. 31:24). The itinerant m. (or *rokhel*) specializing in spices, etc. (Song of Songs 3:6) was also probably a foreigner. Josephus asserts that the Jews of his time had no taste for trade, but there were Jewish m.'s of importance at Alexandria and elsewhere in the early Roman Empire. In the Dark Ages, however, when the Jews were a principal channel of intercourse between the Christian and Islamic worlds, they began to play an important part in international trade, the terms Jew and m. being used almost synonymously in some 9th cent. documents. Jewish m.'s from Baghdad participated also in the India and even China trade at this period. In W Europe, except in Spain, the Jewish m. was eclipsed after the period of the Crusades, when the Jews were forced into moneylending; yet even then many were m.'s also. In the undeveloped areas of E Europe (Poland, etc.), the Jews continued to play an important part as m.'s down to modern times, and trade was from the 17th cent. the economic basis of the Marrano communities in NW Europe and America. Jewish m.'s (at first itinerant, then establishing local stores) were prominent in the 19th cent. in opening up the US South and West.

MERHAVYAH: Israel communal settlement (KA) and also smallholders' village in the Valley of Jezreel. A settlement was founded there in 1911 on the first stretch of land acquired by Jews in the Valley. Originally a *Ha-Shomer* camp, it was the scene of the first attempt to run a workers' cooperative according to F. OPPENHEIMER's experimental plan, which proved unsuccessful. Several groups followed each other at the site. In 1922, the present smallholders' village was founded by settlers from E Europe; and in 1929, a kibbutz was also erected by pioneers from Poland. The settlement is the center of the *Ha-Kibbutz ha-Artzi* movement and houses its printing press. Pop. (1972): settlement, 564; village 227.

MERIBAAL see **MEPHIBOSHETH**

MERODACH (Marduk): Babylonian deity. In mythology he was regarded as the main opponent of the monster Tiamat and as creator of the world and mankind. King of the gods, he determined men's fate at the beginning of the year.

*MERODACH-BALADAN (fl. 8th cent. BCE): King of Babylon. In the reign of Hezekiah he sent envoys to Judah to forge political links with that kingdom directed against Assyria (II Kings 20:12, etc.).

MEROM, WATERS OF: Palestinian site of Joshua's victory over the alliance of northern kings led by Jabin of Hazor (Josh. 11:5). The place is also mentioned in inscriptions of pharaohs of the 18th and 19th dynasties, and of Tiglath-Pileser III who relates that he banished its inhabitants — with the rest of the population of Galilee — to Assyria. The Waters of M. were formerly erroneously thought to be Lake Huleh but are now identified with MERON or Maron near the Lebanese border.

MERON: Ancient town in Galilee. It is mentioned in Egyptian inscriptions from the 2nd millennium BCE. M. was conquered by Tiglath-Pileser in 732 and was fortified by Josephus in the war with Rome. The traditional tomb of R Simeon ben Yoḥai and his son Eliezer situated there became a place of pilgrimage, especially on *Lag ba-Omer*. There are remains of a 2nd — 3rd cent. synagogue in the vicinity. A smallholders' settlement (PM) was founded there on *Lag ba-Omer*, 1949, by veterans of Israel's War of Independence and E European settlers. Pop. (1972): 272.

Ruins of Meron Synagogue.

MERRICK (originally **MILLER**), **LEONARD** (1864–1939): British author. He excelled in novels, dramas, and short stories, his subjects being frequently derived from theatrical life.

MERZBACHER, GOTTFRIED (1843–1926): German explorer. He explored the Caucasus (1891—2), Arabia, Persia, and India (1892—4), and N China (1902—8). M. wrote a standard work about the Caucasus mountains.

MESHA (9th cent. BCE): King of Moab. At first tributary to the House of Omri, he exploited Israel's weakness after the death of Ahab to throw off her suzerainty. Jehoram of Israel, in consort with Jehoshaphat of Judah and the king of Edom, invaded Moab. According to the Bible, their campaign was successful until they besieged the capital Kir-hareseth whereupon M. sacrificed his eldest son, after which the invading armies retreated, for uncertain reasons (II Kings 3). M. exploited the opportunity to regain the land he had lost and even captured the territory of Reuben and part of Gad. His own account of his victories is inscribed on the MOABITE STONE (or Mesha Stele).

MESHARET (Heb. "servant"): In grammatical terminology, accent marks which indicate minor pauses.

MESHED: Town in Iran. In 1839 its Jewish community was forced by the fanatical Shi'ite sect to adopt Islam. Many of them or their descendants succeeded in leaving the country and some have settled in Israel. Others lived as secret Jews known as JEDID EL-ISLAM. In 1967, there were 4,000 Jews in M.

MESHULLAH (Heb.): An emissary sent to conduct propaganda or raise funds for a charitable or pious institution: those formerly sent by the "Four Holy Cities" of Palestine (Jerusalem, Hebron, Safed, Tiberias) were generally termed *Shadar*. The institution goes back to a remote period, the earliest record being the "apostles" sent in the Classical Period to collect contributions for the Palestinian patriarchs. The *meshullahim* sometimes penetrated into very distant places, where their learning and information were greatly prized; they thus helped to knit the Jewish world together, and their travel accounts (e.g. that of H. J. D. AZULAI) are important historical sources. The institution still survives.

MESHULLAM BEN MENAHEM OF VOLTERRA see **VOLTERRA**

MESHUMMAD (Heb): A CONVERT to Christianity; an apostate (used opprobriously).

MESOPOTAMIA see **IRAQ**

MESQUITA: Sephardi family of Marrano origin; prominent in Europe and America. (1) *BENJAMIN BUENO DE M.* (d. 1683), W Indian merchant, was an early settler in New York and the first person known to have been buried in the N. Y. Jewish cemetery. (2) *DAVID BUENO DE M.* (17th cent.), merchant and diplomat; he was agent in Holland for the margrave of Brandenburg (1684), and was entrusted with diplomatic missions to the Sultan of Morocco. (3) *MOSES GOMEZ DE M.* (1688–1751) was Haham in London from 1744.

MESSEL, ALFRED (1853—1909): German architect. Professor at Berlin, M. built many outstanding buildings, his style marking the transition from the late 19th cent. to the modern style of architecture. He left Judaism.

MESSER LEON see **LEON**

MESSIAH (Heb. *mashiah*): The Anointed One; the ultimate deliverer. The word is used in the Bible as an adjective referring to kings, etc. who have been anointed, thereupon receiving Divine sanction and a unique inviolability of status. High priests were also anointed, and in exilic and post-exilic times the word came to imply anyone with a special mission from God (the patriarchs, prophets, the Jewish people, even gentiles such as Cyrus the Mede). After the exile the prophetic vision of the universal establishment of God's kingdom was associated with the ingathering of Israel under a scion of David's house, who would be the Lord's anointed. In the period of Roman rule the expectation of a personal M. acquired great prominence and he assumed the character of a descendant of David who would break the alien yoke and establish a golden age. The messianic figure was the center of a large number of eschatological concepts, and is reflected in the body of hellenistic-Jewish pseudepigraphic literature from the 1st cent. CE. Messianic emotionalism became intense shortly before 70 CE. Numerous false m.'s now appeared, the New Testament vividly reflecting the messianic ferment at this time. The belief in a M. grew even stronger after the destruction of the Second Temple (70 CE), and critical world events affecting the Jews invariably sharpened anticipation of his advent. Frequent predictions as to its timing were based on the Book of Daniel and other biblical passages. The widespread Jewish revolt of 115—117 certainly had a messianic content, and during the last revolt against the Romans, BAR KOKHBA was acclaimed M. (131). In the 5th cent. a pseudo-m. called Moses appeared in Crete. The fall of the Persian and Byzantine empires (7th cent.) again aroused Jewish messianic hopes, and in the 8th cent., three pseudo-m.'s appeared —ABU ISSA AL-ISFAHANI in Persia, Severus or SERENE in Syria, and YUDGHAN in Hamadan. In the 9th cent. ELDAD HA-DANI, though not himself claiming messianic status, announced the existence of the Lost Ten Tribes, whose return was a prerequisite of the messianic era, and thereby stimulated apocalyptic imagination. Maimonides in his Letter to the Yemen (c. 1172) restated in glowing terms the messianic doctrine, and subsequently included confidence in the coming of the M. among the thirteen articles of faith. Elsewhere, he insisted on the rational, unmiraculous nature of the Messianic Age, the distinguishing feature of which

A View of Metullah.

would be merely the breaking of the yoke of political bondage under a scion of the House of David.

Pseudo-m.'s and enthusiasts who claimed to be prophets or precursors of the M. were numerous from the Crusading Period. In 1096, it was believed in Salonica that the deliverance had already begun; and in 1121, a Karaite claimant was reported in Palestine. In 1147, the spectacular David ALROY appeared in Mesopotamia, and similar figures are recorded in Yemen, Fez, Persia, Spain, and France in the 11th and 12th cents. Avraham ABULAFIA was active in Sicily in the 13th cent. and was followed in Spain by his disciples, Samuel and Abraham; in 1295, a m. was expected at AVILA. The Spanish persecution of 1391 produced MOSES BOTAREL; the expulsion (1492) was followed by a number of such figures — Asher LAMLEIN (1503), Solomon MOLCHO (c. 1500—1532), and others. The most important of all pseudo-m.'s was SHABBETAI TZEVI (1626–1676) of Smyrna, who gained wide adherence and an offshoot of whose sect, the DONMEH, still survives. His failure and the universal trend toward rationalism created a reaction against messianic speculation although a few pseudo-m.'s, e.g. Jacob FRANK (1726—1791) and Ḥayyim Malakh, Mordecai Mokhiaḥ, JUDAH ḤASID, and Löbele PROSSNITZ still appeared during the 18th cent. A pseudo-messiah declared himself in Yemen as recently as 1889.

MESSINA: City of Sicily. Jews are mentioned there in the 6th cent. and again in the 12th (when Benjamin of Tudela found Jews in M.). Ritual Murder charges were leveled in 1347 and 1475, and the Jews were expelled in 1492.

METATRON (etymology uncertain): The highest angel in aggadic and kabbalistic texts; identified with the Angel of the Presence and with ENOCH after his translation to heaven. M. appears as the scribe of the Divine court, the keeper of celestial secrets, and (in the Zohar) as the heavenly archetype of man.

Because the numerical value of the name M. is equal to that of the Divine name SHADDAI he is likened to his Master and said to act as a mediator.

METEG (Heb. "Bridle"): Short vertical line placed on the left of a vowel sign, expressing a secondary accent in a word (or series of words joined by *makkeph*). The complicated rules governing the m. were gradually formulated in the Middle Ages.

METEMPSYCHOSIS: Transmigration of souls; the belief that the soul after death may reappear in another person or (in some forms of the belief) in an animal. The idea seems to have originated in India. It appears in Manicheism and derived sects, and is discussed by earlier Jewish philosophers. In Kabbalah it first emerges in the book *Bahir*, and then, from the Zohar onward, was commonly accepted by mystics, playing an important role in Ḥasidic belief and literature.

METHUSELAH: Biblical figure; son of Enoch and father of Lamech. He died at the age of 969(Gen. 5:25–7), the oldest age recorded in the Bible.

METULLAH: Village in the extreme N of Israel. It was set up in 1896 by Baron Edmond de Rothschild who chose young settlers to fight off the warlike Druze of the neighborhood. M. later came under ICA administration.The village suffered from water shortage for 40 years, and its development was severely hampered. Since the 1930's, it has developed as a summer resort. The closing of the Lebanese frontier, after the 1948 War of Independence, separated the settlers from their best land. Pop. (1967): 400.

METURGEMAN (Aram. "interpreter"): Mouthpiece of talmudic rabbis. It was customary for teachers to deliver their lectures through the m. The rabbi, seated, spoke quietly to the latter, who would repeat the teaching to the assembled public in a loud voice.

METZ: Town of Lorraine. Its Jewish community flourished in the 10th cent., suffered severely in the Crusading Period, and was expelled in 1306. The Jews returned in the 16th cent., and in the 18th cent., M. was a leading European community (480 families) and the home of famous rabbis. The French Rabbinical Seminary was founded at M. in 1829, being transferred to Paris in 1859. The Jews of M. left early in World War II, but many returned after 1945. Jewish pop. (1973): 2,500.

MEVASSERET YERUSHALAYIM see **MOTZA**

MEXICAN INDIAN JEWS: Proselytes who seem to derive from the Christian sect of *Iglesia de Dios* (Church of God), though they themselves assert that they are descendants of Marranos. A group of about 8 families lives in the village of Venta Prieta (Hidalgo State); another of c. 12 families in Mexico City. In both places they have a synagogue in which services are mostly conducted in Spanish, with a few prayers and benedictions in Hebrew. In physical type they are Indian or Mestizo.

MEXICO: Central American country. Marranos from Spain arrived with the *conquistadores* early in the 16th cent., two being burned at the stake in 1528. In 1571, an Inquisitional tribunal was set up, and remained active for two centuries. A few European Jews reached M. in the 19th cent., but the community only became sizable after World War I. The Ashkenazi immigrants came mainly from Poland, Russia, and Lithuania, and the Sephardim from Syria, Turkey, Greece. Jewish immigration was severely restricted in 1937. The Jews of M. have played a large part in the industrial development of the country. They number (1973) 40,000 (the great majority in Mexico City) besides the MEXICAN INDIAN JEWS. The Comité Central Israelita represents all groups of the Jewish population. There are six all-day Jewish schools and two Yeshivot in the capital and one each in Guadalajara and Monterey, with c. 4,800 students; about 65% of the Jewish children attend schools, from kindergarten to high school, that offer Yiddish, Hebrew, and general courses. The Colegio Hebreo Tarbut offers a Hebrew and general curriculum. There is also a Jewish Teachers' Seminary. The Yidisher Sport Tzenter has a membership of 20,000. There are 10 Jewish newspapers and periodicals, 5 in Spanish, 3 in Yiddish, and 2 in both. The ten-volume *Encyclopedia Judaica Castellana* is the most ambitious Mexican Jewish cultural achievement.

MEXICO CITY: Capital of MEXICO. A number of judaizing cases were tried there 1574—1645, but the present community (except for the MEXICAN INDIAN JEWS) was refounded by immigrants from Aleppo in 1909, and the first (Sephardi) synagogue was built in 1912. After World War I, there was considerable immigration from E Europe. M. C. has 6 Jewish day-schools and is the hub of Jewish life in the country, with a Jewish Spanish and Yiddish press. Its Jewish pop. (1973) is 30,000, almost half being Sephardim.

MEYER, ANNIE NATHAN (1867—1951): US educator and author. A pioneer advocate of higher education for women, she was a founder of Barnard College, the women's college of Columbia Univ. (1889). She wrote a number of plays and books.

MEYER, EUGENE (1857—1959): US banker and publisher. He was publisher and later chairman of the board of directors of the *Washington Post*. In 1932, he was the first chairman of the Reconstruction Finance Corporation and in 1946, the first president of the International Bank for Reconstruction and Development.

MEYER, LÉON (1868—1957): French statesman. He was mayor of Le Havre from 1919 until deposed by the Vichy regime in 1940, and a rightist Radical deputy from 1921. He was minister of the merchant marine in French cabinets in 1932 and 1933.

MEYER, VICTOR (1848—1897): German chemist. He lectured at Zürich, Göttingen, and Heidelberg, made numerous discoveries, and published many scientific papers. He developed certain types of laboratory equipment, including an apparatus for determining the density of vapors.

MEYERBEER, GIACOMO (originally Jacob Liebmann Beer; 1791—1864): German composer. Son of a leading banker, Herzl Beer, he evinced talents as pianist and composer at an early age. After traveling throughout Europe, he settled in Paris where his opera *Robert le Diable* was successfully performed in 1831. In 1836, *Les Huguenots* received its première. M. was appointed music director to the king of Prussia in Berlin in 1842. His later operas include *Le prophète* and *L'Africaine*.

MEYERHOF, OTTO FRITZ (1884—1951): Physiologist. Born in Germany, M. went to the US in 1940 and taught biochemistry at the Univ. of Pennsylvania 1940—51. He published many important studies in his field and was awarded the 1923 Nobel Prize for medicine in recognition of his research in the chemistry of the muscles.

MEYEROWITZ, WILLIAM (1887—): US artist. He is noted for his landscape, figure, and still-life paintings and etchings.

MEYERSON, ÉMILE (1859–1933): Philosopher: son of Malvina M. (1839—1922), a noted Polish novelist. In 1882, M. settled in France where he worked for the Agence Havas and was active in ICA. At the same time, he prepared philosophical works. He maintained that the principle of causality derives directly from that of identity. As matter is the domain of the irrational, any rational explanation sought by the human mind is ultimately unattainable. His principal works are *Identité et réalité* and *Le Cheminement de la pensée*.

MEZHIRICH: Village in Volhynia, Russia. Its Jewish community came into existence in the 17th cent. Because of its proximity to Lithuania and important Russian centers, it was selected by the Ḥasidic leader DOV BER as his residence, which became the center of Ḥasidism after the death of Israel Baal Shem Tov in 1760. Solomon Maimon in his autobiography gives a vivid description of a visit to the Ḥasidim at M.

MEZUMMAN (Heb. "ready"): Ready cash, money. Also, one of the quorum of three necessary for the public recitation of the grace after meals.

MEZUZAH (Heb. "doorpost"): Parchment scroll placed in a container and nailed to the doorposts (on the right side of the entrance) in rooms occupied by Jews. On the scroll is written Deut. 6:4—9 and 11:13—21 where the injunction of *m.* occurs. The word *Shaddai* ("Almighty") is written on the back of the parchment and is often visible. The rabbis taught that the moral purpose of the *m.* is to teach that all man's material possessions are the gift of Heaven. The ignorant, however, have at times looked upon the *m.* as an

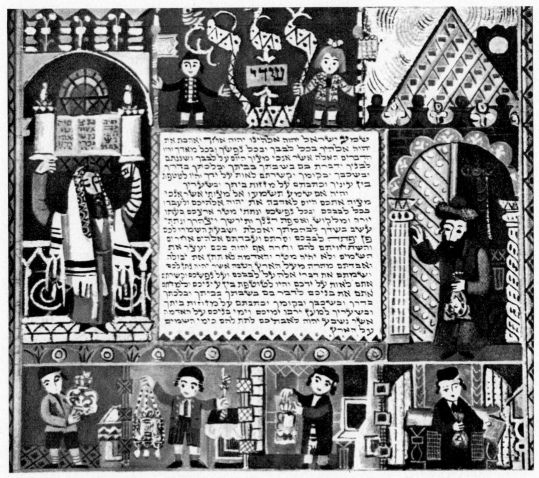

A Mezuzah written and illuminated by Ilyah Shor.

amulet to ward off evil spirits, and it is now often worn round the neck, etc. with this motive. The m.-case sometimes assumes artistic forms.

MEZUZAH: One of the seven minor talmudic tractates. Its two chapters deal with the various regulations pertaining to the writing and the use of the MEZUZAH.

MI ADDIR AL HA-KOL (Heb. "He who is mighty above all"): Ashkenazi alphabetic hymn of unknown authorship, recited before the wedding service.

MI SHE-BERAKH (Heb. "He who blessed"): Opening words of benedictory formula recited for the congregation, or for an individual after he is summoned to the reading of the Torah. It was customary to insert within the m.s. a promise of an offering to the synagogue or to charity in honor of relatives or friends, this being at one time a principal source of communal income.

MIAMI: City in Florida, US. Its first synagogue, B'nai Zion (from 1917 Beth David) was founded in 1912. The community of Miami Beach was organized in 1925, chiefly for winter visitors, but has since become an important all-year community. The Greater M. Jewish Federation was founded in 1938. The weekly *Jewish Floridian* appears in M. The town has the largest and most rapidly expanding Jewish community in the southern US numbering 200,000 (1973).

MIBASHAN see **BRAUNSTEIN**

MICAH (fl. latter 8th cent. BCE): Prophet in Judah, originating from Moresheth-Gath in the Shephelah and apparently of peasant stock. He speaks for the people against the oppression of the ruling-classes, being the first to threaten them with the destruction of the country and exile to Babylon. He foresees, however, a future monarch of the House of David who would bring peace to the world. M. bases human relations on the quality of mercy and the relations of man to God on humility. The prophecy was perhaps edited in M.'s lifetime, possibly by himself; it was already familiar in the reign of Jehoiakim (Jer. 26:18).

MICHAEL (Heb.; lit. "who is like unto God"): The prince of angels, according to Dan. 10:13. As the archangel nearest to God he is the chief Divine messenger and executes God's judgments. M. appears frequently in apocryphal and aggadic literature where he is described as the guardian angel of Israel, the chief antagonist of SATAN, and (as mediator between heaven and man) the keeper of the celestial keys.

MICHAEL, HEIMANN JOSEPH (1792—1846): German bibliophile. A merchant at Hamburg, he amassed an important library (929 mss, c. 5,500 printed books). The mss were acquired in 1848 by the Bodleian Library in Oxford and most of the printed books, by the British Museum.

MICHAELIS, SIR ARCHIE (1889–1973): Australian public figure. He was speaker of the Victorian Legislative Assembly 1950–2.

MICHAL: Younger daughter of Saul; wife of David. She assisted David to escape Saul's jealousy. Saul married her to another man after David fled to Judah, but the latter subsequently insisted on her return. When David danced before the ark on its entry into Jerusalem he was rebuked by M. for debasing himself. She died childless.

MICHELSON, ALBERT ABRAHAM (1852—1931): US physicist. After a few years as a naval officer, M. turned to scientific research, and was professor at the Univ. of Chicago from 1892. He successfully tested the relative velocity of the earth and the ether and also conducted studies in measuring the velocity of light. M.'s experiments broke down the theory of a static ether and laid much of the experimental base for the special theory of relativity. He received the Nobel Prize for physics in 1907.

MICHIGAN: US state. Jewish fur traders went there in the 1760's, and some of them were captured by the Indians during the 1763 uprising. M.'s few Jews were divided in their loyalties during the Revolutionary War. During the first half of the 19th cent., there were Jews in Mackinac. Organized Jewish communities appeared with the advent of immigrants from Germany in the 1840's The first Jewish services were held in Ann Arbor in 1845, and in 1848—9, the Ypsilanti-Ann Arbor community established the first Jewish cemetery in M. Soon, many of the Ypsilanti-Ann Arbor Jews moved to DETROIT where the first services were held in 1850. M.'s Jewry grew slowly until the arrival of E European Jews after 1880. The efforts of the INDUSTRIAL REMOVAL OFFICE to direct immigrants inland laid the foundation for the state's present thriving communities. Next to Detroit, Flint, Grand Rapids, and Ann Arbor have the largest Jewish populations. The total Jewish population of the state in 1973 was 93,400.

MICROCOCCUS PRODIGIOSUS: Scarlet microscopic organism which sometimes forms on stale food kept in a damp place. It is believed that its presence may have led to the medieval belief that the Jews were guilty of the DESECRATION OF THE HOST which miraculously "bled" in consequence.

MIDDOT see **HERMENEUTICS**

MIDDOT (Heb. "Measures"): Tenth tractate (ninth in some codices) in the Mishnah order of *Kodashim*, containing 5 chapters. It has *gemara* neither in the Babylonian nor Palestinian Talmud. It describes the architecture, organization, and dimensions of the Second Temple.

MIDIAN: Beduin tribe related to Abraham (Gen. 25:2). Its members traveled with caravans of incense from Gilead to Egypt, and later to other countries. They were closely connected with the Israelites. Moses fled from Pharaoh to M. and married there the daughter of JETHRO. At the end of the desert period, the princes of M. cooperated with Moab against Israel (Num. 21:29) and at a later period conducted a plundering expedition against the Valley of Jezreel; this was repulsed by Gideon (Judg. 6). They dwelt near the Moabites and Edomites. From Second Temple times, the Land of M. was thought to be located in NW Arabia.

MIDRASH: The finding of new meaning, in addition to the literal one, in the Scriptures. Talmudic tradition has formulated certain rules to deduce such hidden and new meanings (see HERMENEUTICS). In certain cases, the M. established the law; in others, it found scriptural support for laws already accepted. The entire talmudic literature is replete with the midrashic exposition of verses. Nevertheless, there exist certain specific independent midrashic compilations which retain the order of the verses as found in Scripture. The term M. is now applied mainly to M. AGGADAH—i.e., legend and ethics.

MIDRASH RABBAH: Collection of aggadic Midrashim to the Pentateuch and five *megillot*. It is composed of GENESIS RABBAH, EXODUS RABBAH, LEVITICUS RABBAH, NUMBERS RABBAH, DEUTERONOMY RABBAH, SONG OF SONGS RABBAH, RUTH RABBAH, LAMENTATIONS RABBATI, ECCLESIASTES RABBAH, and ESTHER RABBAH. These books stem from different periods and differ among themselves in their general character.

MIDRASHIC LITERATURE: Rabbinic books containing biblical interpretations in the spirit of the AGGADAH. Aggadic literature extends over a thousand years, ranging from tannaitic times to the 10th cent. It can be divided into works connected with the books of the Bible and those the subject of which is taken from the readings for specific festivals, etc. Of the former, the best-known is MIDRASH RABBAH on the Pentateuch and the five Scrolls. There are many differences in character and date of composition between the various parts and each is an independent work, having been gathered into one collection at a late date. The TANHUMA, in which the homilies generally begin with the words *Yelammedenu Rabbenu* "Our Rabbi, teach us") was quoted by early rabbis as *Yelammedenu*. Modern research has shown that there were originally several versions of this work. Other homiletic works on the Bible include Midrashim on Psalms (known as *Shoḥer Tov*), on Proverbs and on Samuel. The groups of Midrashim linked with the festivals and special Sabbaths are called *Pesiktot*. The PESIKTA DE-RAV KAHANA and PESIKTA RABBATI are series of homilies for special occasions in the Jewish year. In a different category are AVOT DE-RABBI NATAN, an expansion of the mishnaic tractate AVOT; DEREKH ERETZ RABBAH—ethical teachings dealing with modesty, table-manners, and conduct in society; DEREKH ERETZ ZUTA advising scholars on their religious and pedagogic activities; TANNA DE-VE 'ELIAHU, moral advice on everyday conduct; SEDER OLAM, a work of historical aggadah; and PIRKE DE-RABBI ELIEZER, stories connected with events from the creation of the world until the wanderings of the Israelites in the wilderness. Subsequent writers collected and arranged aggadic literature in several popular works, e.g. YALKUT SHIMONI (13th cent.: material arranged according to Bible verses). There are, in addition, large numbers of separate Midrashim of various dates on individual books of the Bible, as well as small Midrashim on various subjects (e.g. on the TEN MARTYRS). Many small Midrashim and fragments have been collected and published, especially by A. Jellinek and S.A. Wertheimer.

MIELZINER: (1) *MOSES M.* (1828–1903): Rabbi and talmudic authority. He went to the US in 1865 after occupying pulpits in Germany and Denmark. M. was rabbi in New York, and taught Talmud at Hebrew Union College, Cincinnati, of which he was president 1900–3. M. was an interpreter of rabbinics and Jewish law for the Reform movement. His writings include a standard *Introduction to the Talmud* and *Slavery among the Ancient Hebrews*. His son *LEO M.* (1869–1935) was a versatile artist specializing in portraiture, specimens of which are to be found in leading American museums. *JO M.* (1901–1976), son of Leo is a stage designer whose settings have been highly influential in the American theater. He has left Judaism.

MIGDAL: Israel village near the NW shore of the Sea of Galilee. It was founded in 1910 by Jews from Moscow. In 1924, part of the land was taken over by British Jews and Lord Melchett established a farm there. After the War of Independence, new immigrants were absorbed in the village. Tropical fruit (e.g. bananas, date-palms) are raised. Pop. (1972): 640. The name is historical, a place in this area being mentioned by Josephus as Migdal Nunia. It was perhaps the home of Mary Magdalene (see MAGDALA).

MIGDAL ASHKELON see ASCALON

MIGGO (Aram. "since"): Talmudic phrase for a type of legal proof. For example, if a man pleads a certain argument before the court when he could have chosen a more effective defense, he is believed, "since" he would have used the more conclusive argument had he been pleading falsely.

MIGRATION: The earliest mass-m. of the Jewish people was the wholesale deportation to Babylonia at the close of the First Temple Period, followed by the voluntary return from exile. In Second Temple times, there was a considerable movement of Jewish population, partly compulsory and partly voluntary: from Mesopotamia into Asia Minor and from Palestine to Egypt, where a great Jewish settlement was built up. Later, when Palestine came under Roman rule, the deportation of prisoners of war and the voluntary m. of merchants resulted in the establishment of an important Jewish center in Italy. The Jews were to some extent affected by the general movement of population in the Dark Ages. There seem to have been three main lines of m. into Europe, viz. from Palestine to S Italy, and thence over the Alps into France and Germany; from the Byzantine Empire up the valley of the Danube into Central Europe; and under the Arabs, from Mesopotamia and Egypt through Morocco into Spain. It was thus that between c. 500 and c. 1000, the balance of the Jewish population was gradually transferred from the the Middle East to W Europe. Later, the attractions of trade on the one hand and persecution and, ultimately, expulsion on the other, drove the mass of W European Jewry eastward again from N Europe into Poland, and from Spain largely to the Ottoman Empire. The Chmielnicki massacres in Poland in 1648–9, coinciding in date with the emergence of more favorable psychological and economic conditions in W Europe, resulted in a large-scale westward migration which, to a great extent, conditioned Jewsh history in the 17th–18th cents. Jewish m. differed from that of other peoples in its motivations and its proportions which far exceeded those of general migratory movements in the modern world. In other national migrations, economic factors have generally been decisive, but Jewish m. has generally been that of refugees. More recently, the voluntary return to Zion has been a new factor. Three main epochs of m. can be distinguished. (1) From the destruction of the Second Temple until the 19th cent., when Jews moved under the pressure of persecution and expulsion; (2) from the 1880's to World War I; a period of free m., chiefly to the US, caused by anti-semitism and economic factors; (3) from the 1920's onward, characterized by western restrictions on immigration and its consequent global dispersal, contrasting with the m. to Israel, now the chief country absorbing Jewish migrants. This development is reflected in the following tables:

TABLE I:
TOTAL JEWISH MIGRATION, 1881–1951

Period	Total No. Jewish Migrants	Annual Average
1881—1914	2,370,000	71,000
1919—1932	759,970	54,000
1933—1951	1,551,440	86,000
1881—1951	4,681,410	67,000

TABLE II:
JEWISH MIGRATION (except to Israel), 1881–1951

Period	Total No. Jewish Migrants	Annual Average
1881—1914	2,320,000	70,000
1919—1932	633,720	45,000
1933—1951	484,270	27,000
1881—1951	3,437,990	49,000
(1919—1951 only)	1,117,990	34,000

TABLE III:
IMMIGRATION TO ISRAEL (Palestine), 1881—1951

Period	Total No. Jewish Migrants	Annual Average
1881—1914	50,000	1,500
1919—1932	125,250	9,000
1933—May 1948	389,055	26,000
May 1948—1951	678,116	195,000
1881—1951	1,242,321	18,000
(1919—1951 only)	1,191,421	37,000

From 1952, Jewish m. diminished. Immigration to Israel, which had totaled nearly 700,000 during the previous 3½ years dwindled to 23,375 in 1952, 10,347 in 1953, and 17,471 in 1954. However, with the deterioration of conditions in N Africa and elsewhere the number rose (see ALIYAH). The decline in m. to other lands was more pronounced. The US, which absorbed 1,485,641 Jews between 1899 and 1914, and 129,078 in 1933—1940 was now taking only 5,000 Jewish immigrants a year. In 1963, it rose to 10,750 but in 1965 dropped to 7,800. Canada took in 289,615 Jews in 1920-4, and over 40,000 Jews after World War II, but from the peak figure in this latter period of 8,957 in 1948-9, the number fell to 5,092 in 1952-3 and 3,712 in 1953-4. It was 2,180 in 1963 and 3,113 in 1964. Similarly, Australia absorbed c. 18,000 Jews immediately after World War II, but from c. 1950 its doors—like those of Latin America— were virtually closed to Jewish immigrants. The sum total of m. over the past century is still huge. Of 5,025,000 migrants in the period 1840-1952, 3,154,000 (62.8%) were absorbed in the US and Canada, 1,243,000 (24.7%) in Palestine-Israel, and 628,000 (12.5%) in other countries. The chief results of recent Jewish m. have been: (a) the shifting of the center of gravity of Jewish life from E Europe to the American continent and the state of Israel; (b) the improvement of Jewish civil and economic conditions as a result of the movement from lands of poverty and persecution to free countries with a high standard of living; (c) the progressive diminution of the Jewries of Eastern countries (except Russia); and (d) the hastening of Assimilation as a result of the high cultural standards of the lands of absorption; while on the other hand, the establishment of the state of Israel has given an opportunity to develop Jewish culture.

MIKHMORET: Site of two Israel settlements and a fishing school in the Central Sharon plain. M. was founded by World War II veterans in 1945 as a cooperative settlement. In 1954, Mikhmoret *Bet* was formed in the vicinity, also as a fishing village, by Israelis and immigrants. The fishing school at M. is government-sponsored. An anchorage serves the two settlements and the school. Pop. (1972): 980.

MIKHOELS, SOLOMON (stage name of Solomon Vovsi; 1890—1948): Russian actor. From 1929, he directed the Jewish State Theater in Moscow. During World War II, he visited western countries in behalf of the Jewish Anti-Fascist Committee, but subsequently fell victim to the Stalinist purges.

MIKULOV (Ger. Nikolsburg): Czech city. The construction of a large synagogue in 1450 indicates the presence of a sizable Jewish community. The number of Jews grew steadily until World War I when a decline set in. M. had a famous yeshivah and was the home of a number of noted rabbis. The pre-World War II community of 900 Jews was completely destroyed by the Nazis.

MIKVAOT (Heb. "Ritual Baths"): Sixth tractate in the Mishnah order of *Tohorot*, containing 10 chapters. It has *gemara* neither in the Babylonian nor the Palestinian Talmud. It deals with the regulations of ritual bathing (Lev. 14:8; 15:5).

MIKVEH (Heb. "collection" especially of water): Ritual bath. Persons and some objects (e.g. certain types of new vessels made by a non-Jew) have to be immersed in a bath according to the laws of the Jewish religion. To be ritually fit for use, the *m.* has to contain sufficient water to cover the body of a woman of average size, while the water has to come from a natural spring or a river. Jews are forbidden to reside

Solomon Mikhoels.

Mikveh Israel.

in places where there is no *m.*, and it is permitted to sell even a synagogue to build a *m.* The *m.* is used mainly by the post-menstruous woman, although some observant Jews— especially among the Ḥasidim — immerse themselves on various occasions.

MIKVEH ISRAEL: Israel agricultural school near Tel Aviv. It was founded in 1870 by Charles NETTER in behalf of the Alliance Israélite Universelle, and was the first modern Jewish agricultural undertaking in the country. In the early years of Zionist activity, there was friction between the school's administration and the Zionists, the school for some time insisting on French as the language of instruction. Today M.I. is the foremost agricultural institution in Israel (becoming a government school in 1956), and has to its credit important research and practical work in agricultural research, botany, etc. In 1972, there were 655 teachers, pupils, and residents.

MILAH see **CIRCUMCISION**

MILAN: Italian town. Jews were found in M. in the Roman period, their synagogue being menaced by St. Ambrosius in 388. In the Middle Ages, the Jews were generally excluded from the city, and their main centers in the duchy of M. were at Pavia and Cremona. They were expelled from the entire duchy in 1597 when it was under Spanish rule. A community was established in the early 19th cent., and owing to immigration from the rest of Italy, Germany, Turkey, etc., has become numerically the most important in Italy after Rome, numbering (1973) 9,500. It suffered considerably during the German occupation in World War II.

MILCHIG (Yidd.): Adjective describing milk foods which, according to Jewish dietary law, are not to be consumed with or after meat-dishes (*fleishig*).

MILHAUD, DARIUS (1892–1974): French composer member of an old Provençal family. After World War I, he was a member of the well-known group of composers Les Six. In 1940, he escaped to the US and after World War II divided his time between that country and France. His operas include the large-scale *Christophe Colomb*, *Maximilien*, and *Simon Bolivar*, as well as shorter works on classic Greek subjects.

Darius Milhaud.

M.'s instrumental compositions comprise 6 symphonies, concertos, lighthearted works (some influenced by Jazz rhythms), and music for the stage (notably to works by Claudel), ballets, films, etc. Much of his music is of Jewish interest, including the operas *Esther de Carpentras* and *David*, his setting of *Poèmes Juifs*, *Chants hébraïques*, *Hymne de Sion*, *Cantique de Jérusalem*, and the Sabbath morning service.

MILITARY TITLES: The commonest biblical title is *sar*, particularly *sar tzava* (commander-in-chief), and also *sar gedud* (unit-commander), *sar ha-rekhev*

Nathan Milstein.

COMMISSIONED RANKS

Israel	English	
(Army, Navy, Air Force)	Army	Navy
Rav-Aluph	Major-General	Rear Admiral
Aluph	Brigadier	Commodore
Tat-Aluph	(US: Brigadier General)	
Aluph-Mishneh	Colonel	Captain
Segan-Aluph	Lt.-Colonel	Commander
Rav-Seren	Major	Lt.-Commander
Seren	Captain	Lieutenant
Segen	Lieutenant (US: First-Lieutenant)	Sub-Lieutenant (US: Lieutenant, junior grade)
Segen Mishneh	Second-Lieutenant	(US: Ensign)

NON-COMMISSIONED (Other) RANKS

Israel	English
Rav-Sammal Rishon	Regimental Sergeant Major
Rav-Sammal	Company Sergeant Major (US: First Sergeant) (US: Master Sergeant)
Sammal Rishon	Staff Sergeant (US: Sergeant, 1st Class)
Sammal	Sergeant
Rav-Turai	Corporal
Turai Rishon	Lance Corporal (US: Private, 1st Class)
Turai	Private (US: Recruit).

(captain of chariots), *sar ḥamishim* (captain of 50), *sare alaphim*, *sare meot*, *sare asarot* (commanders of thousands, hundreds, tens). These latter four also appear in the Dead Sea Scroll of the *War of the Sons of Light against the Sons of Darkness*. Other examples are *shalish* (charioteer), sometimes used for an officer; *sar ha-tabbaḥim* (captain of the bodyguard) occurs under Babylonian influence. *Pakid* and *Katzin* were rarer terms for commanders.

The above lists contain the names of the ranks of the Land, Sea, and Air Forces of the Israel Defense Forces, together with their English and American equivalents.

MILLAUD, EDOUARD (1834—1912): French statesman. Founder of the law school at Lyons, M. was a deputy from 1871, senator in 1880, and minister of public works 1886—7.

MILLER, ARTHUR (1915—): US author. His first work, a novel, *Focus*, dealt with anti-Semitism. His plays include *All My Sons*, *The Crucible*, *A View from the Bridge*, and *The Price*. The most important, *Death of a Salesman*, won a Pulitzer Prize, and is a realistically critical expression of popular American ideals. *After the Fall* was inspired by the personality of his ex-wife, the film actress Marilyn Munroe, who adopted Judaism prior to their marriage.

MILLIN: (1) *PHILIP M.* (1888–1952): S African jurist. He was appointed judge of the Transvaal division of the S African Supreme Court in 1937. (2) *SARAH GERTRUDE M.* (1892–1968): Author; wife of (1) She wrote novels of S African life, as well as plays and biographies.

MILLO (Heb. "filling"): Name given to a point — probably a depression — at N end of David's city of Jerusalem, dividing it from the Temple. Solomon is recorded as having "built" M. (I Kings 9:15), which was "strengthened" by Hezekiah (II Chron. 32:5), suggesting that in later days, a fortification was erected on the site.

*MILMAN, HENRY HART (1791—1868): English divine: from 1849, dean of St. Paul's Cathedral, London. In 1820, he published a poem on the Fall of Jerusalem and in 1830, a *History of the Jews* down to his own time that is still widely read.

MILSTEIN, NATHAN (1904—): Violinist. He began his career in Russia but left there in 1925 and has since appeared with many major orchestras in Europe and since 1928, in the US where he has made his home.

MILWAUKEE: City in Wisconsin, US. Jewish settlement there began in 1836. Congregation Emanu-El was formed in 1849; in 1856, it combined with Congregation Ahavath Emunah (organized in 1850) to form

Congregation B'ne Jeshurun. A group seceding from B'ne Jeshurun in 1869 constituted a Reform congregation Emanu-El. These groups were reunited in 1927. E European immigrants arriving in the 1880's laid the foundation for M.'s present Orthodox community. Jews were among the pioneers of many of M.'s commerical and industrial establishments. In 1973, it had 23,900 Jews with 6 synagogues. The weekly *Wisconsin Jewish Chronicle* appears in M. The M. Jewish Welfare Fund was founded in 1938.

MINC, HILARY (1905–): Polish communist statesman. Escaping to the USSR in 1939, he helped to organize the free Polish forces. He became minister of commerce in the 1945 Polish government, controller of the country's economy in 1948, and deputy premier 1952-6.

MINHAG (Heb.): Custom or observance. With reference to the Jewish liturgy, the prayer customs of a given sector of Jewry (e.g. Ashkenazim, Sephardim).

MINHAH (Heb. "offering"): (1) Term applied to various types of meal-offering described in Lev. 2. These could be unbaked, baked in an oven or on a griddle, cooked, or parched with fire. They had to be made with oil and seasoned with salt, but leaven was forbidden as an ingredient. Part was offered on the altar and the rest belonged to the priests. (2) Daily prayer. It was instituted in place of the afternoon Temple meal-offering two and a half hours before nightfall but could be recited any time after midday until sunset. On Sabbath and fasts, a portion of the Pentateuch is read at M. According to the rabbis, the service was initiated by the patriarch Isaac.

MINIM: Talmudic term for sects holding views considered heretical by Pharisaic tradition. The designation was applied variously to early Christians, gnostics, and other dissidents. Commentators and scholars differ as to the philological origin of the term.

MINKOFF, NOCHUM B. (1893—1958): Yiddish poet. Born in Poland, he settled in 1914 in New York where he helped found the *In-Sich* introspectionist movement in Yiddish poetry. In 1926, he reverted to objectivism. He edited the monthly *Zukunft* and published *The Yiddish Pioneer Poets in America*.

MINKOWSKI, MAURICE (1881—1930): Polish artist. Despite being deaf and dumb, he achieved prominence as a realistic chronicler in the Czarist Period, dramatically portraying traditional Jewish life and sufferings.

MINKOWSKY, HERMANN (1864—1909): Mathematician; born in Lithuania. Baptized, he taught at Bonn, Königsberg, Zürich, and Göttingen. M. is noted for his investigations of the mathematical basis of relativity, giving the time dimension equal importance with the space dimensions.

MINKOWSKY, PHINEHAS (1859—1924): Cantor. He officiated at Kishinev (1877), Kherson (1880), and New York (1884). Succeeding his teacher Nisan

Blumenthal at the Broder synagogue, Odessa, he introduced — together with his choir master David NOVAKOVSKY — a modern rite, utilizing an organ and a choir of 40, but in a traditional style which rejected modern cantoral abuses. M. also taught at the Jewish Conservatoire of Music and wrote on the history of Jewish ritual. In 1923, he settled in the US.

MINNEAPOLIS: City in Minnesota, US. Jews from Central Europe settled there in the late 1860's and in 1871, were joined by Jewish refugees from the Chicago fire and the yellow fever epidemic in the South. In 1878, a congregation was formed. After 1880, large numbers of Jews from E Europe settled in M. and founded Orthodox congregations. M. has an outstanding educational system. The M. Federation for Jewish Service was founded in 1931. The weekly *American Jewish World* began appearing in 1912. Jewish pop. (1973): 22,085.

MINNESOTA: US state. Its Jewish settlement dates from the mid-19th cent. when immigrants from Central Europe went to ST. PAUL and in the late 1860's to MINNEAPOLIS. The community in DULUTH originated in the 1870's. Until the arrival of immigrants from E Europe in the 1880's, the Jewish population of M. remained small. In the first decade of the 20th cent. the INDUSTRIAL REMOVAL OFFICE settled 1,371 Jews in 40 M. cities and towns. M.'s Jewish farm population is small. In 1973, there were 34,885 Jews in M. the largest centers being Minneapolis (22,085), St. Paul (10,000), and Duluth (1,100).

MINOR PROPHETS see **PROPHETS, MINOR**

MINORCA: Second of the BALEARIC ISLANDS, belonging to Spain. The Jews occupied an honored place there in the Roman Period but in 418, were forced to adopt Christianity by the attacks of a mob led by St. Severus. The records of Jews in the island in the Middle Ages are sparse, and none survived the expulsion of 1490. A Jewish community was briefly reestablished when M. was under British rule in the 18th cent.

MINORITY RIGHTS: Before and during World War I Jewish bodies concerned with the position of the Jews in E Europe organized a movement for securing in the peace treaties provisions for the religious, civil, and political rights of racial, religious, and linguistic minorities in those countries. They took the lead in approaching the Principal Allied Powers at the Peace Conference in 1919, and obtained their agreement that special treaties should be made with the "successor states" of the Austro-Hungarian and Czarist Empire and the enlarged states of SE Europe. The recognition of "national" minorities was, however, rejected, and a project to include an article in the Covenant of the LEAGUE OF NATIONS concerning the assurance of m.r. was abandoned. Treaties, however, were made by the Principal Allied Powers, first with Poland and then with Rumania, Hungary, Austria,

Lithuania, Latvia, etc. The Polish treaty, which was the most detailed, prescribed that all permanent residents who were not foreign nationals should have Polish nationality, and that all Polish nationals should be equal before the law, enjoying the same civil and political rights. Those who belonged to a minority should be entitled to establish their own charitable and religious institutions and schools with the right to use their own language. Education Committees, appointed locally by Polish Jewish communities, should provide for the distribution of the public funds allocated to Jewish schools. Jews were not to be compelled to perform any act which constituted a violation of the Sabbath, and no election should be held on a Saturday. Poland agreed that these obligations were of international concern and would be under the guarantee of the League of Nations. Any member of the Council of the League of Nations would have the right to bring any infringement to the attention of the Council. Numerous petitions were in fact submitted to the Council of the League about m.r. and it was the regular procedure to refer them to a committee of three members of the Council. Two famous petitions by Jewish bodies were so referred. The first in 1920, and again in 1924, concerned the introduction of the NUMERUS CLAUSUS in Hungarian universities. The second — the Bernheim petition in 1933 — concerned the application of Nazi racial legislation to the Jews in Upper Silesia where the protection of minorities was stipulated in a Polish-German convention. Action was taken in both cases but was only effective for a short time. During the second decade of the inter-war period, the minority treaties were widely disregarded by the nations which had signed them. At the end of World War II, the Charter of the UNITED NATIONS did not revive the provisions about m.r. It was decided to enlarge the international guarantee so as to cover the rights of all individuals, whether of the majority or a minority in the state. The question remained whether and to what extent the old treaties were still in force. A fundamental principle of the UN Charter is to provide and encourage respect for Human Rights without distinction on grounds of race, religion, or language. The Human Rights Commission, established by the Economic and Social Council, has formed a sub-committee concerned with the prevention of discrimination and with the rights of minorities.

MINSK: White Russian town. Jews are first mentioned there in the 15th cent. They received a charter from Stephen Batory of Poland in 1579. The community suffered in the Chmielnicki uprising of 1648, was expelled in 1654, and attacked in 1671. M. was the scene of bitter disputes between Mitnaggedim and Ḥasidim and between the orthodox and *maskilim*. In the 20th cent., it was a center of Jewish revolutionaries, and in the 1920's, of Jewish communists. In the latter period the community of c. 54,000 accounted for 40% of the total population. In 1941—3, M. was a concentration center of Jews prior to extermination by the Nazis. Jewish pop. (1970): 47,057.

MINSKY, N. (pseudonym of Nicholas Vilenkin; 1855—1937): Russian poet. Preaching art for art's sake, he was a prominent literary figure and translated the *Iliad* into Russian. He left Russia after the Communist Revolution.

MINYAN (Heb. "number"): A group of ten male adult Jews, the minimum required for communal prayer. Among Sephardim, "to enter *minyan*" means to become BAR MITZVAH.

MINYAN MAN: One who attends service regularly, for payment, to ensure a *minyan*.

MINYAN SHETAROT see **CHRONOLOGY**

MINZ see **MÜNZ**

MIR: Polish townlet. Its yeshivah, founded in 1817, achieved a reputation throughout the Jewish world. The student body was rescued in World War II and after a period in Shanghai, the yeshivah was transferred to Brooklyn, NY, in 1947 as the Mirrer Yeshivah Central Institute. Some of its leading scholars founded a M. yeshivah in Jerusalem.

*MIRABEAU, GABRIEL-HONORÉ DE RIQUETI, COMTE DE (1749–1791): French revolutionary. His interest in Jewish emancipation dated from 1786, and in the following year, he wrote a work in its favor. In the National Assembly of 1789, he advocated religious liberty for all Frenchmen, including Jews.

MIRACLES: Events attributed to supernatural intervention. In a strict sense the concept of m. as a suspension of or exception to the laws of nature presupposes the notion of nature as a closed system of causal relations. Consequently m. could become a theological and philosophical problem only at a later date: at an earlier stage the distinction was not between natural and supernatural, but between usual, viz. normal, and extraordinary phenomena. Though the normal run of things is Divinely willed and ordered (cf. Gen. 8:22 and Ps. 104), special intervention breaking through this established order is possible and, in fact, characteristic of biblical history. God works "signs and wonders" for Israel to save His people and make them "believe" (cf. Ex. 4:1—10); elsewhere (Deut. 14:2—4) it is indicated that m. must not be considered to prove the truth of any message or teaching but may occur to test steadfastness. Biblical and talmudic legend recount m. wrought by or to (through their merits) many saintly "men of God". Medieval Jewish philosophers attempted to rationalize m. In support of their views they quoted a rabbinic saying (*Avot* 4:6) to the effect that m. were foreordained at the time of creation, i.e., their occurrence does not really constitute a contradiction of the natural order. Rationalists have sought natural explanations for m. described in the Bible, whilst modern scholarship is inclined to regard them as products of creative religious imagination.

*MIRANDOLA, GIOVANNI PICO DELLA (1463–1494): Italian humanist. Of noble family and an eager student of philosophy, he was taught Hebrew by Elijah del Medigo and became convinced that the Kabbalah contained the key to the verities of Christianity. His writings show a considerable range of Jewish knowledge and mark the beginning of the study by Christians of Hebrew as an academic discipline rather than a theological instrument.

MIRIAM (etymology unknown; possibly from Egyptian *Meri*="love"): Elder sister of Moses. She watched her infant brother when placed in a chest on the Nile and on her suggestion, Pharaoh's daughter called the child's mother to nurse him. After the Red Sea crossing, M. led the Israelite women in a triumphal song and dance. The Bible and Jewish literature account her a prophetess. Together with Aaron, she challenged the sole leadership of Moses and as a punishment was temporarily afflicted with leprosy. She died and was buried at Kadesh in the Sinai desert forty years after the exodus. M. figures frequently in aggadah where her merits are emphasized.

MISEH (=**MITAH**) **MESHUNNEH** (Heb. "strange death"): An abnormal or violent death; used as an imprecation.

MISHMAR HA-EMEK: Israel communal settlement (KA) in W Valley of Jezreel. Founded by immigrants from Poland in 1926, it suffered heavy attacks by Arab bands in the disturbances of 1929 and 1936–9. In the War of Independence an army of Arab irregulars under Fawzi Kawukji was routed when it marched against M.H., this constituting the first major Israel victory in the war. M. H., is the regional educational center of *Ha-Shomer ha-Tzair*. Pop. (1972): 923.

MISHMAR HA-YARDEN: Israel settlement. It was founded in 1890 by immigrants from E Europe, aided by Baron Edmond de Rothschild. The settlement did not develop satisfactorily owing to the prevalence of malaria. In the Israel War of Independence the Syrian army established a bridgehead over the Jordan at M. H. and attacked fiercely in an attempt to cut off the Ḥuleh Valley. In the heavy fighting (May–July 1948) the settlement was completely destroyed. After its restoration to Israel, in accordance with the Israel-Syrian Armistice Agreement, two new settlements were erected on its land, a smallholders' village (affiliated to *Herut*) and Ha-Goverim, a communal settlement (KM). Pop. (1972): 229.

MISHNAH: Legal codification containing the core of the Oral Law. It was compiled by R Judah Ha-Nasi on the basis of previous collections and arranged logically. It is divided into six Orders (Heb. *sedarim*): (1) *Zeraim* ("seeds")—dealing primarily with the religious laws pertaining to agriculture. (2) *Moed* ("season")—dealing with the laws of Sabbath, festivals, etc. (3) *Nashim* ("women")—dealing with the laws of marriage and divorce and vows. (4) *Nezikin*

The Tractates of the Mishnah
(for details see entry for each tractate).

ORDER		
1. *Zeraim*		
Berakhot	Sheviit	Hallah
Peah	Terumot	Orlah
Demai	Maaserot	Bikkurim
Kilayim	Maaser Sheni	
2. *Moed*		
Shabbat		Betzah (Yom Tov)
Eruvin		Rosh ha-Shanah
Pesaḥim		Taanit
Shekalim		Megillah
Yoma		Moed Katan
Sukkah		Ḥagigah
3. *Nashim*		
Yevamot	Nedarim	Gittin
Ketubbot	Nazir	Sota
		Kiddushin
4. *Nezikin*		
Bava Kamma	Sanhedrin	Eduyyot
Bava Metzia	Makkot	Avodah Zarah
Bava Batra	Shevuot	Avot
		Horayot
5. *Kodashim*		
Zevaḥim	Bekhorot	Meilah
Menaḥot	Arakhin	Tamid
Ḥullin	Temurah	Middot
	Keritot	Kinnim
6. *Tohorot*		
Kelim	Tohorot	Zavim
Oholot	Mikvaot	Tevul Yom
Negaim	Niddah	Yadayim
Parah	Makhshirin	Uktzin

("damages")—treating of civil and criminal legislation (5) *Kodashim* ("holy things")—describing the laws regulating ritual slaughter, sacrifices, and consecrated objects. (6) *Tohorot* ("purities")—dealing with the laws of ceremonial purity. Every Order is subdivided into tractates, each of which deals with a specific topic. Every tractate is divided into chapters, and these contain smaller paragraph divisions called *mishnayyot* (see LAW, ORAL; TALMUD).

MISHNEH TORAH see **MOSES BEN MAIMON**

MISHPOKHE (Heb. *mishpaḥah*): Family, relatives.

MISSIONS: The medieval Church organizations which were largely devoted to conversionist propaganda, such as the Dominican order, may be regarded as the prototypes for the Christian m. among the Jews. The 17th-18th cents. saw the rise in the Protestant countries of religious m. for the propagation of Christianity among the heathen which inevitably also stimulated similar systematic efforts for the conversion of the Jews. The earliest specific organizations of this nature were founded in Holland toward the end of the 17th cent., later spreading to Germany where the Institutum Judaicum at Halle was founded in 1728. In England, the London Society for Promoting Christianity among the Jews was founded in 1809, partly as a result of the efforts of the apostate Joseph Samuel Frey, who later continued his activities in the US. Though its results were negligible and the few converts frequently men of low character, the organization commanded very wide support and stimulated counter-activity among the Jews, e.g. improved educational facilities. The records of these m. are frequently important as historical sources. The educational and medical facilities set up by these organizations among poor Jewish communities in Europe and in Near Eastern countries (including Palestine) sometimes did useful work but were centers of propaganda. Similar Catholic m. among the Jews began late under the auspices of the order of Notre Dame de Sion founded by the Ratisbonne brothers. Since 1945, some Catholic m., especially since the Second Vatican Council, have adopted a more sympathetic viewpoint and have been prominent in pro-Jewish propaganda.

MISSISSIPPI: US state. There were Jews among the colonists settled in Biloxi and Natchez by John Law's Mississippi Company in 1699. Despite the BLACK CODE enforced from 1724, Jews settled in Biloxi and Natchez in the 1750's. While southern M. was part of British W Florida from 1763, the authorities remained indifferent to the Code but forbade Jews to vote. By the time M. became a state in 1817, there were about 100 Jews living in Natchez and the Gulf Coast towns, most of them peddlers or storekeepers originally from Alsace and Germany. The oldest existing congregation is B'nai Israel, established in Natchez in 1840. In 1841, the Anshe Chesed Congregation was formed in Vicksburg where Jews had settled a decade earlier. Between 1830 and 1850, Alsatian and German Jews founded about 15 communities in M. Between 1870—90, E European immigrants moved into the Delta area. In the years 1901—17, the INDUSTRIAL REMOVAL OFFICE settled 353 Jews in 46 different towns. In 1973, M. had 4,165 Jews living chiefly in Greenville Clarksdale, Jackson, Vicksburg, Meridian, and Cleveland. Greenville, Jackson, and Vicksburg had federations and welfare funds.

MISSOURI: US state. Individual Jews from the East settled in ST. LOUIS, Cape Girardeau, Troy, and Louisiana early in the 19th cent. Jewish peddlers opened stores in new towns along the Mississippi and M. rivers in the 1820's and 1830's. In the general movement westward, many Jews, mostly immigrants from Austria, Bohemia, and Germany, went to M. in the 1840's. M.'s Jewish population increased further with the arrival of persons fleeing from yellow fever epidemics in the South, refugees from the Chicago Fire of 1871, and especially E European Jews who arrived after 1880. The INDUSTRIAL REMOVAL OFFICE settled 6,000 Jews in 51 centers in the early 1900's. The largest Jewish communities in M. are in St. Louis and KANSAS CITY. There were 75,525 Jews in M. in 1973.

MITNAGGEDIM (Heb. "opponents"): Opponents of the Hasidic movement, so called after the issuance of a ban against the Hasidim by the Vilna Gaon in 1772. The reasons for the opposition were (1) the pantheistic tendencies of the Hasidim; (2) their use of the Sephardi liturgy; (3) the establishment by them of separate synagogues; (4) their belief in *tzaddikim*. As a result of the ban, Shneour Zalman of Lyady was arrested and held in S. Petersburg fortress in 1798. After his release, the conflict died down. During the 19th cent. the two groups were largely reconciled, though the term Mitnagged is still widely used.

MITTWOCH, EUGEN (1876—1942): German orientalist. He was professor at Berlin Univ. and director of its Institute of Oriental Languages. Dismissed by the Nazis, he went to London in 1939. His many writings include studies on the life of Mohammed and the influence of Judaism on Moslem prayer and histories of Arab medicine and Moslem art, etc.

MITZVAH (Heb. "commandment"): An injunction of the Torah, which can be positive (*mitzvat aseh*) or negative (*mitzvat lo taaseh*). According to the Talmud (*Makkot* 23*b*), there are 613 PRECEPTS in the Pentateuch (*mitzvot de-orayta*) besides commandments decreed by the rabbis (*mitzvot de-rabbanan*). Various scholars enumerated the list of commandments, and different versions exist. The Talmud (*Yoma* 67*b*) differentiates between two categories of commandments: (1) *mishpatim* ("ordinances")–commandments, the observance of which would have been deducible even if the Bible had not enjoined them; and (2) *hukkim* ("statutes") —commandments which would not have been logically derived unless specifically commanded. Medieval Jewish scholars termed the first category *sikhliyyot* (rational) and the second *shimiyot* ("revealed"). Other distinctions have also been made, such as: commandments performed with the external limbs of the body and those by the heart; commandments regulating conduct between man and his Maker and between man and his fellows; commandments the observance of which are contingent upon a particular time and commandments which are permanently obligatory; commandments applicable only to Palestine and those not depending upon Palestine. The term *m.* is applied colloquially to any good or charitable deed; also to synagogue honors.

MIXED MARRIAGES see **INTERMARRIAGE**

MIZPAH (or Mizpeh): Place in the territory of Benjamin. It was regarded as sacred from the beginning of the period of the Judges; thus, Samuel gathered there the Israelites for prayer before they issued forth against the Philistines, and after their victory, Samuel visited M. annually to judge the people. After the split in the kingdom, M. was in Judah, serving as a fort against Israel. It retained its importance, and was the residence of Gedaliah during his governorship of Judah. Again settled after the return from Babylon,

Judah the Maccabee and his men also assembled there to pray before going out to battle. The place has been identified with Nebi Samwil, 4½ m. NW of Jerusalem, but most scholars now place it at Tel en-Nasbe, 7½ m. N of the city.

MIZRAH (Heb. "east"): A decorated parchment or metal plate hung on a wall to indicate, for purposes of prayer, the direction of Jerusalem. Yidd.—a place of honor.

MIZRAHI (abb. Heb. *merkaz ruhani* —"spiritual center"): Religious Zionist organization. It was founded in 1901 as a reaction to a resolution sponsored by the DEMOCRATIC FRACTION at the 5th Zionist Congress favoring a program of national education to be officially sponsored by the Zionist Movement. In 1903, the first World *M.* conference took place in Pressburg (then Hungary) and was attended by hundreds of delegates from all over the world, including the US. It adopted a program of religious Zionism within the framework of the Zionist movement. Since the establishment of the state of Israel, *M.* has participated in coalition governments. It had 4 seats in the First Knesset, 2 in the Second and—together with HA-POEL HA-MIZRAHI—11 in the Third, 12 in the Fourth and Fifth, 11 in the Sixth, 12 in the Seventh, 10 in the Eighth. Generally *M.* has concentrated on education and, until the institution of State Religious Education, catered, together with *Ha-Poel ha-Mizrahi*, to over 60,000 children in kindergartens, elementary and secondary schools, trade schools, yeshivot, and higher institutions of learning. It created an organization for yeshivot known as *Miphal ha-Torah*. The MOSAD HA-RAV KOOK publishing society, the *Talmudic Encyclopedia*, and the new edition of the Talmud were all initiated by the *M.* BAR-ILAN UNIV. in Ramat Gan is conducted in the spirit of traditional Judaism. The *M.* also maintains economic enterprises including banks and a company for constructing housing quart-

First convention of the Mizraḥi in Poland (Warsaw, 1917).

ers. Together with *Ha-Poel ha-Mizraḥi* it conducts an organization dealing with refugee rabbis, Youth Aliyah etc. Its women section, *Omen*, concentrates on kindergartens, social welfare, and children's homes. M. has branches throughout the world. Since the merger decision of 1955, *M.* has joined with *Ha-Poel ha-Mizraḥi* to constitute the NATIONAL RELIGIOUS PARTY.

MIZRAHI, ELIJAH (d. 1526): Turkish talmudist and mathematician. As *Ḥakham Bashi* of Turkey from c. 1495, he advocated a more tolerant treatment of the Karaites. Among M.'s many works are an important collection of responsa, a super-commentary on that of Rashi on the Pentateuch, and a learned mathematical treatise.

MNEMONICS: Words used as aids in memorizing.

In Hebrew, the most common form of mnemonic is the combination of the initials of a sequence of words (or of the numerical value of numbers) into some easily remembered verbal form. M. of this type, indicating the order of treatment of various subjects, are sometimes interpolated in the Talmud. Psalms and prayers from early times were often written as alphabetic acrostics so that they should be easily memorized. The mnemonic may sometimes constitute actual words, more often meaningless syllables.

MOAB: Country in S Transjordan. The land (or "Field") of M. is bounded by the river Ḥeshbon in the N, and the river Zered in the S, the Jordan and Dead Sea to the W, and the Syrian Desert on the E The Moabites were kindred to the Israelites, being traditionally descended —like the Ammonites —from Lot (Gen. 19:37). Their language was akin to biblical Hebrew. In the patriarchal era, they settled in their land which had been captured from the Rephaim (or Emim; cf. Deut. 2:10—11). During the Exodus Period, part of this territory came under the rule of the Amorite monarch Sihon, but after his defeat by the Israelites was occupied by the latter and become an object of contention between Israel, Moab, and Ammon. Originally divided into small tribes, the Moabites united into a single kingdom, and it was their second ruler BALAK who summoned BALAAM to curse the Israelites. Under their king Eglon, the Moabites extended their territory to the Jericho region until Eglon was killed by EHUD. David conquered M. (II Sam. 8:2) which remained under the suzerainty of the Northern Kingdom down to the rebellion of MESHA of M. (II Kings. 1:1; see also MOABITE STONE). In the reign of Tiglath-Pileser III, M. became an Assyrian province. During the Persian Period, Arabs penetrated the country and assimilated with the inhabitants. M. was conquered by the Hasmoneans and was later incorporated by the Romans into Arabia. The Pentateuch forbids intermarriage with a Moabite (Deut. 23:4). The Talmud interpreted this as referring only to males and the prohibition was abolished in the Mishnaic Period. RUTH was a Moabitess.

Moabite Stone known as the Mesha Stele

MOABITE STONE (also known as the Mesha Stele): Stone inscribed and set up by MESHA, king of Moab, to commemorate his successful revolt against Joram of Israel (cf. II Kings 3:4 ff.). It was found at the Moabite capital, Dibon, in 1868, and is now in the Louvre. It records Omri's subjection of Moab and Moab's liberation from Israel. Its language is closely akin to Hebrew.

MOADIM LE-SIMḤAH ("Holidays for rejoicing"); GREETING (from the festival *Kiddush*) used among Sephardim (now general in Israel) on religious holidays. The reply is *Ḥagim u-Zemanim le-Sason* (= "Festivals and festal periods for joy").

MOBILE: Seaport in Alabama, US. Individual Jews went to M. at the close of the 18th cent. In 1841, lots for a cemetery were purchased by the Shaarai Shomayim Congregation, legally incorporated 3 years later. By 1885, there were about 75 Jewish families in M. A number of Jews from M. served with Alabama regiments during the Civil War. An Orthodox congregation, Ahavas Chesed, was organized by a group of Russian Jews in 1900. In 1973, there were 1,200 Jews in M., which had a Jewish Welfare Federation.

MOCATTA (or **MOCATO**): Sephardi family of Marrano origin. The *Calle Mocato* in the Venetian ghetto still commemorates their presence there.

MOSES M. (formerly Alonso Nuñez Marchena) settled in Holland, c. 1640. Another *MOSES M.* (d. 1693) was among the earliest members of the Sephardi community in London, his descendants still being associated with the firm of Mocatta and Goldsmid, bullion brokers to the Bank of England since the 18th cent. His descendants included *FREDERIC DAVID M.* (1828–1902), philanthropist and bibliophile, who bequeathed the MOCATTA LIBRARY to the Jewish Historical Society of England.

MOCATTA LIBRARY: Library of Jewish history and English Judaica, housed at University College, London, and administered in conjunction with the Jewish Historical Society of England. Its nucleus was the library of Frederic David MOCATTA. Destroyed in a German air-raid in 1940, it has since been reconstituted.

MOCH, JULES SALVADOR (1893–): French politician. He supported the Popular Front and was minister of public works in Leon Blum's 1938 cabinet. During World War II, he worked with Gen. de Gaulle. After the war, he was minister of communications 1945–7, of the interior 1947–50, and for a short period in 1958, and of national defense 1950–1. Nominated premier in 1949, he failed to obtain a majority in the National Assembly.

MODENA: Italian city, formerly the capital of a duchy. The history of the Jewish community dates from 1373, when Jewish loan-bankers were first established. Under the ducal house of Este the Jews at first flourished, but the ghetto system was introduced in 1638. In the 17th–18th cents., it was one of the most important communities in Italy, with Sephardi as well as Ashkenazi and Italian synagogues and a flourishing intellectual life, being a center of Kabbalistical study as well as of support for Palestinian settlement. In the 19th cent., the duchy of M. followed a reactionary policy which lasted until it was united with the kingdom of Italy in 1861. The community was reduced to insignificance by the deportations of World War II. Jewish pop. (1970): 150.

MODENA, AARON BERECHIAH (d. 1639): Italian kabbalist. He composed liturgical collections and the widely-used *Maavar Yabbok* containing prayers for the sick and the dead, mourning regulations, etc.

MODENA, LEONE (1571–1648): Italian rabbi. He lived and taught at Ferrara and elsewhere, but was associated especially with Venice where he spent the greater part of his life. Though not a profound scholar, he was versatile, widely read, remarkably prolific and articulate, famous as a preacher, and published large numbers of books both in Hebrew and Italian. His writings brought him into contact with many of the leading non-Jewish scholars of his time, both in Italy and elsewhere, to whom he represented Jewish scholarship. His personal character was not high, and he was a leader of the gambling

coterie in the Venetian ghetto. He also directed its theater and musical academy. His letters and autobiography (one of the earliest in Hebrew) throw much light on social conditions in Italian Jewry in his day.

MODIGLIANI, AMADEO (1884–1920): Painter. After studying in his native Italy, he went in 1906 to Paris where his artistic career was spent against a background of dissipation and poverty. He first exhibited in 1915. After coming under the influence of Cézanne, the cubists, and medieval art, he evolved a highly individual style, notably in evocative portraits and nudes. Fame came to him only after his death, and he is now considered among the greatest of modern artists.

MODIIN (MODIIM): Ancient Israelite town, SE of Lydda. It was the home of the Hasmoneans and the scene of Mattathias' first rebellion against the officials of Antiochus Epiphanes. His son Simon built there an impressive family mausoleum, remains of which still survive. A burning torch is now carried to Jerusalem from M. each Hanukkah by relay runners.

MOED (Heb. "Set Feast"): Second Order (*Seder*) of the Mishnah, consisting of 12 tractates to all of which there is *gemara* in both the Babylonian and Palestinian Talmuds (except for *Shekalim* which has only the latter). The tractates of the Order deal with the laws concerning the Sabbath, festivals, and fast days.

MOED KATAN (Heb. "Minor Festival"): Eleventh (twelfth in some codices) tractate in the Mishnah order of *Moed*, containing 3 chapters. It has *gemara* in both the Babylonian and Palestinian Talmuds. It is also known as *Mashkin* (after the opening word) or simply *Moed*. It deals with the nature of work

Amadeo Modigliani: *Portrait of Chaim Soutine.*

permitted during the intermediate days of Passover and Tabernacles and also discusses mourning on holidays.

MOETZET HA-POALIM (Heb. "Workers' Council"): In the Israel labor movement, the supreme authority of the HISTADRUT in a given locality. It supervises the enterprises and institutions serving the workers and furthers their economic consolidation. The *M. P.* is elected by the local workers by proportional representation, and in turn elects the secretariat and the local *Histadrut* court.

MOETZET HA-POALOT (Heb. "Women Workers' Council"): Central institution of the women's labor movement in Israel. Its activities include vocational and agricultural training for women, hostels, advice bureaus, work enterprises, etc. It also organizes cultural and information activities and publishes the journal *Devar ha-Poelet*. *M. P.* maintains agricultural and trade schools, evening courses, a training center for children's nurses, and girls' clubs. For children, it runs residential schools, day-nurseries, kindergartens, clubs, feeding centers, and summer camps, attended in all by 20,000 children. *M. P.* also supports a fund for aid to immigrants. The central council is elected at a national conference of female members of the HISTADRUT.

MOGADOR (Essaouira): Moroccan town. The Jewish quarter (*mellah*) was established in 1807 and the authorities appointed a Jewish representative responsible for the payment of special taxes imposed on the Jews. Jewish pop. (1970): 500.

*MOHAMMED (c. 570–632): The prophet of ISLAM. In his early days, he accompanied the Meccan trade caravans, and often met Jews and Christians who probably first turned his interest to religious questions. At the age of about 40, his mind became strongly occupied by meditations on God, the hereafter, and the Day of Judgment which he believed to be close at hand. Knowing that God had revealed Himself to other peoples through His prophets, he became convinced that he had been chosen as the Arab prophet, and publicly proclaimed the revelations which he claimed to experience through the intermediation of the angel GABRIEL; these eventually constituted the KORAN. Scholars have long discussed to what extent M. was influenced by other religions; some emphasize the influence of Judaism, while others maintain a greater and earlier dependence on Christianity. Certainly, Jewish lore and tradition played a significant part in M.'s revelation, in his tenets of faith, and religious precepts. He held that all Holy Books were copies of a heavenly model and that, accordingly, all revelations were essentially one, having, however, been distorted in several ways by the respective people. He therefore repeatedly emphasized that his mission was only to confirm what had been revealed to former prophets and to correct the distortions.

Consequently, he referred with respect to the Hebrew Scriptures and the Jewish prophets, quoting extensively from the Bible and other Jewish sources as far as his scanty and sometimes erroneous knowledge reached. His early conviction that there existed no essential difference between Judaism and Islam led him to the hope that the Jews would welcome his mission and accept the new faith. In his attempt to win over the Jews he adapted, in MEDINA, the ritual of his community to theirs in some points, adding, e.g., a third daily prayer, introducing a day of fast corresponding to the Day of Atonement, fixing a day of public prayer after the model of the Jewish Sabbath, and directing his followers to turn to Jerusalem during prayer. When he realized that his hopes would not be fulfilled, he changed some of the new rites and adopted a hostile attitude toward the Jews of Medina who, gradually, were either annihilated or expelled. The other Jews of ARABIA, however, were treated more leniently, possibly from political and economical considerations. One of his wives (Safia) was of Jewish origin.

MOHAMMEDANISM see **ISLAM**

MOHEL see **CIRCUMCISION**

MOHILEV: White Russian city. Jews living there were expelled and massacred by the Russians 1654–8. Jewish captives from M. formed the basis of the Moscow community. In the 17th–18th cents., M. was a center of Sabbetaism. In 1772, M. was annexed to Russia, which abolished the community organization instituted under Polish rule and imposed a poll-tax. A pogrom occurred in 1904. The 25,000 Jews living there in 1941 fled to the Russian interior or were murdered by the Germans by 1943. Jewish pop. (1959): 28,430 (M. province).

MOHILEVER, SAMUEL (1824–1898): Rabbi and pioneer Zionist. He officiated in his native Glubokoje (near Vilna), Shakin, Suvalk, Radom, and Bialystok. From 1874 he actively supported Jewish settlement in Palestine and in 1881, founded the first society of *Hoveve Zion* in Warsaw. M. helped to interest Baron Edmond de Rothschild and Baron de Hirsch in Palestinian settlement. In 1884, he was among the organizers of the KATTOWITZ CONFERENCE. Later, he enthusiastically supported Herzl.

MOHR, ABRAHAM MENAHEM MENDEL (1815–1868): Hebrew author. A leading member of Galician Haskalah, he participated in the publication of several periodicals in Hebrew and Yiddish. His works include geography books, a lexicon, and biographies of Napoleon I and III.

MOISE: US family. Its first members went to the US in 1791 and they and their descendants played prominent roles in civic and Jewish affairs in several southern states. A distinguished figure in the second generation was *PENINA M.* (1797–1880), teacher and author of numerous widely published poems and hymns.

MOISEWITSCH, BENNO (1890–1963): Pianist. Of Russian birth, he settled in England in 1908 and acquired an international reputation.

MOLCHO, SOLOMON (1500–1532): Pseudo-messiah. Born a Marrano in Portugal, as Diego Pires, he became a royal notary. His imagination fired by the appearance in Portugal of David REUBENI in 1525, he had himself circumcised and made his way to the Levant where he became immersed in kabbalistic study. Going to Italy, he made a profound impression on Pope Clement VII, who welcomed him in the Vatican and protected him from the Inquisition. Ultimately, he came to consider himself the messiah. Rejoining Reubeni, they went to Regensburg in order to interview the emperor Charles V. M. was arrested and handed over to the Inquisition, by whom he was burned at Mantua. His votaries believed that he survived and was later seen in Italy. Despite painstaking research, no record of his trial has been traced.

MOLDAVIA: Rumanian province. Jewish traders from Poland went to M. in 1349. Jews from Poland and Germany began arriving in the early 16th cent. Heavy taxes and other forms of persecution in 1574 were the prelude to their expulsion five years later. In 1612, they were permitted to return. In 1648, Jews arrived from Poland and the Ukraine, fleeing the CHMIELNICKI horrors. Cossacks massacred many Jews in M. in 1648 and 1652. The Blood Libel appeared in M. for the first time at Neamtz in 1710. In the 18th–19th cents., large numbers of Jews arrived at the invitation of the boyars, and were granted exemption from taxes for a number of years and free land for their institutions. During this period, they founded 63 towns and villages. From 1859, M., as part of the new principality of RUMANIA, shared the vicious anti-Semitic atmosphere prevailing until the end of World War I. In 1889, there were 200,000 Jews in M., in most cities of which the Jews then constituted at least one third of the population. In 1900, 4,000 Jews walked from Berlad to Hamburg where they sailed for the US. Before World War II, there were 165,000 Jews in M. with important centers at Iasi (JASSY), Botosani, Dorohoi, Galati, and Roman. In 1970, its Jewish pop. was officially put at 98,072.

MOLECH see **MOLOCH**

MOLEDET see **BENE BERIT**

MÖLLN, JACOB BEN MOSES see **JACOB BEN MOSES**

MOLNAR, FERENC (1878–1952): Playwright, novelist, and short-story writer. He was born in Hungary, and settled in the US in 1940. His fiction, chiefly treating city life, includes *Prisoners*, *The Paul Street Boys*, and *Angel Making Music*. His fame, however, rested chiefly on his plays which combine fantasy and realism and reveal much technical virtuosity: of

Kadia Molodowsky-Lew.

these *Liliom* and *The Guardsman* were the most popular.

MOLOCH (MOLECH, MILCOM): Probably the name of a deity, later a term for one of the aspects of Baal (especially Baal-Melkart, the Sidonian god of hell). The Canaanites and peoples under their influence sacrificed human beings, especially first-born children, to M. by passing them through fire. The practice is strictly forbidden in the Bible (Lev. 18:21; 20:3–5) but nevertheless persisted both in the northern kingdom and even, for a time, in Jerusalem where altars were built to M. at Topheth in the valley of Hinnom (Jer. 7:31, 19:1–5; II Chron. 28:3). The word M. means "vow" in Punic. A deity of the name is found in the Mari scripts (pre-17th cent. BCE).

MOLODOWSKY LEW, KADIA (1894–): Yiddish poet. A sensitive lyricist, she is the author of many poems, novels, short stories, and plays depicting Jewish life in Poland, as well as biblical and historical themes. She has lived in the US since 1935.

MOMBERT, ALFRED (1872–1942): German poet. An outstanding lyricist, much of his work is philosophical in intent, e.g. the dramatic triology *Aeon*. He was elected to the Prussian Academy in 1926. He died in Switzerland after release from a Nazi concentration camp. His poems include *Die Schöpfung* and *Der himmlische Zecher*.

*MOMMSEN, THEODOR (1817–1903): German jurist and historian. In his history of Rome, he dealt fully with the position of the Jews in the Roman Empire. He was strongly opposed to anti-Semitism, countering Treitschke's diatribes in a sympathetic pamphlet.

MONASH, SIR JOHN (1865–1931): Australian soldier. An engineer by profession and volunteer soldier, he held the rank of colonel at the outbreak of World War I. M. served with distinction in Gallipoli and afterward in France, ultimately commanding the Australian contingents there (with the rank of general) and being considered by Lloyd George for the command of all the British forces.

MONATSSCHRIFT FÜR GESCHICHTE UND WISSENSCHAFT DES JUDENTUMS (Ger. "Monthly for the History and Science of Judaism"): German learned periodical devoted to Judaica, founded by Zacharias FRANKEL. Its 83 volumes were published 1851–1939 (with a break 1887–92). It originally appeared in Dresden but after 1861, mostly in Breslau.

MOND: English family, founded by *LUDWIG M.* (1839–1909), chemist, industrialist, and art collector. Born in Germany, he settled in England in 1862 and established its alkali industry. His art collection was subsequently presented to the National Gallery in London. His son *ALFRED M.* (1868–1930), created Lord Melchett in 1928, industrialist and statesman, joined his father's firm and by a series of amalgamations developed it into the Imperial Chemical Industries of which he was chairman. He entered parliament in 1906 and was later first commissioner of works and minister of health. Both as minister and as industrialist he devoted himself to fostering cooperation between employers and employed. Although not brought up as a Jew, M. became profoundly interested in Zionism, generously supported Zionist work, and was joint-chairman of the Jewish Agency. His son, *HENRY M.* (2nd Lord Melchett) (1898–1949), industrialist and economist, although brought up as a Christian, formally embraced Judaism at the outset of the Nazi persecutions. He was a director of Imperial Chemical Industries and chairman of the council of the Jewish Agency. His son *JULIAN EDWARD ALFRED M.* (3rd Lord Melchett) (1925–1973) was in 1967 appointed chairman of the British Steel Corporation.

MONEYLENDING: The Pentateuch prohibits the exaction of interest on a loan to a fellow-citizen but permits it as regards a stranger (Deut. 23:20, etc.). Nevertheless, there was a tendency to forbid all lending at interest, and the Talmud painstakingly forbids even the shadow ("dust") of interest. In the Middle Ages, all wealthy elements in Europe (priests, burghers, Jewish merchants) were approached for loans. The Church, however, basing itself on Aristotle and the New Testament, set its face against all forms of interest, the tendency reaching its climax in the 12th–13th cents. This coincided with the virtual exclusion of the Jews in N Europe from trade and handicrafts. The prohibition of m. not applying to them as stringently as it did to Christians, the open and regulated lending of money in N European countries hence fell into their hands, and they were sometimes specifically forbidden to engage in any other occupation. However, since the greater part of their profit was drained from them by exorbitant taxation, the profession became in effect a government monopoly, which they were compelled to manage for the benefit of the royal treasury. The rates of interest, etc. were carefully regulated, the terms of the unofficial Gentile moneylenders being far more onerous. In a period of credit-scarcity Jewish loans sometimes performed an important function. In S Europe, m. remained the profession of only a minority of the Jews. In Central and N Italy, the Jewish municipal money lenders or loan-bankers were mainly responsible for the establishment of the new Jewish communities in the 13th–14th cents. With the removal of economic restrictions on the Jews, m. has ceased to be a characteristic occupation.

MONIS, JUDAH (1683–1764): Hebraist. Born in Algiers or in Italy, he went to New York in 1716 and to Boston in 1720. After being publicly baptized at Harvard in 1722, he was instructor in Hebrew there, until 1760. His *Dickdook Leshon Gnebreet* was the first Hebrew grammar in America.

MONOBAZ II (fl. mid-1st cent. CE): King of ADIABENE, eldest son of HELENA and Monobaz I. He succeeded his younger brother Izates to the throne, and like him was a proselyte to Judaism, settling with his mother in Jerusalem.

MONOGAMY see **POLYGAMY**

MONOTHEISM: The belief in one sole God. M. is generally held to be a late development in the history of religion, being preceded by polytheism (as is still suggested in Hebrew by the use of the plural form *Elohim* for "God") and by monolatry (the exclusive worship of one God without denying the existence of other Divine powers). Jewish m. is enshrined in the formula (Deut. 6:4) "Hear O Israel, the Lord our God, the Lord is one." The evidence of the Bible suggests that in popular Israelite belief the God YHWH alone was to be worshiped but that other divinities presided over the destinies of other nations (Chemosh over Moab, etc.). In many parts of the Bible (e.g. the latter part of Isaiah), m. appears as a clearly defined and absolute principle. M. was Judaism's main legacy to CHRISTIANITY and ISLAM. The exact definition of Jewish m. was a main problem of medieval Jewish theology; for Maimonides it excluded all Divine ATTRIBUTES whereas for the Kabbalists it included the mystery of the 10 SEPHIROT.

MONSKY, HENRY (1890–1947): US communal leader. A lawyer by profession, he was president of the Supreme Lodge of B'nai B'rith from 1938 until his death, and led it into full participation in Jewish communal and cultural affairs. M. was the convener of the American Jewish Assembly and chairman of the AMERICAN JEWISH CONFERENCE.

MONTAGU: English family. *SAMUEL M.* (formerly Samuel; 1832–1911): Financier. He founded Samuel Montagu & Co., long one of the most important private banks in London. He was a Liberal member of parliament for many years, and was created Lord Swaythling in 1907. Strongly Orthodox and active in communal life, he established the Federation of Synagogues in London in 1887. His heirs, the second Lord Swaythling (1869–1927) and the third (1898–), took a smaller share in Jewish affairs. His second son *EDWIN SAMUEL M.* (1879–1924) entered parliament, became minister of munitions (1916), and secretary of state for India (1917–22). In this capacity he was jointly responsible for the Montagu-Chelmsford report which endeavored to satisfy India's national aspirations within the British Empire. An extreme anti-Zionist, he opposed the BALFOUR DECLARATION in the Cabinet and was responsible for modifying its terms. *LILIAN HELEN M.* (1873–1963), daughter of the first Lord Swaythling, was one of the founders and most enthusiastic supporters of the Liberal Jewish movement in England. *EWEN EDWARD SAMUEL M.* (1901–), son of the second Lord Swaythling, after a distinguished naval career in World War II, took a prominent part in English Jewish life as president of the Anglo-Jewish Association and of the United Synagogue. In 1945, he was appointed judge advocate of the British Fleet. His book, *The Man Who Never Was*, relates his role in a striking episode of World War II psychological warfare tactics.

MONTAIGNE, MICHEL DE (1533–1592): French essayist, one of the great figures in European literature. His mother was Antoinette Loupes, a member of the Marrano family of Lopez de Villanueva (as Jews, the Pazagon family of Saragossa).

MONTANA: US state. Jews were among its first settlers and active in its civic life even before it became a state. The oldest congregation was formed in Helena in 1866. Its synagogue, built in 1891, was presented to the state upon the dissolution of the Jewish community. Butte has 175 Jews with one Orthodox and one Reform synagogue. There are 100 Jews in Billings. In 1973, the Jewish population of Montana was 545.

MONTEFIORE: English family of Italian origin. (1) *CLAUDE JOSEPH GOLDSMID M.* (1859–1939): English scholar. A great-nephew of (4) and grandson of Isaac Lyon GOLDSMID, he inherited considerable wealth and was able to devote his life to philanthropy and scholarship. His principal interest was the New Testament period, and his most important work was on the Synoptic Gospels. Inclining increasingly to religious reform, he was the founder,

Sir Moses Montefiore.

mouthpiece, and inspiration of the Liberal Jewish movement in England. He supported Jewish scholarship of all complexions, brought S. SCHECHTER to England, and financed as well as edited the *Jewish Quarterly Review* 1888–1908. He was active in English Jewish public life and president (1895–1922) of the Anglo-Jewish Association, in which capacity he strenuously opposed Zionism and the Balfour Declaration. (2) *SIR FRANCIS ABRAHAM M.* (1860–1935): English Sephardi leader; grandnephew of (4). He was active in the *Hoveve Zion*, eagerly supported Herzl, and was the first chairman of the English Zionist Federation. (3) *LEONARD GOLDSMID M.* (1889–1961), son of (1), was president (1926–39) of the Anglo-Jewish Association. (4) *SIR MOSES M.* (1784–1885): English philanthropist. He amassed a comfortable fortune as a broker, largely through close collaboration with N. M. Rothschild, and was able to retire from business at the age of forty. In 1837, he was sheriff of the City of London and the first English Jew in modern times to be knighted. Profoundly pious, he became famous throughout the Jewish world by his mission to the Levant with A. Crémieux in 1840 at the time of the DAMASCUS AFFAIR. Henceforth and to the end of his phenomenally long life, he enjoyed an unparalleled status. He interceded personally in behalf of the Jews of Russia (1846, 1872), of Morocco (1863), of Rumania (1867), and of the kidnapped E. MORTARA in Italy (1858), these journeys being regarded almost as official missions in behalf of the British government. He visited Palestine on seven occasions, the last time at the age of 90, and besides his other benefactions there worked to improve the status of the Jews and to organize the first agricultural settlements. M. was president of the Board of Deputies of British Jews 1838–74, in which capacity he strenuously opposed religious Reform tendencies. He spent most of his later years in a country seat at RAMSGATE where he built a synagogue and established a college in memory of his wife Judith (1784–1862). M.'s career exemplified Jewish beneficence at its finest and established the 19th cent. philanthropic predominance of W European Jewry.

MONTEUX, PIERRE (1875–1964): Musician. Of French birth, he conducted orchestras in Europe and the US, including the Boston Symphony 1919–24, the Paris Symphony 1924–8 and the San Francisco Symphony 1935–52. He conducted the Metropolitan Opera, New York, from 1953 and the London Symphony Orchestra from 1961.

MONTEVERDE: A district of Rome where a catacomb from the Imperial Period was found in 1602, further examined in 1885 and 1904, and now destroyed. It contained about 200 inscriptions — many in Greek, some in Latin and a few in Hebrew — and symbols on the gravestones. Most of the finds are preserved in the Vatican Museum.

MONTEVIDEO: Capital of Uruguay. A few Marranos arrived there shortly after the town's foundation (1726) but the Inquisition prevented their increase. The modern influx began in 1905–7 and organized Jewish life in 1909. The community was augmented considerably by immigration from oriental countries in the 1920's and from Central Europe from the 1930's. A Central Jewish Committee was founded in 1940. In 1973, M. had 48,000 Jews (including c. 7,000 Sephardim) with 18 synagogues, 11 Jewish schools, with 2,600 pupils, 2 teachers seminars, 2 Yiddish daily papers, and weeklies in Spanish, German, and Yiddish.

MONTOR, HENRY (1905–): US Zionist. He was assistant editor of *The New Palestine* 1926–30, founder of the *Palcor* News Agency in 1936, executive vice-president of the United Jewish Appeal 1939–50, and from 1951 to 1955 chief executive officer of the State of Israel Bonds in the US. In the latter capacities he was responsible for raising huge sums of money for Israel.

MONTPELLIER: French town. Jews were living there in the 11th cent. and were reported by Benjamin of Tudela (c. 1165) to be generally opulent and devoted to learning. An ancient but unsubstantiated report speaks of Jewish teachers in the medical faculty of the famous university of M. Many distinguished rabbis lived in M. and the ban pronounced there on Maimonides' *Guide* ignited the Maimonist controversy. The community's tribulations began with the annexation to France in 1293, and they were expelled in 1306 and 1394. Although Marranos, etc. settled there in later centuries, the community never regained its former luster. There is now a small community in M., numbering 2,000 in 1970.

MONTREAL: Canadian city. In 1760, a number of Jews arrived with General Amherst's conquering British army, remaining there permanently. They became importers and fur traders. Subsequently small numbers of other Jews arrived. In 1768, the Sephardi congregation Shearith Israel was organized. In 1846, Polish Jewish families settled in M. but their numbers were augmented very slowly and only in 1858, were they able to organize the (Ashkenazi) Shaar Hashomayim synagogue, now Conservative. The emigration from Russia, following the outrage of the 1880's, intensified the growth of the Jewish population. In 1903, a new law provided that Jewish children were to be accorded equal opportunity for education within the Protestant school system. In a later period, M.'s school pattern contributed to the growth and success of Hebrew and Yiddish Day Schools. The Jews of M. are extensively engaged in the clothing industry. Philanthropically, the M. Jewish community has had an outstanding record, maintaining a YMHA, a Jewish public library, a Jewish general hospital, etc. Jewish pop. (1973): 113,000.

MOON, BLESSING OF THE (Heb. *kiddush levanah*): In mishnaic times, the new month was determined by observation of the moon, blessed formally by the head of the Bet Din. The tannaim laid down a benediction to be recited on seeing the new moon: "Blessed is He who renews the months," customarily uttered in Palestine; this was later extended to the poetic version "who by his word created the heavens," etc. It is customary for a quorum of ten adult males to bless the moon. The time of the blessing is when the rays of the moon are strong, i.e., from the 3rd to the 15th day of the month (or from the 7th to the 15th, according to an alternative version). The ceremony usually takes place at the close of the Sabbath in the courtyard of the synagogue.

*MOORE, GEORGE FOOT (1851–1931): US scholar. Professor of the history of religion at Harvard, he was an outstanding authority on the Bible and the talmudic era. His major work was the monumental *Judaism in the First Centuries of the Christian Era* (3 vols., 1927–30).

MOR (FRIEDMANN-YALIN), NATHAN (1913–): Israel public figure. He was born in Poland, reached Palestine in 1941, and joined the underground terrorist movement LOHAME HERUT YISRAEL which he headed from 1943. After the assassination of Count Bernadotte in 1948, he was sentenced by an Israel court to 8 years' imprisonment but was freed in the general amnesty of Feb. 1949. In the first Knesset (1949–51) he represented the Fighters' Party.

Sabato Morais.

MORAIS, SABATO (1823–1897): Rabbi. He was born and educated in Italy, officiated in London 1846–51, and then succeeded Isaac Leeser as rabbi of the Sephardi Mikveh Israel congregation in Philadelphia. M. was a leading opponent of Reform, against which he spoke and wrote. During the Civil War, he was an ardent abolitionist, thus becoming involved in friction with his congregation. In 1886, he led in the establishment of the Jewish Theological Seminary of America and served as its academic head until his death.

MORAVIA: Former province of Bohemia, later Austria, now Czechoslovakia. Jews lived there from the early Middle Ages, suffering in massacres in 1337, and again at the time of the Black Death in 1349. They were partly expelled in 1421. After the Polish persecution from 1648 onward, their numbers increased considerably by immigration. From the 17th cent., there existed a General Council of Moravian Jewry, endowed with authority for taxation, which periodically enacted laws for communal self-government. M., especially its capital town Brno (BRÜNN), was long an important center of rabbinic learning. The Jewish population in 1938 was c. 45,000, most of whom perished at the hands of the Nazis.

MORAVIA (PINCHERLE), ALBERTO (1907–): Italian author. He produced his first novel in 1929, and his work has been widely translated. His books include *The Woman of Rome* and *Two Women*. He is not a professing Jew.

MORDECAI (c. 5th cent. BCE): Benjamite serving as a palace official at Shushan in the reign of Ahasuerus. His niece Esther was wedded to the king and through her intervention, Ahasuerus learnt from M. of an assassination plot against him. M.'s refusal to bow to the vizier Haman instigated the latter to plan vengeance on all the Jews in Persia, but his scheme was frustrated by Esther. Haman was hanged and his position as chief minister filled by M. The name M. is of Babylonian origin, being found in inscriptions (Mardukha).

MORDECAI BEN HILLEL (d. 1298): German codifier. He was martyred in Nuremberg with his wife and five children. His *Mordekhai* is a talmudical compendium quoting large numbers of medieval authorities and containing valuable material on social and intellectual life. He also wrote responsa and liturgical poetry.

MORE JUDAICO see **OATH MORE JUDAICO**

MOREH NEVUKHIM see **MOSES BEN MAIMON**

MORENU (Heb. "our teacher"): Title given to distinguished rabbis. It was introduced in 14th cent. Germany, from where it spread to other countries.

MORGENSTERN, JULIAN (1881–): US biblical scholar. He was professor of Bible and Semitic languages at Hebrew Union College, Cincinnati 1907–49, and its president 1921–47. He has written widely on biblical subjects from an extreme critical viewpoint, especially on Amos and ancient Jewish religious ritual.

MORGENSTERN, LINA (1830–1909): German social worker and educationalist. She worked to promote the welfare of women and children, founding the first Fröbel kindergarten (1860).

MORGENTHAU: (1) *HENRY M.* (1856–1946): US businessman and diplomat. He went from Germany to the US in 1865. Originally a lawyer, he was

Henry Morgenthau Jr.

Moroccan Jewish types.

active in New York real estate and banking. As US ambassador to Turkey 1913–6, he used his influence to protect the Jews in Palestine. In 1919, he was head of a commission to investigate the condition of the Jews in Poland after the pogroms. He was chairman of the League of Nations Refugee Settlement Commission which in 1923 handled the exchange of Greek and Moslem refugees. (2) *HENRY M. JR.* (1891–1967): Statesman; son of (1). He was active in public life as conservation commissioner, and under President Franklin D. Roosevelt, became under-secretary (1933–4) and secretary (1934–45) of the treasury. During this period he was responsible for the financing of the New Deal program and then for the financing of America's war effort. He was general chairman of the United Jewish Appeal 1947–50 and chairman of the Israel Bond drive in the US 1951–5.

MORIAH: (1) District in Palestine. On one of its mountains (apparently identical with Mt. M. in Jerusalem), Abraham prepared to offer Isaac. (2) Hill in Jerusalem; site of the threshing-floor of Araunah the Jebusite purchased by David on which to build an altar. Later the Temple was erected there. The original hill was enlarged in the course of time by embanking.

MORIAH: Hebrew publishing house founded at Odessa in 1912 by Bialik, Ravnitzky, and others for the publication of textbooks. In 1922, it merged with DEVIR.

MORNING FREIHEIT see **FREIHEIT**

MORNING JOURNAL: Yiddish daily, founded in 1901 by Jacob Saphirstein with Peter Wiernik as editor. As a Yiddish organ of American Orthodoxy, it attained its peak circulation of 111,000 in 1916. In 1928, it absorbed the oldest Yiddish daily *Yidishes Tageblatt*, which had been founded in 1872. In 1954, it merged with *Der Tog* but closed in 1971.

MORNING SERVICE see **SHAḤARIT**

MOROCCO: N African state. Jews lived there when it was the Roman province of Mauritania, their position deteriorating after the Empire became Christian. Some Berber tribes, of whom the DAGGATUN still survive, are said to have become converted to Judaism. Under Byzantine rule (7th cent.), all synagogues were destroyed. After the Arab conquest, opposed in battle by the Jewess DAHIA AL-KAHINA, the communities increased in number, FEZ and SIGILMESSA becoming famous seats of learning. The proscription of Judaism under the Almohades (1146–1269) ended this period of achievement, but on their fall, the communities again came out into the open. Refugees from Spain arrived in great number at the end of the 14th cent. and were greatly reinforced after the expulsion from Spain in 1492, much friction resulting between them and the less-cultured native elements. The Jews were ill-treated, confined to MELLAḤS, forced to perform degrading offices, compelled to wear distinctive black clothing, etc., and were periodically subjected to fanatical attacks of violence. From time to time, some would rise to eminence as treasurers or agents of the sultan, but in the end, they generally met with disaster. In the seaports, too, some Jews temporarily prospered as merchants and agents of foreign powers. Conditions further deteriorated under the Rashid dynasty (from 1670). Sir Moses Montefiore's mission to M. in 1864 did a little to improve conditions. Under the French administration (1912–55), order was established, violence ceased, and the Jewish status improved, CASABLANCA becoming a major center of population, and similar condi-

Samson Morpurgo.
(Painting in the possession of the Morpurgo family).

tions prevailed in the Spanish zone, particularly TETUAN. The Jews played an important role also in the international port of TANGIERS. In recent years many Jews have left for Israel and France. According to the 1960 census, there were 159,803 Jews in M. (of which 151,245 lived in 117 urban centers) while in 1965, it was estimated that the total had dropped to c. 75,000 and by 1973 to 31,000.

MORPURGO: N Italian family, ultimately deriving from Marburg (Styria). Its members included: (1) *RACHEL M.* (1790–1871): Hebrew poet. A house-wife in humble circumstances at Trieste, she wrote numerous Hebrew poems and sonnets in the tradi-tional Italian style, some of them directed to her cousin Samuel David LUZZATTO. They were published posthumously under the title *Uggav Raḥel* ("Rachel's Lyre"). (2) *SALAMONE M.* (1859–1942): Literary historian. A Dante expert, he also wrote on the Wandering Jew in medieval Italian literature. He was director of the National Library in Florence. (3) *SAMSON M..*(1681–1740): Rabbi. Born in Gradisca, he settled in Ancona as physician and rabbi. He is remembered for his courageous polemic against the monk Benetelli, his commentary on Bedersi's *Beḥinat Olam*, and his responsa, *Shemesh Tzedakah*, replete with historical data.

MORRIS, IRA NELSON (1875–1942): US diplomat.

A retired businessman, he was entrusted by President Wilson with a special diplomatic mission in Italy (1913), and was minister to Sweden (1914–23).

MORSE, DAVID ABNER (1907–): US public official.

In 1946–8, he was assistant secretary and under-secretary of labor under President Truman. From 1948 to 1970 he was director-general of the International Labor Office.

MORTARA (generally Levi Mortara): Italian family, deriving from a place of that name, mainly centered originally in Verona. *MARCO M.* (1815–1894), rabbi of Mantua from 1842, was the out-standing pupil of S. D. Luzzatto and published many historical monographs, including an Index of Italian Jewish scholars from the beginning of the Christian era. His writings were based largely on his valuable collection of mss which were acquired by D. Kaufmann and passed with his library to the Hungarian Academy of Sciences. His son *LUDOVICO M.* (1855–1937), was president of the Italian Supreme Court.

MORTARA CASE: In 1858, a 7-year-old Jewish child, Edgardo Mortara, was kidnapped from his parents' home in Bologna by the Papal gendarmes

The kidnapping of Edgardo Mortara. (Drawing by Moritz Oppenheim).

Title-page of a polemical work by Saul Levi Morteira.
(Drawn by Michael Lopez).

to be brought up as a Christian. The pretext was that 6 years previously, his Christian nurse, believing him to be on the point of death, had informally baptized him. The episode aroused universal indignation in liberal circles. Sir Moses Montefiore journeyed to Rome in the vain hope of securing the child's release. and in France, the Alliance Israélite Universelle was founded largely as a result of the incident. Edgardo Mortara entered the priesthood, refused the opportunity to return to Judaism after the capture of Rome in 1870 and died in Belgium in 1940.

MORTEIRA, SAUL LEVI (1596–1660): Rabbi and scholar. Of Italian birth, he officiated in the Amsterdam Sephardi congregation from 1616. M. was a member of the Bet Din that excommunicated Spinoza who had formerly been his pupil. His writings include a volume of sermons and unpublished but widely used anti-Christian polemics in Portuguese.

MOSAD BIALIK (Heb. "Bialik Foundation"): Institute in Jerusalem for the publication of Hebrew books, founded in 1935 by the Jewish Agency. Its major projects have included the publication of a biblical encyclopedia, comprehensive collections of the Hebrew classics, and works of Jewish scholarship.

MOSAD HA-RAV KOOK (Heb. "Rabbi Kook Foundation"): Jerusalem religious cultural institution. It was founded in 1937 by the World Center of *Mizrahi*, with the cooperation of the Jewish Agency. It has published or subsidized over 1,000 books as well as the monthly review *Sinai*.

MOSCHELES, IGNAZ (1794–1870): Musician. He was born in Prague and achieved an early reputation as pianist and composer. In 1814, under Beethoven's supervision, he prepared the piano-score for *Fidelio*. From 1826, he lived and taught in London. and from 1846, in Leipzig as professor of piano at the Conservatoire founded by his pupil Mendelssohn. 142 of his works were published, including 8 piano concertos. His interpretations of piano works by classic composers were outstanding. His son *FELIX M*. (1833–1917) made a reputation in England as a painter and was active in the cause of international peace.

MOSCOW: Capital of the USSR. Orders forbidding Jewish settlement there were issued in 1490, 1549, 1610, and 1667. After White Russia was annexed to Russia in 1772, Jewish merchants began to stream to M., chiefly from Shklov. From 1826–56, a ghetto was established; most Jews permanently resident in M. at that time were families of CANTONISTS. The community thereafter expanded rapidly and was a center of the *Hoveve Zion*. In 1891, some 20,000 craftsmen, workers, teachers, etc. were expelled to the Pale of Settlement. The situation improved after the 1905 revolution. After the 1917 revolution, the Jewish population of M. increased enormously and it became the most important Russian Jewish center. Jewish cultural activities (e.g. *Tarbut*, the *Ha-Bimah* and Yiddish theaters) flourished there for a time, though with no corresponding development of religious life. These cultural authorities also came to an end in the last year of Stalin. There are now 1 large and 2 suburban synagogues. Official Jewish pop. (1970) 251,523.

MOSENSOHN, YIGAL (1920–): Israel author. He has published short stories, novels (*The Way of Man*), plays (*In the Steppes of the Negev*), and a series of popular children's stories (*Ḥasambah*).

MOSENTHAL, SOLOMON HERMANN VON (1821–1877): Dramatist. Born in Germany, he wrote in Vienna many successful plays (*Cäcilia von Albano, Deborah*, etc.) and librettos for operas by Rubinstein, Goldmark, etc., stories about Hessian Jews, and a novel *Jephthah's Daughter*.

MOSER (Heb. "betrayer"): Term of obloquy used among Ashkenazim for an informer who denounces fellow-Jews to the secular authority. In S Europe the corresponding term was *Malsin*.

MOSES: Lawgiver, prophet, and founder of the Jewish religion. He was born in Egypt to Amram and Jochebed of the tribe of Levi. The Egyptians, seeking to stem the growth of the Israelites, had decreed the slaughter of new-born males, but M. was hidden among the reeds of the Nile, and later found by Pharaoh's daughter who raised him in her own household. When M. grew up and learned of his origin, he took an interest in his enslaved kindred and killed an Egyptian whom he discovered beating a Hebrew. Fleeing to Midian, he became shepherd to the local priest JETHRO and married his daughter

ואת עָמֵלְנוּ אֵלוּ הַבָּנִים כְּמוֹ
שֶׁנֶּאֱמַר כָּל הַבֵּן הַיִּלּוֹד
הַיְאֹרָה תַּשְׁלִיכֻהוּ וְכָל הַבַּת
תְּחַיּוּן : וְאֶת לַחֲצֵנוּ זוֹ הַדְּחַק כְּמוֹ
שֶׁנֶּאֱמַר וְגַם רָאִיתִי אֶת הַלַּחַץ

The Finding of Moses.
(From the Haggadah illustrated by Joseph Leipnik, 1740,
in the British Museum.)

ZIPPORAH, who bore him two sons Gershom and Eliezer. Eventually, he witnessed God in the BURNING BUSH at Mt. Horeb and received the Divine command to return to Egypt and lead out his people. With the assistance of his brother AARON, he interceded with Pharaoh who — after being smitten with the TEN PLAGUES — released the Israelites. Subsequently changing his mind, Pharaoh set out to pursue them, but his entire army was drowned in the Red Sea which previously had been successfully and miraculously crossed by the Israelites. After several marches and a severe battle with the Amalekites, M. led the people to Mt. Horeb in the Sinai wilderness ("Mt. Sinai"), receiving there the TEN COMMANDMENTS by Divine revelation. As a supplement, he taught the people an entire legal code, expounded the sacrificial practice, gave instructions for the erection of the TABERNACLE and, on the advice of Jethro, organized a judicial system. During the initial period of wandering, he frequently clashed with various sections of the people, some of whom expressed a preference to return to Egypt. His first attempt to penetrate Canaan failed. The Bible is silent on events between the 2nd and 39th year of the Exodus. In the latter year, he endeavored to bring into Canaan the new generation that had grown up in the wilderness and successfully fought the Amorites, the Moabites, the Midianites, and Bashan — all in Transjordania. Before his death, he appointed JOSHUA as his successor and in a public address summarized the events of the preceding 40 years and the main legislation laid down at Sinai. He blessed the people, gave them guidance for their life in Canaan, and died at the age of 120 at a place unknown to posterity. M. was above all a prophetic lawgiver, preparing the nation for a new and unique religion to be observed in its own land. The basis is complete MONOTHEISM and loyalty to God, the Creator and Father of all. Israel is a holy nation and a model to other people. The concept had been nurtured by the patriarchs but M. gave it form and substance. By giving the TORAH, M. created Judaism and was thereby the father of monotheism. Traditionally, the entire Pentateuch was written by M. The Midrash and late aggadah relate many legends about him, and various works were pseudepigraphically ascribed to him (*Assumption of M.*, *History of M.*).

MOSES, ASSUMPTION OF: Apocryphal work extant in Greek, dating from the 1st cent. CE. It relates the revelation of Moses to Joshua including a history of Israel down to the time of Herod, forecasting the messianic era shortly thereafter. An additional section, describing the death of Moses and the war between Satan and the archangel Michael over his body, has been lost. The book seems to have originated with an Essenic group.

MOSES, BLESSING OF: Benediction uttered by Moses over the Israelites before his death (Deut. 33). Its form is poetical and its contents, after a preamble, consist of a blessing for each tribe (except Simeon) and for the entire people.

MOSES, SEAT OF: Referred to in the New Testament (Mat. 23:2) as the synagogue seat occupied by the scribes and Pharisees. It has been conjectured that it was either the place of the rabbi or the stand where the *Sepher Torah* was placed. What is believed to be a S. o. M. has been found in the synagogue ruins of Chorazin and at Delos.

MOSES, SONG OF: Words of Moses before his death (Deut. 32). It foretells the calamities that would result from deserting the Torah and describes God's love for Israel. Among Jews it is known by its initial word *Haazinu* ("Hear ye").

MOSES BEN ENOCH (fl. 10th cent.): Talmudist. One of the Four Rabbis legendarily captured by Saracen pirates after they sailed from Bari (S Italy) in 972, he was ransomed in Cordova where his worth was recognized and he was appointed rabbi. This marked the beginning of talmudic learning in Spain. He was succeeded in his office by his son, ENOCH BEN MOSES.

MOSES BEN ISAAC DI RIETI (1388 — c. 1460): Italian philosopher and poet. He was physician at Rieti until 1422, and then was in Perugia, Narni,

Moses Maimonides:
Plaque in the lobby of the Capitol, Washington, D.C.

Fabriano, and Rome where he officiated as rabbi and was physician to Pius II. His best-known work is *Mikdash Me'at* ("The Lesser Sanctuary"), a long moral and philosophical poem in *terza rima*, which includes a vision of Paradise and an account of Jewish scholars down to his own period, modeled on Dante's *Divine Comedy*. Another section of the poem entered into liturgical use. M. also wrote on medicine and philosophy.

MOSES BEN JACOB OF COUCY (fl. 13th cent.): Codifier. To counteract the inroads of religious indifference, he went in 1235–6 to S France and Spain where his eloquence resulted in a higher standard of observance. In 1240, he participated in the DISPU-TATION of Paris. An opponent of philosophy, he taught high ethical principles toward non-Jews and Jews alike, and was the author of a popular codification *Sepher Mitzvot Gadol* (known as *Semag*) and the "old tosaphot" to tractate *Yoma*.

MOSES BEN JACOB OF RUSSIA (also Moses Ashkenazi; 1449–1520): Rabbinic scholar. He was born in Lithuania, studied in Constantinople, and lived in Kiev and later, as a fugitive, in Lithuania. Taken captive there by the Tartars, he was ransomed by the Jews and Karaites of Solchat, Crimea. He wrote several scholarly works, including a commentary on Ibn Ezra, and compiled a liturgy, according to the rite of Kaffa, Crimea.

MOSES BEN MAIMON (Maimonides; abbr. *Rambam*; 1135–1204): Philosopher, halakhist, and medical writer. At about the age of 13, he left his native Cordova with his family to escape the Almohade persecutions. After a period of wandering in

N Africa, he reached Palestine in 1165, having already written treatises on the Jewish calendar, *Sepher ha-Ibbur* on intercalation (1158), and works on the technical terms of logic, as well as establishing a list of the 613 PRECEPTS. Being unable to settle in Palestine, then still suffering from the aftermath of the Crusades, the family went on almost immediately to Egypt. In a document of 1167, M. appears as one of the signatories of a decree issued by the Egyptian rabbinical authorities and soon became spiritual head of the Cairo community. At first he lived by trading in jewels in association with his brother David, but after the latter's death M. became in 1170, physician to the viceroy of Egypt. He died in his 70th year and, according to tradition, was buried in Tiberias where his tomb still attracts pilgrims. In 1168, he concluded his commentary on the Mishnah, *Kitab as-Siraj* (Heb. *Sepher ha-Maor*), composed during his travels. Its aim was to explain the exact meaning of the text and to indicate which opinions were accepted as halakhah. The prefaces which he wrote to *Avot* (*Shemonah Perakim*) and to the tenth chapter of *Sanhedrin* (*Ḥelek*) are often printed and studied separately. The latter leads up to the famous Thirteen Articles of Faith (see DOGMA). All these earlier books were written in Arabic and translated later into Hebrew (the *Logic* three times). From 1170— 80, M. worked on his Hebrew compendium of the entire halakhah, *Mishneh Torah*, also called *Yad Ḥazakah* ("Strong Hand": *Yad* numerically = 14, the number of parts of the work) "to save himself in his advanced age the trouble of consulting the Talmud on every occasion," as he wrote in a letter. This code covers all halakhic subjects, however minute, discussed in the Talmud; it introduces each subject by a clear explanation, and where several opinions are adduced in the *gemara*, gives only the one M. accepted; M. is thus a decisor (POSEK). The systematic arrangement is unsurpassed. Exception was early taken to the fact that he never mentions the talmudic source of his statements— some have not yet been fully traced—and his decisions were criticized harshly by Abraham ben David of Posquières and others, nor were all universally accepted. The appeal to the general reader is underlined by the first book, the *Fundamentals of the Law*, an exposition of Jewish theology (trans. M. Hyamson, 1937; the whole work is being translated into English in the *Yale Judaica Series*). Meanwhile M. had continued his theological research. In 1190, he completed his *Dalalat al-Ḥa'irin* or *Guide of the Perplexed* (Heb. *Moreh Nevukhim*) in 3 books containing 176 chapters. This presents an exposition of the Jewish faith as complete as that of Jewish practice contained in the *Mishneh Torah*. It begins with a discussion of biblical expressions apt to be theological pitfalls, goes on to discuss the nature of God, especially the vexed question of attributes, then to a proof (against Aristotle) that the

Universe was created, and hence created by God. It analyzes the nature of prophecy, therefore of His Law. M. discusses Divine Providence and the purpose of the Law as a whole, as well as of many individual laws, stressing above all their educational purpose. In the final two chapters, he outlines the higher religion of the "perfect man," which consists in philosophical contemplation of the divine and is identical with "Love of God." The *Guide* is written in the technique and spirit of Aristotelian philosophy in its later Arabic form (which incorporates some features of Neoplatonism), the tenets of which he accepts where they do not conflict with what he regards as principles of Jewish religion. Aristotelianism was then universally accepted by the educated, and M.'s purpose was to prove to Jews with a secular education that Judaism was rational within that framework. In the course of argumentation however, M. does in fact claim that Judaism can be properly understood only through Aristotelian thought, and a belief not so based is therefore a form of idolatry; even the common people must be taught by rote the correct definitions of the nature of God. This comes close to a rejection of the traditional, illogical, and mildly anthropomorphic faith then held by the majority of Jewry. It was therefore not surprising that this aspect of the work raised a storm of protest when the book, in the translation of Samuel Ibn Tibbon (1204) and later of Judah al-Ḥarizi (1205—13), became available to the Jews in Christian countries, especially since irreligious intellectuals soon used its authority to support their laxity in observance. A violent controversy ended only in 1305, when the reading of philosophical works was permitted to those over 25 years old, but forbidden under pain of excommunication to younger persons; subsequently, however, the controversy broke out again. In later centuries, the issues involved lost their relevancy, and the *Guide* is now accepted even by the most Orthodox. During the Haskalah Period, nevertheless, it was again for a time the rallying point of anti-traditional rationalism ("the Bible of the *maskilim*"); Mendel Lepin now adapted the style of the Tibbon translation into current rabbinic Hebrew (Zolkiev, 1829). The Tibbon translation was almost from the first the only one used, in spite of its heavy, arabicized style. There exists also a popular introduction *Ruah Ḥen* (anon.) and even a verse adaptation. Latin translations were made in the 13th cent. (anon.) and in 1629, by J. Buxtorf Jr. Outside Jewish circles, the *Guide* influenced Aquinas, John Spencer, and Leibniz. It was translated into English by M. Friedländer (1881—5). M. also wrote a number of important epistles on theological subjects, responsa, and many private letters preserved in his own handwriting. He was a medical author of note, writing treatises on asthma, hemorrhoids, poisons, healthy living, sexual intercourse, a collection of medical aphorisms, etc. Some of these were translated into Latin, printed frequently, and studied in European universities down to the 17th cent. He often introduces medical subjects into his other writings.

MOSES BEN NAḤMAN (or Naḥmanides; abbr. *Ramban*; in Spanish called Bonastruc de Porta: 1194—c. 1270): Scholar. Rabbi of Gerona (Aragon), his range of knowledge was unrivaled in his day. His glosses on the Talmud similar to, though more practical than, those of the French tosaphists established his reputation as the foremost Spanish talmudist. His *Torat ha-Adam* on the rites of mourning was basically halakhic but dealt with the nature of the super-soul. Opposed to the study of philosophy, though not to Maimonides, he endeavored to mediate between the latter's supporters and opponents in 1238. In 1263, Pablo CHRISTIANI, who had already encountered M. in argument at Gerona, challenged him to a public religious DISPUTATION which took place at Barcelona in the presence of King James I. M.'s own account in Hebrew shows him to have exhibited courage as well as humor, as he did again on the following Sabbath when he replied to the King's conversionist address in the synagogue. Although M. had been promised immunity, he was tried for blasphemy and had to leave Spain. From 1267, he lived in Palestine, where he settled in Acre, reorganizing the Jewish settlement, and writing his popular Bible commentary with its characteristic combination of rational interpretation (sometimes with contemporary allusions) and insistence on kabbalistic implications.

MOSES BEN SHEMTOV DE LEON see LEON

MOSES HA-DARSHAN (i.e., the preacher; fl. 10th—11th cents.): S French biblical commentator who taught in Narbonne. He wrote commentaries on many parts of the Bible utilizing legends selected in some instances from secular sources. His writings were much used by Rashi. His "Midrash" on Genesis (*Bereshit Rabbati*), quoted by Raymund Martini, has only recently been published.

MOSES OF LONDON (d. c. 1268): Grammarian. An affluent businessman, he was also a halakhist and Jewish scholar. His treatise on Hebrew punctuation and accentuation (*Darkhe ha-Nikkud veha-Neginah*) is the most competent work of the sort produced in N Europe at that time. He was the father of the scholars Elijah of London and BERECHIAH OF LINCOLN.

MOSES OF NARBONNE (called Maestro Vidal Blasom; d. after 1362): Philosopher, translator, and physician. His most important commentary is on Maimonides' *Guide*, which he analyzes critically from a strictly Aristotelian-Averroistic point of view.

MOSES (ḤAYYIM EPHRAIM) OF SODILKOV (c. 1737—c. 1800): Ḥasidic leader; son of Israel Baal Shem Tov's daughter, Odel. He grew up in his grandfather's home and later studied under Dov Ber of Mezhirich. For 20 years, he lived modestly as rabbi and preacher in the village of Sodilkov in Volhynia.

In his *Degel Maḥaneh Ephraim*—one of the fundamental works of the Ḥasidic movement—he expounded his grandfather's doctrines, teaching that the goal of Hasidism is extreme humility and self-evaluation. The *tzaddikim* are the "eyes of the community" whose duty is to reprove and reform back-sliders and elevate the people by prayer and religious instruction.

MOSES, ADOLPH (1840—1902): Rabbi in Poland he went to the US in 1870 and served the Reform congregation in Louisville 1881—1902. With his brother Isaac S. Moses and Emil G. Hirsch, he edited the German weekly *Zeitgeist* (1880), in the pages of which appeared notable contributions to Jewish learning by eminent scholars. A collection of his writings appeared posthumously under the title *Yahvism and Other Discourses*.

MOSES, FRANKLIN J. (1804–1877): US jurist. He served in the S Carolina state legislature and senate and was chief justice of the State Supreme Court in the Reconstruction government 1868–77. His son, FRANKLIN J. MOSES JR. (1838–1906), who served a two-year term as Republican governor of the state, was a convert to Christianity. He was assailed for malpractice and retired in disgrace.

MOSES, ROBERT (1888–): US civil servant. He has held numerous positions of importance in the New York area, among them New York City Park Commissioner (from 1934). In 1964–5, he was in charge of the New York World Fair.

MOSHAV see **MOSHAV OVEDIM**

MOSHAV OVEDIM (Heb. "workers' settlement"): In Israel, an agricultural village the inhabitants of which possess individual homes and smallholdings, but cooperate in the purchase of equipment, etc., the sale of produce, and mutual aid. Certain central buildings, equipment, sometimes stock and some productive branches, are also owned in common. The land normally belongs to the Jewish National Fund, and non-employment of wage-labor is a nominal principle. The first experiments in this form were at Beer Yaakov (1907), En Ganim (1908), and Naḥlat Yaakov (1913). During the Third Aliyah (1918–21), a reaction against the early KEVUTZAH led to the foundation of the big *m. o.* Nahalal and Kephar Yeḥezkel. The *moshave ovedim* are organized in TENUAT HA-MOSHAVIM (founded 1928). Since the establishment of the state the *m. o.* has become the commonest form of workers' village and there are 349 in Israel (1974).

MOSHAV SHITTUPHI (Heb. "cooperative settlement"): In Israel, an agricultural village the members of which possess individual homesteads, but where the agriculture and economy, sales and purchases, are conducted as a single cooperative unit. Each family receives a budget on a fixed scale according to its size, and the community regulates the hours which women work on the farm. The land normally is owned by the Jewish National Fund. The form stands intermediate between the KIBBUTZ and the MOSHAV. The first *m. s.* was founded in 1936 at Kephar Ḥittim with the aim of modifying certain elements of the kibbutz. Most such settlements are organized within the TENUAT HA-MOSHAVIM. In 1974, there were 28 *moshavim shittuphiyim*.

MOSHAV ZEKENIM (Heb. "dwelling-place of the old"): The traditional name for a Jewish old age home. The institution is relatively new in Jewish life, the aged poor having been previously cared for either by relatives or in the communal hostel (*hekdesh*).

MOSHAVAH (Heb. "colony"; "settlement"): In Israel, an agricultural village in which farming is conducted on individualist lines on privately owned land. The m. originated during the First Aliyah (1882–1904), the earliest examples being Petaḥ Tikvah and Rishon le-Zion; a number were founded or assisted by Baron Edmond de Rothschild. The majority are plantation colonies based mainly on citriculture; some of the older ones have grown into municipalities. A number of moshavot founded since 1933 cooperate in marketing and supply and are termed *moshavah shittuphit*.

MOSLER, HENRY (1841–1920): US painter. He specialized in genre pictures, telling stories with humor and pathos.

MOSSE, RUDOLF (1843–1920): German publisher and philanthropist. In 1867, he founded a successful advertising business and in 1872, the *Berliner Tageblatt*, which became one of Germany's leading independent liberal newspapers. In 1880, he acquired the ALLGEMEINE ZEITUNG DES JUDENTUMS. His business, which was continued by his family, was appropriated by the Nazis in 1933.

MOSUL: Town in N IRAQ. Jewish settlement in the region dates back to biblical times. A large community existed in ancient NINEVEH, in the immediate vicinity. M. itself, founded in the early Mohammedan era, had 7,000 Jewish inhabitants at the time of Benjamin of Tudela (c. 1170). In the early 13th cent., M. is reputed to have harbored the largest Jewish community in Iraq, at one time being the seat of an exilarch. With the decline of the town in modern times, the number of Jews dwindled, totalling only 1,100 in 1903. In the latter 19th cent., their economic position deteriorated due to persecution, and they were largely reduced to peddling. In and after 1948, under the pressure of political circumstances, all the Jews emigrated, mostly to Israel.

MOSZKOWSKI, MORITZ (1854—1925): Pianist and composer. He was born in Breslau and settled in Berlin, moving to Paris in 1897. His early works (e.g. *Spanish Dances* for piano) which covered a wide musical range, were very popular, but later, he neglected his music and died in poverty.

MOTION PICTURES: Jews have played a prominent role in the development of the motion picture industry, especially as producers and distributors. Outstanding pioneers in this sphere in the US have included Adolph Zukor, Lewis J. Selznick, Carl Laemmle, and Jesse Lasky. Among American Jewish directors who have left their mark on the industry have been David O. Selznick, Marvyn LeRoy, Irving Thalberg, Ernst Lubitsch, Joseph L. Mankiewicz, and William Wyler. There have been many Jewish screen stars, e.g. Theda Bara, Jack Benny, Elizabeth Bergner, Fannie Brice, Eddie Cantor, Kirk Douglas, Melvyn Douglas, Paulette Goddard, Judy Holliday, Al Jolson, Danny Kaye, Paul Lukas, the Marx Brothers, Paul Muni, Luise Rainer, Edward G. Robinson, Joseph Schildkraut, Sylvia Sidney, Conrad Veidt, Jerry Lewis and Lew Weber. Outstanding screen authors have included S.N. Behrman, Moss Hart, Ben Hecht, Lilian Hellman, Garson Kanin, George S. Kaufmann, Sidney Kingsley, Herman J. Mankiewicz, Clifford Odets, Elmer Rice, Irwin Shaw and Budd Schulberg. Successful producers have included William Fox, Samuel Goldwyn, Marcus and Arthur Loew, Nicholas and Joseph M. Schenck, and Warner Bros. In Europe also, Jews have played an important, though not as decisive, role in the motion picture industry. Sir Michael Balcon was knighted for his endeavors and achievements in Great Britain. Many Jews were very prominent in the pre-Hitler film industry of Germany (e.g. Paul Davidson, George Pabst, Erich Pommer); while in France Harry Baur, Anouk Aimée and Simone Signoret were outstanding actors and Jean Benoît-Lévy, Jules Dassin and Claud Lelouch distinguished producers. A number of films have been produced in Yiddish (mostly pre-World War II), and a number of full-length films have been shot in Israel, some of them Hebrew-speaking.

MOTKE ḤABAD (Mordecai Rakover: d. 1875): Jester. A popular figure among Lithuanian Jewry, he had many jokes and anecdotes attributed to him.

MOTOT, SAMUEL BEN SAADYAH IBN see **IBN MOTOT**

MOTTELSON, BENJAMIN R. (1926–): Physicist. Born in the US but worked in Denmark from 1951. With his colleague Aage Bohr, he won the 1975 Nobel Prize for work on the inner structure of the atom.

MOTZA: Israel rural settlement near Jerusalem. The biblical town, belonging to the tribe of Benjamin, existed also in Second Temple times. After the destruction of the Second Temple, Vespasian ordered 800 Roman legionnaires to settle at M., which was now known as Colonia Amasa. The modern settlement was erected nearby. Pop. (1972): 451. In 1956, an additional settlement Mevasseret Yerushalayim was established on neighboring land.

MOTZI see **HA-MOTZI**

Mount of Olives: The Desecrated Jewish Cemetery.

MOTZKIN, LEO (1867—1933): Zionist leader and communal worker. He was born in Russia and, in 1889, helped to found the first Berlin students' Zionist society. He enthusiastically followed Herzl although differing from him sharply on several issues. M. helped to found the DEMOCRATIC FRACTION and TARBUT. During World War I, he directed the Zionist bureau at Copenhagen and, after the war, was secretary and then president of the *Comité des Délégations Juives* at the Paris peace conference. He headed the organization of European National Minorities until 1933, and from 1925—33, was chairman of the Zionist Executive. M. was the author of a history of the Russian pogroms.

MOUNT OF OLIVES: Mountain extending E of Jerusalem, beyond the Kidron Valley. It has three summits, one occupied by the village of et-Tur (ancient Beth Phagi), the second by the Victoria Augusta Hospice, and the third by the Hebrew Univ. (Mt. Scopus; 2,684 ft.). It was called "the Ascent of the Olives" in the time of David, who worshiped on its summit (II Sam. 15:30, 32): the name M. of O. appears first in Zech. 14:4. In Second Temple times, its summit served as the first post of the chain of beacons to Babylonia to communicate events in the religious calendar. Various incidents described in the New Testament are said to have occurred on the M. of O., e.g. the place on which Jesus wept over Jerusalem (*Dominus flevit*), his arrest (Gethsemane, at the foot of the mountain), and the ascension (at its top); in consequence, a series of churches was constructed at various points from the time of Constantine. The Jewish necropolis of Jerusalem has been at the foot of the mountain since the time of the First Temple. From 1948 to 1967, the S part of the mount was in Jordanian hands, while the N part was a demilitarized zone with the Hebrew Univ. and Hadassah hospital buildings under Israel sovereignty. After the Six-Day War the mount was incorporated into the united Jerusalem and plans were made for re-activating and expanding the university campus and the hospital. The Jewish cemetery — extensively desecrated by the Jordanians — was restored as much as possible.

MOUNT SCOPUS see **MOUNT OF OLIVES**

MOUNT VERNON: City in New York state, US. Six-ty families of Jewish immigrants from E Europe settled there between 1869 and 1892. An Orthodox congregation, Brothers of Israel, was founded in 1892. The Jewish Community Council, formed in 1939, represents the city's Jewish organizations, and a monthly paper, the *Westchester Jewish Tribune*, was founded in 1950.

MOUNTAIN JEWS see **CAUCASUS**

MOUNTAINS OF JUDAH see **JUDEAN HILLS**

MOURNERS FOR ZION see **AVELE ZION**

MOURNING (Heb. *avelut*): The customs and natural reactions expressing grief over the death of a relative, friend, etc. M. customs in Israel during the Biblical Period were rooted in common Middle Eastern practice. The Torah forbade some of these (e.g. cutting or tearing the flesh, shaving the head) but there is evidence that they still survived down to talmudic times. Customs that were not forbidden included rending the garments, girding on sackcloth, sitting on the ground, placing earth and dust on the head, weeping, and m. by professional weepers, especially women. M. generally lasted 7 days, but in practice the period varied. Many m customs were also observed for certain catastrophes, e.g. the destruction of the Temple and even for the sickness of a relative. Most of these practices were retained in talmudic times, and several new ones added, e. g. the sounding of the *shophar* to announce a death and the institution of the HEVRAH KADDISHA. The rending of all garments was replaced by the symbolic tearing of one. Apart from dirges during the funeral, a eulogy (HESPED) is generally uttered in praise of the deceased. M. begins after the BURIAL. The mourner dons special garments, takes off his shoes, remains in his home for a week (SHIVAH) and does not go to synagogue (except on Sabbaths), read Scripture (except the laws of m.). It is a duty to visit the mourner during this period to pray with him and to console him with the accepted formula "May God comfort you among the other mourners for Zion and Jerusalem." Parents are mourned 12 months (30 days intensively: see SHELOSHIM), other relatives 30 days. All these customs from the Talmudic Period are collected in EVEL RABBATH. Several alterations took place in m. customs in post-talmudic times but mostly they retained their

ancient forms. The main subsequent innovation was the kindling of a lamp during the m. period and recitation of KADDISH, the sources of which are to be found in the Talmud. The *kaddish* is recited for eleven months after the burial of a parent or child and each year on the anniversary of the death.

MUFTI see **HUSSEINI**

MÜHLHAUSEN, YOMTOV LIPMANN (14th — 15th cents.): Polemist. At Prague in 1399, he was compelled to participate in a disputation with the apostate Peter (Pesah), who alleged that Jews blasphemed Christian beliefs. He was arrested and subsequently released, though 80 other Jews were martyred. M., who knew Latin, wrote a famous anti-Christian polemical work *Sepher Nitzahon* ("A Book of Triumph") at the close of which he summarized the details of the disputation. This work greatly impressed Christian theologians, several of whom attempted a refutation.

MÜHSAM, ERICH (1878 — 1934): German poet and dramatist. A philosophical anarchist, he was influenced by Gustav Landauer to participate in the short-lived Bavarian Soviet Republic, and was imprisoned 1920 — 4. He continued radical political agitation by means of poems and dramas and as editor of anarchist periodicals. In 1933, he was seized by the Nazis and subsequently tortured to death.

MUKACHEVO (MUNKACS): City in the Ukraine, USSR; formerly Hungary. Encouraged by the nobility, Jews settled there in the early 18th cent., serving in the city administration in 1794. The main stream of immigrants consisted of Polish Hasidim. M. became the center of the uncompromising orthodoxy of the Spira dynasty. During the 20 years of Czech rule following World War I, the Jews enjoyed complete civic equality. Before the Nazi invasion, M. had 15,000 Jews (50% of the population), with 30 synagogues, a famous yeshivah, a Hebrew secondary school, and 4 Yiddish newspapers. Jewish pop. (1970): c. 2,000.

MUKDONI, ALEXANDER (pseudonym of Alexander Kappel; 1877 — 1958): Yiddish essayist. Born in Russia and active in Yiddish literature there, he went to the US in 1924. His critical and historical essays on the Yiddish theater appeared in Warsaw (1909ff.), but he is best known as dramatic critic (from 1922) of the New York *Morgen Journal*.

MUKTZEH (Heb. "set aside"): Objects the handling of which is forbidden on Sabbaths, etc. The law prohibits the use on Sabbaths and festivals of anything customarily connected with secular work. It forbids even the touching of objects pertaining exclusively to weekday activities, mainly because they are normally used for a forbidden purpose: e.g. money (used for trade) or matches (for making fire) are not touched or carried by the pious Jew on the Sabbath or a holy day.

MÜLLER, DAVID HEINRICH VON (1846 — 1912): Orientalist. A native of Galicia, he was professor of oriental languages at Vienna Univ. (1885) and at the

Paul Muni in the film "I was a Prisoner in the Chain Gang".

Vienna Rabbinical Seminary. He wrote on the structure of ancient Semitic poetry, the code of Hammurabi, the archeology of S Arabia, etc.

MULLER, HERMAN JOSEPH (1890–1967): US geneticist; professor at Indiana Univ. In 1946 he was awarded the Nobel Prize for Medicine for his discoveries regarding hereditary changes or mutations produced by X-rays. His main works include *Mechanism of the Mendelian Heredity* and *Genetics, Medicine, and Man*.

MÜLLER, JOEL (1827–1895): Scholar. After officiating as rabbi in Moravia and Bohemia, he taught Talmud and codes at the Berlin *Lehranstalt für die Wissenschaft des Judentums*. M. wrote extensively on gaonic and French responsa.

MÜLLER-COHEN, ANITA (1890—1962): Social worker. She was active in the relief of Jewish distress during World War I in Galicia and Bukovina, founding many hospitals, etc. and transferring starving children to western countries. In 1920, she initiated in America the adoption of victims of Russian pogroms. She settled in Palestine in 1936.

MUNI, PAUL (originally Muni Weissenfreund; 1895—1967): US actor. He made his debut on the Yiddish stage in 1908 and joined the Yiddish Art Theater in 1918. He appeared frequently in character roles on Broadway and in such films as *The Story of Louis Pasteur* and *Emile Zola*.

MUNICH: Town of W Germany; capital of BAVARIA. Jews lived there from the early 13th cent., their chief occupation being moneylending. The status of the community was regulated by legislation in the 13th-14th cents. 67 Jews were burned in the synagogue in 1285 as a result of a Blood Libel, and the community was destroyed during the Black Death outbreaks (1349) Jews returned by 1375, were the victims of a Host Desecration allegation in 1413, and were expelled in 1440, only returning in the 18th cent. The first modern synagogue was inaugurated in 1824. Anti-Semitism increased in the 20th cent. — especially after KURT EISNER'S revolutionary Bavarian government — and M. was a stronghold of the Nazi movement in the 1920's. The Jews suffered from the Nov. 1938 pogroms, and their numbers fell from 9,000 in 1933 to 3,000 in 1941 and these were eventually exterminated. After World War II, a community was re-established and numbered 3,611 in 1973.

MUNK, HERMANN (1839–1912): German physiologist. He was a pioneer in cerebral physiology, and published works on the functions of the brain and on nervous impulses.

MUNK, SALOMON (1803—1867): Orientalist. Born in Glogau, he studied in Germany and settled in Paris, working from 1835 in the Department of Manuscripts of the Bibliothèque Royale. He was also secretary of the Central Consistory, but resigned his posts in 1852 on going blind. In 1864, M. was appointed professor of Hebrew at the Collège de France. His books include an encyclopedic work on Palestine, philosophic studies and the Arabic text and French translations of Maimonides' *Guide*. He first established Ibn Gabirol's authorship of *Fons Vitae*.

MUNKACS see **MUKACHEVO**

MUNKACZI, BERNAT (1860—1937): Hungarian philologist and ethnologist. He was president (1893—1910) of the Hungarian Ethnographical Society. His works include a lexicon of the Votyak language (1888-96).

*MÜNSTER, SEBASTIAN (1489—1552): Hebraist. Originally a Franciscan, he taught Hebrew and mathematics at Basle from 1592. M. was the first Christian to edit the Hebrew Bible (Basle 1534—5, with German translation). He translated the Gospel of Matthew into Hebrew (1537) and the grammatical works of his teacher Elijah Levita into Latin. He wrote grammars of biblical Aramaic (1527) and rabbinic Hebrew (1542).

MÜNZ (MINZ): (1) *JUDAH M.* (c. 1409–1509): Rabbi. On the expulsion from Mainz in 1461, he settled in Padua where he established a famous yeshivah and, according to tradition, taught philosophy at the university, where his statue is said to have been erected. There is only an indirect record of his polemic with Elijah DELMEDIGO. His responsa are historically important. (2) *MOSES M.* (fl. 15th cent.): Rabbi; cousin of (1). He was rabbi at Mainz but after the 1461 expulsion, officiated at Posen. His responsa were published in 1617.

MURABAAT: Site of four caves in a wadi near the Dead Sea (in Jordan) where important archeological finds were made in 1952. The caves were the headquarters of a Jewish commander, Yeshua ben Gilgola, during the Bar Kokhba revolt, and many remains of the period were discovered including correspondence with Bar Kokhba. Other documents included Bible fragments and mss of the Roman military post established after the capture of the caves.

MURDER: "Thou shalt not kill" is one of the Ten Commandments. According to traditional Hebrew law, the punishment for premeditated m. witnessed by two proper witnesses who gave forewarning of the seriousness of the crime is beheading by the sword. In order to impose a sentence of capital punishment, however, Hebrew law requires such meticulous proof of the details of the crime that for all practical purposes it becomes impossible to impose the death sentence. Under these circumstances, a man guilty of premeditated m. is sentenced to severe imprisonment. Another precondition for passing a death sentence is that the Sanhedrin sit in the Chamber of Hewn Stones in the Temple. Where the crime was not premeditated, the killer had to flee to a CITY OF REFUGE in order to escape the vengeance of the next of kin and there await the death of the high priest.

MUSAPH: Service comprising a supplementary *Amidah* recited on those days when an additional sacrifice (Heb. *Musaph*) was offered in the Temple (Sabbaths, New Moons, the three pilgrim festivals, the New Year, and the Day of Atonement). It includes a passage describing the offering prescribed for the occasion. In the New Year *m.* the number of benedictions is enlarged to nine; in the Day of Atonement *m.*, a description of the high priest's service is inserted.

MUSAR MOVEMENT: Moral movement developing in the latter part of the 19th cent. among Orthodox Jewish groups in Lithuania. Its founder, R Israel SALANTER, preached the need to strengthen inner piety, and with this object his followers set aside certain periods for studying traditional ethical literature (*musar*) as well as engaging in moral self-criticism. They established throughout Lithuania *musar* institutions—reading rooms containing ethical literature. The movement became influential in yeshivah circles, although many at first opposed it for fear it would detract from the study of the Talmud. Eventually, most of the Lithuanian and US yeshivot came under its influence as their leaders regarded it as a defense against secular incursions. A daily period (generally half-an-hour) was set aside for reading ethical literature and regular lectures were given by a *mashgiah* or spiritual head. Special yeshivot were established by leaders of the movement notably at Kelm, Slobodka, and Novahardok.

MUSEUM: The conception of a m. devoted specifically to Jewish ritual art and objects of Jewish interest originates from the second half of the 19th cent.

The Jewish Museum, NY City.

The pioneer collection of M. Strauss exhibited at the Trocadero in Paris in 1878, was subsequently presented by Baron de Rothschild to the Cluny Museum (but is no longer on exhibition). In 1897, the first specific Jewish m. was established in Vienna. In Germany, the Jewish m. at Frankfort-on-Main was established in 1901, that of Danzig 1903, of Berlin in 1917; there were others in Mainz, Breslau, etc. The London Jewish M. was opened in 1933, and about the same time Gustave Tuck established a m. in connection with the Jewish Historical Society at University College. Meanwhile, the Jewish Theological Seminary of America, New York, had accumulated a large number of m. specimens, which were inadequately exhibited until 1947, when the gift of the Warburg family mansion on Fifth Avenue made possible the organization of the New York Jewish M. under Stephen Kayser, with a section devoted to modern works of art. A Jewish m. based on the collection purchased in 1926 from S. Kirschtein was also organized under F. Landsberger in association with the Hebrew Union College at Cincinnati. Smaller Jewish m.'s are to be found in the US in connection with various communities and temples. In Paris, the Jewish M. organized after World War II has arranged a number of successful exhibitions. The BEZALEL National M. in Jerusalem, including also a picture gallery, founded by Boris Schatz in 1906, was greatly developed by M. Narkis and eventually incorporated in the ISRAEL MUSEUM (established in 1965) which also had an imposing archeological wing. The Tel Aviv M., concentrating on paintings, etc., was established in 1932 by M. Dizengoff, who gave over his own house for the purpose, with the express intention of providing esthetic standards for the city. The Ha-Aretz Museum in Tel Aviv houses special collections (e.g. glass, coins). Another M. of Art is in Haifa (where there is also a naval m.), and there are others elsewhere in Israel, including En Harod and the Wilfred Israel collection at Ha-Zorea as well as many art and regional archeological and natural history collections.

MUSIC: Music is mentioned early in the Bible (cf. Gen. 4:21), but no pictorial sources and no written m. are available to enable a reconstruction of ancient Hebrew playing and song. The singing and dancing of biblical times are often described and generally associated with women (Miriam, Deborah, Jephthah's daughter, etc.) whose songs were accompanied by musical instruments. Six of them are mentioned during the nomadic period: *ugav* (probably a shepherd flute), *kinnor* (a stringed instrument), *toph* (frame drum), *paamon* (bell or jingle), *shophar* (ram's horn), and *hatzotzrah* (trumpet). The soft-sounded flute, lyre, and drum were used to accompany the song; the ram's horn and trumpet were the shrill and resounding instruments of the cult. At the time of the Kings, foreign influences and the development of urban life did away with the former simplicity. Under Egyptian influence, the splendor of orchestral sound and urban dance-m. were introduced, and more powerful musical instruments replaced the flute and lyre — such as the *keren* (horn or trumpet), *mashrokitah* (a loud pipe), *katros* (large lyre), *sabkha* (a kind of harp), and *psanterin* (psaltery). At the same time, m. became a profession practiced by a religious caste in the Temple and by professional women in the houses of kings or nobility. This is also the period in which there developed the Jewish modal system, still basically prevalent in oriental civilization. Jewish popular belief and legends ascribed to David not only the organization of the musical service in the Temple and the creation and singing of the Psalms, but also the invention of musical instruments. The musical instruments played in the Temple were perfected, and new names make their appearance (*halil, abbuv, shalishim, metziltayim,* etc.). The levites were charged with the professional organization and performance of the service; they trained singers, players, and conductors, and had a chorus of at least twelve singers, with an accompanying orchestra probably of 2 to 6 harps, 9 or more lyres, 2 to 12 oboes, and one pair of cymbals. Usually, there were as many singers as instrumentalists. After

The Rubin Academy of Music in Jerusalem.

the Babylonian exile, a decline in the appreciation of instrumental m. set in. Not only was the number of players reduced, but the priests now permitted non-levites to accompany the singers. The trumpets were invariably used separately (and not within the orchestra), while the drum — the typical instrument of the women — was absent. M. served the Temple, the Court, and the country, and accordingly three different styles developed — the organized Temple liturgy, the m. at feasts and celebrations in the nobleman's house, and the pastoral m. of the people in the country. A permanent mutual influence was only natural, but in time instrumental m. lost importance and then disappeared, and only the liturgical song has retained its essential character; its remnants are preserved in the Jewish chants of Yemen, the Babylonian regions, Persia, Syria and N Africa, where Jews lived in seclusion for more than thirteen hundred years. The centuries in which the spiritual heritage of Judaism was assembled in the Talmud also saw the development of the synagogue, the service of which was modeled after ancient Temple practice. The traditional anti-phonal singing was long retained, but the HAZZAN began to undertake the embellishment of the traditional melodies and to perform them impressively. Signs were devised to help the singers memorize the melodies, and these "accents" later influenced the beginnings of musical notation in western m. When Christian service and liturgy developed, much attention was paid to ancient Hebrew practice; the form and organization of the liturgy, the m. of the Psalms and other scriptural passages, and the style of singing were taken over — but later developed in different ways. Instrumental playing was in due course banned in the synagogue, ultimately coming to be despised by the Jews and Moslems alike. More recently, Jewish musicians and theorists have

Members of the Israel Philharmonic Orchestra playing for Soldiers.

contributed considerably to m. in the world, without their contribution necessarily being of a typically Jewish character. In the heyday of Islam's Spanish period, Jewish philosophers wrote on m. (among them Saadyah, Hai Gaon, Isaac Alfasi, Abraham bar Ḥiyya, Maimonides, Levi ben Gershon). While the ancient heritage was preserved in the oriental Jewish communities, it underwent some changes in the European centers of Jewish settlement. There are only isolated early instances of Jewish musicians taking part in the general cultural development—such as the German minnesinger Süsskind of Trimberg. Musical life developed within the Jewish quarters but showed signs of outside influence at an early stage. The use of foreign tunes in the synagogue and at feasts was strictly forbidden by the rabbinical authorities, but the folksong of the countries in which the Jews lived could not but intrude into their own song, in house and synagogue alike. Jewish musical life in the ghetto culminated in the Ḥasidic movement with its ecstatic religious music. An early, and outstanding, instance of Jewish musicians working outside the ghetto is that of Salomone DE' ROSSI in Renaissance Italy. Rossi's free style of liturgical composition was followed two hundred years later by the Reform movement in 19th cent. Germany. As Jewish emancipation developed all over Europe composers were enabled to come into their own; in the work of some of them Jewish traits have been detected and analyzed, but generally these are insufficient to justify the name of Jewish or Hebrew m. Toward the end of the 19th cent., there developed a "National Jewish Music School," basing its works on the folklore of E European Jewry. Ernest BLOCH now created a Hebraic style not connected with actual folk-lore. With the return to Zion, attempts began to create a Palestinian, later an Israel, musical style. In contemporary Israel m., the process of amalgamation is obvious. The elder generation of composers brought a rich musical heritage from Europe and is perpetuating it, though under the impact of the musical language of the Orient; the middle generation listens to the voice of the Orient—that is to say, to the roots of the most ancient m. of Israel—and seeks expression in an "Eastern-Mediterranean" musical style; the youngest composers base their musical language on the inflections of Hebrew. In modern times, Israel fulfils the same role in certain manifestations of m. as it did in antiquity; that of a mediator between East and West and of a bridge between the old and the new. See also CANTOR.

*MUSOLINO, BENEDETTO (1809—1885): Italian Zionist precursor. Politician and philosopher and a comrade of Garibaldi, he wrote a treatise in 1851 from the strictly Catholic viewpoint advocating the re-establishment of a Jewish state in Palestine and anticipating many of Herzl's views. It was published only in 1952.

*MUSSOLINI, BENITO (1883—1945): Founder of Italian FASCISM. His movement was at the outset not explicitly antagonistic to the Jews, some of whom were among his earlier associates. He even showed some interest in Zionism, especially when it afforded a prospect of embarrassing England in the Middle East. His rapprochement with Hitler led him to embrace an anti-Semitic policy in 1938. Even then M.'s regime refused to follow Germany in its worst anti-Jewish brutalities and managed to introduce an element of restraint in the occupied areas of France and the Balkans. In 1943—5, however, M.'s subservient Italian Fascist republic collaborated obediently in the campaign of extermination.

MYERS, SIR ARTHUR (1867—1926): New Zealand public figure. He was mayor of Auckland 1905—8, member of parliament 1910—21, and held cabinet posts in various ministries.

MYERS, CHARLES SAMUEL (1873—1946): English psychologist. Professor at London 1906—9, he was from 1922, principal of (later adviser to) the National Institute of Industrial Psychology, a subject in which he pioneered. He was active in English Jewish communal life.

MYERS, SIR MICHAEL (1873—1950): New Zealand jurist. In 1929, he was appointed chief justice of New Zealand.

MYRTLE: One of the four species which make up the complete LULAV, used while praying on the Feast of Tabernacles. In the Bible the reference is to "a leaf-covered bough of a tree" (Lev. 23:40).

MYSTICISM see **KABBALAH**

NAAMAN (fl. 9th cent. BCE): General of Aram-Dammesek (Damascus), probably in the time of Ben-Hadad III and Jehoram of Israel. Being afflicted with leprosy, he went to Israel to consult Elisha who cured him. N. took back to Syria a load of soil upon which to built an altar to God (II Kings 5).

NABAL: Wealthy Calebite, dwelling at Maon in S Judah. DAVID, who regarded himself as the protector of the local population against attacks from the desert Beduin, asked him for food for his troops. When brusquely refused, David prepared to attack him but was dissuaded by N.'s wife ABIGAIL who secretly conveyed food to David. The news, when broken to N. the next day, caused a mortal stroke.

NABATEANS: People of Arab extraction who occupied Edom in the 6th cent. BCE, establishing their capital at Petra (Rekem). Originally typical nomads, the N. soon learned to develop agriculture under almost desert conditions by an elaborate system of water conservation. They profited from their position astride the Elath-Gaza road and the northern outlet of the Arabian desert by fostering the caravan trade. For this purpose they established a chain of agricultural settlements across the NEGEV. During the decay of the Seleucid Empire, the N. extended their power up to and including Damascus, coming into conflict with Alexander Yannai. Subdued by the Romans in 63 BCE, their country was annexed in 106 CE, and became the Provincia Arabia. The N. developed a remarkable Arab-Hellenistic culture, especially in their "rose-red" rock-cut city of Petra.

NABLUS see **SHECHEM**

NABOTH (fl. mid-9th cent. BCE): Jezreelite whose patriarchal vineyard was situated near the palace of Ahab. The king desired the plot for his kitchen-garden, but when N. refused to sell, Jezebel engineered his execution (I Kings 21). The opposition of the prophetical party under Elijah to this action was a prime motive in their supporting Jehu who wiped out the dynasty of Ahab. "Naboth's Vineyard" has became proverbial.

NACHTASYL (Ger. "shelter for a night"): Title of a play by Gorki, applied by Max Nordau at the Sixth Zionist Congress (1903) to the UGANDA plan.

NADAB AND ABIHU: Eldest sons of Aaron. As priests, they ascended Mt. Sinai to behold the Divine revelation (Exod. 24:1–11) but later sacrificed "strange fire" on the altar, and, in punishment, were mortally struck by "fire from before the Lord" (Lev. 10:1–3).

NADAB: King of Israel c. 913–911 BCE; son and successor of Jeroboam. While fighting the Philistines, he was assassinated — together with the rest of the house of Jeroboam — by his rival Baasha (I Kings 15:25–31).

NADEL, ARNO (1878–1943): Painter, author and composer. Born in Lithuania, he lived in Germany from 1895. N. was a synagogue choir conductor in Berlin, composer and collector of Jewish liturgical and folk music, a portait painter of note, and an author of expressionist poetry. He was murdered in a Nazi concentration camp.

NADIR, BANU see **BANU NADIR**

NADIR, MOSHE (Pseudonym of Isaac Reiss; 1885–1943): Yiddish writer. Arriving in the US in 1898, he participated in many Yiddish publications. Using several pseudonyms, he wrote in most branches of literature (poetry, drama, feuilletons,' etc.).

NAGDELA, IBN see **SAMUEL IBN NAGRELA**

NAGID (Heb. "prince"): Title applied in Moslem (and some Christian) countries in the Middle Ages to a leader recognized by the state as head of the Jewish community. The office may have been intended originally to replace locally the Babylonian EXILARCH. The institution probably originated in Egypt in the 10th cent. and thence spread to Morocco (Jacob ben Abraham, 10th cent.) and Spain, where the most distinguished N. was SAMUEL IBN NAGRELA of Granada. In the 13th cent., the descendants of Moses Maimonides were accorded the rank of N. of the Jews in Egypt where the office persisted until the 16th cent.

NAGRELA, IBN see **SAMUEL IBN NAGRELA**

NAHAL (Heb. abbr. for *Noar Halutzi Lohem* = "Fighting Pioneer Youth"): A branch of the Israel Defense Forces training cadres for agricultural settlements. When half of the *N.* member's term of service in the army expires, he is given an opportunity for permanent settlement along the borders,

Nahal: a new settlement in Golan.

either in existing villages or among the founders of new ones. Members of *N.* are recruited from youth movements, Youth Aliyah, pioneer youth organizations abroad, and the army.

NAHAL MIZRAYIM (Heb. "Brook of Egypt"): According to the accepted identification, first found in the Septuagint and later in Saadyah's Bible translation, Wadi EL ARISH, the largest of the wadis of the Negev and Sinai, which flows into the Mediterranean E of El Arish in the Sinai peninsula. According to the Bible (e.g. Num. 34:5; Jos. 15:4), the S frontier of the Land of Israel follows *N. M.* (referring to its lower sector).

NAHAL SOREK (Heb. "Brook of Sorek" in some mss Shorek): Valley in Judah where Delilah lived (Judg. 16:4) and Samson was captured by the Philistines. It is identified with the valley in the Judean hills where the railroad from Jerusalem to Tel Aviv now runs.

NAHALAL: Israel smallholders' settlement (TM) in the Jezreel Valley. Founded in 1921, it was the first *moshav ovedim.* The settlers drained the malaria-infested swamps in the area and built their farmsteads.

The concentric village-plan designed by R. Kauffman led the way for the rational planning of similar settlements. It is the site of an agricultural training farm. Pop. (1972): 1,043.

NAHARIYYAH: Israel semi-urban settlement on the coast of W Galilee. Founded in 1934 by immigrants from Germany, it was the first Jewish village in the area, being in a precarious position during the disturbances of 1936–9, and again during the War of Independence. The settlers built up a highly intensive gardening and truck-farming economy and also soon developed N. into a seaside resort. After 1948, it grew more rapidly with the absorption of immigrants from many countries (Rumania, Hungary, Yemen, etc.). Traces of Phoenician (Canaanite) settlement have been found at several places in the vicinity. Pop. (1974): 27,900.

NAHAVENDI, BENJAMIN see **BENJAMIN BEN MOSES NAHAVENDI**

NAHMAN BAR ISAAC (fl. 4th cent.): Babylonian amora. He was the RESH KALLAH under Rava in Mahoza and during the last four years of his life headed the Pumbedita academy. N. composed ingenious mnemonics to assist the study of the Talmud.

NAHMAN BAR JACOB (3rd–4th cents.): Babylonian amora. He was an expert on the authority of law courts. Imbued with a special love for Palestine, he hospitably received Palestinian scholars, from whom he learned much of the Palestinian aggadah. He was a son-in-law of the exilarch and headed the Nehardea academy.

NAHMAN OF BRATZLAV (1772–1811): Hasidic rabbi; grandson of ODEL, daughter of the BAAL SHEM TOV. From childhood he absorbed Hasidic doctrine and Lurianic Kabbalah. Of an ascetic temperament, he would isolate himself in the fields and woods to devote himself to the God of nature. N. endeavoured to be a "true *tzaddik*" and renew the inspiration of Hasidism. In 1798–9, he lived in Tiberias studying Kabbalah and on his return to the Ukraine stated that he had "attained to wondrous understanding in Palestine." His enthusiasm aroused antagonism, especially from Aryeh Leib of Spoli who professed to detect traces of Sabbetaism in N.'s doctrines and attitude. In 1802, N. settled in Bratzlav, where his pupil, R Nathan Sternharz, joined him and noted down his teachings. These exalt the position of the *tzaddik* who is the "Divine image of the generation." His own Hasidim confessed their sins to him, asking for repentance. He taught simple faith, emphasizing the importance of prayer – even if recited in Yiddish – and of music (singing and dancing). His parables are famous. In 1810, he settled in Uman where he died. The followers of his teaching still maintain synagogues in Israel and elsewhere.

NAHMANI BAR KAYLIL see **ABBAYE**

NAHMANIDES see **MOSES BEN NAHMAN**

NAHOUM, HAIM (1873–1960): Rabbi and scholar.

Born in Turkey, he studied for the rabbinate in Paris and in 1907, went to Abyssinia to investigate the history and customs of the Falashas. From 1908 to 1920, he was chief rabbi (*Hakham Bashi*) of Turkey; from 1923, chief rabbi of Cairo and from 1925, of Egypt. He was a member of the Egyptian Senate, 1930-4.

NAHSHON: Chief of the tribe of Judah during the Exodus and the wanderings in the desert; brother-in-law of Aaron and ancestor of David. According to the aggadah, he was the first of the Israelites leaving Egypt to have the faith to enter the Reed Sea (*Sotah* 37a).

NAHUM (fl. 7th cent. BCE): Prophet hailing from Elkosh (which some place in Palestine, others near Nineveh). He foretold the fall of Nineveh "the bloody city." N. is one of the great biblical poets – a master of language and of vivid descriptions. The Book of N. contains 3 chapters of which the first is a general introduction.

NAHUM OF GIMZO (fl. 2nd cent.): Tanna, hailing from Gimzo near Lydda. His contribution to midrashic exegesis included the suggestion, adopted and extended by his pupil R Akiva, that in the Pentateuch the untranslated Hebrew particle *et* signifies that the word governed should be given a wide rather than a narrow connotation. His comment on every apparent misfortune was the later proverbial *gam zo le-tovah* ("this too is for good") by which the name Gimzo was explained. In his later years, he suffered from paralysis.

NAIDITSCH, ISAAC (1868–1949): Industrialist and Zionist leader. Of Russian birth, he early joined the *Hibbat Zion* movement and remained active in Zionist affairs throughout his life, being one of the founders and directors of the *Keren ha-Yesod*. He lived in Paris after World War I and moved to the US in World War II.

NAJARA, ISRAEL BEN MOSES (1555–1628): Hebrew poet. He was born and spent most of his life at Safed, where he was a prominent member of the kabbalistic school. A master of Aramaic as well as of Hebrew, he wrote in those languages large numbers of hymns, often to be sung to familiar secular tunes, some of which became very popular. They were assembled in his *Zemirot Israel* and other works. The mystical eroticism of many of his compositions attracted unfavorable comment. N. died as rabbi of Gaza.

NAKDANIM (Heb. "punctuators"): Experts between the 9th and 14th cents. who provided biblical mss with vowels and accents: successors of the MASORETES. They flourished in the Orient and in England, France, and Germany. Some of them wrote treatises on the subject.

NAKHES (Yidd. from Heb. *nahat* from *nahat ruah*): Pleasure.

NAMES: Biblical n. were generally of good omen and were based, in the earliest period, on Hebrew roots many incorporating the name of the deity BAAL. Later, monotheistic principles manifested themselves with names based on the prefixes *Eli, Jeho,* etc., or suffixes such as *El, Eli,* or *Jahu.* Toward the end of the Second Temple Period, Greek n., sometimes used in conjunction with the Hebrew, were common, while at the same time Aramaic forms became frequent both in Palestine and in Babylonia. Later, Latin forms begin to emerge, especially in Italy. In the Middle Ages, vernacular equivalents, very frequently based on the Blessings of Jacob (Gen. 49) or of Moses (Deut. 33), were habitually used by the side of the Hebrew names (e.g. Leon = Judah). For the men, a Hebrew or Hebraized name (frequently out of the Bible) was necessary for synagogal purposes: for the women, vernacular names needed no Hebrew equivalent. Surnames began to emerge in Italy and Spain in the Middle Ages, but elsewhere patronymics only were generally employed at this time. Surnames in the modern sense were invariable in the W European countries (as in America) from the 18th cent.; and from the period of the French Revolution (in E Europe somewhat later) were generally made obligatory by law. There was a tendency for Jewish names to be patronymic (e.g. Jacobs, Jacobson), geographical (e.g. Romano, Englander), or occupational (e.g. Schneider). In the 19th cent., it became increasingly common for Jews to take, sometimes by legal process, n. of an ostensibly non-Jewish character. In Israel, especially since 1948, the tendency has been reversed, Hebrew n. being adopted to replace those of a non-Hebrew type.

NAMES OF GOD see **GOD, NAMES OF**

NAMIER, SIR LEWIS BERNSTEIN (1888–1960): Historian. Of Polish birth, he settled in England in 1907. He was professor of modern history at Manchester 1931–53, and wrote fundamental studies on 18th cent. English political history and international relations in the 19th–20th cents. From 1929–31, N. was political secretary of the Jewish Agency. On his marriage in 1947, he became an Anglican.

NAMIR, MORDEKHAI (1897–1975): Israel labor leader. Born in Russia, N. moved to Palestine in 1924. He was Israel minister to the USSR 1949–50, secretary general of the *Histadrut* 1950–6, minister of labor 1956–9, and mayor of Tel Aviv 1959–69. From 1951, he was a *Mapai* member of the Knesset.

NAOMI: Wife of Elimelech. Together with her husband and sons, Mahlon and Chilion, she left Bethlehem for Moab in a famine period. After several years abroad — in the course of which Elimelech and her sons died — she returned with her daughter-in-law, Ruth, whom she assisted in marrying Boaz.

Medal commemorating the Napoleonic Sanhedrin, 1806/7.

NAPHTALI: Sixth son of Jacob, his second by Bilhah. The inheritance of the tribe descended from him was in the northern part of Canaan, including the entire E coast of the Sea of Galilee and the mountains of Galilee. The tribe was active in the war against Sisera and Gideon's campaign against the Midianites. N. belonged to the northern kingdom of Israel after the split; it was overrun by Arameans in the time of Baasha, while a large section of its inhabitants was exiled by Tiglath-Pileser. From the survivors were derived many of the Jews living in Galilee in Second Temple times.

NAPHTALI, PERETZ (Fritz; 1888–1961): Israel economist. Born in Germany, he was economic editor of the *Frankfurter Zeitung* 1921–6, and manager of the Labor Movement's Economic Research Bureau in Berlin 1926–33. Settling in Palestine in 1933, N. directed the Workers' Bank 1938–49. He was a *Mapai* Knesset member 1949–59, minister without portfolio 1951–2 and 1955–9, and minister of agriculture 1952–5.

NAPLES: Italian seaport. Inscriptions and literary sources attest to the presence of Jews there, and in the neighboring Pozzuoli, in the Classical Period. Jews assisted in the defense of N. when it was besieged by Belisarius in 537. A community existed throughout the Middle Ages, was decimated in an attack about 1290, again flourished in the 15th cent., and received large numbers of Spanish exiles in 1492. A handful of these reconstituted the community after attack and temporary exclusion in 1495/6, and it existed until the general expulsion from the kingdom of Naples in 1541. Jewish settlement was refounded in the 19th cent. under the aegis of Baron Karl von Rothschild and numbers (1969) 450.

*NAPOLEON BONAPARTE (1769–1821): French Emperor. During his Middle Eastern campaign of 1799, he issued an appeal to the Jews vaguely promising the resuscitation of a Jewish state but this met with little response. Protests against Jewish meneylending practices in Alsace led him in 1806 to take an active interest in the Jews. He convoked an Assembly of Jewish Notables in Paris and ordered a temporary moratorium on debts owed to Jews in the Rhineland. The 111 Notables met (July 15, 1806 – April 6, 1807) and discussed problems submitted by the authorities, e.g. Jewish matrimonial status, internal administration, occupations, and duty to the state. The delegates, while insisting on their religious rights, recognized the authority of the civil law, thus in effect transforming the Jews from a sub-national to a purely religious community. To confirm these decisions N. convoked a Sanhedrin (see SANHEDRIN, GRAND), which met Feb. 9 – Mar. 9, 1807, and later set up in France (1808) a central Jewish communal administration, working through CONSISTORIES. At the same time, N. issued several restrictive measures (the "infamous decree"), chiefly relating to commerce and finance, which seriously restricted Jewish rights. N.'s work of admitting Jews to civil rights not only in France but in other areas subject to his political domination (e.g. Italy and Germany) did much to hasten Jewish Emancipation.

NARBONI, MOSES see **MOSES HA-DARSHAN**

NARBONNE: S French town. Jews resided there from at least the 5th cent. but were expelled in the 7th, by the Visigoth king, Wamba. Later in the Middle Ages, the community was headed by a "Jewish King" by virtue of privileges said to have been granted in the 8th cent. by Charlemagne. It remained prominent until the expulsion from France in 1306. N. was the seat of a noted academy and many leading scholars lived there.

NARDI, NAḤUM (1901–): Israel composer. Of Russian birth, he settled in Palestine in 1923 and has written hundreds of songs, many based on the folklore of the oriental communities.

NASH PAPYRUS: A fragment of 24 broken lines taken from Egypt by L. W. Nash and published in 1903. It contains, in square Hebrew characters, the

Ten Commandments followed by the beginning of the *Shema* in a text closely resembling that of the Septuagint. It is most probably pre-Christian. It has been connected with the phylacteries containing the Ten Commandments as used by the KUMRAN Sect.

NASHIM (Heb. "Women"): Third order *(seder)* of the Mishnah, consisting of seven tractates, all of which have *gemara* in both the Babylonian and Palestinian Talmuds. It deals with betrothal, marriage, divorce, the general relationships of husband and wife, vows, and the law of the Nazirite.

NASHN (Yidd.): To lick, to eat a little, intermittently.

NASHVILLE: Capital of Tennessee, US. There were Jews in N. before 1845. A Hebrew Benevolent Society was formed in 1853. A year later, N.'s first congregation (Orthodox), Magen David, was chartered. Congregation B'nai Jeshurun (Reform) was founded in 1862. The vicissitudes of the Civil War forced both congregations to merge in 1868. The Jewish Community Council, incorporating 19 smaller communities in Central Tennessee, was established in 1936. N. had 3,700 Jews in 1973 supporting 3 synagogues. The weekly *Observer* has been published in N. since 1934.

NASI (Heb. "prince"): Talmudic term for the president of the *Sanhedrin,* who was also the spiritual head and later, political representative of the Jewish people. The second in authority to the *N.* was the *av bet din* (or president of the court), and together they composed the ZUGOT ("pairs") recorded in the Mishnah. Some historians have questioned the talmudic traditions and find indications in non-Jewish sources that the president of the Sanhedrin was the high priest. A solution has been found in the theory that there were two Sanhedrins, political and religious, the latter only being presided over by the *N.* before the fall of Jerusalem. From the 2nd cent., the *N.*— henceforth always a descendant of Hillel—was recognized by the Roman authorities as Patriarch of the Jews. Later, the title was used in some centers (e.g. Spain) to designate the lay leader of the Jewish

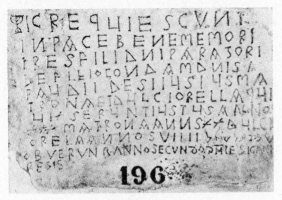

Jewish epitaph, dated 688.
(Narbonne Museum).

Gracia Nasi the Younger.
(Medal by Pastorino de' Pastorini, c. 1555).

community, and ultimately became a surname. In 132–5, Simon Bar Kokhba assumed the title, and it is possible that it was applied to the president of the Sanhedrin only after this period.

NASI: (1) *GRACIA N.* (c. 1510–1569): Jewish leader. Born in Portugal as the Marrano Beatrice de Luna, she married the banker Francisco Mendes, and on his death in 1536, went to Antwerp. Prominent and envied because of her great wealth, she feared religious persecution and escaped first (1544) to Venice, where she was denounced and imprisoned, and then (1549) to Ferrara. There she became known as a Jewess, patronized literature, and controlled an underground organization for the rescue of Marranos from Portugal. In 1552–3, she went to Constantinople, being known as Gracia Nasi; there she was joined by her nephew Joseph N. While continuing her widespread commercial operations, she became the most prominent leader of Turkish Jewry—building synagogues, helping fugitive Marranos, organizing in 1556–7, in the face of opposition, the boycott of the port of Ancona in revenge for the burning of a group of Marranos there, and beginning the project for the colonization of Tiberias associated with Joseph N. She probably died in Palestine. (2) *JOSEPH N.* (c. 1520–1579): Statesman; nephew and son-in-law of (1). Born a Marrano in Portugal as João Miguez, he went to Antwerp in 1536 with Gracia N. When his aunt fled to Italy in 1544, he remained behind to settle her affairs. He joined her in 1554 in Constantinople where he embraced Judaism publicly as Joseph Nasi and married Gracia's daughter Reyna. Owing to his wide knowledge of European affairs, he obtained an entree to the Turkish court and became an intimate of Selim, the heir to the throne. In c. 1561, he received from the sultan a lease of Tiberias and an adjacent area which he endeavored to develop as an autonom-

Title-page of *Ben Porat Yoseph* (against astrology),
by Joseph Nasi, Constantinople, 1577.

ous Jewish center. When Selim became sultan in 1566, N. was created duke of Naxos and the Cyclades, "the premier duchy of Christendom." Promised the crown of Cyprus by the sultan if the island became Turkish, he was partly responsible for the breach with Venice and the disastrous Cyprus war of 1570–3. Although in 1571, he was appointed voivode of Wallachia, his power thereafter waned. N.'s widow established, after his death, a Hebrew printing-press at her palace of Belvedere outside Constantinople; there and at Kuru Cesme (also near Constantinople) several works were published under her auspices 1592–9.

NASSAU: Former German state. Jews are known there from the early 13th cent. Several communities suffered in 1337 during the *Armleder* persecution, in 1349 at the time of the Black Death, and in 1445. After the Thirty Years' War, the area of Jewish settlement increased. In 1806, the degrading LEIBZOLL was abolished. In 1842, the Jews were obliged to choose German surnames and in 1848, were recognized as citizens. In 1866, N., then including 77 small communities (among them, Wiesbaden, Ems, and Dietz), was incorporated in PRUSSIA.

*NASSER, GAMAL ABDUL (1918–1970): Egyptian leader. In 1948, he was an officer in the Egyptian army which invaded Palestine. After becoming premier in 1954, he aspired to lead the pan-Arab

movement and organized anti-Israel activities in the military, economic, and propaganda spheres. His 1955 arms deal with Russia led to the growth of Soviet influence in the Middle East. After the Egyptian defeat in the SINAI CAMPAIGN, Oct.-Nov. 1956, N. expelled stateless Jews from Egypt and proscribed the activities of Egyptian Jewry, most of whom left the country in the following years. In 1967, he stood at the head of an Arab coalition against Israel which decreed the closing of the Straits of Tiran to Israel shipping. In the ensuing Six-Day War, Nasser was rapidly defeated, losing his air force and much of his army, as well as the entire Sinai peninsula. However Russian support enabled him to rearm his forces rapidly and to maintain a belligerent anti-Israel stand.

NASSY: Former Marrano family. (1) *DAVID N.* (alias Joseph Nuñez de Fonseca; fl. 17th cent.) formerly from Brazil, received from the Dutch West India Company tracts of land in Curaçao and later in Guiana for Jewish settlement. He collaborated in Blaeu's *Geography*. (2) *DAVID N. II* (fl. 18th cent.), physician in Philadelphia and then in Surinam, was the intermediary for the opening of relations between the Jews of that place and the Portuguese government. He wrote *Lettre politico-théologico-morale sur les Juifs* pleading for Jewish Emancipation.

NATHAN (fl. 11th-10th cents. BCE): Prophet. He announced to David that his royal house would be perpetually established but also prevented him from building a permanent Temple in Jerusalem. As a protagonist of moral values, he charged David with responsibility for the death of Uriah the Hittite. Later, he was prominent in securing the succession for Solomon. N. wrote a chronicle of David's reign (I Chron. 29:29), which was probably one of the main sources for the Book of Samuel.

NATHAN (fl. 2nd cent.): Tanna. Son of the Babylonian exilarch, he went to Palestine to study. During the Hadrianic persecutions, he was forced to leave Palestine but returned later and was appointed president of the court at Usha, an office second to that of the patriarchate. He was an expert judge in civil suits and also helped the Palestinian scholars in their opposition to the fixing of the calendar outside Palestine by Hananiah son of R Joshua. Because of a dispute with the patriarch, his decisions were not quoted in the academy by his name but as "others say." The amplified parallel to the treatise *Avot*, known as *Avot de-Rabbi Natan*, is popularly attributed to him.

NATHAN BEN ISAAC OF BAGHDAD (fl. 10th cent.): Chronicler. He wrote a graphic account, extant in Hebrew, of the organization of the gaonic academies in Mesopotamia and the disputes at the time of Saadyah. Further fragments of this work have been found in the *genizah*, and it is now believed to have formed part of a comprehensive chronicle of Baghdad written in Arabic, perhaps at Kairouan.

NATHAN BEN JEHIEL OF ROME (c. 1035–1106):
Italian Hebrew lexicographer. In 1101, he completed his *Arukh*, the only medieval lexicon covering the Talmud and Midrashim. The Hebrew and Aramaic words are given under roots: they are often left unexplained, but illustrated by extracts, many of which come from works now lost. The author shows a wide knowledge of languages, quoting passages of historical and folkloristic importance. Several supplements were written, notably by Benjamin Musafia and Isaiah Berlin. It forms the basis of the 12 vol. lexicon *Arukh Completum* by Alexander KOHUT.

NATHAN BEN JOSEPH OFFICIAL (fl. 13th cent.):
French talmudist. His religious controversies with numerous Christian opponents, including bishops and ecclesiastics, were recorded by his son.

NATHAN OF GAZA (Ghazzati; 1643–1680): "Prophet" of Shabbetai Tzevi. After studying in his native Jerusalem, he settled in Gaza, devoting himself to Kabbalah and ascetic practices. Under the influence of a vision he met Shabbetai Tzevi in Gaza and proclaimed the messianic nature of his mission. His belief in Shabbetai Tzevi was not shaken by the latter's apostasy. N. wandered through the Balkans and Italy developing the special theology of Sabbetaianism, basing it upon the Lurianic KABBALAH. He taught that the soul of the Messiah has to descend to the *kelippot* ("husks") to redeem the scattered sparks of Divine light but with the act of *tikkun* ("restoration") it will reappear in a great light. Expelled by the rabbis of Venice, he returned to the Balkans and died at Uskub near Salonica, still venerated by Sabbetaians and still maintaining his views.

NATHAN THE BABYLONIAN see **NATHAN**; **NATHAN BEN ISAAC**

NATHAN THE WISE see **LESSING, GOTTHOLD EPHRAIM**

NATHAN: British family of public servants, including four brothers: (1) *SIR FREDERIC LEWIS N.* (1861–1933), soldier who joined the Royal Artillery in 1879 and became an expert on the manufacture of explosives and, later, on fuel. He was president of the Institute of Chemists 1925–7, and commandant of the Jewish Lads' Brigade 1905–26. (2) *SIR MATTHEW N.* (1862–1939) joined the Royal Engineers in 1880, later entered the Colonial Service, was governor of the Gold Coast 1900–03, of Hong Kong 1904–06, of Natal 1907–10, of Queensland from 1920, and chairman of the Board of Inland Revenue 1911–14. (3) *SIR NATHANIEL N.* (1854–1916), colonial civil servant and lawyer, became judge of the Supreme Court and attorney general of Trinidad. (4) *SIR ROBERT N.* (1866–1921), Anglo-Indian administrator, from 1910 was chief secretary to the govern-

ments of E Bengal and Assam. In World War I, he worked on counteracting the activities of German subversive agents in the US.

NATHAN, ERNESTO (1845–1921): Italian statesman. Born in England of a family closely associated with Mazzini, he settled in Rome in 1871. Of progressive liberal views, he long headed the Italian freemasons and fought fiercely for a secular state. He was mayor of Rome 1907–13.

NATHAN, GEORGE JEAN (1882–1958): US author and drama critic. In dozens of volumes, N. wittily interpreted the growth of the modern American theater. From 1943, he issued an annual *Theater Book of the Year*. He was associated with H. L. Mencken in founding and editing the *American Mercury*, 1924–30.

NATHAN, HARRY LOUIS, LORD (1889–1963):
British public figure. A solicitor by profession, he sat in parliament 1929–35 as a Liberal, and 1937–40 as a Labor member, became a peer 1940, and was minister of civil aviation 1946–8.

NATHAN, ISAAC (1790–1864): English composer. He wrote operettas, etc. and also set to music his friend Byron's *Hebrew Melodies*. In 1841, he settled in Australia. His *Don John of Austria* was the first Australian opera.

NATHAN, MAUD (1862–1946): US social worker. Born in New York City, she achieved fame as a champion of women's suffrage and also fought for decent labor legislation. She was honorary president of the National Consumers' League and a vice-president of the National Institute of Social Science.

NATHAN, PAUL (1857–1927): German philanthropist and public figure. A left-wing liberal, he edited with Theodor Barth the weekly *Die Nation*. He was chairman of the Society Against Anti-Semitism and after 1918, joined the Social Democratic Party. N. participated in many branches of Jewish communal activity, being a founder of the Hilfsverein der Deutschen Juden and its general secretary 1901–14. During World War I, he organized assistance for Jews in the German-occupied zones of Europe, and after the war, fostered agricultural settlement among Russian Jewry.

NATHAN, ROBERT (1894–): US novelist and poet. N. has written numerous short novels, such as *Road of Ages* dealing with the European Jewish tragedy. His other works include *Portrait of Jennie* and are noted for a gentle, satiric style.

NATHANSEN, HENRI (1868–1944): Danish author. He began his literary career by writing novels and then turned to drama, being the author of eight plays, several on Jewish themes. He ceased dramatic activity when his teacher Georg BRANDES (whose biography he wrote) criticized the dramatization of Jewish subjects. His novel *The Life of Hugo David* describes the tragic fate of a Jewish actor. N.'s work emphasizes the tension between the "ghetto" Jew and his emancipated successor, the solution according to his last novel, *Mendel Philipsen and Son,* being Zionism. He committed suicide while a refugee in Sweden.

NATHANSON, MENDEL LEVIN (1780–1868): Economist and journalist. He developed the Danish linen trade by his direct connections with English producers. His works on economics are still in use. N. edited in Copenhagen the *Berlingske Tidende* which he transformed into a modern newspaper. He fought for Jewish rights and advocated secular education for Jews.

NATIONAL AGRICULTURAL COLLEGE: Institution in Doylestown, Pennsylvania, for the preparation of youths for careers in agriculture and allied fields. It was organized in 1896 as the National Farm School by Joseph Krauskopf. In 1948, the NAC was accredited by the Council of Education of Pennsylvania as a four-year senior college. The College accommodates 300 students.

NATIONAL COMMITTEE FOR LABOR ISRAEL: US organization (originally the National Labor Committee for the Organized Jewish Workers in Palestine) assisting the HISTADRUT. It is supported by US trade unions, Labor Zionist groups, Workmen's Circle branches and other bodies.

NATIONAL CONFERENCE OF CHRISTIANS AND JEWS: US organization founded in 1928, comprising Protestants, Catholics, and Jews, with the object of furthering better relations among men of all religions, races, and nationalities. The Conference has 5 national commissions and 62 regional offices. NCCJ sponsors the national observance of "Brotherhood Week" in the US and maintains the Religious News Service in New York.

NATIONAL COUNCIL FOR JEWISH EDUCATION: US organization founded in 1926 in New York City. It aims to promote the growth and welfare of Jewish education and educators. It publishes two professional magazines, *Jewish Education,* in English (3 issues a year) and *Shevile ha-Ḥinnukh,* in Hebrew (quarterly). The membership of the Council is drawn from all Jewish ideological groupings, Orthodox, Conservative and Reform.

NATIONAL COUNCIL OF JEWISH WOMEN: US organization founded in 1893 by Mrs. Hannah G. Solomon. It is dedicated to furthering human welfare in the Jewish and general communities, locally, nationally, and internationally through service, education, and social action. It has 100,000 members in 329 sections (1970) throughout the US, and is a constituent member of the International Council of Jewish Women. National Conventions, originally triennial, have been held every two years since 1953. It maintains various educational projects in Israel.

NATIONAL COUNCIL OF YOUNG ISRAEL see YOUNG ISRAEL

NATIONAL FEDERATION OF HEBREW TEACHERS AND PRINCIPALS: US organization founded in 1944 as the HEBREW TEACHERS FEDERATION. It maintains a placement bureau, has secured retirement and other benefits for teachers and principals, and cooperates with other Jewish educational bodies.

NATIONAL FEDERATION OF JEWISH MEN'S CLUBS: US organization. Founded in 1929, it has (1975) a membership of 40,000 in 350 clubs in the US and Canada. Its clubs and brotherhoods are affiliated with congregations adhering to Conservative Judaism.

NATIONAL FEDERATION OF TEMPLE BROTHERHOODS: US organization founded in 1923 as an affiliate of the UNION OF AMERICAN HEBREW CONGREGATIONS; its membership (1976) is 70,000 in 460 brotherhoods. In 1939, it assumed responsibility for the JEWISH CHAUTAUQUA SOCIETY. The Federation publishes *Brotherhood,* a quarterly magazine.

NATIONAL FEDERATION OF TEMPLE SISTERHOODS: US organization founded in 1913 as the women's agency of the UNION OF AMERICAN HEBREW CONGREGATIONS. It has (1976) a membership of more than 100,000 in some 620 sisterhoods affiliated with Reform congregations, mostly in the US. It helps maintain youth activities programs, subsidizes institutes for religious school teachers, and is the founder (1931) and patron body of the Jewish Braille Institute of America.

NATIONAL FOUNDATION FOR JEWISH CULTURE: US organization founded in 1960 by the COUNCIL OF JEWISH FEDERATIONS AND WELFARE FUNDS. Its objectives are to stimulate the study and growth of Jewish cultural programs in the US. It has supported Judaica courses in general universities and institutions pursuing research into Jewish subjects.

NATIONAL JEWISH COMMUNITY RELATIONS ADVISORY COUNCIL: The joint planning and policy-making agency of a number of US Jewish organizations and community councils. NCRAC coordinates 9 national agencies and 81 local communities.

NATIONAL JEWISH HOSPITAL: Hospital at Denver, Colorado. It was opened in 1899 to provide care for tuberculosis victims who flocked to the climate of Colorado. It has a staff of 400 and maintains 225 beds in 14 buildings. The institution provides free care for victims of tuberculosis and chest diseases, irrespective of race, religion, or nationality. It has the largest research laboratories in the US for such diseases. Its pediatric department is one of the few non-governmental services caring for tubercular infants and children.

NATIONAL JEWISH WELFARE BOARD (JWB): The central organization of JEWISH COMMUNITY

CENTERS. Founded in 1917, it is authorized by the US government to care for the welfare of Jewish military servicemen and for those in Veterans Administration hospitals. During and after World War II, it was a constituent member of the United Service Organizations, providing prayer books, educational services and materials to chaplains of all denominations, and recreational facilities to servicemen. Through its Commission on Jewish Chaplaincy, embracing Orthodox, Conservative, and Reform rabbinates, JWB recruits and serves Jewish CHAPLAINS in the US armed forces. In 1921, JWB merged with the National Council of Young Men's Hebrew and Kindred Associations. In 1974, JWB had some 1,000,000 members in 450 Centers in the US and Canada. JWB is also a founder and principal member of the World Federation of YMHA's and Jewish Community centers. Since the early 1940's it has sponsored the Jewish Book Council of America and the National Jewish Music Council. Through its Jewish Center Lecture Bureau, it fosters adult Jewish education.

NATIONAL LIBRARY see **LIBRARY, NATIONAL**

NATIONAL REFUGEE SERVICE: US organization formed in 1939 to facilitate the adjustment in the US of refugees from Nazi persecution. It conducted a program of relief, economic rehabilitation, resettlement, and integration. It provided over 26,000 refugees with employment and financially assisted over 1,500 each month. Its funds were supplied by the United Jewish Appeal. In 1946, the NRS merged in the UNITED SERVICE FOR NEW AMERICANS.

NATIONAL RELIGIOUS PARTY; Israel political party formed through the merger of HA-POEL HA-MIZRAHI and MIZRAHI.

NATIONAL SOCIALISM (Nazism): Extermination of the Jews was an essential part of the gospel of Nazism and inherent in the core of the Nazi creed. The Aryan decree issued on Apr. 11, 1933 defined as non-Aryan any person having a non-Aryan, particularly Jewish, parent or grand-parent. On Sept. 15, 1935, the NUREMBERG LAWS were adopted by the Reichstag. These racial laws coordinated and regularized Nazi anti-Jewish action. They were reinforced by persecutory decrees, economic and social discrimination, and incarceration in CONCENTRATION CAMPS without legal proceedings or protection. Beginning with the boycott on Apr. 1, 1933, Jewish persecution was stepped up to intolerable proportions. Actions of violence became common after the occupation of Austria on Mar. 13, 1938, with the avowed intention of compelling Jews to emigrate. The pogrom of Nov. 9–10, 1938 followed the killing of Vom Rath in Paris; the brutal assault on Jews throughout the Reich. the demolition of their houses and businesses, the burning of synagogues and the wholesale arrests, violence, and murder roused world-wide protests. Nevertheless, GOERING proceeded with the so-called

"penalties" edicts, including the billion mark collective fine, complete elimination of Jews from German economy (Nov. 12), and the decree on aryanization of Jewish property (Dec. 3). Altogether the massive Jewish emigration between 1933 and Aug. 1939 amounted to about 225,000 from Germany, over 100,000 from Austria, and 35,000 from Bohemia-Moravia before the decree of Nov. 1941 which altogether prohibited Jewish departure. A conference held in HITLER's railroad car on Sept. 12, 1939 decided on the "Final Solution" by the total extermination of the Jews. GHETTOS were set up in various places, while HEYDRICH issued instructions to his police chiefs and *Einsatzkommandos* to herd the Jews at concentration points near railroad junctions, preliminary to deportation. Extermination camps were set up in Belzec, Treblinka, Sobibór, and Maidanek. In 1941, Himmler gave orders to build the mammoth concentration extermination camp in Auschwitz-Birkenau. The "Wannsee Conference" called by Heydrich on Jan. 20, 1942 systematized and coordinated the policy of extermination. In the summer months of 1942, Jewish deportations took on monstrous proportions. Some 300,000 Jews were deported in loaded boxcars from the Warsaw ghetto for extermination, principally to Treblinka. Similar devastating "actions" were conducted in other ghettos, leaving 10–15% "workers" for the 1943 extermination action. The year 1943 was a year of risings and revolts in the Jewish ghettos, initiated by the Warsaw Ghetto's heroic stand. Similar uprisings broke out in other ghettos and concentration camps including Treblinka, Sobibór, Chelmno, and Auschwitz. From all corners of Europe the Nazis dragged the Jews in huge deportation trains to the East, while the security detachments of the *Einsatzgruppen* in Soviet Russia massacred over a million and a half Jews in the wake of the advancing *Wehrmacht* columns. Between May and the middle of July 1944, some 450,000 Hungarian Jews were deported and 350,000 gassed at Auschwitz. Between 1939 and 1945, the total of Jewish victims amounted to some 6,000,000. Adolph EICHMANN estimated that approximately 4,000,000 were killed in the concentration camps, while an additional 2,000,000 met their death in other ways. After the war twelve of the major Nazi leaders were sentenced to death as major WAR CRIMINALS; this was followed by further trials of war criminals. The war did not stamp out Nazism and subsequently Neo-Nazi organizations have been reported from many parts of the world.

NATIONALISM: Jewish n. is the term used to describe the point of view which refuses to attach an exclusively religious connotation to the term "Judaism." It insists that the Jewish people, though losing some of the important characteristics of nationhood in the centuries of exile, has nonetheless

The Kattowitz Conference (1884) which was dominated
by a spirit of nationalism.

remained a nation, as distinct from a purely religious group or "church." In biblical times, the Jews regarded themselves as a group possessed of a national individuality differing from that of its neighbors. The prophets and, subsequently, the scholars of the Talmudic Period thought and spoke constantly in terms of a national spirit. National solidarity was enhanced by the establishment of the monarchy, the capital of which all were to visit thrice yearly. Later, as pressure by external forces increased, the feeling of national distinctiveness permeated the whole existence of the Jew. Jews always regarded themselves as the members of a unique group with each individual member sharing the common destiny. In modern times, this point of view was always implicit in the position and outlook of the Jewish masses in E Europe; but the emancipated Jews of the West, in the process of ASSIMILATION to their non-Jewish environment, came to regard themselves as Jews by religion only and to object to any suggestion of a "national" difference between themselves and their neighbors. This new conception of Judaism was trenchantly criticized by Moses Hess in his *Rome and Jerusalem* (1862), but, broadly speaking, it remained dominant in the western Jewish communities until nearly the end of the 19th cent. It was then challenged not so much on ideological as on practical grounds. The persistence of anti-Semitism in eastern and western countries alike cast doubt on the assumption, implied in the attitude of the western Jewish communities, that the Jewish problem could be solved by EMANCIPATION and assimilation. In 1882, the Russian Jew J. L. PINSKER propounded (in his *Auto-Emancipation*) the idea that the only possible solution lay in the return of the Jewish people to a national life on a territory of its own, but his plea for action on these lines awakened no echo in the west. The same idea

was advanced independently in 1895 by Theodor HERZL in *Der Judenstaat*. The publication of this pamphlet, leading to the establishment of the World Zionist Organization, let loose a flood of controversy on the question of Jewish n., the opponents of which were apprehensive of it's possible political implications. In the early years of the 20th cent., the anti-Zionist socialist BUND became an exponent in E Europe of Jewish Diaspora n., either as a means of bringing Socialism to the masses or as an instrument for assuring the supremacy of Yiddish culture in Jewish life. The belief that Jewish life in the Diaspora could not retain its individuality led to the evolution of TERRITORIALISM in its diverse forms. The success of ZIONISM, culminating in the establishment of the state of Israel, has made the issue academic. Even among the assimilated Jews of the western world, only a minority still maintains that Judaism is, or ought to be, a purely religious differentia. On the other hand, except for a few extremists, Jewish nationalists do not claim that the Jews of the Diaspora do or should form a nation in the political sense of that term, or that in the case of the Jewish people the concept of nationality can be completely divorced from the religious traditions. Herzl's Zionist Organization. though its leadership was western, drew most of its support at the outset from the Jewish masses in E Europe where the *Ḥoveve Zion* had for some years been endeavoring to promote Jewish settlement in Palestine as the basis of a new national life. The so-called "spiritual Zionism" of AḤAD HA-AM, one of the leading *Ḥoveve Zion,* with its insistence on the need for a "spiritual revival" – a return to the Hebrew language and culture and to Hebraic ethical values — as a preliminary to the establishment of a Jewish State, gave the fullest and most uncompromising expression to a conception of Jewish n. for which the fragmentation and the spiritual weakness of the scattered Jewish people posed an even more serious problem than its material ills and its lack of a territory. A contemporary of Aḥad Ha-Am, the Russian historian Simon DUBNOW, went even further; while taking for granted that the Jewish people had never ceased to be a nation, he held that it had outgrown the territorial phase of nationhood and that, instead of seeking to migrate to a land of their own, the Jews should demand the rights of a national minority, especially cultural rights, in those countries (e.g. in E Europe) in which they lived in large numbers. His "diaspora nationalism," or "autonomism", had some short-lived practical success in the Baltic countries during the period between the two world wars. After the disaster in Europe his views, despite their theoretical interest, lost their relevance to present-day conditions. While many Zionists regard Jewish n. as separable from Jewish religion, the Orthodox sections hold that Orthodox Judaism and Jewish n. are inseparable and that national life must be constituted on the basis of the Torah. The attitude of Communism to Jewish n. was declared by Stalin who claimed that as Jews lacked a territory and a language of their own, they were not a nation. After the revolution, however, the Jews of Russia were recognized as a national minority on the basis of Yiddish culture; but the enforced neglect of traditional Judaism, segregation from world Jewry, and, ultimately, also discrimination against Yiddish have made this recognition nugatory.

NATORE KARTA (Aram. "Guardians of the City"):
Group of Orthodox Jewish zealots, numbering some hundreds, chiefly drawn from the "*old yishuv*" in Jerusalem. They oppose political Zionism. all public cooperation with non-Orthodox Jews, and refuse to recognize the state of Israel. Its outlook has been current in Palestine and some parts of the Diaspora (especially Hungary) for several generations. Originally part of AGUDAT ISRAEL, they seceded in 1937, and the difference between the two was accentuated when *Agudat Israel* accepted the state of Israel in 1948. Until 1965, the leader of the *N. K.* was Amram BLAU.

NATRONAI: (1) Gaon of Pumbedita (fl. early 8th cent.), known as Rav Yenuka. He was extremely severe with the scholars of the academy, many of whom left for Sura. (2) Gaon of Sura 853–6. He wrote many responsa, foremost of which is an arrangement of the daily "one hundred" blessings prepared at the request of the community of Lucena, Spain. These, together with many of N.'s other responsa, served as the basis of the first complete Order of Prayer prepared later by Amram Gaon. He took a strong stand against the Karaites and their liturgy. His responsa include notes on tractates of the Talmud.

NAUMBOURG, SAMUEL (1816–1880): German musicologist. In 1845, he was appointed cantor in Paris on the recommendation of the composer Halévy and two years later published *Semirot Jisrael* containing settings of the entire liturgical cycle for cantor, choir, and — to some extent — organ, chiefly in the spirit of the S German cantoral school. His *Agudas Shirim* collected famous traditional melodies, while his edition of the compositions of Salomone de' ROSSI rescued these works from obscurity.

NAVARRE: Former kingdom in the Pyrénées. Its first king, Sanche, installed Jews in towns evacuated by the Saracens, granting them special privileges *(fueros)*. Under French kings in the 13th–14th cents., their lot was harsher and 6,000 Jews were massacred there in 1328 in a series of riots incited by a Franciscan friar. The Jews henceforward were heavily taxed and confined to ghettos. In 1492, Jewish refugees were admitted from Aragon, but in 1498, the whole community was given the choice of baptism or expulsion. The Jews of N. engaged in handicrafts and especially trade, while they included a number of noted doctors, astrologers, etc. The principal communities were those of Pamplona, Estella, and Tudela.

NAVEH: Town in S Bashan (now Nawa, Syria). It is first known in the 16th cent. BCE, and its Jewish community from c. 170 CE although probably originating earlier. N. is mentioned in the Talmud and produced scholars of note. In the 4th cent., it was referred to as a Jewish town but in the 6th cent., was Christian, although the Jewish community persisted at least until the 11th cent. Interesting remains of the Talmudic Period, including a synagogue and 2-story stone Jewish dwellings, have been preserved.

NAVIGATION: Little is known about n. in biblical times, though under Solomon Hebrews collaborated with the Tyrians in maritime voyages (I Kings 9:26–8). It has been conjectured that some members of the northern tribes (e.g. Zebulun) may have been associated with Phoenician expeditions. In the period of the Second Temple, symbols on the coins of the Hasmoneans, etc. suggest maritime ambitions and knowledge, and during the war of 66–70 there were naval engagements both in the Mediterranean and the Sea of Galilee, and in the war of 132–5 in the Mediterranean. Various drawings of ships in Jewish tombs, etc. in the later Second Temple period and after indicate a lively interest in the sea. A Greek writer tells of a journey from Alexandria to Cyrene in a boat wholly manned by Jews who refrained from unnecessary work on the Sabbath. The Jewish

Judean ship of the third century.

Nazareth — view from the west.

merchants of the Dark Ages owned ships which may have had Jewish crews. In the Middle Ages, Jews forwarded n. by the maps made by Cartographers, such as the Cresques family in Majorca, the invention of Jacob's Staff by Jacob ben Makhir, improvements to the Astrolabe, and astronomical tables such as those of Abraham Zacuto. In the age of Emancipation, Jews, e.g. the American Uriah P. Levy, served with distinction in various navies. From the time of the Balfour Declaration determined efforts were made to familiarize Palestinian Jews with n., the Zebulun Society being founded to train boys for the sea, while companies were formed to develop a merchant marine. It is nevertheless only since 1948 that a tradition of n. has become firmly established in Israel Jewry exemplified in its navy (see Tzeva Haganah Le-Israel) and the merchant fleet (see also Zim).

NAVON, JOSEPH (1852–1934): Palestinian philanthropist and pioneer advocate of Jewish colonization. He was instrumental in obtaining permission to establish early settlements, in acquiring vast tracts of land, and in building the Jaffa-Jerusalem railroad.

NAVY see **NAVIGATION; TZEVA HAGANAH LE-ISRAEL**

NAXOS, DUKE OF see **NASI, JOSEPH**

NAZARENES see **EBIONITES; JEWISH CHRISTIANS**

NAZARETH: Israel town in Lower Galilee, 24 m. E of Haifa. It is mentioned several times in the New Testament as the home of the family of Joseph and the place where Jesus was brought up. N. remained a Jewish village until Byzantine times. The first church there was built under Constantine but is not mentioned before 570. In Crusader times, it became an important ecclesiastical center which was destroyed by the Mameluke leader Baybars in 1263. In 1620, the Franciscan monks resettled the site, building a church in 1730 replaced by a larger basilica dedicated in 1969. In 1948, N. was occupied by the Israel forces and has since become the headquarters of the Northern District of Israel. It is the principal Arab city in Israel, most of its inhabitants being Catholic or Greek Orthodox, with a Moslem minority. Pop. (1974): 36,400. Above the ancient town of N. there is now the new Jewish settlement of Upper N. with a pop. (1974) of 18,300 mainly recent immigrants.

NAZIR (Heb. "Nazirite"): Fourth tractate in the Mishnah order of *Nashim*, containing 9 chapters. It has *gemara* both in the Babylonian and Palestinian Talmuds and deals with the biblical prescriptions concerning Nazirite vows (Num. 6:1–21).

NAZIRITE (Heb. *nazir*): Religious devotee who vowed not to drink any intoxicating liquor, nor to have his hair cut, and to avoid ritual uncleanness through proximity to corpses (Num. 6:2, etc.). Special sacrifices were stipulated in cases of pollution and on concluding the period of naziriteship. The undertaking was generally for a limited period (not less than 30 days) but could also be for life. Parents could dedicate their children as Nazirites before birth (cf. Samson, Samuel). The n. vow was common in ancient times and during the Second Temple Period after which — with rare exceptions — it disappeared.

NAZISM see **NATIONAL SOCIALISM**

NEANDER, JOHANN AUGUST WILHELM (as a
Jew, David Mendel; 1789–1850): Protestant
theologian. He was converted to Christianity in
1806 and became professor of church history at Berlin
Univ. N. was a leading ecclesiastical historian, writing
*Allgemeine Geschichte der christlichen Religion und
Kirche; Das Leben Jesu,* etc.

NEBBICH (Yidd. *nie bei eich* — "never with you"):
A word appended (sometimes contemptuously)
to a mention of someone arousing sympathy; or
uttered on hearing of an action evoking such an
attitude.

NEBO: Mountain at the NW extremity of the Mts.
of Moab. Its peak, 2,755 ft. above sea-level,
commands a wide vista. From N., Moses looked on
the Promised Land before his death (Deut. 34:1–3).
Another Mt. N. was in the territory of the tribe of
Reuben (Num. 32:3,38).

NEBRASKA: US state. From 1855, Jewish immigrants from Central Europe went to N., settling
in OMAHA, LINCOLN, Plattsmouth, Columbus, Fre-
mont, Grand Island, and Madison County. Many of
them were storekeepers or professionals. Most of N.'s
current Jewish population is descended from the
2,000 E European Jews sent there between 1900 and
1913 by the INDUSTRIAL REMOVAL OFFICE. There
were 8,290 Jews in N. in 1973.

*NEBUCHADNEZZAR (or Nebuchadrezzar; from
the Babylonian Nabu-kudurri-ussur): King of
Babylonia 605–562 BCE. As a result of his victory
over the Assyrian-Egyptian alliance at Carchemish in
605, he conquered all the lands from the Euphrates
to the Egyptian frontier, including Judah. In 597,
after Judah revolted, he dispatched contingents
which captured Jerusalem, replaced the young king
Jehoiachin with his own nominee, Zedekiah, and
exiled 8,000 of the local aristocracy to Babylon. N.'s
acount of these events is preserved in the British
Museum. Eight years later, Zedekiah rebelled. The
forces of N. under NEBUZARADAN again invaded Judah,
captured Jerusalem in 586, and destroyed the Temple,
laying waste the cities and exiling masses of the
population. The king was taken to Riblah, where N.
had him slain. N. also figures in a number of legends
related in the Book of Daniel.

*NEBUZARADAN (fl. early 6th cent. BCE): Captain
of Nebuchadnezzar's bodyguard, he commanded
the armies which in 586, captured Jerusalem, destroyed
the Temple, and expelled the inhabitants.

*NECHO II: King of Egypt 609–593 BCE. At the
battle of Megiddo (608)', he defeated and slew
Josiah of Judah and appointed Jehoiakim in his
stead. N. was subsequently defeated at Carchemish
by Nebuchadnezzar (605).

NECROMANCY: DIVINATION by aid of the dead.
From the strict biblical injunctions against n.
(Lev. 19:31, 20:6; Deut. 18:11, etc.) and from other
references, it appears that the custom was popular
and widespread. It may have been practiced chiefly
by women. In one type of n. at least, only the diviner
saw the apparition, while the inquirer merely heard
a deep voice. Whereas the Bible classes n. with
idolatry, the Talmud treats it as MAGIC *(Sanhedrin
67 b)*.

NEDARIM (Heb. "Vows"): Third tractate in the
Mishnah order of *Nashim,* containing 11 chapters.
It has *gemara* in both the Babylonian and Palestinian
Talmuds. N. deals with regulations concerning vows,
e.g. expressions considered to be valid as vows, the
annulment of vows, the possible interpretations of
a vow, etc.

**NEDERLANDSCH ISRAELITISCH SEMINAR-
IUM:** Dutch Ashkenazi rabbinical seminary; it
developed from a yeshivah founded in 1708, and was
modernized as a state institution from 1834.

NEDOVEH (Yidd. from Heb.): A charitable contribution; alms.

NEGAIM (Heb. "Plagues of Leprosy"): Third
tractate in the Mishnah order of *Tohorot,* containing 14 chapters. It has *gemara* neither in the Babylonian nor Palestinian Talmud. N. deals with laws
concerning various types of leprosy affecting a person,
clothes, or dwellings (Lev. 13–14).

NEGBAH: Israel communal settlement (KM) in the
S coastal plain. It was founded in 1939 by a group
from Poland, and initiated the drive toward coloniz-

The water tower at Negbah during the
War of Independence.

Granite and slate mountains near Elath.

Experiments in farming.

ing the Negev. During the War of Independence, the defense of N. was a major factor in halting the Egyptian advance toward the north. Partly destroyed in the fighting, it was subsequently rebuilt on a larger scale. Pop. (1972): 429.

NEGEV: The southern "dry-land" of Israel, extending over an expanse of 5,138 sq. m., i.e., 60% of the total area of the country. The N. is defined as the area in which the annual rainfall is less than 200 mm., i.e., the region S of the Mishmar ha-Negev-Masada line. It can be divided into (1) the northern N., where the land is loess, which is flat or gently undulating; this part is cultivable (except where covered by sand) if irrigated; (2) the second zone comprising the valleys and hills of the central N., cultivable in parts; its distinguishing marks are the three circular depressions (MAKHTESH); (3) the southern N. is composed of typical "badlands," eroded rocks; (4) the rift valley depression (Arabah) in which water (mostly salt) can be found and cultivation is possible in places. It continues to the Gulf of Elath with its outlet to the Red Sea. In prehistoric times, the N. was settled in the north, especially near Beersheva where underground Chalcolithic settlements have been found dating to the 5th millennium BCE. At that date the copper mines of the Arabah were already being exploited. Sporadic settlement in the N. continued in the patriarchal period, during which the Beer-sheba-Egypt route was developed. After the Exodus, the southern N. was occupied by nomadic tribes, the Amalekites, while the northern part belonged to the tribe of Simeon, which later amalgamated with Judah. David's conquest of the Amalekites and of Edom opened up Elath and the copper mines to the Israelites under Solomon; at the same time, maritime trade began (with Phoenician assistance) from Elath to Ophir (S Arabia?). The division of the kingdom led to a decline of Judean power in the N.; only in the times of King Uzziah were the N. roads developed (II Chron. 26:10), apparently because the usual way to Elath was blocked by the Edomites. After the fall of Jerusalem, the Edomites moved into S Judah and the N. was occupied by the NABATEANS, who began systematically to develop the Gaza-Elath and Petra-Gaza roads; their caravan stations, including the site of Ḥalutzah and Avdat, started the agricultural exploitation of the N. through a series of dams and channels fanning out the rain water over the fields. The northern N. was temporarily occupied by Alexander Yannai, who cut the Nabatean trade-routes. In early Roman times, the N. declined owing to a re-routing of trade from Elath to Damascus; but it began to flourish again in the Late Roman and Byzantine Period. At that time, trade routes to Elath and the pilgrims' way to Sinai were secured by a series of border fortresses. Behind this zone developed an extensive agricultural area surrounding five towns

(Nessana, Subeita, Elusa, Mampsis, and Eboda) some of which were unfortified. Remarkable water-installations and innumerable cisterns ensured their water supply, and even public baths have been discovered. With the Arab conquest, the N. settlements began to wither away, although maintaining themselves in one form or another down to the Crusader Period, after which, until the early 20th cent., the N. was a desert inhabited only by Beduin. The Turks finally began to extend their power over the N., refounding Beersheba; in World War I, the British and Turko-German armies fought over the N. In the Mandatory Period, various attempts were made to settle it. In the 1947 partition plan, it was allotted to the Jewish state but was occupied by the Egyptians in May 1948, except for the areas already settled by Jews. In the WAR OF INDEPENDENCE the Egyptians were driven out (Oct. 1948–Mar. 1949) and Elath reached. Since that time, the northern N. has been intensively settled, the mines of the central N. developed, copper mining in the Arabah has been resumed, and a port at Elath constructed. Beersheba has been linked to the Israel railroads, a road built to Sodom and two others to Elath. An oil pipeline was constructed across the N. in 1956–7 and another was started in 1968.

NEGINOT see **ACCENTS**

NEGRO JEWS: Several congregations in New York, numbering several hundred families, are composed of Negroes who observe most of the Orthodox Jewish ritual. They call themselves Ethiopian Jews and claim descent from the FALASHAS. Some of them are believed to be descendants of Negro converts to Judaism dating back to American and W Indian slavery days; most adopted Judaism comparatively recently. The main group was first organized as a congregation in 1930 by one of their members, Rabbi Wentworth A. Matthew (1892–), and has grown steadily in numbers. N. J. are found in half a dozen other American cities.

NEHARDEA: Babylonian town situated at the junction of the Euphrates and the Nahr Malka (or "Royal Canal"). Josephus describes N. as a heavily fortified city, one of the two centers (with NISIBIS) in which the Temple offerings were assembled for forwarding to Jerusalem. It contained the "Shaf Veyativ" synagogue, said to have been built by the exiled king Jehoiachin of Judah and described by Abbaye (4th cent. CE) as the seat of the Divine Presence in Babylonia. Benjamin of Tudela reported on the ruins of this synagogue in the 12th cent. In talmudic times, N. was the home of the exilarch and of the senior Babylonian academy, headed in the 3rd cent. by Samuel. The town was destroyed by the Palmyrenes in 259 CE and the academy reopened in Pumbedita under R Judah ben Ezekiel, but a group of scholars called "Nehardeans" continued to exist until savoraic times and, for a while, provided heads of the academy alternately with the Pumbeditans. N. was the capital of the small rebel state set up by the Jewish brothers ANILAI AND ASINAI c. 20 CE.

NEHEMIAH (fl. 5th cent. BCE): Governor of Judah. While serving as a cupbearer to the Persian king Artaxerxes I, he heard of the deplorable conditions in Jerusalem and requested permission from the king to go there. Artaxerxes acceded and appointed him *Tirshata* (governor) of Judah (444). On reaching Jerusalem, he organized the repair of its walls — an activity that was completed in 52 days despite interference by neighboring peoples. N. then devoted himself to social reforms, including the stimulation of Sabbath observance and the cancellation of debts owed by the poor. The leaders of the people had to pledge themselves to maintain the Temple regulations and pay their tithes. The security of Jerusalem was ensured by arranging for a tenth of the people to take up residence there. After 12 years, N. returned to Susa, but later went back to Jerusalem to renew his drastic activity. In 433–2, he took steps against mixed marriages, etc. in conjunction with EZRA. His work was decisive in the rebuilding of Judah. N.'s memoirs form the basis of the biblical Book of N. (which is a continuation of the Book of Ezra) in the Hagiographa.

NEHUNYAH BEN HA-KANAH (fl. late 1st cent. CE): Tanna. He expounded the Torah according to the principle of *kelal u-pherat* ("a general followed by a particular") and transmitted this method to his pupil R Ishmael. He attributed his long life to the fact that he never gloried in the shame of his fellow *(Megillah 28a)*. Several mystical works are ascribed to him, such as the Book *Bahir* and the acrostic prayer *Anna be-koah*.

NEHUSHTAN: Figure of a snake kept in the Temple until smashed by Hezekiah. Traditionally, it was created by Moses as sympathetic magic directed against the fiery snakes sent to bite the people (Num. 21:6–9; II Kings 18:4). In the folklore of other peoples, the snake is connected with the god of healing.

NEILAH (Heb. "closing"): The prayer recited at the time of closing the gates of the Temple, formerly also on public fast-days decreed outside Jerusalem. This service is now only recited on the Day of Atonement, the liturgy of which interprets the name N. as referring to the closing of the heavenly gates as judgment is sealed. The *Amidah,* movingly phrased, does not differ from the other four *Amidot* of the day, but the *Viddui* is different. The Sephardi rite introduces the service by the hymn *El Nora Alilah*. The service concludes with *Avinu Malkenu,* after which the *Shema* and other verses are recited. Finally a single blast of the *shophar* is sounded.

NEISSER, ALBERT LUDWIG SIEGMUND (1855–1916): German dermatologist. He discovered the pus producing bacterium of gonorrhea and identified

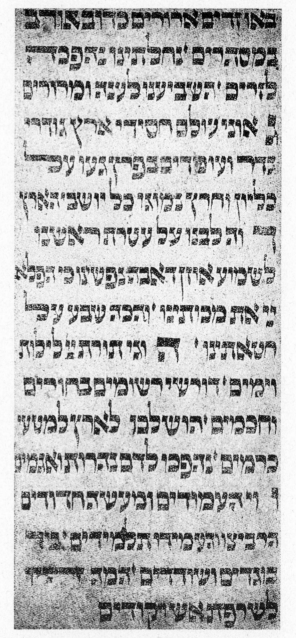

Excerpt from Prayer for Martyrs of Nemirov, 1648.
(Formerly in the possession of Simon Dubnow).

the leprosy bacillus. N. was also one of the initiators of the blood test for syphilis. He founded the earliest society to combat venereal disease and safeguard maternity.

NEMIROV: Ukrainian city, USSR. A flourishing Jewish community in the 17th cent., it was the scene of a ghastly massacre during the Chmielnicki terror when 6,000 of its Jews were murdered. The position improved somewhat under Turkish rule (1672–99), but in 1702, there was further suffering at the hands of the Ukrainians. The Jews were prominent in the town's weaving industry. The community came to an end in World War II.

NEOFITI (It. "neophytes"): Name given locally to the Jews converted by force in S Italy from the close of the 13th cent. and to their descendants, many of whom remained secretly attached to Judaism. Reinforced from time to time by fresh converts, they remained distinguishable until the 16th cent.

NEO-HEBREW LITERATURE see **HEBREW LITERATURE**

NEOPLATONISM: A late Greek philosophy, represented mainly by Plotinus (205–270 CE), Porphyry (233–305), and Proclus (412–485), which became very influential in medieval Judaism. From c. 900–1170, there was a series of Jewish Neoplatonists, e.g. Isaac Israeli, Solomon Ibn Gabirol, Baḥya Ibn Pakuda, Abraham bar Ḥiyya, Joseph Ibn Tzaddik, and Abraham Ibn Ezra. Even in the 12th–13th cents., when Aristotelian philosophy became supreme among Jewish thinkers, it was — as with the Arabs — heavily tinged with Neoplatonic ideas, such as that of Divine emanation. The Kabbalah, too, incorporates important Neoplatonic elements.

NEPHILIM: Semi-legendary race in the antediluvian era begotten, according to Gen. 6:4, by the union of the "sons of God" and the "daughters of man." The term was applied hyperbolically to the inhabitants of the Land of Canaan by the spies dispatched by Moses (Num. 13–33).

NER TAMID (Heb. "perpetual ['eternal'] lamp"): Light kept burning in the synagogue as a symbol of the radiance of faith. Originally it presumably served also to kindle the other lamps on the conclusion of the Sabbath, etc. Normally it hangs before the ark, but in E Europe was often in a niche in a side wall. Similarly, fire was perpetually kept alight on the altar in the Tabernacle (Lev. 6:6).

*NERO: Roman emperor 54–68 CE. His reign coincided with a period of turmoil in Judea culminating in the outbreak of the war against Rome. His wife Poppaea was, however, sympathetic to Judaism. N. is not unfavorably represented in talmudical legend (e.g. *Gittin* 56a).

NES TZIYYONAH: Israel semi-urban settlement in the Judean coastal plain. Founded in 1883 by *Bilu* immigrants from E Europe, its growth received a strong impetus with the success of citrus plantations in the vicinity which attracted large numbers of Arab laborers; these constituted the majority of N. T.'s inhabitants until the War of Independence. New immigrants took their place, bringing its population to 12,600 (1974).

NETANYAH: Israel coastal town. Founded in 1929 by the descendants of veteran Galilean settlers as a village based on large citrus plantations, it developed as a seaside resort. From World War II, it became a center of the diamond-polishing industry and also attracted large undertakings in other industrial branches. Its growth after 1948 was stimulated by the nearby *maabarah* of Shevut Am (Bet Lid), the largest in the country, many of the inhabitants of which found employment and, finally, also permanent housing in N. Pop. (1974): 79,500.

NETHERLANDS see **HOLLAND**

NETHERLANDS EAST INDIES see **INDONESIA**

NETHINIM: Temple servants. They were originally conquered Canaanites who were said to have been allotted by David to the LEVITES for menial service in the Temple. They were exiled to Babylon together with the Jews and returned with them under Zerubbabel and Ezra, being given a special quarter of Jerusalem (Ezra 2:58, 8:20; Neh. 3:26). Although accepting Ezra's covenant, they were still debarred from the Jewish community. N. maintained their identity down to amoraic times.

NETTER, CHARLES (1826—1882): French philanthropist. He left commerce to devote himself to social affairs, especially to the Alliance Israélite Universelle of which he was a founder. In 1870, he started the MIKVEH ISRAEL Agricultural School near Jaffa, the pioneer Palestinian colonization institution. The land was purchased after N.'s personal intervention at the court of the sultan, and he served as the first director 1870—3. He was also active in general Jewish philanthropic work in Europe.

NETZER SERENI: Israel communal settlement (IK) in the Judean plain. It was founded in 1948 by a group called "Kibbutz Buchenwald" composed of survivors of Nazi death camps. After the split in *Ha-Kibbutz ha-Meuḥad*, N.S. absorbed the *Mapai* members of Givat Brenner. Pop. (1972): 509.

NEUBAUER, ADOLPH (1831–1907): Bibliographer. Born in Hungary, he went to Oxford in 1868 to complete the catalogue of Hebrew mss in the

Promenade on Netanyah beach.

Abraham A. Neuman.

Bodleian Library begun by M. Steinschneider, subsequently being appointed sub-librarian. He also reported on the Hebrew mss in St. Petersburg, etc., wrote in French on the geography of the Talmud, published a series of medieval Hebrew chronicles, and was mainly responsible for the history of 14th cent. French rabbinical scholarship edited by E. Renan.

NEUBERG, CARL (1877—1956): Biochemist. He was director of the Kaiser Wilhelm Institute of Biochemistry at Berlin 1913—38, and research professor at New York Univ. 1941—56. He also taught at the New York Medical College. He developed the process for making glycerine from sugar and discovered the enzyme carboxylase and other synthetic products.

NEUBURGER, MAX (1868—1955): Historian of medicine. Originally a neuropathologist, he taught the history of medicine at the Univ. of Vienna from 1904 until 1939 when he moved to England and later (1948), to the US. His history of medicine is one of the fullest and most learned accounts of ancient and medieval medicine.

NEUMAN, ABRAHAM AARON (1890–1970): US rabbi and historian. Taken to the US from Galicia as a child, he became rabbi of the Sephardi congregation in Philadelphia, professor of history and later

(1941–1967) president of Dropsie College, the activity of which he greatly extended. He was the author of *The Jews in Spain* and co-editor of the *Jewish Quarterly Review*.

NEUMANN, ALFRED (1895—1952): Novelist. He lived in Germany, Italy, and France until 1941 when he settled in the US. His novel of France in the time of Louis XI, *The Devil*, was followed by other historical novels. He also wrote plays and poetry.

NEUMANN, EMANUEL (1896—): US Zionist leader; president of the Zionist Organization of America 1947—9 and 1956—60; member of the Zionist Executive in Jerusalem 1931—9, 1946—7, and of the Jewish Agency executive since 1951. N. is a General Zionist leader.

NEUMANN, KARL FRIEDRICH (as a Jew, Bamberger; 1793—1870): Orientalist. Converted to Christianity in 1818, he taught Chinese in Munich, but his liberal views (he participated in the 1848 revolution) brought him into frequent conflict with the academic authorities. In 1829, he brought 12,000 books from China, most of which he donated to the Munich State Library. N.'s works include a history of American literature.

NEUMANN, ROBERT (1897–1975): Author. Of Austrian birth, his earlier work reflected the chaos of post-1918 Europe. After 1933, he left Germany for England and from 1958 lived in Switzerland. His writings include novels (*By the Waters of Babylon*), poetry, plays, and parodies.

Emanuel Neumann.

NEUMANN, SOLOMON (1819—1908): German physician and public worker. He engaged in medical statistics and public hygiene. His refusal to take the special form of medical oath for Jews in 1845 led to its general abolition throughout Prussia. Active in Jewish communal endeavor, he was in particular a patron of scholarship.

NEUMARK, DAVID (1866—1924): Scholar. After a rabbinical and academic career in Europe, he became professor of philosophy at Hebrew Union College, Cincinnati in 1907, serving until his death. His *History of Jewish Philosophy* (in Hebrew) is his major work.

NEVADA: US state. In 1862, there were in N. 200 Jews, who had joined the search for gold and silver. In that year, a B'nai B'rith lodge and cemetery were established in Virginia City. At the same time, a Hebrew Benevolent Society and cemetery were founded in Eureka. By 1869, services were being held in Carson City. Most of the Jews came from Californian coastal towns. Jews played an active part in N.'s commercial and civic life. Few Jewish immigrants went to N. after the 1900's. In 1973, N. had 7,380 Jews, 7,000 of them living in Las Vegas and 380 in Reno.

NEW BEDFORD: City in Massachusetts, US. Its first Jews were of Sephardi origin. By the middle of the 19th cent., a small community of German Jews was living there. E European immigrants began arriving in the 1870's. The first synagogue, Ahavath Achim, was erected in 1899. In 1973, N. B. had 3,100 Jews with 3 synagogues and a Welfare Federation (founded in 1949).

NEW BRITAIN: City in Connecticut, US. Its first Jews settled there immediately after the Civil War. In the early 1890's, Congregation Acheynu B'nai Israel was organized. The N. B. Jewish Federation was established in 1936. In 1973, N. B. had 1,980 Jews with 2 synagogues.

NEW BRUNSWICK: Canadian province. Its earliest Jewish settlers arrived from England and settled in St. John in 1858—60. From the 1890's, settlers were largely from Russia and Poland. In 1896, Congregation Ahavath Achim was established in St. John; subsequently, synagogues were built in Moncton and Fredericton. Jewish pop. (1973): c. 1,250. The largest Jewish communities are in St. John (520), Moncton (300), and Fredericton (230).

NEW CHRISTIANS see **MARRANOS**

NEW HAMPSHIRE: US state. Individual Jews, mostly peddlers and traders, first appeared there at the end of the 17th cent. N. H. was the last of the 13 colonies to grant political equality to Jews (1877), non-Protestants being previously excluded by law from some political offices. The first Jewish community was established by E European immigrants about 1885. The first Jewish organization in N. H. was the Hebrew Ladies' Aid Society of Manchester formed in 1896.

A year later, the state's first synagogue, Anshay Sfard, was founded in the same city. Most of N. H.'s Jewish population of 4,220 (1973) lives in Manchester (1,500), Portsmouth (700), Dover (360), and Nashua (320).

NEW HAVEN: City in Connecticut, US. Jewish settlement dates from 1772, and German Jews arriving in the late 1830's formed the first permanent community. The first congregation, Mishkan Israel (Reform), was organized in 1840. In 1881, a group of recently arrived Russian Jews laid the foundation for a flourishing Orthodox community. Its Jewish Community Council, founded in 1928, sponsors the local Welfare Fund. In 1973, N. H. had 20,000 Jews with 5 major synagogues.

NEW JERSEY: US state. A handful of Jews lived there throughout the 18th cent. No Jewish community developed until the 1840's, when immigrants from Central Europe settled in PATERSON, NEWARK, NEW BRUNSWICK and TRENTON. Between 1858 and 1880, Jewish communities were established in JERSEY CITY, ELIZABETH, Perth Amboy, Hoboken, East Orange, and Bayonne. Large numbers of Jews from E Europe arrived in N. J. in the 1880's. The Jewish farm movement in the US had its origin in colonies established in the S part of N. J. after 1882. There are now flourishing farm and industrial communities grouped around Bound Brook, Freehold, Englishtown, Egg Harbor, Dayton, Farmingdale, Lakewood, Plainfield, Toms River, and WOODBINE. Jewish pop. (1973): 418,000.

NEW LONDON: City in Connecticut, US. Its Jewish settlement dates from the early 1880's. More than 75% of the Jewish population of 4,500 (1973) had its origin in E Europe. The first congregation, Ahavath Chesed, was founded in 1892. Another Orthodox congregation, Ohev Sholom, was organized in 1918 and the Conservative Beth El came into being in 1932. The Jewish Community Council of N. L. was organized in 1951.

NEW MEXICO: US state. Except possibly for isolated Marranos, there were no Jews there until the mid-19th cent. From then on, until its admission to the Union, Jews played a conspicuous role in the life of the territory. Religious services were first held in Santa Fé in 1860. The first Jewish organization was a B'nai B'rith lodge founded in Albuquerque in 1882. N. M.'s first synagogue was built in Las Vegas in 1886. Arthur SELIGMAN was governor of N. M. 1930-3. In 1973, most of N.M.'s 3,060 Jews were living in Albuquerque (2,000), A Jewish Welfare Fund was founded in 1938.

NEW MOON: The first day(s) of the month, (Heb. *Rosh Ḥodesh*), formerly celebrated as a holiday (I Sam 20:18 ff., II Kings 4:23, Is. 1:14) with special sacrifices (Num. 28:11—15). In the Talmudic Period, there were elaborate arrangements for the observation and festive proclamation of the N.M., which then was communicated throughout and beyond Palestine by a system of beacons. Something of this still survives in the ceremony of *birkat ha-levanah* (see MOON, BLESSING OF). For calendarial reasons the N. M. is now sometimes observed for two days, its formal celebration being confined to the recital of the Half HALLEL and the addition of the MUSAPH service to the ritual. The N. M. is announced in synagogue on the preceding Sabbath in a special ceremony (see NEW MOON, BLESSING OF THE).

NEW MOON, BLESSING OF THE (Heb. *Birkat* [popularly *Mevarekhim*] *ha-Ḥoḍesh*): Formula for announcing the day or days to be celebrated as *Rosh Ḥodesh* ("First of the Month"). It is recited solemnly, the reader holding a Scroll of the Law, after the reading of the law on the Sabbath preceding the new moon (except before the NEW YEAR). In addition to the formal announcement, the Ashkenazi formula contains supplication for national redemption and a prayer for a prosperous and blessed month. Among Ashkenazim, the Sabbath is termed *Sabbath Mevarkhim*. The Sephardi form, which is varied before the New Moon of *Av*, is simpler.

NEW ORLEANS: City in Louisiana, US. The first congregation, Shaarey Chesed, was organized in 1828. In 1843, N. O. had about 125 Jewish families, mostly of German origin, and a second congregation, Shaarey Tefilah, was founded in 1845. Spanish and Portuguese Jews established their own congregation in 1847, but the Sephardi element subsequently disappeared. A congregation of Polish Jews was organized in 1857. The Jewish Federation of N. O. was created in 1911, the N. O. Jewish Welfare Fund, in 1933. N. O. had 10,500 Jews in 1973 with 6 synagogues.

NEW ROCHELLE: City in the state of New York, US. A few German Jewish families were living in N. R. when E European immigrants began arriving in the 1880's. Its oldest congregation, Anshe Sholom, was founded in 1898. In 1970, N. R. had 26,000 Jews with 3 synagogues (Orthodox, Conservative, and Reform).

NEW TESTAMENT: An early designation — based on Jer. 31:31 — of CHRISTIANITY, to distinguish it from Judaism, the "former" or "old covenant" (i.e., the covenant of Sinai). The designation was transferred to the Christian Scriptures, the Jewish Bible in contrast being called henceforth by Christians the "Old" Testament. The canon of the N. T. was fixed in the 2nd cent. CE. The language of the N. T. is Greek, although there are scholars who maintain that some books at least were translated from an Aramaic original. As the scene of JESUS' ministry was Palestine and both he and his APOSTLES were Jews, the N. T. abounds in references to contemporary Jewish life which, however, is not always faithfully portrayed. Moreover, the N. T. writings were composed after the rift between the nascent Church and Judaism so that partisanship often appears in the writings — as

is evidenced, e.g. by the N. T. equation of Pharisees with hypocrites. Paul, particularly in his Epistle to the Romans, struggles with the problem of the rejection of Christ by the original Chosen People. The recently discovered Dead Sea Scrolls show many points of contact with certain N. T. doctrines; it is not improbable that the latter represent ideas current in Jewish sectarian circles though deviating from the "normative" Judaism of the rabbis.

NEW YEAR: The opening Mishnah of the treatise ROSH HA-SHANAH lists four dates during the year which have the significance of a New Year for certain calculations: (1) *Nisan* 1 for dating the reign of kings, the order of the festivals, and the counting of the months; (2) *Tishri* 1 (*Rosh ha-Shanah*) for the agricultural year with reference to the observance of the Sabbatical and Jubilee years, etc.; (3) *Elul* 1, for the tithing of cattle; (4) *Shevat* 15, as the NEW YEAR FOR TREES with respect to the tithing of fruit.

NEW YEAR FOR TREES (Heb. *Tu bi-Shevat* i.e., 15th -day of *Shevat*): Date marking a dividing line for fruit tithing; all fruits becoming ready for tithing after this date require a separate tithing. It is popularly celebrated by the eating of various fruits, especially those connected with Palestine. Jewish mystics developed a fruit ritual still widely observed among Sephardi communities. In modern Israel, the day is celebrated as an "Arbor Day" with tree-planting by schoolchildren, etc.

NEW YORK: US state. Jewish traders from NEW YORK City appeared along the Hudson River shortly after 1660, and merchants of Sephardi origin were found there throughout the 17th and 18th cents. Jewish communities, however, did not develop until the 1830's. The first Jewish community in the state N of New York City came into being in 1837 at Wawarsing where 12 families founded a short-lived colony called "Sholom." The first permanent congregation outside of New York City was established at ALBANY in 1838. The next year, several Jewish families settled in SYRACUSE. In the 1840's, communities came into being in BUFFALO, ROCHESTER, UTICA, Oswego, Poughkeepsie, and Plattsburg, where the oldest Jewish community in the Adirondacks was founded. During the decade before the Civil War, additional communities were founded in Elmira, Kingston, Newburgh, SCHENECTADY, and TROY. By the end of the 1860's, there were communities in Amsterdam, Hudson, Ogdensburg, and Niagara Falls. In 1877, 19 cities in the state reported the existence of 53 congregations; by 1890, this figure had risen to 179 (135 in New York City), of which 152 were Orthodox and 27 Reform. A number of farm settlements were established after the turn of the century in Sullivan and Ulster Counties with the aid of the Baron de HIRSCH FUND and the JEWISH AGRICULTURAL SOCIETY. In 1910, there were 1,092 Jewish farm families in the state, most of them in the Catskill Mountains region which is now famous as a Jewish resort area. In 1956, N. Y. state had 1,560 Jewish congregations, 36 of them rural. The largest centers of Jewish population are in New York City, Buffalo, Rochester, and Syracuse. The Jewish population of N. Y. State is estimated (1973) at 2,150,385 or 11.8 per cent of the total state population — by far the highest proportion in the US.

NEW YORK: City in US. Its Jewish community dates from the arrival in 1654 of 23 refugees from Recife, Brazil. Their number grew slowly, and by 1812 did not exceed 400. There were many initial difficulties, e.g., the Jews were denied certain civic rights and permission to engage in crafts. These rights were obtained gradually and the naturalization law accepted only in 1715. The Jews were not at first allowed to erect a synagogue, and the first mention of one dates from 1693; this developed into the (Sephardi) congregation Shearith Israel, which was unique until the Ashkenazi synagogue B'nai Jeshurun was founded in 1825. Immigration from Europe grew greatly in the 1820's and 1830's and the Jewish pop. in 1846 was 10,000. By the end of the 19th cent. there were in N. Y. (including BROOKLYN) 250,000 Jews and by 1940, over 2 million: in 1854, there were 14 synagogues and in 1927, over 1,000. At present the Jewish pop. of N. Y. city is declining numerically: it dropped from 2,130,000 in 1952 to 1,836,000 in 1971 and the

process is likely to continue. This is due to the absence of any considerable immigration, departure to other regions of the US, and especially the movement to suburban areas and neighboring towns. This last factor is general throughout the US and is not confined to N. Y. or to the Jews. Many congregations have developed around N. Y. in recent years; their original members tend to be young couples, mainly from the middle-class. The estimated Jewish pop. for Greater New York is 2,381,000. The birth rate of N. Y. Jews is slightly lower than among the general white population; proportionately there are fewer Jews under 45 and more over 45. Children below 20 account for 25.8% among Jews and 27.4% among the general white population. The average number of members per family is 2.1 among the Jews and 3.2 among the others. The percentage of employed males is about equal: it is lower among Jews in the 14–24 age bracket but higher over 25. Housewives constitute a higher percentage than in the general population. Occupationally, the Jews are prominent among proprietors, managers, salesmen, office workers, and the liberal professions; less in handicrafts, manual labor, and in the services. Over 66% of the Jews engage in non-manual work, while the percentage for the general population in 50%. There is no organized N. Y. community on the lines of many European cities. The central institution is the N. Y. Federation of Jewish Philanthropies, which coor-

Interior of Shearith Israel synagogue, NY.

Prime Minister Golda Meir receives the freedom of the city
of New York from Mayor John Lindsay. (1969).

dinates all charitable institutions, and from which
600,000 people benefit annually. The American
headquarters of all the large Jewish political institutions (the Jewish Agency, the World Jewish Congress,
the American Jewish Committee, the American Joint
Distribution Committee, etc.) are situated in N. Y.,
as are rabbinical colleges of all three trends (Yeshiva
Univ., the Jewish Theological Seminary, the Jewish
Institute of Religion). The N. Y. Public Library
possesses a very rich collection of Judaica. About
250 Jewish books are published in N. Y. annually,
as are most of the American Jewish periodicals
(2 news agencies, 3 Yiddish dailies, 6 weeklies, 4
fortnightlies, 27 monthlies, 17 bi-monthlies, 21 quarterlies, 3 semi-annuals, and 9 annuals), mostly in
English, also in Hebrew, Yiddish, and other languages.
There are some 650 Orthodox synagogues, besides
private prayer-houses, 150 Conservative, and 77
Reform. There are c. 300,000 Jewish children of
school-age (6–15), of whom 140,219 receive a Jewish
education (24% once a week, 31% in day schools,
mostly yeshivot, and 44% in Talmud Torahs and
synagogue schools, generally for 2–5 afternoon hours
a week). Recent years have seen a growth in tension
between Jews and Negroes in New York City despite
the activities of many Jewish organizations and
individuals on behalf of civil rights and for the
betterment of conditions among the Negroes.

NEW ZEALAND: British dominion. One of the
earliest writers on the country was Joel Samuel
Polack who traveled there in 1831–7. English Jews
arrived in the first immigrant ships in 1840. The Jewish
community in WELLINGTON was founded by Abraham
Hort of London under the authority of the chief
rabbi in 1843. Communities were later established in
AUCKLAND and other centers. Jews have actively
collaborated in N.Z. public life and have occupied
the highest positions including those of administrator,
prime minister, and chief justice. The community,
at first mainly English, was reinforced by immigrants
from E Europe from 1882 and Central Europe from
1933 onward. The Jewish pop. of 4,100 (1973) is
distributed among Wellington (2,000), Auckland
(2,000), Christchurch (200), Dunedin (40), and Hastings (60).

NEW ZIONIST ORGANIZATION see **REVI-
SIONISM**

NEWARK: City in New Jersey, US. Jews first settled
there in 1844. The first synagogue in the state was
erected in 1858 by the B'nai Jeshurun congregation
(founded 1848). N.'s second congregation was founded
in 1853. By 1855, N. had about 200 Jewish families,
predominantly of German origin. E European Jews
who began settling there in the 1880's comprised
about half of N.'s 20,000 Jews at the turn of the
century, later rising to about three-quarters. In 1973

The Yiddish Daily "Forverts" building, N.Y.

the Essex County area which included N. had 95,000 Jews. The weekly *Jewish News* is published in N. The Jewish Community Council of Essex County was founded in 1922.

NEWCASTLE-ON-TYNE: English seaport. Jews were excluded from the city in 1234. Jewish resettlement began at the close of the 18th cent., and a community was organized before 1831. There are now 4 synagogues, a Representative Council, etc. Jewish pop. (1973): 3,500.

NEWFOUNDLAND: Island off the NE coast of Canada. The majority of the Jewish population of 253 (1973) is of Russian origin. The first settler arrived in 1892 in St. John's where a synagogue was established in 1924 and where 130 Jews live.

NEWMAN, LOUIS ISRAEL (1893–1972): US rabbi and author; from 1930, rabbi of Temple Rodeph Sholom, New York. He has taught at the Jewish Institute of Religion, New York, and is author of *Jewish Influence on Christian Reform Movements*; *The Jewish People, Faith and Life*; *The Hasidic Anthology*, etc. He also composed music, plays, and cantatas.

NEWPORT: City in Rhode Island, US. The tradition that Sephardi refugees from Brazil settled in N. as early as 1658 is now doubted, but in 1677, a cemetery was purchased — the oldest Jewish burial ground in N America. A beautiful synagogue, designed by Peter Harrison and now a national shrine, was dedicated in 1763. Before the American Revolution, N. was a hub of commerce, in which its handful of Jews were leaders. The community's disintegration began with the British occupation during the American War of Independence. By 1818, there were only 3 Jewish families left, but the maintenance of the synagogue was assured by the endowments of the Touro brothers. The arrival of immigrants from E Europe after 1882 revived the community. In 1973, N. had 1,200 Jews with 2 synagogues.

NEWSPAPERS see **PRESS**

NEXT YEAR IN JERUSALEM (in Heb. *la-shanah ha-baah bi-Yerushalayim*): Traditional conclusion to the *Seder* service on Passover eve and in some communities, to the services of the Day of Atonement. In Israel, the word *Ha-benuyah* (i.e., "in 'rebuilt' Jerusalem") is added.

NEZIKIN (Heb. "Damages"): Fourth order (*seder*) of the Mishnah, consisting of 10 tractates, 8 of which have *gemara* in both Babylonian and Palestinian Talmuds. It is also the original name of the tractate with which the order started, now divided into *Bava Kamma, Bava Metzia,* and *Bava Batra.* The order *N.* is also referred to as *Yeshuot* ("Deeds of Help"). It treats of money matters and all damages which are decided by the courts, criminal law, and oaths. It contains a tractate containing ethical teachings (*Pirke* Avot).

*NICANOR (d. 161 BCE): General who — with Gorgias — commanded the Syrian forces of Antiochus IV against the Hasmoneans in 166–5 BCE, being defeated at Emmaus. He was again sent against Judah the Maccabee in 161 and defeated and killed at Adasa, the date (*Adar* 13) being thereafter commemorated in the Jewish calendar as "Nicanor day."

NICANOR, GATE OF: Gate within the Jerusalem Temple mentioned several times in talmudic sources. It apparently gave access from the Women's Court to the Inner Court. An ossuary found on the Mount of Olives in 1903 bears the name of "N. of Alexandria who made the Gate," perhaps the person in question.

NICARAGUA: Central American republic. Its Jewish Community, stemming from E Europe and Germany, came into being between World War I and 1930 when Jewish immigration was stopped. The great majority of the country's 200 Jews (1973) live in the capital, Managua.

NICE: French (formerly Italian) port. The Jewish community there dates back to the 14th cent. when a special officer (*bailo*) controlled their affairs. Refugees from Rhodes were admitted in 1499. In the 17th cent., the dukes of Savoy encouraged Jews and Marranos to settle in the neighboring port of Villefranche, and conditions in N. were more favorable than elsewhere in the duchy. Restrictions ended temporarily under French rule, 1792–1814, and when N. finally became part of France in the 19th cent., the community expanded. During the Italian occupation 1940–3, N. was a haven for Jews, but great suffering ensued when the town was occupied by the Germans in 1943. There are now both Sephardi and Ashkenazi synagogues and many N. African Jews settled there in the 1950's and 1960's. Pop. (1974): 25,000.

*NICHOLAS: Russian czars. *NICHOLAS I.* reigned 1825–55, aimed at assimilating the Jews by police methods. In 1827, he introduced the system of Cantonists. In 1844, the Jewish community organization was abolished and secular government schools introduced. The Jewish costume was forbidden in 1850. Intellectual life was strictly supervised. Converts were granted several years' exemption from taxation. *NICHOLAS II,* reigned 1894–1917, continued the harsh policies of his father Alexander III toward the Jews. Severe pogroms occurred 1903–7, and the notorious Beilis trial in 1913. When his premier Stolypin presented a plan affording some relief to the Jews, N. replied "As long as I am czar, the Jews of Russia shall not receive equal rights."

*NICHOLAS OF DAMASCUS (b. c. 64 BCE): Historian and philosopher. He was the private secretary of Herod and friend of Augustus. At Herod's suggestion, he wrote a universal history in 144 volumes from the most ancient times down to Herod's reign. N. also was the author of a biography of

Augustus and an autobiography. Josephus largely utilized N.'s works for his descriptions of Herod's reign.

NICHOLS, MIKE (1931–): US director. Born in Berlin, he was taken to the US in 1939. He began his career by appearing in cabaret with Elaine May. His successes have included his stage productions of Neil Simon's *Barefoot in the Park* and Murray Schisgal's *Luv*, and the movies *Who's Afraid of Virginia Woolf?* and *The Graduate*.

NICOLAEV: Ukrainian city. In 1829, it was placed outside the Pale of Settlement, but Jewish residence became possible from 1858. It was the scene of a pogrom in 1905 and a massacre in 1919 perpetrated by the White Russian armies. Before World War II, there were c. 30,000 Jews in N. The majority of them (c. 25,000) escaped to the Russian interior; the rest were annihilated by the Nazis in 1941.

NIDDAH (Heb. "Menstruous Woman"): Seventh (fifth in some codices) tractate in the Mishnah order of *Tohorot*, containing 10 chapters. It has *gemara* in both the Babylonian and Palestinian Talmuds, the latter, however, covering only the first 3 chapters. It deals with the ritual uncleanness conveyed by menstruation (Lev. 15:19–24) and by childbirth (Lev. 12:1–5).

NIEMIROVER, JACOB ISAAC (1872–1939): Rumanian rabbi. After officiating in Jassy 1895–1912 and then in Bucharest, in 1921 he became chief rabbi of Rumania and was the first Jew in the Rumanian Senate. N. helped to obtain the repeal of the special Jewish oath customary in Rumanian courts. For many years, he was chairman of the Rumanian Zionist Organization.

NIETO, DAVID (1654–1728): Rabbi and physician. Born in Venice and for a time officiating in Leghorn, he became Haham of the Sephardi community in London in 1702. He wrote in Italian, Spanish, and Hebrew on many subjects, including a courageous attack on the Inquisition, anti-Sabbetaian polemics, and especially *Matteh Dan*, a philosophical vindication of Judaism modeled on Judah ha-Levi's *Kuzari*. His son *ISAAC N.* (1702–1774) succeeded him as Haham, 1728–1735, but later led a disturbed life. He published Spanish translations of the liturgy.

NIGER, SAMUEL (pen-name of Samuel Charney; 1883–1956): Yiddish author and critic. He was active as editor of Yiddish periodicals in Russia, and in the development of Jewish literary life. After a narrow escape from Polish pogroms, N. went to the US in 1919. He became literary editor of *Der Tog*, and continued his critical work. His critical studies of Yiddish literature appeared in many volumes, notably *Vegen Yiddishe Shreiber*, *Mendele Moikher Sforim*, *H. Leivik*, and *I. L. Peretz*. N. was the principal critic in Yiddish literature, the national and cultural ideals of which he helped to formulate.

David Nieto.
(Engraving by David Estevens).

NIGGUN (Heb.): Traditional air or song, particularly among the Ḥasidim.

NIGHT OF WATCHING see **LEL SHIMMURIM**

NIGHT PRAYER (Heb. *keriat shema al ha-mittah* "reading of the *Shema* on the bed"): The practice of reciting the SHEMA before sleeping is based on a saying of R Joshua ben Levi (*Berakhot* 4b). Mystics regarded it as a protection against evil spirits (*Ibid* 5a). The brief liturgy includes a blessing and prayer texts, most of them taken from the evening service. Some add a confession and ADON OLAM.

NIKOLSBURG see **MIKULOV**

NILES, DAVID K. (1890–1952): US government official. After a career in liberal politics, he was from 1942 to 1951 administrative assistant to Presidents Roosevelt and Truman. During World War II, N. distinguished himself in the mobilization effort.

NILI (Heb. initials of "The Glory of Israel will not lie"; I Sam. 15:29): Pro-British and anti-Turkish Jewish underground organization in Palestine during World War I. Its leader was Aaron AARONSOHN who transmitted information to British warships off the Palestinian coast. The organization also assisted Jews liable for Turkish conscription. The Turks obtained information and arrested many of its members, some (including Sarah Aaronsohn) being executed. Part of the Jewish population opposed the activities of *N*.

NIMES: French town. Count Hilderic in 672 welcomed Jews expelled from Spain, and by the 12th cent., it was an important community and renowned center of learning. Its Jews were expelled in 1306 and 1394. The modern settlement (mainly of Sephardim) dates from shortly before the French Revolution and in 1970 numbered 1,200.

NIMROD: Ancient biblical figure. He was of Cushite origin and regarded as a mighty hunter and strong ruler whose kingdom comprised Babylon, Erech, Accad, etc. Assyria was poetically known as "the land of N." His historical identity with one of the ancient Babylonian kings has not been settled; other identifications have been made with Gilgamesh and with the Assyrian war-god Ninurata.

NINEVEH: Capital of the new Assyrian Empire (from c. 1100 BCE). Of great antiquity, the Bible can be interpreted to ascribe its foundation to Nimrod (Gen. 10:11), but the passage is unclear. Jonah was sent to N. to persuade its citizens to repent.

NINTH OF AV see **AV, NINTH OF**

NIR DAVID: Israel communal settlement (KA) in the Bet Shean valley. Founded by settlers from Poland in 1936, it was the first STOCKADE AND TOWER settlement and the first Jewish outpost in the neighborhood. N. D. pioneered in breeding carp in ponds. Pop. (1972): 551.

NIR ETZYON: Israel cooperative smallholders' settlement (PM) on the W slopes of Mt. Carmel. It was founded in 1950 by survivors of Kephar Etzyon, in the Hebron mountains, which fell to the Arab Legion in May, 1948. Nearby are the Wingate children's village — Yemin Orde — and the artists' colony, En Hod. Pop. (1972): 244.

NIRENBERG, MARSHALL W. (1927–): US scientist; biochemist at the National Institute of Health, Bethesda, Maryland. In 1968 he (and two others) were awarded the Nobel Prize for Medicine for their

Section from the mosaic floor of an ancient synagogue discovered near Nirim.

work on the interpretation of the genetic code and its function in protein synthesis. This provided the key to translating the language of nucleic acids into that of proteins.

NIRIM: Israel collective settlement (KA) in the W Negev. Founded in 1946, it held out against Egyptian attacks in 1948. In 1949, the settlers moved to a new site closer to the border of the Gaza Strip, also named "Nirim," while the original site was occupied by a younger group and renamed Nir Yitzhak. The remains of the mosaic floor of an ancient synagogue were discovered in the vicinity.

NISAN: First month of the religious year, seventh of the civil. In the Pentateuch it is called the month of Abib, i.e., spring. Passover occurs on the 15th of the month and probably for this reason, no public mourning is permitted during N., nor is the penitential *tahanun* recited in the daily prayers.

NISHMAT (Heb. "The soul of" [every living thing]): Doxology recited at the end of the PESUKE DE-ZIMRA on Sabbaths and festivals. R Johanan called it *Birkat ha-Shir* and in the Mishnaic Period it was already recited after *Hallel* on *Seder* night. The *N.* prayer comprises three parts — the section known in mishnaic days, a section which served as a thanksgiving for rain, and a gaonic addition. Its author is unknown, and a curious medieval legend ascribes it to the apostle Peter.

NISIBIS: Mesopotamian city, center for the collection and dispatch of gifts for the Jerusalem Temple under the Herods. In the early 2nd cent., it was the seat of the academy of Judah ben Bathyra. Its Jewish community was massacred in punishment for their fierce resistance to the Romans in 155–7, but in the 12th cent., N. had 1,000 Jews, with 3 ancient synagogues.

NISSENBAUM, ISAAC (1868–1943): Religious Zionist leader. He officiated in the *Hoveve Zion* synagogue in Warsaw. He was active in the founda-

Some members of the Nili underground organisation.
Standing: Nissim Rotman, Sarah Aaronsohn.
Sitting: Tovah Gelberg, Yosef Lishansky.

Yitzhak Rahamim Nissim.

tion of the *Mizrahi* movement (1902) and was the first preacher in the Diaspora to give sermons in Hebrew (from 1907). He contributed to scholarly and popular journals and from 1911 was on the editorial board of *Ha-Tzephirah*. He was killed by the Nazis in the Warsaw ghetto.

NISSIM BEN JACOB BEN NISSIM (Ibn Shahin; fl. 11th cent.): N African talmudist and moralist. He was born in Kairouan, succeeding his father and his teacher HUSHIEL as head of the academy there. He corresponded at great length with Hai Gaon. His chief halakhic work is *Kitab Miftah Maghalik al-Talmud* ("Key to the Locks of the Talmud"), a commentary on and methodology of the Talmud. He also wrote a collection of consolatory tales in Arabic.

NISSIM, RABBENU GERONDI see **GERONDI**

NISSIM, YITZHAK RAHAMIM (1896-): Joint (Sephardi) chief rabbi of Israel. A native of Baghdad, he lived in Jerusalem in a private capacity before his election in 1955. He is a distinguished halakhic authority and has both edited and published volumes of responsa. He served intil 1972.

NISTER, DER see **KAHANOVITZ, PHINEHAS**

NITTAI THE ARBELITE (2nd cent. BCE): Sage. Little is known of him except that he was president of the Sanhedrin when Joshua ben Perahiah was patriarch (see ZUGOT).

NITZANAH (Auja el-Hafir): Police post on the border between Israel and the Sinai peninsula. Built in the Hellenistic Period on the desert fringe and settled by Nabateans, it became a flourishing town in the Byzantine Period and continued to exist some time after the Moslem conquest in the 7th cent. The Israel army captured the place in 1948; in the 1949 Israel-Egyptian Armistice Agreement the region on both sides of the frontier around N was demilitarized.

NO AMON ("city of [the god] Amon": Gk. Thebes): Egyptian city (Nah. 3:8; Ezek. 30:15-16, etc.). The temple of Rameses III there contains a description and illustrations of his campaign against the "peoples of the sea" on the borders of Palestine.

NOACHIAN LAWS see **LAWS OF NOAH**

NOAH: Biblical figure, hero of the FLOOD narration (Gen. 6 ff.). Due to its evil ways God determined to annihilate the human race through the flood. N. was the sole exception, being "a man righteous and whole-hearted," and was hence commanded to build an ark for himself, his family, and specimens of all living species, who were thereby saved. His later years were spent as a husbandman, and he died at the age of 950. From his sons SHEM, HAM, and JAPHETH sprang the first seventy people from whom humanity was derived. The Babylonian Gilgamesh epic contains a parallel flood story, the hero of which is called Utnapishtim. Many midrashic legends were woven round the story of N.

NOAH, MORDECAI, MANUEL (1785-1851): US diplomat and author. He was US consul to Tunis 1813-15 and was subsequently sheriff of New York County and publisher of several newspapers in New York. He was also a prolific playwright. N. was surveyor of the port of New York 1829-33, and associate judge of the New York Court of Sessions 1841-2. He was father of the plan to establish ARARAT, a Jewish city of refuge on Grand Island in the Niagara River. Ceremonies marking the official launching of the project were held in 1825, but the European Jews whom N. had invited to settle never came. In later years, he advocated the need for mass Jewish settlement in Palestine. N. believed that the American Indians were descendants of the Ten Lost Tribes of Israel.

NOB: Priestly city probably situated near Jerusalem on Mt. Scopus. After the destruction of the tabernacle at Shiloh, the priests of the sons of Eli built a high-place in N. where they officiated. As a punishment for the assistance given to the fugitive David, Saul slew all the priests of the place.

NOBEL PRIZE WINNERS, JEWISH: The Nobel Prizes are awarded annually for outstanding contributions in various fields. The following list enumerates winners who are Jews or of Jewish descent:

Joseph Erlanger.

Robert Bárány.

Otto Meyerhof.

Hermann Joseph Muller.

Paul Ehrlich.

Ernst Boris Chain.

Tadeusz Reichstein.

Selman Waksman.

Fritz Albert Lipmann.

Physics	*Date awarded*
Michelson, Albert Abraham	
(1852–1931); American	1907
Lipmann, Gabriel	
(1845–1921); French	1908
Einstein, Albert	
(1879–1955); German	1921
*Bohr, Niels	
(1885–1962); Danish	1922
**Hertz, Gustav	
(1887–1975); German	1925
Franck, James	
(1882–1964); German	1925
Stern, Otto	
(1888–1969); American	1943
Rabi, Isidor Isaac	
(1898–); American	1944
Bloch, Felix	
(1905–); American	1952
Born, Max	
(1882–1970); German	1954
Segre, Emilio	
(1905–); Italian	1959
Glaser, Donald A.	
(1926–); American	1960
Hofstadter, Richard	
(1915–); American	1961
Landau, Lev	
(1908–1968); Russian	1962
Feyman, Richard P.	
(1918–); American	1965
Schwinger, Julian	
(1918–); American	1965
Bethe, Hans Albrecht	
(1906–); American	1967
Gell-Mann, Murray	
(1929–); American	1969
Gabor, Dennis	
(1900–); British	1971
Josephson, Brian	
(1940–); British	1973
Mittelson, Benjamin R.	
(1926–); US-Danish	1975

Medicine and Physiology	
*Metchnikoff, Elie	
(1845–1916); Russian	1908
Ehrlich, Paul	
(1854–1915); German	1908
Bárány, Robert B.	
(1876–1936); Austrian	1914
Meyerhof, Otto	
(1884–1951); German	1922
**Landsteiner, Karl	
(1868–1943); American	1930
**Warburg, Otto Heinrich	
(1883–1970); German	1931
Loewi, Otto	
(1873–1961); Austrian	1936
Erlanger, Joseph	
(1874–1965); American	1944
Chain, Sir Ernst Boris	
(1906–); British	1945
Muller, Hermann Joseph	
(1890–1967); American	1946
*Cory, Gerty Theresa	
(1896–1957); American	1947
Reichstein, Tadeusz	
(1897–); Swiss	1950
Waksman, Selman Abraham	
(1888–1973); American	1952

Lipmann, Fritz Albert	
(1899–); American	1953
Krebs, Sir Hans Adolf	
(1900–); British	1953
Lederberg, Joshua	
(1925–); American	1958
Kornberg, Arthur	
(1918–); American	1959
Bloch, Konrad	
(1912–); American	1964
Jacob, François	
(1920); French	1965
*Lwoff, André	
(1902); French	1965
Wald, George	
(1901–); American	1967
Nirenberg, Marshall W.	
(1927–); American	1968
Luria, Salvador	
(1912–); American	1969
Katz, Sir Bernard	
(1911–); British	1970
Axelrod, Julius	
(1912–); American	1970
Edelman, Gerald Maurice	
(1929–); American	1972
Baltimore, David	
(1938–); American	1975
Temin, Howard Martin	
(1925–); American	1975
Blumberg, Baruch S.	
(1925–); American	1976

Chemistry	
*Baeyer, Adolf J.F.W. von	
(1835–1917); German	1905
*Moissan, Henri	
(1852–1907); French	1906
Wallach, Otto	
(1847–1931); German	1910
Willstätter, Richard	
(1872–1942); German	1915
**Haber, Fritz	
(1868–1934); German	1918
Hevesy, George von	
(1885–1966); Hungarian	1943
Calvin, Melvin	
(1911–); American	1961
Perutz, Max Ferdinand	
(1914–); British	1962
Stein, William Howard	
(1931–); American	1972

Peace	
Asser, Tobias Michael Carel	
(1838–1913); Dutch	1911
Fried, Alfred Hermann	
(1864–1921); Austrian	1911
Cassin, René	
(1887–1976); French	1968
Kissinger, Henry	
(1923–); American	1973

Literature	
*Heyse, Paul J.L. von	
(1830–1914); German	1910
Bergson, Henri Louis	
(1859–1941); French	1927
***Pasternak, Boris	
(1890–1960); Russian	1958
Agnon, Shemuel Yoseph	
(1888–1970); Israel	1966

Sachs, Nelly
　　　(1891–1970); Sweden　　　　　　　　1966
Bellow, Saul
　　　(1915–); American　　　　　　　　　1976

Economics
　Samuelson, Paul
　　　(1915–); American　　　　　　　　　1970
　Kuznets, Simon
　　　(1901–); American　　　　　　　　　1971
　Arrow, Kenneth Joseph
　　　(1921–); American　　　　　　　　　1972
　Kantorovich, Leonid
　　　(1912–); Russian　　　　　　　　　1975
　Friedman, Milton
　　　(1912–); American　　　　　　　　　1976

*half-Jew　　　　**left Judaism　　　　***award not accepted

*NÖLDEKE, THEODOR (1836–1930): German
　orientalist; from 1864 professor in Kiel and in
　1872–1906, in Strasbourg. His pioneer work on the
　Mandean language was a major contribution to the
　study of the history of E Aramaic dialects. He sug-
　gested that the Neo-Syriac Jewish dialects were not a
　continuation of talmudic Aramaic but were bor-
　rowed by Jews from their Christian environment. He
　wrote general surveys of the Semitic languages, Syriac
　grammars, a history of the Koran, etc.

NOMBERG, HIRSCH DAVID (1876–1927): Polish
　author. His first writings were in Hebrew, and he
　participated in several Hebrew journals. He then
　turned to Yiddish, from 1908 writing only on topical
　problems. N. was a founder of the FOLKISTEN —
　whom he represented in the Seym — and was promin-
　ent in the CZERNOWITZ conference.

NONES: US family. *BENJAMIN N.* (1757–1826)
　served in the American army during the Revolu-
　tionary War, rising from private to the rank of major.
　Thereafter he played an active part in politics. His
　14 children and their descendants were prominent
　in US army and navy service.

NORDAU (SÜDFELD), MAX (1849–1923): Author
　and Zionist leader. Born in Budapest, he practiced
　medicine in Paris from 1880. His journalistic career
　began in the Hungarian press, but his name was
　made by his German articles and his book *The
　Conventional Lies of our Civilization* (1883). This
　directed sharp, rationalistic criticism against the
　conventional religious and ethical concepts of his
　time and immensely influenced contemporary throught.
　His subsequent books (e.g. *Paradoxes*; *The Malady
　of the Century*; *Degeneration*, all criticizing con-
　temporary culture) and novels were also popular but
　his dramatic works were not particularly successful.
　His writings won him a commanding position in
　Parisian and European intellectual life. N. drifted
　far from Jewish tradition and his books were as
　critical of Judaism as of other religions. Nevertheless
　— largely as a result of HERZL's personal influence
　and magnetism — he was one of the first adherents of

the ZIONIST MOVEMENT, a participant at all Zionist
Congresses until 1911, and in 1897, active in the
formulation of the BASLE PROGRAM. His brilliant
surveys of the Jewish situation throughout the world
were among the highlights of the early Congresses.
He advised Herzl on Zionist problems, adopting a
"political Zionist" attitude in opposition to the policy
of Jewish penetration into Palestine before the granting of political rights there; accordingly, he supported
the UGANDA plan. He refused to succeed Herzl on
the latter's death but remained political counselor
to the president of the Zionist Organization, David
Wolffsohn. After Wolffsohn's policy was rejected by
the "practical Zionists," N. threw himself into the
opposition and campaigned against the new trends in
the Zionist movement. During World War I, he was
expelled from France as an Austrian subject and took
refuge in Spain. Weizmann invited him to London after
the war but his activism (e.g. his demand for the immediate transfer of 500,000 Jews to Palestine to make
it effectively Jewish) led to dissension, and he spent
his last two years in France.

NORFOLK: City in Virginia, US. Its Jewish settlement
　dates from 1787. The first congregation was or-
　ganized in 1836 by German Jews. At the turn of the
　century, immigrants from E Europe augmented the
　community. The N. Jewish Community Council was
　established in 1837. In 1973, N. had 11,000 Jews with
　4 synagogues.

NORMAN, EDWARD ALBERT (1900–1955): US
　banker and philanthropist. In 1941, he founded
　what became known as the American Fund for Israel
　Institutions (now the AMERICA ISRAEL CULTURAL
　FOUNDATION, also known as "The Norman Fund").

NORMANDY: French province. Many Jews lived
　there in the Middle Ages, as is evidenced by the
　number of rabbinical scholars as well as streets in
　some localities named after the Jewish population.
　They were expelled in 1394, but in the early 17th cent.,
　there was an important Marrano settlement at Rouen.
　The number of Jews grew in the 19th cent. and there
　are now communities at Rouen, Le Havre, and Elbeuf.

NORSA: Italian family, prominent since the 15th cent.,
　ultimately deriving from Nurcia in Umbria: hence
　the Hebrew form *Norzi*. Many were rabbis in Mantua
　where the family had their own synagogue. Outstand-
　ing was *JEDIDIAH SOLOMON BEN ABRAHAM N.*
　(c. 1560–c. 1626): biblical scholar, who established a
　rigorously scientific text of the Bible in his standard
　work *Minḥat Shai*, for which he traveled to the Levant
　and consulted over 900 mss. *RAPHAEL BEN
　GABRIEL N.* (16th cent.) wrote popular ethical
　works.

NORTH CAROLINA: US state. Individual Jews
　lived there in the mid-18th cent. Although a Jew,
　John Henry, was elected to the N.C. legislature in
　1808, it was not until 1868 that Jews were given the

right to hold public office in the state. The first synagogue in N. C. was Temple Israel in Wilmington, dedicated 1876. In 1973, the Jewish pop. was 10,340 notably in Charlotte (2,600), and Greensboro (1,500). There are central Jewish organizations in Ashville, Charlotte, Gastonia, Greensboro, High Point, Hendersonville, and Winston-Salem. *The American Jewish Time-Outlook* has been published in Greensboro since 1935.

NORTH DAKOTA: US state. Most of its Jewish settlers in the 1870's and 1880's came to till the soil. The majority of them were Russian immigrants, of whom a number settled in Bismarck where Jews had been living since 1871. In the same period, Jews settled in Fargo, Grand Forks, and Minot. The first synagogue in N. D. was established in Ashley in 1888. Between 1882 and 1906, 18 Jewish agricultural colonies, of which none survives, were established in the state. There is still a number of farmers among the 1,145 Jews (1973) living in N. D. Most of N. S.'s Jews live in Fargo (700), and Grand Forks (100).

NORTHERN RHODESIA see **ZAMBIA**

NORWAY: European kingdom. There is no record of Jews there before the 17th cent., when a few Sephardim were permitted to settle by the Danish kings. Under Swedish rule (from 1814), Jews were specifically excluded until 1851, when the poet Wergeland successfully headed a movement for the removal of the ban. A small Jewish immigration, largely from Russia, now began. Full emancipation was granted in 1891, a community being formally established in the following year at Christiania (OsLo); others followed in the 20th cent. at Trondheim and Bergen. General conditions were good, although ritual slaughter was prohibited in 1930. In 1939, the Jewish population of N. (in addition to c. 2,000 refugees from Germany) was approximately 1,500, more than one half at Oslo. With the Nazi occupation of 1940–5, the Nuremberg laws were introduced and the Jews who remained were annihilated. Jewish pop. (1973): 900.

NORWICH: English city. Little is known about the Jews in N. until 1144, when there took place the earliest recorded instance of the Ritual Murder accusation, associated with the name of WILLIAM OF N. The royal officers protected the Jews, who were nevertheless attacked in 1190 and 1234–8. The preservation of a great number of Hebrew legal documents regarding N. Jewry in the 13th cent. illustrates its inner history more intimately than that of almost any other medieval English Jewish community. N. was also the residence of scholars such as the poet Meir of N. There is no record of Jews in N. after the expulsion of 1290 until the 18th cent. A community (which has remained small) was founded c. 1750. Jewish pop. (1973): 170.

NORZI see **NORSA**

NOSHEN see **NASHEN**

NOSSIG, ALFRED (1864–1943): Polish author, sculptor, and publicist. In 1902, he founded in Berlin a society for Jewish statistics and, in 1906, an organization to assist Jewish art. An active Zionist, he opposed the policies of Herzl. After World War I, he engaged in world peace propaganda and in 1928, founded a Jewish branch of the Peace Federation of the Religions. N. wrote many books, some of a Jewish national content, and plays in Polish. His sculptures centered largely around Jewish themes. He was killed by the Jewish Underground in the Warsaw ghetto for alleged collaboration with the Nazis.

NOTABLES, ASSEMBLY OF see **SANHEDRIN, GRAND**

NOTARIKON (Gk.): Method of abbreviating Hebrew words and phrases by writing single letters (generally the initials = *Rashe Tevot* ["The Beginning of Words"]). If the *n.* represents a single word, it is marked by an apostrophe at its end; if several words are combined in one *n.*, a double superlinear stroke is inserted before the last letter. It is usual to read a *n.* like an ordinary word by inserting the vowel *a* in several places. Examples: *Tanakh* (Bible) = *Torah*, *Neviim, Ketuvim* (Pentateuch, Prophets, Hagiographa); *Rambam* = Rabbi Moses Ben Maimon.

NOVAKOVSKI, DAVID (1848–1921): Liturgical composer. As choir conductor in the Broder Synagogue (Odessa), he worked in close cooperation with MINKOWSKY. His many synagogal compositions written in a decidedly European style are marked by a characteristic harmony and often by great length.

NOVELLAE (Heb. *ḥiddushim*): Commentaries on the Talmud and later rabbinic works that attempt to derive new facts or principles from the implications of the text. The TOSAPHOT incorporate the n. of most of the early French and German talmudists. In Spain, however, n. were issued as separate works, those of R Moses ben Naḥman, R Solomon Ibn Adret, and R Yomtov ben Abraham of Seville being the best known. From 1520 onward, both Rashi's commentary and the *tosaphot* were printed in most editions of the Talmud and gave rise to a new set of n. Some, like those of R Samuel Edels, R Meir of Lublin, and R Solomon Luria, are themselves now printed together with the Talmud. Others, like the *Pene Yehoshua* of R Joshua Falk or the n. of R Akiva Eger, are separate works. In recent years, the tendency has been to incorporate n. into a few connected discourses on selected themes.

NOVI ISRAEL (Russ. "New Israel"): Jewish-Christian sect formed in Odessa in 1881 by a Jewish teacher, Jacob Priluker, to unite Reform Judaism with Greek Orthodox dissenters and to obtain equality of rights for the Jews. Its bases were acknowledgment of the Pentateuch and rejection of the Talmud, the transfer of Sabbath to Sunday, abolition of circumcision and of the laws of forbidden foods, etc. In 1883, N.I. united with the *Spiritual Biblical Brotherhood* of Jacob Gordin. Its founder became a Christian and, in 1890, emigrated to England. In 1884, the sect was renewed in Kishinev by Joseph Rabinovich who also became a Christian in 1885, when the sect's activity ceased.

*NOWACK, WILHELM (1850–1928): German biblical scholar and theologian. He wrote commentaries on many biblical books and a textbook of Hebrew archeology (1893) and published a translation with commentary of the mishnaic tractates *Shabbat* and *Eruvin*.

NUDNIK (Yidd.; derivation uncertain): A persistent bore; an annoying pedant.

NUMBERS: The Bible shows no tendency toward attributing special significance to n., except for a certain fondness for 7, common in the East and prominent in the Dead Sea Scrolls. Talmudic literature frequently fixed mnemonic n. There is a tendency to regard the occurrence of the same number in different things or events as indicative of a connection between them, e.g. the threefold repetition of the prohibition of seething a kid in its mother's milk corresponds to the three covenants of God with Israel. This idea was extensively developed later in GEMATRIA. Mystical n. appear first in the *Sepher Yetzirah* where the ten first n., the SEPHIROT, and the 22 letters are seen as the forces active in forming the World. Later mysticism retained the same *sephirot* but greatly changed their meaning. Abraham Ibn Ezra uses much Pythagorean number mysticism, but the real flowering of the magic use of n. belongs to Christian "Kabbalah."

NUMBERS: Fourth book of the Pentateuch; in Heb. called *Be-Midbar* ("in the wilderness") after its first distinctive word. It relates the history of the Israelites in the desert from the second to the fortieth year of the Exodus, together with the legislation stemming from this period. Its name (*Arithmoi* in the Septuagint) is based on the census it describes. The book is traditionally attributed to Moses, but some scholars date its final redaction after the Babylonian exile.

NUMBERS RABBAH: Midrash on the Book of Numbers; now part of MIDRASH RABBAH. The first 14 sections comprise a late haggadic composition on Num. 1–7; section 15–23 is essentially the Midrash TANHUMA. The compilation of the work is placed at not earlier than the 12th cent.

NUMERUS CLAUSUS (Lat.): Term applied to the restriction of the number of persons of some category, especially Jews, admitted to educational institutions, particularly universities. Such restriction was normal in Czarist Russia, but the term first became familiar after World War I in Hungary, when the admission of Jewish students to universities was formally restricted to 5% of the total student body; thence, although a contravention of the Minority Treaties, it spread. Similar restriction was applied.

Illuminated page of Nuremberg Haggadah now in Schocken Library, Jerusalem. (Scene from the story of Jonah).

formally or informally, also at some US universities. Although illegal in the US, informal application of the N.C. conception cannot easily be suppressed.

NUMISMATICS see **COINS**

NUN (נ): Fourteenth letter in the Hebrew alphabet; numerical value 50. It is pronounced *n*. When closing an unaccented syllable (except before laryngal letters) it disappears, being replaced by a *dagesh hazak*.

NUN REVERSED: Sign appearing before or after Num. 10:35-6, shaped like an inverted medial *nun*; also (not in all Bibles) before Ps. 107:21–26 (or 23–28) and 40, here mostly shaped like an inverted *resh*. Its significance is unknown.

NUÑEZ (NUÑES): Marrano and Sephardi family. (1) *HECTOR N.* (1521–1591): Physician and merchant. He headed the Marrano community in London in the reign of Elizabeth, providing her government with military and diplomatic information from his agents on the continent. (2) *MARIA N.* (b. 1575): Marrano beauty. Legend tells of her flight from Portugal, adventurous residence in England, and final settlement in Amsterdam where hers was the first Jewish marriage. (3) *PEDRO N.* (1492–1577): Marrano mathematician, cosmographer, and the most distinguished Portuguese nautical astronomer. His *Treatise on the Sphere* (1537) initiated modern cartography. He remained secretly attached to Judaism. (4) *SAMUEL RIBEIRO N.* (18th cent.): American pioneer. Formerly court physician in

Lisbon, he fled from the Inquisition and was an early settler in Savannah, Georgia. See also Costa,Da.

NUREMBERG: German city. Jews are known to have lived there from the latter 12th cent. when their livelihood was derived from moneylending. Their numbers grew in the 13th cent. but the community was destroyed by the 1298 Rindfleisch persecutions, 728 Jews being martyred. After some time, the settlement was refounded by newcomers from Franconia and the Jews again played a major economic role in the city's development. Financial extortion, however, was increased, and social intercourse rigidly restricted. In the 1349 Black Death massacres, 562 Jews were put to death and the remainder expelled. The community was soon refounded but never attained to its previous eminence, although its yeshivah enjoyed an international reputation. Christian moneylenders brought about a further expulsion of the Jews in 1499. Resettlement was permitted only in 1839, and before the Nazi catastrophe, 7,502 Jews were living in N., which was a center of the anti-Semitic movement. No Jews were left there by 1942. Jewish pop. (1970): 290.

NUREMBERG LAWS: Laws approved by the Reichstag at Nuremberg on Sept. 15, 1935. These excluded the Jews from German citizenship and prohibited all marital or extra-marital relations between Jews and non-Jews on pain of severe penalties; Jews were forbidden to employ Gentile domestic servants or to hoist the German flag. A Jew was defined as a person with at least two Jewish grandparents. By a series of subsequent supplementary decrees, the N. L. were extended to place German Jews outside German law and to exclude them from economic life.

NUSAKH (Heb. "version"): Term applied to the various rites of prayer (e.g. *Nusakh Ashkenaz*, etc.), sometimes also to the accepted tradition of synagogal melody.

NUZI: Ancient Mesopotamian city. Excavations have revealed that the town was inhabited by the biblical Horites.

OAK OF WEEPING see **ALLON BACUTH**

OAKLAND: City in California, US. Jews are first mentioned there in 1866, and their first congregation dates from 1874. The principal communal institutions are concentrated in the Jewish Community Center, founded in 1924 by the O. Jewish Federation. The O. Jewish Welfare Federation was founded in 1945. In 1969, O. (with Alameda and Contra Costa counties) had 18,000 Jews with 3 major synagogues.

OATH MORE JUDAICO see **JEWISH OATH**

OATHS: In Jewish jurisprudence, judicial o. are administered only where there is insufficient evidence for a decision. According to biblical law, o. could be imposed solely in cases concerning private (but not sacerdotal) movable (but not immovable) property. Rabbinic law, however, extended the application of o. Biblically, only the defendant could be made to take an oath. The Mishnah, however, rules that under certain conditions the oath should be transferred to the plaintiff. Not all o. are applied the same way, the severity of application varying according to the biblical or particular rabbinic character of the oath. Jewish law imposes no o. in criminal cases (for no one charged with a crime can be believed upon oath), nor upon witnesses. Extrajudicial o. were common in biblical and early talmudic times. These had the nature of vows. The tendency of later practice has been, however, to discourage such o. The pious in all ages were careful to avoid o., especially judicial o. See also JEWISH OATH.

OBADIAH: Fourth of the twelve Minor Prophets. The biblical book containing his prophecy consists of a single chapter. It severely condemns Edom for having refused to assist Jerusalem in her hour of calamity. Its date is unsettled but is generally assigned to the period following the destruction of the First Temple.

OBADIAH OF BERTINORO see **BERTINORO**

OBERMANN, JULIAN (1888–1956): Orientalist. A native of Warsaw, he taught in Hamburg and settled in the US in 1923, becoming professor of Semitic languages at Yale in 1933. He specialized in biblical studies and Arabic and edited the *Yale Judaica Series*.

OCCUPATIONS The Hebrews of the Biblical Period were normally balanced in their o., being mainly peasants, with a handful of craftsmen, and leaving trade to alien "Canaanites." This continued in Palestine in the Second Temple Period, when Josephus emphasized that trade held no attraction for the Jews. Although Jews were favored in Asia and Egypt as agricultural settlers (see AGRICULTURE), the proportion of craftsmen in the Diaspora was probably greater, and in Egypt a few capitalists emerged. After the Barbarian invasions, Diaspora Jewry, now pre-eminently an international element, was very important in wholesale trade between the Moslem and Christian areas, at the same time concentrating on highly technical handicrafts such as glass-making, silk-weaving, and dyeing. However, the Jews in Moslem countries perpetuated until a late date the agricultural society which is reflected in the Babylonian Talmud. In S Europe, trade and skilled handicrafts (see CRAFTS), especially in the various branches of textiles, were long characteristic of the Jews. In N Europe, on the other hand, the increasing monopolistic organization of trade and handicrafts by Christian guilds made it necessary for the Jews to find some other outlet, and in medieval England, France, Germany, and N Italy they were thus driven into MONEYLENDING. In Poland, however,

Pottery making is the occupation
of this young Israeli.

the great mass of the Jews were petty craftsmen, while in Salonica and other parts of the Turkish empire – as previously in Sicily — they were largely engaged in menial occupations and physical labor, e.g. as stevedores. In W Europe, meanwhile, the great mass of the Jews – in the 18th cent. largely peddlers and old-clothes dealers – were now in the category of petty bourgeois and shopkeepers, with special interest in the tailoring industry and an influential element of financiers. Extreme changes have characterized the occupational structure of Diaspora Jewry in the present century. According to the Russian census of 1897, when 60% of world Jewry lived in that country, 3.55% of the Jews engaged in agriculture, 35.45% in industry and handicrafts (chiefly the latter), 38.65% in commerce, 3.98% in transport, 6.61% in domestic services and wage labor, and 11.76% in public services and the free professions. The Russian Jews then were chiefly a group of shopkeepers (middlemen) and craftsmen, and the situation in the second largest Jewish community, – the Austrian Empire – was similar. The first major change in this situation resulted from the mass migration to the US where Jews concentrated mainly in light industry. According to the 1900 census, in seven large cities, 59.6% of the Jews earned their living by labor (largely in the garment industry) and only 20.6% by commerce. The development of a non-Jewish trading class, often coupled with governmental discriminations against Jewish traders, reduced the number of Jews in commerce in many lands. The nationalization of trade and commerce also produced this result. Thus, in the USSR after the Revolution and in the late 1930's, 7.1% of Russia's Jews were engaged in agriculture, 14.3% in handicrafts, 21.5% in industry, 37.2% in clerical work, and 12.8% in the free professions; with commerce having vanished from the list of their o. In Poland during the inter-War period, the percentage of Jews went up in crafts and industry (45.4% in the 1930's) but there was also a considerable section of middlemen (commerce and credit – 38.2%), all other o. being of minor importance. By contrast, in western countries, the Jews concentrated chiefly in commerce and, to a much lesser degree, in industry. In time their share in the free professions grew. Thus, in pre-Nazi Germany, 49.8% of the Jews engaged in commerce, 18.7% in industry, and 9.4% in the free professions. In the US, the children of Jewish immigrant workmen entered commerce in large numbers, and many became professionals. In the early 1930's 50% of American Jews were in commerce, 28% in industry, and 10% in the free professions. In Latin America, the proportion in commerce remained high (55% in Argentina, 66% in Brazil, 68.3% in Mexico) with only a small share in the free professions (7% in Argentina, 6% in Brazil, 2.5% in Mexico).

17th cent. Italian Jewish peddler.
(Museo Correr, Venice).

Since World War II, the Jews of E Europe, and to some extent also of Central Europe, are approaching a similar occupational structure to that of Russian Jewry. In 1948, 46% of the survivors of Polish Jewry were in industry, 19% in clerical jobs, and 15% in free professions, with only 11% in commerce and even this number was diminishing. Only in the backward Middle Eastern countries has the Jewish occupational structure remained similar to what it was in E Europe until the close of the 19th cent. Thus, in French Morocco in 1947, 46.5% of the Jews lived by commerce, 36.1% by handicrafts, 7.6% by free professions and 4.1% by agriculture.

In Israel, the occupational structure approximates more to that among the general population in other countries than to the situation among Jews in the Diaspora.

OCCUPATIONAL STRUCTURE OF DIASPORA JEWS AND OF JEWS IN ISRAEL (percentages)

	Diaspora in the 1930's	Palestine 1947	Israel 1952
Agriculture	4.0	12.6	14.7
Industry, Crafts, Building, Public Works	36.4	35.2	29.8
Free Professions and Public Services	6.3	18.6	20.2
Commerce, Finance, Transport	40.6	25.7	24.9
Others	12.7	7.9	10.4

It will be seen that agriculture, the free professions, etc. are more prominent in Israel at the expense of commerce. Although the percentage in crafts is similar, the internal breakdown is different, as in the Diaspora the emphasis is on handicrafts while in Israel, industry and building are of chief importance. With the transition to the professions in Israel, the middlemen and other abnormal occupations resulting from the Diaspora economy have decreased. The nature of immigration has also affected the occupational structure, particularly in the pre-state period. In British Mandatory days, every 100 immigrants included 15 agriculturists and 55.4 craftsmen and industrial workers. On the other hand, about 2/3 of the mass-immigration since 1948 has been without occupation, and only 4.9 have been agriculturalists. Efforts have been made to correct the distortion and the percentage engaged in agriculture has increased.

OCCUPATIONAL STRUCTURE (JEWS) IN ECONOMIC BRANCHES IN ISRAEL, 1967

Occupation	%
Agriculture, Forestry, and Fishing	12.6
Industry (Factories, Crafts, Quarries)	24.6
Building and Public Works	7.6
Electricity, Gas, and Water	2.2
Commerce and Banking	13.5
Communications and Storage	7.3
Government and Public Administration	2.6
Education and Social Services	16.5
Personal Services and Entertainment	8.1

Bust of Adolph S. Ochs in the *New York Times* Annex.

The percentage of workers in government service has grown with the extension of the civil service in connection with health, education, social assistance, etc.

OCHS: US family founded by *JULIUS O.* (1826–1888), an officer in the Union Army during the Civil War. He was prominent in public affairs in Tennessee, serving as US commissioner, tax assessor, and justice of the peace. Most distinguished of his sons was *ADOLPH SIMON O.* (1858–1935), who after a successful career as newspaper publisher in Chattanooga, went to New York and in 1896, became the publisher of the *New York Times*, then on the verge of bankruptcy. From 1899 the paper was under his control, and under his leadership developed into one of the great independent newspapers of the world. His daughter married Arthur Hays SULZBERGER who succeeded him as head of the paper. A second son of Julius was *GEORGE WASHINGTON O.-OAKES* (1861–1931), who was associated with his brother in the publication of papers in Chattanooga and Philadelphia. Another brother, *MILTON BARLOW O.* (1864–1955), also published newspapers.

ODEL (b. c. 1725): Only daughter of the BAAL SHEM TOV and mother of several *tzaddikim*. A devout follower and favorite of her father, she figures in Ḥasidic legend as the prototype of noble womanhood.

ODESSA: Russian city. The Jewish community founded in 1798, was prominent in the town's development and up to World War I controlled 90 % of its grain trade and 50% of its shopkeeping and banking. In the 19th cent., O. was a center of Russo-Jewish assimilation and simultaneously the focus of Jewish literary and nationalist life. Here were founded the first secular school for Russian Jews (1824), the first Russian synagogue with a choir, the first Russian Jewish newspaper *Rasviet* (1860), and the pioneer Hebrew newspaper in Russia *Ha-Melitz* (1860). Many of the great figures of modern Hebrew literature (Mendele Mocher Sephorim, Aḥad Ha-Am, Bialik, Klausner etc.) were active in O., and in the 1880's, it was the center of Haskalah, Hebrew literature, and the Zionist movement (from 1890–1914, the seat of *Hoveve Zion*). Pogroms occurred in 1821, 1859, 1871, 1881, and 1905. The position of the Jews declined after World War I. After the Nazi occupation of 1941, the community previously numbering c. 180,000 fled or were annihilated, 26,000 being massacred on Oct. 23–25, 1941 alone. Jewish pop. for O. province (1970): 117,233.

ODESSA COMMITTEE see **ḤOVEVE ZION**

ODETS, CLIFFORD (1906–1963): US playwright. In 1935, his reputation was established by the experimental, proletarian plays *Waiting for Lefty*, *Awake and Sing*, and *Till the Day I Die*. His subsequent successes included *Golden Boy* and *The Country Girl*. O. also wrote film scenarios.

*OESTERLEY, WILLIAM OSCAR E. (1866–1950): English Hebraist. A clergyman and professor of Hebrew at King's College, London, he published numerous works on the Bible, Apocrypha, hellenistic Judaism, the Jewish background of the Christian liturgy, etc. and collaborated with T. H. Robinson in a *History of Israel*.

OFFENBACH: German town. Its Jewish community was well-established by the 14th cent. Jacob Frank and his daughter Eve settled there in the 18th cent. and the town became a Frankist center. There were 950 Jews in O. in 1933 but the community ended under the Nazi regime, during which period a great research library of looted Hebraica and Judaica was established there. In 1970, 662 Jews lived there.

OFFENBACH, JACQUES (1819–1880): Composer. His father was a cantor in Cologne, but from an early age O. lived in France where he studied music and in 1849, became conductor of the Théâtre Français. From 1853, he produced his own operettas of which over a hundred appeared including *La grande Duchesse*, *La belle Hélène*, *La Vie Parisienne*, and *Orphé aux Enfers*, distinguished for their musical lilt and satire on contemporary Parisian life. His lyric opera *The Tales of Hoffmann* became an international favorite.

OFFICIAL, JOSEPH see **JOSEPH BEN NATHAN**

Jacques Offenbach

OG: Amorite king of the land of Rephaim in Bashan and Gilead: called "king of Bashan." He was noted for his stature and physique. He attempted to interrupt the march of the Israelites but was defeated (Num. 21:33–35). The "Land of O." was a strongly fortified territory throughout the Middle and late Bronze Ages.

OHALOT (Heb. "Tents"): Second tractate in the Mishnah order of *Tohorot*, containing 18 chapters. It has *gemara* neither in the Babylonian nor Palestinian Talmud. It discusses the ritual impurity conveyed by a corpse (Num. 19:13–20), including that transmitted to anything under the same roof.

OHEL (Heb. "tent," "chamber"): Edifice over a grave – especially that of a *tzaddik* which is visited by the Ḥasidim on the anniversary of the death (*yahrzeit*). A *ner tamid* ("perpetual light") is kept burning at the end of the grave. In time of trouble, persons would sometimes prostrate themselves upon the grave and place upon the coffin a *pitka* ("note") asking for help.

OHEL: Israel workers' theater founded in 1925 by the cultural committee of the *Histadrut* but from 1958, an independent concern. Its center was in Tel Aviv. It disbanded in 1969.

OHEL MOED see **TABERNACLE**

OHIO: US state. From 1817, a few Jews, mostly of British origin, settled in Cincinnati. Jews from Germany began arriving in O. in the late 1830's. Its second Jewish congregation was founded in Cleveland in 1838. Before the Civil War, Jews appeared in Columbus (1838), Dayton (1842), Akron (1850), Elyria (1852), Circleville (1855), Hamilton (1855), Portsmouth (1858), and Piqua (1858). During the Civil War, 1,000 Jews from O. served in the Union Army. In 1877, O. had a Jewish population of 14,600, mostly of German and Hungarian origin. By the end of the 19th cent., 18 cities and towns had at least one Jewish institution. in 1973, O. had 160,900 Jews. There were 125 congregations, concentrated mainly in Cincinnati, Cleveland, Columbus, Toledo, Youngstown, Canton, Dayton, Akron, and Lorain.

OHOLAH and **OHOLIBAH:** Symbolic sisters who in Ezek. 23 represent respectively Israel and Judah.

OISTRAKH, DAVID (1908–1974): Russian violinist. He graduated from the Odessa Conservatoire in 1926 and soon made his reputation, becoming professor in the Moscow State Conservatoire in 1942. O. performed with great success in many countries. His son *IGOR* (1932–) is also a noted violinist.

OKHLAH VE-OKHLAH: Ancient work on the MASORAH, taking its name from the opening phrase of the book which comprises two homophonous words of different grammatical structure. Its purpose is to point out peculiarities and distinctive

Synagogue in Tulsa, Oklahoma.
Designed by Percival Goodman.

elements in the written biblical text, the arrangement being primarily alphabetical. It dates from before the 10th cent., and its origin is probably Babylonian. In its present form, however, it contains additions by both Sephardi and Ashkenazi scholars.

OKLAHOMA: US state. Its first Jewish community came into being during the last quarter of the 19th cent. in Ardmore where the first congregation was organized in 1899. Numbers of Jews went to Guthrie and Oklahoma City after 1889 when new lands were opened to white settlement. Temple B'nai Israel was founded in Oklahoma City in 1903. In 1973, there were 6,060 Jews in O. Tulsa had 2,500 Jews and Oklahoma City 1,500. Ardmore had a Jewish Federation (est. 1934), Oklahoma City, a Jewish Community Council (est. 1941) and Tulsa, a Council (est. 1938). *The Southwest Jewish Chronicle* has been published quarterly in Oklahoma City since 1929, and the Tulsa section of the National Council of Jewish Women has published the *Tulsa Jewish Review* since 1930.

OLAH see **SACRIFICE**

OLAM HA-ZEH; OLAM HA-BA (Heb. "This World"; "The World to Come"): Talmudic terms which have become proverbial. *Olam ha-Zeh* is the material world, while *Olam ha-Ba* refers to (1) the eternal world of the spirit to which the human soul passes after death, and (2) the period following the advent of the Messiah, when all the world will be perfected.

OLD AGE HOMES see **MOSHAV ZEKENIM**

OLD TESTAMENT see **BIBLE**

OLEH (Heb. "ascender"): (1) Immigrant to Israel; see Aliyah. (2) Pilgrim to the Holy Land and Jerusalem for the observance of Passover, Pentecost and Tabernacles (Ex. 23:14–17).

OLGIN (NOVOMISKY), MOSES (MOISSAYE) JOSEPH (1878–1939): Socialist writer. Active in the Russian revolutionary movement and the Jewish

Bund, he wrote in Yiddish on the life of the Jewish working-classes and also literary criticism. O. went to the US in 1914, later becoming the editor of the Yiddish communist newspaper *Freiheit*.

***OLIPHANT, LAURENCE** (1829–1888): English proto-Zionist. His interest in Zionism was partly stimulated by his religious mysticism and partly by his desire to improve economic and cultural conditions in Asiatic Turkey for the sake of the peace of Europe. In 1879, he toured Palestine and in the following year, began vigorous propaganda for Jewish resettlement in Transjordania. He contacted *Hovevei Zion* societies, traveled to Constantinople for political negotiations, settled in Haifa, and wrote *The Land of Gilead* and *Haifa, or Life in Modern Palestine*.

OLIVES, MOUNT OF see **MOUNT OF OLIVES**

OMAHA: City in Nebraska, US. Jews of Austrian, Bohemian, and German origin settled there in the early 1860's. In 1874, Congregation Temple Israel was organized. Large numbers of E European Jews arrived in the 1880's and again at the turn of the century. The Federation for Jewish Service of O., founded in 1903, sponsors the Jewish Welfare Fund (since 1930). In 1973, O. had 6,500 Jews with 5 synagogues. The weekly *Jewish Press* has been published in O. since 1921 by the Federation for Jewish Service.

***OMAR:** The second caliph; ruled 634–44. During his reign, several regions with ancient Jewish communities were conquered, e.g. Palestine, Syria, and Mesopotamia. On his orders, most of the Jews were expelled from N Arabia. To O. is attributed a

Dome of the Rock

"covenant" with Jews and Christians which assured them protection in return for the payment of a special POLL-TAX but also stipulated certain restrictions and disabilities, e.g. exclusion from public office, the wearing of distinctive clothes, prohibition against erecting new houses of worship, etc.

OMAR, MOSQUE OF: Moslem mosque (also called the Dome of the Rock) built in the center of the Temple area (*al-Ḥarim ash-Sherif*) in Jerusalem by Caliph Abd al-Malik c. 738 to replace the temporary structure set up by Caliph OMAR a century earlier. It is situated on the traditional site of Mt. MORIAH.

OMER: The first sheaf cut during the barley harvest, which was offered in the Temple as a sacrifice on the second day of PASSOVER (Lev. 23:15). Before the offering of this sacrifice, it was forbidden to eat the new grain. The seven-weeks beginning from this day and culminating in the Pentecost holiday is known as the period of the Counting of the Omer (see OMER, COUNTING OF). The word *o*. is also a dry measure equal to the tenth part of an *ephah*.

OMER (Heb. "Word"): Israel daily newspaper with vowels, designed to promote the knowledge of Hebrew among new immigrants. It was founded in Tel Aviv in 1951 by *Davar*.

OMER, COUNTING OF THE (Heb. *Sephirat ha-Omer*): 49 days are counted from the day on which the OMER was first offered in the Temple (according to the rabbis, *Nisan* 16th, i.e., the second day of Passover), the 50th day being the Feast of Weeks, SHAVUOT. This period of counting is known as the *Sephirah* period, during a certain part of which special mourning customs prevail and marriages are not solemnized. The number 49 (7×7) inspired the Kabbalists to read mystical meanings into the ritual of the counting, regarding it as marking the period of waiting between the deliverance of the Israelites from Egypt and their betrothal to the Torah at Sinai.

OMNAM KEN (Heb. "Indeed it is true"): Liturgical poem (*seliḥah*) for the eve of the Day of Atonement in the Polish rite. All its verses end with the word *salaḥti* ("I have forgiven"). The author was probably R. YOMTOV of Joigny (killed at York, 1190).

OMRI: King of Israel 887–876 BCE, and founder of a dynasty. As Elah's general, he directed the operations against the Philistine city of Gibbethon. Although the army proclaimed him king after the murder of Elah, his hold on the country was fully established only after a 6-year struggle with Tibni (I Kings 16:16–27). O. seems to have forged the Sidonian alliance which exercised a marked influence on the development of the Israelite religion. According to the MOABITE STONE, he subdued Moab. The Assyrians called the kingdom of Israel by his name for the rest of its existence.

ON (= Gk. Heliopolis): Ancient Egyptian city; also called in the Bible Beth Shemesh (i.e., "House of the Sun" = Heliopolis; cf. Jer. 43:13). The temple of ONIAS was situated in the district.

ONAN: Son of Judah. He married the widow of his brother, but refused to have children by her (whence the term "onanism"), for which he died in Divine punishment.

ONEG SHABBAT (Heb. "Sabbath delight"): A gathering held late on Saturday afternoons for lectures or cultural performances. A modern version of the "third meal" (*seudah shelishit*) customary among the Ḥasidim, it was inaugurated in Palestine by BIALIK whose main concern was to interest Jews in the cultural values of Judaism. The term has been expanded to mean any celebration during the Sabbath.

ONIAS: Name of several high priests during the Second Temple Period. (1) Son of Simon the Just, high priest c. 230 BCE. He refused to pay the 20 talents of silver given annually to Ptolemy III of Egypt thus endangering the safety of Judea. His nephew, Joseph son of Tobias, succeeded in pacifying the king. (2) Son of Simon II; grandson of (1). After the failure of Heliodorus to take the Temple treasury, he was deposed by Antiochus Epiphanes in 174 BCE. O. was later assassinated through the machinations of his brother, Menelaus, who had supplanted him as high priest. (3) Son or grandson of (2). He went to Egypt where many Jews had fled from the religious persecutions of Antiochus Epiphanes. Settling at Heliopolis (ON), he was given permission by Ptolemy IV to build a temple at LEONTOPOLIS.

ONKELOS (fl. 1st cent. CE): Palestinian proselyte. According to the Babylonian Talmud and the Tosephta, he was a pupil of R Akiva and responsible for the best-known Aramaic translation of the Pentateuch (TARGUM). Modern scholars doubt the authenticity of this tradition (which they ascribe to confusion with the name AQUILA) and consider the translation to have been made in Babylon.

ONO: Israel rural settlement (previously *maabarah*) near Tel Aviv. O. is mentioned as a Canaanite town in Egyptian documents from the time of Thutmose III. It was one of the places resettled by the Jews returning from the Babylonian captivity (Ezra 2:33; Neh. 6:2, etc.). It increased in importance after the destruction of the Second Temple. Immigrants began to settle in Kiryat Ono in 1949.

ONOCHI, Z. I. see **ARONSOHN, ZALMAN**

ONTARIO: Canadian province. Jews traded in the region from the earliest period of British occupation. The Franks and Solomons families established fur trading posts at Michilmackinac in 1763. Permanent Jewish settlement dates from 1833. By 1856, Jews of TORONTO had organized their first synagogue. From 1857, Jews settled in several other O. centers, including Lancaster, Hamilton,

Joseph Opatoshu.

OTTAWA, Dundas, North Bay, and Chapleau. By 1970, O. had a Jewish population of over 125,000 of whom 105,000 resided in Toronto; the remainder were scattered among 185 towns notably Ottawa (6,000), Hamilton (4,000), and Windsor (2,600). 16 Jewish communities have synagogues and Hebrew schools.

OPATOSHU (originally Opatovsky), **JOSEPH** (1886–1954): Yiddish author. Of Polish birth, he migrated to the US in 1907 and published his first Yiddish stories in 1910. Hundreds of his stories and novels, dealing chiefly with Jewish life in Poland and America, appeared in the American Yiddish press. O.'s most important works are his historical novels, which have been translated into many languages. They include *In Poilishe Velder* ("In Polish Woods"), which depicts Hasidic life in the mid-19th cent. against the background of the Polish revolt, *Der Letster Oyfshtand* ("The Last Revolt") dealing with the period of Bar Kokhba, and *A Tog in Regensburg* picturing German Jewry in the 16th cent.

OPERATION EZRA AND NEHEMIAH: The airborne transfer of 120,000 Jews from Iraq to Israel under the auspices of the Jewish Agency and the Israel government. The project was initiated in May 1950 and ended in Oct. 1951. At first the Iraqi authorities did not permit direct Baghdad-Lydda flights, compelling the immigrants to fly to Cyprus where they transferred to Israel-bound aircraft. 80% of the Iraqi immigrants were dispersed among MAABAROT, 10% were absorbed immediately in agricultural settlements, and 10% were welfare cases.

OPERATION MAGIC CARPET: Airborne operation conducted by the Jewish Agency and Israel government, which liquidated the Jewish communities in YEMEN and transported nearly 50,000 Jews to Israel. The majority of the Yemenite Jews made their way to Aden from where they were flown to Israel, since Egypt did not permit their passage through the Suez Canal. The project began in the fall of 1949 and lasted for a year.

OPFERPFENNIG (Ger.: "tribute penny"): The tribute exacted from the Jews in Germany from the 14th cent. on by the Holy Roman Emperors as successors to Vespasian and Titus. It perpetuated the conception of the FISCUS JUDAICUS of Roman times. See KAMMERKNECHTSCHAFT.

OPHAKIM: Israel rural center in the NW Negev. It was founded in 1955 according to a scheme for grouping agricultural settlements around a semi-urban center. Pop. (1974): 10,600.

OPHAN: Type of Hebrew medieval liturgical poem incorporated in the Sabbath and festival morning prayers and based on the description of the angels (*ophannim*) in Ezek. 1, etc. These poems describe the recitation of the doxology by the heavenly host.

OPHEL: Part of ancient Jerusalem from the time of the Kings, first mentioned by Michah (4:8) and Isaiah (32:14); according to II Chron. 27:3 Jotham "built much on the wall of O." According to Neh. 3:26, the NETHINIM lived in O. The wall of O., which is mentioned near the Temple area, was apparently discovered by Warren in 1867. The name O. has been extended by modern archeologists to cover the whole area of the City of David S of the Temple Mount.

OPHIR: Country from which Solomon imported precious stones and other valuables. It was famed for its gold and was reached by Ezion-geber.

Yemenite immigrants brought to Israel by "Operation Magic Carpet."

Suggested identifications have included an island in the Red Sea, N Africa, the E coast of the Arabian peninsula, and India.

OPPENHEIM (or Oppenheimer). **DAVID** (1664–1736): Rabbi and bibliophile; nephew of Samuel Oppenheimer. He was born in Worms and served as rabbi in Nikolsburg and, from 1702, in Prague. He built up a library of books and mss, expending enormous sums on their acquisition, but, because of the censorship in Prague, kept them in Hanover. 780 mss and 5,421 printed books from his collection were eventually purchased by the Bodleian Library, Oxford (1829), serving as the basis of its Hebrew section.

OPPENHEIM, HERMANN (1858–1919): German neurologist. He published many studies on the anatomy and pathology of the brain, spinal cord, and peripheral nerves.

OPPENHEIM, JAMES (1882–1932): US poet and novelist. He was one of the inaugurators of the free-verse and psychoanalytic fiction movement. His works include *Dr. Rast* and *The Sea.*

OPPENHEIM, MORITZ DANIEL (1800–1882): German painter. His first subjects were biblical, but later, he concentrated on portraits and popular pictures of German Jewish life.

OPPENHEIMER, DAVID (1832–1893): Canadian public figure. One of the founders of the city of Vancouver, O. served 4 terms as its mayor (the first Jewish mayor in Canada), contributing considerably toward its progress.

OPPENHEIMER, SIR ERNEST (1880–1957): S African mining magnate. Starting business in Kimberley in 1902, O. – who was baptized in middle life – became in 1929, chairman of De Beers' Consolidated Mines and a dominating figure in S African economic life.

OPPENHEIMER, FRANZ (1864–1943): German economist and sociologist. Originally a physician, his work confronted him with social problems and he became a sociologist. He created a theory of liberal (in contrast to Marxist) socialism, fusing agrarian reform and agricultural cooperation. His fight was directed chiefly against landed property, and he participated in several experiments to implement his theories. He was associated with the Zionist movement, and the MERHAVYAH cooperative settlement was founded in Palestine in 1911 according to his theories. In 1919, O. was appointed professor at Frankfort. After the Nazi advent to power, he settled in the US.

OPPENHEIMER, J. ROBERT (1904–1967): US physicist. He was professor of physics at the Univ. of California and the California Institute of Technology, 1929–47, and directed atomic energy research and the manufacture of the atom bomb during World War II. In 1947–66, he was director of the Institute

J. Robert Oppenheimer.

for Advanced Study, Princeton. O. served as chairman of the general advisory committee of the US atomic energy commission until 1954 when he was suspended following allegations of leftwing associations.

OPPENHEIMER, JOSEPH BEN ISSACHAR SÜSSKIND (Joseph Süss or Jüd Süss; c. 1698–1738); Financier. Appointed by Carl Alexander of Württemberg as his finance minister in 1732, he endeavored to consolidate the duchy's finances and free its ruler from dependence on grants from the estates. His "modern" financial methods aroused much opposition and after the death of the duke (1737), he was accused of embezzling state finances and hanged at Stuttgart, nominally for having sexual relations with Christian women. He refused to save his life by accepting baptism. His career is the subject of many books, including the novel *Jew Süss* by Lion Feuchtwanger.

OPPENHEIMER (or **OPPENHEIM**), **SAMUEL** (1630–1703): Philanthropist and Court Jew. The first Jew to settle in Vienna after the 1670 expulsion, he was Leopold I's agent and financier, helping to finance his wars with the Turks and the War of the Spanish Succession. In 1697, he was accused of conspiring to murder his rival Samson WERTHEIMER and imprisoned until vindicated. O. liberally supported the poor, Jewish scholars, and Judah Hasid's movement to settle in Palestine.

OPPERT: (1) *GUSTAV SOLOMON O.* (1836–1906): German orientalist. After working in the libraries of Oxford and Windsor, he became professor of Sanskrit at Madras. From 1894, he lectured in Dravidian languages at Berlin. He wrote on Indian philology and history. (2) *JULES O.* (1825–1905): German orientalist; brother of (1). An outstanding authority on Sanskrit, Persian and Assyriology, he settled in France, became professor of

Assyriology at the Collège de France, and participated in an expedition to the Middle East which identified the site of ancient Babylon. He was the first person to decipher Sumerian inscriptions and wrote the first Assyrian grammar. O. also wrote on Jewish topics and was active in French Jewish communal life.

ORACLE see **URIM AND THUMMIM**

ORAH HAYYIM see **JACOB BEN ASHER**

ORAL LAW see **LAW, ORAL**

ORAN: Town in Algeria. Its Jewish settlement, dating from the 13th cent., was swollen by refugees from Spain in the 14th–15th cents. The Spanish rulers excluded the Jews from the district after 1669, but the Turks permitted them to return in 1792. Although in 1870, the Jews received French citizenship, as elsewhere in Algeria, the town remained a hotbed of anti-Semitism. The Jewish population (numbering 30,000 in 1959) emigrated to France on the eve of Algeria independence (1962).

ORDINATION (Heb. *semikhah* = "placing" [of the hands]): The custom of o., whereby teachers selected their best pupils and conferred on them the title "rabbi" and permission to give decisions in matters of ritual and law, is ancient in Jewish life. The Talmud traces its origin back to Moses who conveyed the leadership to Joshua by placing his hands on Joshua's head. Any scholar who has been ordained has the right to ordain others. Jewish law, nevertheless, recognized the full authority of o. only when conferred in Palestine. For this reason, Babylonian o. was not fully acknowledged, and the recipient, whose authority was restricted to the administration of justice, received the title *rav* in place of the Palestinian *rabbi*. When the Palestinian center declined, the chain of o. was considered broken and even Palestinian authorities in the Middle Ages were not regarded as fully ordained. An attempt by Jacob BERAB to revive Palestinian o. in the 16th cent. failed after arousing a sharp controversy. A new form of o. was established in Germany during the 14th cent. by R Meir Ha-Levi of Vienna who required that all candidates for the post of rabbi should have received a *ketav semikhah* ("writ of o.") and been granted the title MORENU. The custom spread to Italy in the 15th cent. and was eventually adopted also in Poland and Lithuania where great scholars gave such documents to younger scholars whom they deemed worthy. Later, a distinction was made between giving *hattarat horaah* ("permission to lay down a decision") – called by analogy *semikhah* also – and the conferring of the title *morenu* which came to be an honorary title ascribed to a learned or respected person. Today, any applicant for the position of rabbi must possess a certificate of *hattarat horaah*, the wording of which is not definitely determined but which usually embodies the phrase

18th cent. Certificate of Ordination signed by Isaac Lampronti.

yoreh yoreh yadin yadin ("he may surely give a decision and may surely judge").

OREGON: US state. The first Jewish settlers arrived in O. territory in 1849. Mostly German immigrants, they settled in Albany, Corvallis, Salem, Oregon City, Eugene, Willamette, and PORTLAND. The first religious services were held in Jacksonville in 1856. O's first congregation, Temple Beth Israel, was founded in Portland in 1858. The city of Heppner was called after Henry Heppner, who in 1872, was the first permanent settler in the NE part of the state. Until recently, the only organized community ouside Portland was in Albany which maintained a synagogue from 1878 to 1910. O. has had a Jewish governor (Julius L. MEIER) and two Jewish senators. Today, outside Portland there are communities in Salem and Eugene numbering (1968) 200 and 360, respectively. Jewish pop. (1973): 8,685.

OREN (Fr. *orer*; Lat. *orare*): Among German Jews, to pray.

ORGAN: The Talmud states that the Second Temple was equipped with an organ (*magrephah*) possessing 10 pipes, each with 10 holes (*Arakhin* 10b). An o. was in use in the principal Prague synagogue in the 17th–18th cents., though it was not played during Sabbath. In the 19th cent., the question of the introduction of the o. into the synagogue became a main point of contention between the Reform and Orthodox elements in Judaism, the opposition basing itself on the general ban on instrumental music in worship outside the Temple, the objection to imitating Gentile methods, and the rabbinic prohibition of playing any instrument on the Sabbath. The use of the o. is now general in Reform and many Conservative congregations in the US and in most large Italian

Organ in former Leghorn synagogue.

and French synagogues. Elsewhere, it is occasionally used, e.g., for weddings and special services.

ORIENT, DER: German weekly journal, founded by Julius Fürst, and published 1840–51. The organ of German Jewish conservative circles, it included a historical and literary supplement, etc.

ORIENTALISTS, JEWISH: When Jews began to enter European academic life in the 19th cent., many turned their knowledge of Hebrew to account and took up the study of other Semitic languages. Moreover, Near Eastern cultures contributed to a better understanding of Judaism itself; and many Jewish o. specialized in problems of contact between Judaism and other oriental civilizations. The Jewish contribution is most notable in Arabic studies where Joseph and his son Hartwig Dérenbourg, G. Weil, S. Fraenkel, J. Barth, M. Schreiner, H. Reckendorf, I. Goldziher, H. Hirschfeld, G. Jacob, J. Horovitz, and E. Mittwoch belonged to the first rank of scholars; their tradition is continued by many Jewish Arabists. The study of the S Arabian inscriptions was largely made possible by the intrepid Jewish travelers J. Halévy and E. Glaser. Much material was also collected both in S Arabia and elsewhere by L. Burchardt. In Ethiopic studies, Jews played a smaller role, but besides L. Goldschmidt and E. Mittwoch, there was J. Faitlovich who studied the Falashas. At present, W. Leslau is the chief investigator of modern Ethiopian languages. In the beginning of Assyriology, J. Oppert and J. Halévy played an important part; later contributions were made by Morris Jastrow, S. Daiches, H. Zimmern (of Jewish origin), and several living scholars. The field of Semitic inscriptions owes much to the baptized Polish Jew M. Lidzbarski. The young discipline of Ugaritic is largely cultivated by Jews, including M. D. Cassuto, H. L. Ginsberg, and C. H. Gordon; Phoenician by Z. Harris. Aramaic studies are practically an auxiliary of Hebrew, and Jews, such as C. Levias, M. L. Margolis, M. Schlesinger, and Marcus Jastrow, have dominated them. In Egyptian research, few Jews have taken part; exceptions include A. Ember, who compared Egyptian and Semitic, and A. S. Yahuda, who studied Egyptian influence on Hebrew. In Persian, there were J. Darmesteter, A. Kohut, and Sir Aurel Stein. The scientific grammar of Turkish was created in the early 19th cent. by a young English Jew, A. L. Davids and much furthered by the travels and studies of A. Vambéry. Jews in Indian studies include G. S. Oppert, I. Scheftelowitz, and M. Winternitz. A number of Jews in the present generation are important in Chinese studies; these include Arthur Waley, whose translations have done much to make Chinese literature accessible. Near Eastern Oriental studies are intensively cultivated at the Hebrew Univ.

*ORIGEN (c. 184–c. 253 CE): Church Father in Alexandria. A prolific author, he compiled the *Hexapla*, a polygot Bible containing the original Hebrew, a Greek transliteration of the Hebrew, and the Greek translations of Aquila, Symmachus, the Septuagint, and Theodotion. He maintained contact with contemporary Jewish sages, to some of whom he refers.

ORIGINAL SIN: The doctrine that Adam's sin has remained an eternal imperfection in the human race preventing man from doing good. This doctrine is basic to Christianity which teaches that man can be redeemed only by the atoning death of Jesus. Judaism, on the other hand, does not consider man as born in a state of eternal sinfulness. He is ruled by both GOOD AND EVIL and has the power to choose. Judaism teaches that man needs God's help to overcome evil, but this help is axiomatic once man strives to do good.

ORLAH (Heb. "Uncircumcized Fruit"): Tenth tractate in the Mishnah order of *Zeraim*, consisting of 3 chapters. It has *gemara* in the Palestinian, but not the Babylonian, Talmud. It deals with the law forbidding the use of the fruit of trees or vineyards for the first three years after planting (Lev. 19:23).

ORLEANS: French town. There are records of a 6th cent. synagogue, but no traces of the community between the 6th and 10th cents. Thereafter, many distinguished rabbis (notably tosaphists) lived in O. Expulsions were decreed in 1182 and 1306. A Jewish settlement was reestablished on a small scale in the 19th cent. and numbered 500 in 1971.

Hannah Orloff: Mother and Child (Bronze).

ORLOFF, ḤANNAH (1888–1968): Sculptor. Born in the Ukraine, she moved to Palestine with her family at an early age and in 1910, settled in Paris. She sculpted a wide range of subjects including busts, figures, groups, animals, and a series illustrating the theme of motherhood.

ORMANDY, EUGENE (1899–): Conductor. Of Hungarian birth, he settled in the US in 1920, first as a violinist, then as a conductor. Since 1936, he has conducted the Philadelphia Orchestra.

ORPAH: Moabite wife of Chilion and sister-in-law of Ruth; she was dissuaded from returning to Judah with her mother-in-law, Naomi (Ruth 1).

ORPHANS AND ORPHANAGES: The care of o. was considered among the Hebrews a primary act of charity, God being termed "the father of orphans" (Ps. 68:6[5]), and special provision was made for their support (Deut. 14:29; 24:19, 21). Rabbinical law insisted not only on supporting the o. but even gave them special privileges: thus, even if wealthy, they were exempt from taxation for charitable purposes. In the Middle Ages, the number of Jewish o. was disproportionately high, owing to the large families and the recurrent devastation caused by massacres. Most larger communities had special charitable organizations for their care, known by such names a *Giddul Yetomim* (Heb. "Bringing up the o."). Generally, the o. would be taken into the home of a relative or charitable stranger, or foster-parents would be paid to bring them up. Their education was not neglected, the TALMUD TORAH societies primarily busying themselves with the fatherless. It was probably only in the 19th cent. that specific orphanages were instituted in larger communities. Some, such as the Jewish Orphanage in London (founded 1830), became model institutions.

ORT (initials of Russian *Obshtchestvo Remeslenovo Truda* i.e., "Society for the Encouragement of Handicraft"): Jewish organization for the develop-

Opening ceremony of a new Ort school in Tel Aviv, 1958.

ment of skilled trades and agriculture among the Jews. Founded in Russia in 1880 at the initiative of Baron Horace de Günzburg and other Jewish leaders, it established a network of vocational schools and cooperative workshops in Russia after the 1905 Revolution. After World War I, ORT extended its vocational programs throughout Central and E Europe with trade and farm schools, cooperative workshops, etc. The World War ORT Union was created in Berlin in 1921 to centralize all activities and an American ORT was founded in 1922 to provide financial aid. In 1933, the head office was transferred to Paris and ORT schools were set up throughout S America, Canada, Australia, and other areas, especially for European Jewish refugees. In 1943, the head office moved to Geneva and after World War II, ORT schools were founded in displaced persons' camps in Germany and E Europe (until 1949 and Poland again 1957) and activities were extended especially to Israel and N Africa. A Central Teachers' Training Institute was created at Anières, Switzerland. In 1975, the ORT program embraced 700 training units and over 70,000 students operating in 23 countries with an annual budget of $45,000,000. In Israel, there were over 380 schools and courses in 40 towns, with more than 48,000 pupils.

ORTA, GARCIA D' (c. 1500–1568): Portuguese Marrano physician. In 1534, he settled in Goa (India). His monograph on eastern botany, *Colloquios de simples e dragas* (1563), was the first scientific work published in Portuguese and laid the foundation for the study of tropical diseases. He was posthumously condemned by the Inquisition as a Judaizer.

ORTHODOXY: Term designating adherence to accepted traditional Judaism. The rise of REFORM JUDAISM in W Europe brought this term into use to describe those opposed to Reform. Leaders of O. in Central Europe in the 19th cent. included Moses Sopher (Hungary) and Azriel Hildesheimer (Germany). An important part of both Hungarian and German Orthodox Jewry (in the latter case primarily under the influence of Samson Raphael Hirsch) separated themselves from those Jewish communities where Reform had gained the ascendancy and organized separate and independent Orthodox communities. Nevertheless many of the Orthodox opposed this separation and believed that the battle of O. should be fought within the general community (the leader of this group in Germany was Seligmann Bär Bamberger). There was a certain distinction between E European O. and that of Germany and W Europe generally. The former uncompromisingly opposed all innovation, even in speech, dress, or manner of education; the latter, however, adopted the policy of preserving traditional life, while accepting modern dress, use of the vernacular, and general education. The term O. today designates those Jews who differ from the Conservative Reform by insisting on strict adherence to the laws of the SHULHAN ARUKH and the application of its principles and details to modern living as interpreted by leading rabbinic authorities.

OSE see **OZE**

OSHAYAH see **HOSHAYAH**

OSIRIS, DANIEL (1825–1908): French financier. Born in Bordeaux, he amassed a fortune in business and then devoted himself to philanthropy. The chief beneficiaries were the French state (to which he gave La Malmaison and part of the field of Waterloo), the Institut de France, and the Jewish community.

OSLO: Capital of NORWAY, with a Jewish community going back to 1876 when a cemetery was purchased. A congregation was organized in 1892. Many of the Jews of O. were deported to their death during the Nazi occupation 1940–5. Jewish pop. (1973): 700.

OSSUARIES: Small stone caskets closed by stone lids into which bones of the dead were put after the flesh had decayed, the o. being then redeposited in the tomb. The practice is referred to in the Mishnah (*Pesahim* 8:8, *Moed Katan* 1:5, etc). The vast majority of Jewish o. come from Palestine and date between the 2nd cent. BCE and the 3rd cent. CE. They are usually decorated, the chief motifs, possibly symbolic, being zigzags, rosettes, olive-branches, palms, wreaths, columns, and chalices. The names of those whose bones they contained were frequently inscribed in Hebrew, Aramaic, or Greek.

OSTRACON: Ancient potsherd bearing an inscription. Ostraca were used in ancient times for letters, receipts, etc. and hence frequently preserve valuable evidence on social and economic life, alphabetical and linguistic development, etc. Important finds in this respect have been made at Gezer, Samaria, and especially Lachish (the LACHISH LETTERS), etc. and, with Aramaic inscriptions, at Elath. Aramaic ostraca at Elephantine and those in Greek at Edfu (Egypt) have thrown light on Jewish

Stone ossuary from the environs of Jerusalem.

life in the Persian and Hellenistic-Roman Periods respectively.

OSTROG (Ostraha): Russian town. Jews lived there from the 16th cent., and it became one of the chief centers in Volhynia. The community was destroyed in the Chemielnicki massacres of 1648 but was slowly reconstituted and resumed its position of eminence. Prior to its destruction by the Nazis, the Jewish pop. numbered 8,000 (60%).

OSTROPOLER, HIRSCH (fl. 18th cent.): "Court jester" of various leading Hasidic rabbis, including Baruch of Medzibozh. His fluent jests reproved as well as amused, and some became part of Jewish folklore.

OSWIECIM see **AUSCHWITZ**

OTHNIEL: First judge in Israel, son of Kenaz (or a Kenizzite); of the tribe of Judah. In his youth, he captured Debir for his brother Caleb and in return received Caleb's daughter Achsah in marriage. Later, O. led the army which threw off the yoke of Cushan Rishathaim, an unidentified king of Aram-Naharaim who had enslaved Israel for eight years.

OTRANTO: Port in S Italy. Its Jewish community, going back legendarily to classical times, became an important intellectual center in the 10th cent. It continued to exist until the close of the Middle Ages, being revived after the general persecutions of 1494 in the kingdom of Naples until the expulsion of 1541. A separate synagogue was later maintained in Salonica by exiles from O.

OTTAWA: Federal capital of Canada. The first Jewish settlers arrived from Russia in 1857 but the growth of the community was slow until the early 20th cent. It has a Jewish Community Council (Va'ad ha-Ir) with representatives from its four congregations. There is a Modern Jewish School, a day school and a communal *talmud torah*. Jewish pop. (1973): 6,000.

OTTOLENGHI, GIUSEPPE (1838–1904): Italian general and politician. The first Italian Jew to serve on the General Staff, he participated in the Wars of the Risorgimento. later lecturing at the military academy and becoming tutor to the royal family. In 1902–3, he was minister of war.

OTTOMAN EMPIRE see **TURKEY**

OTZAR NEHMAD (Heb. "Thesaurus of Delight"): Hebrew annual of Jewish studies published by Isaac Blumenfeld in Vienna intermittently between 1856 and 1863.

OUMANSKY, CONSTANTIN (1902–1945): Russian diplomat. He was USSR ambassador to the US 1939–41, and during World War II directed the Soviet news agency Tass. He was killed in plane crash while ambassador to Mexico.

OUZIEL BEN ZION MEIR HAI see **UZIEL, BEN ZION MEIR HAI.**

OXFORD: English university city. Jews are first recorded there about 1130. They prospered in the 13th cent., not only lending money but also accommodating students in their stone houses. Between the 14th and 19th cents., a few Hebrew teachers, mostly apostate, found their way to O. A community was established only in 1840. Jews began to enter the university in the 1850's, the number increasing after the removal of religious tests in 1871, and the Jewish student society dates from the early 20th cent. Jewish pop. (1973): 600.

OZE (abbr. of Russian *Obshtchestvo Zdravookhranyenie Evreyev* i.e., "Jewish Health Society"): Society for the protection of the health of the Jewish population. founded in 1912 at St. Petersburg with the object of reducing Jewish mortality and disease. After World War I, O. societies were set up in various countries; these combined in an international federation in 1923. Since 1946, O. has been mainly active in Israel and N Africa.

PABLO CHRISTIANI see **CHRISTIANI, PABLO**

PACIFICO, DAVID ("Don Pacifico"; 1784–1854):
   Gibraltar-born merchant. His claims for compensation, when his property at Athens was pillaged by Greek anti-Semitic rioters in 1847, resulted in Lord Palmerston's famous *Civis Romanus sum* speech in the House of Commons ("A British subject shall feel that the strong arm of England will protect him"; it could not be tolerated that "because a man is of the Jewish persuasion, he is fair game").

PACIFISM see **PEACE**

PADUA: Italian city, with a Jewish community dating back to the mid-13th cent., reinforced by loan-bankers both from the south (Rome) and the north (Germany) in the 14th cent. The Jews did business with the university students. Some of them were, however, permitted to study medicine from the 14th cent., and in the 17th–18th cents., P. was one of the few places in Europe where Jews (some coming specially from Germany and Poland) were permitted to graduate as physicians. The ghetto, established in 1602, made the Jews easy victims of the plague of 1631. They had a narrow escape from massacre during the riots at the time of the siege of Buda, where Jews were alleged to be aiding the Turks (1684). In the 18th cent., the community was so reduced in wealth that it became bankrupt (1761). From 1829 to 1871, the Italian Rabbinical College

Detail from a Padua *ketubbah* of 1694.

was situated at P. The community numbers 200 (1970), and only one of its former synagogues is still in use.

PADUA, MEIR (Katzenellenbogen; known as "Maharam Padua"; 1482–1565): Talmudist. He was born in Germany, studied in Poland, and officiated as rabbi in Padua. An outstanding codifier, he was extensively consulted on halakhic problems.

PAGAN MARTYRS, ACTS OF: Series of Egyptian papyri, dating from the 2nd – early 3rd cent. CE, purporting to describe the trial of Alexandrian Greek leaders by Roman emperors. There is a strong anti-Jewish tendency, and one method adopted of discrediting the emperors is by ascribing to them a pro-Jewish attitude. Some of the fragments detail accusations brought before Claudius against Agrippa I by Alexandrians.

PAKISTAN: Republic in British Commonwealth, formerly part of India. Isolated Jews lived in the area in the Middle Ages, but organized settlement began only in the 19th cent. under British rule. The Jewish community is now much diminished, partly because of the negative attitude of the P. government toward the state of Israel. The Jewish pop. made up partly of BENE ISRAEL, is 250 (1973), mostly in Karachi and Peshawar.

PALACHE: Moroccan family, later associated with Holland. *SAMUEL P.* (d. 1616) was Moroccan envoy in Holland and partly responsible for the sanction of Jewish worship in that country. His brother, Joseph, and his nephew, David, subsequently succeeded him in his diplomatic position, while others of the family were Moroccan diplomatic agents in Denmark and Constantinople. Samuel was ancestor of *ISAAC P.* (1858–1926), *Ḥakham* of the Portuguese community in Amsterdam, whose son *JUDA LION P.* (1886–1944) was professor of Semitics at the Univ. of Amsterdam and was killed by the Nazis.

PALE OF SETTLEMENT: 25 provinces of Czarist Russia (in Poland, Lithuania, White Russia, Ukraine, Bessarabia, and Crimea) where Jews were permitted permanent residence. Permission to live outside its confines was granted only to certain groups, e.g. members of the liberal professions with a high school diploma, big businessmen, skilled artisans, and ex-CANTONISTS. The fate of the Jews found outside the P. without permission depended on the arbitrary decision of the local governor. The system was instituted in 1791 by decree of Catherine II. The borders were arbitrarily restricted from time to time, e.g. by the oppressive "Statute Concerning the Jews" of 1835. In 1882, under the MAY LAWS, Jews were excluded from rural areas inside the P. As a result of these restrictions, Jewish economic development was severely hampered. The P. was abolished in effect in Aug. 1915, and legally in Mar. 1917.

PALEOGRAPHY see **ALPHABET: WRITING**

PALESTINE: The name properly denotes the land of the PHILISTINES, first being applied to its hinterland by the Greeks. The present P. was termed "Palestinian Syria" in classical antiquity, the latter component being omitted in due course. It is probable that the name P. was imposed by the Romans on the former Judea in order to minimize the Jewish association of the country. P. was originally termed in Hebrew [*Eretz*] *Canaan*, later *Eretz Israel*. For history of P., see under ISRAEL.

PALESTINE ECONOMIC CORPORATION (PEC): A public company incorporated in the US in 1926 as the instrument of American private capital for the development of the Jewish Homeland. It is a vehicle through which Americans furnish material aid on a strictly business basis to productive Israel enterprises. It engages in developing and financing enterprises of a banking, credit, industrial, land, agricultural, and utility nature.

PALESTINE ELECTRIC COMPANY: Company founded by Pinhas RUTENBERG in 1923. After establishing power stations in Haifa, Tel Aviv, and Tiberias, the PEC in 1926 obtained a concession for harnessing the waters of the Yarmuk and Jordan rivers for the production of cheap electricity. A plant was constructed at Naharayim in 1932, but destroyed by the Arab Legion during the 1948 War. Electricity in Israel is now run by the government-owned Israel Electric Corporation. Consumption rose from 246 million kwh. in 1948 to 4,093 million kwh. in 1967–8.

PALESTINE EXPLORATION FUND: British society, founded in 1867. Under its auspices, the first modern map of Palestine was made in 1874–8, together with a complete archeological survey. It was active in the excavations of Jerusalem 1894–7, the city mounds of the Shephelah 1899–1900, the mound of Gezer 1902–9, Beth Shemesh 1911–12, and the Ophel in Jerusalem 1923–7. Later it collaborated in the excavations at Jericho. Its Quarterly is a primary source for Palestinian ARCHEOLOGY and history.

PALESTINE FOUNDATION FUND see **KEREN HA-YESOD**

PALESTINE JEWISH COLONIZATION ASSOCIATION see **JEWISH COLONIZATION ASSOCIATION; PICA**

PALESTINE LAND DEVELOPMENT COMPANY see **ISRAEL LAND DEVELOPMENT COMPANY**

PALESTINE OFFICE: First institution founded by the World Zionist Organization (Jaffa, 1908) for the supervision of practical work in Palestine; its director was Arthur RUPPIN. It became the central institution of the Jewish community in the country, financing settlement, organizing a Hebrew school system, and looking after Palestinian Jewry's material needs during World War I. It was dissolved in 1918, its functions devolving on the Zionist Commission.

PALESTINE TALMUD see **TALMUD**

PALGRAVE (originally **COHEN**), **SIR FRANCIS** (1788–1861): British historian. After changing his faith and adopting his wife's name, he became deputy keeper of public records and was the first English scientific historian resorting consistently to original record-sources. His sons included *FRANCIS TURNER P.* (1824–1897), professor of poetry at Oxford and compiler of *The Golden Treasury of English Songs and Lyrics; SIR REGINALD P.* (1829–1904), clerk of the House of Commons; *SIR ROBERT HARRY INGLIS P.* (1827–1919), editor of the *Dictionary of Political Economy*; and *WILLIAM GIFFORD P.* (1826–1888), oriental traveler, missionary, and diplomat.

PALLENBERG, MAX (1877–1934): Actor. Playing from 1914 under Reinhardt in Berlin, he became one of Germany's outstanding comedians, particularly in plays by Molière and Hauptmann. His wife was Fritzi MASSARY.

PALLIÈRE, AIMÉ (1873–1950): French thinker. Intended for the priesthood, he became interested in Hebrew and Judaism with which he eventually identified himself, without formally becoming converted. He worked in behalf of the Jewish community and wrote several books including the autobiographical *Unknown Sanctuary* and *The Raised Veil*. P. helped influence French Liberal Jews toward traditionalism and Zionism and shared the Jewish plight under the Nazi occupation. Thereafter, he recommended the practice of the Catholic ritual, although maintaining his connection with and belief in the teachings of Judaism.

PALMA: Capital of MAJORCA. Its Jewish community, going back to Moslem and perhaps Roman times, was destroyed in the massacres of 1391; reconstituted, it was again wiped out in 1435 in consequence of a Ritual Murder accusation. P. nevertheless remained the main center of crypto-Jews or CHUETAS. Despite the persecutions of the Inquisition (especially in 1691) this element still survives.

Palmaḥ soldiers of the Negev Brigade.

PALMAḤ (abbr. of Heb. *peluggot maḥatz* "shock companies"): The striking arm of the HAGANAH. Set up by the *Haganah* high command in May, 1941, it was maintained underground until May, 1948, thereafter becoming an organic part of the Israel Defense Army. It was commanded by Yitzḥak SADEH 1941–3, Yigal ALLON 1943–8, and Uri Brenner during the WAR OF INDEPENDENCE. Originally established to assist the British in opposing the German advance, the connection was dissolved when the immediate threat passed. The *P.* continued, nevertheless, to exist as an underground permanently-mobilized force executing tasks imposed by the central command of the *Haganah*. Its units (6 companies in 1942; 11 in 1948) were dispersed throughout Palestinian labor settlements and their time was divided between work and training. *P.* numbered a few hundred men in 1942, 2,500 in 1945, and 5,500 in 1948; much of its strength was drawn from the left-wing element of the population. In 1945–7, it concentrated on the struggle against the British notably by the organization of HAAPALAH, by defending settlement projects, and by armed actions against the British. In the War of Independence, the *P.* assumed a foremost role in the military operations; it was organized into the Harel Brigade (under Y. Tabenkin) originally on the Jerusalem front, the Yiphtaḥ Brigade (under Y. Allon; later under S. Cohen) originally on the northern front, the Negev Brigade in the S, and later the Golani Brigade. In Nov. 1948, Gen. Dori, chief of the Israel General Staff, ordered the disbanding of the *P.* 75 members of *P.* fell in action in 1945–7, and 1,000 in 1947–8.

PALMYRA see **TADMOR**

PANAMA: Central American Republic. The first Jews there were Sephardim who arrived from the Caribbean Islands in the mid-19th cent. and played a leading role in trade and the sugar industry. A second Jewish group originated from Middle Eastern countries, and a third from E Europe, mostly Poland and Rumania. The majority of the 2,000 (1973) Jews live in Panama City and Colon. The official body is the Comite Representativo de la Sociedad Israelita.

PANN (PFEFFERMAN), ABEL (1883–1963): Painter. He was born in Russia, trained in Vienna and Paris, and in 1913, settled in Palestine where he was one of the first teachers at the BEZALEL art school. His paintings depicted Bible stories, Israel (especially Yemenite) settlers, etc., adapting a romantic tradition to a modern oriental background.

PAPAL BULLS see **POPE**

PAPAL STATES see **POPE; ROME**

PAPERS see **PRESS**

PAPPA (fl. latter 4th cent.): Babylonian amora. A pupil of Rava and Abbaye he removed to Neresh, near Sura, after the death of the former and established an academy there. His colleague, Huna son of R Joshua, went with him to serve as *Resh Kallah*. P. was a brewer and amassed great wealth, which he spent liberally, supporting many students. His own approach to rabbinical controversy was extremely conciliatory.

PAPPENHEIM, BERTHA (1859–1936): German Jewish women's leader. After directing a Jewish orphanage at Frankfort-on-Main 1881–93, she founded the Society of Jewish Women and was its president 1904–24. P. translated Yiddish classics into German and wrote memoirs and essays on social work.

PAPPUS AND JULIANUS (fl. early 2nd cent. CE): Patriots. According to talmudic tradition, they established banks to assist wayfarers in Jerusalem. They were captured by the Romans at Laodicea in Syria, having apparently been among the leaders of the Jewish rising against Trajan (115–8 CE). According to one account, their execution was averted by the death of Trajan on *Adar* 12, which was therefore declared a semi-holiday.

PAPYRUS: Paper made from reed-like plants, and bearing on it a ms document. The chief area of the discovery of ancient papyri is Egypt, but a few have also been found in Palestine. The Egyptian papyri of Jewish interest include documents in Greek, Aramaic, Hebrew, and Arabic. Aramaic p. from ELEPHANTINE (5th cent. BCE) throw much light on its contemporary Jewish garrison community. The vast majority of Egyptian papyri of Jewish interest (i.e., written by or concerning Jews) are in Greek and belong to the 2nd cent. BCE – 7th cent. CE; these include petitions, proclamations, ordinances, court and municipal proceedings, wills, official correspondence, contracts, registers of people and property, tax-lists, receipts, and personal correspondence. Among the important papyri may be mentioned the so-called. Acts of the PAGAN MARTYRS (Greek) and the NASH P. (Hebrew) containing the decalogue and *shema*. The Greek papyri of Egypt have also thrown much light on Jewish life there. A corpus of Jewish papyri from Egypt has been edited by Avigdor Tcherikover (1957 ff.).

PARABLE see **FABLE**

PARADISE see **HEAVEN**

PARAGUAY: S American republic. Jews from Poland began to enter P. in 1912. Subsequent immigrants were of Sephardi or German origin, but many later left for Argentina. Jewish pop. (1973): 1,200, 90% Ashkenazi, of whom most live in the capital Asuncion. The Alianza Israelita represents the entire community.

PARAH (Heb. "Heifer"): Fourth tractate in the Mishnah order of *Tohorot*, containing 12 chapters. It has *gemara* neither in the Babylonian nor Palestinian Talmud. It deals with the regulations concerning the Red Heifer (Num. 19).

PARAH ADUMMAH see **RED HEIFER**

PARAN: Desert ("wilderness") in the Negev, the home of Ishmael. It was traversed by the Israelites after they left Mt. Sinai. It was apparently situated NE of the traditional Mt. Sinai, S of Kadesh, extending to the shores of the Gulf of Elath and the Arabah. Its name was revived for the former Wadi Jerafi which crosses the Israel Negev.

PARASHAH (Heb. "section"): Denotation of a passage in the Bible dealing with a single topic: (1) in the writing of books ("open" or "closed" according as to whether the next p. is begun after a space or in the following line); and (2) in the reading of the Pentateuch where it denotes the weekly portion (SIDRA) or, especially, the smaller passages read to or by each person called up to the Reading of the Law.

Abel Pann.

Paris: Memorial to the six million Jewish victims of the Nazis.

PARASHIYYOT, THE FOUR: Special portions read on the Sabbaths preceding Passover. In mishnaic times, the regular readings on these Sabbaths were suspended; today the special portions are read from a second Scroll of the Law as *maphtir* and followed by an appropriate *haphtarah*. The portions are (1) *Shekalim* (Exod. 30:11–16), with the injunction to bring contributions for the repair of the Temple; read on the Sabbath preceding the second day of *Adar*; (2) *Zakhor* (Deut. 25:17–19), on the extermination of Amalek; read on the Sabbath before Purim (Haman being traditionally of Amalekite origin); (3) *Parah* (Num. 19:1–22), a warning on general purity as a preparation for the paschal sacrifice; read on the last (or last but one) Sabbath in *Adar*; and (4) *Ha-Hodesh* (Exod. 12:1–20) on Passover regulations; read on the Sabbath preceding *Nisan* 2.

PARDES: Mnemonic word formed by the initials of the four main streams of biblical interpretation current in the 13th cent. viz: *peshat* (literal meaning), *remez* (allegorical – often philosophical), *derash* (aggadic), and *sod* (mystical). BAHYA BEN ASHER based his Bible commentary on all four methods, which were used also by Christian scholars.

PARDES HANNAH: Israel village in N Sharon. It was founded in 1929 by the PICA society on land that was later turned over to the settlers, who originated mostly from E and Central Europe. As a result of the citrus boom in the 1930's, P. H. expanded quickly. Various educational establishments are situated there. In 1969, P. H. merged with KARKUR. Pop. of P. H.-Karkur (1972): 13,821.

PARDO: Sephardi family, originally from Salonica and subsequently found in Italy, Holland, England, and America. *DAVID P.* (1719–1792), born in Venice, was rabbi at Spalato before settling in Jerusalem. He published numerous commentaries on talmudic and rabbinic literature, as well as liturgical poetry. *SAUL P.* (d. 1708), known in business circles as Saul Brown, was the first known *hazzan* of the Jewish community of New York.

PAREVEH: Yiddish expression originating in E Europe, describing a foodstuff which is considered neutral in its relation to milk or meat foods, and may hence be eaten with either.

PARHON, SOLOMON (fl. 12th cent.): Hebrew lexicographer. Born in Aragon, he studied with Judah Ha-Levi and Abraham Ibn Ezra. In 1160, he completed at Salerno (S Italy) a biblical lexicon *Mahberet he-Arukh* with a grammatical introduction.

PARIS: Capital of France. Jews lived there in Roman times and a settlement is recorded throughout the early Middle Ages. Persecutions took place from the 12th cent., and the community was expelled in 1182–98. In 1240, the DISPUTATION of Paris was followed by the public burning of the Talmud. The community underwent further hardships and like the rest of French Jewry, was banished in 1306 and 1394. In the 17th–18th cents., there was an infiltration of Jews from Bordeaux, Avignon, Alsace, etc. At the time of the Revolution, there were c. 500 Jews in P. Settlement being henceforth unrestricted, in the course of the next century there was a considerable influx, and by 1880 the total had risen to c. 40,000. Many of the newcomers, who were from Alsace and Lorraine, established themselves in the city's commercial life, and many Jews achieved prominence in politics, literature, art, the theater, etc. From 1882, P. attracted many emigrants from Russia, while Jews from N Africa and from the former Ottoman Empire were also drawn to the Metropolis. The DREYFUS AFFAIR stirred up the city at the end of the 19th cent., but the anti-Semitism it aroused subsequently abated. Over 70,000 Jews from E Europe settled in P. between the two World Wars as did many German Jews after 1933, making a total Jewish pop. of c. 200,000 in 1939. Many left with the Nazi occupation, and at least 50,000 died in the death camps. The current (1975) community of c. 300,000 contains a variety of groups of whom many are rapidly assimilating and becoming increasingly indifferent to Judaism although the recent influx of Jews from N. Africa, especially Algeria, has tended to provide a counterbalance. P. boasts many monumental synagogues and a wealth of communal institutions, including the administrative center of the ALLIANCE ISRAELITE UNIVERSELLE and the Central CONSISTORY.

PARKER, DOROTHY ROTHSCHILD (1893–1967): US poet and short-story writer noted for her ironic wit. Her verse has been collected in *Not So Deep as a Well* and prose in *Here Lies*.

*PARKES, JAMES WILLIAM (1896–): British clergyman and historian. His special interest in Jewish-Christian relations has expressed itself in a number of Jewish historical studies including *The Conflict of the Church and the Synagogue*, *The Jew in the Medieval Community*, *An Enemy of the*

Baron Lionel de Rothschild takes his seat in the House of Commons, July 20, 1858.
(From *The Illustrated London News*).

People: *Anti-Semitism*, *A History of Palestine* and an autobiography. His library on relations between the Jewish and non-Jewish Worlds was transferred to Southampton University in 1964.

PARLIAMENT, JEWS IN: The earliest instance of a Jew in a modern representative assembly is probably Francis SALVADOR, elected to the Provincial Congress of S Carolina in 1775, and later to the General Assembly of the state. In 1797, two Amsterdam Jews were elected members of the Dutch National Assembly and thereafter, Jews were uninterruptedly active in Dutch political life. In Italy, Moses Formiggini represented Milan in the Legislative Assembly of the Cisalpine Republic, and there were other instances in various parts of Europe during the Napoleonic Period. A. Crémieux was the first Jewish member of the French Chamber of Deputies (in 1842) and after the revolution of 1848, Jews were elected to parliamentary assemblies all over Europe. The controversy over the admission of Jews to the English House of Commons, which began in 1830, ended with the admission of Baron Lionel de Rothschild in 1858, his son becoming the first Jewish member of the House of Lords in 1885. In the British dominions, admission to Parliament was somewhat earlier. Thus, in Canada, though Ezekiel Hart was unable to take his seat in the Quebec legislature in 1808, a bill of 1831–2 extended to Jews the same rights as to Christians. In S Africa, Saul Solomon represented Cape Town in Parliament from 1854. The first Jewish M. P. in modern Italy was Giuseppe Finzi (1881) and the first Jewish senators were appointed in 1876 (Isaac Artom, Tullo Massarani).

In Russia, Jews sat in the First Duma in 1906. In the US, the first Jewish member of the House of Representatives was David L. Yulee (1845) who was also the first Jewish senator. For Israel p., see KNESSET.

PARMA: Italian city, formerly capital of a duchy.

Jews lived in the city of P. in the 15th–16th cents., but thereafter, were restricted to a few of the rural centers, the most important being Busseto. In the 19th cent., a community, now insignificant, was again formed in the capital. P. is noted for the great collection of Hebrew books and mss in the Palatine Library, the nucleus of which was acquired from G. B. de ROSSI. Jewish pop. (1969): 60.

PARNAS (Heb. from *parnes* "to foster, support"):

The chief synagogue functionary. He was at first vested with both religious and administrative functions, but by the 16th cent., the former passed to the religious leadership. It has been an elected office since that time.

PARNOSSE (Heb. *parnasah*): Sustenance, livelihood.

PAROKHET (Heb.): The curtain of the sanctuary in the wilderness, made by BEZALEL, of scarlet, purple, and fine linen, with a woven design which which included cherubim (Exod. 26:31). Josephus gives a more extended description. The term is now applied by the Ashkenazim to the curtain hanging before the Ark in the synagogue.

PARSIISM (also known as Mazdaism): The ZOROASTRIAN religion. According to this, man's task is the fight for the light and the good; evil is conquered not by ascetic abnegation but by truthfulness, justice, and productive work as well as by

Embroidered *parokhet* by Leah Ottolenghi. Italy, 1699. (Jewish Museum, NY).

strict attention to ritual purity. The doctrine of P. also includes belief in an individual judgment after death, a final era of redemption, and the appearance of savior-types (*soshants*). Isaiah (45:6–7; 50:10–11) combats these beliefs, but there was probably some influence of P. on Judaism (e.g. in its conception of angels and demons). In later talmudic times and subsequently, persecutions of Judaism by the *Magi* or "fire-worshipers" — as they were called — were not infrequent.

PARTHIA: Empire of Iranic people, fl. 3rd cent. BCE–226 CE. It ruled over the vast mass of the Jewish population in Mesopotamia, Babylonia and Media. The Parthians restored Antigonus Mattathias to the throne of Judah in 40 BCE. The Jews of the Roman Empire looked on P. as their future savior; in P. itself, the Jews enjoyed considerable autonomy under the exilarch. It was under the rule of P. that the famous rabbinic schools in Mesopotamia began to flourish.

PARTISANS: National guerilla movements in World War II. The scale and size of Jewish participation is difficult to determine, especially as many Jews had to suppress their identity for various reasons. Nevertheless, there is strong evidence that the percentage of Jewish p. was disproportionately high (their number has been estimated at 20,000) and many were honored for their services after liberation. Jews were active in all the conquered countries and Jewish partisan companies were organized in areas with a dense Jewish population. Such groups were already active in White Russia and Polesye in 1941, and by 1942–3, in Lithuania, Poland, the Bialystok region, Lublin, etc. When the Soviet partisan movement was organized, it absorbed almost all the Jewish companies in its zone. The Jewish p. had a function additional to those of their non-Jewish comrades, namely, to protect defenseless Jews – old people, women and children. With this object, they organized family camps in the forests, keeping them supplied and defended.

PARTITION: Term applied to the division of Palestine into autonomous areas proposed at various times before the establishment of the state of Israel. The p. proposal advanced by the PEEL COMMISSION in 1937 was at first accepted by the British government and evoked deep differences of opinion within the Zionist movement. Its opposers objected to any additional contraction within the historic frontiers of the country, while its protagonists held that the establishment of a Jewish state, even in part of the country, would help to solve difficult problems facing the Jewish people. The 18th Zionist Congress (1937) empowered the Jewish Agency Executive to negotiate on the basis of p., but the Council of the Jewish Agency immediately placed reservations on the resolution and requested a further effort to come to terms with the Arabs. The British proposal was received coldly by the League of Nations. In Nov. 1937, the British government appointed the Woodhead Commission to formulate practical proposals for p., obviating the population transfers envisaged by the Peel Commission. The Commission in 1938 submitted three different proposals, none of which was satisfactory, and the subject became academic as a result of the MacDonald WHITE PAPER and World War II. However, the concept of Jewish sovereignty had become current and the Zionist movement in its BILTMORE PROGRAM of 1942 and London conference of 1945 demanded a Jewish State in Palestine. Nevertheless, in 1946, following the report of the Anglo-American Joint Committee, the Jewish Agency Executive agreed to negotiate on the basis of p. A majority of the 1947 UN Committee on Palestine advocated a program of p. coupled with economic union – the minority, a federative state. The UN Assembly on Nov. 29, 1947,

A group of Jewish Partisans.

adopted the majority proposal with minor emendations. The ultimate p. of Palestine was largely a result of military operation and different from the original scheme; Jewish Jerusalem and the Jerusalem Corridor, W Galilee (including Nazareth), Jaffa, and certain sections of the Negev were incorporated in Israel, the proposed Arab state never came into being, the Arab areas being taken over by Jordan and Egypt, and the recommended economic union was not implemented. The changes were incorporated in the RHODES AGREEMENTS.

PARTNERSHIP: This includes both joint ownership and commercial p. A p. is formed by joint acquisition or by inheritance. It can be dissolved on demand either by physical partition if each share will be of useful size or, if not, by one partner offering the other the choice of buying or selling a half share at a named figure. Commercial p., according to Maimonides, is a development of joint ownership and the partners must first become actual joint owners of the invested capital. Other opinions regard symbolic consent (see Ruth 4:7) or verbal agreement as sufficient. Where there is no specific arrangement, capital gains are shared equally "since business capacity is as important as capital." Once both parties are operating, only death or consent can dissolve the p. before the end of the agreed term.

PARTOS, ÖDÖN (1909–): Israel violist and composer. Born in Hungary, he settled in Tel Aviv in 1938. He is leader of the viola section of the Israel Philharmonic Orchestra and directs the Tel Aviv Music Conservatoire. His compositions include *Song of Praise* for viola and orchestra and the symphonic fantasy *En Gev*.

PARVEH see **PAREVEH**

PASCHAL LAMB see **PASSOVER**

PASCIN (formerly **PINCAS**), **JULES** (1885–1930): Painter. Born in Bulgaria of Sephardi parents, he went to Vienna to study art. He worked in Munich and in 1905, moved to Paris, although traveling extensively and living in the US 1914–22. A brilliant and passionate satirist who excelled more as a

Woodcuts depicting the Passover Meal and Paschal Sacrifice. (Venice, c. 1480).

draftsman and etcher than as a painter he was attracted by the exotic, the erotic, and the highly colored. P., who remained eccentrically attached to Judaism, committed suicide.

PASKEN (Yidd. based on the Hebrew *pasok*, i.e., "decide," "declare the law"): To give a decision on a religious question.

PASSAIC: City in New Jersey, US. Individual Jews lived there during the Revolutionary War and after, but no congregation existed until 1893. Nearly all the community is of E European origin. Its Jewish Community Council was founded in 1933. In 1973, P. had 9,200 Jews supporting six major synagogues and a hospital.

PASSFIELD WHITE PAPER see **WHITE PAPER, PASSFIELD**

PASSOVER (Heb. *pessah*): First of the three festivals of pilgrimage to Jerusalem, it begins on *Nisan* 15. The traditional interpretation of the Hebrew name is from the root "pass over" (Exod. 12:13), but some modern scholars take it from the root "dance" or "leap," connecting it with an ancient spring-festival. The festival is observed for 7 days (8 outside Israel). Its origin is probably double — the anniversary of the Exodus and the festival of the barley-harvest (expressed by the bringing of the OMER). Properly, the name applies only to the paschal sacrifice and the first day, the entire festival being called the Feast of the Unleavened Bread. The first and last day (outside Israel, the first two and last two days) are festivals, and the intermediate period, *Hol ha-Moed*. On the eve of the festival, all LEAVEN (*hametz*) is cleared from the home, and it is prohibited to eat or possess leaven for the duration of the festival during which only unleavened bread (*matzah*) is consumed. In Temple times, the paschal lamb was slaughtered on the eve of the festival and eaten on the first night. After the Destruction, the home celebration (SEDER) of the first night (in the Diaspora — two nights) was retained and the HAGGADAH read. In the additional service on the first day, a prayer for dew is inserted. Full HALLEL is recited on the first day (two days in the Diaspora) but only half *Hallel* during the rest of the festival, as the Egyptians — also creatures of God — were traditionally drowned on the seventh day. The Song of Songs is read by Ashkenazim on the intermediate Sabbath.

PASSOVER, SECOND (or Lesser Passover; Heb. *pesah Sheni*): Passover sacrifice offered on *Iyyar* 14 by anyone who had been ritually impure or absent on a journey on the occasion of the PASSOVER festival the previous month. The Talmud extended the privilege to forced converts from Judaism, and to those who had erred as to the date.

PASTERNAK: (1) *BORIS P.* (1890–1960): Russian lyric poet of the symbolic school; son of (2). His works include *Lieutenant Schmidt, Dr. Zhivago*, short stories, criticism, translations (Goethe, Shakespeare, etc.) and an autobiography *Safe Conduct*. P., who was baptized, was awarded the 1958 Nobel Prize in Literature after the publication of *Dr. Zhivago*, but he refused to accept the award. His play *Blind Beauty* dealt with the abolition of serfdom in Russia. (2) *LEONID OSSIPOVICH P.* (1862–1945): Russian painter of genre-subjects excelling in the colored representation of light and shade. In 1905, he was elected to the St. Petersburg Academy of Arts. In 1921, P. left Russia, living in Germany and England. His paintings include portraits of Tolstoy's family and of distinguished Jews (Bialik, Aḥad Ha-Am, Einstein, etc.).

PATAI, JOSEPH (1882–1953): Hungarian writer, poet, journalist, and translator. He was founder and editor of the literary monthly *Mult és Jövö* which he devoted to the Hebrew renascence and Zionism. He translated Hebrew verse and published studies on Hebrew poetry. His son *RAPHAEL PATAI* (1910–) was an anthropologist and editor who in 1936 received the first Ph.D. degree awarded by the Hebrew University. He settled in America, taught folklore and ethnology, and published many studies, including *Hebrew Myths* (with Robert Graves). He edited the *Encyclopedia of Zionism and Israel.*

PATER SYNAGOGAE (Lat. "Father of the synagogue"): Title recorded in Greek and Roman inscriptions of Jewish origin in the Classical Period. They are found in the Diaspora (especially Rome) but not in Palestine. If not an honorary title, the term indicates the holder of an office, but the exact definition is unclear. The term *mater synagogae* ("mother of the synagogue") also occurs.

PATERSON: City in New Jersey, US. Its Jewish community was founded in the 1840's by immigrants from Bohemia, Germany, and Hungary. The first congregation in the state (Reform), B'nai Yeshurun, was organized in P. in 1847. P.'s first Orthodox congregation, B'nai Israel, was formed in 1886 at the beginning of the E European influx. The Conservative Temple Emanu-El, the largest congregation in P., was founded in 1904. The Jewish Community Council was established in 1933. In 1970, P. had 15,000 Jews.

Leonid Pasternak: *Whither?* (Drawing).

PATRIA: French ship to which 1,771 Jewish "illegal" immigrants in Haifa harbor were transferred in 1940 by the British mandatory authority for deportation to Mauritius. On Nov. 25, 1940, an explosion took place on the ship, which sank with the loss of 202 immigrants and 50 members of the crew and police. The explosion was reportedly the work of the Jewish resistance, aimed at delaying the deportation.

PATRIARCHATE see **NASI**

PATRIARCHS (Heb. *Avot*): Name given to the three ancestral fathers of the Jewish people — ABRAHAM, ISAAC, and JACOB. The p. were the recipients of the Divine revelation of MONOTHEISM and of the promise of the land of ISRAEL for their descendants.

*PATTERSON, JOHN HENRY (1867–1947): British soldier. He commanded the ZION MULE CORPS (1915–6) and later the Jewish Battalion which he led in Palestine.

PAUKER, ANA (1890–1960): Rumanian communist leader. The daughter of a rabbi, she joined the Communist Party in 1920 and was imprisoned 1936–41. One of the organizers of the Democratic Front in 1944, she was Rumanian foreign minister from 1947 but was discredited in the 1952 purges, also losing her position as member of the Politburo and of the party secretariat.

PAUL (d. c. 65 CE): Name adopted by Saul of Tarsus after his conversion to CHRISTIANITY. A Jew born in a hellenistic city in Asia Minor, he had some familiarity with Greek philosophy and with the mystery cults popular at the beginning of the Christian era. He is said to have studied in Jerusalem under R Gamaliel the Elder, but his writings show little comprehension of Pharisaic Judaism, and his early zeal in persecuting members of the new Christian sect contrasts with Gamaliel's tolerant attitude. However, as a result of a vision, according to the New Testament, P. himself became a Christian and contributed greatly to the development of a distinctive Christian theology. As the "apostle to the Gentiles," he brought into the young church thousands of new converts who did not adopt Jewish loyalty or Jewish observance, as converts of the other disciples had done. His thinking is dominated by the doctrine of ORIGINAL SIN. All men, he held, were contaminated by the guilt of Adam and can be freed from it only by faith in the atonement consummated by the death of JESUS. The Torah is not (as the Jewish teachers held) a means of achieving righteousness but a Divine measuring rod which reveals to man his hopeless situation since no one can properly obey it. With the atonement made by Jesus, the Law has been abrogated. P. also taught that those who believe in Jesus are "the true Israel" and that Divine election of "Israel after the flesh" was invalidated when the Jews rejected Jesus. He, however, retained an emotional attachment to the Jewish people and hoped that in the future they would accept the Gospel and be reinstated as God's chosen. There is no clear reference to P. in talmudic literature, but many rabbinic utterances must be understood as answers to the Pauline doctrine.

*PAUL: Name adopted by several popes. *PAUL IV* (officiated 1555–9) who, as Cardinal Caraffa, had inspired the anti-Jewish policy of the Catholic reaction, issued in 1555 the bull *cum nimis absurdum* which initiated the ghetto system in Rome and the papal dominions. P. was responsible for the burning of the Marrano refugees in Ancona in 1556. *PAUL VI* (officiated 1963–) visited the Middle East in 1964 and during his stay in Israel was officially received by President Shazar at Megiddo and Jerusalem. The Second Vatican Council, convened by his predecessor John XXIII, concluded during his reign and among various documents adopted a schema on the attitude of the Church to the Jews.

PAUL OF BURGOS see **SANTA MARIA, PAUL DE**

PAYTAN see **PIYYUT; POETRY**

PE: Seventeenth letter of the Hebrew alphabet; numerical value 80. It is equivalent to a *p* sound (פ), but without a dagesh (פ) is pronounced as *f*.

PEACE: The Hebrew term for p. is *shalom*, implying also completeness and well-being: the common Jewish greeting is "peace unto you." The vision of ultimate p. was given to the world as an essential element of the messianic ideal by the Hebrew prophets (cf. Micah 4:3; Is. 2:4; 9:6). The last of the EIGHTEEN BENEDICTIONS is an invocation for p. P. is enhanced in the world by scholars (*Berakhot*, 64*a*), and the rabbis stated that God, one of whose names is p. (*Shabbat* 10*b*), knows no vessel more full of blessing for Israel (*Uktzin* 3:11). Yet the traditional Jewish ideal was not pacifist, and it was always conceded that war can in some circumstances be justified. In modern times, Jews, by virtue of their religious tradition as well as of their unique international position, have played an important part in international peace-movements. Jewish Nobel Peace Prize Winners include T. M. C. ASSER, who represented Holland at international p. conferences, A. H. FRIED, founder of the German Peace Society and the French lawyer-statesman René CASSIN. A society for the abolition of war was founded in 1869 by Eduard LÖWENTHAL. I. S. (Jan) BLOCH gave the first impetus to the establishment of the Hague Peace Tribunal, and S. LEVINSON suggested the Briand-Kellogg Pact of 1929 outlawing war.

PEACE-OFFERING: SACRIFICE, in the form of cattle or sheep, offered as (1) a thanksgiving; (2) in fulfilment of a vow; (3) a free-will offering (Lev. 3; 7:11). After the priests had sprinkled the blood on the altar, sacrificed certain parts of the fat, and taken their own portion (the breast and thigh), those making the sacrifice ate the flesh.

PEAH (Heb. "Corner"): Second tractate of the Mishnah order of *Zeraim*, containing 8 chapters. It has *gemara* in the Palestinian, but not the Babylonian, Talmud. It deals primarily with the setting aside of the corners of the field for the use of the poor (Lev. 19:9; 23:22) but also considers the dues of the poor (Deut. 24:19).

PEEL COMMISSION: Commission dispatched by the British government to Palestine in 1936 to decide whether the country was ripe for constitutional changes. The scope of inquiry was widened after the outbreak of the Arab riots and received the status of a Royal Commission, with Viscount Peel as its chairman. The sessions began in Palestine in Nov. 1936 and were continued in London in Feb. 1937. Its findings recommended the PARTITION of the country into two sovereign independent states, one Jewish, the other Arab, and a small area under British mandate covering historic and strategic sites. The British government accepted the suggestion in principle but the British parliament, the League of Nations, and the Arabs were cool and the Zionists divided. A further commission (the "Woodhead Commission") in 1938 considered the practical implementation of these proposals and made recommendations but the issue was made academic by the 1939 WHITE PAPER.

PEERCE, JAN (1907–): US singer. Born in New York, he appeared as tenor soloist in films, television, and concerts and made his debut at the Metropolitan Opera in 1941. P. also excels in Jewish cantoral music.

PEIERLS, SIR RUDOLF ERNST (1907–): Physicist. Of German birth, he has been professor of mathematical physics at Birmingham since 1937. He has engaged in atomic research.

PEIXOTTO: US family active in religious, medical, diplomatic, and cultural affairs. Founder of the family was *MOSES LEVY MADURO P.* (1767–1828), a merchant in the W Indies and in New York from 1807, who was minister of Congregation Shearith Israel 1816–28. His son, *DANIEL LEVY MADURO P.* (1800–1843), was a leading physician in New York, president of the NY County Medical Society (1830–2) and editor of the *New York Medical and Physical Journal* from 1829. He also engaged in politics as a Jacksonian Democrat. The latter's son, *BENJAMIN FRANKLIN P.* (1834–1890) was sent as the first US consul-general in Rumania 1871–5, where he labored for Rumanian Jewish emancipation. He was also US consul in France 1877–85. P. was president of B'nai B'rith 1863–6. Outstanding in the fourth generation were *GEORGE DA MADURO P.* (1859–1937), a painter noted for his murals and portraits;

A Shop in Pekiin.

JESSICA BLANCHE P. (1864–1941), the first woman professor (social economics) at the Univ. of California (1905–35), and *ERNEST CLIFFORD P.* (1869–1940), painter and illustrator, whose murals hang in many public buildings. He directed mural painting at the Beaux Arts Institute of Design, New York 1919–26.

PEKAH: King of Israel 735–730 BCE. Possibly of Gileadite origin, he was the captain of his predecessor Pekahiah whom he killed after a conspiracy, seizing his throne. Allying himself with Rezin of Aram-Dammesek, he attacked Judah but their initial success led Ahaz of Judah to appeal for help to Tiglath-Pileser III of Assyria. Tiglath-Pileser invaded the allied kingdom, abolished Aram-Dammesek as a state, and stripped Israel of Galilee and Gilead. P. was subsequently murdered by Hosea. According to the Bible, P. reigned 20 years but this is difficult to reconcile with Assyrian records.

PEKAHIAH: King of Israel 736–5 BCE. After a brief reign, he was the victim of a conspiracy led by his captain Pekah. The plot may have been caused by P.'s apparent opposition to the popular desire to resist Assyria.

PEKIIN (Bekiin): Israel village in Upper Galilee, probably identical with ancient Baka, which — according to Josephus — was the N limit of Galilee. Jewish tradition describes P. as the place where

R Simeon ben Yoḥai and his son Eleazar hid from the Romans in a cave for thirteen years. Ancient remains include decorated stones from a synagogue of the 3rd–4th cents. According to local tradition, the Jews of P. never left their village, continuing to live there from the times of the Second Temple; unbroken residence is certain from the 16th cent. Pop. (1972): 2,255 (Druze and Jews).

PELI: Family of Israel publishers, *MEIR P.* (1894–1958) and his wife *BERAKHAH P.* (1893–), who both went to Palestine from Russia in 1921, founded the MASSADAH publishing company. They published the *Encyclopedia Hebraica*, of which their son *ALEXANDER P.* (1915–) is managing director.

PELIA, BOOK OF see **KANAH, BOOK OF**

PELONI ALMONI (Heb.; cf. Ruth 4:1): "Someone or other"; an anonymous person.

*PEÑAFORTE, RAIMON DE (1176–1275): Spanish Dominican. Devoting himself to the conversion of unbelievers, he participated in the Disputation of Barcelona in 1263, induced the Dominican Order to take up the study of Hebrew with conversionist aims, and was responsible for the introduction of censorship and conversionist sermons into Aragon.

PENITENCE, TEN DAYS OF (Heb. *aseret yeme teshuvah*): First ten days of the month of *Tishri*, i.e., from the commencement of the New Year to the close of the Day of Atonement. The rabbis held that mortals are judged at the beginning of this period and judgment pronounced on the Day of Atonement; those whose case is in doubt may obtain clemency by sincere repentance during this period. Each day, penitential prayers (*seliḥot*) are recited, and the extremely Orthodox practice day-long fasts. There are, moreover, various verbal modifications in the liturgy emphasizing the Kingship of God. *Tishri* 3 is the fast of GEDALIAH. On the eve of the Day of Atonement, eating and drinking are regarded as a duty; it is also an occasion for donating to charity, for visiting cemeteries and the graves of the pious and, in some oriental traditions, for flagellation.

PENITENTIAL PRAYERS see **SELIḤOT**

PENNSYLVANIA: US state. Although there were individual Jews — mostly traders — in P. from the middle of the 17th cent., their numbers were small until the first half of the 18th cent. By 1750, there were communities or groups of Jews in PHILADELPHIA, LANCASTER, EASTON, READING, Heidelberg, York, and Shaefferstown. A number of Jews played an important part in the Revolutionary War. In 1812, there were an estimated 100 Jewish families in P., of whom 30 lived in Philadelphia. In 1825, large-scale Jewish immigration from Germany began, and the Jewish communities of PITTSBURGH, SCRANTON, HARRISBURG, and WILKES-BARRE came into being. In 1850, there was a further large influx of German Jews. During the Civil War, 527 Jewish soldiers from P. served in the Union Army. By 1880, there were about 18,000 Jews in P. This figure rose to 100,000 in the following two decades as a result of the E European immigration. In 1973, P. had 470,655 Jews.

PENTATEUCH see **TORAH**

PENTECOST see **SHAVUOT**

PEOT (Ashkenazi *peos*; Heb. "corners"): Earlocks worn by Orthodox Jews in literal obedience to Lev. 19:27. They are now characteristic of Ḥasidim and Yemenite Jews.

PEREA: In hellenistic and Roman times, the region between the Sea of Galilee and the Dead Sea, E of the Jordan. It contained wide areas under direct royal administration in Herodian times; later, these were Roman imperial states. Its population was largely Jewish until the revolt of 66–70.

PERES, SHIMON (1923–): Israel politician. Born in Belorussia, he went to Palestine in 1934. He sat in the Knesset from 1959 (representing successively Mapai, Rafi, and the Israel Labor Party). He was minister of communications 1970–4 and minister of defense from 1974.

PEREIRA (PEREYRA): Sephardi family of Marrano origin. *ABRAHAM ISRAEL P.* (originally Tomàs Rodrigues P.; d. 1699) escaped from the Spanish Inquisition to Holland where he was one of the wealthiest and most liberal members of the Jewish community. He founded a Talmud Torah at Amster-

I. L. Peretz.

dam and the *Ḥesed Abraham* yeshivah at Hebron. An enthusiastic Sabbetaian, he wrote *La Certeza del Camino* to arouse the Marranos to repentance in the messianic age and set out for Palestine to greet Shabbetai Tzevi, but stopped in Italy. *JONATHAN P.* (1804–1853), physician and teacher of medicine in London, compiled numerous medical works, including the standard British pharmocology. For *MOSES LOPEZ P.* see AGUILAR, DIEGO D'.

PÉREIRE (Originally Pereira): French family. *JACOB RODRIGUEZ P.* (1715–1780), born as a Marrano in Spain, was brought as a child to Bordeaux and later settled in Paris. Here he was syndic of the Sephardi Jews and devoted himself to the oral instruction and rehabilitation of deaf-mutes. His grandsons *ÉMILE P.* (1800–1875) and *ISAAC P.* (1806–1880). ardent disciples of St. Simon, were financiers, active in the development of the French railways and banking, and founding the *Crédit Mobilier*. Both were deputies, wrote works on socialist and financial topics, and were active in Jewish affairs, as was Isaac's son *EUGÈNE P.* (1831–1908).

PERELMAN, SIDNEY JOSEPH (1904–): US humorist. A contributor to the *New Yorker*, his works include *Strictly from Hunger* and *Crazy like a Fox.*

PERETZ, ISAAC LEIB (1852–1915): Yiddish author. Reared in the E European religious tradition, he early came in contact with modern learning. Completing his studies of Russian jurisprudence, he practiced law 1877–87, and settled in Warsaw as a subordinate employee in the Jewish Communal

Bureau. P. began to write at the age of 14. After experimenting with Polish and Hebrew, he finally decided upon Yiddish as a literary vehicle in order to reach the Jewish working masses. His first major Yiddish poem "*Monish*" appeared in 1888, and his first collection of Yiddish tales was published in 1890. His literary reputation was enhanced by *Ḥasidic Tales*, begun in 1894. His most active years as a dramatist were 1906–8. P. experienced and gave expression to the ferment that swept Jewish life from the mid-19th cent. to World War I. His social lyrics were recited and his love lyrics sung throughout E Europe. His short stories stirred to pity (e.g. *Bontsie Shvaig*). His heroes and heroines suffer hardship but are never crushed by their lot. They lack knowledge as to why they are subjected to suffering, but they have no doubt that there is a meaning to it – and P. rewards their faith. He pleads the cause of the heart against the claims of the intellect, of the poor against the arrogance of the rich, of the Ḥasidim or mystics against their deriders. P. spoke the language of the common man and expressed the pain, idealism, and messianic hope that lodged in the Jewish heart.

PERIZZITES: One of the seven Canaanite peoples inhabiting Palestine prior to the Israelite conquest under Joshua. Their descendants were made tributary by Solomon.

PERJURY: The rabbis generally considered that even true OATHS should be avoided if possible. False oaths are a breach of the third Commandment and a desecration of the Name of God, bringing calamity on the whole House of Israel. Witnesses are not required by Jewish law to swear to the truth of their evidence.

PERL, JOSEPH (1773–1839): Hebrew author and *maskil*. A wealthy merchant, he founded the first modern Jewish school in Galicia and also a "reformed" synagogue. He advocated the establishment of Jewish agricultural colonies and, in his satirical writings, opposed Ḥasidic influence.

PERLES: (1) *FELIX P.* (1874–1933): German Bible scholar; son of (2). He was rabbi in Königsberg from 1899, lecturer in the university there from 1924, and author of biblical and linguistic studies. (2) *JOSEPH P.* (1835–1894): Rabbi and scholar. Of Hungarian birth, he officiated in Posen from 1861 and Munich from 1871. He wrote on philology, Jewish customs, history, and medieval literature.

PERPETUAL LIGHT see **NER TAMID**

PERPIGNAN: French town, formerly Spanish. Jews lived there from the 12th cent. and from 1251, were confined in a street known as the *Call*. Many distinguished doctors, astronomers, and rabbis belonged to the community. As a result of the attempts to convert the Jews, their numbers dwindled in the 15th cent., and the remnants of the Jewish population were expelled in 1492. A small community

has been established in the past century and in 1967 numbered 750.

PERSIA (IRAN): Middle Eastern state. P. first became a factor in Jewish history as a result of the conquest of the Babylonian Empire by CYRUS (538 BCE). For the next two centuries, both the mass of Jews in EXILE in Mesopotamia and in the homeland in Palestine were under Persian rule. It was under Persian auspices that there took place the return from exile to Palestine which, however, continued to be a Persian province with some degree of local autonomy. Moreover, the political unity of the Middle East under Persian rule made inevitable considerable movements of population from one part of this area to another. The Book of ESTHER envisages Jews living throughout the 127 provinces of the Persian Empire and depicts them as numerous and influential in the capital, Susa (Shushan). The exact period and historical setting of the plot against them described in this work cannot be ascertained. It is, however, certain that at least from the 4th cent. BCE onward, Jews lived in considerable numbers in P. proper, as they continued to do (although little is known about their history) when the area was controlled by PARTHIA, from 250 BCE onward. P. resumed its existence as a state in 225 CE under the Sassanid dynasty, its authority again extending over the ancient centers of intensive Jewish settlement in Mesopotamia. The Babylonian Talmud, which was redacted here under P. rule, evidences a vigorous Jewish life in P. proper, and the Persian queen SHUSHAN DUKHT was of Jewish birth. Though conditions were at first favorable, there were later fierce religious persecutions under Zoroastrian influence, culminating in the attempt to suppress Jewish observances under Yezdegerd II (438–57). There was an even more sweeping persecution in 468 under FIRUZ (459–86) after the alleged murder of two magi by the Jews in the capital ISFAHAN (a city reputedly of Jewish foundation). When Kavadh I (485–531) adopted and endeavored to impose the communistic practices of Zendicism, the Persian Jews joined in the revolt led by the exilarch MAR ZUTRA II in 513–20. The Arab conquest of 641/2 introduced a new, generally tolerant spirit, with certain reservations. The Jews of P. flourished under the Eastern Caliphate of Baghdad; they were controlled by the exilarchs and paid intellectual allegiance to the Gaonim whose influence was strong. P. was, at this period, a nursery of sectarian movements – e.g. that of ABU ISSA AL-ISFAHANI (c. 700). Consequently, Karaism obtained a vigorous hold in P. from the 8th cent., and some of its most influential teachers, such as BENJAMIN NAHAVENDI, came from there. Benjamin of Tudela, toward the end of the 12th cent., found throughout this area numerous and flourishing Jewish communities, which, however,

Page from 17th cent. illuminated Persian Jewish ms (Adler Collection, Jewish Theological Seminary. NY).

had recently been disturbed through the messianic movement of David ALROY. After an interlude under Mongol rule, during which the lot of the Jews was checkered (13th–15th cents.), Persian independence was reasserted in 1499 under the Safavid dynasty. The Shiite form of Islam, henceforth generally dominant, was highly intolerant in theory and practice. The Jews were treated worse than in other parts of the Moslem world, all manner of restrictions being enforced, and in the 17th cent., there were widespread persecutions and forced conversions, particularly in Isfahan. Conditions temporarily improved under the broadminded Nadir Shah (1736–47) who aimed at creating a new religious synthesis. He was responsible for settling a Jewish community at his new capital, Meshed, from which

they had hitherto been excluded. On his death. however, a reaction followed, and Shiite intolerance again became supreme. Nevertheless throughout this period, a fairly vigorous intellectual life persisted, partly expressed in a literature in the Judeo-Persian DIALECT. The old Persian prayer-book, based on Saadyah's ritual, was still current, until in the early 19th cent. it was superseded by the Sephardi rite through the influence of visiting Palestinian scholars. Medieval conditions of intolerance continued in P., and in 1839, the entire Meshed community was forcibly converted to Islam, though retaining secret fidelity to Judaism as JEDID AL-ISLAM. In the 19th cent., Persian Jewry was among the most depressed of the world's Jewish communities, notwithstanding the diplomatic interventions occasionally secured by western Jewry, and intermittent promises of ameliorations by successive shahs were overlooked. From 1898, schools of the Alliance Israélite Universelle did something to introduce a more modern spirit, but progress was slight and the *Jedid al Islam* did not dare to return openly to Judaism. Although equality of political rights has now nominally been introduced into P., the social and economic status of the Jews has changed little. Jewish pop. (1973): 80,000. Between 1948 and 1966, 53,488 Jews left P. for Israel.

PERSKY, DANIEL (1887–1962): US Hebraist. Born in Russia, he settled in New York in 1908 and devoted himself to fostering the Hebrew language and literature in the US. P. was noted as a grammarian and light feuilletonist.

PERTH: Australian town. Its Jewish congregation was founded in 1896 and numbers 3,000 (1973), including a considerable proportion of former Palestinians who went to Australia after World War I.

PERU: Marranos from Portugal played a leading part in the economic life of the country in the early part of the 16th cent. Under the Inquisition (1570–1806), 131 Judaizers were condemned, of whom 24 were burnt at the stake, mainly in a concentrated campaign in 1639–64. A Jewish community was established by immigrants from Alsace after 1870, but these became completely assimilated within a half century. E European Jews went to P. in the 20th cent. Of the Jewish pop. (1973) of 5,300, about 90% reside in Lima. The three major groups — Ashkenazim from Germany, Ashkenazim of E Europe, and Sephardim — are united in the official Association de Sociedades Israelitas del Peru.

PERUTZ, MAX FERDINAND (1914–): Chemist. Born in Vienna he went to England in 1936 and worked in the Cambridge Institute for Molecular Biology. He was corecipient of the 1962 Nobel Prize for Chemistry for his work on the structure and function of proteins and nucleic acids.

PESAḤ see **PASSOVER**

PESAḤ SHENI see **PASSOVER, SECOND**

PESAḤIM (Heb. "Paschal Lambs"): Third tractate in the Mishnah order of *Moed*, containing 10 chapters. It has *gemara* in both the Babylonian and the Palestinian Talmuds. It deals with the regulations appertaining to the Passover holiday, primarily from the viewpoint of the sacrificial service in Second Temple times.

PESARO: Port on the E coast of Italy. Jews are recorded there in the 12th cent., and the community flourished when P. was the principal city of the duchy of URBINO in the 16th cent. In 1556, when Ancona was boycotted to avenge the burning of the Marranos, many Jewish traders transferred their activities to P. The community, with beautiful synagogues for the Italian and Levantine rites, decayed

under papal rule (17th–19th cents.) and is now almost extinct.

PESHAT (Heb.): The simple, literal meaning of Scripture. This is considered as the primary type of interpretation.

PESHER (Heb. "interpretation"): Term used by the authors of the DEAD SEA SCROLLS to introduce their interpretation of Scripture. The term is used now to designate those Scrolls which provide running commentaries on biblical books, e.g. *P. Habakkuk*. *P. Nahum*, *P.* on Psalms, *P. Isaiah*.

PESHITTA (Syriac "simple"): The Syriac translation of the Bible, called "the Simple" in contrast to the Syrohexapla (see SEPTUAGINT). It was made in the 2nd cent. CE into the dialect of Edessa (now Urfa, N Syria), probably with the help of, or by, Jews from a text differing from the Masoretic. It served as the Bible of the Christians of Syria and the Nestorians of Iraq and Persia.

PESIKTA DE-RAV KAHANA: Collection of 32 midrashic homilies for the holidays and special Sabbaths of the year, probably from about the 7th cent. It is probably attributed to the amora R Kahana because he is mentioned in an opening passage, but, according to Theodor was compiled by the gaon of that name. Although mss were not known at the time of Zunz, he was able to reconstruct the work from quotations and references in other sources. His reconstruction was corroborated by mss subsequently discovered and published by Solomon Buber (more recently by B. Mandelbaum). The oldest midrash termed *Pesikta* (i.e., "section," so-called because written in divisions), it is sometimes known simply by that title.

PESIKTA RABBATI: Midrash drawing upon various sources, probably compiled in Palestine, comprising 48 homilies based upon the holidays and special Sabbaths of the year. Its date is disputed but is probably c. 7th cent. 28 of the homilies are of the YELAMMEDENU type. The *P. R.* was scientifically edited by M. Friedmann (1880). An English translation by W. G. Braude appeared in 1968.

PESIKTA ZUTARTA see **LEKAḤ TOV**

PESUKE DE-ZIMRAH (Heb. "passages of songs" called *Zemirot* among the Sephardim): Section of the SHAḤARIT prayer between the morning blessings and the one preceding the recitation of the *Shema*, inserted in accordance with the rabbinical dictum that praise of God should precede prayer. It consists in the main of Ps. 145–150, closing with various verses and the Song of Moses (Exod. 14:30–15:18). The *P. de Z.* are introduced by the blessing *barukh she-amar* and end with *yishtabbaḥ* (preceded on Sabbaths and festivals by NISHMAT). In the Sephardi rite, some of the psalms precede *barukh she-amar*. Additional psalms are added on Sabbaths and festivals.

Petaḥ Tikvah

PETAḤ TIKVAH: Israel town. After an unsuccessful attempt to settle the site in 1878, a plantation colony (vineyards, grain) was founded in 1883 by *Hoveve Zion* pioneers of the First Aliyah. It received the assistance of Baron Edmond de Rothschild, developing rapidly into a center of citriculture. In the course of time, it became an industrial center. P. T. received the status of a municipality in 1937, and is now the head of a district. Pop. (1974): 103,000.

PETHAHIAH OF REGENSBURG (fl. 12th cent.): German traveler. He journeyed from Germany to Palestine through Central Europe, S Russia, Armenia, the Caspian area, and Babylonia. On his return, his account of the journey was written down by Judah the Ḥasid. Although containing many legendary elements, it is of great historical importance, especially for its light on the organization of Jewish life in Baghdad and conditions in the Holy Land.

*PETLURA, SIMON (1880–1926): Ukrainian leader 1918–20. Forces under his command perpetrated 493 pogroms in which 16,706 Jews were murdered; these commenced at Zhitomir in Jan. 1919, and the most extensive – claiming 1,500 victims – was at Proskurov. P. was assassinated by Shalom SCHWARTZBARD.

*PETRIE, SIR WILLIAM MATTHEW FLINDERS (1853–1942): British founder of scientific archeology. He worked in Egypt and Palestine, discovering the stratigraphic method, the chronological value of pottery, etc. His impact on Palestinian archeology was methodological. P.'s works include *Hyksos and Israelite Cities*; *Egypt and Israel*, and *Ancient Gaza*.

PETROGRAD see **LENINGRAD**

*PETRONIUS PUBLIUS (fl. 1st cent. CE): Roman governor of Syria 39–41 CE. Recognizing the potential consequences of Caligula's order for the erection of his statue in the Temple at Jerusalem, he delayed its execution, further complications being prevented by Caligula's death. P. later protected Syrian Jews against gentile attacks.

PFEFFERKORN, JOHANN JOSEPH (1469–after 1521): Apostate. A Moravian butcher, he went to Germany after being caught thieving and was baptized at Cologne in 1505. Maintaining that the obduracy of the Jews was due to the influence of the Talmud, he proposed that rabbinic works be confiscated, Jewish children kidnapped, and adult Jews expelled from the country. In 1509, Emperor Maximilian empowered him to examine Jewish books in Germany and to destroy those "blaspheming" Christianity. Many were confiscated but the Jews, with the support of several humanists, persuaded the emperor to order their restitution. On P.'s appeal, the matter was referred to three scholars – REUCHLIN, a Dominican, and a Jewish apostate. Reuchlin's defense of the Talmud led to a violent polemic with P.

whose material was prepared for him by the Dominicans. The controversy broadened and formed a prelude to the Reformation. The pope ultimately decided against Reuchlin but the ban on Jewish books was not renewed.

*PFEIFFER, ROBERT HENRY (1892–1958): US orientalist, prof. of Semitic languages and history at Harvard. He directed the Harvard-Baghdad School of Archeological Excavations at Nuzi (Iraq) 1928–9, and edited the *Journal of Biblical Literature* 1943–7. His works include a standard *Introduction to the Old Testament* and a *History of New Testament Times*.

PHARAOH: Permanent title of the king of Egypt in ancient times. The word means the "Great House," and was originally applied to the royal palace.

PHARISEES (Heb. *Perushim*, probably meaning "set apart" i.e., avoiding contact with others for reasons of ritual purity): Jewish religious and political party during the Second Temple Period. Their origin, like that of other contemporary parties, is unknown: probably they represent a continuation of the HASIDEANS. Although a relatively narrow body, closed to the masses, their activity was directed to the masses whom they sought to imbue with a spirit of holiness by propagating traditional religious teaching. The gulf between the P. and those ignorant of the Law or not practicing it was complete. The P. used to eat in groups and observe all the rules of purity in the same manner as the priests consuming consecrated food in the Temple. They endeavored to extend their influence over the Temple at the expense of the SADDUCEES, whose control there was absolute. In addition, they incorporated into the cult folk-customs not mentioned in the Bible (e.g. the Water-Drawing Festival), to the dismay of the Sadducees. The antagonism between the two parties extended to many spheres, which some scholars attribute to basic social differences; generally, the P. admitted the principle of evolution in their legal decisions, while the Sadducees were incapable of adaptation to a changing environment. The P. were thus generally lenient in their interpretations, while the Sadducees clung to the letter of the written text. The P. placed the nation's life within a halakhic framework expressed in the ORAL LAW which they regarded as no less vital than the Written Law (the Bible). Their doctrine aspired to embrace the entire life of the community, touching therefore on the theological foundations of life, questions of fate, good and evil, the immortality of the soul, and eschatology. They admitted Divine predestination but also man's responsibility for his deeds. In contrast to the Sadducees, they believed in life after death, the resurrection of the dead, the advent of the Messiah, and the Day of Judgment. Not all P. lived up to their high principles, and the Talmud itself lists seven hypocritical types: nevertheless, in reality they were far removed from the derogatory New Testament picture. In fact, Pharisaism was responsible for strengthening morality and introducing the elasticity which enabled Judaism to withstand its subsequent tribulations; the movement was continued in the stream of historic Judaism.

PHASAEL (d. 40 BCE): Elder son of Antipater; brother of Herod. Appointed governor of Jerusalem by his father, he proved himself a wise and energetic ruler, opposing his brother's violent methods. In 40 BCE, P. accepted a proposal to go with Hyrcanus the high priest to negotiate peace in the Parthian camp, but both were arrested by the Parthians, P. eventually committing suicide. Herod called one of the towers on the wall of Jerusalem after P.

PHILADELPHIA see **RABBATH AMMON**

PHILADELPHIA: City in Pennsylvania, US. Nathan Levy of New York is reputed to be the founder of P.'s Jewish community. In 1738, he bought a private burial plot which later became the city's first Jewish cemetery. The Sephardi congregation Mikveh Israel, the oldest Jewish congregation in the country, was organized in 1745. Members of the FRANKS and GRATZ families played a prominent part in the city's economic life during the third quarter of the 18th cent. The Jewish community grew considerably after the British capture of New York during the Revolution. The second congregation in P. was Rodeph Shalom, organized in 1802 by German Jews. Congregation Beth Israel was formed by German and

Engraving from J. J. Pfefferkorn's *Judenbeichte*, 1508.

Polish Jews in 1840, followed by Keneseth Israel in 1847. By 1850, there were about 2,500 Jews in P. In order to fill the need for a theological seminary, Maimonides College was founded in 1867 and existed for 6 years. By 1918 there were 200,000 Jews in P., mostly of E European origin. A large number of religious, welfare, educational, and civic organizations appeared as the population grew, and the Federation of Jewish Charities (later Agencies) was founded in 1901. The Allied Jewish Appeal for overseas causes was established in 1938. P. is the home of DROPSIE COLLEGE, GRATZ COLLEGE, and the JEWISH PUBLICATION SOCIETY OF AMERICA. Two weeklies, the *Jewish Exponent* and the *Philadelphia Jewish Times*, are published in P. In 1973, P. had a Jewish Population of 350,000.

PHILANTHROPIN: Jewish school at Frankfort-on-Main, founded by Sigismund Geisenheimer in 1804. The P., which was conducted in a liberal religious spirit, was closed down shortly before World War II.

PHILANTHROPY see **CHARITY**

PHILATELY: The collecting and study of postage stamps. The first post offices in Palestine were founded about 1854 by European Powers (France and Austria, later also Russia, Italy, and Germany). Turkey established post offices in Palestine in the 1860's and disputed the right of foreign powers to maintain them, though they existed until 1914. Egypt maintained a post office at Jaffa 1871–2. The Egyptian Expeditionary Force under General Allenby established a network of military post-offices (1917/8) which were shortly put into general use. Stamps of a primitive design were printed, first in Cairo and later, in London. With the establishment of the British Mandate over Palestine in 1920 these stamps received the trilingual overprint "Palestine" in English, Arabic, and Hebrew. The new set of pictorial designs came into use in 1927. At the end of the British Mandate over Palestine, the Jewish People's Administration issued provisional stamps (May 2–14, 1948). The first stamps of the state of Israel appeared on May 16, 1948. Special stamps are issued for important anniversaries, congresses, memorial days, as well as to mark each Jewish New Year and Independence Day.

PHILIP (d. 34 CE): Son of Herod. He was educated at Rome and in his father's last will was appointed tetrarch, receiving the territories of Gaulanitis, Trachonitis, and Bashan and the city of Paneas, which he renamed Caesarea Philippi. In contrast to his father and brothers, he possessed an equable temperament, administering his territories justly. His wife was SALOME.

PHILIPPINES: A group of islands in the Pacific, formerly under Spanish rule. In the 16th–17th cents., a number of Marranos settled there, and some were tried by the Inquisition. Immigrants from Alsace-Lorraine arrived between 1870 and 1880. With the acquisition of the islands by the US in 1898, Jews migrated from the American mainland and Europe. After World War I, a considerable number of Russian Jews came via Siberia. A congregation was formed in Manila in 1919, and the island's first synagogue was built there in 1924. Refugees from Central Europe reached the P. from 1933 on; others came from Japanese-occupied Shanghai after 1937. The Japanese occupation completely disrupted Jewish life. In 1943, the authorities instituted an anti-Semitic campaign, deporting or interning all Jews irrespective of nationality. The community was reconstituted in 1945, numbering some 500 Jews (300 in Manila) in 1973.

PHILIPPSON: German family. (1) *ALFRED P.* (1864–1953): German geographer; son of (3). He was professor of geography in his native Bonn from 1911, surviving deportation to Theresienstadt during World War II. He wrote chiefly on the Mediterranean region, etc. (2) *FRANZ P.* (1852–1929): Banker and public worker; son of (3). From 1866, he lived in Brussels where he founded a bank and was active in Jewish communal affairs. In 1919, P. was elected president of ICA. (3) *LUDWIG P.* (1811–1889): Rabbi and scholar. From 1833 to 1862, he officiated in Magdeburg. A believer in Liberalism, he fought for Emancipation but advocated only minor liturgical reforms, adopting a positive attitude to historical traditions. He initiated several rabbinical conferences and organized that held in 1869 at Leipzig. P. published a German translation of the Bible with commentary and illustrations (1839–53). He founded the ALLGEMEINE ZEITUNG DES JUDENTUMS in 1837 and edited it until his death. In 1855, he established the Institute for Jewish Literature. His best-known book is *Die Entwicklung der Religion im Judentum, Christentum und Islam* ("The Development of Religion in Judaism, Christianity, and Islam"). (4) *MARTIN P.* (1846–1916): Historian; son of (3). From 1875, he taught modern history at Brussels Univ., being appointed rector in 1890, but was forced to resign because he was a German. P. went to Berlin but anti-Semitic propaganda prevented him from entering there on a university career, and he devoted himself to Jewish affairs. From 1896 to 1912, he was chairman of the *Deutsch-Israelitischer Gemeindebund*. In 1904, he helped to found the *Verband der Deutschen Juden*, of which he was the first president. His writings include a history of the Jews in recent times.

PHILIPSON, DAVID (1862–1949): US rabbi. He was a member of the first graduating class from Hebrew College in 1883 and became one of the leaders of Reform Judaism in the US. From 1888 to 1938, he was rabbi of the Rockdale Ave. Bene

Israel Temple in Cincinnati. He wrote extensively on Reform Judaism and on Jewish history, and taught at Hebrew Union College from 1889.

PHILISTINES: Mediterranean people. Apparently originating from Asia Minor and Greek localities, they reached PALESTINE in various waves. One group arrived in the pre-patriarchal period and settled S of Beersheba in Gerar where they came into conflict with Abraham and Isaac. Another group, coming from Crete after being repulsed from Egypt by Rameses III in 1194 BCE, seized the S coastal area of Palestine, where they founded five principalities (Gaza, Ascalon, Ashdod, Ekron, and Gath). By nature a fighting people, they dominated parts of Judah in the period of the Judges. Saul at first repelled the danger but was ultimately defeated. David, however, ended the era of Philistine domination and overran Philistia. When the Israelite kingdom dissolved, the P. re-established their independence but were never thereafter a serious factor. In the Persian and Greek Periods, foreign settlers — chiefly from the Mediterranean islands — overran the Philistine districts. From the time of Herodotus, Greeks called Palestine after the P. (Syria Palæstina); and under Hadrian, the Romans gave the name officially to the former land of Judah.

PHILLIPS: (1) *SIR BENJAMIN P.* (1811–1889) was lord mayor of London 1865–6, and active in Jewish affairs. (2) *SIR GEORGE FAUDEL P.* (1840–1922), son of (1), was lord mayor of London in Queen Victoria's diamond jubilee year, 1896–7.

PHILLIPS, SIR LIONEL (1855–1936): Financier. Born in London, he went to S Africa in 1875, and rose to be a leader of the diamond mining industry, as well as of the British opposition to Kruger. He was fined and deported (at first sentenced to death) for his part in the Jameson raid (1895), but later returned, and was a member of the Union Parliament 1910–5.

PHILO (c. 20 BCE – after 40 CE): Alexandrian philosopher. The only details known of his life are a visit to Palestine and his participation in the deputation of Alexandrian Jews to Caligula during the anti-Jewish outbreaks in 40. His family was one of the wealthiest in Egypt. He received a hellenistic education, his writings evidencing his familiarity with Greek literature, philosophy, etc. His command of Greek stems from his acquaintance with the philosophers, especially PLATO. His Jewish education was slight; it is doubtful if he knew Hebrew, and his knowledge of the Bible appears to be derived from the Septuagint and from hellenistic commentaries current among Alexandrian Jewry. These commentaries were allegorical and P. adopted this approach in his own writings. His literary output was considerable, including metaphysics, ethics, and Bible commentary. He also wrote an historical work,

parts of which survive in his account of the persecution by and retribution of Flaccus, governor of Egypt, during the anti-Jewish disturbances, and in a vivid description of the deputation to Caligula. P. teaches that God created the world from eternal matter but does not influence it directly. The *logos* mediates between God and the world. The human soul is derived from the Divine Source and is hence capable of attaining a conception of the nature of Divinity not through spiritual perception but by self-immersion, either through mystic mediation or the spirit of prophecy: this is the ultimate goal in man's striving for moral self-elevation. Judaism holds the instrument enabling man to attain moral and philosophical perfection — the Torah opening the way to union with the Divine. The way is allegorical: the Pentateuchal stories of non-moral content depict for the philosopher the coarse passions of mankind which are to be avoided; other stories allegorically depict the good which is to be striven for. Generally, P. believes Jewish law to be the purest revelation of Divinity. His philosophy is eclectic, using borrowed elements in an individual fashion, fusing Greek and Jewish elements into one system. The effects of his teaching are discernible not in subsequent Jewish thought but in the Church Fathers and in Neoplatonism.

PHILO VERLAG: German Jewish publishing house, established in 1919 by the *Centralverein deutscher Staatsbürger jüdischen Glaubens.* It published statistical material, apologetic literature, a one-volume lexicon, a bi-monthly journal *Der Morgen* (1925–38), and an historical quarterly *Zeitschrift zur Geschichte der Juden in Deutschland.* It was closed in 1938.

PHILOSOPHY: The study of ultimate reality as distinct from the study of natural phenomena (science, natural p., etc.). In Jewish p. it is necessary to distinguish between (1) the p. of Judaism, i.e., the philosophical effort to elucidate the nature, contents, meaning, presuppositions, and implications of JUDAISM as a religion or as a historical phenomenon; and (2) the contributions made to general p. by Jews. (1) The p. of Judaism is marked by two formal characteristics. In the first place, it overlaps with theology or rather tends to take its place. The study of the contents of the Divine revelation (i.e., theology proper) being the study of Law or HALAKHAH, it was inevitable that the attempts of thinkers to expound the basis and belief of Judaism should result in a p. of religion as the alternative to Jewish theology. Secondly, p. is no immanent "home grown" product of Jewish culture but always appears as the result of contact with the philosophical thought of other civilizations (Greece, HELLENISM, Islamic Aristotelianism, post-Kantian Idealism, modern Existentialism, etc.). It may thus be defined as the attempt of Jewish thinkers to use the categories of their contemporary philosophical systems as a means of arriving at a philosophical understanding of Judaism. Though the BIBLE is essentially non-philosophical in character, its symbols and underlying ideas demand philosophical elaboration: God, creation, revelation, transcendence, monotheism, Divine justice (Theodicy), the meaning of history, etc. In a a way, the biblical practice of using fundamental ideas and symbols in a non-philosophical manner was continued by the rabbis (AGGADAH; cf. also ANTHROPOMORPHISM): often they would raise genuine philosophical problems in epigrammatic form but without discussing them philosophically, e.g. "all is foreseen, yet permission (i.e., free will) is granted" (*Avot* 3:19). Philosophical thinking proper manifested itself for the first time in the orbit of hellenistic culture. Its foremost representative is PHILO of Alexandria whose interpretation of Judaism in terms of Neoplatonic and Stoic thought left, however, little or no mark on Jewish posterity. Of far greater significance was the revival of Greek p. among the Arabs and the use to which it was put by the theological schools of ISLAM (Mu'tazila, Kalam). The fact that two universal religions claimed exclusive validity, sharing in common only their rejection of Judaism, gave an enormous impulse to the rationalist criticism of religion in general and to the theological effort of proving the validity of (one's own) religion by rational means. The first great Jewish philosopher, SAADYAH GAON, still represented the Kalam school as did David ALMUKAMMAS and many others, both orthodox Rabbinites and Karaites. But, whereas the latter remained in the Mu'tazilite tradition, rabbinic thought developed under the decisive influence of the two main streams of Arab-Greek p.: NEOPLATONISM and ARISTOTELIANISM. The former began with Isaac ISRAELI and reached its height in the *Foundation of Life* (*Fons Vitae*) of Solomon IBN GABIROL; it manifested itself also in the moral and ascetic theology in *The Duties of the Heart* of BAHYA IBN PAKUDA, in Joseph IBN TZADDIK's *Microcosm*, and especially in the *Kuzari* by JUDAH HA-LEVI. The other trend, however, proved by far the more powerful. Established by some of the greatest thinkers of Islam, Aristotelianism had already appeared in Abraham IBN DAUD and reached its height in the major work of the most outstanding medieval Jewish philosopher, Moses MAIMONIDES' *Guide to the Perplexed*. The caliber of this work made it inevitable that most subsequent writings were dependent on it, either commenting on and developing its ideas or criticizing and combating them. The Maimonist controversy, which almost rent Jewry into two hostile camps, could not, in the long run, prevent the victory of Maimonides' p., some of the extreme features of which were further accentuated by developments in Arab Aristotelianism (Averroes), and exemplified in the work of Isaac

ALBALAG, LEVI BEN GERSHON, Hasdai CRESCAS, and many lesser figures like Joseph ALBO. The prolific and versatile Isaac ABRAVANEL marks the end of Spanish p., the tradition of which was cultivated, though not really continued, in Italy (Judah Messer LEON, etc.) where Jews had philosophized in a Christian environment since at least the time of HILLEL BEN SAMUEL of Verona. The modern period began with Moses MENDELSSOHN. His p., in many ways typical of the European HASKALAH, was soon superseded by the triumph of German Idealism, applied to Judaism by Solomon Formstecher and Samuel Hirsch. Nahman KROCHMAL was also one of the pioneers of the new *Wissenschaft des Judentums* and in his *Guide to the Perplexed of Our Times* used historical research in the service of an ambitious p. of history. Whereas the Hegelian overtones are distinct in Krochmal, Ludwig Steinheim propounded a decidedly anti-rationalist p. of revelation. The turn of the century witnessed a revival of Kantianism, exemplified by Moritz LAZARUS' *The Ethics of Judaism* and particularly by the work of Hermann COHEN. The modern, anti-idealist (or existentialist) trend came to the fore with Franz ROSENZWEIG's *The Star of Redemption*. The last decades of German Jewry were marked by the activity of other great religious thinkers, in particular Leo BAECK and Martin BUBER. Since the destruction of German Jewry, the centers of gravity of Jewish religious p. have shifted to the US (Abraham HESCHEL, Will HERBERG, etc.) and Israel. Another trend initiated by the "enlightenment" was the growth of a secular attitude in philosophizing about Judaism. Though this trend expressed itself more in literature and journalism (Haskalah), it determined the climate in which the developing Jewish NATIONALISM formulated its ideology and its evaluations of past and present (ZIONISM). The most outstanding of these philosophical essayists was AHAD HA-AM whose doctrine of Zion as a "spiritual center" was opposed both by the historian Simon DUBNOW, basing Jewish existence on the Diaspora-centers, and by Jacob KLATZKIN, preaching a radical "negation of the Diaspora." Others (Ber BOROCHOV) tried to bring Zionism in line with radical Marxist or Socialist views. With the establishment of the state of Israel, problems concerning the Jewish attitude to history, statehood, religion, individual and collective destiny, etc. tend to merge once again.

(2) Until the modern period, Jewish thought exerted its influence mainly in a general way and in the sense that Judaism or the Bible profoundly influenced Christianity, Islam, etc. For the rest, individual writers (Philo, Maimonides, etc.) influenced general p. to the extent that they were available in translations and that gentile thinkers studied them. With the exception of Ibn Gabirol, the pursuit by Jews of non-denominational and strictly general p. only

began in the modern period. The first such writer was one of the greatest minds in the history of p. — SPINOZA. Though his influence on 18th and 19th cent. thinkers increased steadily, Jewish general p. again remained in abeyance until the post-Mendelssohnian period. Not only was Moses Mendelssohn greatly admired by the German philosophical public, but Jews were soon prominent as disciples of Kant (Marcus HERZ, Lazarus BENDAVID, and in particular the brilliant Solomon MAIMON) and of Hegel. Of special significance were the leftist Hegelians and founders of socialism Karl MARX, Ferdinand LASSALLE, Moses HESS, etc. The neo-Kantian revival was also greatly indebted to Jews such as Hermann Cohen and Ernst Cassirer, and so was the new phenomenological school of Eduard HUSSERL, many of whose leading disciples were Jews or converted Jews (Adolf REINACH, Edith Stein, Max Scheler, etc.). Henri BERGSON in France has exerted world-wide influence; Samuel ALEXANDER was one of the leading English philosophers of his day. Moreover, Jewish scholars working in different but related fields (mathematics, sociology, psychology, etc.) have given powerful impulses to modern p.

PHINEHAS: Priest; grandson of Aaron. In reward for his zealous action against ZIMRI, he and his descendants were promised the priesthood (Num. 25), and the Zadokites (see ZADOK) traced their ancestry to him. He received a holding on Mt. Ephraim and was still officiating at the time of the campaign of the tribes against Benjamin (Judg. 20:28).

PHINEHAS: Priest at Shiloh; second son of Eli. He and his brother Hophni — both regarded as unworthy priests — were killed at Ebenezer while accompanying the Ark of the Covenant into battle against the Philistines (I Sam. 4).

PHINEHAS BEN ABRAHAM OF KORETZ (1726–1791): Ḥasidic rabbi. Given a traditional education in Lithuania, he settled in Volhynia, was attracted to Ḥasidism under the influence of the Baal Shem Tov, and drew many to Ḥasidism. P. preached simplicity and humility and opposed *pilpul*.

PHINEHAS BEN JAIR (fl. late 2nd cent.): Tanna; son-in-law of R Simeon ben Yoḥai. All his extant teachings are in the field of aggadah and demonstrate his insistence on purity and holiness in daily life.

PHOENICIANS: Ancient people of Syria. Living along the Syrian-Palestinian coast, their main towns were Arvad, Beirut, SIDON, TYRE, Gebal (Byblos), Simirro, and Sin. At certain periods, they expanded N toward the later Antioch and S to the Carmel and even to Jaffa. Their language, known chiefly from inscriptions, was akin to Hebrew. The script used by them (also utilized by the ancient Hebrews) was transmitted with modifications to the Greeks and thence to other European peoples. The history of the P. is mainly derived from inscriptions,

the Bible, and Greek authors. Gebal had close relations with Egypt from early times and is prominent in Egyptian mythology. The Egyptians controlled Phoenicia from the period after the expulsion of the Hyksos (c. 1500 BCE) down to the time of Rameses III (while the N Phoenician cities were evidently ruled by the Hittites). After a time, the P. attained complete independence; HIRAM of Tyre was closely allied with Solomon, while Ethbaal of Sidon's close cooperation with OMRI influenced Israelite religious life for a time. In the 8th cent. BCE, Assyria subjugated most of the cities. Later, Phoenicia was incorporated in the Persian Empire, and its influence extended southward along the Palestinian coast. With the growth of Greek influence, Hellenization spread rapidly among the P.; many of their cities achieved autonomy and even independence, but Pompey's campaign in 64 BCE brought all of them under Roman rule. Their special ability was expressed (especially in Tyre) in maritime trade, their ships trading with almost the entire known world (see Ezek. 27). They discovered distant lands and disseminated the products of Middle Eastern countries. Their colonies, spreading from Cyprus to Carthage and Spain, paid tithes to Tyre, but the bonds loosened in the face of Greek competition. Outstanding among their home industries were purple-deying and glass manufacture. Artistically they were influenced by their neighbors (Egypt, Greece, etc.). Their religion was the Canaanite faith described in the Bible and in UGARITIC poetry; the chief deities were Baal, lord of fertility and the rains, and Astarte, goddess of fertility. Anat was the goddess of war, and Melkarth the patron-god of Tyre. Worship was conducted under trees and on hills, but there were also temples with images. Their religious practices included the sacrificing of children to MOLOCH and the dedication of religious prostitutes.

PHYLACTERIES see **TEPHILLIN**

PHYSICIANS see **MEDICINE**

PHYSICS, JEWS IN: Although the Jewish contribution to physical research up to the mid-19th cent. was slight, many of the tremendous advances of the past century have been due to Jews, who have been prominent in both the experimental and theoretical fields, several having received NOBEL PRIZES. Heinrich Herz pioneered in research on electromagnetic waves. Albert Einstein with his relativity theory revolutionized the entire scientific approach to the universe. Niels Bohr, who is of Jewish origin, laid the foundations of modern atomic science. Other major contributions came from Albert A. Michelson, Hermann Minkowsky, and Tullio Levi-Civita (who paved the way for Einstein), James Franck and Gustave Hertz (who helped to develop the quantum theory), Vito Volterra, Max Born, Abram F. Joffe, and Sir Franz Simon. Among the

Gregor Piatigorsky.

scientists responsible for the development in nuclear physics in recent years are J. Robert Oppenheimer, Edward Teller, and Lise Meitner. In Israel, research in physics is pursued at the Hebrew Univ., the Weizmann Institute of Science, and the Haifa Technion. See also NOBEL WINNERS, JEWISH.

PIATIGORSKY, GREGOR (1903–1976): Cellist. Born in Russia, he performed with the Bolshoi Theater in Moscow 1917–21, and the Berlin Philharmonic Orchestra 1925–9. P. settled in the US in 1929.

PICA (initials of "Palestine Jewish Colonization Association"): Colonization company founded by ICA after World War I to administer Palestinian colonies supported by Baron Edmond de ROTHSCHILD. In 1957, it was wound up and assets transferred to the Israel national institutions.

*****PICART, BERNARD** (1673–1733): Engraver. His *Cérémonies et coutumes religieuses*, with 261 plates (1723–43), includes vivid representations of religious life in Amsterdam's Jewish community.

PICO DELLA MIRANDOLA see **MIRANDOLA**

PICON, MOLLY (1898–): US actress. A star of the New York Yiddish theater, she has toured the world as an entertainer in both Yiddish and English.

PIDYON HA-BEN see **FIRST-BORN, REDEMPTION OF**

PIERCE, SYDNEY (1901–): Canadian diplomat. He was ambassador to Mexico 1947–9, minister in Washington 1951–3, and ambassador to Brazil 1953–5. In 1955, he was appointed deputy high com-

missioner in London, and in 1958, ambassador to Belgium. Later he was chief Gatt trade negotiator for Canada in Geneva.

PIJADE, MOSHE (1899–1957): Yugoslav statesman. An art teacher and journalist, he was imprisoned for his communist activities 1921–39. In 1941, he joined Tito at partisan headquarters and after World War II, was president of Serbia and of the presidium of the People's Assembly.

PILATE, PONTIUS see **PROCURATORS**

PILGRIMAGE: The Pentateuch enjoins all Israelite males to visit the sanctuary thrice yearly — on the festivals of Passover, Pentecost, and Tabernacles (Deut. 16:16). They had to offer up a special burntoffering on the occasion, together with a holocaust for the festival and other holocausts of rejoicing. The pilgrimage was performed regularly, at first to Shiloh, later to Jerusalem. The institution of p. was recommenced during the time of the Second Temple, Jews even in the Diaspora considering themselves bound to sacrifice in Jerusalem at least occasionally. After the destruction of the Temple, some persons would still go to pray at the Temple site on the occasion of the feasts, especially during Tabernacles. The idea of p. was revived in the Middle Ages, largely under Karaite influences, though now restricted to the pious and adventurous. Special prayers were composed for the pilgrims to recite in Jerusalem and on visits to the graves of biblical figures and talmudic scholars; many records of their travels have been preserved.

PILICHOWSKI, LEOPOLD (1867–1933): Painter. A native of Poland, he settled in England in 1914. His work includes portraits of outstanding Jews, genre scenes, and a panoramic painting of the opening of the Hebrew Univ. in 1925.

PILPUL (= "debate"): In talmudic and rabbinic literature–a clarification; later, a sharp and dialectic intellectual distinction, a certain type of discipline in talmudic study. This discipline, introduced by Jacob POLLAK, was especially dominant in Poland from the 16th cent. and is exemplified in the works of talmudic scholars there. These works are noteworthy for their sharp and casuistic construction of relationship between matters entirely removed one from another. Many rabbinic scholars opposed this discipline, contending that it gave a false perspective.

PINCUS, LOUIS ABRAHAM (ARYEH) (1912–1973): Israel public figure. Born in South Africa and a lawyer by profession, he settled in Israel in 1948. From 1949 to 1956 he was managing director of El Al. In 1961 he was elected treasurer of the Jewish Agency and from 1965 was chairman of its Israel executive.

PINERO, SIR ARTHUR WING (1855–1934): English playwright, descended from a Sephardi family. He exercised a great influence on the English drama, his

J. L. Pinsker.

best-known plays including *The Second Mrs. Tanqueray*, *Trelawney of the Wells*, and *The Magistrate*.

PINES, JEHIEL MICHAL (1842–1912): Zionist pioneer and author. Born in Poland, he contributed to the Hebrew press, wrote against assimilation, and prepared a plan to found an agricultural school. From 1878, he represented the *Mazkeret Mosheh* society in Palestine and played an important role in the early stages of Jewish settlement, encouraging the Bilu. P. was one of the creators of the Hebrew-speaking movement in Jerusalem. Although religious, his opposition to *Halukkah* and fanaticism brought him into conflict with the Jerusalem rabbis.

PINKAS: Popular name among the Ashkenazim for a Jewish communal register. The term is a mispronunciation (due to incorrect vocalization) of *pinaks*, a Greek word used in the Talmud for writing tablets, etc.

PINSK: Town of USSR, formerly Poland. Jews settled there by the 16th cent., receiving privileges in 1581. Their chief occupation was the grain trade with Danzig and Königsberg. The community achieved importance in Polish Jewry but suffered severely in the Chmielnicki massacres of 1648–9 and the Swedish wars of 1700. Later in the 18th cent., P. was the scene of bitter conflict between Mitnaggedim and Hasidim settled in the suburb of Karlin. In 1939, there were 17,500 Jews (75% of the population). They were herded into a ghetto by the Nazis and annihilated in 1942. Jewish pop. (1970): 1,500.

PINSKER: (1) *JUDAH LOEB (LEON) P.* (1821–1891): Pioneer Zionist; son of (2). He taught Russian at the Kishinev Jewish school and then practiced as a physician in Odessa. In 1856, he served as medical officer in the Crimean War. From 1860, he wrote in the Jewish press and advocated Haskalah, but after the Odessa pogrom of 1871, he held that Enlightenment alone would not solve the Jewish question. Under the influence of the 1881 pogroms, he maintained that only national territorial rebirth would provide a solution and the following year published his pamphlet *Auto-Emancipation*, which had strong repercussions, particularly among Russian Jews. P. called on the Jewish nation to aid itself and return to national consciousness and a life of territorial independence. Anti-Semitism was a universal peril and would not be solved by mere migration to minority status in another country. P. did not hold that Palestine should be the Jewish independent territory until influenced by Lilienblum and Hermann Shapira in 1884. That year, he convened the KATTOWITZ CONFERENCE of HOVEVE ZION at which he was elected president of the movement's presidium. (2) *SIMHAH P.* (1801–1864): Russian scholar. He wrote a comprehensive book on the Karaites, showing the important part they played in laying the foundations of medieval Hebrew grammar, lexicography, and poetry. He also published a work on the Babylonian system of Hebrew vocalization.

PINSKI, DAVID (1872–1959): Yiddish dramatist, novelist, and editor. In 1899, he went from E Europe to the US where he edited *Der Abendblatt*, *Die Arbeiterzeitung*, and *Der Kempfer*. In 1928, he joined the editorial staff of *Der Tog*. He was a founder of the Farband Labor Zionist Organization and president of the Jewish National Workers' Alliance (1920–22) and the Jewish Culture Society (1930–53). His most popular comedy *Der Oitzer* (The Treasure) was produced in Yiddish as well as on the German and New York stage. *The Eternal Jew* was staged by Ha-Bimah in Moscow in 1919. His novel *The House of Noah Eden* was a panorama of the decline of Jewishness in America during three generations and voiced a plea for stemming the tide of assimilation. In 1950, P. settled in Israel and began a series of biblical dramas (*Samson, Saul*).

PINTER, HAROLD (1930–): British playwright. His plays (*The Birthday Party*, *The Caretaker*, *The Homecoming*) have been performed in England and the US and some have been made into films.

PINTO: Marrano family, prominent in Holland, England, and America. In the 17–18th cents., the P. family was among the wealthiest in Amsterdam. *AARON ADOLF DE P.* (1828–1915), Dutch jurist, was president of the Supreme Court, part-author of the Dutch penal code of 1886, and organizer of the first Peace Congress.

Camille Pissarro: *Self-portrait*. (Basle Museum).

PIONEER see **HE-HALUTZ**

PIONEER WOMEN: Women's Labor Zionist Organization. Through its sister organization, the MOETZET HA-POALOT, it maintains in Israel a network of social service agencies for women, youth, and children, including agricultural schools, youth villages, kindergartens, nurseries, recreational centers, etc. P. W. groups can be found in many countries.

PIRBRIGHT, LORD (1840–1903): British statesman. As Baron Henry de Worms, he was active in London Jewish communal life and president of the Anglo-Jewish Association 1874–86. He entered parliament as a Conservative in 1880, was under-secretary for the colonies 1888–92, and was raised to the peerage in 1895.

PIRKE AVOT see **AVOT**

PIRKE DE-RABBI ELIEZER: Tannaitic midrash on Genesis (especially the Creation story) and the first chapters of Exodus, considerably enlarged by a commentary, portions of which are believed to be as late as the 8th cent. The first two of its 54 chapters consist of biographical details of R Eliezer ben Hyrcanus for whom the Midrash is named and to whom the anonymous tannaitic portion is ascribed. The commentary describes many customs which are not known from any other source.

PISA: Italian city. One of the few N Italian cities where Benjamin of Tudela found a Jewish community c. 1168, it later attracted loan-bankers and

was the seat of the eminent Da Pisa family in the 15th–16th cents. In 1593, Marranos were invited to settle there as in Leghorn which, however, soon assumed the hegemony. The community, which suffered severely in the German occupation of 1943–4, numbers 210 (1970).

PISGAH: Part of the ridge of the Abarim mts. on the E border of the Dead Sea (Deut. 3:17). According to another view (Deut. 34:1), P. refers solely to the peak of Nebo. Balaam prophesied from one of its summits, while from another summit Moses saw the Promised Land before his death.

PISHON: One of the four streams branching from the river surrounding Eden (Gen. 2:11). The early rabbis identified it with the Ganges. Some have suggested it was in America, others the Blue Nile.

PISSARRO: Family of painters. (1) *CAMILLE P.* (1830–1903) was one of the founders of impressionism. Born in the W Indies of Sephardi ancestry, he went to Paris in 1847. His first decidedly impressionistic works were exhibited in 1874; later, he was influenced by Seurat's pointillism. His main subjects were landscapes and peasant life. All his sons became painters including (2) *GEORGES P.* (1871–1961), known for colorprints and pictures of birds and flowers influenced by Japanese art; and (3) *LUCIEN P.* (1883–1944) who lived chiefly in England and was an impressionist painter (mostly of landscapes) and engraver and greatly influenced English typography.

PITHOM: One of the two places (with Ramses) where the Hebrews built storage cities for Pharaoh during the Egyptian bondage (Exod. 1:11).

PITTSBURGH: City in Pennsylvania, US. Isolated Jews lived there from 1760 when it was called Fort Pitt. Jews from Bavaria arrived from 1830–50,

Mt. Sinai Hospital in Pittsburgh; founded 1903.

and from Poland after 1845. Jewish religious services were first held in 1842; the first congregation was organized 4 years later, and a synagogue erected in 1861. The United Jewish Federation was organized in 1912 and reorganized in 1955. Jewish pop. (1973) 45,000. There is one weekly, the *Jewish Chronicle* (1962) and a monthly, *Jewish Leader* (1889). P. was the scene of a conference of Reform rabbis in 1885 when the "P. Platform" was accepted, while in 1918, the Zionist Organization of America meeting there adopted its basic statement of principles, known as the "P. Program."

PITTUM HA-KETORET (Heb. "The compound forming the incense"): *Baraita* (*Keritot 6a*) on the preparation of incense in the Temple, recited at the end of the morning prayer (among Ashkenazim outside Israel on Sabbaths and festivals only); by the Sephardim, before the afternoon service; and in some rites also as study (*limmud*) after the morning blessings. The mystics attached great importance to the meticulous recital of the passage.

*PIUS: Name adopted by many popes. *PIUS IV* (1559–65) mitigated the anti-Jewish legislation of his predecessor PAUL IV. *PIUS V* (1566–72), as Cardinal Ghislieri, was responsible for the burning of the Talmud in 1554. As pope, he renewed the anti-Jewish policy of Paul IV and by his bull *Hebraeorum Gens* (1569), expelled the Jews from the Papal States (except Rome and Ancona). *PIUS VI* (1775–9) issued in 1775 an "Edict concerning the Jews" of the utmost severity in which he renewed all former restrictions against them. *PIUS VII* (1800–23) renewed after the Napoleonic wars the former repressive legislation against the Jews and restored the ghetto. *PIUS IX* (1845–78) started his regime as a liberal and relieved the Jews of some restrictions (e.g., conversionist sermons, carnival tax, ghetto walls). Later, he became reactionary and was responsible for the maintenance of the repressive regime against the Roman Jews until he lost his temporal power in 1870. *PIUS XI* (1922–39) unsparingly condemned Nazi and Fascist racialism. *PIUS XII* (officiated 1939–1958) came under strong criticism, especially after his death, for his failure to condemn unequivocally the Nazi destruction of the Jews during World War II. His defenders pointed to certain actions designed to save Jews but his critics (e.g., the German playwright Rolf Hochhuth) claimed that much more could have been accomplished had he spoken out.

PIYYUT (from Gk. *poietes*): Form of Hebrew liturgical POETRY which began in Palestine, probably c. 300–500 CE. The great early *paytanim* (i.e., composers of p.) were Yose ben Yose, Yanai, Eleazar Kalir, and Phinehas; nothing is known about their dates. They were almost certainly *hazzanim* who wrote these poems in order to enliven their services. The first non-Palestinian *paytan* was Saadyah. P. reached the west as part of the general Hebrew revival. Between the 10th and 12th cents. there were an Italian school (Solomon ben Judah Ha-Bavli = the Roman; Moses ben Kalonymos; Elijah ben Shemaiah; Shephatiah; Amittai ben Shephatiah), a Provençal school (Joseph ben Solomon of Carcassonne; Zahlal ben Nathanael; Joseph Bonfils), a German — N French school (Kalonymos of Lucca; Meshullam ben Kalonymos; Simeon bar Abun; Gershom ben Judah; Meir ben Isaac; Rashi; Kalonymos ben Judah), and a Spanish school (Joseph Ibn Abitur; Isaac ben Giyyat; Solomon Ibn Gabirol). In the Spanish school, ryhmed metrical poetry on the Arabic pattern gradually took the place of p. to the extent that Abraham Ibn Ezra made fun of p. and its language. Zunz, whose *Synagogal Poesie des Mittelalters* is still the standard work on p., names over 400 *paytanim*; the discoveries in the Cairo *genizah* have brought to light many more. The individual *piyyutim* are inserted in certain portions of the prayer-book and named according to these places. The chief classes are: *Yotzer*, in the first blessing before the morning *Shema*; *Ophan*, in the middle of the same blessing; *Zulat*, in *Emet ve-yatziv* after the *Shema*; and the *Kerovah*, accompanying (in several parts) the first three blessings of the *Amidah*. Insertions in the evening service are called *Maaravot*. These, and some minor types for other prayers, were written for festivals and special sabbaths, but the chief day for p. is the Day of Atonement when in addition to the above types, the *Selihah* is recited; a complete set of p. for the whole day is called *Maamad*. The *Selihah* became the favorite field of p. composers; such poems are recited also on the New Year and during *Elul* and the Ten Days of Penitence. They thus became independent liturgical items, as are also the *Kinot* for the Ninth of *Av* and the *Reshut* poems (introductions recited by the *hazzan* before starting a major section of p.). The poetic devices of p. are manifold: rhyme, fixed number of syllables to the line, repetitions of words, refrains, involved stanzas, and various utilizations of the initial letters of words. Though hardly any p. is devoid of alphabetical devices, these are used without any regularity. The p. is characterized in no less a degree by its language, which is basically mishnaic Hebrew, but (a) includes the whole of the biblical vocabulary and of Aramaic; (b) enriches the Hebrew vocabulary by the creation of new words, numbering several thousands; and (c) is distinguished by certain individual grammatical and syntactical features. It employs allusions to the Bible and to the Midrash extensively; these are often clothed in an intentionally obscure form intelligible only to those expert in midrashic lore. Originally the p. were free additions to the prayers, and could be exchanged or omitted at will; only gradually did the various rites fix the p. to be used, each differently. The attribution among Ashkenazim of special holiness to certain p. (expressed by opening the Ark) is fairly recent. The Reform movements and even some Orthodox groups have tried to reduce the quantity of p. so as to shorten the services, and because the difficult style is unintelligible to most congregants.

PLAGUES, THE TEN: Afflictions suffered by the Egyptians as a result of Pharaoh's refusal to permit the Israelites to leave the country (Exod. 7:14–12:34). They were (1) the waters of the Nile turned to blood; (2) infestation of frogs; (3) lice affecting man and beast; (4) flies (possibly the tsetse fly; according to the Jewish interpretation, ravening wild beasts); (5) murrain affecting the cattle; (6) boils; (7) heavy hail; (8) locusts devouring the crops;

The Plague of Lice (Sarajevo Haggadah).

(9) three days of darkness; (10) death of the firstborn of man and beast. Seven plagues were brought on by Moses or Aaron raising his staff and three sent directly by God. Some scholars have explained the plagues by the natural climatic conditions in Egypt. The episode features prominently in the SEDER service.

PLAIN OF MOREH see **ELON MOREH**

*PLATO (428/7–347 BCE): Greek philosopher. According to some Church Fathers, he either took his teachings from Jewish sources or was a disciple of Moses. Y. Baer has discerned some influence of his political theories on the earlier rabbis (2nd–1st cents. BCE). The only outstanding Jewish philosopher who followed P. was Philo. In the Middle Ages, his views were mainly known at secondhand but were respected, e.g. by Maimonides. Late Greek paraphrases of some of his dialogues circulated in Arabic, but were not translated into Hebrew, except for the *Republic* with Averroes' commentary and selections of the *Laws* (from the Latin). P.'s main influence on Jewish thought was through NEO-PLATONISM.

PLEDGE: Object taken by the lender from the borrower as security for a loan. The Bible prohibits taking as a p. vessels used in the preparation of food. The lender is also obliged to return at night the garment in which the borrower sleeps in the event that this was taken as a p. and this principle applies to any object taken as a p. from a poor man.

*PLEHVE, VYACHESLAV VON (1846–1904): Russian statesman. He was generally believed to have been implicated in the organization of the KISHINEV pogrom in 1903, but afterward received Herzl sympathetically and promised his support. A Jew, Sikorski, was one of his assassins.

PLOESTI: Rumanian town. The community, called "the Jewish corporation," was in existence before the 19th cent. Later, there were two communal superintendents, an Ashkenazi and a Sephardi. The Jews were subject to periodical persecutions (including Ritual Murder allegations). After 1871, they prospered economically, being prominent in trade and industry. There were 15,000 Jews in P. in 1939; they suffered pogroms, spoliation, and forced labor during World War II. Jewish pop. (1970): 120 families.

POALE AGUDAT ISRAEL (Heb. "AGUDAT ISRAEL Workers"): Religious labor movement founded in Lodz in 1922. It operates within the framework of *Agudat Israel* but has joined Israel government coalitions without *Agudat Israel*. Active especially in agricultural settlement, *P.A.I.* has several kibbutzim. The youth movement *Ezra* has been affiliated to *P.A.I.* since 1937.

POALE ZION (Heb. "Workers of Zion"): Socialist Zionist party. Although individual socialists participated in the First Zionist Congress (1897), socialist Zionist groups first began to be formed some three years later. In Berlin, the efforts of Naḥman SYRKIN led to the establishment of an organization called *Ḥerut*. Isolated groups of Zionist workers were organized in Russia under the name of *P. Z.*, and within five years, groups were formed also in other European countries, in the US, and in Palestine. At a conference at the Hague (1907) many of these united to form the World Confederation of *P.Z.* Several theoreticians contributed to the crystallization of the Socialist Zionist ideology and program, the most influential being Syrkin and BER BOROCHOV. Syrkin maintained that Zionism is not only a nationalist movement but also a social ideal. "There can be no Zionism except Socialist Zionism," Syrkin maintained, and he developed a program of "Socialist Constructivism" in which the class-struggle was played down and the idea of cooperative enterprise was stressed. Borochov, on the other hand, diagnosed the Jewish problem and prognosticated its solution in terms of Marxist dialectic. He held that for the Jewish people the realization of Zionism was historically inevitable because each economic group within

Jewry is subject to pressures by the parallel non-Jewish group with whom it is in competition in each country. This leads, on the one hand, to an uneven Jewish economic structure, and on the other, to displacement, and hence the need for emigration. The role of labor is, therefore, to safeguard and extend the interests of the Jewish workers and to turn the national home into a strategic base in the fight for a socialist society. Although the theories of both men agreed in many essentials, there arose schisms because of the differences, with the views of Syrkin predominating in most of the movement, especially in Palestine and America. In the Diaspora, the movement engaged actively in the struggle for the democratization of Jewish communal life, the enhancement of its cultural content, and the development of progressive Jewish education and the pioneering movement. In Palestine, it created collective settlements, the cooperative sector of the economy, and the HISTADRUT. Through a series of splits and reunions over the years, there emerged the present three groupings: one, centered around MAPAI in Israel; a second, around MAPAM; and a third, around AHDUT HA-AVODAH. All have their related groups in other countries.

PODHORETZ, NORMAN H. (1930–): US author and editor. From 1956 he edited the magazine *Commentary* (published by the American Jewish Committee) making it a leading intellectual monthly. He also published an autobiography *Making It* and a collection of essays *Doings and Undoings*.

PODOLIA (Transdniestria): Province of Ukraine, USSR. Jews living there in the 15th cent. traded with Cracow and Lublin. P. received Jewish refugees from Germany and Bohemia during the Thirty Years' War (1618–48). The community was exterminated in the Chmielnicki uprising (1648) and revived during the period of Turkish rule (1672–99). It was a center of Sabbetaianism, the Frankist movement, and Hasidism. The Jews suffered severely during the Russian Civil War 1918–20. In World War II, its Jewish population was annihilated. From 1941, Rumanian Jews were also herded there; some 60,000 died, while 55,000 survived upon liberation by the Russian army.

POETRY: Hebrew p. differs sharply in spirit and technique according to periods, generally resembling the p. of the comtemporary non-Jewish environment. Biblical p. can be divided into (a) ancient epical poems (perhaps parts of popular epics), such as Gen. 4:23–4; Gen. 49; Exod. 15; Num. 21:17–18; Num. 23–25; (b) echoes of popular lyrical poetry, e.g. the Song of Songs or Is. 5:1–6; and (c) prophecies in poetical form. In technique, all these closely resemble Babylonian and Canaanite p.; the essential feature is parallelism, i.e., the verse is divided into two halves (hemistichs), of which the second either repeats the content of the first in different words or forms an antithesis. There seems to have been also some kind of rhythm, but this has not yet been successfully analyzed. The language of biblical p. differs from that of prose in grammar and vocabulary, being mostly more archaic. Some psalms (e.g. 119) begin each verse or group of verses with a successive letter of the alphabet (ACROSTIC). The DEAD SEA SCROLLS contain many poems which continue the use of parallelism but in a much freer form and without rhythm. Occasional rhymes appear and it has been claimed that the use of rhyme (which in antiquity was avoided as ugly) originated with the Jews. The oldest parts of the prayer book observe a rough kind of parallelism and are arranged in short phrases of about four words, with frequent rhymes. They use a language quite different from the mishnaic prose of the time, with ample borrowing from biblical p., and the only sample preserved of the popular p. of the period (*Pesahim* 57a) is of the same type. These features are developed and exaggerated in PIYYUT which employs rhyme, meters, involved strophic arrangements, refrains, and acrostics. All these techniques were also employed at the time by Greek and Syriac church p. The chief *paytanim* were YOSE BEN YOSE, YANNAI, ELEAZAR KALIR, SAADYAH, and KALONYMOS. About the end of the 10th cent., the Arabic meters, based on alternation of short and long syllables, were adapted to Hebrew (which hitherto had not distinguished between long and short vowels) by making use of the sounded SHEVA and the HATEPHS, e.g.

> *adon o-lam | asher ma-lakh |*
> *bete-rem kol | yetzir niv-ra |*

There are twelve meters, differing in the arrangement of heavy and light syllables. Each line is divided into two hemistichs and all lines in a poem have the same rhyme. Though these meters were also used for religious p., the important innovation of the Middle Ages, especially in Spain, S France, and Italy, was secular p. In spirit and style, this was entirely modeled on contemporary Arabic p.: its main themes were praise of others or oneself, love, wine-drinking, and conventional sentiments about the sadness of life. Great store was set by ingenuity and smooth elegance; truly great poems are rare. The Hebrew was strictly biblical. Among the poets of this type the most outstanding were SAMUEL IBN NAGRELA, Solomon IBN GABIROL, Moses and Abraham IBN EZRA, JUDAH HA-LEVI, and IMMANUEL OF ROME. There were hundreds of minor poets. Among oriental Jews such p. has continued until the present day. After the 14th cent., European Jewry (except in Italy) produced little p. in Hebrew, though some was written in YIDDISH. Hebrew p. only reappeared

Warsaw: Memorial to the Jews who fell
in the Warsaw Ghetto Uprising.

there with the HASKALAH. In Italy, from the 16th cent. onward, verses with a fixed number of syllables (as in European p.) were gradually introduced. Such meters were used by Moses Ḥayyim LUZZATTO, Ephraim LUZZATTO, and in N Europe by D. FRANCO-MENDES, and N. H. WESSELY. In the E European Haskalah this type of meter was renounced for modern meters based on word accent. Present-day Hebrew p. uses all the techniques of European and American p., including *vers libre*. In style and content, too, modern Hebrew p. generally follows international trends. One characteristic feature is the popularity of the idyll (TSCHERNIKHOVSKI, SHIMONI). Among the important modern Hebrew poets are Micah Joseph LEBENSOHN, J. L. GORDON, H. N. BIALIK, S. TSCHERNIKHOVSKI, Y. CAHAN, Z. SHNEOUR, RAHEL, A. SHLONSKY, D. SHIMONI, SH. SHALOM, and N. ALTERMAN.

POGROM (Russ. "destruction"): An organized massacre for the annihilation of any body or class, especially with governmental collusion; more specially one directed against Jews. The term was first used in English at the time of the anti-Jewish outbreaks organized by the BLACK HUNDREDS in RUSSIA in 1905, but is often applied to earlier Russian outbreaks from 1881 onward.

POLAND: E European country. Jews lived here from the 9th cent. Whether the first settlers originated from the West (Germany, Bohemia, etc.) or the South (the Kingdom of Kiev and the Byzantine Empire) is uncertain, but in either case they were apparently reinforced by KHAZAR elements. Not very much is known about the early settlers, presumably traders, who in the Dark Ages helped to open up the area to civilizing influences. According to legend, the first charter was granted in 905. Polish coins of the 12th–13th cents. struck by Jewish mintmasters bear Hebrew inscriptions, thus illustrating the significance of the Jews in economic life. The Tartar invasions of 1240/1 utterly devastated P. To restore its economy, the kings encouraged the immigration of merchants from Germany. These were followed and accompanied by Jews, who brought with them their language (see YIDDISH), the ASHKENAZI ritual, and their passionate devotion to Talmud study, all of which became dominant in Polish Jewry. A model charter of protection was issued by Boleslaw the Pious in 1264. This was extended by Casimir the Great to all of P. by the Statute of Kalisz in 1334, to White Russia and Little P., in 1364, and to LITHUANIA, in 1388/9. The charters regulated legal conditions, the framework of economic employment, judicial suits between Jews and Christians, safeguards of Jewish life and property, freedom of trade, etc. The German traders introduced anti-Jewish sentiments and the growth of the Jewish population led to complaints from the clergy. As a result, Vladislaus Jagiello (1386–1434) refused to confirm the Jewish privileges. There were Blood Libels at Posen in 1399 and Cracow in 1407, a host desecration charge in 1400, and in the following year, students in CRACOW began an anti-Jewish riot. In 1454, the Jewish privileges were largely abolished, and in the same period, attacks on the Jews took place in many cities — e.g. Cracow, Lvov, and POSEN — where they were regarded by the merchants as economic competitors; elsewhere, they were expelled, e.g. WARSAW 1483, Cracow 1491. Nevertheless, despite attacks and legal restrictions, the Jews played an important part in commerce. Conditions improved in the 16th cent. under the liberal Sigismund (1500–48) and Sigismund II Augustus (1548–72) when Jewish revenue collectors, bankers, physicians, etc. occupied key-positions in the economic and political life. From this period onward, P. was a renowned center of rabbinic study and its talmudic scholars profoundly affected Jewry as a whole. For fiscal reasons, the foundations were laid for the AUTONOMY of the organized communities. As the community organizations (KEHILLOT) became better situated and economically stronger, the struggle with the cities intensified. The Jews, relying on their charters, appealed for royal protection and — with the mediation of the king — obtained agreements and concessions. Stephen Báthory (1576–86) confirmed Jewish privileges and sharply attacked Blood Libel accusations. Under the influence of the Counter-Reformation, reaction set in under his successor Sigismund III (1587—1632), who, nevertheless, protected Jews from Church (especially Jesuit) persecutions. The *kehillot* joined forces to become provincial councils and reached their climax in the COUNCIL OF THE FOUR LANDS (abolished in 1764).

The strengthening of reaction led to changes in the economic life of Polish Jewry, especially in the villages, where the Jewish lessees were exploited by the nobles to oppress the peasants, especially in the UKRAINE (then Polish). The leasing of estates became a major source of livelihood, and the lessees employed many other Jews as subordinates. This was one of the causes of the massacres at the time of the CHMIEL-NICKI uprising (1648–9) which destroyed hundreds of communities. During the latter 17th cent., the kings of P. endeavored to foster the rehabilitation of the Jewish communities but were frustrated by the general anti-Jewish atmosphere. Economic restrictions, pogroms, and Ritual Murder charges were recurrent. The position was particularly bad under the Saxon kings (1697–1763) when there was a series of Ritual Murder trials, attempts at forced conversion, expulsions, riots, etc. Thousands were killed in the HAIDAMAK Cossack disorders of 1768 in the Ukraine.

The influence of the Kabbalah was strong in P. from the 16th cent. In the 17th cent., Polish Jewry was profoundly influenced by the messianic claims of Shabbetai Tzevi and, thereafter, was a center of the SABBETAIANS. This culminated in the strange movement led by Jacob FRANK, which ultimately resulted in an attack on the Talmud and large numbers of nominal conversions. On the other hand, this atmosphere resulted also in the emergence in the mid-18th cent. of HASIDISM. As a result of the partitions of P. in the late 18th cent., many areas were severed from the kingdom, those of the province of Posen reinforcing Prussian Jewry, those of Galicia going to Austro-Hungary, and those of the E provinces constituting the kernel of Russian Jewry. The national movement which now sprang up in the truncated kingdom discussed the amelioration of the Jewish position, and some degree of emancipation was advocated by the "Quadrennial Diet" in 1790 and granted under Napoleon in 1807; it was not, however, carried into effect. After 1815, the bulk of P. was under the oppressive Russian rule. In 1828, two-thirds of P.'s Jews lived in towns where they constituted 50% of the total urban population. Most of them lived by petty trade, handicrafts, liquor distilling, and domestic industries — particularly textile manufacture. Some Jews participated in the 1830 revolt, the aftermath of which brought rises in taxation and no relaxation of restrictions. Jews played an important role in economic life, particularly in Warsaw and LODZ. The revolutionary rising of 1863 proclaimed equal rights for Jews and its suppression the following year left in its wake a certain trend toward assimilation among the Polish Jewish intelligentsia. Jews now held key-positions in foreign trade, in the timber, grain, and metal trades, in all branches of finance, in industry, and in the free professions. A pronounced anti-Semitic trend prevailed at the end of the 19th cent. Polish anti-Semites supported by the clergy and the press launched a campaign against the Jews, which was supported by the great majority of political groups, and there was a pogrom in Warsaw in 1881. ZIONISM took a strong hold, while the BUND also flourished. Very great numbers of Polish Jews emigrated at this period, particularly to W Europe and the US. The independent state of P. established after World War I undertook to protect its minorities, but its attitude toward the Jews left much to be desired. The economic position of its Jews sharply deteriorated as the new Polish middle-class tended to push them out of trade, handicrafts, and industry. In 1938, 300,000 Jewish breadwinners were unemployed, and emigration continued on a large scale (395,223 Jews left P. 1921–37). Nevertheless, there was great progress in public and cultural life, especially in the field of Jewish education, while Polish-Jewish literature and press flourished. The struggle for the full enjoyment of civic and national rights was tortuous and difficult. In 1939, P. had over 3 million Jews. Under Nazi occupation. they underwent wholesale massacre and suffered martyrdom. Ghettos were set up at Warsaw, Lodz, Bialystok, etc., and these proved the prelude to the CONCENTRATION CAMPS and gas chambers. Great numbers of Jews were brought to P. from other parts of Nazi-occupied Europe for annihilation. Jewish youth participated in the underground struggle of the PARTISANS, while the ghetto risings at Warsaw, Bialystok, and elsewhere produced acts of desperate courage. After World War II, Jews who had escaped to Russia or had been exiled, returned to try and pick up the threads of life in P., mostly settling in Silesia, Lodz, Warsaw, and Cracow.

Jewish Soldiers from Poland visit
the Hebrew University in Jerusalem, 1942.

Despite the opposition of the communist regime, there occurred cases of assault and even pogroms (e.g. at Kielce, 1946) resulting in considerable emigration and a drastic reduction in the size of the new settlement. From 1955, open anti-Semitic activity appeared, certain communist circles deliberately directing discontent against the Jews. After the Gomulka regime came to power in 1956, Jews were permitted to emigrate. Between 1948 and 1958, approximately 140,500 Jews left P. for Israel After the Six-Day War in 1967, a strong anti-Semitic reaction in the government deprived Jews of leading positions in various walks of life and led to a further emigration. The numbers remaining in 1973 were estimated at 8,000.

Polemic between Jewish and Christian
scholars. 16th cent. woodcut.

POLEMICS: Traces of Jewish p. are found in talmudic literature in the record of discussions between rabbis and *minim* (a term sometimes referring apparently to gnostics, sometimes to Christians). On the Christian side, polemical literature, endeavoring to convince or confute the Jews, was common, beginning with Justin Martyr's semi-fictional account of his dialogue with Tryphon (2nd cent.). A general record of early Christian p. is to be found in A. Lukyn Williams' *Adversus Judaeos*, which describes works by (among others) Tertullian and Chrysostom in Greek and by Augustin, Prudentius, Isidore of Seville, Raymund Lutt, etc. in Latin. There are no similar works on the Jewish side (see APOLOGETICS), and the record of religious discussions by Joseph OFFICIAL in 12th cent. France is genial and good-natured. In the 13th cent., Christian anti-Jewish p. took on a more vigorous aspect in the activities of the Dominican Order and the organization of the great DISPUTATIONS at Paris, Barcelona, etc. From this period, specific Jewish polemical writings begin to be preserved. These include both accounts of the various disputations and specific works such as the satirical letter of Profiat DURAN, the *Sepher ha-Berit* of Joseph KIMHI, the closely-argued *Sepher Nitzahon* by Yomtov Lipmann MUHLHAUSEN, and, above all, the classical *Hizzuk Emunah* by the Karaite Isaac of TROKI. Noteworthy, too, are the works produced by ex-Marranos in Amsterdam, etc. The Christian polemical works endeavored to prove the dogmas of the Trinity, Virgin Birth, Messiahship of Jesus, etc.; the Jewish protagonists concentrated on the unqualified Divine unity and the eternity of the Mosaic law. Judeo-Moslem polemical literature is scantier and less systematic, though some works, such as the *Keshet u-Magen* of Simeon Duran, are directed against both Christianity and Islam. In the 19th cent., religious p. against Judaism became secondary to p. against the Jews (see ANTISEMITISM), lacking any religious basis.

POLIAKOFF: Russian family of industrialists headed by the brothers *JACOB P.* (1832–1909), *LAZAR P.* (1842–1913), and *SAMUEL P.* (1837–1888) who were ennobled. Lazar, head of the Moscow community, founded a textile factory at Dobrovna. Jacob headed the St. Petersburg community and was vice-chairman of ICA in Russia. Samuel was a founder of the Academy of Jewish Sciences in St. Petersburg and of ORT.

POLITZER ADAM (1835–1920): Viennese physician. Director of Vienna Univ.'s otological clinic, he initiated the therapeutic treatment of ear diseases.

POLL TAX: The first p. t. on the Hebrews was the levy of half a SHEKEL imposed on all adult males (Exod. 30:12–16) after the Exodus. In the time of the Second Temple, this became an annual levy. The imposition of a p. t. by the Romans in 6 CE led to the rebellion under Judah the Galilean. On the destruction of Jerusalem, the former voluntary levy of half a shekel for the upkeep of the Temple was converted by the Romans into the FISCUS JUDAICUS. This continued to be levied at least until the 4th cent., at first with great harshness. In the Middle Ages, the levy was renewed by the Holy Roman Emperors in Germany, as heirs to the emperors of Rome, under the name OPFERPFENNIG. In other countries, the p. t. was levied only occasionally: thus it was instituted in England, Spain, France, etc. In Turkey (and Moslem states generally), a p. t. was payable by all non-Moslems as a condition of toleration.

POLLAK, JACOB (1470–1541): Rabbi and codifier. He was compelled to leave the rabbinate in Prague after issuing a decision opposed to the views of his colleagues. Nevertheless, he was highly respected in Poland and in 1503, was appointed communal rabbi at Cracow. P. introduced the PILPUL method of Talmud study. Forced to leave Poland, he resided for ten years in Jerusalem before returning to Lublin.

POLNA CASE: Ritual Murder libel. In 1899, a Christian girl was found dead in a wood near Polna (Bohemia), and a Jew, Leopold Hilsner, was accused of the murder. A slander of ritual murder was spread and pogroms occurred in several localities. Hilsner was found guilty and sentenced to death. The verdict aroused a storm of protest from progressive elements (led by Thomas G. Masaryk) as well as further anti-Semitic attacks. The court of appeal quashed the verdict but at a retrial in 1900, Hilsner was again sentenced to death. The Austrian emperor commuted the sentence to life imprisonment. Hilsner was amnestied only in 1916.

POLYGAMY: The Bible reflects, without recommending, a polygamous society. Nevertheless, the household of Isaac, regarded as a model in later Jewish tradition, was monogamous. P.' became general in the luxurious courts of the first Jewish kings (and the number of Solomon's concubines is recorded), but the ideal picture of the housewife in Proverbs 31 seems to picture a monogamous household. The society reflected in the Talmud is essentially monogamous, only a handful of rabbis being recorded as having more than one wife. This ideal governed Jewish life thereafter. The *takkanah* of R Gershom forbidding polygamy (c. 1000 CE) thus gave formal sanction among Ashkenazi Jews to what was already generally accepted. Among the Spanish and oriental Jews, on the other hand, p. continued to be legal, though by no means general. In Italy, down to the 17th cent., a person whose wife was barren was occasionally permitted by papal licence to take a second wife. With the Europeanization of many oriental communities in recent generations, p. has become increasingly rare. In Israel, monogamy is now enforced by law, though existing polygamous marriages are recognized.

POMI (POMIS), DAVID DE' (1525–1588): Italian physician. A native of Spoleto in the Papal States, he had to abandon his brilliant medical practice in that area when the Jews were expelled in 1569, and he settled in Venice. Here he attended the doge and many important magnates, both lay and clerical. His works include a treatise on gynecology, a historical vindication of Jewish physicians, written to forestall an attempt to force them out of practice, and *Tzemah David*, a Hebrew-Latin-Italian dictionary replete with scientific and historical information.

*POMPEY (106–48 BCE): Roman general. Arriving in Syria in 65–3 BCE, he became arbiter in the dispute between Hyrcanus II and Aristobulus for the throne of Judea. Ultimately favoring the former, he captured Jerusalem and the Temple from Aristobulus' supporters. He left the shrine intact, although entering the the Holy of Holies. Judea was made tributary and stripped of the territories acquired by

Lorenzo da Ponte.

the Hasmoneans; Aristobulus and his family were taken to Rome to grace P.'s triumph. P. effectively terminated Jewish independence enjoyed since Simon the Maccabee.

PONTE, LORENZO DA (originally Emanuele Conegliano; 1749–1838): Italian poet, baptized in youth. As poet to the court opera at Vienna, he wrote the libretti for Mozart's *Marriage of Figaro*, *Don Giovanni*, and *Cosi fan tutte*. In 1805, he settled in New York where he laid the foundation for American opera.

PONTIUS PILATE see **PROCURATORS**

POOL, DAVID DE SOLA (1885–1970): Rabbi. Born in England, he went to the US in 1907 as minister of the Spanish and Portuguese synagogue in New York. He published a study of *The Kaddish* and works on the history of his congregation, translations of liturgy, and an edition of the Passover Haggadah

David de Sola Pool.

in collaboration with his wife, *TAMAR DE S. P.* (1893–), who was president of Hadassah 1939–43.

POOR see **POVERTY**

POPES: Heads of the Roman Catholic Church.

The earliest p. – the line legendarily beginning with St. Peter – were inevitably of Jewish birth. Later p. were of importance in Jewish history both because of their spiritual position and influence on the policy of Catholic rulers everywhere, and because of their temporal authority in and around ROME, in Italy, as well as in the COMTAT VENAISSIN in S France. Though some earlier p. are known to have had personal relations with Jews, the first who had significance in Jewish history was GREGORY I ("the great"; 590-604) who laid down the general lines of policy toward the Jews from which the papacy never departed: on the one hand, the safeguarding of the religious privileges which they traditionally enjoyed, including the full practice of Judaism and their protection against violence; on the other hand, their exclusion from any "innovations" not so guaranteed and from any possibility of exercising authority over Christians, as well as the encouragement of their conversion. The fact that Jewish communities always existed under papal rule emphasizes the continuity of the favorable side of the policy. A phrase used in one of Gregory's letters formed the opening to the protective bull *Sicut Judeis*, forbidding the molestation of the Jews and guaranteeing their religious rights, which was first issued by Calixtus II (1119–24) in 1120, and was thereafter regularly confirmed by his successors down to the close of the Middle Ages. On the other hand, INNOCENT III (1198–1216) emphasized the unfavorable aspect of the papal policy, inspiring the anti-Jewish legislation of the fourth LATERAN COUNCIL of 1215, which aimed at Jewish segregation and degradation and provided a somber standard for later generations. But the traditional balance nevertheless continued to be maintained. Thus, Gregory IX (1227–41), while enforcing the Lateran legislation and taking the first steps leading to the condemnation of the Talmud, issued a number of protective bulls: and Innocent IV, three years after sentencing the Talmud in his bull *Impia Gens* (1244), unequivocally condemned the Ritual Murder libel in *Lachrymabilem Judeorum Alemannie* (1247). The Avignonese p. maintained the now conventional attitude, though many Jews were in the employment of the papal court at this time. On the other hand, the anti-pope Benedict XIII (1394-1417) tried to achieve a publicity triumph by presiding in person over the DISPUTATION of TORTOSA in the hope of driving the Jews to baptism. In Italy, Martin V (1417–31) adopted a generally benevolent attitude, but his successor Eugenius IV (1431-47) put into execution the anti-Jewish legislation of the Council of Basle. At the end of the 15th cent., Roman Jewry began a period of well-being under the auspices of the cultured, broadminded p. of the Renaissance Period, especially LEO X (1513–21), who permitted the printing of the Talmud, and his cousin Clement VII (1523–33), the protector of David Reubeni and Solomon Molcho. The Counter-Reformation introduced a new spirit in which the negative side of the papal policy triumphed as never before. PAUL IV (1555–9) persecuted the Marranos of Ancona and instituted the ghetto system with its concomitant horrors by his *Cum Nimis Absurdum* (1555), while Pius V (1566–72) expelled the Jews from the smaller places in the Papal States by his *Hebraeorum Gens* (1569). Moreover, the p. of this and the succeeding period greatly extended the area of the papal territories in Italy in which this legislation was meticulously observed and exerted pressure to have it adopted elsewhere in the peninsula. There was a considerable alleviation under SIXTUS V (1585–90) who wished to use the Jews to relieve the economic distress in the Papal States, but the reaction returned in full under Clement VIII (1592–1604), thereafter knowing little respite. Yet even now, the benevolent aspects of the papal policy toward the Jews were not wholly forgotten: indeed, Clement XIV (1769–74), as Cardinal Lorenzo Ganganelli, had drawn up for the Holy See a notable memorandum condemning the Blood Accusation. On the other hand, his successor PIUS VI (1775–98) renewed all the anti-Jewish legislation of the past down to its most minute and preposterous details in his *Editto sopra gli Ebrei* of 1775. It was in his day that the ideas and, ultimately, armies of the French Revolution burst into Italy depriving the papacy of its former authority for a generation. With the restoration of the temporal rule of the p., Pius VII (1800–23) and, especially, his successor Leo XII (1823–9) enforced again in their dominions the whole of the medieval repressive anti-Jewish code, except for the Jewish Badge. Pius IX (1846–78) began his career as the hope of the liberal element and did a good deal to alleviate the sufferings of Roman Jewry. He was subsequently driven into reaction and in great part perpetuated the ghetto system over his dwindling dominions down to the fall of the Temporal Power in 1870. His successors, such as Leo XIII (1878–1903), tended to associate the Jews with the advance of socialism, as was shown in some of their nervous pronouncements. Pius XI (1922–39), however, took up an attitude of unswerving opposition to Nazi racialism, and under PIUS XII (1939–58), the papacy helped to alleviate the sufferings of the Italian Jews during World War II. although failing to condemn the Nazi atrocities outspokenly. The papacy's attitude to the creation of the state of Israel, and especially to the incorporation in it of Jerusalem, has been on the whole unfavorable, and there are no diplomatic relations between Israel and the Vatican state. JOHN XXIII (1958–1964) modified

Catholic liturgy referring to Jews and initiated the Jewish document which was eventually endorsed in a modified form at the Second Vatican Council under PAUL VI (1963—). In the framework of a pilgrimage to the Holy Land, Paul visited Israel in 1964 and was received by President Shazar.

POPPER, DAVID (1843–1913): Bohemian cellist. He toured extensively and from 1896, taught at the National Academy of Music, Budapest. His compositions include four concertos.

POPPER (LYNKEUS), JOSEPH (1838–1921): Austrian engineer and scholar. He made important innovations in the spheres of electricity and aeronautics. For moral reasons he abandoned science and belles-lettres to devote himself to the problems of human society (prevention of war, reform of criminal law, etc.). The Russian pogroms brought him close to Judaism and Zionism.

POPULATION see **STATISTICS**

PORCIUS FESTUS see **PROCURATORS**

PORGE (Sp. *Porgar*, "Purge"): Among English-speaking Jews, to remove the sinews, etc. of the hind-legs from an animal slaughtered according to the prescriptions of *kashrut*.

PORTALEONE, ABRAHAM BEN DAVID (1542–1612): Italian physician and author. In 1573, he was appointed medical attendant to the duke of Mantua. In 1605, half his body was paralyzed in consequence of a stroke. In a mood of repentance, he wrote *Shilte ha-Gibborim* ("Shields of the Mighty"), which deals with all matters connected with Temple ritual.

PORTLAND: City in Oregon. US. Jews – mostly of S German origin – settled there in the early 1850's, and the first Jewish congregation was founded in 1858. Russian Jews began arriving in the 1880's. Four mayors of the city as well as a state governor and two senators have come from P.'s Jewish community. In 1973, P. had 7,800 Jews with 5 synagogues (one Sephardi). The Jewish Welfare Federation of P. was established in 1920; the Oregon Jewish Welfare Fund has been situated in P. since 1936.

PORTO-RICHE, GEORGES DE (1849—1930): French dramatist. *Théâtre d'amour*, a collection of his plays, includes *Amoureuse* which became a classic of the French stage. His later work was less successful.

PORTSMOUTH: English port. Its community, established in 1747, is the oldest in Great Britain outside London. It flourished during the 18th cent., when P. was the greatest English naval base, and in 1766–89, maintained two rival congregations. The community dwindled in the 19th cent., and the original elements have now been superseded by later immigration. Jewish pop. (1973): 600.

PORTUGAL: European republic. Jews were probably settled in this area while it was still under Arab rule, and when the Christian state was formed,

there were apparently communities in LISBON, Beja, and Santarem. Little is known of them until the 13th cent. Conditions were generally tranquil, notwithstanding riots at Lisbon in 1373, and P. escaped the wave of massacres that engulfed Spain in 1391. The community was closely organized by Alfonso III (1248–79) in his elaborate code, with a chief rabbi (*Arrabi Mor*) at its head. After the expulsion from Spain in 1492, large numbers of the exiles were allowed to enter P. on payment of a poll-tax, but many were subsequently detained in the country and sold as slaves. Manoel II ordered the expulsion of the Jews from his dominion (Oct. 1496) in order to secure the hand of the Spanish Infanta but later changed his mind and had almost the entire community converted by force (1497). Thus, a large body of MARRANOS was created in P. The INQUISITION was introduced in the 16th cent. and the refugees who fled to escape it formed the "Portuguese" synagogues in London, Amsterdam, New York, etc. in the 16th–17th cents. At the close of the 18th cent., Jews from Gibraltar and N Africa established themselves in Lisbon, though freedom of worship was permitted only after the Revolution of 1910. Ashkenazi immigrants from Central and E Europe have arrived in recent years. There was also for a time a tiny community at Faro. Marranos with strong Jewish sympathies are still numerous in northern P. A movement to rescue them was started in 1925, and in 1938, a synagogue was built as their religious center in Oporto. Apart from the Marranos, whose numbers cannot be ascertained, the Jewish pop. of P. is 580 (1973) mostly in Lisbon.

POSEKIM see **LAW, CODIFICATION OF**

POSEN (POZNAN): Town in Poland. Jews from Germany settled there in the latter part of the 14th cent. They were subject to the exclusive jurisdiction of the king who protected them against the townspeople, although in 1399, a Host Desecration allegation resulted in the martyrdom of the rabbi and 13 elders. Anti-Jewish outbreaks occurred in 1468 and 1577, while an attack on the Jewish quarter in 1687 was successfully resisted. From 1532 to 1803 their residence was restricted to 49 dwelling houses. P. was a major center of Jewish scholarship, its rabbis were regarded as chief rabbis of Greater Poland and a Hebrew press operated from the late 16th cent. Under Prussian rule the policy of Germanization led to the Jews' receiving civic equality. The percentage of Jews in P. – 25% (3,000) at the end of the 18th cent. – dropped rapidly in the later 19th-early 20th cents. and most removed to Germany, being replaced by newcomers from Poland. The 2,000 Jews (1939) suffered the same fate as the rest of Polish Jewry in World War II.

POTIPHAR: Chief of Pharaoh's bodyguard. Joseph was sold to him as a slave but became his chief

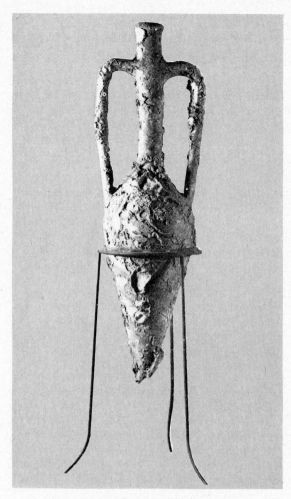

Hellenistic pottery taken from the sea off Caesarea.

official until imprisoned on a false charge of attempted seduction brought by P.'s wife.

POTIPHERA: Priest of On and father of Asenath wife of Joseph. Identification with Potiphar (suggested in the Aggadah and elsewhere) is untenable.

POTOCKI, VALENTIN, COUNT: Legendary convert to Judaism. According to tradition, he belonged to a famous Polish family of magnates, became a proselyte, and was burned at the stake in Vilna in 1749. The legend was first published in Polish in 1842 in a book by the historian and writer Ignaz Kraszawski. No evidence has been found to confirm the truth of this story.

POTOFSKY, JACOB SAMUEL (1894–): US labor leader. Born in Russia, he went to the US in 1908. Since 1946, he has been president of the Amalgamated Clothing Workers' Union.

POTTERY: The first records of p. in Palestine date from the Neolithic Period, when it was handmade. In the Chalcolithic Period, a primitive turntable was used, chiefly for urns and cups with painted geometric decoration. In the Early Bronze Ages, bandslip and geometric decorations were common, the usual forms being urns and beakers. In the Middle Bronze Age, the potter's wheel became prominent, and there was much elaboration of form and decoration, with imitation of metal prototypes, incised decoration, and appliqué bands. In the Late Bronze Age, foreign importations became numerous. During the 12th cent. BCE, Philistine ware, a local version of late Mycenean styles, was to be found in the coastal plain. P. from the period of the Israelite monarchy included handled storage jars, some stamped by the authorities, and wheelburnished bowls. Greek glazed ware became a feature in the 7th cent. In the Hellenistic Period, black glazed and brown-slipped ware was commom; coarse rilled vessels began to appear and remained common until the end of the Byzantine epoch. The Roman age saw the importation of red-glaze, later locally imitated. In the 4th cent. CE, colorcoated p. spread. The Talmud has hundreds of names for various vessels, many of them of Greek derivation. A royal p. industry was maintained by the kings of Judah (I Chron. 4:22–3). Jewish manufacturing centers existed, particularly in Galilee, in mishnaic times, and the sectarians of Kumran made pots which were used as repositories for their documents. The mishnaic tractate *Kelim* treats of the ritual cleanness of earthern vessels. See also ARCHEOLOGY.

POVERTY: Jewish thought regarded p. as a misfortune, not as a virtue: the poor would never entirely disappear (Deut. 15:11) and their relief was a primary religious duty. The triennial "poor man's tithe" (Deut. 26:12) is probably the first statutory poor-relief in history. In the 4th cent., the emperor Julian was inspired by the Jewish example in ordering the establishment of hostels for indigent strangers. In later Jewish history, P. was exceptionally widespread among the Jews. This was due partly to cramping restrictions on their activities, partly to the large numbers despoiled, maimed, or bereaved of support in successive outbreaks. Although there was a handful of well-to-do Jews, the fact that Jewish beggars (Yid. SHNORRER) were seldom seen in public gave the impression of Jewish wealth. Even in W Europe in the 18th cent., it was reckoned that one-third of the total Jewish population received charity and another third was on the verge of destitution. The Jewish social outlook resulted in the development of distinctive charitable institutions such as the *tamḥui* or public kitchen and arrangements to help the poor to become self-supporting rather than subsist on CHARITY, etc.

POZNAN see **POSEN**

POZNANSKI, SAMUEL ABRAHAM (1864–1921): Scholar; from 1897 rabbi in Warsaw. A devoted pupil of Steinschneider, he specialized in the post-gaonic period and Karaite history, editing several medieval commentaries. P. prepared a bibliographical lexicon of Karaite literature and published hundreds of learned studies.

PRACTICAL ZIONISM see **ZIONISM**

PRAEFECTUS JUDAEORUM (Lat. "prefect of the Jews"): Title of the official lay representative of the Jews of Hungary in the 15th–16th cents. The office was held from 1482 to 1539 by successive members of the Mendel family.

Woodcut of a hare-hunt: a traditional depiction of the *yaknehaz* mnemonic (Prague Haggadah, 1527).

PRAGUE: Capital of CZECHOSLOVAKIA. Jews settled there in the 10th cent. and engaged in trade. They resisted the attacks of the Crusaders in 1096. Expulsions, violence, and discrimination were common during the 14th–15th cents. The position improved in the 16th cent. which ushered in the community's cultural golden age, lasting until the 18th cent. In 1512, Gershon ben Solomon Cohen established a Hebrew printing shop in P., however, from 1562, all Hebrew books were subject to censorship. In the 16th–18th cents., it was one of the largest and most important communities in Central Europe, with its large and self-contained Jewish quarter (*Judenstadt*), its ancient synagogues many of which still stand, its world-renowned scholars, its Hebrew printing-press, its highly-developed autonomous institutions, its Jewish craft-guilds, etc. The synagogues (Altneuschul, Pinkasschul, etc.) and vast cemetery are still among the sights of the city, and the legend of the "Hoh Rabbi Löw" and the GOLEM he manufactured have entered into Jewish folklore. The Jews, exiled from 1745–8, were only allowed to return after promising to pay exorbitant taxes. In 1848, the Jews of P. were granted full equality, and four years later the ghetto was abolished. Jews then began taking a large share in German cultural life with only smaller groups showing interest in Czech culture. Under the Czechoslovak Republic between World Wars I and II, the P. community flourished, Jews achieving prominence in all walks of life. After Sept. 1938, 15,000 Jews from the Sudeten district ceded to Germany sought refuge in P. A month later, with the formation of a Nazi regime in the country, the liquidation of the P. community began. There were 65,000 Jews in P.

in 1942, about 25,000 of them refugees, but these were exterminated by 1945. Jewish pop. (1973), 3,000.

PRAYER: Man's appeal to God, whether as a request or in thanksgiving. P. is frequently mentioned in the Bible, which reports the formulas of individual prayers (e.g. Eliezer, Gen. 24:12–15; Jacob, Gen. 32:10–13; Moses, Exod. 32:11–13; Hannah, I Sam. 2:1–10; Solomon, I Kings 8:22–53). Most of the Psalms are prayers, some (e.g. Ps. 17, 86, 90) being explicitly so called. Daniel prayed thrice daily (Dan. 6:11), and this was apparently an ancient Jewish custom. From the beginning of the Second Temple Period, there was a settled p. formula determined by the men of the Great Assembly and recited three times day, viz. morning (SHAHARIT), afternoon (MINHAH), corresponding to the times of the permanent sacrifice in the Temple, and evening (*Arvit* or MAARIV) with an additional prayer (MUSAPH) recited on Sabbaths and festivals corresponding to the additional sacrifice. On the Day of Atonement, a further prayer (NEILAH) was added toward nightfall. The original version of the daily p. includes EIGHTEEN BENEDICTIONS (*Shemoneh Esreh* or *Amidah*) in praise of the Creator and petitioning for the needs of the individual and the community. After the Destruction, p. was regarded as a substitute for sacrifice and until the Temple should be rebuilt, this rebuilding and the concomitant renewal of the sacrificial service would be petitioned for in all the prayers. It is an ancient Jewish custom to turn toward Jerusalem when praying, while those in Jerusalem turn to the Temple site. Many additions have accrued to the liturgy in the course of centuries. The SHEMA and its blessings, formerly recited separately, have been added in the mornings and evenings. A book containing the full text of the prayers is called a *Siddur Tephillah* ("Order of P.") or in brief a *Siddur* or *Tephillah*. Compilation of such works had already begun in the gaonic period and extended through all subsequent epochs. The main text among most Jews is uniform, but there are differences in detail between the various communities (Ashkenazi, Sephardi, Italian, Yemenite, etc.) and also between the Hasidim and their opponents. The Reform (and to lesser extent the Conservative) have introduced prayers in the vernacular and various other modifications (e.g. omission of prayers for the restoration of the sacrificial service or for the return to Zion), although the actual changes differ from country to country. P. may be in solitude or in public, but the latter is preferable and certain parts (e.g., KEDUSHAH, KADDISH) are only said in public, i.e., by a *minyan* (at least ten Jewish adult males). In public, most of the prayers are recited by all participants, only short parts being repeated by the precentor (*Hazzan* or *Sheliah Tzibbur*). Public p. is generally, but not necessarily, recited

Front page of the earliest Hebrew newspaper in the US:
Ha-Tzopheh ba-Aretz ha-Hadashah, June 11, 1870.

in a SYNAGOGUE (*Bet Keneset*). Discussions on p.
rites are to be found in talmudic and rabbinical
literature and on the ethical aspects, in the talmudic
and midrashic aggadah as well as in the religious,
ethical, and philosophical literature.

PRAYER BOOK see **PRAYER**

PREACHING see **HOMILETICS**

PRECEPTS, 613 (Heb. "*taryag* [= 613] *mitzvot*"):
The number of the Divine precepts (Pentateuchal
laws) was computed in talmudic times. They consist
of 248 affirmative precepts (traditionally corresponding in number to the bones of the body) and 365
negative precepts (equal to the days of the year). To
these the rabbis added another seven precepts known
as *mitzvot de-rabbanan* ("rabbinical commandments").
The Divine precepts were first classified by the 8th
cent. Babylonian halakhist R Yehudai Gaon and by
R Simeon Kayyara, and the first detailed list of the
613 precepts is to be found in the HALAKHOT GEDOLOT.
Maimonides later listed and classified the number in
his *Sepher ha-Mitzvot* and adopted it as the basis

of his *Mishneh Torah* code. R Moses of Coucy (13th
cent.) compiled the precepts according to talmudic
tradition in his *Sepher Mitzvot Gadol*, treating the
positive precepts in the first part and the negative
ones in the second. The 613 precepts include many
which have become inoperative since the destruction
of the Temple, e.g., the laws relating to sacrifices,
the Temple service, and the laws of ritual purity.
Several of the precepts are incidental and apply only
to certain categories of people.

PREDESTINATION see **FREE WILL**

PRE-EXISTENCE: The theory that certain objects,
in particular human souls, exist before coming
into being on earth, or even before the creation of
the world. No such belief has been proved to exist
in the Bible, but it is firmly established in Apocryphal
literature and among the Essenes who held that
souls before birth existed in "the finest ether." It was
held also by the rabbis of the Talmud who believed
that all souls pre-existed in an abode called *guph*,
that the Torah, Messiah, etc. existed before Creation,
and that ten or more objects, including the staff of
Aaron and the Tablets of the Law, were precreated
at the end of the days of Creation (*Avot* 5:6). Among
philosophers, Philo (following Plato) and Ibn Gabirol
accepted p. It forms an essential belief of Kabbalah
where it is linked with METEMPSYCHOSIS.

PRESBYTER JUDAEORUM (Gk. and Lat. "Elder
of Jews"): Title of the lay head of medieval
English Jewry, appointed by the king. Six incumbents
of the office are known between 1199 and 1290.

PRESS: The earliest Jewish periodicals were published
to give general news to Jews unaccustomed to reading the language of their countries of residence, and did
not pay specific attention to Jewish matters. The
earliest was the *Gazeta de Amsterdam*, in Spanish
(1678) which was followed by a bi-weekly Yiddish
KURANT issued in the same city 1686/7; other such
Yiddish periodicals appeared in the 18th cent. at
Dyhernfurth (1771–2), Metz (1789–90), etc. Meanwhile, serial publications dealing with rabbinic and
other matters appeared in Amsterdam, Ferrara, etc.,
and in 1784, Moses Mendelssohn founded the literary
monthly, HA-MEASSEPH. In the 19th cent., periodical
newspapers in the modern sense began to appear in
the various countries of W Europe concentrating
on news of Jewish interest accompanied by literary
contributions. The earliest in the English language
was the London *Hebrew Intelligencer* (1823), succeeded by the *Voice of Jacob* (1841–8) and the JEWISH
CHRONICLE (founded 1841) which is now the oldest
surviving Jewish periodical. In Germany, the ALL-
GEMEINE ZEITUNG DES JUDENTUMS established in 1837
survived until 1921, while in France, the *Univers
Israélite* was published 1846–1940. In E Europe, as
Jews became more alert to the world around them,
newspapers in Yiddish began to make their appearance

in the mid-19th cent., beginning with *Kol Mevasser* (1853–72), this tradition being carried by the Russo-Polish immigrants to W Europe and America. This Yiddish p. in turn stimulated the development of a Hebrew p. (see below). In the late 19th cent., the number of periodicals increased, influenced by the renaissance of the Hebrew language, the classics of the new Yiddish literature, the birth of modern Zionism, the first signs of Jewish Socialism, the growth of Jewish parties particularly in E Europe, etc. Before World War II, Europe had the greatest number of Jewish papers, then America took the lead, but now, Israel occupies first place. Hitler exterminated the Jewish p. in all the lands he dominated, but, nevertheless, some secret papers were issued in the ghetto and among the partisans. After the liberation, dozens of papers were published in the camps, mainly in Yiddish. The number of Jewish papers increased everywhere after World War II, except behind the Iron Curtain. In the Diaspora 56.28% of Jewish papers are in English and 15.42% in Yiddish. The number of Hebrew dailies and weeklies has dropped, especially as a result of the liquidation of E European Jewry. The Yiddish press is also declining, circulating mainly among the older generation. There are 629 Jewish papers in 79 countries of the Diaspora and 325 in Israel.

HEBREW PRESS: The first period of the Hebrew p. dates from the publication of Mendelssohn's *Kehillat Musar* (1750) and was characterized by irregularity and lack of continuity. Most of the periodicals were devoted to general studies and literature and lacked a topical approach. A new era was inaugurated in 1856 by the appearance of HA-MAGGID, the papers now being generally weeklies and largely devoted to news and articles on current affairs; literary compositions and studies received disproportionate space but were concomitants to the paper as a whole. It was through the Hebrew p. in Europe, the US, and Palestine that the Hebrew language was molded to everyday needs and the great figures of modern Hebrew literature received their training and found an outlet. *Ha-Maggid* was followed by other weeklies in Europe (HA-MELITZ, HA-TZEPHIRAH, HA-MEVASSER, HA-TZOPHEH BA-ARETZ HA-HADASHAH, etc.), the US and Palestine (HA-LEVANON, HAVATZELET, etc.). In 1886, the first Hebrew daily HA-YOM made a short-lived appearance in S. PETERSBURG, but shortly thereafter *Ha-Melitz* and *Ha-Tzephirah* were converted into dailies. The Zionist movement was served by the Hebrew p. from its outset. The public for the Hebrew p. outside Palestine declined after the early 20th cent., and the pioneer dailies and periodicals were replaced by weeklies. Between the world wars, efforts to maintain Hebrew dailies in Poland (*Ha-Tzephirah*) and the

US (HA-DOAR) lasted only a few years. World War II saw the end of the Hebrew p. in Europe. Many weeklies and monthlies have been established in the US and the weekly *Ha-Doar* has been in existence for 35 years, becoming the central Hebrew mouthpiece of American Jewry. 20 Hebrew periodicals (second only to Israel) now appear in the US. Hebrew journalism in Palestine received an impetus with the arrival of Eliezer BEN-YEHUDAH who, together with his son Ittamar BEN-AVI, helped to give the p. there a European complexion in form and content. This was fortified with the traditions brought by pioneers of the Second Aliyah. Eventually, the Palestinian p. achieved an international standard while embodying the traditional elements of the Hebrew p. More recent developments have been the evening p. and a large number of specialist journals. In 1973, 218 Hebrew periodicals appeared of which 199 were published in Israel (including 12 dailies).

US PRESS: In 1972, there were more than 220 dailies, weeklies, monthlies, and quarterlies issued for the Jewish reader in the US. About 60 of these served local communities only, while most of the remainder were organs of national organizations. The first paper of importance in the American Jewish community was *The Occident*, in English, which appeared between 1843 and 1868. Oldest of the existing papers is *The American Israelite*, founded in Cincinnati in 1854. The first Yiddish papers began to appear as early as 1870, but the increase in immigration from E Europe created a new demand. The *Tageblatt* began as a daily in 1885, the *Forverts* (*Jewish Forward*) in 1897, the *Morgenjournal* (*Jewish Morning Journal*) in 1901, and *Der Tog* (*The Day*) in 1914. Weeklies and even dailies appeared in Yiddish in some of the larger cities, notably Philadelphia, Chicago, and Cleveland. Recent years have witnessed a marked contraction in the circulation of the Yiddish press. In 1973, there were only two Yiddish papers of major national circulation, *Forverts* and the *Tog-Morgenjournal*. The community periodicals, loosely known as the Anglo-Jewish press, devote their columns to news of local interest, as well as events of national and international concern to Jews. Among the serious or scholarly journals are the *Jewish Quarterly Review* (1910), *Jewish Social Studies* (1939), *Commentary* (1945), *Judaism* (1952), *Midstream* (1955), and *Tradition* (1958).

PRESSBURG see **BRATISLAVA**

PREUSS, HUGO (1860–1925): German scholar and Liberal statesman. From 1906, he was professor of public law at the Berlin Institute of Commerce. He became minister of the interior in the German 1918 Republican government, and prepared the draft of the Weimar Constitution. He resigned in 1919 as a result of his opposition to the Versailles treaty.

PRIESTLY BLESSING: Formula for the blessing of the people by the descendants of Aaron (Num. 6:24–6). This blessing was given daily by the priests in the Temple. It passed over to the synagogue service and is still recited daily in synagogues in Israel. In the Diaspora, it is said only on holidays. After washing their hands and removing their shoes, the priests go up before the ark (DUKHAN) and, when the reader comes to the beginning of the last BENEDICTION of the AMIDAH asking for peace, they turn with fingers outstretched in a characteristic arrangement and repeat the biblical formula (ibid.) word for word after the reader to a special chant. The ceremony has been abolished in Reform and some Conservative congregations.

PRIESTS AND PRIESTHOOD: The priest (Heb. *cohen*) was the chosen holy instrument to mediate between man and God. Originally it seems that every Israelite family head was consecrated to serve as p., with the first-born son – regarded as the inheritor of his father's house – in a position of considerable power. This arrangement was maintained until after the Exodus when the first-born became suspect as a result of the Golden Calf incident, and the tribe of LEVI was selected in their stead. Most of the LEVITES were thereafter employed in work connected with the Tabernacle whereas the family of AARON became the actual p., responsible for sacrifices, the supervision of hygienic purity, and instructing the people in the Mosaic Law. The HIGH PRIEST was also charged with DIVINATION through the URIM AND THUMMIM. To prevent the p. acquiring political domination (a normal phenomenon among neighboring peoples, e.g. Egypt), the tribe of Levi was excluded from acquiring its own tract of territory, and its livelihood derived from the contributions of TITHES, while the p. received a tenth of the levites' tithe and also a portion of the sacrifices offered. The priesthood was hereditary and the p. subject to strict laws regarding contamination by corpses and the choice of wife. While worshiping, they wore a distinctive dress. To ensure their presence throughout the country, special cities were assigned to them in the territories of the various tribes. These laws, laid down prior to the conquest of Canaan, evolved differently when the Israelites settled in their land. The descendants of Aaron indeed concentrated around .the Tabernacle, but local shrines were also established – either following a local revelation or to meet needs – and these were serviced by other p., often levites. David (according to I 'Chron. 24) reorganized the priesthood and levites about the future TEMPLE in Jerusalem, arranging 24 watches of p. (and corresponding watches of levites, singers, and gatekeepers); it is not, however, clear to what extent this method was maintained after the division of the kingdom. In the temples established by Jeroboam I in the Northern Kingdom at Dan and Bethel, p. not of the tribe of Levi were permitted to serve and apparently were allowed to continue after Josiah destroyed the high places of Samaria, though not as acting priests. After the construction of the Temple, changes took place in the mode of service. The high priest ceased to go into battle together with the Ark and also no longer gave oracles through the Urim and Thummim. Until the Hasmonean Period, the high priest was derived from the family of ZADOK and headed a sacerdotal hierarchy. He was assisted by a deputy. The ordinary priests were regarded by the sages and prophets as teachers of the people. From the time of Hezekiah, and especially from that of Josiah, all worship was centralized in the Jerusalem Temple and this strengthened the priesthood. The high priests were loyal adherents of the Davidic dynasty. The Temple organization was further strengthened after the return from the Babylonian exile. Although only 4 priestly families returned, the division into 24 watches was soon restored and these were augmented by 24 watches of ordinary Israelites. To systematize the offerings and tithes the peasants were ordered to bring them to special chambers where they were apportioned to their recipients; this practice prevailed until Hasmonean times, but thereafter the tithes were divided on the actual threshing-floor. In Second Temple times the p. exceeded the levites and received part of the levitical tithes, this subsequently contributing to their wealth which became proverbial. From the time of Nehemiah, the high priest was regarded – in the absence of secular leadership – as head of the community. In the early Hellenistic Period, he collected the taxes and dispatched them to the king. This contact with the rulers led to a process of assimilation among large sections of the priesthood. A fringe, however, firmly maintained their religious zeal and from this element emerged the Hasmoneans who renewed the national spirit. Nevertheless the wealthy and powerful priestly families joined the aristocratic SADDUCEE party, while others left to join the ESSENES who eschewed the Temple service. Under Herod the high priesthood ceased to be hereditary and became subject to appointment by the secular ruler. Only the last high priest, Phinehas ben Ḥavta was again elected by the Sanhedrin, as laid down by the rabbis.

PRIMOGENITURE see INHERITANCE

PRINTING: The first mention of Jews in connection with p. is in Avignon, c. 1444–before Gutenberg–when a Jew, Davin de Caderousse, studied the new art. The earliest dated example of Hebrew p. was produced at Reggio di Calabria in 1475, but it is not impossible that some undated specimen preceded this. About 150 Hebrew INCUNABULA are known from Italy, Spain, and Portugal (with single specimens from N Africa and Turkey): in Portugal, as in some oriental countries, Hebrew p. preceded any other.

Printer's Mark of the Soncino family (Italy, 15th cent.).

In Spain, Portugal, and Italy, Jews engaged in the early period also in non-Hebrew p. The most important family in the early history of Hebrew p. was that of SONCINO, famous also as general printers. Daniel BOMBERG made Venice the great center of Hebrew p., which it remained throughout the 16th cent., except for an interval after the burning of the Talmud in 1554. In the 16th cent., there were important

Hebrew p. centers also in Germany (e.g. Augsburg), Poland (Cracow), etc. as well as in the Levant (Constantinople, Salonica, Safed). In 1627, Manasseh ben Israel introduced Hebrew p. to Amsterdam which became the principal center in the 17th–18th cents., the firm of PROOPS being especially famous. The 19th cent. witnessed the pre-eminence of E Europe, the firm of ROMM in Vilna becoming prominent; the former esthetic standards, however, declined. Hebrew p. from blocks was known in England from 1524, protracted texts beginning to appear in the 17th cent. and complete Hebrew books in the 18th. In the US, the earliest specimen of Hebrew p. is in the Bay Psalm Book (Cambridge, Mass. 1640). A commentary on Daniel (Safed, 1563) is the earliest example not only in Palestine but in Asia as a whole. With the destruction of Jewish life in E Europe, Israel is now the main center of Hebrew p. Monotype and linotype machines now set up Hebrew texts complete with vowel points.

PRINZ, JOACHIM (1902—): Rabbi. Born in Germany, he was a rabbi in Berlin until forced to leave in 1937. He went to the US. and has been rabbi of Temple B'nai Abraham, Newark since 1939. Active in Jewish communal affairs, P. was president of the American Jewish Congress 1958–66. He is the author of books on various Jewish subjects.

PROCURATOR: Governor of Judea under the Roman emperors, 6–66 CE. There were 14 altogether, seven between 6 and 41 CE, and the others between 44 and 66. Although having the status of governor with special administrative powers, the p. was subordinate to the Syrian legate. The latter

Procurator	Governed	Leading Events
L. Coponius	c. 6 — 9 CE	Census in Judea leads to Zealot rising.
M. Ambibulus	c. 9 — 12 CE	
Annius Rufus	c. 12 — 15 CE	
Valerius Gratus	c. 15 — 26 CE	Appointed and removed high priests in rapid succession (Ananias, Ishmael ben Pabi, Eleazar ben Hanan, Ben Kemah, Joseph Kaipha).
Pontius Pilate	c. 26 — 36 CE	Executed Galilean patriots without trial; offended popular feeling by introducing Roman military standards into Jerusalem; used Temple funds for the construction of an aqueduct; maltreated the Samaritans for which he was recalled to Rome. Jesus was crucified during his term of office.
Marcellus	36 — 37 CE	
Marullus	c. 37 — 41 CE	In office when Caligula ordered his statue to be placed in the Temple. Superseded when Herod Agrippa became king of Judea.
Cuspius Fadus	c. 44 — 46 CE	Assred custody of the vestments of the high priest; savagely suppressed followers of the pseudo-messiah Theudas.
Tiberius Julius Alexander	c. 46 — 48 CE	Executed sons of Judah the Galilean.
Ventidius Cumanus	48 — 52 CE	Massacred Jews in Jerusalem. Condoned attacks on Jews by Samaritans and in consequence was banished.
Antonius Felix	52/3 — 60 CE	Favored the Samaritans as against the Jews and ruthlessly suppressed Jewish insurgents, including Eleazar ben Dinai and an Egyptian Jew who deluded the masses into believing he would destroy the walls of Jerusalem.
Porcius Festus	60 — 62 CE	Just administrator: supported Agrippa II in a dispute with the priests.
L. Albinus	62 — 64 CE	Enriched himself unscrupulously, taking bribes from all sides.
L. Gessius Florus	64 — 66 CE	His demand for 17 talents from the Temple led to outbreaks in Jerusalem; the resulting massacre touched off the Great Revolt of 66–70.

exercised his authority over the p. if he was charged with abusing his office, with being unduly extortionate in his treatment of the population, and, especially, in the event of rebellion, in which cases the legate would act as final arbiter, and either exonerate or punish the p. Punishment could take the form of dismissal from office, but the p. had to be sent to Rome for trial by the emperor who would either confirm or annul the sentence, as the p.'s appointment was by the latter and independent of the legate. The p.'s of Judea had the administrative status of members of the *equites* class. They governed in place of the legate of Syria. This form of tenure of office, however, was only theoretical, for the p.'s were in fact independent governors armed with full administrative authority. They enjoyed the "right of the sword," i.e., full powers to inflict punishment, including the death penalty. These powers were enforceable only in respect of inhabitants of the province who were not Roman citizens. The latter had the right to demand the transfer of their trial before the emperor in Rome, as in the case of Paul. Jurisdiction in civil matters was vested in the Sanhedrin in Jerusalem, but this was limited by the p.'s surveillance. The influence of the p.'s was exercised particularly in monetary suits where they were in a position to bring pressure to bear upon the litigants. This they were able to do by virtue of the fact that, as officials charged with economic administration, they were responsible for the imperial revenue and for collecting taxes and excise dues. The p.'s of Judea generally resided at Caesarea, the administrative capital of Roman Judea. On special occasions, such as the celebration of Jewish feasts, when many thousands of pilgrims congregated in Jerusalem and there was the danger of riots, the p.'s went there to maintain order. When in Jerusalem, the p. resided in Herod's palace.

PROFIAT DURAN see **DURAN**

PROGRESSIVE PARTY: Israel political party with liberal tendencies. It was founded in 1948 by three factions – the progressive wing of the GENERAL ZIONISTS, *Ha-Oved ha-Tziyyoni*, and the *Aliyah Hadashah* group. 83 agricultural settlements are affiliated. The P. P. was represented in the First Knesset (1949) by 5 members, in the Second (1951) by 4, in the Third (1955) by 5; in the Fourth (1959) by 6; it participated in nearly all the coalition governments. The world youth-movement HA-NOAR HA-TZIYYONI shares its outlook. In 1961, the P. P. and the General Zionists re-united to form the LIBERAL PARTY but in 1965 the former P. P. was reconstituted as the Independent Liberal Party, obtaining 5 seats in the Sixth Knesset and 4 in the Seventh and Eighth.

PROOF see **EVIDENCE**

PROOPS: Firm of Hebrew printers and publishers in Amsterdam, founded at the close of the 17th cent. by *SOLOMON BEN JOSEPH P.* (d. 1734) whose printed catalogue, *Apirion Shelomoh*, was the first publication of its kind in Hebrew.

PROPERTY: Hebrew law recognizes the right of a man over his p. and prohibits others from taking it against his will (see BURGLARY and ROBBERY). There are several ways whereby p. can legally come into the possession of a person, each being termed *kinyan* ("possession"). These forms of possessing are: *meshikhah* ("drawing of the object toward one self"), *hagbahah* ("raising the object"), *ḥazakah* ("taking possession"), as well as whatever is accepted by local custom as symbolizing transfer of p. Objects may also change ownership through INHERITANCE. A man has the right to abandon his p. (HEPHKER) which may then be taken over by anyone else.

PROPHETS, PROPHECY: A prophet is designated by God to convey His message to men and to give guidance for the future. Prophecy is an ancient institution originating in primitive times. It appears among early Semitic peoples (e.g. in Mesopotamia, Phoenicia, Canaan) but in Israel took on a distinctive form. The Hebrews implicitly believed that they had been chosen by God who had sent them p. to point out the right path. The prophet was primarily the protagonist of monotheism and morality, and fulfilled a decisive role in Jewish religious life and development alongside the PRIEST and the sage. Only hints and mutilated information throw light on the pre-Mosaic period but thereafter there were three main periods – the prophecy of MOSES, the charismatic p., and the rhapsodic p. The period of Moses determined the fundamental content of the late prophecies and also – by means of the Torah – the nation's spiritual content, way of life, and mission. The decisive characteristic of Moses' prophecy was that it was continuous and not the result of sudden inspiration. The charismatic p. who followed Moses were religious leaders guiding the nation in times of difficulty, e.g. Deborah, Samuel. With the rise of the monarchy, when policy was handled by rulers and ministers, the prophet became increasingly prominent as a fighter for social morality, where necessary rebuking the King for his moral lapses (Nathan, Ahijah the Shilonite). Together with their disciples ("sons of the p."), they zealously opposed any manifestation of paganism (Elijah, Elisha). The rhapsodic p. appeared early in the 8th cent. BCE, first in Israel and later in Judah. Previously, the p. had mainly contented themselves with the spoken word, while prophetic circles committed accounts of earlier p. to writing. From the time of Amos, the p. wrote their own utterances, generally in a lofty language that constitutes the culmination of biblical poetry. As formerly, the central motif is the attack on religious corruption, but concomitantly the drive against social corruption arises. The prophet foresees national disaster to be followed by consolation. The rhapsodic seers also utter visions concerning the gentiles, but the central subject is still Israel, who – as the elect of the Lord – must set an example and bear the punishment of failure. The eschatological belief is expressed that all evil men will be destroyed at "the end of days" but the righteous remnant of Israel will establish the kingdom of God. Formalism is condemned unless accompanied by good deeds. Much of the popular appeal of prophecy can be attributed to the belief that the p. could foresee the future, and later generations held that the prophecy contained visions down to "the last generation," if interpreted aright. The prophetic utterances were generally oral or written, but sometimes the prophet demonstrated his message with "signs." Prophecy was revealed both in waking and sleeping hours, and the prophet later recapitulated the message before the people. According to rabbinic teaching, the spirit of p. ceased with the last of the Minor Prophets (Zachariah, etc.), the spiritual role of the prophet thereafter being assumed by the "Men of the Great Synagogue" and the sages who succeeded them. These had the faculty of interpreting the Bible prophecies: indeed, "a Sage is higher than a Prophet" (*Bava Batra* 12a). In the messianic age, however, the faculty of p. would be renewed. In the Hebrew Bible the title "Former Prophets" applies to the historical books of Joshua, Judges, Samuel, and Kings (in the Christian tradition, other historical portions of the Bible are also comprised); "Latter Prophets" is applied to Isaiah, Jeremiah, Ezekiel, and the Twelve Minor Prophets.

PROPHETS, MINOR: Twelve prophetical books (Hosea, Joel, Amos, Obadiah, Jonah, Micah, Nahum, Habakkuk, Zephaniah, Haggai, Zechariah, and Malachi) placed in the Hebrew Bible after the Book of Ezekiel. Their dates range between the 8th and 5th cents. BCE. The Dead Sea Scrolls include commentaries on some of these books, endeavoring to discover in them allusions to contemporary events. They are traditionally termed TERE ASAR. (See entries under individual books.)

PROSBUL (Gk. "for the court"): A special form of legal document annulling the cancellation of debts during the Sabbatical year enjoyed by biblical precept. Scripture warns against refusing to lend to the needy because of the approaching Sabbatical year cancellation (Deut. 15). Nevertheless, the tendency prevailed not to make loans as the Sabbatical year approached, and Hillel therefore issued an enactment whereby a lender would not lose his money despite the Sabbatical year if he made a declaration in writing to the court in the following manner: "I hereby make known to you, judges of this place, that I wish to be able to collect all debts due to me at any time I may desire."

PROSELYTES (Heb. *gerim*, sing, *ger*, short for *g. tzedek* "righteous stranger"): The convert to Judaism has been known in all ages since biblical times. During the Second Temple Period, the great expansion under the Hasmonean rulers was rendered possible by the widespread proselytization of the areas around Judea, especially Galilee and Idumea: and in the 1st cent. the royal family of Adiabene embraced Judaism. There were many proselytes to Judaism in the Roman Empire, e.g. the translator Aquila and Flavius Clemens. The rabbis fostered missionary activity during the 1st cent. CE. As conversion to Judaism entailed the rite of circumcision for males, it was forbidden by Hadrian and subsequently by the Christian emperors. It was thus considered a capital offense in Christian Europe in the Middle Ages. Nevertheless, in the 8th–9th cents., there was a widespread conversion movement among the Khazars, led by the king and embracing other classes, and in W Europe too, numerous persons continued to enter Judaism, notwithstanding the danger to which they and those who received them were subjected. They included the French archdeacon Bodo, 893; Robert of Reading, an English Dominican, burned at Oxford in 1222 and Obadiah the Norman, active in Palestine and the neighboring lands (converted in 1102). The ferocity of medieval persecution was responsible for the intensification of the Jewish reluctance to receive p, until this came to be regarded almost as axiomatic. After the Medieval Period, there may be mentioned Nicholas Antoine, burned at Geneva in 1632; Count Valentin Potocki, who traditionally suffered at Vilna in 1749; the German scholars Conrad Victor (Moses Prado, 1607) and Johann Peter (Moses Germanus); Lord George Gordon, the former English Protestant leader; Abraham ben Jacob, illustrator of the Amsterdam Haggadah of 1695; the Dutch rabbi, Aaron Moses Isaac Graanboom, and the American proto-Zionist, Warder Cresson. In the 19th cent. the Subbotnik movement among the Russian peasantry and a similar movement in Transylvania resulted in a widespread conversion to Judaism. Early in the same century an entire proselyte community was living in Safed in Palestine, while a body of converts from San Nicandro in Italy emigrated *en masse* to Israel after the establishment of the state. Recent years have witnessed an increase in the number of proselytes, especially in the US. Most of these are connected with a marriage to a Jewish partner and the majority are women. There have been numerous p. to Judaism from Islam and other faiths.

PROSKAUER, JOSEPH MEYER (1877–1971): US jurist. He was justice of the New York Supreme Court from 1923, serving in its Appellate Division, 1927–30. As president of the American Jewish Committee (1943–9), he led that non–Zionist

Joseph M. Proskauer.
(Painting by Eugene Spiro).

organization into support of the establishment of the state of Israel.

PROSSNITZ, LÖBELE (d. 1750): Self-styled miracle-worker. A poor peddler in Prossnitz, he claimed that Isaac Luria and Shabbetai Tzevi had appeared to him in a dream and taught him their doctrine. He forecast that the latter would return in 1706 and perform wondrous deeds. Outlawed by the Moravian rabbis, he continued to preach in Austria and Germany, in the end declaring himself messiah and extracting vast sums from his followers. In 1725, his frauds became notorious and he fled to Hungary.

PROTEST RABBIS (*Protestrabbiner*): Term applied by Herzl in 1897 to a group of German rabbis who "protested" against the convening of the First Zionist Congress and warned communal leaders and rabbis against participation. The first protest resulted in a change of the Congress' venue, originally fixed for Munich. Unable to prevent the holding of the Congress, the P. R. published a statement in the *Berliner Tageblatt* that Zionism contradicted the Jewish messianic hope.

PROTESTANTISM: The movement in western Christianity which rejected the authority of the Roman Catholic Church. Some of the early leaders of P. had Jewish contacts studied Hebrew (see REFORMATION), and Protestant sects hoped that their presentation of Christianity would win over the Jews. Nevertheless, P. did not immediately affect for good the attitude of its adherents. Indeed, whereas the Catholic Church officially advocated the toleration of the Jews, under rigorous conditions, Martin LUTHER later expressed himself against them in wildly intolerant terms. Some Protestant parts of Germany (e.g. Saxony) excluded the Jews entirely long after the Reformation, as did also various other Protestant countries (e.g. Norway until the 19th cent.). A difference became discernible with the rise of specific forms of P. in the trading countries of the Atlantic seaboard, especially England and Holland. There, religious forms based largely on the Bible induced a more favorable attitude toward the Jews: on the other hand, mercantile expansion necessarily induced a tolerant attitude toward all who could be economically useful. Thus, Puritanism and Toleration became closely interconnected. The same mercantilistic spirit, spreading to the rest of Europe in the 19th cent., was largely responsible for the end of anti-Jewish discrimination in Catholic as well as Protestant countries. In the persecution of the Jews in 1933–45, the German Protestant churches showed themselves on the whole subservient to the state.

PROTOCOLS OF THE ELDERS OF ZION see **ELDERS OF ZION**

PROUST, MARCEL (1871–1922): French novelist. His Jewish mother (née Weill) had a profound influence on him, and he had many Jewish friends. One of the principal figures in *A la recherche du temps perdu* is the intelligent, worldly Jew, Swann, tortured by a love unworthy of him. The Dreyfus trial also plays an important part in the background of this novel.

PROVENCE: French province. Jews lived there from the 5th cent., notably at AIX, ARLES, and MARSEILLES. The liberal regime welcomed Jewish fugitives in the Middle Ages and by the 13th cent., there were many communities. Although conditions differed from place to place, the Jews generally enjoyed a relatively high status, owning land, practicing medicine, and sometimes holding administrative office. The reaction against the Albigenses adversely affected the Jews, and in the 13th cent., the Church intervened, the Jews being henceforth confined to certain quarters, compelled to wear the badge, and restricted within certain professions. In 1348, the Black Death led to a massacre at Toulon but the survivors were protected by the count. The Jewish population at this time included outstanding poets, scholars, and philosophers. At the end of the 14th cent., the king appointed a *conservateur des juifs* who was responsible for taxes and had the right to administer justice, etc. The situation changed with the annexation of P. to the French crown in 1481, and discriminations and expulsions (from the entire province in 1500) ensued. Jewish communities continued henceforth in P. only in the papal possessions (COMTAT VENAISSIN). In 1789, 2,500 Jews, originating from several countries, were living in

P. Many refugees fled to P. during World War II. The only organized community until recently was at Marseilles. But the influx from N. Africa has led to the resuscitation of a number of ancient communities.

PROVERBS (known in Heb. by its first word *Mishle*): Biblical book, the second in the Hagiographa. It is a specimen of the WISDOM literature. Together with Psalms and Job, it has a special system of ACCENTS. The book is a collection of moral sayings, particularly directed to the young, postulating the belief that ultimately due reward will be meted out to the righteous (identified with the wise) and retribution to the wicked (especially the ignoramus). Murder, theft, sloth, anger, gossip, and lechery are particularly denounced, while diligence, caution, respect for elders and teachers, patience, and fear of God are praised. The work is not uniform and is composed of 8 or 9 collections. The first (chap. 1–9) contains a general introduction and a characterization of Wisdom. The second (10:1–22:16) and the fifth (25–39), both ascribed to Solomon, are miscellaneous collections of short sayings. The third (22:17–24:22) and fourth (24:23–24), attributed to "the wise," consist of long stanzas on closely interconnected

themes. The sixth (30), by Agur ben Jakeh (otherwise unknown), contains riddles, while the book ends with the sayings of King Lemuel (also unknown) and a poem praising the industrious wife. The teachings are individual and universal – not national – resembling the Book of AHIKAR and early Egyptian moral collections. Its opening sentence ascribes the authorship to Solomon and parts, at least, may date from that epoch. Its redaction is placed by the Talmud in the period of the Great Assembly.

PROVERBS, MIDRASH TO: A late and incomplete Midrash (10th–11th cents.) to the Book of Proverbs, based on material from earlier midrashic collections and largely in the nature of a commentary. The compiler seems also to have used mystic sources such as the HEKHALOT.

PROVIDENCE (Heb. "*hashgahah*"): Term first used by the Greek philosophers for the power that rationally governs the world and human fate by knowing everything and sustaining the world it has created in conformity with its purposes. This philosophic concept has obvious points of contact with the biblical notion of the Creator, and most biblical stories (e.g. those of the Patriarchs) are

Interior of Temple Beth-El, Providence, R. I.

illustrations of p. Whereas the main stress in biblical literature on p. is in connection with the fate of the people of Israel, rabbinical teaching is more concerned with the influence of Divine p. over individual fate. Philosophical and theological problems connected with p. loom large in the discussions of medieval writers (Saadyah, Ibn Daud, Judah Ha-Levi, Maimonides, etc.). Medieval Aristotelianism allowed that Divine p. was only "general," i.e. concerned with species and not with individuals; Jewish thinkers insisted on "special p." (*hashgahah peratit*) and tried to reconcile this with their philosophical premises. Of special importance is the teaching of Maimonides that p. varies with the individual's nearness to God: p. is nothing but the Divine influx via the "active intellect" into the souls of those who cleave to God in contemplation. Generally, however, religious teaching considered p. as independent of intellectual contemplation, being essentially a characteristic of God's relationship to His creatures.

PROVIDENCE: City in Rhode Island, US. There are indications of Jews in P. in the latter part of the 18th cent., but no congregation existed until 1855. The early Jewish settlers were mainly peddlers, tailors, and clothing merchants; they were of Bohemian, Dutch or German origin. In the last two decades of the 19th cent., large numbers of Jews from E Europe went to P. After 1933, c. 400 Jews from Central Europe settled there. The central communal body is the General Jewish Committee of P., founded in 1945. In 1973, P. had c. 20,000 Jews with 18 synagogues.

PRUSSIA: Former German state. Jews lived in the region before the state was formed, and in 1648 were still living in limited areas, but these were extended in 1671 by Frederick William, the Grand Elector (1640–88). The Court Jews, mint masters, and army purveyors constituted the aristocracy of the community; the rest were largely merchants, peddlers, and moneylenders. The government intervened in their internal affairs but left intact the authority of the rabbis and communal officers. Frederick I (1688–1713) regarded the Jews mainly as a source of revenue; he encouraged additional settlement but at the same time imposed increased protection-dues and appointed a board to supervise Jewish affairs (1703). Frederick William I (1713–40) made the Jews subject to the state's judiciary and defined their economic functions. Frederick the Great's (1740–86) conquest of Silesia increased the state's Jewish population. He gave the Jews a detailed statute, restricting rabbinical juridical competence and prohibiting rural residence, but granting equal rights with Christians in permitted occupations. Social ties were forged between Jews and Christians, and – led by Moses MENDELSSOHN – the HASKALAH made rapid headway. In 1812, the Jews of P. were recognized as citizens, while the remaining powers of the rabbinical courts were abolished. Many Jews were living in countries ceded to P. after 1815 but only in 1847 were these Jews also granted uniform rights. Certain disqualifications from public office remained until 1918. In the late 19th and early 20th cents., Jews rose in the economic scale, many entered the liberal professions, and there was increasing participation in general cultural life and in politics. After 1871, the history of Prussian Jewry is bound up with that of the rest of GERMANY, culminating in the disaster of 1933–45.

PRYLUCKI, NOAH (1882–1944): Yiddish scholar. A lawyer by training, he founded the Yiddish daily *Der Moment* in 1910 and directed its policies until World War II. He was a leader of the *Folkisten* and fought for Jewish autonomous rights in the Polish parliament 1922–8. P. pioneered in Yiddish research and published original contributions on Yiddish philology, folklore, and theater.

PRZEMYSL: Polish city. Jews are mentioned from 1437. The community was granted a charter by Sigismund August in 1559, receiving right of residence and permission to purchase houses from Christians. The relations of the Jews with the burghers were determined by contracts, and after the Jews participated in the defense of P. against the Swedes in 1757, they were permitted to live in the city center. Before World War II there were 17,000 Jews in P. A large ghetto was set up in the city by the Nazis and liquidated in 1943.

PSALMS (in Heb. *Tehillim*): First book in the Hagiographa section of the Bible. It contains 150 p. (divided somewhat differently in the Septuagint from the Hebrew), although the Talmud refers to only 147. There is an inner subdivision into five books, beginning respectively with Ps. 1, 42, 78, 90, and 107, and each concluding with a benediction of thanksgiving. Some of the p. are anonymous but most are attributed to authors: – 74 to David, 18 to Asaph, 12 to the sons of Korah, 2 to Solomon, and one each to Moses, Heman, and Ethan. The book is composed of collections originally constituting independent units (Books II and III originally comprised a single work). Only among p. ascribed to David are the events inspiring their composition mentioned and all the Davidic p. are written in the first person singular. Further collections are marked by the opening words "Hallelujah," "Give thanks," and "A Song of Degrees." The authorship and redaction of the book were traditionally attributed to David. For some time, scholars have tended to deny this tradition and posit later dates down to the Maccabean Period. However, the earlier dating has been corroborated by the study of similar works in other Near Eastern literatures as well as by a profounder appreciation of their contents, and many modern scholars maintain not only that a large number of the p. derive from David's time but that some are even earlier (e.g., 80 and 83, of the period of the Judges). It is thought that the latest examples belong to the Babylonian Exile or shortly thereafter, and the book was redacted within one or two generations (the work was known to Ben Sira, while the Greek translators found the musical notations incomprehensible). The literary and poetic forms are numerous; models of many of them have been found in Ugaritic poems (14th–13th cents. BCE). A number of p. are written as alphabetic acrostics; some have refrains. Various p. are headed by technical terms not yet adequately interpreted; they may include names of musical instruments or musical expressions, or refer to poetical forms. Judging by their content, some of the p. were recited by the congregation, others by the individual; these can be divided into thanksgiving poems (recited when offering sacrifice after a personal deliverance), songs of praise, didactic songs, songs in honor of the kings, war songs, songs connected with festivals or historical events, and songs concerning events in the lives of individuals (e.g. David), including effusions of sorrow and joy. The whole work is an anthology of lyric poems of high artistic standard and suffused with a deep religious feeling which has assured its popularity among Jews and Christians; many of the p. are incorporated into the liturgies of both religions.

PSALMS, MIDRASH ON: Collection of homilies to the Book of Psalms. There seems to be no unified arrangement, the impression being of a varied gathering from diverse sources. A difference is especially discernible between the first part (Psalms 1–118) and the second (119–150). The date is late. It is also known by the name of *Midrash Shoḥer Tov* from its opening words, taken from Prov. 11:27.

PSALMS OF SOLOMON: Pseudepigraphic book, probably written in Palestine in Hebrew shortly after the fall of Pompey in 48 BCE, but preserved only in Greek translation. It contains 18 poems attributed to Solomon (but not, apparently, in the original), in which the author describes the desecration of the Temple by the enemy (Pompey?), condemns immorality and sin, and looks forward to the advent of the Messiah.

PSEUDEPIGRAPHIA see **APOCRYPHA**

PSEUDO-JONATHAN see **TARGUM**

PSEUDO-MESSIAH see **MESSIAH**

PSYCHOLOGY, JEWS IN: The Talmud already speculated as to individual differences among men (*Avot* 5:14), indicated signs by which mental deficiency could be recognized (*Ḥagigah* 3b–4a), and commented upon criteria for analyzing human behavior (*Eruvin* 65b). Centuries of persecution made the Jew unusually sensitive to his environment and the conduct of other men so that Jews played a disproportionate part in

the evolution and progress of the science of the mind. Hugo MUNSTERBERG set up the laboratory for experimental psychology at Harvard Univ. In England, Charles Samuel MYERS was largely responsible for the development of industrial psychology. Max WERTHEIMER founded the Gestalt school in 1912. C. G. SELIGMAN analyzed anthropological data in the light of psychological research. Kurt LEWIN's studies in topology opened a new field in the application of physics to psychological phenomena and investigations into the behavior of children. Joseph BREUER collaborated in the study of catharsis with Sigmund FREUD, the founder of psychoanalysis and the man who did most to illuminate the dynamism of the forces at work in the various levels of the mind. Alfred ADLER founded the school of Individual Psychology. Otto RANK studied the influence of myths and stressed the birth trauma as a source of the neuroses while Theodor REIK applied psychoanalytic concepts to explaining Jewish ceremonials.

*PTOLEMY: Name of the first Macedonian king of Egypt and the originator of the Ptolemaic dynasty, all the kings of which bore this name. *P. I Lagi Soter* (reigned 305–285 BCE) conquered Palestine in 319–8, but withdrew in 315. A number of Jews, including the high priest Hezekiah, accompanied him to Egypt, possibly in 311 after a second invasion. He later retook Jerusalem and is then supposed to have deported a large number of Jews to Egypt. He finally subjected Palestine in c. 301. P. also settled Jews in Cyrenaica. *P. II Philadelphus* (283–246 BCE) is credited with the redemption of numerous Jewish slaves sold in Egypt. The Greek translation of the Bible (SEPTUAGINT) is said to have been made with his encouragement. *P. III Euergetes I* (246–221 BCE) is alleged by Josephus to have sacrificed at Jerusalem. He was served by the Jewish tax-farmers Joseph the Tobiad and his son. *P. IV Philopator* (221–203 BCE), according to III Maccabees, attempted to enter the Temple and persecuted Egyptian Jews, but the charges seem to be mythical. *P. V Epiphanes* (203–181 BCE) lost Palestine in 200. *P. VI Philometor* (181–145 BCE) was served by Jewish generals (Onias and Dositheos) who supported him against his brother Physkon. He allowed Onias IV to build a Jewish temple at Leontopolis (c. 161). He invaded Palestine to interfere in Syria but was friendly to Jonathan the Hasmonean. *P. VII* or *Physkon, Euergetes II* (170–116 BCE including several years jointly with P. VI) is alleged to have persecuted the Jews, but is known to have permitted a synagogue in Egypt to be dedicated to him (c. 160). *P. VIII Soter II Lathyrus* (116–81 BCE) attacked Alexander Yannai but was driven off by his mother Cleopatra (104–3). *P. IX Alexander I* (108–88 BCE, jointly with P. VIII for a number of years) had Jewish generals, who influenced him and Cleopatra III to withdraw from war against Alexander Yannai. Judea owed to the Ptolemies an administrative system which was little altered by the Seleucids and Hasmoneans and survived until Roman times.

PUAH: One of the midwives who disobeyed Pharaoh's orders to kill the Hebrew male children at birth (Exod. 1:15). P. is identified by the rabbis with Miriam.

PUBLISHING: The mechanics of the sale and distribution of Hebrew books after the invention of PRINTING are little known. There were Jewish booksellers (e.g. in Naples) who exported large quantities of books in the 15th cent., and in the 16th cent. the products of the Venetian Hebrew press found their way in large numbers to Poland, Turkey, etc. Occasionally, books were specifically printed for the foreign market. Many works were subsidized by the authors or their patrons, and one method by which books were diffused was by personal solicitation on the part of the authors themselves. In the early 16th cent., Hebrew books were sold in great numbers at the Frankfort fair. The first known catalogue of a Jewish printer was produced at Amsterdam by Manasseh ben Israel in 1652. Occasionally, the printer and publisher were not identical. The better organization of general p, in the 19th cent. did not greatly affect that of Hebrew books because they were marketed in so many lands; thus, the most important names of recent times, such as Romm, remain those of printers rather than publishers. In the 19th cent., Jews began to enter into the general publishing field with important firms such as Ullstein in Germany, Treves in Italy, Calmann-Lévy in France, Rinehart, Simon and Schuster in the US, Gollancz and Routledge in England. The number of books published in Israel is proportionally among the highest in the world; 70 firms are affiliated with the Israel Publishers' Association.

PUERTO RICO: US State. Marranos are recorded there from the 16th cent. The modern community, numbering 3,000 (1972), dates from the 20th cent., originating either from E Europe or the US. Most of the Jews live in the capital San Juan and the neighboring town of Santurce.

PULITZER, JOSEPH (1847–1911): Newspaper owner. A half-Jew, he went to the US from Hungary in 1864 and joined Carl Schwarz's *Westliche Post* in St. Louis. He published the *St. Louis Post-Dispatch* from 1878 and then (1883–1911), the *New York World*. P. established the school of journalism at Columbia Univ. in 1903. The Pulitzer prizes for outstanding achievement in journalism, literature, and music have been awarded since 1917 under the terms of his will. His sons *JOSEPH P.* (1885–) and *RALPH P.* 1879–1939) were also publishers.

PULPIT: Raised platform for a preacher. The traditional synagogue had no p., the sermon being delivered either from the ALMEMAR in the middle

Pulpit of the Florence synagogue.

of the building or from before the Ark. Many modern synagogues have introduced a special raised p., but in America the p. is frequently combined with the reading-desk and ark.

PUMBEDITA: Babylonian city on the Euphrates; seat of a famous academy founded by Judah ben Ezekiel in the middle of the 3rd cent. The destruction of NEHARDEA at about the same time brought P. to the fore as its natural successor. Judah ben Ezekiel's successors as heads of the academy were Rabbah bar Nahmani, Joseph bar Hiyya, and Abbaye. On the latter's death in 338, his successor, Rava bar Joseph, removed the academy to Mahoza. It was returned to P. in 352 by Nahman bar Isaac, and continued to flourish, with a few intervals, down to the end of the Gaonic Period, though ultimately removed to Baghdad. It attained great distinction in the 10th–11th cents. under Sherira Gaon and his son Hai, closing on the latter's death in 1038.

PUNCTUATION see **VOCALIZATION**

PUNISHMENT: Scripture makes provision for both physical and financial judicial penalties. The physical penalties include death in four ways – by stoning, burning, beheading, and strangulation – and exile and flogging. In the last book of his code, Maimonides lists 36 offenses which may entail a death penalty (*Sanhedrin* 15:10–12), 39 offenses for which Scripture indicates either extirpation or death "at the hand of Heaven" but for which the courts were empowered to administer a flogging of up to 39 strokes (cf. Deut. 25:3), and a further 168 offenses for which a similar flogging is the maximum penalty. For death or stripes to be incurred, the offense had to be committed in the presence of eye-witnesses and to be deliberate – i.e., committed after warning of the penalty it would entail. For some cases of inadvertent homicide, the penalty was exile to a City of Refuge. Scriptural material penalties include simple restitution, reparation for any loss inflicted, or, in a few cases which included rape, seduction, theft, and bodily injury, financial compensation for the suffering incurred. All the above penalties were supplemented under rabbinic law. Thus, if murder (but no other offense) was established by eye-witnesses but technical reasons prevented the imposition of the death penalty, the murderer was subjected to a form of imprisonment calculated to hasten death. Repeated wilful transgression of a commandment for which a man had already been flogged twice was punished with the same form of imprisonment. Furthermore, if either the Sanhedrin or the king considered that, as a temporary measure, a particular offense should receive more than the penalty provided for in the law, they had the power to impose death or any other penalty. In post-biblical times, Scriptural law was largely supplemented by rabbinic law, and appropriate physical and financial penalties were devised for its enforcement. Wilful violation of rabbinic prohibitions was dealt with by disciplinary flogging, the severity of which was at the discretion of the court. Even mutilation was not unknown in medieval Spain. As an example of a monetary penalty for an offense not actionable under Scriptural law, the "pound of gold" payable for a verbal insult to a scholar may be cited. In addition, the weapon of EXCOMMUNICATION, or (more exactly) boycott, in a greater or lesser degree (called *herem* and *niddui* respectively), enabled the courts to exert powerful pressure on those who would not obey its behests. So powerful was this weapon that in later times,

when it was almost the sole means possessed by a Jewish court of enforcing discipline, its use was prohibited by the government in many European countries. If other means failed, gentile courts were sometimes asked to punish Jewish offenders and compel them to obey the directives of a Jewish tribunal. For some offenses, for which a penance rather a penalty in the ordinary sense was indicated, an offender was sometimes given the option of fasting or paying a sum to charity instead of suffering physical punishment.

PURIFICATION see **PURITY, RITUAL**

PURIM (Heb. "lots"): Festival commemorating the rescue of Persian Jewry through the mediation of ESTHER from the threat of annihilation engineered by HAMAN. According to the Book of Esther, the extermination was fixed by lot for *Adar* 13, but the Jews escaped, successfully resisting their persecutions on that date and in Shushan, also on the next day. P. is observed on *Adar* 14, and the following day (Shushan P.) is observed as P. in cities which have been walled since the time of Joshua (e.g. Jerusalem). Some critics regard the Book of Esther as a romance written to explain a festival already adopted, but others have found confirmation of elements of the story in Persian sources. The Book of Esther (*Megillat Ester*) is read in the synagogue on the eve and morning of P. The custom arose of making an uproar by sounding rattles, etc. whenever the name of Haman was mentioned and also of wearing fancy-dress or masks, and performing plays based on the story of Esther. The P. banquet became a traditional occasion for merrymaking. It is obligatory to send gifts (*manot*) to friends and give money to the poor. An account of the story of P. inserted into the EIGHTEEN BENEDICTIONS on that day, and a passage referring to the defeat of Amelek (Haman's ancestor) is read from the Pentateuch, as on the previous Sabbath. In modern times, a P. carnival (ADLOYADA)

The main Purim characters. (From a 17th cent. illuminated *megillah*, formerly in the Bersohn Museum, Warsaw).

is held in Israel. In leap years, P. is observed in Second *Adar*, but the 14th of First *Adar* is a minor celebration called Purim Katan.

PURIM KATAN (Heb. "little Purim"): The 14th and 15th days of the first month of *Adar* in a leap year when Purim is celebrated during the second month of *Adar*. On *P.K.*, fasting and funeral eulogies are prohibited and the *Taḥanun* prayer is not recited.

PURIM PLAYS: Although Purim masquerades go back to gaonic times, the custom of presenting plays on Purim originated in Europe in the Middle Ages, probably being influenced by the Christian carnival and morality plays, etc. usual at this season of the year. The essential topic was the story of the Book of Esther; later, other biblical stories too, such as the sale of Joseph. The earliest recorded Purim play was presented in the Venice ghetto in 1531, and the earliest text preserved was written in Portuguese by Solomon Usque in 1559. Yiddish P. P. are extant from a somewhat later date; there are also a Spanish text from Amsterdam from 1699 and a French text from Provence by Jacob de Lunel from the late 18th cent. Later, itinerant actors went from one community to another to perform P. P., this being the nursery of Jewish actors and the origin of the Yiddish drama which emerged in the mid-19th cent.

PURIMS, SPECIAL: Annual celebrations instituted by Jewish communities or individuals in celebration of their deliverance from danger: not all, however, were specifically given the name of P. Sometimes, a Megillah, closely imitating the style and even form of the Book of Esther, was compiled to celebrate the occasion. The oldest such celebration specifically given the name of P. is the Purim of Narbonne, commemorating a deliverance of the Jews there on *Adar* 21, 1236. The P. of Saragossa (properly of Syracuse), commemorating an event of 1380 or 1420, is still observed in the Levant by some families of Sicilian origin. Other P. are those of Cairo (*Adar* 28; instituted 1524), of Hebron (*Tevet* 14), of Buda (observed at Padua on *Elul* 10, instituted 1684), of Winz, at Frankfort-on-Main (*Adar* 20, instituted 1616: see Fettmilch) and of the earthquake at Leghorn (*Shevat* 22, instituted 1743). Several of these (including the last two) were preceded by a local fast-day. In S France, such celebrations (Avignon, Carpentras, Cavaillon) were termed "the *yom-tov* of the community." During the French Revolutionary

Title-page of *Ḥevrah Kaddisha* regulations for purification of the dead, Starakonstantinov, Volhynia.

Wars, almost every Italian Jewish community instituted a local P. to celebrate its escape from attack.

PURITY, RITUAL: Ritual purity and impurity constitute important aspects of biblical and mishnaic law. Rites of purification vary in their elaborateness according to the severity and the degree of impurity contracted. Ritual bathing was considered sufficient to remove the impurity which came with sexual intercourse or seminal emission (Lev. 15:16–18). Purification following childbirth, etc. required, in addition, a sin-offering and a burnt-offering (Lev. 12:6–8; 15:13–15, 28–30). The most severe degree of ritual impurity came through contact with a corpse and the purification ritual required the sprinkling of water mixed with the ashes of the Red Heifer (Num. 19:17–19). Purification after leprosy was even more complicated (Lev. 14:1–32). After menstruation a woman had to offer a sacrifice; in post-Temple times, she had to have a ritual bath (Mikveh). With the destruction of the Temple, those laws of r. p. intrinsically connected with the Temple fell into abeyance. The term Tohorah ("purification") has been transferred to the ritual washing of a corpse before burial.

Q

QIRQISANI see **KARKASANI**

QUEBEC: Canadian province. During French rule no professing Jew could reside in Q. The earliest Jewish settlers arrived with General Amherst's British army in 1760. These settled in MONTREAL, Three Rivers, and Quebec City, and with these places Jewish life in Q. was thereafter most closely associated. The Hart family of Three Rivers was outstanding, and the election of Ezekiel Hart to the Q. Assembly in 1807, although he was not allowed to take his seat, was the first episode in the political emancipation of the Jews of Q. (completed 1831/2). After the Russian persecutions of the 1880's, the number of Jews in Q. greatly increased. Q. was for many years the center of considerable anti-Semitism, especially among the Catholic clergy, making its first organized appearance during the Dreyfus trial in France. After World War I, the *Protocols of the Elders of Zion* gained wide circulation, but anti-Semitism subsided greatly after World War II. Jewish pop. (1974): 115,000. The major Jewish community is in Montreal (113,000), and Quebec City has 495 Jews.

QUEEN OF SHEBA see **SHEBA**

QUERIDO, ISRAEL (1884–1932): Dutch naturalistic writer. In addition to works on the farmers and workers of Holland, Q. wrote novels about the Jewish diamond workers and the poor Jews of Amsterdam. He also wrote the plays *Saul en David* with a biblical background and *Aaron Laguna* about Holland's rich Jews. His essays deal with art and literature.

QUERIDO, JACOB (d. c. 1690): Turkish heresiarch. The follower and spiritual heir of Shabbetai Tzevi, whose surname he later adopted, Q. went over to Islam in 1683 with 300 families of his followers. They continued to observe Sabbetaian and Jewish rites in secret. This was the origin of the DONMEH sect.

QUMRAN see **KUMRAN**

Jewish Public Library, Montreal, Quebec.

RAANANAH: Israel settlement in the S Sharon.
Founded in 1921, it soon became a center of citriculture. The religious children's village, Kephar Batyah,
was founded in R. by Youth Aliyah and the *Mizrahi*
Women's Organization of America. Pop. (1974):
18,500.

RAAYA MEHEMENA (Aram. "The Faithful Shepherd"): Kabbalistic work on the commandments,
dating from the 14th cent. and probably composed in
Spain. Originally an independent work, it was later
incorporated into the ZOHAR, from which it differs,
however, in style and thought. It is called after Moses,
the faithful shepherd, who manifests himself to the
kabbalists to reveal Divine secrets.

RABB, MAXWELL MILTON (1910–): US public
official. As assistant to President Eisenhower from
1953, he was in charge of civil rights, immigration, and
labor problems. He was secretary to the cabinet 1956–8.

RABBAH BAR BAR ḤANAH (3rd–4th cents.):
Amora. He lived in Palestine but frequently visited
Babylonia (probably his birthplace) where he transmitted the teachings of the Palestinian rabbis. A great
traveler, he noted vividly the many and varied incidents
of his journeys, relating with oriental exaggeration the
wonders of Sinai, etc. He has been termed "the Jewish
Sinbad."

RABBAH BAR NAḤMANI (generally known as Rabbah; 3rd–4th cents.): Babylonian amora. A leading halakhist, he headed the Pumbedita academy 308–
30 and was noted for his acumen and scholarship.

RABBAN: Variant form of "rabbi" applied as a title of
special honor in early mishnaic times to certain
outstanding scholars (e.g. Johanan ben Zakkai),
especially heads of the Sanhedrin.

RABBANITES see **RABBINITES**

RABBATH AMMON (or **RABBAH**): Ancient city at
the source of the river Jabbok; now Amman,
capital of Jordan. A city of the AMMONITES, it was
captured by David but the Israelites apparently lost
control after his death. It was subsequently subject to
Assyria, Babylon, and Persia. After the Greek conquest, it became hellenized, its name being changed to
Philadelphia in honor of Ptolemy Philadelphus (285–
46 BCE). From the time of Pompey, R.A. was a city
of the DECAPOLIS and under Trajan was annexed to
Provincia Arabia. Jews lived there from early times, but
since the beginning of the Christian era the city has had
no Jewish settlement. It became the capital of TRANS-
JORDANIA in 1921, and grew rapidly especially after
absorbing refugees from W Palestine in 1948 Pop.
(1971): c. 500,000.

RABBENU TAM see **JACOB BEN MEIR TAM**

RABBI and the **RABBINICAL OFFICE**: The title
rabbi (Heb. for "my master") came into use during
the 1st cent. CE as a mode of address to those authoritative teachers who were ordained members of the
Sanhedrin. Until the Patriarchate was finally suppressed during the 5th cent., the title was used only in
Palestine, scholars in Babylonia being addressed as
Rav ("master"). It is known from the the Talmud that
scholars were entitled to exemption from some taxes
and to certain privileges for their goods and farm produce in the markets, and that butchers had to submit
their slaughtering knives for inspection to the leading
authority of the district. But detailed knowledge of
the religious organization of the communities during
the period is meager and no clear picture can be
formed of the duties of a r. vis-à-vis the public.
Later in Jewish history, men distinguished in Jewish
learning were addressed as "rabbi," the title being
also applied to the appointed spiritual heads of the
communities. Only in N Europe, apparently, was a
system of ORDINATION in vogue. A scholar would
receive from his teacher—himself a r.—permission,
usually in writing, to express opinions on matters of
Jewish law without referring them to his teacher for
decision. The considerable measure of self-government enjoyed by the Jews of medieval Europe gave
the r. substantial power and the communities were
ruled with a firm hand. But neither in Europe nor in
Moslem countries was the office of r.—as distinct
from that of *dayyan* or judge—salaried before the
15th cent. As long as Jewish learning was cultivated
by the laity, the manifold duties of the r. of a large
town, embracing every phase of communal activity,
called for outstanding creative scholarship and wise
statesmanship. The r. in a large community maintained
a yeshivah, while under his supervision *dayyanim*
adjudicated lawsuits and arranged divorces, and
assistants supervised ritual slaughter and the ritual

baths. In the E Mediterranean, the r., mainly responsible for educational and judicial functions, was called *Marbitz Torah*. After the emancipation of the Jews of Europe a period of transition ensued in which efforts, that were only occasionally successful, were made to add secular culture to the full normal equipment of a traditional r. In modern times the r. of primary importance to the individual Jew is the one who serves the congregation of his synagogue and seldom performs the duties mentioned above. Apart from sermons in the synagogue and speeches at functions, his duties may be described as pastoral, social, and educational (usually at primary school level). In America, the title is almost universally applied to the religious leaders of the Jewish communities and is conferred largely by the theological seminaries. whereas in England, etc. those who carry out corresponding functions at the lower level are termed "minister." See also CHIEF RABBI; CROWN RABBI.

RABBI see **JUDAH HA-NASI**

RABBI BINYAMIN (pseudonym of Yehoshua Ha-Talmi, formerly Radler-Feldman; 1880–1957): Hebrew author. He was born in Galicia and lived in Palestine from 1907. B. wrote many books, essays, and articles on current problems and Zionist history. An editor of several periodicals and anthologies, he was an advocate of Arab-Jewish rapprochement.

RABBINERSEMINAR FÜR DAS ORTHODOXE JUDENTUM: The BERLIN RABBINICAL SEMINARY.

RABBINICAL ALLIANCE OF AMERICA (*Iggud ha-Rabbanim*): Orthodox Jewish organization established in 1944, seeking to further traditional Judaism. Intended to serve as the alumni association of the yeshivah Torah Vadaath, it became a representative body of Orthodox rabbis, with a membership of 250. The R. A. supports the Mesivta Torah Vadaath in Brooklyn which has an enrollment of 1,500 students.

RABBINICAL ASSEMBLY OF AMERICA: An association of over 900 Conservative rabbis serving primarily in the US and Canada. The majority (c. 80%) are graduates of the JEWISH THEOLOGICAL SEMINARY. Organized in 1900 as the Alumni Association of the Jewish Theological Seminary, it was reorganized in 1940 as the R. A. It has produced in conjunction with the United Synagogue revised Sabbath and Festival Prayerbooks. It publishes a quarterly journal *Conservative Judaism* and an annual volume of *Proceedings* of its convention. The R. A.'s Committee on Jewish Law and Standards has published a number of responsa.

RABBINICAL CONFERENCES: Records of conferences of Jewish lay and rabbinical leaders to discuss and act upon communal, religious, legal, and political problems go back to the 2nd cent. CE, when two such conferences were held — at Lydda and at Usha — to deal with problems arising from the Hadrianic persecution and the Bar Kokhba revolt.

Later, in the Amoraic and Gaonic Periods the KALLAH conventions were held twice a year. Gatherings were held also in the Middle Ages; thus an assembly of French and German rabbis headed by R Jacob ben Meir Tam met probably at Troyes c. 1165, and councils were convoked in Mayence in 1223 and 1245. The Napoleonic SANHEDRIN sat in 1807. R. C. in the modern sense began to be held in the 19th cent., when grave dissensions within Jewry, as well as external problems stemming from Emancipation, had to be solved. Three conferences were held in Germany: at Brunswick in 1844, at Frankfort in 1845, and at Breslau in 1846. Owing to irreconcilable conflicts over proposals for radical changes in traditional ritual and customs, proposed by advocates of REFORM JUDAISM, these conferences all failed to reach any agreement and no further meetings of the kind were held in Germany. In 1869, a series of conferences of small groups of US Reform rabbis began with a meeting in Philadelphia. This was followed by three called by Isaac M. Wise in Cleveland and in New York in 1870, and in Cincinnati in 1871. All these conferences adopted proposals for radical departures from traditional Judaism. At a meeting in Pittsburgh in 1885, eighteen Reform rabbis adopted a statement of principles including the repudiation of Jewish nationalism and the idea of a return to Zion, the substitution of the concept of spiritual immortality for the traditional doctrines of resurrection, and the proclamation of justice and righteousness as the basis for the solution of social and political problems. These principles, modified from time to time especially in respect of Zionism, became the official platform of Reform Judaism in the US. Four years after the Pittsburgh conference, the CENTRAL CONFERENCE OF AMERICAN RABBIS (Reform) was established, the first rabbinical organization to hold annual conferences. Other American rabbinical organizations that meet annually are the UNION OF ORTHODOX RABBIS of the United States and Canada (*Agudat ha-Rabbanim*), organized in New York City in 1902, and the RABBINICAL ASSEMBLY OF AMERICA (Conservative), established in 1900. In England, the Union (1894) and Conference of Anglo-Jewish Preachers (1923) also hold annual conferences. Leaders of the *Agudat Israel* meet from time to time to discuss problems connected with their work.

RABBINICAL COUNCIL OF AMERICA: Organization, founded 1923, of ordained Orthodox rabbis occupying pulpits in the US, Canada, and elsewhere in N America. Its 900 members come from all official Orthodox theological seminaries in the US.

RABBINICAL COURTS see **BET DIN**

RABBINICAL SEMINARIES: When Jews entered modern European life in the 19th cent., the need was felt for equipping RABBIS with secular and critical scientific training, as the traditional Talmud training of the YESHIVAH could not alone deal with the new circumstances. Moreover, the governments of several European states set up certain standards to be met by those entering the rabbinate. At first, rabbinical students studied at the general universities, continuing their Jewish studies privately. Leading Jewish scholars, however, demanded the establishment of modern r. s. These were founded in the course of the century in almost all W European countries as well as the US. Modern rabbinical schools were also founded in Russia and Poland, but these were imposed from without upon the general Jewish population, which for the most part remained entirely antagonistic to them; their aim was not the inculcation of a proper Jewish training, but the spread of Russian and Polish culture. The following r. s. were established in Europe: Italy, 1829; France, 1829; Netherlands, 1834 (Ashkenazi), 1837 (Sephardi); England, 1855; Germany, 1854 (Breslau), 1870 (Hochschule), 1873 (Berlin); Hungary, 1877; Austria, 1893; Turkey, 1898; Poland, 1928. In the US the four leading r. s. are the HEBREW UNION COLLEGE, Cincinnati (Reform 1875); the JEWISH THEOLOGICAL SEMINARY, New York (Conservative, 1886); the Rabbi Isaac Elchanan Theological Seminary (YESHIVA UNIV., Orthodox 1896); and the Jewish Institute of Religion (Reform, 1922) which merged with the Hebrew Union College in 1950.

RABBINISM and **RABBINITES** (also **RABBA-NITES**): The name Rabbinites was given by the KARAITES to their opponents who accepted the precepts of Jewish law contained in the Mishnah and Talmud. This led to the name Rabbinism being applied to the form which Judaism assumed between the time of Ezra and the modern period. For Rabbinism, authority resides in the continually growing ORAL LAW which interprets and supplements Scripture. This is administered by scholars ("rabbis") whose right to expound the law derives from their knowledge of and loyalty to it. With the virtual disappearance of Karaism, Rabbinism became synonymous with normative Judaism.

RABBINOVITZ, RAPHAEL NATHAN NETA (1835–1888): Russian scholar. An encyclopedic talmudist, his major publications were *Dikduke Sopherim* (16 volumes of variant readings from Talmud mss) and a study on printed editions of the Talmud.

RABBINOWITZ, ISRAEL MICHAEL (1818–1893): Scholar. Of Russian birth, he qualified as a doctor in Paris but gave up medical practice to write on the Talmud, his chief works being: *Législation Civile du Talmud* (5 vols.), *Législation Criminelle du Talmud*, *La Médecine du Talmud*, *Le Traité des Poisons de Maimonide* and an introduction to the Talmud. His later years were spent in London.

RABI, ISIDOR ISAAC (1898–): US physicist. He was awarded the Nobel Prize in 1944 for research in nuclear physics, quantum mechanics, and magnetism. R. has been professor of physics at Columbia Univ. since 1937 and was chairman of the general advisory committee of the US Atomic Energy Commission from 1953.

RABIN, YITZHAK (1922–): Israel soldier. Born in Jerusalem, he served in the PALMAH and in the 1948 War of Independence commanded the brigade which helped to raise the siege of Jerusalem. He served in various capacities in the Israel Defense Army, being appointed chief-of-staff in 1964. He commanded the Israel army during the victorious Six-Day War. He was ambassador to the US, 1968–73, entered the Knesset in 1974, and shortly afterward became prime minister. His 1975 negotiations with Kissinger culminated in the interim agreement with Egypt.

RABINOVICH, OSSIP (1817–1869): Russian journalist. He founded *Rasviet*, the first Jewish Russian weekly, in Odessa in 1860. In the general Russian press he defended the Jews; in the Jewish press, he advocated reforms in Jewish life.

RABINOVITZ, SOLOMON see **SHOLEM ALEI-CHEM**

RABINOWITZ, ALEXANDER SÜSSKIND (known from his initials as *Azar*, 1854–1945): Hebrew author. He was born in White Russia and in 1906, settled in Palestine. His works include stories (many on labor themes), monographs, translations of world literature and Judaica into Hebrew, and textbooks.

RABINOWITZ, JOSEPH (1837–1899): Russian sectarian leader. In 1882, he founded the Jewish-Christian sect NAVI ISRAEL and wrote its book of

Yitzhak Rabin.

statutes in which he explained his adoption of Christianity while retaining Sabbath observance and circumcision. In 1885, he became a Protestant.

RABINOWITZ, LOUIS ISAAC (1906–): Rabbi. Born in Scotland, he officiated in London, was a chaplain in the British army, and in 1945, was appointed chief rabbi in Johannesburg (chief rabbi of the Transvaal, 1948) and professor of Hebrew at Witwatersrand Univ. His books include studies of the Radanites and medieval French Jewry. In 1961, he settled in Israel and was a deputy editor of the *Encyclopedia Judaica*.

RABINOWITZ, LOUIS MAYER (1887–1957): US philanthropist. Greatly interested in Jewish culture, he made many gifts to US educational institutions and libraries, especially that of Yale Univ., and established the Yale Judaica series of translations of Hebrew classics into English.

RABINOWITZ, MORDECAI see **BEN-AMMI**

RABINOWITZ, SAUL PHINEHAS (known as *Shepher*; 1845–1910): Hebrew writer and *Hibbat Zion* leader. Of Lithuanian birth, he lived in Warsaw from 1874, being attracted to Jewish nationalism and then to Zionism under the influence of Smolenskin. After the 1881 Russian pogroms, he was active in organizing the emigration of Jewish refugees. In 1884, he was secretary of the KATTOWITZ CONFERENCE and thereafter, was secretary of the Warsaw office of the *Hoveve Zion*. R. contributed to Hebrew journalism, edited and published the annual *Keneset Yisrael* 1886–8, translated Graetz's history into Hebrew (with much supplementary material), and wrote on the history of the Jews exiled from Spain in the 1490's as well as monographs on Zunz and Z. Frankel, etc.

RABSHAKEH (Assyrian "steward"): Title of high Assyrian army official, the chief spokesman for Sennacherib's embassy to Hezekiah demanding the surrender of Jerusalem (II Kings 18:17).

RACE, RACIALISM: The conception that mankind is divided into different races is found in a vague and imprecise fashion in the Bible where, however, the essential unity of all races is suggested (as the rabbis emphasized) in the story of the Creation and of the common origin of all men. The conception of r. began to take on a new aspect in the 19th cent. The realization of the existence of the Aryan and Semitic families of languages led to the theory of the existence of Aryan and Semitic races and later, to the classification of their subsections, the Teutons exemplifying the former and the Jews the latter. The theory was based on the belief, since rejected by scientists, that (a) Jews were physically homogeneous, and (b) that there was a correlation between physical type and mental-cultural characteristics, Jews (and certain other groups) being regarded as racially "inferior." At the end of the 19th cent., this became a basic conception of the revived anti-Jewish movement in Germany

which, in the new era of tolerance, could no longer base itself exclusively on religion and, moreover, was confronted with large numbers of Jews in whose lives Judaism played no part. Thus, what had hitherto been an innocuous if unsound theory became in the hands of E. DUHRING, Wilhelm MARR, H. S. CHAMBERLAIN, A. ROSENBERG, etc. a deadly weapon. A fundamental principle of the Nazi movement from the outset (see NATIONAL SOCIALISM), it was officially and precisely formulated by the NUREMBERG LAWS in 1935, intermarriage between Jews and "Aryans" being sternly forbidden and the new Jewish disabilities being extended to all persons with two or more Jewish grandparents. This conception was applied somewhat less rigorously in Fascist Italy in 1938 and in various Nazi-occupied countries of Europe in 1939–45. On it was based the extermination policy carried out by the Germans in this period, extending therefore in many instances to persons with only the vaguest Jewish associations and even to Christian clergymen and priests. The alleged "scientific" evidences of racialism, based on craniometry, etc. are wholly untenable.

RACHEL: One of the four matriarchs of the Jewish people; second wife of Jacob. She was the daughter of Laban and lived at Haran in Aram-Naharaim. Jacob wished to wed R. but was tricked into marriage with her elder sister Leah; in return for 7 years' service to Laban, he subsequently received R. also as wife. She was the mother of Joseph and Benjamin and died near Bethlehem in giving birth to the latter (see TOMB OF RACHEL). The biblical image (Jer. 31:15) of the compassionate mother R. weeping for her children driven into captivity became a favorite figure in Jewish folklore.

RACHEL (pen name of Rachel Blovstein; 1890–1931): Hebrew poet. Born in Russia, she went to Palestine in 1909 and worked as a laborer first at Rehovot, later at Kinneret. In her latter years, she suffered from consumption, and the knowledge of her approaching death is reflected in her poems. She wrote simple, autobiographical lyrics imbued with a love for the Palestinian countryside and the work of the pioneers.

RACHEL see **FELIX, RACHEL**

RACHEL, TOMB OF see **TOMB OF RACHEL**

RADANITES: Jewish merchants who, in the 9th cent., traveled between S France and China. They are known mainly from a description by the early Arab geographer Ibn Khordadbeh (c. 846–86) who states that they spoke "Arabic, Persian, Roman, and the languages of the Franks, Andalusians, and Slavs." He describes in detail four trade-routes that they followed. The first was *via* the Mediterranean to Alexandria, overland to the Red Sea, and *via* the Indian Ocean to the China Sea. The second route went overland *via* Damascus, Baghdad, and Basra and then continued as in the previous route. The third of the routes was entirely overland across N Africa to Palestine, Baghdad, and then into the interior óf China, while the fourth went across central Europe.

RADEK (originally **SOBELSOHN**), **KARL** (1885– c. 1939). Russian communist. He participated in the 1917 Bolshevik Revolution, organized the German Communist Party the following year, and in 1920, was made secretary of the Third International. As a Trotskyist he was expelled from the Party in 1927, but was readmitted in 1930, becoming editor of *Izvestia*. In 1937, he was sentenced to ten years' imprisonment and was not heard of subsequently. He was posthumously rehabilitated in 1962. R. wrote a history of the socialist movement.

RADLER-FELDMAN, YEHOSHUA see **RABBI BINYAMIN**

RAFI (Heb. initials of "Israel Workers' List"): Party that broke away from MAPAI in 1965 under the leadership of David BEN-GURION who had retired from the Premiership and was critical of his successor, Levi Eshkol. In the 1965 General Election, R. obtained ten seats in the Knesset. In 1968 it merged with MAPAI and AHDUT AVODAH to form the ISRAEL LABOR PARTY.

RAGOLER, ELIJAH BEN JACOB (1794–1849): Rabbi. He was successively rabbi of Shat, Ragola (whence his surname), and finally Kalish. He held that the movement for religious reform in Germany should be countered by intensive educational propaganda.

RAHAB: Courtesan in Jericho who housed and shielded the spies sent by Joshua (Josh. 2). As a reward, the Israelites spared her and her family (Josh. 6).

RAIN, PRAYER FOR: Special petition in the Additional Service on SHEMINI ATZERET. According to the Mishnah (*Rosh ha-Shanah* 1:2) distribution of the rains is decided on Tabernacles when MASHIV HA-RUAH is inserted in the Eighteen Benedictions and this fact is announced in the synagogue. The liturgical poets wrote a number of appropriate compositions for recitation on this occasion. The best-known example, by Eleazar Kalir, has found its way into the German and Polish rites. The Sephardim chant a different accompanying poem by Solomon Ibn Gabirol. Especially outside Israel, the Ashkenazim recite the prayer with great solemnity and it is customary for the cantor to be clothed in white on this occasion.

RAINER, LUISE (1912–): Actress. She made her theater debut in Germany and in 1935, went to the US where she appeared on stage and screen.

RAISIN, MAX (1881–1957): US rabbi. After serving congregations in Mississippi and Brooklyn, he was rabbi in Paterson N. J. 1921–46. His books include a supplementary volume to Graetz's *History of the Jews*.

RAKAH (Heb. initials of *Reshimah Komunistit Hadashah* "New Communist List): Israel Communist party formed as a result of a split in the Communist party in 1965. *Rakah*, which supports Russian policy in the Middle East and derives most of its support from Israel Arabs, obtained 3 seats in the Knesset elections of 1965, 1969 and 1973.

RAKOSI, MÁTYÁS (1892–1971): Hungarian communist politician. He took part in Béla Kun's Communist Republic (1919) and became secretary of the Comintern (1920). Imprisoned for life in 1933, he was freed in 1940 and went to Russia. He returned in 1945, became secretary of the Hungarian Communist Party until 1956, and was premier 1952–3. In 1962, he was expelled from the Party. From 1956, in USSR.

RAKOVER, MORDECAI see **MOTKE HABAD**

RALBAG see **LEVI BEN GERSHON**

RAMAT GAN: Israel town near Tel Aviv. Founded in 1921, it has become one of the major centers of Israel industry. R. G. has expanded rapidly and is now the fourth city in the country. It is noted for its well-planned development and numerous public gardens, among them the National Park. Pop. (1974): 120,200.

RAMAT HA-GOLAN see **GOLAN**

RAMAT HA-SHARON: Israel settlement in the S Sharon plain. It was founded in 1923 by middle-class settlers, and its economy is based mainly on

Ramat Gan: The Diamond Exchange.

The Jewish settlement of Ramat Raḥel, south of Jerusalem,
after having been shelled by the Arab Legion's guns.

citriculture. After 1948, many immigrants were
absorbed. Now the greater part of the inhabitants has
citriculture. After 1948, many immigrants were
Pop. (1974): 23,000.

RAMAT RAḤEL: Israel communal settlement (IK)
near Jerusalem. It was founded in 1926 by a group
from *Gedud ha-Avodah*. The site was of strategic
importance and underwent ceaseless attacks during
the disturbances of 1929 and 1936–9. Its heroic
resistance in the Israel War of Independence (mainly
against an Egyptian column) determined the fate
of Jewish Jerusalem; the settlement was destroyed
but later rebuilt. An Israelite fortress has been found
there, and the site is believed to be the biblical Neto-
phah or Beth ha-Kerem. Pop. (1972): 92.

RAMAT YOḤANAN: Israel communal settlement
(IK) in the plain of Zebulun; named after Jan
Smuts. It was founded in 1932 by youth from E
Europe, who drained the swamps of the area under
difficult conditions. In the Israel War of Independence,
R. Y. repulsed strong forces, composed mainly of
Druzes, thereby warding off a threat to Haifa. The
settlement has developed new cultural traditions,
notably its ceremony for the gathering-in of the OMER.
Pop. (1972): 542.

RAMATAYIM see **HADAR RAMATAYIM**

RAMBAM see **MOSES BEN MAIMON**
RAMBAN see **MOSES BEN NAḤMAN**
RAMESES (RAAMSES): Ancient Egyptian city in
the Nile Delta area where Jacob and his family
settled (Gen. 47:11, 27). Their descendants were
compelled to build storehouses for the Egyptian king.
R. was the point of departure for the Exodus (Exod.
12:37). Formerly thought to be the city of Pelusion
on the Delta border, modern scholars identify it
with another site further S.

RAMḤAL see **LUZZATTO, MOSES ḤAYYIM**
RAMLAH: Israel town. Founded by Arabs in 716,
it soon became the capital of Palestine, and most
inhabitants of nearby Lydda (the previous capital)
moved to R. Its population in the Middle Ages was
composed of Arabs, Samaritans, and Persians. In
the 10th cent., a Jewish and a Karaite community
were founded. In the 11th cent., the town suffered
from Bedouin attacks and was nearly destroyed by
earthquakes in 1016 and 1033. Built up again, it was
taken by the Seljuk Turks and, later, by the Crusaders
under whose rule the Jewish, Karaite, and Samaritan
communities almost disappeared. After its conquest by
the Mamelukes, and later under Turkish rule, R.
remained an important station on the way to Jerusalem. In the 19th cent., a Christian community

The "White Tower" of Ramla, 13th Century A.D.

began to develop. R. was occupied by Israel forces in 1948. About 1,000 of its Arab inhabitants remained in the town and were soon augmented by large numbers of Jewish immigrants. Pop. (1974): 36,300.

RAM'S HORN see **SHOPHAR**

RAMSGATE: English seaside town, where in the mid-19th cent. a small Jewish community (now numbering 65) was attracted by the Sephardi synagogue built near his residence by Sir Moses Montefiore and by the JUDITH MONTEFIORE COLLEGE which he endowed.

RAN see **GERONDI**

RANK, OTTO (1884–1939): Psychoanalyst. He was founder of the International Psychoanalytic Institute in Vienna and its director 1919–24. At first a disciple of Freud, he broke with him in 1925 over relative importance of the conscious and the unconscious, subsequently developing his central theory of the birth trauma. He settled in the US in 1935.

RANSOM see **CAPTIVES**

RAPHAEL (Heb. compound of *rapha* "heal" and *el* "God"): Archangel and Divine messenger with the special function of healing. He is first mentioned in the apocryphal books of Enoch and Tobit.

RAPHAEL BEN JEKUTHIEL COHEN (1722–1803): Talmudist. Born and educated in Poland, he was rabbi at Minsk 1757–63, Pinsk 1763–71, Posen 1772–6,

and Altona 1776–99. He objected to modernism and bitterly opposed Moses Mendelssohn. His *Torat Yekutiel*, a partial commentary on the first part of the *Shulḥan Arukh*, became a standard work.

RAPOPORT, SOLOMON JUDAH (known from his initials as *Shir*; 1790–1867): Pioneer of WISSENSCHAFT. He was born in Galicia and ordained for the rabbinate but also studied secular subjects. R. was rabbi in Tarnopol, Galicia 1837–40, and in Prague from 1840, and was early attacked by Ḥasidim and the ultra-Orthodox for the enlightened approach reflected in his writings. His researches into Jewish history and culture combined European scientific critical methods and a broad rabbinic knowledge. His methods were cautious and moderate, though not conservative, and his work helped to lay the foundations of modern Jewish scholarship. He wrote brilliant monographs on Jewish scholars of the Gaonic Period, commenced a talmudic encyclopedia (*Erekh Millin*: only part I, comprising the letter *aleph*, appeared), and translated European poetry into Hebrew, notably Racine's *Esther* (as *She'erit Yehudah*). Important mutual influence resulted from his personal friendship with Nachman Krochmal and his correspondence with S. D. Luzzatto.

RAPOPORT, SOLOMON SEINWIL see **AN-SKI**

RAS SHAMRA see **UGARIT**

RASHBA see **ADRET, SOLOMON BEN**

RASHBAM see **SAMUEL BEN MEIR**

RASHBASH see **DURAN, SOLOMON BEN SIMEON**

RASHBATZ see **DURAN, SIMEON BEN TZEMAH**

RASHI (abbr. for R Solomon Yitzḥaki [= ben Isaac]; 1040–1105): French rabbinical scholar. After studying in the Rhineland, he returned to his

Title-page of Rashi's commentary on the Pentateuch, published by Elijah Aboab. (Amsterdam, 1720).

native Troyes where his school rapidly achieved a wide reputation, though he apparently earned his livelihood from his vineyard. Many halakhic queries were addressed to him and his decisions have been preserved in the works of his pupils. He also composed penitential hymns. His chief contribution was his lucid commentary on the Bible and Babylonian Talmud. The commentary on the Bible, particularly the Pentateuch, became universally popular, while his notes on the Babylonian Talmud were responsible for making that work an open book. He had an extensive knowledge of sources and earlier commentaries (although not generally citing them by name) as well as of current grammatical works. He also relies to a considerable extent on Targum Onkelos for his interpretation of the Pentateuch. His style is simple and concise, and his object, to present the direct rational meaning of the text; nevertheless the popularity of his commentary on the Pentateuch can be partly attributed to the admixture of Midrash. His commentary on the entire Talmud (with the exception of a few tractates) made several outstanding contributions: (1) the establishment of a correct text on the basis of mss, oral tradition, and parallels in the Talmud and contemporary sources. His corrections of the text have been incorporated in the printed editions; (2) the definition of terms; (3) the explanations of unusual words and phrases, together with emphasis on the connecting-links in the discussions. The style of his commentary on the Talmud is more "rabbinic" than on the Bible i.e., his Hebrew there is mixed with Aramaic; but it is marked by the same artistic conciseness. He frequently quotes the French equivalent (*laaz*) in Hebrew transliteration for rare words; these notes have proved significant for the study of medieval French philology and pronunciation. His comments on the Mishnah are perfunctory, the main explanations being reserved for the relevant *gemara*. R.'s commentaries served as the basis for later scholars such as Naḥmanides and Ibn Ezra in their interpretation of the Pentateuch.

RASHI SCRIPT: Semi-cursive form of Hebrew characters principally used for writing and printing rabbinical commentaries, especially that of Rashi; termed also *mashket* and technically known as "rabbinic characters."

RASKIN, SAUL (1878–1966): Artist. He was born in Russia and went to the US in 1904. His paintings, etchings, and water colors deal for the most part with Jewish subjects. He published illustrated editions of *Avot*, the Passover Haggadah, Psalms, and other Jewish works.

RASMINSKY, LOUIS (1908–): Canadian economist. R. was associated with various international economic bodies including the economic section of the League of Nations, the International Monetary Fund, and the International Bank for Reconstruction and Development. From 1955 he was deputy governor and in 1961–75 governor of the Bank of Canada.

RASVIET (Russ. "The Dawn"): Name of three Russian Jewish weekly journals: (1) appearing 1860–1 in Odessa under the editorship of Ossip Rabinovich advocated Enlightenment among Jews and also equal rights; (2) appearing 1879–83 in St. Petersburg (ed. Alexander Zederbaum); (3) appearing 1907–18 in St. Petersburg (ed. Abraham Idelson), 1921–33 in Berlin, and 1933–4 in Paris (ed. Vladimir Jabotinsky) was the organ of Russian Zionism.

RATHENAU: (1) *EMIL R.* (1838–1915): German engineer. He organized the German telephone system and directed the *Allgemeine Elektrizitäts-Gesellschaft* (AEG; "General Electric Co."). To R. are due many improvements in the fields of radio-telegraphy, aluminium manufacture, etc. (2) *WALTER R.* (1867–1922): German engineer, economist and statesman; son of (1). He discovered a new method for extracting chlorine and alkalies and built power stations in several countries. In 1915, he succeeded his father as director of the General Electric Co. which became one of the largest enterprises in Germany. In 1921, R. was appointed minister of reconstruction in the German republican government and in the following year, foreign minister; in both positions he strove for a Franco-German rapprochement. He was assassinated by anti-Semites. He was the author of works on politics and philosophy.

RATISBON see **REGENSBURG**

RAV see **RABBI**

RAV (Abba Arikha = Abba the Tall; fl. early 3rd cent.): Babylonian amora; founder of the Sura academy. Descended from an illustrious family, he went with his uncle R Hiyya to Palestine where he studied, primarily with R Judah Ha-Nasi. He rose to prominence in Palestine, but, in later life, returned to Babylonia where he declined the position of head of the Nehardea academy in favor of his colleague Samuel to whom he considered it belonged. Finding abysmal ignorance of Jewish tradition in the outlying areas of Babylonia, he established an academy in Sura which, in a short time, became the leading school in the country, with 1,200 students. He excelled in both halakhah and aggadah, and his influence upon the cultural life of Babylonia was profound and stimulating. He and Samuel are the two scholars whose teachings figure most prominently in the Babylonian Talmud. He is thought to have been the author of the Alenu prayer.

RAVA (fl. mid-4th cent.): Babylonian amora; son of the amora Joseph bar Ḥama and contemporary of Abbaye. He established an academy in his native Maḥoza after Abbaye became head of the academy at Pumbedita and by his analytical and logical manner of teaching attracted many of the latter's students. After Abbaye's death, R. also became head of the

Pumbedita academy which he incorporated into his school at Maḥoza. Thus, until his death, there was only one academy in Babylonia. R. placed study higher than any other virtue, including prayer, and devoted his life to that end. He also laid stress on high moral living. Personally, he was extremely zealous in the observance of ritual. His controversies with Abbaye were famous and with six exceptions, the halakhah was determined according to the view of R. He was also an outstanding homilist.

RAVENNA: Italian city. Its Jewish community goes back to late classical times, a synagogue destroyed by mob-attack having to be rebuilt in 519. Jews were again living there in the early 13th cent., and when the city passed under Venetian rule in 1441, there was a group of Jewish loanbankers there, as elsewhere in the region. R. was the scene of a synod of the Italian Jewish communities in 1442. The Jews were expelled from R. (then under papal rule), as from the rest of the states of the Church, in 1569, and finally, in 1593.

RAVNITZKY, YEHOSHUA ḤANA (1859–1944): Hebrew and Yiddish author and editor. Born in Odessa, he was one of the first *Hoveve Zion* and a founder of *Bene Mosheh*. He became editor of the Yiddish periodical *Der Yid* at Cracow in 1899, and in 1901, cofounded the MORIAH publishing house. In 1922, he settled in Palestine where he helped to establish the DEVIR publishing house. He collaborated with Bialik in publishing the *Sepher Aggadah*, the diwan of Ibn Gabirol, and the poems of Moses Ibn Ezra.

RAWIDOWICZ, SIMON (1897–1957): Philosopher. A native of Poland, he studied in Berlin and lectured at London 1934–40 and Leeds 1941–8. In 1948, he settled in the US where he taught at the Chicago College of Jewish Studies 1948–51, and at Brandeis Univ., 1951–7. R. wrote, mainly in Hebrew, on a wide range of philosophical subjects and thinkers (Saadyah, Maimonides, Mendelssohn, Krochmal, etc.) as well as on contemporary Jewish problems. He was co-editor of *Ha-Tekuphah* (1927–30), editor of the miscellany *Metzudah*, and a founder of the BERIT IVRIT OLAMIT.

RAYMUND, MARTINI see **MARTINI**

RAYNAL, DAVID (1840–1903): French statesman. A deputy 1879–97 and thereafter senator, he was minister of public works 1881–2, 1883–5, and minister of the interior in 1893.

RAYNER, ISIDOR (1850–1912): US senator. He was elected to the Maryland General Assembly in 1878, to the Maryland State Senate in 1885, and to the US Congress in 1888. In 1905, he became senator, in which capacity he devoted himself to domestic issues and to problems of international law. He was considered one of the leading orators of his day.

The Marquess of Reading.

RAZIEL (Heb. literally "mystery of God"): Angelic guardian of Divine secrets. The name first occurs in the Slavonic Book of ENOCH and later in mystical pseudepigrapha.

RAZIEL, BOOK OF: A composite kabbalistic work, supposedly delivered by the angel RAZIEL to Adam (hence known also as "Book of the First Man"). It contains mystical teachings, letter mysticism, descriptions of the heavens and angelological material, as well as magical recipes and formulas for amulets. It was formerly believed that a home containing the Book of R. was secure against fire.

RAZIEL, DAVID (1911–1941): Palestinian extreme nationalist leader. He led the IRGUN TZEVAI LEUMI from 1937. He was killed in a German air-raid at Habbaniya while on a mission for the British to Iraq.

READING OF THE LAW see **LAW, READING OF THE**

READING, MARQUESS OF (Rufus Daniel Isaacs; 1860–1935): English statesman. Born of a middle-class London family, he studied law after an unsuccessful attempt in business. He soon became an outstanding advocate, entered parliament as a Liberal, and was appointed successively solicitor general (1910), attorney general (1910), and lord chief justice (1913). In 1918, he was ambassador to the US and in 1921–6, viceroy of India. He was foreign secretary in 1931. Strongly Jewish in sentiment, though not observant, he was chairman of the Palestine Electric Corporation. R. was created a peer in 1916 and marquess—the only English Jew to have received this honor—in 1926. His son, the *2nd MARQUESS* (Gerald Rufus Isaacs; 1889–1960), after a successful legal, political, and literary career, was minister of state for foreign affairs 1953–7. His wife *EVA VIOLET* (1895–1973), d. of Alfred MOND, embraced Judaism at the time of Nazi persecutions and was president of the British section of the World Jewish Congress.

REBBE: Yiddish form of Rabbi, applied generally to a teacher; also to a Hasidic rabbi.

REBEKAH: Wife of Isaac; daughter of Bethuel, and mother of Esau and Jacob. Her kindness attracted the attention of Abraham's envoy Eliezer who had been dispatched to Aram Naharaim to seek a wife for his master's son Isaac (Gen. 24–8). She later supported Jacob in his struggle with Esau. R. is regarded as one of the four matriarchs of the Jewish people and in legend is the ideal type of Jewish womanhood.

RECANATI, MENAHEM BEN BENJAMIN (c. 1300): Italian kabbalist, living at Recanati in the province of Macerata. He introduced German mysticism and the study of the Zohar into Italy.

RECHABITES: Order organized among his family by Jehonadab ben Rechab, who assisted Jehu in purging Israel of the cult of Baal (II Kings 10:15–17, 23). They undertook to abstain from drinking wine, cultivating vineyards or fields, and living in houses. Apparently they lived first in Samaria and only transferred to Judah after the destruction of the Northern kingdom. The group maintained its identity in the Second Temple Period when they were known as "sons of the waterdrinkers." Every year on *Av* 7, they brought wood to the altar. A modern Anglo-American temperance organization has adopted the name of R.

RECIFE (PERNAMBUCO): City in Brazil. It had a Jewish community, mainly of Marrano origin, from c. 1630 when still under Dutch rule. Its regula-

tions and minutes have been preserved and recently published. The rabbi from 1642 was Isaac ABOAB da Fonseca. The community came to an end with the Portuguese reconquest in 1654, the first 23 settlers in New Amsterdam coming from Recife. There is now again a Jewish community in R. pop. (1970): 1,600.

RECONSTRUCTIONISM: A trend of thought in American-Jewish life, originated by Mordecai M. KAPLAN in 1934, with adherents among the Conservative and Reform Jews as well as among some so-called secularists. It teaches that Judaism is not only a religion, but a dynamic religious civilization, now entering upon its fourth stage in the history of the Jewish people as a result of Emancipation and Enlightenment. It calls for: (a) the reclamation of the Land of Israel as the home of the historic Jewish civilization, and the formation of organic Jewish communities in the Diaspora; (b) the revitalization of Jewish religion through the study of it in the spirit of free inquiry, and through the separation of its institutions from all political authority; (c) the acceptance of diversity in Jewish religious thought and action, as well as respect for traditional ceremonies and way of life as aspects of Jewish civilization; (d) the expansion of the concept *Torah* to include ethical culture, ritual enrichment, and esthetic creativity. The Jewish Reconstructionist Foundation in New York publishes the *Reconstructionist* magazine, and sponsors the Reconstructionist Press. A *Haggadah, Sabbath Prayerbook, High Holiday Prayerbook,* and

View of Recife by Zachariah Wagner (17th cent.).

Reform Temple Emanu-El, NY.

Festival Prayerbook have been issued, bearing a strong resemblance to the Conservative liturgy, but embodying additional medieval and modern devotional material.

RECORDS see **ARCHIVES**

RED HEIFER (Heb. *parah adummah*): A congregational sacrifice whose ashes, when mixed with water, removed impurity created by contact with the dead. The sacrificed animal, a r. h. unblemished and never yoked, was burnt outside the camp (at Jerusalem, on the Mt. of Olives) while those that handled it also required purification (Num. 19). Later generations, finding the ceremony incomprehensible, put forward various explanations, e.g. that the r. h. atoned for the worship of the golden calf or that the color of the heifer symbolized sin.

RED SEA: A branch of the Indian Ocean extending from the Strait of Aden and forking to Suez and Elath. It was early identified (cf. the Septuagint) with the "Reed" Sea (*yam suph*) crossed by the Israelites during the Exodus from Egypt (Exod. 13:18 etc.). It was certainly so called in the period of the Monarchy (I Kings 9:26). It now forms Israel's S outlet to the Indian Ocean by way of Elath.

RED SHIELD OF DAVID see **MAGEN DAVID ADOM**

REDAK see **KIMḤI, DAVID**

REDEMPTION (Heb. *geulah*): Religious and philosophic concept expressing man's striving or desire for personal and social improvement, emphasizing the difference between reality and the ideal. Although most religions place r. "at the end of days" —i.e., at the end of history—others, such as Christianity, have placed it within the framework of history. The outstanding Jewish example is the Exodus from Egypt. The final r. yet to come was considered by earlier Judaism primarily as an historical event, although there was also to be r. from sin (Is. 11:9, 51:5 etc.). The rabbis of the Talmudic Period had a similar view but some transcendental overtones are already seen in certain mystical references, like that of the Divine Presence being in exile with Israel, or in viewing the final r. of Israel as the factor bringing about the r. of the world. With the fuller development of Jewish mysticism, r. came to be associated with a metaphysical change in the order of creation. It meant the complete restoration of the identity of the Godhead. At first this was taken to be outside man's power to influence. Isaac Luria, however, taught that it could be effected by man's actions in bringing about Tikkun Ha-Olam. After the failure of the Sabbetaian movement, r. tended to be limited to the personal salvation of the individual as taught in Hasidism. In modern times, a purely secular interpretation of r. has developed in the Zionist striving for a Jewish national home.

REDLICH, JOSEPH (1869–1963): Political scientist. R., who was baptized, lectured in Vienna and from 1926, at Harvard Law School. He was prominent in Austrian politics, serving as a member of parliament and, for short periods in 1918 and 1931, as minister of finance. R. wrote standard works on constitutional law.

REFORM JUDAISM: Religious movement maintaining that to meet contemporary exigencies, modifications have to be introduced in traditional Jewish thought and practices. Reacting to the Napoleonic Emancipation, the Reform Jewish movement began in Germany with the formation of small synagogues by laymen such as Israel Jacobson who shortened the service, introduced the vernacular, utilized an organ, made the vernacular sermon a regular feature, and instituted the ceremony of group-confirmation. Early German Reform rabbis tended to be extreme in their practices and opinions seeking, at a succession of RABBINICAL CONFERENCES, to break with the tenets which characterized European Judaism of their day. Men like Samuel Holdheim and Abraham Geiger advocated drastic changes in practice and a complete severance from talmudic restrictions. The first congregation in the US to adopt Reform was Beth Elohim in Charleston, S. C. in the early part of the 19th cent., but the movement received its major impetus in the US through the efforts of Isaac Mayer Wise who founded the UNION OF AMERICAN HEBREW CONGREGATIONS (1873), the HEBREW UNION COLLEGE (1875), and the CENTRAL CONFERENCE OF AMERICAN RABBIS (1889). Each of these agencies was the first of its kind in the US. R. J. maintains that "the externals of Judaism may be altered to strengthen its eternals." It declares that historic Judaism continuously adapted itself to its environment in order to strengthen its impact upon society, and modern Judaism should make similar modifications to correspond to the current situation. Reform abandoned the doctrine that it is Jewish destiny to be miraculously transported by the Messiah to the Holy Land, there to have the entire levitical and temple apparatus recreated for him. In its recoil against this belief in the personal Messiah (for which it substituted the belief in a messianic age), early Reform turned against Zionism. Later, however, its attitude toward Zionism became decidedly more favorable. R. J. maintains that it is the mission of the Jew to spiritualize mankind. Hence, those customs designed to separate the Jew from his neighbor may be surrendered. Without altering its feeling that there are deep theological gulfs separating Judaism from Christianity, R. J. nonetheless declares anachronistic such differentiatory practices as covering the head at worship, the dietary laws, the use of the phylacteries, etc. Reform has not eliminated ceremonialism, but holds that all practices should be meaningful and esthetic. In recent years, there has been an increasing tendency to reintroduce traditional ceremonies. Reform synagogues exist in 26 countries with a Jewish community in America it counts a million adherents, members of some 550 Reform temples. The movement is affiliated to the WORLD UNION FOR PROGRESSIVE JUDAISM.

REFORMATION: Term generally used to describe the great religious movement of the 16th cent. that divided western Christianity into the Catholic and PROTESTANT camps. Among the preliminary skirmishes which preceded the R. in Germany was the great dispute between REUCHLIN and the "obscurantists" resulting from the Dominican onslaught on Hebrew literature. Most of the early Reformers, appealing to the authority of Scripture as against the tradition of Rome, attached great importance to the Hebrew text of the Old Testament, and many of them studied Hebrew in order to understand it fully. For this reason, their opponents often accused them of judaizing, and Catholics suspected the Jews of actively fomenting the Reform movements. This was wholly unjustified, although some Jews regarded the schism in the Church as fulfilment of prophecy and as a prelude to messianic days. Martin LUTHER, though hoping at first that the Jews would be won over to Reformed CHRISTIANITY, subsequently vented his disappointment by adopting a ferociously anti-Jewish attitude, and none of the Reformers was in any degree pro-Jewish. Nevertheless, the suspicions of the Catholic Church against the Jews as fomenters of Reform were in part responsible for the stern measures adopted against them by the popes in the Counter-Reformation. The R. otherwise had no immediate effect on the position of the Jews, many Protestant areas of Europe excluding them while

Catholic regions continued to tolerate them. It was only with the subsequent development of a mercantilistic outlook in Puritan England and Holland that a more tolerant attitude began to be manifest in the Protestant world.

REFUGE, CITIES OF see **CITIES OF REFUGE**

REFUGEES: It was after World War I that the protection of r. was first recognized as an international responsibility. Millions left their country because of political, racial, or religious persecutions; and in 1921, Dr. Nansen was appointed by the LEAGUE OF NATIONS as high commissioner for Russian and Armenian r. He devised an identity certificate and a travel document for r. known as the Nansen passport. After his death, the protection of r. was undertaken by the Nansen Office of the League, and an international convention of 1933 prescribed their status. In that year, consequent on Nazi persecution, another high commissioner of the League was appointed for r. (Jewish and other) from Germany. James G. MACDONALD, the first high commissioner, resigned after two years because of inadequate action by members of the League, and his successor was restricted to the juridical protection of r. In 1938, President Roosevelt convened a conference of government representatives at EVIAN to assist the emigration and resettlement of r. In 1939, the high commissioner for German r. became director of that inter-governmental committee and responsible for all r. under the protection of the League. During World War II, he worked to relieve r. who were outside the Nazi-occupied territories and improve the conditions of emigration. In 1947, the League office and the committee were replaced by an instrument of the UNITED NATIONS, the INTERNATIONAL REFUGEE ORGANIZATION which was a non-permanent specialized agency. The Palestine war of 1948 created the problem of Arab r., concentrated mostly in Jordan and the Gaza strip, who are the concern of a non-permanent specialized agency of the UN — the UNWRA.

REGENSBURG (RATISBON): German city. Its Jewish community is among the oldest in Germany, possibly originating in the 5th cent. Until the time of the Crusades, the Jews of R. engaged in trade and moneylending. In 1096, the crusaders forced the Jews into baptism but the emperor Henry IV permitted them to resume their faith the next year. From the 13th cent., the king, the city, the bishop, and the dukes of Lower Bavaria obtained certain rights in regard to the Jews, but the community — although paying taxes to all four — was able to build its internal authority and established a reputation as a center of scholarship; in the mid-15th cent., R. was the leading German community. With the city's subsequent decline, relations between Jews and Christians deteriorated. In 1452, the Jews were forced to wear the Jewish badge and in 1476, a Blood Libel was laid against them by the local bishop. In 1519. the king acceded to a petition of the burghers that they should be allowed to expel the Jews. A few families resettled there in 1695 and about 150 families resided in R. from the mid-19th cent. until the Nazi era. Jewish pop. (1970): 140.

REGGIO DI CALABRIA: Seaport in the extreme S. of Italy, with a Jewish community in the Middle Ages largely dependent on the silk industry. The first dated Hebrew book was printed there in 1475.

REGGIO EMILIA: Town in N Italy to which Jewish loan bankers were summoned in 1413 to curb the "biting usury" of the Christian money-lenders. Later, as one of the principal cities of the duchy of Modena, its Jewish community was among the most important in Italy, producing many scholars of wide reputation. The ghetto was introduced in 1669/71. The community dwindled after emancipation in the 19th cent., suffering during the German occupation in 1943–5, and now numbers less than 100.

REGGIO, ISAAC SAMUEL (abbr. *Yashar*; 1784–1855): Scholar and mathematician. He was a pioneer of Haskalah in N Italy. R. translated the Pentateuch into Italian, appending a commentary with a critical tendency which provoked fierce antagonism, especially from the German rabbinate. He expounded a fusion of the progressive rationalism of his period with the Jewish halakhic tradition in his *Torah and Philosophy* and took the lead in establishing the Padua rabbinical college which incorporated secular studies in its curriculum (1829). In 1846, he succeeded his father as rabbi in Gorizia.

Havivah Reik

REHOBOAM: King of Judah 933–917 BCE; son of Solomon by his Ammonite wife Naamah. As a result of his refusal to accede to a popular demand for relief from taxation, the kingdom split in two shortly after his accession, only the tribes of Judah, Simeon, and most of Benjamin remaining loyal to him. Shishak of Egypt exploited the opportunity to invade the country and plunder the Temple.

REHOVOT: Israel town in the Judean coastal plain. It was founded in 1890 by *Bilu* pioneers from Poland and Russia. The name was derived from the Bible ("Rehoboth"), although the biblical R. (where Isaac dug his wells) is in the Negev. At first, vineyards and almond plantations constituted the main branches of the economy, but citrus groves became the colony's mainstay in the early 1900's. Industrial undertakings have been developed since the 1930's. On the initiative of Chaim Weizmann, who made R. his permanent home, it became the site of the Sieff and Weizmann Research Institutes, of the Jewish Agency's Agricultural Experimental Station and of the Agricultural Faculty of the Hebrew University. Pop. (1974): 46,400.

REICHSTEIN, TADEUSZ (1897–): Organic chemist. Born in Poland, he became head of the organic chemistry department of the Univ. of Basle in 1946. In 1950, he was recipient of a Nobel Prize in physiology and medicine for his work on the suprarenal glands and their hormones.

REICHSVERTRETUNG DER DEUTSCHEN JUDEN: The representative body of German Jewry 1933–39. It concentrated activities in the fields of rehabilitation, occupational training, and education, and also organized emigration.

REIFMANN, JACOB (1818–1895): Polish Hebrew scholar. Although living in poverty in a small townlet. he engaged throughout his life in Jewish historical and philological research, corresponding with the chief scholars of his time. He published numerous Hebrew monographs, including studies on the Talmud and other branches of Judaica.

REIK, ḤAVIVAH (1914–1944): Palestinian heroine. Of Slovak birth, she joined the *Ha-Shomer ha-Tzair* movement and reached Palestine in 1939. In 1944, she volunteered for the Allied forces as a parachutist, and was dropped in Poland where she organized radio communications with the allies and Jewish partisan groups, as well as the escape of refugees. She was taken prisoner and shot.

REIK, THEODOR (1888–1969): Psychoanalyst. After teaching in Europe until 1938, he settled in the US. He wrote books on popular psychology including interpretation of Jewish customs, and from 1946, was president of the National Association for Psychoanalytic Psychology.

REINA, JOSEPH DELLA (fl. c. 1470): Palestinian kabbalist. According to a popular tradition, he endeavored to hasten the Redemption, believed to be imminent, by breaking the power of the angel Samael, but his failure caused the postponement of the date. In some versions, his lack of success is attributed to his pity for Samael; alternatively, R. is said to have been too occupied with combinations of Divine names to carry out the instruction to slay him. The fate of R. in real life does not correspond with the traditions according to which he was baptized, went mad, or committed suicide. The story is influenced by the legends of Theophilus and Faust.

REINACH: French family, including the brothers (1) *JOSEPH R.* (1856–1921): politician. In 1881–2, he was *chef de cabinet* of Gambetta, about whom he wrote several works. He was a deputy (1893–8, 1906–14) and actively vindicated the innocence of Dreyfus, publishing an outstanding work on the affair. He wrote voluminously on politics and history: (2) *SOLOMON R.* (1858–1932): archeologist. He directed the excavations of Carthage in 1883, and in 1886, was appointed curator of the national museums, lecturing at the Louvre School and, from 1902, directing the Museum of National Antiquities at St. Germain-en-Laye. R. wrote extensively on the history of art and of religions, advocating a Jewish-Christian rapprochement through the abolition of the barrier of superstition. He was a vice-president of the Alliance Israélite Universelle: and (3) *THEODORE R.* (1860–1928): historian. After practicing law, 1881–6, he turned to literature, editing the *Revue des études grecques*, 1888–1906 and the *Gazette des Beaux-Arts*, 1906–28. From 1894–1901, he taught at the Sorbonne, from 1903, he was director of studies at the École des Hautes Études and from 1924 professor of numismatics at the Collège de France. He was a member of the Chamber of Deputies, 1906–14. During World War I, he commanded an artillery unit. R. was active in the Société des Études Juives, and some of his writings deal with Hellenism and Judaism (especially *Greek and Latin Texts concerning Judaism*); he also edited the French translation of Josephus.

REINES, ISAAC JACOB (1839–1915): Rabbi and Zionist. He officiated in various Lithuanian centers and evolved an original method of talmudic study positing abstract rules of logic as the basis for all discussions, both halakhic and aggadic. In 1882, at a rabbinical conference in St. Petersburg, he proposed the introduction of secular studies into the syllabus of yeshivah education to counteract the inroads of Enlightenment. The suggestion was not adopted, but he established yeshivot on this basis. One of the first rabbis to join the Zionist movement, in 1901 he founded the religious Zionist *Mizraḥi* movement. His modern attitude to education and Zionism evoked the hostility of the fanatically Orthodox.

Rembrandt: *A Jewish Rabbi.*
(The National Gallery, London).

REINHARDT, MAX (1873–1943): Producer. A theater owner and one of the foremost producers of plays in Germany, his projects included the founding of the Salzburg Festival. His rationalistic productions and decors had a vast influence on the modern theater. After 1933, he worked in the US.

REISEN: (1) *ABRAHAM R.* (1876–1953): Yiddish poet and short-story writer. He achieved early renown for his tales and simple lyrics. R. fought for the recognition of Yiddish as the Jewish national language, helping to convene the Yiddish Language Conference at Czernowitz in 1908. He traveled extensively in Europe and America in behalf of Yiddish cultural activities before settling in New York in 1914. (2) *ZALMAN R* (1888–1941): Yiddish editor and scholar; brother of (1). Influenced by his brother, he specialized in Yiddish philology, publishing *Di Yidishe Gramatik* and his main work *Lexicon fun der Yidisher Literatur un Presse*, an encyclopedia of Yiddish writers. He edited Yiddish newspapers and Yivo publications in Vilna until his arrest by the Soviets in 1939. He perished in Russia.

REJOICING IN THE LAW see **SIMḤAT TORAH**
RELEASE, YEAR OF see **SABBATICAL YEAR**
RELIGIOUS ZIONISTS OF AMERICA: Group formed in 1957, from a merger of the American Mizraḥi and Ha-Poel ha-Mizraḥi organizations. Membership: 150,000.

REMA see **ISSERLES, MOSES**
REMAK see **CORDOVERO, MOSES BEN JACOB**
*REMBRANDT VAN RIJN (1607–1669): Dutch painter. Living in the Jewish quarter of Amsterdam, he became attracted by Jewish types, whom

he depicted with insight and compassion. 37 out of his 200 male portraits are of Jewish personalities or types. He also painted numerous biblical themes. Among his sitters were Dr. Ephraim Bueno and Manasseh ben Israel whose *Piedra Gloriosa* (1655) he illustrated in a series of etchings.

REMEZ (DRABKIN), DAVID (1886–1951): Israel labor leader. Born in Russia, he went to Turkey in 1911 and Palestine in 1913. Active in the labor movement, D. was secretary-general of the *Histadrut* 1926–36, chairman of the *Vaad Leumi* 1944–48, and a *Mapai* member of the first two Knessets, serving as minister of communications 1948–50 and of education 1950–1.

REMNANT OF ISRAEL (Heb. *She'erit Yisrael*): Concept, found in nearly all written Jewish prophecies from the Book of Amos onward, that after God annihilates all sinners of Israel before the Day of Judgment He will leave a remnant of the righteous and repentant who will thenceforward constitute the kingdom of God on earth.

RENAISSANCE: The revival of art and letters under the influence of classical models which took place from the 15th cent., generally referred to as the R., was preceded by the so-called Latin R. of the 12th–13th cents., when Greco-Arab science and philosophy became acclimatized in W Europe. In this process, Jewish translators such as Jacob ANATOLI, FARAJ of Girgenti, KALONYMOS BEN KALONYMOS, etc. played an important part, as did original scholars such as ABRAHAM BAR ḤIYYA. In the 15th cent. R., the role of the Jews was far less pronounced, partly because the movement was based on sources in the Greek language of which their knowledge was slight. Nevertheless, Jews such as ELIJAH DEL MEDIGO were much esteemed as exponents of Aristotelian thought, and important translations were made by him, Jacob MANTINO, and others. In Florence, Jews such as Del Medigo, Johanan ALEMANNO, etc. were familiar in the circle of Pico della MIRANDOLA who was responsible to a great extent for the revival of the study of Hebrew as a third humanistic language by the side of Latin and Greek. The *Dialoghi di Amore* by Judah ABRAVANEL (Leone Ebreo), produced perhaps in this environment, was one of the most popular works of R. philosophy and exercised a wide influence. In the artistic life of the R., the share of Jews was trivial, the only name of any significance being the metal-worker Ercole de' Fedeli (Solomon da Sessa). On the other hand, there were many Jewish instrumentalists, and at the very end of the R. Period, Solomon de' ROSSI of Mantua was an important figure in the musical revival: in Mantua, too, Leone de' Sommi greatly influenced the development of the theater. The Jews of Italy were noticeably affected by the R. spirit, even in some of its less desirable aspects. The wealthy Jewish loan-bankers patronized the arts, supported scholars, and commissioned splendidly illuminated mss. Hebrew poetry, rhetoric, and composition all reflected the standards of the R. and Azariah de' ROSSI introduced its conceptions into Jewish historiography. The Counter-Reformation of the mid-16th cent. confined the Jews in ghettos and interrupted their relations with the outside world, thus effectively preventing the further spread among them of the spirit of the R.

*RENAN, ERNEST (1823–1892): French orientalist and philosopher. Although he gave up his original intention of an ecclesiastical career, his subsequent work is marked by Christian theological tendencies. In 1862, he was appointed professor of Hebrew at the Collège de France, but the publication of his humanized *Life of Jesus* the following year caused a scandal in religious circles and he was deprived of his chair. He continued his writing (*History of the Origin of Christianity*; *History of the People of Israel*) and in 1883, became administrator of the Collège de France. Many of his works are of Jewish interest including biblical studies and monographs (in collaboration with A. Neubauer) on medieval French Jewish scholars.

RENDING OF THE CLOTHES (Heb. *keriah*): A mourning custom, first mentioned in the Bible in connection with the story of Joseph (Gen. 37:29, 34). Rabbinic law makes this practice obligatory after the decease of a father, mother, son, daughter, brother, sister, wife, or husband. The rent must be a handbreadth in depth and in the case of parents should never be completely resewn. Although the Talmud maintains that clothes should be rent also for people of general piety and importance, this has not become orthodox practice. The r. of the c. today is done before the funeral when the *barukh dayyan emet* blessing is recited. It was usual also when a pilgrim first saw Jerusalem or the Temple site.

REPARATIONS and **RESTITUTION:** The former term signifies the payment by one state to another of a sum of money as satisfaction for injury caused by a violation of international law — usually, but not invariably, in war. The latter denotes the restoration of property of which the owner was wrongfully despoiled. Both concepts assumed special significance for Jews after the Nazi persecutions. In 1945, the Zionist movement put forward a claim to a share in reparations, and slight recognition of this was accorded in the Paris Act of 1946 whereby certain heirless German assets abroad and "non-monetary gold" was allocated to (but not fully received by) the Jewish Agency and the American Joint Distribution Committee for relief purposes. Israel formally claimed reparations, at first from the Occupying Authorities and later from each German government. The Federal Republic agreed in 1951 to make good the material damage caused by the Nazis and to meet

Israel's claim for global recompense for the cost of the integration of the refugees. After arduous negotiations, an agreement was signed — by Israel's then foreign minister, Moshe Sharett and the German chancellor and foreign minister Konrad Adenauer at Luxembourg on Sept. 10, 1952, by which the figure was placed at 3,000 million Deutsche Mark ($715 m.) to be paid in goods, mostly of a capital nature, over a period of 12 years. A further 450 m. D. M. ($107 m.) were to be paid to the CONFERENCE ON JEWISH MATERIAL CLAIMS AGAINST GERMANY, for the rehabilitation of Nazi victims outside Israel. The implementation of this agreement, which was meticulously observed, was an important factor in the development of Israel's economy. E Germany refused to make similar reparation. Restitution is not confined to Germany but arises wherever Jews were deprived of their property through anti-Semitic governmental policies. In many countries it has been achieved solely by domestic legislation, following in many cases difficult negotiations between the government concerned and the local Jewish communities and important organizations such as the World Jewish Congress. In the case of W Germany, other agreements signed at Luxembourg stipulated details of what was to be done by the Federal and by the *Land* governments, and this then became a formal international obligation. In E Europe, restitution became confused by the general nationalization policies of the communist governments, and the overall results proved unsatisfactory.

REPENTANCE (in Heb. *teshuvah*, lit. "return"):
The renouncing of sin and the return to righteous living have always been basic to Judaism. The Bible, especially the prophetic writings, consistently call for r. and this is the theme of the days starting on *Rosh ha-Shanah* (the ten days of penitence). The Day of Atonement fast is the climax of this period and prayers on that day center around the theme of r. Forgiveness of sin depends upon true r. while a wrong done to a fellow-man requires rectification and restitution before forgiveness is possible. Jewish writers in the Middle Ages deal extensively with the subject, a special section being devoted to it in Maimonides' *Code*. In the modern period, religious leaders have created movements (e.g. the MUSAR movement) with r. and the constant improvement of man's moral nature as their chief goal.

REPHAIM: Ancient people inhabiting Transjordania in the time of Abraham (Gen. 14:5). Some of them apparently settled near Jerusalem in the "Valley of R."

REPHIDIM: One of the Israelites' stopping-places between the Wilderness of Sin and the Sinai Desert (Num. 33:14–5). While the people were encamped there, Moses struck the rock at Mt. Horeb, and a supply of drinking water issued forth. At R. the Israelites under Joshua repelled a surprise attack of the Amalekites (Exod. 17). The location of R. is uncertain, some scholars suggesting a site in the S of the Sinai peninsula, others in the N.

RESH (ר): Twentieth letter of the Hebrew alphabet; numerical value 200. Pronounced as the Spanish trilled *r* it also has the sound of the uvular *r*. It is one of the letters that cannot take a *dagesh*.

RESH GALUTA see **EXILARCH**

RESH KALLAH ("head of the kallah"): Second in authority to the gaon in Babylonian academies. He was, it is presumed, especially active in the KALLAH months of *Adar* and *Elul*, during which students came from all parts of the country to study at the academies. The *r. k.* was one of the chief expositors of the talmudic treatise selected for study.

RESH LAKISH see **SIMEON BEN LAKISH**

RESHEVSKY, SAMUEL J. (1911–): Chess player. He began his career in Poland as a boy wonder and later settled in the US where he was frequently chess champion and represented the country in many international tournaments.

RESISTANCE MOVEMENT see **PARTISANS**

Title-page of a book of responsa by
Solomon ben Adret (Hanau, 17th cent.).

RESPONSA: Although the Talmud itself contains vestiges of r., the term is usually confined to the written replies (*teshuvot*) given to questions (*she'elot*) on all aspects of Jewish law by qualified authorities from the time of the later geonim to the present day. About a thousand volumes containing more than half a million separate r. have appeared in print. To provide a cultural bond with the distant communities on whom the Babylonian academies were increasingly dependent after the 9th cent., the geonim solicited inquiries on "the Bible, the Mishnah, and the Talmud," and most extant gaonic r. are replies, often discursive, to the questions that resulted. Their practical influence can be traced in the codes of Alfasi and Maimonides

Ezekiel's Vision of the Resurrection. (From a fresco in the 3rd cent. CE synagogue at Dura Europos).

and in the NOVELLAE and compendia of the tosaphists; the gaonic r. are now mainly of historical interest. Many formerly unknown r. in both Hebrew and Arabic were obtained from the Cairo *genizah*. The social and economic development of Europe between the 12th and 15th cents. provided the Jews with many new problems, especially in the commercial field, and the leading scholars of the period (called *rishonim* or earlier authorities) interpreted and extended the talmudic precedents to cover cases for which the Talmud itself contained no exact parallel. In Germany and N France the many-sided correspondence between, for example, Meir of Rothenberg and contemporary tosaphists usually made each decision the consensus of opinion of the outstanding personalities of the locality. Elsewhere, the acknowledged pre-eminence of individual scholars, like Solomon ben Adret in Christian Spain or Isaac ben Sheshet (Perfet) in N Africa, gave their judgments exceptional authority. The great contribution of the r. of this period to Jewish law found its due place in the *Shulḥan Arukh* of Joseph Caro. The r. of Samuel de Modena of Turkey, Ezekiel Landau of Prague, and Moses Sopher of Pressburg, among many others, are important aids to the advanced study of the Talmud and CODES. R. of all periods contain incidental information on religious philosophy, natural sciences, etc., as well as data of social and political interest, and they are accordingly fertile sources of contemporary history. An attempt was made to collect all gaonic r. in the *Otzar ha-Geonim* of B. M. Lewin. An almost complete list of volumes of r. up to the end of the 18th cent. was published in 1930 by Boaz Cohen and selections in English have been published by Solomon Freehof. Each of the recent centuries has produced scholars ready to deal with new problems. Thus, as new a technique as artificial insemination in human beings is already the subject of numerous r. Moreover, the r. of these *aharonim* or later authorities are often short monographs in which every text remotely relevant to the point at issue is quoted and discussed.

RESTITUTION see **REPARATIONS**

RESURRECTION: The belief that at the end of time the bodies of the dead will rise from their graves. Belief in r. was adopted by post-exilic Judaism, particularly by the Pharisees, although rejected by the Sadducees. The Talmud teaches belief in r. as a fundamental of the Jewish faith, and Maimonides incorporated it into his Thirteen Articles of Faith. Its denial was generally considered as heresy until the modern period when various Reform prayerbooks substituted phrases like "eternal life" for the earlier references to r. Although belief in r. seems to contradict belief in IMMORTALITY, the two views were combined in Jewish as well as in Christian and Moslem orthodoxy. See also ESCHATOLOGY.

RETALIATION: The desire to retaliate finds expression in such Scriptural verses as "Eye for eye, tooth for tooth, hand for hand, foot for foot, burn for burn, wound for wound, bruise for bruise" (Exod. 21:24–5; see also Lev. 24:19–20 and Deut. 19:21). No case of the literal application of this law (the *lex talionis*) is known, and Jewish tradition asserts that an injurer could only be required to compensate his victim financially, paying him the estimated value of the injury incurred (i.e., for loss of earning-power and employment, for pain and humiliation inflicted, and for medical treatment) and seeking his forgiveness for the moral wrong.

RETRIBUTION (Divine): The faith in Divine justice requiting every man according to his deeds. This faith could lead to the conclusion that prosperity is of itself evidence of righteousness and Divine approbation, while misfortune is proof of wickedness and Divine wrath. The prevalence of this belief is attested by many Psalms and is sharply attacked in the Book of Job. Rabbinic theology further elaborated the "measure for measure" motif, though insisting that God's punitive justice is tempered by His love. On the other hand, the rabbis also developed the notions of vicarious suffering or "sufferings of grace" to account for the misfortune of the righteous. The biblical books consistently interpret Jewish history as resulting from the operation of the principle of r., but the principle had to face the apparent lack of

Divine justice in both individual fate and the historic suffering of Israel. ESCHATOLOGY (individual reward and punishment in the hereafter, paradise and hell, resurrection, and the Last Judgment) thus became an important adjunct to most theologies upholding r.

REUBEN: Eldest son of Jacob and Leah. R. opposed his brothers' plot against Joseph (Gen. 37) and later volunteered as surety for Benjamin during the latter's visit to Egypt (Gen. 42). Jacob, being informed of R.'s incestuous relations with his concubine Bilhah, transferred R.'s rights as firstborn to Joseph (Gen. 48–9). In the wilderness, the heads of the tribe of R. (Dathan, Abiram, and On) unsuccessfully claimed the right to serve as priests (Num. 16). When the Israelites settled in Canaan, the tribe of R. requested and received territory in Moab (Transjordania), which was fertile but presented political problems, and eventually much of their territory fell into the hands of the Moabites or Ammonites. R. was one of the ten tribes exiled to Assyria by Tiglath-Pileser in 721 BCE. Possibly because of its isolated situation, R. played little part in the history of the Israelite tribes after the settlement in Canaan.

REUBENI see **SEE REUVENI**

*REUCHLIN, JOHANNES VON (1455–1522): German Hebraist. At the suggestion of Pico della MIRANDOLA he intensively studied Hebrew so as to penetrate the secrets of the KABBALAH. The works which he published in consequence are landmarks in the history of Hebrew study in Christian Europe. When in 1509, as a result of PFEFFERKORN's slanders, Hebrew literature (especially the Talmud) was condemned to destruction by the emperor Maximilian, R. wrote strenuously in its defense. A long polemic ensued in the course of which R. was bitterly assailed by the Dominicans under Jacob van Hoogstraaten of Cologne. R.'s intellectual triumph was unmistakable, although ultimately (1520) Pope Leo X gave a formal verdict against him. These polemics, in which the German reactionaries as a group were ranged against R. and the humanists, proved to be the first skirmishes preceding the REFORMATION in Germany.

REUEL see **JETHRO**

REUTER, PAUL JULIUS, BARON VON (1816–1899): News agency founder. Born at Cassel as Josaphat, he settled in London in 1851 and founded there Reuter's Agency which became the greatest organization of its type in the world. He had no connection with the Jewish community.

REUVENI, DAVID (c. 1500–1535): Adventurer. After traversing Palestine and Egypt, he appeared in Venice in 1524 asserting that he had been sent by his brother, the king of the Tribe of Reuben, to obtain help from the Christian powers against the Moslems. Going to Rome, he made a profound impression on Jews and Christians. Pope Clement VII gave him letters of recommendation to the king of Portugal. The effect of his visit there on the Marranos (e.g. SOLOMON MOLCHO, who thereupon embraced Judaism) made it desirable for him to leave the country, and he returned to Italy. In 1532, he and Molcho attended an Imperial Diet at Ratisbon in the hope of enlisting the support of Charles V but were arrested. Molcho was condemned to death by the Inquisition and burned at Mantua. R. was taken to Spain and imprisoned at Badajoz, where he ultimately perished at an auto-da-fè. The travel diary which he left suggests that he was in fact a Central European Ashkenazi Jew.

REVEL, BERNARD (1885–1940): Orthodox leader. Born in Lithuania, he studied in E Europe and went to the US in 1907. He became head of the Isaac Elchanan Yeshiva in New York in 1915, and in 1928, organized Yeshiva College, which offered a program of arts and sciences under orthodox Jewish auspices. He had a great influence on the development of modern Orthodoxy in the US.

REVELATION: The act of communication from God to man and the content of such a communication. Jewish belief holds that man's knowledge of the existence of God came originally from God Himself. When Scripture describes God's r. to Adam, Cain, and to the Patriarchs, it does so without special emphasis. The fundamental laws of human morality

Opening page of diary of David Reuveni.
(Bodleian Library, Oxford).

binding upon all people, expressed succinctly in the seven Noachian Commandments, were also traditionally communicated directly by God. The Mosaic r. and its culmination on Mt. Sinai provided Israel with a Written Law and an Oral Law to determine henceforward, and for all time, the pattern of their conduct, both individually and nationally. The prophets, and their successors, the scribes and the rabbis, were still vehicles of r., but the effect of their r. was merely to increase the knowledge of the Law already received; it was not considered to have provided new Law. The relationship between knowledge obtained by r. — Torah — and knowledge obtained through human reason alone — Wisdom — is discussed at length by Saadyah Gaon and other Jewish philosophers. During the 19th cent., Reform Judaism proposed a doctrine of "progressive r.," maintaining that r. is a continuous process throughout history.

REVISIONISTS (HA-TZOHAR): Zionist party founded in 1925 by Vladimir Jabotinsky. It advocates a Jewish state on both sides of the Jordan. The R. opposed the official Zionist policy toward British mandatory rule as lacking purpose and firmness. They also combated the prevailingly collectivist character of Palestinian Jewish colonization. Increasing independent political action on the part of the R. caused a sharp conflict with the discipline of the World Zionist Organization. This led to a rift in the Revisionist movement and the formation in 1933 of the JEWISH STATE PARTY which abided by the Zionist discipline. In 1935, the R. seceded from the World Zionist Organization and formed the New Zionist Organization which maintained its independence until 1946. From the Revisionist section of the *Haganah* originated the activist resistance forces IRGUN TZEVAI LEUMI and LOHAME HERUT ISRAEL. The R. in Israel became known as HERUT (part of GAHAL) which is affiliated with Revisionist organizations in the Diaspora in the World Union *Herut ha-Tzohar*. Their youth movement is the *Berit Trumpeldor* (BETAR).

REVIVIM: Israel communal settlement (KM) in the Negev. Erected in 1943 as one of three experimental Jewish outposts on the most difficult site in the area, it soon made headway with special techniques for dry-farming and the storage of storm waters. In the Israel War of Independence it was completely isolated and heavily attacked, but held out. Pop. (1972): 451.

REVUE DES ÉTUDES JUIVES (Fr. "Review of Jewish Studies"): Journal of the *Société des Études juives*. It appeared quarterly 1880–1940 and contained many outstanding articles, notably on French Jewish history and literature. Since World War II, it has been produced sporadically.

REWARD AND PUNISHMENT see **RETRIBUTION**

RHODE ISLAND: US state. Its first Jews were Sephardi immigrants who settled in the mid-17th cent. in NEWPORT; here the group was important in the 18th cent. Although the colony had been established on a theoretical basis of complete religious freedom, the naturalization of Jews was later not permitted. Aaron LOPEZ was the most important R. I. merchant in pre-Revolutionary days. In the early 19th cent. the Newport community temporarily became extinct, that of PROVIDENCE now assuming first place. In the early 1880's, E European Jewish immigrants began to arrive in R. I. R. I. is the only state where the consanguineous marriages of Jews are determined solely by biblical law. In 1973, there were 22,000 Jews in R. I., with the main Jewish communities in Providence, Pawtucket, Newport and Woonsocket.

RHODES: Aegean island. Its Jewish community goes back to classical times and in the 12th cent., numbered c. 500. It was able to maintain itself under the rule of the Knights of St. John (1309–1522), though in the end suffering for suspected sympathy with the Turks. Under Turkish rule many Sephardi settlers arrived, changing the composition of the community (formerly Greek). A Ritual Murder accusation in 1840 was averted through the intervention of Sir Moses Montefiore. After the Italian occupation (from 1912), an attempt was made to establish R. as a center for the diffusion of an Italianized Jewish culture among the Jews of the Middle East, and in the Fascist period, a rabbinical seminary was established. In 1938, the Italian anti-Semitic legislation led to a considerable exodus from the island, largely to Rhodesia and the Belgian Congo. The majority of those who remained were deported to their death by the Germans in World War II and few out of a former population of c. 4,000 remain.

RHODES (ARMISTICE) AGREEMENTS: Name given to the complex of armistice agreements signed in 1949 between Israel and Egypt (Rhodes, Feb. 24), Lebanon (Rosh ha-Nikrah, Mar. 23), Jordan (Rhodes, Apr. 3), and Syria (Mahanaim, July 20), by which the military phase of Israel's WAR OF INDEPENDENCE was terminated. The negotiations were conducted under the chairmanship of Ralph Bunche, the acting UN mediator in Palestine. The agreements were recognized by the Security Council (on Aug. 11, 1949) as constituting a step toward the restoration of peace. All the agreements fall into the same pattern. Broadly speaking, the armistice demarcation lines follow the former international frontier of Palestine except those between Israel and Jordan, where, with several adjustments, the fighting lines were taken as the basis, and also in the SW, where Egypt was left in occupation of the GAZA STRIP. As a result, Israel obtained more territory than was allotted under the original PARTITION plan of Nov. 29,

Education center of the Bulawayo Hebrew Congregation, Rhodesia.

1947. Under each agreement a Mixed Armistice Commission was established to supervise the execution of its terms; these consisted of an equal number of representatives of the two parties, under UN chairmanship. The expectation that the agreements would prove to be the starting-point for the restoration of permanent peace in Palestine was frustrated by the refusal of the Arab States to contemplate the normalization of their relations with Israel. Of the remaining Arab states which had taken part in the invasion of Israel, Iraq authorized Jordan to negotiate for its forces; and Saudi Arabia and Yemen withdrew their contingents before the negotiations.

RHODESIA: Country in Africa. The Jewish population of Rhodesia is 4,800, centered mostly in Bulawayo (2,000) and Salisbury (2,500). Jews were associated with R. even before it was annexed (1890) and have played an important role in opening up this territory, and in developing ranching, commerce, and industry. In the early days they were also prominent in mining. The central representative body is the Rhodesian Jewish Board of Deputies. The other national body is the Rhodesian Zionist Council.

RIBALOW, MENAHEM (1895–1953): Hebrew critic and editor. He studied in Odessa and at an early age began to publish poems and essays. In 1921, he settled in the US and the following year became editor of the Hebrew weekly *Ha-Doar* in which many of his own critical articles appeared. R. also edited anthologies of American Hebrew literature.

RIBASH see **ISAAC BEN SHESHET**

RIBICOFF, ABRAHAM A. (1910–): US attorney and public official. He served as a Democratic member of the US Congress 1949–52, as governor of Connecticut from 1955 and as secretary for health, education and welfare in the US government (1961–2). Since 1962 he has been a senator for Connecticut.

RICARDO, DAVID (1772–1823): English economist; author of *Principles of Political Economy and Taxation* (1817), one of the most influential books of the 19th cent. Though he left Judaism upon marriage, he championed religious liberty and advocated the removal of Jewish disabilities.

RICCHI, IMMANUEL HAI (1687–1743): Italian kabbalist. He lived in Safed 1717–9, subsequently at Florence, and then settled in Leghorn. He was murdered by bandits near Modena. R. wrote several works, mostly on Kabbalah.

RICE, ELMER (1892–1967): US playwright. He became the chief representative of expressionist technique in America, notably in *The Adding Machine*. Other plays include *Street Scene*, *Counsellor-at-Law*, and *Not for Children*. R. also wrote novels (e.g. *Imperial City*).

RICHMOND: City in Virginia, US. The first indications of Jews there date from 1769. A congregation, mostly of Sephardi origin, was organized in 1789. In 1841, a congregation of German Jews was formed and one of Polish Jews, in 1856. More than 100 R. Jews served in the Confederate Army during the Civil War. Russian Jews began arriving after 1880. The Jewish Community Council was established in 1935. In 1973, T. had 10,000 Jews with 4 synagogues.

RICKOVER, HYMAN GEORGE (1900–): US nuclear energy expert. As head of the Naval Reactors Branch of the Atomic Energy Commission and an assistant chief in the Navy's Bureau of Ships for Nuclear Propulsion, Vice Admiral R. was responsible for the launching of the world's first atomic submarine.

Hyman George Rickover.

RIDBAZ, YAAKOV (1845–1913): Rabbi; known as the Slutzker Rav. After a rabbinical career in Russia, he lived in the US 1900–5 and then in Safed where he founded and headed a yeshivah.

Gabriel Riesser receiving his laurels as orator.
Contemporary caricature.

RIESSER, GABRIEL (1806–1863): Protagonist of German Jewish Emancipation. He was refused permission to practice his legal profession on account of his Jewishness. His series of memoranda and articles (many appearing in the journal *Der Jude* which he founded and edited 1832–7), demanding civic equality for Jews, aroused the conscience of German liberals. R. was elected in 1848 to the parliament meeting at Frankfurt, of which he was a vice-president. He was also a member of the 1850 "Union" parliament at Erfurt and of the Hamburg City Council (1860–2), and was the first Jewish judge in Germany (appointed 1859).

RIETI, MOSES OF see **MOSES BEN ISAAC OF RIETI**

RIF see **ALFASI, ISAAC**

RIGA: Capital of Latvia, now in USSR. Jews are first mentioned there in 1536, and were expelled in 1593. Under Swedish rule (1621–1710), Jewish residence was forbidden, and only individual Jews lived there until the end of the 18th cent. During the 19th cent., their numbers increased although their presence was not fully legalized. In the period of Latvian independence (1918–40), the community (numbering 42,000 in 1930) supported a network of Hebrew and Yiddish schools. After the German occupation in 1941, a ghetto was established and nearly all the Jewish population of 29,000 (including the historian S. Dubnow) were massacred together with c. 15,000 deportees from Germany. Pop. (1970): 30,581.

RIMMONIM (Heb. "pomegranates"): Name given among the Sephardim, and now more generally, to the finial ornaments for the Scroll of the Law, usually called among the Ashkenazim *Etz Ḥayyim* or in English "bells." Formerly, they were shaped like pomegranates but later were generally in tower form.

RINDFLEISCH MASSACRES: Series of exterminatory attacks on the Jews throughout Franconia and the surrounding regions in 1298, after a Ritual Murder accusation at Röttingen. They were instigated and led by a Bavarian noble, Rindfleisch. 146 communities were annihilated.

RINGELBLUM, EMANUEL (d. 1944), historian. R. taught in Yivo in Vilna and was active in the Poalei Zion movement. In World War II he was in the Warsaw Ghetto where he built up a secret archive documenting what was happening in Warsaw. He and his family were sent to their deaths. The archive was discovered after the War and provided invaluable information on the history of the ghetto.

RIO DE JANEIRO: Former capital of BRAZIL. Marranos settled there in the 16th cent., suffering severely from Inquisitional persecutions. In the early 18th cent., it was the principal Marrano center in Brazil, many persons being sent from there to Cuba for trial. Open Jewish settlement began only in the mid-19th cent. By 1900 R. de J. had a small community which developed rapidly after World War I. The Jewish pop. (1973) is 50,000 with 10 synagogues, 6 Jewish schools, and two Yiddish and three Portuguese Jewish newspapers. R. de J. is the seat of the Brazilian Confederation of Jewish Institutions.

RISHON LE-ZION (Heb. "First in Zion"; cf. Is. 41:27): Title given to the Sephardi chief rabbi of the Holy Land.

RISHON LE-ZION: Israel town in the Judean coastal plain. Founded in 1882 by Russian *Bilu* pioneers; the settlers were rescued from economic ruin by the intervention of Baron Edmond de Rothschild. Vineyards became the mainstay of the village, and a large wine cellar was erected by the Baron. They were supplemented by almonds and citriculture. Industrial projects were developed from the 1930's, and the population rapidly increased. Pop. (1974): 63,400.

RISHONIM (Heb. "first ones"): A general term denoting older authorities. The Talmud uses it to distinguish the earlier from the later prophets (*Sotah* 48b), and the former from the later generations in the Talmudic Period (*Sanhedrin* 11 b). In modern times, *R.* primarily refers to all commentators and codifiers of talmudic law of the Gaonic Period up

The beginnings of Rishon Le-Zion, founded in 1892.

to the time of the compilation of the *Shulḥan Arukh*, subsequent authorities being called AHARONIM ("later ones").

RITUAL MURDER LIBEL see **BLOOD LIBEL**
RITUAL PURITY see **PURITY, RITUAL**
RITUAL SLAUGHTER see **SHEḤITAH**
ROBBERY: Unlawfully taking another person's property by force. In biblical law it is a crime, whoever is robbed. The sole penalty, however, is restitution. False denial of the r. under oath increased by a quarter the restitution payable and also entailed a guilt-offering. Restitution means the restoration either of the property itself or of its value as at the time of the r. if the property has (1) ceased to exist, (2) undergone a radical alteration (cf. *specificatio* in Roman Law), (3) become part of a structure that would have to be demolished to extract it, or (4) been regarded by the original owners as lost beyond recovery and also been alienated by the robber. A penitent robber should be treated leniently, and payment not recoverable at law should be refused. See THEFT.

Wine Cellars in Rishon Le-Zion.

ROBBINS, JEROME (1918–): US choreographer.
He started his career as a dancer, appearing with
success in the New York City Ballet. Later his
choreography for Broadway shows (*West Side Story*,
Fiddler on the Roof) and movies had widespread
success and influence.

ROBINSON, EDWARD G. (1893–1973): Actor.
Born in Rumania, he went to the US in 1903. After
a successful career on the stage he went to Hollywood
and became a star. He often portrayed gangsters or
"tough" characters.

ROCHESTER: City in New York state, US. Jews
were living there in the early 1840's, and in 1848,
immigrants from Germany established the first
congregation. These early settlers founded the city's
ready-to-wear clothing industry. The community
grew considerably in the 1880's as a result of immigration from E Europe, and five Orthodox synagogues were founded within a short time. A community
was founded by Sephardim of Turkish origin in the
1930's. In 1937, all fund-raising activities were concentrated in the United Jewish Welfare Fund. In
1973, R. had 21,500 Jews. The weekly *Jewish Ledger*
has appeared since 1924.

RÖDELHEIM: German town. In 1290, the king
permitted Jewish settlement there but the first
evidence of Jews in R. dates from 1371. From the
mid-18th cent., it had a Hebrew press printing a
number of Haskalah works and in the early 19th
cent., this was acquired by Wolf Heidenheim and
Baruch Baschwitz who produced fine editions of
the Pentateuch, liturgy, etc. 102 Jews were living
in R. in 1925 when the townlet was absorbed into
Frankfort-on-Main.

RODENBERG (originally Levy), **JULIUS** (1831–
1914): German realistic novelist and autobiographer. He is best-known as the editor of the *Deutsche
Rundschau* (1874 ff.).

RODGERS, RICHARD (1902–): US composer. He
wrote the scores for many successes (notably in
collaboration with Lorenz [Larry] Hart and Oscar
Hammerstein II) including *Oklahoma*, *South Pacific*,
and *The King and I*. He also composed music for
motion pictures and ballet.

RODKINSON (FRUMKIN), MICHAEL (1845–
1904): Hebrew and Yiddish author. At first a
fervent Ḥasid in Russia, he wrote works on the
Ḥasidic rabbis. Later, in Germany, he edited the
Hebrew weekly *Ha-Kol* and the Yiddish weekly
Kol la-Am. From 1889 he lived in the US where he
for a time revived *Ha-Kol* and also founded a monthly
Tekhunat Ruaḥ ha-Yisraeli. The principal work of R.
(who is reported to have been baptized) is an abbreviated edition of the Talmud in English.

RODZINSKY, ARTHUR (1894–1958): Conductor.
He began his career as conductor at the Warsaw
Opera House, went to the US in 1926, and succes-

Woodcut from title-page of the Italian translation of
La Celestina by Fernando de Rojas, Venice, 1519.

sively conducted orchestras in Philadelphia, Los
Angeles, Cleveland, New York, and Chicago. He
died a Catholic.

ROGOCHOVER see **ROZIN, JOSEPH**

***ROHLING, AUGUST** (1839–1931): German the-
ologian and anti-Semite. He alleged that the
Talmud commanded Jews to harm — and even kill —
gentiles. R. published various anti-Semitic pamphlets
and was charged by Joseph BLOCH with ignorance
and perjury. R. sued Bloch but had to drop his
suit and resign his teaching post when leading scholars
testified against him.

ROJAS, FERNANDO DE (d. 1541): Spanish Marrano author. It has recently been demonstrated
from the Inquisitorial archives that he was author or
co-author of the tragi-comedy *Calisto e Meliboea*
("La Celestina"), the most important Spanish literary
production before *Don Quixote*, which profoundly
influenced European literature. Members of his
family suffered at the hands of the Inquisition.

ROKAḤ, YISRAEL (1896–1959): Israel public
figure. A member of the Tel Aviv city council
from 1922, he became deputy mayor in 1927 and
was mayor 1936–53. He was a General Zionist member
of the Knesset from 1949, minister of the interior
1953–5, and deputy speaker of the Knesset 1957–9.

ROKEAḤ FAMILY see **BELZ**

ROKEAḤ, ELEAZER see **ELEAZAR BEN JUDAH**

ROMBERG, SIGMUND (1887–1951): Composer.
Born in Hungary, he settled in the US in 1909.
R. wrote over 2,000 popular songs and many suc-
cessful operettas, including *The Student Prince*, *The
Desert Song*, and *New Moon*.

ROME: Capital of ITALY. Its Jewish community is
the oldest in Europe and one of the oldest in the

world with a continuous history, the first reliable record of Jews dating to 139 BCE. The close subsequent relations between R. and Judea and the intermittent wars, with their aftermath of Jewish slaves in R., reinforced the community. In CLASSICAL LITERATURE, there are numerous references to Jews in R. — some of them suggesting a large and influential settlement. Light is thrown on their religious organization by several series of CATACOMBS, which attest the existence of some twelve different Jewish communities in the city in the Classical Period. In the Dark Ages, when R. itself was relatively unimportant, the community dwindled but never died out. This was largely due to the protective policy of the POPES, who — while holding that Jewish "insolence" and influence should be suppressed — insisted that Jewish worship should be protected. Hence, although Catholic rulers all over Europe expelled or maltreated the Jews, they were always treated in the capital of Christendom with a modicum of humanity. At this time, R. was a center of Jewish culture and scholarship (cf. NATHAN OF R., IMMANUEL OF R.). In the 13th cent., R. was the original center from which Jewish loan-bankers spread out into central and northern Italy, thus extending the area of Jewish settlement and establishing numerous communities following the Roman (or, henceforth, Italian) rite of prayer. Notwithstanding occasional vicissitudes and threats (e.g. from John of CAPISTRANO) in the middle of the 15th cent., Roman Jewish history was generally tranquil. A

considerable well-being or even resplendence was attained at the time of the RENAISSANCE, especially under the Medicean popes Leo X and Clement VII. The Expulsion from Spain, etc. in 1492 brought about a considerable influx to R. and the establishment of Aragonese, Catalan, and Sicilian communities by the side of those of the Roman rite. The Counter-Reformation resulted in a drastic reformation of papal policy. Paul IV in his bull *Cum Nimis Absurdum* (1555) renewed all the anti-Jewish legislation of a former age, excluded the Jews from honorable walks of life, and instituted the ghetto, henceforth enforced in a very strict sense. The expulsion of the Jews from the minor places in the Papal States in 1569 greatly increased the pressure of population in the ghetto. Although there was a slight alleviation under Sixtus V (1585–90), the ghetto system with its concomitants (censorship of Hebrew books, forced baptism, badge of shame, conversionist sermons, etc.) henceforth remained in force without interruption. In 1775, the *Editto sopra gli Ebrei* of Pius VI renewed the entire persecutory legislation. Temporary emancipation came during the period of French domination at the time of Napoleon, but after 1815, the former system was renewed in every respect except that the wearing of the Jewish badge was not enforced. Pius IX (1846–78) achieved some improvement in the liberal period at the outset of his pontificate, the gates of the ghetto being now removed. Subsequently, however, he turned reactionary, and the persecutory system

The Synagogue in Rome.

remained in force until in 1870, R. became the capital of united Italy, and its Jews were automatically emancipated. Though for some time its intellectual life was stagnant, the subsequent development of the city attracted numerous Jewish immigrants from other parts of Italy, especially in the mid-20th cent. In 1943–4, over 2,000 Roman Jews were deported by the Germans, the greatest number being rounded up on Oct. 16, 1943. Jewish life in the city was driven underground until the liberation in June 1944. With a population of 15,000 (1973) R. is now the only Italian Jewish community with a considerable Jewish proletariat. In it are concentrated in an increasing degree the main institutions of Italian Jewry.

ROMM: Family of Hebrew printers, founded by Baruch ben Joseph R. (d. 1803) who established in 1789 at Grodno the first Hebrew printing-press in Lithuania which he later transferred to Vilna. He was followed by his son Menahem (d. 1841), who collaborated in producing the first "Vilna Talmud," 1835 ff. Menahem R.'s son Joseph Reuben (d. 1848) and especially his grandson David (d. 1860) developed the activities of the firm. At the end of the century, the imprint of "the widow and brothers R." was to be found on many standard Hebrew works, in particular the magnificent Babylonian Talmud of 1892, etc. The press continued active until after the outbreak of World War II, its productions being marketed by the Germans to obtain dollar currency.

RONALD, SIR LANDON (1873–1938): British musician; son of Henry RUSSELL. A noted conductor, pianist, and composer, he was principal of the Guildhall School of Music.

*ROOSEVELT, FRANKLIN DELANO (1882–1945): President of the US 1933–45. One of his major achievements in the domestic scene was the establishment of a Fair Employment Practices Commission (FEPC) in 1941 to protect the rights of minority groups in the execution of government contracts. In the international scene, R. was concerned over the plight of the Jews in Nazi Germany and in 1938, summoned the EVIAN conference. In Jan. 1944, he set up a War Refugee Board to rescue surviving victims of Nazism. On many occasions, R. expressed sympathy with Zionist aspirations but shortly before his death he was influenced in the opposite direction by a meeting with King Ibn Saud of Saudi Arabia. Many Jews (e.g. Bernard BARUCH, Henry MORGENTHAU Jr., and Felix FRANKFURTER) were associated with R.'s New Deal administration. R.'s wife, ANNA ELEANOR R. (1884–1962) was a patron of Youth Aliyah.

ROSALES, JACOB (c. 1593 — c. 1668): Marrano physician and author, known as Immanuel Bocarro Frances. A friend of Galileo, he wrote a number of works on medicine and astronomy and was created count palatine. He ultimately settled in

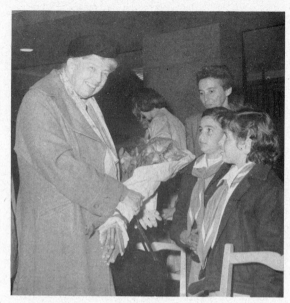

Mrs. Eleanor Roosevelt visiting a Youth Aliyah institution in Israel.

Leghorn as a Jew. His *Anacephalosis*, describing the glories of Portugal, was his best-known work.

ROSANES, SOLOMON ABRAHAM (1864–1938): Historian. A businessman living in needy circumstances (for most of his life in Bulgaria), he devoted himself to Jewish studies and published several Hebrew monographs. His principal study is a six-volume work (1908–45) on the Jews in the Ottoman Empire.

ROSEN, JOSEPH A. (1876–1949): Agronomist. A native of Russia, he went to the US in 1903. In the early 1920's, he supervised the colonization of 250,000 Jews in Crimea and the Ukraine in behalf of Agro-Joint and in 1940, directed Jewish colonization in the Dominican Republic. R. discovered the Rosen winter rye used widely in the US.

ROSEN (ROSENBLÜTH), PINḤAS (Felix; 1887–): Israel jurist. After a legal career in Germany, he settled in Palestine in 1931. R. was active in the *Aliyah Hadashah* party 1941–8 and in 1948, became president of the Progressive Party. He was a Knesset member 1949–68 and was a member of the provisional government 1948–9 and minister of justice in successive coalition cabinets 1949–51 and 1952–61.

ROSENAU, MILTON JOSEPH (1869–1946): US medical scientist. He founded the first school of public health at Harvard Univ. in 1909, directed it until 1925, and was director of the division of public health at the Univ. of N Carolina, 1935–46. His contributions were in hygiene, sanitation, and preventive medicine.

ROSENAU, WILLIAM (1865–1943): US Reform rabbi, author, and educator. He officiated at Congregation Ohel Shalom, Baltimore 1892–1939, and was assistant professor of Semitics at Johns Hopkins Univ., Baltimore, from 1902. R. was one of the founders of the Jewish Welfare Board.

ROSENBACH, ABRAHAM SIMON WOLF (1876–1952): US bibliophile. He was one of the world's leading dealers in rare books and mss. R. was president of Gratz College and of the American Jewish Historical Society to which he left an important collection of American Judaica.

ROSENBAUM, SEMYON (1860–1935): Lawyer and Zionist leader. He was a member of the *Hoveve Zion*, attended the First and subsequent Zionist Congresses, and was among the fiercest opponents of the Uganda plan. He was a delegate to the first Duma (1906). During World War I, R. worked for an independent Lithuania and after the state was established, became deputy foreign minister, representing Lithuania at the Paris Peace Conference. For a time, he was minister of Jewish affairs. In 1924, he settled in Palestine where he acted as chairman of the Jewish Supreme Legal Court.

*ROSENBERG, ALFRED (1893–1946): German Nazi leader. In 1934, he was placed in charge of the ideological indoctrination of the Nazi Party, his main work being *The Myth of the Twentieth Century*, a pseudo-scientific racialist tract owing much to Gobineau and Houston Chamberlain. In 1941, he became minister of occupied territories in E Europe, in which capacity he was responsible for the death of millions of Jews. He was condemned to death at Nuremberg by the International Military Tribunal and executed.

ROSENBERG, ANNA M. (1902–): US public official. Born in Hungary, she went to the US in 1912. She has held many important government positions among them regional director of the Social Security Board 1936–43 and of the War Manpower Commission 1942–5; and assistant secretary of defense, 1950–3.

ROSENBERG, ISAAC (1890–1918): English poet. Born of immigrant parents in Bristol, he was killed in action in World War I. His poems have since gained an increasing appreciation. He also showed considerable promise as a painter.

ROSENBLATT, JOSEPH (1880–1933): Cantor. He began to give concerts in Europe at the age of 9 and officiated as cantor at Munkács, Pressburg, Hamburg (where he published his *Zemirot Yoseph*), and from 1912 in New York. R. was one of the best-known cantors of the 20th cent.

ROSENFELD, MORRIS (1862–1923): Yiddish poet. After leaving Russia in 1882, he worked as a tailor in London and settled in America in 1886. While toiling in sweatshops on the brink of starvation, he wrote, recited, and published sad lyrics of labor. In 1897, his *Song Book* established his literary reputation. Far more than other sweatshop-poets, he sings of specific Jewish sorrows, portraying the Jew as a mendicant who has no resting place but still dreams of Zion.

ROSENHEIM, JACOB (1870–1965): Orthodox leader. From 1906, he edited the extreme religious organ *Der Israelit* in his native Frankfort-on-Main. R. was one of the founders, leaders, and ideologists of AGUDAT ISRAEL, serving as president of its world organization from 1929. From 1940, he lived in the US and Israel and was later influential in securing *Agudat Israel* consent to participation in the Israel government and Knesset. R. wrote extensively on religious topics.

ROSENMAN, SAMUEL IRVING (1896–1973): US jurist. A member of the New York State Legislature 1922–6; justice of the New York Supreme Court 1932–43; and special counsel to Presidents Roosevelt and Truman 1943–6, he edited *The Public Papers and Addresses of Franklin D. Roosevelt* (1928–45; 13 vols.).

ROSENTHAL, HERMAN (1843–1917): Bibliographer. He went to the US as head of the AM OLAM immigrants, with the purpose of founding colonies, but when that venture failed, returned to his literary career. He was head of the Slavonic division of the New York Public Library from 1898.

ROSENTHAL, LESER (1794–1868): Talmudist and bibliophile. Of Polish birth, he taught at Paderborn and then became rabbi in Hanover. His library

Pinḥas Rosen.

was presented by his son, Baron George R., to the city of Amsterdam and is known as Bibliotheca Rosenthaliana.

ROSENTHAL, MORITZ (1862–1946): Pianist. He made his European debut as a child prodigy and soon came under the influence of Liszt. He made his home in Europe until 1938, and for almost 50 years constantly toured Europe and the US.

ROSENWALD: US family. *JULIUS R.* (1862–1932): began his career in the clothing business and in 1895, joined the mail order firm of Sears, Roebuck, and Co. in Chicago. In 1910, he became its president, and under his leadership it developed into a giant enterprise. R. was deeply interested in advancing the education of American negroes and in 1917, established the Julius Rosenwald Fund, to be expended within 25 years of his death, principally for the establishment of schools for negroes. The fund at one time totaled more than $30,000,000. Other beneficiaries of his generosity were Jewish War Relief, the Univ. of Chicago, Jewish agricultural settlement in Crimea and the Ukraine, and the Museum of Science and Industry which he established in Chicago. He aided cultural and agricultural causes in Palestine although he did not favor Zionism. It is estimated that during his lifetime he gave away about $70,000,000. His eldest son, *LESSING JULIUS R.* (1891–), a noted book-collector, succeeded him as chairman of the

Julius Rosenwald.

board of Sears, Roebuck and Co. 1932–9, and was chairman of the Julius Rosenwald Fund 1932–48. Strongly opposed to the Zionist movement, he became president of the AMERICAN COUNCIL FOR JUDAISM in 1943. Another son of Julius R., *WILLIAM R.* (1903–), has been active in many Jewish causes and has held prominent positions in the United Jewish Appeal, HIAS, the Joint Defense Appeal, and the New York Federation of Jewish Philanthropies.

ROSENZWEIG, FRANZ (1886–1929): German philosopher. Born of an assimilated family, R. was on the point of embracing Christianity, when the experience of an Orthodox Day of Atonement service in 1913 brought him back to Judaism. To the teaching of this he now devoted his life. As a soldier in World War I he wrote his chief work *Stern der Erlösung* ("Star of Redemption"). In *Hegel and the State* he repudiated German idealism. Thereafter, his chief preoccupation was with Jewish adult education, which forms the theme of the essays collected in his *Kleinere Schriften.* In 1920, he founded the *Freies Jüdisches Lehrhaus* in Frankfort-on-Main. His translations of 92 poems of Judah Ha-Levi with commentaries and of the Hebrew Scriptures (in collaboration with Martin Buber) further extended his influence. In his latter years, he suffered from a pernicious paralysis which gradually robbed him of almost all powers of communication, but he continued to work to the end. His writings have remained influential among Jewish religious thinkers.

ROSH see **ASHER BEN JEHIEL**

ROSH HA-SHANAH (Heb. literally "head of the year"): Two-day holiday (one day in biblical and early mishnaic days) at the beginning of the month of *Tishri* (Sept.-Oct.; commencing the Ten Days of Penitence, which end on the Day of Atonement). In the Rabbinic Period, it was already regarded as a Day of Judgment for the entire world when the fate of each man for the coming year is inscribed in the Book of Life. Although termed the New Year, the Bible refers to it as the first day of the seventh month (Lev. 23:24), and not all the rabbis considered it as the day marking the creation of the world. The distinctive feature of the religious ritual of the day is the blowing of the SHOPHAR. Other special rituals are the added benedictions in the Additional Service, as well as the ceremony of TASHLIKH in the afternoon of the first day. Traditionally, white vestments are worn during the service. The central theme in the petitional prayers is the request for a "good year." In post-talmudic times various customs developed, such as the eating of honey (or apple dipped in honey) "for a sweet year," or the head of an animal "that we ever be the head and never the tail."

ROSH HA-SHANAH: Eighth tractate in the Mishnah order of *Moed*, containing 4 chapters. It has *gemara* both in the Babylonian and Palestinian

Rosh Pinnah: the first Jewish settlement in Upper Galilee in modern times.

Talmuds. After a general introduction, it discusses the regulations concerning the sanctification of the new moon, with particular reference to that of the seventh month (i.e., *Rosh Ha-Shanah*), the blowing of the ram's horn on the occasion, and the special order of prayer.

ROSH ḤODESH see **NEW MOON**

ROSH PINNAH: Israel village in Upper Galilee. The first Palestinian Jewish agricultural settlement in the modern period, it was founded in 1878 by a number of families from the "Old Yishuv" in Safed who, harassed by malaria, crop failure, and Arab attacks, subsequently had to abandon the place. It was refounded in 1882 by *Bilu* immigrants, mostly from Rumania. The intervention of Baron Edmond de Rothschild ensured the continuation of the village's existence despite the failure of numerous agricultural experiments and the stagnation of the population for decades. Serving as a center for the scattered Jewish settlements in Upper Galilee, R. P. absorbed new immigrants after the Israel War of Independence. Pop. (1972): 830.

ROSHEIM, JOSEL(MAN) OF see **JOSELMAN OF ROSHEIM**

ROSS, BARNEY (1909–1967): US boxer. He held the world lightweight championship 1934–5, and the world welterweight championship 1934–8.

ROSS, LEONARD Q. see **ROSTEN, LEO**

ROSSELLI, CARLO (1899–1937): Italian socialist. He was a strenuous opponent of Fascism, at first in Italy and then abroad, organizing the movement and periodical *Giustizia e libertà* and fighting in the Spanish Civil War. With his historian brother *NELLO R.* (1900–1937) he was murdered in France by Fascist gunmen.

ROSSI, AZARIAH (Bonaiuto) **BEN MOSES DEI** (*Min Ha-Adummim*; c. 1511–1578): Italian scholar, living successively in Bologna, Ferrara, and Mantua. He showed a keen critical sense as well as a wide knowledge of Latin, Greek, and contemporary literature in his *Meor Enayim* (Mantua, 1574), which endeavored to demonstrate how contemporary records (e.g. the Letter of Aristeas, which he first translated into Hebrew) threw light on Jewish history and literature in the Classical Period. His researches were a new phenomenon among Jews and were characterized by the critical spirit of Italian humanism. Like his non-Jewish contemporaries, however, he did not question the veracity of his sources, often blindly following spurious records. His writings aroused opposition from some rabbis and were forbidden to readers under the age of 25. R. was also the author of poems in Italian, Hebrew, and Aramaic.

*ROSSI, GIOVANNI BERNARDO DE (1742–1831): Italian Hebraist. Although a priest, his wide Jewish knowledge enabled him to make important contributions to the study of the text of the Bible and to Hebrew bibliography, his *Historical Dictionary of Jewish Authors* still retaining its importance. He built up a superb collection of Hebrew books and mss, now in the Palatine Library, Parma.

ROSSI, SALOMONE DE' (*Min ha-Adummim*; c. 1560—c. 1632): Instrumentalist and composer at the court of Mantua. He had an orchestra of his own and was permitted to dispense with the yellow badge. R. belonged to a musical family; his sister(?), known as "Madame Europa," sang in opera and her son Anselmo de' R. was also a composer. He published much secular, instrumental, and vocal music and *Ha-Shirim Asher Li-Shelomoh*, a collection of Hebrew religious songs, composed in the madrigal style of the period. R., who collaborated with Monteverdi, has been spoken of as the founder of the symphony.

ROSTEN, LEO CALVIN (pseudonym Leonard Q. Ross; 1908–): US humorist. He wrote *The Education of H*y*m*a*n K*a*p*l*a*n* and *The Return of H*y*m*a*n K*a*p*l*a*n*. His later novels include *Captain Newman M.D.* He also wrote *Joys of Yiddish* and an anthology of Jewish quotations.

ROSTOV-ON-DON: Russian city. Jews settled there c. 1827 and prospered until the reign of Alexander III. Pogroms occurred in 1883 and 1905 and the community suffered greatly in the Russian Civil War 1918–20. In 1941, there were c. 35,000 Jews, most of whom fled before the German occupation; those that remained were exterminated. Jewish pop. (1970): 18,190 (R. province).

ROTENSTREICH, NATAN (1914–): Israel philosopher; son of the Zionist Ephraim Fishel R. (1882–1938). He was born in Galicia, settled in Palestine while a youth, and lectured in philosophy (professor, 1955) at the Hebrew Univ. (rector 1965–9). His writings include studies of Jewish thinkers and a survey of modern Jewish thought.

ROTH: (1) *CECIL R.* (1899–1970): English historian; reader in Jewish studies at Oxford from 1939 to 1964 when he settled in Israel. R.'s studies in Jewish history include a general history of the Jewish people, works on specific communities (notably Italy and England), and biographies (e.g. Manasseh ben Israel, Joseph Nasi, the Rothschilds, and the Sassoons). He also wrote on Jewish art, the Jews in the Renaissance, the Jewish contribution to civilization, and works on general (particularly Italian) history. He was editor-in-chief of the *Encyclopedia Judaica*. (2) *LEON R.* (1896–1963): Philosopher; brother of (1). He lectured in philosophy at Manchester 1923–8, and was professor at the Hebrew Univ. 1928–53 (rector, 1940–3). R. published philosophical works in Hebrew and English (including monographs on Spinoza and Maimonides), translated philosophical classics into Hebrew, and wrote *Judaism* on the Jewish religion.

ROTH, HENRY (1907–): US author. Born in Austria, he grew up in the New York slums which formed the background of his book *Call It Sleep*. This appeared in 1934 but achieved real success 30 years later. Meanwhile R. had ceased writing and devoted himself to farming.

ROTH, JOSEPH (1894–1939): Novelist. Born in Volhynia, he lived after World War I in Austria, Germany, and France. He campaigned against the shallowness of modern civilization, and the uprooting of E European Jewry from their environments. His works include the novels *Job* and *Hotel Savoy* and the essays *Jews in Wandering*.

ROTH, PHILIP (1933–): US author. Born in Newark, he taught at Chicago and in 1962 was appointed writer-in-residence at Princeton. His first success was his book of short stories *Goodbye Columbus*. His novels include *Letting Go* and *Portnoy's Complaint*.

ROTHENBERG, MORRIS (1885–1950): US Zionist leader. He was president of the Zionist Organization of America 1932–6. R. was a magistrate in the New York City courts from 1937.

ROTHENBURG: Town in Bavaria, W Germany. Information on Jewish residence there dates from the latter 12th cent. The community grew in numbers and importance in the second half of the 13th cent. especially due to the influence of R Meir ben Baruch. It was destroyed in 1298 during the Rindfleisch massacres, was renewed shortly thereafter, again destroyed in 1349 during the Black Death massacres, and again renewed. There was a further expulsion following massacres in 1397; the Jews returned in 1402 but were progressively impoverished by taxation. In 1520, the authorities yielded to clerical pressure and expelled the Jews. The modern community dates from 1870; it remained small and was not refounded after the Nazi Period.

ROTHENSTEIN, SIR WILLIAM (1872–1945): English artist. He early made a brilliant reputation in literary and artistic circles in London and became principal of the Royal College of Art. His early paintings include several on Jewish themes. His brother, *ALBERT DANIEL RUTHERSTON* (1881–1953), artist and designer, illustrated a fine edition of the Passover Haggadah. William R.'s son, *SIR JOHN R.* (1901–), director of the Tate Gallery, has no connection with Judaism.

ROTHSCHILD: Family of financiers and philanthropists deriving its name from a house at the sign of the "red shield" at Frankfort-on-Main, where its members lived from the 16th cent. The fortunes of the family were founded by *MAYER AMSCHEL R.* (1743–1812), originally a dealer in antique coins, who became financial agent to the landgrave of Hesse-Cassel during the French Revolutionary wars. His five sons established themselves in different European centers. The various branches of the House of R. are

Baron Edmond de Rothschild.

dealt with individually in the following entries which, however, omit the common title of baron and the suffixes "de" and "von."

(1) *England*: The founder of the English house of R. was *NATHAN MAYER R.* (1777–1836) who settled in Manchester as a textile agent in 1798, moved to London in 1805, and became a dominant figure in English finance in the Napoleonic Wars, partly through his family connections abroad. His eldest son, *LIONEL R.* (1808–1879), financed the English purchase of the Suez Canal shares in 1875 and was the first Jewish member of parliament (1858). He was father of *NATHANIEL, 1st LORD R.* (1840–1915), who succeeded him as head of the banking-house and was the first Jewish peer (1885) and one of the outstanding Jews in his time. *WALTER, 2nd LORD R.* (1868–1937), a distinguished zoologist, was succeeded by his nephew *NATHANIEL MAYER VICTOR 3rd LORD R.* (1910–), scientist and bibliophile; chairman of the Agricultural Research Council 1948–58. *FERDINAND R.* (1839–1898) of the Vienna house, also made his home in England, sat in parliament, and brought together a great art collection which he left to the British Museum. *SIR ANTHONY R.* (1810–1876), the first president of the United Synagogue, and *MAYER R.* (1818–1874), member of parliament and patron of the turf, were brothers of Lionel R.; while *ALFRED R.* (1842–1918), artpatron and *LEOPOLD R.* (1845–1917), philanthropist, were brothers of the 1st Lord R. and with him members of the circle of Edward VII. The descendants of Leopold R. now head the London firm.

(2) *France*: *JAMES R.* (1792–1868), 5th son of Mayer Amschel R., who had been acting as his brother Nathan's agent in Paris from 1812, founded the Paris house in 1817 and with great skill and adroitness maintained his influence in French finance for over half a century notwithstanding successive changes of government. He was active in French railroad development, devoted vast sums to philanthropy, and long headed French Jewry. He was succeeded in this capacity by his sons *ALPHONSE* (1827–1905), *GUSTAVE* (1829–1911), and *EDMOND* (1845–1934), all notable collectors and philanthropists. Edmond (Baron Edmond de R.) was interested in intellectual and artistic pursuits, and built up a great art collection. He and his wife Adélaide (also a R. by birth) were attached to Jewish religious traditions. The first Zionist pioneers in Palestine appealed to him in the early 1880's to save them from financial collapse. He readily answered, continuing to support Palestinian colonization unostentatiously and gradually taking under his protection all the new settlements, which would have had to be liquidated had it not been for his aid. His patronage was expressed in the dispatch of agricultural experts and officials whose activities often led to friction with the settlers. In historical perspective, it may be said that many failures were caused by the officials, but on the other hand, they educated the new agricultural population of Palestine. R. visited the country five times (1887, 1893, 1899, 1914, 1925), each occasion being a great event for the Jewish population. Altogether, he bought 125,000 acres in Palestine and is to be credited with the settlement of Galilee and Samaria. In 1900, he transferred the management of the colonies to ICA (from 1924, PICA). In his last years, he cooperated with Weizmann and Sokolow and in 1929 was honorary president of the Jewish Agency. The remains of R. and his wife were reinterred at Zikhron Yaacov in 1954. *NATHANIEL R.* (1812–1870), son of Nathan Mayer of London, also settled in Paris and was father of *JAMES EDOUARD R.* (1844–1881), a collector and expert on medieval illuminated mss; the latter's son *HENRI R.* (1872–1947), physician and philanthropist, specialized in children's ailments and wrote plays under the name of André Pascal. *GUY EDOUARD ALPHONSE R.* (1909–) became the lay leader of French Jewry after World War II. Edmond's son *JAMES R.* (1878–1957) sat in the British parliament as a Liberal, 1929–45 and left a large bequest for the construction of Israel's new Knesset building.

(3) *Austria*: *SALOMON MAYER R.* (1774–1855), lived in Vienna from 1816 and developed the Austrian branch of the firm, devoting his attention especially to industrial development and railroad construction. He was followed as head of the house successively by *ANSELM R.* (1803–1874) and *ALBERT SOLOMON R.* (1844–1892) whose sons were held for

ransom by the Nazis after their seizure of Vienna in 1938, when the firm ceased to exist.

(4) *Naples*: *KARL R.* (1788–1855) opened a banking-house in 1821 in Naples, then the capital of an independent kingdom, and was instrumental in founding a Jewish community there. His sons moved back to Frankfort.

(5) *Frankfort*: *AMSCHEL R.* (1773–1855), the eldest of the R. brothers, remained in Frankfort and was active there in Jewish communal life. His nephews from Naples, *MAYER KARL R.* (1820–1886) and the strictly Orthodox *WILHELM R.* (1828–1901) succeeded him as head of the parent house, which closed down on the latter's death.

ROTTERDAM: Dutch port. A Sephardi community was established there in the early 17th cent. under the aegis of the Pinto family, soon being outstripped by an Ashkenazi congregation. With the development of the harbor of R. in the 20th cent. the community grew, becoming the second in importance in Holland, and numbering c. 13,000 in 1940. This was reduced by the Nazi occupation and totaled 1,500 in 1973.

ROUSSILLON: French region, formerly subject to Aragon. Jews are recorded there from the 12th cent., and were subject to discriminatory legislation from 1228. Nevertheless, their economic and intellectual life flourished. With the accession of King Martin in 1396, they were afforded legal protection. Alfonso IV in 1427 intervened to prevent the introduction of the Inquisition which was, however, eventually enforced. Refugees from Spain found temporary asylum in R. in 1492, but all Jews were expelled in the following year. The only community now existing is at Perpignan.

ROVINA, ḤANNAH (1892–): Actress. She was among the founders of HA-BIMAH in Moscow, 1917, and in 1928 went with the company to Palestine. R. is the outstanding tragedienne of the troupe, gaining world fame with her performance as Leah in An-Ski's *Dibbuk*.

ROWE, LEO STANTON (1871–1946): US political scientist. He was professor of political science at the Univ. of Pennsylvania 1904–17, assistant secretary of the US treasury 1917–8, chief of the Latin American division of the State Department 1919–20, and director-general of the Pan-American Union 1920–46. He was president of the American Academy of Political and Social Science 1902–30.

ROZIN, JOSEPH ("The Rogochover Gaon"; 1858–1936): Talmudist. From 1899, he was rabbi of the Ḥasidic community of Dvinsk except for 1915–25 when he was in St. Petersburg. His responsa are individualistic and many appeared in his *Tzaphenat Paaneaḥ*. A collection of his unpublished works was rescued from Europe after World War II and taken to the US to be published.

Reuven Rubin: *Self-Portrait*, 1925.

RUBIN, REUVEN (1893–1974): Painter. Rumanian-born, he studied in Italy, France, and Palestine where he ultimately settled, becoming one of the best-known interpreters in art of its scenery and types. He was Israel minister to Rumania 1948–50.

RUBIN, SOLOMON (1823–1910): Polish Hebraist. He wrote extensively about the folk beliefs of the Jews of E Europe through which he traveled widely. His translations include works of Spinoza.

RUBINSTEIN: Russian family of musicians. (1) *ANTON R.* (1829–1894), pianist and composer of operas as well as orchestral and chamber music; founder of the St. Petersburg Conservatoire. (2) *NIKOLAI R.* (1835–1881), pianist and composer, founder of the Russian Musical Society and the Moscow Conservatoire; brother of (1). They were friends of Tchaikovsky, who wrote his piano concerto No. 1 for Anton.

RUBINSTEIN, ARTUR (1889–): Pianist. Of Polish birth, he toured from the age of 12 and settled in the US in 1940. A soloist and recording artist of world renown, he has composed piano works and chamber music.

RUBINSTEIN, ISAAC (1880–1945): Rabbi and communal leader. In 1906, he was appointed government rabbi in Vilna and in 1920, minister of Jewish affairs in the Lithuanian government. After Vilna was annexed to Poland in 1922, R. was elected to the Polish Senate, where he fought for Jewish rights until the Nazi conquest. An ardent Zionist, he was elected joint chief rabbi of Vilna in 1928. When Soviet Russia annexed Lithuania in 1940, he had to leave his post and settled in New York where from 1943, he taught at the R Isaac Elḥanan Yeshivah.

RUBY (RUBINSTEIN), JACK (1911–1967): Dallas nightclub owner who killed Lee Oswald, murderer of President John Kennedy, in 1963. Ruby shot Oswald in a police-station as Oswald was being moved out of his cell under full television coverage a few days after Kennedy's death. He was sentenced to death for the murder but before his appeal was heard, died in prison.

RUFUS TINEIUS see **TINEIUS, QUINTUS RUFUS**

RUMANIA: European republic. Jews have lived in what is now R. since the 4th cent. They were among the first settlers of the city of Roman in 1391, and several Jewish communities existed in R. at the end of the 16th cent. when Joseph NASI and Solomon ASHKENAZI played a part in the history of this area. A century later, the Jews received legal status from the princes. In 1740, there were important communities at Bacau, Barland, Galati, and Roman. The Jews suffered greatly from both sides in the various Russo-Turkish wars taking place in R. between 1769 and 1812. Between the mid-18th and mid-19th cents., large numbers of Jews came from Poland, etc. to the region, especially to MOLDAVIA. They played an important part in transforming the old feudal system into a modern economy. From the temporary Russian occupation in 1828 until 1916, Jews were subject to discriminatory legislation, violence, and arbitrary expulsions. They were divided into "foreign subjects," under the protection of a foreign consul, and "native

Artur Rubinstein.

born," to whom citizenship was also refused. 200 special laws regarding the Jews made it difficult for them to earn a livelihood. After an interlude of liberal treatment in 1860–6, anti-Semitism became a part of internal Rumanian policy. In 1872, the US representative in Paris termed the Rumanian persecution of the Jews "a disgrace to Christian civilization." The provisions of the Berlin Treaty of 1878 which demanded equal treatment for the Jews were evaded on the pretext that even the native-born were not Rumanian citizens. Poor Jews, unable to bribe the officials, were the chief sufferers. The great mass of Jews were Ḥasidim and bitterly fought any attempts at modernization. There was no modern Jewish school until 1860 when one was opened at JASSY. More than 70,000 Jews left R. in 1900–06. Despite enactments of 1918–19 granting equal rights to Jews, discrimination and anti-Jewish agitation persisted. The advent to power in 1937 of Octavian Goga of the National Christian party led to a series of decrees depriving the Jews of citizenship, their Hebrew and Yiddish press, and the opportunity to practice their professions. Massacres took place after 1940, when ordinances patterned on the NUREMBERG LAWS came into effect. Of the nearly 800,000 Jews in R. at the outbreak of World War II, 385,000 had been exterminated before liberation. After the return of deportees from AUSCHWITZ and Transdniestria and the immigration of 50,000 Jews from Soviet-annexed territory, the Jews numbered almost 400,000. Communist domination in 1946 led to a liquidation of Jewish organizational life. From 1948 until 1952, when the government halted emigration, 125,000 had left for Israel. Emigration was resumed in the later 1950's and many of the remaining Jews departed. At first the Rumanian government acted harshly toward the Jews. However as Rumania became more independent, its attitude was more relaxed. This also applied to its relationship with Israel. Not only was Rumania the only E European country which maintained relations with Israel after the Six-Day War, but it even intensified its ties, especially in the economic and diplomatic spheres. Jewish pop. (1973) 90,000.

RUPPIN, ARTHUR (1876–1943): Zionist leader, economist, and sociologist. He directed the Jewish Statistical Bureau in Berlin 1903–7. In 1908, he went to Palestine as representative of the Zionist Organization and opened the PALESTINE OFFICE in Jaffa. He founded various settlement companies of the Zionist Organization (including the Palestine Land Development Company) and in cooperation with the pioneer element originated labor colonization in the country. Deported by the Turks from Palestine in 1916, he returned in 1919, and two years later was appointed director of the Zionist Executive's colonization department in Jerusalem. From 1926, he taught sociology at the Hebrew Univ. R. was the author of many books including *The Sociology of the Jews.*

RUSSELL, HENRY (1813–1900): British singer, organist, and composer. He wrote 800 songs, some of great popular appeal (such as *Cheer, boys, cheer* and *A life on the ocean wave*). His children included William Clarke Russell (1844–1911), famous as writer of fiction for boys; Sir Herbert Russell (1869–1944), war-correspondent; and Sir Landon RONALD (1873–1938), composer.

RUSSIA: Jews have lived within the borders of what is now R. (USSR), especially in the S provinces, since classical times (see CRIMEA, CAUCASUS, KHAZARS, LITHUANIA, TURKESTAN, and UKRAINE). In 986, Jews participated in a disputation on the occasion of Duke Vladimir's conversion to Christianity. A Jewish gate is mentioned in the 12th cent. at Kiev, and the Jewish quarter there was looted in 1113. At this period, Russian Jews attended western yeshivot and addressed queries to the German rabbis. In the late 15th cent., Jewish traders from Lithuania disseminated a Judaizing sect in Novgorod and Moscow and this precipitated a drastic reaction. In 1563, 300 Jews were drowned at Polotsk and Vitebsk on refusing to accept baptism. In 1667, the Jews were expelled from E Ukraine upon its annexation to R. Clauses prohibiting Jews from visiting the country were inserted in treaties signed by R. with foreign

Arthur Ruppin.

powers in 1550 and 1678, while expulsion orders were issued in 1727, 1738, and 1742. In 1753, 35,000 Jews were driven out of R. In 1762, CATHERINE II permitted all aliens to live in R., except Jews. By the partitions of POLAND in 1772, 1793, and especially 1795, the great Jewish masses of WHITE RUSSIA, the Ukraine, Lithuania, and COURLAND became Russian subjects and, for more than a century, the great majority of the world's Jews were under the reactionary rule of the Czars. In 1786, their residence was restricted to towns, thereby laying the foundation of the PALE OF SETTLEMENT; only the Karaites received equality of rights with the Christians (1795). On the authority of the DERZHAVIN report on White Russia, a Council for Jewish Affairs was established in 1802. Two years later, it defined the Pale, restricted Jews in the villages (1807–8), limited the activities of the KAHAL in the spheres of religion and charity, and prohibited the traditional Jewish costume; on the other hand, it took measures to promote agriculture. The Jews remained loyal to R. during Napoleon's 1812 invasion, and ALEXANDER I (1801–25) was at first benevolent. Later, however, he turned reactionary, and some 20,000 Jews were expelled from the provinces of Vitebsk and Mohilev in 1824, and those remaining were forbidden to live near the frontier. Approximately 600 oppressive enactments regarding the Jews were published during the reign of NICHOLAS I who regarded them as an injurious element. In 1827, military service was brutally imposed on Jews (see CANTONISTS). The frontiers of the Pale of Settlement were restricted in 1835 and remained effective until 1915. A censorship was imposed on Jewish books in 1836, and in 1844, the *Kahal* was abolished; ALEXANDER II attempted to Russify the Jews by education and the gradual relaxation of restrictions, while the judicial law of 1864 contained no anti-Jewish discrimination. At this time, 65,000 Russian Jews were engaged in agriculture. Jews became prominent in economics, culture, and left-wing politics; social anti-Semitism now began to replace or reinforce the former religious prejudices. The intensive reaction which followed the assassination of Alexander II in 1881 made the Jews its chief victims. The appalling POGROMS of the early 1880's influenced the official view regarding the Jews as a foreign element to be kept apart from the village population, which was expressed in the MAY LAWS. In 1891, Jews were expelled from Moscow and a NUMERUS CLAUSUS introduced into high schools and secondary schools; they turned increasingly to ZIONISM, Socialism (the BUND was founded in 1897), and the revolutionary movement. An organization advocating equal Jewish rights was founded in 1905, and the following year 12 Jewish deputies were elected to the Duma, most of them representing the Liberal Party. A law proposed by the premier Stolypin

Detail of a mural in a 17th cent. synagogue at Mohilev, Russia.

alleviating the Jewish legal position was vetoed by Nicholas II and conditions steadily deteriorated. Official anti-Semitism reached a peak with the BEILIS case, the most notorious of a long series of Blood Libels. The vast emigration, especially to the US, which began in the 1880's barely offset the natural increase among Russian Jewry. Russian Jewry in the 19th cent. comprised perhaps the most vital elements of the Jewish people. The Pale of Settlement was, with Poland, the world's great center of talmudic study. S Russia (particularly Odessa) was the focus of the Hebrew literary revival and the place of origin of many remarkable individuals in Zionist and contemporary Jewish history. At the outbreak of World War I, 5,600,000 Jews lived in the empire of the Czars (including almost 2 million in Poland). Those residing near war zones were deported *en masse*, and, despite the 300,000 Jews in the Russian army, the community was made the scapegoat for the Russian defeats (expulsion of Jews from Kovno, Grodno, and Courland; prohibition of Hebrew and Yiddish printing). Immediately after the Russian Revolution, the provisional government abrogated all anti-Jewish decrees (Apr. 2, 1917) and Jews were prominent both in the Kerensky regime and later in the Bolshevik Revolution (TROTSKY, ZINOVIEV, SVERDLOV). From 1918, Jewish departments existed

in the commissariats of national affairs and of education. In Apr. 1919, the Soviet government abolished the non-communist Jewish institutions. The civil war was accompanied by a wave of pogroms, and the Soviet government proclaimed anti-Semitism a criminal offense. The policy of the Soviets rapidly changed the basis of the life of the petty traders, etc. who had formerly constituted the great mass of Russian Jewry. Their traditional economic distinctiveness rapidly disappeared. A great number were in due course absorbed by heavy industry. There remained, however, a tendency to concentrate in the administrative and distributive branches of the new system. The anti-religious policy of the Soviet government, the prohibition of public religious teaching, and the economic revolution, which made traditional observances difficult, had an immediate effect on the religious life of Russian Jewry. Although a minority, mostly of the older generation, tenaciously clung to the traditional Jewish way of life, it was abandoned by the vast majority with prodigious rapidity even in the first generation. On the other hand, the Soviet government, not recognizing the Jews as a nationality, discouraged Hebrew and persecuted Zionism. In the 1921–9 period, the Jewish economic position improved. To encourage agriculture among the Jews, the government set up a committee for settling Jews

Conference of the *Hovevei Zion* in Odessa. 1890.

on the land (*Komzet*) which furnished territory in the Ukraine, Crimea, and BIRO-BIDJAN; the means for settlement were supplied by the American Jewish Agricultural Corporation, but the Jewish part in agriculture remained small. From 1930, increasing efforts were made to discourage Jewish practices, and many prominent Jews were removed in the purges of the 1930's. The annexation early in World War II of W White Russia, W Volhynia, E Galicia, N Bukovina, Bessarabia, Lithuania, and Latvia led to the mass-deportation of Jews, especially the intelligentsia, from these regions. The Nazis, who invaded R. in 1941, aimed at exterminating the Jewish population; thus of the 500,000 Jews in White Russia, only half escaped to the interior and up to 200,000 were slaughtered. The Soviet government established the Anti-Fascist Committee to appeal to World Jewry in 1941, but immediately the Nazi peril had passed, an anti-Jewish trend asserted itself; many outstanding Jews "disappeared," including most of the exponents of Yiddish culture. The charge brought in 1952 against Jewish physicians of plotting against the state served to presage a systematic anti-Jewish campaign, but after Stalin's death in 1953, all who survived were released. The government has, however, maintained a policy of restricting Jewish cultural expression. It does however permit the publication of the monthly Yiddish literary journal *Sovietish Heimland*. The large-scale evacuations and flight from the fighting area during the War, reinforcing the Soviet policy of creating new industrial centers in the Ural region, etc., resulted in a vast redistribution of the Jewish population, now spread more evenly throughout the country. In the new centers, on the other hand, Jewish tradition is inevitably even weaker than elsewhere in the USSR. Statistical details are at present uncertain. At the last census Moscow with 251,000 Jews was the greatest center of Jewish population in R. but the communities of Leningrad (162,000 Jews), Odessa (c. 115,000), Kiev (152,000), etc. are now rivaled numerically by new centers. Contacts with the outside Jewish world are slight and seldom spontaneous. Yet, notwithstanding the waning of traditional Jewish life, strong Jewish sentiments persist among a great part of the population. In 1947-8, R. supported the creation of the state of Israel, but — disappointed by the almost complete failure of pro-Soviet elements there — adopted a strong pro-Arab and anti-Israel policy, intensified from 1955 and especially from the period of the 1967 Six-Day War when Russia broke off relations with Israel and came out in unqualified support (material and political) of the Arabs, especially Egypt. The number of Jews in Russia according to the 1959 census was 2,268,000. The 1970 estimate published by the USSR Academy of Sciences was 2,150,707. Taking into account Jews who did not declare themselves as such, the number may well be considerably higher. After 1967, many Russian Jews demanded the right to emigrate to Israel and this was achieved in the early 1970s, and in the following years over 100,000 Jews left R.

RUTENBERG, PINḤAS (1879-1942): Engineer and

Pinḥas Rutenberg

Zionist leader. He participated in the 1905 Russian revolution and later lived in Italy. Returning to Russia in 1917, he played a leading role in revolutionary activities and opposed the Bolsheviks who imprisoned him for a time. He thereafter settled in Palestine and obtained a concession from the British Mandatory government for the hydroelectric project at the confluence of the Yarmuk and Jordan rivers ("The R. Scheme"). To carry out the project he founded the PALESTINE ELECTRIC COMPANY which he headed until his death. In 1929, R. was elected chairman of the *Vaad Leumi.*

RUTH: Moabitess; ancestor of David. After the death of her husband Mahlon, she accompanied her mother-in-law Naomi back to Bethlehem and eventually married Naomi's kinsman Boaz. The story is related in the Book of R., one of the "Five Scrolls" incorporated in the Hagiographa; it is read on the Feast of Weeks. In the Septuagint and Christian tradition, it follows the Book of Judges. Apparently written during the period of the monarchy, its charming idyllic character has ensured its popularity.

RUTH RABBAH: One of the earlier midrashim; part of MIDRASH RABBAH. It is of exegetical character, and the compiler utilized earlier sources, including the Palestinian Talmud, *Genesis Rabbah, Leviticus Rabbah*, and the *Pesikta.*

RUTHENIA: District in Trans-Carpathian Ukraine.

USSR. Until 1918, the Jews of R. shared the vicissitudes of other Jewish communities in the provincial areas of HUNGARY. They were strongly influenced by Hasidism and Orthodoxy, with Zionists in the minority. Their economic situation was always bad, one-third of the wage-earners having no definite occupation. During the period of Czech rule (1918–39), efforts were made to rehabilitate its Jewish population. The Hungarian occupation in 1939 brought immediate discrimination and the expulsion of Polish and recently-settled Jews. Before World War II, the Jewish population was c. 100,000. Only a few hundred survivors of the Nazi persecution remained after the war.

RUTHERSTON, ALBERT see **ROTHENSTEIN**

RUZHIN, ISRAEL OF (1797–1851): Hasidic rabbi; grandson of ABRAHAM MALAKH. At the age of 16, he succeeded his father as *tzaddik* in Ruzhin. He achieved a widespread reputation through his conduct, wisdom, charm, and organizational ability. He lived in luxury, holding that the *tzaddik* must behave like a man of wealth in order to exert influence. The Hasidim regarded his behaviour as befitting a messianic sovereign, a role in which R. also saw himself. He was imprisoned by the Russian authorities for 22 months and after his release settled at Sadagora in Bukovina, which henceforth became a Hasidic center.

SAAD: Israel communal settlement (PM) in the N Negev. It was founded in 1946 by settlers from Central Europe, later joined by immigrants from English-speaking and other countries. The nearest Jewish settlement to Gaza, S. was in danger during the Israel War of Independence. Pop. (1972): 502.

SAAD AL-DAULA (d. 1291): Physician and statesman. Born in Persia, he was a physician in government service in Baghdad, later holding several administrative posts, culminating in the governorship of Baghdad and Iraq. In 1289, he was appointed vizier by the Mongolian ruler Arghun. His success was marred by the enmity both of the Mongol nobility and of the preponderantly Moslem subjects of the Mongol emperor, which resulted in his murder.

SAADYAH BEN JOSEPH (882–942): Gaon. He left his native Egypt in 915, and wandered through Palestine and other countries. While on his way to Babylonia in 921, he became involved in a controversy with the Palestinian gaon Aaron ben Meir on a calendar question. In his *Sepher Zikkaron* he refuted the Palestinian claim to final authority in this matter, thereby establishing the calendar now in use. Appointed gaon of the academy of Sura at a time of crisis in 928, he was in 930 deposed by the exilarch David ben Zakkai, his former patron, whom he had criticized. Riots and the interference of the Moslem government ensued, until in 936, the exilarch reinstated him. S. describes his trials in *Sepher ha-Galui*. His earliest known work (915) was a polemic against the Karaite Anan; this was followed by many writings against various heretics which throw much light on the turbulent intellectual life of the period. His main philosophic contribution is his Arabic *Amanat wa-i'tiqadat* (Hebrew: *Emunot ve-Deot* = "Beliefs and Opinions", English translation by S. Rosenblatt, 1948). This follows the methods of the Moslem *Kalam* in some respects and those of Aristotle in others. It denies any conflict between reason and revealed religion and defines God as Creator possessing eternal life, omnipotence, and omniscience. The book was early translated into a Hebrew reminiscent of the *piyyut* style. The standard translation is by Judah Ibn Tibbon (1186). In halakhah, S. wrote several monographs, mostly in Arabic, and responsa.

His systematic compilation of the prayer book (*Siddur*, published Jerusalem, 1941) with instructions in Arabic is important. He also probably wrote an introduction to the Talmud. In the *Siddur* and elsewhere there are religious poems (*piyyutim*) by S., often very involved and difficult. He wrote much in elegant rhymed biblical Hebrew; his *Sepher ha-Galui* is intended as a model for composition. Besides translating the whole Bible into Arabic, he wrote Arabic commentaries on most books, varying from brief notes to detailed philosophical expositions. S. is the founder of the scientific study of Hebrew. Fragments are still being recovered of his great lexicon, the *Egron*, with Arabic explanations (plagiarized by the Karaite David ben Abraham Al-Fasi), and of his grammar, *Kutub al-Lugha* (in 12 parts in Arabic). He produced an explanatory list of the biblical HAPAX LEGOMENA and a poem giving the number of times each letter of the alphabet occurs in the Hebrew Bible.

SABATH, ADOLPH JOACHIM (1866–1952): US congressman. He was Democratic representative for Chicago in the US Congress from 1907 until his death, consistently supporting the policies of Franklin D. Roosevelt.

SABBATH: The day of rest. The Jewish S. is observed weekly from shortly before sunset on Friday until after nightfall on Saturday. The Friday night meal is preceded by KIDDUSH, recited over a cup of wine, in which the day is acknowledged to be a Divine gift, a memorial of the Creation of the world and of the Exodus from Egypt. There have been many attempts to discover a Babylonian origin for the S. but it is the Jewish conception that has influenced the world. In the Ten Commandments, and in the Pentateuch generally, the emphasis is on the S. as a day of complete rest and abstention from work, "an everlasting sign between me and the children of Israel that in six days the Lord created heaven and earth, but on the seventh day He rested and was refreshed" (Exod. 31:17). Subsequently Jewish law has defined thirty-nine separate types of action which constitute an infringement of the S. and has also legislated extensively to enhance the positive character of the S. rest. Nevertheless, Scripture itself prescribed the offering of sacrifices in the Temple on the S., despite the work involved (Num. 28:9–10). It is a cardinal rabbinic principle that if a human life is in danger (e.g. through illness), everything possible must be done even on the S. to save it. Circumcisions are also performed if the eighth day is a S. The prophets, like religious authorities of later times, complained of S. desecration (see, e.g. Jer. 17:21 ff., Ezek. 20:12 ff.), but they also expressed additional positive ideas for S. observance. The verse of Isaiah (58:13) "And call the S. a delight, and the holy of the Lord honorable" is held to imply that, in order to honor the S., everyone however wealthy or distinguished should participate actively in the preparations for the day, should don clean attire to welcome it, and should make sure that in the home the table is laid and the Sabbath lights are burning. By lighting a special S. LAMP or candles, the mistress of the house ushers in the S. To make the S. delight, the finest food should be prepared, and where appropriate, the rabbis recommended that marital intercourse should be indulged in on Friday night. Although food cannot be freshly cooked on the S., full use should be made of permissible means of storing hot food and drink to ensure that all three meals of the day are thoroughly enjoyed. From ancient times, according to the testimony of Philo and Josephus, the S. was regarded also as an occasion for spiritual and intellectual improvement, and study has always been a feature of the day's observance. The synagogue services, therefore, include readings from the Torah and the Prophets and are followed generally by study of the Law, individually or in groups. After the termination of the S., a valedictory benediction called HAVDALAH is recited.

SABBATH, GREAT (Heb. *Shabbat ha-Gadol*): The Sabbath before Passover: formerly the term was also applied to the Sabbath before Pentecost. It is signalized by reading a special *haphtarah* (Mal. 3:4–24) and by a rabbinical discourse dealing with the laws of the approaching holiday. The Ashkenazim read part of the HAGGADAH during the Afternoon Service. The origin of the name is controversial.

SABBATHS, SPECIAL: Four Sabbaths are named after the special Torah reading (with a corresponding *haphtarah*) which replaces the ordinary *maphtir* of the weekly biblical portion. These are: (1) *Shekalim*: The annual half-shekel poll tax for the purchase of the Temple sacrifices was collected during the month of *Adar*, and so Exod. 30:11–16 is read as *maphtir* on *Adar* 1, or on the preceding Sabbath, to remind worshipers of the ancient tax. (2) *Zakhor*: On the Sabbath before Purim, Deut. 25:17–19 is read in fulfillment of the biblical command to "remember what Amalek did." (3) *Parah*: On the Sabbath preceding *Ha-Hodesh* (see 4). Num. 19:1–22 is a reminder of the commandment to be ritually clean in time for the Passover festival. (4) *Ha-Hodesh*: On *Nisan* 1 or

on the preceding Sabbath, Exod. 12:1–20 is a reminder that Passover is at hand. Three Sabbaths are named after the first word of the prophetical portion. They are: Sabbath *Hazon* (before *Av* 9: Is. 1:1); Sabbath *Nahamu* (the Sabbath after *Av* 9: Is. 40:1), and Sabbath *Shuvah* (between New Year and the Day of Atonement: Hos. 14:2). Sabbath *Bereshit* (the last Sabbath of *Tishri*, when the reading of the Book of Genesis begins) and Sabbath *Shirah* (when the Song of the Red Sea – Exod. 15 – is read) are named for the regular biblical portion of the week. Sabbath *Hol ha-Moed* is the Sabbath during the intermediate days of Passover or Tabernacles. The Sabbath before Passover is termed *Shabbat Ha-Gadol* (possibly "The Great Sabbath").

SABBATICAL YEAR AND JUBILEE (Heb. *she-mittah* i.e., "fallow" and *yovel* i.e., "ram"): The Pentateuch ordains a rest from agricultural work in Palestine once in seven years (Lev. 25:3 ff). Any crops in the seventh year ("year of release") are communal property. The year following seven fallow-years – i.e., the 50th year – is the Jubilee (Lev. 25:8) when cultivation is also prohibited, slaves are freed, and land, purchased since the previous Jubilee, reverts to its original owner. The Jubilee year was proclaimed by sounding the horn on the Day of Atonement. The relevant laws are discussed in the talmudic tractate SHEVIIT. According to halakhah, the commandments of the Jubilee year are valid only when all Jews are resident in their land, each tribe in its territory. Nevertheless, ultra-orthodox Jews in Israel observe the Sabbatical year (e.g. 5726 i. e., 1965–6).

SABBETAIANS: Followers of SHABBETAI TZEVI. After his death in 1676, belief in his messianism revived and his adherents held he would reappear as the savior of Israel. The S. split into various sects. Shabbetai Tzevi was succeeded by Jacob QUERIDO who, together with his son Berechiah, overtly adopted Islam while retaining Sabbetaianism, thus creating the DONMEH sect. The ideologist of the S., Abraham Miguel CARDOZO (d. 1706), traveled through various N African countries preaching belief in the converted messiah. Meanwhile, the ascetic Mordecai Mokhiah of Eisenstadt disseminated Sabbetaianism in Germany and Italy. Many S. joined JUDAH HASID who organized a mass pilgrimage to Palestine; 1,500 set out but most died en route, and many others became converted. The most extreme instance of the development of Sabbetaianism were the FRANKISTS. Eventually, HASIDISM diverted popular attention from Sabbetaianism.

SABEA: Country in S ARABIA, home of a rich culture and a powerful kingdom from the first half of the last millennium BCE to c. 500 CE. Its language was Semitic; there are numerous inscriptions which throw light on biblical institutions and vocabulary.

Albert B. Sabin.

The Sabeans carried the incense of their country, gold, and goods imported from India by caravan to Palestine; S. is frequently mentioned in the Bible under the name of Sheba. The queen of Sheba (I Kings 10) cannot be identified with any historical personality; Bedouin Arab queens are recorded, but no women are known among the rulers of S. At some, as yet undetermined, time – according to legend at the destruction of the First Temple – Judaism reached S. Several inscriptions mention Israel, "their God, Lord of the Jews," and "the Merciful," proving that Judaism had gained adherents among the local landed aristocracy. During the 5th cent. several Jewish kings flourished, the last and most famous being DHU NUWAS.

SABIN, ALBERT BRUCE (1906–): Medical researcher. Born in Bialystok, he moved to the US in 1921. He took up polio research in 1931 and in 1959 developed a live, orally-administered vaccine for anti-polio immunization which was put into mass use two years later. He lived in Israel 1969–1972 when he was president of the WEIZMANN INSTITUTE OF SCIENCE.

SABORA see **SEVORAIM**

SABOT, ELIAS see **ELIJAH BEER BEN SHABBETAI**

SABRA (Arab. "prickly pear" cactus; in Heb. *tzabbar*): Native of Israel. The term refers metaphorically to their alleged characteristic of a prickly exterior with a tender interior.

SACHAR, ABRAM LEON (1899–): US educator; president of Brandeis Univ. which he helped to found in 1948. Prior to that, he was national director of the Hillel Foundations in American universities 1933–48. He has published *A History of the Jews* and an outline of modern Jewish history, *Sufferance is the Badge.*

SACHS, CURT (1881–1959): Musicologist. He taught at Berlin Univ. and the Sorbonne and from 1937 in New York. He wrote on the development of musical instruments, the history of the dance, etc.

SACHS, MICHAEL JEHIEL (1808–1864): Rabbi and preacher. He officiated in Prague 1836–44 and Berlin 1844–64. His powerful orations counteracted the influence of Holdheim and the Berlin Reform congregation. His scholarly works included translations into German of the liturgy and parts of the Bible.

SACHS, NELLY (1891–1970): Poet and Nobel prize laureate. Born in Berlin, she escaped to Sweden on the eve of World War II and settled there. Her prewar poetry is romantic in character but her reputation rests chiefly on her German verse that was inspired by the Nazi holocaust. In 1966 she was corecipient (with S.Y. AGNON) of the Nobel Prize for literature.

SACKLER, HARRY (1883–): Dramatist and novelist. He went to the US from Austro-Hungary in 1902, was secretary of the New York City Kehillah 1917–8, and later of other Jewish organizations. He is

Nelly Sachs.

Sacrifice in the Temple of Jerusalem. From a 15th cent. illuminated ms of Maimonides' *Mishneh Torah* (Private Collection, NY).

best known as the author of Yiddish dramas, short stories in Hebrew and Yiddish, and an English novel *Festival at Meron*.

SACRIFICE: A cultic act giving tangible expression to a feeling of submission to dependence on the deity; s. seeks to obtain the god's favor and atone for the sins of the sacrificer. The Canaanites sacrificed human beings (the cult of Moloch, see II Kings 3:27), but with the story of the binding of Isaac the Bible teaches God's displeasure with human s. To the ancient mind, a cult without s. was unthinkable, but the Jews gave s.'s a monotheistic tendency and concentrated them in the Jerusalem Temple. No animals were slaughtered except by s. until the time of the code of Deuteronomy. The three varieties of s. were animal-s. (*zevah*), meal-offerings (*minhah*), and libations (*nesekh*).

All animal-offerings had to be perfect and unblemished (Lev. 23:20). They were divided into the highest class of s. (burnt-offering, sin-offering, guilt-offering, congregational peace-offering) and s.'s of a minor grade (individual peace-offerings, first-born, animal tithes, paschal lamb). The former category was slaughtered to the N of the altar and eaten by the priests inside the enclosures of the Temple court (except for the burnt-offering which was entirely consumed by fire); the latter group could be killed in any part of the Temple Court and eaten by the sacrificer in any pure place in Jerusalem. Before offering any individual s., the sacrificer placed his hands on the animal and confessed his sin or iniquity; hands were laid on peace-offerings, thank-offerings, and bird-offerings. After this ceremony the animal was slaughtered and its blood sprinkled on the altar. A contribution was given from these s.'s to the priests. The sin-offering of an individual and the s. of a Nazirite had to be a female animal; a peace-offering could be of either sex. Honey and leaven were forbidden with the s. but leaven was offered on the Feast of Weeks and with the thanksgiving s. of the peace-offering. Every meal-offering was seasoned with salt. Meal-offerings were divided into oven-baked oblations, griddle baked oblations, and stewing-pan offerings (Lev. 2:4–7). There was also a first-fruit oblation (Lev. 2:14). Most of the offerings used oil and frankincense, the latter imparting a festal character. An important category of s. was the obligatory offering laid down in the Bible (Num. 28–9) to be offered on Sabbaths and feasts. Other s.'s were offered on special occasions of joy, sorrow, fulfillment of vows, or in thanks or repentance. The daily burnt-offering was sacrificed in the morning and evening, and Nehemiah taxed the people in order to obtain an adequate supply for this s. Thank-offerings and festival s.'s were offered when the people went to Jerusalem. The s. of the burnt-offering was made to the accompaniment of musical instruments and the levitical choir: two priests sounded the trumpets and the people bowed in worship.

The prophetical condemnation of s. can perhaps be connected with its similarities to Canaanite worship and the desire of the prophets to purify the Jewish cult. As explained by Maimonides, the true objective was to attain to the worship that is in the heart.

SACRIFICE OF ISAAC see **AKEDAH**

SACRILEGE: With reference to the Temple service, s. includes not only the actual appropriation for secular use of Temple property but, for example, the imitation of the formula for sacrificial incense for any secular use or copying the candelabrum or other vessels for any but Temple use. With the destruction of the Temple, the principle of s. was still widely applied. Improper use of the synagogue is defined by the rabbis as s.; so, too, is disrespect toward a Scroll of the Law. The imitation of Holy Writ for secular purposes or the recital of the Song of Songs as purely secular poetry is also deemed sacrilegious. In matters pertaining to death and burial, the principle of s. places limitations; cemeteries must be respected and no private gain can be derived from the body of a corpse or from a shroud.

SADAGORA: Townlet in Bukovina, now USSR. In the 19th cent. most of its Jewish settlers were Hasidim. In middle of the century R. Israel Friedman of Ruzhin settled there and his "court" was noted for its luxury. The dynasty he founded – known as the S. "rebbes"–moved to Vienna and later to Tel Aviv.

SADDUCEES (Heb. *tzedukim*): Sect of the Second Temple Period. Its origin is unknown: even the derivation of its name is uncertain but most scholars consider that it comes from the high priest

Yitzhak Sadeh meets the commander of the Egyptian Forces

ZADOK whose descendants served in the same office until 162 BCE. The well-connected priests and prominent aristocrats belonged to the S. who were thus influential in political and economic life. For them religion was primarily the Temple cult without a basis of abstract faith. They differed from the PHARISEES in the nature of their religious outlook and way of life. According to their viewpoint, individuals and groups must aspire to well-being in this world without expecting recompense in the world to come. The S. had no belief in a future world, resurrection, or the immortality of the soul and also rejected the existence of angels and spirits. Their slavish adherence to the Written Law led them to behave severely in cases involving the capital penalty, and they interpreted the *Lex Talionis* literally rather than in the sense of monetary compensation which was adopted by the Pharisees. Their austere conceptions extended to the Temple and its cult, retaining the decisive role of the priest and opposing Pharisaic innovations (e.g. the Water-Drawing Festival) which might have given a foothold to non-sacerdotal circles. Developing into the supporters of the Hasmonean kings from the reign of John Hyrcanus, they lost influence under Salome Alexandra and suffered severely at the hands of Herod. The whole power and existence of the S. was bound up with the Temple cult, and on the destruction of the Temple they disappeared.

SADEH (LANDSBERG), YITZHAK (1890–1952): Israel labor and military leader. He assisted Trumpeldor in founding the Russian HE-HALUTZ movement in 1919 and the following year settled in Palestine. In 1941, he organized the PALMAH which he commanded until 1945, and later served on the HAGANAH staff. With the establishment of the state of Israel, he commanded the Eighth Armored Brigade. Active in the labor movement, S. was a leader of MAPAM. He wrote stories, plays, and memoirs.

SAFED (Heb. *Tzephat*): Town, apparently identical with the fortified village of Sepph in Upper Galilee mentioned by Josephus; in the Talmud it is mentioned as one of the places where beacons were lit to mark the New Year. It first appears to be of importance in crusading times; Fulk of Anjou, king of Jerusalem, built a fortress there in 1140. It became Templar property in 1168 and was destroyed by Baybars in 1266. In Mameluke times, S. was one of the administrative centers of Palestine and Jews already lived there in the 11th cent. In the 16th cent., S. became a most important center of rabbinical and kabbalistic activity. Here lived the kabbalist R Isaac Luria and his pupils, while the rabbinical authorities included R Joseph Caro. A Hebrew press was established in S. in 1588. The administrative decay of the Turkish empire led to a decline in S. which was much affected by the wars between the Bedouin tribes. Epidemics and earthquakes (especially the great earthquake of 1837) brought about the ruin of the community, which in 1845, numbered only 400. In later times, the population fluctuated and in 1948, S. was inhabited by 12,000 Arabs and 1,800 Jews. Despite their numerical superiority and better strategic position, the Arabs fled from S. after some bitter fighting. Its present population (1974) is 14,200. Owing to its height (2,720 ft.) and splendid panorama, it is a summer resort and is being developed as a center of art, especially painting.

SAGERIN see **ZOGERIN**

SAHL BEN MATZLIAH (fl. second half of 11th cent.): Palestinian Karaite. He traveled extensively to disseminate his teachings. His works, which incorporate important information on Karaites and on Palestinian Jewry in his time, include anti-Rabbinite polemics in Hebrew and an Arabic commentary on the Pentateuch.

SAHULA, ISAAC BEN SOLOMON see **IBN SAHULA**

ST. JOSEPH: City in Missouri, US. Jews settled there in the late 1840's, and a congregation was organized in 1859. By 1905, the majority of its Jewish population of c. 1,200 were recent E. European immigrants. The Federated Jewish Charities was founded in 1915. Jewish pop. (1973): 625.

ST. LOUIS: City in Missouri, US. Jewish settlement dates from 1807. In 1836, the first recorded Jewish religious services W of the Mississippi were held there, and shortly afterward, the United Hebrew Congregation was organized. In the 1840's, the

westbound migration brought many Jews to S.L. These were mostly of Austrian, Bohemian, or German origin. In the 1880's, an influx of E European Jews further increased the Jewish population. Its Jewish Federation was established in 1901. The *Missouri Jewish Post and Opinion*, founded 1948, appears weekly. Jewish pop. (1973): 60,000.

ST. PAUL: City in Minnesota, US. Its Jewish settlement dates from the mid-19th cent. In 1857, the Mt. Zion Hebrew Association was formed. Until the arrival of E European Jews in the 1880's, the community remained small. A large number of welfare and social organizations grew up during the early years of the 20th cent., and the United Jewish Fund and Council were created in 1935. The *Jewish News* was founded in 1953. In 1973, S.P. had 10,000 Jews.

ST. PETERSBURG see **LENINGRAD**

SAKEL, MANFRED JOSHUA (1900–1957): Physician. He was born in Austria and settled in New York in 1936. He pioneered in the treatment of mental diseases by insulin shock treatment.

SALAMAN: English family. (1) *CHARLES KENSINGTON S.* (1814–1901), pianist and composer, founded the English Musical Association in 1876. (2) *MALCOLM CHARLES S.* (1855–1940), son of (1), wrote on art and drama and was an expert on English engravings.

SALAMAN, REDCLIFFE NATHAN (1874–1955), scientist, directed the Potato Virus Research Station at Cambridge and wrote many studies in pathology, botany, anthropology, etc. His first wife *NINA S.* (1877–1925), poet, published translations of medieval Hebrew religious poetry.

SALAMANCA: Spanish town. Its Jews were accorded equal rights with Christians when it was captured from the Moors in 1170, and the municipal government was obligated to defend the Jewish quarter in case of emergency. In 1456, S. was the scene of a Ritual Murder accusation.

SALANT, SAMUEL (1816–1909): Rabbi. Born in Poland, he was ordained rabbi at the age of 13. He settled in Jerusalem and became chief rabbi of the Palestinian Ashkenazi communities in 1878. He founded there the Etz Hayyim yeshivah.

SALANTER, ISRAEL (Israel Lipkin; 1810–1883): Founder of the MUSAR MOVEMENT. Born in Zhagory, S. was one of the most active rabbinic personalities in Lithuania and Russia, setting up special "*Musar*-houses" for the study of ethical literature and publishing a journal (*Tevunah*) to disseminate his ideas. Under his pupils' influence the *Musar* movement rapidly developed, particularly among the Torah students of Lithuania. S. also traveled in W Europe to propagate his doctrines. His ethical works were collected by his pupil Isaac Belzer in *Or Israel*.

Jonas E. Salk.

SALEM see **JERUSALEM**

SALINGER, JEROME DAVID (1912–): US novelist.
His *Catcher in the Rye* was widely acclaimed as were the volumes of stories about the Glass family commencing with *Franny and Zooey*.

SALK, JONAS EDWARD (1914–): US scientist.
He was professor of bacteriology and director of the virus research laboratory at the Univ. of Pittsburgh 1949–61, and since 1961 has headed the Institute for Biological Research at the Univ. of California. S. developed the vaccine, known as the Salk polio vaccine, which gives immunity to paralytic poliomyelitis.

SALMON: (1) *SIR CYRIL BARNET S.* (1903–):
British judge. In 1947, he was appointed a High Court judge in 1957, a Lord High Justice of Appeal in 1964 and Lord of Appeal in 1972. (2) *SIR ISIDORE S.* (1876–1941): British restaurant chain proprietor; director of the catering firm of J. Lyons and Co. S., who revolutionized army catering during World War I, sat in parliament as a Conservative for many years.

SALMON, ALEXANDER (1819–1866): Adventurer.
Running away to sea from his home in London, he married the author-princess Arii Taimai of Tahiti, their daughter being the last queen of the island.

SALOME (Heb. *Shelom-Zion*; fl. 1st cent. CE):
Daughter of Herod's son, Herod, and Herodias. She has been identified with the "daughter of Herodias" responsible for the death of JOHN THE BAPTIST (Matthew 14:3–6; Mark 6:17–29): Josephus gives a different account of John's death. She later married her uncle, the tetrarch Philip.

SALOME (Heb. *Shulamit*; d. 10 CE): Sister of Herod. Her ceaseless calumnies against Herod's wife Mariamne led to the latter's execution on charges of adultery. She also incited Herod against Mariamne's sons. Herod regarded her as the only loyal member of his family and in his will bequeathed her many possessions, including the town of Jabneh.

SALOME ALEXANDRA (Heb. *Shelom-Zion*): Ruler of Judea 76–67 BCE. She succeeded her husband, Alexander Yannai, and reversed his inimical policy toward the Pharisees, traditionally by his dying request. According to Josephus, S. handed internal control to the Pharisees while retaining responsibility for the army and foreign policy. Her appointment of her eldest son Hyrcanus as high priest and heir was opposed by his brother Aristobulus. Talmudic sources, which speak of S. as sister of R Simeon Ben Shetaḥ, regard her favorably, but Josephus is critical.

SALOMON (or **SOLOMON**), **EDWARD S.** (1836–1913): US public official. Born in Germany, he went to the US in 1854, was brevet brigadier general in the Union Army in the Civil War, governor of Washington Territory 1870–4, served two terms in the California state legislature, and was district attorney of San Francisco County.

SALOMON, GOTTHOLD (1784–1862): Preacher.
One of the outstanding orators of his day, he officiated from 1818 at the newly-founded Hamburg reform congregation. In 1841, the publication of his edition of the liturgy occasioned widespread controversy.

SALOMON, HAYM (1740–1785): US financier and patriot. Born in Lissa (Poland), he went to America in 1772 and entered the brokerage business. At the outbreak of the War of Independence, he ardently embraced the patriot cause and suffered imprisonment. He subsequently became official broker to the Office of Finance and collaborated heroically with Robert Morris in maintaining public credit, especially in 1781–4. He also aided from his own funds many patriot leaders such as James Madison and Thomas Jefferson. His devoted assistance in the sphere of finance helped to consolidate the American republic in its formative years.

SALOMONE, WALTER L. (d. 1939): Maltese statesman. He was a member of the Maltese parliament 1921–33, and minister of trade and customs 1927–31. A leader of the constitutionalist party, he supported British rule in Malta.

SALOMONS, SIR DAVID (1797–1873): English emancipation pioneer. A founder of the joint stock banking system in England, he fought stubbornly for the admission of Jews into English public life, becoming successively, in the face of opposition, the first Jewish sheriff (1835), alderman (1844), and finally lord mayor of London (1855–6). Elected to the House of Commons in 1851, he assumed his seat without taking the statutory Christological oath and was ejected, thus forcing the problem of Jewish parliamentary disabilities on public notice; subsequently, he sat legally for many years. His nephew *SIR DAVID LIONEL S.* (1851–1925) was an inventor and pioneer motorist.

SALOMONS, SIR JULIAN EMANUEL (1834–1909): Australian statesman. English-born and a distinguished advocate, he was solicitor-general in New South Wales 1869–70, chief justice 1886, and agent-general in London 1886–90 and 1899–1902.

SALONICA (THESSALONIKI): Greek port. Its Jewish community dates back to classical times and was visited by the apostle Paul in 50 CE. Throughout the Middle Ages, the Jews remained in the town under various rulers. In 1098, when they were attacked by the crusaders, S. was the center of a great messianic ferment. Later – especially after the Turkish occupation in 1430 – the textile industry attracted refugees from Central Europe. After the expulsion from Spain in 1492, the community received a vast impetus and became, with Constantinople, the greatest haven for the exiles. The original Greek-speaking inhabitants and immigrants from other

Title-page of *Seder Zemanim* by Saadyah Lungo (Salonica, 1594).

countries became culturally absorbed by the Spanish-speaking immigrants and adopted their language. Some 40 different congregations and synagogues reflected the rites of the cities and provinces from which they derived. In the 16th cent., there was a constant influx of Portuguese Marranos. S. was also noted for its rabbinic scholarship, while at the same time perpetuating the traditions of Spanish culture. It had large numbers of academies, printing presses (from 1515), and schools of poetry. In 1568, through the efforts of Moses ALMOSNINO, the community was made autonomous. Fires caused frequent devastation – e.g. in 1545 and 1617. In the 17th cent., S. was the major seat of activity of Shabbetai Tzevi and many Jews followed him into insincere Islam, thus creating the sect of the DONMEH, whose main center henceforth was in S. The community suffered greatly from this blow but remained the pivot of Sephardi culture. Down to the Greek conquest in 1912, the city, with 80,000 Jews, remained predominantly Jewish, no ship being able to discharge its cargo in the harbor on Saturday. The interchanges of population between Greece and Turkey after World War I resulted in the emigration of the Donmeh and a large Greek influx. The Jewish population, whose condition was now somewhat less favorable, was reduced by 1940 to under 20% (c. 5,000), many having emigrated to Palestine, France, America, etc. During the German occupation of 1941–4 almost all the community, after being despoiled, was deported in 19 convoys to Poland for extermination. There are (1973) only 1,092 Jews in S.

SALT LAKE CITY: City in Utah, US. Individual Jews settled there in the mid-19th cent. and conducted their first organized religious services in 1864. A congregation was formed in 1873. The United Jewish Council and the Salt Lake Jewish Welfare Fund were founded in 1936. Jewish pop. (1973): 1,500.

SALTEN (ZALZMANN), FELIX (1869–1945): Austrian novelist and critic. He wrote feuilletons, plays, and dramatic criticism. His international fame rests on his animal tale *Bambi*. His Jewish interests come to the fore in the novel *Simson* and in the novel based on his Palestine trip *Neue Menschen auf alter Erde*.

SALTING see **DIETARY LAWS**

(EL) SALVADOR: Central American Republic. The first Jews arrived in the 19th cent. but the main period of immigration was 1920–30. Almost all its 300 (1973) Jews live in the capital, San Salvador. The Communidad Israelita is the recognized Jewish body.

SALVADOR see **BAHIA**

SALVADOR, FRANCIS (1747–1776): US revolutionary hero. Son of the English financier and philanthropist Joseph Salvador or Joseph Jessurun

Ruins of the Herodian basilica of Samaria (Sebaste).

Rodrigues (1700–1786), he emigrated from England in 1773, served in S Carolina's colonial legislature, and was scalped by Indians.

SALVADOR, JOSEPH (1796–1873): French historian. At first far from Judaism (his mother was Catholic), he became interested in Judaism at the time of the 1819 Hep! Hep! riots. He wrote about Jewish history and the Jewish mission, holding that the Torah was the ideal law corresponding with the ideals of the French Revolution. He wrote on Roman rule in Judea, a history of "The Institutions of Moses and the Jewish people," and a work on Jesus.

SALZBURG: Austrian town. Evidence of Jewish residence in the bishopric comes from the late 13th cent. and the first mention in the city dates from 1329. The community was massacred during the Black Death outbreak (1349) and following a Host Desecration charge in 1404, and the Jews were expelled by the archbishop in 1498. Resettlement was only permitted in 1813, and a community was organized in 1911. 400 Jews lived in S. in 1938 but they fled or were destroyed by the Nazis. A community was reestablished after the war.

SAMAEL (Heb. perhaps "venom of God"): Prince of DEMONS, identical with Satan and therefore also with the serpent, the tempter, the angel of death, and Lucifer. S. is mentioned frequently in the Slavonic Book of ENOCH and in midrashic and kabbalistic literature. As the principle of evil, he is also identified with the guardian angel of Rome; his opponent is MICHAEL, the guardian angel of Israel. S.'s wife is LILITH, the queen of demons.

SAMARIA (Heb. *Shomron*): Capital of the Northern kingdom of Israel, founded c. 880 BCE by Omri on a hill bought from Shemer (I Kings 16:24). The site, c. 7 m. NW of Shechem (Nablus) was on an isolated elevation dominating a wide countryside. The city occupied 25 acres; it had an acropolis with a casemate wall within which was the royal palace in the Assyrian style; inscribed ostraca were found by excavators in its store-rooms and also ivory inlays recalling the "ivory house" built by Ahab (I Kings 22:39). S. withstood the siege of the Syrians but fell in 721 BCE to Sargon II of Assyria who resettled it with Cutheans; these, intermingling with the remnants of the former population, were the ancestors of the SAMARITANS. It remained an administrative center in the Persian Period and became a Macedonian colony in 331 BCE. John Hyrcanus took S. c. 107 BCE and razed it; it was restored by Pompey. Herod renamed it Sebaste (Gk. for "Augusta") in honor of Augustus Caesar and the name has been preserved in the modern Sabastiya. He also endowed it with a new wall, a temple of Augustus, a forum, a basilica, and an aqueduct. The city flourished in Roman times, especially in the 3rd cent. CE, and impressive ruins still remain. It was the traditional burial place of John the Baptist. S. decayed in Byzantine times and shrank to a village in the Arab period. It was excavated in 1908–10 and 1931–35 by Harvard Univ., the Palestine Exploration Fund, and the Hebrew Univ.

SAMARITAN LANGUAGE AND LITERATURE:
The Samaritan language is the Hebrew of the Torah. Its pronunciation, very different from either Ashkenazi or Sephardi Hebrew, is probably very old. The gutturals are not pronounced nor distinguished from each other. There is a tendency to prefix and suffix *alephs* to words in pronunciation though seldom in writing. Samaritan Hebrew was never influenced by the Masoretes and preserves a variant ancient tradition. Apart from the Torah and parts of the liturgy, there is little extant literature in Hebrew.

The old *Defter* (Liturgy) is in Samaritan Aramaic, as are the *Memar Marka*, a Samaritan haggadic Midrash of the 4th cent. CE, and the Targum. Samaritan Aramaic is a separate dialect, though approximating that of the Palestinian Talmud. The Samaritans possess a considerable literature in Arabic — not classical but their own literary form of the Palestinian colloquial. A relatively varied and extensive Samaritan literature still exists in mss.

SAMARITANS (Heb. *Shomeronim*; in the Talmud *Kutim*): People, with their capital at SAMARIA; originally calling themselves *Bene Yisrael* or *Shomerim* (the "keepers" of the Law). They were descended from the tribes of Ephraim and Manasseh (c. II Chron. 34:9; Jer. 41:5) with an admixture of non-Israelite colonists (cf. II Kings 17:24–41). In the Persian period, Nehemiah foiled the Samaritan SANBALLAT'S attempt to obtain political and religious influence over Judah. When his son-in-law was driven from Jerusalem (Neh. 13:28), Sanballat built a rival Temple on Mt. Gerizim, which was destroyed by John Hyrcanus (c. 128 BCE). However, the territory between Judea and Galilee was still Samaritan. The S. did not participate in the Jewish revolt of 66–70, but rose independently from time to time against the Romans. Zeno in 486 destroyed the second Samaritan Temple on Gerizim, building a Christian church in its stead. In 529, Justinian issued a decree against the S., and thereafter, their autonomous existence practically ended. S., not being considered "People of the Book," suffered under Islam, and their numbers dwindled rapidly. In 1974 there were 250 S. in Nablus and 230 in Holon. Their synagogue, housing the ancient Pentateuch, is at Mt. Gerizim near Nablus and there they hold their annual Passover sacrifice. In addition to the parent body in Palestine, a Samaritan Diaspora existed in Egypt from the time of the Ptolemies and lasted until the 18th cent. A Samaritan synagogue in Rome was destroyed c. 500 CE; there were S. in Babylonia in the Talmudic Period (cf. *Gittin* 45a) and in Syria in the 17th cent.

Samaritan religion is a form of primitive Judaism, except that the whole Bible of the S. is the Pentateuch, which is the same as the Jewish version but represents a pre-Masoretic text with Samaritan variants; claiming, for instance, in the Ten Commandments that the place chosen by God for His sanctuary is Mt. Gerizim. The S. maintain that their text is the original and that the Jewish one was altered by Ezra. The Samaritan religious year has seven feasts: *Pesah, Matzot, Shavuot, Yom Teruah, Yom Kippur, Sukkot,* and *Moed Shemini. Pesah* (Passover) can only be celebrated on Mt. Gerizim where the lambs are sacrificed, roasted, and hastily eaten. On the seventh day of *Matzot* (i.e., Unleavened Bread) they make a *Hag* (pilgrimage) to the Mountain, reciting sections of the Pentateuch. *Hag Shavuot*

(Pentecost) always falls on a Sunday (the morrow of the seventh Sabbath after *Pesah*). *Yom Teruah* ("The Day of Trumpet-Call") is not called *Rosh ha-Shanah*. At *Hag Sukkot* (Tabernacles), the *lulav* and *etrog* are unknown. Twice a year at the semi-festivals of *Tzimmut Pesah* (*Shevat* 15) and *Tzimmut Sukkot* (*Av* 15) the Samaritan priests supply calendars for the ensuing six months. The priests and levites never allowed a class of lay religious scholars to develop as in Judaism. There is practically no halakhic development of the 613 precepts, which are kept literally, but a rigid *haggadah* compensated for lack of halakhic activity. Moses is the one prophet in Samaritan eyes. The minor talmudic tractate *Kutim* treats of the S. and closes: "When will we accept them? When they deny belief in Mount Gerizim and confess Jerusalem and the resurrection of the dead."

SAMBATYON: Mythical river resting on the Sabbath day. The lost ten tribes were supposed to have been transported beyond it. The name occurs in the pseudo-Jonathan Targum to Exod. 34:10 and the historical basis may be a river in Syria called by a name similar to the word Sabbath. Josephus knew of the mythical river, the waters of which ran dry for six days at a time; Pliny, however, came closer to the talmudic view, saying that it was dry only on the Sabbath. R Akiva argued the Divine character of the Sabbath by reference to the phenomenon of the S. (*Sanhedrin* 35b). The traveler Eldad Ha-Dani (9th cent.) gave much information regarding the S., relating that it carried sand and rubble rather than water but with such force that it could crush a mountain. On its other side lived, not the lost ten tribes, but the Children of Moses. Abraham Abulafia (13th cent.) wandered in search of the river, and Shabbetai Tzevi (17th cent.) intended to journey there, marry the daughter of Moses, and restore the ten tribes to the Holy Land.

SAMEKH (ס): Fifteenth letter in the Hebrew alphabet; numerical value 60. It is pronounced *s*.

SAMINSKY, LAZARE (1882–1959): Musician. Of Russian birth, he settled in New York in 1920, becoming music director of Temple Emanu-El in 1924. His compositions include liturgical and symphonic works, choral music, and ballets. He wrote on music and Jewish musicians.

SAMKALDEN, IVO (1912–): Dutch lawyer. He was an official in the Dutch East Indies and was interned by the Japanese in World War II. In 1958 he became professor of international law at Leyden. In 1956–8 and again in 1965–6 he was minister of justice, in which capacity he helped to prepare the new Dutch civil code. In 1967, he was elected mayor of Amsterdam.

SAMOILOVICH, RUDOLPH LAZAREVICH (1884–): Russian Arctic explorer. He discovered the coal-mines of Spitzbergen and explored Novaia Zemlia and the Franz Joseph archipelago. S. is a member of the Arctic Institute of Leningrad.

SAMPTER, JESSIE (1883–1938): Author. After an assimilationist childhood in the US, she was attracted to Jewish life and in 1919, took up permanent residence in Palestine. She wrote books, articles, and poems on Zionist and Jewish themes, and was, with Henrietta Szold, active in Hadassah during its early days.

SAMSON: Israelite judge; son of Manoah of the tribe of Dan (Judg. 13–16). A Nazirite from birth, he excelled in strength and courage, and his feats against the Philistines—although often executed for personal reasons—expressed the Israelites' desire

Samson tearing the lion.

for freedom from the Philistine suzerainty. Ultimately, he fell into Philistine hands as a result of the deceit of DELILAH who betrayed the secret of his strength as lying in his hair; his eyes were put out and S. made to turn the prison mill. When brought as an object of mockery before the Philistines at a festival at Gaza, he destroyed the building and killed the entire assembly, including himself.

SAMSON BEN ABRAHAM OF SENS (c. 1150—c. 1230): French tosaphist; pupil of R Jacob ben Meir Tam. He founded an academy at Sens and was among the leaders of the group of 300 rabbis who settled in Palestine c. 1211. S. wrote talmudical commentaries ("The *tosaphot* of Sens") and also liturgical poems.

SAMUEL (fl. 11th cent. BCE): Prophet and last Israelite Judge. He originated from a levitical family dwelling on Mt. Ephraim and at Ramah (in the land of Zuph). His mother consecrated him before his birth as a Nazirite who would serve the sanctuary at Shiloh. There, he received the Divine call as a child and later foretold the destruction of the House of ELI. After the death of Eli and his sons and the decisive defeat of the Israelites by the Philistines at the battle of Aphek, S. endeavored to restore the traditional religious worship. He resided in Ramah and judged the Israelites in the sacred towns of Bethel, Gilgal, and Mizpeh, preparing the way for national unity. Apparently on his initiative, groups of prophets were formed to guide the people. In his old age, when external pressure grew acute, he reluctantly acceded to the popular demand for a king and selected SAUL. However, tension between S. and Saul eventually reached an open break. Later, S. went to Bethlehem where he anointed David as Saul's successor.

SAMUEL, BOOK OF: Third book of the Former Prophets section in the Bible. It relates the history of the Israelites from the end of the period of the Judges down to the last days of David, with especial emphasis on the biographies of Samuel (chaps. 1–7), Saul (8–31), and David (16 ff). The book is written with a thorough knowledge of the period and its pragmatic historical approach is unique in ancient eastern literature. The main author appears to be a contemporary, and possibly an acquaintance, of David. The editor has added from various sources which relate the stories of Samuel, Saul, and the house of Eli. The printed Bible follows the Septuagint and Vulgate in dividing the Book into two, but in Hebrew tradition it is one work. From an early period it was called after Samuel, the first outstanding personality in the Book. Important textual variations (many corresponding to the Septuagint translation) figure in the Hebrew Bible fragments found among the Dead Sea Scrolls.

SAMUEL, MIDRASH TO: Midrash to the Book of Samuel. It is largely a compilation from old Midrashim, many of which seem to be taken from a prototype. Though composed in Palestine, the final compilation was not made before the 11th cent.

SAMUEL (often called "Mar Samuel"; c. 177–257): Babylonian amora; head of the Nehardea academy. His debates with his colleague RAV on halakhic problems are frequently cited in the Talmud. S. was an authority on civil law, in which his views were accepted as decisive. The Talmud records several basic principles laid down by him, such as "the law of the land (in which Jews live) is binding" (*Gittin* 10*b*). He was an expert astronomer and dealt with questions connected with the Hebrew calendar, claiming that "the paths of the heavens are as clear to me as the paths of Nehardea" (*Berakhot* 58*b*). S. was also a physician and during his younger days, while studying in Palestine, attended R Judah Ha-Nasi. He advocated amicable relationship with non-Jews and was himself on friendly terms with King Sapor I of Persia.

The swearing-in of Herbert Samuel as first High Commissioner for Palestine, 1920.

SAMUEL BEN ALI HA-LEVI (d. c. 1207): Gaon, after the renewal of the gaonate in Baghdad. S. also aspired to the functions of the exilarch and was jealous of the increasing prestige of Maimonides, opposing his *Code* on many grounds.

SAMUEL BEN AVIGDOR (c. 1720–1793): Rabbi. From 1750, he was rabbi of Vilna, where his father-in-law was an influential citizen. After the latter's death, a bitter dispute with the *kahal* began, in which the local lay and ecclesiastical gentile authorities participated and which was never composed. No successor to him was ever appointed.

SAMUEL BEN MEIR (called *Rashbam*; c. 1085 — after 1158): French scholar. Like his grandfather Rashi he was both a Bible exegete and a Talmud commentator. His Bible commentaries aimed at expounding the simple and natural meaning of the text, and he used the Targumim (even referring to the Vulgate), Midrashim, and Talmud to support his views. S. completed Rashi's commentary on *Bava Batra* and *Pesahim*, although he was unable to match his grandfather's conciseness. He also wrote independent works quoted by the tosaphists.

SAMUEL HA-KATAN (i.e., "the small"): Tanna; lived toward the end of the 1st cent. CE. Although no halakhah is recorded in his name in the Mishnah, and little is found in aggadah, much is told of his piety, humility, and spiritual qualities. At the request of the patriarch Gamaliel II, S. composed the *birkat ha-minim*, the extra blessing inserted in the EIGHTEEN BENEDICTIONS against the early Christians and other dissenters. His appellation "the small" is explained as a reference to his humility or to his being only slightly inferior to the prophet Samuel.

SAMUEL HA-LEVI see **ABULAFIA**

SAMUEL HA-NAGID see **SAMUEL IBN NAGRELA**

SAMUEL IBN ADIYA (fl. first part of 6th cent.): Arabic poet. Lord of a castle near Taima in Arabia, he was famous both for his poetic talents and his noble character: "More faithful than al-Samu'il (i.e., Samuel)" was a well-known Arabic proverb. His poems are similar in language, style, and content to those of other pre-Islamic Arab poets, except that some are composed in a religious vein.

SAMUEL IBN NAGRELA (or Ibn Nagdela, also *Ha-Nagid*; 993–1056): Spanish statesman, poet, and talmudist. Belonging to a family which had been reduced to penury by the sack of Cordova, he was for a time a spice-seller at Malaga. By reason of his fine Arabic style he became secretary and, in 1020, successor to the vizier of King Habbus of Granada. On Habbus' death in 1037, S. espoused the cause of his son Badis whom he continued to serve, both administering the kingdom and commanding its armies in the field. Notwithstanding the unpopularity he aroused, he continued in power until his death, when he was succeeded by his ill-fated son Joseph, who was overthrown and killed in 1066. S. was a prolific and capable, if not inspired, poet; his poetical works, which include imitations of the biblical books of Proverbs, Ecclesiastes, and Psalms, have recently been published. He also wrote grammatical works and an introduction to the Talmud now printed in the standard editions. His generosity to scholars, patronage of learning and Jewish devotion earned him the title NAGID, conferred on him as head of the Jewish community of the country.

SAMUEL, HERBERT LOUIS, VISCOUNT (1870–1963): British statesman and philosopher. The first professing Jew to be a member of a British cabinet (from 1909), he held office in the Liberal government 1905–16, and in the national government 1931–2. His memorandum to the Cabinet in 1914 concerning a British trust for the Jewish Home influenced the BALFOUR DECLARATION. In 1920–5, he was the first HIGH COMMISSIONER for Palestine. He also served as chairman of the Royal Commission on the Coal Industry (1925), preparing the way for nationalization. He was leader of the Liberal Party in the House of Commons 1931–5, and in the House of Lords 1944–55. From 1936, he served as president of the Council for German Jewry and in 1939, founded the Children's Movement to bring unaccompanied refugee children from Germany to Britain. S. was president of the Royal Institute of Philosophy 1931–56, and the author of the popular philosophical studies *Practical Ethics, Belief and Action*, and *Physics and Philosophy*.

SAMUEL, SIR MARCUS see **BEARSTED**

SAMUEL, MAURICE (1895–1972): Essayist and novelist. Born in Rumania, he was brought up in England and settled in the US in 1914. He visited Israel on many occasions and accompanied the development of its community with interpretative books *What Happened in Palestine, Harvest in the Desert*, and *Level Sunlight*. His theoretical books on the Jewish question *You Gentiles; I, the Jew; The Great Hatred*, and *The Gentlemen and the Jews* are acute and original. S. wrote books on Sholem Aleichem and Y. L. Peretz, a novel on the Borgias *The Web of Lucifer, Certain People of the Book* on biblical characters and a study of the BEILIS trial.

SAMUEL, SIR SAUL (1829–1900): Australian statesman. Taken from England to Sydney as a child, he prospered in business. Entering politics, he was successively colonial treasurer and postmaster general for New South Wales and from 1880, agent general in London.

SAMUELSON, PAUL (1915–): US economist; professor at the Massachusetts Institute of Technology. In 1970 he received the first Nobel Prize in Economics for work on economic theory.

SAN ANTONIO: City in Texas, US. Jews settled there in 1854, and religious services were first held a year later. In 1856, the Hebrew Benevolent Association (later: Montefiore Benevolent Society) was founded. A Reform congregation was formed in 1874, and an Orthodox congregation organized in 1890. The Jewish Social Service Federation was created in 1924. Jewish pop. (1973): 6,500.

SAN DIEGO: Port in California, US. Jews have lived there since 1850. In 1861, a Reform congregation was formed and an Orthodox congregation organized in 1905 after the arrival of Jewish immigrants from E Europe. The United Jewish Fund was created in 1935 and the Federation of Jewish Agencies in 1950. In 1973 there were 15,000 Jews with 3 synagogues.

SAN DOMINGO see **DOMINICAN REPUBLIC**

SAN FRANCISCO: City in California, US. Two congregations were organized in 1849–50: Sherith Israel representing American, French, and German elements, and Emanu-El, by British and Polish immigrants. In 1850, the Eureka Benevolent Society was founded and, together with the Hebrew Benevolent Association formed at the same time, assisted destitute newcomers. Jews played a prominent part in the city's economic development; a number distinguished themselves in civic affairs and two served in California's first legislature. Jews made up nearly a quarter of the Vigilantes Committee. Julius Eckmann, first rabbi of Congregation Emanu-El, organized a Sabbath school in 1854 and published the first Jewish journal on the Pacific coast, *The Gleaner*, a year later. *The Voice of Israel* and *Jewish Messenger of the Pacific* appeared subsequently. When Emanu-El adopted Reform in the 1860's, many of its members formed a new congregation, Ohabai Shalome. A Federation of Jewish Charities, founded in 1910, was reorganized in 1955 as the Jewish Welfare Federation. A Welfare Fund was established in 1925. Since 1946, the weekly *Jewish Community Bulletin*, consolidated with the privately owned *Emanu-El*, has been the official organ of the community and the *Jewish Star* appears monthly. Jewish pop. (1973): 75,000.

SAN NICANDRO: Small town in S Italy where 23 peasant families adopted Judaism before migrating to Israel in 1949. The spontaneous conversion resulted from the vision (in 1932) of Donato Manduzio, a local vinegrower, in which he was told to return to the faith of Moses. Together with his disciples he became a Jew despite the threats of the local clergy, the dissuasion of the Rome rabbinate, and the opposition of Fascist officials. Manduzio died shortly before the emigration to Israel. The group settled first at Kephar Alma in Upper Galilee but, as a result of internal disputes, subsequently dispersed.

SAN REMO CONFERENCE: Conference meeting in San Remo, Italy, during Apr. 1920, to consider problems arising from the Versailles Peace Treaty. The Zionists proposed that the Jewish right to Palestine should be recognized and that Great Britain administer the country, thus making possible the establishment of a Jewish National Home and eventually an autonomous commonwealth. As a result of the conference, the Palestine MANDATE was awarded to Britain.

SAN SALVADOR see **SALVADOR**

SANAA: Capital of YEMEN. Local tradition dates Jewish settlement there before the destruction of the First Temple. For many centuries, the town harbored the largest Yemenite Jewish community. Until 1679, the Jews lived in their own quarters inside S.; later, after having been expelled and recalled, they had to settle in a special suburb outside the town. In the early 19th cent., c. 10,000 Jews lived in S., and their number steadily increased until the mass exodus of Yemenite Jewry to Israel in 1949-50.

SANBALLAT (fl. 5th cent. BCE): Satrap of Samaria in the reign of Artaxerxes I of Persia; opponent of Nehemiah. He attempted to prevent the rebuilding of the walls of Jerusalem. S. was related by marriage to the high priest Eliashib. Josephus calls him a contemporary of Alexander the Great (reigned 336-323) and associates him with the building of the Samaritan temple on Mt Gerizim, but his chronology must be confused as S. is specifically mentioned in the Elephantine papyri (late 5th cent. BCE).

SANCHEZ, ANTONIO RIBEIRO (1699-1783): Portuguese Marrano physician and philosopher. He was a pioneer of educational and penal reform and also introduced the Russian vapor bath into W Europe. Although spending part of his life as a professing Jew in England, he subsequently returned to Portugal.

SANCHEZ, GABRIEL (fl. 15th cent.): Marrano supporter of Columbus. A member of the wealthy *converso* family Ussuf, of Saragossa, he became high treasurer of the kingdom of Aragon. He befriended Columbus and (with Luis de Santangel) received his first report of the discovery of America.

SANCTIFICATION see **KIDDUSH**

SANCTIFICATION OF THE MONTH see **NEW MOON**

SANCTIFICATION OF THE NAME see **MARTYRS**

SANCTUARY: (1) Place consecrated for Divine worship, e.g. the Tabernacle in the wilderness and at Shiloh, the House of God at Nob and Gibeon, and the Temple. In Shiloh and Jerusalem, the s. contained the ARK, regarded as the site of Divine manifestation. (2) Place of refuge for the accidental killer. The relative avenging the murdered kinsman was forbidden to enter the refuge or harm the slayer. In ancient times down to the period of the monarchy, this function was fulfilled by the altar (Exod. 21:14; I Kings 1:51; 2:28). Moses set aside special CITIES OF REFUGE. The monarchy eventually took over authority to adjudicate such cases.

SANDALPHON: According to later anagelology, one of the highest angels. He plays an important role in Kabbalah as the guardian of prayers and of Israel in exile. In some texts, he is named as the Divine messenger at the time of the Resurrection.

SANDEK see **CIRCUMCISION**

SANHEDRIN: Hebrew word of Greek origin denoting in rabbinic literature the assembly of 71 ordained scholars which functioned both as Supreme Court and as legislature. At its head stood the NASI, who in its later history was usually a descendant of Hillel, and an *Av Bet Din*. Before 70 CE, the S. met in the Temple chamber called the Hall of Hewn

Stone, which could be entered from both the priests' court and the Israelites' court; later, it functioned in various centers successively. Its duties included the monthly proclamation of the New Moon, declaration of leap years, and decisions on state offenses and doubtful questions of Jewish law. The New Testament and some passages in Josephus depict the S. as a council of state presided over by the high priest which also conducted the trials of political offenders. Some scholars believe that there were two different S.'s, one political and the other religious. There is, however, no evidence for the existence of a political body except during the troubled decades which preceded the destruction of the Temple. The S. disappeared from the Jewish scene before the end of the 4th cent. CE. During the 16th cent., an unsuccessful attempt was made by Joseph Caro and Jacob Berab, applying a suggestion of Maimonides, to revive ORDINATION in the land of Israel and so make possible a new S. The rebirth of the state of Israel in 1948 brought a fresh demand for a revival of the S., but authoritative opinion considers the legal and constitutional difficulties at present insuperable. For the Jewish assembly called by Napoleon (1806) see S., GRAND.

SANHEDRIN: Fourth tractate in the Mishnah order of *Nezikin* containing 11 chapters. It has *gemara* in both the Babylonian and the Palestinian Talmuds. It treats in particular of courts of justice and judicial procedure, especially with reference to criminal law. Topics discussed include the four primary methods of execution, the law of the rebellious son (Deut. 21:18-21), and that of the city tempted to evil (Deut. 13:13-15). It includes a list of sins which exclude a man from future life. Scholars dispute whether the description of the courts reflects actuality or an ideal.

SANHEDRIN, GRAND: Body of 71 members convoked by NAPOLEON to confirm the decisions of the Assembly of Notables. It consisted of 45 rabbis and 26 lay-members, meeting Feb. 9 — Mar. 9, 1807 under the presidency of David Sintzheim, rabbi of Strasbourg. Its decisions prescribed adherence to the civil code (subject to the general demands of Judaism).

SANTA MARIA, PAUL DE (Paul of Burgos; c. 1352-1435): Spanish churchman. Born a Jew as Solomon Ha-Levi, he was rabbi in Burgos. He became converted to Christianity and made a brilliant career in the Church, becoming successively bishop of Cartagena and then of his native Burgos and member of the Castilian Council of Regency. He was partly responsible for the anti-Jewish legislation in Castile in 1412, and author of learned controversial works and biblical commentaries.

SANTANGEL, LUIS DE (d. 1498): Marrano financier; chancellor and comptroller of the royal household of Aragon. He was descended from the Jewish family of Chinillo, of Calatayud. He was a staunch supporter of Christopher Columbus, introduced him to Queen Isabella, and advanced 5,000,000 maravedis free of interest to support the expedition. With Gabriel SANCHEZ, he received from Columbus the earliest report of the discovery of America. Another LUIS DE SANTANGEL (d. 1487) was executed at Saragossa for implication in the murder of the inquisitor Pedro Arbues.

SANTIAGO DE CHILE: Capital of Chile. Marranos settling there in the 16th–18th cents. became assimilated. The present Jewish community derives from the 19th–20th cent. immigrations. The main influx followed World War I and continued until 1939 when immigration was severely restricted. In 1973, there were 32,000 Jews in S. de C., the seat of the Central Representative Committee of Chilean Jews.

SANTOB DE CARRION see **CARRION**

SAO PAULO: Brazilian city. Its early Marrano settlers were ultimately assimilated to the general population. The present community derives from immigration in the 19th–20th cents. especially since World War I. The Jews contributed largely to the growth of textile and paper industries. S. P., the seat of a Federation of Jewish Institutions, supports 27 synagogues, 13 schools, Yiddish and Portuguese Jewish periodicals, etc. Jewish pop. (1973): 65,000.

SAPHIR, MORITZ GOTTLIEB (1795–1858): Journalist. Born in Hungary, he lived in Vienna, Berlin, and Munich (where he was baptized). In Vienna, he founded (1837) the satirical *Humorist*, one of the most widely-read journals of the time.

SAPIR: (1) *YAAKOV S.* (Saphir; 1822–1885): Hebrew author and traveler. Born in Lithuania, he went to Palestine in 1833. After teaching and serving as a public official, he left in 1858 on a five-year fund-raising mission in oriental countries (including Yemen, India, Australia, and New Zealand), describing his travels in *Even Sappir*, which contains valuable information on 19th cent. oriental Jewish life and customs, especially in Yemen. (2) *YOSEPH S.* (1902–1972): Israel public figure; grandson of (1). He was prominent in the development of citriculture and was mayor of Petaḥ Tikvah 1940–50. A General Zionist (later Liberal and *Gaḥal*) member of the Knesset from 1949, he was minister of communications 1953–5. In 1967, he joined the national coalition government first as minister without portfolio and in 1969–70, minister of commerce and industry.

SAPIR, EDWARD (1884–1939): US anthropologist and linguist. The results of his researches among the American Indians are to be found in numerous publications. He was chief anthropologist at the Canadian National Museum 1910–25 and thereafter professor in Chicago 1925–31 and at Yale 1931–9.

SAPIR, PINHAS (1906–1975): Israel public figure. He went to Palestine from Poland in 1930. S. was director-general of the Ministry of Defense 1949–51,

Pinhas Sapir.

and of the Ministry of Finance 1963–5, minister of commerce and industry 1955–64 and minister of finance from 1963 to 1968 and 1969 to 1974 when he became chairman of The Zionist Executive.

SARAFAND (Heb. *Tzeriphin*): Village 10 m. SE of Tel Aviv on the Jerusalem road. It is probably the ancient Tzeriphin the gardens of which are mentioned in the Mishnah. In the mandatory period, the British army erected its central camp between this village and Rishon le-Zion; it was captured by the *Haganah* in 1948 and now serves the Israel Defense Forces.

SARAGOSSA: Former capital of Aragon. Jews lived there in the Moorish Period and Jekuthiel Ibn Ḥasan was vizier in the 11th cent. The community flourished under Christian rule, its rights being specifically confirmed, and the Jewish quarter surrounded by a wall. Notarial documents and Hebrew sources provide particularly detailed knowledge of the organization of the community with its textile industry, its guilds of weavers, dyers, goldsmiths, cutlers, tanners, and shoe-makers (maintaining sometimes their own synagogues and guild-halls), its network of charities, its internal controversies, etc. After the massacres of 1391, S. was one of the principal centers of the Marranos who organized the assassination of Pedro Arbues, the first inquisitor, in 1485.

SARAGOSSA, PURIM OF: Special feast with its own imitative MEGILLAH still celebrated on *Shevat* 17–18 by some oriental Jewish families in commemoration of a "miraculous" deliverance in

1380 or 1420. It probably originated at Syracuse (*Saragoza*) in Sicily.

SARAH (originally Sarai; Gen. 17:15): Wife of Abraham, mother of Isaac; one of the four matriarchs of the Jewish people. She was related to Abraham and married him before they left Haran. While accompanying Abraham to Egypt, and later in Philistia, her beauty attracted the local ruler, but she was restored to her husband when it became known she was wedded. After many years of barrenness, she gave Abraham her servant Hagar who bore him Ishmael. Subsequently — at the age of 90 — S. gave birth to Isaac. She died aged 127, and Abraham acquired the Cave of Machpelah for her burial.

SARAJEVO: Town in Yugoslavia. Epitaphs evidence Jewish settlement in 1551, and in 1581 the Jews were assigned a small suburb where a new synagogue was built. Equal rights were received as a result of the Turkish legislation of 1839, 1856, and 1876. Its intellectual center during the period of Turkish rule was at Salonica, while the rabbis of S. were subordinate to the authority of the *Ḥakham Bashi* at Constantinople. In 1941, the Jews of S. numbered 10,500, mainly Sephardim, most of whom were murdered by the Nazis. Jewish pop. (1973): 1,100.

SARAJEVO HAGGADAH: Illuminated codex of the Passover Eve service, executed in N Spain in the 13th cent., and now in the public library of Sarajevo (Yugoslavia). It follows the normal type of Spanish Haggadah ms in the arrangement and choice of the illustrations.

SARASOHN, KASRIEL HERSCH (1835–1905): Founder of the American Yiddish press. He was born in Poland and was a rabbi and merchant until he settled in the US in 1866. He pioneered in Yiddish journalism, founding the weekly *Die New Yorker Yiddishe Zeitung* (1872), which failed. He succeeded with *Die Yiddishe Gazetten* (1874), which later became the first Yiddish daily, *Die Tegliche Gazetten* (1881), and the *Yiddishes Tageblatt* (1885). S. also published a Hebrew weekly *Ha-Ivri*, 1891–8, and was a founder of HIAS.

SARATOV: Town in the USSR. It was the scene of a blood accusation in 1854 and the three accused were sentenced to hard labor. Two committed suicide and the third was released by the Czar in 1867. As a result of the S. affair, a Russian government commission was appointed to investigate the Blood Libel charge in general. S. was the scene of a pogrom in 1905.

SARDINIA: Mediterranean island. Jews were exiled to S. by the emperor Tiberius in 19 CE, and some inscriptions, etc. of the Roman Period are preserved. In 599, a convert led a riot against the synagogue at Cagliari. Later, in the Middle Ages, under Aragonese rule, there were communities at Cagliari, Alghero, Sassari, etc. Their position deteriorated as elsewhere in the Spanish dominions in the 15th cent., and S. was included in the general edict of expulsion from Spain in 1492. No community has since been formed there.

*SARGON: King of Assyria 721–712 BCE. He seized the throne on the death of SHALMANESER III during the siege of Samaria which he brought to a successful conclusion, exiling many of the inhabitants. In 720, he defeated a military alliance which included the remnants of the Israelites of Samaria. His reign was marked by a series of victories. On his assassination, he was succeeded by SENNACHERIB.

SARNOFF, DAVID (1891–1971): US industrialist. Born in Russia, he went to the US in 1900. He began his career as messenger boy and wireless operator (receiving the first message about the sinking of the *Titanic*) and pioneered in the radio industry. From 1921, he was successively general manager, executive vice-president, president and chairman of the board of the Radio Corporation of American (RCA) and from 1953 was president of the National Broadcasting Company. His son *ROBERT S.* (1918–) was president of RCA from 1965 to 1975.

SARUK, ISRAEL (fl. 16th cent.): Kabbalist. He journeyed through Italy, Poland, and Holland disseminating the teachings of Isaac LURIA. His doctrines differed, however, from those of Ḥayyim VITAL who succeeded Luria in Safed. S. was the author of many kabbalistic works.

SASA: Israel communal settlement (KA) in Upper Galilee. It was founded in 1949 on a strategic crossroad near the Lebanese frontier by settlers from

David Sarnoff.

the US 2,850 ft. above sea level, S. is the highest settlement in Israel. The place is mentioned in the Talmud.

SASKATCHEWAN: Canadian province. Its earliest Jewish settlers were farmers. In 1882, the Russo-Jewish Committee of London helped to settle the first Jewish families at Moosomin, and this farm settlement was followed by others at Wapella, Hirsch, Lipton, Sonnenfeld, and Edenbridge, the latter three aided greatly by the Jewish Colonization Association. Most of the immigrant generation remained farmers, but their children left the farm to take up residence in the cities. The Jewish pop. of S. (1969) is c. 2,700 with 1,200 in Regina, 780 in Saskatoon and smaller groups in Prince Albert (98), Melville (62), Moose Jaw (150), and Yorkton (48).

SASPORTAS, JACOB (1610–1698): Rabbi. Born in Oran, he was sent by the sultan of Morocco on an embassy to Spain, but incurred his enmity and settled in Holland. In 1664, he became first *Ḥakham* in London, but left the next year because of the Great Plague, living in Hamburg, Amsterdam, and Leghorn before being appointed *Ḥakham* in Amsterdam in 1681. He was the most unrelenting opponent of Shabbetai Tzevi and Sabbetaianism, and his bitter work *Tzitzat Novel Tzevi* is the primary authority for this period. S. also wrote learned responsa (*Ohel Yaakov*), etc.

SASSOON: Anglo-Indian family, founded by *DAVID BEN SASSON* (1792–1864), member of a distinguished Baghdad family. Settling in Bombay, he built up an enormous business with ramifications all over the Orient and was famous for his philanthropies. His son, *SIR ALBERT S.* (1818–1896), settled in England and, with his brothers *ARTHUR S.* (1840–1912) and *REUBEN S.* (1835–1905), became prominent in English society and among the court circle of Edward VII. Albert's son *SIR EDWARD S.* (1856–1912) was an English-Jewish communal leader and member of parliament. Edward's son *SIR PHILIP S.* (1888–1939), who took little interest in Jewish affairs, was an art-collector and under-secretary of state for air 1924–9 and 1931–7. *DAVID SOLOMON S.* (1882–1942), a grandson of the original David S. and son of the hostess and scholar *FLORA S.* (1859–1936), built up in London a collection of Hebrew mss, learnedly described in his catalogue *Ohel David* and other works: one of its treasures was the *Divan* of Samuel Ibn Nagrela, which he edited. From other sons of the original David S. are descended *SIEGFRIED S.* (1886–1967), poet and novelist (a half-Jew), and *SIR VICTOR S.* (1881–1961), industrialist and philanthropist.

SATAN: Usually identified with the devil, Lucifer, or the prince of DEMONS. This identification is late, and in the Bible, S. (perhaps lit. "he who hinders") is no demon or evil spirit, but belongs to the Divine household like other angelic beings (cf. Job 1:6), his function apparently being that of accuser. He developed into a hostile, destructive, and hence evil spirit, finally becoming the "tempter" (in I Chron. 21:1 he is credited with seducing David — an act ascribed to God Himself in the parallel passage in II Sam. 24:1). Negative or destructive characteristics or actions originally attributed to God were gradually transferred to independent, autonomous demonic beings, and to the extent that these are merely representatives of the principle of evil, S. is their chief or king. In opposition to the radical Persian DUALISM, all systems, that depend on the Bible consider S. and his associates to be in some measure subject to God's rule and sovereignty, although in some sectarian doctrines (including early Christianity) their power was great and the whole world was actually considered to be under the dominion of the devil. In the Kumran texts, S. is known as Belial. In rabbinic literature S. is identified with the tempter, accuser, and ANGEL OF DEATH. In some legends S. appears as the arch-enemy of Israel. In kabbalistic literature he is less prominent, as other names and designations are generally used for the demonic rulers and princes of evil.

SATANOV, ISAAC (1732–1805): Hebrew writer. A native of Podolia, he was attracted to Haskalah and in 1772, settled in Berlin where he studied secular subjects. Throughout his life, he fluctuated between traditional Judaism and Haskalah. He was noted chiefly for his fables (*Mishle Asaph*, etc.) written in a biblical style. S. was a pioneer in demanding innovations in the Hebrew language and opposed the negative attitude adopted by the *maskilim* to mishnaic Hebrew. Many of his books appeared anonymously with ascriptions to ancient authorities, and he was hence accused of literary falsification. His works include poems, linguistic, literary and scientific studies, an imitation of the Zohar, *Sepher ha-Ḥizzayon* (an encyclopedia of the arts and sciences modeled on the style of Al-Ḥarizi's *Taḥkemoni*), and commentaries on Maimonides' *Guide* and Judah Ha-Levi's *Kuzari*.

SATANOWER, MENDEL see **LEFIN**

SATIRE: S. is not absent from the Bible (examples are to be found in Isaiah and Hosea), and many short instances are to be found in the Talmud and Midrash. As a distinct literary genre, it became fashionable, like other Arabic modes of writing, in the Spanish Period. There are numerous works "Against Women" (also "In Defence of Women") and a long lampoon against the communal leaders of Saragossa by Solomon Bonfed, etc., as well as some excellent satirical poetry by Abraham Ibn Ezra. S. looms large in the *Taḥkemoni* of Judah Al-Ḥarizi and dominates the *Maḥbarot* of Immanuel of Rome. Among N European Jews, s. was mainly represented by compositions for Purim. In modern Hebrew literature, it is first represented by two brilliant writers of the Galician school: Joseph Perl with his *Megalleh Temirin*, a collection of letters alleged to have been written by Ḥasidim, and *Boḥen Tzaddik*; and Isaac Erter whose satirical essays were collected in *Ha-Tzopheh le-Vet Yisrael*. To the Galician school belonged also Mordecai D. Brandstätter. A considerable element of s. pervades the works of J. L. Gordon and Peretz Smolenskin; in Mendele Mocher Sephorim, s. is mingled with HUMOR. In Yiddish literature humor is predominant, s. being almost completely absent. In present-day Hebrew literature, s. is rare.

SAUDI ARABIA see **ARABIA**

SAUL (fl. 11th cent. BCE): First king of Israel; son of Kish of the tribe of Benjamin. Bowing to the populor clamor for a king in view of the military threat, particularly from the Philistines and Ammonites, the prophet SAMUEL selected S. who at once organized a trained army and inflicted defeats on the enemy. A spectacular victory at Michmash stemmed the Philistine danger, and punitive expeditions were undertaken against the Moabites, Ammonites, and Arameans. Internally, he carried out a purification of religion (e.g. the elimination of witchcraft). Nevertheless, friction with Samuel grew, and eventually, the prophet appointed DAVID as S.'s successor. David's growing popularity caused intense jealousy on the part of S. who bitterly persecuted David and drove him from the country. When the Philistines launched a united attack, S. was only able to fight

Hermann Tzevi Schapira.

defensively and fell with his three sons (including JONATHAN) in the battle on Mt. Gilboa; a surviving son, ISHBOSHETH was temporarily acknowledged as his successor over part of the country. Though S.'s death led to the temporary domination of the Philistines, the groundwork he laid for national unity eventually proved effective in establishing a strong and independent Israelite monarchy.

SAUL OF TARSUS see **PAUL**

SAVANNAH: City in GEORGIA, US. Jews dispatched by the Sephardi community of London were among the city's earliest settlers in 1733. The first white child born in S. belonged to the Minis family, which, with that of Sheftall, continued prominent through many generations. The original Sephardi community, Mickve Israel, now follows Reform, but Orthodox and Conservative communities are also supported by S.'s 2,900 Jews (1973).

SAVOY: Former duchy. French Jews lived there in the Middle Ages, at Chambéry, etc.; they suffered at the time of the Black Death, and Hebrew literature was burned there in 1426. Ultimately, as rulers of Piedmont, the dukes of S. became intimately associated with the destinies of Italian Jewish communities such as TURIN, etc.

SAXONY: Former German state; now in E Germany. Jews appeared at Meissen in the late 12th cent., LEIPZIG in the 13th., and at Bautzen and Zittau in the mid-14th cent. They suffered from the Black Death persecutions (1348–9) and expulsions in the 15th cent. Many Jews visited the Leipzig fair in the 17th–18th cents. but were forbidden to reside there until 1746. Only in 1837–8 did the government recognize the communities of Leipzig and DRESDEN and permit them to build synagogues. Civil rights were granted in 1848 but at the request of the Christian merchants, restricted in 1852 and only renewed in 1868 when S. joined the N German Federation. 20,584 Jews lived in S. in 1933; the settlement was destroyed by the Nazis. After World War II small congregations were reorganized in Dresden, Leipzig, Chemnitz (now Karl Marxstadt), and Plauen. In 1966 there were 613 Jews in lower S.

SAYINGS OF THE FATHERS see **AVOT**

SCAPEGOAT see **AZAZEL**

SCHALKOWITZ, ABRAHAM LEIB see **BEN AVIGDOR**

SCHANZER, CARLO (1865–1953): Italian statesman. After a legal background, he was minister of posts 1906–9, finance minister in 1919, and foreign minister in 1922. S. represented Italy at the League of Nations 1920–4. He was remote from Judaism.

SCHAPIRA, HERMANN TZEVI (1840–1898): Mathematician and Zionist leader. When already an ordained rabbi, he developed an interest in mathematics and became professor at Heidelberg (1887). At the First Zionist Congress (1897), he proposed the

Solomon Schechter.
(Painting by Leo Mielziner, 1910).

establishment of a Hebrew university and also the foundation of a JEWISH NATIONAL FUND to redeem the soil of Palestine. His suggestion that this fund should be based on the biblical principle of leasing the land and not selling it to individuals was adopted when the Jewish National Fund was established in 1901.

SCHAPIRO, ISRAEL (1882–1957): Librarian and author. Born in Russia, he went to the US in 1911, after teaching in Jerusalem. He was the first to head the Semitics division of the Library of Congress when it was created in 1913. He was professor of Semitics at George Washington Univ. 1916–27, and wrote numerous studies on Hebrew literature.

SCHARFSTEIN, ZVI (1884–1972): US educator. Born in Russia, he emigrated to the US in 1914. From 1915, he taught Jewish education and Hebrew literature at the Teachers' Institute of the Jewish Theological Seminary, New York. S. wrote Hebrew text-books and a history of Jewish education.

SCHATZ, BORIS (1866–1932): Artist. Born in Latvia, he studied with Antokolsky in Paris, and soon made a reputation with his statues and reliefs, many on Jewish topics. In 1895, he was appointed professor at the Academy of Visual Art at Sofia. S. went to Jerusalem in 1906 to found the BEZALEL School of Arts and Crafts, also laying the foundation for the Bezalel Museum. His ideas on art, especially Jewish art, had a profound influence in Palestine. His son *BEZALEL S.* (1912–), his daughter *ZAHARAH S.* (1916–), and his daughter-in-law *LOUISE S.* (c. 1913–) are all painters.

SCHECHTER, SOLOMON (1850–1915): Scholar and founder of CONSERVATIVE JUDAISM. Born in Rumania, he studied in Vienna and Berlin. C. G.

Montefiore invited him to England in 1882 to assist him in his studies. There, he rapidly acquired a remarkable mastery of English, became a notable figure in intellectual life, and was appointed lecturer in Talmud at Cambridge in 1890. His identification of a Hebrew fragment brought from Egypt as part of the lost Hebrew original of Ecclesiasticus resulted in his journey in 1896–7 to Cairo, whence he removed the remaining contents of the GENIZAH to Cambridge. His remarkably fruitful work on these materials enhanced his reputation. In 1901, he was appointed president of the Jewish Theological Seminary of America, New York. Under his direction, this became a scholastic institution of the first rank. He developed the Seminary and its associated organizations, such as the UNITED SYNAGOGUE OF AMERICA, as the institutions of Conservative Judaism, the philosophy of which he elaborated in a series of works and addresses. Besides his editing of important scholarly texts (*Aboth de R Nathan*; *Documents of Jewish Sectaries*; etc.) he published in English several works combining scholarship with popular appeal, such as his *Some Aspects of Rabbinic Theology* and especially his *Studies in Judaism* (3 vols.).

SCHEFTELOWITZ, ISIDOR (1875–1934): Orientalist. He was rabbi at Cologne 1909–26, and professor of Sanskrit and Iranian philology at Cologne Univ. 1920–33. S. wrote extensively on comparative religion.

SCHENECTADY: City in the State of New York, US. Jews settled there in the mid-19th cent. In 1856 an Orthodox congregation was formed. The Jewish Community Council, established in 1938, coordinates all community activities and sponsors the Federated Welfare Fund. The comprehensive and progressive program of Jewish education has become known as the "S. plan." In 1973, there were 4,500 Jews in S.

SCHERMAN, HARRY (1887–1969): US publisher. From 1931, he was president of the Book-of-the Month Club in the US. He wrote on economics and other topics.

SCHICK, BARUCH see **BARUCH OF SHKLOV**

SCHICK, BÉLA (1877–1967): Immunologist. Of Hungarian birth, he taught pediatrics at the University of Vienna. In 1913, he discovered the test, named for him, to determine susceptibility to diphtheria. He went to New York in 1923 and became clinical professor of diseases of children at Columbia Univ.

SCHIFF, DAVID TEVELE (d. 1791): Rabbi. Head of the Bet Din in Frankfort, he went to London in 1765 as rabbi of the Great Synagogue, being recognized throughout Great Britain, after some difficulties, as chief rabbi. His responsa *Leshon Zahav* were published posthumously.

SCHIFF, JACOB HENRY (1847–1920): Financier and philanthropist. Born in Germany, S. went to the US in 1865 and in 1885, became head of the

Jacob Schiff.

banking firm of Kuhn, Loeb, and Co. For many years, he was virtual lay head of American Jewry. Deeply hostile to Czarist Russia for maltreating its Jews, he consistently obstructed its attempts to obtain loans. A founder of the American Jewish Committee (1906), he was a leader in its successful effort in 1911 to abrogate the US–Russian commercial treaty because of Russian discrimination against Jewish holders of US passports. The range of his philanthropies, Jewish and non-sectarian, was immense (e.g. the Semitic Museum at Harvard, the Jewish Theological Seminary, the Montefiore Home in New York, etc.). Although a Reform Jew, he retained much of the piety and observance that he had learned in his early years and generously supported the religious, educational, and scholarly work of all branches of Judaism. While opposing Zionist nationalism and secularism, he felt that Palestine was needed as a refuge and as a spiritual and cultural center. He therefore supported educational institutions in Palestine and, before World War I, sided with the Hebraists in the dispute over the language of instruction in the Haifa Technion.

SCHIFF, MEIR (known as Maharam Schiff: 1605–1641): German talmudist. In 1622, he became rabbi of Fulda and whilst there, wrote notes on the Talmud distinguished by their brevity and depth.

SCHIFFER, EUGEN (1860–1954): German statesman and lawyer. He was minister of finance 1919, minister of justice 1919–20 and 1921, and head of the administration of justice in E Germany 1945–8. S. renounced Judaism.

SCHILDKRAUT, RUDOLPH (1872–1930): Actor. After starring in Vienna and Berlin, he appeared on the Yiddish stage in New York and thereafter, on Broadway and in films. His son *JOSEPH S.* (1896–

1964) was also a distinguished actor on stage and screen.

SCHILLER-SZINESSY, SOLOMON MAYER 1820–1890): Rabbi and Hebraist. Sentenced to death for participating in the Hungarian rising of 1848, he escaped to England where he was rabbi in Manchester. Subsequently, he became reader in rabbinics at Cambridge where he published scholarly monographs.

SCHINDLER, KURT (1882–1935): Choral conductor. Born in Germany, he settled in the US in 1905. He created the *Schola Cantorum* in New York. S. was associated with music publishing as critic and editor and wrote *The Folk Music and Poetry of Spain and Portugal*, etc.

SCHIPPER, IGNACY (1884–1943): Polich historian. He devoted himself to the history of Polish Jewry, particularly in the sphere of law and economics, and also to the study of the economic history of European Jewry. His works in Polish, Yiddish, and Hebrew include *The Economic Conditions of Medieval Polish Jewry*, *The History of Jewish Economy* (4 vols.), and *A History of Jewish Theatrical Art and Drama*. S. was one of the founders of *Poale Zion* and published numerous studies of Socialist-Zionist ideology. He also participated in Polish political life, being a deputy in the *Seym* 1919–27. From 1939, he lived in the Warsaw ghetto until transported to his death in Treblinka.

SCHLEGEL, DOROTHEA see **MENDELSSOHN, DOROTHEA**

SCHLETTSTADT, SAMUEL BEN AARON (fl. 14th cent.): Rabbi and scholar. An informer whom he condemned to death at Strasbourg saved himself by baptism and S. was forced to flee from the wrath of the burghers. He spent several years in a castle near Colmar, later wandering to Babylonia. Eventually he returned to Strasbourg but his fate is uncertain. He was author of an abridgment of *The Book of Mordecai* by Mordecai ben Hillel.

SCHLOSSBERG, JOSEPH (1875–1971): US labor leader. He was secretary-treasurer of the Amalgamated Clothing Workers' Union 1914–40; chairman of the National Committee for Labor Israel from 1934.

SCHMITZ, ETTORE (1861–1928): Italian novelist of Jewish descent writing under the name "Italo Svevo." His involved psychological novels, culminating in *La conscienza di Zeno* (1923), led critics to refer to him as "the Italian Proust" and influenced James Joyce.

SCHNABEL, ARTUR (1882–1951): Pianist and composer. Born in Austria, S. settled in the US in 1938. He had an international reputation as an interpreter of Beethoven, Mozart, and Schubert. His compositions were expressionistic.

SCHNEERSOHN, ISAAC (1882–1969): French Jewish public figure. Born in Kamenetz-Podolsk, he acted as crown rabbi in Gorodnya from 1906 and eventually settled in France. While living in concealment in 1943, he founded the CENTRE DE DOCUMENTATION JUIVE CONTEMPORAINE and later launched the project of the "tomb of the unknown Jewish martyr."

SCHNEIDERMAN: (1) *HARRY S.* (1885–1975): US editor and organization executive. He edited the *American Jewish Year Book* 1920–48 and was assistant secretary of the American Jewish Committee 1914–45. He was co-editor of *Who's Who in World Jewry*, 1955. (2) *ROSE S.* (1882–1972): US labor leader; sister of (1). She was president of the New York Women's Trade Union League 1918–49; was the only woman member of the Labor Advisory Board of the National Recovery Administration 1933–5; and was secretary of the New York State Department of Labor 1937–44.

SCHNITZER, EDUARD see **EMIN PASHA**

SCHNITZLER, ARTHUR (1862–1931): Austrian dramatist and novelist. He began by practicing medicine, became interested in psychotherapy, and ended as a literary psychologist. The influence of his early calling is reflected in his novels and dramas. His wisest comments are put into the mouths of physicians. Illness is a favorite theme with him and the consciousness of death constantly haunts his characters. His views on the place of the Jew in modern life can be gleaned from his autobiographical novel *Der Weg ins Freie* and from his play *Professor Bernhardi*.

SCHOCKEN: (1) *GUSTAV GERSHOM S.* (1912–): Israel publisher; son of (2). Of German birth, he settled in Israel in 1933 and since 1937, has published and edited HA-ARETZ. He also directs the Schocken Publishing House in Israel and represented the Progressive Party in the Knesset 1955–9. (2) *SHELOMOH SALMAN S.* (1877–1959): Publisher and philanthropist. Born in Germany, he pioneered in the establishment of chain stores. From 1927, he published Hebrew and German books, subsequently extending this activity to the US and Palestine. In 1930, he founded the INSTITUTE FOR THE STUDY OF HEBREW POETRY. S. settled in Palestine in 1933, later moving to the US.

SCHOFFMAN, GERSHON (1880–1972): Hebrew novelist. He edited literary journals in Poland and (chiefly) Austria before settling in Palestine in 1938. His chief work consists of short sketches and novels.

SCHOLEM, GERSHOM GERHARD (1897–): Scholar of mysticism. Born in Germany, he has lived in Jerusalem since 1923 and became professor of Jewish mysticism at the Hebrew Univ. in 1933. He is president of the Israel Academy of Arts and Sciences. His work is devoted to the study and interpretation of the Jewish esoteric tradition in all its forms and aspects; by his strict historical and philological methods he has inaugurated a new era in the study of KABBALAH and Jewish mysticism, placing it on a firm scientific basis. His main writings include *Major Trends in Jewish Mysticism* and *Shabbetai Tzevi*.

SCHONBERG see **BELMONT**

SCHÖNBERG, ARNOLD (1874–1951): Composer. Largely self-taught as a composer, he attracted the attention of Gustav Mahler who defended him against the opposition aroused by the innovations he introduced after his initial post-romantic works (*Verklärte Nacht*, String Quartet No. 1, etc.). S. held teaching posts in Vienna, Berlin, and Amsterdam and settled in Berlin in 1924. In 1933 he left Germany and went to live in the US. He returned to Judaism (which he had left). In addition to his symphonic and chamber works, he composed operas (including *Moses and Aaron*), the Psalms *De profundis* to the original Hebrew words, *Kol Nidre* for chorus, speaker, and orchestra, *A Survivor from Warsaw* for chorus, speaker and orchestra, etc. He expounded his theory of atonality in several books on musical theory.

SCHOOLS see **EDUCATION**

SCHOR, ILYA (1904–1961): US artist and silversmith. Born in Poland, he studied in Warsaw and Paris. S. settled in the US in 1941 and gained a reputation for his outstanding work on religious objects made of silver, and also for his book illustrations. His art depicts Jewish life in E Europe.

SCHORR, FRIEDRICH (1888–1953): Opera singer. Of Hungarian birth, he appeared in Europe and in 1922, went to the US. From 1924, he was a leading singer at the Metropolitan Opera, notably in Wagnerian roles.

SCHORR, JOSHUA HESHEL (1814–1895): Galician Hebrew publicist, satirist, and philologist. He established in 1852 the periodical *He-Ḥalutz* and published 13 issues until 1889. Although rich, he lived as a recluse in hunger and misery but left his precious library and a large legacy to the Vienna Rabbinical Seminary. In his numerous articles, he fought Orthodoxy by Bible criticism and by asserting inconsistency and foreign influences in the Talmud. In spite of his tendentiousness, much of his work has real value, e.g. his study of Zoroastrian influences on Judaism and his editions of medieval authors.

SCHORR, MOSES (1874–1942): Rabbi and scholar. He was born in Galicia and taught at LVOV until taking up (1923) a rabbinical appointment in Warsaw where he helped to found the Institute of Jewish Studies. He was professor of Semitic languages at Warsaw Univ. and a member of the Polish senate in 1936–9. Before 1910, he wrote a number of important works on Polish Jewish history, tracing in particular the development of the communal organization. Thereafter, he concentrated on Semitic history and philology, especially the history of Babylonian and Assyrian culture. He died in a Soviet prison.

SCHRAMECK, ABRAHAM (1867–1948): French statesman. At the outbreak of World War I, he was governor-general of Madagascar, and from 1920 to 1940, sat in the senate as a leader of the democratic (radical) left. S. was several times minister of the interior (notably under Painlevé) and also minister of justice.

SCHREIBER, ABRAHAM SAMUEL BENJAMIN (1815–1875): Hungarian rabbi; son of R Moses SOPHER and his successor as head of the Pressburg yeshivah. He was a leader in the fight against religious reform. S. became widely known as *Ketav Sopher* after his collection of responsa, Bible commentaries, and talmudic glosses of that name.

SCHREINER, MARTIN (1863–1927): Rabbi and historian of Judeo-Arabic religion and literature. He taught in his native Hungary and from 1894 in Berlin but from 1902 suffered from mental disease. He wrote on Moses Ibn Ezra, the history of the Kalam in Jewish literature, etc.

SCHULBERG, BUDD (1914–): US novelist. His works include *What Makes Sammy Run?* and *The Disenchanted*, based on the life of Scott Fitzgerald.

SCHULMAN, KALMAN (1819–1899): Hebrew author. He was born in White Russia and from 1843 lived in Vilna. S. helped to foster education among Hebrew readers by his many popular editions and translations into a pure and flowery Hebrew. His translation of Sue's *Secrets of Paris* was particularly influential as one of the first novels to appear in Hebrew. He published a universal history, a world geography, a history of Jewish scholarship, a translation of Josephus, etc.

SCHULMAN, SAMUEL (1864–1955): US rabbi. He served in the pulpit of Temple Beth El, New York, from 1899 and continued as rabbi after the amalgamation of that congregation with Temple Emanuel. He was a leader in the US Jewish Reform movement.

SCHULMANN, ELEAZAR (1837–1904): Hebrew author; lived in Odessa and Kiev. He wrote stories and studies, the latter including the lives of Heine and Börne and a work on Yiddish and its literature. His tales satirize life in the Pale of Settlement.

SCHUMAN, WILLIAM HOWARD (1910–): US composer. In 1945–61 he was president of the Juilliard School of Music, New York. Since 1961, he has been president of the Lincoln Center for the Performing Arts in New York. His compositions include symphonies, chamber works, the ballet *Judith*, and stage and film music.

*SCHÜRER, EMIL (1844–1910): German Protestant theologian and historian. His history of the Jewish people from the Hellenistic Period to 135 CE (3 vols., also in English translation), though written from the Christian point of view and with little reference to talmudic literature, remains a standard work.

SCHUSTER: English family, deriving from Frankfort. They included the brothers (1) *SIR ARTHUR S.* (1851–1934), astronomer and physicist, who headed four solar eclipse expeditions and was professor of applied mathematics, and later of physics, at Manchester. (2) *SIR FELIX S.* (1854–1936), banker, finance member of the Council of India and chairman of the National Provincial Bank; and (3) *ERNEST S.* (1850–1925), an authority on international law, economics, and political science and author of several works on these subjects. None of the brothers, whose children have continued to play an outstanding part in English life, was associated with the Jewish community.

SCHUSTER, MAX LINCOLN (1897–1970): US publisher. He was co-founder of the publishing firm of Simon and Schuster, and edited literary anthologies.

SCHUTZJUDE (Ger. "protected Jew"): Term used in 17–18th cent. Germany to designate Jews who were tolerated and given special privileges for residence, travel, etc. because of their peculiar utility to various rulers. They were inferior in status to the *Hofjude* (COURT JEWS).

SCHWAB, MOISE (1839–1918): French scholar. He worked in the Bibliothèque Nationale, Paris, from 1868. S. translated the Palestinian Talmud into French (11 vols., 1871–90), wrote on Jewish history and Hebrew incunabula, and edited collections of Hebrew inscriptions in France and Spain.

SCHWABE, MOSHEH DAVID (1889–1956): Classical scholar; of German birth. He was principal of a Hebrew High School at Kovno before settling in Palestine in 1925. S. taught classical studies at the Hebrew Univ. (of which he was rector 1950–2) and was a leading authority on Greek and Greco-Jewish inscriptions.

SCHWARTZ, JOSEPH J. (1899–1975): US communal leader. Born in Russia, he went to the US in 1907. S., who graduated as a rabbi, went in for a career of public service. From 1939 he was associated with the American Joint Distribution Committee and during and after World War II played an important role in rescue activities on behalf of European Jewry. He was executive vice-chairman of the UJA 1951–5 and from 1955–70 vice-president of the Israel Bond Organization.

SCHWARTZ, MAURICE (1888–1960): US actor. As producer, director, and actor he was one of the leading figures of the American Yiddish stage. In 1918, he founded the Yiddish Art Theater in New York and produced more than 150 plays by noted Jewish authors, as well as international classics in Yiddish translations.

SCHWARTZ, RUDOLF (1902–): Conductor. Of Viennese birth, he became conductor of the Düsseldorf Opera in 1920. From 1936 to 1941, he directed the Jüdischer Kulturbund's musical activities in Berlin and then he was imprisoned by the Nazis. He later settled in England where, after conducting

Joseph Schwarz.

at Bournemouth and Birmingham, he was conductor of the BBC orchestra (1957–62).

SCHWARZ, ADOLF (1846–1931): Talmudic scholar.

He was born in Hungary, officiated as rabbi at Karlsruhe 1875–93, and then directed the Israelitisch Theologische Lehranstalt in Vienna. His studies dealt largely with talmudic hermeneutics.

SCHWARZ, DAVID (1845–1897): Austrian inventor.

In 1890, he devised and in 1892, constructed the first rigid dirigible airship. His designs were subsequently utilized by Zeppelin.

SCHWARZ, JEHOSEPH (1804–1865): Rabbi and Palestinographer. Of Bavarian birth, he settled in Jerusalem in 1833. His works include maps of Palestine and *Tevuot ha-Aretz* (English edition by Isaac Leeser, *A Descriptive Geography of Palestine*, 1850) devoted to the biblical and talmudic topography of the country.

SCHWARZBARD, SHALOM (1886–1938): Russian soldier and poet. In 1919, he organized an international battalion (composed chiefly of Jews) to fight PETLURA'S forces. In 1926, he shot Petlura in Paris in revenge for his pogroms against the Jews of Ukraine. After a sensational trial he was acquitted. S. wrote lyrical poetry, memoirs, and moving accounts of the Russian Revolution.

SCHWARZ-BART, ANDRÉ (1928–): French author.

His parents were gassed in World War II and he fought in the French underground. A great impression was made by his book *The Last of the Just*, based on the theme of the Jewish martyrdom. Together with his W. Indian wife, he embarked on a 7–volume history of the W. Indies.

SCHWARZBART, ISAAC IGNACY (1888–1961): Communal leader. He was elected to the *Seym* in 1938, and was a member of the Polish National Council 1940–5, later settling in the US. Until 1960,

he headed the organization department of the World Jewish Congress which he helped to found. S. was the founder of the World Union of General Zionists (1931).

SCHWARZSCHILD, KARL (1873–1916): German astronomer and mathematician. From 1901, he taught at Göttingen directing the observatory there and at Potsdam (1909). S. left Judaism.

SCHWINGER, JULIAN (1918–): US physicist.

Professor at Harvard Univ., he was a co-recipient of the 1965 Nobel physics prize for his work on transforming the "exchange play" between elementary particles to mathematical facts.

SCHWOB, MARCEL (1867–1905): French author.

He was both a literary historian, specializing in the period of Villon, and an accomplished author whose works were influential at the beginning of the 20th cent. (*Mimes* [poetry], *Vies imaginaires*, *La Lampe de Psyché*).

SCIENCE OF JUDAISM see **WISSENSCHAFT, JÜDISCHE**

SCOPUS, MT. see **MOUNT OF OLIVES**

SCOTLAND: There is barely any evidence of Jews in medieval S., but Jewish merchants are encountered in EDINBURGH and GLASGOW in the 17th cent. In the 18th, some Jews studied medicine at Scottish universities. There are indications of a Jewish community in Edinburgh in 1780, but it was properly organized only in 1816, one following in Glasgow in 1823. The Russian Jewish immigration resulted in the growth of the latter, which with 13,400 Jews is the fourth in size in Great Britain. Edinburgh on the other hand has only 1,400. There are small communities also in Aberdeen, Ayr, and Dundee. Jewish pop. (1971): 15,000.

*SCOTT, CHARLES PRESTWICH (1846–1932): English journalist. Editor of the influential liberal *Manchester Guardian*, he was greatly impressed with the personality of Chaim Weizmann and unswervingly supported the implementation of the Zionist ideal in the Balfour Declaration.

SCOUT MOVEMENT: International youth organization. Jewish youth movements accepted the organization forms current in their various countries. Thus, in Germany and Central Europe, they were free youth-movements and in the English-speaking countries, they tended to take the form of English scouts. The Israel scout organization (*Ha-Tzophim*) fused both types: it is based on the Baden-Powell scouting program with the additional values of self-management (its instructors graduate from the s.m.) and of pioneering labor (*halutziut*); its graduates have founded several *kibbutzim*. It has groups in both the Jewish and Arab areas of Israel, all organized in the Israel Boy and Girl Scout Federation with 20,130 members in 1968. Jewish scouts exist in almost every democratic country, but independent Jewish

The Kibbutz En Gev and Mount Susita, on the eastern shore of the Sea of Galilee.

scout organizations in only a few (France [Éclaireurs Israélites], Switzerland, Italy, and Mexico). In the US, a Jewish Committee for Scouting fosters Jewish traditional values among Jewish scouts. In England, a voluntary committee of Jewish scout-leaders is organized in a Council of Jewish Scouters.

SCRANTON: City in Pennsylvania, US. Jewish immigrants from Germany settled there in the mid-19th cent., and a Reform congregation was organized in 1860. In the 1880's immigrants from E Europe together with a small number of Turkish Sephardim settled in S. In 1943, over 95% of the community were of E European origin. The Jews of S. are chiefly merchants, professional workers, and owners of small industries. The S. Lackawanna Jewish Council, was founded in 1936. In 1973, there were 5,010 Jews with 5 synagogues.

SCRIBE (Heb. *sopher*): In the Judean monarchy the "s. of the king" is the highest official in the land. Ezra is described as "s. of the law of the God of Heaven," possibly equivalent to secretary for Jewish affairs in the Persian administration, and is always called "Ezra the S." In his time or soon after, the word changed its meaning. Ben Sira (38:24, 39:1–11) depicts the s. as the literate man, occupied in particular with the study of the Jewish law. In the New Testament the "scribes" occur in company with the "Pharisees." For the Mishnah "Words of the Scribes" are ancient post-biblical regulations, but the rabbis are never called "scribes," a term then reserved, as now, for those who wrote Scrolls of the Law, etc., and also preserved the tradition of the correct text. The tractate *Sopherim*, an addition to the Babylonian Talmud, describes the rules for writing sacred documents. The "scribes" introduced 18 emendations into the Pentateuch text, mostly to avoid gross anthropomorphisms.

SCRIPTURES see **BIBLE**

SCROLL OF THE LAW see **LAW, SCROLL OF**

SCROLLS, FIVE: Comprehensive name for five works of the biblical Hagiographa read on special occasions; the *SONG OF SONGS* on Passover (by Sephardim on Friday afternoons and *Seder* nights), *RUTH* on the Feast of Weeks, *LAMENTATIONS* on *Av* 9, *ECCLESIASTES* on Tabernacles (not by Sephardim), and *ESTHER* on Purim.

SCULPTURE see **ART**

SEA OF GALILEE (Lake Kinneret): The second of the lakes formed by the Jordan river. It is 14 m. long and 8 m. wide and is situated 680 ft. below sea level, its maximum depth being 156 ft. The lake is traversed by the Jordan from N to S. In the Bible it is called the Sea of Chinnereth after a city on its NW shore; it marks the E boundary of the Promised Land (Num. 34:11; Josh. 13:27). In the Maccabean Period, the name of Chinnereth was changed to Ginosar and the name of the lake is altered accordingly; hence the form Lake of Gennesaret found in the New

Testament (Luke 5:1). The name source contains also the appellations "Sea of Galilee" (Mat. 4:18, etc.) and "Sea of Tiberias" (John 21:1, also in Josephus and the Talmud). The lake was an important center of the fishing and salting industry during and after the Second Temple Period. In Christian eyes it is hallowed by the activities of Jesus and the apostles, many of whom were from the villages bordering the sea, such as Capernaum (Kephar Nahum). In modern times, the shores of the sea were gradually occupied by Jewish colonies, beginning with Deganyah in 1909. Under the arrangement made between Mandatory Palestine and Syria the whole lake as well as its shores (narrowing to a strip 32 ft. wide along its NE shore) belonged to Palestine; this passed to Israel under the 1949 Armistice Agreement. These sovereign rights — disputed, sometimes violently, by the Syrians — led to frequent friction until the Six-Day War when Israel forces captured the commanding eastern heights. The Israel National Water Carrier derives its waters from the Sea conveying it as far as the Negev for purposes of irrigation.

SEA OF SAMKHO see **ḤULEH**

SEALS: The act of sealing is mentioned frequently in the Bible, and more than one hundred actual s. of the period of the Monarchy, bearing the owner's name in the old Hebrew characters, sometimes together with decorative features, have been discovered: a few of them belonged to women. S. were used not only for documents, but also to secure and attest the contents of jars, etc. A number of Jewish s. and impressions of the Classical Period, many of them bearing representations of the *menorah*, etc. are known: subsequently they were generally incorporated in signet rings. In the Middle Ages, these often bore the personal emblem (e.g. a lion) and initials of the owner. To seal with a representation of the human head was, however, disapproved of, as this act created a new impression of the human likeness. Many Jewish communities also had their s. The official emblem of the state of Israel consists of a *menorah* flanked with olive branches.

Seal of Shema (8th cent. BCE) found at Megiddo.
(Formerly in the Archeological Museum, Constantinople).

SEATTLE: City in the state of Washington, US. Individual Jews first settled there in 1858 but the congregation Ahabath Shalom was organized only in 1887. A number of Sephardi Jews from the Near East settled in S. early in the 20th cent. and more arrived after World War I, creating the third largest Sephardi community in the country. The community's Federated Jewish Fund and Council was established in 1937. The bi-monthly *Transcript* serving Washington's Jews has been published in S. since 1942. In 1973, S. had 13,000 Jews with 7 synagogues.

SEBASTE see **SAMARIA**

SECOND TEMPLE see **TEMPLE**

SECTS see **CONTROVERSIES, RELIGIOUS**

SEDEH BOKER: Israel kibbutz in the Negev, 25 m S of Beersheba. Its economy is based on agriculture and quarrying. It was founded in 1952 and at the end of 1953 David Ben-Gurion became a member.

SEDER (Heb. "order"): Ceremony observed in the Jewish home on the first night (outside Israel, first two nights) of Passover when the HAGGADAH is recited. The structure of the ritual is based on the Mishnah (*Pesaḥim* 10) and to some extent resembles the feasts customary in Palestine during the Hellenistic and Roman Periods, although here regularized according to rabbinic injunction. All the requirements of the ceremony are traditionally kept in a receptacle containing three pieces of unleavened bread, together with an egg and a shankbone commemorating the Temple sacrifice.

SEDER ELIYAHU see **TANNA DEVE ELIYAHU**

SEDER OLAM (RABBAH): The earliest postbiblical Hebrew chronicle. It comprises a brief chronological record, demonstrated from the Bible, from the Creation to Alexander the Great, with a fragmentary appendix extending to Bar Kokhba. It is mentioned repeatedly in the Talmud, etc. The name *S.O. Rabbah* (= Greater *S.O.*) is applied to distinguish it from the SEDER OLAM ZUTA (= "smaller *S.O.*"). The traditional Jewish chronology is largely based on the *S.O.R.*

SEDER OLAM ZUTA: Chronological work listing the names and dates of the 50 generations from Adam to Jehoiakim and 39 exilarchs in Babylonia descended from Jehoiakim through Zerubbabel. Its main object is to prove that the exilarchs up to (but excluding) Bostanai were of the Davidic dynasty. It probably dates from the 8th cent. The last portion is historically valuable. (See SEDER OLAM RABBAH.)

SEDEROT see **SHEDEROT**

SEDOM see **SODOM**

SEDOT YAM: Israel communal settlement (KM) near CAESAREA. Founded in 1940, by Youth Aliyah graduates and young Palestinians, its settlers fish in the Mediterranean. The cultural center has been named after Hannah SZENES who was a member of the settlement; there is also a collection of antiquities

Sedeh Boker.

from Caesarea. The government fishery research station is located at S. Y. Pop. (1972): 555.

SEE: French family (also known as ZAY) living at Metz from the 16th cent. Leading members have included *CAMILLE S.* (1827–1919), lawyer, secretary of the Ministry of the Interior in the 1870 government, and deputy 1876–81; *EDMOND S.* (1875–), dramatist and theater critic; *GERMAIN S.* (1818–1896), physician and professor of pathology in Paris; *HENRI S.* (1864–1936), historian, especially of the French rural classes; and *LEOPOLD S.* (1822–1904), soldier, who eventually reached the rank of general.

SEERS see **PROPHETS**

SEGAL, MOSHEH TZEVI HIRSCH (1878–1968): Biblical scholar. Of Lithuanian birth, he was minister in Oxford and elsewhere in England until 1926 when he settled in Palestine, becoming professor of Bible at the Hebrew Univ. He wrote Bible commentaries, a grammar of mishnaic Hebrew, etc. and the standard Hebrew edition of Ecclesiasticus.

SEGALL, LASAR (1891–1957): Painter. Born in Vilna, he settled in Berlin and from 1913, his work became increasingly somber under the influence of the Jewish position in E Europe. He helped to found the Dresden *Secession* group which was prominent in experimentation after World War I. In 1923, he moved to Brazil where his work became more cheerful and included colorful landscapes and lyrical portraits.

SEGOL: The short *e* vowel, written (⸱⸱). In Yemenite pronunciation and the Babylonian pointing it is not distinguished from PATTAḤ.

SEGOVIA: Town in Castile with a Jewish community dating back to the Moorish Period, of considerable importance down to the close of the 14th cent. The massacre of 1391 drove many of its Jews into baptism, and thereafter, the city was a main center of Marranos, many of whom were killed there in 1474. In 1410, a charge of desecrating the Host resulted in the execution of the physician, Meir ALGUADES, and the confiscation of the principal synagogue which was turned into the Church of Corpus Christi, still extant. On the expulsion in 1492, the Jews are said to have taken refuge in caves in the surrounding hills.

SEGRÈ: Italian family which provided rabbis for many Piedmontese communities from the 17th cent. Its members included (1) *CORRADO S.* (1863–1924): Mathematician; professor of higher geometry at Turin from 1888. He was responsible for many engineering discoveries and developments. (2) *DINO S.* (Pitigrilli; 1893–1954): Author. A gifted and daring writer, he became a Fascist informer and apostatized. (3) *EMILIO S.* (1905–): Physicist. A pioneer in atomic research, he taught at Palermo 1936–8, and then at Berkeley Univ., being among those responsible for the first atomic explosion at Los Alamos. He was awarded the 1959 Nobel Prize for physics (jointly) for discovery of the antiproton. (4) *GINO S.* (1864–1942): Jurist. He taught at Turin Univ. 1916–39, was a member of the commission for the reform of the legal code, and wrote on problems of common ownership, etc. (5) *JOSHUA BEN-ZION S.* (1720–1809): Rabbi, landowner, and municipal councillor at Vercelli, was first vice-president (*av bet din*) of the

Gershom Mendez Seixas.

Napoleonic Sanhedrin of 1807. (6) *ROBERTO S.* (1872–1936): Soldier. He was in effective command of the Italian artillery in the chief actions of World War I.

SEIBER, MATYAS (1905–1960): Composer. Born in Hungary, he went to England in 1935 and became lecturer at Morley College, London. He wrote orchestral and chamber works, film music, and a cantata based on Joyce's *Ulysses*.

SEIR: Term for the mountainous country of EDOM (Gen. 33:14; Num. 24:18). The descendants of Esau — the Edomites — replaced the Horites as inhabitants of the region.

SEIXAS: US Sephardi family founded by *ISAAC MENDES S.* (1708–1780), who emigrated to America from Portugal in 1730. His son *GERSHOM MENDEZ S.* (1745–1816) was minister of Congregation Shearith Israel in New York for some 50 years. When the British occupied New York City in 1776, he took the scrolls and other religious objects from the synagogue and went to Stratford, Conn. and thence to Philadelphia where he helped found the first Jewish congregation (1780). After the British left New York, he returned to his duties there. He was one of thirteen clergymen to participate in George Washington's first inauguration. S. was a trustee of Columbia College 1787–1815. Of his sons, *DAVID G. S.* (c. 1788 – c. 1880) achieved prominence as an educator of the deaf and introduced the daguerrotype into America, while *BENJAMIN MENDEZ S.* (1747–1817) was a founder of the New York stock exchange.

SEJERA see **ILANIYYAH**

SELAH: Term found frequently in the Book of Psalms (both in the middle of psalms and at their conclusion) and in other psalms. The Septuagint translates it as *diapsalma* which may mean "change of melody" but already in the time of Aquila it was taken as a blessing meaning "forever" and this remained the traditional interpretation.

*SELDEN, JOHN (1584–1654): English jurist and Hebraist. His books (in Latin) include several on Jewish topics; these include an attempt to relate natural and international law back to the seven Noachian commandments. He also wrote a short historical treatise on the Jews of England.

SELDES: (1) *GEORGE S.* (1890–): US journalist. He wrote a life of Mussolini and books exposing suppressions by the press. (2) *GILBERT S.* (1893–1970): US critic; brother of (1). He wrote *The Seven Lively Arts.*

SELEUCIA: Ancient city on the Tigris; the main center of HELLENISM E of the Euphrates. It contained a large Jewish community which was temporarily swollen after the destruction of the principality of ANILAI AND ASINAI. This resulted in a wholesale massacre in 40 CE, but, nevertheless, Jews continued to reside there.

SELEUCIDS: Hellenistic royal dynasty founded by Seleucus Nicator, one of Alexander the Great's generals. Scholars doubt Josephus' information that Seleucus granted civic rights to Jewish settlers in the Ionian cities of Asia Minor, but it is certain that ANTIOCHUS III settled Babylonian Jews in the cities of Phrygia and Lydia, entrusting them with an important role in securing those regions of his empire. Antiochus III conquered Palestine c. 200 BCE and granted privileges to the Temple. In the time of Seleucus IV, relations between the Jews and the S. deteriorated as the Seleucid kingdom was compelled to resort to all possible financial extortions to meet its depressed monetary situation. The religious and cultural policy of ANTIOCHUS IV (Epiphanes) led to the HASMONEAN revolt as a result of which the Jews freed themselves from the S. Antiochus VII Sidetes invaded the country in the time of Simon the Hasmonean (138 BCE) and again with greater success in 134. On Antiochus' death in 129 the Jews revolted, and S. rule in Palestine ended in 128.

SELIGMAN, ARTHUR (1873–1933): US public official. He was mayor of Santa Fe, New Mexico, for six years and governor of that state 1930–3.

SELIGMAN, CHARLES GABRIEL (1873–1940): British anthropologist and ethnologist. He conducted expeditions to New Guinea, Sudan, and Ceylon. He was professor of Ethnology at London Univ. and president of the Royal Anthropological Institute 1923–5. He wrote studies of various races and works on Chinese and Japanese culture.

SELIGMAN, EDWIN ROBERT ANDERSON (1861–1939): US economist. Faculty member at Columbia Univ. from 1885, he was economic adviser to the US Congress and some foreign governments, specializing in problems of taxation. S. wrote a number of works on economics, and edited the *Encyclopedia of the Social Sciences*.

SELIGMANN, CAESAR (1860–1951): German Reform leader. He preached in Hamburg (1889) and Frankfort-on-Main (1902). S. was one of the founders of the Society for Liberal Judaism in Germany and joint-editor of Reform liturgy which was widely accepted in Germany. From 1938, he lived in London.

SELIHOT (Heb. "penitential prayers"): A special type of PIYYUT requesting forgiveness for sin and mercy. The THIRTEEN ATTRIBUTES, prefaced by standard liturgical introductions, form the foundation of the *s.* prayers. In early times, these, together with appropriate verses from Scripture, were all that preceded the CONFESSION. The entire order of the *s.* was brought into the framework of the Eighteen Benedictions which became the place also for reciting *piyyutim* written later in this connection. In Palestine, the early *paytanim* connected the *s.* with the KEROVAH, and this connection has remained in certain rituals for fast days. Fast days (including the Day of Atonement) were especially dedicated to supplication and prayer, and *s.* were written for such occasions. Only during the Middle Ages did *s.* become particularly associated with the penitential period leading up to *Rosh ha-Shanah* and the Day of Atonement. These *s.* constituted a special service of their own recited at or before dawn and without any connection with the regular service. The content of most *s.* is similar. The desperate plight of the Jews during the Middle Ages is looked upon as punishment for transgression, and they call for repentance in the hope that God will have mercy upon His people. The Sephardim begin their *s.* from *Elul* 1; the Ashkenazim from the beginning of the week preceding *Rosh ha-Shanah* (if this falls on a Monday or Tuesday in the previous week). Many *s.* rituals according to the various rites have been published. The corresponding service is termed *Tahnunim* ("supplications") in the Italian rite, *Ashmorot* ("watches") in the Avignonese, etc.

SELZNICK, DAVID OLIVER (1902–1965): US film producer. He was associated with various Hollywood firms and produced films which won international awards.

SEMAG see **MOSES BEN JACOB OF COUCY**
SEMAHOT see **EVEL RABBATI**
SEMAK see **ISAAC BEN JOSEPH OF CORBEIL**
SEMIKHAH see **ORDINATION**
SEMINAIRE ISRAÉLITE (formerly *École Rabbinique*) **DE FRANCE**: Rabbinical college founded at Metz in 1829 and transferred to Paris in 1859. It graduates rabbis after a 5-year course.
SEMITES see **SHEM**
SEMITIC LANGUAGES: The language family comprising the following tongues (with approximate dates of written documentation):

E Semitic = Akkadian Branch
Old Akkadian (2500–1950 BCE): Babylonian (—200 BCE); Assyrian (—600 BCE).

N W Semitic
Amorite (Syria-Mesopotamia, 18th-17th cents.) known only through personal names; Ugaritic (NW Syria, 14th cent. BCE), discovered 1929.

Canaanite Branch
Hebrew; Phoenician (18th–3rd cents.) and Punic (Carthage — 4th cent. CE); Moabite (one inscription 9th cent. BCE).

Aramaic Branch
Various old Aramaic dialects (9th–6th cents.); Imperial Aramaic (Persian Empire, 6th–4th cents., known mainly from Egypt); Biblical Aramaic; Nabatean (Transjordan and Negev, 1st cent. BCE — 3rd cent. CE); Palmyrenian (E Syria, 1st–3rd cent. CE); Palestinian Jewish Aramaic (Targums and Palestinian Talmud); Samaritan; Christian Palestinian Aramaic (died out before 1000 CE); Syriac (2nd–13th cent.); Jewish Babylonian (talmudic) Aramaic; Mandean (S Iraq); Modern Syriac; Modern Aramaic of Malula (Lebanon).

South Semitic
Various proto-Arabic dialects (6th cent. BCE — 5th cent. CE); Arabic (since 5th cent. CE), with many modern dialects. Ancient S Arabian languages (4th cent CE). Minean, Sabean, Katabanian, etc. Modern S Arabian languages: Mehri, Shkauri, Botohari in Hadharamaut; Sokotri on the Isle of Sokotra. Ancient Ethiopic (since 3rd cent. CE); Amharic (since 15th cent. CE); Tigre, Tigrinya, Harari, Gafat, Gurage, Argobba (all in Abyssinia).

The connection between Hebrew, Aramaic, and Arabic was demonstrated by Judah Ibn Kuraish (10th cent.): the relationships were systematically described first by W. Wright in 1890, most completely by C. Brockelmann in 1908–13. The name "Semitic" for the family is based on Gen. 10 and was suggested by A. L. Schlözer in 1781. The Semitic family forms a branch of the Hamito-Semitic family, to which belong also Ancient Egyptian, Somali, the Cushitic languages of E Africa, and the Berber dialects of N Africa. Relationship with the Indo-European language family has been frequently suggested, but is not proved. The connection of the S. L. among themselves is demonstrated by the following table:

HEBREW	Aramaic	Akkadian	Arabic	Ethiopic
ehad (one)	*had*	*êdu*	*ahadu*	*ahadu*
shalosh (three)	*tlât*	*shelâshu*	*thalâthu*	*shalâsh*
ab (*av*) (father)	*ab, abba*	*abu*	*abu*	*ab*
em (mother)	*em, imma*	*ummu*	*ummu*	*emm*
ah (brother)	*ah*	*akhu*	*akhu*	*ekhw*
ahot (sister)	*hât*	*akhâtu*	*ukhtu*	*akhât, ekht*

Comparison with words known from other S. L. has often helped to define the meanings of biblical words, just as comparison with the grammar and syntax of other S. L. affords a better understanding of Hebrew grammar, and has assisted the discovery of the development of Hebrew forms, since the underlying assumption is that all S. L. have arisen in course of time from a common proto-Semitic language, the forms of which can be reconstructed at least hypothetically. The question as to where this proto-Semitic language was spoken is unsolved. Though evidently the language must have been transmitted by continuous groups or peoples, these were in the course of history mixed with many elements. There is no such thing as a Semitic race; but there are certain cultural traits common to all or several S. peoples, which may partly be due to common inheritance, partly to constant contacts. Today — apart from remnants of Aramaic and S Arabian — the S. L. are represented by Arabic, Hebrew, and the Abyssinian languages, in all spoken by c. 57 million people.

SENIOR, ABRAHAM (c. 1422 — c. 1500): Spanish financier; principal tax-farmer in Castile (with Isaac Abravanel) at the time of the siege of Granada. Living at Segovia, he was active in Spanish Jewish life and was appointed court rabbi. Previously, he had helped to arrange the marriage of Ferdinand and Isabella. To avoid expulsion in 1492, he was baptized and assumed the name of Fernando Perez Coronel.

*SENNACHERIB: King of Assyria 705–681 BCE; son of Sargon II. Until 689, he was engaged in constant wars with Elam and Babylon. When the kings of Phoenicia and Palestine led by Hezekiah rose in revolt, S. invaded Judah (701), captured 46 cities (but not Jerusalem), and many prisoners. A plague that broke out in his camp compelled his retreat. According to one view, S. led two campaigns against Judah; the first resulted in Hezekiah's surrender, while the second, when the latter withheld his tribute, was cut short by the plague.

SEPHARAD, SEPHARDIM: Sepharad was an Asiatic region, probably N of Palestine, to which exiles from Jerusalem were deported on the destruction of the First Temple (Obad. 1:20). In the Middle Ages, the term was applied to Spain, while the name Sephardi was given to the Jews of Spain, and thereafter to their descendants, wherever resident. The term was used particularly for the Jews expelled from Spain in 1492; these settled all along the N African coast (especially in Morocco) in smaller numbers in Italy, Egypt, Palestine, and Syria and above all in the Balkans and the central provinces of the Turkish Empire where considerable communities were established in places such as Salonica and Constantinople. In the course of time, they assimilated to themselves the other elements — either earlier residents or immigrants from other lands — who adopted their language, customs and practices,

and henceforth became part of the Sephardi group. After 1497, they were reinforced by refugees from Portugal. Later, Marranos established fresh Sephardi communities in Amsterdam, London, Hamburg, Bordeaux, Bayonne, and elsewhere in W Europe, as well as in the W Indies and on the mainland of N America. This wider nexus of Sephardi communities was not so important numerically but of great economic and political significance. The differentiation between Sephardim and ASHKENAZIM became very marked from the 16th cent. onward. Basically, the difference was one of synagogal rite and tradition, that of the Sephardim going back ultimately to Babylonian Jewry, and that of the Ashkenazim to Palestine. It was reflected also in the pronunciation of Hebrew, social habits, literary fashions, costume, etc. The Sephardim of the Mediterranean countries spoke Judeo-Spanish, or LADINO, in which a considerable literature grew up. The great cultural center of Sephardi life down to modern times was Salonica, which was however annihilated by the Nazis in 1943. Of late, there is a tendency to consider as Sephardim all members of the oriental communities (many of which have adopted the Sephardi ritual) or even all non-Ashkenazim. Some confusion has been engendered by the fact that the E European Hasidim adopted the basic S. ritual though not its pronunciation, etc. Nevertheless, the relative importance and significance of the Sephardim in Jewish life has dwindled since the Middle Ages. The non-Ashkenazi communities number c. 2,250,000 (1974) or 17% of the world Jewish population.

SEPHARAD: Spanish learned periodical for Jewish, biblical, and allied studies appearing at Madrid twice yearly since 1944 under the auspices of the School of Jewish Studies which is supported by the Spanish government. It has published many important articles on Spanish Jewish history, etc.

SEPHARDI, SEPHARDIM see **SEPHARAD, SEPHARDIM**

SEPHARDIC JEWISH BROTHERHOOD OF AMERICA: US friendly organization. A number of small Sephardi groups were founded in New York, some in the early part of the 20th cent., merging into the SJB in 1947. The society now has branches in New York, New Jersey, and Florida with a total family membership of c. 10,000. Its objects are to promote the welfare of its members and encourage the unification of American Sephardi groups.

SEPHER MITZVOT GADOL see **MOSES BEN JACOB OF COUCY**

SEPHER MITZVOT KATAN see **ISAAC BEN JOSEPH OF CORBEIL**

SEPHER TORAH see **LAW, SCROLLS OF**

SEPHER YETZIRAH (Heb. "Book of Creation"): An obscure mystical work dealing with cosmology, written probably between the 3rd–6th cents. in

Palestine or Babylonia. It derives the structure of the cosmos from the Hebrew alphabet and the 10 primary numbers (SEPHIROT). Gnostic and Neopythagorean influences are discernible in the book which was later ascribed to the patriarch Abraham and considered to embody the "mysteries of creation." Knowledge of these mysteries, particularly of the letter combinations, was supposed to confer magical power; hence the GOLEM was legendarily created by means of formulas from the *S. Y.* Treated as a canonical text by later kabbalists, it greatly influenced their thinking and terminology. From gaonic times it was the subject of commentaries — e.g. by SAADYAH and DONNOLO.

SEPHIROT: Technical term of Kabbalistic mysticism used (from the 12th cent.) to designate the 10 potencies or emanations through which the Divine manifests itself. Kabbalistic theosophy used the term to describe the dualism between the hidden, non-manifest, inaccessible, and transcendent Godhead (*En Soph*) and the manifest, dynamic, and creative aspect of GOD ("World of S."). The concept is indebted to Neoplatonic and Gnostic thought. The S. (for which many other synonyms are used in kabbalistic literature, e.g. crowns, attributes, steps, principles, names) mediate between the hidden, mystical "Cause above all Causes" and the world of plurality and matter. The precise nature of the S. is a matter of controversy in kabbalistic literature and forms its major subject-matter. Kabbalistic writings up to the 16th cent. were mainly concerned with the symbolism of the S. as the mystery of the Godhead. They usually distinguished between the 3 highest S., which are too remote and exalted for mystic contemplation, and the lower 7. The doctrine of S., regarded by kabbalists as the great "mystery of the faith," has been subjected to frequent criticism as heretical and incompatible with strict Jewish MONOTHEISM. See also KABBALAH.

SEPPHORIS (Heb. *Tzippori*): Ancient city in Galilee.

It appears in history at the beginning of the reign of Alexander Yannai as a Jewish city. S. was the capital of Galilee in late Second Temple times; its inhabitants favored peace with the Romans and surrendered in 67. It was the seat of the patriarchate from the time of Judah Ha-Nasi until its removal to Tiberias in the early 3rd cent. After the war of Bar Kokhba, a non-Jewish municipality was established there but did not survive; however, a Roman garrison remained in the Castrum dominating the city. From the 2nd cent., S. was renamed Diocaesarea but remained a Jewish city in Byzantine times, serving as the center of revolt in 315 and having a Jewish majority well into the 6th cent. The Crusaders built a fortress there and apparently expelled the Jews; restored, it served as a stronghold of the Arab village Saffuriye which was replaced in 1949 by a Jewish settlement. Pop.

(1972): 183. Excavations in 1931 unearthed the remains of a Roman theater and aqueduct.

SEPTUAGINT (Lat. "the Seventy," often written LXX): A Greek translation of the Bible, so named because its oldest part, the Pentateuch, was — according to legend — translated at the command of Ptolemy II (285–246 BCE) by seventy Jewish scholars, each working independently, whose translations agreed in every word. In fact, it appears that the S. gradually grew up through the practice of oral translation in the synagogues of Alexandria though some books may have been translated or edited by individuals. There is no single S. version, but every ancient ms presented a somewhat different text, departing in its own way from the masoretic Hebrew. The mss of the S. include the "Great Codices" or Uncials, among them the Alexandrinus (5th cent.), the Sinaiticus (4th cent.) — both now at the British Museum — and the Vaticanus (4th cent.) at Rome, and the minor codices or cursives, of which there are hundreds. In the early 3th cent. ORIGEN re-edited the S. — together with the Hebrew text and 3 other Greek translations (by AQUILA, SYMMACHUS, and THEODOTION) — in his Hexapla, adding renderings of words in the Hebrew text which did not appear in the S. Besides this recension, two others, ascribed to Lucian and Hesychius, were known by the 4th cent. Remnants of what seems to be a Palestinian Jewish recension of the S. were found about 1952 in the vicinity of the Dead Sea. The S. was translated into Latin (the "Old Latin" version of *Vetus Latina* — as opposed to the VULGATE), into three Coptic dialects, Ethiopic, Arabic, Armenian, Georgian, Church-Slavonic, and Gothic. Parts were translated into the Christian Palestinian Aramaic dialect. The S. column of the Hexapla, with selected notes from other columns, was translated into Syriac ("Syro-hexapla"). As the oldest of all ancient versions, the S. is important for the text and interpretation of the Bible. Of its many deviations from the masoretic text, some evidence a different Hebrew text, traits of which are also preserved in Hebrew in the Dead Sea Scrolls. Others are due to misreadings, mistranslations, and subsequent internal corruption of the S. text. The transliteration of names and Hebrew words in the S. is a valuable help in reconstructing the history of Hebrew pronunciation.

SERAPHIM: Class of ANGELS, similar to CHERUBIM, OPHANNIM, etc.; perhaps originally mythological figures represented by winged serpents (*saraph* = "serpent"). In Is. 6:2, they appear as members of the celestial court surrounding the Divine majesty. In medieval writings, they are classed as one of the 10 hierarchical orders of angels.

SERBIA see **YUGOSLAVIA**

SEREKH (Heb.): A term used frequently in the DEAD SEA SCROLLS meaning "rule, order, arrangement" and the like. *Serekh ha-Yaḥad* is the name given to the DISCIPLINE SCROLL.

SERENE (fl. 8th cent.): False messiah; his real name was probably Severus. About 720, in Syria, he declared himself messiah, attracting many followers and creating a stir in the Jewish world as far as Spain.

SERENI, ENZO (1905–1944): Palestinian hero. Born in Italy, he settled in Palestine in 1927 and was among the founders of Givat Brenner. In 1943, he organized the Jewish parachutists to be dropped by the British army into Nazi-controlled territory to help Jews and organize resistance. He himself was dropped in N Italy, captured, and shot.

SERKES, JOEL BEN SAMUEL (known as the *Baḥ* from the initials of his books; 1561–1640): Codifier. He officiated as rabbi in various Polish and Lithuanian communities. His book *Bayit Ḥadash* is a commentary on the *Turim* of Jacob ben Asher, demonstrating its halakhic basis from talmudic and early rabbinical sources. He also wrote numerous responsa and talmudic glosses, which have been incorporated into most editions of the Talmud.

SERKIN, RUDOLF (1903–): Pianist. He was born in Bohemia and began his concert career in 1920. He was particularly noted for his association with his father-in-law Adolf Busch in programs of sonatas and chamber music. S. made his US debut in 1933 and has taught at the Curtis Institute of Music, Philadelphia, since 1941 (director, 1968).

SERLIN, YOSEPH (1906–1974): Israel politician. Of Polish birth, he went to Palestine in 1933. Among the founders of the General Zionist Party, he sat in the Knesset since 1949, was its deputy-speaker 1951–2, and minister of health 1952–5.

SERMONS: The regular exposition of religion, morality, and human conduct is an old institution in Judaism, going back to the prophets (cf. Amos 5:10). During the Second Temple Period, the need arose for a regulated and permanent system of teaching and preaching. This was filled by scholars who utilized the innovation of reading the Torah and selections from the prophetical books on Sabbaths and festivals. Various means were used, one of which was to translate, during the public reading, the biblical passages into the Aramaic vernacular. By the end of this time, teaching and preaching on Sabbaths and festivals had become an important feature of Jewish life, as is evidenced by many New Testament stories of Jesus and his apostles. After the destruction of the Temple, this instruction received a new impulse, for the synagogue and the religious service became the center of Jewish life. The MIDRASH embodies to a great extent the substance of such ethical discourses delivered by famous rabbis. As time went on, the sphere of the sermon was widened to include special events in Jewish life, such as weddings and funerals: in connection with the latter,

a special type of sermon was produced known as the *hesped* (funeral oration). During the Medieval Period, preaching played a very important role in Jewish life, especially in Spain and Provence. In the 11th cent., some famous scholars were known as DARSHANIN ("preachers"), e.g. MOSES HA-DARSHAN and JUDAH HA-DARSHAN. In Germany, however, where people were accustomed to study the aggadic midrashim on their own, preaching was less prevalent. Formal s. were delivered only on certain occasions, especially on *Shabbat ha-Gadol* (before Passover) and *Shabbat Shuvah* (before the Day of Atonement). In the Renaissance Period in Italy, s. were developed to a high pitch of perfection by famous synagogal orators such as Judah Moscato. The introduction of s. in the vernacular was regarded by the Orthodox in Germany in the early 19th cent. as a dangerous innovation, and Leopold ZUNZ wrote his *Gottesdienstliche Vorträge* (1832) to demonstrate that it was in fact a continuous Jewish institution of immemorial antiquity. Subsequently, the sermon assumed great importance in Jewish religious life in W Europe. The general decline of Jewish learning and the impact of modern culture on Jewish life made the pulpit address the main means of imparting Jewish knowledge and inspiration. Outstanding preachers emerged such as Noah MANNHEIMER (1793–1865) and Adolf JELLINEK (1821–1893). The case was different in E Europe, especially in the Polish-Russian center. Jewish learning and study were widespread and consequently the sermon in the western sense did not attain prominence in Jewish life. In its place there developed lengthy ethical discourses, partly intended for the women and the unlearned, which were delivered by itinerant preachers known as MAGGIDIM; the most distinguished of these was JACOB BEN WOLF KRANZ (d. 1815). In the latter part of the 19th cent., with the rise of the Jewish national movement, a number of effective preachers, such as Tzevi Hirsch MASLIANSKI, contributed greatly to the spread of that movement. In the English-speaking countries, the synagogue sermon, readjusted in accordance with the fashions of the religious life of the country, has become a significant factor in Jewish life, and pulpit addresses are regarded as the most important function of the rabbi or minister. In the US especially, the sermon has become the most prominent feature of the main synagogue services. See also HOMILETICS.

SERP see **SEYMISTS**

SERPENT: From the period of Genesis, the s. symbolized an ancient and wise power. For provoking Eve to eat the fruit of the Tree of Knowledge, it was cursed to crawl on its belly and be in an eternal state of feud with man (Gen. 3). Although poisonous and harmful, the s. was also regarded as a curative power; Moses made a brass serpent which cured men suffering from snake-bite (NEHUSHTAN); a similar symbol was known to other ancient peoples. The bronze s. was smashed by Hezekiah for fear of idolatry (I Kings 18:4). The s. was forbidden to Jews as food (Lev. 19:26).

SERVANT OF THE LORD: Term used by Isaiah. According to Is. 42:2-4 the S., chosen by God, is to preach Divine truth to the gentiles. Is. 52:12-13 depicts the S. suffering vicariously; this passage has evoked considerable controversy. The S. has been identified with Israel, the Messiah, the prophet Isaiah, and—by Christian tradition—with Jesus.

SETER, MORDEKAI (1916–): Israel composer. Born in Russia, he settled in Palestine in 1926. Since 1950 he has been professor of composition at the Israel Academy of Music, Tel-Aviv. His main compositions include *Sabbath Cantata*, the oratorio *Tikkun Hatzot*, and the ballet music *The Legend of Judith*, written for the Martha Graham company.

SETH: Adam's third son. He is said to have lived 912 years. The "Sons of S." mentioned by Balaam (Num. 24:17) have been identified with the nomadic Sutho(?) tribes mentioned in the neighborhood of the Palestine-Syria frontier, c. 15th cent. BCE. They seem to have been related to the Hebrews.

SETTLEMENT, SETTLEMENTS see **AGRICULTURAL SETTLEMENTS**

SETZER, SAMUEL HIRSH (1882–1962): Yiddish and Hebrew journalist. After serving as literary editor of Nahum Sokolow's *Ha-Tzephirah* in Warsaw, he turned to Yiddish and became editor-in-chief of the Warsaw daily *Der Telegraph*. From 1912, he lived in New York and in 1960 settled in Israel. His biographical and historical studies include books on Lassalle, Judah HaLevi, Baal Shem Tov and Nahman of Bratzlav.

SEUDAT MITZVAH (Heb. "feast of the fulfilment of a commandment"): A meal which accompanies a religious celebration such as a wedding, circumcision, the redemption of the first-born, or the completion of the study of a talmudic treatise.

SEVEN BENEDICTIONS (Heb. *sheva berakhot*):(1) Blessings recited under the canopy in the wedding ceremony, and traditionally during the seven subsequent days of feasting if new guests are present. (2) The benedictions of the AMIDAH on the Sabbath and festivals.

SEVILLE: Town in S Spain. Jews lived in the region in the Roman Period, and there was an important community when it was a powerful Moorish emirate in the 11th cent. In 1391, S. was the scene of the inflammatory preaching of Ferrand MARTINEZ and a wave of massacres which then swept the country and created the Marrano problem. In consequence of this, the Inquisition began its operations in S. in 1480 and the Jews were expelled in 1483 (before the general expulsion from Spain). The former Jewish quarter is now the Barrio de Santa Cruz. There is a small Jewish community.

SEVORAIM (Heb. "reasoners"): Name given to the Babylonian scholars between the amoraim and the gaonim, that is, approximately 500–700. According to R SHERIRA Gaon, the S. refrained from new legislation but demonstrated the implication of the old by logical argument. He says, further, that the first section of the treatise *Kiddushin* of the Babylonian TALMUD was composed by the later S. Some modern scholars have ascribed to S. most of the compilation of the Talmud; others credit them with only a few scattered passages. It is not improbable that they are responsible for most of the anonymous dialogues typical of the Babylonian *gemara*. R Geviha of Be-Katil, Rava of Rov, and R Aḥai of Be-Ḥattim are three of the earlier S. whose names have been preserved.

SEX: While recognizing the normality of the sexual appetite, Jewish law insists that it should find satisfaction within the marriage bond and makes extensive provision for its regulation and control. Males must "be fruitful and multiply," that is, beget at least one male and one female each, and so the male must find a wife. This does not, however, apply to a woman who may remain unmarried, if she so desires. Early marriage encourages chastity. Cohabitation is prohibited during the menstrual period, usually, for twelve days from the beginning of the monthly blood flow, and the wife must take a ritual bath before conjugal life is resumed. But at most other times cohabitation is permissible, and even praiseworthy—above all on the Sabbath eve— as long as it is a voluntary act. Modesty and moderation are enjoined. Conduct and situations which stimulate illicit desire must be avoided. Wilful refusal of sexual relations by either husband or wife is punished by an increase or a decrease of the marriage settlement and, if persisted in, is a ground for divorce. Although all intimacy outside marriage is illicit, only the offspring of unions which could not be confirmed by marriage —because of consanguinity or because the woman is already married—are *mamzerim* (bastards). All prostitution is abhorrent. While homosexual relations between females are only scandalous and not criminal, relations between males, or between humans and animals, are capital crimes in biblical law.

SEYMISTS (Polish: *Seym*, "diet"): Members of an E European Jewish political party also known as the *Serp* or *Jüdisch-Sozialistische Arbeiterpartei*. Derived from the VOZROZHDENIA group, they were formed in 1905, and adopted a non-Zionist program of Diaspora nationalism involving regional autonomy through the medium of local diets. In May 1917, they merged with the Jewish "Socialist-Zionists" (Territorialist) Party but subsequently joined the communists.

SFORNO, OBADIAH BEN JACOB (c. 1475–1550): Italian physician and Bible commentator. In 1498, he taught Reuchlin Hebrew in Rome. After many wanderings, he settled at Bologna where he conducted a yeshivah. His biblical commentaries rely on plain meaning (*peshat*) and sometimes on philosophy but include no linguistic observations. He also wrote a commentary on *Avot*, grammatical and geometrical compositions, and a philosophical work *Or Ammim* championing the Bible against Aristotle; this he translated into Latin, with a dedication to the king of France.

SHAAR HA-GOLAN: Israel communal settlement (KA) in the Central Jordan Valley. Pop. (1967): 575. It was founded in 1937 as a "stockade and tower" settlement by pioneers from Czechoslovakia. In the Israel War of Independence, the Syrians overran it and its neighbor Massadah but the settlements were later recaptured after being almost completely destroyed. S. ha-G. was subsequently rebuilt. A prehistoric settlement of the Neolithic Period (c. 10,000 BCE) has been uncovered there and the finds collected in a local museum.

SHAATNEZ (word probably of Egyptian origin): An admixture of wool and flax, the wearing of which is prohibited (Lev. 19:19; Deut. 22:11). The commentators give several explanations for this prohibition. Some explain that kinds which by their very nature are essentially different should not be mixed, while Maimonides connects it with the ancient customs of idolatrous priests who wore such garments for cultic purposes.

SHABBAT see **SABBATH**

SHABBAT (Heb. "Sabbath"): First tractate in the Mishnah order of Moed, containing 24 chapters. It has *gemara* both in the Babylonian and Palestinian Talmuds. It develops and formulates the general rules of the Sabbath and its observance, enumerating 39 specific categories of prohibited work and dealing with each in detail. Chapter II is devoted to the regulations concerning the Sabbath Lamp.

SHABBAT HA-GADOL see **SABBATH, GREAT**

SHABBAZI, SHALOM (fl. late 17th cent.): Yemenite poet, living in Taiz, S of Sanaa. A weaver by profession, he occupied himself with kabbalistic literature and gained a saintly reputation, his tomb becoming a place of pilgrimage for the Jews of Yemen. He composed many Hebrew and Arabic poems and hymns which are still widely recited by his countrymen both for liturgical and secular purposes. In some of his poems Hebrew and Arabic are used alternately.

SHABBES GOY (Yidd.): A non-Jew employed by Jews on the Sabbath to carry out tasks prohibited by orthodox Jewish practice to Jews on that day.

SHABBETAI BEN MEIR HA-COHEN (known as *Shakh* after the initials of his book; 1621–1662): Codifier. He officiated in Dresin and later Holleschau (Moravia). He suffered in the Chmielnicki massacres of 1648 and composed commemorative *selihot*. His *Siphte Kohen* (1647) on the code *Yoreh Deah* immediately became a standard work. A similar, but less useful, commentary on *Ḥoshen Mishpat* was published posthumously in 1667.

SHABBETAI TZEVI (1626–1676): Pseudo-messiah. Born in Smyrna, he was attracted to Kabbalah in his youth and early manifested manic depressive traits which grew more pronounced throughout his life. After the horrors of the Chmielnicki massacres (1648/9), he was moved by a "messianic spirit" and a "heavenly voice" proclaiming that he would redeem Israel. Thenceforward, his actions assumed antinomistic features — he pronounced the Ineffable Name, anounced the abolition of fasts, etc. As a result of the opposition of the Smyrna rabbis, he left in 1654 for Salonica where he declared his messiahship in a solemn ceremony of "marriage with the sacred Law." The masses were won over by his emotional sermons and fresh doctrines. In 1662, he traveled to Rhodes, Tripoli, and Egypt, where he wedded an imaginative young survivor of the Polish massacres, called Sarah, who desired to marry the Messiah. The same year, he returned to Palestine and in 1665, was hailed as king-messiah by NATHAN OF GAZA but excommunicated by the rabbis of Jerusalem. Returning to Turkey, S. was joyfully received by the masses and heaped with honors. The fervor spread throughout the Jewish world and rumors were current of a Jewish army which would advance from the Arabian desert to conquer Palestine. In 1666, he went to Constantinople to "depose the sultan" but was arrested and confined in the fortress of Gallipoli. Here he held court and royally received thousands of followers. S. transformed his birthday, the fast of *Av* 9, into a feast, while Nathan of Gaza published regulations for repentance and special liturgies for the hastening of redemption. Messianic expectations ran high throughout Europe and the rabbinate was sharply divided on the issue. However, S.'s behavior evoked the wrath of the Turkish authorities and to save himself from death, he accepted the Islamic faith. Jewry was shaken by his conversion. Nevertheless, S. and his followers continued to adhere to Jewish rites and elaborated a philosophy according to which the suffering and conversion of the Messiah were a form of atonement for Israel. The SABBETAIANS quoted the Zohar as saying that the Messiah would be "good within and evil without." S. had therefore changed his religion in accordance with the kabbalistic doctrine of descending to the husks to redeem the scattered sparks of Divine light (see KABBALAH). In consequence of S.'s Jewish way of life and the veneration with which he was still regarded by the Jews, he was banished to the citadel of Dulcigno in Albania. Nevertheless, he kept in touch with his admirers until his death, which they held would precede his return as Messiah and Redeemer. The

17th cent. Italian *Shaddai*.
(Victoria and Albert Museum, London.)

history of S. and his movement has been investigated in particular by Gershom Scholem.

SHABBETAIANS see **SABBETAIANS**

SHADAR see **MESHULLAH**

SHADDAI: Divine name found frequently in the Bible (e.g. Exod. 6:2); etymology doubtful, but usually interpreted as "Almighty." The name S. figured prominently in kabbalistic formulas and is often found among the Sephardim, etc. on amulets, which are therefore given the name S. It is also generally displayed on the *mezuzah*. See GOD, NAMES OF.

SHADKHAN (Heb. "negotiator"): Marriage broker.
The institution, which goes back to antiquity, was a practical necessity in the Middle Ages when the Jews lived in small, scattered communities. The profession was therefore regarded as highly meritorious, and many scholars of great reputation (e.g. JACOB BEN MOSES MÖLLN) were proud to engage in it. The fee payable for the service, usually a recognized percentage of the dowry, was regulated by custom and sometimes discussed in rabbinic responsa. The profession still survives and performs a useful function in some environments.

SHAFFER, PETER (1926–): English playwright. His first success was *Five-Finger Exercise*. He also wrote the ambitious *Royal Hunt of the Sun* set in Peru, *Black Comedy*, and the one-act plays *The Private Ear and the Public Eye*.

SHAHAM, NATAN (1925–): Hebrew author; son of Eliezer STEINMANN. He has written plays (*They Will Arrive Tomorrow*) and stories, many with a background of settlement life or the Israel struggle for independence.

SHAHARIT (Heb. "dawn [prayer]"): The first prayer of the day, traditionally decreed by Abraham: historically, a substitute for the daily-sacrifice offered at dawn (TAMID). It consists of (1) the dawn benedictions (*birkhot ha-shahar*), originally intended to be recited by the individual: these are followed by biblical verses related to the sacrificial system and rabbinical passages for study; (2) PESUKE DE-ZIMRAH (Psalms) with appropriate benedictions; (3) the SHEMA and its benedictions; (4) the AMIDAH (19 blessings on weekdays; 7 on Sabbaths and festivals) recited by the individual silently and then repeated aloud by the *hazzan* together with the recitation of the KEDUSHAH; (5) TAHANUN: On Mondays, Thursdays, and special occasions, the Reading of the Law takes place after (5), on Sabbaths and festivals (when (5) is not recited) after (4); and (6) concluding prayers, including ALENU.

SHAHIN (fl. end of 13th cent.): Judeo-Persian poet.
He wrote an epos on biblical themes in imitation of the classical Persian "Book of the Kings of Firdausi," divided into a Genesis Book, Moses Book, Ezra Book, and Ardashir Book.

SHAHN, BEN (1898–1969): US artist. He was born in Russia and went to the US in 1906. He is noted for outstanding graphic work. His realistic paintings and murals are satirical and politically slanted. He illustrated the Passover Haggadah.

SHAIKEVITCH, NAHUM MEIR (pseudonym Shomer; 1849–1905): Yiddish novelist and dramatist. S. wrote primarily to entertain and satisfied the taste of his readers; the good hero is always rewarded and the villain punished. First publishing in the 1870's he immediately outstripped all other Yiddish writers in the quantity, though not in the quality, of his narratives. In 1889, when he had already published between 100 and 150 best-sellers, leading Yiddish and Hebrew writers launched violent attacks upon him and his imitators as corruptors of literary taste. S. then left E Europe for the US, where he continued to publish voluminously. After his death, his popularity waned rapidly.

SHALE SUDES see **SHALOSH SEUDOT**

SHALIAH (Heb. "emissary"): A MESHULLAH; in modern times, an emissary from Israel to Jewish communities abroad for the purpose of fund-raising, education, etc.

SHALLUM: King of Israel, 743 BCE. He conspired against and slew Zechariah, son of Jeroboam II, and seized the throne. After five months, he was killed and succeeded by Menahem.

SHALLUM: King of Judah, son of Josiah. Probably an alternative name for JEHOAHAZ.

*SHALMANESER: Kings of Assyria. (1) *S. III*, reigned 860–825 BCE, though not mentioned in the Bible, fought against an Alliance of Damascus,

Hamath, and Israel headed by Ahab and against other peoples at Karkar in Syria (854, 853) but returned home unsuccessful. Later, he ravaged the territory of Hamath, and — on his own testimony — received tribute from Jehu. (2) *S. IV*, reigned 728/7–722 BCE, fought against Sidon, Tyre, and Acre. Hoshea, king of Israel, revolted against S. but fell into his hands. S. died during the siege of Samaria.

SHALOM (SHOLEM) ALEIKHEM (Heb. "peace unto you"): The usual Jewish greeting; in Israel generally abbreviated to *Shalom*.

SHALOM SHABBAZI see **SHABBAZI, SHALOM**

SHALOMZION, ALEXANDRA see **SALOME**

SHALOSH SEUDOT (Heb. "three meals"): According to the Talmud, three meals are to be eaten on the Sabbath (Friday evening, Saturday morning and afternoon). According to R Hidka, a fourth meal is also compulsory. The Kabbalah finds mystical meaning in the Sabbath meals, especially the third. Isaac Luria wrote special Aramaic hymns for these meals. The Hasidim composed melodies for hymns chanted during the third meal, consumed toward evening. The meal taken after Sabbath is called MELAVVEH MALKAH.

SHAMGAR (fl. 13th cent. BCE): Israelite Judge. He defeated the Philistines with an ox-goad, thereby delivering Israel (Judg. 3:31). The name appears to be Hurrian.

SHAMIR: Legendary worm which could split stone and metal. It was used by Moses in engraving the names of the tribes on the high priest's breastplate and, later, by Solomon in the construction of the Temple, no tool of iron being heard in the house (I Kings 6:7). The word *s.* occurs several times in the Bible where it has the meaning of "hard stone."

SHAMIR, MOSHEH (1921–): Israel author. His novel *He Walked in the Fields*, based on life in the *kibbutz* and the *Palmah*, was successfully dramatized. His historic novel *A King of Flesh and Blood* deals with Alexander Yannai, a subject he resumed in his play *The War of the Sons of Light against the Sons of Darkness.*

SHAMMAI (fl. 1st cent. BCE): Rabbi; contemporary of HILLEL, forming together with him the last of the ZUGOT. Living during the troubled times of Herod's reign, he foresaw the dangers of Roman hegemony and therefore enacted many rules intended to keep the Jews from mixing with the heathen. S. took a rigorous point of view in moral and religious matters, at the same time being of a friendly nature, teaching "receive every one graciously" (*Avot* 1:15). Although the School of S. is famous for its disputes with the School of Hillel, S. himself differed on only three points with Hillel (*Eduyot* 1:1). Very few halakhic teachings have survived in his name. S. is possibly identical with the Pharisee Sameas who rallied the Sanhedrin against Herod's attempt at intimidation in 47 BCE.

SHAMMASH (Heb. "one who serves"): A synagogue beadle. The term is used also to denote the additional candle, etc. used in kindling the Hanukhah lights.

SHANGHAI: Chinese port. Sephardim mainly of Baghdadi origin established themselves there — largely under the aegis of the SASSOON firm — shortly after it became a treaty port in 1841. They were followed by Russian Jews, especially after 1917. For a time, S. was among the most prosperous Jewish communities in the world. In the period immediately preceding World War II, S. was one of the few places to which access was possible without a passport, and very large numbers of refugees settled there. During the Japanese occupation in 1914–5, modified anti-Semitism was introduced and most Jews were interned. The community later re-established itself but after the Chinese occupation, S.'s special status ended and its Jews emigrated.

SHAPIRA, CONSTANTIN ABBA (1840–1900): Russian Hebrew poet. Settling in St. Petersburg, he prospered as a photographer, especially in court circles. As a result of his hard life he had become a Christian but, tortured by pangs of remorse, he expressed his feelings in Hebrew poems imbued with melancholy and national pride. He died before his

Mosheh Hayyim Shapira.

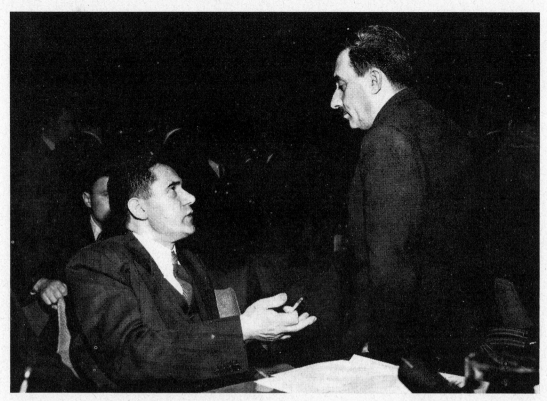

Moshe Sharett (*right*) in conversation with Andrei Gromyko, head of the Soviet delegation to the UN. (Nov. 1947.)

plans to settle in Palestine and return to Judaism were realized. His rich library was bequeathed to the Midrash Abravanel (forerunner of the National Library, Jerusalem).

SHAPIRA, M. W. (c. 1830–1884): Forger. Born in Poland, he dealt in antiques in Jerusalem. Portions of an apparently ancient scroll of Deuteronomy, allegedly discovered near the Dead Sea, were offered by S. to the British Museum in 1882 and created a sensation until pronounced fraudulent by the French archeologist Clermont-Ganneau. S. then committed suicide. In recent years, a few scholars have expressed the opinion that his Dead Sea Scroll may have been genuine.

SHAPIRA, MOSHEH ḤAYYIM (1902–1970): Israel public figure. Born in White Russia, he was a founder of the *Mizraḥi* youth movement (1919). In 1925, he settled in Palestine. S. was elected to the Jewish Agency Executive in 1935. He represented the National Religious Party (formerly *Ha-Poel Ha-Mizraḥi*) in the Knesset from 1949. In successive Israel coalition governments, he served as minister of immigration, health (1948–9), the interior (1949–52 and since 1959), religious affairs and social welfare (1952–8) and minister of health (1961–70).

SHAPIRO: Family of Ḥasidic *tzaddikim* and printers in Volhynia. *PHINEHAS S.* of Koretz (d. 1791), a pupil of the Baal Shem Tov, was the author of the Ḥasidic classic *Midrash Pinḥas*. His son, *MOSES S.* (c. 1758–1838) was from 1808 *tzaddik* at Slavuta where he printed the Talmud at his own press.

SHAPIRO, KARL JAY (1913–): US poet. His works include *V-letter and Other Poems, Essay on Rime*, and *Trial of a Poet*. Since 1956 he has been professor of English at the university of Nebraska.

SHAPP, MILTON J. (1912–): US public figure. He was the first Jew elected governor of Pennsylvania (1970).

SHAPRUT see **IBN SHAPRUT**

SHAREF, ZEEV (1906–): Israel public figure. Born in Rumania, he settled in Palestine in 1925. He was the first secretary of the Israel government (1948–57). He served in various positions (civil service commissioner; director, state revenue) being elected to the Knesset in 1965 on the alignment (Mapai) list. He was a minister in the Israel government 1966–73 (commerce, housing, etc.).

SHARETT (originally **SHERTOK**): (1) *MOSHE S.* (1894–1965): Israel statesman. He went to Palestine from Russia in 1906. Active in Socialist circles, he succeeded Chaim Arlosoroff as head of the Jewish Agency's political department in 1933. He led the campaign against the British 1939 White Paper policy. In June-Nov. 1946, he was among the leaders of the Jewish Agency interned at Latrun. S. was

Sharm e-Sheikh, view from the air.

appointed foreign minister of the provisional government in 1948 and led the Israel delegation to the UN assemblies of 1949 (when Israel was accepted as a member) and 1950. He served as foreign minister in successive coalition governments and in 1953–5, also as prime minister. Noted for his moderation, he resigned from the cabinet in 1956 as a result of differences with Ben-Gurion. From 1961, he was chairman of the Jewish Agency executive. (2) *YEHUDAH S.* (1901–): Israel composer; brother of (1). His works include the setting of the Passover eve service used in many settlements.

SHARM E-SHEIKH: Point on the southern tip of the SINAI peninsula. Because of its strategic position controlling the Straits of Tiran, it was a prime target for the Israel army in the SINAI CAMPAIGN (1956) and the Six-Day War (1967) having on each occasion been fortified by the Egyptians with the intention of preventing shipping sailing to Elath.

SHARON: Part of the Israel coastal plain, extending from Caesarea to Jaffa. In ancient times, it was proverbial for its fertility and was partly covered with oak forests (*Saronis* = oak in Greek, being a possible derivation), pasture-land, and swamps, the result of the gradual choking of the river mouths

and of the neglect of outlets cut through the coastal ridge. In Israelite times, it belonged to the tribe of Ephraim. The Assyrians conquered it in 732 BCE and established there the district of Duru (DOR); the Persians gave it to the Sidonians. Greek and Roman cities flourished in the S. until its gradual decay in the Arab and Mameluke Periods. The deserted and swamp-ridden S. was transformed by Jewish settlement in the nineteen-thirties.

SHAS (Heb. initials of *shishah sedarim*, the "six orders" of the Mishnah forming the basis of the TALMUD): The Talmud. The term became current after the 16th cent. when the Catholic censorship objected to the word "Talmud."

SHAVING: Biblical law prohibits the s. of the "corners of the head" and of the BEARD (Lev. 19:27). The rabbis held that these "corners" of the beard are five in number, although they differ as to where they are. Talmudic tradition interprets s. as removal of the hair with a knife or razor. Other methods of s., such as with a depilatory, are neither biblically nor rabbinically prohibited. Biblical commentators, seeking a rational basis for the prohibition of s., connect it with idolatry and its priesthood. The beard may, however, be clipped with scissors, etc., hence the use of an electric razor is permitted. S. (and trimming the hair generally) is forbidden on holidays and during the period of mourning (*shivah* and *sheloshim*); and by custom during the *Omer* period and the "Three Weeks" before *Av* 9.

SHAVUOT (Heb. "weeks"): One of the three pilgrim festivals. It is observed on *Sivan* 6 (in the Diaspora also on *Sivan* 7) on the occasion of the wheat-harvest. In Temple times, this was expressed in the bringing of two loaves to the priests and the offering of first-fruits (*bikkurim*). The Mishnah and Talmud call it *atzeret*, apparently meaning "termination," i.e., of the Passover period inasmuch as fifty days (Gk. Pentecost) had elapsed and been counted (see OMER). After the destruction of the Temple, the tradition was emphasized that S. commemorates the giving of the law on Mt. Sinai on *Sivan* 6, and this aspect permeates the prayers of the festival. From the 16th cent. on, kabbalists have observed the eve of S. in study (TIKKUN *lel Shavuot*). The Book of Ruth, which mentions the barley and wheat harvests, is read in the synagogue on S.

SHAW, IRWIN (1913–): US playwright and novelist.
He made his reputation with the anti-war play *Bury the Dead*, short stories and the novels *The Young Lions* and *The Troubled Air*.

SHAZAR (RUBASHOV), SHNEOUR ZALMAN (1890–1974): Third president of Israel. Russian-born, he went to Palestine in 1911 and after a further period in Europe, finally settled there in 1924. From 1925, S. was on the editorial board of *Davar*. He sat in the Knesset in behalf of *Mapai* 1949–57, was minister of education and culture in the Israel government 1949–50, and a member of the Jewish Agency Executive from 1951. In 1963, he was elected to succeed Yitzhak BEN-ZVI as president of the state and he was reelected in 1968. He wrote extensively on historical, political, and literary topics. His wife RACHEL (née Katznelson) (1888–) was born in Russia and moved to Palestine in 1912 where she was active in the woman's labor movement. She was a founder of the Working Women's Organization and editor of *Davar ha-Poelet*.

SHEAR-JASHUB (Heb. "The remnant shall return"):
Name given by Isaiah to his son (Is. 7:3) to symbolize the remnant which would return to God after suffering at the hands of the enemy. On the "Day of the Lord," it would constitute the perfect Israel, cleansed of sin (Is. 10:21). A moshav called S. was founded in N Galilee in 1949. It was affiliated to Ha-Oved ha-Tziyyoni and had 150 members in 1967.

SHEBA see **SABEA**

SHEBA, QUEEN OF: Ruler of S Arabian kingdom who visited Solomon and returned to her country full of admiration for his wisdom (I Kings 10). The circumstances were much elaborated in Jewish and even more in non-Jewish legend (the Bilqis of Arab folk tales). The Ethiopian royal family claims descent from a legendary union of the queen and Solomon.

SHECHEM (NABLUS): Ancient Canaanite town, originally situated between Mt. Gerizim and Mt. Ebal; its identification was established by excavations under German auspices on the site in 1913–34. It was in Jordanian territory 1948–67 and since then has been controlled by Israel. Its earliest walls date from c. 2000 BCE; it was under Egyptian control as early as the period of the 12th dynasty. The biblical patriarchs camped under its walls and it was pillaged by Simeon and Levi (Gen. 34). Later, S. was in the territory of Ephraim, a levitical city and a city of refuge, as well as the center of the House of Joseph, Joseph himself being buried there. Abimelech presumably tried to establish his kingdom at S., while the northern tribes who broke away from Rehoboam encamped there when Jeroboam was made king. In later centuries, S. was overshadowed by Samaria, but remained the cult center of the Samaritans. In 72, Vespasian founded the nearby Neapolis (modern Nablus), which became an important Roman city; most of its inhabitants remained Samaritans. In Crusader times, S. (called Naples) was a royal city with a palace and fortress. The present town (with 44,000 inhabitants in 1967) is overwhelmingly Moslem (with a tiny Samaritan community) and has for

Shneour Zalman Shazar.

General view of Shechem.

decades been a center of fanatical Arab nationalism. A small Jewish community formerly existed there.

SHEDIM see **DEMONOLOGY**

S(H)EDEROT: Israel development town. Founded in the N. Negev in 1951 it was settled by new immigrants working in development industries. Pop. (1974): 8,400.

SHE'ELOT U-TESHUVOT see **RESPONSA**

SHEFTALL, MORDECAI (1735–1795): US Revolutionary patriot. He was actively engaged in revolutionary activities in Georgia from the outbreak of the rebellion, took part in the defense of Savannah, and was captured by the British.

SHE-HEḤEYANU see **BENEDICTIONS**

SHEḤITAH (Heb. "slaughtering"): Term usually applied to the ritual slaughtering of animals in accordance with Jewish law. It is carried out by means of a special knife called *ḥallaph* and is entrusted only to a properly qualified person (SHOḤET).

SHEITEL: Wig worn by very Orthodox Jewish married women as a covering for the hair. Jewish law requires married women to cover their hair, and the *s.* was introduced in fairly modern times as a way of permitting a woman to show herself with hair. However, it met with opposition among many rabbinic authorities who felt this to be a violation of the spirit of the religious prohibition.

SHEKALIM (Heb. "Shekels"): Fourth tractate (fifth in some codices) in the Mishnah order of *Moed*, containing 8 chapters. It has no *gemara* in the Babylonian Talmud, but the *gemara* in the Palestinian Talmud is usually printed in editions of the Babylonian Talmud. It deals primarily with the half-shekel tax collected in the time of the Second Temple for the maintenance of the Temple worship.

SHEKEL: A silver unit of weight, later a permanent accepted coin among the Jews. It was divided into units called the *beka* and the *gerah* — two *bekaim* or 20 *gerah* making one *s.* In addition, a coin called the "holy s." was worth double that of the normal s., according to the rabbis. The s. became current as a coin in the time of the Maccabees. In accordance with Exod. 30:13, the Hebrews in the wilderness paid a levy of a ½ s. for the maintenance of the Sanctuary. In the period of the Second Temple, this was revived as an annual levy paid by the Jews of Palestine and of the Diaspora. Special arrangements were made for the transmission of the levy to Jerusalem, and one of the charges against the Roman procurator of Asia Minor, Flaccus, was that he had confiscated the sums collected at Cos for this purpose. The Mishnah tractate *Shekalim* deals with the collection of this levy. After the destruction of the Temple in 70 CE, the voluntary tribute of the s. was converted by the Romans into the compulsory levy of the FISCUS JUDAICUS. The concept of the s. was revived in modern times by the Zionist Organization, the members of which pay a small annual levy called a s., which entitles them to participate in elections to the World Zionist Congress. This s. was introduced at the First Congress in 1897 to indicate support of the BASLE PROGRAM and affiliation with the Zionist Organization.

SHEKHINAH (Heb. "Divine Presence"): From the verb *sh-kh-n* ("dwell"), which in the Bible frequently implies God's dwelling in the midst of the children of Israel, there developed the noun *s.* signifying the presence of God in the world, in the midst of His people, or with individual men. As a counterpart to the principle of Divine Transcendence, *s.* represents the principle of Divine Immanence. The *s.* is described as sharing Israel's suffering and exile; more particularly, it suffers on account of human sinfulness. In kabbalistic literature *s.* became a technical term for the tenth *sephirah* which represents the "feminine" aspect of the Godhead in kabbalistic symbolism.

SHEKOAH see **YISHAR KOAH**

SHELIAH TZIBBUR (Heb. "emissary of the congregation"): Term applied to the person reading the public prayers in the synagogue on any occasion, whether or not a professional. Frequently applied to the HAZZAN, its abbreviated form gave rise to the Ashkenazi surname *Shatz*, etc.

SHELKOWITZ, A. L. see **BEN AVIGDOR**

SHELOM-TZIYYON, ALEXANDRA see **SALOME**

SHELOSHIM (Heb. "thirty"): The thirty-day period of MOURNING following the death of a near relative (on the analogy of the 30-day mourning for Moses; Deut. 34:8). Some of the customs of mourning observed during the SHIVAH period remain in force, such as letting the hair and beard grow. Similarly, marrying or participating in any joyful celebration is prohibited. Among Sephardim, a public discourse was sometimes delivered at the end of the period.

SHEM: One of the three sons of Noah. From S. originated, according to the Bible, the nations of Elam, Asshur, Arpachshad, and Aram. Arpachshad was in turn father of Eber and ancestor of Abraham. Peoples speaking tongues akin to HEBREW are accordingly called Semitic peoples and their languages SEMITIC LANGUAGES.

SHEM HA-MEPHORASH see **GOD, NAMES OF**

SHEMA YISRAEL (Heb. "Hear O Israel": Deut. 6:4): Judaism's confession of faith, proclaiming the absolute unity of God. The *s.* is recited twice in daily worship — in the evening and the morning ("when thou liest down and when thou risest up" Deut. 6:7). Liturgically it consists of three quotations from the Pentateuch (Deut. 6:4–9; 11:12-21; Num. 15:37–41), preceded by two blessings and followed by a further benediction in the morning, or two (three in some Diaspora rites) in the evening. In accordance with the Talmud (*Berakhot* 4b) the *s.* is also recited in bed (*al ha-mittah*) before going to sleep (see NIGHT PRAYER). An early synagogal custom was to take out the Scroll of the Law while reciting the first verse. Possibly during a Byzantine persecution, when the recitation of the *s.* was forbidden, the first and last verses were inserted in the KEDUSHAH. The accepted practice of concluding the Day of Atonement service with the solemn recital of the first verse of the *s.* is first mentioned in medieval French sources. The *s.* is also uttered by or in behalf of a dying Jew. Myriads of Jewish martyrs met their death staunchly professing this summary of the creed of Judaism.

SHEMAIAH (fl. 5th cent. BCE): False prophet hired by Tobiah and Sanballat to incite Nehemiah to hide in the Temple from alleged enemies. The intention was thereby to discredit him as a sacrilegious coward (Neh. 6:10).

SHEMAIAH: Head of the Sanhedrin at the end of the Hasmonean Period in the second half of the 1st cent. BCE. He and Avtalion constituted the fourth of the ZUGOT. Legend describes both Shemaiah and Avtalion as proselytes, descended from Sennacherib (*Gittin* 57b). No *halakhot* are directly recorded as given by them, although several are quoted in their name by others.

SHEMINI ATZERET (Heb. "eighth day of solemn convocation," Lev. 23:36): The final day (in the Diaspora the final two days) at the conclusion of the festival of Tabernacles. It is nominally a separate holiday; thus, there is no partaking of meals in the tabernacle, nor use of the *lulav* and *etrog*, and like all individual holidays, it requires the *she-heheyanu* benediction. The special prayer for RAIN is recited during the *musaph* service. In Ashkenazi rituals, the *yizkor* memorial prayer is said. See also SIMHAT TORAH.

SHEMITTAH see **SABBATICAL YEAR**

SHEMONEH ESREH see **EIGHTEEN BENEDICTIONS**

SHEMOT see **EXODUS**

SHEMOT RABBAH see **EXODUS RABBAH**

SHENHAR (SHENBERG), YITZHAK (1905–1957): Hebrew author. Born in the Ukraine, he went to Palestine in 1924 and from 1942 edited the Schocken publications there. His realistic novels encompass Jewish life in E Europe and Israel. S. translated extensively from European literature.

SHEOL: According to the biblical conception, the dwelling of the dead (Gen. 37:35; Is. 38:10), situated far below the earth (Is. 57:9), whose inhabitants will not give thanks to the Lord. S. is more especially the dwelling of the wicked (Ezek. 32:15). The name in the Bible is synonymous with *shahat* and *avaddon*.

SHEPHARAM: Israel town in Lower Galilee, inhabited by Druze and Christian Arabs. For a short period in the 2nd cent. CE, it was the seat of the Sanhedrin under R Judah Ha-Nasi. The crusaders fortified the town, and later it was Saladin's base in his siege of Acre. In the 16th cent., Dahir el-Amr, the governor of Galilee, resided in the town and called it Shafa Amr. Pop. (1974): 12,700 (Arabs and Druze).

SHEPHATIAH BEN AMITTAI (d. 886): Italian *paytan*. He is reported to have saved his fellow-Jews in S Italy from the forced conversion decreed by the Byzantine emperor Basil I about 873–4. His exploits are described in the *Chronicle* of his descendant AḤIMAAZ. Among his hymns is *Yisrael nosha* in the Ashkenazi *Neilah* service of the Day of Atonement.

SHEPHELAH (Heb. "lowland"): Southern part of the coastal plain of Israel, extending from Lydda to Gaza; in the Bible, the lower hills are called S.

SHEPHEYA (Meir Shepheyah): Israel agricultural school on the Carmel range. It was founded as a colony by Baron Edmond de Rothschild in 1892, and in 1904, Israel Belkind opened an agricultural school for orphans of the Kishinev pogroms nearby. The colony and, later, the school were abandoned before World War I. In 1923, a new school was opened at S. In the nineteen thirties, it became an institution of Youth Aliyah and was adopted by Junior Hadassah of America. Pop. (1972): 362.

SHERIRA (906–1006): Gaon of Pumbedita 968–998. His father Ḥanina and his grandfather Judah had also served as geonim in Pumbedita. S. restored for a time the waning prestige of the Babylonian center, fast being superseded by the new centers in the west. Together with his son HAI he maintained contact through numerous responsa with N Africa, Spain, etc. The most famous of these is the lengthy and important historical Epistle written c. 992 in response to an inquiry from Kairouan. This chronicles the origins of the Mishnah and Talmud and the continuing tradition of the sevoraim and geonim. It is a chief source of information for the history of the Oral Law and especially for the Gaonic Period. S. also wrote commentaries to the Bible and various talmudic tractates, only isolated passages of which have survived. During the last years of his long life he suffered at the hands of the caliph Kadir who had him imprisoned and his property confiscated.

SHESHBAZZAR: Jewish official appointed by CYRUS over Judah in 538 BCE. He was entrusted with the Temple vessels which he returned from Babylon to Jerusalem. He also laid the foundation for the building of the Second Temple (Ezra 1:8, 11; 5:14–16). His identity is not established; it has been suggested he was Shenazzar, grandson of Jehoiachin, but others consider him identical with ZERUBBABEL.

SHESHET (fl. late 3rd cent.): Babylonian amora. His main place of residence was at Shilhi on the Tigris. He was familiar with all the tannaitic literature and always found an appropriate tannaitic source to answer questions. In his later years, he became blind.

SHESTOV, LEV (pseudonym of Lev Isakovich Schwarzman; 1866–1938): Russian philosopher. After the Russian Revolution in 1917, he was an emigré in France. An admirer of Kierkegaard, he was also influenced by Dostoievski and Nietzsche. Denying the existence of absolute truth, he was apparently sceptical of everything except the suffering of the individual and opposed classical abstract philosophy which took no account of the human being. God is above good and reason, and the quest for Him is the main object in life. His later works approached the "existentialist" viewpoint. Although an assimilationist, he adopted a positive attitude toward Judaism in his last years.

SHETAR see **DEED**

SHEVA: The sign: in Hebrew pointing. It expresses absence of any vowel (*s. quiescens*) or a very short vowel (*s. mobile*); the latter, which formerly was pronounced with varying colorings, is now sounded as short *e* (but see ḤATAPH). In the middle Ages (especially in poetry), in all Ashkenazi variations of Hebrew pronunciation, and in modern Israel pronunciation it has often been neglected.

SHEVA BERAKHOT see **SEVEN BENEDICTIONS**

SHEVAT: The 11th month of the ecclesiastical year and 5th of the civil year. It has 30 days and corresponds to Jan.-Feb. The NEW YEAR FOR TREES is celebrated on the 15th of the month.

SHEVAT, FIFTEENTH OF (TU BI-SHEVAT) see **NEW YEAR FOR TREES**

SHEVIIT (Heb. "Seventh Year"): Fifth tractate in the Mishnah order of *Zeraim*, containing 10 chapters. It has *gemara* in the Palestinian, but not the Babylonian, Talmud. It deals with the laws of the Sabbatical year (Exod. 23:11; Lev. 25: 1-7). The last chapter considers the release of debts (Deut. 15:1-6) and the rabbinic institution of PROSBUL.

SHEVUOT (Heb. "Oaths"): Sixth tractate in the Mishnah order of *Nezikin*, containing 8 chapters. It has *gemara* both in the Babylonian and Palestinian Talmuds. It deals with the various types of oath (Lev. 5:4) and the laws applying to one who becomes aware of being unclean (Lev. 5:2-3).

SHEWBREAD: Twelve loaves of fine white flour which were laid in two rows on the golden table in the inner shrine of the temple. They were placed on chalices filled with spices and remained there from one Sabbath to the next, when they were divided among the priests (Lev. 24:1-9).

SHIBBOLETH (Heb. "sheaf of corn"): Word used by Jephthah to test the nationality of wayfarers near the fords of the Jordan. In Ephraimite dialect, the word was pronounced *sibboleth*, and this enabled him to identify the Ephraimites, with whom he was in strife. The term has been proverbial, and is used in English as "slogan" or "test-word."

SHIDDUKH (Heb. from Aram.): In the Talmud, the preliminary conversations with a potential bride or her parents before betrothal. By extension, a BETROTHAL or actual marriage.

SHIELD OF DAVID see **MAGEN DAVID**

SHIKKER (Yidd. from Heb. *shikkor*): Drunk; a drunkard.

SHIKKUN (Heb. from *shakken*, to house): In Israel a housing project; colloquially, a residence.

SHILOAḤ see **SILOAM**

SHILOH: The first cult-center of the Israelite religion after the conquest of Palestine under Joshua. It was situated 25 m. N of Jerusalem in the Mts. of Ephraim. The Ark and Tabernacle were kept there during the period of the Judges, serving as the central national shrine and object of pilgrimage, especially during the long priesthood of ELI. The Town and the Tabernacle were destroyed by the Philistines after the battle of Aphek (c. 1050 BCE), when the Ark was captured. S. thereafter was insignificant. It was settled from the Hellenistic Period down to the 12th cent. CE. The site was excavated by a Danish expedition 1926-8.

SHIMEI: Benjamite. A zealous supporter of Saul, he resented David's accession and cursed the latter when he was fleeing from Absalom's revolt. David spared S. on his return but later he was put to death by Solomon (I Kings 2:35-46).

SHIMONI (SHIMONOVITZ), DAVID (1886-1956): Hebrew poet. Of Russian birth, he settled in Palestine in 1920. His early verse was lyrical and individualistic and expressed his distress at the rootlessness of Jewish youth in the Diaspora. His Palestinian poetry is brighter, dealing chiefly with the idyllic character of the Palestinian landscape and the life of the pioneers. S. also wrote parables, satires, meditations, and memoirs.

SHIN see **SIN**

SHIN SHALOM (pen-name of Shalom Shapira; 1904 —): Hebrew poet. The son of the Ḥasidic rabbi of Drohobycz, he lived in Vienna 1914–22 and then in Palestine. Much of his poetry strikes a mystical religious note. S.S. has also written an autobiographical novel, stories, and plays and translated Shakespeare's sonnets into Hebrew.

SHINAR: Country mentioned in the Bible. Formerly thought to be Sumer, modern scholars identify it as a land called Shanḥar mentioned in cuneiform documents. This was situated either in N Mesopotamia or in the plain of Babylon. Rulers of S. included Nimrod (Gen. 10:10) and Amraphel (Gen. 14:1-9). Exiles from Judah were banished there after the destruction of the First Temple (Is. 11:11).

SHINWELL, EMANUEL, BARON (1884–): English politician. A founder of the Marine Workers' Union (1920), he was a Labor member of parliament 1922–70 and was minister of fuel 1945–7, secretary of war 1947–50, and minister of defense 1950–1.

SHIR HA-KAVOD (Heb. "Hymn of Glory): Hymn (opening words *Anim Zemirot*) recited by the Ashkenazim after the morning service and Sabbath additional service, the Ark being opened during its recitation. It is in the form of an alphabetic acrostic, dating perhaps from the 11th cent., and reflects the outlook of the Rhineland mystics. Some congregations omit it.

SHIR HA-MAALOT see **SONG OF DEGREES**

SHIR HA-SHIRIM RABBAH see **SONG OF SONGS RABBAH**

SHIRAYIM (Heb.) Food left over by the *tzaddik* and competed for eagerly by his Ḥasidim during the Sabbath and festival meals. These "left-overs," according to Ḥasidic belief, partake of the holiness belonging to that part of a sacrifice not consumed upon the altar.

SHIRAZ: Persian town. Traditionally, its first Jewish settlement dates to an early, but unspecified, period. Benjamin of Tudela (c. 1170) found 10,000 Jews in S. Their number dwindled considerably in consequence of the persecutions suffered by Persian Jewry in general from the 15th cent. at the hands of the Moslems. Very many were forced to embrace Islam, and in 1850, only 500 were left. In 1973, the Jewish population was 8,000, (the number emigrating to Israel having been more than replaced by the influx from rural districts.)

*SHISHAK (Egyptian: Sheshonk; fl. c. 925 BCE): Egyptian king of Libyan origin. When Jeroboam fled from Solomon, he found refuge with S. In the fifth year of Rehoboam's rule, S. overran Judah and plundered the Temple treasure in Jerusalem. Archeological evidence indicates that his conquests also included the kingdom of Israel.

SHITREET, BEHOR SHALOM (1895–1967): Israel politician. A police official during the British Mandate, he was minister of police, 1948–66 in various coalition governments, sitting in the Knesset until 1951 as a Sephardi Party representative and thereafter for *Mapai*.

SHIUR KOMAH (Heb. "measurement of stature"): Hebrew mystical work containing a physical description of the Divinity. Known in the Gaonic Period (c. 8th cent.), it was opposed by the Orthodox because of its extreme anthropomorphism and its affinity to gnosticism.

SHIVAH (Heb. "seven"): The "seven days" MOURNING following the burial of a relative; mentioned in Ecclesiasticus 22:12. It is also known in the Talmud as *avelut* ("mourning"). During this period, all ordinary work is prohibited, the mourners sit unshod on low stools or the floor ("sitting s."), sexual intercourse is forbidden, and visits by friends are made to the mourners' home for prayer and condolence. The prohibition of SHELOSHIM naturally also apply to this period.

SHLEMIEL (Yidd.; cf. Num. 7:36): Ne'er-do-well, a feckless person.

SHLIMMAZEL (Yidd. *shlimm* "bad" and Heb. *mazzal* "luck"; in English-speaking countries, cor-

Avraham Shlonsky.

rupted to *Shlimozel*, etc.): A mishap or failure.

SHLONSKY, AVRAHAM (1900–1973): Hebrew poet. Of Russian birth, he resided in Palestine from 1921. His poems are stormy and rebellious, his style revolutionary, and his politics tended toward Marxism. Many of Israel's young authors have been influenced by his work, which sought to create a new poetic language to replace that of the previous generation. S. is regarded as one of the finest translators in modern Hebrew literature and rendered classics from several languages into Hebrew. He was a founder and editor of SIPHRIYYAT HA-POALIM and from 1951 edited its literary quarterly *Orlogin*. His sister *VERDINA S.* (1905–), is a composer.

SHMUSS (Heb. *shemuot*, rumors): Chat.

SHNEERSOHN: Hasidic dynasty, with centers at Lyady, LIUBAVICH, Kapost, etc., which helped to disseminate the *Habad* school of Hasidism. The founder of the line was SHNEOUR ZALMAN OF LYADY. He was succeeded by *DOV BER OF LIUBAVICH* (d. 1828), founder of the *Habad* settlement in Hebron and advocate of Jewish agricultural settlement in Kherson province, Russia. His son-in-law and successor *MENAHEM MENDEL S.* (d. 1866) composed the halakhic work *Tzemah Tzedek*. After him came *SAMUEL S.* (d. 1883) and his son *SHALOM DOV BER* (d. 1920). The son of the latter, *JOSEPH ISAAC S.* (d. 1952) was imprisoned by the Soviets for his activity in strengthening religion. Released after a short time (1927), he settled in Otwock (Poland), but went to New York after the outbreak of World War II. There, he established a chain of yeshivot and schools in the *Habad* tradition. The present head is *MENAHEM MENDEL S.* (1902–).

SHNEOUR ZALMAN BEN BARUCH OF LYADY (1747–1813): Founder of the HABAD movement in HASIDISM. Joining the Hasidim at the age of 20 as a pupil of Dov Ber of Mezhirich, he became the ideologist of the movement. In 1777, he succeeded R Menahem Mendel of Vitebsk as its leader. He took a leading part in the bitter controversy with the Mitnaggedim led by the Vilna Gaon. As a result of accusations by his opponents in 1799, he was arrested by the Russian authorities and imprisoned in St. Petersburg. He was released when the charges were disproved but was rearrested for a short period the next year following further allegations by the Mitnagged rabbi Avigdor of Pinsk. In 1804, S.Z. settled in Lyady where he devoted himself to teaching and writing. On the approach of Napoleon's army, he fled to the interior of Russia but died on the journey. His teaching affirmed the spiritual pre-eminence of the *tzaddik* but differed from the popular Hasidism of Volhynia and Podolia by rejecting the *tzaddik*'s ability to work wonders and decrying the emotional aspects of Hasidism. Emphasizing a rational approach, he taught the importance of intensive study and contemplation. His works included a liturgy, a code of laws known as *Shulhan Arukh*, a mystic commentary on the Pentateuch, and *Likkute Amarim*, popularly known as the TANYA, S.Z.'s interpretation of the Kabbalah which has become the standard work of the *Habad* movement.

SHNEOUR, ZALMAN (pen name of Zalkind Shneour; 1887–1959): Hebrew author. Of White Russian birth, he lived in Vilna 1904–6. After a period of travel, he lived in Berlin, Paris (from 1924), the US (from 1941), and Israel (from 1951). His poetry is vivid and sensual, covering a vast range of general as well as specifically Jewish problems. His satirical attitude to modern culture was displayed in several

Shneour Zalman of Lyady.

of his poems exposing its shortcomings. On Jewish topics, some of his verse expressed admiration for Jewish communities in the Diaspora, while his poetic cycle *Luḥot Genuzim* ("Hidden Tablets") criticizes the moral development of Judaism as reflected in biblical literature. Jewish life in the Pale of Settlement served as background for many of his stories, notably the cycle of tales *Peoples of Shklov* and the well-known novel *Noah Pandre*. S. also wrote considerably in Yiddish, especially prose-works.

SHNODER (Yidd. from Heb. *she-nadar* = "because he vowed"): To make an offering in the synagogue. The term derives from the *mi sheberakh* formula.

SHNORRER (Yidd.; etymology obscure): A professional beggar. This figure, characteristic of the Jewish life of E and Central Europe in the 19th and earlier 20th cents., has been immortalized by Yiddish writers and in English by Israel Zangwill. The classical S., despite his profession, is distinguished by his wit, resourcefulness, and even learning.

SHOHAM (initials of *Sherute ha-Yam*; Heb. "maritime services"): Israel shipping company founded 1949 by the *Zim* company. S. acts as agents of ships owned by *Zim* and its affiliates and attends to all activities necessary to operate their ships. Its main office is in Haifa.

SHOHAM (POLAKEVICH), MATTATHIAS (1893—1937): Polish Hebrew author. He lived in Warsaw and wrote plays and verse. His plays (*Tyre and Jerusalem, Thou shalt not make gods of iron*) are based on the conflicts of Judaism and idolatry, sensualism and spirituality, and love of war and the desire for peace.

SHOHER TOV: Popular name for Midrash to Psalms, being derived from the opening verse quoted. See PSALMS, MIDRASH TO.

SHOHET: Ritual slaughterer of animals and poultry. According to talmudic law any normal person not a minor may slaughter, provided this be done in accordance with the provisions of Jewish law. Later Jewish custom and law limited slaughtering to people properly educated and trained. The *s.* in modern times is learned in matters of Jewish law and, as a rule, is a man of piety.

SHOKHEN AD (Heb. "He who inhabits eternity"): Commencement of last section of the NISHMAT prayer; in Ashkenazi tradition these are the first words recited by the reader of the morning prayer on Sabbaths and festivals.

SHOLEM (SHOLOM) ALEICHEM (pseudonym of Shalom Rabinovich; 1859—1916): Yiddish novelist and humorist. Encouraged by his father, he began at an early age to compose poems, novels, and dramas in Yiddish, Hebrew, and Russian. In 1888—9, while temporarily enjoying wealth, he published at his own expense *Die Yiddishe Folksbibliotek*, an annual in which the most prominent Yiddish writers partici-

Sholem Aleichem.

pated, but shortly after he met with financial disaster on the stock exchange. In his most difficult years, he created the character of *Tevye der Milchiger* (Tevye the Milkman), a lighthearted pauper who drives his rickety wagon in search of a pittance but whose thoughts traverse the world and reach up to God. S.A.'s predecessors, even his model Mendele Mocher Sephorim, had used humor and mockery as instruments for reform; he, however, held that the primary need was to make the Jew a happier human being. Kasrilevke, the scene of many of his sketches, is a town of poor but jolly Jews who are always rushing about trying to earn enough for the Sabbath. S.A. went to the US for the first time in 1906 and again upon the outbreak of World War I. The sketches of his last years afford penetrating insight into the immigrant generation on American soil.

SHOMER see SHAIKEVITCH

SHOMRON see SAMARIA

SHOOL (Yidd. from German *schul* "school"): A synagogue.

SHOPHAR: Horn of the ram (or of any clean animal other than the cow). Biblical law prescribes its sounding for the memorial blowing on the New Year, as well as to proclaim the year of release (Lev. 25:9). At various periods the *s.* was sounded also on fast days, at the time of the proclamation of a rabbinic edict, in

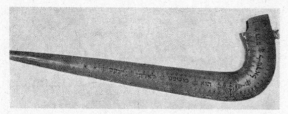

Engraved *shophar*, 18th cent.

the ceremony of excommunication, before the entry of the Sabbath, and at times of famine or plague. The customs of blowing the s. during the synagogue services in the month of *Elul* and on Hoshanah Rabbah (among Sephardim etc.) and at the conclusion of the Day of Atonement, are late.

SHOPHETIM see **JUDGES**

SHOREK, BROOK OF see **NAHAL SOREK**

SHOVAL: Israel communal settlement (KA) in the N Negev. It was founded by settlers from S Africa and Palestine in 1946. Pop. (1972): 502.

SHOWBREAD see **SHEWBREAD**

SHREVEPORT: City in Louisiana, US. About a dozen Jewish families, mostly of Alsatian and German origin, arrived in the mid-19th cent., and a congregation was organized in 1857. A number of immigrants from E Europe settled in S. between 1880 and 1890, leading to the formation of an Orthodox congregation. In 1973, S. had 1,500 Jews. The Jewish Federation was founded in 1941.

SHTADLAN (Heb. from Aram. "persuader"): Title applied to a Jewish representative adroit in negotiation and with access to dignitaries of state who worked at royal courts, etc. in behalf of the Jewish community. The prototype in Jewish history is Josel of Rosheim (15th—16th cents.). In 18th cent. Poland, the S. became a formal and sometimes salaried agent, and unauthorized persons were forbidden to attempt similar activity.

SHTETL (Yid. "small town"): Jewish small-town or village community in E Europe.

SHTIF, NOCHUM (pseudonym: Baal Dimyon; 1879—1933): Yiddish critic and philologist. A fervent protagonist of Yiddish culture, he published many Yiddish essays and translations and fought for the supremacy of Yiddish over Hebrew. In 1908, he took up the scientific study of the Yiddish language and literature, publishing important researches in this sphere. S. was a founder of Yivo in Vilna. In late life, he came to terms with communism and accepted the Yiddish chair at the Kiev State Academy.

SHTILLE KHUPPEH (Yidd. and Heb. *huppah*): A secret wedding, i.e., one conducted in conformity with the Jewish, but not the civil regulations.

SHTUSS (Heb *shetut*): Foolishness, nonsense.

SHULAMITE: Name or soubriquet for a young woman mentioned in the Song of Songs. It has been variously interpreted as Shunammite (i.e., from

SHUNEM), Jerusalemite (Salem being an abbreviation of Jerusalem), the "perfect maiden" (Heb. *shalem*= "perfect"), or as a personal name. From the Talmudic Period—and especially in *piyyut*—it was applied to the Jewish people in its relations to God, resulting from the allegorical interpretation of the Song of Songs. Christian tradition interpreted S. as referring to the Church.

SHULḤAN ARUKH see **CARO, JOSEPH**

SHULKLAPPER (Yidd.): The official (normally the beadle) who in former days aroused the worshipers for early morning service at the synagogue (*shul*) by knocking (*klappen*) at their doors. In E Europe an artistically carved hammer was sometimes used for the purpose.

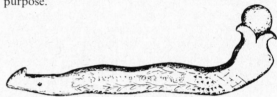

Shulklapper's hammer with the inscription "I rejoiced when they said unto me 'Let us go unto the house of the Lord.'" (Lemberg, 18th cent.).

SHUM: Heb. abbr. for the neighboring Jewish communities of Speyer, Worms, and Mainz. The regulations of their synod (*takkanot Shum*) were binding on all German Jews.

SHUNEM: Ancient Palestinian place in the territory of the tribe of Issachar, mentioned prior to the Israelite conquest in Egyptian inscriptions and in the Tel el Amarna letters. It was the home of the wealthy woman ("the Shunammite") whose dead son was revived by Elisha (II Kings 4). The site is near the modern Afula.

SHURUK: The long *u* vowel, written (ו). In biblical spelling the *vav* is often missing and *kubbutz* is is written instead of *s*.

SHUSHAN (Susa): Capital of Elam and subsequently of Persia. Excavations carried out last century revealed the royal palace probably mentioned in the book of Esther (Est. 2:18; 3:9).

SHUSHAN PURIM see **PURIM**

SHYLOCK: The central Jewish character of Shakespeare's *Merchant of Venice*. Though filling the conventional unsympathetic role of the 16th cent. stage Jew, he is by the author's genius instilled with a human pathos. The first sympathetic interpretation of the role was given by Charles Macklin in 1741. Attempts have been made unsuccessfully to establish a Hebrew origin for the name. The play was written close to the time of the execution of Rodrigo LOPEZ when there was an anti-Jewish atmosphere in England.

SIBERIA: Asiatic region of the USSR. Jews may have been exiled there as early as the 17th cent. In 1827, Jews were prohibited from going there to follow exiled relatives. A government plan was evolved in 1836 for the settlement of Jews in the regions of Tobolsk and Omsk; after its abandonment, a year later, Jewish criminals were no longer deported to remote regions of S. Jewish emigration to S. was prohibited in 1899, though political exiles continued to be sent there. The Jewish population of S. (numbering 50,000 in 1926) increased under Soviet rule, notably as a result of the establishment of the Jewish autonomous region in BIROBIDJAN and the industrial development of the region and, from 1940, the Soviet policy of exiling Jews from the Baltic countries, White Russia, the Ukraine, and later the satellite states.

SIBYLLINE ORACLES: Series of verse prophecies in Greek hexameters of pagan, Jewish, Christian, or mixed Jewish-Christian authorship ranging from the 2nd cent. BCE to the 4th cent. CE. Many of the S. O. are Jewish or Christian propaganda under a pagan mask. These books mostly sketch the history of the Mediterranean world in prophetic form, attack the enemies of Israel (chiefly Rome) for greed and immorality, threaten disaster to the peoples that have wronged the Jews, and foretell messianic judgment and redemption after wars and natural cataclysms.

SICARII: Rebel group in the late Second Temple Period. They were called after the dagger (*sica* in Latin) they carried beneath their clothes. Mixing with pilgrims on the Temple hill, they murdered their political opponents, i.e., those desiring peace with Rome. The best-known S. included Menahem ben Jair and ELEAZAR BEN JAIR who held Masada until 73 CE.

SICILY: Mediterranean island, formerly an independent kingdom. There is literary and archeological evidence that Jews lived in S. in Roman times, perhaps as early as the 1st cent. BCE. The correspondence of Pope Gregory I, who protected them, shows an active settlement in the 6th cent. It continued during the period of Arab occupation (9th–11th cents.), which left a profound impression on the language and culture of Sicilian Jewry. The Jews reached the acme of their prosperity under the Norman rulers. In the later Middle Ages, Jews were thickly settled throughout S., and numbered about 40,000. In the 15th cent., their head was the DIEN-CHELELE appointed by the king. From 1282, the island was ruled by the House of Aragon and closely influenced by Spanish ideas and events, so that in 1391 there was a devastating wave of massacres, and another in 1474; the Inquisition was introduced in 1479. As part of the Aragonese territories S. was included in the edict of expulsion from the Spanish dominions in 1492. Most of the exiles ultimately found their way to the Italian mainland and the Levant. In 1745, an unsuccessful attempt was made to attract Jewish settlers again to S. The Jewish population is now insignificant.

SICK, VISITING THE see **VISITING THE SICK**

Page from the *siddur* (1803) of the Auras synagogue, Lower Silesia.

SIDDUR (Heb. "order"): Among Ashkenazim, the volume containing the daily prayers, in distinction to the MAHZOR containing those for the festivals. Among Sephardim, the term *tephillah* ("prayer") is used instead of *s*.

SIDE-LOCKS see **PEOT**

SIDON: Ancient Syrian coastal city, now in the Lebanon. It was regarded as the capital of the Phoenicians who are termed Sidonians in the Bible and in Homeric verse. The city is mentioned in the Tel el Amarna letters. JEZEBEL was of Sidonian origin and introduced its Baal cult into Israel. S. was occupied on several occasions by the Assyrians, was subject to Persia, and was captured by Alexander the Great. After falling under Roman domination, it finally lost its independence.

SIDRAH (Heb. "order," "arrangement"; Yidd. *sedre*): A section of the Pentateuch ("portion of the week") read in the synagogue on the Sabbath. There are 54 such divisions, this arrangement permitting the reading of the entire Pentateuch annually. Old Palestinian custom, however, was to divide the Pentateuch into approximately 175 *sedarot*, completing the reading of the Pentateuch in a three or three-and-a-half year cycle. Each *s*. has a distinctive name, taken from the first important word in its text.

SIEDLCE: Polish town. Its first Jews settled there in 1547 and the town became an important Jewish center. 31 Jews were killed there in a pogrom in 1906. In 1939, the community numbered over

16,000 (40% of the total), nearly all of whom were annihilated in the following years.

SIEFF, ISRAEL MOSES, BARON (1889–1972): British Zionist and industrialist. A collaborator of Weizmann, he was secretary of the Zionist commission to Palestine in 1918. He contributed generously to Zionist funds and founded the Daniel Sieff Research Institute at Reḥovot in 1934. His wife, *REBECCA S.*, (1890–1966) sister of Baron MARKS, was founder of WIZO and president until 1963.

SIEFF INSTITUTE see **WEIZMANN INSTITUTE**

SIENNA: Former city-republic in central Italy. Jews are first mentioned there in 1229, and it later attracted many loan-bankers who lived under affluent circumstances. It became a center of scholarship in the 16th cent. through the lavish support of the wealthy Ishmael da Rieti. A ghetto was established in 1571 when S. was annexed to the grand duchy of Tuscany, and thereafter, the condition of the Jews deteriorated. In 1799, during the reaction against the French Revolution, the ghetto was attacked and 13 persons killed, an annual memorial fast subsequently being instituted. In the 19th cent., the community dwindled and the ancient synagogue is now used irregularly. Jewish pop. (1970): Under 100.

SIGILMESSA (now *Rissani*): Town and oasis in Morocco. In the early centuries of Moslem rule it was an important Jewish center and seat of scholarship.

SIHON: Amorite king. He ruled in Transjordan between the rivers Jabbok and Arnon, his capital being at Heshbon. S. conquered much of this area from the Moabites (Num. 21:21 ff). He was defeated and killed by the Israelites after refusing them passage across his territory, and his land was partitioned between the tribes of Reuben and Gad.

SILBERMANN, ELIEZER LIPMANN (1819–1882): Hebrew journalist and editor. By profession a cantor and ritual slaughterer, he lived in the E Prussian town of Lyck. In 1856, he started the first Hebrew weekly HA-MAGGID and helped to found MEKITZE NIRDAMIM.

SILESIA: Region of Europe, now divided between Czechoslovakia and Poland. There was Jewish settlement from the 12th cent., and anti-Jewish legislation was introduced at the Synod of BRESLAU (1267), where the largest community developed. Expulsions from various other towns occurred during the 14th cent. The general position deteriorated during the Hussite War and in 1453, CAPISTRANO preached against the Jews, instigating a Ritual Murder charge at Breslau. As a result of expulsions in the 16th cent., Jews remained only in Glogau and Zülz. In 1740/5, most of S. became part of PRUSSIA, and in 1746, Jews were again banished. After the close of the 18th cent., the Jewish community greatly increased through immigration. In 1918, part of S.

became Polish. After World War II, Jewish survivors settling chiefly in Breslau (Wroclaw), Münsterburg (Ziebice), and Kattowitz (Katowice) numbered c. 10,000 but nearly all left after 1967.

SILKIN, LEWIS, LORD (1889–1972): British public figure. A lawyer, he was a Labor member of parliament 1935–50, and minister of town and country planning 1945–50. His son *JOHN ERNEST S.* (1923–) has been labor member of parliament, minister of public buildings and works 1969–70, minister of planning and local government 1974–6, of agriculture 1976. Another son *SAMUEL CHARLES S.* (1918–) has been a labor member of parliament since 1964 and attorney general from 1974.

SILKINER, BENJAMIN NAHUM (1883–1934): Hebrew poet. His verse dealt with native American as well as Jewish themes. He translated *Macbeth* into Hebrew and collaborated in a Hebrew-English dictionary.

SILOAM (Heb. *Shiloah*): Pool in the vicinity of Jerusalem receiving water from the GIHON spring. In c. 700 BCE, to assure the city's water supply in case of siege, Hezekiah cut a tunnel through which the water of the Gihon spring (outside the old city walls) flowed into the pool at S. (II Kings 20:20). The work was cut from two directions and when the workmen met they commemorated the event in an inscription carved on the wall. This is one of the most ancient Hebrew epigraphic documents (now in

The Pool of Siloam.

Abba Hillel Silver.

the Istanbul museum). The surrounding area, also known as S. (modern Silwan) formerly included a settlement of Yemenite Jews.

SILVA, DA: Sephardi and Marrano family. (1) *ANTONIO JOSE DA S.* (1705–1739): Portuguese playwright. Brazilian born, he was one of the most prolific and popular Portuguese dramatists in his day. Penanced by the Inquisition in 1726, he was rearrested in 1737 and burned at an auto-da-fè at Lisbon two years later, one of his comedies being presented at the principal theater the same night. (2) *FRANCISCO MALDONADO DA S.* (c. 1592–1639): Marrano martyr. A physician in Chile, he was attracted to Judaism and circumcised himself, adopting the name Eli Nazareno. After arrest by the Inquisition, he practiced Jewish rites and conducted religious propaganda even in prison, until burned at an auto-da-fè in Lima. He was venerated as one of the outstanding Marrano martyrs. (3) *SAMUEL DA S.* (17th cent.): Marrano physician and controversialist. Born in Oporto, he returned to Judaism in Amsterdam. His Portuguese *Treatise on the Immortality of the Soul* (1623) was written to combat the views of Uriel Acosta. Another *SAMUEL DA S.* (fl. c. 1750) was an early English-Jewish artist.

SILVER, ABBA HILLEL (1893–1963): US rabbi and Zionist leader. Born in Lithuania, he was taken to the US as a child. From 1917, he was rabbi of the Temple, Cleveland, Ohio. He was at various times between 1938 and 1948 head of the Zionist Organization of America, American Zionist Emergency Council, United Jewish Appeal, United Palestine Appeal, and Central Conference of American Rabbis. As chairman of the American section of the Jewish Agency he was one of the chief Zionist spokesmen before the UN in the Palestine hearings of 1947. His writings include *Messianic Speculations in Ancient Israel* and *Where Judaism Differed.*

SILVERMAN, MORRIS (1894–1972): US Rabbi. From 1923, he was rabbi in Hartford, Conn. The Sabbath, Festival, and High Holiday prayer books which he edited and published have become popular in the Conservative movement in the US.

SILVERMAN, SAMUEL SYDNEY (1895–1968): British politician. A lawyer by profession, he sat in the House of Commons as a Labor member from 1935, and was largely responsible for legislation abolishing capital punishment in Britain.

SIMA, MIRON (1902–): Painter. Of Russian birth, he settled in Palestine in 1933. He excels as an expressionist painter of landscapes and portraits in oils and gouache.

SIMEON: Second son of Jacob. Out of zeal for the good name of his sister Dinah, he and Levi tricked the citizens of Shechem, captured the town, slaughtered its male inhabitants, and took captive the women and children (Gen. 34). Jacob objected to these acts and in his final benediction prophecied the dispersion of the descendants of S. and Levi among the other tribes. The tribe of S. received territory in Palestine within the lot of Judah in two distinct localities of the Negev but was of minor importance. In the reign of Hezekiah, they took possession of the Arab areas of Seir (1 Chron. 4:24–43). Some of them apparently settled in the Mountains of Ephraim (II Chron. 15:9).

SIMEON BAR GIORA see **BAR GIORA**

SIMEON BEN ELEAZAR (fl. 2nd–3rd cents. CE): Tanna: pupil of R Meir. He is mentioned only seven times in the Mishnah but figures prominently in the Tosephta. Many differences of opinion are recorded between him and his contemporary R Judah Ha-Nasi. A characteristic of his teaching was to lay down general rules, and many *halakhot* are recorded with the opening formula: "This is the general rule, said R Simeon ben Eleazar." He was also noted as aggadist and polemist.

SIMEON BEN GAMALIEL: (1) Patriarch, fl. 1st cent. CE. He succeeded to the patriarchate about 20 years before the destruction of the Temple. Initially a leader of the revolt against Rome in 66 CE and a member of the revolutionary government, he later inclined to moderation and became unpopular with the war-party. He is listed among the "Ten Martyrs" but it is possible that he fell at the hands of the zealots. His name does not occur frequently in tannaitic sources, but many of his teachings have been recorded anonymously in the name of the "School of Hillel." (2) Patriarch, fl. 2nd cent. CE. During the period of the Bar Kochba rebellion he had to go into hiding, but was subsequently elected patriarch, setting up his center at Usha in Galilee. Other scholars established rival centers of learning, leaving him with relatively few students. His decisions, quoted in the Mishnah and Tosephta, were moderate and gave much force to local custom; with 3 exceptions, they were accepted as halakhah.

SIMEON BEN ISAAC BEN ABUN (d. c. 1015): Liturgical poet, living in Mainz, known as S. the Great: uncle of Rashi. Many of S.'s hymns, which are of great spiritual force, are included in the Ashkenazi liturgy, especially for the New Year, etc. He was reputed father of the legendary pope ELHANAN.

SIMEON BEN LAKISH (known as Resh Lakish; c. 200 — c. 275): Palestinian amora; colleague and brother-in-law of R JOHANAN BAR NAPPAHA through whose influence he returned to Jewish study after a roving life. He taught at the Tiberias academy and became prominent as an aggadist. S. was noted for his physical strength.

SIMEON BEN MATTATHIAS see **SIMON THE HASMONEAN**

SIMEON BEN SHETAH (fl. 1st cent. BCE): Reputed president of the Sanhedrin. A brother of Queen SALOME ALEXANDRA, he was largely responsible for making Pharisaic influence dominant in public and private life during her reign (76–67), when he turned the Sanhedrin into a Pharisaic body. Together with Judah ben Tabbai he constituted the third of the ZUGOT. His period of leadership is pictured in legend as one of peace and prosperity.

SIMEON BEN TZEMAH DURAN see **DURAN**

SIMEON BEN YOHAI (fl. mid-2nd cent. CE): Tanna. He was a pupil of R Akiva, even following him for instruction after Akiva's imprisonment by the Romans. S. himself expressed opinions which the authorities thought rebellious and was forced to hide in a cave with his son Eleazar for 13 years. This incident was the background for attributing to him authorship of the ZOHAR. He was unworldly, teaching that Torah study should take precedence over the pursuit of a livelihood; he even regarded a man who paused in his study to admire nature as deserving death (*Avot* 3:7). S. was noted as a miracle-worker. In later life, he was sent on a mission to Rome where he succeeded in obtaining the withdrawal of a persecutory decree. He had an intense love for the Holy Land and considered emigration from there a grievous sin. His pupil R Judah Ha-Nasi frequently quotes him in the Mishnah. Kabbalists have long made his traditional tomb at Meron a center of pilgrimage, especially on LAG BA'OMER, the traditional date of his death.

SIMEON HA-DARSHAN see **KAYYARA, SIMEON**

SIMEON KAHIRA see **KAYYARA, SIMEON**

SIMEON SON OF JUDAH THE GALILEAN (1st cent. CE): Zealot leader. He and his brother Jacob, who led the Zealots after their father's death, were captured and crucified as rebels by the procurator Tiberius Alexander (46–8 CE). They were succeeded as leaders of the sect by their younger brother MENAHEM.

SIMHAH BEN SAMUEL OF VITRY (d. 1105): French scholar; pupil of Rashi. He compiled the *Mahzor Vitry*, a principal authority for the prayerbook, synagogal customs, and hymnology of medieval French Jewry.

SIMHAT TORAH (Heb. "Rejoicing of the Law"): Holiday marking the annual completion of the synagogue reading of the Pentateuch. It is observed on SHEMINI ATZERET (outside Israel as a separate celebration on the following day). The name is comparatively modern. It is customary to take out all the Scrolls of the Law and to carry them seven times or more round the synagogue, sometimes with dances which may be continued for hours. All male worshipers are called up for *aliyah* at the time of reading. The last section of Deuteronomy is read by (or for) the Bridegroom of the Law (*Hatan Torah*); he is followed by the Bridegroom of Genesis (*Hatan Bereshit*) who reads (or has read for him) the first verses of Genesis. Sweets are usually distributed to the children and the "bridegrooms" act as hosts to the community.

SIMMEL, GEORG (1858–1918): German philosopher, professor at Berlin and Strasbourg. He was one of the first to apply philosophy to history and sociology, basing himself on Bergson and William James. He attempted to establish the relation of spiritual life and metaphysics, further emphasizing the impact of human attitudes on the development of human institutions. Besides works on abstract philosophy, S. wrote studies of individuals and was a recognized authority on Goethe. S. was baptized.

SIMON OF TRENT see **TRENT**

SIMON THE HASMONEAN (called Thassi or Tarsi; d. 135 BCE): Second and last surviving son of Mattathias the HASMONEAN. He succeeded his brother JONATHAN in 142 BCE as head of the Jewish state. S. captured Gezer, secured the evacuation by the Greek troops of the Acra which dominated Jerusalem, and received exemption from tribute from Demetrius II. He was now elected hereditary high priest, ethnarch, and general (142/1). He renewed the treaty with Rome in 138 and at Jabneh defeated Antiochus VII who was attempting to reimpose tribute (135). S. was murdered by his son-in-law Ptolemy the same year. It was he who finally established Jewish independence, under a hereditary dynasty of high priests. S. was succeeded by his son John Hyrcanus.

SIMON THE JUST (Heb. *Shimon Ha-Tzaddik*): High priest; one of the last survivors of the Great Assembly (according to *Avot* 1:2). Opinions differ as to whether the title "the Just" was given to Simon I (4th–3rd cents. BCE) or to Simon II (3rd–2nd cents. BCE). If the talmudic account of his meeting with

Alexander the Great (*Yoma* 69*a*) is accepted, then the former identification must be adopted. The second theory, which is less likely, is based on the hypothesis that S. was the subject of the panegyric of the high priest Simon, son of Onias, in *Ecclesiasticus* 50. The Talmud praises S. highly and describes seven wonders that occurred during his priesthood (*Yoma* 39*b*). Despite the legendary nature of the tradition, the figure of a strong and saintly personality emerges.

SIMON: (1) *SIR LEON S.* (1881-1965): British civil servant and scholar. He became director of telegraphs and telephones in the British post office (1931) and then, of national savings (1935). He was a member of the 1918 Zionist Commission. S. lived in Israel, 1946–53, being active in the Hebrew Univ. administration and establishing the Israel postal savings bank. His books include several on Ahad Ha-Am and Hebrew translations of Greek classics. (2) *MAURICE S.* (1874–1955): Scholar; brother of (1). He was co-editor of the English translation of the Zohar and wrote works of Jewish interest.

SIMON, ERNST AKIVA (1899–): Educator. He was born in Germany where he co-edited *Der Jude* with Martin Buber (1923–5). Since 1928 he has been living in Palestine, teaching pedagogics at the Hebrew Univ. from 1940, and writing books on education, philosophy, etc.

SIMON, SIR FRANCIS EUGEN (1893–1956): Physicist. He taught at Berlin, Breslau, and (after 1933) Oxford. His work in the field of low temperature physics was of fundamental importance in atomic research.

SIMON, JAMES (1851–1932): German cotton merchant and philanthropist. He was a member of the directorate of the Reichsbank and vice-president of the Berlin Chamber of Commerce. He donated many valuable works of art to Berlin museums and helped to finance several archeological expeditions in the Middle East. In 1901, he was one of the founders of the HILFSVEREIN DER DEUTSCHEN JUDEN.

SIMON, SIR JOHN (1818–1897): British lawyer. Born and educated in Jamaica, he practiced successfully at the English Bar and was made serjeant-at-law in 1868. As a Liberal member of parliament 1872–92, he championed Jewish causes outspokenly in the House of Commons, especially at the time of the Russian persecutions. He was active in the London Reform Synagogue and was a founder of the Anglo-Jewish Association.

SIMON, JOSEPH (1851–1935): US public official. He served in the Portland city council 1877–80, in the Oregon State Senate 1880–98, in the US Senate 1898–1903, and as mayor of Portland 1909–11.

SIMON, JULIUS (1875–1969): Zionist leader and economist. Of German birth, he was early connected with the Jewish Colonial Trust. In the US

from 1922, he founded the PALESTINE ECONOMIC CORPORATION taking charge of its work in Palestine in 1934, and directing various other major economic projects there.

SIMON, NEIL (1927–): US playwright and TV writer. With his brother Danny he wrote *Come Blow Your Horn*. His other successes included *Barefoot in the Park* and *Plaza Suite*.

SIMONSEN, DAVID JACOB (1853–1932): Danish rabbi, bibliophile, and orientalist; chief rabbi of Copenhagen 1891–1902. His copious writings on oriental studies included a work on Palmyrene sculpture and inscriptions. He was an organizer of the MEKITZE NIRDAMIM society. His great collection of books, still bearing his name, is now at the Royal Library, Copenhagen.

SIMSON, MARTIN EDUARD VON (1810–1899): German jurist and statesman. In 1849 as head of the German parliament he headed the deputation which offered the crown of the German Empire to Frederick William of Prussia. S. sat in subsequent parliaments and in 1870, led the Reichstag delegation which asked the king of Prussia to accept the crown offered by the princes. He presided over the first Reichstag of the Reich 1871–4, and from 1879–1891 was the first president of the German Supreme Court. B. was baptized in his youth.

SIN: Twenty-first letter of the Hebrew alphabet; numerical value 300. In pointed script distinguished from *shin* (שׁ), by having a dot over its left shank (שׂ), undistinguishable in unpointed script. Though no doubt it had a distinct sound in ancient times, *sin* has in all Hebrew dialects the same sound as *samekh*, namely *s*. Confusions of spelling in the Masoretic Bible text show that this dates from very early times.

SIN: Any violation of righteous actions, whether toward God or one's fellow man, is considered sinful by Judaism. There are variations in the degree of s., the three prime categories being (in ascending order): *het* (unwillful s.), *avon* (knowledgeable s.), and *pesha* (rebellious s.). No man is free of s., although he has the free will to reject it. REPENTANCE and forgiveness, therefore, are inextricably linked in Judaism with the subject of s. No s. is unpardonable. Sacrifice, repentance, the Day of Atonement, and death bring forgiveness. For a s. against a fellow-man, restitution and placation are essential. Biblical narrative invariably links individual punishment and national calamity to s. CONFESSION of s. is important in the Jewish conception of atonement. This confession, however, is made directly to Heaven and not to any intermediary. Moreover, it is considered improper to confess private sins aloud, and for this reason the Day of Atonement ritual has all confessions in the plural.

SIN OFFERING: Sacrifice brought in atonement for a sin committed unwittingly (Lev. 4:1–3). It

Stone from the Sinai peninsula bearing Aramaic inscriptions in Nabatean characters.

was also brought after childbirth, leprosy, and completion of the Nazirite vow, as well as on certain public occasions. According to circumstances it was either animal or bird.

SIN, WILDERNESS OF: Desert traversed by the Israelites during the Exodus Period on the journey from the Red Sea to Rephidim (Exod. 15:1; 17:1). It is thought to lie in the Sinai peninsula.

SINAI: Mountain where MOSES received the Law.

The name is also applied to the surrounding desert where the Israelites encamped and received most of the Pentateuchal legislation (Exod. 19:2), and later to the entire peninsula between Egypt and Palestine. The exact location of the mountain is undetermined, but the monastery of St. Catherine purports to be built on the site.

SINAI DESERT: Peninsula extending between the two branches of the Red Sea. Throughout its history it has been settled only at its oases and by Bedouin. It was crossed by the children of Israel after the Exodus from Egypt. It was captured by Israel from Egypt at the time of the SINAI OPERATION of 1956 but evacuated shortly thereafter. It was again captured by the Israel army in the SIX-DAY WAR of 1967.

SINAI INSCRIPTIONS: Inscriptions in an alphabetic script discovered by Flinders Petrie in 1906 in the S Sinai peninsula. The date is disputed but is now generally placed in the 15th cent. BCE. The writing is regarded as a prototype of the ancient Hebrew (Phoenician) script.

SINAI OPERATION: Israel military operation directed against Egypt, Oct. 29–Nov. 5, 1956. Its objectives were to break the ring of encirclement

Military formation among the Sand-dunes of the Sinai Desert.

The Egyptian destroyer "Ibrahim el-Awal" is tugged into
Haifa port after her surrender to the Israeli naval forces.

Israeli forces 15 km east of the Suez Canal, in 1956.

created by the anti-Israel alliance of Egypt, Jordan, and Syria, to destroy the menacing concentration of Egyptian armaments, and to eliminate marauder bases in the GAZA STRIP. Within a few days, Israel forces conquered the entire Sinai peninsula, with the exception of a 10-mile strip along the E side of the Suez Canal (not occupied in accordance with an Anglo-French ultimatum), and took possession of the Gaza Strip. Large quantities of Russian-manufactured material and 5,600 Egyptian prisoners were captured in this operation, as well as an Egyptian destroyer which attempted to shell Haifa port. Israel losses were 171 dead, 700 wounded, and one prisoner. The operation took on a new aspect from Nov. 2, when British and French bombers attacked strategic Egyptian positions before occupying Port Said. Under pressure from the United Nations, Britain and France soon evacuated the points they had captured. The Israel withdrawal was slower, but was reluctantly completed with the evacuation of the Gaza Strip and Sharm e-Sheikh at the S tip of the Sinai peninsula in March 1957. Notwithstanding this, the S. O. resulted in the opening of the Gulf of Elath to Israel shipping and the temporary decline of Nasser's prestige after his military defeat.

SINGAPORE: Far Eastern port. The Jewish community was founded c. 1840 by Baghdad Jews (later reinforced from India and Europe), the first synagogue being built in 1878, and the second in 1904. David MARSHALL was the chief minister of S. 1955–6. Jewish pop. (1973): 500.

SINGER: (1) *CHARLES S.* (1876–1960): English historian of science; son of (3). He was professor of the history of medicine at London Univ. 1932–7, co-edited the *Legacy of Israel* and *The History of Technology*, and was author of many works on the history of science. (2) *DOROTHEA WALEY S.* (1882–1964), wife of (1), also wrote extensively on the history of science. (3) *SIMEON S.* (1848–1906): English rabbi. Minister in London synagogues, renowned preacher, and author of scholarly studies, he published in 1890 a new edition and translation of the Daily Prayer Book, of which 25 editions (over 500,000 copies) had appeared by 1956.

SINGER: (1) *ISAAC BASHEVIS S.* (1904–): Yiddish novelist. Born in Poland, he went to the US in 1935. His novels, which achieved wide popularity in English translation, include *The Family Moskat, Gimpel the Fool, The Magician of Lublin*, and *The Manor*. (2) *ISRAEL JOSHUA S.* (1893–1944): Yiddish novelist; brother of (1). Born in Poland, he settled in the US in 1934. Beginning as a writer of short stories about Polish Jews, his reputation was established by his play *Yoshe Kalb*. S.'s finest novel *Di Brider Ashkenazi* ("The Brothers Ashkenazi"), an epic of the Jewish textile industry in Lodz, was also dramatized.

SINGER, ISIDORE (1859–1939): US scholar. He was born in Moravia and was a journalist in Paris before going to New York in 1895. S.'s great achievement was his plan of the *Jewish Encyclopedia* (appearing 1901–06), of which he was managing editor. He also wrote extensively on Jewish life and thought.

SINZHEIM, JOSEPH DAVID (1745–1812): French rabbi. Rabbi of Strasbourg, he was a leading participant in the Assembly of Notables and president of the Great Sanhedrin (1807). Napoleon appointed him chief rabbi of the Central Consistory on its inception. S. was author of *Yad David* (unfinished) on parts of the Babylonian Talmud.

SIPHRA (Aram. "The Book"): Halakhic Midrash of Leviticus; also known as *Torat Kohanim* ("Law of the Priests") and *Siphra de-ve Rav* ("The Book of the School of Rav"). It is a product of the school of R Akiva and reflects primarily the views of Akiva's pupil R Judah (*Sanhedrin* 86a).

SIPHRE (Aram. "The Books"): Midrash on Numbers and Deuteronomy. The section on Numbers is primarily halakhah and that on Deuteronomy, mostly aggadah. Almost all of this tannaitic work comes from the school of R Ishmael, R Akiva's contemporary and opponent, except for the commentary on the strictly legal part of Deuteronomy (Chaps. 16–26) which derives from the school of R Akiva.

SIPHRE ZUTA (Aram. "The Small *Siphre*"): Halakhic Midrash on Numbers, stemming from the school of R Akiva. This work records the differences between the Schools of Shammai and Hillel. Although quoted by writers of the Middle Ages, it was subsequently lost and manuscript fragments have only recently been found and a reconstruction rendered possible.

SIPHRIYYAT POALIM (Heb. "Workers' Library"): Israel publishing house. Founded in 1940 at Merhavyah by *Ha-Kibbutz ha-Artzi*, by 1975 it had brought out over 1,780 Hebrew titles. It publishes the *Encyclopedia of Social Sciences*.

SIRA see **BEN SIRA**

SIROTA, GERSHON (d. 1943): Cantor. He officiated in Vilna and Warsaw and achieved an international reputation. He was killed by the Nazis in the Warsaw ghetto.

SISERA: General of Jabin, Canaanite king who dwelt at Hazor. He conducted the war against the Israelites under Barak and Deborah. In the battle by the river Kishon, S. was defeated, and subsequently killed by Jael the Kenite, in whose tent he had sought refuge (Judg. 4–5).

SIVAN: Ninth month of the Jewish civil year, and third of the ecclesiastical one. It has 30 days. Feast of Weeks (*Shavuot*) occurs on the 6th of the month (6th–7th in the Diaspora). *Megillat Taanit* mentions S. 15, 16, and 25 as days on which auspicious historical events occurred. Later, the festive aspect

Israeli forces preparing for the conquest of the Golan-plateau.

of the month was overshadowed by the many tragedies which occurred in this period, especially during the Crusades.

SIX-DAY WAR: War between Israel and Egypt, Jordan, and Syria in 1967. It had been preceded by a building-up of tension, largely due to over two years of sabotage activities inside Israel and border incidents, mostly undertaken by the Syrians, who were interested in involving the other Arab states in a further war with Israel. Fearing Israel retaliation against Syria and in an effort to deflect it Egypt began moving its army into the Sinai peninsula on May 15, 1967. Nasser demanded the removal of UN troops who had been posted along the Gaza Strip and at Sharm e-Sheikh and when the UN secretary-general, U Thant immediately acceded, Nasser decreed a blockade of the Straits of Tiran so that no Israel shipping would be permitted to go to the port of Elath. Israel inaugurated diplomatic activity to try and prevent the situation from deteriorating into war but Nasser moved 100,000 men and 1,000 tanks into Sinai while the other Arab states rapidly made their preparations and coordinated their moves for a unified attack on Israel, including an agreement between Nasser and King Hussein of Jordan. The Arab world was seized with war hysteria and in a preemptive move, Israel struck on June 5. The Israel Air Force went into action, attacking mainly grounded Egyptian planes, over 300 of which were destroyed in 3 hours. Similar attacks virtually wiped out the Syrian and Jordanian air forces. At the same time, Israel troops attacked Egyptian positions along the Gaza Strip and in the Sinai Desert. By June 8, Israel had overrun the Gaza Strip and the entire Sinai peninsula as far west as the Suez Canal and as far south as Sharm e-Sheikh. A few hours after the fighting had begun, Jordan attacked Israel, despite a message sent to Hussein by the Israel prime minister Levi Eshkol that if she remained out, she would not be attacked. Israel Jerusalem and border settlements were heavily shelled by the Jordanians. Late on June 5, Israel troops began their moves against Jordanian positions and in a pincer-move, starting from the Latrun salient, cut off Jordanian Jerusalem (including the Old City) which fell on June 7. The entire area W. of the Jordan river, including Bethlehem, Hebron, and Nablus fell to the Israel army. Particularly emotional scenes were witnessed when the Israel troops first reached the Western Wall, access to which had been barred to Jews for almost 20 years. In the North, Syria had shelled border settlements and made a couple of unsuccessful attempts to advance beyond the frontier during the first four days of the fighting. Only after the fighting on the southern and eastern fronts ended did Israel troops move to attack the Syrian positions. The terrain here proved particularly difficult inasmuch as the Syrians were entrenched in the heights overlooking the Israel positions. However after three days of bitter fighting (June 8–10), the Golan Heights were cleared of Syrian troops and Israel accepted the UN demand for a cease-fire. The immediate effects of the War were to remove the Arab openly-voiced threat of destruction of the State of Israel; to break Arab military strength (which, in

Israeli paratroopers in front of The Wailing Wall.

the case of Egypt and Syria, was speedily built up again by the Russians); to reopen the Straits of Tiran to Israel shipping; to remove the constant threat of bombardment from settlements along the Syrian border and in the center of the country; and to leave Israel with more easily defensible boundaries, farther removed from the main centers of population. It also left Israel ruling a further million Arabs — a situation which presented a variety of political, security, and administrative problems. Parallel to the Six-Day War, intense diplomatic activities were carried on in various parts of the world and especially at the UN. Here the efforts of the Arab states and their supporters — notably Russia and the East European states (who with the exception of Rumania had broken off all relations with Israel) — to cancel Israel's military victory through political pressure were largely nullified due to US support of Israel. A disappointment to Israel was the stand of De Gaulle's France — previously friendly to Israel — which now adopted an outright anti-Israel stance. The debate lasted for several months and a resolution was finally passed calling both on Israel to evacuate territories she had occupied and the Arab States to end their state of belligerency with Israel. Despite continuing diplomatic activity, no progress was made in the implementation of this resolution. The Six-Day War period witnessed a tremendous upsurge of feeling among Jews in all parts of the world. Contributions to Israel reached record levels, thousands of volunteers reached Israel to undertake civilian jobs vacated by those who had been called to military duty, and a hitherto unsuspected profundity of identity between the Jewish people and Israel was revealed.

SIYYUM (Heb. "termination"): The completion of the writing of the Pentateuch scroll or more particularly of the study of a tractate of the Talmud. Both are recognized occasions for joyful celebration. In the former case, a few lines are left in outline, to give various people an opportunity to indite at least one letter of the Torah. In the second, a special meal is held where a *hadran* ("conclusion lecture") is delivered. First-born often forego their traditional fast on Passover eve by organizing the celebration of a talmudic *s.* on that day.

SKOSS, SOLOMON LEON (1884–1953): Orientalist. Of Russian birth, he went to the US in 1907 and became professor of Arabic at Dropsie College, Philadelphia. S. made important contributions to the study of early Hebrew philology by his researches on Saadyah's grammatical works and his edition of the dictionary of the 10th cent. Karaite David Alfasi.

SLANDER (Heb. *leshon ha-ra*): The spreading of malicious reports to damage another person's reputation. This is regarded as the greatest of crimes for, as the Midrash puts it, "the slanderer speaks in Rome and kills his victim in Syria." To listen to s.

is equally forbidden. Scripture cites only the case of a husband who falsely questions his newly-married wife's virginity (Deut. 22:13 ff), his punishment including both a flogging and a heavy fine. Later rabbinic law made stringent enactments to punish all slanderers, giving the courts the power to fine and excommunicate the offender until he apologizes to the satisfaction of the person he has injured. In some cases, fasting was required as an additional penance. False s. (see MALSHIN) must be distinguished from *leshon ha-ra* (damaging gossip, possibly based on fact).

SLANSKY TRIAL: Communist "purge" trial, 1952–3, in which the central figure was Rudolf Slansky, till 1950 general secretary of the Czech Communist Party and till 1951 vice-premier of Czechoslovakia. In Nov. 1952, Slansky and 13 of his associates were charged with "Trotskyite-Titoist-Zionist activities in the service of American imperialism." They were also alleged to have maintained espionage contact with Israel diplomats. In Dec. 1952, S. and 10 others (including 7 Jews) were found guilty and executed.

SLAUGHTER, RITUAL see **SHEHITAH**

SLAVES AND SLAVERY: Jewish law recognized the institution of slavery, which existed in parts of the world until the 19th cent., but made detailed provision for its humane regulation. Scriptural law allowed an Israelite to become another Israelite's slave only for a limited period, with manumission at the seventh year of service or at the jubilee year; the freed slave, moreover, was to receive a suitable parting gift. Even this limited form of slavery became impossible after the Babylonian Exile. Non-Jewish ("Canaanite") slaves were normally acquired by purchase from neighboring peoples. These slaves were proselytes of a kind, the males having to undergo circumcision, and the women being subject to the laws binding Jewish women. A slave's marriage was arranged by the master, and the offspring were the property of the owner. Although a master could beat a slave, to kill him was considered murder, and if a master destroyed his slave's eye, tooth, etc., the slave went free. A slave who escaped was not to be handed back to his master, and according to rabbinic law, one who reached Palestine automatically regained his freedom. Freed slaves were considered proselytes in every respect. In the Middle Ages, Jewish merchants engaged to some extent in the slave trade, but because of the danger entailed, especially in Christian lands, the slaves generally remained non-Jewish. Nevertheless, the benediction to be recited on the occasion of the circumcision of a slave continued to figure in some Sephardi prayer books down to the 17th (or in India to the 19th) cent.

Although there were Jewish slave-owners, (e.g. in the W Indies and the southern states of the US), many Jews were prominent in the struggle which finally led to the abolition of slavery. Individual Jews in the

US such as Judah Touro were among the first to free their slaves. American Jews as a whole took no stand in the slavery debates which preceded and continued through the American Civil War. But many individuals were active in the abolitionist cause, e.g. Michael Heilprin, August Bondi, and Rabbis Einhorn, Felsenthal, Adler, and Szold. On the other hand, Rabbi Morris J. Raphaell of New York City declared publicly (1861) that the Bible sanctioned slavery. A number of Jews assisted in the "Underground Railway" that smuggled slaves to free states and Canada. Jews who fought for abolition on the political front included Sigismund Kaufman, Philip J. Joachimsen, and Abraham Kohn.

SLAVUTA see **SHAPIRO**

SLIOSBERG, HENRY (1863–1937): Russian barrister and communal leader. Head of the St. Petersburg community, he frequently intervened with the Russian government on Jewish matters and appeared in several Jewish *causes célèbres*. S. wrote a history of Russian legislation concerning Jews, a history of the Günzburg family, and memoirs.

SLOBODKA: Suburb of Kovno, Lithuania, famed for its yeshivah (founded 1881) conducted in the spirit of the MUSAR MOVEMENT. In 1925, some of its students founded a yeshivah at Hebron, from where they removed to Jerusalem in 1929. Former leaders of the S. yeshivah founded the Bene Berak yeshivah in 1947. A second important yeshivah was opened in S. in 1897 but left during World War I, eventually establishing itself in Kamenetz (Lithuania).

SLONIMSKY: E European family. *HAYYIM SELIG S.* (1810–1904), editor and mathematician, directed the government rabbinical college at Zhitomir from 1862. He invented a calculating machine, made improvements in the telegraph, and wrote in Hebrew on mathematics, astronomy, and the calendar. In 1861, he founded the periodical HA-TZEPHIRAH. His son *LEONID S.* (1850–1918) was a liberal Russian journalist and his grandsons included *ANTONY S.* (1894–1976), Polish poet (baptized), *ALEXANDER S.* (1881–), Russian literary critic, *MIKHAIL S.* (1897–1972), Russian poet, and *NICOLAS S.* (1894–) composer and musicologist, resident in the US since 1923, *HENRY S.* (1884–1970) philosopher, taught at the Jewish Institute of Religion, New York.

SLOUSCHZ, NAHUM (1872–1966): Author and scholar. Born in Lithuania, he spent his youth in Odessa and was early associated with the Zionist movement. In 1903, he wrote the first history of modern Hebrew literature. The next year, he became lecturer in modern Hebrew at the Sorbonne. S. traveled extensively in N Africa, taking special interest in Jewish antiquities and the position of the Jews there, which he described in several volumes. His other works include a book on the Portuguese Marranos and a corpus of Phoenician inscriptions. He

lived in the US 1916–18, and from 1919 in Palestine.

SLOVAKIA: Region in Central Europe. Its Jewish community dates from the 12th cent. In 1291, the Jews received a special charter from Andrew III; they were expelled in 1360 but allowed to return in 1368. S. was the center to which representatives of Jewish communities came to submit their petitions to' the Seym. Anti-Jewish outbreaks occurred in 1848, 1850, 1887, and 1889 in Pressburg which was the home of the first Hungarian anti-Semitic organization and newspaper. In the 20th cent., the Jews of S. established a federation. They numbered c. 100,000 in 1939; some escaped from the Germans but over 60,000 were sent to death-camps in Poland and Germany. After World War II many Jews concentrated in S. and the 1968 Jewish population was estimated at c. 9,000.

SMILANSKY, MOSHEH (1874–1953): Israel author and planter. He went to Palestine from Russia in 1890 and from 1893, lived in Rehovot. As an owner of citrus plantations, he was active in developing the Jewish economy, being a founder and for many years president of the Palestine Farmers' Association, editor of its journal *Bustanai* (1929–39). He was a prolific author of stories, memoirs, the history of modern Palestinian colonization, etc. His tales of Arab life — the first in Hebrew — appeared under the pseudonym "Khawaja Musa." His great-nephew *YIZHAR S.* (pen-name S. Yizhar; 1918–) is a Hebrew novelist writing against a modern Israel background. His best known work is *Yeme Ziklag*. He has represented *Mapai* and *Rafi* in the Knesset.

SMOLENSKIN, PERETZ (1842–1885): Hebrew author. Born in White Russia, he left home at the age of 12 and, after several years of wandering, lived in Odessa 1862–7 and thereafter in Vienna. His translation of Goethe's *Faust* appeared in 1867. In 1868, he founded the Hebrew monthly HA-SHAHAR which until 1885 (with interruptions) was the central organ of Hebrew literary activities and Jewish national thought; it contained most of S.'s stories and articles. In 1878, he started the weekly *Ha-Mabbit*, but only 26 numbers appeared. His romances and stories are marked by dramatic tension and a realistic description of E European Jewish life, their motives being to denounce moral blemishes and inculcate national Hebrew secular ideology. These works were widely circulated and exerted a strong influence on the Hebrew-reading public. His articles developed a Jewish national theory which was opposed to religious Orthodoxy and Haskalah. He maintained that the Jews are "a nation of intellect" whose national life is not dependent on a country of its own, on political power, or on a spoken language, but on intellectual values which must be transmitted to all nations. Jews must foster the ideals of historical national culture, the Hebrew language, and the hope of redemption. His theories were later developed by DUBNOW. After the 1881 pogroms, S. joined the *Ḥibbat Zion* movement and enthusiastically advocated emigration to Palestine.

SMUSHKEVICH, YAKOV (1902–c. 1949): Russian soldier. He fought in the Bolshevik forces during the Revolution and in 1921–31, served in the Soviet air force as commissar and political officer. In 1931, he became commander of an aviation brigade and in 1940, head of the Soviet military air force. He was killed in the Stalinist purges.

*SMUTS, JAN CHRISTIAN (1870–1950): S African statesman. As a member of the British War Cabinet in 1917 he was one of the authors of the Balfour Declaration, which he consistently supported thereafter.

SMYRNA see **IZMIR**

SNEH (KLEINBAUM), MOSHEH (1909–1972): Israel politician. In Poland he was a General Zionist leader. In 1940, he reached Palestine and as a member of the *Haganah* staff conducted its resistance and "illegal" immigration operations, becoming a member of the Jewish Agency Executive in 1945. In 1947, he resigned and joined *Mapam*. In 1953, he formed an independent left-wing group which later merged in the Israel Communist Party. He sat in the Knesset 1949–65 (from 1949 for *Mapam*, from 1955 as a communist). When the Communist Party divided, S. was a leader of the MAKI faction.

SOBELOFF, SIMON ERNEST (1893–1973): US jurist. After a noted legal career in Maryland, he served as US solicitor-general from 1954 to 1956 when he was appointed judge of the Circuit Court of Appeals.

SOCIALISM: The participation of Jews in the Socialist movement varied according to time and place. In 19th cent. France, Jews (e.g. the brothers Pereire) were conspicuous in the Saint-Simonian movement. In Great Britain, the role played by the Jews in the Socialist movement was insignificant. Jews assumed importance only in the Socialist movements of Germany, Austria, and Russia. In Germany, the outstanding founders of the Socialist movement were Jews (Moses Hess, Ferdinand Lassale) or converted Jews (Karl Marx). Eduard Bernstein, the spiritual father of German revisionism, was a Jew. In Austria, Victor Adler and Otto Bauer were the most important Jewish leaders of Social Democracy. In Russia, Jews were prominent both among the Menshevik and Bolshevik leaderships. The number of important socialists (and anarchists) who at one time or another in their career fought against persecution of the Jews or against political anti-Semitism is high, although some were not entirely free of anti-Jewish bias. A number of great socialists showed a hostile attitude toward the Jews

because they considered all Jews (and not only the Jewish bourgeoisie) as an incarnation of social parasitism; thus, Charles Fourier regretted that the Jews were granted civil equality and proposed discriminatory measures against them, while for Pierre Joseph Proudhon, the Jewish people personified intellectual incapacity, parasitism, and lust for domination. In the eighteen-sixties, a new variety of socialist Jew-hatred appeared; racial anti-Semitism, first propagated by the Blanquists, and later by the Fourierist epigones. In Germany, the great socialists were biased against the Jewish people. Lassalle in his early years showed some attachment to Judaism but developed Jew-hatred in time, although his anti-Jewish statements were almost all made in private. No trace of such restraint is found in Marx who throughout his life never ceased to be an anti-Semite, as is clearly shown in his published writings as well as in his private correspondence. Engels indulged in anti-Jewish utterances during more than thirty years but noting the danger which anti-Semitism involves for s., he changed his attitude. Many socialist anti-Semites were Jews, e.g. Marx, Lassalle, Victor Adler, and Bernard Lazare (in the earlier stage of his career). The Socialist movement was almost always officially opposed to political anti-Semitism. However, anti-Semitic trends existed not only among individual socialists but also in Socialist parties, organizations, and in the Socialist press. The leading Socialist organ *La Revue Socialiste* frequently printed anti-Jewish material in the eighteen-eighties and -nineties, and a similar attitude was adopted in other countries. Anti-Jewish trends within the International Association of Workingmen (the First International) were chiefly represented by Bakunin and some of his friends. The *Narodnaya Volya* issued a proclamation in 1881, urging the masses to revolt against the "Jewish Czar," the Jews, and the nobles. The Jewish question was discussed at the International Socialist Congress in Brussels in 1891: Abraham Cahan, representing the Hebrew Trades of New York, asked the Congress to vote a declaration of sympathy for the Jewish workers. The Congress rejected his motion and voted instead a resolution condemning both "anti-Semitic and philo-Semitic excitations." At the end of the 19th cent., anti-Semitism within the Socialist movement of W Europe became increasingly weak but remained fairly strong in E European countries. During World War I, the Socialist International changed its attitude toward the Jewish people and became increasingly friendly toward the Jewish cause. It finally recognized the Jews as a nationality, and their right to create a national center in Palestine (1919). Moreover, some of the most prominent members of the International gave moral support to Zionism. The Jewish Socialist attitude to the Jewish problem can be divided historically into 4 outlooks:

Accommodations for the workers of The Israel Potash Works at Sodom.
In the background, Mount Sodom, a mountain built of salt and gypsum.

(1) The assimilationist: this was adopted, e.g. by Jewish communists who held, after World War I, that all Jewish problems would be solved automatically by the dictatorship of the proletariat; later special attention began to be paid to Jewish problems (partly on a territorial basis—c. BIROBIDJAN), but never on a basis of Jewish independence. (2) The Territorialist: the Jewish masses required productivization to create s., and therefore an autonomous territory was necessary. This school, flourishing 1904–14, virtually disappeared after 1917, except for brief resurgences. (3) The BUNDIST: Jewish problems would be solved with the general Socialist (Social-Democratic) revolution in each land, but cultural Jewish (generally Yiddishist) AUTONOMY was favored. Allied was the SEYMIST view, which advocated Jewish local autonomy based on representative councils. Both views declined between the World Wars. (4) The Zionist Socialist, stressing national territorial concentration and economic productivization in Palestine (Israel) as a prerequisite of s. See also TRADE UNIONS.

SOCIÉTÉ DES ÉTUDES JUIVES: French organization founded in 1880 to encourage the study of Jewish history and literature. It has been responsible for the publication of the REVUE DES ÉTUDES JUIVES and scholarly works.

SOCIETY FOR THE ADVANCEMENT OF JUDAISM: US organization founded in 1922 by Mordecai M. KAPLAN, sponsoring the advancement of Judaism as a religious civilization. The Society, located in New York City, carries on all the activities of a religious congregation, together with support of the RECONSTRUCTIONIST Foundation.

SOCIETY FOR THE DISSEMINATION OF ENLIGHTENMENT: Society founded at St. Petersburg in 1963 for the propagation of secular education in the Russian language among the Jews. It sponsored Russian translations of the Bible, of Graetz's *History of the Jews*, etc. Later, it organized Jewish schools with Russian as the language of instruction. In 1891, it founded a society for Jewish history and ethnography. It possessed considerable resources and attracted thousands of members. All activities ceased with the advent of the Soviet regime.

SODOM (Heb. *Sedom*): Chief of the five cities ("Pentapolis") of the Jordan plain (the others being Gomorrah, Admah, Zeboiim, and Zoar). Lot and his family settled in S. but escaped its destruction caused by the wickedness of its inhabitants (Gen. 19).

The site of the five cities of the plain has been disputed, some scholars assigning them to the northern end of the Dead Sea, while tradition expressed by the location of Jebel Usdum ("Mountain of S.") and the vicinity of Zoar (where Lot and his daughters took refuge) suggests the south. This latter region was once dry land and might have been overwhelmed by a catastrophe within human memory. The name of S. has been revived for the site of the Israel potash works at the southern end of the Dead Sea.

SOFIA: Capital of Bulgaria. A community of Greek-speaking Jews was living there in the 10th cent. Jews arrived from Hungary in 1376, Bavaria in 1470, and Spain in 1492: the Sephardim eventually constituted the predominant element. An Ashkenazi synagogue was founded after 1878 by Russian and Rumanian refugees. During World War II, the community was deprived of civil rights but escaped deportation. Jewish pop. (1973): 4,000.

SOKOLNIKOV (pseudonym of Grigorii Briliant; 1888–?): Russian communist leader. He was a member of the Soviet peace delegation at Brest-Litovsk in 1918, finance minister 1922–6, and Soviet minister in London 1929–33. In 1937, S. was condemned to 10 years' imprisonment and was not heard of again.

SOKOLOW, NAHUM (1860–1936): Zionist leader and Hebrew journalist. Polish born, in 1884 he joined the editorial board of *Ha-Tzephirah* in Warsaw, and was soon its manager, laying the foundation of the Hebrew periodical press in E Europe. He adhered to Zionism only after the First Congress, largely under the influence of Herzl. He was general secretary of the World Zionist Organization 1905–9,

Nahum Sokolow.

and in that capacity traveled extensively, edited the Organization's central journal *Die Welt*, and founded its Hebrew weekly *Ha-Olam*. He resigned his offices in 1910 because he supported "practical Zionism" against the "political Zionism" advocated by Wolffsohn. On the outbreak of World War I, he moved from Berlin to London where he was a key figure in the negotiations leading to the Balfour Declaration. During the Paris Peace Conference, he presided over the *Comité des délégations juives*. S. was chairman of the Zionist Executive from 1921 to 1931, when he was elected to succeed Weizmann as president of the World Zionist Organization and of the Jewish Agency. In 1935, when Weizmann returned to these offices, S. was elected honorary president and also president of the *Keren ha-Yesod*. His many books include a *History of Zionism*.

SOLA, DE: Sephardi family of Marrano origin. *DAVID AARON DE S.* (1796–1860), born in Holland, was minister of the Sephardi congregation in London and translated the liturgy (Sephardi and Ashkenazi) into English. His son *ABRAHAM DE S.* (1825–1882) was minister in Montreal and his sons were prominent in Canadian life. *JUAN ISAAC DE S.* (1795–1860), born in Curaçao, emigrated to the S American mainland and, after engaging in journalism, was a general in the Colombian forces in the war of independence against Spain.

SOLDIERS see **ARMED FORCES**

SOLEL BONEH see **COOPERATIVES (ISRAEL)**

SOLIELI (SOLOVEICHIK), MAX (1883–1957): Zionist. A member of the Lithuanian parliament in 1919–22, he was minister for Jewish affairs in the Lithuanian government. He settled in Palestine in 1933 and held various official positions. S. wrote several books of biblical scholarship.

SOLIS-COHEN: US family. Three brothers established its eminence: *JACOB S.-C.* (1838–1927), a pioneer of laryngology which he taught at Jefferson Medical College and the Philadelphia Polyclinic; *DAVID S.-C.* (1850–1928), who was police commissioner of Portland, Oregon, and its mayor 1896–8; and *SOLOMON S.-C.* (1857–1948), professor of clinical medicine and diagnostician, translator of medieval Hebrew poetry, founder of the *American Hebrew*, and from 1929–40 a member of the council of the Jewish Agency. Children of Jacob S.-C. included *JUDITH S.-C.* (1876–1927), writer of short stories and columnist; *MYER S.-C.* (1877–), physician and assistant director of public health in Philadelphia 1944–52; and *JACOB S.-C. JR* (1890–1968), president of the Jewish Publication Society 1933–49. *EMILY S.-C.* (1890–1966), daughter of Solomon, was a versatile writer.

SOLOMON: King of Israel c. 961–c. 920 BCE; son of David and Bathsheba. He succeeded to the throne before his father's death through the maneuvering of Bathsheba and the prophet Nathan. After consolidating his position, he rid himself of his elder brother, Adonijah, and other potentially dangerous individuals and built the TEMPLE in Jerusalem in cooperation with architects and builders sent him by Hiram of Tyre. The work was completed in the 11th year of S.'s reign and ensured the central position of Jerusalem in the kingdom. Administratively, S. divided the country into 12 districts and constructed a series of fortresses, store-cities, and chariot-cities (e.g. Megiddo, Hazor). To develop trade and commerce, he built a harbor at Elath on the Red Sea and, together with Hiram, sent a great fleet ("ships of Tarshish") to the land of OPHIR. Another source of wealth consisted of gifts from foreign monarchs, e.g. the queen of SHEBA who herself came with a large retinue to visit S. In addition, trade prospered with neighboring states. Large smelting furnaces in the S areas produced copper and iron. The royal house and court were built up with oriental magnificence, and sumptuous buildings housed the royal family and harem (consisting of 1,000 wives and concubines). Politically, S. rested on David's achievements; the realm extended from Egypt to the Euphrates and was the most energetic in the entire region. In the cultural sphere, the arts of historiography, parable, and elegant writing were developed, and several biblical works (e.g. Song of Songs, Ecclesiastes, Psalm 72) were later attributed to S., who himself achieved a widespread reputation for his wisdom. Despite all these successes, the first signs of the country's subsequent deterioration can be traced back to his reign. The forced labor connected with the extensive building program impoverished the country. Several subject peoples, such as the Edomites and Arameans, began to revolt, and there is evidence of malcontent inside Israel. These problems came to a head with S.'s death which was quickly succeeded by territorial loss and internal division. S. was called JEDIDIAH by Nathan (II Sam. 12:25).

SOLOMON, PSALMS OF see **PSALMS OF SOLOMON**

SOLOMON, SONG OF see **SONG OF SONGS**

SOLOMON'S POOLS: Name given to three rock-cut and walled pools S of Jerusalem. The two upper pools were constructed by Herod or Pontius Pilate and the third in the 15th cent. by the Mameluke sultan Qaitbay.

SOLOMON BEN ADRET see **ADRET**

SOLOMON BEN ISAAC see **RASHI**

SOLOMON BEN JEROHAM (fl. first half of 10th cent.): Karaite scholar. He lived in Egypt and Jerusalem, dying at Aleppo. His writings include Arabic commentaries (later translated into Hebrew) on several biblical books. He also wrote in rhyme a sharp Hebrew polemic against Saadyah Gaon.

SOLOMON HA-LEVI OF BURGOS see **SANTA MARIA, PAUL DE**

SOLOMON: S African family. *SAUL S.* (1777–1853) coming from Canterbury (England) was Napoleon's intimate in exile on St. Helena. His nephew, *SAUL S.* (1817–1892), was leader of the Liberal Party in Cape Colony; a great-nephew, *EDWARD S.* (d. 1914), was cabinet minister; another great-nephew, *SIR WILLIAM HENRY S.* (1852–1930), was chief justice. The family left Judaism.

SOLOMON: English family of artists; children of *MICHAEL S.* (b. 1779), the second Jew to obtain the Freedom of the City of London (1831). *ABRAHAM S.* (1824–1862) attained considerable distinction as a painter of genre scenes. He died on the day of his election as an associate of the Royal Academy. His younger brother *SIMEON S.* (1834–1905) was a promising member of the pre-Raphaelite group but became a pervert and passed his last years in misery. Their sister *REBECCA S.* (d. 1886) was also an artist of merit.

SOLOMON, EDWARD S. see **SALOMON**

SOLOMON, SOLOMON JOSEPH (1860–1921): English painter. He was noted for his portraits and also for his figure compositions, many with Jewish motifs. During World War I, he was a pioneer of "camouflage".

SOLOMON, VABIAN (1853–1908): Australian politician. He was prime minister of S Australia in 1899, and a member of the convention that framed the Commonwealth constitution.

SOLOMONS, ADOLPHUS SIMEON (1826–1910): US philanthropist. The American Red Cross was founded in Geneva in 1881 largely as the result of his initiative, and he was the first American vice-president of the International Red Cross.

SOLOVEICHIK: (1) *HAYYIM S.* (1853–1918): Lithuanian talmudist; son of (2). He taught at Volozhin yeshivah 1880–92, and developed a method of talmudic study based on an analysis of fundamental concepts which is still practiced in many yeshivot. S. was rabbi of Brest-Litovsk in succession to his father, 1892–1914. (2) *JOSEPH DOV S.* (1820–1892): Lithuanian talmudist. After teaching at Volozhin 1853–65, he became rabbi at Slutzk 1865–75, and Brest-Litovsk 1875–92. An outstanding scholar, he fought strongly against the Haskalah movement. His *Bet Ha-Levi* deals with both halakhah and aggadah. (3) *JOSEPH B. S.* (1903–): US rabbinic scholar. Head of the R. Isaac Elchanan Theological Seminary at Yeshiva University, S. is chairman of the Rabbinical Council *Halakhah* Commission and the outstanding Orthodox authority in the US.

SOMMERFELD, ARNOLD (1868–1951): German physicist; professor at Aachen and Munich. He extended knowledge of the atom by utilizing the theory of relativity. He explained the structure of spectrum lines by amplifying the quantum theory of the atom and, by developing the electronic theory, was able to explain electric conductance. He left Judaism.

SOMMERSTEIN, EMIL (1883–1957): Polish politician. In 1922–39, he was a deputy in the *Seym*. He was a founder of the Jewish cooperative movement in Poland. During World War II, S. lived as a refugee in Russia. For a short time he was minister of Jewish affairs in the Polish government at Lublin. In 1946, he settled in the US.

SON OF GOD: Term applied in the Bible to demi-gods, angels, and similar mythological beings (cf. Gen. 6:2–4 and Ps. 82:6) as well as to human beings standing in a relation of special intimacy to God such as kings (cf. Ps. 89:27–8) or the people of Israel (Exod. 4:22; Hos. 11:1). In the Apocrypha, the term is also applied to the Messiah. Rabbinic literature uses the term referring to Israel or man generally, but as a rule implies it indirectly by speaking of God as the "Father in Heaven." In Christian theology S. of G. has become a technical term, denoting the divinity of Jesus.

SON OF MAN: Epithet applied in the books of Ezekiel and Daniel to a man of God in his relation to God. Ezekiel is termed S. of M. in the vision of the Divine chariot (Ezek. 2:1) and Daniel is so called by the angel Gabriel (Dan. 8:17). According to the gospels, Jesus frequently called himself by this epithet.

SONCINO: Small town in N Italy, where in 1483 the physician Israel Nathan S. set up the Hebrew printing press with which the name is now mainly associated. His work was carried on by his son Joshua Solomon S. and especially by his grandson Gershon ben Moses S. During its activity in Italy, the press functioned at Casalmaggiore, then returned to S. and later moved to Naples, Brescia, Barco, Fano, Pesaro, Ortona, and Rimini, now printing in Latin and Italian as well as in Hebrew. Nearly one half of the known Italian Hebrew INCUNABULA were produced by members of the S. family. Gershom helped to introduce the italic type into printing. In 1526, he was driven by competition—especially from Daniel BOMBERG in Venice—to emigrate to Turkey where he and other members of the family took up printing in Salonica (1526–9) and Constantinople (1530–47). The prominence of the S. family in early Hebrew printing led to the adoption of the name by the *Soncino Gesellschaft* founded in 1925 in Berlin as a society of Jewish bibliophiles, which produced an annual miscellany and several independent publications (including some facsimiles). From 1929, the name was used in England by the Soncino Press which published a number of finely-produced books of Jewish interest, including the English translation of the Talmud (1935ff).

SONG OF DEBORAH see **DEBORAH**
SONG OF MOSES see **MOSES, SONG OF**

Song of Songs from a Passover Maḥzor.
(Adler Collection, Jewish Theological Seminary, NY).

SONG OF SONGS (Canticles; Heb. *Shir ha-Shirim*): First of the five SCROLLS incorporated in the biblical Hagiographa. The contents comprise love-poems written in dialogue form, and the composition is attributed to Solomon. Various interpretations have been suggested. Some regard it as a dramatic poem with several actors (the maiden Shulamit, the daughters of Jerusalem, and the shepherd-boy) relating the love of Solomon for a country-girl who herself loved a shepherd. Others hold it to be a collection of bridal songs written for festal days or perhaps simply a collection of love-poems. The Talmud and medieval commentators interpret the S. of S. as an allegory depicting a dialogue between God and Israel containing mystical songs of holiness. Christian tradition saw in it a dialogue between Jesus and the Church.

SONG OF SONGS RABBAH: Midrash to the Song of Songs, known also as *Midrash Ḥazita* after its opening verse (Prov. 22:29). It draws upon older works but contains much that is original. It is a late Midrash, probably of the 9th cent.

SONG OF DEGREES: Description attached to fifteen psalms (120–134). Various interpretations have been suggested including songs of ascent recited from Babylon to Palestine, songs of pilgrims to Jerusalem, and songs recited in the Temple by the levites on the 15 steps leading from the Court of the Israelites to the Women's Court (*Sukkot* 5:4) at the Water-Drawing Festival.

SONNEMANN, LEOPOLD (1831–1909): German banker and politician. In 1856, he founded the liberal newspaper the *Frankfurter Zeitung*. He was identified with the federal wing of the anti-Prussian S German Democrats and represented the People's Party in the Reichstag 1871–6 and 1878–84.

SONNENFELS, JOSEPH FREIHERR VON (1733–1817): Political scientist. A lawyer, baptized in youth, he founded several literary journals in Vienna. S. was professor of political science at Vienna and wrote textbooks on the subject. His advocacy of legal reforms led to a number of alleviations in the Austrian penal code.

SONNENTHAL, ADOLF, RITTER VON (1832–1909): Actor. He was leading actor and subsequently director (1887–90) of the Vienna Hofburg theater.

SONNINO, SIDNEY, BARON (1847–1922): Italian economist, diplomat, and statesman; of Jewish paternity. An ardent nationalist, he was prime minister in 1906 and 1909–10, and foreign minister in 1915–9.

SONS OF LIGHT: In the DEAD SEA SCROLLS, those who are on the side of God and governed by the "Prince of Light," i.e., according to the WAR SCROLL, the pious Jews. Their opponents, the gentiles and the Jewish sinners, are "Sons of Darkness," led by the "Prince of Darkness," i.e., Belial or Mastema, the devil.

SOPHER see **SCRIBE**

SOPHER (or SCHREIBER), MOSES (1762–1839): Rabbi; known after his most distinguished work as *Hatam Sopher*. From 1803, he officiated in Pressburg where he founded a noted yeshivah. At first devoted to *pilpul*, his method of instruction later became more direct and simple. His fame as a halakhic authority brought him legal inquiries from all parts of the Jewish world. A powerful preacher, he bitterly fought the Reform movement, and uncompromisingly opposed innovation in Jewish religious practice. His *Hatam Sopher* (6 vols.) contained responsa and novellae, while his other published writings included poems in a kabbalistic spirit and notes on the Pentateuch.

SOPRON (Ödenburg): Hungarian city. Jews are first known there in the 14th cent. Expelled together with the rest of the Jews of Hungary in 1360, they returned in 1365, but their economic activities were circumscribed and they were again forced to leave in 1526. In 1840, Jews were again allowed to live permanently in S. From 1920–30, the Jewish population decreased rapidly as a result of the annexation of S.'s economic hinterland to Austria. The medieval synagogue has recently been restored. Jewish pop. (1970): 40.

SOTAH (Heb. "Errant Wife"): Sixth tractate (fifth in some codices) in the Mishnah order of *Nashim*, containing 9 chapters. It has *gemara* in both the Babylonian and Palestinian Talmuds. The first 6 chapters deal with the laws concerning the woman suspected of adultery (Num. 5:11–31). The remaining chapters include a discussion of which liturgical readings may be recited in any language and which only in Hebrew, and the rite of the heifer whose neck is broken in the event of unusual murder (Deut. 21:1–9). The last chapter refers to the decline of standards since the destruction of the Temple and the anarchy that will precede messianic times.

SOUL: The biblical expressions denoting s. (*nephesh, ruah, neshamah*) all understand life as the animation of the body and derive from roots meaning "wind," "breath," etc. (cf. Gen. 2:7); after death there is merely a shadowy existence in the underworld (*sheol*). Only in the last centuries BCE did the soul-body dualism and the concept that the s. was an independent substance joined to the body gain general credence: the s. originates in heaven and descends to earth, joining a material body at the moment of conception or birth and losing its original perfection. This dichotomy, fully developed in hellenistic literature (Philo, etc.), is also accepted by the Talmud where it is said that all s.'s exist from the creation of the world and are stored in heaven until their time comes to join the bodies destined for them. The rabbis do not merely equate s. and body with good and evil; it is always the s. which sins and not the body. In medieval philosophy the main problem concerning the s. was that of IMMORTALITY. The Neoplatonic tradition which assumed an independent spiritual soul-substance could entertain a belief in immortality more easily than the Aristotelian philosophers for whom s. was the "form" of the organic body. Maimonides and other Jewish Aristotelians assumed that only that part of the s. which man develops by his intellectual efforts (the "acquired intellect") is immortal; other thinkers defined the s. in such a way as to extend immortality also to non-philosophers. Kabbalists generally accepted the belief in METEMPSYCHOSIS (*gilgul*). The desire to express one's love for departed s.'s and, if possible, to improve their lot in the hereafter has given rise (to a large extent under non-Jewish influence) to various rites, some of which (e.g. YIZKOR, HASHKAVAH, KADDISH) have become permanent features of the synagogue service.

SOUL, TRANSMIGRATION OF see **METEMPSYCHOSIS**

SOUTH AFRICA see **AFRICA, SOUTH**

SOUTH AMERICA see **AMERICA**

SOUTH CAROLINA: US state. A number of Sephardi Jews from London and the W Indies settled there prior to 1700. The Jewish population of the state steadily increased during the first half of the 18th cent. In 1755, Joseph Salvador purchased 100,000 acres of S. C. land part of which he re-sold to other Jews. These came to be known as the "Jews' lands." S. C.'s Jews played an active part in the American Revolution, serving on both sides. For a time CHARLESTON was the largest, most cultured, and wealthiest Jewish community in N America. In 1822 a congregation was established at Columbia. During the Civil War, 182 S. C. Jews — of whom 25 fell — served with the Confederate Army. During the Reconstruction Period, many S. C. Jews moved northward. In the last two decades of the 19th cent., immigrants from E Europe brought new life to the dwindling Jewish communities of S. C. In 1973, there were 7,485 Jews in S. C., leading Jewish communities being in Charleston (3,000), Columbia (2,000), and Greenville (600).

SOUTH DAKOTA: US state. Jewish settlement dates from the mid-1870's when small communities sprang up in Deadwood, Custer City, Lead, and Yankton. Most of the pioneer Jews were merchants. After 1880, there were Jews among the homesteaders who settled in Eureka, Sioux Falls, Aberdeen, and Mitchell. In 1882, 200 Jews established the short-lived Crémieux Colony on a former Indian reservation 20 miles from Mitchell. By 1889 unsuccessful homesteaders had scattered throughout the state. In 1910, there were still 365 Jews living on farms. 635 Jews lived in S.D. (1973). Since 1938 there has been a Jewish Welfare Fund in Sioux Falls (Jewish pop: 280), where the state's first congregation was established in 1909.

SOUTHERN RHODESIA see **RHODESIA**

SOUTHWOOD, JULIUS SALTER ELIAS, BARON (1873–1946): English newspaper proprietor and philanthropist. As chairman and director of Odham's Press, he was responsible for the development of the Labor Party newspaper *The Daily Herald*.

SOUTINE, CHAIM (1894–1943): Painter. Born in Lithuania, he settled in 1913 in Paris where he lived a recluse's life in poverty. His portraits (which achieve remarkable psychological insight), landscapes, and still-lifes express the violence of his own emotions.

SOVIET RUSSIA see **RUSSIA**

SOYER: Family of Russian origin, in the US from 1913. *ABRAHAM S.* (1867–1940), author of Hebrew and Yiddish essays, stories, and textbooks, was father of the artists *ISAAC S.* (1907–), *MOSES S.* (1899–1974), and *RAPHAEL S.* (1889–). They belong to the Realist school and are noted for their portrayal of the life of the lower middle-class.

SPAIN: SW European country. According to legend, S is the biblical SEPHARAD in which Jews were settled from the period of the destruction of the First Temple. It is certain that they were to be found in the 1st cent. CE and were specifically mentioned in the canons of the Church Council at Elvira in 312. Some tombstones of the Classical period have been found. After the fall of the Roman Empire, the Jews were favorably treated by the Visigoths so long as the latter followed the Arian form of Christianity, but when they embraced Catholicism in 589 there was a reaction. From 612 onward, a relentless persecution took place under the direction of successive Councils of Toledo, and over a great part of the period the practice of Judaism was completely prohibited. Freedom was brought in 711 by the invasion of the Arabs. In the course of the next two centuries, S. became one of the greatest centers of Jewish life. Its communities were Arabized in language, nomenclature, and outlook: and though Islamic law prescribed a rigid anti-Jewish discrimination, some Jews rose to positions of great influence in the state, as evinced in the careers of Hasdai Ibn Shaprut in Cordova and Samuel Ibn Nagrela, vizier to the king of Granada. Simultaneously, HEBREW LITERATURE began to flourish in the country, largely on Arab models especially as regards poetry and philosophy, and Spanish Jewry served as a channel through which classical science reached Christian Europe. In 1136, the invasion of the ALMOHADES brought about a reaction, and the practice of Judaism was forbidden in Andalusia. In the N of the country, however, the expanding Christian kingdoms had adopted a more tolerant policy, finding the Jews useful as diplomats, financiers, and agricultural colonists. Henceforth, the great centers of Jewish life were in the areas under Christian rule. In the court of Alfonso the Wise of Castile (1252–84) Jewish savants played an important part in intellectual activity, especially as translators and astronomers. Samuel Abulafia in the 14th cent. and Isaac Abravanel in the 15th cent. typify the important place which Jews played in public life, especially as court financiers. But with the waning of Moslem domination, a more intolerant spirit began to spread from N Europe. In the middle of the 13th cent., the Dominican Order in particular initiated constant anti-Jewish propaganda, which had its fruit in the DISPUTATION of Barcelona, etc., conversionist sermons, the implementation of the persecutory code of the fourth LATERAN COUNCIL, and some scattered physical outbreaks. In 1391, a wave of massacres beginning at Seville swept through the entire Peninsula, as a result of which very large numbers of Jews accepted baptism in order to escape death: this was repeated in the following years. These "New Christians" or MARRANOS, ostensibly Christians but Jewish at heart and attracting jealousy through their remarkable social and economic progress, henceforth constituted a serious problem. After a series of popular outbreaks against them, the INQUISITION was introduced in 1478. This procedure against the secret Jews encouraged further action against those remaining true to their faith who were alleged to have provoked the other element to infidelity. In 1492, the Jews were therefore expelled from the country by an edict of Ferdinand and Isabella. The number of exiles is reckoned at

150,000 who found refuge mainly in N Africa and the Turkish Empire where their descendants (SEPHARDIM) have continued to preserve the Spanish traditions and language. In the country, there remained only the Marranos — sometimes fervently Jewish at heart — against whom the Inquisition continued its activities until the close of the 18th cent. The expulsion from S. was succeeded and completed by those from PORTUGAL (1497) and NAVARRE (1498). A limited immigration into S. took place in the 19th cent. The law prohibiting the establishment of synagogues having been abolished in 1909, small congregations now exist in Madrid and Barcelona. The expulsion was officially revoked in 1931, and in 1968, when the Madrid synagogue was formally dedicated, it was officially abolished. Jewish pop. (1973): 8,500, nearly all in Barcelona and Madrid.

SPALATO see **SPLIT**

SPASSKY, BORIS (1937–): Russian chess master. He defeated Petrosian for the world championship in 1969 but lost his title to Bobby FISCHER in 1972.

SPECTOR, MORDECAI (1858–1925): Yiddish novelist. A prolific writer of feuilletons, travel sketches, and short stories, he edited *Der Hausfreund* (1888–9), and in 1894, joined Y. L. Peretz in editing *Yom-Tov Bletlech* in Warsaw. S. participated in many Yiddish literary ventures in E Europe until emigrating to the US in 1921.

SPEISER, EPHRAIM AVIGDOR (1902–1965): Orientalist. A native of Galicia, he settled in the US in 1920. He conducted excavations in various Middle Eastern countries and wrote extensively in the fields of Near Eastern history and philology. He taught at the Univ. of Pennsylvania from 1928.

SPEKTOR, ISAAC ELHANAN (1817–1896): Russian rabbi. He officiated in various Lithuanian and White Russian towns and from 1864 was rabbi in Kovno where he founded a noted yeshivah. An outstanding authority, he sent responsa to halakhic queries from all parts of the Diaspora, tending to leniency especially on problems of the *agunah*. S. was active in Russian Jewish communal life. The Isaac Elhanan Yeshiva (now incorporated in Yeshiva Univ.) in New York was named after him.

SPEYER see **SPIRE**

SPEYER: Family of bankers, originating in Frankfort-on-Main where the philanthropists *JOSEPH MICHAEL S.* (d. 1729) and *GEORG S.* (1834–1902) were noteworthy. *GUSTAV S.* (1825–1883), who lived in the US 1845–63, was a partner in the firm of Speyer & Co., which flourished until its voluntary liquidation in 1939. It helped the Union cause during the Civil War by floating US government bonds and was prominent in the financing of leading American railroads and industries. Gustav's son, *JAMES S.* (1861–1941), was senior partner of the firm 1899–1939. He founded the Provident Loan Society in New York.

contributed more than $2,000,000 to numerous educational and philanthropic enterprises, and left an even larger amount to these causes upon his death. His younger brother, *EDGAR S.* (1862–1932), was in charge of the firm's London office. He was made a baronet and member of the Privy Council, but because of anti-German prejudice during World War I settled in the US. *HERBERT S.* (1870–1942) was professor of jurisprudence at the Univ. of Brussels and vice-president of the council of the Jewish Agency.

SPICES (Heb. *besamim*): Aromatic woods were among the ingredients of the incense used in the Temple. They, or s. in the more specific sense, were inhaled after meals. This is probably the basis for the practice of smelling s. at the close of the Sabbath, later interpreted as a fortification of the body after the departure of the "additional soul" enjoyed on the Sabbath. The spice boxes used on this occasion were the object of a specific form of Jewish ritual art. Separate benedictions were prescribed to be recited on smelling aromatic woods or cloves. In the Middle Ages, Jews played some part in the enormously lucrative spice trade between Asia and Europe, and this formed at the beginning of the 16th cent. the foundation of the prosperity of the Mendes and other Marrano firms in Antwerp.

SPIEGEL, SHALOM (1899–): US scholar. Born in Austro-Hungary, he taught in Palestine 1922–8 and thereafter, at the Jewish Institute of Religion and the Jewish Theological Seminary in New York. He is author of *Hebrew Reborn*; *Ezekiel or Pseudo-Ezekiel*; *Noah, Daniel, and Job*; *The Last Trial* (about the *Akedah*), etc.

SPIELMAN(N): English family, represented especially in the three brothers (1) *SIR ISIDORE S.* (1854–1925), director for art at the Board of Trade, who from 1897 organized the British exhibits at international art exhibitions. He was largely responsible for the Anglo-Jewish Historical Exhibition of 1887. (2) *MARION HARRY S.* (1858–1948): Art critic and connoisseur. He wrote on the portraiture of Shakespeare and on Chaucer, Vesalius, and the history of *Punch* and many works on art. (3) *SIR MEYER S.* (1856–1936), educator, was inspector of the Home Office schools and held many public positions in connection with education, child delinquency, etc.

*SPINA, ALFONSO DE (d. 1468): Spanish priest. General of the Franciscans, rector of the Univ. of Salamanca, and confessor to Henry IV of Castile, he was partly responsible for the introduction of the Inquisition into Spain. His *Fortalitium Fidei* (1459) contains, besides venomous anti-Jewish invective, some important historical material.

SPINGARN, JOEL ELIAS (1875–1939): US author and publisher. As professor of comparative literature at Columbia Univ. 1904–11, he wrote *A*

Benedict Spinoza. Medallion by Hendrik van der Spyck.
(Royal Museum, The Hague.)

History of Literary Criticism in the Renaissance and *The New Criticism* in which he adhered to the esthetics of Croce. He later became a publisher. S. was a founder and president of the National Association for the Advancement of Colored People.

SPINOZA (de Spinoza or Espinoza), **BENEDICT** (Baruch or Bento; 1632–1677): Dutch philosopher. He was descended from a family of Portuguese Marranos, his grandfather and father having escaped to Amsterdam, returned to Judaism and become leaders of the community. S. had a traditional education, his teachers including Manasseh ben Israel. He accepted the influences of Renaissance thought and studied philosophy, especially Descartes. His unorthodox religious views led to his formal excommunication by the Sephardi community in 1656. From 1660, he lived away from Amsterdam, partly earning his living as a lenspolisher. His *Theologico-Political Treatise* (published anonymously 1670) initiated modern Bible criticism, pointing to internal contradictions. In it he draws the difference between theology, the obedient knowledge of faith and piety, and philosophy, the independent rational discovery of truth in nature. He opposed clerical authority and the claims made in behalf of revelation and argued that the state must ensure free thought. His posthumous works included the *Ethics* in which, following his conception that a rational institution is the highest degree of knowledge, he applied Euclidean methods to demonstrating a metaphysical concept of the universe with ethical corollaries. The one infinite substance is cause of itself — it is Nature or God. Nothing is supernatural and even God's transcendence is denied. He is both Creating Nature

— i.e., the One — and Created Nature — i.e., the All. Each finite thing is in God and He is immanent in all things (this is the metaphysics of pantheism). Will is a necessary cause but not a free one, and the system is thus a vigorous determination. He concludes with the concept of the wise man's freedom, which is virtue or the power of the most perfect intellect; this is the power of intellectual love of God and it constitutes man's true happiness. S.'s system profoundly influenced subsequent philosophy, especially German thinkers. His thought was influenced by medieval and Renaissance Jewish philosophy, including Maimonides, Ḥasdai Crescas, and Leone Ebreo.

SPIRE (Speyer): Rhenish town. The first definite information on a Jewish community in S. dates from 1070; its Jews freely practiced commerce under the protection of Bishop Rodiger who regarded them as valuable subjects and invited refugees from Mayence to settle there. A Jewish judge was permitted to exercise jurisdiction, and the Jews defended their quarter in times of siege. In 1096, the bishop of S. protected the Jews from the crusaders, but some were killed. The town at this period was a center of Jewish scholarship, and associated with Worms and Mayence in rabbinical synods. The situation deteriorated in the 12th cent., improved in the 13th, but the Black Death massacres of 1348–9 led to murder and expulsion. A series of banishments and recalls ensued until the expulsion order of 1455. Jews lived there again 1689–1714, and again in modern times, when the community of 400 was destroyed under the Nazis.

SPIRE, ANDRÉ (1868–1966): French poet. He was drawn to Jewish interests by the Dreyfus affair and represented the French Zionists at the Paris Peace Conference in 1919. An exponent of free verse, his works include *Poemes juifs* and *Quelques juifs et demi-juifs*. During World War II he resided in the US.

SPITZ, MARK (1950–): US swimmer. He won 4 gold medals at the 1968 olympics and an unprecedented 7 gold medals at the 1972 olympics.

SPLIT (Spalato): Dalmatian port. Formerly a Venetian possession, its great development as a free port in the 16th cent. was due to the former Marrano, Daniel Rodriguez. The Jewish community, which greatly developed in consequence, was nevertheless confined in a ghetto in 1738 and suffered restrictions. First emancipated by the French in 1797, it dwindled in the 19th cent., and was almost annihilated during the German occupation when the old synagogue was destroyed. Jewish pop. (1970): 120.

SPORT: Ancient Jewish history reveals no special attitude toward s. as existed among the Greeks or Romans, but there are indications of physical training and athletic activity among the Jews. Archery and exercise in weapons (e.g. lance, sword, sling) were widespread. The Bible also mentions individuals noted as runners. Late Hellenism made inroads among the Jews and a gymnasium was founded in Jerusalem c. 170 BCE to educate youths in physical culture. Herod built stadia and organized Palestinian delegations to the Olympic Games. The amora RESH LAKISH was originally a gladiator. Life in the Diaspora and especially the enforcement of the ghetto system prevented normal developments and robbed the Jews of opportunities for physical training. Nevertheless Maimonides wrote on the importance of physical exercise to prevent illness, and in the 15th cent. Jews took part in the athletic contests at Rosenau and one, named Ott, was the champion wrestler of the country. Tennis was widely played in the Italian Jewish communities and fencing masters were commonly Jews. In the 18th cent. Jews such as D. Mendoza, S. Belasco, etc. began to figure prominently in the English prize-ring. With the advent of the Enlightenment Period Jews were able generally to indulge in sporting activities, and in the first modern Olympiad (Athens, 1896) a Hungarian Jew Hache won the 100 meter freestyle swimming contest. By 1964 Jews had won 211 Olympic medals. Zionism fostered s.; before 1897 Jewish sports societies existed only in Constantinople and Budapest, but by 1910 over 50 had been founded. In 1898, the first federation of Jewish s. societies, *Die Jüdische Turnerschaft* (from 1921, the MACCABI movement), was set up. A leading Jewish sports club was HA-KOAH of Vienna. International gatherings of Jewish sportsmen have been held since 1932 under the auspices of the MACCABIAH. Jews have achieved national and international renown in s. Many Jews have been world boxing champions including Benny Leonard (lightweight champion 1917–25), Max Baer (heavyweight champion 1934), and Barney Ross (lightweight 1933–5 and welterweight 1933–7). Other Jewish world champions have included Joe Choynsky, "Battling" Levinsky, Max Rosenbloom, Gus Lesnevich, Solly Krieger, Toni Zeil, "Young" Peretz, Abe Goldstein, Charlie Rosenberg, Al Phillips, and Robert Cohen. Leading boxing promoters have included Mike Jacobs (US) and Jack Solomons (England). The Hungarians N. Cohen, Fuchs, Kabos, Petschauer, and Elek won Olympic fencing titles as did the German Helene Mayer. In wrestling, outstanding names have included Leucht (Germany), Hirschl (Austria), Weiss (Hungary), Wittenberg (US), and Oberlander (Canada). Tennis stars have included Richard Savitt and Herbert Flam (US), Tom Okker (Holland), and Abraham Segal (S Africa). In light athletics, outstanding Jewish sportsmen have included Myer Prinstein of the US, the Abrahams brothers of England (Harold Abrahams winning the 100 meters in the 1924 Olympic Games), the Finnish Hello Katz and Agnes Kelethy of Israel (formerly Hungary). Johnny Kling, Hank Greenberg, Al Rosen, and Sandy Koufax have been leading baseball figures.

Richard Bergmann (England) and Victor Barna (originally of Hungary) were noted in table tennis, Irving Jaffe (US) in ice-skating and Morris Zimmerman, Louis Babow, and "Ocky" Geffen (of S Africa) in rugby. In US football, Benny Friedman and Harry Newman have been prominent as has Nat Holman in basketball. Jews have been especially outstanding in CHESS and bridge. Israel s. organizations, apart from *Maccabi*, include *Hapoel* (run by the workers' movement), *Betar* (of *Ḥerut*), and *Elitzur* (of the religious parties). Israel teams have played in various international tournaments with particular success in basketball, association football, and chess. In 1976, Israel won the women's chess Olympics.

SPRINGFIELD: City in Massachusetts, US. Its Jewish community began in 1881 with the arrival of immigrants from Lithuania. Smaller groups also came from Galicia and Poland. The first congregation was organized in 1888. The Jewish community Council, founded in 1938, sponsors the United Jewish Welfare Fund. The *Jewish Weekly News* has appeared since 1945. Jewish pop. (1973): 11,000 with 7 congregations.

SPRINZAK, YOSEPH (1885–1959): Israel public figure. He was born in Russia, where he was among the founders of *Tzeire Zion* in 1905. In Palestine from 1908, he was active in labor politics, being among the founders of the *Histadrut* and *Mapai*. From 1949 he was a *Mapai* representative and speaker of the Knesset.

SRI LANKA see CEYLON

S. S. (1) (initials for Russ. "Zionist Socialists"): Jewish socialist TERRITORIALIST party. Organized in 1904 after the split over UGANDA in the Zionist movement, it became the strongest territorialist group, particularly in Russia, Austria, and the US. In 1917 it merged with the Seymists but disappeared shortly afterward with the advent of the Balfour Declaration and the Russian Revolution. It held that Jewish socialism could only be obtained through industrialization, for which colonization in an independent territory was essential. (2) (initials for Ger. *Schutzstaffeln* "bodyguard"): Nazi formation directed by HIMMLER. It was responsible for control of the CONCENTRATION CAMPS and was the main instrument for the deportation and extermination of European Jewry.

STAHL, FRIEDRICH JULIUS (1802–1861): German jurist and political scientist. Baptized in 1819, he taught at several universities and in 1840, was brought to Berlin by Frederick William IV. He was a member of the Supreme Church Council and the Prussian Upper Chamber from 1849. A theoretician of the Prussian Conservative Party, he influenced its program (which contained a clause opposing equal rights for Jews). His teachings emphasized the function of the monarchy, the legal basis of the state, and the right of the individual to a just law.

STAMFORD: City in Connecticut, US. A few Jews, mostly of German origin, settled in the city in the 1860's. E European Jews began arriving in the 1880's. An Orthodox congregation was incorporated in 1889, and a Conservative congregation was formed in 1920. In 1973 there were 10,800 Jews in S. served by 3 synagogues.

STAMPS see **PHILATELY**

STAR OF DAVID see **MAGEN DAVID**

STARER, ROBERT (1924–): Israel composer. He has written chamber music, vocal works, the *Kohelet* cantata and symphonies.

STARR, JOSHUA (1907–1949): US historian. He published important studies especially on the Jews in the Byzantine Empire.

STATE OF ISRAEL see **ISRAEL**

STATISTICS, JEWISH: Statistical data are difficult to obtain among Jews owing to the lack of public sources. Jews early recognized the importance of s., and the Bible records several instances of a CENSUS. In subsequent generations, attempts were made at numbering the Jews, and Benjamin of Tudela in the 12th cent., for example, indicated the Jewish population in each place he visited or of which he heard.S. as a science were only utilized from the 18th cent. ZUNZ attempted to define J. S., and later in the 19th cent., scientific studies were published by Alfred Nossig, Joseph Jacobs, etc., while important work was carried out by ICA and the German *Büro für Statistik der Juden*, which published a journal until the 1920's. Prominent modern Jewish statisticians have included Liebmann Hersch, Jacob Lestschinsky, Arthur Ruppin and Roberto Bachi. A Jewish Statistical Office was established in the US early in the 20th cent. and carried out pioneer work, chiefly in the sphere of demography. From the mid-1920's, YIVO devoted much attention to J. S., and a Yiddish statistical periodical *Bletter far Yiddische Demographie, Statistik un Economik* appeared in Berlin. Current research is conducted through leading Jewish organizations (World Jewish Congress, American Jewish Committee, American Joint Distribution Committee, the Hebrew University's Institute for Contemporary Jewry), and useful material is contained in the *American Jewish Year Book* and the *Annual of the Institute of Jewish Affairs*. A systematic sta-

The General and Jewish Population in Europe in the 1930's

Main Countries	Total Population	Jews
	(Thousands)	
Austria	6,760	191
Belgium	8,092	60
Bulgaria	6,090	48
Czechoslovakia	14,729	356
France	41,905	260
Germany	65,988	503
Great Britain	46,189	300
Greece	6,200	73
Holland	7,935	112
Hungary	8,688	444
Italy	42,500	48
Latvia	1,950	93
Lithuania	2,028	155
Poland	32,183	3,113
Rumania	18,052	758
Russia (USSR incl. Asiatic Russia)	169,789	3,021
Switzerland	4,066	18
Turkey (European)	1,266	52
Yugoslavia	13,394	69
Total for Europe	536,139	9,654

The General and Jewish Population in Europe in 1973

Main Countries	Total Population	Jews
	(Thousands)	
Austria	7,456	12
Belgium	9,695	40
Bulgaria	8,579	7
Czechoslovakia	14,481	8
Denmark	4,963	7
France	51,720	550
Germany	76,000	32
Great Britain	55,788	418
Greece	8,851	5
Holland	13,379	30
Hungary	10,405	90
Italy	54,345	33
Poland	33,130	8
Rumania	20,470	110
Russia (USSR incl. Asiatic Russia)	246,309	2,151
Sweden	8,132	15
Switzerland	6,253	20
Turkey (incl. Asiatic Turkey)	37,010	23
Yugoslavia	20,858	7
Total for Europe	758,770	4,091

Distribution of the Jewish People according to Continents (in Thousands)

	1900		1939		1954		1973	
	Total	%	Total	%	Total	%	Total	%
Europe (incl. Asiatic Russia)	8,900	80.9	9,650	57.9	3,348	28.7	4,090	29
America (N & S)	1,200	10.9	5,500	32.9	5,925	50.8	6,901	49
Asia (without Russia)	510	4.6	850	5.2	1,645	14.0	2,907	20
Africa	375	3.4	625	3.8	707	6.0	177	1.5
Australia and New Zealand	15	0.2	33	0.2	60	0.5	76	0.5
Total	11,000	100	16,658	100	11,685	100	14,152	100

The General and Jewish Population in the Americas in the 1930's

Main Countries	General Population	Jews
	(Thousands	
Argentina	12,402	320
Brazil	40,273	80
Canada	11,506	170
Mexico	16,522	20
Uruguay	1,903	30
US	131,669	4,850
Other Countries	28,293	29
Total for America	242,568	5,499

The General and Jewish Population in the Americas in, 1973

Main Countries	General Population	Jews
	(Thousands)	
Argentina	24,290	475
Brazil	101,710	155
Canada	22,130	305
Chile	10,230	30
Colombia	23,210	12
Mexico	54,300	40
US	210,400	5,800
Uruguay	2,990	50
Venezuela	11,290	15
Total for America	460,550	6,882

The General and Jewish Population in Asia in the 1930's

Main Countries	General Population	Jews
	(Thousands)	
India	352,837	24
Iran	15,000	70
Iraq	3,561	150
Palestine	1,467	475
Syria & Lebanon	3,630	16
Turkey (Asiatic)	14,935	30
Yemen	2,000	50
Other Countries	657,753	31.5
Total for Asia	1,051,183	846.5

The General and Jewish Population in Asia in 1973

Main Countries	General Population	Jews
	(Thousands)	
India	574,220	12
Iran	31,300	80
Israel	3,302	2,806
Lebanon	3,060	1
Total for Asia	611,882	2,899

The General and Jewish population in Australia and New Zealand in 1973

Total Population	Jews
(Thousands)	
16,090	76.2

The General and Jewish Population in Africa in 1973

Main Countries	General Population	Jews
	(Thousands)	
Ethiopia	26,080	12
Morocco	16,310	30
Rhodesia	5,500	5
South Africa	22,990	118
Tunisia	5,510	8
Total for Africa	76,390	173

The Chief Jewish Communities of the World (1967)

Community	Number of Jews	Community	Number of Jews
New York	2,381,000	San Francisco	75,000
Los Angeles	463,000	Bene Berak	74,000
Tel Aviv	394,000	Netanyah	70,000
Buenos Aires	350,000	Sao Paolo	65,000
Philadelphia	350,000	Marseilles	65,000
Paris	300,000	Budapest	65,000
Moscow	285,000	St. Louis	60,000
London	280,000	Johannesburg	58,000
Jerusalem	266,000	Rishon le-Zion	52,000
Chicago	253,000	Rio de Janeiro	50,000
Haifa	210,000	Kishinev	50,000
Miami	200,000	Teheran	50,000
Boston	180,000	Montevideo	48,000
Kiev	170,000	Givatayim	48,000
Leningrad	165,000	Minsk	47,000
Odessa	117,000	Pittsburgh	45,000
Ramat Gan	117,000	Ashkelon	43,000
Montreal	113,000	Herzlia	41,000
Washington	112,000	Ashdod	41,000
Bat Yam	100,000	Bucharest	40,000
Holon	98,000	Tashkent	40,000
Toronto	97,000	Cernauti	37,000
Baltimore	94,000	Hadera	32,000
Newark	94,000	Santiago	32,000
Petah Tikvah	92,000	Riga	31,000
Beersheba	84,000	Casablanca	30,000
Cleveland	80,000	Acre	30,000
Detroit	80,000	Melbourne	30,000
Kharkov	80,000	Istanbul	22,000

tistical machinery was maintained in Palestine from the early 1920's by the mandatory government and the Zionist Organization. After 1948, their work passed to the Statistical Bureau in the Prime Minister's Office. The chief difficulty concerning J. S. in the Diaspora is the problem of gathering adequate basic material. More aspects have to be examined than is the case with the non-Jewish population, while the data is extremely limited, as most countries do not list separate s. about Jews. Moreover, the changes in Jewish life tend to be far more frequent and striking than among the rest of the population; thus, in the last two generations, mixed marriages have become a striking phenomenon, natural increase has dropped to a remarkable extent, migration has been converted into settlement in Israel, etc. Political and social factors also hamper the statistician, e.g. there are few details on the large Jewish community of the USSR.

STEIN, EDITH (1891–1942): German philosopher. A pupil of Husserl, she was converted to Catholicism and in 1933 became a Catholic nun known as Sister Teresa Benedicta. In World War II she requested the Pope in vain to issue an encyclical on the Jewish question. She was gassed at Auschwitz. Her collected works were published posthumously in 5 volumes.

STEIN, GERTRUDE (1874–1946): US writer. From 1903, she lived in Paris. Her highly individualized use of language, especially in *Three Lives* and *The Making of Americans*, endeavored to reproduce the "stream of consciousness."

STEIN, LUDWIG (1859–1930): Philosopher and sociologist. He taught at Zurich (1886–9), Berne (1890–1910), and Berlin (1911–24). In his works he proposed a social philosophical system which he called "social optimism."

STEIN, SIR MARC AUREL (1862–1943): Explorer. Of Hungarian birth, he went to Britain and then to India. His explorations and discoveries threw new light on the early civilizations of India, Turkestan, China, etc.

STEIN, WILLIAM HOWARD (1931–): US chemist. He won the 1972 Nobel Prize for his work on coupled chemical reactions which constitute the concept of life and living organisms.

STEINACH, EUGEN (1861–1944): Physiologist: professor at Vienna Univ. After experimentation with animals in conjunction with other scientists, he eventually transplanted sex glands on human beings, and proved the general reactivation that followed this operation.

STEINBERG, ISAAC NACHMAN (1888–1957): Public figure. A member of the Russian Social Revolutionary Party, he was minister of justice in 1917–8, but left the country in 1923, eventually settling in the US. He was prominent in the Yiddishist and Territorialist ("Freeland") movements and published several books on the Russian revolution and Jewish problems.

STEINBERG, JUDAH (1863–1908): Hebrew author. He lived in Bessarabia until 1906 when he moved to Odessa. He wrote textbooks, stories, feuilletons, fables, etc., excelling in tales of Ḥasidic life. S. was one of the creators of children's literature in Hebrew.

STEINBERG, MILTON (1903–1950): US rabbi. A talented lecturer and teacher, he officiated at the Conservative Park Ave. Synagogue, New York from 1933 until his death. His books include *The Making of the Modern Jew* and a novel based on the life of Elisha ben Avuya.

STEINBERG, SAUL (1914–): US artist. An outstanding cartoonist and magazine illustrator, his work is represented in several leading American museums.

STEINBERG, YAAKOV (1887–1947): Hebrew author. He lived in Odessa, Warsaw, Switzerland, and from 1914 in Palestine. His poetry is pessimistic and imbued with a mood of solitude. His stories, mostly set against his native Ukrainian background, emphasize the sorrows of Diaspora life, especially for the Jewish woman. Several collections of S.'s essays appeared in his latter years. He also wrote in Yiddish.

STEINHARDT, JAKOB (1887–1968): Artist. He was born in Posen and settled in Palestine in 1933, becoming director of the New Bezalel School of Arts and Crafts, Jerusalem (1953–7). His works include woodcuts on Jewish and biblical themes, colorful Palestinian landscapes, etc.

STEINHARDT, LAURENCE ADOLF (1892–1950): US lawyer and diplomat. He was US minister to Sweden 1933–7; ambassador to Peru 1937–9; to the Soviet Union 1939–41; to Turkey 1942–5; to Czechoslovakia 1945–8; and to Canada from 1948 until his death in an air-crash.

STEINHEIM, SOLOMON LUDWIG (1789–1966): German religious philosopher. A physician by profession, S.'s *Offenbarung nach dem Lehrbegriff der Synagoge* attempts to show the superiority of revelation to reason. Israel is the bearer of revealed truths and this is the main factor in the survival of the Jews.

STEINITZ, WILLIAM (1836–1900): Chess master. He began his chess career in 1862, being the first world champion 1866–94. Of Czech birth, he became a naturalized British subject, but settled in New York in 1893. He was editor of *The International Chess Magazine*, 1885–1900.

STEINMAN, DAVID BARNARD (1886–1960): US bridge engineer. Among his 400 bridges are the reconstruction of Brooklyn Bridge, New York, and the five mile long Mackinac Bridge, in Michigan.

STEINMANN, ELIEZER (1892–1970): Author. Born in Russia, he lived in Odessa and Warsaw writing for the Hebrew and Yiddish press. In 1924, he settled in Palestine and contributed regularly to *Davar*. His novels are psychological and often topical. He translated into Hebrew works by Dostoievsky, Strindberg, etc., and wrote versions of Ḥasidic stories.

STEINMETZ, CHARLES PROTEUS (1865–1923): Electrical engineer. Of German birth, he went to the US in 1889, and taught electrical engineering at Union College, Schenectady, from 1903. His inventions include dynamos, electric motors, and devices making possible the transmission of electricity at high voltage over long distances. He was for many at high voltage over long distances. He was chief consulting engineer of the General Electric Co.

STEINSCHNEIDER, MORITZ (1816–1907): Bibliographer and orientalist. He lived much of his life at Berlin where he taught, was director of its Jewish girls' school, and from 1869, assistant librarian at the Berlin State Library. He is the outstanding figure in Jewish bibliography, his works including

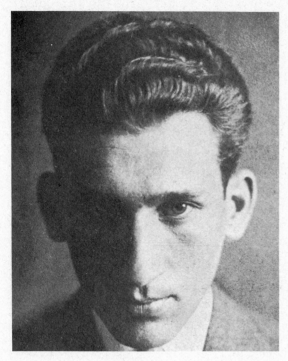

Avraham Stern.

catalogues of the Hebrew books at the Bodleian Library, Oxford (in Latin), and of the Hebrew mss at Leyden, Munich, Hamburg and Berlin, and books on apologetic literature in Arabic, Judeo-Arabic literature, Jewish mathematical and historical literature, etc. S. wrote pioneer studies of the history of Jewish literature and of Hebrew typography. He founded the periodical *Hebräische Bibliographie* which he edited 1858–82. Particularly interested in the reciprocal relationship between the culture of the Jews and that of the peoples among whom they dwelt, he wrote an important study on medieval Hebrew translators and on the Jews as interpreters.

STEINTHAL, HEYMANN (Hayyim; 1823–1899): German philologist and philosopher. Together with his brother-in-law, Moritz Lazarus, he founded the system of the "Psychology of the Nations." From 1850, he lectured on philology at Berlin Univ. and from 1872, taught Bible and the philosophy of religion at the Berlin *Lehranstalt für die Wissenschaft des Judentums*. In Jewish life, he devoted special efforts to improving religious teaching in the small provincial communities. His studies on the psychology of language are basic.

STEKEL, WILHELM (1868–1940): Austrian psychoanalyst. S. was one of Freud's earliest adherents and published many treatises on sexual aberrations and psychoanalysis. He founded the first psychoanalytical society.

STERN, ABRAHAM JACOB (1762–1842): Polish mathematician and inventor. He invented calculating machines and also agricultural machinery. He was appointed by the authorities to the censorship and as inspector of Jewish schools. S. was the only Jewish member of the Warsaw Society of Friends of Science and for a time headed the Warsaw Rabbinical College.

STERN, AVRAHAM (pseudonym—Yair; 1907–1942): Nationalist. In 1939–40, he left the *Irgun Tzevai Leumi*, of which he had been a leader, because of its refusal to continue anti-British activities in Palestine during World War II. He formed an underground organization later known as LOHAME HERUT ISRAEL (by the British, as the "S. Gang") which carried out acts of sabotage, etc. S. was killed by British police while being arrested.

STERN, GLADYS BRONWYN (Mrs. G. L. Holdsworth; 1890–1973): English novelist and playwright. Some of her novels deal with Jewish themes (*Tents of Israel, Mosaic*) chronicling the life of a cosmopolitan Jewish family in England. She was baptized.

STERN GROUP see **LOHAME HERUT ISRAEL**

STERN, ISAAC (1920–): US violinist. He made his debut at the age of 11 and went on to establish a reputation as virtuoso, with successful concert appearances in many parts of the world.

STERN, JACQUES (1882–1949): French politician. He was elected a deputy in 1914 and in 1935–6, was minister for the merchant marine, later for the colonies. In 1942, he took refuge in the US where he committed suicide.

STERN, LINA (1878–1968): Latvian physiologist. She was educated and taught in Switzerland until 1925, when she returned to Russia where she organized the Soviet Institute of Physiology, and in 1939, was made full member of the USSR Academy of Sciences. Her many works deal mainly with endocrinology and the chemical and physiological basis of nervous activity.

STERN, OTTO (1888–1969): Physicist. He taught at Frankfort-on-Main 1914–21, at Hamburg 1923–33, and was research professor of physics at the Carnegie Institute of Technology at Pittsburgh from 1933. In 1943, he was awarded the Nobel Prize for his contribution to the development of the molecular ray method of detecting the magnetic momentum of protons.

STERN, WILLIAM (1871–1938): German psychologist and philosopher. S. taught psychology and philosophy at the Univ. of Hamburg from 1897, and in 1934 became professor at Duke Univ., N Carolina. His early experiments and observations on various aspects of child behavior served as the basis of his *Psychology of Early Childhood*. S. also developed a system known as personalism. It was S. who, in 1912, after an extended study of individual differences, introduced the idea of an intelligence quotient (IQ).

STERN-TÄUBLER, SELMA (1890–): Historian; wife of Eugen TÄUBLER. Working originally in Germany, she has written extensively on the history of German Jewry, including monographs on the Court Jews, Jew Süss, etc. She was archivist of the American Jewish Archives in Cincinnati 1947–56.

STERNBERG, ERICH WALTER (1898–1974): Composer. German by birth, he lived for a time in Palestine before going to the United States. His works include string quartets, orchestral variations, *The Twelve Tribes of Israel*, and songs for chorus after Judah ha-Levi.

STERNE, MAURICE (1878–1957): US painter and sculptor. A native of Latvia, he went to the US in 1890. He was predominantly a classicist painter, using restrained colors. His works include frescos in the Department of Justice in Washington and the monument to the early settlers of New England in Worcester, Mass.

STIEBEL (Yidd. "small room"): Side-room of a synagogue used for public prayer; also applied to the gathering-chamber of Ḥasidim.

STIEGLITZ: (1) *ALFRED S.* (1864–1946): US art pioneer. A master of the photographic art, he edited various periodicals dealing with the subject. (2) *JULIUS OSCAR S.* (1867–1937): US chemist; brother of (1). Professor at Chicago, he was one of the first to establish the interdependence of chemistry and medicine. He was president of the American Chemical Society.

***STILES, EZRA** (1727–1795): US Hebraist. While minister of the Congregational church in Newport, RI, in 1772, he befriended the Palestinian R Ḥayyim Isaac CARIGAL with whom he had numerous discussions. When S. was inaugurated president of Yale in 1778, he delivered a Hebrew oration and later he made the study of Hebrew compulsory for freshmen.

STOBI: Ancient Greco-Roman town of Macedonia, today Gradsko, Yugoslavia. Excavations have revealed remains of an ancient synagogue, including a column with a Greek inscription, probably of 163–5 CE, recording its reconstruction.

STOCKADE AND TOWER see **ḤOMAH U-MIGDAL**

***STÖCKER, ADOLPH** (1835–1909): German anti-Semite. In 1878, while preacher at Berlin royal court, he founded the Christian Social Workers Party to fight socialism and the Jews, who he claimed undermined the foundations of religion and morality. He sat in the Reichstag 1881–1908 (with interruptions). S. founded the Society of German Students through which he disseminated anti-Semitism in intellectual circles.

STOCKHOLM: Capital of SWEDEN. The community was founded in 1774 by the engraver Aaron Isak. Riots which took place there in 1838 resulted in the withdrawal of a measure for the removal of Jewish disabilities. These restrictions were removed in the latter part of the 19th cent. and communal life developed tranquilly. Jewish pop. (1973): 7,000.

STOKES, ROSE PASTOR (1879–1933): US labor agitator. Born in Russian Poland, she went to the US as a child. She collaborated with Margaret Sanger in promoting birth control, and played an important part in organizing women members into the Hotel and Restaurant Workers' Union. She was a founder and for some time served on the central executive committee of the Communist Party in the US.

STONE, ELIHU D. (1888–1952): US Zionist. He was founder of the New England Zionist Region and the outstanding Zionist leader in that area until his death. From 1922–34, he was assistant US attorney for Massachusetts.

STONE, IRVING (1903–): US author. He has written novels and successful historical fiction such as *Lust for Life* (on Vincent Van Gogh) and *The Agony and the Ecstasy* (on Michelangelo).

***STRACK, HERMANN LEBERECHT** (1848–1922): Hebraist. Professor at Berlin, he founded the Berlin *Institutum Judaicum* with a missionary object but strongly fought anti-Semitism and the Blood Libel. He published biblical and mishnaic texts and wrote introductions to the Bible, the Talmud, and the Midrash.

STRASBOURG: Town in Alsace, France. Jewish settlement dates from the Dark Ages and was first protected by the lords and clergy. In the First Crusade (1096), the Jewish quarter was burned and many Jews were killed. At the beginning of the 12th cent., the Jews received protection as "serfs" of the emperor. Their condition deteriorated in the 13th and 14th cents., many being ferociously massacred in 1349, and in 1388, the new community was expelled. Resettlement started in 1771, and the rabbi of S. (David Sintzheim) was president of the Napoleonic Sanhedrin. The Jews had to leave during World War II, but 8,000 were living there again in 1973 and maintaining an active communal life.

STRASHUN, SAMUEL (1794–1872): Lithuanian talmudist. He earned his livelihood from a liquor distillery and refused to accept an official post. His glosses on the Babylonian Talmud (*Hagahot ha-Rashash*) are printed in all complete editions.

STRAUS: US family (1) *JESSE ISIDOR S.* (1872–1936): Public figure; son of *ISIDOR S.* (1845–1912). A New York merchant, he was president of the firm of R. H. Macy and served as US ambassador to France 1933–6. (2) *NATHAN S.* (1848–1931): Philanthropist. He and his brother Isidor became heads of the R. H. Macy store in New York in 1896. He was New York park commissioner 1889–93 and president of the New York Board of Health 1898. He was deeply interested in public health, and campaigned for the compulsory pasteurization of milk.

Nathan Straus.

He built pasteurization plants at his own expense and distributed the milk among the poor of New York from 1892 until 1914 when the necessary legislation was passed. He made possible the construction by Hadassah of child welfare stations and health centers in Palestine which bore his name. It is estimated that he gave over $2,000,000 for health causes in Palestine. (3) *OSCAR SOLOMON S.* (1850–1926): Public official; brother of (2). He was US minister to Turkey 1887–9, and again 1898–1900, and American member of the Court of Arbitration at The Hague in 1902, 1908, 1912, and 1920. S. was the first Jew to serve in an American cabinet, being secretary of commerce and labor under Theodore Roosevelt 1906–9. In 1909–10.. he returned to the diplomatic service as ambassador to Turkey. He was also actively interested in many Jewish organizations, among them the American Jewish Historical Society, of which he was president 1892–8.

STRAUS, OSCAR (1870–1954): Composer. He was born in Austria and lived in Germany, France, and the US, returning to Austria after World War II. He composed operas, orchestral works, and chamber music before specializing in operetta. His famous operettas include *Waltz Dream*, *The Chocolate Soldier*, and *The Last Waltz*.

STRAUSS, GEORGE RUSSELL (1901–): British politician. A labor member of parliament since 1929, he was minister of supply 1947–51.

STRAUSS, JOSEPH BAERMANN (1870–1938): US bridge engineer. He participated in the building of more than 500 bridges in every part of the

world and designed the Golden Gate Bridge, San Francisco.

STRAUSS, LEO (1899–1973): Philosopher. He taught in Germany until the Nazi era when he moved to the US and taught at the New School for Social Research, New York, 1938–49, and then at the Univ. of Chicago. His main subjects were political philosophy and the relations of philosophy and theology, with particular reference to Spinoza, Maimonides, and Hobbes.

STRAUSS, LEWIS LICHTENSTEIN (1896–1974): US public official. Member, banking firm of Kuhn, Loeb, and Co., 1919–47, he served as special assistant to the secretary of the navy in World War II, becoming rear-admiral in 1945. He was a member of the US Atomic Energy Commission 1946–50, and its chairman 1953–8. S.'s appointment as Secretary of Commerce in 1958 was not confirmed by the Senate in 1959.

*STREICHER, JULIUS (1885–1946): German anti-Semite. He participated in Hitler's Munich *putsch* (1923), and edited the notorious pornographic anti-Semitic paper *Der Stürmer* 1923–45. Gauleiter of Franconia, he was one of the architects of the Nazi anti-Jewish Campaign. He was condemned to death by the International Military Tribunal at Nuremberg and hanged.

Barbara Streisand.

STREISAND, BARBARA (1944–): US actress. She made a hit in 1964 in the musical *Funny Girl* (based on the life of Fanny Brice), repeating her success in the movie, for which she was awarded an Oscar.

STRICKER, ROBERT (1879–1944): Zionist leader. A co-founder of the first academic Zionist society in his native Moravia, he later moved to Vienna where he edited the Zionist organ *Jüdische Zeitung.* He presided over the Austrian Jewish national council 1919–20, and was a member of the Austrian parliament which drafted a constitution for the republic. Active in Zionist politics, he was co-founder of the Jewish State Party, 1933. S. edited the Zionist daily *Wiener Morgenzeitung*, 1919–27, and the weekly *Neue Welt*, 1928–38. He refused to leave his community after the Germans took over Austria in 1938, and perished in an extermination camp.

STRIPES or **FLOGGING** (Heb. *malkut*): CORPORAL PUNISHMENT inflicted by the court for the willful transgression of a negative commandment after a previous warning delivered in the presence of witnesses has been ignored. The biblical basis for such punishment is Deut. 25:1–3, while the talmudic discussion is in the treatise MAKKOT. Pietists voluntarily submitted to the 39 stripes as a token of penitence before the Day of Atonement.

STRAND, OSCAR (1879–1935): Austrian architect and stage designer. He was noted for his revolutionary domestic decorations, designs of communal flats, and scenery and costume for stage and screen initiating a new tradition in theater architecture.

STROOCK: (1) *ALAN MAXWELL S.* (1907–): US attorney and communal leader; son of (2). He has been active in the Jewish Theological Seminary (chairman since 1944), the American Jewish Committee, and various legal associations. (2) *SOLOMON MARCUSE S.* (1873–1941): US communal leader. An expert in corporation law, he was active in the Jewish Theological Seminary and the American Jewish Committee of which he became president shortly before his death.

STRUCK, HERMANN (1876–1944): Artist. Born in Germany, he lived in Palestine from 1922. A skilled graphic artist, S. was also a noted teacher. His book on etching, *Die Kunst der Radierung*, is a standard work.

STRUMA: "Illegal" immigrant ship which late in 1941 left Rumania for Palestine carrying 769 refugees. They reached Istanbul but were turned back when it was learned that the British Mandatory government had refused them entry into Palestine. The boat foundered in the Black Sea (Feb. 1942) with the loss of all on board.

STRUNSKY, SIMEON (1879–1948): US journalist. He edited the New York *Evening Post*, 1920–4, and thereafter was on the editorial staff of the *New York Times*. He was a popular essayist, with a straightforward, witty style. His books included *Belshazzar Court or Village Life in New York City* and *No Mean City.*

STUDENT ZIONIST ORGANIZATION: US student body. Organized Zionist activity on US campuses was crystallized with the creation of AVUKAH, which for almost 20 years carried on a vigorous educational program. In 1945, it was superseded by the Intercollegiate Zionist Federation of America (IZFA). The latter was in turn replaced in 1954 by the SZO, and that by American Students for Israel.

STUTTGART: W German city. In 1348, the Jews of S. were burnt on a charge of well-poisoning. In succeeding centuries there were small settlements and a number of expulsions. The modern community dates from the 18th cent. The 4,408 Jews living there in 1933 escaped abroad or were destroyed in the Nazi Period. Jewish pop. (1969): 480.

STYRIA: Austrian province. Jews lived there from the 11th–12th cents. and by the 14th, enjoyed judicial autonomy and other privileges. These aroused the hostility of the masses who pressed for their expulsion, finally executed in 1496. Jewish settlement was resumed after 1848, a community being established at GRAZ in 1863. In 1938, the Jews of S., numbering 2,500, were expelled or exterminated in death-camps by the Nazis.

SUARÈS, ANDRÉ (Yves Scantrel, pseudonym, Caedral; 1866–1948): French author of Jewish origin. His works, notable for their lofty thought and style, included *Images de la grandeur*, *Sur la vie*, and *Le Voyage du Condottière*. Although regretting the Jews' rejection of Jesus, he admired their passion for justice and reason and rallied to their defense after the advent of Nazism.

SUBBOTNIKI (Russ. "Sabbatarians"): Russian sabbatarian movement, widespread from the end of the 18th cent. in Caucasus, Siberia, and the Volga and Don regions. Practicing Jewish customs, some of its followers acknowledged the New Testament in addition to the Old, while others accepted only the Old Testament but not the Talmud. Under Nicholas I, they were banished to Siberia and sent to the army. From 1905 they enjoyed religious freedom. Their number was estimated at several tens of thousands before 1917. Some of their descendants fully embraced traditional Judaism and settled in Palestine.

SUDAN: Jews visited the Sudan from remote times. In 1885, the Mahdi compelled all Jews and Christians to embrace Islam. The community, numbering 50 in 1973, dates from the end of the 19th cent. and is mostly in Khartoum.

SUEZ CAMPAIGN see **SINAI OPERATION**

SUEZ CANAL: Waterway linking the Mediterranean with the Gulf of Suez and the Red Sea. Thanks to the activity of Benjamin DISRAELI, it was secured

Professor Eliezer Lipa Sukenik.

by a British-controlled company which held it until 1956. In the SINAI CAMPAIGN that year Israel troops stopped short of the Canal but in the 1967 War, they moved up to take positions along its eastern bank. All shipping ceased along the canal which in the following years became the scene of prolonged hostilities. It was recaptured by Egypt in the 1973 YOM KIPPUR WAR and reopened to shipping in 1975.

SUICIDE: Deliberate self-destruction is regarded by Judaism as a crime equivalent to murder, and the deliberate s., like a convicted murderer, was denied normal burial and mourning. But it was realized that most s.'s result from mental unbalance and that some could not be condemned at all. Biblical s.'s include Samson (Judg. 16:30) and Saul (I Sam. 31:4). In 73 CE, the garrison of Masada killed themselves rather than be taken by the Romans, while in 1190, the Jews of York killed themselves to avoid falling into Christian hands. The toll of suicides in Nazi lands and concentration camps was heavy. Except when the action was the result of mental disturbances, the s. was buried in a plot at the side of the cemetery.

SUKENIK, ELIEZER LIPA (1889–1953): Archeologist. Of Polish birth, he settled in Palestine in 1912 and lectured on archeology at the Hebrew Univ. from 1935 (professor, 1938). He excavated the Third Wall of Jerusalem, Samaria, Bet Alpha,

etc., and his most distinguished work concerned ancient synagogues and Second Temple funerary inscriptions. In 1947, S. realized the importance of the Dead Sea Scrolls, some of which he succeeded in acquiring for the Hebrew Univ. and partly published before his death.

SUKKAH (Heb. "tabernacle"): Booth erected for the Feast of Tabernacles when, for seven days, religious Jews "dwell" or at least eat in it (Lev. 23:42). It commemorates the special protection given the Israelites during their 40-year wandering in the desert (when according to the rabbis, the "nimbuses of glory" surrounded them on all sides like a tent): it also recalls the booth-like structures in the fields in which the peasants lived during the harvest in Palestine. The Mishnah and Talmud treatise *Sukkah* deals with the special regulations governing its construction, especially the roof covering which must be of certain materials (normally leafy boughs, sometimes straw, etc.) with the shaded area exceeding the unshaded. Walls may be of any material, and only two need be complete. It is customary to decorate the *s.* with curtains, fruits, and symbols of the holiday. In western countries, a *s.* is generally constructed near the synagogue, a token meal (with *kiddush*, etc.) being eaten there after the service.

SUKKAH (Heb. "Booth"): Sixth tractate in the Mishnah order of *Moed*, containing 5 chapters. It has *gemara* both in the Babylonian and Palestinian Talmuds. It deals with the various laws connected with the Feast of Tabernacles and also contains a description of the water libation festival.

SUKKOT (Heb. "Tabernacles"): One of the three pilgrim-festivals. It begins on *Tishri* 15 and lasts for seven days, the eighth day SHEMINI ATZERET being

Detail of *Parokhet* for Sukkot, 1810.
(Jewish Museum, Prague.)

technically a separate holiday (in Israel combined with, but in the Diaspora followed by, SIMḤAT TORAH). Work is only prohibited on the first day (two days in the Diaspora) and on *Shemini Atzeret* (and on *Simḥat Torah* in the Diaspora). The festival is also known as *ḥag ha-asiph* ("the festival of harvest," Exod. 23:16) or simply *ḥag* ("the festival," II Chron. 7:8). It is celebrated by taking the FOUR SPECIES (palm [*lulav*], citron [*etrog*], myrtle, and willow) and carrying them in procession in the synagogue; also by "dwelling" (i.e., at least eating all meals) in the SUKKAH. In Temple times it was also celebrated as a water libation festival, surviving to some extent in the seventh day (HOSHANA RABBAH).

SULZBACH: German town, site of a Hebrew press, 1669–1851, which printed traditional Jewish literature (Bible, Talmud, Zohar, etc.), and works in Yiddish.

SULZBERGER: US family. *LEOPOLD S.* (1805–1881) and his brother *ABRAHAM S.* (1810–1880) emigrated to the US from Germany during the first half of the 19th cent. Of Leopold's three sons, *DAVID S.* (1838–1910) was interested in education and communal work, and *CYRUS LEOPOLD S.* (1858–1932), was prominent in New York as merchant, philanthropist, and Jewish community leader. He was especially active in cultural affairs and aid to immigrants. Of the latter's two sons, *ARTHUR HAYS S.* (1891–1968) was president (until 1957) and publisher of the *New York Times* from 1935, and *LEO S.* (1885–1926) was a textile merchant and noted philanthropist. His son, *CYRUS LEO S.* (1912–), was chief foreign correspondent for the *New York Times*, 1944–54, and subsequently, foreign affairs columnist. Of Abraham's sons, *MAYER S.* (1843–1923), was judge of the Court of Common Pleas, Philadelphia, 1895–1916, and first president of the American Jewish Committee, 1906–12. Another brother, *SOLOMON S.* (1839–1918), was president of B'nai B'rith 1875–6, and treasurer 1878–1915. The latter's son, *MYRON S.* (1875–1956), was a member of the New York state legislature 1902–3, and a municipal court judge 1927–41.

SULZER, SOLOMON (1804–1891): Austrian cantor and composer; founder of the modern school of Jewish liturgical music. From 1826, he was *ḥazzan* in Vienna. His principal work is *Song of Zion* in two vols., the first in the German romantic spirit and the second according to Jewish cantoral art. These compositions spread rapidly throughout Europe and were extensively imitated, although opposed by the E European cantoral school.

SUMERIA: Region of S Babylonia named after a non-Semite people which migrated there in prehistoric times and founded a series of city-states. Its culture was the basis of Babylonian civilization and influenced the Semitic inhabitants of ACCAD to their

N. S. is not specifically mentioned in the Bible but some early names (e.g. Nimrod, Cush) are connected with Sumerian tradition.

SUMPTUARY LAWS: Name given to regulations restricting extravagance in dress, festivities, etc. These were known among the Jews from talmudic times and in the Middle Ages became common, partly because ostentation aroused gentile enmity. S.L. are found in most countries, and specific codes under the title (*Seder*) *Pragmatica*, etc., were drawn up at frequent intervals in various Italian communities. They laid down the maximum number of guests that might be invited to private festivities, the dishes that could be served, the amount of jewelry that women might wear, the dress of both sexes, the nature and number of wedding gifts, etc. These codes throw much light on social history.

SUN, BLESSING OF THE: Ceremonial blessing, recited once every 28 years (e.g. 1981) during the month of *Nissan*, when the sun is supposed to stand in the same spot in the heavens as at the Creation.

SUPERSTITION: In the Biblical Period it is not easy to distinguish s. from heathen practices which persisted among the Israelites, as is illustrated by a recently-discovered Hebrew AMULET dating back to the period of the monarchy and intended against night-demons. Later, the rabbis characterized such usages as "Amorite customs." Nevertheless, belief in DEMONS, etc. was rife in the Talmudic Period. In the Middle Ages, s. was affected by kabbalistic practices, and amulets based on permutations of the Divine names, biblical verses, etc. became very common from the 16th cent. Apart from this, numerous s.'s were current among Jews, some of them native, or even resulting from the desire to avoid gentile practices. Moreover, religious customs were sometimes given a superstitious importance: the MEZUZAH, for example, has been used as a good-luck charm. Widely-observed Jewish s.'s include the use of the *aphikoman* to still a storm, moistening the eyes with *havdalah* wine, burning nail-parings for fear of demons, etc.

SUPPLICATION see **BAKASHAH**

SURA: Babylonian city where Rav founded an academy in the early 3rd cent. The academy endured, with only occasional interruptions, for eight centuries. Its most brilliant periods were during the period of office of RAV and his pupil R HUNA, during the incumbency of R ASHI, and during the Gaonic Period, especially under the incumbency of SAADYAH (928–942). The academy was ultimately transferred to Baghdad, merging in the end with the rival institution of PUMBEDITA.

*SURENHUYS (Surenhusius), **WILLIAM** (1698–1763): Dutch orientalist. His major work was a Latin translation of the Mishnah with the commentaries of Maimonides and Obadiah of Bertinoro.

SURINAM (Dutch Guiana): Dutch settlement in S America. Its Jewish community was established by Marrano refugees after the Portuguese occupation of Brazil and was reinforced by settlers, both Sephardi and Ashkenazi, from Europe. Apart from the community in the capital Paramaribo, there was in the 17th–18th cents. a flourishing and quasi-autonomous Jewish agricultural settlement at Jodensavanne, up the river. Surinam Jews were active in the military defense of the colony against the French and bush-negroes in the 17th–18th cents. The Paramaribo community maintains an active life with a Central Committee for Jewish Affairs in Surinam, a synagogue in Paramaribo serving both the Sephardi and Ashkenazi congregations, a Jewish school, and a monthly *Teroenga*. Jewish pop. (1973): 500.

SUSA see **SHUSHAN**

SUSANNAH AND THE ELDERS: Book of the Apocrypha. It relates the story of a plot laid by two elders against the chaste Susannah and how the contradictions in their allegations were brought out on cross-examination by the wise Daniel. The book may have been originally written in Hebrew and possibly relates to the controversy in Alexander Yannai's time between Pharisees and Sadducees on the subject of conspiring witnesses (c. 90–80 BCE).

Süsskind von Trimberg. (13th. cent. Manasser Codex, University Library. Heidelberg.)

SUSHAN-DUKHT (fl. 5th cent.): Persian queen. Daughter of the exilarch, she married King Yezdegerd I (399–420), was mother of Bahram V (420–38), and was reputed founder of the Jewish settlement in Isfahan and Hamadan.

SUSITA: Ancient Palestinian town on the E shores of the Sea of Galilee. It was renamed Hippos in the Hellenistic Period and Antioch under the Seleucids. S. was captured by Alexander Yannai and reconstructed as a free town by Pompey, then becoming a member of the DECAPOLIS. Its Jewish population suffered in the Roman war. The Talmud mentions it as a gentile enclave in Jewish territory. Recent excavations on the site have revealed Byzantine buildings.

SÜSS, JUD see **OPPENHEIMER, JOSEPH**

SÜSSKIND VON TRIMBERG (c. 1250 — c. 1300): German minnesinger. His lyrical poems in Middle High German, six of which are preserved, are typical of German minstrelsy of his time. His Jewish origin has been questioned.

SUTRO, ADOLPH (1830–1898): US engineer. He accumulated a fortune from real estate in San Francisco, where he was mayor. His great library, given to the city of San Francisco, included many Hebrew mss.

SUTRO, ALFRED (1863–1933): English playwright. Son of a physician and grandson of a rabbi, he turned from journalism and translation (Maeterlinck's *Life of the Bee*, etc.) to the drama and wrote some 20 popular plays (e.g. *The Walls of Jericho*).

SUTZKEVER, AVRAHAM (1913–): Yiddish poet. Born in Lithuania, he belonged to the "Young Vilna" school of Yiddish poets. In 1941–3, S. was in the Vilna ghetto from which he escaped to the partisans. In 1947, he went to Palestine. S. edits the Yiddish quarterly "*Goldene Kait*". Much of his poetry deals with the European holocaust.

SVERDLOV, JACOB MIKHAILOVICH (1885–1919): Russian revolutionary. He was active in the Social Democrat party, being twice exiled to Siberia. After 1917, he was on the central Soviet committee. His work was chiefly organizational.

SVEVO, ITALO see **SCHMITZ, ETTORE**

SWAYTHLING see **MONTAGU**

SWEDEN: European kingdom. In 1745, the government attempted to encourage the settlement of Portuguese Jews from Amsterdam and London, but without tangible results. The engraver Aron Isak was permitted in 1774 to settle in STOCKHOLM and hold religious services. In 1779, the permission was extended to Gothenburg and Norrköping. The Jews of S. suffered from considerable disabilities. A measure for relieving them of the worst of these in 1838 led to riots and was withdrawn. Emancipation was thereafter granted slowly (1860/70), but Jews were still debarred from some positions. The Jews of S.

have played an important part in the life of the country, particularly in the arts. There was an influx of refugees from Germany after 1933, and especially during World War II. The Jewish pop. (1973): 15,000.

SWINE: Listed in the Bible (Lev. 11:7; Deut. 14:8) among those animals forbidden as food, it became particularly obnoxious to Jews. Antiochus Epiphanes used the refusal to eat its flesh as a test for Judaism (II Macc. 6:22). The rabbis cursed those who raised s. (*Sotah* 49*b*), and referred to it contemptuously as *davar aḥer* ("other thing"). In Israel, local authorities have been empowered to ban the raising of s. and the sale and serving of pork products.

SWITZERLAND: Jews lived in the German areas of what is now S. in the Middle Ages, holding the same status and suffering the same treatment as in Germany. In 1294, there was an accusation of Ritual Murder followed by expulsion at BERNE, and in the period of the Black Death particularly gruesome massacres took place (1349) at BASLE, ZURICH, etc. The communities reestablished in S. in the later 14th cent. were short-lived, and the Diet excluded Jews from the country in perpetuity in 1622. Jewish communities existed, however, in the villages of Lengnau, Klingnau, and Endingen in the Aargau canton, which did not join the Swiss Confederation until 1803. Jews also lived from 1780 in Carouge, a suburb of GENEVA ruled by the dukes of Savoy. The majority of the Swiss cantons maintained their exclusion policy into the 19th cent. Political complications ensued with England, the US, and especially France, which objected to the exclusion of one category of its citizens from rights of trade and residence in S. These protests resulted in the gradual removal of restrictions against the Jews in individual cantons beginning with Graubünden (1861), the Federal Constitution of 1874 finally abolishing all Jewish disabilities. In 1893, however, *sheḥitah* was forbidden in S. ostensibly on humanitarian grounds. Surrounded on all sides by German-controlled territories, S. gave shelter to many Jewish fugitives during World War II although she was also criticized for not having done more. The Jewish population is 20,000 (1973), the largest communities being those of Zurich, Basle and Geneva.

SWOPE, GERARD (1872–1957): US industrialist. He was head of the International General Electric Company 1919–33, and president of the General Electric Company 1922–39, 1942–4. S. was a member of the general staff of the US army in World War I, author of the "Swope Plan" for the stabilization of industry (1931), and assistant to the secretary of the treasury in 1942. He left a considerable legacy to the Haifa Technion. His brother *HERBERT BAYARD S.* (1882–1958), journalist, edited *The World* 1920–9.

SYDNEY: Capital of New South Wales, AUSTRALIA. Jews from England settled there in the early 19th cent. regular religious services being held before 1828

and a congregation constituted in 1831. It prospered during the Australian gold rush in the mid-19th cent., remaining closely affiliated to English Jewry. Many members of the community attained high distinction in civic and political life. There was a considerable influx from Russia after 1882. Immigration from Central and E Europe after 1945 has also greatly strengthened the community, which now has nineteen synagogues (one Reform) and a network of charitable and cultural institutions. Pop. (1973): 25,300.

SYKES-PICOT TREATY: Series of secret agreements between Britain, France, and Russia (with the later addition of Italy) entered into between 1914 and 1916, and providing for the postwar partition of the Turkish Empire. Insofar as it affected Palestine and Syria, the "Treaty" consisted of an Anglo-French memorandum initiated on Mar. 9, 1916, after protracted negotiations between Sir Arthur Nicolson and later Sir Mark Sykes (for Britain) and Georges Picot (for France). It provided for the complete dismemberment of Palestine, with Upper Galilee under French control, the Hauran a French-protected Arab State, Transjordan and the Negev a British-protected Arab State, the Haifa Bay area under British control, and the remainder of central Palestine (from Nazareth to Hebron) an Anglo-French-Russian condominium. The Zionist leaders discovered the terms of this arrangement early in 1917, and sharply protested both against the condominium (which they believed would expose the Jewish population to the dangers of a constant power conflict) and against the radical dismemberment of the country. The "treaty" was partly responsible for the form of the post-war frontiers of Palestine.

SYLVESTER, JAMES JOSEPH (1814–1897): English mathematician. The first professing Jew to enter Cambridge Univ., he taught at London 1837–41, Virginia 1841–55, the Woolwich military academy 1855–76, and was professor at Johns Hopkins Univ., Baltimore 1876–83 and Oxford 1883–97. He helped to evolve the theory of invariants and made a study of algebraic forms. S. founded the *American Journal of Mathematics*.

SYMMACHUS (fl. latter 2nd cent. CE): Translator of the Bible into Greek. His exact dates and place are unknown. According to one tradition, he was an Ebionite, another regards him as a Samaritan proselyte to Judaism, while some Jewish scholars consider him a pupil of R Meir. His translation — unlike that of Aquila — was more faithful to the content than the form.

SYNAGOGUE (Gk. "assembly"; Heb. *bet keneset*): Building for Jewish public prayer. Sources of the 1st cent. CE show that the s. was already then an ancient institution. Attempts to detect reference to it in the Bible are conjectural and it is widely believed to have originated among the Babylonian exiles as a

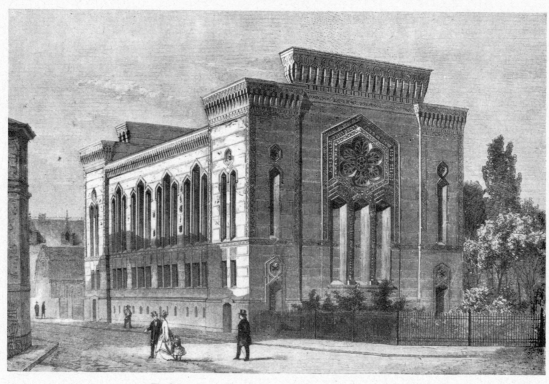

The Synagogue in Stockholm. (Architect: F. W. Scholander.)

substitute for the Temple. There were s.'s throughout Palestine before the destruction of the Second Temple, including several in Jerusalem (one even on the Temple hill). In the Diaspora, evidence in Egypt goes back to the 3rd cent. BCE, where a contemporary inscription refers to right of asylum in the s. The great s. of Alexandria, with separate sections for each trade-guild, was famed in Roman times. S.'s are known throughout Greece and the Greek islands, Syria, Cyprus, Asia Minor, and Cyrenaica. After the destruction of the Second Temple, they increased in importance, and beautiful examples have been excavated in Palestine and Syria from the ensuing period (Bet Alpha, Capernaum, Dura-Europos, Nirim, etc.). At this time, they were frequently placed on a high spot, sometimes outside the city, one end of the building being oriented toward Jerusalem. They served as places of prayer, study, and public assembly, and some had accommodation for travelers. Special accommodation was made for women, which in the 3rd cent. CE took the form of a gallery above the hall. From this period, many s.'s were decorated with figured carvings, mosaics, and frescos. In classical times, the s. was governed by an ARCHISYNAGOGUS and other officers, variously named, e.g. *gerontes* ("elders"), *patres synagogue*, and ḤAZZAN. Synagogues belonged to corporate communities or else to the individuals who had built them. The protection they received was shaken by the Christianization of

the Roman Empire. Many were now destroyed, others converted to churches, and further construction or enlargement was forbidden. After the Arab conquest, s.'s were built in the lands under Moslem rule. In the Orient, there were famous examples at Baghdad, Fostat, Damascus, and Aleppo. Outstanding medieval European examples were at Toledo (12th and 14th cents.), Worms (built 11th cent.; destroyed 1938), Regensburg (13th cent.), the *Altneuschul* in Prague (14th cent.; still extant); the largest in Europe was at Cracow (13–14th cents.). In the Middle Ages, the s. was of particular significance as a center of study. From this period, the ARK was often built in the wall facing Jerusalem, instead of being a movable cupboard. A partition divided men from women unless special architectural provision was made to accommodate them. Many s.'s had an adjacent courtyard where law-cases were heard, marriages celebrated, and even markets held. In more modern times (16th–17th cents.), many Polish s.'s were built by government order as fortresses, affording the opportunity for defense. The officers were the *gabbai*, the *ḥazzan* (now a precentor), and the *shammash* (responsible for order and cleanliness). Institutions (e.g. the communal hall, the ritual bath) were housed in the courtyard in the modern period, while the separate gallery for women was reinstated. The Ḥasidic movement was responsible for the KLAUS. The 19th cent. REFORM MOVEMENT introduced an organ, moved the platform for the reader from the center to the E wall combining it with the Ark, gradually abolished the women's section: some of these innovations were later adopted by the more moderate Orthodox. In the US, the modern tendency has been to restore the s. (or "Temple") as a communal and social center.

PLAN AND DESIGN: Many of the early examples in Palestine are basilical with a gallery and often decorated; the doors are at the end or in the larger side; others consist of a single hall with portico and apse opposite it on the long side. The s. at HAMAM-LIF is a complex of 15 rooms. The 3rd cent. s. at DURA-EUROPOS was adorned with biblical frescos. The majority of medieval s.'s consisted of halls subdivided by one or more rows of columns. From the Middle Ages, some Spanish examples, later preserved as churches (e.g. at Toledo), reflect Moorish influence. Early Italian s.'s were much altered in the course of time; the influence of Spanish exiles upon their architecture is noticeable from the 16th cent. The interiors frequently reflect Renaissance and Baroque styles, as do Sephardi examples in other W European countries (including Amsterdam, 1675 and Bevis Marks, London, 1701) and America (Newport, 1763). The Worms s. was a long vaulted hall that was copied elswhere in Central and E Europe. Very many timber synagogues were constructed in E Europe, but none now survives; they often had second stories, towers, external galleries, etc. and the interiors were adorned with paintings. The type spread to S Ger-

many and Bohemia in the 18th cent. With the 19th cent., greater attention was paid to the exterior, but there tended to be a lack of unity between function and appearance. In the 20th cent., functionalism increasingly influenced s. design building (e.g. those designed by Erich Mendelsohn in Baltimore and St. Louis in the US).

SYNAGOGUE COUNCIL OF AMERICA: Body established in 1926 for the purpose of overall Jewish religious representation. The organization acts in behalf of Orthodox, Conservative, and Reform Judaism in the US. It participates in inter-faith activities, plays an important part in opposing missionary attempts to convert Jews, and is active in fighting religious prejudice.

SYNAGOGUE, THE GREAT see **GREAT ASSEMBLY**

SYNOD see **COUNCILS**

SYNTHETIC ZIONISM see **ZIONISM**

SYRACUSE: City in the state of New York, US. Jews from New York City and Albany settled there and organized a congregation in 1839. 9 congregations were established by 1900. There is a Jewish Communal Center, and, besides religious schools affiliated with the various congregations, the community maintains the daily Hebrew Free School, incorporated in 1899. Jewish pop. (1973): 11,000.

SYRIA: E Mediterranean country; in the Bible called ARAM. The kings of Aram did not succeed in creating a homogeneous state, while the coastal strip was settled by the Phoenicians. As described

Synagogue of the Hebrew University. (Architect: Rau: 1957.)

Nachman Syrkin

in the Bible (I and II Kings), there was constant friction with the kingdoms of Israel and Judah until the 8th cent, when S. was overrun by the Assyrians. Its Jewish population, especially at ANTIOCH, was of special importance in the SELEUCID era but suffered from the hostility of the Greeks. There were few Jews there in the Talmudic Period and under Theodosius II (408–50), their religious freedom was restricted, many synagogues being converted to churches. The situation improved with the Arab conquest (634–7), when Jews were allowed to maintain their faith but were forced to pay poll-tax. The largest communities in the 12th cent., according to Benjamin of Tudela, were at ALEPPO (5,000), DAMASCUS (3,000), and Palmyra (2,000). The Jewish settlement was increased after 1492 by refugees from Spain and Sicily and was important in the transit trade between Europe and Asia. The DAMASCUS BLOOD LIBEL in 1840 evoked worldwide reaction. Under the French mandate (1920), Jews obtained equal rights, but these were infringed during World War II under the Vichy regime. A considerable emigration to the US and the Lebanon, as well as to Israel, reduced the Jewish population from nearly 30,000 in 1943 to c. 14,000 in 1947, and a further exodus was caused by terrorization during the Israel War, material decline, and moral isolation. The Jews in recent years have been confined to their own quarter, notably in Damascus. By 1973, the number of Jews was down to 4,000. Syria has been consistent in the virulence of its anti-Israel policy and has continued acts of hostility since it joined the Arab invasion of 1948. Its extremism was largely responsible for the SIX-DAY WAR in the

course of which Israel defeated the Syrian army and occupied the GOLAN HEIGHTS from which the Syrians had been bombarding Israel settlements.

SYRKIN, NACHMAN (1867–1924): Zionist socialist leader and author. Born in Russia, he went to study in Germany where he was a founder of the Russian Jewish Students' Society at Berlin Univ. In this circle, from which many modern Zionist concepts developed, S. advocated socialist Zionism. He participated in the First Zionist Congress but supported Territorialism from 1905 until 1909 when he rejoined the Zionist Organization. In 1907, S. settled in New York, where he contributed to Yiddish journals and was active in Zionist work. During World War I, he helped to found the American Jewish Congress and in 1919 was a member of the *Comité des délégations juives* at the Paris Peace Conference. He wrote extensively on Socialist Zionism, of which he was one of the pioneer theoreticians. His daughter *MARIE S.* (1900–) has written biographies of Hannah Szenes, Golda Meir, etc. She taught English literature at Brandeis Univ. and was a member of the Jewish Agency Executive.

SZENES, HANNAH (1921–1944): Palestinian heroine. Born in Budapest, she went to Palestine in 1939 and joined the kibbutz Sedot Yam. Volunteering for the British army in 1943 as radio operator, she was parachuted into Yugoslavia in 1944 with the object of reaching Hungary to rescue prisoners and organize Jewish resistance. She was captured, tried at Budapest, and shot. S. wrote some moving Hebrew poems, notably *Blessed is the Match*.

SZIGETI, JOSEPH (1892–1973): Violinist. Born in Hungary, he performed from the age of 13 and taught at the Geneva Conservatoire 1917–24. In 1925, he settled in the US.

SZOLD: US family. (1) *BENJAMIN S.* (1829–1902): Rabbi. He served Congregation Oheb Shalom in Baltimore for more than 40 years and edited a popular revised prayer-book. (2) *HENRIETTA S.* (1860–1945); daughter of (1). She was active in assisting the integration of Jewish immigrants in the US. She was secretary of the Jewish Publication Society 1892–1916, editing and translating many of its books, and served also as associate editor of the *American Jewish Year Book* (1895 ff.). As a result of her visit to Palestine in 1909 she decided that health, sanitation, and welfare work were necessary prerequisites for Zionist development and in 1912, organized HADASSAH, the Women's Zionist Organization of America. In 1918, she was responsible for the dispatch of the American Zionist Medical Unit to Palestine. She was the first woman to become a member of the Zionist Executive (1927), with responsibility for education and health, and three years later was named to the *Vaad Leumi* in charge of social welfare. After the Nazi rise to power, she became the energetic and

Henrietta Szold.

active leader of YOUTH ALIYAH and was responsible for saving thousands of European Jewish youth. She was deeply interested in fostering friendly relations between Jews and Arabs in Palestine. (3) *ROBERT S.* (1889–): Zionist leader. He was associated with the Brandeis-Mack group in American Zionism and was among the founders of the Palestine Economic Corporation and chairman of its board. In 1930–1, S. was president of the Zionist Organization of America.

SZTERÉNYI, JOZSEF (1861–1939): Hungarian economist, statesman, and journalist. The son of a Reform rabbi, S. early adopted Christianity. In 1890, he joined the ministry of commerce, later organizing home industries and craft training. He was elected to parliament, became minister of commerce in 1918, and in 1927, a member of the upper house. S. represented Hungary at the League of Nations.

SZYK, ARTHUR (1894–1951): Artist. Born in Lodz, he studied in Paris and later specialized in book-illumination, in which he acquired outstanding proficiency. His illuminated versions of the Statute of Kalish, the Passover Haggadah, and the US and Israel Declarations of Independence are among the leading modern achievements of their type. After living for some years in France and England, he emigrated in 1940 to the US, where he became noted for book illustrations and satirical caricatures, especially in anti-Nazi drawings.

Synagogue in Kephar Tabor at the foot of Mt. Tabor.

TAANACH: Site of a Canaanite fortress in the Jezreel Valley; now the Arab village Ti'innik which was in Jordan territory 1948–67, near the then-border with Israel. On the Israel side of the border, 11 immigrants' villages were erected in 1954–7, according to the "T. regional settlement plan." An important center in the Early Bronze Period, T. also flourished in the Late Bronze Age. It was allocated to the tribe of Manasseh but continued as an independent Canaanite town and participated in the battle against the Israelites under Deborah. It is not mentioned after the destruction of the First Temple.

TAANIT (Heb. "Fast"): Ninth tractate in the Mishnah order of *Moed*, containing 4 chapters. It has *gemara* in both the Babylonian and Palestinian Talmuds. It deals with the designation of fast days in time of drought, as well as with the time and form of prayers for rain. Other communal fasts are incidentally discussed.

TABERNACLE (Heb. *mishkan*): The portable sanctuary set up by Moses in the wilderness according to Divine instructions (Exod. 26–7). Its chief architects were Bezalel and Oholiab. The frame was constructed of acacia wood overlaid with gold. Various layers of curtains and animal skins gave it a tent-like appearance (hence its other name *ohel moed* i.e., "tent of meeting"). The most important part of the t. — the Holy of Holies — was separated by a curtain; it contained the Ark, the seven-branched *menorah*, the table of Shewbread, and the golden altar for incense. The name t. is generally applied in English also to the Sukkah.

TABERNACLES see **SUKKOT**

TABLETS OF THE LAW see **COMMANDMENTS, TEN**

TABOR: Mountain (1,921 ft.) in Lower Galilee, Israel. Because of its prominence, it served as a boundary point for several tribes. Here, Deborah and Barak concentrated their forces before their decisive battle with Sisera. In hellenistic times, it served as a royal fortress (Atabyrion); it was refortified by Josephus and stormed by the Romans under Titus. According to Christian tradition Jesus was transfigured on T. before the eyes of his disciples (Matt. 17:1 relates the events merely as occurring on "a high mountain"). A Byzantine church was erected on the top of the mount and in the Crusader Period, a Benedictine abbey, which ceased to exist in 1187. In 1873, the Franciscans established themselves on T. by the side of a Greek Orthodox church; the present church was built in 1924.

TADMOR: Ancient Syrian city, known to the Romans as Palmyra. According to a biblical tradition, it was founded by Solomon. Palmyrenes served in the Roman armies, 66–70, and hostility to the city is expressed in the Talmud. Jews served in the Roman military units raised from T. in the 3rd cent., and converts from T. are recorded in Palestine. Many Palmyrene Jews are buried in the catacombs of Bet Shearim. Benjamin of Tudela found 2,000 Jews in T. in the 12th cent.

TADSHE: Late Midrash so-called from its opening word. It is also known as the *Baraita* of R Phineas ben Jair. It deals principally with the symbolism of numbers.

TAGIN (Aram. "crowns"): Dagger-like strokes added to the tops of various letters when written in the Torah and other parts of the Bible. They do not appear in printed texts. According to the Masorah, the seven letters *shin, ayin, tet, nun, zayin, gimel,* and *tzade* require three crown strokes; the others take one or none. According to one opinion, the *t.* formerly had varying forms with exegetical implications. They are referred to in the New Testament as "tittles."

TAHANUN (also *tehinnah*; Heb. "supplication"):
Prayer following the week-day EIGHTEEN BENEDIC-
TIONS. Halakhic literature calls it *nephilat appayim*
("falling upon the face") after the original custom
of prostration during its recitation; this was later
modified to bowing the head over the arm. The
wording of the prayer was finally established only
after the Gaonic Period and the *t.* was lengthened on
Mondays and Thursdays. Some communities preface
the prayer with penitential prayers (*Selihot*). *T.* is not
recited on joyful days, in the presence of a bridegroom,
or on the day of circumcision.

TAHARAH see **PURITY, RITUAL; TOHORAH**

TAHKEMONI see **AL-HARIZI**

TAIROV (KORNBLÜT), ALEXANDER (1885–1950):
Russian producer; of Jewish extraction. He
headed the Moscow Chamber Theater 1914–50, and
was noted for his realistic productions.

TAKHLIS (Heb. *takhlit* = "purpose"): A practical
material end; in a bad sense, devotion to material
self-seeking.

TAKHRIKHIM (Heb.): The shroud in which a
corpse is wrapped.

TAKKANAH: A regulation which supplements the
law of the Torah. Such regulations have been
executed since earliest times, and the total number
incorporated into current Jewish law is extremely
large. Instances (in reported chronological order) of
takkanot are: the Torah is to be read on Sabbaths, etc.
(ascribed to Moses); residents of a courtyard must
pool their domains (by means of an *eruv*) if they wish
to transfer articles freely between their houses and the
courtyard on the Sabbath (Solomon); courts are to
sit every Monday and Thursday (Ezra); a wife's
marriage settlement (*ketubbah*) is to be a general
mortgage on the whole of her husband's property
(Simeon ben Shetah); communities must appoint
elementary school teachers (Joshua ben Gamala); a
father must support his minor children (the Sanhedrin
at Usha); debts are recoverable from a deceased
debtor's movable property (the geonim); prohibition
of bigamy (R Gershom) applying to Jews living in
Christian Europe (in Moslem countries an alternative
regulation made bigamy subject to the first wife's
consent); prohibition against opening a private letter
(R Gershom); the husband cannot retain the dowry
if his wife dies within a year of marriage (R Tam).
The inner life of communities and congregations
was similarly governed by *takkanot*. Thus, some
communities prevented by *t.* lavish displays of wealth
at weddings, etc. (see SUMPTUARY LAWS); such
takkanot either lapsed with the passage of time or
disappeared with the community itself.

TAL see **DEW**

TAL, MIKHAIL (1937–): Russian chess master
native of Riga. In 1960–1, he was the world chess
champion.

TAL (originally **GRÜNTHAL), YOSEPH** (1910–):
Israel musician. He studied in Berlin and settled
in Palestine in 1934. His compositions include
operas two symphonies, six ipano concertos,
the choreographic poem *Exodus* the cantata *The
Mother of the Sons Rejoiceth* and pioneer compositions
in electronic music.

TAL SHAHAR: Israel smallholder settlement (TM)
in the Judean foothills, founded in 1948 and
named for Henry Morgenthau Jr. Pop. (1972): 398.

TALLIT (Heb.): Prayer shawl. It is donned by adult
males (among the Orthodox, often only by
married males) during the morning (and additional)
prayers (on *Av* 9 in the afternoon, and on the Day of
Atonement at all services). It is a four-cornered
garment, usually made of wool, upon the corners
of which TZITZIT have been knotted in accordance
with the biblical prescription (Num. 15:37–41).
Occasionally the head-piece is adorned with a strip
of worked silver or gold called the *atarah* (crown).
A smaller form, the *Tallit Katan* (small *t.*) or *Arba
Kanphot* ("four corners") is worn perpetually under
the outer garment during waking hours.

TALMID HAKHAM (Heb. "wise pupil"; or properly
"disciple of the wise"): Person learned in talmudic
study. In Jewish tradition the *t. h.* was the ideal
toward which every individual was expected to strive.

TALMUD (Heb. "Teaching"): Name applied to
each of two great compilations, distinguished respectively as the Babylonian T. and the Palestinian
T., in which are collected the records of academic
discussion and of judicial administration of Jewish
LAW (see also HALAKHAH) by generations of scholars
and jurists in many academies and in more than one
country during several centuries after 200 CE (the
approximate date of the completion of the MISHNAH).
In external form, each T. consists of the Mishnah
together with a *gemara*, which is both a commentary
on and a supplement to the Mishnah. Both T.'s also
contain non-legal or aggadic digresssions. The authorities mentioned by name in the Palestinian T. all lived
before c. 400 CE; those mentioned in the Babylonian
T. lived before c. 500 CE. In addition to material
by named authors, each T. — but more especially the
Babylonian — contains material of unknown authorship that appears to be later in date than the latest
of the named authorities. The Babylonian T. has
been estimated to contain about two and a half
million words and is rather more than three times as
long as the Palestinian T. The *gemara* of the Babylonian T. is in Hebrew and eastern Aramaic (a grammar
in English of this Aramaic dialect was published by
C. Levias in 1900), while the *gemara* of the Palestinian
T. is in Hebrew and Western or Palestinian Aramaic
(the standard grammar being by G. Dalman in German; 2nd ed. 1905). A French translation of the
Palestinian T. (by M. Schwab; 11 vols.) was published

Page from the Munich manuscript of the Talmud.
the only almost complete Talmud-manuscript.

toward the end of the 19th cent. During the present century complete translations have appeared of the Babylonian T. into German (by L. Goldschmidt; 12 vols.) and English ("Soncino Talmud" edited by I. Epstein; 35 vols). Translations of single treatises into various languages, including Hebrew, also exist. Both because of its greater length and because of its greater subsequent influence on Jews and Judaism, the Babylonian T. is by far the more important of the two compilations.

The Palestinian (or Jerusalem) Talmud. Almost nothing is known of the history of this T. between the date of its compilation and its emergence toward the end of the gaonic era, almost six centuries later, as an aid to the study of the Babylonian T. After this time, however, it is quoted by many commentators on the Babylonian T., etc. Only one complete ms is known; this is now at Leyden in Holland and was used for the first printed edition (Venice, 1522). The Vatican Library in Rome possesses a partial ms and there are also numerous *genizah* fragments. There is, however, no continuous textual tradition such as exists for most of the Babylonian T. Quotations by authors who possessed ms copies are thus particularly valuable. Most of their quotations from *Zeraim* and *Moed* are collected in Ratner's *Ahavat Zion Vi-*

Yrushalayim. The Palestinian T. possesses *gemara* on all the tractates of the Orders *Zeraim*, *Moed*, *Nashim*, and *Nezikin*, and on the tractate *Niddah*; *Niddah* and *Makkot* are incomplete because the Leyden ms is defective at these two points. Many scholars believe that a *gemara* on *Kodashim* was compiled but is now lost. All agree that the supposed version of *Kodashim* issued early in this century is spurious. The *gemara* is arranged lemmatically, i.e., the opening words of a sentence or paragraph of the Mishnah are cited and the relevant *gemara* follows. If the *gemara* on a section of the Mishnah consists of several paragraphs, these are recorded in turn, and if, as happens often, *gemara* on other sections of the Mishnah is also relevant, this is repeated next. No attempt is made, however, to combine the consecutive paragraphs of *gemara* into a connected whole, and this fact both explains the greater brevity of the Palestinian T. and indicates its earlier compilation (considerable space in the Babylonian T. is taken up by attempts of comparatively late date to establish connections between originally distinct passages of *gemara* and to combine them into continuous discourses). A significant part of the *gemara* of the Palestinian T. consists of a comparative study of the Mishnah and analogous BARAITOT, the majority of which are also to be found in the TOSEPHTA and halakhic MIDRASHIM. Among the post-mishnaic authorities, called AMORAIM, those of Palestinian origin naturally predominate. Nevertheless, a considerable contribution is due to the earlier generations of Babylonian amoraim, e.g. Rav and Samuel and their pupils. Investigation into the history of the compilation of the Palestinian T. has hitherto produced only a few results of value. Maimonides' statement that the Palestinian T. was edited by R Johanan is enigmatic if his reference is to the famous head of the academy of Tiberias, R Johanan ben Nappaḥa, for much of this T. is due to amoraim who lived during the century following this R Johanan's death in 279 CE. Appreciable differences in style and content between the *gemara* of the Order *Nezikin* and that of the other Orders have led S. Lieberman to conclude that the former originated as a legal handbook in Caesarea c. 350 CE, while the rest of the T. was edited at Tiberias c. 400 CE. Most commentaries on the Palestinian T. date from the 18th cent. and after, and are influenced by the advanced stage reached in the study of the Babylonian T. All the important commentaries to the date of publication are contained in the Vilna edition of 1922 (7 vols.; supplementary volume, 1926). Many additional commentaries and elucidations of difficult passages have been published since. A simple readable consecutive commentary, similar to that of Rashi on the Babylonian T., has still to appear.

The Babylonian Talmud. The history of this T. is only briefly obscured, for quotations from it in the *Sheeltot de-Rav Aḥai* and in the *Halakhot Pesukot*

Order	Tractate	No. of chapters	Gemara in Palestinian Talmud	Gemara in Babylonian Talmud
Zeraim	Berakhot	9	X	X
	Peah	8	X	
	Demai	7	X	
	Kilaim	9	X	
	Sheviit	10	X	
	Terumot	11	X	
	Maaserot	5	X	
	Maaser Sheni	5	X	
	Hallah	4	X	
	Orlah	3	X	
	Bikkurim	3	X	
Moed	Shabbat	24	X	X
	Eruvin	10	X	X
	Pesahim	10	X	X
	Shekalim	8	X	
	Yoma	8	X	X
	Sukkah	5	X	X
	Betzah	5	X	X
	Rosh Ha-Shanah	4	X	X
	Taanit	4	X	X
	Megillah	4	X	X
	Moed Katan	3	X	X
	Hagigah	3	X	X
Nashim	Yevamot	16	X	X
	Ketubbot	13	X	X
	Nedarim	11	X	X
	Nazir	9	X	X
	Gittin	9	X	X
	Sotah	9	X	X
	Kiddushin	4	X	X
Nezikin	Bava Kama	10	X	X
	Bava Metzia	10	X	X
	Bava Batra	10	X	X
	Sanhedrin	11	X	X
	Makkot	3	X	X
	Shevuot	8	X	X
	Eduyyot	8		
	Avodah Zarah	5	X	X
	Avot	5		
	Horayot	3	X	X
Kodashim	Zevahim	14		X
	Menahot	13		X
	Hullin	12		X
	Bekhorot	9		X
	Arakhin	9		X
	Temurah	7		X
	Keritot	6		X
	Meilah	6		X
	Tamid	7		X
	Middot	5		
	Kinnim	3		
Tohorot	Kelim	30		
	Oholot	18		
	Negaim	14		
	Parah	12		
	Tohorot	10		
	Mikvaot	10		
	Niddah	10	X	X
	Makhshirin	6		
	Zavim	5		
	Tevul Yom	4		
	Yadayim	4		
	Uktzin	3		

show that it was substantially in its present state by the middle of the 8th cent. CE. Only its history between 500–700 is uncertain, the meaning of the information contained in the famous historical letter of R Sherira Gaon being the subject of dispute among historians. The Babylonian T.'s own statement (*Bava Metzia* 86a) is that R Ashi and Ravina mark the end of *horaah* ("instruction"), although R Ashi and Ravina were certainly not responsible for all the anonymous material it contains. The Babylonian T. possesses *gemara* on *Berakhot* and *Niddah* and on the Orders of *Moed* (except *Shekalim*), *Nashim*, *Nezikin* (except *Avot* and *Eduyyot*), and *Kodashim* (except *Middot* and *Kinnim*). During the Middle Ages, the Babylonian T. was stated, chiefly by Jewish apostates, to be blasphemous and inimical to Christianity and this led to large numbers of copies being seized and burnt. Consequently, only one complete ms of the whole of the Babylonian T. is now known, a 14th cent. codex in Munich, which has been reproduced in facsimile. Many other ms copies of single treatises and groups of treatises exist and the very considerable amount of material available is being collated and assembled in Jerusalem for the publication of a critical edition in the near future. At present, the best edition available is the Vilna edition (1902) which contains a large number of commentaries and has been reprinted many times. Invaluable textual information is contained in R. N. Rabbinowitz's *Dikduke Sopherim* (16 volumes covering *Zeraim*, *Moed*, *Nezikin*, and part of *Kodashim*). There are thousands of volumes of commentaries on the whole or on parts of the T. Although the Babylonian T. is no longer the chief direct source of Jewish law — for ultimate authority has long since passed to the Codes and subsequent compilations, especially Responsa — it is nevertheless still the most important Jewish legal source-book and, as such, continues to provide the foundation of religious education among observant Jews. It has been estimated that about a seventh of the Palestinian T. and about a third of the Babylonian T. consist of non-legal or aggadic digressions not strictly relevant to the commentary or to the Mishnah. These digressions are replete with historical, scientific, and medical information, anecdotes, proverbs, religious and moral sermons, essays in biblical exegesis and interpretation, and folklore. It can be inferred from the T. itself (*Shabbat* 30a) that a halakhic discourse in the time of the amoraim would normally include also an appropriate aggadic section. Which literary works were drawn upon for this material, however, is still only a matter for conjecture. The aggadah of the Babylonian T. is also published separately in a work entitled *En Yaakov*, the Palestinian aggadah being contained in a supplement entitled *Yepheh Mareh*. (See also entries on individual treatises).

TALMUD, BURNING OF: The first official destruction of rabbinic literature by the Catholic Church took place in Paris on June 17, 1242, when 24 cartloads of Talmud mss were burned as a sequel to the religious DISPUTATION there two years earlier. Minor onslaughts of the same type recurred intermittently thereafter (e.g. in Italy in 1322). The full-scale offensive was resumed in the 16th cent., vast numbers of volumes comprising all types of Jewish literature being destroyed in Rome on Sept. 9, 1553. This example was soon followed all over N Italy, though deferred at Cremona until 1559. Rabbinic works found in raids on the Jewish quarters were thereafter burned sporadically. Thousands of volumes of the Talmud were burned in Poland by order of Bishop Dembowski after the disputation between the rabbis and the "Zoharists" led by Jacob Frank at Kamenetz-Podolsk in 1757.

TALMUD COMMENTARIES: The first T. c. are to be found in the isolated textual comments of the later geonim, starting with Paltoi. Full commentary is found in the explanations of SHERIRA, HAI, and SAMUEL BEN HOPHNI. Two major commentaries appeared in 11th cent. N Africa: NISSIM BEN JACOB OF KAIROUAN in his *Sepher ha-Maphteah shel Manule ha-Talmud* ("Key to the Locks of the Talmud") clarifies difficult passages by references to parallels elsewhere in the Talmud, while HANANEL BEN HUSHIEL made extensive use of the Palestinian Talmud in his commentary to the Babylonian Talmud. Germany and France were the next great centers for commentary. GERSHON BEN JUDAH wrote in the early 11th cent. and his commentary was the foundation for that of RASHI, the most accepted and influential of all Talmud commentators whose explanations have become an integral feature of Talmud study. Rashi was followed by the TOSAPHISTS who added dialectic method to Rashi's clear and simple logic. From France and Germany, the dialectic method passed to Spain where important commentaries were written by MOSES BEN NAHMAN and SOLOMON BEN ADRET. The next great period of T. c. was in 16th cent. Europe. Here a new approach was developed, that of PILPUL, originating with Jacob Pollak of Poland; this remained the accepted method of study in E Europe and centers coming under E European influence. The three great commentaries of the 16th cent. are *Hokhmat Shelomoh* of Solomon LURIA, *Hiddushe Halakhot* and *Hiddushe Aggadot* of Samuel EDELS, and the *Meir Ene Hakhamim* of MEIR LUBLIN. The Vilna Gaon (ELIJAH BEN SOLOMON) influenced Talmud study in Lithuania as did more recently Hayyim SOLOVEICHIK. A fresh approach resulted from the rise of scientific study in the 19th cent. but it produced no new commentary to the Babylonian Talmud. The writing of commentaries to the Palestinian Talmud as a distinctive work came late. Solomon Sirillo and Joshua Benveniste wrote commentaries to great parts of it in the 17th cent. They were followed in the 18th cent. by Elijah Fulda. Later in the same century David Fränkel and Moses Margalioth wrote the commentaries which became part of the standard editions. The latter wrote a commentary to the entire Palestinian Talmud. Scientific commentaries on parts of the Palestinian Talmud have begun to appear, notably by Louis GINZBERG and Saul LIEBERMAN.

TALMUD TORAH (Heb. "study of the Law"): Term applied generally to Jewish religious (and ultimately talmudic) study. It was regarded as one of the primary good deeds which brought a man his reward both in this world and the next (*Peah* 1:1). The name was adopted by the voluntary associations ("*Hevrot T. T.*") established to foster religious education; later, it was also applied to the schools set up under their auspices, and ultimately to Jewish religious public schools as a whole. The *T. T.* is to be distinguished on the one hand from the private HEDER, the scope of which was more elementary, and on the other, from the advanced ACADEMIES for talmudic study. The *T. T.* flourished especially in E Europe and among the immigrant communities in W countries. A separate *T. T.* for girls is reported in 15th cent. Rome.

TAM, JACOB BEN MEIR see **JACOB BEN MEIR**

TAMAR: Wife of Er, eldest son of Judah, and later Er's brother, Onan. After Onan died, Judah refused to wed her to his third son, Shelah, and in protest at this break of tradition, T. disguised herself as a prostitute and conceived twins by Judah. The story illustrates the ancient obligation to marry a deceased brother's wife.

TAMAR: Daughter of David and sister of Absalom. She was raped by her stepbrother Amnon (II Sam. 13) who was slain for his action by Absalom.

TAMID (Heb. "Perpetual Offering"): (1) The daily morning and evening WHOLE OFFERING sacrificed in the Temple (Num. 28:1-8). (2) Ninth tractate (tenth in some codices) in the Mishnah order of *Kodashim*. It contains 7 (originally 6) chapters, and has *gemara* in the Babylonian, but not the Palestinian, Talmud. It deals with the prescriptions for the daily burnt-offerings (Exod. 29:38; Num. 28:1-8) and also discusses the Temple organization.

TAMMUZ: Babylonian-Sumerian deity. Legendarily carried off to the underworld, all life on earth withered until he was brought back to life by Ishtar. The cult of T. under various names (Adonis, Osiris, etc.) was widespread in the Middle East and reached Palestine (Ezek. 8:14).

TAMMUZ: Tenth month of the Hebrew civil year and fourth of the ecclesiastical. It corresponds to June-July and has 29 days. Its most important date is the 17th, observed as a fast commemorating the breaching of the Temple walls by Titus as well as by Nebuchadnezzar.

TAMPA: City in Florida, US Jews went there with the development of the cigar industry in the late 19th century. The first congregation Shaarai Zedek was incorporated in 1894 (it became Reform). Conservative and Orthodox Congregation followed. A Community Council was established in 1969. Jewish pop. (1973): 7,000.

TANAKH (from the initial letters of Heb. *Torah Neviim Ketuvim*: "Pentateuch, Prophets, Hagiographa"): The Hebrew Bible.

TANGIERS: Port in NW Africa. Some 50 Jews were living there when it passed under English rule in 1662 but were expelled in 1683. After its capture by the Arabs in 1684, many Jewish families settled in T. Under the international regime in the 20th cent., the Jews played an important part, and in the period of Expansion after World War II. Jewish pop. (1973): 3,000.

TANHUM BEN JOSEPH OF JERUSALEM (fl. 13th cent.): Biblical commentator. In his commentaries, mostly in Arabic, philology is stressed, and philosophical subjects are treated according to the ideas of Maimonides. He wrote a lexicon to Maimonides' *Mishneh Torah* and to the Mishnah.

TANHUMA: Midrash attributed to R TANHUMA BAR ABBA; also known as *Yelammedenu* from the characteristic opening phrase in each sermon *yelammedenu rabbenu* ("Let our master teach us"). Every discourse has a similar structure, beginning with a halakhic question from which the preacher goes on to the main aggadic discussion. The discourses usually centered around the opening verse of the portion of the week, according to the triennial Palestine cycle. The various collections coming under the name T. or *Yelammedenu*, although compiled relatively late, utilized early sources.

TANHUMA BAR ABBA (fl. latter 4th cent.): Palestinian amora, generally called simply R Tanhuma. He developed the art of homiletics. He is considered the author of many of the Midrashim which begin with the words *yelammedenu rabbenu* including Midrash TANHUMA. His home was in Antioch, although Bacher identified him with R Tanhum of Naveh.

TANNA: (1) A teacher mentioned in the Mishnah or BARAITA living during the first two centuries CE. The Tannaitic Period begins with the death of Hillel and Shammai (the last of the ZUGOT) and ends with the generation after R Judah Ha-Nasi. Scholars enumerated five or six generations of tannaim with inevitable overlapping: those of the sixth generation are mentioned only in the *Baraita*, and for this reason are considered apart from the general category of tannaim (see AMORA). (2) Term applied throughout the Talmudic Period to the academy reader of tannaitic texts. Written texts of the oral law being interdicted, he served as the "living library" of the academy.

TANNA DE-VE ELIYAHU: Midrash also known as *Seder Eliyahu*. It consists of two parts: *Seder Rabbah* ("Major Order") and *Seder Zuta* ("Minor Order"). Scholars differ as to its date and place of origin; thus, some place it in the Talmudic Period, others consider it to have originated in 9th cent. Italy. Traces of outside influence, including the Apocrypha, can be detected.

TANSMAN, ALEXANDRE (1897–): Composer. Born in Lodz, Poland, he settled in Paris. In 1941–6, he was in the US. He has written symphonies, operas, the oratorio *Isaiah*, and chamber and piano music.

TANTURA see **DOR**

TANYA: (1) Code of laws abbreviated from Zedekiah ben Abraham ANAU's *Shibbole ha-Leket*. Prepared in Italy probably in the 14th cent., it is known after its initial word. (2) Hasidic work (real name: *Likkute Amarim*) by SHNEOUR ZALMAN OF LYADY, founder of the HABAD movement. It guides the believer to the attainment of DEVEKUT and is based mainly on Kabbalah but also draws from talmudic literature and medieval Jewish philosophy. In *Habad* circles, the *T.* is studied daily.

TARBUT (Heb. "culture"): E European Hebrew educational and cultural organization operating between the two World Wars. The Polish branch was founded in 1919 under the auspices of the Zionist Organization. Progress was spectacular in Lithuania and Poland where an advanced Hebrew educational system was established. Despite governmental opposition, considerable achievements were made in Rumania. The T. organization also promoted Hebrew culture in Britain from 1929.

TAREPH see **TEREPHAH**

TARGUM (Aram. from Assyrian *targumanu* "interpreter", cf. "dragoman"): The Aramaic translation of the Bible. The Talmud (*Megillah* 3a) concludes from Neh. 8:8 that the custom of adding an Aramaic translation to the public reading of the Bible goes back to Ezra; it was certainly well-established in the Second Temple Period. This oral T. was both a translation and an interpretation adding legal and midrashic details to the text and studiously avoiding anthropomorphism. All T.'s are written in a somewhat artificial ARAMAIC, half-way between biblical Aramaic and the spoken language of Palestine. There are three T.'s to the Pentateuch: *T. Onkelos* (according to some so called after the proselyte AQUILA) showing the most archaic type; *T. Jonathan* (erroneously so called); and *T. Yerushalmi* (or Palestinian T.), known only in a fragmentary form until 1956 when a complete ms was discovered. The T. to the Former and Latter Prophets is called after Jonathan ben Uzziel; it is mainly a paraphrase emphasizing the teachings of the text. The T.'s to the various books of the Hagiographa are midrashic in character, especially those to the Five Scrolls; they are considerably longer than the text they render and often show little connection with the literal sense. An exception is the T. to Proverbs, which is literal and couched in a language close to Syriac. The T. (especially T. Onkelos) has long enjoyed a sanctity second only to the Hebrew text. The Talmud enjoins the reading of the weekly passage "twice in Hebrew, once in T." (*Berakhot 8a*). The T. is cited as an authoritative interpretation by Rashi and other commentators, and like the Hebrew text, has a Masorah and numerous commentaries. There is also a Samaritan Aramaic T. *Targum* is the word used by the Jews of Kurdistan to denote their spoken Aramaic language.

TARGUM SHENI (Heb. "Second Targum"): An extensive Aramaic paraphrase to the Book of Esther, additional to the ordinary Targum but more midrashic. It was written between 500 and 1000 CE.

TARNOPOL: Galician town. Jews settled there shortly after its foundation in 1540. The community was well-organized and in 1648, participated in the defense of the town against the Cossacks. Joseph PERL founded a Jewish School in the spirit of Enlightenment, greatly influencing the cultural development of the T. Jews who later played important parts in the Haskalah and Zionist movements. The Jews were also active in T.'s public life. The community numbered 18,000 on the Nazi occupation in 1941. A ghetto was established and systematically liquidated by July, 1943. On liberation in May, 1944, only 139 Jews survived. Jewish pop. (1970): c. 500.

TARPHON (fl. late 1st cent. CE): Tanna. In his youth, he served with his priestly family in the Temple. He studied with R Johanan ben Zakkai and R Gamaliel I, although leaning personally to many teachings of the school of Shammai. T. took a leading part in the discussions at Jabneh. The Mishnah records halakhic differences of opinion between himself and his beloved pupil R Akiva. Occasionally harsh in manner of expression and severe in his attitude toward dissident sects, T. was personally humble and charitable.

TARSHISH: Son of Javan (Gen. 10:4). The name was applied apparently to the region of the town Tarsus in Cilicia, to the N of which were situated large forests and copper mines; possibly the "ships of T." were made there. Some scholars maintain that the "ships of T." refer to vessels traveling to the Phoenician colonies in Sardinia and Spain.

TARTAKOWER, ARYEH (1897–): Sociologist. He taught at the Institute of Jewish Sciences in Warsaw, 1923–39, and lived in the US during World War II. In 1946 he settled in Palestine. He became co-chairman of the World Jewish Congress Executive in 1946, and in 1948, chairman of its Israel section. T. has written on the Jewish labor movement, migration problems, the history of Polish Jewry, anti-semitism, and the Jewish communities of the Diaspora.

TARYAG MITZVOT see **PRECEPTS**

TASHKENT: Capital of Uzbekistan S.S.R. A number of the Jews of T. are Bukharan and they numbered 3,000 at the beginning of the 20th century. During World War II many Jews were sent there from W Russia, Poland, etc. and by 1942 there were 40,000 Jews there. Some returned after the war but after an initial decrease, the Jewish population again rose and in 1970 numbered 55,758.

TASHLIKH (Heb. "thou wilt cast"): Custom observed on the first day of the New Year (or the second when the first falls on Sabbath). Prayers are recited near a stream or body of water, preferably where there are fish, symbolizing protection against the evil eye. Originally, bread crumbs were thrown to the fish as part of the ritual. The prayers derive chiefly from Micah 7:10–20 ("Thou wilt cast their sins into the sea"). Scholars believe that the ritual originated in Germany during the 14th cent., possibly adopted from the non-Jewish environment.

TASMANIA: Island-state of Australia. In the mid-19th cent., a sizable Jewish community lived there; the Hobart synagogue, opened in 1845, is the oldest in the Southern Hemisphere. Jewish pop. (1973): c. 200, mainly in Hobart (130) and Launceston (50).

TAUBER, RICHARD (1892–1948): Musician. Austrian by birth, he became a British subject in 1940. A conductor and composer, he was mainly famed as a tenor in lieder and operettas, especially those of Lehar.

TÄUBLER, EUGEN (1879–1953): Historian. He was co-founder and director of the Central Archives of the Jews in Germany 1906–19 and was professor of history at Heidelberg until 1933, later going to the Hebrew Union College, Cincinnati. In addition to works on Roman history, T. wrote on German Jewish history.

TAUSSIG, FRANK WILLIAM (1859–1940): US economist. He was on the faculty of Harvard University from 1892–1935 and a founder of the Harvard Graduate School of Business Administration. In 1917–9, he was chairman of the US Tariff Commission. In 1896–1937, T. edited the *Quarterly Journal of Economics*

TAV (ת): Twenty-second and last letter of the Hebrew alphabet; numerical value 400. Without the dagesh (ת) its classical pronunciation was *th* as in "thin," still preserved in the Yemenite and Iraqi readings. Ashkenazim pronounce it *s* without the dagesh and *t* with it, while Sephardim and modern Israelis give it the sound of *t* in either case.

TAXATION: Not much is known about the system of tax-exaction in biblical times, except for the POLL-TAX imposed in the wilderness (Exod. 30:11–16), etc., (see also SHEKEL) though there was a regular system of t. in kind by the system of TITHES for the

Tashlikh service in Poland. (Painting by Strykowski).

maintenance of the Temple and the priesthood, and additional levies (e.g. *Peah*) to assist the poor. The t. necessitated by the building-projects in the reign of Solomon was so heavy as to precipitate the revolt of the northern tribes. The poll-tax formerly devoted to the Temple was continued by the Romans after its destruction in 70 CE as the FISCUS JUDAICUS, but there was then no other special t. incumbent on the Jews as Jews. In the Middle Ages, however, disproportionate t. was levied on the Jewish community in every city, or sometimes on the Jews in an entire country, the Jewish community as a whole answering for its collection. This resulted in a considerable degree of Jewish AUTONOMY, exemplified in institutions such as the COUNCIL OF THE FOUR LANDS. The general burden was enhanced by the fact that rulers would sometimes exempt favorite individuals from t.: on the other hand, similar exemption was traditionally extended by the Jewish communities to scholars. In Italy, in the 17th–18th cents. communal dues were exacted by a tax on capital known as *Capella*, the assessment being made by every individual under oath in the synagogues; essential ghetto services (sanitation, etc.) were defrayed from the proceeds, as well as the amounts due to the government as the price of toleration. One of the distinguishing features of the modern Jewish community, as it evolved from the 17th cent. in Europe and America, was that no special t. was imposed on Jews or on Jewish congregations as such. On the other hand, in countries such as Germany and Italy, where the Jewish communities were regulated by law, they had the right to impose t. on all members for ,the maintenance of essential communal institutions. In the Moslem countries, all unbelievers including the Jews had to pay the *Jizya* or poll-tax as well as a levy in lieu of military service.

TAZ see **DAVID BEN SAMUEL HALEVI**

TCHERIKOVER, AVIGDOR (Victor; 1894–1958):
Historian. He was born in Russia, studied in Germany, and settled in Palestine in 1925. From 1926, he taught ancient history at the Hebrew Univ. (professor, 1947). His main work was on the Jews in Palestine and Egypt in the Hellenistic and Roman Periods, including a *Corpus Papyrorum Judaicarum.*

TCHERNIAKOV, ADAM see **CHERNIAKOV**

TCHERNIKHOVSKI see **TSCHERNIKHOVSKI**

TCHERNOWITZ see **CERNAUTI**

TCHERNOWITZ, CHAIM (1871–1949): Rabbinic scholar and writer. He was crown rabbi in Odessa 1900–12 and established there a Hebrew-speaking yeshivah. He was professor of Talmud at the Jewish Institute of Religion, New York, from 1923 and founded (1939) the Hebrew monthly *Bitzaron.* Under the pseudonym *Rav Tzair* ("young rabbi"), he published many scholarly works on rabbinic literature, including an abridgment of the Talmud, and histories

The Winston Churchill auditorium of the Haifa Technion.

of the Halakhah and codifiers. His memoirs vividly illustrate the circle of Hebrew scholars and writers of Odessa. His brother *SAMUEL T.* (1879–1929) was a noted Hebrew writer.

TEACHER OF RIGHTEOUSNESS (Heb. *moreh hatzedek*): The founder and leader of the sect of the DEAD SEA SCROLLS. He was perhaps a priest, and was persecuted by the WICKED PRIEST. It is possible that he was the author of the THANKSGIVING PSALMS.

TEACHERS see **EDUCATION**

TEBA, TEVA (Heb. "chest, coffer"): see **AL-MEMAR; ARK**

TECHNION, HAIFA ("Israel Institute of Technology"): Israel technological university. It was founded in 1912 on the initiative of the *Hilfsverein der deutschen Juden* and with funds provided by Jacob Schiff of New York and the Wissotsky estate of Moscow. Even before the institution opened, it was the center of a dispute between proponents of German and Hebrew with regard to the language of instruction. After World War I, the controversy was settled in favor of Hebrew. The war delayed the beginning of classes until 1924. Successive presidents have been: Arthur Blok (1924–5), Mosheh Hecker (1925–8), Aharon Tcherniavsky (1928–9), Yoseph Breuer (1929–31), Shelomoh Kaplansky (1931–50), Yaakov Dori (1951–65), Alexander Goldberg (1965–73) and Amos Horev (from 1973). In 1954, the Institute began development of a new 300-acre campus on Mt. Carmel ("Technion City"). It possesses a highly specialized technical library. In 1974, the T. had an enrollment of 7,200 students on the university level and its graduate school, and an additional 1,650 students in its affiliated technical high school. It offers a B.Sc. degree after 4 years of study, and a professional degree of Ingenieur following a fifth year. Master's and Doctorate degrees are offered in the graduate school. Faculties and Departments comprise civil engineering. architecture, mechanical engineering, electrical engineering, chemistry, physics, mathematics, nuclear science, chemical engineering, agricultural engineering, aeronautical engineering, mining, management and industrial engineering, and food and bio-technology.

TEHERAN: Capital of Iran. Its Jews resided for centuries in their own quarter, living largely as dealers, silversmiths, and wine merchants. Frequent persecutions reduced them to a state of misery and ignorance. Toward the end of the 19th cent., there were 4,000 Jews in T.; in 1968, the community numbered 50,000. Because of a considerable influx from other places their number has not been diminished notwithstanding large-scale emigration to Israel. Some renaissance of Jewish life has taken place this century. A Society for the Propagation of the Hebrew Language was founded and published Hebrew books and periodicals. In 1930, a Jewish school teaching modern Hebrew was established.

TEHILLIM see **PSALMS**

TEITEL, JACOB (1851–1939): Russian judge and communal leader. A member of the Saratov district court, 1904–12, he was the only Jewish judge in Russia at that time. Refusing to become baptized, he was forced to resign. T. left Russia in 1921 and was chairman of the Federation of Russian Jews in Germany.

TEITELBAUM, MOSES (1769–1841): *Tzaddik*. Originally a Mitnagged, he turned to Hasidism under the influence of R Jacob Horowitz of Lublin. He settled in Ujhely, Hungary, and won fame for his piety, learning, and wonderworking. He originated the dynasties of Satmar and Sigut in Carpathian Russia.

TEIXEIRA or **TEXEIRA**: Sephardi family of Marrano origin, allied with that of De Mattos. *ABRAHAM SENIOR T.*, formerly Diego Texeira de Sampayo (c. 1578–1666), after serving in the Low Countries as paymaster-general for the Spanish government, embraced Judaism in 1647 in Hamburg where he enthusiastically supported Jewish causes and became agent for Queen Christina of Sweden. His son *ISAAC ḤAYYIM (MANOEL) SENIOR T.* (1625–1705), who had accompanied his father into Judaism, succeeded him in this office. Later, he became head of the Portuguese community in Amsterdam. He unsuccessfully interceded in behalf of the Jews of Austria when they were threatened with expulsion in 1670. *PEDRO T.* (c. 1570–1650). Portuguese Marrano explorer, circumnavigated the world and described his experiences in a famous book of travel (1610), which is one of the most important sources for conditions in the Orient in his day. He is believed to have reverted to Judaism in his last years.

TEKOA: (1) Town S of Bethlehem, after which the neighboring Desert of T. was called. AMOS was born there. The place was also known in the Crusading Period. (2) Town in Upper Galilee, noted in Second Temple times for its olives and oils.

TEL (TELL) (Heb. and Arab.): In the Middle East, a mound, especially one formed by the accumulation of successive layers of settlement (see ARCHEOLOGY). It is a frequent component of Middle Eastern place-names.

TEL AVIV: Israel city. It was founded in 1909 as a garden suburb of JAFFA and named after the title of the Hebrew translation of Herzl's novel *Altneuland* (cf. Ezek. 3:15). This quarter, containing about half-a-dozen streets, was selected as the site of the Herzliyyah secondary school and this contributed to its development. In World War I, the inhabitants of T. A. were exiled by order of the Turks. The city developed rapidly under the British Mandate, especially as Arab riots forced most Jews to abandon Jaffa. In 1921 T. A. became a separate town. As a result of the 1936 Arab riots, a harbor was inaugurated (closed 1965). In 1947–8, fighting broke out between T. A. and Arab Jaffa which ended with the capitulation of Jaffa on the eve of the establishment of the state of Israel. The state itself was proclaimed on May 14, 1948 at T. A. which remained the seat of the government and the Knesset until 1949. In the meantime, Jaffa had been abandoned by most of its Arab inhabitants and resettled with new immigrants; the two cities were amalgamated in 1949 under the name T. A.–Jaffa. The population (1974) was 357,600. It houses the principal theaters of the country; all the Hebrew daily newspapers have their homes there as do most of the publishing-houses. Its industries are mostly small as compared with those in Haifa, but their number and the number of workers employed exceeds that of the

Illuminated *ketubbah* of the Teixeira-De Mattos family. (Hamburg. 1690).

View of Tel Aviv from the air.

In a Tel Aviv art gallery.

The University of Tel Aviv.

other cities of Israel. T. A. is connected by road and rail with Jerusalem. Haifa, and Beersheba; it is planned as the central railway junction of the country. The city, which initially was inadequately planned and therefore suffers from traffic congestion and crowding, has expanded rapidly northward and straddles the YARKON river. Principal buildings include the Shalom skyscraper, the Habimah theater, and the Mann concert hall. The sea front has been developed as a major tourist area.

TEL AVIV UNIVERSITY: University in Tel Aviv.

In 1974 it had an enrollment of 11,100, an academic staff of 1,900. It has faculties in the social sciences, natural sciences, and humanities as well as a medical school. Its presidents have been George S. Wise, Yuval Neeman, and Haim Ben-Shahar.

TEL EL AMARNA see **AMARNA**

TEL ḤAI see **KEPHAR GILADI**

TEL MOND: Israel village in the S Sharon plain.

founded in 1929 and named for Sir Alfred Mond. Laborers' villages with auxiliary farms erected in the neighborhood during succeeding years developed into full-fledged smallholders' settlements forming a well-organized regional bloc ("the T. M. bloc"). Pop. (1972): 3,011.

TEL YOSEPH: Israel communal settlement (IK) in the E Jezreel Valley. It was founded in 1921 by immigrants from E Europe belonging to the GEDUD HA-AVODAH. The group suffered a political split in 1926–27, part of its members leaving for other places. Pop. (1972): 534.

TELLER, EDWARD: (1908–): Physicist. He went from his native Budapest in 1934 via England to the US where he became professor at the universities of Washington, Chicago, and California. T. served on the advisory board of the American Atomic

Energy Commission and worked on the development of the hydrogen bomb.

TELS: Lithuanian townlet. It was noted for its yeshivah which flourished from its foundation in 1881 until World War II. After the war, its surviving teachers founded a yeshivah at Cleveland.

TEMESVAR see **TIMISOARA**

TEMIN, HOWARD MARTIN (1925–): US medical researcher; teacher at the University of Wisconsin, Madison. He was awarded a 1975 Nobel Prize for work on genetics.

TEMPLE: The central edifice for Divine worship in Israel until 70 CE; situated on Mt. Moriah in Jerusalem. The First T., built by Solomon, was a shrine for the Ark, the sacred vessels, and offerings, with a court for worshipers. It consisted essentially of a hall, shrine, and inner sanctum ("holy of holies"); exact contemporary parallels do not exist among oriental shrines, although tripartite Canaanite temples have been discovered at Lachish, Bet-Shean, etc. A close replica is the t. found in Syria near a royal palace (9th–8th cents. BCE). Solomon's T. measured $113\frac{3}{4} \times 32\frac{1}{2}$ ft. (the hall $16\frac{1}{4} \times 32\frac{1}{2}$ ft., the shrine $65 \times 32\frac{1}{2}$, and the holy of holies $32\frac{1}{2} \times 32\frac{1}{2}$) and was oriented E-W. It was surrounded outside by an abutting 3-storey structure divided into cells and rooms used to store vessels and treasure. The main worship was performed in the shrine which was entered from the hall (*hekhal*) through two internal cedar doors. The holy of holies (*devir*), containing the ARK, had a raised floor and was windowless. A small cedar altar overlaid with gold stood at the entrance to the holy of holies, but the main bronze altar (15 ft. high) was in the court before the hall and surrounded by a ditch. In the SE of the court stood the Brazen Sea, a huge cauldron resting on the figures

The Temple according to the vision of Ezekiel.
(Reconstruction by Charles Chiplez).

of bulls. Also in the court stood bronze bases for the lavers. The two columns BOAZ and JACHIN stood at the entrance to the hall. The T. was constructed of hewn stone and cedarwood, i.e., masonry laced with beams, the internal coffering being of cedar. It served for the offering of SACRIFICES but was also a center of popular worship to which the masses came to sacrifice, atone, and confer, especially on holidays (notably the three PILGRIMAGE FESTIVALS when attendance at the T. was obligatory on all males). Its income was derived from grants by royalty and aristocracy, individual contributions, war-booty, and the half-SHEKEL contributed by every adult Jew which from the time of Joash was devoted to the repair of the T. Service in the T. was performed by the PRIESTS, LEVITES, and certain NETHINIM. The division of the kingdom and the struggle against the HIGH PLACES strengthened rather than weakened the T. as the central shrine of Judah. On several occasions the vessels and equipment were despoiled by conquerors or surrendered as tribute, but the position of the T. was consolidated, particularly by Hezekiah. It was, however, completely destroyed by Nebuchadnezzar in 586 BCE. The T. was rebuilt 538–515 (the "Second T.") and major reconstructions were carried out in the periods of Simon the Just, Judah the Maccabee,

Simon the Hasmonean, and Herod but detailed information is available only for the last (which included the WESTERN WALL). The Herodian wall surrounding the T. hill measured $913 \times 1,515 \times 1,586 \times 1,050$ ft. and the extensive area enclosed was partly obtained by leveling and filling between the Tyropoeion and Kidron valleys. The T. was entered by a number of gates and approached by 4 bridges (2 in the E, 2 in the W). The court was surrounded by internal porticoes which were connected on the NW with the tower of ANTONIA, the largest of these (the "Royal Portico") forming a basilica where money-changers and merchants had their business. The Women's Court in the E communicated via the Nicanor Gate with the Court of the Israelites, in effect part of the Court of the Priests and the scene of mass-assembly on the festivals. The Court of the Priests, which surrounded the T. proper, was entered by the laity only for purposes of sacrifice: it contained the main altar and was surrounded by chambers used for various purposes connected with sacrifices, ablutions, etc. Also adjoining were the Chamber of Hewn Stone, where the Sanhedrin sat, and the priests' quarters. The T. itself was divided into the hall, the shrine (containing the incense-altar, shewbread table and candelabrum); and the holy of holies (which was empty and entered only by the HIGH PRIEST on the Day of Atonement). The building was constructed of white stone, profusely adorned with gold, and a roof of cedarwood. The priests serving in the T. were divided into 24 watches; the levites into assistants of the priests, musicians and doorkeepers; menial tasks were performed by the Nethinim. Laymen were associated in the regular cult through the organization of 24 MAAMADOT, each accompanying a corresponding watch of priests to participate in the public sacrifices and the bringing of the first fruits. The high priest was responsible for the service on the Day of Atonement and on other occasions of his choice. His deputy supervised the cult and under him served the financial officers of the T. Income was derived from the half-shekel, donations by Jews, converts and foreign rulers, and deposits from the rich, etc. In the siege of Jerusalem during the Roman war, the T. served as a center of military activity, and was destroyed by the conquering Romans in 70 CE. A Roman t. was later built on the site, and since the Moslem Period a mosque has stood there (Mosque of OMAR). The area around the western and southern walls of the (Herodian) Temple compound has been extensively excavated by B. MAZAR since 1968 with many discoveries from the time of both Temples.

TEMPLE see **SYNAGOGUE**

TEMPLE OF ONIAS see **ONIAS**

TEMPLE SCROLL: One of the DEAD SEA SCROLLS. It contains lengthy quotations from the Bible but rewritten so that God speaks throughout in the first person singular. Much of this scroll is devoted to a description of Jerusalem and the Temple. It came to light in 1967.

TEMPLO, JUDAH see **LEON TEMPLO**

TEMURAH (Heb. "Exchange"): (1) Term denoting an animal which is *hullin* (not holy) placed as an exchange for one which is *kodesh* (holy, i.e., having already been set aside for sacrifice). The law in such cases is that both animals become holy. (2) Sixth tractate in the Mishnah order of *Kodashim*, containing 7 chapters. It has *gemara* in the Babylonian, but not the Palestinian, Talmud. It deals with the regulations concerning the exchange of an animal consecrated for sacrifice (Lev. 27:10, 33).

TEN COMMANDMENTS see **COMMANDMENTS, TEN**

TEN DAYS OF PENITENCE see **PENITENCE, TEN DAYS OF**

TEN MARTYRS, THE (Heb. *asarah haruge malkhut*): Ten rabbis executed, according to talmudic tradition, by the Roman government after the Bar Kokhba revolt for defying the prohibition of Jewish observances and Jewish religious teaching. The names figure differently in various compilations and are not all contemporary, martyrs of various periods having apparently been brought together in folk-memory;

the list normally includes: Akiva ben Joseph, Ishmael ben Elisha, Eleazar ben Dama, Hanina ben Teradyon, Judah ben Bava, Hutzpit the interpreter, Yeshevav the Scribe, Eleazar ben Shammua, Hanina ben Hakhinai, Simeon ben Gamaliel, and Ishmael the high priest. A late Midrash and several dirges, for recital on *Av 9*, are devoted to the T. M.

TEN PLAGUES see **PLAGUES**

TEN TRIBES see **TRIBES, LOST TEN**

TENANCY: Talmudic law distinguishes between agricultural t. and urban t. In the former case, two types of tenant are specified, the *aris* and *hokher*. The *aris* gives the landlord a percentage of the produce, while the *hokher* pays a fixed amount, which may be either in money or produce. Local custom is the prime deciding factor in determining the law regulating landlord and tenant relationship in agricultural t. Urban t. is treated separately in the Mishnah, where the tenant is called *sokher* ("hirer"). Where a lease is made, the property belongs to the tenant during the period of the lease. Acceptance of advance payment has the binding character of a lease. In the absence of specific terms of time, it is presumed that rental is for the winter season or for the shorter summer period. In a large town, however, as well as in the case of shops, 12 months' notice to vacate is required.

TENNESSEE: US state. Except for a few individuals who reportedly settled near the Holston River in 1778, there are no traces of Jewish settlement in T. during the 18th cent. The first congregations, composed of Austrian, Bohemian, and German immigrants, were organized in MEMPHIS and NASHVILLE, where there were Jews before 1845. In the 1850's, Jews settled in CHATTANOOGA. A Jewish community came into being in KNOXVILLE toward the end of the Civil War. In Dec. 1862, General Grant issued an order expelling all Jews from the military department of T. This was immediately rescinded by Lincoln. After the Civil War, many Jews from the NE and S went to T. In the 1880's, large numbers of E European immigrants arrived. In addition to the four leading communities, there are congregations in Jackson, Johnson City, and Oak Ridge. Jewish pop. (1973): 17,360.

TENUAT HA-MOSHAVIM (Heb. "the moshav movement"): Movement of Israel workers' cooperative smallholders' settlements (MOSHAVE OVEDIM) comprising (1976) 242 villages and 230,000 acres of land with a population of over 90,000.

TENUVAH see **COOPERATIVES (ISRAEL)**

TEPHILLAH (Heb.): A prayer. Among Sephardim, a prayer-book.

TEPHILLAT HA-DEREKH (Heb. "prayer for the journey"): Prayer recited before embarking on a journey. The full version is to be found in the Talmud (*Berakhot* 29b): "May it be Thy will... that Thou leadest me in peace and settest my steps. . . . Blessed art Thou Who hearest prayer." Under kabbalistic influence, a number of additional verses were added.

TEPHILLIN (Aram. "attachment"; popularly connected with Heb. *tephillah* = prayer): Phylacteries, i.e., two black leather boxes fastened to leather straps, containing four portions of the Pentateuch written on parchment (Exod. 13:1–16; Deut. 6:4–9; 11:13–21). They are bound ("laid") on the arm and the head (cf. Deut. 6:8). An ancient dispute as to the arrangement of the pentateuchal portions (illustrated by variant examples found in the Kumran and Merubaat caves) was renewed in the 12th cent. between Rashi and his grandson, R Tam. The views of Rashi were accepted, but some Orthodox Jews put on two sets of *t.* corresponding to the two traditions. *T.* are laid by adult male Jews on weekdays but not on Sabbaths and festivals (customs differ as to the intermediate days of festivals). Originally worn all day, they are now donned only during the morning prayer (on *Av* 9, during the afternoon prayer).

TEPHILLIN: A minor pseudo-talmudic tractate not in the ordinary editions of the Talmud. It discusses in a single chapter laws pertaining to the wearing of *t.* as well as to their preparation. Most of this material is found in the Talmud proper.

TERAH: Father of Abraham. He left Ur of the Chaldees to travel to the land of Canaan with his son and nephew Lot but on the way they settled in Haran where T. died. The aggadah depicts T. as a devout idolator challenged in his beliefs by Abraham.

TERAPHIM: Images of domestic deities used principally for divination. Scholars believe that possession of them indicated rights to general property-ownership, hence they were stolen by Rachel from her father's house (Gen. 31:19). Although denounced by the Israelite religion, their use persisted into the period of the monarchy.

TERE ASAR (Aram. "twelve"): Traditional name for the twelve MINOR PROPHETS.

TEREPHAH (Heb. from *taraph*, "tear" — Exod. 22:30): Food that is not KASHER. The Sephardi form is *Tareph*.

TERRITORIALISM see **JEWISH TERRITORIAL ORGANIZATION**

TERRY (NEILSON), JULIA (1868–1957): British actress. She first appeared in 1888 and thereafter starred in many successful productions in England and the US.

TERTIS, LIONEL (1876–1975): British violist. His brilliant playing was responsible for the re-emergence and recognition of the viola as a solo instrument.

TERUMOT (Heb. "Heave-Offerings"): Sixth tractate in the Mishnah order of *Zeraim*, containing 11 chapters. It has *gemara* in the Palestinian, but not Babylonian, Talmud. It deals with the heave-offerings

Donning the Tephillin. (Painting by Edward Moise).

due to the priest from both the Israelite (Num. 18:8; Deut. 18:4) and the levite (Num. 18:25 ff.).

TESTAMENTS OF THE TWELVE PATRIARCHS: Pseudepigraphic work of the Second Temple Period, purporting to give the testaments of the sons of Jacob to their descendants. Its tone is moral, while containing an injunction to heed the anointed who shall come forth from Judah and Levi at the end of days. The book originated in the sect which wrote the First Book of Enoch and the Book of Jubilees, and it is cited in the Dead Sea Scrolls, notably in the Damascus Document. It has been preserved in Greek but an extended Testament of Levi in Aramaic was discovered in the Cairo *genizah* and a Testament of Naphtali in Hebrew at Kumran. The date of composition is generally put at the 1st cent. BCE.

TET (ט): Ninth letter in the Hebrew alphabet; numerical value 9. It has a plosive velarized *t* sound.

TETRAGRAMMATON (Gk. "four-lettered"): Term generally used to designate the Divine Name (יהוה) (YHVH) traditionally not pronounced by Jews and formerly misread Jehovah by Christians. See also GOD, NAMES OF.

TETRARCH (Gk): Literally: Ruler of a fourth part. Term applied in the Roman Period to the ruler of a sub-division of a country, e.g. PHILIP, son of Herod.

TETUAN: Moroccan city. Jews arrived after the expulsion from Spain and a local Purim was introduced in 1578 to commemorate the military disaster to the Portuguese invaders. In 1729, the community was the largest in Morocco, with 5,000 Jewish inhabitants and 7 synagogues. The Jews were persecuted in the late 18th cent., while anti-Jewish riots broke out during the Moroccan-Spanish war of 1860. The community dwindled during the late 19th–20th cents. In 1968, there were c. 1,000 Jews.

TEVET: Fourth month of the Hebrew civil year and tenth of the ecclesiastical. It has 29 days and falls in Dec.-Jan. The most notable date in the month is the 10th ("fast of *T.*") commemorating the besieging of Jerusalem by Nebuchadnezzar (II Kings 25:1).

TEVUL YOM (Heb. "One Who Has Bathed That Day"): Tenth tractate (eleventh in some codices) in the Mishnah order of *Tohorot*, containing 4 chapters. It has *gemara* in neither the Babylonian nor Palestinian Talmud. It deals with the minor degree of ritual uncleanness which remains until sunset after ritual bathing (Lev. 15:7–18).

TEXAS: US state. Its first known Jewish settler was Samuel Isaacs who went to Austin in 1821. In the next decade, Jews established themselves in Velasco and Nacogdoches where they engaged in commerce and the professions and served in the government. They played a part in the various struggles for Texan independence. In 1836, Jews settled in GALVESTON. Henry CASTRO brought Jews from France and Germany to T. in 1842. Public religious services were held in T. for the first time in HOUSTON in 1854. 103 Jews from the state served during the Civil War, being represented in both armies. Between the 1850's and 1870's more Jews from Germany settled there. From the 1880's to 1914 many arrived from E Europe, partly as a result of the GALVESTON SCHEME for diverting immigrants from the New York area. Jews have served prominently in both houses of the T. legislature. In 1973, the following cities and towns had Jewish populations of 1,000 or more: DALLAS (20,000), Houston (22,000), SAN ANTONIO (6,500), EL PASO (4,500), FORT WORTH (2,850), Austin (1,900) and Corpus Christi (1,030). Jewish pop. (1973): 66,510.

TEXTUAL CRITICISM see BIBLE CRITICISM

THANKSGIVING OFFERING (Heb. *todah*): Sacrifice brought by an individual as a token of thanks to God. Such sacrifice was brought, for instance, after traveling the seas or the desert, after recovery from illness, and after release from prison.

THANKSGIVING PSALMS (Heb. *Hodayot*): One of the DEAD SEA SCROLLS containing a number of prayers many of which open with the words "I thank Thee, O Lord."

THEATER, JEWS IN THE: Jewish playwrights, and perhaps actors, were known in Alexandria in the 2nd cent. BCE. During the Roman period, the Jewish sages denounced the theater as a source of immorality, but Jewish actors (e.g. Aliturus) were not unknown even then. From the Medieval Period, Purim farces were performed in Central and W Europe; while from the 16th cent. Marrano poets wrote plays in Spanish and Portuguese. In 16th çent. Italy, the Jews — especially of Mantua — began to take an active part in the theater, and the playwright Leone de Sommi wrote one of the earliest treatises on stagecraft. In Venice an attempt was made in the early 17th cent. to establish a permanent ghetto theater. Leone Modena was also a playwright, and the convert Lorenzo da Ponte wrote librettos for Mozart. From the 18th cent., there were outstanding Jewish actors in many W European countries, including in 19th cent. France "Rachel" and Sarah Bernhardt. Sir Arthur Wing Pinero, who was of Jewish descent, played a prominent role in shaping British drama and stagecraft. German Jewry produced many famous critics and dramatists, including Arthur Schnitzler, Richard Beer-Hofmann, Hugo von Hoffmannsthal, Ernst Toller, Franz Werfel, Karl Wolfskehl, and Arnold and Stefan Zweig. Otto Braham and Max Reinhardt achieved eminence as producers and directors. Jews also played some part in the theater in France (e.g. Henri Bernstein, Georges de Porto-Riche), Holland (e.g. Heijermans), the Scandinavian countries (e.g. Brandes), Italy (Sabbatino Lopes), and Russia. Yiddish players presented dramatizations based on the life of Joseph at the beginning of the 18th cent. By 1830, Cracow had a Yiddish theater giving nightly performances to large audiences. In the middle of the 19th cent., a professional troupe was headed by Abraham Goldfaden. From E Europe, Yiddish companies followed the waves of Jewish immigration to the US which soon became the major center of the Yiddish theater. Jacob P. Adler, Sigmund Mogulescu, Boris Thomashefsky, and Jacob Gordin became by-words of Jewish cultural life there. In 1921, Maurice Schwartz organized the Yiddish Art Theater which marked the supreme achievement of the Yiddish drama in the US, presenting a wide variety of original and translated plays, while Yiddish musicals also flourished. In Europe, the Vilna Troupe set the tone for a number of companies functioning until World War II which marked the end of the ten state Yiddish companies in the USSR. Beginning with David Belasco, Jews figure prominently in the dramatic arts in the US from the legitimate theater, through MOTION PICTURES, radio and television. Eminent playwrights include Elmer Rice, George S. Kaufman, Moss Hart, Lilian Hellman, Sidney Kingsley, S. N. Behrman, Clifford Odets, Arthur Miller and Neil Simon. In England a number of Jewish playwrights came to the fore in the 1950's including Arnold Wesker, Harold Pinter, and Lionel Bart. The last wrote musicals, a genre in which a number of Jews have excelled. The removal of the HA-BIMAH Company to Palestine in 1927 marked a turning-point in that company's theatrical life. The OHEL company made its appearance in 1925 to be followed by the satirical company *Matateh*, the CHAMBER THEATER, the Haifa Municipal Theater, etc.

THEFT: In Jewish law, a thief is one who takes another's property secretly (as opposed to ROB-BERY). T. is considered a crime, whoever the victim may be, even t. as a joke being forbidden. If there are witnesses to the t., the thief pays double its value — fourfold in the case of a sheep or fivefold for an ox afterward sold or slaughtered. Spontaneous confession by the thief before the witnesses testify exempts him from this fine. The value of the t. and the fine are civil debts recoverable from the present or future property of the thief. An exception is a male thief who cannot pay the balance, provided that this balance, excluding the fine, is at least equal to his market value; in Bible times, he was sold into slavery for six years. It is forbidden to buy stolen property, and it is also forbidden to buy from an employee property he might have stolen from his employer. An innocent purchaser receives the benefit of market overt and can recover from the owner the amount he paid before giving up his purchase.

THEOCRACY: Form of government based upon acknowledgment of God as ruler of the state and his commandments as the law of the land. Priests or prophets are usually recognized as serving as agents of the Divine rule. Josephus was apparently the first to use the term in his description of the Jewish people under Moses. The Bible posits this form of government when it speaks of "a kingdom of priests and a Holy people" (Exod. 19:6). Samuel's reluctance to establish a monarchy was partly motivated by the desire to safeguard theocratic rule. The Jewish king was always considered to rule by God's appointment, and is bound therefore to heed the voice of the prophet speaking in the name of God. The Persian and hellenistic kings formally recognized the high priest as the supreme Jewish authority in Judea and the Torah as the country's legal code, a position maintained by the Maccabees and *de facto* ended by Herod.

THEODORA: Bulgarian czarina, reigned 1335–1355. She belonged to a Byzantine Jewish family and her original name was Sarah. After baptism, she married the Czar Ivan Alexander. Her son, Czar Ivan Shishman III of Bulgaria, permitted Jews from Hungary to settle in Nicopolis, Plevna, and Murad.

THEODOTION (fl. 2nd cent.): Translator of the Bible into Greek. His exact date is unknown but he lived after Aquila. According to Christian tradition, he was a proselyte originating from Ephesus or perhaps Pontus. His translation draws from the Septuagint and is less slavishly literal than Aquila's version.

THEOLOGY see **GOD; JUDAISM,** etc.

THERAPEUTAE (Gk. "healers"): Jewish religious sect in Egypt in the 1st cent. CE, known only from a description given by Philo. Its members, male and female, lived in solitude and poverty. Celibacy was regarded as desirable but not essential. They spent their time in meditation on the sacred writings and ate only at sunrise. Every fifth day, they gathered in white garments for a common meal and spent the night in religious singing and dancing. Unlike the Essenes, the members did not engage in handicrafts but concentrated entirely on study.

THERESIENSTADT (Terezin): Bohemian garrison town transformed into a ghetto by the Nazis in Nov. 1941. The non-Jews were evacuated in July, 1942, and the Jews herded there maintained a semblance of autonomous Jewish life with a nominated Council of Elders, a bank, special currency, etc. The Nazis considered it a "model" ghetto, to which were sent prominent personalities and other "privileged" Jews. Altogether, 139,654 Jews were sent to T., of whom 86,934 were deported to extermination camps in E Europe. On liberation there were 17,320 survivors. See CONCENTRATION CAMPS.

THESSALONIKI see **SALONICA**

THEUDAS (d. 44 CE): False messiah. Promising to part the waters of the Jordan, he gathered a multitude who were attacked and almost annihilated on the orders of the procurator Cuspius Fadus. T. was beheaded.

THIRTEEN ATTRIBUTES (Heb. *middot*) **OF MERCY:** The Divine ATTRIBUTES of mercy enumerated in Exod. 34:6–7 "The Lord, the Lord, God, merciful and gracious long-suffering and abundant in goodness and truth; keeping mercy unto the thousandth generation, forgiving iniquity and transgression and sin. . ." etc. The number 13 is a rabbinic tradition (though there exist other traditions, particularly among the Karaites, listing 9, 10, or 11 attributes). The exact numeration is controversial. Commentators agree with Maimonides that they are not qualities inherent in GOD but attributes of action. The T. A. are of great importance in the liturgy, particularly in the penitential prayers recited on fasts, in the *selihot* days before and after the New Year, and in the service of the Day of Atonement, when they are repeatedly recited.

THIRTEEN PRINCIPLES OF FAITH: Formulation by Maimonides, in his Mishnah commentary to *Sanhedrin*, of the primary DOGMAS of the Jewish creed. These are: 1. God exists; 2. His unity is absolute; 3. He is without material form; 4. He is eternal; 5. Only He may be worshiped; 6. He has revealed His Law through the prophets; 7. Moses is the chief of His prophets; 8. His Law was given at Mt. Sinai; 9. The Torah is immutable; 10. God has foreknowledge of men's actions; 11. God will reward the just

Café on the shores of the Sea of Galilee at Tiberias.

and punish the wicked; 12. He will send the Messiah; and 13. He will resurrect the dead. The formulation immediately became popular and found its way into the prayer book both in full and in poetic form (see YIGDAL).

THOMASHEFSKY, BORIS (1866–1939): Yiddish actor. Of Ukrainian birth, he went to the US in 1881. He produced, wrote, adapted, and acted in many successful plays performed at New York's Yiddish theaters.

THON: (1) *OSIAS T.* (1870–1936): Zionist. He was rabbi in Galicia and a dominant figure in Polish Zionism. In 1919, he was vice-president of the *Comité des délégations juives* at the Paris Peace Conference. T. sat. in the *Seym*, 1919–35, and for several years, headed its Jewish members' organization. His books include a biography of Herzl and essays on Zionist ideology. (2) *YAAKOV T.* (1880–1950): Zionist; brother of (1). Of Galician birth, he studied in Germany and worked under Ruppin in the Bureau for Jewish Statistics in Berlin, the Palestine Office in Jaffa, and the Palestine Land Development Company, which he later directed.

THRONE OF GOD: The Divine seat; in a secondary sense, the representative symbol of Divine majesty and glory. Visions of the T. are reported in various biblical books (I Kings 22:19; Is. 6:1; Ezek. 1; 10). Ezekiel's vision in particular was of major significance in "throne mysticism" (see MAASEH MERKAVAH) which flourished from tannaitic to gaonic times. It cultivated ecstatic states in which the soul of the mystic left the body and ascended in a perilous journey to heaven, there to behold the overwhelming vision of the Throne of Glory. The influence of the *merkavah* mystics is discernible in the *kedushah* prayer and in some of the hymns of the Ashkenazi New Year service.

TIBBON see **IBN TIBBON**

TIBERIAS: Israel town on the W shore of the Sea of Galilee. It was founded probably in 18 CE by Herod Antipas and named in honor of the emperor Tiberius. T. soon became the principal Jewish city on the lake. Its inhabitants took part in the war with Rome but without enthusiasm, surrendering to Vespasian at the first opportunity. The seat of the patriarchate was transferred to T. in the 3rd cent., and the town was a center of talmudic scholarship and capital of Jewish Palestine until the transfer of the academy to Jerusalem in the 7th cent., being known at this period as Maaziah. It was a main center of the activity of the MASORETES. In 1099, it was taken by the Crusaders and after the 13th cent., remained a fishing village until rebuilt in the 18th cent. by the emir Dahir el-Omar, N of the Roman site; a previous attempt of Joseph Nasi to re-establish it as a Jewish center had failed. As a result of the earthquake of 1837, part of the population of Safed moved to T. which thereafter had a Jewish majority. The development of Jewish colonies around the Sea of Galilee and of the hot springs S of the city has enhanced its importance. Pop. (1974): 25,200.

*TIBERIUS: Roman emperor, reigned 14–37 CE. In 19, he expelled the Jews from Rome on account of a fraud perpetrated on a Roman matron sympathetic to Judaism; 4,000 young Jews were sent to Sardinia to fight the brigands. Palestine was harshly administered under his rule, during which the crucifixion of Jesus occurred.

TIFLISI, ABU IMRAN A- (or Musa az-Zafarani; fl. 9th cent.): Founder of a dissident Karaite sect. He was born near Baghdad and was influenced by his teacher the Karaite scholar Ishmael al-Ukbari, although T. inclined to the view of certain Moslem sects which denied the resurrection of the dead and demanded reward and punishment in this world. His

Copper extraction works at Timna.

followers, known as Abu-Imranists or Tiflisists, persisted until the end of the 12th cent.

*TIGLATH-PILESER III: King of Assyria 745–726 BCE. He reformed Assyrian administration and introduced the policy of exiling hostile inhabitants of conquered countries. In 743, he invaded N Syria and levied tribute on Menahem of Israel. In 734, T. P. invaded Philistia, conquered Damascus (733), and seized a large part of the kingdom of Israel, banishing the population of Galilee to Transjordania. He then exacted tribute from Ahaz of Judah (who had appealed to him for aid against Israel and Aram) and from Ammon, Moab, and Edom. Later he gained control of Babylon where he ruled under the name of Pul.

TIGRIS (Heb. *Ḥiddekel*): River in SW Asia. It was regarded as one of the four rivers emerging from the Garden of Eden (Gen. 2:14). On its banks stood the town of Maḥoza, one of the major Jewish Babylonian settlements in the Talmudic Period.

TIK (properly *tek*; rabbinic Hebrew from Gk. *theke* = "casing"): The wooden or metal case in which the Scroll of the Law is generally enclosed in oriental communities.

TIKKUN see **KABBALAH**

TIKKUN (Heb.): A selection of biblical, mishnaic, and kabbalistic passages instituted by the Kabbalists for reading on certain occasions. The *tikkun ḥatzot* (Heb. "midnight service") consists of selections from Psalms (137, 79, 42, 43, 111, 51, 126), lamentations, and petitions read at midnight in mourning for the destruction of the Temple. The

practice is kabbalistic and first spread in circles close to Isaac Luria. It was particularly prevalent among the Sephardim and in Italy. The *tikkun lel shavuot* is a selection of biblical, mishnaic, and kabbalistic passages read on the night of the Festival of Pentecost, preceding the day which celebrates the giving of the Torah. The custom of spending this entire night in study is mentioned in the Zohar (*Emor 89a*), although the first known actual practice was by the Safed kabbalists of the 16th cent. This consists of excerpts from the beginning and end of every book in the Bible and Mishnah, certain biblical passages (e.g. the Ten Commandments recited in full), the *Sepher Yetzirah*, and the 613 commandments as enumerated by Maimonides. The *tikkun hoshana rabbah* incorporates readings from Deuteronomy, Psalms, the Zohar, as well as special kabbalistic prayers, recited on the night of *Hoshana Rabbah*. Already in the 13th cent. Abudarham refers to the custom of reading the Pentateuch on this night. A similar *t.* was observed in some communities on the night of *Adar* 7, the legendary anniversary of the birth and death of Moses, and on *Av* 5, the anniversary of the death of Isaac Luria.

TIKKUN SOPHERIM (Heb. "scribal emendation"): Term applied to 18 emendations of the Bible, mostly of pronominal suffixes, attributed to the SCRIBES. Their object was to prevent expressions which appeared to represent the Deity irreverently. The name *T. S.* (or *tikkun*) is also applied to an unpointed copy of the printed Pentateuch used for practice in reading the Scroll of the Law.

TIKTIN: Rabbinical family in Breslau. *SOLOMON T.* (1791–1843) was a leader of German Orthodoxy and engaged in a bitter feud with Abraham GEIGER. His son, *GEDALIAH T.* (1810–1886), succeeded him as chief rabbi of Breslau and continued the feud with Geiger until the latter left Breslau in 1863.

TIME, DIVISION OF: No word for "hour" occurs in the Bible, but this may be accidental. The Mishnah counts in hours of 24 to the day, but of unequal length, as the daytime was divided, as was usual in antiquity, into 12 hours whatever the duration of the day. Since the exact division of time is most important for calculating the CALENDAR, the times of the beginning and end of the Sabbath and festivals, and the times during which the three daily prayers may be said, more refined methods were evolved in talmudic times. The hour (now of fixed length) was divided into 1080 parts (each roughly equalling 3 seconds) and each part into 76 moments.

TIMISOARA: Rumanian city. Many Spanish Jews settled there from the mid-16th cent. until 1716 when the Turks lost T. to Hungary and the position of the Jews suddenly deteriorated. They were subjected to numerous restrictions which were not lifted until the late 18th cent. Jews were not permitted to settle freely in T. until 1840. Rumanian deportations in 1942 depleted the community which was reconstituted after the war. 8,000 Jews lived there in 1959 but only 3,000 remained in 1971.

TIMNA: Name of a *Wadi* descending to the Arabah N of Elath. One of Solomon's copper mines was known by this name and from 1958 to 1976 copper-mining was resumed there.

*****TINEIUS RUFUS, QUINTUS** (fl. 130 CE): Roman governor of Judea and commander of the Tenth Legion from 130. Taken by surprise by the Bar Kokhba revolt (132) he had to evacuate Jerusalem and appeal to the legate of Syria for aid. Non-Jewish sources attribute to him ruthless repression and the replowing of the Temple site; he probably retained command of his legion throughout the war although replaced as governor by Julius Severus.

TIOMKIN, VLADIMIR (1860–1927): Russian Zionist leader. T. was one of Herzl's early supporters and participated in the First Zionist Congress. In 1917, he was regarded as the leader of Ukrainian Jewry. As a result of Bolshevik rule he left Russia and moved to Paris where he devoted much time to assisting Jewish refugees. In his last years he supported the Revisionist movement.

TIRADO, JACOB (c. 1560–1625): Founder of the Amsterdam Jewish community. Born in Portugal as a Marrano under the name Jacomo Lopes da Costa, he settled in Amsterdam c. 1596 and is said to have acted as spokesman for the Jews in Latin when they were arrested on suspicion during a Day of Atonement service. He subsequently migrated to Jerusalem.

TIRAN see **YOTBAH**

TIRAT HA-CARMEL: Israel suburban settlement W of Haifa. Formerly the large Arab village Tira, it was conquered by Israel forces in 1948, and abandoned by its inhabitants. It was settled by new immigrants and, from 1949, large immigrant camps and *maabarot* were erected there. Most of the inhabitants work in the Haifa area. Pop. (1974): 15,500.

TIRZAH: Capital of Samaria, before the time of Omri (I Kings 15:21, etc.). It was Menahem's base of operations in his successful rising against Shallum.

TISH (Yidd. "table"): The meal taken by the *tzaddik* with his Ḥasidim. It is held thrice on Sabbaths, holidays, and the death anniversaries of *tzaddikim*. The Ḥasidim look upon the *t.* as an altar atoning for sins. The *tzaddik* gives a discourse and sings hymns with his followers. He also distributes SHIRAYIM, and on the Sabbath the proceedings are concluded by his dancing with his followers.

TISHA B'AV see **AV, NINTH OF**

TISHBI see **ELIJAH**

TISHRI: First month of the Jewish civil, and seventh of the religious, year. In biblical times there is reference to the feast of Ethanim, i.e. the seventh month (I Kings 8:2). Because of the many holidays in T. it is known as "the month of holidays." There are: *Rosh ha-Shanah* ("New Year"), observed on the first and second; *Yom Kippur* ("Day of Atonement"), on the 10th; *Sukkot* ("Tabernacles") from the 15th to the 21st; *Shemini Atzeret* ("Eighth Day of Solemn Assembly") on the 22nd (in the Diaspora observed also on the 23rd as *Simḥat Torah*, i.e., "Rejoicing of the Law"). The Fast of Gedaliah falls on the 3rd. T. has 30 days and corresponds to Sept.-Oct.

TISZAESZLAR: Hungarian town; scene of Ritual Murder accusation in 1882. On false testimony extracted by intimidation and the torture of the two sons of the synagogue sexton, 15 Jews were accused of the murder of a 14-year-old Christian girl for ritual purposes. Anti-Jewish agitation in Hungary reached fever pitch. Six months later, the Hungarian attorney-general released some of the prisoners, and a commission of Budapest professors confirmed their innocence. After 15 months in prison, the remaining prisoners were acquitted amid anti-Jewish outbreaks in various parts of the country.

TITHES (Heb. *maaserot*): A tenth part of the produce. This used to be set aside as a religious offering. This custom has ancient origins, Abraham giving a "tenth of all" to Melchizedek (Gen. 14:18–20). Jewish law lists various obligatory t. (1) First tithe (Num. 18:24), given to the levites, after separation of *terumah* ("heave-offering") for the priests; in Second Temple times this was also given to the priests.

Reconstruction of the Tobiad palace at Arak al-Amir (2nd cent. BCE).

The Mishnah treatise *Maaserot* deals with this tithe. (2) Second tithe (Lev. 27:30–1; Deut. 14:22–6), i.e. an additional tenth taken after the first tithe. This was eaten by the owner himself in Jerusalem. It applied only during the 1st, 2nd, 4th, and 5th years of the Sabbatical cycle. Particulars are in the treatise *Maaser Sheni*. (3) Poor tithe (Deut. 14:28–9; 26:12), given to the poor and replacing the second tithe in the 3rd and 6th year of the Sabbatical cycle. (4) T. of the animals (Lev. 17:32) selected in the thrice yearly counting and offered as a sacrifice by the owner (see the tractate *Bekhorot*). The levites had to pay a tithe of what they themselves received (Num. 18:26).

*TITUS: Roman emperor 79–81 CE; son of VES-PASIAN. He took over command of the Roman army in Judea from his father in 70, when he destroyed Jerusalem after a 5-month siege. According to Josephus, T. endeavored — although unsuccessfully — to preserve the Temple, but other sources relate that the destruction was deliberate with the object of eliminating the national religious center of the Jews. Jewish tradition recalls him as "T. the wicked." Despite the bitter battle in Judea, he did not interfere with Jewish rights elsewhere and refused to accede to the demand of the inhabitants of Antioch to abolish Jewish privileges there. This may have been due to the influence of his mistress BERENICE.

TITUS, ARCH OF: Arch at Rome erected by the Senate in honor of VESPASIAN and TITUS. The original structure has not survived and the present one dates from the reign of Domitian (81–96 CE). The reliefs depict the goddess of victory crowning Titus; the march of Jewish captives bearing the Temple vessels, the shewbread table, seven-branched candlesticks, and the trumpet; the Jordan; and the sacrificial procession.

TOBIADS: The descendants of Tobiah, an estate-owner and apparently petty prince of Transjordania in the mid-3rd cent. BCE, who married the sister of the high priest ONIAS II. His son, Joseph (d. c. 181), leased the taxes of Coele-Syria. Joseph's younger son Hyrcanus was a dynast in Transjordan, building himself a stronghold (Arak al-Amir, near Amman), the remains of which still survive. Hyrcanus supported the Ptolemies, whereas the other sons of Joseph went over to the Seleucid Antiochus III who had conquered Coele-Syria and Judea from the Ptolemies. When Antiochus IV Epiphanes came to power, Hyrcanus committed suicide. The other T. headed the hellenizing movement which supported Antiochus IV, and assisted by their influence Antiochus replaced the high priest ONIAS III with JASON, deposing him in turn in favor of MENELAUS, who was probably a Tobiad. Menelaus' unbridled behavior in the Temple led to a rising in Jerusalem and Jason — receiving a rumor of Antiochus' death — endeavored to regain power. Menelaus and his faction fled to Antiochus, and their stories of an anti-Seleucid revolt in Judea led to Antiochus' persecution of Judaism. Menelaus continued to cooperate with the Syrians but in 163 BCE, was executed by them. The success of the HASMONEAN rising put an end to the hellenizing party and to the status of the T. as a political and social factor.

TOBIAH BEN ELIEZER (fl. 11th cent.): Bulgarian talmudist and poet. He wrote LEKAH TOV or *Pesikta Zutarta*, a midrashic commentary on the

Pentateuch and the Five Scrolls. Four of his poems are extant.

TOBIAS THE DOCTOR see **COHEN, TOBIAS**

TOBIT, BOOK OF: Book of the APOCRYPHA. It relates how the blind Tobit, a pious exile at Nineveh of the tribe of Naphtali, dispatches his son Tobias to Persia to collect a debt. On the way, Tobias visits a relative whose daughter, Sarah, has been wed seven times, but the demon Ashmedai, in love with her, has killed each bridegroom on the wedding night. With the help of the archangel Raphael, the demon is exorcised, Tobias marries Sarah and Tobit's blindness is cured. The work was probably composed in the 2nd–1st cents. BCE. It incorporates the GOLDEN RULE in the negative form. Several of its elements are obviously non-Jewish. The work is extant in Greek, Aramaic, Syriac, and Latin. The original language was perhaps Hebrew, but no early Hebrew version is preserved.

TOCH, ERNST (1887–1964): Composer. A native of Vienna, he worked in Europe until settling in the US in 1934. He taught composition at various American universities. His works include operas, symphonies, stage and film music, and chamber works.

TOG, DER (Yidd. "The Day"): New York Yiddish daily, founded in 1914 with Herman Bernstein as its first editor. It consistently espoused Zionism and American cultural pluralism. In 1919, it absorbed the daily *Wahrheit*, established in 1905, and in 1954, merged with the MORGEN-JOURNAL to become *The Day-Jewish-Journal* which closed in 1971.

TOGARMAH: One of the seventy peoples listed in Gen. 10. The country has been identified with Tagarmah on the Central Euphrates mentioned in Hittite inscriptions (in the Talmud as Germanike). The Armenians and Georgians were traditionally descended from the people of T. Later, the name was applied to Turkey.

TOHORAH (Heb. "purification"): The ceremony of washing a corpse before BURIAL. It is carried out according to a prescribed ritual by members of the ḤEVRAH KADDISHA, who recite appropriate biblical verses while washing the various limbs. After the cleansing, water is poured over the body. The washing (and even bathing) of the dead is an ancient Jewish practice.

TOHOROT (also *toharot, teharot*): (1) General term referring to the rules of ritual cleanliness. (2) Certain foods to be eaten only in a state of cleanliness, obligatory both in regard to the food and to the person partaking.

TOHOROT ("Purifications"): (1) The sixth and last Order (*Seder*) of the Mishnah. The name is a euphemism for ritual uncleanliness, and all the treatises of the Order deal with laws concerning impurity. It consists of 12 tractates, none of which (except *Niddah*) has *gemara*. (2) The name of the fifth

tractate (seventh in certain codices) in the Order T., containing 10 chapters. It deals with minor degrees of ritual uncleanliness, the effects of which last only until sunset.

TOLEDANO, YAAKOV MOSHEH (1880–1960): Israel rabbi and scholar. Born in Tiberias, he was rabbi in Alexandria 1935–41, chief Sephardi rabbi of Tel Aviv from 1941 and minister for religious affairs in the Israel government from 1958.

TOLEDO: Spanish town. Its Jewish community, which dates back to Roman times, was the most important in Spain under the Visigoths, and in the 7th cent., successive Councils of T. formulated the legislation aimed at extirpating Judaism in Spain. Under the Arabs (who are said to have been admitted to T. by the surviving Jews) the community continued to flourish, though outstripped now by Cordova, Granada, etc. Jewish rights were guaranteed after the Christian reconquest in 1085, and when the Almohades suppressed Judaism in Moslem Spain (1146–7) it became the most important community in the peninsula. In the 14th cent., there were in T at least 9 synagogues and four academies. Intellectual life flourished with poets, translators, and talmudic scholars. In the civil war between Pedro and Henry II the Jews of T. supported the former and the *juderia* was sacked. The massacres of 1391 claimed many victims in T. and left behind large numbers of converts.

13th cent. Toledo synagogue.
(Now the Church of Santa Maria la Blanca).

T. was henceforth one of the great centers of the
Marranos, who were attacked and massacred in 1449
and 1467, and later was the seat of a very energetic
Inquisitional tribunal, which remained active after
the expulsion of 1492. Much of the former *juderia*,
including two beautiful synagogues, still stands.

TOLEDO: City in Ohio, US. Jews lived there from
1837. Public religious services were first held in
1863 and a congregation formed 3 years later. The
Jewish Community Council was organized in 1936.
There are 3 Orthodox, 1 Conservative, and 1 Reform
synagogues. Jewish pop. (1973): 7,500.

TOLEDOT YESHU (Heb. "History of Jesus"):
Hebrew work, dating from the early Middle Ages,
which describes Jesus as the illegitimate son of one
Joseph Pandera. The book relates that Jesus wrought
miracles but was vanquished by an emissary of the
rabbis and condemned to death by stoning. The dates
do not correspond with those of Jesus of Nazareth.

TOLERANZPATENT (Ger. "Edict of Toleration"):
Law issued by JOSEPH II on Jan. 2, 1782, relieving
the Jews of the Austrian dominions from ecclesiastical
and other disabilities, encouraging them to engage
in handicrafts and agriculture, and granting them
educational facilities. Its effects were negligible in
changing the way of life of Austrian Jewry.

TOLLER, ERNST (1893–1939): German playwright
and poet. He was active in the 1919 Bavarian
Soviet Republic and was imprisoned for five years
upon its collapse. He left Germany in 1933, and later
committed suicide in the US. His extremely expressionist plays include *Die Wandlung* ("The Change"),
Masse Mensch ("Man and the Masses"), and *Maschin-
enstürmer* ("The Machine Wreckers").

TOMB: Jewish t.'s in Palestine resembled those of
the non-Jewish inhabitants of the country. The
commonest form is the rock-cut chamber: this was
an underground room approached from the surface
by a vertical shaft, the entrance below being closed
by a large stone. In the Late Bronze Age (1500–1100
BCE), the shaft became a flight of steps: later, shelves
were cut round the chamber for the bodies, and niches
appear in the Hyksos Period. In the hellenistic and
Roman eras, the common form is the rock-cut chamber
approached by a sunken forecourt, sometimes
fronted by a columned or ornamental façade and
forehall: the chambers are multiplied and linked by
doors or passages, the bodies lying on ledges, in cists,
sarcophagi, or in galleries. Arched niches containing
cists appear in the 3rd cent. CE. Large complexes
of this type (e.g. at BET SHEARIM) are known as
CATACOMBS. The freestanding surface tombs or
mausolea (see MAUSOLEUM) originated in the Hellenistic Period. Jewish catacombs were known also
in Rome, etc. in the Classical Period (see ARCHEOLOGY).
Later, individual tombs were usual, marked by
upright or (mainly among Sephardim) recumbent

Interior of the Tomb of Rachel.

tombstones, bearing inscriptions (sometimes lengthy)
in Hebrew (later in other languages). The elaborate
family t., mausoleum, etc. has appeared in western
countries in recent years.

TOMB OF RACHEL: According to Gen. 35:19,
Rachel died and was buried on the way to Ephrath
"which is Bethlehem." At least from the Byzantine
Period onward her tomb was shown 5 m. S of Jerusalem. An 18th cent. domed building stands on the
traditional site where Jews used to pray, especially
in the month of Elul. Another tradition (Sam. 10:2,
Jer. 31:15) places the tomb at Ramah, N of Jerusalem.
Until 1948, the domed structure near Jerusalem was
the only recognized HOLY PLACE in Jewish hands to
which it returned after the Six-Day War in 1967.

TOMBS OF THE KINGS: Large tomb found near
Jerusalem dating from Second Temple times. It is
situated N of the present wall of the Old City and
consists of an imposing staircase, a rock-cut court,
a porch, and six tomb-chambers in two stories with
dozens of sepultures. The portico has a finely sculptured frieze. The tomb is closed by a rolling stone;
is was once surmounted by three pyramids. From
Josephus it appears that this was the mausoleum
of the royal family of ADIABENE; the sarcophagus of
Queen HELENA was found there in 1863.

TOMBSTONES see **EPITAPHS**

TOPHETH: High Place in the Valley of Hinnom
on which children were sacrificed to Moloch
(Jer. 7:31). In medieval Hebrew literature, T. was
used for "hell."

TOPOL, CHAIM (1935–): Israeli actor; made
his debut with the revue-troupe *"Batzal Yarok"*
("Green Onions") and then joined the Haifa Municipal
Theatre, where he achieved remarkable success. He
also played the leading roles in several Israeli films,
particularly *"I like Mike"* and *"Sallah Shabati."*
His performances in London in *"Fiddler on the Roof"*

and Brecht's *"The Caucasian Chalk-Circle"* brought him international fame as did the film version of "Fiddler on the Roof."

TORAH (Heb. "teaching," "law"): In its narrow meaning, the Pentateuch, known also in Jewish tradition as "the Written Law." Traditionally, this was given to Moses at Sinai together with a detailed oral exposition of the Torah and its commandments (see LAW, ORAL). Thus, T. has the broad meaning in Jewish tradition of both the Written and Oral Law, together with every exposition of this Law, including the entire talmudic literature and commentaries. T. is often used for SEPHER T.

TORAH ORNAMENTS: Special wraps for the Torah-scroll are mentioned in the Talmud, but only in the Middle Ages did they assume the present form — a binder (*mappah*) to fasten the scroll and a mantle (*meil*) to place over it afterward. The surmounting of the scroll with a silver crown (*keter, atarah*) was common in gaonic times, and specially-made ornaments in this form are known from the Middle Ages: ultimately, they were used mainly in Central and E Europe. In medieval Spain, it became usual to decorate the ends of the staves with fruit-shaped ornaments, known at first as *tappuhim* (=apples) and later as *rimmonim* (=pomegranates). The latter name was retained, though in due course, especially in N Europe, these objects often assumed architectural and other forms. In Italy, the crown and *rimmonim* were used together. In Ashkenazi communities, a silver plaque (*tas*) was placed on the scroll to indicate the occasion or holiday for which it was made ready; subsequently, this was increased in size and became purely ornamental. A pointer (*yad*) of precious metal was provided for indicating the place during the reading (among Sephardi communities, this was kept in the ark; among the Ashkenazim it was hung over the scroll as an additional ornamentation). In oriental and some Sephardi communities, the Torah-scroll was kept in a wooden or metal case (*tik*), sometimes very splendid, other ornaments being then unnecessary.

TORAH, READING OF see **LAW, READING OF**

TORAH U-MESORAH: US society for Orthodox Hebrew Day Schools. Founded in New York in 1944, it is primarily devoted to establishing all-day Hebrew schools.

TORAH VA-AVODAH (Heb. "Law and Labor"): Group inside the MIZRAHI movement proclaiming the basic importance of Religious Labor.

TORONTO: Canadian city. Its earliest Jewish settler arrived in 1833 and the first synagogue (Pirchey Kodesh), originally Orthodox but later Reform, was established in 1856. The small community increased rapidly with the influx of Russian and Polish immigrants after 1882. These formed a number of Orthodox congregations with affiliations strongly

Topol performing for wounded soldiers.

based on *landsmannschaft* ties. In 1968, there were 46 main Orthodox, 5 Conservative, and 3 Reform congregations and also two *yeshivot*. Jewish organizational life is strong, and the central division of the Canadian Jewish Congress has its headquarters there. The United Jewish Welfare Fund (established 1937) is the central fund-raising agency for local and overseas purposes. Jewish pop. (1973): 97,000.

*TORQUEMADA, THOMAS DE (1420–1498): Spanish Dominican, appointed grand inquisitor in Spain in 1483. His personal influence was largely responsible for the expulsion of the Jews from Spain in 1492.

TORRES, LUIS DE (fl. c. 1492): Interpreter to Columbus' first expedition, the first European to set foot in America, and the first known to have used tobacco. A Jew by birth, he was baptized immediately before Columbus' expedition sailed.

*TORREY, CHARLES CUTLER (1863–1956): US Semitic scholar; professor at Yale from 1900. He published important studies on the Bible, the Apocrypha, and Jewish influences upon Mohammed. T. maintained that the New Testament Gospels were originally written in Aramaic.

TORT: An infringement of the primary rights of a human being. Rabbinic law holds that a man is liable for his actions whether they be intentional or not. Unintentional damages are not recompensed except where the injury has been committed in the domain of the injurer. Betrayal of a fellow Israelite, whether in person or property, to the hands of an *annas* (official of the oppressive Roman rule) was also considered a t., regardless of whether the betrayer received any gain or not. Rabbinic law is unique in that it generally provides no money damages for slander, although that is considered a major sin. The talmudic tractate NEZIKIN includes legislation dealing with t.'s

TORTOSA: City in N Spain, with a Jewish community going back to the Roman Period. It is memorable in Jewish history as the seat of a DISPUTATION in 1413–4. This was forced on representatives of Spanish Jewry by the anti-pope Benedict XIII, who presided over it in person. The Christian protagonist was the apostate Geronimo de Santa Fè, formerly Joshua Lorca (Lorki), who claimed to demonstrate the truth of Christianity from the Talmud and Hebrew literature. Foremost among the 22 Jewish representatives were Zerachiah Levi, Astruc Levi, Mattathias Ha-Yitzhari and Joseph Albo. There were 69 sessions spread over 21 months, the last being transferred to the fortress of San Matteo. During the course of the disputation, the pope exerted constant physical and moral pressure on the Jews to apostatize. The process contributed to the breaking of the spirit of large sections of Spanish Jewry and prepared the way for mass conversions. The community of T. was thereafter unimportant.

TOSAPHISTS see **TOSAPHOT**

TOSAPHOT (Heb. "addenda"): Critical and explanatory notes on the Talmud by French and German scholars of the 12th–14th cents. (known as *baale tosaphot* or tosaphists). Initially supplementary to Rashi's Talmud commentary, which they frequently criticize and modify, they soon developed a new independent mode of Talmud study. Interest had previously been centered almost entirely on the law actually expressed in the Talmud, but the tosaphists also investigated in detail the form and content of the talmudic discussions and demonstrated that these too contained implicitly a considerable body of law which they proceeded to render explicit. The *t.* studied most widely are those printed opposite Rashi's commentary in most editions of the Talmud. They were produced in several different schools. Thus the *t.* on *Bava Kamma* are by R Eliezer of Touques, on *Shabbat* by R Samson of Sens, on *Berakhot* by R Moses of Evreux, and on *Betzah* by R Peretz ben Elijah of Corbeille. All of them include quotations from earlier scholars such as R Tam, R Samuel ben Meir, and R Isaac of Dampierre.

TOSEPHTA: A supplement to the Mishnah. The Talmud (*Sanhedrin 86a*) mentions a *T.* and associates it with R Nehemiah, a disciple of R Akiva, but does not give any description. The one extant has six Orders with the same names as those of the Mishnah, and its treatises correspond to all but four (*Avot, Kinnim, Middot, Tamid*) of the mishnaic treatises. Some of its paragraphs, called BARAITOT, are alternative versions of mishnaic paragraphs, others supplement or elucidate them, while others are independent of any mishnaic law. Innumerable *baraitot* are either identical with, or are evidently

versions of, *baraitot* quoted in the two Talmuds. The *T.* is the subject of commentaries. Interest in its literary history is more recent. The view of M. S. ZUCKERMANDEL that the *T.* is the Palestinian version of the Mishnah and the view of H. ALBECK that it was unknown to the redactors of the Babylonian Talmud are extremes between which almost every possibility has been suggested. A critical text based on a manuscript was published by Zuckermandel in 1880–2. A new critical edition with commentary by S. Lieberman began to appear in 1955.

TÖTBRIEF: Name given in Germany to the royal edicts canceling debts due to the Jews or the interest on them. Under King Wenceslaus (1378–1400: especially in 1385 and 1390), they were among the terrors of Jewish life. Similar cancellations on a smaller scale were known elsewhere — e.g. in Spain, where they were called *moratoria*.

TOULOUSE: French city. Jews lived there from at least the 8th cent. The custom of smiting an elder of the community on the cheek on Good Friday was abrogated in the 12th cent. Conditions were subsequently favorable under the heretical Albigensian Counts, but the general expulsion of 1306 was strictly executed. Some Jews returned in 1315 but were annihilated in the Shepherds' Crusade (1321). T. was a Marrano center in the 16th cent. The modern community dates from the early 19th cent. It was reorganized in 1907 and grew considerably in population as a result of the N African immigration in the 1950's and early 1960's. Jewish pop. (1973): 18,000.

TOURO, JUDAH (1775–1854): US philanthropist. Born in Newport, R. I., where his father Isaac T. (1740–84) was minister, he became a prosperous merchant in New Orleans and gave generously to Jewish and Christian charities. He and his brother *ABRAHAM T.* (1774–1822) were responsible for the preservation and maintenance of Newport's 18th cent. synagogue. Judah T.'s will made possible the construction of the first residential units in what became the new city of Jerusalem.

TOUROFF, NISSAN (1877–1953): Educator. He was director of the Bureau of Hebrew Education in Palestine 1914–19, dean of the Boston Hebrew Teachers' College 1921–26, taught at the Jewish Institute of Religion, New York 1926–33. T. greatly influenced Hebrew education in America.

TOWER OF BABEL see **BABEL, TOWER OF**

TOWER OF DAVID: Popular name for the principal tower of the Jerusalem citadel, S of the Jaffa Gate. Its base contains the foundation of the Phasael tower, erected by Herod in memory of his brother. Herod's towers were left standing after the siege of Titus and served to protect the Roman camp in Jerusalem; later buildings on the site were the Crusader royal palace and the Mameluke and Turkish citadel. The identification with David's Tower dates back to the

The Tower of David.

Byzantine Period. Excavations were commenced there in 1969.

TRACHONITIS: Territory in NE Transjordania. It was colonized from 23 BCE by Herod after he had eliminated the robber bands which had formerly controlled the region. It was part of the territory of Agrippa II and after his death reverted to the province of Syria.

TRADE UNIONS: The earliest specific Jewish T.U. was a short-lived tailors' union founded in London in 1874 by a Polish immigrant, Lewis Smith, who went to England after participating in the Paris commune of 1871. Jewish trade unionism in the proper sense, however, originated about this time in Russia and Poland, initially among tailors and printing workers, sometimes in association with synagogues. In contrast to gentile bodies the main Jewish T.U. developed from political organizations. In Europe generally the political character of Jewish T.U. remained pronounced until World War II. Thus, the BUND, organized in 1897 from various pre-existent groups, became a political body regarding itself as the Jewish wing of the Social Democratic Party. The first POALE ZION unions were formed after 1900, and were strong among the small craftsmen of Austro-Hungary. In Poland between the two World Wars Jewish T.U. fell into three main groups according to their Social Democratic (*Bund*), *Poale Zion*, or Communist

affiliations. They were highly militant and struck frequently, but owing to their concentration in numerous places of work under small Jewish employers and in limited trades (e.g. clothing, food), and their relative isolation from the gentile organizations, their achievements were seldom permanent. The Jewish T.U. movement was particularly strong after unions became legal in Poland, where in 1939 membership was about 120,000. From E Europe the Jewish T.U. spread to England, France, Holland, the US, Argentina, Uruguay, and Palestine. In England, the *Bund* and *Poale Zion* continued until World War I, but unions of preponderant Jewish membership were restricted to a few trades (furniture, fur, clothing) in London, Manchester, and Leeds. Generally they amalgamated with the gentile unions. In Holland, strong unions were formed by Jewish diamond and cigar workers. In the US, organization began with the mass immigration of the 1880's, and the growth (as in England) of "sweated" industries (chiefly the needle trades). The predominantly Jewish United Garment Workers' Union was formed in 1891. This was the forerunner of the International Ladies' Garment Workers' Union (1900) and the Amalgamated Clothing Workers' Union. Several Jewish T.U. formed the United Hebrew Trades in 1888. The Jewish bodies fought a prolonged struggle for abolition of "sweatshop" conditions, terminated in 1919;

subsequently they assimilated into the general labor movement. The larger part of the Jewish unions tended to support the crafts form of organization owing to the numerous small Jewish projects. Because of the immigrant character of the membership until World War II, mutual aid (health and life insurance, originally also unemployment relief) became a strong feature of Jewish Trade Unionism in the US. In Palestine, Jewish T. U. struck root in 1905–7, being organized first along party lines (following *Poale Zion* and *Hapoel ha-Tzair* respectively); the first considerable overall body was the Agricultural Workers' Organization. The relative paucity of Jewish capitalists diverted these organizations to tasks of pioneer settlement, mutual aid, cooperation, etc. As a result the HISTADRUT was not established until 1940. The unique feature of Palestinian (now Israel) Trade Unionism is its integration into a body devoted to the satisfying of all the workers' needs. It also functions as colonizer and industrial entrepreneur. See also SOCIALISM.

TRADITION: Teachings or regulations handed down by word of mouth from one generation to another. This was applied especially to the ORAL LAW traditionally given to Moses but only committed to writing in the 2nd cent. CE. For the t. of punctuating the Bible text, see MASORAH.

*TRAJAN: Roman emperor; reigned 98–117. Although there is no evidence that he was personally hostile to the Jews, his oriental policy led to a major clash. In 105/6, he annexed the Nabatean kingdom including the Negev and Transjordan. In 115–7, while he was engaged in his Parthian war, Jewish risings occurred in Cyrenaica, Egypt, and Cyprus, and in Alexandria the Greeks attacked the Jewish population. As a result, in 116 he ordered a preventive massacre of the Jews in Mesopotamia. Judea itself was kept under firm control by his general Lucius Quietus. The suppression of the various risings ended the prosperity of the Jewish settlements in Egypt, Cyrenaica, and Cyprus.

TRANI: Italian port. Its Jewish community goes back to the Dark Ages when it was an important seat of rabbinic learning. The Jews were forced to accept Christianity at the end of the 13th cent. after which T. was the center of a body of "New Christians" (NEOFITI) secretly loyal to Judaism. A renewed Jewish community came to an end with the attacks on the Jews in the kingdom of Naples in 1497. The medieval synagogue (built 1247) still stands and is now a church in the former main street of the Jewish quarter, named after Isaiah di Trani.

TRANI, DI: Family of scholars. *ISAIAH (BEN MALI) DI T.* (the first; fl. 12th cent.): Italian talmudist, probably born in S Italy but lived later in N Italy. His copious talmudic commentaries carried the conception of the contemporary French

tosaphists into Italy. He is said to be the first European to mention the handkerchief. His grand-children included HILLEL BEN SAMUEL OF VERONA and *ISAIAH (BEN ELIJAH) DI T.* (the second; fl. 13th cent.) also a notable Talmud commentator. Descended perhaps from this family were the Turkish rabbis *MOSES BEN JOSEPH DI T.* (*Ha-Mabbit*; 1505–1585), rabbi of Safed and then of Jerusalem, a colleague of Joseph Caro, whose responsa are of great importance for Palestinian history of the age; and his son *JOSEPH DI T.* (1573–1644), rabbi of Constantinople and a noted homilist. Members of the family are still known by the Hebrew form of the name "Mitrany": *DAVID MITRANY* (1888–) is a noted British economist.

TRANSDNIESTRIA see **PODOLIA**

TRANSJORDAN: Name applied to the area of Palestine E of the JORDAN. Geographically it is divided into five parts, separated by deep river valleys: these are (from N to S): (1) GOLAN, Bashan, and Hauran; a level plateau bordered on the E by the Jebel Druze (Mount Hauran) and reaching on the S to the river Yarmuk; (2) GILEAD, between the Yarmuk and the Jabbok, a mountainous area, still wooded; (3) AMMON between the Jabbok and the Arnon; (4) MOAB, between the Arnon and the Zered, which is a high plateau; and (5) the mountains of EDOM (Mount Seir), S of the Zered, extending to the Gulf of Elath. The Jordan Valley borders the T.-J. plateau on the W and the high lands fall gradually to the Arabian desert on the E. Cultivation in T.-J. has fluctuated in area in various historical periods, extending in times of prosperity and strong government, and shrinking whenever authority has weakened. After cultivation in the Chalcolithic-Early Bronze Ages, the area became desert until the 15th cent. BCE when the Amorite kingdoms of Sihon and Og were founded in the N and Ammon, Moab, and Edom in the S. The Israelites defeated the northern kingdoms and the cattle-keeping tribes of Reuben, Gad, and half of Manasseh established themselves in their stead. David conquered the whole of T.-J. including the rich copper mines of the Arabah; under the weak successors of Solomon these areas were lost again or only held temporarily. W Ammon was held for a time by a Jewish family, the TOBIADS. In the period after the destruction of the First Temple, the Edomites moved into S Judah and their place was taken by the NABATEANS. A series of Greek towns was established in northern T.-J. in hellenistic times. The Hasmoneans, from Jonathan to Alexander Yannai, conquered Golan, Gilead, and Moab, but after the Roman intervention only a strip facing Judea on the east remained Jewish (Perea). The Herodian dynasty ruled in northern T.-J. and many Jews settled in Golan and Bashan under its protection. Trajan annexed the Nabatean kingdom (106) and transformed it into the

Provincia Arabia; his governor built the road from Elath to Bostra on the line of the ancient "King's (i.e., Pharaoh's) Way" (cf. Num. 20:17). In the Byzantine Period T.-J. began to decline, a process accelerated by the Arab conquest; from the 8th to the 19th cents. it was mostly left to the Bedouin, except for a time when the crusaders established themselves in *Oultre Jourdain*. The present-day T.-J. is mostly contained in the kingdom of Jordan ruled by the Hashemite dynasty; it replaced the kingdom (former emirate) of T.-J. established in 1921. Its population of c. 2,000,000 includes 85% Moslem Arabs, 8% Christians, and 7% Circassians (Moslems). The capital is Amman (pop. c. 500,000).

TRANSLATIONS AND TRANSLATORS: The rise of Aramaic- and Greek-speaking Jewish communities during the Second Temple Period created the need not only for translations of the BIBLE. but also of the Apocrypha and Pseudepigrapha, most of which are now known only in translations. Josephus, who first wrote his *Wars* in "the language of the fathers," later had it translated into Greek. There is no evidence for translations from other languages into Hebrew. In early medieval times, apart from the translation of the Bible into ARABIC by Saadyah, the Latin translations of two treatises of Abraham bar Ḥiyya and one of Abraham Ibn Ezra, the Book of Yosippon, and some fragments, there was no translation from Hebrew. Aramaic Midrashim seem to have been translated into Hebrew by the 7th cent. Saadyah's *Emunot ve-Deot* was early translated into a curious paytanic Hebrew, and some grammatical and legal works were translated before 1150. The great period of translation followed the expulsion from Moslem Spain in 1148, which brought to S France the Tibbon family and other scholars. It opened with Judah Ibn Tibbon's translation of *Ḥovot ha-Levavot* by Baḥya Ibn Pakuda. Until 1200, the bulk of translations was of Arabic works by Jewish authors; the 13th cent., which produced the largest number, concentrated on philosophical and scientific texts from Arabic, and after 1250 also from Latin. Medieval translations from Arabic started c. 1270 in Italy; among the works translated from Latin, medicine also held an important place. Translations from Arabic diminished after the 14th cent., while translation from Latin still flourished in the 15th cent. Altogether, over 160 translators are known to have made over 1,000 translations (many books were translated three and more times), those from Latin being perhaps more numerous than from Arabic. The style created by the first Tibbonids closely imitated Arabic syntax and idiom to the detriment of the Hebrew but also enriched Hebrew by creating many new words — some still current. Readers became so accustomed to this "astronomers' language" that it was used also for translations from Latin and for

original Hebrew composition. Jews also played an important role as interpreters for Christian scholars wishing to translate from Arabic into Latin; the Latin version was often prepared from an oral translation by the Jewish assistant into Spanish or another vernacular. In Renaissance times, the renewed interest in philosophy, as well as the rise of interest in Kabbalah, produced numerous translations of Hebrew works into Latin, some by Christians, others by Jews such as Jacob Mantino. From the Reformation Period onward, Hebrew grammars and works of rabbinic literature (e.g. the whole Mishnah in 1698–1703) were also translated into Latin. A highly technical introduction to the Talmud by Moses Rohatyn, published in Galicia in 1693, appeared as early as 1714 in Latin at Hanau, Germany. Scientific translations into Hebrew began in 1784 with a work on trigonometry by Baruch Schick based on English sources. M. A. Günsburg translated works on history from 1823 onward. Literary translation starts with M. H. Luzzato's drama *Migdal Oz* (1727, in part original) and D. Franco Mendes' *Gemul Atalyah* (1770, based on a French play and an Italian opera). Many individual poems appeared in Hebrew translation in the *Measseph*. Kalman Schulman published 1857–60 the first (somewhat abbreviated) translation of a complete novel, Eugène Sue's *Mysteries of Paris*. Subsequently a number of English classics were also translated. The rise of a Hebrew-speaking community and Hebrew education speeded up translation activity, which in present-day Israel is considerable: about 25% of the 1,500 books published in 1957–8 were translations. T. from the Hebrew into modern European languages began in the 16th cent. T from modern Hebrew literature is still in its beginnings.

TRANSLATIONS OF THE BIBLE see **BIBLE**

TRANSMIGRATION OF SOULS see **METEMPSYCHOSIS**

TRANSVAAL: S African province. Jews flocked there on the discovery of gold in Johannesburg in 1886. The disenfranchisement of the Jews in the Boer Republic led many of them to espouse the cause of the "Uitlanders" which preceded the Boer War (1899–1902), and at the outbreak of the War, most of the Jewish population left the T. for the British territories. Nevertheless, many Jews supported the Boer cause and fought in the Republican Army. After the war, the development of the Jewish community was resumed, immigration from Lithuania being very marked. Jews are to be found in most of the towns and villages of the T., and despite their small numbers, in most centers maintain a vigorous communal life. The largest communities are JOHANNESBURG (57,490), Pretoria (3,750), Benoni (1,237), Springs (1,049), and Krugersdorp (2,240). Apart from 5 Reform congregations in Johannesburg and one each in Pretoria, Germiston, and Springs, all congregations are Orthodox and are organized in the Federation of Synagogues of the T. The Bet Din of the Federation of Synagogues has jurisdiction over the Transvaal, Orange Free State, Natal, and the Ashkenazi communities of Rhodesia. In 1970, there were 76,440 Jews in T.

TRANSYLVANIA: Rumanian province. A community of Sephardi Jews originating from Turkey lived there in the late 15th cent. By the mid-18th cent. large numbers of Jews from Poland and Moldavia had settled in T. Until 1867, when its history became identical with that of HUNGARY, the Jews of T. led a relatively peaceful existence. With the transfer of T. to Rumania after World War I, Rumanian anti-Semitism spread in the province, and under pro-Nazi governments in Rumania, the Jews of T. were deprived of all civil and political rights. Following the division of T. between Hungary and Rumania in 1940, many of the Jews of both areas were destroyed by the respective regimes. The Rumanian government deported many Jews from T. to Ukraine. Some returned after the war, but Jewish spiritual life has been at a low ebb with most synagogues closed. Jewish pop. (1971): c. 7,000.

TRAUBE, LUDWIG (1816–1876): German pathologist. Director of the Berlin State Hospital, he was the founder of experimental pathology in Germany. His son *LUDWIG T.* (1861–1907) specialized in Latin paleography and taught medieval Latin at Munich Univ.

TRAVELERS: Jews were prompted to undertake long journeys from early in their history either by the desire for travel and thirst for knowledge or for commercial and political purposes. Their dispersion over the whole populated world facilitated such travels. In the 9th cent., Jewish merchants, called RADANITES, regularly undertook distant journeys from Europe to the Orient, from Franconia to China. The emperor Charlemagne sent a deputation to the caliph Haroun al-Raschid which included a Jew Isaac, who alone returned. ELDAD HA-DANI made adventurous journeys, but the historical value of his reports is disputed. About 970, the caliph of Cordova sent a deputation to Germany, incorporating a Jew, Ibrahim ibn Jakub, who wrote an account of his journey. The most famous Jewish traveler was BENJAMIN OF TUDELA who, about 1160–73, journeyed from Spain to France, Italy, Greece, Syria, Palestine, Mesopotamia, and Persia. His account gives much information about the Jewish communities visited. Later (1178–85) a German Jew, PETHAHIAH OF REGENSBURG, traveled through Poland, Russia, Crimea, the land of the Khazars, Armenia, Media, Babylonia, Mesopotamia, Syria, and Palestine, his travels serving as material for a book. Many Jews undertook journeys to Palestine, and others went in search of the Lost Ten Tribes. Other notable t.

were ABRAHAM IBN EZRA, Judah AL-HARIZI, and ESTORI HA-PARHI (who wandered through Palestine for seven years and wrote a valuable book on its topography). In the 15th–17th cents., individual Jews played some part in the expeditions of the Portuguese and the English. The crew of Christopher Columbus is known to have included at least one former Jew. At the end of the 18th cent., Samuel ROMANELLI of Mantua described his travels from Gibraltar to Algiers and Morocco; and in the 19th cent., the missionary Joseph WOLFF traveled to Bokhara, Nathaniel ISAACS explored Zululand and Natal, Arminus VAMBERY penetrated to Central Asia, and EMIN PASHA investigated Central Africa. See EXPLORERS.

TREBLINKA: Polish village; site of one of the largest Nazi extermination camps. From 1942, 200,000 – 300,000 Jews from Warsaw and an unknown number from other ghettos were sent there for extermination. The camp was blown up and leveled by the Germans in Nov. 1943.

TREE OF LIFE: One of the two trees specified in the Garden of Eden (Gen. 2:9). Whoever ate of it lived forever. After Adam and Eve ate of the forbidden Tree of Knowledge of Good and Evil, God expelled them from the Garden lest they eat also of the t. of l. The concept of the t. of l. is known among other ancient peoples and was developed in various mythologies.

*TREITSCHKE, HEINRICH VON (1834–1896): German historian. Frenziedly nationalistic, he gave the support of his name and powerful pen to anti-Semitism after 1878, alleging that "the Jews are our misfortune."

TREMELLIUS, JOHN IMMANUEL (1510–1580): Hebraist. He was born in Ferrara and converted to Christianity in 1540. T. taught Hebrew at Strasbourg (1542), Cambridge (1549), Heidelberg (1561), and Sedan. He published a Latin translation of the Hebrew Bible and of the New Testament from the Syriac.

TRENDEL see **DREIDEL**

TRENT(O): Town in N Italy. A small Jewish community established itself there in the first half of the 14th cent. In 1475, it was exterminated on the charge, instigated by BERNARDINO DA FELTRE, of having put to death a Christian child named Simon for ritual purposes at Passover. Relics of the tragedy are preserved in the cathedral of T. where Simon, beatified in 1582, was venerated until 1965 when the Catholic Church announced that the anti-Jewish accusation was false.

TRENTON: City in New Jersey, US. A group of Philadelphia Jews lived there temporarily in 1793. Jewish immigrants from Bohemia, Germany, and Hungary settled there in the 1840's, and the first congregation was founded in 1860. Between 1880 and

World War I, large numbers of E European Jews went to T. in 1973, 9,900 Jews lived in T., with 6 synagogues. The Jewish Federation of T. was formed in 1929.

TRESPASS-OFFERING (Heb. *asham*): Sacrifice brought by an individual for trespasses committed intentionally or unintentionally. The T. O. consisted of a 2-year old ram and was consumed by the priests. There were "definite" T. O.'s for prohibitions violated and "suspended" T. O.'s when it was uncertain whether the law had been broken.

TREVES see **TRIER**

TREVES: Family deriving from Trier (Treves) in Germany. *MATTATHIAS BEN JOSEPH T.* (c. 1325–1387), author of a work on talmudic methodology, was chief rabbi of France by royal appointment from c. 1360 on the return of the Jews to the country. He was succeeded by his son *JOHANAN T.* (d. 1429) who continued in office in the face of fierce opposition from Isaiah ben Abba Mari and Meir ben Baruch of Vienna until the final expulsion of the Jews from France in 1396, after which he settled in Italy. Many members of the family were prominent in Italy.

TRIBES, LOST TEN: The quest for the Ten Tribes of Israel (who constituted the northern kingdom in the Biblical Period and were taken into captivity by the Assyrians in 721–715 BCE) assumed great importance because of the prophecies (e.g. Ezek. 37:16) which associated the final Redemption with the reunion of the whole House of Israel. As long as the earth's surface was imperfectly explored, the Jewish world was periodically excited by reports of the discovery of the L. T. T. in various regions. ELDAD HA-DANA reported them, apparently in the mountains of Africa. BENJAMIN OF TUDELA heard of them in Central Asia; David REUVENI claimed to be the brother of one of their rulers in some region of Arabia; Antonio de Montezinos stimulated Manasseh ben Israel's political activity in England by his reports that he had found them in S America; SHABBETAI TZEVI appointed rulers over the various tribes. One story associates them with the Japanese, while the votaries of the Anglo-Israel theory place them in the Anglo-Saxon countries. In historic fact, some members of the Ten Tribes remained in Palestine, where apart from the SAMARITANS some of their descendants long preserved their identity among the Jewish population, others were assimilated, while others were presumably absorbed by the last Judean exiles who in 597–586 were deported to areas adjacent to the place of exile of the Ten Tribes (Media, Assyria, and Mesopotamia).

TRIBES, THE TWELVE: Twelve clans into which the Israelites were divided in the biblical epoch, particularly during the earlier period. They derived from the sons of Jacob — Reuben, Simeon, Levi, Judah, Issachar, Zebulun, Joseph, Benjamin, Dan, Naphtali, Gad and Asher. Moses conferred the priestly office on the tribe of Levi and, to maintain the number of tribes receiving territory at twelve (a sacred number), divided the tribe of Joseph into the tribes of Ephraim and Manasseh. Under Joshua, Reuben, Gad, and half the tribe of Manasseh received territory in Transjordan; Naphtali and Asher on the Sidonian frontier in Galilee; Issachar and Zebulun in the Valley of Jezreel area; Ephraim and the other half of Manasseh in the mountains of Samaria, with Benjamin to their S, and Judah further S, Dan along the seacoast around Jaffa, and Simeon in the Negev. The Danites were expelled from their original inheritance by the Amorites and moved on to the sources of the Jordan. Some other tribes also did not succeed in occupying the entire areas assigned to them. Under the monarchy the men of Simeon seized further land in Seir and the territory of the Amalekites. The tribal division was maintained under the Judges but Solomon adopted a fundamentally different administrative division of the country. After Solomon's death, the country split into two with the tribes of Judah, Simeon, and most of Benjamin constituting the southern kingdom. As a result of the invasion of the Assyrian kings, Tiglath-Pileser III (732) and Sargon (721), the northern tribes (see TRIBES, LOST TEN) were exiled, chiefly to Assyria, Media, and the lands neighboring Aram-Naharaim. A large section of the population of the southern kingdom was exiled by Nebuchadnezzar to Babylon in 586 (see EXILE, BABYLONIAN).

TRIBUNALS: In early biblical times, the t. for judging civil cases among the Hebrews were constituted by the "rulers" of groups of 10, 50, 100, and 1,000 families, reportedly established by Moses who, however, retained jurisdiction in cases of doubt (Exod. 18:21–6). Later, the elders sitting in the city gateway constituted the normal tribunal, presumably subject to the superior jurisdiction of the "judges" (*shophetim*). In due course, in the period of the Second Temple at the latest, the BET DIN of three or (as a regional tribunal, for major cases) 23 persons was evolved, the SANHEDRIN of 71 (a late addition) having an overriding authority. The BET DIN of three scholars remained the normal Jewish tribunal throughout the Middle Ages, still retaining authority among Orthodox Jews for religious purposes at least, and in Israel for matters within the competence of the Rabbinate. In the Ghetto Period, however, the lay leaders of the community sometimes constituted themselves into a tribunal for compulsory ARBITRATION on civil cases in order to keep them out of the gentile courts. Such T.'s exist in the US (e.g. JEWISH CONCILIATION BOARD OF AMERICA).

TRIENNIAL CYCLE see **LAW, READING OF**

TRIER (TREVES): Town in Germany. There is proof of Jewish settlement since 1066. They were under the authority of the Bishop until 1794. In 1096 they suffered martyrdom or became converted, the latter returning to Judaism 5 years later. Their rise to importance in the 13th cent. culminated in the elevation of individuals to positions in the 14th cent. unparalleled in Germany. During the Black Plague (1349), however, the community was destroyed. After their return in the 1350's, they were expelled in 1418, returning in 1500. Regarded as a juridical unit, they received charters for specified periods (usually 12 years). The Jews themselves convened a "Council of State" to further study and strengthen the position of the wardens and state rabbi. Equal rights were accorded them during the period of French occupation (from 1794). In 1933, there were 800 Jews in the city; in 1966, 70.

TRIER, HERMANN MARTIN (1845–1925): Danish parliamentarian. A teacher by profession, he was a Liberal member of parliament from 1884, and served as speaker of the house 1901–5, and vice-president of the upper chamber 1918–20. He was mayor of Copenhagen 1898–1907. T. wrote on pedagogics advocating the introduction of handicrafts into schools.

TRIESTE: Italian seaport. Its Jewish community goes back to the 14th cent. despite a spurious document relating to the 10th cent. After the Counter-Reformation, the (Austrian) regime was somewhat more liberal than in other parts of Italy, though the ghetto system was instituted in 1693/7. From the 18th cent., the community developed rapidly, with Sephardi immigration from Turkey, etc. The T. Jews worked strenuously in favor of union with Italy but this did not save them from great suffering in the last period of Fascist rule during World War II. Pop. (1973): 1,200.

TRIETSCH, DAVIS (1870–1935): Zionist writer and statistician. He was born in Germany, lived in the US 1893–9 and there turned his attention to Jewish migration on which he wrote several works. He participated in the First Zionist Congress. T. advocated Jewish settlement in Cyprus and the Sinai peninsula, and later published schemes for mass Jewish settlement in Palestine. He went from Europe to Palestine in 1932. He was a founder of the journals *Ost und West* and *Palästina* and of the *Jüdischer Verlag*.

TRILLING, LIONEL (1905–1975): US author and teacher; prof. of English at Columbia Univ., New York, from 1948. His *Matthew Arnold* placed him in the front rank of contemporary literary critics. His other volumes include *E. M. Forster*, *The Liberal Imagination*, *The Opposing Self*, and the novel *The Middle of the Journey*. T. edited *The Letters of John Keats*.

TRINIDAD: W Indian island. Although under British rule since the 17th cent., organized Jewish life began on the island only in 1930 with the arrival

of Central European refugees. Jewish pop. (1973): 300, nearly all in Port-of-Spain.

TRIPOLI (Tripolitania): N African country, now part of LIBYA. Jews lived there probably from the 3rd cent. BCE. Their numbers increased in Roman times, and in the 7th cent., some local tribes practiced Judaism. The community increased under the Moslems and there was immigration from Spain (14th–15th cents.). Under Italian rule from 1911, their position improved until the Fascist reaction of 1938. They suffered at the hands of the Germans in 1941–2 and from Arab attacks in 1945 and 1948. These, together with the establishment of the kingdom of Libya, led to extensive migration to Israel. In 1948, T. had 28,600 Jews, reduced to 3,000 by 1956. Most of the Jews lived in the town of Tripoli, but others were in rural areas, including some who dwell in caves. On *Tevet* 24, T. Jews observed the Purim Sherif to celebrate an escape from massacre in 1705. The Jewish community came to an end when the Jews remaining in Libya left the country following attacks on them by the mobs during the 1967 Six-Day War.

TROKI: Lithuanian townlet near Vilna. Grand Duke Witold of Lithuania settled 330 Karaite families from Crimea there at the end of the 14th cent. In 1441, the Jews of T. were granted considerable autonomy by Casimir IV, and they continued to enjoy favorable treatment during the succeeding centuries. Rabbinite Jews were excluded from T. on the instigation of the Karaite Firkovich, 1832–62. The Karaite community, Tataric-speaking, is engaged chiefly in vegetable-growing.

TROKI, ISAAC BEN ABRAHAM (1525 or 1533–1586 or 1594): Karaite scholar. From a familiarity with Christian polemical writings sprang his book *Ḥizzuk ha-Emunah* ("Strengthening of the Faith"), which was already popular in ms (printed posthumously in Amsterdam, 1654). The Latin translation of Christian Wagenseil included in *Tela ignea Satanae* aroused much interest among all classes of Christians. Two liturgical poems by T. appear in the Karaite prayer book.

TROTSKY (BRONSTEIN), LEV DAVIDOVICH (1879–1940): Russian communist leader. Born to a family of Ukrainian farmers, he was exiled to Siberia for revolutionary activity in 1898, but in 1902, escaped to England. He became a Marxist and a founder of the Russian Social Democratic Party. Returning to Russia during the 1905 Revolution, he was soon exiled and again escaped, this time to Vienna where he edited left-wing journals. After the Revolution of 1917, he returned to Russia from America and joined the Bolsheviks, playing an active part in the organization of the Communist Revolution. He became commissar for foreign affairs and chief negotiator of the Brest-Litovsk Treaty with Germany. T. then became war commissar and organized the

Trumpeldor Joseph

Red Army. His differences with Stalin, Zinoviev, and other leaders grew more pronounced, and after Lenin's death in 1924 he was given subordinate positions and eventually expelled from the Communist Party in 1927, being exiled to Turkestan, expelled from the USSR and settling in Constantinople. In 1937, he went to Mexico where he was murdered. His attitude to Jews and Judaism was negative and even antagonistic.

TROY: City in the state of New York, US. Jews first settled there in the 1840's, and a permanent congregation was organized in 1853. Immigration from E Europe after 1881 strengthened the Orthodox element in the city. In 1936 the T. Jewish Community Council was formed. In 1968, T. had 2,400 Jews with 3 synagogues.

TROYES: NE French town. A Jewish community existed there from the 10th cent., its prosperity founded on the local fairs as well as wine-growing. They were protected by the counts of Champagne. T. was the home of RASHI and a major center of Jewish learning in his time and the period of the tosaphists. The T. prayer-ritual has been preserved and published (by Max Weiss in Budapest, 1905). 13 Jews were put to death there in 1288 on a Ritual Murder charge: two remarkable elegies in Old French commemorate this episode. After the 1306 expulsion, the community never reattained its former position; Jews again lived in T. during the 14th cent. and from 1794, and numbered about 80 families in 1930. Half the Jews of T. were deported under the Nazi occupation, but the community was reconstituted after the liberation. Jewish pop. (1973): 1,130.

TRUMPELDOR, JOSEPH (1880–1920): Zionist leader. He studied dentistry but volunteered for the Russian army, losing an arm during the fighting around Port Arthur in 1904–5. After release from Japanese captivity, he was made an officer. In 1912, he settled in Palestine, attempting unsuccessfully to found a cooperative agricultural settlement. In Egypt during World War I, he worked with JABOTINSKY for the establishment of a Jewish unit to fight with the British against the Turks in Palestine. He helped raise the ZION MULE CORPS but this was dispatched to Gallipoli. As an ex-Russian officer, T. was excluded from the JEWISH LEGION. In 1917, he went to Russia to organize Jewish settlement-groups for Palestine and from his activity the HE-ḤALUTZ movement emerged. In 1919, he returned to Palestine as leader of a pioneer group and unsuccessfully endeavored to reconcile the antagonisms between the various workers' parties inside the country. He organized volunteers to protect exposed Jewish settlements in Upper Galilee and was killed in the defense of TEL ḤAI.

TSCHERNIKHOVSKI, SHAUL (1875–1943): Hebrew poet; born in the Crimea. His first published poem appeared in 1892 and his first books of poetry in 1898–1900. A physician by profession, he served in the Russian medical corps during World War I:

Shaul Tschernikhovski.
(Painting by Leonid Pasternak).

from 1922–31, he lived in Germany and thereafter, in Palestine. His work covered all types of poetry, especially the idyll and sonnet; he also wrote stories, essays, philological studies, children's poems and stories, and translations of ancient (chiefly Greek, e.g. The *Iliad* and *Odyssey*) and modern verse (the Finnish epic, *Kalevala*). Like Bialik, he was responsible for important innovations in the content and form of Hebrew poetry. T. revolted against the moral and didactic motifs hitherto characteristic of Hebrew verse. His own compositions are based on observations of nature, on the expression of the emotions of love and joy of living, and on artistic portrayals of landscapes, etc. His attitude to nature is pantheistic, and his optimism stems from his conception of the unity of plant and animal life and hence the eternity of creation. He accepted the earthly, nationalist secular ideology propounded by J. L. Gordon and Micah Joseph Bin-Gorion, denouncing the historical spiritual path which he maintained had led to decay and the weakening of the national will. T. advocated a territorial political renascence involving a return to the pristine, pre-spiritual period of the "conquerors of Canaan." His poetry profoundly influenced Jewish youth.

TSCHLENOW, JEHIEL (1863–1918): Russian Zionist leader. A physician by profession, he was one of the first *Ḥoveve Zion* in Russia. During the Uganda dispute, he was among the leaders of the TZIYYONE ZION who opposed the scheme. In 1906, he convened the HELSINGFORS CONFERENCE. From 1915, he lived in Copenhagen and London, playing a prominent role in Zionist political activity. T. returned to Russia for a short period after the 1917 Revolution in an endeavor to convene a Russian Zionist conference.

TU BI-SHEVAT see **NEW YEAR FOR TREES**

TUBAL-CAIN: The first craftsman in iron and copper (Gen. 4:22); son of Lamech. The name is connected with the tribe of Tubal whose members were noted as copper miners and workers.

TUCHMAN, BARBARA (1912–): US historian; niece of Henry MORGENTHAU Jr. Her main works include *The Zimmerman Telegram*, *The Guns of August* (about World War I), and *The Proud Tower*.

TUCKER, RICHARD (1916–1975): US singer. A successful synagogue cantor, he turned to opera and from 1945, appeared as tenor with the Metropolitan Opera in New York.

TUCKER, SOPHIE (1889–1966): US entertainer. A popular night-club and musical-comedy singer, she popularized the song *A Yiddishe Mamme*.

TUDELA: Town in N Spain, former chief city of Navarre. Its Jewish community antedated the Christian reconquest of 1114, when it was promised protection. A large number of documents illustrate its organization and wide economic interests. The Jewish quarter (*juderia*) was situated in the fortified area of the city. Attacked during the disorders of 1235, the Jews again suffered severely during the Shepherds' massacres in 1321, from which they never fully recovered. By the end of the 14th cent., the community was greatly reduced and impoverished. Refugees from Spain temporarily swelled the population in 1492, but when in 1498, the Jews were expelled from Navarre, the community came to an end. BENJAMIN OF TUDELA began his travels from T. c. 1165.

TUDESCO: Sephardi expression meaning literally "German," applied to Ashkenazim.

TUGENDHOLD, JACOB (1794–1871): Pioneer of Haskalah. He lived in Warsaw where he acted as government censor and organized Jewish elementary schools for the state. From 1852, he directed the Warsaw rabbinical college. His books, in Polish and Hebrew, advocated assimilation. T. translated a number of Hebrew classics into Polish.

TUMARKIN, YIGAL (1933–): Israeli painter and sculptor. His provocative paintings and vigorous drawings aroused considerable interest and controversy. His sculptural creations, mostly original assemblies of discarded objects and pieces of scrap metal, tend to express particularly the cruel aspects of modern civilization. He has produced a number of projects for monuments and a series of suggestive scenic decorations.

TUNISIA: N African country. Jewish settlement goes back to Roman times (see CARTHAGE). It finds frequent mention in responsa of the Gaonic Period when KAIROUAN was the greatest center of rabbinic scholarship in the west. The position deteriorated under the Almohades (1146 ff.) when many Jews accepted Islam. Spanish refugees who settled in T. differed in their customs and way of life from the native Tunisian Jews and founded separate com-

Portrait of the Artist as a Young Man. (By Tumarkin).

Professor Naphtali Herz Tur-Sinai.

munities; the two groups, however, merged in the course of time. When T. was temporarily under Spanish rule (1535–74), many Jews perished or were sold into slavery. Discriminatory legislation was gradually modified in the course of the 19th cent. T. passed under French protection in 1881, and its Jews were permitted to acquire French citizenship from 1910, many of them availing themselves of the opportunity. The community suffered from the Vichy laws and German occupation during World War II. The members of the BET DIN in Tunis are appointed by the bey and their decisions executed by the authorities. The Great Council of T. contains 3 Jewish representatives. There were 67,000 Jews in T. in 1959 of whom 55,000 were in the town of Tunis. Most of the Jews are merchants, storekeepers, and office workers, but by 1973 the total for the country had dropped to 8,000 as a result of the large emigration, mainly to France.

TUNKEL, JOSEPH (1881–1949): Yiddish poet and humorist. Born in Russia, he established his reputation as a humorist during a stay in the US, 1906–10. In 1908, he founded the illustrated Yiddish comic magazine *Der Kibitzer*, which evolved into the more influential *Der Groisser Kundes*. Returning to Europe, he participated in many publications in E Europe under the pseudonym *Der Tunkeler*. He returned to New York in 1940.

TUR MALKA: The Aramaic appellation of the Hebrew *Har ha-Melekh* (king's mountain), i.e. the administrative district of Jerusalem in Second Temple times. Its Greek equivalent is Oreiné, the mountain toparchy which succeeded the district (*pelekh*) of Jerusalem of Nehemiah's time. In the Mishnah and Talmud, the T. M. represents the municipal area of AELIA CAPITOLINA. Talmudic sources contain many references to the fertility of this area and the special laws applying to it.

TUR-SINAI (TORCZYNER), NAPHTALI HERZ Harry; 1886–1973): Hebrew Semitic and Bible scholar. Born in Galicia, he taught in Jerusalem 1910–12, at the *Hochschule für die Wissenschaft des Judentums* in Berlin, 1919–33, and was professor of Hebrew language at the Hebrew Univ. from 1933. He was co-chairman of the Hebrew Language Council 1943–55 and first president of its successor organization, the Academy for the Hebrew Language. His works include a German translation of the Bible, *Zur Entstehung des Semitischen Sprachtypus* which propounded a revolutionary theory of the development of language in general, an edition of the LACHISH LETTERS, and philological studies. His contributions to lexicography began with a German-Hebrew dictionary (1927) and from 1934, he edited the lexicon of Eliezer Ben-Yehudah (vol. 11 ff.).

TURIM see **JACOB BEN ASHER**

TURIN: City in N Italy. Jews first settled there in 1424. As capital of Piedmont, the community, styling itself "the Commonalty of the Jews of the Estates of His Most Serene Highness," dominated the others of the region, reaching a population of 1,500 in the 18th cent. A ghetto was established in 1679. In the 19th–20th cents., the community became one of the most important in Italy. It suffered greatly in World War II (when its beautiful synagogue was destroyed) but recovered and now has a rabbinical seminary and communal institutions. Pop. (1970): c. 2,000

TURKESTAN: Asiatic region between the Caspian Sea and China, embracing the Soviet republics of Kazakhstan (N), Uzbekistan, Turkmenia, Tadzhikstan, and Kirghizia (S). Its Jews are partly of native BOKHARAN and partly of European origin. The Bokharans arrived in T. from Persia and speak Judeo-Tajik, a Persian dialect with Turkish and Hebrew admixture. Benjamin of Tudela (c. 1170) related that there were 50,000 Jews in Samarkand. According to Joseph WOLFF, 10,000 Jews lived in T. in 1844, most of them dyers and silk-merchants. Their costume differed from that of the Moslems and they dwelt in ghettos. The European Jews settled there from the 1860's. In 1939, there were 19,000 Jews in Kazakhstan and 50,000 in Uzbekistan. Large numbers of Jews fled from the advancing German armies to Uzbekistan in World War II but most subsequently returned to their previous homes.

TURKEY: Jews lived in ASIA MINOR when the Ottoman Empire was established there, a synagogue being authorized in the old capital of BRUSA in 1326. Later, as a result of conquest, many other important Jewish communities were incorporated in T., the climax coming with the capture of SALONICA (1430) and of CONSTANTINOPLE (1453). After 1492, the sultans opened the gates of the Ottoman Empire generously to the refugees from Spain (later from Portugal and other lands) and the Turkish Jewish community, now predominantly Sephardi, became of great importance. The Jews were favored as a valuable trading and artisan element and also as a counterpoise to the potentially disloyal Christian minorities. Unusually flourishing were the communities of Istanbul (Constantinople), ADRIANOPLE, SMYRNA (Izmir), and especially Salonica where the intellectual traditions of Sephardi Jewry were centered. Palestine, too, was from 1517 part of the Turkish Empire, as were Egypt, the Yemen, Iraq, etc. The sultans applied the normal Moslem code against the Jews but not strictly. Thus persons such as Joseph NASI and Solomon ASHKENAZI were able to exercise great influence in the state. After the 16th cent., circumstances were not quite so favorable, anti-Jewish restrictions being applied more rigidly, but nevertheless there was no general reaction. Even the pseudo-messianic movement of SHABBETAI TZEVI, which might have entailed charges of disloyalty, did not undermine the position of Turkish Jewry, though the outcome much weakened it spiritually. Down to the 19th cent., the position of the community remained almost unchanged, although its treatment no longer seemed especially enlightened as compared with other countries. Numerically, it was the third largest in the world (after Russia and Austro-Hungary), numbering 350,000 in 1900. From then on, the gradual disintegration of the Turkish Empire brought numbers of its Jewish population in the Balkans, etc. under other authorities, the changes generally being for the worse. The process culminated with the first Balkan War and World War I, when the Turkish Empire was destroyed. T. was now reorganized on nationalist lines, the former minorities largely disappearing through the exchanges of population with Greece. In the remaining territories, the position of Turkish Jewry, no longer an especially favored minority but from certain points of view a recalcitrant one, was henceforth more difficult. There was some discrimination, actual rather than legal, and 37,000 Jews emigrated to Israel after 1948. There are 30,000 Jews in the country (1973), with 22,000 in Istanbul, 2,000 in Izmir, and smaller communities in Edirne, Brusa, and Ankara. The spiritual and cultural distinction of former days is, however, ended.

TUV ELEM see **BONFILS**

TUWIM, JULIAN (1894–1953): Polish poet. His early work was distinguished for its satirical note. He founded a group of young writers who fought against outmoded forms of literature and society. T. became the champion of Polish lyrical poetry, outstanding for its national and social aspects. He lived in the US during World War II after which he returned to Warsaw and became a leader of Polish literary and cultural life. T. translated many Russian classics into Polish.

TWELVE MINOR PROPHETS see **PROPHETS, MINOR**

TWERSKY: Hasidic dynasty, living at Chernobyl, founded by R Menahem Nahum (1730–1797), a pupil of the Baal Shem Tov who was known as the *maggid* of Chernobyl. He was succeeded by his son R Mordecai (d. 1837) whose place was filled by his eight sons.

TWERSKY, YOHANAN (1900–1967): Hebrew novelist. Belonging to a Ukrainian Hasidic family, he studied in Germany, lived and taught in the US. and in 1947, settled in Israel. T. was a prolific author chiefly of biographical works, e.g. on Uriel Acosta, Ahad Ha-Am, Dreyfus, Freud, Rashi, and M.M. Noah.

TYPOGRAPHY see **PRINTING**

TYRE: City founded in the third millennium BCE on an island $1\frac{1}{2}$ m. off the shore of PHOENICIA. It profited from a double harbor and was the rival of SIDON. Hiram of T. sent artisans and cedar-wood to Solomon to help build the Temple; the two kings jointly exploited the commerce between Elath and Ophir via the Red Sea. As a result of the marriage of the Tyrian princess Jezebel to Ahab, the religious and cultural influence of T. penetrated to Israel and even to Judah. In Assyrian and Babylonian times T., denounced by Ezekiel (Ch. 27), suffered a series of sieges and in 332 BCE, was captured by Alexander the Great. Under the Romans T., which had been endowed with a temple by Herod, was a center of commerce and purple dyeing, and its Jewish population included rabbis. The Palestinian Gaonate was transferred to T. after 1071. Benjamin of Tudela (c. 1170) found there about 500 scholarly Jews, some owning ships, others engaged in glass-manufacture. T. was held by the crusaders 1124–1291 but subsequently declined and is now a small Lebanese port with a population of 10,000.

TYROL: Former Austrian crownland. Jews are recorded there in the 14th cent. and were accused of well-poisoning at the time of the Black Death. As the result of the Ritual Murder accusation in 1475, the community in Italian-speaking TRENT was destroyed, as were those at Rinn and Lienz in the German-speaking areas shortly afterward. In 1520, the Jews were expelled from T., and though the exclusion was incomplete, organized Jewish life was not renewed until the 19th cent. The community of Innsbruck came to an end under the Nazis; at Bolzano (formerly Bozen) there has been sporadic Jewish life under Italian rule (i.e., since 1918).

TZADDIK (Heb. "righteous man"): Appellation given to a person outstanding for his faith and piety. The type is praised in the Bible (Hab. 2:4;

Prov. 20:7), while the Talmud states that the merits of (at least) 36 *tzaddikim* in each generation keep the world in existence. The concept of *t.* is of special significance in HASIDISM where it was developed by Dov Ber of Mezhirich and Jacob Joseph of Polonnoye. The Ḥasidim regarded the *t.* as the intermediary between God and man; originally one of his pupils was chosen to succeed him but the title eventually became hereditary. According to Ḥasidic doctrine, the *t.* is the foundation — the "soul" — of the world, who brings down Divine blessings. His words are regarded as miraculous and prophetic. Many of the *tzaddikim* (e.g. the dynasties of Rozhin and Chernobyl) adopted a luxurious mode of life; others, especially in Poland and Galicia, lived simply and charitably, opposing rich living. At the entrance to the room of the *t.* stood a *gabbai* ("collector") or *shammash* ("beadle") who would write the *pitka* ("note") containing the name of the supplicant Ḥasid together with his spiritual and material requests. The *t.* would give his visitor advice, counsel on treatment for illness, and *segullot* ("mystical formulae") for his success. After the visit, the Ḥasid would donate a sum of money to the attendant for *pidyon nephesh* ("redemption of the soul") to be used for the *t.*'s household and charitable allotments. Some *tzaddikim* refused to take the *pidyon*, and instead the Ḥasid contributed a kind of annual tax (*maamadot*). Occasionally, the *t.* would tour the province, visiting the Ḥasidim. On Sabbaths and festivals, multitudes of Ḥasidim would gather at the festive table (TISH) of the *t.*

TZADE (**צ**): Eighteenth letter of the Hebrew alphabet; numerical value 90. Originally an emphatic velarized *ss* sound, it is pronounced today as *ts* by most Jewish communities.

TZARA, TRISTAN (1896–1963): French writer. Rumanian by birth, he founded the literary movement of Dadaism in 1916 at Zurich. After World War II, his works evidenced concern with social and moral issues.

TZARFATI (transcribed also Zarfatti, Sarfatti, etc.): Surname of S European families deriving from France. (1) *JOSEPH T.* (known as *GIUSEPPE GALLO*; d. 1527): Italian poet and physician; son of (2). He was active in Jewish life in Rome where he succumbed from his sufferings in the sack of the city. His poems, some erotic, covered a wide variety of subjects, and his translation of the Spanish comedy *Celestina* initiated Hebrew drama. (2) *SAMUEL T.* (or Gallo; d. c. 1520): Italian physician, reputed to be the most able practitioner in Italy in his day. He was in the service in the Medici in Florence and of several successive popes in Rome where he played a prominent part in Jewish communal life.

TZEDAKAH (Yid. = *tzedokeh*; Heb. "righteousness"): charity, philanthropy.

TZEDAKAH BOX: Synagogue receptacle for alms, often of artistic form. It was usually affixed near the door, with separate divisions for local and Palestine charities, etc. Sometimes a movable box was used for collections during the week-day services or at funerals. It was occasionally divided into two parts — one for receiving, the other for dispensing alms.

TZEIRE ZION (Heb. "Young men of Zion"): Zionist socialist youth movement. It originated in isolated groups formed in Russia and Galicia from 1903 on; by 1911, it existed all over Russia and E Europe. After World War I, it became the backbone of the HE-ḤALUTZ movement. After 1920, it split, one section joining HA-POEL HA-TZAIR, while the left wing moved to affiliation with AHDUT HA-AVODAH (1924). Both wings merged as one movement (HITAHDUT) in 1932.

TZEMAḤ, NAHUM DAVID (1890–1939): Theatrical producer. In 1913 in Vienna he formed an itinerant Hebrew dramatic goup which developed into the HA-BIMAH company. His greatest success was the production of An-Ski's *Dibbuk*. T. directed the Tel Aviv *Bet Am* 1930–37.

TZEMAḤ, SHELOMOH (1886–1974): Hebrew author. Polish-born, he lived in Palestine 1903–9 and again from 1921, working as an agricultural expert. The themes of his stories are generally taken from life in Israel.

TZ'ENAH U-RE'ENAH see **ASHKENAZI, JACOB**

TZERE: The long *e* vowel, written ֵ or ֵ and pronounced like *a* in *name* or like French *é*. Many Sephardim and Israelis do not distinguish it from SEGOL, with which it is often interchanged in some mss.

TZEVA HAGANAH LE-ISRAEL (Heb. "Israel Defense Army"; abbr. *Tzahal*): Israel army. It grew out of the underground organizations — notably the HAGANAH — which safeguarded Jewish life and property in Mandatory Palestine. Tz. H. L. was officially established on May 14, 1948, with the proclamation of the state of Israel. At first it was only an ill-equipped force with experience of guerrilla and counter-guerrilla fighting, the bare beginnings of an army staff, and a skeleton navy and air force. Its expansion was extremely rapid and by the end of the WAR OF INDEPENDENCE in 1949 it had been transformed into a regular army. After the war, the ARMED FORCE was further expanded and reorganized to meet a security problem of unusual complexity caused by the disproportionately long Israel frontier, by the fact that few places in Israel are beyond the range of enemy fire, and by the fierce antagonism against Israel of all its neighbors. Tz. H. L. is partly regular and partly conscripted. The regular army is recruited voluntarily, officers being chosen by technical selection boards from men trained at cadet officer courses. The reserves comprise the remainder of the able-bodied nation, all men and women — with certain

David Ben-Gurion, when Minister of Defense visiting a Naval training camp.

exceptions — being called up at 18 (the men for three years' service, the women for two) under the Conscription Law enacted in 1949. Between 20 and 39, the conscript in reserve is called up for any period up to 90 days' service annually, and between 40 and 55, for four weeks' service annually. The able-bodied manhood of Israel numbers well over 250,000, nearly a third of whom are available for combatant service in case of war. Land, sea, and air forces are not independent but part of the Army, under the authority of a general staff, headed by the chief of staff who in turn is subordinate to the Minister of Defense. The president of Israel is the commander-in-chief of the whole Defense Force. The army is divided into three territorial commands (Northern, Central, Southern), each headed by a brigadier-general (*allooph*). Training is carried out by a network of military schools, the highest being the Command and Staff College, established in 1954. There is also a cadet school at Haifa and a naval school at Acre. The lack of heavy armament which hampered the Israel army led the army authorities to the development of shock forces and combined air-ground operations spearheaded by armor. The original striking force of the Israel Defense Army, the PALMAḤ, was disbanded in 1948,

but its tradition is kept alive by the various assault units (paratroopers, armor, armored infantry). Special attention has been given to the development of the Air Force which has had a number of striking successes to its credit. The army has seen action in the War of Independence, the SINAI OPERATION, a number of frontier reprisal raids, the Six-Day War and in the subsequent War of Attrition, the YOM KIPPUR WAR, in the areas occupied in 1967 whose inhabitants are all Arabs, and guarding against sabotage acts inside the country. The army conducts an extensive education program, publishes its own weekly journal *Ba-Maḥaneh* and runs its own radio station *Galle Tzahal*. See also CHAPLAINS.

TZIDDUK HA-DIN (Heb. "justification of the judgment"): Term applied to (1) the "acknowledgment" of the justice of any evil happening, especially death; (2) the BURIAL service.

TZIMTZUM see **KABBALAH**

TZIPPORI see **SEPPHORIS**

TZITZIT (Heb. "fringes"): Threads intertwined with blue cord. The Bible commands the wearing of *t*. (Num. 15:37–41) on the corners of garments. Originally every male garment had *t*,, but later, a special undergarment the *arba kanphot* ("four corners") of *tallit katan* ("little TALLIT") was devised for daily use, the large *tallit* being worn only during morning prayer and the *Kol Nidre* service. The dye for the *t*. was obtained from a Mediterranean mollusc (ḤIL-LAZON) but owing to various difficulties (including the uncertainty as to which particular type of molusc contained the appropriate dye), the Talmud taught that all fringes may be white (*Menaḥot* 38*a*).

TZIYYONE ZION (Heb. "Zionists of Zion"): Zionist political group, founded in 1904 as a result of the Uganda controversy and against Herzl's tendency to accept territory outside Palestine. Based chiefly on the Russian Zionists, the group was active in its opposition to TERRITORIALISM at the 7th Zionist Congress (1905), and its members subsequently headed the drive for practical colonizational work in Palestine as opposed to purely political activity. Its activities ended when the Territorialists left the Zionist Organization in 1905.

TZOM (Heb. "fast"): Hebrew term used as a component in such terms as *Tzom Gedaliah* (see GEDALLIAH, FAST OF).

TZUR, YAAKOV (1906–): Israel public figure. Born in Vilna, he went to Palestine in 1921. He worked in the head office of the Jewish National Fund, 1929–48 and after the establishment of the state represented Israel in various countries (Argentine and other S American countries 1949–53, France, 1953–9). He then returned to Israel where he was appointed director of the Jewish National Fund and also served as chairman of the Zionist General Council. He wrote an autobiography, *Sunrise in Zion*.

Tzeva Haganah Le-Israel: Israel army commanders after taking oath of allegiance to the state, May 1948.

Standing (*l. to r.*): David Shaltiel, Shlomoh Shamir, Dan Even, Mosheh Tzadok, Shimon Avidan, Mosheh Carmel, Yitzhak Sadeh, Shaul Yaffe, Michael Ben-Gal, Gershon Zack, Mishael Shaham, Mordecai Makleff, Mordecai Schumacher, Yisrael Amir.

Center row (*l. to r.*): Yoseph Avidar, Tzevi Ayalon, Yoseph Yaakovson, Levi Eshkol, David Ben-Gurion, Mrs. Paula Ben-Gurion, Israel Galili, Yohanan Ratner, Yigal Allon.

On grass (*l. to r.*): Shalom Eshet, Yehezkel Sachar, Nehemiah Argov, Yigael Yadin, Eliyahu Ben-Hur.

Soldiers from an African country completed their training as paratroopers in Israel.

U

UGANDA: Country in Africa. In 1903, the British colonial secretary Joseph Chamberlain officially offered Herzl an area of what became the neighboring colony of Kenya for Jewish settlement: this was called the "Uganda Scheme." The proposal caused sharp controversy at the Sixth Zionist Congress that year and was finally rejected, after Herzl's death, by the Seventh Congress in 1905.

UGARIT: Canaanite city of the N Syrian coast; today Ras Shamra. It was a commercial center in the mid-2nd millennium BCE but was destroyed in the 12th cent. BCE. Archeological discoveries there have added much to knowledge of ancient Canaanite culture and religion. Of special interest are the poems and cult documents written in an ancient alphabetic cuneiform (Ugaritic) in a Canaanite closely akin to biblical Hebrew. These have aided biblical studies and provided striking parallels to ancient Hebrew religious poetry and observances, which are now seen in a new historic setting. Moreover they use terms which occur in the Bible and which biblical critics formerly considered to be inconsistent with an early date.

UKRAINE: Soviet republic. Jews immigrated to the U. in waves from Khazaria, the Caliphate, and Byzantium between the 9th and 12th cents., from Central Europe in the 14th-15th cents., and from Poland in the 16th-17th cents. Severe massacres occurred there during the Chmielnicki and Haidamak uprisings (17th–18th cents.).. The Frankist and Hasidic movements originated in the 18th cent. in the U. which was also closely associated with the early development of Zionism in the 19th-20th cents. In the 19th cent., the main influxes were from Galicia and White Russia. Always an anti-Semitic center, the U. was the scene of pogroms in 1905 and 1918-20. The Russian government encouraged Jewish agricultural settlement in southern U. 1804-59, so that by 1897, there were 21 Jewish colonies in Kherson province and 16 in Yekaterinoslav with 26,326 inhabitants. The Soviet government in the 1920's promoted Jewish settlement in the U., with funds of the American Joint Distribution Committee, in the regions of Kalindorf, Zlatopol, and Stalindorf; and in 1930, there were 90,000 Jewish agriculturists there. In Jan. 1918, a regime of national autonomy was established in the U.

and the following served as ministers for Jewish affairs: M. Silberfarb (1918), A. Revutzki and W. Latzki (1919), and P. Krasny (1920). Jewish economy and culture suffered under Soviet rule. About half of Soviet Russia's 3 million Jews lived there before World War II, but under Nazi rule, the Jewish inhabitants who had not fled to Russia were wiped out by the Germans and Ukrainians (1941-2). The Jewish pop. was officially put at 777,126 in 1970.

UKTZIN (Heb. "Stalks"): Twelfth and last tractate of the Mishnah order of *Tohorot*, as well as of the entire Mishnah, containing 3 chapters. It has *gemara* in neither the Babylonian nor the Palestinian Talmud. It deals with the conveyance of ritual impurity to a harvested plant when its roots, stalks, or pods come into contact with an unclean person or thing.

ULLSTEIN: German publishing house founded in 1877 by Leopold U. (1826—1899) and carried on by his descendants. It published 4 daily newspapers (including the *Vossische Zeitung*) and 13 weeklies and monthlies, besides cheap editions of books. The firm was aryanized by the Nazis but returned to the U. family after World War II.

ULPAN (Heb. "study"): Institute for advanced study; particularly applied to intensive Hebrew courses for new immigrants in Israel.

UNBESCHRIEEN (Yidd. "without evil omen"): Phrase said after praising someone in order to ward off the evil thought to result from excessive good fortune.

U-NETANNEH TOKEPH see **AMNON OF MAINZ**

UNGER, JOSEPH (1828–1913): Austrian statesman. He took a prominent part in the 1848 Revolution and after baptism, was professor of civil law at Prague, 1853-5, and at Vienna from 1855. U. was a member of the Austrian parliament in 1867, and from 1869, sat in the Upper Chamber, heading the Liberal Party. From 1871 to 1879, he was minister without portfolio and from 1881, president of the Supreme Court of Administration. He wrote many legal works.

UNION CITY: City in New Jersey, US. A mutual benefit society organized in 1883 was the first Jewish organization in the city. In 1973, there were 7,000 Jews in North Hudson county.

UNION OF AMERICAN HEBREW CONGREGA-TIONS: American Reform Jewish body, founded in Cincinnati in 1873 largely through the efforts of Isaac Mayer WISE. Originally numbering 28 synagogues, it comprised in 1967, 650 affiliates with a membership of over a million. Its headquarters have been in New York since 1951. Under its auspices the HEBREW UNION COLLEGE was founded in 1875. The Union's major departments, many of them organized in conjunction with the CENTRAL CONFERENCE OF AMERICAN RABBIS are: education, audio-visual aids to education, synagogue administration, new congregations, public information, synagogue services, and interfaith activities. It is divided into sixteen regions, each with a director and a regional council. The governing body of the UAHC is the assembly of delegates which meets in convention biennially, and there is a national board of trustees. The Union is part of the WORLD UNION FOR PROGRESSIVE JUDAISM. It has fathered various auxiliary groups: the National Federation of Temple Sisterhoods (1913), the National Federation of Temple Brotherhoods (1923), the National Federation of Temple Youth (1939), the National Association of Temple Secretaries (1943), and the National Association of Temple Educators (1955). The Union's various publications include *American Judaism*.

UNION OF ORTHODOX JEWISH CONGRE-GATIONS OF AMERICA: US Orthodox synagogue body founded in 1898 with c. 1,500 affiliated synagogues, 15 major yeshivot, and 238 day schools. The Union publishes a quarterly magazine *Jewish Life* and pamphlets on Jewish topics. The "U" national *kashrut* supervision and certification is widely used. The Women's Branch was founded in 1924. The National Conference of Synagogue Youth (1954) serves youth groups.

UNION OF ORTHODOX RABBIS OF US AND CANADA (Agudath Harabonnim): Organization fostering Orthodox Judaism in America. The UOR works to assist yeshivot and promotes Orthodox observance in Jewish communities. In 1970 it had c. 600 members. Its headquarters are in New York.

UNION OF SEPHARDIC CONGREGATIONS: Organization founded in New York City in 1929, to promote the interests of Sephardi Jews throughout the US. It also supports students training for the rabbinate. One of its main projects has been the preparation of prayerbooks and textbooks.

UNION OF SOVIET SOCIALIST REPUBLICS see **RUSSIA**

UNITED HEBREW TRADES: A central body representing half a million organized workers in New York. Established in 1888, UHT is active in union and labor affairs, and is among the organizations working for the elimination of discrimination in the fields of employment, housing, etc.

UNITED HIAS SERVICE see **HIAS**

UNITED ISRAEL APPEAL: US Zionist fund-raising organization founded in 1927 as the United Palestine Appeal. In 1939, the United Palestine Appeal and the American Jewish Joint Distribution Committee merged their fund-raising efforts to establish the UNITED JEWISH APPEAL. Its funds are utilized to finance immigration and resettlement in Israel.

UNITED JEWISH APPEAL: US organization established in 1939 to coordinate the fund-raising campaigns of the United Palestine Appeal, the AMERICAN JOINT DISTRIBUTION COMMITTEE, and the NATIONAL REFUGEE SERVICE. It became the central American Jewish fund-raising organization for the resettlement of Jews in Israel and elsewhere and for aid to needy Jews throughout the world. Since its inception, the UJA has raised almost two billion dollars (1967), and through its constituent and beneficiary organizations (United Israel Appeal in behalf of the Jewish Agency, Joint Distribution Committee, New York Association for New Americans and the United Hias Service as a participant in the Emergency Rescue Fund) it has helped two and a half million Jewish refugees and victims of war, persecutions, and poverty. Of great historical importance were the large amounts of money raised by the UJA since the establishment of the state of Israel, which enabled the Jewish Agency to help over a million Jews to immigrate to and settle in Israel. The UJA has also developed widespread educational activities.

UNITED NATIONS: The chief specific interest of Jews in the UN has centered on its role in the establishment of the state of Israel, in efforts to resolve the latter's differences with its Arab neighbors, and its influence on the status and concerns of Jews in other parts of the world. In Apr. 1947. 1947, at the request of the United Kingdom, which acknowledged its inability to implement the MANDATE, the General Assembly established a Special Committee on Palestine (UNSCOP) to inquire into the question and submit recommendations. The UNSCOP'S report formed the basis for the Assembly's Partition Resolution of Nov. 29, 1947, which recommended the establishment, in Palestine, of both a Jewish and an Arab state. The state of Israel was proclaimed by the Palestine Jewish authorities on May 14, 1948, on the eve of the day Great Britain relinquished its control. When the Arab armies invaded Israel, no concrete help was afforded by the UN in implementing its resolution but UN mediators negotiated the subsequent cease-fire and armistice agreements supervised by a Truce Supervision Organization with headquarters in Jerusalem. Israel's application for admission to the UN was approved by the General Assembly on May 11, 1949. In the following months, Israel became a member of the various UN agencies. Israel's most pressing foreign problems — those arising from her relations with the

Session of UN General Assembly at which the resolution to partition Palestine was passed, Nov. 1947.

Arab states–have been repeatedly on the agendas of the UN's main organs. Israel-Arab relations reached a climax in the fall of 1956 with the SINAI OPERATION. On March 1, 1957, Israel—under pressure—announced its intention to withdraw its troops from the Gaza Strip and Sharm-e-Sheikh with the reservation that it would exercise its right of self-defense under the UN Charter if its ships were again interfered with in the Gulf of Akaba. In the meantime, in compliance with a Canada-sponsored resolution, adopted on Nov. 4, the Secretary-General submitted a plan for the creation of a UN armed force (UNEF) "to secure and supervise the cessation of hostilities . . ." The plan was quickly adopted. The UN was occupied at times with Israel complaints against the Egyptian blockade in the Suez Canal. A security Council resolution of Sept. 1, 1951 called upon Egypt to terminate the blockade. Proposals to redraw Israel's boundaries to conform to the 1947 Partition Resolution were repeatedly broached in the UN by the Arab states and as often rejected by Israel. Another climax was reached in May 1967 when an Egyptian demand to withdraw UNEF troops was immediately acceded to. The discussion on the Six-Day War at the UN lasted until November when a

resolution was passed calling on the Arabs to end their state of belligerency with Israel and for Israel to withdraw its troops. In subsequent years Israel-Arabs relations were constantly before the UN Security Council with Israel having little faith in that body where an anti-Israel bloc of votes was automatically ensured. The Arabs were unable to have extreme anti-Israel resolutions automatically passed in the General Assembly and in 1974 Yasser Arafat, chief of the Palestine Liberation Organization, was invited to address that body. In 1975 an anti-Israel motion was put through describing Zionism as a form of racisism. The Jerusalem question was repeatedly debated in the UN. The 1947 Partition Resolution had proposed the establishment of an international regime for Jerusalem, to be administered by the UN Trusteeship Council. The General Assembly's resolutions on this subject in Dec. 1948, and again later, were rejected by Israel. The question was raised frequently after 1967. The Arab refugee question was also frequently debated in the General Assembly. The Arab states requested full rights of repatriation while Israel insisted that the bulk of the refugees be resettled in the neighboring Arab states. Israel's cooperation in UN regional projects was impeded by the Arab states' refusal to sit together with

Israelis. Apart from the Israel question, Jews, particularly in the W Hemisphere, W Europe, and Israel were concerned with the UN's activities in other fields, especially relating to the safeguarding and promoting of human rights. They expressed their views on issues in these fields through membership in both national and international nongovernmental organizations. Several Jewish international organizations have been granted consultative status, including the AGUDAT ISRAEL World Organization, the Consultative Council of Jewish Organizations, the Coordinating Board of Jewish Organizations, the World Jewish Congress, the World Union of Progressive Judaism, and the World Union of Jewish Students. Jewish organizations accredited to the UN organization meeting at San Francisco in 1945, urged successfully the inclusion of human rights clauses in the UN Charter. Subsequently, they made suggestions concerning the provisions of the Universal Declaration of Human Rights. Thereafter, they carried on programs intended to publicize and interpret the Declaration and the Genocide Convention, adopted by the UN Assembly in Dec. 1949. Subsequently they have supported the draft Covenants on Human Rights. They have supported also the adoption of conventions on the rights of refugees and on the reduction and elimination of statelessness.

UNITED SERVICE FOR NEW AMERICANS:

Organization with headquarters in New York City, founded in 1946, as a result of a merger between the National Refugee Service (1939) and the National Office of the Service to the Foreign-Born, which had been sponsored by the National Council for Jewish Women. For eight years USNA aided Jewish displaced persons and immigrants in the US, where it arranged

United States: Congregation Beth Israel, Lebanon, Penn.

their reception, resettlement, and rehabilitation and provided family and vocational services and child care. In 1954, it merged with the Hebrew Immigrant Aid Society and the Emigration Services of the American Jewish Joint Distribution Committee into the United HIAS Service.

UNITED STATES: Although individual Jews had been in what is now the US as early as 1621, the first Jewish community was established in 1654 at New Amsterdam (now New York) by a group of 23 Sephardi Jews who left Dutch Brazil after the Portuguese reconquest. Notwithstanding the Dutch India Company's grant of privileges assuring them the right to reside and trade in the New Netherlands (Apr. 26, 1655), they had to contend with the despotic governor, Peter Stuyvesant. However, they succeeded in winning the right to serve in the militia (Nov. 5, 1655); trade and travel (Nov.-Dec. 1655); establish a Jewish cemetery (Feb. 22, 1656); own property (June 14, 1656); and burghership (Apr. 14, 1657). Soon, other Jews came from Holland, England, Germany, and Poland, and Marranos from the Iberian Peninsula. They settled in Delaware (1656), Rhode Island (1658), Connecticut (1659), Carolina (1665), and Georgia (1733), becoming merchants, peddlers, Indian traders, shipowners, skilled artisans, physicians, and even indentured slaves. The first Jewish congregations were founded in Newport (1658), Savannah (1734), Philadelphia (1745), and Charleston (1750). While most early settlers were Sephardi Jews, there were also Yiddish-speaking Ashkenazim and before the Colonial Period ended these had become the majority, though the synagogues followed the Sephardi rite. During the American Revolution, some 2,000 Jews lived in the colonies; most opposed the British. They signed Non-Importation Resolutions, helped finance the revolution, and served in militias. While most anti-Jewish restrictions had been removed prior to and during the American Revolution, others were not eliminated until 1785 (in Virginia), 1816 (in Maryland), and 1868 (in N Carolina). In 1825, there were about 6,000 Jews in the US, and 9 congregations functioned. In 1848, after the revolutionary movement in Europe had been suppressed, Jewish emigration to America received new impetus. Some immigrants settled in New York and Boston; others pushed onward across the continent through Talbotton, Georgetown, Paducah, Cleveland, Cincinnati, Detroit, Chicago, La Crosse, St. Louis, Mitchell, Portland, etc. to San Francisco. They joined in the California gold rush of 1849. They helped build cities and towns, founded Jewish communities, and developed Jewish social life. In 1859, the Board of Delegates of American Israelites was formed and Jews became active in a renewed fight for the separation of Church and State, the protection of persecuted Jews in other countries, etc. They provided relief for Jews in Palestine and established a periodical

United States: Temple Beth-El, Providence, R. I.

German-and English-Jewish press. For the German Jews, Reform Judaism was the dominant faith, and they created the Hebrew Union College, the first US rabbinical seminary, in Cincinnati (1875). When the American Civil War broke out, there were about 150,000 Jews throughout the US; they included ardent abolitionists as well as staunch supporters of slavery. An estimated 6,000 Jews served in Union armies, and more than 1,000 in Confederate forces. The war period was marked by anti-Semitic outbursts both in the N and the S. But when General Grant, commanding the department of Tennessee, charged Jews with illegal activities and issued general order No. 11 (1862), barring Jews "as a class" from that military department, his order was rescinded by President Lincoln. In 1862, a Federal law was passed authorizing the appointment of rabbis as military chaplains. After 1871, when German Jewry was emancipated and some 250,000 Jews lived in the US, immigration from that country dwindled. Jewish immigrants henceforth were chiefly Yiddish-speaking from Eastern and Central Europe. From 1881 to 1914, more than two million Jews emigrated to the US. Immigration — spurred by Russian pogroms — was curtailed during World War I, resumed afterwards, and restricted in 1924 by quota legislation. The immigrants were mainly Orthodox Jews, but included also atheists, radicals, intellectuals, anarchists, and revolutionaries. They settled principally in New York, Chicago, Philadelphia, and Boston and were important to the growth of these cities. Yiddish was used in Jewish schools and found further expression in the development of Yiddish literature, press, and theater. Many E European Jews went to work in the needle trades, while others became cigar and cigarette makers, house painters, glaziers, carpenters, "custom peddlers," or small businessmen. They pioneered in trade unionism and industrial relations and brought to the US rich traditions of community and self-help organizations. At the height of mass immigration, the *landsmanschaften*, benevolent societies whose members came from the the same town in Europe, were the primary units of community organization. Orthodoxy developed into the strongest branch of Judaism and Conservative Judaism began to develop around the Jewish Theological Seminary of America (1886). Institutions of higher learning such as the Isaac Elhanan Yeshiva (1896) and the Hebrew Theological College of Chicago (1922) took on new significance. The growth of active anti-Semitism in Europe heightened interest in Zionism, socialist movements, and secular Yiddishism. The US Jewish community became a primary arena for these contending ideologies. New Jewish organizations were formed to meet and reflect the new interests and needs, relief committees for overseas Jewry were founded, and the Zionist Organization of America (1897) emerged as an important group. The American Jewish Committee (1906), the American Joint Distribution Committee (1914), and the first American Jewish Congress (1917) were formed and invigorated Jewish life. Already in the 1870's, US Jews had begun to face social discrimination. The 1929 depression paved the way for renewed anti-Semitism in the US, concomitant with the rise of Hitler. In the 1930's, US Nazi sympathizers began publishing newspapers and formed anti-Semitic organizations under direction from Berlin. The Jewish Labor Committee (founded in 1935) joined older major national organizations—the American Jewish Committee, the Anti-Defamation League of B'nai B'rith (1913), and the second American Jewish Congress (1922)—in combating the calumnies. Soon, the influx of refugees from Hitler Germany necessitated the creation of the United Service for New Americans (1946) which supplemented the Hebrew Immigrant Aid Society (HIAS; founded 1884) and the National Council of Jewish Women (1893) as well as numerous new organizations and self-help groups. US Jews also sought to improve relations with their Christian neighbors through such organizations as the National Conference of Christians and Jews (1928). Simultaneously, need for overseas relief and domestic educational and recreational requirements spurred the growth of local welfare funds in hundreds of communities. Local Jewish community councils were formed and the Council of Jewish Federations and Welfare Funds was founded in 1935 to service these agencies. When the US entered World War II, the National Jewish Welfare Board (1913) helped establish United Service Organization centers and mobilized chaplains for military service. Some 550,000 US Jews served in military forces during World War II (250,000 in World War I). US Zionists played a vital role in the development of Zionism, especially in the events leading to the Balfour Declaration (1917) and the UN Palestine partition resolution (1947). In 1939, the American Zionist Emergency Council was formed and American public opinion was influenced in favor of the establishment of a Jewish homeland in Palestine. A New York meeting in 1942 adopted the Biltmore Program. The next year saw the organization of the American Jewish Conference which called for the re-establishment of "Palestine as a Jewish commonwealth." With the establishment of the State of Israel, US Jewry's generous financial aid (United Jewish Appeal, Israel Bond Drive, and other campaigns) helped support the economy of the Jewish state. The US Jewish

population is estimated at 5,731,000 (1973). It participates fully in all aspects of American and American-Jewish life. The largest communities have central agencies for Jewish education and fund-raising, teacher training and college-level schools, and regional offices of national agencies. Most communities have coordinating agencies such as federations, welfare funds, and community councils. Community hospitals and other welfare agencies, as well as national institutions, often function on a non-sectarian basis. A number of community relations agencies coordinate their activities through the National Community Relations Advisory Council. Nationally, religious groupings are united in the Synagogue Council of America. Rabbinical bodies include the Central Conference of American Rabbis (Reform), the Rabbinical Assembly of America (Conservative), the Union of Orthodox Rabbis, and the Rabbinical Council of America (Orthodox). The central congregational bodies are the Union of American Hebrew Congregations (Reform), the United Synagogue of America (Conservative), and the Union of Orthodox Jewish Congregations (Orthodox). Orthodox Judaism was strengthened again by emigration from Europe during and immediately after World War II and many rabbinical and all-day schools were established in the larger communities. Another new development is Jewish sponsored universities—Yeshiva Univ. in New York City, which has its own medical school and women's college, Dropsie University for Hebrew and Cognate Learning in Philadelphia (1907), and Brandeis Univ. (1948) in Waltham, Mass., a non-sectarian institution under Jewish auspices. The US has two Yiddish daily newspapers, a Hebrew weekly, more than 200 Jewish periodicals in English, and numerous cultural and scholarly periodicals in English, Hebrew, and Yiddish. (See also entries on the individual communities, states etc.).

UNITED SYNAGOGUE: Federation of Ashkenazi synagogues in London, established in 1870 and authorized by Act of Parliament. The five original member-bodies have increased in number to 23, supplemented by 23 "district" and 35 "affiliated" synagogues, comprising in all over 40,000 families or over 100,000 individuals. Since World War II, the U.S. has extended its activities outside London, but it remains essentially metropolitan. It is the main supporter of the office of the chief rabbi and of the London Bet Din and a primary source of income for other religious and charitable institutions.

UNITED SYNAGOGUE OF AMERICA: US association of Conservative congregations. Originally organized by Solomon Schechter in 1913, it numbers 802 affiliated synagogues in the US and Canada. It guides its member congregations and their affiliates, to this end maintaining a Department of Jewish Education, Department of Youth Activities, a National

Academy of Adult Jewish Studies, Commission on Social Action, Department of Music, Kashrut Commission, Commission on Congregational Standards, a Ramah Commission etc. Associated with the U.S. are the RABBINICAL ASSEMBLY, the Cantors' Assembly, the Educators' Assembly, and the National Association of Synagogue Administrators, as well as its National Women's League, National Federation of Jewish Men's Clubs, United Synagogue Youth, and *Atid* (for young people of college age). See CONSERVATIVE JUDAISM.

UNITED ZIONISTS-REVISIONISTS see **REVISIONISTS**

UNIVERSITIES: The earliest European university in the modern sense was the medical school at Salerno, with the foundation of which in the Dark Ages Jews were legendarily associated. A few Jews studied medicine from the 14th cent. in medieval u. such as Montpellier, and there are persistent though unconfirmed reports of their association with teaching there. As Arab medicine lost its predominance, the Jews became increasingly apt to enroll in u. to study but some theologians considered it improper for them to take degrees as the dignity of doctorate was equivalent to that of knighthood. Presumably for this reason, the Sicilian Jews obtained royal authorization to set up their own u. in 1466, but it does not not seem to have become effective. From the 16th cent. onward, many Jews from Italy and abroad received medical training at the Univ. of Padua, which introduced special ceremonials to enable them to take degrees; approximately 220 were graduated there between 1517 and 1721. The gentile students here and elsewhere compelled the Jews to pay special tribute to escape attack on the occasion of the first snowfall of the year, etc., and Jewish graduates had to entertain the student body. From the 17th cent., Dutch and from the 18th., German u. opened their doors to the Jews; in England, the older u. excluded them until the middle of the 19th cent., the University Tests Act of 1871 abolishing the remaining discriminations. From this period (as also occasionally in Renaissance Italy), Jews are found in some numbers in teaching posts, though in Germany professing Jews were excluded unofficially from professorial chairs. In the US, there has never been any official discrimination against Jews in u., but no Jewish graduates were known until the American Revolution. The influx of Jewish students in the 19th and 20th cents. led in some Central and E European countries to the limitation of their numbers by the NUMERUS CLAUSUS in Hungary, etc. after World War I —at first informally, later officially. A Jewish university, the YESHIVA UNIVERSITY, was established in New York and the non-denominational BRANDEIS UNIV. in Waltham, Mass., is under Jewish auspices. It is now a general phenomenon for Jews to attend u. and their

Issar Yehudah Unterman.

numbers both as students and teachers are frequently disproportionate to their percentage in the population. In Israel, the HEBREW UNIVERSITY was opened in 1925; BAR ILAN UNIVERSITY in 1955; while the TEL AVIV UNIVERSITY campus was dedicated in 1964.

UNLEAVENED BREAD see **PASSOVER**

UNTERFIRER (Yidd.): Person, usually a close relative, who conducts the bride or groom under the wedding canopy.

UNTERMAN, ISSAR YEHUDAH (1886–1976): Rabbi and scholar. Born in Lithuania, he settled in Palestine in 1947 after serving as communal rabbi of Liverpool. He was chief rabbi of Tel Aviv from 1947 and from 1964 to 1972 was Ashkenazi chief rabbi of Israel.

UNTERMEYER: (1) *JEAN STARR U.* (1886–): US poetess; former wife of (2). Her volumes of verse include *Growing Pains, Dreams out of Darkness,* and *Love and Need.* (2) *LOUIS U.* (1885–): US author. He has written poems (e.g. *Challenge, Roast Leviathan*), criticism, and parodies, while his anthologies of British and American poetry are standard. He has translated works of Heine into English.

UR OF THE CHALDEES (probably Ur of the Cassites): Ancient Babylonian city. It was the home of Abraham before his family's departure for Haran

Modern excavations in the ruins, conducted by Sir Leonard Woolley, have revealed the highly-civilized nature of the city in Abraham's time as well as evidence of an extensive flood at an earlier date.

URBACH, EPHRAIM ELIMELECH (1912—): Israel talmudist. Born in Poland, he went to Palestine in 1938 and in 1953 became professor of talmudic literature at the Hebrew University, Jerusalem. His main work is a study of the tosafists and their methods.

URBINO: Italian city. Its Jewish settlement, dating back to the 14th cent., was brilliant when U. was the capital of an independent duchy, but later the center of Jewish life was transferred to Pesaro. Under papal rule (17th—19th cents.) the community was reduced to miserable poverty and is now virtually extinct.

URFA see **EDESSA**

URI PHOEBUS BEN AARON LEVI (1623—1715): Dutch Hebrew printer, active from 1656 in Amsterdam and 1693—1705 in Zolkiev. A grandson of Moses Uri Ha-Levi, the German Jew who first gave religious instruction to the Marranos in Amsterdam, he wrote an account of the latter's achievement, published in Portuguese.

URIAH BEN SHEMAIAH: Prophet, contemporary of Jeremiah. After foretelling the destruction of Jerusalem and Judah, he was persecuted by Jehoiakim and fled to Egypt but was brought back and put to death by the king (Jer. 26:20 ff.). Some scholars have suggested that he is the "prophet" mentioned in the LACHISH LETTERS.

URIAH THE HITTITE: One of David's warriors. David became enamored of his wife, Bathsheba, and consequently engineered U.'s death in battle. The prophet Nathan denounced the crime (II Sam. 11—12).

URIEL: According to mystical literature and the Midrashim, one of the four ANGELS of the Presence.

URIM AND THUMMIM: Sacred means of divination used by the early Hebrews. Their nature has not been exactly determined, but they were attached to the breastplate of the high priest. The divination apparently involved the use of two stones or tablets which, according to ancient Hebrew belief, could answer questions on occasions fateful for the nation or its rulers. It seems that this method could only choose between two—and not several—possibilities. After the time of David, with the growth of prophetic influence, their usage is not mentioned.

URIS, LEON (1924–): US author. His best-selling novels include *Battle Cry* about World War II, *Exodus* about Israel, and *Mila 18* about the uprising of the Warsaw ghetto.

URUGUAY: S American country. Jewish immigration, mainly from Central and E Europe, dates only from the 20th cent. Nearly all the country's 50,000 Jews (1973) live in MONTEVIDEO, the capital, most of them being merchants. They are organized in four com-

munities: the E European, German, and Hungarian Ashkenazi communities, and the Sephardim. All four maintain religious, educational, and social institutions, but they are united in the Comite Central Israelita, the official representation of all Jewish groups. U. Jewry supports schools with Yiddish and Hebrew instruction attended by 2,000 children and two Yiddish daily newspapers and two weeklies, one in Spanish, one in German and Spanish, and a Yiddish monthly.

Lesser Ury: *Self-portrait*, 1928.
(En Harod Museum).

URY, LESSER (1861—1931): German artist. He was an accomplished impressionistic painter of landscapes and café life, excelling also in biblical and other illustrations.

USHA: Israel communal settlement near Haifa. The ancient U., in the vicinity, was settled in Bible times. After the suppression of the Bar Kokhba revolt, a synod was held at U. where far-reaching legislation was enacted (*Ketubbot* 49*b* — 50*a*, etc.). It was also for a time the seat of the Sanhedrin. Its academy was led by distinguished scholars including R Meir and R Yose ha-Gelili. The modern settlement (IK) was founded in 1937 by General Zionist youth. Pop. (1972): 319.

USHPIZIN (Aram. "visitors"): Seven "guests" (Abraham, Isaac, Jacob, Joseph, Moses, Aaron, and David) who, according to the Zohar, successively visit the tabernacle of every pious Jew during the festival of Tabernacles to participate in his meal. The custom arose of reciting before the meal a fixed text inviting the guest. Impecunious scholars are sometimes invited to the table to symbolize the guests.

USQUE: Family of Marrano origin, prominent in Ferrara in the 16th cent. (1) *ABRAHAM U.* (formerly Duarte Pinhel), printer. His press at Ferrara

1552—8 produced a number of important books, both in Hebrew and in Spanish-Portuguese, including a Spanish translation of the Bible ("The Ferrara Bible"). (2) *SAMUEL U.*, poet and historian. In 1553, he published at the press set up by (1) a work in dramatic form in Portuguese, *Consolaçam as Tribulaçoens de Israel* ("Consolation for the Sorrows of Israel"), written to strengthen the steadfastness of the Marranos. It contains valuable material for contemporary history. He later lived in Safed. (3) *SOLOMON U.* or Salusque Lusitano (c. 1530—1595), poet. He translated Petrarch's sonnets into Spanish, composed a Purim play on Esther (later translated into Italian by Leone Modena), and also wrote verses in Italian. He finally·settled in Constantinople.

USSISHKIN, MENAḤEM MENDEL (1863—1941): Zionist leader. He was among the founders of the *Bilu* in 1882, of the *Bene Zion* society in 1884, and the following year was secretary of the Moscow United Zionist Societies. An early supporter of Herzl, he was a delegate to the First Zionist Congress. In 1903, his pamphlet *Our Program* advocated a synthetic Zionism fusing political activity with practical work in Palestine. The same year, he convened an assembly of Palestinian Jews at Zikhron Yaakov which was the first endeavor to organize the Jewish community of the country. He also called a Teachers' Conference, thereby laying the foundation of the Israel Teachers' Association. Returning to Russia, he organized the TZIYYONE ZION to combat the Uganda proposal and was successful in his struggle. Settling in Odessa in 1906, he headed the *Hoveve Zion* there until their dissolution by the Bolsheviks in 1919, when U. moved to Palestine as president of the Representative Council. On his initiative, the ASEPHAT HA-NIVḤARIM was convened and the VAAD LEUMI elected. From 1923 until his death, he was chairman of the JEWISH NATIONAL FUND and was responsible for purchasing large tracts of land in the Jezreel Valley, tha plain of Zebulun, the plain of Ḥepher, etc.

USURY see **MONEYLENDING**

UTAH: US state. Jewish settlement dates from 1854. Merchants who had gone west with the gold seekers settled in SALT LAKE CITY in the 1860's, and in Corinne in 1869. There are (1973) 2,000 Jews in U. mostly in Salt Lake City (1,800). The first non-Mormon governor of U. was Simon BAMBERGER. The United Jewish Council and Salt Lake Jewish Welfare Fund was formed in 1936.

UTICA: City in the state of New York, US. Jews went from Prussia and Poland to U. in the mid-1830's. A congregation was formed in 1848. One Conservative and two Orthodox synagogues now exist there. A Jewish Community Council was organized in 1933. Jewish pop. (1973): 2,800.

Menaḥem M. Ussishkin.

UZBEKISTAN see **BOKHARA**

UZIEL (OUZIEL) BEN ZION MEIR HAI (1880—1954): Rabbi. Born and educated in Jerusalem, he was ḤAKHAM BASHI at Jaffa in 1912, and in 1939, RISHON LE-ZION (Sephardi chief rabbi of Palestine later of Israel). He was a prolific writer on halakhic and other topics.

UZIEL, ISAAC BEN ABRAHAM (d. 1622): Rabbi. Born in Fez, he was brought to Amsterdam in 1606 as rabbi of the *Neveh Shalom* congregation. He had a great share in establishing the traditions of the Amsterdam community, his pupils including scholars such as Manasseh ben Israel. His writings comprise poems, a Hebrew grammar, and a recently published translation of the parables ascribed to Aristotle.

UZZIAH (or Azariah): King of Judah c. 780—c. 740 BCE. Succeeding to the throne at the age of 16, U. conquered Philistia and defeated the Arabians and Mehunians to the S of his kingdom. He also headed a league of kings who opposed Tiglath-Pileser of Assyria. U. rebuilt the Red Sea port of Elath, and under his reign Judah reached the zenith of its development. Toward the end of his life he suffered from leprosy and had to hand over power to his son Jotham. An inscription has been discovered in Jerusalem relating that U.'s remains were transferred outside the city upon the construction of the Third Wall in the time of Agrippa I.

VAAD ARBA ARATZOT see **COUNCIL OF FOUR LANDS**

VAAD HA-LASHON HA-IVRIT (Heb. "Hebrew Language Council"): Institution concerned with the development of the Hebrew language. It was founded in Jerusalem in 1890 by Eliézer Ben-Yehudah, David Yellin, and others as a branch of the *Saphah Berurah* Hebrew-speaking society and was reorganized as an independent body in 1904. It helped to establish modern Hebrew terminology and usage. In 1953, its functions were transferred to the ACADEMY OF HEBREW LANGUAGE.

VAAD HATZALA REHABILITATION COMMITTEE: Organization set up in the US in 1939 to rescue Jewish victims of Nazism. It established branches in Switzerland, Sweden, and Iran and rescued thousands of Jewish families, particularly of religious leaders. It supplies outlying settlements and rabbinical schools in Israel with religious literature.

VAAD LEUMI see **KENESET YISRAEL**

VAKHNAKHT (Yidd. "watchnight"): The night preceding the circumcision ceremony formerly called *Shavua ha-Ben* ("The Week of the Son"; see *Sanhedrin* 32b). It was customarily spent in feasting and the recitation of special prayers, originally perhaps to ward off evil spirits. This observance was later transferred to the Sabbath eve preceding the circumcision. The feast was called *zakhar* or *shelom zakhar*, after the initial word of a hymn recited on the occasion.

VALENCIA: Spanish port. Jewish settlement antedated the Christian reconquest of 1238, when a separate section of the city (walled for protection in 1390) was assigned to the Jews. The community of V. was active in the textile industry and overseas trade. After the massacres of 1391, the surviving members of the community, said to number 11,000, all accepted Christianity. V. was subsequently the seat of an Inquisitional tribunal.

VALENTIN, GABRIEL GUSTAV (1810—1883): Swiss physiologist; professor at Berne for 45 years. He conducted research on the epithelium of the eye, the circulation of the blood, animal electricity, digestion, and brain fibers.

VALLADOLID: Spanish city with an important Jewish community in the Middle Ages privileged by Ferdinand IV of Castile (1295—1312). During the Civil War between Pedro I and Henry of Trastamara, the populace sacked the Jewish quarter and destroyed eight synagogues. Many Marranos were killed in a riot in 1473 in V. which later became the seat of an active Inquisitional tribunal.

VALLEY OF THE KINGS: Central area of the Kidron valley, facing Jerusalem. It was apparently already a royal domain in the time of David, since Absalom built himself a tomb in the "King's dale" (II Sam. 18:18). Here was situated the "King's pool" (Neh. 2:13—14) which irrigated the royal gardens nearby.

VAMBÉRY, ARMINIUS (Hermann Vamberger; 1832—1913): Hungarian orientalist and traveler. Dressed as a dervish, he traveled from the Middle East to Afghanistan and Bokhara. On his return (1864), he became professor of oriental languages at the Univ. of Budapest. He wrote numerous works on linguistics and anthropology. Although baptized, V. was an early supporter of Zionism.

VAN RIJK, etc. see **RIJK**, etc.

VANCOUVER: Canadian city. Jews settled there soon after its foundation in 1855. The first synagogue, Beth El, was established in 1887 as an Orthodox congregation, but eventually became Conservative. A second Orthodox congregation, Shaarey Zedek, came into being in 1905. Jewish communal endeavor is coordinated in the Jewish Administrative Council, which sponsored the weekly *Jewish Western Bulletin*. Jewish pop. (1973): 8,000.

VARNHAGEN VON ENSE, RACHEL see **LEVIN, RACHEL**

***VARUS, PUBLIUS QUINTILIUS** (d. 9 CE): Roman governor of Syria 6—4 BCE. He tried Herod's son Antipater in 4 BCE and later in the same year, suppressed with much brutality a revolt against Roman rule.

***VASHTI**: Persian queen, wife of Ahasuerus. The Book of Esther relates that she was divorced after having refused to answer the king's summons to appear before him at a banquet.

VAV(ו): Sixth letter in the Hebrew alphabet; numerical value 6. Originally (and still in certain oriental dialects) its phonetical value was *w*, but today it is pronounced *v* in all the Western dialects and in Israel. It is also a vowel letter representing long *oo* (וּ) as in "soon" and *o* (וֹ) as in "short" in the current Israel pronunciation; long *o ey ow oi öy* in other pronunciations.

VA-YIKRA see **LEVITICUS**

VA-YIKRA RABBAH see **LEVITICUS RABBAH**

VAZSONYI, VILMOS (1868—1926): Hungarian politician and lawyer. He founded the Democratic Party which he represented in parliament several times from 1901. He was minister of justice briefly in 1917, then minister of franchise and again of justice. He strongly advocated assimilation and opposed Zionism.

VECCHIO, GIORGIO DEL (1878—): Italian jurist. He taught law at various universities; from 1920, at Rome where he was rector 1925—7. His interpretation of law and legal custom as the outcome of historical development led him to sympathize with Fascist nationalism. Nevertheless, he was dismissed in 1939.

VECINHO, JOSEPH (c. 1450—1520): Portuguese astronomer. A royal physician, he was consulted regarding Columbus' plans, and invented an improved astrolabe which he tested on the Guinea coast in 1495. He also prepared Abraham Zacuto's tables for publication. Forcibly converted in 1497, he adopted the name of Diego Mendes Vecinho. His descendants returned to Judaism in Italy.

VEIL, SIMONE (1927–): French public figure. As a child she was deported by the Germans and survived concentration camps. She worked as a magistrate and in 1974 became minister of health.

VEIT, PHILIPP (1793—1877): German painter; son of Dorothea MENDELSSOHN. Working in Rome 1815–30, he was a leader of the German Romantic school, the "Nazarene Brotherhood," which preceded the Pre-Raphaelites. V., who became a Catholic, painted ambitious religious and historical compositions.

VEKSLER, VLADIMIR YOSSIPOVICH (1907—1966): Soviet physicist. His most significant work was on cosmic radiation, particularly in the theory of acceleration, i.e., instruments to produce artificial energy required for the production of atomic nuclei.

VELIZH: Town of White Russia, USSR. It was the scene of a Blood Libel in 1823, the accused being eventually vindicated and compensated by royal privy council. In 1941, half of its population of 11,000 were Jews, who fled or were massacred.

VENEZUELA: W Indian Sephardim were the first Jews in V., arriving about 1850; there were anti-Semitic outbreaks at Coro in 1855 and 1902. In the 20th cent., E European and German Jews entered the country until barred after World War II. They played a leading role in developing the country's trade and in modernizing the capital, Caracas. Jewish pop. (1973): 15,000, mostly in Caracas. Educational facilities are sponsored by the Union Israelita.

VENICE: Former Italian republic. Jews lived there in the 12th cent., but the commercial jealousy of the Venetians prevented any permanent settlement. In

1509, the German invasion of the Venetian *terra firma* drove large numbers of Jewish refugees, mainly of German origin, into V. Since it proved difficult to expel them, they were segregated in 1516 in the New Foundry (*Ghetto Nuovo*) which later gave its name to Jewish quarters throughout Italy (see GHETTO). In 1541, the Jewish traders from the Levant were segregated in the adjacent Old Foundry (*Ghetto Vecchio*), where they were joined toward the end of the century by "Ponentines" or Westerners—i.e., Marranos who were permitted to settle in V. after 1589. The Venetian ghetto was for the next century the most populous in Italy (perhaps c. 5,000 souls) and had the most vigorous intellectual life. The Venetian government, while enforcing the Jewish hat, etc. would not allow forced sermons or child baptisms and kept the Inquisition in check. As the Venetian patricians gave up overseas trade, it was largely left in Jewish hands. In the 18th cent., the city decayed and the community dwindled. With the entry of the French Revolutionary forces in 1797, the ghetto gates were destroyed and the community emancipated, but their condition deteriorated under subsequent Austrian rule. The Jews took a prominent part in 1848–9 in the revolutionary regime of the half-Jew Daniel MANIN, and were fully emancipated when V. was annexed to the kingdom of Italy in 1866. The community suffered severely during the German occupation of 1943–5. Only one of the five surviving synagogues is now regularly open for services, but the ghetto is still a showplace. Jewish pop. (1973): 800.

VENOSA: Town in S Italy. It had a Jewish community in the Classical Period and early Middle Ages. It is noteworthy for its 3rd–8th cent. CATACOMB—the most important in Italy outside Rome.

VEPRIK, ALEXANDER (1899—1952): Russian composer. He was active in the Russian Folk-Music Society and many of his works are on Jewish themes (e.g. *Songs and Dances of the Ghetto*; *Kaddish*; *Jewish Popular Songs*).

VERBAND DER VEREINE FÜR JÜDISCHE GESCHICHTE UND LITERATUR (Ger. "Federation of Societies for Jewish History and Literature"): Organization founded in Germany in 1893 with the object of resuscitating the former *Bet ha-Midrash* tradition by arranging lectures and discussions on Jewish life and literature. Over 200 societies were affiliated in 1914. It was headed by Gustav Karpeles until 1909, and then by Ismar Elbogen. The *V.* was dissolved under the Nazis.

VERGA, IBN see **IBN VERGA**

VERMONT: US state. Jews were living in Poultney shortly after the end of the American Civil War. A congregation now extinct was founded there in the early 1870's. The oldest extant community is in Burlington where Sabbath services were being held in 1880. In the early 1900's, a congregation was founded in

West Rutland which also served the 18 families in Rutland. The 1973 Jewish population of V. was 1,855) with 1,225 in Burlington and 280 in Rutland.

VERONA: Italian city. Though Jews are mentioned there sporadically from the 10th cent., the present community dates from the settlement of Jewish loan-bankers from Germany in the 14th cent. They were protected and flourished under Venetian rule, a Sephardi community being founded in addition to the original Ashkenazi one; the establishment of the ghetto in 1603 was considered a boon and was celebrated annually. The Jewish population is now under 100 (1972).

VERSAILLES TREATY: Term covering various settlements after World War I. At the preceding Paris Peace Conference, the Jews were represented by the Zionist Organization and the COMITÉ DES DÉLÉGATIONS JUIVES, as well as several minor bodies, including the Alliance Israélite Universelle and the Joint Foreign Committee (of British Jewish organizations). The Zionist Organization, after preparatory talks with the emir Feisal (to prevent conflicting Jewish-Arab claims), presented its case asking for the establishment of a Jewish National Home protected by a Mandatory power, with generous frontiers in the north and east to make proper development and settlement possible. The *Comité des délégations juives* dealt with the future of those Jews who would remain in the Diaspora, demanding a solution of all minority problems in E and SE Europe by means of constitutional guarantees as well as civil, political, and national rights of minorities, including, above all, language and autonomy rights; Jews were to be formally recognized as a

Ketubbah from Verona, 1655.

"national minority." The demands of the Zionist Organization (with the exception of the suggested frontiers) were accepted and became the basis of the Treaty of Sèvres with Turkey in 1920 and of the Palestine MANDATE. The demands of the *Comité des délégations juives* became the basis of the Minority Treaties concluded with the new states of E and SE Europe.

*VESPASIAN: Roman emperor 69–79. Nero sent him in 67 to subdue the Judean rebellion and by 68 he had conquered Galilee, Transjordan, and the Judean coast before suspending operations on receiving the news of Nero's death. In 69, he became emperor, and the campaign was concluded by his son, TITUS. He patronized Josephus and the Talmud speaks of his favorable treatment of R Johanan ben Zakkai.

VETUS LATINA see **SEPTUAGINT**

VICHY GOVERNMENT: Regime at V. headed by Marshal Pétain during the German occupation of France, 1940–4. Anti-Jewish legislation was introduced in 1940. A commissariat for Jewish affairs, aimed at outlawing Jews, was directed by Xavier Vallat (1941–2) and Darquier de Pellepoix (1942–4). The Vichy authorities did not hinder the deportation of Jews by the Germans to extermination camps. It carried out its policy through the *Union Générale des Israélites de France*, founded in 1941.

VIDDUI see **CONFESSION**

VIENNA: Capital of Austria. Jews were living there at the beginning of the 10th cent. They received a special dwelling quarter near the ducal palace and were permitted to acquire houses elsewhere in the city. The medieval community was a famed center of scholarship. In the 13th cent., their situation deteriorated under pressure from the burghers, and a ghetto was instituted. In 1406, the Jewish quarter was burnt, and in 1421, the Jews were killed or expelled as the result of a Ritual Murder accusation ("Wiener Geserah"). A number of Jews lived there during the 16th cent., and a community was again formed at the beginning of the 17th cent., maintaining trade connections with Poland, Italy, and Turkey, but they were again banished in 1670. The Jews returned slowly under special license after 1675, but no synagogue could be established until 1826. They participated in the 1848 revolution and finally received equal rights in 1867. Many of them were prominent in the political, economic, cultural, and scholastic life of the city in the 19th–20th cents. Anti-Semitism began to spread from the 1880's under the leadership of Karl LUEGER. In the same period, Zionism attracted many adherents among the Jews under the influence of HERZL, whose home was in V. During World War I, refugees from Galicia, Hungary, and Bukovina swelled the Jewish poulation. The affairs of the community were conducted by a council 1918–38. At this time there were 17 major synagogues (one of them Sephardi), as well as a rabbinical seminary, a Jewish museum, a school network, and

Herzl's funeral procession in Vienna. July 1904.

other institutions. There were c. 180,000 Jews in V. before the Nazi invasion of 1938, when a ferocious persecution immediately began; about a third succeeded in emigrating, almost all the rest being deported to extermination camps. After World War II, survivors from Hungary, Poland, and Czechoslovakia went to V. Jewish pop. (1973): 9,400.

VIENNA, CONGRESS OF see **CONGRESS OF VIENNA**

VIENNA RABBINICAL SEMINARY see **ISRAELITISCH-THEOLOGISCHE LEHRANSTALT**

VILLAGES, CHILDREN'S see **YOUTH SETTLEMENTS**

VILNA: Town in Lithuania, now incorporated in the USSR. Jews were resident there at the end of the 15th cent. but were banished in 1527 by Sigismund I at the request of the burghers. A number returned but were the victims of a riot in 1592; the following year, Jews were formally allowed to settle, acquire houses, and lend money. In 1633, permission was granted to trade in precious stones, meat, and livestock and to be craftsmen. An anti-Jewish riot occurred in 1635, while in 1655, those members of the community who had not fled were massacred by the Cossack army. 4,000 Jews were among the victims of famine in V. in 1709-10. From the 18th cent., the city became a center of rabbinical study, being dubbed the "Lithuanian Jerusalem"; its best-known scholar ELIJAH BEN SOLOMON ZALMAN was universally known as the V. Gaon. Many Haskalah leaders also lived there. An important Hebrew press over several generations was that of the family ROMM, whose edition of the Talmud became standard ("the V. *Shass*"). V. was a Zionist center and also the birthplace of the BUND. The Jews suffered from famine under German rule in World War

I and from a pogrom at the hands of the Polish troops in 1919. YIVO had its headquarters there 1925-41. The Jewish population numbered 140,000 at the end of the 19th cent. but by 1941 had dropped to 65,000 (besides 15,000 refugees from Poland). The Germans established two ghettos in V. and 30,000 Jews were killed there by the end of 1941. The 12,000 remaining were augmented in 1943 by transports from White Russian rural districts. Deportations to extermination camps began in Aug. 1943 and there was some resistance. When the Russians entered V. in 1944, they found 600 Jews hiding in the sewers. Jews from other areas began converging on V. after the war. Jewish pop. (1970): 16,491.

VILNA GAON see **ELIJAH BEN SOLOMON**

VIMPEL (Yidd.): The binder round a Scroll of the Law (also MAPPAH); often presented to the synagogue to commemorate a male child's birth and inscribed with his name.

VINAVER, MAXIM (1862—1926): Advocate and statesman; one of the founders of the Russian liberal Constitutional Democratic Party (Cadets) and a member of the 1906 Duma. He was foreign minister of the anti-Communist government of the Crimea in 1918. From 1919, he lived in France.

VIRGIN ISLANDS: Formerly part of the Danish W Indies, now US territory. Gabriel Milan, member of a Hamburg Jewish family, was governor of St. Thomas, 1684-7. A Sephardi community of 500 existed to the mid-19th cent. The numbers dwindled but rose again in the 1960's. In 1971 there were 450 Jews, with a Sephardi synagogue in St. Thomas.

VIRGINIA: US state. Isolated Jews are first mentioned there in the mid-17th cent. After the middle of the 18th cent., there were Jewish merchants, artisans, and traders in V. A congregation was organized in RICH-MOND in 1789. Many Jews arrived there after 1880, and by 1900, 13 cities and towns had a Jewish communal organization. In 1973, V. had a Jewish population of 58,550 the major centers being Alexandria (11,000 with environs), Richmond (10,000) NORFOLK (11,000), Portsmouth (1,085), and Newport News (2,550).

VISITING THE SICK (Heb. *bikkur holim*): One of the most important commandments of Judaism. Although not directly commanded in the Bible, the rabbis derived its importance from God's visit to Abraham (Gen. 18:1) which, they maintained, was during the illness caused by his circumcision. The rabbis also taught that visiting the sick is one of the things "the fruit of which a man enjoys in this world while the capital remains for the world to come." The purpose is not only to cheer the sick, but to help the invalid if needed and to pray for his recovery. Gentile, as well as Jewish, sick are to be visited. Visiting was discouraged where this would be a strain upon the patient or where the nature of the illness would shame him in the presence of visitors.

VITAL, HAYYIM (1542–1620): Palestinian kabbalist; born of a S Italian family and known as "Calabrese" (= of Calabria). A pupil of Moses Cordovero and Moses Alshekh, he was closely associated with Isaac Luria during the latter's last years in Safed (1570–2), and after Luria's death, V. claimed that he alone possessed an accurate account of his teaching. He boasted to his pupils that his soul was that of the Messiah, son of Joseph, and he became known in oriental countries as a wonder-worker. During an illness, his notes on the Lurianic Kabbalah were extracted from their box, transcribed, and published as *Etz Hayyim*. From 1590, he lived in Damascus where he continued to write kabbalistic works and preach the advent of the Messiah. The rapid diffusion throughout the Jewish world of Lurianic Kabbalah probably owed more to V. than to Luria himself.

VITEBSK: White Russian city, USSR. Jews were living there in the mid-16th cent. V. was conquered by the Russians in 1654 and its Jews banished to Russia until 1667. The citizens continued hostile but the community grew and by the end of the 19th cent., Jews (numbering over 34,000) constituted a majority. The Jewish pop. in 1941 numbered 40–45,000; those who did not escape were deported or herded into a ghetto which was liquidated by the end of the year. Jewish pop. (1970): c. 20,000.

VITKIN, YOSEPH (1876—1912): Zionist pioneer. At the end of the 19th cent., he left Russia for Palestine. His appeal to Russian Jewish youth to settle in Palestine laid the foundations for the Second ALIYAH.

VITRY (V.-le-Brûlé): NE French townlet. Its Jewish community was martyred in 1317 on a charge of well-poisoning. Rashi's disciple, SIMHAH of Vitry after whom *Mahzor* V. was called—lived in V.

A kabbalistic amulet against pestilence from Hayyim Vital's *Shaar ha-Yihudim* (Lemberg, 1855).

VOCALIZATION: The indication of vowels in Hebrew script. At first, Hebrew was written with indication of consonants only. Gradually, toward the end of the First Temple Period, long *i* and *e* came to be indicated by the letter *yod* and long *u* and *o* by *vav*. This is still inconsistent in the spelling of the Hebrew Bible, which in this respect represents the practice of the Second Temple Period, the same form or word being written sometimes with, sometimes without, these *matres lectionis*. In the late Second Temple Period, the use of these indicators increased, and they were also sporadically employed for short vowels; *aleph* was used rarely to indicate *a*. This is the usage in the Dead Sea Scrolls and in early mss of talmudic literature, etc. After the end of the Talmudic Period (c. 500), a method of indicating v. by separate signs added to the consonants began to develop, parallel with similar attempts in Syriac and later in Arabic. This crystallized in three distinct systems: (1) the Babylonian Punctuation, which uses partly letters and partly combination of dots all placed above the line between the letters. The simple Babylonian V. indicates 6 vowels and *sheva mobile*, and the complicated Babylonian V. differentiates between stressed and unstressed vowels.

A simplified form of the Babylonian V., influenced by the Tiberian, is still employed by the Yemenite Jews; (2) the Palestinian Punctuation, indicating 7 vowels by combinations of dots and short lines, placed above the line and between the letters; and (3) the Tiberian Punctuation, indicating 13 vowels and *sheva*. Other systems were the Samaritan V., close in character to the Palestinian, and the Karaite V., employing the Arabic vowel signs. The Babylonian and Palestinian, and at first also the Tiberian systems, were not fixed, but every scribe used the available vowel-signs in his own way, so that no two mss are identical. The differences affect not only the representation of the vowels, but also indicate grammatical variations. The Tiberian system became fixed c. 800 in two definite forms, associated with the masoretic schools of Ben Naphtali and Ben Asher; the Ben Asher system passed into common use and is that of the printed Bibles. The signs of the Tiberian V. are differently interpreted by Ashkenazim, Sephardim, and other communities; their original sound-value is still a matter of controversy though they most probably represent a pronunciation close to the modern Ashkenazi and Yemenite pronunciations, not differentiating between long and short vowels. In the Middle Ages the Ben Asher system was used only for Bibles, the Mishnah and prayer books being pointed according to different rules. Only after invention of printing was the biblical v. extended to all texts.

VOGEL, SIR JULIUS (1835–1899): New Zealand statesman. English-born, he emigrated to Australia in 1852 and thence to New Zealand, where he entered political life and was prime minister 1873–5 and 1884–7. Afterward, he was agent-general for New Zealand in London.

VOLCANI see **ELAZARI-VOLCANI**

VOLHYNIA: Province of NW Ukraine. USSR. Jewish communities were in existence in the 15th cent. and were brought under a centralized organization in the 17th cent., participating in the COUNCIL OF THE FOUR LANDS. V. was then a seat of Jewish learning but this came to an end during the Cossack massacres of 1648–9. In the 18th cent., the province was a Hasidic center. There were 133 Jewish townlets in V. in the 19th cent. The Jews who did not escape in 1941 were exterminated by the Germans, in many cases with the assistance of the Ukrainians.

VOLKISTEN see **FOLKISTEN**

VOLOZHIN: Lithuanian townlet, known for its yeshivah (1802–1892) which attracted students from many countries. The principals were R HAYYIM OF V., 1802–21, his son R Isaac of V., 1821–49, R Eliezer Isaac Fried, 1849–53, and R Naphtali Tzevi Judah BERLIN, 1853–92. From that time, the yeshivah was closed on the orders of the Russian authorities. In 1899, it was refounded, but on a small scale, and was no longer the central institution of rabbinic studies. Its students perished during World War II.

Naphtali Tzevi Judah Berlin, principal of Volozhin yeshivah 1853–92.

VOLTERRA, MESHULLAM (BONAIUTO), DA (15th cent.): Traveler. Son of the Florentine loan-banker Menahem (Manoello) da V., he went to Palestine via Naples, Rhodes, and Egypt in 1481 in fulfillment of a vow, returning via Cyprus, Rhodes, and Greece. His graphic Hebrew account of the journey is a valuable historical source.

VOLTERRA, VITO (1860–1940): Italian physicist, mathematician, and senator; professor at Turin and Rome. His functional calculus has been termed the most important advance in modern mathematical science.

VOLYNOV, BORIS (1934–): Soviet cosmonaut; Commander of the spaceship Soyuz 5 which participated in the first space link-up in 1969 and went into space again in 1976 in Soyuz 21. Born in Siberia, Volynov graduated from the Volgogrod pilot school in 1956 and was in the Soviet air force academy of aviation engineering.

VORONOFF, SERGE (1866–1951): Russian surgeon and physiologist. Working in France, he developed gland transplantation and thus increased the growth of wool on sheep. He also stimulated sex activity by transplanting glands of apes to human beings, claiming that human life could thus be increased to 140 years.

VOSKHOD (Russ. "Dawn"): Jewish monthly journal in Russian, appearing at St. Petersburg 1881–1906 under the editorship of A. Landau (1888–98) and S. Gruzenberg (1898–1906). Until 1904, it was the sole

Russian-Jewish periodical in the Russian language; it fought for Jewish equality of rights, was skeptical regarding Jewish emigration from the country, and rejected Zionism. A weekly *New V.* appeared 1908–10 in the spirit of its predecessor.

VOWELS see **VOCALIZATION**

VOWS: Religious obligations undertaken by an individual voluntarily as additions to the duties imposed on him by the Torah. In talmudic law there are two basic types: (1) a promise to provide Temple sacrifices or to make gifts of property to the Temple or to charity; (2) a resolve not to eat specified food or not to derive any benefit from specified property. V. are binding even if no special formula or Divine name is used. They should be avoided altogether unless the intention is to curb greed or immoderation that the votary is unable to control in any other way; hence pious Jews add the Hebrew phrase *beli neder* ("without a vow") when they express a future intention. If a Jew finds a vow of the second type difficult to fulfill, the rabbis say he should consult a scholar who will, if possible, find some way to absolve him. The v. of children have no validity. Scripture has given a hausband the power to annul his wife's v. (and a father a limited power to annul those of his daughter) when he hears of them (Num. 30:4 ff.).

VOZROZHDENIE (Russ. "Rebirth"): Russian Jewish socialist party, existing 1903–5; precursor of the SEYMISTS. It advocated an autonomous Jewish culture in the Diaspora.

VULGATE: A Latin translation of the Bible made in Palestine in 390–405 by the Church Father JEROME. His initial intention, at the command of Pope Damasus, was to revise the Old Latin version, but after going to Palestine (385) he realized the necessity of basing himself on the Hebrew original. Jerome learnt Hebrew and utilized the assistance of Jewish scholars. The V. became the Bible of the Catholic Church until the 1940's, when it was replaced in official use by a new Latin version from the Hebrew.

WADI KUMRAN see **DEAD SEA SCROLLS; KUMRAN**

*WAGENSEIL, JOHANN CHRISTOPH (1633–1705): German Hebraist; from 1667, professor at Altdorf. He published a number of Latin works pronouncedly anti-Jewish in tone, on various aspects of Hebrew studies, in which he showed considerable competence. The most important is his collection of Jewish polemical writings (with the original Hebrew texts, some of them from mss) *Tela Ignea Satanae* (1681).

WAHL, SAUL (1541–1617): Financier. His father, Samuel Judah ben Abraham (Katzenellenbogen) was rabbi at Venice and then Padua. W. became court-agent to Sigismund III in 1589. He led the Jewish community and used his influence in behalf of his coreligionists in Poland and Lithuania, obtaining for the latter rights of autonomous jurisdiction. An 18th cent. legend, devoid of historical foundation, recounted that during an interregnum he was chosen king of Poland for a day. His son *MEIR W.* (or Katzenelbogen; 17th cent.) was a noted talmudist who in 1623, founded the COUNCIL OF LITHUANIA.

WAILING WALL see **WESTERN WALL**

WAKSMAN, SELMAN ABRAHAM (1888–1973): US microbiologist. He taught at Rutgers Univ. from 1925, and headed its Institute of Microbiology since 1949. In 1944, he isolated streptomycin and thereafter, other antibiotics. He was awarded a Nobel Prize in 1952.

WALD, GEORGE (1906–): US scientist. Born in New York, he has been professor of biology at Harvard since 1948. An authority on the biochemistry of perception, he shared the 1967 Nobel Prize for medicine. Among his discoveries was the presence of Vitamin A in the human eye. W. has often been identified with radical causes.

WALD, LILLIAN D. (1867–1940): US social worker. In 1893, she founded the Henry Street Settlement in New York and was its director until 1933. She organized the first non-sectarian public health nursing system, and the first public school nursing system, and also pioneered in the movement to establish playgrounds in the US.

WALDMAN, MORRIS DAVID (1879–1963): US communal worker. He was director of the GALVESTON Movement 1906–8, and secretary of the American Jewish Committee 1928–43.

WALES: Isolated Jews — though no communities — were to be found in the 13th cent. in those parts of W. under English influence (Chepstow, Caerleon) though the charters of the new N Welsh boroughs explicitly excluded Jews. German Jews settled in Swansea from 1731–41, and its community may be dated from 1768. Later, communities were founded in mining centers in S Wales such as Cardiff (1840), Merthyr Tydfil (1848), Pontypridd (1867), Tredegar (1873), etc. Several others were set up by Russian refugees after 1882. They filled a useful economic function, but during the strikes of 1911, anti-Jewish rioting developed. In recent years there has been considerable shrinking of the smaller communities, which have in some cases been abandoned, and Cardiff, with 2,500 Jews, now contains three-quarters of the total Jewish population.

WALEY: English family, legendarily descended (in the female line) from Saul Wahl. (1) *ARTHUR DAVID W.* (formerly Schloss; 1889–1966): Orientalist. Formerly assistant keeper in the British Museum, he was an expert on oriental art and literature, known especially for his delicate translations from the Chinese. (2) *JACOB W.* (1819–1873): Professor of political economy at University College, London. Active in Jewish communal work, he was the first president of the Anglo-Jewish Association (1871–3).

WALEY COHEN see **COHEN**

WALLACH, OTTO (1847–1931): German chemist and Nobel Prize winner who specialized in aniline dyes. He was professor at Göttingen and was responsible for pioneer work in organic chemistry.

*WALLENBERG, RAOUL (1912 – c. 1947): Swedish diplomat. During World War II he was stationed in Hungary where he was instrumental in saving thousands of Jewish lives. After the Russians conquered Budapest he was taken away by them and never heard of again.

WALSTON (WALDSTEIN), SIR CHARLES (1856–1927): Archeologist and author. Of American birth, he taught archeology at Cambridge 1880–1911.

Herman Goering (*seated*) on trial for war crimes, Nuremberg 1946.

W., who was baptized, also directed the American Archeological School in Athens 1889–96, supervising the excavations of ancient Plataea, the "Tomb of Aristotle" at Eretria, and the Heraion at Argos.

WALTER, BRUNO (1876–1962): Conductor. After conducting in various German opera-houses, he became director of the State Opera in Vienna in 1935. In 1939, he went to the US and conducted many orchestras, including the New York Philharmonic and the Metropolitan Opera. W. wrote on the philosophy of music, Gustav Mahler, etc. He left Judaism.

WANDERING JEW: Central figure of a medieval Christian legend. This tells of a Jerusalem cobbler called Ahasuerus who was condemned to wander eternally for taunting Jesus on his journey to the crucifixion. The legend first appears in the 13th cent. in England. The concept has entered Christian literature (Goethe, Sue, Byron, etc.) but there is no trace in older Jewish literature. David PINSKI wrote a drama *The Wandering Jew* in which he gave the term a Jewish interpretation and depicted the Jew wandering from country to country in search of the Messiah.

WAR see **ARMED FORCES**

WAR CRIMINALS: During World War II, the Allied Powers issued a declaration (Moscow, Nov. 21, 1943) that those Germans responsible for atrocities and massacres would be sent back to the countries in which the abominations had occurred in order to be judged and punished. After the surrender of Germany, the allies, by an agreement in London (Aug. 1945), set up an International Military Tribunal for the trial of the major war criminals whose offenses

had no particular geographical location. Crimes against the Jews were among the specific charges brought against many of the 24 heads of the Nazi government and armed forces, including GOERING, Ribbentrop, STREICHER, and FRANK, who were tried at Nuremberg. Judgment was given on Oct. 1, 1946, and eleven were sentenced to death; three were acquitted by a majority, the Soviet judge dissenting. The Tribunal found also that Nazi organizations, like the SS and SA, were criminal, and membership was a ground for trial before national and military or occupation courts. Besides the International Military Tribunal, the Control Council set up national military courts in the occupied zones. The US Court at Nuremberg tried, between 1946 and 1949, 12 groups of criminals for war crimes and crimes against humanity, including 22 members of the *Einsatzgruppen* which carried out the extermination of Jews. Of the accused, 4 were executed. In the British Zone, military courts were set up by royal warrants for the trial of war criminals, including members of the staff of the Bergen-Belsen concentration camp. In many other countries, national and military courts tried and convicted subjects of the Axis for actions committed in those countries, including atrocities against the Jews.

WAR OF INDEPENDENCE, ISRAEL: War in Palestine 1947–9. After the UN resolution of Nov. 29, 1947, to partition the country into Jewish and Arab states with Jerusalem as a *corpus separatum*, Palestinian Arabs (including veterans of the 1936–9 disturbances, members of Arab youth organizations, and police) initiated hostilities against the Jewish

Review of troops during Israel War of Independence.

Bombardment of Jerusalem by Arab Legion.

Artillery in the Negev.

Israel Forces in Sinai for the first time.

population. They were soon joined by volunteers from neighboring Arab states. Jewish forces were organized mostly in the HAGANAH (underground militia) with a fulltime component of about 4,000, mostly members of the PALMAH. The early attacks resembled the disturbances of 1936–9, the Haganah restricting itself to defense of settlements and communications and limited retaliation. Early in 1948, the first attack on a Jewish village (Tirat Tzevi) occurred which proved unsuccessful. In the cities, the Arabs employed terrorist methods. During March, they concentrated on roads and on towns with a mixed population. The Jerusalem-Tel Aviv road was fiercely attacked and eventually, Jewish Jerusalem was cut off, except for communication by a few light aeroplanes. Meanwhile, the Jews had received a first consignment of arms from Czechoslovakia and the road to Jerusalem was eventually reopened. A volunteer "Arab Liberation Army" led by the Syrian Fawzi el Kawukji failed in its attack on Mishmar ha-Emek in the Jezreel Valley, while a battalion of volunteers from Jebel Druze was routed when attempting to attack Ramat Yohanan near Haifa. In April, the Haganah counter-attacked, overrunning Tiberias, opening the road to Galilee, and capturing Haifa and the Katamon suburb in Jerusalem. Early in May, Safed and the S Huleh district came into Jewish hands, together with Acre and most of W Galilee. Internal Arab resistance was thus ended. But on May 15, with the termination of the Mandate, the states of the Arab League (armies from Jordan, Syria, Lebanon, Iraq, Egypt, and a token force from Saudi Arabia) invaded the country. The Arab Legion overran the Etzion bloc of settlements S of Jerusalem, two Jewish settlements N of the city, as well as the Sheikh Jarrah district of the city and the Jewish quarter of the Old City; the new city of Jerusalem was now under siege. However, Arab attempts to reach the center of the New City failed, largely because of the successful resistance of the outlying settlement of Ramat Rahel and the Notre Dame compound. The siege was eventually circumvented by the secret construction of a road ("Burma Road") for the transport of food and ammunition from the Jewish-held Plain of Aijalon. The Egyptians, attacking through the Negev, at first advanced rapidly, occupying Gaza and Beersheba, but were held back by a chain of Jewish settlements (Kephar Darom, Nirim, Beerot Yitzhak, and Negbah) and at Ashdod, 21 m. S of Tel Aviv. Plans for an Egyptian landing in the vicinity of Tel Aviv were foiled by the hastily-improvised Israel navy cooperating with the fledgling air force, and the Egyptians thereupon limited their objective to an unsuccessful endeavor to isolate the Negev. The main Syrian attacks S of the Sea of Galilee were checked at Deganyah after an initial advance and driven back. Further N, however, the Syrians captured

Mishmar ha-Yarden. Iraqi attacks in the N sector were met by stiff Israel opposition and were not pressed. The Lebanese entered Galilee but made little headway. On June 11, a general truce came into effect which ended on July 8. During this time, a fundamental change had occurred in the balance of forces. The newly-established Israel Defense Army now cleared Lower Galilee and captured Nazareth, took Lydda and Ramleh in the central sector, widened the Jerusalem corridor (but failed to capture Latrun despite repeated attempts), and continued to hold the Egyptians in the S. The UN Security Council enforced a second cease-fire on July 19. This lasted until October when, in a week of heavy fighting, Beersheba was taken, the Egyptians driven back, and an Egyptian brigade surrounded at Faluja. In the N Kawukji unsuccessfully attacked the settlement of Manara; Israel forces, in 2½ days, cleared Upper Galilee and captured villages inside the Lebanon. Fighting in the Negev was resumed in Dec. when the Egyptian front collapsed and Israel forces occupied almost the entire Negev, with the exception of the GAZA STRIP; they also entered the Sinai peninsula, but a British ultimatum led to the withdrawal of Israel forces from Egyptian territory. The Egyptians then agreed to discuss armistice terms and an agreement was signed at Rhodes in Feb., 1949 (see RHODES AGREEMENTS). Subsequently, the Israel army occupied Elath at the S tip of the Negev after its evacuation by the Arab Legion. In the ensuing months, separate armistice agreements were signed with Jordan, the Lebanon, and Syria; no agreement was, however, signed with Iraq or Saudi Arabia.

WAR SCROLL: One of the DEAD SEA SCROLLS, also named "The War of the Sons of Light against the Sons of Darkness."

WARBURG: German family with branches in Scandinavia, England, and the US. The European family included *ABY W.* (1866–1929): German art historian. He sought to establish the connections between art and other cultural manifestations of each period. He founded the W. Library at Hamburg to study the classical tradition in European civilization, especially in the field of art. Transferred to England after 1933, it is now—as the W. Institute—part of the Univ. of London. *EMIL W.* (1846–1931): German physicist. He was professor at Berlin from 1905 and headed the Technical Physical Institute at Charlottenburg. He was baptized. *KARL JONAH W.* (1852–1918): Swedish historian of literature. He was professor at Gothenburg from 1891 and Stockholm from 1906. W. sat in the Swedish parliament 1905–8. *MAX W.* (1867–1946): German banker. He was a German delegate to the Versailles Peace Conference and was active in Jewish affairs. From 1939, he resided in the US. *OTTO W.* (1859–1938): Botanist and Zionist. A native of Germany, he studied tropical

Otto Warburg.

flora, traveling extensively in S and E Asia in connection with his researches. From 1892, he was professor in Berlin. He was an active Zionist, leading the Practical Zionist fraction, and in 1908, was instrumental in founding the Palestine Office at Jaffa. W. was president of the World Zionist Organization 1911–20. From 1920 he headed the Jewish Agency's experimental station at Tel Aviv (later Reḥovot), and was professor at the Hebrew Univ. *OTTO HEINRICH W.* (1883–1970): German physiologist; son of Emil. Director of the Kaiser Wilhelm Institute for Physiology at Dahlem, Berlin, he made important discoveries in the fields of respiration and fermentation and studied the metabolism of malignant tumors. W., who was baptized, received a Nobel Prize in 1931. Several members of the W. family settled in the US. *PAUL MORITZ W.* (1868–1932), in the US from 1902, was a member of the Federal Reserve Board during President Wilson's administration (later, of the Board's Advisory Council). His son, *JAMES PAUL W.* (1896–1969) wrote books on economics and foreign policy. *FELIX M. W.* (1871–1937), brother of Paul M. W., also engaged in banking, but became known primarily for his leadership in the Jewish community and his philanthropy. He was chairman of the American Joint Distribution Committee 1914–32, one of the founders of the Palestine Economic Corporation, and chairman of the administrative committee of the enlarged Jewish Agency when it was formed in 1929. Beneficiaries of his generosity included the Hebrew Union College, the Jewish Theological Seminary, and various other Jewish and non-Jewish educational institutions. His son, *EDWARD MORTIMER MORRIS W.* (1908–) was chairman of the American Joint Distribution Committee from 1946, and has been a leading figure in the United Jewish Appeal since 1951.

WARNER (originally **EICHELBAUM**): The four W. brothers who formed a motion picture producing company of that name were *HARRY MORRIS W.* (1881–1958), *ALBERT W.* (1883–1967), *SAMUEL L. W.* (1887–1927) and *JACK LEMAND W.* (1892–). Their company pioneered in the development of full-length motion pictures, and later in talking pictures and color films.

WARSAW: Capital of POLAND. Jews lived there in the 15th cent., were persecuted in 1454 as a result of CAPISTRANO's incitement, and expelled in 1483. A number of families resided there in the 18th cent. (initially on payment of bribes). The number grew during the early 19th cent. despite continued wrangling over their rights, which were granted to them in full in 1862. They assisted the city's economic development, their success in this sphere intensifying the already latent anti-Semitism of the non-Jewish inhabitants. After World War I, when Poland received independence, although cultural life was rich and flourishing, the economic situation of the Jews con-

Detail from monument to fighters of Warsaw Ghetto Revolt
(Sculptor: Nathan Rappaport).

tinued to deteriorate. From the early 20th cent., W. was a center of Hebrew and Yiddish culture and scholarship. Many Jewish journals were published there (83 in 1930) and there was much activity in the fields of Jewish drama, music, and art. W. Jews also made their contribution to general Polish culture. In 1939, there were 360,000 Jews in W. supporting several school networks, an institute of Jewish Studies, and many religious institutions. In Oct. 1940, the occupying Germans established a crowded ghetto in which they concentrated the Jews of W. as well as deportees from other parts of Poland. Their numbers reached half-a-million. Anti-Jewish legislation was instituted with the German occupation and enforced through the JUDENRAT, the nominally-autonomous Jewish organization. The inhuman living conditions and starvation diet led to a high death rate, claiming 85,000 victims by July 1942. Over 300,000 persons were sent to Treblinka extermination camp, July-Sept. 1942. Jewish resistance appearing at the renewed expulsions of Jan. 1943 was crushed and 70,000 inhabitants killed and captured during the epic revolt of April 19–May 16, 1943 when armed Jews sold their lives dearly in a tenacious house-to-house struggle against German troops using tanks and artillery. Some of the surviving fighters later assisted the Poles in their ill-fated revolt of August 1, 1944 when many Jews perished. The ghetto itself was demolished. After the war, some Jews returned to W. and in 1973, 2,000 Jews were living there.

WASHINGTON: US state. Jewish settlement dates from the 1850's. Jews from Portland, Oregon, and Vancouver went to SEATTLE, Port Townsend, Olympia, and Walla Walla. Edward S. Solomon became governor of W. in 1870. Jews settled in Spokane in the early 1870's. In the next two decades, communities were established in Tacoma, Bellingham, and Everett. The INDUSTRIAL REMOVAL OFFICE settled 967 Jews in 13 cities and towns — chiefly Seattle and Spokane — in the decade following 1909. Of the 15,890 Jews in W. in 1973, 13,000 lived in Seattle, 700 in Tacoma, and 800 in Spokane.

WASHINGTON: Capital of the US. Its Jewish settlement dates from the 1830's. A number of Jewish immigrants from Bavaria and Hungary arrived in the late 1840's, and a congregation was organized in 1852. President Grant and his Cabinet were present at the dedication of W.'s second synagogue in 1878. President McKinley and his cabinet participated in 1897 in the cornerstone-laying ceremony for a new building for the city's first synagogue established in 1863. Many Jewish business and professional men went to W. in the period after the Civil War. The Jewish population increased rapidly in the 20th cent., and in 1973, numbered 112,500 (Greater W.). The Jewish Community Council was founded in 1938 and sponsors a Board of Jewish Education.

WASSERMANN, AUGUST VON (1866–1925): German biologist and bacteriologist. He was director of the Kaiser Wilhelm Institute for Experimental Therapy in Berlin and professor at Berlin Univ. A distinguished research worker, his most important discovery was the "Wassermann reaction" for diagnosing syphilis. He conducted other important bacteriological and serological investigations, mainly in the field of the hereditary transference of infectious diseases, antitoxic sera, and bacteria.

WASSERMANN, JAKOB (1873–1934): German novelist. At first he negated Jewish nationalism and hoped that the symbiosis of German and Jew was possible on a high level; his autobiography *My Life as a German and Jew*, however, evidences his disillusionment. His chief works include *The Jews of Zirndorf*, *Caspar Hauser*, *The Goose Man*, and *The Maurizius Case*.

WASSERMAN, OSCAR (1869–1934): German banker and community leader. Director of the Disconto-Gesellschaft, he was deprived of this position as well as of membership in the General Council of the Reichsbank by the Nazis in 1933. Active in Jewish affairs, W. was president of the KEREN HA-YESOD in Germany.

WATER-DRAWING, FESTIVAL OF THE (Heb. *simḥat bet ha-shoevah*): Festival of water-libation observed at the end of the first day of the Feast of Tabernacles. Advocated by the Pharisees, it was not acknowledged by the Sadducees since it had no authority in the Pentateuch, but the populace nevertheless observed it enthusiastically. The ceremonies are elaborately described in the Mishnah (*Sukkah* 5). It fell into abeyance with the destruction of the Temple but has been revived in an altered form in modern Israel.

WATERBURY: City in Connecticut, US. Jewish immigrants from Germany settled there in the 1840's, and the community was swollen by arrivals from E Europe in the late 1880's. Temple Israel (Reform) was established in 1870. Jewish pop. (1973): 2,600, with 3 synagogues. The Jewish Federation of W. was formed in 1938.

WAXMAN, MEYER (1887–1969): Scholar. Born in Russia, he went to the US in 1905. He served as a rabbi and in 1917, founded the *Mizraḥi* Teachers' Institute. From 1925, he was professor at the Hebrew Theological College, Chicago. His major work is a 5-volume *History of Jewish Literature*.

WEBER, MAX (1881–1961): Painter. Born in Russia, he went to the US in 1909. His one-man exhibition in 1911 was bitterly attacked for its "modernism." W. was in turn formist, cubist, and expressionist. Eventually, he received full recognition for his talent, and his works hang in many major museums and galleries.

WEDDING see **MARRIAGE**

WEEKS, FEAST OF see **SHAVUOT**

WEICHMANN, HERBERT (1896–): German public figure. W. was born in Saxony and became a high court judge in Breslau before joining the Prussian ministry of Justice in Berlin. When Hitler came to power, he went to France and in 1941 reached the US. He returned to Germany in 1948 settling in Hamburg where he was active in local politics, being elected lord mayor (burgomeister) in 1965. A Social Democrat representative in the Bundesrat, he became its president.

WEIGHTS AND MEASURES: 1. *Weights.* Excavations have brought to light a number of SHEKEL weights. These differ in weight — by wear, or because of local variations — but average c. 3/8 oz. There are also examples of the *pim* (c. $\frac{1}{4}$ oz.) and *netzeph* (c. 3/10 oz.). The Bible mentions: *gerah* = 1/20 *shekel*, *beka* = $\frac{1}{2}$ *shekel*, *pim* = 2/3 *shekel*, maneh = 50 *shekalim*, *kikkar* (talent) = 3,000 *shekalim* (c. 76 lbs.). In the Talmudic Period, the biblical w. were equated with standard w. of the time. For sacred purposes "holy shekel" was equated with the Tyrian unit (nearly $\frac{1}{2}$ oz.). The *maneh* was equivalent to the Roman pound. Other w. (*denarius, unkiah*, etc.) were taken over from outside systems.

2. *Measures of length.* There were two systems, based upon the ordinary *ammah* (cubit) = 45.8 cm. (18.1 in.) and the large *ammah* = 52.5 cm. (20.8 in.) respectively. The ordinary *ammah* was divided into: *zeret* "span" = $\frac{1}{2}$ *ammah*; *tephah* or *tophah* ("handbreadth") = 1/6 *ammah*; *etzba* "finger" = 1/24 *ammah*. In talmudic times the main unit was the *tephah*, established at 9.3 cm. (3.7 in.); of the cubit there were many local varieties. The mile (*mil*) of 1,255 yards was Roman.

3. *Hollow measure.* There were many such measures, the more important being the *ephah* (bath) = 10.7 gallons, *seah* = 1/3 *ephah*, hin = 1/6 *ephah*; the *homer* "ass-load" = 10 *ephah*, the *omer* = 1/100 *homer* (1/10 *ephah*), the *kav* = 1/3 *hin*, and the *log* = 1.4 *kav* (a little less than a pint). In talmudic times, the unit was the *betzah* "egg", the *log* being 6 eggs, the *kav* 24. *Ephah*, *hin*, and *kav* are Egyptian words.

4. For ritual purposes, the measures "olive-sized" (= $\frac{1}{2}$ "egg") and "egg-sized" are used. The "egg" is reckoned by many as equal to two normal eggs. The *revi'it* ("quarter") = $1\frac{1}{2}$ "eggs". The *tephah* is reckoned as equal to four times the width of an average man's thumb.

5. In modern Israel, the metric weights and measures (kilo, gram, meter, centimeter, cubic meter, liter) are employed. For land-measure, the *dunam* = 1,000 sq. meters (about $\frac{1}{4}$ acre) is used.

WEIL, GOTTHOLD (1882–1960): Orientalist and librarian of German origin. From 1918, W. was director of the Oriental Department of the Berlin State Library which he founded. He taught post-biblical Jewish history and literature at Berlin Univ. 1912–31 (professor, 1920) and was professor of Semitic languages at the Univ. of Frankfort-on-Main, 1931–33. He became director of the National and Hebrew University Library at Jerusalem in 1935. An authority on Arabic and Turkish he wrote on these subjects and lectured at the Hebrew Univ.

WEIL, GUSTAV (1808–1889): German orientalist. Acquiring a thorough knowledge of Persian and Turkish while teaching French in Cairo, W. taught at Heidelberg from 1835 (professor, 1861). He was the first to investigate Jewish elements in the Koran. W. wrote on Moslem history and Arabic literature and translated the *Arabian Nights* into German.

WEIL, SIMONE (1909–1943): French social and religious thinker. She studied philosophy and became a teacher. As a culmination of her sympathy with the workers, she herself lived the life of an industrial laborer, and this experience profoundly affected her. She fled from the Germans to France in 1940 and afterwards to England where she wrote *L'Enracinement*, a program for the regeneration of France. In the meantime, "waiting for God" had become the very center of her experience of suffering, her realistic thought, and her profound insight. She hated Judaism, and sharply criticized the Church's teachings too in spite of her affinity in life and thought with Catholicism.

WEILL, KURT (1900–1950): Composer. After writing symphonic and chamber music, he turned to the stage and had a great success with his *Dreigroschenoper* (text by Berthold Brecht) in Berlin. He left his native Germany in 1933 and settled in 1935 in the US where he wrote scores for plays and films (e.g. *Lady in the Dark, Lost in the Stars*).

WEINBERG, JACOB (1879–1956): US composer. He toured Russia and European countries as a pianist, lived in Palestine 1922–7, and settled in the US in 1928. His compositions include the Hebrew folk-opera *The Pioneers, The Gettysburg Address* for chorus and orchestra, *The Dead Sea Scrolls* for baritone and organ, as well as liturgical settings, chamber music, etc.

WEINBERGER, JAROMIR (1896–1967): US composer. Born in Czechoslovakia, he settled in the US in 1939. He wrote instrumental works (e.g. *Variations on Under the Spreading Chestnut Tree*), operas (notably *Schwanda the Bagpiper*), and music on biblical motifs.

WEINER, LAZAR (1897–): US composer. Born in Russia, he went to the US in 1914. His works include a setting of the Friday Evening Service and other liturgical compositions.

WEININGER, OTTO (1880–1903): Austrian philosopher. He was baptized in 1902, and the following year committed suicide shortly after the publication of his *Sex and Character*.

WEINREICH, MAX (1894–1969): Scholar. A founder of YIVO, he was its research director in Vilna from 1925, and in New York from 1939, and edited many of its publications. He pioneered primarily in Yiddish linguistics, folklore, and literary history but also contributed studies in psychology, pedagogy, and sociology. From 1947 W. was professor at City College, New York. His son *URIEL W.* (1926–1967) was also a distinguished scholar of the Yiddish language who taught at Columbia Univ. from 1951 and published many studies in Yiddish linguistics.

WEINRYB, BERNARD DOV (1900–): Educator. Born in Poland, he settled in the US in 1940. W. has taught Jewish history and economics at Columbia and Yeshiva Univs. and Dropsie College. He has written prolifically on Jewish life and history.

WEISGAL, MEYER WOLF (1894–): Zionist. He went to the US from Poland in 1905, and was secretary of the Zionist Organization of America, 1921–30, during which time he edited *The New Palestine*. Closely associated with Chaim Weizmann, he settled in Israel in 1949 as chairman of the executive council of the Weizmann Institute of Science of which he was president 1966–9 and chancellor, 1970.

WEISS, ERICH (Harry Houdini; 1874–1926): US entertainer. The son of a rabbi, he specialized in magic, acrobatics, etc. attaining a legendary reputation.

WEISS, ISAAC HIRSCH (1815–1905): Talmudic scholar and historian. A native of Moravia, he received a traditional education and then devoted himself to the scientific study of talmudic literature. From 1861, he lectured at the Vienna *Bet ha-Midrash*. He published editions of the *Siphra* and *Mekhilta*. His chief work was the 5-volume *Dor Dor ve-Doreshav* (1871–91), a history of the development of the Oral Law down to the Middle Ages. Although criticized by the Orthodox for its Haskalah tendencies, it exerted a great influence on E European Jewish youth, for whom it represented the first critical approach to talmudic literature.

WEISS, PETER (1916–): German playwright. W., who had a Jewish father, lived outside Germany during the Nazi period. After the war he became one of the outstanding German dramatists, his plays including...*Marat*...*Sade* and a drama *The Investigation* based on the Auschwitz trial.

WEIZEL (WEISEL), NAPHTALI HERZ see **WESSELY**

WEIZMANN, CHAIM (1874–1952): Chemist, Zionist leader, and first president of the state of Israel. Born at Motel, near Pinsk, he pursued his chemical studies at German and Swiss universities and in 1904, was appointed lecturer in biological chemistry at Manchester. In 1916, he became director of the British Admiralty Chemical Laboratories. W. grew up in an atmosphere of *Ḥibbat Zion* and was deeply influenced by Haskalah. He was early associated

Chaim Weizmann

with Herzl's movement, joining the group led by Ussishkin and the DEMOCRATIC FRACTION. W. criticized Herzl's exclusively diplomatic policy, advocating the democratization of the Zionist Organization and emphasizing the movement's cultural and popular content. In 1902, jointly with Berthold Feiwel, he proposed the foundation of a Hebrew university and, opposing the UGANDA program (1903), became a supporter of synthetic Zionism, i.e., the combination of political, colonizational, and cultural activity, which he propounded in 1907. As a result of the fragmentation of the movement during World War I, W. moved into the political leadership and became chairman of the London committee. His personality was largely responsible for winning the support of A. J. Balfour, Lloyd George, C. P. Scott, H. L. Brailsford and others, and in securing the cooperation in the US of Justice Brandeis. In 1917, he succeeded in obtaining the BALFOUR DECLARATION. W. became chairman of the Zionist Commission which went to Palestine in 1918 to prepare the implementation of the National Home; the same year he laid the cornerstone of the Hebrew Univ. in Jerusalem and obtained an agreement with the emir Feisal. In 1919, together with Ussishkin and Sokolow, he represented the Zionist movement at the Peace Conference and convened the London Zionist Conference in 1920 to mobilize resources for constructive work in Palestine. This conference resulted in the

A building of the Weizmann Institute of Science.

foundation of the *Keren ha-Yesod* and also in W.'s election as president of the WORLD ZIONIST ORGANIZATION. In 1919, he became chairman of the newly extended JEWISH AGENCY but the Arab riots of that year, the growing anti-Zionist policy of Britain, and the reaction in the Zionist movement led to the collapse of the extended Agency and the replacement of W. as president of the World Zionist Organization in 1931. He remained active in the movement, and was re-elected in 1935, continuing to base his policy on faith in Britain and leading Zionist support for the British war effort during World War II. After the war, with the development of the activist struggle with Britain, he became progressively at variance with influential elements in the movement and in 1946, disillusioned by the British Labor government's refusal to honor its pre-election pledges, quit the post of president of the world organization. He retired to Reḥovot in Palestine to work at the WEIZMANN INSTITUTE which he had helped to form. On the establishment of the state of Israel in 1948, he was elected its first president but his health was failing and he took little active part in subsequent developments. W. was a master diplomat and a man of vision, deeply rooted in the Jewish environment, an unimpassioned but impressive orator, and a keen debater. As a scientist he had an international reputation for his discoveries in organic chemistry relating to the fermentation of acetone-butyl, the manufacture of dyes and cancer-producing substances, and the production of synthetic rubber from organic substances and of digestible proteins from vegetable matter. Besides numerous political writings, he published an autobiography *Trial and Error*. He is buried at Reḥovot where a national project Yad Chaim Weizmann has been erected in his memory.

WEIZMANN, EZER (1924–): Israel soldier; nephew of Chaim WEIZMANN. A pilot in the R.A.F. in World War II, he was one of the first pilots in Israel's air force. In 1958, he was appointed its commander and effected its change to jet planes. In 1966 he was appointed chief of operations of the Israel general staff. On leaving the army he joined the Gaḥal party and was minister of transport, 1969–70.

WEIZMANN INSTITUTE OF SCIENCE: Research institute at Reḥovot, Israel. Dedicated in 1949, it is an extension of the Daniel Sieff Research Institute, which opened in 1934 under the direction of Chaim Weizmann. The Institute engages in fundamental and applied research in the exact sciences. It comprises units for applied mathematics, nuclear physics, electronics, isotope research, polymer research, biophysics, X-ray crystallography, organic chemistry, and experimental biology, biological ultrastructure, cell biology, biochemistry, spectroscopy, and plant genetics; comprehensive scientific libraries, and precision instrument and glass-blowing workshops. There are 400 scientists and another 1,000 members of the administrative and technical staffs. The Graduate School has a student body of 500. Yad Chaim Weizmann, which includes the W. I. and Dr. Weizmann's residence and grave, was established in 1952 as a memorial foundation to develop cultural and scientific projects. Abba EBAN was appointed president in 1958, Meir WEISGAL in 1966 and Albert I. SABIN in 1969, Israel Dostrovsky in 1971 and Michael Sela in 1975. A number of international conferences have been held under the auspices of the Institute to examine the problems of developing nations.

WELENSKY, SIR ROY (1907–): Rhodesian statesman. Of mixed parentage, but a professing Jew, he began his career as an engine-driver and formed the N Rhodesian Labor Party in 1941, being elected to parliament as its leader. He became deputy-premier of the Central African Federation at its inauguration in 1953, and premier from 1956 until the break-up of the Federation in 1963.

WELLESZ, EGON (1895–1974): Musicologist and composer. Born in Vienna and later baptized, he taught at Oxford from 1938. He showed the affinity of early Church chant with ancient Jewish cantillation.

*WELLHAUSEN, JULIUS (1844–1918): German orientalist and Bible scholar. He founded a trend in extreme biblical criticism which commanded wide support until more conservative tendencies prevailed. He propounded the documentary theory of the Hexateuch (i.e., the Pentateuch and Joshua) and regarded pre-exilic Judaism as a religion traceable by the study of early Semitic religions.

WELLINGTON: Capital of NEW ZEALAND. The Jewish community was founded under the authority of the British chief rabbi in 1843. The Jewish population is (1973) 2,000.

WELT, DIE (Ger. "The World"): Journal of the World Zionist Organization 1897–1914. Founded and originally edited by Herzl, it appeared at Vienna 1897–1905, Cologne 1906–11, and Berlin 1911–4.

WENGEROFF, PAULINE W. (1833–1916): Authoress, whose epic autobiography conveys an authentic picture of Russian Jewish life in the mid-19th cent. She had Zionist sympathies and was grieved by the conversion of her children who included *SEMYON W.* (1855–1920), literary critic and historian of Russian literature, and *ZINAIDA W.* (1867–1941), literary critic and translator into Russian.

WERFEL, FRANZ (1890–1945): Author. He was born in Prague and served in the Austrian Army 1914–8. W. was one of the outstanding lyric poets of the German expressionist movement and wrote plays including *Goat Song, Juarez and Maximilian, The Eternal Road* (a Jewish allegory), and *Jacobowski and the Colonel.* His best-known novels were the *Forty Days of Musa Dagh* and *The Song of Bernadette.* From 1940, W. lived in the US.

WERNER, ERIC (1901–): Musicologist. Born in Vienna, he taught in Germany and from 1939 at the Hebrew Union College, Cincinnati. Since 1951, he has also headed the faculty of the School of Sacred Music in New York. W. has worked on early Christian, medieval, and renaissance music and on the relationship between ancient Greek and Hebrew hymnology and musical theories.

WERTHEIMER: (1) *JOSEPH VON W.* (1800–1887): Austrian educator and author. Although a businessman, W. studied educational problems and established the first kindergarten in Vienna (1830). He also founded a society for developing handicrafts among the Jews (1840), a children's home (1843), and a society for the care of orphans (1860). To support the struggle for equal rights, he wrote comprehensive accounts of the Jews in Austria. He published the *Jahrbuch der Israeliten* (1854–65) and was the author of popular plays. (2) *SAMSON W.* (1658–1724): Financier. Born in Worms, he went to Vienna in 1684 to join the bank of his uncle Samuel OPPENHEIMER and soon became court banker. He leased royal revenues, was one of the chief purveyors to the imperial forces, and together with his son Wolf lent large sums to the emperor. In 1719, Carl VI appointed him chief rabbi of Hungary with judicial authority. He used his connections to assist Jewish communities and obtained an order from the emperor Leopold prohibiting the publication of Eisenmenger's anti-Jewish work *Entdecktes Judentum.* W. established a fund to assist paupers in Palestine, which existed until 1914. Some of his Sabbath homilies have been preserved.

WERTHEIMER, MAX (1880–1943): Psychologist. He taught in Germany until 1933 and then went to New York where he taught at the New School for Social Research. He was a founder of the Gestalt theory of psychology.

WESKER, ARNOLD (1932–): British dramatist. His plays have included *Chicken Soup with Barley, Roots,* and *Chips with Everything.*

WESSELY, NAPHTALI HERZ (1725–1805): German Hebrew author and Haskalah pioneer. His first work investigated Hebrew roots and synonyms. Next, he published a commentary on *Avot* and an annotated Hebrew translation of the *Wisdom of Solomon.* W. participated in Mendelssohn's Pentateuch commentary, contributing the volume on Leviticus. His notes on Genesis have been only partly published. These biblical commentaries are conservative in spirit and devote considerable space to determining the meaning of Hebrew roots. In *Divre Shalom ve-Emet* ("Words of Peace and Truth"), written under the influence of Joseph II's Edict of Tolerance, he suggested an educational program for Jewish youths in the spirit of Haskalah, extending also to secular subjects; this aroused great opposition and resulted in a long and widespread controversy. In his old age, he began to publish the biblical epic *Shire Tipheret* ("Song of Glory"), relating the events of the Exodus down to the Sinaitic revelation which considerably influenced neo-Hebrew poetry.

Archeological Excavations at Western Wall

WEST INDIES: Archipelago off Central America.

Although at least one Jew was among the companions of Columbus when he discovered the W. I., there was no permanent Jewish settlement until the mid-17th cent., when refugees (mainly ex-Marranos) settled there after the Portuguese reconquest of Brazil from Holland. It was at this period that Jews first went to CURACAO and SURINAM under Dutch rule, BARBADOS, etc. under the English. Communities were set up in JAMAICA after the English conquest of 1655. At one time there were Jewish settlements in the French possessions (especially Martinique), but they were expelled by the Black Code in 1685. The W. I. communities were later recruited partly from the Sephardi Jews of London and Amsterdam, partly direct by fugitive Marranos from Spain and Portugal. In the 18th cent., a considerable Ashkenazi immigration, mainly via Amsterdam or London, established separate communities in Jamaica and Surinam. The Jews were important in the establishment and development of the sugar industry. When

that declined in the 19th cent. the Jewish communities dwindled, largely in favor of N America and Great Britain, some of them (e.g. St. Kitts, Barbados) becoming extinct. After World War I, and especially from 1933 onward, new Ashkenazi settlers arrived in CUBA, PUERTO RICO, and HAITI. These are now the most important in this area.

WEST VIRGINIA: US state. Jewish settlement dates from the 1840's, and a congregation was organized in Wheeling in 1849. Charleston's first congregation was formed in 1873. Jewish settlers engaged in the milling, pottery, and tobacco industries. After 1880, E European Jews arrived, some via E Ohio and W Pennsylvania. In 1973, there were 4,125 Jews in W. V., the leading communities being in Charleston (1,125), Wheeling (775), and Huntington (350), each of which had a central Jewish body.

WESTERN (or Wailing) **WALL** (Heb. *kotel maaravi*):

Part of the wall enclosing Herod's Temple still standing in the Old City of Jerusalem. The five lower courses, each over 3 ft. high, date from the time of Herod; the wall continues over 60 ft. underground. Owing to its proximity to the Holy of Holies (which was at the W end of the Temple) this part of the wall was regarded as sacred in popular legend as far back as the Talmudic Period; since at least the 10th cent., regular services were held before it. As the area in front of the W.W. is Moslem property, a serious dispute broke out between Jews and Moslems in 1929, and in 1931, a special commission of the League of Nations regulated the rights of the parties. From 1948 Jews were cut off from the W.W., which was under Jordanian control, despite a paragraph in the Israel-Jordan 1949 Armistice Agreement affirming Jewish right of access. As a result of the Six-Day War (1967) Jews could again visit the Wall which now came under Jewish sovereignty for the first time since the Second Temple period. On the first day after the War, when the Wall could be visited by the public, 200,000 people went there and since then it has been a focal point for Jews from all parts of the world. Considerable work has gone into landscaping the vicinity and since 1968 excavations in the area, directed by B. MAZAR, have uncovered many remains dating from Temple times.

WESTPHALIA: Former Prussian province, now part of the German Federal Republic. Jewish moneylenders were known in W. from the beginning of the 13th cent. There were small communities or isolated families in 40 towns. Although the Jews of W. suffered as a consequence of the BLACK DEATH, they subsequently returned. During the kingdom of W. (1807–13), they were the first Jews in Germany to receive equal rights (1808). Israel JACOBSON, president of the Jewish consistory, then introduced reforms in education and worship. The 1933 Jewish population of 18,819 disappeared during the Nazi period. After the war, several hundred returned. In 1970, there were 924 Jews nearly a third in DORTMUND.

WHITE PAPER, CHURCHILL: British state document issued in June 1922 following a statement by Winston CHURCHILL, then secretary for the colonies. It stated that the MACMAHON LETTERS did not refer to Palestine, that the aim of the BALFOUR DECLARATION was to establish a Jewish National Home but not Jewish domination, but that the Jews were there by right and not on sufferance. It also made Jewish immigration into Palestine dependent on absorptive capacity. As a direct result of the W. P., Transjordania was excluded from the area to which the Balfour Declaration applied.

WHITE PAPER OF 1939: British government statement of Palestine policy. It was submitted by the British colonial secretary Malcolm MacDonald after the failure of conversations conducted by the British with Jewish and Arab delegations. The W. P. declared the British intention of setting up after ten years an independent Palestinian state in which Jews and Arabs would participate in the government proportionately to their numbers. 75,000 Jews would be allowed to enter over 5 years to 1944 after which Jewish immigration would be dependent on Arab agreement. Land sales to Jews would be restricted or forbidden in the majority of the country. The document aroused the fierce opposition of the Zionist movement but guided British policy in ensuing years.

WHITE PAPER, PASSFIELD: British political document issued October 1930 by the colonial secretary, Lord Passfield (Sydney Webb). Based on the Hope-Simpson report which followed the 1929 Arab riots, it maintained that Jewish land acquisition and settlement were creating a landless Arab peasantry and widespread Arab unemployment. The paper concluded that Jewish immigration and land-purchase must be severely restricted. Weizmann thereupon resigned from the presidency of the World Zionist Organization (1931) thus eliciting a letter from the British premier, Ramsay MacDonald, which in fact canceled the anti-Zionist recommendations of the W.P.

WHITE RUSSIA (Belorussia): Soviet republic. Jews went there originally from Poland. They were living in GRODNO in the 12th cent., at BREST-LITOVSK in the 14th cent., and at PINSK from 1506. In eastern W. R., Jews appeared in the 16th cent., but owing to opposition from the local burghers, the communities were long unrecognized. Massacres occurred at POLOTSK in 1563, at HOMEL in 1649, at MOHILEV, etc. in 1655. The Jewish population suffered severely at the end of the 17th cent. from the Polish-Cossack and Swedish wars. The partition of Poland in the latter 18th cent. brought the Jews of W. R. under Russian rule and led to the abolition of their organized communal framework. In 1804, the Moscow government accepted the views of DERZHAVIN, after his visit to W. R., that the Jews must be indoctrinated with crafts and general education and resettled in S Ukraine. W. R. was an important center of Jewish scholarship, Hasidism (especially of the *Habad*), and Haskalah. The community suffered during World War I when W. R. was a war area and many Jews were expelled to the interior. In 1921, W. R. was partitioned between Russia and Poland. In 1939, the entire area fell under Russian rule and many of the Jewish intelligentsia and wealthier classes were exiled. Under German occupation, 1941–4, those Jews who did not escape into Russia were almost entirely exterminated by the Germans in cooperation with Belorussians and Lithuanians, although a considerable number fought with the partisans. Official 1970 Jewish pop.: 148,011.

WHITEHALL CONFERENCE: Conference of leading lawyers, divines, and merchants convened by Oliver Cromwell to consider Manasseh ben Israel's petitions for the recall of the Jews to England. It had five sessions in Dec. 1655. Although legal opinion was favorable, the merchants were antagonistic and the clergy divided. Cromwell dissolved the conference to prevent it from presenting a negative report.

WHOLE OFFERING (or holocaust; Heb. *kalil*): (1) Any offering consumed entire. (2) Specifically, the meal-offering consumed entire (Lev. 6:15–6). In this sense it is a parallel term to "burnt" offering (*olah*), except that the latter is used only for animal offerings.

WICHITA: City in Kansas, US. Individual Jews went there in the 1860's and 1870's, followed by immigrant groups from Germany and settlers from other parts of the US. In 1885, a Reform congregation was established. The arrival of Jews of E European origin led to the formation of an Orthodox congregation in 1917. Jewish pop. (1973): 1,200.

WICKED PRIEST, THE (Heb. *ha-kohen ha-rasha*): An opponent of the TEACHER OF RIGHTEOUSNESS in the DEAD SEA SCROLLS, according to which he was at first on the side of Truth but later betrayed the Law for gain and persecuted the Teacher of Righteousness. This figure, according to the various dating proposed for the Scrolls, has been identified with the high priests Jason or Menelaus, with Alexander Yannai, etc.

WIDAL, GEORGES FERNAND (1862–1929): French physician. Of Algerian birth, he was professor of pathology at Paris Univ. He devised the diagnosis of typhoid by serum (1896), originated the diagnosis of inflammatory discharges by cystodiagnosis and identified the dysenterial bacillus.

WIDOW: The Bible regards the w. as a privileged person and contains strict injunctions ensuring her protection and maintenance (e.g. Exod. 22:21; Deut. 27:19). A w. has the right to receive the sum stipulated by her husband in the marriage-contract or to be supported from the property of her husband's heirs. Her own movable property cannot be confiscated by creditors. The high priest was not allowed to marry a w. but no such restrictions applied to other priests. God is spoken of (Ps. 68:6) as "judge (i.e. protector) of widows."

WIENER: (1) *LEO W.* (1862–1939): US philologist.

Born in Poland, he settled in the US in 1882. He went to Harvard in 1890, becoming professor of Slavic languages. W. was the first to introduce Yiddish to the American public with his *History of Yiddish Literature in the Nineteenth Century* (1899) and other studies in literature and folklore. He became a Unitarian. (2) *NORBERT W.* (1894–1964): US mathematician; son of (1). A child prodigy, he received his doctorate from Harvard at the age of 18. W. taught mathematics at the Massachusetts Institute of Technology from 1919. He created the new science of cybernetics which deals with the operations of human and electronic brains.

WIENER NEUSTADT: Town near Vienna, Austria.

Jews lived there from shortly after its foundation in 1192. Their position deteriorated from the late 13th cent. culminating in the expulsion of 1496. During this period, it was the home of famous scholars. No further community was founded until the 18th cent. and then only for a brief period. Jews returned after 1848. The modern community, numbering 1,300 in 1927, ended with the Nazi occupation.

WIENIAWSKI, HENRI (1835–1880): Polish violinist and composer. From 1850, he traveled with his brother *JOSEPH W.* (1837–1912), who accompanied him at the piano. From 1874–7, he taught at the Brussels Conservatoire. W. wrote many works for violin and his two concertos are still often performed.

WIERNIK, PETER (1865–1936): Yiddish writer.

Born in Lithuania, he emigrated to the US in 1885. He became editor of the Yiddish daily *Morgen Journal* soon after its foundation in 1901 and also of the weekly *Der Amerikaner*. His English *History of the Jews of America* (1912) was a pioneering work in its field.

WIESEL, ELIE (1928–): Author. Born in Hungary, he was deported to Auschwitz and after the liberation went to Paris where he was a newspaper correspondent and began to write novels. These novels, including *The Gates of the Forest*, *Night* and *The Town beyond the Wall* received wide critical acclaim. Later he moved to New York and his interpretation of the significance of the holocaust had a great influence. His *Jews of Silence* describes a visit to Jews in the USSR.

WIGS: The wearing of w. by women as an adornment or to make up for deficiency of hair was familiar among Jews from the Talmudic Period (cf. *Sanhedrin* 112*a*, etc.). The wearing of a wig (SHEITEL) by married women as a religious prescription in order to prevent the exposure of the natural hair does not go back beyond the 15th cent. In the 17th–18th cents., when w. were fashionable in Europe, Jewish men wore them like their neighbors, though this was forbidden in S France by SUMPTUARY LAWS.

WILENSKY, MOSHEH (1910–): Composer. A native of Warsaw, he went to Palestine in 1932. W. has written many of Israel's popular songs.

WILKANSKY see **ELAZARI-VOLCANI**

WILKES-BARRE: City in Pennsylvania, US. Jewish settlement dates from 1838 and a congregation was organized in 1845. An Orthodox congregation came into being in 1870. The arrival of E European Jews in the 1880's led to the establishment of 4 additional Orthodox congregations. Jewish pop. (1973): 4,735.

*WILLIAM OF NORWICH (d. 1144): Alleged victim of the earliest recorded medieval Ritual Murder accusation. W., a skinner's apprentice of Norwich (England), was subsequently revered locally as a saint, but was not officially recognized as such by the Catholic Church.

WILLS: In Jewish law, INHERITANCE is always by intestacy, i.e., the property which a person possesses at the time of his death passes, after all debts have been paid, to the next of kin as defined in Num. 27:8–11. Nevertheless, it is possible to make provision for an estate to be distributed differently. Thus, a person in his last illness can dispose of all or any part of his property without formality, verbal instructions before witnesses being final and binding after the testator's death. Until death actually occurs, the dispositions may be revoked or varied freely, but if the donor recovers, they are usually void automatically. For this reason, a will made in ordinary form by a healthy person cannot have absolute validity in Jewish law — for it may have been revoked — although it is sometimes possible to proceed under the rule that there is a duty to carry out the wishes of a person who has died. It is, however, possible for a person in normal health to make a will which will ensure that his wishes are carried out after his death but, as is also the case under all other legal systems, the document must embody the correct and somewhat complicated legal formulas. W. often embodied instructions or advice to the dead man's children for the conduct of their lives (see ETHICAL WILLS).

WILLSTÄTTER, RICHARD (1872–1942): German chemist. He directed the Chemical Institute of the Kaiser Wilhelm Society at Berlin from 1912 and was professor at Munich Univ. from 1915 until 1925 when he resigned in protest against the university's anti-Semitic policy. His last years were spent in Switzerland. For his work on the determination of the composition of chlorophyll and hematin he was awarded the Nobel Prize in 1915. Of equal importance was his work showing life to be a chemical process to which the key is the study of enzymes.

Wine bottle with Hebrew inscription
(Feinberg Collection, Detroit).

WILMINGTON: City in the state of Delaware, US. Individual Jews resided there from the second decade of the 19th cent. The present community dates from the arrival of E European immigrants in 1880. A congregation was formed in 1889. Jewish pop. (1973): 9,000 The *Jewish Voice* has been published in W. since 1931.

*WILSON, WOODROW (1856–1924): President of the US, 1913–21. In 1918, he endorsed the BALFOUR DECLARATION, and at the peace conference following World War I, fought for the inclusion in treaties of clauses to protect the rights of minorities.

WIMPEL see **VIMPEL**

WINCHELL, WALTER (1897–1972): US journalist. From 1929, he wrote a popular gossip column for the *New York Mirror*, and broadcast similar material over radio and television.

WINCHEVSKY, MORRIS (1856–1933): Yiddish poet and essayist. Of Lithuanian birth, he suffered imprisonment and banishment from Germany and Denmark for socialist agitation and went to London in 1879 and to New York in 1894. W. contributed brilliant poems and feuilletons to Yiddish periodicals, using them as media for the infiltration of revolutionary socialist ideas. He was the founder of Yiddish socialist literature, and also occasionally wrote in Hebrew.

WINDSOR: Canadian city. Its Jewish community began in 1891 with 61 Jews residing there. After the turn of the century two synagogues were established. Jewish pop. (1973): 2,600.

WINE: In early Israel, w. was the common drink at meals or to create merriment. On the other hand, the Bible contains warnings against overindulgence. The NAZIRITES refrained from drinking w. as did the RECHABITES. W. was poured on the altar with the sacrifices, while it played an important part in later ritual (KIDDUSH; HAVDALAH; HAGGADAH, etc.), and a special benediction was recited before and after drinking it. The vine leaf and grapes figure on Jewish coins of the Second Temple Period and in synagogal art in talmudic times. On the festival of Purim, overdrinking was jocularly encouraged (as later also on the festival of the Rejoicing of the Law). Drunkenness, however, has been a rare phenomenon among Jews. The rabbis enacted strict laws prohibiting the drinking of w. belonging to pagans (Heb. *yen nesekh*); this is traditionally one of the 18 prohibitions legislated at the end of the Second Temple Period to keep Jews apart from pagans. Later codifiers differed as to whether this ban extended to non-pagan gentiles, but the stricter view prevailed. Hence, viticulture was practiced by Jews extensively in medieval Europe (e.g. by Rashi). Many medieval Jewish poets composed poems in praise of w. W.-drinking occupies an important place in Ḥasidic ritual. Viticulture was promoted by the early Zionist settlers in Palestine (notably at Zikhron Yaakov and Rishon le-Zion), and w. is still a significant Israel product.

*WINGATE, CHARLES ORDE (1903–1944): British soldier. While serving in Palestine during the Arab riots of 1936–9, he organized formations of

Charles Orde Wingate.

Jewish volunteers, known as the Special Night Squads, to defeat Arab terrorist activity. A keen Bible student, W. remained an ardent supporter of Zionism to the end of his brilliant military career.

WINNIPEG: City in MANITOBA, Canada. In 1877, its first Jews arrived from Alsace-Lorraine. Services were held from 1879, and in 1883, two congregations — Bethel and the Children of Israel — came into being, merging in 1889 to form Shaarey Zedek. The Congregation Rosh Pina was established in 1892. W. has a Jewish population of 19,750 (1973) and maintains a number of Jewish (including 2 Yiddish) schools. 2 weekly English-Jewish and one Yiddish newspaper appear.

WINTER, LEV (Leo; 1876–1935): Czech statesman. He represented the Bohemian Social Democratic Workers' Party in the Austrian Reichsrat in 1907. W. was minister of social welfare in the Czech cabinet 1918–20 and 1925–6.

WINTERNITZ, MORITZ (1863–1937): Sanskrit scholar. Of Austrian birth, he was librarian of the Oxford Indian Institute (from 1895) and became professor of Sanskrit at Prague in 1911. His main work was a history of Indian literature.

WINTERNITZ, WILHELM (1835–1917): Physician. A native of Bohemia, he was professor at Vienna Univ. and pioneered in hydrotherapy.

WISCHNITZER: (1) *MARK W.* (1882–1955): Historian. He taught history in Russia until 1913, was secretary of the Hilfsverein der Deutschen Juden in Berlin 1921–38, and professor of Jewish history at Yeshiva Univ., New York, 1948–55. He wrote on Jewish history, especially in E Europe. (2) *RACHEL W.* (1892–): Art critic, wife of (1). She was born in Minsk, educated as an architect, and has written extensively on aspects of Jewish art and synagogue architecture. From 1933–8, she was curator of the Jewish Museum in Berlin.

WISCONSIN: US state. Jewish settlement dates from 1792, but, until the arrival in 1836 of Jews in MILWAUKEE, where a congregation was formed in 1847, was limited to traders and peddlers. In the 1840's and 1850's, large numbers of Bohemian and German Jews settled in W. Jewish merchants and businessmen went to MADISON, La Crosse, Green Bay, Racine, Fond du Lac, and a number of smaller towns. W.'s second congregation came into being in La Crosse in 1857, existing until the 1920's. The advent of E European Jews after 1850 increased the Jewish population, and the INDUSTRIAL REMOVAL OFFICE placed 3,700 Jews in 74 W. cities and towns. In 1973, there were 31,930 Jews in W., the largest communities being in Milwaukee (23,900), Madison (2,900), and Racine (800).

WISDOM: In the Bible, a human characteristic Divinely conferred but also resulting from education and experience. The w. of SOLOMON is traditional.

George S. Wise.

W. is not restricted to Israel but is also found among pagan peoples. The Book of PROVERBS devoted special attention to the subject, stressing its moral character. W. is also the subject of panegyrics by Job (28:12) and Ben Sira (21:13). In the post-exilic period, it is identified with knowledge of the Torah and of Law, and a specific WISDOM LITERATURE developed.

WISDOM LITERATURE: Term applied to certain biblical books (Proverbs, Job, Ecclesiastes, and Psalms 37, 49, and 73) and apocryphal works (Ben Sira, Wisdom of Solomon, IV Maccabees). Wisdom, a central feature of this literature, is not abstract knowledge but is based on fear of God and knowledge of the commandments. In application, it leads to the right life. The "Wisdom of God" is described as the sum-total of Divine characteristics on which rests the world order, both moral and physical.

WISDOM OF SOLOMON: Apocryphal book, belonging to the WISDOM LITERATURE. Its contents praise wisdom and are ascribed to Solomon. Chaps. 1–5 counsel wisdom in human life and emphasize the supremacy of the wise over the wicked; 6–9 describe Solomon's wisdom; and 10–19 glorify wisdom as the guide of mankind and extol its role in Jewish history. The book was originally written in Greek, possibly by an Alexandrian Jew. Its date is uncertain; some assign it to the 2nd cent. BCE, others maintain that it refers to the persecution under Caligula (37–41 CE).

WISE, GEORGE S. (1906–): US business executive and administrator. Born in Poland, he went as a child to the US. He headed a large paper corporation

Isaac Mayer Wise.

and was also active in Jewish community life, being chairman of the Hebrew University's board of governors 1953–62. From 1963 he was president (chancellor, 1971) of TEL AVIV UNIVERSITY.

WISE, ISAAC MAYER (1819–1900): Father of Reform Judaism in the US. Born in Bohemia, he emigrated to the US in 1846 and became rabbi of Congregation Beth El in Albany, N.Y., where he began to alter the Orthodox form of service. Opposition arose and the congregants split; one group followed Wise, while another continued to adhere to traditional Judaism. In 1854, he became minister to the Orthodox congregation Bene Yeshurun in Cincinnati. There, he installed an organ and gradually modified the services, so that it became before long one of America's leading Reform temples. In Cincinnati, he founded an English-Jewish weekly, *The Israelite*, and a German language weekly, *Die Deborah*, editing both with great vigor for many years. He compiled an American Reform prayerbook, *Minhag America* (1857), in English and German editions. In 1855, he attempted to found a rabbinical seminary, Zion College, but it failed for lack of funds. Determined to organize the REFORM MOVEMENT in the US, he toured the country and in 1855, called a conference of rabbis in Cleveland. He summoned other conferences in 1869 and 1871, when he began to plan the UNION OF AMERICAN HEBREW CONGREGATIONS eventually organized in Cincinnati in 1873. Two years later, the HEBREW UNION COLLEGE was founded there, and W. became its first president. In 1889, W. organized the CENTRAL CONFERENCE OF AMERICAN RABBIS.

WISE, STEPHEN SAMUEL (1874–1949): US rabbi and Zionist leader. In 1907, he established the Free Synagogue in New York to serve as an example of a pulpit unfettered by the opinions of the lay board, and was its rabbi until his death. In 1922, he founded the JEWISH INSTITUTE OF RELIGION to train rabbis in his own spirit of progressive Judaism, Zionism, and political liberalism. W. was a founder and the first secretary of the Federation of American Zionists, which later became the Zionist Organization of America (ZOA), and held numerous positions of leadership in the Zionist movement. As chairman of the Provisional Committee for Zionist Affairs 1916–9, and friend of President Wilson, he played a significant role at the time of the Balfour Declaration. W. energetically supported the domestic and foreign programs of President F. D. Roosevelt. He was a founder of the American Jewish Congress and its President 1925–9 and 1935–49. W. was a consistent friend of organized labor and an advocate of social legislation, and raised his voice courageously in many battles against injustice to the worker. A powerful orator, W. was one of the most influential American Jews of his time. His wife, *LOUISE WATERMAN W.* (d. 1947), artist, was founder and president of the women's division of the American Jewish Congress. Their son, *JAMES WATERMAN W.* (1901–) edited *Opinion*, has held organizational positions, and has written on contemporary Jewish topics. Their daughter *JUSTINE WISE POLIER* (1903–) has since 1935 been a justice of the Domestic Relations Court of New York City.

Stephen Samuel Wise.

WISSENSCHAFT DES JUDENTUMS (Ger. "Science of Judaism"): Scientific inquiry into Jewish history, literature, and religion developed in Europe in the 19th cent. The movement arose as an indirect by-product of religious Reform, but many Orthodox scholars participated. Its basic assumptions were (a) that Jewish institutions and ideas evolved by the same laws as those of other societies, and (b) that at each stage they were no worse than those of contemporary societies, and could not, therefore, be made an excuse for denying the Jews equal rights. The *W.* did not clearly keep apart political, ideological, and literary development, but rather treated the history of literature as an essential aspect of general Jewish history, and the history of ideas as the main feature of the history of literature, so that to a large extent Jewish history became a history of ideas. Economic and social history were accorded a minor place in accordance with 19th cent. German Idealistic philosophy. A large element of apologetics was always present. Despite its limitations, the *W.* succeeded (a) in establishing within a short period the facts and trends of Jewish history and literature (save for periods for which documentary evidence came to light only later); and (b) in imbuing the educated westernized Jew with a well-founded pride in his past and his inherited institutions. It prepared the ground for the "Jewish Studies" in the 20th cent., which differ from it in being properly divided into disciplines and in being devoid of the apologetic tendency. L. Zunz may be considered, together with A. Geiger, the founder of *W.* Its other major exponents in Germany and Austria included Z. Frankel, M. Joel, and M. S. Zuckermandel, who investigated the Tannaitic and Amoraic Periods, W. Bacher, who besides important work in the same periods contributed also to the opening up of later literary periods. L. Dukes, A. Jellinek, J. Muller, S. Eppenstein who studied medieval literature, and M. Steinschneider, the great bibliographer. The achievements of the German school are crowned by the monumental historical synthesis of H. Graetz. While these wrote in German, S. J. Rapoport and N. Krochmal created a parallel school in Hebrew, joined in Russia by I. B. Levinsohn, M. A. Günzburg, and especially A. Harkavy. One of the greatest contributions of the W. was perhaps the series of text editions *Mekitze Nirdamim.* In Italy S. D. Luzzatto and I. Reggio, and in France, E. Carmoly and S. Munk founded the modern study of Jewish philosophy. In England, where the movement started later, its representatives included A. Neubauer, I. Abrahams, E. N. Adler, M. Gaster, and the two last representatives of *W.*, S. Schechter (!ater in the US) and A. Büchler. An important role in the *W.* was played by its scholarly journals (e.g. Monatsschrift fur die Geschichte und Wissenschaft des Judentums, Jewish Quarterly Review, Revue des Etudes Juives, Bikkure ha-Ittim, Kerem Hemed, Otzar Nehmad).

WISSOTZKY, KALONYMOS ZE'EV (1824–1904): Russian merchant and philanthropist. He founded a tea-business which rapidly became the largest in Russia. An active Zionist, he visited Palestine, supported religious settlers, and contributed toward the foundation of the Haifa Technion. In 1896, he founded Ha-Shiloah.

WITCHCRAFT: The use of supernatural power obtained from association with evil forces; in a wider sense, it includes Magic, sorcery, Divination, and similar practices. A capital offense in biblical law (Exod. 22:17), its practice and belief in its efficacy were difficult to eradicate. Its main manifestations in Israel were resort to necromancers, etc., the casting of lots and oracles, and "charming" in connection with illness. The medieval philosophers and theologians either denied w. altogether or connected it with Demonology (particularly in Kabbalah and folklore). Nevertheless, alleged Jewish witches are sometimes encountered in medieval and post-medieval sources.

WITNESS: A person who is in possession of testimony is obliged to give Evidence before the court and testify. False testimony is punished according to the rule: "Then shall ye do unto him, as he had purposed to do unto his brother" (Deut. 19:19). The testimony of only one w. is sufficient in civil cases to obligate the accused to take an oath that he is not liable for the claim made against him. The testimony of one w. is also valid in matters of purely religious law, regarding things permitted or prohibited. Otherwise, two witnesses are required.

WITZENHAUSEN, JOSEPH see **URI PHOEBUS BEN AARON HA-LEVI**

WIZO (abbr. of "Women's International Zionist Organization"): Women's Zionist organization founded in London in 1920 to further (1) the training of Jewish girls and women in Palestine and the Diaspora for work in the National Home and (2) mother and child care in Palestine. The organization was at first headed by executives in London and Palestine, but after 1948, the direction was concentrated in Israel and is composed of 42 members (22 in Israel, 20 in other countries) meeting annually. Its supreme body is the Conference which convenes every 4 years. Branches of W. are active in 50 countries (but not in the US where the Women's Zionist organization is Hadassah) and number 250,000 members (90,000 in Israel). Its practical work in Israel includes (1) child care from infancy to school age, covering 5,000 children in 90 institutions; (2) agricultural and vocational training for 3,500 young people in 12 schools and after-school clubs for boys and girls aged 6-17; (3) agricultural instruction, home sciences, job guidance, etc. for women and their families.

*WOLF, JOHANN CHRISTOPH (1683–1739): German Hebraist; professor of oriental languages at Hamburg from 1712. His *Bibliotheca Hebraea* (4 vols., 1715–33), based largely on the collection of David OPPENHEIMER which was then in Hamburg, is still a basic work of Hebrew bibliography.

WOLF, LUCIEN (1857–1930): English historian, journalist and Jewish public worker. He entered journalism, at first in the Jewish sphere, and became known as an expert on foreign (especially Russian) affairs. From 1890 he was foreign editor of the (then) influential *Daily Graphic*, and was also editor of *The Jewish World* 1906–8. He took an active part in arousing British public opinion to the persecution of the Jews in Russia, and for this purpose edited the periodical *Darkest Russia* 1912–4. He was profoundly opposed to Zionism, but collaborated with his friend Israel Zangwill in the ITO movement. On the outbreak of World War I, anti-Russian journalistic activity became impossible in England, and in 1917 he became Secretary of the Joint Foreign Committee of the Board of Deputies of British Jews and the Anglo-Jewish Association. In this capacity he attended the Peace Conference in Paris (1919), was secretary of the skeleton organization set up by the Jewish delegation, and was partly responsible for the Minorities' Treaties which were expected to safeguard the rights of the Jews in Central and Eastern Europe. He was subsequently a familiar figure at the League of Nations. From his early days keenly interested in English Jewish history, he published a series of articles and works dealing with the "Middle Period" (between the expulsion and the resettlement) and with the mission of Manasseh ben Israel to Oliver Cromwell.

WOLF, SIMON (1836–1923): US communal leader. A resident of Washington, DC, he frequently intervened with presidents and other government leaders to obtain equity for Jews in America or abroad who were subjected to discrimination or persecution. He was chairman of the standing committee of the Board of Delegates of Civil and Religious Rights 1878–1911, president of B'nai B'rith 1904–5, and consul general to Egypt 1881–2.

WOLFE, HUMBERT (1885–1940): English poet and civil servant. Born at Bradford of a cultured German background described in his autobiography *Now a Stranger*, he published many volumes of poems, including *London Sonnets*, as well as translations from the Greek and from Heine.

WOLFF, BERNHARD (1811–1876): German newspaper owner. After engaging in the translation of scientific works from French and English, he became proprietor of a periodical on economics. In 1848, he founded the Wolff Telegraphic Agency which later became the official German News Agency. It was expropriated by the Nazis.

WOLFF, JOSEPH (1795–1862): Missionary. Son of a German rabbi, he was baptized in 1812, and traveled extensively through Russia and Asia on missionary activities. In 1828, he journeyed from Turkey to Cabul in search of the Lost Ten Tribes. He also visited Yemen, Abyssinia, and Bokhara. In 1845, he settled in England as a country vicar. He married the daughter of the Earl of Orford, their son being *SIR HENRY DRUMMOND W.* (1830–1908), politician and diplomat.

WOLFF, THEODOR (1868–1943): German journalist. Chief editor of the *Berliner Tageblatt* from 1906, he was associated with the newspaper from 1889–1933. Active in the Democratic Party, he was indifferent to Jewish affairs. W. emigrated to Paris in 1933 and died in a concentration camp in S France.

WOLFFSOHN, DAVID (1856–1914): Zionist leader. A native of Lithuania, he settled in Cologne as a timber merchant. He was early drawn to Zionism and in 1893, was co-founder of a society to promote Jewish agricultural work and handicrafts in Palestine. After the publication of HERZL'S *Judenstaat*, he enthusiastically joined the political Zionist movement and remained a devoted assistant to Herzl who entrusted him with the preparations for the founding of the JEWISH COLONIAL TRUST. W. accompanied

David Wolffsohn

Herzl on his journey in 1898 to Palestine where they met Kaiser William II. Elected in 1905 to succeed Herzl as president of the World Zionist Organization, he concentrated on consolidating the ranks of the movement and on safeguarding its political character. Opposition to his purely political direction grew, especially among the Russian Zionists who demanded greater emphasis on practical work in Palestine. He was not re-elected in 1911, but retained the chairmanship of the Jewish Colonial Trust. In this capacity he attempted to prevent the new leadership from spending money on colonization experiments in Palestine before political rights had been attained.

WOLFSKEHL, KARL (1869–1948): German poet. Exiled as a result of Nazi rule, he wrote in Italy a series of poems *Die Stimme spricht* giving voice to the German Jewish tragedy. From 1938, he lived in New Zealand.

WOLFSON, HARRY AUSTRYN (1887–1974): Philosopher. Born in Russia, he emigrated to the US in 1903. He taught Jewish literature and philosophy at Harvard Univ. 1915–58 (professor 1925). W. wrote works of fundamental importance on Jewish philosophy, notably *Crescas' Critique of Aristotle*, *The Philosophy of Spinoza*, and *Philo*.

WOLFSON, SIR ISAAC (1897–): British businessman. Heading a number of chain stores, etc., W. has been active in philanthropic and educational institutions in Great Britain (e.g. W. College, Oxford) and Israel. He is president of the UNITED SYNAGOGUE and largely financed the building *Hekhal Shelomoh* (the Religious Center and seat of the chief rabbinate in Jerusalem).

WOLLEMBORG, LEONE (1859–1932): Italian economist and statesman. He founded and propagated agricultural credit cooperative societies in N Italy and sat in the Italian parliament 1892–1913 and in the senate 1913–32. In 1901, he was minister of finance. He made considerable contributions to economic legislation. In later years, he strongly criticized the economic policy of the Fascist regime.

WOLMARK, ALFRED (1877–1961): Painter. Of Polish birth, he settled in England as a boy and was a pioneer in the "New Movement" in art. A versatile artist, he at one time turned his attention to stained glass and interior decoration, while his portraits of famous Shakespearians hang in the Stratford-on-Avon Memorial Theater.

WOMEN: Although the Hebrews were inevitably affected by oriental standards and outlook in their attitude toward w., the role of w. in early Jewish society as reflected in the Bible is not infrequently one of importance. This emerges not only in the picture of the matriarchs but also in the characterization of MIRIAM, DEBORAH, HULDAH, or (with obvious differences) the queens JEZEBEL of Israel and ATHALIAH of Judah. The Book of Proverbs warns men against

female wiles, but also depicts the "woman of worth" who is the mainstay of her household. In the Second Temple Period, Queen SALOME ALEXANDRA ruled Judea. In hellenistic times the Jewish woman's status in Palestine was superior to that of the Greek woman, insofar as she was an independent legal personality permitted to own property. This continued to be her position, crystallized in talmudic law according to which she can own property when single or widowed and retains certain property after marriage, though increments go to her husband. She could not, however, give evidence except in cases of AGUNAH. The Talmud is nervously aware of the sexual power of the woman, but among the rabbis, too, some w. (e.g. BERURIAH) exercised great personal influence. Rabbinic Judaism concentrated and nearly restricted the w.'s position to the home, exempting them from the performance of many precepts, although the domestic religious rites (e.g. connected with food) were left mainly in their hands. Nevertheless, the general establishment of MONOGAMY (c. 1000 CE) enhanced the position of the woman; polygamy remained legal for oriental Jewries, though it is now illegal in Israel. Moreover, the healthy rabbinic attitude toward SEX and the insistence on the positive virtue of the marital relationship implied that the woman's dignity was recognized notwithstanding her legal inferiority. It was remarked in Spain that at times of persecution, w. set the example of martyrdom for the faith. In the 17th cent., w. such as Benvenida ABRAVANEL or Gracia MENDES were prominent in Jewish life. On the other hand, the education of w. was seriously neglected. In E Europe it was a tradition for the w. to work in order to facilitate the husband's studies. In the last 50 years, w. have been prominent in Zionist pioneering and also in Jewish public life (e.g. Golda MEIR) and organizations such as HADASSAH and WIZO occupy a foremost position in the community. W. in Israel have received the franchise, equal education, etc. although still suffering from certain inequalities in matters of personal status, which are subject to the rabbinical courts.

WOMEN'S INTERNATIONAL ZIONIST ORGANIZATION see WIZO

WOMEN'S LEAGUE FOR ISRAEL: Organization founded in New York in 1928 to aid young women newcomers in Israel. Since its inception, it has built and maintains hostels for immigrant girls in Haifa, Jerusalem, Tel Aviv, and Netanyah (where it maintains a special project for blind girls). It has also built the Women's Student Residence Center at the Hebrew University in Jerusalem. It has housed and provided vocational and professional training for 50,000 young women.

WOODBINE: Town in New Jersey, US. It was founded by the BARON DE HIRSCH FUND as a Jewish agricultural colony with an industrial annexe.

The first 60 families, mostly from S Russia, arrived in 1892, and an agricultural school was established in 1895. In 1903, the colony became the first all-Jewish municipality in the US. Failure of the colony's original plans led to a predominance of industry. In 1942–3, the Hirsch Fund withdrew support from W. The Jewish pop. has declined steadily and in 1968, numbered 140.

WOOLF, LEONARD SIDNEY (1880–1969): English author and socialist. Together with his (non-Jewish) wife the authoress Virginia W., he founded the Hogarth Press in 1917. W. was active in the Fabian Society and edited various literary and political periodicals. He was the author of sociological, political and autobiographical works.

WORCESTER: City in Massachusetts, US. Its Jewish community dates from the decade after the Civil War, the first settlers being peddlers who later opened stores. In 1877, a synagogue was organized. The community increased in the early years of the 20th cent., many Jews working in industry. Jewish pop. (1973): 10,000. The Jewish Federation, formed in 1947, sponsored the Jewish Welfare Fund: The *Jewish Civic Leader*, established in 1923, appears weekly in W.

WORKMEN'S CIRCLE (in Yidd. *Arbeiter Ring*): Fraternal insurance society in the US and Canada with 60,000 members in 400 branches. It was formed by Jewish immigrant workers in 1900 and actively assisted in the formation of unions in the needle and other trades in which Jewish immigrants were pioneers. In 1933, it helped to create the JEWISH LABOR COMMITTEE. It sponsors a system of Jewish education (schools, camps, etc.) using the Yiddish language.

WORLD CONFEDERATION OF GENERAL ZIONISTS see **GENERAL ZIONISM**

WORLD HEBREW UNION see **BERIT IVRIT OLAMIT**

WORLD JEWISH CONGRESS: International organization founded in 1936 at Geneva to succeed the COMITE DES DELEGATIONS JUIVES. Its constituents are mostly federations of Jewish communities or central territorial organizations. 65 countries are represented, while all Israel parties (except *Agudat Israel* and the Communists) are affiliated. The WJC protects Jewish rights and interests in all lands, fosters unity of action between its affiliates, supports Jewish cultural activity, and appears in a representative capacity. It is recognized by the UN as an advisory body. Its directorate is divided into three parts; an American section (headquarters in New York), a European section (headquarters in London) and an Israel section (headquarters in Jerusalem and Tel Aviv). Stephen WISE was president of the Congress until his death in 1949; he was eventually succeeded by Nahum Goldmann. The WJC set up the Institute of Jewish Affairs in 1940 to handle research into Jewish problems; many of its findings have been published.

WORLD LITERATURE, JEWS IN: World literature has been enriched by Jewish authors ever since the holy books began to be translated from the Hebrew. In the secular field, JOSEPHUS and others wrote their works in Greek for non-Jewish readers in the hellenistic and Roman Empire. In the Middle Ages, a few Jews made their contributions in the vernacular: e.g. Süsskind von TRIMBERG who composed German ballads, IMMANUEL OF ROME whose Italian poems were of considerable significance; or, in Spain, Judah Bonsenyor of Barcelona, author of Catalan aphorisms and SANTOB DE CARRION whose *Moral Proverbs* were dedicated to the king of Castile. There were also some baptized Jews or persons of Jewish origin, such as the French astrologer Nostradamus or the German cleric Johannes Pauli, whose writings were important. After the forced conversions in Spain and Portugal, numerous Marranos contributed to Spanish and Portuguese literature, outstanding among them being Fernando de Rojaz, author of the famous tragi-comedy *Calisto e Meliboea* which greatly influenced European literature. Other Marranos continued their literary work in the vernacular after their return to Judaism abroad, e.g. poet S. USQUE or the playwright Antonio Enriquez GOMEZ. A little later, other persons belonging in the main to this element, e.g. the English poet Moses MENDES, began to make a feeble contribution to the literature of their various countries. Yet it was only after the modern Emancipation of European Jewry that Jewish authors entered into the stream of the principal national literatures on a large scale. Moses MENDELSSOHN was an important literary figure of the German Enlightenment. Heinrich HEINE sang the swan-song of German Romanticism and, together with the polemic essayist Ludwig BÖRNE, paved the way for the realism of "Young Germany." Among German realists, Berthold AUERBACH was the chief exponent of the *Dorfnovelle* ("Village Tale"). In England, Benjamin DISRAELI was a novelist of distinction before he became prime minister. But while Disraeli took his Jewish hero from the Sephardi element, Israel ZANGWILL chose his heroes from E European Jewry and popularized the ghetto-novel. In this literary genre, he had been preceded by Leopold KOMPERT in Bohemia and Karl FRANZOS in Germany. Vienna felt most strongly the impact of Jewish esthetes such as Arthur SCHNITZLER, Richard BEER-HOFMANN, Theodor HERZL, Felix SALTEN, Peter ALTENBERG, and Stefan ZWEIG and, outside Vienna, writers who rose to prominence in the dying days of the dual monarchy included the Hungarian dramatist Ferenc MOLNAR and the Prague novelists Franz KAFKA and Max BROD. The rise of Expressionism in Central Europe brought to the fore the dramatists Ernst TOLLER and

Franz WERFEL and the novelists Alfred DOBLIN and Jakob WASSERMANN. On the eve of Hitlerism, Emil LUDWIG, Lion FEUCHTWANGER, and Arnold ZWEIG were commanding a world-wide audience. In no other European tongue did Jews command as great an influence in recent generations as in German; Denmark could boast of Georg BRANDES, Holland of Hermann HEIJERMANS, England of Humbert WOLFE, Louis GOLDING, and Siegfried SASSOON, France of Henri BERNSTEIN, Tristan BERNARD, André MAUROIS, Jean Richard BLOCH, and André SPIRE, Soviet Russia of Isaac BABEL, Boris PASTERNAK, Ilya ILF, and Ilya EHRENBURG, Rumania of Rosetti Roman, and Italy of Italo SVEVO and Alberto MORAVIA. In 19th cent. American literature only the poetess Emma LAZARUS rose above mediocrity. Recently the impact of Jews has been felt most strongly in the works of Elmer RICE, Clifford ODETS, Ben HECHT, S. N. BEHRMAN, Irwin SHAW, George S. KAUFMAN, Norman MAILER, Arthur MILLER, J. D. SALINGER, Philip ROTH, Isaac Bashevis SINGER, and Saul BELLOW. They did not, however, specialize in Jewish themes as did the novelists Ludwig LEWISOHN, Maurice SAMUEL, and Bernard MALAMUD.

WORLD UNION FOR PROGRESSIVE JUDAISM: Organization founded in London in 1926 to coordinate Liberal Jewish groups and establish new centers of Liberal Judaism. Every two years, it holds an international conference devoted to a specific topic. In 1955, it established an international theological training center in Paris of Progressive rabbis and teachers. Bodies affiliated with the WUPJ are to be found in 26 countries, representing well over 1,000,000 members. The Union was recognized as a non-governmental organization in consultative status with the UN and Unesco.

WORMS: German town. Its first Jews probably arrived in the 10th cent. The community was well established by the 11th cent. Emperor Henry IV, in return for financial assistance, rewarded them with substantial privileges in 1074 and 1090, granting them freedom of commerce, security of property, and imperial protection. The community was annihilated in the First Crusade, re-established shortly afterward and again destroyed in the Black Death outbreaks (1349). There was an expulsion in 1615, restrictions were imposed in 1641, and a massacre was carried out by the soldiers of Louis XIV in 1689. Emancipation was conferred after the French Revolution. W. was a famous center of Jewish scholarship in the Medieval Period and Rashi studied there 1055-65. It was closely associated with the communities of Speyer and Mainz (the three together being called SHUM). Its cemetery dates from the 11th cent., while its synagogue originally built in 1034 (and close to it the "Rashi chapel" of 1624 and the ritual bath of 1186) stood until they were destroyed

in Nov. 1938. The 1933 community numbering 1,200 ended under the Nazis. Jewish pop. (1965): 50.

WOUK, HERMAN (1915–): US author. He wrote *The Caine Mutiny*, a novel of the US Navy in World War II; *Marjorie Morningstar*, which treats the milieu of the Jewish middle class of New York, *This is my God* on orthodox Judaism, and *Winds of War* on World War II.

WRITING: The way to mass literacy was prepared by the invention of the ALPHABET in Canaan around the 18th cent. BCE. The story in Judg. 8:14 shows that boys were taught w.; the GEZER CALENDAR (c. 1000 BCE) may be a school exercise. While with neighboring peoples, personal seals usually bore a picture for easier identification, most Hebrew seals contain solely the owner's name, another sign that the ordinary man was expected to be able to read, though this was not always the case (Is. 29:12). W. was done with pen and ink, on potsherds (the LACHISH LETTERS) or on leather scrolls (*sepher*, *megillah*) in columns (*delet*, cf. Jer. 36:23). It was usual in the upper classes to dictate to a scribe (*sopher*) and not to read oneself, but to have the scribe read aloud (Jer. 31:21; Lachish Letter 3:9–10). In the Tannaitic Period, too, the ordinary man could usually read. There were elaborate rules for w. holy books; these are strictly observed in the DEAD SEA SCROLLS. The parchment (*kelaph*) was ruled with a stylus and the letters written suspended from the line (a usage followed until recently in many communities). There was a fixed orthography, and in w. the Bible, no deviation from any peculiarities of the inherited text was allowed. In the Middle Ages, Jews were the most literate people in the world. Until modern times, Hebrew script was used by Jews also for w. other languages, e.g. Arabic, Spanish, Provençal, Italian, German, Yiddish, Persian, and Turkish. Yiddish is still written in Hebrew characters, while nowadays Ladino (Judeo-Spanish) is frequently printed in Latin script. The use of Latin script for Hebrew has been advocated in modern times but without success. The shortcomings of Hebrew w. are generally acknowledged: absence of VOCALIZATION, lack of capital letters, the excessive similarity of several letters, and the limited possibilities of connecting letters in handwriting. Attempts to express vowels in unpointed text by adding *yod* and *vav* have led to anarchy in present-day spelling. While Jews were quick to take advantage of PRINTING, Scrolls of the Law, Scrolls of Esther for use in the synagogue, *Tephilin, Mezuzot*, and divorce documents must still be written by hand, and marriage documents are also often handwritten.

WRITING ON THE WALL see **MENE MENE TEKEL U-PHARSIN**

WRITTEN LAW (Heb. *Torah she-bi-khetav*): The law received by Moses in written form. Strictly speaking, this is limited to the Pentateuch; but

Interior of the Rashi Chapel of the Synagogue of Worms with the traditional chair of Rashi.

The Synagogue of Worms which was destroyed by the Nazis in 1938 and was reconstructed after the war.

by extension it is also used for the Prophetical Books and the Hagiographa, which are also recorded in written form. The latter are nevertheless not binding in character, and are therefore called *divre kabbalah* ("words of tradition"). Complementary to the W. L. is the Oral Law also given to Moses at Sinai, according to tradition. It is regarded as the key to the correct understanding of the former. (See LAW ORAL.)

WROCLAW see **BRESLAU**

*WÜNSCHE, AUGUST (1839–1913): Christian scholar of Hebrew literature. W. translated into German legends from the Babylonian and Palestinian Talmuds, Midrash Rabbah, Pesikta De-Rav Kahana, and other Midrashim. He wrote books and articles on the Bible and Talmud and collaborated in a work on post-biblical Jewish literature.

WÜRTTEMBERG: German state, now part of the German Federal Republic. Jews were known in W. from the beginning of the 13th cent., living in 70 places. Although they suffered during the RIND-FLEISCH and BLACK DEATH disorders, there were Jews in W. until 1521, when they were expelled by law Resettlement began at the end of the 17th cent. Fol lowing the hanging of Joseph OPPENHEIMER in 1738, all the Jews were expelled for a short period. They received equal rights in 1864. The 1933 Jewish population of 10,023 was reduced to 713 in 1966.

WÜRZBURG: Town in Bavaria. Jews lived there from the beginning of the 12th cent. A mob of Crusaders and townspeople killed a number of Jews and forced others into baptism in 1147. The growing Jewish population at first belonged to the king, later to the bishop. R. ELIEZER BEN JOEL HA-LEVI and R ISAAC BEN MOSES OF VIENNA were rabbis there. R MEIR OF ROTHENBURG and MORDECAI BEN HILLEL studied in the local yeshivah. This community was destroyed in 1298 and 1349. A revived settlement was expelled in 1567 to be restored in the 18th cent. A number were killed or driven out during the HEP HEP riots in 1819. In 1933, there were 2,200 Jews. The community ceased to exist in 1943. Jewish pop. (1968): 150.

WYOMING: US state. Jewish settlement dates from the late 1860's when peddlers and storekeepers settled in Cheyenne. More Jewish merchants went to W. in the 1880's and 1890's. Although public worship was initiated in Cheyenne in the 1880's, there was no synagogue until 1915. In 1973, there were 345 Jews, mostly of E European origin, in W., 280 of them in Cheyenne.

YAALEH (Heb. "may it arise"): A synagogue hymn patterned on the prayer Y<small>AALEH</small> <small>VE</small>-Y<small>AVO</small> and recited in the evening service of the Day of Atonement in the Italian and Ashkenazi rites, and in an altered form in the Polish rite. It serves as an introduction to the *seliḥot*. The author is unknown.

YAALEH VE-YAVO (Heb. "may it arise and come"): First words of paragraph added to the *amidah* and Grace after Meals on New Moons and Festivals: in the Spanish and Yemenite rites, also in the *amidah* of the additional service for the New Year and Day of Atonement.

YAARI: (1) *AVRAHAM Y.* (1899–1966): Scholar. Born in Galicia, he settled in Palestine in 1920 and worked in the National Library from 1925. He published numerous works on Hebrew bibliography and on the history of Palestine. They include anthologies of Palestinian travelers' accounts, memoirs and letters describing Palestinian life, and a history of the emissaries (*sheliḥim*) from Palestine to the Diaspora. (2) *YEHUDAH Y.* (1900–): Hebrew novelist; brother of (1). He too went from Galicia to Palestine in 1920. Y. has written stories and romances, chiefly of E European life during the 20th cent. and of pioneer youth in Israel.

YAD (Heb. "hand"): Pointer for indicating the place during the Reading of the Law.

YAD AVSHALOM see **ABSALOM**

YAD CHAIM WEIZMANN see **WEIZMANN INSTITUTE**

YAD HA-ḤAZAKAH see **MOSES BEN MAIMON**

YAD MORDECAI: Israel communal settlement (KA). Founded in 1943 by a group from Poland and named for Mordecai A<small>NILEWICZ</small>, it was captured by the Egyptians in June, 1948, and rebuilt after its liberation 4 months later. As a result of its situation on the border of the G<small>AZA</small> S<small>TRIP</small>, its settlers suffered severely from infiltrators in subsequent years.

YAD VA-SHEM (Heb. "Monument and Name"): Israel official authority for the commemoration of the massacre of the Jews in the Nazi era and of the manifestation of heroism at that time. It was in-

Yad va-Shem shrine in Jerusalem

Professor Yigael Yadin.

stituted by a Knesset bill in 1953 which authorized *Yad va-Shem* to establish commemorative projects, collect and publish documents relating to the catastrophe, etc. Its seat is on Memorial Hill adjoining Mt. Herzl, Jerusalem, which is the site of a shrine, archives, a library, etc. The institution publishes books about the catastrophe. Represented in the directorate of the organization are the Israel government, the Jewish Agency, the Jewish National Fund, and the Conference on Jewish Material Claims against Germany.

YADAYIM (Heb. "Hands"): Eleventh tractate (tenth in some codices) in the talmudic order *Tohorot*, containing 4 chapters. It has no *gemara* in either Talmud. It deals with rabbinic enactments concerning the ritual impurity of hands and the proper manner for their ablution. Other topics include the canonicity of the Song of Songs and Ecclesiastes, the Aramaic language in Ezra and Daniel, the ancient Hebrew script, and disputations between the Pharisees and Sadducees.

YADIN, YIGAEL (1917–): Israel soldier and scholar; son of E. L. SUKENIK. He served as chief of operations during the Israel War of Independence and as chief of staff of the Israel army 1949–52. Since 1952, he has lectured in archeology at the Hebrew Univ. (professor 1959), published basic researches into the Dead Sea Scrolls (*Wars of the Sons of Light against Sons of Darkness*; *A Genesis Apocryphon*, etc.) and the Bar-Kokhba letters, and directed excavations at Hazor (1955–1968) and Masada (1963–5).

YAGUR: Israel communal settlement (KM) near Haifa. Founded in 1922 by a group of E European origin who drained the swamps in the vicinity, it developed into one of the country's largest kibbutzim, combining intensive agriculture with industrial undertakings. Pop. (1972): 1,161.

YAH, YAHWEH see **GOD, NAMES OF**

YAHAD (Heb. "unity"): A term which the sect of the DEAD SEA SCROLLS used to designate its own organization; also the spirit uniting it.

YAHRZEIT (Yidd. from Ger. "year-time"): Anniversary of the death of a close relative, observed by the kindling of a light and the recital of KADDISH; in some communities, also by fasting. Though German in origin, the term has become widely current even in N Africa, Yemen, India, etc. The corresponding Sephardi terms include *hazkarah* ("remembrance") and *petirah* ("passing").

YAHUDA, ABRAHAM SHALOM (1877–1951): Orientalist. Born in Jerusalem, he was professor in Berlin 1905–14 and Madrid 1915–22, and lectured thereafter at various universities. From 1942, he taught at the New School for Social Research in New York. A delegate to the First Zionist Congress (1897), Y. took an active interest in Jewish national affairs. He was author of biblical and philological works, sought to establish Egyptian affinities for the Pentateuch, and edited the Arabic original of Bahya's *Hovot ha-Levavot*.

YAHYA see **IBN YAHYA**

YAKHINI, ABRAHAM HA- (fl. 17th cent.): Sabbetaian; lived in Constantinople. Y., who loyally followed Shabbetai Tzevi even after his conversion, wrote psalms, sermons, and a commentary on the Tosephta. He has wrongly been considered the author of a prophecy of the advent of Shabbetai Tzevi published in the name of a medieval scholar.

Woodcut of a hare-hunt illustrating *yaknehaz* (Augsburg Haggadah, 1534).

YAKNEHAZ: Mnemonic for the order of blessings for *kiddush* recited on a festival beginning on Saturday night. They are *yayin* (wine), *kiddush* (sanctification), *ner* (light), *havdalah* (end of Sabbath blessing), and *zeman* (*she-heheyanu* benediction). Folk-humor associated the word *y.* with the *German* "*jag den Has*" ("chase the hare") and artists illustrated

The Yarkon River.

the formula in Passover Haggadot by a hare-hunting scene.

YAKNEHAZ (pseudonym of Isaiah Nisan Goldberg; 1858–1927): Hebrew and Yiddish author. From 1880 he was a Hebrew teacher in Lithuania and he became a permanent assistant on the Hebrew newspaper *Ha-Melitz*. Y. published some 500 stories and sketches in the Hebrew and Yiddish press. His simple narration and popular subjects won him a wide audience.

YALKUT SHIMONI: A midrashic collection relating to all the books of the Bible, compiled by Simeon Ha-Darshan presumably of Frankfort-on-Main in the 13th cent. The work preserves many sections from Midrashim which are no longer extant.

YAMIM NORAIM (Heb. "Days of Awe"): Term applied to the New Year and Day of Atonement, when — according to Jewish tradition — all mankind stands before the Divine throne of judgment.

YANAIT, RACHEL see **BEN-ZVI**

YANNAI see **ALEXANDER YANNAI**

YANNAI: Name of several talmudic rabbis, the best-known being a Palestinian amora (fl. mid-3rd cent.), pupil of R Judah Ha-Nasi and R Ḥiyya, who established his academy at Akhbara in Upper Galilee. The traditions and teachings of the academy, which continued in existence long after his death, are cited in the Palestinian and Babylonian Talmuds as *de-ve Rabbi Yannai* ("School of R Yannai"). His two chief pupils were R Johanan and R Simeon ben Lakish.

YANNAI (6th cent.?): Hebrew liturgical poet. Little is known of his life, even his period and country of residence being disputed, although it is almost certain that he was Palestinian. He introduced rhyme into religious poetry and was the first-known Hebrew poet to sign his name acrostically. T. wrote *piyyutim* related to the weekly Bible portion and determined the final form of the KEROVAH. With the exception of *Az rov nissim* in the Ashkenazi Passover Haggadah, his *piyyutim* were forgotten until the 19th cent., when scholars discovered surviving poems which were supplemented by further examples from the Cairo *genizah* and were comprehensively edited by M. Zulai (1938).

YARKON: Israel river rising at Rosh ha-Ayin and flowing into the Mediterranean N of Tel Aviv; its length is 20 m. The waters of the Y. have been partly directed to the Negev for irrigation purposes since 1955.

YARMOLINSKY, AVRAHM (1890–1975): Author and librarian. Born in Russia, he went to the US in 1913. He headed the Slavonic division of the New York public library from 1918. Y. wrote, translated, and edited many volumes, mostly from and about Russian literature. He was married to Babette DEUTSCH.

YARMUK (from Gk. Hieromychos, i.e., the "sacred gorge"): Affluent of the Jordan in Transjordania; total length—70 km. (50 mi.). It falls from 1,950 ft. above to 829 ft. below sea level. Its waters were utilized by the Palestine Electric Company, but since 1948 the power-plant at Naharayim on the Israel-Jordan

The Yarmuk River near El-Hammah.

frontier has been unused. The Y. was the scene of a battle in which the Byzantines lost Syria and Palestine to the Moslems (636).

YARMULKE (derivation uncertain): Skull-cap worn for prayer, and, by religious Jews at all times.

YASHAR, SEPHER HA- see **BOOK OF JASHAR**

YAVNEEL see **JABNEEL**

YAVNEH see **JABNEH**

YEAR see **CALENDAR**

YEB (ELEPHANTINE): Ancient island, fortress town on the Egyptian-Ethiopian frontier, on the Nile opposite Aswan. From the end of the Egyptian royal period (c. 590 BCE) and throughout the Persian era, a military garrison of Jewish soldiers, with their own temple, was stationed there. It is thought that the Jewish community reached Y. with refugees from Judah after the destruction of the First Temple. The temple at Y. was destroyed by an Egyptian mob incited by the priests of the local god, but apparently rebuilt as a result of the Jews' request to the satrap of Judah, Bagoas. The episode is described in the contemporary Elephantine papyri, written in Aramaic, which were discovered on the site in the early 20th cent.

YEHOASH see **BLOOMGARDEN**

YEHUD: Israel urban settlement near Lydda. The town existed in Bible times (Josh. 19:45) and was resettled by Jews returning from the Babylonian captivity. It was an Arab village until 1948 and was subsequently occupied by new immigrants mostly working in the Tel Aviv area. Pop. (1974): 9,700.

YEHUDAI: Gaon of Sura 750–4. A native of Pumbedita, he succeeded Solomon bar Hasdai as head of the Sura academy. He was the first to enter systematically into relations with the growing Jewish communities of N Africa and strove to enforce Babylonian usages even in Palestine. Over a hundred of his responsa have survived. His chief literary legacy is the code HALAKHOT PESUKOT which was written for him by his pupils, as Y. himself was blind.

YEHUDI BEN SHESHET (fl. late 10th cent.): Grammarian. A pupil of DUNASH BEN LABRAT, Y. wrote a venomous rejoinder to the polemic which the pupils of MENAHEM BEN SARUK directed against Dunash after the latter's attack upon their teacher.

YEIVEN see **YEVIN**

YEKOPO (initials of Russ. "Committee for Jewish Assistance"): Society founded in 1915 to assist Jews expelled by the Russian military command

A letter from the Jews of Yeb to the satrap of Judah (5th cent. BCE).

David Yellin.

from the Baltic provinces, etc. It was liquidated by the Soviet authorities in 1920.

YEKUM PURKAN (Heb. "may redemption come"):

First words of two Aramaic prayers, one for the welfare of the communal and scholastic heads of Palestine and Babylonia and the other, of the general community. They were composed during the Gaonic Period and are recited in Ashkenazi communities after the reading of the Law on Sabbaths, sometimes with modifications to remove anachronisms.

YELAMMEDENU see **TANḤUMA**

YELGAVA (Mitau): Town in Latvia, now USSR. An organized Jewish community existed there from 1730, except for 1759–70 when Jews were excluded. In 1840, 863 Jews left Y. to settle on the land in S Ukraine. Its community was destroyed during the German occupation in World War II.

YELLIN, DAVID (1864–1941): Palestinian scholar.

He was one of the first teachers of secular Hebrew in his native Jerusalem where he later headed the Hebrew Teachers' College and was one of the organizers of the national Hebrew educational system. He became a central figure in the Palestinian Jewish community, helping to found the *Vaad Leumi*, Jewish Teachers' Organization, B'nai B'rith in Palestine, etc.; he served as deputy-mayor of Jerusalem 1920–5, president of the *Asephat ha-Nivharim* and head of the *Vaad Leumi* 1920–8. His literary researches centered on medieval Jewish poetry (on which he lectured at the Hebrew Univ.) and Hebrew philology. Y.'s publications include a monograph on Maimonides, Bible studies, a Hebrew dictionary and grammar, and an edition of the poems of Todros Abulafia.

YEMEN: Arabic name of SW ARABIA; today an independent state. Various traditions trace the settlement of Jews in this region back to biblical times and even to the era of the First Temple. Immigration on a larger scale (from Palestine and also from Mesopotamia, etc.) does not appear to have preceded the 2nd cent. CE. Inscriptions discovered in the Bet Shearim catacombs evidence the existence of Jewish communities in Y. in the early 3rd cent., and Byzantine sources testify to them from the 4th cent. At first, their number was probably small (estimated at 3,000 for the first centuries), but they made many converts among the native population. According to Moslem tradition, conversion to Judaism started under Abu Karib Asad (ruled c. 390–420), who became a Jew himself and propagated his new faith among his subjects. Arabic sources expressly state that Judaism became widely spread among Bedouin tribes of S Arabia and that Jewish converts were also found with the Hamdan, a N Yemenite tribe. At this time, many of the upper strata of society also embraced the Jewish faith. The position of Judaism in Y. reached its zenith under DHU NUWAS; after his death and the downfall of his kingdom, Christianity rapidly gained ground in S Arabia, especially among the former converts to Judaism; but even then, some Yemenite rulers were of the Jewish faith. After the rise of ISLAM, the Jews of Y. were spared the fate of their coreligionists in HEJAZ. Against payment of the taxes imposed on all non-Moslems, MOHAMMED assured them protection and freedom of religion. No information is extant on Yemenite Jews for the subsequent centuries, but their position must have been precarious, especially after the establishment of Shi'ite rule in the country (early 10th cent.). The men only were educated in Jewish traditional studies, knowing Hebrew and Aramaic well. The Kabbalah was popular among them. They produced several liturgical poets, the most celebrated being Shalom SHABBAZI. The sectarian rulers of Y. proved more oppressive to their Jewish subjects than orthodox sovereigns in other Moslem countries. The restrictions imposed by Mohammedan law on non-Moslems were always rigidly enforced in Y., and up to modern times, its Jews were strictly forbidden, e.g. to ride on animals or wear the same clothes as Moslems. They were deprived of their property on the pretext that any semblance of wealth was incompatible with the status assigned to the Jews by God. They constantly suffered insults and abuses, since religious law was interpreted to the effect that unbelievers should be disgraced. Orphans were converted by force. The Jews usually lived in villages or quarters of their own, but in the late 17th cent., after they had been expelled and on their recall not allowed to re-enter their former homes inside the walls, Jewish suburbs sprang up outside the Moslem cities. Down to the 19th cent. Yemenite Jewry experienced a number of messianic movements, the best-known of which occurred in the late 12th cent., when a false prophet proclaimed the amalgamation of Judaism and Mohammedanism; to counter him, Maimonides wrote his

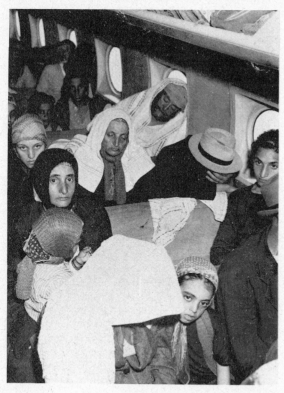

Operation Magic Carpet.

Epistle to Yemen (1172) in which he exhorted the Jews to abide by the faith of their fathers despite compulsion and persecutions. The late history of Yemenite Jews consists mainly of a series of persecutions. The Jews of Y. achieved renown as excellent artisans. chiefly silversmiths. In the early 19th cent., Yemenite Jews are said to have numbered 30,000, about one third living in SANAA. Systematic Yemenite Jewish immigration to Palestine began c. 1910 and attained fairly large proportions despite constant difficulties. This continued until 1948 by which time there were 18,000 Yemenite Jews in Palestine. Virtually the whole Jewish community, numbering about 46,000, was transferred to Israel in 1949–50 in OPERATION MAGIC CARPET.

YEROHAM: Urban settlement in the N. Negev, Israel. Founded in 1951, most of its inhabitants work in the Great Crater and in the Dead Sea Works at Sodom. The name is mentioned in an Egyptian source of the 10th century BCE. concerning Shishak's war with Israel. Pop. (1974): 6,300.

YESHIVA UNIVERSITY: University in New York, US. The first American university under Jewish auspices, it traces its origins to the Etz Chaim yeshivah founded in 1886 and the R Isaac Elhanan Theological Seminary founded in 1896. The two merged in 1915. added Yeshiva College in 1928, and became Y.U. in 1945. With its main center in the Washington

Heights area of New York city, it also maintains educational facilities in the Bronx and Manhattan and has an enrollment of over 7,000 students taking courses leading to graduate and undergraduate degrees. Its staff numbers 1,150. Y. U. includes the R Isaac Elhanań Theological Seminary, Yeshiva College for Men, College of Arts and Sciences, College for Women, Teachers' Institutes for Men and Women, Graduate School, School of General Jewish Studies, School for Higher Jewish Studies, Graduate School of Education, School of Social Work, Institutes of Mathematics, Cantorial Training, and Israel Studies, the Albert Einstein College of Medicine and the Graduate Division of Medical Sciences. Its auxiliary services include a psychological center, educational service, audio-visual service, community service and West Coast Division. Its library system has over 600,000 volumes of which 150,000 are Judaica. It published the Hebrew periodicals *Horeb, Talpioth,* and *Sura* as well as *Studies in Judaica* and *Studies in Torah Judaism* and the mathematical journal *Scripta Mathematica.*

YESHIVAH (Heb.): Jewish traditional school devoted primarily to the study of the Talmud and rabbinic literature. The y. is a direct continuation of the ACADEMIES which flourished in Palestine and Babylonia

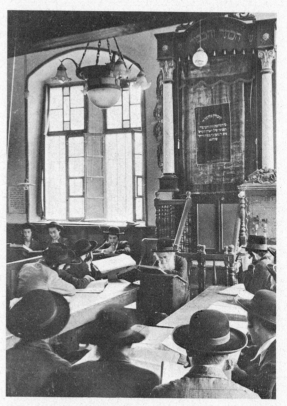

Talmud lesson in the "Tiphereth-Zion" synagogue, in the Old City of Jerusalem.

in the Talmudic and Gaonic Period and which were later established in various parts of Europe and elsewhere. Lithuania is the country most noted for the growth of the y. in modern times, beginning with the establishment of the y. of Volozhin in 1803. Famous yeshivot founded in the 19th cent. include Tels, Slobodka, Mir, and Kamanetz. World War II brought to an end yeshivot in E Europe; many of them transferred to America or Palestine. Almost all the American yeshivot, as well as most of the newly-established ones in Israel, maintain a secular program of study on the intermediate level simultaneously with the traditional grounding in talmudic scholarship.

YESHIVATH TORAH VODAATH AND ME-SIVTA: Orthodox educational institution founded in 1918 in Brooklyn, New York. It consists of elementary and high schools, as well as a teachers' and a rabbinical seminary. Y. T. V. has an enrollment of 1,500 students.

YESUD HA-MAALAH: Israel village in the Upper Jordan Valley. Founded in 1883, its settlers—originating from Mezhirich in Russia—suffered severely in the early years from malaria. Baron Edmond de Rothschild took the settlement under his protection, but development was nevertheless extremely slow, irrigation not being introduced until shortly before 1948. Pop. (1972): 477.

YETZER HA-RA and **YETZER HA-TOV** (Heb.): The evil and the good inclination. *Yetzer ha-Ra* is frequently used in a restricted sense to refer to the sexual urge: see also GOOD & EVIL.

YETZIRAH, SEPHER see SEPHER YETZIRAH

YEVAMOT (Heb. "levirates"): First tractate in the talmudic order *Nashim* containing 16 chapters. It has *gemara* in both the Babylonian and Palestinian Talmuds. Y. deals with the status of the widow of a man who has died childless and whose brother must contract LEVIRATE MARRIAGE with her or grant ḤALITZAH.

YEVIN, SHEMUEL (1896–): Archeologist. Of Russian birth, he settled in Palestine before World War I and participated in many archeological expeditions. Y. was secretary of the *Vaad ha-Lashon* 1935–42, and directed the Israel Department of Antiquities 1948–59. He has written on the Bar Kokhba revolt and is an editor of the *Entziklopedia Mikrait* ("Biblical Encyclopedia").

YEVSEKTZIA (abbr. from Russ. "Jewish branch"): Jewish branch of the Russian Communist Party 1918–30. It was responsible for the liquidation of communal organizations and Jewish institutions, boycotting of synagogues, and activities against Hebrew and Judaism. In 1926 it initiated territorial plans in Crimea and later in BIROBIDJAN. Its organ was the daily EMES. Many of its leaders were executed in the purges of 1936–8.

Page from a 16th cent. ms collection of Yiddish tales.

YEZIERSKA, ANZIA (1885–1970): Author. Born in Russia, she was in the US from 1901. Her stories and novels depict the experiences of Jewish immigrants in America.

YIDDISH: Language spoken by a majority of Ashkenazi Jewry from the Middle Ages. Four main components entered into the formation of Y.: Hebrew, Loez (the Jewish correlates of Old French and Old Italian), German, and Slavic. Of these, medieval German of the Middle Rhine region was the most important. German words, many in new applications, have supplied about 85% of the vocabulary and the basic grammatical structure. Hebrew words predominate in the religious and intellectual sphers. English words have become increasingly significant during recent decades in English-speaking countries and many neo-Hebrew words have been added since the rise of Israel. The structure of the language, however, has hardly been affected by vocabulary changes. Since the formation of Initial Y., 1000–1250, the language has undergone constant growth and may be divided chronologically into Old Y., 1250–1500; Middle Y. 1500–1750; and modern Y., from 1750 on. Y. may also be divided spatially into western Y., now almost extinct, and eastern Y., subdivided into a northern dialect centered in Lithuania and a southern dialect extending from Poland to the Ukraine and Rumania. In the US, the southern dialect dominates on the stage and the northern dialect on the lecture platform, but in daily speech every variety of pronunciation is found. The standard pronunciation is based on the northern dialect. Y. is written in Hebrew characters. Spelling was standardized in 1937 by YIVO, but some newspapers still adhere to older spelling and in the Soviet Union, the traditional spelling of the Hebrew words in Y. has been abandoned. At the outbreak of World War II, Y. speakers numbered between ten and twelve million. Extermination has, however, more than halved this number. In W Europe and America, Y. once predominant among Jews, is now comparatively little spoken by the native-born.

YIDDISH LITERATURE: The first important Yiddish literary works were produced in the 16th cent. and included Arthurian romances, of which the most popular was the *Bovo-Buch* or *Bovo-Maase*, a verse epic of the adventures of Prince Bovo of Antona (= Bevis of Hampton), composed by Elijah Levita in 1507–8. The best heroic epic of Old Yiddish with a Jewish hero was the *Shmuel-Buch*, which centered about King David. The *Maase-Buch* was a prose collection of talmudic legends and folktales in which the lore of many peoples and of countless centuries were recorded in the transformations effected by the Jewish mind. The *Tzenah u-Reenah*, a combination of stories and moralistic teachings based on the Bible, was the Yiddish book most widely read by women. *Tekhines*, Yiddish devotional prayers, were also especially composed for women and still retain their vogue. Yiddish literary production declined in the 17th and 18th cents. During the first half of the 19th cent., Yiddish was used as a medium of enlightenment by Haskalah writers, such as Solomon Ettinger, Abraham Ber Gottlober, and Isaac Meir Dick. They paved the way for the classical masters — Mendele Mocher Sephorim, Isaac Leib Peretz, and Sholem Aleichem. In fiction, the most gifted contemporaries of the classicists were Jacob Dinesohn, Mordecai Spector, and S. An-Ski, although none of them attained the popularity of the prolific Shomer,

pseudonym of Nahum Meir Shaikevitch. The wedding bards Berl Broder, Velvel Zbarzher Ehrenkranz, Eliakim Zunser, and others paved the way for Abraham Goldfaden, father of the Yiddish theater. The drama, which began in Rumania and Russia in the 1870's, reached its climax on American soil in the first quarter of the 20th cent. with Jacob Gordin, Leon Kobrin, Peretz Hirschberg, and David Pinski. The undidactic Yiddish lyric of quality began with S. S. Frug and continued with Jehoash (pseudonym of Solomon Bloomgarden, a master stylist who also rendered the Bible into lucid Yiddish), Abraham Reisin, and H. Leivick. The socialist lyric of Morris Winchevsky, Morris Rosenfeld, and Abraham Liessin was far more effective on the American Jewish scene than the anarchist lyric of David Edelstadt and Joseph Bovshover. The golden glow of Y. L. in Russia was best reflected in the sad, impressionistic tales of David Bergelson, while the most widely read Yiddish novelist of Poland and America was Sholem Asch. Asch and Isaac Bashevis SINGER became known to an international public through translation. In lyric poetry more than in any other medium, literary schools arose and fell, from the Yiddish Introspectivists who centered about the periodical *In Sich* — Jacob Glatstein, A. Glanz-Leyeles, and N. B. Minkoff — to the group *Yung Vilna*, which included Abraham Suzkever, Chaim Grade, and Shmerke Katcherginsky. The Jewish tragedy of 1939–45 in E Europe, together with the Soviet repression, has annihilated the former creative centers of Y. L. On the other hand, the survivors have implanted its influences — it is yet to be seen whether or not with permanent results — more widely than ever before, e.g. in S Africa, Australia, and S America, as well as in England, Israel, and the US. In the 1960's, the outstanding organs for creative Y. L. were *Die Goldne Keht*, published in Tel Aviv, *Die Zukunft* published in New York and *Sovietishe Heimland* published in Moscow. The YIVO, founded in 1925 in Vilna and having its main center in New York since World War II, is the principal institute for the study of Y. L.

YIDDISHE GESELLSHAFTEN KOMITET (Yidd. "Jewish public committee"; abbr. Yidgazkom): Organization founded in 1920 by the Jewish Commissariat and the American Joint Distribution Committee to care for Jewish relief and social activities in Soviet Russia. For the first year representatives of ORT, OSE, and other relief groups also participated. With the liquidation of the Jewish Commissariat in 1923, the Y. G. K. continued to function with funds supplied by the Joint Distribution Committee, but ceased all its activities in 1924.

YIDDISHKEIT (Yidd.): The knowledge and habits of Judaism; Jewish culture.

YIDGAZKOM see **YIDDISHE GESELLSHAFTEN KOMITET**

Yigdal

(Traditional)

Yigdal elohim haive yub-tab-bah nim tza re-en   et   el metzi-u-to e-

had re-en ya bid ke-yi--hu--do ne lam vegannen soph le-ah du-to

YIGDAL (Heb. "may he be magnified"): Liturgical hymn based on an enumeration of Maimonides' THIRTEEN PRINCIPLES OF FAITH. It originated in Italy c. 1300 and its author seems to have been R Daniel bar Judah, dayyan in Rome. In the Sephardi and Italian rites Y. is read on Sabbath eves; the Ashkenazim use it as an opening hymn for the daily morning service. It is not recited by the Hasidim. On High Holy Days, especially the Day of Atonement, it is chanted to a special melody.

YIHUS (Heb. "connection"): Distinguished descent or family connections, especially from or with a scholar.

YISHAR KOAH or **YISHAR KOHAKHA** (Heb. "may your strength increase"): Congratulatory phrase to one who has publicly read, spoken, etc. Corrupted to *Shekoah*.

YISHUV (Heb.): A settlement or population-group: more specifically, the Jewish community of Israel.

YITZHAKI, SOLOMON see **RASHI**

YIVO (Yidd. *Yidisher Visenshaftlikher Institut* = 'Institute for Jewish Research'): Institute founded in Vilna in 1925 for the scientific study of Jewish life throughout the world but with particular emphasis upon E European Jewry and its Yiddish-speaking heirs on all continents. By 1939, branches of Y. were functioning in thirty countries. At the outbreak of World War II, its main center was transferred to New York and at the end of the war, part of the Vilna Library and Archives, salvaged from the Nazis, was brought to the US and added to the American collections of YIVO. In 1956, the English name was changed from Yiddish Scientific Institute to YIVO Institute of Jewish Research. Yivo's publications included, *Yivo Bleter* in Yiddish, the *Yivo Annual of Jewish Social Science* in English, *Yidishe Shprakh*, and monographs in Yiddish and English embodying research in Jewish linguistics, literature, history, sociology, economics, statistics, psychology, and folklore.

YIZHAR S. see **SMILANSKY**

YIZKOR (Heb. "He shall remember"): Opening word of the prayer in commemoration of the dead recited in Ashkenazi communities on the last days of the Three Festivals and on the Day of Atonement. The phrase is popularly applied to the service on these occasions, when congregants honor departed relatives. The rite, medieval in origin, is unknown among the Sephardim.

YIZREEL see **JEZREEL**

YOD (י): Tenth letter in the Hebrew alphabet; numerical value 10. It has the consonantal value of *y*. Yod is one of the vowel letters, י = *ee*; י = *ey* as in *they*; י, long *i* as in "*mind*".

YOFFE, ABRAM FEODOROVICH (1880–1960): Russian physicist. A pupil and assistant of Röntgen, he taught at St. Petersburg Univ. and was a founder of its X-ray and Radiological Institute. He directed the Physico-Technical Institute in Leningrad 1932–51 and was president of the Society of Soviet Physicists. In 1942, he was awarded a Stalin Prize. His researches were mainly in the field of electrotechnics and included work on the physical properties of crystals and the characteristics of dielectrics and half-conductors.

YOFFE, ADOLPH (1883–1927): Russian politician. Forced to leave Russia on account of his revolutionary activities, in 1908 he founded the newspaper *Pravda* at Vienna together with Trotsky. Returning to Russia, he was banished to Siberia in 1912 but released after the 1917 Revolution, when he was appointed head of the Russian delegation to the Brest-Litovsk peace conference (1918) and led various Bolshevik missions. Because of his Trotskyist sympathies, he was removed from public life. He committed suicide the day after Trotsky was expelled from the Communist Party.

YOKNEAM see **JOKNEAM**

YOM ATZMAUT (Heb. "Independence Day"): Anniversary of Israel's declaration of independence which was signed on *Iyyar* 5, 5708 (May 14, 1948). The Hebrew date is observed annually in Israel as a public holiday.

YOM KIPPUR see **ATONEMENT, DAY OF**

YOM KIPPUR WAR: On Yom Kippur, Oct. 6, 1973, Egyptian and Syrian forces attacked Israel, and full-scale war erupted. The Syrians initially overran much of the Golan Heights, but, despite support from Iraqi and Jordanian troops, etc., they were stopped and driven far behind the lines from which they had attacked. The Egyptians crossed the Suez Canal in the first hours of the war and seized the Israel forward positions (the "Bar-Lev line"). As a result of wide-ranging tank battles, however, they were unable to progress through the Sinai Desert. Both sides suffered severe losses in equipment, but when a Soviet airlift replaced Arab *matériel* the US countered with a major arms airlift, starting on Oct. 14. Two days later, an Israeli force crossed the Suez Canal and in a few days cut off the Egyptian Third Army. The USSR, concerned about the possibility of a major Arab defeat, invited US Secretary of State Henry Kissinger to Moscow to work out terms for a ceasefire, which were accepted by the UN on Oct. 22 and became operative on Oct. 25. Israel's overall military victory notwithstanding, the war had grave repercussions within the country because of the initial defects revealed, the loss of more than 2,600 men, and the

"Independence Day" Parade in 1968.

effectiveness of the Arab oil weapon, used internationally for the first time.

YOM KIPPUR KATAN (Heb. "Minor Day of Atonement"): The fast observed on the day before the New Moon. The custom to fast on this day was in existence in Palestine in the 16th cent. (possibly originating in circles close to Isaac Luria) and was brought by Moses Cordovero from there to Italy whence it found its way to Germany. A special order of prayer (consisting of psalms and *selihot*) is added to the regular afternoon service where this custom is observed. In certain communities, the special prayers are recited although the fast is not kept.

YOMA (Aram "The Day"; original Heb. name *Kippurim* called *Yom ha-Kippurim* in the Tosephta): Fifth tractate (fourth in some codices) in the talmudic order *Moed*, containing 8 chapters. It has *gemara* in both the Babylonian and Palestinian Talmuds. It describes the Temple service of the high priest on the Day of Atonement. The regulations regarding the fast and the general significance of atonement and repentance are discussed in the last chapter.

YOMTOV see **FESTIVAL**

YOMTOV BEN ABRAHAM ISHBILI (i.e., of Seville; known as *Ritba*; b. before 1270 — d.c. 1330): Spanish talmudist. In his lucid talmudic commentaries, summaries of the views of previous authorities preface his own contributions. He also wrote a commentary on the Passover Haggadah and a defense of Maimonides.

YOMTOV BEN ISAAC OF JOIGNY (d. 1190): Tosaphist and liturgical poet. His hymns include *Omnam Ken*, which has been incorporated in the Ashkenazi service for the eve of the Day of Atonement. He died in the YORK massacre.

YOMTOV LIPMANN see **MÜHLHAUSEN**
YOREH DEAH see **JACOB BEN ASHER**
YORK: English city. On the Sabbath before Passover (Mar. 16) 1190, the Y. Jews, headed by R Yom-Tov of Joigny, were besieged in the Castle Keep by a bloodthirsty mob and killed one another rather than surrender. A small community was subsequently re-established and continued until the expulsion of 1290. The present congregation (numbering 45) was organized in 1892.

YOSE BEN HALAPHTA (generally called R Yose; 2nd cent. CE): Palestinian tanna; pupil of R Akiva. He headed the academy in his native town of Sepphoris, and was among the leaders of the assemblies at Usha and Jabneh after the abolition of the Hadrianic decrees. He was greatly respected by the patriarchs, Judah Ha-Nasi and Simeon ben Gamliel, who accepted his opinion in all halakhic matters. Y. was noted as a mediator who put forward compromises to reconcile conflicting viewpoints. He is traditionally the author of the chronological work SEDER OLAM, and many historical traditions are quoted by the Talmud in his name.

YOSE BEN JOEZER (2nd cent. BCE): Rabbi; together with Yose ben Johanan the first of the "pairs" (ZUGOT). A pupil of Antigonus of Sokho, he served as president of the Sanhedrin during the generation preceding the Maccabean revolt. In his fight to preserve Judaism against hellenistic inroads, he decreed lands outside Palestine as unclean.

YOSE BEN YOSE (fl. 5th cent.): Poet. The first *paytan* known by name, he probably lived in Palestine. Some of his poems, which were highly regarded by the Babylonian geonim, have been introduced into the High Holiday liturgy, particularly the *Avodah* of the Sephardi rite for the Day of Atonement. They are without meter or rhyme and are constructed on the basis of a double alphabetic acrostic. The language is biblical but mingled with midrashic and late expressions.

YOSE HA-GELILI (i.e., "the Galilean"; fl. 2nd cent. CE): Palestinian tanna. He was a leading figure in the Jabneh academy where he often disputed with R Akiva. Many halakhot are recorded in which he differed from his colleagues. Y. was known for his high moral standards.

YOSEF, OVADIAH (1920–): Israel rabbi. Born in Baghdad, he was taken to Jerusalem as a child. In 1947–50 he served in Egypt. In 1968 he was elected Sephardi chief rabbi of Tel Aviv and in 1972 Sephardi chief rabbi of Israel.

YOSEPH (JOSEPH), DOV (Bernard; 1899–): Israel public figure. A native of Canada and a lawyer by profession, he settled in Palestine in 1921. He was a member of the Jewish Agency Executive 1945–8 and military governor of Jerusalem during the War of Independence. He represented *Mapai* in the Knesset

Ben Shemen children's village.

1949–65 and held several cabinet positions (notably minister of commerce and industry 1951–3, of development 1953–5 and minister of justice 1961–6). In 1957–61, Y. was treasurer of the Jewish Agency.

YOTBAH (modern Tiran): Small island at the mouth of the Gulf of Elath (Akaba). In the 5th cent., it was settled by Jewish traders and cattle-breeders. The Jewish settlement retained autonomy under Persian suzerainty until subjected by Justinian (c. 535).

YOTBAT see **JOTAPATA**

YOTZER (Heb. "createth"): Designation still used in some rites for the morning prayer (SHAḤARIT), taken from words of the opening blessing in the framework of the SHEMA. It is also applied to a hymn preceding the *Shema* and, more loosely, to denote all the special hymns (*piyyutim*) added to the blessings of the *Shema* on Sabbaths and Festivals (the individual names of these hymns being: *yotzer, ophan, zulat,* and occasionally also *meorah, ahavah, mi khamokha, geullah*). Y. is also mistakenly applied in the plural (*yotzerot*) to the additional liturgical hymns included throughout the entire morning service.

YOUNG ISRAEL: US organization established in 1912 in New York to advance Orthodox Judaism and study of the Torah. It has a membership (1970) of 35,000 families (one-half in New York) in 106 branches in the US, Canada, Holland, and Israel. The National Council, formed in 1922, establishes the policies of the movement. Most branches maintain a synagogue, rabbi, Hebrew school, adult study group, and youth activities. The National Council projects include: an Institute for Adult Jewish Studies, with enrollment of 7,000; an Employment Bureau which places nearly 1,000 Sabbath-observers yearly; a monthly periodical, *Young Israel Viewpoint*; and support for yeshivot and other Orthodox cultural institutions in Israel.

YOUNG JUDEA: US Zionist youth movement. It runs summer camps, week-end institutes, etc. Its membership in 1971 was 12,000.

YOUNG MEN'S (WOMEN'S) HEBREW ASSOCIATIONS see **JEWISH COMMUNITY CENTER**

YOUNGSTOWN: City in the state of Ohio, US. Jewish settlement dates from 1837 with the arrival of immigrants from Alsace and Bavaria. A congregation was formed in 1867, and the first Orthodox congregation in 1887. Jewish pop. (1973): 5,400.

YOUTH ALIYAH: Organization for transferring young persons to Israel and educating them there. The movement was initiated by Recha Freyer in the early 1930's as a result of the intensified German anti-Semitism. It was headed 1933–45 by Henrietta Szold. The first group reached Palestine from Germany in 1934; by May, 1948, 29,000 children and youths had been transferred, absorbed, and educated by Y. A. in Palestinian labor villages, agricultural institutions, and specially established centers. These included German-Jewish children, refugees, and orphans of World War II. A further 93,000 had arrived by the end of 1971 from Asia, N Africa, the Balkans, and Europe, while an additional 19,000 were taken under Y. A. auspices in Israel within the framework of the "Town to Country" scheme. More recently, an additional form of absorption has been the regional youth center which the young people attend only during the day. Of the 248 Y. A. centers for education and absorption, 150 are agricultural settlements and the remainder YOUTH VILLAGES and educational institutions. The main educational direction is toward rural settlement. Social education is combined with the reconstruction of the personality. Y. A. wards have originated from 72 countries and at the end of 1971, 10,000 individuals were under its care. The annual budget totals IL. 30,000,000 of which more than half is met by voluntary contributions, notably from the American Hadassah Organization and other Zionist women's groups; the remainder is covered by the Jewish Agency. The project belongs to several international organizations for child education and welfare, etc. The enterprise was administered by Mosheh Kol 1947–66. Its managing committee is appointed by the Jewish Agency Executives. Y. A. publishes the bi-monthly *Dappim* as well as textbooks and educational literature.

YOUTH VILLAGES: Educational and agricultural settlements for young people. There are about 50 Y. V. in Israel, the vast majority being associated with YOUTH ALIYAH. Their educational system is based on study within an elementary school framework, and many also maintain agricultural secondary schools. Practical work is mainly in agriculture, but artistic and musical education is also fostered. The pupils receive their education within the social framework of the children's and youth groups, with the object of preparation for group settlement. The Y. V. average about 200 pupils, although some have 400 or over. The first youth settlement in the country was the agricultural school of MIKVEH ISRAEL. MEIR SHEPHEYAH and BEN SHEMEN are the oldest villages. The types of Y. V. include independent villages with developed farms; villages connected with established agricultural settlements or institutions (for pedagogic therapy, etc.); and those in the vicinity of cities where handicraft education is stressed. The Ministry of Social Welfare also maintains Y. V. for difficult, backward, and disturbed children. Many Y.V. were built by women's Zionist organizations (WIZO,

HADASSAH, etc.). They are associated through Youth Aliyah with an international organization of Y. V. under the patronage of Unesco.

YUDGHAN (fl. early 8th cent.): Founder of a Jewish sect called after him (Yudghanites). He lived in Hamadan and was a disciple of ABU ISSA AL-ISFAHANI, founder of the Issawite sect. Unlike his teacher, he did not claim to have been Divinely charged with the restoration of the Jews to political independence but maintained that he was a prophet. Influenced by the doctrines of Moslem Sufism, he advocated a mystic or spiritual interpretation of the Torah and declared that all traditional religious symbols are mere allegories. He maintained the prohibition on wine and animal food which had already been introduced by the Issawites. The sect he founded was short-lived.

YUGOSLAVIA: Jews were settled in the present Y. from Roman times, as is evidenced by the synagogue inscription found in STOBI and relics at Salona. Little or nothing is known of the relations of medieval Serbia with the Jews. On the Dalmation coast, however, there were communities in Ragusa (Dubrovnik) and Spalato (Split). Inland, refugees from Spain began to settle after the expulsion of 1492, the most important centers being BELGRADE and SARAJEVO, where the Sephardi traditions were preserved. When Serbia re-established her independence in the 19th cent., the treatment of the Jews was bad. But the new state punctiliously observed the conditions of the Berlin treaties of 1878 regarding religious equality, and the "Jewish Problem" rapidly disappeared. The same conditions were extended to the areas conquered by Serbia in the Balkan War of 1912–3 and the former Austrian territories acquired after World War I, which added an Ashkenazi element to the community. In World War II the Germans and their native Ustashi adherents (supported by the Bosnian Moslems instigated by Haj Amin el HUSSEINI) carried out deportations and massacres on a vast scale. After the war, only some 10,500 Jews out of a former total of 72,000 were left in Y. 8,000 Jews from Y. immigrated to Israel after 1948. Jewish pop. (1973): 7,500.

YULEE (LEVY), DAVID (1810–1886): US legislator. He represented Florida in the 27th and 28th Congress and in the Senate 1845–51 and 1855–61 being the first Jew to sit there. During the Civil War he was a member of the Confederate Congress.

YUSHKEVICH, SEMYON (1868–1927): Russian novelist and playwright; of Jewish origin. He left Russia after the 1917 Bolshevik Revolution and died in Paris. He belonged to the group around Gorki and his works described poverty, prostitution, and licence in Jewish life of the large cities.

ZABARA, JOSEPH see **IBN ZABARA**

ZACUT(O), ABRAHAM (c. 1450–1515): Spanish astronomer and historian. He studied and taught in his native Salamanca. His Hebrew work on astronomy *Ha-Ḥibbur ha-Gadol* (written 1473–8) was translated into Spanish and Latin. Z. was the first to make a metal Astrolabe and he drew up improved astronomical tables which were invaluable as guides to navigation and were used by Columbus (a copy with the explorer's own annotations is preserved in Seville). On the expulsion from Spain in 1492, Z. became astronomer and astrologer at the court of John II of Portugal. Here he was consulted by Vasco da Gama before the latter's momentous voyage to India in 1497/8. Shortly afterward, the Jews were expelled from Portugal, and after many wanderings, Z. settled in Tunis. Here he completed his *Sepher Yuḥasin* on the history of rabbinic scholarship. Little is known of Z.'s later years; in 1513, he was in Jerusalem, and in 1515, in Damascus.

ZACUTO (ZACUT), MOSES BEN MORDECAI (c. 1625–1697): Poet and mystic. Born in Amsterdam, he set out on a pilgrimage to Palestine but was persuaded to remain in Italy as rabbi, first in Venice and then in Mantua. A devotee of the Kabbalah, he composed mystical and devotional poems many of which entered into Italian synagogue usage. In addition, he wrote responsa, a poetical vision of the after-life, *Tophteh Arukh*, and a drama on Abraham, *Yesod Olam*.

ZACUTUS LUSITANUS (i.e., Zacuto the Portuguese, properly Abraham Zacuto; 1576–1642): Marrano physician. After a distinguished career in Portugal under the name Manoel Alvares, he fled to Amsterdam in 1625 and declared himself a Jew. His medical writings were of great importance.

ZADOK: Priest. A descendant of Aaron, he may have first officiated at the altar in Gibeon but after Saul's death, went to David at Hebron and—together with Abiathar—was David's chief priest. He remained loyal during Absalom's rebellion and on David's command, anointed Solomon as king. Solomon appointed Z.'s son a high priest in the Temple and from that time the high priesthood remained in the Zadokite family until the period of the Hasmonean rising. Even after their deposition from their high office, many aristocratic priestly families claimed kinship with this family (see Sadducees). It is not known whether the sons of Z. mentioned in the Dead Sea Scrolls have any connection with this family. Z. was also the name of one of the Pharisees who with Judah the Galilean founded the Sect of Zealots in 6 CE.

ZADOKITE FRAGMENTS ("Damascus Document," "Cairo Damascus Covenant"): Two *genizah* manuscripts, first published in 1910 by S. Schechter. Fragments of other copies were found in 1952 in a cave near Khirbet Kumran. From this, it is certain that the Z. F. form part of the literature to which the Dead Sea Scrolls belong; it is still unknown how they came to be copied about 1000 CE. The Z. F. preserve parts of two works. One is a sermon on the history of mankind and of the sect, the other a collection of sectarian laws and rules. Apart from matters also known from other Scrolls, the sermon alludes to an emigration of the sect to the "Land of Damascus" (perhaps the sect's name for an entirely different place) and a "New Covenant" there.

ZAGREB: Yugoslavian town. Jews were living there in the 14th cent. but had left the town by the 16th cent. The community grew after Joseph II's edict of Toleration in 1781. Religious Reform introduced in 1840 led to the secession of the Orthodox who founded a separate congregation in 1846. Equal rights were granted by the Croatian Sabor in 1873. After 1918, it was the main Ashkenazi center in Yugoslavia. A Sephardi community existed until World War II. The 12,315 Jews in Z. in 1941 were deported to forced labor and the concentration camp of Jasenovac. Jewish pop. (1973): 1,342.

ZAIRE see **CONGO**

ZALINSKI, EDMUND LOUIS GRAY (1849–1909): US soldier and inventor. Born in Poland, he went to the US in 1853, fought in the Union Army in the Civil War, and taught military science at the Massachusetts Institute of Technology 1872–6. His inventions include a pneumatic dynamite torpedo-gun and a telescopic sight for artillery.

ZAMBIA: African country. Jews played an important part in opening up the country, especially in the Copperbelt where most of them still reside. About 180 live in Lusaka. Jewish pop. (1973): 400.

ZAMENHOF, LUDWIG LAZARUS (1859–1917):
Creator of Esperanto. An oculist by profession,
he lived in Warsaw and published in 1887 his artificial
auxiliary language, based chiefly on Latin roots and
possessing a minimal grammar, as an instrument to
increase international understanding. The first international Esperanto congress was held in 1905. Z.
translated a number of classics into Esperanto and
also published an Esperanto handbook in Hebrew.

Israel Zangwill.
(Painting by Solomon J. Solomon).

ZANGWILL, ISRAEL (1864–1926): English author.
Born of poor Russian parents in London, he
began to make his name as a writer while teaching
at the Jews' Free School. In 1892, his *Children of the
Ghetto* delineating East End Jewish life with humor
and sympathy became an outstanding success, being
succeeded in the same vein by *Ghetto Tragedies,
Ghetto Comedies, Children of the Ghetto, The King
of Schnorrers*, etc. Later, Z. turned with somewhat
less success to the non-Jewish scene and to play-
writing, though in this field only his *Melting Pot*
achieved a fair measure of success. His mordant
essays on Jewish themes (collected in *The Voice of
Jerusalem*) also attracted great attention, while his
verse translations of Jewish liturgical poetry and of the
poems of Solomon Ibn Gabirol were sometimes
brilliant. Approached by Herzl in 1895 as an outstanding Jewish man of letters of the day, Z. became
an enthusiastic Zionist. In 1905, however, after the
rejection of the UGANDA scheme, he founded the
Jewish Territorial Organization, to the work of
which he devoted himself for many years. He was
active in England also in the suffragette and (during

World War I) the pacifist movements, the Jewish
Historical Society, etc.

ZAREPHATH: Coastal town N of Palestine, near
Sidon, mentioned in I Kings 17:9–10, and in
Obadiah 1:20. In the Middle Ages, the name was
applied to France (excluding Provence) for which it
is also the modern Hebrew term.

ZARFATTI see **TZARPHATI**

ZARITSKY, YOSEPH (1891–): Painter. Of Russian
birth, he settled in Palestine in 1923. At first, he
concentrated on highly-colored landscapes; later his
style became abstract, and he was among the founders
of the "New Horizons" group of Israel painters.

ZAVIM (Heb. "Sufferers from Flux"): Ninth tractate
in the talmudic order *Tohorot*, containing 5 chapters. It has no *gemara* in either Talmud. It deals with
the ritual uncleanness caused by a flux, whether in
man or woman, as described in Lev. 15, and discusses
how persons and things can be rendered unclean
through contact with a person affected with an issue.

ZAY, JEAN (1904–1944): French politician; of
Jewish origin. Minister of education in Léon
Blum's 1936 cabinet, he participated in all subsequent
French governments until 1939 when he volunteered
for the army. He was imprisoned by the Vichy
government and murdered shortly before the
Liberation.

ZAYDE (Yidd.): An old man; grandfather.

ZAYIN (ז): Seventh letter in the Hebrew alphabet;
numerical value 7. It is pronounced *z*.

ZBAHRZ, VELVEL OF see **EHRENKRANZ,
BENJAMIN**

ZEALOTS (Heb. *kannaim*): Jewish political party
in Second Temple times. It was founded in 6 CE
by Judah the Galilean and Zadok the priest who
demanded non-compliance with the Roman demand
for a census (i.e. the assessment of property) on the
grounds that this would constitute an acknowledgment
of subjection. They developed their own theological
and messianic outlook, proclaiming God as the sole
ruler of the Jewish nation. Their struggle was directed
both against foreign rule and those Jews who accepted
it (the latter generally belonging to the wealthy
classes). Bitterly suppressed by the procurators, the
number of Z. increased. One of their most renowned
leaders was Eleazar ben Dinai who was executed by
Felix. The Z. engendered the SICARII. During the
period immediately preceding the revolt against
Rome (66 CE), the Z. won adherents from all social
strata. After the conflict with Rome had been sparked
off, MENAHEM, son of Judah the Galilean, a member
of the Sicarii, went to Jerusalem, appears to have
claimed messianic status, and was slain by the captain
of the Temple, Eleazar ben Hananiah. His comrades,
led by his kinsman ELEAZAR BEN JAIR, fled the city
to MASADA. Their omission from the revolutionary
government came as a great disappointment. The

Roman successes in Galilee weakened the government and strengthened the position of the Z. in Jerusalem who terrorized their opponents, deposed the high priest, and elected his successor by lot. The rest of the populace rose against this regime of terror and drove the Z. under ELEAZAR BEN SIMON into the inner court of the Temple. The Z. summoned the support of the Idumeans who entered Jerusalem and massacred many of its citizens. The Z. under the leadership of JOHN OF GISCHALA regained control of the city and resumed their terrorization. Although they were driven back into the Temple for a time by SIMON BAR GIORA, they were in control of the city when the final siege began in 70. After the destruction of Jerusalem, some of the Z. fled to the forest of Jardes where they were annihilated by the Romans; those in Masada committed suicide in 73. Others fled to Egypt and Cyrene where they tried to stir up disorders but were largely wiped out; however, the N African revolt of 115–117 may have been caused by their descendants. Attempts have been made to identify the sect of the Dead Sea Scrolls with the Z.

ZEBULUN: Sixth son of Jacob and Leah. His descendants — the tribe of Z. — received territory in central Palestine (the Valley of Jezreel), although its exact extent is unclear. The status of the tribe declined during the period of the monarchy, but it maintained its identity and its territory and is mentioned by Isaiah (8:23) and Ezekiel (48:26–27). The rabbis associated Z. with trade, the scholarly descendants of ISSACHAR being supported by the tribe of Z.

ZEBULUN, PLAIN OF (Heb. *Emek Zevulun*): Common, but historically unjustifiable, name for coastal plain between Haifa and Acre. In ancient times, it was settled by Canaanite, and later Israelite, cities. Subsequently, the area was almost uninhabitable until the swamps were drained by Jewish pioneers (1935 ff). It now contains an industrial zone and several suburbs of Haifa with a population of over 80,000 (1956). Various agricultural settlements are situated on its N side.

ZECHARIAH (d. 744 BCE): King of Israel; son of Jeroboam II. The last king of the house of Jehu, after a 6-months' reign he was assassinated by Shallum who succeeded him.

ZECHARIAH (fl. first half of 6th cent. BCE): Prophet living during the period of the return from the Babylonian Exile. Probably a priest (Neh. 2:4, 16), his prophecies are concerned with contemporary events and foretell material prosperity, the ingathering of the exiles, liberation from foreign yoke, and the expansion of Jerusalem. He frequently describes his visions and their interpretation by an accompanying angel. Z. was instrumental in encouraging the people to conclude the rebuilding of the Temple. Many scholars ascribe the latter sections of the

Traditional tomb of the prophet Zechariah.
Kidron Valley, Jerusalem.

book (chaps. 9–14) to another author or authors (possibly of the First Temple Period), on the basis of their language and content.

ZEDEKIAH: False prophet who wrongly foretold that Ahab would be successful in his invasion of Ramoth Gilead and fashioned iron horns to symbolize Ahab's victory.

ZEDEKIAH: King of Judah 597–586 BCE. Son of Josiah, he was originally called Mattaniah but adopted the name of Z. when appointed king by Nebuchadnezzar to succeed the exiled Jehoiachin. He ascended the throne at the age of 21 and swore allegiance to Nebuchadnezzar; in the early years of his reign he refused to join an anti-Babylonian coalition of neighboring kingdoms and in 594, visited Babylon (Jer. 51:59). In the ninth year of his reign, however, he conspired with Egypt; in consequence the Babylonians invaded his kingdom and eventually captured Jerusalem. Z. was overtaken while attempting to flee, and brought for trial before Nebuchadnezzar. His sons were killed before him, his eyes were put out, and he was imprisoned in Babylon until his death (II Kings 25; Jer. 52).

ZEDERBAUM, ALEXANDER (1816–1893): Editor. He founded and edited *Ha-Melitz* (1860), the first Hebrew journal in Russia, and also *Kol Mevasser* (1862), the first Yiddish periodical in the country, which became the popular organ of the rising Yiddish literature. When *Kol Mevasser* was banned in 1871, he fought for a decade to obtain permission for another Yiddish journal and in 1881, founded *Yiddishes Folksblat*. Z. was an influential pre-Herzlian Zionist and a moderately competent novelist.

ZEIRA (Palestinian form of the Babylonian name Zera): Name of several amoraim of whom the best-known lived in the early 4th cent. Born in Babylonia, he later became one of the outstanding scholars in Palestine. His teachers in Babylonia were R Huna and R Judah through whom he received many of the traditions of Rav and Samuel.

James D. Zellerbach.

ZEIRA, MORDEKHAI (1905–1968): Composer. Of Russian birth, he settled in Palestine in 1932. Z. wrote many of Israel's most popular songs.

ZEIT, DIE (Yidd. "The Times"): Yiddish journals. (1) A New York monthly, appearing 1897–8. (2) A New York daily run by the *Poale Zion*, appearing 1920–2. (3) A London daily, founded in 1913 and edited by Morris Myer. It closed in 1950.

ZEITLIN, HILLEL (1872–1942): Author and philosopher. Born in Russia, he settled in Homel in the early 1890's and commenced to write, initially in Hebrew. At first an active Zionist, under the impact of the KISHINEV pogrom he became a supporter of TERRITORIALISM. Settling in Vilna, Z. began to publish mostly in Yiddish from 1906, opposing assimilatory and anti-religious trends in the Jewish environment. In the 1920's, he resumed his support of Zionism. Many of his writings raised religious problems and Z. is regarded as the outstanding representative of Ḥasidic thought in modern Yiddish literature. He was killed in the Warsaw ghetto. His son, *AARON Z.* (1898–) is a Yiddish and Hebrew writer and journalist and professor of modern Hebrew literature at the Jewish Theological Seminary, New York.

ZEITLIN, SOLOMON (1892–): Rabbinic scholar and historian. Born in Russia, he settled in the US in 1915. Since 1925, he has been professor of rabbinical literature at Dropsie College, Philadelphia. Z., who is co-editor of the *Jewish Quarterly Review*, is the author of numerous critical studies on rabbinics and the Second Temple ("Second Commonwealth") Period. He has violently contested the early date generally assigned to the Dead Sea Scrolls.

ZEKHOR BERIT (Heb. "remember the covenant"): Penitential hymn (*seliḥah*) composed by R GER-SHOM BEN JUDAH. In the Ashkenazi ritual it is recited on the eve of *Rosh ha-Shanah*, and consequently the day preceding the New Year is called Z. B. It is also recited during the Concluding Service on the Day of Atonement.

ZEKHUT AVOT (Heb. "merit of the fathers"): Phrase implying the Jewish concept that the pious deeds of the fathers help to secure protection and salvation for their descendants. The example *par excellence* is the lasting merit of the patriarchs Abraham, Isaac and Jacob, continually cited in the Jewish liturgy.

ZELLERBACH, JAMES DAVID (1892–1963): US industrialist and diplomat. He was chief of the American Economic Cooperation Administration in Italy, 1948–50, and US ambassador in Rome 1956–61.

ZELOPHEHAD: Israelite of the tribe of Manasseh who died in the wilderness. He left five daughters and no son, and his daughters claimed their paternal portion in the Promised Land. Accordingly, new legislation was proclaimed permitting daughters to inherit (in the absence of sons) but only when married to a member of their father's tribe (Num. 27, 36).

ZEMIROT (Heb. "songs," hymns"): (1) In the Sephardi and Yemenite rituals the designation for the PESUKE DE-ZIMRA. (2) Among Ashkenazi Jews the term refers to the hymns and songs sung at table during the Sabbath meals and at the end of the Sabbath. The printed prayer books include such collections for Sabbath eve, for Sabbath day, and for the end of the Sabbath. They were mainly composed during the 16th and 17th cents., but also contain the works of well-known early poets such as Abraham Ibn Ezra. Some of these are widespread both in Ashkenazi and Sephardi communities, being sung either recitatively or to the popular tunes characteristic of each particular group.

ZENO PAPYRI: Collection of papyri discovered during World War I at the site of ancient Philadelphia in Egypt. Z. was a treasury official under Ptolemy II and visited Palestine in 259 BCE. His letters throw considerable light on conditions in the country at that time, on the Tobiads in Transjordan, and on commercial relations between Palestine and Egypt.

ZEPHANIAH (fl. 7th cent. BCE): Prophet; member of a noble family of Judah. His prophecies, uttered during the early part of Josiah's reign, were mainly eschatological. He describes the Day of the Lord when God will punish the wicked among the remnant of Israel, the poor will inherit the land, and the Divinity of God will be universally acknowledged (Zech. 3:9–10). The Book of Z. is the 9th in the Minor Prophets section of the Bible.

ZERAHIAH LEVI (known as Ferrer Saldin; fl. c. 1414): Spanish scholar and poet. Rabbi at Saragossa after Ḥasdai Crescas, he was author of sermons, responsa, and verses. He was one of the leading Jewish spokesmen at the Disputation of TORTOSA.

ZERAIM (Heb. "Seeds"): First order of the Mishnah and Talmud. It consists of 11 tractates, the first dealing with the laws of prayer, and the remainder with agricultural laws. There is *gemara* in the Palestinian Talmud to all the 11 tractates but in the Babylonian Talmud, only to the first (*Berakhot*).

ZERUBBABEL (b. c. 480 BCE): Grandson of JEHOIACHIN. He was one of the first Jews to return to Judah from Babylon with the assent of Cyrus. The version related by Ezra, that he was a bodyguard of Darius from whom he obtained permission to rebuild Jerusalem, conflicts with other biblical accounts. He was appointed satrap after the death of SHESHBAZZAR with whom, however, some scholars identify him. He set up an altar, re-established the festivals, and took steps toward the rebuilding of the Temple. Z. is associated with the political revivals in Judah in Darius' reign; but his actual role is conjectural. He was the last satrap of Davidic descent in Jerusalem and after his time, the high priest increased in influence, possibly as a consequence of Persian apprehension concerning the renewal of the Davidic dynasty. Some authorities believe that he was actually removed from office and recalled to Persia.

ZEVAHIM (Heb. "Animal Sacrifices"): First tractate in the talmudic order *Kodashim*, containing 14 chapters. It has *gemara* in the Babylonian, but not the Palestinian, Talmud. The original name of the tractate was *Shehitat Kodashim* ("slaughtering of consecrated animals"); in the Tosephta, it is called *Korbanot* ("Sacrifices"). It discusses the laws governing the offering of sacrificial animals. A historical discussion of the successive places of sacrifice figures at the end.

ZHITLOVSKY, CHAIM (1865–1943): Philosopher and essayist. He participated in the revolutionary activities of the NARODNIKI, but when this group favored assimilationism, he broke away to found a Jewish section of the Socialist Revolution Party (1885), stressing socialism, Jewish national emancipation, and Yiddish as the language of national rebirth. He fled from Russia in 1888 and from 1893 edited in Switzerland the *Russian Worker*. Z. returned to Russia after the 1905 revolution, founded the Jewish *Seymist* party, and was elected to the Duma but not seated on account of his revolutionary past. In 1908, he settled in New York where he edited *Dos Neie Leben* advocating Diaspora nationalism, socialism, and Yiddishism.

ZHITOMIR: Town in Ukraine, USSR. Jews lived there from the end of the 18th cent. In 1845, Z. and Vilna possessed the sole Hebrew printing-presses in Russia. Like Vilna, it was the seat of a Russian governmental rabbinical college (1848–73). A state college for Jewish teachers was situated there 1813–85, and from 1862 to 1884, a state Jewish crafts school — the only one in the country. Z. was the scene of a pogrom in 1905. Its Jewish community of 35,000 was massacred by the Germans in the latter part of 1941. Jewish pop. (1970): 35,706 (Z. province).

ZIDFELD, SIMEON see **NORDAU, MAX**

ZIEGFELD, FLORENZ (1869–1932): US theatrical producer. Chief of his lavish Broadway productions was the annual series known as the "Ziegfeld Follies" (1907 ff.).

ZIKHRON YAAKOV: Israel village on Mt. Carmel. It was founded in 1882 by immigrants from Rumania. Soon after its establishment, Baron Edmond de Rothschild came to its aid, furthering viticulture as the central branch in the village's economy and erecting its large wine-cellars. Its holdings, transferred to the ICA Association in 1900 and enlarged by it, later became the property of the settlers. In 1955, the remains of Baron and Baroness de Rothschild were re-interred at Z. Y. Pop. (1972): 4,276.

ZIKHRONO LI-VERAKHAH (Heb. "of blessed memory"): Phrase uttered when mentioning a deceased person.

ZIKLAG: Ancient Palestinian city in the territory of the tribe of Simeon. In Saul's time, Z. was held by the Philistines who handed it to David and it remained thereafter in the territory of Judah (I Sam. 27:6).

ZILPAH: Handmaid of Leah who gave her to Jacob as wife. She was the mother of Gad and Asher (Gen. 30:9–13).

ZIM see **SHOHAM**

Chaim Zhitlovsky.

ZIMBALIST, EFREM (1889–): Violinist. A native of Russia, he toured extensively and settled in the US in 1911. From 1941, he headed the Curtis Institute of Music in Philadelphia.

ZIMRA, DAVID BEN SOLOMON IBN AVI (known as *Radbaz*; fl. 16th cent.): Talmudist and kabbalist. Born in Spain, he studied in Safed, Fez, and Cairo where he was chief rabbi for 40 years. He then returned to Safed and acted as *dayyan* for 20 years, leaving a collection of over 3,000 responsa. His writings include a commentary on Maimonides' *Mishneh Torah*, kabbalistic works, and talmudic novellae. He died in extreme old age. His pupils included Isaac LURIA.

ZIMRI: Israelite. The head of a clan in the tribe of Simeon, he consorted with a Midianite woman. They were stabbed by Phinehas the grandson of Aaron, and this action ended a plague visited on the Israelites for "committing harlotry" with Midianite women and worshiping Baal Peor (Num. 25).

ZIMRI (d. 887 BCE): King of Israel. A general in the service of Elah, he murdered his master and seized power. When news of the conspiracy reached the Israelite army fighting the Philistines, they declared Omri king. Omri thereupon besieged Tirzah, the capital city, and after a seven-day reign, Z. set his palace on fire and himself with it (I Kings 16:8–18).

ZIN, WILDERNESS OF: One of the four wildernesses of the Sinai peninsula. It was situated SW of the Dead Sea. The spies sent by Moses visited Z. (Num. 13:21) and when the Israelites were here they murmured against God (Num. 27:14).

ZINBERG, ISRAEL (1873–1943): Yiddish literary historian. A chemical engineer in Leningrad, he devoted his leisure to research, completing 8 vols. of a monumental history of Jewish literature from the Middle Ages to the Haskalah Period.

ZINOVIEV, GRIGORI EVSEYEVICH (1883–1936): Russian communist leader. He joined the Bolshevik Party in 1903. He was exiled from Russia but returned in 1917, becoming head of the Comintern in 1919 and one of the triumvirate which ruled Russia after Lenin's death. A supporter of Trotsky, he was expelled from the Communist Party in 1927, returned in 1929 after recantation, but in 1936 was charged with plotting against the regime and shot.

ZION: Jebusite stronghold in Jerusalem, captured by David and identified with the city of David (II Sam. 5:6–7); its site is still disputed. The prophets called Jerusalem "Z." when wishing to stress it as a spiritual symbol. In Maccabean times, Mt. Z. was identified with the Temple Mount and the City of David together, in opposition to the hellenistic quarter on Acra hill. Josephus, on the other hand, identified Z. with the Upper City, and its identification with the eastern hill (Josephus' "Lower City") was forgotten. Since the Crusader Period, the TOMB OF DAVID on "Mt. Zion" became an established Jewish tradition, which has continued into modern times; it was especially stressed 1948–67 when this hill was the only part of ancient Jerusalem in the possession of Israel. On the other hand, scientific opinion is now unanimous in looking for Z. on the hill of the Temple Mount, wrongly called "Ophel." Christian tradition places the scene of the Last Supper in the Coenaculum on the western "Mt. Z." and consequently, the first church in Jerusalem was erected here; the "Dormition" of Mary, mother of Jesus, is also located on this hill.

ZION: Hebrew quarterly founded in 1936 (previously an annual) and devoted to Jewish history; it is published by the Israel Historical Society. Its editors are Yitzhak Baer, Benzion Dinur, and Israel Heilprin. Originally it was devoted to the history of the Jews in Palestine and the neighboring lands.

ZION MULE CORPS: Company in the British army enrolled in World War I in Egypt, on the initiative of Jabotinsky and Trumpeldor, from Jews expelled from Palestine by the Turks. The British authorities rejected the proposal to establish a military formation of these Jews and only agreed to organize companies of mule-drivers to serve as ammunition carriers on the Gallipoli front. The corps was commanded by Colonel Patterson, with Trumpeldor as his second-in-command. After having performed its duties in Gallipoli, the corps was disbanded in 1916.

ZIONIDES see **JUDAH HA-LEVI**

ZIONISM: Movement to secure the Jewish return to the Land of Israel. The term was coined in 1893 by Nathan Birnbaum but expressed aspirations as ancient as the Babylonian Exile. Until the 19th cent., its form was religious and expressed most commonly in the traditional liturgy, pseudo-messianic movements, and in limited ALIYAH. In the latter 19th cent. Z., especially among Jews in E and SE Europe, obtained more specific expression through the HIBBAT ZION movement, which produced an extensive literature, besides encouraging the migration of Jews to Palestine and the foundation of settlements there. Z. crystallized in the political Zionist movement and organization created by HERZL at the First ZIONIST CONGRESS in 1897. The Congress defined its political aspirations as the establishment for the Jewish people of a national home in Palestine guaranteed by public law (BASLE PROGRAM). Z. proceeds from the assumption that the Jews are still a people or nation, many of whom cannot or will not assimilate themselves to other peoples, and wish to retain their identity as a national community. Although arousing mass support, it has encountered widespread opposition inside Jewry — the extreme religious factions claiming that only Divine Providence could restore the Jews to their land, while many liberal Jews denied the nationhood of the Jews whom they maintained to be only

Herzl opening the second Zionist congress. Basle, 1898.

a community united by religion. This opposition has weakened since the establishment of the state of Israel in 1948, but is still not extinct.

In the second half of the 19th cent., *Ḥibbat Zion* had evoked the BILU movement among Russian Jewish students who initiated agricultural settlement in Palestine (1882 ff). A further step was taken at the KATTOWITZ CONFERENCE where the *Ḥoveve Zion* founded a society for the promotion among the Jews of agriculture and handicrafts in behalf of Palestine. In the 1890's Baron Edmond de ROTHSCHILD undertook the support of Jewish colonies which were suffering severely through financial difficulties and lack of technical experience. The methods of the Baron's officials led, however, to considerable friction. Meanwhile, Herzl was creating the World Zionist Organization and its institutions, notably the JEWISH COLONIAL TRUST (1898) and the JEWISH NATIONAL FUND (1901) for the purchase of land in Palestine as the perpetual property of the Jewish people. Herzl made repeated attempts to win support from Turkey (then ruling Palestine) and the great European powers — notably Germany, Britain, and Russia. His failure in Turkey coupled with the renewed intensity of Russia's persecution of its Jews led to his seeking a temporary solution (NACHTASYL) in countries other

than Palestine. Nevertheless, a scheme for settlement near UGANDA was rejected by the majority of his colleagues. After the death of Herzl in 1904, the movement was rent by controversy over its direction. The new president, David WOLFFSOHN, and his supporters wished to maintain Herzl's tradition of diplomatic Z., but the Russian Zionists energetically demanded the immediate beginning of practical colonization work ("practical Z.") in Palestine. A compromise ("synthetic Z.") was accepted by the 1911 Congress. The headquarters of the movement was now transferred from Cologne to Berlin, under Otto WARBURG. The new executive began to implement colonization activity through the PALESTINE OFFICE in Jaffa, and the first AGRICULTURAL SETTLEMENTS of the World Zionist Organization were founded, urban development undertaken (e.g. the foundation of TEL AVIV), and progress recorded in the growth of Hebrew language and culture which had been urged by those who advocated the importance of "cultural Z." World War I divided the Zionists into three camps, in the two belligerent blocs and in neutral states. Zionist leaders continued their work in each of these groups, though setting up an international office at Copenhagen ("Copenhagen Bureau"). But while the Central European Zionists only received vague pledges from Turkey, WEIZMANN in England was able to induce the British government to issue the BALFOUR DECLARATION (1917) approving the Jewish national home in Palestine. SOKOLOW succeeded in securing endorsement of the Declaration from certain European powers (e.g. France and Italy) while US Zionists obtained the agreement of President Wilson. Henceforth, the task of Z., implemented through the newly-created JEWISH AGENCY FOR PALESTINE, consisted firstly in working for the implementation of the Balfour Declaration and in opposing the British policy of restricting its application; secondly in promoting Jewish immigration to Palestine.

The Zionist movement continued its activities after the establishment of the state of Israel in 1948. Much of the financial responsibility for the mass-immigration and absorption of newcomers in Palestine was undertaken by Zionists outside Israel, and the Zionist leadership is still responsible for the organization and financing of immigration and agricultural settlement, as well as for Zionist education in the Diaspora.

Structure of World Zionist Organization (WZO): The supreme legislative institution of the WZO is the Zionist Congress elected by the democratic vote of all SHEKEL-holders. The Congress is composed of elected delegates and members of the advisory and executive institutions of the WZO (the latter without voting rights). Congresses were originally held annually but later less frequently; in the interim, the supreme advisory and supervising institution is the Zionist General Council ("Actions Committee"), the

PRESIDENTS OF THE WZO

1897–1904   Theodor Herzl
1905–1911   David Wolffsohn
1911–1920   Otto Warburg
1920–1931   Chaim Weizmann
1931–1935   Nahum Sokolow
1935–1946   Chaim Weizmann
1956–1968   Nahum Goldmann

CHAIRMEN OF THE ZIONIST EXECUTIVE

1920–1931   Nahum Sokolow
1931–1948   David Ben-Gurion
1948–1956   Berl Locker and Nahum Goldmann
1956–1961   Zalman Shazar and Rose Halprin
1961–1965   Moshe Sharett and Rose Halprin
1965–1968   A. Pincus, Rose Halprin, and Emanuel Neumann
1968–1973   Louis A. Pincus
1974–1975   Pinhas Sapir
1976–   Yoseph Almogi

ZIONISTS PARTIES IN THE WZO

(1)   World Federation of General Zionists
(2)   World Union of *Poale Zion–Hitahdut*
(3)   *Mizrahi* and *Ha-Poel Ha-Mizrahi*
(4)   World League of *Herut* movement and Zionist Revisionists
(5)   World League of *Mapam*
(6)   World League of *Ahdut ha-Avodah–Poale Zion.*

composition of which reflects that of the previous Congress. The size of the Council varies—on occasions it has been 25–30 members, but after the 1956 Congress numbered 142, including 42 *virilists* (i.e., members elected on the basis of their personal services to the movement) and 100 representatives of Zionist parties. The Council supervises the work of the Zionist Executive of 18 (the Jewish Agency Executive) and meets regularly in Jerusalem for the routine supervision of Zionist activities.

Many of the parties are united in national Zionist federations. The Zionist parties in each country hold. annual conferences to determine their policy and elect their institutions.

ZIONIST COMMISSION: Commission appointed in 1918 by the British government and sent to Palestine in April of that year to advise the British military authorities in Palestine on the implementation of the Balfour Declaration and to act as intermediaries between them and the Jewish population. The Z. C., which was led by Chaim Weizmann, was composed of Zionists and non-Zionists from the countries which had occupied Palestine during World War I. Enthusiastically received by the Jewish population, it encountered marked opposition from the British military administration. The Commission organized offices at Jaffa to replace the former PALESTINE OFFICE and also established a center in Jerusalem to handle food-supplies, immigration, education, etc. When Weizmann returned to England, his place was taken by David Eder and then by Harry Friedenwald. After the Twelfth Zionist Congress (1921), the functions of the Z. C. were transferred to the Zionist Executive in Palestine.

ZIONIST CONGRESSES: Regular conferences of representatives of the Zionist movement, instituted by Theodor Herzl in 1897. The Z. C. constitute the supreme legislative body of the Zionist Organization. The participants are composed of the Executive and leading officials of the World Zionist Organization and delegates elected by national constituencies. Every person purchasing a shekel has voting rights. The elections are based on the proportional method, with lists of candidates submitted by the Zionist parties. The function of the Z. C. are: (1) to receive reports from the administrative institutions of the Zionist Organization and to supervise their work; (2) to determine the policy of the executive institutions; (3) to fix the budget; and (4) to elect the Organization's Supreme Institutions.

No.	Year	Site	
1	1897	Basle	Created the World Zionist Organization; formulated the Basle Program; elected Herzl as president.
2	1898	Basle	Founded the Jewish Colonial Trust.
3	1899	Basle	Dealt with problems of Hebrew culture.

Z.O.A. (Zionist Organization of America) House, Tel-Aviv.

4	1900	London	Discussed Zionist propaganda.
5	1901	Basle	Established the Jewish National Fund.
6	1903	Basle	Discussed El-Arish and Uganda Scheme.
7	1905	Basle	Rejected Uganda scheme. Elected Wolffsohn as president.
8	1907	The Hague	Decided to commence practical work in Palestine.
9	1909	Hamburg	Discussed the consequences of the Turkish revolution and the establishment of cooperative settlements in Palestine.
10	1911	Basle	Elected Warburg — representing "synthetic Zionism" — as president.
11	1913	Vienna	Decided on principle of founding Hebrew Univ. in Palestine.
12	1921	Carlsbad	Thanked Gt. Britain for the Balfour Declaration. Elected Weizmann as president.
13	1923	Carlsbad	Discussed the establishment of the Jewish Agency.
14	1925	Vienna	Introduced the unified (in place of party) shekel.
15	1927	Basle	Considered unemployment in Palestine and economic problems.
16	1929	Zürich	Resolved to establish expanded Jewish Agency.
17	1931	Basle	Replaced Weizmann with Sokolow as president.
18	1933	Prague	Discussed murder of Arlosoroff and associated questions
19	1935	Lucerne	Rejected British proposal to establish legislative council in Palestine. Re-elected Weizmann as president.
20	1937	Zürich	Rejected partition proposal.
21	1939	Geneva	Rejected MacDonald White Paper.
22	1946	Basle	Discussed The European catastrophe. Rejected new British proposals. Failed to re-elect Weizmann.
23	1951	Jerusalem	Discussed relations between Zionist movement and state of Israel: formulated Jerusalem program (consolidation of the state of Israel; ingathering of exiles; unity of the Jewish people).
24	1956	Jerusalem	Discussed immigration and absorption into Israel, and education in the Diaspora.
25	1960	Jerusalem	Relations between Israel and the Diaspora.
26	1964	Jerusalem	Organizational revision
27	1968	Jerusalem	Stressed immigration; revised Jerusalem Program (Aliyah; Jewish and Hebrew education; centrality of Israel in life of Jewish people).
28	1972	Jerusalem	Obligated Zionists to immigrate

ZIONIST ORGANIZATION OF AMERICA (Z.O.A.): Organization founded in 1897. It has a shekel membership of c. 100,000 exclusive of its affiliates, Young Judea and the fraternal order B'nai Zion. The Z.O.A. is affiliated to the World Confederation of General Zionists. In Israel it has built and maintains the Z.O.A. — Daniel Frisch House in Tel Aviv and the Kfar Silver Agricultural Training Institute at Ashkelon. In the US, its fields of activity include public relations, education, the promotion of investment in and tourism to Israel, community relations, fund-raising, etc. Its publications include *The American Zionist.*

ZIPPORAH: Wife of Moses and daughter of Jethro, priest of Midian. On traveling to Egypt with Moses, she saved her son's life by circumcising him (Exod. 4:24-6). Later she returned to her father with her two sons, Gershom and Eliezer, rejoining Moses at Mount Sinai (Exod. 18:1).

ZIRELSOHN, JUDAH LÖB (1859–1941): Rabbi and public figure. He became rabbi at Kishinev in 1909 and the following year was appointed to the rabbinical commission of the Russian ministry of the interior. Z. was a Rumanian deputy from 1922 until 1926 when he was nominated for the senate. He was prominent in *Agudat Israel* and published rabbinical responsa.

ZITRON, SAMUEL LÖB (1860–1930): Russian writer. An early Zionist, he wrote a history of the *Ḥibbat Zion* movement and a Zionist lexicon and contributed prolifically to the Hebrew and Yiddish press. He translated Pinsker's *Auto-Emancipation* into Hebrew and wrote a biography of Herzl, but most of his writings were devoted to literary subjects.

ZODIAC: Imaginary zone or belt in the sky containing the twelve signs or constellations within which lie the paths of the principal planets and the sun. The signs of the Z. assumed outstanding importance in ASTROLOGY; and midrashic literature — besides reproducing much of the current astronomical lore — also adds a specific symbolism of its own, e.g. the correlation of the twelve constellations with the twelve tribes. The signs of the Z. constituted a popular subject of Jewish art, figuring on the mosaic floors of ancient Palestinian synagogues and in many prayer-books, marriage contracts, etc.

ZOGERIN (Yid. "sayer"): Woman who reads the prayers in synagogue in the vernacular for the benefit of those women unable to read Hebrew. The practice was common in Russia and Poland.

ZOHAR (Heb. "Brightness"): The chief work of the Spanish Kabbalah, most of which is in the form of a commentary on sections of the Pentateuch and parts of the Hagiographa (Song of Songs, Ruth, Lamentations). In the work, authorship of the Z. is ascribed to the tanna Simeon ben Yoḥai (2nd cent.), his colleagues, and disciples. They discuss the mysteries of the Torah in a kabbalistic spirit. Lengthy homiletic passages, reminiscent of medieval exegesis, alternate with short discourses and parables. The work consists of a number of sections, most of them apparently written by one hand. Their external form varies greatly, but the inner content is, on the whole, uniform. The material can be divided into four strata: (1) *Midrash ha-Ne'elam* ("The Hidden Midrash"); (2) the Z. proper; (3) *Raaya Mehemana* ("The Faithful Shepherd" i.e., Moses, who discusses the Heavenly Academy with R Simeon); (4) *Tikkune ha-Zohar* ("Amendments to the Z."), usually published separately. Each part has a different conception and aim. The second portion, which is the main body of the work, contains *Siphra di-Tzeniuta* ("Book of Mysteries") in the form of an ancient *baraita*; *Idra Rabba* and *Idra Zuta* ("The Larger Assembly" and "The Smaller Assembly"), comprising dramatic stories of mystic revelations by R Simeon and of the latter's death: and fragments entitled respectively *Sitre Torah, Matnitin, Tosephta*, and *Raze de-Razin*. This section is the work of one author. *Midrash ha-Ne'elam*

Title-page of the first printed edition of the *Zohar*, Mantua, 1558.

contains little Kabbalah and much mystical exegesis. *Raaya Mehemana* was written by a different author, and gives mystical reasons for the biblical commandments. The same writer was probably responsible for *Sepher ha-Tikkunim* which contains a detailed commentary on the first chapters of Genesis. All these sections are written in an artificial Aramaic which blends the style of the Babylonian Talmud with that of Targum Onkelos. Behind the veil of Aramaic, the Hebrew of the medieval era can be clearly detected. There are divergent opinions regarding the origins of the Z. Some defend its early authorship, or at least the antiquity of certain sections; others regard it as the result of a lengthy development; others consider it to have been written as late as the end of the 13th cent. by the Spanish kabbalist Moses de Leon; while others are of the opinion that Moses de Leon utilized ancient material, adding his own contributions. It seems that the two earliest strata were composed between 1280 and 1285 in Spain and the third between 1290 and 1300 by another kabbalist who was acquainted with the Z. proper and attempted to imitate it. From the main body of the work there emerges the figure of a strong personality belonging to the kabbalistic school reflecting the development of Jewish mysticism in the 13th cent. The oldest portion appeared between 1280 and 1290, and during the 14th cent. the Z. secured a firm place in kabbalistic literature, though it was not yet widely accepted. It was mainly influential in the period after the expulsion from Spain (1492) when it came to be regarded as the most important Jewish religious classic after the Bible and talmudic literature. It is still venerated as a sacred book by large numbers of Jews from oriental and Ḥasidic communities. All the works of the later kabbalists were based on it, and it exerted a profound influence even beyond these circles, making its impact on Judaism as a whole and on popular beliefs and customs over a long period of Jewish history. The most important commentaries on the Z. are: *Ketem Paz* by Simeon ben Lavi, *Or ha-Ḥammah* by Abraham Azulai, and *Mikdash Melekh* by Shalom Buzaglo. The Z. was first printed in 1558–60 and has been reprinted about eighty times. An English translation appeared in 1931–4.

*ZOLA, ÉMILE (1840–1902): French novelist. He threw himself into the defense of DREYFUS and his article *J'accuse* (appearing in Clemenceau's journal *L'Aurore* on Jan. 13, 1898) caused a sensation throughout France. The author himself was sentenced to imprisonment but took refuge for a time in England, from where he continued the struggle.

ZONDEK, BERNHARD (1891–1966): Gynecologist. He taught obstetrics and gynecology at Berlin Univ. where he was co-discoverer of the first reliable pregnancy test. He went to Israel in 1934 to become professor of obstetrics and gynecology at the Hebrew University.

ZOROASTRIANISM: Religion founded by Zoroaster (?7th cent. BCE), the prophet of ancient Iran. Both the eschatological tendency of Z. (belief in light and righteousness) and its actively ethical character (commendation of marriage and agriculture, turning the earth from a waste into God's kingdom) bear some resemblance to Judaism which, however, unqualifiedly rejected its DUALISM; cf. the polemical utterance of Isaiah (45:7): "I form the light and create darkness; I make peace and create evil: I am the Lord, that doeth all these things." (See also PARSIISM).

ZUCKERMAN, SOLLY, BARON (1904–): Scientist. Born in S Africa, he became research anatomist to the London Zoological Society in 1928, lecturer at Oxford in 1934, professor of anatomy at the Univ. of Birmingham, 1945 and chief scientist, Ministry of Defense, 1960.

ZUCKERMANDEL, MOSES SAMUEL (1836–1917): Talmudist. He was rabbi of various congregations in his native Moravia and in Germany. His chief research was on the TOSEPHTA of which he published a standard scientific edition (1880–2).

ZUCKMAYER, CARL (1896–): German author. He achieved fame with his comedies *Der fröhliche Weinberg* and *Der Hauptmann von Köpenick*. Because his mother was Jewish and his politics anti-Nazi, he lived in the US 1939–1946. His play *The Devil's General* (1949), which has a Jewish theme, was an international success.

ZUGOT (Heb. "pairs"): Term applied to five generations of scholars preceding the tannaim: They are listed in pairs in *Avot*, 1. According to tradition, the first named was president (*nasi*) and the other senior judge of the court (*av bet din*). They were:
1. Yose ben Joezer and Yose ben Johanan.
2. Joshua ben Peraḥiah and Nittai the Arbelite.
3. Judah ben Tabbai and Simeon ben Shetaḥ.
4. Shemaiah and Avtalyon.
5. Hillel and Shammai.
(See also under individual entries).

ZUKOR, ADOLF (1873–1976): US film producer. He went to the US from Hungary in 1888 and in 1903, established the "Penny Arcades." A pioneer of motion picture production, he founded the Paramount Picture Corporation (1917).

ZUKUNFT: US Yiddish monthly, founded 1892. During its most influential years it was edited by Abraham Liessin. It paralleled the approach of the socialist Yiddish daily *Forverts*, which sponsored it. After suspending publication in 1940, it was revived the following year by the CENTRAL YIDDISH CULTURE ORGANIZATION (CYCO) to advance its philosophy.

ZULAI, MENAḤEM (1899–1954): Scholar. Of E Galician birth, he worked from 1930 in the Institute for the Study of Hebrew Poetry, at first in Germany and later in Palestine. He studied and edited the *piyyutim* discovered in the Cairo *genizah*, especially the poetry of YANNAI.

ZUNSER, ELIAKUM (1836–1913): Yiddish poet. As an outstanding BADḤAN, Z. entertained at weddings and festivals with popular songs that preached Enlightenment and Zionism to the Yiddish masses. He published many booklets of his poems from 1860 on. His only dramatic work *Mekhiras Yoseph* (1874) was performed by guilds of artisans in the manner of medieval morality plays. In 1889, he migrated to the US, where social justice became the main theme of his poetry.

ZUNZ, LEOPOLD (1794–1886): German scholar; chief founder of *Jüdische* WISSENSCHAFT. In 1818, he published his first booklet *Etwas über die rabbinische Litteratur* which contained the germ of his plans for the study of Jewish lore. The following year, he helped to found the *Verein für Kultur und Wissenschaft* in Berlin, under the auspices of which he produced a life of Rashi — the first scientific biography in Jewish studies — and a work on Jewish statistics. In 1832, there appeared his monumental history of Jewish homiletics *Gottendienstliche Vorträge der Juden*

Leopold Zunz.

which established his fame. The result of his research into aggadic Midrash published in this work are still considered fundamental. At the request of the Berlin community, he wrote a survey of Jewish names from biblical times (1837). From 1840 to 1850, Z. was principal of the Teachers' Seminary newly opened in Berlin. His later works included a history of Jewish geographical literature, a history of the Jewish liturgy, three books on medieval *piyyutim* and their authors (based on research in the great European libraries), and Bible studies. He also edited the literary remains of Naḥman Krochmal. The *Festschrift* issued on his 90th birthday was the first Jewish collection of its type. In the conflict between Orthodox and Reform Judaism, Z. stood midway, inclining to religious innovation but retaining profound admiration for the historical values of Judaism. In the realms of Midrash, liturgy, and medieval hymnology, Jewish scholars still depend to a great extent on his pioneer researches.

ZÜRICH: Swiss city and canton. Jews, chiefly from S Germany and France, are known in the city from the 14th cent. when they were mainly restricted to moneylending. In 1436, they were expelled. Jews who arrived from Alsace, Germany, and Poland were compelled to remove to village areas in 1774.

With emancipation, the number of Jews in Z. increased, a congregation being founded in 1870. Zionist Congresses were held in Z. in 1929 and 1937. Jewish pop. (1973): 6,000.

ZUTRA, MAR (II; d. 520): Babylonian exilarch. At the age of 15, he succeeded his father Huna, who had been killed in the religious persecutions instigated by Firuz of Persia. Revolting in 513 against King Kobad, Z. established an independent Jewish state in the district of Maḥoza, which lasted for seven years, with the assistance of non-Jewish as well as Jewish elements of the population. After his defeat, he and his grandfather, R Ḥananiah, were crucified. His son, MAR ZUTRA III, born on the day of his death, was taken to Palestine, where an unsuccessful attempt was made to revive the Patriarchate for him.

ZWEIFEL, ELIEZER TZEVI (1815–1888): Russian Hebrew author and teacher. He taught Talmud in the Zhitomir rabbinical college 1853–74. He was one of the first authors of the Haskalah period to write in midrashic language, but his Hebrew style contains numerous linguistic innovations. In his main work, *Shalom al-Yisrael* ("Peace on Israel"), he defended the Baal Shem Tov and Ḥasidism, demonstrating its kabbalistic roots and affinities with philosophical pantheism, particularly that of Spinoza. Z.'s optimistic *Ḥeshbono shel Olam* was influenced by Samuel Smiles' *Self Help*.

ZWEIG, ARNOLD (1887–1968): German novelist. His war novel *The Case of Sergeant Grischa* (1927) was an international success, while his other works include several dealing with Jewish topics. His play *Die Sendung Semaëls* deals with the Tisza-Eszlár Blood Libel. Exiled from Germany by the Nazis, he lived in Palestine from 1933 but returned to E Germany after World War II. In 1957, he was appointed president of the E Berlin Academy of Arts.

ZWEIG, STEFAN (1881–1942): Austrian author. He first composed sensitive neo-romantic poems and then produced distinguished psychological novelettes (*Erstes Erlebnis*; *Amok*). In 1918, he wrote the pacifist drama *Jeremiah*. After publishing a series of critical analyses of 19th cent. writers, he turned to biographies, achieving popular success with *Marie Antoinette*, *Mary Queen of Scots*, *Joseph Fouché*, etc. His pathetic autobiography *The World of Yesterday* appeared after his suicide in Brazil where, after living for a while in England, he had sought refuge from the Nazis. His fiction included *The Buried Candelabrum* on the fate of the Temple treasure and the sensitive *Beware of Pity*.